The Encyclopedia of Philosophy

Volumes 3 and 4
Complete and Unabridged

The
ENCYCLOPEDIA
of
PHILOSOPHY

PAUL EDWARDS, *Editor in Chief*

VOLUME THREE

Macmillan Publishing Co., Inc. & The Free Press
NEW YORK
COLLIER MACMILLAN PUBLISHERS
LONDON

The Encyclopedia of Philosophy

E

[CONTINUED]

EPICTETUS (c. 50–c. 130), the enormously influential teacher of Stoicism, was born in Hierapolis, a city in Phrygia, Asia Minor, and died an exile from Rome in Nicopolis, in northwestern Greece. He was born of a slave woman and was for years a slave himself; he was given his freedom sometime after the death of Nero, in 68. His master was Epaphroditus, himself a freedman of Nero who apparently was Nero's administrative secretary. Epaphroditus sent the young Epictetus to perhaps the most powerful Stoic teacher and theoretician since the early Stoa, C. Musonius Rufus, none of whose works survive. Epictetus was banished from Rome by Domitian in 89 or 93. In the Epirus, his place of exile, he drew around him a large, thriving school where the logic, physics, and ethics of Stoicism were taught to people from many lands. In his old age he married in order to bring up a child whose parents, friends of his, were going to expose it. In Rome and in Nicopolis he lived in a house with only a rush mat, a simple pallet, and an earthenware lamp (after the iron one was stolen). He was a man of great sweetness, as well as personal simplicity, who was humble, charitable, and especially loving toward children, but he was also possessed of great moral and religious intensity. This disciplined fervor was an excellent example of Stoic tranquillity, which is not simply the absence of feeling but the presence of principled moral and religious tension (*tonos*).

The facts that Epictetus was lame much of his life (some say because of maltreatment when he was a slave) and was for so long a slave have led some commentators to see him as somebody whose only motto was "Anechou kai apechou" ("Bear and forbear"). Indeed, there is in his philosophy a large amount of submissiveness to the inexorable, of seeing all events in a total view and as God's gifts. He was not a political or even a religious activist, as were Zeno and Cleanthes in the early Stoa, and he was not a poised gentleman and a political leader, as was Panaetius in the middle Stoa; he accepted the religion and government of his day without much criticism.

But all of this is only one pole of Epictetus' philosophy, as it is only one pole of the Stoic philosophy throughout its history. Epictetus was a moral activist, insisting on rigorous, continuing moral instruction and effort. Thus, he required daily self-examination, whose ultimate purpose was to learn how to judge one's actions clearly and firmly;

he wanted each man to see that he alone was totally responsible for his deeds because he had given his assent to the external circumstances of the deed. The faculty of choice and refusal, the power to use our external impressions, was of immense importance in his philosophy; it was a power even Zeus himself could not interfere with, as Epictetus tells us in the *Discourses*. And when a man finds a fault in his way of using external circumstances, he must root out that fault as ruthlessly and as promptly as a surgeon roots out a dangerous growth. With all his submissiveness Epictetus was one of the great defenders of the *prosopon*, or proper character and personality of a man. He insisted that each man was free to mold it and had an obligation to the rest of the world to display it once it was molded.

Epictetus was in many respects very close to the Cynics, the proletariat, as E. V. Arnold puts it, of the Greek world, who thought of men as citizens of the universe, not products of local convention, who practiced and preached a simple personal life, and who praised and exemplified *autarkeia*, the independence of the virtuous man from external circumstances. And he shared the Cynics' disdain for theory, though he did not fly in the face of convention and law as they did, nor was he as severe in his asceticism as some of the early Cynics were.

Since Epictetus did not publish anything (in this, as in other things, imitating Socrates), we are confined to the class notes of his pupil Flavius Arrianus, taken in Koine Greek, though Epictetus gave them in Attic. One will not find in these notes the typical Stoic emphasis upon system. The *Discourses* and *Manual* Arrianus recorded, did not constitute the texts for formal instruction of the school. The result, however, is felicitous; the *prosopon* of Epictetus himself, with its moral power and personal gentleness, emerges as perhaps the most important lesson he taught.

Bibliography

Epictetus, translated by W. A. Oldfather, 2 vols. (New York, 1926–1928), is the best edition and one of the best translations into English.

E. V. Arnold, *Roman Stoicism* (London, 1958), is especially informative on Epictetus. See also his article "Epictetus," in James Hastings, ed., *Encyclopedia of Religion and Ethics* (Edinburgh, 1937); this is an excellent article, although it is marred by too heavy an emphasis on Epictetus' doctrine of submissiveness.

A. F. Bonhöffer, *Epiktet und die Stoa* (Stuttgart, 1890), is a crucial work on Epictetus which should be translated into English. It shows how close to the early Stoa Epictetus was in some ways.

PHILIP P. HALLIE

EPICUREANISM AND THE EPICUREAN SCHOOL. The Epicureans perpetuated their founder's teaching with little change. Of Epicurus' immediate circle, the most distinguished was Metrodorus of Lampsacus (c. 330–277 B.C.), who predeceased his master. Metrodorus was elevated by Epicurus to a position of eminence—he alone shared the appellation "wise" (*sophos*), and his works were regarded as authoritative statements of doctrine. He wrote on epistemology, ethics, religion, poetry, and rhetoric, and he composed polemics against Plato's *Gorgias* and *Euthyphro*, and against Democritus.

Colotes of Lampsacus, another member of the original circle, published a comprehensive refutation of other schools under the title "That the Doctrines of the Other Philosophers Actually Make Life Impossible." Our knowledge of it comes from Plutarch's *Reply to Colotes*. His other writings included attacks on Plato's *Lysis* and *Euthydemus* and on the myth of Er in the *Republic*.

Hermarchus of Mytilene (325–c. 250 B.C.) was Epicurus' successor as head of the school. His chief work, in 22 books, was on Empedocles. He also wrote on the arts (including rhetoric), attacked Plato and Aristotle, and left a collection of letters.

Polystratus succeeded Hermarchus. Two of his works have been recovered in part from the library at Herculaneum; the better preserved is "On Unreasonable Contempt for Popular Opinion."

In the second and first centuries B.C. the school continued to flourish. One member, Philonides, enjoyed the friendship of Antiochus Epiphanes (king of Syria, 175–164 B.C.) and attained some standing as a mathematician. Later in the second century Zeno of Sidon lectured in Athens on logic, rhetoric, poetry, and mathematics; and he introduced into his ethical teaching many of the commonplaces of the popular moral essays developed by rival schools, including the use of moral examples drawn from literary sources. Zeno's older contemporary, Demetrius of Laconia, also composed popular moral essays and wrote on logic and poetics. These men's rivals were chiefly Stoics, and under the pressure of controversy they occasionally gave new formulations to Epicurean teaching. Whether they were concerned to any great extent with the atomic theory is uncertain; it appears that they did align themselves more closely than did their predecessors with the traditions of Greek *paideia*, perhaps for the added prestige it gave them as they spread their doctrine to the east and west. (Both Zeno and Demetrius counted Romans among their students.) Yet there were a few diehards; one of the rare schisms in the school developed over the question of whether rhetoric is an art. The use of literary embellishment as a means of persuasion was contrary to the principles of the strict Epicureans, who seem to have been influenced by Plato's *Gorgias*. Yet one group accepted epideictic oratory as a legitimate pursuit.

In the first half of the first century B.C. Philodemus of Gadara (in Syria), who had attended the lectures of Zeno in Athens, founded at Naples an Epicurean group with liberal tendencies. The Epicurean library at Herculaneum has yielded extensive passages from his many writings, which included moral treatises, biographies of philosophers, a history of the philosophical schools, and such polemical works as "On the Gods" and *On Methods of Inference*. Among his followers were persons of considerable eminence, notably Piso Caesoninus, Roman consul in 58 B.C., who was his principal patron. To such as these, we may suppose, he addressed "On Wealth," "On the Management of Property," and "On the Good King in Homer." This last piece is remarkable, not so much for its concern with a political matter (Epicurus had written "On Kingship") as for its use of Homer as an authority. (The Epicureans' rejection of the traditional Greek education led them to minimize the importance of the Homeric poems and to challenge the wisdom of Homer.)

Philodemus' treatises "On Rhetoric," "On Poems," and "On Music" were orthodox to the extent of maintaining that these arts are not suitable media for philosophical teaching or moral training; yet Philodemus conceded to them a positive value as art forms. Indeed, he himself had literary pretensions and composed a number of short poems. As a philosopher he won a qualified respect from Cicero. With Siro, his colleague, he attracted to the school a group of young Latin poets, among them Vergil; there is, however, no evidence to connect the school at Naples with the Roman Epicurean Lucretius (see LUCRETIUS).

Under the empire the Epicureans, true to their own precept, withdrew from public view. The last conspicuous member of the school was Diogenes of Oenoanda (a town in Lycia), who about A.D. 200 published the wisdom of Epicurus for his fellow townsmen by having a number of Epicurean writings inscribed on a wall at the entrance to the town. Most of the texts, apparently, he composed himself; two are on natural science, the remainder on ethics. He also included some of Epicurus' sayings and a letter from Epicurus to his mother.

Bibliography

A. Koerte, "Metrodori Epicurei Fragmenta," in *Jahrbücher für classische Philologie*, Supplementband 17 (1890), 531–570, assembles the ancient evidence about Metrodorus' life and writings. W. Croenert, *Kolotes und Menedemos* (Leipzig, 1906), includes the evidence relating to Colotes and contains an account of Zeno of Sidon's work.

For information on Hermarchus, see K. Krohn, *Der Epikureer Hermarchos* (Berlin, 1921). See also *Polystrati Epicurei Peri Alogou Kataphroneseos*, C. Wilke, ed. (Leipzig, 1905), which is the Greek text of Polystratus' "On Unreasonable Contempt for Popular Opinion." For a study of the life and works of Philonides, see W. Croenert, "Der Epikureer Philonides," in *Sitzungsberichte der preussischen Akademie der Wissenschaften* (Berlin, 1900), pp. 942–959.

For further literature on Demetrius of Laconia, see V. de Falco, *L'Epicureo Demetrio Lacone* (Naples, 1923). R. Philippson, "Philodemos," in Pauly-Wissowa, *Realencyclopädie der classischen Altertumswissenschaft*, Vol. 19, 2444–2482, contains a general account of Philodemus' life and work. C. O. Brink, "Neoptolemus of Parium," in *Horace on Poetry* (Cambridge, 1963), Ch. 1, discusses Philodemus' "On Poems." His poems were edited by G. Kaibel, *Philodemi Gadarensis Epigrammata* (Greifswald, 1885),

A. Grilli, *Diogenis Oenoandensis Fragmenta* (Milan, 1960), contains the fragments recovered from Diogenes' wall.

G. D. Hadzsits, *Lucretius and His Influence* (London, 1935), is a general survey of the influence of Epicurean ideas, especially in postclassical times.

P. H. DE LACY

EPICURUS (341 B.C.–270 B.C.) was born of Athenian parents on the island of Samos. At an early age he began his philosophical studies on the islands of the Aegean and the coast of Asia Minor, where he encountered followers of Plato and Democritus. He first taught at Mytilene, on Lesbos, about 311 B.C.; soon he moved to Lampsacus, a city on the Hellespont, where he recruited a loyal following that included several future leaders of the Epicurean school. In 307–306 B.C. he established at Athens an Epicurean community called the Garden. It was the center of his activity until his death.

The Garden became the prototype of Epicurean groups. Its members included women and at least one slave. The retirement in which the Epicureans lived and their acceptance even of *hetaerae* (courtesans) into their circle exposed them to the ridicule and abuse of their opponents. Yet even their enemies granted a grudging admiration to their cultivation of friendship. Something of Epicurus' affection for his followers and their veneration of him can be gathered from the extant fragments of his extensive correspondence. After his death his school celebrated his memory at a monthly feast, and his teaching spread rapidly through the Greek-speaking world.

Three letters containing summaries of Epicurean doctrine have been preserved in Diogenes Laërtius' *Life of Epicurus* (Book x of the *Lives*): *To Herodotus,* on the atomic theory; *To Pythocles,* on astronomy and meteorology; and *To Menoeceus,* on ethics. Diogenes also preserved a collection of forty *Kuriai Doxai (Cardinal Tenets)*, presumably formulated by Epicurus for the guidance of his followers. Epicurus' many other writings, now lost, included *Symposium* (a dialogue), *On the Gods, On the Highest Good, Canon* (on the criterion of truth), and, most important of all, *Peri Physeos (On Nature)*, in 37 books. Fragments of *On Nature* have been recovered from the charred remnants of an Epicurean library at Herculaneum, buried by the eruption of Vesuvius in A.D. 79; they can now be conveniently consulted in Arrighetti's *Epicuro*.

THE PHILOSOPHY OF EPICURUS

Epicurus' system, like his Garden, undertook to establish something sure and secure in a world of uncertainty. The social and political changes that followed the death of Alexander had their counterpart in the artistic and intellectual life of Greece; a new skepticism was challenging old ideals and institutions. Epicurus' aim was to build his system on a firm foundation that made no concessions either to skepticism or to idealism. He found his point of departure in the incontestability of immediate experience. Sense data are "true" because they are the ultimate evidence to which all questions must be referred; to question them is to make life itself impossible. The feelings of pleasure and pain that accompany sense experiences are

the ultimate good and evil; all statements about good and evil are meaningful only by reference to these feelings.

Theory of knowledge. The Epicureans gave the name "canonic" to their theory of knowledge. Knowledge arises from sense experience on several levels. First, repeated experiences preserved by memory give rise to "anticipations" (*prolepseis*), which are equivalent to general notions or concepts. These *prolepseis* make possible the use of language; when we hear the word *man* we "anticipate" the kind of object to which the name refers. The *prolepseis* thus classify experiences and fix the limits of variation. The *prolepsis* of man, for instance, is broad enough to include all sorts of men but excludes cattle, trees, gods, etc. And since our *prolepseis* merely register the similarities and differences found in immediate experience, they are themselves "true" and may be used as criteria. Thus Epicurus set up a correspondence among words, notions, and the data of experience without invoking Platonic ideas or Aristotelian essences and accidents. In general, he had little use for logic. We do not need to define words in order to exploit their "natural" meaning, and analysis of the formal aspects of language and thought tells us nothing. No less alien to philosophical inquiry is the language of poetry and myth, which obscures meaning and confuses thought.

Once we are equipped with *prolepseis* we can proceed to form opinions. The truth of opinions is tested in two ways: Where the opinion is about something by nature observable but removed in time or space, the test is verification by actual inspection. Where the opinion is about something by nature unobservable (*physei adelon*), the test is absence of conflict with observable things; if this absence of conflict is such that the denial of a judgment about the unobservable (*adelon*) is incompatible with the data of experience, then the judgment must be true.

Physics. The basic propositions of Epicurean physics are by this means established as necessarily true. Nothing comes from nothing, and nothing returns to nothing; for the denial of these propositions would remove all restraints on what can happen, and the very persistence of uniform patterns in observable similarities and differences is incompatible with the abolition of restraints. Persistence of patterns, in turn, implies some persisting entity, and as the components of experience are all subject to change, there must be something nonexperienceable that is impervious to change. But since changes do occur, the persisting entities must be multiple and capable of interaction. They are, therefore, bodies, for only bodies can act and be acted upon. Bodies interact, moreover, only by blows and rebounds, for they can affect each other only by contact; they have no power of attraction or other means of acting at a distance. How Epicurus defended this last principle we do not know. It created great difficulties for him, for instance, in the explanation of magnets. The physician Asclepiades (first century B.C.), who was influenced by Epicurean atomism, experienced similar difficulty in his physiology, in explaining the function of the kidneys, for example (see Galen, *Natural Faculties*, i.13). Opponents, notably Galen, made much of these difficulties.

Thus Epicurus built his atomic theory, shaping it by reference to the demands of the phenomena it was to explain and overriding theoretical difficulties by appeal to experience. The atoms have parts because they are extended, but they must not be infinitely divisible if they are to provide a secure foundation for the world we know. They lack sensible qualities (colors, tastes, and the like) but produce these qualities by their combinations. Such qualities do not exist per se; they belong either permanently (as properties) or temporarily (as accidents) to atomic compounds. They are, however, no less real than the atoms, for there are no degrees of reality. Life, consciousness, and the flow of experience are as real as the atoms whose movements produce them. Time is an accident of the moving and changing objects that we see around us. Space, however, exists per se, since change requires that the atoms move, and movement requires empty space. The uniformities of experience put limitations on atomic movement, but these limitations must not be so severe that they produce a completely determined system, for experience is not completely determined. The source of indeterminacy is the "swerve" of atoms, a doctrine that accounts also for the crossing of their paths, for by nature they fall downward at a uniform speed. (The atomic swerve is not mentioned in the extant fragments of Epicurus; it is attested to by Lucretius, in *On the Nature of Things,* ii.216–293; and by Philodemus, in *On Methods of Inference,* col. xxxvi.13; cf. Usener, *Epicurea,* pp. 199–201.) Experience sets no limits to space and time; the supply of atoms, then, must also be limitless if they are not to be separated from each other by infinite distances. But the varieties of atoms and their ability to combine must be limited. Most of Epicurus' departures from the atomism of Democritus arose from such considerations as these, inspired in large part by Aristotle's criticisms of Democritus (see, for example, *De Caelo* iii.4 [303a19–20] on the need for limiting the kinds of atoms).

The infinite supply of atoms moving in infinite space and time has formed every possible combination, however rare. Everything possible is somewhere actual; indeed, Romano Amerio has suggested, in *L'Epicureismo* (Turin, 1953, pp. 42–44), that the Epicurean doctrine of *isonomia* (equilibrium) rests on the principle that in an infinity of space and time it is not possible to say that any one kind of event occurs more often than any other. The number of coexistent universes is infinite because there is nothing to prevent this (*To Herodotus,* 45). And there is nothing to prevent the existence of innumerable gods, for the gods are compounded of atoms, situated in the intervals between the universes and living forever in a state of supreme bliss because they possess the wisdom and power to protect themselves against all disturbances.

The close tie between the actual and the possible serves also as a principle of method: the actual defines the limits of the possible. The Epicureans recognized that our human experience does not exhaust the range of the actual, and the very variety we observe points to further variety beyond. Other universes need not be exactly like ours. But on another level experience does set limits. It is not possible (to use Lucretian examples) for an animal to be half horse and half man, for a tree to grow in the sky, or for a man to be large enough to wade across the sea.

Changes in the combinations of atoms occur in regular sequences, such as the life cycle of an animal and the disintegration of a universe. These sequences constitute a principle of order: no event occurs apart from the series of events that prepare for it. It is the task of the sciences to discover these sequences, for they provide the causal explanation of all that occurs. The philosopher does not need to know the complete details of a chain of events so long as he knows that it occurs according to fixed principles, that there is no hierarchy of ends or final cause, and that no divine agent guides events or interferes with their course. The existence of evil in the universe is sufficient refutation of the doctrine of an omnipotent and beneficent deity.

When the precise cause of an event cannot be discovered, no possible cause can be rejected. Alternate explanations, therefore, may be entertained, and every possible cause is somewhere operative, if not in our universe then in some other. For the most part the Epicureans used multiple explanations in areas where close observation was not possible, for example, meteorology. Because of their relative indifference to specific details of natural processes, the Epicureans failed to exploit the scientific advances being made in their own times, especially in astronomy and physiology.

Man. The human organism, for Epicurus, is composed of atoms undergoing characteristic patterns of change. Body and soul are interdependent; neither can survive without the other. The soul's atoms are of four kinds. Three are the same as the atoms that constitute air, wind, and heat; the fourth, the smallest and most mobile, is *sui generis* and nameless. That part of the soul which transmits sensation is spread throughout the body; that which thinks and feels is centered in the region of the heart. There is no nonempirical self. All functions of the human organism are the results of atomic processes. Sight, for example, is caused by atomic films separating from the surfaces of objects and entering the eye. Films of very fine texture, such as those emitted by the gods, are able to impress the mind directly, without the agency of a sense organ. Films that have become scrambled in transit and no longer correspond to stable physical objects account for dreams and fantasies.

Like all other atomic compounds, men come into being when the necessary conditions have been met. They have no creator and no destiny. Their good is pleasure, their highest good a life of secure and lasting pleasure. United by no bond of nature, they form alliances for mutual advantage, and they acquiesce in the restraints of law and government as a protection against injury by their fellows. These measures, however, do not achieve a good life, because of men's false opinions. Men's empty fears of the gods and of death destroy their peace of mind, and in pursuing wealth, power, and fame they seek security where it cannot be found.

Ethical doctrines. The good life is attainable only by the philosopher. The immediate experience of pleasure, although good in itself, does not bring with it a guarantee of permanence. Intelligent choice is also needed, and practical wisdom (*phronesis*), Epicurus said, is more to be prized than philosophy itself. Practical wisdom measures pleasures against pains, accepting pains that lead to greater pleasures and rejecting pleasures that lead to greater pains. It counts the traditional virtues (justice, temperance, courage, etc.) among the means for attaining the pleasant life; they have no other justification.

The philosopher distinguishes further between "kinetic" pleasures (for example, eating choice foods), which attend on a motion and cease when the motion ceases, and "catastematic" pleasures (for example, not being hungry), which arise from a state, or stable condition, and are capable of indefinite prolongation. The good life requires catastematic pleasures; kinetic pleasures are mere embroidery. The mind as well as the body has its kinetic and catastematic pleasures. The pleasures of the mind are related more or less directly to physical sensations (a doctrine cited by opposing schools in support of the charge of sensualism); it feels *chara*, delight (a kinetic pleasure), at the well-being of the body, and with the removal of pains and cares it enjoys *ataraxia*, peace of mind (its catastematic pleasure). Peace of mind is achieved when the study of natural philosophy has removed fear of the gods, when death is recognized to be merely the limit of experience and therefore irrelevant to the quality of experience, and when the gratification of desires that go beyond what is necessary and natural is seen to result in greater pains than pleasures.

The mind has also the role of building up a reserve of pleasure to be used as a protection against the onslaughts of fortune. The body lives in the present, but the mind, through memory and expectation, contemplates also the past and the future. Furthermore, the mind is able to select the objects of its attention. The wise man stores up the memory of past pleasures and looks forward to pleasures to come. With such resources he overcomes present distress, as Epicurus overcame the suffering of his final illness with the memory of past conversations with his friends.

Way of life. Thus Epicureanism becomes a way of life, with a set of prescriptions for the guidance of the initiates. Epicurus rejected much of traditional education. Geometry does not describe the world as we actually experience it, and rhetoric is an abuse of language. Music and poetry are not fit subjects even for an after-dinner conversation, and happiness does not depend on knowing what side Hector fought on. Epicurus also warned against the assumption of heavy responsibilities and serious involvements, whether public or private, and praised the life that escapes men's notice. These negative features no doubt repelled the intellectual and social elite, but they put the Epicurean life within the reach of the much wider circle of persons who did not enjoy the advantages of wealth, station, and education. To such as these Epicurus recommended the suppression of desires that go beyond natural needs, the cultivation of friendship, the enjoyment of carefree pleasures, and even attendance at religious festivals in order to remind themselves of that complete tranquillity of which the gods are the perfect exemplars.

Texts and Fragments From Epicurus

Arrighetti, G., ed., *Epicuro, Opere*. Turin, 1960. Contains, along with older material, the first complete collection of the papyrus fragments of Epicurus' *On Nature*. With Italian translation, notes, and a partial *index verborum*.

Bailey, C., ed., *Epicurus, the Extant Remains*. Oxford, 1926. A smaller collection than Usener's (see below), but including the *Vatican Fragments*, discovered soon after Usener's book was published. Bailey supplies an English translation and commentary.

Diano, C., ed., *Epicuri Ethica*. Florence, 1946. An important collection, incorporating material from papyri and from Diogenes of Oenoanda, as well as the *Vatican Fragments*. Contains a useful commentary and a partial *index verborum*.

Usener, H., ed., *Epicurea*. Leipzig, 1887. Still the basic collection of Greek and Latin texts bearing on Epicurus and his school. It contains 607 numbered fragments and much more that is unnumbered.

General Accounts of Epicurean Philosophy

Bailey, C., *The Greek Atomists and Epicurus*. Oxford, 1928. A fundamental work.

Bignone, E., *L'Aristotele perduto e la formazione filosofica di Epicuro*, 2 vols. Florence, 1936. A revolutionary work, portraying Epicureanism as directed primarily against the Platonism of Aristotle's early dialogues, as reconstructed by W. Jaeger.

Cornford, F. M., *Principium Sapientiae*, W. K. C. Guthrie, ed. Cambridge, 1952. The chapter "Epicurus" (pp. 12–30) stresses the deficiencies of Epicureanism viewed as a scientific system.

DeWitt, N. W., *Epicurus and His Philosophy*. Minneapolis, 1954. A sympathetic and at times extravagant account, emphasizing Epicurus' saintly character and his opposition to Platonism.

Festugière, A. J., *Epicurus and His Gods*, translated by C. W. Chilton. Oxford, 1955. A perceptive and rather sympathetic study of Epicurean ethics and religion.

Kleve, Knut, *Gnosis Theon: Die Lehre von der natürlichen Gotteserkenntnis in der epikureischen Theologie*. Symbolae Osloenses Fasc. Supplet. XIX. Oslo, 1963. A careful examination of a problem much discussed in recent years: how the Epicureans explained, in terms of their theory of knowledge, men's knowledge of the gods.

Schmid, W., "Epikur." *Reallexikon für Antike und Christentum*, Vol. 5 (1961), 681–819. An authoritative article, with extensive bibliography. Especially good on the fortunes of Epicureanism in the early Christian period.

P. H. DE LACY

EPISTEMOLOGY. In addition to the long survey article EPISTEMOLOGY, HISTORY OF, the Encyclopedia contains the following articles on topics of epistemology: ANALYTIC AND SYNTHETIC STATEMENTS; APPERCEPTION; A PRIORI AND A POSTERIORI STATEMENTS; BASIC STATEMENTS; CATEGORIES; CAUSATION; CERTAINTY; COHERENCE THEORY OF TRUTH; COMMON SENSE; CONCEPT; CONTINGENT AND NECESSARY STATEMENTS; CORRESPONDENCE THEORY OF TRUTH; CRITERION; CRITICAL REALISM; DOUBT; EMPIRICISM; EPISTEMOLOGY AND ETHICS, PARALLEL BETWEEN; ERROR; EXPERIENCE; HEAT, SENSATIONS OF; IDEALISM; IDEAS; ILLUSIONS; IMAGINATION; INDEXICAL SIGNS, EGOCENTRIC PARTICULARS, AND TOKEN-REFLEXIVE WORDS; INNATE IDEAS; INTENTIONALITY; INTUITION; IRRATIONALISM; KNOWLEDGE AND BELIEF; LINGUISTIC THEORY OF THE A PRIORI; MEMORY; MUST; NEW REALISM; OTHER MINDS; PARADIGM-CASE ARGUMENT; PERCEPTION; PERFORMATIVE THEORY OF TRUTH; PHENOMENALISM; PHENOMENOLOGY; POSSIBILITY; PRAGMATIC THEORY OF TRUTH; PRECOGNITION; PRESUPPOSING; PRIMARY AND SECONDARY QUALITIES; PRIVATE LANGUAGE PROBLEM; PROPER NAMES AND DESCRIPTIONS; PROPO-

SITIONS, JUDGMENTS, SENTENCES, AND STATEMENTS; PSYCHOLOGISM; RATIONALISM; REALISM; REASON; REASONS AND CAUSES; RELATIONS, INTERNAL AND EXTERNAL; SELF-PREDICTION; SENSA; SENSATIONALISM; SKEPTICISM; SOLIPSISM; SOUND; THINKING; TIME, CONSCIOUSNESS OF; TOUCH; UNIVERSALS, and VISION.

EPISTEMOLOGY AND ETHICS, PARALLEL BETWEEN.

Usually, actions are taken and policies adopted to realize evisaged goals, and they are undertaken because of belief that they will probably realize the goals. Actions and policies may be criticized, then, on one of two grounds: that the goals are ill-chosen or that the belief that the actions or policies will probably achieve the goals is ill-founded. It is interesting, and perhaps indicative of the facts to be examined below, that many words of appraisal—such as "justified," "warranted," "reasonable," "right"—are used, although possibly in slightly different senses, to indicate the acceptability or unacceptability of both goals and beliefs. Moreover, such appraisals obviously have two features in common. First, the appraisal of a particular goal or belief can be made only in view of some general principle or standard; second, the standards and principles in question are not self-certifying, and their rational justification must be a serious question for a thoughtful person. The appraisal of actions and policies thus raises two questions about both goals and beliefs: What are the proper principles or standards to be used in appraisals, and what is the rational basis for regarding any principle or standard as proper?

Historically, ethics has been the philosophical discipline concerned with these two questions about goals. (However, "goals" must be taken broadly to include not only the question of ultimate values but also the question of moral obligations and moral rights.) And historically, epistemology has been the discipline concerned with the same questions about beliefs. (Again, "beliefs" must be taken broadly to go beyond mere predictions of consequences of the use of certain means to include theories, explanations, and systems of mathematical thought.)

In order to develop the parallel between ethics and epistemology, it is convenient to identify ethical and epistemological statements. Ethical statements are those that imply a statement that could be expressed by some English sentence containing essentially "is a good thing that," "is a better thing," or "is morally obligatory that" (on the assumption that "morally obligatory" does not introduce special concepts different from a phrase such as "it is morally wrong not to"). The class of statements thus specified will be identical with the class of statements that moral philosophers have traditionally been concerned with. Similarly, epistemological statements are those that imply a statement which could be expressed by some English sentence containing essentially "It is reasonable (or warranted) for a person S to place more confidence in h than in i," in which it is understood that for h and i can be substituted expressions of the form "its being true that . . . ." The class of statements thus specified is identical with the class of statements that epistemologists have been concerned with. It is useful to identify as ethical terms those phrases whose occurrence in a sentence distinguish it as an ethical statement and to identify as epistemic terms those phrases whose occurrence in a sentence characterize it as an epistemological statement.

Problem of ethics and epistemology. Moral philosophers have not, at least qua moral philosophers, been concerned with the acceptability of particular ethical statements such as "It would be a good thing if Jones learned to play the piano." Rather, moral philosophers have attempted to arrive at acceptable universal ethical statements which could serve as standards for the appraisal of particular situations. Thus, moral philosophers have defended or criticized such statements as "Enjoyment is always a good thing, abstracted from all consideration of consequences; nothing else is so" and "An action is morally right if and only if it will produce consequences as good as those of any other action the agent could have performed instead." The formulation of such generalizations, together with the proposal of reasons in support of them, is generally called normative ethics. Like moral philosophers, epistemologists are not concerned with the acceptability of particular epistemological statements such as "It is now highly probable that viruses are the cause of some forms of cancer." Instead, they have attempted to arrive at acceptable universal epistemological statements to be used as standards in appraising particular statements. Thus, they have examined the acceptability of such statements as "If at a time t person S seems to remember that he had the experience E at an earlier time, then he is initially warranted in believing that he did have the experience E" or "If at time t person S believes the statement h about his own experience at t, then it is reasonable for S to place at least as much confidence in h as in any other statement." The formulation of statements like these and the proposal of reasons in support of them have traditionally been the main occupation of epistemologists. In order to distinguish this task from other concerns of epistemologists, we may call it epistemology proper.

Some minor points of similarity. If it is morally wrong for a person to take action A, but he takes that action, then in the absence of any excuse we attribute to him a fault of character and say he is morally blameworthy. Similarly, if a person has good reason for believing a certain statement but he doesn't, then in the absence of any good excuse we attribute to him an intellectual fault and characterize him as intellectually open to criticism. (The excuse in either case might be much the same; for instance, a person might plead that he was very upset, not "himself.") It is sometimes said that the parallel extends further in another direction, that just as there are several senses of "morally obligated," so there are corresponding senses of "reasonable to believe." For instance, it is widely believed that "morally obligatory" is sometimes used to mean the act which a being omniscient about the facts of the case and about moral principles would be morally blameworthy for not doing if he were in the place of the agent; this is said to be a sense of "morally obligatory" different from that employed when a person with possibly faulty information about the facts and imperfect clarity about moral principles is said to be morally obligated to do something. Correspondingly, it is sometimes suggested that there is a sense of "reasonable to believe" in which we may say that it is reasonable for a person to believe that any statement is *true;* this sense is contrasted with the sense in which we say it is reasonable for a man to believe what is supported by the evidence he has. Whether there are such different senses in either case we must leave an open question here.

Epistemology reducible to ethics? Some philosophers (R. M. Chisholm, for example) have thought that there is more than just a parallel between epistemology and ethics. They have thought that epistemic terms are properly defined by means of ethical terms. If this is correct, epistemological statements are complicated ethical statements, and, presumably, epistemology is a branch—doubtless a somewhat special one—of ethics. In accordance with this view, for example, the statement "It is warranted for *S* to place more confidence in *h* than *i*" might be taken to mean "For any good thing *G*, if *S* had to choose between risking it by a wager on the truth of *h* or risking it by a wager on the truth of *i*, he would be obligated to wager on *h*." If sound, this definition has the advantage of reducing the number of undefined terms in one's total system of concepts. The disadvantages of the definition are (1) that it is doubtful whether there is any useful sense of "obligated" in which the implied equivalence is true, (2) that the definition seems to be more obscure than the definiendum, and (3) that it does not seem that the meaning of "warranted belief" involves the notion of moral obligation but, conversely, that a person's being obligated to do something, in one ordinary sense, can be explained only by reference to the propositions it is reasonable for him to believe about his situation.

Theories of meaning and verification. If epistemology is not reducible to ethics, there is still a parallel between the higher-order questions and theories to which epistemology proper leads and those to which normative ethics leads. The discipline dealing with these epistemological questions and corresponding to the discipline of metaethics we may call metaepistemology. The central question of these disciplines, roughly, is how the statements of normative ethics and epistemology proper, respectively, can be supported, what is their "logic." The task of showing this is different, of course, from the task of producing a specific line of reasoning in support of specific ethical or epistemological principles. Can such principles be supported in the same way that propositions in the empirical and mathematical sciences can be? Whether they can be depends in part on what the meanings of the special epistemological or ethical terms are. Moral philosophers recognize three main views about the meaning of ethical terms and, correspondingly, about the ways in which ethical principles may be justified. Three very similar views have been given by epistemologists for the meaning and support of epistemological principles.

Nonnaturalism. The first view, which we may call nonnaturalism in epistemology and ethics alike, affirms two things. It affirms (1) that epistemic and ethical terms are meaningful and that epistemological and ethical statements are true or false and (2) that epistemic and ethical terms do not name observable qualities (such as color or shape) and that their meanings cannot be defined, even partially, by citing a relation between them and names of observable qualities. Epistemic and ethical terms can be explained only by way of other epistemic and ethical

terms. Hence, neither epistemic nor ethical principles can be confirmed by observation in the way that principles in the empirical sciences can be. This means that when we know ethical and epistemological statements that are not analytically true (as contrasted with ones like "A person ought to do his duty" or "One cannot know something unless it is reasonable for him to believe it"), our knowledge is synthetic a priori knowledge. A clear example of this view is the theory of probability held by J. M. Keynes, who thought that "probable" is an indefinable concept and that the axioms of probability theory are a priori synthetic knowledge.

Naturalism. The second view can be called naturalism or "definism." It agrees with the first affirmation of nonnaturalism but denies the second. It holds that epistemic and ethical terms can be explained without the use of other epistemic or ethical terms, that they can be explained exclusively by use of empirical and logical concepts. As a result it holds that nonanalytic epistemological and ethical principles have the same logical status as the principles of the empirical sciences and can be appraised ultimately by reference to the data of observation or introspection. For example, according to one such definition of an epistemic term, the statement "It is reasonable for *S* to believe *h*" means just "*S* believes *h*." A more plausible theory defines "know" as follows: "*S* knows that *h* at time *t*" means that *h* follows logically from the propositions *S* believes about his own experience at *t* (including what he seems to remember), plus the following (enumerated) principles of inductive logic and principles about the truth or probability of memory beliefs. Examples of parallel definitions in ethical naturalism are familiar. If the second definition given were accepted, it would be an analytic proposition that the principles of deductive and inductive logic are known by everyone, just as, given a utilitarian definition of "right," the principle of utilitarianism is analytic. Parallel to the claim of the ethical relativist that conflicting basic ethical principles may be affirmed with equal warrant by different persons or social groups, is it possible that conflicting basic epistemological principles may also be affirmed with equal warrant by different persons, even if a naturalistic analysis of epistemological terms is adopted? For instance, just as the ethical relativist may affirm that different assessments of the ethical obligation of making a promise may be made with equal warrant by different persons, may someone claim with reason that different assessments, say, of the weight of an additional observation in support of some general law may be made with equal warrant by different persons? Such questions must be left unanswered here. It is obvious, of course, that given different evidence, it may be reasonable for a person *S* to believe some propositions which it would be unreasonable for person *S'* to believe.

Noncognitivism. The third view, which may be called noncognitivism, denies the thesis common to naturalism and nonnaturalism that epistemological and ethical statements are true or false but agrees with nonnaturalism that epistemic and ethical terms cannot be defined by means of empirical and logical concepts. Noncognitivism holds, however, that epistemic and ethical terms have a function and, in a sense, ideas in meaning. Ethical terms have been assigned various functions by different writers (functions like expressing the speaker's attitudes, changing the audience's attitudes, issuing prescriptions, declaring one's principles, giving advice, entreating, urging, exhorting, and so on). Somewhat similar proposals have been made for epistemic terms. "It is probable that *h*," for example, is sometimes said to be a guarded way of affirming *h* or a cautious way of encouraging others to believe *h*. Again, "it is probable that *h*" is suggested not to assert that the speaker believes *h* but to express his belief in *h*. A more complex suggestion is to say that "it is reasonable to believe *h*" declares or expresses the speaker's own somewhat guarded inclination to believe and usually, at the same time, as a result of people's conditioning in the use of the language, strengthens the beliefs of others in *h*. Further, parallel to ideas in C. L. Stevenson's ethical theory, one might say that epistemic terms also have some rather indefinite descriptive meaning, perhaps to the effect that acceptance of the proposition in question would conform to generally recognized standards—the standards, perhaps, of scientists. One could say, as P. H. Nowell-Smith does in his ethical theory, that epistemic terms have various functions in various contexts and that it is a mistake to look for some single function performed by them on every occasion. It could be added that the use of epistemic words (similar to the suggested parallel to Stevenson's theory) carries special contextual implications which distinguish them from nonepistemic terms. Since the noncognitivist does not think that epistemic and ethical statements are either true or false, his view does not contain any theory about how the truth of such statements may be established, although it often contains a descriptive account of various ways in which persons do or could try sensibly, in view of the kind of statement in question, to remove their disagreements. Defenders of the noncognitive view in epistemology include R. M. Chisholm, Stephen Toulmin, and J. N. Findlay. Although they have been popular, noncognitive views, in epistemology and ethics alike, appear to face some difficulties. (For instance, in conditional clauses, such as "If it were known that . . . , then . . ." or "If it were a good thing to . . . , then . . . ," the ethical and epistemological terms seem to be used in their normal sense, but obviously nothing is being urged or expressed. Again, whatever specific function one assigns to terms of either type, it seems possible to find affirmations which employ the terms and cannot plausibly be said to be performing that function.) Moreover, it is doubtful whether there are conclusive reasons for rejecting "definism" (naturalism) in all its possible forms.

Some broader perspectives. One feature of both ethical and epistemic terms is that even very educated people do not have any clear idea of their meaning or of how to support their applicability in, for example, the way they are able to support the assertion that someone is a bachelor. Nor is it clear how an appeal to whatever vague meaning there is could be used reasonably to require anyone, on pain of inconsistency, to accept a corresponding ethical or epistemological principle; the fact that a person rejected such a principle would always be good reason for saying that his use of the epistemic or ethical term does not correspond to the sense needed in order to require the principle. It would appear that one of the functions of moral philosophy and epistemology is, rather, to propose helpful and clarifying uses for these terms.

What would be a helpful and clarifying use for these terms must presumably be decided by a broad view of human nature and society, a view of action and the requirements of reliable prediction for the purpose of action, the need of informal social controls in a complex society, and the necessity for impartial and general rules for such control, given that human beings are for the most part intelligent, self-interested creatures. However this may be, it is likely that reflection on the functions of science (reasonable beliefs) and conscience in society may provide, in the case of science at least as well as in the case of ethics, a guide for the philosopher's reconstruction of the meaning of ethical and epistemic terms and a basis for the appraisal of epistemic and ethical principles.

It should be noted that metaethics and metaepistemology both have another part. That part is the explanation of various concepts necessary for the understanding of terms and statements of both epistemology and ethics and for an understanding of theories about how epistemological and ethical statements may be supported. Among the concepts that are epistemologically important are "meaning," "truth," "reference," "analytic," and "a priori." Some of these concepts are also important for ethics; other concepts important for ethics are "action," "choice," "free choice," "voluntary," "intention," "motive," and so on. Both metaethics and metaepistemology, then, have branches devoted to these auxiliary concepts.

If there is a parallel between ethics and epistemology, should we go on to say that there is a parallel between ethics and science since, after all, to assert any statement in science is at least to imply that there is evidence for what is stated, that it is generally known, and so on? Is not every scientific statement, at least covertly, an epistemological statement? It seems clarifying not to go this far. Epistemological statements are of the form "It is warranted for *S* to believe that . . . ," and we should note that what comes after the "that" is the sort of statement that occurs in the textbooks of science. If the meaning of this statement also has to be construed as somehow epistemological, difficulties arise.

Bibliography

Atkinson, R. F., "'Good' and 'Right' and 'Probable' in *Language, Truth and Logic*." *Mind*, Vol. 64 (1955), 242–246.

Austin, J. L., *Philosophical Papers*. Oxford, 1961. Pp. 67–71.

Chisholm, R. M., *Perceiving*. Ithaca, N.Y., 1957.

Chisholm, R. M., "Evidence as Justification." *Journal of Philosophy*, Vol. 68 (1961), 739–748.

Firth, R., and Chisholm, R. M., "Ultimate Evidence." *Journal of Philosophy*, Vol. 53 (1956), 722–739. A symposium.

Lewis, C. I., *The Ground and Nature of the Right*. New York, 1955. Chs. 2–3.

Toulmin, Stephen, "Probability," in A. G. N. Flew, ed., *Essays in Conceptual Analysis*. London, 1956.

Urmson, J..O., "Some Questions Concerning Validity," *ibid.*

RICHARD B. BRANDT

EPISTEMOLOGY, HISTORY OF. Epistemology, or the theory of knowledge, is that branch of philosophy which is concerned with the nature and scope of knowledge, its presuppositions and basis, and the general reliability of claims to knowledge. The pre-Socratic philosophers, the first philosophers in the Western tradition, did not give any fundamental attention to this branch of philosophy, for they were primarily concerned with the nature and possibility of change. They took it for granted that knowledge of nature was possible, although some of them suggested that knowledge of the structure of reality could better come from some sources than from others. Thus, Heraclitus emphasized the use of the senses, and Parmenides in effect stressed the role of reason. But none of them doubted that knowledge of reality was possible. It was not until the fifth century B.C. that such doubts began to emerge, and the Sophists were chiefly responsible for them.

During the fifth century B.C. human practices and institutions came under critical examination for the first time. Numerous things which had previously been thought to be part of nature were seen not to be. Thus, a general antithesis was drawn between nature and human convention or custom, and the question of where the line was to be drawn between them arose. The Sophists asked how much of what we think we know about nature is really an objective part of it and how much is contributed by the human mind. Indeed, do we have any knowledge of nature as it really is? Protagoras, for example, seems to have held, if Plato's report is to be believed, that everything is as it appears to a man, that appearances are the only reality. This is the meaning, or part of it, of his famous dictum "Man is the measure of all things." Gorgias was, if anything, more radical, claiming that there was no such thing as reality, that if there were, we could not know of it, and that even if we could know of it, we could not communicate our knowledge of it.

This general skepticism led to the beginning of epistemology as it has been traditionally known—the attempt to justify the claim that knowledge is possible and to assess the part played by the senses and reason in the acquisition of knowledge. Before Plato, Democritus, the Greek atomist, had already drawn a distinction between those properties ordinarily attributed to things which, in his view, really belong to them—for example, size and shape—and those which, as he put it, are a matter of convention (*nomos*), a function of the mind—for example, color. It was Plato, however, who can be said to be the real originator of epistemology, for he attempted to deal with the basic questions: What is knowledge? Where is knowledge generally found, and how much of what we ordinarily think we know is really knowledge? Do the senses provide knowledge? Can reason supply knowledge? What is the relation between knowledge and true belief?

THE NATURE OF EPISTEMOLOGY

Epistemology differs from psychology in that it is not concerned with why men hold the beliefs that they do or with the ways in which they come to hold them. Psychologists can, in principle, give explanations of why people hold the beliefs they do, but they are not necessarily competent, nor is it their province, to say whether the beliefs are based on good grounds or whether they are sound. The answer to these questions must be sought from those who

are experts within the branches of knowledge from which the beliefs are drawn. The mathematician can give the grounds for believing in the validity of Pythagoras' theorem, the physicist can give the grounds for believing in, say, the indeterminacy principle, and an ordinary but reliable witness can provide the grounds for believing in the occurrence of an accident. Normally, when the beliefs are true and the grounds sufficient, it is permissible to claim knowledge, and whether a particular truth can be said to be known may be determined by reference to the grounds which are appropriate to the field from which the truth is drawn. The epistemologist, however, is concerned not with whether or how we can be said to know some particular truth but with whether we are justified in claiming knowledge of some whole class of truths, or, indeed, whether knowledge is possible at all. The questions which he asks are therefore general in a way that questions asked within some one branch of knowledge are not.

Role of skepticism. To characterize the questions asked by the epistemologist as extremely general is not, however, sufficient. Interest in very general questions of this sort and in the nature of general concepts is typical of philosophy as a whole. What distinguishes epistemology other than the fact that its interests center on the concept of knowledge? When a philosopher asks whether something is possible, the question must be set against the consideration that this thing may not be possible. It must be set against a general skepticism concerning the matter in question. To be called upon to justify the possibility of knowledge or of certain kinds of knowledge makes sense only on the supposition that it or they may not be possible. It is no coincidence that epistemology began in the context of a form of the Sophists' general skepticism about knowledge, for until such doubts had been raised, the possibility of knowledge was bound to be taken for granted. Once the doubts had been raised, they had to be answered. How they were to be answered depended on the nature of the doubts and on the degree to which any particular philosopher was susceptible to them.

Views on the nature of knowledge. Perhaps the most characteristic form of skepticism about knowledge has been based upon the premise that we ought not to claim knowledge about anything unless we are absolutely sure about it, unless there is no possibility of our being wrong. Once given this, it is possible to point out that it is at least logically possible to be wrong about most, if not all, the things which we ordinarily claim to know. Philosophers who have been impressed by this argument have generally tried to show that there are at least some things that we can claim to know, about which we cannot be wrong. Even so, most of the things that we normally think we know cannot, on this view, be said to be known at all. This consequence can be mitigated, although not removed, if it can be shown that the things accepted as known in the strict sense give reasons for believing the things that we normally take ourselves to know. Philosophers who have taken this course have differed both on what this "certain knowledge" is and on how it is connected with what we ordinarily suppose ourselves to know. Rationalists have generally attempted to show that the primary truths that constitute this certain knowledge are related to other truths somewhat as the axioms of a formal or geometrical system are related to the theorems. Empiricists, on the other hand, have taken the view that the truths which constitute ordinary knowledge can be constructed out of the primary truths, as a building is built up from its foundations. They have differed again on the nature of the primary truths themselves. Rationalists have looked for them among the deliverances of reason, whereas empiricists have claimed that sense experience alone can provide such truths. Other philosophers have accepted part of the skeptical argument to the extent of denying the status of knowledge to some class of truths, reserving that status for some privileged class. Plato is a case in point in that for at least part of his life he maintained that sense experience never provides knowledge at all, this being reserved for a kind of awareness of or acquaintance with a world of quite distinct entities called Forms. In respect to the world of sense experience we have only opinion or supposition. This view of sense experience has not been uncommon among philosophers.

The concept of knowledge. A quite different way of dealing with the skeptical argument would be to question the initial premise that knowledge requires absolute certainty. One would not normally claim knowledge about something unless one were sure about it, but that is very different from asserting that a man could not be said to know something unless what he claimed to know was absolutely certain. Knowledge does not actually require this; it requires only that there be the best of grounds for what is claimed. To say this is to say something about what knowledge is, about the concept of knowledge itself. Hence, the skeptical arguments and the answers to them are not entirely independent of the conceptual question about the nature of knowledge. An understanding of the concept of knowledge is a prerequisite of embarking upon any attempt to answer other epistemological questions. Most philosophers have had something to say about the nature of knowledge, although many have taken its nature for granted. From this have stemmed a number of traditional epistemological difficulties.

GREEK PHILOSOPHY

Plato. Plato (c. 428–347 B.C.) was influenced by several views—the moral teaching and philosophical practices of his master Socrates, the views of the Sophists already mentioned, and such pre-Socratic views about the nature of reality as the Heraclitean view that the sensible world is in a state of flux and the Eleatic view that reality is one and unchanging. He came to·hold that reality cannot be changing or imperfect and that it must therefore consist of a world of Forms or Ideas independent of the sensible world. The exact reasons why Plato postulated a world of Forms are not altogether clear. But probably, as Aristotle says, he was influenced by Socrates' search for the essences of, for example, moral virtues. But because justice, for instance, is never found in this world in a proper and perfect form, he postulated its separate, ideal existence in order to provide the standard by which sensible instances of justice might be judged. The Forms might be known by reason, not by the senses. Whether there was a Form for

every sensible particular is arguable, with respect to Plato's earlier philosophy. However, it is clear at any rate that by the time he came to write the *Timaeus* he believed this to be the case. Thus, in the first place the Forms were probably standards or exemplars of which sensible things were imperfect copies. At the same time, however, they functioned as universals, entities meant to explain how it is possible to think generally about things of one kind and how it becomes possible to attach a meaning to common names. The fact that the Forms had to fill both these roles gave rise to certain logical difficulties which Plato himself pointed out in the dialogue *Parmenides* and which he tried to deal with in the later dialogues. The Forms were always objects of knowledge and, in his earlier thought, the *only* objects of knowledge. Sensible things were, in his view, objects of opinion only.

Knowledge and true belief. The distinction between knowledge and true belief is first made by Plato in the *Meno* in the context of another Platonic epistemological doctrine—the theory of recollection (anamnesis). In this dialogue Socrates claims to elicit from a boy without instruction the answer to a geometrical problem. Since the problem is a geometrical one, it is one that cannot be answered by an appeal to the senses. Socrates therefore claims that he is enabling the boy to recollect something that he had known in a previous existence. He maintains that it is a doctrine well known to priests and poets that the soul has long ago experienced all things in its various existences. Hence, in a sense the soul knows all things, but because it has forgotten them, it has to be reminded of them. The example suggests that Plato may intend the doctrine, at least in part, as an explanation of our knowledge of a priori truths. Indeed, in the *Phaedo* he uses the doctrine to explain how we see things as instances of the Forms: Sensible things remind the soul of what it already knows and what it cannot know from sense experience —the perfect Forms. The *Meno* does not claim so much. Indeed, Plato goes on to suggest that merely arriving at the right answer to a problem may not constitute knowledge but only true belief. Knowledge requires an ability to give the grounds (logoi) on which the answer rests. Nevertheless, Plato says, true belief may sometimes be, in its practical effects, as good as knowledge.

This distinction between knowledge and true belief is retained by Plato in later dialogues, although he is not always so charitable to belief as such. At the end of Book 5 of the *Republic* Plato begins a long argument, involving the famous similes of the sun, line, and cave to show how the soul may be drawn up by education to a true knowledge of the Forms, the final stage in the process that Plato calls dialectic. At the outset Plato makes a threefold distinction between knowledge, ignorance, and an intermediate state which he calls belief. Each of these states of mind has, he says, an object. The object of knowledge is what exists; the object of ignorance is, paradoxically, what does not exist; and the object of belief is that which is between existence and nonexistence. The last seems to be identified with the sensible world. Plato appears to think of these states of mind as forms of acquaintance with some kind of object, although the allocation of the objects in question is puzzling on any account. He rejects the identification of knowledge and belief on the grounds that belief is liable to error, whereas knowledge can never be. His conception of knowledge is thus a strict one.

Knowledge and sense perception. Plato's reasons for maintaining that we cannot have knowledge of the sensible world are that we should be in error if we attributed properties to sensible things absolutely. A thing is beautiful, heavy, or good only in relation to other things; hence, Plato concludes, nothing is really beautiful, heavy, or good except the standards of beauty, heaviness, and goodness themselves, and they cannot be sensible things. When we judge that sensible things are beautiful, heavy, or good, we are in error and cannot therefore be said to have knowledge.

There are two objections to this argument. First, if we realize that terms like "beautiful" are relative terms, we shall not necessarily be in error in saying that sensible things are beautiful; error will arise only if we are tempted to think that they are beautiful absolutely. Second, not all terms are relative in this way; "red," for example, is not. Perhaps Plato eventually took account of both of these points, but it seems clear that he tried to deal with the second by reference to the Heraclitean doctrine that the sensible world is in a state of flux. If this doctrine is true, it is impossible to attribute any property to sensible things unequivocally. This position is put forward in the *Cratylus* and most fully expressed in the *Timaeus*. It depends, of course, on whether the Heraclitean doctrine is true and free from unpalatable consequences. It is examined in Plato's most extensive consideration of knowledge, the *Theaetetus*, a dialogue probably written at about the same time as the *Parmenides* with its criticism of the traditional theory of Forms.

In the *Theaetetus* Socrates engages in a discussion with a young mathematician, Theaetetus, concerning the nature of knowledge. Theaetetus first answers the question "What is knowledge?" in a manner typical of the dialogues, by giving examples of knowledge, but is then prevailed upon to give the answer that knowledge is esthesis (perception or sensation; the Greek word from which it comes is ambiguous). This view is identified with that of Protagoras, the Sophist, to the effect that everything is what it seems to a man and that esthesis is of what is and must be infallible—that is, what seems to a man is so and cannot be wrong. If knowledge is esthesis, it is thus an incorrigible awareness of something purely relative to the perceiver. Socrates enlarges on this view, indicating the extent to which our judgments about empirical things are relative in this way. Finally, the point of view is made absolutely general by the introduction of the Heraclitean doctrine of the flux. The joint effect of the doctrines is that all judgments about empirical things are relative—the classic Platonic point of view. This conclusion is reinforced by reference to various versions of what has become known as the argument from illusion—an argument stating that we cannot be said to perceive the real properties of things because of the possibility of illusion or because of the causal aspects of perception itself.

Having expounded the view that all empirical judgments are relative, Socrates sets out to refute it. He refutes the pure Protagorean view that appearances are the only real-

ity by pointing out that there are acknowledged experts in different fields of knowledge concerning objective phenomena; moreover, the Protagorean view is in essence self-refuting because no absolute truth can be claimed for it on its own terms. He refutes the Heraclitean doctrine of flux by claiming that if it were true, it would be impossible to say anything about anything, a consideration which he treats as a *reductio ad absurdum*. This section of the dialogue ends with the consideration that certain properties of things—the existence of things, their identity with themselves, and their difference from other things—are ascribable to them only as a result of a judgment by the mind. Knowledge of the sensible world cannot therefore be a simple matter of having sense impressions, of esthesis in the sense specified; it must also involve judgment by the mind.

Possibility of false beliefs. In the next section Theaetetus suggests that knowledge consists of true judgment or belief. This suggestion is eventually refuted by the consideration that it is possible to believe something truly when one's grounds are insufficient. Most of the section, however, is given up to a discussion of false belief or judgment, for Socrates wonders whether this is possible. False belief cannot be a belief in what is not, for, as Parmenides showed, there is no such thing as what is not. On the other hand, if false belief consists in erroneously taking one thing for another, it is difficult to see how it is possible, for the believer must know one or both of the things in question if he is to be in the position of taking one for the other. However, if he knows at least one of the things, how can he mistakenly take it for the other? Socrates considers various possibilities, but the only cases in which he will allow the possibility of error are those in which a man fails to recognize something correctly because he has fitted the wrong sense impression to the wrong memory impression. (It is in the context of this discussion that Socrates introduces the analogy of the wax and the seal to illustrate the nature of the mind; the mind literally receives impressions from things outside it.) Since this account will not cope with judgments like $7 + 5 = 11$, where there is no question of erroneous recognition of a sensible thing, Socrates introduces another analogy, likening the mind to an aviary, with pieces of knowledge represented by the birds. A man may know something in the sense that the idea of it is in his mind as a bird is in the aviary, but he may not have it at hand. That is, he may know it implicitly but not explicitly. Even here the original difficulties recur, however. How can he mistake an explicit piece of knowledge for something else?

The difficulties in this section of the dialogue depend upon construing errors of judgment as mistakes of identity and equating knowledge with direct awareness. The mistakes allowed by Plato are not strictly mistakes of identity but mistakes in matching one thing with another, the sense impression with the memory impression. Plato returns to the matter in the *Sophist*, where he tries to provide a new logical analysis of the nature of judgment. He distinguishes between judgments of identity and existential judgments and probably between both of these and subject–predicate judgments (as they were later called). Judgments generally assert that one thing participates in another (at least the latter being a Form), but judgments of identity and existence assert the participation of something in certain especially important Forms—those of sameness and existence. These Forms are two of a list of five to which Plato gave special attention, the others being difference, rest, and motion. To say that something is identical with another thing is to say that it participates in the Form of sameness in relation to that other thing. Mistakes of judgment can arise over whether something really participates in another thing, and to that extent the difficulties of the *Theaetetus* are resolved, although it may be questioned whether Plato has given a really adequate account of judgment.

True beliefs and logoi. In the last section of the *Theaetetus,* it is suggested that knowledge may consist of true belief together with the giving of a logos. It will be remembered that knowledge was associated with the ability to give a logos in the *Meno.* Here Socrates recounts a "dream" according to which the elements of reality are perceptible but unknowable and without a logos, whereas the compounds which are formed from them are knowable and have a logos. The notion of a logos is a vague and possibly ambiguous one, but its connection with knowledge seems to imply at least that knowledge must be expressible in propositions. Socrates rejects the "dream view" (which may possibly be attributable to Antisthenes) on the ground that knowledge of compounds would not be possible unless there was already knowledge of the elements. Propositional knowledge must depend upon a knowledge by acquaintance of something, in Plato's view presumably a knowledge of the Forms. But what is the logos which, when added to belief, may turn it into knowledge? Three suggestions are considered. First, that a logos is simply the manifestation of the judgment in speech (a possible meaning of the word) is clearly insufficient. Second, that it consists of the recounting of the elements of the thing known is insufficient in that this may not actually amount to knowledge of how the elements are put together. Third, that it consists in the identification of the thing in question is rejected on the ground of circularity, for if being said to know something requires that one know the distinguishing mark of the thing in question, the account is manifestly circular. But nothing less than this is sufficient. The dialogue therefore ends inconclusively.

It is clear that in this dialogue Plato was working toward a view of knowledge which is not too far from the ordinary one. His thought, however, was never entirely free from ambivalence in this respect, and perhaps he never entirely lost his distrust of the senses. The ideal of knowledge as a kind of apprehension of a system of Forms remained. It was the task of the philosopher to investigate this system by means of dialectic, the techniques of logical division and classification. For Plato knowledge was always a state of mind and had to be accounted for accordingly. This presupposition lies behind the inconclusiveness of the *Theaetetus.* Yet most of the traditional epistemological problems arise in the course of Plato's argument, and it is worth attention for this reason alone.

Aristotle. Aristotle (384–322 B.C.) was not so affected by skeptical arguments as Plato was. He does, it is true, try to answer Protagoras (*Metaphysics* Γ 5 ff.), and he does so in a way very much like that of Plato in the *Theaetetus,* by pointing to the standard case in each class of judgment. Even in his early (and now fragmentary) work the *Protrepticus,* he had emphasized the necessity of an appeal to the expert in deciding issues in any particular art or science. This remained his approach throughout his life. Aristotle's preoccupations with epistemology appear in two provinces in particular—in his theory of science and in his theory of the mind and its faculties. But his approach to epistemology was not so much the attempt to justify the claim that knowledge exists as the description of what knowledge and its presuppositions are.

Universals. Like Plato, Aristotle held that knowledge is always of the universal. Insofar as we can be said to know particular things, we know them as instances of a universal; we know the universal in the particular. But it must be emphasized that for Aristotle universals are inherent in particulars; he vehemently rejects the Platonic notion of a world of separate universals or Forms. (The only exceptions to the inherence of forms in matter and God and the most divine part of us, reason in the highest sense.) Knowledge therefore depends ultimately on the soul's or mind's reception of the forms of things. The soul itself, as he made clear in *De Anima,* is not a distinct, spiritual entity but the set of faculties possessed by the body insofar as it has organs to manifest them.

Means of knowledge. Sense perception is the receiving by the sense organ, the faculty of which is the respective sense, of the sensible form of a thing, as he puts it, without its matter. He also describes sense perception as an actualizing of the potentiality which the sense organ possesses as its faculty. It is not easy to see how this account of the matter can be worked out in detail. Granted that the hand becomes hot when it touches a hot object, what happens to the eye when we perceive color? Aristotle thinks that each sense is affected in a way peculiar to it, so that each sense has its own special sense object. The eye has color, the ear, sound; and so on. In addition to the special senses, there is a common sense, which has no sense organ peculiar to it. It is a faculty of all the sense organs or at least of those which are capable of perceiving the same qualities of objects; for example, size and shape are perceptible by both sight and touch. Aristotle speaks of both the special sensibles, such as color, and the common sensibles, such as shape, as essential to the respective senses. Apart from these there are the incidental sensibles, which are the things which possess these properties. Aristotle speaks of them as incidental sensibles because if we use our eyes, we are bound to see color; it is not essential that we see a particular object—to use Aristotle's example, the son of Diares. At any given time he may be the object of our vision, but he does not have to be. Some interpreters have spoken of these incidental sensibles as perceived indirectly, but there is no warrant for this interpretation in *De Anima.* As Aristotle points out, it is possible to see indirectly that sugar is sweet if we know that what we see directly is sweet. But this is quite different from perception of the incidental sensibles.

With this rather passive account of perception Aristotle gives a more active account when he stresses the role judgment plays in perception. Indeed, in the *Posterior*

Analytics he speaks of the senses themselves as discriminative capacities. It is through such judgment that perceptual errors, such as mistaking the identity of a thing, can arise. Aristotle tends to say that when a sense is concerned simply with its own special object—for instance, sight with something white—there is the least chance of error. On occasion, however, he seems to imply that here error is impossible because the reception of the form in this case is something purely passive, so that there is no question of judgment. His position is not altogether clear, and there may be some confusion in his mind on this matter.

The same combination of passive impression and active judgment can be found in Aristotle's account of such faculties as imagination and memory, and to some extent there is a parallel account of the intellect itself. The persistence of the exercise of the sense faculty after its actualization by a sense object leads to the setting up of images. But imagination cannot exist in the full sense without the exercise of some form of judgment. Likewise, memory must depend not only on having images but also on a referring to the past.

It is in the account of the intellect that the parallel with sense perception comes out most clearly. There is, first, a reception of form, in this case not sensible form but intelligible form. This corresponds to having concepts. Second, there is the combination of concepts in judgment, and it is only here that the possibility of error arises. Because the higher faculties depend for their existence on the lower, the exercise of the intellect, which is in itself nothing but a mere faculty, depends on the prior exercise of sense perception. Hence, Aristotle says, the soul never thinks without an image. Owing to the influence of St. Thomas Aquinas, this has often been interpreted as the basis of empiricism. If the issue had been raised by Aristotle, the outcome might have been this doctrine, but it is not clear that he did raise it. To say that the activities of the intellect are always dependent on the workings of the lower faculties is not in itself to say that the only ideas we can have are provided by sense experience. Finally, Aristotle distinguishes between an active and a passive intellect. The intellect thus far described is the passive intellect; the active intellect, something purely actual and without potentiality, is necessary in order to make possible the actualization of the faculties of the soul. In Aristotle's thought it is given no other function.

What knowledge is. Since knowledge is concerned with the universal—with form—any knowledge which is expressible in judgment must consist of an apprehension of an essential connection between forms. To know something about a thing is to be able to subsume it under species and genus and thus to know what is essential to it. It is matter which is responsible for what is accidental, and matter is in the last analysis—as prime matter—unknowable. To a large extent Aristotle's conception of knowledge in the full sense—that is, scientific knowledge—is coincident with Plato's. For Aristotle knowledge implies order; sense experience without this is something less than knowledge. This notion of order or organization is akin to Plato's notion of logos. Similarly, the idea that knowledge consists of classification in terms of genus and species and thus of a charting of the essential connections between forms is akin to Plato's conception of dialectic as concerned with the structure of the world of Forms.

Knowledge and definition. The connection in Aristotle's thought between knowledge and classification in terms of genus and species also entails a connection between knowledge and definition, for definition itself is in terms of genus and species. Aristotle distinguishes between nominal and real definition, the first being designed to give knowledge of terms only, the second giving knowledge of the essence of the thing itself. The difference turns largely on the fact that giving the essence of the thing involves the explanation of its cause. Thus, Aristotle says that we think that we have knowledge in the primary sense when we can give the cause of the thing. To give the cause of a thing involves the demonstration of its essence from first principles, and this is the function of science. The first principles themselves can be known only by a form of intuition; one sees their truth in their instances. It is possible to explain the principles of one science in terms of another science, but this process must come to a stop somewhere. It is the mark of a foolish man, Aristotle says, to think that everything can be proved. Principles such as the law of contradiction, which are implied in all demonstration, can be proved only dialectically. A dialectical proof is one which starts not from necessary first principles but from what is commonly accepted. In this case the proof consists in getting the man who denies the law of contradiction to say something and then to show him that what he says implies the law; he is thus convicted by his own testimony.

Aristotle thus presents us with a concept of an ideal of scientific knowledge and gives some account of what is presupposed by it. The difference between knowledge and true belief is, in his account, presumably dependent on whether what is claimed is essentially and necessarily true, a part of science as he sees it. But Aristotle gives little in the way of a justification of the claim that knowledge is possible at all, for he clearly feels no need to do so. To that extent he is out of the main stream of epistemological thinkers.

Hellenistic philosophers. If anyone in the ancient world was an empiricist, it was Epicurus, the leading Greek atomist.

Epicurus. In the view of Epicurus (341–270 B.C.) all knowledge resulted from contact with the atoms of which the soul is composed by atoms from outside. It is true that he said atoms could sometimes stimulate the soul directly without affecting the senses, providing men with visions of the gods, but in general the senses had to be involved. Atoms affecting the sense organs produced sensations; mass stimulation of the sense organs resulted in a presentation or appearance (*phantasia*) to the soul. Sense experience in the more general sense occurs when an incoming presentation is fitted to a general conception or abstract idea, which itself results from repetition of sensations. This is the nearest thing to judgment in Epicurus' system, and this is the most usual source of error. Epicurus insists that all sensations are true and that they are the ultimate standard to which we must refer all our judgments; they admit of no other check. Since they are the ultimate standard of judgment, there is no other source for a metaphysical theory about the world. This, it has often been pointed out, does not fit in very well with the claims that Epicurus makes in order to give an atomistic picture of the world.

It is not altogether clear what Epicurus meant in saying that all sensations are true, especially since he also maintained that *phantasmata,* dreams or the delusions of the mad, are true. In the context of the atomist conception of the physical basis of perception, however, the view seems to imply a doctrine, common in the history of the subject, that anything in the mind which is caused cannot be liable to error. In reality questions of truth and falsity do not arise in such circumstances, a consideration implicit in Epicurus' statement that sensations are without a logos (not the sort of thing to involve judgment), but the conclusion that error is impossible has frequently been drawn.

Stoics. The rival Stoic school was founded by Zeno (fl. c. 300 B.C.), but the main figure was, perhaps, Chrysippus (c. 280–c. 204 B.C.). The Stoics were also empiricists to a large extent, although there is doubt whether at least some of the school did not admit innate ideas. The central notion of Stoic epistemology was intuition or apprehension (*katalepsis*). This, as is put by the Skeptic critic Sextus Empiricus (c. A.D. 200), was their standard of truth. Like the atomists the Stoics thought that things make impressions on the soul, although they differed from the atomists over which physical processes were involved. They made no suggestion, however, that these impressions were necessarily veridical. This was true only of those impressions which were clear and distinct (*enarges*). Whenever an impression is received in the soul, the soul has to register it by a process known as assent, but there cannot be said to be knowledge until there is apprehension, until the soul is gripped by the impression (*katalepsis* literally means "gripping"). When this apprehension can properly be said to exist is clearly open to question, and this was pointed out by the Skeptics. Hence, later Stoics were forced to say that apprehensive impressions were a guarantee of truth as long as there was no objection.

Skeptics. Meanwhile, the Skeptics were making attacks upon the dogmatic schools, as they called them. The general tendency of this school was to accept the doctrine of impressions and *phantasiae,* but to maintain that there was no ground for going beyond them. Thus, it was necessary to be content with appearances and not to seek for the hidden truth about reality. The arguments against dogmatism were probably unsystematized initially, but they were gradually put into order. Probably under Aenesidemus (first century B.C.) a list of ten (or eight) arguments (tropes) was drawn up. Some of these were forms of the argument from illusion, stressing the possibility of illusion and error in order to suggest that there was no reason to think that we ever gain knowledge of the real truth about things. Perceptions, they said, are always relative to the circumstances, the perceiver, and so on. Hence, no *phantasia* is a criterion of truth, and nothing else can be. A later Skeptic, perhaps Agrippa (first century A.D.), systematized the arguments even further by constructing general forms of skeptical argument. The final form stated that because of the earlier arguments nothing could be known in itself but only in relation to other things; however, something could be known relatively to other things only if these other things could be known absolutely. Because this had already been shown to be impossible, nothing could be known.

Some Skeptics came to see that this conclusion, put so baldly, was too dogmatic. When Arcesilaus of the Academy (the New Academy of the third century B.C.) was sufficiently influenced by Skepticism to claim that knowledge was impossible, perhaps claiming Socratic practice as a precedent, the Skeptics still thought that this view was a species of dogmatism. Carneades (214–129 B.C.), a later academic who tried to meet the arguments of Chrysippus of the Stoa, not only maintained that absolute knowledge was impossible but also tried to substitute a theory of probability for it. He distinguished three grades of probability in respect to perceptions: (1) the simply probable, (2) the probable and confirmed by its consistency with its concomitants, and (3) the probable, confirmed and tested for inconsistency with the system to which it belongs. The last grade is science as we ordinarily know it. But even this would have been too much for the pure Skeptic. Skepticism as a system received its fullest expression in the works of Sextus Empiricus in the second century A.D.

Neoplatonists. In the third century A.D. Platonism was revived by Plotinus, the founder of the Neoplatonic school. This was Platonism in its more mystical aspects, although Plotinus often uses Aristotelian notions, sometimes with a Platonic twist. The soul, as opposed to the body, is given pre-eminence, so that perception and knowledge are made a function of the soul. The soul has its own activities, which are manifested in perception and memory; the body and its impressions are merely instruments for the soul to use. The main function of the soul qua intellect is to contemplate the Forms, above which is the supreme principle or entity, the One. Unity with the One is the soul's goal.

MEDIEVAL THOUGHT

It was Neoplatonism which, according to St. Augustine (354–430), brought about his salvation from Manichaeism in theology and skepticism in philosophy. Neoplatonism offered a supposedly positive doctrine in both metaphysics and epistemology and one which St. Augustine could largely accept, thus ignoring the other, heterodox views. St. Augustine's thought is therefore Neoplatonic in its essentials. As a result he took it for granted that knowledge—and, most importantly, knowledge of God—was possible, and he felt no further need to question this assumption. The same is true of most other medieval thinkers. Since philosophy was closely linked with theology, it was axiomatic that knowledge of God was possible in some sense, and skepticism about knowledge in general was rejected by an appeal to whatever philosophical system was thought best able to explain that knowledge. Insofar as there was argument, it was about the presuppositions and sources of knowledge, not about whether it existed.

Knowledge of a thing involves, it is commonly thought, knowledge of its general characteristics and, therefore, its subsumption under a universal. Medieval thinkers differed according to their philosophical tradition, according to whether they were Platonists or, after the

Aristotelian revival in the thirteenth century, Aristotelians. But the main dispute was over theories of universals. Since the dispute had theological implication, it was heated. The argument had its source in certain questions put by Porphyry, a disciple of Plotinus, about the exact status of species and universals. These questions, the answers to which Porphyry thought were obscure, were discussed by Boethius in a commentary. The main schools of thought on the subject were the realists, conceptualists, and nominalists. Realists thought that universals had an objective existence, although their view of this existence depended on whether they were Platonists or Aristotelians. Conceptualists held that universals existed only as concepts in the mind; nominalists held that the only universal things were words. Such theories, however, were rarely found in their pure form.

Realist theories of universals. The division among realists is best seen in the differences between St. Augustine and St. Thomas Aquinas (1225–1274).

Augustine. St. Augustine gave pre-eminence to the soul, in Neoplatonist fashion. In his view the soul has its own functions and is not directly influenced by the body. Perception is based on the impressions produced by the soul when the body is stimulated. Experience, however, involves inference, as the soul subsumes its impressions under concepts. To have such concepts is, for St. Augustine, to be aware of Forms in the Platonic sense, the one difference being that in his view the Forms are thoughts in the mind of God. Thus, universals have a real existence in the mind of God, and all knowledge, even sense knowledge, involves some awareness of God. There is an ascent from lower forms of knowledge, like perception, to higher forms, with knowledge of God at the peak.

Aquinas. The Aristotelian revival in the thirteenth century led to St. Thomas Aquinas' acceptance of a more Aristotelian point of view than Augustine's. Like Aristotle, Aquinas rejected self-subsistent universals, maintaining that universality is a function of the mind. Nevertheless, there are real similarities between things because of their common form. Hence, species have more than a mere mental existence.

The Thomist theory of knowledge consists largely of an explanation of how knowledge of Forms is possible. When the senses are stimulated, the soul's potentiality is actualized; a sensory image, or *phantasma,* is set up, corresponding to the object of perception. But since the universal aspects of such objects can be apprehended only by the intellect, they must be transferred from the *phantasma* to the intellect. Indeed, *phantasmata* as such are not objects of awareness on our part. The mind is aware only of the universal aspects of things, not their particularity, which is available only to the senses. Something has to illuminate the *phantasmata* in order to make clear their universal characteristics. Aquinas employs Aristotle's distinction between the active and passive intellects here. The active intellect abstracts the universal or species from the *phantasma,* and this is imposed upon the passive intellect as a concept, which is then verbalized. Concepts thus exist only as the result of an abstraction of the universal aspects of things, and the essence of Aquinas' empiricism is that

all knowledge depends on sense experience in this way. Even knowledge of self-evident truths, which Aquinas admits, as well as knowledge of the essential nature of things, is in the last resort dependent on sense experience, and all our thoughts must be based on experience. Aquinas can be looked on as the founder of empiricism in the sense that he held that all the materials for knowledge come ultimately from experience and from nowhere else. Unlike the later philosopher Locke, however, he did not set out to justify the doctrine in detail.

Conceptualist theories of universals. Although Aquinas may be classed as a realist in his theory of universals because he maintained that there are objective similarities between things by virtue of their common form, he could not do so without the notion of concepts in the mind.

Abelard. Peter Abelard (1079–1142) had previously held a conceptualist theory of universals, emphasizing the extent to which universality is a function of the mind. He held that universals are really concepts (*sermones*) involved in judgments that particular things have something in common. They are arrived at by abstraction from particular things, by attending to features of things considered in themselves. Abelard even used the notion of a generic image—that is, an image not of any particular thing but, supposedly, of what is common to a whole class of things—in order to account for our ability to think of things generally. He was anxious to reject both realism and the contemporary nominalism held by Roscelin of Compiègne (died c. 1125), who maintained that universals were just words or even names. He did not, however, deny that concepts had a basis in things. Hence, in a sense Thomist realism and Abelardian conceptualism are very much two sides of the same coin.

Nominalist theory of universals. Similar considerations apply to the great nominalist thinker of the fourteenth century, William of Ockham.

Ockham. Even Ockham (c. 1285–1349) did not quite maintain that the only universal things are words, for he held that words are conventional signs corresponding to concepts which are natural signs of things. Universality lies in the sign–significate relation, in the fact that both words and concepts can be signs of a class of things. To the question "What are universals?" Ockham initially replied that they had only a logical existence; they were meanings, the contents of the mind when thinking generally. For Ockham the term "universal" was what he called a term of second intention. A first intention is the state of mind involved in the apprehension of particular things; a second intention is that involved in the apprehension of first intentions. The term "universal" thus picks out the content of our apprehension of our first-order apprehensions of a class of things. "Redness" is not the name of an entity but of the content of the relation which exists between the sign or concept "red" and particular red things. Ockham later took another step toward conceptualism by holding that universals had a mental, not just a logical, existence. He then held that universals are the concepts which the mind has and which are the natural substitutes for things themselves. Ockham probably took this step for reasons of economy, for in the earlier account universals were a sort of intermediary between the mind and particular things. The place given to generality remained the same, however. There was nothing general in the world; generality depended on the relationship between the mind and particular things.

The real novelty of Ockham's approach lay in his holding the view, new to medieval thought, that the mind itself could have apprehension of particular things. Aquinas, for example, had denied this, holding that the mind could be concerned only with universal characteristics abstracted from *phantasmata*. The consequent gap between the mind and the senses inevitably involved a representative theory of perception; the mind was confronted only with the representatives of things. Ockham denied all this. He held that the mind could be concerned directly with the particular by means of intuitions. Intuitive knowledge is a direct knowledge of a thing or its existence. The senses provide an intuition of a thing's existence, and the intellect provides an intuition of its nature. Duns Scotus (1265–1308) had held that intuition of a particular was a necessary condition of the abstraction of the universal from it, but he had also held that this intuition must, in this life at any rate, be confused. Ockham denied this. In his view intuitions may be perfect or imperfect respectively, according to whether they are dependent merely on present experience or whether they also involve past experience. The possibility of imperfect intuitions, however, depends on the possibility of direct, perfect intuitions.

Although Ockham thought that this kind of direct knowledge does exist, he did not claim that all intuition was equally clear; clarity, moreover, was not always enough to guarantee truth. In the first respect, he claimed, as St. Augustine had done earlier, that we have clearer knowledge of our own mind than of other things. In the second he maintained that God can give us an intuition of something that does not in fact exist (a consideration which looked forward to Descartes's suggestion that God might be a deceiver). This is not the natural course of things, however.

Much of Ockham's thought is in the Stoic tradition, and to some extent this can be said about Descartes, the first of the rationalist thinkers of the seventeenth century. By this time, however, the questioning of the accepted points of view of the Middle Ages had led to increased skepticism. Descartes's theory of knowledge is therefore in the fullest sense the beginning of that "search for certainty" whose elements were found in Plato but had not been prominent after him.

SEVENTEENTH-CENTURY RATIONALISM

Descartes and Cartesianism. The emergence of science during the Renaissance and the disputes which it produced led to a certain skepticism about claims to knowledge and to the search for a method, like that of science, which would determine the truth once and for all. Descartes (1596–1650) was the pioneer in this new tradition, and although his roots were in the Middle Ages, he was to a large extent an innovator. Being a mathematician of distinction, he saw the solution to problems of epistemology in the systematization of knowledge in geometrical form, although he did not carry out the full program himself. This involved starting from axioms whose truth was clear and distinct. He describes the ideal method in the second chapter of the *Discourse on Method* as (1) not to accept as true anything of which we have not a clear and distinct idea, (2) to analyze the problem, (3) to start from simple and certain thoughts and proceed from them to the more complex, and (4) to review the field so thoroughly that no considerations are omitted. Of what do we have clear and distinct ideas? To deal with this problem, Descartes employs the method of doubt—a form of skepticism. This method involves setting on one side anything that can be supposed false until one arrives at something that cannot be supposed false.

That there is a goal to this skepticism is, it might be objected, prejudged, for Descartes points to the fact that he has often been deceived to suggest that he may always be deceived. This conclusion is not, however, admissible, since to establish his premises, he must at least know that he has sometimes been deceived. The truth is that Descartes has a definite conception of what knowledge must be, and most of what we ordinarily call knowledge does not fit that conception. His approach is therefore not strictly that of the general skeptic. It consists in setting on one side anything that does not possess the mark of genuine knowledge, this mark being that we should have clear and distinct ideas of the thing in question. We have a clear idea of a thing when it is open to the mind, when we are clearly aware of it; an idea is also distinct when we have a full knowledge of the nature of its object and of the means whereby that object can be distinguished from other things. Many philosophers have believed that we do not have certain knowledge of empirical truths but that we do have it of mathematical truths. Descartes agrees to the extent that he maintains that we can have clear and distinct ideas of the objects of mathematics, but he also maintains that if God were a deceiver, he might have caused us to have false beliefs even here. Hence, it is at least a possible hypothesis that there is an archdeceiver who brings it about that I am mistaken in all my beliefs. Is there anything which is free from this contingency?

"Cogito ergo sum." The result of Descartes's inquiry into this matter is that there is at least one proposition which is indubitable in the sense that I cannot be wrong in maintaining it. This is the proposition "I think, therefore I exist" (*Cogito ergo sum*). Descartes is definite that this is not to be treated as an argument despite its form; it is an indubitable proposition. (In a sense Descartes had been anticipated in this by St. Augustine's "If I am mistaken, I exist" [*Si fallor sum*], but St. Augustine had not used the proposition for exactly the same purposes.) It is reasonably clear that I cannot deny either "I think" or "I exist" without absurdity, although this is not enough to show that the *cogito* is in any way a logical truth. Yet for Descartes it must have the kind of necessity which is generally attributed to logical truths; it must be logically impossible for the proposition to be false. Moreover, it must have content such that its truth entails the existence of something with a specific nature—namely, a spiritual or thinking substance

which has certain ideas, particularly those of God and material objects. Only then can Descartes go on to justify belief in such objects.

In effect, therefore, Descartes says that I can doubt everything except that I doubt. Since doubting is a form of thinking, I cannot doubt that I think, and since thought requires a thinker, I cannot doubt the existence of myself as the thinker. It might be objected that even if there is no reason to reject this position, it has not been shown to be necessary. If I cannot doubt that I doubt, this may be a contingent matter, not a logical necessity. Once given the *cogito*, however, Descartes can go on to use it as the premise of an argument whose outcome will be the justification of our belief in a world independent of ourselves.

The status of perception. Granted that we have ideas of a world of material things, what prevents those ideas being mere figments of the imagination? Ideas in themselves are purely mental entities (although Descartes is never very clear about their exact nature); they may or may not represent the things they purport to represent. Ideas can be innate, adventitious, or fictitious. To say that they are adventitious is to say that they come from things outside us; to say that they are fictitious is to say that they are produced by the mind itself. Innate ideas are a priori, inborn. Which ideas these are, if any, may be disputed. But, at all events, our ideas of material things are clearly not innate. Why, however, are they not merely fictitious?

To say that an idea is fictitious is not to say that is is impossible for it to be an idea of something objective. To some of our ideas perhaps nothing could possibly correspond; these would be logical impossibilities and would have no objective validity in Cartesian terms. For an idea to have objective validity, the reality in it must be caused by something that has the same reality, either formally or eminently, in itself. A machine, to use Descartes's example, may be formally the cause of a man's idea of it; his idea may be a copy of the machine, the two having the same form. But if the man conceives of the machine himself, then he or his mind is eminently the cause of his idea; the idea is not a mere copy of its cause, for the source of the idea is something higher. If, then, our ideas of material things are to be objectively valid or have objective reality, they must either be copies of actual material things or be produced by something higher. If they are produced by something higher, they were produced either by our minds or by God. To show that our ideas of material things do correspond to those material things, Descartes has to show that they are not produced in this way either by our own minds alone or by God.

Now, ideas in themselves, Descartes maintains, cannot be strictly true or false; it is the use we make of them that can be true or false. Hence, truth and error are functions of judgment. Nevertheless, we have a natural disposition to believe that our ideas are veridical. In Meditation III, Descartes points to this natural disposition and to the fact that our perceptions do not depend on the will as reason for believing in the veridicality of our perceptions, although he rejects these considerations as insufficient. In Meditation VI, however, he has recourse to the same considerations, although they must now be viewed in the context of the view that perception is a faculty of the mind plus body and does not express the essence of the mind alone, which is concerned solely with thinking. The passivity of our perceptual ideas thus seems to be invoked in order to reject the notion that our ideas of material objects could be a product of our own minds. Ideas of material objects, however, might still be caused by God. Yet if this were true and if nothing answered to those ideas, God would be a deceiver, for he would be giving us a natural disposition to believe in the existence of things which do not exist in fact. God, Descartes maintains, is not a deceiver. This point is taken as axiomatic and provides the ultimate guarantee of our belief that we do perceive an objective world.

Existence of God. The existence of God is therefore a cardinal point in the chain of argument. Descartes produces two sets of arguments designed to demonstrate his existence as a necessary truth. The first argument, in Meditation III, is based on the same considerations about the causes of our ideas as those adduced in connection with ideas of material things. The idea of God, which Descartes takes to be objectively valid, could be produced only by something having the same reality formally or eminently in it. We, being inferior creatures, could not produce it, and it could not come from any other source except God himself. Hence, there must be a God. This argument is a version of the so-called Cosmological Argument.

The other argument, to be found in Meditation V, is a version of the Ontological Argument first invoked by St. Anselm. God must through his essence possess all positive attributes in perfection. Existence is a positive attribute; hence, God must exist. It is now generally recognized that neither argument is sufficient to demonstrate the necessary existence of God. However, the necessary existence of God must be demonstrated if the argument concerning the existence of material things is to have any cogency.

If Descartes's argument for the existence of God had been sound, he would have shown that all the reality in our ideas must be in their causes. More is required if it is to be shown that our ideas are, at least in some cases, copies of their causes. This is a problem for any representative or causal theory of perception, any theory which holds that our ideas and perceptions are mental entities which are, at best, only representatives of things outside them. From Descartes's point of view there is the general consideration that God is not a deceiver; any errors or illusions to which we are subject are the results of judgments we make because of the ideas we receive. This makes it incumbent on us, if we are to avoid error, to take due account of the clarity and distinctness of our ideas. We are right in judging that our ideas correspond to their causes only if those ideas are clear and distinct.

Primary and secondary qualities. In Descartes's opinion there is a big difference between primary qualities, such as figure, magnitude, and motion, and secondary qualities, such as color. Primary qualities can be known by an intuition of the intellect (*inspectio mentis*). Our ideas of them are clear and distinct because of the part they play in mathematics, and in mathematics, therefore, the intellect can be regarded as having a proper knowledge of reality.

This is not to say that we cannot make mistakes concerning the primary qualities of objects; judgment can be as liable to error here as elsewhere. However, since the ideas of them are clear and distinct, we have the assurance that in general objects do have such qualities. We have no such assurance in the case of secondary qualities. The intellect is not involved here, but since the senses were, Descartes maintains, provided only for the conservation of life, it does not matter very much whether our ideas of secondary qualities correspond to the actual qualities of objects.

It would not be generally admitted today that mathematics does provide the kind of knowledge of reality that Descartes requires. The question of the exact connection between mathematics and the world is a complicated one. Granted, however, that mathematical ideas have a precision not possessed by other ideas, it does not follow that we have a precise knowledge of any qualities of physical objects. For it remains an open question to what extent such ideas are applicable to physical objects. There is a genuine distinction between primary and secondary qualities in that the first are measurable in a way that the second are not. This, however, is not sufficient to justify the claim that knowledge of primary qualities is knowledge of reality in a way that knowledge of secondary qualities is not. In some places—for instance, *Principles*, Part IV, Section XI, and *Dioptric*, Section VI—Descartes tries to reinforce this view by arguing that since the effects in the brain caused by the stimulation of our senses possess only the properties of motion, figure, and extension, there is no means whereby we could come to apprehend any other properties of objects. There is a circularity in this argument, since its premise is that we do know of the primary qualities possessed by brain processes, whereas all ideas, being the effects of physical processes, should be in the same position.

In sum, Descartes's theory of knowledge is essentially one of a representative kind. It is based on the idea that the mind or soul, being something very different and distinct from the body, can have as its contents only ideas, which are, at best, representatives of physical things. The mind has its own activities, and its nature is to be active. Through these activities it can come to have knowledge of abstract mathematical truths. But all sense knowledge, as opposed to intellectual knowledge, can come only through the medium of ideas, and that these ideas correspond in any way to the physical objects presented to the senses is inevitably open to question. The justification of our belief that they do depends, in the long run, on the affirmation that there is a God and that he is not a deceiver. Descartes thinks that he can demonstrate that there is a God, taking as true by definition that he is no deceiver and that our natural disposition to trust our senses is therefore justified.

Occasionalism. Since Descartes conceived of the soul and the body as distinct substances with distinct essences—that of the soul being thought and that of the body extension—he was inevitably faced with the problem of how one could act on the other. He was never very clear on this point, although he came to insist that there must be some quasi-substantial union between the two. In some places—for example, the *Dioptric*—he speaks of brain processes' giving "occasion" to the soul to have sensations or ideas. Some of his followers, who thereby became known as occasionalists, took up this notion and tried to explain the apparent link between soul and body by saying that God puts ideas into the soul on the occasion of the bodily processes. Geulincx (1625–1669) said that God puts the ideas there by means of the bodily processes; Malebranche (1638–1715) said that God acts directly on the mind on the occasion of the bodily processes. Since Malebranche had leanings toward the views of St. Augustine, he interpreted this occasionalism in terms of the Augustinian doctrine that we know all things in God.

Malebranche. In other respects Malebranche tends to follow Descartes, although often with greater emphasis. He, too, insists that we have clear and distinct ideas of figure, extension, and movement, since these qualities, being conceivable in mathematical terms, are open to the intellect. He also lays great emphasis on our liability to error in anything connected with the senses, especially if we think that the senses provide us with knowledge of things as they actually are. In one respect, however, he adds a certain sophistication to the Cartesian distinction between the ideas or sensations that arise in the mind without any intervention on our part and the judgments that we make and which depend on our will. Sometimes what we see differs from what would be expected on the basis of the sensations resulting from the stimulation of our senses. We may see a thing in its right size, for example, although the actual pattern of stimulation received in the eyes is different; alternatively, we can be subject to illusion when the conditions of stimulation are not abnormal. In such circumstances we are not generally aware of making any judgment in order to correct the sensations received. Malebranche therefore distinguishes between natural judgments, or judgments of sense, and free judgments. Free judgments depend on our will, but natural ones do not; they are, he says, a kind of complex sensation in that they do not depend on us. They are, he explains, made by God in us, in consequence of the laws of the union between soul and body. As judgments they can be true or false, but as sensations they may occur against our will and are certainly not due to our will. Malebranche is in an ambivalent position here, but his difficulties show a certain honesty.

Spinoza. It has often been remarked that what makes the thought of Spinoza (1632–1677) especially interesting is that it combines the quite different and, as generally conceived, quite disparate traditions of nominalism and extreme rationalism. In his nominalism he belongs to the tradition of William of Ockham and, more particularly, of Hobbes (1588–1679). Hobbes maintained that only names were universal. Although names were signs of images of things which constitute our conception of them, there was nothing universal in the conceptions themselves. Only the use to which names are put was universal, for they are taken as signs of many things. Hobbes used this to mount an aggressive attack on the paraphernalia of Scholasticism—essences, substance, and the like. He was a tough-minded mechanist who thought that reality consisted solely of corporeal bodies in motion.

Although he did not have the same motive, Spinoza was similarly opposed to the apparatus of Scholasticism. Indeed, he may have been influenced by Hobbes. In his *Ethics*, Part II, Spinoza held that as a result of the stimulation of our bodily senses by many things, confused, composite images arise, and it is these images that general words represent. There is no place for universals existing in things. Since these images may be set up differently in different men, "universal notions," as Spinoza calls them, may differ from man to man. The knowledge that is expressed by their means can only be confused. Spinoza is not content to leave knowledge there, however; he has the conception of knowledge of a much higher kind, and his working out of this conception is in effect the systematizing of Cartesianism. To make Cartesianism consistent, however, he had to change much in it.

Monism. Although according to Descartes's view the clarity and distinctness of an idea was a necessary condition of its truth, it was not a sufficient condition of its truth. It was always possible to raise the question of whether any particular idea did correspond to reality and, in particular, to its cause. This was a consequence of the dualism between the mind and its ideas and the physical world, a dualism inherent in Cartesianism. Spinoza replaced this dualism by a monism according to which the mental and the physical were two aspects of one thing—ultimately, God or Nature. In adopting this view, he was again carrying out the implications of Cartesianism, for Descartes had asserted that in the proper sense the concept of substance belongs only to God, for only God is self-subsistent, or *causa sui*. Hence, in Spinoza's view everything is a modification or mode of the one true substance, depending on God for its existence. The Cartesian distinction between mental and material substance becomes a distinction between the two infinite attributes of God in Spinoza's theory. Bodies are modifications of God qua extended, and minds are modifications of God qua thinking. They are not distinct things; they are merely parallel aspects of the one true substance. The order of ideas in the mind is the same as the order of things. Hence, the objects, or *ideata,* of ideas, insofar as these have reference to God, are always truly represented by them. No ideas can be absolutely false, and insofar as they refer to God, they must be true. Ideas can be considered false only from the point of view of what we ordinarily call a single human mind, not from the point of view of God.

Truth and falsity. Because everything can be deduced from the essence of God, everything is subject to necessity, and this applies to ideas as much as to everything else. There is no room in Spinoza's theory for the Cartesian distinction between ideas and the will; for him the will and the intellect are the same. Falsity cannot therefore arise from the exercise of our will in the employment of ideas. For Spinoza the exercise of the will in judgment is not something additional to having ideas, and he emphasizes that it is wrong to think of ideas as simple pictures which may or may not correspond to their objects. To have an idea of something and to make a judgment about it are one and the same, and it is by virtue of this composite conception that ideas, not only judgments, can be true or false. Considered as part of God's thinking, ideas cannot, of course, be false, for in that case they must always correspond, qua modifications of God as thinking, to the modifications of God as extended. But considered as ideas in a single human mind, they can represent their objects confusedly or inadequately. In having a confused idea of an object, we fail to see it as following necessarily from the nature of things. Such ideas, Spinoza says, are like consequences without premises.

In the *Ethics*, Part II, Definition 4, Spinoza defines an adequate idea as "an idea which, insofar as it is considered in itself without relation to an object, has all the properties or intrinsic marks of a true idea." If an idea is confused, it cannot be adequate. Therefore, truth must have an intrinsic criterion, not just the extrinsic criterion of the correspondence of an idea to its object. In other words, the clarity and distinctness which Descartes had looked to for the foundations of knowledge is the mark of every true idea. Truth and adequacy thus merge. For full truth an idea must be seen to be true, and this is possible only insofar as it is seen to follow from the nature of things. Truth, Spinoza says, is its own criterion. This is connected with another of Spinoza's epistemological views—that knowledge must ultimately be reflexive. Anyone who really knows something must know that he knows. If a man knows that something is necessarily so, he must know that he knows this, since the truth of what he knows must be manifest.

The doctrine of truth which Spinoza presents is commonly referred to as the coherence theory of truth, and it is normally associated with the doctrine of degrees of truth, knowledge, and reality. The distinctions between grades of reality which exist between the one true substance and its various modifications is paralleled by distinctions between kinds of knowledge. True knowledge, the having of adequate ideas, entails seeing things as following from the essence of God. Knowledge can be more or less inadequate or confused to the extent that a thing is not seen as following necessarily from that essence. Absolute truth consists in having adequate ideas, although every idea has some degree of truth since it must have a counterpart in the order of things. In other words, an idea, although necessarily true in some respect, has greater truth to the degree that it is adequate and to the degree that its object is seen as fitting in with the order of things. Like most versions of the coherence theory of truth, this is really not a theory of what truth is or what is meant in calling an idea or judgment true, but, rather, a theory of when or under what conditions an idea or judgment can be seen to be true. A judgment can be seen to be true if it coheres with the system of judgments which characterize reality. But coherence theorists tend to say that any judgment which can be seen to cohere with other judgments in this way is thereby "more true" than those which do not cohere. In effect, they tend to use the word "true" so that it is more or less equivalent to "verified." A judgment which has a higher degree of verification by virtue of its coherence with other judgments is said to be *ipso facto* more true. The coherence theory of truth is thus a genuine epistemological theory, a theory of the conditions under which we can be said to know a proposition as true.

Kinds of knowledge. Spinoza distinguishes three grades of knowledge. Full knowledge Spinoza refers to as the third kind of knowledge and characterizes it as intuition.

This kind of knowledge, he says in the *Ethics*, Part II, "proceeds from an adequate idea of the formal essence of certain attributes of God to an adequate knowledge of the essence of things." To have this knowledge is the goal of philosophy—to see things *sub specie aeternitatis,* as conforming to a kind of necessity. The right method in philosophy as set out in the *Treatise on the Correction of the Understanding* is to rid the mind of confused and inadequate ideas and to lead it to ideas which are adequate. It is significant that Spinoza calls this kind of knowledge intuition, because in its essence it consists of seeing the world as a coherent whole bound by necessary connections. Most rationalists have ended up with some such conception, and for them reason is inevitably second best. So it is for Spinoza.

What Spinoza calls reason is the second kind of knowledge, below intuition. This is best described by distinguishing it from the first kind of knowledge, which is knowledge derived from vague experience and is also called opinion or imagination. This corresponds roughly to sense experience. (Knowledge from hearsay, the fourth kind of knowledge, added in the *Treatise* to the bottom of the list, is of little importance for present purposes.) From sense experience we gain confused ideas of things without respect to their place in the general order of things. We may obtain knowledge of a similar status from signs—that is, from reading or hearing words which allow us to form ideas similar to those of the imagination. Both of these sources may lead to the setting up of the universal notions referred to earlier, notions which vary from man to man and cannot provide genuine knowledge. In the course of our experience, however, we may light upon notions which are common to all men, such notions as those of extension and other general attributes of reality. These notions Spinoza calls common notions, to be sharply distinguished from the universal notions already discussed. These common notions correspond to the ideas of primary qualities which Descartes had allowed to be clear and distinct because they were the objects of intellectual intuitions. For Spinoza, too, they provide the starting point of the sciences, and as such our ideas of them are adequate. They can be seen to be true of reality inasmuch as they reflect all-pervasive features of reality. It is for this reason that they are common to all men; they are not subjective like the universal notions.

Reason or science thus consists in elaborating the essential features of the attributes of which we have common notions. Like Descartes, Spinoza conceived of science as based on the model of mathematics in general and geometry in particular. His conception of the right method in philosophy itself is modeled on the geometrical method. Indeed, Spinoza had tried to set out the Cartesian philosophy in a geometrical fashion according to the rules that Descartes had preached but had not practiced as well. Thus, although science, the systematization of knowledge, is ultimately derived from sense experience, it reflects the actual order of things more truly than experience does. Nevertheless, the goal of all knowledge is not just this systematization but the seeing of things as a whole, *sub specie aeternitatis.* For this reason intuition stands above reason.

Because the second and third kinds of knowledge involve adequate ideas, they cannot give rise to falsity. Sense experience alone can be the source of falsity. Through sense experience we can have only confused ideas, since ideas reflect particular modifications of reality in some finite respect, not in relation to the infinite attributes of God. Sense experience is ordinarily thought of as a passive form of knowledge, as opposed to forms of knowledge which demand the use of reason. This passivity, Spinoza thinks, is only a sign of the inadequacy of our ideas in this case. Activity on the part of the mind is, conversely, adequacy in its ideas. Spinoza points out that the human mind is part of the infinite intellect of God. Hence, "when we say that the human mind perceives this or that, we say nothing else than that God, not in so far as he is infinite, but in so far as he is explained through the nature of the human mind, or in so far as he constitutes the essence of the human mind, has this or that idea" (*Ethics,* Part II). Just as the ideas of sense experience are confused and inadequate only in relation to our mind, although when considered as God's ideas they are true, so the ideas of sense experience are passive in relation to our mind but are nevertheless part of God's active thoughts.

In sum, for Spinoza the goal of all knowledge is seeing the world as a single whole. On the way to this lies reason or science, which attempts to reveal things as subject to necessity by means of self-evident, necessary truths about things. All else, although not absolutely false, is the source of illusion. But, as in everything else in Spinoza, an adequate understanding of his theory of knowledge also involves an adequate understanding of his complete metaphysics or theory of reality. This is true of philosophers in general but never more so than in Spinoza's case.

Leibniz. In many ways Leibniz (1646–1716) is Spinoza with a strong dash of common sense. Spinoza's monism, especially its assertion of the necessity of things and the apparent consequence that free will is impossible, was anathema to Leibniz. In these respects Leibniz revolted against Spinoza, but in other respects he was very much like Spinoza. He, too, drew no distinction between the will and the intellect and made activity and passivity in the mind a function of the clarity and distinctness or otherwise of our ideas. Furthermore, although common sense told him that there must be a plurality of things, not just one, he had to conceive of each ultimate thing as a simple substance possessing all the properties of Spinoza's one substance.

Leibniz' simple substances had to have a unity in plurality in that, although simple, each one had to be capable of reflecting the whole universe from its point of view. Since Leibniz took as axiomatic that in every true proposition the predicate is contained in the subject, everything that can be said about a substance is so because of the nature of that substance, and all the relations which it has to other things must arise from the nature of that substance and be internal to it. It is for this reason that every true substance must reflect the universe from its point of view and in this way be a microcosm of the macrocosm. The only thing, Leibniz thought, which could be both simple and capable of reflecting the universe in this way was something like the soul. In consequence, he postulated the existence of a plurality of simple substances, spiritual in nature, which he called monads. But for the monads, he said, Spinoza would be right.

Necessary and contingent truths. Since the properties of each monad were internal to it, it might be thought that Leibniz, like Spinoza, would have maintained that everything was a matter of necessity. However, although Leibniz maintained that all the properties of a substance are internal to it and thus follow from the nature of the substance, for other reasons he maintained a clear distinction between truths which are necessary in the logical sense and truths which are dependent on the facts. He was thus perhaps the first to draw a clear distinction between necessary or logical and contingent or factual truths. The first he called truths of reason, the second truths of fact. These truths had different principles as their basis. Truths of reason were dependent on the principle of contradiction, since their necessity turned on the fact that their denial would result in a contradiction. Leibniz thought that such truths, when their terms are defined, could be reduced to identical propositions of the form "*A* is *A*." The reduction to such identical propositions would therefore proceed by means of chains of definitions. Mathematical truths are of this kind, and Leibniz was one of the first to seek a basis for mathematics in logic.

Truths of fact, on the other hand, could not be justified by reduction to identical propositions; their basis had to be found in a separate principle, the principle of sufficient reason. This principle received different formulations at different stages of Leibniz' thought. Insofar as it was meant to allow for the contingency of matters of fact while providing a rationale for them, Leibniz tended to formulate the principle by reference to the choice of God. In creating this universe, God could choose from a number of possible worlds each having a different order or structure. Since, as Leibniz thought, for various different reasons, the number of monads is infinite, the number of such possible worlds is also infinite. Any contingent truth about *this* world has for its justification the fact that in choosing this world, God chose it as the best of all possible worlds. The truth remains contingent because it is dependent on God's choice, but a sufficient reason for its truth is that God chose it as part of the best of all possible worlds. At other times, however, Leibniz' appeal to God's choice has fewer theological implications. For example, in his correspondence with Samuel Clarke, he tries to refute the idea of an infinite absolute space by saying that in such a space God would have no sufficient reason for putting the universe here rather than there. This means that there would be no way of telling where the universe was and that it would, in consequence, make no sense to speak of it as being in one place rather than another. This use of the principle of sufficient reason amounts to something like the use of the verification principle by logical positivists—the meaning of a proposition lies in the method of verification.

When Leibniz maintains, however, that in every true proposition the predicate is included in the subject, he seems to undermine the distinction between truths of reason and truths of fact. For this doctrine would make all propositions into what Kant was later to call analytic propositions or judgments, propositions which are logically necessary. In consequence, it has been maintained (for

example, by Louis Couturat) that in some of Leibniz' writings the principle of sufficient reason merely states that all true propositions are analytic, whereas the principle of contradiction states that all analytic propositions are true. In fact, this is probably a consequence of Leibniz' main views rather than a statement of it. If every proposition about a substance attributes to it a property which is part of its essence, then all such propositions must be analytic even if they are to be characterized as truths of fact on other grounds.

Leibniz accepted this conclusion but tried to evade the contradiction implicit in characterizing a truth of fact as analytic by explaining that the number of properties possessed by any substance must be infinitely great, as the points of view from which a thing can be regarded are endless. We, being finite creatures, cannot complete the analysis of any given substance. Hence, we cannot know for certain whether any given attribute really does belong to it; we cannot, without completing the analysis, even know whether it is possible for this substance to possess the property; it may be a contradiction to suppose it. God, being infinite, can complete the analysis, and so for him all propositions about things are analytic or logically necessary. We, on the other hand, can know only that if a proposition is true, it is necessarily true, but we cannot know for certain whether any given proposition is true. In our judgments about the truth of propositions, we have to depend on probabilities—that is, we have to estimate what reasons are sufficient for our conclusions. Thus, for us any judgment of fact is contingent. For God contingency enters only in that he has chosen what substances there should be, which of all possible worlds should exist. For him everything thereafter is necessary. Hence, the principle of sufficient reason comes into consideration in two related ways—first, in that it guides, without determining, God's choice of a world and, second, in that it guides our decision concerning which world God has chosen.

Perception and appetition of monads. So much for the logical consequences of Leibniz' point of view. Given the metaphysical system according to which there exist an infinite number of spiritual entities or monads, other consequences also follow. According to Leibniz, every monad has perception and appetition—the apparent passive and active features of mental life. Since everything about a monad is internal to it, these features can indeed be only apparent. Appetition is that aspect of a monad responsible for internal change and development. No monad can affect or be affected by any other monad. A perception is any property of a monad which results from its development but which may reflect changes in other monads. (This use of the term "perception" is, although influenced by Leibniz' metaphysics, clearly very general, but its use was very general throughout the seventeenth century.) What may seem to be activity on the part of one monad with respect to another is really having distinct perceptions, whereas passivity is having confused perceptions. Here Leibniz sides with Spinoza.

Self-consciousness of monads. Leibniz' criterion of a distinct idea of a thing is the ability to list the characteristics which distinguish the thing from other things. This clearly involves a degree of self-consciousness, and this is possessed only by the monads constituting the human soul. Although all monads have perceptions in that other things are represented in them, not all have apperception. To have apperception, the monad must be conscious of what is involved in its perceptions, and those perceptions must therefore be distinct. The distinction between perception and apperception means that perceptions can sometimes be unconscious. Leibniz brings forward a number of arguments in support of this view, ranging from the argument that reflection upon perceptions must come to a stop with perceptions that are not self-conscious to the argument that there must be what he calls *petites perceptions*. When we hear the roar of the sea, he argues, we are not aware of hearing each little ripple despite the fact that the waves are made up of ripples. Since the over-all perception must correspond in complexity to its object, he concludes that there must be perceptions corresponding to the ripples, and these little perceptions are therefore unconscious. This is not a psychological discovery but a philosophical analysis the premises of which are open to dispute. Like Descartes, Leibniz accepts the representative theory of perception in thinking that perception consists in having ideas which are, or may be, representative of objects. If this theory is rejected, Leibniz' argument about *petites perceptions* loses much of its force.

Error in perception. Just as Leibniz sides with Spinoza in maintaining that activity and passivity are to be explained in terms of the distinctness of our ideas, so he agrees with him, against Descartes, over the explanation of error. There is no room for the individual will in Leibniz' system. Appetition is only the impulse which provides the development of the monad's perceptions; it in no way corresponds to the will. Error is merely a matter of having confused ideas, and since these are correlated with passivity, the passive aspects of mental life—sense perception and the like—are the source of error.

Innate ideas. Yet although Leibniz can distinguish between ideas of perception and ideas of reason, or the understanding, it remains true that according to his view in a sense all ideas are innate. None is literally produced by things affecting our sense organs. Yet the distinction between ideas in terms of their clarity and distinctness does mean that it is possible to say that some ideas are what Kant called a priori—in no way derived from the senses. These are ideas such as those of mathematics, and Leibniz criticized his empiricist adversary Locke for failing to take sufficient account of these ideas. Indeed, to the empiricist principle that there is nothing in the intellect that was not first in the senses Leibniz replied, "Except the intellect itself."

Rationalism generally tends to emphasize the part played by the intellect in contradistinction to that played by the senses. It holds that real knowledge is that provided by the intellect, for only there is the certainty which knowledge requires. Moreover, it is by means of the disciplines which are peculiarly the province of the intellect that knowledge is to be obtained and preserved.

BRITISH EMPIRICISM

In general, empiricism stands in opposition to rationalism both in its views about the main source of our ideas and in its views concerning the source of true knowledge. Thus, it is often, historically speaking, a reaction against rationalism. The so-called British empiricists of the seventeenth and eighteenth centuries, however, were empiricists only in tendency. The first, Locke, was a complete empiricist concerning the source of our ideas, but he was often a rationalist in allowing other than empirical knowledge. Locke's new way of ideas, as it was called, was an attempt to show that all the materials for knowledge are derived from sense experience. Locke did not claim, however, that all knowledge was founded on experience in any other sense. Berkeley, who carried on Locke's new way of ideas and even sharpened some of Locke's claims, especially on the subject of abstract ideas, was fundamentally a metaphysician with a special way of looking at the world. Hume, the last of the trio, claimed to introduce the experimental method into philosophy, following in the steps of Newton, and of the three he had by far the best right to be counted an empiricist. Indeed, his empiricism led him extremely close to skepticism concerning a number of claims to knowledge; such skepticism, he believed, could be avoided only by "inattention" to philosophical issues. But all three of these philosophers were united in their opposition to any doctrine of innate ideas.

Locke. Book I of Locke's *Essay Concerning Human Understanding* is devoted to an attack on the doctrine of innate ideas, and the positive doctrine begins only in Book II. At the outset Locke (1632–1704) had claimed that he was following the "historical plain method," the object of which was to "set down any measures of the certainty of our knowledge." This historical plain method consists in classifying our different ideas and plotting their source as a prelude to an assessment of claims to different kinds of knowledge. Despite appearances this is not a psychological method; it is a method of philosophical analysis designed to discover the logical character of different ideas. In this way Locke distinguishes between ideas of sense and ideas of reflection. Ideas of reflection result from the operation of the mind itself upon ideas of the sense. There is no other source of ideas.

Locke also distinguishes between simple and complex ideas of both kinds, complex ideas being formed by the mind in compounding simple ideas. He seems to think that what it is to have a simple idea of sense is fairly obvious; it is to be aware of a particular quality of an object mediated by a single sense. The criterion of simplicity was, however, a problem for all British empiricists. In having simple ideas the mind is passive, but some activity is allowable in the forming of complex ideas.

Primary and secondary qualities. Among simple ideas of sense Locke makes an important distinction—already implicit in Descartes and others—between ideas of primary and ideas of secondary qualities. Primary qualities, such as bulk, number, figure, and motion, are, Locke thinks, inseparable from the bodies in which they are found. Bodies could not exist without them. Secondary qualities, such as color, sound, and taste, are, on the other hand, "nothing in the objects themselves but powers to produce the various sensations in us by their primary qualities." In other words, the primary qualities of things produce sensations in our minds which are ideas of secondary qualities, but "secondary quality" is a misnomer to the extent that there is really no such quality in things. Thus, our ideas of primary qualities actually correspond to the things which produce them, whereas our ideas of secondary qualities, although produced by things, resemble nothing in those things, being purely subjective. Locke brings forward a number of arguments for this conclusion, arguments based mainly on the assimilation of our perception of secondary qualities to sensations of pain. That is, he takes the perception of, for example, warmth or color to be the same kind of thing as feeling pain.

Account of perception. He thinks of perception in general as identical with merely having sensations, and he thus fully embraces the causal theory of perception according to which perceiving is having sensations caused by things. He goes further than this in respect to primary qualities, for here he also accepts the representative theory of perception according to which our ideas represent the things which cause them. This theory, as we have seen, was the stock in trade of seventeenth-century philosophy. Like most theorists of this pattern, Locke can give no good reason for the view that any of our ideas resemble their causes, and he cannot take the rationalist course of appealing to an intellectual intuition of some properties of things. It is a fair guess that he, like Descartes and others, was influenced by the success of physical science in maintaining that physical properties like extension—properties which are measurable—are *the* properties of things. There is also the connected fact that these properties are perceptible by more than one sense, as Aristotle had noted in his theory of common sensibles.

Modes, substances, and relations. Complex ideas may be exhaustively subdivided into ideas of modes, substances, and relations. Ideas of modes are ideas of things that depend on substances for their existence—for example, the idea of a triangle or a murder. Ideas of substances are ideas of particular things taken as existing by themselves—the complex idea of substance, he goes on to say, consists mostly of powers. Ideas of relation, finally, result from a comparison of one idea with another. Locke came to have some dissatisfaction with this classification of complex ideas, and in the fourth edition of the *Essay* he introduces a fourfold classification of ideas—simple ideas, complex ideas, ideas of relation, and general ideas. However this may be—and there is room for dissatisfaction with Locke's second classification, too—all ideas other than simple ones are in some way formed by the mind out of simple ideas.

Locke classified ideas of space, time, and number as ideas of modes. That is to say that they are ideas of entities which depend for their existence on particular things. We build up our ideas of these entities out of our ideas of particular things when seen in the appropriate relations. Kant later showed that such a view of the source of our ideas of space and time was untenable; Leibniz commented on the fact that Locke failed to take account of the a priori nature of the ideas of space and time and attributed the failure to Locke's inexperience with mathematics.

Locke maintained that our ideas of physical substances are mostly ideas of powers and that the idea of power is an idea of another mode. Since what we know of physical substances is largely due to their effects on us or on other substances, ideas of physical substances all mainly ideas of power. The effects, Locke thinks, are due to the motions of the invisible parts of things, but owing to the weakness of our senses, we are unable to perceive the nature of these causes. We have little or no knowledge of the "real essences" of things. What we do know of things is of their "nominal essences"—their nature merely in respect of the classifications into which we fit them. Such classifications may not correspond to the real nature of things. Here Locke clearly shows how much he was influenced by the physical sciences. He thought that classifications show the way to the nature of things, but that owing to the weakness of our senses, we are unable to do more than gain a general impression of the nature of those physical processes. Therefore, we have to be content with an ordering of things according to their effects rather than as they are themselves.

Theory of general words. Locke adds to the account of ideas a discussion of language and of the words corresponding to the various ideas. It is in the context of this discussion that he puts forward his theory of the meaning of general words, a theory which was to come under attack from Berkeley. This theory—that the meaning of general words is given by the general or abstract ideas to which they correspond—is in effect Locke's theory of universals. He expresses the problem by asking, "Since all things that exist are only particulars, how come we by general terms; or where find we those general natures they are supposed to stand for?" His answer is that words are general by being signs of general ideas, and we form general ideas by abstraction, "separating from them the circumstances of time and place, and any other ideas that may determine them to this or that particular existence." Thus, words become capable of representing a number of individuals by standing for an abstract idea. Locke's view is therefore a form of conceptualism in that the universal or general element lies in our ideas or concepts, not in anything non-mental. Given a liberal enough interpretation of the word "idea," there is perhaps no great difficulty in understanding what Locke is getting at, although the implication that the meaning of words must always consist in their standing for something (in this case an abstract idea) is certainly wrong. The idea terminology is a vague one, common though it was in the seventeenth and eighteenth centuries, but most of those who employed it would have denied that ideas were simple images of things. Moreover, such an interpretation is far from consistent with much that Locke says about ideas. Nevertheless, the use of the term "abstract idea" is not without its difficulties, especially since Locke says that such ideas must represent things.

Kinds of knowledge. In his account of ideas and their classification Locke is the strict empiricist, maintaining that all ideas must be ultimately derived from simple ideas of sense, either directly or as a result of the operations of the mind upon these. His account of knowledge, given in the last book of the *Essay,* is less empiricist in character; indeed, it owes an obvious debt to Cartesianism. He begins with the claim that knowledge is nothing but "the perception of the connexion of and agreement or disagreement and repugnancy of any of our ideas." This agreement or disagreement can be classified into four kinds: (1) identity or diversity, (2) relation, (3) coexistence or necessary connection, and (4) real existence. It is the fourth kind which presents the difficulties. How can the knowledge of the existence of a thing be a matter of the perception of the agreement or disagreement between our ideas alone? This could be so only if our knowledge of the existence of things could be a priori. Locke thinks that some knowledge of this sort can be shown to be a priori, but it is knowledge of the existence of sensible things that presents the greatest difficulties.

Locke distinguishes between three degrees of knowledge in a manner which is reminiscent of Spinoza's distinction between the three kinds of knowledge. There is, first, intuitive knowledge; second, demonstrative knowledge; and, third, "sensitive" knowledge of particular finite existences. The last Locke adds almost as an afterthought on the ground that it has by no means the certainty which belongs to the first two, although it goes beyond mere probability and is commonly thought of as knowledge. (Locke's conception of the standard to which knowledge must attain is noteworthy here.) Apart from the different degrees of certainty that are to be attached to these kinds of knowledge, they also differ in that intuitive and demonstrative knowledge can be concerned with relations between ideas (we can see that white is not black, and we can reason from one idea to another) but sensitive knowledge is concerned only with the existence of the objects of ideas. This is not to say that there cannot be intuitive and demonstrative knowledge of existence, too. Locke thinks that we have intuitive knowledge of our own existence (compare Descartes's *cogito*) and demonstrative knowledge of God's existence (by means of a version of the Cosmological Argument; Locke distrusts the Ontological Argument). But how can the existence of anything be known from ideas alone? Locke sometimes appears to say that such knowledge consists in the perception of the agreement of certain of our ideas with the idea of existence, but in general he acknowledges that more is required than this—real existence and not merely conceived existence. The difficulties here are especially evident in connection with sensible knowledge.

Existence of external world. In Book IV of the *Essay* Locke tries to justify the claim that we have knowledge of the existence of particular sensible things by showing that our ideas do correspond to the things that cause them. Whereas complex ideas may not always correspond to things because of the part played by the mind in forming them, simple ideas receive no contribution from the mind; they are entirely passive. Unfortunately, it does not follow from this that they are necessarily veridical. He adduces further considerations, stressing the passivity of the mind in receiving ideas and the way in which the senses may cohere in their reports. None of these considerations is really sufficient, and Locke admits that they do not amount to proof. In fact, by simultaneously embracing a general empiricist approach and a representative theory of perception, Locke cannot provide a guarantee of, or even any general argument for, the veridicality of the senses. He cannot provide any independent access to the objects of perception other than that provided by the senses themselves. Like most empiricists, Locke accepts the correspondence theory of truth in that the truth of a proposition consists in its correspondence to the facts. (Truth, he says, signifies "the joining or separating of signs, as the things

signified by them do agree or disagree one with another.") But he has no general warrant for the belief in the correspondence of ideas to things.

Berkeley. The main aim of Bishop Berkeley (1685–1753), as he conceived it, was to defend common sense and religion against skepticism and atheism. But both his metaphysics and his theory of knowledge, connected as they are, can be partially regarded as attempts to rid Locke's theory of impurities. Locke's view of the world involved, besides minds and their contents (ideas), material substances, for the most part unknowable. Berkeley wished to get rid of material substances precisely because they were unknowable. In his view the existence of material objects consists only in their being perceived; their *esse* is *percipi* (their existence is to be perceived). In consequence, they must be regarded as complexes of ideas whose cause cannot be any substance underlying them but must be a spirit, the only active thing. Some of our ideas may be caused by ourselves qua spirits, but insofar as ideas have what we normally think of as an objective order, they must be caused by the supreme spirit, God. The laws of nature according to which ideas are ordered are guaranteed by God, and our ordinary way of looking at and talking about the world obscures this fact. Berkeley therefore thought that it was necessary to rid Locke's views of those elements which prevented this insight. The main issues concerned the notion of substance as the cause of our ideas, with the connected doctrine of the distinction between primary and secondary qualities. Berkeley also found fault with Locke's doctrine of abstract ideas, partly for its own sake but also because he thought it one of the main supports for the doctrine of substance. We might, that is, have an idea of substance by abstraction; it had to be shown that this was impossible.

Knowledge of the external world. At first, in the *New Theory of Vision*, a work on both optics and philosophy, Berkeley maintained that physical objects are primarily objects of touch. Vision, he asserted, could provide us with no direct perception of the distance of things, for the retina of the eye is only a two-dimensional surface. Our sensations of sight (and, like others of his time, Berkeley thought that perception fundamentally consists in having sensations) can only be of expanses of color. When we perceive things as at a distance from us, what really happens is that the visual sensations which we have suggest to us certain ideas derived originally from touch and connected with the visual sensations by experience. The *New Theory of Vision* consists largely in the working out of this theory in detail. Berkeley came to see, however, that there was no reason for making this distinction between sight and touch. All senses should be alike in these respects. Insofar as we have knowledge of what we take to be physical things, it is because we have, as the result of experience, so connected ideas that having certain sensations or ideas suggests other sensations or ideas. These ideas make up a collection which we identify as an object. Thus, for Berkeley objects are, in some sense, identical with collections of ideas.

In the beginning of the main part of his *Principles of Human Knowledge*, Berkeley flirts with the view, now known as phenomenalism, that all we mean when we say, for example, that there is a table in our study when we are not there is that if we were there, we should perceive it. But he adds as an alternative the suggestion that what we mean is that "some other spirit actually does perceive it," and this is his main view. What we ordinarily take to be things are really bundles of ideas in some spirit's mind; they have a certain stability even when we are not perceiving them because God still is. Indeed, it is God's having ideas according to a certain order that guarantees the order of our ideas.

Sensations and ideas generally (for although sensations are, strictly speaking, one species of idea, Berkeley often uses the terms interchangeably) are entirely passive. Their *esse* is *percipi*. On the other hand, spirits—God or ourselves—can be active. We cannot have ideas of spirits, although we have a notion of them, since we can understand the word "spirit" and at least know that we are the source of some of our ideas. There is no room in this for any substance's underlying our ideas, since we have no idea of such a thing. Furthermore, the special place that Locke had given to primary qualities—that of being the properties essential to material substance—is untenable, and if what Locke said about secondary qualities is right, there are no grounds for making any distinction between them and primary qualities. They are equally dependent on the mind, so that if secondary qualities are subjective (and Berkeley accepts and adds to Locke's arguments for this conclusion), they must all be. All qualities are ideas in the mind.

Theory of universals. Berkeley's fiercest attack upon Locke was directed against his doctrine of abstract ideas. Berkeley interpreted Locke as asserting the existence of ideas or images which possess contradictory properties. The abstract idea of a triangle must be simultaneously scalene, isosceles, and equilateral. This is clearly impossible. It is doubtful whether Berkeley is right in this interpretation, but he clearly thought that if such ideas were admitted, there could be little objection to the admission of the idea of substance, too—that is, the idea of a physical but in principle imperceptible object.

In the place of abstract ideas, Berkeley introduced a theory of universals which was nominalist in character. Universals are merely particular ideas that are representative of other ideas in the same class in the way in which a particular man may be representative of other men; hence, their universality lies only in their power of representation. There is no need to assume the existence of general ideas since general words need not correspond to general ideas in order to have meaning. In other words, Berkeley challenged the theory of meaning which asserts that all words are names and refer to something—*unum nomen, unum nominatum* (one name, one thing named), as the Scholastics put it. In his view general words stand for a number of particular ideas belonging to the same class. General words are different from names in that general words represent a number of things indifferently. It must be confessed, however, that it is difficult to see clearly what, according to Berkeley's view, is involved in understanding a general word. Certainly, it involves having an idea which indifferently represents a whole class of things, but what is it to see that it does so?

Refutation of skepticism. Berkeley's general view has certain consequences. It means, for example, that important sections of mathematics have to be abandoned. There must, Berkeley believed, be a least perceptible size. Since all our ideas are ultimately derived from sensations, there can be no ideas of infinitesimals or points. For the most part, however, Berkeley considers himself to be defending common sense against the attacks of the metaphysicians. The vulgar, he maintains, believe that "those things they immediately perceive are the real things" (that is, not imperceptible substance), but philosophers believe that "the things immediately perceived are ideas which exist only in the mind." Berkeley characterizes his own view as the joining of these two notions in that he equated real things and ideas. He thinks that given his view that ideas, which are the objects of immediate perception, are the real things, there is no room for doubt concerning the real nature of things—a doubt which Locke had expressed. Moreover, since what is immediately perceived is by definition free from error, only the wrong use of ideas in judgment can give rise to error. Error is thus a product of the imagination. Insofar as we rely upon our sense perceptions as directly given, we must be free from error. Thus, Berkeley claims, his view prevents skepticism and "gives certainty to knowledge."

Concept of knowledge. Apart from the reference to God and spirits, Berkeley is a strict empiricist not only in the sense that he believes that all the materials for knowledge are derived from sense perception (as Locke, too, believed) but also in the sense that knowledge is itself founded on sense perception. Locke was not such a complete empiricist; he thought that knowledge in the strict sense is founded on intuition and demonstration, and he made skepticism possible to a certain extent over sense perception because he thought that its veridicality could not be completely shown. According to Berkeley, knowledge derived from reasoning must ultimately be founded on knowledge based on sense perception. Sense perception, in turn, is no longer conceived of as having ideas that are produced by objects and may not always represent their causes. Berkeley has given up the representative theory of perception with its assumption that something so underlies our ideas that they may be representative of it. His rejection of the representative theory of perception is the basis of his claim to combat skepticism. Yet, as Hume asserted, it has often seemed a claim that fails to produce conviction, because the claim that what is directly perceived is free from error is true by definition. The question of how we know when we have direct perception still remains, however. Not all ideas are objects of immediate or direct perception; some are ideas of the imagination. According to Berkeley, these are less regular, vivid, and constant than ideas of perception, and they are more "dependent on the spirit"; they can be distinguished from ideas of sense by these criteria. But are all ideas of perceptible things ideas of things immediately perceived, and if not, how do we tell which are?

In the first of the three *Dialogues Between Hylas and Philonous*, Berkeley argues that by sight we immediately perceive only light, colors, and figures; by hearing, only sounds; by taste, only tastes; by smell, only odors; and by touch, only tangible qualities. Here he appears to be arguing from the premise that these things are the special or proper objects of the senses. Although it is difficult to know what, if anything, is special to sight and touch, it is easy to see what is meant in the case of the other senses. Even if we grant that we hear only sounds, taste only tastes, and smell only odors, it does not follow, however, that we cannot be mistaken about the characteristics of these objects in particular instances. Are we necessarily free from error in hearing when we hear that a sound is loud or soft? Nor is our attribution of colors necessarily free from inference as it should be if the perception of color is immediate. What, then, really counts as an object of immediate perception? In answering this question, Berkeley is subject to the same difficulties which have beset more modern philosophers when they have sought to base the philosophy of perception on the notion of sense data. If the foundations of knowledge are found in the deliverances of the senses, there must be certain perceptions which are incorrigible in the sense that they cannot logically be subject to doubt. But what counts as incorrigible perception? Berkeley tries to answer this question by assimilating perception to having bare sensations. Sensations, however, are not the sort of thing which can be right or wrong. The mere passivity of sensation, as opposed to the will, does not show that error arises from the will. If this criticism is valid, Berkeley's theory does not satisfactorily prevent skepticism in the way that he supposes.

Hume. Locke thought that his inquiry had revealed the limitations of the understanding by showing that there are parts of nature that our senses cannot discern. Berkeley, on the other hand, thought that there was nothing which our understanding could not grasp. Sense perception gives us complete knowledge of reality, and we have in addition notions of spirits, including God. Indeed, we could regard our ideas as a sort of divine language by means of which God speaks to us, so that our senses, if viewed correctly, continually reveal the glories of God. Hume (1711–1776) agreed with Berkeley in thinking that there is nothing in nature that lies beyond the reach of our senses, but, contrary to Berkeley, Hume reached the conclusion that our understanding is very limited and that skepticism is the only reasonable attitude toward knowledge. That Hume was intentionally a skeptic has been disputed, but there is no doubt that this is the logical outcome of his views. He thought that whatever Berkeley's claims, his arguments were in fact skeptical: "They admit of no answer and produce no conviction." In effect, therefore, Hume's position is that of following the principles of empiricism to their conclusion without any ancillary claim to knowledge of the inner workings of nature or of God. His conclusions are also something of a *reductio ad absurdum* of empiricism.

Nature of ideas. Hume begins by drawing a sharp distinction between impressions and ideas, impressions being the perceptions of sense and ideas the perceptions of the imagination or memory. In this he claims to be restoring the term "idea" to its original use. Every simple idea must have a corresponding impression—the idea of red, for example, resembling the impression of red—and complex ideas may be formed out of simple ideas. As with Locke, both impressions and ideas may be divided into those of

sense and those of reflection, impressions and ideas of reflection being impressions and ideas of the mind's reflection on impressions or ideas of sense.

The criteria of the simplicity of an impression or idea are as much a problem here as with Locke. To have a simple impression is to have an elementary perception which cannot be further broken down into other perceptions, and this will function as a building block out of which the rest of knowledge may be constructed. Hume takes very strictly the principle that to every simple idea or perception of imagination or memory there must correspond an impression, or perception of sense, although at the very outset he admits a possible exception in the idea of a color in a series. We may have the idea of such a color from the principle of a series without ever having seen it. This possible exception, however, Hume refuses to take as important.

The principle that every simple idea must correspond to an impression is vital for a delimitation of the understanding and as a weapon against rationalism. Impressions and ideas can, however, be distinguished only by the superior force and vivacity of impressions; they cannot be distinguished in terms of their relations to physical objects or minds, for our knowledge of physical objects is derived solely from impressions, if at all. Likewise, among ideas, ideas of memory have a superior liveliness to ideas of the imagination. It is extremely doubtful whether this is always true, and this, in turn, casts doubt on any attempt to characterize remembering and imagining on empiricist lines by reference to the contents of the mind alone.

Theory of universals. Hume follows Berkeley in his theory of abstract ideas or universals. In his view there are no abstract ideas, strictly speaking; however, ideas can be particular in their nature and general in their representation. Hume's only addition to Berkeley's account is his attempt to indicate how this can happen through the association of ideas. The occurrence of one idea may dispose the mind to call up all other ideas associated with it. Hence, the understanding of a general word lies in the disposition of the mind to have the ideas of those things to which it may be applied. This is not a very plausible account in itself since the notion of understanding cannot be analyzed in terms of habits or dispositions of minds, but it is at least an attempt to tackle the problem. The solution is in accord with Hume's general approach; his account of belief is similar.

Space and time are difficult notions for an empiricist to deal with, for, as Kant pointed out, particular phenomena seem to presuppose space and time rather than vice versa. Hence, it is difficult to see how our ideas of space and time can be derived from our ideas of particular phenomena. Locke had nevertheless classified our ideas of space and time as ideas of modes. Hume attempts to deal with our perception of spatial extension and temporal duration in terms of the order in which impressions or ideas appear. But in consequence he has to admit that ultimately the impressions which are ordered in this way cannot themselves be extended or of extended objects, nor can they take time. In general, Hume's treatment of space and time is one of the more puzzling parts of his work.

Causality. Hume's greatest reputation derives from his treatment of causality, although his approach to this subject is similar to his approach to the problem of our knowledge of the external world or of ourselves. His approach is founded upon a distinction between different kinds of relation. There are "relations of ideas," which depend completely on the ideas related, and factual relations, which can be changed without changing the ideas. This is a distinction between logical and matter-of-fact relations, and it leads to a distinction between logical truths and factual truths that parallels Leibniz'. Hume is interested in the causal relation because he believes that it is the only matter-of-fact relation that can lead us from one idea to another. Causality is not a logical or a priori connection, but it is a connection. This assertion is of the utmost importance. Why, however, do we think that there is some necessity in causal connections? It cannot be a logical necessity; also, it cannot be derived from a more general necessity such as might be provided by a principle of universal causality, for Hume believes that such a principle must be contingent and that the evidence for it must be derived from our knowledge of particular causal connections.

He therefore proposes to "beat about the neighbouring fields." He notes that we generally take a cause to be antecedent to its effect and contiguous to it in space. More important, in experience there is a constant conjunction between cause and effect. In a sense these factors provide the basis for our belief in the necessity of the causal connection. Hume takes belief to be a lively idea associated with a present impression, and here the principles of the association of ideas again play a part. What makes an idea a belief is the feeling of being determined by habit or custom to pass from the impression to the associated idea. This feeling is an impression of reflection. It is in such an impression that Hume finds the source of our idea of necessary connection between cause and effect, for the "experimental method"—the resort to experience—should show us that there is no impression of power as such. It is due to habit or custom that we pass from cause to effect, and our belief in the necessity of doing so arises from the impression of a reflection of being determined to do it.

It is important to note just what Hume has achieved here. He has not in any way justified our belief in the necessity of the causal connection; he has merely attempted to explain the origin of the belief by giving a psychological explanation, not a philosophical justification, of the belief. But he has rejected all theories of occult powers in things, so that in one sense he may be considered to have said that what we mean by calling one thing the cause of another is that it is a uniform and contiguous antecedent of another event. To this extent his account is a reductive analysis; he analyzes our notion of cause by reducing it to notions that we understand. Yet Hume can find no justification for inferring the occurrence of one event from that of another; certainly, one event does not logically imply the occurrence of the other, but what other justification is there? Hume's conception of justification fails just because he recognizes no other kind of justification except that one thing logically implies another. Although Hume is commonly said to have raised the problem of induction, he made no real attempt to solve it himself, nor could he within his framework.

Knowledge of the external world. In Hume's account of knowledge of the external world the skepticism already implicit in his account of causality comes to the fore. Like Berkeley, Hume distinguishes between the beliefs of the "vulgar" and of the "philosophical system." The vulgar believe that we are aware of perceptions only, but they also believe that some of them—our perceptions of primary and secondary qualities—have permanent existence. The philosophical system holds that there is a distinction between objects and perceptions and that only objects are permanent. Hume claims to side with the vulgar, but he sees no reason to distinguish any perception from any other. The mind is like a theater in which scenes come and go. Yet he does admit that it is natural to believe in a world of permanent objects. Reason can provide no justification of this belief, but we can give a psychological explanation of it like the account of our belief in the necessity of causality.

Our impressions have a certain coherence and constancy—that is, they fit together and recur in the same order after intervals. As a result, the imagination tends to carry on by custom or habit, and it attributes more regularity to objects of perception than they actually possess. Thus, we come to believe in a world of permanent objects, and we tend to reconcile what reason tells us of the interrupted nature of perceptions and what our imagination suggests about their regularity by a "philosophical" (as opposed to a common-sense) belief in a world of permanently existing objects. Nevertheless, a "direct and total opposition betwixt our reason and our senses" remains. Hume often speaks as if objects were just bundles of perceptions, but he has to deal with the belief that they are more than this. For such a belief he can give no justification, although he offers an explanation of its origin. In the last resort he can only recommend inattention to both our senses and our understanding. This is nothing if not skepticism.

Personal identity. Very much the same account is given of our knowledge of ourselves, a fact which may seem even more paradoxical. Once again, Hume uses the appeal to experience to indicate that we have no impression of the self. He rejects once and for all Berkeley's suggestion that we have a notion of the self. Belief in the self must therefore be parallel to belief in an external world, and Hume proceeds similarly. Belief in our identity through time must result once again from the coherence and constancy that exists between our impressions and ideas, as a result of which the imagination takes them to be impressions and ideas of a single self. Once again, however, no reason can be given for this belief, a fact which worried Hume more than his other tendencies toward skepticism. He returned to the topic in an appendix to the *Treatise of Human Nature,* but in the end he could find no way of ridding himself of his worry except a game of backgammon and a good dinner.

Account of perception. Hume rejected Lockian substance, with the result that perceptions—impressions and ideas—become the substantial entities in his ontology (as he in effect admits in *Treatise,* Book I, Part 4, Ch. 5). In retaining the terminology of perceptions, especially that of impressions, Hume clung to the skeleton of the causal or representative theory of perception. But the skeleton no longer had flesh, despite the suggestiveness of the terminology. Thus, Hume is forced to take his starting point from perceptions that are logically independent of any owner and any object. In one place he says that there is nothing objectionable in the idea of an unperceived perception—a very odd notion. From this he has to build a world which fits the common supposition that there are physical objects and persons. The premises from which Hume derives his position are unacceptable, but given them, he can provide no reason whatsoever for belief in such a world and has to say that the belief is just a product of the imagination. This is skepticism with a vengeance, but it is the logical outcome of his approach.

Reid's criticism. Hume's contemporary Thomas Reid (1710–1796) thought, rightly enough, that Hume's conclusions were manifestly absurd. Finding nothing wrong with the arguments presented by Hume, he concluded that the fault must lie in the premises and proceeded to attack the whole "way of ideas" which was the source of these premises. Reid maintained that it was necessary to make a strict distinction between sensation and perception, a distinction which the doctrine of impressions and ideas blurred. Reid was quite right about this, and his account of the nature of sensation and perception is interesting for its own sake. Sensation, he said, is an act of the mind which has no object distinct from that act, its prototype being pain. Perception is a much more complicated affair, involving a conception of an object and a belief in its existence. In many cases we fail to note the distinction because most of our perceptions are accompanied by sensations. Sensations provide in themselves no basis for inference about the nature of perceived qualities of things, although things cause the sensations. Reid expresses the relation between perception and sensations by saying that the sensations suggest the perceptions; sensations are natural signs of perceived qualities. This suggestion and the sign relationship involved are not a matter of experience, for we do not experience sensations in the same way that we perceive things (to have a sensation is not to perceive anything in itself). The relationship is a natural one like, he says, that between expressions of emotions and the emotions themselves.

Whatever the worth of this account, it is certainly a completely different analysis of perception from that of other philosophers of the period. In claiming to defend our ordinary beliefs by this account against the skepticism introduced by Hume, Reid set himself up as a philosopher of common sense, a position adopted by G. E. Moore in the twentieth century. Reid did retain some of the features of British empiricism, however, especially in a distinction between original and derived perceptions, a distinction which is in some respects very similar to that between simple and complex ideas or impressions. Moore similarly employed much of the apparatus of sense data invoked by modern empiricists.

KANT

Kant (1724–1804) represents the juncture of seventeenth-century rationalism and British empiricism. Brought up in the tradition of post-Leibnizian rationalism, he was, as he put it, awakened from his dogmatic slumber as a result of a reading of Hume. His critical philosophy, as expressed in the *Critique of Pure Reason,* can be characterized as an attempt to draw the boundaries between the proper use of the understanding and the improper use of reason in making assertions of speculative metaphysics and as an attempt to show how the understanding can provide objectively valid knowledge of those things which Hume left to the imagination.

Classification of judgments. Kant bases his approach upon a twofold distinction between types of judgment. There is, first, a distinction between a priori and a posteriori judgments, the first being judgments whose truth can be known independently of experience, the second being judgments whose truth can be known only through experience. A priori judgments are pure when they involve only concepts that are themselves independent of experience. On the other hand, it is not a necessary condition of a judgment's being a priori that it should involve only such concepts. The concepts which are involved in a posteriori judgments, however, must be derived from experience, must be empirical.

The second distinction, that between analytic and synthetic judgments, is different. Analytic judgments are judgments about a thing which give no information about the thing, although they may serve to analyze or explain the concepts involved. This is because the concept of the predicate is contained, albeit covertly or obscurely, in the concept of the subject. The denial of these judgments involves a contradiction; hence, they correspond to what Leibniz called truths of reason. Synthetic judgments, on the other hand, do give information about a thing; in them the concept of the predicate is not included in that of the subject, and their denial does not involve a contradiction.

Kant now combines the two distinctions. Analytic a posteriori judgments are clearly impossible, but there is no difficulty, Kant thinks, about analytic a priori judgments or about synthetic a posteriori judgments. There remains the class of synthetic a priori judgments. It is on these, Kant thinks, that the claims for metaphysics rest, and it is these in particular that empiricists refuse to admit. Kant's program is to show whether and to what extent such judgments exist. The outcome of the program is that although metaphysics in the traditional sense is impossible, synthetic a priori judgments are admissible—first, in mathematics and, second, in the form of the presuppositions of objective experience or science. This program, which constitutes the critical philosophy is Kant's substitute for traditional metaphysics.

Synthetic a priori knowledge. The possibility of synthetic a priori knowledge means that not all knowledge about things can be derived from experience. Nevertheless, Kant thinks that all such knowledge is based on experience. It starts from what he calls intuitions, but since knowledge involves the possibility of making judgments about things, it cannot consist of intuitions alone; it must also involve concepts. To have a sensible intuition is to have a simple awareness of something by means of the senses. This awareness Kant analyzes in a way which derives much from the British empiricists. A sensible intuition consists, first, of a sensation as the content of the intuition. Its form consists of spatial or temporal extension. Hume had to admit that impressions have an order, but he drew the consequence that the impressions themselves were unextended and nontemporal when at their simplest. Kant generally argues that sensations have only intensive qualities, qualities that can vary only in degree. Nevertheless, since the intuition consists of the sensation plus the form—that is, its relations to other sensations—spatiotemporal form is something which is a necessary part of our experience. One cannot, as Locke seemed to suppose, build up ideas of extension from first impressions. Spatiotemporal form is a necessary, a priori characteristic of experience. Since Kant, however, has assumed a theory of perception similar to the representative theory, this a priori spatiotemporal form applies only to things as they appear to us—to phenomena. It does not apply to whatever may be thought to lie behind our experiences (things-in-themselves). This fact Kant expresses by saying that spatial and temporal characteristics (and primary qualities in general) are empirically real but transcendentally ideal. The characteristics in question are not merely subjective; they are objective—valid for all men—but only in relation to phenomena, not to things-in-themselves. (Throughout, Kant's criterion of objectivity is the criterion of intersubjectivity—validity for all men; he is pointing out that from the point of view of the critical philosophy something may be objective in this sense without being a feature of something independent of the mind.)

Pure a priori intuitions. Kant goes on to argue that we have not only a sensible intuition involving a priori spatiotemporal features but also a pure a priori intuition of space and time themselves. It is by virtue of this that the science of mathematics is possible. In order to do geometry, for example, it must be possible to make constructions in space, an idea which presupposes that we have an intuition of space. (Kant insists that this is an intuition, not a concept, but his reasons for this are complex and difficult to understand.) Arithmetic similarly presupposes an intuition of time. It is for this reason that mathematical judgments are both synthetic a priori and possible. Kant took it for granted that Euclidean geometry was *the* geometry of space, so that his account provided the justification of that geometry. It has often been suggested that the discovery of other geometries has undermined his case, and to some extent it has. But Kant would still have insisted that some intuition of space is a necessary condition of the possibility of any geometry, and there is something to be said for this position. Our concepts of space and time are not concepts which can be simply abstracted from experience.

Categories of understanding. Space and time, then, provide the form of all experience, just as sensation provides the content. What is given in this way must be subsumed under concepts in judgment if knowledge is to result. "Thoughts without content," Kant says, "are empty, intuitions without concepts are blind." But in itself the formation of judgments is not enough for knowledge. The judgments which we make might be just the work of the imagination, as Hume in effect supposed in considering our knowledge of the external world. What criteria, then, have to be observed in the case of objectively valid judg-

ments? Kant's answer is that such judgments have to conform to certain principles of the understanding and that these principles are derived from the pure or formal concepts, which Kant calls categories, of the understanding. Only insofar as our judgments conform to these principles can the judgments which we make about appearances be intersubjective, true for all men. Objectivity can be a question of this intersubjectivity alone because no valid judgments can be made about things-in-themselves. What, then, are these principles, and what are the categories?

In the section of the *Critique* known as the "Transcendental Analytic" Kant puts forward two arguments for categories. The first, the "metaphysical deduction," tries to argue for the existence of the categories directly, by finding the key to the list of categories in the traditional table of judgments provided by formal logic. To each of the traditional headings under which judgments can be classified logically, there corresponds, Kant believes, a concept which provides the principle of construction of an objectively valid judgment. The second argument the "transcendental deduction," attempts to show that the existence of categories of the understanding is a necessary condition of possible experience. The two arguments are complementary in that the transcendental deduction depends upon the metaphysical deduction for the actual list of categories, while the metaphysical deduction does not really show that categories are necessary to objective experience. It is true that later, in discussing the principles derived from the categories, Kant brings forward specific arguments in each case, so that it might be said that the case for accepting each of these principles does not depend entirely on an acceptance of the metaphysical deduction. Yet, it is the metaphysical deduction alone that provides the guide to which categories and which principles we should seek. Today, the metaphysical deduction is almost universally rejected. There can be no validity in the attempt to derive a table of categories for objectively valid judgments from a table of judgments classified according to purely logical principles. It remains, therefore, that if the transcendental deduction is valid, it is possible to accept some categories as necessary, but apart from arguments for specific cases one cannot determine which categories are necessary by reference to any general rule.

Transcendental deduction. The argument of the transcendental deduction is very complex, and only the most general outline will be given here. First, the senses provide us with a manifold of sensations set out in space and time. Second, in order that they may form a unity, the understanding, with the aid of the imagination, has to synthesize them. The imagination helps us to see the manifold as a manifold in space, and in the form of memory it ensures that we also see it as a unity over a temporal period. Kant calls these two forms of synthesis the synthesis of apprehension and the synthesis of reproduction. Third, in the synthesis of recognition the manifold has to be given a principle of unity by subsumption under a concept, so that we see the manifold as a such-and-such. The results of this, however, could still be only subjective. In order to attain objective validity, the understanding must enable us to conceive of the manifold as united in an object. What Kant calls the transcendental unity of apperception is the awareness of experiences as part of one consciousness and as having an object, although neither the owner nor the object of those experiences can be found in the experiences as such. Objective experience presupposes these features; otherwise, the situation would be, as Hume in effect supposed, a mass of experiences whose connection with a person or objective world is merely contingent.

Fourth, the judgments we make about the manifold of experience thus unified must themselves conform to certain principles of unity. It must be possible, for example, to see certain connections within experience as that of ground to consequent, and our judgments must presuppose such connections in the things joined in them. Thus, we arrive at the idea that if objective experience is to be possible, it must conform to such categories as ground and consequent. The categories are concepts of the principles of connection of things in judgment, if that connection is to be more than a mere subjective one. They are categories because they are applicable to anything.

Transcendental judgment. The categories derived from the logical table of judgments according to the metaphysical deduction are purely formal. For example, Kant believes that the category of ground and consequent is derivable from the logical notion of a hypothetical judgment. This purely formal category of ground and consequent can be given content only by being applied to phenomena in such a way that it emerges in more material form in terms of the particular relation of ground and consequent that is applicable in the case of phenomena—that is, in terms of the relation of cause to effect. Kant formulated a doctrine of schematism to explain how we can apply the purely formal categories to experience. A schema is a kind of principle for the construction in the imagination of anything that falls under a given concept. It is that which enables us to identify a given object as an instance conforming to the concept. Thus, the schema for each of the categories can be thought of as the principle for the application of the pure category to phenomena in time. The notion of ground and consequent applied to phenomena in time emerges, as we have seen, as the notion of cause and effect (an essentially temporal notion). It is only from these schematized categories that it is possible to derive the principles of the understanding according to which all objectively valid judgments must be viewed. These principles Kant discusses and argues for separately.

In all this Kant believes he has explained how judgments about mere phenomena can be objectively valid although they are confined to these phenomena. The judgments in question are by no means applicable to things-in-themselves, to whatever lies behind phenomena. Such notions as those of a world lying behind phenomena and of a real self which is aware of them are noumena, and as such they must be thought of as limiting concepts. To treat such concepts as if they were concepts of an ordinary kind and to use them in a systematization of knowledge, as is done in speculative metaphysics, is wrong and is liable to produce fallacies. A noumenon is merely a "nonphenomenon," and the concept of a noumenon is essentially a negative one, but reason tends to treat such concepts as positive, and from this the illusions of speculative metaphysics stem.

Critique of metaphysics. The judgments that the understanding allows us to make are conditional in that they are relative only to possible experience. Pure reason tends to assume an absolute, something unconditional, which provides the basis of the unity of all judgments of the understanding. It thus provides us with ideas whose proper use is only regulative, in that they are ideas of the goals or limits toward which the understanding may strive without being able to apply them directly to experience. To use these ideas, as speculative metaphysics does, as ideas under which we can directly subsume reality—such ideas as those of the absolute unity of the thinking subject, the absolute unity of the world in space and time, and the absolute unity of the conditions under which anything can be thought at all, the entity of entities or God—is the source of antinomies and other forms of contradiction or fallacy. Kant sets out to expound these contradictions and their resolutions in detail, but it is impossible to follow the argument here. The section of the *Critique* known as the "Transcendental Dialectic" is a critique of rational psychology, speculative cosmology, and metaphysical theology with its attempts at a demonstration of the existence of God. Although there is much other material in the *Critique,* this section essentially completes the critical philosophy in its attempt to show that the understanding can provide objectively valid knowledge of phenomena and to reveal the limitations of the proper use of the ideas of reason.

An assessment of Kant's work in the theory of knowledge is difficult to give. It contains many extraordinary insights, although their detailed development often leaves much to be desired. Above all, perhaps, it takes as its starting point the analysis of experience provided by the British empiricists, and this undoubtedly limits it.

POST-KANTIAN IDEALIST PHILOSOPHY

Fichte. German philosophy after Kant is in many ways a commentary upon Kant's philosophy, either as further development or opposition. The idealism which was so characteristic of nineteenth-century philosophy was begun when Fichte (1762–1814) found fault with the Kantian view of things-in-themselves that are beyond the reach of knowledge and proceeded to reject the notion on grounds similar to those which are commonly used against any causal or representative theory of perception—there can be no good reason for believing in such things. With the rejection of things-in-themselves, even as a limiting concept, we are left merely with experiences or phenomena, and it is of these that, in the idealist view, reality must consist. The general problem of idealism which Fichte thus introduced was how it was possible to distinguish among experiences those which are purely subjective and those which are really objective. The problem is how we can distinguish between what is contributed by the mind and what is not, between the self and not-self, as Fichte put it. In Kant's view objectivity was equivalent to validity for all men, but that it was at all possible to distinguish between what was due to the mind and what was not seemed guaranteed only by the existence of things-in-themselves. With the rejection of the latter, experiences and experiencer became only two sides of the same coin. For this reason the general trend of idealism was toward the coherence theory of truth—the view that experiences and judgments are true to the extent that they cohere with one another, forming a coherent system. This view was naturally associated with the doctrine of degrees of truth—that judgments have varying degrees of truth to the extent that they cohere with each other. This more or less intelligible view was, however, complicated by being involved with the view that judgments about the empirical world have a very low degree of truth because they bring with them paradox and contradiction. The sensible world is therefore only appearance, and reality must be something else.

Hegel. The belief that the sensible world is only appearance is perhaps less marked in Hegel (1770–1831) than in some of his idealist successors—for example, F. H. Bradley. Hegel was influenced not only by Kant but also by Greek thought, especially by Platonist and Neoplatonist conceptions of an intelligible world of Forms with a structure of its own. Nevertheless, Hegel's relation to Kant may be roughly characterized by saying that he attempted to restore the functions of reason that Kant had forbidden. Whereas Kant had tried to justify the processes of the understanding while underlining the contradictions involved in an improper use of reason, Hegel tries to show that the understanding involves its own paradoxes, which can be resolved only by the use of reason; this, in Hegel's view, is by no means improper.

Dialectical method. Contradictions arise during the application of philosophical categories like those of the One and the many, so that the philosopher finds himself asserting both a thesis and its antithesis, in a manner similar to that expounded in Kant's antinomies. There is, Hegel thinks, a method which reason can pursue in order to resolve any such contradiction. Reason has to find a synthesis, some category which will reconcile those which produce the apparent contradiction. But the resolution may, in turn, find itself opposed to a further antithesis which demands another synthesis and so on. This method Hegel calls dialectic. According to him, it provides the key to understanding how the ideas of reason may be charted. In the end they will be seen to be dependent on the ultimate, absolute idea which provides the ground for everything else. Thus, the idea of something absolute and unconditional which Kant had rejected is restored.

It must be confessed, however, that as a method in the strict sense, Hegelian dialectic is sadly defective in that there appear to be no rules for its use. Hegel presents a series of insights, sometimes real, sometimes imaginary, into the relationships between very general and abstract philosophical ideas, like those of being and essence or consciousness, self-consciousness, and reason. Dialectic provides the architectonic according to which these relationships may be charted, and Hegel is excessively thoroughgoing in its use. The result—the Hegelian system—is a complete map of all forms of knowledge and of all philosophical ideas, constructed on a single plan. The attempt is ambitious; the ground for its validity, slender in the extreme. It would be foolish, however, to deny the incidental insights.

Theory of knowledge. Hegel's theory of knowledge may be found partly in his *Science of Logic* and partly in his

Phenomenology of Mind. In the *Science of Logic* he explains his view of Kant, criticizing Kant's trust of the understanding and Kant's, to Hegel's own mind, undue restriction of the functions of reason. Then, through the dialectic he charts the notions most central to reason, beginning with the opposition between the categories of Being and Nothing, the synthesis of which he finds in Becoming. These are notions which reason finds indispensable for any account of the world and upon which logic must depend.

In the *Phenomenology* Hegel sets forth his view of perception most clearly. There Hegel begins by pointing out that consciousness appears to be an apprehension of what is immediate, of what *is*, which is, it appears, a confrontation of the ego with something else (as Fichte also supposed). But sense knowledge proper must involve a subsumption of this immediate consciousness under universals or concepts, and, moreover, there is no way of grasping the particular which is thus subsumed under concepts except by reference to other concepts. Proper names and even words like "this" are, in Hegel's view, general words, since they apply to a multitude of different things (Hegel here ignores or fails to appreciate the way in which they so apply); hence, they furnish us with no means of identifying a particular independently of universals. Sense knowledge thus turns out to be a mediated knowledge, a knowledge which is possible only through the medium of universals and which is not a direct knowledge of reality.

There is, however, Hegel argues, a contradiction between the fact that we take ourselves to perceive things which are unitary entities and the fact that our knowledge of them can exist only through a plurality of universals which are themselves unconnected. This contradiction is resolved only because the intellect provides us with a higher universal which constitutes the basis or condition for applying the lower-order universals in sense perception. This higher universal is force, the idea of "lawlikeness." The unity of the objects of perception is due to the lawlike connections which exist between the universals under which they are subsumed. This is something which can be discerned only by the intellect, which thus produces the synthesis of the contradictions apparent within consciousness. This, of course, does not end the matter for Hegel, as the phenomena of consciousness are equally phenomena of self-consciousness. The opposition between consciousness and self-consciousness requires a synthesis by reason.

Bradley. The kind of general argument that Hegel used can also be found in the English idealist Bradley (1846–1924), although he was far less attached to Hegel's method, referring to the dialectic as "the bloodless ballet of the categories." (In spite of being chronologically out of order, emphasis is placed on Bradley here because Bradley, although often difficult to understand, is generally easier than Hegel for English-speaking readers. The slight differences between Hegel and Bradley matter little in light of their essential similarity of purpose.) In his *Principles of Logic* Bradley argues that all judgments are only conditionally true in that the identification of the portion of reality which is their subject involves subsumption under universals. The judgment as a whole therefore says that some universal can be ascribed to reality only on condition that some other universal or universals may be ascribed to reality. All judgments, although categorical in that they are concerned with reality (reality being the subject of all judgments), are also hypothetical in this sense. Hypotheticals must likewise rest upon a ground; their truth is dependent upon connections within reality (Hegel's force). In Bradley, however, there is greater emphasis on the idealism. For Bradley universals correspond to ideas, so that in judgment we are attaching an idea to reality. However, since what is known can be connections between ideas only, reality as we know it is a system of ideas joined by what he calls internal relations. A judgment is true to the extent that the ideas which it ascribes to reality cohere with the whole system of ideas. By an internal relation, as opposed to an external relation, Bradley means a relation which is more than a contingent one. The relations which form the system that constitutes what we know of reality are more than mere contingent relations, although they are not so close as to be logical entailments. All that we can know of reality apart from the ideas under which we subsume it is that it is experience; it is the bare fact of consciousness from which Hegel starts. Bradley is indeed Hegel made more palatable for English tastes.

It is only fair to add that in his most explicitly metaphysical work, *Appearance and Reality*, Bradley finds paradoxes in the notion of relations in general. The idea that two things may stand in a relation gives rise, he claims, to an infinite regress. What is relational must be set down as appearance only. It follows that judgment can never amount to absolute truth, for all judgment involves the setting of ideas in relation; all judgment, in other words, involves inference. No judgment can therefore furnish more than a limited degree of truth or be about something which has more than a limited degree of reality.

Judgments about the Absolute, the sum total of reality, may have a certain intellectual incorrigibility, since they will in effect ascribe to the absolute reality what is merely part of itself, but they cannot add up to truth itself. This is inevitable, since Bradley takes all judgment to be asserting the identity of subject and predicate, of reality and idea, while maintaining an unbridgeable gap between them—between the "that" and the "what," as he puts it. The notion of judgment therefore involves a contradiction in itself, and for this reason the understanding is condemned. Intuition or immediate awareness gives us the bare fact of experience as constituting reality. What it is unconditionally and absolutely only reason can tell us. Whereas Kant had maintained that reason can tell us nothing of what is absolute and unconditional and that only paradox can result from the attempt to make it do so, the Hegelian doctrine espoused by Bradley is that the limitations of the understanding can be seen only by going beyond its limits to what is not finite and not conditioned but absolute. The claims for reason had never been pushed so far before, nor have they been since.

Schopenhauer. With Schopenhauer (1788–1860) there was a partial return to Kant. Schopenhauer thought that Hegel's dialectical method was barren because it ignored Kant's insights into the nature of reason and the under-standing. Yet he retained Hegel's idealist approach. Kant's phenomena became presentations or ideas in a sense similar to Berkeley's; that is, they became subjective experiences. Schopenhauer thought that the world consists of ideas or presentations and that necessary connections judged to exist between them are, as Kant thought, merely conditional; however, Schopenhauer does not accept the paraphernalia of Kant's categories for justifying such judgments. In his view all justifications for claiming objective experience rest on the principle of sufficient reason, which takes various forms according to the form of knowledge involved. It acts as a logical ground (the *ratio cognoscendi*) in connection with logical truths, as a ground connected with the features of space and time (the *ratio essendi*) in connection with mathematical truths, and as causality (the *ratio fiendi*) in connection with ordinary empirical phenomena. Thus, the notion of causality is made to play the role of all Kant's categories in relation to empirical phenomena; causality is their only ground for necessity in this sphere. Schopenhauer finally looks to the will as the only ground for action, for moral necessity. As one class of phenomenon, action finds its explanation only in the will.

Will as the thing-in-itself. The world as idea or presentation is only one half of Schopenhauer's philosophy (his main work is entitled *The World as Will and Idea*). Although he accepted the idealist framework, he thought that the demand for a thing-in-itself as the basis of all our ideas was inescapable. He finds the nature of the thing-in-itself in the will. Reality consists of the manifestations of one force, the will, which uses consciousness as an instrument for its own self-promotion. Only in art is there anything like freedom from it, for only there does the mind achieve a state akin to the contemplation of Platonic Ideas, a sort of permanency which is foreign to the general manifestations of the will.

Although the last part of Schopenhauer's thought had some influence upon the romantic movement in nineteenth-century German thought, it has not received much welcome from the main stream of philosophers. However, Schopenhauer's theory of knowledge, contained in the part of his philosophy devoted to the world as idea, contains much of interest along lines which are, in origin, Kantian.

LATE NINETEENTH-CENTURY PHILOSOPHY

Philosophical thought in Germany during the nineteenth century tended to be either romantic or neo-Kantian. Neo-Kantian philosophy came under empiricist influences from Britain, and at the end of the century under Brentano and Meinong this finally led to a return to realism, a movement which not only produced phenomenology (perhaps the dominant philosophy in Europe today) but also to some extent influenced Russell and other realist philosophers in the English-speaking world.

Brentano. Brentano (1838–1917) held that the objects of psychology were mental acts. Each mental act had an immanent object—what Brentano called an intentional object—thus reviving scholastic terminology. These objects were a kind of internal accusative to the relevant act, as a judgment is to the act of judgment. They provide the content of the act. But what is the status of these objects?

Clearly, the question is especially pertinent because it is possible to think of or make judgments about things that do not exist. How can a real act have an unreal object?

Meinong. This was the problem which Meinong (1853–1920) took up. He postulated nonexistent objects to explain the possibility of our thinking, for example, of things that do not or cannot exist. Similarly, false judgments were said to correspond to what he called objectives—nonexistent states of affairs which would be facts if only the corresponding judgments were true. Objectives could not be said to exist, for they were not things, but they might subsist. From a linguistic point of view, this doctrine implied a realist theory of meaning, according to which the meaning of any expression was given by a corresponding entity. The fact that these entities were not themselves mental entities (although they gave content to what is mental) implied a return to realism in a more general sense. Objects could be real, according to Meinong, without being actual.

Husserl. Husserl (1859–1938), another disciple of Brentano, started from very much the same point of view as Meinong, maintaining that the proper philosophical task was to investigate the essence of mental acts and their objects. Philosophy consisted, in his view, in an inquiry into the essence of different manifestations of consciousness and the essences with which they are concerned. To study this, it was necessary to strip off all presuppositions, metaphysical or otherwise. Husserl later emphasized this aspect increasingly. He adopted the method of *epoch*—the bracketing of presuppositions—in a manner akin, as he pointed out, to the Cartesian method of doubt. This would lead to pure consciousness as the one absolute, the one firm thing, and from this the philosopher may turn back to investigate the essence of different phenomena as they appear to consciousness. Thus, in effect the initial realist point of view led back to one which was more like idealism. But this belongs, properly speaking, to the twentieth century.

J. S. Mill. Meanwhile, in Britain the predominant philosophy at the beginning of the nineteenth century was sensationalism with its attendant associationism. James Mill (1773–1836) took a radically empiricist point of view, trying to reduce perception to merely having sensations and other mental phenomena to sensations plus the ideas associated with them. His son J. S. Mill (1806–1873) brought greater sophistication to this point of view and, in so doing, led to its downfall. Like his father, J. S. Mill wished to reduce all knowledge to experience, to the association of certain ideas with basic sensations. He expressed a great admiration for Berkeley's *New Theory of Vision* and its explanation of how we come to see things as at a distance. He thought it possible to explain in a similar way how we come to think of ourselves as perceiving a permanent world of things. We have expectations which take us beyond the immediate sensations because of the associations built up in experience between our immediate sensations and ideas of "permanent possibilities of sensation." Our ideas of material things are simply ideas of these permanent possibilities of sensation. Like Hume, Mill approaches this problem psychologically; he seeks to explain why we believe in an external world. To the extent, however, that he is inclined to add that things are simply these permanent possibilities of sensation, his view is the extreme empiricist doctrine of phenomenalism, the doctrine that all we mean by "material object" is something about our experiences.

Mill's main contributions to philosophy perhaps lie in logic, ethics, and politics. His general approach, however, is psychological, based on a conception of experience as atomistic sensations which could be linked to derivative ideas by the processes of association. Mill's general point of view is perhaps nowhere more obvious than in his account of such necessary propositions as those of mathematics. These are, in his view, simply very highly confirmed generalizations. The only necessity is psychological necessity.

Mill's view of knowledge came under attack in the latter half of the nineteenth century from many sources in Britain and elsewhere. In Britain perhaps the main attack came from the returning idealism, particularly as represented by F. H. Bradley. His main line of thought, as already discussed, was Hegelian with less emphasis on the dialectic and greater emphasis on the idealist point of view, according to which reality consists of experience organized in thought by attaching ideas to it in judgment. In *Appearance and Reality* Bradley sought to show that all features of the empirical world are only appearance and that reality must consist of a form of experience which is absolute and unitary and transcends all the contradictions of appearance. His criticism of Mill is that the pure sensory given is a myth; all the content of our knowledge must come by way of ideas—that is, through thought—and association "marries only universals." Experience in itself is nothing.

Bergson. Criticisms of a different kind came from France and America. In France there were few philosophical developments of interest during the nineteenth century until Bergson (1859–1941). Bergson was an anti-intellectualist who emphasized life against thought. Much of his approach was therefore biological. The space and time of which we are conscious, Bergson thought, are continuous; the division of it into things and processes is due to the intellect, which carries out the division according to our biological needs. Perception involves an awareness of the possible moves which our body can make in relation to an object; in contrast, sensation corresponds to a simple response to a stimulus. Like Bradley, Bergson thought that the atomistic sensations of the sensationalist were a product of intellectual analysis. There are actually no basic experiences of this sort. We perceive things as our biological needs cause us to do so. Similarly with memory; our body acts like a sieve. Without the body our mind might remember everything, and this would be both useless and even disastrous biologically. Our body saves us from this, causing us to select only that which is biologically useful.

Because of this emphasis on biological utility, there is a relativism inherent in Bergson's point of view, and it has much in common with American pragmatism as instituted by William James. Bergson went further than James in his emphasis on life, however. His starting point was a thesis about time which is really outside the scope of this article. Roughly, his view was that the time of consciousness (*la durée*) is continuous; the ideas which thought presents to us are or seem discontinuous. The continuity of consciousness must be due to an interpenetration of those ideas, and as a result, they form a developing series in which, given that each member developed from what has gone before, each member must be unique. The development itself is due to a vital spirit, and the same is true of the universe at large.

James. Bergson's emphasis upon the continuity of consciousness has its counterpart in James's thesis of the stream of thought. In his *Principles of Psychology* William James (1842–1910) insisted, in opposition to the sensationalists, that there were no atomic sensations or ideas; distinct ideas are selected phases of one stream of consciousness, and these phases make up a continuity because each idea has a fringe which overlaps that of its neighbors. Thus far, however, James was content to argue that our ideas are determined by what things there are. We must, he maintained, distinguish between knowledge by acquaintance and knowledge about something (not to be confused with a somewhat similar but really different distinction made by Russell). The baby is acquainted with the universe but he has not yet selected anything from the mass of sensation with which he is confronted. Thus, he knows nothing *about* anything. James was later to go further in Bergson's direction. In *Essays in Radical Empiricism* he rejected the distinction between thought and things, embracing a thesis which is known as neutral monism, the thesis that reality consists of one stuff (in this case experience) out of which both the mental and the physical are to be constructed according to the principles which govern each. From this continuous experience a plurality of thoughts and objects can be developed, a plurality of things related by concatenation only, as experience tells us they are. In this James set himself in opposition to his other bête noire, idealism, with its emphasis on internal relations and its denial of plurality.

Peirce and Dewey. James's special claim to fame (although some would say notoriety) is perhaps his status as the founder of pragmatism, although this, too, has Bergsonian affinities. The original source for the pragmatist point of view was C. S. Peirce (1839–1914), a rather isolated figure. A man with a great wealth of ideas, Peirce, as a nonprofessional philosopher, was to some extent outside the main stream of philosophical thought. He came to philosophy as a mathematician and scientist. He was opposed to all intuitions of the Cartesian type, largely because of his belief in the power of hypothesis and his disbelief in ultimate inexplicables. Perhaps his greatest contribution, however, lies in his theory of signs and meaning. In this connection Peirce maintained that our conception of anything is determined by our conception of the practical bearings of that thing. In sum, meaningfulness is a question of practical utility, and the meaning of any given concept or expression is given by its precise utility.

James turned this theory of meaning into a theory of truth, much to Peirce's disgust. He maintained that the test of the truth of any belief was its fruitfulness. To say that a belief is true is to say that it is good in this sense. Such is the pragmatic theory of truth.

For John Dewey (1859–1952) it is knowledge that is successful practice; propositions are merely instruments which may take us to the goal toward which experimental inquiry is directed. There is no final truth; instead, there is "warranted assertability" when the judgments which we make lead us to the abstract goal of science in accordance with scientific method.

TWENTIETH-CENTURY REALISM

The course of twentieth-century philosophy is not smooth, and it is therefore not easy to chart. No more than a sketch will be attempted here. Undoubtedly, however, the main philosophical event at the turn of the century was a swing from idealism to realism. In America there were the neorealists, such as E. B. Holt, W. B. Montague, and R. B. Perry, influenced by James and his theory of neutral monism; in England there was Samuel Alexander, and in Germany there was Meinong. The most important figures in this revolution were G. E. Moore and Bertrand Russell at Cambridge, and of these Moore was the originator in this respect.

Moore. G. E. Moore (1873–1958) began with a criticism of Bradley. Moore thought that Bradley had not taken far enough his rejection of the view that we abstract our ideas from experience. Insisting that concepts or ideas should be regarded as the objects, the meanings, of our thoughts, Moore went on to argue that there must be propositions as the objects of beliefs. Things are merely collections of concepts and as such enter into propositions as their constituents. Propositions are what we believe when we hold any belief, true or false. This amounts to an insistence upon a distinction between any mental activity or form of awareness and its object. Moore's article "Refutation of Idealism" in his *Philosophical Studies* is founded on just this point, for he finds the refutation of the doctrine that *esse est percipi* in a distinction, somewhat after the manner of Brentano, between the act of awareness in perception and the object of awareness, between consciousness and its object. Idealists, he maintained, failed to notice the distinction.

Moore was later to give up his doctrine of propositions, for in considering the problem of false belief, he said that "there do not seem to be propositions at all, in the sense in which the theory demands them." If there were, there would have to exist something corresponding to false beliefs, and the fact of its existence would make the beliefs true, not false. Belief cannot therefore consist in a relation between ourselves and an object. The rejection of propositions in this objectively existing sense may look like the abandonment of the very foundations of his realism, and so in a sense it is. But Moore did not give up the view that we do know of a reality independent of our minds, and when he abandoned the account of false belief which implied the existence of objectively existing propositions, he nevertheless maintained categorically that we must not give up the view that truth somehow consists in correspondence with reality.

Existence of the external world. Moore sometimes said that he never doubted that we do know things about reality which we ordinarily think that we know. Therefore, he was not influenced by the usual skeptical arguments against this position. In his view the real philosophical problem was to analyze what we mean when we say that we have this knowledge. Moore has generally been one who raises the difficulties about this problem rather than one who gives the answers. He has definitely maintained, however, that we do have knowledge of many different kinds of thing, and in his notorious "Proof of an External World" (*Proceedings of the British Academy,* 1939) he gave as a good argument for the existence of such a world the fact that we can point to objects in it. Thus, he held up his hands, saying, "Here is one hand, and here is another," to prove the existence of an external world. Moore's thought moved toward the view that what requires defending is common sense, ordinary beliefs such as the belief that there are objective things, like his hand, in the world. When metaphysicians say such things as "Time is unreal," this is an affront to common sense and demands explanation. Wittgenstein later said that the view defended by Moore was not strictly common sense, since it was a philosophical point of view. This seems correct; what Moore meant by common sense was a general realist point of view.

Account of perception. In his analyses of what we mean when we claim knowledge, however, Moore's discussion follows the lines of those which have been more influenced by skepticism. Thus, in his account of perception he brings in sense data as what we actually see or directly apprehend when we look at something. Characteristically, he distinguishes between the sense datum (the object which we actually see) and the sensation which we might be said to have of it. But in using the words "direct apprehension" and "actually seeing," he suggests that he wants that indubitability which other philosophers have sought as an answer to the skeptic. Direct apprehension cannot be of the physical object, for, he argues, when an envelope is held up, it cannot be this that we actually see, since some people may fail to identify it as such. There is room for error about the identity of the object but not, perhaps, about its color or even shape as seen, so it must be these that we actually see. Moore's main worry is about the exact relation which exists between sense data and physical objects, both of which, he thinks, certainly exist. The answer that he would like to give is that sense data are parts of the surfaces of physical objects, but the fact that different people may have conflicting views of these objects prevents him from giving this answer. The right answer, and, for the same reason, the precise nature of sense data were always a puzzle to him.

It may be wondered why Moore felt it necessary to bring in sense data at all. The answer must be that for Moore there had to be things which we just know, and although we may know of the existence of physical objects, we may not be so sure of their exact qualities. Hence, the possibility of error plays a part in Moore's thought just as it has done in that of others, even if the influence of skepticism is not so explicit. Direct apprehension fills the same role in his philosophy of perception as intuition in his ethics. The notion has its parallel in the conception of knowledge employed by his Oxford contemporary John Cook Wilson and his disciples, such as H. A. Prichard. They thought

the trouble with idealism lay in its failure to see that there was a distinct state of mind, knowledge, in which there was no possibility of error.

Russell. Bertrand Russell (born 1872) was first an idealist but was converted to realism by Moore. From his early study of Leibniz, Russell took the view that philosophy consists in the analysis of propositions, and his interest in logic also brought him to a concern with language. During the early 1900s he became interested in Meinong, whose realism seemed to confirm Moore in Russell's line of thought. However, he came to think that Meinong's supposition that there had to exist objects to explain our ability to think of things which do not exist in fact, such as round squares, showed, as he put it, an insufficiently robust sense of reality. Partly in response to this and partly in response to a more complex theory of meaning put forward by the mathematical logician Frege, Russell set forth the theory of descriptions.

According to the theory of descriptions, phrases of the form "the so-and-so" are incomplete in meaning. They have no meaning (in the form of an object of reference) in themselves; to give their meaning, it is necessary to analyze the meaning of the whole sentence in which they occur. Sentences of the form "The so-and-so is *F*" are really tantamount to composite sentences including as a part the sentence asserting that something exists corresponding to the description "the so-and-so." Where nothing of the kind exists, the whole proposition is false ("proposition" here being equivalent to "statement," not the objectively existing object of beliefs). The theory of descriptions became a tool of analysis, and Russell used it in many connections.

Theory of knowledge. The main importance of the theory in epistemology is connected with Russell's distinction between knowledge by acquaintance and knowledge by description. Knowledge by acquaintance is Moore's direct apprehension, but Russell has always been more concerned with the justification of claims to knowledge than was Moore. For Russell it was important that all knowledge be founded on knowledge by acquaintance, if it was to be possible at all, for only in knowledge by acquaintance is error absolutely impossible. In *Problems of Philosophy* Russell gave a list of entities of which we have knowledge by acquaintance—sense data, memory data, the self, and universals. Of physical objects we have only knowledge by description because here error is possible. Russell also declares that "every proposition which we can understand must be composed wholly of constituents with which we are acquainted." (By "proposition" he meant the objectively existing entity in the early Moorean sense.) This is possible only if anything of which we have knowledge by description is reducible to things of which we have knowledge by acquaintance. Physical objects, for example, must be reduced to sense data or, since they are not always being perceived, to a combination of sense data and sensibilia—actual and possible sense data. They must, as Russell puts it, be considered as logical constructions from sense data; they are simply bundles of sense data and sensibilia. From the logical point of view, names of physical objects are disguised descriptions, and the theory of descriptions shows that it is not necessary to suppose the existence of a special class of entities called physical objects in order to give propositions about them a meaning. What we are acquainted with when we perceive a physical object is a number of sense data; the physical object we know only by description, and any statement expressing a fact about it is a statement about a description. This statement is analyzable, so that it contains an existential proposition about something answering to that description, according to the theory of descriptions; it is, that is, about something falling under a set of universals, and these are objects of acquaintance as much as sense data are. The notion of an object of acquaintance is closely connected with that of a logically proper name, an expression which cannot fail in its reference. Descriptions can, of course, fail in that there may be nothing answering to them. With the reduction of physical objects to sense data, knowledge of physics is preserved, and this has always been a cardinal point in Russell's program. On the actual status of sense data, Russell's opinion varied, but when most impressed by physics, he made them, paradoxically enough, entities in the brain.

Logical atomism. At the beginning of World War I, when Russell had come under the influence of Wittgenstein, he held that the ultimate constituents of the universe are atomic particulars, which are terms of relations in atomic facts. All other facts were to be built up from atomic facts by the processes of logic. The atomic particulars are sense data, and the relations supply the universal element in the fact.

The theory of logical atomism is a metaphysical theory rather than an epistemological one, and this is even more obviously true of Wittgenstein's version in his *Tractatus Logico-philosophicus.* Russell differs from Wittgenstein in his more explicit interest in the nature of the constituents of atomic facts, and it is clear that his choice of these constituents was determined by his desire to found all knowledge on knowledge by acquaintance. The one exception to the program which Russell found at this stage was that of mental states like belief, for he could not see how statements about beliefs could be reduced to more elementary statements. In order to deal with the problem, he has flirted with behaviorism, since if belief is analyzable only in terms of behavior, this, in turn, may conceivably be explained in terms of sense data.

Russell changed his mind over the details of his logical atomism, especially when he was influenced by the logical positivists, but the framework remained the same. His account of memory is similar to that of perception; it is founded on memory experiences only contingently related to the past, although they may have a feeling of familiarity. The memory data are objects of acquaintance, but the past itself is not. In one general respect, however, Russell acknowledges that empiricism fails—in our knowledge of the postulates on which, in his opinion, inductive inference and, therefore, science rest. Induction, he thinks, is founded on habit, and the principles implicit in such habits cannot themselves be derived from experience. Despite his belief in the limitations of empiricism, Russell has never wavered in his defense of realism. He has always embraced and keenly defended the correspondence theory of truth.

Nature of mathematics. Nothing has been said thus far of Russell's work on the foundations of mathematics, especially his great contribution, written with Whitehead, in *Principia Mathematica*, although this is in a sense part of his epistemology. In *Principles of Mathematics* Russell held that mathematical propositions were synthetic, but when, influenced by Frege, he embarked on the attempt to reduce mathematics to logic by deriving it from a small number of axioms containing only logical notions, he held mathematical propositions to be analytic. This is too complicated a matter for discussion here. The exact nature of mathematical propositions is still a matter of dispute, but the attempt to reduce them to logic may now be seen to be a great and splendid failure.

Whitehead. It may be noted briefly that Russell's partner in *Principia Mathematica*, A. N. Whitehead (1861–1947), took a very different road in epistemology. He tried to explain the properties of things in terms of their relations to one another. In perception the mind tries to grasp—or in Whitehead's term to "prehend"—a part of the system of nature around it; it is reacting to the environment in biological fashion. There are no atomic sense data; to suppose that there are is to be liable to the "fallacy of misplaced concreteness"—the view that because science has a concept (such as that of an instant), there must be entities of this sort in experience. To some extent Whitehead's thought is in the idealist tradition, but it also contains a certain Platonism. The particulars of which nature is composed, he thought, are events; the permanent characteristics which we recognize in them are objects. The objects are, as he puts it, ingredient "into events," not into just one event but through an indefinite neighborhood of events. We do not, that is, see single things with isolated characteristics; we view them as part of a system. Whitehead's thought is, however, difficult, and little can be done to make it intelligible in a short space.

LOGICAL POSITIVISM

Wittgenstein's *Tractatus* influenced a group of philosophers in Vienna who were mainly interested in the philosophy of science after the empiricist fashion of Ernst Mach. Wittgenstein had said that to understand a proposition is to understand what it would be like for it to be true. The Vienna circle, as this group became known, wrongly interpreted this as a general criterion of significance, and so the verification theory of meaning was born. According to this theory, meaningful propositions must be either analytic or empirically verifiable. The propositions of mathematics and logic were thought to belong to the first class, and the propositions of science to the second. Metaphysical propositions, belonging to neither group, were declared meaningless.

The members of the group differed over the details of this scheme, and a progressive relaxation in its rigor gradually took place. One of the biggest problems was the status of the verification principle itself, for on the face of it it is neither analytic nor empirically verifiable. The eventual outcome for some members of the group was to view it as a recommendation only. There were also other problems. The initial aim of the movement was, above all, to lay the foundations of science. Scientific propositions had to be preserved and metaphysics excluded. It became apparent that it was difficult, if not impossible, to provide a formulation of the verification principle which fulfilled both goals.

Moritz Schlick (1882–1936), the original leader of the group, felt compelled to interpret scientific laws as rules rather than statements. Another problem lay in the meaning of the phrase "empirically verifiable." Schlick held that ultimately there had to be a direct confrontation with experience. Other members of the movement—for example, A. J. Ayer (born 1910)—held that there had to be basic propositions which were directly and strictly verifiable (and thus absolutely incorrigible), although others could be indirectly verified by reference to these. This led to a distinction between strong and weak verification; propositions about physical objects, for example, might be only weakly verifiable, since an indefinite number of propositions about immediate experience would have to be invoked in order to verify them conclusively. In this, positivism was associated with the thesis of phenomenalism that statements about physical objects are analyzable into a collection of statements about sense experiences. The fact that such an analysis must be indefinitely long has resulted in a progressive modification of the thesis on the part of its main proponents—for instance, Ayer.

Truth. Schlick's view brought with it the correspondence theory of truth. Otto Neurath (1882–1945), on the other hand, held that this involved an attempt to go outside the web of language and ran the risk of a lapse into metaphysics. Neurath maintained that there had to be "protocol propositions"—observation reports on which science might be founded—but that these need not be reports of immediate experience. The truth of a protocol proposition was determined by its coherence with other propositions making up the language of science. Thus, Neurath embraced a coherence theory of truth. This general line was developed by Rudolf Carnap (born 1891) into a form of conventionalism. He put forward a "principle of tolerance," maintaining that logic had no morals; verificationism thus became a proposal for the best way of developing the language of science. Whereas Schlick and the earlier Carnap had maintained that basic propositions must be about immediate experience, Neurath had maintained the thesis of physicalism that protocol propositions must be in the language of physics. In line with his relaxation of the criteria, Carnap came to accept what he called the "thing-language"—the language of the common-sense world—as the basis for scientific language. Today, positivism in its strict form is more or less a thing of the past.

Nature of science. It is noteworthy that Karl Popper (born 1902), who was not a member of the movement but who was influenced by it and influenced it, held that the key to an understanding of science lay not in verifiability but falsifiability. He put this forward, however, not as a theory of meaning but as a criterion for the demarcation of science from metaphysics. The generalizations of science are, because of their very form, unverifiable, but they *are* falsifiable, whereas the propositions of metaphysics are not. Popper has developed these views into a thesis about science as based on the hypothetico-deductive method.

The aim of science is to put forward bold hypotheses, the deductive consequences of which must be subject to rigorous testing and criticism. This view is associated with a form of skepticism, for Popper sometimes maintains that we can never *know* the truth. The best that we can do is to put forward hypotheses and subject them to rigorous tests, for this is the way in which science progresses. Truth itself is just an illusion.

CONTEMPORARY MOVEMENTS

Contemporary philosophy is in an untidy state of nonuniformity. In Europe perhaps the most prevalent philosophy is a phenomenology deriving from Husserl. This movement is also associated with existentialism, originally a reaction against the superrationalism of Hegel and, therefore, to some extent a form of irrationalism. Existentialists have added little to epistemology; they tend to take for granted the existence of an objective world, aiming only to present a picture of it and of man's place in it. Those existentialists who derive something from Husserl—for example, Jean-Paul Sartre and Maurice Merleau-Ponty—are concerned mainly with descriptions of forms of consciousness, with phenomenology as descriptive psychology.

Ordinary-language philosophy. Perhaps the most significant movement, apart from latter-day positivism and pragmatism, is the so-called ordinary-language philosophy, today most closely associated with Oxford. The leading spirit of the movement is, however, the Cambridge philosopher Ludwig Wittgenstein (1889–1951), who has had an immense influence. His work is not easy to summarize; it is in part a series of comments upon his earlier logical atomist views and the theory of meaning which it espoused. Only a small part of his work can be mentioned here. He has criticized the attempts implicit in much sense-datum philosophy to construct a private language by arguing that the results of such attempts would lack the essential conditions of a language. There would be no way of distinguishing between the occasions on which one was following a rule in applying an expression and those on which one was making a new decision so to apply it. He has also stressed the importance of bringing back terms to the language game (as he calls possible languages) that is their original home—ordinary language. This, he maintains, is perfectly in order as it is; the important thing is to examine the uses to which expressions are put, with the recognition that language is a form of life and must be treated accordingly. Among other things this has led to the recognition of truths which are necessary but not analytic, truths which he calls "grammatical." These are truths which express nonanalytic connections between concepts. The emphasis upon such truths and the arguments which lead to them on the part of followers of Wittgenstein is in a sense a partial return to Kant. (The distinction between analytic and synthetic truths in general has in any case come under fire from several quarters, especially from the American logician W. V. Quine [born 1908]. But his emphasis on the necessity of assessing the status of propositions only within a system is something more of a move toward the idealist point of view.)

The appeal to ordinary language has been used for many

purposes. Gilbert Ryle (born 1900), for example, has used it in order to plot, as he puts it, the logical geography of mental concepts such as mind, belief, or will. He, too, has attacked the notion of sense data, and he has made and emphasized an important distinction between knowing how and knowing that. For present purposes the main importance of the appeal to ordinary language lies in its confrontation of the skeptic. The most stringent appeals to usage (rather than merely to the functions of language, as in Wittgenstein's case) have been made by J. L. Austin (1911–1960), who has emphasized the extent to which many philosophers including skeptics, have departed from our ordinary use of words. It is clear, however, as Austin in effect admitted, that an appeal to what we ordinarily say cannot settle these issues, however much it may be a good first move. Arguments are first required in favor of our ordinary way of speaking.

It has been argued, for example, that anyone who says that we never know anything but only believe or suppose it robs the concept of belief of an essential contrast with knowledge, without which it would be meaningless. This argument—the so-called argument from polar concepts—is invalid, because a philosopher can use the concept of belief as long as he has the concept of knowledge, as long as he knows what it would be like to know; he does not have to admit that anyone knows anything as a matter of fact.

Another argument is that we can never deny that we have knowledge altogether, because this would be denying the existence of the paradigm case by reference to which we have learned the meaning of the word "knowledge." This argument—the so-called paradigm-case argument—fails, in the opinion of the present writer, because it assumes that meaning is given by the applications of a term. Whereas it might be difficult to see how we could have come to attach meaning to a term unless we had learned some of its applications, it is not logically impossible that we should have done so. Hence, more complicated arguments are required.

This is the situation. Most philosophers would agree that if we are to be said to know a proposition *p*, we must believe *p*, *p* must be true, and we must have good reasons for believing in *p*. There is perhaps little argument over the first two conditions, although there might be some hesitation over the details. The problem is what counts as good reasons for believing in *p*. In the ordinary way we recognize different reasons according to the nature of the proposition involved. The skeptic denies that any of these are sufficient, and it is impossible to produce any knock-down argument which will dispose of the skeptic's claim. Each application of this claim must be assessed on its own merits, and the answer to the skeptic must therefore be a dialectical one in the Socratic sense. But the very existence of recognized forms of knowledge presupposes that there must be such knowledge. This is, however, only a presumption, not a proof.

Traditionally, and for good reason, skepticism has had biggest sway in connection with claims to knowledge of objects of perception, knowledge derived from memory, knowledge of other minds, and inductive knowledge. In each of these cases the skeptic may present too high a standard of knowledge, which cannot, in the ordinary way, be attained. But the temptation to accept such a standard may be increased by adopting certain views about the nature of—for example, perception or memory. If perception is thought of as merely having sensations or memory as merely having images or ideas in the mind, there is necessarily a gap to be crossed from our own minds if there is to be objective knowledge in these fields. Hence, the talk of knowledge of an external world, external to our own minds. With a different conception of memory or perception, in which an essential connection is recognized between memory and the past or perception and an objective world, this gap is removed. This is not to get rid of the skeptical problem at one fell swoop, since it remains a question whether and under what conditions these concepts of perception and memory can be applied. This, however, is merely the general problem of how knowledge is possible in different fields; it can be dealt with dialectically. In other words, an incorrect conceptual analysis can worsen the skeptical problem, but a correct one cannot solve it. But the presumption remains that objectivity is possible in these fields, even if it is incapable of proof. Each doubt can be alleviated only by argument; there is no over-all answer. Finally, the supposition that an answer can be provided by showing that there are forms of knowledge in which error is logically excluded and which are therefore absolutely indubitable is an illusion. First, there is no indubitable knowledge; second, it is not necessary for the general possibility of knowledge that there should be. Much of the history of epistemology has depended on this illusion.

Bibliography

For the texts of individual philosophers see the separate articles devoted to them.

INTRODUCTORY BOOKS

Ayer, A. J., *The Problem of Knowledge.* London, 1956.
Russell, Bertrand, *The Problems of Philosophy.* Oxford, 1912.
Woozley, A. D., *Theory of Knowledge.* London, 1949.

GENERAL HISTORIES

Copleston, Frederick, *A History of Philosophy,* 7 vols. London, 1947——.
Hamlyn, D. W., *Sensation and Perception.* London, 1961. A history of the philosophy of perception; contains bibliography.
O'Connor, D. J., *A Critical History of Western Philosophy.* New York, 1964.

D. W. HAMLYN

EQUALITY, MORAL AND SOCIAL. The proposition "*A* and *B* are equal" may be descriptive or normative, but in either case it is incomplete without a statement of the respects in which the objects or persons compared are deemed to be equal. In instances where this appears not to be so, either the context supplies the complement or the comparison is of pure quantities, as in pure mathematics. Two objects equal in weight, or height, or value may be unequal in other respects; apart from the abstractions of mathematics and logic, no two objects could ever be said to be equal in *all* respects, only in all relevant respects. Correspondingly, to say that two candidates are equal in merit would usually mean that with respect to their performances in some understood competition or examination, they deserve to be treated alike; it does not rule out treating them differently if they are unequal in other respects. Aristotle's celebrated account of justice in Book III of the *Ethics* amounts to this: no distinction ought to be made between men who are equal *in all respects relevant to the kind of treatment in question*, even though in other (irrelevant) respects they may be unequal. On the other hand, in any matter in which they are in relevant respects unequal, they ought to be treated in proportion to their relevant inequalities.

These analytical distinctions are of considerable importance in dealing with equality as a moral and social ideal. Thomas Jefferson's claim that "all men are created equal" cannot be rebutted by pointing to the obvious fact that some are taller, stronger, or more clever than others. The claim is intelligible only as a prescription, as saying that there is *some* respect, at least, in which no difference ought to be made in the treatment or consideration given to all men, whatever differences there might be in their qualities and circumstances.

HISTORY OF EQUALITY AS AN IDEAL

Plato preached the political equality of the sexes, Aristotle that of all free citizens; nevertheless, both laid more stress on not treating unequals equally than on any general conception of equality. Aristotle believed that some men were slaves by nature, Plato that some souls were not merely capable of higher development than others but more valuable on that account. The political egalitarianism of Pericles' Athens, described by Thucydides, was concerned only with the equality of Athenian citizens and excluded slaves and foreigners. The first generalized egalitarianism was that of the Stoics, who stressed the natural equality of all men as rational beings with an equal capacity for virtue: "Virtue closes the door to no man; it is open to all . . . the freeborn, the freedman, the slave and the king . . . neither family nor fortune determines its choice—it is satisfied with the naked human being" (Seneca).

The New Testament doctrine of the equality of all souls in the sight of God (Galatians 3.26–29) is a religious expression of a similar principle: "Ye are all one in Christ Jesus." It was profoundly modified, however, by the Augustinian doctrine of election. Men were equal only in the sense that by sin all were totally, and therefore equally, unworthy; God in his mercy extended grace to some but not to others. Aquinas qualified the equality of all men in the sight of God by the doctrine that slavery is the consequence of sin. Though there are signs of a crude social egalitarianism in some of the protest movements of the later Middle Ages, such as the Lollards and the Hussites, medieval social theory was, on the whole, antiegalitarian, deeming hierarchy to be natural both to society and to the whole universal order.

Modern egalitarianism had its beginnings in the seventeenth century. It is related in part to Calvinist doctrine, which, although it admittedly drew a sharp distinction between the saved and the damned, insisted at the same time on the equality of the elect, whether clerical or lay. This view of equality came to be associated with a theory of church government—and indirectly of secular government—that derived legitimate authority (i. e., the right of superiors to command inferiors) from the voluntary agreement of natural equals to submit to such of their number as they chose. These doctrines were given their first completely secular expression—associated with theories of natural right and social contract—by some of the Parliamentarians in the English civil war, particularly the Levelers. Colonel Rainborough's declaration in the General Council of the Army in 1647, that "the poorest he that is in England hath a life to live as the greatest he" and that no one can have a duty to obey a government that "he hath not had a voice to put himself under" is a classic expression of democratic political egalitarianism.

The idea of a natural equality of all men was a dominant theme from the seventeenth century on. Hobbes took it for granted that in the state of nature men are equal in right because roughly equal in strength and cunning. Locke argued that by nature men are equally free, are subject only to natural law, and enjoy the same natural rights. This turns the problem of political authority and obligation into a search for reasons why free and equal men should accept the limitations of civil society. Political inequality, of ruler and ruled, must be justified as a conventional device for the better safeguarding of the rights and advantages that all men already possess but cannot securely enjoy, in a state of nature.

In eighteenth-century philosophy the idea of a natural equality of rights was reinforced by a theory of human nature, as put forth by Condillac and Helvétius, maintaining that all differences of character, talent, and intelligence are due to differences in environment and experience. By nature men are equal in the sense that at birth they have a limitless potentiality without natural characteristics to differentiate one from another. Consequently their diverse natures are, in fact, contingent; in principle all men are equally perfectible, given the appropriate social arrangements. Rousseau explained social inequality by the pressures of a sophisticated way of life; in the state of nature men's needs are simple, none need rely on anyone but himself, so none can exploit another or make him subject. For Rousseau the key problem for social philosophy, to which the sovereignty of the general will could provide a solution, was to reconcile the natural equality and autonomy of men with the social condition and political authority. Without this reconciliation men cannot realize their potentiality as *morally* self-governing persons. Kant offered a philosophically sophisticated version of a very similar moral position: all human beings must be treated as ends, not merely as means; all men are equally "legislating members of the kingdom of ends," because all are equally capable of realizing the good will, the only thing in the world good in itself.

These doctrines permeated the great revolutionary movements in America and Europe at the end of the century and were made explicit in their declarations of rights. In America the doctrine of equality was a denial that any authority imposed on unwilling subjects could be legitimate merely on grounds of law or prescription; in France *l'égalité* repudiated privileges of prestige and opportunity based solely on noble birth. But alongside these broad popular movements were others, such as Babeuf's Conspiracy of the Equals, which challenged economic inequalities. Protests of this kind became increasingly important in the nineteenth century, in the evolution of socialist and communist thinking.

The target of modern egalitarianism, however, is by no means solely, or even primarily, economic inequality. Such inequality is objectionable to many socialists not so much as an unequal distribution of goods but as a source of unequal power, prestige, and regard. Other forms of differentiation have been as strongly attacked—in particular, differentiation by race and color and by sex. Again, egalitarians may make very general claims, such as that in the Universal Declaration of Human Rights (adopted by the UN General Assembly in 1948), that "all human beings are born free and equal in dignity and rights," or they may claim, more specifically, "equality before the law" or "equality of opportunity."

This history has two noteworthy features. First, there is a recurrent theme, the idea of a universal but imprecisely defined equality; behind all differences of talents, merits, and social advantages there is some characteristically *human* nature by virtue of which all men are equal. Second, the focus of egalitarianism has shifted continuously, now attacking the differential treatment of barbarian and Greek, now of freeman and slave, noble and commoner, black and white, rich and poor, male and female. Egalitarianism might be said not so much to assert equality as to deny the justice of some existing inequality of treatment based on some allegedly irrelevant differences of quality or circumstance.

UNIVERSAL EQUALITY AS AN IDEAL

The notion of universal equality as an ideal is difficult to pin down. Many egalitarians have tried to argue that despite the many points of inequality, all men are alike in possessing reason, or a soul, or some other essentially human characteristic or nature, by virtue of which they stand equal. The difficulty, however, is to find an important characteristic that all men possess in *precisely the same degree*, so that whatever differences their other inequalities might justify, this fundamental equality would make them equal *qua* men. And even if one could identify such a characteristic, what would follow from it? If all men are alike in having souls, in what respect should they therefore be treated alike? After all, God is widely believed to punish wicked souls and to reward virtuous ones.

The ideal of universal equality can often be reduced to the principle that all men ought to be equally considered. This does not mean that there is any respect in which they are all alike and by virtue of which they should all be *treated* alike; it is rather a principle of procedure: that all men ought to be treated equally, despite *all* their differences, until a case has been made for saying that some particular difference between them is relevant to the matter at hand. The onus of proof rests on whoever wants to make distinctions. And up to a point this might be said

to be implicit in the notion of rational decision, because it would be irrational, within a given class of cases, to treat some differently from others if no relevant grounds could be found for distinguishing between them.

Nevertheless, the principle of equal consideration does presuppose an initial commitment or decision, for it takes for granted whose interests are to count. No one claims equal consideration for all mammals—human beings count, mice do not, though it would not be easy to say *why* not. The Greeks made a similar distinction between themselves and barbarians, Aristotle between natural slaves and naturally free men, the slaves counting only as tools for the free men. It is not easy to see how anyone who seriously held that white men mattered but black did not could be *reasoned* out of this position, any more than one could argue for the equality of men and mice. Of course, many people who practice discrimination profess to believe that black men are in some way inferior to white, in intelligence, sensibility, responsibility, or some such quality, and on this account ought to be treated differently. But this is to admit the principle of equal consideration for all men, that all men count, and that an argument has to be made to justify discriminating against some among them. The man who denies that they count at all is not bound to show reasons, any more than we feel the need to show reasons for treating inanimate objects, plants, or primitive organisms, such as amoebae, according to our pleasure. Although we hesitate to inflict unnecessary pain on sentient creatures, such as mice or dogs, we are quite sure that we do not need to show good reasons for putting human interests before theirs. The boundaries of moral consideration are enlarged in practice by awakening sympathy and imagination; moral reasons presuppose an initial moral concern.

The principle of equal consideration may be more, therefore, than what is necessarily implied by the concept of rational action. The notion of acting with good reason does not in itself rule out *any* inequality of treatment, for it may always be possible to argue that there is some relevant difference between members of a given class. But the principle that *all men* should be treated as members of the class whose equality is procedurally presupposed is not necessarily implied by the notion of rational action.

However, to some philosophers universal equality has meant more than equal consideration for all men. John Plamenatz, for instance, has tied the notion closely to natural rights and has argued that there are some rights "so much more important than others that these others ought always, or nearly always, to be sacrificed to them, should the need arise" ("Equality of Opportunity," in Bryson et al., eds., *Aspects of Human Equality*, pp. 79–107). The purpose of this equality of rights is to ensure equality of freedom and opportunity: "the equal right of all men to live the kind of life that seems good to them . . . equality of opportunity to be oneself, to live as one pleases." This is attractive, but it hardly touches the problem of what is to be done when what pleases one man interferes or competes with what pleases another. Nor does it cope with the diversity of inclinations—can one be said to have, on a given income, an equal opportunity to become a collector of Picassos or of seashells? Or does equality of opportunity require differential provisions, so that the chance of fulfillment matches the aspiration? Does it envisage open competition or a handicap? Plamenatz has attached very great weight to the principle that every individual's view of where his own interests lie should be given equal consideration. He thus closely associates equality and freedom, denying both that one man's interest might legitimately be subordinated to another's and that anyone can be the proper judge of someone else's interest.

For some philosophers (D. D. Raphael and Gregory Vlastos, for example) the ideal of universal equality requires that the inequalities of nature be mitigated or rectified. By this view, precisely because men born with superior talents or social advantages can claim no merit on that account, it should be the aim of social policy to compensate for such advantages by differentiating between men to redress the balance. It is of course true that modern welfare states commonly do provide special amenities, such as wheel chairs for the crippled or hearing aids for the deaf, to bring naturally handicapped people up to some minimum standard of well-being. But an account in terms of meeting needs or deficiencies is more accurate than one in terms of rectifying inequalities, for the policy is not so much to remedy a handicap that one man suffers in comparison with another (wheel chairs are not meant to enable cripples to compete in races with runners) as to provide conditions necessary to his well-being, understood in the light of some presupposed standard of what a good life requires. This standard will no doubt be governed by the advantages commonly enjoyed by most people in the community, so that in an affluent society a person will be taken to have more needs than in an impoverished one; however, the claim will still be grounded on his *own* needs and interests, not on the greater advantages enjoyed by those more fortunate.

SPECIFIC EGALITARIAN IDEALS

The demand for equality is very often directed against some specific inequalities in social arrangements. It may take the form of a protest either against distinctions based on some specific ground (for example, racial equality, sexual equality) or against discriminations in a particular field (for example, equality before the law, economic equality). Each consideration necessarily involves the other; complaints of sexual inequality imply that sex is made a ground of distinction in some fields, unspecified but understood, where it is considered by the critic to be inappropriate (for example, salaries, jobs in the public service, voting rights). On the other hand, the claim to equality before the law implies that in legal relations or in relations between persons appearing before a court, some unspecified but understood difference (perhaps of sex, or of color, or of wealth) is made a ground of distinction and ought not to be.

The meaning of these ideals changes with their context. No one means by "equality before the law" that *no* distinctions should be legally recognized. A social system consists necessarily of different roles, such as father, son, tenant, landlord, and congressman, each with its own appropriate qualifications and characteristic rights and duties, established and supported by law. A system is said to be unequal only if the differences in privileges are considered unjustifiable because they are irrelevantly grounded or because the qualifications for assuming a role are unduly restrictive (for instance, if a white skin is a necessary condition for voting rights). These ideals change their focus over time. "Equality before the law" in eighteenth-century France meant ending the disabilities of the members of the third estate as compared with the privileges of the nobles and clergy. Today it may mean abolishing racial disabilities, such as exist in South African law, or seeing that prejudice does not interfere with the administration of law (the problem of the southern states of the U.S.). It may also mean eliminating the advantages of wealthy litigants over poorer ones, by public legal aid schemes, or making certain that no one is prevented by poverty from getting a fair trial (see Justice Black's opinion in *Griffin* v. *Illinois*, 351 U.S. 12, 1956).

Equality very rarely means treating everyone alike; usually it means getting rid of one system of distinctions and replacing it with another. Thus, equality of opportunity in education hardly ever means giving everyone exactly the same education; rather, it means eliminating some hitherto determining factor such as ability to pay school or university fees and substituting a test of proficiency. More ambitiously, it might aim at a system with various arrangements, each meant for an appropriate grade of intelligence or type of aptitude. Those who call this equality do so on the ground that the treatment accorded to each is equally appropriate to his needs. Thus, R. H. Tawney argued that "the more anxiously a society endeavours to secure equality of consideration for all its members, the greater will be the differentiation of treatment which, when once the common human needs have been met, it accords to the special needs of different groups and individuals among them" (*Equality*, p. 39). The greater the equality of consideration, the greater the differentiation in treatment. If the latter is not called "inequality in treatment" it is because the word "inequality" has acquired, in this sort of context, a pejorative force; "inequalities" have come to mean *indefensible* differences in treatment.

Bibliography

HISTORY OF EGALITARIAN IDEAS

Abernethy, George L., ed., *The Idea of Equality*. Richmond, Va., 1959. An anthology, from the Old Testament and Herodotus to the present. Contains bibliography.

Bouglé, Celestin, *Les Idées égalitaires*. Paris, 1899.

Lakoff, Sandford A., *Equality in Political Philosophy*. Cambridge, Mass., 1964.

Locke, John, "Second Treatise on Civil Government" (1690), in P. Laslett, ed., *Two Treatises of Government*. Oxford, 1960.

Rousseau, Jean-Jacques, *Discours sur l'origine et les fondements de l'inégalité parmi les hommes* ("Discourse on the Origin of Inequality"). Amsterdam, 1755. Various modern editions have been published.

Stephen, Sir James Fitzjames, *Liberty, Equality, Fraternity*. London, 1873. A classic nineteenth-century criticism of radical and egalitarian ideals.

Thomson, David, *Equality*. Cambridge, 1949. Surveys the principal modern egalitarian ideals against a historical background—a useful, brief general introduction.

RECENT DISCUSSIONS

Benn, S. I., and Peters, R. S., *Social Principles and the Democratic State*. London, 1959. Reissued as *Principles of Political Thought*. New York, 1964. See especially Chs. 5–7.

Brandt, Richard B., ed., *Social Justice*. Englewood Cliffs, N.J., 1962. Essays by K. E. Boulding, Paul A. Freund, William K. Frankena, Alan Gewirth, Gregory Vlastos.

Bryson, L., et al., eds., *Aspects of Human Equality*. Fifteenth symposium of the Conference on Science, Philosophy, and Religion. New York, 1956. Nineteen papers on various aspects. See especially J. Plamenatz, "Equality of Opportunity."

Carritt, E. F., *Ethical and Political Thinking*. Oxford, 1947.

Hobhouse, L. T., *Elements of Social Justice*. London, 1922.

Margolis, J., "'That All Men Are Created Equal.'" *Journal of Philosophy*, Vol. 52, No. 13 (1955), 337–346. Argues a "fundamental and actual equality of all men."

Raphael, D. D., "Justice and Liberty." *PAS*, Vol. 51 (1950–1951), 167–196.

Spiegelberg, Herbert, "A Defence of Human Equality." *Philosophical Review*, Vol. 53, No. 2 (1944), 101–124. Interprets the concept in terms of compensation.

Williams, Bernard, "The Idea of Equality," in Peter Laslett and W. G. Runciman, eds., *Philosophy, Politics and Society, Second Series*. Oxford, 1962.

Wollheim, R., and Berlin, Isaiah, symposium on "Equality." *PAS*, Vol. 56 (1955–1956), 281. Reprinted in F. A. Olafson, ed., *Justice and Social Policy*. Englewood Cliffs, N.J., 1961.

ECONOMIC AND SOCIAL EQUALITY

Dahrendorf, R., "On the Origin of Social Inequality," in Laslett and Runciman, *op. cit.* A sociological approach.

Harris, R. J., *The Quest for Equality*. Baton Rouge, La., 1960. "Equality" in American constitutional history and law.

Jouvenel, Bertrand de, *Ethics of Redistribution*. Cambridge, 1952. A critical analysis of egalitarianism.

Lampman, R. J., "Recent Thought on Egalitarianism." *Quarterly Journal of Economics*, Vol. 71, No. 2 (1957), 234–266. Surveys economic doctrines.

Myers, H. A., *Are Men Equal?* Ithaca, N.Y., 1955. The American egalitarian tradition.

Tawney, R. H., *Equality*, rev. ed. London, 1952.

STANLEY I. BENN

ERASMUS, DESIDERIUS (1466–1536), the great Renaissance humanist and scholar, was born at either Rotterdam or Gouda in Holland, the illegitimate son of a priest. As a child he studied at Gouda, and from 1475 to 1483 he studied at Deventer with the Brethren of the Common Life, a pious, modernist–humanist order. Next he studied at s'Hertogenbosch, then became an Augustinian friar at St. Gregory's (near Gouda) and in 1492 was ordained a priest. Disliking monastic life, in 1494 he became Latin secretary to the bishop of Cambrai. The next year he went to the University of Paris to study theology, but he found both the life and the scholastic philosophy distasteful. In 1499 Erasmus went to England, where he became a close friend of the humanists John Colet and Thomas More and devoted himself to the study of the classics and sacred literature, desiring to combine the new humanistic spirit based on the revival of interest in the classics with Christian learning. In 1500 he returned to the Continent and devoted himself to the study of Greek. One of his first famous works was published in this period, the *Enchiridion Militis Christiani* (1501), an appeal for a return to the simple spirit of early Christianity.

In Belgium in 1504 Erasmus came across a manuscript of Lorenzo Valla's *Annotationes* on the New Testament, in which Valla criticized the Vulgate (Latin) version of the Bible and set forth a critical method for arriving at a correct text of Scripture. Erasmus was tremendously impressed and published an edition of Valla's work in 1505, after which he returned to England and copied the Greek New Testament from the manuscripts available to him there. He then went to Italy as tutor to the sons of Henry VIII's doctor and took his doctorate of divinity at Turin in 1506. He lived in various Italian cities for the next three years and began publishing the famous edition of his *Adagia*, a collection of 3,000 proverbs from classical writers, at Venice in 1508. As a result of this work he was soon recognized as the foremost scholar of northern Europe. In 1509 he returned to England and stayed with Sir Thomas More. There he wrote the *Moride Encomium* (*In Praise of Folly*), a witty satire on worldly learning and activities and a presentation of simple, pious, nontheological Christianity. While in England he lectured at Cambridge on Greek and on St. Jerome's epistles. In 1514 he went to Basel to assist the publisher Johann Froben in preparing an edition of his works. While there he received a summons to return to monastic life, which he resisted strongly, and finally Pope Leo X granted him a dispensation allowing him to live in the world.

In 1516 he published one of his most influential works, the Greek edition of the New Testament. Comparing various manuscripts and citations from the Church Fathers, he presented a more accurate text than the Vulgate, along with his own elegant Latin version and many learned and critical notes. This edition became a model and inspiration for the new learning and for critical scholarship. Theologically, its omission of an interpolated passage in I John 5.7–8 stating the doctrine of the Trinity greatly influenced liberal reformers like Michael Servetus, and its emphasis on St. Paul and the Greek Fathers strongly affected those early reformers and those who antedated the Reformation who were anxious to turn from the opulence of the Church of Rome and from the intricacies of late Scholasticism to the spirit of primitive and early Christianity.

From 1517 to 1521 Erasmus stayed chiefly in Louvain, where he was involved with the new college for the study of the sacred languages, Greek, Hebrew, and Latin. He corresponded with humanistic scholars all over the world and became perhaps the leading figure of the northern Renaissance. His influence was great in all Europe, especially in southern France and Spain (where he was offered a chair at the new University of Alcalá). Liberal and reformist theologians and classical scholars looked to him for inspiration. In 1521 he went back to Basel, where with Froben he published a lengthy series of works on the Church Fathers (editions of Jerome, Cyprian, Pseudo-Arnobius, Hilary, Irenaeus, Ambrose, Augustine, Chrysostom, Basil, and Origen), all of which helped center attention on the theology of the early Fathers rather than on that of the medieval Scholastics. His *Colloquies*, first published about 1518 and in many revised and expanded editions thereafter, is an excellent example of the revived and revitalized Latin style of the Renaissance; the several editions include biting and satirical attacks on various human institutions and beliefs, especially those connected with the church and with popular superstition.

Erasmus' merciless and witty critiques of church practices, monastic activities, Scholasticism, popular religion, and so on, as well as his scholarly efforts toward establishing the Greek text and the meaning of the New Testament and the doctrines of the early Church Fathers, had made him outstanding in the movement for church reform. As the reform movement became more revolutionary, however, Erasmus tried to stay aloof from the struggles. Both orthodox and reformist theologians pressed him to take a stand, while he sought means for mediation and reconciliation. When Luther became more aggressive and violent in his words and actions, and when various early reformers criticized Erasmus for his refusal to join them, he, always hypersensitive to criticism, withdrew more and more. Finally, in 1524 Erasmus spoke out against Luther in his work *De Libero Arbitrio (On Free Will)*, in which he tried to show that Luther had dogmatically decided that man had no free will, even though (1) the issue was so complex that no human could really find a satisfactory solution to the problem and (2) the Biblical texts were so obscure that no one could really tell what they asserted. Erasmus maintained that he preferred to recognize the inability of man to discover adequate answers to such theological problems and to rest content with the decisions of the church on such matters. Luther's furious reply, *De Servo Arbitrio* (1525), cried out against Erasmus' gentle humanistic skepticism and his willingness to accept church teachings uncritically. Christianity, Luther insisted, requires certainties, not opinions or probabilities. Salvation cannot be based on doubts. He concluded that if Erasmus wished to remain a skeptic, he should remember that *Spiritus sanctus non est scepticus* (the Holy Spirit is not a skeptic) and that judgment day is coming. Erasmus wrote another answer, the *Hyperaspistes* (1526), and to a great extent broke with his former reform-minded friends. When the reformers took control at Basel in 1529, Erasmus left for Freiburg im Breisgau, where he stayed almost until his death (which occurred in Basel seven years later as he was preparing to return to the Netherlands). During his last years he continued to use his vast scholarship, his pen, and his influence to bring about religious and political peace. Attacked by both the radical reformers and the conservative churchmen, he tried to find a moderate solution before both sides became so rigid that a compromise maintaining the unity of Christendom was impossible. He advocated making sufficient internal reforms within the church to satisfy the less extreme Reformers. Various popes and some Reformation leaders took him seriously (Pope Paul III is supposed to have wanted to make him a cardinal), while the Sorbonne theologians condemned some of his works and views. The Spanish Inquisition stamped out the influence of his followers in Iberia, and the leading reformers attacked him both as a petty, self-serving person and as a heretical religious thinker.

Thought. Erasmus' ambiguous position in the religious struggles was probably the result of his peculiar nondogmatic point of view and his cautious attitude toward developments in human affairs. He claimed to advocate the "philosophy of Christ," in contrast with the various kinds of scholastic theories put forth by the Thomists, the Scotists, the Ockhamites, and others. Their technical discussions about the nature of baptism, grace, and the freedom

of the will left him entirely unmoved. Rather than take their arguments and analyses seriously and present refutations, Erasmus attempted to undermine the whole scholastic approach with the force of his ridicule.

In place of the philosophical and theological systems of the time Erasmus set forth his "philosophy of Christ," to be arrived at by pious study rather than by disputations. This "philosophy" was supposed to represent the simple and essential message of Christianity in its spirit rather than its letter; it was a message to be lived, not to be formulated in abstract systems. It was a nondoctrinal religion, a religion without a theology, which could be approached through the early Church Fathers and the morality of the New Testament but not through the morass of distinctions, terminology, and theory built up in the Middle Ages. This outlook had a great impact on the most liberal reformers and the nondoctrinal mystics.

Erasmus, who was so fully aware of the foibles of man, was also extremely cautious about the genuine possibilities for reform or constructive improvement in man and his institutions. This may account for his refusal to leave the Church of Rome (although he died without receiving the sacraments). Some have interpreted this refusal as due to personal fears, but it seems more probable that Erasmus remained within the church because he believed that it was better to preserve and improve what already existed than to risk the even greater abuses that might follow the destruction of the current order. Erasmus saw the Church of Rome as fossilized, in much the same manner that he portrayed the Jewish synagogue. On the other hand, he saw the reformers as revolutionists who, intentionally or not, were destroying the very fabric of human existence. He told Luther, "I always freely submit my judgment to the decisions of the Church whether I grasp or not the reasons which she prescribes." He also declared, in the midst of the early Reformation struggles, "I will put up with this Church until I shall see a better." He apparently felt that, given the human condition, it was very important to retain the (far from ideal) way that Christ's message had been institutionalized; at the same time he urged a revival of concern for the substance of this message and a revitalization of the church through the correction of as many abuses as possible and the encouragement of scholarly and moral efforts to recapture the original Christian spirit. Otherwise, he feared, the frail human world might be torn entirely asunder. But, for better or worse, the course of events carried the division of Christendom to a complete rupture; each side became more and more rigid and dogmatic rather than compromising on a vague or undefined Erasmian position.

Influence. Although Erasmus can hardly be classified as a professional philosopher, he influenced the course of philosophy in many ways. His humanistic scholarship greatly affected the European educational system and, both personally and through his many writings, Erasmus greatly encouraged the teaching and study of Greek, Latin, and Hebrew—the languages that were most important to intellectual achievement. The upheavals in the curriculums that occurred in most of the major institutions of higher learning at that time were in large measure due to Erasmus' influence and spirit, and the study of the hitherto unknown or neglected classics of both the Greco–Roman and the Judeo–Christian worlds (many in the editions prepared by Erasmus himself) that resulted from this was the source of many new ideas and theories that became part of the intellectual revolutions of the Renaissance.

Erasmus' ridicule of Scholasticism, although hardly a philosophical refutation of either its methods or its doctrines, created the generally accepted view that the medieval approach to philosophical questions was trivial and useless; he made it difficult for many intellectuals to take seriously the views of Thomas Aquinas, Duns Scotus, William of Ockham, and such later Scholastics as Suárez.

Besides teaching future generations to scoff at the achievements of the school philosophers, Erasmus also had a major role in creating the critical spirit that culminated in the Enlightenment. Through his satire, his critical scholarship, and his undogmatic spirit Erasmus popularized a critical and questioning attitude toward accepted mores, institutions, opinions, and texts that was to flourish in many forms in the next centuries, undermining confidence in almost every area of traditional achievement.

Thus Erasmus, who was essentially conservative by nature and who shunned almost all theoretical or philosophical discussion, not even wishing systematically to oppose dogmatism with skepticism, as Montaigne later did, was one of the most influential figures of the sixteenth century in changing the entire intellectual climate of opinion and in establishing the direction in which modern thought developed.

Works by Erasmus

Omnia Opera, Beatus Rhenanus, ed., 9 vols. Basel, 1540–1542.

Opera Omnia Emendatiora, Jean LeClerc, ed., 10 vols. Leiden, 1703–1706. Photoreproduction ed., Hildesheim, 1961. A new edition is now being undertaken, directed by Dr. C. Reedijk.

The Epistles of Erasmus, edited and translated by F. M. Nichols, 3 vols. New York, 1901–1908; reprinted New York, 1962. Contains letters up to 1517.

Opus Epistolarum, P . S. Allen, H. M. Allen, and H. W. Garrod, eds., 12 vols. Oxford, 1906–1958.

The Praise of Folly, edited and translated by Leonard F. Dean. Chicago, 1946.

Inquisitio de Fide, edited with introduction and commentary by Craig R. Thompson. New Haven, 1950.

Discourse on Free Will, edited and translated by Ernst F. Winter. New York, 1961. Selections from Erasmus and Luther.

The "Adages" of Erasmus. Cambridge, Mass., 1964. A study with translations by Margaret M. Phillips.

The Colloquies, edited and translated by Craig R. Thompson. Chicago, 1965. The first complete English translation since 1725.

A bibliography of editions of Erasmus' works is Ferdinand van der Haeghen, *Bibliotheca Erasmiana*, 12 vols. (Ghent and Brussels, 1897——.

Works on Erasmus

Allen, P . S., *The Age of Erasmus.* Oxford, 1914. Essays on the background of Erasmus' life and works.

Allen, P . S., *Erasmus; Lectures and Wayfaring Sketches.* Oxford, 1934. Essays on Erasmus.

Bataillon, M., *Érasme et l'Espagne.* Paris, 1937. Translated into Spanish by Antonio Alatorre as *Erasmo y España*, 2 vols. Mexico City, 1950. An important study of the impact of Erasmus' work in sixteenth-century Spain. The Spanish edition contains much new material.

Bouyer, Louis, *Autour d'Érasme; études sur le christianisme des humanistes catholiques.* Paris, 1955. On Erasmus' theology and humanism.

Feugère, Gaston, *Érasme, étude sur sa vie et ses ouvrages.* Paris, 1874. A good biography.

Froude, J. A., *Life and Letters of Erasmus.* London, 1894. Well-known nineteenth-century study.

Huizinga, Johan, *Erasmus and the Age of Reformation*, translated by F. Hopman. Reprinted New York, 1957. Excellent intellectual biography.

Kaiser, Walter J., *Praisers of Folly: Erasmus, Rabelais, Shakespeare.* Cambridge, Mass., 1963.

Popkin, Richard H., *The History of Scepticism from Erasmus to Descartes.* Assen and New York, 1964. Ch. 1 deals with Erasmus' role in the history of modern skepticism.

Renaudet, Augustin, *Érasme, sa pensée religieuse et son action d'après sa correspondance (1518–21).* Paris, 1926. Erasmus' life and thought as drawn from his enormous correspondence.

Renaudet, Augustin, *Érasme et l'Italie.* Geneva, 1954. Important study of Erasmus' influence on the Italian Renaissance.

RICHARD H. POPKIN

ERIGENA, JOHN SCOTUS, or John the Irishman (*Scotus*), commonly called Erigena, was born in Ireland about 810. Educated in an Irish monastery, he became an able Greek scholar and a distinguished interpreter of Greek thought to the Latin West, and by 850 he was teaching at the court of the Frankish emperor, Charles the Bald. The mind of the age was dominated by the Augustinian interpretation of Christianity, and Erigena's first important work, *De Praedestinatione*, inspired by the principal theological controversy of his day, aroused suspicions of heresy because of its libertarian arguments, which were based on Greek sources. In 858 Erigena began to translate the writings of the Christian Neoplatonist known to us as the pseudo-Dionysius and to prepare a series of commentaries on them. He also translated works by the Greek theologians Gregory of Nyssa and Maximus the Confessor, and wrote commentaries on the Gospel according to St. John and on several works of Boethius. His own great systematic treatise, *De Divisione Naturae*, was probably produced between 862 and 866. The place and date of his death are not known.

Erigena was the one important philosophical thinker to appear in Latin Christendom between Augustine in the fifth century and Anselm in the eleventh. His indebtedness to his great predecessors in the tradition of Christian Neoplatonism, notably to Gregory of Nyssa, Maximus the Confessor, and, above all, the pseudo-Dionysius, must not be minimized, but his own mind was original and powerful. His doctrinal system, for all its marked ambiguities, which have led to widely divergent assessments of his intentions, unmistakably reveals a notable constructive ability and depth of insight. The considerable influence of his major work on later medieval thought would undoubtedly have been still greater if the exploitation of the book by both the Albigensian heretics and the exponents of a philosophical pantheism had not resulted in its condemnation by Pope Honorius III in 1225.

Philosophy and theology. The later scholastic distinction between philosophy and theology is foreign to Erigena, and in his system philosophical and theological elements are inextricably intermingled. He aims at providing a complete rational explanation of the substance of the Christian message as embodied in Scripture and dogma. It is incorrect to read his assertions of the claims of reason as a denial of the reality of divine revelation or as a repudiation of Biblical and ecclesiastical authority, since he never questions Scripture or creed, as he understands them.

What he does question is the notion that the opinions of the Church Fathers are above rational criticism; in his view, the theologian is free to adopt that interpretation of Scripture which best commends itself to his reason. (In any given case, of course, there may be some patristic precedent for the truly rational interpretation, and in fact Erigena frequently appeals to Ambrose and Augustine, as well as to his favorite Greek Fathers, in support of his own teaching.)

Thus far, Erigena apparently remained within the accepted limits of the Catholic Christianity of his time. Eventually, however, his Christian rationalism proved to be incompatible with orthodoxy. In assuming that the content of divine revelation and the conclusions of correct metaphysical reasoning are ultimately identical, he already posed at least one obvious threat to traditional Christian teaching. If, as he seemed to suppose, Christian doctrine in its entirety can be presented as a logically interconnected structure in which each element is rationally demonstrable, no room is left for the affirmation, integral to Biblical faith no less than to Augustinian theology, of the divine freedom in creation and redemption. That is to say, Erigena's essential methodological principle, taken with full seriousness, calls into question the fundamental Christian conviction of the transcendence or total independence of God with respect to the created world.

Furthermore, even if the methodology of Erigena's Christian rationalism could be reconciled with the world view of Christian orthodoxy, the same issue would be raised by the substance of his rational explanation of revelation. It is true that his philosophy—a form of Neoplatonism, derived from Plotinus and Proclus through the pseudo-Dionysius and others—is in some ways well adapted to his theological purpose. For example, it emphasizes the mystery of deity in a way which seems to exclude any confusion between God and creatures. Thus, in Erigena's treatment of theological knowledge, where he closely follows the pseudo-Dionysius, he insists that no terms applicable to creatures can be predicated of God. At most, superlatives (for example, "super-Essential") can be used to express the truth that God is indescribably more than our creaturely concepts can represent. Apart from such indirect affirmations, which do not really violate the basic rule, theological discourse is essentially negative (apophatic). This view of theological predication clearly presupposes the sharpest possible distinction between God and the created world. At the same time, to the extent that Erigena (still in the Neoplatonic tradition) finds the origin of things in a process of emanation from God, in whose essence creatures participate insofar as they truly are, he seriously threatens the Biblical doctrine of the Creator and his creation. Since, in fact, emanationist language keeps recurring throughout his *De Divisione Naturae*, it may be said that his entire metaphysic is marked by a failure to distinguish clearly between a sophisticated pantheism and Biblical theism.

Doctrine of nature. Nature (*natura*) is the unifying notion of Erigena's system. The term stands for the totality (*universitas*) of reality, comprising both God and the world of creatures in which he is manifested. Erigena's explanations of the notion of nature reflect the inherent ambiguity of his philosophy. On the one hand, he explicitly denies that creatures are a part of God; on the other hand, he often seems to think of God as the one comprehensive reality in which all limited and transitory realities participate.

Erigena's development of his doctrine of nature reflects two traditions which he readily assimilates to each other: the Christian doctrine of creation and its fulfillment, and the Neoplatonic conception of the procession (*exitus*) of creatures from the divine and their return (*reditus*) to it. The complete scheme includes four levels or stages: nature which creates and is not created; nature which is both created and creative; nature which is created but does not create; and nature which neither creates nor is created.

Nature which creates and is not created is God in his eternal reality, the primary principle of all things. God is self-existent and unchanging, the uncaused Cause of the world. He alone truly is, and all other beings exist only as dependent upon or participating in him.

Nature which is both created and creative consists of archetypes or exemplary causes of creatures existing in the divine mind. These archetypes came into being through the eternal generation of the Word (*Logos*) or Son, and can thus be described as created only in an unusual sense of the term. Because the Word is logically prior to them, they are not strictly coeternal with him; however, he has never existed without them. As exemplary causes, they may be said to perform a creative function.

Nature which is created but does not create consists of the world of creatures existing outside the divine mind. In statements which cannot readily be reconciled, Erigena describes these creatures as participating in God's reality and as created out of nothing (*de omnino nihilo*). They constitute the divine self-disclosure or "theophany"—in Erigena's own words, the "manifestation of the hidden," the "form of the formless," and the "body of the incorporeal."

Finally, nature which neither creates nor is created is God as the end and goal of the creative process, God with his creatures perfectly reunited to him, God become all in all. In the end, the whole world of creatures—including fallen man, redeemed through the incarnation of the Word—is to achieve fulfillment in union with God. In that union creatures are not to be simply reabsorbed into God but will be transmuted and spiritualized.

Bibliography

Erigena's works may be found in J. P. Migne, ed., *Patrologia Latina*, Vol. CXXII, pp. 125–1244.

For discussions of Erigena, see H. Bett, *Johannes Scotus Erigena: A Study in Mediaeval Philosophy* (Cambridge, 1925), and M. Cappuyns, *Jean Scot Erigène, sa vie, son oeuvre, sa pensée* (Brussels, 1964).

EUGENE R. FAIRWEATHER

EROS. See LOVE.

ERROR. When we engage in discursive thought and declarative speech, we may attain various forms of success: intelligibility, precision, correctness, and so on. These felicities are best explained by contrast with the corresponding mishaps that threaten our beliefs, assertions, and especially our claims to know something. A person's thinking may be inadequate because he is ignorant, and what he says may be deficient because it is incoherent, rough, or, perhaps most important of all, downright false.

Many philosophers have been troubled in attempting to account for the occurrence of falsity in people's assertions and opinions, that is, in trying to understand how there could be such a thing as error at all. In examining these difficulties, we shall assume a man's statement is erroneous in case it is false and it reflects his belief. Thus, if a man lies, he may speak falsely, but not erroneously. We shall also assume that a person holds a false belief when he is inclined to express it in a statement that would be false. The statement would be erroneous; consequently we can say the belief it mirrors is erroneous as well.

Our inquiry will focus on a pair of famous knots:

(1) Do we believe anything when our belief is false? If a surgeon is convinced his patient will die, and he is correct, there is something he expects: the patient's demise. But if he is mistaken, there is no such event as the patient's death. Did the surgeon then expect nothing? Depicted thus, erroneous thinking seems impossible. Plato inherited this perplexity from Parmenides and finally resolved it.

(2) Granting that error can occur, is it ever voluntary? Clearly we are to blame for some of our mistakes, yet who knowingly and willingly goes in for false beliefs? This puzzle comes from Descartes.

The possibility of error. Parmenides' maxim was that only being—what is—can exist. From this he argued that we cannot "know that which is-not . . . nor utter it; for the same thing can be thought as can be." In other words, "You will not find thought without what is, in relation to which it is uttered . . ." (G. S. Kirk and J. E. Raven, *The Presocratic Philosophers*, Cambridge, 1957, pp. 269–278). According to Plato, the Sophists drew an incredible doctrine from these enigmas: They argued that error is asserting and believing "what is not," specifically, talking and "thinking contrary to the things that are" (*Sophist* 240C, D, F. M. Cornford translation). To state and think what is not is, however, to state and think nothing, which is not stating or thinking.

What could have led the Sophists to this paradoxical view? Naturally, it reinforced other logically quite independent doctrines of theirs regarding truth and falsity, for example, their claim that whatever seems true to any man is true for him and therefore *is* true (*Theaetetus* 161C–179C). The only direct support for their denial of error, however, derives from analogies. In *Euthydemus* (283E–288A) the stating of what is not is compared with impossibilities such as doing but doing nothing or gesturing although there is no gesture one performs. The parallel with sense perception in *Theaetetus* (188D–189B) is renowned. If you see, hear, or touch, then there is something you perceive. To see what is not, is not seeing.

Plato's theory of error. In reply, Plato suggests alternative models which will incline us to regard falsehoods as full-fledged (though incorrect) assertions. His most promising comparison is with spelling, where misspelling is the natural counterpart to stating falsely. This analogy is central to Plato's unsuccessful third definition of knowledge in *Theaetetus* (201D–208B), and it reappears in his successful treatment of falsity in *Sophist* (242D–253, 261D–264B). We should imagine a student who tries to spell syllables and words as his teacher says them or inscribes them. When he answers, aloud or in writing, with the right letters in the right order, he uses letters to represent a thing "that is," the teacher's utterance or inscription. According to conventions of spelling, the correct sequence of letters corresponds to what the teacher said or wrote. When the student misspells, he fails to represent the teacher's utterance or inscription, and nothing corresponds to the misspelling. Does the pupil therefore spell nothing? We describe his failure more accurately by saying: "When he misspells, what he spells is not; that is, not anything said or written by the instructor." How shall we describe cases where he gets some letters right and thus represents phonetic or graphological elements of what the instructor said or wrote? Clearly he does not *spell* those elements. For suppose he answers, "w-i-n" after the instructor says "wine." It makes no sense to claim: "He misspelled the word, but he correctly spelled some sounds the teacher made." Further, if the student happens to give the correct spelling of another word (as in this case), we must realize that the other word "is not," because the teacher did not say it. All this is secondary, however; the significant point is that when he misspells, the pupil is nevertheless engaged in the activity of spelling. This suggests that incorrect statements are statements after all.

Let us develop this parallel. If we restrict ourselves to the simplest paradigms—Plato used the true statement "Theaetetus is sitting" and the false statement "Theaetetus is flying"—we notice how words in declarative speech function like letters in spelling. Individual letters may represent sounds but do not spell them. Similarly, the name "Theaetetus" stands for a thing that is, but saying the name "Theaetetus" is not stating anything. Spelling words requires you to conjoin letters of different types, consonants and vowels, in appropriate patterns. Speech, too, is fitting words together. "If you say 'lion stag horse' or any other names," Plato remarks, "such a string never makes up a statement"; but joining a noun with a verb "gets you somewhere" and of such a compound "we say it 'states,' not merely 'names' something" (*Sophist* 262B–E).

Now if you proclaim, "Theaetetus is flying," when he is not airborne, you refer by name to something that is, in the course of *stating* what is not. There is no aerial activity of Theaetetus to correspond to what you state. If you declare, "Theaetetus is sitting," and his posture is appropriate, then something corresponds to what you state. In Plato's words, the true statement "states about [Theaetetus] the things that are"; whereas "the false statement states about [him] things *different* from the things that are," and therefore states "things *that are not* as being" (*Sophist* 263B).

This correspondence theory of true and false statements may be extended to thought by our assumption that a man thinks falsely in case he is inclined to express his thought in a statement that is false. So formulated, the Platonic theory illustrates how error, even though it is believing what is not, hardly consists in believing nothing. Therefore, Sophists cannot maintain that thinking erroneously is not thinking.

Plato's account is, however, needlessly anchored to the type of counterexample he used against the Sophists. The falsehood "Theaetetus is flying" happens to be "about" an existing thing, but Plato makes this feature a prerequisite for every statement, true or false. He writes: "Whenever there is a statement, it must be about something" that exists (*Sophist* 262E; cf. 263C). Even if this ruling allows statements about things which do not exist now but did or will exist, it excludes too much. For instance, it would be impossible for me to state falsely, "There are flying saucers." By Plato's rule, saying this is not stating unless there are flying saucers for me to talk about. So if I *state* that there are flying saucers, I speak truly.

Here we should invoke Plato's orthographic model. The student does not cease to spell when upon occasion he misses every letter and thus fails to represent any sounds his teacher made. By analogy, why disqualify my utterance simply because I fail to refer to existing things? A correspondence theory still explains why it is false to state, "There are flying saucers": nothing corresponds to what is stated; that is, nothing corresponds to the existence of flying saucers, because none exist.

But the correspondence theory needs elaboration before it will transform Plato's view into a general account of correct and incorrect assertion. What "things that are" would I depict if I conceded "Flying saucers do *not* exist"? Does the nonexistence of flying saucers correspond to what I state? How can there be such a thing? Again, what "things that are" differentiate a true subjunctive conditional, for example, "If I had watered the lawn, it would not have died," from its false contrary, "Even if I had watered the lawn, it would have died"? Does the same withered grass make one statement true and the other false?

Because of these obscurities it appears that Plato has demonstrated how incorrect belief and assertion can occur, but he has not produced an exhaustive analysis of them. Plato's demonstration shows awareness of the distinctive features of assertion, sensitivity to the differences between referring and asserting, and perspicacity about the ontological status of what a person believes; indeed, treatments of error by such twentieth-century philosophers as G. E. Moore and Bertrand Russell are not more satisfactory in these respects.

Moore and Russell. Moore's *Some Main Problems of Philosophy*, adapted from lectures he delivered in 1910–1911, appears to contain two incompatible theories: (1) The dyadic theory, according to which believing pairs believers and propositions. "Error," writes Moore, "always consists in believing some proposition which is false" (p. 66). (2) For complicated reasons Moore later contends that "there simply are no such things as propositions" for people to believe (p. 265), and he renounces his "attempt to analyse beliefs" (p. 266). Nevertheless, he characterizes truth and falsity of beliefs as follows: "To say that a belief is true is to say that the fact to which it refers is or has being; while to say that a belief is false is to say that the fact to which it refers is not" (p. 267). In technical terminology: " 'To say that [a] belief is . . . false is to say that there is *not* in the Universe any fact to which it corresponds" (p. 277).

In his 1953 preface, Moore comments that his two theories may after all be consistent; perhaps he used the term "proposition" in different senses when he first maintained and later denied their existence as targets for believing (p.

xii). Apart from this problem, fundamental questions arise concerning Moore's treatment: are there any facts for mistaken beliefs to be about? are they nonexistent facts "in the Universe," or perhaps existent ones outside it? Besides, the very notions of "proposition" and "fact" are notoriously obscure.

Moore hints at a different analysis when he considers a person's belief that we are now listening to a brass band. What the person erroneously believes is a "combination of us at this particular moment with the hearing of that particular kind of noise"—a combination which "simply has no being" (p. 255)

Russell's multiple relation theory, in his *Problems of Philosophy*, develops such an analysis. Concerning Othello's mistaken belief that Desdemona loves Cassio, Russell says: "The relation called 'believing' is knitting together into one complex whole the four terms Othello, Desdemona, loving and Cassio" (p. 126). This belief is mistaken because there does not exist another "complex unity, 'Desdemona's love for Cassio,' which is composed exclusively of the *objects* of the belief, . . . with the relation [loving] which was one of the objects occurring now as the cement that binds together the other objects of the belief" (p. 128).

The snags in this analysis are well known. How does loving cement things? In case Desdemona is indifferent to Cassio, how does believing sew them together with loving and Othello? Can believing stitch together any collection of objects? Russell noted the last two problems in his 1918 lectures, "The Philosophy of Logical Atomism" (in *Logic and Knowledge*). He recognizes that the structure of Othello's belief requires that "loves" should "occur as a verb"; but he is afraid that admitting the syntactical unity of "Desdemona loves Cassio" is tantamount to "assuming the existence of the non-existent . . . [namely,] a non-existent love between Desdemona and Cassio" (p. 225). But as Plato saw, there can be units of speech—statements—and thought without correspondents in reality.

Error and volition. Plato did not need to convince us that false belief is possible. But Descartes's thesis, that error is always voluntary, seems a contrived solution to an entirely gratuitous theological muddle. This appearance is deceptive.

Descartes begins his *Meditations* with a survey of dreaming, sensory illusion, and the errors they occasion; next he shows we can prove a few things for certain, including God's existence. Then he reasons: The deity "cannot have given me a faculty [of thinking] whose right employment could ever lead me astray"; however, "it seems to follow that therefore I can *never* go wrong" (*Meditation* IV, in *Descartes' Philosophical Writings*, translated by P. T. Geach and G. E. M. Anscombe, p. 93). Descartes's answer to this puzzle is that men have false beliefs, but through their own doing, not God's. Men are endowed by God with such power of will that they can assent to propositions they do not know to be true—that is, to "ideas" that are not "clear and distinct." Is God to blame for this disharmony between our limited capacity for knowledge and our unlimited power of assenting? No, "will is just a single thing; it is incompatible with its nature that anything should be subtracted from it" (*Meditation* IV, p. 99). Besides, although we are free to, we do not have to believe propositions for which we lack conclusive proof. In order to avoid "unsuspected error," we must restrain our desire for truth and withhold assent until we know for certain. (Descartes's *Principles of Philosophy* XXIX, XXXII, XXXV, XXXIX, XLII explain these points in detail.)

Now if we put aside Descartes's theological preoccupations, and his advice that we should only believe what is obvious, at least two genuine questions arise:

(1) Do we exercise any control over our convictions and opinions, as Descartes's concept of "assenting" requires? Clearly, people may decide to make statements. Some criminals voluntarily confess their misdeeds, and others are forced, against their will, to admit guilt. How about belief? Can we choose to reject a proposition that seems most likely, according to available evidence, and believe another that seems less plausible? Perhaps not. But we often make decisions as we form our opinions, as we collect or neglect data and seek or ignore expert testimony. Men who undergo brainwashing are deprived of this control over the formation of their beliefs. The same holds, incidentally, for knowledge. It is absurd to say the investigator decided *to know* but not absurd to say he resolved *to find out* for certain who robbed the grocer. Moreover, children are compelled *to learn* things. In acquiring knowledge and forming opinions, we pursue rather obvious goals: conclusive proof and correct information.

(2) Even so, is it intelligible to suppose that people act deliberately and knowingly when they settle upon *false* beliefs? One everyday case should dispel the appearance of contradiction: I study the racing form, mull over the evidence, and conclude that Wayfarer is bound to take the handicap. I willingly commit myself to this belief by wagering my paycheck. I realize, however, that even well-grounded expectations like mine can prove erroneous. Consequently, if my horse loses, it is true to say, "I formed my erroneous belief willingly, after deliberation, with the intention of predicting the handicap winner; furthermore, I was aware that I could be mistaken." It was not my goal to be wrong, but it was within the scope of my intention. Anyone who aims at truth is prepared for falsity, just as a marksman is prepared to miss the bull's-eye. Can we say I erred "knowingly"? A man who punches another is hardly ever certain that his victim will be injured, but from a legal standpoint he knowingly inflicts harm if he has reason to think injury might result from his blow.

There remains another type of error, fortunately quite infrequent, where such awareness is impossible. This is the unusual situation where you are convinced you know something, banish doubt from your mind, and still turn out to be wrong. Perhaps you acted deliberately and followed your inclinations in pushing your investigation until you believed you could not be wrong. But with this degree of conviction, you cannot have the least awareness that you are mistaken. Your error, then, is not fully voluntary.

Bibliography

PLATO

Plato's *Theaetetus* and *Sophist,* along with excellent commentary, are translated by F. M. Cornford in *Plato's Theory of Knowl-* edge (London, 1935). For further analysis of Plato's theory, see Gilbert Ryle, "Letters and Syllables in Plato," *Philosophical Review,* Vol. 69, No. 4 (1960), 431–451; D. Gallop, "Plato and the Alphabet," in *Philosophical Review,* Vol. 72, No. 3 (1963), 364–376; and Raphael Demos, "Plato's Philosophy of Language," with comments by J. L. Ackrill, in *Journal of Philosophy,* Vol. 61, No. 20 (1964), 595–613.

MOORE AND RUSSELL

The views of Moore and Russell can be found in G. E. Moore, *Some Main Problems of Philosophy* (London, 1953), especially Chs. 3 and 13–16; and Bertrand Russell, *Problems of Philosophy* (London, 1912; reset 1946), Ch. 12, and "The Philosophy of Logical Atomism," in R. C. Marsh, ed., *Logic and Knowledge* (London, 1956). For a view opposed to those of Moore and Russell, see Alexius Meinong, *Untersuchungen zur Gegenstandtheorie und Psychologie* (Leipzig, 1904), translated by Isaac Levi, D. B. Terrell, and Roderick Chisholm as "The Theory of Objects," in R. M. Chisholm, ed., *Realism and the Background of Phenomenology* (Glencoe, Ill., 1960).

There is a brilliant discussion of the connection between negative judgments and falsity in Gottlob Frege's essay "Negation," in Max Black and P. T. Geach, editors and translators, *The Philosophical Writings of Gottlob Frege* (Oxford, 1952).

DESCARTES

See *Descartes' Philosophical Writings,* translated by P. T. Geach and G. E. M. Anscombe (Edinburgh, 1954). Spinoza's objections to Descartes's theory that belief necessarily involves assent can be found in the *Ethics,* Part I, Props. 29, 32, and Appendix, and all of Part II; see also the lucid analysis of Descartes and Spinoza by J. L. Evans, "Error and the Will," in *Philosophy,* Vol. 38 (1963), 136–148.

IRVING THALBERG

ESCHATOLOGY, a doctrine or theory (*logos*) of the end (*eschaton*). "End" here can have two meanings. First, it can mean the end of each individual human life. Second, it can mean the end of the world—or, more narrowly, of the human race. In the first, the individualistic, sense eschatology is an account of the destiny that awaits each person after death. In the second, the cosmic or social, sense it is a description of a goal (*telos*) in which history will be fulfilled. This goal may be of either a this-worldly or an otherworldly kind.

The distinction between these two senses is important, for it is possible to have an eschatological doctrine in one sense without having any in the other. Plato held that the soul, being immortal, would face judgment after death, that it would receive rewards and punishments according to the goodness or badness of its earthly life, and that it would be given an opportunity to choose the condition of its next existence (*Republic* 608c to end). However, he did not believe that there was any purpose to history as a whole. Conversely, a Marxist believes in a purpose of history although he disbelieves in personal survival.

It is doubtful whether eschatology in the second sense is to be found anywhere outside Zoroastrianism and Judaism—together with the religious and philosophical systems that have drawn inspiration from them: Mithraism from the first, Christianity and Islam, and Western thought in general, from the second. According to Greek and Indian thinkers history moves in cycles. Just as the seasons recur within each solar year, so all events recur in a sequence of "Great Years." By contrast, the Persian Zend-

Avesta and the Bible state that history is nonrepeatable and that it is destined for a divine fulfillment in which good will triumph over evil.

In the Bible the second sense predominates. The Old Testament contains only a few vague references to a personal afterlife. But it often refers to a future time when God will establish his everlasting reign of righteousness and peace (for example, Isaiah 11.1–9). The New Testament affirms that this divine end or goal has been reached by the exalted Christ, who defeated the powers of evil on the cross (see, for example, Acts 2.14–36; Colossians 2.8–15; Ephesians 2.11–22; Hebrews 2.5–18). Those who believe in Christ have eternal life here and now (John 3.36; 5.24). While living in "this age," this spatiotemporal order that is still subject to sin and death, they have a foretaste of "the age to come," a renewed cosmos that will be wholly subject to the will of God.

This view of history stands in contrast, first, to the Graeco-Roman theory of recurrent cycles—a theory condemned by Origen and Augustine—second, to the humanistic dogma of inevitable social progress, and, third to Marxism. Although the Marxist philosophy of history owes its form to Hegel's dialectic, its content has often been called a secularization of Christian eschatology. Materialistic determinism would be equivalent to a personal providence, the proletariat to the "chosen people," and the "classless society" to the kingdom of God.

During the early centuries of the church most theologians taught that there will be a universal resurrection of the dead for a final judgment at the end of history, when Christ will appear again "in glory." As a result of this judgment, it was also generally taught, some, the saved, will pass to paradise, where they will enjoy the beatific vision, but others, the damned, will be punished with everlasting torment. Four comments on this scheme are necessary:

(1) One must distinguish between belief in the immortality of the soul and belief in the resurrection of the body. The first belief is derived from Plato, who held that the soul will survive in an incorporeal state. The second belief is based on Biblical revelation. Aquinas held both beliefs. He considered the immortality of the soul to be rationally demonstrable. He also thought that the dogma of a bodily resurrection could be rationally justified on the ground that since soul and body constitute (as Aristotle taught) a single substance, the soul requires the body for its self-expression and beatitude. (To account for the obvious fact that the flesh decays at death, Origen proposed the theory that although the resurrected body will have the same "form" as its earthly counterpart, it will have a different "matter.")

(2) Origen maintained that all spiritual creatures—angels, men, and devils—will be saved in a final "restoration" (*apocatastasis*). But although his doctrine (known as Universalism), which was shared by Gregory of Nyssa, could claim Biblical support, it was attacked by Augustine and formally condemned.

(3) Even orthodox Christian Fathers (such as Irenaeus), as well as Gnostics and Montanists, were millenarians. They believed that Christ would reign on earth for a thousand years before the end of terrestrial history. But since the fifth century millenarianism has been almost wholly confined to minor sects.

(4) Although Clement of Alexandria and Origen spoke of a fire that would purge guilty souls, the full doctrine of purgatory (as a place of temporary punishment preparatory to the beatific vision) was not developed until the Middle Ages.

There has lately been a new attempt to understand the eschatological teaching of the New Testament (especially in the light of Albert Schweitzer's thesis that Jesus expected an imminent end of history and therefore intended his moral teaching solely for an interim). On the other hand, Rudolf Bultmann has attempted to "demythologize" Biblical eschatology, to restate it in existentialist terms that will make it intelligible to modern man. These instances indicate a twofold revival of interest in eschatology among professional theologians in this century.

Bibliography

Bultmann, R., *History and Eschatology, the Presence of Eternity.* Edinburgh, 1957.

Charles, R. H., *Eschatology.* London, 1913. The standard work on Jewish and early Christian eschatology.

Cullmann, O., *Christ and Time,* translated by Floyd V. Filson. London, 1951. An excellent study on the New Testament.

H. P. OWEN

ESP PHENOMENA, PHILOSOPHICAL IMPLICATIONS OF. The Society for Psychical Research (SPR) was founded in London in 1882 by a group of distinguished scientists and scholars for the purpose of investigating, among other things, the alleged acquisition of knowledge without use of any known sense organ. Its first president was Henry Sidgwick. The American SPR was founded in 1885, with William James as one of its leaders. Other philosophers who have served as president or vice-president of one or the other of these societies are A. J. Balfour, Henri Bergson, F. C. S. Schiller, William McDougal, Hans Driesch, C. D. Broad, H. H. Price, and C. J. Ducasse.

One of the first achievements of the SPR was the publication, in 1886, of *Phantasms of the Living,* a collection of what would now be called spontaneous cases of telepathy. The society's next project, a census of hallucinations, attempted to show that the first work was not just a collection of coincidences. About seventeen thousand answers were obtained to the question "Have you ever, while believing yourself to be completely awake, had a vivid impression of seeing or being touched by a living or inanimate object, or of hearing a voice; which impression, so far as you could discover, was not due to any external physical cause?" Those who answered in the affirmative (about 10 per cent of the total) were questioned further. Attention was focused on "death-coincidences"—that is, cases where the subject, *A*, recognized his hallucination at the time as an appearance of another person, *B*; where *B* died within a period of 12 hours before or after the hallucinatory experience; and where *A* had no reason to expect *B*'s death. It was calculated, on cautious assumptions, that the ratio of hallucinations that were death-coincidences (1 in 63) was much larger than expected by chance (1 in 19,000). This laborious method of trying to exclude an explanation in terms of chance is not likely to be repeated, because however impeccable the statistical analysis, the data consist of testimony, and a skeptic's doubts about the honesty of the witnesses or the reliability of their memories cannot be laid to rest merely by the compilation of more testimony.

Rhine's experiments. Controlled experiments were required, but it was not until the 1930s that adequate experiments were successfully performed on an extended scale. The leading pioneer of the now common technique of card guessing was J. B. Rhine, of Duke University. Rhine introduced special cards ("Zener cards") bearing five simple symbols—circle, square, cross, star, and wavy line—a pack comprising five cards of each symbol. The mean chance expectation (MCE) was thus five hits per run. The probability that a subject's score occurred by chance could be calculated by standardized statistical methods. (In this article the probability of the scores in quoted experiments will be symbolized in this manner: $p = .001$ or 10^{-3}. This example states that a score of at least the observed deviation from MCE would be expected to occur by chance once, on the average, in 1,000 such experiments, or, more briefly, that the odds against chance are 1,000 to 1.)

Rhine's first and most important book, *Extra-sensory Perception*, appeared in 1934. A surprising feature of his early work was the number of high-scoring subjects found among college students. Eight achieved scores that in each case gave odds against chance of millions to one. In much of Rhine's early work the conditions did not completely preclude sensory cues. However, the best experiments at Duke meet this requirement. For example, in J. G. Pratt's experiments in which the subject, Pearce, was located in a different building from the target cards, out of 1,825 trials Pearce averaged 7.5 hits per run ($p = 10^{-20}$).

Soal's experiments. Rhine's book stimulated S. G. Soal, a mathematician at London University, to repeat such card-guessing experiments. Between 1934 and 1939 Soal tested 160 subjects but found only chance-scoring. In 1939, however, Whately Carington told Soal about some experiments he had just completed, which were later published. Carington's method was as follows: On ten successive evenings he made and hung up in his study in Cambridge drawings of familiar objects, such as a hand, using a different drawing each evening. The drawing remained there from 7 P.M. to 9:30 A.M. the next morning, and during this period a number of subjects in England, Scotland, America, and Holland attempted to reproduce it "by telepathy." The results were matched by a third party. No significant resemblance was found between the drawings produced by subjects on a given evening and the drawing hung that same evening. There was, however, a striking tendency for the subjects' drawings to resemble the drawings hung on one of the two previous evenings and on one of the two following evenings ($p = 10^{-4}$). On the strength of this temporal displacement effect, Carington persuaded Soal to re-examine the records of his 160 subjects. (Soal had matched their guesses only with the cards they had been aiming at, the 0 card position.) Soal then found that two of his subjects, tested in 1936, had been getting high scores of the kind that Carington had predicted—that is, on both the preceding, or −1, and the ensuing, or +1, card positions.

With each of these subjects Soal later carried out prolonged experiments, taking elaborate precautions to preclude sensory cues or fraud on the part of experimenters or subjects. With one, Basil Shackleton, Soal worked for two years (1941–1943). Throughout this period Shackleton got high scores on the card that was exposed two to three seconds after he had recorded his guess. Normally this was the +1 card, but when the rate of guessing was doubled the high scoring was on the +2 card. Disregarding the various conditions in which Shackleton regularly got chance scores, his average level of scoring was just over 7 hits per run. If we include *all* the experiments, the total excess of +1 hits is such that p is about 10^{-35}.

Soal's experiments with the second subject, Mrs. Gloria Stewart, lasted four years (1945–1949). In her case the temporal displacement did not reappear; her high scoring was on the 0 card. Her average rate of scoring was 6.4 hits per run, but owing to the length of the series, p is about 10^{-70}.

However, amassing astronomical odds against chance was not Soal's chief aim. The main value of his experiments lay in his attempts to discover, by varying the experimental conditions, the factors necessary for or conducive to success.

KINDS OF ESP

In this section some crucial experiments will be described, since it is unprofitable to theorize about ESP unless one is acquainted with the relevant facts and has decided what the irreducible species are. To facilitate description, this article will provisionally adopt one of the commonest definitions of "ESP": the acquisition of information without use of any known sense organs. Two main species of ESP are usually labeled "telepathy" and "clairvoyance." These terms are ill-chosen, especially "clairvoyance," which was originally adopted because mediums and subjects of spontaneous ESP commonly claim to "see" remote objects. Since such reported experiences often involve modes of sense other than sight, "telesthesia," a term suggested by F. W. H. Myers, would have been better.

In the pre-experimental era cases of spontaneous ESP were usually classed as telepathic or clairvoyant according to the content of the information imparted. The question now asked concerns the source of the information. "Telepathy" is used to designate ESP in which the information originates from the mind of another person, and "clairvoyance" ESP in which the information originates from physical objects. It follows that information acquired by telepathy need not be about a person's state of mind as such; it may be about physical events he is observing or has observed. It also follows that information acquired by clairvoyance may be about a person's state of mind, for if by clairvoyance a subject can identify the pattern on a concealed card, presumably he can likewise identify the overt behavior by which another person displays fear or anger.

The third main species of ESP is precognition. To psychical researchers "precognition" means ESP in which the information is about *and originates from* future events. As this definition makes explicit, the concept involves either the notion, self-contradictory within our present conceptual scheme, of effects' preceding their causes or the notion of future states of affairs' being objects of noninferential awareness.

Isolation of telepathy and clairvoyance. One of the first tasks attempted by Rhine was to isolate by experiment telepathic and clairvoyant phenomena. The few attempts made earlier had been inconclusive. Of Rhine's clairvoyance tests the simplest and most convincing was his "Down Through" (DT) method. A pack of cards was shuffled, cut, and placed face down on a table. The subject had to guess the symbols on each card from top to bottom. No one touched the pack until the subject had recorded all his guesses. While the guesses were being made, no one observed or was in a position to infer the order of the cards, so presumably the subject, when successful, was getting his information from the cards.

In Rhine's telepathy test no cards were used. The subject had to guess which of the Zener symbols another person (the "agent") was thinking of at that moment. The agent concentrated on one of the five symbols, chosen at random. After the subject had recorded each guess, a signal was transmitted to the agent, who then recorded the symbol he had just been thinking of. When the subject recorded his guess, no physical object or sign was available, as a possible target for clairvoyance, to indicate which symbol the agent was then thinking of, so presumably the subject, when successful, was getting his information from the mind of the agent. Rhine reported that seven of his eight star subjects scored equally well in both types of test, the eighth succeeding only in the telepathy test.

Rhine's findings have been confirmed by other investigations. D. R. Martin and F. P. Stribic carried out extensive experiments with the DT method at the University of Colorado, adding the precaution, not always adopted by Rhine, of screening the target cards from the subject. Five of their 322 subjects achieved very significant scores ($p < 10^{-8}$ in each case). Soal's star subjects, Shackleton and Stewart, succeeded only in the tests for telepathy. Though the subjects were not told so at the time, Soal interspersed clairvoyance tests with the telepathy tests, arranging for the agent merely to touch the back of the target card, instead of lifting it and looking at it, as he normally did. Chance scores were consistently obtained in these clairvoyance tests.

Such facts would establish that telepathy and clairvoyance are distinct species of ESP, were it not for the possibility of precognition, for which there is evidence that is prima facie impressive. This possibility undermines the results of Rhine's telepathy test, since the subject might be getting his information by precognitive clairvoyance from the sign the agent was to write down a few seconds later. Equally, the results in the DT tests could be ascribed to precognitive telepathy, since the subject might be getting his information from the thoughts or visual experiences of the experimenter, who was to inspect the cards to check the score at the end of the run. This reasoning led experimenters to devise methods that closed the loophole. Success was achieved by Soal for telepathy and by G. N. M. Tyrrell for clairvoyance.

Soal's "pure telepathy" experiment was as follows: The order in which the agent (Soal) thought of the five symbols was determined jointly by a random series of the digits 1 through 5, which was objectively recorded, and by a private code linking digits and symbols, which the agent has never recorded or formulated in spoken words. The subject's guesses were scored by the agent, who recorded only the total number of hits on each sheet. He did not mark correct guesses or let his eyes linger on them, since this would, in theory, permit the subject to identify the code by precognitive clairvoyance. So that those who studied the experiment would not have to rely only upon Soal's memory and testimony, he got a collaborator, an old friend, to infer the code he was using by making indirect allusions to their past shared experiences. His collaborator was thus able to check and confirm the scoring. In the 40 runs done with this method Mrs. Stewart averaged 7.3 hits per run ($p = 10^{-11}$).

In Tyrrell's pure clairvoyance experiment his subject, Miss G. M. Johnson, sat beside five small light-tight boxes, each containing a tiny electric lamp. Her task was to lift the lid of the box in which the lamp had just been (or was about to be) lighted. The operator (Tyrrell), screened from the subject, made a lamp light by pressing one of five keys. The connections between the keys and the lamps were "scrambled" by a commutator enclosed in a box, so that when this box was shut no one could tell by observation what the connections were. The results were recorded automatically by lines drawn on a moving tape. A line was drawn while any one (but not more than one) of the boxes was open. When the correct box was opened, a second line was drawn on the tape parallel to the first. Because the record on the tape gave no indication of which box was opened at any trial, precognitive telepathy could not help the subject. Even if she could have discovered by telepathy from the visual experience of someone who later inspected the tape that her next trial was to produce a hit, this would not have helped her to decide which box to open. To eliminate the possibility that Miss Johnson might have been succeeding by hyperesthesia to radiation from the lighted lamp, Tyrrell introduced a delay switch. The pressing of a key then merely determined that a certain lamp would light if the correct box was opened. Under these conditions (commutator concealed and delay switch used), Miss Johnson, in a series of 855 trials, scored at her usual level, 26 per cent, as against the MCE of 20 per cent (p = nearly 10^{-6}).

Whether or not we allow the possibility of precognition, the experimental evidence for clairvoyance seems as strong as that for telepathy. This must be emphasized, because the contrary view is widely held, and nearly all scientists and philosophers who have tried to explain ESP have ignored clairvoyance.

Isolation of precognition. Shackleton's +1 and +2 scoring provided prima-facie evidence of precognition. However, the method Soal first used to determine the order of the target series permitted another interpretation. In a room adjacent to the one occupied by Shackleton were the agent, *A*, and an experimenter controlling the agent, *EA*. On a table in front of *A* lay five target cards; these were reshuffled after every 50 trials. *A*'s task was to attend to the card in the position indicated by a visual signal from *EA*, who could not see the cards. Two different methods were used for determining the order of the signals given by *EA*.

With the first method, *EA* had to follow a random series of the digits 1 through 5 prepared in advance by Soal. Here the +1 or +2 scoring need not be ascribed to precognition, since Shackleton might, by telepathy, have ascertained both the contents of the list of random numbers and the current position of the target cards and from this have inferred the +1 or +2 card symbols. To generalize, any precognition experiment must rule out the possibility that the subject could infer the target from facts ascertained by nonprecognitive ESP. (Precognition, as conceived in psychical research, must be noninferential; otherwise the information does not originate from future events.)

Soal sought to eliminate this possibility by introducing a second method for determining the target series. *EA* was given a cloth bag or a bowl containing 200 bone counters, 40 of each of 5 different colors, mixed together. Each color represented one of the 5 card positions. *EA* had to select a counter solely by touch and show it to *A*. In the experiments using this procedure and the rapid rate of calling, Shackleton scored high on the +2 cards, although the counters determining which cards these were had not yet been selected when he made his guesses. (The same may not have been true of the +1 cards at the normal rate of guessing, for while *EA* was showing one counter to *A* she was already delving for the next counter with her other hand.) This procedure precludes attributing the high scoring to Shackleton's drawing inferences from data acquired by nonprecognitive ESP. A critic might suggest here that Shackleton clairvoyantly perceived the counters in the bag and *EA*'s hand movements and was thus able to discover *EA*'s habits of selection and make better-than-chance inferences about the next counter to be selected. This explanation, however, fails to account for the fact that Shackleton's scoring, under these conditions, was high from the start and showed no improvement with practice.

There are other explanations that must be eliminated before precognition can be established. The +2 scoring might be explained by the supposition that *EA* learned by ESP the guesses Shackleton had made, the current positions of the cards, and the current arrangement of the counters in the bag and used this information to select counters of colors that would give +2 hits. This is implausible, since there is no evidence that *EA* had ESP powers; still, this sort of explanation remains possible in any experiment in which selection of the targets depends on somebody's free choices. To eliminate such a possibility, the targets can be selected by mechanical randomization after the guesses have been made.

But the subject's guesses (or wishes) may conceivably influence the card-shuffling machine. Rhine, in particular, could not dismiss this possibility, for he claimed to have found evidence for psychokinesis (PK) in experiments in which subjects had tried to influence the fall of dice simply by willing. ("PK" is defined, in the glossary of the *Journal of Parapsychology*, as "the direct influence exerted on a physical system by a subject without any known intermediate physical energy or instrumentation.") Rhine set out to eliminate this possibility by an experiment in which the cards would be shuffled mechanically for a period to be determined by the daily temperature extremes recorded in a specified newspaper on specified future days (J. B.

Rhine, "Evidence of Precognition in the Covariation of Salience Ratios," in *Journal of Parapsychology*, Vol. 6 [1942], 111–143). Rhine argued that it would be incredible that the subjects should, by PK, influence "the temperature itself." This experiment did not give clearly significant scoring, but even if it had the critic could reply that if card-shuffling machines can be influenced by PK, why not thermometers?

It appears to be impossible to design a precognition experiment that will conclusively eliminate explanation in terms of both (1) the exercise of nonprecognitive ESP plus unconscious inference by the subject or by others, and (2) the exercise of PK by the subject or others. G. L. Mangan has attempted to meet this challenge ("Evidence of Displacement in a Precognition Test," in *Journal of Parapsychology*, Vol. 19 [1955], 35–44). In his experiment the target order was determined several days after the guesses were made by throwing dice to select, from a table of random numbers, several groups of digits, upon which a series of complex mathematical operations was then performed by a calculating machine. With this method, to avoid invoking precognition we should apparently have to ascribe to the subject or others the ability to influence dice falls by PK *and* clairvoyant perception of the contents of the table of random numbers *and* prodigious powers of unconscious inference.

Mangan did get positive scoring on the +1 cards ($p < .001$). But does *one* such experiment oblige us to carry out the conceptual revolution involved in accepting precognition as conceived by psychical researchers? If we allow that future states of physical objects may influence a person's present responses or may be objects of his present noninferential awareness, we seem obliged to conceive of the physical world as, literally, a four-dimensional continuum, the future part of which is "there" waiting for us to "come across it" as we "journey through time," time being conceived as a fourth dimension of space. This way of thinking seems to be respectable in recent physics, but have its implications been recognized? It destroys the basic concepts in terms of which we do (and must?) interpret our experience: our concept of a physical thing as a three-dimensional object capable of moving and changing in many respects, our concept of a physical event as a change in physical things or in a physical thing, and our concept of physical causation as a relation between physical events. These concepts can have no application in the four-dimensional physical continuum theory, for in this conceptual scheme a physical object *is* a four-dimensional solid. It cannot (logically) move or change, unless in a time dimension distinct from the one that has been spatialized, and such motion or change is not observable to us since we cannot observe four-dimensional solids. What we now describe as our experience of "things changing" would have to be ascribed to our successive awareness of adjacent three-dimensional cross sections of the four-dimensional manifold (and the succession in question would involve a time distinct from the one that has been spatialized). So this theory implies that all the changes we experience are merely changes in the states of consciousness of subjects who are not in physical space time.

No empirical facts could oblige us to accept precognition, with its extremely paradoxical implications. Even if we do not invoke PK (and the experimental evidence for PK is not nearly so good as that for ESP), we can always say, like Max Black ("Why Cannot an Effect Precede Its Cause?," in *Analysis*, Vol. 16 [January 1956], 54), that ostensible precognitions exert "a causal influence of an esoteric sort" upon the events that fulfill them.

Critique of accepted definitions. The distinction between telepathy and clairvoyance is made to depend on whether the source of the information is mental or physical. Such a distinction presupposes that behaviorism is false. This need not detain us, for insofar as behaviorism claims that all statements about a person's experience are really about his overt behavior, it is false. But an important question is being begged. What right have we to assume that the source of telepathic information is the mind or experiences of an agent? That all experiences are correlated with and determined by brain processes is a widely accepted hypothesis for which the evidence, though limited, is growing, and telepathy experiments provide no evidence against it. If in telepathy tests the source of the information is in fact processes in the agent's brain, the phenomena constitute clairvoyance, according to the accepted definitions. The accepted definitions are defective, therefore, in that they make telepathy unverifiable, until or unless physiologists discover that certain types of experience are not correlated with brain processes and we then find that such experiences can be telepathically communicated. Meanwhile, to make the occurrence of telepathy verifiable, we must redefine it as ESP in which the information originates from another person (his mind or his brain), and clairvoyance must then be defined as ESP in which the information originates from physical objects other than a brain. The terms must be understood in this way in the statement that telepathy and clairvoyance have been experimentally isolated.

The phrase "extrasensory perception" implies that the phenomena are to be assimilated to sense perception. This is liable to be misleading. There are important differences between ESP phenomena and sense perception. Even the most successful card-guessing subjects cannot tell which of their guesses are successful or whether they are producing high or chance scoring. Furthermore, as Antony Flew has asked, what would we think of eyes that gave results better than chance only 2 or 3 times out of 25? Such differences do not, however, show that perception is necessarily inappropriate as a model. John Beloff has pointed out that the features in which successful card guessing differs from normal perception are found also in experiments on subliminal perception. If figures are exposed to a subject, but so briefly or in such dim light that the subject insists he cannot see them, and if he is induced to keep guessing which of several alternative figures is being exposed, he may score a little above MCE.

There is another respect in which ESP resembles sense perception: information—at least in the sense in which "information" is used in communication theory—is acquired thereby. In the everyday sense of the term, we may have qualms about saying that card-guessing subjects are "acquiring information," since they have no idea which of their guesses are successful. If, for this reason, anyone

wishes to avoid the term "information," he can adopt an alternative definition of ESP as responding appropriately to objects or events that one has not observed or inferred. The problem of explaining the phenomena is unaltered.

An operationalist definition of "ESP," based solely on card-guessing experiments, like that proposed by Flew— "the factor which gives rise to significant deviations from mean chance expectation *in a series of guesses*" (*A New Approach to Psychical Research*, p. 118)—is not acceptable. As Flew admitted, this makes it meaningless to ask if a single concurrence of a guess with a card is a case of ESP. Yet guessing experiments were introduced to confirm that spontaneous cases are not merely coincidences. Flew's definition precludes our saying that the experiments have done or can do this. It would also debar us from saying that an individual message conveyed by a medium is a case of ESP, and this is something that many wish to be permitted to say.

Empirical evidence for survival. For some of its pioneers—Myers, for example—the main goal of psychical research was to obtain evidence for the Platonic–Cartesian conception of man by showing that men survive death. The traditional approach is to treat ESP and mediumistic communication as distinct phenomena and then to debate whether the latter can be explained in terms of the former. The question ought to be framed differently, for by any definition of ESP (except Flew's), veridical mediumistic communications that are not susceptible of a normal explanation are cases of ESP. Even if they are also what they commonly purport to be, messages from people who have died, they must still be classed as telepathic. The proper question is whether in addition to telepathy between living people there is telepathy originating from deceased people. The latter type will here be labeled "spirit telepathy" (telepathy$_{(S)}$), and the former "human ESP" (ESP$_{(H)}$).

The case for accepting the occurrence of telepathy$_{(S)}$ seemed at one time formidable, but it has since been very much weakened by the study of ESP$_{(H)}$. Mediumistic communications can be evidence for telepathy$_{(S)}$ only insofar as they are verifiable. (This excludes descriptions of the afterlife, which are in any case scanty.) To be verifiable such messages must concern facts known by, or physical things observable to, living people. Therefore, it is always possible to ascribe information conveyed by mediums to their exercise of ESP$_{(H)}$, telepathic or clairvoyant. No informed students of psychical research would now deny this, but some, including C. D. Broad and C. J. Ducasse, have judged this explanation to be less plausible in some cases than telepathy$_{(S)}$, though Broad makes the qualification that what survives death need not be a mind or personality but can be merely some component of the latter that carries memory traces and may combine temporarily with a medium's body to form a "mind-kin." The relevant facts are so complex that it is impossible to give a balanced discussion of all the pros and cons. All that can be done here is to summarize briefly the three chief arguments used by Broad and Ducasse and to indicate the lines on which these may be answered.

The arguments for ascribing some mediumistic communications to telepathy$_{(S)}$ are as follows:

(1) Such communications are less frequently concerned

with the sitter's living friends than with those who have died (Broad).

(2) There are cases where the medium impersonates the ostensible communicator, speaking with a voice and behaving with mannerisms recognizably similar to those of the ostensible communicator, whom the medium has never met (Broad and Ducasse).

(3) The alternative explanation involves ascribing to the medium powers of $ESP_{(H)}$ for which we have no independent evidence, in particular the power to select relevant bits of information from varied sources, people he has never met, and places he has never visited (Broad and Ducasse).

Broad rightly did not attach very much weight to the first argument. In Britain and America nearly all mediums and their clients are spiritualists. In France belief in spiritualism is less widespread among mediums and their clients, and many of the mediums studied by Eugène Osty gave the same sort of information about living people as about dead ones, without claiming in either case that it came from spirits.

The second argument would have considerable weight were it not for the remarkable Gordon Davies case. During some sittings held by Soal in 1922 with Mrs. B. Cooper, a medium whose messages were spoken in what purported to be the voice of the "communicator," a new "communicator" appeared, calling himself Gordon Davies. Soal remembered Davies as a boy whom he had known slightly at school over twenty years earlier and whom he had not met since, except for a chance half-hour encounter in 1916. Soal recorded at the time that he was much impressed by Mrs. Cooper's "lifelike reproduction of the mannerisms of speech, tone of voice and accent" of Davies. At that time Soal believed that Davies had been killed during the war. In 1925, Soal discovered that Davies was alive and was then able to confirm from him that Mrs. Cooper's "messages from Gordon Davies" had contained many correct and specific statements of fact about Davies unknown to Soal and that the messages contained scarcely any incorrect statements. This case clearly undermined the argument that a medium's impersonation of an ostensible communicator needs to be explained in terms of telepathy$_{(S)}$ rather than $ESP_{(H)}$.

The third argument for telepathy$_{(S)}$ is the strongest. To appreciate its force it is necessary to take account of the method of "proxy sittings," designed to prevent the medium from getting information by telepathy from the sitter. There is good evidence that mediums sometimes do this at proxy sittings. The only person present with the medium is a note-taker (the proxy), who is not acquainted with the deceased person, D, from whom messages are sought and has only very limited knowledge about D, such as D's name or the fact that D once owned an object contained in a parcel that was given to the medium. Though no such experiments are wholly immune to methodological criticism, some have given impressive results. To attribute these results to $ESP_{(H)}$ we should have to suppose that the note-taker functions, so to speak, as a signpost, directing the medium's ESP to whichever of D's friends or relations it was who initiated the proceedings and from whose memories information about D can be obtained.

Admittedly there is little experimental evidence that anyone can employ ESP in this way. One experiment that seems relevant is Soal's "split-agent" experiment. Two agents were placed in different rooms. One knew the order in which five target cards were laid out; the other focused on numbers representing one or another of the five card positions. Neither knew which symbol was the current target. Mrs. Stewart scored high, at her usual rate.

Since Mrs. Stewart was able to piece together information possessed by different people, it is not unreasonable to suppose that a medium can, by $ESP_{(H)}$, tap information possessed by both the proxy (note-taker) and whoever appointed the proxy. In the Gordon Davies case it seems clear that the medium's ESP was directed to the real Gordon Davies by Soal's memory of Davies (and Soal's belief that Davies was dead?). The medium gave much correct information about the house that Davies was, at the time of the sitting, negotiating to buy and about its furnishings when he later occupied it. This information must presumably have been gained by telepathy from Davies himself. Osty has cited analogous cases where the medium has given information not possessed by the sitter about a person known slightly, or only by description, to the sitter.

In the light of such facts, the third argument for telepathy$_{(S)}$ seems after all to be weak. Attributing mediumistic communications to $ESP_{(H)}$ is, ontologically, the simplest hypothesis. The alternative involves attributing ESP to spirits as well as living people. Broad's suggestion that what survives death is merely a trace-bearing component of a mind does not suffice to explain mediumistic phenomena, for the messages refer frequently to events that occurred after the death of the alleged communicator. If such messages come from spirits, these spirits must be credited with the capacity to continue observing the terrestrial scene.

ATTEMPTS TO EXPLAIN ESP AWAY

Attempts to explain ESP away concentrate on either alleged fraud on the part of the investigators or criticism of the statistical methods employed.

Fraud. Sidgwick said in 1882, in his first presidential address to the SPR, "We have done all we can when the critic has nothing left to allege except that the investigator is in the trick. But when he has nothing else left to allege, he will allege that." The best experiments are so designed that several people would have to be "in the trick." G. R. Price and C. E. M. Hansel have tried to work out systems whereby Soal's results could be explained by fraud. Hansel's, which could explain most (though not all) of the data, is detailed and ingenious. It postulates cheating by both subjects and agents. However, there were in the Shackleton series 3 successful agents and in the Stewart series 15, several of them senior teachers at London University. Supposing Shackleton and Stewart were in the trick, it is hard to imagine why they conspired in 1936 to produce displaced scoring that they had no reason to think would ever be noticed. If critics like Price and Hansel were correct, the annals of psychical research would be of philosophical interest at least in providing a fund of illustrations for Hume's thesis about men's gullibility and the unreliability of testimony when the "love of wonder" is excited.

Inapplicability of statistical methods. Criticism of the statistical methods used in psychical research was initially silenced in 1937, when the American Institute of Mathematical Statistics issued a statement that Rhine's statistical analyses, assuming his experiments had been properly performed, were essentially valid. In 1953, however, D. Spencer Brown claimed, in letters to the magazine *Nature* (July 25 and September 26, 1953), that ESP experiments showed only that there is something wrong with the probability calculus. Many took this claim seriously because Brown said that he had found significant correlations simply by matching numbers selected from published tables of random numbers. What Brown did was to try various ways of dividing a table of random numbers into two equal subseries and to match these subseries and count the number of occasions on which the corresponding digits had the same value. When Brown subsequently published a book, *Probability and Scientific Inference* (London and New York, 1957), containing the details of his experiments, it appeared that his own matching tests had not, after all, yielded any significant correlations.

Meanwhile A. T. Oram and J. Fraser Nicol made similar tests on two widely used tables of random numbers and published their results. These passed all tests for randomness applied by their authors, but Brown applied others and found one test on Oram's data that yielded the very low probability of .0002. (This test involved comparing the scores in the top left and bottom right quarters of the pages.) On the strength of this he maintained that the statistical evidence for ESP is an artifact.

Brown's thesis breaks down for three reasons.

First, though it seems surprising to find a correlation whose probability is only 1 in 5,000 by matching subseries selected from a table of random numbers, this probability ought to be multiplied by the number of such tests applied to tables, from which this correlation was selected as the best (from Brown's viewpoint), for in 100 independent tests the probability of finding one such correlation, by chance, increases to 1 in 50. Oram did 10 independent tests. We do not know how many Brown did in the years he spent looking for such correlations.

Second, Brown's theoretical arguments, notably his attempt to show that the concept of randomness used in the probability calculus is self-contradictory, have been shown to be invalid (see C. W. K. Mundle, "Probability and Scientific Inference," in *Philosophy*, Vol. 34 [1959], 150–154; and C. D. Broad, *Lectures on Psychical Research*, pp. 74–91). However, if his arguments had been sound, they would have invalidated the widespread use of tests of statistical significance, not only in psychical research, but in *all* sciences.

Finally, the best ESP experiments are obviously immune to Brown's criticisms. For example, in all Soal's experiments with Shackleton and Stewart he did "cross-checks." Each run of guesses was matched not only with the run of targets at which it was "aimed" but also (the cross-check) with the ensuing or succeeding run of targets.

The scores yielded by the cross-checks were consistently very close to MCE.

Oram's and Brown's discovery, in matching random numbers, of a correlation that was presumably due to chance, for which $p = .0002$, represents a significant warning to all scientists who rely on statistical measurement. Correlations of about the conventional level for statistical "significance" ($p = .01$) should not be regarded as *dependable* evidence of causal connections.

METAPHYSICAL IMPLICATIONS OF ESP

The view that ESP has metaphysical implications is widely held. It has been endorsed by H. H. Price, who argued that ESP cannot be explained by physics and that it therefore disproves materialism and supports the case for psychophysical dualism—though not for Descartes's version, which Price rejected. This thesis must be examined, but first the very different view advocated by Flew should be noted.

Flew claimed that ESP has no important implications for philosophy or even for science. He wrote, ". . . apart from the anomalous set of very weak effects . . . everything else is just as it was before. Once the correlations are admitted as exceptions to the various general principles against which they offend . . . there seems no reason why most sciences (scientists) should be upset further" (*A New Approach to Psychical Research*, p. 124). He argued that we should not abandon scientific postulates violated by ESP but, instead, interpret these postulates as heuristic maxims that, as such, remain sound. In view of the comparative rarity and inconstancy of ESP phenomena, it is tempting to conclude that these awkward facts should be segregated and disregarded as a sphere in which nature unfortunately provides no discoverable laws. But this surely is an unscientific attitude to adopt. Science as we know it would never have developed had scientists ignored rare phenomena that conflicted with their current theories. If physicists had ignored magnetic phenomena or the results of the Michelson–Morley experiment and had been content to say that the principles of Newtonian mechanics remained sound as heuristic maxims, physics would be very different from what it is today.

Incompatibility with physics. Those, Price among them, who argue that ESP is incompatible with physics usually start with the question-begging definition of "telepathy" as the action of one mind upon another. But their main case is that for ESP to be explainable by physics it must, by analogy with radio transmission, be attributed to a physical radiation, and that this theory will not work, for three reasons.

First, the inverse-square law applies to all known forms of physical radiation. (The only exception is radiation concentrated in a beam, which will have little attenuation with distance. However, this does not seem relevant, since there have been many successful ESP experiments with a group of subjects scattered in different directions.) On the physical radiation theory we should, it is argued, find a marked decline in scoring level when the subjects' distance from the source of radiation is much increased. But all investigators agree that there is no covariation between distance and scoring level, and successful experiments have been performed over distances of several hundred miles. The critic may reply that since ESP is being likened to radio and radio sets have amplifiers and volume controls, we can suppose that the brain possesses an automatic volume control that amplifies weak ESP signals. (The many misses in ESP tests must then be ascribed to factors other than weakness of the signals, but such factors can be postulated.)

Second, physical barriers do not affect ESP, as one would expect on the radiation theory. The most thorough experiments yet done on screening were those of L. L. Vasiliev at the Institute of Physiology at Leningrad. The Russian research team set out with the assumption that ESP must be due to electromagnetic radiation. To verify this, their subjects and/or agents were completely enclosed in metal containers that blocked all electromagnetic waves of wavelengths between 1 millimeter and 1 kilometer. ESP was not impaired. Vasiliev conceded that there were very strong grounds for rejecting the hypothesis that ESP is due to electromagnetic waves outside this range.

Third, electrical "brain waves" are too weak to explain telepathy, according to W. Grey Walter, an authority on brain physiology. Discussing the radiation theory of telepathy, he wrote, "If we consider the largest [electrical] rhythms of the brain as . . . radio-signals, we can calculate that they would fall below the noise level within a few millimetres from the surface of the head" (*The Living Brain*, p. 176).

These three objections together seem to eliminate the possibility of ascribing ESP to electromagnetic radiation. But attempts have been made to reconcile ESP with physics by other means.

Unorthodox materialist theories. Hans Berger, the physiologist who discovered the technique of recording brain waves with the electroencephalograph, recognized, as did Grey Walter, that electrical changes in the brain are too weak to explain telepathy. He suggested that electrical energy in the agent's brain is transformed into "psychic energy," which can be diffused over any distance, passing through obstacles without attenuation. On reaching the subject's brain it is transformed back into electrical energy, thus producing neural patterns and experiences corresponding to those of the agent. Though Berger talked of "psychic energy," he was not a dualist; he conceived of psychic energy as a form of physical energy.

Ninian Marshall, like Berger, held the epiphenomenalist view that all experiences are determined by patterns of cortical activity. His theory was more revolutionary than Berger's, involving "action at a distance." Marshall suggested that in telepathy the state of the agent's brain affects the state of the subject's brain, without any continuous chain of intervening events, and indeed without any transmission of energy. To render this suggestion intelligible Marshall offered his "hypothesis of resonance," that "any two substances exert an influence on each other which tends to make them become more alike. The strength of this influence increases with the product of their complexities, and decreases with difference between their patterns" ("ESP and Memory: A Physical Theory," in *British Journal for the Philosophy of Science*, Vol. 10 [1959–1960], 266). This hypothetical force he labeled the "eidopoic influence." He argued that this influence had hitherto produced observable effects only in the form of ESP, because the human brain is by far the most complex structure in the world; he predicted, however, that telepathic interaction would be detectable between computing machines if or when the machines could be made sufficiently complex in structure. This is a bold and intriguing speculation, though Price would be entitled to protest against Marshall's describing as a physical force one that involves no energy transfer: for physicists a physical transaction, by definition, involves a transfer of energy.

Physics and clairvoyance. We need not discuss whether physics could accommodate Marshall's revolutionary theory, for, as was stressed earlier, the evidence for clairvoyance is as strong as that for telepathy. Berger and Marshall both ignored clairvoyance, and their theories must be rejected because they preclude clairvoyance. Both assumed that the source of information in ESP is a brain, but in cases of clairvoyance there is no agent, no brain in which the relevant information has been recorded.

There seems no hope of amending Marshall's theory to cover clairvoyance. He attributed telepathy to resonance between different brains because of their structural complexity and similarity. But Zener cards are extremely simple in structure and unlike brains, so there should be no resonance between them and brains.

To accommodate Berger's theory we would have to postulate that some form of physical energy is emitted by all physical objects (for it is not only cards that have been used in successful clairvoyance tests) and that physicists have overlooked this energy in their theories and calculations (which they will find hard to believe).

There are further formidable difficulties in reconciling physics and clairvoyance. How are we to explain the subject's selectivity, his ability to discriminate the signals coming from the target objects? This problem is acute in the case of Rhine's DT test, for the cards lie bunched together, and one would expect signals emitted by the several cards to interfere with each other.

Again, whatever the nature of the hypothetical radiation, it must, since it penetrates screens, be very different from light. But the information conveyed by clairvoyance concerns (*inter alia*) the visible properties of things, such as the shape or color of a diagram. We should thus have a remarkable and unintelligible coincidence: the radiation, though physically very different from light, carries modifications corresponding to just those features of things that differentially affect light waves and make us see different colors.

Because physical barriers do not impede ESP, we must, unless we reject the principle of conservation of energy, suppose that only brains (or organisms) absorb and are affected by the hypothetical radiation whereas other physical things are, so to speak, transparent to it. Since we have had to suppose that all physical things emit such radiation, this would be an extreme paradox.

Enough has been said to show that it is too facile to dismiss Price's thesis that ESP is incompatible with physics as merely an argument from our present ignorance. To

explain clairvoyance physics would have to undergo a major revolution. Price would have been entitled to argue thus: The case for materialism (or epiphenomenalism or the theory that psychic states are identical with brain states) rests largely on scientific discoveries that make it plausible to claim that all mental powers can be explained in principle by physics, by reference to transmission processes and brain mechanisms. This case is weakened by the fact that ESP cannot be explained thus even in principle. But Price's claim that ESP disproves materialism can be challenged.

It may be argued that "*x* cannot be explained by physics" does not entail "*x* disproves materialism," unless "materialism" means, among other things, that the current theories of physics are correct and complete, which no one would claim. A materialist may define his position this way: that nothing exists except physical things and their states, that experiences are (or are inner aspects of) states of higher organisms, "physical things" here meaning what ordinary men mean by it, things that are both visible and tangible. "Materialism" need not be defined so as to entail that physical things can interact only by contact or by means of physical radiations or fields. A materialist is free to maintain that the "interphenomena" of physics (radiations, the "force" of gravity, etc.) are logical constructs, and that the failure, so far, to construct interphenomena to explain ESP need not cause ontological discomfort. It may eventually be necessary to conclude that ESP involves action at a distance, but physicists may revert to saying the same about gravity.

Psychical theories. Price's further claim, that ESP supports dualism, goes too far. If materialism is rejected in favor of dualism because physics cannot explain ESP it must be shown that ESP can be explained in terms of minds or mental forces. But there do not seem to be sufficient grounds for inferring that the unknown entities or forces responsible for ESP are mental. Dualists have offered various theories at about the same level of generality as the physicalist theories of Berger and Marshall. The most common move is to postulate a collective unconscious mind, a concept expressed poetically by William James: "There is a continuum of cosmic consciousness, against which our individuality builds but accidental fences, and into which our several minds plunge as into a mother-sea." The reason for postulating a collective unconscious may be either to suggest that one person's experiences can directly influence those of another, because all experiences are really contents of one all-embracing Mind, or to suggest that one person's experience can affect another's indirectly, via modifications in a substratum called the "common unconscious."

But then, as Broad has observed, we must ask what grounds there are for assuming that this substratum is mental. There have been many variations on the theme of the "common unconscious," by Price, Tyrrell, and Carington, for example, but all such theories, when combined with dualism (as they usually are), are open to the fatal objection that they can apply only to telepathy, not to clairvoyance.

There seem to be only two dualist theories that would cover clairvoyance. The first is Bergson's theory about normal memory and perception—that each person is at each moment potentially aware of all concurrent events and of all his past experiences and that to prevent his being overwhelmed by useless knowledge the brain suppresses all information except that which is relevant to his present practical needs. It is a short step to equating with ESP the knowledge suppressed by the brain, and Bergson took this step. It seems extravagant, however, to explain a few people's sporadic exercise of ESP by supposing that potentially we are all almost omniscient.

The second dualist theory is that of R. H. Thouless and B. P. Wiesner ("The Psi Processes in Normal and 'Paranormal' Psychology," in *Proceedings of the SPR*, Vol. 48 [1947–1949], 177–196). It postulates that when a person exercises clairvoyance or PK his mind is being influenced by or is influencing physical things outside his body in the same way as his mind normally interacts with his own brain. In this theory Cartesian dualism is taken for granted, but dualism involves notorious problems concerning mind–body interaction which the proposed account of clairvoyance and PK does not seem to render more intelligible.

Many writers have argued that ESP provides evidence for dualism. However, no philosopher seems to have claimed that it supports Berkeleian idealism, although Berkeley's theory can accommodate the phenomena of clairvoyance. It already involves telepathy (if not by that name), for Berkeley held that our perceptual experiences are caused directly by volitions in the divine mind. The phenomena of clairvoyance would also have to be attributed to telepathy, with God as the agent, since material objects, when unobserved by human minds, consist, for Berkeley, in ideas or archetypes in God's mind. But an idealist or a theosophist who used this argument would have to explain why the Deity should vouchsafe trivial information about card symbols to a select few.

ESP phenomena obviously concern philosophy if, as Broad has argued, one of the main tasks of philosophy is synthesis, or "the attempt to supply a coherent set of concepts and principles which shall cover satisfactorily all regions of fact" ("The Relevance of Psychical Research to Philosophy," pp. 292–293). Philosophers' theories have nearly always been influenced by recent scientific theories, and philosophers should particularly take into account facts (including the phenomena of clairvoyance as well as telepathy) that science cannot yet explain even in principle, or at least they should recognize that there are such facts.

(For a discussion of the relevance of ESP to materialism, see MATERIALISM. See also PRECOGNITION.)

Bibliography

JOURNALS

The journals in the field are indispensable sources, especially the *Proceedings* (from 1882) and the *Journal* (public from 1949) of the London Society for Psychical Research, the *Journal of the American Society for Psychical Research* (New York, from 1907), and the *Journal of Parapsychology* (Duke University Press, from 1937). Some important papers have appeared in the *International Journal of Parapsychology* (Parapsychology Foundation Inc., New York, from 1959).

IMPORTANT BOOKS

Serious students of ESP should read all of the following:

Broad, C. D., *Lectures on Psychical Research.* London and New York, 1962. A lucid critical study of a few of the best experiments, of spontaneous cases, and of the psychological aspects of trance-mediumship. Apart from the question of survival, it does not pursue philosophical problems.

Carington, Whately, *Telepathy.* London, 1945. Develops an interesting theory of telepathy that had some value in guiding Carington's experiments.

Gurney, Edmund; Myers, F. W. H.; and Podmore, Frank, *Phantasms of the Living.* London, 1886. A classic collection of spontaneous cases of ESP.

Myers, F. W. H., *Human Personality and Its Survival of Bodily Death.* London and New York, 1903. Surveys all the facts, normal, abnormal, and paranormal, which Myers believed to support psychophysical dualism.

Rhine, J. B., *Extra-sensory Perception.* London and Boston, 1934. Reports on the pioneer card-guessing experiments at Duke University.

Soal, S. G., and Bateman, Frederick, *Modern Experiments in Telepathy.* London, 1954. The best survey of experimental work in ESP, with a detailed account of Soal's own work. Fully documented.

Tyrrell, G. N. M., *Science and Psychical Phenomena.* London, 1938. Covers all aspects of psychical research, with a short account of Tyrrell's experiments.

Vasiliev, L. L., *Experiments in Mental Suggestion,* translated by C. C. L. Gregory. Church Crookham, Eng., 1963. First published in Russian (Leningrad, 1962). Report of experiments carried out between 1921 and 1938 at the Leningrad Institute of Brain Research.

CONTRIBUTIONS BY PHILOSOPHERS

Bergson, Henri, "Presidential Address." *Proceedings of the SPR*, Vol. 26 (1912–1913), 462–479.

Broad, C. D., *The Mind and Its Place in Nature.* London, 1925. Ch. 12 discusses the empirical evidence for survival.

Broad, C. D., "Normal Cognition and Telepathy." *Proceedings of the SPR*, Vol. 43 (1935), 397–438. Reprinted in *Religion, Philosophy and Psychical Research.* London, 1953. A penetrating study of the implications of assimilating ESP and sense perception.

Broad, C. D., "The Relevance of Psychical Research to Philosophy." *Philosophy*, Vol. 24 (1949), 291–309. Reprinted in *Religion, Philosophy and Psychical Research* (see above). Argues that the criterion for distinguishing "paranormal" phenomena, and their importance to philosophy, consists in the fact that they violate what Broad called "Basic Limiting Principles." He listed nine such principles that "we"—presumably modern educated Europeans and Americans—were said to take unhesitatingly for granted. But some of these principles are not accepted by behaviorists or epiphenomenalists, and others are rejected in quantum physics.

Broad, C. D., *Lectures on Psychical Research* (see above).

Ducasse, C. J., "The Philosophical Importance of 'Psychic Phenomena.'" *Journal of Philosophy*, Vol. 51 (1954), 810–823. A reply to J. B. Rhine's "The Science of Non-physical Nature," in the same volume.

Ducasse, C. J., *The Belief in Life After Death.* Springfield, Ill., 1961.

Flew, A. G. N., *A New Approach to Psychical Research.* London, 1953. This book treats the experimental work cursorily but is philosophically interesting in the chapters on survival and "Describing and Explaining."

Kneale, Martha; Robinson, Richard; and Mundle, C. W. K., "Is Psychical Research Relevant to Philosophy?" *PAS*, Supp. Vol. 24 (1950), 173–231. A symposium. See also the critical comments of the chairman, C. D. Broad, in *Journal of Parapsychology*, Vol. 15 (1951), 216–223.

Mundle, C. W. K., "The Experimental Evidence for PK and Precognition." *Proceedings of the SPR*, Vol. 49 (1949–1952), 61–78.

Mundle, C. W. K., "Some Philosophical Perspectives for Parapsychology." *Journal of Parapsychology*, Vol. 16 (1952), 257–272.

Mundle, C. W. K., "Does the Concept of Precognition Make Sense?" *International Journal of Parapsychology*, Vol. 6 (1964), 179–198.

Murphy, Gardner, and Ballon, R. O., eds., *William James on Psychical Research.* London, 1961.

Price, H. H., "Presidential Address." *Proceedings of the SPR*, Vol. 45 (1938–1939), 307–343.

Price, H. H., "Psychical Research and Human Personality." *Hibbert Journal*, Vol. 47 (1948–1949), 105–113. Argues that ESP is incompatible with materialism.

Scriven, Michael, "New Frontiers of the Brain." *Journal of Parapsychology*, Vol. 25 (1961), 305–318. Argues that ESP is compatible with physicalism.

Sidgwick, Henry, first "Presidential Address." *Proceedings of the SPR*, Vol. 1 (1882–1883), 7–12.

OTHER WORKS REFERRED TO IN THE ARTICLE

Beloff, John, *The Existence of Mind.* London, 1962. Ch. 7.

Berger, H., *Psyche.* Jena, 1940. See also the review of this book by W. G. *Roll in Journal of Parapsychology,* Vol. 24 (1960), 142–148.

Besterman, T.; Soal, S. G.; and Jephson, I., "Report of a Series of Experiments in Clairvoyance." *Proceedings of the SPR*, Vol. 39 (1930–1931), 375–414.

Carington, Whately, "Experiments on the Paranormal Cognition of Drawings." *Proceedings of the SPR*, Vol. 46 (1940–1941), 155–228, and Vol. 47 (1942–1945), 34–151.

Dodds, E. R., "Why I Do Not Believe in Survival." *Proceedings of the SPR*, Vol. 42 (1934), 147–172.

Hansel, C. E. M., "A Critical Review of Experiments with Mr. Basil Shackleton and Mrs. Gloria Stewart." *Proceedings of the SPR*, Vol. 53 (1960), 1–42. See Soal's reply in the same volume.

Jephson, I., "Evidence for Clairvoyance in Card-guessing." *Proceedings of the SPR*, Vol. 38 (1929), 223–268.

Martin, D. R., and Stribic, F. P., "Studies in Extra-sensory Perception." *Journal of Parapsychology*, Vol. 4 (1940), 159–248.

Nicol, J. Fraser, "Randomness: The Background and Some New Investigations." *Journal of the SPR*, Vol. 38 (1955), 71–87.

Oram, A. T., "An Experiment with Random Numbers." *Journal of the SPR*, Vol. 37 (1954), 369–377.

Osty, Eugène, *Supernormal Faculties in Man,* translated by Stanley de Brath. London, 1923. Originally published in French as *La Connaissance supra-normale.*

Price, G. R., "Science and the Supernatural." *Science*, Vol. 122 (August 26, 1955).

Rhine, J. B., "Some Basic Experiments in ESP." *Journal of Parapsychology*, Vol. 1 (1937), 70–80.

Rhine, J. B., *The Reach of the Mind.* New York, 1947.

Rhine, J. B., and Pratt, J. G., "A Review of the Pearce–Pratt Distance Series of ESP Tests." *Journal of Parapsychology*, Vol. 18 (1954), 156–177.

Saltmarsh, H. F., "Report on the Investigation of Some Sittings With Mrs. Warren Elliott." *Proceedings of the SPR*, Vol. 39 (1930–1931), 47–184.

Sidgwick, Mrs. Henry, and Johnson, Alice, "Report of the Census of Hallucinations." *Proceedings of the SPR*, Vol. 10 (1894), 25–422.

Soal, S. G., "A Report on Some Communications Received Through Mrs. Blanche Cooper." *Proceedings of the SPR*, Vol. 35 (1926), 471–594.

Soal, S. G., and Goldney, K. M., "Experiments in Precognitive Telepathy." *Proceedings of the SPR*, Vol. 47 (1942–1945), 21–150.

Tyrrell, G. N. M., "Further Research in Extra-sensory Perception." *Proceedings of the SPR*, Vol. 44 (1936–1937), 99–167.

Walter, W. Grey, *The Living Brain.* London, 1953.

C. W. K. MUNDLE

ESSENCE. See DEFINITION; ESSENCE AND EXISTENCE; UNIVERSALS.

ESSENCE AND EXISTENCE. It will avoid misunderstanding if the topic of essence and existence is expounded in an order other than chronological.

Seventeenth-century view. Hobbes and Locke insisted that definitions are not of things but of names. In so doing, they conceived of themselves as breaking with Aristotelianism. Hobbes said that the essence of a thing is "that accident for which we give a certain name to a body, or the accident which denominates its subject"; he had earlier denied that "the definition is the essence of any thing"; and his example of an essence is that "extension is the essence of a body" (*De Corpore*, II, 8, 23).

Locke distinguished the real essence from the nominal essence; the nominal essence is the idea of the property or properties the possession of which justifies the application of a given name; the real essence is as it is understood by "those who look on all natural things to have a real but unknown constitution of their insensible parts, from which flow those sensible qualities which serve us to distinguish them one from another, according as we have occasion to rank them into sets under common denominators" (*Essay* III, 3, 17).

The mistake which Hobbes and Locke ascribed to Aristotelianism was that of confusing the meaning of an expression with the nature of the object which the expression characterizes. In the empiricist tradition this separation of questions of meaning from questions of characterization continued to be influential. One consequence is that the concept of the real essence is dropped altogether. Another is that philosophy itself becomes defined as the study of meaning, as a linguistic inquiry. But will the Lockean separation of the real and the nominal, from which so much of this derives, bear scrutiny? Did Aristotle commit the error ascribed to him? Is it an error?

Aristotle and Aquinas. For Aristotle, the essence of an object (τὸ τί ἦν εἶναι) was what finds expression in the concept which the object embodies, the concept under which it must be identified if it is to be identified as what it is. The natural response of someone trained in the empiricist tradition is to question this concept of an object. In any particular case the question "What is *this?*" can have more than one correct answer—for instance, "a coat" or "a piece of cloth." To ask further what the essence of the thing indicated is, is to miss part of the Aristotelian point, which is best brought out by considering problems of identity. If I ask whether this is the same coat that you wore last year, I am not asking the same question that I would be asking if I inquired whether this is the same cloth made up into trousers that you used to wear in the form of a coat. "The same coat" and "the same cloth" pick out different identities. When I pick out "this" as an object, I can do so only by identifying it under some description, and the object does not have a nature apart from being identified under a description. For otherwise I could not identify what was to be characterized. In other words, we cannot identify an object solely by means of pronouns like "this" or by pointing.

It might be thought a fatal objection to this view that I can apparently identify an object without knowing what it is (a case which Aristotle allows for). Suppose I pick up something in your room and simply ask, "What is this?" The range of possible answers includes "a piece of stone," "a carving," "an image of a saint." My ignorance may extend as far down the range of specificity as you please; I must still be able to find some description to add to my use of "this" or to my pointing. For if I pick it up twice, I must be able to identify it as the same object; and it is a condition of my identifying it as an object at all that I should be able in principle to pick it up, or otherwise indicate it, more than once. Possible reidentification is a necessary condition of identification. But if this is so, then I must, in picking it up, be able to characterize it, even if only as "that small colorless lump" or some such description. There is a limit to vagueness, at which such purely formal concepts as "thing" and "object" lie.

Insofar, then, as Aristotle is concerned with the minimal conditions for identifying and characterizing objects, he is justified in a view which makes understanding what something is, inseparable from understanding the meaning of the description which must be applied to it if it is to be identified as what it is. The nominal and the real cannot be entirely divorced. But Aristotle expresses all this in terms of the concepts of substance and of matter and form, and in so doing he appears to lay himself open to the Hobbes–Locke type of criticism. What Aristotle meant by τί ἦν εἶναι is the subject of disagreement among translators and commentators. Hugh Tredennick (in translating *Metaphysics* 1031a15 ff.) uses "essence"; Joseph Owens invents an arbitrary phrase, "the What-Is-Being" of a thing, and explains it in terms of the being of a thing which is the being of its form. The form is the necessary and unchanging element in a thing, in contrast with the matter and the composite, which may change, and the generic characteristics, which may belong to some other species (*Doctrine of Being in the Aristotelian Metaphysics*, p. 94).

Aristotle thus made the concept, under which an object must fall if it is to be identified and characterized as what it is, express a timeless and necessary element in the nature of the object itself. And insofar as Hobbes, for example, wished to deny that this timeless and necessary element was what a definition could refer to, it would be difficult to disagree. But any further discussion of Aristotle could only proceed by analysis of the doctrine of matter and form (see ARISTOTLE).

What is clear is that Aristotle inherited from Plato the notion of a range of fixed and timeless Forms, natures or essences which are embodied in the changing physical world. Less pessimistic than Plato about the possibility of knowledge of the nature of particular material objects, he retained the view that what the intellect grasps is always a form which could have been embodied in other matter. The name given to the being that the intellect grasps is οὐσία, which W. D. Ross renders as *essence*, following Quintilian and Seneca, who translated it as *essentia*. *Essentia* comes to mean the nature of a thing, the answer to the question *quid sit*. Augustine used *substantia* and *essentia* without difference of meaning, and Boethius translated οὐσία as *substantia*. From then on the word *substantia* was used in this sense and *essentia* was reserved for a new context which was first found in explicit form in Giles of Rome. This contrast is that between essence and existence, which received its completest statement in the work of Aquinas.

Aquinas. A substance is composite; it is an essence upon which existence has been conferred. When existence is conferred on an essence, what was hitherto merely possible becomes actual. In the case of physical bodies, a form receives matter. Thus the concepts of essence and existence, potency and act, form and matter are mutually correlative. The notion of *esse* being conferred upon an *essentia* so that a substance is brought into being was foreign to Aristotle because the notion of creation was foreign to him. For Aristotle, analysis in terms of essence or substance was a way of approaching what already exists or is in the process of change. For Aquinas, that anything at all exists must itself be explained. It is a purely contingent fact that any particular essence is an embodied existent. The only exception to this is God, in whom essence and existence are identical. But it does not follow that by grasping what God is, we can grasp that he is, as Anselm had supposed in his vision of the Ontological Argument. For we cannot grasp the divine essence.

Modern views. The vocabulary of essence and existence was preserved after the seventeenth century both by late Scholasticism and by its intellectual first cousin, rationalist metaphysics. Christian von Wolff inherited, perhaps from Francisco Suárez, whose influence he acknowledged, a view of the universe as a system of essences on which God has chosen to confer existence. But his view of essence as what can be conceived as a clear and distinct idea points to the influence of Descartes and in his version of the Ontological Argument we can see the confluence of Duns Scotus and Leibniz. Knowledge of essences is expressed in propositions which are necessary truths. But these necessary truths are truths about possibilities, and it is a contingent matter of God's will being what it is that these particular essences have been actualized.

A line of thought which is only superficially like that of rationalist metaphysics runs from Spinoza to Hegel. In Spinoza the essence which entails existence is that of the single substance. But this version of the Ontological Argument is only part of Spinoza's whole set of theorems determining the all-inclusive *Deus sive natura* (see SPINOZA). Hegel treated the transition from essence to existence as part of the logical play with concepts that is an essential preliminary to the world of becoming. Of course we cannot deny that being is; but that, for Hegel, is only because the assertion is so bare and empty. When we deal with the realm of becoming, we have the sharpest of contrasts between the *Was-sein* (essence) and the *Das-sein* (existence), as Schelling, the enemy of all clear distinctions, complained.

The notion of an essence as a fixed possibility whose character may be delimited apart from our acquaintance with the existence which embodies it was inherited from Scholasticism by Franz Brentano and Edmund Husserl, whose phenomenology is concerned with essences insofar as it is a study of what is involved in *any* act of judgment, belief, feeling, or willing, independently of the context of particular acts. The use of "essence" and "existence" by Sartre is partly derived from phenomenology and partly from Scholasticism. The latter influence is apparent in the way in which Sartre uses the formula that existence precedes essence in order to deny that men are created by God. Sartre identifies such a conception of creation with the notion of God creating beings with fixed, already determinate natures who would therefore be unfree. Nothing of this appears to be entailed by Aquinas' use of "essence" and "existence," but Leibniz and Wolff could be more convincingly convicted on this charge. Sartre wishes to convey by his formula that men do not have determinate natures, fixed in advance of their choices. By this he means that Smith does not have an existence determined for him which if he did not live out he would not be Smith; so it is Leibniz or Wolff, and not Aquinas, whose propositions he is in fact denying.

What, then, is Sartre asserting? The contention that existence precedes essence may be interpreted as entailing various consequences, not all of which were necessarily intended by Sartre. Sartre clearly does believe that his contention not only constitutes the denial of one species of determinism, as has already been noted, but also involves the invalidity of any version of the Ontological Argument, whether Anselmian, Cartesian, or Hegelian. That is, no essence is such that it is a necessary truth that there must exist some individual embodying that essence. But unfortunately the Sartrian contention is so loosely stated that he might also be taken to imply—what he certainly would not want to imply—that there are no essences, that is, no meanings, apart from existences. This is plainly false. Many meaningful expressions do not name or denote anything that exists, many descriptions do not characterize anything that exists, as the common examples of "unicorn" and "glass mountain" make clear. The chief difficulty with the Sartrian thesis, however, is not that it plainly entails absurd consequences. It is, rather, that the thesis is stated so generally, and is so inadequately developed, that it is not at all clear what does or does not follow from Sartre's contention.

Bibliography

PRIMARY SOURCES

Aristotle, *Metaphysics*, translated by Hugh Tredennick. Cambridge, Mass., 1945.

Aristotle, *Metaphysics*, W. D. Ross, ed. Oxford, 1948.

Sartre, Jean-Paul, *L'Être et le néant, essai d'ontologie phénoménologique*. Paris, 1943. Translated by H. E. Barnes as *Being and Nothingness, an Essay on Phenomenological Ontology*. New York, 1957.

Sartre, Jean-Paul, *L'Existentialisme est un humanisme*. Paris, 1946. Translated by P. Mairet as *Existentialism and Humanism*. New York, 1948.

Thomas Aquinas, *De Ente et Essentia*, M. D. Roland-Gosselin, ed. Le Saulchoir, 1926. Translated by Armand Mauer as *Being and Essence*. Toronto, 1949.

Thomas Aquinas, *In Metaphysicorum Aristotelis Commentaria*, M. R. Cathala, ed. Turin, 1935.

Thomas Aquinas, *Summa Theologica*. Ottawa, 1941–1945.

Translated by the Dominicans of the English Province, 3 vols. New York, 1947.

Wolff, Christian von, *Philosophia Prima Sive Ontologia*. Frankfurt and Leipzig, 1730.

SECONDARY SOURCES

Anscombe, G. E. M., and Geach, P. T., *Three Philosophers*. Oxford, 1961. Discussions of Aristotle, Aquinas, and Frege.

Ayer, A. J., "Some Aspects of Existentialism." *Rationalist Annual* (1948).

Bobik, Joseph, *Aquinas on Being and Essence, a Translation and Interpretation*. Notre Dame, Ind., 1965.

Owens, Joseph, *The Doctrine of Being in the Aristotelian Metaphysics*. Toronto, 1951; 2d ed., 1957.

ALASDAIR MacINTYRE

ESTHETICS. See AESTHETICS, HISTORY OF; AESTHETICS, PROBLEMS OF.

ETERNAL RETURN is the doctrine that every event in the universe, in all its details and in its whole cosmic context, will recur an infinite number of times in exactly the same way that it has already occurred an infinite number of times in the past. This doctrine must be distinguished from the belief in the general periodicity of nature, according to which the main features—but not the specific details—of human and cosmic history recur.

The pre-Socratics. The periodicity of various phenomena is a fact of daily experience; the alternation of day and night, of lunar phases and of the seasons of the year, and the rhythm of breathing and heartbeats were known to primitive man. Even the idea that cosmic history repeats itself in its general features appeared in various forms in mythological thought. Among the pre-Socratics the idea was held by Anaximander, Empedocles, and the atomists. The existing universe was regarded as a result of the differentiation of an original chaos—watery, fiery, or qualitatively undetermined—into which it would eventually return and from which a similar universe would emerge. This idea of the periodicity of worlds soon became associated with the belief that not only the general features but also the most specific details would recur in the same order that they had occurred countless times in the past. According to Eudemus of Rhodes, this was the belief of the Pythagoreans: "Everything will eventually return in the self-same numerical order, and I shall converse with you staff in hand, and you will sit as you are sitting now, and so it will be in everything else, and it is reasonable to assume that time too will be the same" (H. Diels and W. Kranz, *Fragmente der Vorsokratiker*, 58B34).

The same idea of the cyclical nature of time was present, according to Pierre Duhem, in the thought of another Pythagorean, Archytas of Tarentum, who defined time as "the interval of the universe." The length of this cosmic cycle, called the Great Year or Perfect Number, was variously estimated by different thinkers who were influenced by Pythagoreanism. For Heraclitus it was equal to 10,800 years (according to another source 18,000 years). According to the testimony of the Stoics and of Simplicius (whose reliability on this point has been doubted by Friedrich Schleiermacher, Ferdinand Lassalle, John Burnet, and

G. S. Kirk), it measured the period separating two successive conflagrations in which an old world perishes and a new one is reborn.

Plato and Aristotle. Plato associated the period of the Great Year not with a periodically recurring cataclysm but with a return of all the celestial bodies to the same relative positions. Nor did Aristotle accept a universal conflagration, which was clearly incompatible with his idea of the incorruptible celestial realm. Nevertheless he did, if we accept his authorship of the *Problemata*, uphold eternal return in its most radical form: "Just as the course of the firmament and each of the stars is a circle, why should not also the coming into being and the decay of perishable things be of such a kind that the same things again come into being and decay?" (*The Works of Aristotle*, Vol. VII, p. 916a). Aristotle realized that the circularity of becoming would imply a relativization of succession: If the Trojan War will inevitably recur, in a sense we are living "prior" to it. The author of *Problemata*, however, was reluctant to accept the ultimate consequence of the idea of cyclical becoming: "To demand that those who are coming into being should always be numerically identical, is foolish" (*ibid.*).

The Stoics. The problem of cyclical becoming was faced by the Stoics, who believed that at the end of each cosmic cycle a universal conflagration (ἐκπύρωσεις) that dissolves the universe into the original fire will occur. This will coincide with the beginning of another cycle; the events of the previous cycle will then be reconstituted in all their details and in the same order. But Stoics followed Aristotle by claiming that another Socrates who will marry another Xantippe and be accused by another Meletus will not be numerically identical with the previous Socrates, since numerical identity implies an uninterrupted existence. Some younger Stoics, in conceding small differences between successive Socrateses, gave up the circularity of becoming in all but name.

Plotinus. A curious argument for eternal return was given by Plotinus in the *Fifth Ennead* (Book VII, Chs. 1, 2). According to Plotinus, the intelligible world contains the ideal patterns not only of genera but also of all individuals, each of which successively finds its embodiment in the realm of change. But since the supply of these patterns is finite, a time will come when the same pattern—for example, of Socrates—will have to be incarnated again, and this will be possible only in the next identical cosmic cycle. Thus the successive cycles are identical, but there is no repetition within each cycle.

Jewish and early Christian thought. Both Judaism and Christianity, with their emphasis on the finiteness and irreversibility of cosmic history, were strongly opposed to the doctrine of eternal return. According to both the Jewish and the Christian view, the history of the world is bounded by two unique and unrepeatable events: its beginning (the Creation) and end (the Last Judgment). Every individual human life is similarly unique.

Origen, while accepting with the Neoplatonists the eternity of the world and even metempsychosis, rejected the identity of successive cosmic cycles because such a concept was incompatible with human freedom. Nemesius

(*De Natura Hominis*, Ch. 38) and St. Augustine (*De Civitate Dei*, Book XII, Chs. 11, 13) rejected the doctrine, Nemesius on the ground that the Resurrection cannot take place periodically, Augustine because the incarnation of Christ occurred only once.

Medieval thought. A decree of 1277 threatening excommunication of those who accepted the Neoplatonic idea of a Great Year lasting 36,000 years demonstrates the survival of this belief into the Middle Ages. Although St. Thomas rejected the cyclical view of time by claiming that the re-creation of numerically identical individuals would be contradictory, and as such was beyond even God's power, his view was not shared by Duns Scotus and William of Ockham. Nicolas Bonet and François de la Marche explicitly insisted on God's power to restore any past motion, and therefore a corresponding past interval of time, since there was no difference between motion and time.

Early modern thought. Thus, at the threshold of the modern era two of the central ideas of the modern cyclical view of time were present—the reversibility of motion and the relational theory of time. The third essential ingredient of the cyclical theory—the finiteness of the material universe—was excluded by Giordano Bruno's vision of innumerable worlds and limitless space. This may explain the absence of the idea of eternal recurrence in Bruno's contemporaries despite their Neoplatonic leanings. For if the number of constituent parts of the universe is infinite, the number of possible combinations is also infinite, and recurrence of the same configuration is not inevitable.

In Newton and his successors there was an additional motive for not considering the cyclical view. They regarded time as absolute, as intrinsically irreversible, irrespective of its content. Even a complete restoration of the content of the past moment would not make this moment itself present.

Descartes came very close to the cyclical view when he wrote that matter must successively pass through all its possible forms, but since matter to him was coextensive with infinite space, the number of its configurations was inexhaustible. Furthermore, the pagan and astrological associations of the ancient cyclical theory made it thoroughly suspect.

Nineteenth-century views. Interest in eternal return was revived only with the development of modern cosmogony. The nebular hypothesis of Kant (1755) and Laplace (1796) implicitly raised the question of the origin of any primordial nebula: Did it represent a truly initial stage preceded by an act of supernatural creation, or was it merely one of the countless stages in an unending cycle of successive worlds? The principle of the uniformity of nature in time, anticipated by Bruno's and Spinoza's belief in the eternity of the universe, strongly favored the second answer. Although the law of entropy suggested the irreversibility of the whole cosmic process, because of its statistical character it did not exclude the general periodicity of nature. Various hypothetical mechanisms were invented to provide a "rewinding of the cosmic clock," at least on a local scale. The most popular one was that of cosmic clashes by which two stellar masses that had lost their heat could be transformed into another nebula, which would then develop into another world "ever the same in principle, but never the same in concrete results," as Herbert Spencer wrote in his *First Principles* (p. 550).

Such a new world could be the same even in concrete details only if the cosmic mass did not contain an infinite number of units. Eugen Dühring, in various writings (heavily annotated copies of which were found in Nietzsche's library), rejected the concept of actual infinity as self-contradictory and inapplicable to the physical world.

In Nietzsche's thought the concept of a finite universe and of the discrete structure of matter implied a finite number of possible successive configurations, and therefore an inevitable recurrence of a configuration defining a state of the universe that had already occurred an infinite number of times in the past; and this recurring cosmic state must, according to the then accepted deterministic scheme, generate the series of the same events in the same order as in the previous cosmic cycles. This view, formulated by Nietzsche at the end of the fourth book of *Fröhliche Wissenschaft* (1881), became central to his philosophy. The intensely lyrical way in which this view was expressed in *Thus Spake Zarathustra* hid its intellectual origins, which are far more obvious in the posthumously published fragments of *The Will to Power* (see *The Complete Works of Friedrich Nietzsche*, Vol. XV, Ch. 2, esp. p. 430). Prior to Nietzsche only a few nineteenth-century thinkers held the same view: Louis A. Blanqui (*Éternité par les astres*, 1871), Gustave Le Bon (*L'Homme et les sociétés*, 1881), Jean Marie Guyau (*Vers d'un Philosophie*, 1881). It was not held, however, by Dühring, who claimed that the continuity of space admitted an infinite number of configurations even if the number of atomic units was finite (*Cursus der Philosophie*, pp. 84–85). The same objection against eternal return was raised by Alois Riehl and Alfred Fouillée; against this view Franz Selety pointed out that concrete processes were discrete and not mathematically continuous, and therefore, he claimed, eternal recurrence was unavoidable; and G. N. Lewis claimed that the attempt at avoiding an exact recurrence by assuming a whole continuum of possible values is eliminated by the quantum theory.

Henri Poincaré, although he formulated the theorem of phases, according to which any mechanical system of a finite number of particles will in a sufficiently long time pass through a configuration infinitely close to the previous one, nevertheless dismissed the application of the theorem of phases to cosmogony in his *Leçons sur les hypothèses cosmogoniques* (p. 23) as "the dream of eternal return." C. S. Peirce (*Collected Papers*, Vol. I, pp. 498–500) held the cyclical view on the unusual ground that "since every portion of time is bounded by two instants, there must be a connection of time ringwise." Furthermore, this view was entirely incompatible with the rest of his philosophy. The arguments of Abel Rey in favor of the cyclical view were not essentially different from those of Nietzsche, since they were based on the classical corpuscular–kinetic scheme of nature.

Contemporary thought. The contemporary crisis of the classical scheme of nature makes the doctrine of eternal return extremely questionable. The doctrine was based on four fundamental assumptions: (*a*) that the universe is made up of distinct atomic units which persist through time without any intrinsic change, so that they may be identified in successive moments; (*b*) that the number of atomic units is finite; (*c*) that it is meaningful to speak of a definite "state of the universe" at each instant; (*d*) that one such particular state (embodied in a definite atomic configuration) causally determines all future states (Laplacean determinism).

Except for the thesis that the size of the universe is finite, which is favored by some cosmologists, none of these theses remains unchallenged by the recent developments in physics. The atoms of modern physics do not have the rigidity and permanence of classical atoms; and without permanent elements there can be no recurring configurations. The ontological status of "state of the universe at an instant" is challenged by the relativization of simultaneity, and the validity of rigorous determinism has been seriously questioned since the formulation of the indeterminacy principle in 1927.

Moreover, there are ambiguities and discrepancies within the theory of eternal return itself. The assumption of a completely identical repetition of cosmic situations makes the theory intrinsically unverifiable. Moreover, either the successive identical cycles are distinguished by their positions in time—which means that we surreptitiously introduce an irreversible time as their container— or we insist on the numerical identity of the cycles. But we then have only one cosmic cycle, and it clearly becomes meaningless to speak of a "succession of cycles" or of their "repetition." Although it is self-contradictory to speak of numerical identity of genuinely successive events, the two views have often been held jointly, as by the Scotists and Nietzsche.

The eternal return is rejected by all thinkers who insist on the irreversibility of becoming, genuine novelty, and the immortality of the past. Mircea Eliade regards the theory as a manifestation of "ontology uncontaminated by time and becoming" (*The Myth of the Eternal Return*, p. 89); Émile Myerson saw in it an attempt to eliminate becoming (*L'Identité et réalité*, Ch. 8). The emotional effect of the doctrine is equally ambiguous. Thus Nietzsche's mystical ecstasy over "the ring of eternity" was tinged by a note of anxiety and even despair. Gustave Le Bon compared the recurring cosmic cycles to the labors of Sisyphus, and Miguel de Unamuno, in *The Tragic Sense of Life*, regarded the doctrine as a poor substitute for personal immortality.

Bibliography

CLASSICAL AND MEDIEVAL

Diels, H., and Kranz, W., *Fragmente der Vorsokratiker*, 6th ed. Berlin, 1951.
Duhem, Pierre, *Le Système du monde*. Paris, 1954. Vol. I, pp. 65–85, 164–169, 275–296; Vol. II, pp. 447–461; Vol. VII, pp. 441–461. On the idea of the Great Year in Greek and medieval thought.
Mugler, Charles, *Deux Thèmes de la cosmologie grecque: Devenir cyclique et la pluralité des mondes*. Paris, 1953.
Ross, W. D., ed., *The Works of Aristotle*. Oxford, 1923. Vol. VII.
Sambursky, Samuel, *The Physical World of the Greeks*, translated by Merton Dagut. New York, 1956. Ch. 8. On Greek cosmogony.

NIETZSCHE ON ETERNAL RETURN

The Complete Works of Friedrich Nietzsche, translated by A. M. Ludovici. Reissued New York, 1964. Vol. XV, Ch. 2, esp. p. 430.
Andler, Charles, *Nietzsche, sa vie et sa pensée*, 5th ed. Paris, 1958. Vol. II, pp. 402–424; Vol. III, pp. 284–294. Vol. II discusses mythological, Greek, and modern influences on Nietzsche.
Batault, Georges, "L'Hypothèse du retour éternel devant la science moderne." *Revue philosophique*, Vol. 57 (1904), 158–167.
Bois, Henri, "Le 'Retour éternel' de Nietzsche." *Année philosophique*, Vol. 24 (1913), 145–184.
Danto, Arthur, *Nietzsche as Philosopher*. New York, 1965. Ch. 7.
Heidegger, Martin, *Nietzsche*. Pfullingen, 1961. Vol. I, Ch. 2; Vol. II, Ch. 3.
Horneffer, Ernst, *Nietzsches Lehre von der ewigen Wiederkunft und der bisherige Veröffentlichung*. Leipzig, 1900.
Löwith, Karl, *Nietzsches Philosophie der ewigen Wiederkunft des Gleichen*. Stuttgart, 1956.
Schlechta, Karl, *Nietzsches grosser Mittag*. Frankfurt, 1954.
Stambaugh, Joan, *Untersuchungen zum Problem der Zeit bei Nietzsche*. Haag, 1959.
Steiner, Rudolf, *Friedrich Nietzsche. Ein Kämpfer gegen seine Zeit*, 3d ed. Dornach, 1963. Pp. 187–197. On the relation of Nietzsche to Dühring.

GENERAL

Čapek, Milič, "The Theory of Eternal Recurrence in Modern Philosophy of Science." *Journal of Philosophy*, Vol. 57 (1960), 289–296.
Couturat, Louis, "De l'évolutionnisme physique et du principe de la conservation de l'énergie." *Revue de métaphysique et de morale*, Vol. 1 (1893), 564–572.
Denbigh, K. G., "Thermodynamics and the Subjective Sense of Time." *The British Journal for Philosophy of Science*, Vol. 4 (1953–1954), esp. p. 187.
Dühring, Eugen, *Cursus der Philosophie*. Leipzig, 1875.
Eliade, Mircea, *The Myth of the Eternal Return*. New York, 1954.
Lewis, G. N., "Symmetry of Time in Physics." *Science*, Vol. 31 (1930), 569–577.
Marbe, Karl, *Die Gleichförmigkeit der Welt*. Munich, 1916. Chs. 8–11.
Meyerson, Émile, *L'Identité et réalité*, 5th ed. Paris, 1951.
Peirce, C. S., *Collected Papers*, Charles Hartshorne, Paul Weiss, and Arthur W. Burks, eds., 8 vols. Cambridge, Mass., 1931–1958.
Poincaré, Henri, *Leçons sur les hypothèses cosmogoniques*. Paris, 1911.
Rey, Abel, *Le Retour éternel et la philosophie de la physique*. Paris, 1927.
Riehl, Alois, *Zur Einführung in die Philosophie der Gegenwart*. Leipzig, 1903.
Selety, Franz, "Über Wiederholung des Gleichen im kosmischen Geschehen." *Zeitschrift für Philosophie*, Vol. 5 (1914).
Spencer, Herbert, *First Principles*, 4th ed. New York, 1896.
Weber, Louis, "L'Évolutionnisme physique." *Revue de métaphysique et de morale*, Vol. 1 (1893), 425–452.
Whitrow, G. J., *The Natural Philosophy of Time*. London, 1961. Ch. entitled "Cyclic Time," esp. pp. 40–41.
Zawirski, Zygmunt, *L'Évolution de l'idée du temps*. Cracow, 1936. Pp. 336 ff.

MILIČ ČAPEK

ETERNITY. The word "eternal" is derived from the Latin *aeternus*, a contraction of *aeviternus*, which, in turn, is derived from *aevum*, a word from the same root as the English words "ever" and "aye." In Greek the corresponding adjectives are even more obviously connected with the notion of everlasting existence. This is the original sense of the word "eternal" and probably also the sense that is still the most common in ordinary language.

But in certain philosophical contexts the notion of ever-lasting existence is expressed rather by "sempiternal," "eternal" being reserved for the sense of "timeless."

The "timeless present" in science. In English and other Indo-European languages there is a usage described by grammarians as the timeless present. When, for example, we say, "Seven is a prime number," we do not intend our use of the present tense to convey anything about the present as distinct from the past or the future. For this reason we find something very curious in the sentences "Seven was a prime number" and "Seven will be a prime number." Existential statements of a mathematical kind do not refer to the time of speaking. An assertion such as "There is a prime number between 5 and 10" could never be countered sensibly by the remark "You are out of date." For this reason the entities discussed in mathematics can properly be said to have a timeless existence. To say only that they have a sempiternal or omnitemporal existence (that is, an existence at all times) would be unsatisfactory, because this way of talking might suggest that it is conceivable they should at some time cease to exist, an absurdity we want to exclude.

Mathematics, however, is not the only study in which use of the timeless present is appropriate. The same idiom can be found in all studies that are concerned with necessary truths as distinct from matters of fact. It may occur, for example, even in empirical studies when the propositions we formulate involve the notion of necessary connection. Thus, we say "The hydrogen atom contains only one proton" because we do not wish to allow that hydrogen atoms may in the past have contained or may in the future come to contain more than one proton. Here, however, our use of the timeless present is certainly not intended to suggest that hydrogen atoms exist out of time. What we wish to call timeless is simply the connection between being a hydrogen atom and containing a single proton. Sometimes such connections have been called eternal verities, most commonly when it has been thought they could.be known a priori, as in mathematics.

Greek thought. A different conception of timelessness appears in Parmenides' poem "The Way of Truth," where he says of the One, "It neither was at any time nor will be, since it is now all at once [ὁμοῦ πᾶν] a single whole." Since Parmenides and his pupil Zeno argued against the reality of change, we must suppose that this remark does not represent the One as existing merely for a moment but says rather that the One cannot be described in a language that employs tenses. The One exists all at once because it involves no temporal succession of earlier and later. But why should anyone talk in this way? Perhaps Parmenides accepted the religious teaching of Xenophanes, that the Whole is an everlasting god, and tried to defend it against Heraclitus' doctrine of universal flux by maintaining that the Whole is spherical in all respects—that is, temporally as well as spatially. For such a Whole could not itself be in time, and if we talk about it at all we must employ the timeless present. This is only a guess, but there is evidence to show that a conception of cyclical time order was current in the Pythagorean school with which Parmenides is said to have been connected in his youth.

From Parmenides the notion of a mode of existence that allows no distinction between past, present, and future passed to Plato, who applied it to his Forms, or Ideas. The most influential passage of his works dealing with this subject is in the *Timaeus* (37E6–38A6), where he contrasts the created world with the eternal living being, its timeless archetype.

The language of the passage is poetical, and it seems that we are not expected to take all the details seriously. In particular, Plato can scarcely have meant us to believe that time was an afterthought of the creator. Rather, we are to understand that time is to the perceptual world of becoming what eternity is to the intelligible world of being. For Plato said later (*Timaeus* 38B5), "Time was created with the heaven," and he seems to have held that it is identical with the movements of the heavenly bodies, which are commonly said to measure its passage. In many of his works Plato glorified the eternal and spoke of the temporal as something inferior, but he did not, like Parmenides and Zeno, deny the reality of time. The most he said in this regard is that temporal things never have being but are always in a state of becoming, as Heraclitus had argued. However, this seems to be no more than a recognition that we cannot talk of temporal things in the timeless present as we talk of Forms and mathematical objects.

The connection with necessity that Plato had claimed for timeless eternity Aristotle claimed for sempiternity. For having rejected Plato's doctrine of the creation of time (*Physics* 251b14), he did not wish to say that anything was wholly severed from it. Thus, in one place he explicitly associated the objects of mathematics with the universe, which he certainly did not regard as timeless (*Nicomachean Ethics* 1112a22). In his view the objects of mathematics are eternal (ἀΐδια), but only in the sense that they exist always— that is, are sempiternal. He held that among sempiternal things there is no difference between possibility and actuality and also that there is nothing merely accidental (*Physics* 203b30, 196b10). In one place he even said that sempiternal things, insofar as they are sempiternal, are not in time, because they are not bounded by time or subject to aging and the other conditions of time (*Physics* 221b30). Apparently he had in mind not only mathematical objects, such as numbers, but also God and the sun and stars and the whole heaven. For he said elsewhere that the heavenly bodies, unlike perishable things, are not wearied by their motion. The sun is active forever, and there is no danger that it will give out, as some philosophers feared (*Metaphysics* 1050b24). Spinoza may have been influenced, even if only indirectly, by Aristotle's doctrine when he used the word *aeternitas* to signify both necessity and sempiternity.

Christian theology. The doctrine of Plato's *Timaeus* passed into Christian theology, with emphasis on the notion of timeless *life*. As early as the St. John Gospel (8.58) there is a curious passage in which Jesus is represented as saying, "Before Abraham was I am." But it is fairly clear that the author of this gospel knew something of Greek philosophy, possibly at second hand through the works of the Jewish theologian Philo of Alexandria, and also that his narrative is no mere historical record of the life of Jesus. By the end of the fifth century there was nothing at all strange in the use of Platonic thought for the exposition of

Christianity, and St. Augustine, when commenting, in his *De Civitate Dei* (xi, 21), on the sentence in Genesis "God saw that it was good," referred to the passage of the *Timaeus* cited above. In his *Confessions* (xi, 13) he wrote also of God's "ever-present eternity" and said that for God "all years stand at once" (*omnes simul stant*). A century later Boethius, in his *De Trinitate* (4), said that our "now," by running as it were (*quasi currens*), makes time and sempiternity, whereas the divine "now," by abiding, unmoved and immovable, makes eternity; in the final chapter of his *De Consolatione Philosophiae* he discussed this at greater length.

Eternity is the complete possession of eternal life all at once—a notion that becomes clearer from comparison with things temporal. For whatever lives in time moves as something present from the past to the future, and there is nothing placed in time that can embrace the whole extent of its life at once. It does not yet grasp tomorrow, and it has already lost yesterday. And even in the life of today you do not live longer than in the transitory moment. That, then, which is subject to the condition of time, even if (as Aristotle thought of the world) it has no beginning or end and its life extends through endless time, is still not such as may be rightly judged eternal. For though its life be endless, it does not grasp and embrace the extent of it all at once [*totum simul*] but has some parts still to come. . . . And so, if, following Plato, we wish to give things their right names, let us say that God is eternal, but the world everlasting.

All these notions reappeared in the Middle Ages. Aquinas, for example, quoting Boethius as his authority, said in his *Summa Theologica* (I, x, 1) that there are two marks of eternity, namely, that the eternal has neither beginning nor end and that eternity contains no succession, being all at once (*tota simul existens*). This last phrase, though Aquinas could scarcely have known as much, is a rendering of words Parmenides had used over 17 centuries earlier. Not content, however, with the old distinction of time and eternity, medieval theologians sometimes spoke of *aevum*—that is, everlastingness—as something intermediate that was appropriate to the heavens and to angels. This was conceived by some as having a beginning but no end and by others (probably influenced in part by Aristotle's account of God and the heavenly bodies) as possessing earlier and later, but without innovation and aging. Aquinas regarded the latter view as self-contradictory, since, he held, there could be no succession without aging. *Aevum* does not necessarily include earlier and later, according to Aquinas, though these can be joined with it, as is the case with angels, who have changeless being as well as the capacity of change according to choice (*Summa Theologica* I, x, 5).

Criticism of the theological use. Anyone who, like Boethius, speaks of eternity as "the complete possession of eternal life all at once seems to be running together two incompatible notions, that of timelessness and that of life. For we can attach no meaning to the word "life" unless we are allowed to suppose that what has life acts. No doubt the word "acts" may be taken in a wide sense. Perhaps it is

not essential that a living thing produce changes in the physical world. But life must at least involve some incidents in time, and if, like Boethius, we suppose the life in question to be intelligent, then it must also involve awareness of the passage of time. Purposeful action is action with thought of what will come about after its beginning. It is difficult to decide how much of this Plato was prepared to admit when he wrote the *Timaeus*. In his earlier works (for example, the *Meno* and the *Phaedo*) he tried to explain the possibility of a priori knowledge by a doctrine of reminiscence, which involves the hypothesis that before this life the human soul lived among timelessly existent Forms and contemplated them directly as in this life it sees things belonging to the realm of becoming. But he probably came to realize that there is something absurd in the suggestion that a soul can pass part of its time in a timeless realm and then at a certain date enter the temporal realm, for he appears to have dropped the doctrine of reminiscence in his later dialogues, where instead of glorifying the soul by treating it as something akin to the timeless Forms he praised it as the source of motion. In the *Republic*, which belongs to the middle of his literary life, he spoke of God, who is presumably alive, as having created one and only one Form of each kind. But the wording of the passage (*Republic* 597C) seems to be obviously playful, and it is unlikely that Plato ever meant to suggest seriously that the Forms had been created. In the *Timaeus*, as we have seen, the Forms are said to be the timeless model used by the demiurge, or craftsman, who made the temporal world. Yet this same timeless model is said to be itself alive (*Timaeus* 37E6). Is this to be taken seriously? Unlike medieval theologians, for whom things predicated of the eternal were to be interpreted analogically, Plato maintained (*Timaeus* 29B) that discourse about the eternal is to be understood in the strict and primary sense of the words it employs.

How did the theologians come to commit themselves to talk about timeless life? The influence of Plato's style counts for a lot, but not for everything. One might say in the case of Aquinas that the surprising thing is that he held to Plato's account of time and eternity though he must have known it had been criticized by Aristotle. Probably the explanation is to be found in a peculiarity of Christian doctrine. Aristotle, though a theist of a sort, not only rejected the Platonic notion of the creation of time but also maintained the sempiternity of the heavens. To a theologian who had to produce a metaphysical scheme concordant with Biblical revelation (which denied the sempiternity of the cosmos) this must have made Aristotle's criticism of Plato's doctrine of eternity seem unsatisfactory. But apart from that, Plato's doctrine had the positive merit of seeming to provide for the necessity of God's existence. If it is correct, once we have admitted that we understand the meaning of the word "God" and that it involves no inconsistency, we cannot sensibly deny that God exists. Another manifestation of this theological interest in the necessity of God's existence is Anselm's ontological argument. Admittedly, this was rejected by Aquinas, but for epistemological reasons concerned with the limits of our capacities, not for the assumption it involves that divinity, by definition, entails existence. On the contrary, Aquinas, following Boethius, said that God's essence and existence are one.

Other philosophical uses. In later European thought Spinoza and various idealist philosophers used the word "eternity" to describe the existence of their God or Absolute. Spinoza, for example, said in his *Ethics* (I, Definition viii), "By *eternity* I mean existence itself in so far as it is conceived necessarily to follow solely from the definition of that which is eternal. Existence of this kind is conceived as an eternal truth, like the essence of a thing, and therefore cannot be explained by means of duration or time, though duration may be conceived without a beginning or an end." Here there is no longer any verbal connection of eternity with life, but there is still a wish to maintain that something concrete exists with the timeless necessity of which we speak in mathematics. Similar assertions have been made in Indian philosophy, which does not in any way derive from Parmenides or Plato, and we must therefore suppose that they correspond to a widespread demand of religious thought. In modern times even the Pythagorean notion of a cyclical time order has again been considered seriously, by Kurt Gödel.

Bibliography

Brabant, F. H., *Time and Eternity in Christian Thought.* New York, 1937.

Cushman, R. E., "Greek and Christian Views of Time." *Journal of Religion* (1953), 254–265.

Festugière, A.-J., "Le Sens philosophique du mot αἰών." *La parola del passato*, Fasc. 11 (1949), 172–189.

Gödel, Kurt, "A Remark About the Relationship Between Relativity Theory and Idealistic Philosophy," in P. A. Schilpp, ed., *Albert Einstein: Philosopher-scientist.* New York, 1951.

Guitton, J., *Le Temps et l'éternité chez Plotin et chez Saint Augustin.* Paris, 1933; 2d ed., 1956.

Guthrie, W. K. C., "Time and the Unlimited," in *A History of Greek Philosophy*, Vol. I. Cambridge, 1962. Pp. 336–340.

Haldane, J. B. S., "Time and Eternity." *The Rationalist Annual* (1946), 33–38.

Kneale, W. C., "Time and Eternity in Theology." *PAS*, Vol. 61 (1960–1961), 87–108.

Mondolfo, Rodolfo, *L'infinito nel pensiero dei Greci.* Florence, 1934. 2d enl. ed. published as *L'infinito nel pensiero dell'antichità classica.* Florence, 1956.

Wolfson, H. A., "Duration, Time, and Eternity," in *The Philosophy of Spinoza*, Book I. Cambridge, Mass., 1934. Ch. 10.

WILLIAM C. KNEALE

ETHER. The notion of ether originated among the Greeks as a popular view that there is above the air surrounding the earth a rarefied kind of air, thought to be alive and divine and having the nature of fire. Anaxagoras explained that this ether fills the outer part of the universe, leaving no void anywhere; and Democritus, although holding that there is void between material atoms, nevertheless also held that there is an ether consisting of small atoms in the heavenly spaces and that the motion of this ether carries the stars and planets along in their orbits.

In Aristotle, ether is distinguished both from air and from fire, and becomes the fifth, or heavenly, element. He held that, unlike the other four elements—earth, water, air and fire—ether is incorruptible and unchanging and is found only in the region outside the sphere of the moon; its natural motion is that which is nearest the perfection of rest, namely a uniform rotation about the center of the

earth. The planets, sun, moon, stars, and the rotating spheres in which they are embedded are all composed of ether, and so are the intervening transparent spaces, for in Aristotle's universe there is no void. Just as no ethereal substance can exist below the moon, so none of the earthly elements can rise above it; and thus no change of any kind can occur in the heavens, except the uniform circular motion of ethereal bodies. Such phenomena as shooting stars, which appear to imply change in the heavens, and the shadows on the moon, which appear to modify its heavenly perfection, are to be explained as "meteorological" phenomena, occurring below the sphere of the moon.

This cosmic scheme was almost universally adopted in western Europe after the revival of learning in the twelfth century; but meanwhile, in the last centuries of the Classical period, the Stoics had already introduced a radical change in the conception of the ether. They identified it with a quasi-material *pneuma*, or spirit, which not only occupies the heavenly spaces, but also pervades all matter in the earthly region and interacts with matter as a universal transmitter of force. Pneuma retains the ether's traditional function of regulating the circular motion of the heavenly bodies and also the ether's traditional characteristic of near-divinity. In addition, it provides a fundamental category of Stoic terrestrial physics and is appealed to in explanation of such phenomena as the cohesion and hardness of matter, and the transmission of light and of gravitational attraction.

Ether in seventeenth-century science. In face of the prevailing Aristotelianism of the later Middle Ages, mechanical theories, such as those of the Stoics and atomists, were not widely influential until the seventeenth century. Then, however, a mechanical or corpuscular philosophy became the general presupposition of science, and within this philosophy two main types of theory can be distinguished. There were first the plenum theories, according to which matter is continuous and indefinitely divisible and there is no void. These theories required a material ether to preserve the continuity of matter in the heavens, and also in spaces which have been evacuated of air and all other sensible matter, for example, by air pumps. And, second, there were the atomist theories, which postulated discrete, indivisible atoms as the fundamental constituents of matter and held that these atoms move in a surrounding void. In the atomic theories there might or might not be a place for an ether consisting of a very rarefied collection of atoms; but generally an ether of this kind was appealed to in explanation of particular processes, and in that case it was the invisible and intangible nature of the ethereal medium that was exploited, rather than its continuity and all-pervasiveness, as in the plenum theories.

Ether theory was given definitive form for the seventeenth century in the philosophy of Descartes. The immediate consequence of Descartes's identification of matter with spatial extension was that wherever there is space, there is matter of some kind, and where there does not appear to be gross matter, or even air—as in Evangelista Torricelli's vacuum experiments—Descartes postulated "subtle matter," corresponding to the ether of other theories. He distinguished, in fact, three elementary kinds of matter. The first element consists of luminous particles which have been rubbed by continual impacts into spherical shape and which make up the sun and the stars. The second element is the insensible, transparent subtle matter, which is derived from the rubbed-off corners of the luminous particles and which offers no resistance to the motion of larger bodies. The third element is gross matter in large, opaque pieces, which makes up the earth and planets. The natural motion of a free body in Descartes's system is always uniform linear motion, but the predominantly circular motion of the heavenly bodies is explained by the fact that space is a plenum, and hence the natural linear motion of subtle matter in interplanetary space is converted by outside pressure into vortical motion. Thus, Descartes arrived at his general picture of the universe as a system of contingent and interlocking vortices, of which the solar system is one. The ethereal element in this system also has the function of transmitting light, which consists of an instantaneous pressure in the subtle medium, caused by the centrifugal force of rotation of luminous particles. Heat is an agitation of particles of the subtle medium.

Subtle matter, as well as being the medium of interactions in the heavens, also pervades all gross and luminous bodies, filling their interstices. This provides Descartes with explanatory pictures of many natural processes, in accordance with his general program of explanation of all qualities of bodies in terms of primary mechanical motions, impacts, and pressures. The most influential of his explanations was perhaps that of the gravitation of bodies toward the earth. Descartes postulated a vortical motion of subtle matter around the earth, setting up a centrifugal pressure tending to make the subtle particles fly outward. When gross bodies are left unsupported in this vortex they fall toward its center, just as one can see floating twigs and leaves coming to the center of a water eddy, in which the water particles are tending to fly outward. This was the first of many attempts to explain gravitation by means of differential ether pressures, and such attempts, though unsuccessful, were not abandoned in serious scientific publications until the abandonment of the mechanical ether itself in the late nineteenth century.

Descartes's notion of an otherwise homogeneous spatial extension differentiated by the motion of its parts was a difficult one and was the subject of much immediate philosophical criticism. From the point of view of the seventeenth-century natural philosophers, however, difficulties about the ether were of a more practical kind. Ether was generally introduced as the necessary medium of transmission of such influences as heat, light, and magnetism in spaces otherwise void of matter; in this sense it was understood in terms of an analogy with the transmission of sound in air. It was also invoked to save the mechanical theory that all physical interactions are by "push" of contiguous bodies, rather than by "pull" or by action at a distance; thus, external ether pressure was used in mechanical explanations of cohesion, capillarity, and surface tension on the analogy of the explanation of the rise of liquids in barometric tubes by external air pressure. But it was objected by many writers in the middle seventeenth century, including Robert Boyle, that such an ether is unobservable and its existence unverifiable and that it therefore ought not to appear as an ingredient in experimental science.

Newton's attitude on the existence of ether was ambiguous. On the one hand, he rejected ether as a material interplanetary medium on the grounds that any medium, however subtle, would eventually cause perceptible slowing of the motions of the planets, and no such slowing had been observed. But on the other hand, he seems to have hoped that gravitational force would be shown to be transmitted by some sort of medium, if not material, then perhaps—as his disciple Clarke explicitly suggested in his correspondence with Leibniz—immaterial and "of a different nature from mechanism." Neither Newton nor Clarke would admit that action might take place at a distance without a medium of some kind. Again, Newton invoked the ether in particular physical explanations. For example, in his theory accounting for the colors produced by refraction of light in thin films, he came close to a wave theory of light by explaining the periodic character of this phenomenon in terms of vibrations in the neighboring ether. Newton's eighteenth-century disciples, however, found less need for the ether hypothesis, for it came to be accepted that gravitational force acting at a distance is typical of physical forces; and the seventeenth-century picture of matter interacting by mechanical impact was replaced by a picture of particles of matter interacting by forces at a distance—forces not only gravitational in nature but also cohesive, elastic, magnetic, electric, and chemical, and not only attractive but also repulsive. The fundamental model for an agent of force ceased to be interacting billiard balls and became, rather, "elastic fluids," gaslike substances whose constituent particles repelled one another, giving the whole the property of expansiveness and elasticity. Ether, along with material gases, phlogiston, the matter of heat and light, and electric and magnetic fluids, was regarded as an elastic fluid. Ether was sometimes distinguished from all the rest and sometimes identified with one or more of them.

The medium of light waves. At the end of the eighteenth century the nature of matter was clarified by Antoine Lavoisier's new classification of chemical elements and compounds, which were thereafter distinguished by the property of weight from the imponderable fluids of earlier physics. The ether was not included as a material in this new chemical sense. But developments in optics at this time greatly strengthened the case for the existence of the ether as the medium of transmission in the wave theory of light revived by Thomas Young and Augustin Fresnel. There was, however, one puzzling difficulty in using ether to explain the transmission of light. Interference effects were satisfactorily explained in any wave theory, but the polarization of light demanded that wave displacements should be transverse, not longitudinal as had previously been assumed on the analogy of sound waves. Transverse displacements, however, can be propagated only in a solid or very viscous fluid medium, and it was hard to imagine how any material ether could have the resistance to shear required for transverse waves and yet be capable of transmitting light waves at the required speed, without impeding the passage of such material bodies as the planets.

Various ether models were suggested as solutions to this problem, but it should not be assumed that these models were meant to be interpreted in a naively realistic sense.

Rather, a new view of the relation between phenomena, theories, and models was developed in which it was assumed only that the phenomena and their laws could be expressed as special cases of the general laws of motion, in particular the laws of Joseph Louis Lagrange's analytical mechanics. Any system satisfying these equations was mechanical in the very general sense that it satisfied the principle of least (or stationary) action, and also the principle which, in the middle nineteenth century, came to be called the principle of conservation of energy. The problem, then, was primarily to show that the phenomenal laws, for example those of light transmission, could be seen without contradiction as special cases of Lagrange's equations, and only secondarily to describe a mechanism in terms of familiar materials (for example, spheres, cogwheels, levers, or fluid vortices), which in turn could be described by the same phenomenal laws. But it was only assumed of such a mechanism that it would transmit waves in a manner similar to the transmission of light by the ether, which is very different from claiming that the ether is actually constructed of such a mechanism. Even William Thomson (Lord Kelvin), who most desired mechanical explanations, in the form of mechanical analogues of the ether, hardly ever claimed that such analogues were to be identified with the real structure of the ether. The clearest discussion of this kind of explanation by models or analogues is to be found in J. Clerk Maxwell, who explicitly admitted in his paper of 1864 on the electromagnetic field that such terms as "strain," "elasticity," and "momentum," used in connection with the ether, are to be regarded as illustrative and not explanatory. In speaking of the energy of the field, however, he said he wanted to be understood literally, and indeed it might be said that all Maxwell wished to claim for the ether at that stage was that it was a carrier of energy and possibly also of electric "displacement current." Subsequently, ether was not understood as a structure made of matter, but rather as a continuous energy field in which matter was to been seen as a certain kind of singularity.

Ether in modern physics. Toward the end of the nineteenth century it still appeared meaningful to attribute rest and motion to the ether and to consider the motion of material bodies relative to the ether. These concepts were used in connection with light transmission between moving bodies. The attempt was made to specify an absolute space framework by reference to the ether (which thus corresponded with the so-called "Body Alpha"—a term introduced by Carl Gottfried Neumann to designate the absolute standard of rest). But attempts to measure velocities, particularly the velocity of the earth, relative to the ether by means of optical experiments were all unsuccessful. The most famous of these attempts was the Michelson–Morley experiment, first described in 1887, whose well-known negative result provided one incentive for the development of theories in which "motion relative to the ether" became in principle an unobservable concept. One such theory was the contraction hypothesis of George Francis FitzGerald, in which material bodies were supposed to contract in the direction of their motion relative to the ether in the ratio $\sqrt{(1-v^2/c^2)} : 1$, in which case the effects of the motion and the contraction would cancel out

and make both processes unobservable. Meanwhile, Hendrik Lorentz had given mathematical expression to such a hypothesis in the equations known as the Lorentz transformation, which express both length and time measures in a given coordinate system in terms of those in another system moving relative to it with uniform velocity. According to these equations, a rod moving in a coordinate system S appears to an observer who is at rest in S to be shorter than it does to an observer moving with the rod, and a clock moving in S appears to the stationary observer to run slow.

The Lorentz transformation could be supported by other theoretical considerations arising from Maxwell's electrodynamic theory, and in itself it explained, or at least gave mathematical expression to, the negative results of such experiments as the Michelson–Morley without mentioning the ether at all. To these considerations Einstein added the positivist assumption (derived from study of Ernst Mach, but abandoned by Einstein in his later philosophy of science) that if a quantity is unmeasurable or unobservable, it is meaningless in physics and ought not to remain an integral part of a physical theory. The ether and its properties had become unobservable in this sense, and Einstein proposed, in his first paper on special relativity of 1905, the hypothesis that there is no ether providing an absolute standard of rest and that the velocity of light in empty space is always the same relative to any moving coordinate system. He showed that this hypothesis implies the Lorentz transformation and hence explains the results of the Michelson–Morley and other similar experiments.

Apparently the concept of the ether was dead, but fundamental physical concepts are seldom so decisively disposed of. The transformation necessary to enable the concept of ether in a certain sense to survive this apparent death blow had in fact already taken place in Maxwell's work, and the abandonment of the ether as a standard of rest was only the culmination of this development. As long as electromagnetism is understood in terms of a field theory, it is always necessary to speak of energy distributions in otherwise empty space; and when electromagnetic theory was incorporated into general relativity theory, space itself had to be described by means of a mathematical energy-tensor containing terms representing both the gravitational potential and the electromagnetic potential at every point. Such a space contains energy and is "potentially active"; it is therefore certainly not "void" in anything like the ancient atomists' sense. And it is not too far from the traditional use of "ether," as the name of that which is present when matter is not present, to say that even in general relativity theory the ether is retained, although of course it is not in the old sense a material ether.

Retention of the ether is even clearer in more recent quantum field theory. It is now experimentally well confirmed that in high-energy fields particle-pairs may be created or destroyed in collisions, provided that the total mass–energy and total charge are conserved throughout on the macroscopic scale. Thus, for example, a collision between an electron and its antiparticle, the positron, may result in the annihilation of both, with emission of equivalent energy, or, given sufficiently high energy in the field, such a pair may be created, acquiring energy from the field. Moreover, these creations and annihilations do not take place only when charged particles are initially present, but also in what has previously been called *vacuum*, so that the conception of vacuum as understood in classical theory is radically modified. The picture is now one of continuous short-term creations and annihilations of particle-pairs, and thus a continual fluctuation of the number of particles present, and even short-term fluctuations in the total quantity of energy present, so long as these energy fluctuations remain below the limits of detectability consistent with the quantum uncertainty principle. The active vacuum field resulting from this conception may perhaps be regarded as the nuclear theory's equivalent of an ether.

Bibliography

Hesse, Mary B., "Models in Physics." *British Journal for the Philosophy of Science*, Vol. 4 (1958), 198–214. A philosophical account with examples from ether theories.

Huygens, C., *Traité de la lumière*. Leiden, 1690. Translated by S. P. Thompson as *Treatise on Light*. Chicago, 1945. On the light-ether.

Maxwell, J. C., "Ether," in his *Scientific Papers*, 2 vols. Cambridge, 1890. Vol. II, pp. 763–775.

Samburdsky, S., *Physics of the Stoics*. London, 1959.

For additional bibliography, see ACTION AT A DISTANCE.

MARY HESSE

ETHICAL NATURALISM. It has been widely accepted that there is a prima facie distinction between establishing the facts on any matter and evaluating them. It seems evident that in order to perform the latter task properly, one must first perform the former; if one makes one's evaluation without adequate knowledge of the facts, one is likely to do this incorrectly. One should know all the relevant facts before one makes a moral assessment. From this it appears to follow that establishing the facts and making moral assessments of the facts are two totally different things, and that a complete account of the former will make no mention whatsoever of the latter. This is presupposed in the quite commonly accepted view that it is the business of the empirical scientist to give a complete description of what the world is like, but no part of his business to say whether or not this world is good. When it comes to describing the universe, we must take the empirical scientist's expert opinion; when it comes to evaluating it, however, his judgment is no more authoritative than anybody else's. The view that denies this prima facie distinction between establishing facts about the world as it is and making a word estimate of those facts is called "ethical naturalism." According to ethical naturalism, moral judgments just state a special subclass of facts about the natural world. To take just examples, according to one naturalistic theory, judgments about the rectitude of actions are factual judgments about the quantity of pleasure they produce, and, according to another naturalistic view, judgments about the morality of human institutions are judgments about whether they conduce to the survival of the community to which the institutions belong. Some Utilitarians, such as Jeremy Bentham and possibly John Stuart Mill, have held that judgments about the rectitude of actions are factual judgments about the quantity of pleasure these actions produce. Evolutionary theorists like Herbert Spencer have held, roughly, that moral pronouncements upon a practice or an institution are factual judgments about whether these pronouncements are conducive to the survival of the institution that has them. Pragmatists, such as John Dewey, have held, again roughly, that judgments about goodness are factual judgments about what leads to a permanent satisfaction of conflicting wants.

A number of rather facile (although frequently accepted) objections to ethical naturalism may first be disposed of. It is sometimes supposed that because it does not follow from the fact that a man is doing something that he ought to be doing it, and because it does not follow from the fact that a man or an institution exists that he or it is good, it must be concluded that something that is good or ought to be done is not identical with any matter of fact about it. All that may be concluded, however, is that the fact that something ought to be done is not identical with the fact that it is being done and that the fact that something is good is not identical with the fact that it exists. Nothing has yet been said to show that these may not be identical with any facts at all. It has also been supposed that because there is a perfectly good sense in which it is proper to distinguish between questions of fact and questions of right, questions of right cannot be questions of fact. Questions of right are certainly not questions of fact in the sense of "fact" in which it is proper to contrast questions of fact with questions of right; it does not follow, however, that there is not another wider sense of "fact" in which questions of right *are* questions of fact. Analogously, although it is also quite proper to distinguish between questions of fact and questions of law, it does not at all follow that a question of law is not itself a question of fact in some wider sense of "fact"; it is possible that it is just as much a matter of fact that the law says that such-and-such ought to be done in such-and-such a situation, as that such-and-such a situation actually obtains. Lastly, although it is true, in a sense, that one must find out all the facts of the situation before passing a moral judgment upon it, this can simply be interpreted as meaning that one must find out all the nonmoral facts of the situation before asserting any ethical facts about it.

The naturalistic fallacy. G. E. Moore, in *Principia Ethica* (1903), rejected all forms of ethical naturalism on the ground that they committed what he called "the naturalistic fallacy" (his arguments were anticipated by Richard Price in his *Review of the Principal Questions in Morals*). Moore contended that goodness was a unique, unanalyzable, nonnatural property (as opposed to natural properties, such as yellowness or anger, that are perceived through the senses or through introspection). Therefore, any attempt to define goodness in terms of any natural property must be a mistake that is one form of what he called the "naturalistic fallacy." It is not wholly clear from his writings, however, precisely what the naturalistic fallacy is. It has been suggested that he may have meant one or another of the three following. (1) The naturalistic fallacy is the fallacy of defining goodness, which is indefinable; (2) The naturalistic fallacy is not just the fallacy of defining goodness, but the fallacy of defining it in terms of natural properties and thus implying that it itself is a natural property; and (3) The naturalistic fallacy is the fallacy of defining goodness in terms of some property, say happiness, and at the same time asserting that happiness is good, as though this were an important nonverbal contention. Moore contended that many philosophers in the past had wished to maintain that happiness is in fact good on the grounds that "good" simply means happiness; Moore himself argued that, on the contrary, it was inconsistent to maintain both that "good" means happiness and that happiness is good, for the truth of the first contention would make the second trivial.

Although Moore from time to time spoke as if by the naturalistic fallacy he meant one or another of the three alleged mistakes described above. At other times it appears that he must have meant something different. It is doubtful whether he could have meant the first statement, for he probably would not have regarded a definition of goodness as, say, what ought to be desired as committing the naturalistic fallacy, since it defines one ethical concept in terms of another. Nor is it likely that he meant the second statement, because he treats the defining of ethical terms according to metaphysical terms (for example, the theory that "good" means "desired by one's true self") as committing the naturalistic fallacy even though metaphysical theories do not define ethical concepts in terms of natural concepts. And although Moore certainly would regard the sort of definition mentioned in the third statement above as committing the naturalistic fallacy, it appears that he would have regarded a theory as committing this fallacy even if the theory only defined goodness in terms of some natural property and did not also say that those things which possessed this property were good.

Are any of the above three views really fallacies? Moore does produce fairly cogent arguments for the idea that it is a fallacy to define goodness; in what is sometimes called the "open question" argument, he suggests that whatever the property one attempts to say is identical with goodness, the question can always be raised, Are things which possess this property good? The fact that this question can be raised shows, he thought, that possessing this property cannot be just what I mean by "good." It is also plausible to suggest that the third of these alleged mistakes is a fallacy, but Moore's case is perhaps not as convincing as he thought it was. If "good" just means possessing a certain property, then, of course, the statement that things which possess this property are good is true by definition. But this does not necessarily mean that when we say that things which possess this property are good, we are not making an important assertion, for some propositions which are true by definition *are* important. Nor does the fact that we can raise the question of whether things which possess this property, alleged to be identical with goodness, are good or not constitute a fatal objection to the claim that the property and goodness are identical. Although puppies are identical with young dogs, it does nevertheless make sense to raise the question "Are puppies young dogs?"

Moore appears to have thought that if good could not be defined in terms of any natural property, this must be because it was itself not a nonnatural property. Other philosophers have held that the reason why goodness cannot be defined in terms of any natural property is not that it itself is a nonnatural property, but because it is not a property at all: I no more attribute a property to something when I say that it is good than I attribute a property to something when I say "ugh" upon smelling a rat. Even if goodness *is* a property, it still does not follow from the fact that it is not definable in terms of any natural property that it is a nonnatural property. Moore's argument could be parodied by substituting yellowness for goodness; because yellow cannot be defined as round, square, or made of wood, and so on for all the natural properties one can think of, it might be argued, it must be a nonnatural property; but the reason that yellow cannot be defined in any of these ways is not that it is a nonnatural property, but that it is an indefinable property. Similarly, for all Moore shows to the contrary, goodness could be an indefinable natural quality.

One of the reasons why so many people have been convinced by Moore is perhaps that they are inclined to think of the naturalistic fallacy as the fallacy of defining goodness (which is an ethical property) in terms of some nonethical property. If it seems axiomatic to them that this is impossible, perhaps this is because they make it part of the meaning of "nonethical property" that no ethical property can be defined in terms of it. This, however, does not rule out the possibility of defining ethical properties. All it does mean is that if one *can* define goodness, say, in terms of conduciveness to survival, then conduciveness to survival is an ethical property. And why, after all, *should* one make it part of the meaning of "nonethical property" that no ethical property can be defined in terms of it? This may be no more reasonable or convenient than making it axiomatic that biological concepts cannot be defined in terms of nonbiological (for example, biochemical) concepts.

"Is" and "ought." Closely connected with the problem of whether ethical properties are natural properties is the question of whether it is possible to deduce an "ought" from an "is." Hume, in the last paragraph of Book III, Part I, Section I of the *Treatise of Human Nature*, says, "For as this *ought*, or *ought not* expresses some new relation or affirmation, 'tis necessary that it shou'd be observ'd and explain'd; and at the same time a reason should be given, for what seems altogether inconceivable, how this new relation can be a deduction from others, which are entirely different from it."

Some philosophers have accused Hume of being inconsistent in that in the treatise he himself subsequently produces reasons for accepting ethical propositions. However, all he meant when he said that it was impossible to deduce an "ought" from an "is" was that it was impossible to produce a deductively valid argument with factual premises and an ethical conclusion. Hume, along with other philosophers who hold the same view, can quite consistently give nondeductive reasons for ethical conclusions.

Arthur Prior, too, recently argued that it is possible to deduce an "ought" from an "is." Prior maintains that a proposition such as "He is either a fool or a knave" is either an ethical proposition or it is not. If it is nonethical then it, together with the nonethical proposition "He is not a fool," entails the ethical proposition "He is a knave." If, on the other hand, it *is* an ethical proposition, then it is (logically) entailed by the nonethical proposition "He is a fool." This argument may perhaps be countered by saying that it is a mistake to regard all propositions as either ethical or nonethical. A compound proposition, composed of propositions of which at least one is ethical and at least one nonethical, is neither an ethical proposition nor a nonethical one: it is simply mixed, and the fact that there may be a relation between such a partly ethical proposition and nonethical propositions need cause no particular concern. Finally, it must be emphasized that questions like these can only be settled after a careful consideration of a mass of detailed and inconclusive argumentation. It is dangerous to use "you cannot deduce an 'ought' from an 'is'" as a slogan.

Bibliography

Adams, E. M., *Ethical Naturalism and the Modern World View*. Chapel Hill, N.C., 1960. Naturalism critically examined.

Bentham, Jeremy, *The Principles of Morals and Legislation*. London, 1789. Contains some good examples of the sort of thing Moore was complaining about.

Blanshard, Brand, *Reason and Goodness*. London, 1961.

Brandt, R. B., *Ethical Theory*. Englewood Cliffs, N.J., 1959. Chs. 7–8.

Dewey, John, *Human Nature and Conduct*. New York, 1922.

Dewey, John, *The Theory of Valuation*. Chicago, 1929.

Ewing, A. C., *The Definition of Good*. New York, 1947. Ch. 2.

Foot, Philippa, "Moral Arguments." *Mind*, Vol. 67 (1958), 502.

Foot, Philippa, "Moral Beliefs." *PAS*, Vol. 59 (1958/1959), 83. This and the preceding constitute a persuasive attack on some modern forms of nonnaturalism.

Frankena, W. K., "The Naturalistic Fallacy." *Mind* (1939).

Hare, R. M., *The Language of Morals*. Oxford, 1950.

Hume, David, *Treatise of Human Nature*, L. A. Selby-Bigge, ed. Oxford, 1888; reprinted 1955. Bk. III, Pt. I, Sec. I. This contains the classic statement of the view that moral conclusions cannot be deduced from factual premises.

Mill, J. S., *Utilitarianism*. London, 1863.

Moore, G. E., *Principia Ethica*. Cambridge, 1903. Chs. 1–4.

Moore, G. E., "Reply to My Critics," in P. A. Schilpp, ed., *The Philosophy of G. E. Moore*. Evanston and Chicago, Ill., 1942. This contains the classic account of the naturalistic fallacy.

Nielsen, Kai, "Ethical Naturalism Once Again." *Australasian Journal of Philosophy*, Vol. 40 (1962), 313.

Nielsen, Kai, "On Human Needs and Moral Appraisals." *Inquiry* (1963).

Price, Richard, *A Review of the Principal Questions in Morals*, edited, with introduction, by D. Daiches Raphael. Oxford, 1948. Ch. 1. Price anticipates many of Moore's views.

Perry, R. B., *General Theory of Value*. Cambridge, Mass., 1926. Another influential naturalistic theory.

Prior, A. N., *Logic and the Basis of Ethics*. Oxford, 1949.

Prior, A. N., "The Autonomy of Ethics." *Australasian Journal of Philosophy*, Vol. 38.

Rynin, David, "The Autonomy of Morals." *Mind*, Vol. 66 (1957), 308.

Searle, J. R., "How to Derive 'Ought' from 'Is.'" *Philosophical Review*, Vol. 73 (1964), 43. An interesting criticism of some orthodox views.

Spencer, Herbert, *The Data of Ethics*. London, 1879–1880.

Stace, W. T., *The Concept of Morals*. New York, 1937.

Waddington, C. H., *The Ethical Animal*. London, 1960. A modern evolutionary theory.

Walsh, W. H., "The Autonomy of Ethics." *The Philosophical Quarterly*, Vol. 7.

Zimmerman, M., "The 'Is–Ought': An Unnecessary Dualism." *Mind*, Vol. 71 (1962), 53.

JONATHAN HARRISON

ETHICAL OBJECTIVISM. The word "objective," like the word "subjective," is far from being clear. We shall, however, call an ethical theory objective if it holds that the truth of what is asserted by some ethical sentence is independent of the person who uses this sentence, the time at which he uses it, and the place where he uses it. The theory that what I mean when I say an action is right is that it arouses in me, personally, a feeling of approval, does not count as an objective theory, because, according to it, the truth of what an ethical sentence asserts will always depend upon who uses the sentence in question. Used by some people, the sentence "I disapprove of women who spank their children" will convey a truth; used by other people, it will convey a falsehood. No ethical theory ought to maintain that the truth of the assertions made by ethical sentences is *never* dependent on the person who makes them and the time and place at which he makes them; one can always make an ethical sentence depend for its truth upon the time at which it is uttered, for example, by inserting the word "now." The sentence "It is now right to marry one's deceased wife's sister" is now true, although it can be argued that in the nineteenth century it would not have been. It should not be overlooked that with this definition of objective, a theory which is not objective is not the same thing as a theory which is subjective. A theory is subjective if it holds that moral judgments are about actual people's thoughts or feelings, and such a theory can also be objective. For example, the theory that what I mean when I say an action is right is that it is approved of by the person who did it, is subjective in that it holds that moral judgments are about someone's feelings, and also objective in that the assertion that the agent approved of his action does not depend for its truth upon the person who made the assertion or the time or place at which he made it.

Ethical logicism. There is a theory—it might be called ethical logicism—which holds that true ethical judgments are true because they cannot be denied without self-contradiction. No one seems to have held this theory unequivocally, but it is at least suggested by some of the things Thomas Aquinas says about natural law, and John Locke came near to holding it. It was essentially this theory that was one object of Hume's attack in Book III of *The Treatise of Human Nature*, when he contended that moral distinctions were not derived from reason. If ethical logicism were true, our knowledge of moral distinctions would be the work of reason in the sense that all we would need in order to know the truth of the fundamental principles of morals would be a capacity to reason logically.

The view is perhaps not implausible with some ethical generalizations; for example, it may be that we cannot say that murder is sometimes right without contradicting ourselves—it may be that "murder" means "wrongful killing," and it is beyond question that wrongful killing cannot be right. Similarly, "stealing" might be alleged to mean" the wrongful taking of what is not one's own," and "lying" might be alleged to mean "the wrongful assertion, with intent to deceive, of what is not the case." Indeed, there is a tendency for all commonly accepted ethical generalizations to become true by definition—for, once it is generally agreed that something, say, adultery, is wrong, people become reluctant to call anything adultery if they think that it is right.

Although such a theory has the advantage of making moral generalizations logically unimpeachable, this advantage is obtained only at the cost of making them trivial and useless. If it is true by definition that murder is wrong, because we would not call anything murder unless we were convinced that it was wrong, then the generalization that murder is wrong will no longer guide us in any practical decision. Let us suppose I am wondering whether it is right to kill Jones, who is a burglar threatening my wife with a gun. Although if murder means wrongful killing, and the statement that it is wrong to murder is certainly true, this does not allow me to argue that to kill Jones would be murder and thus wrong; I do not know whether to call killing Jones murder or not until I have first made up my mind whether it is wrong. Indeed, someone who thinks that the assertion that murder is wrong is true by definition may, without inconsistency, hold that it is right to slaughter Jews, Arabs, Negroes, or communists, simply by maintaining that doing so is not murder.

Although some ethical generalizations come very close to being true by definition, not all such generalizations can be. It may be true that the statement that murder is wrong cannot be denied without contradiction, but the generalization that killing is wrong certainly can be. If one tries to make a proposition like "fornication is wrong" logically unassailable by defining fornication in such a way that what is not wrong is not fornication, one in fact fails to guarantee the truth of what was originally meant to be asserted by the sentence that fornication was wrong. The proposition that is now true by definition does not make the same assertion that the original proposition did. What is more, the new proposition is trivial, while the original proposition was one of substance. It may be that the feeling that there can be moral rules both guaranteed by logic and of some material significance is due to an unconscious conflation of the two propositions: the proposition that was originally meant by the sentence "fornication is wrong"—which is not trivial but which is also not logically unassailable—and the proposition that is now meant by that sentence—which is logically unassailable but also, unfortunately, trivial. Hence, although it is an interesting fact that some moral generalizations are or tend to become true by definition, this is no help whatsoever with the problem of how we know which ethical generalizations, if any, are true.

Intuitionism. By "intuitionism" we shall mean the theory that, although ethical generalizations are not true by definition, those of them which are true can be seen to be true by any person with the necessary insight. According to this view, a person who can grasp the truth of true ethical generalizations does not accept them as the result of a process of ratiocination; he just sees without argument that

they are and must be true, and true of all possible worlds. To hold this theory one must, of course, reject the now frequently accepted view that there are no synthetic a priori propositions, for, if the theory is correct, ethical generalizations would be both synthetic and a priori.

It is most unfortunate that the word "intuitionism" is used ambiguously by moral philosophers. As defined above, it is the name of an epistemological theory about the nature of moral judgments and the manner of our coming to know them. Sometimes, however, intuitionism is the name of a moral theory, according to which there are a number of moral rules, all of them obligatory or with some tendency to be obligatory independently of the goodness or badness of the consequences of our acting on them. There is no logical connection between the two theories.

It cannot be shown that intuitionism is false by appealing to the fact that different communities have had very different moral beliefs and that the same communities have had very different moral beliefs at different times. The intuitionist may simply reply that the difference is more apparent than real. For one thing, the same fundamental principles, when applied to different circumstances, may lead to different results—for instance, one ought to drive on the left-hand side of the road in England and on the right-hand side in the United States, but in both countries one should observe the law and drive without endangering life. For another thing, moral beliefs in some communities are based on mistakes about matters of fact; some communities, for example, have disapproved of praising children to their faces because they have believed that this would bring them bad luck. Doubtless, if we shared their belief, we would share their disapproval. There is no reason why an intuitionist should not admit irresoluble differences of opinion on moral matters, provided he says that when there is such a difference, one of the parties believes he is intuiting when he is not.

Although intuitionism, in the epistemological sense, is a difficult theory to believe, it is still more difficult to refute. It may be that intuitionism has in the past gained support from an analogy with one theory of the nature of mathematical judgments. It has been alleged that one can grasp intuitively that promise-keeping always has some tendency to be right in the same sort of way that one grasps, without argument, that if two things are each equal to a third thing, they are equal to each other. It may be, however, that when a mathematician lays down as an axiom that if two things are each equal to a third thing, they are equal to each other, he is not claiming insight into a necessary truth about reality; perhaps he is just stipulating that he proposes to use the "equals" sign in such a way that from $X = Y$ and $Y = Z$ he may, if he likes, pass to $X = Z$. There would be neither point nor plausibility, however, in claiming that someone who maintained that promises ought to be kept was simply saying how he proposed to use the word "promises."

There is a sense of intuition in which intuition is certainly necessary in mathematical and other reasoning: whenever we infer one proposition q from another proposition p, we must see without argument that q does follow from p; if argument were necessary, and it could be shown that the proposition that q followed from p could be deduced from some third proposition r, intuition would still be necessary to see that the proposition "q follows from p" followed from r. This sense of intuition, however, is so wide as to make the contention that intuition is involved in ethics scarcely controversial.

Moral-sense theories. According to moral-sense theories, one perceives the difference between right and wrong much as one perceives the difference between a red thing and a blue one. Just as I know that that letter box is red because I see it is, so I know that what Smith is doing is wrong because I perceive that it is.

It has been objected to moral-sense theories that there is no sense organ connected with our perceiving that things possess moral qualities. *Pace* Wittgenstein, however, it is only a contingent fact that we perceive by means of sense organs; indeed, it would be possible to see without eyes if the relevant areas of the brain were appropriately stimulated. A moral-sense theory, nevertheless, is one which is very difficult to believe. Normally, when we perceive that anything possesses some property, it is because we perceive the thing which possesses that property. If we could not see the letter box, for example, we could not perceive that it is red. It is obviously untrue, however, that if I cannot see Smith, I cannot tell whether he is good or not. A moral-sense theorist might reply that just as I can see Smith without hearing him, or touch Smith without seeing him, so I can perceive Smith with my moral sense, even though I cannot perceive him with any of my other senses. If so, they must hold that I can perceive Smith with my moral sense even when he is many miles distant, or perhaps even after he is dead. Alternatively, the moral-sense theorist might say that I know that unperceived men are good just as I know that unperceived crows are black. The crows I have perceived have all been black, so I conclude that the crows I do not perceive are also black. Similarly, the honest men I have perceived have all been good, and so I conclude that the honest men I have not perceived are good too. Presumably, on a moral-sense theory, in order to know whether actions are right or wrong I need at some time to perceive people performing them; but this is obviously untrue.

There is an important difference between a thing's being right or wrong, or good or bad, and its possessing certain perceptual qualities; for ethical properties depend upon the other qualities of a thing, while the perceptual qualities do not. If I am given enough information about Jones or his actions, I can decide for myself whether Jones is good or whether what he does is right, but no amount of information about Jones will enable me to decide what color his hair is, or whether he used a chopper or arsenic to murder his wife. Or, rather, I may be able to decide this, but only because in the past I have been able to make an inductive generalization to the effect that men with crinkly hair are always dark-haired, or that wives are always murdered with choppers; and this, of course, presupposes that I have previously directly perceived instances of men with crinkly dark hair or of wives being murdered with choppers. One does not, however, directly perceive that certain men are bad or that certain acts are wrong. One pronounces them to be bad or wrong by virtue of certain other information one possesses about them; one says that this man is dishonest, cruel, and avaricious, and consequently bad; that this action was a case of wanton malice and consequently was wrong. It would be absurd, however, to say that this cricket ball is spherical and made of leather and consequently is red; it might perfectly well have been spherical and made of leather but not red. Hence, it is quite possible to know the color of some unidentified object in front of me but not to know anything else about it, for I do not pronounce upon its color by virtue of the other things I know about it. Where ethical properties are concerned, this is not the case. I cannot say I know nothing at all about this man except that he is bad, or nothing at all about this action except that it is wrong. Unless I had a reasonable amount of information about both, I could not know whether or not the man was bad, or whether or not the action was wrong. Again, if I find out that what I took to be a red cricket ball is not a cricket ball after all, there is no need for me to withdraw my judgment that it was red, for I did not base it upon other pieces of information which I believed myself to possess. But if I find that I am grossly mistaken about Jones or about the nature of his actions, I do have to reassess the ethical judgments I have made about him. It follows from what has been said that if one man is good, then any man who precisely resembles this man in all other respects must also resemble him in being good, and that if this action is right, then any action which precisely resembles this action in all other respects must also resemble this action in being right. With qualities like red this is not so. One of two otherwise precisely similar letter boxes might be red and the other green. For these reasons it is very unlikely that moral properties are properties like redness or roundness, which we simply perceive certain things to possess, and it is very unlikely, therefore, that a moral-sense theory could be true. (For additional discussion, see MORAL SENSE.)

Theological theories. According to theological theories, there is an objective criterion of what is right or wrong which is provided by what God wishes us to do, approves our doing, commands us to do, and so on. If the criterion of right is provided by God's commands or wishes, then it is not possible for two people, one of whom says that an action is right and the other of whom says that the same action is wrong, both to be correct; for if the one is right in thinking that God wishes us to act in a certain way, then the other must be wrong in thinking that he does not.

There are three ways in which God's commands could be relevant to man's duties. The fact that God commands us to perform a certain kind of action might be what makes this kind of action right. On the other hand, it might be the fact that an action is right that causes God to command us to perform it. Finally, it might be the case that the fact that an action is right and the fact that God commands it are one and the same fact; it might be that all we meant when we said that an action was right was that it was commanded by God.

The first of these theories has been criticized on the ground that it entails that if God commanded us to perform absolutely anything—human sacrifice, for example—this would be right; consequently, it magnifies God's power at the expense of detracting from his morality. The second theory has been criticized on the ground that it seems to suggest that God is determined by an antecedently existing moral law, independent of his will, and so detracts from his omnipotence. The third view has been criticized because it entails that it is impossible for anyone to hold that there are certain things which it would be wrong for human beings to do and at the same time to hold that there is no God—for, obviously, God can prohibit nothing if he does not exist.

Objective naturalism. According to objective naturalism, not only are ethical statements objective in the sense that covert reference is made to the speaker; they are the kind of objective statement which can be ascertained by some scientific, empirical investigation of the natural world. For example, if, as some objective naturalists hold, the word "right" simply means "conducive to the survival of mankind" or "productive of the maximum amount of pleasure for human beings," then it is a matter of empirically ascertainable fact what actions are right or wrong. Some evolutionary ethical theories have held that the first of these definitions is correct; some utilitarians have maintained the validity of the second. (It is, incidentally, possible to be a hedonistic utilitarian, without holding that "right" means "productive of the maximum possible amount of pleasure," so long as one holds that right actions are productive of the maximum possible amount of pleasure in fact.)

Scientific naturalism is not very popular at the moment. It is fairly evident that, whether ethical words can be defined or not, they do not mean what these theorists say they mean. It is possible for many people to hold, quite sincerely, that some actions which would certainly be conducive to human survival in certain circumstances—for example, polygamy—would nevertheless be wrong; and it is possible for people to hold the same of certain actions which would certainly maximize pleasure. It is very difficult to see how these people could maintain this if what they meant by "right" was "conducive to survival" or "productive of the maximum amount of pleasure," for in that case their views would be patently contradictory. A similar argument would show that by "right action" we cannot just mean "action in accordance with the conventions of the community or approved of by the community in which it is performed." This is not to say, of course, that what is conducive to survival or what is productive of pleasure or what is in accordance with convention is irrelevant to what is right or wrong; it would be surprising indeed if this were so. But these things are certainly not relevant in the way in which objective naturalism maintains they are relevant, moral judgments are not merely assertions about what is productive of pleasure or conducive to survival, and so these forms of objective naturalism are false.

Ideal observer theories. Ideal observer theories, which originated in Adam Smith's *The Theory of Moral Sentiments*, have the advantage over subjectivist ethical theories in that they do not hold that moral judgments are about the sentiments of any actual fallible human being or group of human beings; and they also have the advantage over theological ethical theories in that they do not imply that some perfect being exists. Moral judgments are about what some "ideal" being would feel if he existed. An ideal observer theory overcomes the difficulties encountered by subjectivism, for it can be held that the question whether an ideal observer would approve of something is independent of the question whether Tom, Dick, or Harry, or their community approves of it. If Tom says something is right, his statement is inconsistent with Dick's statement that it is wrong, for it cannot be the case that an ideal observer would approve of something and also not approve of it. The approval of an ideal observer cannot change from one time to another; neither can it be based upon ignorance or mistake concerning the matters being morally assessed.

The main difficulty with an ideal observer theory is this: Either it is made part of the definition of an ideal observer that he always approves of what is right, or it is not. If it is, then the proposition that an ideal observer always approves of what is right is true by definition, but the theory is circular; all it maintains is that an action is right if a being who always approved of what is right would approve of it. On the other hand, if it is not part of the meaning of "ideal observer" that he always approves of what is right, then how does one know that an ideal observer would approve of what is right rather than what is wrong?

The answer is that an ideal observer must approve of what is right because it is part of the meaning of "right" that an ideal observer would approve of it. The statement that an action is right if an ideal observer would approve of it, then, is rather like the statement that an object is red if it would look red to a standard observer. Just as an object can look red to me, or to a certain group of people, but not be red because it would not look red to a standard person, so an action can be approved of by me, or by a certain group of people, but not be right because it would not be approved of by a standard or ideal person (there is not as much difference between the two as there might appear to be at first sight).

The chief difficulty with this not implausible theory is that it makes it too much a matter of accident what actions are right and wrong. It is just a brute fact that bananas are yellow; it is conceivable that they might look red to all normal people, in which case they would be red. But it does not seem to be so much an accident that cruelty is wrong. It is conceivable that cruelty might arouse approval in a standard or ideal observer. Even if it did, one would not feel bound to say that cruelty is right. Hence, it does not seem to me that by "right" I do mean "capable of arousing approval in a standard or ideal observer," and the theory, however ingenious, must be rejected.

Bibliography

ETHICAL LOGICISM

Hume, David, *Treatise of Human Nature*, L. A. Selby-Bigge, ed. Oxford, 1888; reprinted 1955. Bk. III, Pt. I. A classic criticism of objectivism.

Kant, Immanuel, *The Moral Law, or Kant's Groundwork of the Metaphysic of Morals*, translated by H. J. Paton. London, 1948. One of the most influential objectivist theories.

Locke, John, *Essay Concerning Human Understanding*, J. W. Yolton, ed., 2 vols. London, 1961. Bk. III, Ch. 11, and Bk. IV, Ch. 3.

Selby-Bigge, L. A., ed., *The British Moralists*. Oxford, 1897. A mine of literature on moral epistemology.

Thomas Aquinas, *Summa Theologica*, translated by the Fathers of the English Dominican Province, 24 vols. London, 1920–1924. Question 94.

INTUITIONISM

Carritt, E. F., *The Theory of Morals*. London, 1928.
Ewing, A. C., *The Definition of Good*. New York, 1947.
Price, Richard, *A Review of the Principal Questions in Morals*, edited, with introduction, by D. Daiches Raphael. Oxford, 1948. Also contains information on theological theories. This is a classical defense of objectivism that has greatly influenced modern British objectivist philosophers.
Prichard, H. A., *Moral Obligation*. Oxford, 1949.
Ross, W. D., *The Right and the Good*. Oxford, 1930. Perhaps the best modern statement of objectivism.
Ross, W. D., *The Foundations of Ethics*. Oxford, 1939. A more detailed and slightly revised statement of the views contained in *The Right and the Good*.

MORAL-SENSE THEORIES

Broad, C. D., "Some Reflections on Moral Sense Theories in Ethics," in Wilfrid Sellars and John Hospers, eds., *Readings in Ethical Theory*. New York, 1952.
Raphael, D. D., *The Moral Sense*. London, 1947.

THEOLOGICAL THEORIES

Butler, Joseph, "Fifteen Sermons," in his *Works*, W. E. Gladstone, ed., 2 vols. Oxford, 1896.
Paley, William, *The Principles of Moral and Political Philosophy*. London, 1785.

OBJECTIVE NATURALISM

Bentham, Jeremy, "The Principles of Morals and Legislation," in his *Works*, J. Bowring, editor, 11 volumes. Edinburgh, 1838–1843.
Moore, G. E., *Principia Ethica*. Cambridge, 1903.
Spencer, Herbert, *The Data of Ethics*. London, 1879–1880.

IDEAL OBSERVER THEORIES

Brandt, R. B. *Ethical Theory*. Englewood Cliffs, N.J., 1959.
Firth, Roderick, "Ethical Absolutism and the Ideal Observer." *Philosophy and Phenomenological Research*, Vol. 12 (1952).
Smith, Adam, *The Theory of Moral Sentiments*. London, 1759.

JONATHAN HARRISON

ETHICAL PRINCIPLES. See ULTIMATE MORAL PRINCIPLES: THEIR JUSTIFICATION.

ETHICAL RELATIVISM. The term "ethical relativism" is always used to designate some ethical principle or some theory about ethical principles, but within this limitation different authors use it quite differently. Contemporary philosophers generally apply the term to some position they disagree with or consider absurd, seldom to their own views; social scientists, however, often classify themselves as relativists. Writers who call themselves relativists always accept the first and second and sometimes accept the third of the theses described as descriptive relativism, metaethical relativism, and normative relativism, respectively.

Descriptive relativism. The first thesis, without which the others would lose interest, is that the values, or ethical principles, of individuals conflict in a fundamental way ("fundamental" is explained below). A special form of this thesis, called "cultural relativism," is that such ethical disagreements often follow cultural lines. The cultural relativist emphasizes the cultural tradition as a prime source of the individual's views and thinks that most disagreements in ethics among individuals stem from enculturation in different ethical traditions, although he need not deny that some ethical disagreements among individuals arise from differences of innate constitution or personal history between the individuals.

Fundamental disagreement. The most important and controversial part of the first thesis is the claim that diversities in values (and ethics) are fundamental. To say that a disagreement is "fundamental" means that it would not be removed even if there were perfect agreement about the properties of the thing being evaluated. (If disagreement is nonfundamental then it may be expected that all ethical diversity can be removed, in principle, by the advance of science, leading to agreement about the properties of things being appraised.) Thus it is not necessarily a case of fundamental disagreement in values if one group approves of children's executing their parents at a certain age or stage of feebleness whereas another group disapproves of this very strongly. It may be that in the first group the act is thought necessary for the welfare of the parent in the afterlife, whereas in the second group it is thought not to be. The disagreement might well be removed by agreement about the facts, and indeed both parties might subscribe, now, to the principle "It is right for a child to treat a parent in whatever way is required for the parent's long-run welfare." The disagreement might be simply about the implications of this common principle, in the light of differing conceptions of the facts. There is fundamental ethical disagreement only if ethical appraisals or valuations are incompatible, even when there is mutual agreement between the relevant parties concerning the nature of the act that is being appraised.

Metaethical relativism. A person might accept descriptive relativism but still suppose that there is always only one correct moral appraisal of a given issue. Such a position has been widely held by nonnaturalists and by some naturalists (see, for example, the interest theory of R. B. Perry). The metaethical relativist, however, rejects this thesis and denies that there is always one correct moral evaluation. The metaethical relativist thesis is tenable only if certain views about the meaning of ethical (value) statements are rejected. For instance, if "A is right" *means* "Doing A will contribute at least as much to the happiness of sentient creatures as anything else one might do," it is obvious that one and only one of the two opinions "A is right" and "A is not right" is correct. Thus, the metaethical relativist is restricted to a certain range of theories about the meaning of ethical statements. He might, for instance, subscribe to some form of emotive theory, such as the view that ethical statements are not true or false at all but express the attitudes of the speaker. Or he might adopt the naturalist view that "is wrong" means "belongs to the class of actions toward which I tend to take up an impartial attitude of angry resentment" (held by the relativist E. A. Westermarck) or the view (suggested by the anthropologist Ruth Benedict) that the phrase "is morally good" means "is customary."

Ethical reasoning. At the present time metaethical relativists do not wish to rest their case solely on an appeal to what ethical statements mean; nor would their critics. The point of active debate is rather whether there is some method of ethical reasoning whose acceptance can be justified to thoughtful people with force comparable to the force with which acceptance of inductive logic can be justified. Is there any such method of ethical reasoning that can be expected in principle to show, when there is a conflict of values or ethical principles, that one and only one solution is correct in some important and relevant sense of "correct"? Metaethical relativists deny that there is any such method, and their denial may take either of two forms: They may deny that there is any method of ethical reasoning that can be justified with force comparable to that with which scientific method (inductive logic) can be justified. Or they may agree that there is such a method but say that its application is quite limited, and in particular that the fullest use of it could not show, in every case of a conflict of ethical convictions or of values, that one and only one position is correct in any important sense of "correct."

Use of the term "relativism." Many writers, both in philosophy and in the social sciences, accept a combination of descriptive relativism and metaethical relativism. Philosophers who hold this view, however, seldom label themselves "relativists," apparently because they think the term confusing in this context. There is seldom objection to "cultural relativism" as a descriptive phrase, for it can be taken to mean that a person's values are "relative" to his culture in the sense of being a function of or causally dependent on it. But if "ethical relativism" is construed in a similar way, to mean that ethical *truth* is relative to, in the sense of being dependent on or a function of, something (for example, a person's cultural tradition), then this term is thought to be confusing since it is being used to name a theory that essentially denies that there is such a thing as ethical "truth."

One frequent confusion about what implies ethical relativism should be avoided. Suppose metaethical relativism is mistaken, and there is a single "correct" set of general ethical principles or value statements. It may still be true, and consistent with acceptance of this "correct" set of principles, that an act that is right in some circumstances will be wrong in other circumstances. Take, for instance, the possible "correct" principle "It is always right to do what will make all affected at least as happy as they could be made by any other possible action." It follows from this principle that in some situations it will be right to lie (for instance, to tell a man that he is not mortally ill when one knows he is, if he cannot bear the truth) and that in other situations it will be wrong to lie. Thus, even if metaethical relativism is false there is a sense in which the rightness of an act is relative to the circumstances or situation. The fact that the rightness of an act is relative to the circumstances in this way does not, of course, imply the truth of metaethical relativism.

Normative relativism. Neither descriptive nor metaethical relativism commits one logically to any ethical statement. The former is simply an assertion about the diversity of moral principles or values actually espoused by different

persons; the latter is only a general statement about whether ethical principles are ever "correct." Nothing in particular about what ought to be, or about what someone ought to do, follows from them. Of particular interest is the fact that it does not follow that persons, depending on their cultural attachments, ought to do different things. In contrast, a person who holds to some form of what I shall call "normative relativism" asserts that something is wrong or blameworthy if some person or group—variously defined—thinks it is wrong or blameworthy. Anyone who espoused either of the following propositions would therefore be a normative relativist:

(*a*) "If someone thinks it is right (wrong) to do *A*, then it *is* right (wrong) for him to do *A*." This thesis has a rather wide popular acceptance today but is considered absurd by philosophers if it is taken to assert that what someone thinks right really is right for him. It is held to be absurd because taken in this way, it implies that there is no point in debating with a person what is right for him to do unless he is in doubt himself; the thesis says that if he *believes* that *A* is right, then it *is* right, at least for him. The thesis may be taken in another sense, however, with the result that it is no longer controversial, and no longer relativist. The thesis might mean: "If someone thinks it is right for him to do *A*, then he cannot properly be condemned for doing *A*." This statement merely formulates the view, widespread in the Western world, that a person cannot be condemned morally for doing what he sincerely believes to be right. (In order to receive universal approval, some additions must doubtless be added to the thesis, such as that the person's thoughts about what is right must have been the product of a reasonable amount of careful reflection, not influenced by personal preferences, and so on.) The thesis is not relativist, since it is not asserted that any person's or group's belief that something is blameworthy is either a necessary or a sufficient condition of its being blameworthy.

(*b*) "If the moral principles recognized in the society of which *X* is a member imply that it is wrong to do *A* in certain circumstances *C*, then it *is* wrong for *X* to do *A* in *C*." This principle says, in effect, that a person ought to act in conformity with the moral standards of his group. Like the preceding principle, this one has a good deal of popular acceptance today, is espoused by some anthropologists, and has some plausibility; it will be discussed below.

Difficulties in the relativist positions. The following appear to be the most important questions about the various relativist theses: (*a*) Is descriptive relativism supported by the scientific evidence? There are methodological obstacles in the way of answering the question whether there is fundamental diversity of ethical views. Such diversity would be established by producing two individuals, or cultures, who attribute identical properties to an act but nevertheless appraise it differently. But it is not easy to be sure when one has produced two such individuals or cultures. First, it is difficult to demonstrate that an act is believed to have identical properties by individuals or groups who appraise it differently. Is theft the same thing in societies where conceptions or systems of property differ? Is incest the same thing in societies with different kinship terminologies, different ways of counting lineage, and different beliefs about the effects of incest? It is possible to question members of different cultural traditions in an abstract way so that such differences in conception are ruled out, but then it is likely that the informant will not grasp the question and that his answer will be unreliable. The second difficulty is that there is no simple test for showing that groups or individuals really conflict in their appraisals. We may know that we think it morally wrong to do so-and-so, but it is not clear how to determine whether a Navaho agrees with us. Perhaps we have first to determine whether the Navaho language contains an expression synonymous with "is morally wrong." Or can we show that a Navaho does not think it morally wrong to do *A* by the fact that he feels no guilt about doing *A*? Or perhaps a mere conflict of *preferences* is sufficient to establish a disagreement in personal values. These questions deserve more discussion among anthropologists than they have received.

The evidence for descriptive relativism consists mostly of reports from observers about what is praised, condemned, or prohibited in various societies, usually with only scanty information on the group's typical conception of what is praised or blamed. In some instances projective methods and dream analysis have been utilized, and discussions with informants have elicited fragments of the conceptual background behind the appraisals. On the basis of such material most social scientists believe there is some fundamental diversity of values and ethical principles. A few years ago some investigators (among them W. G. Sumner and Ruth Benedict) supposed that the extent of diversity was practically unlimited, but today it is believed that there is also considerable uniformity (for example, universal disapproval of homicide and cruelty). One reason for believing there is considerable uniformity is that it appears that it would be difficult for a social group even to survive without the presence of certain features in its value system. (A social system must provide methods for rearing and educating the young, for mating, for division of labor, for avoiding serious personal insecurity, and so on.) Uniformity of evaluation is the rule in areas that pertain to survival or to conditions for tolerable social relationships; in other areas there are apt to be fundamental differences. Psychology adds some support to this construction of the empirical data. It offers a theory of enculturation that explains how fundamentally different values can be learned, and it also suggests how some universal human goals can set limitations to diversity among value systems.

(*b*) Does descriptive relativism support metaethical relativism? It is evident that from descriptive relativism nothing follows about what ethical statements mean or could fruitfully be used to mean. It is also evident that nothing follows about whether there is some method of ethical reasoning that can correctly adjudicate between conflicting ethical commitments, at least in some cases. Descriptive relativism may very well have bearing, however, on whether a justifiable method of reasoning in ethics (assuming there is one) could succeed in adjudicating between all clashes of ethical opinion. To be sure about this we would need to have an account of the reasonable method of ethical reflection before us. But let us take an example. Suppose we think that the only reasonable way to correct a person's ethical appraisal is to show him that it does not coincide with the appraisal he would make if he were vividly

informed about all the relevant facts and were impartial in his judgment. Then suppose the descriptive relativist tells us that some people are simply left cold by the ideal of equality of welfare and that others view it as a basic human right, when both groups have exactly the same beliefs about what equality of welfare is and what its consequences would be. In this case we might be convinced that both parties were already impartial (if the views were not just typical of different social or economic classes) and that further information probably would not change their views. Doubtless much more analysis of the situation is necessary, but it is clear that given the described assumption about actual ideals and the assumption about the limitation of ethical argument, one might be led to a cautious acceptance of the view that not all ethical disputes can be resolved by this justifiable method of ethical reasoning.

(*c*) Are cultural and metaethical relativism necessarily committed to any form of normative relativism? Neither the cultural relativist nor the metaethical relativist is committed logically to any form of normative relativism. It is consistent to assert either of these positions and also to affirm any value judgment or ethical proposition one pleases. However, the second proposition cited under normative relativism (that a person ought to act in conformity with the moral standards of his group) at least presupposes the acceptance of cultural relativism. There would be no point in asserting this normative principle if cultural relativism were not accepted.

How strong are the arguments that can be advanced in favor of this form of normative relativism? Suppose that in *X*'s society it is a recognized moral obligation for a person to care for his father, but not for his father's siblings (at least to anything like the same degree), in illness or old age. Suppose also that in *Y*'s society it is recognized that one has no such obligation toward one's father or his siblings but does have it toward one's mother and her siblings. In such a situation it is hard to deny that *X* seems to have some obligation to care for his father and that *Y* seems not to have, at least to the same degree. (Some philosophers hold that there is no obligation on anyone, unless one's society recognizes such an obligation for the relevant situation.) So far, the principle seems intuitively acceptable. In general, however, it appears less defensible, for the fact that *X*'s society regards it as wrong to play tennis on Sunday, to marry one's deceased wife's sister, and to disbelieve in God does not, we should intuitively say, make it wrong for *X* to do these things. Thus, our principle seems valid for some types of cases but not for others. The solution of this paradox probably is that for those cases (like an obligation to one's father) where the principle seems acceptable, the reasons for which it seems acceptable are extremely complex and are not based simply on the fact that society has asserted that an obligation exists. When society recognizes a moral obligation, there are many repercussions that basically affect the types of responsibility the individual may have toward other members of his society. For instance, one result of a society's recognizing a son's moral obligation to care for his father is that no one else will take care of the father if the son does not. Another is that a kind of equitable insurance system is set up in which one pays premiums in the form of taking responsibility for one's own father and from which one gets protection in one's old age. So it is at least an open question whether it can seriously be claimed that the moral convictions of a society have, in themselves, any implication for what a member of the society is morally bound to do, in the way our suggested principle affirms that they do.

Bibliography

Aberle, D. F., et al., "The Functional Prerequisites of a Society." *Ethics*, Vol. 60 (1950), 100–111.

Asch, S. E., *Social Psychology*, Chs. 12, 13. Englewood Cliffs, N.J., 1952. An excellent critique of the evidential basis for descriptive relativism.

Benedict, Ruth, "Anthropology and the Abnormal." *Journal of General Psychology*, Vol. 10 (1934), 59–82. A graphic account of some ethnological data in support of a rather extreme type of relativism.

Brandt, R. B., *Hopi Ethics*. Chicago, 1954. An analysis of the values of the Hopi Indians with special reference to relativism. Methodologically oriented.

Brandt, R. B., *Ethical Theory*, Chs. 5, 6, 11. Englewood Cliffs, N.J., 1959. A cautious review and assessment of the evidence.

Firth, R., *Elements of Social Organization*, Ch. 6. London, 1951. A learned survey of anthropological material by an anthropologist with leanings toward relativism.

Ginsberg, Morris, *Essays in Sociology and Social Philosophy*, Vol. I. New York, 1957. A learned survey of the evidence by a sociologist.

Herskovits, M., *Man and His Works*, Ch. 5. New York, 1948. One of the most vigorous contemporary defenses of relativism by an anthropologist.

Kluckhohn, C., "Ethical Relativity." *Journal of Philosophy*, Vol. 52 (1955), 663–677. A cautious assessment of the evidence by an anthropologist who stresses the uniformities of value systems.

Ladd, J., *Structure of a Moral Code*. Cambridge, Mass., 1956. A fine study of the Navaho, emphasizing methodological problems.

Linton, R., "Universal Ethical Principles: An Anthropological View," in R. N. Anshen, ed., *Moral Principles of Action*. New York, 1952. An excellent statement, by an anthropologist of the middle-of-the-road position, emphasizing both uniformities and diversity.

Westermarck, E. A., *The Origin and Development of the Moral Ideas*, Vol. I, Chs. 1–5. New York, 1906. One of the most influential statements of the relativist position, with encyclopedic documentation; however, it is methodologically somewhat unsophisticated.

Westermarck, E. A., *Ethical Relativity*, Ch. 5. New York, 1932. A shorter defense of the relativist position, intended primarily for persons interested in philosophy.

RICHARD B. BRANDT

ETHICAL SKEPTICISM. See EMOTIVE THEORY OF ETHICS; ETHICAL RELATIVISM; ETHICAL SUBJECTIVISM.

ETHICAL SUBJECTIVISM. A subjectivist ethical theory is a theory according to which moral judgments about men or their actions are judgments about the way people react to these men and actions—that is, the way they think or feel about them. It follows that moral predicates are not possessed by actions or actors in the absence of people who pass judgments upon them or who respond to them with such feelings as admiration, love, approval, detestation, hate, or disapproval. It follows from this definition that nonpropositional or noncognitive ethical theories are not subjective, for according to them there are no moral propositions at all, and thus moral judgments cannot be propositions about people's feelings. This definition is also intended to exclude views according to which moral judgments are judgments about how people

behave; hence, views such as that "wrong" means "contrary to the accepted code of the society in which the action is performed" will not count as subjective, even if, as seems likely, statements about moral codes are statements about the prohibitory or permissory behavior of the communities possessing these codes. Although this distinction is not hard and fast (for statements about moral codes might often turn out to be statements about how the people possessing these codes think or feel), we shall maintain it in order not to trespass too far into the subject of ethical relativism, which is treated elsewhere. Elements of subjectivism can be found in so many ethical theories that it is almost impossible to give an account of them. The greatest, though not the most consistent, subjectivist was the eighteenth-century Scottish philosopher David Hume. The theory has also been popular among anthropologists, of whom Edward Westermarck was probably the most outstanding.

Subjectivist theories can provisionally be classified according to whether moral judgments are alleged to be about the speaker's thoughts or feelings, about the thoughts or feelings of some group of people, or about the thoughts or feelings of men as such.

Moral judgments state what the speaker feels. The view that moral judgments are about the feelings of the person making the judgment—that what I mean when I say that an action is right or that a man is good is that the thought of that man or action evokes in me, personally, at this moment, a feeling of approval—has been subjected to an enormous number of objections. It has been argued that, so far from its being possible to identify moral judgments as those judgments that are about feelings of approval, it is in fact only possible to identify feelings of approval as those feelings that are evoked by the judgment that an action is right, and argued that if we feel approval of an action because we judge it to be right, our thinking that it is right cannot be identical with our approving of it. It has also been objected that if the theory is true, all I need do to settle any doubt I have concerning the rectitude of someone else's action is to introspect, and that it is very difficult, if not impossible, to be mistaken about one's feelings, although it is very easy to make a mistake about whether an action is right. More plausibly, it has been alleged that the theory implies that one can only criticize someone else's moral judgment on the ground that the other person is mistaken about how he himself feels.

Some of the worst difficulties for the theory arise from the fact that sentences offered as definitions of moral judgments contain words like "I," "now," and "here," whose reference depends upon who uses them, at what time, and in what place. From this it follows that one person's moral judgments can never be incompatible with any other person's moral judgments; the sentence "I do not feel disapproval of divorce," when used by one speaker, does not express a judgment incompatible with that expressed by the sentence "I do feel disapproval of divorce," uttered by a different speaker. It would appear, however, that when one person says, "Divorce is wrong," he does mean to say something incompatible with what someone else means when he says, "Divorce is not wrong." From the fact that moral judgments are alleged to have a covert reference to the feelings the speaker now has, it follows that if at one time he judges an action (say, Brutus' assassination of Caesar) to be right, his judgment is not incompatible with the judgment he may make at a later time when he judges Brutus' assassination of Caesar to be wrong. For according to this theory, what he meant on the first occasion was that he did not then feel disapproval of Brutus' assassination of Caesar, and what he meant on the second occasion was that he now does. Clearly there is no reason why *both* judgments should not be true.

G. E. Moore, in a famous argument, attempted to deduce that the subjectivist theory led to the paradoxical conclusion that the same action could be both right and wrong, and that one and the same action could change from being right to being wrong. (It is important to remember that Moore thought classes of actions—for example, marrying one's deceased wife's sister—could change from being right to being wrong, that is, that an instance of a class of actions, performed at one time, might be right, while another instance of the same class of actions, performed at a later time, might be wrong.) First, Moore argued as follows. If Jones approves of Brutus' assassination of Caesar and says Brutus was right, it follows from the theory that Brutus *was* right. Similarly, if Smith disapproves of Brutus' assassination of Caesar and says Brutus was wrong, then Brutus *was* wrong. Hence Brutus was both right and wrong to assassinate Caesar. Second, to show that Brutus' assassination of Caesar can change from being right to being wrong, all Moore thought he need do was to point out that if Jones says (at a time when he approves of Brutus' action) that Brutus was right, then according to the theory, Brutus was right; if he later comes to disapprove of Brutus' action, then, if he says Brutus was wrong, according to the theory, Brutus *was* wrong. If Jones can truly judge at one time that Brutus was right and at a later time that Brutus was wrong, it must follow that Brutus' action has changed from being right to being wrong.

C. L. Stevenson has criticized Moore's argument in the following manner. Although Jones can truly say that Brutus was right to assassinate Caesar and Smith can truly say that Brutus' action was wrong, neither Jones nor Smith nor anyone else can say that this action is both right and wrong. For anyone to be able to say it is both right and wrong, someone would have both to approve of it and disapprove of it. Hence, although Jones, who approves of Brutus' action, can say it is right, and Smith, who disapproves of it, can say it is wrong, neither can say it is both right and wrong. Moore's mistake, perhaps, consisted in construing the theory we are considering as maintaining that "right" is a predicate like "disapproved of by *someone*" (from which it would follow that the same action can be both right and wrong), whereas "right" is alleged to be a predicate like "disapproved of by me, the speaker," from which it follows that the same action cannot be both right and wrong, since the speaker cannot both approve and disapprove, on the whole, of one and the same action.

A free exposition of Stevenson's criticism of Moore's argument (that if the view that moral judgments are statements about the speaker's feeling is true, one and the same action can change from being right to being wrong) might take the following form. Moore supposes that if ten years ago I could truly say Brutus was right to assassinate Caesar (because at that time the thought of this action did arouse

approval in me) and now I can truly say that Brutus was wrong to do this (because at this time the thought of his action arouses disapproval in me), it follows that the action must have changed from being right to being wrong. Stevenson, however, points out that the statement "Brutus' action has changed from being right to being wrong" is equivalent to the conjunction of statements "Brutus' action was right a while ago" and "Brutus' action is now wrong." Although the truth of the second of these statements is entailed by the fact that I now feel disapproval of Brutus' assassination of Caesar, the first of them is not entailed by the fact that I earlier felt approval of Brutus' assassination of Caesar. Although Moore supposes "Brutus' assassination of Caesar *was* right" to mean "I once approved of Brutus' assassination of Caesar," what it actually means is "I *now* approve of Brutus' erstwhile assassination of Caesar," and, *ex hypothesi*, "I do not now approve of Brutus' action, I disapprove of it." Moore's mistake is to suppose that the word "was" in the sentence "Brutus *was* right to assassinate Caesar" shows that the sentence is about my past approval, whereas in fact its function is to show that it is the action I am disapproving of, not my disapproval, that is past.

Although Stevenson's detailed criticisms of Moore are valid, it is possible to restate Moore's arguments in a way that avoids them. To take the second of Moore's arguments first, it would plainly be absurd for me to say that Brutus was wrong to assassinate Caesar and at the same time to say that I was correct many years ago when I judged that Brutus was right to assassinate Caesar. If I now say he was wrong, I am bound to say that when, earlier, I said he was right, I was mistaken. In regard to the first argument, although it does not follow from this subjectivist theory that anyone can say that an action is both right and wrong, it does follow that if Jones says that Brutus was right to assassinate Caesar, he is not saying anything incompatible with what Smith is saying when he says that Brutus was wrong to assassinate Caesar. Clearly, however, Jones and Smith think they are saying something incompatible, and it is unlikely that they have such a poor understanding of how to use their own language as to be mistaken on this point. In other words, according to the subjectivist theory, if Jones says Brutus was right to assassinate Caesar, Smith can say to Jones that Brutus was wrong and at the same time agree that Jones is making a true statement when he says that Brutus was right. This is absurd. Stevenson has tried to overcome this particular difficulty by saying that although insofar as Jones and Smith are making assertions, their assertions are not incompatible with one another, they are doing something over and above asserting things—namely, Jones is trying to evoke in Smith an attitude of approval toward Brutus' action, and Smith is trying to evoke in Jones an attitude of disapproval toward Brutus' action. Hence, although their beliefs are compatible, their interests clash. Jones aims to achieve something that is incompatible with what Smith aims to achieve. A consideration of this view of Stevenson's, however, would take us away from subjectivism to a consideration of nonpropositional ethical theories.

The difficulties already mentioned may well be fatal to the type of subjectivist theory we are considering, at any rate as long as it is not bolstered by the nonpropositional theory. Moreover, there is a further difficulty which seems to settle the issue. Suppose Jones says that the death penalty for murder ought to be retained in Great Britain, and he says this because he wrongly supposes that abolishing the death penalty would lead to an increase in the number of murders. According to this kind of subjectivism, all Jones means when he says that the death penalty ought to be retained is that the thought of retaining it arouses in him feelings of approval, and since it does do this, his statement that it ought to be retained is true, however mistaken he may be about the facts of the situation. He is under no obligation to withdraw his statement, therefore, when he discovers his mistake. Again, this is absurd.

Moral judgments state the speaker's thoughts. So far we have considered the view that moral judgments are judgments to the effect that the action under judgment arouses certain feelings in the person making the judgment. It is possible, however, to think that what someone making a moral judgment is asserting is that the action or person being judged arouses in the person making the judgment certain thoughts or beliefs. The most natural view is that someone who asserts that an action is wrong is saying that the thought of the action arouses in him personally the belief that it is wrong, or in other words, that all we mean when we say that an action is wrong is that we personally think it is wrong. This view is circular because even though it offers a definition of "wrong" (that is, it maintains that "X is wrong" just means "I think X is wrong"), the word "wrong" still occurs in the definition (compare "'thoroughbred horse' means 'horse both of whose parents are thoroughbred horses'"). It is obviously impossible to get rid of the circularity by again substituting "thought wrong" for "wrong" in the definition, however many times we do it.

Objective and subjective senses of "right." It is quite commonly held that whenever one thinks one is acting rightly, one is acting rightly. Philosophers who hold this view, however, are not properly regarded as subjectivists. Clearly, if the word "right" is being used twice in the same sense when it is asserted that one is doing rightly if one does what one *thinks* is right, the view is contradictory. According to it, one would be acting rightly even if one did what one mistakenly thought was right: from the fact that one *mistakenly* thought it was right it follows that it is wrong, and from the fact that one is acting rightly if one does what one thinks is right, it follows that the act is right. Those philosophers who have held this view, however, have generally distinguished two senses of the word "right," sometimes called an objective sense and a subjective sense, and have held that an action is right, in the subjective sense, if it is thought to be right in the objective sense. This removes both the contradiction and the suggestion that the property of being right depends on being thought to be right; the property of being subjectively right depends on the different property of being thought to be objectively right.

Moral judgments state what a community feels. Next to be considered is the view that when men make moral judgments they are talking not about the way they themselves think or feel about the things they are judging, but of the way some group of people thinks and feels about these things. Presumably the group of people might be named by a proper name—for example, "Englishmen" or "Melanesians," or more plausibly (to avoid the difficulty that Englishmen cannot be supposed to be talking about the feelings of Melanesians and vice versa) by a descriptive phrase such as "my group" or "the community to which I belong." The theory that moral judgments are about the feelings of the speaker's own community is open to a large number of the objections to which the private reaction theory is open and a few more besides. Although two people, one of whom says a given action is right and the other of whom says that the same action is wrong, will be saying incompatible things if they belong to the same community, if they belong to different communities their statements will be perfectly compatible. Again, if a man says at one time that an action is right and at a later time that the same action is wrong, there is no need for him to withdraw his first assertion, provided that the attitude of the community to which he belongs has changed during the interval. In that case there is no reason why both his first assertion and his second assertion should not be true. It follows, too, that however ignorant or mistaken a given community may be concerning the nature of the action being morally assessed, the statement by a member of that community that the action is right will be true as long as his community does approve of it. For example, if a community disapproves of giving eggs to pregnant women because it believes that this will cause them to give birth to chickens, the statement by a member of the community that it is morally wrong to give eggs to pregnant women will be a true one, because this community really does have the feelings it is alleged to have. Over and above these quite fatal objections, the theory that moral judgments state how members of a community feel about the actions under judgment is exposed to two difficulties, to which the view that they state how the speaker feels is not exposed. Although one might just accept the conclusion, implied by the latter theory, that one discovers a given action is right by introspection (in Hume's language, by looking inside one's breast and discovering there a sentiment of approval or disapproval), it is quite impossible to accept the view that one discovers a given action is right simply by asking other members of one's community whether they approve of it. The theory also leads to the quite unacceptable consequence that anyone who believes, for example, that most of his community approves of retaining a law against homosexuality and at the same time believes that the law against homosexuality ought to be abolished believes two logically incompatible things; for, according to this theory, what he is believing when he believes that the law against homosexuality ought to be abolished is just that most of his community would feel approval of its abolition.

A variant of this last theory would be the view that what we mean when we say that an action is right is that it is approved of by the agent's community, not the speaker's. This is more plausible because it means that instead of condemning actions performed in distant places or times because they do not accord with the moral attitudes of our community, we may praise them because they do accord with the moral attitudes of the community to which the man who performed them belonged. Hence, it appeals to a tendency in some modern moral philosophers to be rather absurdly uncritical of the moral attitudes of communities other than their own. They may be less willing to accept this variant theory, however, when they realize that if it is true, they must be equally uncritical of the morals of their own community. It must be pointed out that according to this theory, if one says, "Introducing racial segregation into University *X* was wrong," one means that introducing segregation into the university was disapproved of by the community in which the action was performed. It is perfectly obvious, however, that one might perfectly well think that it was wrong and at the same time know that it was not disapproved of by the community in which it was performed. Again, this theory has the difficulty that even when a community disapproves of some practice only because the community is grossly mistaken concerning its nature (as in the case of the women and the eggs), we are still bound to say that the practice is wrong, providing the community does in fact disapprove of it.

Moral judgments state what most men feel. The objections that have already been raised against earlier types of subjectivism can be applied without much difficulty to the view that what we mean when we say an action is right is that most men approve of it. This theory does imply that any two men (whoever they are), one of whom condemns an action and the other of whom judges it to be right, really will be saying incompatible things, for it cannot be that most men approve of an action and at the same time disapprove of it. However, since men may change from approving of something to disapproving of it, the theory does entail that a man may judge an action to be right and later judge the same action to be wrong without having to retract his first judgment. The theory means that an action is wrong if most men feel disapproval of it, however ignorant or mistaken they may be about the nature of the action. It also means that it is impossible for a man to make up his mind concerning the rectitude of any action unless he has decided whether mankind in general would approve of it; it is obvious, however, that we can make up our minds on such questions without having the least idea what the attitude of most men would be. In view of what has already been said about the theory that what we mean when we say that an action is right is that the speaker thinks it is right, nothing need be said about the analogous views that an action is right if the speaker's community thinks that it is right, or that an action is right if most men think that it is right.

It is fairly obvious from what has been said that all subjectivist theories need to be amended, at least to exclude the possibility that the attitude of the people we are alleged to be describing when we make moral judgments is not based on ignorance or mistake. Hence, a consideration of subjectivism may lead to the view that an action is right not if it is approved of by any actual person or group of people, but only if it would be approved of by a person of a very special kind—for instance, one who, at the very least, is never ignorant of or mistaken about any relevant matter of fact concerning the action toward which his attitude of approval is directed. Hence, a consideration of subjectiv-

ism must inevitably lead to a consideration of ideal observer theories; these, however, are best treated as a variety of ethical objectivism.

Bibliography

Carritt, E. F., *Ethical and Political Thinking*. Oxford, 1947.
Carritt, E. F., *The Theory of Morals*. London, 1928.
Edwards, Paul, *The Logic of Moral Discourse*. Glencoe, Ill., 1955. An acute discussion of various kinds of subjectivism.
Ewing, A. C., *The Definition of Good*. New York, 1947. Ch. 1.
Hume, David, *Treatise of Human Nature*, L. A. Selby-Bigge, ed. Oxford, 1888; reprinted 1955. Bk. III, Pt. I, Secs. I–II.
Hume, David, *Inquiry Concerning the Principles of Morals*, C. W. Hendel, ed. New York, 1957. Ch. 1, Appendix I. The classical criticism of objectivism.
Kant, Immanuel, *The Moral Law, or Kant's Groundwork of the Metaphysic of Morals*, translated by H. J. Paton. London, 1948.
Moore, G. E., *Ethics*. London, 1912. Chs. 3–4. An important criticism of subjectivism.
Plato, *The Republic*, translated with an introduction by A. D. Lindsay. New York, 1907; paperback ed., 1958. Bk. I.
Price, Richard, *A Review of the Principal Questions in Morals*, edited, with introduction, by D. Daiches Raphael. Oxford, 1948. Excellent defense of objectivism.
Ross, W. D., *The Right and the Good*. Oxford, 1930. This work and the following are two modern versions of Price's theory.
Ross, W. D., *The Foundations of Ethics*. Oxford, 1939.
Stevenson, C. L., "Moore's Arguments Against Certain Forms of Ethical Naturalism," in P. A. Schilpp, ed., *The Philosophy of G. E. Moore*. Evanston and Chicago, Ill., 1942. A reply to some of Moore's criticisms.
Westermarck, Edward, *Ethical Relativity*. New York, 1932. A well-known version of subjectivism.

JONATHAN HARRISON

ETHICS. The Encyclopedia features two detailed survey articles, entitled ETHICS, HISTORY OF and ETHICS, PROBLEMS OF. It also contains separate articles on the following topics and theories of ethics: ASCETICISM; CAN; CHOOSING, DECIDING, AND DOING; CONSCIENCE; DEONTOLOGICAL ETHICS; DETERMINISM; DUTY; EGOISM AND ALTRUISM; EMOTIVE THEORY OF ETHICS; ENDS AND MEANS; EPISTEMOLOGY AND ETHICS, PARALLEL BETWEEN; EQUALITY, MORAL AND SOCIAL; ETHICAL NATURALISM; ETHICAL OBJECTIVISM; ETHICAL RELATIVISM; ETHICAL SUBJECTIVISM; GOLDEN RULE; GOOD, THE; GUILT; HAPPINESS; HEDONISM; HISTORY AND VALUE JUDGMENTS; LIFE, MEANING AND VALUE OF; LOYALTY; MORAL SENSE; MOTIVES AND MOTIVATION; NATURAL LAW; NIHILISM; PESSIMISM AND OPTIMISM; PUNISHMENT; RELIGION AND MORALITY; RESPONSIBILITY, MORAL AND LEGAL; RULES; SUICIDE; TELEOLOGICAL ETHICS; ULTIMATE MORAL PRINCIPLES: THEIR JUSTIFICATION; UTILITARIANISM; VALUE AND VALUATION; VOLITION; and VOLUNTARISM.

ETHICS, DEONTOLOGICAL. See DEONTOLOGICAL ETHICS.

ETHICS, EMOTIVE THEORY OF. See EMOTIVE THEORY OF ETHICS.

ETHICS, HISTORY OF. The term "ethics" is used in three different but related ways, signifying (1) a general pattern or "way of life," (2) a set of rules of conduct or "moral code," and (3) inquiry *about* ways of life and rules of conduct. In the first sense we speak of Buddhist or Christian ethics; in the second, we speak of professional ethics and of unethical behavior. In the third sense, ethics is a branch of philosophy that is frequently given the special name of metaethics. The present discussion will be limited to the history of philosophical or "meta" ethics, for two reasons. First, because it is impossible to cover, with any degree of thoroughness, the history of ethics in either of the first two senses. Practices and the codification of practices are the threads out of which all of human culture is woven, so that the history of ethics in either of these senses would be far too vast a subject for a brief essay. Second, although ethical philosophy is often understood in a broad way as including all significant thought about human conduct, it can well be confined within manageable limits by separating purely philosophical thought from the practical advice, moral preaching, and social engineering which it illuminates and from which it receives sustenance. This distinction, while somewhat artificial, makes sense of the common opinion that philosophy in general, and ethical philosophy in particular, was invented by the Greeks.

The central questions of philosophical ethics are: What do we or should we mean by "good" and "bad"? what are the right standards for judging things to be good or bad? how do judgments of good and bad (value judgments) differ from and depend upon judgments of value-neutral fact? But when these questions are answered, it is important to find out the differences between specific types of value judgments that are characterized by such adjectives as "useful," "right," "moral," and "just." We may therefore divide our subject matter into the search for the meaning and standards of good in general, and of well-being, right conduct, moral character, and justice in particular. Needless to say, these are not watertight compartments. Many philosophers reject sharp distinctions between them. But provisional separation of these topics, subject to reunification in accordance with particular philosophical views, will prove helpful in disentangling the various issues on which philosophers have taken opposing stands, so that the history of ethics can be seen as irregular progress toward complete clarification of each type of ethical judgment.

GREEK ETHICS

Ethical philosophy began in the fifth century B.C., with the appearance of Socrates, a secular prophet whose self-appointed mission was to awaken his fellow men to the need for rational criticism of their beliefs and practices.

Greek society of the fifth century was in a state of rapid change from agrarian monarchy to commercial and industrial democracy. The religious and social traditions that had been handed down from one generation to the next through the natural processes of social imitation and household training were brought into question by the accession to power of a commercial class, whose members were untrained in and scornful of the ancestral way of life. New rules of conduct were required by a market economy in which money counted more than noble birth and in which men had to be considered equals as buyers and sellers. Men who wished to be elected to public office, but

had not been trained at home as rulers of serfs and household servants, needed a more explicit and general code of conduct than was embodied in the sense of honor and *esprit de corps* of the landed aristocracy. Occurring with the rapid political and social transformation of Greece, and interacting with it as both cause and effect, was the development of basic industrial arts and a scientific technology. These forces both expressed and intensified the developing interest in rational evaluation of beliefs. As Henry Sidgwick put it:

> This emergence of an art of conduct with professional teachers cannot thoroughly be understood, unless it is viewed as a crowning result of a general tendency at this stage of Greek civilization to substitute technical skill for traditional procedure. . . . If bodily vigour was no longer to be left to nature and spontaneous exercise, but was to be attained by the systematic observance of rules laid down by professional trainers, it was natural to think that the same might be the case with excellences of the soul. (*Outlines of the History of Ethics*, p. 21)

Early Greek thinkers drew frequent comparisons between medicine and ethics, describing ethics as the "art of living" and the "care of the soul." Socrates' motto, "A sound mind in a sound body," suggests the medical image of ethics as mental hygiene. Many thinkers took a special interest in medicine, and, recognizing the interdependence of mind and body, they practiced a rudimentary psychiatry. Alcmaeon of Croton, Empedocles, and Democritus were renowned for their psychotherapeutic skills. This biological conception of mind and soul led to a more critical and scientific approach to problems of ethical judgment. Philosophers began to search for reasons for established modes of conduct and, where no reasons were found, to suggest that action could be directed toward individual goals in defiance of tradition. The professional teachers known as Sophists, whose social role was to prepare the uncultivated *nouveaux riches* for positions of power in the rising democracies, employed the new-found weapon of logic with devastating effect against the code of honor of the declining aristocracy. Protagoras, Gorgias, and Thrasymachus taught methods of self-advancement and of attaining virtue. They stressed the difference between subjective values and objective facts, arguing that good and evil are matters of personal decision or social agreement (*nomos*) rather than facts of nature (*phusis*).

Socrates. Socrates stood midway between the unexamined, traditional values of the aristocracy and the skeptical practicality of the commercial class. Like the Sophists, he demanded reasons for rules of conduct, rejecting the self-justifying claim of tradition, and for this reason he was denounced as a Sophist by conservative writers like Aristophanes. But unlike the Sophists, he believed that by the use of reason man could arrive at a set of ethical principles that would reconcile self-interest with the common good and would apply to all men at all times.

The central questions of ethical philosophy were raised for the first time by Socrates and the Sophists, but only Socrates realized the difficulty, bordering on impossibility, of finding adequate answers. In this respect, Socrates may be regarded as the first philosopher, in the strictest sense of the term. While the Sophists, after exposing the impracticality of traditional rules of conduct, then offered glib formulas in their place—such as "Justice is the rule of the stronger" (Thrasymachus) and "Man is the measure of all things" (Protagoras)—Socrates applied the same logical criticism with equally devastating results to both aristocratic and market-place morality. He did not find the universal and self-evident code he searched for, but it was his memorable achievement to have revealed to mankind that without such a code its actions will lack justification and that moral perfection is therefore an ideal to which we can only approximate. Perfect clarity about what constitutes moral perfection is no more of this world than is moral perfection itself.

Our knowledge of Socrates is primarily derived from the dialogues of Plato, so it is not possible to draw a sharp line between the ideas of the two men. But since Plato's early dialogues are considerably different in style and content from those which he wrote later in life, one may take the early as fairly representative of Socrates and the late as more expressive of Plato's own thought. The chief differences discernible are the following: the more Socratic dialogues are devoted to the criticism of conventional beliefs and to the demonstration of the need for further inquiry, while the later dialogues argue for positive conclusions; the early dialogues search for definitions of ethical concepts, while the later dialogues are concerned with justifying a contemplative way of life in which pleasures of the senses are spurned in favor of pleasures of the mind; finally, the Socratic style is conversational and argumentative, while that of the later years is more didactic and abstract.

The Socrates of the early dialogues raises questions about the meaning of ethical terms, such as "What is justice?" (*Republic*), "What is piety?" (*Euthyphro*), "What is courage?" (*Laches, Charmides*), "What is virtue?" (*Protagoras*). The answers offered by others to these questions are then subjected to a relentless cross-examination (Socratic dialectic), exposing their vagueness and inconsistency.

Although Socrates did not separate judgments of value from judgments of fact, the negative results of his line of questioning suggest a distinction that was made explicit only in modern times by Hume and Moore. In each of his discussions of ethical concepts like courage or justice, Socrates refutes all efforts to define them in terms of ethically neutral facts. For example, when, in the *Protagoras, Laches,* and *Charmides,* courage is defined as resolute facing of danger, Socrates observes that a man who faces dangers that he would be wise to avoid is a fool rather than a hero. The generalization toward which Socrates points the way, although he does not arrive at it himself, is that ethical concepts can never be adequately defined in terms of observable facts alone. Many philosophers, beginning with the Sophists, have believed that this principle leads to ethical skepticism. Plato attempted to escape such skepticism by means of his theory of Forms, and the modern school of intuitionism proposes a similar way out. Indeed, all the ethical theories developed since Socrates may be considered as alternative explanations of the relation between facts and values, naturalistic theories stressing their interdependence and nonnaturalistic theories stressing their differences. Socrates, in demanding rational grounds for ethical judgments, brought attention to the problem of tracing the logical relationships between values and facts and thereby created ethical philosophy.

Plato. Plato's thought may be regarded as an endeavor to answer the questions posed by Socrates. From the *Republic* on through the later dialogues and epistles, Plato constructed a systematic view of nature, God, and man from which he derived his ethical principles. The foundation of this metaphysical view was the theory of Forms, whose most succinct formulation may be found in the discussion of the Divided Line, toward the end of Book VI of the *Republic.* Plato divides the objects of knowledge into two main categories and each of these into two subcategories symbolized by unequal sections of the line. The main division is between the realm of changing, sensible objects and that of unchanging, abstract forms. Knowledge of sensible objects acquired by sense perception is inaccurate and uncertain, for the object of sense, like the river of Heraclitus, is in continual flux. In contrast, knowledge of timeless forms is precise and rigorously provable. The realm of sensible objects is subdivided into shadows and images, in the lower section, and natural objects in the upper section. The realm of forms is subdivided into mathematical forms and ethical forms. At the apex of this ascending line is the Form of the Good, in relation to which all other objects of knowledge must be defined if they are to be adequately understood. Thus, ethics is the highest and most rigorous kind of knowledge, surpassing even mathematics, but it is also the most difficult to attain. Mathematics leads us away from reliance on visual images and sense perception, and ethical philosophy demands an even greater effort of abstraction. The objects of ethical knowledge are even less visualizable than geometrical forms and numbers—they are concepts and principles ultimately unified under the all-encompassing concept of the Good.

Although Plato suggests in this and other passages that ethical truths can be rigorously deduced from self-evident axioms, and thus introduces the mathematical model of knowledge that has guided many philosophers ever since, he does not employ a deductive procedure in his discussions of specific ethical problems, perhaps because he did not feel that he had yet attained an adequate vision of the Good that would supply him with the proper axioms from which to deduce rules of conduct. His actual procedure follows what he calls an ascending dialectic, a process of generalization through the give and take of conversation and the consideration of typical cases, a process designed to culminate in an intellectual vision of the structure of reality, from which, by a "descending dialectic" or deduction from general principles, particular judgments of value can be deduced. Plato's main goal in his ethical philosophy is to lead the way toward a vision of the Good.

The Socratic–Platonic ethical theory identifies goodness with reality and reality with intelligible form and thus concludes that the search for value must lead away from sense perception and bodily pleasure. This suggests an ascetic and intellectualistic way of life which is spelled out in full detail in the *Republic,* in the description of the training of the guardians. Some difference in the degree of intensity of the preference for mind over body may perhaps be discerned in the increasing severity of tone from the early dialogues to the later. In the *Protagoras* and *Symposium,* Socrates argues for rational control over the body for the sake of greater pleasure in the long run, but he does not oppose pleasure as such. In the *Symposium* the unity of body and mind is a luminous thread throughout the discussion. Love is regarded as a search for the pleasure that consists in possession of what is good, and it is shown to exist on many levels, the lowest being that of sexual desire and the highest that of aspiration toward a vision of eternity. While still under the influence of Socrates, Plato distinguishes noble pleasures from base pleasures, rather than condemning pleasure in itself. The image he draws of Socrates is of a man who eats and drinks heartily and enjoys himself on all levels of experience, but in rationally controlled proportions. Socrates enjoys the wine at the symposium as much as anyone else, but unlike the others he remains sober to the end. While the poet Agathon becomes drunk with his own rhetoric, Socrates employs richly sensual language and metaphor in a way sufficiently controlled to make a philosophical point and so remains master of his rhetoric as well as of his body.

In the extraordinarily beautiful dialogue *Phaedo,* which describes the day of Socrates' execution, the theme of superiority of soul to body is dealt with directly, as might be expected of a philosopher who is about to die. Here Socrates commits himself unequivocally to a rejection of the body and its pleasures, maintaining that a wise man looks forward to his own death, when the soul is freed from its corporeal prison. Whether this is an exact expression of Socrates' attitude toward life may, however, be doubted in view of other dialogues, such as the *Protagoras.* In any case, it is natural for a man confronting death to try to set the best possible light on it. But it was this more somber, otherworldly strain in Socrates that Plato in his later works elaborated into a mystical vision of a timeless higher world. Plato has Socrates say, in the *Philebus,* ". . . no degree of pleasure, whether great or small, was thought to be necessary to him who chose the life of thought and wisdom" (translated by B. Jowett, New York, 1933, Para. 33).

In the *Timaeus,* where, significantly, the protagonist is no longer Socrates but the Pythagorean Timaeus, pleasure is described as "the greatest incitement to evil," and Timaeus places the "inferior soul" below the neck, separating it from the intellect. Plato's severe castigations of bodily pleasures, his sharp separation of soul from body and of the eternal from the temporal, and his mystical cosmology entail a more extreme asceticism than that preached or practiced by Socrates.

Plato's mistrust of bodily pleasure and perceptual judgment led him to take an unfavorable view of public opinion and, consequently, of democratic institutions. In the *Republic,* and still more emphatically in the *Laws,* he proposed that society be ruled by an intellectual elite who would be trained to govern in accordance with their vision of eternal forms. He proposed, in the *Laws,* a ruthless system of punishments and the propagation of ideologically useful myths that would preserve social harmony and class distinction. Yet despite his support of severe punishment for social transgressions, Plato followed Socrates in holding, in the *Protagoras, Timaeus,* and *Laws,* that evil is due only to ignorance or madness and that "no man is voluntarily bad," a paradox that Aristotle later tried valiantly to resolve.

Aristotle. One might expect that Aristotle, who studied at Plato's Academy for many years, would take the same view of nature and human conduct as his mentor. But the differences between Plato and Aristotle are more fundamental than the resemblances. Although Aristotle naturally used a similar terminology and shared with Plato certain principles and attitudes expressive of the rationality of Hellenic culture, his method of inquiry and his conception of the role of ethical principles in human affairs were different enough from Plato's to establish a rival philosophical tradition. Plato was the fountainhead of religious and idealistic ethics, while Aristotle engendered the naturalistic tradition. Throughout the subsequent history of Western civilization, ethical views that looked to a supranatural source, such as God or pure reason, for standards of evaluation stemmed from the metaphysics of Plato, while naturalistic philosophers who found standards of value in the basic needs, tendencies, and capacities of man were guided by Aristotle.

Aristotle was born in Stagira, Macedonia, the son of Nicomachus, court physician to Amyntas II. He received early training in biology and physiology and in methods of careful observation and classification, a fact that may account for his later differences with Plato on the role of sense perception in the acquisition of knowledge. While Plato was guided by mathematics as a model of scientific knowledge, Aristotle modeled his system on biology, stressing the importance of observation of recurrent patterns in nature. Thus Plato's goal for philosophical ethics was to make human nature conform to an ideal blueprint, while Aristotle tailored his ethical principles to the demands of human nature.

Aristotle's ethical writings, consisting of the *Eudemian Ethics,* the *Nicomachean Ethics,* and the *Politics,* all edited by his disciples from his lecture notes, constitute the first systematic investigation of the foundations of ethics. Since the *Eudemian Ethics* is superseded by the *Nicomachean Ethics* and the *Politics* is an extension of his ethical principles to social regulation, this discussion will be confined to the ideas contained in the *Nicomachean Ethics.*

In the latter work, Aristotle's main purpose was to define the subject matter and methodology of philosophical ethics. In doing so, he both drew upon and revised the beliefs and values of the Greek society of his time. Aristotle begins his study by searching for the common feature of all things said to be good and, in contrast with Plato, who held that there is a Form of Good in which all good things "participate," Aristotle concludes that there are many different senses of "good," each of which must be defined separately for the limited area in which it applies. Each such "good" is pursued by a specific practical art or science, such as economics, military strategy, medicine, or shipbuilding. But the ends of these particular disciplines can be arranged in order of importance, so that the supreme good can be identified with the goal of the most general practical science to which the others are subordinate. On an individual level, this all-inclusive science is ethics; on a social level, it is politics. The end of ethics is personal happiness and that of politics is the general welfare, and since the good of the whole ranks above that of the part, personal ethics is subordinate to politics. However, this principle does not entail, for Aristotle, that the individual must sacrifice his interests to those of the community, except under unusual conditions such as war, because he assumed that the needs of both normally coincide.

Aristotle identifies the supreme good with "happiness," which he defines as the exercise of natural human faculties in accordance with virtue. His next task is to define virtue as a skill appropriate to a specific faculty, and he distinguishes two classes of virtues—intellectual and moral. There are five intellectual faculties, from which arise art, science, intuition, reasoning, and practical wisdom. He offers a long list of moral virtues, defining each as the mean between the extremes of either emotion or tendencies to action. For instance, courage is the mean between the excess and the deficiency of the emotion of fear, temperance is the mean between the tendencies to eat and drink too much or too little, justice is the mean with respect to the distribution of goods or of punishments. The bulk of the *Nicomachean Ethics* contains detailed analyses of the criteria of specific moral virtues. The final result of Aristotle's investigations is the definition of happiness or the good life as activity in accordance with virtue, and thus as the harmonious fulfillment of man's natural tendencies.

Summary: Socrates, Plato, and Aristotle. Returning to the central problems of ethical theory, one may hazard an estimation of the contributions of Socrates, Plato, and Aristotle to their clarification. Socrates was the first to recognize the importance of analyzing the meaning of good, right, just, and virtuous, and of articulating the standards for ascribing these properties. Plato charted a spiritualistic direction for finding the answers in a realm of timeless ideals, while Aristotle located the answers in the scientific study of biology, psychology, and politics. Good, for Plato, means resemblance to the pure Form, or universal model of goodness, which serves as the standard for all value judgments. Actions are right, laws are just, and people are virtuous to the degree to which they conform to the ideal model. For Aristotle, good means the achievement of the goals at which human beings naturally aim, the balanced and rational satisfaction of desires to which he gives the name "happiness." Right action, just laws, and virtuous character are the means of achieving individual and social well-being. All three philosophers agree in identifying individual good with social good and in defining moral concepts such as justice and virtue in terms of the achievement of good.

Moral responsibility. The concept of moral responsibility that acquired crucial importance in later Christian thought was only obliquely considered by Plato and more fully, although inconclusively, dealt with by Aristotle. Plato, who identified virtue with philosophical understanding, concluded that "no one does evil voluntarily," so that wrong action is always due to intellectual error. Aris-

totle recognized that intellectual error must be distinguished from moral vice, since the former, unlike the latter, is involuntary. In order to distinguish punishable evil from innocent mistakes, he explained vice as due to wrong desire as well as poor judgment. The will, for Aristotle, is rationally guided desire, formed by moral education and training. But since even voluntary action is determined by natural tendencies and early training, Aristotle searched for an additional factor to account for the freedom of choice necessary for moral responsibility. He thought he found that factor in deliberation, the consideration of reasons for and against a course of action. The further question, as to whether, when an agent deliberates, he has any choice of and consequently any responsibility for the outcome of his deliberation, was not considered by Aristotle and remains an unsettled issue between determinists and libertarians. In general, the concepts of free will and moral responsibility did not become matters of great concern until the rise of Christianity, when people became preoccupied with otherworldly rewards and punishments for moral conduct.

HELLENISTIC AND ROMAN ETHICS

During the two millennia from the death of Aristotle in the fourth century B.C. to the rise of modern philosophy in the seventeenth century A.D., the interests of ethical thinkers shifted from theoretical to practical ethics, so that little advance was made in the clarification of the meanings of ethical concepts, while, on the other hand, new conceptions of the goals of human life and new codes of conduct were fashioned. The philosophical schools of Skepticism, Stoicism, Epicureanism, and Neoplatonism that set the ethical tone of Hellenistic and Roman thought offered a type of intellectual guidance that was more like religious teaching than like scientific inquiry and paved the way for the conquests of Christianity. The popular conception of philosophy as an attitude of indifference to misfortune applies best to this period, in which philosophy and religion were nearly indistinguishable.

The subtlety of Socrates' thought is attested to by the variety of schools that developed out of his teaching. Plato and, through Plato, Aristotle probably represent the Socratic influence most completely. But the Stoics, Epicureans, and Skeptics also owed their guiding principles to Socrates. Aristippus of Cyrene, at first a disciple of Socrates, founded the school of Cyrenaicism, which followed the simple hedonistic principle that pleasure is the only good. Antisthenes, another Socratic disciple, founded the Cynic school on the apparently opposite principle that the good life is one of indifference to both pleasure and pain. The Cynics, of whom Diogenes was the most renowned, rejected the comforts of civilization and lived alone in the forests, like the dogs after whom they named themselves. Cyrenaicism developed into Epicureanism, and Cynicism into Stoicism. Soon after the death of Aristotle, Pyrrho of Elis initiated the philosophy of Skepticism, influenced by both the Sophist and the Socratic criticisms of conventional beliefs. According to Skepticism, no judgments, either of fact or of value, can be adequately proved, so that the proper philosophical attitude to take toward the actions of others is one of tolerant detachment, and toward one's own actions, extreme caution. In the second century B.C., the leaders of Plato's Academy, Arcesilaus and Carneades, adopted Skepticism, and Carneades developed a theory of probability which he applied to ethical judgments. During this period, the Peripatetic school at Aristotle's Lyceum continued the Aristotelian tradition until it merged finally with Stoicism.

Epicureanism. Epicurus (c. 341–270 B.C.) founded one of the two dominant philosophical schools of the era between the death of Aristotle and the rise of Christianity. The other dominant school was, of course, Stoicism. These two traditions are often thought of as diametrical opposites, yet it may plausibly be argued that the differences between them were more verbal than substantial. Both views of life were fundamentally pessimistic, directed more toward escape from pain than toward the positive improvement of the human condition. Both encouraged individual withdrawal from the public arena of struggle for economic and political reform, in favor of personal self-mastery and independence of social conditions. The later Roman Stoics modified this extreme individualism and placed more stress on civic duties, but even they preached resignation to the imperfections of social organization rather than efforts at improvement.

Epicurus based his ethics on the atomistic materialism of Democritus, to which he added the important modification of indeterminism by postulating a tendency of the atoms that make up the human body—and particularly its "soul atoms"—to swerve unpredictably from their normal paths, resulting in unpredictable human actions. In this way, Epicurus thought he could account for freedom of the will. He assumed that freedom of choice of action is incompatible with the deterministic principle that all events are necessary results of antecedent causes. But this identification of freedom with pure chance seems to entail that a capricious person is more free than a rational and principled person, and such a conclusion would contradict Epicurus' own vision of moral life. For Epicurus' main difference with his Cyrenaic predecessors lay in his conviction that, by the use of reason, one could plan one's life and sacrifice momentary pleasures for long-run benefit. Like the Cyrenaics, Epicurus held that pleasure is the single standard of good. But he distinguished "natural pleasures," which are moderate and healthful, from "unnatural" satiation of greed and lust. His name for moderate and natural pleasure was *ataraxia,* gentle motions in the body which he regarded as the physiological explanation of pleasure. He proposed, as the ideal way of life, a relaxed, leisurely existence, consisting in moderate indulgence of the appetites, cultivation of the intellect, and conversation with friends, which is how Epicurus himself lived and taught in his famous garden. Two centuries later, Epicureanism was established in Rome by Lucretius (c. 99–55 B.C.), whose influential poem, *On the Nature of Things,* helped to spread Epicureanism among the Roman aristocracy.

Stoicism. Stoicism was by far the most impressive intellectual achievement of Hellenistic and Roman culture prior to Christianity, providing an ethical framework within which metaphysical speculation, natural science,

psychology, and social thought could flourish to such a high degree that Stoicism has not unjustly been identified in the public mind with philosophy itself, that is, with the distinctively "philosophical" attitude toward life. Like every great tradition, Stoicism evolved through many stages and thus comprehends a great variety of specific beliefs. Historians generally distinguish three main stages of its development:

(1) The early Stoa—which derived its name from the portico, or porch, on which the early Stoics lectured—whose important figures were Zeno of Cyprus, Cleanthes, and Chrysippus. Chrysippus made the most substantial contributions to Stoic logic and theory of knowledge. The early Stoics remained close to Cynicism in recommending withdrawal from community life so as to render oneself independent of material comforts, social fashions, and the opinions of one's fellow men. Their ethical goal was the achievement of apathy, the state of indifference to pleasure and pain. They considered reason to be the distinctive nature of man and proposed that one should live "according to nature" and thus according to rational principles of conduct.

With the Stoics, the concept of duty acquired a central place in ethics, as conformity to moral rules which they identified with laws of human nature. The later Roman Stoics developed this doctrine into the theory of natural law on which Roman jurisprudence was largely based. Most of the Stoics were materialists, yet imbued with natural piety, and many identified God with the Logos of Heraclitus, as a universal "fire" or energy of nature embodied in its lawlike processes. Many were fatalists, maintaining that man can control his destiny only by resigning himself to it, a principle that contrasted vividly with their emphasis on rationality and self-control. They sought to reconcile this extreme determinism with freedom and moral responsibility by means of the Aristotelian distinction between external and internal causation, thus suggesting that the free man is one who, in understanding the necessity of what befalls him, accepts it and thus freely chooses it, a solution echoed in modern thought by Hegel's definition of freedom as the recognition of necessity.

(2) The middle Stoics, notably Panaetius and Posidonius, brought Stoicism to Rome, shaping the doctrine to the political-mindedness of the Romans by modifying its extreme individualism and stressing the importance of social duties.

(3) The late Stoics, Seneca, Epictetus, Marcus Aurelius, and, to some extent, Cicero—who accepted only certain parts of Stoic doctrine—developed the ideal of a "cosmopolis," or universal brotherhood of man, in which all men would be recognized as having equal rights and responsibilities, an ideal which Christianity absorbed into its conception of the "City of God" and which, in the modern age, Kant made the cornerstone of his system of ethics.

Neoplatonism. Epicureanism offered a way of life that was open only to the leisure class. Stoicism appealed to highly reflective men of all classes, as evidenced by the fact that the two great figures of late Stoicism were the educated slave Epictetus and the emperor Marcus Aurelius. However, both philosophical views could interest only those of a sufficiently high level of education and thoughtful temperament to place intellectual values above all others. As the Roman Empire declined, and reason seemed powerless to solve the intense economic and social problems of the empire, an atmosphere of pessimism and disaffection with reason began to prevail, a situation which Gilbert Murray has described as "a failure of nerve." Interest increased in finding supernatural routes to salvation of the kind offered by various religious cults, and even in the intellectual schools the study of logic and natural science declined in favor of a search for psychological means of escape from suffering. The philosophy of Neoplatonism fashioned by Plotinus (c. 204–270) offered an intellectual road to salvation, while early Christianity paved an emotional and ritualistic highway toward the same destination. Later, these two roads converged.

Plotinus lectured in Rome and, after his death, his notes were edited by his disciple Porphyry, forming the work entitled *Enneads*—so called because of its division into chapters of nine sections each. Plotinus developed one strain of Plato's thought, the ascetic mysticism of the passages on the Form of the Good in the *Republic* and the *Symposium* and the pantheistic metaphysics of the *Timaeus*. According to Plotinus, the world is a series of emanations or overflowings of the One, the ineffable and ultimate reality of which every determinate thing is a part. The One is so transcendent as to be indescribable, "the One, transcending intellect, transcends knowing." But if the One cannot be described, it can at least be negatively characterized in terms of what it is not, namely, that it is not limited by any finite properties. This negative characterization of the One was the source of Christian "negative theology," the description of God in terms of the denial of all modes of limitation.

The One emanates intelligible Forms or Platonic Ideas, out of which the World Soul produces individual souls which in turn emanate lower beings in a process that approaches, but does not quite reach, pure matter. Matter, as total formlessness, is so far from true being that it does not exist. Identifying evil with matter or formlessness, Plotinus concluded that evil does not exist in an absolute sense, but only as incompleteness or lack of good. This account of evil as having no positive existence was later adopted by Augustine and most subsequent theologians.

Since Plotinus, following Plato, equated goodness with reality and evil with unreality or distance from the One, it followed that virtue consists in purging the soul of reliance on sensual pleasures and imagery, so that it can ascend the ladder of being and return to its source in the One. The culmination of this process of purification through self-denial is the mystical experience of reunion with the One, which Plotinus describes—having experienced it himself at least four times—as "the flight of the Alone to the Alone." Thus virtue, for Plotinus as later for Augustine, is not its own reward but is a means to a metaphysical state of blessedness. In the words of the historian W. T. Jones, "Like other men of his time, Plotinus found this world a sea of troubles and a vale of tears; like them he sought to leave it; and like them he found perfect peace only in otherworldliness." How much of this view was absorbed into Christian, Islamic, and Judaic theology can hardly be overestimated, although the influence of Platonism on Judaism was mainly through Philo Judaeus (fl. 20 B.C.– A.D. 40), an Alexandrian Jew and contemporary of Jesus, who combined elements of Stoicism with a Platonistic interpretation of Judaic theology and ethics.

(The above section on Hellenistic and Roman ethics was prepared in collaboration with Professor Richard O. Haynes of the University of Hawaii.)

MEDIEVAL ETHICS

The rise of Christian philosophy, out of a fusion of Greco-Roman thought with Judaism and elements of other Middle Eastern religions, produced a new era in the history of ethics, although one that was prepared for by Stoicism and Neoplatonism. The Stoic concern with justice and self-mastery, and the Neoplatonic search for reunion with the source of all being, were combined in early Christian philosophy with the Judaic belief in a personal God, whose commandments are the primal source of moral authority and whose favor is the ultimate goal of human life. Two sources of ethical standards, human reason and divine will, were juxtaposed in one system of ethics, and the tension between them was reflected in conflicting sectarian interpretations of theological principles.

From the second to the fourth century, Christianity spread through the Roman Empire, offering the poor and the oppressed a hope for otherworldly happiness in compensation for their earthly suffering, and thus a way of life with which the more pessimistic and intellectualist schools of philosophy could not compete. By the fourth century, Christianity dominated Western civilization and had absorbed the main ideas and values of the secular schools of thought, as well as rival religions such as Manichaeism, Mithraism, and Judaism. Having converted the masses, it was time to win over the intelligentsia, and doing this required the hammering out of an explicit and plausible system of metaphysical and ethical principles. This task was performed by the Church Fathers, Clement of Alexandria, Origen, Tertullian, Ambrose, and, most completely and authoritatively, by Augustine.

Augustine. St. Augustine (354–430), born near Carthage, the son of a pagan father and a Christian mother, was first a Manichaean and later became converted to Christianity. He rose in the church to become bishop of Hippo and helped to settle the doctrinal strife among the many Christian sects by constructing a system of theology, ethics, and theory of knowledge that soon became the authoritative framework of Christian thought, modified but not supplanted by subsequent church philosophers. Augustine's major works, *Confessions, The City of God, Enchiridion,* and *On Freedom of the Will,* wove together threads of Stoic ethics, Neoplatonic metaphysics, and the Judaeo-Christian doctrine of revelation and redemption into a many-colored fabric of theology. With Augustine, theology became the bridge between philosophy and revealed religion, the one end anchored in reason and the other in faith, and ethics became a blend of the pursuit of earthly well-being with preparation of the soul for eternal salvation.

Like the Neoplatonists, Augustine rejected almost entirely the claims of bodily pleasures and community life, maintaining, as St. Paul had done, that happiness is impossible in this world, which serves only as a testing ground for reward and punishment in the afterlife. Augustine inherited the Neoplatonic conception of virtue as the purgation of the soul of all dependence on material comforts in preparation for reunion with God. Against the Stoic and Aristotelian reliance on reason as the source of virtue, Augustine maintained that such apparently admirable traits as prudence, justice, wisdom, and fortitude—the four cardinal virtues identified by Plato and stressed by Stoics and Christians—are of no moral worth when not inspired by Christian faith. With the pessimistic view of life characteristic of an era of wars, political collapse, and economic decline—a view already apparent in the Stoic, Epicurean, and Neoplatonic modes of withdrawal from social responsibilities—intensified by his personal sense of guilt and worthlessness, Augustine saw life on earth as a punishment for Adam's original sin. "For what flood of eloquence can suffice to detail the miseries of this life?" he laments in *The City of God*.

Nature. The tension between natural and supernatural values in Augustine's ethical thought shows itself most clearly in his ambivalent attitude toward nature. Nature, as God's creation, must be unqualifiedly good. Natural evils are only apparently evil, and in the long run they contribute to the fulfillment of divine purpose. Natural evil is simply imperfection that makes variety possible and thus, when viewed on a cosmic scale, does not exist at all. On the other hand, since man must be held morally responsible for his sins, human sin cannot be so easily explained away as incompleteness that promotes the cosmic good. Moreover, it is man's bodily desires that tempt him to sin. Without the aid of divine grace, the promptings of human nature, whether impulsive or rational, lead only to vice and damnation. Augustine resolves this paradoxical view of human nature by holding that man, unlike other natural species, was endowed by his Creator with free will and thus with the capacity to choose between good and evil. Through the original sin of Adam he has chosen evil, and it is for this reason, rather than because of any flaw in his original construction, that he is irresistibly inclined to further sin.

Free will and divine foreknowledge. If Augustine's dual conception of nature is explained by his concept of free will, the latter contains new difficulties. The problem of free will is critical in Christian ethics, which emphasizes responsibility and punishment. The Greek ideal of practical reason ensuring physical and mental well-being was supplanted by the ideal of purification of the soul through suffering, renunciation, and humble obedience to divine will.

Where the practice of virtue produces well-being as its natural consequence, as in the Greek view, virtue carries with it its own reward in accordance with the causal processes of nature, so that causal necessity and moral desert are not merely compatible; they normally coincide. But in the Christian view, causal necessity and moral responsibility seem incompatible, for the choice between good and evil is made by the soul, independently of natural processes, and its reward or punishment is independent of the natural effects of human actions. Man is punished or

rewarded to the degree to which he voluntarily obeys or disobeys the commands of God. In the Greek view, man suffers from the natural consequences of his mistakes, but in the Christian view, no matter what the natural consequences of his actions, he is held to account for the state of his soul. It is his motives and not his actions that count in assessment of his moral responsibility, and the primary motive is his desire for, or his turning away from, God.

Responsibility is thus transferred from the consequences of a person's actions to the state of his soul. Yet if the soul is created by God, and not subject to its temporary owner's control, then in what sense can man be said to have freedom of choice between good and evil? Augustine describes the soul that chooses evil as "defective," but if so, is not the Creator of the defective soul responsible for its deficiency? In absolution of God, Augustine argues that a defect is not a positive entity, thus not a created thing and not attributable to a creator—a terminological escape that is vulnerable to the objection that, on such grounds, a man who stabs another produces in his victim a deficiency rather than a positive state and therefore is not responsible for his "nonexistent" product.

Augustine's concept of free will is further complicated by his support of the theological principle of divine omniscience, which entails foreknowledge by God of human decisions. The term "predestination," used by later theologians and notably by the Protestant reformers, suggests a determinism that Augustine rejects in his criticism of fatalism. For Augustine, God knows what man will choose to do and makes it possible for man to act on his free choices but does not compel him to any course of action. To the obvious question of how God can know in advance what has not been destined or causally necessitated, Augustine replies by means of his subtle analysis of time. God has knowledge, not of what we are compelled to do but of what we freely choose to do, because his knowledge is not the kind of advance knowledge that is based on causal processes but is due to the fact that, in the mind of God, we have already made our decisions. All of past and future time is spread out in the specious present of the divine mind, so that what, from our limited standpoint, would be prediction of the future is, for God, simply direct awareness of contemporaneous events.

Distinctions among ethical concepts. While Augustine's ethical writings are mainly concerned with the substantive problem of how to achieve redemption, rather than with the clarification of ethical concepts, much of his writing is philosophical in our strict sense, in that it suggests solutions to conceptual or metaethical problems of meaning and method. Augustine opposed the classical tendency to define the moral concepts of rightness and virtue in terms of individual and social well-being and interpreted moral right and virtue as obedience to divine authority. The concept of good is split into a moral and a practical sense. Good as fulfillment of natural tendencies is subordinated to eternal beatitude, the fulfillment of the aspirations of the virtuous soul. Freedom and responsibility are interpreted as internal states of the soul and as excluding, rather than (as for Aristotle) presupposing, causal necessity.

Fourth to thirteenth centuries. From Augustine in the fourth century to Abelard in the eleventh century, Christian, Islamic, and Judaic philosophy was dominated by Neoplatonic mysticism and preoccupied with faith and salvation. The outstanding figure of this period was John Scotus Erigena (c. 810–c. 877), whose conception of good was the Platonic one of approximation to timeless being and whose view of life as issuing from and returning to God bordered on heretical pantheism.

By the eleventh century, interest in rational philosophical speculation had revived, and even those Schoolmen like Bernard of Clairvaux (1091–1153), who continued to defend religious mysticism and denounced reliance upon reason as inimical to faith, nevertheless employed philosophical arguments to refute contrary opinions. Augustine had asserted that one must "believe in order to understand," and St. Anselm (1033–1109) took this to mean that faith is not incompatible with reason but, rather, prepares the soul for rational understanding. The main issues among philosophers of this time were the relation between faith and reason, and the nature of universals.

However, Peter Abelard (1079–1142), an extraordinarily original and independent thinker whose vibrant personality reveals itself in his philosophical writings, rediscovered some of the unsolved problems of ethical philosophy. Abelard brought into clear view the distinctive features of Christian ethics implicit in Augustine's work, in particular, the split between moral and prudential concepts that sharply separates Christian ethics from Greek ethics. Abelard held that morality is an inner quality, a property of motive or intention rather than of the consequences of one's actions, a principle that was later stressed by the Reformation and attained its fullest expression in the ethical system of Immanuel Kant. A somewhat heretical corollary follows from Abelard's principle, namely that, as Étienne Gilson puts it, "Those who do not know the Gospel obviously commit no fault in not believing in Jesus Christ," and it seems clear from all this that Christian faith need not be the foundation for moral rules. Abelard concluded that one can attain to virtue through reason as well as through faith.

Thomas Aquinas. The towering figure of medieval philosophy is, of course, Thomas Aquinas (c. 1225–1274), whose philosophical aim was to reconcile Aristotelian science and philosophy with Augustinian theology. The way to this achievement had already been prepared by the revival in western Europe of interest in Aristotle, whose thought had been preserved and elaborated by Muslim and Jewish scholars such as Avicenna, Averroës, and Maimonides and had been brought to the attention of Christendom by the commentaries of Albert the Great. It remained for Aquinas to prove the compatibility of Aristotelian naturalism with Christian dogma and to construct a unified view of nature, man, and God. This he undertook with remarkable success in his *Summa Theologica* and *Summa Contra Gentiles*.

To a large degree, Aquinas' union of Aristotelianism with Christianity consisted in arguing for the truth of both and in refuting arguments of his predecessors and contemporaries that purported to show their incompatibility. Aristotle's ethics was relativistic, rational, and prudential; Augustinian ethics was absolutist, grounded on faith, and independent of consequences. Now one of these views is

totally misguided, or else there must be room for two different systems of ethical concepts and principles. Aquinas adopted the latter alternative and divided the meaning of ethical concepts into two domains, "natural" and "theological." Natural virtues, adequately accounted for by Aristotle, can be attained by proper training and the exercise of practical reason, while theological virtues—faith, hope, and love—require faith and divine grace. Similarly, he distinguished two highest goods, or paramount goals of life, worldly happiness and eternal beatitude (which has precedence); the former is achieved through natural virtue and the latter is achieved through the church and its sacraments. Aquinas thus expressed a considerably more optimistic attitude than did Augustine toward the possibility of improving man's lot on earth through knowledge of nature and intelligent action. This helped to prepare the climate for the rebirth of natural science, whose first stirrings were felt in the thirteenth century.

Natural law. At the center of Thomistic ethics was the concept of natural law. The medieval doctrine of natural law, stemming from Aristotle's teleological conception of nature and from the Stoic identification of human reason with the Logos, was a fusion of naturalistic Greek ethics with monotheistic theology. On this view, the promptings of informed reason and moral conscience represent an inherent tendency in the nature of man, and conformity to this nature fulfills both the cosmic plan of the Creator and the direct commands of God revealed in the Scriptures. Natural law is the divine law as discovered by reason, and therefore the precepts of the church and the Bible, and scientific knowledge of the universal needs and tendencies of man, provide complementary rather than competing standards of ethical judgment. Where conflicts between science and religious authority arise, they must be due to inadequate understanding of science, since church authority and dogma are infallible.

The Thomistic unification of scientific and religious ethics in the doctrine of natural law—further elaborated in subtle detail by Francisco Suárez and other legalists—was an effective way of making room, within the religious enterprise of achieving salvation, for the practical business of everyday living in pursuit of personal and social well-being. The ideological supremacy of theology was maintained, but the doctrine of natural law purported to guarantee reliable knowledge of nature, psychology, and political economy. The weakness in this system was that it placed religious barriers in the way of scientific advance, tending to sanctify and render immune from revision whichever scientific principles seemed most congenial to theology, such as instinct theory in psychology, vitalistic biology, and geocentric astronomy.

Free will. Aquinas' account of freedom and moral responsibility was, in general form, similar to that of Augustine, maintaining the compatibility of free will with predestination or divine foreknowledge. Aquinas also maintained the compatibility of free will with causal determinism, thus dealing with the problem on the level of prudential ethics as well on as the theological level of grace and salvation. Aquinas' solution makes effective use of Aristotle's analysis of choice and voluntary action in terms of internal causality and deliberation, and it identifies free will with rational self-determination rather than with the absence of causal influences. On the other hand, Aquinas' concept of freedom is, as a result, more relativistic than Augustine's, and, while it explains the conditions under which an agent may be held responsible for his *actions*—namely, the conditions of desire, knowledge, and deliberation—it does not meet the further issue of whether these faculties that determine action are within the control of the agent, that is, whether a person can freely choose the habits and desires that determine his actions. Later writers, particularly Protestant theologians, tended to interpret Augustine as stressing predestination and Aquinas as stressing free will, but it may be argued to the contrary, that Augustine's conception of free will as an inexplicable and supernatural thrust of the soul allows the agent more independence of his formed character than does Aquinas', but by that very token, Aquinas' account is more congenial to a scientific view of man.

Subsequent scholastic philosophy, from the fourteenth to the seventeenth centuries, added little to the clarification of metaethical problems, but it probed further into the relation between intellect and will as sources of human and divine action. John Duns Scotus (c. 1266–1308), William of Ockham (c. 1285–1349), and Nicholas of Autrecourt (fl. c. 1335) developed the voluntaristic doctrine that the will is free in a more absolute sense than that accounted for by Aquinas, in that it is independent both of external causality and of determination by the intellect—that is, by the agent's knowledge of what is right and good. Their view in one way strengthened the case for religious faith as against scientific reason, at least in matters of ethical judgment, but, in another way, it helped stimulate an attitude of individualism and independence of authority that prepared the ground for the secular and humanistic ethics of the modern age.

EARLY MODERN ETHICS

Philosophy seems to flourish best in periods of rapid social transformation, when the conceptual framework of a culture crumbles, requiring a re-examination of basic concepts, principles, and standards of value. The sixteenth and seventeenth centuries, which saw the demise of medieval feudalism and ushered in the modern age of industrial democracy, were, like the fifth and fourth centuries B.C., a period of intense philosophical ferment. In both cases, the preceding century witnessed the demolition of traditional beliefs, while the succeeding century was one of systematic reconstruction. The development of commerce and industry, the discovery of new regions of the world, the Reformation, the Copernican and Galilean revolutions in science, and the rise of strong secular governments demanded new principles of individual conduct and of social organization.

In the sixteenth century, Francis Bacon demolished the logic and methodology of medieval Scholasticism. Erasmus, Luther, and Calvin, while attempting to strengthen the bond between religion and ethics, undermined the elaborate structure of canon law based on the moral authority of the medieval church, and Machiavelli dynamited the bridge between religious ethics and political science. The task of reconstruction in philosophy was performed in the seventeenth century by Descartes, Hobbes, Leibniz, Spinoza, and Locke.

Hobbes. Modern ethical theory began with Thomas Hobbes (1588–1679). The advent of Galilean natural science had challenged the traditional notions, supported by authority, of purpose, plan, and value in the physical world; it cast into doubt the doctrine of natural law and nullified the anthropomorphic assumptions of theology. New standards of ethical judgment had to be found, not in the cosmic plan of nature or in scriptural revelations of the divine will but in man himself, either in his biological structure, or in his agreements with his fellow men, or in the social and political institutions that he creates. Thus were born, simultaneously and to the same parent, the ethical philosophies of naturalism, cultural relativism, and subjectivism, respectively.

Born in a time of international and domestic strife, Hobbes regarded the preservation of life as the paramount goal of human action and constructed his system of ethics and political science in his major work, *Leviathan,* with the principle of self-preservation as its cornerstone. His enthusiasm for Galileo's physics and his conviction that all fields of knowledge could be modeled on this universal science (following the method of Euclid's geometry) may have suggested to him that the drive to self-preservation is the biological analogue of the Galilean principle of inertia. Hobbes conceived of man as a complex system of particles in motion and attempted to deduce ethical laws from the principle of self-preservation. He offers, however, two formulations of this principle, the first of which is his foundation of ethics, while the second is, in effect, the repudiation of ethics.

The tendency to self-preservation, according to Hobbes, expresses itself in the quest for social harmony through peace-keeping institutions and practices or, alternatively, in the aggressive drive toward power over one's fellow men. Thus he formulates his "first and fundamental" principle in two parts, the "law of nature" to the effect that "Every man ought to endeavor to peace as far as he has hope of obtaining it," and the "right of nature," that "when he cannot obtain it, he may seek and use all the helps and advantages of war." Which of these two forms of the principle of self-preservation should be applied depends, for Hobbes, on whether the agent finds, himself in a well-organized society or in a "state of nature" in which he cannot expect cooperative behavior on the part of his fellow men. Thus, the concept of ethical law applies to social agreements and commitments, while that of rights applies to the exercise of natural powers. In the state of nature one has a right to do whatever one has the power to do.

From his fundamental law of nature, Hobbes derives a number of specific rules that prescribe the means of establishing and maintaining a peaceful society, the primary means being the willingness to make or, if already made, to maintain the social contract in which individual rights or powers are surrendered to a sovereign in return for the guarantee of personal security. The state is thus the artificial creation of reasonable men, a "Leviathan" that maintains peace by means of power relinquished to it by its citizens. Once such a commonwealth has been established by contract or conquest, other general rules of conduct follow in accordance with Hobbes's theory of psychology. To restrain the natural human tendencies to envy, mistrust, self-aggrandizement, and aggression, the virtues of accommodation, gratitude, clemency, obedience to authority, and respect for the equal rights of others are recommended by "laws of nature" as effective means of ensuring social harmony.

Reason and ethical laws. Hobbes's use of the term "laws of nature" in referring to ethical principles is to be distinguished sharply from the medieval concept of natural law that he rejected. There is, for Hobbes, no moral order in the cosmos, nor any natural prompting toward justice and sympathy for others in human nature. Man, like the rest of nature, is a system of particles perpetually moving and colliding in accordance with physical laws whereby direction and intensity of motion are determined solely by preponderance of force. Yet reason plays a role in human action that distinguishes man from the rest of the world machine. Ethical rules are "precepts, found out by reason, by which a man is forbidden to do that which is destructive of his life or taketh away the means of preserving the same."

In his mechanistic physiology, Hobbes explained reason as a mechanical process in the brain consisting in the combining and separating particles that serve as representations of objects and qualities; thus, cognitive processes are a special type of physical process, governed by the same laws. But on this mechanistic view of man, it is difficult for Hobbes to account for the prescriptive character he attributes to ethical laws as distinguished from physical laws. Throughout his discussion, Hobbes vacillates between a conception of ethics as a branch of physical science that describes the behavior of human mechanisms and the quite different conception of ethics as rational advice on how to get along with one's fellow men by consciously restraining one's aggressive impulses. Both sides of the *nomos–phusis* controversy between the Sophists and Plato are represented in Hobbes's thought, and he cites both social authority and prudential reason as sources of ethical obligation. Moral virtue consists in conformity to custom and law, in opposition to the natural aggressiveness that equips a man for survival in the state of nature, yet the "precepts found out by reason" provide a natural basis for the establishment of customs and laws.

Desire and will. Hobbes's account of desire and will is designed to bridge the gap between rational directives and physical laws. He defines good as "any object of desire" and desire as the motion toward an object that results from physiological processes ("endeavors") within the body. To act rationally does not entail freedom to act contrary to one's physiological impulses, since rationality or deliberation is simply the mediating processes of the central nervous system. The will is not a supernatural power controlling desires but simply the last stage of deliberation that eventuates in overt action, and thus is itself a neurological process governed by laws of physics. Freedom of the will from causal influences is, for Hobbes, a senseless combination of concepts; freedom is the "absence of external impediments" to the will. It is the person who is free or unfree, and not his will, since his freedom consists in the determination of his overt actions by his will rather than by external forces. Yet this mechanistic account of the will seems in paradoxical contrast with his subjectivist account of civil law as deriving its obligatory force from the arbitrary will of the sovereign, an account which comes dangerously close to the Aristotelian and Augustinian notions of the will as a "first cause."

Naturalism and nonnaturalism. The importance of Hobbes to modern ethical theory is inestimable. In freeing ethics from bondage to revealed theology and its anthropomorphic view of nature, Hobbes brought philosophy back to the problems with which it had begun to wrestle in the time of Socrates and the Sophists, and of which it had lost sight for a millennium. At the same time, he raised the understanding of these problems to a higher level, profiting both from the Christian insight that moral principles have an obligatory force and from the refinements of scientific method introduced by Bacon, Galileo, and Descartes.

If ethics was to become a body of reliable knowledge, it must be grounded on objective laws of psychology and biology, rather than on tradition, sentiment, and church authority. On the other hand, if nature and its scientific description are ethically neutral, then ethics is to be contrasted with science and purged of references to nature, just as natural science must be purged of references to ethical values. In that case, ethical principles must be understood as subjective expressions of emotion and desire, and not as objectively verifiable laws. This dilemma has plagued philosophy ever since, and, if it was not resolved by Hobbes, at least his thought was not completely impaled on either horn but only a bit on both.

Early intuitionists. Reaction to Hobbes's attack on the objectivity of ethical judgment was immediate. The doctrine of natural law and its vision of nature as a moral system were defended in a new form by a group of scholars at Cambridge who became known as the Cambridge Platonists, principally Ralph Cudworth (1617–1688) and Henry More (1614–1687). They maintained that moral principles are self-evident truths, as certain and immutable as the laws of mathematics. Richard Cumberland (1631–1718) attempted to deduce all the principles of ethics from a single "Law of Nature" that later became the cornerstone of utilitarian ethics, namely, the law that all actions should promote the common good. Nicholas Malebranche (1638–1715) developed the Cartesian theory of ethics as a deductive system but gave it an Augustinian slant, attributing to God the sole power to translate knowledge of ethical truth into action. Malebranche realized that the analogy between ethics and mathematics fails to explain the connection between ethics and action, and so he made a virtue of this defect by means of his "Occasionalist" account of causality as divine intervention. Samuel Clarke (1675–1729) developed an intuitionist theory of "natural religion" similar to that of Cudworth and More, holding that the quality of right or "fitness" is an intrinsic property of actions that the mind can perceive as directly as it perceives geometrical relations.

Spinoza. Born in the Netherlands of Jewish refugees from the Spanish Inquisition, Benedict Spinoza

(1632–1677) combined Descartes's faith in the capacity of reason to govern action with Hobbes's mechanistic theory of psychology to express a scientific vision of nature as a unified system of laws. In his *Ethics Demonstrated in the Geometric Manner* Spinoza, like Hobbes but with more formal precision, derived the principles of physics, psychology, and ethics from metaphysical axioms.

The first principle of psychology for Spinoza, as for Hobbes, is the drive to self-preservation and self-aggrandizement, corresponding to the physical principle of inertia. But Spinoza's unique achievement was to derive, as the logical corollary of this egoistic psychology, a rational, humane, and cultivated way of life. A strict determinist in his metaphysics and a thorough naturalist in his ethics, Spinoza held that every event is deducible from antecedent causes and concluded that ethical right is identical with causal necessity. The rules of conduct are therefore laws of human nature, obeyed by all but obeyed blindly by the selfish person enslaved by his passions while understood and accepted by the free man who, in achieving a vision of the necessary order of all things, experiences the "intellectual love of God" that provides both happiness and moral virtue.

While Spinoza tried more consistently than Hobbes to reduce ethics to psychology and thus to make it a branch of natural science, it has often been contended that his program was self-defeating. For if men cannot help acting in accordance with their desires, and if nothing is objectively good or bad but only appears so to those who do not understand the necessity of all events, then what sense can there be to either prudential or moral rules of conduct? Having banished values from nature, Spinoza, like Hobbes, had to relocate them in human consciousness. But then consciousness must be either a supranatural force that interrupts the causal order of nature—as it was for Descartes—or a part of nature and thus ethically neutral, in which case ethics becomes senseless; or, finally, consciousness is an illusory reflection of physical processes in the body, in which case ethics, too, is illusory. Spinoza and Hobbes vacillated between the last two alternatives although, as we have seen, Hobbes's prescriptivist account of moral right as stemming from the will of an authority may be suspected of having slipped an element of supranatural agency back into the picture.

In their social and political theories, both Spinoza and Hobbes argued for the appraisal of institutions and policies in terms of the satisfaction of human needs rather than of conformity to religious tradition. But Hobbes's conception of force as the basis of law led him to support political authoritarianism, while Spinoza's identification of value and right with rational self-interest enabled him to argue, like Locke, for representative government and maximum civil liberty.

Locke. John Locke (1632–1704) is generally regarded as the founder of modern utilitarianism, although his applications of utilitarian ethics to social and political theory were more influential than his analysis of standards of individual conduct. He combined the mathematical model of ethical judgment suggested by Descartes and the Cambridge Platonists with a hedonistic theory of psychology according to which pleasure is the goal of all human action

and consequently is the fundamental standard of evaluation. In his *Essay Concerning Human Understanding,* Locke criticizes the doctrine of innate ideas of Descartes and Leibniz, in defense of the principle that all knowledge is founded on experience; he then, somewhat paradoxically, offers an account of ethics as a deductive science in which specific rules of conduct are derived "from self-evident propositions, by necessary consequences as incontestable as those in mathematics." The appearance of paradox dissolves, however, on noting that, for Locke, the formation of the ideas of goodness and justice is due to the sensations of pleasure and pain, and thus ethical *concepts* are derived from experience although their logical relations are then discoverable by reflective analysis.

Locke follows Hobbes in defining good as the object of desire, but then, assuming that the only property of things which provokes desire is their tendency to produce pleasure or reduce pain, he also defines good as "what has an aptness to produce pleasure in us." Again, like Hobbes, Locke defines moral virtue as conformity to custom and law, but he differs from Hobbes in maintaining that custom and law can in turn be evaluated by the more fundamental standards of utility and natural rights. It is in terms of these more basic standards that Locke justifies representative government and civil liberty.

Locke's main contribution to the clarification of the meaning of ethical concepts was in his distinction between "speculative" and "practical" principles. Speculative knowledge is independent of action, while practical principles (including ethical principles) can be said to be believed and known to be true only insofar as they are acted upon. This distinction accounts for the obligatory force of ethical principles and eliminates the need for a supernatural agency, "free will," to translate belief into action, although it makes it difficult to explain why, if practical principles are "self-evident propositions," we do not all behave in a morally impeccable way. Like Hobbes, Locke ridicules the notion of free will as a semantical absurdity similar to the questions "whether sleep be swift or virtue square." Will is the power of the mind to decide on action, and freedom the power to carry out one's decisions, that is, to get what one wants.

Moral-sense theories. The seventeenth-century philosophers found the connection between self-interest and morality in the threat of punishment—divine, natural, or civil—that coerces the individual to be moral for the sake of self-interest. But it was soon noticed that this connection breaks down wherever the expected benefit to the individual of immoral conduct outweighs the likelihood of punishment and that, if morality is grounded in psychology, then human nature cannot be as aggressively self-centered as the apostles of self-preservation and pursuit of pleasure maintained.

The third earl of Shaftesbury (1671–1713) and Francis Hutcheson (1694–1747) proposed that moral obligation has its source in benevolent affections, such as love and pity, that are as natural and universal as the more aggressive tendencies ("self-affections"), such as envy, greed, and the impulse to self-preservation. Moreover, there is a "moral sense" in man that finds unique satisfaction in actions directed toward the common good. This moral sensibility turns us from the pursuit of pleasure toward the performance of duties toward others and explains our admiration of self-sacrifice independently of external reward or punishment.

Bernard Mandeville (c. 1670–1733), in *The Fable of the Bees,* defended egoistic psychology against this attack and ridiculed the concept of moral conscience as a hypocritical device for maintaining social privileges, a view later echoed by Holbach, Marx, and Nietzsche. Bishop Joseph Butler (1692–1752), whose sermons in defense of Christian morality against the cynicism of Hobbes and Mandeville reveal extraordinary analytical power, argued that benevolence and conscience are as deeply rooted in human nature as is self-love. In adding conscience or intuition of duty to benevolence as the psychological source of moral obligation, Butler lessened the stress of earlier moral-sense theorists on emotion and gave more recognition to the role of rational judgment.

Moral-sense theory, refined further by David Hartley (1705–1757) and Adam Smith (1723–1790), who applied utilitarian ethics to economic theory, achieved its most persuasive formulation in the writings of David Hume.

Hume. David Hume (1711–1776), like Hartley and Smith, combined an emotional account of morality with a utilitarian theory of good. Hume's discussions of ethics in the third part of his *A Treatise of Human Nature* and, more fully, in his *An Enquiry Concerning the Principles of Morals* are attempts to answer the metaethical questions of the meaning of good, right, justice, and virtue; by what standards they are attributed to persons and actions; how it is psychologically possible for men to admire and cultivate morality at the expense of self-interest; and by what rules ethical disputes can be decided in favor of one judgment against another. Despite the clarity and good sense that Hume brings to bear on these topics, his discussion shifts inadvertently from one type of question to another, particularly from questions of meaning to questions of motivation, a shift characteristic of moral-sense theories.

Hume begins his studies of ethical judgment with a search for the meanings of ethical terms. Finding no observable facts or logical relations that answer to our concepts of goodness, justice, and moral virtue, Hume concludes that the function of ethical terms is not to denote qualities or relations but to convey a "sentiment of approbation," so that their meaning is to be found in the feelings of the judge rather than in the object judged. We call things good for the same reason that we call them beautiful: because we find them agreeable. An object is good if it is immediately pleasant, or if it is a useful means for attaining something else that is pleasant. Virtues are qualities that render a person agreeable or useful to himself or to others, whether they are "natural virtues" such as talent, wit, and benevolence or "artificial virtues" like honesty and justice. While judgments as to what is useful in producing pleasure, insofar as they rest on knowledge of causal facts, are within the competence of reason, nevertheless they depend, for their distinctively ethical import, on feeling or taste, since rational knowledge alone is "not sufficient" to produce any moral blame or approbation. "Utility is only a tendency to a certain end; and were the end totally indifferent to us, we should feel the same

indifference toward the means. It is requisite a certain *sentiment* should here display itself . . ." (*Enquiry Concerning the Principles of Morals,* Appendix I).

Thus, according to Hume, there are two possible grounds or standards of evaluation, utility and feeling, the one objective and subject to rational confirmation, the other subjective and personal. The objective standard, unfortunately, applies only to instrumental values and not to ultimate ends. However, the subjectivity of feelings is not cause for despair about achieving agreement on ethical judgments, since the sentiment that motivates them, the disinterested pleasure and approval that we feel in contemplating actions directed toward the welfare of others, is, for Hume as for Butler, a universal tendency in human nature.

Moral reasons and psychological motives. In common with Hobbes and Locke, who justified moral conduct by the fear of punishment, and the earlier moral-sense theorists, who explained moral obligation in terms of the benevolent affections, Hume identifies the psychological motives that influence and often prejudice moral judgments with the logical grounds or reasons for moral judgments. From the premise that, were it not for our natural benevolence, we would not care enough about moral issues to make moral judgments, Hume draws the ***non sequitur*** that the only evidence that supports such judgments lies in the feeling of approval or disapproval that motivates them.

Hume tends to equate moral virtue with the artificial quality of justice, artificial because it is required only for the protection of property rights in a society in which goods are neither too scarce nor sufficiently abundant. The importance for social harmony of strict conformity to laws renders it dangerous and undesirable to make exceptions in the name of expediency. Consequently, the utility of strict justice outweighs the utility of any possible exceptions. But Hume realized that this rather abstract utilitarian consideration can hardly explain our sense of moral obligation and our admiration for those who demonstrate high moral character. He therefore supplements this account with the notion of "disinterested interest" that resembles the rational moral sense appealed to by Butler, Price, and Reid (see below).

However, Hume is not positing any occult faculty, for he explains disinterested moral approbation as a combination of the natural quality of sympathy for others (pain at witnessing another's pain) and the habit of following rules. Since natural sympathy alone would lead us into injustices and considerations of utility alone would seem to justify exceptions to general rules, we come to agree on general principles of conduct and transfer to these principles the sentiment of approbation that we originally felt toward the happiness or release from pain usually produced by following such principles. Thus arises the sense of moral duty and the capacity for disinterested approval. Here again, Hume offers a psychological description of the motivating processes that cause us to approve of moral virtue as an answer to the question of what criteria we use to judge persons and actions to be worthy of moral approval. Once this identity of psychological motive and logical ground is presupposed, it becomes impossible to distinguish between correct and incorrect moral judgments. The question as to whether action that meets with general approbation actually merits such approbation cannot even be raised, since merit has already been identified with the mere fact of approbation.

Freedom. On the issue of free will and its relation to moral responsibility, Hume argued persuasively that responsibility presupposes the causal efficacy of threat of punishment. He developed further the arguments of Hobbes and Locke that freedom is not a quality of the will but a relation between desire, action, and environment, such that a man is free when his actions are caused by his own desires and unimpeded by external restraints, a view that William James later baptized "soft determinism."

Common-sense intuitionism. Hume's subjective account of moral judgment was countered by the common-sense intuitionism of Thomas Reid (1710–1796) and Richard Price (1723–1791), who explained the moral sense, or conscience, that enables man to distinguish right from wrong as a combination of benevolent emotion and rational intuition. Both argued, like Butler, that moral principles are not in need of utilitarian justification but are as natural to man as self-love and desire for pleasure. Reid argued that moral qualities are as directly perceived as physical properties are and thus exist in the object judged rather than in the feelings of the subject who judges. Ethics is as much a matter of objective fact as science is, except that its principles are self-evident and can be discovered by "common sense" alone, uncorrupted by bad philosophy. Reid also defended the belief in freedom of the will as the ground of moral responsibility, arguing that we are introspectively aware of our ability to choose between good and evil independently of our desires.

The French Enlightenment. Ethical thought in eighteenth-century France paralleled developments in Great Britain, although the French philosophers failed to establish as strong traditions as their British contemporaries. French thought subsequent to the eighteenth century added little to moral philosophy as compared with that of Germany and Great Britain. Due to their intense involvement in political issues, the French writers placed rhetorical effectiveness above clarity and consistency as a standard of philosophical value.

Voltaire (François Marie Arouet, 1694–1778) and Jean-Jacques Rousseau (1712–1778) led the revolt against Cartesian rationalism as well as against political and religious superstition, so transforming philosophy into ideology that *idéologue* became a popular French synonym for *philosophe*. Voltaire employed acid satire in attacking religious and philosophical obscurantism in *Candide, Zadig,* and his *Philosophical Dictionary,* while Rousseau inaugurated the romantic style of soul-stirring emotional intensity, in place of detached analysis and rigorous argument. Denis Diderot (1713–1784) raised philosophical writing to the highest level of literary grace and subtlety since Plato, criticizing conventional morality and religious beliefs in his remarkable essay-novels *Le Neveu de Rameau, Jacques le fataliste,* and *Rêve de d'Alembert.* Yet while appreciating their extraordinary intellectual qualities and the permanence of their place in Western culture, it must be noted that they provided few new concepts and principles on which later ethical philosophers could build.

Rousseau. Rousseau's celebrated exaltation of untutored human nature in his two *Discourses* attributed genial and cooperative tendencies to man's innate disposition and aggressively self-serving tendencies to the harmful influence of civilization. This coincided with the British moral-sense theorists' attacks on Hobbesian egoism. However, unlike Hume (his friend and benefactor prior to their notorious public quarrel), Rousseau considered custom and law to be arbitrary restraints on natural impulses rather than rational methods of channeling self-interest toward the common good. Whatever justification can be given for control of the individual by social institutions lay, for Rousseau, in their claim to represent the "general will," that is, the desires of the majority, independently of whether what is so desired is good. While Rousseau argued forcefully, in *The Social Contract,* for popular sovereignty and the right of revolution, he justified the use by the state of extremely repressive measures, such as the death penalty for atheism. His rather mystical notion of the state as the embodiment of the general will helped to inspire the overthrow in France of absolute monarchy in favor of representative government, yet half a century later it was employed by Fichte, and a century after that by Lenin, in the justification of authoritarianism.

Although Rousseau's religious mysticism and his preference for feeling over rational prudence were contrary to the general tone of the Enlightenment, his most lasting contribution to ethical philosophy was his insistence that good and evil tendencies are due to social causes, a principle that he shared with Montesquieu, Voltaire, and the Encylopedists. The soundness of this principle is subject to question, but there can be no doubt that it served as a useful guide in the reform of social institutions.

Montesquieu. Charles Louis de Secondat, baron de la Brède et de Montesquieu (1689–1755), in *The Spirit of the Laws* founded the relativistic conception of moral and political principles as grounded in the traditions of particular societies. The "spirit of the laws" is the system of social practices in relation to which new laws are to be evaluated. Western European governments require a division of functions and compensating checks and balances to fulfill the partly republican, partly monarchical values of European society. In treating values as historical and sociological facts, rather than as divine principles or natural laws, Montesquieu developed further the scientific approach to ethics and politics begun by Machiavelli and Hobbes.

The Encyclopedists. Denis Diderot, Claude Helvétius (1715–1771), and Baron Paul Dietrich d'Holbach (1723–1789) derived, from a materialistic theory of nature, an ethical view based on the self-centered pursuit of pleasure as the sole rational motive for action. A well-ordered society, on their view, is one in which the pursuit of personal well-being is unhindered by social authority. Insofar as there are conflicts between morality and self-interest, these are due to defects of social organization and perverse education, rather than to the moral defects of individuals. These Encyclopedists, and kindred spirits in other countries, such as the Italian legal philosopher Beccaria, employed utilitarian moral theory in political campaigns for representative government and humane laws and punishments.

Kant and the German Enlightenment. The Enlightenment attack on tradition and authority in favor of individual reason took a nonutilitarian form in the philosophy of Immanuel Kant (1724–1804). The utilitarians identified reason with practical intelligence in the pursuit of happiness. Kant, however, inherited the Cartesian and Leibnizian conception of reason as the intellectual recognition of abstract truths. In fashioning an ethical theory that became the main rival of utilitarianism, Kant combined the Augustinian emphasis, revived by Butler, Price, and Reid, on the internal sense of moral obligation with the rationalistic ideal of knowledge as a deductive system. In his *Critique of Pure Reason,* he attempted to show that the laws of science are imposed by the mind on the objects of its perceptions and can thus be known with certainty through reflection on the a priori structure of knowledge. In his *Critique of Practical Reason* he applied the same analysis to ethics, founding morality on the a priori laws with which "practical reason" regulates action. While Kant defended religious faith against the utilitarian freethinkers, he shared their view that ethics is independent of theology, and he followed the deistic tradition of interpreting God as a scientific and ethical ideal, rather than as a supernatural source of revelation and authority.

In his most influential work on ethics, *The Foundations of the Metaphysics of Morals,* Kant made the most thorough attempt by any philosopher to clarify and explain the difference between ethical principles and laws of nature. The difference lies both in our subjective sense of obligation to obey moral laws, as contrasted with laws of nature, toward which we feel no such obligation, and in the practical—that is, prescriptive—meaning of moral laws, in contrast with the "theoretical"—that is, descriptive—meaning of laws of nature. In virtue of this difference, moral rules are expressed in the imperative mood and laws of nature in the declarative mood. To account for this disparity, Kant distinguished two realms of knowledge dealing with two metaphysically distinct subject matters. Natural science, including scientific psychology, formulates laws of nature that the mind imposes on the objects of perception in accordance with the principle of causal determinism. Ethics articulates the "laws of freedom" that a rational being imposes on his own actions and expects other rational beings to recognize and obey. The justification for these rules lies in the logical fact that to be rational means to act in accordance with general rules and that moral rules are those which can be followed consistently by all rational beings. Thus, insofar as man is moral, he is rational and, in this sense, free; insofar as he is immoral, he is an irrational slave to his natural inclinations. The reward of virtue is not happiness but dignity and freedom.

Moral virtue: the supreme good. Kant's system of ethics is built on three pillars: the examination of the facts of moral experience, the analysis of the logic of ethical judgment, and the formulation of the metaphysical principles presupposed by ethical judgments, as distinct from scientific generalizations. In the first part of the *Foundations* Kant argues, like Reid, that common-sense reflection, uncorrupted by the dialectics of philosophers, informs us with unwavering certainty that duty is distinct from pleasure and utility, that moral virtue or "good will" is the supreme good to which all other values are subordinate, and that moral worth is not measured either by the consequences of a person's actions or by his natural benevolence but by the agent's intention to obey moral laws.

Categorical imperatives. In the second section of the *Foundations,* Kant attempts to explain the distinctive character of moral laws by clarifying the logical differences between three types of rules or imperatives: technical "rules of skill," prudential "counsels" as to how to achieve happiness, and moral duties. The first two, he argues, are "hypothetical imperatives" whose directives are contingent on the desires of the agent. Naturalistic ethics mistakes counsels of prudence for moral laws because the desire for happiness is so universal that directives toward this end have the superficial appearance of unconditional laws. But the generalization that all men seek happiness is a law of nature, not a rule commanding action, and the very possibility of a moral code entails that this psychological generalization is subject to exception. For moral duty requires that the agent sacrifice his personal happiness and even the welfare of his community rather than violate a "categorical imperative."

A moral or genuinely categorical imperative is a rule that commands a type of action independently of any desired end, including happiness. Kant accepts the utilitarian account of hypothetical imperatives but argues that the peculiar obligatoriness of moral principles can be explained only by their unrestricted universality and thus by their independence of any facts of human nature or circumstance. It is not in virtue of what satisfies human needs, but in virtue of the demand of reason that action be in accordance with universal law, that we feel obligated to obey moral principles.

Universalizability criterion. To the question of whether any rule of action can qualify as a moral principle, Kant's answer was in the negative. He maintained that there is one general or "fundamental" categorical imperative from which all specific moral duties can be derived: "Act only on that maxim which you can will to be a universal law." All maxims or specific rules of conduct can be judged morally right or wrong according to this general criterion. If universal obedience to a proposed rule would contradict the very purpose of the rule, as is the case for rules that under certain circumstances permit lying, stealing, or taking life (somewhat inconsistently, Kant approved of capital punishment), then the rule cannot be part of a true moral code. In contrast, a rule such as "Do not make false promises" can in principle be followed without exception and thus qualifies as a moral duty.

This criterion of universalizability, that is, the logical or psychological possibility of requiring universal obedience to a rule of action (logical for "strict" duties and psychological for "meritorious" duties), was undoubtedly Kant's most original and important contribution to ethical theory. It expresses more precisely and unambiguously the "golden rule" to be found in all the great religions, and it has been incorporated, in one form or another, in most modern systems of ethical theory. Countless writers since Kant have attempted to reformulate the criterion of universalizability in a way sufficiently qualified to avoid reasonable objections, but without complete success.

The obvious objection to Kant's formulation is that no

one would want *any* specific rule of action to be followed without exception. No one would want the truth to be told on occasions when unmitigated harm would result—for example, when a murderer demands to know where his intended victim is hiding. Kant's own reply to this objection is that, while one may not be psychologically inclined to tell the truth on such occasions, there is no logical contradiction in willing—that is, commanding—that it be told, come what may.

A second objection is that Kant assumes, for any rule of action, that either it or its negation must be a moral law, and yet there are few rules, if any, which we would care to have followed universally in either positive or negative form. Kant argues that, since it would be self-defeating to will that every person may make false promises when it suits his purposes, we ought to will that false promises never be made. Yet on the same reasoning one could justify all sorts of absurd laws, such as that everyone at all times wear heavy clothing, since we would not and could not will the universal prohibition of heavy clothing.

A third weakness of Kant's theory is that it provides no grounds for deciding what is right in a situation where apparent moral duties collide and one must be sacrificed in favor of another. With respect to this problem, utilitarianism seems clearly superior to Kantian ethics.

Autonomy of the will. The third part of Kant's ethical theory consists in the metaphysical account of the rational will as a source of action outside the sphere of causal determinism and thus not an object of scientific investigation. The autonomy of the will—that is, the capacity to obey laws of its own conception in defiance of natural causes—is, Kant argues, a necessary presupposition of any moral code. For if all actions were necessary effects of natural causes, then moral evaluation would be pointless. "Ought" implies "can," that is, the obligation to do what is right entails the ability to do it and the ability not to do it. Since science rests on the regulative principle of universal determinism, there can be no scientific proof of freedom of the will. But this only shows the radical difference between science and ethics and the folly of attempting to derive ethics from psychology. Man as an object of scientific inquiry is an organic phenomenon obeying laws of biology and psychology. But man as an object of ethical evaluation is a noumenal being, free to obey or disobey the dictates of practical reason. From this dual conception of man as both inside and outside nature, Kant derives an ideal way of life impressive in its purity and its faith in human perfectibility. Man as a rational agent is a member of a "kingdom of ends" in which he is both subject and sovereign, legislating for himself and for others. The highest goal of human life is to realize this ideal "kingdom" in individual and social practice.

NINETEENTH-CENTURY ETHICS

Nineteenth-century ethical thought became a battleground for two rival traditions. Utilitarianism, stemming from Locke, Hume, and the French Encyclopedists, dominated British and French philosophy, while idealistic ethics was supreme in Germany and Italy. Both traditions took root in the United States, with idealism appealing to the religious vision of Emerson and Royce, while utilitarianism answered to the developing faith in technology that found philosophical expression toward the end of the century in the pragmatic ethics of James and Dewey.

Utilitarianism. Christian ethics based on divine authority and natural law was given a utilitarian interpretation by William Paley (1743–1805) in his *Principles of Moral and Political Philosophy.* The source of moral obligation, he agreed with Hobbes, lies in the "violent motive resulting from the command of another," while the ground of goodness is pleasure or utility. But moral duty and self-interest coincide because God, as the paramount authority, commands us through the Scriptures and the promptings of conscience to seek the general good as well as our own happiness. Moral obligation is supported both by natural pleasure in the welfare of others and by the fear of divine punishment which provides the selfish but rational person with a good reason to sacrifice his pleasure for the common good. Paley's psychological account of morality, like that of earlier moral-sense theories, failed to explain why anyone who lacks natural benevolence ought to have it. His alternative justification of morality in terms of the fear of divine punishment equally fails to explain why such punishment would be just and why a nonbenevolent nonbeliever in Christian theology can nevertheless be expected to behave morally.

Bentham. The mainstream of utilitarian thought was anticlerical. Jeremy Bentham (1748–1832) and James Mill (1773–1836) formed a political movement that helped bring about legislative reforms by criticizing social institutions in terms of their utility in producing "the greatest happiness for the greatest number." In his influential *Introduction to the Principles of Morals and Legislation,* Bentham formulated a theory of ethics and jurisprudence remarkable for its clarity and consistency. The great appeal of Bentham's theory lay in its apparent simplicity and ease of application, although these virtues may have been more apparent than real. Bentham attempted to make ethics and politics scientifically verifiable disciplines by formulating quantitative standards of evaluation. He began with the psychological generalization that all actions are motivated by the desire for pleasure and the fear of pain: "Nature hath placed mankind under the governance of two sovereign masters, *pain* and *pleasure.* It is for them alone to point out what we ought to do, as well as to determine what we shall do. On the one hand the standard of right and wrong, on the other the chain of causes and effects, are fastened to their throne" (*Principles,* London, 1823, p. 1). From this equation between ethical obligation and psychological necessity, Bentham derived the general principle of utility which "approves or disapproves of every action whatsoever, according to the tendency which it appears to have to augment or diminish the happiness of the party whose interest is in question" (*ibid.*), happiness being understood as the predominance of pleasure over pain.

The most original but also the most dubious part of Bentham's theory is his "hedonic calculus" for measuring pleasures and pains, in computing the over-all value of alternative policies. If such a procedure were feasible, ethical judgments would be as scientific as meteorological forecasts, even though both are subject to considerable error, due to the complexity of the factors involved. But Bentham's ideal of a science of ethics runs afoul of two internal difficulties, the resistance of pleasure to measurement and the impossibility of predicting the long-range consequences of actions. Aside from these internal defects, there remains the general objection that pleasure, unlike pain, is not a bodily sensation but a favorable response to an object grounded on the perception of value in the object, as Thomas Reid had argued. To conclude that an object is good from the fact that it pleases us involves the circular reasoning that it is good because it is judged to be good, a principle too vacuous to provide a guide to ethical judgment. If, on the other hand, pleasure is understood in a more narrow, technical sense as desirable bodily sensations, then Bentham's identification of happiness and welfare with pleasure is unacceptable because it reduces human experience to the level of animal existence. The plausibility of Bentham's theory may be due to the ease with which he shifts inadvertently from one of these senses of "pleasure" to the other.

Despite its theoretical defects, Benthamite utilitarianism, which was more socially oriented than that of Locke and Hume, had a salutary effect on social legislation. His analysis of pleasures into factors of intensity, duration, propinquity, certainty, fecundity, and "extent" (number of persons affected) offered reasonable criteria by which alternative social programs and laws can be evaluated and was a marked improvement over the sanctification of existing laws and customs by which Hobbes, Locke, and Hume had made the transition from self-interest to morality. But there is a missing link in Bentham's chain of reasoning that may not be reparable within the confines of his hedonistic psychology, namely, the link that should connect the desire for one's own pleasure with the willingness to consider "extent" or pleasure of others in deciding on a course of action. Is desire for the pleasure of others also a "sovereign master under which nature hath placed us?" If so, then desire for one's own pleasure cannot be sovereign as well. If not, then on what ground are we required to consider the factor of extent?

Mill. John Stuart Mill (1806–1873) recognized the defects in Bentham's formulation of utilitarianism, and in his essay "Utilitarianism" he offered a more sophisticated version that sought to incorporate the moral insights of rival ethical systems. Realizing that Bentham's emphasis on quantitative aspects of pleasure reduces pleasure to bodily sensation and tends to justify an uncultivated mode of life, Mill proposed a new factor by which pleasures could be compared, the factor of quality. Some pleasurable experiences, notably intellectual, aesthetic, and moral achievements, are qualitatively superior to the satisfaction of bodily needs: "Better to be Socrates unsatisfied than to be a fool satisfied." But like Epicurus' preference for "natural" over "unnatural" pleasures, Mill's criterion of quality introduces a standard of value other than pleasure, by which pleasure itself can be evaluated, and thus contradicts the principle of utility, that pleasure is the single standard of good.

Mill also tried to make room in utilitarian theory for the appreciation of the saintly virtues, renunciation and self-sacrifice, by arguing along Humean lines that such virtues are originally valued for their social utility but that we later become attached to them for their own sake, and that this psychological shift from appreciation of virtue as a social instrument to admiration of virtue for itself is a good tendency because it, too, is socially useful. For the appreciation of moral qualities independently of their immediate consequences ensures the social reliability of the agent and, in the long run, produces more good than harm. This utilitarian defense of moral principles rested on an optimistic belief in the generally beneficial tendencies of man. In applying it to political theory, Mill argued for democratic institutions, minimum state interference in social life, and free economic competition. Assuming a general convergence of individual and social benefit, Mill, like Hume and Bentham, left unanswered the question why, in cases of conflict, one *ought* to place public over private interest and confined himself to explaining why we admire the person who does so. Yet if the social utility of moral self-sacrifice is the only rational ground for favorable judgment of it, then it would seem to follow that each of us has reason to approve of self-sacrifice in others but not in himself. If the step from individual happiness to the greatest good for the greatest number is justified only by the long-range coincidence of the two, then whenever we are assured that they will not coincide, we have no reason to prefer public welfare to our own other than the irrational habit of doing so, a habit which, in such case, it would be wise to break. In Kantian terms, utilitarianism, even in Mill's sophisticated version, fails to provide a logical bridge between inclination and obligation, between "is" and "ought."

Later intuitionists, beginning with Henry Sidgwick (1838–1900), attempted to supply this bridge by combining the Kantian theory of rational duty with the utilitarian theory of value, maintaining that we are intuitively aware of the duty to obey moral principles at the expense of self-interest but that moral principles, in turn, are justified by their utility in promoting the common good.

Idealist ethics. Kant's distinction between man as noumenon, legislating and obeying "laws of freedom," and man as phenomenon, governed by laws of nature, was incorporated into new ethical systems by later German idealists, who assimilated the phenomenal side of the distinction to a part of the noumenal side, making natural science subordinate to ethics. Johann Gottlieb Fichte (1762–1814) extended the noumenal will into a universal force that creates the material world out of its own force and expresses itself partially in the free rational will of the individual conscience but more fully in social institutions and laws. The individual thus achieves self-realization in identifying himself with the universal will and voluntarily accepting his *Beruf* (vocation) as part of the social order.

Fichte. In his early work *Wissenschaftslehre* (*Theory of Science*, 1794) Fichte enlarged Kant's ethical concept of man into a metaphysical picture of the universe. Rejecting Kant's notion of things-in-themselves, Fichte reduced reality to the projections of an absolute mind, and he reduced mind itself to will. The criterion of reality became a practical one: that is real which it is right or good to believe and to act upon (the beginning of pragmatism).

Fichte went even further than Kant in stressing moral duty as the goal of life. Kant had sharply separated duty from self-interest in criticizing positions of the kind later referred to as utilitarianism, but Fichte moved full circle by reidentifying moral duty with a higher form of self-interest, the self-realization of an absolute will of which each person is a temporary embodiment. The logical problem created by Fichte's voluntaristic idealism is caused by the fact that it begins with Kant's primacy of moral good over prudential good but concludes with a form of supernatural utilitarianism in which prudential good of a higher self reappears as the ground of morality.

Fichte explained the function of the state as the regulation of conflicts among individuals in protection of their natural rights, and on this basis he supported democratic government. But he advanced the view, later elaborated by Hegel, that governmental restraints on individual action are not limitations of personal freedom but expressions of the higher freedom of the absolute will.

In *The Vocation of Man* (1800) Fichte, who had been accused of atheism, developed a less rationalistic and more religious view of human life. He identified the absolute will with the personal God of Christianity and moral duty with the vocation imposed on man by God. In his later *Addresses to the German Nation* (1808) he applied his notion of divinely ordained vocation to the German nation, which he claimed was destined to raise civilization to a higher level. The evolution of Fichte's thought from austere moralism to religious mysticism and then to chauvinistic nationalism provides an instructive example of the lengths to which thought can go in denying the basic distinctions from which it begins, such as that between self-interest and moral duty or between individual rights and social restraints.

Hegel. G. W. F. Hegel (1770–1831) developed Fichte's social basis of ethics further and in more historical terms. For Hegel value, morality, and law are among the highest forms of self-realization of absolute spirit. The Enlightenment doctrine of abstract rights is only the first stage in the development of ethical consciousness. A higher stage is reached in the Kantian sense of moral duty, which recognizes the conflict between individual rights and social responsibilities, subordinating the former to the latter. But the highest stage of self-realization of "objective mind" involves the incorporation of rights and duties in a rational system of social and political institutions which the individual citizen recognizes as the embodiment of the national will. The perfect freedom that consists in rational self-determination is achieved when individual conscience coincides with custom and law, so that will and reason, subjective motivation and objective necessity, become identical. But this is possible, according to Hegel, only in the modern age of the national state, Christian conscience, and constitutional law. In earlier stages of human history, whatever was necessary for historical progress was, for that age, necessary and therefore right, as, for example, the institution of slavery was necessary and right in ancient Greece. "World history," he declared, "is world justice."

Post-Hegelian theories. The impact of Darwin's theory of natural evolution produced naturalistic echoes of Hegelian historical relativism in the utilitarian "survival of the fittest" doctrine of Herbert Spencer (1820–1903), the

Marxist philosophy of class conflict, and the cultural elitism of Nietzsche.

Marx. Karl Marx (1818–1883) transformed Hegel's theory of the dialectical self-realization of mind into a doctrine of dialectical development of history through class conflict. In the Marxist theory, moral principles represent the sanctification of the interests of the ruling class at each stage in the development of progressively superior modes of economic organization. Marx criticized both utilitarian and Kantian ethics as variant expressions of bourgeois market-place procedures. Subordinating rules of individual conduct to the historical imperatives of "revolutionary praxis," the *Communist Manifesto* of Marx and Engels called for revolutionary action to achieve a classless society in which "the free development of each is the condition for the free development of all," a society that would require neither the internal repressions of conscience nor the external repessions of laws and punishments. Both morality and the state would "wither away."

Schopenhauer. Arthur Schopenhauer (1788–1860), like Fichte, located the source of both egoistic pursuit of pleasure and moral obligation in the universal will. The morality of equal rights for all represents a higher development of consciousness than that of self-interest, but a still higher stage is reached in the philosophical understanding that the will, in any form, produces illusion and suffering and that the extinction of desire is the only salvation. Schopenhauer gave the Stoic and Buddhist ethic of ascetic renunciation an idealistic metaphysical basis.

Kierkegaard. Søren Kierkegaard (1813–1855) rejected the rationalistic and socially oriented ethic of Hegel in favor of religious individualism. While, like Hegel, he regarded the conflict between self-interest (the "aesthetic attitude") and duty (the "ethical attitude") as reconciled and transcended in a higher stage of consciousness, he denied that this stage could be achieved by reason and described it as a "leap of faith" preceded by tragic anguish. As the contemporary existentialists who have rediscovered Kierkegaard have put it, "The world is absurd" because there are no objective grounds for human decisions. What is right, according to Kierkegaard, is what the individual asserts with the total commitment born of faith, but it is right only for him. Emotional authenticity rather than conformity to rules is the proper guide to action.

Nietzsche. Friedrich Nietzsche (1844–1900) proposed a less mystical but equally individualistic transcendence of moral codes. Like Hobbes and Mandeville, he regarded altruism as contrary to natural impulse and denounced moral restraint as a device created by religion to contravene the natural order of dominance of the strong over the weak. The true source of value lies in the creative self-assertion of the artist and the man of genius who produce new and positive forms of good, while moral prohibitions produce only resentment, envy, and dull conformity.

American developments. In the United States, the transcendentalists, led by Ralph Waldo Emerson (1803–1882) and the pragmatic idealist Josiah Royce (1855–1916), fashioned still other variations on the idealist theme of self-realization as the goal of human life. The transcendentalists identified the self with the creative force of nature, the "oversoul." Royce, following Hegel, defined the fully realized self as a unity of personal and community interests. All of these post-Hegelian philosophies rejected the Kantian morality of strict adherence to general rules of conduct and proposed ways of transcending the conflict between duty and self-interest through a higher mode of consciousness in which the conflict allegedly disappears.

Toward the end of the nineteenth century, William James and John Dewey developed the philosophy of pragmatism, in which all of human knowledge is regarded as essentially ethical. They rejected both the Kantian separation of ethics from natural science and the traditional conception of scientific knowledge as disinterested contemplation of value-neutral truths. The split between value and fact was bridged by reinterpreting both so that they became indistinguishable. James (1842–1910) combined utilitarianism with a creative individualism similar to that of Nietzsche and the prescriptivism of Hobbes, by identifying the source of value with the human act of making a claim, thus bestowing value on the object claimed. Ethical judgment is a rational process of determining by empirical investigation which policies are likely to satisfy the maximum number of such claims. James defended the indeterminist concept of free will, criticizing what he called the soft determinism of Hume and Mill as a purely verbal escape from the embarrassing consequences of scientific determinism.

British idealism and intuitionism. In the last quarter of the nineteenth century the vitality of idealism began to attract even the sober British intellect, and the ethics of self-realization became a powerful rival to utilitarianism through the influence of Green, Bosanquet, and Bradley.

Green. Thomas Hill Green (1836–1882) introduced Oxford students to the lofty vision of idealist metaphysics. In his *Prolegomena to Ethics* (published posthumously) Green derived liberal ethical and political principles from his conception of the individual self as part of a universal and divine self. He criticized both utilitarianism and moral-sense theories for downgrading the role of reason in moral judgment and for reducing human motives to natural causes. A motive, he argued, is a goal previsioned by a rational consciousness, not an event or process in the body. Value is therefore logically prior to desire rather than a product of desire. One can desire or find pleasure only in what one has judged to be good. The source of evil must therefore be found in defects of the understanding, in the failure of the human mind to realize its identity with the universal mind. The highest good is thus as much an object of self-interest as any other, but it is the kind of self-interest that also constitutes morality.

Green was active in social and political controversies, supporting the North in the American Civil War and supporting liberal legislation in England. Green rejected laissez-faire individualism, insisting on the more positive role of government in promoting social welfare.

Green's ethical theory was sharply criticized by Henry Sidgwick in *The Ethics of Green, Spencer and Martineau* (1902). Sidgwick argued that Green's identification of morality with higher self-interest obliterates the all-important distinction between prudence and duty and thus fails to provide a basis for moral responsibility, a defect that, as we have seen, goes all the way back to Plato.

Bosanquet. Bernard Bosanquet (1848–1923), like Green, grounded ethics and politics on idealist metaphysics. Bo-

sanquet stressed somewhat more than Green the uniqueness of individual values while at the same time taking a Hegelian view of the state as the embodiment of objective mind. Like Green, Bosanquet actively supported liberal political causes.

Bradley. Francis H. Bradley (1846–1924), generally considered the most distinguished ethical theorist among the British idealists, criticized both utilitarianism and Kantian formalism and favored a Hegelian conception of the community as an organic unity whose needs, expressed in social institutions, transcend those of individual citizens, a conception which he applied in the defense of conservative social policies. Bradley was probably more consistent than Green and Bosanquet. If law and custom are the expression of a higher self, then only internal inconsistencies can justify reforms, and individual rights are subordinate to group or national interests. In his *Ethical Studies* (1876) Bradley supported retributive punishment on the ground (which he held to be self-evident to common sense) that punishment is unfair unless it is deserved and that moral desert is independent of social utility. He attempted to reconcile freedom with causal determinism in the notion of an all-encompassing Reality that determines itself in accordance with rational laws. Recognizing that idealism faces the problem of accounting for evil and that its traditional solution—claiming that evil does not exist—is contrary to the judgment of common sense on which Bradley himself always relied, he employed a subtle distinction between existence and reality in holding that evil, though it exists, is unreal. From the standpoint of the totality of knowledge, evil may be seen to contribute to cosmic harmony. This "solution" was later castigated by Bertrand Russell as a morally untenable justification of evil.

Sidgwick. Henry Sidgwick (1838–1900) combined the social utilitarianism of Mill with the intuitionism of Butler and Kant. In *The Methods of Ethics* (1875), a work described by C. D. Broad as "the best treatise on Moral Philosophy that has ever been written," Sidgwick raised ethical analysis to a new level of precision and logical rigor. Setting aside practical moralizing as not the business of objective philosophical analysis, Sidgwick interpreted the task of moral philosophy to be the clarification of the logic of moral judgment, a conception of philosophy that was continued by the contemporary British school of linguistic analysis.

Sidgwick held that there are just three approaches to ethics worth philosophical consideration: egoistic hedonism, utilitarianism, and intuitionism. He pointed out that neither the self-centered ethics of Hobbes and the French Encyclopedists nor the socially oriented ethics of Bentham and Mill can justify the step from psychology to ethics, that is, from the description of human motivation to judgments of moral obligation. Even those who declare that one ought to pursue one's own interests must justify their use of "ought," and this cannot be done on the grounds of psychological facts alone. Sidgwick therefore insisted on distinguishing psychological hedonism from ethical hedonism and grounding the latter on intuition. His argument is reminiscent of Hume's claim that values cannot be deduced from facts, and it anticipates G. E. Moore's later analysis of the "naturalistic fallacy."

All three "methods of ethics" rest, according to Sidgwick, on principles held to be self-evident, and thus intuitionism is, to some extent, inescapable. The egoist must assume the self-evident rightness of pursuing one's own pleasure, and the social utilitarian must assume the rightness of maximizing the common good. Intuitionists differ from utilitarians and egoists only in holding many principles and duties to be self-evident as well, and thus they expose themselves to inevitable counterinstances. The more numerous and specific the rules claimed to be self-evident, the more subject to exception and vulnerable to disproof. Sidgwick concludes that social utilitarianism offers the correct standard of moral judgment but that this standard is in turn grounded on direct awareness of moral obligation. Thus at least one, and probably at most one, moral intuition is essential for moral judgment.

Sidgwick could not finally decide between the conflicting claims of self-interest and social utility. He leaned toward the latter as definitive of moral duty, but he recognized that one's self-interest rightly carries a special weight, other things being equal. Perhaps he would have been able to reconcile these two "intuitions" more easily had he considered utilitarianism in a somewhat weaker form, as the principle that one ought always to refrain from causing unnecessary suffering, rather than the stronger claim that one ought always to aim at maximizing happiness. For while one's own welfare seems naturally to outweigh that of others, it is very close to being self-evident to any morally sensitive person that he ought not to pursue his interests at the cost of substantial suffering to others.

It would appear from our brief glance over the history of ethics through the nineteenth century that philosophers failed to find any conclusive ethical truths and merely argued, more persuasively and with a more impressive display of learning than most, for whatever way of life and standards of conduct they happened to prefer. In some respects this impression would be justified, and it serves to remind us of the differences between scientific knowledge and ethical wisdom. The perennial character of the problems, the lack of general agreement on proposed solutions, and the return of later doctrines to principles advanced by earlier ones all contrast strikingly with the irreversible progress of scientific discovery. It has been suggested by some contemporary philosophers that the endless disputability of ethical issues is rooted in the very nature of ethical language, so that it is not a defect of philosophy to have failed to achieve general agreement on ethics. As W. B. Gallie has put it (*Philosophy and the Historical Understanding*, New York, 1964), ethical concepts are "essentially contestable." It is essential to their meaning that they evoke continual disputes as to the correct standards for their application. But if we cannot find historical progress in the form of final settlement of issues, we can at least discern some degree of gradual, if irregular, advance toward greater clarity in the formulation of the issues.

On the central issue of the logical relation between facts and values, ethical theories have provided increasingly clear and sophisticated statements of two fundamental positions, naturalism and nonnaturalism (sometimes called teleology and deontology). Naturalistic theories relate values to facts by defining "good" and related concepts in terms of observable criteria, such as fulfillment of natural tendencies (Aristotle), satisfaction of desire (Hobbes and Spinoza), production of pleasure for the greatest number (utilitarianism), conduciveness to historical progress (Spencer and Marx), or efficiency of means to ends (Dewey). Nonnaturalistic theories stress the fact that the meaning of ethical terms goes beyond the observable facts on which ethical judgments are grounded, and they locate the additional component of meaning outside nature. Plato located it in a realm of abstract Forms, Christianity in the will of God, the intuitionists in the direct recognition of the quality of rightness, the moral-sense theorists in the feeling of approbation. Each of these accounts of value and moral right has revealed an additional dimension of the complex logic of ethical judgment. Naturalistic theories have brought to light various ways in which ethical judgment is grounded on the fulfillment of biological and social needs, while nonnaturalistic theories have revealed prescriptive aspects of moral concepts that are independent of prudential considerations. The main effort of twentieth-century ethical philosophy has been to weave together in a consistent pattern all the threads, both naturalistic and nonnaturalistic, that constitute our philosophical heritage.

CONTEMPORARY NONNATURALISM

In much of the English-speaking world G. E. Moore's *Principia Ethica* (Cambridge, 1903) is taken to be the starting point of contemporary ethical theory. But it is important to recognize that this primacy is to a considerable degree local and distinctive of the tradition of analytical ethics. On the Continent and in Latin America the work of Max Scheler and Franz Brentano has been a preeminent influence. For much of American thought until fairly recently, the work of John Dewey or Ralph Barton Perry provided the starting point. But, for all that, it is reasonable to begin with G. E. Moore.

Moore. It is the critical side of Moore's work in ethics that has had the most lasting effect. His delineation of the subject matter of ethics and his very careful effort to show that any form of ethical naturalism involves a fundamental conceptual mistake—the work of the first three chapters of *Principia Ethica*—has been the part of Moore's work that has deeply affected contemporary ethical thought. However, Moore's own positive nonnaturalistic cognitivism, with its reliance on nonnatural characteristics, has found few adherents. Most philosophers—C. L. Stevenson and R. M. Hare are typical—who have been convinced that in essence Moore's case against naturalism is sound have not followed Moore's lead but have adopted some form of noncognitivism.

It was Moore's belief that if moral philosophers simply interest themselves in good conduct, they are not really starting at the beginning, for we cannot know what good conduct is until we know what goodness is. Moore's concern was with a "general enquiry into what is good." Our first question must be "What is good and what is bad?" Such knowledge of good and evil, Moore claims, is the "goal of ethical investigation"; but, he stresses, "it cannot be safely attempted at the beginning of our studies, but only at the end." First we must consider how "good" is to be defined.

Moore clearly is not interested in giving a stipulative definition of "good," and from his disclaimers in *Principia Ethica* about being interested in a merely verbal point, it would seem that he is not interested in a lexical definition either. What he is after, in seeking a definition of "good," is just this: what property or set of properties is common to and distinctive of anything that could conceivably be properly called intrinsically good, for instance, "answering to interests." Moore thinks "good" stands for a property, and he seeks to determine what it is. Moore's answer, which he is aware will cause discontent, is that "good" is not definable. All we can finally say correctly is that good is good and not anything else. "Good," like "red," is, in the appropriate sense, indefinable. Good is a simple, unanalyzable, nonnatural characteristic. We are either directly aware of it or we are not, but there is no way of defining it or analyzing it so as to make it intelligible to someone who is not directly aware of it.

Such a radical claim on Moore's part would have little force if he could not thoroughly refute naturalistic and metaphysical theories which do purport to give the kind of characterization of intrinsic goodness that he takes to be impossible.

Moore's case against naturalism. Let us consider Moore's case against ethical naturalism. An ethical naturalist holds that moral judgments are true or false empirical statements ascribing an empirical property or set of properties to an action, object, or person. "Good" is defined in terms of this property or set of properties. But, Moore argues, we will *not* come to know what good is simply by "discovering what are those other properties belonging to all things which are good." Those who commit what Moore calls the naturalistic fallacy think that when they have "named those other properties they were actually defining good; that these properties, in fact, were simply not 'other,' but absolutely and entirely the same with goodness." But to identify good with any other property is to commit the naturalistic fallacy. The naturalists confuse the question of the meaning of the concept of good with the quite different question of what kinds of things are good.

In a famous argument, which has been dubbed the open-question argument, Moore points out that for whatever naturalistic value we substitute for the variable *x* in a proposed definition of "good," we can always significantly ask if it is good. If a man says "Happiness is good," or "Self-realization is good," or "The object of any interest is good," we can always significantly ask "Is happiness good?," "Is self-realization good?," "Is the object of any interest good?" Even though we agree, let us say, that happiness is good, it is an evident fact of language that these questions are not without significance. But they would be without significance if "good" did *mean* "happiness," or "self-realization," or "the object of any interest," just as it is pointless to ask if a father is a male parent or a puppy is a young dog. For whatever naturalistic definitions we offer—whatever naturalistic values replace the variable *x*—it always makes sense to ask if that thing is good. Since this is so, these naturalistic definitions can be seen to be inadequate.

This can be seen in another way as well. If a statement like "The satisfaction of desire is good" were a definition of the sort Moore was searching for, it would be analytic and it would be self-contradictory to assert "This satisfies desire but it is not good." For whatever naturalistic definition one proposes, however, one can assert without self-contradiction "This is *x* but it is not good," but if *x* meant the same as "good" this would be impossible, for "*X* is good" would then be analytic. But since this is possible it is clear that the proposed statement is synthetic.

Moore's influence. The above arguments of Moore's, together with his famous argument in Chapter 3 of *Principia Ethica* against Mill's alleged naturalism, have provided the background for much of the controversy in contemporary ethical theory. While few have accepted all the details of Moore's case against ethical naturalism, it has been felt by many that Moore's essential case is well taken. R. M. Hare in his *The Language of Morals* (Oxford, 1952), P. H. Nowell-Smith in his *Ethics* (Harmondsworth, 1954), and A. C. Ewing in his *Second Thoughts in Moral Philosophy* (London, 1959) try to restate these Moorean insights in such a way as to present a decisive case against ethical naturalism.

It should be noted, however, that the reception of Moore's case against naturalism, even on the part of such eminent nonnaturalists as A. N. Prior and E. W. Hall, has not been that favorable. It is generally thought now that (1) the naturalistic fallacy is not, strictly speaking, a fallacy but is at best a mistake and (2) that it is not really distinctive of naturalism but should be called the definist fallacy, that is, the belief that moral terms are capable of definition in nonmoral terms.

Criticisms of Moore. It is easy to see that someone, though at a certain price, could be a consistent ethical naturalist and that Moore's naturalistic fallacy would not really point to anything necessarily fallacious in such a naturalist's reasoning. An ethical naturalist who is also a hedonist could argue: By "intrinsic good" I am just going to mean "pleasure." This is a stipulative definition on my part and I am making no claim that it squares with ordinary usage, but it will give a clear and consistent definition of "good" that fits well with my preanalytic insight that pleasure and pleasure alone is intrinsically good. It is indeed true that on my theory "Pleasure is good" is a tautology and "Is pleasure intrinsically good?" is a self-answering question. Still, there is a normatively vital question that I can and do ask with perfect conceptual propriety. The vital open question is this: Should an individual seek pleasure and only pleasure as the thing that, morally speaking, he ought always to do? If a man takes this position, Moore's arguments, given above, do not show anything fallacious in his thinking, that is, he has committed no formal or informal fallacy, though it can be shown by some additions to Moore's arguments that he has said something that is mistaken.

There is a further criticism of Moore that can be made with considerable plausibility. Though it is indeed true that "good" taken in isolation cannot be defined, the term "good" is in reality always used in specific contexts, with context-dependent meanings and with such riders as "good at" and "good for." But in such a context "good" can be defined. "A good car," "good teacher," "good at ballet," or even "good man" can be naturalistically defined, even though "good" *sans phrase* cannot. Finally, and perhaps most importantly, it has been pointed out that the open-question and noncontradiction arguments are not conclusive. At best they show why all the naturalistic definitions hitherto proposed do not work. They do not show that naturalistic definitions are impossible.

Deontological nonnaturalists. There are other nonnaturalists who, while holding cognitive metaethical theories, reject Moore's ideal utilitarianism. Moore thought that Bentham and Mill were mistaken in trying to define "good" naturalistically, but that they were not mistaken in regarding good as the fundamental moral concept and were not mistaken in arguing that it is always our duty to seek to bring the greatest total good possible into being. H. A. Prichard, W. D. Ross, E. F. Carritt, and C. D. Broad all agree with Moore that intrinsic good is a unique, nonnatural quality that is indefinable and can only be known directly. But they reject Moore's claim that "right" means "productive of the greatest possible good." "Right," they argue, is also *sui generis;* it is not reducible to "good" or to any teleological concept. To say "This is a right act" means, according to Ross, "This act ought to be done." Furthermore, even what *makes* an act right is not to be completely determined by teleological concepts. An act, even though it may be productive, everything considered, of the best consequences, may still not be the right thing to do. Even Broad, who makes the most concessions to the utilitarians of any of the deontologists (as they are called), argues that in determining what is suitable to the actual situation, we must consider both the total fittingness of the events that are relevant to the act in question and the utilities in question, and then without any precise measure of what is suitable to the situation, we must decide what we are to do. The utilitarians, including Moore, the deontologists agree, oversimplify the situation here.

In 1909 H. A. Prichard, in his celebrated article "Does Moral Philosophy Rest on a Mistake?," set forth in perceptive but uncompromising form the deontological position. But it is W. D. Ross, taking Prichard's position as a starting point, who has been the most influential of these deontological nonnaturalists. Ross's *The Right and the Good* (Oxford, 1930) and his *Foundations of Ethics* (Oxford, 1939) present the classical statement of these views.

Prichard. In "Does Moral Philosophy Rest on a Mistake?" Prichard argued that it was an endemic mistake of moral philosophy to try to give reasons for our obligations. Moral obligation cannot be reduced to acts which ought to be done because by doing them, more good is likely to result than by doing any alternative act. We do not, Prichard contended, come to appreciate an obligation by argument, but in a particular situation we are either directly aware of what it is we ought to do or we are not. Moral philosophy cannot justify these obligations; it can only (1) help us to come to understand the nature of this immediate type of awareness and (2) help us to see through the confused attempts to exhibit the "truly rational foundations" of these obligations by showing how they are grounded in human interests.

Ross. Ross accepted the Prichardian belief that we have an intuitive insight into our obligations, but he went on from certain hints in Prichard to develop a concept of prima-facie duty. A prima-facie duty is a conditional duty of a very distinctive kind. What is meant by saying that it is "conditional" is that it is something which always would be an actual duty were it not for the fact that in certain circumstances there are more stringent moral considerations that outweigh it. But prima-facie duties are always actual duties unless such conditions obtain. Ross takes it as "self-evident that a promise, simply as such, is something that prima facie ought to be kept, and it does not, on reflection, seem self-evident that production of the maximum good is the only thing that makes an act obligatory." Like Cook Wilson and Prichard before him, Ross takes as his data "the moral convictions of thoughtful and well-educated people." They serve as his point of departure and his check on all theorizing concerning morals.

Reasoning from this base, Ross can show that we do not always reason as utilitarian moralists would have us reason. We often have duties of special obligation that conflict with the utilitarian principle that we should always maximize good. If we carefully attend to the data of ethics—our actual moral experiences—we will note that we have prima-facie duties to fidelity, reparation, gratitude, justice, beneficence, nonmaleficence, and self-improvement. Some of these prima-facie duties are more binding than others. *Ceteris paribus*, the duty of nonmaleficence outweighs our obligation to keep a promise. But Ross stresses—as does Broad—that it is not always the case that we have a rule, a general principle, for deciding what to do when there is a conflict in prima-facie duties. Sometimes we simply have to appreciate or come to "see" what is suitable to the situation.

Criticisms of deontology. Many, though by no means all, philosophers would agree that the deontologists have shown that moral reasoning is not as simple as the classical utilitarians took it to be. But it has been thought by many that consequences play a far larger role in determining what makes an act right than the deontologists have been willing to admit. Their rather antiquated epistemology of intuitions, synthetic a priori judgments, and so forth, and their misleading use of mathematical analogies have stood in the way of an acceptance of deontology. It is, however, quite feasible to argue that such appeals are not essential to a deontological view.

It has also been repeatedly argued that a deontological position, with its list of prima-facie duties and its appeal to the convictions of the thoughtful and the well-educated, is thoroughly ethnocentric. To these objections it is reasonable to reply that most of Ross's prima-facie duties are very similar to the kind of generalities that the anthropologists Ralph Linton and Robert Redfield (among others) have claimed to be cross-culturally sanctioned "universal values." Moreover, the appeal to thoughtful and well-educated people surely need not and should not limit itself to people in one cultural circle.

Rather more important criticisms of deontology have been that it gives us no criteria for deciding what laws, practices, rules, or institutions are worthy of our acceptance. Here the kind of quasi-utilitarian reasoning concerning practices characteristic of the good-reasons approach seems to have decided advantage.

Ewing. It should be mentioned that A. C. Ewing in two closely reasoned books, *The Definition of Good* (New

York, 1947) and *Second Thoughts in Moral Philosophy* (London, 1959), works out a theory that in many respects tries to find a middle ground between Moore and Ross. Ewing takes "ought" as his fundamental term, and in the second work he makes far more concessions to the naturalists and noncognitivists than in the first, without abandoning what he takes to be the core of his nonnaturalism.

Phenomenological views. Moore, Ross, Broad, and Ewing are not the only nonnaturalists and intuitionists who have exerted a considerable influence on contemporary ethical thought. During a roughly comparable period, Franz Brentano, Nicolai Hartmann, and Max Scheler had a comparable influence on the Continent.

It is necessary to mention that in contemporary philosophical thought there is a fundamental cleavage that divides the English-speaking and Scandinavian countries, on the one hand, from the Continent, Latin America, and the Near East and Far East, on the other. In these latter areas of the world the influence, either direct or indirect, of the philosophers so far discussed has been slight, while the influence in intellectual circles of the philosophers to be discussed in this section and in the section on existentialism has been considerable. Even though Moore, Ross, and Ewing opposed empiricism, their techniques remained analytical, while the work of the philosophers about to be discussed is philosophy in the grand manner; that is, it is comparatively speculative and metaphysical.

Brentano. Franz Brentano's *The Origin of Our Knowledge of Right and Wrong* (Leipzig, 1889) and his later *Grundlegung und Aufbau der Ethik* (F. Mayer-Hillebrand, ed., Bern, 1952) mark the beginning of contemporary Continental ethical theory. In 1903 G. E. Moore remarked that Brentano's work more closely resembled his own than that of any writer with whom he was acquainted. Like Moore, Brentano rejected naturalistic definitions of ethical terms, regarded fundamental moral concepts as *sui generis,* and thought judgments of intrinsic value incapable of being proved.

To gain an adequate understanding of Brentano's ethical theory, it is essential to understand the rudiments of what he called descriptive psychology (the latter, in Husserl's hands, was to become phenomenology). Brentano classified mental phenomena into three fundamental classes: ideas and sensory presentations (images and the like), judgments, and emotions. That is to say, there are three fundamental ways in which one may be intentionally related to something. One may simply think of it, one may take an intellectual stance toward it by either accepting or rejecting it, or one may take an emotional or attitudinal posture toward it. To do the last is a matter of loving or hating it. (Brentano, of course, uses "love" and "hate" here in a very stretched manner.) Brentano regarded emotions as intentional; he maintained that "certain feelings refer unmistakably to objects and language itself signifies this through expressions which make use of it." Moreover, emotions, like judgments but unlike ideas, can properly be called either correct or incorrect. In this way Brentano differed radically from the emotivists.

How do we decide whether a given emotion is correct or incorrect? Here Brentano, who like Ross was a careful student of Aristotle, was very Aristotelian. We can come to understand what a correct emotion or, for that matter, a correct judgment is only by contrasting actual cases of emotions and judgments taken to be correct by experienced and thoughtful people with cases that are not so regarded.

To say that something is good—where we are talking about "intrinsic good"—is to say that it is impossible to love it incorrectly. To say that something is intrinsically evil is to say that it is impossible correctly to love whatever is in question. "Good" and "evil" are what Brentano called synsemantic terms: they do not refer to concrete particular things, either physical or mental. But such ethical concepts were, on Brentano's view, objective because of the impossibility of loving correctly whatever is hated correctly and of hating correctly whatever is loved correctly. The truth of these fundamental moral judgments is directly evident to the mature moral agent. Any question about the empirical evidence for them is as impossible as it is unnecessary.

Scheler. Max Scheler attempted to apply Husserl's phenomenological method to moral concepts. His major works in ethics, *Formalism in Ethics and the Ethics of Intrinsic Value* (Halle, 1916) and *The Nature of Sympathy* (Bonn, 1923), are among his earlier writings (*The Nature of Sympathy* is simply a second and enlarged edition of the early *Zur Phänomenologie und Theorie der Sympathiegefühle,* Halle, 1913); but his later work in philosophical anthropology, *The Forms of Knowledge and Society* (Leipzig, 1926), also has important implications for his ethical theory.

Scheler's ethics is best understood by setting it in relation to that of Kant. Scheler accepted Kant's critique of naturalistic and utilitarian ethical theories. But while he took the categorical imperative as pointing to an essential feature of morality, he thought that such Kantian formalism was incomplete. Like Husserl, Scheler believed that Kant was mistaken in limiting the a priori to the purely formal. The phenomenological method shows that we have a *Wesensschau* (an intuition of essences) in virtue of which we know certain fundamental a priori but nevertheless nonformal moral truths, such as "Spiritual values have a higher place in the scale of values than vital values, and the Holy a higher place than the spiritual."

Given this very extended sense of "a priori," it is correct to say, according to Scheler, that there are objective nonformal moral judgments which are universal, necessary, and synthetic. These moral judgments are said to have an intrinsic content that is given in our intuition of essences.

Scheler argued that there is a hierarchy of objective values, all open to our intuitive inspection. There is, he would argue, nothing subjective about this ordering. In the hierarchy of values phenomenologically given to man, we have at the top religious values, then cultural values (aesthetic, speculative, scientific, and political), and finally, at the bottom, material values (useful things, things that satisfy needs, desires, etc.). All of these values are thought to have an ethical dimension. Questions concerning moral obligation arise when there is a conflict of values. Moral obligation is that which binds us, in such a situation, to take as the order of our incentives the values as they are ordered in the value hierarchy. Scheler was, however, sufficiently Kantian to believe that the ultimate ground of moral obligation lay not in the consequences of moral acts but in the intentions of moral agents. To someone who has studied Mill, Sidgwick, or Ross, this seems like a plain confusion between the moral "grades" we would give a person and an objective consideration of what acts are morally right.

There is another aspect of Scheler's moral theory that should be mentioned, namely, his claim that love and sympathy are the sole means by which we gain an intuitive insight into moral reality. Like Brentano, he thought that these feelings had intentional objects, and like Pascal, he thought that there was a "logic of the heart"—that through the feelings we gain a type of cognition into essential value structures that can be had in no other way.

Hartmann. Nicolai Hartmann's massive work *Ethics* was published in Berlin in 1926. It shows the influence of Scheler and Husserl and is without doubt the most extensive phenomenological discussion of value in the literature. Ethics, for Hartmann, is part of a general theory of value, though, as might be expected, ethical values are the highest values. "Value" for Hartmann, as for Scheler, is a general predicate, and under it there are more specific predicates for determinate values, for instance, "beauty" is to "value" as "red" is to "colored." Values are said to be essences, and we have a direct though emotionally tinged intuition of essences. Being essences, values, like numbers, are thought by Hartmann to have an ideal self-existence (*Ansichsein*). But unlike numbers, values have a "material essence."

Like Scheler, Hartmann believes that if we will but attend patiently to our feelings, we will be able to discern, though vaguely, some hierarchical ordering of those things which are valuable. Putting aside as far as possible our theoretical preconceptions concerning values, we should reflect carefully on our actual experience until we achieve a clear and evident insight into value phenomena. This, of course, is a desideratum that will never be completely achieved, for "morally no age entirely comprehends itself." The real ethical life is "a life deeper than consciousness." But there is a capacity on the part of the human animal to appreciate the valuable, and by ever more carefully attending to this, we can attain both a clearer view and a more purified form of the moral life.

Though values are material essences, they are not, as in Plato, identical with being. Hartmann, no more than Moore or Sartre, will identify what is good or what has worth with what exists. That would destroy the autonomy of ethics and obscure the nature of value. But although values are independent of existence, they are related to existence by a "tendency to reality" which Hartmann calls the ideal Ought-to-Be. We have many different values, but it always remains the case that values ought to be. The criteria for what is good or for what is valuable vary from context to context, but the ought-to-be remains the same: "The ideal Ought-to-Be is the formal condition of value, the value is the material condition of the Ought-to-Be." In contrast with the ideal Ought-to-Be there is the more practical, more directly morally relevant "Ought-to-Do." Here "ought" implies "can," and here practical moral questions arise about making something the case that is not the case.

Recent developments in Germany. Finally, a brief note is in order about more recent developments in ethics among German philosophers. Heidegger, whose influence is completely overshadowing in Germany, took a dim view not only of the relevance of logic to philosophy but also of philosophical ethics. This has impeded systematic work in ethics in Germany, but nonetheless it is going on. There has been a reaction against the work of Scheler and Hartmann. O. F. Bollnow has argued for a *Situationsethik* and Richard Schattländer has contended that the Scheler–Hartmann approach is too speculative and theoretical and does not adequately handle the moral agent's question: what ought I to do? But the Scheler–Hartmann school is hardly dead, for Hans Reiner, in his *Das Prinzip von Gut und Böse* (Freiburg, 1949), gives us a detailed and vigorous restatement of such a position. Against Heidegger, he defends the philosophical importance of a general theory of value. But in an effort to blunt Heidegger's criticism that such investigations are morally and humanly irrelevant, Reiner concerns himself primarily with moral values. In his concern with moral value, he examines in some detail the problem of ethical relativism, and in this examination he stresses the importance of anthropological investigations to our understanding of morality.

NATURALISM IN AMERICA

While ethical naturalism seemed to have received its quietus in England from Moore and Ross and certainly could not be considered a major force on the Continent, in America in various forms it was, until shortly after World War II, the dominant form of ethical theory.

Perry. R. B. Perry developed a general theory of value with specific applications to questions of normative ethics, law, politics, economics, and education in his *General Theory of Value* (Cambridge, Mass., 1926) and *Realms of Value* (Cambridge, Mass., 1954). "Value" is used by Perry in a very broad sense as a generic term to group together such terms as "desirable," "good," "worthwhile," "right," "beautiful," "holy," "obligatory," and the like. Perry defines "value" as follows: "a thing—anything—has value, or is valuable, in the original and generic sense when it is the object of an interest—any interest." In an attempt to make his contention overtly verifiable, Perry in turn defined "interest" quasi-behavioristically as "a train of events determined by expectation of its outcome." "Interest" for Perry was an umbrella term for such terms as "like," "desire," "preference," and "need" and their opposites. For something to have positive value, it must be an object of a favorable interest; for something to have negative value, it must be an object of aversion, disapproval, or dislike: in short, it must be an object of negative interest.

It should be understood that this definition of "value" is not taken by Perry to be either a lexical or a purely stipulative definition. It is, rather, a reforming definition. That is to say, it is a deliberate proposal concerning the use of a term in the language, but the proposal is not simply a stipulation, for it has some antecedent basis in the usage in question. It is proposed that this use be adopted as the standard use in order to clear up what are taken to be confusions allegedly resulting from unclear and vacillating usage. By such maneuvers Perry hoped to escape from Moore's arguments concerning the naturalistic fallacy.

Such a theory, initially at least, is extremely attractive, for it holds out a promise for a genuine "normative science" and thus for some objective, if not absolute, knowledge of good and evil. It holds out the promise that we will eventually use the emerging sciences of man to gain some cross-cultural and interpersonally confirmed, and thus objective, knowledge of right and wrong.

The crucial problem for the naturalist is to show how all statements containing ethical terms can be translated into statements that do not contain such terms and are directly or indirectly confirmable or disconfirmable by empirical observation. What must be achieved to develop such a naturalism is to show the tenability of some set of naturalistic definitions of key moral terms.

Working from his initial definition of "value," Perry developed his system from the following definitions:

(1) "X has value" equals "X is the object of any interest."

(2) "X is bad" equals "X has negative value."

(3) "X is good" equals "X has positive value."

(4) "X is intrinsically good" equals "X is the object of a favorable interest for its own sake."

(5) "X is extrinsically good" equals "X is the object of a favorable interest because X, directly or indirectly, is the most efficient means to something which is intrinsically good."

(6) "X is morally good" equals "X is the object of interests harmoniously organized by reflective agreement."

(7) "X is the highest good" equals "X is the object of an all-inclusive and harmonious system of interests."

(8) "X is morally right" equals "X is conducive to the moral good."

(9) "X is morally obligatory" equals "X is a social demand that, of any alternative demand, is most clearly called for by the ideal of harmonious happiness."

A theory based on these definitions should, Perry would argue, provide us with a systematic account of our normative concepts and exhibit the rationale of our moral judgments. However, it would be queried by many, including many who are not intuitionists, just how it can be that all moral statements are really a subspecies of empirical statement and how they all could, even in principle, be empirically confirmed or disconfirmed. To take moral statements as empirical statements asserting that so-and-so is the case seems to miss their distinctive, dynamic, and guiding function in the stream of life.

Dewey. For John Dewey, moral philosophy had a definite normative ethical function. Dewey wanted to criticize normative standards and hoped to indicate more reasonable moral goals. "Philosophy's central problem," he wrote, "is the relation that exists between the beliefs about the nature of things due to natural science and beliefs about values—using that word to designate whatever

is taken to have rightful authority in the direction of conduct."

His basic proposal was that we should use what he called experimental intelligence in morals. This means that in moral inquiry we should use the same methodological principles we use in scientific inquiry. We should develop a scientific critique of our institutions and of the patterns of conduct designated "moral." In order to do this we must show the untenability of what Dewey took to be an unjustified but ancient philosophical preconception that injects a divorce or dichotomy between scientific knowledge, on the one hand, and moral, philosophical, or religious knowledge, on the other. There is but one kind of knowledge, with one reliable method of fixing belief, the experimental method, though this knowledge and method of fixing belief must be applied to different subject matters.

To most people, the use of the experimental method in ethics heralds a drop of any normative ethical standards. In trying to establish that this is a misconception, Dewey tried to establish a severe contextualism. A central mistake of traditional moral philosophies, both naturalist and non-naturalist, was that of looking for one bedrock *summum bonum* or one ultimate moral criterion rather than realizing that there is an irreducible plurality of moral standards and that moral problems are fully intelligible and rationally resolvable only in a definite context. Moral standards are a part of a cultural context in which means and ends are qualitatively continuous and functionally interactive.

This reference to a continuum of means and ends leads to another main element in Dewey's moral philosophy. He argues against the specialist's conception of ethics. To hold this conception, which is traditional with philosophers as different as Plato and Russell, is to stress the distinction between intrinsic good and instrumental good and to contend that intrinsic good is the sole object of philosophical interest. This, according to Dewey, is a mistaken dichotomy rooted in the ancient Greek dichotomy between theory and practice. It is not only intellectually bankrupt but it can, Dewey argues, have vicious social consequences. It even makes for irrationalism in ethics, for given this conception, we are easily led to the assumption that while science can deal with mundane instrumental goods, the highest goods—the basic ends, namely, intrinsic goods—must be grasped by intuition, be vouchsafed by revelation, or be merely a matter of the whims of mortal will. Dewey argued that in concrete moral contexts, answers concerning means actually transform ends. In reasoning morally it is not a matter of discovering the most efficient means to attain a fixed end. If in considering the means it becomes apparent that our ends are utopian, we will, if we are behaving rationally, often give them up or modify them in view of this discovery. Here intelligence has a major role to play in morality. Ends cannot rationally be divorced from means. In fact, they are always functionally interactive. Furthermore, what is an end in one problematic situation is a means in another, and so on. There are never any actual normative goals or ends that are simply intrinsic goods. Ideals are always transformable in the light of what we discover about our world, and they are always imbedded in a network of other ideals.

Such considerations, it will surely be objected, hardly show that there are no intrinsic goods—but it could be contended that they effectively argue against Aristotelian final ends, or against the belief that in moral appraisal we can justifiably consider intrinsic goods independently of their consequences—and this, after all, is the major point Dewey wanted to establish.

Here we hardly have the metaethical concerns that are so distinctive of the work of Moore and Perry. But Dewey—though he didn't call it that—also had a metaethical theory.

Dewey argued that moral judgments are judgments of practice. That is to say, they are made in problematic situations of choice in which a moral agent is trying to decide what to do. This gives them their distinctive normative or *de jure* force. But at the same time they remain *de facto* empirical statements. It is this puzzling amalgam that we must understand if we are to get clear what Dewey was claiming.

Dewey asserted that value judgments are not mere prizings and disprizings. They are predictions about the capacity or incapacity of actions, objects, or events to satisfy desires, needs, and interests. As such they are confirmable and disconfirmable. They predict that certain ends in view will satisfy certain vital impulses under certain conditions. Not everything that is desired is desirable, but those things which are desired "after examination of the relations upon which the object depends" are desirable. In short, to say of something that it is valuable, desirable, or good is to say that it is something which would be desired or approved after reflection upon its relevant causes and consequences.

Criticism of Dewey. Dewey's theory has been subject to some trenchant criticisms by Morton White and Charles Stevenson and has been stanchly defended by Sidney Hook, Gail Kennedy, and Gertrude Ezorsky. The basic considerations here are as follows: even if X is desired after an examination of the causes and consequences of desiring X, it still does not follow that X is desirable or that X ought to be desired. However, to carry out Dewey's program of identifying moral statements as a subspecies of empirical statement, some such identity of meaning must be established.

But the admission that Dewey is wrong in claiming that moral statements are empirical statements or hypotheses is not destructive to his over-all program about the place of reason in ethics. If we ask how we justify our ethical evaluations, it seems that much of Dewey's method of criticism, including much of his use of science, could still be reasonably instituted. Dewey's great failure in talking about morality was in not realizing how very different "values" and "facts" are; his great success was in seeing the extensive relevance of scientific knowledge and scientific method to the making of intelligent moral appraisals.

CONTEMPORARY NONCOGNITIVISM

Both naturalism and nonnaturalism are cognitive theories. That is to say, they regard moral utterances in the declarative form as statement-making utterances that assert the existence of certain moral facts and are thus either true or false. But first in Sweden, and later in England and America, a quite different kind of metaethical theory developed that has been called a noncognitive theory. According to this theory, moral statements do not assert moral facts; they are neither confirmable nor disconfirmable, and there is nothing to be known by "moral intuition." It is even characteristic of this view to argue that it is either mistaken or at least misleading to characterize moral utterances as true or false.

Emotive theory. The noncognitive view, which has subsequently been called the emotive theory, received its first formulation in 1911, when the Swedish philosopher Axel Hägerström drew the outlines of such a theory in his inaugural lecture, "On The Truth of Moral Propositions." In 1917 Hägerström developed his ideas with particular attention to the concept of duty in his *Till Frågan om den Gällande Rättens Begrepp* (Uppsala, 1917). Similar statements of the emotive theory have been developed in Scandinavia by Ingmar Hedenius and Alf Ross. Independently of its Scandinavian formulation, the emotive theory was first stated in the English-speaking world by I. A. Richards and by Bertrand Russell, but it was developed in the Anglo-Saxon world by A. J. Ayer and by Charles Stevenson. There have also been interesting if somewhat atypical statements of it by Richard Robinson, Rudolf Carnap, and Hans Reichenbach.

The emotivists were convinced that moral statements are not a subspecies of factual statement, and they were further convinced that it was impossible to derive a moral statement from a set of purely factual statements. As Hägerström put it, "There is no common genus for the purely factual and the 'ought.' By using the predicate 'ought to happen' we refer an action to an altogether different category from the factual. That an action 'ought to be done' is regarded as something which holds true altogether without reference to whether it actually is done or not." The whole notion that there is a determinate character of an action that would make a moral statement true or false is, Hägerström argues, an illusion. There is nothing there for an "unmoved spectator of the actual" to observe that would either confirm or disconfirm his moral statements. Moral statements characteristically take a declarative form, but they actually function not to assert that so-and-so is true but to express an attitude toward an action or a state of affairs.

The emotive theory developed as a *via media* between intuitionism, on the one hand, and ethical naturalism, on the other. Both of these ethical theories displayed crucial difficulties. "Nonnatural qualities" and "nonnatural relations" were obscure, fantastic conceptions, to say the least, and the notion of intuition remained at best nonexplanatory. Furthermore, it was plain that moral judgments are closely linked to one's emotions, attitudes, and conations. But, as Moore in effect showed, neither "A cup of tea before bed is good" nor such general utterances as "Pleasure is good" and "Self-realization is good" are empirical or analytic.

The function of ethical statements. The emotivists maintained that while the grammatical function of a sentence like "A swim before bed is good" is indicative, its actual logical function is much closer to that of an optative or imperative utterance, such as "Would that we could go swimming before bed" or "Swim before bed." Because of this, emotivists have claimed that it is misleading to say that ethical sentences can be used to make statements: they do not function to assert facts.

Similarly, it is a mistake to treat all words as simply functioning to describe or designate some characteristic or thing. Some words so function; but there are other words, like "nasty," "saintly," "graceful," and "wise," that function primarily or in part to express the attitudes of the utterer or to evoke reactions on the part of the hearer. The emotivists claim that "good," "ought," "right," and the like are also emotive words. This gives them their normative function.

Ethical argument. Hägerström and Ayer contend that the fact that there are no moral facts carries with it the corollary that there can be no genuine moral knowledge. There are no moral facts to be learned; there is no moral information to be gained or forgotten. It makes clear sense to say "I used to know the difference between a pickerel and a pike, but by now I've forgotten it," but what is meant by "I used to know the difference between right and wrong, but by now I've forgotten it"? The word "forgotten" could hardly do its usual job here. The utterance is so deviant that without explanation and a very special context, we do not understand it. Considerations of this sort bring us to the realization that moral utterances are not used to state facts or assert truths; their essential role is a noncognitive one. They typically express emotions, attitudes, and conations and evoke actions, attitudes, and emotional reactions.

Because of this fact about the logical status of moral utterances, it always remains at least logically possible that two or more people might agree about all the relevant facts and disagree in attitude—that is, disagree about what was desirable or worth doing.

We do, however, as Ayer and Stevenson stress, give reasons for moral judgments. If I say "MacDonald did the right thing in killing Janet," it is perfectly in order to ask me to show why this is so. If I say "I don't have any reasons. There aren't any reasons, but all the same I just know that MacDonald did the right thing," I am abusing language. I am saying something unintelligible, for we can't "just know" like that. The person who claims that an action is right *must* always be prepared to give reasons for his moral claim.

Ayer and Stevenson grant all that. This is indeed how we do proceed when we are being reasonable about a moral disagreement. But Ayer says: ". . . the question is: in what way do these reasons support the moral judgments? They do not support them in a logical sense. Ethical argument is not formal demonstration. And they do not support them in a scientific sense either. If they did, the goodness or badness of the situation, the rightness or wrongness of the action, would have to be something apart from the situation, something independently verifiable, for which the facts adduced as the reasons for the moral judgment were the evidence." But this is just what we cannot do. There is *no* procedure for examining the *value* of the facts, as distinct from examining the facts themselves.

If we cannot demonstratively prove or inductively establish fundamental moral claims, then what can it mean to say that a factual statement *F* is a good reason for a moral

judgment *E*? The emotivist's answer is very simple: if *F* causes the person(s) to whom *E* is addressed to adopt *E*, to share the attitude expressed by *E*, then *F* is a good reason for *E*. It is Ayer's and Stevenson's claim that whatever in fact determines our attitudes is *ipso facto* a good reason for a moral judgment.

Criticisms of emotive theory. It has been argued by many moral philosophers (W. D. Falk, Richard Brandt, Errol Bedford, Paul Edwards, and Kai Nielsen, among others) that so to characterize what is meant by "a good reason" in ethics is persuasively to redefine "a good reason" in ethics. As Bedford has well argued against the emotive theory, "we do use logical criteria in moral discussion, however inexplicit, unanalyzed, and relatively vague these criteria of relevance may be." Remarks like "It doesn't follow that you ought to" or "That's beside the point" are just as common and just as much to the point in moral argument as elsewhere. There is no reason to think that these remarks about relevance differ in any essential way from their use in nonevaluative contexts. We don't just seek agreement when there is a moral dispute, but we try to justify one claim over another and we rightly reject persuasion as irrelevant to this task of justification.

Stevenson has replied that to answer in this way is in effect to confuse normative ethical inquiries with metaethical ones. "Good" and "relevant" are normative terms and have their distinctive emotive force. To say that such and such are good reasons is to make a moral statement. Making such a statement involves leaving the normative ethical neutrality of metaethical inquiry. One answer to this is that to say what is *meant* by "good reasons" in ethics is to *mention* "good reasons" and not to *use* them.

Existentialism. Noncognitivism is not limited to emotivism. The existentialists do not call themselves noncognitivists, nor do they write metaethical treatises. But reasonably definite metaethical assumptions are implicit in their writings. Their contention that "men create their values," their stress on decision, commitment, and the impossibility of achieving ethical knowledge, strongly suggests a noncognitivist metaethic. We shall limit the examination here to two major figures, Albert Camus and Jean-Paul Sartre.

Camus. Unlike Sartre, Albert Camus wrote no technical philosophy, but in his *Myth of Sisyphus* (Paris, 1942), *The Rebel* (Paris, 1951), and his plays and novels he did articulate an ethical view that has been called the ethics of the absurd. To read Camus is to be immediately thrown into normative ethics via what has been called philosophical anthropology. We are immediately confronted with a picture of man and man's lot. Man is divorced from the world yet is paradoxically thrust into it. The world as we find it—given our hopes, our expectations, our ideals—is intractable. It is incommensurate with our moral and intellectual demands. Life is fragmented. We seek to discover some rational unity amidst this diversity and chaos. We discover instead that we can only impose an arbitrary unity upon it. *L'homme absurde,* as distinct from *l'homme quotidien,* sees clearly the relativity and flux of human commitment and the ultimate purposelessness of life. Yet man has a blind but overpowering attachment to life as something more powerful than any of the world's ills or any human intellectualization. But the world is ultimately unintelligible and irrational, and man's lot in the world is absurd.

Given this situation, all moral commitments are arbitrary. There is no escaping this: reason will only show us the arbitrariness of human valuations, and a Kierkegaardian leap of faith in the face of the absurd is evasive. It is evasive because it is to consent to absurdity rather than to face up to it, recognizing it for what it is. Man's dignity comes in his refusing to compromise. His very humanity is displayed in his holding on to his intelligence and in recognizing, contra Kierkegaard, that there is no God and, contra Jaspers, that there is no metaphysical unity that can overcome the absurdity of human existence.

Yet paradoxically, and some would claim inconsistently, in his novel *The Plague* (Paris, 1947), and in his essays, collected and published in English under the title *Resistance, Rebellion and Death* (New York, 1961) Camus writes with passion and conviction in defense of human freedom and intelligence. Camus's rationale for this is that we become *engagé* because we see that life has no ultimate meaning and that, finally free from a search for cosmic significance, we can take the diverse experiences of life for what they are in all their richness and variety. Yet beyond that and perhaps because of that, Camus, as a humanist, is espousing the cause of man. By this is meant, as is very evident in *Resistance, Rebellion and Death,* that Camus repeatedly defends human freedom, equality, and the alleviation of human misery and deprivation. We must become involved, but in this involvement Camus urges a reliance on human intelligence in facing the problems of men.

What might be taken to be a conflict between the more theoretical side of Camus's thought and his more directly normative ethical side comes out in his fourth "Letter to a German Friend." Camus agrees with his "German friend" that the world has no ultimate meaning, but he does not and will not conclude from this, as his "German friend" did, "that everything was equivalent and that good and evil could be defined according to one's wishes." Camus then goes on to remark that he can find no valid argument to answer such a nihilism. His only "answer" is "a fierce love of justice, which after all, seemed to me as unreasonable as the most sudden passion." Camus felt he could only resolutely refuse to accept despair and "to fight against eternal injustice, create happiness in order to protest against the universe of unhappiness." Camus concludes with a cry of the heart that while "the world has no ultimate meaning . . . something in it has a meaning, namely man because he is the only creature to insist on having one."

Sartre. Jean-Paul Sartre's views on man's condition are in many important respects like those of Camus, but to a far greater degree than Camus, Sartre in *Being and Nothingness* (Paris, 1943) and *Critique de la raison dialectique* (Paris, 1960) sets his ethical theorizing in the murky atmosphere of metaphysics. The promised systematic work on ethics that was to follow *Being and Nothingness* has not been forthcoming, but in one way or another all of Sartre's works are concerned with ethics. It can be said that there are two Sartres, or at least that the Sartre of *Critique de la raison dialectique* has moved from his earlier existential-

ism over to a kind of Marxist materialism. Here we shall for the most part (except where specifically noted) be concerned with the earlier Sartre, whose philosophical endeavor centered on his massive *Being and Nothingness*.

Sartre, like Camus, finds man's lot in the world absurd. Since there is no God, life can have no ultimate meaning and there can be no objective knowledge of good and evil. We cannot "decide a priori," or find out by investigation, what we are to do. Man in his forlornness and freedom imposes values. The choices man makes, the projects he forms for himself, and the sum of his acts constitute his values. There is no good and evil to be intuited or in any way discovered by the human animal. Man in anguish creates his values by his deliberate choices, and, to add to his anguish, in making his choices "he involves all mankind." That is to say, Sartre stresses the Kantian claim that moral judgments, in order to be moral judgments, must be universalizable, but, as Sartre adds in his lecture "Existentialism Is a Humanism" (1945), though their "form is universal . . . the content of ethics is variable" and there is no rational way of justifying the acceptance of moral principles with one content rather than another.

Sartre thinks this position is simply a matter of drawing out in a nonevasive manner the implications of a consistent atheism. Only if there were a God could values have an objective justification, but without God "everything is permissible" and "as a result man is forlorn, because neither within him nor without does he find anything to cling to." In this, Sartre is surely mistaken. It does not follow that if there is no God, nothing matters, or that everything is permissible. It is not a contradiction to assert, "Though there is no God, the torturing of children is still vile," and the nonexistence of God does not preclude the possibility of there being an objective standard on which to base such judgments.

Sartre asserts flatly, in good Moorean spirit, "Ontology itself cannot formulate ethical precepts. It is concerned solely with what is, and we cannot possibly derive imperatives from ontology's indicatives." (All the same, his account of morality in *Being and Nothingness* and his account of human action relevant to morality are immersed in "the language of being.") In fact, Sartre goes on to point out that ontology and what he calls existential psychoanalysis can in a given situation constitute "a moral description, for it presents to us the ethical meaning of various human projects." This method of description—though hardly the descriptions themselves—is very like the phenomenological method practiced by Scheler and Hartmann. Yet to proceed in this way hardly constitutes a violation of the is/ought distinction, since Sartre's descriptions of moral evaluations—descriptions of man's ethical life—need not themselves be evaluative, though given the language Sartre uses, they often are.

"Man," he tells us, "pursues being blindly by hiding from himself the free project which is this pursuit." Existential psychoanalysis can reveal to man the real goal of his pursuit. Horrified by the "death of God," man attempts in his anguish to be God. He flees from his freedom—he does not wish to be a creator of values—but in what Sartre ironically calls the spirit of seriousness, he seeks to deny human subjectivity and attributes to value some independent cosmic significance. To the extent that we are caught up in this spirit of seriousness, we will try to fuse "being-for-itself" with the brute facticity of "being-in-itself." (The odd phrase "being-in-itself" is simply the label for the self-contained reality of a thing, while its mate, "being-for-itself," is the label for the realm of consciousness that perpetually strives to transcend itself.) But if we pursue this line, we still condemned to despair, for we "discover at the same time that all human activities are equivalent . . . and that all are on principle doomed to failure." Phenomenological analysis reveals to man that though he perpetually tries to become a thing, a brute existent, the fact that he has consciousness makes this impossible. Given this ability to think and to feel, man, whether he likes it or not, is slowly led to see that without God he can have no essential nature; that is, though he may form his own projects, there is and can be no purpose to life.

It should be noted that Sartre's view of man's lot is even grimmer than Camus's, for Sartre contends that even in community with others there is no surcease from suffering and alienation, for human relations are essentially relations of conflict and estrangement.

In *Critique de la raison dialectique,* Sartre tries to work out a new kind of Marxism and a new materialist conception of man. But he wishes to integrate his existentialist conceptions into a Marxist materialism in such a way that the latter can come to have a truly "human dimension." Marxism, he argues, must purge itself of its deterministic conceptions of man and acknowledge a rational conception of human freedom. Sartre, in a reversal from *Being and Nothingness,* now argues that there is nothing intrinsic in human nature that makes conflict, war, and a reign of terror inescapable, though, like a good Marxist, he does argue that conflict is a basic factor in human history. It is scarcity, scarcity of goods and materials, that triggers human conflict. Only under these conditions of scarcity is social conflict inescapable and a rational social order impossible. Men make their own history by the choices they make in the face of problems created by history. But man remains the rider, not the horse. Human choices—human projects—are still free choices for which men remain responsible.

RECENT VIEWS ON MORAL DISCOURSE

Linguistic philosophy. As has frequently been noted, there are at least superficial resemblances between the existentialists and the otherwise very different, self-consciously metaethical theories of such linguistic philosophers as R. M. Hare, P. H. Nowell-Smith, Bernard Mayo, Alan Montefiore, and John Hartland-Swann.

There is, indeed, this much similarity between these linguistic philosophers and the existentialists. All of the former make the following contentions, all of which would be welcome to the latter:

(1) Moore was essentially right about the naturalistic fallacy. That is to say, moral statements cannot be deduced from any statement of fact, whether biological, historical, psychological, sociological, or religious.

(2) No moral choice or question of value can ever be guaranteed by logical rules.

(3) We are free, as far as language or logic is concerned, to apply evaluative or prescriptive terms to anything we wish to commend or condemn, criticize or approve, prescribe or forbid.

(4) Moral utterances are generalizable decisions, resolutions, or subscriptions.

Given that a man accepts certain moral principles, other moral principles can, together with certain factual statements, be derived from the above principles. But like Ayer and the existentialists, these linguistic philosophers hold that there must be some moral principles which are not derived from any other principles—moral or otherwise—and, being fundamental moral principles, they are not even verifiable in principle. They express moral commitments and can have no rational ground, for what is deemed worthy of acceptance ultimately depends on the very commitments (generalizable decisions, resolutions, or subscriptions) an agent is willing to make.

Many people have thought that such a view of morality is either directly or indirectly nihilistic—that both the linguistic philosophers and the existentialists espouse what is in effect an irrationalism that would undercut the very possibility of a rational normative ethic.

If we consider a reply linguistic philosophers typically make to such criticisms, we will become aware of a crucial dissimilarity between them and the existentialists and a fundamental defect in existentialist ethics.

Linguistic philosophers have frequently claimed that the existentialists have merely dramatized a logical point. That moral principles are expressions of commitment or choice, that man cannot simply discover what is good or evil or know a priori that a certain thing must be done but must "create his own values," is not a worrisome fact about the human predicament; it is a conceptual truth concerning the nature of moral discourse. It is not a fact of the human condition that man is born into a world alien and indifferent to human purposes. What is a fact is that the phrases "the universe has a purpose" and "value and being are one" are unintelligible phrases. To say "man creates his own values" is in reality only to say in a dramatic way that a judgment of value is an expression of choice. This statement, it is argued, is not an anguished cry of the human heart but is merely an expression of a linguistic convention.

To say "If x is a judgment of value, then x is an expression of choice" is not to say "Any choice at all is justified," "Anything is permissible," or "All human actions are of equal value." These latter statements are themselves value judgments and could not follow from the above-mentioned statement, for it is not itself a statement of value but a nonnormative metaethical statement about the meaning of evaluative expressions, and, as Sartre himself stresses, one cannot derive an "ought" from an "is." In general, Hare and Nowell-Smith, as well as Ayer and Stevenson, stress the normative neutrality of metaethical statements.

Hare. R. M. Hare in two very influential books, *The Language of Morals* (Oxford, 1952) and *Freedom and Reason* (Oxford, 1963), has developed a very closely reasoned metaethical analysis of the type that has been discussed. In *The Language of Morals,* Hare views moral utterances as a species of prescriptive discourse, and he feels that we can most readily come to understand their actual role in the stream of life if we see how very much they are like another form of prescriptive discourse, namely, imperatives. Imperatives tell us to do something, not that something is the case. Moral utterances in their most paradigmatic employments also tell us to do something. Imperative and moral utterances do not, as the emotivists thought, have the logical function of trying to *get* you to do something. Rather, they *tell* you to do something. Furthermore, there are logical relations between prescriptive statements, just as there are logical relations between factual statements.

Moral judgments are viewed as a kind of prescriptive judgment but, unlike singular imperatives, moral judgments (as well as all value judgments) are universalizable. Hare means by this that such a judgment "logically commits the speaker to making a similar judgment about anything which is either exactly like the subject of the original judgment or like it in the relevant respects."

Hare stresses that while almost any word in certain contexts can function evaluatively, "good," "right," and "ought" almost always so function. The evaluative functions of these terms are distinct from their descriptive functions and are an essential part of their meaning. In fact, the distinctive function of all value words is that they in one way or another commend or condemn. But while "good" is a general word of commendation, the criteria for goodness vary from context to context and are dependent on what it is that is said to be "good."

The meaning of "good" or any other value term is never tied to its criteria of application. There is nothing in the logic of our language to limit the content of a moral judgment. As far as logic is concerned, any universalizable prescription that expresses a deep concern or commitment is *ipso facto* a moral prescription, and we can decide without conceptual error to do anything that it is logically or physically possible to do. If we treat the resulting decision as a decision of principle, that is, a universalizable prescription, then it is a value judgment that is in good logical order. As Nowell-Smith has well put it in discussing Hare's theory, "Nothing that we discover about the nature of moral judgments entails that it is wrong to put all Jews in gas-chambers."

Criticism of Hare. Probably the most persistent dissatisfaction with Hare's theory has resulted from the belief that it makes moral reasoning appear to be more arbitrary than it actually is. To say "Nothing that we discover about the nature of moral judgments entails that it is wrong to put all Jews in gas-chambers" is, it will be argued, a *reductio* of such a position. Hare would reply that to argue in such a way is to fail to recognize that he is talking about entailment, and that he is simply making the point that from nonnormative statements one cannot deduce normative ones.

Hare argues that his thesis about the logical status of moral utterances does not commit him to the position that there can be no rational resolution of basic conflicts in moral principle. Returning, in *Freedom and Reason*, to a stress on decisions (though with a new attention to inclinations), Hare contends that to have a morality we must have freedom. Specifically, we must have a situation in

which each man must solve his own moral problems. (This is not to moralize about what we should do but to state a logical condition for the very existence of moral claims.)

Philosophers who have criticized Hare, including someone as close to him as Nowell-Smith, have suggested that Hare still has a far too Protestant conception of moral discourse. He fails really to take to heart the Wittgensteinian claim that here, as elsewhere in human discourse, we must have public criteria for what could count as a logically proper moral claim. As F. E. Sparshott—whose book *An Enquiry into Goodness* (Chicago, 1958) deserves more attention than it has received—notes: Hare's individualism leads him to neglect the fact that a morality, any morality, will necessarily incorporate "those rules of conduct that seem necessary for communal living." It is not the case that just *any* universalizable set of prescriptions can constitute a morality or a set of moral judgments.

The good-reasons approach. The last metaethical theory we shall discuss has been dubbed the good-reasons approach. Stephen Toulmin, Kurt Baier, Henry Aiken, Marcus Singer, Kai Nielsen, A. I. Melden, A. E. Murphy, and John Rawls may be taken as representative figures of this point of view. It is an approach which obviously has been deeply affected by the philosophical method that we have come to associate with the work of the later Wittgenstein. These philosophers have centered their attention on the logic of moral reasoning. Their central question has been "When is a reason a *good* reason for a moral judgment?" Accordingly, the crucial problems center on questions concerning the nature and limits of *justification* in ethics. These philosophers agree with the noncognitivists that moral sentences are used primarily as dynamic expressions to guide conduct and alter behavior. And they would also agree with ethical naturalists that moral utterances usually, at least, also make factual assertions. But they believe that the primary use of moral utterances is not theoretical or just emotive but practical. Hare and Nowell-Smith are right in stressing that they are designed to tell us what to do.

Yet while moral utterances typically tell us what to do, language with its complex and multifarious uses does not neatly divide into "the descriptive" and "the evaluative," "the constative" and "the performative," "the cognitive" and "the noncognitive." These are philosophers' specialized terms, and they do not help us to understand and clearly characterize moral discourse but actually distort our understanding of it. There can be no translation of moral terms into nonmoral terms, and the ancient problem of bridging "the is – ought gulf" is a muddle, for there is no clear distinction between such uses of language and no single function that makes a bit of discourse normative. Some moral utterances indeed bear interesting analogies to commands or resolutions, but they cannot be identified with them. It is a mistake to think ethical judgments are like scientific ones or like the judgments of any other branch of objective inquiry; yet cognitivist metaethicists were correct, not in pressing this analogy but in maintaining that there is a knowledge of good and evil and that some moral claims have a perfectly respectable objectivity. No matter how emotive or performative moral utterances may be, when we make a moral judgment, it must—logically must—satisfy certain requirements to count as a moral judgment. In making a moral judgment, we must be willing to universalize the judgment in question, and it must be possible to give factual reasons in support of the moral claim.

The advocates of the good-reasons approach in the general tradition of the later Wittgenstein did not take it to be incumbent on the philosopher to translate moral utterances into some clearer idiom. They did not believe that there was some other favored discourse or form of life that moral discourse or morality should be modeled on. What was expected of the philosopher was that he should describe morality so as to perspicuously display the living discourse at work. In particular, philosophers should concern themselves with a conceptual cartography of the nature and limits of justification in ethics. Before we can reasonably claim that moral judgments are at bottom "all subjective" or that no moral claim can be "objectively justified," we must come to understand what can and what cannot count as a good reason in ethics and what the limits of moral reasoning are.

Toulmin. Two books, Stephen Toulmin's *An Examination of the Place of Reason in Ethics* (Cambridge, 1950) and Kurt Baier's *The Moral Point of View* (Ithaca, N.Y., 1958), have most single-mindedly attacked the problem of moral reasoning. They may be taken as paradigms of the good-reasons approach. Toulmin argues that moral rules and moral principles are to be justified by discovering which of these rules or principles, if consistently acted upon, will most likely lead to the least amount of avoidable suffering all around. Those social practices which probably will cause the least amount of suffering for mankind are the social practices which ought to be accepted. Classical utilitarians maintained that a moral rule is justified if it tends to produce greater happiness all around than any alternative rule, but Toulmin favors the negative formulation because (1) though it is very difficult to determine what will make people happy or what they want, it is less difficult to determine what causes suffering, and (2) it is less the function of morality to tell men what the good life is than to tell them what *not* to do so that their interests, including their differing conceptions of the good life, can be realized to the maximum extent.

This theory about moral reasoning, while purporting to be metaethical, is very close to the normative ethical theory sometimes called rule utilitarianism.

Toulmin argues that if we examine closely the way moral reasoning is actually carried on, it will become evident that moral rules and practices are characteristically judged by roughly utilitarian standards, while many individual actions are judged by whether or not they are in accordance with an accepted moral rule or social practice. Utilitarians point out that it is of the greatest social utility that we characteristically judge moral acts in this seemingly nonutilitarian fashion. However, frequently a decision concerning how to act involves conflicting moral rules with no clear order of subordination, and in some situations there seems to be no moral rule—unless the principle of utility is taken as a moral rule—that is readily applicable. In such a situation, the thing to do is to act on a utilitarian basis when it is at all possible to make some reasonable

judgment of the probable beneficial consequences to the people involved of doing one thing rather than another. If that is not possible in a given situation, then we should act as a reasonable man would act. (The concept of a reasonable man, we should not forget, is itself very much a moral concept.)

Criticism of Toulmin. There certainly are a host of objections that spring to mind concerning Toulmin's account. First, it will be said that this is normative ethics, not metaethics: it tells us what we should do, what a good reason is, and how we can justify basic moral rules. Moreover, why should we accept it? Once we see through its modish trappings, it will become apparent that it has all the difficulties attendant on classical utilitarianism.

It could be replied that though the speech is in the material mode and sounds like normative ethics, in reality it is a brief description of how moral reasoning is actually carried on.

Even if this reply is accepted, there are difficulties here too, for viewed this way, Toulmin's account surely looks like an account of a basically sociological sort of how certain people in fact reason. That is to say, it appears to be an impressionistic bit of descriptive ethics and hardly a metaethical account of the *logic* of moral reasoning. It covertly and persuasively redefines as "moral" only a very limited pattern of reasoning—reasoning that expresses the historically and ethnographically limited views of a determinate group of people. The ethnocentric character of this linguistic analysis makes it implicitly, but surreptitiously, normative.

This contention will be rejected by many. It will be argued that moral reasoning, like any other mode of reasoning, is limited. To determine what the moral point of view is and what it is to reason morally, we need first to determine the function (purpose, over-all rationale) of morality.

The function of morality, Toulmin tells us, is to adjudicate conflicting interests and to harmonize desires (that is, moderate our impulses and adjust our demands) so as to reconcile them with our fellows, in such a way that everyone can have as much as possible of whatever it is that, on reflection, he wants.

Given this conception of the function of ethics, something like Toulmin's account of moral reasoning is very plausible, but it has been objected that morality has no *one* such function. Many people have ideals of human excellence that have nothing to do with such a conception of the function of ethics: many Jews and Christians, with their ideals of the love of God, do not conceive the function of moral living in this way, and the Buddhist community with its ideals of *arhat*ship certainly would not accept, either in theory or in practice, such a conception of the function of ethics. Morality is a much more complicated and varied activity. There are diverse and often conflicting functions of morality. Any attempt to claim one function or rationale of morality as *the* function or *the* purpose of morality so circumscribes what can count as moral considerations that its effect is unwittingly to advocate one limited moral outlook as the moral point of view.

Finally, even if Toulmin could make out a case for claiming that the function of morality, or the primary function of morality, is such as he claims it to be, one could still ask, concerning this descriptive account of morality, "Why keep it as the sole or primary function of morality?" If altering the function of morality somewhat alters the meaning of "moral," then why should we be such linguistic conservatives? What is so sacred about that function of morality and its attendant conception of morality?

Toulmin could claim that now his critic has confused normative issues with metaethical ones. The issues here are complex and lead us into the heart of current discussion about the nature of moral reasoning. Yet a strong case can be made for the contention that there is more to be said for a general approach such as Toulmin's and Baier's than has commonly been thought.

It seems evident that much contemporary thinking about ethics, while devoted to Moore's exacting standards of making perfectly clear precisely what is being claimed, is concerned not with the very general question of the meaning of "good" or, for that matter, "right" or "ought" but with the rich texture of moral reasoning. This brings once more to the foreground the kind of detailed descriptions of the moral life distinctive of such phenomenologists as Scheler and Hartmann, but given the present care for actual conceptual distinctions, we may develop a kind of linguistic phenomenology which may be of major importance to an understanding of morality. Perhaps the most exciting endeavors from this point of view have been those of John Rawls, Philippa Foot, and Georg von Wright. Rawls, in a series of distinguished essays, has shown the central role of considerations of justice in moral deliberation and the way such considerations modify utilitarian patterns of reasoning; Philippa Foot, also in a series of much-discussed essays, has shown the importance of a discussion of the virtues and the vices and has reinvigorated ethical naturalism. Georg von Wright's recent masterful discussion of the varieties of goodness in his *The Varieties of Goodness* (London, 1963) has contributed immensely to our understanding of morality.

(See also ETHICS, PROBLEMS OF.)

General Histories of Ethics

HISTORICAL AND SOCIAL CONTEXT OF ETHICAL BELIEFS

Brinton, C. C., *A History of Western Morals*. London, 1959. A very readable history of ethical beliefs and practices.

Bruce, A. B., *The Moral Order of the World in Ancient and Modern Thought*, 4 vols. London, 1899. A detailed study of the literary and religious background of ethical thought from ancient Greece to the Reformation.

Dittrich, Ottmar, *Geschichte der Ethik*, 4 vols. Leipzig, 1926. A scholarly study of the literary and religious origins of Western ethical ideals.

Harkness, G. E., *The Sources of Western Morality*. New York, 1954. An exploration of the ancient origins of modern ethics. Useful comparisons of primitive with Old Testament ethics and of Greek with Christian ethics.

Kropotkin, P. A., *Ethics, Origin and Development*, translated by L. S. Friedland and J. R. Piroshnikoff. New York, 1924. A Marxist account of the development of ethics from primitive to modern Western society.

Lecky, W. E. H., *History of European Morals*, 2 vols. New York, 1919. A justly celebrated study of how moral values reflect, but fail to keep up with, actual practices in the Western world. Vol. I, Ch. 1, discusses modern British ethical philosophy.

Mencken, H. L., *Treatise on Right and Wrong*. New York, 1934. Perceptive and often caustic comments on the evolution of moral ideas in philosophy and religion; a critique of authoritarianism.

Robertson, J. M., *A Short History of Morals*. London, 1920. A relativistic view of the history of ethics, stressing the sociological sources of morality.

Westermarck, Edward, *The Origin and Development of Moral Ideas*, 2 vols. London, 1908. A monumental work of historical and anthropological scholarship.

HISTORIES OF ETHICAL PHILOSOPHY

Broad, C. D., *Five Types of Ethical Theory*. London, 1930. A critical study, by a distinguished intuitionist, of the ethical systems of Spinoza, Butler, Hume, Kant, and Sidgwick.

Kautsky, Karl, *Ethics and the Materialist Conception of History*, translated by J. B. Agnew. Chicago, 1907. A brief sketch of the evolution of ethical thought by a noted Marxist.

MacIntyre, Alasdair, *A Short History of Ethics*. New York, 1966. An important discussion by a contemporary analytic philosopher.

Mackinnon, D. M., *A Study in Ethical Theory*. London, 1957. A comparison of the theories of Kant, Butler, and the utilitarians as alternatives to religious ethics.

Maritain, Jacques, *Moral Philosophy*, translated by M. Suther. New York, 1964. A critical evaluation of secular ethical theories from the standpoint of Catholic theology.

Martineau, James, *Types of Ethical Theory*, 2 vols. Oxford, 1898. Vol. I evaluates the metaphysical and ethical views of Plato, Descartes, Malebranche, Spinoza, and Comte. Vol. II criticizes utilitarian and moral-sense theories.

Rogers, R. A. P., *A Short History of Ethics*. London, 1911. A brief survey of the history of ethical theory. Incomplete but clear and readable.

Sidgwick, Henry, *Outlines of the History of Ethics*. London, 1886. A brief but illuminating discussion of the most important schools of ethical thought from ancient Greece to nineteenth-century England.

Swabey, W. C., *Ethical Thought From Hobbes to Kant*. New York, 1961. A useful summary of several philosophical systems.

Plato

GENERAL EXPOSITIONS

Dickinson, G. L., *Plato and His Dialogues*. New York, 1932.

Field, G. X., *The Philosophy of Plato*. London, 1951.

Friedländer, Paul, *Plato*, translated by Hans Meyerhoff. New York, 1958–1964. A multivolume work of tremendous scholarship on the cultural background of Plato's writings.

Shorey, P., *What Plato Said*. Chicago, 1933.

Taylor, A. E., *Plato, the Man and His Work*. London, 1908.

SPECIALIZED STUDIES

Lodge, R. C., *Plato's Theory of Ethics*. New York, 1928. A thorough study limited to Plato's ethical ideas.

Nettleship, R. L., *Lectures on the Republic of Plato*. New York, 1962. An extraordinarily illuminating study of Plato's most important dialogue.

RELATION OF PLATO TO OTHER GREEK THINKERS

Burnet, John, *Platonism*. Berkeley, 1928. Distinguishes sharply between Socratic and Platonic views.

Cornford, F. M., *Before and After Socrates*. Cambridge, 1960.

Demos, R., *The Philosophy of Plato*. New York, 1939. Rejects any systematic interpretation of Plato.

Field, G. C., *Plato and His Contemporaries*. London, 1948.

Gould, J., *The Development of Plato's Ethics*. Cambridge, 1955.

Hampden, R. D., *The Fathers of Greek Philosophy*. Edinburgh, 1862.

Merlan, Philip, *From Plato to Platonism*. The Hague, 1960.

PLATO'S ETHICS AND POLITICS

Crossman, R. H., *Plato Today.* London, 1937. Critical.
Fite, W., *The Platonic Legend.* New York, 1934. Critical.
Koyré, Alexandre,*Discovering Plato.* New York, 1945. Favorable.
Levinson, R. B., *In Defense of Plato.* Cambridge, Mass., 1953.
Wild, J. D., *Plato's Modern Enemies.* Chicago, 1959. Favorable.

Aristotle

ARISTOTLE'S ETHICS

Gauthier, R. A., *La Morale d'Aristote.* Paris, 1958.
Grene, Marjorie, *A Portrait of Aristotle.* London, 1963.
Marshall, T., *Aristotle's Theory of Conduct.* London, 1906.
Mure, G. R. G., *Aristotle,* London, 1932.
Oates, W. J., *Aristotle and the Problem of Value.* Princeton, N.J., 1963.
Randall, J. H., *Aristotle.* New York, 1960. Chs. 11–14.
Ross, W. D., *Aristotle.* London, 1930.
Veatch, H. B., *Rational Man.* Bloomington, Ind., 1962.
Walsh, J. J., *Aristotle's Conception of Moral Weakness.* New York, 1963.

ARISTOTLE AND OTHER ETHICAL PHILOSOPHERS

Cornford, F. M., *Before and After Socrates.* Cambridge, 1960.
Hampden, R. D., *The Fathers of Greek Philosophy.* Edinburgh, 1862.
Merlan, Philip, *Studies in Epicurus and Aristotle.* Wiesbaden, 1960.
Taylor, A. E., *Aristotle.* London, 1943.

Hellenistic and Roman Ethics

EPICUREANISM

DeWitt, N. W., *Epicurus and His Philosophy.* Minneapolis, Minn., 1954.
Hadzsits, G. D., *Lucretius and His Influence.* New York, 1935.
Merlan, Philip, *Studies in Epicurus and Aristotle.* Wiesbaden, 1960.

STOICISM

Arnold, E. V., *Roman Stoicism.* Cambridge, 1911. Middle and late Stoa.
Bréhier, Émile, *Chrysippe et l'ancien Stoicisme.* Paris, 1951. Early Stoa.
Brussell, F. W., *Marcus Aurelius and the Later Stoics.* New York, 1910.
Murray, Gilbert, *Stoic, Christian and Humanist.* Boston, 1950.
Wenley, R. M., *Stoicism and Its Influence.* Boston, 1924.

NEOPLATONISM

Elsee, C., *Neoplatonism in Relation to Christianity.* Cambridge, 1908.
Feibleman, J., *Religious Platonism.* London, 1959.
Pistorius, P. V., *Plotinus and Neoplatonism.* Cambridge, 1952.
Switalski, B., *Neoplatonism and the Ethics of St. Augustine.* New York, 1946.
Whittaker, T., *The Neoplatonists.* Cambridge, 1918.

COMPARISONS

Hicks, R. D., *Stoic and Epicurean.* New York, 1910.
Zeller, Eduard, *Stoics, Epicureans and Sceptics,* translated by O. J. Reichel. London, 1880.

Medieval Ethics

GENERAL HISTORIES OF MEDIEVAL PHILOSOPHY

Copleston, F. C., *A History of Philosophy,* Vols. II and III. Westminster, Md., 1950–1953.

Gilson, Étienne, *The Spirit of Medieval Philosophy,* translated by A. Downes. New York, 1936.
Gilson, Étienne, *Reason and Revelation in the Middle Ages.* New York, 1938.
Hawkins, D. J. B., *A Sketch of Medieval Philosophy.* London, 1945.
Husik, I., *A History of Medieval Jewish Philosophy.* New York, 1916.

AUGUSTINE

Gilson, Étienne, *Introduction a l'étude de saint Augustin.* Paris, 1943.
Switalski, B., *Neoplatonism and the Ethics of St. Augustine.* New York, 1946.

AQUINAS

Copleston, F. C., *Aquinas.* London, 1955. Ch. 5.
D'Arcy, M. C., *St. Thomas Aquinas.* Dublin, 1953. Ch. 9.
Gilson, Étienne, *The Philosophy of St. Thomas Aquinas,* translated by E. Bullough. St. Louis, 1934.
Maritain, Jacques, *St. Thomas and the Problem of Evil.* Milwaukee, Wis., 1942.
Mullane, D. T., *Aristotelianism in St. Thomas.* Washington, 1929.

ERIGENA AND ABELARD

Bett, H., *Johannes Scotus Eriugena.* Cambridge, 1925.
Sikes, J. G., *Peter Abailard.* Cambridge, 1932. Chs. 2 and 8.

Seventeenth-century Ethics

HOBBES

Laird, John, *Hobbes.* London, 1934.
Peters, R. S., *Hobbes.* London, 1956.
Stephen, Leslie, *Hobbes.* Ann Arbor, Mich., 1961.
Taylor, A. E., *Hobbes.* New York, 1908.

SPINOZA

Bidney, D., *The Psychology and Ethics of Spinoza.* New Haven, 1940.
Broad, C. D., *Five Types of Ethical Theory.* London, 1930. Ch. 2.
Hampshire, S., *Spinoza.* Harmondsworth, England, 1951. Chs. 4 and 5.
Joachim, H. J., *A Study of the Ethics of Spinoza.* London, 1901.
McKeon, R., *The Philosophy of Spinoza.* New York, 1928.

LOCKE

Aaron, R. I., *John Locke.* Oxford, 1955.
Lamprecht, S. P., *The Moral and Political Philosophy of John Locke.* New York, 1918.

CAMBRIDGE PLATONISTS

Cassirer, Ernst, *The Platonic Renaissance in England,* translated by J. P. Pettegrove. Austin, Texas, 1953.
Powicke, F. J., *The Cambridge Platonists.* Cambridge, Mass., 1926.

Eighteenth-century Ethics

MORAL-SENSE THEORIES

Bonar, J., *Moral Sense.* New York, 1930.
Raphael, D. D., *The Moral Sense.* London, 1947.

CLARKE

Le Rossignol, J. E., *The Ethical Philosophy of Samuel Clarke.* Leipzig, 1892.

BUTLER

Broad, C. D., *Five Types of Ethical Theory.* London, 1930. Ch. 3.

Duncan-Jones, A. E., *Butler's Moral Philosophy.* Harmondsworth, England, 1952.

SHAFTESBURY AND HUTCHESON

Fowler, Thomas, *Shaftesbury and Hutcheson.* London, 1882.

HUME

Basson, A. H., *David Hume.* Harmondsworth, England, 1958. Ch. 5.

Broad, C. D., *Five Types of Ethical Theory.* London, 1930. Ch. 4.

Smith, Norman Kemp, *The Philosophy of David Hume.* London, 1941.

Stewart, J. B., *The Moral and Political Philosophy of David Hume.* New York, 1963.

PRICE AND REID

Raphael, D. D., *The Moral Sense.* London, 1947.

FRENCH ENLIGHTENMENT

Becker, C. L., *The Heavenly City of the Eighteenth Century Philosophers.* New Haven, 1932.

Cassirer, Ernst, *The Philosophy of the Enlightenment,* translated by F. Koelln and J. P. Pettegrove. Princeton, N.J., 1951.

Crocker, L. G., *Nature and Culture.* Baltimore, 1963.

Halévy, Élie, *The Growth of Philosophic Radicalism,* translated by M. Morris. New York, 1928.

Rouston, M., *The Pioneers of the French Revolution,* translated by F. Whyte. London, 1926. A study of the social and political involvements of the Encyclopedists.

KANT

Broad, C. D., *Five Types of Ethical Theory.* London, 1930. Ch. 5.

Jones, W. T., *Morality and Freedom in the Philosophy of Immanuel Kant.* Oxford, 1940.

Körner, S., *Kant.* Harmondsworth, England, 1955. Chs. 6 and 7.

Lindsay, A. D., *Kant.* London, 1934.

Paton, H. J., *The Moral Law, or Kant's Groundwork of the Metaphysic of Morals.* New York, 1948.

Paton, H. J., *The Categorical Imperative.* Chicago, 1948.

Teale, A. E., *Kantian Ethics.* London, 1951.

Nineteenth-century Ethics

UTILITARIANISM

Halévy, Élie, *The Growth of Philosophic Radicalism,* translated by M. Morris. New York, 1928.

Stephen, Leslie, *The English Utilitarians,* 3 vols. New York, 1900.

GERMAN IDEALISM

Dewey, John, *German Philosophy and Politics.* New York, 1942. Highly critical.

Hook, Sidney, *From Hegel to Marx.* New York, 1936.

Löwith, Karl, *From Hegel to Nietzsche,* translated by D. Green. New York, 1964.

Marcuse, Herbert, *Reason and Revolution.* London, 1941.

Royce, Josiah, *The Spirit of Modern Philosophy.* New York, 1896.

FICHTE

Adamson, Robert, *Fichte.* Edinburgh, 1881.

Royce, Josiah, *The Spirit of Modern Philosophy.* New York, 1896. Part I, Ch. 5.

HEGEL

Findlay, J. N., *Hegel.* London, 1958. Chs. 5 and 11.

Marcuse, Herbert, *Reason and Revolution.* London, 1941.

Stace, W. T., *The Philosophy of Hegel.* New York, 1955.

Royce, Josiah, *The Spirit of Modern Philosophy.* New York, 1896. Part I, Ch. 8.

SCHOPENHAUER

Copleston, F. C., *Arthur Schopenhauer, Philosopher of Pessimism.* London, 1947.

McGill, V. J., *Schopenhauer, Pessimist and Pagan.* New York, 1931.

Mann, Thomas, *Schopenhauer.* Stockholm, 1938.

NIETZSCHE

Brinton, C. C., *Nietzsche.* Cambridge, 1941.

Copleston, F. C., *Friedrich Nietzsche.* London, 1942.

Lefebvre, Henri, *Nietzsche.* Paris, 1939.

MARX

Berlin, Isaiah, *Karl Marx.* London, 1939.

Hook, Sidney, *From Hegel to Marx.* New York, 1936.

MacIntyre, A. C., *Marxism, an Interpretation.* London, 1953.

Marcuse, Herbert, *Reason and Revolution.* London, 1941.

Tucker, R., *Philosophy and Myth in Karl Marx.* Cambridge, 1961.

AMERICAN TRANSCENDENTALISM

Pochmann, H. A., *New England Transcendentalism and St. Louis Hegelianism.* Philadelphia, 1948.

Schneider, H. W., *A History of American Philosophy.* New York, 1946.

ROYCE AND JAMES

Santayana, George, *Character and Opinion in the United States.* New York, 1920.

Smith, J. E., *Royce's Social Infinite.* New York, 1950.

BRITISH IDEALISM

Pfannenstill, Bertil, *Bernard Bosanquet's Philosophy of the State,* translated by Bert Hood. Lund, Sweden, 1936.

Sidgwick, Henry, *The Ethics of Green, Spencer and Martineau.* London, 1902.

Wollheim, Richard, *F. H. Bradley.* Harmondsworth, England, 1959. Ch. 6.

SIDGWICK

Broad, C. D., *Five Types of Ethical Theory.* London, 1930. Ch. 6.

Twentieth-century Ethics

ASSESSMENTS OF MOORE

Adams, E. M., *Ethical Naturalism and the Modern World-view.* Chapel Hill, N.C., 1960. Careful discussion of naturalism–nonnaturalism debate.

Broad, C. D., "G. E. Moore's Latest Published Views on Ethics." *Mind* (1961).

Field, G. C., "The Place of Definition in Ethics." *PAS* (1932). Key discussion of difficulties in Moore's conception of definition.

Frankena, W. K., "The Naturalistic Fallacy." *Mind* (1939). Classical source for discussion of naturalistic fallacy.

Hall, E. W., *Categorial Analysis,* E. M. Adams, ed. Chapel Hill, N.C., 1964. Important defense of Mill against Moore.

Prior, A. N., *Logic and the Basis of Ethics.* Oxford, 1949. Crucial for history of the naturalistic fallacy.

Taylor, Paul, *Normative Discourse.* Englewood Cliffs, N.J.,

1961. Is/ought carefully discussed and a general theory of value developed along linguistic lines.

Warnock, Mary, *Ethics Since 1900*. Oxford, 1960.

Wellman, Carl, *The Language of Ethics*. Cambridge, Mass., 1961. Clear statement of difficulties in ethical naturalism.

DEONTOLOGICAL NONNATURALISM

Broad, C. D., *Five Types of Ethical Theory*. London, 1930.

Broad, C. D., "Review of Julian S. Huxley's Evolutionary Ethics." *Mind* (1944).

Broad, C. D., "Some Reflections on Moral-sense Theories in Ethics." *PAS* (1944/1945).

Broad, C. D., "Some of the Main Problems of Ethics." *Philosophy* (1946).

Broad, C. D., "Critical Notice of H. A. Prichard, *Moral Obligation*." *Mind* (1950).

Broad, C. D., "Imperatives, Categorical and Hypothetical." *The Philosopher* (1950).

Broad, C. D., *Ethics and the History of Philosophy*. London, 1952.

Carritt, E. F., *The Theory of Morals*. Oxford, 1928.

Carritt, E. F., "Moral Positivism and Moral Aestheticism." *Philosophy* (1938). Less important than Prichard or Ross but still influential.

Ewing, A. C., *The Definition of Good*. New York, 1947.

Ewing, A. C., *Ethics*. London, 1953.

Ewing, A. C., *Second Thoughts in Moral Philosophy*. London, 1959.

Ewing, A. C., "The Autonomy of Ethics," in I. T. Ramsey, ed., *Prospects for Metaphysics*. London, 1961.

Hall, E. W., *What Is Value? An Essay in Philosophical Analysis*. New York, 1952.

Hall, E. W., *Our Knowledge of Fact and Value*. Chapel Hill, N.C., 1961.

Hall, E. W., *Categorial Analysis*, E. M. Adams, ed. Chapel Hill, N.C., 1964.

Prichard, H. A., *Moral Obligation*. Oxford, 1950. Posthumously collected essays. Primary source for deontology.

ASSESSMENTS OF DEONTOLOGICAL NONNATURALISM

Edwards, Paul, *The Logic of Moral Discourse*. Glencoe, Ill., 1955.

McCloskey, H. J., "Ross and the Concept of a *Prima Facie* Duty." *Australasian Journal of Philosophy* (1963).

Monro, D. H., "Critical Notice of *Second Thoughts in Moral Philosophy*." *Australasian Journal of Philosophy* (1960).

Schilpp, P. A., ed., *The Philosophy of C. D. Broad*. New York, 1959. Note essays by Frankena, Hare, and Hedenius and Broad's reply. Broad's work, though largely critical of other philosophers, represents a key statement of deontology.

Strawson, P. F., "Ethical Intuitionism." *Philosophy* (1949).

ASSESSMENTS OF PHENOMENOLOGICAL NONNATURALISM

Hook, Sidney, "A Critique of Ethical Realism." *International Journal of Ethics* (1929).

Jensen, O. C., "Nicolai Hartmann's Theory of Virtue." *Ethics* (1942).

Schlick, Moritz, "Is There a Factual *A Priori*?," in Herbert Feigl and Wilfrid Sellars, eds., *Readings in Philosophical Analysis*. New York, 1949.

Walker, Merle, "Perry and Hartmann, Antithetical or Complementary?" *International Journal of Ethics* (1939).

ETHICAL NATURALISM

Dewey, John, *Essays in Experimental Logic*. Chicago, 1916.

Dewey, John, *Human Nature and Conduct*. New York, 1922.

Dewey, John, *The Quest for Certainty*. New York, 1929.

Dewey, John, *Theory of Valuation*. Chicago, 1939.

Dewey, John, "Ethical Subject Matter and Language." *Journal of Philosophy* (1945).

Dewey, John, *The Problems of Men*. New York, 1946.

Findlay, J. N., *Values and Intentions*. London, 1961.

Findlay, J. N., *Language, Mind and Value*. London, 1963.

Foot, P. R., "Moral Arguments." *Mind* (1958).

Foot, P. R., "Moral Beliefs." *PAS* (1958).

Foot, P. R., "Goodness and Choice." *PAS*, Supp. Vol. (1961).

Pepper, Stephen, *A Digest of Purposive Values*. New York, 1947.

Prall, D. W., *A Study in the Theory of Value*. Berkeley, 1921.

Reid, J. R., *A Theory of Value*. New York, 1938.

Reid, J. R., "The Nature and Status of Values," in R. W. Sellars, V. G. McGill, and Marvin Farber, eds., *Philosophy for the Future*. New York, 1949.

Rice, P. B., *On the Knowledge of Good and Evil*. New York, 1955.

Stace, W. T., *The Concept of Morals*. New York, 1937.

Westermarck, Edward, *Ethical Relativity*. London, 1932.

ASSESSMENTS OF ETHICAL NATURALISM

Ezorsky, Gertrude, "Inquiry as Appraisal: The Singularity of John Dewey's Theory of Valuation." *Journal of Philosophy* (1958).

Frankena, William, "Ethical Naturalism Renovated." *The Review of Metaphysics* (1957).

Frankena, William, "Obligation and Motivation in Recent Moral Philosophy," in A. I. Melden, ed., *Essays in Moral Philosophy*. Seattle, Wash., 1958.

Frankena, William, "Lewis' Imperatives of Right." *Philosophical studies* (1963).

Frankena, William, "C. I. Lewis on the Ground and Nature of the Right." *Journal of Philosophy* (1964).

Frankena, William, "Three Comments on Lewis's Views on the Right and the Good." *Journal of Philosophy* (1964).

Hare, R. M., *The Language of Morals*. Oxford, 1950.

Kennedy, Gail, "Science and the Transformation of Common Sense: The Basic Problem of Dewey's Philosophy." *Journal of Philosophy* (1954).

Wellman, Carl, *The Language of Ethics*. Cambridge, 1961.

White, Morton, *Social Thought in America*. New York, 1949.

White, Morton, "Value and Obligation in Dewey and Lewis." *Philosophical Review* (1949).

(See also the works by Moore, Ross, Ewing, and Hall previously cited.)

CONTEMPORARY NONCOGNITIVISM

Ayer, A. J., *Language, Truth and Logic*. London, 1935.

Ayer, A. J., "On the Analysis of Moral Judgments," in his *Philosophical Essays*. New York, 1954.

Carnap, Rudolf, *Philosophy and Logical Syntax*. London, 1935.

Cassirer, Ernst, "Axel Hägerström: Eine Studie zur schwedischen Philosophie der Gegenwart." *Goteborgs Hogskolas Arsskrift* (1939).

Edwards, Paul, *The Logic of Moral Discourse*. Glencoe, Ill., 1955.

Hedenius, Ingemar, *Om Rätt och Moral* ("On Law and Morals"). Stockholm, 1941.

Hedenius, Ingemar, "Values and Duties." *Theoria* (1949).

Hedenius, Ingemar, "Etikens Subjecktivitet," in *Tro och Moral*. Stockholm, 1955.

Reichenbach, Hans, *The Rise of Scientific Philosophy*. Berkeley and Los Angeles, 1951.

Richards, I. A., *The Meaning of Meaning*. New York, 1933.

Richards, I. A., *Speculative Instruments*. Chicago, 1957.

Robinson, Richard, "The Emotive Theory of Ethics." *PAS*, Supp. Vol. (1948).

Robinson, Richard, *An Atheist's Values*. Oxford, 1964.

Ross, Alf, *Kritik der sogenannten praktischen Erkenntniss*. Copenhagen, 1933.

Ross, Alf, "On the Logical Nature of Propositions of Value." *Theoria* (1945).

Ross, Alf, *On Law and Justice*. Berkeley and Los Angeles, 1959.

Ross, Alf, "On Moral Reasoning." *Danish Yearbook of Philosophy* (1964).

Russell, Bertrand, *Religion and Science*. Oxford, 1935.

Schilpp, P. A., ed., *The Philosophy of Rudolf Carnap*. La Salle, Ill., 1964.

Stevenson, Charles, *Ethics and Language*. New Haven, 1944.
Stevenson, Charles, "The Scientist's Role and the Aims of Education." *Harvard Educational Review* (1954).
Stevenson, Charles, *Facts and Values*. New Haven, 1963.

ASSESSMENTS OF THE EMOTIVE THEORY

Bedford, E., "The Emotive Theory of Ethics," in *Proceedings of the Eleventh International Congress of Philosophy*, Vol. X. Amsterdam, 1953.
Brandt, Richard, "The Emotive Theory of Ethics." *Philosophical Review* (1950).
Falk, W. D., "Goading and Guiding." *Mind* (1954).
Foot, P. R., "The Philosopher's Defense of Morality." *Philosophy* (1952).
Nielsen, Kai, "Bertrand Russell's New Ethic." *Methodos* (1958).
Nielsen, Kai, "On Looking Back at the Emotive Theory." *Methodos* (1962).
Tegen, Einar, "The Basic Problem in the Theory of Value." *Theoria* (1944).

ASSESSMENTS OF EXISTENTIALISM

Ayer, A. J., "Albert Camus, Novelist-philosopher." *Horizon* (1946).
Ayer, A. J., "Novelist-philosophers: Jean-Paul Sartre." *Horizon* (1946).
Ayer, A. J., "Philosophy at Absolute Zero." *Encounter* (1955).
Beauvoir, Simone de, *The Ethics of Ambiguity*, translated by Bernard Frechtman. New York, 1948. Important in its own right and in relation to Sartre.
Cranston, Maurice, *Sartre*. Edinburgh and London, 1962. General discussion of the range of Sartre's work. Elementary but clear.
Cruickshank, John, *Camus and the Literature of Revolt*. New York, 1959. Contains a detailed and sympathetic account of Camus's thought.
Cruickshank, John, ed., *The Novelist as Philosopher*. London, 1962.
Hochberg, Herbert, "Albert Camus and the Ethic of Absurdity." *Ethics* (1965). Important analytical criticism.
Jeanson, Francis, *Le Problème moral et la pensée de Sartre*. Paris, 1947. Sympathetic and informal discussion of Sartre's moral theory.
Murdoch, Iris, *Sartre: Romantic Rationalist*. New Haven, 1955. Relates Sartre to English thought.
Warnock, Mary, *Ethics Since 1900*. Oxford, 1960.
Warnock, Mary, *The Philosophy of Sartre*. London, 1965. Challenging but sympathetic assessment of Sartre.
Wollheim, Richard, "The Political Philosophy of Existentialism." *Cambridge Journal* (1953).
Wollheim, Richard, "Modern Philosophy and Unreason." *Political Quarterly* (1955).

LINGUISTIC NONCOGNITIVISM

Hare, R. M., "Universalizability." *PAS* (1954).
Hare, R. M., "Descriptivism." *Proceedings of the British Academy* (1963).
Hartland-Swann, John, *An Analysis of Morals*. London, 1960.
Mayo, Bernard, *Ethics and the Moral Life*. London, 1958.
Montefiore, Alan, *A Modern Introduction to Moral Philosophy*. New York, 1959.
Montefiore, Alan, "Goodness and Choice." *PAS*, Supp. Vol. (1961).
Nowell-Smith, P. H., *Ethics*. Harmondsworth, England, 1954.
Nowell-Smith, P. H., "Morality: Religious and Secular." *Rationalist Annual* (1961).
Nowell-Smith, P. H., "Contextual Implications and Ethical Theory." *PAS*, Supp. Vol. (1962).
Nowell-Smith, P. H., "Review of *Freedom and Reason*." *Ratio* (1964).

ASSESSMENTS OF LINGUISTIC NONCOGNITIVISM

Binkley, Luther, *Contemporary Ethical Theories*. New York, 1961.

Castañeda, Héctor-Neri, "Imperatives, Decisions and 'Oughts. A Logico-metaphysical Investigation," in Héctor-Neri Castañeda and George Nakhnikian, eds., *Morality and the Language of Conduct*. Detroit, 1963.
McCloskey, H. J., "Hare's Ethical Subjectivism." *Australasian Journal of Philosophy* (1959).
McCloskey, H. J., "Nowell-Smith's Ethics." *Australasian Journal of Philosophy* (1961).
Monro, H. D., "Are Moral Problems Genuine?" *Mind* (1956).
Monro, H. D., "Impartiality and Consistency." *Philosophy* (1961).
Monro, H. D., "Critical Notice of *Freedom and Reason*." *Australasian Journal of Philosophy* (1964).
Sparshott, F. E., "Critical Study of *Freedom and Reason*." *Philosophical Quarterly* (1963).

GOOD-REASONS APPROACH

Aiken, H. D., *Reason and Conduct*. New York, 1962.
Baier, Kurt, "Decisions and Descriptions." *Mind* (1951).
Baier, Kurt, *The Meaning of Life*. Canberra, 1957.
Falk, W. D., "Morals Without Faith." *Philosophy* (1944).
Falk, W. D., "Obligation and Rightness." *Philosophy* (1945).
Falk, W. D., "'Ought' and Motivation." *PAS* (1947/1948).
Falk, W. D., "Morality and Nature." *Australasian Journal of Philosophy* (1950).
Falk, W. D., "Goading and Guiding." *Mind* (1953).
Falk, W. D., "Moral Perplexity." *Ethics* (1956).
Falk, W. D., "Action-guiding Reasons." *Journal of Philosophy* (1963).
Falk, W. D., "Morality, Self and Others," in Héctor-Neri Castañeda and George Nakhnikian, eds., *Morality and the Language of Conduct*. Detroit, 1963.
Gauthier, David, *Practical Reasoning*. Oxford, 1963.
Ladd, John, "Reason and Practice," in John Wild, ed., *The Return to Reason*. Chicago, 1953.
Ladd, John, *The Structure of a Moral Code*. Cambridge, Mass., 1957.
Ladd, John, "The Issue of Relativism." *The Monist* (1963).
Melden, A. I., "Two Comments on Utilitarianism." *Philosophical Review* (1951).
Melden, A. I., *Rights and Right Conduct*. Oxford, 1959.
Murphy, A. E., *The Uses of Reason*. New York, 1943.
Murphy, A. E., "Blanshard on Good in General." *Philosophical Review* (1963).
Murphy, A. E., *The Theory of Practical Reason*, A. I. Melden, ed. La Salle, Ill., 1965.
Murphy, A. E.; Hay, William; and Singer, Marcus, eds., *Reason and the Common Good*. Englewood Cliffs, N.J., 1963.
Nielsen, Kai, "The Functions of Moral Discourse." *Philosophical Quarterly* (1957).
Nielsen, Kai, "Justification and Moral Reasoning." *Methodos* (1957).
Nielsen, Kai, "Is 'Why Should I Be Moral?' an Absurdity?" *Australasian Journal of Philosophy* (1958).
Nielsen, Kai, "The 'Good Reasons Approach' and 'Ontological Justifications of Morality.'" *Philosophical Quarterly* (1959).
Nielsen, Kai, "Appraising Doing the Thing Done." *Journal of Philosophy* (1960).
Nielsen, Kai, "Can a Way of Life Be Justified?" *Indian Journal of Philosophy* (1960).
Nielsen, Kai, "Conventionalism in Morals and the Appeal to Human Nature." *Philosophy and Phenomenological Research* (1962).
Nielsen, Kai, "Why Should I Be Moral?" *Methodos* (1963).
Nielsen, Kai, "The Good Reasons Approach Revisited." *Archiv für Rechts- und Sozialphilosophie* (1965).
Rawls, John, "Outline of a Decision Procedure for Ethics." *Philosophical Review* (1951).
Rawls, John, "Two Concepts of Rules." *Philosophical Review* (1955).
Rawls, John, "Justice as Fairness." *Philosophical Review* (1958).
Rawls, John, "Constitutional Liberty and the Concept of Justice," in *Nomos*, Vol. VI, *Justice*, Carl J. Friedrich and John W. Chapman, eds. New York, 1963.

Rawls, John, "The Sense of Justice." *Philosophical Review* (1963).

Rawls, John, "Legal Obligation and the Duty of Fair Play," in Sidney Hook, ed., *Law and Philosophy.* New York, 1964.

Singer, Marcus, *Generalization in Ethics.* New York, 1961.

Singer, Marcus, "The Golden Rule." *Philosophy* (1963).

Singer, Marcus, "Negative and Positive Duties." *Philosophical Quarterly* (1965).

Taylor, Paul, "Four Types of Ethical Relativism." *Philosophical Review* (1954).

Taylor, Paul, *Normative Discourse.* Englewood Cliffs, N.J., 1961.

Taylor, Paul, "On Justifying a Way of Life." *Indian Journal of Philosophy* (1961).

Taylor, Paul, "The Ethnocentric Fallacy." *The Monist* (1963).

Toulmin, Stephen, "Knowledge of Right and Wrong." *PAS* (1949/1950).

Toulmin, Stephen, *An Examination of the Place of Reason in Ethics.* Cambridge, 1950.

Toulmin, Stephen, "Is There a Fundamental Problem of Ethics?" *Australasian Journal of Philosophy* (1955).

Toulmin, Stephen, "Principles of Morality." *Philosophy* (1956).

Wright, Georg von, "On Promises." *Theoria* (1962).

Wright, Georg von, *The Logic of Preference.* Edinburgh, 1963.

Wright, Georg von, *Norm and Action.* London, 1963.

Wright, Georg von, "Practical Inference." *Philosophical Review* (1963).

Wright, Georg von, *The Varieties of Goodness.* London, 1963.

(Ethics through the nineteenth century)
RAZIEL ABELSON
(Twentieth-century ethics)
KAI NIELSEN

ETHICS, PROBLEMS OF. What ethics or moral philosophy is, and at best ought to be, has always been variously conceived by philosophers. There is no uncontroversial Archimedean point from which ethics can be characterized, for the nature and proper office of ethics is itself a hotly disputed philosophical problem. But there are some things which can be said on the subject that will elicit a wide measure of agreement, although in any description of ethics the emphasis and organization will display a particular philosophical orientation.

P. H. Nowell-Smith, in his widely read and influential book *Ethics* (1954), argues that in the past moral philosophers sought to give us general guidance concerning what to do, what to seek, and how to treat others. That is not to say that such philosophers as Plato, Aristotle, Epicurus, Hobbes, Spinoza, and Joseph Butler functioned like parish priests or a citizens' advice bureau: they did not seek to give detailed practical advice as to how we should behave on a particular occasion, but they did believe that they could communicate some general but crucial knowledge of good and evil. It was their belief that there is such a thing as a true moral code or a normative ethical system and that philosophers could show what it is. The philosopher's task, in their view, primarily consists in setting forth systematically the first principles of morality and in showing how it is possible to justify these principles. Such an exposition would include not only the philosopher's theoretical conception of the limits of moral justification but also his conception of the good life for man.

Traditionally, moral philosophy had a practical purpose; moral knowledge was not conceived as purely theoretical knowledge of moral phenomena but as practical knowledge about how we ought to live. The goal was not that we should simply know what goodness is but that we should become good. (Some argued that to know what goodness really is, is to become good.)

Yet this still does not adequately characterize what is distinctive about moral philosophy, for novelists, poets, dramatists, and sometimes even historians, social scientists, and psychologists have functioned, in one way or another, as moral sages and have claimed to give us, in some manner, some knowledge of good and evil. It would be difficult to deny that such men as Tolstoy and Dostoyevsky, Sophocles and Shakespeare, Thucydides and Montaigne have sometimes been very perceptive in what they have said about morality. What distinguishes a specifically philosophical account of morality is its generality, its systematic nature, and its attempt to prove its claims.

Even within this traditional conception of the task of ethics, important disagreements have arisen. Such philosophers as Kant and Henry Sidgwick, unlike Bentham and Nietzsche, stressed the fact that it is not the philosophers' aim to discover *new* truths. Moral philosophy, they thought, should give a systematic account of the knowledge man already possesses; it should try to unify and show the ultimate rationale of the moral knowledge and practices man already has. There should be no wholesale rejection of practical moral claims, but an attempt should be made to unify and show the objective justification of most of these claims. Subjectivists, however, would challenge the latter aim, although in an important way there is less conflict between them and philosophers like Kant and Sidgwick than might at first be supposed. Subjectivists did not so much question specific moral practices as attempt to show, as did Edward Westermarck in his *Ethical Relativity* (1932), that the alleged objective foundations of these practices are in shambles. They maintained that common expectations notwithstanding, there is, and in reality can be, no such thing as ethics as a body of knowledge demonstrating how we ought to live. Traditional moral philosophers have been concerned to refute such general skeptical conclusions.

In attempting to do this, they tried to set forth a true moral code, that is, to determine the objective foundations of ethics and to show the sole grounds on which we can justify our moral beliefs. Skeptical moral philosophers tended to leave common-sense moral beliefs intact but questioned whether it was possible to give an objective underpinning to them.

Nietzsche stands out as stark exception to this in his conception of the task of a moral philosopher. He not only questioned the general methods of moral reasoning; he questioned, criticized, even rejected certain common-sense moral beliefs as well. He would not take morality itself as something given; he stressed the diversity of morals and did not seek to supply a rational foundation for our very common moral convictions but, rather, sought to discover new moral truths.

Yet, in spite of these differences, the writings of nearly all of these philosophers fit Nowell-Smith's over-all characterization of the traditional task of moral philosophy. They did not simply seek to clarify the use of moral discourse or to enable us to gain knowledge of moral phenomena but, skeptics and subjectivists apart, sought to give us objective practical knowledge about how we should live.

Even the skeptics and subjectivists lived in the shadow of this goal, for their primary purpose was to show that the moralists could not achieve it.

NORMATIVE ETHICS AND METAETHICS

Contemporary analytic philosophers, when they consider moral philosophy, usually construe their task quite differently. In relation to traditional moralists, Nowell-Smith himself is, in the words of R. M. Hare, "their champion, not their imitator." His *Ethics* is an example of the contemporary approach and is described as "a study of the words and concepts that we use for making decisions, advising, warning, and appraising conduct." The direct object of Nowell-Smith's study is not practice but knowledge: knowledge of the distinctive uses or roles of moral language or, to use another idiom, knowledge of the meanings of moral concepts.

Philosophers like Nowell-Smith and Hare do not set forth a moral system and try to show how it is rationally justified; instead, they analyze moral concepts, including moral systems such as hedonism and utilitarianism. They do not, in their philosophical essays, make moral statements themselves (except incidentally); rather, they discuss the meaning and function of such statements—in their works, moral words and statements occur in mention, not in use. Of course, traditional moral philosophers also analyzed moral concepts, but what distinguishes contemporary ethicists is that many regard analysis as their sole philosophical task.

In developing this distinction, we shall call the body of ethical statements, or the actual normative argument, of the moral philosopher his *normative ethics;* discussions of the meanings or uses of moral terms and utterances about the nature of moral concepts will be called *metaethics.* (Other philosophers use different terminologies. Normative ethics is sometimes called substantive ethics or morals. What we shall call metaethics has been referred to as analytical ethics, critical ethics, theoretical ethics, the epistemology of ethics, the logic of ethics, or ethics.)

We should first further distinguish between normative ethical and metaethical statements. Normative ethical statements are actual moral statements: "The treatment of Negroes in Harlem is a glaring evil," "John's leaving her without a word was cruel," "You ought to be more considerate." There are also more abstract and general normative ethical statements that are apt to occur in traditional philosophical treatises. The following are typical examples: "Pleasure and pleasure alone is intrinsically good, and pain and pain alone is intrinsically evil." "One ought not to use one's head but one's feelings in deciding what one ought to do." "Those rules and practices ought to be adopted which harmonize most fully the interests of as many people as possible."

Metaethical statements, by contrast, are about the uses or meanings of normative ethical statements, utterances, or terms, about the logical status of moral claims, about the nature of moral argument, or about what constitutes a morality. The following are typical examples: "Moral utterances are neither autobiographical statements nor statements of nonnatural fact but expressions of emotion."

" 'Good' is the name of a simple, unanalyzable, nonnatural quality." "The truth of fundamental moral statements can be known only through intuition." "The criteria for what can count as 'a good reason' for a moral claim can be determined only by determining the over-all rationale of that discourse."

Not all discussion of normative ethical talk or belief is metaethical, for there are also statements of fact about people's moral opinions, and there are sociological and psychological descriptions of normative ethical beliefs and language, explanations of why people use moral language in the way they do, and accounts of its origin. The following are examples:

Descriptions of moral beliefs: "Most people believe that nuclear warfare under any circumstances is evil."

Descriptions of moral language: "For many children 'cooperative' and 'uncooperative' come to have the same force as 'good' and 'bad.' "

Explanations of moral language: " 'Cooperative' and 'uncooperative' come to have the same force as 'good' and 'bad' because they are used in the same contexts that 'good' and 'bad' are used in and with the same approbative/disapprobative force."

Accounts of the origin of moral language: "Moral discourse arose because people felt the need for some over-all method of control over the native egoism and aggressive impulses of human beings."

Such descriptive talk about moral discourse is not about the meaning or use of moral terms or utterances, the logical status of such utterances, or the method of validation of moral statements—and thus cannot be properly called metaethical. Sociological or psychological questions of fact about moral discourse, or more generally about people's moral beliefs or attitudes, can conveniently be called questions of descriptive ethics. Descriptive ethics can, in various ways, be relevant to metaethics or normative ethics, but it is most certainly distinct from both.

It is sometimes difficult to tell from mere inspection whether a given statement is a part of descriptive ethics, but the following criterion can be utilized: The truth of a statement in descriptive ethics depends on what moral opinions are actually held by the people referred to, or by what beliefs they have about how people actually behave (purely linguistic behavior apart); the truth of a metaethical statement depends on the kind of utterance people would actually be making if they made a certain moral claim, or on the uses or meanings of the terms in the utterance.

For example, the claim that a moral statement is really a statement about the likes and dislikes of the person making the statement is a metaethical assertion. In order to test its truth one might consider whether the utterances "I like to do it" and "I ought to do it" express the same meaning. To show that the claim is false, we need only point out that the sentence "I don't like to do it, but I ought to do it" is not self-contradictory. We do not need to know anything about the actual moral opinions of the people involved; we need only to know what they and we believe counts as an intelligible or possible moral utterance or expression. By contrast, "Most young Catholics do not really believe that birth control is wrong and hope the hierarchy will change its position about this" can be known to be true or false only by knowing something about the actual moral convictions of people.

A normative ethicist tries to set forth a system of true normative ethical statements or at least to show how certain fundamental normative ethical statements are rationally supported. Some ethicists are iconoclasts and moral critics like Nietzsche and Camus, and seek to show that at least some of our actual normative ethical ideals are irrational. Some, like Kant and Sidgwick, are concerned to exhibit the rational foundations of common-sense normative ethics; they seek to state the heterogeneous claims of common-sense morality in some systematic order, to state its fundamental principles, and to show how they can be rationally justified. Some, like Bentham and Dewey, pursue both courses, with emphasis on the latter. (It is important to note that in doing these tasks a very considerable amount of metaethics also is done.)

A metaethicist tries to analyze and perspicuously display normative ethical discourse. He typically starts with everyday first-order moral (normative ethical) talk, but he also concerns himself with the claims and systems of normative ethicists. His object is not to engage directly in moral argument, reasoning, or normative ethical discourse at all but, as a kind of conceptual cartographer, to give a clear description and/or account of that discourse. His effort is not, even in the most general terms, to tell us how to live or to justify living in a certain way but to make clear what morality is all about and, particularly today, to ask whether normative ethics is really possible as a rational inquiry. If it is, how can it be rationally pursued?

RELATION OF NORMATIVE ETHICS TO METAETHICS

Two questions naturally arise: What is the relationship between normative ethics and metaethics? Why should philosophers concern themselves with metaethics at all?

Many philosophers who are antagonistic to analytic philosophy think that contemporary moral philosophy has regressed in so exclusively concerning itself with metaethics. On the other hand, a few purists among analytic philosophers think that since the sole proper concern of philosophy is with the logical analysis of language or the analysis of concepts, philosophers ought *not*, as philosophers, to do normative ethics. Philosophers, they argue, are not seers; they have no special insight into "moral truth," and therefore they have no right at all to preach to their fellow men or tell them how they ought to live. But this, it is argued, is in effect just what they do when they engage in normative ethics.

Many moral philosophers, including this writer, take the less extreme position that to engage in normative ethics properly is not to preach or in a direct, specific, and casuistic way to tell one's fellow man how to order his life. It is, rather, to criticize irrational moral beliefs and to search for certain general, rationally justifiable moral principles. Its aim is finally to discover and articulate a sound normative ethical system. A moral philosopher should do both metaethics and normative ethics; the crucial thing is not to confuse them and to be clear about their intermural relations.

Yet there is a conviction on the part of many philosophers, and perhaps justifiably so, that a philosopher's main task is to do metaethics. This conviction has been engendered by several considerations. There has been the recognition that philosophical attempts to set forth a rational and objective normative ethic have not been notably successful in spite of the fact that philosophers have been engaged in that activity for the last 24 centuries. Furthermore, the arguments for moral skepticism—skepticism about the feasibility of articulating an objective normative ethic—have been very telling. Finally, and most importantly, it is felt by many philosophers that the logical status of moral utterances and the nature of moral reasoning are so unclear that we cannot profitably do normative ethics until we have a far more adequate metaethic than we have at present. Because of such convictions, a central and pervasive question in metaethics is whether normative ethics is possible. If it is, then it is reasonable to argue that the articulation of a rational normative ethical system is, as G. E. Moore believed, the ultimate aim of moral philosophy. If such a system is impossible, then the task of moral philosophy is to show why this is so and to limit itself to metaethical analysis.

Even if we conclude that in some way it is possible to articulate a sound normative ethic, questions still arise about the relevance of metaethics to normative ethics. What is the logical relationship between metaethical statements and normative ethical statements, or between a normative ethic and a metaethic? And what (if anything) is the normative relevance of metaethical analysis? What, in short, is the proper role of a metaethic with respect to the moral life?

It is frequently claimed that metaethical theories and metaethical statements are all normatively neutral (the neutrality thesis). This is taken in different ways. To ask if they are normatively neutral is to ask at least one of the following questions: (1) Do metaethical statements or theories entail any normative ethical statements or theories? (2) Do normative ethical statements or theories entail any metaethical statements or theories? (3) Do at least some metaethical theories presuppose certain specific normative ethical doctrines? (4) Do at least some normative ethical theories or doctrines presuppose certain specific metaethical beliefs? (5) Do metaethical theories have a normative ethical role? (6) Do one's metaethical beliefs sometimes alter (causally impinge upon) one's normative ethical beliefs or attitudes?

If in claiming that metaethical contentions are all normatively neutral, one answers (6) in the negative, then one is surely mistaken. Most philosophers no doubt overestimate the extent to which conceptual considerations have causal effects on practical matters—including moral beliefs—but many people, perhaps foolishly, have altered their normative ethical beliefs upon accepting a noncognitive metaethic.

However, most analytic philosophers who have wanted to maintain the neutrality thesis have wanted to contend that (1), (2), (3), and (4) should be answered in the negative. Some, however, have wanted to maintain that only (1) and (2) should be answered in the negative.

The belief that normative ethical statements are about

what ought *to be done* or ought *to be* the case, that they are about what is right or good to *do* or good to *make* the case, and that metaethical statements, by contrast, are about what *is* the case strongly inclines one to the neutrality thesis on the ground that a normative statement can never be derived from any nonnormative statement or subset of purely nonnormative statements. Thus there can be no entailment either way.

It might be argued that so to deny an entailment between normative ethical statements and metaethical statements is to presuppose a number of metaethical theses that are themselves quite questionable: that one cannot derive an "ought" from an "is," that there is a clearly demarcated line between factual statements and normative statements or between descriptive discourse and prescriptive and evaluative discourse.

It is, of course, trivially true that if we can make no fundamental or clear demarcation between fact-stating or descriptive discourse and normative discourse, or if normative discourse is a subspecies of factual discourse, then there will be no general reason to deny an entailment between metaethical statements and normative ones. Whether there is such a demarcation in discourse is one of the central issues of contemporary ethical theory.

Some who would answer (1) and (2) in the negative would answer (3) and/or (4) in the affirmative. There is no entailment between normative ethical claims and metaethical claims, but normative ethical claims presuppose a certain metaethic, or any given normative ethic, is compatible only with a particular metaethic or at least with a certain range of metaethical theories. Where we have an entailment between two statements, *p* and *q*, then if *p* is true, *q* is true; and if *q* is false, *p* is false. But if *p* is presupposed by *q*, then if *p* is false, *q* as well as not-*q* is void; but *q* can be false without *p* being false. If "Bentley has some students" (*p*) is presupposed by "Bentley's students are Irish" (*q*), then "It is false that Bentley's students are Irish" does *not* show that Bentley has no students; but if *p* is false and Bentley has no students, then neither "Bentley's students are Irish" nor "Bentley's students are not Irish" is false, for both statements are voided when such a condition obtains.

Let our ethical case be "Moral statements can be true or false" (metaethical statement *p*). Let us try to assert that *p* is presupposed by normative ethical statement *q* ("It is patently false to claim that the innocent under certain circumstances ought to be punished"). If *p* is false, *q* is not false but in an important sense is meaningless or void, for the falsity of *p* shows that the very labels "truth" and "falsity" are not applicable to *q*. In this way the intelligibility, and thus also the truth, of a given normative ethical claim presupposes the truth of a given metaethical statement. If the metaethical statement is false, we cannot assert the normative ethical statement. But it still remains the case that the adoption of that metaethic would not constitute a good reason for accepting the normative ethic or normative ethical statement in question rather than some conflicting normative ethic or normative ethical statement, for if *q* presupposes *p*, so does not-*q*. Since "John's children are bald" presupposes that John has children, so does "John's children are not bald."

The converse does not hold. It is not the case that a given metaethical theory or statement presupposes the correctness of a given normative ethical theory or statement. Consider this case: "Moral utterances are expressions of emotion" does not presuppose "Communism is a glaring evil" or "One ought to experience one's emotional life to the full." These normative statements could be rejected without voiding the metaethical statement. Such a metaethical claim is not voided by any normative ethical statement, no matter how general. Even the falsity of "People ought to do what they are emotionally disposed to do" does not void "Moral utterances are expressions of emotion." The metaethical statement in question only asserts that if an utterance is moral, it expresses the emotions of the speaker; it does not tell one what one ought or ought not to do. It does not say one ought or ought not to do what one is emotionally disposed to do. It only implies that when a speaker asserts "People ought never to do what they are emotionally disposed to do," this utterance, like any moral utterance, expresses the speaker's emotions.

Here we can see in a specific case that a metaethical statement does not presuppose a given normative ethical statement and appears not to presuppose any specific metaethical statement or type of metaethic. It would quite generally appear to be the case that no metaethical statement or metaethic presupposes a normative ethical statement or a given type of normative ethic. If there were no normative ethical claims at all, there could be no metaethics, but that is a different matter.

If correct, the above line of reasoning has important consequences, for it makes it apparent that a given metaethic or metaethical theory does not entail any normative ethical claim, statement, or theory; and the converse relationship also holds. It is also the case that no metaethical theory presupposes any given normative ethics. In these very important respects the defenders of the neutrality thesis seem to be correct. But it would also appear to be the case that we can make certain normative ethical claims only if certain metaethical claims are true. The truth of these metaethical claims does not insure the truth of the normative ethical claims, but the normative ethical claims cannot be true unless the metaethical claims are. In this respect metaethics does not seem normatively neutral.

Finally we consider (5): Do metaethical theories have a normative ethical role? From the above discussion we can see that we are in a position to make one important assertion, namely, that from the truth of any given metaethic or metaethical statement we cannot conclude that a given normative ethic or normative ethical statement is true. But metaethical theories do have normative implications. If "No moral statements can be true or false" is true, then we cannot assert as a normative ethical statement that it is false to say that communism is evil. Thus there are normative functions of metaethical statements, but it is important to determine just what they are and how they work, for on this turns the pragmatic value of metaethics.

It is sometimes argued that metaethics has normative implications because, without being a normative activity itself, it can still serve as an instrument for greater rationality in our actual moral life. Given the fact that we want to be more rational in our moral thinking, and given the fact that we can be more rational, metaethical analysis can be extremely useful.

There are some important ways in which the above contention is true. Metaethical analysis can undermine certain obscure beliefs about morality and in that way can further the moral life. This is not to say that if a man changes his metaethical beliefs, there is any reason for him to change any given normative ethical belief (such as that the infliction of pain is evil). But metaethical analysis of the meaning of "*x* is wrong" or "*x* is right" may enable him to be clearer and more certain in the organization of his moral beliefs and in his efforts to justify them. To take obvious examples, the man who believes that "*x* is right" means "*x* is commanded by God" may in certain situations be unsure of how to decide or demonstrate what it is that God has commanded. On the other hand, a man who believes that "*x* is right" means simply "the speaker feels that *x* is right" may have difficulty in justifying or finding convincing reasons for doing what he feels is right. However, further metaethical analysis may show that moral judgments do not require special insight into the mind of God or into some nonnatural realm, and moreover that there are rules of valid reasoning appropriate to moral argument. To reason morally may be to reason in accordance with a rule of inference that says "If something causes pain, it is, *ceteris paribus* (all things being equal), not to be done." Thus, moral beliefs may be represented in what is presumably a more coherent and perspicuous way, and one no longer need feel mystified about them and uneasy about their having an objective rationale.

That metaethical beliefs can be helpful in this way assumes that metaethical theory can attain the kind of clarity that would enable us, with some justification, to claim that certain metaethical beliefs are true or at least probable. This is not easy to establish; yet, if it can be shown that some metaethical beliefs are well warranted, then, in the way we have exhibited above, we will have shown how they can clarify normative ethical thought and in this way have an important normative ethical function.

DISCOURSE IN NORMATIVE ETHICS

We must now consider the familiar Kantian question: "Is normative ethics possible?" That is, is it possible to state and rationally defend a normative ethic in such a way that all rational men, after carefully reflecting on the considerations pro and con, would find it acceptable? Is philosophical normative argument possible?

To see, or at least to begin to consider, whether it is or not, let us examine some important normative ethical claims and see if they can be so defended. As this examination proceeds, it will become apparent why so many contemporary philosophers have concerned themselves almost exclusively with metaethics, for when we push normative inquiries to a certain stage, the conclusion often turns to some considerable degree on metaethical issues.

Normative ethics tries systematically to establish the general principles for determining right and wrong or good and evil. In attempting to produce such an answer, many ethical questions are asked, but they can all be subsumed under three general questions: (1) What is right and

wrong? (2) What is blameworthy and praiseworthy? (3) What is desirable or worthwhile? Here (2), which presupposes an answer to (1), will be ignored (see EPISTEMOLOGY AND ETHICS, PARALLEL BETWEEN), and we shall concentrate on (1) and (3).

It is important to see that (1) and (3) are distinct questions, for while it may be that everything that is desirable to do is also something that one is obligated to do, it is still not the case that to *say* that something is worthwhile or desirable is the same as saying that one is obligated to do it. Questions about what is desirable to do, what is worthwhile, or what is good in itself may not even strike one as moral questions. If a woman struggles with herself about whether it would be more desirable to be a dentist or a doctor, she is not, at least in typical situations, facing a moral dilemma, although it may be a very crucial personal problem for her; but if a woman struggles over whether to tell her husband that she is going to have a child by another man, she is, in our society at any rate, definitely involved in a moral problem. Yet it is surely not implausible to argue that morality exists for man and not man for morality; that those practices which should be thought of as involving duties and obligations are so labeled because it is believed (perhaps mistakenly) that in the long run they will bring about a better or more desirable life for more people than would the institution of any alternative set of practices. This is not to urge the metaethical thesis that "*x* is right," "*x* is obligatory," or "*x* ought to be done" means "*x* is the most desirable thing for everybody" or "*x* is the best possible or most worthwhile act under the circumstances." It is, rather, designed to show the ethical relevance of questions of the third type.

In asking "How should we live?" it is certainly not unreasonable to argue that one ought always to do that act which under the circumstances would have the best or most desirable consequences for everyone involved. After all, what better, more worthwhile thing could we do than to do what is best for everyone? This does not settle the issue in favor of teleologists over deontologists, but it does make the teleological position sufficiently plausible to make it worthwhile to give careful consideration to (3). A teleologist in ethics argues that the only thing we have to know in order to decide whether or not an act is right is whether the act, among all the alternative acts we might perform, would bring about the best total state of affairs. Deontologists, by contrast, assert that there are at least some other considerations, besides the goodness or badness of the consequences of actions or attitudes, that make actions or attitudes right or wrong. Yet even a deontologist can quite consistently consider (3) an ethical question.

Granted that it is crucial in knowing how we ought to live to determine what is worthwhile, desirable, or good in itself, just how would we do it? This issue is a central one in moral philosophy. But before we consider some of the central positions and issues involved in any decision here, it is essential to make an important distinction. In asking our question we are asking what it is that makes something *intrinsically* desirable, good, or worthwhile. That is, what (if anything) is worthwhile for its own sake or in itself, quite irrespective of its consequences?

To say that *x* is intrinsically desirable (good, worthwhile) is to say that, *ceteris paribus*, the existence or occurrence of *x* is more desirable (better, more worthwhile) than its nonexistence or nonoccurrence because of its own nature alone, completely apart from any positive or negative desirability possessed by things to which *x* is conducive. To say that *x* is extrinsically desirable (good, worthwhile) is to say that *x* is conducive, directly or indirectly, to something else, *y*, which is intrinsically desirable (good, worthwhile).

This distinction, like most distinctions made by philosophers, has been vigorously attacked. There are serious questions concerning whether it is a clear distinction; questions concerning its applicability and importance in moral assessment; and, to say the least, it certainly must be questioned whether intrinsic and extrinsic are all the fundamental varieties of goodness. But, historically at least, this distinction has been of considerable moment, for most of the classical normative ethical theories have been theories about what is intrinsically desirable or worthwhile.

Normative ethical theories about what is intrinsically desirable can be conveniently divided into monistic and pluralistic theories. Monistic theories, like hedonism and self-realizationism, claim that one, and only one, kind of experience or reality is intrinsically desirable or good; pluralistic theories maintain that there can be more than one kind of intrinsic desirability or good.

The respective merits of these views will become somewhat more apparent if we examine what could be said for and against ethical hedonism.

Ethical hedonism. One of the strongest and most persistent theories about what things are intrinsically good is ethical hedonism. An ethical hedonist contends that pleasure, and pleasure alone, is intrinsically good. But hedonism is not just a theory about what is intrinsically good; it also attempts to be a complete normative ethical theory. It aims to tell us which moral principles are justified, what general types of moral rules we should follow, and, in principle at least, it aims to tell us what general types of action are good and what attitudes are desirable. It would, in short, supply us with a complete normative ethical theory, but the whole edifice of such a theory rests on its doctrine about what is intrinsically good. This doctrine is not sufficient to establish hedonism as a complete normative ethic, but it is necessary.

The hedonist's contention is that pleasantness is either identical with or a criterion for intrinsic goodness. To establish either claim involves establishing (1) that pleasure or pleasant (enjoyable) experiences are always intrinsically good and (2) that *only* pleasure or pleasant (enjoyable) experiences are intrinsically good. Neither (1) nor (2) is sufficient by itself.

What can be said for (1)? There is no serious question about whether sometimes a pleasant experience is intrinsically good; the question is whether it is always intrinsically good. There are bad pleasures or evil pleasures, it will be argued. The Klan member who takes pleasure in beating a Negro to death or the sadistic doctor who takes pleasure in hurting his patients does something that is evil. To take pleasure in deliberate acts of cruelty is evil.

To this the hedonist replies that there is nothing wrong with such pleasure per se. Its effects, namely the pain it brings to others, is bad; but if we consider the pleasure in isolation from its effects, it will be seen that there is nothing bad about it taken by itself. It is intrinsically good but extrinsically bad because it is conducive to something that is intrinsically bad, namely pain.

Some will argue that taking pleasure in giving pain to others is both intrinsically and extrinsically evil. Even in the case where an act inspired by sadistic motives has good effects, they will still hold that the act is intrinsically evil. (An example might be a sadistic doctor who enjoys giving shock therapy because he likes to watch his patients suffer but who administers this therapy only in cases where it is the best available treatment to cure the patient.) The nonhedonist may also appeal to majority opinion and maintain that most people will agree that it would be a better world if doctors didn't take pleasure in giving pain. The hedonist will reply that it is not opinion which determines what is intrinsically good or bad. He will point out that the sadistic doctor's pleasure slightly lessens the sum total pain in the world, so in such a situation a world in which he took pleasure in his work would be intrinsically better than a world in which he did not, for the more intrinsic good there is in the world, the better. Those who deny this are either being irrational or are making a miscalculation, for character traits that accompany such sadism usually cause a good deal of unnecessary suffering. But if such behavior has exactly the same effects all around as the behavior of the doctor who does his job with repugnance or just as a matter of routine, then, if one carefully and impartially reflects on it, one will come to appreciate not only that a world with such sadists is not a worse world but is actually a better world, for there will be more pleasure (more intrinsic good) in it than in a world in which this is not so.

The dialectic of this normative ethical argument gives rise, quite naturally, to two metaethical issues. In the first the nonhedonist in effect argues that if *x* is ordinarily believed to be intrinsically good, then *x* is intrinsically good—or at least that this ordinary belief is a necessary condition for *x*'s being intrinsically good. The hedonist rejects this and claims instead that only what the clearheaded, impartial, and informed man believes to be intrinsically good is intrinsically good. Both are in reality arguing about what it means to call something "intrinsically good" and about the logic of justification of claims of intrinsic goodness. To do this is to do metaethics.

Suppose the nonhedonist grants that there would be more total pleasure in the sadist's world but still maintains that such pleasure is intrinsically evil and the hedonist, recognizing this, continues to assert it is intrinsically good. How, if at all, could we rationally resolve this issue? Both claims are apparently synthetic, and they are in conflict. To say they are essentially contested or that neither is true or false—for they merely exhibit a disagreement in attitude—is to assume without argument a metaethical position; and exactly the same thing is true if one asserts that one is immediately aware of the truth of the hedonist's or the nonhedonist's claim. Further progress toward resolving this normative issue calls for clarification of the meaning of the terms "good" and "pleasure" and of the logical status of "Pleasure is intrinsically good."

We have noted some, but by no means all, of the difficulties in establishing that pleasure is *always* intrinsically good. But let us assume that we have in some way established its truth. We still have not established the truth of hedonism, for we must also establish what is much harder to establish, that *only* pleasure is intrinsically good. Here most people part company with hedonism and adopt some form of pluralism.

Ethical pluralism. G. E. Moore argues that the claim of the hedonist is absurd, for it commits him to the belief "that a world in which absolutely nothing but pleasure existed—no knowledge, no love . . . no moral qualities—must yet be intrinsically better worth creating—provided only the total quantity of pleasure in it were *the least bit greater* [italics added], than one in which all these things existed *as well as* pleasure." There are many things of great value. It is, it is argued, absurd to think that only one of them should be classified as worth having for its own sake. Many people who have reflected on the matter regard knowledge, freedom, conscientiousness, a sense of identity, and awareness to be intrinsically good as well.

The hedonist can reply to Moore's argument by agreeing that a world with knowledge and love in it is better than a world without such knowledge, but he will argue that it is not *intrinsically* better. A world with love and knowledge in it will, in the long run, lead to a world with greater happiness in it. We so readily assent to Moore's remarks because we all, on good grounds, believe this; but such a belief is quite compatible with the truth of hedonism.

Part of the difficulty in this argument stems from confusions on both sides about the concept of pleasure. Some critics of hedonism think of pleasure as consisting in delightful sensations. They think that a hedonist is claiming that the only things desirable for themselves alone are things like being rubbed, stroked, or massaged. But this, of course, is an absurd parody of the claims of hedonism. The hedonist does not identify pleasure with such delectable sensations. His use of "pleasure" is identifiable with enjoyable states of consciousness. He claims that something is intrinsically good if, and only if, it is an experience that is enjoyable whenever a person has it. But this is not to treat pleasure, as one treats pain, as a sensation. It is, in a way that is very hard to characterize correctly, a dimension or quality of experience.

Is it true that the only kind of experiences we want for their own sake are enjoyable experiences? (If true, is it logically true or contingently true?) Are these experiences the only things that are intrinsically desirable? Most philosophers have remained pluralists on these questions. How, for example, does the hedonist know that knowledge always has only extrinsic value? Why not, at least for some kinds of knowledge, both?

Again metaethics becomes relevant. Suppose a man says: "I don't find self-knowledge or scientific knowledge intrinsically desirable at all. If it leads to happiness, it is worthwhile; if not, not. Similarly, a sense of one's humanity or a sense of identity has no intrinsic merit. To have a sense of identity and an understanding of oneself is valuable only if it leads to happiness; if it does not, it is without intrinsic worth. Pleasure, enjoyment and pleasure, or enjoyment alone is intrinsically good." But, let us further

suppose, the ethical pluralist continues to claim that self-identity and some kinds of knowledge are intrinsically good. How, if at all, can we settle this issue? How, if at all, can man either *know* or even have good reason to believe he is right? Here again fundamental metaethical issues lurk behind the scenes.

It is very natural for people to argue here, unwittingly switching to a metaethical argument, that what it *means* to say that something is intrinsically good is that it is enjoyable, pleasant, or productive of pleasure. This is to make a metaethical claim that can be countered by metaethical arguments—that it is an intelligible question to ask if all those things which are enjoyable are intrinsically good; that it is not self-contradictory to assert "It's pleasant but it has no intrinsic worth"; and that it can be pointed out that "Those things which are fecund sources of pleasure are worth seeking for their own sake" is not an analytic statement. We could, by a suitable stipulative redefinition of this last statement, make it true by definition, the one before it self-contradictory, and the question self-answering. But this does not settle the question(s) of why these definitions should be accepted as normative and how a stipulation can reveal "normative truth."

If instead we claim that all men desire or seek pleasure (enjoyment, satisfaction of desire), and only pleasure, for its own sake, this would be, depending on how we took it, either a most questionable psychological claim or a disguised tautology. Whether tautologically true or empirically true, the claim would still not constitute a *normative* claim. That people desire or seek pleasure only for its own sake does not *eo ipso* establish that what they seek is desirable or intrinsically good; and, if the only thing people *can* seek is pleasure or satisfaction of desire, then it makes no sense to say that it is good that they do so, for they cannot do otherwise. But if they do always in fact seek pleasure for its own sake but might seek something else instead, then it is appropriate to ask why they should continue to seek it or why it is good to seek it at all.

If the hedonist, like Sidgwick, claims that on careful reflection he is aware, through immediate or intuitive insight, that only enjoyable states of consciousness are intrinsically good, then he is again engaged in metaethics. He is relying on the possibility and, granted the possibility, the correctness of some intuitions. Sidgwick is not alone in having or claiming to have intuitions, and others, after careful reflection, have intuitions or what they take to be intuitions that conflict with Sidgwick's. Are they all genuine intuitions? How can we know which "intuitions" (if any) are correct? W. D. Ross, for example, has intuitions that are diametrically opposed to Sidgwick's. How can we tell who is right, or is there in reality no right and wrong—no moral truth—here? Are they not both simply expressing their preferences and trying to get others to adopt their attitudes? In trying to assess this normative ethical dispute, we are ineluctably led into fundamental metaethical controversies.

If the hedonist tries to resolve the argument in his favor in another way, he is also led into metaethical controversy and he also, if he so argues, shows how in the interests of his theory he has arbitrarily extended the meaning of "pleasure." Suppose he says that the man who judges some knowledge to be intrinsically good says he *wants* that knowledge for its own sake and not simply because of the pleasure or power it will give him. Similarly, the man who says that, painful or not, he *wants* to keep his self-identity shows that he is, after all, unwittingly reasoning as a hedonist, for in judging knowledge and self-identity to be intrinsically good, he shows that he *wants* them for their own sake; and to say that *x* is pleasant is to say that *x* is a part of experience that all people or most people want to continue on its own account. To be a hedonist is to argue that something is intrinsically desirable if, and only if, it is an experience that the person who has it *wants* to prolong for its own sake.

If this is so, hedonism appears to become true by definition, in which case pluralist theories are unintelligible rather than false. But this may be an arbitrary redefinition of the word "pleasure" in the interests of a normative ethical theory, for ordinarily it would seem that one could understand someone's contention that, even though an experience is painful, he wishes to continue having it because he regards it as having intrinsic value. Such a wish may be irrational, but it certainly does not appear unintelligible. This gives us some reason to believe that such a hedonist is operating with an arbitrarily extended definition of "pleasure."

The hedonist could reply that this is not so, for if we stress, as we should, intrinsic value (that is, an experience worth having "on its own account"), it is not so evident that it makes sense to say that we seek painful experiences on their own account or for themselves, or that we seek nonpleasurable experiences on their own account or for themselves.

Whoever is right here, it is again apparent that to adjudicate this normative ethical issue between the hedonist and the nonhedonist, we must resolve a metaethical dispute about the meaning of "pleasure" and about the relation of "pleasure" to "good."

The hedonist may take yet another tack in his own defense, but again he is led into another metaethical controversy. He may grant, given ordinary moral consciousness and the moral discourse that reflects that consciousness, that it is of course correct to assert that knowledge, self-identity, and many things other than pleasure are intrinsically good. But he still may argue that ordinary moral consciousness is, in many respects, irrational and parochial, and that we cannot rely on it or the discourse it enshrines to give us an understanding of what morality is really about. This raises a cluster of metaethical issues about the nature of justification in ethics.

The point of the discussion about the question of what is intrinsically good or worthwhile has not been to settle this ancient issue in favor of hedonism or in favor of any pluralistic theories, but to show how these normative ethical issues will, when pursued relentlessly, finally turn to a considerable degree, although not entirely, on conceptual controversies. It is these controversies that metaethics is designed to handle.

Normative ethics is actual, so in one plain but trivial sense it is possible; but normative ethical issues lead to metaethical ones, and whether a sound normative ethic is possible turns on the proper answer to certain metaethical questions. (That the relation is not quite that simple will become apparent later. The final constraint on any metaethics is living moral language.)

To settle what is intrinsically good or what is worth seeking for its own sake does not, by any means, exhaust the normative ethical questions that deserve careful treatment. Even the teleologist must go on to determine what is the best thing to do. If he is a pluralist, he must determine which one of various conflicting intrinsic goods is most desirable; and a hedonist must decide what is most pleasurable and *whose* pleasure is to be considered. Other ethical monists have similar problems. But if we are teleologists we will reason in this way, unless we are also egoists: whatever is intrinsically good should be promoted. If the greatest amount of good to everyone involved is realized, then we will have achieved what should be done. Our obligation, as moral agents, is always to promote the greatest possible net good. But, as deontologists and others have been quick to bring out, there are all kinds of questions about this position. Most pressing, perhaps, is the question of whether the rightness of an act depends entirely on its consequences. Is it really the case that an act is right if, and only if, it maximizes intrinsic good?

Suppose act *A* or rule or practice *A* involves breaking a promise or lying, while act *B* or rule or practice *B* does not; but act *A* or rule or practice *A* has *slightly* better consequences. Is it clear that we do the right thing in performing act *A* rather than *B*? It is not so clear. Many moralists would claim that the right thing to do here is *B*. This, they say, is even clearer if the consequences of *A* and *B* both lead to the same amount of total intrinsic good. Where this last situation obtains, teleologists would say that there is no reason for saying one act or one rule is right and the other wrong; but surely an act or rule that involves lying or breaking a promise is, *ceteris paribus*, morally inferior to an act or rule that does not involve lying or breaking a promise. In determining what is right and wrong, it is important to determine what things are intrinsically good and what contributes to a maximum amount of intrinsic good, but such knowledge is not by itself sufficient to give us knowledge of what is the right or wrong thing to do. Moreover, we seem to have a further and independent criterion for justice, for it is not clear that we should always seek the maximum net good; we should be concerned with the equity of its distribution as well. It would seem that we should seek that state of affairs which will, as far as possible, realize the maximum net good for *everyone* involved.

There are a host of questions here about what is the right, just, or fair thing to do that any sound normative ethic must answer. We cannot here examine them in detail, but it should be reasonably apparent that satisfactory answers to them again lead to making a decision about appropriate answers to metaethical questions. Can "right," "ought," "just" be defined or explicated in terms of "good"? Is discovery of the criteria for good also discovery of the criteria for right? Are there independent objective criteria for rightness or justice? What is the logic of justification in ethics? What is (are) the meaning(s) of "moral"? This discussion would again show that normative ethics, pursued diligently, naturally leads, when pressed to a certain level of abstraction, to the conceptual inquiry called metaethics.

In this section we have sought to establish that many fundamental normative ethical disputes require for their resolution an examination of metaethical issues. Our primary means of achieving this has been through examining some of the conflicts that arise in normative ethics between ethical hedonism and pluralistic theories. In trying to resolve certain fundamental issues in normative ethics, disputes quite naturally arise concerning the intelligibility of the concept of intrinsic goodness, its exact nature, and its centrality in moral reasoning. As we have seen, disputes which arise between ethical hedonists and nonhedonists over whether pleasure and only pleasure is intrinsically good lead to metaethical disputes over the meaning of "pleasure" and over the logical status of such claims as "Pleasure alone is good." Furthermore, even if the normative ethical beliefs of a given normative ethical theory (such as ethical hedonism) conflict with ordinary moral beliefs, it will only follow that this normative ethical theory is in error, if it is true that a normative ethical theory is sound only if it is in accord with ordinary moral beliefs. But this is also a thesis in metaethics and requires metaethical analysis for its rational resolution. Finally, as we have also seen, when normative ethicists consider what is the best thing to do and what ought, everything considered, to be done, metaethical questions concerning the meaning, criteria, and intermural relations of "right," "good," "just," and "ought" come to the fore. To know whether a rational normative ethic is possible, we must have some reasonable answer to such metaethical questions.

METAETHICAL RELATIVISM AND SUBJECTIVISM

Given the difficulty in justifying any normative system, we should now examine various forms of the familiar assertion that moral claims, unlike factual claims, are all subjective. There are confusions here and distinctions that must be made before we can profitably pursue some of the metaethical questions that have been central to moral philosophy.

The difficulty in discussing the charge that moral claims are all relative or all subjective is in knowing exactly what the charge is. People who have made such claims have meant many very different things. (See ETHICAL RELATIVISM for distinctions between descriptive relativism, of which cultural relativism is a subspecies; normative relativism; and metaethical relativism. As the article makes apparent, it is metaethical relativism that is at the bottom of the most serious perplexities connected with the assertion that all moral claims are fundamentally relative or conventional.)

To understand clearly what is involved in a conventionalist's challenge concerning morals, a few remarks about metaethical relativism, its cousin ethical skepticism, and subjectivism are in order.

Relativism and skepticism. Metaethical relativism claims that there are no objectively sound procedures for justifying one moral code or one set of moral judgments as against another code or set of moral judgments. Ethical skepticism claims that no one can ever say with any justification that something is good or bad, right or wrong. Some actions may be right and others wrong, but there is no way of knowing which is which.

Ethical skepticism at first appears to be a normative ethical doctrine, but it is difficult to understand it as anything other than a claim about the logic of justification in ethics and thus as a part of metaethics. The skeptic leaves open the possibility that some actions or principles are right or wrong, but he claims we can never be in a position to know that this is so. This claim refers to what is logically possible to do and thus is about the nature of moral concepts. This means that if we are to find good arguments for ethical skepticism, they must be found in some metaethical argument about the meaning of ethical terms and/or the nature of moral argument.

Subjectivism. It is here that subjectivism becomes relevant. Subjectivism, as it is construed by philosophers, is a metaethical contention about the logical status of moral utterances. It is usually taken to mean any one of the following. (1) A moral utterance is merely an autobiographical statement about the attitudes or feelings of the person making the statement. (2) Moral utterances merely express the attitudes or feelings of the utterer and are used by him to evoke or invite similar attitudes in others. (3) Moral judgments *purport* to refer to something outside the speaker's mind, but in reality they only express, although in a disguised way, his approbations and disapprobations. (4) There is no way of rationally resolving *fundamental* moral disputes, for fundamental moral judgments, or *ultimate* moral principles, cannot correctly be said to be true or false independently of the attitudes of at least some people. (A fundamental moral dispute is a dispute that would not be resolved even if there were complete agreement about the nonmoral facts relevant to the dispute. Ultimate moral principles are those which would divide people in such situations of moral dispute, and fundamental moral judgments are the conflicting moral judgments people would make when they disagreed morally, even when they were in complete agreement about the nonmoral facts relevant to the dispute.)

All four of these metaethical claims are to be contrasted with a fifth sense of "subjectivism" that is not metaethical but probably is closer to what most nonphilosophers would mean by "subjectivism in ethics." This is the contention that the moral judgments people make are all formed or at least very strongly influenced by their emotional biases or prejudices. In short, (5) asserts that all moral judgments are prejudiced judgments.

It is evident that many moral judgments are unwittingly biased and thus are subjective in sense (5), but, unless "bias" and "prejudice" are to be evacuated of all their content, it is clear that this form of subjectivism presupposes the possibility that *some* moral judgments are not subjective in that way. Sometimes people make moral judgments in a calm, impartial way after a due consideration of the facts; and even if this empirical truism would turn out to be false, this would be of a considerably less strictly philosophical consequence than might at first be thought because we would still be able to conceive what it would be like for moral judgments to be objective. The problem would not cause philosophical bewilderment, although it would surely lead to social chaos.

The first characterization of subjectivism given above is a typical way in which analytic critics of subjectivism state the position they are criticizing. Such a subjectivism is plainly untenable. To say (*a*) "One ought never to lie" is not to say (*b*) "the idea of never lying, as a matter of psychological fact, arouses in me a pro-attitude toward never lying." I could surely say, without contradicting myself, that the idea of never lying arouses in me a pro-attitude toward never lying, but all the same I ought to suppress that pro-attitude. But since this is not self-contradictory, (*a*) and (*b*) cannot be identical in meaning; and if they are not identical in meaning, subjectivism in sense (1) is false. What would establish the truth of (*b*) is reasonably evident, but what, if anything, would establish the truth of (*a*) is not at all evident; however, if they have the same meaning, what would establish the truth of one would establish the truth of the other. Nevertheless, we have no reason at all to think they have the same truth-value.

A good case, however, can be made for the claim that this first kind of subjectivism is but the straw man of certain analytic philosophers and that in this form it is seldom maintained by serious philosophers.

Some philosophers, who wish to limit subjectivism to (1) or perhaps to (4), say (2) is not subjectivism at all but a simple and very unsatisfactory variety of emotivism. Others have wished to call emotivism a new subjectivism. It is a moot point whether all forms of emotivism should be called subjectivistic, but (2) would deny any interpersonal validity to moral claims and would deny that they could be true. This would seem enough to warrant calling this form of emotivism a subjective metaethic; later we shall examine whether it is an adequate metaethic. But such a paradoxical claim, if true, would surely give us a negative answer to the Kantian question "Is a normative ethic possible?" It would not entail the impropriety of any normative ethical claim, but if true, there could be no question about justifying a normative ethical claim or a normative ethical system. However, (2) is highly implausible.

Subjectivism in senses (3) and (4) is a far more serious threat. If (3) were true, no rational normative ethic would be possible; and if (4) were true, it would seem questionable whether we could answer the Kantian question affirmatively. Yet there are powerful considerations favoring (3) and (4). They give substance and greater precision to the frequently voiced and very confused claim that *alles ist relativ*. We could, of course, raise difficulties about (3) and (4), but we would always be faced with the possibility that (3) or (4), more adequately stated or modified, could avoid these difficulties. A more direct approach would be to state an adequate metaethic that was not subjective in any of the above senses and that clarified the nature of the problem about justification in ethics and treated how it could be answered by showing how moral disagreements can be rationally resolved and how they have certain formal and perhaps nonformal conditions of adequacy. Before considering the adequacy of certain traditional nonsubjectivist metaethical theories, we must explain these formal requirements and state the problem of justification somewhat more fully.

FORMAL FEATURES OF MORAL DISCOURSE

Most fundamentally, the question of justification in ethics is the question of stating, elucidating, and defending a sound procedure for determining the truth of conflicting moral claims and the soundness of moral arguments. In everyday life we are barraged with a variety of moral claims and counterclaims; the moral arguments in support of them are diverse and conflicting. How are we finally to decide among them? Is it really the case that metaethical relativism or some variety of subjectivism is correct? Moralists have traditionally claimed objectivity for their moral principles, and this claim of objectivity seems to be embedded in our everyday moral discourse. But is this claim actually justified? Can we show that there are objectively true moral judgments or that there are sound moral arguments?

Such a question clearly calls for a characterization of what could be meant by calling a moral judgment objective. A moral judgment is objective if, and only if, it is either true or false and if its truth or falsity does not depend on the peculiarities of the person who makes the judgment or on the culture to which he belongs, but shall be determinable by any rational agent who is apprised of the relevant facts.

It should be noted that there are some metaethicists who claim that there are objective moral judgments and yet deny that moral judgments or statements can properly be called true or false. They recognize that moral judgments do not have the kind of necessary truth characteristic of mathematics, and they argue with considerable plausibility that moral statements are not true or false in the way that empirical statements are true or false—there are no ethical characteristics, rightness and wrongness, goodness and badness, that are either directly or indirectly observable. Since this is so, they conclude that there are no objective moral facts which would make moral judgments true or false; because of this, "truth" and "falsity" are not correctly applicable to moral judgments.

Even if it is true that moral judgments differ from factual judgments in this way, it does not follow that we cannot correctly say that moral judgments are true or false. To assert that a judgment or statement is true is to give a warranted endorsement of that judgment or statement, but what makes the judgment warranted varies according to what we are talking about. To be capable of being true, a statement need not state a fact or assert that certain empirically identifiable characteristics are part of an object or an action. Rather, what is necessary is that the statement in question be publicly warrantable, that is, that it admit of some publicly determinable procedure in virtue of which rational men could come to accept it. If a given statement has a sufficiently powerful warrant to justify our claiming that we are certain of it, then we can properly say it is true. But what and how we warrant what we are talking about depends on *what it is that* we are talking about. We can properly call a statement or judgment in any area objectively true if it would be endorsed without doubt by informed, reasonable, reflective, and careful observers.

Such a publicly determinable judgment, whether true or false, is objective. If, by contrast, its acceptability depends on some cultural or individual idiosyncrasy of the person(s) involved, then the statement is subjective and cannot have the kind of truth required for an objective moral judgment.

There are some features other than the claim to objectivity that are held to be formal requirements of all moral judgments. Moral judgments all make a claim to universality—if I judge that I have a right to disregard a certain regulation or that I ought to do a certain thing, I implicitly judge that relevantly similar persons in relevantly similar situations also have a right to do it or ought to do it. Similarly, if I say that it would be a good thing if x would do y, I give one to understand that it would be a good thing for anyone relevantly like x and similarly situated to do y. And if I say of something, "It's a good one," I must say, on pain of incoherence, that anything exactly like "it" is also a good one. What, exactly, counts as a relevant similarity or a relevant respect cannot be determined apart from the context and nature of what we are discussing, but what constitutes a relevant similarity is often evident enough in a given context. At any rate, this kind of universality or generalizability is built into the very use of moral expressions and helps govern what can count as a moral judgment.

Moral discourse is also a form of practical discourse; its primary use is not that of asserting, questioning, or reaffirming that something is the case but that of making something the case, of criticizing or appraising something that is the case, or of molding attitudes toward certain states of affairs or actions. This is what is meant when we say that moral discourse is essentially action-guiding and attitude-molding.

Beyond the claims to objectivity, universality, and practicality, it is also frequently, but not always, asserted that moral discourse is an autonomous mode of discourse. This means that no moral or normative claim is derivable from, or depends for its validity on, purely nonmoral or nonnormative statements alone. Certain inessential and unimportant qualifications apart, no moral statement is entailed by any set of purely nonnormative statements. Morality, no matter how carefully elaborated, can never become or be reduced to an empirical science. We cannot discover what we ought to do or what is desirable from a knowledge of nonmoral facts *alone,* including the facts about human nature and conduct. (For further discussion, see ULTIMATE MORAL PRINCIPLES: THEIR JUSTIFICATION.)

METAETHICAL THEORIES

Metaethical theories, where they are not explicitly subjectivistic, attempt to account for four central features of moral discourse: that moral judgments claim universality, autonomy, and objectivity, and that moral discourse is a form of practical discourse—it guides conduct and tends to alter behavior. In handling the problem of justification, these various theories divide on what form the justification of ethical judgments can take, but with one exception about autonomy they agree that a clear characterization of moral discourse must square with the fact that moral discourse in some way satisfies these four conditions.

Not all metaethical theories will be discussed; rather, concentration will be on some of the central aspects of naturalism, intuitionism, and noncognitivism. (For a fuller account of contemporary metaethical theories, see ETHICS, HISTORY OF.)

Naturalism. As a distinctively metaethical theory, naturalism contends that moral terms are completely definable in nonmoral terms and that moral judgments are a subspecies of empirical judgments. In reality, moral terms stand for purely natural characteristics.

Naturalism is an attractive theory, for, if correct, ethical theory could become an empirical science. We would have finally uncovered a perfectly objective method for confirming or disconfirming moral judgments, including fundamental moral judgments. There would be no need to appeal to intuition or to regard moral judgments as essentially contested, incapable of rational resolution because ethical naturalism, if true, shows us how we can have a purely empirical knowledge of good and evil.

Whether this desideratum can be realized depends on whether the naturalist can show that all moral terms are actually equivalent in meaning to terms standing for purely empirical characteristics—qualities or relations capable of either direct or indirect observation by empirical methods. It is here that certain objections, first formulated in the twentieth century by G. E. Moore, become relevant. Moore's most central argument has been dubbed the open-question argument.

A naturalist may, for example, try to define "intrinsic good" as "that which satisfies desire," or "moral good" as "that which promotes human survival." But we can intelligibly enough ask, "Is that which satisfies desire intrinsically good?" This is not a senseless question equivalent to asking, "Is that which satisfies desire that which satisfies desire?" We can also with perfect linguistic propriety ask if all those things which promote human survival under any circumstances, cannibalism or incest, for example, are morally permissible. But if the above naturalistic definitions were correct, we could not sensibly ask such questions any more than we can sensibly ask if a father is a male parent. More generally, the argument is this: for any proposed naturalistic definition x we can always, unless x itself contains some normative terms (and thus is not genuinely naturalistic), ask—without making a purely verbal mistake—if x is good, right, or obligatory. This shows that such moral terms are not equivalent to empirical terms. Furthermore, for whatever naturalistic value satisfies the variable x, to assert that x is good, right, or obligatory is not to assert a statement that cannot be denied without contradiction.

There are many counters to such antinaturalist arguments. One is to claim that moral terms have many contextually dependent meanings and that it is only this, and not the impossibility of naturalism, that the open-question argument shows. It is also argued that there may be a *covert* synonymity between terms, particularly where the correct definition of a term is very complex. Consider this definition of "good": to say "*x* is good" is to say that if there were an omniscient, disinterested, and dispassionate observer, he would approve of *x*. If someone were to inquire whether it made sense to ask if what an omniscient, disinterested, and dispassionate observer would approve is good, we might not know, even after careful reflection, whether such a question is or is not a closed question. In short, a question actually may be closed when it appears to be open. The open-question argument is thus far from decisive.

The critic of naturalism could grant that the open-question argument is not decisive and still argue that nevertheless it counts heavily against naturalism. The criteria for a good woman, a good chisel, and a good horse differ significantly. In this way "good" is a context-dependent word, but as J. O. Urmson has remarked, "good" is not a punning homonym; it has a common use in all these contexts. Furthermore, we can significantly ask, using "good" in a more specific manner, "Is pleasure *intrinsically* good?" or "Is what one's society approves of and regards as having overriding social importance *morally* good?" Thus, even when the kind of normative concept is specified, the moral term in question still is not naturalistically definable. Finally, given the fact that naturalists are trying to define "good" in such a way that their definition, if correct, will show that there are some purely empirical terms that have the same meaning as "good," we must, to have good grounds for asserting such an equivalence, show that an ethical term and its proposed empirical equivalent cannot be used to form an open question. If, after careful reflection, it is possible for someone well acquainted with the language in question to assert that the question is open or even that he is unsure whether it is open or not, we are in no position to assert that the naturalistic definition works. (If the naturalist makes the equivalence a matter of stipulation, he has done something quite arbitrary.) We have very good grounds for believing that all simple naturalistic definitions allow open questions, and the more complex ones also appear to do so.

A more fundamental and perhaps more telling argument for naturalism consists in pointing out that the nonnaturalist assumes something that is quite questionable—that there are two distinct classes of terms: ethical terms and nonethical terms. But the nonnaturalist's distinction has little philosophic value, for no one has given a clear criterion for what counts as an ethical or "evaluative" term, as distinct from a nonethical term. This objection is a two-edged sword, for, if correct, we would have no basic naturalistic or empiricist language made up of terms, logical constants apart, standing for purely empirical realities; and thus we would have no way of knowing whether the naturalist's program could be carried out.

From the above it should be evident that naturalism has not been decisively refuted. If it were a correct metaethic, it would in nonsubjectivist forms show the objectivity and universality of moral discourse. What is, however, very questionable is whether naturalism can adequately account for the practical nature of moral discourse, and naturalism also denies the autonomy of moral claims.

Intuitionism. Intuitionists make negative points against naturalism, but they also develop positive contentions of their own. As much as they differ among themselves, they all agree that morality is autonomous: that there must be at least one primitive ethical term that is the vehicle for a nonnatural quality, relation, or concept. This primitive ethical term is indefinable, and the reality it stands for is an objective reality that we must cognize directly. We cannot prove that there is such a reality or confirm or disconfirm its existence by empirical observation. We are either directly aware of it or we are not. It is in this manner that we gain our fundamental knowledge of good and evil.

Moore took "good" as his primitive ethical term. Others have taken "right," "ought," or "fitting" as such a term. Still others have allowed two primitive terms, "right" and "good," but the fundamental point is that there must be at least one such term standing for a unique and unanalyzable object of thought that must simply be apprehended to be known.

There are different types of intuitionism—according to one variety, we intuit the intrinsic goodness of actions; according to another, what we intuit is the obligatory character of an act. Some intuitionists stress that we are directly aware of the rightness, goodness, or obligatoriness of specific actions or attitudes; others argue that we are directly aware only of the self-evidence of certain general, highly abstract principles of conduct. But they all agree that such truths are both necessary and synthetic and that to say we intuit their truth is to say we have a direct, nonsensory, cognitive awareness of the necessary truth of certain moral claims.

If someone reports that he is not aware, on honest reflection, of such a nonnatural characteristic when he judges something to be good or obligatory, but only of a feeling that so and so is good or a feeling that something is obligatory, it will not do for the intuitionist to reply that he must then be morally blind, for, unlike color blindness, there is no agreed-upon criterion for moral blindness. We have physical tests for tone deafness or color blindness, but not for moral blindness. The intuitionist claims to be aware of a nonnatural quality or relation—to see, in a way that is not literal observing, that so and so is good or ought to be done. But what counts as a nonnatural quality? To be told it is not an empirical quality or relation, directly or indirectly given as a sense constituent, is not to be told what it is. The intuitionist has not given us an intelligible description of what it is we must apprehend in order to apprehend a nonnatural quality or relation. His account has all the defects of the *via negativa*. If we are told we just see that it is wrong to kill little children, in the same way that we see that two plus two equals four, the reply must be that we do not see this to be so in a way analogous to our apprehension of logical or mathematical truths; "two plus two equals four," like all logicomathematical truths, is analytic, while the moral statement, as intuitionists are the first to insist, is synthetic.

There are, it is argued, two even more fundamental errors common to both naturalism and intuitionism. They both operate with a very inadequate conception of how language functions. According to both theories, a word, logical constants apart, is meaningful if, and only if, it stands for something. Naturalists claim that a meaningful word stands for a natural characteristic(s) and intuitionists, noting that it does not seem to stand for a natural characteristic(s), conclude, since moral terms are obviously intelligible, that it *must* stand for a nonnatural characteristic. The mistake is to assume that, to be intelligible, a term must stand for something. Not all terms, not even all adjectives, are property-ascribing words. "Good" and "right" do not stand for properties at all or, more conservatively, do not simply stand for properties, natural or nonnatural; they have a different but distinctive role in that form of social intercourse we call language.

The second error (or alleged error) common to naturalism and intuitionism is that neither can account properly for the practical functions of moral discourse. To know that one ought to do something involves setting oneself to do it. Moral utterances guide conduct and alter behavior, but naturalism and intuitionism in effect treat moral utterances as property-ascribing theoretical utterances. To regard moral utterances in such a way is to miss their distinctive function. In using moral language we do not, at least typically, tell someone *that* something is the case; we tell someone *to make* something the case. If knowledge of good and evil were simply an apprehending that something is the case, then it would remain inexplicable why to know that one ought to do x is to know that one must, if one is a moral agent, *try* to do x.

Noncognitivism. When we consider the common difficulties in naturalism and intuitionism, some form of noncognitivism is likely to become an attractive possibility. ("Noncognitivism," although it has become a fairly standard label, is in a way an unfortunate one, for it suggests what few noncognitivists would affirm, namely that there is no knowledge of good and evil.) Noncognitivists deny that moral utterances are simply, or sometimes even at all, purely property-ascribing utterances, and they likewise deny that moral terms simply or at all stand for characteristics of any sort. We must not, noncognitivists argue, confuse fact-stating and normative discourse. What makes an utterance normative is precisely its dynamism, its trigger function; a normative utterance is an utterance that guides conduct and molds or alters attitudes.

Noncognitivists differ greatly among themselves. Some model moral utterances on imperatives; others model them on decisions of principle, resolutions, or declarations of intention; still others believe that what marks an utterance as moral or normative is that it expresses the attitudes of the speaker and tends to evoke or invite similar attitudes in the hearer. Noncognitivists with greater philosophical sophistication contend that moral utterances are multifunctional. Some function in one way and some in another, but the sophisticated noncognitivists continue to contend that all the various primary functions of moral utterances are always, directly or indirectly, action-guiding.

Some, including A. J. Ayer, maintain that it is misleading to say that statements made by using moral utterances are true or false, for they are not factual statements; others, including C. L. Stevenson, maintain that in virtue of their declarative form and in virtue of the fact that "true" and "false" are typically used to back up or warrant declarative statements of various types, it is perfectly proper to follow everyday usage and say of such moral statements that they are true or false. But all noncognitivists agree that fundamental moral judgments cannot be verified (confirmed or disconfirmed) and that we can never have an a priori or purely conceptual warrant for claiming that fundamental moral conflicts can be resolved by empirical methods alone. It will always remain at least a logical possibility that we might agree about all the facts and still disagree about what we ought to do or about what is good or worth having for its own sake. On these issues the noncognitivists side with the intuitionists against the naturalists. But like the naturalists they deny that we have any intuitive knowledge of good and evil. Fundamental moral claims are not matters of knowledge but expressions of attitude, decisions of principle, or declarations of intention. Hence the label noncognitivist. The intent of moral language is not simply to describe what is the case but to prescribe that something be done or to evaluate something that is, has been, or may be the case.

Since not all noncognitivist views are the same, different difficulties will apply to different views. If the noncognitivist is an emotivist and contends that to be a moral utterance, an utterance must be attitude-expressing and attitude-evoking, a question immediately arises about the logical status of this claim. Presumably it must be analytic. (If it were empirical, it would not show what makes an utterance a moral utterance.) The statement "His attitudes and emotional reactions are those of a segregationist, but he knows segregation to be wrong" does not appear to be self-contradictory, and as children we are not taught any rule of language to the effect that an utterance must be attitude-expressing to be moral. We know that there is a close link between attitudes ("the passions") and morality, but this is perfectly compatible with a cognitivist metaethic. How, then, do we know that moral utterances must be attitude-expressing? We are tempted to say that moral dispute is at an end when, and only when, we attain agreement in attitude; but this does not appear always to be so. Two people may have the same attitudes concerning the white power structure vis-à-vis Harlem; they both, let us say, disapprove of the behavior of the city officials, yet they still disagree morally about the issue because they have different reasons for their disapproval of the city officials. And it is not the case that any consideration that leads the hearer to share the expressed attitude of the speaker will *ipso facto* count, as the emotivists claim it will, as a morally relevant reason for adopting that attitude. Emotional appeals and nonrational persuasion are irrelevant in moral reasoning. What motivates one to act in a certain way or to adopt a certain attitude may or may not justify one in so acting, and what justifies one in doing it may or may not so motivate one to do it.

Other noncognitivists, such as Hare, argue that moral utterances are much more like imperatives than expressions of attitude. It is their primary logical function to tell us to do something, to guide our actions; whether or not they actually succeed in persuading us or goading us into so acting, they still remain perfectly intelligible moral utterances. But there are also difficulties in such an imperativist view. Imperativists claim that all moral utterances entail imperatives, but while "You ought to vote Socialist" functions very like an imperative and entails "Vote Socialist," no imperative is entailed by "He ought to have voted Socialist" or "He will come to appreciate that he ought to vote Socialist." Furthermore, the contradictories of moral utterances entailing imperatives do not themselves entail imperatives, although surely the moral terms in both utterances have the same meaning.

Besides, whether we liken moral utterances to imperatives, resolutions, declarations of intention, or decisions of principle, it remains the case that the "ought" in the antecedent clause of conditional sentences does not have any of the above noncognitive functions. The "ought" in "If he ought to be told, he should be told now" has the same meaning as the "ought" in "He ought to be told," but the "conditional ought" clearly does not entail an imperative, declare an intention, or express a resolution. Thus, the "ought" in the latter sentence cannot have as an essential part of its meaning any such function.

Lastly, any form of noncognitivism would in effect undermine the objectivity of moral judgments. (This should not be taken to mean that noncognitivists do not have moral principles they are willing to stand by or that they advocate that everything be permitted. To take the remark in this way is to confuse metaethical claims with normative ethical ones.) We have seen that the minimal requirement for the objectivity of a judgment is that it can be interpersonally validated; in the case of moral judgments, this means that an objective moral judgment is a judgment that every rational agent will accept if he reasons disinterestedly, is apprised of the nonmoral facts, and takes the matter to heart. But if moral utterances are essentially resolutions to act in a certain way, declarations of intention, expressions of attitude, or decisions of principle, it follows that moral utterances do not, given such a logical form, require such interpersonal agreement. A man may resolve or decide, even as a matter of principle, to do what no one else does or would resolve or decide to do after careful reflection, and yet there would be nothing logically inappropriate about his decision or resolution.

MORAL REASONING

Those philosophers who tried to bridge the "is/ought gap" were trying, although perhaps in a mistaken way, to do something that is very important. It is a fact of moral reasoning that certain facts are good reasons for moral judgments. Without at all committing oneself to ethical naturalism, and without denying the insight of the noncognitivists that one cannot demonstratively prove or inductively establish fundamental moral claims, it remains the case that we do conclude from "He is my father" that "He has a right to special consideration from me" or from "He promised to return" that "He is under an obligation to return." It is an obvious fact of moral discourse that we give reasons for moral claims, that these reasons are typically statements of fact, and that sometimes we can conclude that if a given factual statement, *F*, is true, then a certain moral conclusion, *E*, follows.

It does not, however, follow from this that there is no logical gap between facts and norms. Such ethical conclusions hold only in virtue of certain canons of relevance; when these canons of relevance are explicitly stated, they will be found to invoke normative principles. Moreover, there must be some normative principles used in our judgments of relevance that will not be derived from, or even made in accordance with, other higher-order normative principles.

Such neonaturalists as Philippa Foot and A. I. Melden are perfectly right in claiming that certain matters of fact constitute good and sometimes even conclusive reasons for acting in a certain way, *given* the assumption of the conceptual structures constitutive of our ordinary moral reasoning. But in accepting these we accept a structure that has as constitutive elements certain normative principles, such as "Similar cases are to be treated similarly," "In deciding what is to be done, every person concerned has a right to equal consideration," and "There can be no arbitrary inequalities." It is in virtue of certain very general but still normative principles that we can derive certain moral conclusions from certain factual premises and that certain factual statements become good reasons for certain moral conclusions.

It is also crucial to see, as such philosophers as Stephen Toulmin, Kurt Baier, and Marcus Singer have stressed, that in morality, as in science, we have a limited but distinctive mode of reasoning with its own pragmatic point. If we are ever to understand the nature of moral reasoning, we must not simply fix our attention on the meaning of moral terms or expressions taken in isolation; we must seek to grasp the over-all point or rationale of the discourse in question. Subservient to the over-all purposes for which we have the discourse, each mode of discourse has its distinctive procedures, and in accordance with these procedures we judge whether something is or is not good evidence for or a good reason for a certain claim. Without such ground rules we cannot correctly speak of the evidence or reasons for or against any contention.

If we examine actual moral discourse when it is being conducted, we will come to see that there is a complicated network of procedural rules connected with morality that limit and partially specify what can count as good reasons for a moral claim. Furthermore, if we reflect on why we have a morality, any morality at all, moral discourse and moral action will be seen to have a point; and the procedural rules that help define morality will be found to be instrumental to the continuance of this activity.

Moral discourse is a form of practical discourse. Moral questions are fundamentally questions about what we are to do. The primary intent of moral utterances is not to assert that so and so is the case, but to advise, admonish, suggest, proclaim, or protest that so and so be done. Moral knowledge is knowledge about what to do or about what attitude to take toward what has been done, is being done, or is intended. In pointing out that moral judgments do not assert something to be the case and thus are not confirmable, Ayer and the emotivists in effect are showing that moral utterances are not theoretical statements about what is the case but are bits of practical discourse about what to *make* the case. As we want and need to know what is the case, so we want and need to know what to do. Indeed, we could not know what to do if we did not know something about what is the case—something about how the world goes--but we also need to know what to do. There are no grounds for assuming that questions about what we should do are more subjective than factual questions or that moral language is more untrustworthy than theoretical discourse. It is just different. In life we need both these activities and the diverse uses of language embedded in them.

Many might concede that morality has its distinctive procedural rules and still object that this does not give it the required objectivity. It has been argued that while the procedural rules connected with the making of factual judgments are cross-culturally valid, the procedural rules connected with moral discourse are purely conventional.

Moral rules, such a conventionalist or metaethical relativist will argue, are rationalizations of custom. Morality is constituted by certain social rules and the actions and attitudes appropriate to those rules. Any attempt to appraise these rules as sound or unsound will at best be question-begging.

In challenging metaethical relativism, we must show how it is possible to assert correctly and objectively that certain social practices either are or are not morally justifiable; and in a like manner we must show how it is possible to assert correctly that the whole moral order either does or does not have a rational claim to our assent.

The metaethical relativist is indeed on solid ground when he points out that morality is a rule-governed activity that guides conduct and molds and alters actions and attitudes. In determining the content and structure of a strange tribe's morality, we would have to discover the social practices to which that tribe was most deeply committed and elicit the rules defining these social practices. We would have to know much more as well, but we would have to know at least that.

Morality necessarily involves a cluster of practices. "Practices" here refers to social activities that contain a set of rules which specify rights and duties, permissible and impermissible steps. The rules that so define a practice we may call procedural rules. Games and ceremonies are good examples of practices. If in playing baseball I hit into center field, I cannot wonder if I really must go to first before I go to second, but I can deliberate about whether to hold up at first or try for second. That a runner must go to first before going to second is a rule of procedure which helps define the practice of baseball. Although not so strictly codified, moral behavior is also a rule-governed activity, a complex cluster of practices with procedural rules that define those practices.

Promising is one such practice. It involves public rules of procedure, rules that are readily taught. We can say that a person has made a promise only when he acts in accordance with certain procedural rules. If I have promised to meet a friend, it is not open to me to excuse my failure to meet him simply on the ground that I had subsequently thought it through and decided that slightly more good would be served by not meeting him. I cannot offer that excuse and still act in accordance with the practice of promise-keeping, any more than I can have three strikes

and still be at bat. We could, of course, deliberately change the practice, but given the practice and given the fact that I accept the practice, there are some things I must do. My failure to do these things would, exceptional circumstances apart, show that I either did not really accept the practice or did not properly understand it. There are, of course, legitimate excuses, but the very rules of the practice itself specify what is to count as a legitimate excuse for not acting in accordance with the practice. There are, for example, conditions that excuse fulfilling a promise, but they are built into the very practice of promise-keeping.

If my action falls under an existing practice that I accept, and if my action does not also fall under a conflicting practice that I also accept, then I have no moral alternative, while accepting the practice, but to try to act in accordance with it. In a contrasting situation where conflicting practices are involved, I must see if there are any principles which I accept that give some moral priority to one or another of the conflicting practices. Where there is such priority, I must acknowledge it and try to act in accordance with it. There are indeed moral questions that cannot without strain and ambiguity be answered by subsumption under any procedural rule, but this does not disconfirm the claim that there are practices which specify and limit how we are to act while acting as moral agents.

What has been said so far might be taken as giving aid and comfort to metaethical relativism, but so far only a very partial account of moral reasoning has been given. The justification of moral beliefs does not terminate in the statement of rules that partially codify our social practices; we can reason about and ask for a justification of the practices themselves. There is a whole battery of objective tests for evaluating social practices, and they are clearly recognizable as a part of our first-order moral discourse. Understanding what morality is involves knowing how to use these procedures for appraising social practices.

Morality has developed in such a way that it is now correct to say that in morality we are concerned with the reasoned pursuit of the interests of all rational agents. That is to say, from the moral point of view, we are concerned with the most extensive welfare of all concerned. When, as with the Nazis or the segregationists, there is both an overriding of some individuals' rights and a pretension to moral rectitude, this oppression is accompanied by rationalization. The victims are thought of in such a way that they are not regarded as fully human, that is, they are not regarded as rational agents capable of the sensibilities of moral agents. That even Nazis and segregationists are committed to act in accordance with such a conception of morality is evidenced by the fact that they must depersonalize their victims in order to justify to themselves their treatment of them. From the moral point of view, we are concerned with the most extensive welfare of all persons concerned. In theory, such racists do not reject such a principle but through rationalization convince themselves that Jews or Negroes are not fully human.

Terms such as "human welfare" and "well-being" are not so vague that certain states of affairs could not be said to be incompatible with them. Social practices that drastically frustrate our need for sleep, food, sex, drink, or elimination; or practices that pointlessly diminish self-esteem, the appreciation of and concern for others, creative employment and diversion; or practices that seek to destroy our tendencies to prize integrity, conscientiousness, knowledge, and the contemplation of beautiful things are practices which must be said to be morally inferior to social practices which do not so frustrate us. This is not to deny the obvious, namely that there are sharp disagreements over the value of some things and that there is even considerable disagreement about the moral priority of those very things we universally prize, approve of, or admire. But even with our less than exact conception of human welfare, we can still show that there are many sets of social practices both imaginable and actual that intelligent and correctly informed people judge without equivocation to be morally inferior to comparable sets of practices. As our knowledge of man develops and as our superstitions—particularly our religious superstitions—diminish, it is reasonable to expect that moral deliberation will enable us to achieve a greater understanding of and agreement about those attitudes and styles of behavior that are taken to be desirable or admirable.

There is a further procedural rule to be considered. In a moral situation we cannot be concerned only with the maximum welfare; we must also be concerned with the welfare of everyone involved. Quite independently of what we judge human welfare to be, these distinctively human values must, from a moral point of view, be distributed as equitably as possible to all the people involved. If I decide I have a right to do x, I must, if I am reasoning morally, be prepared to grant that others relevantly like me and similarly situated have a right to do x as well. As Marcus Singer has shown in his *Generalization in Ethics* (1961), what count as "relevantly like me" and as "similarly situated" cannot be specified apart from a determinate context. Too much depends on who I am and what I am doing, but in determinate contexts there frequently are criteria for an objective determination of these matters.

It is also a procedural rule of morality that the moral agent (as well as the moral critic) must, in making moral judgments, try to assume the viewpoint of an impartial but sympathetic observer. *Ideally,* moral judgments are made in the light of full knowledge and appreciation of the relevant facts; and they *must* be made in the light of the facts that the moral agent can be reasonably expected to have in his possession when he makes the judgment. In making moral judgments we must attempt to make impartial judgments in the light of the relevant facts, using the relevant consideration-making beliefs; but to gain the moral insight that mature morality requires, we should also, before rendering judgment, vividly imagine and emphatically rehearse and review what we know. We should strive to enter unreservedly into the feelings and attitudes of the persons involved in the action; we should seek to see the situation as they see it. After this exercise in imagination, we should then make our moral appraisals as impartial but understanding observers. The attempt to view the situation impartially is a minimum requirement for correct moral appraisal, but mature moral thinking requires sympathy and imagination as well. In utilizing these methods, we have additional checks on our moral beliefs. Any man who will take the trouble to attend carefully to moral discourse will find procedures for its critical appraisal and correction built into its very use.

We have tried to show that while morality involves reasoning in accordance with certain practices, there remain generally acknowledged ways of appraising these practices. This being so, metaethical relativism or subjectivism cannot be true.

The metaethical relativist or subjectivist may well claim by way of rebuttal that all these tests are conventional and that the rationality of the whole moral enterprise is spurious. Only our conditioned virtue—our psychological involvement with morality—blinds us to the fact that it is merely a matter of convention or arbitrary decision whether we accept the requirements of the moral order or become nonmoral rational egoists.

Against the conventionalist claim one can point out that there are good Hobbesian reasons for rational and self-interested people to accept the moral point of view. A rational egoist will naturally desire the most extensive liberty compatible with his own self-interest, but he will also see that this is most fully achievable in a context of community life where the moral point of view prevails. Thus, in a quite nonmoralistic sense of "reasonable," it is reasonable for men, even self-interested men, to acknowledge that it is better for people to behave morally than amorally or immorally.

It is not the case that there is no logical limit to what could count as a valid moral judgment. If what we have claimed is correct, there are unequivocal material procedural rules that help define morality. They limit the scope of what counts as a moral judgment, and they have a rational point. Thus, under certain conditions certain moral judgments are objectively true and others are false. That is to say, there are certain moral truths that do not at all depend on the personal idiosyncrasies or cultural perspective of anyone but would be affirmed by any rational agent apprised of the relevant facts. If this is so, neither metaethical relativism nor any form of subjectivism can be an adequate account of moral reasoning. Although moral utterances express attitudes and have a moving appeal, moral reasoning remains a rule-governed activity with an objective rationale.

Bibliography

CLASSIC SOURCES

Plato, *The Republic,* translated and edited by F. M. Cornford. Oxford, 1941; New York, 1945.
Aristotle, *The Nichomachean Ethics,* in *The Basic Works of Aristotle,* R. M. McKeon, ed. New York, 1941.
Epicurus, *Letter to Menoceus,* in *Epicurus, the Extant Remains,* translated and edited by Cyril Bailey. Oxford, 1926.
Thomas Aquinas, *Summa Theologica,* translated by the Fathers of the English Dominican Province. London, 1920–1924; New York, 1947. Part II.
Butler, Joseph, *Sermons.* London, 1726.
Hume, David, *An Inquiry Concerning the Principles of Morals,* C. W. Hendel, ed. New York, 1957.
Spinoza, Baruch, *Ethics,* in *The Chief Works of Spinoza,* translated and edited by R. H. M. Elwes. New York, 1955. Especially Parts III–V.
Selby-Bigge, L. A., ed., *British Moralists,* 2 vols. Oxford, 1897; New York, 1965. An important collection of the principal writings of the classical British moralists of the eighteenth century.

Bentham, Jeremy, *The Principles of Morals and Legislation.* London, 1789. Reprinted in Hafner Library of Classics and edited by L. J. Lafleur. New York, 1948.

Mill, J. S., *Utilitarianism.* London, 1861.

Kant, Immanuel, *The Moral Law, or Kant's Groundwork of the Metaphysic of Morals,* translated with analysis and notes by H. J. Paton. London, 1948; 3d ed., 1956.

Kant, Immanuel, *Critique of Practical Reason,* translated and edited by L. W. Beck. Chicago, 1949.

Hegel, G. W. F., *The Philosophy of Right,* translated by T. M. Knox. Oxford, 1942.

Kierkegaard, Søren, *The Concept of Dread,* translated by Walter Lowrie. London, 1944.

Schopenhauer, Arthur, *The Basis of Morality,* translated by A. B. Bullock. London, 1903.

Marx, Karl, *Capital,* translated by Samuel Moore and Edward Aveling. Chicago, 1912.

Kamenka, Eugene, *The Ethical Foundations of Marxism.* London, 1962. Classical examination of Marx's scattered writings on the problems of ethics.

Sidgwick, Henry, *The Methods of Ethics.* London, 1874–1878; 7th rev. ed. by Constance Jones, Chicago, 1962.

Nietzsche, Friedrich, *The Genealogy of Morals,* in *The Complete Works,* Oscar Levy, ed. Edinburgh and London, 1909–1913.

Bradley, F. H., *Ethical Studies.* Oxford, 1876; New York, 1954.

MODERN WRITINGS

Baier, Kurt, *The Moral Point of View.* Ithaca, N. Y., 1958. A much-discussed account of the logic of moral reasoning.

Blanshard, Brand, *Reason and Goodness.* New York, 1961.

Brentano, Franz, *The Origin of the Knowledge of Right and Wrong,* translated by Cecil Hague. London, 1902.

Broad, C. D., *Five Types of Ethical Theory.* London, 1930.

Dewey, John, *Human Nature and Conduct.* New York, 1922.

Dewey, John, *The Quest for Certainty.* New York, 1929.

Edwards, Paul, *The Logic of Moral Discourse.* Glencoe, Ill., 1955. An attempt to square crucial features of the emotive theory and a modified ethical naturalism. Important discussion of previous contemporary metaethical theories.

Ewing. A. C., *The Definition of Good.* London, 1947.

Ewing, A. C., *Second Thoughts in Moral Philosophy.* London, 1959. A cognitivist, nonnaturalist analysis that tries to develop a *via media* between Moore and the deontologists.

Gauthier, David, *Practical Reasoning.* Oxford, 1963. An analysis of the logic of moral reasoning from the point of view of linguistic analysis.

Ginsberg, Morris, *On the Diversity of Morals.* New York, 1957.

Ginsberg, Morris, *On Justice in Society.* Ithaca, N.Y., 1965. An account by a distinguished British sociologist of the problem of relativism and some of the central problems of justice.

Hägerström, Axel, *Inquiries Into the Nature of Law and Morals,* translated by C. D. Broad. Stockholm, 1953.

Hägerström, Axel, *Philosophy and Religion,* translated by Robert T. Sandin. London, 1964.

Hare, R. M., *The Language of Morals.* Oxford, 1952.

Hare, R. M., *Freedom and Reason.* Oxford, 1963. A much-discussed and closely reasoned statement of nondescriptivist metaethic.

Hartmann, Nicolai, *Ethics,* translated by Stanton Coit. London, 1932.

Lewis, C. I., *An Analysis of Knowledge and Valuation.* La Salle, Ill., 1947.

Lewis, C. I., *The Ground and Nature of the Right.* New York, 1955. An important statement of a general theory of value and a discussion of the unique role of the concept of right.

Mayo, Bernard, *Ethics and the Moral Life.* New York, 1958. An important examination of the logic of moral reasoning from the point of view of linguistic analysis.

Moore, G. E., *Principia Ethica.* Cambridge, 1903.

Moore, G. E., *Ethics.* London, 1912.

Nowell-Smith, P. H., *Ethics.* London, 1954. A book, covering a wide range of metaethical topics, that is characteristic of contemporary linguistic philosophy.

Perry, R. B., *General Theory of Value.* Cambridge, Mass., 1926.

Perry, R. B., *Realms of Value.* Cambridge, Mass., 1954. A classical statement of ethical naturalism.

Prichard, H. A., *Moral Obligation.* Oxford, 1949. A collection of crucial essays from a deontological point of view.

Prior, A. N., *Logic and the Basis of Ethics.* Oxford, 1949. A careful statement of the central issues between naturalism and nonnaturalism. The history of the dispute is displayed.

Raphael, D. D., *Moral Judgment.* London, 1955. An analysis of the meanings of certain central moral concepts and a discussion of the ground of obligation and the problem of free will.

Rice, Philip B., *On the Knowledge of Good and Evil.* New York, 1955. A restatement, in the light of the criticisms of it by noncognitivism, of a variety of ethical naturalism. Important discussions of contemporary metaethical theories.

Robinson, Richard, *An Atheist's Values.* Oxford, 1964. A lucid discussion of important normative ethical problems by a distinguished British philosopher.

Ross, W. D., *The Right and the Good.* Oxford, 1930.

Ross, W. D., *The Foundations of Ethics.* Oxford, 1939. The major statement in contemporary philosophy of the deontological position.

Russell, Bertrand, *Human Society in Ethics and Politics.* New York, 1955. An attempt to combine a utilitarian account of moral reasoning with an emotive metaethic. Interesting discussion of specific normative ethical issues.

Scheler, Max, *The Nature of Sympathy,* translated by Peter Heath. New York, 1954.

Singer, Marcus, *Generalization in Ethics.* New York, 1961. A careful study of the force of the generalization argument in moral reasoning. Important discussions on Kant and the utilitarians.

Sparshott, F. E., *An Enquiry Into Goodness.* Chicago, 1958. An attempt to develop a theory of moral reasoning and an explication of the concept of goodness. A useful discussion of the nature of moral philosophy.

Stevenson, Charles, *Ethics and Language.* New Haven, 1944.

Stevenson, Charles, *Facts and Values.* New Haven, 1963. A much-discussed and complex statement of an emotive metaethic.

Toulmin, Stephen, *The Place of Reason in Ethics.* Cambridge, 1950. A pioneer account, from the point of view of linguistic analysis, of the nature of moral reasoning.

Wellman, Carl, *The Language of Ethics.* Cambridge, Mass., 1961. A discussion of contemporary ethical theories and a careful cataloguing of the meanings of ethical sentences.

Westermarck, Edward, *Ethical Relativity.* London, 1932; Paterson, N.J., 1960.

Wright, G. H. von, *The Varieties of Goodness.* New York, 1963. A very careful account of the varieties of goodness, together with important remarks about justice and duty.

ANTHOLOGIES

The following books are excellent selections of recent and original work in analytical ethics.

Brandt, Richard, ed., *Social Justice.* Englewood Cliffs, N.J., 1962.

Castañeda, Héctor-Neri, and Nakhnikian, George, eds., *Morality and the Language of Conduct.* Detroit, 1963.

Melden, A. I., ed., *Essays in Moral Philosophy.* Seattle, 1958.

Olafson, Frederick, ed., *Justice and Social Policy.* Englewood Cliffs, N.J., 1961.

Ramsey, I. T., ed., *Christian Ethics and Contemporary Philosophy.* London, 1965.

Sellars, Wilfrid, and Hospers, John, *Readings in Ethical Theory.* New York, 1952.

The following anthologies contain good selections from classical and contemporary sources.

Brandt, Richard, ed., *Value and Obligation.* New York, 1961.

Dewey, Robert E.; Gramlich, F. W.; and Loftsgordon, Donald, eds., *Problems of Ethics.* New York, 1961.

Katz, Joseph; Nochlin, Philip; and Stover, Robert, eds., *Writers on Ethics: Classic and Contemporary.* Princeton, N.J., 1962.

Melden, A. I., ed., *Ethical Theories,* 2d ed. Englewood Cliffs, N.J., 1955.

Mothersill, Mary, ed., *Ethics.* New York, 1965.

Munitz, Milton K., ed., *A Modern Introduction to Ethics.* Glencoe, Ill., 1958.

Taylor, Paul, ed., *The Moral Judgment.* Englewood Cliffs, N.J., 1963. Contemporary sources only.

TEXTS

Baylis, Charles, *Ethics: The Principles of Wise Choice.* New York, 1958. Elementary.

Brandt, Richard, *Ethical Theory.* Englewood Cliffs, N.J., 1959. Advanced. A detailed and careful text that examines the central metaethical and normative ethical theories.

Dewey, John, *Theory of the Moral Life.* New York, 1960. A description of classical ethical theories, together with a complex evaluation of them by a famous pragmatist.

Ekman, Rosalind, ed., *Readings in the Problems of Ethics.* New York, 1965. Important collection of contemporary writings on ethics.

Ewing, A. C., *Ethics.* London, 1953. Elementary.

Frankena, William, *Ethics.* Englewood Cliffs, N.J., 1963. Elementary.

Hospers, John, *Human Conduct.* New York, 1962. A full discussion of classical and contemporary ethical theories. Readable and full of examples.

Montefiore, Alan, *A Modern Introduction to Moral Philosophy.* New York, 1959. An analytical introduction to ethics by a linguistic philosopher.

Wilson, John, *Reason and Morals.* Cambridge, 1961. An attempt to state contemporary metaethical analysis in a popular form and show its moral relevance.

Wilson, John, *Logic and Sexual Morality.* Harmondsworth, England, 1965. Attempts to use the techniques of modern analysis to say something about the problems of sexual morality.

KAI NIELSEN

ETHICS, TELEOLOGICAL. See TELEOLOGICAL ETHICS.

ETHICS AND ECONOMICS. See ECONOMICS AND ETHICAL NEUTRALITY.

ETHICS AND EPISTEMOLOGY. See EPISTEMOLOGY AND ETHICS, PARALLEL BETWEEN.

ETHICS AND RELIGION. See RELIGION AND MORALITY.

EUCKEN, RUDOLF CHRISTOPH

(1846–1926), German philosopher of life, was born in Aurich, East Friesland. He studied philology and philosophy at the University of Göttingen; after attaining his doctoral degree, he taught several years at Frankfurt Gymnasium. In 1871 he became professor of philosophy at the University of Basel, and in 1874 at Jena, where he remained until his death. In 1908 he received the Nobel prize in literature.

Eucken was not a systematic philosopher. He began with life as man experiences it. Life inevitably tends to organize into "systems of life" that are organic or institutional. The function of philosophy is to make the meaning of each system explicit and, by explicating each, to raise the question, Which is to be preferred? But philosophy does not merely explicate; it also helps to transform existing life systems. Men assess these explications practically, in terms of their fruitfulness for life or for a particular life system. Each man chooses a life system, but he does not choose one simply for himself. Every act of such choosing inevitably involves other men. There is no escape for any man from this social involvement.

Life is a process, an evolution; it cannot be contained within the boundaries of any philosophy or life system. The strains and stresses created when life breaks its established boundaries raises the deep need for a new philosophy or new philosophies, and inevitably men develop them. Eucken believed that every significant new philosophy is more comprehensive and clearly defined than any past philosophy.

The elaboration of new philosophies comes only through action (i.e., activism), through man's relentless affirmation of life—an affirmation which recognizes both the good and evil inherent in life. No significant philosophy is ever purely intellectualistic, for life is more than an idea or a theory. At its best, life is creative energy bursting into expression and molding past and present experience into a higher, more spiritual unity and order. For Eucken, life is neither noological nor psychological nor cosmological; its basis and meaning are to be found in man.

Life in man is self-conscious; as such, it goes beyond the subjective individual to bind together all conscious beings. Through this transcendence, it becomes the "independent spiritual life," or man reaching through action toward the absolute truth, beauty, and goodness. This "independent spiritual life" is attained only as personality is developed, but it is never a final achievement, since it is always a process that evolves as history. It is not rooted in the external world but in the soul, and it manifests itself more and more completely as the soul becomes independent of this world, self-willed yet subordinate to the ultimate trinity of truth, beauty, and goodness. These ultimates are not theoretical abstractions; they are concrete human experiences that push man beyond cosmic nature to something transcendentally spiritual.

Man has his beginning in nature, but through his soul evolves beyond it. His soul raises questions such as "Why?" and "Whence?" and opposes nature at all points. His soul seeks to become timeless and above nature, even as it feels helpless in the grasp of nature. In spite of this feeling of helplessness, it continues to seek freedom—a freedom realized through the creation of a consistent philosophy that makes possible man's physical and spiritual survival. For Eucken, thought is not something intrinsic to itself but a means, or organ, of life itself.

The need for a new philosophy, Eucken felt, arises from two social conditions—modern man's drive for a "broader, freer, cleaner life, a life of greater independence and spiritual spontaneity" and his drive for a "naturalistic culture . . . which limits all its activity to the world around us" (*Can We Still Be Christians?*, p. 51).

The first drive provides modern man with a basis for radically transforming classical Christianity. Man's new problems, created by science, transcend the theological and ritualistic solutions that Christianity offered for millenniums. The eternal contribution of Christianity is its religious affirmation of universal redemption. But redemption must be combined with new elements of faith (science as the true complement of religion; religious democracy, or the political equality of all religions before man; complete separation of church and state) if Christianity is to help give birth to the new spiritual philosophy needed by man.

Eucken was very critical of naturalism. A naturalistic culture imposes false limitations upon man's essential spirituality. The conception of a naturalistic culture is a result of the impact of science upon man's life—an impact that is essentially good, but dangerous if it leads to the restriction of man's potentialities to the realm of nature only. In two works, *Individual and Society* (1923) and *Socialism: An Analysis* (1921), Eucken clarified the grounds of his criticism of naturalism. The naturalistic approach opens the door to individual freedom, but it is unable to guide man in the proper use of his freedom, since it lacks an overarching conception of unity. It fails to understand the necessity of social cooperation and social cohesion. Intellectualistic idealism understands the necessity for cooperation, cohesion, and unity, but fails to understand the need for individual freedom. The only proper answer, Eucken believed, is spiritual autonomy. Autonomy gives primacy to the whole of which the individual is a part, but it never reduces him to a state of utter subordination to that whole. The individual realizes his own unique freedom through this whole.

In *Socialism: An Analysis* Eucken also offers six criticisms of socialism: it cannot give unity to the life process; it fails to understand man's need for an inner life; it makes the present the only significant moment in man's life and thus cuts him off from the past and future; by reducing men to mathematical equality, it fails to appreciate genuine cultural and spiritual differences among men; espousing no higher faith than naturalism, it reduces social life to a struggle of man against man; and by considering man in purely economic terms, it stunts and aborts his true nature.

Eucken illustrated the attainment of freedom in terms of science and the peaceful society. In science the primary objective is to give man control over nature, but this task can be accomplished only when scientists cooperate by working together. Science, in other words, is essentially social, but it accomplishes its task through the freedom to investigate that is given to scientists. The peaceful society, although not yet attained, plainly depends upon human cooperation, upon no man raising his hand against another.

However, spiritual autonomy is not possible in a naturalistic culture. It rests upon a faith that goes beyond naturalism—the spiritual belief that man can produce a better and a freer world for all of humanity. Such a belief cannot find support in external circumstances alone. It requires the presence in each man of an inner life, a life constantly struggling to attain the good.

Works by Eucken

Geschichte und Kritik der Grundbegriffe den Gegenwart. Leipzig, 1878.

Die Einheit des Geisteslebens in Bewusstsein und Tat der Menschheit. Leipzig, 1888.

Der Sinn und Wert des Lebens. Leipzig, 1908. Translated by Lucy Judge Gibson and W. R. Boyce Gibson as *The Meaning and Value of Life.* London, 1909.

Grundlinien einer neuen Lebensanschauung. Leipzig, 1907. Translated by Alban G. Widgery as *Life's Basis and Life's Ideal.* London, 1911.

Können wir noch Christen sein? Leipzig, 1911. Translated by Lucy Judge Gibson as *Can We Still Be Christians?* London, 1911.

Erkennen und Leben. Leipzig, 1912. Translated by W. Tudor Jones as *Knowledge and Life.* London, 1913.

Sozialismus und seine Lebensgestaltung. Leipzig, 1920. Translated by Joseph McCabe as *Socialism: An Analysis.* London, 1921.

Lebenserinnerungen. Leipzig, 1921. Translated by Joseph McCabe as *Rudolf Eucken: His Life, Work and Travels.* London, 1921.

The Individual and Society. Translated by W. R. V. Brade, London, 1923.

Works on Eucken

Gibson, W. R. B., *Rudolf Eucken's Philosophy of Life.* London, 1907.

Jones, W. T., *An Interpretation of Rudolf Eucken's Philosophy.* London, 1912.

RUBIN GOTESKY

EUSEBIUS (265–339 or 340), church historian and Christian apologist, was bishop of Caesarea (Palestine) early in the fourth century. He is best known for his enthusiastic support of the emperor Constantine and for his pioneering *Historia Ecclesiastica,* intended to show how the church expanded but always remained the same because of its leaders' fidelity to tradition. Though Eusebius was essentially a historian rather than a philosopher, he did produce one work of significance for the history of philosophy. This is his *Praeparatio Evangelica* ("Preparation for the Gospel"), probably written between 312 and 318. It consists of 15 books, perhaps because Porphyry's treatise, *Kata Christianon* ("Against the Christians"), contained the same number. Eusebius claimed that his treatise went beyond earlier works of controversy or exegesis; the novelty seems to have lain in the method of quoting passages in which philosophers contradict one another, although he obviously found materials for this technique in some of his pagan sources.

The *Praeparatio* may be outlined thus: the earliest cosmogony (I. 7–8); the earliest theology (I. 9); Phoenician theology (I. 10); Egyptian theology (II. 1); Greek mythology (II. 2–8); Greek "physical" theology (III. 1–17); Greek oracles (IV–VI), leading on to the doctrines of Greek philosophers on fate, free will, and foreknowledge (VI); Hebrew doctrines (VII–IX); the chronological priority of Hebrew learning to Greek (X); the agreements and disagreements of Greek philosophy with the Hebrew oracles (XI–XIII); and the inconsistency of Greek philosophy, culminating with a transcription of part of the treatise "On the Doctrines of Philosophers" ascribed to Plutarch (XIV–XV).

The sources used by Eusebius reflect the predominantly Platonic character of the books assembled in church libraries, especially at Caesarea, by Origen and others. Eusebius made extensive use of Plato and Philo, but not of Aristotle. His other sources include the textbooks by Arius Didymus and Pseudo-Plutarch, as well as works by eclectic Platonists of the second Christian century (Atticus, Numenius, Plutarch, Severus) and a few of their contemporaries (the Peripatetic Aristocles, the Epicurean Diogenianus, the Cynic Oenomaus). From the third century he used the treatise "On Fate" by Alexander of Aphrodisias, the school text of Plotinus (earlier than that found in Porphyry's edition), several works by Porphyry ("On Abstinence," "Letter to Anebo," "Against the Christians,"

"Philological Lectures," "On the Philosophy to Be Derived from Oracles," "On the Soul Against Boethus," "On Statues"), and a fragment by a Christian Neoplatonist named Amelius.

His basic viewpoint is that of a Christian ecclesiastic and a historian; he has considerable sympathy for his favorite philosophers (especially Plato), but he is not really at home with them. Indeed, in his later work, *Theophania* ("On the Theophany"), written after 337, his attitude toward philosophy is markedly hostile.

In later times the *Praeparatio* was used as a mine of philosophical quotations by such Christian apologists as Theodoret and Cyril of Alexandria (Cyril often looked up Eusebius' sources and provided slightly different quotations). It would appear that this is its principal value.

Works by Eusebius

The best Greek texts are in *Die griechischen christlichen Schriftsteller der ersten drei Jahrhunderte*, published by the Berlin Academy from 1902 on, although the first volume needs to be re-edited (see F. Winkelmann, *Die Textbezeugung der Vita Constantini des Eusebius von Caesarea*, Berlin, 1962). Translations include H. J. Lawlor and J. Oulton, *Eusebius: The Ecclesiastical History and the Martyrs of Palestine*, 2 vols. (London, 1928), valuable commentary; W. J. Ferrar, *The Proof of the Gospel (Demonstratio Evangelica)*, 2 vols. (London, 1920); and E. H. Gifford, *Eusebii Pamphili Evangelicae Praeparationis Libri XV*, 4 vols. in 5 (Oxford, 1903).

Works on Eusebius

Full bibliography in J. Quasten, *Patrology* (Utrecht, 1960), Vol. III, pp. 309–345 (on the *Praeparatio*, pp. 329–331). Later titles include D. S. Wallace-Hadrill, *Eusebius of Caesarea* (London, 1960) and J. Sirinelli, *Les Vues historiques d'Eusèbe de Césarée* (Dakar, Senegal, 1961). On early use of Eusebius' works see Pierre Canivet, *Histoire d'une entreprise d'apologétique au Ve siècle* (Paris, 1958); R. M. Grant, "Greek Literature in the Treatise *De Trinitate* and Cyril *Contra Julianum*," *Journal of Theological Studies*, Vol. 15 (1964), 265–279.

ROBERT M. GRANT

EVIL, THE PROBLEM OF. The problem of evil concerns the contradiction, or apparent contradiction, between the reality of evil on the one hand, and religious beliefs in the goodness and power of God or of the Ultimate on the other. In a very general classification, the religions of the world have offered three main types of solution: (1) There is the monism of the Vedanta teachings of Hinduism, according to which the phenomenal world, with all its evils, is *maya*, or illusion. A confused echo of this doctrine is heard in contemporary Western Christian Science, which affirms that "evil is but an illusion, and it has no real basis. Evil is a false belief" (Mary Baker Eddy, *Science and Health*, auth. ed., Boston, 1934, p. 480:23,24). Considered as a response to the problem of evil as stated above, this view is defective in that it redescribes the problem but does not attempt to solve it, for it leaves unexplained the evil of our suffering from the compulsive illusion of evil. (2) There is the dualism exemplified most dramatically in ancient Zoroastrianism, with its opposed good and evil deities, Ahura Mazdah and Angra Mainyu. A much less extreme dualism was propounded by Plato (*Timaeus* 30A and 48A) and is found in various forms in the finite deity doctrines of such modern Western philosophers

as J. S. Mill (expounded in "Attributes," *Three Essays in Religion*, London, 1874) and Edgar Brightman (*A Philosophy of Religion*, New York, 1940, Chs. 8–10). (3) There is the distinctive combination of monism and dualism, or of an ethical dualism set within an ultimate metaphysical monism (in the form of monotheism) that has been developed within Christianity and that represents the main contribution of Western thought to the subject.

Since the terms of the problem of evil vary with the character of the religious beliefs which give rise to it, a separate study is required for each of the great religious systems. In the present article, however, the problem will be treated only in the context of the Christian tradition.

Christianity (like Judaism and Islam) is committed to a monotheistic doctrine of God as absolute in goodness and power and as the creator of the universe *ex nihilo*. The challenge of the fact of evil to this faith has accordingly been formulated as a dilemma: If God is all-powerful, he must be able to prevent evil. If he is all-good, he must want to prevent evil. But evil exists. Therefore, God is either not all-powerful or not all-good. A theodicy (from *theos*, god, and *dike*, justice) is accordingly an attempt to reconcile the unlimited goodness of an all-powerful God with the reality of evil.

The kinds of evil distinguished in the literature of theodicy are (1) the evil originated by human beings (and angels), that is, moral evil or sin; (2) the physical sensation of pain and the mental anguish of suffering, which may be caused either by sin or by (3) natural evil, that is, disease, tornado, earthquake, and so forth; and (4) the finitude, contingency, and hence imperfection of all created things which some have called metaphysical evil. The last two topics will be treated in the course of discussing the others in response to the questions: "Why has an infinitely powerful and good God permitted moral evil in his universe?" and "Why has an infinitely powerful and good God permitted pain and suffering in his universe?"

THE PROBLEM OF MORAL EVIL

The traditional Augustinian theodicy. The problem of evil was a lifelong preoccupation of Augustine (354–430), and the main lines of thought which he established have been followed by the majority of subsequent Christian thinkers. Before his conversion to Christianity, Augustine was attracted by Manichaeism, a powerful contemporary religious movement with Eastern and Gnostic roots, which affirmed an ultimate dualism of good and evil in the forms of light, or spirit, and darkness, or matter. In turning from this doctrine to Christianity, Augustine rejected a final dualism in favor of belief in a good God as the sole ultimate reality, and rejected the Manichaean disparagement of matter in favor of an acceptance of the material world as reflecting the goodness of its creator.

But if the sole ultimate power is unambiguously good, what is evil and whence does it come? In answer to this question, Augustine develops two interlocking lines of thought, presenting the *privative* and the *aesthetic* conceptions of evil.

Evil as privation. Augustine counters the Manichaean conception of evil as an independent reality and power coeternal with good by his analysis of evil (derived from Plotinus, *Enneads*, I, Eighth Tractate) as the privation, corruption, or perversion of something good. Evil, he taught, has no independent existence, but is always parasitic upon good, which alone has substantival being. "Nothing evil exists in itself, but only as an evil aspect of some actual entity" (*Enchiridion*, Ch. 4). Thus, everything that God has created is good, and the phenomenon of evil occurs only when beings which are intrinsically good (though mutable) become corrupted and spoiled.

Augustine expresses the same thought from another perspective when he equates being with goodness. God, as the highest, richest, and most intensely real being, is the supreme good, and everything that he has brought into existence is *ipso facto* good. For this reason the corruption which we call evil can never be complete; for if a thing becomes so vitiated in nature that it ceases to exist, the evil which is parasitic upon it must also cease to exist. Hence, there can be no wholly evil being.

How does this spoiling of God's initially good creation come about? Augustine's answer is that evil has entered into the universe through the culpable volitions of free creatures, angels and men. Their sin consisted, not in choosing positive evil (for there is no positive evil to choose), but in turning away from the higher good, namely God, to a lower good. "For when the will abandons what is above itself, and turns to what is lower, it becomes evil— not because that is evil to which it turns, but because the turning itself is wicked" (*City of God*, XII, 6). Augustine holds that natural evils, such as disease, are divinely ordained consequences of the primeval fall of man, and thus traces all evils either directly or indirectly to a wicked misuse of creaturely freedom: "There are two kinds of evil, sin and the penalty for sin" (*Against Fortunatus*, 15).

When we ask what caused man to fall, Augustine's answer is his doctrine of deficient causation. There is no efficient, or positive, cause of evil willing. Rather, evil willing is itself a negation or deficiency, and to seek for its cause "is as if one sought to see darkness, or hear silence" (*City of God*, XII, 7). Perhaps the best way to interpret this obscure teaching is as an assertion of the inexplicability, in principle, of free volitions; for "what cause of willing can there be which is prior to willing?" (*Free Will*, III, xvii, 49). Augustine is saying that the origin of moral evil lies hidden within the mystery of human and angelic freedom. The freely acting will is an originating cause, and its operations are not explicable in terms of other prior causes.

Aesthetic conception of evil. The other main theme in Augustine is the aesthetic conception of evil, which is also derived from Plotinus (*Enneads*, III, 2, 17). According to this view, what appears to be evil, when seen in isolation or in a too limited context, is a necessary element in a universe which, viewed as a totality, is wholly good. From the viewpoint of God, who sees timelessly and as a whole the entire moving panorama of created history, the universe is good: "To thee there is no such thing as evil, and even in thy whole creation, taken as a whole, there is not" (*Confessions*, VII, 13).

The presupposition of this aesthetic view is the ancient conception, deriving from Plato (*Timaeus*, 41 B–C), which Arthur Lovejoy has called the principle of plenitude (*The Great Chain of Being*, Cambridge, Mass., 1936). According to this principle, a universe in which all the varied potentialities of being are realized and which contains as many different kinds of entity as are possible (lower as well as higher, lesser as well as greater), is a better universe—one which more adequately expresses the infinite creativity of God—than would a universe which contains only the highest type of created beings. There is thus an immense hierarchy of forms of created existence, and each creature, in its own proper place in the scheme of nature, is good and glorifies its Maker. Those that are lower in the scale of being are not on that account evil; they are just different goods, contributing in their different ways to the perfection of the universe. Again, things that are transitory by nature, appearing and then perishing within the ever-changing pattern of nature's beauty, contribute, even by their death, to the perfection of the created order. As a very minor subtheme within this aesthetic conception, Augustine sometimes also uses the notion of evil as providing a contrast by which good shines the more brightly.

As an application of the principle of plenitude, Augustine holds that the universe must contain mutable and corruptible creatures, compounded of being and nonbeing. It is better that the universe should include free beings who may, and do, fall than that it should omit them. Thus, Augustine brings even moral evil within the scope of his aesthetic conception. In doing so, he employs the further principle (later invoked by Anselm, in his atonement theory) that as long as sin is exactly balanced by just punishment, it does not upset the moral harmony of the universe. "Since there is happiness for those who do not sin, the universe is perfect; and it is no less perfect because there is misery for sinners. . . . So, whatever a soul may choose, ever beautiful and well-ordered in all its parts is the universe whose Maker and Governor is God" (*Free Will*, III, 9, 26–27).

Influence of the Augustinian analyses. Both of these main Augustinian themes reappear in the thought of Thomas Aquinas in the thirteenth century (*Summa Theologica*, I, 47–49).

Luther and Calvin, the Reformers of the sixteenth century, were not interested in developing a general theodicy, although they followed Augustine in his doctrine that all the evils of human life flow ultimately from the culpable fall of man.

Leibniz, in his *Théodicée* (1710), employed the two Augustinian themes, the privative and aesthetic conceptions, in the course of his argument that this is the best of all possible worlds (or, more strictly, the best of all possible universes, for he uses "world" in its most comprehensive sense)—a notion pointedly satirized in Voltaire's *Candide* (1759). It is the best, not because it contains no evil, but because any other possible universe would contain more evil. The eternal possibilities of existence are individually present to the Divine Mind which, like an infallible calculating machine, surveys all possible combinations and selects the best, to which it then gives existence.

Summary and criticism of the Augustinian theodicy. The traditional Augustinian theodicy in respect to moral evil asserts that God created man with no sin in him and set him in a world devoid of evil. But man willfully misused his God-given freedom and fell into sin. Some men will be redeemed by God's grace, and others will be condemned to eternal punishment. In all this, God's goodness and justice alike are manifested.

This traditional theodicy has been criticized for its accounts of the origin and of the final disposition of moral evil.

The origin of moral evil. It is urged that the notion of finitely perfect beings willfully falling into sin is self-contradictory and unintelligible (cf. Friedrich Schleiermacher, *Der christliche Glaube*, 2d ed., Berlin, 1830–1831, par. 72). A truly perfect being, though free to sin, would in fact never do so. To attribute the origin of evil to the willful crime of a perfect being is thus to assert the sheer contradiction that evil has created itself *ex nihilo*.

There appears, further, to be a disharmony between this theodicy and Augustine's doctrine of predestination, which in effect sets the origin of moral evil within the purpose and responsibility of God. Augustine's doctrine (*City of God*, XI, 11 and 13, and XII, 9) refers to the fall of the angels. Calvin (*Institutes*, III, 23, 7 and 8,) has a parallel doctrine referring to the fall of man.

The assumption of the traditional theodicy that it is logically impossible for God to have created men such that they would always freely make right moral choices has recently been attacked under the name of "the free will defense." Defining a free action as one which flows from the nature of the agent, without external compulsion, recent writers have claimed that, without logical contradiction, God might initially have given men a nature which would always freely express itself in right actions. (See J. L. Mackie, "God and Omnipotence," *Mind*, April, 1955, and Antony Flew, "Divine Omnipotence and Human Freedom," *New Essays in Philosophical Theology*, 1955. For an important critical comment on these two articles, see Ninian Smart, "Omnipotence, Evil and Supermen," *Philosophy*, April, 1961, and replies in the same journal by Flew, January, 1962, and Mackie, April, 1962.) Three of the questions involved in this debate are: (1) In denying that we do what we do because we are what we are, and that therefore we might have been made so that we would always freely act rightly, can we avoid equating free behavior with merely random behavior? (2) Is there any important difference between a good will which has been created ready-made as such, and one which has become steadfastly good as the outcome of a history of moral endeavor and struggle? (3) If God's primary purpose for men is to evoke in them a free and uncompelled love and trust in relation to himself, would this purpose be frustrated by his creating men so that they cannot do other than make this response?

The final disposition of moral evil. The criticism of the eschatological aspect of the traditional Augustinian (and also, on this point, the Calvinist) theodicy has been expressed as a dilemma. If God desires to save all his human creatures, but is unable to do so, he is limited in power. If, on the other hand, he does not desire the salvation of all, but has created some for damnation, he is limited in goodness. In either case, the doctrine of eternal damnation stands as an obstacle in the way of Christian theodicy.

The Irenaean type of theodicy. Prior to Augustine and the development of his theology by the Latin fathers of the Christian church, a significantly different conception of the fall of man was prevalent among many of the Greek-speaking fathers, chief among them Irenaeus (c. 120–202). Whereas Augustine held that before his fall, Adam was in a state of original righteousness, and that his first sin was the inexplicable turning of a wholly good being toward evil, Irenaeus and others regarded the pre-Fall Adam as more like a child than a mature, responsible adult. According to this earlier conception, Adam stood at the beginning of a long process of development. He had been created as a personal being in the "image" of God, but had yet to be brought into the finite "likeness" of God. His fall is seen, not as disastrously transforming and totally ruining man's situation, but rather as delaying and complicating his advance from the "image" to the "likeness" of his Maker. Thus, man is viewed as neither having fallen from so great a height of original righteousness, nor to so profound a depth of total depravity, as in the Augustinian and Calvinist theologies; rather, he fell in the early stages of his spiritual development and now needs greater help than he otherwise would have required. (The contrast between the Latin and Greek doctrines of the Fall is most fully presented in N. P. Williams, *The Ideas of the Fall and of Original Sin*. London, 1927.)

In much of the British theology from the mid-nineteenth to the mid-twentieth century, which has been influenced by Schleiermacher's discussion of evil, this earlier, less dramatic conception of the Fall has been carried further. The Fall is regarded as a virtually inevitable incident in man's development as a child of God. If man is to enter into a genuinely personal relationship with his Maker, he must first experience some degree of freedom and autonomy. For only a relatively independent being can enter into a relationship of love and trust with his Creator, and man's fall is seen as a fall into this independence. It is thus analogous to the phase of disobedience which signals a young child's assertion of his own individuality in relation to his parents.

This line of thought may be carried further on the basis of the awareness in much modern theology that the "Fall" does not refer to a historical or prehistorical, but rather a mythological event. That is to say, man has never actually existed in a state of pre-Fall perfection. The Fall story is an analysis of man's present condition of estrangement from God, but not an account of how he came to be in this condition. Using our knowledge of the early state of mankind, we may say that man, as he emerged from the lower forms of life, was endowed with only dim and rudimentary conceptions of his Maker. He existed at an epistemic distance from God, which allowed him to respond to modes of divine revelation that do not coerce the human mind but which preserve man's relative autonomy. Man's existence at this epistemic distance from God constitutes his fallen estate, and from this flows the moral and spiritual cleavage and estrangement which is traditionally called "original sin." In this type of theodicy, God bears the *ultimate* responsibility for (in other words, is the necessary and knowing cause of) man's existence as a fallen creature, although, on his own level, man remains individually responsible for his personal choices and actions. Further, though the significance of this cannot be pursued here, the God who has thus created man as imperfect but perfectible has also entered into human life, in Christ, to bring about man's redemption.

THE PROBLEM OF PAIN AND SUFFERING

Human pain and suffering. Some instances of suffering—for example, those caused by war, injustice, and the many forms of "man's inhumanity to man"—are traceable to human wrongdoing, and thus fall within the problem of moral evil. But other sources of pain, such as disease, earthquake, flood, drought, and storm, are built into the structure of the world itself. Surely, it is urged, they make it incredible that the world should have been designed by a Creator who is both perfectly good and infinitely powerful. The theist's reply is that this reasoning presupposes that God's purpose in making the world must have been to produce a hedonic paradise for man to inhabit. (This is the assumption, for example, of David Hume in his *Dialogues concerning Natural Religion*, XI.) It is assumed by the critic of Christian theodicy that the Creator's problem was analogous to that of a human being who is making a cage for a pet animal. He will naturally make it as safe and agreeable as he can, and any remaining sources of danger or discomfort are evidences of either his want of care or want of means. But the Christian conception of the divine purpose in creation differs from the one which is presumed in such a criticism. According to the Augustinian and Calvinist theologies, nature was created free from defect, and its present perils and hardships are punishments which man has brought upon himself. According to the Irenaean type of Christian theodicy, the purpose of the world is to be a place of "soul-making," an environment in which the higher potentialities of human personality may develop. To this end, it is claimed, nature is an autonomous system operating by its own laws, which men must learn to obey. If God had created a world in which natural law were continuously adjusted for the avoidance of all pain, the more heroic human virtues would never be evoked. Indeed, a great part of our present moral language would be meaningless. There would be no such thing as "doing harm," for no one would be able to suffer any kind of injury; there would be no such thing as "doing good," for there would be no needs, deficiencies or occasions for improvement; there would be no such thing as a crime or a benefaction, an act of generosity or of meanness, of kindness or unkindness; and there would be no situations to which such qualities as courage, fortitude, loyalty, honesty, and the caring and protective aspects of love would be appropriate responses. There would thus be no occasions for moral choice. Such a world would be ill-designed to evoke many of the human traits which we value most highly. Indeed, it would seem that the "rough edges" of the world—its challenges, dangers, tasks, difficulties, and possibilities of real failure and loss—constitute a necessary element in an environment which is to call forth man's finer qualities.

But might not men have been created by God already possessed of these virtues? This is one of the points of contemporary debate. On the one side it is argued that, in principle, there are no limitations to an omnipotent God's capacity to create beings endowed with specific personal characteristics. On the other side it is argued that a virtue which has been formed as a result of making real decisions in real situations of moral choice is of greater value than the analogous virtue created by divine fiat, and that it is reasonable to suppose that the Creator is not content to build into men the merely ready-made and unearned qualities.

However, the discernible connection between the more heroic human virtues and the kind of world in which we live remains a very general one. It does not by any means amount to a one-to-one correspondence between each item of evil in human experience and some moral gain accruing to those who undergo it. Further, it appears that evil has crushed the human spirit as often as it has developed it, and that men have collapsed before life's challenges and opportunities as often as they have risen triumphantly to meet them. Accordingly, this type of theodicy demands completion in an eschatology. It points toward the eternal happiness of human beings in society with one another and in communion with God, which is symbolized by the "Kingdom of Heaven"; and its fuller claim is that the final fulfillment of God's purpose for his creatures in his heavenly kingdom constitutes a good so great and enduring that it justifies all the pains which have been experienced in order to reach it. (At this point, again, theodicy excludes the notion of eternal torment, for such torment could never serve any good end beyond itself, and would thus constitute precisely the kind of unredeemed evil which would make a theodicy impossible.)

A fundamental objection which is raised against this appeal to eschatology is that there is a contradiction between justifying a first-order evil, such as danger, as being required for the second-order good of courage, and then justifying the process by which courage is produced out of evil by reference to a future heavenly state in which, presumably, there will no longer be any dangers, and hence no need to have developed the virtue of courage in the first place. More generally, if heaven is free from "rough edges," how will virtues, so dearly bought in this world, survive within it?

Possibly the difficulty might be met in terms of heavenly analogues of earthly virtues, created by the development of the latter but no longer requiring the situations which evoked them; or in terms of the transmutation of a particular virtue (courage, for example) into an aspect of faith in God. However, Christian theology has not developed any definitive answer to this question.

Animal pain. Thus far this article has been concerned with evil as it directly affects mankind in the forms of sin, pain, and suffering. There is also, however, the baffling problem of animal pain beneath the human level. Throughout the animal kingdom, one species devours another, and painful accidents and lingering diseases disable and then kill. How is this spectacle of "nature, red in tooth and claw" to be reconciled with the religious belief in an omnipotent and perfect Creator?

Certain solutions of the problem have been proposed. It is claimed that the lower animals live wholly in the present moment and lack the high-level capacities of memory, anticipation, and conscience which give rise to the human experience of suffering as distinct from the experience of physical pain; that the pain mechanism is a necessary warning device in bodily organisms that move about within a material environment; and that an animal's life, even though violently terminated, is predominantly active and pleasurable.

Solutions of a more speculative nature have been sought in two main directions. From the viewpoint of the Augustinian type of theodicy, it has been suggested that the premundane fall of Satan has had cosmic consequences, perverting the entire evolutionary process to a savage struggle for existence (see for example, C. S. Lewis, *The Problem of Pain*, pp. 122–124). The criticisms which have been made of the Augustinian account of the origin of evil apply also to this extension of it.

From another point of view, which adopts a theme of Eastern thought, it has been suggested that there may be a continuous reincarnation of souls through the levels of animal existence up to self-consciousness in human life. Thus, the pain of the animals is not wasted, but is part of a long constructive process (see Nels Ferré, *Evil and the Christian Faith*, pp. 62–65). The aspect of this suggestion which is most readily open to criticism is its entirely speculative and unverifiable character.

Bibliography

STATEMENTS AND HISTORIES

The problem of evil is forcibly stated in J. S. Mill, "Nature," *Three Essays on Religion* (London, 1874) and David Hume, *Dialogues concerning Natural Religion*, edited by N. Kemp Smith, 2d ed., X and XI (London, 1947).

For historical treatments of the attempts to meet the problem, see Julius Müller, *Die Christliche Lehre von der Sünde*, 3d ed., 2 vols. (Breslau, 1849), translated by William Urwick as *The Christian Doctrine of Sin* (Edinburgh, 1868); F. Billicsich, *Das Problem des Übels in der Philosophie des Abendlandes*, 3 vols. (Vienna, 1952–1959); Charles Werner, *Le Problème du mal dans la pensée humaine* (Paris, 1944); R. A. Tsanoff, *The Nature of Evil* (New York, 1931); A. G. Sertillanges, *Le Problème du mal*, Vol. I (Paris, 1948); and N. P. Williams, *The Ideas of the Fall and of Original Sin* (London, 1927).

PLOTINUS AND AUGUSTINE

Plotinus deals with the problem in the *Enneads*, First Ennead, Eighth Tractate, and Third Ennead, Second Tractate, which appear in *The Enneads*, translated from Greek by Stephen Mackenna (London, 1917–1921). See also B. A. G. Fuller, *The Problem of Evil in Plotinus* (Cambridge, 1912). Augustine's main discussions of evil are in *De Libero Arbitrio*, *De Vera Religione*, and *De Natura Boni*, among his anti-Manichaean works, translated by J. H. S. Burleigh in *Augustine: Earlier Writings* (London and Philadelphia, 1943); and in his *Confessions*, Bk. VII, Chs. 3–5 and 12–16, and *Enchiridion*, Chs. 3–5 in *Confessions and Enchiridion*, translated and edited by A. C. Autler (London and Philadelphia, 1955); and *De Civitate Dei*, Bk. XI, Chs. 16–18 and Bk. XII, Chs. 1–9, translated and edited by Marcus Dods (Edinburgh, 1871). See also M. L. Burton, *The Problem of Evil: a criticism of the Augustinian point of view* (Chicago and London, 1909); Régis Jolivet, *Le Problème du mal d'après saint Augustin* (Paris, 1936).

THOMAS AQUINAS

Thomas Aquinas deals with the problem of evil in his *Summa Theologica*, First Part, Questions 47–49, and *De Malo* (second of the Quaestiones Disputatae); see A. C. Pegis, ed., *The Basic Writings of Saint Thomas Aquinas* (New York, 1945). See also Jacques Maritain, *St. Thomas and the Problem of Evil* (Milwaukee, Wis., 1942).

LEIBNIZ

Leibniz' famous work is entitled *Essais de théodicée sur la bonté de Dieu, la liberté de l'homme, et l'origine du mal* (Amsterdam, 1710), translated by E. M. Huggard as *Theodicy; essays on the Goodness of God, the freedom of man, and the origin of evil* (London, 1951). For a contemporary theological critique of Leibniz, see Karl Barth, *Die Kirchliche Dogmatik* (Munich, 1932), Vol. 3, Part 1, par. 42,3; translated into English as *Church Dogmatics*, T. F. Torrance and G. W. Bromiley, eds. (Edinburgh, 1959–1960).

HELLENISTIC THEODICY

For origins, see Irenaeus, *Adversus Haereses*, W. W. Harvey, ed., 2 vols. (Cambridge, 1857), Bk. IV, Chs. 37–38, also found in A. Roberts and J. Donaldson, eds., *The Writings of the Ante-Nicene Fathers* (Edinburgh, 1867; Grand Rapids, Mich., 1885), Vol. I; and A. Harnack, ed., *Epideixis* (Leipzig, 1807), translated by J. P. Smith as *Proof of the Apostolic Preaching* (Westminster, Md., 1952).

JEWISH WRITINGS

Some major Jewish writings on the problem of evil are Maimonides, *Guide of the Perplexed*, translated by M. Friedländer, 3 vols. (London, 1881–1885), Book III, and Martin Buber, *Bilder von Gut und Böse* (Koln, 1952), translated by Michael Bullock as *Images of Good and Evil* (London, 1952).

NINETEENTH-CENTURY STUDIES

The Idealist treatment of the problem is found in Josiah Royce, *Studies of Good and Evil* (New York, 1898). Arthur Schopenhauer's views are in his *Parerga und Paralipomena* (Berlin, 1851), from which T. B. Saunders has assembled and translated passages under the title "On the Sufferings of the World," in *Studies in Pessimism* (London, 1890).

TWENTIETH-CENTURY DISCUSSIONS

The following are some modern Augustinian discussions: A. G. Sertillanges, *Le Problème du mal* (Paris, 1951), Vol. 2; Paul Siwek, *The Philosophy of Evil* (New York, 1951); François Petit, *Le Problème du mal* (Paris, 1958), translated by C. Williams as *The Problem of Evil* (New York, 1959); Charles Journet, *Le Mal* (Paris, 1961), translated by Michael Barry as *The Meaning of Evil* (London, 1963); Mark Pontifex, "The Question of Evil" in *Prospect for Metaphysics*, Ian Ramsey, ed. (London and New York, 1961); and among Protestant writers, C. S. Lewis, *The Problem of Pain* (London, 1940); Austin Farrer, *Love Almighty and Ills Unlimited* (New York, 1961).

The Irenaean type of theodicy finds classic expression in Friedrich Schleiermacher, *Der Christliche Glaube*, 1st ed. (Berlin, 1821), Part I, 3, and Part II, translated and edited by H. R. Mackintosh and J. S. Stewart as *The Christian Faith* (Edinburgh, 1928). More recent writers who tend in this direction include F. R. Tennant, *Philosophical Theology*, Vol. 2, Ch. VII (Cambridge, 1930); William Temple, *Nature, Man and God*, Ch. XIV (London, 1934); and Nels Ferré, *Evil and the Christian Faith* (New York, 1947); J. S. Whale, *The Christian Answer to the Problem of Evil* (London, 1939). John Hick, *God and Evil* (London, 1966) traces the two types of theodicy, Augustinian and Irenaean, and presents an Irenaean theodicy for today.

Some philosophical discussions are: A. C. Ewing, *Fundamental Problems of Philosophy*, pp. 247–250 (London, 1951); J. E. MacTaggart, *Some Dogmas of Religion* (London, 1906), Chs. 6 and 7; C. H. Whiteley, *An Introduction to Metaphysics* (London, 1950), Ch. 11. In addition to the articles referred to in the body of this article, see John Wisdom, "God and Evil," in *Mind*, Vol. 44, No. 173 (1935), 1–20, and H. D. Aiken "God and Evil," in *Ethics*,

Vol. 68, No. 2 (1958), 77–97, (1949), reprinted in Aiken's *Reason and Conduct* (New York, 1962).

More purely theological discussions occur in P. T. Forsyth, *The Justification of God* (London, 1916) and Karl Barth, *Die Kirchliche Dogmatik* (Munich, 1932), Vol. 3, Pt. 3, par. 50, translated as *Church Dogmatics*, T. F. Torrance and G. W. Bromiley, eds. (Edinburgh, 1959–1960). A book discussing Karl Barth's views on the problem of evil is Kurt Lüthi, *Gott und das Böse* (Zurich, 1961).

See also C. G. Jung, *Antwort auf Hiob* (Zurich, 1952), translated by R. F. C. Hull as *Answer to Job* (London, 1954). On the problem of animal pain, see the relevant chapters in the works cited by Ferré, Farrer, and Lewis.

JOHN HICK

EVOLUTION. See DARWINISM; EMERGENT EVOLUTIONISM.

EXISTENCE. Philosophical discussion of the notion of existence, or being, has centered on two main problems which have not always been very clearly distinguished. First, there is the problem of what we are to say about the existence of fictitious objects, such as centaurs, dragons, and Pegasus; second, there is the problem of what we are to say about the existence of abstract objects, such as qualities, relations, and numbers. Both problems have tempted philosophers to say that there are inferior sorts of existence as well as the ordinary straightforward sort, and they therefore often suggest that we use the word "being" to cover both kinds but restrict "existence" to "being" of the common, nonfictitious, nonabstract sort. (Sometimes the term "reality" is proposed for "existence" or for "being.") The problems of fiction and abstraction are different, however, for there are both real and fictitious abstractions. For example, the integer between two and four is real, but the integer between two and three is fictitious. On the other hand, there are both concrete and abstract fictions; for example, the winged horse of Bellerophon and the integer between two and three. Accordingly, philosophers have often dealt with the two problems in quite different ways and perhaps ought to do so.

While these are the two main problems, there are others, for example, that of what we are to say of the being of objects which have not yet begun, or have now ceased, to exist. The history of this subject, moreover, has been tangled with theological issues, to which it will be necessary to refer at certain points. Most of what follows will concentrate on the question of fictitious existence, with some consideration of past and future existence and with a final section on the being sometimes ascribed to abstractions. (For rather different questions concerning existence, see ESSENCE AND EXISTENCE; EXISTENTIALISM.)

FICTIONS

Ancient and medieval. It is clear from Aristotle's earliest works that there was current among the Greeks a sophism to the effect that whatever is thought of must exist in order to be thought of. Countering this, Aristotle distinguished between "to be A" (for instance, to be thought of) and "to be" without qualification. He made the same remark about the "being A" of that which has "ceased to be"; for instance, from "Homer is a poet" it does not follow that "Homer is."

Some such distinction seems necessary, since among the A's that one can be is "dead" or "no longer existent." The Aristotelian view is not simple, however, for elsewhere he suggested that propositions equivalent to "Socrates is ill" and "Socrates is well" imply the plain "Socrates is"; "neither is true if Socrates does not exist at all."

The various facets of the Aristotelian position were reproduced by the Scholastics. They distinguished, for example, between *est secundi adiecti* ("is" added as a second element in a simple sentence, as in "Socrates is"), and *est tertii adiecti* ("is" added as a third element, as in "Socrates is ill"), a distinction made by Aristotle in substantially the same terms; they also had the rule that from "being A" we may infer plain "being." But the Scholastics questioned and qualified this rule with the other Aristotelian examples in mind; from *Chimaera est opinabilis*, "The chimera can be thought of," the plain *Chimaera est* does not follow, nor does *Caesar est* follow from *Caesar est mortuus*. Some predicates, they said, presuppose *esse simpliciter*, and some do not. (*Chimaera* itself, incidentally, they put in the first class, and were thereby led to say that even "The chimera is the chimera" is false—the chimera, since it "isn't," isn't anything, even the chimera.) In this connection they sometimes distinguished between "objective" and "formal" being; "objective" not having its modern sense but rather the opposite—for a thing to exist "objectively" it sufficed that it be an object of thought; "formal" being was, as it were, serious being.

Anselm's Ontological Argument for the existence of God hinged on this notion of "objective" being, which he called existence in the mind. The Psalmist's fool who says in his heart that God does not exist must in that very act be thinking of God, so that God exists in his mind. But by definition God is that than which nothing greater can be thought of (if this definition is objected to, we can simply say, "Never mind—that than which nothing greater can be thought of, whether you give this the name "God" or not, can be thought of, and therefore exists in the mind even of one who denies its existence anywhere else"). And to exist outside the mind as well as in it is a greater thing than to exist in the mind only; we can also think of a being that does this, so if it exists in the mind only, the *maximum cogitabile* isn't the *maximum cogitabile* at all; it is therefore self-contradictory to deny real existence to that than which nothing greater can be thought of. "Greater" in this argument means, in part, better, so it is no answer to say that of some things it might be better for them not to exist. If God is by definition everything that a being ought to be, then such a being ought to be, among other things, real; and to think of him as not being real is therefore to think of him as not being all that he ought, and thus is not to be really thinking of God. The thought of an unreal God is internally incoherent, so if God can be thought of at all (and the man who thinks he doesn't exist does think of him), he must, if we are to be consistent, be thought of as real. But it is clear that this type of argument, if valid, has other than theological applications; as Anselm's opponent Gaunilo pointed out, there would be a similar contradiction in ascribing merely mental existence to the greatest (and best) conceivable island.

The notion of "weak" forms of being entered into another medieval theory, that of the "ampliation," or widening, of the "supposition," or reference, of certain terms in certain contexts. If we say "Some men are running," it is understood that we mean some men now existing; but if we say "Some men were running" or "Some men will be running," it will be enough to verify the former if some formerly existing men were running, and the latter if some men who will then exist will be running; and if we say "Some men are thought of as running," it will do if some merely thought-of men (Sherlock Holmes and Dr. Watson, say) are thought of as running. The pool of objects on which we may draw to verify our statements may in some cases extend to objects whose being is comparatively shadowy yet is substantial enough for them to be genuine subjects of affirmative discourse.

It is noteworthy, however, that at least one medieval thinker, Thomas Aquinas, quite firmly refused to avail himself of the notion of substandard existence at a point where it might have been thought to be helpful: in dealing with objections to the doctrine of creation out of nothing. Creation out of nothing, Aquinas insisted, is not creation out of a peculiarly tenuous material; to be created out of nothing is simply not to be created out of anything, and God himself is "created out of nothing" in this sense. But to be created (as God of course is not), yet not created out of anything, is to be given existence; and to what is existence given if there is literally nothing there to give it to? To give existence to nothing, surely, is just not to give existence to anything, and thus not to create at all. That there already are "creatables" whose capacity to exist in the full sense is made actual in their creation is explicitly denied; the only power involved is that of God to create, and creating is denied to be a genuine action on an object. All that Thomas could say positively is that the receiver of existence starts to be simultaneously with the giving of that existence—*Deus simul dans esse, producit id quod esse recipit: et sic non oportet quod agat ex aliquo prae-existenti* (*De Potentia Dei*, Q.2, A.1). Leibniz' later talk of God as conferring actual existence upon a selected few of an infinite number of *possibilia*, each with its own eternally complete individuality, seems much less perceptive. Creating out of *possibilia* is not creation out of nothing at all.

Eighteenth and nineteenth centuries. The rejection of halfway points between existence and nonexistence which characterized Aquinas' treatment of creation found wider applications in the works of the eighteenth-century philosopher Thomas Reid. In discussing "conception," Reid distinguished this "operation of the mind" from others by the fact that whereas "the powers of sensation, of perception, of memory, and of consciousness [introspection] are all employed solely about objects that do exist, or have existed . . . conception is often employed about objects that neither do, nor did, nor will exist" (*Essays on the Intellectual Power of Man*, Essay IV). It is important, he said, to "distinguish between that act or operation of the mind, which we call conceiving an object, and the object that we conceive." The former always exists; the latter need not. The notion that it must has led some philosophers to interpose between the act and the object an entity called an idea, which is the "immediate" object of concep-

tion and exists even when the "remote" object does not. According to Reid's view, there are no such entities, and "having an idea of" is just a circumlocution for "conceiving."

> The philosopher says, I cannot conceive a centaur without having an idea of it in my mind. . . . He surely does not mean that I cannot conceive it without conceiving it. This would make me no wiser. What then is this idea? Is it an animal, half horse and half man? No. Then I am certain it is not the thing I conceive. . . . This one object which I conceive is not the image of an animal—it is an animal. I know what it is to conceive an image of an animal, and what it is to conceive an animal; and I can distinguish the one of these from the other without any danger of mistake. (*Ibid.*)

Not only is there no reason to believe in the existence of "ideas" (apart from the sheer "prejudice" that all acts of the mind must have existent objects); postulating them does not help, and only gives rise to an infinite regress.

> In every work of design, the work must be conceived before it is executed—that is, before it exists. If a model, consisting of ideas, must exist in the mind, as the object of this conception, that model is a work of design no less than the other, of which it is the model; and therefore, as a work of design, it must have been conceived before it existed. (*Ibid.*)

The point that the idea or copy theory just doesn't help seems unanswerable. But Reid's own position has serious difficulties. Every act of conception, he said, "must have an object; for he that conceives must conceive something"; thus, to conceive nothing—not to conceive anything—is not to conceive at all. But if what is conceived—for example, a centaur—does not exist in any sense, is this not simply conceiving without any second term? The object of conception in all cases is something, as Reid claimed; it would therefore seem that "somethings" ("beings," "objects," in a wide sense) are divisible into two sorts, ones with existence over and above their mere objecthood, and ones without. Reid said as much when he spoke of a man as acquiring sufficient judgment to "distinguish things that really exist from things that are only conceived." Reid was trying to slip this statement past as if it were not the theory of weak and strong modes of "being." But if it is not, what is it? He said that men six feet tall and men sixty feet tall are both "things," even if he said it under his breath. The theory of weak and strong being is not easily avoidable, and in the present century it was stated in these terms in Bertrand Russell's early work and in Reid's terms by Alexius Meinong.

There is a rather different strand in postmedieval philosophy, starting perhaps with Pierre Gassendi. Replying to the Cartesian version of Anselm's Ontological Argument, Gassendi said that existence is not a "perfection," not because it is sometimes an undesirable property but because it is not a property at all; it is, rather, a prerequisite for the possession of any properties. In itself this looks like merely accepting one side of Aristotle's dilemma and ignoring the other (must a thing exist in order to possess the property of being thought of?). Later writers, however, took the thought further. David Hume, in particular, held that existence is a nugatory notion. "When after the simple conception of any thing we would conceive it as existent, we in reality make no addition or alteration on our first idea" (*Treatise of Human Nature*, Book I, Part 3, Sec. 7 and note). The notion of an existent God, man, or centaur is simply the notion of a God, a man, or a centaur. The common view of judgment as "the separating or uniting of different ideas" is therefore mistaken; the judgment that God exists, for example, involves only one idea, that of God. The real difference is not that between a God and an existent God but that between conceiving God's existence (which is the same as conceiving God) and believing in his existence; this is a difference in our mode of thought, not in what is thought of. Kant made the same point in his treatment of the Ontological Argument; existence, he said, is not a genuine predicate, and the conception of a hundred real dollars has no more "content" than that of a hundred merely possible dollars.

Hume's denial that the object of judgment is necessarily complex was taken further by Franz Brentano. Since the time of Aristotle, logicians had divided propositions or judgments into simple "existential" assertions and denials, of the forms "X is" and "X is not," and "predicative" ones, of the forms "X is Y" and "X is not Y," and had tended, when assimilating the two, to treat existential assertions as a special case of predicative ones—"X is" amounts to "X is existent" or "X is a being." Brentano reversed this, treating the difference between the two types as merely a difference in the complexity of what is asserted or denied to be— "X is Y" amounts to "XY is" and "X is not Y" to "XY is not" (for instance, "Horses don't fly" amounts to "Flying horses do not exist"). He avoided the infinite regress that would appear if "XY is" was further transformed into "Existent XY is," and "XY is not" into "Existent XY is not" by denying, with Hume, that existence is a feature of the object of thought. "X is" and "XY is" simply express the mind's acceptance of the concept X or XY, as opposed to the mere entertainment of it, and "X is not" and "XY is not" similarly express the mind's rejection of "X" and "XY."

An obvious objection to the theories of Hume, Kant, and Brentano is that they are concerned not with the notion of existence but with that of believing in something's existence, and the account given of this latter—that to believe that what is before the mind exists is simply to accept this object—is such that the notion of the object's existence apart from our belief disappears. It is like the account of "believing X to be good" that reduces it to "liking X"; the notion of X's being good, outside of its being believed to be so, vanishes. However it may be with beliefs about goodness, beliefs about the existence of things are surely true or false; and they are true only if the things in question exist in fact. Brentano's answer was to define what really exists as the object of right affirmative judgment, but this seems to reverse the matter—the judgment that X exists is a right one if and only if X does exist (see CORRESPONDENCE THEORY OF TRUTH).

However, the treatment of predicative judgments as complex existential ones can easily be disentangled from Brentano's subjectivism; and it is also found in writers, notably John Venn, whose interests were less in metaphysico-psychological questions than in developing formal logic by algebraic means. If we are to do this, it is natural to write "No X is a Y" as "XY = 0" and to read this as "XY's are nonexistent." Similarly "Some X is a Y" becomes "XY ≠ 0"; "Some X is not a Y," "X$\bar{Y}$ ≠ 0" (writing "$\bar{Y}$" for what is not a Y; that is, "non-Y"); and "Every X is a $\bar{Y}$," "X$\bar{Y}$ = 0," or "X's that are not Y are nonexistent." This, as Brentano and Venn observed, has the odd consequence of making both universal forms true of what does not exist, for if there are no X's at all, there are none that are Y and none that are not Y, so that "No X is a Y" is true in the sense of "XY's are nonexistent" and "Every X is a Y" is true in the sense of "X's that are not Y are nonexistent." This is sometimes expressed as the dictum that the null (or empty) class is included in every class; the class of centaurs, for example, is included in that of tables because, since there are no centaurs at all, there are no centaurs that aren't tables.

This leads to divergences from the scholastic rule that affirmative predications imply the existence of their subject while negative predications do not; and the late nineteenth-century discussions of this problem of the "existential import" of the Aristotelian predicative forms were very elegantly summed up by J. N. Keynes in his *Studies and Exercises in Formal Logic*. The scholastic rule, it should be noted, was subject to qualification in the light of the doctrine of "ampliation" already mentioned; "All centaurs are said to be musical," for example, was not falsified by there being no real centaurs because in this context the reference of "centaur" was extended to centaurs merely spoken of. A nineteenth-century counterpart of this doctrine was the theory of the "universe of discourse." "Existence," according to this theory, always means membership in some collection of objects taken as real for the purposes of the discussion, and this might be either the actual universe or, for instance, the world of Homeric mythology. Taken seriously, this would seem to be a variant of the theory of weak and strong modes of being.

Brentano's account of predicative judgments as complex existential ones is reversed in Alexander Bain's theory that all intelligible assertions of existence have complex subjects and therefore can be restated in the predicative form. For example, "when we say there *exists* a conspiracy for a particular purpose, we mean that at the present time a body of men have formed themselves into a society for a particular object" (*Logic*, Book I, Ch. 3, Sec. 23), and in general, "XY's exist" = "Some X's are Y's." In the present century this view was enlarged upon by John Anderson. According to Anderson, statements are meaningful (and thus true or false) only if all terms occurring in them are real; that is, only if they have objects answering to them. This means, in view of the Bain–Anderson analysis of assertions of existence, that these terms must be implicitly complex and that the statements in which they occur must presuppose other statements in which this implicit complexity is made manifest; these in turn presuppose others, and so on without end. "All X's are Y's" (for instance, "All albinos are short-sighted") is meaningful only if there are X's and Y's (albinos and short-sighted individuals), and this condition is itself meaningful only if "X" and "Y" are implicitly complex—if an *X*, for example, is an *AB* (an albino is an animal with white hair and pinkish eyes), so that "*X*'s exist" means "Some *A*'s are *B*'s" ("Some animals with white hair have pinkish eyes"); and similarly for these statements in their turn.

The apparent predicate "exists" disappears from this system, without any subjectivism (the plain "*X*'s exist," or at all events "*XY*'s exist," has been given a meaning, and not just "*A* judges that *XY*'s exist"). But the system completely wrecks such simple rules of construction as the one that if "*X*" and "*Y*" can both figure as terms in a meaningful sentence, so can "*XY*" ("what is at once an *X* and a *Y*").

Russell's theory of descriptions. The most extensive and fruitful discussions of existence in the present century have been those initiated by Russell, in works written after his abandonment of the theory of weak and strong modes of being. On the meaning of "all" and "some" Russell stands squarely in the tradition of Venn; he reads "Some *X*'s are *Y*'s" as "*XY*'s exist" and "All *X*'s are *Y*'s" as "*X*'s that are not *Y*'s do not exist"; but he also insists, in the tradition of Kant, that "exists" is not a genuine predicate. For Russell the fundamental form of prediction is the singular or "atomic" proposition, "*x* *φs*," where "*x*" is a proper name of an individual and "*φs*" is a genuine predicate or verb. "Lions exist" and "Tame lions exist" (or "Some lions are tame") are respectively analyzed as "For some individual *x*, *x* is a lion" and "For some individual *x*, *x* is a lion and is tame"; the predicates are "is a lion" and "is a lion and is tame"—"exist" has disappeared into the prefix, or "quantifier," "For some individual *x* . . . ." To predicate "exists" of an individual directly named is meaningless; but Russell makes a sharp distinction between genuine, or "logically proper," names and spurious ones. A genuine proper name (Russell usually takes the demonstrative "this" as an example) contributes nothing to the meaning of a sentence except the identification of some individual as its subject; in John Stuart Mill's terminology, it "denotes" but does not "connote." Anything it tells us about the individual, if it is being used as a genuine proper name, is no part of what is being said; and if there is no individual that it identifies, then nothing is being said at all. A singular, or "definite," description of the form "the so-and-so," or a grammatical proper name with the sense of such a description (such as "Scott" used to mean "the author of Waverley"), is quite a different matter. When analyzed, "the so-and-so," like "some so-and-so" and "every so-and-so," disappears into a complex of predicates and quantifying prefixes; for example, "The present king of France is bald" amounts to "For exactly one individual *x*, *x* is now king of France, and for any *x*, if *x* is now king of France, *x* is bald." "The so-and-so exists," unlike "This exists," has a perfectly clear meaning; it means "For exactly one individual *x*, *x* is a so-and-so."

This apparatus yields a neat solution to the Aristotelian problem of when "*X* is *Y*" entails "*X* is" and when it does not. When "*X*" is a genuine proper name, in Russell's view, the question does not arise ("*X* is" being simply meaningless). But when it is a definite description or has the sense of a definite description, and the predicate is complex, it is often possible to read "*X* is *Y*" in different

ways; and whether it entails "*X* is" will depend on how it is read. For example, "The present king of France is not bald" may assert that someone is the present king of France but is not bald, which does entail that someone is the present king of France—that the present king of France exists; but if it means only that it is not the case that someone is the present king of France and is bald, then it does not entail either that there is or that there is not a unique present king of France. Similarly, "The present king of France is believed to be bald" may be read as asserting that someone is the present king of France and it is believed of this person that he is bald, and this does entail the existence of the present king of France; or it might merely mean that it is believed that someone is the present king of France and is bald, and this could be true even if there were in fact no present king of France. Where the whole means something of the form "Someone is the present king of France and . . . ." (the complexity, if any, coming after the "and"), the description "the present king of France" is said to have primary occurrence; where a whole sentence of this form is preceded by or embedded in some qualifying context, the occurrence of the description is said to be secondary. Only primary occurrences of descriptions entail that there really is something answering to them; that is, that the thing described exists. Russell, incidentally, agrees with Buridan that "The chimera is the chimera" entails "The chimera exists" and thus is false, although where "*x*" represents a genuine proper name, "*x* is (identical with) *x*" is always true.

The Russellian apparatus removes the necessity for postulating weak and strong modes of being, at least where definite descriptions are involved. We do not need to suppose, when we imagine the Hydra, that there is a Hydra that we imagine, even in a weakened sense of "is," or that there is some real thing that we imagine to be the Hydra. Two prefixes, "I imagine that" and "For exactly one individual *x*," are involved here; and which governs which greatly affects the interpretation. "I imagine that for exactly one individual *x*, *x* is a Hydra" makes one assertion, and "For exactly one individual *x*, I imagine that *x* is a Hydra" makes quite another; and neither assertion entails that for exactly one individual *x*, *x* is a Hydra. The second form, indeed, asserts a relation between me and a certain real individual (the one which I imagine to be the Hydra); but the first form does not assert any relation between me and any individual whatever, real or imaginary—it just asserts that I imagine that there is such a thing as the Hydra. These forms are sufficient to describe what might be going on; there is no need whatever to suppose that if I imagine that there is a real individual of such and such a sort, then there really must be an "imaginary individual" of whom I imagine these things; that is, there is no need whatever to twist the first form around to "For exactly one imaginary individual *x*, I imagine that *x* is the Hydra," or to talk about "imaginary individuals" at all. There is, indeed, a merely imagined state of affairs involved, so that one might say that this solution merely removes the problem one step further. But the existence of states of affairs is part of a different problem, that of the existence of abstract rather than fictitious objects, and is, perhaps, soluble.

Russell's insistence that "exists" has no sense in which it can be a genuine predicate—that is, in which it can attach directly to a genuine proper name—seems a little arbitrary and not at all essential to his position as a whole. As G. E. Moore has pointed out, all that follows from this position is that a sentence like "This exists" is bound to be true; and one like "This does not exist" is bound to be false, if it says anything at all (for if "This exists" were false, "this" would not be picking out any object, and nothing would be being said). Russell's own formal system does in fact contain predicates—for instance, "_____ is identical with itself"—which have just this property, and he uses such predicates to define the class of individuals, or "things," that is, the "universal" class. He himself, moreover, reads the proposition "For some *x*, *x* is in the universal class" (which follows from "For some *x*, *x* is identical with itself") as "At least one individual exists," and he considers it a defect of *Principia Mathematica* that this proposition is provable in it. Such a proposition is scarcely avoidable in a system which has symbols for logically proper names; and its derivation is not, as some might fear, a revival of the Ontological Argument. "It is necessary that there should be something" does not mean or entail "There is something that 'is' necessarily," any more than "There is bound to be someone who wins" entails "There is someone who is bound to win." Nor can the Ontological Argument arise in its original form even if existence is a predicate, for it is blocked by the illegitimacy of the passage from "I am imagining that God really is" to "There is an imaginary God (a being in the mind) of whom I imagine this."

Nevertheless, there is a genuine problem about contingent and necessary being in this context. One of Moore's arguments for the meaningfulness of "This exists" is that it must have some meaning because "This might not have existed" often does have meaning and in general is true. The suggestion is that "This might not have existed" is analyzable as "It might have been the case that (it is not the case that (this exists))," and this could have no meaning if its innermost component did not. The odd thing, however, is that when it is thus analyzed, the statement does not appear to be true. "It is not the case that this exists" is just "This does not exist," but under what circumstances might this have been true, if "this" is being used as a genuine proper name? Under none at all, it would seem, according to Moore's own argument above. Some of Russell's followers—Wittgenstein in the *Tractatus* and F. P. Ramsey—have argued that in fact the only possible states of affairs alternative to the actual one are ones in which the objects that in fact exist have properties and relations different from those which they in fact have. This is to make all individuals what the Scholastics thought God was, "necessary beings." However, the formulation "This need not have existed," read as "It is not the case that (it is necessary that (this exists))," does not seem open to these difficulties, since its verification does not require that there be states of affairs in which we could truly say of the object in question "This does not exist"; it is enough if there are states of affairs in which nothing can be said of the object in question at all (for then not all states of affairs will be ones in which we can say of it "This exists," that is,

"This exists" will not be a necessary truth). This solution makes a distinction between "possibly not" and "not necessarily," which in most logical systems are equivalent; however, it is possible to develop systems of modal logic in which they are not equivalent.

Russell's distinctions also throw some light on Aquinas' problems about creation out of nothing. Thus, P. T. Geach claims that "God has created a man out of something" amounts to "For some *x* (God has brought it about that (*x* is a man))"; but in the case of creation out of nothing we have only "God has brought it about that (for some *x* (*x* is a man))." In the first form, where "For some *x*" governs "God has brought it about that," what is said is that there is an already existing object on which God has so acted as to make it a man; in the second form, where "God has brought it about that" governs "for some x," it is not said that there is something that God makes into a man, but only that he brings to pass the state of affairs expressed by "Something is a man." But it is only the creation of something under a certain description ("a man") that could be construed in this latter way; the creation of individuals as such out of nothing (as opposed to their creation out of, say, "possible individuals") still seems impossible, since they have no identity until they are "there," and a divine "Let there be this man" would be senseless before that time.

ABSTRACTIONS

Turning from the supposed existence of fictitious objects to that of abstract ones, it will be useful to make some preliminary grammatical distinctions. Besides the proper names of individuals, most languages contain common nouns, adjectives, and verbs which apply to various individuals without actually naming any of them, and abstract nouns which seem to name the qualities, relations, states, and actions of individuals as if they were themselves individuals of a tenuous sort. We may say that a verb "*φs*" applies to an individual *x* if in fact *x* *φs*, that an adjective "*A*" applies to *x* if in fact *x* is *A*, and that a common noun "*C*" applies to *x* if in fact *x* is a *C*. Current logic tends to treat the verb form of a predicate as fundamental and adjectives and common nouns as always implicitly functioning as parts of verbal phrases like "is *A*" or "is a *C*." Where common nouns appear as grammatical subjects, as in "All men are liars," and adjectives as directly qualifying nouns, as in "All white men are liars," a little twisting will usually set the word in the basic verb context ("Whatever is-a-man is-a-liar," "Whatever is-a-man and is-white is-a-liar"). As verbs do not even look like names of objects, there are no very serious problems.

Abstract nouns, however, do look like names of objects, and so do common nouns in certain rather special uses, as in "Man is the noblest of animals" and "Man is a species." The objects which they appear to name are sometimes called universals; here they shall be called abstract objects or abstractions. Numerals also appear to name abstract objects—numbers—and noun clauses like "that Caesar conquered Gaul" and equivalent phrases like "Caesar's conquest of Gaul" also seem to name abstract objects—

states of affairs or (in one use of the term) "propositions." Other apparent names frequently used in recent times are phrases of the form "the class of so-and-so's."

Some of these linguistic suggestions were taken very seriously by Plato and others have been taken seriously by other writers, and it is now common to describe as Platonism the view that abstract objects "exist" in a perfectly literal sense as part of the "furniture of the universe" alongside tables and chairs. If the Platonist admits that their being has something peculiar about it, and perhaps calls it subsisting rather than existing, he will nevertheless say that there is a single being which both subsisting and existing objects possess. The opposed Aristotelian tradition is to say that there is no single being which is common to objects of all different categories (things, qualities, relations, etc.), and that they are not just different sorts of beings but rather that they "are" in different but related ("analogous") senses of "are." In the fundamental sense of "are," only substances or things really "are"; qualities "are" also, but only in a secondary sense—their reality consists simply in their qualifying real things; the reality of relations consists similarly in their relating real things, and so on. On the Aristotelian view, one might say there are weaker and stronger senses of "be" but no sense so weak as to cover, unambiguously, the subjects of all the others. The view that there is no necessity to attribute existence in any sense to anything but concrete individuals is generally called nominalism (after the medieval view that "universals" are no more than empty names).

Most abstract nouns have verbs, adjectives, or common nouns related to them in meaning, and the nominalist's problem could be described as that of paraphrasing statements ostensibly about abstract objects in such a way that the abstract nouns disappear into the corresponding verbs or allied forms. Often this can be done quite easily. "Caesar is a member of the class of men" and "Caesar has the attribute of manhood," or "Manhood characterizes Caesar," seem no more than pompous ways of saying that Caesar is human (or human and male). Similarly, "The class of men is included in the class of mortals" and "Manhood is always accompanied by mortality" seem to mean simply that whatever is human is mortal. But other cases are trickier—"Red is a color," for example. This means more than "Whatever is red is colored"; we may presume that all red things, and only red things, occupy a certain set of regions of space (or of space–time), so that it is true that whatever occupies these regions is colored (just as all red things are colored) but not that the occupation of those regions is a color—it is not a color but a location. "Being red is a way of being colored" is more like it, but "being red" and "way of being colored" are as nounlike in form (the one a name of one thing and the other a common noun applying to many) as "red" and "color" themselves. If we write "being red" as "redding" and "being colored" as "coloring," we can perhaps say that "_____ing is a way of _____ing" builds a sentence out of two verbs just as "Whatever _____s, _____s" does and that the suffix "-ing" does not form real names but is an inseparable part of complexes like "_____ing is a way of_____ing." But some might say that rather than be driven to *ad hoc* solutions

such as this last, it is better to admit the existence of abstractions and be done with it.

In comparatively recent history both Platonism and nominalism have run into difficulties of a rather technical sort. (For some of these, including special problems about the existence of classes and numbers, see RUSSELL, BERTRAND ARTHUR WILLIAM).

Bibliography

The key texts in Aristotle are *De Sophistici Elenchis* 167a1 ff.; *De Interpretatione* 19b18 ff. and 21a26 ff.; and *Categories* 13b16 ff. and 29 ff.

Anselm's Ontological Argument is stated in his *Proslogium* and *Monologium,* and Gaunilo's answer is in his *Pro Insipiente;* Aquinas' summary and answer are in his *Summa Theologica* I, 1, 2; Descartes's variant is in his *Meditations;* Gassendi's criticism is in the Objections appended to Descartes's *Meditations;* and Kant's criticism is in his *Critique of Pure Reason,* Transcendental Dialectic, Book II, Ch. 3, Sec. 4. The key passages in Anselm, Descartes, and Kant are included in Charles Hartshorne and W. L. Reese, *Philosophers Speak of God* (Chicago, 1953).

For Aquinas on creation out of nothing and problems arising out of the notion of "giving existence," see his *De Potentia Dei* Q. 2, A. 1, Objections 2, 7, 11, and 17 and answers. For comments on this, see Antonin Sertillanges, *L'Idée de création et ses retentissements en philosophie* (Aubier, 1945), especially pp. 45–48; A. N. Prior, "Identifiable Individuals," in *Review of Metaphysics,* Vol. 13 (1960), 684–696; and P. T. Geach, "Causality and Creation," in *Sophia* (1962), 1–8. Problems about the identifiability of as yet nonexistent individuals are also acutely discussed in Jonathan Edwards, *Freedom of the Will,* Paul Ramsey, ed. (New Haven, 1957), Part IV, Sec. 8, and in G. E. Moore, *The Commonplace Books,* Casimir Lewy, ed. (London and New York, 1963), p. 329. Leibniz' solution in terms of pre-existent *possibilia* is developed in his correspondence with Arnauld (edited by Geneviève Lewis, Paris, 1952), which arose out of his *Discourse on Metaphysics* (translated and edited by P. G. Lucas and L. Grint, 2d ed., Manchester, 1963), and in the dialogue at the end of his *Theodicy* (translated by E. M. Huggard, London and New Haven, 1952).

For Thomas Reid's views, see his *Essays on the Intellectual Powers of Man* (Edinburgh, 1785), Essay IV ("On Conception") and Essay VI ("On Judgment"). For Russell's early position, see *The Principles of Mathematics* (Cambridge, 1903), especially pp. 43 and 71. The best and most accessible treatment of Meinong's views is in J. N. Findlay, *Meinong's Theory of Objects* (Oxford, 1933; reprinted with additions, Oxford, 1963), Ch. 2.

For Hume, the key passage is in his *Treatise of Human Nature,* Book I, Part 3, Sec. 7 and note; for Brentano, his *Psychologie vom empirischen Standpunkt* (Leipzig, 1874), Vol. I, Book II, Ch. 7, Sec. 15. J. N. Keynes's discussion of possible responses to the challenge of Brentano and Venn is in his *Studies and Exercises in Formal Logic* (London, 1884; 4th ed., London, 1906), Ch. 8. Bain's views are in his *Logic,* 2d ed. (London, 1873), Book I, Ch. 3, Sec. 23, and are discussed in a footnote to J. S. Mill's *System of Logic,* 9th ed. (London, 1875), Book I, Ch. 5, Sec. 5.

Russell's later theories are most clearly developed in his 1918 lectures "The Philosophy of Logical Atomism" (included in *Logic and Knowledge,* London, 1956), Lectures V and VI, and in Ch. 16 of his *Introduction to Mathematical Philosophy* (London, 1918). The latter contains, on pp. 168–170, his splendid and rather Reid-like appeal for a "robust sense of reality," G. E. Moore's agreements and disagreements with Russell are in his Aristotelian Society paper "Is Existence a Predicate?," reproduced in his collected *Philosophical Papers* (London, 1959). The same collection contains another relevant Aristotelian Society paper, "Imaginary Objects," which may be compared with pp. 243–245 o, Moore's *Commonplace Books.* F. P. Ramsey's development of the consequence that Russell's theory allows for no contingency of existence is in *The Foundations of Mathematics* (London, 1931), p. 285; see also the ingenious argument on p. 155.

On the "grammatical" solution to the problem of universals, see

Russell's 1924 essay "Logical Atomism," also included in *Logic and Knowledge*, and Tadeusz Kotarbiński's article "The Fundamental Ideas of Pansomatism," translated by David Rynin, in *Mind*, Vol. 64 (1955), 488–500.

Much current discussion takes its start from W. V. Quine's paper "On What There Is," included in his *From a Logical Point of View* (Cambridge, Mass., 1953).

A. N. PRIOR

EXISTENCE AND ESSENCE. See ESSENCE AND EXISTENCE.

EXISTENTIALISM is not easily definable. Its protagonists have traced it back to Pascal, to St. Augustine, even to Socrates. It has been alleged in our time to be the doctrine of writers as various as Miguel de Unamuno and Norman Mailer. At first sight, characteristics of the doctrine are almost as various. That two writers both claim to be existentialists does not seem to entail their agreement on any one cardinal point. Consequently, to define existentialism by means of a set of philosophical formulas could be very misleading. Any formula sufficiently broad to embrace all the major existentialist tendencies would necessarily be so general and so vague as to be vacuous, for if we refer to a common emphasis upon, for example, the concreteness of individual human existence, we shall discover that in the case of different philosophers this emphasis is placed in contexts so dissimilar that it is put to quite different and incompatible uses. How then is existentialism to be defined?

EXISTENTIALIST THEMES

Existentialism may perhaps be considered most fruitfully as a historical movement in which connections of dependence and influence can be traced from one writer to another. Thus, even if two writers who are both rightly called existentialist differ enormously in doctrine, they can be placed in the same family tree. But this only throws the question of definition one stage back. How do we select our philosophical pedigrees? The answer must be in terms of a number of recurrent themes that are in fact independent of one another but have, as a matter of philosophical history, been associated in a variety of patterns. The key themes are the individual and systems; intentionality; being and absurdity; the nature and significance of choice; the role of extreme experiences; and the nature of communication.

The individual and systems. Søren Kierkegaard chose for his own epitaph the words "that individual." The concept of the individual for Kierkegaard was contrasted both with the concept of philosophical system and with the concepts of the stereotype and the mass. Between these contrasts there is a connection. A philosophical system was for Kierkegaard an attempt to understand individual existence within a conceptual scheme of a kind that would exhibit a logically necessary connection between every individual part and the conceptual scheme of the whole universe. People in the mass, or those who live out a stereotyped role, are people who understand themselves in terms of some concept or concepts they happen to em-

body. In both cases the individual is secondary to the concept it embodies. In fact, however, what exists comes first; concepts are necessarily inadequate attempts to grasp individual existence, which always evades complete conceptualization. One of the difficulties in understanding what Kierkegaard and his later followers have meant by assertions of this kind is that none of their detailed arguments appear to entail their conclusion. Consider two of these arguments.

The first is a revival of Kant's argument against the so-called Ontological Proof. Like Kant, Kierkegaard argued that existence is not a property and that no concept of a given object entails the existence of that object. Also, Kierkegaard anticipated some modern writers in arguing that action and choice can be understood only if viewed from the standpoint of the agent rather than from that of the spectator. What is puzzling, however, is that Kierkegaard assumed that the notion of philosophical system is inextricably bound up with the viewpoint of the spectator and the refusal to admit that existence is not a property. In consequence, he concluded that justice can be done to the nature of the individual only if philosophical system building is condemned. The explanation for this particular line of thinking is that Kierkegaard equated the construction of philosophical systems with Hegelianism, and he interpreted Hegelianism as a form of rationalist metaphysics. It is noteworthy that some kind of metaphysical rationalism is almost always the background for existentialism. In countries where empiricism has a long history existentialism does not seem to flourish, even in the form of a reaction to the prevailing moods of thought.

Thus, it is perhaps instructive to regard existentialists as disappointed rationalists. When they announce that reality cannot be comprehended within a conceptual system or, more particularly, that individual existence cannot be so comprehended, they identify the role of a conceptual system with the notion of an all-embracing set of necessary truths derived by deduction from some axiomatic starting point. It may seem, therefore, that existentialists are sometimes doing no more than reformulating the empiricist protest against rationalism (namely, that no matter of fact can be expressed as a necessary truth) in an unnecessary and misleadingly dramatic way. The drama, however, has at least one independent source.

The nineteenth century witnessed a series of very diverse protests against the notion that the universe is a total system, whether one presided over by a Creator God or a purely rational one developing in an evolutionary progress toward higher and higher goals. That the universe does not make sense, that there are no rational patterns discernible in it, is a theme central, for example, to Dostoyevsky's *Notes From the Underground* (1864). Dostoyevsky is often cited as a forerunner of existentialism precisely because in his disillusionment with rationalist humanism he stressed the unpredictable character of the universe and because his individuals appear face to face with pure contingency. Any established connection between things may break down at any minute. Order is a deceptive mask that the universe, especially the social universe, wears. The individual thus confronts the universe with no rational scheme by means of which he can hope to master it. Reason will only lead him to formulate generalizations that will, if he relies upon them, let him down.

Existentialism sometimes gives expression to this kind of view of the limitations of reason. But it is not thereby necessarily committed to irrationalism. At least some existentialist philosophers have been prepared to argue the case for the limits of reason on rational grounds—indeed, on grounds that are partly Kantian. Moreoover, when existentialist philosophers speak of the limits of reason they are usually careful to explain that they wish in no way to trespass upon the territory of the natural sciences or of mathematics. Karl Jaspers goes so far as to accept positivism as a valid account of the sciences, illegitimate only when it aspires to give an account of reasoning as such. Moreover, Jaspers would claim that the areas with which existentialism concerns itself are not outside the competence of reason but only demand that reason be understood in new and less restrictive ways.

The claims, therefore, that the individual cannot be comprehended within a rational system and that the universe which the individual confronts is absurd turn out to have a less striking content than might at first sight have appeared. What has led to their exaggeration is perhaps in part an association with two other philosophical traditions, phenomenology and the kind of philosophy that treats ontology as a central philosophical discipline. Each of these provides existentialism with characteristic themes, which will be considered below.

Intentionality. With the exception of Kierkegaard, existentialist philosophers often make use of a conceptual scheme derived from the phenomenologists Franz Brentano and Edmund Husserl and, through them, from Descartes. In attempting to answer such questions as What is belief?, What is an emotion?, and What is an act of will? phenomenologists wished to combat the associationist psychology that aspired to explain beliefs and emotions in purely naturalistic terms. In contrast, phenomenology emphasized that belief is always belief that . . . and anger is always anger about . . . . The object of belief or of emotion is not an object or a state of affairs in the external world. I may believe what is false or be angry about what did not in fact happen. So the object of belief or emotion is internal to the belief or emotion. It is, in the language of phenomenology, an intentional object.

Brentano concentrated on the isolated individual only in order to describe accurately the central features of believing, feeling, willing, and so on. Husserl treated the individual's consciousness of his own acts as having a primary role not unlike that which Descartes gave it. Among post-Husserl existentialists, notably Sartre, the doctrine of intentionality is used to underline a fundamental difference between my knowledge of myself and my knowledge of others. Other people, so it is asserted, are viewed not as they are but as intentional objects of my perceptions, my beliefs, my emotions. But to myself I can never be such an object, nor am I in fact an object, and if they regard me as such their view of me is necessarily falsified. The obvious criticism of this is to say that the word "object" has been used as a pun. To say that my beliefs have intentional objects is to say neither that they

are necessarily false nor that my beliefs about other people commit me to viewing them as things rather than people. But no existentialist writer is in fact making so simple a mistake. There is always some additional premise to the argument which provides a basis for the existentialist claim that to make others the object of my perceptions or beliefs is to view them as other than they are. In the writings of Sartre and Simone de Beauvoir, for example, specific theses about the character of love and hate play an important role.

What is clear, however, is that although the doctrine of intentionality need not be understood in an existentialist way, this doctrine does add a dimension to the existentialist concept of the individual. Only through the notion of intentionality could the themes in Kierkegaard (which were partly an inheritance from the individualism of Protestantism and partly a reaction against Hegel) have become in Heidegger part of a theory of knowledge and of a metaphysics.

Being and absurdity. Existentialists, believing as they do that reality always evades adequate conceptualization, are especially apt to treat "Being" as a name, the name, in fact, of the realm which we vainly aspire to comprehend. "What the philosophers say about Reality," wrote Kierkegaard, "is often as disappointing as a sign you see in a shop window which reads: Pressing Done Here. If you brought your clothes to be pressed, you would be fooled; for only the sign is for sale" (*Either/Or*, 1843).

In Kierkegaard we get little or no systematic treatment of this kind of theme. In some of his successors, however, we find a systematic ontology, which owes more to the influence of scholastic metaphysics and of rationalism than it does to Kierkegaard. Heidegger took up Leibniz' question, Why are there the things that there are rather than nothing? For Leibniz this question could be answered only by producing the Cosmological Argument for the existence of God. For Heidegger the question itself is misleading, because the posing of it relies upon an inadequate analysis of the notions of being and of nothing. Heidegger treats "Being" and "Nothing" as if they were both names, sometimes the names of powers, sometimes the names of realms. It is not that he is entirely unaware of the logical difficulties encountered in so doing. But he treats such difficulties as evidence of the exceptionally elusive character of Being and Nothing rather than as a sign of his own mistakes. He also accepts the fact that scientific thought never uses such concepts or language, but this he treats as a testimony to the inadequacy of science as a method for understanding reality and to the need for poetry and philosophy. He distinguishes Being (*Sein*) from beings (*die Seiende*) and from modes of being. At times his writing is reminiscent of scholastic ontology, but it is more often aphoristic and oracular.

In Sartre, too, there is an implicit relation to metaphysical rationalism of the kind mentioned above. The thesis that existence is absurd, which is especially important in French existentialism, turns out to be a denial of the principle of sufficient reason. There is no ultimate explanation of why things are as they are and not otherwise. What is curious here is that on the one hand the fact that this is so is seen as a flaw in the nature of things. It belongs to what

Heidegger calls their "fallenness"; the experience of it arouses in us anxiety and perplexity. Yet on the other hand that it is so is the guarantee of human freedom. Both German and French existentialists distinguish sharply between the beings that exist for themselves (*pour-soi*), which have consciousness and freedom, and the beings that exist in themselves (*en-soi*), which are simply things. Now, for existentialism all the important possibilities of human life are bound up with the fact of human freedom, so that to lament the absurdity of existence is in a way odd. But what this lament does reflect is the ambiguous attitude of existentialists to human freedom.

Freedom and choice. If any single thesis could be said to constitute the doctrine of existentialism, it would be that the possibility of choice is the central fact of human nature. Even the thesis that existence precedes essence often means no more than that men do not have fixed natures that limit or determine their choices, but rather it is their choices that bring whatever nature they have into being. As existentialists develop this thesis, they are involved in at least three separate contentions.

The first is that choice is ubiquitous. All my actions imply choices. Even when I do not choose explicitly, as I may not do in the majority of cases, my action bears witness to an implicit choice. The second contention is that although in many of my actions my choices are governed by criteria, the criteria which I employ are themselves chosen, and there are no rational grounds for such choices. The third is that no causal explanation of my actions can be given.

The first thesis is given varying interpretations. For Kierkegaard a person's actions will always form part of a coherent way of life: the aesthetic, in which pleasure is pursued, or the ethical, in which principles are treated as binding, or the religious, in which God is obeyed. Between these one must choose, and it is in this sense that behind any action there lies a choice. For Sartre it sometimes appears as if each separate action expresses an individual choice. Even if I do not choose, I have chosen not to choose.

The second thesis is fundamental to existentialism. But it is plausible to hold that I am free to choose the criteria by which I discriminate true from false beliefs only if this contention is restricted to the field of morals and religions. Kierkegaard sometimes, although not always, allowed for this restriction.

The third thesis, which seems to be logically independent of the others, is often treated by existentialist writers as though it were entailed by the first two. This is less surprising when it is recognized that one of the impulses behind existentialism seems to be a dissatisfaction with the kind of nineteenth-century materialism which held that if human actions can be causally explained, then determinism is true in a sense that excludes the possibility of human agents' being responsible and free. However, instead of denying that causal explanation entails this kind of determinism, the existentialist takes the unnecessary step of denying the probability of causal explanations of human action.

Anxiety, dread, and death. Kierkegaard argued that in certain psychologically defined moments truths about human nature are grasped. One such moment would be when we realize that we do not just fear specific objects but experience a generalized dread. Of what? Of nothing in particular. What is this nothing, this void we confront? Kierkegaard interpreted it in terms of original sin. Heidegger sees it as an ontological constituent of the universe. Sartre sees it as a confrontation with the fact of freedom, of our unmade future.

The variety of interpretations suggests that perhaps different experiences are being discussed or that the ratio of interpretation to experience may be too high. But stress on the extreme and the exceptional experience is common to all existentialism. Everyday experience, by contrast, is thought of as a conventionalized, predigested aid to complacency, conformity, and self-deception. Heidegger gives a very special place to the continuous awareness of one's own future death; Jaspers lays a more generalized stress on a range of situations in which the fragility of our existence is brought home to us.

The form of communication. Since the existentialist writer acknowledges the sovereignty of individual choice and the importance of the concrete situation, he cannot address himself to his audience in the manner of traditional philosophy, for *ex hypothesi* the reader has to make his own choices in the light of his own experiences. Argument will be powerless unless the reader chooses to agree with the author's premises. As a matter of fact, existentialist writings do commonly argue with the reader. But Kierkegaard, for example, was usually careful to frame his arguments in a hypothetical way: "If you choose this starting point, then that logically follows. . . ." He was also in the habit of writing different works under different pseudonyms, so that what the reader was confronted with would be a continuing debate between rival standpoints rather than a single argued case.

Later existentialist writers have developed in two differing ways. All the major existentialist philosophers have written systematic treatises. But they have also made large contributions to imaginative literature, and the content of existentialist philosophy makes it clear that dramatic dialogue, whether in plays or in the novel, is probably a form of expression more consistent with the author's intentions than deductive argument would be.

Such, then, are the shared themes of existentialism. But at this point one ought also to stress, even if briefly, the large differences that are compatible with the thematic resemblances between individual authors.

EXISTENTIALIST AUTHORS

Since the major existentialist philosophers are all treated in separate articles, what is delineated here is their interconnections insofar as they influence one another and above all the way in which the same themes recur in quite different social and philosophical contexts.

Søren Aabye Kierkegaard elaborated all his fundamental doctrines in order to expound and to defend what he took to be true Christianity. The philosophers upon whom he drew were Hegel (though only to attack), Kant, Aristotle (purely as understood through the writings of Friedrich Trendelenburg), and the Platonic Socrates. In contrasting philosophy from Plato to Hegel with authentic Christianity, Kierkegaard emphasized the concepts of the individual, of choice, of dread, and of paradox. He thus originated all the fundamental themes of existentialism.

These themes have been put to a quite new use by Karl Jaspers, who is concerned with criticizing positivism rather than Hegelianism. He has undertaken this with a view to defending a generalized spirituality that Christianity shares with other religions, rather than to defending specifically Christian doctrines. Where Kierkegaard spoke of paradox, Jaspers speaks of contradictions, and in this he is influenced as much by Nietzsche as by Kierkegaard.

Martin Heidegger, too, has felt the influence of Nietzsche. But St. Augustine and Husserl have also been important for his synthesis of existentialism and phenomenology. As a result of this synthesis Heidegger has outlined a systematic ontology which, as such, stands at the opposite pole to Kierkegaard's enterprise. Heidegger's world is one from which God is absent (in this, too, he contrasts with Kierkegaard), but he has denied that he is therefore an atheist. This has no doubt made it easier for theologians to utilize his writings but makes it all the more surprising that his key concepts should have been so easily integrated into yet another existentialist system, that of Jean-Paul Sartre.

In Sartre the concept of choice, which for Kierkegaard was a decision between fundamentally different ways of life, has become a ubiquitous presence behind every human action, and the being of people, which Heidegger has distinguished from the being of things in terms of the relationship of consciousness in its various modes to the world, is now defined essentially in terms of such choices.

Sartre brings together other threads from the earlier history of existentialism. He employs psychological analyses similar to Kierkegaard's analysis of dread but sets them out in terms borrowed from phenomenology. These analyses are carried through for their own sake in Sartre's philosophical writings but are put to work in his novels and plays. They are employed, too, in the novels of Simone de Beauvoir, whose moral and political writings also use the Sartrian concept of choice.

Of parallel psychological interest are the novels of Albert Camus, but the atheism that for Sartre is a consequence of his views of human nature and the world was basic in the thought of Camus. Human life is represented in the myth of Sisyphus, who was doomed eternally to roll up a hill a vast stone that would always fall back just as he was about to reach the top. The dignity of life derives from mankind's continual perseverance in projects for which the universe affords no foothold or encouragement.

Gabriel Marcel is linked to Sartre and Camus by his critique of their atheism. He is an existentialist in his stress on key experiences and on the impossibility of adequately conceptualizing the important features of human life. But the features upon which he lays stress are those of hope and relationship, and his philosophy derives from Royce's personal idealism and even from F. H. Bradley, rather than from any existentialist predecessors.

The range of views expressed by existentialist writers has made it all too easy for the most multifarious authors to claim the title and for the most widespread ancestry to be found for existentialism. Someone like Unamuno, whose book on the tragic sense of life belongs to the same climate as Kierkegaard and Dostoyevsky, could scarcely for that reason be called an existentialist, but those influenced by him in Spain today might well make use of the term. Karl Heim, the German writer on the philosophy of physics, has defined existentialism so widely that almost everything not strictly in the area of science becomes the subject matter of existentialism. Such examples could be multiplied indefinitely. Therefore, it seems wise now to consider the diffused influence of existentialism in the fields of theology, politics, and psychoanalysis.

EXISTENTIALIST THEOLOGIANS

There is a variety of theological systems which in some way are in debt to existentialism. The multiplicity of conclusions which theological writers have drawn from existentialist premises is perhaps testimony both to the ambiguity of those premises and to an underlying failure to analyze adequately some of the basic concepts involved.

Barth. The earliest theological developments are to be found in Kierkegaard's thought, not surprisingly, since he was a theologian in his own right. When Karl Barth repudiated the optimistic liberal theologies of pre-1914 Protestantism, he did so in a commentary on the Epistle to the Romans (*Der Römerbrief*, 1919), which draws quite as heavily on Kierkegaard and Dostoyevsky as it does on St. Paul. From Kierkegaard, Barth took the view that God is totally other than man. Finite reason cannot hope to grasp or comprehend infinite deity. From both Dostoyevsky and Kierkegaard, Barth inherited the thesis that nature and human life are enigmatic, that nothing in the world is reliable.

Barth used these doctrines in two ways. In one direction he repudiated all attempts to find a rational foundation for Christianity, whether in the rational theology of Roman Catholicism or in the philosophical idealism of nineteenth-century Protestantism. In another he used his arguments to revivify the orthodox Protestant theory of the Reformation period. It is worth noting that although Barth repudiates the possibility of any rational ground for revelation, he has, like Kierkegaard, used philosophical argument when it suited his purposes.

Tillich. Paul Tillich, unlike Barth, used existentialist materials in constructing a system that has analogies with Heidegger's but, in contrast with Heidegger's, reaches theistic conclusions. As with Heidegger, the terms "Being" and "Not-being" or "Nothing" played a key role in his thought. God is Being-itself, but in Tillich's interpretation this characterization of God has a quite different sense from that which the same form of words would bear in medieval theology. For according to Tillich we discover "Being-itself" through self-affirmation; we discover that what we call "God" or "Being-itself" represents our ultimate concern with overcoming doubt and anxiety in the face of nothingness. The message of theology is that we can overcome the meaninglessness of contemporary existence by taking up certain types of attitudes to that meaninglessness. It is pertinent to ask whether Tillich was trying to provide Christian conclusions with a new set of existentialist premises from which they may validly be derived or was trying to provide those Christian conclusions with a new sense, which enabled him to repeat some of the traditional forms of language but gave them a quite unorthodox meaning. Support for the latter alternative can be derived from the fact that Tillich was quite content to admit that the God of traditional theism does not exist. What remains unclear is whether the word "God" is an appropriate name for the concept of Being-itself as it figures in Tillich's thought.

Bultmann. Rudolf Bultmann, by contrast with Tillich, is avowedly concerned with reconstructing Christianity. Bultmann is a historical critic of the New Testament who believes that in the New Testament a genuinely existentialist message is distorted by being presented in terms of a prescientific cosmology. This cosmology, Gnostic in origin, is a myth from which the kernel of the gospel must be extracted. The Gnostic cosmology pictures a three-tiered universe with human life on the earth occupying a place midway between the divine realm above and the powers of darkness below. The message concealed is that men are poised between the possibility of an "authentic" (Heidegger's term) human existence, in which the individual faces up to the limits of human existence and especially his own death, and the possibility of inauthentic existence, in which the individual retreats from death and *Angst* and *Sorge* and so becomes their victim. The charge made against Bultmann by orthodox theologians is that he turns Jesus Christ into a mere precursor of Heidegger. Bultmann's reply is that his interpretation of the gospel is still distinctively Christian because of his insistence that the decision in which man chooses between authentic and inauthentic existence is one that the rational man does not have the power to make for himself. But here either Bultmann is bringing in a supernaturalism which he otherwise disowns or he means simply that the choice of authentic existence is an action of which no account can be given in terms of the life of "rational man," of inauthentic existence. But to suppose that the traditional Christian assertion of the need for grace and the necessity of Christ's work is even a disguised version of the Heideggerian account of the choice of authenticity seems highly implausible.

Two of Bultmann's followers, Wilhelm Kamlah and S. N. Ogden, have argued that there is a deep inconsistency between Bultmann's Heideggerian themes and his Christian interpretations. Kamlah has argued that not only belief in the historical Jesus but also belief in a God who intervenes in history is inconsistent with Heidegger and draws atheistic conclusions. Ogden, who remains a Christian, believes that the role of the historical Jesus must be less important than either Bultmann or traditional orthodoxy suggests if justice is to be done to existentialism. It is notable that for all the writers of this kind, existentialism is above all else a characterization of the human condition as such, sharing much of the generality and the theoretical character of the Hegelian doctrines which Kierkegaard condemned.

Bultmann's references to God always appear to be external to his central concerns. When his critics ask him how he justifies belief in and speech about God, he tends to reply in traditional Christian terms that have little to do with existentialism. This perhaps provides some confirmation of the view that existentialism is in fact a theologically neutral doctrine. Its neutrality derives from its stress on ultimate commitment and the unjustifiable character of any particular commitment. If the only justification for *any* belief is, in the last analysis, that I have chosen to believe, then the same justification is equally available for all beliefs, whether theistic or atheistic. But insofar as existentialism is a doctrine about human nature, its themes are very close to those of traditional theology, and it is therefore not surprising, quite apart from any impulses originating from Kierkegaard's special concerns, that most existentialist philosophers have taken up well-defined positions in relation to theology.

An existentialist vocabulary is often used by theological writers who are not in any strong sense existentialists. So the Russian Orthodox thinker Nikolai Berdyaev and some Catholic theologians, in their discussions of anxiety, guilt, and man's relation to God, have used existentialist concepts. But these uses reflect the fashionable character of existentialism rather than any of its philosophical characteristics.

EXISTENTIALISM AND POLITICS

As in theology so also in politics existentialism appears to be compatible with almost every possible standpoint. Kierkegaard was a rigid conservative who viewed with approval the monarchical repression of the popular movements of 1848; Jaspers is a liberal; Heidegger was for a short time a Nazi; and Sartre was over a long period a Communist party fellow traveler. However, at least three systematic political themes can be discerned in existentialism.

The first is a form of religious humanism designed to counteract what is believed to be an unsatisfactory value system at the basis of modern society. Both Jaspers and Marcel maintain that the growth in technology and bureaucracy is creating in Europe a cult of mediocrity, conformism, and loss of individuality, with the inner life of the individual sacrificed to external forms. Heidegger, too, sees the individual as threatened by impersonality. But although Jaspers and Marcel plead for a greater recognition of transcendent and religious values in general, neither has a specific program of social reform to offer.

Second, the existentialist stress on commitment and irrationality of choice has sometimes been used in support of irrationalistic extremism. The most notorious but not the only example is Heidegger's brief excursion into politics. Needless to say, advocates of Nazism tend to ignore the existentialist stress on the importance of the individual.

Commonly, existentialism may be associated with communism, and this is largely due to the influence of Sartre. However, Sartre has occupied more than one position. His prewar writings contain scarcely any reference to politics. During the war and immediately after, his political aims—those of a radical democrat—were expressed in terms that seem largely independent of his existentialism. At that time, in his analysis of political activity he found himself at odds with orthodox Marxism because Marxism offered causal explanations of behavior that Sartre wanted to explain in terms of choices and purposes. But in his later writings he has accepted a Marxist framework for both political theory and political practice and has presented existentialism as merely a corrective to a too rigid and too deterministic Marxism. Yet his account of political life is, in fact, still far more psychological than any a Marxist would give.

EXISTENTIALISM AND PSYCHOANALYTIC TOPICS

There are several points at which existentialism touches on psychiatric themes. Karl Jaspers originally practiced as a psychiatrist, and in *Allgemeine Psychiatrie* (1913) he criticized ordinary scientific psychology and the psychotherapy based upon it. He did so on the ground that what he regards as the positivistic approach of conventional psychotherapy is unnecessarily and misleadingly deterministic. It treats the actual outcome of the patient's life as the inevitable outcome. Jaspers concedes that scientific examination will not reveal the fact of human freedom of choice. The personality available for empirical scrutiny is simply what it is, but the assumption that there is nothing to personality but what empirical scrutiny will reveal is groundless and arbitrary. Behind the empirical self there is, in Jaspers' view, a true self of which we are made aware in what Jaspers calls "boundary-situations"—that is, in situations of an extreme kind where we confront despair, guilt, anxiety, and death. In these moments of awareness we realize our own responsibility for what we are, and the reality of freedom of choice is thrust upon us.

The name "existential psychiatry" has been taken, however, by another tradition of thought, which derives from Heidegger and whose most important exponent is Ludwig Binswanger. Binswanger, who calls his system of analysis *Daseinsanalyse*, criticizes two of Freud's central concepts. Freud saw the neurotic symptom of the adult as caused by a past traumatic event, the memory of which has been repressed into the unconscious, from where it exerts its causal power upon present behavior. According to Binswanger, however, the neurotic symptom is to be explained not in terms of the content of the patient's unconscious but in terms of his mode of consciousness, and the key concept involved in the explanation is not that of causality but that of meaning. When an adult reacts to a situation neurotically it is because his consciousness confers upon that situation a meaning he does not recognize as deriving from the nature of his own consciousness. Certainly, past traumatic events are relevant. But they are relevant precisely because in them a like meaning was given to a like situation. Attention is thus focused upon the patient's whole mode of consciousness, the way in which he approaches, attends to, and comprehends the world. The explanation of behavior lies in the present, in the mode of consciousness, not in the past or in the unconscious.

Binswanger's understanding of the different possible modes of consciousness is derived directly from Heidegger. He speaks of "Being-in-the-world" and its modes and of the contribution of existentialist philosophy to psychiatry as consisting in the a priori analysis of all possible modes of "Being-in-the-world." He very largely discounts the biological determination of human behavior, although he allows it a minor role. But he tends to insist on interpreting behavior, even at the biological level, in terms of the meaning it has for the agent.

This emphasis is reiterated by Sartre, who uses the doctrine of intentionality to criticize all causal theories of emotion and behavior. Sartre attacks both the James–Lange theory of the emotions and the Freudian theory of the unconscious because he holds that they cannot allow for the intentional (in the Husserlian sense) and purposive aspects of emotion and behavior. It has already been suggested that it is unclear why Sartre believes that if emotions, for example, must be understood in terms of their intentional object and aim, they cannot also be explicable in causal terms. Like Binswanger, Sartre approves of much in Freudian technique, and in his writings on Baudelaire and Flaubert he has emphasized the formative experiences of early childhood. Perhaps his most extensive treatment of these themes is his book on Jean Genet (*Saint Genet: Comédien et martyre*, 1952).

Both Sartre's earlier and his later writings have been utilized by R. D. Laing in the study of schizophrenia (*The Divided Self*). Sartre's account of experiencing another person as a free agent for whom one exists only as an object and by whom one is reduced to the status of an object (in *L'Être et le néant*, III, 1943) is used by Laing to throw light on case histories of the kind where the decisive actions of another person have resulted in a loss of identity on the part of the patient. Laing's work does, in fact, strongly suggest that Sartre has sometimes offered us not, as he purports to do, a description of what is basic to human consciousness as such but a description of certain abnormal types of consciousness, to which we are all sometimes prone but which become dominant in mental illness. However, Laing himself does not make this criticism of Sartre and has used in the study of normal family life some of the concepts that Sartre elaborates in the *Critique de la raison dialectique* (1960).

CRITICISM AND EXPLANATION

The suggestion that existentialism is a form of disappointed rationalism has already been made. It may now be extended to the charge that existentialism's dissatisfaction with the concepts of traditional rationalist metaphysics has been insufficiently radical. If the thesis that the universe is absurd is simply a denial that the universe has a Leibnizian sufficient reason, then it relies as much as Leibniz did on the adequacy of the concept of a sufficient reason. When the existentialist could profitably have questioned the very terms with which the rationalist characterized the world, he has all too often simply taken over the rationalist scheme of concepts and denied what the rationalist affirmed. Moreover, he has mistaken his own denials for a positive characterization of the nature of things.

It has also been suggested that the existentialist often makes the same logical points against rationalism that the empiricist did but invests them with more drama. Perhaps the explanation of this is that the discovery that there are no sufficient reasons or ultimate justifications, of the kind offered by rationalist metaphysics and allied types of theology, is not private to existentialist philosophers. Questions of ultimate justification remain unimportant and unexamined by most people so long as social life is relatively stable and social conflict is not disruptive. When, however, the conventional supports of civilized life are withdrawn, as they have been too often in Europe since 1914, ordinary people are forced to ask questions about justification that normally do not arise for them. The loneliness and self-questioning of a Kierkegaard become far more common. Moreover, people find that their normal responses are put in question; deception and self-deception become pressing topics. What were publicly approved acts with established utilitarian justifications become signals into a darkness where there are no answering lights.

It is a commonplace that it is people living in loneliness and doubt who provide the characters for existentialist novels, but it is less remarked that the existentialist's conceptual psychology rests equally upon examples drawn from extreme situations. How, indeed, could it be otherwise for those who assert that it is only in extreme situations, in what Jaspers calls boundary situations, that authentic human nature is revealed? But existentialist writers remain open to the criticism that they treat the exceptional as the typical. Indeed, because the contrast between the exceptional and the typical has been obliterated, the force of the notion of the boundary situation tends to be lost.

When existentialists come to construct their own systems, the most obvious criticism they are subject to is that they are insensitive to the syntactic and semantic properties of the language they employ. So Kierkegaard spoke of a dread of nothing in particular as though this implied that such dread had an object whose name was "Nothing." So Heidegger hypostatizes Being and Nothing as substantial entities. So Jaspers discards the traditional framework for metaphysics but writes of "the transcendent" as though this were an expression whose meaning raised few difficulties. A. J. Ayer has accused Sartre of a systematic misuse, in his ontology, of the verb "to be."

Ayer has suggested that when a philosophical criticism of existentialism has been carried through it is not improper to ask for a sociological explanation of its use and vogue. He himself has pointed to the fact that German existentialism followed on the defeat of 1918, whereas French existentialism is a sequel to 1940. But, in fact, Sartre took up all his main existentialist positions before 1939. And the purely philosophical ancestry of later existentialism must be allowed for.

This is not to say that we should look for an account of existentialism only in terms of philosophical antecedents. It would be more illuminating to see existentialism as the fusion of a certain kind of dramatization of social experience with the desire to resolve certain unsolved philosophical problems. The unsolved problems are those of traditional epistemology and metaphysics. In the period between Descartes and Bacon, on the one hand, and Kant and Hegel, on the other, certain philosophical problems were posed but not solved. Within the framework of assumptions in which they were posed they could not, in fact, have been solved. Foremost among these assumptions is that the whole of knowledge has to be reconstructed out of the epistemological resources of the single, isolated

knowing subject. Also, there is the search for first principles, based either upon an indubitable, because logically undeniable, proposition or upon an incorrigible set of reports of immediate experience. There is the treatment of the first principles as axioms and their employment as a basis for a deductive model within which all human knowledge is to be set forth. There is the invocation of God or Nature to bridge the gulfs too great for argument on its own.

Hegel abandoned all these assumptions, as Wittgenstein did later on. But where Wittgenstein placed epistemological problems in the context of an understanding of language as a social phenomenon Hegel placed them, in the end, in the context of a metaphysical system. Those who rejected his system retreated to the epistemological assumptions of the earlier period, but with this difference: after Hume and Kant they could no longer believe in guaranteed first principles. So Kierkegaard's choice between the ethical and the aesthetic reproduces the Kantian choice between duty and inclination but lacks its rational basis. More generally, Kierkegaard's individual resembles the Cartesian ego without the *cogito*. Sartre inherited from phenomenology an explicit Cartesianism. In Sartre the individual as the knowing subject is the isolated Cartesian ego; the individual as a moral being is a Kantian man for whom rational first principles have been replaced by criterionless choices. Neither God nor Nature is at hand to render the universe rational and meaningful, and there is no background of socially established and recognized criteria in either knowledge or morals. The individual of existentialism is Descartes's true heir.

According to Marxist critics, especially Georg Lukács, the debased individualism of the existentialist is a symptom of the malaise of the bourgeois intellectual. Bourgeois man can no longer find his values incarnated in the social life that surrounds him; therefore, he makes a fetish of his own inner experience and tries by the fiat of his own choice to legitimate the values that in public life no longer appear to have validity. This theory of Lukács's has two central weaknesses: it appears to suggest a correlation between holding existentialist views in philosophy and having certain highly specific political and social attitudes, and it assimilates all existentialism to one rather restricted model. The suggested correlation is not warranted by the evidence, and the preceding discussion points to the dangers of assimilating different existentialisms too closely to one another.

A more relevant criticism might be phrased as follows. Certain philosophical attitudes are embedded in the matrix of existentialism; in general, existentialism embodies a distrust of metaphysical rationalism. Insofar as existentialist philosophers elaborate conceptual analyses in such fields as ethics and the philosophy of mind, their work can be understood and assessed in the same way as the work of analytical philosophers. Paradoxically, however, when they go beyond conceptual analysis it is usually not only to stress the inevitability of choice or the importance of dread but also to construct systems of the kind that existentialists originally protested against. The outcome of these systems on the whole lends further weight to the protests.

Finally, the doctrine of choice itself stands in need of

closer scrutiny than existentialist philosophers have given it. This doctrine depends on the relationship between choice and criteria for judging between true and false and right and wrong. In existentialist writings this relationship remains, on the whole, unscrutinized.

(See also ALIENATION; BEING; DEATH; ESSENCE AND EXISTENCE; EXISTENTIAL PSYCHOANALYSIS; "MY DEATH"; NIHILISM; and NOTHING. See Existentialism in Index for articles on existentialist figures.)

Selected Bibliography

Works by individual existentialist philosophers are included only if they contain discussions of existentialism.

Ayer, A. J., "Some Aspects of Existentialism." *Rationalist Annual* (1948).

Barrett, William, *Irrational Man*. New York, 1958.

Binswanger, Ludwig, "Daseinsanalyse und Psychotherapie." *Acta Psychotherapeutica et Psychosomatica*, Vol. 8, No. 4 (1960), 258. Translated as "Existential Analysis and Psychotherapy," in Frieda Fromm-Reichmann, ed., *Progress in Psychotherapy*. New York, 1956.

Blackham, H. J., *Six Existentialist Thinkers*. London, 1951; New York, 1952.

Brock, W., *Introduction to Contemporary German Philosophy*. Cambridge, 1947.

Bultmann, Rudolf, *Glauben und Verstehen*, Vol II. Tübingen, 1952. Translated as *Essays: Philosophical and Theological*. London, 1955.

Collins, James, *The Existentialists: A Critical Study*. Chicago, 1952.

Gilson, Étienne, ed., *Existentialisme chrétien*. Paris, 1947.

Grene, Marjorie, *Introduction to Existentialism*. Chicago, 1959.

Grimsley, R., *Existentialist Thought*. Cardiff, 1960.

Heidegger, Martin, *Existence and Being*, translated by D. Scott, R. Hull, and A. Crick. Chicago, 1949. Translation of *Was ist Metaphysik?*; *Vom Wesen der Wahrheit*; *Höderlin und das Wesen der Dichtung*: and *Andenken an den Dichter: "Heimkunft—an die Verwandten."*

Kaufmann, Walter, ed., *Existentialism From Dostoevsky to Sartre*. New York, 1956. Selections with introductions.

Kolnai, A., "Existence and Ethics." *PAS*, Supp. Vol. 27 (1963).

Laing, R. D., *The Divided Self*. London, 1960.

Lukács, Georg, *Existentialismus oder Marxismus?* Berlin, 1951.

MacIntyre, Alasdair, "Existentialism," in *A Critical History of Western Philosophy*. London and New York, 1964.

Manser, A., "Existence and Ethics." *PAS*, Supp. Vol. 27 (1963).

Marcel, Gabriel, *The Philosophy of Existence*, translated by Manya Harari. New York, 1949. Republished as *Philosophy of Existentialism*. New York, 1961.

Molina, Fernando, *Existentialism as Philosophy*. Englewood Cliffs, N.J., 1962.

Mounier, E., *Introduction aux existentialismes*. Paris, 1947.

Ogden, S. N., *Christ Without Myth*. New York, 1961.

Ruggiero, Guido de, *Existentialism*. London, 1946.

Salvan, Jacques, *To Be and Not to Be*. Detroit, 1962.

Sartre, Jean-Paul, *L'Existentialisme est un humanisme*. Paris, 1946. Translated by P. Mairet as *Existentialism and Humanism*. New York, 1948.

Sartre, Jean-Paul, "Questions de méthode," in *Critique de la raison dialectique*, Vol. I. Paris, 1960. Translated by Hazel E. Barnes as *The Problem of a Method*. New York, 1963.

Sartre, J.-P.; Garaudy, R.; Hyppolite, J.; Vigier, J.-P.; and Orcel, J., *Marxisme et existentialisme*. Paris, 1962.

Tillich, Paul, *The Courage to Be*. London and New York, 1952.

Weigert, E., "Existentialism and Its Relation to Psychotherapy." *Psychiatry*, Vol. 12 (1949).

ALASDAIR MACINTYRE

EXISTENTIAL PSYCHOANALYSIS

EXISTENTIAL PSYCHOANALYSIS is a trend in psychology and psychiatry best understood as a reaction against the theoretical and philosophical presuppositions of the psychologies based on natural science in general and of Freudian psychology in particular. The phenomenology of Edmund Husserl and the existentialism of Martin Heidegger, Jean-Paul Sartre, and Martin Buber, rather than the mechanistic world view of natural science, are seen by existential psychoanalysts as providing the proper philosophical and methodological route to a more complete understanding of man. In its original form, therefore, existentialist psychoanalysis was not a countermovement to Freudian psychoanalysis, unlike Jungian or Adlerian psychoanalysis, for example. Its criticism always focused on the philosophical theory of man implicit in Freud's work, and it offered itself as a philosophical complement to Freud. The main burden of its criticism is that a full understanding of the patient's experience and world is impeded if the patient is approached on terms derived from the hypotheses of natural science rather than on his own specifically human terms.

The pioneer of existential psychoanalysis, Ludwig Binswanger, sought to describe the experiential world of his patients with the help of the conceptual scheme of Heidegger's ontology of man's being. However, his work contained few major differences from Freud in therapeutic technique. Indeed, another existential analyst, Medard Boss, has claimed that existential analysis "enables psychotherapists to understand the meaning of Freud's recommendations for psychoanalytic treatment better than does his own theory" (*Psychoanalysis and Daseinsanalysis*, p. 237). The implication is, of course, that a fuller understanding of the patient will result in more efficacious treatment, but that the methods of treatment will not differ fundamentally from Freud's. The result is to separate Freud's dealings with his patients from the mechanistic scientific constructs by which he sought to explain psychic functioning.

However, those persons in the United States who call themselves or who are called existential psychoanalysts are a very heterogeneous group. Perhaps the most significant change in the United States is that existential psychoanalysis is seen by many practitioners as a substitute for Freudian psychoanalysis. The phenomenological method of describing and hence understanding the patient's world is looked upon as itself a therapeutic measure, something far from the minds of the movement's originators. Certain notions of Sartre or Buber concerning the existential encounter between human beings are taken as replacements for the classical analyst–patient relationship. On this point, Binswanger had simply argued that the full human meaning of the doctor–patient relationship be realized in therapy; he did not seek to eliminate the classical relationship. The result of these changes has been that almost any therapy that departs from the general Freudian mold is called existentialist—particularly those which place emphasis on unusual therapeutic intervention and those which reject the scientific element in psychoanalysis, for good and bad reasons. It is therefore essential to understand the philosophical core of the original movement.

The subject – object split. The shortcomings attributed to psychoanalysis emanate from the scientific tradition in which psychology has sought to place itself. Natural science since Galileo can be understood as a mode of approaching the world in which one aspect of the phenomenal world, the aspect of pure corporeality, is given the privileged position of basic substance, of primitive, irreducible fact. The notion of pure corporeality as the reality to which all phenomena are to be reduced is the concomitant of a dictate that the perceiver remove himself as much as possible from the world in the attempt to gain knowledge of that which is perceived. The roots of this dictate lie in the philosophy of Descartes, which isolates the realm of consciousness from that of the body and the perceived world. Thus, the concept of pure corporeality is the product of a methodological dictate: Keep the self out of its world as it investigates its world.

This famous Cartesian sundering of the world into two isolated regions, *res cogitans* (the thinking substance, the world of consciousness, purpose, telos, will, quality) and *res extensa* (the world of pure extended matter, undifferentiated, quantitative), has been attacked by phenomenologists and existentialists as the most disastrous event in four centuries of Western thought. Nevertheless, this subject–object split had the immeasurable value of disciplining a new kind of human self-awareness, in the air since the Renaissance: man's awareness of his self-sufficiency and his urge to master nature, or the universe, which had revealed itself as a radical other. The split furthered man's alienation from his world, but at the same time it gave him, in the methods and the objective attitude of natural science, the means to bridge the separation in action if not in philosophical comprehension.

But psychology, the most recent child of this attitude, is in a strained position. On the one hand it seeks to be objective, to take its place as one of the natural sciences along with biology, physics, and chemistry. On the other hand it seeks to study that which science since Descartes and Galileo has demanded be ruled out of the field of investigation—the soul, psyche, consciousness. Psychology is thus faced with the apparently self-contradictory task of investigating consciousness as part of the realm of the *res extensa*, although the *res extensa* is that which exists independently of consciousness. To investigate consciousness scientifically, psychology must eliminate from consciousness its essential element. Freud's doctrine of the unconscious can be conceived of as an attempt to overcome this contradiction by viewing the essence of consciousness as that which lies in the realm of *res extensa*. His success is due to the fact that his scientific psychology, unlike others, does not reduce the experienced meanings in the field of consciousness to a level below the level of meaning. In Freudian psychology, meanings are reduced not to physiology or to objectively perceptible spatiotemporal processes, but to another kind of meaning, instinctual meaning.

All explanation involves the reduction of that which is explained to something taken as more basic. The ever-present danger is that that to which the phenomena are reduced may become so alien to the phenomena that there is no returning to them without circularly invoking previous knowledge. Freudian psychoanalysis seems to avoid this danger by focusing on a basic reality, instinctual meaning, which is not totally alien to the phenomena to be explained.

Intentionality. Existential philosophy denies the subject–object split that defines the whole attitude of natural science. The mind, consciousness, is not a strange and unprecedented *thing* whose workings are somewhat more puzzling than those of its neighboring objects, the things of this world. Nor is it, as Descartes held, a distant spectator, alien and sufficient unto itself, moving like a ghost on the earth. For existential philosophy, the problem of how the mind reaches over to the object is a pseudo problem that results from the gratuitous and erroneous presupposition that consciousness can be understood independently, apart from that which it intends or is conscious of. Mind, or consciousness, is to be defined as simply this intentionality, this reference-to. Consciousness is not viewed as something that intends an object; consciousness is the intention.

Existentialist–phenomenological psychology maintains, therefore, that the phenomena with which psychoanalysis is concerned are intentional acts, conscious phenomena, not the nonintentional, nonreferring phenomena of the world of objects. Whereas other psychologies, in emulating science, stripped consciousness of that very quality which constitutes its essence, namely intentionality, the minimum level of reduction in psychoanalysis is an intentional act—instinct, a psychic act that intends pleasure.

However, the implications of the definition of consciousness as intentionality militate against the psychoanalytic notion of the unconscious. If consciousness is always consciousness of something, then what appears to consciousness is all of consciousness; there cannot, by definition, be an intentional act below the level of consciousness. To speak of "unconscious" acts is therefore a contradiction if the intentionality of these acts is to be preserved. If intentionality is not to be preserved, there is no contradiction; but then, of course, psychoanalysis would slip below the acceptable level of reduction. Thus Freud, according to existential philosophy, did not avoid the contradiction of placing the *res cogitans* in the *res extensa*, however brilliantly and extensively he refined his definitions of instinctual meaning.

Being-in-the-world. The issue of intentionality springs directly from the work of Husserl, the founder of phenomenology. Husserl, as a pure phenomenologist, did not seek to discover anything about the natural world. He was concerned purely and simply with ascertaining the essence of phenomena as they appear to consciousness. The question whether these phenomena correspond to the natural and real world he left to the explanatory disciplines of philosophy and science. Relations to the real human self he left to psychology. His student Heidegger, however, was interested in that oldest of philosophical questions, the nature of Being. For Heidegger, the essential structure of *human* being turns out to be an extension of the concept of intentionality. Just as consciousness is defined as consciousness-of, human being is characterized by Heidegger as being-in-the-world. The hyphens are deliberate; they represent an effort to undercut the subject–object split. Just as consciousness is not a separate entity that subsequently relates to objects, so man is not a separate being who then encounters his world. Rather, he is essentially in-the-world, he *is* his disclosure of world.

One essential that differentiates this basically human mode of being from that of the objectively known world is, for Heidegger, the element of possibility. The essence of man is always his possibilities, which he "has" in a more inclusive sense than the way an object has properties. An account of the factual content of an object can never express the essence of man, because that essence has yet to be his being as his own. Human time and space differ from "objective" time and space in that they are essentially related to man's determination of himself and his world. The essence of man, for Heidegger, is his appropriation of his essence, his making it his own. Thus the categories that describe human being are not qualities, but matrices within which qualities are to be appropriated.

We have noted how psychoanalysis seeks to place the *res cogitans*, or intentionality, into the *res extensa*, or sphere of pure corporeality. Existentialists object to the way in which psychoanalytic theory attempts to give man an essence in the way that an object has an essence. For psychoanalysis instinct, or libido, constitutes a residue that is taken a priori as the irreducible limit of investigation. Man has instinct as an object has its essence. It is not to the credit of psychoanalysis that this instinct is an intentionality of a sort; the existentialists maintain that the whole notion of intentionality is perverted when one particular class of intentional acts is singled out a priori as the basis of all classes. The meaning of psychic acts, intentions, is to be arrived at on their own terms, phenomenologically; they are not to be given meaning, as are the objects of natural science. Since, for the existentialists, human existence precedes essence, the task of an existential psychoanalysis must be, in Sartre's words, to uncover in each individual "a veritable irreducible; that is, an irreducible which would not be presented as the postulate of the psychologist and the result of his refusal or his incapacity to go further. . . . This demand . . . is based on the refusal to consider man as capable of being analyzed and reduced to original givens, to determined desires (or 'drives'), supported by the subject as properties [are] by an object" (*Being and Nothingness*, pp. 560–561). The task of existential psychoanalysis is to apprehend the essence of each individual's life and world. If existence precedes essence, the analyst must apprehend the matrix within which essence is yet to be determined in each individual. Sartre calls this matrix the original choice or original project; Binswanger calls it the transcendental category that is the individual's mode of being-in-the-world.

Thus the critique of Freudian theory offered by existential psychoanalysis differs from that of the various revisionists in that it questions the theoretical root of all major movements in contemporary psychology: the assumption that the study of man can be wholly a natural science, that the notion of *homo natura* (man as a creature of nature) most fully expresses the essence of human being. The practical implications for psychiatry involve, among other things, wresting the concepts of mental health and illness away from analogies with purely somatic medicine, and thereby redefining the over-all goal of any psychotherapy.

Bibliography

SOURCES

Binswanger, Ludwig, *Grundformen und Erkenntnis menschlichen Daseins.* Zurich, 1942; 2d ed., 1953.

Binswanger, Ludwig, *Ausgewahlte Vorträge und Aufsätze,* 2 vols. Bern, 1947–1955.
Binswanger, Ludwig, *Drei Formen missglückten Daseins.* Tübingen, 1956.
Binswanger, Ludwig, *Schizophrenie.* Pfullingen, 1957.
Boss, Medard, *Meaning and Content of Sexual Perversions,* translated by L. L. Abell. New York, 1950.
Boss, Medard, *Psychoanalyse und Daseinsanalytik.* Bern and Stuttgart, 1957. Translated by Ludwig B. Lefebre as *Psychoanalysis and Daseinsanalysis.* New York, 1963.
Boss, Medard, *The Analysis of Dreams,* translated by A. J. Pomerans. New York, 1958.
May, Rollo; Angel, Ernest; and Ellenberger, Henri F., eds., *Existence.* New York, 1958. Translations of important works by Binswanger, Straus, Minkowski, von Gebsattel, and Kuhn.
Merleau-Ponty, Maurice, *Phénoménologie de la perception.* Paris, 1945. Translated by Colin Smith as *Phenomenology of Perception.* London, 1962.
Sartre, Jean-Paul, *Esquisse d'une théorie des émotions.* Paris, 1939. Translated by B. Frechtman as *The Emotions.* New York, 1948.
Sartre, Jean-Paul, *L'Imaginaire: Psychologie phénoménologique de l'imagination.* Paris, 1940. Translated by B. Frechtman as *The Psychology of the Imagination.* New York, 1948.
Sartre, Jean-Paul, *L'Être et le néant.* Paris, 1943. Translated by Hazel Barnes as *Being and Nothingness.* New York, 1956.
Straus, Erwin, *The Primary World,* translated by Jacob Needleman. New York, 1963.

CRITICAL STUDIES

Lyons, Joseph, *Psychological Reports,* Monograph Supplement 5. 1959. Extensive bibliography of works in English.
Needleman, Jacob, *Being-in-the-World.* New York, 1963. The first half is a comparative and interpretive study of Binswanger and Freud.
Sonnemann, Ulrich, *Existence and Therapy.* New York, 1954. A searching presentation, in a difficult prose style, of the issues and their relevance to the several schools of psychology. Bibliography.
Van den Berg, J. H., *The Phenomenological Approach to Psychiatry.* Springfield, Ill., 1955. A simple, clear, and quite elementary introduction.

JACOB NEEDLEMAN

EXPERIENCE. As the plain man understands this term, it means no more than familiarity with some matter of practical concern, based on repeated past acquaintance or performance. The experienced doctor or soldier knows his trade, not by the book merely, but by long practice under a variety of circumstances. The older philosophical meaning of the word differs but little from this, denoting as it does the capacity to do something, learned in the habit of doing it and guided rather by rule-of-thumb precept than by theoretical understanding (cf. the well-known passage in Aristotle, *Posterior Analytics* II, 19). It is in this fashion—by retention of individual memories and their gradual hardening into principle—that the craftsman acquires his skill, the scientist his knowledge, and the practical man his wisdom. But (save in the last case, perhaps) it represents at best only a stage on the way to real understanding in terms of universals and is thus by most ancient writers despised as a makeshift and uncertain form of knowledge. The mere empiric cuts, and continues to cut, a poor figure even into the modern period, though by that time associated, rather (as in Bacon), with the trial-and-error experimenter in alchemy or medicine who endeavors by persistence alone to filch Nature's secrets from her without first gaining insight into her laws. The preference for rational certainty over mere empirical generalization is in fact endemic among philosophers and can be seen not merely in avowed rationalists (such as Descartes), but also, for example, in those whose uneasiness over the principle of induction has led them to seek ways of validating it as the major premise for a quasi-deductive treatment of science.

The experience from which the empiric draws his conjectures is, of course, the homely and substantial experience of a world of public objects, which forms for all sane and unreflective persons the basis of ordinary life. It has been regularly insisted, however, since the earliest times, that experience in this sense is nothing ultimate: the alleged paradoxes of motion and change and the more familiar facts of perceptual error and illusion are enough (it is thought) to show that it cannot be straightforwardly identified with the real. Hence, in addition to the rejection of habit-learning as a road to knowledge, there arises that further prejudice against the deliverances of the senses and in favor of necessary reasoning from first principles, of which the Parmenidean distinction between the "ways" of truth and opinion is an early and famous example.

The "given." The uncertainty of sense experience leads, by this route, to a further important conclusion. Since perceptual illusion and mistake seem essentially to be the fault of the observer, he must himself contribute something to his experience by way of inference, interpretation, or construction. Experience must, in part at least, be the work of the mind. For all that, the individual certainly does not create or invent his experience and in certain respects is powerless to alter it at will, it seems, therefore, equally undeniable that some part of it is simply "given" and is only thereafter subject to adulteration by its recipient. This given is generally referred to as the object of "bare" or "immediate" experience, in contrast to the more "solid" or developed experience of which it is held to be an essential ingredient. The legitimacy of the contrast is seldom, indeed, disputed, for though immediate experience has often been denounced as a myth, the usual motive for doing so has been to stigmatize it as a mere abstraction got by analysis and not something that could occur, psychologically, by itself. *All* experience, on this view, involves interpretation, and it is thus senseless to suppose any unvarnished, direct acquaintance with the given. But since it would be equally senseless to suppose an interpretation with nothing to interpret, it is commonly admitted that an "epistemic" given must nonetheless be present in experience, though impossible to view independently, since this would *ipso facto* be to construe it in some fashion under the auspices of thought.

For writers who accept either a psychological or an epistemic given, a number of problems arise. What does it consist of? What marks or features does it exhibit? How is it related to the everyday experience built upon it? And how, once the latter has been derived, is it possible to proceed from thence to the realities which presumably underlie, occasion, and explain the whole? The last is essentially a metaphysical question, but the remainder (to which we here confine ourselves) are staple topics of epistemological dispute.

As to the content of immediate experience, there are characteristic differences of opinion. At one extreme lie the theories of direct realism, whose claim is that material objects are immediately given, so that no real difference arises between naked and clothed experience, sensation and perception, or for that matter appearance and reality; apart from perceptual error there is thus no "problem of knowledge" at all. At the opposite pole are the theories of William James and F. H. Bradley, for whom immediate experience presents only an undifferentiated mass of feeling or sensation in which nothing is discriminated or related and in which even the contrast between subject and object has not begun to appear. Of this "blooming, buzzing confusion" (in James's well-known phrase), it is obvious that nothing can be said, even to distinguish its modes. *Ex hypothesi*, it is merely the residue left after elimination of all processes involving association, memory, judgment, thought, and language; it is free from error because it says nothing; but as such, however indispensable, it has little to contribute to knowledge.

Writers in the empiricist tradition, less anxious to make knowledge the sole work of the mind, have been correspondingly averse to such unstructured versions of the experiential given, though the argument from illusion has equally deterred the majority from claiming direct acquaintance with a world of things. For most of them the given includes at least simple sense-qualities of color, taste, sound, etc., together with organic sensations, feelings, and images, it being generally assumed that these are presented individually and even as "atomic" cognitive units (impressions, ideas, sense data, etc.) to a consciousness distinct from themselves. Beyond this, however, there is little agreement. Some have asserted, while others have denied, that spatial, temporal, causal, or other relations are given in this fashion. Some have been prepared to admit associative or sign material as part of the given; others have not. Visual impressions, for example, have been held (most notably by Berkeley) to be initially two-dimensional; but in other writers (for example, H. H. Price) the claim is that they are presented in, or as having, depth. Images, memory impressions, and feelings have all been ascribed to the given, but again it is disputed as to whether all images belong in this category or only those of simple qualities (as with impressions of sense). There is similar contention as to whether the "pastness" of the memory image is intrinsic to it or imputed on the strength of some other feature, and whether, in general, the "inner" and "outer" character of feelings and images, on the one hand, and sense impressions on the other, are marks of the data themselves, or a construction imposed upon them.

Criteria of "givenness." The foregoing differences and others like them are not, as they seem, due to want of regard for the facts, nor would closer attention suffice to dispel them. They arise from a failure in agreement as to the formal characteristics of "givenness" itself, and hence as to the criteria for its identification. What are these criteria? The commonest answers seem to be that the given is private; that it is adventitious (in Descartes's sense); that it is simple, as involving no element of thought or inference; and that it is incorrigible. Too often these tests are also assumed to coincide in yielding the same result or to be sufficient rather than necessary conditions for givenness. Many of the historic uncertainties surrounding the description of the given would appear to have arisen in this way.

Privacy, for example, is inconsistent with simplicity, inasmuch as every variety of thought and feeling, imagery, or sensory seeming is necessarily private, however obvious it may be that it belongs to a sophisticated rather than a primitive level of consciousness. Adventitiousness, as a criterion, would similarly include within the given all phenomena not under the subject's voluntary control, including the appearance and causal behavior of objects, but excluding some part of his thoughts and feelings—though how much it seems impossible to say. In both cases the given seems too generously defined to serve as a foundation for knowledge. If the given is limited to experience uncontaminated by "inference," the difficulty is to know what counts as such and hence where analysis is to stop. Even the lowliest amoeba can react to sensory cues and so "transcend the given," but who is to say if it thinks or not?

The psychological given, on this showing, may well be accounted a myth. The epistemological arguments, however, are harder to put aside. Their main support has been the belief that the data they point to represent the only foundations for knowledge that could be called certain or incorrigible. The judgments of perceptual experience, concerning the existence, properties, and relations of objects, are all (it is said) subject to error, and so open to correction. But reports of what seems merely, of the presence of sense qualities to consciousness, make no such claim about real existence and so run no risk of mistake. The "sense datum" theories popular from 1900 onward, like their eighteenth-century predecessors, attempted to erect on this basis a theory of knowledge more stable and concrete than that underwritten by the necessary truths of rationalism. Their vogue has declined, however, and that for two reasons. On the one hand it has been argued that no sense datum statement, however guarded, can fail (if it says anything at all) to make some conceptual commitment that might later call for retraction; and on the other, that a great many factual statements are quite as certain as those they are alleged to depend on. Given a sufficiently straightforward case of perceptual contact with an object, there is no ground for treating it as a judgment based on the "evidence" of sense data, since it is beyond the power of any future evidence to enforce its withdrawal. It is as certain as anything could be, and nothing is gained, therefore, by an appeal to supposedly more primitive certainties to provide it with support.

Ordinary experience. The above argument is not beyond question, but it illustrates the difficulties not merely of characterizing the sensory given but even of securing agreement as to its existence. It is more profitable, perhaps, to turn for a moment to those writers who, having accepted a given of some sort from the outset, have occupied themselves with the second stage of the problem, namely, the manner in which this given is elaborated into the fullness of ordinary experience. Here the issue lies chiefly between those who maintain (with Locke, and still more, with Condillac) that the concepts employed in the construction of developed experience are themselves derived (by abstraction, association, composition, or induction) from immediate experience, and those who argue

(as do all rationalists) that this elaboration depends on principles contributed by the mind a priori, and not first learned from experience itself. The rationalist does not thereby deny the fact of immediate experience any more than does the empiricist. His claim, rather, is that this experience does not make itself intelligible by any natural process and that it is only the logical activity of the mind that brings order and coherence into the result.

The most celebrated statement of this position is doubtless that of Kant, for whom the "manifold" of sensory intuition, though spatiotemporally ordered insofar as it is presented at all, is unified into a world of empirical objects only insofar as it is brought under the a priori rules, or categories, of the understanding. Experience in the full sense is thus a synthesis, part given and part made, though in some of Kant's idealist successors the creative aspect is so far emphasized at the expense of the given as to tend toward that extreme of rationalism in which the world of experience is construed as an exclusively mental product, with no element of "brute fact" in it at all. For the modern "logical empiricist" the position is, in effect, reversed, his typical doctrine being (as already noticed) that the content of all empirical propositions can be reduced without remainder to "protocols" recording actual or possible fragments of immediate experience. But the attempt to reconstitute ordinary experience out of a mixture of sense data and formal logic, though long and ably sustained, has met in the end with little more success than the search for certainty that led to the introduction of these data in the first place. Recent work on the subject has shown signs of impatience with this starting point and seeks to discredit it by attacking the whole distinction between sensation and perception—the two-level theory of experience—and the argument from illusion on which that distinction so largely depends. Whether this rejection of the traditional premises of the problem offers any hope of solving (or dissolving) it is a question that time alone can answer. If experience teaches anything, it is that success is unlikely; but then, even in philosophy (or so philosophy tells us), experience is not always or necessarily a reliable guide.

Bibliography

The literature on this subject is endless. The following is a short list of representative works by Anglo-American authors, published in this century.

Austin, J. L., *Sense and Sensibilia.* Oxford, 1962.

Ayer, A. J., *Foundations of Empirical Knowledge.* London, 1940.

Ayer, A. J., *Problem of Knowledge.* London, 1956.

Hamlyn, D. W., *Sensation and Perception.* London, 1961. A history of the problem.

Hirst, R. J., *The Problems of Perception.* London, 1959.

Lewis, C. I., *Mind and the World-Order.* New York, 1929.

Lewis, C. I., *Analysis of Knowledge and Valuation.* La Salle, Ill., 1946.

Moore, G. E., *Philosophical Studies.* London, 1922.

Moore, G. E., *Some Main Problems of Philosophy.* London, 1953.

Pasch, A., *Experience and the Analytic.* Chicago, 1958.

Price, H. H., *Perception.* London, 1932.

Price, H. H., *Thinking and Experience.* London, 1953.

Russell, B. A. W., *Our Knowledge of the External World.* Chicago, 1914.

Ryle, G., *Concept of Mind.* London, 1949.

Stace, W. T., *Theory of Knowledge and Existence*. Oxford, 1932.
Walsh, W. H., *Reason and Experience*. Oxford, 1947.
Yolton, J. W., *Thinking and Perceiving*. La Salle, Ill., 1962.

P. L. HEATH

EXPLANATION. See EXPLANATION IN SCIENCE; FUNC-
TIONALISM IN SOCIOLOGY; HISTORICAL EXPLANATION;
HOLISM AND INDIVIDUALISM IN HISTORY AND SOCIAL SCI-
ENCE; LAWS AND THEORIES; NEWTONIAN MECHANICS AND
MECHANICAL EXPLANATION; REASONS AND CAUSES; WHY.

EXPLANATION IN SCIENCE. The aim of scientific
research is not only to discover and describe events and
phenomena in the world but also, and more importantly, to
explain and understand why these events and phenomena
occur as they do. Why did the Tacoma Narrows Bridge
collapse in 1940? Why do the planets move in elliptical
orbits? Why are protons stable and neutrons unstable? The
fact that the scientist is primarily and predominantly concerned with explanation was aptly observed by Aristotle:
"Men do not think they know a thing till they have
grasped the 'why' of it."

What, then, is the logical structure of explanation? Is
there a single pattern to all explanations, or are there logically distinct types of explanation, each appropriate to
some particular area of science? What are the conditions of
adequacy for explanations? How is explanation related to
such other scientific procedures as prediction and confirmation? These are some of the logical and methodological questions that call for philosophical analysis.

Probably the first systematic attempt by a philosopher to
raise and answer these questions was made by John Stuart
Mill in his *A System of Logic*, where he proposed and
elaborated a model of explanation. This model, now generally known as "the deductive model," has been refined
extensively in the twentieth century by such philosophers
as Richard Braithwaite, Carl Hempel, Ernest Nagel, and
Karl Popper. The most detailed statement and defense of
the deductive model is presented in a paper by Hempel
and Paul Oppenheim, "Studies in the Logic of Explanation." This study has stimulated most of the recent discussions on the concept of explanation.

COVERING-LAW THEORY OF EXPLANATION

The orthodox view of explanation as represented by
these philosophers also recognizes, with varying degrees
of emphasis, "the probabilistic model." The two models
will be called "the covering-law models of explanation";
the thesis that explanations in science are analyzable in
terms of these two models will be called "the covering-law
theory of explanation."

The deductive model. Why did the walls of a room
painted in white blacken? A possible explanation of this
phenomenon is that (C_1) the paint contained lead carbonate, (C_2) sulfur was contained in the gas used for lighting in
the room, and (L) lead carbonate combines with sulfur to
form lead sulfide, which is black. In logical form, the explanation is a deductive argument whose premises are the
singular statements C_1 and C_2, describing antecedent
conditions, and the general law of nature L, and whose

conclusion is the statement of the phenomenon to be explained, the assertion to the effect that the paint covering
the walls of the room blackened.

The fundamental idea in the covering-law analysis of
explanation is the view that the occurrence of an event
is explained when it is subsumed under or covered by a law
of nature, i.e., when it is shown to have occurred in accordance with some general regularity of nature. Thus, the
logical form of an explanation can be exhibited as follows:

$$\frac{C_1, \cdots, C_n}{\underline{L_1, \cdots, L_m}} \quad \textit{The explanans}$$
$$E \qquad \textit{The explanandum}$$

The explanans consists of two sets of premises: (1) a set
of singular statements, $C_1, \cdots, C_n$, describing relevant
initial conditions, and (2) a set of general laws, $L_1, \cdots, L_m$.
The explanandum statement (briefly, the explanandum),
E, which describes the phenomenon to be explained, is
logically deduced from the explanans. The phenomenon
to be explained is called the explanandum event. The derivation of E from the C's and L's may involve principles of
higher mathematics as well as the usual rules of logic.
This, in essence, is the deductive model.

According to the covering-law theory, every explanation must invoke some general law of nature, and this
leads to the following logical requirement for deductive
explanations: The explanandum, E, must be a logical consequence of the C's and the L's, but not of the C's alone.
This condition, however, does not exclude obviously nonexplanatory arguments, such as the following: (L) All
copper conducts electricity. (C) The Tacoma Narrows
Bridge collapsed, or the Tacoma Narrows Bridge is non-
conducting copper. Therefore, (E) the Tacoma Narrows
Bridge collapsed. A precise characterization of the logical
relation between the explanans and the explanandum is
not an easy problem; various proposals have been made for
explanations in languages with simple formal structure,
but the general problem is still open.

A deductive explanation is sometimes called "a causal
explanation," and in this case the conditions referred to by
the singular premises, C's, of the explanans may jointly be
called a cause of the explanandum event. There are, however, deductive explanations in which some of the initial
conditions occur later than the explanandum, and in these
cases it would not be proper to call the former a cause of
the latter. Such an explanation can result when a law of
"variational" form, such as Fermat's principle that the
path of a light ray between two points is such as to minimize or maximize the time required in its passage, is used
in the explanans. As an explanation of why a light ray
passed through a point P, we may say that the light ray
originated at point P_1 at time t_1 and was absorbed at P_2 at t_2,
and that its passage through P at t, where $t_1 < t < t_2$, was
required by Fermat's principle.

There are other cases for which our intuition does not
seem to provide a clear guide, as when the macro-property
of a substance (for example, the fragility of a piece of glass)
is explained on the basis of the substance's micro-properties (for example, the molecular structure of the glass). The
difficulty here is that the conditions referred to by the

singular premises are not earlier than the explanandum, whereas it is normally taken as a truism that cause precedes effect. Such an explanation can perhaps be called a causal explanation, but it is not clear that the initial conditions can be called a cause of the explanandum.

A deductive explanation of an individual event requires in its explanans laws of universal form, which affirm, in simple cases, that every event of kind F is followed invariably by an event of kind G. Universal laws, however, are rare except in physical science, and even here statistical laws are countenanced among the basic laws of nature. Thus, if statistical laws are to function as explanatory laws, a model of explanation other than the deductive model must be recognized.

The probabilistic model. A simple statistical law has the following form: "The statistical probability (roughly, the long-run relative frequency) of the occurrence of an event of kind G under the conditions of kind F is r" (briefly, $p(G,F)=r$) where $0 \leqq r \leqq 1$. The statistical probability of throwing a 6 with a given die may be approximately $\frac{1}{6}$; the statistical probability of a birth in a given population being the birth of a male may be approximately 0.492, and so on. When the value, r, of statistical probability is close to 1, such a law can be used to explain why an event of kind G occurred on the basis of the additional information that an event of kind F occurred. This simple probabilistic explanation has the following form:

$$\frac{b \text{ is an } F \text{ (briefly, } F_b)}{b \text{ is a } G \text{ (briefly, } G_b)} \quad p(G,F)=r$$

where b is some individual case. Thus, the emergence of a muon–neutrino pair might be explained by pointing out that a pion decayed and that an overwhelming percentage (roughly 99.986 per cent) of pion decays result in the creation of muon–neutrino pairs.

The explanans of a probabilistic explanation does not logically imply the explanandum: the former only gives a more or less high degree of inductive support or confirmation to the latter. Thus, the truth of the explanans is compatible with the falsehood of the explanandum. In this sense, the explanatory connection effected by a probabilistic explanation may be said to be weaker than that effected by a deductive explanation. This fact has led some philosophers to deny the explanatory efficacy of probabilistic explanations; it has led others to claim that probabilistic explanations, although acceptable as temporary stop-gap measures, are eventually to be replaced by fully deductive ones as our knowledge of relevant causal factors grows. Both of these views, however, must be reconsidered in the light of the fact that some basic laws of science as we now know them are essentially statistical, it is a piece of philosophical speculation that these laws will some day be superseded by universal ones.

Suppose that we have a probabilistic explanation of the phenomenon as given by G_b in accordance with the simple schema cited earlier. It may be that the object b satisfies another set of conditions, F^*, such that $p(\text{non-}G, F^*)$ is very high, in which case a probabilistic argument can be constructed whose premises confer a high degree of prob-

ability upon the conclusion non-G_b. For instance, we might explain Jones's recovery from a surgical operation by pointing out that (1) the operation was the removal of his appendix and (2) the recovery rate from operations of this kind is very high. However, we also find that (1′) Jones is 90 years of age and (2′) the recovery rate of patients over 90 from an internal surgical operation is very low. In this case, the original explanation of Jones's recovery is no longer acceptable: on the basis of our total knowledge concerning the situation there is a strong ground for expecting that Jones would not recover. A probabilistic explanation, therefore, must meet the following requirement of total evidence (as pointed out by Carl Hempel in "Deductive–Nomological vs. Statistical Explanation"): the explanans must include all the available information that is inductively relevant to the explanandum, i.e., all the available evidence that affects the probability of the explanandum. This requirement is automatically satisfied by deductive explanations.

Explanation of laws. A simple example of explanation of a law is the following: Any solid whose density is less than that of the fluid in which it is placed floats in the fluid. The density of ice is less than that of water. Therefore, ice floats in water. The law that ice floats in water is explained by deduction from two other laws. The three laws in this explanation share the characteristic that the concepts contained in them refer to broadly observable features of the world; that is, the terms occurring in them are exclusively "observational terms." As a result, the laws are amenable to inductive confirmation by observation of their instances. Laws of this sort are called "inductive generalizations" or "experimental laws." A theoretically more fruitful kind of explanation is obtained when experimental laws are explained by deduction from theoretical laws or principles. Theoretical laws, unlike experimental laws, contain terms that ostensibly refer to unobservable entities and properties, such as electrons, genes, and the unconscious. Consequently, these laws cannot be confirmed directly by observation; their confirmation is indirect—they are confirmed by confirmation of the experimental laws deduced from them. Further, theoretical laws and principles are not isolated statements but often form organized systems of interconnected laws with comprehensive explanatory and predictive power. Science in its advanced theoretical stage has as its primary objective a comprehensive integration and systematization of diverse experimental laws within a simple and powerful system of theoretical laws.

For example, the Newtonian system of physics is a theoretical system of this kind. Such diverse regularities as the behavior of freely falling objects near the surface of the earth, the motion of the planets as given by Kepler's laws, the correlation between the ocean tides and the phases of the moon, and the behavior of bodies in collision can all be explained by deduction from the theoretical principles of the Newtonian system in conjunction with specific factual information. When such deductive explanation is effected, we often speak of "reduction of laws"; we say that Kepler's laws are reduced to Newtonian physics and thereby explained.

One important variety of theoretical explanation is "micro-reduction," whereby the macro-properties of an object are explained by reference to its micro-properties, i.e., the properties and relationships of its constituent parts. The Boyle–Charles law, which relates the macroscopic properties—temperature, pressure, and volume—of gases, is explained on the basis of certain theoretical postulates concerning the behavior of the molecules of gases (the kinetic theory of gases); the electrical properties of a substance may be explained in terms of the atomic structure of the substance. Certain biological phenomena are explained by reference to the internal physicochemical processes of organisms. Further, some phenomena characteristic of social groups are held to be explainable in terms of the behavior patterns of the individual members of the group. Some thinkers hold that the ultimate goal of science is the micro-reduction of all the separate domains of science to a single theory, presumably a physical theory of elementary particles. Whether this goal is ever to be achieved is a matter of speculation, but micro-reduction has undeniably been a powerful explanatory procedure in science, with an impressive list of accomplishments.

Symmetry of explanation and prediction. One important corollary of the covering-law theory is the thesis that explanation and prediction share identical logical structures. That a covering-law explanation could have been used to predict the explanandum event if its premises had been known before the occurrence of the event is a simple consequence of the fact that the explanation is an argument in logical form. If the premises are known, there is a sufficient warrant, either deductive or inductive, for the assertion of the explanandum as a prediction. In fact, the symmetry in this sense goes deeper: a more sweeping symmetry can be asserted between explanations and *projective* arguments in general, whether predictive or retrodictive. If E is an explanatory argument explaining an event e, then E can be used to predict e before the occurrence of e, to retrodict e after it, and to infer the occurrence of e simultaneously with it. Recall the explanation of the blackening of the wall as given earlier. This explanatory argument can be used to retrodict that the wall of the room blackened at some time in the past, provided we have the information that the initial conditions of the argument were fulfilled at the time (i.e., gas containing sulfur was being used in the room, etc.). It can be used to predict the same phenomenon, provided we have the information that the initial conditions are being fulfilled or will be fulfilled. It can be used to infer that the phenomenon is now taking place, provided we have the information that the conditions are now being fulfilled. For the actual use of an explanation as a projection, its premises may have to be ascertained by independent predictive or retrodictive arguments, which may be practically impossible, but this does not detract from the generality of the thesis.

The thesis can be extended to explanations of laws: a deductive explanation of a law could be used to justify the "prediction," or the positing of the law, if the laws used in the explanans were known independently of the law being explained.

Is every projective argument potentially explanatory? The purpose of a projective argument is merely to justify or warrant a projection, and therefore any deductively or inductively sound argument can be used as a projective

argument. Thus, reference to general laws is not essential; a valid projection can be based on "accidental generalizations" of limited scope or statistical data with no explanatory efficacy. The failure of a complete symmetry is due to the fact that grounds for warranted assertion are not necessarily grounds for explanation.

Epistemic conditions. An argument conforming to the logical requirements of either of the two models may be called a potentially explanatory argument, but not necessarily an explanation. There are certain nonformal conditions to be broadly termed "epistemic conditions," whose satisfaction is essential. The requirement of total evidence is one such condition. There are others.

Truth and confirmation. The explanation of the phenomenon of combustion as provided by the phlogiston theory qualifies as a potentially explanatory argument but fails as an explanation, because the laws invoked in its explanans, i.e., the phlogiston hypotheses, are false. More generally, statements constituting the explanans of a true or correct explanation must be true. Further, one cannot explain a nonexistent event or fact, for example, why the orbit of the earth is perfectly circular. Taking this into consideration for probabilistic explanations, the requirement of truth can be put thus: Every statement in an explanation must be true.

The guarantee of truth, however, is difficult to attain, and the acceptability of an explanation must be assessed on the basis of the degree to which the explanans as a whole is supported by factual evidence. This requirement of factual confirmation excludes theological or metaphysical explanations of empirical phenomena; whatever the intrinsic value and interest of these explanations may be, they surely cannot be regarded as scientific explanations.

Ex post facto explanation. Some philosophers require that the explanatory premises be adequately supported by evidence other than the explanandum itself. The intent of this requirement is to exclude the so-called ex post facto explanations, some of whose explanatory premises are established on the basis of knowledge that the explanandum event has occurred.

This requirement, however, would be too restrictive. When a request for an explanation is made—"Why P?"—the truth of P is known or at least presumed to be known; thus, P is part of our total evidence, and there is no reason to exclude P from our evidence base in ascertaining suitable initial conditions and laws that would constitute an explanans for P. When an ex post facto explanation is unsatisfactory, the reason is often simply that the premises introduced ex post facto are not adequately confirmed, their only credential being that they would explain the explanandum if they were true. There are other possibilities, however. The explanandum statement, when taken together with some known law or statistical regularity, may deductively imply or strongly confirm the desired statements of initial conditions, and in this case we can legitimately use these as part of an explanans for the given explanandum.

Suppose we want to explain, on the basis of the Mendelian laws of heredity, the phenotypical features of a given generation of pea plants. In providing such an explanation, it is essential to have information concerning the allelic structure of the genes of the parent generation. It is not, however, generally possible to obtain such information merely on the basis of the phenotypical features of the parent generation. But in suitable circumstances the Mendelian laws enable us to infer this information on the basis of the phenotypical features of both the parent and the given generations. In this case our knowledge of the explanandum event (i.e., the phenotypical features of the given generation) is used essentially for ascertaining the desired initial condition (i.e., the allelic structure of the genes of the parent generation).

Familiarity and explanation. Some influential thinkers have maintained that to explain is to reduce the unfamiliar to the familiar. Need for an explanation typically arises when a "surprising" or "unexpected" phenomenon is observed, and an explanation of such a phenomenon is held to consist in eliminating this element of surprise. This conception of explanation leads to the requirement that the explanans be more "familiar" than the explanandum. Two interpretations of this condition are possible: (1) the explanans must be psychologically more familiar than the explanandum; and (2) the explanans must itself be explained. Under neither interpretation is the condition acceptable. Under the first, it quickly leads to a psychological relativization of the concept of explanation. Under the second, it commits us to a vicious explanatory regress; in any scientific theory there are certain basic principles that have the status of axioms or postulates, and these cannot be explained within the system. If we require that everything be explained, we explain nothing.

OBJECTIONS TO THE COVERING-LAW THEORY

Is the covering-law theory too wide? Consider the following argument conforming to the deductive model: All copper expands when heated. This piece of copper did not expand. Therefore, it was not heated. Is this an explanation of why the piece of copper was not heated? Our intuitive answer would be in the negative. Notice that examples of this kind can be generated systematically. One would be ill-advised to attempt to exclude this apparently nonexplanatory argument by invoking the condition that the initial conditions not be later than the explanandum. For this would exclude too much: it would rule out, for example, the explanation based on Fermat's principle given above.

The covering-law theorist might argue that the example cited is explanatory, perhaps not in the ordinary sense, but in the sense that it systematizes separate events under a lawful pattern and hence increases our scientific understanding of the situation. He might also argue that the concept of explanation as explicated by the covering-law theory is a "rational reconstruction" and cannot be expected to conform to our ordinary notion of explanation at every point.

Are laws invariably invoked in explanations? There are three main objections to the requirement that an explanation include general laws essentially in its explanantia. (1) It may be argued that laws and theoretical principles should be construed not as premises of an explanatory argument, but rather as rules of inference by means of which the explanandum is deduced from the explanans. The re-

quirement of a law, however, can be restated to suit this instrumentalist view of scientific laws and theories—for example, by stating that the derivation of the explanandum from the explanans must make essential use of some "physical (or material) principle of inference." (2) Some philosophers have argued that laws as such are not part of an explanation, though they may be invoked as "a justifying ground" for an explanation. This objection is largely verbal. The covering-law theorist may require that all explanations be justified by appeal to known or adequately confirmed laws. Moreover, the objection is seen to have absurd consequences when applied to explanations of laws, for these explanations contain only laws in their explanantia. (3) It is claimed by some that laws need not be involved at all in explanations, either as premises, as inferential rules, or as justifying grounds. When we explain why a person contracted measles by pointing out that he was in the company of another person with measles, there is no law that can be invoked to effect the required deductive or probabilistic connection. (This kind of example, incidentally, is often used as an argument against the thesis of symmetry between explanation and prediction. It is supposed to exemplify a situation where an explanation is possible but a corresponding prediction is not.) It is also pointed out that sometimes an explanation consists of a redescription of the phenomenon to be explained. We might explain certain lines on a photographic plate by saying that they are paths of electrons; we are explaining what they are, and this involves a redescription of the phenomenon but no laws.

The covering-law theorist answers these objections by pointing out that the measles case can be construed as either (1) a weak probabilistic explanation, or (2) an incomplete explanation that is perhaps deductive in intent but fails to specify all the relevant initial conditions and general laws. As for the second case, it will be said that much more than a redescription of the phenomenon is involved in the alleged explanation. The given redescription is explanatory only because certain laws and initial conditions are tacitly presupposed, including those concerning the mechanism of a cloud chamber, the law that electrons are ionizing emissions, the law that ionized particles in a gas serve as condensation nuclei of water vapor, and the law that a rapid expansion of a gas containing water vapor results in the formation of water droplets on condensation nuclei.

Acceptability of the deducibility requirement. When the laws of planetary motion as given by Kepler are deduced from Newtonian physics, certain simplifying assumptions must be made—for example, that the planets move in central force fields. But these assumptions are not strictly true. Planets do not move in central force fields because of the mutual interactions of the planets themselves. Hence, if all the relevant initial conditions are taken into account, what can be deduced from Newton's laws is a set of laws slightly different from Kepler's original laws. Does this show that the requirement of deducibility is incorrect? The answer is in the negative. Kepler's laws, as originally stated by him, are, strictly speaking, false, and false laws cannot be explained. The deduction from Newtonian physics gives us, not an explanation of Kepler's laws, but an explanation of laws of planetary motion very similar to Kepler's. When we speak of an explanation of Kepler's laws, our assertion must be understood in this sense.

Are the two covering-law models adequate? Although granting the adequacy of the covering-law analysis for explanations in the physical sciences, some critics have argued that the analysis is not adequate for certain types of explanation to be found in other branches of science. For instance, teleological explanation and functional analysis in the biological and social sciences are held not to conform to the covering-law models. It is also argued that history and some areas of psychology deal with actions of rational agents, and that these actions cannot be explained by subsumption under general laws—they are explained by reasons, not causes. There are two avenues open to the covering-law theorist in meeting these points. He may try, first, to fit these explanations to the covering-law patterns and, second, if there are any that resist such reduction, to exclude them as pseudo explanations. There is an obvious methodological advantage in having a unitary concept of explanation valid for all branches of science. However, this by itself does not, of course, guarantee that such a unitary concept of explanation can be found.

Anthologies

Baumrin, Bernard, ed., *Philosophy of Science: The Delaware Seminar.* New York, 1963. See especially the following articles: Adolph Grünbaum, "Temporally Asymmetric Principles, Parity Between Explanation and Prediction, and Mechanism Versus Teleology"; and Carl G. Hempel, "Explanation and Prediction by Covering Laws."

Feigl, Herbert, and Brodbeck, May, eds., *Readings in the Philosophy of Science.* New York, 1953. With a bibliography.

Feigl, Herbert, and Maxwell, Grover, eds., *Minnesota Studies in the Philosophy of Science.* Minneapolis, 1962. Vol. 3. See especially Paul K. Feyerabend, "Explanation, Reduction and Empiricism"; Carl G. Hempel, "Deductive–Nomological vs. Statistical Explanation," which contains a bibliography; and Michael Scriven, "Explanations, Predictions, and Laws."

Feigl, Herbert, and Sellars, Wilfrid, eds., *Readings in Philosophical Analysis.* New York, 1949.

Books

Braithwaite, Richard B., *Scientific Explanation.* Cambridge, 1953. Contains a good discussion of teleological explanation.

Campbell, Norman, *What Is Science?* London, 1921.

Dray, William, *Laws and Explanation in History.* London, 1957. Critical of the covering-law theory.

Duhem, Pierre, *La Théorie physique, son objet et sa structure.* Paris, 1906. Translated by Philip P. Wiener as *The Aim and Structure of Physical Theory.* Princeton, 1953.

Hanson, Norwood Russell, *Patterns of Discovery.* Cambridge, 1958. A Wittgensteinian approach to explanation and other problems in philosophy of science.

Mill, John Stuart, *A System of Logic.* London, 1843. See Book III, which contains a classic statement of the deductive model.

Nagel, Ernest, *The Structure of Science.* New York, 1961. An excellent and comprehensive account of explanation in the various branches of science from the viewpoint of the covering-law theory.

Popper, Karl, *The Logic of Scientific Discovery.* London, 1959.

Scheffler, Israel, *The Anatomy of Inquiry.* New York, 1963. A critical but basically sympathetic account of the covering-law theory.

Toulmin, Stephen, *The Philosophy of Science.* London, 1953.

Articles

Eberle, Rolf; Kaplan, David; and Montague, Richard, "Hempel and Oppenheim on Explanation." *Philosophy of Science,* Vol. 28

(1961), 418–428. A valuable discussion of the logical problems of the deductive model.

Hempel, Carl G., and Oppenheim, Paul, "Studies in the Logic of Explanation." *Philosophy of Science,* Vol. 15 (1948), 135–175. Reprinted with omissions in Feigl and Brodbeck, *op. cit.*

Hospers, John, "On Explanation." *Journal of Philosophy,* Vol. 43 (1946), 337–356. Reprinted in A. Flew, ed., *Essays in Conceptual Analysis.* London, 1956. An elementary but lucid account of deductive explanation.

Kaplan, David, "Explanation Revisited." *Philosophy of Science,* Vol. 28 (1961), 429–436. Presents a rigorous logical characterization of the deductive model.

Bibliographic Work

Kahl, Russell, ed., *Studies in Explanation.* Englewood Cliffs, N.J., 1963. In addition see bibliographies cited above.

JAEGWON KIM

EXPRESSIVE MEANING. See EMOTIVE MEANING.

EXTENSION. See MATTER; PRIMARY AND SECONDARY QUALITIES; SPACE.

EXTERNAL RELATIONS. See RELATIONS, INTERNAL AND EXTERNAL.

EXTREMAL PRINCIPLES. In physics the laws of motion and change assume one of two forms: a differential form, in which a given process is described as it unfolds, or an integral form, in which the details are inferred from the properties of the complete process. The differential form is usually expressed in a differential equation, but however it is expressed, it provides a means for following a process from one moment in time to another moment infinitesimally removed from the first, and thence to the next moment, until the motion as a whole has been described. Because this form of law gives a subsequent state in terms of an immediately preceding state, it is often discussed in terms of efficient cause (cause and effect). The integral form is usually expressed in an integral equation, describing in detail the properties of the entire process. Because this form gives each particular intermediate state in terms of the total process, there is an appearance of teleology (final cause), each detail being determined by the grand pattern.

In fact, the quantitative description of motion and change is the same regardless of the type of law used to make calculations. Although the form of law actually used in any given instance depends on mathematical convenience and on the preferences of the person doing the work, the numerical results obtained in that instance are always the same. In this sense, all expressions of the laws of motion are equivalent.

An extremal principle is a particular kind of integral law of motion—one which sets apart the process actually taking place from all other processes that might have taken place (had the laws of motion been different) by assigning the actual motion some "extreme," or "stationary," value. By this is meant a maximum or minimum value (or, possibly, simply an unchanging intermediate value) relative to other adjacent values of the property under consideration. (Examples will be given later.) The extremal principle itself does not distinguish between maxima, minima, and unchanging intermediate values; any one of the three is a possible actual motion. Historically, it was first thought that extremal principles pick out minima; hence the word "least" in the title of many of the early principles (Principle of Least Time, Principle of Least Action). It was soon realized that the actual values picked out by the principles are extreme values rather than minimum values.

Historical development. Over the centuries a great many different extremal principles have been enunciated. The first one recorded is that given by Hero of Alexandria, who wrote that light "strives to move over the shortest possible distance" and who showed that the correct laws of propagation and reflection of light follow from this principle. In the fifteenth century Leonardo da Vinci noted that a body falling freely in a straight line takes the shortest path possible. At that time it was generally accepted that nature always acts through the shortest path possible. In the seventeenth century Pierre de Fermat announced his Principle of Least Time for light: Light travels from one point to another in such a way that the time taken is a minimum. He was able to derive from this principle the correct laws for the propagation, reflection, and refraction of light.

From the middle of the eighteenth century on, extremal principles increasingly came to occupy the attention of physicists. In the 1740s Pierre de Maupertuis formulated his Principle of Least Action: "When a change takes place in nature, the quantity of action required to effect the change is the least possible." Exactly what Maupertuis meant by "action" was not quite clear; he felt that it must depend on mass, velocity, and distance traversed, and he took it to be their product. Leonhard Euler took up Maupertuis's less than precise formulation and turned the Principle of Least Action into an unambiguous, mathematically clear law, capable of yielding exact information on the motion of bodies. In fact, Euler was one of the key figures instrumental in developing the calculus of variations, that branch of calculus which treats extremal problems and provides methods for their solution. Subsequently, Joseph Lagrange extended the principle to complex systems containing many interacting particles. Lagrange also introduced another extremal principle, the "Principle of Stationary *Vis Viva* [Kinetic Energy]," a variant of the Principle of Least Action.

These extremal principles had built into them the assumption that the paths being compared (relative to which the *actual* path was an extremum) were all paths on which the system had constant total energy. This restriction introduced an extraneous element, energy, into the considerations. In the early nineteenth century Sir William Rowan Hamilton introduced an "Action Principle" ("Hamilton's Principle") in which the energy restriction was dropped, and the only requirement was that all paths being compared be traversed in the same length of time. (Even the time element was removed in a later reformulation of the Action Principle by Karl Jacobi.) The Action Principle has proved to be the most useful of all extremal principles, and it has been adapted to meet the needs of all revisions of physical theory: as they were developed, electrodynamics, relativity, quantum theory, quantum mechanics, and quantum field theory were all formulated in terms of an Action Principle similar in form and conception to the one introduced by Hamilton.

Metaphysical implications. Superficially, extremal principles seem to imply a grand teleological plan for physical systems. It appears that we are being told that a system undergoing change picks out, from all processes, that particular process for which the action (or some other property) is a minimum (or extremum); and that to enable the process to take place, the choice must be made at the outset, in full knowledge of all that will happen in the future. Such apparently prior knowledge of the entire process obviously can be taken to have all sorts of philosophical and theological implications. Maupertuis thought he had found in this a strong additional proof of the existence of God, whose perfection requires simplicity and a minimum expenditure of effort. Euler saw in his principle a verification of the idea that all processes in nature must obey certain maximum or minimum laws. Much has been written on the simplicity, grandeur, and purposefulness supposedly mirrored in one or another extremal principle.

In fact, there is neither more nor less of the metaphysical in this realm of physics than in any other. Some people have felt that the simplicity and elegance of extremal principles as general laws governing change in the universe lends support and plausibility to the idea of a pervading cosmic order or of a grand cosmic Orderer, even if it does not prove their existence. To such people it appears that universal design, if it exists, almost demands expression in principles having exceptional brevity and unity. But there is no reason to single out extremal principles in this context. The laws of motion and change as expressed in differential form are just as elegant and simple; and indeed *any* formulation of basic laws governing the behavior of the physical world *must* appear simple and elegant by virtue of the fact that these laws must encompass in a brief statement an endless variety of phenomena.

Extremal principles are simply another precise formulation of the laws of motion, from which exact numerical consequences can be derived. That systems conform to these principles need imply no purposeful action; to say that a particle moves in a circle need not imply that it decided at the outset to choose from among all possible paths the one that is most perfect. There is no question that the philosophical outlook of physicists affects their attitude toward these principles and largely determines their interest in using such principles and creating new ones of the same type. However, this is true of all principles—extremal, differential, or others—and should not be construed to contradict the ever-present aim of physics to provide quantitative explanations of natural phenomena.

Bibliography

Very little has been written on the subject of extremal principles. The only book-length historical survey is Wolfram Yourgrau and Stanley Mandelstam, *Variational Principles in Dynamics and Quantum Theory*, 2d ed. (New York, Toronto, and London, 1960). Useful information can also be found in Cornelius Lanczos, *The Variational Principles of Mechanics* (Toronto, 1949) and in Ernst Mach, *The Science of Mechanics*, translated by T. J. McCormack, with an introduction by Karl Menger (La Salle, Ill., 1960).

DANIEL A. GREENBERG

F

FACTS. See ANALYSIS, PHILOSOPHICAL; CORRESPONDENCE THEORY OF TRUTH; PROPOSITIONS, JUDGMENTS, SENTENCES, AND STATEMENTS.

FAITH. In discourse concerning religion, "faith" has two rather different meanings. As a trusting and confident attitude toward God, faith (*fiducia*) may be compared with trust in one's fellow human beings. As a cognitive act or state whereby men are said to know God or to have knowledge about him, faith (*fides*) may be compared with our perceptual awareness of our material environment or our knowledge of the existence of other persons. This article will deal with the notion of faith as putatively cognitive, as this has operated in Western religious thought.

FAITH IN CLASSIC CATHOLIC AND PROTESTANT THOUGHT

Aquinas. The key thinker for the discussion of faith in Roman Catholicism is Thomas Aquinas, who wrote on the nature of faith in his *Summa Theologica*. Aquinas' main points may be summarized as follows:

(1) Faith is belief in revealed truths. Ultimately the object of faith is God himself, who is not, however, known by the human mind in his divine simplicity but only discursively and by means of propositions. These revealed truths are authoritatively presented in the creeds. Thus, to have faith means to believe the articles of faith summarized in the credal affirmations of the church.

(2) In its degree of certainty, faith stands between knowledge (*scientia*) and opinion. It ranks below knowledge, for although the objective cause of faith—divine truth—is in itself more certain than the product of any human reasoning, yet faith's grasp of its object—since it lacks cogent demonstration—is less certain than rational knowledge. On the other hand, faith ranks above opinion, for while opinion is accompanied by doubt and by fear that the opposite opinion may be true, faith is firm and free from all such hesitations.

(3) The objects of faith on the one hand, and of sight and demonstration on the other, are different: "the object of knowledge [*scientia*] is something seen, whereas the object of faith [*fides*] is the unseen." There can thus be no faith concerning matters which are objects of rational knowledge, for knowledge excludes faith.

However, some truths may be objects of faith to one person and of knowledge to another. In particular, some of the preliminary articles of faith—such as the existence, unity, and incorporeality of God—are capable of being philosophically demonstrated and are revealed as objects of faith only for the sake of those many who are unable to follow the path of abstract reasoning. Those matters which are of faith absolutely are above reason—incapable of being arrived at by human reasoning, however expert.

Aquinas' account of the relation between faith and reason is, accordingly, that they apprehend different sets of truths, the truths of faith being above reason. However, this statement must be qualified by adding that there is an area in which faith and reason overlap, since the basic theological propositions—those of natural theology—are held to be both demonstrable and revealed.

(4) Faith is "an act of the intellect assenting to divine truth at the command of the will moved by the grace of God." That is to say, whereas in knowledge the intellect is moved to assent by the object itself, known either directly or by demonstrative reasoning, in faith the intellect is moved to assent "through an act of choice, whereby it turns voluntarily to one side rather than to the other." Faith does not, however, represent an arbitrary or unmotivated decision. It is a response, under the influence of divine grace, to certain external evidences, particularly miracles. As such, it is sufficiently determined by the evidence to be rational and yet sufficiently undetermined and free to be meritorious.

Modern Catholicism. The doctrine of faith in modern Catholicism is essentially Thomist, although a fuller apologetic context is developed than was necessary in the medieval period. Faith is defined by the first Vatican Council (1870) as "a supernatural virtue, by which, guided and aided by divine grace, we hold as true what God has revealed, not because we have perceived its intrinsic truth by our reason but because of the authority of God who can neither deceive nor be deceived" (*Constitution on Faith*, Ch. 3). Such a definition provokes a query, for faith, characterized as belief in various truths on divine authority presupposes a knowledge both that God exists and that he has revealed the propositions in question. How is this prior information gained? The question is answered by the doctrine of the *preambula fidei*. The preambles to faith consist in the acceptance of God's existence, established by philosophical proofs, and of the validity of the Biblical revelation and the authority of the Catholic church as the divinely appointed guardian of revelation. These latter are authenticated by a variety of visible signs, such as miracles, fulfillments of prophecy, holy lives, and the growth and durability of the church. The believer's appreciation of the weight of this evidence is not an exercise of faith but of reason: "The use of reason precedes faith and must lead us to it" (Denzinger, *Enchiridion* No. 1626, *cf.* No. 1651). Thus, the whole structure of belief rests originally upon the historical evidences of miracles and other manifestations of divine activity which do not establish the articles of faith themselves, but rather the fact that the omniscient God has revealed these articles. Although it is denied by Catholic apologists, the comment of John Locke in his *Essay Concerning Human Understanding* would still seem pertinent: "Though faith be founded on the testimony of God (who cannot lie) revealing any proposition to us, yet we cannot have an assurance of the truth of its being a divine revelation greater than our own [rationally acquired] knowledge; since the whole strength of the certainty depends upon our knowledge that God revealed it."

It should be noted that in some of the more recent Catholic discussions, such as that by Eugène Joly in the article "Faith" in the *Twentieth Century Encyclopedia of Catholicism* (Paris, 1956), there is a tendency to move beyond a narrowly propositional conception of faith and to be hospitable to the idea of an encounter with God mediated through man's religious experience.

Protestantism. For Martin Luther (1483–1546), the chief moving spirit of the Reformation, faith was not primarily belief in the church's dogmas but rather a wholehearted trust in the divine grace and love revealed in Jesus Christ. Thus, Luther considered faith as primarily *fiducia* rather than *fides*. Indirectly it included all the fundamental Christian beliefs, but Luther's main emphasis was upon faith as a total reliance upon God's omnipotent goodness. He was not concerned with the logically prior question of our knowledge that God exists. In this he was at one with the Biblical writers, who were so vividly conscious of the reality and presence of God that their writings take his existence for granted. In the Bible, as in the thought of Luther, faith is not the belief that God exists, that he is three in one, and so on, but is an attitude of trust and self-commitment to him. In a distinction that Luther himself drew, it is not belief *that* but belief *in*.

John Calvin (1509–1564), the first and greatest systematizer of Reformed theology, gave greater prominence to the cognitive aspect of Christian faith, defining it in the *Institutes* as "a firm and certain knowledge of God's benevolence toward us, founded upon the truth of the freely given promise in Christ, both revealed to our minds and sealed upon our hearts through the Holy Spirit." That to which faith responds is the Bible as the inspired Word of God: "there is a permanent relationship," Calvin says, "between faith and the Word." Thus, in Reformed theology acceptance of the authority of Scripture replaces the *preambula fidei* of Thomism.

The philosophical question raised by this conception of faith is similar to that raised by the Roman Catholic conception: what is the nature of our knowledge that the God whom we are invited to trust in fact exists, and that he has inspired the writings which he is alleged to have inspired?

Two subsequent Protestant contributions to some extent address themselves to this question. In the early nineteenth century Jakob Friedrich Fries, influenced by Friedrich Heinrich Jacobi in the previous century, described faith as *Ahnung* (or *Ahndung*), by which he meant an unconceptualized feeling, hunch, or presentiment as to the reality of the supernatural. Friedrich Schleiermacher also regarded faith as a kind of feeling (*Gefühl*), a sense of absolute dependence upon a higher reality. In a different vein altogether Søren Kierkegaard, the father of modern existentialism, emphasized the objective uncertainty of the religious realm, which can be entered only by a leap of faith. He stressed the tremendous risk involved, like being "out upon the deep, over seventy thousand fathoms of water."

MODERN THEORIES OF FAITH

The Thomist doctrine contains most of the elements which have, in varying proportions, characterized subsequent theories of faith. The Thomist analysis treats faith as (*a*) a form of propositional belief but as (*b*) belief which rests upon weaker evidence than scientific knowledge, and (*c*) regards it as requiring an act of will.

Voluntarist theories. Nearly all subsequent epistemological discussions of faith assume that it is a cognitive attitude directed toward religious propositions. Widespread in modern discussions is the rationalist definition of faith as (to quote a typical formulation) "very firm belief, either unsupported or insufficiently supported by evidence" (C. J. Ducasse, *A Philosophical Scrutiny of Religion*, New York, 1953, p. 74). Some such definition as this is used by a large number of religious philosophers as well as by many of those who reject religious belief.

How, from the believer's point of view, is the evidential gap supposed to be filled? Here the voluntarist theme, first stressed by Aquinas, reappears.

Pascal. In the famous Wager passage in his *Pensées* (No. 233) Blaise Pascal (1623–1662) recommends a purely voluntarist route to religious belief, assuming that reason can find no grounds on which to determine whether there is a God. One must decide to believe or to disbelieve; and regarding the decision as a wager, it is prudent to decide to believe.One will then gain eternal life and felicity if God indeed exists and will lose nothing if he does not; whereas if one decides to disbelieve, one will gain nothing if he does not exist but will forfeit eternal life if he does.

William James. The idea briefly adumbrated by Pascal appears in an elaborated form in William James's well-known essay "The Will to Believe" (1895). He points out that there are cases in which we may come into contact with some aspect of reality only by acting, prior to any adequate evidence, as if it existed; in these instances our faith helps to bring its object into being. For example, in the realm of personal relationships faith in an individual's good will or honesty may on occasions elicit these qualities when otherwise they would have been wanting. Precursive faith of this kind is justified by its subsequent verification rather than by prior evidence.

James then proceeds to consider religious faith. Here we have what is for many people a living, momentous, and—James emphasizes—a forced option, for to refuse to say "Yes" to the claim of religion is in effect to say "No" to it. It is to miss the good that follows from believing the religious gospel, if it be true, as decisively as if one had positively rejected it. Therefore we have the right to choose for ourselves between the risk of falling into error by adopting a faith which may turn out to be false, and the risk of missing our highest good by failing to adopt a faith which may turn out to be true.

Furthermore, James adds, the Judaeo-Christian religious hypothesis refers specifically to a personal God; and in our dealings with a cosmic Thou, as with our fellow humans, a venture of faith on our part may be necessary if we are to establish any positive relationship. To respond as a person to another person involves showing a certain trustfulness and willingness to "give the benefit of the doubt" and thereby anticipate proof and verification. It may be that God can or will disclose himself only to one who shows such an initial faith and is willing to venture in trust beyond what has been established by scientific proof or philosophical demonstration. In other words, it is possible that in order to gain the religious knowledge upon which our personal good depends, we must give rein to our "passional" desire to believe. Hence, James concludes, we cannot reasonably be required to adopt a methodology which would prohibit us from finding this good: for "a rule of thinking which would absolutely prevent me from acknowledging certain kinds of truth if those kinds of truth were really there, would be an irrational rule."

James's argument has been criticized at a number of points, chief among them being the following:

(1) His basic assumption is that there are no grounds of either reason or evidence which might lead one to accept or reject the "religious hypothesis." There is nothing to make it significantly more probable either that there is or that there is not a God; and in such a situation, says James, we are entitled to follow our desires. But many, both theists and atheists, claim that there are substantial arguments or evidences for (or against) the existence of God, and that we ought to attend to these rather than to our personal predilections. Furthermore, whatever conclusion we arrive at should be held only with the degree of conviction that is warranted by the evidence.

(2) The "precursive faith" which helps to create that in which it believes, although a genuine phenomenon, is irrelevant to belief in the existence of God or in the reality of eternal values; for if these exist, they exist independently of man's belief or lack of belief in them. In the social situations which James cites, our willingness to trust someone in advance of proof of his trustworthiness may help to make him trustworthy but does not bring him into existence, and faith in the existence of a divine creator of the universe cannot bring such a being into existence.

(3) James's argument ought not to be applied only to our current live options, since "live option" is a psychological category having no necessary relation to the truth or falsity

of hypotheses. We ought to heed equally every momentous and forced option. However, we cannot act upon them all, since they demand incompatible responses. We shall act, then, only upon that which we should most *like* to be true. So stated, the "right to believe" argument stands revealed as an invitation to wishful thinking.

(4) From the side of religion, an unfavorable comparison is made between the kind of faith recommended by James and that already possessed by the religious believer. James presumes a complete absence of grounds for belief and, in this situation, he proposes a prudent gamble. However, the religious believer—as we meet him, for example, in the pages of the Bible—is convinced that he is aware of God acting toward him in and through the events of the world around him, so that at all times he is having to do with God and God with him. His concern is to draw others into this direct awareness of God, rather than to induce them to make James's gamble.

Tennant. F. R. Tennant (1866–1958) has provided the fullest recent voluntarist apologetic for theistic faith. Faith in general, according to Tennant, is the conative element in the acquisition of knowledge. In every advance from sense data to the perception of an ordered world or from the projection of a scientific hypothesis to its observational verification, as in every successful voyage of discovery or in the invention of some new kind of machinery, there must be not only an act of theorizing or of insight but also a sustained effort of will which carries the operation through to completion. In both of these respects religious cognition shares a common structure with knowledge in the sciences and in personal life. First, there is the creation of a hypothesis: Scientific hypotheses satisfy the inclination to explain the structure and order of the universe by quantitative laws, while theological and ethical hypotheses satisfy the inclination toward teleological explanation. Second, there is the volitional investment, the venture of faith, which may eventually be rewarded with a dividend of verified knowledge. The faith venture in secular contexts is continuous in kind with that of the religious prophets and apostles. Thus, faith is the indispensable volitional component within the process of acquiring knowledge, and it plays a basically similar role in both religion and nonreligious life.

However, the kinds of verification that are possible in science and religion are importantly different, although Tennant wavers between stressing their similarity and their dissimilarity. Scientific verification consists in observing that predictions deduced from a hypothesis are fulfilled in the experimenter's observations. Religious verification, on the other hand, consists in the valuable effects of faith in the life of the believer—in strengthening him as a moral agent and in his attainment of heroic life. Thus, while scientific verification leads to objective certainty, or at least to a high degree of objective probability, religious verification leads only to subjective certitude. "Nevertheless," Tennant adds, "verification such as religion claimed for its faith will satisfy most men."

It is noteworthy that the basic features of the classic Thomist analysis of faith reappear, although in a very different setting, in Tennant's theory: (1) Faith, as acceptance of the religious hypothesis, is propositional. (2) Faith is of the same cognitive order as scientific knowledge but is based upon a lower degree of evidence. (3) Faith is not concerned with the material world itself, which is an object of knowledge, but with its teleological meaning. (4) Faith is distinguished by the conative element within it from ordinary belief and knowledge. Whereas the act of will can, in Thomism, appeal for rational justification to such external evidences as miracles and fulfilled prophecies, in Tennant's philosophy it appeals to a comprehensive teleological argument for the existence of God.

This propositional and voluntarist tradition, which has so largely dominated the scene since the time of Aquinas, has been criticized on the following grounds: (*a*) Actual religious faith is not, from the believer's point of view, analogous to a scientific hypothesis but with a weaker verification. It is a direct awareness of God, with its own assurance which is not dependent upon philosophical argument. (*b*) As (putatively) a direct awareness of God, faith is not primarily a form of propositional belief; rather, it is a form of religious experience. Theological beliefs naturally grow out of it but are not themselves the primary objects or content of faith.

Faith and freedom. A very important connection has long been recognized between faith and what may be called the cognitive freedom of the human mind in its relation to God. The first writer to note this connection was the second-century Christian writer Irenaeus, who said, "And not merely in works, but also in faith, has God preserved the will of man free and under his own control" (*Adversus Haereses*, IV, 37, 5). The theme is continued in Augustine and in Aquinas' view that faith is a sufficiently free act to be meritorious. Pascal stated that God's self-revelation in the Incarnation took a deliberately veiled form, so that no one could be compelled to find God in Jesus Christ, and yet so that all who were willing to find God there might do so: ". . . willing to appear openly to those who seek him with all their hearts, and to be hidden from those who flee from him with all their hearts, he so regulates the knowledge of himself that he has given signs of himself, visible to those who seek him, and not to those who seek him not" (*Pensées*, No. 430). Kierkegaard also spoke of the divine incognito in the Incarnation. The same theme is continued by the twentieth-century Protestant theologian Emil Brunner and by many other writers.

The basic thought behind this emphasis, at any rate in the modern writers, is that God, having created man as personal, always acts toward him in ways which respect and preserve man's freedom and responsibility. For this reason God does not reveal himself to man in his unveiled glory, for in a direct, unmediated awareness of infinite perfection man's frail moral autonomy would be destroyed. Therefore, the divine presence is always mediated through the events and circumstances of a world which God has created to be a relatively independent sphere of interaction with his human creatures. Man's personal autonomy is protected by the fact that he can become conscious of God's activity toward him only by an uncompelled response of faith. Thus, men are not only free to obey or disobey God; they also have the prior and more fundamental freedom to be conscious of God or to refrain from being conscious of him. The human mind displays a natu-

ral tendency to interpret its experience religiously, but this tendency acts only as an inclination which can be resisted and inhibited. Man is thus cognitively free in relation to God. Faith is the correlate of freedom and is related to cognition as free will is to conation.

Faith as interpretation. Closely related to this emphasis upon man's cognitive freedom is a contemporary theory which regards faith as the interpretative element in religious experience—that which constitutes it as *religious* experience in distinction from any nonreligious experiencing of the same field of data. Here "interpretation" does not mean intellectual interpretation or theory construction, but something more akin to the interpretative processes which take place in sense perception. From the point of view of epistemology, faith is thus analogous to the phenomenon of "seeing as," which was brought to the attention of philosophers by Ludwig Wittgenstein in his *Philosophical Investigations* (II, xi). We may look at a puzzle picture, seeing it now as a meaningless disarray of lines and now as the outline of, say, a human face. This is an instance of purely visual interpretation. But the concept of "seeing as" can be expanded into that of "experiencing as," referring to the way in which a situation apprehended through our sensory apparatus as a whole is experienced as having some particular kind of significance; that is, as rendering appropriate some particular dispositional response on our part. To cite religious examples, when the Old Testament prophets experienced the events of contemporary Israelite history as mediating the presence and activity of God and as speaking a divine imperative to them, they were undergoing a religious mode of "experiencing as." Again, the apostles whose witness constitutes the message of the New Testament saw, but were not compelled to see, Jesus as the Christ. Indeed, it is always true of the religious mode of "experiencing as" that the data in question are in themselves ambiguous and capable of being responded to either religiously or naturalistically. More strictly, the two types of interpretation are not alternatives on the same level but are different orders of significance found in the same field of data. The religious significance of events includes and transcends their natural significance. Those events which the prophets saw as acts of God can also be seen as having proximate natural or human causes; and the person of Christ, seen by Christian faith as divine, is depicted in the New Testament as being at the same time genuinely human. From a theological point of view, this systematic ambiguity, which is the precondition of faith, serves to protect man's freedom and autonomy as a finite personal being in relation to the infinite God.

Bibliography

The article on πίστις by Rudolf Bultmann and A. Weiser in Vol. VI of Kittel's *Theologisches Wörterbuch zum Neuen Testament* (Stuttgart, 1959) treats authoritatively the various Biblical concepts of faith; it was translated by Dorothea M. Barton as *Faith* (London, 1961). Historical treatments of the idea of faith occur in D. M. Baillie, *Faith in God* (Edinburgh, 1927) and W. R. Inge, *Faith* (London, 1909). The distinction between faith as trust and as congition is developed in Martin Buber, *Zwei Glaubensweisen* (Zurich, 1950), translated by Norman P. Goldhawk as *Two Types of Faith* (London, 1951). The congitive aspect of Christian faith is defined in John Calvin, *Institutio Christianae Religionis* (Basel, 1536; 5th ed., 1559), translated by F. L. Battles as *Institutes of the Christian Religion*, 2 vols. (London, 1861). Aquinas' teaching on the nature of faith occurs in *Summa Theologica* (II–II, 1–7), translated by Anton C. Pegis in *The Basic Writings of Saint Thomas Aquinas*, Vol. II (New York, 1945). Aquinas' teaching on the relation between faith and reason is contained in *Summa Contra Gentiles* (I, 3–8), which was translated by Anton C. Pegis as *On the Truth of the Catholic Faith* (Garden City, N.Y., 1955–1957).

Contemporary Roman Catholic discussions of faith include G. D. Smith, "Faith and Revealed Truth," in *The Teaching of the Catholic Church* (New York, 1956), Vol. I and Eugène Joly, *Qu'est-ce que croire?* (Paris, 1956); the latter was translated by Illtyd Trethowan as *What Is Faith?* (New York, 1956). Also see H. J. D. Denzinger, *Enchiridion Symbolorum* (Freiburg, 1952).

Protestant neo-orthodox conceptions of faith are represented by Karl Barth, *Kirchliche Dogmatik* (Zurich, 1932), Vol. I, Part 1, translated by G. T. Thompson as *The Doctrine of the Word of God* (Edinburgh, 1936); H. F. Lovell Cocks, *By Faith Alone* (London, 1943); and F. Gogarten, *Die Wirklichkeit des Glaubens* (Stuttgart, 1957), translated by Carl Michalson and others as *The Reality of Faith* (Philadelphia, 1959).

The conception of faith as *Ahnung* occurs in F. H. Jacobi, *David Hume über den Glauben, oder Idealismus und Realismus* (1787), in *Werke* (Leipzig, 1815), Vol. II; and J. F. Fries, *Wissen, Glaube und Ahnung* (Jena, 1805), edited by Leonard Nelson (Göttingen, 1905). See also R. Otto, *Kantisch Fries'sche Religionsphilosophie und ihre Anwendung auf die Theologie* (Tübingen, 1909), translated by E. B. Dicker as *The Philosophy of Religion* (London, 1931).

Christian existentialist views of faith occur in Søren Kierkegaard, especially in *Philosophical Fragments*, translated by David F. Swenson (Princeton, 1936) and *Concluding Unscientific Postscript*, also translated by David F. Swenson (Princeton, 1941); and in G. Ebeling, *Das Wesen des Christlichen Glaubens* (Tübingen, 1959), translated by Ronald Gregor Smith as *The Nature of Faith* (London, 1961).

The classic attempt to base faith on a moral foundation is in Kant's *Critique of Practical Reason*. W. R. Sorley, *Moral Values and the Idea of God* (Cambridge, 1918); D. M. Baillie, *Faith in God* (Edinburgh 1927); and J. Baillie, *The Interpretation of Religion* (Edinburgh, 1929) contain more recent endeavors to the same end.

Modern voluntarist theories of faith are found in William James, *The Will to Believe* (New York, 1897); James Ward, *Essays in Philosophy* (London, 1927); and F. R. Tennant, *Philosophical Theology*, Vol. I (Cambridge, 1928) and *The Nature of Belief* (London, 1943).

The view that faith operates not only in religion but also in many other spheres of life has an extensive literature, including Arthur Balfour, *The Foundations of Belief* (London, 1885); W. R. Inge, *Faith* (London, 1909); B. H. Streeter, ed., *Adventure: The Faith of Science and the Science of Faith* (London, 1927); Alan Richardson, *Christian Apologetics* (London, 1947), Raphael Demos in the symposium *Academic Freedom, Logic and Religion* (New York, 1953); and H. R. Niebuhr, *Radical Monotheism and Western Culture* (New York, 1960).

J. H. Newman's Illative Sense theory (*A Grammar of Assent*, London, 1870) is discussed in M. C. D'Arcy, *The Nature of Belief* (London, 1945). Paul Tillich's view of faith as "ultimate concern" occurs in *Dynamics of Faith* (New York, 1957).

The conception of faith as the interpretative element in religious experience is expounded in J. H. Hick, *Faith and Knowledge* (Ithaca, N.Y., 1957).

JOHN HICK

FALLACIES. A fallacy, in the strict sense, is an invalid form of argument. Thus fallacy, or unsoundness in reasoning, is distinguished from simple falsity in that a single statement or belief may be false, but what is fallacious is the transition from a set of premises to a conclusion. However, this distinction is often slurred over; and we call other kinds of mistakes or confusion that are more or less closely related to faults in reasoning fallacies, in an extended sense. Indeed, we sometimes give the title of "fallacy" to what is little more than a particular type of false belief. At the same time, we usually count as fallacies only those invalid forms of argument, or related kinds of error, that are plausible and into which people frequently and easily fall. Fallacy is different from sophistry, which is the deliberate use of unsound reasoning or of related errors. A fallacy used with intent to deceive or to win an argument unfairly, to carry conviction without justification, or to defeat proper discussion becomes a sophistic device.

This article will survey and classify the main kinds of fallacies, explaining and illustrating many that have been traditionally recognized and named, and noting especially those that are of particular importance in philosophy; and it will touch on the conditions in which fallacies flourish and the means by which they may be avoided or detected.

In classifying fallacies, we shall take first fallacies in the strict sense, forms of argument in which the conclusion does not follow from the premise or premises. These are divided into formal fallacies, errors in the formal reasoning itself, and informal fallacies, in which the reasoner either argues invalidly without using any precise logical form or goes wrong in putting a thought or an ordinary language statement into logical form or in translating back from logical form into thought or ordinary language. (It is a consequence of this division that if anyone commits an informal fallacy, there would be a formal fallacy somewhere in the argument that would be obtained if his intended premises, conclusion, and intermediate steps were put correctly and consistently into some logical form; but it is useful to distinguish informal fallacies in order to indicate how the mistakes have occurred.)

Next we shall take fallacies in nondeductive reasoning and in observation. We cannot speak accurately of fallacies in this case, since we no longer have strictly valid arguments with which to contrast them; but in a looser way we can contrast good procedures and patterns of reasoning that confirm hypotheses with ones that fail to confirm or are likely to produce errors.

Third, we shall examine fallacies in discourse. Such faults as inconsistency, circularity, prejudice, irrelevance, and unfair interrogation—which include some of the best-known fallacies—are not mistakes in reasoning from premises, or evidence, to a conclusion but are to be condemned on some other ground. Philosophical fallacies do not constitute a special group apart from those already mentioned, but some of these have been singled out for special notice.

FALLACIES IN THE STRICT SENSE

Formal fallacies. Formal fallacies may be arranged by reference to the logical systems, or parts of a logical system, whose valid argument forms they mimic or distort.

Hypothetical and disjunctive reasoning. Hypothetical and disjunctive reasoning is systematized by the calculus of propositions. The p, q, and other terms in the forms given below stand for variables that range over complete statements or propositions, and the phrases "If . . . then" and "Either . . . or" stand either for the corresponding truth operators or for any operators that, with respect to the arguments into which they enter, obey substantially the same calculus. The following fallacies are common in reasoning of this kind.

Asserting the consequent: If *p* then *q*, and *q*, therefore *p*.

Denying the antecedent: If *p* then *q*, and not *p*, therefore not *q*.

Converting a conditional: If *p* then *q*, therefore if *q* then *p*. For example, "If this equation holds, so does that one; therefore, if that equation holds, so does this one."

Negating antecedent and consequent: If *p* then *q*, therefore if not *p* then not *q*. For example, "If the nations disarm, there will be peace; so if the nations do not disarm, there will not be peace."

These invalid forms of argument are plausible partly because they are distortions of valid forms. The first two are distortions of *modus ponens* (If *p* then *q*, and *p*, therefore *q*) and *modus tollens* (If *p* then *q*, and not *q*, therefore not *p*). Similarly, the third and fourth both mimic the valid form transposition (If *p* then *q*, therefore if not *q* then not *p*). However, concrete arguments of these invalid forms may also be explained as informal fallacies due to ambiguity (discussed under "Ambiguous Words and Phrases" below). An expression that actually asserts only a proposition of the form "If *p* then *q*" may be wrongly taken as asserting "*q* if and only if *p*," and if each of the conditionals above were replaced by the corresponding biconditional, each fallacy would become a valid form of argument.

It is also easy to fall into these fallacies when one is working in a field in which corresponding statements of the forms "If *p* then *q*" and "If *q* then *p*" are frequently both true or both false. This is the case in certain areas of mathematics, and indeed this fact is used in the procedure for discovering proofs that is sometimes called geometrical analysis. We assume the truth of what we wish to prove, and work out its consequences; if among these we find something that is already known or that can be proved independently, we try to construct a proof by retracing the previous steps. We assume that *p*, we deduce in a series of steps that *q*, we prove independently that *q*, and hence, reversing the previous deduction, that *p*. However, this final proof will be valid only if each of the steps in the analysis is reversible. Geometrical analysis is a useful heuristic procedure because this is often the case, but this utility in many geometric arguments may tempt us to assume, wrongly, that such steps are always reversible and that wherever we have established "If *p* then *q*," we are entitled to infer, from this alone, "If *q* then *p*."

Another common fallacy is that of *asserting an alternative:* Either *p* or *q*, and *p*, therefore not *q*. This is a distortion of the disjunctive syllogism (Either *p* or *q*, and not *p*, therefore *q*). However, concrete examples may also be explained as due to the ambiguity of disjunctive expressions, for if "Either *p* or *q*" were replaced by the strong disjunction "Either *p* or *q* but not both," this would be a valid form of argument.

There are also fallacies that are distortions of De Morgan's rules. Thus, "Not both *p* and *q*" is equivalent to "Either not *p* or not *q*," but we may invalidly infer from it "Both not *p* and not *q*"; and from "Either not *p* or not *q*" we may invalidly infer "Not either *p* or *q*."

Use of arguments. If a conclusion follows validly from a premise or set of premises, we can use this fact correctly in either of two ways. Given that the premises are true, we can infer that the conclusion is true; or, given that the conclusion is false, we can infer that at least one of the premises is false. However, these correct inferences may be replaced by the following fallacious ones:

(1) The conclusion is true; therefore the premise is true (or therefore all the premises are true).

(2) The premise (or at least one of the premises) is false; therefore the conclusion is false.

The first of these can contribute to confusion between the confirmation of a hypothesis and a proof of it; for when a hypothesis is confirmed, a conclusion drawn from it as a premise is found to be true, and the fallacy would make us infer from this that the hypothesis is itself true.

(3) The conclusion is false; therefore all the premises are false.

We might take as a variant of the above inference a fallacy noted by Aristotle and inappropriately named *non causa pro causa*. In this variant, an assumption is rejected because an argument in which it is used as a premise leads validly to a false or self-contradictory conclusion. This unsatisfactory conclusion is not due to this assumption, however, and would have followed from the other premises used without this assumption. In practice, one may slip into such an improper *reductio ad absurdum* (or *ad falsum*) either through not noticing that other premises besides the assumption are used, or through too easily taking them to be correct.

There are also fallacious ways of using the fact that an argument is invalid, such as:

(4) The argument from this premise (or these premises) to that conclusion is invalid; therefore the conclusion is false.

Examples of the first and fourth fallacies in the use of argument can also be explained in another way. The correct inference in each case is that the conclusion is not supported by the proposed argument, and we may confuse "not supported" with "false." Indeed, where the conclusion is the subject of controversy and we have previously had both arguments tending to show that it is true and arguments tending to show that it is false, the demolition of a supporting argument will shift the balance between the opposing views and will leave our reasons for denying this conclusion relatively stronger than they were before.

Traditional logic. The *simple conversion of an A-proposition* (or universal affirmative) is a common fallacy having the form "all *P* are *Q*, therefore all *Q* are *P*." For example, having agreed that whatever is conceivable is logically possible, we are liable to infer from this that anything that is logically possible is conceivable. An equivalent error is the negating of terms in an A-proposition, that is, arguing from "All *P* are *Q*" to "All not-*P* are not-*Q*": "Whatever is conceivable is logically possible; therefore, anything that is not conceivable is not logically possible."

A similar fallacy is the *conversion of an O-proposition:* "Some *P* are not *Q*, therefore some *Q* are not *P*." An example is "Some states with parliamentary government are not democratic; it follows that there are genuinely democratic states which lack parliamentary government."

We can give a complete list of the possible formal fallacies in the traditional syllogism and sorites because the following set of four rules (one of them in two parts) is such that every argument that has the form of a syllogism or a sorites is valid if it obeys all these rules and is invalid if it breaks any of them.

Rule I. Not more than one premise may be negative.

Rule II. If one premise is negative, the conclusion must be negative, and vice versa.

Rule III. Each middle term must be distributed at least once.

Rule IV. If a term is distributed in the conclusion, it must be distributed in the premise in which it occurs.

In interpreting these rules, we take the subjects of universal propositions and the predicates of negative propositions to be distributed, and the subjects of particular propositions and the predicates of affirmative propositions to be not distributed.

There are, then, the following possible formal fallacies:

Two negative premises.

Negative conclusion with no negative premise.

Negative premise with no negative conclusion.

Undistributed middle. A middle term is not distributed in either of the premises it is meant to connect.

Illicit major. The major term, the predicate of the conclusion, is distributed in the conclusion but not in its premise.

Illicit minor. The minor term, the subject of the conclusion, is distributed in the conclusion but not in its premise.

Fallacies of the last three kinds are the most common and important. The argument "All machines work in accordance with causal laws, and all human beings work in accordance with causal laws; therefore all human beings are machines" commits the fallacy of undistributed middle because the middle term, "things that work causally," is undistributed in each of the premises as the predicate of an affirmative proposition. This fallacy is more plausible if the reasoning is expressed hypothetically: "Machines are causally determined, so if human beings were causally determined, they would be mere machines."

The fallacy becomes yet more plausible if the argument is extended to form a sorites: "Machines are causally determined, and they are not morally responsible for what they do; therefore, if human beings were causally determined, they would be no more morally responsible than machines are." The syllogism "All matters of taste are subjective, and no moral judgments are matters of taste; therefore no moral judgments are subjective" contains the fallacy of illicit major, for the term "subjective" is distributed in the conclusion but not in its premise. The fallacy is not obvious here, and it is still less obvious in the sorites "Matters of taste are subjective, but we do not dispute about matters of taste; since we do dispute about moral judgments, they cannot be subjective." However, the fallacy may be easily seen in an argument of the same form on another subject, such as "All birds are egg-layers; no insects are birds; therefore no insects are egg-layers." Similarly, the argument "All Victorian Gothic buildings have nonfunctional features, and they are all ugly; there-fore all buildings with nonfunctional features are ugly" is an example of the fallacy of illicit minor, for the term "buildings with nonfunctional features" is distributed in the conclusion but not in its premise.

There are fallacies that consist in the mishandling of complex (conjunctive and disjunctive) terms. These include distortions of the De Morgan rules for terms, corresponding to fallacies noted above. Thus, it is fallacious to argue from "No policy will both defend freedom and insure peace" (*PeDI*, which is equivalent by obversion to *PaDI̅*) to "Every policy both fails to defend freedom and fails to insure peace" (*PaD̅I̅*).

Two traditionally recognized fallacies are the *fallacy of the accident* and the *converse fallacy of the accident*, which is also called the fallacy *a dicto secundum quid ad dictum simpliciter*. The latter consists in going invalidly from a qualified statement to an unqualified one—for example, in arguing from "It is always wrong to take another person's property without his permission" to "It is always wrong to take another person's property." (It is similarly fallacious to go from a statement qualified in one way to a like statement qualified in another way; both these errors, when they occur in moral reasoning, amount to neglect of the principle that circumstances alter cases.) Considered formally, the converse fallacy of the accident consists in invalidly dropping a conjoined term, in arguing from "All *PQ* are *R*" to "All *P* are *R*." It is always fallacious to drop a conjunct from a distributed term, and we might therefore extend the traditional name to cover all cases of this sort. But what, then, is the fallacy of which this is the converse? Adding a conjunct to a distributed term is generally valid, but it is always a fallacy to add a conjunct to an undistributed term—for example, to argue from "Some snakes are poisonous" to "Some snakes native to Madagascar are poisonous"—and we may give this fallacy the traditional name of the fallacy of the accident. However, supposed examples of this are often really examples of the converse fallacy.

Parallel with the fallacies of dropping a conjunct from a distributed term and adding a conjunct to an undistributed term are the fallacies of dropping a disjunct from an undistributed term (All *P* are *Q* or *R*, therefore all *P* are *Q*) and adding a disjunct to a distributed term (No *P* are *Q*, therefore no *P* are *Q* or *R*).

Relational arguments. We may recognize certain arguments involving relations as being valid on account of some formal feature of these relations, such as symmetry or transitivity. There will then be a kind of fallacy that consists in treating a certain relation as if it had some formal feature that it does not have. Thus, it is fallacious to argue "Even an experienced doctor may be unable to distinguish diphtheria at an early stage from tonsillitis, or tonsillitis from an ulcerated throat; even an experienced doctor, therefore, may be unable to distinguish diphtheria at an early stage from an ulcerated throat," because the relation "is indistinguishable from" is not transitive. This invalid argument is plausible because this nontransitive relation can be confused with the transitive one "is exactly like."

Multiple and nonextensional operators. In multiply quantified statements, the order of two successive universal quantifiers can be changed. Thus, "Every man is always selfish" (which we can symbolize as $\Pi m \Pi t Smt$—"For every man, for every time, that man is selfish at that time") is equivalent to "At every time all men are selfish" ($\Pi t \Pi m Smt$). Similarly, "Someone at some time is selfish" ($\Sigma m \Sigma t Smt$) is equivalent to "There is a time at which someone is selfish" ($\Sigma t \Sigma m Smt$). However, "Every man is sometimes selfish" ($\Pi m \Sigma t Smt$) is not equivalent to "Sometimes every man is selfish" ($\Sigma t \Pi m Smt$—"There is a time such that every man is selfish at that time"); the latter implies the former but not vice versa. It is, therefore, a fallacy to change the order of successive quantifiers from universal–particular to particular–universal. Aristotle would have been guilty of this fallacy if he had argued directly from "Every activity aims at some good" to "There is a good at which every activity aims."

There are similarly invalid ways of changing the order of successive operators one or both of which are not quantifiers. "It is certain that someone will win" (which may be symbolized as $V \Sigma x Wx$) does not imply "There is someone who is certain to win" ($\Sigma x VWx$), although the invalid inference from the first to the second is facilitated by the fact that "Someone is sure to win" is ambiguous between the two. Berkeley's central argument (in Section 23 of the *Principles of Human Knowledge* and in the first of the *Three Dialogues*) contains an example of this fallacy. He showed, correctly, that a statement which we can formulate as follows is necessarily false: "There is something which someone truly believes not to be thought of" ($\Sigma m \Sigma m BmNTx$). However, he thought he had demonstrated the necessary falsity of the different statement "Someone truly believes that there is something which is not thought of" ($\Sigma m Bm \Sigma x NTx$). Berkeley argued invalidly from the denial of the former statement to the denial of the latter, and so to the conclusion that it is absurd to maintain that material objects exist unconceived.

We should recognize, then, a *fallacy of rearranging operators*. Indeed, we could bring under this heading many fallacious forms of argument. Thus, the fallacies due to distortions of De Morgan's rules noted above consist in reversing the order of negation and conjunction, or of disjunction and negation. The invalid argument from "You are not obliged to resign" to "You are obliged not to resign" reverses the order of the deontic operator and negation; the fallacious "logical" proof of determinism, "Necessarily either you will go or you will stay; so either you will go necessarily or you will stay necessarily," reverses the order of the modal operator and disjunction; and so on.

Some operators set up nonextensional contexts, contexts in which terms or propositions that are extensionally equivalent cannot be validly substituted for one another. Whereas "Mrs. Jones shot the man in her bedroom," together with the fact that the man in her bedroom was her husband, entails "Mrs. Jones shot her husband," "Mrs. Jones intentionally shot the man in her bedroom" does not similarly entail "Mrs. Jones intentionally shot her husband." And even if "p" is logically equivalent to "q," "Smith believes that p" does not entail "Smith believes that q." It is still a matter of dispute how such contexts should be explained and classified, and what kinds of substitution are valid in each sort of context; however, we

can recognize, as a further type of fallacy, *extensional substitution in nonextensional contexts*.

Informal fallacies. Many informal fallacies are due to ambiguity or vagueness of expressions used to make statements. If the terms used are vague or ambiguous, the expressions in which they are used will be correspondingly vague or ambiguous. However, the whole expression may be vague or ambiguous even if the terms are not, principally because a sentence form may be indeterminate as to the logical form it represents. We may, therefore, distinguish fallacies that arise from the ambiguity or vagueness of expressions in representing logical form from those that arise from other sorts of ambiguity or vagueness. Ambiguity or vagueness is not in itself a fallacy, but it may lead to fallacy. For example, someone may move invalidly from one assertion to another, but not notice that he has made any move at all because he uses the same ambiguous expression for his premise and for his conclusion. Or he may use an ambiguous expression to assert a premise, and thus infer a conclusion that would follow from one possible sense of that expression but does not follow from the sense he intends to assert. Or, having validly inferred a certain conclusion, he may assert a different conclusion, using an expression ambiguous between the validly derived conclusion and the one asserted.

Indeterminacy of expressions. A sentence such as "Men are unwise" may be ambiguous between "All men are unwise" and "Some men are unwise." It suffers from suppressed quantification. Similarly, if someone says "Courage and wisdom go together" (or "always go together," or "are constantly conjoined"), is he saying that all the courageous are wise, that all the wise are courageous, or both of these? Some philosophical terminology is ambiguous in just this way. If we say that one thing is a criterion of another, do we mean that it is a necessary criterion, a sufficient one, or both? Such indeterminacy may facilitate an invalid move from one meaning to the other, and in actual cases we may be unable to decide whether an arguer has committed the formal fallacy of simply converting an A-proposition or the informal fallacy of going from one sense to the other of an ambiguous expression.

Conditional expressions are often similarly indeterminate. "You will succeed if you make an effort" may say what it would be literally taken as saying ($m \supset s$), but with a different emphasis or in a different context it may mean "You will succeed only if you make an effort" ($s \supset m$), or perhaps the conjunction of these two ($s \equiv m$). Disjunctive expressions, while they are commonly used to express a weak disjunction, can be ambiguous between weak and strong disjunction; but logicians have themselves often fallen into a fallacy in supposing that whenever two disjoined terms are mutually exclusive, either necessarily or as a matter of fact, the disjunction is itself a strong (exclusive) disjunction. The truth is that when the disjoined terms are known to exclude one another, it makes no practical difference whether the disjunction itself is weak or strong.

The name of the *fallacy of division* has been given, by some modern writers, to attempts to argue from the premise that something is true of some whole, or of some class considered collectively, to the conclusion that the same is true of the parts of that whole, or of the class considered distributively (that is, of each of its members); and the name of the *fallacy of composition* has been given to arguments in the reverse direction. Either of these fallacies may be covered by an ambiguity of the word "all" between its collective and its distributive sense. This ambiguity of "all" leads us to commit the fallacy of division when we argue, for example, from the fact that all the citizens are strong enough to resist a tyrant (meaning that the citizen body considered as a whole has sufficient strength to do this) to the conclusion that all the citizens are strong enough to resist a tyrant (meaning that every citizen, considered individually, has sufficient strength to do this). We are in this case arguing from the statement made by a sentence in which "all" is used collectively to the statement made by the same sentence when "all" is used distributively. We are committing the fallacy of composition when we argue from the premise that every man can decide how he will act to the conclusion that the human race can decide how it will act (for example, with regard to the rate of increase of population or the choice between war and peace). In this case we move from the distributive to the collective sense of "all" in "All men can decide on their actions." This, or a similar fallacy, is committed whenever we assume, without adequate reason, that we can speak about groups in the same ways in which we can speak about their members, that we can speak of a nation having a will or interests, or of a society having problems. Of course, it may be possible to do this; there may be predicates applicable (in the same sense) to a group and to its members, but this cannot be assumed without evidence. It may also be possible to introduce a different but useful sense in which a predicate normally applied to individuals may be applied to a group; but if so, the new sense must be explained.

However, what Aristotle called the fallacies of division and composition are different from these. He was speaking about changing the ways in which words are combined; for example, from "John is able-to-write while he is not writing" to "John is able to write-while-he-is-not-writing." In all such cases there is an ambiguity that conceals a fallacy of rearranging operators (the former example may be symbolized as $\Sigma t K M W a t N W a t$—"At some time both it is possible that John is writing at that time and John is not writing at that time"—and the latter as $M \Sigma t K W a t N W a t$—"It is possible that at some time both John is writing at that time and John is not writing at that time"). The ambiguity of "All the men pushed, but could not move the stone" is really of this sort; the first clause is symbolized in one sense as $\Sigma t \Pi m P m t$—"There is a time such that every man pushed at that time"—and in another sense as $\Pi m \Sigma t P m t$—"For every man, there is a time such that the man pushed at that time." There need not be any question of ascribing the activity of pushing to a totality of men. In either case there are only individual pushings; but the statement in one sense says that these were simultaneous and in the other sense it does not. This contrast might also be referred to as a distinction between collective and distributive senses. There are, therefore, at least two distinct pairs of fallacies that have been called fallacies of composition

and division, but if we speak about collective and distributive senses we tend to run the two pairs together.

Ordinary language seems to lend itself to ambiguities about operator order. Does "You can fool all of the people some of the time" mean that there are times at which the whole populace can be deceived ($\Sigma t M \Pi m D m t$—using M for "It is possible that" and $D m t$ for "that man is deceived at that time")? Or that every person is occasionally foolable ($\Pi m \Sigma t M D m t$)? Does "You can fool some of the people all of the time" mean that some people are capable of being permanently deceived ($\Sigma m M \Pi t D m t$), or that at every time it is possible to fool some people ($\Pi t \Sigma m M D m t$ or $\Pi t M \Sigma m D m t$, these two being perhaps equivalent)?

However, in all the cases considered here, and in some of those to be considered in the next subsection, it may be questioned whether we should say simply that the fallacy is due to ambiguity or vagueness. We may fail to distinguish two kinds (or forms) of situations because we use the same expression to describe them, but it could also be that we use the same expression because we commonly fail to distinguish the two things. Informal fallacies, as considered here, are due to confusion as much as to ambiguity. We can conveniently explain them in terms of the ambiguity of various expressions, but we should not assume that the linguistic fact of ambiguity (or vagueness) is the sole or the primary cause of these errors.

Ambiguous words and phrases. Ambiguity is extremely common, but it is likely to lead to fallacy only in cases in which the different meanings of a word or phrase are close enough to be confused. One fallacy that can then arise is that of the *ambiguous middle*, that is, an argument may appear to have the form of a syllogism, but the expression we take as standing for a middle term may have different meanings in the two premises. For example, an authority on theology is more likely than other people to be right about theology, and a learned divine is an authority on theology. Does it follow that a learned divine has a better than ordinary chance of being right about theology? Not if the phrase "an authority on theology" means in the second premise an authority on the body of theological assertions but in the first premise means an authority on that which theological assertions are about. In such cases there is really no term common to the two premises, and therefore there is no genuine syllogism. There are also similar fallacies in which an expression is used in different senses in a premise and in the conclusion. Ambiguity often gives rise to these fallacies when the meaning of a word is fixed by its context, and the two different contexts give the word two different meanings. All these are instances of equivocation.

Some words are systematically ambiguous in a troublesome way. An observation may be either what is observed or the observing of it; a perception may be either a perceiving or what is perceived. There are similar indeterminacies about "experience," "sensation," and "belief." Such ambiguities constantly create difficulties in epistemology, the philosophy of science, and philosophical psychology.

There are also forms of speech that tempt us to confuse what we can say about words with what we can say about the corresponding things. A cause necessarily produces an effect, but only in the sense that it would not be called a cause if it did not. Similarly, murder is necessarily wrong, but not in the sense that there is a necessary connection or a rationally discoverable link between the kind of act called murder and its being wrong.

Sometimes when words are not ordinarily ambiguous, we perversely make them so; for example, by giving a word, in addition to its ordinary meaning, another meaning that is borrowed from a cognate word or a similarly formed word. If John Stuart Mill confused "is desirable" (meaning "ought to be desired") with "can be desired," deriving this second sense from the use of "is visible" to mean "can be seen" and "is audible" to mean "can be heard," he was making a mistake of this kind. Similar results are produced by an idiosyncratic use of language. It is hard to keep to a sense specially assigned to a word, and we are always liable to slip back into some more conventional use. When a psychologist has redefined "learning" in relation to some special procedure by which "learning" can be measured, he or his readers may think that what he then discovers is true also about learning in its ordinary, much broader sense.

Such unwarranted generalization, considered formally, exemplifies the fallacy *a dicto secundum quid;* in practice, however, it is aided by various ambiguities and confusions. Thus, the words "class" and "set" may be confined to finite collections or may embrace infinite ones as well. We are liable to argue from the fact that something holds for all finite classes or sets to the conclusion that it holds for all classes or sets, including infinite ones, partly because the words are ambiguous, partly because we fail to notice that the wider concept is a different one, and partly because we generalize from specimen cases and choose specimens that are more easily visualized but are not fully representative.

As we have noted, errors may arise not only from ambiguity as such but also from the confusing of things that, although similar or related, are different. A classic example of this, of great importance in philosophical discussion, is the confusing of separation with distinction. Thus the distinction between analytic and synthetic statements may be attacked, fallaciously, on the ground that actual statements are difficult to assign, without reservations, to one category or the other. Confusion here is due partly to failure to see what sorts of things are being distinguished—not verbal forms, not sentences, but ways of using sentences to make statements.

When this obscurity is removed, however, we may still have to defend the distinction against the critic who says that because of indeterminacies in the use of component words, every concrete use of a sentence in order to make a statement lies somewhere between being analytic and being synthetic. Even if this critic were right, this would in no way count against the distinction. Indeed, such a status makes it particularly important to draw the distinction, in order to expose the common fallacy of arguing from a statement in which words are so used as to make the statement analytically true to a synthetic statement made by the same words in a different sense (as might be done with the statement "A change in the moral code means social disintegration").

This confusion can also be used in the opposite way. It may be argued that because two things can be distinguished, they must be separate—for example, to argue that since we can distinguish a motive from a cause, things that have causes cannot have motives, or that a person's having a certain motive cannot be a cause of his action.

FALLACIES IN NONDEDUCTIVE REASONING AND IN OBSERVATION

Outside the sphere of deductive reasoning, we can speak of fallacies only in an extended sense. For example, we can contrast genuine confirmation of hypotheses with something that is mistaken for it, probable arguments that give some support to their conclusions with ones that do not, and, in general, techniques and procedures that tend to give correct results with ones that tend to produce error. However, it would be pointless and misleading to call a piece of inductive reasoning, say, fallacious merely because its conclusion turned out to be false.

Induction and confirmation. We may note two fallacies *about* induction or confirmation: the mistaking of confirmation for proof, and the demanding of proof where no more than confirmation is possible. There are also fallacies *in* induction and confirmation. Where scientific or common-sense reasoning follows the lines of one of the eliminative methods of induction (see MILL'S METHODS OF INDUCTION), failure to observe the requirements of that method will count as a fallacy. Thus, in reasoning along the lines of the method of agreement, it will be a fallacy to conclude that there is a causal relation between the phenomenon P and a certain feature A, merely because occurrences of P are repeatedly found to be accompanied or preceded by occurrences of A, without trying to discover other possibly relevant features common to these occurrences of P or, what amounts to the same thing, without trying to find occurrences of P that are as relevantly diverse as possible and then seeing whether A is present in them all. Thus, it is fallacious to conclude that William is allergic to strawberries from the evidence that his allergic symptoms have repeatedly appeared after he has eaten strawberries, if William has eaten strawberries only in one particular house, at a particular sort of gathering, and so on.

Similarly, in reasoning along the lines of the method of difference, it will be a fallacy to conclude that A is even an indispensable part of a sufficient condition for P from a comparison of a case in which P and A are both present and a case where they are both absent, without checking that the two cases are otherwise relevantly alike, that no likely-to-be-relevant feature except A differentiates the case in which P occurs from the one in which it does not. In other words, it is fallacious to use a control case that differs from the experimental case in some unwanted respect. Thus, it is fallacious to infer that John's having recovered more rapidly than James is due to a drug that was given only to John, if John was also told that he was having a new treatment and the doctors and nurses all took special care of John because they were interested in the experiment. There can be correspondingly unsound experimental procedures, and corresponding errors in reasoning, in applications of the method of concomitant variation.

Post hoc ergo propter hoc is traditionally listed as a fallacy; but much respectable inductive reasoning would fall under this heading, and it is not to be condemned because it is not deductively valid. We argue, reasonably, that the one likely-to-be-relevant change causes the result that follows. We are, in effect, taking the "before" situation as the control case and the "after" situation as the experimental case. This is a fallacy only if we ignore other likely-to-be-relevant changes.

All such mistakes can be summed up as consisting in failures to test the hypothesis in question—that A is (in some sense) the cause of P—that is, in failure to look for what, if the hypothesis were false, would be most likely to reveal its falsity. If A is not the cause of P, we are most likely to reveal this by finding cases of P so diverse that A is not present in them all, or a control case so like the experimental case that P occurs in both, or occurs in neither, in spite of A's being present in one and absent from the other.

Another inductive fallacy is to take a hypothesis as being confirmed by observations to which it is irrelevant, when without this hypothesis our other knowledge and beliefs would explain what is observed equally well. Further, since it is a basic principle of inductive reasoning that alternative hypotheses should be considered, and that to confirm one hypothesis we must eliminate its rivals or show them to be improbable, it is a fallacy to take a hypothesis as being confirmed by observations that are equally well confirmed by an intrinsically more probable alternative hypothesis—for example, to take the Michelson–Morley experiment as confirming the theory of relativity without eliminating the FitzGerald–Lorentz contraction and the emission hypothesis of the velocity of light.

We may add a fallacy of saving hypotheses. It is certainly a fault for a thinker to be so attached to a hypothesis that he notices only evidence that agrees with it and ignores or denies unfavorable evidence. Popular superstitions of all kinds are protected by this fallacy, but it is also common among scientists, historians, and philosophers. It may also be a mistake, when one finds evidence that is prima facie unfavorable, to introduce supplementary *ad hoc* hypotheses in order to protect the original one from falsification. Carried to an extreme, this procedure constitutes a linguistic change that makes the original hypothesis analytically true, and it can generate the fallacy described above of oscillating between an analytic and a synthetic use of the same expression. In less extreme cases, how can we systematically mark off this error from the respectable procedure of interpreting new observations in the light of an established theory? Perhaps in two ways: first, in the respectable procedure, we are working with a hypothesis that is already well confirmed, but it is a fallacy to "save" a hypothesis for which there is no strong independent support; and second, even if the original hypothesis was well confirmed, it may be appropriate to consider, after it has been "saved" by additional hypotheses (after the new observations have been interpreted in the light of the original hypothesis) or has been modified and qualified in various ways, whether some alternative hypothesis would account better for the whole body of evidence.

Analogy. All arguments from analogy are fallacious in the sense that they are not deductively valid. However, we often want further to distinguish weak analogies from strong ones and to suggest that a weak analogy is completely fallacious but that a strong analogy has at least some force. In an analogy we compare two things, A and B; we find some resemblances, say X, Y, Z, between them; and then we argue that since A has some further feature P, it is likely that B also has this feature. We are inclined to say that if the points of resemblance X, Y, Z are few or trivial, the analogy is weak or far-fetched but that it is a strong analogy if there are many important points of resemblance. An alternative way of looking at the distinction is that to use this analogy is implicitly to frame and then use the hypothesis that all things that have the features X, Y, Z also have the feature P. The analogy will be weak if we already have evidence that falsifies this hypothesis or makes it implausible, but it will be strong if we have no such evidence and what we know about A somehow constitutes good inductive evidence for a connection between X, Y, Z, and P.

Classification. Faults in classification can in several ways give rise to fallacies in either the strict or the extended sense. If things are classified under headings where they simply do not belong, the classification implicitly asserts false propositions which may be used as premises in arguments that, even if formally valid, will therefore give no real support to their conclusions. If a classification is based on unimportant resemblances, this may give rise to weak analogies and to the framing of unlikely hypotheses, and inductive reasoning that uses such a classification—in the methods of agreement and difference, for example—will give an appearance of support to conclusions that are not really supported by the evidence as a whole. Again, if the division of a class into subclasses is not exhaustive, it may be wrongly taken to be so, and this will provide a false premise for a disjunctive argument. Thus, if we divide trees into conifers and deciduous trees, we may infer that since eucalypts are not conifers, they are deciduous. Similarly, a division that is not exclusive may be wrongly taken to be so; the same division of the class "trees" may lead us to infer that larches, being conifers, are not deciduous.

Two important fallacies concerned with classification arise from the attempt to draw sharp distinctions where the facts show a continuous (or near continuous) gradation. Is a man bald if he has one hair on his head? or two? or three? And so on. Just what degree of mental disorder is to count as insanity? One fallacy consists in assimilating every intermediate case to one or the other of the extremes and is exemplified in the black-and-white thinking that divides people into normal individuals and lunatics or states into peace-loving nations and warmongers. The contrary, and more subtle, fallacy consists in arguing that because there is no break in the gradations, there is no distinction even between the extremes—concluding, for example, that we are all insane—as if the problem about when a man is bald showed that there is no difference between a man with a completely smooth scalp and one with a full head of hair.

Statistics. We can deal here only with some elementary mistakes in statistical reasoning. One of these consists in paying attention to simple frequencies or proportions rather than to correlations. If a high proportion of atheists are honest, this in itself does not indicate any sort of causal connection between atheism and honesty; the first thing to discover is whether the proportion of honest people is higher among atheists than among nonatheists. Similarly, the frequency of persons who have both mathematical ability and artistic talent may be small in the population as a whole; but if only one person in ten has mathematical ability and only one in ten has artistic talent, then only one in a hundred would have both, even if there were no natural opposition between these gifts. Before we conclude that these abilities tend to occur separately, we must find whether artistic talent is more or less common among the mathematically able than among the rest of the population.

Another common statistical fallacy consists in directly inferring a causal connection from a positive correlation: given a positive correlation between cigarette smoking and lung cancer, it is a further question whether this is to be explained by a causal connection between them. An associated fallacy of confusion, which is becoming more common, is simply not to talk about causation but to use the word "correlation" as if it meant causal connection, for example, to infer predictions and practical recommendations directly from correlation statements. Another fallacy is the neglect of the requirements of significance. Essentially, this consists in taking as causally informative, or as representative of a similar correlation in a larger population, a correlation within a sample that could equally well be explained as a chance result. This is, therefore, an instance of the neglect of alternative hypotheses.

Even when there is good statistical evidence for a causal connection between two features *A* and *B*, it is a mistake to conclude immediately that one, say *A*, is the cause of the other without having considered and excluded the possibilities that *B* may tend to produce *A*, that *A* and *B* may be joint effects of some other cause, and that there may be causation in more than one direction. For example, a positive correlation between poverty and ill health might be due to the fact that poverty causes ill health, to the fact that ill health diminishes earning capacity and wastes resources, to the fact that stupidity, idleness, or drunkenness tends to produce both poverty and ill health, or to a combination of more than one of these causal tendencies.

Probability. Fallacies in reasoning about probability arise mainly from failure to attend to the fact that a probability is relative to certain evidence and changes as the evidence changes. The best-known is the gambler's fallacy. For example, since it is unlikely that a penny will fall heads up five times in a row, the gambler reasons, when it has fallen heads four times, that it is unlikely to fall heads at the next throw. But although the probability of five heads, relative to the knowledge that an unbiased penny is tossed in a random manner five times, is 1/32, the probability of this result, relative to the conjunction of this knowledge with the knowledge that it has fallen heads on the first four throws, is 1/2.

Observation. It is questionable whether we should follow Mill and speak of fallacies of observation. Many of the items so described consist of errors in reasoning rather than in observation, and so fall under other headings. We may, however, note the following principles.

First, there are errors of nonobservation, which may be due to deficiency of one's senses or sense apparatus, to carelessness, or to the tendency to see only what we want to see. This may include the nonobservation that is one way of saving hypotheses.

Second, any of the above-mentioned causes may equally produce misobservation.

Third, it is impossible to separate, and difficult even to distinguish, observation from interpretation: we always have some conceptual framework, some expectations that determine how we shall observe what we observe. For example, we expect an object that looks like an adult human being to be between five and six feet tall, and we therefore tend to see any such object as being at a distance that would agree with this. The actual material to which our prior concepts are applied may not conform to them, however, and then we may make wrong judgments through using these concepts. Also, if we do not realize how observation and interpretation are mixed together, we may give the authority of an observed fact to a judgment that really rests on our preconceptions.

Fourth, our perceptual mechanisms automatically allow for factors which have been constant or to which it is inconvenient to attend, and errors arise when allowances are made for what is no longer there; for example, the illusion that the land is moving when we first go ashore after becoming used to the rolling of a ship.

Fifth, we may in perception confuse relations, say of comparison, with intrinsic qualities. This explains the illusions of contrast. For example, if after having had one's left hand in cold water and one's right hand in hot water, one puts both hands into lukewarm water, the lukewarm water feels hot to the left hand and cold to the right hand because it really is *hotter than* the left hand (or than what it has just been feeling) and *colder than* the right hand (or than what it has just been feeling).

Sixth, we may mislocate what we observe. In particular, we have a tendency to project and to treat as objective, as belonging to some external state of affairs, the feeling that the state of affairs arouses in us (the *pathetic fallacy*) or to mistake connections within our thoughts for connections between the corresponding objects. There is no room here for a full discussion of perceptual illusion and observational error, but it seems that many varieties of these can be explained by reference to one or more of these principles.

FALLACIES IN DISCOURSE

Inconsistency. A position or a system of thought cannot be sound if it contains incompatible statements or beliefs, and it is one of the commonest objections to what an opponent says that he is trying to have it both ways. Inconsistency has many possible sources, but one that is of special importance in philosophy is the case in which a thinker, in order to solve one problem or deal with a particular difficulty, denies or qualifies a principle he has previously adopted, although in other contexts he adheres to the principle and uses it without qualification.

Inconsistency is a formal feature and can be formally checked, although it may also be concealed by the use of different expressions with a single meaning. It is not the same as invalidity, however; indeed, any argument with incompatible (or self-contradictory) premises will be formally valid. It is particularly important to detect inconsistencies in a set of premises, for an argument with inconsistent premises, even though valid, gives no support to its conclusion; and using one is not a satisfactory way of establishing anything or of convincing an audience.

On the other hand, it is a formal fallacy to suppose that because your opponent has tried to have it both ways, he cannot have it either way—that every part of an inconsistent position must be false.

"Petitio principii." An argument that begs the question, that uses the conclusion as one of the premises, is always formally valid. A conclusion cannot fail to follow from a set of premises that includes it. This is also a fallacy only in the extended sense that such an argument gives no support to its conclusion. One kind of *petitio principii* consists in arguing in a circle, when one proposition is defended by reference to another, and the second is defended by reference to the first. For example, we may argue that a certain historian is trustworthy because he gives a balanced account of some episode, but also rely on that historian's account in order to decide what actually occurred in this episode, and hence to decide what would be a balanced account of it.

The larger and more complex a circle of argument is, the harder it is to detect the fallacy. One result of circularity is that the propositions that have been proved from one another appear to have been conclusively established, although no empirical evidence has been given for either of them. This can create an illusion that there are synthetic propositions which have no need of empirical support. This may be combined with a fallacy of confusion, of failing to distinguish the coherence or consequential character of a system from its truth—a confusion that has developed into the coherence theory of truth and that is still encouraged by some eccentric uses of the word "true" or of such a phrase as "true within the system."

Circularity is common in moral reasoning, and here, too, it may make us think that moral conclusions can be rationally established without reliance on observations, intuitions, choices, or decisions. The exposure of such circularity compels us to give a more adequate account both of how moral judgments are to be supported and of how they are to be interpreted.

A priori fallacies. Under the heading of a priori fallacies Mill listed a number of natural prejudices, including the popular superstition that words have a magical power and such philosophical dogmas as that what is true of our ideas of things must be true of the things themselves; that differences in nature must correspond to our received (linguistic) distinctions; that whatever is, is rationally explicable; that there is no action at a distance; that every phenomenon has a single cause; and that effects must resemble their causes. These are all errors, but we can go further and recognize a general apriorist fallacy, which consists in trying to base knowledge of fundamental synthetic truths on anything other than empirical evidence. These examples illustrate how once we start looking for a priori truths, we are led to try to distill them from language or from our ideas (giving each of these an authority to which it is not entitled), or to confuse continuity with intelligibility and necessity, or to dignify with the title of a priori truths what are no more than sweeping generalizations from the simplest and most familiar observations.

More generally still, we can recognize a fallacy of prejudice, which consists in believing without evidence, in adopting or adhering to views on any subject without any relevant reason. It is worth noting that adopting a method of argument (other than a deductively valid form) is tantamount to adopting an assertion. For example, regularly to judge the rightness of actions by their utility is tantamount to adopting the principle that whatever maximizes utility is right; and, again, regularly to argue that because a statement cannot be verified, it is meaningless, is tantamount to adopting a verifiability theory of meaning. This is a particularly easy way of committing the fallacy of prejudice.

"Ignoratio elenchi." The fallacy of *ignoratio elenchi* consists in missing the point, in arguing for something other than what is to be proved. However, we can speak in this way only if the context somehow determines what is to be proved. In the first place, the context may be a discussion between *A* and *B*, and *B* will commit this fallacy if he claims to be replying to what *A* has said but fails to come to grips with *A*'s argument—for example, if he tries to disprove some proposition that *A* has not asserted either as a premise or as a conclusion. *B* is also guilty of this fallacy if he bluntly denies something that *A* has claimed to prove but does nothing to rebut *A*'s proof. Alternatively, it may be a thinker's general position or some long line of argument that makes it imperative for him to establish some point, and makes him guilty of irrelevance if he establishes something else instead.

There are a number of common and important types of irrelevance in discussion. If the question is whether a certain view is true or false, it is irrelevant to argue that adopting this view will be beneficial or pernicious. Thus, a body of religious doctrine may be irrelevantly defended on the ground that it makes people happier or better behaved. Similarly, the origin of a belief is in general irrelevant to the question of its truth; but if the fact that a belief is widely held has been used as evidence of its truth, then this reasoning may be relevantly rebutted by showing that the belief has come to be held for reasons or from causes that are independent of its truth. The truth of the belief and the account of its origin are in this case alternative explanatory hypotheses. That a view is held by certain people is also in general irrelevant to its truth, so that appeals to authority are usually examples of *ignoratio elenchi*. Cases in which the authority appealed to can be independently shown to be an authority in the sense of being likely to be well-informed about the point at issue are exceptions. Irrelevancy shades into prejudice; we may readily accept the doctrines of "our party" and reject those of "the enemy." In this, there may also be present a fallacy of confusion, in that we treat factual beliefs as if they were items of another category—principles to which we can adhere or subscribe, or which we can reject, by choice.

Another form of irrelevance is the *tu quoque*, or "two wrongs" technique. If some action or view of one's own is criticized, one may reply by attacking some action or view of one's critic that is equally hard to defend. The *argumentum ad hominem* is similar—we reject what someone says on the irrelevant ground that *he* is in no position to say it. However, an *argumentum ad hominem* may quite properly point to an inconsistency, and may validly establish the limited conclusion that this man cannot consistently hold this view—a conclusion that may be of special interest in a moral discussion, where the problem may well be that of finding a policy which is both coherent and acceptable.

Related fallacies of irrelevance have been named *argumentum ad verecundiam* (appeal to authority or to feelings of reverence or respect), *argumentum ad personam* (appeal to personal interest), and *argumentum ad populum* (appeal to popular prejudice). Sometimes an *argumentum ad ignorantiam* or *ad auditores* is grouped with these, but these names seem to refer not to any specific fallacy but to the use of any unsound argument which is likely to deceive the actual audience.

Fallacies of interrogation. There are two forms of the *fallacy of many questions*. In one, two or more questions are asked together, and a single answer is demanded to all of them. This is fallacious in that it unfairly prevents the person asked from giving different answers to the different questions. In the second form, the question asked has a presupposition which the answerer may wish to deny but which he would be accepting if he gave anything that would count as an answer. Thus, an answer of either "Yes" or "No" to the question "Have you left the party?" would be an admission of having been a party member, and any answer to the question "Why does such-and-such happen?" presupposes that such-and-such does happen. There is no fallacy, however, in merely asking a question that has a presupposition; the fallacy lies in demanding an answer in the narrow sense, in not permitting or in discouraging a reply that denies the presupposition. Again, it is an instance of the fallacy of prejudice to ask a question that has a presupposition without first investigating whether that presupposition is correct.

Fallacies in explanation and definition. Just as a circular argument fails to give support, so a circular explanation fails to explain. There are concealed circularities of explanation; for example, some mental performance is explained by reference to a faculty, but further inquiry shows either that to say that this faculty exists is only to say that such performances occur or that, although more may be meant, there is, apart from such performances, no evidence for the existence of the faculty. Words like "tendency," "power," "disposition," and "capacity" lend themselves to circularities of this sort.

Similarly, a circular definition, in which the term to be defined recurs within the definiens, fails in its task. If it is intended as a stipulative definition, it fails to assign a meaning; and if it is intended as a reportive definition, it fails to inform anyone of the meaning with which the word is used.

Stipulative definitions can create ambiguity when we assign one meaning to a word but also retain another meaning. This amounts to an assertion that the two meanings go together, disguised as the innocent procedure of stipulation. Persuasive definition is an instance of this in which the retained meaning is an emotive one.

It is a fallacy, in the extended sense, to use words without meaning. But it is not a fallacy not to have defined one's terms, provided that they have a meaning that is known to the audience and is precise enough for the pur-

pose in hand. On the contrary, since it is impossible to define all one's terms, it is a fallacy in discourse to demand that in all terms should be defined; a demand for definition can be a sophistic device for preventing the discussion of substantive issues.

PHILOSOPHICAL FALLACIES

The naturalistic fallacy. What G. E. Moore called the *naturalistic fallacy* is the identifying of goodness with any natural characteristic, such as pleasantness or being the object of desire. If there is a distinct property, goodness, it will of course be an error to identify it with any other feature, even if the two are coextensive, and this would be an example of the refusal to distinguish what we cannot separate; however, it must first be shown that there is such a property as Moore's goodness. Alternatively, if it is a question of how the word "good" is commonly used, then it would be an error to say that it is used to convey some natural description. However, if the naturalist is not trying to report the ordinary use, but is saying that this ordinary use is somehow unsatisfactory (and also that there is no such property as the one of which Moore speaks) and is therefore proposing a different use, where is his mistake? It is true that if he redefines "good" as the name of some natural characteristic, but still also uses the word in its ordinary evaluative or prescriptive sense, he will be slipping into a fallacy of ambiguity; but a consistent ethical naturalist may be committing no fallacy at all.

Arguing from "is" to "ought." An error exposed by Hume, but still frequently committed, is that of arguing from premises that contain only descriptive terms, and no copula except "is," to a conclusion that contains an "ought." This is a fallacy in the strict sense; arguments of this sort cannot be valid, but they are often made plausible by the ambiguous use of such words as "reasonable," "fitting," "authority," "desirable," "beneficial," "courageous," "temperate," "just," "right," and "good" itself, any one of which may be used first in a purely descriptive sense and then interpreted in a sense that is partly descriptive and partly prescriptive. A currently popular version of this fallacy combines it with one or more of the a priori fallacies. Since our concept of, say, courage or our ordinary use of the word "courage" combines a certain natural description with a certain prescription or evaluation, it is concluded that behavior that conforms to this natural description must be recommended or valued in just this way; that is, the move from "is" to "ought" is covered by an appeal to the supposed authority of our language or our ideas.

Confusing relations with things or qualities. A group of philosophical errors that is less well known than the two just mentioned but at least as widespread and harmful consists in identifying a quality with a relation, in treating a relation as if it were an intrinsic quality of one of its terms, or in constructing fictitious entities out of relational situations. Presented linguistically, this means that a term is treated as standing both for a thing or a quality and for a relation, and this, like other ambiguities, can make synthetic connections appear necessary. Thus, an idea or a sense datum is supposed to be an object of which someone can be aware and to have this relation—someone's being aware of it—as part of its nature. This conflation generates a supposed matter of fact about which one can have infallible knowledge and thus gives rise to the pseudo problem of bridging the gap between this direct and infallible knowledge and ordinary fallible knowledge of objects that do not have being known built into their natures. Similarly, minds (or consciousness) have been treated as things that have as part of their nature the relation of being aware of something, and this generates difficulties in philosophical psychology. Also, errors which the naturalistic fallacy was meant to cover are better dealt with in this category. Goodness may be both treated as an intrinsic quality (natural or nonnatural) of, say, states of affairs and identified with or taken as logically including the relation of being pursued, aimed at, or recommended; indeed, it seems that it is just such a conflation of features that makes a quality nonnatural. Similarly, beauty may be both treated as an intrinsic quality and identified with or taken as logically including such relations as pleasing or being admired.

Category mistakes. Philosophers now carefully distinguish different uses of language, different "language games"; the contrasting error is to confuse different ways of using words, to treat a term that belongs to one category as if it belonged to another. However, the concept of a *use* of language is itself ambiguous. In distinguishing uses, we may be noting differences that lie within language, differences in the relations between words and things, differences in the things to which our expressions apply; and it will be a mistake to confuse one kind of distinction with another. There is also a tendency to think that, at least in philosophy, we cannot employ this distinction between words and things; this view is supported by a variant of Berkeley's fallacy: since we cannot talk about something except by using words in relation to it, it is supposed that we cannot talk about things as they are, apart from relations to words.

AVOIDANCE AND DETECTION OF FALLACIES

Popular discussions of fallacies rightly lay great stress on the psychological or emotional aspect of fallacious arguments. Under the influence of violent passions, thinking becomes more purely associative and less consequential, and we are more than usually ready not only to employ arguments, however unsound, that appear to support whatever cause we espouse but also to extend our favor to anything linked, however loosely, with what we already like, respect, or admire, and to extend our hostility to anything linked with what we already dislike, despise, or fear. Ridicule can also be used to brush aside relevant considerations and to condemn a person or a view without a hearing. All sorts of attachments, passions, and emotional prejudices can foster fallacies, and one of the chief means for the avoidance or detection of fallacies is to consider a problem calmly.

Precise formal statement often helps in the detection not only of fallacies in the strict sense but also of inconsistency, circularity, and irrelevance. However, since it is too laborious a task to state all our reasonings formally, we can use this device only when we already have reason to sus-

pect a fallacy. Also, in cases involving equivocation or a category mistake, there is a danger that inaccurate formulation will conceal the fallacy instead of exposing it.

As Richard Whately remarked, ". . . a very *long* discussion is one of the most effective veils of Fallacy; . . . a Fallacy which when stated barely . . . would not deceive a child, may deceive half the world if *diluted* in a quarto volume" (*Elements of Logic*, p. 151). Consequently, an important weapon against fallacy is condensation, extracting the substance of an argument from a mass of verbiage. But this device too has its dangers; it may produce oversimplification, that is, the fallacy *a dicto secundum quid*, of dropping relevant qualifications. When we suspect a fallacy, our aim must be to discover exactly what the argument is; and in general the way to do this is first to pick out its main outlines and then to take into account any relevant subtleties or qualifications.

Bibliography

The pioneer work on fallacies is the *De Sophisticis Elenchis* of Aristotle. Medieval and later logicians followed and expanded his account. Many textbooks on logic include a chapter on fallacies. Jeremy Bentham, throughout his writings, paid much attention to fallacious reasonings by which views that he opposed were supported, and he collected many of them in *The Book of Fallacies,* which is in Vol. II of his *Works,* J. Bowring, ed. (Edinburgh, 1843). Richard Whately, in Ch. 3 of his *Elements of Logic* (London, 1826), gave a much improved classification and analysis of fallacies. John Stuart Mill devoted Book V of *A System of Logic* (London, 1843) to an account of fallacies, developing a new classification and concentrating on a priori fallacies (prejudices) and mistakes in observation and generalization.

Augustus De Morgan, in Ch. 13 of *Formal Logic* (London, 1847), rejected the attempt to list all possible ways of going wrong but gave a penetrating and well-illustrated analysis of many of the traditionally listed fallacies. Arthur Schopenhauer, in "The Art of Controversy," in *Essays from the Parerga and Paralipomena,* translated by T. B. Saunders (London, 1951), described stratagems that may be used in disputes, that is, both sophistic devices and ways of countering them. H. W. B. Joseph included in *An Introduction to Logic* (London, 1906) an appendix on fallacies based on the Aristotelian account.

M. R. Cohen and Ernest Nagel, in Ch. 19 of *An Introduction to Logic and Scientific Method* (New York, 1934), emphasized abuses of scientific method. R. H. Thouless in *Straight and Crooked Thinking* (London, 1930), Susan Stebbing in *Thinking to Some Purpose* (Harmondsworth, England, 1939), and W. W. Fearnside and W. B. Holther in *Fallacy—The Counterfeit of Argument* (Englewood Cliffs, N.J., 1959), gave lively and readable accounts, illustrated with many examples of popular errors and of sophistry in practice, concentrating on political and social debate and propaganda, and stressing the emotional basis of a great deal of fallacy.

J. L. MACKIE

FĀRĀBĪ, AL-, more fully Abū-Nasr Muhammad al-Fārābī (c. 873–950), known in Latin as Alfarabius or Avennasar, was one of the greatest Muslim philosophers. He was widely known as "the second master," Aristotle being the first, and ibn-Khaldūn rates him above Avicenna and Averroës. He was of Turkish origin, and his name indicates that he came from the district of Fārāb, on the middle Jaxartes River (now Syr Darya).

One of al-Fārābī's teachers was the Nestorian Christian Yuhannā ibn-Haylān, who was noted as a logician; it is uncertain whether al-Fārābī studied with him in Merv (Persia) or Harran (Syria) or Baghdad. His principal teacher was Abū-Bishr Mattā ibn-Yūnus, the most prominent member of the school of Christian Aristotelians in Baghdad. Here al-Fārābī studied not merely the various branches of philosophy, but also physics, mathematics, astronomy, and music, even becoming a skilled musical performer. He spent the last few years of his life at the court of the ruler Sayf-ad-Dawla at Aleppo. He did not seem to have had any regular occupation by which to earn a livelihood and lived frugally, even ascetically, often in solitude.

Al-Fārābī's philosophy is based on the teachings of Plato and Aristotle as they were interpreted in the school of Baghdad in the tenth century. Like all writers in Arabic he assumed there were no essential differences between the two, but he preferred the metaphysics of Aristotle, as interpreted by Neoplatonists. Plato, however, he regarded as superior in practical matters, and he wrote commentaries on the *Republic* and the *Laws*. What is often regarded as his major work is reminiscent of these books; it has the clumsy title "On the Principles of the Views of the Inhabitants of the Excellent State," often shortened in practice to "Der Musterstaat," or "The Ideal City" (*al-madīna al-fadila*). The first third of this work sets out al-Fārābī's metaphysical system, the second third his psychology (largely Aristotelian), and the concluding third his views on the ideal state and various imperfect states.

To those familiar with the intellectual environment in which al-Fārābī lived, it is immediately apparent that he wrote in such a way as to commend his views to as many different groups of people as possible. It has been alleged that he supported the Shī'ite sect of Islam, and certainly his last patron Sayf-ad-Dawla was a Shī'ite; features of his "ideal city," such as the dependence of all on the head, resemble Shī'ite conceptions. Yet it is also clear that he wrote in such a way as not to offend the Sunnite majority; for example, by avoiding such a technical Shī'ite term as "imam." Indeed, his view of the relation of philosophy and religion led him to attach positive value to the religions, although he regarded them as inferior to philosophy. Philosophy was the supreme exercise of human reason and therefore the primary requirement of an ideal city. By it, man came to know the one ultimate truth about the universe. To this ultimate philosophical truth the symbolic representations of it found in the several religions stand in varying degrees of proximity and remoteness. Al-Fārābī paid particular attention, of course, to the forms of the main Islamic states of his time and developed his conception of the ideal city in such a way that the actual states he knew were within measurable distance of the ideal.

His metaphysics, similarly, resembles that implicit in the Qur'ān (Koran) and Islamic theology. God is the One or the First from whom all existence proceeds; and in this sense he accepts the Islamic doctrine that God is the creator of the world, although he also holds the heretical view that the world is eternal. In the relation of existent things to God there is a hierarchical order. Similarly in the ideal city there is a head (*ra'īs*) who is the source of all authority and who assigns men to their appropriate grades. This head is also described as commanding but not obeying; all the intermediate grades obey those above and command those below, and the lowest grade only obeys.

Interest has been shown, especially in recent times, in al-Fārābī's theory of prophecy; that is, in particular, how it was possible for Muḥammad to receive the Qur'ān from God. Philosophic knowledge, the highest of all, he regarded as coming to the passive intellect of the philosopher from the Active Intellect, an existent below God in rank. Prophetic revelations also come from the Active Intellect but are received by the imagination of the prophet. In this al-Fārābī was able to accept the Qur'ān as coming from God and yet to place philosophy above it.

Works by al-Fārābī

The "Ideal City" has been translated as *Der Musterstaat von al-Fārābī* by Friedrich Dieterici (Leiden, 1900) and as *Idées des habitants de la cité vertueuse* by R. P. Jaussen, Youssef Karam, and J. Chlala (Cairo, 1949). A critical edition of the Arabic text and an English translation by Richard Walzer is in preparation.

See also *Al-Fārābī's Short Commentary on Aristotle's Prior Analytics*, translated by Nicholas Rescher (Pittsburgh, 1963); *Al-Fārābī's philosophische Abhandlungen*, short essays translated by Friedrich Dieterici (Leiden, 1892); and *The Fusul al-Madani: Aphorisms of the Statesman of al-Fārābī*, with an English translation, introduction, and notes by D. M. Dunlop, ed. (Cambridge, 1961).

Works on al-Fārābī

De Boer, T. J., *The History of Philosophy in Islam*, London, 1903. See especially pp. 106–128.

Rescher, Nicholas, *Al-Fārābī: An Annotated Bibliography*. Pittsburgh, 1962.

Rescher, Nicholas, *Studies in the History of Arabic Logic*. Pittsburgh, 1964.

Quadri, G., *La Philosophie arabe dans l'Europe médiévale*. Paris, 1947. See especially pp. 71–94.

Walzer, Richard, *Greek into Arabic*. Oxford, 1962. See especially pp. 18–23, 206–219.

W. Montgomery Watt

FARADAY, MICHAEL (1791–1867), British chemist and physicist, came from a poor family and had no formal schooling beyond the elementary level. While a bookbinder's apprentice, he became interested in chemistry and electricity. Faraday took notes on a series of lectures given by Sir Humphry Davy, the leading British chemist, presented them to Davy, and soon afterward, at the age of 21, was appointed laboratory assistant to Davy at the Royal Institution (London). He became director of the laboratory in 1825 and Fullerian professor of chemistry at the institution in 1833. His early scientific work in chemistry included the discovery of several new compounds and the liquefaction of chlorine and other gases. In 1831, Faraday discovered electromagnetic induction, or the creation of electric currents in a conductor by changing currents or moving magnets in the vicinity; this phenomenon is the basis of the electrical generator. This was followed by a series of investigations demonstrating with greater certainty than had been previously achieved the identity of the nature of the electricity generated by friction, voltaic cells, electromagnetic induction, and other means. Extensive experiments in electrochemistry led Faraday to the enunciation of his laws of electrolytic decomposition in 1833. The source of the power of the voltaic pile, or battery, was the object of his subsequent research. He investigated the electrical properties of insulators, or dielectrics, in 1837. In 1845 he discovered that the plane of polarization of light was rotated on passing through a transparent diamagnetic substance in the direction of externally applied lines of magnetic force. At the same time he began his investigation of diamagnetism. In his last years he suffered from loss of memory, and he ceased his researches in 1855. He was a member of a small Christian sect, the Sandemanians, and was noted for his gentleness of character.

Faraday is generally regarded as one of the greatest of all experimental scientists. The truth of this, adequately attested to in the three-thousand-odd paragraphs of the *Experimental Researches in Electricity*, should not be allowed to obscure the fertility of his imagination and conceptualizing powers and the guiding role of theoretical principles in sustaining his persistent research. His most important contribution to physics is probably the concept of lines of force, which was the beginning of the development of field theory. The accepted approach to electrodynamical phenomena at the time was to express the forces between charges mathematically as direct actions at a distance, an approach which was to prove unfruitful. Faraday was not trained in the mathematics necessary for this tradition. In order to represent the action of electromagnetic induction, he envisaged the space surrounding magnets to be filled with lines of magnetic force representing everywhere the direction of the force which would be experienced by a magnetic pole introduced from outside in the manner of the lines formed by iron filings sprinkled on a paper resting on a magnet. The lines of magnetic force have not only direction but also sense—that is, a north magnetic pole is pushed one way along them, and a south pole is pushed in the opposite sense; furthermore, their concentration near a given point represents the intensity of the magnetic force at that point. Each such line forms a closed loop, beginning or ending nowhere, but in the case of a magnet passing through its substance from one pole to the other. In these terms the law of electromagnetic induction may be expressed: "The quantity of electricity thrown into a current is directly as the amount of curves intersected" (*Experimental Researches in Electricity*). In James Clerk Maxwell's famous words:

> Faraday, in his mind's eye, saw lines of force traversing all space where the mathematicians saw centres of force attracting at a distance: Faraday saw a medium where they saw nothing but distance: Faraday sought the seat of the phenomena in real actions going on in the medium, they were satisfied that they had found it in a power of action at a distance impressed on the electric fluids. (Preface to the first edition of the *Treatise on Electricity and Magnetism*)

In most of Faraday's researches the concept of lines of force was used merely as a "representative aid" and was not meant to include "any idea of the nature of the physical cause of the phenomena." This cautiousness was a mark of Faraday's methods; in the choice of terminology to describe new phenomena, for example, he carefully attempted to avoid suggesting anything more than they warranted. However, at times Faraday allowed himself to speculate, and in 1852 he considered "the possible and probable *physical existence* of such lines" ("On the Phys-

ical Lines of Magnetic Force"). On the basis of arguments which can be characterized only as suggestive (such as that the magnetic lines are curved) he hypothesized that magnetic lines of force have physical existence and contrasted this with gravitation, where there was no evidence that the lines of force are anything but abstract and ideal. In a charming talk published in 1846 ("Thoughts on Ray-vibrations") Faraday speculated that the atoms of matter might be simply point centers of force, as Boscovich had suggested in the eighteenth century, or, in Faraday's terms, points from which lines of force spread into space. The extension of the atom may be identified with the extent of these lines, so that each atom would occupy all space and atoms would be mutually penetrable. Light might consist of vibrations in these lines, possibly obviating the need for an ethereal medium for its propagation; on the other hand, he suggested elsewhere that the lines might represent a condition of the ether, "for it is not at all unlikely that, if there be an ether, it should have other uses than simply the conveyance of radiations."

Faraday's geometric–intuitive representation was in particular rejected by the Continental electrodynamicists, and in 1846 Wilhelm Weber developed a theory of forces acting directly at a distance between charges which included the phenomena of electromagnetic induction. The validity of the lines of force concept was vindicated by the theoretical researches of William Thomson and particularly of James Clerk Maxwell, who regarded his task to be putting Faraday's ideas into mathematical notation. It was with this motive that Maxwell developed his electromagnetic field theory, which, reinterpreted in quantum terms, remains the accepted theory of electromagnetic action and which was the prototype of all the field theories that dominate physics today. Maxwell's early representation of the lines of magnetic force as vortexes in the ether spinning about these lines as axes was in part suggested by Faraday's discovery of the magnetic rotation of the plane of polarization of light. The existence of this magnetic effect upon light had confirmed others in their speculations that light was some sort of propagated electromagnetic phenomenon, and the rotation of the plane of polarization suggested to Thomson and Maxwell that magnetism was in some way a rotatory effect, or, in contemporary terminology, the magnetic field is a pseudovector field.

Faraday was one among many who gave adumbrations of the generalized principle of conservation of energy, the clear expression of which is credited to Julius Mayer, James Joule, and Hermann von Helmholtz. His convictions regarding the interconvertibility of forces led him, from Hans Christian Oersted's generation of magnetism by an electric current, to seek that generation of a current from magnetism which he found. In a lecture of 1834, Faraday spoke explicitly of this mutual convertibility, but he did not proceed further to specify how he conceived of the "forces" or "powers" which might be conserved or to discover quantitative relations. In connection with his investigations in 1840 of the source of the action of the voltaic pile he cited this principle against the contact theory, according to which the mere contact of two metals was the source of the current so that there would be a "creation of power" out of nothing, and in favor of the chemical theory, which found the source in the chemical actions occurring in the pile.

Bibliography

Faraday's work in electricity, including electrochemistry, is to be found in his *Experimental Researches in Electricity*, 3 vols. (London, 1839, 1844, 1855); his chemical work is collected in *Experimental Researches in Chemistry and Physics* (London, 1859). Of particular interest are the speculative papers "Thoughts on Ray-vibrations," in *Philosophical Magazine*, Vol. 28 (1846), 345–350, reprinted in the *Experimental Researches in Electricity*, Vol. III, pp. 447–452, and "On the Physical Lines of Magnetic Force," in *Royal Institution Proceedings*, June 11, 1852, reprinted in *Experimental Researches*, pp. 438–443. The standard biography is H. Bence-Jones, *The Life and Letters of Faraday*, 2 vols. (London, 1870). See also L. P. Williams, *Michael Faraday* (New York, 1965). A brief and lucid treatment of the development of his researches is given by John Tyndall in *Faraday as a Discoverer* (New York, 1868).

ARTHUR E. WOODRUFF

FARIAS BRITO, RAIMUNDO DE (1862–1917), was the philosophic forerunner of Brazilian modernism. A profound sense of crisis underlies the work of Farias Brito. Individual existence is a precarious struggle against despair and death, and social order is threatened by moral disintegration and anarchy. Knowledge of man's role in his world is necessary to confront this crisis. Intellectual pursuit of the truth is the primary ethical obligation. Lacking certainty, man establishes a relative morality through conviction, involving both philosophy and religion. Metaphysics attempts to embrace the truth theoretically through formulation of world views; religion embraces the truth practically through acceptance and appropriation of a given world view. This free acceptance of common convictions creates community, informing and giving thrust to the total culture of which it serves as a focus. The theoretical task is a permanent activity of the human spirit; the practical task, a permanent necessity. Convinced that modern philosophy was not adequate to its task, largely because of its predominantly skeptical mood grounded in phenomenalism, Farias Brito hoped to establish a new dogmatism capable of providing convictions that could give both courage for withstanding suffering and despair and the bases for re-establishing social order and direction. There was a transition in his thought from an early attempt to provide grounds for a naturalistic religion, inspired by German monism, to the articulation of his philosophy of spirit, influenced by French spiritualism. The naturalism is expressed in an incomplete series of volumes entitled *A finalidade do mundo* (1895–1905). The new series, *Filosofia do espírito* (1912–1914), was initiated after Farias Brito had moved to Rio de Janeiro in 1909 to accept the chair in logic at Colégio Pedro II.

The spirit, "a live principle of action, capable of modifying . . . the order of nature; . . . of dominating itself; . . . of exercising dominion over things" is the "foundation of all reality and the basis of all experience." Psychological data are therefore indispensable to the metaphysician. Physiological psychology deals solely with the physical base of spirit; psychology proper ought to be concerned with subjective psychic phenomena. Its method is introspective, direct introspection supplemented by indirect introspection, a study of the manifestations of

consciousness through which men achieve expression and communication. "Transcendent psychology" is the method employed for utilizing psychological data in metaphysics. From the felt fact of human existence, it is possible to rise to the level of transcendence, seeking knowledge concerning essence. The introspective operation of the individual consciousness reveals two facets of experience—consciousness itself and that which is presented to consciousness; both constitute existential reality. Through abstraction and analysis of each, pure consciousness is seen to have priority. Understanding man as essentially conscious spirit, the method of "transcendent psychology," leads to the postulation of divine spirit.

Bibliography

Other works by Farias Brito are *Verdade como regra das ações* ("Truth as the Rule of Action"; Rio de Janeiro, 1905), *Base física do espírito* ("Physical Base of Truth"; Rio de Janeiro, 1912), and *Mundo interior* ("Inner World"; Rio de Janeiro, 1912).

For a study on Farias Brito, see Fred Gillette Sturm, "Farias Brito: Brasilian Philosopher of the Spirit," in *Revista interamericana de bibliografia*, Vol. 13 (1963), 176–204.

FRED GILLETTE STURM

FASCISM, the ideology of the movement which, under the leadership of Benito Mussolini, seized power in Italy in 1922 and held power until the Allied invasion of Italy in World War II. Mussolini was a socialist until 1915, and fascism is a paradoxical but potent mixture of extreme socialist, or syndicalist, notions with a Hegelian or idealist theory of the state.

An attempt to provide fascism with a fully articulated theory was made by an Italian Neo-Hegelian philosopher of some distinction, Giovanni Gentile, who was converted to fascism after Mussolini's coup. But as a former liberal and collaborator of Benedetto Croce, Gentile was opposed by the anti-intellectual wing of the Fascist party, and his draft for a manifesto of fascist ideology was rewritten by Mussolini himself and published in 1932 in the *Enciclopedia italiana* as *La dottrina del fascismo*. However, no adequate conception of fascism could be derived from these theoretical sources alone; the actual behavior of the Italian fascists during their twenty years of power must also be taken into account.

The word "fascism" is often used, especially by left-wing writers, not only for the Italian doctrine but also for the similar, if more fanatic, national socialism of Hitler and for the altogether less coherent ideologies of Franco, Perón, Antonescu, and other such dictators. But however justifiable the wider and looser use of the word, the present article is confined to the system and ideology which called itself *Fascismo* and which flourished in Italy under Mussolini.

Gentile in his two books *Che cosa è il fascismo* (1925) and *Origini e dottrina del fascismo* (1929) stressed, as one might expect, the Hegelian elements in fascism. He argued that fascism was essentially idealistic and spiritual. Whereas liberalism, socialism, democracy, and the other progressive movements of the nineteenth century had asserted the rights of man, the selfish claims of the individual, fascism sought, instead, to uphold the moral integrity and higher collective purpose of the nation. And whereas liberalism saw the state simply as an institution created to protect men's rights, fascism looked on the state as an organic entity which embodied in itself all the noblest spiritual reality of the people as a whole. Fascism opposed the laissez-faire economics of capitalism and the bourgeois ethos which went with it. But fascism equally opposed socialism, which preached class war and trade unionism and thus served only to divide the nation. Fascism could tolerate no organized sectional groups which stood outside the state, for such groups pressed the supposed interests of some against the true interests of all. Hence, in place of trade unions, employers' federations, and similar organizations, fascism set up corporations which were designed to integrate the interests of particular trades, industries, professions, and the like into the wider harmony of the state.

Fascism, said Gentile, understood all the defects of bourgeois capitalism which had led to the rise of socialism, but fascism revolutionized society in such a way that the socialist critique was no longer relevant. For fascism replaced the old, competitive, hedonistic ethos of liberalism with an austere, stern, rigorous patriotic morality in which "the heroic values of service, sacrifice, indeed death itself were once more respected." Fascism did not deny liberty, but the liberty it upheld was not the right of each man to do what he pleased but "the liberty of a whole people freely accepting the rule of a state which they had interiorised, and made the guiding principle of all their conduct."

Fascism was proud of its comprehensive nature, of its totalitarian scope. For fascism, Gentile argued, was not just a method of government; it was a philosophy which permeated the whole will, thought, and feeling of the nation. "The authority of the state," Gentile wrote, "is absolute. It does not compromise, it does not bargain, it does not surrender any portion of its field to other moral or religious principles which may interfere with the individual conscience. But, on the other hand the state becomes a reality only in the consciousness of individuals." The state was "an idea made actual."

When Mussolini revised Gentile's draft for his *La dottrina del fascismo,* he retained most of the Neo-Hegelian idealistic talk about the ideal nature of the state, but he had more to say about fascism's debts to the more extreme and fanatic elements of the nineteenth-century left wing. Mussolini named Georges Sorel, Charles Péguy, and Hubert Lagardelle as "sources of the river of Fascism." From these theorists, especially from Sorel, Mussolini derived the idea that "action is more important than thought"; by "action" he meant, as Sorel meant, violence. The extremists of the anarchist movement in the nineteenth century were obsessed by what they called *la propagande par le fait* ("propaganda by deed"); this "deed" tended to take the form of undiscriminating acts of revolutionary violence, such as throwing bombs into crowded cafés. The exhilaration of this policy soon blinded several of its champions to the end they were supposed to be pursuing—overthrowing the state—so that anarchism produced a movement of revolutionary disciplinarianism which Mussolini recognized as the source of his own inspiration.

Fascism was thus a movement which not only accepted, but also rejoiced in, violence. It had no patience with parliamentary or democratic methods of changing society. Indeed, Mussolini believed that the violent seizure of power, such as his own movement accomplished when it marched on Rome in 1922, was a necessary part of the moral rejuvenation of the nation; it was needed in order to create that "epic state of mind" (a phrase of Sorel's) which fascism prized so highly. Thus rejoicing in violence, fascism was, as Mussolini explained, hostile to all forms of pacifism, universalism, and disarmament. Fascism frankly acknowledged that "war alone keys up all human energies to their maximum tension, and sets a seal of nobility on those persons who have the courage to fight and die." The fascist state would have nothing to do with "universal embraces"; it "looked its neighbour proudly in the face, always armed, always vigilant, always ready to defend its integrity." Schemes such as that of the League of Nations were anathema to fascism.

With some reason Mussolini also claimed that fascism derived historically from the nationalistic movement of the nineteenth century. Nationalism, he insisted, owed nothing to the left. The German nation was not unified by liberals but by a man of iron, Bismarck. The nation of Italy, too, had been created by such men as Garibaldi, a man of revolutionary violence; the first great prophet of Italian unity was Machiavelli, the archenemy of liberal, pacifist scruples. Mussolini had the highest regard for the author of *The Prince.* Machiavelli's desire to rekindle in modern Italy all the military virtues and military glory of ancient Rome was also Mussolini's ambition, but Mussolini's version of Machiavelli's dream was a much more vulgar one, and his achievements would have struck Machiavelli as tawdry, shabby, and corrupt.

Mussolini argued that it was the Italian state that had created the Italian nation. Indeed, it was the state, as the expression of a universal ethical will, which created the right to national existence and independence. Mussolini rejected the racism which was so central a feature of Nazi teaching in Germany. "The people," he wrote, "is not a race, but a people historically perpetuating itself; a multitude united by an idea." It must be recorded in favor of fascism that it never taught race hatred, and even when Mussolini entered the war on Hitler's side and introduced anti-Semitic legislation to please his ally, the Italian fascists were far from zealous in the enforcement of the laws against Jews.

Indeed, Mussolini's glorification of war and violence had never more than a limited success with the Italian people. Accustomed to rhetoric and appreciative of any kind of display, the Italians accepted the showier side of fascism more readily than the "austere, heroic way of life" which it demanded. Slow to conquer the backward Ethiopians in Mussolini's colonialist war against Abyssinia in 1935, the average Italian conscript soldier was even less eager to meet the Allied forces in World War II. Likewise, despite the cruelty of Mussolini's henchmen to his numerous political prisoners, there was never in Italy anything approaching the genocide which was faithfully enacted by Hitler's followers in Germany; even at its worst Fascism never robbed the Italians of their humanity.

Mussolini earned a reputation, even among critical foreign observers, for the "efficiency" of his administration; he was popularly supposed abroad "to have made the

Italian trains run on time." This achievement was largely mythical, for economic growth was minimal, but Mussolini was able, by forbidding strikes and subordinating industries to his state corporations, to prevent any of the more easily discernible manifestations of economic disorder. In any case his rule was never a mere personal dictatorship. He built up a powerful party with an elaborate hierarchy of command which served him much as the Soviet Communist party served Stalin. Fascism was in a very real sense the dictatorship of a party, and the effectiveness of the party organization in a country by no means notable for good organization was one secret of fascism's twenty years of success.

Bibliography

Ambrosini, G., *Il partito fascista e lo stato*. Rome, 1934.
Finer, Herman, *Mussolini's Italy*. New York, 1935.
Gentile, Giovanni, *Genesi e struttura della società*. Florence, 1946.
Germino, Dante L., *The Italian Fascist Party in Power: A Study in Totalitarian Rule*. Minneapolis, Minn., 1959.
Landini, Pietro, *La dottrina del fascismo*. 1936.
Lion, Aline, *The Pedigree of Fascism*. Florence, 1927.
Mussolini, Benito, *Scritti e discorsi*, 12 vols. Milan, 1934–1939.
Mussolini, Benito, *The Doctrine of Fascism*, translated in Michael Oakeshott, ed., *Social and Economic Doctrines of Contemporary Europe*, 2d ed. New York, 1942.
Pitigliani, Fausto, *The Italian Corporative State*. London, 1933; New York, 1934.
Rocco, Alfredo, *Political Doctrine of Fascism: Recent Legislation in Italy*. New York, 1926.
Salvatorelli, Luigi, *Storia del fascismo*. Rome, 1952.
Salvemini, Gaetano, *Under the Axe of Fascism*. New York, 1936.
Spencer, H. R., *The Government and Politics of Italy*. Yonkers-on-Hudson, N.Y., 1932.

MAURICE CRANSTON

FATHERS OF THE CHURCH. See PATRISTIC PHILOSOPHY.

FECHNER, GUSTAV THEODOR (1801–1887), German philosopher, founder of psychophysics, and pioneer in experimental psychology. He was born in Gross-Saerchen, Prussia, and studied medicine at the University of Leipzig, where he passed his examinations at the age of 21. His interests, however, led him into physics, and by 1830 he had published over 40 papers in this field. He also wrote a number of poems and satirical works under the pseudonym of "Dr. Mises," which he also used for some of his later metaphysical speculations. A paper on the quantitative measurement of electrical currents (1831) led to his appointment as professor of physics at Leipzig. Fechner's incipient interest in psychology is shown in papers of 1838 and 1840 on the perception of complementary colors and on subjective afterimages. His experiments on afterimages, however, had tragic consequences. As a result of gazing at the sun he sustained an eye injury, and his subsequent blindness led to a serious emotional crisis. Fechner resigned his professorship in 1839 and virtually retired from the world.

A seemingly miraculous recovery, three years later, stimulated Fechner's interest in philosophy, particularly in regard to the question of the soul and the possibility of refuting materialistic metaphysics. In a work entitled *Nanna oder das Seelenleben der Pflanzen* ("Nanna, or the Soul-Life of Plants," Leipzig, 1848) he defended the idea that even plants have a mental life. This book is indicative of the panpsychistic bent of Fechner's thought, which was the major cause of the direction taken by his further work.

Psychophysics. In 1848 Fechner returned to the University of Leipzig as professor of philosophy. His desire to substantiate empirically the metaphysical thesis that mind and matter are simply alternative ways of construing one and the same reality was the main motivation for his pioneering work in experimental psychology. His *Elemente der Psychophysik* (Leipzig, 1860) was intended to be an outline of an exact science of the functional relations between bodily and mental phenomena, with a view to showing that one and the same phenomenon could be characterized in two ways. Fechner divided his new science of psychophysics into two disciplines: inner psychophysics, which studies the relation between sensation and nerve excitation; and outer psychophysics, to which Fechner's own experimental work was devoted and which studies the relation between sensation and physical stimulus. Psychophysics became one of the dominant fields within experimental psychology.

Fechner's work on the relation between physical stimuli and sensations led to a mathematical formulation that he called the law of intensity, which states that the intensity of a sensation increases as the logarithm of the stimulus, that is, by diminishing increments. When Fechner realized that his principle corresponded to the findings of E. H. Weber (1795–1878), he called it "Weber's Law," a name now reserved for the vaguer statement that a barely noticeable difference in stimulus has a constant ratio to the stimulus. Fechner's studies in psychophysics included a number of classical experiments on the perception of weight, visual brightness, and distance.

Panpsychism. Fechner's psychological studies were meant to confirm his theory of panpsychism. He maintained that the whole universe is spiritual in character, the phenomenal world of physics being merely the external manifestation of this spiritual reality. That which *to itself* is psychical is *to others* physical. In his *Atomenlehre* he argued that physics requires us to regard atoms only as centers of force or energy, as Leibniz had argued; it is not necessary to suppose them to be material or extended. These atoms are only the simplest elements in a spiritual hierarchy leading up to God. Each level of this hierarchy includes all those levels beneath it, so that God contains the totality of spirits. Consciousness is an essential feature of all that exists, but this assertion does not mean, as Leibniz had supposed, that every physical entity or phenomenon has its own soul. Only certain systems, namely, organic wholes, give evidence of possessing souls, and those bodies which do not are only the constituents of besouled bodies. The evidences of soul are the systematic coherence and conformity to law exhibited in the behavior of organic wholes. Fechner regarded the earth, "our mother," as such an organic besouled whole. The stars and the physical universe as a whole are also bodies of this kind. God is the soul of the universe; He is to the system of nature as that system is *to itself*.

To regard the whole material universe as inwardly alive and conscious is to take what Fechner called the "daylight view" (*Tagesansicht*). To regard it as inert matter, lacking in any teleological significance, is to take what he called the "night view" (*Nachtansicht*). Fechner ardently advocated the daylight view and hoped that it could be supported inductively by means of his psychophysical experiments. But he also argued for the daylight view on pragmatic grounds, offering the sort of arguments that William James later found highly congenial. Fechner urged that any hypothesis which cannot be positively proved but which does not contradict scientific findings be accepted if it makes us happy. The antimaterialistic daylight view is such a hypothesis. Fechner also defended his theory by means of analogical arguments. When certain qualities are found to be present in several types of objects, we are justified in assuming hypothetically that these objects share other, undetected qualities. Entities which exhibit the sort of order that our own bodies do may therefore be assumed to be alive and inwardly spiritual as we are.

Immortality. Fechner's argument for immortality is based on the observation that many individual experiences which are forgotten or unnoticed may later be recalled into consciousness. If the soul as a whole is treated on the analogy of its individual experiences, then, since these do not vanish utterly but often return in the form of memory, the soul itself may likewise continue to exist in God's memory. Mind and body are not parallel aspects of some third substance, as in Spinoza; they are identical. The persistence of mind is therefore no more difficult to entertain than the persistence of the material universe itself, which is only the outward manifestation of an all-inclusive soul.

Aesthetics. Between 1865 and 1876 Fechner turned his attention to aesthetics. He published a paper on the golden section, the supposedly ideal proportion, and several papers on the controversy over two Holbein paintings of the Madonna. These two paintings, one in Dresden, the other in Darmstadt, were the subject of serious debate among art critics and aestheticians. Fechner hoped to settle the question of their relative excellence by means of a public preference poll when the paintings were exhibited together.

The desire to put aesthetics on an empirical, scientific footing and to bring philosophical speculation into some sort of accord with experimental science is shown further in Fechner's *Vorschule der Aesthetik* ("Propaedentic to Aesthetic," Leipzig, 1876), a work of considerable significance for the history of experimental aesthetics. In the preface to this work Fechner stated that previous aestheticians such as Schelling and Hegel had theorized "downward" from universal principles to particulars. Fechner proposed to reverse this procedure, to build aesthetic theory "from below," on a foundation of empirical evidence. The word "beauty," he maintained, denotes the approximate subject matter of aesthetics. It is a word applicable to everything that has the property of arousing pleasure directly and immediately. (Pleasure aroused by thoughts of the consequences of an object is nonaesthetic.) Our experiences of aesthetic pleasure are simple, unanalyzable psychic atoms. The aim of an experimental aesthetics is to discover the objects that produce such atoms, that is, the causal laws connecting aesthetic experiences with the characteristics of outer objects.

Experimental methods. Fechner suggested three experimental methods for carrying out this program: the method of selection or choice, the method of production or construction, and the method of measuring common objects. The first of these methods is illustrated by Fechner's experiments with rectangles. Ten rectangles of varying dimensions but equal areas were spread at random on a table. The subject was asked to make a selection, ranking the rectangles in the order of his aesthetic pleasure and displeasure. A record was kept of his responses, with allowance being made for variation in hesitation of response. Fechner's results seemed to support the hypothesis that there exist certain ratios of length to width that possess specific aesthetic value. Most of the people tested tended to reject as unpleasant both the square or nearly square and the extremely elongated figures, with the largest number of favorable responses going to the rectangle whose proportions were 34:21. Fechner took this as empirical confirmation of the special aesthetic status of the golden section.

In the second of Fechner's methods, the subject was confronted, for example, with four vertical lines of various lengths and asked to place a dot over each line at the distance that seemed to him most aesthetically pleasing. The results were that the average distance was proportional to the length of the line. This experiment was referred to as the "inquiry into the letter 'i.'" Fechner's third experimental method involved measuring such objects as books, visiting cards, etc., and here too he found the ratio of the golden section in a large percentage of cases.

Laws of psychological aesthetics. A number of psychological laws formulated by Fechner are relevant to aesthetic experience. His principle of aesthetic threshold states that a stimulus must acquire a certain intensity before it can produce pleasure or pain. The effect will then increase gradually until it reaches a maximum point, whereupon it will decrease to the point of indifference. In the case of pleasure but not in that of pain, the effect may, after the maximum is reached, change to its opposite. Aesthetic reinforcement refers to the fact that several conditions of pleasure may, when combined, produce a total satisfaction greater than the sum of these conditions taken separately, for example, melody and harmony in music, meaning and rhythm in poetry. The principle of "uniform connection within the manifold" states that we prefer objects which are both unified and complex over objects which are homogeneous or excessively diverse. The principle of "absence of contradiction" claims that harmony and truth are aesthetically preferable to disagreement, contradiction, or error. Vagueness and ambiguity are aesthetically displeasing, as the principle of "clarity" announces. The recollection of an event portrayed in some aesthetic object may bring pleasure or displeasure, depending on whether the event reminds us of something pleasant or unpleasant: the principle of "aesthetic association." The principle of "minimum effort" states that pleasure is derived from the smallest possible expenditure of energy relative to a given end in view and not simply from the minimum expenditure of energy as such.

Conclusion. These "laws of the mind" illustrate the spirit of Fechner's philosophizing. He was one of the most versatile thinkers of the nineteenth century, laboring to reconcile an idealistic view of reality with the methodology of modern science and, in so doing, providing some of the groundwork for further developments in a number of areas of experimental psychology. His somewhat fantastic metaphysical speculations disclose a mind of poetic sensitivity, whose visions, however, he insisted on subjecting to scientific scrutiny.

Additional Works by Fechner

Büchlein vom Leben nach dem Tod. Dresden, 1936. Translated by John Erskine as *Life After Death.* New York, 1943.

Zend-Avesta oder über die Dinge des Himmels und des Jenseits ("Zend-Avesta, or Concerning Matters of Heaven and the World to Come"), 3 vols. Leipzig, 1851.

Über die physikalische und philosophische Atomenlehre ("On Physical and Philosophical Atomic Theory"). Leipzig, 1850.

Über die Seelenfrage. Ein Gang durch die sichtbare Welt, um die Unsichtbare zu finden ("On the Question of the Soul. A Path Through the Visible World in Order to Find the Invisible"). Leipzig, 1861.

Die Tagesansicht gegenüber der Nachtansicht ("The Daylight View as Opposed to the Night View"). Leipzig, 1879.

Die drei Motive und Grunde des Glaubens ("The Three Motives and Grounds of Faith"). Leipzig, 1863.

Note: A bibliography of 175 of Fechner's writings can be found in *Elemente der Psychophysik;* 2d ed. Leipzig, 1889. Vol. 1.

Works on Fechner

IN ENGLISH

Boring, E. G., *History of Experimental Psychology.* New York, 1929 and 1950. Ch. 14.

James, William, *A Pluralistic Universe.* New York, 1909. Lecture 4.

James, William, *Principles of Psychology.* New York, 1890. Vol. 1, pp. 553–549.

Külpe, O., *Die Philosophie der Gegenwart in Deutschland.* Leipzig, 1902. Translated by M. L. Patrick and G. T. W. Patrick as *The Philosophy of the Present in Germany.* London, 1913. Pp. 147–160.

Murphy, G., *Historical Introduction to Modern Psychology.* New York, 1949. Pp. 82–94.

Perry, R. B., *Philosophy of the Recent Past.* New York, 1926. Pp. 82–86.

IN GERMAN

Hermann, J., *Gustav Theodor Fechner.* Munich, 1926.

Kuntze, J. E., *Gustav Theodor Fechner.* Leipzig, 1882.

Lasswitz, K., *Gustav Theodor Fechner.* Stuttgart, 1896.

Meyer, F. A. E., *Philosophische Metaphysik und Christliche Glaube bei Gustav Theodor Fechner.* Goettingen, 1937.

ARNULF ZWEIG

FEELING. See EMOTION AND FEELING.

FÉNELON, FRANÇOIS DE SALIGNAC DE LA MOTHE (1651–1715) French bishop and author, was born in Périgord of an ancient noble but impoverished family. He received his education in Cahors and then in Paris, where he entered the seminary of Saint-Sulpice and was ordained priest about 1675. First in Paris and then in Saintonge he was made responsible for securing the conversion of Protestants, and in this, especially after the revocation of the Edict of Nantes (1685), he had to offset the effects of brutal military repression. He was certainly firm and successful, but opinions vary on how gentle he

was. By 1689 he enjoyed the favor of Bishop Bossuet and Mme. de Maintenon and had been appointed tutor to Louis XIV's grandson, the duc de Bourgogne.

Fénelon's association with Mme. Guyon, the exponent of quietism, dramatically changed his career. In 1694, mainly on Bossuet's initiative, she was censured by an official inquiry and temporarily put under his supervision at Meaux. Both Fénelon and Mme. de Maintenon were implicated with Mme. Guyon in a devotional group, but when Bossuet consecrated Fénelon archbishop of Cambrai in 1695 it seemed that he had averted potential scandal by using promotion as a pretext for removal. Fénelon, however, had become personally committed to mysticism and the doctrine of pure love (the disinterested love of God, divorced from any act of will, or even concern for one's salvation). Learning that Bossuet planned a crushing (and unfair) attack on Mme. Guyon and, through her, on all mysticism, Fénelon tried to forestall him by publishing a reasoned defense of mystical spirituality, *Les Maximes des saints* (1679). Bossuet then embarked on a campaign of slander, falsification, and corruption, which resulted in Fénelon's banishment from the court (1697) and his condemnation by the pope (1699). Fénelon, who had always been fragile in health, remained in exile at Cambrai, conscientiously ruling his war-ravaged diocese, earning a reputation for sanctity, and pursuing a relentless, and ultimately successful, struggle against Jansenism in high places.

Though he owed much of his early success to Bossuet, whom he had at first admired, Fénelon was by temperament so different that a subsequent breach was inevitable. In his attitude to the theater Fénelon had a breadth and humanity of outlook that led him to praise Racine and even Molière, who had been mercilessly attacked by Bossuet (*Lettre à l'Académie,* 1714). Fénelon had been deeply influenced by Greek culture, and much of his thinking bore the mark of Plato. He combined sensitivity and idealism with a strong vein of practicality, but he echoed neither the authoritarianism nor the moral grimness of Bossuet.

In philosophy Fénelon was enthusiastic rather than original. In 1687 he undertook for Bossuet a *Réfutation du système de la nature et de la grâce* against Malebranche, but he soon espoused a form of Cartesianism—best represented in his *Traité de l'existence de Dieu* (1712 and 1718)—that came very close to Malebranche's position. Fénelon also wrote *Lettres sur divers sujets de métaphysique et de religion* (1718).

His early *Traité de l'education des filles* (1687) is humane and sensible, arguing that to neglect the education of one half of the human race can only have adverse effects on the other. Basing his system firmly on Christian teaching, he emphasized the need for a moral education deriving from love of virtue, rather than from fear of punishment. In addition to general literacy and elocution, Fénelon advocated the teaching of such practical matters as sufficient knowledge of law to enable women to protect their much-abused interests.

Fénelon's principle of developing rather than repressing character appears in *Télémaque,* written for his pupil about 1694 and semiofficially condemned on publication (1699).

The transparent veil of Homeric legend does nothing to conceal the author's detestation of royal absolutism in its contemporary manifestations. Wars of aggression fought in the name of national prestige, territorial aggrandizement and extravagant luxury at court are condemned, not only for the misery they cause for impoverished subjects, but also as evils in themselves. For Fénelon a good king is one whose people enjoy prosperity based on industry and commerce and who accepts the duty of ensuring not only their material but also, through his example, their moral welfare. Fénelon's fundamental political axiom was that kings and their policies are subject to and judged by the moral law, as embodied in Christian teaching, and that the true interests of a state can never conflict with this law. Similar views occur in the *Dialogues des morts*. Had it not been for the premature death of the duc de Bourgogne (1712), Fénelon's teaching, so contrary to Louis XIV's practice, might well have become official policy.

Works by Fénelon

Oeuvres complètes, J. Gosselin, ed., 10 vols. Paris, 1848–1852. Numerous editions of separate works.

Works on Fénelon

Adam, A., *Histoire de la littérature française au XVIIe siècle*, Vol. V, Ch. 5. Paris, 1956. Excellent chapter on Fénelon.
Bremond, H., *Apologie pour Fénelon*. Paris, 1910.
Carcassonne, E., *Fénelon, l'homme et l'oeuvre*. Paris, 1946.
Goré, Jeanne-L., *L'Itinéraire de Fénelon*. Paris, 1957.
Hazard, P., *La Crise de la conscience européenne*, 2d ed. Paris, 1961. Translated by J. L. May as *The European Mind*. London, 1953; Harmondsworth (paperback), 1964.

A. J. KRAILSHEIMER

FERGUSON, ADAM (1723–1816), Scottish historian and philosopher of the school of Thomas Reid and the philosophy of common sense. Ferguson was born at Logierait, Perthshire, and educated at Perth Grammar School, St. Andrews University, and Divinity Hall, Edinburgh. Ordained in 1745, he served until 1754 as chaplain to the 42nd Regiment (the Black Watch) and saw active service in Flanders. In 1759 Ferguson became professor of natural philosophy at Edinburgh and, in 1764, professor of pneumatics and moral philosophy, holding the latter post for over twenty years. He then accepted a nominal appointment as professor of mathematics which enabled him to lead a semiprivate literary life in Edinburgh until 1796. Thereafter he moved to Neidpath near Peebles, where he lived for four years before retiring to St. Andrews. In good health almost to the last, Ferguson died in his 93rd year and was buried in the grounds of the old cathedral.

Social history. Ferguson is remembered today for his *Essay on the History of Civil Society* (1767) rather than for his contributions to moral philosophy or Roman history; he was what we should now call an intellectual historian, tracing the gradual rise of the human mind from barbarism to political and social refinement. Regarded in this way, his life's work reveals a unity based on his conviction that the interrelation of man and society is of prime importance. Debates between Reid, Dugald Stewart, Hume, Adam Smith, Lord Kames, and Ferguson himself reveal

Scottish philosophy, in general, to be important sociologically. Ferguson's thought was part of a general eighteenth-century movement, stimulated by the French, built upon English empirical traditions, and hostile to Cartesian speculation. The most characteristic tendency of this movement was inquiry into the nature and origin of society as the hub around which philosophy revolves. Ferguson is sometimes considered the father of modern systematic sociology, and although he himself was soon forgotten amidst the antiempirical reactions of Hegelian disciples, the influence of the philosophical group to which he belonged was attested to by such nineteenth-century political thinkers as Comte, Mill, and Marx. Like his contemporaries, however, Ferguson believed that society was approaching a state of perfection and that such a state could be maintained, so that, in general, his philosophy had little to offer his successors. Nevertheless, his discussions of politics, economics, history, aesthetics, literature, and ethnology were a synthesis of the thought of his time. He emphasized the role of observation and treated his subject phenomenologically, not evaluatively.

Another estimate of Ferguson is less flattering. He offered no distinct sociological method or any quantitative or statistical approach; at no point did he try to analyze society's psychology; instead he proposed a psychological interpretation of a dynamic process. It must be admitted that he was essentially a historian, or historical sociologist, who attempted few generalizations and in no way anticipated the nineteenth-century view of social evolution as a part of cosmic or universal evolution. Ferguson's philosophy of social development looked back to the early sixteenth century, and his role of polyhistor totally involved him in the speculative fashions of Augustan Edinburgh. The movement of which he and his contemporaries brought up the rear guard was a positive, factual, and intellectual endeavor, based on the methodology of scientific discovery and treating human affairs on mechanistic assumptions, practically in the manner of physics.

The interdependence of all human institutions and all functions of society was the center of Ferguson's philosophy; he said, "Social appetite in human souls is the great spring and source of moral actions." In this he diverged from Hobbes and Hume, who founded morals in utility, from Adam Smith's theory of sympathy, and from the moral sense of Shaftesbury and Hutcheson; but he did try to reconcile all three systems of morals and to incorporate them into his own principle of perfection ("the desire of something better than is possessed at present"), which, controlled by man's functional intelligence, governs standards of conduct.

Ethics and politics. Ferguson's doctrine of ethics, although not original, is a noteworthy attempt to establish a comprehensive system based on a perfectionist principle of moral approbation. The sanctions of this fundamental law of morality are of two kinds: those which need to be enforced and those which may be left to operate on the free will of the agent. The first are the subject of jurisprudence, the laws of peace and war; the second relate to the duties of man, founded on natural law. In his treatment of politics, Ferguson upheld the liberal spirit and opposed despotism. His egalitarian views, stimulated by Montesquieu, were modified after his early enthusiasm for the French Revolution had waned. In *Principles of Moral and Political Science* (1792), he admitted that certain inequalities protested against by the advocates of "liberty" and a rankless society were after all necessary. Like Montesquieu, Ferguson ascribed to climate and situation a great influence on the literature, commerce, and policy of nations. His moral system was a Stoic one, and his idealization of the Roman warrior spirit marks his emphasis on the role of conflict in social life, a factor which, although perceptible in earlier political theories such as those of Machiavelli and Hobbes, was not stressed before Ferguson.

Principal Works by Ferguson

A Sermon Preached in the Ersh Language. London, 1746.
The Morality of Stage Plays Seriously Considered. London, 1757.
History of the Proceedings in the Case of Margaret commonly called Peg, only lawful Sister to John Bull, Esq. London, 1761.
Analysis of Pneumatics and Moral Philosophy. London, 1761.
"On the Principle of Moral Estimation: a Discourse between David Hume, Robert Clerk and Adam Smith," E. C. Mossner, ed. *Journal of the History of Ideas*, Vol. 21, No. 2 (1960), 222–232. An unpublished manuscript by Ferguson, written probably in 1761.
An Essay on the History of Civil Society. Edinburgh, 1767.
Institutes of Moral Philosophy. Edinburgh, 1769.
Remarks on a pamphlet lately published by Dr. Price, entitled Observations on the Nature of Civil Liberty. London, 1776.
History of the Progress and Formation of the Roman Republic. London, 1783.
Principles of Moral and Political Science. Edinburgh, 1792.
Minutes of the Life and Character of Joseph Black. London, 1801.

Works on Ferguson

Chastaing, Maxime, "Reid, la philosophie du sens commun et le problème de la connaissance d'autrui." *Revue philosophique de la France et de l'étranger*, Vol. 144 (1954), 352–399. Examines the distinctive qualities of Scottish philosophy.
Cousin, Victor, *Cours d'histoire de la philosophie morale au dix-huitième siècle.* Paris, 1839–1840. Contains an exhaustive appreciation of Ferguson's political philosophy.
Graham, H. G., *Scottish Men of Letters in the Eighteenth Century.* London, 1901. Devotes part of a chapter to Ferguson's literary life.
Lehmann, W. C., *Adam Ferguson and the Beginnings of Modern Sociology.* New York, 1930. Contains a selective bibliography.
Mossner, E. C., *The Life of David Hume.* Edinburgh and London, 1955. Gives a general account of the period.
Small, J., *Transactions of the Royal Society of Edinburgh.* 1864. Vol. 23, Ch. 3. A biographical memoir by the then librarian of the university.

A. M. KINGHORN

FERRARA, FRANCIS SYLVESTER OF. See SYLVESTER OF FERRARA, FRANCIS.

FERRI, LUIGI (1826–1895), Italian epistemologist and historian of philosophy, was born in Bologna. He studied at Paris and was professor of the history of philosophy at Florence and at Rome. A self-styled disciple of Terenzio Mamiani, Ferri contributed to Mamiani's journal, *La filosofia delle scuole italiana*, and continued editing the journal, under the title *Rivista italiana di filosofia*, from the death of Mamiani in 1885 until his own death in Rome in 1895.

Ferri's philosophizing moved within the framework of Italian ontologism, which saw in man the capacity for a direct and "intuitive" relationship with the Absolute (Being or God), but his interest focused principally on the psychological conditions in which this relationship takes shape. His investigations, therefore, had as their object man's interior experience, the "inner (or intimate) sense" of which Maine de Biran spoke. To the latter Ferri owed his basic inspirations. Reproving associationist psychology for reducing the spirit, or self, to an associative mechanism that takes no account of the activity of consciousness, Ferri tried to bring to light the function of this activity. He saw this activity as a kind of force or energy that "by making itself its own object, determines its modes according to rules proper to itself, proposes goals, directs and oversees its own work, and frees itself finally from the influence of sensation and emotive impressions so as to find truth with the intellect and to reproduce in itself, with ideas and the evidence of experience, the world of phenomena."

Ferri used the term *dynamism* to refer to the conception that the substance of both the physical and the spiritual worlds is energy and that in both of these worlds energy is regulated by the same laws of conservation. Thus there is a "permanence in the quantity, quality, and relationships of the spiritual world" just as there is a permanence in the amount of matter and energy. Ferri also held that only the energy regulating the spiritual world is known or immediately given to man in the act of consciousness; the actions of energy operating in the external world are known to man only indirectly, i.e., by the effects they have upon this act through sense perception. The unity of the universal energy is, however, the sole theme of metaphysics.

Works by Ferri

Essai sur l'histoire de la philosophie en Italie au dix-neuvième siècle, 2 vols. Paris, 1869. Traces the development of Italian philosophy from the sensationalism of the eighteenth century to the ontologism or idealism of the nineteenth, represented by Rosmini, Gioberti, and Mamiani.
La psicologia di Pietro Pomponazzi. Rome, 1877. Contains a previously unpublished commentary by Pomponazzi on Aristotle's *De Anima.*
La Psychologie de l'association depuis Hobbes jusqu'à nos jours, histoire et critique. Paris, 1883.
In the *Atti dell'Academia dei Lincei*, of which Ferri was a member: *Analisi del concetto di sostanza e sue relazione con i concetti di essenza, di causa, e di forza; contributo al dinamismo filosofico* (1885); *Il fenomeno sensibile e la percezione esteriore ossia i fondamenti del realismo* (1886); *Dell'idea del vero e sue relazione con l'idea dell'essere* (1887); *Dell'idea dell'essere* (1888).

Works on Ferri

Barzellotti, G., "Luigi Ferri." *Nuova Antologia* (1895).
Gentile, G., *Le origini della filosofia contemporanea in Italia*, Vol. 1, pp. 215–233. Messina, 1917.

NICOLA ABBAGNANO
Translated by *Nino Langiulli*

FERRIER, JAMES FREDERICK (1808–1864), Scottish metaphysician, was born in Edinburgh into a wealthy family of lawyers. After studying at the universities of Edinburgh and Oxford, he spent some months in Germany. He settled in Edinburgh in 1832 as an advocate, becoming active in the intellectual circle of Sir William

Hamilton, which included Thomas De Quincey and "Christopher North" of *Blackwood's Magazine*. Under this stimulus Ferrier contributed to *Blackwood's* between 1838 and 1843 the 11 long articles that fill most of the second volume of his *Lectures and Remains* (2 vols., Edinburgh and London, 1866). In 1845 he was appointed professor of moral philosophy and political economy at the University of St. Andrews. Ferrier issued a drastically revised version of his philosophy in the *Institutes of Metaphysic* (Edinburgh and London, 1854; 2d ed., 1856). The *Institutes* was to some extent affected by Ferrier's commitments in the political and ecclesiastical struggles that then divided Scotland. This social influence is still more marked in the pamphlet defending his position, *Scottish Philosophy, the Old and the New* (Edinburgh, 1856). Meanwhile, Ferrier elaborated, until incapacitated in 1861, on an impressive series of lectures on Greek philosophy, posthumously published as Volume I of *Lectures and Remains*.

The first seven *Blackwood's* articles constitute a unitary work on the philosophy of consciousness. Its starting point is a critique of Thomas Brown's doctrine that it is wrong to regard states of mind, such as emotions, as objects of consciousness. Brown argued that to speak of being conscious of feeling angry is the same thing as to speak of feeling angry. Ferrier pointed out that there is a marked difference between speaking of someone as boiling with rage and speaking of him as being conscious of the boiling rage within him. In the latter case, instead of looking outward at the injustice and brooding on the affront, he looks inward at the consequent irritation in his heart and ceases to brood.

Thus far Ferrier was merely making an intelligent use of the doctrine of the inverse variation of feeling and knowledge proposed by his friend Sir William Hamilton. But as Sir William noted with approval, Ferrier then went beyond the customary limits of British philosophy by asking what is involved in the shift from unself-conscious anger to self-conscious anger. This self-knowledge does not arise straightforwardly out of ordinary experience. The use of the first personal pronoun, which is the mark of self-knowledge in the proper sense, is something that cannot be learned from the experience of other people and their talk in the same imitative way as the use of a word like "table" can. The indubitability of self-knowledge arises just because it is not based on observation in the same way that our knowledge of mountains is. Therefore, Ferrier concluded, there is something anomalous about the foundations of self-knowledge. What is it?

In his four *Blackwood's* articles on the subject of sense perception, contributed between 1841 and 1843, Ferrier gave his problem a definite form by limiting it. To gain light on the nature of self-knowledge he looked into the foundations of the ordinary distinction between act of sense and object of sense. Ferrier's discussion is brilliantly original. The key to the difficulty is that as long as we view each sense field in isolation, no proper distinction can be drawn between the act and the object of sense. Within the visual field alone vision does not stand out as empirically separable from the colors seen; within the tactual field the effort of feeling presents itself as indistinguishable from the solids felt. But when the sense fields are viewed in correlation with one another, seeing separates itself from the colors seen as being connected with something tangible but not visible: the eye. Similarly, feeling distinguishes itself from solidity by being vested in an organ of touch revealed by vision rather than by touch. Ferrier thus argued that the key to self-experience is the peculiar experience of appropriating one's own body in the sense of correlating one's own sense organs. This is reminiscent of Merleau-Ponty and Sartre. Like them, Ferrier developed the theme of human freedom, first by reference to the contrast between reflective experience and prereflective experience, then by reference to the contrast between the experience of one's own body and the experience of foreign bodies.

Ferrier was stimulated by Schelling and Hegel, but there is a distinctive originality to his position in his attempt to give life and definiteness to their ideas by viewing them in terms of the problems of philosophy posed by Hamilton and Thomas Brown. As De Quincey said, Ferrier's philosophy is "German philosophy refracted through a Scottish medium."

Ferrier's highly original early efforts have been overshadowed for posterity by the respectable academic contributions of his later life. In his *Institutes of Metaphysic* he moved from a "phenomenological" standpoint, inherited from Reid by way of Hamilton and Victor Cousin, to a narrowly a priori point of view which, distinguishing sharply between necessary and contingent truth, would restrict philosophy to necessary truth. As a result, the *Institutes of Metaphysic* omits the analysis of self-knowledge and the experience of one's own body that distinguishes the *Blackwood's* articles, confining itself to well-worn doctrines that can be expounded in an a priori way, such as the Cartesian *cogito* and a verifiability principle not unlike that of modern positivism. But Ferrier's later work should not be underestimated. It contains remarkably illuminating discussions of the relations of universals and particulars (rather like that in Mansel), which is carried further in the *Lectures on Greek Philosophy*. In this work there is also an extremely impressive analysis of the experience of change and movement that in one way anticipates Bergson and in another way looks back to Hegel.

Ferrier's later work was very influential in the late nineteenth century in the English-speaking world and to some extent in France. In particular, the *Institutes of Metaphysic* provided Shadworth Hodgson with his starting point and most of his leading ideas. Ferrier's early work, unfortunately, escaped notice in the nineteenth century, but a re-evaluation of it has begun.

Works by Ferrier

Ferrier's works are collected in the three-volume *Philosophical Works* (Edinburgh, 1875).

Works on Ferrier

Arthur Thomson's article "The Philosophy of J. F. Ferrier," in *Philosophy*, Vol. 39 (1964), 46–62, re-evaluates Ferrier's early work. There is a short biography by E. S. Haldane, *James Frederick Ferrier* (Edinburgh, 1894). See also *The Democratic Intellect*, by G. E. Davie (Edinburgh, 1961).

GEORGE E. DAVIE

FEUERBACH, LUDWIG ANDREAS (1804–1872), German philosopher, theologian, and moralist, was born in Landshut, Bavaria. He studied theology at Heidelberg and Berlin and then, in 1825, under the influence of Hegel, transferred to the faculty of philosophy. He received his doctorate in 1828 at Erlangen, where he remained to teach as docent until 1832. In 1830 he published anonymously at Nuremberg a work—*Gedanken über Tod und Unsterblichkeit*—that created a minor scandal by interpreting Christianity as an egoistic and inhumane religion. When his authorship of this book became known, he was dismissed from the faculty. In 1836 he retired to Bruckberg, where he lived on a modest pension from the Bavarian government, income from his writings, and revenue provided by his wife's interest in a pottery factory.

Between 1836 and 1843 he collaborated with Arnold Ruge on Ruge's *Hallische Jahrbücher für deutsche Wissenschaft und Kunst*, in which many of Feuerbach's most important early writings on religion and philosophy first appeared. He broke with Ruge when the latter began collaboration with Karl Marx on the *Deutsch-französische Jahrbücher*, although he contributed to the one issue of that journal. He reappeared briefly in academic life in 1848–1849, lecturing to audiences of intellectuals and workers at Heidelberg at the request of students, for whom he had become a symbol of liberal thought.

With the failure of the Frankfurt Assembly and the defeat of liberalism in Germany, Feuerbach retired once more to Bruckberg, where he devoted himself to the study of the natural sciences, the composition of a monumental *Theogonie* (Leipzig, 1857), and a voluminous correspondence with friends and admirers all over Europe. In 1860 his wife's pottery factory failed, and Feuerbach removed his family to Nuremberg, where he was forced to live off the generosity of his friends. In 1867 he suffered the first of a number of strokes that finally killed him.

Works. Feuerbach's most important works—"Zur Kritik der Hegelschen Philosophie" (in the *Hallische Jahrbücher*, 1839), *Das Wesen des Christentums* (Leipzig, 1841; translated by M. Evans [George Eliot], London, 1854), *Grundsätze der Philosophie der Zukunft* (Zurich and Winterthur, 1843), and *Das Wesen der Religion* (Leipzig, 1846)—were produced in his early years. They were meant to expose the contradictions in Hegelian philosophy, to establish the "illusionistic" character of all religious belief, and to plead for a "new philosophy," based on anthropology and physiology, that would provide the foundation of a naturalistic–humanistic ethic. His criticism of Hegelianism served as the point of departure for the so-called left Hegelians, of whom Marx and Engels were the most important representatives.

Criticism of Hegelianism. Feuerbach's critique of Hegelianism proceeded not from sympathy for "obtuse materialism," under which term he grouped Newtonian science, empiricism, and positivism alike, but rather from his discovery of contradictions in Hegel's own system. The resolution of these contradictions would, he believed, allow the establishment of a "new philosophy," which, while remaining thoroughly materialistic, would accommodate those insights into the operations of human consciousness that constituted Hegelianism's definitive contribution to human self-knowledge.

Feuerbach viewed Hegelianism as the culmination of modern rationalism, and he believed that "the secret of Hegel," as of all rationalism, lay in an essentially religious spirit concealed beneath an apparent denial of all transcendence. This hidden religious element accounted for the degradation of the material world, of man, and of the senses that was characteristic of Hegel's metaphysics, ethics, and epistemology, respectively. In Hegel's thought, however, the means were provided for finally transcending all of the religious residues in modern philosophy. For Hegel's attempt to sustain simultaneously the primacy of intellect and the necessity of reason's realizing itself in matter results in the negation of the Hegelian system itself in the interest of a materialistic metaphysics, a humanistic ethics, and a sensible (*sinnliche*) epistemology, the bases of the "philosophy of the future."

Development of modern philosophy. Feuerbach believed that modern philosophy had followed a pattern of development set by theology. The attempt of theology to establish the relationship between the sensible attributes of God and the extrasensible sphere in which he exists necessarily led to pantheism, which makes matter an attribute of God or defines God (as did Spinoza) as "extended essence" and thus ends by deifying matter itself. In fact, pantheism is "theological atheism," the discovery by theology that matter is the sole reality, and hence it foreshadows the ultimate self-dissolution of religion.

Empiricism had already discovered that matter was the sole reality, but only in a practical, not in a theoretical, sense, for in making "mere" matter the sole reality it was unable to deal with the data of human consciousness. Rationalism, however, of which idealism was the necessary outcome, underwent a secularized development from theism as a divinization of spirit to pantheism as the self-dissolution of spirit. Idealism was nothing but an attempt to salvage God by vesting full epistemic authority in consciousness, intellect, or reason at the expense of the senses. Yet because it was overtly secularist, rationalism had to account for the world discovered by the senses. It could do this only by affirming, as Kant did, an absolute hiatus between the world of intellect, to which it ascribed all truth, and the world of sense, to which it granted reality. Hegel tried to close this gap between truth and reality, but he could do so only by extending the Cartesian divinization of Reason to the world as a whole. The result was a transition from Kantian "rational theism, theism rationalized" to Hegelian "pantheistic idealism."

Reason in Hegel. In affirming the rationality of the real and the reality of the rational, Hegel, according to Feuerbach, elevated reason to the status of "absolute essence." Then, to account for the existence of the spatiotemporal world, he had to hold simultaneously that matter is the negation of thought and that thought can only "realize itself" by becoming matter. To Feuerbach this showed that on Hegel's own terms "thought presupposes, without being aware of it, that truth is reality, sensibility independent of thought." On the one hand Hegel viewed sensibility as "an attribute of the idea," whereas on the other he maintained that it is "an attribute without which thought has no truth"; that is, he had to hold that it is "at one and the same time central and marginal, essence and accident."

According to Feuerbach, idealism knew implicitly that "truth, reality, and sensibility are identical," but it suppressed this truth in order to subordinate the sensible world to an absolute being endowed with the attributes of the human ego, that is, with consciousness and reason. This led idealism to assert that the thinking of the absolute being is real, whereas that of the finite sensible being, man, is not. According to Hegel, human reason is nothing but the self-revelation of the absolute being to itself. Thus, Feuerbach exclaimed, Hegel "alienates and expropriates from man his typical essence and activity!"

Primacy of human consciousness. Feuerbach's own "new philosphy" began with the axiom "Only a sensible being is a real, true being," standing the Hegelian position on its feet so that its truth could be seen aright. "The true relation of thought to being is only this," he wrote in the *Vorläufige Thesen*: "being is the subject, thought the predicate. Thought is a product of being, not being of thought. . . . The essence of being as being is the essence of nature." The consciousness deified by Hegel, like the reason deified by Descartes and Kant and the Matter deified by Spinoza, "is our ego, our intellect, our essence: and this God is no God in itself, but only the appearance of ourselves to ourselves." Hence, the lasting contribution of idealism to philosophy is its analysis, under the aspect of an examination of the absolute being, of the operations of human consciousness, the reality of which is denied by simple empiricism. Hegelianism, like all metaphysics, is nothing but "esoteric psychology."

Materialism and idealism. Unlike conventional materialism the new philosophy granted ontological and epistemological status to consciousness and intellect, and unlike idealism it accorded reality to matter. But it deified neither matter nor consciousness. For according to Feuerbach, it is wrong to say, with the materialist, that "man is distinguished from the brute *only* by consciousness"; in fact, "in a being which awakes to consciousness, there takes place a qualitative change, a differentiation of the entire nature." Yet this "qualitative change" in no way justifies the idealist contention that man is consciousness alone, "for as man belongs to the essence of Nature,—in opposition to common materialism; so Nature belongs to the essence of man,—in opposition to subjective idealism."

Man. Every attempt to specify the essence of man by deriving his material from his spiritual nature, or vice versa, is therefore mistaken, in Feuerbach's view. The task of philosophy is to encounter man in his situation, as that part of nature endowed with consciousness which seeks to realize its own peculiar essence through specific kinds of relationships with the rest of nature and with other members of its species. Feuerbach's philosophy assumed only that "I am a real, sensible essence: the body is constituted of my essence; indeed the body in its totality is my ego, my existence itself." It recognized that man's essence reveals itself quintessentially in the impulse toward union with other men: "The essence of man is contained only in community, in the unity of man with man—a unity which however is founded only on the reality of the differences between I and thou." To comprehend human action and thought one must take account of man's capacity to transcend the limited responses of the lower animals to their environment.

Philosophy, properly studied, then, is "the complete, coherent, and absolute resolution of theology into anthropology. . . ." It takes man as the culmination of the natural process and defines him as "universal essence" and then concentrates on the study of the totality of his responses to the rest of the world. Among these responses will be found the passions, especially the emotion of love, the impulse toward "union" with the "other" that is peculiar to man. The capacity to create communities of shared emotive contents is the secret of man and therefore the secret of all thought and action; for what men are really seeking in every imagined absolute is nothing but the "unity of I and thou."

Religion. All of this is assumed in Feuerbach's studies of religion and lies at the base of his "unmasking" of Christian beliefs in *Das Wesen des Christentums,* his most celebrated work.

Feuerbach regarded religion as one of the forms of human thought and action by which man raised himself above the animal. Beginning with the assumption of D. F. Strauss that religion, myth, ritual, and dogma tell us more about the inner lives of individual men than about their presumed object of worship, Feuerbach tried to determine the purely human significance of all mythological thought. He professed to be a uniformitarian in religious matters—that is, he denied that past religious experiences differ from those that can be observed in the present—thus anticipating the approach to religious experience of both James and Freud. Like them, he claimed to be rigidly empirical in method. "I found my ideas on materials which can be appropriated through the senses," he wrote in the 1843 preface to *Das Wesen des Christentums*; "I do not generate the object from the thought, but the thought from the object; and I hold that alone to be a proper object which has an existence beyond one's brain. . . . I am nothing but a natural philosopher in the domain of the mind."

His study led him to conclude that religion is a form of the projective spirit in man, the means by which man "projects his being into objectivity, and then again makes himself an object to this projected image of himself thus converted into a subject, he thinks of himself not as an object to himself but as an object of an object, of another being than himself." Thus, religion is "the dream of the human mind"; properly understood, it is a dream of human, not divine, development: "it is and can be nothing else than the consciousness which man has of his own—not finite and limited—but infinite nature." Man, then, unlike the animal, is self-transcending, and religion is one of man's means of objectifying his own essence in ideal terms, of spinning out visions of what he might be. For example, the Christian idea of the Incarnation is nothing but a reflection of the dream of man to become God and the realization that this can be achieved only through a transcendent love of one's fellow man.

Religious feelings thus depend on an alienation of man

from himself. Religion generates belief in an objective "other" in which all of man's best qualities are vested, his worst qualities being designated as the true human essence. Philosophy must therefore "destroy an illusion" that deprives man of the power of a free life as well as a genuine sense of truth and virtue, "for even love, in itself the deepest, truest emotion, becomes by means of religiousness merely ostensible, illusory, since religious love gives itself to man only for God's sake, so that it is given only in appearance to man, but in reality to God." In short, for Feuerbach religion is the uncontrolled and unconscious exercise of a human faculty that with the aid of the sciences of anthropology, physiology, and psychology can be controlled, raised to consciousness, and turned toward the attainment of genuine health, well-being, and community here on earth. For "the consciousness of God is nothing but the consciousness of the species."

Influence. Feuerbach was little concerned with political polemics, for which Marx and Engels vehemently criticized him, but his work served as an inspiration for those who were trying to work out a realistic program of reform in Germany during the middle decades of the century. Many of his dicta became dogmata for the radical movement, as for example the 1850 statement: "The doctrine of foods is of great ethical and political significance. Food becomes blood, blood becomes heart and brain, thoughts and mind-stuff. Human fare is the foundation of human culture and thought. Would you improve a nation? Give it, instead of declamations against sin, better food. Man is what he eats" (quoted in Höffding, *History of Modern Philosophy*, London, 1900, Vol. II, p. 281). But his main concern remained the mystery of the transformation of "human fare" into human thought. This mystery was the basis of his naturalistic humanism, which Marx and Engels regarded as merely a vestige of the old idealism. According to Marx's "Theses on Feuerbach," Feuerbach resolved "the essence of religion into the essence of *man*," and Marx protested that "the essence of man is no abstraction inherent in each separate individual. In its reality it is the ensemble of social relations." The judgment was basically correct. Feuerbach, though he resolved Hegelianism into psychology, made of consciousness itself a mystery, if not a miracle.

By 1850 Feuerbach's star had already set. The future of materialism in Germany lay with mechanists such as Büchner on the one hand and with Marx on the other. Engels was right in saying, "With one blow, [Feuerbach] pulverized the contradiction [of idealism] and without circumlocutions . . . placed materialism on the throne again. . . ." But he was also right in noting that Feuerbach "stopped halfway; the lower half of him was materialist, the upper half idealist. . . ." Feuerbach's "destruction" of Hegelianism was less important than the way he carried it out, since this destruction was the sport of almost every significant thinker in the Germany of his day. But because he generated materialism out of Hegel himself, Feuerbach provided the means by which German thought could become "scientific" while still indulging its overriding interest in historical processes. Thus, his work inspired both Marx and Engels, but it also laid the foundation for that phenomenological anthropology that has made him a source of information and insights for such modern philosophers as Heidegger, Sartre, and Karl Barth.

Works by Feuerbach

Ludwig Feuerbach Sämtliche Werke, Wilhelm Bolin and Friedrich Jodl, eds., 10 vols. Stuttgart, 1903–1910. New and augmented ed., 12 vols. Stuttgart, 1959–1960. The complete works of Feuerbach, accompanied by a full *apparatus criticus* and biographical and bibliographical information on writings both by and about him.
The Essence of Christianity, translated by M. Evans, new ed. New York, 1957. Contains a chapter on Feuerbach from Barth's *Theologie und die Kirche*.

Works on Feuerbach

Barth, K., *Die protestantische Theologie im 19. Jahrhundert*. Zurich, 1952. Translated by Brian Cozens as *Protestant Thought from Rousseau to Ritschl*. New York, 1959.
Barth, K., *Die Theologie und die Kirche*, Vol. II, pp. 212–239. Zurich, 1928. Translated by L. P. Smith as *Theology and Church*. New York, 1962.
Chamberlain, W. B., *Heaven Wasn't His Destination: The Philosophy of Ludwig Feuerbach*. London, 1941.
Cornu, A., *Moses Hess et la gauche hégélienne*. Paris, 1934.
Engels, F., *Ludwig Feuerbach und der Ausgang der klassischen deutschen Philosophie*. Stuttgart, 1888. Translated as *Ludwig Feuerbach and the Outcome of Classical German Philosophy*, C. P. Dutt, ed. New York, 1934.
Grégoire, F., *Aux Sources de la pensée de Marx*. Paris, 1947.
Grün, K., *Ludwig Feuerbach in seinem Briefwechsel und Nachlasse*, 2 vols. Leipzig, 1874.
Hook, S., *From Hegel to Marx*. New York, 1936.
Jodl, F., *Ludwig Feuerbach*. Stuttgart, 1904.
Lévy, A., *La Philosophie de Feuerbach*. Paris, 1904.
Löwith, K., *Von Hegel zu Nietzsche*. Stuttgart, 1941.
Marcuse, H., *Reason and Revolution*. London and New York, 1941.
Nüdling, Gregor, "Die Auflosung des Gott-Menschenverhältnis bei Ludwig Feuerbach," in *Der Mensch vor Gott*. Düsseldorf, 1948.
Nüdling, Gregor, *Ludwig Feuerbachs Religionsphilosophie*. Paderborn, Germany, 1936.
Rawidowicz, S., *Ludwig Feuerbachs Philosophie*. Berlin, 1931.
Tucker, R., *Philosophy and Myth in Karl Marx*. Cambridge, 1960.

HAYDEN V. WHITE

FICHTE, JOHANN GOTTLIEB (1762–1814), German philosopher and exponent of ethical idealism, was born in Rammenau, Lusatia, and died in Berlin. The son of a ribbon-maker, he was the eldest of a large family of children. As a child he herded geese. However, he gave very early promise of a remarkably retentive mind, and a fortunate incident gave him a chance for an education. A Baron von Miltitz had arrived in Rammenau one Sunday too late for the sermon, but someone suggested to him that little Fichte could "re-preach" it to him verbatim. The child did this so well that Miltitz decided to adopt him and send him to school. After several years of private instruction at the home of a pastor, the boy was sent to the school of Pforta. His first years there were trying, on account of harsh discipline and unsatisfactory personal relations, but later he gained the good will of his teachers and schoolmates, graduated with distinction in 1780, and proceeded to the University of Jena, and from there to the universities of Wittenberg and Leipzig. Baron von Miltitz had died, inadequately providing for the young man's education, and eventually Fichte was thrown upon his own resources. Thus began a career clouded by serious economic privation, with intervals of academic and literary success, first at Jena and later in Berlin.

Influences on Fichte. Fichte had always had a strong moral and religious turn of mind, and at Jena he had registered as a student of theology, but his free and critical approach to all ideas increasingly directed him toward philosophy. Of the three thinkers who had the greatest influence upon his mental development (namely, Lessing, Spinoza, and Kant), the third proved decisive. Lessing's championship of untrammeled freedom of thought and of an education and social culture of tolerance inspired Fichte's mental attitude and plan of action. Even more influential in Fichte's development was Lessing's stress on the supreme importance of creative spiritual endeavor. The study of Lessing led Fichte to Spinoza, whose pantheism made a lasting impression upon his own systematic philosophical development. But by far the most vital influence upon Fichte resulted from his somewhat later study of Kant, especially of Kant's moral philosophy.

"Critique of All Revelation." At the conclusion of his university studies Fichte experienced financial difficulties and some downright indigence, from which he got temporary relief in 1788 by securing employment as a tutor in the home of a rich hotelkeeper in Zurich. Beyond providing him with temporary self-support, his years in Zurich expanded his social contacts. He became intimate with the leading pastor, Johann Kaspar Lavater, with whom he shared moral and religious ideals and an enthusiasm for the poetry of Klopstock. Lavater introduced him to the family of Inspector Rahn, whose daughter Johanna immediately inspired Fichte's love. But no academic post was in sight, and his plans to edit a journal were no more promising than his other literary projects.

While his personal prospects were disheartening to him and to his hopes of marrying Johanna, the direction of his lifework as a thinker reached a decisive turn at this time with a study of Kant, and particularly of the *Critique of Practical Reason* (1788). With great anticipation, Fichte journeyed to Königsberg to meet Kant and to learn further from him, but the aged philosopher proved at first disappointingly unresponsive. Fichte resolved to gain Kant's interest with a sample of his own philosophical work; by summoning intense concentration he wrote his *Critique of All Revelation* (*Versuch einer Kritik aller Offenbarung*, Königsberg, 1792) and inscribed it to "The Philosopher." In this work Fichte applied Kant's ethical principle of respect for duty, which he had adopted as central to his own moral philosophy, to the interpretation of religion. Fichte maintained that revealed religion expressed the recognition in ourselves of an imperative spiritual principle not derived from our empirical nature but sovereign in our lives. This is the true supernatural revealed in our natures, the divine authority of the moral law; the practical acknowledgment of it in our obedience to God's will strengthens our moral resolution and is exalted in divine worship.

Professorship at Jena. When Kant had read Fichte's manuscript, he received the young disciple most graciously and expressed an interest in the publication of the new

work. Through some mischance that has never been explained, Fichte's *Critique* appeared anonymously, but this mishap actually proved the turning point in his career. The reading public mistook the work for a fourth *Critique* by Kant, and it gained immediate wide reception. Kant disavowed authorship, but wrote very favorably of the young author. Goethe's newly aroused interest in Fichte was shared by his fellow councilors at the court of Weimar, and, as there was a vacancy on the philosophical faculty of Weimar's University of Jena, in 1794 the 32-year-old Fichte received and accepted a call to a professorship. Meanwhile, during the previous October he and Johanna Rahn had married.

Thus began the second period in Fichte's life. From the outset he found a hearty welcome from the university community. The poet Friedrich Schiller, professor of history, proved a friendly colleague. Fichte's lectures were highly successful; in two semesters, his classes grew from attendance by a bare score to some two hundred, so that he needed the largest available classroom. His letters of the period reflect great satisfaction and bright hopes for the future. But this early success was brief; before long, it was shaken by growing resistance from students, colleagues, and clerics. In their judgment, Fichte was too rigorous in his moral demands and too radical in his political and religious ideas. His censures alienated disorderly students and lax professors. His sociopolitical ideas—expressed during the last decade of the century, the decade of the French Revolution—alarmed the conservative monarchists. In his Zurich years he had already responded vigorously to the spirit of republicanism with which multitudes of German youths and many of their elders later hailed the collapse of the French monarchy. He had endeavored to justify and defend the true principles and motives of the revolution against its detractors in terms which had impressed many of his readers as being subversively democratic. Now in Jena he was reported as having declared from his professorial chair that kings and princes would cease to exist within twenty or thirty years.

Atheismusstreit. Fichte's religious views were equally disturbing to traditional orthodoxy. In his *Critique of All Revelation* he had explored the basis of religion in the imperative supremacy of the moral law. This ethical conception of religion led him to a reinterpretation of the idea of God. Belief in God, he held, is essentially a recognition of the fundamental and sovereign moral dynamic in reality. The exposition of these ideas in Fichte's lectures and writings aroused severe opposition. His ambiguity regarding a personal deity and his apparently pantheistic leanings did not shock Goethe, who had for years carried Spinoza's *Ethics* in his pocket; but in the judgment of many Lutheran theologians, the Jena professor was headed for atheism. While he was admonishing students against their unseemly revels and duels, his own teachings were apparently misleading many sons of godly families into paths of infidelity. Instead of going to church they attended his Sunday lectures. Ecclesiastic and civic officials pressed first for a restriction and then for a termination of Fichte's activities in Jena. He stood his ground, unyielding both on principle and by temperament, rejecting the charge of atheism and refusing to alter his course of teaching and the publication of his ideas. The conflict could not be resolved and in 1799 Fichte was forced to leave the university. Some of the students supported him actively, but their appeals in his behalf were unavailing. His friends, among them Goethe, while admiring his personal integrity and his intellectual mastery, deplored his unbending rigor. (For a more detailed account of Fichte's career and conflicts at the University of Jena, see ATHEISMUSSTREIT.)

Fichte's remaining years. It was now the period of Germany's struggle of resistance to Napoleon's spreading power. In Fichte's career, these years of professional insecurity were also years of the most resolute devotion to his chosen purposes, both in the systematic development of his philosophy and in his popular and eloquent appeals to the German nation to sustain and reaffirm itself in its cultural and spiritual vitality. During a temporary residence in Berlin he was at first welcomed by the circle of romantics typified by Friedrich Schlegel, but he could not accept their emotionalism. He demanded of himself and others stern moral commitment.

Eventually Fichte undertook a second important, though brief, academic career. After two short terms of lecturing at the universities of Erlangen and Königsberg and offers from Russian Kharkov and Bavarian Landshut, he was appointed in 1810 as dean of the philosophical faculty at the newly established University of Berlin. The following year he was chosen as rector, but he found the administrative duties of his office uncongenial. More particularly, in Berlin, as at Jena, he showed more rigor than academic statesmanship in dealing with problems of student discipline. He resigned his office as rector and returned to his classroom and public lectures. During the fateful years 1812 and 1813, both he and his wife joined in the national struggle against Napoleon. Johanna, who was serving as a war nurse, fell ill with typhus, from which she recovered; Fichte, however, caught the disease and died from it.

ETHICAL FOUNDATIONS

Fichte's philosophy reflected his personal character, and vice versa; indeed, their interplay determined his career. "The kind of philosophy which one adopts," he wrote, "depends upon the sort of man one is; for a philosophical system is not a lifeless piece of furniture that one might take or discard . . . but it is animated by the soul of the man who has it" (*Werke*, Vol. I, p. 434). In Fichte's own case, the basic motives of his systematic philosophy were the actual dynamics of his personal experience, both in his theoretical activity and in his practical conduct. His career and the resulting crisis at Jena were chapters in his philosophy as well as in his biography. Even before he had formulated his systematic theses of ethical aspiration and commitment, his own spirit was possessed by a demand for an august ideal. He had found this ideal in Kant's ethics of duty, and Fichte himself might have been called a living exemplar of the categorical imperative. His philosophy had a metaphysical basis, but its motivation could not have issued from formally attested principles, but only from inexpugnable convictions of the upright will. To Fichte, the Kantian primacy of practical reason was decisive in metaphysics as well as in ethics. He told Mme. de Staël,

"Grasp my metaphysics, Madame; you will then understand my ethics." He might have explained that his ethics was integral to his view of ultimate reality and expressed the fundamental tenor of his idealism. Both the characteristic worth of his philosophy and certain of its limitations are due to this imperative direction.

METAPHYSICS AND THEORY OF KNOWLEDGE

In Fichte's judgment, the primary truth of idealistic philosophy is that it recognizes the primacy of spiritual activity and its significance. All other philosophies are varieties of what he called dogmatism; they begin with substances—material or mental—with varied contents, from the investigation of which they expect to attain knowledge of the fundamental nature of reality. But basic unity and nature and meaning cannot be comprehended in this derivative way. The unity is itself the immediately real, and it requires initial recognition. Thus, the pre-eminent truth of idealism is that it begins with the ideal activity itself. As Goethe's *Faust* expressed it, "In the beginning was the *Act*."

Fichte designated the theory of knowledge and metaphysics together as the science of knowledge (*Wissenschaftslehre*). His first works on this subject, *Über den Begriff der Wissenschaftslehre* and *Grundlage der gesamten Wissenschaftslehre*, were written in 1794, during his Jena period, and published the same year in Leipzig. These works were revised and developed in a number of other versions with various titles, some of which were published posthumously. The later versions were more idealistic than the earlier ones. One volume was translated by A. E. Kroeger as *The Science of Knowledge* (Philadelphia, 1868, and London, 1889).

Fichte's three fundamental principles. The ethical tone of Fichte's idealism found expression in his fundamental view that reality is ideal activity, underived, and prior to any specific or definable thing, substance, or process. The primary reality of self-existence is in its ideal self-affirmation. As Fichte formulated it, "The Ego posits itself." This is a sort of metaphysical version of the logical law of identity: "A is A." The really and basically existent Ego is the Ego in its self-affirming activity. The absolute and infinite activity evokes and sets for itself a field in which it is to act. In Fichte's terms, "The Ego posits a non-ego." This second positing in no way nullifies the basic and absolute self-affirmation of the Ego, but it involves further differentiation within both the Ego and the non-ego, in the absolute ideal activity, and in its field of operation. In thus setting or positing a range for its activity, the Ego has in fact limited itself. We now have the conditions for definite knowledge, but already we have an opposition-in-relation of the knower and the known, a subject–object dualism. Out of the fundamental metaphysical "opposing" expressed by the second principle, the specific limitations and distinctions of our world, the world that we know, have made their appearance. The conditions of finitude and definition have emerged out of the undefinable ultimate self-activity of the infinite Ego. Therefore Fichte formulated his third principle: "The Ego posits a limited ego in opposition to a limited non-ego."

Moral activity and the limitations of cognitive experience. The subjective "limited ego" of Fichte's third principle is the subject of empirical knowledge. It is always limited by the objective non-ego of its cognitive experience. The limitation is a condition of its more definite manifestation, but it is also a "splitting" (*Spaltung*), a schism in the metaphysical unity of the infinite Ego. We have come home, empirically, but we have come to a divided house. For cognition cannot weld this cleavage of subject and object and achieve a meaningful unity. The object (*Gegenstand*) is also a resistant (*Widenstand*). Only in moral activity can we see the way to a true synthesis. A moral act spans the subject–object dualism. The endeavor to achieve justice is an objective event; it is a striving to overcome that to which we object, namely, injustice; and in its active expression it is the subject's self-revelation and self-affirmation. In every moral action spirit molds nature as it resists nature, and nature is aroused to manifest spirit; the two are radically, that is, at root, one.

Metaphysical voluntarism. The activistic and dynamic voluntarism of the doctrine is evident in the first principle, which expresses the essential reality of the Ego, its primal self-existence as manifested in its self-affirmation. Fichte has been criticized for his second principle because of his inadequate recognition of the objective metaphysical factor, Nature, which in his view is but the Ego's evoked field of operation. But the second principle reaffirms the ethical point of view of Fichte's idealistic metaphysics. The positing of the non-ego is a step in the self-affirmation of the Ego, in its essentially moral-ideal fulfillment. It must be remembered that Fichte's belief in God was belief in an ethical world order, a conviction of a moral dynamic of reality, essentially spiritual in character, which posits an objective range of its self-manifestation. In his third principle, Fichte's quandary of a seeming self-splitting or schism of the Ego only serves to re-emphasize the ethical tenor of his metaphysics. Viewed cognitively, the basic unity of the primal Ego is apparently undone in the subject–object dualism, and the limited non-ego of our knowing consciousness no longer manifests its primal archetype. But here again, in our moral activity the ideal unity is reaffirmed. Fichte traced reality in a voluntaristic metaphysics, from the primal self-affirmation of the absolute Ego to the subject–object integration achieved by the moral will. My will, in its striving and in its unending pursuit of the ideal, expresses both its own limited character, as an empirical ego, and also, in activity according to duty, its essential oneness with the infinite Ego. This communion and union, Fichte's fundamental ideal, was expressed in the successive versions of the *Wissenschaftslehre* with a growing religious emphasis. The conclusion of the *Wissenschaftslehre* of 1810 declared that our real, realized life is not in the blind drive of our empirical impulses but in the higher self-insight and self-commitment to the godly life. Likewise Fichte wrote in *Die Anweisung zum seligen Leben, oder auch die Religionslehre*, "Divinity itself enters again into thee, in its first and original form, as life, as thine own life that thou shouldst live and wilt live."

MORAL PHILOSOPHY

The ethical idealism of Fichte's theory of knowledge and metaphysics found more specific expression in his moral philosophy, notably in such works as *The Science of Ethics as Based on the Science of Knowledge* (*Das System der Sittenlehre nach den Principien der Wissenschaftslehre*, Jena and Leipzig, 1798; English translation by A. E. Kroeger, 2d ed., London, 1907). Moral activity, in his view, is the free, purely dutiful commitment of the will in ideal devotion. The conviction of duty is a challenge to any mere wants or empirical conditions. The dutiful will is the will of our true self, pursuing in unremitting endeavor an expanding goal. In the recognition of any course of action as my duty, I am also expressing a more fully realized recognition of myself. I should never disavow the fulfillment of my duty as being beyond my ability. The true moral reflection is quite the opposite; it takes the form "If I ought, I can."

Freedom and duty. Man's true vocation is to achieve in ever fuller freedom an ever more loyal devotion to his spiritual ideals. Freedom and loyalty alike are unique and personal. The duty to which I am devoted is my duty; the endeavor to recognize and fulfill it is my true being and career. This insight and commitment constitute my conscience, my own self-recognition and my self-expression. The categorical imperative in Fichte's ethics is formulated explicitly in terms of conscientious activity: "Act always in accordance with your best conviction of your duty; or act according to your conscience." As I thus forthrightly play my role in the drama of reality, I also reach towards godliness. True religion is the consummation of moral piety: in our aspiration towards the divine, the Divine itself is actively manifest in us.

The nature of evil. To this view of the moral life as free, dutiful endeavor, Fichte contrasted the actual defectiveness of the empirical self. Evil essentially consists in the laxity or disloyalty of the moral will. Any placidity or routine self-contented stagnation is a denial of our moral career. Any easygoing or cowardly compromise with our bounden duty is a betrayal of our quest. These two evils are in corrupt kinship: laxity and laziness lead to cowardice, and from these two basic vices issues the third, falseness. Fichte's ethics made no concession to the least departure from unqualified veracity: "I positively owe every man absolute frankness and truthfulness." Any plea that a true answer in many cases may have undesirable consequences is a surrender of right principle to expediency and seeming advantage, and such a surrender is never in any circumstance justified.

SOCIAL AND ECONOMIC PHILOSOPHY

Fichte's moral philosophy emphasized the self-achievement of the dutiful will, in utter devotion to ideal ends. But Fichte also viewed this unique career of each person as involved and participating in a social institutional milieu. In the system of actual human conduct one's duties are not merely one's own; they imply acknowledgment of others and of their rights. The purposes and projects of my career cannot be realized in a social vacuum; they affect others and others' claims and rights. These claims and rights, and my relation to them, are not only personal; they affect objective natural conditions in which ethics involves economics. Moral respect for my neighbor precludes violation of what belongs to him, that is, his property rights.

In this ethics of social-economic values, Fichte seems to have been balancing two purposes. One of them was to safeguard the personal moral will from being engrossed and engulfed in cramping material enterprises. That was the ascetic note in his morality: the admonition to hearken, in any circumstances, to the still small voice of conscience, and to observe dutiful integrity in self-expression. His other purpose was to secure for the individual, as well as for the society and the nation, the external conditions of satisfactory self-reliant operation. With this purpose, Fichte advocated, in "The Closed Commercial State" (*Der geschlossene Handelsstaat*, Tübingen, 1800) economic autarchy, the closed commerical state. A nation should balance its economic supply and demand within its own social economy. To prevent any disturbance of that balance by unregulated imports and exports, all foreign trade should be directed by the government. By avoiding both surpluses and scarcity, and using the labor of all to provide for the needs of all, the state can wipe out unemployment and poverty and assure to each citizen the conditions for humane fulfillment.

PHILOSOPHY OF HISTORY

Fichte's ethical idealism also found expression in his philosophy of history. His lectures, *The Characteristics of the Present Age* (*Die Gründzüge des gegenwärtigen Zeitalters*, Berlin, 1806; English translation by W. Smith, London, 1844), traced the historical struggle between instinctive pressures and ideal purposes, and contemplated the progressive, though arduous, increasing influence of reason over instinct. He distinguished five epochs of these contending historical processes: first, unreflective quasi-reasonable conduct; second, authoritarian imposition, by a minority, of laws to control the behavior of the masses; third, the upsurge of lawless instinct defying the restraint of laws; fourth, the gradual recognition and adoption of rational policies in an age of enlightenment; and finally, the full noontide of spiritual humane fulfillment of society. In this historical purview Fichte contemplated his own epoch: was it an age of resistance to authority without the freedom of self-control based on sovereign rational principles, or did it perhaps manifest the higher stage of rational fulfillment? His judgment differed, depending upon his exposition of the decisive marks of historical progress: the subjection of appetites and impulses to laws and principles, and the dynamic conviction of imperative ideal goals. Thus, in his *Addresses to the German Nation* (*Reden an die deutsche Nation*, Berlin, 1808; English translation by R. F. Jones and G. H. Turnbull, Chicago, 1922), which advocated the cultivation of philanthropic devotion as the guiding aim of national university education, he declared that the moral ideal, always sovereign, is never actualized in any historical period: it "never is, but eternally ought to be." Fichte was not concerned with the historical fortunes of social projects or institutions, but rather with their moral worth. What matters is not whether I succeed, but whether I deserve to prevail, whether the end to which I bend my duty really merits my loyal devotion.

FICHTE'S INFLUENCE AND AN EVALUATION

While Fichte's influence upon the course of philosophical thought cannot be compared with that of Kant and Hegel, the ethical emphasis of his idealism, as expressed especially in his popular works, aroused active response in Germany during the crisis of Napoleon's invasions, and also later during the unrest of the mid-century. His moral philosophy of life made a deep impression on Thomas Carlyle and guided the motivation of the latter's gospel of work, notably in *Sartor Resartus*. The distinctive merit, but also some of the shortcomings of Fichte's philosophy, may be ascribed to his moral rigorism. His inflexible commitment to his sovereign principle enabled him thoroughly to explore and elicit the significance of a prevailingly ethical interpretation of reality. But that interpretation did not do justice to the modern scientific view of nature. Fichte's ethical idealism was as one-sided as the materialism which he opposed. The philosophical demand for a rational correlation of causal mechanism and the realm of values required a different cosmic outlook.

Works by Fichte

Sämmtliche Werke, I. H. Fichte, ed., 8 vols. Berlin, 1845–1846.
Nachgelassene Werke, I. H. Fichte, ed., 3 vols. Bonn, 1834–1835; reprinted, Berlin, 1962.
Werke, F. Medicus, ed., 6 vols. Leipzig, 1908–1912 (incomplete), reprinted 1954——.
Briefwechsel, F. Schulz, ed., 2 vols. Leipzig, 1925; 2d ed., 1930.

ENGLISH TRANSLATIONS

Grundlage des Naturrechts. Jena and Leipzig, 1796; English translation by A. E. Kroeger, *The Science of Rights*. Philadelphia, 1869 and London, 1889.
Popular Works, translated by William Smith, ed., 2 vols. London, 1848–1849; 4th ed., London, 1889. Includes translations of *Die Bestimmung des Menschen* and *Die Anweisung zum selingen Leben*.

Biographies and Critical Studies

Adamson, Robert, *Fichte*. Edinburgh and London, 1881.
Everett, C. C., *Fichte's Science of Knowledge; A Critical Exposition*. Chicago, 1884.
Fichte, I. H., *J. G. Fichte's Leben und litterarischer Briefwechsel*. Sulzbach, 1830–1831.
Fischer, Kuno, *Fichtes Leben, Werke und Lehre*, 4th ed. Heidelberg, 1914.
Gurwitsch, Georg, *Fichtes System der Konkreten Ethik*. Tübingen, 1924.
Léon, Xavier, *Fichte et son temps*, 2 vols. bound in 3. Paris, 1922–1927.
Medicus, Fritz, *Fichte*. Berlin, 1905.
Medicus, Fritz, *Fichtes Leben*. Leipzig, 1914; 2d. revised ed., Leipzig, 1922.
Talbot, E. B., *The Fundamental Principle of Fichte's Philosophy*. New York, 1906.
Thompson, A. B., *The Unity of Fichte's Doctrine of Knowledge*. Boston, 1895.

RADOSLAV A. TSANOFF

FICINO, MARSILIO (1433–1499), founder of the Florentine Academy, was born the eldest son of a physician in Figline, near Florence. He studied the humanities, philosophy, and medicine in Florence but apparently did not obtain an academic degree. About 1456 he began to study Greek. In 1462 he received from Cosimo de' Medici a house in Careggi, near Florence, and several Greek manuscripts; this is regarded as the date the Platonic Academy of Florence was founded. Having earlier taken minor orders, Ficino was ordained in 1473; he held several ecclesiastic benefices and became a canon of Florence Cathedral in 1487. After the explusion of the Medicis from Florence in 1494, Ficino, who had been closely associated with several generations of the family, apparently retired to the country. He was honored after his death in a funeral oration delivered by a chancellor of the republic of Florence.

Ficino became interested in Platonist philosophy at an early age, presumably through studying Augustine. His earliest extant writings also show familiarity with Aristotle and his commentators and with Lucretius. Among Ficino's Latin translations from the Greek, the first that attained a wide circulation was his version (1463) of the works attributed to Hermes Trismegistus. Ficino's translation of Plato, the first complete rendering of all his dialogues in any Western language, was begun in 1463, probably completed in 1469, subsequently revised, and first printed in 1484. His influential commentary on Plato's *Symposium* was written in 1469; the other Platonic commentaries, some of them extensive, belong to different periods of Ficino's life. The translation of and commentary on Plotinus was begun in 1484 and printed in 1492. Translations of Porphyry, Iamblichus, Proclus, and other philosophers appeared in 1497. Ficino's chief philosophical work, *Theologica Platonica de Immortalitate Animarum* ("Platonic Theology—On the Immortality of the Souls") was written between 1469 and 1474 and was printed in 1482. Aside from this work and his commentaries, the most important source for Ficino's philosophy is his letters, which he began to collect around 1473 and finally published in 1495. Important also are his apologetic treatise *De Christiana Religione* (1474) and his work on medicine and astrology, *De Vita Libri Tres* (1489), which is often wrongly referred to as *De Vita Triplici*.

Ficino's work as a translator of and commentator on Plato and the Neoplatonists, and his avowed intention of reviving Platonism, led many older historians to treat his doctrine merely as a repetition of ancient Neoplatonism. More recently, however, a closer study of his known and unpublished works has shown that in restating the doctrines of Plato and his ancient followers, Ficino showed a good deal of originality. In addition, his writings show the influence of medieval and Byzantine Platonism, early Italian humanism, and also the tradition of scholastic Aristotelianism, which had a strong impact upon his terminology and method. He was familiar with Dante and other Italian poets and wrote or rewrote several of his own works in the Tuscan vernacular.

Ficino was the founder and for many years the head and guiding spirit of the Platonic Academy of Florence, which has remained famous as a symbol and institutional center of Renaissance Platonism. The academy was not a firmly established institution in the manner of later academies but a rather loosely organized spiritual community of friends. We hear of informal discussions between the older members of the circle and of philosophical banquets celebrated on Plato's birthday. There were recitals of edifying orations before a small audience, private readings of Plato and other texts given by one or a few younger disciples, and public lectures on Plato and Plotinus delivered in a church or auditorium. Distinguished visitors from other Italian cities and abroad called upon Ficino or participated in the meetings, and Ficino's correspondence served as a vehicle both for maintaining contact with the members of the academy and for arousing the interest of strangers in the academy's activities. The catalogue of his pupils, which he gives in one of his letters, and the list of the persons with whom he was in correspondence, whom he mentions, or who owned the manuscripts and printed editions of his writings are ample evidence of the wide influence he exerted during his lifetime.

Ficino's writings present a highly complex system of ideas, embroidered with similes, allegories, and lengthy quotations from his favorite authors. We can mention but a few of his more important and influential doctrines.

Hierarchy. In his description of the universe, Ficino took from Neoplatonic and medieval sources the conception of a great hierarchy in which each being occupies its place and has its degree of perfection, beginning with God at the top and descending through the orders of the angels and souls, the celestial and elementary spheres, the various species of animals, plants, and minerals, down to qualityless prime matter. In spite of Ficino's indebtedness to earlier schemes, it appears on closer examination that his hierarchy differs in significant details from those of his predecessors. It is arranged in a final scheme of five basic substances: God, the angelic mind, the rational soul, quality, and body. This scheme comes fairly close to that of Plotinus but differs from it in various ways. Above all, quality did not constitute a separate level of being for Plotinus, who instead assigned separate places to the sensitive and vegetative faculties of the soul. It can be shown that Ficino intentionally revised the Plotinian scheme, partly to make it more symmetrical and partly to assign the privileged place in its center to the human soul, thus giving a kind of metaphysical setting and sanction to the doctrine of the dignity of man, which he had inherited from his humanist predecessors. The soul is truly the mean of all things created by God, Ficino tells us. It is in the middle between higher and lower beings, sharing some of its attributes with the former and some with the latter.

Ficino was not satisfied with a static hierarchy in which each degree merely stands beside the others and in which the relationship of degrees consists only in a continuous gradation of attributes. He was also convinced that the universe must have a dynamic unity and that its various parts and degrees are held together by active forces and affinities. For this reason, he revived the Neoplatonic doctrine of the world soul and made astrology part of a natural system of mutual influences. Since thought for Ficino has an active influence upon its objects, since love is an active force that binds all things together (as in Plato's *Symposium*), and since the human soul extends its thought and love to all things, from the highest to the lowest, in Ficino's writing the soul becomes once more and in a new sense the center of the universe. The soul is the greatest of all miracles in nature because it combines all things, it is the center of all things, and possesses the forces of all things. Therefore the soul may rightly be called the center of nature, the middle term of all things, the bond and juncture of the universe.

Contemplation. Ficino's cosmology, which was very influential during the sixteenth century, offers some points of intrinsic interest; however, it constitutes only one side of his thought. The other and even more profound component is his analysis, based on direct inner experience, of the spiritual or contemplative life, and analysis that links him with some of the medieval mystics and, again, with Neoplatonism. In the face of ordinary daily experiences, the mind finds itself in a state of continuous unrest and dissatisfaction, but it is capable of turning away from the body and the external world and of concentrating upon its own inner substance. Thus purifying itself of things external, the soul enters the contemplative life and attains a higher knowledge, discovering the incorporeal world that is closed to it while it is engaged in ordinary experience and in the troubles of the external life. Ficino interpreted this contemplative life as a gradual ascent of the soul toward always higher degrees of truth and being, an ascent that finally culminates in the immediate knowledge and vision of God. This knowledge of God represents the ultimate goal of human life and existence—in it alone the unrest of our mind is satisfied—and all other modes and degrees of human life and knowledge must be understood as more or less direct and conscious preparations for this end. In accordance with Plotinus, Ficino was convinced that this highest experience could be attained during the present life, at least by a few privileged persons and for a short while, although he never explicitly claimed to have attained this state himself.

In describing the various states and the ultimate goal of inner experience, Ficino used a twofold terminology, and in this he was influenced by St. Augustine and by the medieval philosophers. The ascent of the soul toward God is accomplished with the help of two wings, the intellect and the will; accordingly, the knowledge of God is accompanied and paralleled on each level by the love of God; and the ultimate vision, by an act of enjoyment. Ficino also considered the question of whether intellect and knowledge or will and love are more important in this process, and although he seemed to come to different conclusions in different parts of his writings, in general he leaned toward the superiority of will and love over intellect and knowledge. Yet the question was not so important for him as might be expected, since he regarded the knowledge of God and the love of God as merely two different aspects or interpretations of the same basic experience—namely, the contemplative ascent of the soul toward its ultimate goal.

This experience and the manner in which it is interpreted hold the key to both Ficino's metaphysics and his ethics. It is the inner ascent of contemplation, through which the reality of incorporeal things—of the ideas and of God himself—is discovered and verified. Since this inner ascent constitutes the basic task of human existence, Ficino was not interested in specific moral precepts or in casuistry, but only in the general identification of the human good and man's moral excellence with the inner life. His whole moral doctrine, as expressed in his letters, may

be said to be a reduction of all specific moral rules to a praise of the contemplative life. He who has attained this life is exempt from the blows of fortune; and, animated by his inner certainty and insight, he will know and do the right thing under any given circumstance.

Intimately related to the doctrine of the contemplative life are two other theories of Ficino's, both of great historical importance: his theory of the immortality of the soul and his theory of Platonic love.

Immortality. Ficino's main work, *Theologia Platonica de Immortalitate Animarum*, consists for the most part of a series of arguments in support of the soul's immortality. It appears from a famous passage twice repeated in Ficino's writings that, in direct contrast with the teachings of the Aristotelian philosophers of his time, he considered this doctrine the central tenet of his Platonism. It is true that the immortality of the soul had been defended by Plato and Plotinus, by Augustine and many other Christian writers, and that Ficino borrowed many specific arguments from them. It may also be granted that Averroës' doctrine of the unity of the intellect in all men, which had been widely discussed and often accepted by Aristotelian philosophers from the thirteenth to the fifteenth century, made a defense of individual immortality imperative. In addition, the humanists had attached great importance to the individual human being, his experiences, and his opinions; and the belief in personal immortality was, as it were, a metaphysical counterpart of this individualism and an extension of it into another dimension.

Yet it seems evident that for Ficino the doctrine of immortality was a necessary complement and consequence of his interpretation of human existence and of the goal of human life. If it is our basic task to ascend, through a series of degrees, to the immediate vision and enjoyment of God, we must postulate that this ultimate goal will be attained, not merely by a few persons and for a short while but by a great number of human beings and forever. Otherwise, man's effort to attain this ultimate end would be in vain, and the very end for which he had been destined would remain without fulfillment. Thus, man would be unhappier than the animals, which do attain their natural ends, and this would be inconsistent with the dignity of the place man occupies in the universe. Moreover, if a natural end corresponding to a natural desire implanted in all men could not be attained, this would contradict the perfection of the order of nature and the wisdom of God, who created that order. In his "Platonic Theology," and in other parts of his writings, Ficino never tired of repeating these and similar arguments. It seems obvious that they reflect the real intent and motivation of his thought, for his whole interpretation of human life as a contemplative ascent toward God would lose its meaning unless this ascent were to find its permanent fulfillment in the eternal afterlife of the immortal soul. This alone would explain why the doctrine of immortality assumed such a central place for him. All other arguments are merely auxiliary to this central one.

Ficino's doctrine of immortality, and his arguments for it, made a profound impression on many thinkers of the sixteenth century; and it may very well be due to his indirect influence that the immortality of the soul was formally pronounced a dogma of the Catholic church at the Lateran Council of 1512.

Theory of love. Of equal historical importance, although different in character, is Ficino's doctrine of human love. In this doctrine, as in many of his others, Ficino combined elements from several different sources and traditions. He took over and reinterpreted Plato's theory of love as expressed in the *Symposium* and *Phaedrus*, and combined it with other ancient theories of friendship that were known to him primarily through Aristotle and Cicero; he also tried to identify it with the Christian love (*caritas*) praised by St. Paul. He even added some touches from the tradition of medieval courtly love as it was known to him through Guido Cavalcanti, Dante, and other early Tuscan poets. This doctrine of love, which exercised a tremendous influence during the sixteenth century, and for which Ficino himself coined the terms "Platonic love" and "Socratic love," was first expressed by him in his commentary on Plato's *Symposium* and further developed in many of his letters and other writings. The term "Platonic love" means love as described by Plato, according to Ficino's interpretation; more frequently, he spoke of it as divine love. The basic point is that he regarded love for another human being as merely a preparation, more or less conscious, for the love of God, which constitutes the real goal and true content of human desire and which is turned toward persons and things by virtue of the reflected splendor of divine goodness and beauty that may appear in them. Ficino insisted that true love or friendship is always mutual. A genuine relationship between two people is a communion founded on what is essential in man, that is, it is based in each of them on his original love for God. There can never be only two friends; there must always be three—two human beings and one God. God alone is the indissoluble bond and perpetual guardian of any true friendship for a true lover loves the other person solely for the sake of God. True love and friendship between several persons is derived from the love of the individual for God; it is thus reduced to the basic phenomenon of the inner ascent, which constitutes the core of Ficino's philosophy.

It appears from Ficino's letters that he considered true friendship in this sense to be the bond that united the members of his academy with each other and with himself, their common master, and that he liked to think of the academy not merely as a school but as a community of friends.

This conception of Platonic love was to exercise a strong influence on Italian and European literature throughout the sixteenth century. Many lyric poets spoke of their love in terms that reflected the influence of Ficino, as well as that of the old Tuscan poets and Petrarch; and there was a large body of treatises and lectures on love that derived much of their inspiration, directly or indirectly, from Ficino's commentary on the *Symposium*. In this literature the concept of Platonic love was separated from the philosophical context in which it had originated with Ficino, and so it became more and more diluted and trivial. For this reason, the notion of Platonic love has acquired a slightly ridiculous connotation for the modern reader.

Yet we should try to recapture its original meaning, remembering that the true meaning of an idea is best understood in the context of the thought in which it originated and which, in a sense, made its formulation necessary. If we trace Platonic love back to its origin in Ficino—back to the context of an individual's love of God—it may still seem a strange and remote concept, but we shall at least understand that it had a serious content and that it was related to the central ideas of his philosophy.

A further aspect of Ficino's thought that requires mention is his conception of religion and of its relationship to philosophy. Ficino was a priest and a canon of Florence Cathedral; he had an adequate knowledge of Christian theology; and he even wrote an apologetic treatise on the Christian religion as well as several other theological works. There is not the slightest doubt that he intended to be orthodox, although some of his doctrines may seem to have dubious implications and although he was in danger of an ecclesiastical condemnation for the views on astrology and magic expressed in his work *De Vita* (1489). He insisted on his Christian faith and submitted to the judgment of the church. He was even willing to abandon the opinions of his favorite Platonist philosophers when they seemed to contradict Christian doctrine. Thus, we are not surprised to find that he regarded Christianity as the most perfect of all religions. At the same time, he saw some merit in the variety of religions and insisted that any religion, however primitive, is related indirectly to the one true God. In his implicit tolerance toward other religions, Ficino came very close to a concept of natural religion, a position that made him a forerunner of Herbert of Cherbury, the deists, and other advocates of a universal religion. Divine worship, he said, is almost as natural for men as neighing is for horses or barking is for dogs. A common religion of all nations, having one God for its object, is natural to the human species. This religion, which is again based on man's primary knowledge and love of God, is not shared by the animals but is peculiar to man, a part of his dignity and excellence and a compensation for the many defects and weaknesses of his nature.

As to the relation between religion and philosophy, Ficino was convinced that true religion (that is, Christianity) and true philosophy (that is, Platonism) are in basic harmony with each other; and he was inclined to treat them as sisters instead of trying to make one subservient to the other. He believed that it is the task of Platonic reason to confirm and support Christian faith and authority, and he even considered it his own mission, assigned to him by divine providence, to revive true philosophy for the benefit of true religion. He believed that those who will not be guided by faith alone can be guided toward truth only through reason and the most perfect philosophy.

In the light of this relationship, the continuity of the Platonic tradition assumed a new significance for Ficino. Since this tradition was thought by him to go back to Hermes and Zoroaster, whose apocryphal writings Ficino treated as venerable witnesses of early pagan theology and philosophy, he considered the tradition to be as old as the religious tradition of the Hebrews. Thus, the religious tradition of the Hebrews and Christians, and the philosophical tradition of the Hermetics and Platonists, seemed to run a parallel course in human history from the early beginnings through antiquity and the Middle Ages down to the modern period. It is in accordance with this view of Ficino's that Augustinus Steuchus, a Catholic theologian of the sixteenth century, wrote his *De Philosophia Perenni* ("On the Perennial Philosophy," 1542).

Influence. Ficino's influence was considerable, both during his lifetime and for a long time afterward. As a metaphysician in the proper sense of the word, Ficino added an element to Florentine culture that had been largely absent from it before and left a new imprint on that culture that was to last for several generations. Among his associates and pupils we find Cristoforo Landino, author of the *Camaldulensian Disputations* and of an influential commentary on Dante's *Commedia*, and Lorenzo de' Medici, famous not only as a statesman but also as one of the best Italian poets of his century. Whereas Pico della Mirandola developed an independent position, another pupil, Francesco da Diacceto, carried the Platonic tradition of Ficino into the first decades of the sixteenth century; and later in that century, Platonic philosophy was cultivated both at the new Florentine Academy of 1540 and at the University of Pisa. This Platonist climate of opinion in Florence and Pisa accounts for some of the opinions and preconceptions of Galileo. In the rest of Italy, poets and prose writers drew on Ficino's theory of love, and theologians and philosophers upon his doctrine of immortality as well as some of his other ideas. His influence appears in the works of such leading philosophers as Patrizi and Bruno; even thinkers who opposed his views, such as Pomponazzi, were impressed with his learning and acumen.

During his lifetime, Ficino's influence was already growing, through his correspondence and through the circulation of his writings, in most European countries. His admirers included Reuchlin and Colet, Gaguin and Lefèvre d'Étaples. During the sixteenth century his writings were reprinted, collected, read, and quoted all over Europe. His medical and astrological treatises were especially popular in Germany. In France, he was repeatedly quoted and plagiarized by Symphorien Champier, and admired in the circles of Queen Marguerite of Navarre and of the Pléiade. There, some of his writings and his Latin translations of Plato were translated into French. Elements of his Platonism appear in Bovillus and Postel, and not so much in Peter Ramus as in his mortal enemy Jacques Charpentier. Even in Descartes there are strong elements of Platonism. Outside of France, Erasmus, Thomas More, Sebastian Fox Morcillo, Paracelsus, Cornelius Agrippa, and finally Kepler exemplify the importance of Platonism in sixteenth-century thought, an importance that is closely linked with the writings, translations, and commentaries of Ficino.

In the seventeenth century, after Galileo and Descartes, the speculative cosmology of the Renaissance was no longer possible within the framework of a natural science based on experiments and mathematical formulas. The influence of Platonism persisted, however, in the metaphysics and epistemology of Spinoza and Leibniz, Malebranche and Berkeley; and it gained a new life in the school of Cambridge Platonists. And, since the authority of Plato himself remained a powerful force with many thinkers, we find even in Kant and Goethe several theories associated with the name and prestige of Plato (and Plotinus) that actually belong to his Florentine translator and commentator. Coleridge wrote in his autobiography that as a youth he read Plato and Plotinus, together with the commentaries and the *Theologia Platonica* of the illustrious Florentine. It was only in the nineteenth century that Ficino lost even this anonymous or pseudonymous influence, after a new school of philological and historical criticism had begun to make a rigorous distinction between the genuine thought of Plato and that of his successors and commentators in late antiquity and during the Renaissance. On the basis of this distinction, it has become possible again to understand Ficino's thought in its own right—to appreciate its indebtedness to sources other than Plato, its close connection with the thought and scholarship, art and literature of its time, and its own peculiar style and originality.

Bibliography

Of Ficino's main works, only the commentary on Plato's *Symposium* has been reprinted in modern editions. See *Marsilio Ficino's Commentary on Plato's Symposium*, translated and edited by Sears R. Jayne, Vol. XIX, No. 1, in The University of Missouri Studies (Columbia, Mo., 1944), and *Commentaire sur le Banquet de Platon*, Raymond Marcel, ed. (Paris, 1956). For the others, the Basel editions of his collected works, *Opera Omnia*, 2 vols. (1561 and 1576), are still the only source; the second edition is slightly more complete and has been reprinted recently (Turin, 1959). Also see *Supplementum Ficinianum*, Paul Oskar Kristeller, ed., 2 vols. (Florence, 1937), with lists of manuscripts and editions and a chronology of Ficino's works, and P. O. Kristeller, *Studies in Ficino's Thought and Letters* (Rome, 1956), with a number of papers discussing Ficino's life, sources, influence, and thought. Aside from the commentary on the *Symposium*, only the short *Five Questions Concerning the Mind* (from Ficino's *Letters*) has been translated into English, by Josephine L. Burroughs, in Ernst Cassirer and others, eds., *The Renaissance Philosophy of Man* (Chicago, 1948), pp. 193–212.

For Ficino's life and the history of the Platonic Academy, see Arnaldo Della Torre, *Storia dell'Accademia platonica di Firenze* (Florence, 1902), which is still indispensable, and Raymond Marcel, *Marsile Ficin* (Paris, 1958).

For discussions of Ficino's philosophy, see Giuseppe Saitta, *La filosofia di Marsilio Ficino* (Messina, 1923; 3d ed., Bologna, 1954); Sears R. Jayne, *John Colet and Marsilio Ficino* (Oxford, 1963); Paul O. Kristeller, *Il pensiero filosofico di Marsilio Ficino* (Florence, 1953), translated by Virginia Conant as *The Philosophy of Marsilio Ficino* (New York, 1943)—the Italian edition is superior because of its additional indices and original text quotations.

Also see Michele Schiavone, *Problemi filosofici in Marsilio Ficino* (Milan, 1957), and Ernst Cassirer, *Individuum und Kosmos in der Philosophie der Renaissance* (Berlin and Leipzig, 1927; reprinted Darmstadt, 1962), translated by Mario Domandi as *The Individual and the Cosmos in Renaissance Philosophy* (New York, 1963).

Ficino's influence on the theory and iconography of Renaissance art has been discussed by Erwin Panofsky—*Idea* (Leipzig and Berlin, 1924; 2d ed., Berlin, 1960) and *Studies in Iconology* (New York, 1939; reprinted 1962)—and by E. H. Gombrich and others; see especially André Chastel, *Marsile Ficin et l'art* (Geneva, 1954). For a discussion of Ficino and magic, see D. P. Walker, *Spiritual and Demonic Magic From Ficino to Campanella* (London, 1958).

Literature on the influence of Ficino's theory of love includes A. M. J. Festugière, *La Philosophie de l'amour de Marsile Ficin et son influence sur la littérature française du XVIe siècle* (Paris,

1941); John C. Nelson, *Renaissance Theory of Love* (New York, 1958). See also Nesca A. Robb, *Neoplatonism of the Italian Renaissance* (London, 1935), and Raymond Klibansky, *The Continuity of the Platonic Tradition During the Middle Ages* (London, 1939 and 1950).

Paul Oskar Kristeller

FIDEISM is the view that truth in religion is ultimately based on faith rather than on reasoning or evidence. This claim has been presented in many forms by theologians from St. Paul to contemporary neo-orthodox, antirationalist writers, usually as a way of asserting that the fundamental tenets of religion cannot be established by proofs or by empirical evidence but must be accepted on faith. Some forms of fideism denigrate or deny the value of reason and science, and these amount to a kind of irrationalism, as indicated in Hume's ironic statement at the end of his essay "Of Miracles":

> [The] *Christian Religion* not only was at first attended with miracles, but even to this day cannot be believed by any reasonable person without them. Mere reason is not sufficient to convince us of its veracity; and whoever is moved by *Faith* to assent to it, is conscious of a continued miracle in his own person, which subverts all the principles of his understanding, and gives him a determination to believe what is most contrary to custom and experience. (*Essay Concerning Human Understanding*, L. A. Selby-Bigge, ed., Oxford, 1951, p. 131)

Extreme fideism. Extreme fideists like J. G. Hamann and Søren Kierkegaard have praised Hume's formulation as a proper characterization of religious orthodoxy.

Starting with St. Paul's contention that the central doctrine of Christianity was nonsensical by Greek philosophical standards and with Tertullian's announcement *credo quia absurdum* (I believe that which is absurd), there have been theologians who have insisted that religious truths are contrary to those which might be supported or justified by reasonable evidence and that rational activities are not proper means to arrive at such truths. Some have insisted that there are suprarational or extrarational ways, such as mystical or revelatory experiences that provide the "knowledge" of fundamental truths. Such writers have tended to ignore rational arguments or standards, and often, as St. John of the Cross did, they have offered means by which one could train oneself to escape the confines of rationality in order to intensify religious experience and belief.

Others have tried to show the inability of reason to establish any fundamental or absolutely certain truth. Usually employing skeptical arguments, they have contended that ultimate principles are open to question or rational standards, and also that these standards can themselves be questioned. In view of this, they have contended, basic truths are to be accepted on faith. Montaigne, Pierre Charron, and other so-called Christian skeptics set forth this form of fideism.

Others, like Pierre Bayle, Kierkegaard, Félicité Robert de Lamennais and L. I. Shestov, went further and asserted that religious truths were of such a nature that they were contrary to the kinds of assertions that were probable, plausible, or even possible on rational or reasonable standards and that such truths could therefore be believed or accepted only on faith. Bayle insisted that religious tenets were not only above and beyond reason but also were in opposition to it and that the strongest faith was that which denied the truths based on natural light and embraced those most incomprehensible to or contrary to reason. (For a discussion of the nature of Bayle's skepticism and fideism, see BAYLE, PIERRE.) Kierkegaard first accepted the type of skepticism developed by Bayle and Hume about rational knowledge and then insisted that the fundamental tenet of Christianity, the Incarnation, is not only contrary to rational evidence but is even a self-contradiction on rational standards: "No knowledge can have for its object the absurdity that the eternal is the historical" (*Philosophical Fragments, or A Fragment of Philosophy*, p. 50). Kierkegaard held Hamann's view that Hume had summed up the nature of religious belief—that it really is contrary to reason, custom, and experience. For Kierkegaard the very absurdity of the Christian claim makes it worthy of belief, and it is only by total commitment, or "the leap into faith," that it can be accepted. There can be no reasons for the leap, no justification for it. In the words of Bayle's opponent, Pierre Jurieu (also an irrationalist), all the believer can say is, "I believe it because I want to believe it."

In the twentieth century, among the fideists who have advanced Kierkegaard's view, one of the most striking is the Russian Orthodox theologian Shestov, who has insisted that the rejection of all rational standards is a part of true belief. In a commentary on Dostoyevsky he contended that the refusal to accept that $2+2=4$ and the ability to believe that $2+2=5$ are intimately connected with attaining religious truth.

Moderate fideism. In contrast to irrationalist or antirationalist fideism, a more moderate kind has developed, especially within the Christian Augustinian tradition. Rather than insisting that all ultimate certitude rests on faith in contrast to reason, this tradition has admitted that faith precedes reason in establishing certain fundamental truths but that reason and evidence can play some role both in the search for these truths and in the explanation and comprehension of them. The Augustinian slogan, *credo ut intelligam* (I believe in order to know), places the primary emphasis on faith. However, as Augustine's philosophical dialogues show, the recognition of the basic fideistic element may be (and perhaps must be) preceded by a rational search for truth. Once rational inquiry has revealed the need to accept some fundamental principles or beliefs on faith, then it may be possible to show that these commitments are reasonable, probable, or plausible. Purported proofs of the existence of God, metaphysical systems interpreting what is accepted on faith, and historical and psychological evidences about the nature of religion and its effects on believers can all be offered as rational explanations or even justifications of what has already been accepted on faith.

Pascal's presentation in the *Pensées* illustrates this form of fideism. He forcefully argued that the natural capacities of man are inadequate to lead him to any completely certain truth. A man can show that it is unreasonable or unwise to be an atheist but not that it is reasonable to be a theist. Once one has realized the human predicament—man's fundamental need for ultimate truths and his inability to find them—then one is ready to hear God and to accept his revealed Word on faith alone. Once one has faith, one can see the force of the apologetic and psychological evidence for the truth of the Christian religion. Such evidence might then constitute "good reasons" for believing what one has already accepted fideistically.

Fideism in philosophy. A nonreligious analogue of moderate fideism appears in various skeptical philosophical views, such as those of Hume, Russell, and Santayana. Hume's contention that it is belief that "peoples the world," and that everybody lives within his own private belief system, could be considered as a kind of fideism. The ultimate presuppositions by which we live cannot be justified by reason or evidence and are accepted not on religious faith but (to use Santayana's term) on "animal faith." Russell, in his *Human Knowledge,* insisted (on the basis of Hume's arguments) that the fundamental assumptions of science cannot be justified but must be accepted on faith. However, even if one has the mystical skeptical experience Santayana described, of seeing all in doubt, it is still rational investigation that led Hume and his successors to the recognition of the belief factor involved in rational activities. Having discovered this, Hume then showed that one can study the causes of beliefs and that beliefs can be explained even though they can never be justified; working from the basis of a set of "reasonable" beliefs, one can evaluate other beliefs in terms of psychological factors. The philosophical tradition emanating from Hume, then, can be considered as a kind of fideism, sharing some of the characteristics of the moderate fideism of the Augustinian tradition.

Contemporary developments. At present irrationalistic fideism, especially of the Kierkegaardian variety, is extremely popular, especially among Protestant theologians (partly in reaction to liberal, rationalistic theological tendencies of the nineteenth century). Many theologians have been concerned with man's apparent inability to find any ultimate answers through science, secular political movements, and so forth, and his need to base his ultimate commitment on faith alone. The existentialist stress on the fundamental absurdity of man's world is part of this movement. The official Catholic position from the time of the Council of Trent to the present remains opposed to the central fideistic thesis, that ultimate beliefs can be established not by reason or evidence but only by faith. However, in a world in which so many optimistic, "reasonable," scientifically supported views have been undermined by the cataclysmic events of the twentieth century, fideism may provide one of the main avenues to some kind of significant belief for the present age. William James's analysis, in his "Will to Believe," of the psychological need for commitment and belief despite the lack of evidence may represent much of the present mood. The religious fideists, however, find James's own faith too tepid, and they seem to be moving more and more to the irrationalist fideism of Kierkegaard, Dostoyevsky, and Shestov.

Bibliography

Bartley, William W., *Retreat to Commitment.* London, 1964. A critique of some contemporary fideistic views.

Bayle, Pierre, *Historical and Critical Dictionary, Selections,* translated by R. H. Popkin. Indianapolis, 1965. "Pyrrho" and the "Third Clarification" deal especially with fideism.

Harent, S., "Foi," in *Dictionnaire de théologie catholique,* Vol. VI. Paris, 1920. Cols. 55–514.

Herberg, Will, *Judaism and Modern Man.* Philadelphia, 1951.

Herberg, Will, *Four Existentialist Theologians, A Reader From the Works of Jacques Maritain, Nicolas Berdyaev, Martin Buber and Paul Tillich.* New York, 1958.

Kierkegaard, Søren, *Philosophical Fragments, or A Fragment of Philosophy,* translated by David F. Swenson. Princeton, N.J., 1946.

Kierkegaard, Søren, *A Kierkegaard Anthology,* Robert Bretall, ed. New York, 1959.

Popkin, Richard H., "Theological and Religious Scepticism." *The Christian Scholar,* Vol. 39 (1956), 150–158.

Popkin, Richard H., "Kierkegaard and Scepticism." *Algemeen Nederlands Tijdschrift Voor Wijsbegeerte en Psychologie,* Vol. 51 (1959), 123–141.

Santayana, George, *Scepticism and Animal Faith.* New York, 1955.

Sauvage, G. M., "Fideism," in *Catholic Encyclopedia,* Vol. V. New York, 1909. Pp. 68–69.

Shestov, Lev I., *In Job's Balances,* translated by Camilla Coventry and C. A. Macartney. London, 1932.

Shestov, Lev I., *Kierkegaard et la philosophie existentielle,* translated by T. Rageot and Boris de Schloezer. Paris, 1936.

Tillich, Paul, *Dynamics of Faith.* New York, 1957.

Richard H. Popkin

FIELD THEORIES. See Action at a distance and field theory.

FILMER, ROBERT (c. 1588–1653), English political writer and theorist of the divine right of kings, early expositor of the patriarchal account of the state and of society. He was a country gentleman of the county of Kent but also belonged to the intellectual society of London and had some connection with the Court. He was an associate of prominent lawyers and historians, such as John Selden and Sir Henry Spelman, of the orthodox clergy, and of the Jacobean poets and literati too, including George Herbert and possibly John Donne. His absolutist views on political matters may have been acquired while he was at Trinity College, Cambridge, or at the Inns of Court and were developed well before the outbreak of the Civil War between the king and Parliament in 1642. In this he resembles Thomas Hobbes, his contemporary, but Filmer wrote his works for circulation in manuscript among his London acquaintances and the manor houses of Kent rather than for publication in print. Although his family was engaged on the side of the king in the struggle with Parliament in the 1640s and although he himself suffered considerable losses, Sir Robert never actually fought with the royalist forces and even pleaded neutrality, which has since been looked upon as inconsistent in the conduct of an extreme defender of royalist claims. His neutrality did not prevent his being sent to prison for a time.

Filmer's importance in the history of thought rests almost entirely on the fact that John Locke's work on political theory, the famous *Two Treatises of Government,* was directed against him, though it was not published until 1689, nearly forty years after Filmer's death. (See LOCKE, JOHN, section on political thought.) It has only recently been shown how extensive was Locke's preoccupation with Filmer, in the second of his treatises as well as in the first. But the social theorists of the present day are also interested in Filmer's thinking as an expression of traditional patriarchal attitudes toward authority and social structure. The relationship between Locke and Filmer has become the classic example of a rationalist–critical political system (the Lockian) confronting an ideological–determinist outlook (the Filmer view).

It has not been possible, however, to see in Filmer simply a "codifier of unconscious prejudice," as he has been called. He was remarkably enlightened in some of his views, especially as to witchcraft, and wrote with surprising urbanity rather as a critical reviewer of the political works current in his time than as the solemn expositor of outraged orthodoxy. Those of his works which he himself had printed, mainly reviews of Aristotle, Milton, Grotius, and Hobbes, are brief and pointed, and it is, perhaps, significant that he refused to publish the only concerted exposition of his political theory, the famous *Patriarcha; or the Natural Power of Kings* (London, 1680), from which all the others derive. He may have thought his political theory too extreme in its earlier, positive form.

Patriarcha, which was composed for the gentry of Kent in the 1630s, asserts that every individual is absolutely bound to obey the political authority established in his country because that authority enjoys by divine decree the powers originally conferred on Adam at the creation over his wife, his children, and their descendants eternally. From this view of the Old Testament it follows that males are always superior to females, the elder to the younger, and that all humans are naturally—physiologically—related to each other. Society is a family, descended from one single male individual. All men are born, and always remain, unfree and unequal, and consent is irrelevant to political association. Political society is also universal, for there are no humans who are not descended from Adam. A prepolitical state of nature makes no sense at all, nor does any idea of a contract to replace such a condition by political society. Property as well as political power is distributed according to God's patriarchal decrees and belongs absolutely to the person who inherits it or to whom it has been given.

These social and political doctrines are original only in the sense that Filmer combined together many positions held by his predecessors, notably those of the French legal theorist Jean Bodin, those of the bishops of the Anglican church, and especially those of its royal head, King James I. These views are acceptable only to a naively fundamentalist believer in the Christian scriptures, and Locke had no difficulty in demolishing all the "glib nonsense," as he called it, about the kingship of Adam and its descent to the Stuart kings, to the usurper Oliver Cromwell, to any man or group lucky enough to seize power. Nevertheless, there was rather more to Filmer's "rope of sand" than Locke wished to admit, and in Filmer's shrewd remarks about the historical absurdities of a state of nature and in his very acute analysis of majority rule he raised difficulties which Locke never satisfactorily overcame.

Filmer demanded to know how an assembly convened for the purpose of making a universal contract could ever proceed to a valid vote of everyone with the right to vote. There would be bound to be absentees, and when it came to original multitudes voting to set up a government, the rights of some individuals would inevitably be overrun. What about servants, women, children, and the sick? Locke blandly responded by dogmatically asserting that in "one Body Politick the Majority have the Right to act and conclude the rest" (*Second Treatise,* 95). Filmer's doctrine of property seems to have impelled Locke into the formulation of the labor theory of value, with all its enormous consequences in social thinking.

Filmer's doctrines by no means disappeared with the Glorious Revolution of 1688 and the victory of Lockian rationalism. His arguments were persuasively restated by Jonathan Boucher in championship of the Tories at the American Revolution, and again by George Fitzhugh in defense of the South in the 1850s. Filmer remains the most valuable literary source for traditional European preindustrial patriarchal political attitudes.

Bibliography

For Filmer's works, see Peter Laslett, ed., *Patriarcha and the Other Political Works of Sir Robert Filmer* (Oxford, 1949); it contains a bibliography. For American attitudes, see C. Vann Woodward's introduction to his edition of *Cannibals All, or, Slaves Without Masters,* by George Fitzhugh (Cambridge, Mass., 1960).

PETER LASLETT

FINNISH PHILOSOPHY. See SCANDINAVIAN PHILOSOPHY.

FISCHER, KUNO (1824–1907), German philosopher and historian of philosophy, was born at Sandewalde in Silesia. He studied philology at Leipzig and theology and philosophy at Halle. In 1850 Fischer was appointed *Privatdozent* in philosophy at the University of Heidelberg, but his pantheistic views caused his dismissal three years later. In 1856 he qualified as *Privatdozent* at the University of Berlin, and in the same year he was invited to Jena as professor of philosophy. In 1872 he returned to Heidelberg, where he taught with great success until 1903.

Fischer's major work is his *Geschichte der neueren Philosophie* (1852–1877). This widely reprinted history of modern philosophy owed its success in large part to Fischer's splendid gift for exposition. Endowed with a remarkable capacity for sympathetic understanding, Fischer was able to reproduce the great philosophical systems in a literary form of exemplary brilliance and clarity, as well as to unravel their basic themes and subtlest ramifications and to illuminate and reconstruct them systematically. At the same time, he sought to place these systems in their larger cultural and historical context and thus to understand the historical development of philosophy as the progressive self-knowledge of the human mind.

Fischer was the author of the first large German monograph on Kant, *Kants Leben und die Grundlagen seine*

Lehre (Mannheim, 1860), and it is from Fischer that Neo-Kantianism received its decisive impulse.

Apart from Kant, Hegel was the chief object of his interest. In its equating of logic and metaphysics, Fischer's *System der Logik und Metaphysik oder Wissenschaftslehre* (Stuttgart, 1852) exhibited the strong influence of Hegel. In this work an attempt was also made to bring Hegel's principle of dialectical development into harmony with modern evolutionism in the sense of a teleological idealism. Fischer held that the dialectical development ran from Being through Essence to purpose. The system of logical and, at the same time, metaphysical categories that he outlined culminated in the idea of finality, which guaranteed a purposeful development that goes beyond the merely given. In the second edition (Stuttgart, 1865), Fischer attempted to mediate between Kant and Hegel and to do justice not only to Hegelianism but also to Kantianism and empiricism.

Schopenhauer also influenced Fischer. In the study *Das Verhältnis zwischen Willen und Verstand im Menschen* (Heidelberg, 1896), Fischer distinguished between the will that is guided by knowledge and the unconscious volition that precedes all knowledge and conscious behavior. He also claimed that just as the essence of nature is "force," so the essence of man is "will" and the essence of the body is the manifestation of volition.

Fischer was also an extremely productive literary aesthetician. His conception of art is to be found in his early publication *Diotima: Die Idee des Schönen* ("Diotima: The Idea of the Beautiful," Pforzheim, 1849). In this work Fischer defined the aesthetic attitude as one of "playing," characterized by a concentration and uniting of all our faculties. He devoted later works to the origin and development of humor and to the classical poetry of Shakespeare, Lessing, Goethe, and Schiller.

Additional Works by Fischer

Fischer's chief work is the *Geschichte der neueren Philosophie* (Stuttgart, Mannheim, and Heidelberg, 1852–1877). Originally published in six volumes (on Descartes, Spinoza, Leibniz, Kant, Fichte, and Schelling), it was later extended to ten volumes, with a second volume on Kant, one on Schopenhauer (1893), and one on Hegel (1901); and it also included Fisher's early work on Francis Bacon and his school (Leipzig, 1856). Other writings include *Kleine Schriften*, 8 vols. (Heidelberg, 1888–1898), which contains *Über den Witz* ("On Humor"), *Über die menschliche Freiheit* ("On Human Freedom"), *Das Verhaltnis zwischen Willen und Verstand* ("The Relationship Between Will and Understanding"), and other essays. See also *Philosophische Schriften* ("Philosophical Writings"), 6 vols. (Heidelberg, 1891–1892; 6th ed., 1908–1909).

English translations of Fischer's works include the following: J. Oxenford, *Francis Bacon* (London, 1857); J. P. Mahaffy, *A Commentary on Kant's "Critick of the Pure Reason"* (London and Dublin, 1866); F. Schmidt, *Benedict Spinoza* (Edinburgh, 1882); J. P. Gordy, *Descartes and His School* (New York, 1887); W. S. Hough, *A Critique of Kant* (London, 1888).

Works on Fischer

For literature on Fischer, see Hugo Falkenheim, *Kuno Fischer und die literarhistorische Methode* (Berlin, 1892); Wilhelm Windelband, *Kuno Fischer* (Heidelberg, 1907), a memorial address; and Ernst Hoffmann, *Kuno Fischer* (Heidelberg, 1924).

FRANZ AUSTEDA
Translated by *Albert E. Blumberg*

FISKE, JOHN (1842–1901), American philosopher, advocate of evolutionary theory, was born in Hartford, Conn., and baptized Edmund Fisk Green; he changed his name to John Fisk shortly after his mother remarried in 1855 (the "e" was added in 1860). He grew up in Middletown and attended the Congregational church, but he became dissatisfied with orthodox Christianity and found himself drawn to the philosophical and theological implications of modern science. He early declared himself an "infidel," meaning by the word "non-Christian" rather than atheist. While he was a student at Harvard, he was punished by the college faculty for reading Auguste Comte in church.

Fiske's main philosophical work, *Outlines of Cosmic Philosophy*, developed from lectures given at Harvard in 1869 and 1871, and was completed in London during 1873 and 1874. In it he acknowledged himself a disciple and expositor of the philosophy of Herbert Spencer, the importance of which, he believed, would in time be seen to surpass that of Isaac Newton. This judgment did not appear extravagant to Fiske, since Spencer's law of evolution was "the first generalization concerning the concrete universe as a whole." According to Fiske's formulation of this law, "The integration of matter and concomitant dissipation of motion, which primarily constitutes Evolution, is attended by a continuous change from indefinite, incoherent homogeneity to definite, coherent heterogeneity of structure and function, through successive differentiations and integrations." He illustrated the law's operation at great length with examples drawn from organic processes, the nebular origin of the solar system, comparative philology, and the development of civilization.

Fiske maintained that at some time in the past, human evolution had reached a stage in which man's brain alone continued to evolve; ultimately, a level was achieved at which the individual's brain continued to develop after his birth. This process, which necessitated a period of prolonged infancy accompanied by the evolution of strong parental affection, provided the physical setting for the evolution of the resulting family into clans and society; for the origin of morality in the altruism demanded by family care; and for cultural progress, through the enhanced receptivity of yet developing minds. Prolonged infancy was the cornerstone of an evolutionary explanation of civilization; indeed, Fiske believed that this theory was his most important contribution to philosophy.

Fiske aimed to show the unity of all knowledge, the inevitability of progress, and the ultimate harmony of science and religion. He appealed to the law of evolution to accomplish the first two aims and to "Berkeleian idealism" to accomplish the third. All knowledge is "relative" in the sense that it consists only of classifying and discovering regularities among phenomena. What underlies and creates our experience or phenomena Fiske calls the "Unknowable," "Deity," and "Absolute Power." This "Deity" is the only proper concern of religion, while the regularities discoverable among the phenomena in which Deity manifests itself are the scientist's laws of nature. Thus Fiske's "cosmic theism" reconciles religion and science. Religious dogmas which intrude upon the scientist's world of phenomena are vestiges of primitive, anthropomorphic stages of religious development. Miracles must therefore be rejected, and the doctrine of special creation must give way to Darwin's theory of natural selection. Pantheism, which according to Fiske identifies Deity with the phenomenal world, is rejected, since Fiske's Deity is an "unconditioned existence" which is "something more than the universe." He rejects Comte's Religion of Humanity as a mere conceit. Materialism is rejected because it is at least conceivable that matter is reducible to mind or feeling, but inconceivable that feeling should evolve from matter; thus, the view that Deity is "Spirit" is plausible.

The major difference between Fiske and Spencer is Fiske's greater emphasis on the religious implications of evolutionary philosophy. Whereas Spencer was guarded, Fiske was unambiguous in calling what lay behind the phenomenal world "Spirit," and he took pains to prove that it was a plausible object of earnest religious contemplation. A further difference between the two thinkers is that Fiske, unlike Spencer, brought evolutionary philosophy to the defense of social conservatism, in the belief that inevitable progress obviated the need for radical social and religious change.

Fiske greatly enjoyed living in Cambridge, Massachusetts, and as late as 1878 he retained the hope of gaining a permanent position at Harvard in either the department of history or of philosophy. He declined job offers from other universities, but at Harvard he could obtain only temporary positions as a lecturer and as assistant librarian of the college. Early in life Fiske sought to make a living from his writing. Later he was always short of money and tried to make ends meet by going on the lecture circuit; however, he achieved genuine popularity both as a writer and lecturer only in the last decade of his life.

Throughout his life Fiske retained an earnest religious attitude, which he expressed in his later popular lectures in terms which were more and more conciliatory toward New England Protestantism. Thus "The Unseen World" (1876), the title essay of his first collection of essays, merely urged that science could not refute the immortality of the soul and that "a simple act of trust" in immortality was not unreasonable. In "The Destiny of Man" (1884), another title essay, Fiske said that the human soul was not merely the end product, but the goal of the great evolutionary process contrived by God. Finally, in *Through Nature to God* (1899), Fiske argued, in reply to T. H. Huxley's Romanes lecture "Evolution and Ethics" (1893), that nature is not morally indifferent but, on the contrary, that evolution "exists purely for the sake of moral ends." He also argued that science offered confirmation of the existence of God and of immortality.

After 1887 Fiske wrote nearly twenty volumes on American history. He was never an original philosopher, but through his clear writing and well-phrased public lectures he helped to advance American religious liberalism. He was a competent popularizer of Darwin's theory of evolution at a time when most religious writers were attacking evolution with frenzy.

Bibliography

Fiske's more philosophical works include *Outlines of Cosmic Philosophy; Based on the Doctrine of Evolution, with Criticisms on the Positive Philosophy*, 2 vols. (Boston, 1874); *The Unseen World, and other Essays* (Boston, 1876); *Darwinism, and other Essays* (London and New York, 1879); *The Destiny of Man Viewed in the Light of His Origin* (Boston, 1884); *Excursions of an Evolutionist* (Boston, 1884); *The Idea of God as Affected by Modern Knowledge* (Boston, 1885); *A Century of Science, and other Essays* (Boston, 1899); and *Through Nature to God* (Boston, 1899). Josiah Royce examines Fiske's philosophy in the introduction to the 1902 edition of *Cosmic Philosophy*. Milton Berman's *John Fiske, The Evolution of a Popularizer* (Cambridge, Mass., 1961) includes an extensive bibliography.

ANDREW OLDENQUIST

FLORENSKY, PAUL ALEXANDROVICH, Russian theologian, philosopher, and scientist, and a leading figure in the development of the twentieth-century Russian religious philosophy inspired by Vladimir Solovyov. Florensky was born in 1882, raised in Tbilisi, Georgia, and received his early education there before entering Moscow University. At the university he worked primarily in mathematics but also studied philosophy under S. N. Trubetskoy and L. M. Lopatin. After his graduation in 1904, he did advanced work in philosophy and the history of religion at the Moscow Theological Academy, and subsequently joined the staff as a lecturer. In 1908 he was named professor of philosophy at the academy, and in 1911 he was ordained a priest in the Russian Orthodox church. During the Russian Revolution he was exiled to Russian Turkestan, but in 1919 he was allowed to return to Moscow, where he assumed important positions in scientific research and administration for the Soviet government, chiefly in the fields of physics and electrical engineering. Florensky persistently rejected Soviet demands that he renounce holy orders, and he was imprisoned several times. Finally, in the mid-1930s, he was exiled to Siberia. Nothing certain is known of his subsequent fate, but he is thought to have died in Siberia in the 1940s.

Renowned as a universal genius whose gifts extended to poetry, painting, and music, as well as philosophy and science, Florensky first gained fame in 1914 through the publication of his chief philosophical work, *Stolp i Utverzhdeniye Istiny* ("The Pillar and Ground of the Truth"). An existential critique of rationalism in theology, the work builds on Solovyov's concept of "pan-unity" (*vseyedinstvo*) in metaphysics and gives theological elaboration to Solovyov's "sophiology." It is credited with inaugurating a new period in Russian religious thought through its influence on such thinkers as Sergey Bulgakov and Nicholas Lossky.

Florensky maintained that truth is a living whole which transcends the logical laws of thought. Reason loses itself in antinomies when attempting to fathom this whole; but through direct religious experience, one can perceive the integral truth and can reconcile, superrationally, such contradictions as those between Divine Unity and Trinity, free will and predestination, universal salvation and eternal damnation. Thus, theology must take its departure from spiritual experience. Florensky emphasized the mystical and personal character of cognition, and gave much attention to occult phenomena.

Florensky's view of cognition was rooted in the metaphysics of pan-unity, according to which all created beings are consubstantial with one another. In cognition the knower escapes from his isolation and, contravening the logical law of identity, he achieves identity with his "other"—the known. Denying the doctrine of representative perception, Florensky held that the perception of an object involves the direct unification of perceiver and object. Cognition is intrinsically connected with love, the end of which is, according to Florensky, "that two should become one." Love is a manifestation of the consubstantiality of created beings, and in the self-centeredness or separateness which represents a failure of love, lies error, ignorance, sin, and metaphysical dissolution.

Following Solovyov, Florensky maintained that the metaphysical unity of created beings is rooted in "Sophia," the principle of Divine Wisdom; Sophia thus represents a kind of mystical, integrating substratum of the cosmos. The focus of the Divine prototypes in accordance with which the cosmos is created, Sophia is a "fourth hypostasis" in the Divine nature. According to Florensky, Sophia has many aspects and thus can be interpreted in many ways—as the "ideal substance" of the created world, as the Church, as the Mother of God, and so on.

In addition to his major work Florensky published essays on idealism and on the philosophy of A. S. Khomyakov. He also published a volume of poetry, and numerous books and monographs in mathematics, physics, and art.

Principal Works by Florensky

"Obshchechelovecheskiye Korni Idealizma" ("The Universally Human Roots of Idealism"). *Bogoslovsky Vestnik*, No. 2 and No. 3 (1909), 284–297, 409–423.

Stolp i Utverzhdeniye Istiny. Moscow, 1914.

"Smysl Idealizma" ("The Meaning of Idealism"), in *Sbornik Statey v Pamyat' Stoletiya Imperatorskoy Moskovskoy Dukhovnoy Akademii* ("Collected Articles Commemorating the Centenary of the Imperial Moscow Theological Academy"). Sergiyev Posad, 1915.

"Alexey Stephanovich Khomyakov." *Bogoslovsky Vestnik* (July–August, 1915), 516–581.

Works on Florensky

Florovsky, George, *Puti Russkovo Bogosloviya* ("Paths of Russian Theology"). Paris, 1937.

Lossky, N. O., *History of Russian Philosophy.* New York, 1951.

Zenkovsky, V. V., *Istoriya Russkoy Filosofii*, 2 vols. Paris, 1948–1950. Translated by G. L. Kline as *A History of Russian Philosophy*, 2 vols. New York and London, 1953.

JAMES P. SCANLAN

FLORENTINE ACADEMY, or Platonic Academy of Florence, is the name usually applied to the circle of philosophers and other scholars who gathered around Marsilio Ficino, under the auspices of the Medici, in Careggi, near Florence, between 1462 and 1494. These scholars were engaged in the study and discussion of the works of Plato and his followers and of Platonic philosophy. The name "academy" was adopted in memory of Plato. There is no direct link between this Platonic Academy and other academies active in Florence at a later date.

According to Ficino, the academy was founded by Cosimo de' Medici because his enthusiasm for Plato had been aroused by the lectures of Gemistus Pletho at the time of the Council of Florence (1438). In 1462 Cosimo placed a villa in Careggi at the disposal of Ficino, the promising young son of his physician, and lent him several Greek manuscripts of Plato and other ancient philosophers, assigning him the task of studying, translating, and interpreting these writings. This event may be considered the founding of the Florentine Academy. Unlike most later academies, Ficino's Platonic Academy had no formal organization, charter, or fixed membership, and its activities must be inferred from contemporary sources, mainly the letters and other works of Ficino and his associates.

The chief products of the academy are the numerous writings of Ficino and his associates. Whether the public lectures given by Ficino on Plato, Plotinus, and St. Paul were considered part of the work of the academy we do not know. Its activities probably included some regular readings of the Platonic texts and some lectures about them, and surely Ficino gave individual instruction to some of his pupils. On many occasions he addressed edifying sermonlike speeches to his gathered friends and pupils, and this fact, along with a few others, suggests a link between the academy and some of the lay religious associations of the same period. The most famous events of the academy are the banquets celebrated on Plato's reputed birthday, November 7, in 1468 and in 1473, and perhaps in other years. The banquet of 1468 provided the setting for Ficino's commentary on Plato's *Symposium.* The academy also held discussions on philosophical and other subjects on numerous occasions, and it was customary for learned or otherwise distinguished visitors to Florence to attend some of the meetings. The study in which Ficino talked to his pupils contained a painting that represented the globe, with the crying Heraclitus and the laughing Democritus on either side. The often repeated story that Ficino kept an ever-burning lamp before a bust of Plato must be rejected as a legend.

There is no philosophical doctrine common to the Florentine Academy distinct from that of Ficino, but the thought of all its members was influenced to a greater or lesser degree by his teachings. The circle included such philosophers as Giovanni Pico della Mirandola and Francesco Cattani da Diacceto, and such philosophically inclined scholars and poets as Cristoforo Landino, Lorenzo de' Medici, Angelo Poliziano, and Girolamo Benivieni, to mention only some of the better-known members whose writing showed the impact of the academy. The meetings of the academy became famous during its own time, and its intellectual influence, through its visitors and through Ficino's correspondence, spread to the rest of Italy and Europe. Thus, in spite of its informal and fluctuating character, the academy became, and has remained in history and tradition, the most tangible center of Renaissance Platonism. (For the nature of its teachings, see FICINO, MARSILIO.)

There is a close link between Ficino's philosophical doctrine and the structure of the academy as he conceived it. Following the model of the ancient philosophical schools, Ficino considered the academy as a community of friends, and his philosophy included an elaborate theory of friendship which he identified with Platonic love. The members of the academy were, he felt, linked with each other and with their master through a "divine" friendship that was based on their common concern with the contemplative life and with the spiritual ascent toward the knowledge and enjoyment of God.

The goal of the academy was philosophical and, in a broader sense, spiritual and cultural rather than political. Although Ficino and the academy were closely identified with four generations of Medici rulers, it cannot be proved that he was their political tool or that his personal and scholarly attachments were limited to their partisans. Nonetheless, although Ficino lived until 1499 and remained active as a scholar throughout his later years, we hear next to nothing of the activities of the academy after 1494, the year in which the Medici were expelled from Florence, Poliziano and Pico died, and Ficino's published correspondence stopped. There is no direct evidence that the meetings of the academy were discontinued, but it is easy to understand that the illness and old age of its leader, the death of some of its most prominent members, and the political and religious climate that prevailed in Florence after 1494 must have put an end to the academy or at least reduced its activities to a strictly private character.

Bibliography

Della Torre, Arnaldo, *Storia dell'Accademia Platonica di Firenze.* Florence, 1902. This work is still indispensable.
Kristeller, Paul Oskar, "The Platonic Academy of Florence." *Renaissance News,* Vol. 14 (1961), 147–159. Reprinted in Kristeller's *Renaissance Thought II.* New York, 1965. Pp. 89–101.
Marcel, Raymond, *Marsile Ficin.* Paris, 1958.

PAUL OSKAR KRISTELLER

FLUDD, ROBERT (1574–1637), or Flud, also known as Robertus de Fluctibus, was an English physician, author, and occultist. The son of Sir Thomas Fludd, paymaster to Queen Elizabeth's forces in France and the Low Countries, Fludd was born at Milgate House, Bearsted, Kent. At the age of seventeen he entered St. John's College, Oxford, then a center of high Anglicanism. After taking his M.A. degree in 1598, Fludd spent some years abroad, studying medicine. On returning to Oxford, he entered Christ Church. He took the degrees of M.B. and M.D. in 1605, but had considerable difficulty obtaining from the College of Physicians the right to practice medicine, which was not granted until 1606. It was alleged that he had spoken with contempt of Galen. Nevertheless, he was admitted as a fellow of the College of Physicians in 1609.

As a London doctor Fludd prospered; he was able to provide himself with an amanuensis, to whom he dictated his numerous treatises. His first book, *Apologia Compendiaria Fraternitatem de Rosea Cruce* (1616), was a defense of the ideas of the "Fraternity of the Rosy Cross." About the origins and character of the Rosicrucian Fraternity there is considerable dispute. Although allegedly introduced into Europe in the fifteenth century, Rosicrucian ideas, in fact, derive from two anonymously published tracts written by the Lutheran theologian Johann Valentin Andreä in the early seventeenth century. These, for motives which are somewhat obscure, purported to be of fifteenth-century origin. Whether even in the seventeenth century there actually was a Rosicrucian Society as described by Andreä remains a matter of dispute. But these tracts provided a common point of reference for like-minded occultists.

It is impossible to take Fludd seriously as a philosopher; however, he did give expression to a system of ideas which was very influential in the seventeenth century. This can most succinctly be described as an attempt to uphold allegorical interpretation of the Bible, and the established pseudo sciences—astrology, chiromancy, alchemy, and sympathetic magic—against the scientific spirit.

Fludd attacked scientific inquiry mainly in its Greek form, as represented in Aristotle and Galen, but certainly with an eye on what was happening around him. His point of departure was St. Paul's attack upon philosophers who try to discover the truth by their own efforts rather than by the interpretation of what God has chosen to reveal. Fludd's criticism of science can be summed up in the familiar phrase: "What is true isn't new; what is new isn't true." He argued that so far as science has any truth in it, it teaches doctrines which careful interpretation will reveal in Genesis (Like Henry More, Fludd was greatly influenced by cabalistic writings). For the most part, however, the teachings of science have to be rejected. Fludd attacked Aristotle's meteorological writings, for example, because Aristotle gives a naturalistic account of lightning and thunder; whereas lightning, according to Fludd, "is a fire burning from the face and presence of Jehovah."

Yet, strangely enough, there is a good deal of contemporary science incorporated into Fludd's work. His contemporaries, he complained, demanded "ocular demonstrations" of divine truths and he used the thermometer—the invention of which is sometimes ascribed to him—and the lodestone for that purpose. Like many of his fellow occultists, Fludd had a passion for diagrams, and some of his optical diagrams remained in physics textbooks up to the present century.

His general approach, however, is cosmogonical, in the manner of the mythmaker, rather than cosmological, in the manner of the scientist. His ideas are most fully presented in *Utriusque Cosmi, Maioris Scilicet et Minoris, Metaphysica, Physica atque Technica Historia* (An Account, Metaphysical, Physical, and Technical, of Both Worlds, Greater and Lesser"), which was published as a series of volumes from 1617 to 1621, and was even then left unfinished. Fludd makes great play with the general concepts of light (heat) and darkness (cold)—hence his interest in optics; rarefaction and condensation—hence the thermometer; sympathy and antipathy—hence the lodestone. His theory can be described in this way: in the beginning God created a void by withdrawing into himself (contraction), and the void appeared as darkness because God is light. Expanding again as light into the void, God created all the substances of the world. Thus, the world we live in is ruled partly by light (God) and partly by darkness (the kingdom of the devil). Since everything is of the same nature—that is, a mixture of light and darkness—there are secret sympathies and secret antipathies everywhere, marked by signs which the adept can discover with God's help. The practice of medicine depends entirely on understanding these forces, as do the practices of chiromancy and astrology.

Fludd's works were published in Latin, and circulated

on the Continent, where they attracted a considerable amount of attention. In 1623 Marin Mersenne attacked Fludd as an "evil magician"; and when Fludd replied, Gassendi, at Mersenne's request, criticized his occultism at length. Fludd also engaged in controversy with Kepler, who had criticized Fludd in the appendix to his *Harmonice Mundi* (1619).

Bibliography

Fludd's works were brought together as *Opera* (Gouda, 1638); *Philosophia Moysaica* appeared posthumously in an English version—Fludd's own—in London (1659); his short alchemical essay "Truth's Golden Harrow" was published in *Ambix*, Vol. III, Nos. 3 and 4 (April, 1949), 91–150, with an introduction by C. H. Josten.

James Brown Craven, in *Doctor Robert Fludd, the English Rosicrucian* (Kirkwell, 1902) summarizes Fludd's works enthusiastically, but without much insight. Craven's book includes details of the Fludd–Mersenne–Gassendi controversy.

Other writings on Fludd include Serge Hutin, *Robert Fludd: Le Rosicrucien* (Paris, 1953) with a bibliography; Walter Pagel, "Religious Motives in the Medical Biology of the Seventeenth-Century," in *Bulletin of the Institute of the History of Medicine*, Vol. III, No. 4 (1935) 265–312; Robert Theodore Gunther, *Early Science in Oxford*, Vol. XI (Oxford, 1937); Sherwood Taylor, "The Origins of the Thermometer," in *Annals of Science*, Vol. 5, No. 2 (December, 1942), 129–156; Lynn Thorndike, *History of Magic and Experimental Science*, Vols. VII and VIII (New York, 1958). See also Denis Saurat, *Milton: Man and Thinker* (London, 1944), Ch. 3, pp. 248–267.

JOHN PASSMORE

FONSECA, PETER (1528–1599), Neo-Scholastic Aristotelian philosopher, was born at Proença-a-Nova, Portugal, and died at Lisbon. He entered the Society of Jesus at the age of 20, completed philosophical and theological studies in that order, and spent most of his life as a professor of philosophy at Coimbra, where he was the leader of a group of scholars who produced a famous series of textbooks (*Cursus Conimbricensis*). Fonseca has been called the Aristotle of Portugal. His *Institutionum Dialecticarum* ("Eight Books on Logic," Lisbon, 1564), was widely used as a textbook throughout Europe, and in 1625 it was in its 34th printing. Basically an interpreter of the philosophy of Aristotle, Fonseca corrected the Aristotelian text then in use, using Greek manuscripts, and started the process of improving the Renaissance Latin versions. His logic is the traditional syllogistic which continued to be taught in Europe until J. S. Mill and the nineteenth-century mathematicians broadened the scope of the subject. As a student Fonseca had, of course, been taught a modified form of Thomism, but he showed a great deal of independence on specific questions. In theory of knowledge he maintained that a singular thing is directly known by the human intellect (contrary to Aquinas), and he seems to have felt (with the later Ockhamists) that the theory of intelligible species as intellectual determinants of the process of conceptualization is useless. Fonseca placed great emphasis on the unity of the formal concept of being (influencing Francisco Suárez) and taught that this concept is univocal and not analogical in its reference to individual realities. However, he approximated the Thomistic real distinction of essence and existence by treating essence as an ultimate intrinsic mode of the nature of a thing and existence as a contingent addition to this nature. He is, then, partly responsible for the introduction of the terminology of modes into early modern metaphysics. Fonseca abandoned Thomism in denying that matter is pure potency and in rejecting quantified matter as the principle of individuation in bodies. He explained individuation as due to a positive difference (*differentia*) added to the essence of a thing, a theory reminiscent of Duns Scotus.

Works by Fonseca

Commentariorum in Libros Metaphysicorum Tomi IV ("Commentary on Aristotle's Metaphysics"). Vols. I and II, Rome, 1577–1589; Vol. III, Evora, 1604; Vol. IV, Lyons, 1612.

Isagoge Philosophica ("Introduction to Philosophy"). Lisbon, 1591.

Works on Fonseca

Giacon, C., *La seconda scolastica*. Milan, 1946. Vol. II, pp. 31–66.

Nedelhofen, M., *Die Logik des Petrus Fonseca*. Bonn, 1916.

VERNON J. BOURKE

FONTENELLE, BERNARD LE BOVIER DE (1657–1757), French author, forerunner of the Enlightenment, was born in Rouen and died in Paris, having lived one month short of a century. Schooled by the Jesuits, he also studied law, but soon abandoned the career of advocate to follow in the literary footsteps of his uncles, Pierre and Thomas Corneille. Neither then nor later was he to distinguish himself as a poet or dramatist but, in 1683, with the appearance of the *Dialogues des Morts* (*Dialogues of the Dead*), he achieved immediate success as a man of letters. The witty paradoxes and sparkling conversations in these imaginary dialogues of illustrious and notorious figures of the past confirmed the reputation of their 26-year-old author as a seventeenth-century *bel-esprit*; more important, they revealed him as a singularly independent thinker, skeptical of traditional values and, as such, a potential enemy of seventeenth-century orthodoxy. Judging his literary fame firmly established, Fontenelle turned to the study of mathematics, physics, and astronomy and published *Entretiens sur la pluralité des mondes* (*Conversations on the Plurality of Worlds*, 1686), a brilliantly successful popularization of the Copernican system which, until that time, had achieved very limited acceptance.

The following year his *Histoire des Oracles*, ingeniously adapted from the ponderous Latin of van Dale, appeared anonymously. Ostensibly an exposure of imposture and charlatanism in religious practices of pagan antiquity, the work was soon recognized for what it really was: a bold attack on credulity and superstition in all ages. Equally daring was *De l'Origine des fables* ("The Origin of Fables"), composed by Fontenelle before 1680, but fear of persecution invited prudence, and it was not published until 1724. One of the first modern studies in the field of comparative religion, it based early man's belief in the supernatural on his ignorance of natural phenomena. But it was obvious that the criticism was intended to apply equally as well to Christianity and other revealed religions.

The quarrel over the relative literary merits of the Ancients and Moderns had been raging for some years when, in 1688, Fontenelle entered the fray with his *Digression sur les Anciens et les Modernes*. His thesis was that since the question also included the problem of man's progress, the recent accumulation, organization, and dissemination of scientific knowledge proved the superiority of the Moderns. Because of his position in the dispute, entry into the French Academy was denied him on four occasions; and he was not elected a member until 1691.

In 1697 Fontenelle was elected to the Academy of Science, and two years later he became its secretary. His clarity and intelligence, the cool impartiality of his judgment, his wide range of scientific knowledge, and his gift for expression made Fontenelle ideally suited for the post, and he came to be considered as spokesman for his fellow academicians. He contributed a great deal to the widespread popularization of the scientific spirit at home and abroad with his remarkable series of *Éloges* for departed academy members, written over a period of forty years. These essays provided an impressive, constantly renewed picture of accomplishments in science on various fronts, written with the same lucidity and ease of expression that marked all of Fontenelle's serious writing. They were admirably complemented by the *Histoire de l'Académie royale des sciences* which alone, with its masterful preface and original views, would have assured Fontenelle's reputation throughout eighteenth-century Europe as one of the great historians of the philosophy of science.

In the field of mathematics, Fontenelle was particularly interested in the differential calculus of Newton and Leibniz and the analytical geometry of René Descartes. One of his own mathematical treatises is the *Préface des éléments de la géométrie de l'infini* ("Elements of Infinitesimal Calculus," 1727). The last book he wrote was also scientific in nature. Entitled *Théorie des tourbillons cartésiens* ("The Theory of Cartesian Vortices," 1752), it showed him to be a disciple of Descartes in physics, if not in metaphysics.

Concerning Descartes, Fontenelle said that he should be held in esteem at all times but followed only now and then. Nevertheless, Fontenelle can be considered a Cartesian in two respects. First, his own skepticism was closely bound up with Descartes' principle of methodical doubt. Second, as a stout believer in the purely mechanical philosophy of nature, he found the Cartesian theory of vortices far closer to reality than Newton's laws of attraction, according to which it was necessary to hold that some invisible, seemingly supernatural force operated across vast stretches of space.

Among a number of audaciously conceived, anonymous works on religion and metaphysics ascribed to Fontenelle is the *Traité de la liberté*, which appeared in 1745 together with four other pamphlets under the title of *Nouvelles Libertés de penser*. The work, a few copies of which escaped police seizure, purports to reconcile divine foreknowledge with human free will, but, in fact, casts doubt on the existence of either.

Immediately following Fontenelle's death in January 1757, the general opinion of his accomplishments was summed up by Frédéric-Melchior Grimm: "The philosophic spirit, today so much in evidence, owes its beginnings to M. de Fontenelle" (*Correspondance littéraire*, February 1, 1757).

Although there were serious lapses in Fontenelle's knowledge and, hence, in his scientific judgment, his works nevertheless served as the single most important bond between the philosophico-scientific revolution in progress during his life and the *philosophe* movement just getting under way. He was one of the great forerunners of the French Enlightenment, and no small part of his success in this role lay in the fact that he exploited, as had never been done before, a technique for the popularization of science that was still to have its effects some two centuries later.

Principal Works by Fontenelle

Oeuvres, G.-B. Depping, ed., 3 vols. Paris, 1818.
Entretiens sur la pluralité des mondes; Digression sur les Anciens et les Modernes, Robert Shackleton, ed. Oxford, 1955.

Works on Fontenelle

Carré, J.-R., *La Philosophie de Fontenelle ou le sourire de la raison*. Paris, 1932.
Cosentini, John W., *Fontenelle's Art of Dialogue*. New York, 1953.
Maigron, Louis, *Fontenelle, l'homme, l'oeuvre, l'influence*. Paris, 1906.
Marsak, Leonard M., "Bernard de Fontenelle, The Idea of Science in the French Enlightenment." *Transactions of the American Philosophical Society*, New Series, Vol. 49, Part 7 (1959), 64.

OTIS FELLOWS

FORCE. In the most general sense, force denotes the faculty of action or the power to overcome a resistance. In the physical sciences it is that entity which changes, or tends to change, the state of rest or of motion of a body. Consequently, it may also be defined as the cause of motion, or more precisely—assuming the validity of the principle of inertia, according to which unaccelerated motion and rest are dynamically and causally equivalent and correspond merely to different choices of the reference systems—as the cause of acceleration.

The metric unit of force in science is the *dyne*, which is the force necessary in order to give a mass of one gram an acceleration (increase of velocity) of one centimeter per second in each second. The British unit of force is the *poundal*, which is the force necessary to give a mass of one pound an acceleration of one foot per second each second. The practical unit is the *gram force*, that is, the force which the earth exerts on one gram of mass at sea level and 45° latitude; it equals 980.616 dynes. Another common unit is the *newton*, which is the force necessary in order to give a mass of one kilogram an acceleration of one meter per second each second, and is therefore equivalent to 10^5 dynes.

Apart from being used in a figurative sense, such as "force of habit," "police force," or "economic forces," the word "force," especially in the natural philosophy of the eighteenth and nineteenth centuries and in the early writings on the principle of conservation of energy (R. Mayer,

H. von Helmholtz) signified action and energy. This homonymic use caused considerable confusion at the time.

Originally taken as an analogy to human will power, muscular effort, and spiritual influence, the concept early became projected into inanimate objects and played an important role in ancient thaumaturgy, occultism, and medieval sorcery.

Concept of force in ancient philosophy. The early Greek hylozoism of the Milesian school (Thales, Anaximander, Anaximenes) conceived nature as a living, animated, and self-moving being, and consequently did not see a problem in the origin of motion. The concept of force gained prominence only with Heraclitus' doctrine of opposing tensions, according to which force is a primary constituent of physical reality and a regulative element in the universe. In Empedocles' philosophy of love (*philia*) and strife (*neikos*), forces, although still conceived in analogy to human affections, became efficient causes of change and motion. In spite of the fact that Plato's natural philosophy relegates the principle of motion ultimately to the existence of a world soul and corresponds in this respect to early hylozoism rather than to the dynamistic teachings of Empedocles and Anaxagoras, the term *dynamis*, signifying not only transitive activity but also passive susceptibility or receptibility, plays an important role in his doctrine. Although Aristotle, in his conception of nature as "physis," still recognized the Platonic notion of force as something inherent in matter, in *De Caelo* he also approached the formulation of a more mechanical conception of force as a physical emanation from one substance to another: through push and pull, bodies affect each other and generate motion in extraneous objects. This Aristotelian notion of emanating kinematic effects, although restricted to contiguous modes of action, is the first instance of the modern dynamical conception of force. In his *Physics* Aristotle subjected this cause of compulsory motion to a quantitative investigation: a force A which moves a mobile B through a distance D during the time T could move half the mobile ($\frac{1}{2}B$) through twice the distance ($2D$) during the same time (T), or could move half the mobile ($\frac{1}{2}B$) through the distance D during half the time ($\frac{1}{2}T$), and so forth. In modern terminology Aristotle's dynamical law of motion may be stated as follows: the velocity of a mobile is proportional to the ratio of the motive force and the resistance of the medium. Nowhere did Aristotle employ units in which these quantities were to be measured. Although it is fairly obvious that forces were practically measured in terms of weight (the early use of the balance is an evidence of this), Aristotle's conception of weight as a manifestation of natural motion and not as a cause of compulsory motion precluded, on theoretical grounds, the possibility of using the units of weight as units of force. Since, according to Aristotle, contiguity between the motor and the mobile was an indispensable prerequisite for the occurrence of dynamical action, force as an action at a distance had no place in his conceptual scheme. Hence, an explanation of planetary motion required the assumption of an external agent or astral intelligence as a "motor" attached to the star, unless the star was thought to be endowed with a life of its own.

With Posidonius' investigations at Gades of the connection between the tides and the movements of the sun and the moon and his doctrine of a universal tension, the concept of force was generalized as something able to pervade all space. Stoic philosophy thus abandoned the Aristotelian restriction of an immediate linkage between the mover and the moved, and conceived force as a mutual correspondence of action between objects, even when the objects were separated in space. In fact, the Stoics were probably the first to formulate the idea of a field of forces and to regard the universe as a vast system ruled by the interaction of forces.

Medieval philosophy. Arabian and Christian medieval philosophy, in general, adhered to the Aristotelian conception of force. The exceptions were mostly inspired by Neoplatonic ideas. Thus, in al-Kindi's treatise *On the Tides* (*Fi-l-madd wal-jazr*), his notion of force is wholly Aristotelian except that he holds that force can be propagated by means of optical rays, a theory conducive to astrological exploitation. Roger Bacon's conception of forces as "species"—isolated entities, detached from their subject and spreading through space in accordance with specific laws of propagation—showed similar features.

The Aristotelian law of motion, already criticized by John Philoponus in the sixth century A.D. and by Avempace in the twelfth century, was shown by Thomas Bradwardine in the middle of the fourteenth century to contradict experience in the case of equality between the motive force and the resistance, so that the ratio is one but the velocity zero. Bradwardine consequently modified the law, claiming that the velocity, in modern terms, depends on the logarithm of the ratio between motive force and resistance.

In the fourteenth century the Stoic conception of a field of forces was also revived, probably independently of the ancient school. In his *Quaestiones Super Libris Quattuor de Caelo et Mundo* ("Questions on the Four Books of the Heaven and the Earth") John Buridan postulates a celestial force which permeates all space and exerts its influence on physical bodies, in contrast to the Peripatetic dictum, *Causa agens est simul cum suo effectu proximo et immediato.* However, the revolutions of celestial bodies, according to Buridan, are not the result of a constant activity of special intelligences, but rather of an original rotational impetus communicated to these bodies by the Creator at the beginning of time.

Kepler. A decisive stage in the development of the concept of force was reached in Johannes Kepler's search for a quantitative determination of dynamic activity. In his early writings, such as the *Mysterium Cosmographicum* (1596), Kepler still refers to force as a soul animating the celestial bodies. His correspondence, however, and particularly his letters addressed to David Fabricius, show clearly that his use of the term *anima* ("soul") in his writings was merely a metaphor to express the immateriality of the principle that governs the mutual movements of celestial bodies. In 1605 Kepler was already convinced that the force of attraction could be subjected to a mathematical formalism. In the third part of his *Astronomia Nova* (1609), Kepler discusses the causes of planetary motion and insists for the first time on a mathematical definition of force, even if it is not a push or pull. "For we see that these motions take place in space and time and this virtue emanates and diffuses through the space of the universe, which are all mathematical conceptions. From this it follows that this virtue is subject also to other mathematical necessities." Having discovered that the planets move in their orbits with velocities that vary with the distance from the sun, Kepler inquired into the physical cause of this mathematical relation and was thus led to assume the existence of a regulative force whose magnitude decreases with the distance. However, attraction was not yet seen as a radial force, but rather as a tangential drag, and Kepler, under the influence of William Gilbert's *De Magnete* (1600), suggested an analogy with magnetism. But in spite of this, Kepler's conception of a gravitational force of attraction is a typical example of the fact that the existence of forces is, and has to be, inferred from the phenomenological aspects of regularities in the variations of motion. It also exemplifies the fact that the postulation of forces as causes of motions and their kinematic variations is a methodological process which finds its philosophical justification in the reduction of numerous cases of functional dependence to one single agency. Kepler's procedure thus became the prototype for the introduction of forces in the various branches of physics: gravitational, elastic, electromagnetic, nuclear forces, and so forth.

Newton. Newton's conception of force can be traced to two originally disparate classes of mechanical or dynamical phenomena which, however, finally found their logical unification in his *Principia* (1687), through its very definitions of force and mass. Documentary evidence seems to show that his earliest conception of force originated from the study of impact phenomena. Thus Newton's "Waste Book 1664" (Ms. Add. 4004, Portsmouth Collection, University Library, Cambridge, England) starts with a definition of the quantity of motion of a body as the product of its "quantity" (mass) and its velocity, and continues: "Hence it appears how & why amongst bodys moved some require a more potent or efficacious cause others a lesse to hinder or helpe their velocity. And ye power of this cause is usually called force. And as this cause useth or applyeth its power or force to hinder or change ye perseverance of bodys in theire state, it is said to Indeavour to change their perseverance." In another document (Ms. Add. 3965, Portsmouth Collection), force is implicitly defined by the statement: "The alteration of motion is ever proportional to ye force by wch it is altered." Considering the exact text of Newton's Second Law of Motion in the *Principia*, "The change of motion is proportional to the motive force impressed," one is led to the conclusion that "force" in these statements denotes more or less what we mean today by "impulse" (which, in fact, is equal to the change of momentum). Newton's original conception of force was consequently that of a thrust, a kick, or a push, as exhibited in collision phenomena, which at that time were the subject of extensive studies by Galileo, Marcus Marci, John Wallis, and Christian Huygens. On the other hand, in his search for a derivation of the phenomenological aspects of planetary motions from the hypothesis of an inverse-square law, Newton needed the time rate of change of momentum as the primitive notion, and thus identified the change of momentum with its rate of change for astronomical applications. Later commentators, therefore, interpreted Newton as stating that force is measured by the product of mass and acceleration, a product which for constant mass equals the time rate of change of momentum. Thus, although not rigorously impeccable, Newton's definition of force led to a unified treatment of terrestrial and celestial mechanics, and the notion of force became a fundamental concept of physics. Whereas Newton's First Law of Motion or Law of Inertia, according to which every body, unaffected by a force, persists in a state of rest or of uniform motion, may be regarded as a qualitative definition of force (namely, as change of state of motion), the Second Law quantified the concept and provided a meaning for the notion of mass. The Newtonian characterization of force is completed with the Third Law, which states, in essence, that every force manifests itself invariably in a dual aspect: it has a mirror-image twin. For it claims that if *A* acts on *B*, then *B* acts on *A* with equal magnitude in the opposite direction; or in other words, to every action there is always opposed an equal reaction. Forces, consequently, arise only as the result of a combined interaction of at least two entities. In a universe composed of only one body, no forces are conceivable.

Having thus explored the quantitative aspects of force, and of gravitational force in particular, Newton does not specify the metaphysical nature of force; as far as physical science is concerned, force is an ultimately irreducible notion. Newton's contribution may thus be regarded as the culmination of a conceptual development in a search for a quantitative determination of an otherwise obscure and indiscernible, yet necessary, notion—a development whose philosophical necessity had already been stressed by Bacon, Hobbes, and even by Descartes.

The scientific legitimacy of a force such as gravitation, which could act at a distance without the intermediacy of an intervening medium, was early called into question. Newton himself, particularly in his *Opticks* (1704), referred to certain speculations, primarily to the notion of an ether, in order to reduce such actions at a distance to contiguous effects compatible with the corpuscular-kinetic theory prevalent at that and later times. Yet, in spite of early opposition (as voiced particularly by Leibniz, who rejected action at a distance as a scholastic obscure quality), the notion of force as conceived by Newton became the basic concept of classical theoretical mechanics. Pierre de Laplace, in his *Mécanique céleste* (1799–1805) considered the reduction of all mechanical phenomena to forces acting at a distance as the ultimate objective of the physical sciences, and Joseph Louis Lagrange's *Mécanique analytique* (1788), the highlight of classical mechanics, was written in the same spirit. The mechanics of action at a distance gained further support through its successful applications by Laplace, Siméon Denis Poisson, and Wilhelm Weber in the classical theories of electricity and magnetism. Even capillary phenomena—contact phenomena par excellence—were treated by Laplace and Karl Gauss as subject to actions at a distance.

Criticisms of action at a distance. The great mathematical success of these theories of force as an action at a distance did not suppress doubts as to the philosophical legitimacy of such conceptions, and alternative mechanistic or kinetic-corpuscular theories, especially for gravitation, were proposed in great number. One of the earliest attempts in this direction, George Louis Lesage's theory of "ultramundane particles" (1747), was typical of similar hypotheses which gained great popularity in the nineteenth century. Particles were assumed to move in all directions through space and to be rebounded by macroscopic bodies; the resulting screening effects were supposed to produce the mutual "attractions" of "gravitating" bodies. The main criticism of the Newtonian conception of force from the philosophical point of view, however, was directed against the hypostatization of force as a metaphysical entity of an autonomous ontological status. Berkeley, in his *De Motu* ("On Motion," 1721) opposed this approach and viewed the notion of force as a convenient auxiliary fiction with which to work; for the notion had the same status in science as the concept of epicycle has in astronomy. Terms like force, gravity, and attraction, he admitted, are convenient for purposes of reasoning or computation; for an understanding of the nature of motion itself, however, Berkeley regards them as wholly irrelevant. They should not lead us to the fallacy that they could throw any light on the real efficient causes of motion, for the only objective of physical science is the establishment of the regularities and uniformities of natural phenomena; to account for particular phenomena means "reducing them under, and shewing their conformity to, such general rules" (*Siris*, 1744). Hume, Pierre de Maupertuis, and especially the early proponents of modern positivism (Gustav Kirchhoff, Heinrich Hertz, Ernst Mach) followed Berkeley in asserting that force is merely a construct in the conceptual scheme of physics and that it should not be confounded with metaphysical causality. Most radical in this respect was Mach's antimetaphysical attitude, in accordance with which he tried to divest mechanics of all conceptions of cause and force and to adopt a purely functional point of view. Following Kirchhoff's *Lectures on Mechanics* (*Vorlesungen über Meckanik*, 1874–1876), Mach, in his *Science of Mechanics* (*Die Mechanik in ihrer Entwicklung, historisch-kritisch dargestellt*, 1883), identified force with the product of mass and acceleration and thus reduced it to a purely mathematical expression relating certain measurements of space and time.

But even after this process of purification and divestment of all causal or teleological implications, the concept of force was not eliminated from the conceptual scheme of physics. Its methodological justification lies in the fact that it enables us to discuss the general laws of motion irrespective of the particular physical situation with which these motions are associated. In contemporary physics the concept plays somewhat the same role as does the middle term in the traditional syllogism; it is a methodological intermediate in terms of which we can study the kinematical behavior of a physical body independent of the particular configuration in which it is found.

Psychological origins of the concept of force. The advancement of the critical attitude toward the concept of force, initiated by Berkeley and Hume and culminating in the logical and metaphysical point of view held by Kirchhoff and Mach, brought in its wake a study of the psychological origin of the notion. The first to deal at length with this problem was Thomas Reid, Hume's immediate successor and founder of the Scottish school. He derived the concept of force from the consciousness we have of the operations of our own mind, and especially from the consciousness of our voluntary exertions in producing effects. Reid concluded that if we were not conscious of such exertions, we would not have formed any conception of force and consequently would not have projected this notion into nature and the changes in it which we observe. Kant's younger contemporary, Maine de Biran, whose personalistic philosophy has many points in common with Reid's empirical intuitionalism, considered our own will as the source of the notion of force; in his view, the resistance to muscular effort felt in the case of voluntary activity makes us aware that certain actions are not involuntary acts, but the results of our ego as a source of force. From the twofold nature of the ego as an individual source of action and as inseparably united to a resisting organism, we aquire the universal and necessary notion of force. While the Berkeley–Hume criticism led almost to the exclusion of the concept of force from science and natural philosophy, at the same time it supplied to the more psychologically and physiologically oriented philosophy important arguments to oppose such elimination. For it was claimed that the concept of force stands in the same relation to the sensation of muscular effort as the concept of motion to visual perception, and science without the concept of motion is inconceivable. Moreover, if one kind of sensation is to be preferred to the others, it should certainly be muscular sensation, the nearest to the psychological experience of volition. Even William James, who, in "The Feeling of Effort," in *Collected Essays and Reviews* (1920), rejected the so-called feeling of innervation and opposed the view that the resistance to our muscular effort is the only sense that brings us into close contact with reality, contended that reality reveals itself in the form of a force like the force of effort which we exert ourselves. The concept of force, according to James, thus remains "one of those universal ideas which belong of necessity to the intellectual furniture of every human mind."

Bibliography

Ellis, Brian D., "Newton's Concept of Motive Force," in *Journal of the History of Ideas*, Vol. 23 (1962), 273–278.

Hesse, Mary B., *Forces and Fields*. London, 1961.

James, William, "The Feeling of Effort," in *Collected Essays and Reviews*. New York, 1920.

Jammer, Max, *Concepts of Force (A Study in the Foundations of Dynamics)*. Cambridge, Mass., 1957; reprinted in paperback, New York, 1962.

Mach, Ernst, *Die Mechanik in Ihrer Entwicklung, historisch-kritisch dargestellt*. Leipzig, 1883. Translated by T. J. McCormack as *Science of Mechanics*. La Salle, Ill., 1960. With introduction by Karl Menger.

Margenau, Henry, *The Nature of Physical Reality*. New York, 1950. Ch. 12.

Röhr, Julius, *Der Okkulte Kraftbegriff im Altertum*. Leipzig, 1923.

Weyl, Hermann, *Philosophy of Mathematics and Natural Science*. Princeton, N.J., 1949. Pp. 148 ff.

M. JAMMER

FOREKNOWLEDGE. See PRECOGNITION.

FORM. See MEDIEVAL PHILOSOPHY; PLATO; UNIVERSALS.

FORM, AESTHETIC. See AESTHETICS, HISTORY OF; AESTHETICS, PROBLEMS OF.

FORMALISM IN MATHEMATICS. See MATHE-MATICS, FOUNDATIONS OF.

FORMAL SYSTEMS AND THEIR MODELS. See SYSTEMS, FORMAL, AND MODELS OF FORMAL SYSTEMS.

FOUCHER, SIMON (1644–1696), one of the foremost critics of Cartesian philosophy, was born in Dijon, France, where, after taking orders, he was made honorary canon of the Sainte Chapelle. He took a bachelor's degree in theology at the Sorbonne and spent his adult life as a chaplain in Paris, where he died. His published works include a long poem showing the compatibility of Greek and Christian morals, an experimental work on hygrometry, and three major dissertations concerning the value of Academic skepticism in the search for truth. He was the first to publish criticisms of both Malebranche's occasionalism and Leibniz' monadism, and it is for these critiques that he is best known.

Academic method. Foucher considered himself the reviver of Academic philosophy, by which he meant Socratic ignorance combined with the reasonable doubt of Philo of Larissa and Antiochus of Ascalon, who said that they knew some things and were ignorant of others; he considered this the middle way between dogmatism and Pyrrhonism. The primary maxim of his Academic philosophy is to recognize only *vérité évident* as a rule of truth. The Academic laws are (1) to proceed only by demonstrations in philosophy; (2) to avoid unanswerable questions; (3) to admit when one does not know; (4) to distinguish what one knows from what one does not know; and (5) always to seek after knowledge. There are three important axioms: (1) true knowledge cannot come from sense experience; (2) opinion is not knowledge; and (3) words must presuppose concepts. Foucher said the goal of philosophy is to find a criterion of truth with which to avoid error in judgment. The criterion can be used to obtain knowledge of the essence of things and also to put this knowledge into a necessary order. However, Foucher built no system; his talents were primarily critical. His method was that of the traditional skeptic; he assumed the suppositions of the system under analysis and then reasoned to what he considered were contradictory conclusions.

Criticisms of Malebranche and Cartesianism. Foucher claimed that Descartes, to his credit, took his rules of method from the Academics but that it was a major mistake on Descartes's part to assert that clear and distinct ideas represent things external to us. Foucher professed that he could not understand how we could have knowledge of the external world if no such knowledge came through the senses. He further insisted that Descartes's claim that the knowledge of properties of extension comes only through the reason, and not the senses, was unintelligible. Beyond this, Foucher made four basic criticisms of Cartesianism.

First, Foucher argued that if mind and matter differ in essence, this allows no possibility of essential likeness between the two substances, which is necessary for causal interaction. Therefore, Cartesian mind and matter cannot interact.

Second, interaction between mind and matter obviously takes place, yet this interaction cannot be accounted for by Cartesian principles. Consequently, the Cartesians cannot know the true essences of mind and matter. The principle that likeness is necessary between cause and effect is self-evident, Foucher said, so mind and matter cannot be essentially different.

The third criticism concerns the ontological similarity between sensations and ideas, both of which were said by the Cartesians to be modifications of the mind. Both also are caused by the interaction of the mind with material things. However, ideas are said to represent objects external to the mind, whereas sensations do not. Foucher argued that if ideas are mental modifications representative of the material things that cause them, then why cannot sensations, which are also modifications of the mind, represent the material things that cause them? Or conversely, if sensations cannot represent material things, then how can ideas do so? This objection of Foucher's seems to be based on the Cartesian dictum that the cause of an idea must have at least as much formal or eminent reality as the idea has objective reality. He believed this meant that it was necessary for there to be a likeness between the formal or eminent reality of the material thing and the objective reality of its idea. Because of this likeness, the material thing could cause the idea to resemble it and, hence, to represent it. Since sensations are caused by the same objects that cause ideas, why would sensations not also be like their causes, and hence representative of them?

Fourth, if mind and matter are substances that differ in essence, then there can be no similarity or resemblance between them or their respective modifications. And, Foucher claimed, it is obvious that if there is no resemblance, there can be no representation. Unextended ideas cannot *represent* extended material things or material modifications because ideas are mental modifications that can in no way *resemble* material things or material modifications. Hence, Cartesian ontology precludes an intelligible epistemology.

Such Cartesians as Jacques Rohault, Pierre-Sylvain Régis, Robert Desgabets, Louis de La Forge, and Antoine Le Grand denied that ontological likeness or resemblance is necessary for an idea to represent its object. Foucher persisted in asking for an explication of this nonresembling representation that is as intelligible as the notion that representation depends on resemblance, but he received little more in reply than that God assures it. Foucher was himself a faithful Christian, but he insisted against the Cartesians and Malebranche that declarations of faith in God's power and wisdom cannot be used as principles in philosophy.

Foucher took Malebranche, as well as Descartes, to be saying that both sensations and ideas are modifications of the soul, which is a substance differing in essence from body. Malebranche denied that his ideas were mental modifications, but Foucher suggested that Malebranchian ideas external to the mind would be as difficult to know as are material objects external to the mind. Despite Malebranche's derision and the fact that Foucher could never see him as anything but a Cartesian, Foucher's criticisms touch a vital point in Malebranche's system as well as in the systems of nonoccasionalist Cartesians. The epistemological failure of Cartesianism stems from the inability of Cartesians to give an explication of how ideas represent material things that is compatible with their dualistic ontology.

Correspondence with Leibniz. In a correspondence noteworthy for the clearness with which each philosopher stated his views, Leibniz agreed with Foucher that Academic principles are useful and that once in a lifetime a philosopher should follow his suppositions to their ground. But Foucher insisted that philosophy is primarily the examination and establishment of first principles, whereas Leibniz contended that very few philosophers are needed for this task; the important work is to follow out consequences. Foucher agreed that mathematics and hypothetical systems based on propositions of identity allow the deduction of internal truths, but he was concerned with the relation of these conceptual systems to the external world. Before a deductive natural philosophy is possible, it must be determined that the physical world is truly represented by our concepts and axioms.

Extracts from the correspondence appeared in the *Journal des sçavans* from 1692 to 1696. In these, Leibniz first placed his new system before the public and Foucher gave it its first published critique. Foucher saw Leibniz' new system as little more than pre-established Malebranchian occasionalism, and he asked why God should go to such trouble to make it appear that mind and body interact if they really do not. Leibniz objected to occasionalism on the grounds that God should not continually be involved in making adjustments; Foucher argued that pre-established harmony, with all adjustments made at once, is no better. He said that Leibniz, like Malebranche, retains matter that is useless in his system because everyone experiences the interaction between mind and body. The task is to explain how interaction *does* take place, not merely how it *seems* to take place and how we can talk as though it does.

Foucher approved of Leibniz' denial of the Cartesian contention that extension is the essence of matter, and the closest he came to outlining a positive system of his own was in his suggestion to Leibniz that interaction between body and mind can be explained if it is assumed that their essences are similar. But he was not assured that any first principles apply to the world, and therefore he criticized Leibniz for building a system on uncertain foundations. Foucher's closing words are a reiteration that, after all, the infallible mark of truth has not yet been discovered.

Simon Foucher is important in the history of modern philosophy as a skeptic who originated epistemological criticisms that are fatal to the Cartesian way of ideas. Leibniz considered him a valued critic. His arguments against the distinction between ideas and sensations were utilized to destroy the Lockean distinction between primary and secondary qualities by Bayle (*Dictionnaire*, "Pyrrhon," Remark B), Berkeley (*Principles* 8–15; *Three Dialogues* I), and Hume (*Treatise* I, IV, ii).

Bibliography

WORKS BY FOUCHER

Dissertation sur la recherche de la verité, ou sur la logique des academiciens . . . . Dijon, 1673.

Critique de la Recherche de la verité où l'on examine en même-tems une partie des Principes de Mr *Descartes . . . .* Paris, 1675.

Réponse à la Critique de la Critique de la Recherche . . . . Paris, 1676.

Réponse pour la Critique à la Preface du second volume de la Recherche . . . . Paris, 1676.

Nouvelle dissertation sur la recherche de la verité. Paris, 1679.

De la sagasse des anciens . . . . Paris, 1682.

Traité des hygrometres . . . . Paris, 1686.

Dissertation sur la recherche de la verité, contenant l'apologie des academiciens . . . . Paris, 1687.

Dissertations sur la recherche de la verité, contenant l'histoire et les principes de la philosophie des academiciens. Avec plusieurs réflexions sur les sentimens de M. Descartes. Paris, 1693.

"Extrait d'une lettre de M. Foucher chanoine de Dijon, pour repondre à M. de Leibniz sur quelques axiomes de philosophie." *Journal des sçavans*, Vol. 21 (Mar. 16, 1693), 365–369.

"Reponse de M. S. F. à M. de L. B. Z. sur son nouveau sisteme de la communication des substances, proposé dans les journaux du 27 juin & du 4 juillet 1695." *Journal des sçavans*, Vol. 23 (Sept. 12, 1695), 639–645.

ANSWERS TO FOUCHER

Desgabets, Robert, *Critique de la Critique de la Recherche de la vérité.* Paris, 1675.

Gerhardt, C. J., ed., *Die Philosophischen Schriften von Gottfried Wilhelm Leibniz*, 7 vols. Berlin, 1875–1890. Vol. I, pp. 363–427. Leibniz–Foucher correspondence.

Malebranche, Nicolas, "Préface pour servir de réponse à la Critique du premier volume," in his *Recherche de la vérité*, Vol. II. Paris, 1676.

WORKS ON FOUCHER

Gouhier, Henri, "La Première Polémique de Malebranche." *Revue d'histoire de la philosophie*, Vol. 1 (1927), 23–48, 168–191.

Popkin, Richard H., "L'Abbé Foucher et le problème des qualités premières." *XVII*[e] *Siècle*, No. 33 (1957), 633–647.

Rabbe, Félix, *Étude philosophique. L'Abbé Simon Foucher chanoine de la Sainte Chapelle de Dijon.* Paris, 1867.

Watson, Richard A., *The Downfall of Cartesianism, 1673–1712.* The Hague, 1965.

RICHARD A. WATSON

FOUILLÉE, ALFRED (1838–1912), French philosopher and sociologist, was a prolific writer, especially on political, social, and historical subjects. He was a lecturer in *lycées* at Douai and Montpellier, at the University of Bordeaux, and finally, from 1872 to 1875, at the École Normale in Paris. When he had to retire because of ill health, he devoted his time to his writings. Through most of his varied output there ran a common thread. This was a concern to reconcile the values of traditionally metaphysical or spiritualistic philosophy—above all, liberty and free will—with the deterministic and antimetaphysical findings of contemporary work in the natural sciences, a concern, that is, to reconcile philosophical idealism with scientific naturalism. Fouillée, who was not closely identified with any formal school of thought, thus represented a further step in the direction indicated before him by some of the later disciples of the spiritualistic school of Victor Cousin, such as Paul Janet and Étienne Vacherot, who aimed at absorbing or coming to terms with, rather than combating, the rising power of natural science and scientific philosophy.

Fouillée's outstanding and most original contribution to this enterprise was the idea that thought could lead to action, which he embodied in his concept of *idée-force,* or "thought force." This concept contains in itself the essence of Fouillée's consciously eclectic, conciliatory method and aim, for it borrows the notion of "force" from contemporary physical science and applies it to mental states, to consciousness. Force, defined as a tendency to action, becomes a universal fact of consciousness; conversely, every idea is a force which has a potential for realizing itself in action. Thus ideas, whether or not they are themselves caused, are causes; and since ideas are mental phenomena, mind is an efficient cause of physical action. The *idées-forces* are intermediaries between the private existence of consciousness and the objective existence of things. They enabled Fouillée to preserve spiritual values within the conditions imposed by natural science by developing what has been called a "positive metaphysics," that is, a metaphysics within the limits of the physically conceivable. Thus he undertook to refute the central tenet of materialism that mind or consciousness is merely an epiphenomenon. Specifically taking up the crucial concept of liberty, Fouillée argued that the consciousness of liberty amounts to the existence of liberty, since it gives rise to ideas formulated in terms of freedom of choice and since these ideas can in fact exert an effect on the outside world.

Fouillée's system is based primarily on psychological analysis, resembling, again, the spiritualism of the school of Cousin. This orientation was indicated by Fouillée himself when in his last work he labeled his philosophy "voluntaristic idealism." The will is the most immediate reality of consciousness, although not sharply separated from the intelligence or reason; ideas in Fouillée seem scarcely distinguishable from intentions. Yet, since he was attempting a comprehensive philosophical synthesis, Fouillée also constructed ontological categories on his psychological foundations. Causation, for instance, was established as an objective reality because it is one of the conditions necessary for the exercise of will, for the efficacy of the *idées-forces.* In like manner he developed an ethics with a strong social orientation. Consciousness, he taught, is aware not only of its own existence but of the consciousness of others (in this connection he suggested the emendation of Descartes' famous dictum to read "Cogito ergo sumus"). Altruism is a necessity, since isolation is impossible; moral choice is explained in terms of the attractive or repulsive power of *idées-forces* in the form of ideals; and ethical conduct is defined in terms of social beneficence.

It is doubtful whether a system like Fouillée's, developed from a defensive posture, could ever prove generally acceptable. The concept of *idées-forces* is suggestive and useful as a tool of psychological analysis, but dubious if elevated to the status of ontological reality. It is ultimately a merely verbal concept or device, seeking to bridge the gap between internal or mental processes and physical actions by, as it were, inserting a hyphen between them. But it will not bear the weight it is meant to carry, and as a result, the system as a whole remains merely suspended between idealism and naturalism. Though he struck a responsive chord and was widely read in his day, Fouillée had, in the end, few if any important followers.

Bibliography

Among the most important of Fouillée's works are *La Liberté et le déterminisme* (Paris, 1872); *La Science sociale contemporaine* (Paris, 1880); *L'Évolutionnisme des idées-forces* (Paris, 1890); *Critique des systèmes de morale contemporains* (Paris, 1883); *L'Avenir de la métaphysique* (Paris, 1889); *Psychologie des idées-forces,* 2 vols. (Paris, 1893), perhaps the central work; *Le Mouvement idéaliste et la réaction contre la science positive* (Paris, 1896); *Les Éléments sociologiques de la morale* (Paris, 1905); *Morale des idées-forces* (Paris, 1908); *La Pensée et les nouvelles écoles anti-intellectualistes* (Paris, 1911); *Esquisse d'une interprétation du monde* (Paris, 1913).

For literature on Fouillée, consult Augustin Guyau, *La Philosophie et la sociologie d'Alfred Fouillée* (Paris, 1913), a laudatory view; Harald Höffding, *Moderne Filosofer* (Aarhus, 1904), translated by Alfred C. Mason as *Modern Philosophers,* pp. 82–88 (London, 1915); D. Parodi, *La Philosophie contemporaine en France,* pp. 40–48 (Paris, 1919); Elisabeth Ganne de Beaucoudrey, *La Psychologie et la métaphysique des idées-forces chez Alfred Fouillée* (Paris, 1936), a massive and judicious work.

W. M. Simon

FOURIER, FRANÇOIS MARIE CHARLES (1772–1837), French social critic, utopian socialist, and eccentric. Charles Fourier was born into a merchant family in Besançon. Except during the French Revolution, Fourier led a quiet and isolated life as a minor business employee and bachelor in Paris, Lyons, Rouen, and elsewhere in France, with occasional trips abroad. Shortly after the turn of the nineteenth century, Fourier began to develop his doctrine, publishing his first major work, *Théorie des quatres mouvements et des destinées générales,* in 1808. He continued throughout his life to elaborate and propagate his views with a single-minded devotion, acquired some followers, and was able to dedicate his last years entirely to his self-appointed task.

After a superficial classical secondary education in a Jesuit school in Besançon, Fourier was entirely self-taught. His reading was confined largely to contemporary periodicals and often apparently to bits of articles or merely to headlines. His views reflect many ideas of the Enlightenment and of the early nineteenth century, with strong Rousseauistic and physiocratic strains.

Fourier believed that, because the world had been created by a benevolent deity and yet wallowed in misery, men had obviously failed to carry out the divine plan. The plan was discovered by Fourier, and it had to be translated into practice. Happiness would then replace misery, unity would replace division, Harmony would replace Civilization. The transformation would occur through the release of man's thirteen passions, instilled by God but repressed in Civilization: the five senses; the four "group," or social, passions of ambition, friendship, love, and family feeling; the three "series," or distributive, passions, that is, the "cabalist," or passion for intrigue, the *papillone* ("butterfly"), or passion for diversification, and the "composite," or passion for combining pleasures; and, finally, the passion for harmony, which synthesizes all the others. With the passions released, existence would become intense joy, and a lifetime would seem but a moment.

To accomplish the release of the passions, humanity would have to be organized into phalanxes of about eighteen hundred men, women, and children. In each phalanx different characters and inclinations would be scientifically combined in a complex and finely graded system of groups and series so that each person could give full expression, in his work and in his other activities, to all his passions, tastes, and capacities, and avoid everything that did not suit him. The economies accomplished by communal work and living and by finding the right place for every talent, and the enormous enthusiasms and energies mobilized by the new order, would make phalanxes extremely successful economically as well as in terms of human happiness. Indeed, a single trial phalanx would prove its absolute superiority within a few weeks or, at the most, months and, through imitation, abolish Civilization in a year or two. Moreover, the savages and barbarians who had stubbornly resisted Civilization would eagerly join Harmony. The result would be one world of happy phalanxes, linked vaguely by a hierarchy of monarchs and more effectively by temporary industrial armies for special tasks and similar touring bands of poets, actors, and musicians. Fourier's life became a constant search for the means to establish a trial phalanx, and his political, social, and other preferences were all subordinated to this one great purpose. Fourier believed his main enemies to be the *philosophes* of all sorts, with their "400,000 false volumes."

Fourier's ideas for transforming society were linked to peculiar views on man's past and to strange cosmological beliefs and "analogical" methods (Fourier argued "by analogy" in dealing with all elements of the cosmos). Because the world was one, the coming of Harmony would lead to new, beneficial creations on earth and would result in the appearance of new satellites, in the regaining of health by our planet, and in more distant desirable cosmic repercussions. At the moment, however, earth remained deplorably behind other planets, and Fourier hoped that sufficiently powerful telescopes would enable men to observe the system of Harmony as practiced by the Solarians or the inhabitants of Jupiter. Fantastic details of many kinds abound in Fourier's writings, and the very form of the writings is frequently bizarre.

In addition to giving rise to Fourierist communal experiments and anticipating cooperatives, Fourier has exercised a broad general influence as social critic, early socialist, and man of many insights, especially psychological ones. Fourier's criticism, appreciated by Marx and Engels among others, is notable for its fundamental character, its incisiveness, its richness, and its lack of compromise or nuance. It ranges from magnificent denunciations of exploitation and sham in family, society, church, and state, through striking discussions of fraudulent business practices (in particular of fraud in commerce, Fourier's bête noire), and of the appalling conditions of the masses, to a listing of dozens of different kinds of cuckoldry. Fourier was a moralist and believed that Harmony would establish truth as well as happiness among men, for truth rather than deception and hypocrisy would then become the profitable and accepted way of life.

Fourier's socialism is *sui generis;* he would have retained some private property, and he regarded inequality and discord as necessary for the construction of graded series and groups and the exercise of all passions. He stressed gastrosophy (the science of cuisine), opera, and

horticulture rather than large-scale agriculture or industry. Far from desiring to mold man to a social purpose, he essayed to create a society where every individual whim would be satisfied. But Fourier did define man in social terms (the natural unit for lions, he said, is the couple, and for man, a phalanx, for only in a phalanx could man truly be man); and he charted an extremely complicated and interdependent socialist society, in which men own property, work, and live in common, in their specially built phalansteries, one for each phalanx.

This vision, together with his criticism of the existing system and many of his specific doctrines, places Fourier as one of the most inspired preachers and prophets of modern socialism. Fourier's remarkable psychological insights, such as his championing of brief sessions and variety in work, his quickness to see oppression no matter how veiled, and his at times penetrating concern with different character formations and problems, link him, for instance, to modern pedagogy, the emancipation of women, and personnel management. Fourier can also be described as a brilliant exponent of the idea of alienation or as a premature theoretician of the affluent society. Especially notable are his emphasis on the repression of passions as the source of all evil, as well as the foundation of Civilization, and his vision of that insane world of repressed passions.

Works by Fourier

Fourier's *Oeuvres complètes,* 6 vols. (Paris, 1841–1845) consists of his three major works, *Théorie des quatre mouvements et des destinées générales,* 2 vols. (Lyons, 1808); *Théorie de l'unité universelle* (Paris, 1822), originally known as *Traité de l'association domestique-agricole;* and *Le Nouveau Monde industriel et societaire* (Besançon, 1829). Fourier also published *La Fausse Industrie morcelée, répugnante, mensongère, et l'antidote: l'industrie naturelle, combinée, attrayante, véridique, donnant quadruple produit,* 2 vols. (Paris, 1835–1836), and numerous booklets and articles. There are also quantities of archival material, the bulk of which, including 98 *cahiers* in manuscript, is in the Archives Nationales in Paris. (See Émil Poulat's indispensable descriptive work, *Les Cahiers manuscrits de Fourier,* Paris, 1957.)

Works on Fourier

The standard work on Fourier remains Hubert Bourgin, *Fourier, Contribution à l'étude du socialisme français* (Paris, 1905). A very rich and up-to-date bibliography with listings in original languages can be found in a recent Soviet study of Fourier by I. I. Zilberfarb, *Sotsialnaia Filosofiia Sharlia Fure i Ee Mesto v Istorii Sotsialisticheskoi Mysli Pervoi Poloviny XIX Veka* (Moscow, 1964). For an excellent brief treatment in English see Frank E. Manuel, *The Prophets of Paris* (Cambridge, Mass., 1962).

NICHOLAS V. RIASANOVSKY

FRANCK, SEBASTIAN, also known as Franck von Word (1499–1542), was an outstanding figure among the spiritualists of the Reformation. His basic spiritualist concept of the conflict in each human being and in the world between the Inner Word (Son of God; eternal, invisible Christ), which is ultimate reality, and the outer word (law, flesh, selfishness), which is only appearance, shadow or phantom, was developed in all his philosophical, theological, historical, and cosmographical works. Franck was born in Donauwoerth, Germany, and died in Basel. After studying at the University of Ingolstadt, Franck entered the Dominican Bethlehem College in Heidelberg in 1518. As a priest he officiated in the diocese of Augsburg. He turned to the Lutheran faith about 1526 and became Lutheran pastor in Buchenbach near Ansbach and then in Gustenfelden near Nürnberg. Franck resigned his pastorate in 1528 or early 1529 to become an independent writer and lived in Nürnberg until 1529 or early 1530.

Nürnberg, a cultural center, offered ample literary resources and personal contacts, especially with Theophrastus Paracelsus and the many followers of Hans Denck. Among Denck's followers were Albrecht Dürer's famous pupils the brothers Hans Sebald and Barthel Beham, whose sister Ottilie became Franck's wife. When Franck left Nürnberg, three of his controversial books were already written. Two of them were free translations from Latin into German (with many of his own unorthodox ideas injected) of Andreas Althamer's *Diallage* (1528), a Lutheran attack against Anabaptism, and of an unknown author's *Chronica und beschreibung der Türkey mit yhrem begriff* (Nürnberg, 1530), in which his ideas on the invisible church were already outlined. The first book wholly his own, *Von dem grewlichen laster der trunckenheyt* (1528), is a notable contribution to the literature on alcoholism.

From Nürnberg he moved to Strassburg, where he had occasion to meet Johann Buenderlin, Caspar Schwenckfeld, Melchior Hofmann, Jacob Ziegler, Michael Servetus, Johann Campanus, and, again, Paracelsus. There he wrote a universal history, extending from the creation of the world to the reign of Emperor Charles V and of Pope Clement VII, entitled *Chronica, Zeytbuch und geschycht bibel* (Strassburg, 1531), famous for its numerous penetrating spiritualistic comments on many ecclesiastical and secular personalities and events. Its chronicle of heretics included Erasmus of Rotterdam as a Roman heretic. Because of this and his adverse remarks about Charles V, Franck was arrested and banned from Strassburg in 1531.

After living in Esslingen, Franck settled in Ulm as a printer and wrote most of his books there. His spiritualistic interpretation of the Scriptures can be found in his *Paradoxa ducenta octoginta* . . . (Ulm, 1534), *Die guldin Arch* . . . (Augsburg, 1538), and *Das verbütschiert mit sieben Siegeln verschlossen Buch* (Basel, 1539). *Die vier Kronbüchlein* (Ulm, 1534) contains Erasmus' *Das thèur und kunstlich Buochlein Morie Encomion, das ist, ein Lob der Thorhait* and Cornelius Agrippa's *Von der Heylosigkeit Eitelkeit und ungewissheit aller Menschlichen Kunst und Weissheit* (both of which he freely translated from the original Latin texts), *Vom Baum des Wissens Guts and Böss* . . . , in which he tries to prove that awareness of good and evil can impair one's goodness, and *Encomion, ein Lob des Thorechten Gottlichen Warts* . . . . His *Weltbuch, Spiegel un bildtniss des gantzen Erdbodens* . . . (Tübingen, 1534), a cosmography with one of the first German descriptions of America and with one chapter dealing with the different religious movements of his time, which initiated systematic comparison of religion on Reformation soil, became one of his most popular books. His *Germaniae Chronicon* (Augsburg, 1538) has been used as an important source for historical research. In his *Das Krieg büchlein des Friedens* . . . (1539) Franck tried to

prove that war not only contradicts Christ's teaching but is also "a devilish, inhuman thing, an abhorrent plague . . . an open door for all vices and sins and destruction of land, soul, body and honor . . . ." Most of these works made Franck the defendant in a trial before the city council that was instigated by Martin Frecht, main preacher in the cathedral of Ulm, Philipp Melanchthon, Martin Butzer, and Landgrave Philip of Hesse. It resulted in his expulsion from Ulm.

Franck, his wife, and their six children went to Basel in July 1539. There, after the death of his wife, he married Barbara Beck of Strassburg. His famous collection, with his interpretation, of *Sprichwörter* . . . (Frankfurt, 1541) was partially republished by G. E. Lessing. The last years of his life were devoted mostly to his Latin paraphrase of the *Deutsche Theologie*, which was never published, and to several posthumously published tractates (*Van het Ryke Christi*, Gouda, 1611; *Een Stichtelijck Tractaet van de Werelt des Duyvels Rijck*, Gouda, 1618; *Sanctorum Communio*, Gouda, 1618), all of which survive only in the Dutch translations. They prove that dualism of God and world fully dominated his thoughts before his death.

Franck's world view is primarily panentheistic, with heterogeneous elements drawn from Lutheranism, medieval mysticism, Neoplatonism, Renaissance speculation, humanism, Anabaptism, and rationalism, with ample citation of the Church Fathers and non-Christian philosophers. This comprehensive syncretism makes Franck an almost unique figure in the Reformation era and therefore a major figure in the history of ideas. As a religious philosopher he will be remembered for his radical spiritualistic tendency to replace exterior authority with inner illumination by God's spirit. The deep spiritual meaning of the Bible (outer word)—which is allegorical, not historical but typological, full of contradictions and merely testimonial to the eternal truth—can be comprehended only by those who have already accepted the Inner Word: "Unless we listen to the word of God within ourselves, we can make nothing of Scripture . . . for everything can be decked and defended with texts" (*Das verbütschiert mit sieben Siegeln verschlossen Buch*). In the light of his spiritualism none of the churches and sects, with their outgrown external disciplines, dogmas, sacraments, ceremonies, and festivals can be the true church. The true church is his *ecclesia spiritualis*, where only inward enlightenment is sufficient; it is the universal invisible church of the spirit, to which even those non-Christians who without knowledge of the incarnate Word have accepted the Inner Word can belong: "I love any man whom I can help and I call him brother, whether he be Jew or Samaritan . . . I cannot belong to any separate sect . . ." (*ibid.*).

As a historian Franck placed the Reformation in the stream of historical development and thus relativized it. He is credited with recognizing the historic force that externalizes the spiritual ("The world must have a papacy even if it has to steal it."). He also observed the typical recurrent rise and fall of kingdoms and peoples, and by recognizing this change of fortune as God's punishment for disobedience of his Inner Word, Franck saw history as interaction between God and the world, as the struggle between the spirit and the forces which resist it.

As one of the most ardent advocates of religious liberty in the sixteenth century, Franck insisted on toleration not only among the individual members of the different churches and sects in Christendom but also toward Jews, Muslims, heathens, and even heretics, since all men, created by God, descended from Adam, and accessible to the Holy Spirit, are equal.

Luther, Philip Melanchthon, and Martin Butzer were especially aware of the danger of Franck's unorthodox thoughts to the new Protestant position. Luther called him "the devil's most cherished slanderous mouth." The convention of Protestant theologians at Schmalkalden in 1540 issued a resolution of condemnation of both Franck and Schwenckfeld, which the latter called a (Protestant) papal bull.

Franck's extraordinarily well written books had a great influence on German prose style. They were widely read in German, Dutch, Swiss, and even English editions until the end of the seventeenth century. There exist at least ten editions of his *Chronica* and as many of his *Sprichwörter*. His *Weltbuch* went through at least six editions, as did his *Vier Kronbüchlein* or parts of it.

While Franck's specific traceable influence was restricted in Germany to Valentin Weigel and Gottfried Arnold, and in Basel to Sebastian Castellio, his spirit and ideas found ardent followers in Holland (Dirk Volkerts Coonhert, Menno Simons, David Joris, and the Franckists or Sebastianists). Although he had strong roots in the late Middle Ages, much of Franck's thought carried the seed of what was to become important in modern thinking. Wilhelm Dilthey rightly testifies that "the ideas of Franck flow toward modern times in a hundred streamlets."

Additional Works by Franck

Klagbrieff oder supplication der armen dürftigen in Englandt an den könig daselbst gestellt wider die reychen geystlichen Bettler. Strassburg, 1529.

Dass Gott das einig ain und höchstes Gut sey . . . . Ulm, 1534.
Sechshundertdreyzehn Gebot und Verbot der Juden. Ulm, 1537.
Des Grossen Nothelffers und Weltheiligen Sant Gelts oder S. Pfennings lobgesang . . . . Ulm, 1537.
Was gesagt sei: Der Glaub tuts alles: Und warumb im die Rechtfertigung alleyn werde zugeschriben . . . . Ulm, 1539.
Schrifftliche und gantz gründtliche ausslegung des LXIIII Psalm . . . . Ulm, 1539.
Handbüchlein Siben Haubtpunken aus der Bibel gezogen und zusammengebracht, darin angezeigt ist leben und todt, Himmel und Hell . . . durch Sebastian Franck gemacht . . . . Frankfurt, 1539.
"A Letter to John Campanus by Sebastian Franck, Strassburg, 1531," translated by G. H. Williams, in *Spiritual and Anabaptist Writers.* The Library of Christian Classics, Vol. XXV. Philadelphia, 1957.

Works on Franck

Bainton, R. H., "Concerning Heretics (Castellio)," in *Records of Civilization XXV.* New York, 1935. Pp. 93–104. Republished New York, 1966.
Barbers, Meinulf, *Toleranz bei Sebastian Franck.* Bonn, 1964.
Becker, Bruno, "Nicolai's Inlasshing over de Franckisten." *Nederlandsch Archief voor Kerkgeschiedenes,* N.S. Vol. 18 (1925), 286–296.
Dilthey, Wilhelm, "Auffassung und Analyse des Menschen im 15. und 16. Jahrhundert," in his *Gesammelte Schriften,* Vol. II. Stuttgart and Göttingen, 1957.
Gritsch, E. W., "The Authority of the Inner Word. A Special Study of the Major German Spiritual Reformers in the 16th Century." Dissertation. Yale University, 1959.
Hegler, Alfred, *Geist und Schrift bei Sebastian Franck.* Freiburg im Breisgau, 1892. The most important work on Franck.
Hegler, Alfred, *Sebastian Francks lateinische Paraphrase der deutschen Theologia und sein holländisch erhaltenen Traktate.* Tübingen, 1901.
Hegler, Alfred, "Beitrage zur Geschichte der Mystik in der Reformationszeit," in *Archiv für Reformationsgeschichte,* Vol. I. Berlin, 1906.
Jones, R. M., *Spiritual Reformers in the 16th and 17th Centuries.* London, 1917. Pp. 46–64. Republished Boston, 1959.
Krahn, Cornelius, and Zijpp, N. van der, "Sebastian Franck," in *The Mennonite Encyclopedia,* Vol. II. Pp. 363–367. Scottdale, Pa., 1956.
Koyré, Alexandre, *Mystiques, spirituels, alchimists du XVIᵉ siècle allemand.* Paris, 1955. Pp. 22–43.
Oncken, Hermann, "Sebastian Franck als Historiker," in *Historisch-politische Aufsätze und Reden,* Vol. I. Munich and Berlin, 1914. Pp. 273–319.
Peuckert, W. E., *Sebastian Franck, ein deutscher Sucher.* Munich, 1943. The only recent interpretation of all aspects of Franck's thought.
Raeber, K., *Studien zur Geschichtsbibel Sebastian Francks.* Basel, 1952.
Raumer, Kurt von, *Ewiger Friede.* Freiburg im Breisgau and Munich, 1953. Pp. 23–60, 249.
Rieber, Doris, "Sebastian Franck (1499–1542)." *Bibliothèque d'humanisme et Renaissance,* Vol. 21 (1959), 190–204.
Schottenloher, Karl, *Bibliographie zur deutschen Geschichte im Zeitalter der Glaubensspaltung,* Vol. I. Leipzig, 1933. Pp. 263–266. Lists all books on Franck to 1932.
Teufel, Eberhard, "Luther und Luthertum im Urteile Sebastian Francks," in *Festgabe für D. Dr. Karl Müller zum 70. Geburtstag dargebracht von Fachgenossen und Freunden.* Tübingen, 1922. Pp. 132–144.
Teufel, Eberhard, "Die 'Deutsche Theologie' und Sebastian Franck im Lichte der neueren Forschung." *Theologische Rundschau,* N.S. Vol. 11 (1939), 304–319, and Vol. 12 (1940), 99–129.
Teufel, Eberhard, *Landräumig; Sebastian Franck, ein Wanderer an Donau, Rhein und Neckar.* Neustadt an der Aich, 1954.
Troeltsch, Ernst, *The Social Teachings of the Christian Churches,* Vols. I and II. Republished London, 1956.
Williams, G. H., *The Radical Reformation.* Philadelphia, 1964.

JACQUES J. WHITFIELD

FRANK, ERICH (1883–1949) studied philology and classics at the universities of Vienna, Freiburg, and Berlin. In 1907 he turned to philosophy, which he studied in Heidelberg under Heinrich Rickert and Wilhelm Windelband. His philosophical career in Germany was brief but distinguished. In 1923 he became professor at Heidelberg, and five years later he was appointed Heidegger's successor in Marburg. Three years after his dismissal from Marburg in 1936, he came to Harvard on a research fellowship and made America his second home. Almost all of Frank's works reflect his double interest in philosophy and history and his efforts to combine historical knowledge and philosophical thought: *Plato und die sogennanten Pythagoreer* (Halle, 1923); *Aristotle's Testimony on Pythagoras and the Pythagoreans,* edited by Emma J. Edelstein (scheduled for publication in 1966); *Wissen, Wollen, Glauben* ("Knowledge, Will, Belief"), a collection of English and German historical and speculative essays, edited with an appreciation by Ludwig Edelstein (Zurich, 1955), of which the title essay represents Frank's most original contribution to philosophy; *Philosophical Understanding and Religious Truth* (New York, 1945).

As a student, Frank felt dissatisfied with current attempts to model philosophy on science and to eliminate the traditional questions of metaphysics, ontology, and religion. Nor was he long satisfied with the post-Kantian idealism which was offered as an alternative and which for a time attracted him. When in 1914 he discovered Kierkegaard, at that time almost unknown in philosophical circles, he thought he had found the beginning of a new and fruitful approach to the problem of the subject–object dialectic. He shared his discovery with Karl Jaspers, and five years later, with the publication of Frank's essay *Wissen, Wollen, Glauben* and Jaspers' *Psychologie der Weltanschauungen* the foundations of German existentialism were laid. The major theme of Frank's essay is that the unity of the subject in self-consciousness is achieved not in the act of knowing or in the act of willing, but only in the act of faith. This knowledge of the self is logically unprovable but is also incontrovertible. The act of faith is neither blind belief nor a "will to believe," but arises out of the immediate awareness both of oneself as free and of a transcendence of oneself. Faith is thus both the condition and the result of the subject's freedom, and all theoretical and practical activity has its source in this freedom. Frank believed he had found in the act of faith the unity of the subject which Kant sought but could not find in the act of judging.

Later Frank came to question the subjective direction in which existentialist philosophy was developing. In his review of Jaspers' *Philosophie* (1933) he not only criticized what he called the "atheistischer Nihilismus" (atheistic nihilism) of Heidegger, but he also pointed out the insufficiency of Jaspers' existential ontology (the *Chiffre*), which, he claimed, bears no analogical relation to Being. Existentialism, he argued, has not succeeded in combining existential concerns with metaphysical objectivity. The freedom of the subject is not threatened by his encounter with the objective. Indeed, that freedom which does not express, historically and analogically, a truth concerning objective Being, is an empty, irrational freedom.

In *Philosophical Understanding and Religious Truth*, which grew out of the Flexner lectures he gave at Bryn Mawr in 1943, Frank considered the question of analogical terms through which alone, in his view, philosophy could adequately express the subjective, existential experience of objective reality. All philosophical truth, he argued, is analogical in that it recounts, in and for each historical period, the relation of man to Being. Philosophical analogy is possible only because there is an objective reality to which our thinking bears a relation. Just as in *Knowledge, Will, Belief* Frank argued that the freedom of the subject always presupposes a transcendence of it, so he now maintained that philosophical thought presupposes an object beyond itself which is its content and its substance. Thus, philosophy shares with religion the belief that there is an objective reality to be known; and the task of philosophy is, in part, the rational elucidation of religious truths. However, philosophy must not take the place of the revealed mystery of religion. In every historical period philosophical truths have a different starting point and find a different expression, but their content—Being—is eternal. Philosophical analogy is possible only because there is Being;

and Being becomes part of our thinking only in analogy. The purpose of philosophy is to present in rational terms the existential dialectic of the subjective and the objective, the temporal and the eternal.

Bibliography

In addition to the works cited above, the reader may wish to consult Frank's "Das Prinzip der dialektischen Synthese und die Kantische Philosophie," in *Kant-Studien*, Ergänzungsheft No. 21 (1911), and his "Mathematik und Musik und der griechische Geist," in *Logos*, Vol. 9, No. 2 (1920), 222–259. See also his editions of Fichte's *Die Anweisung zum seligen Leben* (Jena, 1910) and of the so-called *Nachtwachen von Bonaventura* by Clemens Brentano (Heidelberg, 1912), and his literary and philological studies of Schelling and Brentano in *Sitzungsberichte der Heidelberger Akademie der Wissenschaften, Philosophische–Historische Klasse*, 1 Abh. (1912); and *Germanisch–Romanische Monatsschrift*, Vol. 4 (1912), 417–440.

EVA GOSSMAN

FRANK, SIMON LYUDVIGOVICH (1877–1950), Russian philosopher and religious thinker, was trained in law at Moscow University (1894–1898) and in economics and philosophy at the universities of Berlin and Munich (1899–1902). As a student in Moscow he was a member of a Marxist group headed by P. B. Struve; his first published work was a critique of Marx's theory of value (1900). Between 1902 and 1905 (during which years he moved back and forth between Moscow and Germany) he was a principal contributor to Struve's journal *Osvobozhdeniye* ("Liberation"), published in Stuttgart.

Frank joined a number of other young ex-Marxist intellectuals—among them Struve, Nikolai Berdyaev, and Sergey Bulgakov—in publishing three important symposium volumes: *Problemy Idealizma* ("Problems of Idealism," Moscow, 1903); *Vekhi* ("Signposts," Moscow, 1909); and *Iz Glubiny* ("De Profundis," Moscow, 1918). This last work was printed but because of Soviet censorship was never released.

In 1906 Frank settled in St. Petersburg; in 1912 he joined the Russian Orthodox church and began to teach philosophy at St. Petersburg University. In 1915 (at St. Petersburg) he published, and in 1916 defended, his master's thesis, *Predmet Znaniya* ("The Object of Knowledge"); in 1917 he published his doctoral dissertation, *Dusha Cheloveka: Opyt Vvedeniya v Filosofskuyu Psikhologiyu* ("Man's Soul: An Introductory Essay in Philosophical Psychology," Moscow), but was unable to defend it because of political events. From 1917 to 1921 Frank was professor of philosophy and dean of the newly organized faculty of history and philosophy at Saratov University. In 1921 he was named professor of philosophy at Moscow University. He was among the group of non-Marxist intellectuals expelled from the Soviet Union in the summer of 1922. He settled in Berlin, where he gave university lectures (in German) on Russian literature and culture. In 1937, forced to leave Germany, he moved to France. In 1945 he moved to London, where he died.

From Solovyov—and ultimately from Plotinus—Frank took his central doctrine of positive "total-unity" (*vseyedinstvo*). His epistemological intuitivism was close to that of his older colleague Nicholas Lossky. His characteristic emphasis on the "metalogical unity" of the real, and its transcendence of the Aristotelian laws of thought, was drawn mainly from Nicholas of Cusa. Frank always identified himself as a Platonist.

Although Frank's thought exhibits many Hegelian strands, and although he regularly used terms like *moment* (*das Moment*) in Hegel's special sense (as "dialectical phase" or "component of a totality"), he employed one crucial pair of terms in a very un-Hegelian way. To the absoluteness of *realnost* (reality) he opposed the relativity of *deistvitelnost*, not "actuality" in the sense of Hegel's *Wirklichkeit* (the common meaning of *deistvitelnost* in Russian philosophy) but the merely empirical or factual. Frank distinguished between conceptualizable and objectifiable "factuality" and the nonconceptualizable, metalogical "dual-unity" (*dvuyedinstvo*) of "reality." The real is fully related and concrete; the factual is isolated and abstract: "Being is a total-unity, in which everything particular exists and is conceivable only in its relation to something else . . ." (*Nepostizhimoye*, p. 51). We apprehend reality as a "mono-dual" coincidence of opposites, as both "distinct from all particular determinate contents" of knowledge and as "containing and permeating" every such content (*Realnost i Chelovek*, pp. 93–94). The real is both "transdefinite" and "transfinite"; and in both respects it eludes conceptualization. "Everything finite," Frank declared, "is given against a background of infinity. . . . The knowable world is surrounded on all sides by the dark abyss of the unfathomable" (*Nepostizhimoye*, pp. 29, 35).

Frank agreed with Descartes that, although the *term* "finite" is prior and positive in meaning, and the term "infinite" is derived from it by negation, "it is precisely the infinite as the 'fullness of all' that is given as primary and positive, while the concept of finitude is formed by negation of that fullness" (*Realnost i Chelovek*, p. 57).

Forms, or "ideal elements," are determinate aspects of factuality. The totality of such determinations is grounded in what Frank, following Solovyov, called the primordial unity or total-unity of the real. Although reality is unfathomable, it is not hidden; rather, it is "entirely evident, being mysterious only in the sense that it is inexplicable, irreducible to anything else, and inaccessible to logically analytic thought. It is what Goethe called *ein offenes Geheimnis*" (*ibid.*, p. 78). "Objective factuality" is something alienated and abstract, a "rationalized, i.e., logically crystallized, part of reality." Like a nut's shell, it forms a "hard and relatively distinct outer layer, produced by the inner saps and energies of a living organism" (*ibid.*, pp. 106 ff.).

Reality in its wholeness is graspable only in the integral intuition of "living knowledge" (*zhivoye znaniye*), of which conceptual knowledge is only a derivative product or superstructure: "All particular knowledge is partial knowledge of a whole."

The "I" of the Cartesian *cogito* is a "reality in which subject and object coincide—a "self-revealing" and "self-transparent being-for-itself," accessible to "living knowledge." Sounding rather like Heidegger, whose general position he repudiated, Frank wrote, "We are conscious of ourselves only as a self-revelation of [being] in us" (*Nepostizhimoye*, p. 93). He also offered a more emphatic version of Heidegger's doctrine of *Mitsein*: "No finished 'I'

exists prior to the encounter with the 'thou.' . . . It is in this encounter . . . that the 'I' in a genuine sense first comes into being" (*ibid.*, pp. 148, 154). Frank also suggested Heidegger's category of impersonal "itness" (*das Man*): "The 'we' appears in the form of an 'it' . . . which constitutes the basis and first source of objective being . . . " (*ibid.*, p. 177). Although there can be no "I" apart from its relation to a "thou," "every 'I' has a special root of its own, lying in secret depths inaccessible to others" and "the most essential part of me remains solitary and inexpressible." The more one is aware of oneself as a person, the more one withdraws into "metaphysical solitude," for "we are wholly open only to ourselves and to God" (*Realnost i Chelovek*, pp. 127, 129).

In religious—and especially mystical—experience, "I encounter God as a 'thou' for me, only in . . . that ultimate and essentially solitary stratum of my 'I' in which I am . . . inaccessible to everyone except myself—and God (as Kierkegaard rightly insisted). I encounter God in the utter solitude in which I encounter death" (*ibid.*, pp. 215 f.).

Like Solovyov, Frank generalized the notion of "God-manhood" (Solovyov's term was *Bogochelovechestvo*; Frank's somewhat more abstract term, *Bogochelovechnost*) beyond its Christian context. Its primary reference is not to the Incarnation, but to the basic ontological category of "divine–human reality." In Frank's words, "The dual-unity of Godmanhood is logically prior to the conceptions of both God and man" (*ibid.*, p. 249).

Works by Frank

Predmet Znaniya: Ob Osnovakh i Predelakh Otvlechyonnovo Znaniya ("The Object of Knowledge: On the Foundations and Limits of Abstract Knowledge"). St. Petersburg, 1915. Abridged French translation by Kaffi; Oldenbourg; and Fedotoff, *La Connaissance et l'être*. Paris, 1937.

Dukhovnye Osnovy Obshchestva: Vvedeniya v Sotsialnuyu Filosofiyu ("The Spiritual Foundations of Society: An Introduction to Social Philosophy"). Paris, 1930.

Nepostizhimoye: Ontologicheskoye Vvedeniye v Filosofiyu Religii ("The Unfathomable: An Ontological Introduction to the Philosophy of Religion"). Paris, 1939.

Realnost i Chelovek ("Reality and Man"). Paris, 1956. An English translation by N. Duddington is scheduled for publication in 1966. Excerpts from this translation, together with a hitherto unpublished essay, "Of the Two Natures in Man," appear in James M. Edie, James P. Scanlan, Mary-Barbara Zeldin, and George L. Kline, eds., *Russian Philosophy*. Chicago, 1965. Vol. III, pp. 281–314.

Works on Frank

Lossky, N. O., *History of Russian Philosophy*. New York, 1951. Pp. 266–292.

Zenkovsky, V. V., *Istoriya Russkoi Filosofii*, 2 vols. Paris, 1948, 1950. Translated by G. L. Kline as *A History of Russian Philosophy*, 2 vols. London and New York, 1953. Pp. 852–872.

Zenkovsky, V. V., ed., *Sbornik Pamyati Semëna Lyudvigovicha Franka* ("A Collection of Essays in Memory of Simon Ludvigovich Frank"). Munich, 1954. Reminiscences and critical essays by Zenkovsky and others. Contains a bibliography of Frank's writings, compiled by L. A. Zander, pp. 177–192.

GEORGE L. KLINE

FRANKLIN, BENJAMIN (1706–1790), United States statesman, scientist, and author. Franklin was born in

Boston, where he attended school for less than a year. He learned the printer's trade, and at 17 he ran away to Philadelphia. After two years in England (1724–1726) he returned to Pennsylvania, where, prospering in his trade, he began publishing *The Pennsylvania Gazette* in 1729 and *Poor Richard's Almanack* in 1732. He had already formed a tradesman's self-improvement club, the Junto, and soon began civic and educational promotions, including the founding of the American Philosophical Society.

Franklin retired from business in 1748, turned to science, and in 1751 published *Experiments and Observations on Electricity.* The same year he entered the Pennsylvania Assembly, where he was a leader in opposing the influence of Proprietor Thomas Penn and in advocating colonial union. In 1757, as agent for the assembly, he went to England, where, except for 18 months, he lived until 1775, enjoying English society and the friendship of Hume, Lord Kames, Richard Price, and other British philosophers. At first he worked loyally for the expansion of the British Empire and sought to exchange proprietary for royal government in Pennsylvania, but after 1765 he became the leading colonial spokesman in resisting British measures in North America. Although he opposed every act of oppression, he sought until the very end to reconcile differences; but in 1775 he returned home, signed the Declaration of Independence, and worked for a united war effort. In 1776 he went to France, where he signed the French Alliance (1778), secured loans and supplies for the Revolutionary War, and helped negotiate the Treaty of Paris (1783).

He was lionized by Voltaire, Madame Helvétius, Condorcet, La Rochefoucauld d'Enville, and other *philosophes,* and returned home in 1785. He served for three years as president of the Pennsylvania Executive Council, attended the Constitutional Convention of 1787, sought the abolition of slavery, and worked on his *Autobiography* in the five years preceding his death.

Franklin's greatest popular fame is as a moralist. The aphorisms of Poor Richard and the example of his *Autobiography* have served as a philosophy of life for millions. In these two works Franklin sought deliberately to set down the rules of conduct that would enable anyone, however humbly born, to prosper and live more meaningfully. The emphasis was unashamedly on the mundane virtues: thrift, hard work, diligence, prudence, moderation, honesty, and shrewdness. For this, Franklin has been denounced by D. H. Lawrence and others as a "snuff-colored man" who impoverished life by "fencing it in" with a stifling, despiritualizing morality. In fact, Franklin knew the precepts of Poor Richard were but a partial philosophy; in his own career and in his other writings he showed abundantly how full and imaginative human life can be.

Like many deists of his day, Franklin believed "in one God, Creator of the Universe, that he governs it by his Providence . . . [and] that the soul of Man is immortal" (letter to Ezra Stiles, March 9, 1790).

As a scientist, Franklin formulated important and influential laws concerning the nature of electricity. By proving that lightning is an electrical discharge, he placed electricity beside heat, light, and gravity as one of the primordial forces in the universe and hypothesized a new dimension or quality possessed in some measure by all matter. Characteristically, Franklin turned readily from electrical theory to a useful invention, the lightning rod. His scientific attitude is summarized in the statement "Let the experiment be made," and in the observation that electrical experiments would "help to make a vain man humble."

As a public philosopher, Franklin assumed that the traditional personal values have political relevance. He shared the Aristotelian belief that government exists for the sake of the good life and that its powers can be used to that end. A good citizen, guided by the virtues Franklin encouraged in *Poor Richard's Almanack* and in his *Autobiography,* would undertake civic improvement and participate disinterestedly in government. In an expanding country filled with opportunity, Franklin saw individual initiative as the essential engine of progress, but he did not hesitate to seek whatever seemed required for the public good through government. His confidence in the virtue of the citizens of the United States caused him to favor government by consent, but he was not a simple democrat who believed majority will should be omnipotent. He accepted democracy because he thought it would yield good government; if it did not, he readily rejected it.

Franklin thought freedom's dynamism would cause its spread around the world, and therefore that the United States, as a leading free nation, would be influential without being predatory. At the same time he understood the anarchic character of international relations and counseled the nation to maintain its strength, protect its national interest, and act to maintain a balance between France and Great Britain. His essential faith was that, from tradesmen's juntos to the court of Versailles, good men working together could improve the condition of mankind.

Bibliography

For Franklin's writings, see L. W. Labaree and others, eds., *The Papers of Benjamin Franklin,* 8 vols. (New Haven, 1959——) and *The Autobiography of Benjamin Franklin* (New Haven, 1964); and A. H. Smyth, ed., *The Writings of Benjamin Franklin,* 10 vols. (New York, 1905–1907).

For his life and thought, see Carl Van Doren, *Benjamin Franklin* (New York, 1938); Carl Becker, *Benjamin Franklin* (New York, 1946); and R. L. Ketcham, *Benjamin Franklin* (New York, 1965).

On his scientific thought, see I. B. Cohen, *Franklin and Newton, An Inquiry Into Speculative Newtonian Experimental Science and Franklin's Work in Electricity as an Example Thereof* (Philadelphia, 1956). For his political thought, see R. L. Ketcham, ed., *The Political Thought of Benjamin Franklin* (New York, 1965). For his place as an Enlightenment philosopher, see Frank L. Mott and Chester E. Jorgenson, eds., "Introduction," in *Benjamin Franklin: Representative Selections* (New York, 1936).

C. L. Sanford, ed., *Benjamin Franklin and the American Character* (Boston, 1955), reprints a good collection of critical essays on Franklin.

RALPH KETCHAM

FREEDOM. In the history of philosophical and social thought "freedom" has a specific use as a moral and a social concept—to refer either to circumstances which arise in the relations of man to man or to specific conditions of social life. Even when so restricted, important differences of usage are possible, and most of the political or philosophical argument about the meaning or the nature of freedom is concerned with the legitimacy or convenience of particular applications of the term.

Absence of constraint or coercion. It is best to start from a conception of freedom that has been central in the tradition of European individualism and liberalism. According to this conception, freedom refers primarily to a condition characterized by the absence of coercion or constraint imposed by another person; a man is said to be free to the extent that he can choose his own goals or course of conduct, can choose between alternatives available to him, and is not compelled to act as he would not himself choose to act, or prevented from acting as he would otherwise choose to act, by the will of another man, of the state, or of any other authority. Freedom in the sense of not being coerced or constrained by another is sometimes called negative freedom (or "freedom from"); it refers to an area of conduct within which each man chooses his own course and is protected from compulsion or restraint. J. S. Mill's essay *On Liberty* is perhaps the best-known expression in English of this individualistic and liberal conception of freedom.

Some writers take the view that the absence of coercion is the sufficient and necessary condition for defining freedom; so long as a man acts of his own volition and is not coerced in what he does, he is free. Other writers wish to widen the concept in one or both of two ways. They argue that natural conditions, and not only the will or the power of other men, impose obstructions and restraints on our capacity to choose between alternatives and that therefore the growth of knowledge or anything else that increases our capacity to employ natural conditions for the achievement of our purposes *ipso facto* enlarges our freedom. They also sometimes argue that whether or not it is the will of other men or natural obstacles that are considered as limiting or constraining our actions, we cannot truly be said to be free to choose some preferred alternative unless we have the means or the power to achieve it, and thus the absence of means or power to do X is equivalent to absence of freedom to do it. For those who take this view the necessary conditions for the existence of freedom would be (a) the absence of human coercion or restraint preventing one from choosing alternatives he would wish to choose; (b) the absence of natural conditions preventing one from achieving a chosen objective; (c) the possession of the means or the power to achieve the objective one chooses of one's own volition. Many of the assertions frequently made about liberty in recent political thought assume that possession of the means or power to realize preferred objectives is part of what it means to be free. For example, the contention that men who suffer from poverty or have a low level of education cannot really be free, or that they cannot be as free as the well-to-do and the well educated, relies on the assumption that "to be free to do X" includes within its meaning "to be able," "to have the means," and "to have the power" to do X.

What are the objections to thus connecting "being free to" with "having the capacity or the power to"? It can be said that, at least in many cases, equating freedom with possession of power will involve a distortion of ordinary language. If I ask, "Am I free to walk into the Pentagon?"

the question will be clearly understood; but if I ask, "Am I free to walk across the Atlantic Ocean?" the appropriate answer will be "You are free to, if you can." This suggests the main argument: The linking of "being free to" with "having the capacity or power" deprives the word "free" of its essential and unequivocal function, which is to refer to a situation or state of affairs in which a man's choice of how he acts is not deliberately forced or restrained by another man. As de Jouvenel points out, if we say that to be free to achieve chosen ends requires the possession of the power and the social means necessary for their achievement, then the problem of freedom coincides with (or becomes confused with) the quite different problem of how satisfactions are to be maximized. It may be true to say that the poor man is as free to spend his holidays in Monte Carlo as the rich man is, and true also to say that he cannot afford to do so. These two statements, it is argued, refer to two distinct states of affairs, and nothing is gained by amalgamating them.

Meaning of "coercion." Even if we confine ourselves to saying that a man is free insofar as his action is not coerced by another, it is evident that the concept of coercion itself requires some consideration. An important point may be made by examining Bertrand Russell's often-quoted sentence: "Freedom in general may be defined as the absence of obstacles to the realization of desires." This hardly goes far enough. Let us imagine an authoritarian society in which rulers have for years been so successful in controlling and manipulating what members of the community read and what views they encounter, and in which the educators have been able so subtly and skillfully to mold the minds and dispositions of the very young, that almost all citizens naturally desire what their rulers desire them to desire, without its ever occurring to them that there are alternatives to what they are accustomed to or that their freedom to choose has been in any way circumscribed. They are not conscious of any obstructions to the satisfaction of desire and, indeed, no obstructions may exist to the satisfaction of any desires they experience. This is a limiting case, but it points to conditions which exist more or less in all societies. We would scarcely concede that the members of such a society enjoyed any or much freedom. The society described may be one in which coercion in the usual sense does not occur and has in fact become unnecessary.

Two important points follow from this. First, if absence of coercion is a necessary condition of being free, coercion must be understood as including not only the direct forms—commands or prohibitions backed by sanctions or superior power—but also the many indirect forms—molding and manipulation or, more generally, forms of control which are indirect because they involve control by certain persons of the conditions that determine or affect the alternatives available to others. This is an important extension of the notion of coercion. Second, if liberty means the right of individual choice between alternatives, then this right in turn implies that the alternatives can be known by those who are to choose; that individuals have the opportunity to understand the character of available alternatives and can make a deliberate or informed choice. The freedom that members of a society enjoy will be connected, therefore, with the extent to which competing opinions, objectives, modes of behavior, ways of living, and so on are, so to speak, on display; on how freely they can be recommended, criticized and examined; and thus on the ease with which men can make a deliberate choice between them.

For this reason, since literacy or education enlarges the capacity or faculty of choice and decision, it is an important precondition of the existence of freedom: knowledge extends the capacity for acting freely. Similarly, not only suppression but also distortion and misrepresentation, any kind of dishonest propaganda which gains its effect from privileged control over sources of publicity, may restrict the freedom of others; insofar as it succeeds in concealing or misrepresenting the character of certain of the available alternatives, it will tend to restrict or manipulate the range of choice no less effectively than direct coercion or constraint may; and thus it will also tend to limit the exercise of freedom in a particular society. It is not sufficient to consider only the presence or absence of coercion in the more literal and direct sense. Freedom in its positive aspect is the activity or process of choosing for oneself and acting on one's own initiative, and choice can be manipulated as readily as it can be coerced.

Does it follow from this that the extent of freedom is related to the number of available alternatives, in that the more alternatives there are for choice, the freer a man is? Clearly there can be no simple or direct relationship between the range of available alternatives and the extent of freedom. However numerous the alternatives between which a man may choose, he will not admit himself to be free if the one alternative that he would most prefer is the one which is excluded. In a society that forbids the preaching of Catholic doctrine and the practice of Catholic forms of worship, Catholics will not concede that they are free just because they are still free to be either Anglicans, Methodists, or Buddhists. In certain circumstances the extent of the range of available alternatives may be relevant to a judgment of the extent of freedom; but in general we can talk profitably about both the existence and the extent of freedom in a particular society only by taking into account the individual and social interests, the capacities, the modes of behavior, and the ways of living on behalf of which freedom is claimed.

Kinds of freedom. When men speak of their being free or claim freedom for themselves, they are referring not only to the absence of coercion and restraint imposed by others (freedom *from*) but also to that on behalf of which freedom is being claimed (what they are claiming freedom *for*). This is another sense in which we can speak about a positive aspect of freedom. In political and social discussion a claim to freedom is almost invariably (albeit usually implicitly) a claim to a particular liberty, a claim to freedom for or in the exercise of some particular interest or form of activity. Although Russell says that freedom is the absence of obstacles to the satisfaction of desire, probably no serious philosophical or social thinker has defended freedom in the sense of absence of obstacles to the satisfaction of *any* desire; what has been defended, and what freedom has been identified with, is the absence of obstacles to the exercise and satisfaction of specific interests and

forms of activity which are accepted as possessing especial moral and social significance.

Thus, freedom in the abstract is a class comprising many species—freedom of thought and speech, freedom of association, freedom of assembly, freedom of worship, freedom of movement, freedom in the use or disposal of one's property, freedom in the choice of one's employer or occupation, and so on. In every case there is, of course, a reference to the absence of coercion or interference and to an area within which one can choose or act on one's own initiative; not to an abstract or indeterminate possibility of choosing but instead to a specific sphere of individual or social activity within which the right to make one's own choices and decisions, to follow one's own course, is regarded as being of particular importance in the moral life of the individual. This seems to be one way in which positive notions of freedom (as contrasted with the more abstract idea of bare immunity from coercion or interference by others) have emerged, namely, in the attempt to identify (and thus to identify with freedom) those specific spheres of human activity within which what Mill calls individuality, the right and capacity for individual choice and initiative, really matter.

Some of the particular freedoms which have been much emphasized in recent times (freedom from want and freedom from fear are important examples) seem at first sight to refer neither to the absence of coercion nor to any specific interest or form of activity for which freedom is being claimed. It might appear that what *is* being claimed is, rather, the institution of political and economic arrangements by means of which men may be made immune from feelings and circumstances which they find to be evil. If this is all that is meant, then this is to employ freedom in a sense different from the one we have been discussing; this is shown by the fact that freedom from want and fear could conceivably be attained by the setting up of political and social arrangements under which the amplitude of choice within important spheres of activity would be drastically restricted and under which there might be a considerable measure of coercion and constraint; in other words, freedom from want and freedom from fear might well be compatible with a very authoritarian regime, just as in contemporary China freedom from flies is said to have been achieved by very authoritarian methods. Thus, if "freedom from want" and "freedom from fear" are taken simply in that way, the freedom involved is logically and socially distinct from that which has so far been taken as being central and fundamental in the tradition of liberal thinking. However, this may be to interpret these two freedoms superficially. For a more sympathetic interpretation we must return to what has been said about manipulation.

Freedom and power. In modern societies manipulation in various forms is at least as important as the processes we normally identify as coercive. It is well known that, within a society, a group of men may enjoy such control over property or the means of production, or over an educational system or the media of communication, that they are able to determine within a fairly narrow range the alternatives between which their fellow citizens can choose. It is not only true that less privileged men often lack the means or the power to attain their preferred alternative but also that others can exploit their lack of power in order to prevent them from attaining what they would wish to attain; sometimes the less powerful can even be prevented from knowing what alternatives there are and from knowing that some of them might be capable or worthy of being pursued. It is this argument which can justify notions like "freedom from want" or "freedom from economic insecurity" and which links them with what has been taken to be the central sense of freedom, the absence of constraint. Even though we refuse to conclude that the mere absence of the means or the power to attain a preferred alternative goal is equivalent to not being *free* to pursue it, it is a different situation when means and power are controlled and manipulated by others in order to secure compliance with their demands. Thus, if "want" and "insecurity" describe a condition in which there is unequal control over the means and conditions of choice and action, in consequence of which some men can manipulate the range of choice available to others, then freedom from want and insecurity belongs with freedom from coercion; in that case, freedom from want and insecurity is the condition of the ability to act on one's own initiative, which is the positive side of liberty.

There is, then, this connection between freedom and power: When there is conflict between individuals and groups for possession or control of scarce means and conditions of action, control over means is a condition of the availability of alternatives, and hence of choice and freedom. It follows, therefore, that when men have unequal power, this will often mean that they will also be unequal with respect to the freedom they enjoy—not merely in the sense that the man who is better off has the means to choose more widely and live more abundantly than his poorer brother (although this is also true) but in the more relevant sense that the more powerful man can restrict the range of choice and the freedom of the less powerful in order to satisfy his own interests more fully. Obviously this relation between inequality of power and inequality of freedom provides one of the connections that exist between liberty and democracy. If we define democracy as being a form of political organization in which all adult members of the community share in making decisions about the common arrangements of the society (including those decisions about the use and distribution of the resources which affect the choices of acting available to men), then the right to participate in the making of these decisions is a liberty that will affect (or at least may very substantially affect) the range and character of the alternatives that are available in very important areas of social and private life.

Political participation. Thus, we may say that political participation, or sharing in the process of government, will enter into the meaning of "liberty" in society in at least two different ways. First, political activity and participation in government is an interest and mode of activity to which many men attach great importance, and thus the existence of the right and opportunity to engage in this form of activity is one of the liberties that some men cherish highly. Second, it is in addition a liberty that forms part of a wider structure of liberties because the extent to which this liberty is accorded and exercised will usually also affect the extent to which liberty is available in other areas of social life. This is not to say, of course, that the more democratic a society is (the less men are restrained or restricted in their participation in the activity of government), the more freedom there will be in other areas of social life; it is possible for democracies to be exceptionally coercive, restrictive, or intolerant in certain areas of living and, apart from this, it is also true that expansion of particular liberties (or of liberty in particular areas) often entails the curtailment of others. The point is, rather, that political liberty in the sense specified forms part of a more complex system of liberties in any developed society; both logically and causally, political liberty is connected with the liberties that are established in other spheres of individual activity.

Freedom and choice. We have seen that liberty has its negative and its positive sides—"negative" referring to the absence of obstructions, interference, coercion, or indirect control; "positive," to the processes of choosing and acting on one's own initiative, and more concretely and less formally to the general types of human interests or forms of activity for the expression and exercise of which liberty is claimed. Some writers, concentrating particularly on the positive aspect, have been inclined to assert that a man is being free only when he is actually choosing, exercising initiative, and acting deliberately or responsibly. Mill, in what he says in *On Liberty* about "individuality," "individual spontaneity," the "despotism of custom," and related matters, comes very close to asserting this, although he never quite does so. The same kind of view is hinted at in Graham Wallas' "Freedom is the capacity for continuous initiative," but it would be difficult to accept this as a general position. For the devotee of a religious faith, the religious freedom he claims and believes himself to enjoy may be no more than the freedom to practice unmolested a form of worship he has inherited and which he has never felt the faintest temptation to question; in such a case it is a fiction to speak of a process of choice. The same can be said of the man who is content to follow narrowly, uncritically, and unadventurously the established customs and conventions of his society. Even though there may be a sense in which we can intelligibly talk of such men as being slaves to customs, habits, or orthodoxies, it would still be straining the point to maintain that they are not free.

On the other hand, the man who has been so molded and manipulated that he always wants what his ruler or superior wants him to want is scarcely free. This case suggests that freedom will exist only where there exists the *possibility* of choice, and the possibility of choice in turn implies not only the absence of direct coercion and compulsion but also that the availability and the characteristics of alternatives must be capable of being known. Thus, whatever the situation of any particular individual may be, it is most likely that there will be a large measure of individual freedom within a society when there exists what Mill calls a variety of conditions—where a wide variety of beliefs are in fact expressed and where there is a considerable diversity of tastes and pursuits, customs and codes of conduct, ways and styles of living. And, because of the connection between inequality of power and inequality with respect to the enjoyment of freedom, a society in which power is widely distributed is also likely to be the one characterized by the existence of wide possibilities for choice and individual initiative.

Bibliography

Adler, M. J., *The Idea of Freedom*, 2 vols. New York, 1958–1961.

Bay, Christian, *The Structure of Freedom*. Stanford, 1958.

Berlin, Isaiah, *Two Concepts of Liberty*. Oxford, 1958.

Cranston, Maurice, *Freedom; A New Analysis*. London, 1953.

Friedrich, C. J., *Man and His Government*. New York, 1963.

Fuller, Lon, "Freedom: A Suggested Analysis." *Harvard Law Review*, Vol. 68 (1955), 1305–1325.

Hayek, F. A., *The Constitution of Liberty*. London, 1960.

Jouvenel, Bertrand de, *Sovereignty: An Inquiry Into the Political Good*. Cambridge and Chicago, 1957.

Knight, Frank, *Freedom and Reform*. New York, 1947.

Malinowski, Bronislaw, *Freedom and Civilisation*. London, 1947; Bloomington, Ind., 1960.

Mill, J. S., *On Liberty*. London, 1859.

Oppenheim, F. E., *Dimensions of Freedom*. New York and London, 1961.

Russell, Bertrand, "Freedom and Government," in Ruth N. Anshen, ed., *Freedom: Its Meaning*. New York, 1940.

P. H. PARTRIDGE

FREETHINKERS. See DEISM.

FREGE, GOTTLOB (1848–1925), German mathematician and philosopher and the founder of modern mathematical logic. His entire professional career was spent in the mathematics department of the University of Jena. Half of Frege's published work belongs to philosophy rather than to mathematics, and even in mathematics he did very little work outside logic. His philosophical work, too, was severely restricted in scope, being confined to philosophical logic and the philosophy of mathematics.

Frege's work in philosophical logic probably represents his greatest contribution to philosophy. His introduction of the quantifier–variable notation for expressing generality caused the sharp break between modern logic and the older logical tradition, to which George Boole and his followers still belonged. There is no such clean division in the philosophy of mathematics—unless one makes the criterion of distinction the use of mathematical logic as a tool. Still, it is not unreasonable to characterize Frege as the first of the modern philosophers of mathematics.

When, in the first quarter of the twentieth century, mathematical logic began to develop, few were aware of how much credit was due Frege for having initiated it. Although his founding of modern mathematical logic makes him a major figure in the history of mathematics and of philosophy, his first publication on the subject, *Begriffsschrift* (1879), met with general incomprehension, and his fundamental ideas were propagated chiefly in the works of other writers, often with no acknowledgment of their source.

His work in philosophy was as little known and appreciated as his work in mathematical logic. Apart from those whose philosophical work was confined to the philosophy of mathematics, three great figures—Edmund Husserl, Bertrand Russell, and Ludwig Wittgenstein—studied Frege and were influenced by him, but the general philosophical public was largely unaware of him. At present there is intense interest in his work among philosophers in Britain and the United States, an interest that is almost wholly directed toward his philosophical logic. This concentration is entirely natural. All of Frege's ideas in mathematical logic have either been exploited or rediscovered—in either case, absorbed and made common currency. His work in the philosophy of mathematics, though still interesting, is in a fundamental respect archaic. Partly because of discoveries made since his time with mathematical logic, the instrument of research he invented, questions he did not even pose now appear crucial. In particular, the meaning of quantification over an infinite domain and the validity of two-valued logic for statements involving such quantification never appeared to him as problematic, although these later became the central problems of mathematical philosophy. Nor did he raise the question of the relation between the notions of truth and provability for a mathematical statement. For Frege the foundations of a mathematical theory comprised the elucidation and justification of its axioms; the rest would take care of itself. It is perhaps a measure of how little advance has been made by philosophical logic, in contrast to the philosophy of mathematics, that Frege's ideas on this subject appear as fresh as any contemporary writing and as much concerned with questions that now seem relevant.

In a history of philosophy Frege would have to be classified as a member of the realist revolt against Hegelian idealism, a revolt which occurred some three decades earlier in Germany than in Britain, and as a realist he can now be recognized as having been considerably more sophisticated than Alexius Meinong or the early G. E. Moore or Russell. But such a classification, though correct, would be very misleading. Frege launched a strong attack on what he called "psychologism" (see PSYCHOLOGISM) —the thesis that an account of the meanings of words must be given in terms of the mental processes which they arouse in speaker or hearer or which are involved in acquiring a grasp of their sense (or the stronger thesis that these mental processes are what we are referring to when we use the words). This psychologistic outlook was at least as deeply embedded in British empiricism as in post-Kantian idealism, but apart from his assault upon psychologism, Frege barely troubled to attack idealism at all; he simply passed it by.

What enabled Frege to bypass idealism was that feature of his philosophical approach in which his modernity principally consists. It is evident that some branches of philosophy are logically prior to others; questions which are the subject matter of the prior branch have to be answered before any advance can be made in the subordinate one. Thus, metaphysics is prior to natural theology and philosophy of mind to ethics. Philosophers have differed, however, in what they take to be the starting point of philosophy, the branch that is prior to all others. Perhaps the most far-reaching aspect of Descartes's revolution in philosophy was to give this place to the theory of knowledge, which had never occupied it before.

From the time of Descartes until very recently the first question for philosophy was what we can know and how we can justify our claim to this knowledge, and the fundamental philosophical problem was how far skepticism can be refuted and how far it must be admitted. Frege was the first philosopher after Descartes totally to reject this perspective, and in this respect he looked beyond Descartes to Aristotle and the Scholastics. For Frege, as for them, logic was the beginning of philosophy; if we do not get logic right, we shall get nothing else right. Epistemology, on the other hand, is not prior to any other branch of philosophy; we can get on with philosophy of mathematics, philosophy of science, metaphysics, or whatever interests us without first having undertaken any epistemological inquiry at all. It is this shift of perspective, more than anything else, which constitutes the principal contrast between contemporary philosophy and its forebears, and from this point of view Frege was the first modern philosopher. The change of perspective was not yet to be found in Frege's junior, Russell; the first work after Frege's to display it was Wittgenstein's *Tractatus Logico-philosophicus*. It is for this reason that Frege, for all the narrowness of his interests, is of such significance for present-day philosophy.

DEVELOPMENT OF FREGE'S THOUGHT

Frege's career fell into five clearly demarcated periods. The first covered the publication of *Begriffsschrift* and some brief articles written in explanation of it. *Begriffsschrift* presented for the first time a modern logical system, with negation, implication, the universal quantifier, and identity as primitive: it is a formulation of classical second-order predicate calculus whose first-order fragment constitutes a complete formalization of first-order logic (and, indeed, whose sentential fragment constitutes the first complete formalization, in the modern manner, of classical sentential logic). The notation differs from what is now customary, the differences, in principle, being the exploitation of the two-dimensional character of the printed page (with antecedent and consequent of a conditional written on separate lines) and the absence of (defined) symbols for alternation, conjunction, and the existential quantifier. The work also contains the famous definition of the "ancestral" of a relation as the method for transforming an inductive definition into an explicit one by the use of second-level quantification; another version of this definition was later given independently by Richard Dedekind. Frege's primary object in devising this logical system was to achieve the ideal of that rigor to which all nineteenth-century mathematics had been tending: if proofs were completely formalized, then no appeal to intuition would be required in assessing the correctness of a proof, and hence there would at last be certainty that proofs were cogent and rested only on the assumptions explicitly stated.

The second stage of Frege's career ended with the publication of his masterpiece, *Die Grundlagen der Arithmetik* (1884). After *Begriffsschrift* his first intention was to apply his program to the most fundamental of mathematical theories, the theory of numbers. For this it would be necessary first to present arithmetic as an axiomatic theory, which had not yet been done. But in attempting to isolate the necessary primitive notions and fundamental laws of arithmetic, Frege thought he discovered that it was unnecessary to ascribe to that theory any irreducible notions peculiar to it or to assume any axioms special to it: all arithmetical notions could be defined in terms of notions required for logic in general, and all arithmetical laws

could be proved from principles likewise required. This was the famous logicist thesis subsequently espoused, in a weakened form, by Russell (see MATHEMATICS, FOUNDATIONS OF). It should be noted that Frege at no time held this thesis for the whole of mathematics. He applied it to analysis (the theory of real numbers) as well as to elementary arithmetic, but throughout his career he held a Kantian view of geometry as resting on synthetic a priori truths not reducible to logic.

In order to provide a preliminary account of his view of arithmetic Frege wrote *Grundlagen*. It is in this book that he appeared for the first time, and to best advantage, as a philosopher and not merely as a logician. After an introductory announcement of his program the book contains a long, destructive attack on the views of his predecessors and contemporaries on two questions: What are numbers? What is the nature of arithmetical truth? The attack is brilliantly successful: the views Frege criticized are totally annihilated. He then outlined his own method of defining the basic notions of arithmetic in purely logical terms and proving the basic laws of arithmetic from purely logical principles. This account was deliberately formulated without the use of symbolism (other than letters for variables). The work is fascinating even for those quite uninterested in the philosophy of mathematics, since in the course of it many ideas are presented which are of significance for the whole of philosophy.

The third period of Frege's career extended to the publication, in 1903, of the second volume of his great, but uncompleted, work, *Die Grundgesetze der Arithmetik*. After the publication of *Grundlagen*, Frege became aware of certain deficiencies in the philosophical logic underlying that work and set out to remedy them in a series of articles. In these he gradually developed a highly articulated system of philosophical logic, comparable in coherence and complexity, though not in scope, to some of the great metaphysical systems of the past. This system contains much that is absent from *Grundlagen*, above all the distinction between sense and reference that is his most celebrated contribution to philosophy. Although nothing in *Grundlagen* is recanted, the spirit of Frege's writing is very different. The freshness and insight of the purely philosophical sections of *Grundlagen* are replaced by a doctrinaire approach: several of the tenets of his later system are advanced solely as derivable from other doctrines contained in the system (and being implausible in themselves, they serve only to weaken the credibility of those other doctrines), whereas in *Grundlagen* nothing is asserted save on the basis of intrinsic acceptability. Moreover, if there is no demonstrable incompatibility, there definitely is severe tension between certain of the later doctrines and some of the most important philosophical theses of *Grundlagen*.

Simultaneously with the construction of this edifice of philosophical doctrine Frege was at work writing *Grundgesetze*, in which the program sketched in *Grundlagen* was to be carried out in detail with the use of symbols, with proofs set out as derivations within a formal system. The first volume was published in 1893. The formal system differs from that of *Begriffsschrift* in possessing more rules of inference (and correspondingly fewer axioms) in order to shorten the formal proofs; for all that, it is tedious to follow them through. A more important difference is that the system embodies a theory of classes—namely, the naive set theory within which Russell first discovered Frege's contradiction. Apart from divergences due to an unrestrained use of classes, the development follows with remarkable faithfulness that outlined in *Grundlagen*. The long informal prolegomenon to the book represents the most precise of all Frege's statements of the system of philosophical logic developed in this third period.

Because of the lack of attention paid to the first volume of *Grundgesetze*, delayed publication of the second until 1903. The second volume completes the development, as far as Frege was concerned with carrying it, of the theory of cardinal numbers (he never treated ordinals) and commences a construction of the theory of real numbers, which he preferred to develop without passing through the intermediate stage of a theory of rationals. The formal development is preceded by a long critical study of the theories of other mathematicians concerning real numbers, evidently intended to do for analysis what the first part of *Grundlagen* does for number theory. But though it scores a number of hits, the tone becomes carping and the wit ponderous. The formal treatment is carried far enough to present a theory which anticipates the theory of ordered groups, but it breaks off before "real number" has been defined. Frege obviously meant to complete it in a third volume; however, while the second volume was in press he received a letter from Russell informing him of the discovery of the contradiction. Frege hastily devised a weakening of his naive comprehension axiom, which blocked the straightforward derivation of the Russell paradox, and inserted it into an appendix. After Frege's death Stanisław Leśniewski proved that even the modified axiom yielded a contradiction. There is no reason to suppose Frege knew that it did so, but he must have asked himself whether the proofs still went through under the weakened axiom and discovered that the crucial theorem about the infinity of the series of natural numbers could no longer be proved.

The years 1904–1917 were totally uncreative; Frege's only publications were polemical, and he probably spent these years in a condition of depression. The third volume of *Grundgesetze* remained unwritten. In 1918 he began (for the sixth time) to write a book on philosophical logic, of which the first three chapters were published as articles; they contain some new ideas and have some of the freshness of style of his best writing. However, in 1923 he became convinced that the whole project of founding arithmetic on logic was in error and that the theory of classes constituted the nub of the error: set theory was an intellectual aberration which had led him and others astray. Since mathematics still needed to be unified, geometry would have to be taken as the fundamental mathematical theory and analysis and even number theory derived from it; all mathematical truth was thus synthetic a priori. Frege began some work expounding this new philosophy of mathematics, but he was unable to carry it far and published none of it.

WAS FREGE A LINGUISTIC PHILOSOPHER?

Many of the philosophical problems which Frege posed were, or easily could be, expressed by asking after the

sense of some range of expressions or sentences, thus: What do number words mean? What is the analysis of statements of number (statements answering the question "How many?")? What is the logical status of arithmetical theorems? How are we to explain statements of identity? What is the function of the negation sign? But though it may be significant to divide philosophers into those whose questions can be framed in this way and those whose questions cannot, the former category comprises too many (including Plato and Aristotle) for membership in it to be the criterion for being a linguistic philosopher. Frege's celebrated distinction between sense (*Sinn*) and reference (*Bedeutung*) has overshadowed a distinction he made between sense and "coloring" (*Färbung*). The sense is that part of the meaning of an expression which is relevant to the determination of the truth-value of a sentence in which the expression may occur; the coloring is that part of its meaning which is not (for instance, that which distinguishes "chap" from "guy" and from "man"). Frege made this distinction only as a preliminary to an exclusive concentration on the senses of words, coloring being, in his view, philosophically unimportant. In this he stands opposed to much modern linguistic philosophy, both of the J. L. Austin and of the Wittgenstein schools. For these philosophers our utterances, even when grammatically they constitute statements, can serve many purposes besides the expression of assertions with determinate truth-conditions, and the neglect of this fact has caused philosophers fatally to misconstrue many concepts.

Within the philosophy of mathematics it was necessary for Frege to give a number of analyses of particular mathematical notions, but elsewhere he was more concerned with giving a general account of the structure of language, and therewith a general theory of meaning, than with explaining the senses of particular words. His development of the quantifier–variable notation determined his orientation toward the philosophy of language. The subtle and elaborate theories of the scholastic logicians had failed to give a coherent account of a fundamental feature of language—the expression of generality—and since the Renaissance, logicians had simply given up the problem as too hard, at least as far as sentences involving multiple generality were concerned, while maintaining the fiction that the problem did not exist. When Frege solved this hitherto intractable problem, he did so not by analyzing the devices employed in natural language for the expression of generality but by inventing a totally distinct method of expressing it, operating on a mechanism that was easily explained and governed by rules of inference that could be simply formulated. This discovery of a new method implanted in Frege a permanent distrust of natural language, certain features of which he was ready to dismiss as merely incoherent. This attitude of Frege's is still not always fully grasped—for instance, his thesis that a sentence containing what he called a "proper name" (a singular term, in a sense that includes definite descriptions) which lacked a reference was itself devoid of truth-value. This stands opposed to Russell's theory of descriptions, but it was not intended by Frege as a theory in the same sense. On the contrary, the possibility of forming a proper name without a reference and a sentence without a truth-value represented for him a basic defect of natural language that ought to be remedied in any properly constructed language, such as that of his formal system. This was not a mere aesthetic preference, or a matter of convenience, as is often claimed; Frege really meant that no coherent account (what we would call a semantic account) could be given of a language containing well-formed sentences which were neither true nor false. In constructing a philosophy of language we need not be shackled by the inadequate instrument with which we are forced to make do in everyday discourse; we can construct a more perfect instrument and base our account upon that.

PHILOSOPHICAL LOGIC OF "GRUNDLAGEN"

Meaning and linguistic practice. Frege based his investigation of the theory of numbers on three fundamental theses, which are plainly enunciated in *Grundlagen*. The first is the rejection of psychologism. The mental images which a word may arouse in the mind of speaker or hearer are irrelevant to its meaning, which consists, rather, in the part played by the word in determining the truth-conditions of sentences in which it occurs. This is the first clear statement in the history of philosophy of a basic principle which must underlie any adequate theory of meaning. The vague conception, common, for instance, to both the British empiricists and Aristotle, whereby a word represents an "idea," and a phrase or sentence accordingly represents a complex of ideas, is simply too crude to serve even as a starting point; it virtually forces us to adopt the conception whereby the meaning of a word is embodied in a mental image. No progress can be made until we take the step, first taken by Frege, of seeing the meaning of a word as connected with our actual practice in the employment of language; Frege's severance of mental images from meaning is thus the first move in the direction of Wittgenstein's dictum that "the meaning is the use." But whereas the weakness of Wittgenstein's dictum lies in its extreme generality, the conception of linguistic practice employed by Frege in *Grundlagen* is excessively schematic: for him everything was a matter of the utterance of sentences with determinate truth-conditions.

Words and sentences. The above principle is closely connected to the second one which dominates *Grundlagen* —namely, that "it is only in the context of a sentence that a word has meaning." This dictum, repeatedly emphasized in *Grundlagen,* was endorsed by Wittgenstein both in the *Tractatus* and in the *Philosophical Investigations,* but it never occurs again in Frege's works, for a reason discussed below. It is inaccurate to interpret the dictum, with W. V. Quine, as advancing the view that "the sentence is the unit of meaning." Frege nowhere suggested the absurd idea that a language is conceivable in which the thoughts expressed by sentences like "The earth is round," "$5+17=22$," and even "There are fewer saucers than cups in the cupboard" could be conveyed by a single, noncomplex sign, and he expressly said that the sense of a sentence is built up out of the senses of its constituent words—that is, that not only do we in fact attain an understanding of the sentence by our understanding of the words which make it up, but this sense is intrinsically complex. Rather, Frege was aiming at what Wittgenstein

expressed by saying that only by the utterance of a sentence, and not of any smaller linguistic unit, do we succeed in "making a move in the language-game," do we perform a linguistic *act*; Frege's dictum conveys that the meaning of a word consists wholly in the contribution it makes to precise determination of what particular linguistic act may be effected by the utterance of each sentence in which the word may occur.

If we do not observe this principle, Frege said, we shall commit the fallacy of "asking after the meaning of a word in isolation," and except in the few cases where the word stands for some concrete object, the attempt to concentrate on the meaning of a word without adverting to the kind of sentence which contains it will lead us to fix on some mental image as its meaning. What we ought to be doing instead is characterizing the truth-conditions of the most general form of sentence in which the word occurs. Since such a characterization relates to complete sentences, there is no reason why it need proceed via an explicit definition of the word in question. When *Grundlagen* is read in its natural sense, without the importation of views stated only in Frege's subsequent writings, it is plain that he regarded his principle that words have meaning only in the context of sentences as justifying contextual definition and took this to be one of its most important consequences.

Concept and object. Frege's third basic principle is the distinction between concept and object and between concepts of second and of first order. The distinction cannot be appreciated until Frege's rather definite conception of an object is grasped. This notion is correlative with that of what Frege called a proper name, by which he meant what is more generally called a singular term. There is no implication, for Frege, that a proper name should be logically simple, and thus what Russell distinguished as definite descriptions Frege included in the general category of proper names. This category of expressions assumed a peculiar importance for Frege because of the analysis of the structure of sentences which for him underlay the quantifier–variable notation for expressing generality. In order to explain the sense of sentences containing quantifiers it is necessary to give the most general characterization possible of the sort of expression to which a quantifier can be attached. This can be done either (as Frege did) by regarding a quantifier as capable of being attached only to a one-place predicate (so as to form a complete sentence) or by allowing, more generally, that it can be attached to an $(n+1)$-place predicate to form an n-place predicate. In either case it is necessary to explain the relevant notion of a predicate, and it is essential that this notion cover logically complex expressions. The simplest way to do this is to explain a one-place predicate as something which results when one or more occurrences of some one singular term (proper name) are removed from a sentence; an n-place predicate is explained similarly. (This method removes the necessity for introducing operations that have the effects of permuting and identifying variables and at the same time allows any device used in sentence formation also to contribute to the formation of complex predicates without the need for special explanation.) The variables bound by the quantifier attached to such a predicate will then fill the gaps in that predicate so that a complete sentence is formed (in the case of an $(n+1)$-place predicate the relevant gaps are filled so that an n-place predicate is formed); at the same time it must be explained that the predicate is also regarded as occurring in any sentence that results when all those gaps are filled by one and the same arbitrary proper name.

Proper names. Frege's notion of a one-place predicate, and a two-place relational expression, is explained in terms of the prior notion of a proper name; hence, what we recognize as constituting a predicate will depend upon what we recognize as constituting a proper name. An object is, as has been stated, the objective correlate of a proper name: it is that which we use a proper name to talk about. No other general characterization of an object, save via the linguistic notion of a proper name, is possible. Frege gave no completely precise rules for determining whether or not an expression is to be regarded as a proper name, but he said enough to make it clear that the criteria are to be what we may loosely describe as formal; that is, they concern the most general features of the logical functions of the expression. Hence, objects, which are what proper names stand for, may be of the most varied types—human beings, heavenly bodies, points in space, proofs of a theorem, and directions, for instance. In *Three Philosophers,* Peter Geach has written that in calling numerals proper names Frege was not stretching the notion of a proper name; the term is justified if we accept his view that numbers are objects. This is the wrong way round: we cannot first determine from what we know of an entity that it is an object and then accordingly confer on a term for it the status of a proper name; we have to see whether the term behaves like a proper name in order to decide whether it stands for an object. If Geach means to hint that Frege's thesis that numbers are objects shows, not the comprehensiveness of his notion of an object, but rather the singularity of his conception of numbers, the suggestion is tendentious; the ordinary notion of an object, apart from being far vaguer than Frege's, is surely much less inclusive. In *Grundlagen,* Frege not only stated generally that he wished to countenance abstract as well as concrete objects but also devoted a whole section to the consideration of a large range of abstract objects, among which are directions and shapes, and his whole theory of classes was founded on the proposition that classes are objects. Against this background the thesis that numbers are objects does not appear in the least bizarre; what, if anything, is to be questioned is the legitimacy of so extensive a category of "objects."

Identity. Often in his writings Frege made use of rather superficial grammatical tests for whether an expression is a proper name. He thus did not adequately protect himself from the gibe that he would be forced to admit such objects as the whereabouts of the prime minister or the manner in which General Eisenhower putts. In *Grundlagen* he did, however, introduce a line of thought which if pursued would extricate him from this absurdity: he said that there has to be associated with every object—and therefore with every expression for an object—a "criterion of identity," a criterion for "recognizing the object as the same again." This does not entail, Frege insisted, that there is no single absolute relation of identity or that the expression "the same" is equivocal, assuming different senses in different

contexts. Rather, in stipulating the criterion of identity associated with a proper name, or a range of proper names, we are taking the general sense of "the same" as given and are carrying out an essential part of the stipulation of the sense of that proper name (or of the proper names of that range). This doctrine reappeared in the *Investigations* as a cornerstone of Wittgenstein's whole later philosophy.

Frege never adequately elucidated this notion of a criterion of identity, and if we attempt to do so, we are at once forced to distinguish between two cases. One case is that principally considered in the *Investigations,* of the sort of object which can be the target of an ostension—that is, the sort which is capable of being referred to by a use of the demonstrative "this." Here a question of the form "Is this the same as that?" (or ". . . as the one which . . . ?") is genuinely ambiguous, the answer depending on the reply to the counterquestion "This *what?*" This counterquestion is sufficiently answered by a criterion of identity, which may in this case be thought of as the criterion for the truth of an affirmative answer to the original question—that is, of an identity statement involving only demonstratives. (Because of his almost total neglect of such expressions as demonstratives, Frege nowhere explained the notion of a criterion of identity in anything like this manner.) The case with which Frege was concerned in *Grundlagen,* however, is that of objects which in general cannot be the targets of any ostension, objects which are referred to by complex names of such forms as "the direction of the line *a*" and "the shape of the figure *B*." Such names are formed by means of an operator like "the direction of . . ." or "the shape of . . . ," where it would not be possible for anyone to conceive of the range of objects in question without understanding the sense of the relevant operator. (Thus, such an operator is quite different from one like "the wife of . . . .") In this case the criterion for identifying the direction of the line *a* with the direction of the line *b* is to be given as a condition that some already understood relation should obtain between the lines *a* and *b,* to give this criterion is part, at least, of what is required in introducing the operator "the direction of . . . ."

Bound variables and the domain of objects. Such substantival phrases as "the whereabouts of the prime minister" are to be excluded from the category of proper names, which stand for objects, on such grounds as that there is no criterion of identity associated with them. It is also clearly essential to Frege's conception of an object that although for an entity to be an object it is a sufficient condition that the entity be a possible target of an ostension, with a corresponding criterion of identity, this is not a necessary condition. We may well wonder how there could be actual philosophical error in Frege's constructing so wide a logical category as that of his objects. True, there may be many significant logical distinctions to be made within that vast category—a fact already recognized in his acknowledgment of a distinction between those which are concrete and those which are not—but by first picking out the supercategory he did not impede such further distinction. The answer lies in Frege's understanding of bound individual variables. Unlike modern logicians, Frege did not regard an interpretation of a formula of first-order predicate logic as involving a special stipulation of the range of the variables; rather, he saw these as in all contexts ranging over the domain of all objects—that is, of all entities which could be the bearers of proper names. But the paradoxes of set theory reveal that it is impossible coherently to interpret bound variables as ranging simultaneously over all objects which could be comprised within a domain over which bound variables could coherently be interpreted as ranging. The importance of Frege's assignment of any one given range of entities (numbers, for instance) to the category of objects lies less in the consequent treatment of expressions for them as proper names (singular terms) than in the inclusion of those entities in the one domain over which his individual variables are then taken as ranging. This is especially important when terms for those entities are formed, as is the case with numbers and classes, by means of an operator which attaches not to the name of an object of another kind but to a predicate. For Frege all terms for (cardinal) numbers are ultimately formed (perhaps via definitions) by means of the operator "the number of x's such that . . . x . . . ," where the gaps in this expression are to be filled by predicates, not names. If numbers are objects, then the predicate in question may legitimately be taken as applying to numbers. Indeed, it is by this means that Frege was able to give a proof, apparently from purely logical assumptions, of the existence of infinitely many distinct numbers, and therefore it is precisely at this point that his reduction of number theory to logic collapses, since, of course, pure logic cannot guarantee the existence of a domain of objects over which an operator having the properties demanded of the operator "the number of . . ." can be defined. There is no way to save Frege's system from incoherence, because, after all, it was within it that the contradiction arose; what is important is to locate the incoherence precisely. It arises not out of his notion of an object as such but rather out of his conception of the totality of objects.

Universals. Frege's distinction between objects and concepts cuts clean across the traditional method of posing the problem of universals. Traditionally a particular is that which can only be named (in order to have something predicated of it), whereas a universal can either be predicated of a particular or have some higher-level universal predicated of it; the dispute concerns whether, and in what sense, universals are "real." From this standpoint, therefore, the universal, redness, is denoted by the word "red" equally when it is used as an adjective, as in "The carpet is red," and as a noun, as in "Red is a primary color." (This perspective is to be found even in so recent a work as P. F. Strawson's *Individuals*.) For Frege such an approach was erroneous from the outset. The word "red" used as a noun is a proper name and must stand for an object; a predicate like ". . . is red," on the other hand, is an expression of such a totally different kind that we cannot suppose it to be correlated with an entity of the same sort at all. (Admittedly, Frege nowhere cited colors as examples of objects, but the noun "red" acts as a singular term just as the noun "two" does, and the operator "the color of . . ." is analogous to "the shape of . . . .") Just as objects can in general be characterized only as the objective correlates of proper names, so "concept" can be explained only as applying to that which corresponds, in reality, to (one-place) pred-

icates and "relation" to that which corresponds to (two-place) relational expressions. Because predicates and proper names fulfill totally different linguistic roles, the entities which correspond to them must be equally dissimilar.

It might be asked why it is not enough to regard as different the relations in which these two types of expression stand to their nonlinguistic counterparts without supposing the second terms of the relations to be different also. Frege did indeed hold that the relation of a proper name to an object was different from, though analogous to, the relation of a predicate to a concept. However, the fact is that in general it is not appropriate to suppose that something having the characteristics an object must possess corresponds in any way to an arbitrary predicate. In view of this the example of the word "red" is misleading, in that there is a definite criterion of identity for colors and a range of properties which only colors can have and of relations in which only colors can stand; the abstract nouns which can be formed from such predicates as ". . . is slimy" or ". . . is shiny"—not to speak of the awkward abstract substantival phrases formed from complex predicates—have no such criterion of identity associated with them and no special range of predicates attachable to them, and hence they cannot seriously be considered as standing for objects.

Predicates. Notoriously, the traditional approach to the problem of universals repeatedly stumbled over the relation which obtains between an entity and a universal truly predicated of it (and to an even greater extent over the ternary relation between two entities and a relational universal truly said to subsist between them). If the predicate, as well as the subject, is thought of as referring to an object which is capable of being denoted by a singular term, then it is difficult to see how by merely referring to two objects in turn we can succeed in saying something true or false. For Frege there was no corresponding difficulty. It is characteristic of a concept that what alone can stand for it is an expression with gaps which yields a sentence when the gaps are filled by a proper name (for the predicate was formed by removing some occurrences of a proper name from a sentence). So the concept must be thought of as having a corresponding kind of incompleteness; if it did not, there would be no reason why it should not be denoted by some proper name. Frege's theory of predicates as referring to concepts is not intended, like the traditional theory of universals, as an explanation of what predication is; rather, it is by already understanding how predicates are used that we come to grasp what sort of entity they stand for. In fact, for the understanding of sentences not containing quantifiers we do not need the general notion of a predicate at all, and hence we do not need the general notion of a concept. For instance, to understand (know the truth-conditions for) the sentence "John is dark, and John is handsome" we have indeed to understand the simple predicates ". . . is dark" and ". . . is handsome," but we need have no idea of the possibility of seeing the sentence as obtainable by completing the predicate ". . . is dark, and . . . is handsome" with the name "John." The incompleteness of a predicate does not reside merely in the fact that it is to be regarded not as directly constructed out of its constituent parts but as formed from a sentence which has been so constructed by removing an expression from it; more particularly, it resides in the fact that it is not, in general, a separate *piece* of the sentence but is, rather, a *feature* of the way in which the sentence is constructed. The above complex predicate, for example, occurs also in the sentence "Charlie is dark, and Charlie is handsome" but not in "John is dark, and Charlie is handsome," though there is no *part* of the first two sentences which does not also occur in the third. A predicate is thus something which literally cannot be exhibited separately. The description of the concept for which the predicate stands as likewise incomplete registers the fact that only an expression which has just this kind of incompleteness can be regarded as standing for a concept. The concept is an entity whose being is to be true of some objects and false of others (or, as Frege said, to have some objects falling under it and others not), and it could not be conceived in any other way.

Higher-order incomplete expressions. Frege did not deny that something can be predicated of a concept; that it can be so predicated is a result of the fact that a sentence can be formed from a predicate otherwise than by filling the predicate's argument place with a proper name—that is, by attaching a quantifier to it—but a predication about a concept takes an altogether different form from a predication about an object. This is because in order for the predicate to continue to be a predicate, and thus still to refer to the concept, it must retain its incomplete character; that is why the quantifier carries with it bound variables for insertion into the argument place of the predicate. A sentence like "Some people are both dark and handsome" says something about the concept for which the predicate ". . . is dark, and . . . is handsome" stands, but in accordance with the totally different nature of concepts and objects, it says about that concept a completely different sort of thing from anything which could meaningfully be said about an object. We thus arrive at the notion of a concept of second order; this is what is referred to by a new kind of incomplete expression—namely, one which is obtained from a sentence by omitting one or more occurrences of a (first-order) predicate (here some care is needed in specifying when such a predicate is said to "occur in" a sentence). In fact, we have a whole hierarchy: second-order concepts under which first-order concepts fall, second-order concepts under which first-order relations fall, second-order relations between first-order concepts, etc. Just as the recognition of the general category of first-order concepts was needed only to explain operators (such as quantifiers) which were to be attached to expressions for them, so the recognition of some types of second-order concept is really necessary only when we want to introduce operators (such as higher-order quantifiers) attachable to expressions for *them*. Frege has no reservations about the use of such higher-level quantification. Given his insistence that concepts and relations are distinguished from objects by their incompleteness and are distinguished among themselves by the kinds of incompleteness they have, his notational rule that signs or variables for concepts and relations should never appear without their accompanying argument places (with the sole exception of the bound variable that

is adjoined to the quantifier) is a natural requirement. If that requirement is observed, then it becomes literally impossible to infringe his prohibition on saying about an object what it makes sense to say only about a concept or conversely, or on saying about a first-order concept what can meaningfully be said only about a second-order one. Since an expression for a concept is incomplete, the attempt to use it to fill the gap in another predicate, so as to say about that concept what the second predicate can be used to say about an object, yields not a sentence but an expression that still has a gap in it, and the attempt to fill the gap in an expression for a second-order concept with a proper name leaves us with a bound variable which cannot be inserted anywhere.

FREGE'S LATER PHILOSOPHY

"Sinn" and "Bedeutung." The two most striking additions that Frege made to the philosophical logic of *Grundlagen* greatly add to its coherence; indeed, it is difficult to set out the doctrine of *Grundlagen* without appealing to these amplifications. The first is the distinction between *Sinn* (sense) and *Bedeutung*. The standard translation of the German word *Bedeutung* is "meaning," but Frege's use of it is conventionally rendered as "reference" (with "stand for" as the cognate verb). The rendering has this much justification, that it is certainly incorrect to say (as is occasionally said) that Frege's distinction is between two ingredients in the meaning of an expression (as his distinction between sense and coloring is). Rather, if "meaning" is taken as the mechanism or rule determining the use of an expression, then Frege's "sense" is (the main) part of an expression's meaning, whereas his *Bedeutung* is not part of it at all but is what is meant by the expression in an altogether different use of the word "mean." From here on "meaning" will be used only as the translation of Frege's *Bedeutung* and "mean" as that of *bedeuten;* any awkwardness in this use of the English words is matched by Frege's use of the German ones. In place of "meaning" in the sense of what is known when an expression is understood (Frege himself had no word for this) "significance" will be used; significance thus includes, but is not exhausted by, sense. The "meaning" of a name, in Frege's use, is its bearer, that which we use the name to talk *about.* He insisted that two proper names may have different senses but the same meaning: the same object is the bearer of both names, although the criterion for identifying an object as the bearer of the one name differs from that for identifying it as the bearer of the other. This is evident for complex proper names, and Frege held it to be true also for proper names in the strict sense—that is, those which are logically simple. Only by acknowledging that names with the same meaning may have different senses is it possible to understand how an identity statement may be true and yet informative. Armed with this distinction, Frege was able to clarify his notion of a concept: he used "concept" to apply not to the sense of a predicate but to the entity which the predicate means.

Frege hardly ever bothered to argue for the existence of anything that is meant by an incomplete expression such as a predicate, and in this his instinct was correct: the question whether there are any such entities in reality is a misconceived one. Frege intended the notion of a concept to be understood in such a way that the existence of concepts which are the meanings of predicates is generally as unproblematic as the existence of objects which are the meanings of proper names generally is (or at least as unproblematic as is the legitimacy of quantifying over concepts, which is clearly involved in stating that there is something which a predicate means—admittedly, for Quine though not for Frege, a severe qualification), and in his unpublished writings he succeeded, after a struggle, in expressing the doctrine in such a way as to make this clear. What is problematic is the role played by meanings in the determination of the truth-values of sentences, and this depends on what, exactly, we take the senses of proper names, predicates, etc. to be. It has often been observed that on this matter Frege was remarkably silent. A natural picture would be the following: To know the sense of a proper name is to know the criterion for identifying any given object as the meaning of that name; to know the sense of a predicate is to know the criterion for deciding whether it is true of an arbitrary object. Thus, in determining the truth-value of a simple subject–predicate sentence we would proceed by finding the object which the name meant and then deciding whether or not the predicate was true of it. This would need modification for those objects which cannot be given by means of an ostension; perhaps in such cases we could think of an object as given by means of a term from some special class (for example, Arabic numerals in the case of natural numbers). It is evident that this picture is too crude to be plausible: we could hardly hold that the sense of the name "Cleopatra," for instance, consists in a criterion for identifying an arbitrary human being as Cleopatra. In any case, Frege's *Grundlagen* thesis that names have meaning only in the context of sentences appears to go against this as being the interpretation of the notion of sense he intended, for this thesis surely entails that the sense of a name may be given by means of a rule for determining the truth-conditions of a sentence containing it otherwise than via the identification of an object as the meaning of the name. But insofar as this picture approximates the correct one there is a lack of analogy between the ascription of meaning to proper names and to predicates, for we can attach very little significance to the notion of identifying a concept as the meaning of a predicate, and hence we can hardly view the process of deciding the truth-value of a sentence formed by attaching a quantifier to a predicate as consisting of first finding the relevant concept and then determining whether or not the quantifier was true of it. (On the other hand, in order that such sentences should have definite truth-values we have to know which concept the predicate means, and if we do not suppose that our language contains a name for every object, this involves more than just knowing the truth-conditions of all sentences formed by putting a name in the argument place of the predicate.)

The meaning of a complex name depends only on the meaning, not on the sense, of its constituent parts, and the truth-value of a sentence only on the meaning, not on the sense, of the words in it. The many apparent counter-examples to this latter principle Frege dealt with by saying

that in such contexts the words do not have their ordinary meanings but mean what are ordinarily their senses. This is not a mere dodge: what is true of an object must remain true however the object is referred to. Thus, when the truth-value of a sentence alters when one name of an object is substituted for another, it cannot be that object which is being talked about, and hence, if "meaning" is defined as above, it cannot be that object which the names mean in that sentence. If, now, we do not remember that the meaning of an expression (in Frege's use) is not any part of its significance, we shall lose the notion of sense altogether, for sense was distinguished from coloring as that part of the significance of an expression which alone is relevant to the truth-conditions of sentences containing the expression. The difference in sense between two names which mean the same object is a difference in the criteria for recognizing that object as the meaning. But Frege's whole point in insisting that names have sense as well as meaning was just that the sense of a name could not consist merely in its meaning the object which it does mean; there must also be some particular way in which we recognize the object as the meaning. For expressions which cannot be defined, or explained verbally in any way, Frege did not say what he regarded the conveying of their sense as consisting in, but when we give a definition we do not have to state separately what the sense of the expression is—we state only its meaning, even though it is sense which determines meaning, not the converse. We can give different, though equivalent, definitions; although these assign the same meaning, they confer distinct senses, just because they *are* different. Difference in sense consists in the different ways in which the meaning is assigned. The *Tractatus'* distinction between saying and showing might have been useful to Frege here: when we define a word, what we say is what its meaning is, and by the way in which we say this we show what its sense is.

Assertion. The second main ingredient of Frege's philosophical logic that does not appear in *Grundlagen* is the theory of the force carried by an utterance, which was already sketched in *Begriffsschrift*. If it is to our linguistic practice that we must look in giving an account of the senses of our words, and if this account turns on the truth-conditions of the sentences we utter, then we must be able to give a general description of the connection between the truth-conditions of an arbitrary sentence and what we effect by uttering that sentence. When we make an assertion we are not merely uttering a sentence with determinate truth-conditions understood by the hearer, and hence with a particular truth-value; that, after all, we would do if the sentence expressed only part of what we were asserting—for instance, if it were the antecedent of a conditional. We are also, rightly or wrongly, saying that the sentence is true. This activity of asserting that the thought we are expressing is true is *sui generis:* it is not a further determination of the truth-conditions of the sentence, which remain unchanged whether we are asserting it to be true or not, but rather something which we *do* with a sentence whose truth-conditions have already been fixed. This is not the only thing we can do with a sentence: we can use it in giving a definition, in asking a question (of the kind requiring the answer "Yes" or "No"), or in the course of telling a story. (Other uses can easily be thought of, but the ones listed are those actually admitted by Frege.) It is only in the case of questions that the use being made of the sentence actually affects the form the sentence takes in natural language. We distinguish the other cases by the context; in particular, the linguistic form of a sentence being used, on its own, to make an assertion is indistinguishable from that of the same sentence occurring as a subordinate clause. But whether it is expressed or not, here is a third feature of an utterance which needs to be understood if communication is to succeed, something which, like sense and coloring, is ordinarily counted as part of the significance of the utterance. Frege called this the "force" of an utterance. In a language that is to express everything we wish to convey, we need some special signs for this element; in his symbolic language Frege employed two special signs to convey the force, one for assertion and one for definition. These signs may be attached only to complete sentences; there is no room for an assertion sign within a subordinate clause, such as the antecedent of a conditional, since such a clause serves to determine only partially the truth-conditions of the whole sentence.

Such a doctrine, whether ultimately tenable or not, provides a first reply to those who have criticized, for example, Frege's account of number words on the ground that he explained them only as they occur in "statements." The truth is that Frege's account does not relate in any special way to the use of number words in sentences used to make assertions; his concern is to explain the truth-conditions of sentences containing them and hence to explain their use in any utterance whose force can be described in terms of the truth-conditions of some sentence. (On the other hand, since Frege, surprisingly, said of imperatives that unlike interrogatives, they do not differ from the corresponding assertoric sentences only by their force or by their sense, he left unexplained the use of number words in imperatives.)

Meaning of a sentence. The two supplementations of the *Grundlagen* doctrines are in complete conformity with the original doctrines and make them more coherent; it was quite different with the rest of the theoretical structure erected by Frege in his third period. The crucial step was the identification of a sentence's truth-value with its meaning. Frege argued, convincingly, that the meaning of a sentence cannot be considered the thought which the sentence expresses (and thus not the proposition, as Russell or Moore would use the term), which is, rather, its sense, for the meaning of the whole cannot alter so long as the meanings of its parts remain constant, whereas the thought expressed can alter. But Frege gave no direct argument for ascribing a meaning to a sentence, and such an ascription proves to have very implausible consequences. Admittedly, the most immediate consequence is a striking elegance and economy. Sentences are evidently complete expressions, and hence truth-values are objects; sentences thus become a particular kind of complex proper name. Now, besides concepts and relations, Frege also admitted functions, as incomplete entities which are the meanings of functional expressions. But if sentences are proper names, then concepts and relations are only functions of a special kind (of one and two arguments respec-

tively)—those, namely, whose value is always a truth-value. This idea is incorporated into the formalism of *Grundgesetze* and confers on it a notable smoothness; at the same time, it is of value in explaining Frege's notion of the incompleteness of concepts, for the incompleteness of a function is something we can grasp more easily. But if an expression, say "Ruritania," has no meaning, then a complex name of which it is part, say "the capital of Ruritania," has no meaning either; if a sentence's meaning is its truth-value, a sentence containing a name without meaning will have no truth-value. This already sunders the notion of falsity from that of not being correctly assertible: if someone seriously asserts, "Queen Elizabeth I's husband was Dutch," his assertion is clearly incorrect, although according to Frege he is saying nothing false. (Note that Frege did not deny that such a sentence has a sense.) Moreover, not only is such a sentence neither true nor false; if that were all, we could ascribe to it a third truth-value and devise for a language containing such sentences a three-valued logic preserving as much of the classical logic as is feasible. But for Frege these sentences lack *any* truth-value, and this means that any complex sentences of which they are constituents must also lack truth-value. The mere fact that we could treat such sentences as having a third truth-value and could stipulate plausible truth tables for the sentential operators in the three-valued system is enough to show that a sentence does not stand to its truth-value in the same relation as a name does to its bearer. But given Frege's assumption that once a name without meaning gets into a sentence anywhere it infects the whole sentence and deprives it of truth-value, he was consistent in drawing the otherwise baseless conclusion that there can be no coherent account of a language containing sentences which are neither true nor false, and hence none of a language containing terms without meaning.

From this one false step most of the more extraordinary doctrines of Frege's later period follow; those that do not follow are connected. Since from the admission of terms without meaning, incoherence results, every functional expression from which complex proper names can be formed must mean a function which is defined for every object as argument: we must admit something to be the capital of the moon and something else to be the square of the sun. By the same token, every predicate must also be defined for every argument. if we are going to introduce the predicate ". . . is prime," we must do so in such a way as to provide a truth-value for a sentence like "Julius Caesar is prime." In harmony with this is Frege's later animus against any form of conditional, stepwise, or contextual definition. The opposition to contextual definition wars against the *Grundlagen* thesis that it is only in the context of sentences that words have meaning, which, in *Grundlagen*, is used to justify contextual definition; indeed, this thesis, never reiterated though never repudiated, has no place in Frege's later philosophy, since it accords a distinctive position to sentences which he was no longer prepared to recognize. There is a trace of it left in *Grundgesetze*, where he in effect advanced the thesis that names do not have to be given a meaning save in context—the context, namely, of more complex names in which they occur. This amounts to saying that we can bestow a meaning on some names by bestowing one on other names; no general principle is provided by which we can judge which names are to have a meaning directly stipulated for them. Insofar as this doctrine can be justified, it is in virtue of the special role of sentences. If we can succeed in specifying the truth-conditions of the sentences of a language without assigning a meaning to some of the terms in them, all will still be in order because it is the sentences, not any briefer expressions, which we use to perform those linguistic acts—in particular, those acts of assertion—which it is the purpose of the language to make us capable of effecting.

ARITHMETIC

Frege held that the true statements of what he called "arithmetic" (the theories of natural and of real numbers) are analytic, by which he meant that they are logically deducible from purely logical laws with the help of definitions of the arithmetical notions (thus, he tacitly assumed every true arithmetical statement to be provable). This in itself entails not that arithmetic involves no primitive notions not reducible to extra-arithmetical ones but only that it would be unnecessary to appeal to the understanding of any such primitive notions in order to establish the truth of arithmetical statements. Yet in fact Frege held that this is so and that all arithmetical notions are definable in terms of purely logical ones.

Comparison of cardinality. Frege held that the natural numbers constitute the finite members of the totality of cardinal numbers, which are those numbers that answer questions of the form "How many objects of such-and-such a kind are there?" He rightly maintained that the central notion for the conception of cardinal number is expressed by "just as many as" (as the central notion for the conception of length is expressed by "just as long as"). That is, the notion "just as many" is prior to the notion involved in giving any particular answer to the question "How many?" in that (1) we can tell that there are just as many things of one kind as there are of another without knowing *how* many of each kind there are (for instance, if on a table each plate has just one knife on it and each knife is on just one plate, we know that there are just as many knives as plates on the table), and (2) any answer to a question of the form, "How many *F*'s are there?" amounts to saying "Just as many as there are things of some standard kind" (for instance, to count up the *F*'s and find that there are six of them is to establish that there are just as many *F*'s as numerals from "1" to "6"). Frege's logical definition of "just as many," anticipated one year earlier by Georg Cantor, is that there are just as many *F*'s as *G*'s if and only if there is some one-to-one relation *R* which correlates the *F*'s with the *G*'s. It is thus a notion which involves second-level quantification, over relations. "*R* is one-to-one" means, in turn, that for all objects x, y, and z, if xRy and xRz, then y is the same as z, and also if yRx and zRx, then again y is the same as z; "*R* correlates the *F*'s with the *G*'s" means that for every object x, if x is *F*, then for some y, xRy and y is *G*, and likewise for every y, if y is *G*, then for some x, xRy and x is *F*.

This definition has long been canonical. There are only

two questions that can be raised concerning it (which there is no space here to discuss). First, in view of what is now known (but was not known to Frege) about the incompletability of the theory of second-order quantification, should we regard the notion "'just as many" as being not absolute but relative to a selection of a particular domain for relation variables? Second, can we be sure that whenever there are, intuitively, just as many *F*'s as *G*'s, there actually is a relation which correlates them one to one, or should we explain "just as many" as meaning that there *could be* such a correlation? (And if so, can the relevant sense of "could" be specified without circularity? Here we might regard applications of the axiom of choice to yield proofs of cardinal equivalence as such a specification: we show by means of it that even when there is no actual correlation, this is not due to there not being enough objects of the given kind.)

Definition of an operator class. In arithmetic we need not only a vocabulary for comparing sets of objects in respect of cardinality but also one for referring to cardinal numbers, since here the expressions we use for cardinal numbers play the logical role of singular terms (for example, in "19 is prime," where "19" is grammatically a noun, not an adjective as in "There are 19 books on the table"). Frege thought that all numerical terms were to be analyzed by means of the operator "the number of *F*'s" (henceforth called the numerical operator) and that this obviated the need for a special explanation of the adjectival uses, since "There are 19 books on the table" is equivalent to "The number of books on the table = 19" and every sentence containing "19" as a number adjective can be converted into one with the form "There are just 19 . . ." or with a constituent of that form. (Note that for Frege the equals sign always denotes the relation of identity, to be read "is the same [object] as" or, simply, "is.") The problem thus becomes one of defining the numerical operator. An obvious condition is that a statement of the form

"The number of *F*'s = the number of *G*'s"

shall be equivalent to

"There are just as many *F*'s as *G*'s."

In *Grundlagen*, Frege asked whether an outright stipulation of this equivalence could serve as a partial definition of the numerical operator, to be supplemented by explanations of other contexts in which numerical terms could occur. (As has been observed, at the time of writing *Grundlagen*, Frege had not yet developed his later opposition to contextual and to piecemeal definition; in fact, he even advanced a general defense of it.) Frege compared the introduction of the numerical operator with the introduction of any of a large range of other operators, such as "the direction of *a*," "the shape of *A*," and so on; thus, we can define "the direction of *a*" contextually, beginning with a stipulation that "the direction of *a* = the direction of *b*" is to mean "*a* is parallel to *b*." Frege did not spell out the range of operators he had in mind, but analysis of his text shows that they must satisfy two conditions: (1) if "*O*" is such an operator, then an identity statement of the form "$Oa = Ob$" is to be equivalent to a statement of the form "aRb" where "R" stands for some particular equivalence relation (one which is reflexive, symmetrical, and transitive), and (2) there should be no intuitive demand that terms formed by means of the operator be taken as standing for objects customarily denoted by terms of any other form (for instance, we do not normally require a direction to be identified with an object that is something other than a direction). Frege here evidently regarded it as unimportant that the numerical operator differs from the other examples in being attached to a predicative expression (such as "planets in the solar system") rather than to another term (such as a term standing for a line).

Frege eventually rejected the possibility of a contextual definition for such terms, on the ground that it would be powerless to determine the truth-value (presumably false) of statements of identity which involve only one term formed by means of the operator to be defined—such sentences as "Julius Caesar is the number of planets" and "England is the direction of the earth's axis." But it would be straightforward to provide by direct stipulation for the falsity of such sentences. The serious difficulty, which Frege did not expressly acknowledge, relates to the fact, noted earlier, that "the number of F's," unlike "the direction of a," is an operator of second level. If we can eliminate terms of the form "the direction of a," then we can also eliminate quantification over directions, by reducing "For some direction $d, \ldots d \ldots$" to "For some line $a, \ldots$ the direction of $a \ldots$." In the same way we can reduce "For some number $n, \ldots n \ldots$" to "For some concept $F, \ldots$ the number of F's $\ldots$," but this forms part of a genuine translation of statements involving the notion of number into those which do not involve this notion only if the domain of objects required for interpreting the statement after translation does not include numbers (and so the concept variable "F" is not taken as ranging over concepts under which numbers fall). In particular, we should have to prohibit the formation of terms of the form "the number of A's" whenever "A" was a predicative expression itself containing the numerical operator. Without such restrictions the proposed manner of introducing the numerical operator would not provide us with a means of eliminating it and hence could count not as a definition of the operator but only as an axiom governing it (which would be insufficient for Frege's program of demonstrating that arithmetical truths are analytic according to his definition of "analytic"). But with such restrictions Frege's proof of the infinity of the number series would break down.

Frege's way out of the difficulty which he professed to find in the proposed contextual definition of any such operator was to give an explicit definition by means of the notion of classes. Where "$Oa = Ob$" is required to be equivalent to "aRb," "Oa" will be defined as "the class of objects x such that aRx"; likewise, "the number of F's" will be defined as "the class of concepts G such that there are just as many F's as G's." Thus, cardinal numbers are to be classes of concepts. (The notion of a class of concepts is unusual, but in *Grundlagen*, Frege was scrupulous about reducing his employment of the notion of class to a mini-

mum. In *Grundgesetze* no such care was taken, and in place of the operator "the number of F's," Frege defined an operator attaching to singular terms and meaning intuitively "the number of members of a," this being defined as "the class of classes x such that there are just as many members of x as there are members of a"; "a" need not here be taken to stand for a class.)

This technique has since become known, rather unhappily, as definition by abstraction. It is not at all clear that it gets Frege out of the difficulty he believed himself to be in, for in order to use the technique to demonstrate that Julius Caesar is not the number of planets, we have to know that Julius Caesar is not a class of concepts, and the question arises how we know this. In *Grundlagen*, Frege did not make explicit the required assumptions concerning classes. In *Grundgesetze*, however, the axiom governing classes is of exactly the same general form as the rejected contextual definition of the numerical operator (that is, "The class of F's = the class of G's if and only if all and only those objects which are F are G"), and Frege expressly denied that this axiom by itself determines the truth-value of statements of the form "a is the class of F's," where "a" is a term formed without the use of the class operator. He proposed an additional stipulation that would accomplish this, but if an additional stipulation would serve the purpose for the class operator, a similar one would do the same for the numerical operator, without the need for explicitly defining the latter in terms of classes.

Definition of natural numbers. Frege defined the number 0 as the number of objects not identical with themselves and the relational expression "n is an immediate successor of m" as "For some concept F and some object a, a is an F, n is the number of F's, and m is the number of objects other than a which are F" (this expresses the relation "$n = m + 1$," so that every transfinite cardinal is its own immediate successor). He applied to this relation his definition, given in *Begriffsschrift*, of the ancestral of a relation, so as to yield a relation $S^*(n,m)$ expressed by "n falls under every concept F such that m is an F and such that for every j and k, if k is an immediate successor of j and j is an F, then k is an F" (if m is a finite cardinal, then $S^*(n,m)$ holds if and only if n is a finite cardinal $\geq m$). Frege then defined "n is a natural number" as "$S^*(n,0)$." He thus held, as did Russell, that the principle of mathematical induction—far from being a special principle of inference peculiar to the theory of natural numbers, whose validity is to be apprehended by mathematical intuition—is part of the definition of "natural number"; the natural numbers are to be defined as just those objects for which mathematical induction is valid.

Frege, in effect, succeeded in deriving, on the basis of these definitions, all the propositions that have subsequently become known as the Peano axioms for the natural numbers. The crucial theorem is the one guaranteeing the infinity of the number series, which states that every natural number has an immediate successor. To prove this, on his definitions, Frege had to show that for every natural number n there exists a concept F such that the number of F's is an immediate successor of n. For each given n this condition is satisfied by the concept "natural number $\leq n$," which Frege was able to express by "$S^*(n,m)$."

Mathematics and logic. It is often maintained that Frege's attempt to demonstrate that arithmetical truths are analytic by reducing them to truths of logic fails because of his use of the notion of class, which is said to be a mathematical rather than a logical notion and also, in view of the paradoxes, a problematic one. So far as Frege's treatment of the theory of real numbers is concerned, this is not unreasonable, since it requires a fairly heavy use of the notion of class to advance from the theory of natural numbers to that of real numbers, but as a diagnosis of the failure of Frege's program for the theory of natural numbers, it is very superficial. Only the weakest conceivable assumptions concerning classes are required for the construction of the theory of natural numbers expounded in *Grundlagen* to succeed, and it seems absurd to appeal to the paradoxes in order to bring these assumptions into question. Indeed, it is doubtful that even these assumptions can be reckoned to belong to the laws of logic, but it does not appear that the proper way to inquire into this question is by asking whether the notion of class is a logical or a mathematical one. Rather, the assumption that certain class terms can be formed and treated as having a reference is an existential assumption and can hardly be grounded on logic alone. The minimal assumption Frege needed in *Grundlagen* is that there is a mapping by which each concept F is mapped onto a class of concepts containing just those concepts G such that there are just as many F's as G's. When classes are taken, as Frege took them, to be objects—that is, to be in the domain over which the concepts in question are defined—this is tantamount to the assumption that there are at least denumerably many objects. From this point of view it does not much matter whether the numerical operator is taken as primitive or as defined in terms of classes: the existential assumption is the same. Now, admittedly, if numbers (or classes) are taken to be objects, then it is reasonable to assert that there are infinitely many objects (far more reasonable than Russell's "axiom of infinity," which asserts that there are infinitely many *individuals*—objects that are neither classes nor numbers—and is probably not even true). But then the recognition of the truth of the statement that there are infinitely many objects cannot be held to precede a grasp of the notion of number, which is required for the understanding of the domain over which the individual variables are taken as ranging.

It might be claimed in defense of Frege that since he did not take the numerical operator as primitive but defined it in terms of class, the understanding of his notion of object presupposes a grasp not of the notion of number as such but only of that of class, so that the acknowledgment of principles from which the existence of infinitely many objects can be derived may be prior to the grasp of any specifically *arithmetical* notions. However, the only classes whose existence is required by *Grundlagen* are equivalence classes of objects or concepts under some equivalence relation. To anyone who does not already possess the notion of classes (which Frege explained is *not* to be identified with that of aggregates or wholes made up of parts) there seems to be no more cogent manner of making the conception of such equivalence classes intuitively clear than by reference to the kind of operators which

Frege defined in terms of equivalence classes in his procedure of definition by abstraction. That is, the equation of the direction of the line a with the class of lines parallel to a may be taken more plausibly as informing someone familiar with the concept of a direction what sort of thing an equivalence class is to be taken to be than as telling someone familiar with the idea of an equivalence class what sort of thing a direction is. From this point of view definition by abstraction simply gives the general form of a method of concept formation with which we are extremely familiar, both in everyday discourse and in mathematics, that method by which we pass from an expression "R" for an equivalence relation between objects of a given kind to an operator "O" which forms terms denoting objects of a new kind, where for any objects a and b of the old kind, $Oa = Ob$ if and only if aRb. Frege succeeded in pointing to an analogy between transitions of this kind and the transition from using the notion "just as many as" to speaking of numbers as objects, effected by the introduction of the operator "the number of F's." What he overlooked is that if, as he wanted (and as he needed if he was to be able to prove the infinity of the number series), the "new" objects—in this case, numbers—are to be taken as already belonging to the original domain of objects, then their introduction depends upon an existential assumption about the size of the original domain, and that the unrestricted introduction of such operators, attaching to predicative expressions, would lead to contradiction, as in fact it led Frege. In any case, from this point of view the definition of cardinal numbers as equivalence classes of concepts (under the equivalence relation "just as many as") is not exactly a reduction of the notion of number to some other, independently given notion, since the notion of an equivalence class has itself to be explained by reference to the same sort of transition as that which we make when we pass from using the notion expressed by "just as many . . . as . . ." to the conception of the cardinal numbers as objects.

At two points in his construction—in defining "just as many as" and in defining "n is a natural number"—Frege had to employ higher-level quantification. Although there is an important difference between the logic of quantification over objects and that of quantification over concepts and relations, it is implausible to make this difference the boundary between logic and mathematics. Frege was able to demonstrate that certain principles which we should acknowledge as belonging to logic require higher-level quantification for their expression. His demonstration of the analyticity of arithmetical truths breaks down at the point where he needed to prove, from purely logical principles, the existence of infinitely many natural numbers. We may accordingly divide arithmetical truths into those for whose statement or proof we need to invoke the infinity of the number series and those for whose statement or proof we do not (the exact dividing line will vary according to the particular way we choose to frame our definitions of arithmetical notions). Frege's claim to have shown that arithmetical statements are analytic is to be upheld only for statements for which we do not need to invoke the infinity of the number series. Thus, even though Frege himself displayed no uncertainty about the meaning of quantification over infinite totalities, his work reveals very clearly why this became one of the principal preoccupations of later philosophers of mathematics.

Works by Frege

Rechnungsmethoden, die sich auf eine Erweiterung des Grössenbegriffes gründen. Jena, 1874.

"Über eine Weise, die Gestalt eines Dreiecks als complexe Grösse aufzufassen." *Jenaische Zeitschrift für Naturwissenschaft,* Vol. 12, Supplementar-Heft (1878), 17 ff.

Begriffsschrift, eine der arithmetischen nachgebildete Formelsprache des reinen Denkens. Halle, 1879. Ch. 1 translated by Peter Geach as "Begriffsschrift," in Peter Geach and Max Black, eds., *Translations From the Philosophical Writings of Gottlob Frege.* Oxford, 1952.

"Über Anwendungen der Begriffsschrift," in *Sitzungs-Bericht des Jenaischen Gesellschaft für Medizen und Naturwissenschaft für das Jahr 1879.* Pp. 29–33.

"Über die wissenschaftliche Berechtigung einer Begriffsschrift." *Zeitschrift für Philosophie und philosophische Kritik,* Vol. 81 (1882), 48–56. Translated by J. M. Bartlett as "On the Scientific Justification of a Concept-script." *Mind,* Vol. 73 (1964), 155–160.

"Über den Zweck der Begriffsschrift." *Jenaische Zeitschrift für Naturwissenschaft,* Vol. 16, Supplementar-Heft (1883), 1–10.

Die Grundlagen der Arithmetik. Eine logisch-mathematische Untersuchung über den Begriff der Zahl. Breslau, 1884. Translated by J. L. Austin as *The Foundations of Arithmetic: A Logico-mathematical Enquiry Into the Concept of Number.* Oxford, 1950; 2d rev. ed., 1953. Includes German text.

"Über formale Theorien der Arithmetik." *Jenaische Zeitschrift für Naturwissenschaft,* Vol. 19, Supplementar-Heft (1886), 94–104.

Funktion und Begriff. Jena, 1891. Translated by Peter Geach as "Function and Concept," in Geach and Black, *op. cit.*

"Über das Trägheitsgesetz." *Zeitschrift für Philosophie und philosophische Kritik,* Vol. 98 (1891), 145–161.

"Über Begriff und Gegenstand." *Vierteljahrsschrift für wissenschaftliche Philosophie,* Vol. 16 (1892), 192–205. Translated by Peter Geach as "On Concept and Object," in Geach and Black, *op. cit.*

"Über Sinn und Bedeutung." *Zeitschrift für Philosophie und philosophische Kritik,* Vol. 100 (1892), 25–50. Translated by Herbert Feigl as "On Sense and Nominatum," in Herbert Feigl and W. S. Sellars, eds., *Readings in Philosophical Analysis.* New York, 1949. Also translated by Max Black as "On Sense and Reference," in Geach and Black, *op. cit.*

Grundgesetze der Arithmetik. Begriffsschriftlich abgeleitet, 2 vols. Jena; 1893–1903. Parts translated by P. E. B. Jourdain, J. Stachelroth, Peter Geach, and Max Black, in Geach and Black, *op. cit.* First part of Vol. I translated by Montgomery Furth as *The Basic Laws of Arithmetic: An Exposition of the System.* Berkeley, 1965.

Review of Husserl's *Philosophie der Arithmetik. Zeitschrift für Philosophie und philosophische Kritik.* Vol. 103 (1894), 313–332. Parts translated in Geach and Black, *op. cit.*

"Kritische Beleuchtung einiger Punkte in E. Schröders Vorlesungen über die Algebra der Logik." *Archiv für systematische Philosophie,* Vol. 1 (1895), 433–456. Translated by Peter Geach as "A Critical Elucidation of Some Points in E. Schroeder's *Algebra der Logik,*" in Geach and Black, *op. cit.*

"Le Nombre entier," *Revue de métaphysique et de morale,* Vol. 3 (1895), 73–78.

"Lettera di signore G. Frege all'Editore" (dated September 29, 1896). *Revue de mathématique/Rivista di matematica,* Vol. 6 (1896–1899), 53–59.

"Über die Begriffsschrift des Herrn Peano und meine Eigene." *Bericht des mathematische-physische Class des königliche Sächsische Gesellschaft der Wissenschaft,* Vol. 48 (1897), 361–378.

Über die Zahlen des Herrn H. Schubert. Jena, 1899.

"Über die Grundlagen der Geometrie I." *Jahresbericht der Deutschen mathematiker Vereins,* Vol. 12 (1903), 319–324, 368–375, and Vol. 15 (1906), 293–309, 377–403, 423–430. First two sections translated by M. E. Szabo as "On the Foundations of Geometry." *Philosophical Review,* Vol. 69 (1960), 3–16.

"Was ist eine Funktion?," in *Festschrift Ludwig Boltzmann gewidmet zum sechzigsten Geburtstage 20 Februar 1904.* Leipzig, 1904. Pp. 656–666. Translated by Peter Geach as "What Is a Function?," in Geach and Black, *op. cit.*

"Antwort auf die Ferienplauderei des Herrn Thomae." *Jahresbericht der Deutschen mathematiker Vereins,* Vol. 15 (1906), 586–590.

"Die Unmöglichkeit der Thomaeschen formalen Arithmetik aufs Neue nachgewiesen." *Jahresbericht der Deutschen mathematiker Vereins,* Vol. 17 (1908), 52–55.

"Schlussbemerkungen." *Jahresbericht der Deutschen mathematiker Vereins,* Vol. 17 (1908), 56.

"Der Gedanke." *Beiträge zur Philosophie des deutschen Idealismus,* Vol. 1 (1919). Translated by A. Quinton and M. Quinton as "The Thought: A Logical Inquiry." *Mind,* Vol. 65 (1956), 289–311.

"Negation." *Beiträge zur Philosophie des deutschen Idealismus,* Vol. 1 (1919), 143–157. Translated by Peter Geach as "Negation," in Geach and Black, *op. cit.*

"Logische Untersuchungen. Dritter Teil: Gedankengefüge." *Beiträge zur Philosophie des deutschen Idealismus,* Vol. 3 (1923), 36–51.

Works on Frege

Anscombe, G. E. M., and Geach, Peter, *Three Philosophers.* Oxford, 1961.

Bergmann, Gustav, "Frege's Hidden Nominalism." *Philosophical Review,* Vol. 67 (1958), 437–459.

Caton, Charles E., "An Apparent Difficulty in Frege's Ontology." *Philosophical Review,* Vol. 71 (1962), 462–475.

Dummett, Michael, review of Geach and Black's *Translations From the Philosophical Writings of Gottlob Frege. Mind,* Vol. 63 (1954), 162–165.

Dummett, Michael, "Frege on Functions." *Philosophical Review,* Vol. 65 (1956), 229–230.

Dummett, Michael, "Frege's 'The Thought.'" *Mind,* Vol. 66 (1957), 548.

Jackson, Howard, "Frege's Ontology." *Philosophical Review,* Vol. 69 (1960), 394–395.

Kneale, William, "Gottlob Frege and Mathematical Logic," in A. J. Ayer et al., *The Revolution in Philosophy.* New York and London, 1956.

Kneale, William, and Kneale, Martha, *The Development of Logic.* Oxford, 1962. Ch. 8.

Marshall, William, "Frege's Theory of Functions and Objects." *Philosophical Review,* Vol. 62 (1953), 374–390.

Nidditch, Peter, "Peano and the Recognition of Frege." *Mind,* Vol. 72 (1963), 103–110.

Quine, W. V., "On Frege's Way Out." *Mind,* Vol. 64 (1955), 145–159.

Rudner, Richard, "On 'Sinn' as a Combination of Physical Properties." *Mind,* Vol. 61 (1952), 82–84.

Russell, Bertrand, *The Principles of Mathematics.* Cambridge, 1903. Appendix A, "The Logical and Arithmetical Doctrines of Frege."

Searle, J. R., "Russell's Objections to Frege's Theory of Sense and Reference." *Analysis,* Vol. 18 (1957–1958), 137–143.

Stoothoff, R. H., "Note on a Doctrine of Frege." *Mind,* Vol. 72 (1963), 406–408.

Walker, Jeremy, *A Study of Frege.* Oxford, 1965.

Wells, Rulon E., "Frege's Ontology." *Review of Metaphysics,* Vol. 4 (1951), 537–573.

Wells, Rulon E., "Is Frege's Concept of Function Valid?" *Journal of Philosophy,* Vol. 60 (1963), 717–730.

Wienpahl, P. D., "Frege's *Sinn und Bedeutung.*" *Mind,* Vol. 59 (1950).

MICHAEL DUMMETT

FRENCH ENCYCLOPEDIA, THE. See ENCYCLOPÉDIE.

FRENCH PHILOSOPHICAL LITERATURE. See
CLANDESTINE PHILOSOPHICAL LITERATURE IN FRANCE;
ENCYCLOPÉDIE.

FRENCH PHILOSOPHY. French philosophy proper,
as distinguished from earlier philosophy written in what is
now modern France, may be said to begin in the sixteenth
century. For that is the period in which the practice arose
of writing philosophy in the vernacular rather than in Latin
and in which there began to develop a point of view that
did not derive from Scholasticism. The use of Latin did
not, of course, die out in lay circles until two hundred
years later, but the mere possibility of expressing serious
thought in a language that was not sanctified by tradition
and sonorous with theological overtones gave to philosophy new directions that in turn suggested new problems.
This innovation ran parallel to the rise of the new nations.
And nowhere was there a greater awareness of what was
going on politically than in France. By the end of the
sixteenth century the frontiers of France were almost what
they are today, and though power was not so centralized as
it was to be under Louis XIV, the struggle for centralization was under way and its outcome fairly certain.

A philosophy of opposition. The sixteenth century in
France was also the century of the Wars of Religion. Few
civil wars have ever been more brutal and destructive. The
Lutheran Reformation had demonstrated that the authority
of the church could be not only challenged but overthrown. This was both an ideological and a political victory. But whereas the Lutherans in the Germanies could
count on protection from the princes, the Calvinists in
France had only their own resources to rely on. Their main
resource was stubborn resistance. But it was backed up by
literature in the form of theological and philosophical
debates. One must therefore think of French philosophy in
this period as determined not only by its inner logical
structure but also by a revolutionary temper. It was
definitely a philosophy of opposition, and that character
remained true of philosophy in France well into the twentieth century. In the early days we find opposition to
ecclesiastical authority, to Scholastic authority, and to the
authority of a traditional method of thinking. In the seventeenth century we find opposition to Aristotle and opposition to attacks on Aristotle. In the Encyclopedists we find
opposition to the church and to absolute monarchy, and in
Rousseau and his followers opposition to the rationalists.
Many, in fact most, of the philosophers who have survived
were not members of the teaching profession. Montaigne,
Descartes, Voltaire, Rousseau, Maine de Biran, Cournot,
Auguste Comte held no university posts. It was not until the
university system was organized under Victor Cousin that
eminent philosophers were also professors. And when
that happened, a strong opposition was formed against them
by men like Taine and Renan.

Breadth of interest. Though the assignment of causes to
historical events is always precarious, it may be surmised
that one of the effects of this situation has been the breadth
of French philosophical interests. Political, social, pedagogical, and aesthetic problems have been living issues
among French philosophers. Whereas in Great Britain the
philosophers in the main narrowed their field to the limits
of epistemology and seldom ventured farther abroad than
ethics and political philosophy, a man like Descartes could
become an authority in mathematics and physics as well as
in technical philosophy; a Voltaire could write plays and
poems and novelettes, as well as a philosophical dictionary
and a treatise on Newton; Rousseau became as famous for
La Nouvelle Héloïse as for his *Contrat social*. Ravaisson
could figure in a history of archaeology, just as Sartre could
figure in a history of the drama.

Philosophy and the schools. Whatever the cause may be,
a tradition has developed in France of searching out the
underlying philosophical problems in matters of daily life.
The French child for some generations has begun his
philosophical initiation in the *lycée*. His very training in
rhetoric is also a training in logic, for he is drilled in the
preparation of outlines from his earliest years. When
presenting his lessons in elementary arithmetic, he propounds his reasoning process rather than merely his results. He is thus accustomed to the analysis of his own
thoughts as well as those of others, and if his insistence on
the uncovering of *les principes* is sometimes annoying to
foreigners, it must be granted that it has given his writing a
kind of clarity both in meaning and in structure which is
unique.

Breakdown of traditional thought. Until the French
Revolution education was in the hands of the church. But
this educational monopoly had a weakness: it indoctrinated
its pupils in a technique of thinking that had been effectively challenged by Italian and English scientists and
could not be applied to the most pressing problems of the
times. Though the syllogistic method was excellent for
testing one's reasoning, its plausibility rested on the plausibility of its premises; and the great question that was
disturbing the keener minds of the French Renaissance
was precisely how fruitful the traditional premises were.
By the middle of the sixteenth century the New World had
been discovered and partly explored. The past had been
unearthed. The Copernican system was replacing that of
Ptolemy. Printing had been invented. The story has been
told too often to need repeating; but it is hardly likely that
any inquisitive youngster of that time would have been
satisfied with a set of syllogisms drawn from St. Thomas
Aquinas when he wanted to know what was on the other
side of the ocean or why, if the earth was round, the waters
did not run off it. Whatever the explanation of this
effervescence of curiosity, it appeared in country after
country. In France its most influential result was a wave of
skepticism about received opinions.

SIXTEENTH-CENTURY SKEPTICISM

In Renaissance France, as in Italy and England, philosophers began by examining the grounds of authority. In
matters of religion the authority was revelation, as found in
the Bible and supported by the Fathers and tradition. It
was official doctrine that this was a body of truth based
upon supernatural sources and therefore never to be questioned. In scientific matters the authority was usually Aristotle and his commentators, supplemented by Plato's
Timaeus. The metaphor of matter and form, the theory of
the four elements, the dogma of natural positions and the

finite universe, explanation of teleology—all had been questioned, yet never successfully. But the sixteenth century was the century of Luther, Calvin, Erasmus, Melancthon, Theodore Beza, and Lefèvre d'Étaples, and no one could any longer entertain the belief that the message of either revelation or of science was clear. Textual criticism indicated problems in the interpretation of Scripture itself; the Fathers disagreed, as did the commentators. The doctrines of Aristotle were variously expounded, and tradition was seen to be a growing process with accretions, the sanctity of which was far from certain. This is not the place to examine all the disputes that arose over the meaning of any of these sources of information, but it can at least be pointed out that when a man is conscious of a conflict of authorities, he will, if a philosopher, try to settle it in a rational manner or give up the job as hopeless.

Rabelais. Whatever else a skeptic may doubt, he will never doubt his critical method. If he doubts the efficacy of reason, he may substitute for it something which he will call nature or common sense or tradition or experience or intuition, or some similar term. This is inevitable if he is to avoid the self-defeating position of denying the truth of any assertion whatsoever. Regardless of that, no skeptic on record ever denied that some knowledge was possible, and in general, skepticism has been based on a set of ideas or a choice of premises which are held as certain. Thus Rabelais (1494?–1553), who ridiculed monasticism, marriage, current education, and pedantry in *Gargantua* (1534), nevertheless held to the fundamental rightness of human nature when uncorrupted by institutionalism. His Abbaye de Thélème with its famous motto, *Fais-ce que vouldras,* in spite of its fantastic details, preaches the need of self-knowledge and self-command and lays down freedom as its foundation. The value and the possibility of these are never doubted. One must not read a consistent and theoretical structure into the buffoonery of Rabelais, for his book is, as Montaigne put it, *simplement plaisant.* But it would not have been *plaisant* had there not glowed through the caricatures a spirit of hedonism which was itself a protest against pretentiousness and authoritarianism. The book was the assertion of man's native ability to know his own ends and to discover his own values. This ability, however, was constantly threatened by the pedants and the *chats fourrés* ("stuffed shirts").

De Bruès. Another vein of skepticism appeared in the work of Guy de Bruès (fl. 1554–1562), *Les Dialogues . . . contre les nouveaux académiciens* (1st ed., 1557). The spokesman for skepticism in this work based his argument largely on the diversity of opinions, which ought not to arise if there were a certain basis for knowledge. He substituted for reason a power which he called nature. The term, which has served a large number of different purposes, here meant the uninstructed sentiments of an individual; and though the author deprecated the use of nature as a standard, nevertheless he presented the arguments in its favor so clearly that a reader is likely to be persuaded by them. The skeptic of this type never asks what human nature would be if it were not educated either in the schoolroom or through association with other human beings. On the contrary, he takes it for granted that we possess a kind of insight into moral and other values

which can be, and usually is, perverted by education. But he never hesitates to utilize the same type of argument as that which would be used by an authoritarian. Bruès was not himself a skeptic and his book had very little influence. It is of some historical value, however, in showing that skepticism had a certain vogue in intellectual circles of that period. Moreover, it was in Montaigne's library, and its influence on him, if any, must have been in a direction antithetical to that which its author intended.

Sanches. Usually the skeptics of this period in France doubted the efficacy of reason in order to put faith in place of reason. But this was not the purpose of such a man as Francisco Sanches (c. 1551–1623), who taught at Toulouse. His *Tractatus de Multum Nobili et Prima Universali Scientis Quod Nihil Scitur* (1581) appeared just a year after the first edition of Montaigne's *Essays.* Sanches' underlying purpose was to show that since nothing can be known by the traditional methods, a new method must be developed. This method was to be based on the indubitable facts of inner experience. He failed to develop this method, however, and his book ended without resolving the questions it raised. Yet he too, while deprecating the use of reason, did so in a rational manner and seems to have had no doubts either about the validity of his criticisms or the results of introspection.

This type of skepticism arose from the observation that philosophers fail to agree. The conclusion was drawn that if they had as sound a method as that of the mathematicians or natural scientists, agreement would be possible. But the difficulty of finding a correct and fruitful method was so great that some philosophers threw up their hands in despair, and the nescience of a man like Sanches seemed better than the extravagances of fifteenth-century Scholasticism. The revolt against the schools was as pronounced as it had been in Italy and was beginning to be in England. The solution of Sanches was a retreat into self-knowledge. That was also the solution of Montaigne.

Montaigne. Michel de Montaigne (1533–1592) went further than his contemporary. He doubted not only the utility of formal reasoning but also, in some of his moods, that of authority. To these he added doubts about the value of civilization itself and was thus one of the most potent influences in modern times toward cultural primitivism. His skepticism regarding reason appears in his insistence that he was engaged only in a self-portrait; he was describing an individual, neither classifying types of human nature nor deducing any conclusions from self-evident premises. He was willing to go along with custom as far as faith and morals were concerned, for that was easier than protest; he had, moreover, lived through the Wars of Religion and felt that little good had been accomplished by strife. Nevertheless, two of his theses became scandals in the succeeding century—that of natural theology, as it appeared in the "Apology for Raimond Sebond" (*Essays,* II, 12), and that of cultural primitivism in his essay "On the Cannibals" (I, 31). The "Apology" was an exposition and defense of the cosmological argument for the existence of God. It was not Montaigne's intention to maintain that this argument could supplant faith in either revelation or tradition. On the contrary, it was simply additional support for one's faith. If one of his readers were to say that reason alone would suffice for religious belief, Montaigne was prepared to reply that even the beasts could reason. Indeed, he went further in this direction than was required, for he assigned to the animals not only the power of ratiocination but also morals superior to those of men. Here he was bound to come into conflict with the church; for it was an essential part of the Catholic tradition that men alone had souls, that they were not animals but a special kind of creature, and that they alone could reason. But the lesson that Montaigne drew from his observations was that humility and submission to God are the sole appropriate attitudes of man. The desire for knowledge comes from pride and it was pride that led to the Fall of Man in the Garden of Eden.

Just as the beasts are our superiors in intelligence and morals, so are the savages. Montaigne's point was that Christian virtue does not depend on erudition but on simplicity of soul and intuitive insight. The savages of whom he was writing were American Indians. They were, he was informed, inhabitants of well-policed states and lived in accordance with perfect religious precepts. And yet they had not received the Gospels. They simply obeyed the law of nature and knew nothing of commerce, letters, science, law, slavery, wealth, agriculture, metallurgy, or viniculture. They had no conception of mendacity, treason, dissimulation, avarice, envy, belittlement, or pardon and hence had no words for them. Their regimen was simplicity itself, and they could do without any of the luxuries which European man demanded. This idyllic life, which is of course purely legendary, Montaigne admitted, was tempered with warfare and cannibalism. But, as he said, he had seen similar things in the recent civil wars. The admission of these defects in an otherwise perfect existence was used to show that the savages are no worse than their European contemporaries. In short, the example of the savages proved that nature is as good a teacher as reason.

Charron. Praise of the animals and savages for their innate wisdom is sometimes merely a paradox without serious intention, but sometimes, as a satire on humanity, it takes on greater importance. The anti-intellectualism of Montaigne was organized into something resembling a system by his disciple, Pierre Charron (1541–1603), whose *De la Sagesse* went into 32 editions before 1664. This work clarified the significance of Montaigne's *Essays*, making the point that if one attacked reason, it was in order to justify faith. Doubt in defense of belief thus became a mode of philosophizing that could be used by profoundly religious people as well as by scoffers. And the scoffers could always maintain for their own protection that their anti-intellectualism was proreligious. This has seemed to some historians to have been the strategy of the seventeenth-century thinker, Pierre Bayle. However, there is no cause to believe that Charron's contrast between wisdom (*sagesse*) and reason was anything but sincere. It was analogous to Pascal's distinction between reason and the heart, and no one would doubt the sincerity of Pascal.

Pious skepticism. A thread of pious skepticism ran through French philosophy from the time of Charron at least to the early nineteenth century, when Bautain's *fidéisme* was condemned by Pope Gregory XVI. At that time the position of the church was declared to be that reason is sufficient to prove the existence of God and that faith is posterior to revelation; in short, a nonbeliever cannot be asked to accept the tenets of the church without rational proof. In the twentieth century a tendency analogous to pious skepticism appeared in the writings of both Bergson and the Christian existentialists. In these thinkers reason was shown to be either irrelevant to vital concerns (Bergson) or incapable of exploring individual existents (Gabriel Marcel).

Pious skepticism appeared in defense of deism as well as of traditional Catholicism. In Rousseau's "Profession of Faith of the Savoyard Vicar" (*Émile*, Book IV), it is said that reason in the form of science will disprove the existence of God, the immortality of the soul, and freedom of the will, but that feeling (*sentiment*) will restore them all. Hence one could be a skeptic and yet believe, on no evidence other than that of some nonrational power within us, called by various names.

One group of writers, frequently called libertines, developed a more radical skepticism. The best known of these men is probably La Mothe Le Vayer (1588–1672), whose ideas may be summed up in his own sentence, "The more knowledge, the more grief" (*Qui addit scientiam addit atque dolorem*). Common sense, he maintained, would do all that is needed in the way of religious and moral instruction, and there is nothing more presumptuous than seeking the "inner purposes" of the Creator. But this tendency easily became generalized into the condemnation of all knowledge, for it was soon seen that once a pronouncement of the heart, the spirit, or the feelings was put into words, it would be subjected to exactly the same kind of rational investigation as any other pronouncement.

The anti-intellectualistic tradition continued well into modern times. In the followers of Rousseau, in the traditionalists—who maintained that tradition is in itself evidence of truth—and in Bergson's theory of intuition we find continued defenses of a nonrational source of truth. And in André Gide's *acte gratuit* the very absurdity of the act, the complete absence of conscious motivation, gives value to what is done. Similarly in surrealism and its derivatives the fact that the artist is supposed to be totally unaware of what he is making confers upon his work of art a deeper meaning than it would have if he had deliberately and rationally planned it.

THE RETURN TO RATIONALISM

In 1617 appeared the *Banquet des sages* and in 1624 the *Doctrine curieuse de beaux-esprits de ce temps,* both by the Jesuit Père François Garasse (1585–1631). These works were violent attacks on Charron and his school for what Garasse believed to be their central thesis, that man need rely on nothing more than nature for all wisdom and guidance. The attack was as unjust as it was violent, but its author saw the danger to ecclesiastical authority in any doctrine that located the source of truth within the individual. To him, the enemy was maintaining that something identified with nature sufficed to direct men in both their thinking and their practice, and this led to pantheism, sensuality, and hedonism, all equally accursed. It was true that Montaigne and his followers did urge men to follow nature, but the advice involved rejecting the disputes and hairsplitting of the pedants rather than the teachings of religion. Nevertheless, since there had been a long standing opposition between Nature, on the one hand, and God or the Supernatural, on the other, there were grounds for feeling that to follow nature was to turn away from God. Natural theology, the discovery of God's purposes in nature, had long been recognized as a legitimate enterprise, but it was never held by authority to be sufficient. It might lead to deism, but not to Christianity.

Descartes. Hence any attempt to reinstate reason was welcome. And it was one role of René Descartes (1596–1650) to show that even if one doubted everything that could possibly be doubted, still reason would reassert its rights in that very process and re-establish the existence of God and the authority of his divine commandments. Descartes's famous method of universal doubt was not so integral as he thought. He never doubted the necessity of an agent for all acts, of the ancient causal principle that there must be a similarity between causes and their effects, nor the efficacy of what had been called the natural light. His rationalism consisted in deducing from a few elementary principles, some of which were never made explicit, a whole system of metaphysics. His ideal, in his own terms, was first to establish a technique which would lead to absolute certainty. But the technique itself was based upon a metaphysics which he never attempted to justify, probably because it was itself the metaphysics of common sense or the natural light. At the risk of doing him an injustice, one might say that he assumed without question that ideas are atomistic; that when an idea is logically primitive, it corresponds to a fact that is elementary; and that the universe is of such a nature that its entire character can be inferred logically from a few elementary propositions. But more striking to his readers than all this was the obvious fact that by assuming the method of his antagonists, he showed that it would lead to results antithetical to theirs.

Descartes's assumptions would have been accepted by any of his contemporaries, and they were instrumental in molding subsequent French philosophy and in raising new problems which seventeenth-century rationalists debated for at least two generations after Descartes's death. For example, the causal postulate implied that if two things said to be related as cause and effect have no discoverable identity between them, one cannot be the cause of the other. Descartes himself used this to prove that God himself must be the cause of the idea which we have of him.

Occasionalism. On the other hand there was one apparently causal situation in which no common identity could be found. It seemed that a purely material being, an air wave, for instance, was the cause of sensation, which, however, Descartes had demonstrated to be immaterial. There was nothing shared by an air wave and a sound, nothing in common—to use Descartes's language—between extended and thinking substance. How then could an air wave cause a sensation? And in reverse order, how could a volition cause the movement of a muscle? Géraud de Cordemoy (1620–1684), Nicolas de Malebranche (1638–1715), and the occasionalists in general decided that causation was itself a mystery. To the occasionalist the apparent interaction between minds and bodies was only

apparent, not real; God produces the sensation on the occasion of a bodily impetus and the motion on the occasion of a volition. Cordemoy, in fact, maintained that though we could observe the contact between two bodies in collision, we could not observe the causative power which was transferred from one to the other. By extension this could be asserted of all cases of causation. Its implications led Spinoza, for instance, to redefine Cartesian substance and make mentality and materiality two of the infinite attributes of God, rather than two substances. They could not interact, but whatever happened in one would be found in another form in the other. Thus the influence of Cartesianism went well beyond the frontiers of France, and it was not until the work of John Locke had made itself felt on the Continent that French philosophers gave up the Cartesian method.

Cartesianism in art and literature. Cartesianism, like Freudianism, Bergsonism, Marxism, and existentialism, was a movement which extended well beyond the limits of technical philosophy. It was not so much the method of doubt that was accepted by the seventeenth century in general, but rather the insistence upon analysis, on seeking clear and distinct ideas, the use of what came to be known as the geometrical method. We find the effect of this in the aesthetic practices of both the painters and the poets. It requires no carefully trained eye to see in the paintings of such a man as Nicolas Poussin the simple geometrical grids upon which they were constructed, and there is scarcely a play of Racine in which the main characters do not analyze their states of mind and deliver their analyses to the audience in beautifully balanced alexandrines. Though Bossuet's *Art poétique* owes as much to Horace as to Descartes, yet it fits in with the Cartesian principles as if it had been directly drawn out of them. The cataloguing of the emotions, which became a standard practice of the French drama and novel, derives obviously from Descartes's *Treatise on the Passions*, which in turn goes back at least to the Peripatetics. And the notion of consistency of character, which also had its ancient analogues, became not only a literary device but an ethical norm. It was not until Marcel Proust became widely read, after World War I, that this notion was abandoned by writers of fiction. But by then various forms of anti-intellectualism had become predominant in nonacademic circles in France.

THE ANTI-CARTESIANS

Though Cartesianism and the geometrical method were the dominant forces in seventeenth and early eighteenth-century France, there were powerful forces opposing them as well. The opposition to Cartesianism came from both religious and secular writers.

Pascal. On the religious side the most important attack came from Blaise Pascal (1623–1662). Pascal saw clearly that a God who simply started the world's motions and then stepped back to observe results was hardly one who would bring much support to a suffering and sinful humanity. One might with reason say that Pascal made a distinction between the metaphysical First Principle—Aristotle's Unmoved Mover—and the God of the Bible. Or, as he himself said, "God of Abraham, God of Isaac, God of Jacob, not of the philosophers and scholars." The existence of the former might be a necessity of reason, but the latter was known by something higher than reason, the heart. The heart's cognitive power had to be recognized if God was to be accessible to all men, the simple as well as the learned. The number of the latter is always much smaller than that of the former, and it was inconceivable to Pascal that God would be available only to the élite. In this he was following a tradition that went back at least to Tertullian.

Along with the distinction between reason and the heart went another, equally famous, between the *esprit de géometrie* and the *esprit de finesse*. It would be futile to attempt an analysis of what the *esprit de finesse* consisted in, but certain of its traits can be set down without much fear of error. First, it is an apprehension of particulars, not the power of abstracting general characteristics. Second, it is an apprehension of existents, not of possibles. Third, it is more important than reasoning, for it gives us insight into nature or reality, whereas the universals of the reason are constructed by art. And fourth, it alone can discover first principles of religious and moral relevance. When one thinks of these traits as a whole, one sees in them a weapon against the kind of program into which Cartesianism had evolved. Science is lowered in rank; its systematizations become a falsification of reality; it tends to be antireligious and to substitute theology or metaphysics for the religious experience. As is too well known to require much comment here, Pascal's thoughts have no order; their order has been given to them by their various editors. They are the expression of a series of insights which came to him at various moments of his life. That there is no logical passage from one to the other would not have been a fault in his eyes. Their importance as a literary source lies in the extraordinary series of maxims, thoughts, observations, and reflections, which have come from French authors since the seventeenth century. One has only to think of La Rochefoucauld, La Bruyère, Vauvenargues, Chamfort, and Joubert, to say nothing of their imitators, to realize the vogue of this form of writing. Its effectiveness comes from the flash of insight which produces it and the flash of authenticity it produces.

Huet. An attack on Cartesianism from within the clergy came from Pierre Daniel Huet (1630–1721), bishop of Avranches. His disagreement with Descartes arose first over the principle of methodical doubt. He argued that if the truth of a proposition is doubted, the truth of its contradictory is asserted. Thus, if I doubt the existence of an external world, I am asserting that an external world does not exist. One cannot doubt both the truth of a proposition and that of its contradictory at the same time. But to believe in the falsity of a proposition is not to doubt. Descartes might have escaped this attack by pointing out that one can suspend judgment and in that sense doubt a given proposition without committing oneself to the truth of any other proposition, even its contradictory. He was, however, more vulnerable to Huet's second argument: there is no self-evidence in the belief that thinking requires a subject, an ego to do the thinking. When Descartes in his famous *cogito* asserted that he was intuitively aware of himself in the act of doubting, Huet challenged him on the ground that the distinction between agent and act is not given in the consciousness of the act. Huet did not deny that the distinction is valid, but merely contended that it does not arise in the process of thinking.

The very word "thinking," he said, has a threefold sense. It may mean the thinking mind, or the subject matter of a thinking mind, or the relation between a thinking mind and its subject matter. The point of this distinction was that since Descartes used the term in all these senses without differentiating among them, he could argue that there was an external world in the subject matter of thought without having recourse to God as its Creator. Huet insisted, moreover, that there are two separate mental acts involved in thinking and in the awareness that one is thinking, whereas Descartes believed them to be identical. "I think" and "thinking" are two separate ideas, says Huet, not one, and when one asserts that one is aware of thinking, one is relying on more than simple awareness, here and now, of a process of thought.

But Huet's more radical disagreement with Descartes lay in his assertion that there are some beliefs which we hold with absolute certainty and of which we can have no rational knowledge. These are the truths of religion. They also are no more empirical than they are rational, and when they are judged by either experience or reason, they fall to the ground. Since Descartes himself had said that he would never sustain a thesis that contradicted the truths taught by the church, Huet had the upper hand in this skirmish.

Gassendi. The most influential of the French anti-Cartesians was Pierre Gassendi (1592–1655). He too was an antirationalist, but his attacks on reason arose from several sources: his profound dislike of having recourse to pagan philosophers (though he did revive the atomism of Epicurus); his belief that things have both an "inner" and an "outer" nature; his argument that the syllogism was always a *petitio principii*; and his assumption that the inner natures of things were inevitably unknowable. Against the *cogito* he maintained that the natural light would suffice to prove one's own existence. Against the dualism of the two substances, mind and body, he argued that the mind or soul could be envisioned as simply a sort of sublimated spirit. Sublimated spirits exist in space. And for that matter Descartes himself had used the animal spirits to move the muscles. Against the doctrine that the beasts are simply machines with no feelings whatsoever, he argued that since they have organs like our own, there is no more reason to deny them the feelings appropriate to such organs than there is in our own case.

But there was also a constructive side to Gassendi's philosophy. Assuming that the end of philosophy is human happiness, which in his opinion consists in tranquillity and lack of pain, he found a basis for such a position in Epicureanism. He elaborated an epistemology that distinguished three kinds of knowledge, to each of which corresponded a kind of truth. Truth might be found in immediate experiences, in reasoning, and in judgments of value. The first is always obtained when we are confronted with sensory data and make simple assertions about what we observe. The second occurs when we interpret these data or when we draw out of them conclusions implicit in them. The third is based exclusively on the hedonistic principle that the greater pleasure should always be preferred to the lesser. But he also maintained that reason alone would tell us what pleasures are great and what small, for few are unmixed with pain.

Gassendi's Epicureanism did not stop with hedonism. He also revived the theory of atomism. His universe is composed of conglomerates of atoms of a certain magnitude, shape, solidity, and weight. The notion that solidity was a matter of degree allowed him to conclude that some material objects could have their atoms so widely separated as to be what in modern terminology would be called gaseous. It was in this way that spirits could be both material and apparently nonspatial. The effect of Gassendi's atomism, however, was not profound. It was only his hedonism and empiricism that survived.

Molière and La Fontaine. As there are echoes of Cartesianism in Racine, so there are echoes of Gassendi in Molière. The satire against philosophy that is found in *Les Femmes savantes* is not a repetition of anything in Gassendi but is certainly directed against the notion that body and soul are utterly separate. Similarly, the insistence to the point of absurdity upon precision of statement, as well as the suggestion of the absolute evil of the erotic passions, could be satires either on Cartesianism or on Jansenism. (The two could be easily confused in the last decades of the seventeenth century.) If Molière is not easily to be called a disciple of Gassendi, the same cannot be said of La Fontaine, who in his *Discours à Mme de la Sablière* and the fable of *Les Souris et le chathuant* clearly attacked some of the Cartesian theses.

THE "PHILOSOPHES"

The last years of Louis XIV saw a return to traditional piety, while the reign of his successor, the regent, and of the regent's ward, Louis XV, saw a return to licentiousness. Jansenism was dead and what was produced by men who could be called philosophers was of no lasting importance. The contrast between the state of affairs in England and in France turned the minds of French thinkers toward the land which they believed to be freer, happier, and better governed than their own, and men began to write about matters of more practical importance than the possibility of knowledge, the test of truth, the conflict between faith and reason, or the control of the passions. It is at this time that two new interests appeared, an interest in the foundations and structure of government and an interest in collecting information. Though at various times in the Middle Ages the question of sovereignty had been raised, along with the "regimen of princes," the source of royal power, and the duty of subjects, and though such questions had been discussed by Machiavelli as well as by Marsilius of Padua before him, the investigation was relatively new in France. It might be said to have been initiated in the sixteenth century by Jean Bodin (1530–1596), but it reached a kind of popularity in the work of Montesquieu.

Bodin. Bodin had been in England during the reign of Elizabeth, but whether his experiences there had given him any new ideas about government is not certain. At any rate his *De la République* (1577) is a defense of monarchy based on the metaphor of paternalism, and his main contribution to political philosophy seems to have been his frank assertion that sovereignty comes not from God but out of the requirements of social life. Society as Bodin conceived it was a constellation of families in each of which the father had absolute power; and clearly such a collection of autonomous princelings could not continue to exist without some "super-prince" to control them. Less interesting systematically but more interesting historically was Bodin's correlation of kinds of governments with kinds of climates, for it was an attempt at least to find some observable cause for observable differences in a homogeneous group of individuals. This attempt anticipated a movement which was making itself felt in philosophy as well as in science and which reappeared in the writings of the much more influential Montesquieu.

Bayle. The tendency to ground philosophy in observable facts and to subject all problems to rational scrutiny is also found in Pierre Bayle (1647–1706). Bayle's *Dictionnaire historique et critique* was by its very nature a compilation of information, but it was information which had been passed through the sieve of criticism, regardless of its source. Bayle had no more respect for authority and tradition than he had for irresponsible gossip, and thanks to his highly developed critical sense and his vast erudition he was able to present to the public a mass of information upon which the new philosophy could be built. His skeptical spirit was such that his readers were freed from the compulsion to accept tradition when it could not stand the same tests as new discoveries in science. Bayle was one of the great liberating forces of the eighteenth century.

Montesquieu. But the first fruits of the liberation were found in the writings of Charles de Secondat, baron de Montesquieu (1689–1755). His *Lettres persanes* (1721) showed an author capable of looking at his own civilization from an objective point of view, without prejudice either for or against it. This was clearly the attitude needed for political philosophy and had been previously exemplified in the two major works of Machiavelli. One of the effects of the *Lettres persanes* was the clarification of cultural differences, with the consequent suggestion that the human race is far from being all of a piece in spite of their common descent from Adam and Eve. It made little sense in the eighteenth century to write a universal history in the manner of St. Augustine or Bossuet, for exploration had shown Europeans that there were races of men who were so vastly different from their European contemporaries that they might just as well have been of radically different descent. These people were, moreover, well governed, moral, highly civilized at times, at others living a life "in accordance with nature," and all this in spite of the obvious fact, controlled by observations made on the spot, of their having been cut off from Biblical knowledge from extremely remote times. It is not beyond the bounds of probability that the spread of colonialism had some influence in making an appreciation of such peoples essential for the sake both of efficient government and of trade.

Montesquieu's *Esprit des lois* (1748) was of greater importance than the *Lettres persanes* in that it concentrated its attention upon government and did not wander over social customs and manners. The laws whose spirit Montesquieu was describing varied, he maintained, with customs, climate, religion, and commerce; and there seemed to be no intention on its author's part to search for a single law which would describe all governments or the inner nature of government in general. There are certain laws, the laws of nature, in terms of which one can predict how a people will be governed, but these laws prescribe the variables of which governmental systems are the functions. All men feel themselves to be weak in the face of natural forces, desire mates, food, and social life. But in every situation the ability to combat the forces of nature varies and the kind of available food, the virility of men, and the type of social organization will inevitably vary too. Variation in such matters is ultimately a function of climate, but one will also find variations in religion, laws, administrative traditions, and manners. Climate is the one factor which is given in a state of nature.

Montesquieu knew that government is artificial, not natural, and the government which he most admired was that of England. For in the separation of powers, as he saw it, there are sufficient checks and balances to permit the subjects to be as free as is humanly possible.

The emphasis on freedom was what marked off Montesquieu's work from its rivals, such as they were. It was freedom in the sense of liberation, not in the naked sense of liberty. And it is not unfair to say that the two features of society from which men most wanted to be liberated were the church and the absolute monarchy. To bring this about required education. And here men like Bayle and the Encyclopedists were of the greatest help. They all seemed agreed that once these shackles were removed from human behavior, all would know how to employ their freedom profitably.

The "Encyclopédie." The group of thinkers usually called the *philosophes* disagreed among themselves on a variety of subjects, but they agreed on the general principle of the educational value of philosophy, a term which in the eighteenth century still denoted the sciences. *Les lumières* were to be made the common property of all society, and the spread of true information was presumably to aid in the pursuit of happiness. This program was strengthened by the actual experience of relatively free inquiry in religion and above all by the technological innovations that science had made possible. The influence of Bacon is obvious.

This movement reached its climax in the *Encyclopédie* of Diderot and d'Alembert. The work began to appear in 1751, three years after the publication of Montesquieu's "Spirit of the Laws." One of its main theses was the essential interdependence of the arts and sciences, which entailed the assumption that the distinction between the liberal and the manual arts was trivial. In its "Preliminary Discourse," written by d'Alembert, the source of all knowledge is assigned to sensation. Sensation not only tells us what is real and what unreal, but also what is good and what bad. But, as had been pointed out by Gassendi, raw sensations must be organized and their effects must be induced from them by a reasoning process. The ultimate purpose of knowledge is self-preservation, which can be achieved only through a thoroughly empirical approach to our problems and, what is equally important, by the cooperation of our fellows. This thesis runs through the *Encyclopédie*, though—as is inevitable in a work written by so many hands—its emphasis varies.

Self-preservation depends not only on bodily health but also on the steady improvement of technology. On the other hand, its attainment is the aim of all knowledge, even of that which seems most remote from practical ends, for though some sciences, such as mathematics, do not seem to cater to utility, yet the satisfaction of curiosity is itself a great pleasure and in producing that, mathematics may be thought of as practical. Who, moreover, knows when the most abstract thought might stimulate a useful discovery?

Philosophy and science. This practical point of view was common to all the *philosophes*. They might be atheists like Holbach, or deists like Voltaire. They might be materialists like La Mettrie or sensationalists like Condillac. But they never seemed to disagree about the basic purpose of thinking. They anticipated the naturalism of the nineteenth and twentieth centuries in basing all philosophy on natural science. And it was this, rather than the details of their various theories, that alienated them from some of their contemporaries.

Freedom of inquiry. If the program of the *philosophes* was to be fulfilled, it was clear that education had to be taken out of the hands of ecclesiastics and that governmental censorship of books must cease. In the France of the eighteenth century the functions of church and state were so closely intertwined that if one were to be changed, the other would change too. The *philosophes* were not antimonarchical; their admiration for England convinced them that monarchy and freedom could live in peace together. Their polemics were fundamentally aimed at the church as an educational institution and as the propagandist of beliefs which were contradicted by science. Even when the French Revolution broke out, there was no intention of deposing the king, to say nothing of setting up a republic. That came later.

But the notion of freedom expanded until in the nineteenth century there emerged a doctrine of philosophical anarchy.

RETURN TO ANTI-INTELLECTUALISM

Rousseau. A major intimation of the self-destroying dialectic of philosophical anarchy appeared in the work of Jean-Jacques Rousseau (1712–1778). His *Contrat social* (1762) opened with the ringing statement that man is born free but is everywhere in chains. The purpose of the work, therefore, was to discover a way of regaining man's natural freedom. But one is astonished to find out before the end of the work that the government of the common ego (*le moi commun*) is just as absolute as that of a king, for though we all participate in it, the participation is of a metaphysical kind. The individual substitutes for his instincts his sense of justice. At this point Rousseau argued dialectically that if a will is general, it must be the common property of all capable of willing. The general will takes on all the prerogatives of Machiavelli's prince or Hobbes's king, for it cannot do wrong. It determines what is right and what is wrong. Thus, when man has regained his freedom, it is to be absorbed in a spirit larger than his own.

Though Rousseau started out as a member of the philosophical circle of the French Enlightenment, he became its worst enemy. He agreed with the *philosophes* in their attacks on authority, but he sharply disagreed with their theory of knowledge. To him science was antitheistic by its very nature and an instrument of despair. The clearest expression of his epistemological position is in the fourth book of *Émile*, "The Profession of Faith of the Savoyard Vicar." Here Rousseau stated that if one follows the path of the scientists, one will end up by denying the existence of God, the freedom of the will, and the immortality of the soul. But belief in these three principles is essential to living a good life; for if there is no God, if we are determined by material causes in all that we do, or if this terrestrial life is all we possess, then we might just as well throw in the sponge and eat, drink, and be merry. But such a hedonistic regimen was repulsive to Rousseau. Brought up as a Calvinist in Geneva, he could not believe that man was merely a beast, an animated machine. Hence he had to find some justification for his belief which would be neither "scientific" nor ecclesiastical. The source of knowledge must lie within the individual, and it must be possessed by all men, not merely by the learned.

The source turned out to be sentiment, a faculty similar to Pascal's heart, the inner light, or common sense. Regardless of what the scientists might say, one feels the existence of God as one feels one's own existence. One needs no argument to prove that one exists; one knows it immediately. So too, one knows without demonstration that God exists. Yet Rousseau also attempted to prove that God existed as the first cause of motion, a proof that goes back at least to St. Thomas Aquinas. And he also argued to some of God's characteristics; for instance, the fact that there is order and harmony in the universe shows that God is a cosmic intelligence, a cosmic power, and a cosmic will. Rousseau added to these the character of goodness. But then, as if ashamed of his concessions to rationalism, he insisted that all these gave him no clear idea of God's nature, that he was satisfied to perceive God in his works, to feel God within himself, and to see God all about him. That was sufficient.

Rationalism and sentimentalism. One does not look for great precision of statement in Rousseau. But his style convinced some of his readers that rationalism would not be able to prove what they desired to believe and that the only alternative to rationalism was what was later to be called sentimentalism. In any event, after Rousseau French philosophy split into two camps, that of the rationalists and that of the sentimentalists. The next generation labeled the two camps the Voltaireans and the Rousseauists. The labels were not accurate, for among the former were men who were far from agreeing with everything that Voltaire stood for, such as his defense of conscience and his anticlericalism, and among the latter were some whose hearts told them things which their master's heart had overlooked. At the end of the century the target of the discussion shifted. For after the French Revolution the main question was whether the source of truth lay within the individual or

in the group. While the traditionalists, Joseph de Maistre and the vicomte de Bonald, could properly be called rationalists, they maintained that the reason on which they relied was not that of any one man but that of society as expressed in tradition. The sentimentalists argued analogously that it was the feeling of the group, not that of the individual, which counted. Thus Chateaubriand (1768–1848), Pierre Simon Ballanche (1776–1847), and even the Abbé Bautain (1796–1867), supported by men like Pierre Paul Royer-Collard (1763–1845), Theodore Jouffroy (1796–1842), and Victor Cousin (1792–1867) turned toward the conception of a collective mind for a solution to their problems. This return to the ancient Stoic principle of the *consensus gentium* raised more problems than it could solve, and its course was abandoned soon after the turn of the century.

Sensationalism. Meanwhile a group of more technical philosophers had begun to write. Under the influence of Condillac an investigation was begun into the operations of the mind. Étienne Bonnot de Condillac (1715–1780) had maintained that everything the soul knows comes to it from sensation. Sensations are like the tesserae of a mosaic and are built up into patterns of various sorts according to definite laws. We are limited in our knowledge by what such groups of sensory material can tell us; but Condillac, of course, claimed to know—though he did not say on what evidence—just what kind of information they could give him. Thus, whatever ideas we may have can be analyzed into the sensory components from which they arose.

There seem, therefore, to be in our faculties two sorts of things: passively received sensations and the active power of composing, judging, and analyzing them. Since Condillac's major emphasis was on the passive side of knowledge, his successors were moved toward explaining how we become active. This problem was tackled by the *idéologues*—Pierre-Jean Georges Cabanis (1757–1808) and Destutt de Tracy (1754–1836)—and developed further by Pierre Laromiguière (1756–1837). But it was Maine de Biran who explored the problem most carefully and whose work gave rise to a new development in French philosophy of the nineteenth century.

SPIRITUALISM

Maine de Biran. In his early work Maine de Biran (1766–1824) had noticed that we are aware of the external world by the resistance which it makes to our muscular effort. The fact that we can exert pressure upon things was to him evidence that there is something within the human soul that is not merely an effect of the external world upon it. This obviously was what had always been called the will. But he also perceived that the traits of our will are projected into the external world in the phenomena of mobility, in which we believe that a cause effectuates a change in things. We cannot actually perceive causal efficacy—here Maine de Biran harked back, though unconsciously, to Cordemoy and Malebranche—but in our own volitional efficacy we have immediate knowledge of it. The primordial cognitive experience is, in fact, our intuition of our own activity, not our awareness of received sensory data. Maine de Biran's preoccupation with this peculiar experience led him to attempt to derive the categories of existence from it. The mind by intuition finds itself to be a substance, a cause or force, a unity, and to be self-identical through time. It uses these characters as categories and interprets everything that it knows in these terms. Thus the concept that we have of a "thing" is that of something which is substantial, acting upon other things, unified, and inherently unchanging, that is, unchanging in its inner nature.

This conception led Maine de Biran to sever his connection with the *idéologues*. For if there is such a faculty as the will, known only through intuition, and if the will is the ego itself, then as a purely active force it must be free and insusceptible to analysis. It becomes an ineffable being, since it is an individual, and its nature can be fully explored only by the act of mystical union, which gives us our first idea of its existence. But as one proceeds on this path, one discovers a progression in human experience from the initial stage at which one is conscious only of the external world, to a stage at which one withdraws from the external world in order to observe and judge it, and finally to a stage where both the external and the internal worlds disappear and one exists for God alone. Effort disappears in this third stage and one is lost in God, the cosmic will.

Ravaisson. The voluntarism—or spiritualism as it was called in France—of Maine de Biran was developed by Félix Ravaisson-Mollien (1813–1900). Reverting to the problem of habit, which Maine de Biran had examined in his earliest published work, Ravaisson argued that habit is peculiar, since it can determine the future regardless of the number of choices open to us. This is obviously not true of mechanical causation. In classical physics there is repetition, of course, but the mere fact that a billiard ball has on several occasions rolled downhill is not the reason why it continues to roll downhill. Habit in human affairs, however, can determine what a man will do even when that which it determines is undesirable or inappropriate. This peculiarity of animate beings led Ravaisson to make a sharp distinction between the world of space, in which there are no true individuals but only collections of homogeneous things, and the world of heterogeneous individuals, in which there is life and growth. In the former reign the laws of necessity; in the latter there is spontaneity, or what he called "nature." Things in the world of space can be thoroughly understood "from without" and can be adequately described in the theorems of physics. In the world of individuals there is action upon the world of physics, action which modifies it and does so spontaneously. The two worlds, which are cut off from each other conceptually, are in reality connected when vitality appears, for life cannot exist without a material world, though as life develops, it becomes (or can become) less and less dependent upon that world. The tree of life exhibits a steady alienation from matter in the sense that as we mount its branches, we find more and more spontaneity and complexity.

Ravaisson added to this a distinction between the nontemporal world of matter and the temporal world of life, which shows a "definite and continuous duration," terms that Bergson was to employ in the next period. Because of this second differentia the material world is known through the categories of diversity and quantity, whereas the vital world has a kind of unity which we discover in our own nature. This is not the unity of an arithmetical sum, but is *sui generis* and is called "organic." We are not, then, entirely free from the material world, but we always make an effort to escape its limitations. This effort, said Ravaisson, was the discovery of Maine de Biran.

Bergson. Ravaisson provided future philosophers with a new start. Instead of beginning with sensations caused in us by material forces, he followed the lead of Maine de Biran and began with our internal life. This clue was pursued by Ravaisson's most distinguished disciple, Henri Bergson (1859–1941).

For Bergson the only true knowledge we have is that of immediate experience. But experience is always of our inner life, since sensory data *as observed* are subjective. We conclude to their objective sources by inference. The one trait common to all immediate experience is its duration, in his own language the *durée réelle*. The flow of consciousness, in which nothing is cut off from anything else, in which the past is retained to grow into the future, is the essential part of our being. But since it is unique, it cannot be conceptualized, and the only way to know it is to identify oneself with it. In any given individual's case this is no problem. The problem arises when we attempt to know someone else. Then we have to cease conceptualizing and to live the lives of those whom we would understand. But this is true of all that lives. Concepts are useful, he maintained, for understanding the material, spatial, analyzable world. Intuition alone can penetrate into the vital, the qualitative, the temporal. The great error of philosophers has been to treat the latter with tools which are suitable only for the treatment of the former.

The outcome of Bergson's philosophy is the conception that the two realms that are given to us, the mechanical and the vital, are not walled off from each other by an impenetrable barrier but melt into each other by degrees. Thus, space turns out to be arrested time, matter becomes the effect of habit, concepts are dead intuitions. He generalizes the push of life with his concept of *élan vital*, which is common to all that is animate, whether vegetable or animal. Within each type of life there is a swing from lethargy to activity, from rigid patterns to creativity, from dogged persistence in the road of tradition to lyrical experimentation. Though Bergson never denied that the intellect was able by itself to handle the problems of science, he always insisted that it was incapable of dealing satisfactorily with those of life, whether they arise in the fields of morals, art, or religion. In these fields intuition alone is sovereign. Hence it is fair to say that Bergson's anti-intellectualism was only partial. The sciences which deal with matter and space must be intellectualistic; it is only those disciplines which have the vital as their subject matter that are the domain of intuition.

PHILOSOPHY OF SCIENCE

No account of French philosophy would be complete if it omitted the philosophy of science. As early as Descartes one finds an attempt to discover the rules which guide scientific inquiry, and the "geometrical method" was itself a philosophy of science in germ. It was certainly Descartes's belief that all science could be deduced from a few simple principles, and we find that method surviving as late as 1750 in the works of the German philosopher Christian Wolff. But even in Wolff's day the *Encyclopédie* turned from Descartes to Bacon and Locke, taking from Bacon the thesis that all science is essentially a tool for increasing human welfare and from Locke the thesis of sensory empiricism. By the end of the century the *idéologues* had developed a substitute for logic in the analysis of ideas, while retaining the practical interests of the Encyclopedists.

Comte. By 1822 Auguste Comte (1798–1857), following Saint-Simon, had developed his "law of the three stages," according to which it was possible to understand the technique of thinking employed by our intellectual ancestors and also to predict the future. As far as this part of Comte's philosophy was concerned, civilization was determined by the way men thought. All thinking passed from a condition in which events were explained in anthropomorphic terms to a final condition in which positivistic descriptions of phenomena would suffice. But each stage was also homogeneous in that the technique of thinking was paralleled by methods of production, of religion, of art, and of government. Comte also maintained that all knowledge tended toward mathematics in its progress and that, consequently, when the positivistic period would be fulfilled in the future, engineers would replace priests and mathematicians would replace philosophers.

Later positivists. The most celebrated direct disciple of Comte was Émile Littré (1801–1881), compiler of the famous *Dictionnaire de la langue française*. But Littré confined his positivism to the methodological theses. Pierre Lafitte (1823–1903), however, retained his faith even in Comte's more fantastic religious and political doctrines and was more influential than Littré in spreading the religion which Comte called "humanism." This cult spread well beyond the borders of France into Great Britain and even Brazil, but seems to have few if any logical roots in positivism more strictly defined. There are traces of Comte's influence in Hippolyte Taine (1828–1893) and Ernest Renan (1823–1892), but not strong enough to mark them as members of the school.

In the case of Lucien Lévy-Bruhl (1857–1939) the influence of Comte is more evident. It induced Lévy-Bruhl to try to found a science of ethics on perceptual data, the manners and customs of human beings, rather than on unobservable ideals. This same tendency appeared in his studies of primitive mentality. Thus, for Lévy-Bruhl ethics became "social physics" and ethnology in part a study of the theological stage of human thinking. It is fair to say that the religious and social ideas of Comte died out in France and that what remained alive was positivism as a technique of investigation.

Cournot and Boutroux. Though Comte became the leader of a school, the work done in the philosophy of science by men who did not ally themselves with him was in many ways more important than that of his disciples. Among these other philosophers of science was Antoine Augustin Cournot (1801–1877). His *Essai sur les fonde-ments de nos connaissances* (1851) and *Considerations sur la marche des idées et des événements dans les temps modernes* (1872) emphasized the dependence of philosophy upon the natural sciences and upon the mathematical method but departed from the principles of positivism by proposing a clear defense of chance as a real existent. Cournot never denied that all events were caused, but he maintained that causal series were independent of one another and that, consequently, their interactions as series could not be foretold. They could be predicted only on the basis of the calculus of probabilities. Chance therefore is not simply human ignorance but an essential part of the universe. He was far from believing that all events are the effects of chance, but that chance must be seen to be a true cause of certain events which he was able to define. His views on chance had a greater influence on economics than in philosophy, though the works of Émile Boutroux (1845–1921) reflect his probabilism; and it is likely that Bergson's *élan vital* with its inherent indeterminism was, if not the child, at least the grandchild of Cournot.

Bernard. Meanwhile there came from a scientific contemporary of Cournot, Claude Bernard (1813–1878), a work which not only influenced scientists and philosophers but also novelists. Bernard was a physiologist and physician, and in his famous *Introduction to Experimental Medicine* (1865) he asserted a doctrine that emphasized the role of hypotheses in science as the corrective of simple positivistic observation. According to this theory, the collection of perceptual data is of no value whatsoever unless it is made with a view to answering questions previously put to experience by the scientist. The formulation of the proper questions depends on the creative imagination of the questioner. Experimentation is always carried on with the purpose of answering such questions and is never self-substantiated or self-initiated. It was this work of Bernard's that gave Émile Zola the idea of the experimental novel, an idea which became the program of the naturalistic school of novelists. For just as the scientist put questions to nature and through his experiments found the answers, so the novelist imagined situations in which his characters would be placed and sought their reactions through the spectacles of science.

Poincaré. In a similar vein the mathematician Henri Poincaré (1854–1912) emphasized the role of the imagination in the formulation of hypotheses. The sciences follow certain conventions, which are the creation of the human mind. Poincaré, like Bernard, presented a strong criticism of that side of positivism which maintained that perceptual data were the stuff of science. From such data nothing of scientific value could emerge without the organizing methods of the scientist. These methods are the scientist's contributions to the so-called facts. Poincaré never set clear limits to the use of conventions nor gave a definition of the kind of utility which conventions might have, but his strong assertion of the part played by the imagination of the scientist impressed philosophers of science not only in France but also in the Anglo-Saxon countries.

Milhaud. The name of Gaston Milhaud (1858–1918) should not be omitted even in a brief sketch of the philosophy of science. Milhaud's *Essai sur les conditions et les* *limites de la certitude logique* (1894) was outstanding as a critique of positivism and a defense of the subjective status of science. Scientific concepts, he held, were enclosed within the limits of the human mind's contributions. The human equation can never be subtracted from knowledge, and even our basic ideas have a fictional character. This suffices to prevent absolute certainty in any sense other than logical consistency. The similarity to the views of Poincaré is obvious.

Meyerson. In more recent times the work of Émile Meyerson (1859–1933) has attracted wide attention. For Meyerson the history of the sciences showed a persistent technique of explanation, which could be reduced to finding an identity between cause and effect. This identity is never complete, for certain qualitative differences are always observable in the effect which were not present in the cause. These differences constitute an irrational element. But in order to establish the identity that is sought, they are discounted either as trivial or as mere "appearance." Genuine identity is conceived by science as that which is measurable, and the one measurable entity discoverable in both cause and effect is mass. When, therefore, an equivalence of mass is established, an explanation is said to be complete. In a series of erudite volumes Meyerson was able to illustrate his thesis on a historical basis. The first of these books, *Identité et réalité* (1908), contained the nucleus of his theory and exemplified his method.

Brunschvicg. One of the assumptions of Meyerson was that the essential forms of thought are to be found in the history of thought. It is these which he called the historical a priori. A similar assumption appeared in the philosophy of Léon Brunschvicg (1869–1944). In his early work *La Modalité du jugement* (1897) he envisioned knowledge as constituting a realm of its own in which the object and the subject are integrated into a unity. It is therefore the purpose of philosophy to raise all knowledge to self-consciousness, and this is done by a thorough study of the technique of thinking as exemplified not only in the sciences but also in the arts. For truth to Brunschvicg was intelligibility, and that is rather a trait of knowledge than of things. In science one makes the world of things intelligible by transforming it into a set of harmonious concepts.

The tendency to find the nature of the mind in our ways of thinking is characteristic of the French philosophers of science. They usually admit that these intellectual methods are modified in history, but they seek behind the varieties of method a common unity. Thus Brunschvicg in *L'Idéalisme contemporain* (1905) granted that there is a movement of thought in the history of the sciences which "gives to thought an increasing approximation to reality." But this increase is due to the inner dialogue which the mind has with itself, operating through the perception of contradictions and our efforts to adjust our concepts to crude experience. Brunschvicg insisted that experience cannot be divorced from human beings, for experience is always human experience, modified to be sure by the techniques of observation and reasoning upon which we are operating. His philosophy thus is neither a pure intellectualism or idealism nor a pure empiricism. It is empirical in that it grants to the objective world the power of presenting us with problems to be solved, and it is intel-

lectualistic in that the solution is always found by and determined by the human intellect and its needs.

EXISTENTIALISM

Existentialism entered France through the work of both Søren Kierkegaard and Edmund Husserl. It is best known in the writings of Jean-Paul Sartre, though Gabriel Marcel and Maurice Merleau-Ponty should not be overlooked. Sartre flatly denied the distinction between inner and outer natures, a distinction which had obtained in philosophy for centuries. All is equally appearance and appearances have nothing "behind" them. But all appearances appear to a human being who exists in time and, hence, is himself in a constant state of change. A man selects out of all possible appearances those which for one reason or another are of interest to him. But our awareness or experience of an appearance is itself our consciousness. There is, then, no consciousness apart from such. Consciousness is not something added to experience or possessive of experience.

We are, then, minds confronted with external appearances. But we are also able to expect certain appearances to be experienced. When such expectations are not fulfilled, we assert nonbeing. Nonbeing in this sense conditions our judgments. The "nothing" (*le néant*) is the failure of our expectations. But since we are conscious both of individual existences and of their failure to appear when our expectations are frustrated, it is existence and not essence which presents the human being with his problems. Essences are made by man; they do not exist in nature. Hence when we look for the exemplification of an essence and fail to come upon it, we can be filled with anguish and hatred and a sense of frustration. And since we start with doubt, in a quasi-Cartesian manner, there is more chance of frustration's being the rule than the exception. The thesis that experience is the source of problems rather than the answer to them is a point of view shared by all existentialists. But the interpretation of the situations given by a man like Gabriel Marcel differs radically from that of Sartre. To Marcel the situation is identical with that of the religious man who cannot find his answers by observation but must make a decision by fiat.

The outcome of Sartre's existentialism rests as much upon his theory of the temporality of consciousness as upon the "priority of existence." For as we proceed in and through time, we are creating ourselves by negating our past to make our present and negating our present to create our future. Thus Sartre demanded that a person make choices, choices which, to be sure, may fail but which depend for their goals upon him alone. These choices, since they are directed toward individual, localized, and dated historical occurrences, cannot be determined logically. We thus exert our freedom, a freedom which is a logical surd and may end in disaster. Yet the price of not making a choice is to fall into the condition of an inert mass of matter. The similarity of this point of view to that of Bergson is as clear as its derivation from Husserl. It might even be thought of as the dramatic culmination of French philosophy since Montaigne. For it has within it many themes which had been anticipated: the theme of self-scrutiny, of universal doubt, of dialectical analysis, of the reality of chance, of phenomenalistic empiricism, and of temporalism. Each of these themes can be traced back to a French predecessor.

(See also CAROLINGIAN RENAISSANCE; CARTESIANISM; CHARTRES, SCHOOL OF; CLANDESTINE PHILOSOPHICAL LITERATURE IN FRANCE; ENCYCLOPÉDIE; ENLIGHTENMENT; EXISTENTIALISM; and POSITIVISM. See French Philosophy in Index for articles on French, Swiss, and Belgian philosophers.)

Bibliography

Baladi, Naguib, *Les Constantes de la pensée française*. Paris, 1948.

Benrubi, J., *Les Sources et les courants de la philosophie contemporaine en France*, 2 vols. Paris, 1933.

Boas, George, *French Philosophy of the Romantic Period*. Baltimore, 1925.

Boas, George, *Dominant Themes of Modern Philosophy*. New York, 1957. Chs. 3, 4, 5, 9, 11, 12, 18.

Bréhier, Émile, *Histoire de la philosophie*. Paris, 1928. Vol. 2, Fascicle 2.

Charlton, D. G., *Positivist Thought in France During the Second Empire, 1852–1870*. Oxford, 1959.

Höffding, Harald, *Den nyere Filosofis Historie*. Copenhagen, 1887. Translated by B. E. Meyer as *A History of Modern Philosophy*. London, 1900; New York, 1955. Vol. 1, Bks. 3 and 5.

Lévy-Bruhl, Lucien, *A History of Modern Philosophy in France*. Translated by G. Coblence. London and Chicago, 1899.

Martin, Kingsley, *French Liberal Thought in the Eighteenth Century*. London, 1929.

Randall, John Herman, Jr., *The Career of Philosophy: From the Middle Ages to the Enlightenment*. New York and London, 1962. Bk. 3, Sec. 2; Bk. 4, Secs. 12–16.

Smith, Colin, *Contemporary French Philosophy*. London and New York, 1964.

Soltan, Roger, *French Political Thought in the Nineteenth Century*. New Haven, 1931.

GEORGE BOAS

FREUD, SIGMUND (1856–1939), the founder of psychoanalysis, was born in Freiberg, Moravia (now Czechoslovakia). When he was three years old his family moved to Vienna, and in 1873 Freud entered the University of Vienna, where he studied medicine. He specialized in neurology and contributed to the field valuable laboratory researches, which were published in 1885 and 1886. He also published several clinical studies. Under the influence of J. M. Charcot, with whom he studied in Paris in 1885, and of Josef Breuer, an older colleague and friend in Vienna, Freud turned his attention to the psychological aspects of neurology.

Charcot had been the first to recognize hysteria as a distinctive disorder, and Breuer, in treating a hysterical patient, had discovered that when she talked about the earliest occurrence of her symptoms they began to disappear. Charcot used hypnotism not only to treat his patients but also to demonstrate how hysterical symptoms could be produced. Although neither Breuer nor Freud ever doubted that nervous disorders had a neurological basis and a neurophysiological explanation, they became interested in treating patients by discovering sources of hysterical symptoms in the patients' ideas and in changing those ideas by talk. The catharsis that such patients achieved is classically described in their joint *Studies in Hysteria* (1895).

Breuer, however, could not follow Freud in the empha-

sis that he was coming to place on the sexual origin and content of neuroses. It was therefore left to Freud alone to pursue in the years up to 1900 the questions of the traumatic origin of neuroses, of the sexual content of the libido, and—through his own self-analysis from 1897 onward—of the method of the discovery and treatment of neuroses.

Freud had married Martha Bernays in 1886, and they had six children. (Anna Freud, the youngest child, became a distinguished psychoanalyst.) Freud's ability to endure both the loneliness to which his originality condemned him and the conflicts in which it involved him certainly owed much to the extraordinary stability and happiness of his family life.

Late in 1899 *The Interpretation of Dreams* was published, but it was not until the next decade that Freud achieved recognition both in Vienna and abroad. The first International Psycho-analytical Congress, held at Salzburg in 1908, marks the point at which psychoanalysis became not only a theory and a therapy but also a movement. The publication of a series of theoretical essays in 1915 and of the *Introductory Lectures in Psycho-analysis* in 1916 mark the point at which Freud gave the fullest expression to the theoretical interests already manifest in 1895.

In 1911 Alfred Adler separated himself from Freud, in 1912 so did Wilhelm Stekel, in 1914 Carl Jung, and in 1924 Otto Rank. But it would be wrong to suppose that either in the psychoanalytic movement or in Freud's own thought a static and monolithic orthodoxy was being maintained in the face of heresy and schism. Freud made important theoretical innovations in *Beyond the Pleasure Principle*, *The Ego and the Id*, and *Group Psychology and Analysis of the Ego* in the years immediately following World War I. By no means were all of these accepted by his colleagues and collaborators, but sustained disagreement was not necessarily incompatible with continued friendship and collaboration. Freud's relationship with the Swiss pastor Oskar Pfister was a supreme example of this.

The later years of Freud's life were marked contrastingly by widespread international recognition of his greatness and by exile in London after Austria was occupied by the Nazis; his four aged sisters, who could not leave, were all murdered by the Nazis. At his death he left unfinished a new short theoretical statement, *An Outline of Psychoanalysis*. His remarkable vigor persisted almost up to the last days of his life.

Basic ideas. Of the doctrines Freud developed in the years up to 1915, there is first the recognition and description of recurrent features of abnormal adult behavior, hysterical, obsessional, and depressive; what was new in Freud was not merely his description of these traits but the form of description that he employed. Instead of treating the behavior in question as simply pointless and meaningless, so that the only task for the psychiatric inquirer is to seek for antecedent physiological conditions producing the neurotic behavior, Freud treated neurotic behavior as a form of human action of which it is appropriate to ask for the point and purpose. That is, Freud treated neurotic behavior as being goal directed. Until the purposes of the neurotic are understood, his behavior will necessarily be misdescribed. When we understand these purposes we discover that in adult neurotic behavior there are elements of a re-enactment of childhood episodes, and even when the adult behavior is not a re-enactment of specific episodes, the neurotic symptoms can be understood as the expression of essentially childish fears and anxieties. But in characterizing neurosis in this way we point to the second main feature of Freud's doctrines, the view that the early life of children has been misconstrued and misunderstood.

Freud's discovery of infantile sexuality was in part an enlargement of the concept of sexuality, as well as a factual discovery about small children. Anal and oral pleasure become intelligibly related to genital pleasure in Freud's scheme of development, where different zones of the body are at different stages focuses for sexual attention. At the same time the child's instinctual reaching after satisfaction is continually checked and redirected in encounters with the parents and the social environment generally. Child development is thus not a smooth and uncontradictory evolution but a more or less successful movement through a series of conflicts, in which not only actual events but also the child's own phantasies play key roles. Freud's discovery of the importance of childhood phantasy was a product of his first refinements upon an initial picture of the causation of a neurotic symptom. According to his picture of the development of neurotic symptoms, a childhood trauma brought about repression of the memory of the traumatic event laden with painful emotion, and a difficult situation in adult life reawakened the now unconscious complex of memory and emotion. Questions concerning the traumas suffered by his patients seemed to reveal that Viennese girls were extraordinarily often seduced in very early childhood by older male relatives; doubt about the actual occurrence of these seductions was soon replaced by certainty that it was descriptions of childhood phantasy that were being offered. It is the sexual content of such descriptions that is one of the clues to the character of childhood. Consequently, when Freud characterized the key Oedipal situation as one in which the child's wish is to kill his father and marry his mother, he was not merely offering a vivid metaphor, for it is under some such description that the wish must be envisaged if the later expressions of the guilt and anxiety aroused by it are to be intelligible.

It is of course impossible to describe either Freud's characterizations of adult traits or his scheme of child development without making clear that the core of Freudian theory lies in his view of the relation between these two. Freud was first of all committed to the view that there is an empirical correlation between the occurrence of certain types of event in early childhood and the exhibition of certain traits in adult life. Thus, an obsessional character that manifests itself in overscrupulosity or miserliness or an intense concern with cleanliness or tidiness is in Freud's view correlated with certain anal experiences and more particularly with a certain kind of toilet training.

These alleged empirical observations require explanation. The key concepts in the Freudian theory include those of repression, of sublimation, and of the unconscious itself. What is repressed is what is too painful for consciousness to continue to hold in view; the human organism, which naturally seeks pleasure, is continually forced to adapt to external social and physical reality. Drives which cannot find an outlet are consequently rechanneled; this is called sublimation. Not all that is unconscious is repressed, for the unconscious has its own dynamic patterns, and both repressions and sublimations take place in accordance with laws of transformation that are native to the unconscious. The unconscious is thus a theoretical entity, in principle unobservable, without which the connections between early childhood and adult life would remain unintelligible. Freud's early association of repression with peculiarly traumatic events in the life of the deeply neurotic person was replaced by a picture of normal human development in which repression plays an indispensable role. In repressing what is felt as a threat to the personality, the ego defends itself against disruption. The concept of defense, of the ego resorting to strategies, became increasingly important in Freud's thought.

He elaborated a scheme in which the *ego's* fundamental task is to reconcile the instinctual, biologically given demands of the *id*, the socially desired internalization of parental control that constitutes the *superego,* and the demands of reality itself. The price that the ego must pay for its defense against the pain of external reality, the conflicts within, or both, may of course be too high: either modes of behavior that are essentially neurotic and which disable the ego in its relations with reality or even a psychotic withdrawal from reality. The mature ego denies the demands of neither id nor superego but translates them into terms in which the admission of these demands is no longer destructive. To reach this stage is at one level the task of every child who grows up; at another level it is the task of psychoanalytic therapy.

Psychoanalysis as therapy. The technique of psychoanalysis is to enable the patient to become aware of motives hitherto unconscious. The method used is that of free association. The analyst from time to time offers the patient interpretations of what the patient says or does. The aim is to enable the patient to recover lost memories in which his unconscious motives are rooted and by so doing to return to the point at which conflict or weakness became embedded in his character in such a way as to produce the inabilities and the neuroses of later life. This is not easy—it is necessarily a prolonged process—because there are no unconscious motives or wishes for which the patient does not possess a strong unconscious desire that the motives remain unconscious. The analyst therefore has to help the patient to encounter, understand, and overcome his own resistances.

It is a great mistake to suppose that what is involved in the awareness of unconscious motives and in the recovery of hitherto repressed memories of forgotten incidents and phantasies that analysis provides is simply an intellectual apprehension. The painful emotions and scenes have to be revisited in feeling as well as in thought, and in the whole process there is a strong element of regression. It is because of this that the patient may first have to get worse in order that later on he may get better. Freud originally laid some store by acquiring independent evidence to confirm the patient's memory claims; however, as he became persuaded of the importance of phantasy as well as of actual incidents, he ceased to attach importance to this. Finally he concluded that the key to the process lies in what he called transference; the patient transfers to the analyst and projects onto the analyst attitudes and emotions which were originally directed in childhood at the parental figures. Indeed, it is from the nature of the transference that the analyst gets some of his most important clues about the patient; a successful transference is a condition of a successful analysis.

Dreams, culture, and religion. The claim that psychoanalytic theory is a theory of normal, as well as of abnormal, behavior and development entails and is partly founded upon a claim to be able to explain the character of many pervasive elements in human life. Freud's treatments of dreams, culture, and religion particularly illuminate the nature of these claims. The narration of dreams is important in analysis because in the dream the manifest content, what the dream is apparently about, is an expression in symbolic form of a latent content, an unconscious wish or motive. The unconscious wish is too strong for its expression to be altogether denied, but its direct expression encounters censorship in the form of the internalized prohibitions and repressions which demand that the wish take on a symbolic form if it is to be acknowledged at all. The dream is thus an attempt at a surrogate wish fulfillment. The sexual character of our basic wishes—which we cannot acknowledge to ourselves because of the prohibitions of adult culture—and above all the incestuous character of our desires result in a proliferation of sexual symbolism in our dreams.

This theme of a tension between the instinctual sexual drives and the demands of culture was basic to Freud's whole world view. The world of cultural achievement is won only by denying to the instincts the direct gratifications which they seek and by using the energy so released in sublimated forms for the tasks of art and science. The myth that Freud believed in abandoning all inhibition and constraint on instinctual drives is at the opposite pole from the truth. Freud was at times in danger of treating art as a substitute for more elemental gratifications; the artist has converted his withdrawal into the satisfactions of phantasy into a new way of encountering reality by giving to his phantasies the form of painting, poetry, or sculpture only, so Freud seemed to say, because initially the artist could not secure more direct gratifications. However, especially in his later writings, Freud saw cultural activity as having an independent value for the ego.

Freud regarded religion differently. It too is the product of wish fulfillment. In its monotheistic forms it replaces the fallible father of reality by projecting onto the heavens an omnipotent and infallible father. By this means the status of a child can be retained into adult life. But this is to say that religion perpetuates infantile behavior patterns, notably in relation to guilt and forgiveness. The falsity of religious beliefs is not, of course, entailed by their being the product of wish fulfillment. Freud believed in their falsity on independent grounds. But he thought of religion as a particularly damaging species of illusion, precisely because it militates against the scientific effort to distinguish between what reality in fact is and what we want it to be.

Conceptual innovation. By speaking of unconscious motives and unconscious desires Freud compelled us to clarify the concepts of motive and desire in more than one way. To describe a piece of behavior as the outcome of an unconscious motive is initially to redescribe the behavior so that we understand it as goal-directed action and not as mere physical movement. But in ascribing a motive to the behavior are we merely redescribing and reclassifying the behavior or are we also asserting a connection between it and a hidden cause, the unconscious motive, identifiable somehow independently of the behavior? How do unconscious motives stand in relation to our ordinary distinctions between motives, reasons, and causes? Freud himself wrote of unconscious motives as of a kind of cause, and philosophical critics have been perhaps too hasty in supposing that he must be mistaken. For since it is clear that there may well be a criterion for identifying the presence of an unconscious motive, a criterion independent of the behavior that the motive is invoked to explain, the presence or absence of a motive may indeed function as a causal factor. That is, at one and the same time the motive may be seen as a reason guiding the agent's behavior and the presence of the motive as a cause of that behavior, and this without any logical incongruity.

Further, there is the question of how Freud could speak intelligibly of motives and wishes which *ex hypothesi* are unconscious. Here it is important neither to overrate nor to underrate the extent of his innovations. On the one hand there is a well established pre-Freudian usage whereby it is recognized that others may see at work in an agent's behavior motives of which he himself is unconscious: ambition, jealousy, and the like. On the other hand, others are able to construe the behavior because it, so to speak, wears its meaning on its face; this is palpably true of the kind of obsessional or hysterical behavior to which Freud ascribed unconscious motives. For an unconscious motive is not merely a motive of which the agent happens to be unaware, as he may be unaware of the workings of his respiratory or digestive system. An unconscious motive is one that the agent refuses to acknowledge or one that he finds intolerable to acknowledge; that is, it is a motive which the agent has a motive for not recognizing. Thus, there are always two unconscious motives at work together, not just one. Moreover, the consequent behavior is not such that others would recognize, except in the light of psychoanalytic theory. Freud brought within the range of behavior to which motives are ascribed a whole group of types of behavior hitherto thought to be explicable at best only in neurophysiological terms. Not that the truth of psychoanalytic explanations is logically incompatible with the truth of neurophysiological explanations; Freud always believed that a physiological and biochemical basis for his discoveries must exist.

Ethics. It is commonly assumed that the logical distinction between reasons and causes guarantees moral beliefs against their being in any way discredited by genetic accounts of how they come to be held. But the Freudian explanation of the imperatives issued by the superego as the internalization of the parental commands and the Freudian contrast between the essentially immature morality which consists in the appeal to such imperatives and the mature morality of the ego ideal in which the agent looks for justification of his moral beliefs in terms of certain goals and desires provide a framework within which certain moral beliefs no longer appear plausible. For if it is true that the kind of morality which makes the contrast between duty and desire as sharp as possible is in fact a morality in which the appeal to duty is an appeal to unconscious desire, and indeed unconscious desire of an infantile and authoritarian kind, then the claims of that kind of morality can no longer be convincing. The categorical imperative announces itself not as the claim of a law grasped by pure practical reason but as the ghost of the voice heard not on Sinai but in the nursery.

Moreover, if the grasp of this fact depends, as Freud claimed, on the discovery of the roots of the agent's morality in the agent's childhood, then the value of self-knowledge takes its old Socratic place—first place—in the scheme of the values. Freud is sometimes presented as a crude moral hedonist. It is, however, in transcending the pleasure principle in the name of the claims of reality, of truthfulness, that the core of the Freudian ethic lies. Part of what we learn from Freud morally is the extent to which the possession of reasonableness and of truthfulness are necessary preconditions for the true possession of any other virtues at all.

Psychoanalysis and determinism. Freud's discovery of the causation both of neurotic symptoms and of normal character traits fatally weakened any attempt to maintain that human behavior was essentially exempt from explanation in causal terms or that the line between responsible rational behavior and nonresponsible irrational behavior could be drawn in terms of the applicability of the notion of cause. Later attempts to show that human actions cannot be caused (as, for example, that by A. I. Melden in *Free Action*, London, 1961) have had to ignore not only the fact of but even the logical possibility of psychoanalytic explanations of action in terms of predisposing childhood causes. Yet the interest of Freud's discoveries for traditional discussions of determinism and free-will is much greater than just this.

If we try to define responsibility and freedom in terms of the absence of coercion and constraint, or if we try to introduce the concept of "knowing what one is doing" as part of the analysis of "free action," then relevant questions are raised by psychoanalysis. If my present behavior is the inevitable result of my early upbringing, does that upbringing function as a constraint? Or if I am unconscious of what moves me to do what I do, do I know what I am doing? It is instructive at this point to note that one criterion by means of which the psychoanalyst identifies behavior as irrational and unconsciously motivated is the degree of the agent's inability either to bring rational criticism to bear on his own actions or to respond to rational criticism of them. The extreme case is that of compulsive behavior of a trivial and arbitrary sort. This criterion enables us to understand that the familiar line between responsible and nonresponsible behavior is best drawn in terms of a distinction between conduct which the agent can and conduct which he cannot control. It is not because my behavior is caused that I am not responsible for it; it is because and insofar as the causes of its being what it is are

outside my control by any ordinary means. For it is only certain kinds of causes which render behavior unalterable by the agent.

Psychoanalysis is in practice an attempt to extend the area of rational control and therefore of responsibility. The contribution it makes at the theoretical level is that of assisting in showing that the indefinite extension of causal discoveries in the realm of human behavior in no way of itself necessarily narrows the limits within which we assign human responsibility.

Verifiability. Are Freud's doctrines in fact true? Here we must distinguish three separate issues. First and most easily, it is clear that Freud brought to light and described a huge variety of hitherto unrecognized types of behavior. Whatever we believe about his explanations, since Freud psychology has had a new subject matter to explain. But when we come to the tasks of theory and explanation, there arise two possible criticisms of Freud which must be taken very seriously. The first is that in fact a great deal of Freudian theory remains untested and that where there *is* experimental or clinical evidence on particular points Freud is sometimes clearly mistaken (for example, Freud's claim that girls feel penis envy). It would of course be curious if it were not so.

More interesting are the large-scale differences in theory between Freud and some other analysts, such as Wilhelm Reich. Reich's claim that what Freud presented as the unconscious is in fact a secondary formation, a deformation of a basically social and nonaggressive human nature, puts into sharp relief the need to state both doctrines so that the issue between them becomes settleable by means of experimental and clinical attempts at falsification. And at this point one must confront the suggestion that psychoanalytic theory is in principle unfalsifiable, untestable, and therefore empirically vacuous (see PSYCHOANALYTIC THEORIES, LOGICAL STATUS OF). The refutation of this claim rests essentially on the fact that Freudian theory does entail a wide range of predictions about human behavior in a variety of conditions. Bruno Bettelheim's revisions of Freud, for example, begins from the observations that in concentration camps men under extreme stress do not behave in the ways that a Freudian would have predicted. Thus, in large and small ways the continual transformation of Freudian theory is not so much one of its defects as one of its virtues. Nor is this transformation anything other than what Freud himself expected. (See UNCONSCIOUS, PSYCHOANALYTIC THEORIES OF THE.)

Works by Freud

The Standard Edition of the Complete Psychological Works of Sigmund Freud, James Strachey, ed., in collaboration with Anna Freud, assisted by Alix Strachey and Alan Tyson, 24 vols. London, 1953–1964. In English translation.

Works on Freud

Brown, J. A. C., *Freud and the Post-Freudians*. London, 1961.
Fine, R., *Freud: A Critical Reévaluation of His Theories*. London, 1963.
Jones, Ernest, *The Life and Work of Sigmund Freud*, 3 vols. London, 1957.
Nelson, B., ed., *Freud and the Twentieth Century*. New York, 1957.

Rieff, Philip, *Freud: The Mind of the Moralist.* New York, 1959.

Sears, R. R., *Survey of Objective Studies of Psychoanalytic Concepts.* Social Science Research Bulletin No. 51. New York, 1943.

Thompson, C., *Psychoanalysis: Its Evolution and Development.* New York, 1950.

ALASDAIR MacINTYRE

FRIES, JAKOB FRIEDRICH (1773–1843), German critical philosopher, was born in Barby, Saxony. An avowed follower and elaborator of Kant's philosophy, Fries emphasized the analytical, descriptive, and methodological aspects of the critical philosophy as against the constructive and speculative idealism of such contemporaries as K. L. Reinhold, Fichte, Schelling, and Hegel. He received his secondary and college education at the Moravian Academy in Niesky. From his Pietistic Moravian background Fries preserved a conviction of the importance of "pure feeling" as a manifestation of "the infinite in the finite." At Niesky he was given a thorough grounding in mathematics and in the natural sciences. There he was also introduced to a version of Kant's philosophy based on Reinhold's, which he early sought to correct and supplement by secretly reading in Kant's own writings. In 1795 he went to Leipzig, where he studied under the philosopher-physician Ernst Plattner. The influence of Plattner and of F. H. Jacobi accounts for Fries's emphasis on the concept of self-observation. From 1797 on, Fries continued his studies in mathematics and physics at Jena, where he also attended Fichte's lectures. "I listened to Fichte, took notes, then rushed home and wrote rebuttals," he later recalled. These critical notes were incorporated into his polemical writings. As early as 1798, in the article "Über das Verhältniss der empirischen Psychologie zur Metaphysik" ("On the Relation of Empirical Psychology to Metaphysics," in *Erhard Schmids Psychologische Magazin,* Vol. 3), he argued that the task of philosophy is essentially descriptive rather than speculative.

Following his studies at Jena, Fries served as a private tutor in Switzerland, then returned to Jena as a docent in 1801, submitting a habilitation thesis on intellectual intuition. The polemical tract *Reinhold, Fichte und Schelling* (Leipzig, 1803) established his reputation as a critic of the romantic orthodoxy in German philosophy. From Jena he was called to a professorship in philosophy and mathematics at Heidelberg. That year he published *Wissen, Glaube und Ahndung* ("Knowing, Faith and Presage," Jena, 1805), a popular exposition of his doctrine of a threefold approach to reality. This was followed, during the year 1896–1897, by his chief work, the three-volume *Neue Kritik der Vernunft* ("New Critique of Reason," Heidelberg, 1807; 2d ed., *Neue oder anthropologische Kritik der Vernunft,* Heidelberg, 1828–1831), in which he attempted to correct and restate the Kantian critique of speculative and practical reason as a program of psychological self-observation or "anthropology."

Progressive political views. A decisive shift in Fries's career occurred in 1816, when he returned to Jena to a professorship in theoretical philosophy. Under the tolerant and liberal regime of Duke Karl August, he published his *Ethik* (Heidelberg, 1818), a work in which he stressed the ideal of individual liberty and political equality as a consequence of the Kantian doctrine of the dignity proper to a human being. In pamphlets and lectures and at student gatherings during this period, Fries argued for constitutional and representative government, extolled the political wisdom of the "people," opposed the conservatism of student secret societies, and advocated German unification. This activity, climaxed by his participation in the Wartburg Festival of October 18, 1817—a demonstration by student liberals that included a ceremonial burning of "reactionary" books—inevitably incurred the wrath of the Austrian and Prussian governments. It also elicited scornful comments from the politically more orthodox Hegel, who in his *Philosophy of Right* (translated by J. M. Knox, Oxford, 1942) downgraded Fries as "a ringleader of those hosts of superficiality, of these self-styled 'philosophers,'" and attacked his Wartburg speech as "the quintessence of shallow thinking . . . a broth of 'heart, friendship, and inspiration.'" By 1819 the conservative opposition had prevailed upon Karl August, and Fries was suspended from his position at Jena. He had earlier lost hope that he would be offered the chair of philosophy at Berlin, which in 1818 went to Hegel.

Although Fries was eventually allowed to resume teaching at Jena (he taught science from 1824 and philosophy from 1825 on) and held this post until his death, the 1819 suspension was the final turn in his estrangement and isolation from the intellectual currents of the period. From then on, supported by a small following, he devoted his life to studies of mathematics, physics, and psychology, to systematization of his metaphysics and ethics, and to a rewriting of the history of philosophy on the theme of "progress in scientific development." To this period belong *Die mathematische Naturphilosophie* (Heidelberg, 1822); *System der Metaphysik* (Heidelberg, 1824); *Handbuch der psychischen Anthropologie* (2 vols., Jena, 1820 and 1821); and *Die Geschichte der Philosophie* (2 vols., Halle, 1837–1840).

Approaches to reality. Fries followed Kant in the over-all architectonic of his philosophy and in specific doctrines. Corresponding to Kant's three Critiques, he distinguished three approaches or attitudes toward reality—knowing, faith, and presage, or presentiment (*Ahndung*). We know things only as appearances to a peculiarly human sensibility and understanding. But we have faith in the reality of a world of real moral agents under eternal moral laws. Our understanding is aware of this world only negatively, as a limitation of the empirical world, through the Ideas of Reason. Finally, through presage or presentiment, a pure and disinterested feeling akin to the experience of the beautiful and the sublime, we are given the assurance that the world of appearances and the real world are not two worlds but one, and that the former is a manifestation of the latter—a finite projection of the infinite into the finite.

Types of knowledge. Within the sphere of knowing, Fries distinguished two levels: original or immediate knowledge, and reflective or mediate knowledge. The types of mediate knowledge are given in the Kantian forms of judgment: analytic, synthetic a posteriori, and synthetic a priori. We must also distinguish three types of immediate knowledge. An empirical intuition is a direct awareness of the sensory given; a pure intuition is a direct awareness of space and time as empty containers of sensible entities; and an immediate metaphysical cognition is the direct but nonintuitive awareness of principles involving the categories of the understanding (for example, the principle of causality or the principle of the permanence of substance). No attempt to reduce cognitions of the second and third types to cognitions of the first type can ever succeed. Space and time are the forms of our empirical intuitions; the categories are the forms of human understanding. Fries thus shared with Kant the critical solution of the problem of a priori knowledge. He also shared with Kant the rejection of both the empiricist and the intellectual intuitionist solutions of the problem.

Metaphysical knowledge. Fries departed from Kant, however, in his interpretation of the basis for the critical solution in the case of a priori metaphysical knowledge. Fries found inconsistency and circularity in Kant's attempt to validate categories and to "prove" the principles of the understanding by referring them to "the possibility of experience." If these are indeed principles, no proof could be required and none would be sufficient. Kant succumbed, in Fries's judgment, to the ancient rationalist prejudice that everything can be proved and that all truths can be reduced to a single principle—in Kant's case, the concept of possible experience. All that is possible, Fries objected, is to display the status of certain cognitions *as* a priori and necessary. "I do not prove," he explained, "that all substance is permanent; rather I point to the fact that the principle of the permanence of substance lies in every finite mind" (*Neue oder anthropologische Kritik der Vernunft*, 2d ed., Vol. I). In Kant's language, only a "metaphysical deduction" (the answer to the question, "What is the case?") is possible.

Discovery of metaphysical principles. The regression to metaphysical principles is not an easy task, for unlike empirical and pure intuitions, which are clear and readily available to consciousness, metaphysical principles lie "concealed and obscure" in the depths of human reason. Fries described this regression as a process of self-observation or "psychic anthropology," and likened it to experimental physics insofar as the latter aims to discover the general law involved in specific physical phenomena. Kant, accordingly, misunderstood the function of critical philosophy and the status of the judgments that constitute it, for whereas the truths that critical philosophy aims to uncover are nonempirical and necessary, the critique itself is empirical and fallible. Fries admired the long "subjective" deductions of the categories in the first edition of Kant's *Critique of Pure Reason* but was skeptical of the short "objective" deductions of the second edition.

Proof. A complete theory of proof must, therefore, distinguish three kinds: (1) demonstration, or the reduction of a "reflective" or "mediate" congition to an intuition (pure or empirical); (2) proof, or the reduction of one mediate cognition to another; and (3) deduction, or a regressive analysis that traces a given cognition to its ground in immediate metaphysical knowledge. Just as in the case of demonstration, in which no question can arise concerning the validity of the intuitions themselves, so too, in the case of deduction, no question can possibly arise as to the va-

lidity of our immediate metaphysical knowledge. A deduction is, of course, something fallible; closer scrutiny may later reveal a disparity between a given cognition and its supposed ground. But the same danger exists for demonstration—in this case minimally.

Truth. Truth is a matter of correspondence between thought and object, but the object is not something transcendent; it is simply an immediate cognition. Truth is a relation between two levels of cognition. With regard to immediate knowledge itself we must accept the principle of "Reason's self-reliance" (*Selbstvertrauen der Vernunft*), that is, that we possess such knowledge and that it is intrinsically valid.

Fries's "psychologism." Fries's restatement of the Kantian deduction has often been attacked as psychologism. If psychologism is understood as the attempt to find the validity of human beliefs in their psychological causes and in the laws of association, the charge is unfair. Fries was not a proponent of psychologism in that sense: for him, the validity of immediate knowledge lay in its logical character, universality, and necessity, not in its causal origins. Indeed, Fries wrote critically against such contemporary advocates of psychologism as Friedrich Eduard Beneke, with whom he was sometimes mistakenly compared. On the other hand, he did seem to suggest that logical character can be gathered from mere psychological observation of our mental processes. And in this connection he has been justly criticized for confusing a mental act with its logical content. Certainly the process that Fries described as "anthropology" would be more accurately described today as "logical" or "phenomenological" analysis. Fries was perhaps misled by the analogy between a logical regress to presuppositions in philosophy and the heuristic regress (induction) to general hypotheses and theories in physics.

Science and mathematics. In the fields of mathematics, physics, and psychology, Fries's thought was highly original and expertly worked out. He had a clear conception of a philosophy of mathematics and physics as an independent discipline, and anticipated the modern distinction between a theory and a metatheory. In his theory of nature he attacked Kant's concessions to teleology and argued for a thoroughgoing mechanism that would also encompass the biological sciences. His psychological investigations extended into the study of pathological phenomena. He took note of the distinction between inherited and acquired, as well as between continuous and periodic, mental disorders and argued for the physiological basis of mental illness—concepts that were by no means as current in Fries's time as they are in ours and that were unfortunately ignored by the psychiatric practitioners of his day.

Fries's influence. Fries was succeeded at Jena by his pupil E. F. Apelt, who published a masterly textbook of Friesian metaphysics and in 1847 established the journal *Abhandlungen der Fries'schen Schule*, which served for two years as a forum for critical, scientifically oriented philosophy. There was a revival of interest in Fries and in his approach to Kant in the years preceding and immediately following World War I, centering about Leonard Nelson at Göttingen, who shared Fries's scientific outlook and reacted to the idealist Neo-Kantian orthodoxy in the

German universities of his time much as Fries had reacted to Fichte, Schelling, and Hegel. The theologian Rudolf Otto, an early associate of Nelson, developed Fries's concept of "presage" in his influential book *Das Heilige* (*The Idea of the Holy*, Gotha, 1917). In 1904 Nelson established a new series of the *Abhandlungen der Fries'schen Schule* of which six volumes appeared before publication was discontinued in 1937. National Socialism proved itself as inimical to Nelson's school as Metternich's political reaction had been to Fries's. In 1958 Julius Kraft, a student of Nelson's, founded the philosophical journal *Ratio* as a continuation of the *Abhandlungen*.

Although Fries's influence was and remains limited, part of the interest that his philosophy holds for the modern reader lies in its analogues with, and anticipations of, positions and problems that have been central in twentieth-century thought, especially in England and the United States. There is, first, an obvious but quite unexplored analogy between Fries's psychological method and Husserl's phenomenology. Moreover, the view that metaphysical principles can only be exhibited as such but not proved has been variously defended by R. G. Collingwood and by representatives of the Oxford school of linguistic analysis. There are also apparent counterparts of Fries's "self-reliance of Reason" in G. E. Moore's appeal to common sense, in the positivists' appeal to a level of incorrigible knowledge, and in Wittgenstein's famous dictum that "the propositions of our ordinary language are in perfect order." Indeed, the question of the status of the propositions employed by the critical or analytical philosopher, which was first raised by Fries, has come under much discussion in recent years, under the heading "the problem of analysis."

Bibliography

There are no English translations of Fries's works. A list of all his writings will be found in *Abhandlungen der Fries'schen Schule*, N.S. Vol. 6 (1937), 473–495.

On Fries's life and writings, the fundamental work remains E. L. T. Henke, *Jakob Friedrich Fries* (Leipzig, 1867). The last detailed study of Fries's theory of knowledge is in Alfred Kastil, *Fries' Lehre von der Unmittelbaren Erkenntnis*, a monograph that constitutes *Abhandlungen der Fries'schen Schule*, Vol. 4 (1912). For a short critical assessment of the same subject, see Ernst Cassirer, *Das Erkenntnisproblem in der Philosophie und Wissenschaft der neueren Zeit* (Berlin, 1923), Vol. III, Ch. 7. A stimulating but partisan account of Fries's philosophy will be found in Leonard Nelson, *Fortschritte und Rückschritte der Philosophie* (Frankfurt, 1962). In connection with Fries's theory of law and religion, especially interesting are Julius Kraft, *Die Methode der Rechtstheorie in der Schule von Kant und Fries* (Berlin, 1924) and Rudolf Otto, *Kantisch-Fries'che Religionsphilosophie und ihre Anwendung auf die Theologie* (Tübingen, 1909), translated by E. B. Dicker as *The Philosophy of Religion Based on Kant and Fries* (London, 1931).

ALEXANDER P. D. MOURELATOS

FROEBEL, FRIEDRICH (1782–1852), German philosopher of education, was born at Oberweissbach in Thuringia. He studied forestry and related fields at the University of Jena, came in contact with Johann Heinrich Pestalozzi in 1808, and participated as a volunteer in the war of liberation against Napoleon. In 1816 he established a school, which soon was moved from Griesheim to Keil-

hau, and in 1837 he founded his first kindergarten at Blankenburg in Thuringia, which became the model of many similar institutions. However, these institutions had to be closed in Prussia in 1851 because the government, as well as the clergy, suspected Froebel of liberal political and religious leanings. The prohibition lasted for ten years, but afterward the kindergarten movement spread rapidly throughout the European countries.

Froebel's whole educational theory and practice was determined by his conviction of the ultimate oneness of life, of nature and spirit. According to him it is the destiny of all things to unfold their divine essence and to reveal God in their transient being.

As Froebel's autobiography shows, he was, as a child, deeply troubled by the contrast between "spirit" and "the flesh" in the Christian supernaturalism and moralistic dualism of his father, a pastor, until he discovered the pervasive beauty of nature and the mystery of sex life in the whole creation. His conviction about the inner unity of the cosmos was confirmed by his scientific studies, his reading of the Zend-Avesta, and his acquaintance with Friedrich Schelling's philosophy of identity.

In conformity with his metaphysics, Froebel conceived of education as a continuation of the world's unceasing evolution on the level of consciousness, with the child's play being the first sign of life's urge toward purposeful activity. Thus, he wrote in *The Education of Man* (pp. 1 ff.), "Education consists in leading man, as a thinking, intelligent being, growing into self-consciousness, to a pure, unsullied, conscious and free representation of the inner law of divine unity, and in teaching him means thereto." Out of respect for the "inner law of unity" or for life as an "unbroken whole in all its operations and phenomena" (*The Education of Man*, p. 238), the educator should organize the instructional process in such a way that the order of the subjects to be taught supports the learner's inner development, while the whole program of studies should help the student to realize the reflection of the unity of life in the unity of knowledge.

Froebel's educational principles may be summarized as follows:

(1) That the development of nature reveals itself in the development of the individual mind should be demonstrated in the teaching of science, the humanities, and religion

(2) Education should be structured to harmonize with the natural inner development of the pupil.

(3) Education should unfold the whole man in each person. Religion should be taught in order to cultivate the emotions, nature should be studied because it is the self-revelation of God, and mathematics should be appreciated as the symbol of universal order. Language, too, connects man with the order and rhythm of things and should therefore take its part in education.

(4) The arts should be taught, for art is a general human talent and conducive to the harmonious unfolding of a person's inner life.

The central theme in Froebel's educational work is most evident in *The Education of Man*, which presents a unique attempt to provide an ontological explanation of the process of human learning.

Historically, Froebel must be understood as being in the tradition of John Comenius, Rousseau, and Pestalozzi. His ideas have been criticized for many and sometimes contradictory reasons: for their pantheistic naturalism, their romanticism, their individualism and neglect of discipline, their sentimentality and their one-sided emphasis on early childhood. But there can be no doubt that the work with which his name is mainly connected, the kindergarten, has been an inestimable blessing to mankind, and many of his psychological insights, like those of Pestalozzi, have been increasingly confirmed by modern psychology.

Bibliography

Froebel's *Gesammelte pädagogische Schriften* was edited by Richard Lange (Berlin, 1862–1874). Of the many translations of this work, the following are most important: *Froebel's Chief Writings on Education,* translated by S. S. F. Fletcher and J. Walton (New York, 1912); *Education by Development,* translated by J. Jarvis (New York, 1899); and *The Education of Man,* translated by W. N. Hailmann (New York, 1887).

For literature on Froebel, see Robert Ulich, *History of Educational Thought* (New York, 1950), and his *Three Thousand Years of Educational Wisdom* (Cambridge, Mass., 1959).

ROBERT ULICH

FUNCTIONAL EXPLANATIONS IN BIOLOGY.
See BIOLOGY and TELEOLOGY.

FUNCTIONALISM IN SOCIOLOGY.

In sociology and social anthropology the term "functional analysis" is used not only in the mathematical sense, where a function expresses a correspondence between two variables such that for every value of the one there are one or more determinate values of the other, and the second, or dependent, variable is, in a less technical use of the term, said to be a function of the first. Sociologists, of course, like all scientists, are interested in establishing such dependencies. The term "functional analysis" in their work also has a special connotation analogous to the use of the notion of "function" in describing biological systems or such artifacts as are self-organizing systems—for example, a heat engine with a thermostat. Such a system can be considered as a unitary whole; it is differentiated into elements, and the function of the elements can be said to be the part they play in maintaining the system in a persisting state or (in the case of artifacts) in maintaining the efficiency of the system for the purpose for which it has been set up. There are, however, differences between the use of the notion in sociology and the use as applied to biological and artificial systems, and these have become more apparent as sociologists have worked with and reflected on "functional methods." The differences hinge on the questions of whether a society should be taken to be a single integrated system or whether it may be so diversified that what is "functional" for one part may not be so for others, and whether the only "end" to which an element of a social system should be shown to contribute is the maintenance of the system as a whole in its environment.

Function and cultural facts. Functional notions were used by the pioneers of modern social anthropology and sociology, Émile Durkheim and W. Robertson Smith. The term "functionalism," however, was first put forward as the name of a special method and approach by Bronislaw

Malinowski in the article "Anthropology" in the *Encyclopaedia Britannica* (13th ed., supp. I). The article reads as something of a manifesto, in which functionalism is said to be "the right method" in social anthropology. Functional analysis is said to be "explanation of . . . facts . . . by the part they play within the integral system of culture, by the manner in which they are related to each other within the system, and by the manner in which this system is related to the physical surroundings. . . . The functional view . . . insists therefore upon the principle that in every type of civilisation, every custom, material object, idea and belief fulfils some vital function, has some task to accomplish, represents an indispensable part within a working whole" (*Ibid.,* pp. 132–133). Thus, the function of magic is said to consist in its being "a remedy for specific maladjustments and mental conflicts, which culture creates in allowing man to transcend his biological equipment" (*Ibid.,* p. 136), and myth is said to perform an "indispensable function" in strengthening the traditions on which a cultural life depends.

These claims for the "functional method" were both vague and grandiose. Later exponents and critics of a functional method in the social sciences have been concerned to state more precisely what it does and what it does not claim to assert. (See especially Merton, 1957, and Nagel, 1956.) Malinowski's account left the notion of the "needs" to which a function was said to be related insufficiently clear; his use of the word "indispensable" left it uncertain whether the "needs" themselves were indispensable to the society in question or whether the particular cultural item held to be the means of satisfying them was indispensable in the sense of not admitting of a substitute.

Malinowski's statement of the method was also far more than a recommendation to anthropologists to look for functions; it was a dogmatic assertion that "an object . . . appears as 'inessential,' 'arbitrary,' 'devoid of function' only as long as we do not understand the function of that detailed feature or object" (*Ibid.,* pp. 138–139). It also implied that every cultural item was necessary to the working of the social system as a whole. Of course, if the social system is defined as the total complex of all its cultural items, this becomes tautological. Malinowski avoided this by speaking of "vital needs" that the elements in the system are held to fulfill. But the notion of "needs," interpreted biologically and psychologically, is so extremely general that it is not shown why they can be fulfilled only by particular cultural arrangements.

Function and social structure. The next leading anthropologist to use and also to write about "functional methods" was A. R. Radcliffe-Brown. (See especially his *Structure and Function in Primitive Society.*) Radcliffe-Brown worked with an even more "organic" notion of a society than did Malinowski, since the latter held that practices in a society should be seen as functional for the biological and psychological needs of its *members,* while Radcliffe-Brown was interested in seeing the function of a particular social usage as the contribution it makes to the *total social life,* which is unified as a social system. Radcliffe-Brown regarded a social system as a set of interconnected features of social life, while he defined a social structure as "an arrangement of persons in institutionally controlled and defined relations." This definition appears insufficiently abstract: "social structure" surely should not be used to refer to persons in relationships, but to the distinguishable pattern of recurrent sets of relationships described by social roles. But Radcliffe-Brown's account helped to link the notion of function with that of structure; that is, the uses studied were not those of separate cultural items, but of persistent forms of social relations, such as those shown in marriage arrangements.

The linking of function with structure helps to strengthen the biological, organic analogy behind this way of thinking. Thus, Radcliffe-Brown spoke of a social system as though it were a unitary whole in which every part is internally related to every other, and where it is possible to speak, by analogy with a biological organism, of the structure as serving a "total life." Following this analogy, the use so served is seen as the survival of the total society as an on-going concern. This way of looking on a society was no doubt made more plausible by the fact that the societies so studied were small-scale primitive ones, where the society might seem to be a whole of integrated parts that, it was thought, could be exhaustively enumerated. It becomes much less plausible when applied to larger, more flexible societies comprising a number of subgroups that often are hostile to one another. This may also explain why it appeared that the "function" served was the survival of the society in its traditional given form and why, therefore, functional theory has been held to support a conservative ideology.

The context of a function. That functional theory need not be conservative was shown by Merton, who defined its central orientation as "the practice of interpreting data by establishing their consequences for larger structures in which they are implicated." Merton pointed out that although the notion of function is related to that of some end or need served, this end may not be the perpetuation of the existing social system. Subgroups may have radical interests served by certain social practices that would thus be functional within the context of those interests. Hence, it is not meaningful to speak of a cultural element or institutional practice simply as "functional." It must be shown to be functional in some specific context and in some specific respect; that is, it must have designated consequences for designated properties of designated units, but these units need not be "the society as a whole." However, the notion does presuppose some complex context in which it is possible to show how certain elements have certain consequences contributing to the complex being maintained in a certain state or to the furthering of some interest to which one "function" is related. That an element has such a function relative to such a context or interest can be stated as a matter of descriptive fact, and it need have no ethical implication to the effect that the interest itself (or the function) is thereby commended. Still less need it imply that persons or groups in a society are of consequence only because of such alleged functions.

Explanations and descriptions. How far can the direction of attention to consequences be a form not only of description but also of explanation? Malinowski spoke of such functional analyses as "explanations," though he also remarked that explanation, to the scientific thinker, is nothing but the most adequate description of a complex fact (*A Scientific Theory of Culture*, New York, 1944, p. 117). Whether or not this is a satisfactory view of scientific explanation, there remains the question of whether a functional analysis is the most adequate description of a complex fact *tout court*, or rather a description of the effects of certain elements in the complex on certain other elements; that is, a partial description from the point of view of a particular interest. Merton indeed used the word "interpretation," which is presumably weaker than "explanation," and he spoke throughout his work of "functional analyses."

A functional analysis would be an explanation only if the answer to the question "What is the effect of x in context a, b, c?" could also be seen as an answer to the question "Why does x occur?" or "Why does x have the character it has?" It could be so put if the effect of x is the intended effect of an intentional action (the effect of my turning the key is to unlock the door, and the reason I turn the key is to unlock the door); that is, if the explanation is explicitly teleological, so that it is said that x occurs in order to produce the effect y.

The interest of sociologists is, however, largely directed to detecting the unintended and unanticipated consequences of actions (what Merton called their "latent" as distinct from their "manifest" functions). In such cases, can an effect y be cited as an explanation, or partial explanation, answering the question "Why does x occur?" Can functional statements in contexts where conscious purpose is presumably absent be looked on as explanations? Jonathan Cohen has defined a functional explanation as one in which the fact to be explained—for example, the beating of the heart—is a necessary condition for that which is cited as explaining it—for example, "to circulate the blood" ("Teleological Explanation," *PAS*, Vol. 51 (1950–1951), pp. 255–292; *cf.* D. M. Emmet, *Function, Purpose and Powers*, pp. 48 ff.)

This definition describes the form of a functional statement, but does it show that it is a different kind of explanation from a causal one? Nagel claimed that the factual content of such functional statements can be exhaustively translated into causal terms (*Logic Without Metaphysics*, pp. 250–251); for example, "the beating of the heart is a necessary condition for maintaining the circulation of the blood." Similarly Kingsley Davis, in "The Myth of Functional Analysis as a Special Method in Sociology and Anthropology," maintained that such statements simply assert that certain phenomena have certain consequences. To direct attention to consequences, especially unintended but interconnected consequences, is, he held, the distinctive approach of sociologists. "Functional" analysis is therefore not a special method in sociology, but just sociological method; and the name "functionalism," as supposedly that of a special movement or school, had better be dropped.

From this it would appear that functional statements can be explanations where they can be interpreted teleologically in terms of purpose; that is, where to say an element in a system has a function is to say that it is as it is because it has been so designed with reference to a purpose for which the system has been set up. Where this reference to purpose cannot be made, functional statements would be a form of causal statement in which the interest is directed not to the cause of a phenomenon itself, but to its effects considered as causes within a wider context. However, the reference to a wider context and the need for this to be a context within which some systematic interconnections can be shown distinguish such statements from those presenting unilinear sequences of cause and effect.

Self-regulating system. Functional statements are also particularly appropriate in those systematic contexts in which "return effects" on the cause itself can be shown; that is, where some of its consequences react back on it, so that the consequences can be invoked to explain, in part at any rate, why it is as it is. Thus, Nagel held that functional statements are most appropriately used in describing self-maintaining or self-regulating systems. His formulation for such systems can be briefly summarized as follows: Let S be a system and E its environment, and let S be functional, self-maintaining, or directively organized with respect to a trait (property, state, process), G. Let S undergo a series of alterations terminating in G. Let there then be some fairly extensive class of changes either in E or in certain parts of S. Then, unless S contains some mechanism that produces effects compensating for these changes, S will cease to exhibit G or the tendency to acquire G.

The system S must be specified to show how its parts are causally relevant to the state G, and if the "function" of a part in maintaining G against changes is to be cited as a cause of the state of S, the return effects of this part on other parts of S must be specified. The instantaneous values of the state coordinates must be independent at any given time, although the values of one set at one time will not be independent of those of another set at another given time (that is, the values in one set will change according to previous changes in another set). Nagel held that the relations between the elements in a functional system need to be thus precisely specified, and that very few "functional analyses" in sociology satisfy these requirements.

Latent and manifest functions. Nevertheless, sociologists may be said to produce analyses in which they seek to approximate this model even if they do not entirely satisfy it. This is true particularly where the data studied are shown to have consequences in some larger context, and the consequences are return effects upon the data themselves, so that there is a mutual reinforcement. For instance, Malinowski claimed that the "function" of myths was to strengthen the traditions that help to maintain a social way of life. This may not have been the original reason for the creation of the myth (whatever this may have been, it was said by Malinowski to be sociologically unimportant). But it may be the case that the fact that the myth now performs this perhaps originally unintended function strengthens people's interest in the myth and its hold upon them, and so serves to perpetuate it. Perhaps in some cases what was a "latent" function of some activity, such as recounting a myth, can thus be made the "manifest" function, the explicit purpose of the activity, without disturbing the disposition of its practitioners to go on doing it. But in some cases this may not be true. When, for instance, Malinowski said that "the function of religion is to relieve anxiety," or others (such as Radcliffe-Brown) said that the function of religious ritual is to strengthen the

will to maintain the common values on which the society depends, it is at least open to question whether the adherents of a religion would be able to go on practicing it if they came to look on these functions as the "real reason" for doing so. Thus in some cases the change of a latent into a manifest function will be self-frustrating.

Certain conclusions can be drawn. First, it is misleading to speak of *the* function of a practice, belief, or institution *tout court*. It may have *a* function in relation to a certain interest in a certain context, and this itself may be a disfunction in relation to other interests. Thus, the fact that religion can sometimes relieve anxiety might be a disadvantage in contexts where interest lay in religion as a challenge to complacency.

Further, if such statements of "function" are to do more than merely describe consequences, it should be possible to show that the alleged function also reinforces the practice of the activity. But this must not be taken to imply that this is the sole or "real" reason for the practice. Thus, it may well be that, because of the complexity of human motivation, religious practices sometimes (not necessarily or always) relieve anxieties or promote loyalty to common values; if so, this can strengthen inducements to perform them.

The fact that activities performed with one interest in view can have unanticipated consequences in satisfying other interests can add to the survival value of these activities. Thus, Max Weber's well-known view that there was a nexus between the Calvinistic ethic and the pursuit of capitalist enterprise should not be taken to imply that "the function" of Calvinistic religion was to promote money-making (or vice versa), still less that the pursuit of the former was a hypocritical cloak for the latter. Rather, Weber's view implies that a particular kind of moral outlook, stressing diligence, thrift, and abstinence, was appropriate to the furtherance of capitalist enterprise, so that two independent and strong human interests, the religious and the economic, reinforced each other and thus helped to establish a way of life with considerable survival value. (It is worth noticing that this particular nexus could probably become established only under social and environmental conditions where there were opportunities for the entrepreneur who could save capital. But this is not to interpret these probably necessary conditions as sufficient conditions for explaining the Calvinistic way of life.)

A functional approach in sociology can therefore be taken not as the assumption that every cultural item has a function, but as a directive to watch for "functions," particularly in the unintended consequences of a form of social action, above all for those functions that react back on the form of social action itself, so as to produce a mutually reinforcing nexus. But the analogy with biological or with self-organizing systems must not be pressed too far, since behind forms of social activity are persons or groups capable of entertaining a variety of values and interests. Functional statements in sociology, even if they are not themselves teleological, carry an indirect teleological implication in that if something is said to have a function, it has one in relation to some value, interest, or purpose held by some person or group within the society (though not necessarily by the sociologist himself, who may simply be reporting the fact that some form of activity promotes this value). Where no value is stated, the presumption tends to be that what is served is the preservation of the society as an on-going concern. That it is desirable to preserve the society (though not necessarily just in its existing form) is taken for granted by almost everyone. Thus, when something is said to have a "function" in maintaining the society, although the point is not always recognized, one ingredient in the complex notion of function is a value judgment.

Bibliography

There is an extensive literature discussing functional methods in sociology. Most of it is surveyed by Robert K. Merton, "Manifest and Latent Functions," in his *Social Theory and Social Structure* (Glencoe, Ill., 1949; revised and enlarged, 1957), pp. 19–84.

Discussions of the use of functionalism in anthropology up to 1954 are considered by Raymond Firth, "Function," in *Year Book of Anthropology* (Glencoe, Ill., 1956).

See especially Bronislaw Malinowski, "Anthropology," in *Encyclopaedia Britannica*, 13th ed., supplement I (Chicago, 1926); A. R. Radcliffe-Brown, *Structure and Function in Primitive Society* (London, 1952), which contains some papers and addresses written some 20 years before publication; and Talcott Parsons, *Essays in Sociological Theory, Pure and Applied* (Glencoe, Ill., 1957).

Other discussions include Ernest Nagel, "Formalization of Functionalism," in his *Logic Without Metaphysics* (Glencoe, Ill., 1956), pp. 247–283, and *The Structure of Science* (New York, 1961), pp. 520–535; D. M. Emmet, *Function, Purpose and Powers* (London, 1957); Kingsley Davis, "The Myth of Functional Analysis as a Special Method in Sociology and Anthropology," in *American Sociological Review*, Vol. 24 (1959), 757 ff.; C. G. Hempel, "The Logic of Functional Analysis," in Llewellyn Gross, ed., *Symposium on Sociological Theory* (New York, 1959).

DOROTHY M. EMMET

G

GALEN (129–c. 199), Greek physician and writer, was a native of Pergamum. He is well known in medical history, in which he occupies a virtually unique pre-eminence among its writers; but philosophy's debt to him is not commonly acknowledged. While his was not a first-rate philosophic mind, Galen was an ardent champion of philosophy and did much to promote it in his own time, as did his writings in subsequent centuries.

Galen's father Nikon was an architect and a trained mathematician who wished to give his son a sound philosophical education. Accordingly, after having personally instructed him in the rudiments of mathematics, he sent him at the age of 14 to attend the lectures of the four major schools of philosophy (Platonic, Peripatetic, Stoic, Epicurean). Even at this early age Galen must have been an extremely conscientious student of philosophy, for he drew up outlines of Stoic logic for his own use. He chose a medical career at the age of 16, and went to study at Smyrna (where he heard the Platonist Albinus) and finally at Alexandria, where he completed his education. About 161 he sought his fortune in Rome, where he healed the Peripatetic philosopher Eudemus and gained a reputation that brought him to the attention of Emperor Marcus Aurelius. While in Rome, Galen gave public demonstrations of anatomy. A plague drove him back to his native city, but Marcus Aurelius called Galen to accompany him on the campaign against the Germans. Galen managed instead to assume the supervision of the emperor's son in Rome, and he put the time to good use by writing his major works. He died in Rome at the age of 70.

Galen was an immensely prolific writer; many of his works, of course, are strictly medical, but even these frequently contain remarks about scientific method or philosophy that make them a storehouse of information on Hellenistic philosophy. They give us a picture of an alert, receptive Greek mind of the second century, selecting what he finds valuable in the philosophy of classical and Hellenistic times. Galen's judgments were, on the whole, remarkably sound. He held "the ancients" in great respect and admired the theory of science he found in Aristotle and Theophrastus. This, however, did not prevent him from subscribing with even greater enthusiasm to the ethics and anthropology of Plato, whose views on the nature of man he expounded, along with those of Hippoc-

rates, in a treatise, *Peri tōn Hippokratous kai Platōnos Dogmatōn* ("On the Doctrines of Hippocrates and Plato"), which has not yet received the attention it deserves from scholars.

From the point of view of professional education, Galen was a passionate advocate of careful training in philosophical analysis and logical method for would-be medical men. He constantly exhorted his readers and students to greater exertions on behalf of learning and mathematical studies. Diligent practice is demanded, so he maintained, of anyone who wishes to become proficient in the healing art, or in any other discipline.

Galen's doctrine of scientific demonstration was at least partly an attempt to salvage human knowledge from the corrosive acids of skepticism. For example, his short treatise, "On the Best Teaching," is directed against the contemporary skeptic teacher Favorinus, who taught his pupils to argue on either side of any point. Galen held that it was absurd of Favorinus to leave his pupils free to judge for themselves while destroying all confidence in the starting points of human knowledge. "For if there is nothing evident to the intellect or worthy of credence in itself, all judgment (*krisis*) is wrecked," he remarked. The most effective teaching is based upon the teacher's seeing intellectual things more clearly than others do.

This concern for scientific demonstration establishes Galen as a leading theorist of science in antiquity. Aristotle's *Posterior Analytics* was a calm, dispassionate attempt to incorporate the results of his researches in logic into a picture of scientific knowledge, and his concern to put the syllogism to work may have unduly preoccupied Aristotle in his examination of science. Galen was under no such commitment: instead, while recognizing the occasional usefulness of syllogistic reasoning, he insisted upon the superiority of what he called the linear proof (*grammikē apodeixis*) of geometry. The possibility of such proof alone, he tells us, kept him from lapsing into a total skeptical uncertainty caused by the welter of philosophical doctrines to which he had been exposed. Having achieved with considerable effort a pattern of truly scientific proof, Galen had no patience with slipshod reasoning in medicine.

So concerned was he with the subject that he devoted to it a long treatise, *Peri Apodeixeōs* ("On Demonstration"), unfortunately lost sometime after the sixth century. In this work he argued that all scientific knowledge must begin with what clearly appears to the senses or with what is evident to the mind. What Galen says about the basis of science is much more forceful than anything to be found in Aristotle's *Posterior Analytics*, where the matter of sense perception is rather casually treated. Probably the main inspiration for Galen's line of thought was Theophrastus, Aristotle's immediate successor, but Stoic elements may have entered in as well. At any rate, the result is an astonishingly modern doctrine of logical empiricism, differing from more recent versions mainly in his taking the axioms of science to be self-evident rather than hypothetical. Even his teleology, while it sometimes runs away with him, is more often employed by Galen in the service of strictly controlled scientific explanation. He never tires of admiring the structure and purposiveness of the human body, but this is an attitude shared by many who have investigated human anatomy and physiology.

Galen also wrote in the field of moral philosophy and was especially interested in those aspects of psychology that have a bearing upon ethics. He adopted an essentially Platonic view of the soul, recognizing the three parts distinguished in the *Republic*. But, unlike Plato, Galen marshaled evidence from animal and child psychology to support his view that the native endowment of humans is set at birth and can be modified by education only within limits. Against Chrysippus the Stoic, Galen held that our characters are to be assigned to the irrational rather than to the rational soul. Small children and animals, in whom reason is not yet highly developed, display strongly individual characteristics that, in the case of children, carry through into adult life. This does not absolve adults from the responsibility they bear for their moral traits: these may, and must, be shaped by training and education. By nature some people are good; others, bad, and still others, somewhere in between. Galen argued that the in-between class can be corrupted or improved by association with others. While none of this is strikingly original, Galen's treatment of moral themes bears the stamp of an acute observer oriented toward facts, an attitude so rare in moral philosophizing as to merit notice.

We are indebted to Galen for the preservation of many fragments of the pre-Socratic and Hellenistic philosophers and also, incidentally, for some most interesting observations upon the then obscure sects of Jews and Christians.

Historically, Galen's influence on the progress of medical science and philosophy was predominantly beneficial. His pleas to follow no sect blindly, but to think and look for oneself, did not fall upon deaf ears. It is no accident that Galen's influence reached its all-time high during the Renaissance, when his manifesto of philosophical independence was badly needed—and was heard. For his contributions we can easily forgive Galen his combativeness and long-windedness. Were it not for the combined effect of these two faults, we would not possess nearly so much information as we do on Hellenistic philosophy and science.

Bibliography

A miserable nineteenth-century Greek and Latin edition of Galen's works, edited by C. G. Kuhn, is slowly being replaced by the *Corpus Medicorum Graecorum* (Leipzig, 1908——). In the Teubner series, see Galen's *Scripta Minora*, 3 vols. (Leipzig, 1884–1893) and *Institutio Logica* (Leipzig, 1896). The *De Placitis Hippocratis et Platonis* is partly available in a critical edition by Iwan Mueller (Leipzig, 1874). In the Loeb series one may find Galen's *On the Natural Faculties*, translated by A. J. Brock (New York, 1916). *On the Passions and Errors of the Soul* has been translated by P. W. Harkins, with an introduction and interpretation by W. Riese (Athens, Ohio, 1964).

An indispensable discussion of Galen is Iwan Mueller's "Über Galens Werk vom wissenschaftlichen Beweis," in *Abhandlungen der philosophisch-philologischen Classe der königlich Bayerischen Akademie der Wissenschaften*, Vol. 20 (1897), 405–478. Richard Walzer's books, *Galen on Jews and Christians* (Oxford, 1949) and *Greek into Arabic* (Oxford, 1962), contain much new information. See also Donald Fleming, "Galen on the Motions of the Blood in the Heart and Lungs," in *Isis*, Vol. 46 (March 1955), 14–21, and John S. Kieffer, *Galen's Institutio Logica, English Translation, Introduction, and Commentary* (Baltimore, 1964). On Galen's scientific methodology, see N. W. Gilbert, *Renaissance Concepts of Method* (New York, 1960), pp. 13–24.

NEAL W. GILBERT

GALILEO GALILEI (1564–1642), Italian astronomer and physicist, was born at Pisa. Although he created no systematic philosophy, his influence on the trend of modern philosophical thought is very marked. To it may be traced the definitive separation of physical science from philosophy, the abandonment of authority as a criterion of scientific truth, the distinction between objective and subjective qualities in observable phenomena, and the introduction (or reintroduction) of empirical and skeptical elements into philosophical investigations. The seventeenth-century revival of atomism and the removal of occult qualities from the concept of causation owed much to Galileo. His writings marked the beginning of an antimetaphysical movement in philosophy, exemplified in later times by Positivism and operationalism, and they remained relatively free from such concealed ontological assumptions as are to be found in some ostensibly nonmetaphysical systems; for example, in philosophical empiricism, mechanism, and phenomenalism. The events of Galileo's personal life involved him in an active struggle for freedom of thought, and this in turn underlay those scientific and philosophical convictions for which he became a symbol to his contemporaries and followers.

After a meager, conventional preparatory education, Galileo was enrolled in the school of medicine at the University of Pisa in 1581. His interests turned to mathematics about 1583, and he left the university in 1585 without having received a degree. For a time he continued his studies alone, giving lessons at Siena and Florence, and in 1589 secured the chair of mathematics at Pisa. His early investigations in physics, particularly mechanics, set him in sharp opposition to the views prevailing among professors of philosophy, who, as followers of Aristotle, looked with disfavor upon the introduction of mathematics into physics. In 1591 Galileo left Pisa to become professor of mathematics at the University of Padua. Here he continued his mechanical researches, undertook the manufacture of mathematical instruments for sale, and composed several useful treatises that were circulated in manuscript among his pupils and friends.

In 1604 he disclosed, in a letter to Fra Paolo Sarpi, the mathematical law of freely falling bodies. He had made substantial progress toward a rational mechanics when, in 1609, his attention was diverted from those studies by the invention of the telescope in Holland. Galileo promptly duplicated and improved the device, producing an instrument suitable for astronomical observation, and early in 1610 he published *Sidereus Nuncius* ("The Starry Messenger"), in which he described the mountainous character of the moon, the existence of countless previously unobserved stars, and the discovery of four satellites of Jupiter. These discoveries provoked widespread controversy among philosophers and astronomers. Shortly after "The Starry Messenger" was published, Galileo resigned his post and returned to Florence as chief mathematician and philosopher to Cosimo II de' Medici, grand duke of Tuscany. Late in 1610, he detected the curious appearance of Saturn (although he could not account for it) and the phases of Venus, and shortly thereafter he noted the phenomenon of sunspots.

Strong philosophical opposition was aroused by his publication in 1612 of *Discourse on Bodies in Water*, in which he ridiculed the Aristotelian theory of the elements, advocated observation and experiment as the chief criteria of physical truth, and gave some support to the views of Democritus. Publication in 1613 of his *Letters on Sunspots* aroused theological opposition by its open support of the Copernican theory, which appeared to contradict the Bible by asserting the motion of the earth and the stability of the sun. Toward the end of that year certain philosophers and priests, in the presence of members of the ruling family, attacked Galileo and Copernicanism on religious grounds. Galileo replied in a long letter addressed to his former pupil Benedetto Castelli, who had defended him in his absence. In this letter Galileo contended that Biblical passages had no authority in scientific controversies, and that the language of the Bible should instead be interpreted in the light of man's knowledge of natural phenomena, gained through reason and observation.

Early in 1615, Galileo was violently attacked from the pulpit in Florence, and a copy of his earlier letter, together with a denunciation of the Galileists, was sent to the Inquisition at Rome. Rumors spread that the Catholic church would soon officially condemn the Copernican theory and silence Galileo. He countered by greatly expanding the arguments of his previous letter to Castelli, and widely circulated the new version in manuscript copies ostensibly addressed to Grand Duchess Christina, the mother of Cosimo de' Medici. At the end of the same year Galileo went personally to Rome in an attempt to stem the anti-Copernican tide. In this he was unsuccessful, for the church officially moved to condemn the views of the motion of the earth and stability of the sun as contrary to the Scriptures. Galileo was instructed not to hold or defend these views, but no action was taken against his person or his previously published books.

After a period of silence, Galileo entered into a polemic with a Jesuit professor at Rome over the nature of comets, and in 1623 he published *The Assayer* (*Il saggiatore*), ridiculing the Aristotelian philosophy and expounding his methodological ideas. This book was dedicated to the new pope, Urban VIII, who as cardinal had been very friendly toward Galileo. In 1624, Galileo visited Rome and obtained permission to write on the Copernican and Ptolemaic systems, provided that the treatment was impartial. The composition of his next book, *Dialogue Concerning the Two Chief World Systems*, occupied Galileo intermittently for several years. After great difficulty in getting a license to publish it, he brought it out at Florence in 1632. Five months later the printer was ordered to issue no more copies, and Galileo was summoned to Rome to face the Inquisition. Despite remonstrances of the Tuscan ambassador and of Grand Duke Ferdinand II, he was eventually compelled to appear and stand trial. In June 1633 the book was condemned, and Galileo was sentenced to life imprisonment. He was, however, permitted to reside first at Siena with the archbishop, his friend and former pupil, and then under house arrest at his own villa near Florence. There he managed to compose and smuggle out his most mature work, a treatise on physics known as *Two New Sciences*, which was printed in Holland in 1638. Galileo died four years later.

PHILOSOPHICAL ROOTS

The conditions of Galileo's education and career led to his intimate familiarity with the works of Aristotle. There is little evidence, however, that he ever preferred to read the works of any particular philosopher. His personal library was scanty, and his correspondence is devoid of philosophical references or discussions. In polemic works he refers often to Aristotle, usually with disfavor. His occasional references to Democritus, Socrates, Plato, and Seneca are more favorable but superficial, and appear to express general anti-Aristotelianism rather than allegiance to any other philosopher. Near contemporaries such as Girolamo Cardano and Bernardino Telesio were dismissed by Galileo with the remark that he had read but little of their work. Although there is extant a Latin treatise in Galileo's handwriting that contains references to scores of ancient and medieval philosophers, this dates from his student days (1584) and is not demonstrably original or representative of his own views.

It is evident that during most of his life Galileo's favorite reading was literary rather than philosophical. He is said to have known Ariosto by heart; he lectured on Dante, annotated Tasso, delighted in the rustic dialect writings of Ruzzante (Angelo Boelco), and frequently cited Homer, Vergil, Pulci, and other poets in his works. Nowhere in his writings is there an overt expression of allegiance to any of his philosophical predecessors. However, the question of Galileo's true metaphysical position has been much debated in recent decades. His emphasis on the mathematical element in physics has induced many excellent scholars, led by Alexandre Koyré, to classify him unequivocally as a Platonist. On the other hand, Galileo's insistence on the power of observation to refute any reasoned conclusion has caused others, notably Ludovico Geymonat, to resist this conclusion and even to stress a strong Aristotelian element in Galileo's own work. In opposition to both these views, Edward Strong has questioned the propriety of reading any metaphysical position into Galileo's work and emphasizes his evident preoccupation with methodological considerations, to the exclusion of dogmatic philosophy. Finally, Alistair Crombie has aptly remarked that it is precisely the absence of systematic philosophy in Galileo that has made it possible for adherents of nearly every philosophical school to find some support for their views in his works.

Galileo's anti-Aristotelianism makes its first appearance in his early studies of motion. In order to defend a theory of motion (later abandoned) founded on Archimedean conceptions, he was obliged to demolish several prevailing Aristotelian assertions: that the speed of free fall is proportional to the weight of the falling body and inversely proportional to the density of the medium; that the motion of projectiles depends on some action of the medium; and that motion is impossible in the void. Galileo's attack on Aristotle widened with his adoption of the Copernican astronomy and his abandonment of the distinction between elemental and celestial matter, so essential to Aristotle's world view. In the end he questioned the reliability of Aristotelian logic and asserted that rigorous demonstration was to be found only in mathematics. Thus, it may be argued that Aristotle's physical errors led Galileo to distrust logical deduction as a basis for physics, and his famous dictum that "the book of nature is written in mathematical characters, without a knowledge of which men cannot understand it" probably represents a methodological canon rather than a metaphysical position.

Galileo's opposition to Aristotle was also to some degree a literary pose rather than a true philosophical position. In later years he often declared himself a better Aristotelian than his contemporary Peripatetic adversaries, and in the opening sections of the *Dialogue* he made extensive use of Aristotelian arguments to secure assent to essential points in the Copernican theory. Perhaps the chief significance of Galileo's anti-Aristotelianism is its intimate relation to his consistent rejection of authority of any kind in matters of science. His unwillingness to accept any intermediary between himself and nature was the motivation of his bold warning to the church against the utilization of scriptural authority in scientific disputes. In short, Aristotle was not so much the philosophical opponent as the historical symbol in Galileo's unremitting battle against authority as a criterion of truth.

Separation of physics from philosophy. Until Galileo's time, physical science (including theoretical astronomy) was regarded as a proper part of philosophy and was so taught in the universities. Aristotle's principles of motion supplied the axioms, and the science was purely deductive. Several of Galileo's predecessors had questioned those principles as being in apparent contradiction with experience; Galileo continued these attacks and undertook experimental investigations of the actual phenomena of motion. In this way he came upon some new results and sought principles from which both the old and new phenomena might be deductively established. If he was not entirely successful in this quest, that was not a matter of deep concern to him. Descartes later criticized Galileo sharply for his investigation of physical effects without a prior knowledge of their causes, and Cartesian physics was made an integral part of Descartes's systematic philosophy. In the end, however, the example of Galileo, and not that of Descartes, was followed by scientists. Physics became first a distinct branch (the "natural philosophy" of Newton) and ultimately a separate discipline from philos-

ophy. The philosophical effects of this separation have been enormous. The emphasis on physics that prevailed in philosophy at Galileo's time has vanished; in its place, the theory of knowledge has risen to pre-eminence in modern philosophy, where from time to time it has threatened to subordinate or even to expel metaphysics. It is very doubtful that this would have come about without the separation of physical researches from philosophical investigations, in which separation Galileo was the pioneer.

Nor was Galileo content merely to remove terrestrial physical phenomena from the realm of speculative philosophy. Telescopic observation suggested to him a direct analogy between terrestrial and celestial matter, a conception that was antagonistic to Aristotle's entire scheme. The mountainous chararacter of the moon's surface refuted the axiom of perfect sphericity of celestial bodies; the appearance and disappearance of sunspots destroyed the axiom of celestial immutability and perfection. Galileo did not hesitate to attribute terrestrial qualities to all celestial bodies, thus laying the basis for physical astronomy, even though this had grave religious implications and challenged the traditional cosmological and cosmogonical assumptions of the Peripatetics, who dominated the philosophical thought of the time.

ABANDONMENT OF AUTHORITY

The age into which Galileo was born was one in which the power of authority was uppermost in every sphere of activity—political, religious, and philosophical. It was therefore virtually impossible to attack that power in one sphere without disturbing it in others. To Galileo it was clear that in matters of scientific investigation, authority as such could not be allowed any weight; observation, experiment, and reason alone could establish physical truth. Accordingly, he disputed the right of philosophers and theologians to exercise control over scientific investigations or even scientific theories. Confronted with almost overwhelming opposition in this dispute, he was compelled to adopt, if not to formulate systematically, an alternative criterion of truth that might have some hope of acceptance. In so doing he avoided the error of such philosophers as Telesio and Bacon, who in effect had called for reliance solely upon sensory evidence, for Galileo was well aware of the possibility of illusion or of misinterpretation. It appeared to Galileo that mathematics alone had the kind of certainty that could be completely trusted, and he took the position that only to the extent to which men can detect mathematical regularities in phenomena can they be certain they have reached the truth in physical matters: "Without mathematics, one wanders about in a dark labyrinth." This dictum of Galileo's is often taken today as the expression of a fundamentally Platonic viewpoint, but there is no evidence that Galileo believed in a world of Platonic forms as distinguished from that of events. He appears to have been concerned with relationships rather than essences, and it is in this sense that his mathematical conception of the world is to be taken. He expressly stated that the failure of a physicist to describe the real world was not the fault either of that world or of mathematics, but was merely a result of the limited competence of the physicist, analogous to the shortcomings of a merchant or an accountant who had failed to take into account the weights of the containers in computing the value of his merchandise. Galileo held that although we must be satisfied with limited objectives, we may achieve complete certainty with regard to them.

Galileo's battle for free inquiry, independent of the interference of authority, was, in his own time, doomed to defeat. Nevertheless, the practicability of his alternative criterion of truth gained him a substantial number of followers whose intelligent application of his suggestions was eventually beneficial not only to physical science, but to philosophy as well. The systematic search for solutions to physical problems within pre-established limits of inquiry, under the rule that the demands of sense data, reason, and mathematical interpretation must be simultaneously satisfied, led to the development of a body of dependable knowledge of the physical world that philosophers could no longer ignore in their speculations about underlying reality. At the same time, this complex criterion of physical truth gave rise to a more serious examination of epistemological problems that had been relatively neglected in previous ages of untrammeled speculative philosophy. "We must deal with the real world, and not one on paper," Galileo proclaimed in his *Dialogue*.

It should be noted that Galileo did not extend his demands beyond the domain of physical science. In order to reconcile his scientific position with his acceptance of religious authority, he distinguished sharply between the two uses of language, or even the two languages, of faith and science. This position was expounded at length in his *Letter to Christina* (1615, published 1636). Wherever natural phenomena are involved, the language of the Bible is to be interpreted by the findings of science, while the exposition of supernatural texts is to be left to theologians. This concept of duality of language was given an interesting extension in his *Two New Sciences;* the purely mathematical sections are written in Latin, while the physical and more general sections are in Italian. It is reasonable to assume that Galileo's attitude toward the difficult question of why mathematical relations prevail in physics, and indeed toward metaphysical questions in general, was similar to his expressed opinion with regard to supernatural assertions of any kind: that they were outside the domain of science.

OBJECTIVE AND SUBJECTIVE QUALITIES

It is well known that Galileo clearly set forth the distinction, later made into a fundamental principle by the philosophical empiricists, between primary and secondary qualities. In accordance with his conception that only mathematics afforded complete certainty, he believed that to the fundamental particles of matter one must attribute size, shape, number, and rate of motion; but that one is under no compulsion to invest them with color, sound, odor, and the like. This separation of subjective qualities from those capable of mathematical treatment was a decisive step in the removal of man from his traditionally central place in the entire scheme of things. It is also noteworthy that Galileo showed no interest whatever in pursuing an analysis of subjective (or secondary) qualities; he did not (as did Aristotle and Descartes) compose books on the mind, the spirit, or man in general. Thus, Galileo's treatment of this fundamental principle of empiricism is by no means indicative that he subscribed to an empiricist philosophy in the technical sense. His distinction of objective–subjective was simply an integral part of his separation of physics from philosophy; and if it had any metaphysical implications, they were lost to Galileo. The source of inspiration for this fundamental notion was certainly Greek atomism; but if any classifiable system of philosophy is to be found in Galileo's own writings, it is that of naive realism—a recurrent theme in physical science and the philosophy of science from Galileo's time through the nineteenth century.

Highly important philosophically in Galileo's physical investigations was his insistence on the doctrine of relativity of motion. On the one hand, this removed the earth from its privileged position in astronomy, and in this regard was little more than an extension of the Copernican revolution. On the other hand, it began a new revolutionary movement in which the investigation of natural laws as mathematical relationships was to replace traditional inquiries into the natures or essences of physical entities. Thus, the way was opened to a coherent science of dynamics, while the accepted world view based on the doctrine of "natural places" was rendered untenable.

SKEPTICISM AND THE SCIENTIFIC METHOD

It is worth noting briefly that Galileo introduced (or rather reintroduced) into Western philosophy certain traditions of skepticism which had lapsed during the reign of authority. He often said that it was easier for him to determine that something was false than to discover the truth of any matter, and he openly contended that it was less shameful to be ignorant than to argue on the wrong side. He was accustomed to advise his pupils freely and candidly to confess "I do not know" rather than to offer merely verbal explanations. Thus, among his followers it became once more respectable for a philosopher to acknowledge ignorance. The effects of this were very noticeable in the activities of his disciples and in the Galilean school they created. Establishment of the first great experimental scientific society, the Academy of the Cimento, with its motto of "Test and test again," would scarcely have been possible before Galileo. It was his habit to stress the infinite amount that must remain unknown, no matter how deeply one might penetrate into any subject of inquiry.

Methodological views. Galileo's philosophical importance is nowhere clearer than in his contributions to the method of scientific investigation. His suggestions and his example in this field laid the basis for procedures in physical science that have enriched epistemology as much as science itself. Yet Galileo's conceptions of scientific method, like his other philosophic views, make their appearance in his books only implicitly and incidentally to other considerations. They are first apparent in his polemic work on floating bodies (1612), in which experiments are designed for and applied to the refutation of verbal explanations and arguments. This book marked a definite epoch in the philosophy of science, inasmuch as it is perhaps the first systematic exposition of physical experiments specifically designed to refute a philosophical position. In classical form, it presents the Peripatetic theory and Galileo's countertheory, with a set of experimental tests to show the falsity of the former and the truth of the latter. Although methodological considerations are not discussed in the abstract, the work is a model of the "experimental philosophy" carried on by the school of Galileo.

The work on sunspots published in the following year is also rich in methodological material; here Galileo destroyed the arguments of his anonymous Jesuit adversary by establishing the analogy of terrestrial phenomena to solar phenomena and by applying mathematical reasoning to the problem of the location of the spots. In this instance the use of experiment was precluded by inaccessibility of the phenomena, but observational data were correctly applied in its stead. It thus constituted a methodological continuation of the book on floating bodies, although the points at issue were in this case strictly scientific and not philosophical, at least in modern terms. Particularly noteworthy are certain semantic critiques directed against arguments based upon purely verbal deductions made by Galileo's adversary in this controversy.

Because of the prohibition against discussion of Copernicanism, ten years elapsed before the publication of Galileo's next acknowledged work, *The Assayer*, which differed markedly from his earlier works. Ostensibly a polemic over the nature of comets, it was in reality a detailed critique of the then prevailing treatment of astronomical phenomena. Instead of adopting a specific theory of comets, Galileo undertook to refute his opponent by showing that all his arguments depended upon assumptions that could not be demonstrated or upon confusions of a linguistic character. It is probable that he was motivated at least in part by a desire to place in the hands of his readers a method by which they might themselves arrive at conclusions that he had been forbidden to advocate. Among the principal themes of this work are the proper and improper use of observation and experiment, the distinction between primary and secondary qualities, the necessity for clarification of language in dealing with physical concepts, and the infinite scope of natural phenomena.

In his ill-fated *Dialogue* of 1632, Galileo developed the last-named theme at length. It was his view that physical truths are boundless in number but perfectly consistent; that human knowledge at any time can comprise but a finite part of this infinite whole; that sense experience, indispensable though it is to a knowledge of the world, can be deceptive or misleading in any given instance. Thus, the concept of physical science as essentially a process of successive approximations is already implicit in the teachings of Galileo. At each stage of inquiry, sense experience must be combined with reasoning and with mathematics to afford a sound basis of deduction. Galileo noted that the method used in proof is rarely the same as that used in making a discovery, and held that unless the proof is mathematical, it lacks absolute certainty.

The *Two New Sciences* of 1638, Galileo's chief contribution to physics, was of less direct philosophical importance. Its indirect importance lies in the fact that it definitively established physics as a distinct discipline on the basis of its own methods of investigation, methods that have persisted virtually unchanged. Of particular importance to later philosophical developments were the introduction in this work of the concept of one-to-one correspondence in the analysis of the arithmetical infinite and Galileo's suggestions relating to the roles of physical and mathematical indivisibles in the explanation of observable phenomena.

In conclusion, it should be observed that a profound difference existed between the methods by which Galileo and his contemporary, Johannes Kepler, applied mathematical reasoning to physical science, particularly to astronomy. Kepler's thought was pervaded by the conviction that numerical relationships determined the structure of the universe in the sense of Pythagorean mysticism. Accordingly, he attempted, repeatedly to deduce that structure from a priori numerical hypotheses. As a result, he was early led into fantastic speculations from which he was sometimes able to extricate himself only after years of labor. Galileo, on the other hand, regarded mathematics as an indispensable practical tool and as the definitive test in the quest for physical certainty; but he was not inclined to follow wherever mathematical deduction might lead. His errors, unlike Kepler's, are usually to be found in attempts to create mathematical proofs for physical laws of which he had previously made certain, in the desire to achieve the unique degree of certainty that he ascribed to mathematical demonstration.

Works by Galileo

Edizione nazionale delle opere di Galileo Galilei, A. Favoro, ed. Florence, 1890–1909; reprinted 1929–1939.

Discorso intorno alle cose che stanno in su l'acqua. Florence, 1612. Translated by T. Salusbury as *Discourse on Bodies in Water*. Urbana, Ill., 1960.

Istoria e dimostrazioni intorno alle macchie solari ("Letters on Sunspots"). Rome, 1613. Translated by S. Drake in *Discoveries and Opinions of Galileo*. New York, 1957. Introduction and notes by S. Drake.

Il saggiatore. Rome, 1623. Translated by S. Drake in C. D. O'Malley and S. Drake, eds., *Controversy on the Comets of 1618*. Philadelphia, 1960.

Dialogo sopra i due massimi sistemi del mondo. Florence, 1632. Translated by S. Drake as *Dialogue Concerning the Two Chief World Systems*. Berkeley, 1953.

Nov-antiqua . . . Doctrina . . . de Sacrae Scripturae Testimoniis. Strasburg, 1636. Translated by S. Drake as "Letter to the Grand Duchess Christina" in *Discoveries and Opinions of Galileo*. New York, 1957.

Discorsi e dimostrazioni matematiche intorno a due nuove scienze. Leiden, 1638. Translated by H. Crew and A. De Salvio as *Dialogues Concerning Two New Sciences*. New York, 1914.

Works on Galileo

Aliotta, A., and Carbonara, C., *Galilei*. Milan, 1949.

Banfi, A., *Galileo Galilei*. Milan, 1948.

Burtt, E. A., *Metaphysical Foundations of Modern Physical Science*. London, 1925.

Cassirer, Ernst, *Substance and Function*. Chicago, 1923.

Crombie, Alistair, *Galilée devant les critiques de la posterité*. Paris, 1956.

Fazio-Allmayer, V., *Galileo Galilei*. Milan, 1911.

Geymonat, Ludovico, *Galileo Galilei*. Milan, 1957. Translated, with notes, by S. Drake; foreword by G. de Santillana. New York, 1965.

Giua, M., *Storia delle scienze ed epistemologia*. Turin, 1945.
Goldbeck, E., *Der Mensch und sein Weltbild*. Leipzig, 1925.
Grimaldi, V., *La mente di Galileo Galilei*. Naples, 1901.
Höffding, H., *History of Modern Philosophy*. London, 1900.
Koyré, Alexandre, *Études galiléennes*. Paris, 1939.
Lasswitz, K., *Geschichte der Atomistik*. Hamburg, 1890. Vol. II.
Natorp, P., "Galilei als Philosoph," in *Philosophische Monatshefte*. Heidelberg, 1882. Vol. XVIII.
Olgiati, F., Rovighi, S., Campo, M., et al., *Nel terzo centenario della morte di Galileo*. Milan, 1942.
Olschki, L., *Galilei und seine Zeit*. Halle, 1927.
Romao, M., *Galileu e o método scientifico*. Lisbon, 1944. Vol. I.
Rossi, G., *Galileo Galilei ed il suo metodo*. Bologna, 1880.
Strong, Edward, *Procedures and Metaphysics*. Berkeley, 1936.
Wohlwill, E., *Galilei und sein Kampf für die Kopernische Lehre*. Hamburg, 1909. Vol. II.

S. DRAKE

GALLARATE MOVEMENT. The name "Gallarate movement" applies to an organization called the Centro di Studi Filosofici fra Professori Universitari, established in 1945 at Gallarate, Italy, as well as to the basic philosophical orientation of its members and to the enterprises undertaken to advance its ideas. The leading original members of the movement were Felice Battaglia (Bologna), Carlo Giacon (Padua), Augusto Guzzo (Turin), M. F. Sciacca (Genoa), and Luigi Stefanini (Padua). Among adherents in other countries are Romano Guardini and Helmut Kühn in Germany, Jean Wahl and Régis Jolivet in France, Adolfo Muñoz Alonso in Spain, and A. Robert Caponigri in the United States.

The Gallarate movement accepts the basic Christian affirmation, but no schema of propositions allegedly deduced from it. The philosophy of the movement is that of a Christian who is philosophizing from his own existential position. The movement is committed to no philosophical position, but encourages a dialogue among all points of view. The participants in this dialogue have tended to think along two lines of speculation: the restoration of transcendence as the cardinal principle of philosophy and the restoration of value to its ontological, as well as to its operative, status. According to this analysis, the principle that has controlled modern thought has been immanence, which inevitably leads to various forms of positivism, ethical relativism, and problematicism. The movement does not reject these aspects of modern thought, but accepts and builds upon them. It is claimed that the direct experience of immanence leads directly to the need for a metaphysical affirmation of the Absolute, in order to restore rationality to being and existence as well as an ontologically grounded realm of objective value effective in action and in history. Philosophical reconstruction is thus seen, not as a dogmatic imposition upon the modern philosophical situation, but as a response to the needs of modern thought itself. The Christian affirmation is taken as being among the immediate contemporary data from which philosophy must take its point of departure.

The Gallarate movement sponsors annual congresses, among the most important of which have been the initial conference of 1945 on contemporary Christian philosophy, that of 1947 on Maurice Blondel and the point of departure for philosophy, and that of 1956 on the problem of value.

The movement also edits and publishes works of philosophical scholarship, among the most important of which are the *Bibliografica filosofica italiana* (4 vols., 1950–1956), the *Enciclopedia filosofica* (4 vols., Venice and Rome, 1956–1960), and collections of texts of philosophical classics.

Bibliography

The proceedings of the Gallarate movement conferences are published, usually at Brescia, in the annual ATTI. See also Carlo Giacon, *Il movimento di Gallarate* (Padua, 1955); P. dalla Nogare, "I convegni filosofici di Gallarate," in *Divus Thomas*, 3d series, Vol. 4 (1949), 408–421; Luigi Stefanini, "Il movimento filosofici di Gallarate," in *Ragguaglio* (1953); G. Galetti, "Nel decenale de centro di studi filosofici di Gallarate," in *Gregorianum*, Vol. 25 (1955), 100–124.

A. ROBERT CAPONIGRI

GALLUPPI, PASQUALE (1770–1846), Italian epistemologist and moral philosopher, was born in Tropea, Calabria. He began the study of law in Naples but soon switched to theology and philosophy. At first Galluppi was strongly influenced by Christian Wolff. In 1800 he began to read Condillac and Locke, and his first published work, *Sull'analisi e sulla sintesi* ("On Analysis and Synthesis," Naples, 1807), was an attack on sensationalism. From 1807 until 1815 Galluppi studied Kant. Although he was strongly attracted by Kantianism, he finally rejected it as "skepticism," and, through an examination of Descartes and Locke, he arrived at a position strongly resembling that of the Scottish common-sense school as it had been interpreted by the French eclectics.

The publication in 1819 of the first volume of his *Saggio filosofico sulla critica della conoscenza* ("Philosophical Essay on the Critique of Knowledge," 6 vols., Naples, 1819–1823) brought Galluppi widespread recognition. Between 1820 and 1827 he published his best-known works: the *Elementi di filosofia* (4 vols., Messina, 1820–1827), in which he expounded his theories, and the *Lettere filosofiche sulle vicende della filosofia relativamente ai principi delle conoscenze umane da Cartesio sino a Kant inclusivamente* ("Philosophical Letters on the Events in Philosophy Concerning the Principles of Human Knowledge From Descartes to Kant Inclusive," Naples, 1838), a remarkable history of human thought. In October 1831 Galluppi was named professor of philosophy at the University of Naples. He corresponded with Victor Cousin, whose *Fragments philosophiques* he translated into Italian (2 vols., Naples, 1831–1832), and in 1838 he was named foreign correspondent of the Academie des Sciences Morales et Politiques.

Galluppi held that the only method of philosophy is analysis, a regressive movement in which reflective thought goes back over its own development. The starting point is consciousness: the existence of the conscious ego is "an original experimental truth" and an immediate intuition. The conscious ego consists in the immediate apprehension which the existing ego has of itself. This apprehension simultaneously produces apprehension of the object (which is sensation) and apprehension of the subject that perceives the object (which is feeling). Galluppi expressed this originating act in the formula "I feel (*sento*) a me which senses (*sente*) something" outside of me. Consciousness, in other words, is the awareness that the ego has of itself and of a separate, independently existing reality. On the basis of this indisputable testimony of consciousness Galluppi proclaimed the reality of both the ego and things, in opposition to Berkeley's idealism and Hume's analyses.

Using the same procedure, and by means of the evidence provided by internal consciousness, Galluppi found in the ego the universal ideas which had been denied by the empiricists: these ideas are proved by inner experience, which affirms the existence of God and, by revealing that the conscious ego can only be the effect of a divine intelligent cause, invariable and absolute, also attests the validity of causal relations. True knowledge, knowledge which is adequate to reality, consists in rearranging, by a real synthesis, the objective unities of beings just as they are. The existence of God, proved in the same way that Descartes did, by means of consciousness ("I think, therefore I am; therefore God exists"), proves that the self-evident relationships are valid. (This last argument differs from the Cartesian principle of divine truth.)

Galluppi adhered to the same theory in moral philosophy. In moral philosophy also it is the testimony of consciousness that tells us we are free and that makes us feel the necessity of moral good and thus the presence of a natural moral law: our duty is affirmed to us by our innermost sense.

Additional Works by Galluppi

Lezioni di logica e metafisica. 4 vols. Naples, 1832–1834.
Filosofia della volontà. 4 vols. Naples, 1832–1840.
Considerazioni filosofiche sull'idealismo trascendentale e sul razionalismo assoluto. Naples, 1841. A paper presented at the Institut de France in 1841.
Lettere filosofiche. Augusto Guzzo, ed., 2d ed. Florence, 1925. Contains an ample bibliography.

Works on Galluppi

Di Napoli, Giovanni, *La filosofia di Pasquale Galluppi.* Padua, 1947. Contains a complete bibliography, including an exhaustive list of manuscripts and editions.
Gentile, Giovanni, *Dal Genovesi al Galluppi.* Naples, 1903.
Guzzo, Augusto, *Idealisti e empiricisti.* Florence, 1937.
Lastrucci, Vincenzo, *Pasquale Galluppi, studio critico.* Florence, 1890.
Spaventa, Bertrando, *Prolusione e introduzione alle lezioni di filosofia nell'Università di Napoli.* Naples, 1862; 2d ed. edited by Giovanni Gentile as *La filosofia italiana nelle sue relazioni con la filosofia europea.* Bari, 1908; 3d ed. Bari, 1926. Pp. 133–145.

EUGENIO GARIN
Translated by *Robert M. Connolly*

GAMES, THEORY OF. See DECISION THEORY.

GARRIGOU-LAGRANGE, RÉGINALD MARIE
(1877–1964), notably influenced the revival of Thomism in some European and American philosophical circles. He was born Gontran-Marie Garrigou-Lagrange at Auch, France. His first university studies were in the faculty of medicine at the University of Bordeaux. After two years, however, he chose to embrace the priesthood and on May 20, 1900, made his profession as a Dominican, receiving the name Réginald Marie.

In addition to the regular course of philosophy as a Dominican, he pursued graduate studies at the Sorbonne, where he had the opportunity to attend the lectures of Henri Bergson. In 1909 Garrigou-Lagrange entered into what proved to be a long career as professor at the international university of philosophical and theological studies in Rome, now called the Universitas Studiorum Pontificia S. Thomae Aquinatis in Urbe. He remained in this position until 1959. Although his courses were primarily in the theological faculty, it is significant that throughout his teaching life he lectured each week on the metaphysics of Thomas Aquinas. Garrigou-Lagrange was also a founding member of the Academia Pontificia Academia Romanae S. Thomae Aquinatis.

An accurate view of the philosophical thought of Garrigou-Lagrange must take into account the fact that he was not simply a philosopher; his professional labors as well as his writings are preponderantly theological. However, because his concern was with the teachings of Thomas Aquinas, his work has a philosophical import on two counts. First of all, the Thomistic theological synthesis is characterized by its employment of the speculative resources of human intelligence. In this concentration on theology, then, Garrigou-Lagrange necessarily devoted himself to the exposition of the basic Thomistic philosophical positions. Second, from the beginning of his career Garrigou-Lagrange was faced with a challenge to the relevance and the validity of Thomism, or indeed of any metempirical assertions of the human mind. It is to this challenge that his purely philosophical labors and writings are principally addressed.

His first book, *Le Sens commun, la philosophie de l'être et les formules dogmatiques,* is a rejoinder to the position taken by Édouard Le Roy in a series of articles (*Revue de métaphysique et morale,* 1899–1901). Le Roy alleged all expressions of truth by the human mind to be totally relative, mutable, and conditioned. Human thought is simply the expression of *de facto* acceptations, significant according to that natural and subjective orientation of the human mind which for Le Roy is the *sens commun.* Against this Bergsonian usage, Garrigou-Lagrange used the term *sens commun* to designate the commonly assumed character of the human mind, namely, its extramental orientation toward objectively existent and intelligible reality. He set himself the task of vindicating this realism, of defending the objective validity and transcendental range of human thought.

The basic themes of his position are readily discernible. The human intelligence has "being" as its connatural object. In its attainment of being the human mind surpasses sense knowledge, goes beyond mere phenomena. The first principles of human reason—identity, contradiction, causality, and finality—are not mere subjective thought patterns; they are grounded in being. The human evaluation of the data of experience in virtue of such principles, then, has an ontological validity; the human mind is capable of assertions concerning the real that are objectively true and absolute. Because in its attainment of being the mind goes beyond mere phenomena, the principles of philosophical inquiry have a transcendental validity. Man is able, consequently, to achieve true judgments, not only about the entitative structure of experienced reality, but also about the nonexperienced but necessarily affirmed primary cause of the beings of experience. The connaturally realistic orientation of human intelligence, therefore, provides the capacity for objectively valid metaphysical evaluations of reality and even for a true natural theology.

Garrigou-Lagrange maintained that Aquinas presented a philosophy of being that was an effectively enunciated and developed expression of the natural metaphysical orientation of human intelligence in which the *sens commun* has its scientifically articulated realization. Garrigou-Lagrange's principal philosophical contribution, then, was a forceful and clear exposition of the basic Thomistic insights. In his writings there is a clear and honest confrontation of Thomistic realism with both nominalist empiricism and Kantian subjectivism.

An evaluation of the work of Garrigou-Lagrange must place it in relation to the so-called Neo-Scholastic movement. Since his career began well after the early attempts to reassert Thomism, his writings are free of the alien influences present in the work of the restoration's pioneers. His chief concern, the basic critical problem of the validity of human intelligence, is a central issue in all Neo-Scholastic philosophy. In the light of subsequent developments among Neo-Scholastic philosophers, and even among Thomists, concerning the critical problem, the approach of Garrigou-Lagrange may be designated as somewhat simplified. He strove to set forth directly the positive statements of a philosophy of being against a philosophy of becoming, to manifest the human mind as a faculty of truth, not an amasser or coordinator of data. Later Thomists have sought by more reflective methods to show how being manifests itself in the very process of cognition as the evidential justification of human knowledge. Their efforts are a refinement of the task to which the efforts of Garrigou-Lagrange were directed. His work, then, was a necessary stage in a vital development. Because of his dedication to the thought of Aquinas, he directed that development to a more fruitful use of Thomas' understanding of the problems of being and intelligence.

Works by Garrigou-Lagrange

BOOKS

Le Sens commun, la philosophie de l'être et les formules dogmatiques. Paris, 1909; 4th ed., Paris, 1936.
Dieu, son existence et sa nature. Paris, 1915; 6th ed., Paris, 1950. Vols. I and II translated by Dom Bede Rose as *God, His Existence and His Nature, a Thomistic Solution of Certain Agnostic Antinomies.* St. Louis, 1934.
Le Réalisme du principe de finalité. Paris, 1932.
La Synthèse Thomiste, Paris, 1946. Translated by Dom Patrick Cummins as *Reality, a Synthesis of Thomistic Thought.* St. Louis, 1950.

ARTICLES

Angelicum, Vol. 14 (1937), 5–37. A complete bibliography of Garrigou-Lagrange's numerous articles through 1937.
Bulletin Thomiste. For the discussion of the critical problem

among Thomists during the height of Garrigou-Lagrange's career, see the following: Vol. 3 (1932), 451 ff; Vol. 4 (1935), 400 ff., Vol. 5 (1938), 365 ff.; Vol. 6 (1940–1942), 236 ff.

THOMAS C. O'BRIEN, O.P.

GARVE, CHRISTIAN (1742–1798), German "popular philosopher," was born in Breslau. After studying at Frankfurt an der Oder, Halle, and Leipzig, he became extraordinary professor of philosophy at Leipzig in 1770, but in 1772 he resigned on account of ill health and moved to Breslau. In 1779 Frederick II called him to Charlottenburg, where he remained until his death.

Garve's interests were mainly in practical morality and empirical psychology. He sought useful knowledge and was averse to abstract speculation. He drew inspiration from La Rochefoucauld and Helvétius, and especially from the British moralists. His translations of Adam Ferguson, Edmund Burke, Alexander Gerard, Adam Smith, and other British authors were important in popularizing British moral philosophy and aesthetics in Germany. He also translated and commented on the moral and political works of Aristotle and Cicero.

In his own writings Garve studied the individual characteristics and inclinations of different men, and their interrelation in society. He explained their differences by a difference in the degree of clarity and vividness of the ideas they possessed. Interest—the participation of an individual in the feelings, ideas, and actions of another— was a central notion in his psychology. It was derived from the "benevolence" and "sympathy" then current in British thought. In Garve's works psychology, sociology, and ethics were interwoven. His goal was that of a social psychologist, moralist, and educator. Kant drew from Garve some elements of his moral and religious philosophy.

Works by Garve

Über die Verbindung der Moral mit der Politik. Breslau, 1788.
Über verschiedene Gegenstände aus der Moral, Literatur und dem gesellschaftlichen Leben, 5 vols. Breslau, 1792.
Vermischte Aufsätze, 2 vols. Breslau, 1796–1800.
Über Gesellschaft und Einsamkeit, 2 vols. Breslau, 1797–1800.
Übersicht der vornehmsten Principien der Sittenlehre. Breslau, 1798.
Einige Betrachtungen über die allgemeinen Grundsätze der Sittenlehre. Breslau, 1798.
Sammlung einiger Abhandlungen, 2 vols. Breslau, 1802.

Works on Garve

Manso, S. J. C., *Chr. Garve in seinem schriftstellerischen Charakter.* Breslau, 1799.
Müller, P., *Christian Garves Moralphilosophie und seine Stellungnahme zu Kants Ethik.* Erlangen, 1905.
Schelle, G. G., *Briefe über Garves Schriften und Philosophie.* Leipzig, 1800.
Stern, A., *Ueber die Beziehungen Christian Garves zu Kant.* Leipzig, 1884.

GIORGIO TONELLI

GASSENDI, PIERRE (1592–1655), French skeptical and Epicurean philosopher, was born at Champtercier, a Provençal village. He studied at Digne and at Aix and was appointed professor of rhetoric at Digne at the age of 21. In 1614 he received a doctorate in theology at Avignon and was ordained a priest in 1616. From 1617 to 1623, as professor of philosophy at Aix, he developed a critique of Aristotelianism that formed the basis of his first published work, *Exercitationes Paradoxicae Adversus Aristoteleos* (Grenoble, 1624). This work was intended to be followed by six more parts, of which only the second part, published posthumously, was written. It contains both a massive attack on Aristotle's thought and portions of Gassendi's "mitigated skepticism."

After a year in Digne, during which he performed various ecclesiastical duties, Gassendi visited Paris for a brief period in 1625 and became friendly with such avant-garde thinkers as La Mothe Le Vayer and Marin Mersenne. He continued the astronomical researches that he had begun in Provence, and, with the mathematician Claude Mydorge, observed a lunar eclipse. (Gassendi's careful astronomical records from 1618 to 1655 were published after his death.) Gassendi returned to Paris in 1628, remained there until August 1629, and then spent nine months in Flanders and Holland, where he met many leading scientists and scholars. He spent the next years partly in Paris and partly in Provence, publishing scientific works on astronomy and physics and presenting skeptical attacks on Herbert of Cherbury and the Rosicrucian Robert Fludd. He undertook an intensive study of Epicurean atomism, a subject in which he had been interested for some time. The results of this study were to form a basic part of his later writings.

In 1634, Gassendi was elected provost of the Cathedral of Digne. In 1641 he was sent to the assembly of the French clergy in Paris and during this visit taught philosophy to the young Molière. Gassendi was appointed to the chair of mathematics at the Royal College (now the Collège de France), in 1645, but because of ill health he was away from his post from 1648 to 1653. He fell ill in 1654 and died the following year.

Except for his early attacks on Aristotelianism, Fludd's Rosicrucianism, and Herbert of Cherbury, Gassendi's philosophical works date from the 1640s onward. In 1641, at the request of Mersenne, Gassendi wrote his objections to Descartes's *Méditations* ("Fifth Set of Objections"). Descartes's testy answer led Gassendi to expand his criticism into the bulky *Disquisitio Metaphysica*, finished in 1642 and published in Amsterdam in 1644. He published three works on Epicurus and his philosophy between 1647 and 1649—*De Vita et Moribus Epicuri* (Lyons, 1647), *Animadversiones in Decimum Libri Diogenis Laertii, qui est de Vita, Moribus Placitisque Epicuri* (Lyons, 1649), and *Syntagma Philosophiae Epicuri, cum Refutationibus Dogmatum, Quae Contra Fidem Christianum ab eo Asserta Sunt* (Lyons, 1649). His most important philosophical writings appeared only posthumously, in the 1658 edition of his complete works. His over-all treatment of philosophical problems appears in *Syntagma Philosophicum* (*Opera*, Vols. I and II) and in the second part of his first work, the *Exercitationes*, which presents his "constructive skepticism."

"Exercitationes." Gassendi's thought developed from a fairly thoroughgoing skepticism, strongly influenced by

Sextus Empiricus, Montaigne, Pierre Charron, and Francisco Sánchez, to what he called a *via media* between skepticism and dogmatism. The *via media* involved both a fundamental epistemological skepticism and a hypothetical form of Epicurean atomism that was modified to eliminate those aspects of Epicurus' thought that conflicted with Christian doctrine. In the first part of the *Exercitationes*, Gassendi, following in the tradition of Francesco Patrizi and Petrus Ramus, tried to show all of the erroneous or dubious aspects of Aristotelianism. The second part set forth an attack upon all those who claimed to have discovered necessary and indubitable knowledge of the real nature of things. Our knowledge of the world, Gassendi insisted, comes only from sensory experience. We are unable to arrive at absolutely true first principles and real or essential definitions, since inductions from experience can never yield certain universal propositions. No matter how much data is gathered, a negative instance may still turn up in the future. Even if we somehow managed to discover some genuine definitions and first principles, no further scientific knowledge about nature could be gained by employing syllogistic reasoning, since, as the Greek Pyrrhonists had shown, the truth of the premises of a syllogism depends upon antecedent knowledge that the conclusion is true. Either the conclusion is part of the evidence for the premises or the syllogism establishes nothing, since it is not known whether the premises are true.

In the concluding section, Gassendi launched his strongest attack upon the possibility of gaining necessary knowledge about the world. Using the arguments of the ancient skeptics, he tried to show that all that we can know is how things appear, not how they really are in themselves. We can know that honey seems sweet, but we cannot find out if it really is sweet. On the basis of appearances, we cannot tell what the real nature of things must be that produces such effects on us. Sense experience varies too much to provide any means for determining what reality is like on the basis of what is perceived. We lack any means of reasoning from experience to what has caused it. We are not even able to establish any criterion of true knowledge. Hence, we can only conclude that nothing can be known about reality. However, in this early work, Gassendi insisted that we can develop useful sciences about appearances. As long as we restrict our conclusions to the world of experience, we will neither come in conflict with divine truth, nor accept any dubious dogmatic theory about unperceived reality. Such theories, whether metaphysical or mathematical, are presumptuous conjectures that have no value whatsoever.

Objections to Descartes. In his middle period, Gassendi challenged those who claimed to have discovered some means of knowing the real nature of things. He employed various skeptical arguments against Renaissance naturalists and against such leading "new philosophers" as Herbert of Cherbury and Descartes. Gassendi's two letters against Herbert's *De Veritate* (in which the latter claimed to have refuted skepticism) used arguments about diversity of experience and disagreements among men to counter Herbert's common notions and common consent theory. In the "Fifth Set of Objections" and the *Disquisitio Meta-*

physica, Gassendi turned skeptical argumentation against Cartesianism. He tried to show that Descartes's method of doubt illustrated what the skeptics had claimed for centuries. Then Gassendi challenged Descartes's positive dogmatic conclusions. Gassendi contended that the vaunted Cartesian criterion of true knowledge (that of clarity and distinctness) was useless, since people often think that they clearly and distinctly perceive something and then turn out to be wrong. Hence, in order to employ this criterion, another criterion would be needed to determine when something really is clear and distinct and does not merely appear to be so. In addition, another criterion would be necessary in order to employ this second criterion, and so forth. The culmination of Gassendi's attack, which Descartes called the objection of objections, was his posing the possibility that all knowledge, even if it were clear and distinct, might not be about anything outside of our minds. If this could be the case, then all the knowledge purported to be found by Descartes might be imaginary or fictitious. Descartes saw this suggestion as a fundamental challenge to his system and as a denial of the possibility of gaining knowledge about any reality other than our own thoughts. (His reply consisted in refusing to take the objection seriously, since if one did, "it follows that there is nothing that we can in any way comprehend, conceive or imagine, that should be accepted as true, that is to say that we have to shut the door completely on reason, and be content to be monkeys, or parrots, and no longer men"; Descartes, *Oeuvres,* C. Adams and P. Tannery, eds., Vol. IXA, p. 212.)

Mitigated skepticism. In his later writings, Gassendi attempted to develop a mitigated skepticism that would show how we could possess worthwhile knowledge about the world of appearances and how a science of this world could be developed, using Epicurean atomism as a hypothetical model.

The full presentation of this view appears in the *Syntagma Philosophicum.* This work begins with what Epicurus had called canonics, the philosophy of logic and the theory of knowledge. After summarizing the Pyrrhonian view, Gassendi set forth his compromise theory. He asked whether there is any absolutely certain criterion for distinguishing truth from falsehood. Some matters are obvious at certain times, such as that "it is day." Everybody, including the skeptics, accepts what is obvious, evident, or apparent. Difficulties only arise in regard to those things that the Pyrrhonists had classified as "nonevident"—that is, those matters that are concealed from us. Some of these are absolutely nonevident and can never be known under any conditions. Gassendi gave the classical Pyrrhonian example—namely, whether the number of stars is odd or even. Other matters are naturally nonevident; we cannot perceive them. However, we are able to know about them by means of signs. The example that Gassendi used is that of the existence of pores in the skin, which we are able to infer from perceiving sweat. Finally, some things are temporarily nonevident: they can be perceived, but sometimes they are not perceived because of temporary conditions.

The ancient skeptics admitted that temporarily nonevident things could be known through "suggestive signs"—events that are regularly conjoined with others, so that if one is observed, then we think of the other. Smoke is a suggestive sign of a fire even if the latter is temporarily not seen. The Pyrrhonists regarded knowledge of the nonevident through suggestive signs as important and valuable in ordinary life. The disagreement between skeptics and dogmatists is about whether there are any signs by which we can gain knowledge about naturally nonevident matters. The skeptics doubt that we can know more about things than how they appear to us. The dogmatists contend that knowledge of naturally nonevident matters can be attained through "indicative signs"—signs that reveal things beyond all possible experience.

The dogmatists, Gassendi claimed, exaggerated the power of the human mind, since things-in-themselves, or the real natures of things, are actually concealed from us. The skeptics, however, overemphasized the barriers to knowledge. Since it is obvious that something exists and that some things both can be and are known, there is no need for complete doubt. We know appearances, and we also know some things about naturally nonevident objects by means of a kind of indicative sign. Through our senses, we become aware of apparent signs, which our reason is able to interpret. In this way we find out about unperceivable objects. Even though our senses are sometimes in error, this situation can be corrected by careful reasoning. Our reasoning and our knowledge about naturally nonevident things can be tested experientially, by seeing if the predictions that result can be verified. The skeptical objections about our reasoning can be ignored, since there are certain principles of reasoning that no one questions and that are sufficiently evident to employ as means of drawing inferences.

Atomism. Gassendi did not claim we could discover the real nature of objects by experiential reasoning. Rather, he claimed that we could find scientific explanations of the causes of our experience—laws or reasons explaining, for example, why honey seems sweet to us, why objects appear to have certain colors, or why our experiences vary according to conditions in us and in the outside world. This kind of knowledge, which is more extensive than the skeptics admitted and far less extensive than the knowledge that the dogmatists claimed to possess, results from a most careful examination of appearances and a most cautious rational evaluation of the data derived from them. This evaluation is not based on knowing the real nature of things, but on a consideration of the conditions that would make our experience both possible and intelligible. For Gassendi, the best explanatory system was atomism, which can account for the sense qualities we experience and can provide a model for the known data about the observable world.

Gassendi's atomism, derived from a study of the classical Epicurean texts, was not advanced as a metaphysical theory about the true nature of things. The atomic world is inferred from experienced indicative signs. It is confirmed by verifying predictions about atomic effects in the observable world. Gassendi limited his descriptions of the characteristics of atoms to sensory qualities found in experience. Rather than conceiving of them as mathematical objects, he portrayed them as having various shapes. Gassendi rejected the conception of the unseen world as being composed of pure mathematical forms as another danger-ous and unnecessary metaphysical theory, a kind of Pla-tonism or Pythagoreanism.

Gassendi avoided those points on which atomism conflicts with Christian doctrine. By eliminating any meta-physical features of the theory and presenting it as a hypo-thetical explanation for the observable world, Gassendi could claim that his version of Epicureanism was compat-ible with a universe that is divinely created and run. Fur-ther, he maintained that atomic explanations did not ex-tend to the human soul and that he accepted on faith the doctrine of the immortality of the soul. He insisted that his Christian Epicureanism in no way denied or cast doubt on any articles of Catholicism and led to no heretical conclu-sions.

Influence and significance. Gassendi's mitigated skep-ticism and limited Epicureanism was one of the major and most influential theories of the scientific and philosophical revolutions of the seventeenth century. Gassendism rivaled Cartesianism as a new alternative to Scholasticism and as a way of interpreting the findings of the scientists. When the Jesuits were demanding the suppression of Descartes's views, some of them insisted that Gassendi's philosophy was much to be preferred. Locke was in-fluenced to some degree by the empirical aspect of Gas-sendi's thought. Gassendi's separation of science from metaphysics and his presentation of atomism as a hypothe-sis or model for explaining the phenomenal world had a great and lasting impact on the development of modern scientific theory. In many ways, his thought is closer to twentieth-century conceptions of the scientific outlook than that of almost any other seventeenth-century thinker.

On the negative side, although Gassendi himself made some important contributions in the areas of astronomy and physiology, neither he nor his followers were able to use the atomic theory to produce major scientific results. This was partly because of the state of scientific research during this period, and partly because of Gassendi's ex-treme caution and his studious reliance on tradition and ordinary experience. Gassendi lacked the daring of the great innovators of the time. He was also too immersed in classical humanism to present his views without enormous citations, endless references, and inordinate detail. As a result, none of his works (with the exception of his shorter answers to Descartes) are still read, and he was neglected in favor of later empiricists and skeptics. Thus, Gassendi's ideas survived more in the presentations of others than in his own works, and his later philosophical and scientific influence resulted chiefly from second-hand versions of his thought by Bayle, Locke, Voltaire, and others.

Religion. A major problem in interpreting Gassendi's contribution is that of assessing his intentions and actual beliefs. He has been seen both as the founder of modern materialism and a leading skeptic and libertine, and as a serious Christian trying to find a *via media* between his faith and the new science. He was not a metaphysical materialist, nor was he a skeptic in the sense of doubting that anything can be known, but he was a skeptic about whether human beings could gain any necessary and cer-tain knowledge about reality. Gassendi was a priest all of his life. He was friendly with the most orthodox and the

most unorthodox figures of his time. He was always careful to state his views so that they did not conflict with those of his church. He may have seen, as few others of his time did, the importance of the values of his religious tradition, of the classical heritage, and of the new science, and at the same time fully appreciated what the skeptics had shown about man's fallible nature. Unlike Montaigne, Charron, and La Mothe Le Vayer (all of whom he admired), he did not wish to destroy the fruits of human efforts along with man's presumptuous and dubious claims. More like Sán-chez, he wanted to find a constructive resolution to the skeptical crisis of the Renaissance, but not in the form of the new dogmatisms of Herbert of Cherbury or Descartes. Living within a major religious tradition, he tried to show that by discarding Aristotelianism and by accepting the wisdom of the skeptics along with certain elements of Epicureanism, faith and the new scientific discoveries could coexist. He apparently lacked the fervent need to harmonize these worlds, as Kepler did, or to preserve the religious one at all costs, as Pascal did, but he offered a way of living simultaneously in both of them. In so doing, he developed an interpretation of science and human knowledge that came closer to certain dominant modern views than any interpretation that was achieved by any of his contemporaries.

Works by Gassendi

Opera Omnia, 6 vols. Lyons, 1658. Photoreproduction ed., Stuttgart, 1964.

Exercitationes Paradoxica Adversus Aristoteleos (1624), edited and translated by Bernard Rochot as *Dissertations en forme des paradoxes contre les aristotéliciens.* Paris, 1959.

Lettres familières à François Luillier pendant l'hiver 1632–1633, Bernard Rochot, ed. Paris, 1944.

Disquisitio Metaphysica (1644), edited and translated by Ber-nard Rochot as *Recherches métaphysiques.* Paris, 1962.

Works on Gassendi

Bernier, François, *Abrégé de la philosophie de Gassendi,* 7 vols. Lyons, 1678. Popular seventeenth-century presentation, by a disciple, of Gassendi's atomism.

Berr, Henri, *An Jure Inter Scepticos Gassendus Numeratus Fuerit.* Paris, 1898. Translated by Bernard Rochot as *Du Scepti-cisme de Gassendi.* Paris, 1960. An important discussion of Gas-sendi's compromise between skepticism and dogmatism.

Brett, George, *The Philosophy of Gassendi.* London, 1908. Only full-scale treatment of Gassendi in English, mainly on his atom-ism. Outdated by modern studies.

Centre international de synthèse, *Pierre Gassendi, 1592–1655, sa vie et son oeuvre.* Paris, 1955. Lectures on Gassendi by Bernard Rochot, Alexandre Koyré, Georges Montgrédien, and Antoine Adam. Some excellent discussions of his philosophical and scientific views.

Gregory, Tullio, *Scetticismo ed empirismo—Studio su Gas-sendi.* Bari, 1961. Important study.

Hess, Gerhard, "Pierre Gassend. Der Französische Späthuman-ismus und das Problem von Wissen und Glauben." *Berliner Beiträge zur Romanischen Philologie,* Vol. 9 (1939), 1–199. Im-portant study of Gassendi's views on faith and reason.

Kiefl, F. X., "Gassendi's Skepticismus und seine Stellung zum Materialismus." *Philosophisches Jahrbuch des Görres-Gesell-schaft,* Vol. 6 (1893), 23–34, 295–311, 361–373. A criticism of the view that Gassendi was the father of modern materialism.

Lange, Friedrich A., *The History of Materialism and Criticism of its Present Importance,* translated by E. C. Thomas, 3d ed. London, 1957. Book I, Sec. 3, Ch. 1 of this mid-nineteenth-century work is on Gassendi.

Lasswitz, Kurd, *Geschichte der Atomistik vom Mittelalter bis*

Newton, 2 vols. Leipzig, 1926. Vol. II, pp. 126–188. Evaluation of Gassendi's views in terms of the history of atomism.

Pintard, René, *Le Libertinage érudit dans la première moitié du XVIIe siècle*. Paris, 1943. Gassendi is examined in relation to the *libertins*, and an irreligious interpretation of his views is offered.

Popkin, Richard H., *The History of Scepticism from Erasmus to Descartes*. New York, 1964. Chs. 5 and 7 deal with Gassendi's mitigated skepticism.

Rochot, Bernard, *Les Travaux de Gassendi sur Epicure et sur l'atomisme*. Paris, 1944. A very important study of Gassendi's development. Contains a critical bibliography.

Rochot, Bernard, "Le Cas Gassendi." *Revue d'histoire littéraire de la France*, Vol. 47 (1947), 289–313. A defense of Gassendi's religious sincerity against the accusations of Pintard.

Rochot, Bernard, "Gassendi et le Syntagma Philosophicum." *Revue de synthèse*, Vol. 47 (1950), 67–79. A study of Gassendi's philosophy of science and scientific method.

Sortais, Gaston, *La Philosophie moderne depuis Bacon jusqu'à Leibniz*. Paris, 1922. Vol. II. Presents a detailed summary, analysis, and evaluation of Gassendi's philosophy and his influence.

RICHARD H. POPKIN

GAUNILO

GAUNILO was an eleventh-century Benedictine monk of Marmoutier, who attacked Anselm's Ontological Proof for the existence of God shortly after its appearance in the *Proslogion*. Anselm had undertaken to show that the fool of the *Psalms*, who says in his heart that there is no God, is truly a fool since his denial contradicts itself. Gaunilo's reply was entitled *Pro Insipiente* ("In Behalf of the Fool").

Gaunilo urged a variety of objections to Anselm; they turn, however, mainly on one central point, which may be put—however little in Gaunilo's terms—as follows: in no case does the sense of a concept imply that it has a reference; in no case does the sense of a concept imply that there is an existent to which it is applicable. Gaunilo supports this by an argument from analogy. All sorts of objects exist in the understanding. Nevertheless, they are understood to be unreal, and, further, their (hypothetical) excellence has no bearing on the question of whether they really exist. For example, the Islands of the Blessed, which are conceived to be the most excellent of lands, are not thereby conceived to exist. Anselm's argument is invalid because it contains an illicit transition from the conceptual order to the real order.

Gaunilo's argument found favor with St. Thomas Aquinas (*Summa Theologica*, Q. II., Art. I., Reply Obj. 2) and for that reason continues in some quarters to be urged as an objection to Anselm. Yet it is difficult to understand why, for it is not an argument but, as Anselm pointed out in his reply to Gaunilo, a mere *petitio*. One cannot assume that no concept implies its own applicability in order to refute a proof that there is one concept that does. Nor can an argument from analogy be used to refute a proof whose conclusion implies that the terms in question are not analogous. The concept of that than which a greater cannot be conceived, Anselm thought, differs from ordinary concepts precisely because it can *not* be conceived not to exist.

Bibliography

Deane, S. N., *St. Anselm*. La Salle, Ill., 1962. Includes Gaunilo's reply to Anselm in an English translation.

Schmitt, F. S., ed., *S. Anselmi Opera Omnia*. Seckau, 1938. Vol. I.

R. E. ALLEN

GAY, JOHN (1699–1745), English moral philosopher, was a fellow of Sidney Sussex College, Cambridge, and later vicar of Wilshampstead, Bedfordshire. His short "Dissertation Concerning the Fundamental Principle of Virtue or Morality" was first published as a preface to Edmund Law's translation of William King's Latin *Essay on the Origin of Evil* (1731). (Law was bishop of Carlisle and King was archbishop of Dublin.) The "Dissertation" is one of the seminal works in the history of English utilitarianism. In the eighteenth century its influence may be found in the works of the theological utilitarians, Abraham Tucker (*The Light of Nature Pursued*, 7 vols., 1768–1778) and William Paley (*Principles of Moral and Political Philosophy*, 1785). David Hartley said that Gay's assertion of the importance of psychological association in human nature was the origin of his *Observations on Man* (1749).

Gay hoped to eradicate confusion in moral philosophy and to harmonize the competing theories about the criterion of virtue. In his survey of candidates for the criterion of virtue, Gay noticed acting agreeably to nature; acting agreeably to reason; conformity to the fitness of things; conformity with truth; promoting the common good; and conformity to the will of God. In opposition to the claim that a criterion of virtue can be stated, Gay noticed the protagonists of the moral sense who claim that our judgments of virtue and vice are but the instinctive determinations of a moral sense. Gay set himself the task of showing that all of the above-mentioned criteria of virtue are compatible and not inconsistent with our having a moral sense.

Gay insisted upon the difference between a definition and a criterion, claiming that one must know what a thing is before one can measure it. Therefore, he first defined virtue as conformity to a rule of life. He expanded on the concept of "rule of life" by saying that it is a rule directing the actions of all rational creatures with respect to each other's happiness and that the rule must be understood to be obligatory for everyone in all cases.

Gay next turned to the question, What is it that can oblige everyone in all cases to follow a rule of life? He argued that a full and complete obligation can only arise from the authority of God, because only God can in all cases make a man happy or miserable. Gay then said that the criterion of virtue is the will of God. But what rule of life does God will that we follow? Attending to God's nature, we find him supremely happy. From God's goodness we infer that he has designed men to be happy and that he has willed the means to human happiness. Therefore, a person should always behave so as to be a means to the happiness of mankind. Arguing from the will of God, Gay thus arrived at a criterion of virtue once removed.

The above account covers what might be called the first part of Gay's system. In it he found the clues for harmonizing the several criteria of virtue he had collected from earlier writers. He found conformity to the will of God to be the fundamental criterion of virtue, but the other criteria are necessary to explicate this one. Thus the criterion of the will of God with respect to virtue is whatever promotes the happiness of mankind or the common good. Gay defined things which are fitting and agreeable to nature as those things or actions which may be used to bring about the happiness of mankind. He complained about earlier writers who left the phrases "fitness of things" or "agreeableness to nature" empty of meaning by not seeing that they must be used in relation to some end, namely, the happiness of mankind.

To account for agreeableness to reason as a criterion of virtue, Gay included under his notion of reason not only reason—that is, the foreseeing of the inconveniences of certain things and actions by contemplating their natures—but also experience, or the perceiving of these inconveniences when they happen. Reason in this extended sense is the criterion of the fitness and unfitness of things and actions, as they contribute to human happiness. Gay added that when reason conforms to things as they really are, we say that we have the "reason" of things, or the "truth" of things. Thus, he fit in conformity with truth as yet another criterion of virtue. But while he succeeded in fitting all these criteria into an account of virtue, he also warned that some are more remote criteria than others.

Gay brought the moral sense into his account of virtue by denying that it is innate, or that it operates instinctively. Men must acquire the moral sense, notably by learning to be pleased by those actions which promote human happiness and to be displeased by those which do the contrary. Gay allowed that once it is learned, the operation of the moral sense may be habitual. He also allowed that much of mankind may learn what virtue is by example and observation, without being able to reason out their judgments.

Gay also explained why a person may be virtuous. Curiously enough, he made little of man's obligation to obey the will of God. Rather he appealed to the universality of man's inclination to seek pleasure and to avoid pain; and he equated a person's happiness with his being pleased. There are two motives, then, for virtuous behavior. First, when I see that my own happiness depends on the happiness of others, I will seek to promote their happiness in the hope that they will in turn promote mine. Second, since esteem and merit are associated with virtue, I may behave virtuously in order to enjoy the pleasure of being esteemed. Similarly, I will esteem those who promote my happiness, in order to encourage them.

Bibliography

The "Dissertation" is reprinted in *British Moralists*, Vol. 2, L. A. Selby-Bigge, ed. (Oxford, 1897). Gay also wrote a preface to Edmund Law's *Enquiry into the Idea of Space, Time, Etc.* (London, 1734). For critical discussion, see Ernest Albee, *A History of English Utilitarianism* (New York, 1902).

ELMER SPRAGUE

GEHLEN, ARNOLD, German social psychologist, was born in 1904 in Leipzig. In 1934 he succeeded his teacher, Hans Driesch, as professor of philosophy at the University of Leipzig. He went to Königsberg in 1938 and from 1940 to 1944 was at the University of Vienna. In 1948 he became professor of sociology and psychology at the Hochschule für Verwaltungswissenschaften at Speyer. Since 1962 he has been at the Technische Hochschule in Aachen.

Gehlen, a leading representative of the movement known as philosophical anthropology, seeks to reinterpret the concepts of mind and intelligence in biological and sociological terms. His eclectic thought has partial affinities with the pragmatism of G. H. Mead and F. C. S. Schiller, with the integrationalism of Rudolf von Ihering, Maurice Hauriou, and Carl Schmitt, and with the cultural criticism of Oswald Spengler, Hans Freyer, and Martin Heidegger. At the same time, he rejects ontology and metaphysics. He rejects the traditional dualisms of soul and body, mind and matter, theory and practice. He emphasizes the predominant role of collective, or institutional, values as against those of individuals. He discards rationalism and regards present-day civilization as one of late-period decline.

Method and task of philosophy. Gehlen rejects the experimental methods of the natural sciences as leading to materialism and rejects the "understanding" approach of the advocates of the *Geisteswissenschaften*, because it employs contemporary intellectual standards in the analysis of heterogeneous situations. The method of philosophy, Gehlen claims, is the intuitive or phenomenological method that he himself uses to interpret the significance of sociocultural institutions. According to Gehlen the task of philosophy differs from that of science. Disregarding the factual inferences of the sciences as irrelevant, philosophers should "unravel" (*freilegen*) the realities that are their proper concern. These realities, or "categories," are the basic qualities of man and of institutions that remain intact after the fullest cultural, social, and historical analyses. Gehlen conceives of such a study of reality as empirical and thus envisages no complete system of categories.

Man's nature and power. Gehlen defines man as an "acting, anticipatory, nondetermined, self-delimiting being—a product of culture." Like other philosophical anthropologists, Gehlen views man, compared with other animals, as a vulnerable, deficient being, lacking the powerful instincts and natural weapons of survival of other animals. Man's fabled power of thought is an artificial substitute for his weak instincts. He is reduced to dependence on technical means for his survival. For survival and to liberate himself from anxiety he has had to develop tools and techniques including language, myth, and magic, and has had to create a common, habitual, and stable cultural environment.

This cultural environment is perpetuated in institutions, the historically evolved realities of state, family, law, economy, and so forth. To be "legitimate" an institution need not be useful but must be derived from man's nature as expressed in the cultic, nonutilitarian experiences of ecstasy, trance, and asceticism. Institutions are comprehensive and abstract structures that, through their principle of order, impart autonomy to the individuals participating in the collective *entente secrète*. The utility of social and cultural institutions is a secondary by-product of their development. Gehlen contrasts unreflective, spontaneous, self-sacrificing action, which he describes as noble (*vornehm und edel*), with self-interested and utilitarian action (including its sublimated forms in art, philosophy, and literature), which he designates as base (*gemein*).

Theory of truth. Like certain pragmatists, Gehlen stresses action as the determinant of valid thought. While defining truth in terms of inner coherence and correspondence with facts, Gehlen also distinguishes another aspect of truth, which he calls "inner truth." "Essentially irrational, non-scientific and not directly controllable experience has *its* truth: that is certainty. And it has *its* form of acting: non-experimental action based on tradition, instinct, habit and conviction" (*Der Mensch*, p. 330). These illogical, ethical certainties are valid without rational or experimental justification—as a matter of mere "appositeness" or inner sanity. Rational knowledge (*Wissenschaft*) cannot take over the function of the *idées directrices* of society that are the product of *Urphantasie*, the divinity and energy of the animal component of man.

Pessimism. Gehlen's analysis of the present age is unrelievedly somber. Our times, according to Gehlen, are marked both by the dissolution of institutions and a shift in individual and social consciousness from irrational certainty to an anarchic intellectualization. This change takes place against a historical background in which organic agrarian society is giving way to organized industrial society. The cultural rupture transforms social organisms into "colonies of parasites" riddled with subjectivism, mechanization, a turn toward abstract and mathematical methods in art and science (desensualization), and experimental thinking. Rising living standards, far from representing progress, create new urges for limitless satisfactions. Such changes lead away from ethical obligation deriving from man's nature to goal-directed efficiency deriving from man's method. These changes entail making the spiritual sphere political and robbing the political sphere of its religious aura. Since science is esoteric, the mass of the people are condemned to be primitive. The eclipse of the nation-state and the trend toward supranational organization and peace will leave a legacy of unresolved conflicts that may lead to a complete loss of individual freedom. Only two very unlikely circumstances could reverse the trend: an unexpected return to legitimate, nonrational values that are not amenable to conscious volition or the rise of a creative personality to provide a new kind of institutional leadership.

According to Gehlen, the philosopher's task in such a world situation is to point to signs of decline and to emphasize the "legitimate" elements in national heritages as expressed in the institutions of state, church, and law. Although present-day society is increasingly alienated from these heritages, they alone represent society's legitimate "reality." Reality has therefore to be sought in the archaic forms of the past.

Works by Gehlen

Theorie der Willensfreiheit. Berlin, 1933.
Der Staat und die Philosophie. Leipzig, 1935.
Der Mensch, seine Natur und Stellung in der Welt. Leipzig, 1940; 6th ed., Bonn, 1958.
Urmensch und Spätkultur. Bonn, 1956.
Die Seele im technischen Zeitalter. Hamburg, 1957.
Anthropologische Forschung. Hamburg, 1961. A collection of articles. Bibliography, pp. 144–145.
Zeitschrift für philosophische Forschung, Vol. 6 (1951/1952), 589–593. A bibliography.

Works on Gehlen

Ballauf, Theodor, Review of *Der Mensch. Zeitschrift für philosophische Forschung*, Vol. 6 (1951/1952), 566–589.
Haering, Theodor, "Zu Gehlens Anthropologie." *Zeitschrift für philosophische Forschung*, Vol. 6 (1951/1952), 593–598.
Mahn, Anneliese, "Über die philosophische Anthropologie von Arnold Gehlen." *Zeitschrift für philosophische Forschung*, Vol. 6 (1951/1952), 71–93.

H. O. PAPPÉ

GEISTESWISSENSCHAFTEN. The term *Geisteswissenschaften* was coined in Germany in the middle of the nineteenth century to translate John Stuart Mill's phrase "the moral sciences." The English phrase is rarely used now, and a modern equivalent is not easy to find. The range of disciplines covered by the term is, however, quite clear; it includes history, philology, economics, sociology, social anthropology, comparative jurisprudence, comparative religion, and, at least in part, psychology. More recently established subjects such as criminology, semantics, and communication theory can be classed with these. This list is wider than that covered by such terms as "the humanities" or "the social sciences"; therefore the translation "the human studies" is gaining ground, although it is by no means universally accepted. Terminology apart, the grouping is not particularly startling—subjects are grouped in a similar way in English and American universities.

The German tradition. The German term *Geisteswissenschaften* is rooted in a particular tradition of thought and carries philosophical and methodological implications that raise substantial issues. *Wissenschaft* (*scientia*, science) covers every kind of disciplined research that aims at knowledge; it is subdivided into two branches, *Geisteswissenschaften* and *Naturwissenschaften* (the physical sciences, or simply the sciences). The human studies are therefore thought of as sciences; and the notion that they are not sciences and can only become scientific by modeling themselves on the physical sciences is not suggested by the German name as it is by the English.

Geist. It is difficult to translate the term *Geist* and impossible to indicate succinctly in English relationships between words that are obvious in German. A tradition of spirituality, inwardness, and cultural refinement—in contrast to the more pragmatic and down-to-earth approach of the English-speaking world—is reflected in the German idiomatic usages. They identify the spiritual with the intellectual and cultural, and no translation can render this complex meaning. *Der Heilige Geist* is translated as "the Holy Ghost"; *der Geist der Zeit* as "the spirit of the age"; *Geistesgeschichte* as "the history of ideas", "*geistreich*" means "witty in a refined sort of way." In some contexts *Geist* means "mind," but *die geistige Welt* cannot be translated as "the world of mind" because the English phrase is used to refer to the psychological processes within individuals, their fantasies, their fears; the German is more aptly translated as "the cultural world." The *Geisteswissenschaften* are, as was suggested above, best described as the human studies. To call them the studies of the mind would seem absurd; even calling them the cultural studies would be a little odd, since they include such disciplines as economics. The transparent connection between the *Geisteswissenschaften* and the *geistige Welt* that is the product of the operation of *Geist* cannot be shown in English.

The notion of *Geist* acquired additional meaning as a key term in the works of Hegel and other idealist philosophers, who treated the realm of *Geist* not only as an autonomous sphere but as fundamental reality. The supporters of *Geisteswissenschaften* were influenced by this tradition; but Wilhelm Dilthey, who introduced the term, and his disciples transformed the concept of *Geist* from a metaphysical to an empirical concept employed in classifying certain data and serving other methodological needs.

According to this view the phenomena of *Geist*, comprising such entities as languages, games, poems, religions, and institutions, constitute one class of objects of knowledge, the other two being physical objects and mental processes. A poem, a pen, and a pain are different types of things, each belonging to one of the three classes; they do not exist side by side like three chairs in a room. Each of the classes of phenomena presents itself in a different way, and they are complexly related to each other. When I see a table I perceive a physical object, but my seeing is a mental process; at the same time the concept "table" by which I classify what I see belongs to the sphere of *Geist*.

The ontological and epistemological status of these spheres is a matter of metaphysics, and different philosophers have interpreted it differently. Here we are concerned only with the methodological value of the distinction. We want to say, for example, that a particular poem is a good illustration of the Elizabethan sonnet, that it is popular, or that it has influenced Smith. Clearly there are physical manifestations—marks on paper or sounds in the air—by means of which the poem is conveyed; and clearly the poem has been created by a particular mental process and mental processes are involved in its appreciation. Without these physical manifestations and mental events there would be no poem. Yet, to speak of the sonnet in terms of these physical and mental entities would, if it were possible at all, be infinitely tedious. It is, therefore, methodologically convenient to refer to it as an independent entity, an objectification of mind (*Objektivation des Geistes*) that forms part of the sphere of objective mind (*der objektive Geist*). The nearest English equivalent to the term "objective mind" is "culture" as used in modern cultural anthropology.

The products of human activity are the objectifications of *Geist;* the human consciousness that creates the products is *Geist* itself. We speak of *Geist,* and not merely of mental processes, because the thoughts of individuals are embedded in and dependent on a superindividual sphere of language, logic, and tradition. Cats and dogs share with man the possession of mental processes; but they do not have *Geist* because they do not think and act in terms of general ideas. The presence of *Geist*—the capacity to use symbols to create language, and to communicate—makes tradition, history, religion, law, and art possible and is the characteristic and pervasive feature of all human life. Therefore the *Geisteswissenschaften*, which deal with the manifestations of *Geist*, have the life of mankind as their common subject matter.

The human world consists of innumerable individuals who have entered upon various relations to each other and formed different groups and associations, and also of the products of their activity. Because this world is permeated by thought, illuminated by interpretations and valuations, and organized in terms of purposes, it is meaningful. To grasp systematically the various meanings embodied in it is the specific task of the human studies.

This definition of the nature and task of the human studies cuts across some traditional subject boundaries. Insofar as psychology explains human behavior in terms of valuations, social goals, and the use of language, it is a human study; but insofar as it deals purely with physiologically based processes it is a physical science.

DILTHEY'S THEORY

Rickert and Dilthey. The chief architect of the theory that the *Geisteswissenschaften* can be significantly distinguished from the physical sciences was Wilhelm Dilthey. His theory was further elaborated and systematized by his disciples Erich Rothacker, Eduard Spranger, and Theodor Litt. The classification of disciplines attempted by Heinrich Rickert, who systematically developed suggestions made by Wilhelm Windelband; also made significant contributions to the clarification of the subject. Rickert's approach was based on different theoretical assumptions and appeared to result in a rival theory, but even though differences of emphasis and terminology remain, the final conclusions of Rickert and Dilthey converge.

Rickert insisted that method, not subject, should be the basis of a significant classification of disciplines. Therefore, he distinguished the monothetic (or generalizing) from the ideographic (or individualizing) sciences. The monothetic sciences are the systematic sciences that aim at the establishment of general laws; the ideographic sciences—the historical studies—are concerned with the discovery and exploration of individual facts. This distinction cuts across that between physical and human disciplines (astronomers may deal with the history of the solar system; psychologists may aim at generalizations). However, Rickert argued that the study of individual sequences in the physical sciences ultimately subserves the establishment of general laws and that therefore these sciences are by and large monothetic, whereas human studies are largely ideographic because the understanding of individual phenomena remains one of their intrinsic goals. According to Rickert, facts are selected for study in the ideographic sciences in terms of their relevance to cultural values and in the monothetic sciences in terms of their relevance to the laws to be established. Not everything that happens is a historical fact—only what affects an existing value structure. For example, in a society that considers Christianity of supreme importance a damaging attack on that religion would constitute a relevant fact.

Rickert supplemented his classification by method with classification by subject matter and so distinguished the physical sciences from the *Kulturwissenschaften*, or cultural sciences. He chose the term *Kulturwissenschaften* in preference to *Geisteswissenschaften* because he believed that the latter misleadingly suggested a concern with psychological processes. Dilthey's use of *Geisteswissenschaften* in his earlier writings is open to this interpretation, but in his mature works *Geisteswissenschaften* means precisely what Rickert, and Ernst Cassirer after him, called *Kulturwissenschaften*.

Dilthey arrived at his position by a route different from

Rickert's. Dilthey considered a classification of disciplines by subject matter more fundamental than one by methods. The common subject matter of the physical sciences is the physical world; the subject matter of the *Geisteswissenschaften* is the human world pervaded by *Geist*—by thoughts, valuations, and purposes objectified in languages, beliefs, and institutions. The disciplines dealing with man are meaningfully related to each other, and even when they can be differentiated into the historical and the systematic, as they were by Rickert, they supplement each other. (For example, economic history provides the empirical evidence for economics, and economics provides the laws by means of which the connection between individual events can be grasped.) Dilthey, therefore, considered it more appropriate to use Rickert's classification to subdivide the two main classes, the *Geisteswissenschaften* and the *Naturwissenschaften*.

Understanding through expressions. Dilthey, like Rickert, believed in a profound methodological difference between the *Geisteswissenschaften* and the physical sciences. What distinguished his position from Rickert's was his conviction that this difference is imposed on the *Geisteswissenschaften* by the nature of their subject matter. The manifestations of *Geist* can only be grasped by a distinctive cognitive process which Dilthey called "understanding" (*Das Verstehen*). This concept came to play a crucial part in the work of Dilthey's disciples and in that of eminent practitioners of the *Geisteswissenschaften* who cannot be described as disciples, such as Max Weber. It is, therefore, important to consider Dilthey's comprehensive and systematic account of his theory of understanding.

Understanding is a perfectly familiar process. We understand a letter or a traffic signal and, through them, either what a person is thinking or the traffic rule that is to govern our behavior at a particular road junction. There seems to be nothing very difficult here, nothing mystical; no flash of intuition is involved. We are merely confronted with one type of cognitive process that has some distinctive features.

All understanding is based on the observation of a special class of physical manifestations that Dilthey called *Ausdruck* ("expression"). Dilthey also used *Erlebnisausdruck* and, as a wider term, *Lebensäusserung* (the finer distinctions between these terms cannot be easily reproduced in English). Expressions can be defined as objects or events that, apart from possessing physical characteristics, express or refer to some mental content. Expressions as a class (and Dilthey painstakingly subdivided them) embrace facial expressions, gestures, words, works of art, actions, and the products of deliberate actions, such as factories or universities. (Obviously a university is not only an expression, in the sense in which thumbing one's nose is; but it is an expression insofar as social and cultural purposes are expressed in its make-up.) Used in this sense, expressions represent the whole range of the empirically given subject matter of the *Geisteswissenschaften* and can serve to define these studies.

Certain other conditions have also to be fulfilled if understanding of expressions is to take place. We must be familiar with what it is to have an intention, to be in pain, to feel, to think, and so on (as in fact we are, because we share a common human nature). Without this familiarity there could be no communication and no language would be meaningful to us. Before we can even know that something is a word we must first recognize the intention to convey some meaning that lies behind the word. We must also know the rules and conventions that govern the use of many—though not, perhaps, all—expressions. The context in which an expression stands is also relevant. The meaning of a word is determined or colored by the sentence in which it occurs; that of an action, by the situation to which it is a response. The extent of understanding depends upon how well these conditions are fulfilled. The more familiar we are with the basic features of human consciousness and the better we know the context and the cultural background of rules and conventions, the more complete our understanding can be.

There are, obviously, different forms of understanding; to understand a person is not the same as to understand a code of law. The approach will vary with the nature of the expressions given. Other methods of thought and research will inevitably be involved, although these cannot be easily disentangled from the process of understanding. An investigation may start with the eliciting, collecting, and classifying of responses, say to a questionnaire. This corresponds to procedures in the physical sciences; however, this empirical material is not something merely perceived, like shapes under a microscope, but consists of answers that have to be understood. The further process of investigation, such as the framing of hypotheses, aims to deepen that original understanding.

In conformity with this theory of understanding, the *Geisteswissenschaften* treat the human world in terms of meaningful entities (expressions) such as actions, valuations, beliefs, and traditions, and this treatment represents a coherent and distinctive conception of the nature and tasks of the human studies.

Positivist criticisms. Influential though Dilthey's theory of understanding has proved, it is far from uncontroversial. There is a rival theory, usually described as positivism, which denies that the distinction between the human studies and the physical sciences is more fundamental than that between any two scientific disciplines, such as physics and biology. Positivists believe that instead of insisting on the uniqueness of the human studies we should concentrate on those features of man that can be treated by the methods so spectacularly successful in the physical sciences. Only by adopting a behavioristic or near-behavioristic approach, by eliminating subjectivity, by controlled observation, and by achieving precision through quantification can the human studies become scientific and take their place in a unified edifice of science. These beliefs deserve respect, although there is at present some justification for the suspicion that the choice of problems suitable for such treatment leads to the neglect of complex and important issues and that a behavioristic approach denies itself a valuable source of knowledge by rejecting introspection. There may be room for both the positivistic approach and the "understanding" approach; ultimately each has to justify itself pragmatically by the light it can throw on human affairs. Without deciding between these two approaches, we can clear up some of the misunderstandings that have colored the attacks made by positivists on the theory of understanding. This may also serve to clarify some aspects of the theory.

Richard von Mises (in *Positivism*) and G. A. Lundberg (in *Foundations of Sociology*), for example, have argued that understanding is not a distinctive method but the common goal of all methods. They have failed to appreciate that understanding is used by Dilthey and his school as a technical term referring to a special type of comprehension, namely that of the content of expressions. It seems perfectly plausible to distinguish the process of understanding a poem—grasping the thoughts or feelings expressed in it—from that of comprehending the relation between physical things—say the effect of water on sugar.

The trouble taken by Ernest Nagel (in *The Structure of Science*), von Mises (in *Positivism*), and Carl G. Hempel (in "The Function of General Laws in History") to demonstrate that the human studies use the same procedures as the physical sciences also resulted from a misunderstanding. Their arguments appear to be marshaled as an attack on the theory of understanding. Yet when Dilthey insisted that understanding was an indispensable method in the human studies he did not imply that it was the only method or that it took the place of classification, generalization, the forming and testing of hypotheses, and other methods of the physical sciences.

Even when the distinctive role of understanding is acknowledged it is often treated as something mysterious, a knack of having hunches, or a form of intuition. Lundberg spoke of it as a "mysterious method," Hempel conceded that it might serve as a "heuristic device." Even writers opposed to positivism have found it obscure. Talcott Parsons, in *The Structure of Social Action*, called it "this somewhat difficult concept" (p. 484) and H. Stuart Hughes described it as "the most difficult intellectual problem" (*Consciousness and Society*, p. 187). This reaction is probably produced by the literature on the subject (vast and only partly translated) rather than by the concept itself. Attention to obvious examples of understanding—understanding a poem, or why a person is sad—should dispel much of this air of mystery.

EXPONENTS OF THE GEISTESWISSENSCHAFTEN

The division of the realm of knowledge into the physical sciences and the *Geisteswissenschaften* is not merely a matter of classification. Acceptance commits us to a way of looking at the human world and to the use of certain methods of investigation. Some of the philosophers who forged the concept or helped to clarify it applied their point of view to actual research in the *Geisteswissenschaften*. Dilthey engaged in extensive biographical and historical research and Cassirer explored such subjects as myth, language, magic, and the evolution of religions. Max Scheler, though first and foremost a philosopher, contributed to the development of the sociology of knowledge.

Werner Sombart, Max Weber, Ferdinand Tönnies, Ernst Troeltsch, Eduard Spranger, and others have applied the method of understanding to economics, sociology, anthropology, and psychology. The influence of their work on contemporary research is so extensive that an account of it would amount to a survey of modern social science. Even among thinkers who are not direct or indirect disciples, the challenge of these ideas has produced modifications in theory and method.

A brief reference to the influential work of Max Weber may highlight the way in which a philosophic theory can prompt the development of methodological tools. Weber's assumption that social actions were the ultimate units of analysis for the sociologist and his definition of action as "that type of human conduct . . . to which a meaning is assigned by the acting person or persons" (in his *Wissenschaftslehre*) are characteristic of an approach that stands in sharp contrast to behaviorism. He concluded that the "patternings and regularities of human conduct differ from all other patterns in one important respect; they alone may be "understandingly" interpreted. To promote this understanding he used the concept of "ideal types." These are theoretical constructions of rationally coherent patterns of ideas or actions in which the connections between the elements are understandable. Actual bodies of beliefs (often inconsistent and confused) an empirically given human behavior (often irrational) can then be understood by considering how they diverge from these ideal patterns.

By this method he analyzed systems of religious ideas that provided an intelligible purpose for action (in *The Protestant Ethic and the Spirit of Capitalism*, for example). His concept of rationally purposive (*zweckrational*) conduct is also an ideal type. He defined it as "completely centered upon means *subjectively* viewed as adequate for the attainment of ends *subjectively* conceived to be unambiguous" (*Wissenschaftslehre*).

The extensive and fruitful influence of Weber's methods on modern sociology underlines the continuing importance of the philosophic theories behind the concept of the *Geisteswissenschaften*.

Bibliography

BASIC THEORY

Cassirer, Ernst, *Naturalistische und humanistische Begründung der Kulturphilosophie*. Göteborg, 1939.

Cassirer, Ernst, *Zur Logik der Kulturwissenschaften*. Göteborg, 1942.

Cassirer, Ernst, *An Essay on Man: An Introduction to a Philosophy of Human Culture*. New Haven, 1945.

Dilthey, Wilhelm, *Gesammelte Schriften*. Vol. 7, *Der Aufbau der geistigen Welt in der Geisteswissenschaften*. Leipzig and Berlin, 1927. Selected passages in translation in H. P. Rickman, *Meaning in History* (London, 1961; New York, 1962).

Rickert, Heinrich, *Die Grenzen der Naturwissenschaftlichen Begriffsbildung*. Freiburg, 1896–1902.

Rickert, Heinrich, *Kulturwissenschaft und Naturwissenschaft*. Freiburg, 1899.

Rothacker, Erich, *Logik und Systematik der Geisteswissenschaften*. Munich, 1927.

Znaniecki, Florian, *Cultural Sciences*. Urbana, Ill., 1963.

HISTORICAL AND SYSTEMATIC ACCOUNTS

Hayek, F. A., *The Counter-Revolution of Science: Studies in the Abuse of Reason*. Glencoe, Ill., 1952.

Hughes, H. Stuart, *Consciousness and Society: The Reorientation of European Social Thought*. New York, 1958.

POSITIVISTIC CRITIQUES

Hempel, Carl G., "The Function of General Laws in History." *Journal of Philosophy*, Vol. 39 (1942), 35–48. Reprinted in Patrick Gardiner, ed., *Theories of History* (New York, 1959), pp. 344–356.

Lundberg, G. A., *Foundations of Sociology*. New York, 1939.

Mises, Richard von, *Kleines Lehrbuch des Positivismus*. The Hague, 1939. Translated by Jerry Bernstein and R. G. Newton, with the help of the author, as *Positivism: A Study in Human Understanding* (Cambridge, Mass., 1951).

Nagel, Ernest, *The Structure of Science*. New York, 1961.

THE GEISTESWISSENSCHAFTEN APPROACH

Litt, Theodor, *Individuum und Gemeinschaft*. Leipzig, 1919.

Scheler, Max, *Die Wissensformen und die Gesellschaft*. Leipzig, 1926.

Sombart, Werner, *Die drei Nationalökonomien*. Munich and Leipzig, 1930.

Sombart, Werner, *Vom Menschen: Versuch einer Geisteswissenschaftlichen Anthropologie*. Berlin, 1938.

Spranger, Eduard, *Lebensformen: Geisteswissenschaftliche Psychologie und Ethik der Persönlichkeit*. Halle, 1914.

Tönnies, Ferdinand, *Gemeinschaft und Gesellschaft*. Leipzig, 1887. English translation by C. P. Loomis as *Community and Association* (London, 1955).

Troeltsch, Ernst, *Die Sociallehre der christlichen Kirchen und Gruppen*. Tübingen, 1912. Translated by Olive Wyon as *The Social Teaching of the Christian Churches*, 2 vols. (London and New York, 1931).

Weber, Max, *Gesammelte Aufsätze zur Wissenschaftslehre*. Tübingen, 1922. Three essays translated by Edward Shils and H. A. Finch as *Max Weber on the Methodology of the Social Sciences* (Glencoe, Ill., 1949).

Weber, Max, *Wirtschaft und Gesellschaft*, 2 vols. Tübingen, 1922. First part translated by A. M. Henderson and Talcott Parsons as *The Theory of Social and Economic Organization* (London, 1947; New York, 1957).

H. P. RICKMAN

GENERAL WILL, THE.

The general will is the name given to a set of related concepts in political philosophy which have as their model the attribution to the collectivity of a faculty of willing, corresponding to the will in the individual. This way of thinking makes it appropriate to discuss the possibility of a real personality in a society or a state, something which does the willing. It suggests a distinction not only between the general and the individual will but also between the general (collective, unitary) will and the united wills (pooled individual wills) of sets of persons within the collectivity, often called the "will of all." It has prompted some writers to claim that the general will, which is general not only in its origins but also in its ends, is the "real will," and that of individuals or groups of individuals only an "apparent will." It presents the problem of political and social obedience as a choice between the requirements of the general will, which is by definition directed toward social and ethical ends, and the individual will, which need not be so directed.

History. The simple model of a will belonging to the collectivity has understandable attractions for the understanding of political institutions as well as for the analysis of political ethics. From the time of Jean-Jacques Rousseau and his treatise *Du Contrat social* (1762), the classic formulation of the general will, until the decline of the idealist philosophical tradition in the early twentieth century, the general will occupied an important and sometimes a predominating position in discussions of the individual, the state, and society. The democratic process, which was developing and spreading from nation to nation all this time, was looked upon as the search for the expression of the general will through the electoral machinery and through the other devices which instituted and maintained government by consent. The argument usually proceeded as if it could and must be shown that in obeying the collectivity, a man was obeying himself—himself under another identity.

The general will was used to attack despotic and irresponsible rule by compelling it to submit to radical questioning of its basis and objectives. Nevertheless, the theorists of the general will were critical of individualism, and the whole idealist philosophical position was hostile to the notion of the collectivity as the result of a specified and limited agreement between independent persons such as was presumed by those who had developed the idea of the social contract (see SOCIAL CONTRACT). Some idealists went so far as to claim that the individual himself, as well as the individual will, was apparent rather than real. "All sound theory and good practice are founded on the faith that the common self or moral person of society is more real than the apparent individual," wrote Bernard Bosanquet in 1899. It was found in practice that the general will arguments about consent and responsibility needed neither representation, nor constitutionalism of any kind, nor even the rule of the people in any factual sense. Once the general will could be shown to be embodied in the rule of a traditional monarchy or of a particular elite or party, even in the rule of a dictator of the kind so lamentably common in the twentieth century, the moral issue of obedience and the right of resistance seemed to have been disposed of.

For this and other reasons the concepts associated with the general will have come to occupy a curious position in contemporary political thinking. Idealism, as expounded by Rousseau, by Hegel, by Kant, and by such English thinkers as T. H. Green and Bosanquet, has ceased to be persuasive, and the general will has come to be regarded as embodying the implications of idealism for political life, very unfortunate implications indeed, since they have occasionally ended in fascism and other forms of totalitarianism. On the other hand, political scientists go on trying to develop methods which will make governments as responsive as possible to the expressed will of the people. In fact, the new and flourishing study of political and electoral sociology (psephology in England) makes notable use of the general will concept. "Voting," it is said, "is not a device whereby each individual expresses his personal interest, but rather whereby each individual gives his opinion of the general will."

At the same time, the theory of games has begun to be applied to these problems. Mathematical studies have vindicated the possibility of unanimity concerning social ends, if only under very narrow and specific conditions, and the drive to act upon this unanimity has been called the general will. It has been shown that the distinction between the general will and the will of all does correspond to an objective possibility in political life. Rousseau's notorious claim that in being required to pursue the general will, men are only being "forced to be free" can be given a plausible meaning; a game has even been devised which justifies his prohibition of political parties as contrary to the general will. It is interesting to see that these studies combine the contractual model with the model of the general will.

Analysis. In view of the revival of the concept of the general will, it is important that the concept be separated as far as possible from its unfortunate historical associations and from the misleading implications of the word "will" and the language of will. Recent philosophers are disposed to dispense altogether with the will as a faculty of the personality and with the view that a decision is an act of obedience to that faculty (see especially the work of Gilbert Ryle). Moreover, the general will is understandably regarded as representative of metaphysics and metaphysical argument in political theory, which makes its status equivocal to many contemporary philosophers, especially the logical analysts. At least some of these difficulties can be cleared up by drawing certain distinctions.

First, the general will can be either literal or hypothetical, either descriptive or normative. If it is literal, if a society or a state really has a will of its own, then it is important to understand the nature and functions of that will, and it even makes sense to look for a body which does the willing, a real personality in the state or in society. Norms, rights, and duties may also be derived from such a literally existent general will, although it does not necessarily follow that there is no other source of norms. If, on the other hand, the general will is hypothetical only, if it is a decision on the part of the theorist to discuss state and society *as if* some general will existed, then no willing body comes into question; and the disadvantages of the language of will may also be circumvented. The metaphor may be adopted both because it has descriptive advantages and because it seems to be the proper way of approaching the problems of obedience, rights, and duties, but the one reason does not entail the other. Social scientists and political theorists seem often to overlook these distinctions. They argue as if the existence of a literal or hypothetical consensus, and hence of a will, in a political body must imply a particular system of allegiance and duty or as if the usefulness of the metaphor of will in the discussion of ethics must imply the existence of a willing body. Some even talk as if the absence of proof of a literal will disposed of its metaphorical possibilities.

Second, the general will need not, in any of its senses, be thought of as absolute or total—as based, for example, on a consensus which covers all the issues a state or society may be faced with or as providing the one and only correct way of analyzing every possible problem of political obligation.

These distinctions and limitations nevertheless cannot be said to overcome the objections to the general will as a "metaphysical" entity. Its function in political analysis has been, and is, to relate long-term, fully informed decisions and policies framed for the benefit of every affected individual with short-term, often ignorant decisions made by individuals or groups for their own benefit. Therefore, the concept can belong only to a world of the kind Kant de-

scribed as a "kingdom of ends." We must not be surprised to find, then, that the objectives demonstrated by the welfare economist as beneficial to everyone in short term and with restricted information may seem to, or in fact do, damage the interests of certain individuals (talking in Kantian terms). In his view such a kingdom, where everyone treats everyone as an end in himself, is to be called "in our terminology a society with a satisfactory social welfare function" (K. J. Arrow).

Rousseau made none of these distinctions and imposed no limitations on the general will; to him it was total and absolute. He assumed that there was an objective consensus, covering every conceivable decision, to be found in a properly constituted political society and that this was what made it a state. For that reason it seemed to Rousseau impossible that any large-scale state could be rightfully constituted. It has been urged against him and against all subsequent exponents of the absolute general will that the doctrine can have only a tangential relevance to the life of the nation-state proper because, like so many of the concepts used to discuss it, the general will depends on face to face relationships (see Laslett's essay). Nevertheless, Rousseau went on to insist that only when the general will was embodied in the collectivity could citizens live in accordance with their consciences and recognize that in obeying the state, they were not restricting but enlarging their freedom. His champions in our own day have repeatedly claimed that his general will can be arrived at only after the most exhaustive discussion and criticism and cannot be called totalitarian.

Reinterpretations. It is perhaps doubtful that Rousseau was the first to clothe the consistent aims and policy of constituted states with these characteristics, since the model of willing was not uncommonly used in the vast literature which thinkers in the natural-law tradition consecrated to the discussion of political association. In the contractual system of the most rigorous of them, Thomas Hobbes, the will of the sovereign, "or to speak more reverently, of that mortal god," seems sometimes to approach what Rousseau might have expected of his institutionalized general will.

Rousseau's successors were, on the other hand, entirely unable to accept any sort of contractual model for political analysis; historians of thought look upon the general will as appearing in Kant as the categorical imperative and in Hegel as the progressive emanation of that reason in which the individual will is universalized by the state. Neither of these entities could conceivably have appeared out of mere agreement between individuals.

The successive reinterpretations of the general will in the direction of representative government by subsequent thinkers, especially by the English idealists, have to a large extent lost their interest for the contemporary political thinker. T. H. Green looked upon natural rights as a delusion and upon the law as "the expression of general will in favour of the rules which maintain rights," but he did not believe in the sovereignty of the general will in the sense of a coercive force. Bosanquet's extremist exposition of general will principles, with its strange claims about reality and unreality, was discredited before twentieth-century totalitarianism ever became formidable (see the book by Hobhouse). Nevertheless, various recensions of general will principles of a modified absolutist character survived into the middle decades of the twentieth century, and the works of Mary Parker Follett, A. D. Lindsay, and Ernest Barker represent the progressive refinement of the older views so as to accommodate and safeguard the principles and machinery of representative government. It was the political experience of the 1940s, together with the effects of logical atomism and analytic philosophy on the idealist tradition, which joined forces with political sociology to give rise to the position summarily described above.

Bibliography

The classical study of general will theory in its historical context is C. E. Vaughan, *Studies in the History of Political Philosophy, Before and After Rousseau* (Manchester, 1925, 1939). The same writer's *Political Works of Rousseau* (Manchester, 1915; Oxford, 1962) and T. H. Green's *Lectures on the Principles of Political Obligation* (London, 1895) are important texts, as is Bernard Bosanquet's *The Philosophical Theory of the State* (London, 1899; reprinted up to 1951). L. T. Hobhouse published his critique of general will theory as *The Metaphysical Theory of the State* (London, 1918; 5th impression, 1951); Mary Parker Follett published her *New State* (with an introduction by Bosanquet) in the same year. A. D. Lindsay propounded his general will theory in *The Modern Democratic State* (London, 1943) and Ernest Barker in *Principles of Social and Political Theory* (Oxford, 1951). For an analysis of the language of will see Gilbert Ryle, *The Concept of Mind* (London, 1949). K. J. Arrow, *Social Choice and Individual Value* (New York, 1951; 2d ed., 1963), is the important authority on the theory of games and the general will. See also the series *Philosophy, Politics and Society*, No. 1 (Oxford, 1957), edited by Peter Laslett (articles by Bernard Mayo and Laslett), and No. 2 (Oxford, 1962), edited by Laslett and W. G. Runciman (article by John Rawls).

The above analysis owes much to S. J. Benn and R. S. Peters, *Social Principles and the Democratic State* (London, 1959), and to W. G. Runciman and A. K. Sen, "Games, Justice and the General Will," in *Mind*, 1965.

PETER LASLETT

GENOVESI, ANTONIO (1713–1769), Italian philosopher and economist. Genovesi (the name was originally Genovese) was born in Castiglione, Salerno. After studying literature and rhetoric and then philosophy, he attended the lectures of the aged Giambattista Vico. In 1741 he began to teach metaphysics at the University of Naples as extraordinary professor. In 1743 he published the first volume of his *Elementa Metaphysicae Mathematicum in Modum Adornata* (5 vols., Naples, 1743–1745), for which he was accused of rationalism and atheism. In 1745 he began to teach ethics. In that year he published his *Elementa Artis Logico-criticae* and an important historical introduction to the Neapolitan edition of Pieter van Musschenbroek's *Elementa Physicae*. In the same year his *Universae Christianae Theologiae Elementa* was accused of heterodoxy; it was not published until after his death (Venice, 1771). Discouraged, Genovesi turned to other, less philosophical studies. He was offered the new chair of civil economy (economics), the first in Europe, by the University of Naples and began his lectures in 1754 (*Delle lezioni di commercio ossia di economia civile*, Naples,

1765–1767). The problems of practical philosophy which occupied his final years are discussed in *Diceosina o sia filosofia del giusto e dell'onesto* (2 vols., Naples, 1766–1777).

In Genovesi's judgment, modern philosophy began when Francis Bacon and Galileo freed Europe from abstract and sterile inquiry. "Dialectics and metaphysics," he proclaimed, "are the Don Quixote of the Republic of Letters." According to him, it is impossible to know true reality, substance, that which "underlies" the phenomena that we can observe. (He asked, "Who lifts the skirt of nature to see that which ὑπάρχει [underlies]?") Although his thought had some similarities to Berkeley's idealism and Leibniz' monadism, as time went on his interest turned from logic and metaphysics and was oriented toward the moral disciplines, particularly toward economics, which he considered as affecting "our present comfort and tranquility." He sought to determine in a rational system "the primary, simple, and universal laws" of economics. He arranged in a similar framework the *Discorso sopra il vero fine delle lettere e delle scienze* (Naples, 1753), in which he argued against all inquiries "that remain exclusively in the shadow of the school, and never transgress into the acquisition of something useful for mankind."

Works by Genovesi

Opere scelte. Milan, 1824.
Illuministi italiani, Vol. V, *Riformatori napoletani*, Franco Venturi, ed. Naples and Milan, 1962. Pp. 1–330. Contains an important introduction and bibliography on Genovesi's influence in Italy.
Autobiografia, lettere e altri scritti, Gennaro Savarese, ed. Milan, 1962.

Works on Genovesi

Gentile, Giovanni, *Storia della filosofia italiana*, Vol. I, *Dal Genovesi al Galluppi*, 2d ed. Milan, 1930. Pp. 1–23.
Garin, Eugenio, *La filosofia italiana*. Milan, 1947. Vol. II, pp. 392–402.
Villari, Lucio, *Il pensiero economico di Antonio Genovesi*. Florence, 1959. Contains an excellent bibliography.

EUGENIO GARIN

GENTILE, GIOVANNI, was one of the major figures in the resurgence of Hegelian idealism in Italy at the beginning of the twentieth century. His "actual idealism," or "actualism," represents the subjective extreme of the idealist tradition in that the present activity of reflective awareness (*l'atto del pensiero, pensiero pensante*) is regarded as the absolute foundation on which all else depends. The act of thinking is the "pure act" that creates the world of human experience.

Life and works. Gentile was born on May 30, 1875, at Castelvetrano in Sicily. He began his university education as a student of Italian literature under Alessandro d'Ancona at Pisa in 1893, but was quickly drawn into the study of philosophy by Donato Jaja, a pupil of the Neapolitan Hegelian, Bertrando Spaventa. Of the two main threads that run through all of Gentile's work, one—his concern with the theory and practice of education—is rooted directly in his own temperament and his strongly felt vocation as a teacher; but the other—his almost chauvinistic interest in the Italian philosophical tradition and its relation to the general European tradition—reflects the life-long influence of Spaventa on his mind. His degree thesis, *Rosmini e Gioberti* (Pisa, 1898), in which he emphasized points of contact and agreement between the native Catholic thinkers and the German Idealists, was meant to illustrate Spaventa's thesis regarding "the circulation of European philosophy."

His second book was a critical examination of Marx (*La filosofia di Marx*, Pisa, 1899) from an orthodox Hegelian standpoint. While writing it, Gentile became acquainted with Benedetto Croce, who was similarly occupied at the time. Thus began a friendly alliance that lasted more than twenty years. Gentile was the younger by nine years, but it seems clear that in these early formative years it was he who influenced the development of Croce's philosophy rather than vice versa, as most of their contemporaries assumed. Gentile was always more of a Hegelian than Croce ever became, and was more exclusively interested in the traditional problems of philosophy.

In 1900 Gentile wrote his important essay "The Concept of Education" ("Il concetto scientifico della pedagogia") and began his long campaign for the reform of the Italian school system. He became *Privatdocent* at Naples in 1903 and professor of the history of philosophy at Palermo in 1906. But the "reform of the Hegelian dialectic" and the "method of immanence" that led to actual idealism (in a paper of 1912) were worked out amid controversies with Modernists and polemics for religious instruction in elementary schools; and Gentile's philosophy was first fully expounded in the two-volume work *Sommario di pedagogia come scienza filosofica* ("Summary of Educational Theory," 2 vols., Bari, 1913–1914).

In 1914 Gentile succeeded to Jaja's chair at Pisa, where he wrote the one book through which he is internationally known, *Teoria generale della spirito come atto puro* ("The General Theory of the Spirit as Pure Act," Pisa, 1916). In 1917 he moved to the University of Rome; and the first volume of his *Sistema di logica come teoria del conoscere* ("System of Logic as Theory of Knowing," Pisa, 1917), the most systematic statement of his view, appeared. The second volume followed at Bari in 1923.

In 1922 Gentile became minister of education in Mussolini's first Cabinet, and in this capacity he reformed and reorganized the whole Italian school system. After his resignation in 1924 he became the first president of the National Fascist Institute of Culture; he remained for the rest of his life the most prominent publicist of the regime and the self-styled "philosopher of fascism." Gentile continued until his death to lecture at Rome, but in the fascist period his only important philosophical work was the *Filosofia dell'arte* (Milan, 1931). He was directing editor of the *Enciclopedia italiana* from its inception in 1925 to its completion in 1937. After the fall of Mussolini in 1943, Gentile went into retirement and wrote a short but important book on the genesis and structure of society which was published only after his death (*Genesi e struttura della società*, Florence, 1946). Subsequently persuaded to return to public life as a supporter of the Fascist Social Republic set up by the Germans, Gentile was assassinated by Italian communist partisans at Florence on April 15, 1944.

Conception of philosophy. Gentile justifies his "theory of the spirit as pure act" in two ways. First, he strives to show that it is the logical outcome of the whole movement of Western philosophical thought since Descartes; and, second, that the "method of pure immanence," when we arrive at it, provides an adequate and coherent way of explicating our actual experience. It is impossible to give more than the briefest indication of the line of his historical argument, although it bulks very large in most of his systematic works.

In any case, the significance of his theory emerges more clearly through an examination of his analysis of actual experience. The claim that actual idealism is the logical outcome of the main tradition of modern philosophy is interesting chiefly because it throws light on Gentile's conception of the essential problem of philosophy and the conditions for its solution. Philosophy for him, as for Fichte, was *Wissenschaftslehre*, the science of knowledge, the science that, without presupposing anything itself, provides an a priori ground for the presuppositions actually made in other sciences. Descartes's method of universal doubt can quite naturally be viewed as the first approach to this problem, and Berkeley's doctrine that *esse est percipi* is a vital step toward its solution. However, the genesis of actual idealism begins with Kant; and although Gentile arrived at his view through the progressive elaboration of a "reform of the Hegelian dialectic" that had been initiated by Spaventa, he remains fundamentally a Kantian in his determination to confine philosophical speculation to the task of exhibiting the logical structure of actual experience. He is at one with Kant and Fichte in his resolute rejection of any "dogmatic metaphysics" that posits or presupposes a reality transcending actual consciousness.

Theory of self-constitution. There is a temptation to say at once that it is a mistake to conceive of the task of philosophy in this way, as the exhibition of the logical structure of actual experience, and that the ideal of a "philosophy without presuppositions" is a chimera. The most primitive postulate of ordinary common sense is that a physical world exists prior to and independent of our consciousness of it. However, Gentile's theory is not meant to be taken as a denial of this assumption, but as a thesis about logical priority. The temporal pre-existence of the object of awareness is itself something that we take ourselves to be aware of, and in this sense the common-sense assumption is a product of our attempt to organize our experience in thought. Actual idealism must properly be judged as a theory about this process of rational organization or "concrete logic."

The most primitive level of the process for which we have ordinary words is sensation. We normally distinguish the objective cause of a sensation from the subjective feeling (pleasant or unpleasant) that it arouses in us. According to Gentile, this is a mistake. The sensation as a whole is our act of self-awareness, and the pleasure or pain is an aspect of this whole, not a reaction of the self to an object. He agrees emphatically that there cannot be any actual consciousness without the distinction of the subject of the awareness from the object of which it is aware. But he holds that since what has to be understood is the integral unity of the self, it is a mistake to look for the cause of experience within the content of experience. At the ideal limit, pure sensation can be thought of as an encounter with something absolutely other than the self; but it can also be thought of as a spontaneous activity of self-affirmation. Gentile does in fact employ "sensation" in both ways. Spontaneous self-affirmation is in his view the ideal aim of the artist, and loss of self in the contemplation of an absolute object is the typical concern of religious experience. But actual experience is always a synthesis, so that pure art and pure religion are nowhere to be found; and the actual understanding of any type of artistic or religious experience will involve restoring the suppressed aspects of the synthesis, that is to say, discovering the philosophy behind it.

Actual sensation is a process of self-constitution (*autoctisi*) in which the subject preserves its own past and relates it to present sensation. Language is abstractly the instrument and concretely the form through which this is done. It is neither the clothing nor the vehicle, but the embodiment of our thought. But we are able to think of it abstractly, as an inheritance shared by all who are able to use it, because the thought embodied in it has universal import. Thus the self that comes to consciousness when we express our thoughts in language is a spiritual universe, a system of meanings in which all other thinking beings can share. This is the absolute subject of experience, the transcendental Ego whose being (like the God of Aristotle and St. Thomas) is "pure act." The abstract form that Kant called the "transcendental unity of apperception" is given concrete existence, or brought to life, so to speak, in Gentile's conception of the "pure act" of "self-founding." My reflective awareness is on the one hand exactly what is essential to my existence as an independent personality; but on the other hand, so far as I achieve reflective awareness, I enter the world of thought in which nothing belongs, or can belong, to me personally. When I claim to *think* something, I must be able to communicate my thought; I must be able to show others the path by which I arrived at it so that, insofar as they can follow in my footsteps, they can share it. *Reflective* awareness is already communication, for my own thought is a dialogue within myself. The obvious fact that man is a social animal and that the peculiarly human institution of language is a collaborative production has its absolute or philosophical ground in the fact that the founding of the self is the founding of a transcendental society.

When we understand the fundamental concept of self-constitution in this way, Gentile's thesis about the unity of thought and action, which was the chief bone of contention between him and Croce, falls naturally into place and is easily understood. There appears to be a contrast between thought and action because in cognitive thinking we presuppose the reality we are concerned about, whereas our action is directed toward the creation of some object. However, all thinking and acting is in reality part of the same activity of self-conquest in which nothing is *absolutely* presupposed *theoretically*, and some things *must* be accepted (or presupposed) *practically*, if there is to be a

line between the self and the not-self, the conquering subject and the nature or world that is to be conquered: " . . . the spiritual act is never a self-creation that must be contemplated and watched over afterward; it is always simultaneously a self-creation that is self-awareness and vice versa" (*Opere* I, 84). The establishment of truth is the self-establishment of the transcendental Ego; and the establishment of the Ego is the establishment of an ideal community that Gentile, like Hegel, calls "the State."

The State is on the one side that complex of social institutions, cultural traditions, and ethical values that appears to the individual as the actual fabric of his own moral personality; on the other side it is all the ideals that have still to be striven for and achieved in the actual world in which he lives. Gentile often insists on this latter Mazzinian side of his doctrine, but in practice he tended to subordinate it to his conservative Hegelian faith in the rationality of the actual social structure. In his fascist apologias it often seems as if whatever is done in the name of the existing State must be patiently, even joyfully, accepted and endured as a condition for any further advance—an attitude that is more reminiscent of Hobbes than of Mazzini. There can be no question that this attitude is false to the spirit of his doctrine.

Gentile's logic and the forms of value. The unity of theory and practice means that in Gentile's work "logic"—the concrete logic of the self-concept—becomes inseparable if not indistinguishable from ethics, and philosophy itself is seen as the critical self-awareness of actual political life. His major theoretical problem was to show how the nonpolitical values of human experience could be integrated into his view. This problem came to Gentile in the form that Hegel gave it when he made art and religion the moments of the final triad of the Absolute Idea, subordinate only to philosophy itself. Gentile solved it by regarding art and religion as the moments of his own Absolute, the act of thought. Thus art and religion, instead of being ultimate, become primitive; they are the essential moments of all experience. They have their joint origin, as has been shown, in the opposite aspects of the sensation or "self-feeling" in which consciousness originates. As distinct modes of experience they are attempts to achieve the impossible by aesthetically recapturing or mystically losing oneself in that ideal point of origin.

Thus the seeming independence of aesthetic and religious values arises from the one-sided consciousness of the artist or worshiper. In reality the self-willed artist is dedicated to the production of an object of universal value and significance; art is not just the release of feeling, but the disciplined expression of it. And the proclaiming of the glory of God or the doing of his will is the work of a human voice or the task of a human hand. The "private" world of the artist and the "other" world of the believer get their meaning and fulfill their function in the actual society of the transcendental Ego. When we view the artist's work, we must strive to comprehend the ideal to which he has devoted his skill; and when we seek to interpret a religious doctrine, we must express its meaning for humanity and in terms of our own actual lives. It thus becomes the task of the critic to interpret the work of art or the religious doctrine philosophically. Gentile wrote a number of books and essays—mainly but not exclusively about literary artists—in which he endeavored to do just this; and on the religious side he maintained that his "humanistic conception of the world" was a philosophical expression of the Christian revelation.

In the concrete logic of the act of thought, the moment of spontaneous self-expression is prior to the consciousness of the object, which necessarily appears as a limit upon the self. Hence, in the progressive development of consciousness, which is the subject of Gentile's philosophy of education, an aesthetic phase of free, spontaneous play is succeeded by a religious phase that it is the main task of the elementary school to establish and govern. On this basis a properly philosophical conception of the world, a sense of the autonomous moral responsibility of the self-conscious citizen, should then be built up in secondary education.

Abstract logic. It should by now be clear that actual idealism can be interpreted as primarily a theory about the logical structure of our experience of values. But this theory does contain within it a theory about the ordinary logic of factual propositions. Formal logic, whether mathematical or conceptual, is the logic of presupposition, the logic of "nature," the abstract logic of any object that any actual concrete consciousness may assume as its content. Gentile thought of this *logo astratto* as being essentially static and unchanging. Spinoza's system was for him the perfect philosophical expression and *reductio ad absurdum* of it; and his own conception of natural science was strictly Kantian. "Nature" was for him an a priori concept with a fixed logical structure, not an idea that evolves in the dialectic of actual research. But this is only a reflection of his own personal background and interests. The "idea of nature" has a history, and a full development of the theory of mind as pure act would seem to require that the history of science be incorporated as an essential aspect or complement of the history of theoretical philosophy.

Gentile's own use of the category of the *logo astratto* in the sphere of practical philosophy was quite fluid and dialectical. In ethics, for example, it appears as the nature that we must conquer and subdue, but it appears also as the abstract law to which we must submit. When we remember that the transcendental Ego itself, the *logo concreto*, is both the organic unity of all prior achievement and the ideal of a perfect harmony still to be achieved, this becomes quite easy to understand. The concrete self-concept has its abstract content under each aspect—there is sinful nature and there is the law in virtue of which we are aware of it as sinful; the act of self-constitution is the resolution of the conflict that produced the two opposed abstractions.

Negative values. Finally, Gentile holds that error, pain, and sin are in some sense "unreal." This doctrine follows logically from the fact that they belong to the category of the *logo astratto*. They are things that we are conscious of, and they have already been overcome or surpassed in the very consciousness of them. It is quite easy to exhibit, as a mere matter of logic, how "truth" is the concrete category of which "error" is only the abstract content. For to be actually aware that some proposition is or may be an error is to hold that a proposition about that proposition is true—namely, the proposition that it is or may be an error.

In the case of sin, something more than a logical rela-

tionship of propositions is involved. If I say, "I am a sinner," I am setting myself up as a supposedly just judge of my own conduct; but I do not thereby cease to be a sinner. Rather, the question is posed of how a single self is to be constituted out of this divided consciousness. This is the key to the only defensible interpretation of Gentile's doctrine, which then asserts that when I truly say, "I am a sinner," I must be on the road to redemption and that the test of whether I do actually think I am a sinner is my consciousness of repentance.

Gentile's view that "pleasure" is the concrete and "pain" or "grief" the abstract category is more difficult to interpret. If I am conscious of being in pain, I have certainly "overcome" the pain; i.e., isolated it and objectified it as a fact. But to argue that because of this it is not really I who am in pain is sheer sophistry. It is certainly true that the consciousness of pain is a complex activity (including, for example, the active seeking of a remedy or a distraction), while the pain in itself is an abstract element. But pain is "unreal" only in the sense in which art and religion are unreal. That is to say, there cannot be a pure pain-consciousness, for this is just the point at which consciousness disappears.

Gentile's influence. Actual Idealism was the dominant philosophy in Italian state schools and universities throughout the last twenty years of Gentile's life. In this period his students, like Hegel's, split into two main parties. There was first the "right," led by Armando Carlini, who emphasized the Christian origin and Augustinian character of much of Gentile's thought, and identified the transcendental Ego with the God of Catholic theology. After Gentile's death this group joined with the religious existentialists to form the contemporary movement known as Christian Spiritualism.

On the other side, a group of younger disciples, led by Ugo Spirito, formed the Gentilian "left," which from the first devoted itself to social problems and provided much of the economic and political theory of the fascist corporate state. Since World War II this group has been aligned with the political left and has shown some affinities with orthodox Marxism. But in the current work of both groups it is the mystical spirit of Gentile's philosophy rather than the logical structure that has survived. Outside of Italy, Gentile's influence can be seen most notably in the work of R. G. Collingwood.

Bibliography

The Gentile Foundation was established in Rome in 1947, with the *Giornale critico della filosofia italiana* (founded by Gentile in 1920) as its official organ. The foundation is issuing the definitive edition of Gentile's *Complete Works* in 55 volumes (of which 30 had appeared by August 1964). Three of his books have been translated into English: *The Theory of Mind as Pure Act* (London, 1922); *The Reform of Education*, lectures to the schoolteachers of Trieste (New York, 1922); and *Genesis and Structure of Society* (Urbana, Illinois, 1960). This last includes a complete bibliography and critical survey of everything by or about Gentile in English.

For critical studies of Gentile, see the following: H. S. Harris, *The Social Philosophy of Giovanni Gentile* (Urbana, Illinois, 1960) surveys the whole range of Gentile's practical philosophy, including his "philosophy of fascism," which has been largely ignored above. R. W. Holmes, *The Idealism of Giovanni Gentile* (New York, 1937) is a detailed and critical study of the *System of*

Logic and a work of fundamental importance. P. Romanell, *The Philosophy of Giovanni Gentile* (New York, 1938) provides a general survey.

H. S. Harris

GEOMETRY is thought to have had its origin in the practical work of surveying land. According to Herodotus, the Egyptians became skilled at surveying because the flooding waters of the Nile annually inundated their fertile lands, obliterating the boundary markers of their fields; thus, each year their *harpenodapts* ("rope tiers") had to lay out the boundaries anew. The Greeks saw what the Egyptians could do, and they must have learned from them a number of useful laws about lines, angles, and figures—laws which the Egyptians had presumably arrived at by empirical generalization. To this knowledge the Greeks gave the name of geometry, that is, earth measurement. The more laws of geometry one knows, however, the more awkward it becomes to continue using empirical generalization as the means of learning additional laws; deduction of further laws from those already known is a more reliable and more efficient method. The Greeks took the decisive step of embracing deduction as their method of discovering new laws, and finding it a delightful method, they began to construct deductive proofs even of geometrical propositions that were not doubtful. Tradition ascribes to Pythagoras the further achievement of having made the study of geometry a theoretical science. This achievement involved introducing systematic order into the subject by selecting a few particular laws as basic and attempting to deduce from them all other known laws; it also involved introducing more abstract geometrical conceptions, such as the notion of lines being without width and the notion that a line can be tangent to a circle, thus having but one point in common with it. The Greeks prized this theoretical study of geometry for its own sake, not merely for its useful applications; Pythagoras and, after him, Plato exalted the intellectual importance of geometry because in its abstract timeless purity it seemed to them to have a close kinship with metaphysics and religion.

EUCLIDEAN GEOMETRY

About 300 B.C. Euclid wrote *The Elements,* in which he drew together and presented systematically all the geometrical knowledge then available. This great book raised the Greek science of geometry to a new level, and it also became one of the most influential classics in the literature of Western thought. Through ancient times, through the medieval era, and in the modern period up into the nineteenth century, Euclid's *Elements* served both as the textbook of geometry and as the paradigm of rigorous scientific thinking.

Euclid's procedure in *The Elements* was to develop geometry in a systematic deductive fashion: he employed five unproved principles about lines, angles, and figures, which he called postulates; from them, with the aid of axioms and definitions, he deduced a large number of further propositions (theorems). Euclid postulated the following:

(1) A straight line can be drawn from any point to any other point.

(2) Any straight line can be extended continuously in a straight line.

(3) Given any point and any distance, a circle can be drawn with that point as its center and that distance as its radius.

(4) All right angles are equal to one another.

(5) If a straight line crosses two other straight lines so that the sum of the two interior angles on one side of it is less than two right angles, then the two straight lines, if extended far enough, cross on that same side.

Besides the postulates, Euclid stated five other unproved principles which are called axioms (or common notions), such as, "Things which are equal to the same thing are also equal to each other." The main difference between the postulates and the axioms seems to be that the postulates deal specifically with the subject matter of geometry (lines, angles, and figures), whereas the axioms have to do with the more general notion of equality of magnitude—a notion that is used in almost every subject. Modern mathematicians and logicians do not generally make any such distinction between axioms and postulates; the terms "axiom" and "postulate" are now used interchangeably.

It was also a cardinal point of Euclid's method to try to define each geometrical term that he used. Below are some of his definitions, numbered according to their order in *The Elements:*

(1) A *point* is that which has no part.

(2) A *line* is breadthless length.

(4) A *straight line* is a line which lies evenly with the points on itself.

(14) A *figure* is that which is contained by any boundary or boundaries.

(23) *Parallel* straight lines are straight lines which, being in the same plane and being produced indefinitely in both directions, do not meet one another in either direction.

From the postulates, together with the axioms and definitions, Euclid aimed to deduce all his other geometrical propositions, first those of plane geometry and then those of solid geometry. In *The Elements* the propositions proved are of two kinds. Some are universal laws; for instance, Proposition 47 of Book I says "In right-angled triangles the square on the side subtending the right angle is equal to the squares on the sides containing the right angle." But many others are expressed as tasks to be performed; thus, Proposition I of Book I is "On a given finite straight line to construct an equilateral triangle." A method for performing the task by means of straightedge and compasses is worked out in a way that makes it possible to prove that following the method will accomplish the task (here is involved the notion of construction, which later became central in Kant's philosophy of mathematics).

Modern criticism. For more than two thousand years Euclid's *Elements* survived all challenges and stood as a supreme mathematical achievement, the rigor of its proofs being admired as perfect. During the nineteenth century, however, mathematicians' standards of rigor rose sharply, and it came to be realized that Euclid's work, admirable though it is, does contain logical gaps. There are places in Euclid's proofs where his stated assumptions are not sufficient to make his conclusions follow by formal deduction alone, as he had intended them to do. The assumptions needed to close these gaps are not more trivial in content or less worthy of being explicitly stated than are the postulates that Euclid did state.

Another respect in which Euclid's system falls short of modern standards of rigor is with regard to definitions. Although he recognized the need for distinguishing clearly between theorems that are proved in the system and postulates that are unproved, Euclid did not see that strict rigor also demands a clear distinction between terms that are defined within the system and terms that are not. Euclid attempted to define all the geometrical terms he used; nevertheless, his definitions are not all alike. Some of them (such as 1, 2, and 4) are vague elucidations in which terms that occur in his postulates and theorems are partially explained by means of other terms that do not. These definitions are never made use of by Euclid in his proofs. But many other definitions (such as 23) explicitly relate some terms of his system to others also occurring in the system, and these definitions are used in proofs. We may think of the terms introduced by the former sort of definitions as being Euclid's primitive terms. Unfortunately, however, in some cases (such as 14) it is not clear which kind of definition is being offered, and this makes the structure of the system somewhat obscure.

From a more modern point of view, there are two basic decisions to be made, and made clear, in drawing up a system like this. First, with regard to terms, some geometrical terms must be chosen to serve as primitive, and all the other geometrical terms occurring in theorems must be definable in terms of these. Second, thinking of the totality of laws that can be expressed by using our primitive and our defined terms, we must select a limited list of these laws to serve as our unproved assumptions, on the basis of which our theorems are to be proved.

How much leeway is it legitimate to allow in the choice of primitive terms, of definitions, and of postulates? Contemporary thought holds that considerable leeway may be permitted here. There may well be alternative choices of primitive terms, of definitions, and of postulates that will lead to differing yet equally legitimate formulations of the same subject matter. Thus, in the modern axiomatization of Euclidean geometry devised by David Hilbert, the six primitive terms are "point," "line," "plane," "incident," "between," and "congruent." In a different axiomatization worked out by Oswald Veblen a little later, only the terms "point," "between," and "congruent" are used, and his set of axioms is different from Hilbert's. Still different is the axiomatization by E. V. Huntington, who used only the terms "sphere" and "includes" as primitive and whose axioms had to be different too. All these axiomatizations are different, yet all are formulations of the same subject matter, since in all of them the same Euclidean theorems can ultimately be proved. From a modern point of view, all these axiomatizations are perfectly legitimate, although progressively more economical in regard to their basic sets of terms.

THE TRADITIONAL VIEW OF GEOMETRICAL KNOWLEDGE

Euclid's motives in axiomatizing geometry must have included the pure mathematical desire to exhibit logical connections between geometrical laws, for some of the theorems he proves are no more doubtful than are his postulates. But surely he also felt that his procedure had value in making clearer and more certain our whole grasp of geometrical truth: for Euclid must have regarded his postulates as truths about lines, angles, and figures; therefore, theorems deduced from them will also have to be acknowledged as true. Now, when some further postulates are added to fill the gaps mentioned above, Euclid's theorems can indeed be made to follow strictly by formal logic from his postulates. This does explain how the theorems are known to be true—provided the postulates are known to be true. But how, if at all, do we know that the postulates are true?

From ancient times until the nineteenth century, there was a large measure of agreement among philosophers about this. They regarded Euclid's postulates as true and as knowable with the utmost clarity and certainty. They felt that these laws are known to be absolutely universal and strictly true, in a manner incompatible with their being empirical generalizations; hence, they regarded them as a priori and necessary. Moreover, most traditional philosophers would have thought that Euclid's postulates are synthetic rather than analytic statements; that is, these postulates are not knowable merely through knowledge of the laws of formal logic and of definitions but must be known by some other means. How can we possess knowledge attained neither through sense experience nor through formal logic and definitions? The usual traditional answer was that it is through some kind of rational insight that this synthetic a priori knowledge is attained. Plato suggested that we see with the eye of reason into an eternal realm of Forms; Kant held that in knowing geometry the mind is apprehending a priori the structure of its own faculty of sensibility.

The view that the postulates of Euclidean geometry are true is the least venturesome component of this traditional position. In maintaining that they are true, traditional philosophers would have meant to hold that these postulates are true when the geometrical terms occurring in them are understood in ordinary fashion. But what is it to understand geometrical terms in ordinary fashion? Let us focus our attention on the terms "line" and "straight," for these are key terms in the sense that once their meanings are characterized it becomes comparatively easy to ascribe related meanings to the other geometrical terms, such as "point" and "figure."

The terms "line" and "straight." The term "line" is thought of as meaning any continuous pathway through space or any protracted boundary between one area and another. Even if all actual boundaries and pathways have breadth, we can understand what it means to speak of breadthless boundaries, such as the boundary between northern and southern hemispheres, for to speak of a breadthless boundary is to speak of the limit which actual markings of the boundary approach as surveying and marking techniques become more and more refined.

What is ordinarily meant, however, by saying of a line segment that it is straight? There is a noteworthy ambivalence in our ordinary notion, for we have various different criteria of straightness. One way of telling whether a line is straight is to sight along it, as the carpenter does; here the idea is that for a line to be straight is for it to be the path of a ray of light (of course the medium through which the light travels must be of uniform refractive index). Another idea is that of the Egyptian "rope tiers," that for a line to be straight is for it to be the path along which a stretched cord tends to lie as its tension is increased without limit. Still another idea is that for a line to be straight is for it to be the case that however the line is divided into overlapping subsegments, each of them will be a path between its endpoints along which a correctly handled measuring rod need be laid down the fewest times (of course, if temperature variations are present, a correction must be made to take account of thermal expansion of the rod). The criteria of straightness mentioned so far are akin in a way to be noted later. There are other criteria, however, that form a separate group. Thus, another way of telling whether a line segment is straight is to investigate whether there is any other line segment with the same end points and as short a length as the given segment; if there is no such other segment, then the given segment is straight. This notion of length may be thought of as operationally defined by reference to correct procedures with measuring rods, but with the proviso here that every influence that distorts rods must be corrected for. Still another way of telling whether a line segment is straight is to see whether, when a circle is drawn through one end point with the other end point as center, the ratio between the length of the circumference of the circle and the length of the line segment is twice π. Here again length can be understood as being determined by such procedures as the use of measuring rods, but with the proviso that all distorting influences must be corrected for.

In differing circumstances, different ones of these criteria would be practical to employ, but each of these criteria (and there are others, too) expresses an aspect of how we use the term "straight" in its ordinary sense. Someone may object, "Surely *one* of these criteria must express the essence of what 'straight' ordinarily means; surely there must be one correct definition." However, a single unambivalent definition has not been needed, for in all ordinary experience the various criteria of straightness march together: a line that is straight according to any one of these criteria proves to be straight according to all of them. All these various criteria of straightness go together to constitute our ordinary notion of what "straight" means.

When the terms "line" and "straight" are understood in this ordinary fashion, with other geometrical terms being understood in normal associated ways, what is the status of Euclid's postulates? The reasonable view in Euclid's time and in Newton's time was that these postulates are strictly true, for experience afforded no ground whatever for doubting them.

NON-EUCLIDEAN GEOMETRY

Euclid's fifth postulate is more intricate to state and less easy to comprehend than are the other four. Through the centuries a number of different commentators on Euclid, including Greeks, Arabs, and moderns, feeling that the fifth postulate was less self-evident than the others, attempted to devise ways of proving it as a theorem, so that it would no longer have to be regarded as a postulate.

Their efforts always failed to be satisfactory; in each case, either the supposed proof contained some outright logical fallacy or else it covertly assumed some geometrical law just as intricate as Euclid's fifth postulate itself.

However, such attempts did succeed in showing that there are various other geometrical laws capable of doing the same logical job of yielding theorems that Euclid's fifth postulate does. One is the law that from a point not on a given line, one and only one line can be drawn parallel to the given line (this law, called Playfair's postulate, was substituted for Euclid's fifth postulate in a widely used eighteenth-century version of Euclidean geometry; for this reason Euclid's fifth postulate itself is sometimes misleadingly referred to as "the parallel postulate"). The law that the sum of the angles of a triangle equals two right angles could also do the job of Euclid's fifth postulate, as could the law that given any three points not on a straight line, there is just one circle that passes through them. Any one of these laws could replace Euclid's fifth postulate without altering the array of theorems ultimately provable, but none is significantly simpler than Euclid's postulate.

Lobachevskian and Riemannian geometries. It was not until the nineteenth century that mathematicians came to understand the logical situation and to realize that Euclid's fifth postulate is independent of his others, so that there can be formally consistent systems of geometry that substitute for Euclid's fifth postulate something contrary to it. N. I. Lobachevsky and Farkas Bolyai independently published the first accounts of non-Euclidean geometry. In Lobachevskian geometry (Bolyai's is the same), through a point not on a given line, more than one line can always be drawn parallel to the given line. The sum of the angles of a triangle is always less than two right angles, the amount by which it is less being proportional to the area of the triangle; triangles of different sizes can never be similar. The ratio of the circumference of a circle to its diameter is always greater than π, the amount by which it is greater increasing with the area of the circle. As in Euclidean geometry, a straight line can always be extended farther and farther without limit; so, like Euclidean space, the space envisaged by Lobachevskian geometry is infinite in extent.

Later in the nineteenth century G. F. B. Riemann developed another type of non-Euclidean geometry, in which both Euclid's fifth postulate and the assumption that a straight line can be extended to any desired length are denied (the latter assumption is suggested by Euclid's second postulate but not strictly implied by it). In Riemannian geometry there is a maximum length to which any straight line can be extended; thus, the envisaged space is finite. In this geometry, through a point not on a given straight line, no straight line can be drawn parallel to the given line. Through two given points more than one straight line can always be drawn. The sum of the angles of a triangle is always greater than two right angles, the excess being proportional to the area of the triangle. The ratio of the circumference of a circle to its diameter always is less than π and decreases as the area of the circle increases.

The development of Lobachevskian and Riemannian geometries came as a shock. It had been supposed that there is only one true geometry, whose laws are necessarily Euclidean. But if Euclid's postulates and theorems are all necessarily true, then it would seem that any non-Euclidean geometry must contain some postulates and theorems that are necessarily false; this might be thought to mean that the non-Euclidean systems must be inconsistent. Yet their opponents were never able to show that either Lobachevsky's or Riemann's geometry violates formal consistency by yielding a pair of theorems one of which is the negation of the other. Later it was established that both Lobachevskian and Riemmanian geometries have Euclidean models; that is, there are ways of interpreting the terms of a non-Euclidean geometry so that all its laws become laws of Euclidean geometry. A partial example of such a model is provided if we consider the surface of a sphere and if we interpret Riemann's term "straight line" to mean "great circle"; then every two such straight lines intersect, the sum of the angles of a triangle constructed of such lines will exceed two right angles, and so on. Here we have a model of the two-dimensional part of Riemannian geometry, that is, a way of interpreting part of the laws of Riemannian geometry so that they turn into Euclidean laws. In more intricate ways the whole of Riemannian geometry can be given a Euclidean model, as can the whole of Lobachevskian geometry. This establishes that both Lobachevskian and Riemmanian geometries must be formally consistent if Euclidean geometry is so; that is, neither type of non-Euclidean geometry can have a theorem whose negation is also a theorem unless Euclidean geometry also does so. Since no one questions the formal consistency of Euclidean geometry, we may safely regard these three forms of geometry as formally consistent.

MODERN VIEWS OF GEOMETRICAL KNOWLEDGE

Granting that both Euclidean and non-Euclidean types of geometry are formally consistent, does this mean that these geometries all are somehow equally true? To be sure, there are standpoints from which they may be regarded as equally true. For instance, it is possible to think of Euclidean geometry as saying merely that if the Euclidean postulates hold, then the Euclidean theorems hold, and of Lobachevskian geometry as saying merely that if the Lobachevskian postulates hold, then the Lobachevskian theorems must hold. From this standpoint all geometries are equally true, for each merely expresses true assertions about the logical deducibility of theorems from postulates. From another standpoint the various geometries should be regarded as abstract uninterpreted systems in which no meaning has been assigned to the primitive terms and in which, therefore, no question of the truth of postulates or theorems can arise. Then the only proper questions in geometry pertain to the formal deducibility of uninterpreted theorems from uninterpreted axioms. This view makes any geometry as true as any other, in the degenerate sense that truth is irrelevant to them all.

Either of these ways of viewing geometries accords well enough with the practice of pure mathematicians, who concern themselves only with such logical relations. These mathematicians need not attach any specific meanings to geometrical terms and need not ask whether the postulates and theorems with which they deal are in any sense true descriptions of space as it actually is. Indeed, so far as pure mathematics is concerned, geometry may be regarded merely as the study of certain kinds of abstract order; there is no need to think of it as connected, except historically, with the study of the space of the world. Although this approach is mathematically legitimate, it omits the question that is philosophically most challenging, namely, which set of postulates is true, that is, true when the geometrical terms in them are understood in their normal ways.

Each non-Euclidean geometry must be presumed to be formally consistent, and therefore there must be ways of interpreting its terms so that its postulates all become truths. But these ways of interpreting its terms may all be remote from the ordinary meanings of the terms. Thus, the rise of non-Euclidean geometries as formally consistent systems worthy of mathematical study by no means suffices to refute the view that Euclidean geometry is the one geometry that is true of actual space.

Geometry and relativity theory. The most serious challenge to the traditional view of Euclidean geometry as the one true description of space is provided by Einstein's theory of relativity. According to Einstein's theory, which must now be regarded as well established, we have to make some predictions that differ surprisingly from those of classical physics. Suppose a closed three-sided figure is laid out, its sides being determined by light rays, or by paths along which measuring rods need be laid down the fewest times, or by paths along which stretched cords tend to lie. According to the theory of relativity, we must predict that in the presence of a gravitational field the sum of the angles of this figure will be greater than two right angles. We must also predict that between any two separate points there will, in the presence of gravitational fields, be more than one path along which light rays can travel, more than one path divisible into overlapping subsegments along each of which a measuring rod need be laid down a minimum number of times to get from end point to end point, and so forth. However, it is only where the distances involved are astronomical that these differences between what Newtonian physics predicts and what the theory of relativity predicts become large enough to be detectable. The Newtonian theory remains accurate enough for ordinary terrestrial phenomena.

How shall these findings be described? We must not say that these findings show that straight lines bend or that triangles have curved sides, for these would be self-contradictory descriptions. Many philosophers of science would describe these as the findings that the sum of the angles of a triangle is greater than two right angles and that between any two separate points there is more than one straight line. They would choose these descriptions because of their belief that any path which is the path of a light ray, which is a path divisible into subsegments along each of which a measuring rod need be laid down a minimum number of times, and which is the path along which a taut cord would tend to lie, must necessarily be a straight line. They would regard this as central to the meaning of the term "straight." That is, the criteria of straightness belonging to the first group mentioned above are regarded by them as the important ones, the ones that govern the term. Hence, they would say that the theory of relativity proves space to be Riemannian rather than Euclidean in its general form. Einstein himself is the outstanding representative of this viewpoint, which he expressed in more generalized form in his often quoted dictum, "As far as the laws of mathematics refer to reality, they are not certain; and as far as they are certain, they do not refer to reality." In uttering this dictum he was surely thinking primarily of geometry and was expressing his view that any specific assignment of plausible meanings to the terms of a geometry must make the laws of that geometry empirical hypotheses about the behavior of measuring rods, light rays, and taut cords.

However, that is not the only possible view of the matter. An alternative description would involve saying that what Einstein's theory shows is that gravitation bends light rays and shrinks rods and cords. This means that in a gravitational field the path of a light ray or the path laid out by means of a rod or cord can fail to be a straight line and that a closed three-sided figure laid out by such means need not be a triangle. It was already known that light rays do not travel straight through media of varying refractive index, and that measuring rods expand and contract with varying temperature; according to this view what the theory of relativity shows is just that gravitational fields, too, can affect the paths of light rays and the lengths of rods and cords. In spite of the distorting influence of gravitation, light rays and measuring rods can still be used to lay out straight lines—but when they are so used an appropriate correction must be introduced to take account of the distortion. Underlying this viewpoint is the supposition that the criteria belonging to the second group mentioned earlier are the ones that are of central importance to the straightness of a line. Those who adopt this viewpoint feel that for a line to be straight is for there to be no other path as short between its end points, and they understand the notion of length in a way that preserves Euclidean laws. Viewed in this way, the findings of relativity theory do nothing to refute Euclidean geometry. Indeed, no findings of physics could do so, for the criteria that are regarded as fundamental to the meaning of "straight" are so understood as to express Euclidean laws. When we understand geometrical terms in this spirit, all the sentences of Euclidean geometry become necessary statements knowable a priori, rather than empirical statements knowable only through experience.

Here someone may object, "The laws of Euclidean geometry cannot all be necessarily true, for some of them have consistent contraries in non-Euclidean geometry." This objection fails to distinguish adequately between a geometrical sentence and the various statements that it can express when its terms are understood in various ways. To be sure, non-Euclidean geometries are consistent, in the sense that there are ways of interpreting their sentences so as to make them true; and Euclid's fifth postulate does have its contraries in the other geometries. But the objection neglects the fact that if we adopt a specific interpretation of the geometrical terms that makes all the sentences of Euclidean geometry into true statements, then any non-Euclidean geometry must have some of its sentences made into false statements by that interpretation; and if we adopt an interpretation of the geometrical terms that makes all the sentences of Euclidean geometry into necessarily true statements, then any non-Euclidean geometry must have

some of its statements made into necessarily false statements by that interpretation.

However, even though the postulates and theorems of Euclidean geometry are necessarily true according to the way of understanding their terms that we have been considering, there is no need to regard our knowledge of them as resulting from some queer kind of synthetic a priori insight. The knowledge here involved can best be regarded as based on an understanding of the intended senses of the terms: The proposition that the sum of the angles of a triangle must equal two right angles reflects our determination not to call anything a triangle unless it has this character.

Misunderstandings about this situation often arise because people have the impression that if the laws of some non-Euclidean geometry are true (as Einstein held), then the laws of Euclidean geometry cannot in any sense all be true. They have the impression that Euclidean and non-Euclidean geometries are totally incompatible with one another and so cannot both be correct. As has already been indicated, this is not so. People who have this impression fail to realize that the laws of a geometry are capable of truth or falsity only when their terms are understood in particular ways, and that each consistent geometry admits of some interpretations of its terms under which all its laws are true and of other interpretations of its terms under which not all its laws are true. If we want to avoid being misled, we should say that when the term "straight line" is interpreted as meaning the path of a ray of light through a medium of uniform refractive index, and when the other geometrical terms are interpreted in normal associated ways, then the laws of Euclidean geometry are not all true, but the laws of a form of Riemannian geometry are true. We should add that when geometrical terms are given any sort of interpretation that builds the Euclidean postulates into their very meaning, then of course all the Euclidean laws are necessarily true under that interpretation, and each non-Euclidean geometry under that interpretation contains some necessarily false propositions.

The choice between Euclid and Riemann. Two different viewpoints have now been considered from which the findings of the theory of relativity can be differently described. Which of these two viewpoints is more correct? Should the laws of Euclidean geometry be regarded as empirical hypotheses about light rays and measuring rods, hypotheses that have now been refuted? Or should they be regarded as necessary conceptual truths that hold simply by virtue of the meanings of geometrical terms? To ask this question amounts to asking whether it is the first group or the second group of criteria of straightness that more truly embodies the normal meaning of "straight."

The best answer seems to be that neither group of criteria is more central than the other to the normal meaning of "straight." The criteria of both groups belong to its meaning, and its meaning is therefore ambivalent in this noteworthy way. Prior to Einstein's theory of relativity there was no need for the ambivalence to be resolved, for the criteria of the two groups were believed always to march together. Now we see that they diverge, and, if we wish to speak clearly, we must make a decision to allow one group of criteria rather than the other to govern our use of the term. Neither way of speaking would appear to be more correct than the other; each way of speaking seems to grow out of real tendencies genuinely present in the past usage of the term. The decision will have to be an arbitrary choice about how we shall henceforth use the term "straight."

Sometimes the notion of simplicity is invoked at this point, and it is said that by giving up Euclidean geometry in favor of Riemannian, a simpler over-all theory of geometry-*cum*-physics is attained, and this is offered as a strong reason for so doing. To this it must be replied that the kind of simplicity involved here is not the kind of simplicity that is relevant to truth. It is not simplicity in the sense in which we might say that since the hypothesis that smoking exacerbates heart ailments is the simplest explanation of the known data correlating smoking with deaths from heart disease, therefore the hypothesis is probably true. Instead, it is simplicity of the kind relevant to convenience, the kind of simplicity that is involved when we say that the metric system is simpler than are English measures.

The choice between Euclidean and Riemannian geometries is a matter of two different descriptive schemes, each of which is capable of describing the scientific facts. Any hypothesis, prediction, or explanation that can be expressed in one of these descriptive schemes can be expressed just as accurately in the other; to this extent the situation is like that of Fahrenheit and centigrade descriptions of temperature or that of Cartesian and polar coordinates. If some people decide to take the first group of criteria of straightness as central, they will say that the laws of Euclidean geometry are empirical hypotheses and have been refuted. If others decide to take the second group of criteria as central, they can say that the laws of Euclidean geometry are necessary truths immune to any refutation from physics. Each way of speaking will have its respective conveniences and inconveniences, but both are legitimate ways of speaking, both are equally rooted in ordinary language.

The conception being advocated here is akin to the "conventionalism" in geometry espoused by Poincaré. He fully recognized the mathematical legitimacy of non-Euclidean geometries, yet he held that discoveries in physics cannot dictate to us what form of geometry we must accept for describing the world. He held that if we retain Euclidean geometry, we do so "by convention," by a free decision—a decision to which we can adhere if we wish, come what may in physics. Poincaré's own preference was for retaining Euclidean geometry, because it is mathematically simpler than any non-Euclidean geometry, and he felt that science would retain it. However, Poincaré, writing before Einstein's general theory of relativity, naturally was not in a position to appreciate the convenience and attractiveness that Riemannian geometry would come to possess as a way of describing spatial phenomena in terms of that theory.

Bibliography

The edition by Sir Thomas Heath of *The Thirteen Books of Euclid's Elements* (New York, 1956) provides Euclid's text together with extensive historical commentary. A historical account of non-Euclidean geometry is given by Roberto Bonola, *Non-Euclidean Geometry* (New York, 1955). A modern axiomatic treatment of Euclidean geometry is David Hilbert, *The Foundations of Geometry* (Chicago, 1902). Two introductory mathematical treatments are Leonard M. Blumenthal, *A Modern View of Geometry* (San Francisco, 1961) and Stefan Kulczycki, *Non-Euclidean Geometry* (Warsaw, 1961).

Three excellent statements of the philosophical interpretation that is now most widespread are Hans Reichenbach, *The Philosophy of Space and Time* (New York, 1958); Carl G. Hempel, "Geometry and Empirical Science," in *American Mathematical Monthly*, Vol. 52 (1945), 7–17, and reprinted in Herbert Feigl and May Brodbeck, eds., *Readings in the Philosophy of Science* (New York, 1953); and Ernest Nagel, *The Structure of Science* (New York, 1961), Chs. 8 and 9. Valuable criticisms of this position are offered by R. D. Bradley, "Geometry and Necessary Truth," in *The Philosophical Review*, Vol. 73 (1964), 59–75, and by Adolf Grünbaum, *Philosophical Problems of Space and Time* (New York, 1963). A statement of the view of Henri Poincaré can be found in his *Science and Hypothesis* translated by W. J. Greenstreet (New York, 1955), Chs. 3, 4, and 5.

STEPHEN F. BARKER

GERBERT OF AURILLAC, educational reformer and pope (Silvester II) of the eleventh century, was born in Auvergne about 938, became a monk of St. Gérard d'Aurillac, and was educated there and in Catalonia. He later visited Rome, where Pope John XIII (965–972) introduced him to Emperor Otto I. Gerbert shortly left Otto's court to study at Rheims, where he later became master of the schools. His fame led Otto II to make him abbot of Bobbio about 980, but in 983 Gerbert returned to Rheims, where he engaged in political and antipapal controversies. In 991 he became archbishop, and after many vicissitudes he was transferred to Ravenna in 998. His old friend and patron Otto III secured his election as Pope Silvester II in 999; as pope he established the church in Hungary and strongly asserted papal claims. He died in 1003.

Despite the intrigues and restlessness of his later public life, Gerbert was—and was recognized as—the most learned, versatile, and influential master of his age. Rheims during his first stay (c. 966–980) became a principal center of the educational revival that was beginning to inspire the cathedral schools of France and that from them passed to the universities. Fulbert, founder of the school of Chartres, was Gerbert's pupil.

Gerbert's greatest achievement was to give new life to the skeleton of the ancient *trivium* and *quadrivium*. In rhetoric he restored the careful study of Terence and Vergil, the satirists Horace and Persius, Lucan, and the critics Seneca and Quintilian; in dialectic, which he reestablished as the goal of a literary education, he developed what was to become the classical syllabus of the *Isagoge* of Porphyry, the *Categories* and *De Interpretatione* of Aristotle, the *Topics* of Cicero, and the whole dialectical corpus of Boethius. He rescued the *quadrivium* from its bookish decadence and injected a real, practical orientation. In mathematics, his forte, Gerbert revived the ancient Greek tradition and replaced clumsy Roman numerals with the Indian numerals 1 through 9; he produced a simplified abacus, with instructions for its use; and he wrote at length on methods of multiplication and division. In astronomy he taught by means of a sphere showing the movements of the planets.

It is uncertain how much these innovations were the result of his early experiences in Spain and his contacts there with Arabic science and thought. Save for a short disputation on human reason, in which he showed an attraction toward the Platonic Ideas, he wrote no philosophical work. His only authentic scientific writings are mathematical. His letters, some of which contain discussions of mathematics, illustrate his political activity and the events of his age. In his later life he had little influence on the intellectual and spiritual life of his age. His earlier work as a teacher, however, marked an epoch.

Works by Gerbert

"Opera," A. Duchesne, ed., in J. P. Migne, ed., *Patrologia Latina*. Vol. 139, pp. 201–264. There is a more recent version edited by A. Olleris. Clermont-Ferrand, 1867.

Gerberti Opera Mathematica, N. Bubnov, ed. Berlin, 1889.

Lettres de Gerbert, J. V. Havet, ed. Paris, 1889. The best Latin text. Translated by H. P. Lattin as *The Letters of Gerbert With His Papal Privileges as Sylvester II*. Records of Civilization. Sources and Studies, Vol. 60. New York, 1961.

Works on Gerbert

Amann, E., "Silvestre II," in *Dictionnaire de théologie catholique*. Paris, 1939. Vol. XIV, cols. 2075–2083.

Leflon, J., *Gerbert: Humanisme et chrétienté au Xᵉ siècle*. Abbaye Saint Wandrille, 1946.

Picavet, F., *Gerbert, un pape philosophe*. Paris, 1897.

Uhlirz, M., *Untersuchungen über Inhalt und Datierung der Briefe Gerberts von Aurillac*. Schriftenreihe der historischer Kommission bei dem bayerischen Akademie der Wissenschaft, Vol. II. Göttingen, 1957.

DAVID KNOWLES

GERMAN PHILOSOPHY.

Although the earliest person mentioned in the histories of philosophy who is known to have been born in what is now Germany was St. Ambrose (340–397), the beginnings of German philosophy must be placed long after him. The ninth century saw the introduction of philosophy into Germanic lands through Charlemagne's establishment of schools; the thirteenth century first saw Germans as Germans begin to take an independent (although still minor) role in philosophical work.

THE BEGINNINGS, 800–1200

The schools established by Alcuin under Charlemagne's sponsorship had a political task—to provide civil administrators—and in comparison with the earlier monastic schools, they had a humanistic character. Hrabanus Maurus (776/784–856), a pupil of Alcuin and the first preceptor of the school in Fulda, established the *trivium–quadrivium* curriculum and prepared textbooks for the schools; and he participated in what was, so far as is known, the first philosophical controversy on German soil. The subject was Augustine's doctrine of predestination, and his opponent was the monk Gottschalk (Gotescalc, 808–867). The successor to Hrabanus in Fulda, Candidus (fl. 822), is credited with the first philosophical proof of the existence of God to have been invented in the Middle Ages, the "proof" that a hierarchy of perfections must have a highest member.

Decline of education. The division of the Carolingian Empire in 843 separated the more advanced western lands from the more primitive eastern marches; and the educa-

tional reforms instituted by Hrabanus and continued, at least intermittently, by his successors were not so successful as were like reforms made earlier by Alcuin in the West. Perhaps the long period of Latinate influence in what is now France and Belgium had had a slowly civilizing effect and provided a better basis for the later, still Latin educational reforms. Whatever the reasons, the schools in Fulda and St. Emmeram, the best in Germany, cut a poor figure in comparison with those at Paris and Tours. By the eleventh century even knowledge of Latin had declined so far that Notker Labeo (c.950–1022) translated Boethius, Martianus Capella, and some Aristotle into German for his students, who would not otherwise have been able to read them. Notker had to create a German philosophical vocabulary almost out of nothing, and he did so with great skill; but because he had no immediate followers, a similar creation had to be accomplished again in the fourteenth century by Meister Eckhart. So great was the decline of learning that by the twelfth century all the monks at St. Emmeram were said to have been illiterate, and German monastic life was hardly susceptible to the Cluniac reforms that had been so successful in France. Hence, Germany was largely left out of the early developments of Scholasticism, and the few Germans who desired an education had to go to other countries for everything beyond the most elementary study. The most notable of these gifts of Germany to France was Hugh of St. Victor (c.1096–1141), whose work has seemed to some to anticipate the later mixture of natural empiricism and supernatural mysticism sometimes thought to characterize the most representative German philosophers.

Intellectual climate. Since the few German philosophers there were, were studying in Paris or Italy, the church and schools in Germany rejected the little philosophy they were exposed to. Wandering dialecticians from Italy, called *peripatetici*, performed rhetorical feats in public that remind one of those of the Sophists in Athens and Rome; and they sowed doubts in sensitive minds about dogmas of the church. But the *peripatetici* succeeded only in bringing contempt upon the dialectical art and hence upon philosophy; and in the minds of the few in whom they did plant doubts, out of which philosophical examination might have grown, the doubts were eradicated through an effort to return to the simplicity of primitive Christianity, a morbid sense of sin, hatred of the intellect, and ignorant piety. Otloh of St. Emmeram (1010–c.1070) described his own wrestling with intellectual temptation in one of the first spiritual autobiographies written by a German; similarly Manegold of Lautenbach (c.1060–1103), who showed himself a good dialectician in the investiture dispute between Pope Gregory VII and Emperor Henry IV, at one time was as antiphilosophical as Otloh (see J. A. Endres, "Die Dialektiker und ihre Gegner," *Philosophisches Jahrbuch*, Vol. 19, 1906, 20–33).

Thus it was that in the larger issues of the time, which concerned the relative importance of faith and reason, German thinkers were of negligible importance, in spite of the fact that the political analogue of this philosophical issue—the respective claims of empire and papacy—was fought out in Germany itself. The main line of the political conflict runs through German history; but the main line in the history of philosophy runs through France, where the questions were debated on a high level by Anselm (1033–1109) and Abelard (1079–1142), who were able to reconcile faith and reason and to make the latter serve the former. The full development of Scholasticism in Germany did not take place until the time of Albertus Magnus, over a century after the Concordat of Worms in 1122 had settled, at least for a time, the political issues that paralleled this intellectual issue.

FIRST PERIOD OF ARISTOTELIANISM, 1100–1300

When philosophy did come to life in Germany, it was under two influences: the political and clerical forces locked in the continuing investiture conflict between the papacy and the empire, and the introduction of hitherto unknown writings of Aristotle.

Otto of Freising. The political-clerical and Aristotelian influences met first in one man, Otto of Freising (c.1114–1158), an uncle of Frederick II and probably a pupil of Hugh of St. Victor. Otto's conception of history was based largely on St. Augustine's philosophy, which gave form to his own historical works. In these works German national consciousness and Hohenstaufen pride were put into a philosophical framework that shows the style of a man of the world, not a monk. As a churchman, Otto assigned a superior status to the church, but he thought of the empire as having the divine mission of protecting the church; and therefore he feared that if the papacy triumphed over the empire, the church would be left defenseless. Deeply pessimistic, he saw the end of the world coming if the pope triumphed.

Introduction of the "Organon." Otto of Freising was the first and the chief philosophical spokesman for the Ghibelline conception of the state later defended by Dante. However, his principal contribution to philosophy lay in his making known the whole of Aristotle's *Organon*. He introduced into Germany the *logica nova*, logic based on the whole *Organon* instead of on only the parts that Boethius and Notker had translated. (Otto erroneously believed, however, that the translations he used were by Boethius.) Manuscript copies of Aristotle that he obtained in Italy were widely distributed in Germany, and they provided the basis for Albertus Magnus' knowledge of Aristotle, which at that time was unmatched in Europe. These translations did not immediately provide the shock felt when the differences between Plato and Aristotle became evident in the thirteenth century. Otto himself thought of Plato as "the philosopher" of the pair, and of Aristotle only as a logician and a fellow student, with Plato, of Socrates.

Controversy over Aristotle. The situation changed markedly in the thirteenth century, as translations of Aristotle's works other than the *Organon* became available from Spain and Aristotle's Arabic commentators became known in Europe. The physical works were the first to be widely used because they filled a real vacuum in knowledge; the metaphysical and ethical works, on the other hand, conflicted with well-established Platonic and Augustinian doctrines. Efforts to forbid and, when they failed, to restrict the study of Aristotle were repeatedly made during the early part of the century; they were probably less successful in Germany than in Paris. Arnold of Saxony had composed a commentary on Aristotle's *Physics* by 1230, only twenty years after the study of this book had been banned in Paris. Albertus Magnus (Albert of Bollstedt, 1193–1280) used all of Aristotle's writings on nature and made considerable progress in distinguishing between genuine Aristotelian and Neoplatonic doctrines. His last journey to Paris, in 1277, was made in order to protest against the condemnation there of Averroism insofar as this condemnation seemed also to threaten the kind of Aristotelianism propounded by Albert and his recently deceased pupil, Thomas Aquinas. He was not able to prevent the condemnation, but by that time Dominican Aristotelianism already dominated philosophical thought in Germany.

Philosophy and theology. The controversy among Albert, the Averroists, and the bishop of Paris was complicated by many circumstances that had little to do with philosophical issues and that may very well have been the real source of the bitterness of the dispute. The philosophical issue itself, however, was clear: Were Aristotle's writings authoritative in philosophy just as they stood, or were they to be corrected in the light of the higher truth of revelation? The Averroists upheld the former alternative, and to avoid open conflict they maintained (at least according to their opponents) the doctrine of double truth. Albert and Thomas Aquinas upheld the latter alternative: the conception of philosophy as being only the highest natural knowledge and ancillary to theology. This use of Aristotle was not condemned in 1277, no doubt largely through Albert's efforts to distinguish the two conceptions; and although Averroism continued in Paris despite the ban, the Albertine or Thomistic conception of the relation of philosophy to theology was maintained in Germany.

Thus, the effect of Albert's work in Germany was to maintain the scholastic hierarchy of philosophy and theology and to delay their separation or opposition, which had been effected in Paris by the Averroists. In this respect once again Germany appears to have lagged behind the developments to the west. German Dominicans tended to follow Albert's Aristotelianism with its mixture of Neoplatonism rather than the purer Aristotelianism of Thomas Aquinas, and they were often called Albertists rather than Thomists. The most important of the Albertists were Dietrich of Freiberg (1250–?1310), noted for his researches in optics and his explanation of the rainbow; Ulrich of Strassburg (d. 1277/1278); Hugh of Strassburg (Hugo Ripelin, fl. 1300); and Berthold of Mossburg (fl. 1318). More Thomistic were John of Lichtenberg (Joannis Picardi de Lucidomonte, fl. 1303–1313), Heinrich of Lübeck (fl. 1325), Heinrich of Gorkum (1386–1431), Nicolas of Strassburg (the first inquisitor of Meister Eckhart in 1326), Gerhard and Johann Sterngasse (fl. 1310), and Thomas of Strassburg (d. 1357).

REACTIONS AGAINST SCHOLASTIC ARISTOTELIANISM, 1300–c. 1551

The adjustment of the claims of philosophy and theology as achieved by Albertus Magnus was too delicate to stand the theological and political storms of the fourteenth century. Gregory VII's reform of the church had produced an extreme bureaucratism, ultramontanism, and formalism that left the religious needs of the people largely unsatisfied, thus opening the way to schism, anticlericalism, heresy, and nonsacramental forms of religious life. These movements were also favored by the development of free towns, which gave an opportunity for cultural developments not otherwise available in the continuing struggle between the imperial and spiritual powers. Within the framework of Scholasticism there arose the Franciscan teachings of Duns Scotus against the Dominican teachings of Albert and Thomas Aquinas; but Duns Scotus died shortly after coming to teach at Cologne, and his thought was far less influential in Germany than that of Aquinas.

The influence of the nominalism of Duns Scotus' fellow Franciscan, William of Ockham, however, was fateful for the entire history of German thought. And in opposition to the whole enterprise of Scholasticism (whether Franciscan or Dominican) there stood the mystics, the natural philosophers, and the humanists. Nominalism, mysticism, naturalism (and occultism), and humanism contributed in their own ways and times to dismantling the medieval balance of faith and reason by a division of labor and purpose between theology and philosophy. As a result of these four countermovements, diverse and antithetical as they were, theology was banished to, or took refuge in, the recesses of faith and mystery, and philosophy was, for the first time, free to follow its own course without constant and humble adjustment to the requirements of theology. How, and how little, this freedom was used by each of these antischolastic movements of the fourteenth to the sixteenth centuries will be briefly traced.

Mysticism. Fourteenth-century mysticism was not entirely new, nor was it directly related to the Protestant movement of the sixteenth century. Johannes Eckhart (1260–c.1327) followed in an already old tradition and was a faithful son of the church who, apparently, renounced what the church found heretical in his teaching. However, he inspired a religious life that was not easily accommodated to the established institutions of the church, and this was what was both new and portentous in his life and teaching. Mysticism among medieval philosophers was usually Neoplatonic in origin; but the mysticism among female orders (*Frauenmystik*) of Germany (as in Mechthild of Magdeburg [1212–1282]) was, on the other hand, not philosophical at all. Both kinds of mysticism contributed to Eckhart's thought, the latter especially and in a peculiar way. Eckhart was a trained scholastic philosopher who did not indulge in the erotic *Frauenmystik* but spoke the language of Platonism; but—and this is the peculiarity—he spoke this Neoplatonic language to philosophically untrained women (particularly to the women who were members of the semimonastic order of the Beguines, in which there was a tradition of mysticism). One of the chief duties of the Dominicans was the instruction of the Beguines, which explains the homely German of Eckhart's sermons and much of the form his preaching took. Eckhart de-eroticized and Platonized the traditions and lore of *Frauenmystik*, and there was a fruitful meeting of Neoplatonism

and Scholasticism in his work. The Scholasticism showed in the degree of precision he achieved in polemics with his accusers; and 28 of his theses that suggested pantheism and antinomianism were condemned.

This condemnation made the rest of fourteenth-century German mysticism of little importance to the history of philosophy. Johann Tauler (1300–1361) and Heinrich Suso (or Seuse, 1300–c. 1365) were not courageous or original philosophers like Eckhart. Avoiding speculations of the kind that brought about Eckhart's condemnation, they exerted a chiefly practical influence in the establishment of lay houses and schools in the Rhineland that were unusually independent of ecclesiastical authority.

Jan van Ruysbroeck (1293–1381) in Brabant, the unknown author (Thomas of Kempen?) of the *Imitatio Christi*, and the unknown author of the *Theologica Germanica* showed an independence from and even opposition to Scholasticism; from them came the *devotio moderna*, a movement emphasizing personal devotion that had its later Protestant counterpart in the Pietistic rejection of Protestant scholasticism in the seventeenth century. In their school at Deventer, the Brethren of the Common Life educated Nicolas of Cusa, Erasmus, and other philosophers and theologians of the following centuries.

Cusanus. Nicolas of Cusa (1401–1464) cannot be classified only as a mystic, for he markedly represented almost every contemporary movement away from Scholasticism. He has been claimed as a protohumanist and a natural philosopher; as the first Renaissance philosopher north of the Alps and as the final medieval thinker of importance. He does not fit into any one of the various types to the exclusion of the others. But as a philosopher Cusanus was closer to Eckhart than to any other figure in Germany, and his interest in mathematics and astronomy and his concern with ecclesiastical polity (he was perhaps the first real ecumenist in the history of the church) were brought into a quite remarkable synthesis with his mysticism. "Learned ignorance" was his path to mystical union and contemplation, and the kind of ignorance he propounded was reached through a study of mathematical paradoxes and scientific puzzles. Nature was itself thereby spiritualized, almost deified, and not cast off from God as a mere symbol or emanation. Cusanus is thus often considered by Germans of a like turn of mind (members of the school of Schelling, for example) to be the first genuinely German philosopher. While his contributions to astronomy have no doubt been exaggerated, he did influence Giordano Bruno and a long line of thinkers who have wanted to use the knowledge of nature for metaphysical and theological purposes.

Nominalism. The interconnection of the fate of philosophical ideas with political and social events is shown more vividly in the history of German nominalism than in almost any other chapter in the history of philosophy. In 1329 William of Ockham, the English Franciscan studying in Paris, escaped from Avignon, where he was being held for trial on charges of heresy, and took refuge with the excommunicated Emperor Ludwig II in Pisa and then in Munich. Like Marsilius of Padua, who was also at the court of Ludwig, Ockham engaged in the defense of the emperor against Pope John XXII; he formulated a political theory defending the rights of the emperor and challenged papal authority in political matters; as a founder of the conciliar theory (to which Nicolas of Cusa at one time adhered), he proclaimed the supreme authority of the Bible, tradition, and revelation as interpreted by church councils and claimed the right of councils even to remove a pope.

General influence of Ockhamism. The principal center of learning in Germany—the Dominican school in Cologne—was loyal to the papacy, and Ockham, being connected with the Court instead of with a school, seems to have had little or no direct personal influence on German philosophical thought. However, his influence in Paris was great, partly because of certain harmonies between his nominalist teaching and Averroism; one consequence of both was to make theology depend exclusively upon revelation and thus to make philosophy free from subservience to theology. Combined with Ockham's voluntarism, his nominalism made the will of God so inscrutable that even natural theology was only probabilistic. Ockham himself, as a theologian, found faith quite sufficient in theological matters; he was no skeptic. As a consequence, philosophy's connection with theology was loosened, and philosophy could go its own way.

"Its own way," of course, then meant "the way of Aristotle," not the way of Bacon or Descartes three centuries later, for at that time Aristotle gave the only large-scale nonreligious picture of the world. Hence, nominalistic Scholasticism, freed from narrow devotion to theological matters but not from the equally heavy hand of Aristotelian authoritarianism (except in the persons of a few outstanding men, none of them Germans), became the theory opposed by theologians (as well as humanists) for logomachy, logic-chopping, bad Latin, and triviality. Nominalism did make some contribution to the study of nature, but this grew more out of either an intelligent reading of or a criticism of Aristotle than out of a lively empiricism.

A combination of Aristotle and theology had proved victorious in the thirteenth century, and the separation of them by the Averroists and nominalists was the first step toward the replacement of Aristotelianism by other philosophies in the centuries ahead. What has here been described was a widespread phenomenon in the fourteenth century, not peculiar to—indeed not even prominent in—Germany, although its ramifications were felt there.

Nominalism in German universities. The Great Schism of 1378 put the Germans in Paris in a very difficult position, since France accepted Clement VII as pope and Germany sided with Urban VI. If they remained in Paris, they could not expect political preferment in Germany, so a general exodus from Paris commenced. Such nominalist teachers as Marsilius of Inghen (c.1330–1396) and John Buridan (d. c. 1358) had already been driven out of Paris, and now German students (among whom there were naturally many nominalists) also had to leave. Some went to the University of Prague, the first German university (founded in 1347 in opposition to papal wishes); others went to Vienna (founded 1365), Heidelberg (founded 1385), and Erfurt (founded 1392), all established as bulwarks against the French influence, and to Cologne, where the civil authorities had converted the Dominican school

into a *studium generale* about 1388. Marsilius of Inghen became the first rector of Heidelberg; Albert of Saxony ("Albertus Parvus," 1316–1390), a pupil of Buridan and one of the founders of the impetus theory in mechanics, became rector at Vienna (he had been rector in Paris). He was followed by Heinrich of Hainbuch (1325–1397), who expounded Ockham's conciliar theory.

In 1409 there was a sudden exodus of over a thousand German students and masters from Prague, in revolt against the university's favoring of Bohemians and of Hussite realism over the Ockhamism they had brought from Paris. Many of them organized themselves into the University of Leipzig, while others strengthened the nominalist parties in Heidelberg, Erfurt, Vienna, and Cologne.

Germany was now ready to participate fully in the intellectual, philosophical, and theological life of Europe. In each university (except Cologne and Prague) there was established the curriculum known as the *via moderna* (the study of the classical texts according to the logic of Ockham, with its excessive attention to their logical analysis); in some there were two curricula, the *via moderna* and the *via antiqua*, with a separate faculty for each. (The *via antiqua* was the study of the classical texts from the point of view represented by Thomas Aquinas and, in some instances, Duns Scotus, in which the *realia* and not the logical form was emphasized.) In all universities (with the two exceptions mentioned) the *via moderna* triumphed, but the battle went on with great bitterness, and from time to time the civil authority attempted to dictate the terms of victory or the terms of peace. For example, under Albertist influence the *via antiqua* won in Cologne, but the civil authorities argued that the Council of Constance had, in condemning Hus, also condemned his realism (the *via antiqua*); and therefore the university should forbid the teaching of *via antiqua*. The faculty replied that it was not the realists but Wycliffe who had led Hus into heresy and that the Council of Constance had not condemned realism; the faculty added that if they forbade the *via antiqua*, they would lose their students. They won their point.

Biel. Except for work in mechanics by Marsilius of Inghen and Albert of Saxony, and in theology by Gabriel Biel (1430–1495), the German Ockhamists cannot be regarded as philosophers of European standing, important though they were as formers of German university life. Biel, often called (erroneously) the last of the Scholastics, had great influence on theology. It was the theology of his followers (known as Gabrielists) that Luther learned in Wittenberg and developed to its bitter, anti-intellectual end. The impotence of human reason to penetrate the inner core of faith, taught by the excommunicated Ockham, thereby became one of the fundamental theses of Protestantism two centuries later. Thus, both mysticism (through the *devotio moderna*) and nominalism (*via moderna*) pointed toward Lutheranism.

Humanism. "Humanism" means many things in the history of philosophy. "Carolingian humanism" was obviously something quite different from the later movements, but even the German and Italian humanisms of the Renaissance are quite different phenomena. German humanism, so far as the historian of philosophy is concerned, was a reaction against Scholasticism under the initial influence of Italian Platonism. But whereas Italian humanism turned to Greek sources for its primary inspiration, German humanism added to this an even deeper concern for the origins of Christianity. Where Italian humanism remained literary and philosophical, or at most abstractly theological, German humanism became embroiled in theological – political controversies and prepared the way for the rejection of Catholicism.

Almost any generalization about the German humanists, however, fails to cover the rich diversity of the versatile men who called themselves humanists. Some even had good things to say about Scholasticism and remained in the priesthood; others were friendly to the scientific study of nature; some were nationalistic patriots, while others were citizens of the world; some were Catholics and some were Lutherans. However, they were united in their opposition to the bad Latin, the oversubtle logic, the pedagogical presumption, and the practical fruitlessness of the Schoolmen as being inadequate to both the religious and the secular needs of the time. Hence, if they were in universities, they emphasized the studies in the lower faculty as opposed to those of the higher faculties, preferring rhetoric to logic, moral philosophy to metaphysics, and classical Latin to school Latin. (Few of them, however, ventured to write in the vernacular, and thus they failed to avail themselves of their best weapon.) Where the Italian humanists could appeal to the golden age of Rome and Athens, the German humanists turned either to the values of primitive Christianity or to those values of barbarian Germany that had resisted the spread of Christianity; they mixed the gentleness of the *devotio moderna* with some of the fiercest chauvinism known to that century.

In the beginning, humanism was hardly more than a program for the reform of the universities through improving the arts curriculum by adding the study of the profane classical writers. Secular circles of humanists sprang up over Germany in the late fifteenth century, just as circles of the Friends of God had appeared outside the ecclesiastical establishment in the fourteenth century. The rapid development of the arts faculty produced a situation in which many men who had completed their baccalaureate degrees, but had not gone into the higher faculties, established private Latin schools without any theological or scholastic connections. All this set the stage for the most effective (because most bitterly amusing) attack ever made on Scholasticism, the *Letters of Obscure Men* (1515) by the humanists Crotus Rubeanus and Ulrich von Hutten. With the "return to the sources" emphasized by Erasmus of Rotterdam (1467 – 1536), Conrad Wimpfeling's history of Germany (1505), and the cabalistic studies of Johann Reuchlin (1455 – 1522), there was a convergence of humanist thought on opposition to the state of the church in Germany. Luther was no humanist, and most humanists did not embrace Protestantism, but humanism made the Reformation possible.

For this reason the German humanists deserve a place in the history of philosophy that they did not earn by their eclectic, unoriginal, and uncritical concern with philosophical issues. Their satires, lampoons, orations, and editions had a greater, though indirect, effect on German philosophy than any continuation of scholastic subtleties

could have had. However, if Nicolas of Cusa is not considered a humanist, no great system or synthesis of "humanistic philosophy" was achieved in Catholic Germany, and nowhere in Germany before the Enlightenment.

Natural philosophy and theosophy. In Europe it was not until the seventeenth century that natural science achieved a degree of autonomy and dignity that provided a basis for a philosophy in opposition to that based on revelation or the works of Aristotle. However, a devotion to a tutelary nature was possible before scientific knowledge of nature was gained, so that a "nature mysticism" developed long before there was any natural science or natural philosophy. When the latter replaced the former, it did so in the West, not in Germany; and the scientific revolution that determined the course of philosophy in France and England in the seventeenth century was not felt in Germany until the eighteenth. It is, therefore, only with caution that one can speak of science as playing a role in the German opposition to the medieval synthesis of faith and reason. The few authentic German scientific students of nature—Witelo (1230 – 1275), Copernicus (1473 – 1543), and Kepler (1571 – 1630)—had little influence upon German philosophical thinking. The great and revolutionary impact of Copernicus' work did not come until long after Scholasticism had lost its dominant position, and it was first effective in Italy, France, and England—not in the land of its birth.

The other sixteenth-century adepts in the study of nature, who neglected the mathematical methods that had been characteristic of Witelo, Albert of Saxony, and Nicolas of Cusa, were so far from the main scientific movements of the following centuries that they have little or no role in the history of science. Neoplatonic mysticism and occultism appeared in the work of Agrippa of Nettesheim (1486 – 1535), who later renounced such speculations for skepticism (*De Incertitudine et Vanitate Scientiarum*, 1527) and earned himself a place in the early history of the Faust legend. More important was Theophrastus Bombastus of Hohenheim (or Paracelsus, 1493 – 1541), who used his alchemical knowledge more for the improvement of medicine than for the transmutation of elements. He was influenced by Neoplatonism and perhaps by Nicolas of Cusa in developing the analogy between man and the whole universe in order to replace the doctrine of the humors of the body with an alchemical theory of the balance of elements in man and the world. Although he bombastically insisted on the authority of his own senses to understand nature and undoubtedly was skillful in observing health and disease, his speculations were as little controlled by fact as Agrippa's were; and his philosophical influence was not on the modest and objective study of nature that might have led to science but on the nature mysticism of Jakob Boehme and the natural philosophy of Schelling.

All of the movements sketched above made some positive contribution to the breakdown of scholastic philosophy; all but the last contributed mightily to the breakdown of the church in Germany and to the establishment of Lutheranism. Mysticism and nominalism passed into Protestant thought; humanism, although rejected by Luther, helped prepare his way and was quickly reinstated by

Melanchthon; but the philosophical impact of science was not felt until a later age.

THE REFORMATION, 1515–1680

The Reformation was not an event that belongs intrinsically to the history of philosophy; but since philosophizing never occurs in a political, social, or religious vacuum, and great spiritual changes do not occur in isolation from philosophical thought, it is not incorrect to refer to the "philosophy of the Reformation" as a distinct period and type in German philosophy. At first there was remarkably little distinctive of philosophy in Lutheran circles, so that one can hardly speak of a characteristic Protestant philosophy. However, two changes were to have important repercussions in philosophy: the establishment of new universities, and the special Lutheran and Calvinist teachings concerning the importance and dignity of work (vocation, *Beruf*) that gave a religious cast and urgency to scholarship outside the churches—in this respect continuing the antiecclesiastical trend begun by the humanists.

Luther began with Biel's theology and moved backward through Ockham and the late medieval mystics (including the author of the *Theologica Germanica*, which he published in German) to St. Augustine and finally to St. Paul, bypassing or denouncing the most important philosophical work of the period of high Scholasticism, the exploitation of the philosophy of antiquity for the purposes of Christian theology. Luther was no philosopher, and his hatred of Aristotle and "that whore, reason" inhibited philosophizing among most of his closest followers; this also had the effect of leaving an empty place in Protestant thought that could be filled with the most diverse philosophies. After Luther, therefore, four movements of thought are discernible in Germany: (*a*) Gnesio-Lutheranism, a rigorously dogmatic development in the predominantly Lutheran states and universities after the misnamed Formula of Concord (1577), which formula articulated dogma so rigidly that heresy-hunting replaced philosophizing (reason was denounced as "one of the women on whom silence in church is enjoined"); (*b*) Counter Reformation Catholic philosophy, centered in the Catholic states and universities, especially in Silesia, and mainly under the Spanish influence of Suárez and Molina, vigorously disseminated by the Jesuits; (*c*) Protestant mysticism; and (*d*) Protestant scholasticism, both Lutheran and Calvinist. Since Gnesio-Lutheranism was antiphilosophical, and since in Counter Reformation Catholicism the Germans were mere beneficiaries of a Europe-wide movement, they will not be discussed here. Protestant mysticism will be discussed briefly and Protestant scholasticism in some detail.

Protestant mysticism. Protestant mysticism was undoubtedly influenced by Luther's loosening of the established theological structure, by humanism's extrasacramental religious thought, by natural philosophy and theology, and, perhaps most of all, by those intense private religious feelings that had provided a principal motive for the Reformation itself. Although Luther translated the *Theologica Germanica*, he later renounced it, and mysticism (and in general private, noncommunal forms of religious life) was as vigorously fought by the Lutherans as similar movements in Catholicism had been fought two

centuries earlier. The most important Protestant mystics of this period were Sebastian Franck (1499–1543), Valentin Weigel (1533–1588), and Kaspar Schwenkfeld (1489–1561). The most original Protestant mystic was Jakob Boehme (1575–1624), whose fantastic nature mysticism lies in the line of development from Eckhart and Nicolas of Cusa to Schelling. Another later mystic was Johannes Scheffler (or Angelus Silesius, 1624–1677), who became a Catholic.

Protestant scholasticism. Protestant scholasticism was founded by Luther's most immediate disciple, and Reuchlin's nephew, Philipp Schwarzert (or Melanchthon, 1497–1560). Melanchthon began his career as a humanist and came to Wittenberg as professor of Greek; for a time he was influenced by Luther's hatred of Aristotle but then recovered his independence (that is to say, his native dependence on Aristotle). His mild and irenic disposition and his humanistic education served him well in the task he assumed, that of establishing a Lutheran educational system based on humanistic learning, and codifying Protestant doctrine for the purpose of unifying opposing religious views. By his efforts in the latter direction, however, Melanchthon opposed the victorious Gnesio-Lutherans, and his followers, notably Georg Calixtus (1586–1656), were accused of both crypto-Catholicism and crypto-Calvinism. Indeed, some did become Catholics, and many became Calvinists; but in the long run the full fruit of Melanchthon's labors was found in Calvinism rather than in Lutheranism, where Gnesio-Lutheranism triumphed.

The development of Protestant scholasticism from Melanchthon's humanism went through three stages. First, Melanchthon saw the need of an essentially Protestant educational system. He was one of the principal figures in the establishment of the University of Jena (1556) (some of the older universities became Protestant). The basis of Protestant education was Aristotelian and humanistic; it emphasized the logical, ethical, and psychological works of Aristotle rather than his metaphysics.

In the second stage, this nonspeculative humanistic education was met by a renewal of scholasticism during the Counter Reformation, and the curriculum of the Jesuit schools and even some of their textbooks were adopted by the best Protestant schools. Hence, when metaphysics was reintroduced, it was largely Catholic (Suarezian) metaphysics. (See Ernst Lewalter, *Spanisch-jesuitische und deutsch-lutherische Metaphysik des 17. Jahrhunderts*, Hamburg, 1935). But whereas the Suarezian influence on a largely uniform body of Catholic thought was so strong and pervasive that original Catholic philosophizing in Germany almost ceased, Catholic scholasticism represented only one step toward a genuine Aristotelian metaphysics among the Protestants, who were greatly influenced at this time by the Aristotelian renaissance in Italy of Zabarella, Piccolimini, and Scaliger. Commentaries on Aristotle for use as university textbooks began to reappear (Daniel Cramer's was the first in 1594).

This new enthusiasm for Aristotle was strongly criticized by Nicolaus Taurellus (Öchslein, 1547–1606), who showed a new spirit in not only condemning the appeal to authority but also being largely independent of Aristotelian teachings. His iconoclasm brought him into sympathetic relations with the followers of Peter Ramus at a time when other Lutherans, led by Jakob Schegk (1511–1587) and Philip Scherb (d. 1605), were attacking Ramism and attempting to keep it out of Germany. In his theory of knowledge (a very moderate empiricism), his cosmology (a deterministic theory that compared the universe to clockwork), and his minimal theology (an attempt to cut the articles of faith to a bare minimum), Taurellus was before his time and, indeed, in advance of the representatives of the third and last stage of Protestant scholasticism.

The third stage, that of autonomous metaphysics, was reached when scholastic metaphysics was developed in at least putative independence of Aristotle. The principal writers in this stage were Christoph Scheibler (1589–1653, called the Protestant Suárez), Cornelius Martini (1568–1621), Jakob Martini (1570–1649), Daniel Stahl (1589–1654), Georg Gutke (1589–1634), and Abraham Carlov (1617–1686). However healthy this development seems in the narrow world of Lutheran scholasticism, these men were contemporaries of Bacon, Hobbes, Descartes, and Spinoza, who were "modern" to a quite different degree. These Germans were untouched by the scientific and mathematical thought that gave a new direction to European philosophy. In addition, the devastation of the Thirty Years' War (1618–1648), from which Germany did not fully recover for another century, contributed to the backward condition of Germany during the greatest period of English, French, and Dutch philosophizing. Among the scholastics, only Erhard Weigel (1625–1699) in Jena showed any appreciation of the decisive importance of mathematics and science for metaphysics.

Calvinist philosophy. Contemporaneous with the above movements was the development of philosophy among the Calvinists. Although Zwingli's humanism was Platonic rather than Aristotelian, and Calvin's theology more Scotist than Ockhamist, it is difficult to see any simple correlation of philosophical differences with genuine theological points of difference; the principal points of difference between Calvinist and Lutheran philosophy seem to reflect general and pervasive differences of *Weltanschauung* rather than technical theological differences. Calvinism was more sympathetic than Lutheranism to humanistic and this-worldly concerns; it appealed to the rising middle classes of the towns instead of to the conservative peasantry; its congregational organization gave it more freedom from direct political control; and it was fortunate in the enlightenment of some of the Calvinist princes who were its protectors.

The outstanding philosophical differences between Lutheranism and Calvinism, therefore, lay in Calvinism's more vigorous humanism, its earlier separation of theology from philosophy, and its earlier concern with purely philosophical issues, especially those of gnoseology (epistemology). Thus Calvinism reached its third stage sooner than Lutheranism did, in the representative work of Clemens Timpler (1568–1624).

As might be expected, Calvinism proved more open than Lutheranism to the anti-Aristotelian teachings of Peter Ramus, who had been a student of the Calvinist Johannes Sturm (1507–1589) and was himself converted to Calvinism during his time in the Palatinate. While Lutheran universities were condemning and forbidding Ramism

(Leipzig, 1591; Helmstedt, 1597; Wittenberg, 1603), the leading teachers in the Calvinist universities—Rudolf Goeckel (Goclenius, 1547–1628), Bartholomäus Keckermann (1571–1609), and Johann Heinrich Alsted (1588–1638)—were Ramists or Philippo-Ramists (the latter, under the influence of Melanchthon, gave a more prominent place to Aristotle).

Although the Calvinists developed epistemological interests earlier than the Lutherans, their principal work in philosophy lay in the theory of politics, a field almost wholly neglected by the Lutherans. Johannes Althusius (1557–1638) at the University of Herborn taught natural law's independence of divine law, a doctrine that did not appear in Lutheranism until the work of Samuel von Pufendorf (1632–1694), whom the Calvinists had to protect from Lutheran persecution.

Reactions to Protestant scholasticism. Repeatedly in the history of philosophy the same types of reaction against scholasticism occur: mysticism, humanism, and naturalism. So it was at the end of the seventeenth century. There was a revival of nonsacerdotal and nonsacramental religious life and "practical mysticism" among the Pietists—Philipp Spener (1635–1705) and August Hermann Francke (1663–1727); a revolt against scholasticism in the name of practical, this-worldly (courtly) education, as in Jacob Thomasius (1622–1684) and his son Christian (1655–1728); and a turn to the study of nature. While the first two were primarily the work of Lutherans, the Calvinists were responsible for the third.

German Calvinism was almost confined to the Rhineland and the Netherlands in the sixteenth century; during the Spanish war (c. 1570) German Calvinism was strengthened by an influx of Calvinists from the Low Countries into the Palatinate, where the University of Heidelberg became the stronghold of Calvinism until the Thirty Years' War, during which it became Catholic. After a short restoration of Calvinist teaching following the Treaty of Westphalia (1648), which gave inadequate guarantees to the Calvinists, Louis XIV made the Palatinate and its re-established university in Heidelberg again Catholic. Calvinists in the Palatinate then returned to Holland, while Huguenots from France settled in Brandenburg, whose elector had become Calvinist. The exodus of German Calvinists to Holland brought them into contact with Cartesian and other Western influences; and German students (especially from Silesia and Saxony) went to Holland as they had gone to Paris centuries before. Thus the Lutheran and Catholic repression of Calvinists had the unexpected effect of exposing Germany to the new movements that Louis XIV unsuccessfully attempted to stamp out in France and opened a new chapter in the history of German philosophy. (See Herbert Schöffler, *Deutsches Geistesleben zwischen Reformation und Aufklärung*, Frankfurt, 1956, on the important Dutch influences.)

PENETRATION OF WESTERN IDEAS, 1650–1700

Scholasticism was largely unaffected by the developments of science and the problems the new scientific world view created for Aristotelian metaphysics. The beginnings of modern philosophy, in contrast to scholasticism, were marked by the prerogatives accorded to epistemology over metaphysics; although modern philosophy did not, in its earliest phases, deny metaphysics, it did not, on the other hand, take the possibility of metaphysics for granted. While German scholasticism went almost unchallenged in the German universities, such Western nonacademics as Bacon, Descartes, and Hobbes were bringing the whole scholastic and metaphysical system under scrutiny and attack. Calvinism was open to Ramist teaching in Germany, but it was not until the dissemination of Cartesian teaching in the Low Countries that Germans were affected by Western concern with the implications of natural science and mathematics for metaphysics. Since it was mostly German Calvinists who were in Holland, Calvinist teaching was the first to be affected. By the last quarter of the seventeenth century, therefore, Cartesianism was being taught in Calvinist universities—by Johann Christoph Sturm (1635–1703) in. Altdorf; by Christophorous Wittich (1625–1687) and Johann Clauberg (1622–1665), both of whom taught in Herborn and Duisberg; and by Johannes Sperlette (1661–1725), a Frenchman in Halle, which had been established as the Prussian university in 1694. All these men taught a mixture of Cartesianism and scholasticism. Daniel Sennert (1572–1637) followed Gassendi, and Sennert's pupil Joachim Jungius (1587–1657) developed the corpuscular philosophy still further; they were not scholastic, but because their kind of philosophy needed the sustenance of a community of scientific interest, which was lacking in Germany, their work had little effect.

The teachings of Spinoza were brought to Germany by Friedrich Stosch (1646–c. 1704) and by Ehrenfried Walther von Tschirnhaus (1651–1708), whose attempt to do philosophy *more geometrico* makes his work a transition between Spinoza and Christian Wolff. An effort to modify scholastic teaching by mathematical methods was made in Jena by Erhard Weigel (1625–1699), who influenced Leibniz and Wolff.

Leibniz. The first great German thought to show the influence of Western ideas was, of course, the philosophy of Leibniz (1646–1716). In Leibniz all the intellectual currents of his time except mysticism and Pietism flowed together, and from him came the principal line of thought of the German Enlightenment. His influence was felt in all the fields in which he worked and in which he had been influenced by the scientific and philosophical thought of England, France, and Holland. But unlike his contemporaries in these countries—Descartes, Spinoza, Locke, Hobbes, Newton—Leibniz was also deeply and positively influenced by scholasticism, and there was a strain of active piety in him quite unlike anything found among the Western philosophers, except Pascal and Malebranche. The work of Leibniz that was best known in his lifetime was the *Théodicée,* hardly the work of a revolutionary spokesman for a new age. His solid scientific work had no followers in Germany, and his philosophy was destined to triumph in Germany only in the form of Wolff's pedantic scholasticism. His indirect influence on learning, as an entrepreneur of ideas in learned journals and academies and as a friend of those high in church and state, was greater than his direct contribution to the corpus of German philosophy. In fact, his direct influence was greater

after his death, following the publication of his *Nouveaux Essais* (1765), than in his own lifetime.

THE GERMAN ENLIGHTENMENT, 1700–1780

Protestant scholasticism suffered a fate in the seventeenth century like that of Catholic scholasticism in the fifteenth because both failed to satisfy the religious, intellectual, and practical needs of their time. Both led, by reaction, to nonsacramental and even anticlerical forms of religious life and to humanistic, this-worldly concern; both were helpless against the advance of science and the improvements in technology made possible by science. However, Germany was nearly a century behind the Western countries in throwing off the yoke of scholasticism, all its intellectual apparatus, and its educational and quasi-political manifestations. When the Enlightenment finally did dawn in Germany, it was marked by three differences from the corresponding movements in France and England. First, it was not initiated or sustained by successful scientific work; second, it did not focus on needed political reforms; third, it was immersed in an atmosphere of religiosity.

In regard to the lack of scientific work, Newtonianism, the most characteristic scientific thought of the century, was little known until the middle of the century. In addition, Germany was isolated from the science of the future both by the absence of worthy followers of Leibniz and by the reputation of Leibniz himself. Second, the profusion of small German states neither permitted nor inspired high political thought or earnest political criticism in the universities; also, the princelings did not need to employ men of imagination and intellect (as was the case especially in England). There was no original and fundamental political thinking until France shocked Germany with her Revolution; before there had been some ineffective propaganda but philosophically little more than innocuous repetitions of Grotius, Pufendorf, and Althusius; a shocked horror at Hobbes; passive acceptance of absolutism; and a pious hope that absolutism would be enlightened and beneficent. As to the third characteristic of the German Enlightenment, just as German humanism was religious, so also was the German Enlightenment. German thinkers were, by French and English standards, timid in their religious thought, and none went to the extremes of, say, Voltaire. There were perhaps two reasons for this.

One was that Germany, unlike France, had a great variety of religious forms, with Calvinism, Lutheranism, and Catholicism existing side by side. One could reject the religion of his youth without having, as in France, to become radically antireligious; one could always move to a neighboring state or university. It was no accident that the center of the German Enlightenment lay in those parts of Germany (Saxony, Silesia, Brandenburg, and Prussia) where the various confessions had learned of necessity to tolerate each other.

The other reason was that the Enlightenment was coeval with a religious revival and was, so to speak, the secular arm of Pietism. Pietism as a religious doctrine and Enlightenment as a cultural *Weltanschauung* have much in common: a recourse to the healthy understanding of the common man, a commitment to the dignity of one's profession outside the church, and a concern with the *Bildung*—a certain dignified passivity in the face of oppression—of the populace. Pietists and Enlighteners were not always congenial, however. Their relations were marred by disgraceful conflicts (such as those of August Francke and Christian Thomasius and of Streigel and Wolff), and Pietists did not share the Enlighteners' optimism about secular education. The pervasive effect of Lutheranism was to keep the German Enlightenment from reaching the radical and explosive stages of the French Enlightenment, and much of the later German reaction against the Enlightenment in general was a reaction against what were regarded as the excesses of the French Enlightenment.

Thomasius. The German Enlightenment had its principal sources in two men, Christian Thomasius and Christian Wolff. Thomasius is chiefly remembered as the first university professor to declare his independence of scholastic education by announcing his lectures in German. In 1688 he founded the first learned journal to be published in German. In 1690 he moved to the Ritterliche Akademie in Halle, which was raised to the status of a university by Frederick I of Prussia as a school for his civil service. Thomasius was in every respect a forerunner of the "popular philosophy" of the mid-eighteenth century, except that for a while he was a fervent Pietist until he was cured of "enthusiasm" by reading Locke.

Followers of Thomasius. Thomasius was not an original philosopher, but he was a spokesman for a new period in German thought. Education was to be for the man of the world, the *honnête homme*. Instead of fighting heresies, Thomasius fought the persecutors of witchcraft: he fought skepticism not by epistemological criticism but by appeal to "healthy human reason." His teaching, keeping its eclecticism but going more deeply into philosophical issues (in defending itself from Wolffian subtleties), was continued by Johann Franz Buddeus (or Budde, 1667–1729), Joachim Lange (1670–1744), and Nikolau Hieronymous Gundling (1671–1729) in Halle; by Budde and his son-in-law Johann Georg Walch (1693–1775) in Jena; and by Andreas Rüdiger (1673–1731) and Johann Burkhard Mencke (1674–1732) in Leipzig. But the full fruition of Thomasius' thought was not achieved until the development of "popular philosophy" in the middle of the eighteenth century; the first half belonged to the Wolffians.

Wolff. Christian Wolff (1679–1754) was, like Thomasius, eclectic rather than original; but he was fortunate in having Leibniz as his archetype. Wolff's career had four periods. From 1703 to 1710 he worked primarily as a mathematician; and although he was not a creative mathematician, his clearly written works reformed German mathematics instruction. From 1710 to 1723 he taught philosophy in Halle and wrote his principal German works. Driven from Halle in 1723 through a Pietistic cabal, he took refuge in the Calvinist University of Marburg, where he repeated his basic philosophical writing in Latin. In 1740 he was recalled to Halle by Frederick the Great and continued his Latin writings, mostly on natural law; but his influence was spent by then.

Wolff's deadly style and his unmatched prolixity make it difficult to understand his immense popularity. His writing combines the worst features of scholastic pedantry and a specious mathematical form; but he must be praised, as Kant did, for his thoroughness (*Gründlichkeit*), and he must be regarded as the principal coiner of the German philosophical vocabulary. Wolff's philosophy is a highly systematized form of Leibnizianism. It contains a much more restricted version of the doctrine of pre-established harmony but a much less restricted appeal to the principle of contradiction in Wolff's attempts at a priori proofs, in excruciating detail, of all sorts of propositions, including the true, the false, and the trivial. Yet Wolff was obviously motivated by an immense intellectual good will and a real pedagogical passion; he was Germany's archetypal schoolmaster, and he deserves the name *praeceptor Germaniae* just as much as Hrabanus Maurus or Melanchthon.

Wolff's influence. Before Wolff was recalled to Halle, his influence in Germany was very extensive. His pupil Georg Bernhard Bilfinger (1693–1750) coined the epithet "the Leibniz–Wolffian philosophy," to the displeasure of both Leibniz and Wolff; Johann Christoph Gottsched (1700–1766) wrote a popular presentation of Wolff's system that became the most widely used philosophy textbook during the second quarter of the century; G. F. Meier (1718–1777) and Alexander Gottlieb Baumgarten (1714–1762) extended Wolff's system to include aesthetics, which thus appeared for the first time as a distinct philosophical discipline; Martin Knutzen (1713–1751) was Kant's teacher; and Johann August Eberhard (1739–1809) fought Kant on Wolffian grounds until the end of the century. Joachim Georg Darjes (1714–1791), one of the most influential teachers in Germany at the time, taught Wolffianism at Jena, although he rejected some parts of it. Wolff's Latin works brought him the approval of the Jesuits, and they were used in Jesuit schools in Germany even in the nineteenth century. Although Wolff returned to Halle in personal triumph, he was not able to sustain his great intellectual influence in his old age, and he died almost ignored.

The Berlin Academy. Toward the middle of the eighteenth century the intellectual climate of northern Germany underwent a marked change that was largely attributable to the tolerance, enlightenment, and personal example of Frederick the Great (1712–1786), "the philosopher of Sans Souci." In 1750 Frederick re-established Leibniz' academy in Berlin, an act that had manifold effects on German intellectual life. It attracted philosophically-minded scientists from other countries to Berlin—Leonhard Euler (1707–1783) from Switzerland; Johann Heinrich Lambert (1728–1777) from Alsace; and Pierre de Maupertuis (1698–1759) from France—thereby bringing German philosophy into fruitful contact with science for the first time since Leibniz. The academy had a division, unique at that time, for speculative philosophy; and its whole spirit was opposed to the dominance of any single dogmatic system, favoring worldly rather than systematic and rigorous philosophy—Samuel Formey (1711–1797), a Wolffian and the permanent secretary, nevertheless wrote a "popular"-style work entitled *La Belle Wolfienne*. Through its membership and its prizes to nonmembers, the academy favored the publication of eclectic, critical, and historical books and papers bearing on the intellectual issues of the times. Because of the many French thinkers in Berlin and Potsdam—including Julien Offroy de La Mettrie (1709–1751)—and also because of a certain similarity in the intellectual climate, Berlin at the time was called Paris on the Spree.

However, with the exception of Gotthold Ephraim Lessing (1729–1781), who preferred English literary models to French ones, and the speculative metaphysics of the previous century (Spinoza's and Leibniz' in particular) to the rather jejune mixtures of eudaemonism, impiety, and free thinking that were common in Berlin, Germany produced no thinker or writer to be compared with any of a half-dozen French contemporaries.

Göttingen. Another new center of Enlightenment thought was the University of Göttingen, established in 1737 by George II, king of England and elector of Hanover. This university, with a function comparable to that of Halle in the previous century, was open to English influences that to some extent counterbalanced the French influence in Berlin, and many translations of English philosophers came from the Göttingen circle. Because it was conceived as both a research and teaching institution, Göttingen has often been called the first modern university. In systematic philosophy, however, it carried no great weight; only Johann Georg Feder (1740–1821), a critic of Kant and a widely respected publicist, and the physicist Georg Christoph Lichtenberg (1742–1799), known for his aphorisms, need be mentioned.

Popular philosophy. A third factor contributing to the change in intellectual climate, closely related to and in part including the French influences at Berlin and the English influences at Göttingen, was the universal acceptance of the Wolffian and Thomasian ideals of popular education and enlightenment in contrast to ecclesiastic and courtly education. As in other countries, this was a period of newspapers and "moral weeklies," of popular didactic poetry, of sentimental and empirical psychology, of the influence of Rousseau and the English novelists, of educational reform—Johann Bernard Basedow (c. 1724–1790) and Johann Heinrich Pestalozzi (1746–1827)—and of such societies as the Illuminati and the Freemasons.

Decline of orthodox religion. A final factor in the change in the intellectual climate was the decline of the Pietism and orthodoxy of the early part of the century, in part occasioned by French free thought and English deism and in part by earnest historical and philosophical criticism in Germany by such writers as Hermann Samuel Reimarus (1694–1768), Johann Salomo Semler (1725–1791), and Lessing.

Common characteristics. It would not be possible to categorize many philosophers, as some historians have done, as representing only one aspect of the German Enlightenment to the exclusion of the others. Few of them were sufficiently systematic to be definitely one kind of thinker and not another; "eclectics" represents a miscellaneous classification that cannot be neatly divided into schools and movements. To varying degrees all the thinkers of the period, including Frederick the Great, Moses Mendelssohn (1729–1786), Ernst Platner (1744–1818), and even Euler can be called popular philosophers; there

is no need to reserve this as a term of opprobrium for only the most superficial of them. All of these men represented and spread the individualistic, bourgeois, intellectualistic, optimistic doctrines that were characteristic of the English, French, and German Enlightenments. German thinkers were, on the whole, much more cautious in their social and religious criticism than the French *philosophes* were, and they lacked the commitment to science that one finds in Diderot. But however much they differed among themselves in the selections they made from other people's ideas, and however much the synthesis and style showed the character of the individual thinker, they were united in holding to the *Bildungsideal* that has stereotyped our conceptions of the eighteenth century.

KANT, 1724–1804

The death of Lessing and the publication of the *Critique of Pure Reason* occurred in the same year, 1781. The conjunction of these two events was significant, for Lessing had been one of the most typical and also the wisest and deepest of the Enlightenment thinkers, and Immanuel Kant was to put almost every fundamental concept of the Enlightenment into jeopardy. Although Kant's essay "What Is Enlightenment?" was the best propaganda for the whole movement and its most forthright manifesto, Kant was also, in Mendelssohn's words, "the all-destroyer." He denied the theory of a unitary source of knowledge (against both rationalists and empiricists), the possibility of speculative metaphysics and theology (against both the theologians and their opponents), the materialistic interpretation of living nature, and a simple theodicy of inanimate nature. He rejected the optimistic illusion of an automatic and unending progress in history. He condemned utilitarianism and eudaemonism in ethics but at the same time refused to admit any religious foundation of ethics to take the place of eudaemonism. In the philosophy of art he destroyed the Gottschedian notion of rule-governed craftsmanship as sufficient without genius to produce a work of art, yet he heaped contempt on the pretensions of unschooled genius as a way of life. In politics he despised the theory of enlightened despotism and was a partisan of the French and American revolutions, unshocked by their violence; he spoke with a compassion, rare in the German Enlightenment, of "respect for the common man" while rejecting the theory of "sound human sense"; and he remained, at least in his personal ethos, a Pietist. From Wolff Kant got his ideal of *Gründlichkeit;* and publication of Leibniz' *Nouveaux Essais* gave him access to a level of rationalism that his predecessors had not known. The acute criticisms of Wolff by Christian August Crusius (1715–1775), Kant's "recollection of Hume," and his near enthusiasm for Rousseau gave his whole thought a dialectical tension lacking in the Wolffians and the popular philosophers in Berlin and Göttingen.

Critics of Kant. A great philosopher has a polarizing effect on the intellectual world; he forces others to become critics, or epigoni, or creative explorers of the new horizons he has seen. So it was at the end of the eighteenth century. Kant had critics who supported the metaphysics and popular philosophy he attacked: Feder in Göttingen, Christian Garve (1742–1798), Eberhard, and Platner, to name only the most important.

There was a much more significant group of critics who rejected Kantianism because of its intellectualism and rationalism. These philosophers were critics of the Enlightenment in general and saw Kant as continuing the inadequate Enlightenment conceptions of man, God, and nature. They anticipated the ideas that were important after Kant, whereas the first group defended an already lost cause. The most important men in this second group were Johann Gottfried Herder (1744–1803), Friedrich Heinrich Jacobi (1743–1819), and Johann Georg Hamann (1730–1788). No doubt the rejection of rigorous intellectual discipline among these thinkers (for which Kant chided his former pupil Herder) can be attributed to some of the same factors that, in literature, led to a rejection of classical restraint and rule-governed art among the writers of the *Sturm und Drang*. This anti-Kantian movement, obvious in Herder, was undoubtedly one of the influences that favored the romantic movement in literature toward the end of the century.

The philosophers of feeling of the nineteenth century, such as Franz von Baader (1765–1841) and, to some extent, Friedrich Schleiermacher (1768–1834)—the former a Catholic and the latter a Protestant—present a like rejection of Kant's intellectualism. Jean Paul Richter (1763–1825) was directly influenced by Jacobi but remained closer to Kant than Jacobi and the others were. Although differing among themselves, they were all committed to a doctrine of the superiority of some kind of direct insight—feeling, intuition, faith, *Ahnung* (presentiment)—over the Kantian analytic and critical transcendental method; and thus they thought they were justified in claiming knowledge where Kant had denied it was possible.

Although he was not a philosopher of feeling, another critic of Kant who anticipated later thought, and was not an apologist for the earlier popular and metaphysical systems, was the Göttingen philosopher Gottlob Ernst Schulze (1761–1833), whose criticism of Kant seemed to arise from the skepticism he discerned to be implicit in Kantianism. Schulze's work was not in the spirit of the times, neither hailing Kant as a savior nor seeing him as only a relic of Enlightenment; and its full value was not recognized until much later.

Disciples of Kant. The faithful disciples of Kant, writing in the journals, teaching his doctrines in various universities, making outlines and textbooks based on his writings and lectures, editing anthologies of his works, and conducting salons in Berlin (where Kantianism was the topic of lively talk) included Marcus Herz (1747–1803), Johannes Schultz (1739–1805), Karl C. E. Schmid (1761–1812), Gottlieb Benjamin Jäsche (1762–1842), Wilhelm Traugott Krug (1770–1842), J. G. K. C. Kiesewetter (1766–1819), Georg Samuel Albert Mellin (1755–1825), Christian Jacob Kraus (1753–1807), Johann Heinrich Tieftrunk (1759–1837), and Lazarus Bendavid (1764–1825). They earned praise—some from Kant, all from later writers and students—for their work in making Kant's difficult teachings more widely known and intelligible than they would have been if seen only through the eyes of his critics.

"Semi-Kantians." Finally, there were the "semi-Kantians," who were forced by difficulties in Kant's position to criticize, reconstruct, and ultimately to some extent to transcend it. Kant's views on many important matters were either unclear (as on the relation of phenomena to things-in-themselves), inadequately worked out (as on the relation of various mental "faculties" to one another), or, in the eyes of many of his followers, clearly wrong (as on the relation between formal and transcendental logic, between moral law and sentiment, and between morality and religion). Depending upon the interests of the semi-Kantian, one or the other of these problems became decisive, and the solution proposed for it forced changes and adjustments in the rest of the system, so that what sometimes began as a reconstruction of Kant ended as the construction of a somewhat new, but still Kantian, philosophy. Men who went through such a procedure were Friedrich Schiller (1759–1805); Karl Leonhard Reinhold (1758–1823); Jakob Friedrich Fries (1773–1843), through whom Jena became a principal center of Kantianism; Friedrich Eduard Beneke (1798–1854); Jakob Sigismund Beck (1761–1840); Salomon Maimon (1752–1800); Friedrich Bouterwek (1765–1828); and Christoph Bardili (1761–1808). This group anticipated many later developments of Kantianism in Germany—idealistic Kantianism (Maimon and Beck), realistic Kantianism (Reinhold), and psychological Kantianism (Fries). Fries's philosophy was so comprehensive that he may well deserve a place among the great system builders instead of among the semi-Kantians; but political persecution delayed his achieving much influence in the universities, and the later developments in nineteenth-century German philosophy were not influenced in any marked degree by his thought.

THE GREAT SYSTEMS, 1790–1830

Both the semi-Kantians and the speculative idealists of the period from about 1790 to 1830 began with Kant, and both went beyond him. However, the idealists went so far beyond him that it is barely justifiable to call them Kantians at all. Kant denounced the first of them, Fichte, but he was generally friendly with the semi-Kantians he knew; and only Schopenhauer among the truly independent philosophers was careful to remind his readers how much he and they owed to Kant.

There is much in Kantian philosophy that is reminiscent of the Faust legend as interpreted by Goethe, and Kant has appeared to some historians as a tragic figure who repeatedly drew boundaries he could not cross and left empty spaces he could not fill because he found that the human mind was not capable of doing either. While the semi-Kantians were troubled by inconsistencies or fallacious arguments in the Kantian corpus, the speculative idealists were impatient with the whole conception of a mind that constantly reminded itself of its limits and the dangers of speculation. The speculative philosophers have been called fanatics for totality (*Ganzheitsfanatiker*) for to their Faustian yearnings for the infinite in contrast to Kant's "bathos of experience," which seemed to them as obsolete as anything else left over from the days of Frederick the Great—Hegel contemptuously said that for Kant experience meant "a snuff box here, and a candlestick there."

Thus, there were two factors in the philosophical movements of this period, a set of technical philosophical problems left unsolved by Kant and a new cultural climate in which Kantian objectivity and matter-of-fact thinking was no longer in the spirit of the times.

Search for a metaphysics. The strictly philosophical problem, recognized equally by the semi-Kantians and the speculative idealists, was to develop a metaphysics that would replace the rationalist metaphysics Kant had destroyed and that would be the transcendental philosophical system to which Kant had only written prolegomena, foundations, *Anfangsgründe*. (Hence it was young Fichte's claim that *he* was the systematic Kantian, not Kant himself.) Such a metaphysics entailed at least the following: (1) denial that there is a substantial, unknown, and unknowable thing-in-itself; (2) denial of the sharp demarcation between faith and knowledge; (3) denial of sharp divisions between the various "faculties" (between understanding and reason, thinking and sensing, intellectual intuition and sensuous intuition, imagination and understanding) and an effort to replace them with concepts from a more "organic" psychology; (4) complete exclusion, so far as possible, of the individualist psychological structuring of experience and its replacement with a much vaguer transcendental apparatus (by Fichte) or by structures of objective (not psychological) *Geist* ("spirit, mind") as developed in history (by Hegel); (5) denial of the intellectual frameworks of classical logic, mathematics, and Newtonian science as being fixed, given, Procrustean beds to which philosophy had to be fitted; (6) denial of the validity of universal, and hence empty, moral laws conceived abstractly, apart from historical, social, and even idiosyncratic personal contexts; and (7) denial of abstract formalism in the theory of art, the isolation of aesthetic from other values, and the restriction of genius to the creation of works of fine art. While many of these seem to be internal philosophical problems of the kind that would concern any student of Kant even today, it is readily seen that all of them, with the possible exception of the first, have ramifications throughout the intellectual life of the early nineteenth century.

Widening the scope of philosophy. The general, rather than technically philosophical, factors in the intellectual life of the post-Kantian period were perhaps of even more importance, but they are harder to define. The word "romanticism," because of its ambiguity, signifies most of the important factors in German cultural life of that time. Romanticism had a pervasive effect on philosophy that was by no means adequately manifested in the individual philosophers, such as Friedrich Schlegel (1772–1829) and Novalis (1772–1801), who are classed in the "romantic school." Romanticism—a cult of feeling, a love of antiquity, a nurturing of idiosyncratic individuality, a satisfaction with ambiguity, a warm feeling of brotherhood, a contempt for bourgeois virtue but a love of bourgeois maidens, *Wanderlust* but a longing for hearth and home, a patriotism based on quixotism, and traditions created for the occasion—this conflation of ideas alone cannot sustain

an integral philosophy, but its emotional richness can widen philosophers' horizons. Even more than in the time of Wolff, philosophical meditation and contemplation and argumentation became omnipresent, and it was perhaps during this period that the Germans got the reputation of being a "philosophical" people; they could philosophize about anything, and their *Ganzheitsfanatismus* immeasurably broadened the scope of technical, professional philosophical concern. There came into philosophy a concern with folk art, the Middle Ages, mythology, the Orient, music, mysticism, and all manner of things the Enlightenment had either ignored or rationalized; history and philology became sciences without losing their philosophical moorings; comparative studies of various cultures were carried on, empirically and systematically. Hence, when Hegel spoke of the *Phenomenology of Mind* as his "voyage of discovery," he was not using the words "phenomenology" and "mind" in a sense that Kant would have understood, and his whole conception of his task as a philosopher was not unlike that of Faust: to know, and hence to be, all things, and not to let them utterly pass away but to save them up in some eternal vision of process.

Opposition to Western ideals. The enrichment of the fund of experience for which the philosopher was to provide a phenomenology and a metaphysics was, however, restricted by an opposing force that grew out of the French Revolution. Goethe was the best representative of the synoptic goal of thought and art, but the ideals of eighteenth-century cosmopolitanism did as much as Greece and Italy to keep him from being (or at least remaining) a romantic (hence also his indifference to the Wars of Liberation). But the romanticists, being in full revolt against Enlightenment, naturally reacted against what was regarded as the final outcome of Enlightenment, the French Revolution and Napoleon. The apparently unlikely confusion of Napoleon with the ideals of the Enlightenment led them to a confusion of Germanism with ideals opposed to the Enlightenment. This confusion was present throughout the period of German idealism and was definitely fostered by the idealists; this is why German idealism is looked upon by many Germans as the climax of the cultural life of their country but with dismay by many critics of Germany. It was then, when Germany almost for the first time acted as a political unity against the West, that Germany also set itself against Western (Enlightenment) thought. (See Hajo Holborn, "Der deutsche Idealismus in sozialgeschichtlicher Beleuchtung," in *Historische Zeitschrift*, Vol. 174, 1952, 359–384).

Meister Eckhart and Jakob Boehme, or at best Spinoza, replaced Descartes and Locke as philosophical mentors; Adam Müller (1779–1829) put Burke ahead of both Hume and Adam Smith as a social philosopher; the Middle Ages (and even German antiquity, in the person of the Teutonic warrior Arminius) were re-evaluated and placed above the Age of Reason. Fichte's Closed Commercial State could not have Schiller's "Ode to Joy," with its glorification of universal brotherhood, as an anthem. Schelling's *Naturphilosophie*, which stood in no fruitful relation to the natural sciences; K. C. F. Krause's almost incomprehensible pantheism; Schleiermacher's emotional and romantic religiosity; Jacobi's and Franz von Baader's philosophy of faith; Schopenhauer's pessimism and anti-intellectualism; Hegel's Prussianism and panlogism; and, a little later, Richard Wagner's sophisticated primitivism—all these were results of a philosophical and emotional movement that escaped not merely from Kantian reserve in epistemology and metaphysics but also from the ideals of the Age of Reason.

The great idealists. If there is such a thing as a "German national philosophy," a philosophy clearly distinct from and proudly independent of the philosophical traditions of other nations, so persuasive that it influences almost all phases of the cultural life—in a word, if there is a philosophy that expresses the "German soul" and puts into a comprehensive metaphysics the "German experience"—then it is the philosophy of German idealism, by which is meant primarily the philosophy of Hegel, Schelling, and Fichte. The philosophies of Schleiermacher (although his most important work was not in metaphysics), Schopenhauer (although his influence came later), and Krause (on strictly metaphysical grounds) could be included, although none of these men ever had the popular influence of the great triumvirate. When critics of or apologists for Germany say "German philosophy," this is the philosophy they mean. It is by reading into earlier centuries some of the characteristic doctrines of these men that such earlier philosophers as Eckhart, Cusanus, Boehme, and Paracelsus have been identified as *echt deutsch* long before there was a Germany; and when historians complain about the low state of philosophy in the middle of the nineteenth century, they mean the low state of German idealism at that time.

Later idealists. It should not be denied that the great idealists had much in common, both in their specific metaphysical teaching and in their *Weltanschauung*. On the basic idealist point they were at one: The empirical world for all of them was the appearance of the real world; the real world was not to be reached by plodding empiricism and cold reason but by mystical experience or intuition or *Vernunft* or dialectic; the real world was spiritual in nature, not material, and supported man's highest cultural aspirations in morals and religion (and, for some of the thinkers, in art and politics). Into this formula can be put the variables for each of the early nineteenth-century idealists; when this is done, most of the viable possibilities for idealism have been exhausted. As a result, German idealists since that time have seemed to repeat the teachings of the idealists of the romantic period and either to fall into patterns established at that time (even though no direct influence of even detailed similarities can be established in every instance) or to be eclectic (with a little taken from all).

Immanuel Hermann Fichte (1796–1879), Hermann Ulrici (1806–1884), and Christian Hermann Weisse (1801–1866) were theistic idealists opposed to Hegel's "pantheism"; Gustav Theodor Fechner (1801–1887) was a panpsychist whose views much resembled some aspects of Schelling's *Naturphilosophie;* Rudolph Hermann Lotze (1817–1881) and Wilhelm Wundt (1832–1920) came to philosophy through the natural sciences (biology and psychology, respectively) and were concerned with the relation of phenomenal to numenal reality, the

mind–body relation, and the mechanism–teleology controversy; with Hans Driesch (1867–1941) they fought materialism by showing the teleological implications of the best natural science of their day. Except for his pessimism, which was uncharacteristic of most idealism, Eduard von Hartmann (1842–1906), who further developed the voluntarism of Schopenhauer, was another typical figure among the epigoni of the great idealists at the beginning of the twentieth century.

In their opposition to materialism and to the obvious extravagance of *Naturphilosophie* as practiced by Hegel and Schelling, the later idealists were undoubtedly aided by the development of Aristotelian studies in Berlin under Adolf Trendelenburg (1802–1872), who also directly influenced his pupil Rudolf Eucken (1846–1926). Eucken's philosophy had more kinship with Fichte's than with Hegel's; and with the exception of the metaphysical idealists of the Neo-Kantian schools (see H. Levy, *Die Hegelrenaissance in der deutschen Philosophie*, Berlin, 1927), the most important direct influence that Hegel had on German philosophy was not on the professional metaphysical idealists.

DISSOLUTION OF THE GREAT SYNTHESIS, 1830–THE PRESENT

The recent history of any discipline is not likely to show the sharp contours of its more remote history. A history of German philosophy suffers especially from this lack of perspective, since there can be no doubt that the number and variety of significant figures in its history has increased since 1800 and that, with the possible exception of Nietzsche, no single philosopher has given, in the manner of a Leibniz, a Kant, or a Hegel, a vantage point from which a uniquely significant path can be discerned. This section, then, must deal with a variety of equally significant but very divergent directions in German philosophy. Besides the continuing line of idealists, there have been the "young Hegelians," materialisms and positivisms, Neo-Kantianism, various forms of realism, the philosophy of life and culture (including Nietzsche), and the philosophy of the *Geisteswissenschaften*.

Right and Left Hegelians. Hegel was one of the great intellectual jugglers in the history of philosophy. The number of theses, antitheses, and syntheses he could keep suspended in the air was unmatched by any other philosopher: "The truth," he said, "is thus the bacchanalian revel, where not a member is sober; and because every member no sooner becomes detached than he collapses, the revel is also a state of transparent, unbroken calm" (*Phenomenology of Mind*, Preface). But members did become detached, and they did live their independent lives. Hegel's most important disciples went beyond and against him, and against each other.

Right Hegelians. The most important issue in the interpretation of Hegel at the time of his death (1831) was that of the relation of his conception of philosophy to his conception of religion. The Right Hegelians held that Hegel taught the identity of the truth of religion and the truth of philosophy; hence, his philosophy as a whole had to be interpreted supernaturalistically, transcendentally, and theistically. No philosopher of the first rank held this view, but it triumphed in the German universities, which were strongholds of political conservatism and religious orthodoxy. The strict identification of Hegelianism with ideological forces opposed to social and political reform was no doubt responsible for the low esteem in which Hegel was held especially after the Revolution of 1848. Right Hegelians did, however, distinguish themselves through continuing the master's work in the history of philosophy. Much of the most important work in this field was done by Johann Eduard Erdmann (1805–1892), Karl Rosenkrantz (1805–1879), Karl von Prantl (1820–1888), and Kuno Fischer (1824–1907).

Left Hegelians. The Young Hegelians or Left Hegelians are much more important in the history of the nineteenth century and in contemporary philosophy. Their interpretation, or rather their use, of Hegel, although important for future philosophy prevented them for the time being from exercising a direct influence by keeping important university posts closed to them; indeed, Karl Marx (1818–1883), Heinrich Heine (1797–1856), and Arnold Ruge (1802–1880) had to live in exile.

The Left Hegelians rejected the orthodox theistic interpretation of Hegel, but for the most part they accepted the dialectic features of Hegel's thought while rejecting the idealistic. Doing so also meant transcending Hegelian philosophy as such, rejecting the Hegelian claim that philosophy, and a fortiori Hegelian philosophy, represented a final stage in dialectic. Thus it came about that the most important work of the Left Hegelians was not in philosophy proper, or at least not in a philosophy aiming at understanding the world, but in a philosophy whose task it was to change the world. It was obvious that religious obstacles had to be surmounted before this change could occur, and this was the work attempted by David Friedrich Strauss (1808–1874) and Ludwig Feuerbach (1804–1872) in their historical and psychological studies of religion. Anarchism was the natural consequence of the solipsistic teachings of Max Stirner (1806–1856). While Feuerbach tended naturally in the direction of metaphysical materialism, he did not go so far as the metaphysical materialists, who worked solely from science without any Hegelian inspiration, or as far as Marx and Friedrich Engels (1820–1895), who in their dialectical materialism "stood Hegel on his head."

The work of Marx and Engels best illustrates the point that the important influence of the Left Hegelians was on social and political life, not on academic philosophy. All the philosophers mentioned (with the exception of Strauss) were committed to social and political reform, and Ferdinand Lassalle (1825–1864), the founder of the Social Democratic party in Germany, was a Hegelian. There is something paradoxical about Hegelianism being archly conservative and at the same time the source of most of the revolutionary movements of the nineteenth century; it is a paradox Hegel might have enjoyed working out had he lived to see it. But it is not difficult to resolve: *Any* philosophy taken statically becomes conservative, even if the philosophy itself is a philosophy of change; but no philosophy of the nineteenth century before Nietzsche's was more Heraclitean, dynamic, or evolutionary than Hegel's.

Thus the dialectic, not the idealism, inspired social criticism and change. It remains, of course, a difficult question whether Hegel's peculiar dialectic depends upon his idealistic logic, and whether dialectics of the sort attempted by Engels and Marx have anything in common with Hegel's except the name.

Recent Marxism. Since the division of Germany, dialectical materialism has been the outstanding philosophical movement in the eastern portion. Much reinterpretation of the history of German philosophy has been undertaken in order to revive the memory of almost forgotten German materialists or naturalists of the eighteenth and nineteenth centuries and to emphasize the social and economic, as well as the political, motives of many of its leading figures. Georg Lukacs is the leader in this revisionism.

Metaphysical materialism. In contrast to dialectical materialism, metaphysical materialism did not come from the internal tensions of Hegelianism but arose (as materialism often does) in reaction to philosophy itself—as if philosophy necessarily meant speculative idealism, a priori methods, and the like. Although Feuerbach and Engels became metaphysical materialists, the main impetus toward materialism came from such natural scientists as Robert Mayer (1814–1878) or from men trained in the natural sciences—Jacob Moleschott (1822–1893), Ludwig Büchner (1824–1899), Karl Vogt (1817–1895), and Heinrich Czolbe (1819–1873). Although they did not call themselves materialists, two significant natural scientists with a speculative drive, Ernst Haeckel (1834–1919) and Wilhelm Ostwald (1853–1932), belong in this group.

The widespread popularity of the writings of all these men was undoubtedly caused by the spread (for which some of them deserve the credit) of Darwinian ideas among the general public and by the respect for science and technology that was one of the new features of German life after the rapid industrial revolution. Certainly the traditional idealism oriented around the humanistic studies now had a rival in scientific materialism that it had lacked previously in German philosophy.

Positivisms and the philosophy of the physical sciences. One effective response to the new anti-idealistic and antireligious philosophy was found by professional philosophers in the revival of the critical concern with epistemological problems in the manner of Kant and Beneke; the word *Erkenntnistheorie* was invented during the mid-nineteenth century. The movement of thought symbolized by this new word clipped the metaphysical wings of science by a critical examination of its methods, suppositions, and limits; and it helped the sciences do their proper job by providing them with a rigorous methodology and—perhaps inadvertently—the modicum of metaphysics they needed. For the first time since Kant and Leibniz, there was sophisticated and sympathetic understanding of the problems of the actual sciences, a real philosophy of science instead of speculative philosophies of nature.

Hermann von Helmholtz (1821–1894), the most important scientist in Germany, found that his scientific studies of vision had important implications for scientific theorizing about the world; for example, in the development of possible applications of non-Euclidean geometries and of the theory of perception as a system of signs. From Helmholtz, who thought his psychological work pointed in Kantian directions, came one of the incentives for the Neo-Kantian movement. Friedrich Albert Lange (1828–1875) studied the history of materialism and pointed out its psychological and, in some sense, its idealistic presuppositions; and studies by Hermann Cohen (1842–1918) of the foundations of the integral calculus also pointed to the necessity of a "return to Kant." Later contributors to the epistemology of the exact sciences were Hans Vaihinger (1852–1933), whose fictionalism showed some resemblance to American pragmatism, and Ernst Cassirer (1874–1945), whose work in the philosophy of science had marked resemblances to later logical positivism.

Positivisms. Ernst Laas (1837–1885) gave the most systematic presentation of positivism, but without the Kantian predilections of Helmholtz and Lange. Richard Avenarius (1843–1896) developed his theory of "empirio-criticism," which had much in common with the sensationalistic positivism of Ernst Mach (1838–1916), who directly influenced the development of the logical positivism of Moritz Schlick (1882–1936) and his pupils and colleagues. Views somewhat similar to those of Avenarius were presented by Theodor Ziehen (1862–1950), Wilhelm Schuppe (1836–1913), and Johannes Rehmke (1848–1930). Eugen Dühring (1833–1921) related positivism to social reform and was himself attacked by Engels.

Realisms. At the risk of considerable oversimplification, German realism since Kant has been either Cartesian (asserting the existence of things-in-themselves as substances), Aristotelian (asserting the naturalistic teleological features of cognition and other mental processes), or Platonic (asserting the intrinsic subsistence [*Ansichsein*] of ideal entities, such as meanings and values). Cartesian realism, implicit in Kant, was emphasized by some of the semi-Kantians, most systematically by Johann Friedrich Herbart (1776–1841); among the Neo-Kantians the same view was developed by Alois Riehl (1844–1924), and against the Neo-Kantians it was propounded by Oswald Külpe (1862–1915).

Aristotelian realism. Aristotelian realism was strengthened by the historical work of Adolf Trendelenburg in Berlin, and Neo-Thomist realism was maintained by such orthodox Catholic philosophers as Josef Kleutgen (1811–1883) and Josef Geyser (1869–1948). In non-Catholic circles the Aristotelian teleological theories became associated with such "philosophies of life" as those of Rudolf Eucken and Hans Driesch, who may equally be claimed by the idealist schools.

Platonic realism and the rejection of psychologism. What has here been called Platonic realism for lack of a more accurate name was formulated by the Bohemian Catholic Bernard Bolzano (1781–1848). Bolzano, whose metaphysics of spiritual substances resembled those of Leibniz and Herbart, is most important in the history of philosophy for his abortive effort to free logic from dependence on or confusion with psychology. He made logic the study of judgments and concepts *an sich;* that is, without regard to whether they are thought or not. In this, Bolzano was far in advance of his time; and most German logic continued to be a mixture of logical and psychological, theoretical and practical notions—the work of Chris-

toph Sigwart (1830–1904) was typical. When Edmund Husserl (1859–1938) turned, about 1900, against his own earlier psychologistic work in logic and mathematics, he formulated a theory that resembled Bolzano's in many respects and also showed the profound effects of the teachings of another Catholic philosopher, Franz Brentano (1838–1917), on the relations between logic and psychology. Somewhat similar realisms and antipsychologisms were found in the works of Alexius von Meinong (1853–1920), Christian von Ehrenfels (1859–1932), and Carl Stumpf (1848–1936).

Phenomenology and existentialism. Husserl's own philosophizing began as an attempt to give a presupposition-less description of the essential structure of cognitive consciousness, without any specific metaphysical consequences, but it later tended more and more in the direction of transcendental idealism, and many who followed his conception of the proper phenomenological method either continued to reject metaphysics or maintained metaphysical positions different from his and from each other's, although most of them were realistic in various senses. Max Scheler (1874–1928) and Nicolai Hartmann (1882–1950) remained Platonic realists in value theory; Hartmann's realistic ontology was perhaps the last great systematic metaphysical synthesis accomplished in Germany.

Influenced, at least at first, by Husserl were Martin Heidegger and, in his work in psychotherapy, Karl Jaspers. A close connection between phenomenology and existentialism was maintained in France, but in Germany the two movements, although both were influenced by Husserl, became opposed to each other. Husserl's claim that phenomenology could make philosophy a "rigorous science" was rejected by both Jaspers and Heidegger, who were interested in philosophizing from an individual existential starting point and did not aspire to the kind of universal objectivity Husserl believed could be achieved by "pre-suppositionless description" (see Herbert Spiegelberg, "Husserl's Phenomenology and Existentialism," *Journal of Philosophy*, Vol. 57, 1960, 62–74). Jaspers never attained the influence within German philosophy that Heidegger achieved, Heidegger being without doubt the most influential philosopher in Germany from the 1920s almost to the present; there are many signs, however, that Heidegger's influence is now beginning to wane.

Geisteswissenschaften and philosophy of culture. The rapid growth of the natural sciences in Germany was matched by perhaps the even more important development of the human studies (*Geisteswissenschaften*), especially history and philology, as putatively rigorous disciplines. The practitioners of these sciences, beginning with Herder, Wilhelm von Humboldt (1767–1835), and Friedrich Karl von Savigny (1779–1861), had been concerned with the methodology of history, language study, and jurisprudence; and the historians Heinrich von Treitschke (1834–1896) and Leopold von Ranke (1795–1886) had dealt with (and created problems for) the critical philosophy of history. The question of the proper and peculiar methods of the social sciences was raised to a new level, however, when the method of the natural sciences was brought to full consciousness by the positivists and the

Neo-Kantians. The contrasting categories and methods of the natural and social sciences were among the principal interests of the Heidelberg Neo-Kantians—Wilhelm Windelband (1848–1915) was the most prominent—and by Georg Simmel (1858–1918). The most important and influential thinker on these problems was Wilhelm Dilthey (1833–1911). Folk psychology, class structure's influence on patterns of thought, social and economic concepts in relation to religion, the persistence and change of value systems, and the problems of historicism and historical objectivity and relativism were dealt with by Wilhelm Wundt (1832–1920), Ernst Troeltsch (1865–1923), Max Weber (1864–1920), Max Scheler (1874–1928), Eduard Spranger (1882–1963), and Karl Mannheim (1893–1947). Toward the end of his life Ernst Cassirer turned his attention from natural science and intellectual history to the philosophy of the social and moral sciences.

Nietzsche. By philosophy of culture is meant the philosophical study of culture as it is manifested in history and social organization, not the study of the philosophical presuppositions of our study of culture itself. Obviously no sharp line of demarcation can be drawn between these two inquiries, although some philosophers are remembered chiefly for their contributions to one rather than the other. The outstanding philosopher of culture of the nineteenth century was undoubtedly Friedrich Nietzsche (1844–1900), whose teaching was a violent reaction against the commonly accepted ideals of the latter part of the nineteenth century (liberalism, democracy, utilitarianism, and nationalism), built upon a voluntaristic philosophy in which values were seen as created by the heroic or slavish human will distorted by various forms of social pressures. Nietzsche's philosophy is not easily categorized (a feature of which he would have been proud), and like other philosophers who have held opposing principles in a state of dialectical tension, he has been seen as holding quite diverse and incompatible views by almost all later students of his work, among whom the most important and influential have been Karl Jaspers, Martin Heidegger, and Alfred Bäumler, the last of whom represented Nietzsche as a proto-Nazi.

Spengler and other nonacademic writers. The other important philosopher of culture was Oswald Spengler (1880–1936), whose work enjoyed world-wide popularity during the period between 1918 and 1939 but had little or no impact on professional philosophy except perhaps to strengthen the historicism and relativism that emerged from much of the work on the foundations and limits of the *Geisteswissenschaften.* In fact, philosophy of culture, as this term is understood here, has been most effectively practiced by nonacademic writers with an especially urgent and messianic, or equally urgent but practical, concern with political and social problems, such as Hermann von Keyserling (1880–1946), the poet Stefan George (1868–1933), the statesman Walther Rathenau (1867–1922), and the proponents of racial and national socialist ideologies, including Houston Stewart Chamberlain (1855–1927), Arthur Moeller van den Bruck (1876–1925), Alfred Bäumler, and even Alfred Rosenberg (1893–1946), whose work was earnestly and enthusiastically discussed by professional philosophers during the period of national socialism.

Since the end of World War II, philosophy in West Germany has begun to be concerned with modern logic, the philosophy of language, and the methodology of science; and the great gap that separated it from Anglo-Saxon philosophy during the first half of the twentieth century now seems to be growing narrower.

"GENIUS" OF GERMAN PHILOSOPHY

German philosophers since 1800 have been deeply concerned to discover those features of German philosophy that distinguish it from that of other European nations. More than any other people, Germans have not only done philosophy but have also talked about doing philosophy; although they did not invent the word "metaphilosophy," metaphilosophy has been one of the principal interests of German philosophers at least since Fichte, and perhaps since Wolff. However, the concern with the nature of German philosophy has not been confined to Germans. Philosophers of other countries have repeatedly discussed what it is that has made Germany "a nation of poets and philosophers," and many of them have found the explanation of what they do not like about German political life in the philosophical proclivities of the German mind.

A great deal of dangerous nonsense has been written on all sides of this question. A suitable selection of heroes or villains can be made to justify the claims that it lies in the "nature of the German soul" to develop philosophies that are mystical, idealistic, monistic, transcendental, nonempirical, absolutistic, intuitive, pantheistic, naturalistic, *volkisch*, étatistic, Protestant, or Faustian, among many others. Such efforts at summary, description, and evaluation of a long and complicated philosophical tradition have been quite unconvincing in their results and have usually followed contemporary stereotypes and served as propaganda. But the very fact that German philosophers have put so much time and effort into the project of a national typology is of some importance, and an understanding of that fact may lead to an understanding of what is indeed peculiar to German philosophy.

Cultural isolation. In any search for distinguishing characteristics, it is difficult to discern clearly the difference between cause and effect, between the essential and the accidental. But perhaps the central reason for the large quantity of German metaphilosophy carried out along nationalistic lines lies in two closely related features of German life—Germany's relatively high degree of isolation from Western intellectual, and specifically philosophical, movements throughout much of its history, examples of which have been given in abundance; and the fact that through most of German history the universities have been the most effective, and sometimes the only effective, all-German institutions, the only institutions that could, and from time to time did, speak for Germany. These two factors together contributed to the form of German intellectual life as a whole, and especially of German philosophy.

German philosophers before about 1650 were cut off, or cut themselves off, from Western influences. Part of this isolation can be attributed to Lutheran orthodoxy and political intolerance. Some of it was perhaps owing to the fact that the intellectual base for modern philosophy, which lay in mathematics and natural science, had not been laid in Germany, so that German philosophers simply had little interest in, and no understanding of, the problems that were transforming philosophy in France, Holland, and England. Later nationalistic writers have imagined that the moral and philosophic genius of Germany intentionally quarantined itself from the infection of rationalism and empiricism (see, for example, Franz Böhm, *Anticartesianismus: Deutsche Philosophie im Widerstand*, Leipzig, 1938). Another name for such a *Widerstand*, of course, is "provincialism," and many a German philosopher has expressed a contempt for the work of his non-German confrères that is equaled only by his ignorance of their work.

If one grants the belief in a uniquely German philosophy that is the creation of the German soul uninfected by foreign influences (except those that came from Greece), and yet finds that the actual variety of systems of philosophy produced in Germany is at least as great as that in other countries, one would expect that diversities in philosophy would be handled much more bitterly than in countries in which either philosophy is not taken so seriously or the individual philosopher does not presume to be the spokesman for the soul of the nation. This is indeed the case. On the one hand, at any time (with the exception of parts of the century between 1830 and 1930) there has been one overwhelmingly representative system of philosophy—whether Wolffianism, Kantianism, idealism, Neo-Kantianism, or Heideggerism—with other rival systems neither enjoying the prestige nor getting the hearing of the dominant system. (Consider, for example, the systematic and successful efforts to people the universities with Wolffians in one century, with Hegelians in the next.) On the other hand, differences of philosophic teaching, even minor differences, have been magnified and debated in the manner of hairsplitting theologians on whose interpretation of a text may hang the fate of mankind.

Role of the universities. The role of the universities in the history and shaping of German philosophy cannot be overemphasized. Whereas the strictly philosophical importance of Oxford, Cambridge, and even Paris has been comparatively small during much of their histories, German philosophy has been intimately related to German university life. The founding of new universities (such as Leipzig in 1409, Halle in 1694, Berlin in 1809) has often symbolized important changes in the philosophical climate. The variety of competing German philosophies is, no doubt, partly attributable to the large number of universities (large compared to that of England, France, or Italy), in each of which the *professor ordinarius* was expected (even in Wolffian and Hegelian times) to produce his own multivolume system and to start his own school.

Most German professors of philosophy have produced philosophies, and most philosophies in Germany have been produced by professors of philosophy. This has given German philosophy a peculiar form that appears in other modern national philosophical traditions only very late in their course. The form is generally didactic, systematic, encyclopedic, prolix, humorless, and not for the layman; the philosophy grows out of, and is compressed back into, textbooks, encyclopedias, histories of philosophy, professional journals, school manifestoes, proceedings of academies and learned societies, debates between the disciples

of the great masters, and *Festschriften* on the masters' birthdays. Masters and disciples alike show symptoms of *furor academicus*, and the epigoni feel a loyalty to a philosophical school (such as Marburg Neo-Kantianism) that an Englishman might well feel for Cambridge but hardly for Cambridge Platonism.

Philosophy remained an important professional and professorial craft because of the persistence of the scholastic ideals and practices well into the eighteenth century, long after Scholasticism had disappeared from the major universities elsewhere. It became a *Fach* (discipline, or university department) in the modern sense early in the nineteenth century, long before it did elsewhere, because practice of the *Geisteswissenschaften* in seminars and research groups was established when the philosophical faculty, with its seminars in the *Geisteswissenschaften*, became the dominant educational factor in Germany, with research regarded as one of its major functions. In this great change to the modern conception of the university, with its attendant professionalization of disciplines (including philosophy), the University of Berlin led the way. Thus, an almost unbroken line of university philosophy connects Albertus Magnus (in the *Studium generale* in Cologne), Melanchthon (professor in Wittenberg and first professor, temporarily, in Jena), Thomasius (first professor in Halle), and Fichte (first rector of Berlin) with the present-day members of the Allgemeine Gesellschaft für Philosophie. Only Cusanus, Leibniz, Schopenhauer, and Nietzsche among the great philosophers were not primarily known as professors.

This complex set of facts serves to explain some of the peculiarities of German philosophy rather more simply than theories of the German "soul" or race. While one cannot categorically deny that one people may have a more philosophical turn of mind than another, and must grant that it has been commonly believed—at least since 1800—that Germans are uniquely endowed with good philosophical minds, the circumstances adduced here serve to explain, to some extent at least, the form and style of German philosophy.

(See also ATHEISMUSSTREIT; GEISTESWISSENSCHAFTEN; GERMAN PHILOSOPHY AND NATIONAL SOCIALISM; HEGELIANISM; LOGICAL POSITIVISM; NEO-KANTIANISM; PANTHEISMUSSTREIT; PHENOMENOLOGY; and PHILOSOPHICAL ANTHROPOLOGY. See German Philosophy in Index for articles on German, Austrian, and Swiss thinkers.)

Bibliography

Good general histories of German philosophy are Eduard Zeller, *Geschichte der deutschen Philosophie seit Leibniz* (Munich, 1873); J. E. Erdmann, *Grundriss der Geschichte der Philosophie*, 2 vols. (Berlin, 1866), translated by W. S. Hough as *History of Philosophy*, 3 vols. (London, 1890), Vols. II and III; and Frederick Copleston, *History of Philosophy*, Vol. V, *From Wolff to Kant* (London, 1960), and Vol. VI, *From Fichte to Nietzsche* (London, 1963). Essential for scholarly work is the encyclopedic T. K. Österreich, Max Frischeisen-Köhler, and Willy Moog, eds., *Überwegs Grundriss der Geschichte der Philosophie*, 12th ed. (Berlin, 1924), Vol. III (through Kant) and Vol. IV (the nineteenth and twentieth centuries in Germany). Werner Ziegenfuss, *Philosophen-Lexikon*, 2 vols. (Berlin, 1949), is a useful reference work, especially on minor philosophers, Émile Bréhier's *Histoire de la philosophie allemande* (Paris, 1921), is too brief to be very useful. The history of German philosophy as seen in one university is excellently treated in Max Wundt's *Die Philosophie an der Universität Jena* (Jena, 1932); Friedrich Paulsen's *Geschichte des gelehrten Unterrichts* (Leipzig, 1885; 2d ed., 2 vols., Leipzig, 1896), is an indispensable work.

Three good intellectual histories of Germany in English are W. J. Bossenbrook, *The German Mind* (Detroit, 1961); Frederick Hertz, *The Development of the German Public Mind*, 2 vols. (London, 1957–1962), which covers to the end of the Enlightenment; and Hans Kohn, *The Mind of Germany* (New York, 1960), which deals mainly with the nineteenth and twentieth centuries.

Medieval philosophy is treated by Hans Henning, *Der Ursprung der nordischen Philosophie* (Berlin, 1933); and A. Richter, *Der Übergang der Philosophie zu den Deutschen im VI.–XI. Jahrhundert* (Halle, 1879–1880). Michael Seidlmayer's *Weltbild und Kultur Deutschlands im Mittelalter*, translated by D. Barker as *Currents of Medieval Thought With Special Reference to Germany* (Oxford, 1960), gives useful background information. Nominalism is studied by Gerhart Ritter, *Studien zur Spätscholastik*, Vol. II, *Via antiqua und via moderna auf den deutschen Universitäten des XV. Jahrhunderts* (Heidelberg, 1922); and in Georg Kaufmann's *Geschichte der deutschen Universitäten*, 2 vols. (Stuttgart, 1888–1896). The standard work on mysticism is W. Preger, *Geschichte der deutschen Mystik im Mittelalter*, 3 vols. (Aalen, 1874–1893); J. M. Clark, *The Great German Mystics* (Oxford, 1949), is also of value. On humanism, see R. Newald, *Probleme und Gestalten des deutschen Humanismus* (The Hague, 1962); and L. W. Spitz, *The Religious Renaissance of the German Humanists* (Cambridge, Mass., 1963). Albertists and Thomists are discussed in G. M. Löhr, "Zur Geschichte der kölner Dominikanerschule im 14. Jahrhundert," in *Divus Thomas*, Vol. 23 (1945), 57–84; and in Martin Grabmann, "Der Einfluss Alberts des Grossen auf das mittelalterliches Geistesleben," in *Zeitschrift für katholische Theologie*, Vol. 25 (1928), 153–162, 313–356. Grabmann's work also appears in his *Mittelalterliches Geistesleben*, Vol. II (Munich, 1936), pp. 325–412.

The philosophy of the Reformation period is treated in Erich Franz, *Deutsche Klassik und Reformation* (Halle, 1937); Josef Bohatec, *Die cartesianische Scholastik in der reformierten Dogmatik des XVII. Jahrhunderts* (Leipzig, 1912), Vol. I (only volume published); Peter Petersen, *Geschichte der Aristotelischen Philosophie im protestantischen Deutschland* (Leipzig, 1921); and Max Wundt, *Die deutsche Schulmetaphysik des XVII. Jahrhunderts* (Tübingen, 1939).

The philosophy of the Enlightenment is studied in Max Wundt, *Die deutsche Schulphilosophie im Zeitalter der Aufklärung* (Tübingen, 1945); Cay von Brockdorff, *Die deutsche Aufklärungsphilosophie* (Munich, 1926); and Max Dessoir, *Geschichte der neueren deutschen Psychologie* (Berlin, 1894; 2d ed., Berlin, 1902), Vol. I (only volume published). General intellectual histories of the period are Karl Hillebrand, *Six Lectures on the History of German Thought from the Seven Years' War to the Death of Goethe* (New York, 1880); and H. M. Wolff, *Die Weltanschauung der deutschen Aufklärung* (Bern, 1949).

On the period immediately after Kant, see Ernst Cassirer, *Das Erkenntnisproblem in der Philosophie und Wissenschaft der neueren Zeit*, Vol. III, *Die nachkantischen Systeme* (Berlin, 1920); Wilhelm Dilthey, *Gesammelte Schriften*, Vol. IV, *Die drei Grundformen der Systeme im ersten Hälfte des XIX. Jahrhunderts* (Berlin, 1921); Rudolf Haym, *Die romantische Schule* (Berlin, 1870; 5th ed., Berlin, 1928); Nicolai Hartmann, *Die Philosophie des deutschen Idealismus*, 2 vols. (Berlin, 1923–1929; 1-vol. ed., Berlin, 1960); Moritz Kronenberg, *Geschichte des deutschen Idealismus*, 2 vols. (Munich, 1909–1912); Richard Kroner, *Von Kant bis Hegel*, 2 vols. (Tübingen, 1921–1924; 2d ed., Tübingen, 1961); Willy Moog, *Hegel und die Hegelische Schule* (Munich, 1930); Josiah Royce, *The Spirit of Modern Philosophy* (Boston, 1892); and Leonard Nelson, *Fortschritte und Rückschritte der Philosophie* (Frankfurt, 1962). Older works still of interest are Heinrich Heine, *Religion and Philosophy in Germany*, translated by J. Snodgrass (London, 1882; Boston, 1959); and Mme. de Staël, *De l'Allemagne*, 3 vols. (London, 1813), translated by O. W. Wight as *Germany*, 2 vols. (New York, 1887).

The remainder of the nineteenth century is dealt with in the following: Ernst Cassirer, *The Problem of Knowledge; Philosophy,* *Science, and History Since Hegel*, translated by W. H. Woglom and C. W. Hendel (New Haven, Conn., 1950); Sidney Hook, *From Hegel to Marx* (New York, 1936); Karl Löwith, *Von Hegel zu Nietzsche* (Zurich and Stuttgart, 1941), translated by D. E. Green as *From Hegel to Nietzsche* (New York, 1964); Georg Lukács, *Die Zerstörung der Vernunft* (Berlin, 1955); Otto Siebert, *Geschichte der neueren deutschen Philosophie seit Hegel* (Göttingen, 1898); Carl Siegel, *Geschichte der deutschen Naturphilosophie* (Berlin, 1890; Leipzig, 1913); and Wilhelm Windelband, *Die Philosophie im deutschen Geistesleben des XIX. Jahrhunderts*, 3d ed. (Tübingen, 1927). J. T. Merz's *History of European Thought in the Nineteenth Century*, 4 vols. (Edinburgh and London, 1912–1923), although not restricted to Germany, has valuable information on the German intellectual life.

Twentieth-century philosophy is surveyed by E. von Aster, *Die Philosophie der Gegenwart* (Leiden, 1935); Werner Brock, *Introduction to Contemporary German Philosophy* (Cambridge, 1935); W. T. Jones, *Contemporary Thought of Germany*, 2 vols. (New York, 1931); Oswald Külpe, *Die Philosophie der Gegenwart in Deutschland* (Leipzig, 1902), translated by M. L. Patrick and G. T. W. Patrick as *Philosophy of the Present in Germany* (New York, 1913); Ludwig Landgrebe, *Philosophie der Gegenwart* (Bonn, 1952); Paul Menzer, *Deutsche Metaphysik der Gegenwart* (Berlin, 1931); Hans Meyer, *Geschichte der abendländischen Weltanschauung*, Vol. V, *Die Weltanschauung der Gegenwart* (Würzburg, 1950). Gerhard Lehmann, *Die deutsche Philosophie der Gegenwart* (Stuttgart, 1943), is not without useful information and valuable insights, although the book as a whole is marred by national socialist propaganda; it may be contrasted with Klaus Zweiling, ed., *Die deutsche Philosophie*, 3 vols. (Berlin, 1961–1962), which is made up of essays on German philosophy since the death of Engels, prepared for the five-volume history of philosophy to be published by the Academy of Sciences of the U.S.S.R.

Valuable work on specific movements is given in the following books: on Neo-Kantianism, Mariano Campo, *Schizzo storico della esegesi e critica kantiana*, Vol. I (Varese, 1959) and Wolfgang Ritzel, *Studien zum Wandeln der Kantauffassung* (Meisenheim, 1952); on phenomenology, Herbert Spiegelberg, *The Phenomenological Movement*, 2 vols. (The Hague, 1960) and R. M. Chisholm, ed., *Realism and the Background of Phenomenology* (Glencoe, Ill., 1960); on the development of the *Geisteswissenschaften*, Carlo Antoni, *Dallo storicismo alla sociologia* (Florence, 1940), translated by H. V. White as *From History to Sociology* (Detroit, 1959); on logical positivism, Viktor Kraft, *Der wiener Kreis* (Vienna, 1950), translated by Arthur Pap as *The Vienna Circle* (New York, 1953). An extremely useful collection is Raymund Schmidt's *Die Philosophie der Gegenwart in Selbstdarstellungen*, 8 vols. (Leipzig, 1921–1929), which contains autobiographical statements by many German philosophers.

Works purporting to bring out the "essence" of German philosophy are Magdalene Aebi, *Kants Begründung der "deutschen Philosophie"* (Basel, 1947); Émile Boutroux, *Études d'histoire de la philosophie allemande* (Paris, 1926); John Dewey, *German Philosophy and Politics* (New York, 1915); Ferdinand Lion, *Lebensquellen der deutschen Metaphysik* (Frankfurt, 1960); Mario Pensa, *Il pensiero tedesco; saggio di psicologia della filosofia tedesca* (Milan, 1938), translated by Walter Meckauer as *Das deutsche Denken* (Zurich, 1948); George Santayana, *Egotism in German Philosophy* (New York, 1916); and Wilhelm Wundt, *Die Nationen und ihre Philosophie* (Leipzig, 1915). The last-named book is war propaganda that may well be compared with the Boutroux, Dewey, and Santayana books.

National socialism's coordination (*Gleichschaltung*) of German philosophy may be seen in Hermann Glockner, *Vom Wesen der deutschen Philosophie* (Stuttgart, 1941); Theodor Haering, *Die deutsche und die europäische Philosophie* (Stuttgart, 1943); and in the essays in Theodor Haering, ed., *Das Deutsche in der deutschen Philosophie* (Stuttgart, 1941). Perhaps the most extraordinary work of this kind by a reputable scholar is Max Wundt, *Die Wurzeln der deutschen Philosophie in Stamm und Rasse* (Berlin, 1944), which "proves" by means of maps and portraits that different racial mixtures in Germany have produced different philosophies. R. O. Gropp, *Das nationale philosophische Erbe* (Berlin, 1960), represents an almost equally extreme Marxistic estimation of the true inner nature and cause of German philosophy. One welcomes the injection of fact and common sense to be found in Morris Ginsberg, "German Views of the German Mind," in G. P. Gooch, ed., *The German Mind and Its Outlook* (London, 1945).

LEWIS WHITE BECK

GERMAN PHILOSOPHY AND NATIONAL SOCIALISM. The national socialist movement, born in the turmoil that followed the defeat of Germany in 1918, first undermined and then overthrew the German Republic and won its ephemeral and disastrous victories in the name of an ideology. Its propagandists were aglow with the conviction that they had to deliver a saving message—the gospel of a rebirth of German nationhood after a humiliating defeat. From its very inception national socialism aimed at things greater than the formation of a political party among other parties. It claimed to bring to the German people a new *Weltanschauung*. The political measures it advocated were inspired by a comprehensive outlook on life, expressed in impassioned addresses and manifestos and embraced with a fanatical faith. A revolution rather than a reform was intended. Not only political procedures and institutions, but also the manner of life and modes of thinking, were to be reshaped from the bottom. This project of a radical reconstruction of German life was dominated by a dazzling vision of the future, evoked in the mind by the mystic slogan of the Third Reich. Under the sway of this ideological dream, all political realities were overlaid with an ideological tinge. Even the leader of the movement, Adolf Hitler, who was the object of a rapturous hero worship and the ultimate and uncontested authority in all matters of ideology, was looked upon as the embodiment not only of the German people and the Aryan master race but also of a principle—the *Führerprinzip*—that was the antithesis of democratic cooperation.

THE DOCTRINE OF NATIONAL SOCIALISM

As a totalitarian mass movement inspired by an ideological faith, national socialism fits into a pattern set by Marxism and foreshadowed to some extent by the French Revolution. But whereas Marxism was based on a doctrine that called for serious examination, even though it was erroneous both as a system of economics and as a philosophy of history, national socialism, far from developing a political theory, espoused an irrational creed and rejected theory as a guide to action. It had no doctrine in the proper sense of the word. It was fundamentally hostile to philosophy, and the ideas of orthodoxy and heresy remained foreign to it. While one can conceive of Marxism surviving all existing communist states, national socialism was bound to vanish when the National Socialists went down in defeat. A creed has to be composed of ideas. The ideas—few in number, and crude as well as shallow—that formed the hard core of the national socialist creed had hardly sufficient logical coherence to deserve the name of an ideology. Only the violent emotions out of which it grew and which it was designed to foster prevented it from appearing as the sorry patchwork which it in fact was.

The official program of the National Socialist German Workers' party (NSDAP) was vague and elusive, and there never existed an authoritative document defining the basic concepts of the national socialist message. Yet a scrutiny of the *Führer*'s speeches reveals a persistent pattern of ideas that can be identified as the ideological nucleus of the movement. According to the Italian fascist catechism, the *Duce* is always right. Similarly, the political and ideological infallibility of Hitler was the first maxim of national socialist loyalty. Hence, Hitler's own utterances hold a unique rank as historical evidence for a canon of approved ideas.

Aryanism. Hitler's thinking was fundamentally pervaded by a crude and unreflective naturalism, occasionally veiled by unctuous references to the Lord God or to "destiny." Life, for him, was a struggle for superiority. The combatants on the historical stage were peoples and races rather than individuals; and in this deadly struggle the stronger and better race would prevail in the end, although the tragic possibility that the superior race could be outnumbered and overwhelmed by a conspiracy of the inferior rabble could not be excluded. The chosen people were the Aryans and, in the first place, the Aryan elite—the German people. Awakened by its *Führer* to a consciousness of its true mission, the Germanic master race would cast off the shackles of foreign masters and alien ideas to which it had been subservient, and establish the rule of those who were born to rule. In this scheme the state itself was subordinated to the race or people. The dynamic quality of the people was embodied in the party, which in its turn was the movement transformed into an organization. The individual person derived his worth from his membership in the racial community of the *Volk*. In addition to the self-denying service that he owed to the nation, the individual was the transient vessel of the precious Aryan blood, which antedated its incarnation in him and was destined to survive him. Compared with the real issue of history, the private interest of the individual seemed of little account, and economic and industrial life had to minister to the state.

Nihilism. Unlike nineteenth-century nationalism, this novel system of thought owed its tremendous potency, in the first place, not to the affirmation of national superiority but to a grand negation. Hitler addressed himself not to a people triumphant and self-confident but to one smarting from its wounds and unable to come to terms with its recent past—the military defeat, the collapse of imperial rule, the enforced peace treaty of Versailles, the little understood and less loved Weimar Republic. While magnifying and deepening the public consciousness of prevailing misery, he had to provide a diagnosis before offering his saving prescription: he had to discover and to name the cause of the evil—the enemy. The great adversary rather than the greatness of his nation was Hitler's dominant obsession. In his table of commandments hatred took precedence over love. The swastika became the symbol of a nationalism born of resentment, of a faith springing from despair.

Anti-Semitism. The enemy was the Jew. On the one hand, this enemy was a concrete group of human beings defined by their descent, discoverable by bureaucratic methods, and liable to expulsion, imprisonment, and, eventually, extinction. Indirectly, this definition of the Jew furnished the only concrete conception of the Aryan available: he was identified as a non-Jew. The Jew, on the other hand, became the avatar of evil. There were numerous hostile concepts that inspired the eloquence of the leader and that, taken together, formed the antithesis of the triumphant *Reich:* communism, capitalism, liberalism, democracy, humanitarianism, Freemasonry, rationalism—to mention only some of the chief targets of abuse. But ultimately, all these inimical powers that plotted against the rightful victory of the Aryan race were nothing but puppets moved about by the sinister master player—the wicked one himself—who artfully hid his odious Jewish face behind many masks. Anti-Semitism, far from being merely an ingredient, was the very substance of national socialism. National socialism—a degraded metaphysics involving a gnostic concept of evil—called for the concrete manifestation of anti-Semitism in secret police and concentration camps. The murder of millions, effected by government action with the help of a modern extinction industry, was its logical outcome.

Hitler shrewdly avoided endorsing further ideas which, congenial though they appeared, would have given his program a more tangible content and a sharper outline than seemed politically desirable. *Der Mythus des 20. Jahrhunderts* ("The Myth of the Twentieth Century"), an amateurish book in which the party's chief ideologist, Alfred Rosenberg, tried to harness German mystics—especially Meister Eckhart—to the war chariot of his nationalist myth, never received the official approval of the *Führer*. In the years preceding the seizure of power, when the party needed substantial gifts from industrialists to balance its budget, Hitler checked the importunity of zealous friends who remembered too vividly the socialist phraseology of the early propaganda. Likewise, he kept at arm's length the champions of Nordic paganism, the worshipers of Wotan, who flocked around General Ludendorff and his wife Mathilde, the high priestess of the cult. Otherwise, the Christian churches, which, though sorely vexed by a policy of subdued hostility, still managed to derive some comfort from the "positive Christianity" avowed by the party program, might have prematurely taken alarm. Unimpressed by the ideological gifts offered him by a host of prophets and professors, Hitler guarded the amorphousness of his program as an invaluable political asset. By consistently using a language specific on questions of principle and vague on particular issues, he succeeded in channeling all the resentment, both private and national, scattered throughout the German fatherland into the mighty stream of the revolutionary movement.

GERMAN PHILOSOPHICAL TRADITION

National socialism is a perversion of philosophy rather than a philosophy. Yet this perversion is not devoid of philosophical interest. The contributions that it received from philosophy—mostly though by no means exclusively from German philosophy—may conveniently be discussed under three headings. (1) Philosophy removed or weakened the barriers that should have checked the rising tide. (2) Philosophy helped to create an intellectual atmosphere favorable to the growth of national socialism. (3) Philosophy furnished an apology for the victorious movement and produced national socialist philosophies. To discuss the first contribution one must go back as far as German classical idealism.

German thought, throughout the nineteenth century and down to our own time, has been dominated, even in its moments of rebellion, by an idealist philosophy—by Kant's critical idealism and its transformation into absolute idealism through Fichte, Schelling, and Hegel. Nietzsche substituted "life" for the idealist key word *Geist* (mind or spirit). But even his great anti-idealist revolt was dependent on what he attacked. And the philosophy of life (*Lebensphilosophie*), with its characteristic leaning toward historicism, that ruled supreme in German intellectual life during the 1920s was a variety of Hegelianism, modernized in the spirit of vitalism and relativism.

The individual and the Absolute. The greatness of German idealism sprang from the zeal with which its exponents tried to put the human mind in contact with the Absolute. It was animated by a metaphysical ardor, and its metaphysics verged on religion. But the idealist Absolute was conceived as a dynamic force, rather than as a supposedly more static concept of being in classical metaphysics. In order to effect contact with this transcendent reality, trust in reason had to be stretched to the utmost. Reason was raised high above understanding—the lower faculty that has no other counters to play with but fixities and definite things. But this superrational reason ultimately became irrational. Philosophy of life, the source of the antidemocratic and anti-Western thought rampant in the 1920s, retained the metaphysical ardor of idealism and combined it with faith in the irrational. *Vernunft* ("reason") became a term of obloquy. In a similar manner, the concept of the human person in the idealist scheme of thought was dangerously poised between two diametrically opposed positions. Fichte endowed the ego with world-creating powers. At the same time, he demanded the annihilation of the individual—the empirical person—and dreamed of a "Republic of the Germans" in which every male, from his twentieth year to his death, had to be a soldier.

The same dialectic was thought and lived through in the 1920s; the spokesmen of the German intelligentsia—individualists to the point of eccentricity—at the same time yearned to be submerged in a communal order. The height to which idealist speculation had risen in the early nineteenth century—a danger of which Kierkegaard and other contemporary critics were keenly aware—bade fair to create a metaphysical giddiness in the minds of its latter-day followers. There was too much uncertainty about the dividing line between the infinite mind and the finite one. In his *Geständnisse* (1854), with sardonic humor Heinrich Heine remembered his own past Hegelianism as the blissful time when he believed he was God on earth (*Werke*, Leipzig, 1915, pp. 174–177).

The idealist philosophers considered themselves the rightful heirs of the Protestant reformation. But since their religious inspiration derived partly from Neoplatonism, partly from Jakob Boehme, Louis Claude de Saint-Martin, Emanuel Swedenborg, and other troubled sources rather than from Luther or Calvin, they failed to instill fresh life into a languishing theology, in spite of Schleiermacher's heroic efforts. Instead, they carried on the critical work of the Enlightenment they despised, and helped to found the invisible church of those educated Protestants who substituted religious feeling for religion and Christian humanism for Christian dogma, substitutions which later permitted Paul Tillich and other modern theologians to celebrate Nietzsche as a great Protestant. Theirs was the rarefied faith that under Bismarck's chancellorship was cherished by the majority of patriots as the "religion of our forebears" and that survived as a subtle aura among the antibourgeois nationalists and socialists of the Weimar Republic.

Freedom. The idealist faith or philosophy, sublime but amorphous, revering as its founding fathers Herder, Kant, Goethe, and Schiller, together with Fichte, Schelling, Hegel, and Schopenhauer, grew and developed at some distance from active life and the responsibilities of citizenship. It idolized Hellas and was oblivious of Rome. Its cradle was the Protestant vicarage. Its creators and its later adherents were the sons of the German third estate (*des Bürgertums*) whose struggle for active and full participation in the business of government ended in frustration. When finally, in October 1918, parliamentary government was granted, the democratic zeal had long evaporated, and national disaster was close at hand.

The remoteness of the idealists from the seats of political responsibility did not, however, divert their attention from the political destiny of mankind. The outbreak of the French Revolution filled them with enthusiasm for liberty. But the subsequent reign of terror disillusioned them, and in horror they turned their backs on active political life. From then on, their philosophy of freedom suffered a twofold deformation. On the one hand, it was lifted above the sphere of historical reality: freedom for Hegel, though the ultimate goal of the historical process, was the freedom of the *Geist* rather than of the individual, and as such, it was identical with "infinite necessity" (*Die Vernunft in der Geschichte*, Philosophische Bibliothek, Hamburg, 1955, p. 63). On the other hand, freedom as an actualization within history, according to Hegel, existed only as the state. Between these two poles, no room was left for *eleutheria*—the Greek conception of the liberty of the citizen who, by definition, was both ruler and subject in one person.

The state. The fruit of the idealist philosophy of freedom was an idolization of the state. "One must worship the state as a terrestrial divinity," according to Hegel (*Philosophie des Rechts*, Sec. 272). In the name of true liberty, romantic philosophers lent their moral support to the Holy Alliance by which Metternich tried to safeguard autocratic forms of monarchy in the face of a growing nationalist and democratic movement. Behind this bourgeois revolutionary wave the socialist movement, led by the advocates of the new class of industrial workers, pressed forward, also armed with a political philosophy derived from Hegel. Marx, their prophet, succeeded in kindling from the embers of revolution smoldering under the weight of the Hegelian system a mighty fire. Meanwhile, under Bismarck's German Empire, the church of the unchurched, called cultural Protestantism, moved the altar closer to the throne while removing it farther from Calvary and the

Sermon on the Mount. German intellectualism abandoned its revolutionary fervor to lapse into pious or cynical respectability under a thriving modern state with an antiquated political and social order.

The contact with the Absolute by means of either Kant's categorical imperative, the intellectual intuition of the post-Kantian idealists, or the Hegelian dialectic was ambiguously related to practical and especially to political life. It might create an aloofness of mind that fastidiously eschewed the humdrum, the dust, and the passionate confusion of everyday existence as well as the responsibilities of communal life. But once these philosophers were forced to descend into the practical world, either by inward or by outward necessity, the same preoccupation could result in actions more single-minded, more uncompromisingly determined, and more ruthlessly inhuman than any activity animated by less high-flown ideas. Roquairol in Jean Paul's *Titan* is all the more wicked for being the angelic Albano's spiritual twin brother. More clearly than anyone else, Heinrich Heine saw this ambiguity and expressed it in words that have a prophetic ring. In 1834 he wrote:

[The German revolution] will not turn out milder or gentler for having been preceded by the Kantian critique, Fichte's transcendental Idealism or even the Philosophy of Nature. Thanks to these doctrines revolutionary forces have developed which only bide their time to break out one day and to fill the world with dismay and admiration. Kantians will step forth who, casting aside holy fear in this our phenomenal world, will dig up mercilessly, with sword and axe, the soil of European life to eradicate the last remnants of the past. Armed Fichteans will strut onto the scene whose fanaticism of will can be restrained neither by fear nor by considerations of utility . . . But more terrible than all would be the Natural Philosopher . . . He will make a pact with the aboriginal forces of nature so as to conjure up the demoniacal power of ancient Germanic pantheism. In him that lust for battle will awaken which we find in the ancient Germans, and which does not fight to destroy or to win but to fight (*Zur Geschichte der Religion und Philosophie in Deutschland*, in *Werke*, Vol. VII, pp. 350–351).

Dismissal of practical reason. In the decisive decades of the French Revolution the disintegration of classical metaphysics reached its completion with the fading away of the idea of practical reason from the minds of philosophers—a process in which German philosophy took the lead. It was symptomatic that ethics, one of the traditional disciplines of philosophy, either dropped out of the systematic scheme of absolute idealism altogether, or was assigned (as by Hegel) a subordinate status within a philosophy of right. In Hegel, morality (*Moralität*) figured only as the subjective moment of the good which, together with law (the abstract moment of the good) had to be integrated into the concrete system of *Sittlichkeit*—that is, of the state which, in its turn, was considered an essentially historical reality. According to this view, the ultimate judgment on right and wrong, good and evil, rested with the state or, in the era of intellectual maturity, with the philosophy of history that translated into human science the mystery of divine providence and thus knew the purpose allotted at a given moment to a particular state. It is true that Hegel was not oblivious of the human conscience as a sanctuary that it would be an outrage to violate. But because of its subjective and formal character it was, he thought, continually on the verge of perversion into evil, and therefore the state could grant it no recognition (Hegel, *op. cit.*, Secs. 137 and 139).

In post-Kantian idealism, the immediate relationship between speculative thought and the Absolute was reaffirmed, but the moral immediacy of the human agent suffered curtailment. Between the individual and the good as revealed by the voice of conscience two mediating authorities that tolerated neither argument nor resistance interposed themselves; they were the state as the social materialization of freedom and the demands of the historical moment. Since the latter could be deciphered only in the light of a philosophy of history, for the man in doubt as to the course of action to take, everything depended on being privy to the counsels of history. Instead of asking "What is right?" he must ask "What is timely?" or, more grandiloquently, "What does world history at its present juncture expect me to do?" Such teaching, addressed to mankind in general, might seem preposterously at variance with man's actual perplexities. Yet the ideologies of the modern mass movements sought to supply a credible answer to these perplexities in terms of such questions. They all taught the same sort of lesson: "Such is the route mankind is fated to travel toward the terrestrial fulfillment of its hopes. Keep in step with history, and all will be well with you." But by such exhortations the ideologies pointed in different directions, and instead of uniting mankind, they split it into hostile parties animated with crusading zeal. Each ideology, without avowing it, denied the practical reason. The question of right or wrong had forfeited its claim to priority. A sublime opportunism took the place of philosophical wisdom, and the adage of the ancient philosophers: "Live in conformity with nature " was replaced with the modern maxim: "Live in conformity with history."

The importance of German idealist philosophy as a formative element of German life can hardly be overrated. It was to color the thoughts and attitudes even of those who lacked the talent for abstract argument and sophisticated reflection. While it held great promise, it was at the same time fraught with grave dangers. It was better fitted for uplifting the mind than for securely balancing it. High-strung energy rather than poise seemed to be its natural effect on its votaries. It justly prided itself on the profundity and comprehensive boldness of its leading concepts. But these lofty ideas were afflicted with a perilous instability. The cult of a reason that towered infinitely above mere understanding paved the way for irrationalism. The speculative flight that took the thinker to a realm far beyond the labor and sweat of communal life eventually sent him back to earth with a blueprint for radically remodeling life on earth. There was no more ardent champion of freedom than the speculative idealist. But since he believed he discerned in human history the footprints of God in his passage through time, and in the state the divine instrument for conferring on liberty a concrete form, his very concern for freedom could make him an advocate of unreserved submission. He believed in Christianity but he disbelieved Christ's teachings. His twentieth-century heirs put his beliefs to a test in the years of trial that followed World War I and found them unfit to ward off a suicidal error.

THE ERROR OF THE SCRIBES

The suicidal error was committed by German intellectuals under the Weimar Republic at the time when national socialism, thanks to the master demagogue Hitler, developed from an insignificant lower-middle-class group of disgruntled patriots into a mass movement of unparalleled intensity and ruthlessness. These intellectuals, because of their cultural fastidiousness, were constitutionally unable ever to become authentic national socialists and they despised a movement that reeked of vulgarity. Yet they believed they could use national socialism and its tremendous might for their own purposes, which they judged to be akin to those pursued by national socialism. But in the end the movement used them for its own purposes. Instead of attaining positions of real influence, they only succeeded in conferring a sham intellectual respectability upon national socialism; and thereby they helped the mass of educated Germans to overcome the moral squeamishness that had long prevented them from donning the brown shirt of Hitler's storm troops. Some of the deceived deceivers paid for their mistake with their lives; others made up for it by joining one of the resistance groups; and others went into hiding and reappeared after 1945, trying as best they could to live down their ideological past. There were three distinct but converging movements among these intellectuals: the new conservatism, legal decisionism, and philosophical existentialism.

New conservatism. The new conservatism, arising immediately after World War I, took shape in the minds of a group of writers gathered around a rather modest figure, Arthur Moeller van den Bruck, author of a book that appeared in 1923 under the ominous title *Das dritte Reich*. Its message was particularly well received by the more intellectual war veterans, by the youth movement and by the younger generation in general. At first it was discussed and developed in small esoteric groups. After 1929 the conservative ideas won favor with a wider public, largely because of the brilliant periodical, *Die Tat*, ably edited by Hans Zehrer.

A number of well-known authors, among them Oswald Spengler, Ferdinand Fried, Edgar J. Jung, G. F. Jünger, and Ernst Jünger, spread the gospel of a refined and highly sophisticated though impassioned nationalism. None of these writers could be described as a philosopher, but each was animated by philosophical ambitions. To regard them as heirs of the idealist philosophers of the past would have seemed absurd to them. They were all disciples of Nietzsche and flaunted a violently anti-idealist realism that they liked to think of as heroic and that was keyed to the maxim: the harder on us and the more repellent to our moral feelings and sanguine hopes, the more real. The idealist philosophy of spirit had reached them chiefly through Schopenhauer's irrationalist version or in the modern garb of a philosophy of life. From Dilthey and his school. they had inherited a historical relativism that was oddly at variance with their militant fervor.

Aesthetic vision of the state. Living and thinking at a considerable distance from the actual problems of political life, the new conservatives were animated by political passion. The focus of their thinking was the state—a state, however, that their hopes projected into a future envisaged as the apogee of a philosophically interpreted world history. Theirs was the vision of the aesthete rather than of the politically minded man. At the age of 19 Otto Braun, a German volunteer who lost his life in World War I, had expressed a similar vision in a letter to his parents:

My inmost yearning, my purest, though most secret flame, my deepest faith and my highest hope—they are still the same as ever, and they all bear one name: the State. One day to build the state like a temple, rising up pure and strong, resting in its own weight, severe and sublime, but also serene like the gods and with bright halls glistening in the dancing brilliance of the sun—this, at bottom, is the end and goal of my aspirations (*Deutsche Briefe des 20. Jahrhunderts*, Munich, 1962, p. 87).

The same enthusiasm, with less purity, burned in the minds of the new conservatives.

The conservative revolution. "Conservative revolution," the paradoxical watchword that best expressed the state of mind of the new conservative writers and propagandists, was probably coined by Thomas Mann and was given wide currency by the Austrian poet Hugo von Hofmannsthal, who used the term in an address to students of the University of Munich in 1927. This ill-matched pair of words was intended to voice, first, a longing that ran counter to the great movement of modern history—a nostalgia for discipline and subordination rather than for freedom, for command and obedience as the elements of a well-balanced order. By "conservative," no conservation of time-honored institutions was intended—little was left for conservation after the havoc wrought by war and revolution. Instead, the new conservatives aimed at a restitution of those elements on which, in their opinion, the permanence of communal life itself was predicated. On the basis of this reinterpretation the qualifying word "conservative" could be affixed to "revolution," and insofar as these men had any contact with political actuality, it was through the latter term. As revolutionaries they scorned and hated the existing order of things, the Weimar Republic. Hence they applauded the destructive activities of the national socialists, and occasionally even those of the communists.

Hatred of the West. The intellectual hostility against the Weimar Republic raised this unfortunate state to the rank of a symbol. In the eyes of its enemies it was a debased copy of Western democracy; and Western democracy, together with capitalism, commercialism, and industrialism, was abhorred as a product of the disintegration of Western culture and, in fact, as a world in decline and doomed to imminent self-destruction. During World War I,

Max Scheler had utilized Nietzsche's ferocious criticism of modern civilization to build up a German myth, a counterpart to the anti-German myth invented and publicized at the same time by John Dewey and George Santayana. According to Scheler's myth, Germany was destined to save the threatened values of the Occident. It would set faith against skepticism, metaphysics against science, the organic whole against atomism, life against mechanism, heroism against calculation, true community against commercialized society, a hierarchically ordered people against the mass leveled down by egalitarianism. This philosophy, an unpalatable mixture of national arrogance, legitimate criticism of the foibles of the modern democracies, and blindness to their unabated strength, was thoroughly exploited by the postwar critics of the Weimar Republic. Simultaneously other riches of dubious value were derived from various sources: from Ferdinand Tönnies, author of *Gemeinschaft und Gesellschaft* (1887), which exalted genuine community at the expense of mere society; from Julius Langbehn, author of *Rembrandt als Erzieher* (1890), apostle of a mystic nationalism and generally referred to as *der Rembrandtdeutsche;* from Paul de Lagarde, who exacerbated his nationalist creed with a goodly dose of anti-Semitism; and finally from a contemporary scholar, the Viennese sociologist Othmar Spann, a bitter enemy of individualism and inventor of a theory of "organic totality" that formed the romantic German companion piece to the holism developed by the South African statesman Jan Christiaan Smuts. Further ideological ingredients were furnished by a number of non-German authors belonging to the antirevolutionary, Machiavellian, and irrationalist tradition, such as Donoso-Cortés, Charles Maurras, Vilfredo Pareto, and Arthur Graf Gobineau.

In spite of a certain affinity to the romantic political philosophers of the period of the German-Austrian Restoration, the men of the conservative revolution had little in common with the old conservatives and nationalists of the right-wing party that in 1932, with the help of Hindenburg and the cabinet of barons, vainly tried to stem the Nazi brown flood. For these official representatives of wealth and tradition, with their lingering nostalgia for the shining armor of the Wilhelmine empire, the new conservatives had nothing but scorn. They were as violently antibourgeois as they were antiliberal. They considered the ideas of class rule and class struggle antiquated, and a strong ingredient of socialism went into the making of their nationalist views. Although the majority of them were anti-Marxist, Georges Sorel's syndicalism, amalgamating the idea of political myth with that of violence, appealed to their partiality for revolutionary truculence. In one respect at least they stood on common ground with national socialism: the political distinction between right and left had become meaningless to them, and their nationalism had a tendency to shade off into national bolshevism. Ernst Niekisch, a former social democrat influenced by Moeller van den Bruck's ideas, founded the National Bolshevik Resistance Movement, whose emblem combined hammer and sickle with the Prussian eagle.

There was an obvious lack of a constructive and practicable conception in this mixture of ideas, but the revolutionary conservatives made up for their lack of a positive ideology by maintaining a strong sense of being carried forward by the torrent of historical events. Suspended between the dread of an approaching cataclysm and the apocalyptic anticipation of a future grandeur beyond hope, they desperately sought to interpret their diagnostic observations and their forebodings in terms of a prophetic philosophy of history. But as their attempts in this direction ended in failure, they made up for it by constructing a myth, an imaginative picture of a state of things to come, half forecast of a future development and half utopia. The embodiment of a paradoxical dream, the myth was a nightmare envisaged wistfully—unbearably inhuman and yet a challenge to the adventurous mind, a fiction designed to produce a reality. Of the numerous mythmaking books written, two in particular caught the imagination of contemporary readers: Oswald Spengler's *Preussentum und Sozialismus* (Munich, 1920) and Ernst Jünger's *Der Arbeiter, Herrschaft und Gestalt* (1932). Spengler prophesied the partnership and fusion of two traditions hitherto violently opposed to one another. The virtues of a high sense of duty, of obedience, and of self-abnegation, as cultivated by the Prussian kings and their armies, would be wedded to the equally militant discipline of the battalions of the socialist revolution to form the mighty body social of the postindividualist and postliberal era. In Jünger's vision of the future, the worker was the architect and master of the new state. But the heroic worker he portrayed bore even less resemblance to the real worker of the industrial age than Spengler's idealized Prussian to the actual *Junker.* The lineage of Jünger's worker was traceable in literature rather than in life—he was Nietzsche's superman reborn out of the spirit of ecstatic collectivism. These highly intelligent authors succeeded in intoxicating both themselves and others with their fantastic dreams. When they awoke, they stood aghast before the real future that had meanwhile taken shape in Hitler's Third Reich.

Legal decisionism. Under the pretext of quelling a rebellion of the SA (storm troops) allegedly engineered by Colonel Röhm, Hitler ordered a massacre on June 30, 1934. Among the victims was Edgar J. Jung, one of the best-known exponents of the new conservatism. This act of lawless savagery was hailed as a saving deed not only by the intimidated and demoralized *Reichstag* but also by an eminent legal philosopher, Carl Schmitt, whose thinking ran closely parallel to that of Jung and his friends. In an article entitled "The Leader Protects the Law" (in *Positionen und Begriffe*, 1940, pp. 200 ff.), he maintained that the murder of a large number of men without indictment or process of law signified the creation of a new order of law and justice. But Schmitt was not an ordinary sycophant; he merely applied the principles of antiliberalism to a case that happened to involve another antiliberal. In fact, the astute jurist had thought through the antiliberal ideas much more thoroughly than the dilettantes of the conservative revolution. Although he too was an admirer of Sorel's invention, the political myth, he preferred for his own use a paradoxical but perfectly logical theory he called decisionism. With its help he became Hitler's legal–philosophical stirrup-holder. Schmitt accompanied with

legal comments each phase of the turbulent development that led from the paralysis of parliamentary rule and the government by the president through emergency orders to Hitler's chancellorship and the triumph of the national socialist revolution, and at every juncture he was found on the winning side.

What constitutes the legitimacy of a legal order? The ultimate source of legitimacy, Schmitt maintained, is in the act of decision. By this term he meant the fiat of the passionate will, life itself breaking through the crust of the repetitive routine of normal existence, the human response to an emergency, the *extremus necessitatis casus.* The maker of this creative decision was, of course, not the individual as such but the sovereign. In fact, Schmitt defined sovereignty by reference to the extreme situation. The sovereign, he wrote in 1922, "is one who decides in an emergency" (*Politische Theologie, 4 Kapitel zur Lehre von der Souveränität*, quoted from the 2d ed., Munich and Leipzig, 1934, p. 11). This decision is twofold: The sovereign decides both whether an emergency exists and what is to be done about it. The decision is not determined by an existing order, for the rules defining that order are annulled by the exceptional situation; but conversely, every order is based on a decision. In other words, decision is an extralegal act rendering possible a legal order—any legal order. From this Neo-Hobbesian point of view, article 48 of the German constitution of 1919, which explained the special powers granted to the president in an emergency and by means of which Hitler in 1933 transformed a parliamentary democracy into a totalitarian autocracy without formally repealing the constitution, appeared as fundamental.

This decisionist theory was well fitted for conferring a semblance of legality upon the violent and even criminal policy Hitler was determined to pursue. The *Führer* did even better than Professor Schmitt's philosophy foresaw; thanks to his superb demagogy he was able to create the emergency that in decisionist doctrine figured as an event on the order of an earthquake or volcanic eruption. After Hitler's seizure of power, Schmitt did his best to exploit the potentialities of theoretical decisionism and to adapt it to the new state of things. His three constituents of sovereignty—the norm, the decision, and the institutions (with the primacy belonging to decision)—he equated with the triad state – movement – people, thus effecting a *rapprochement* between his own language and that of the party. But no conceptual alchemy could transform the decisionist into an authentic national socialist. Hitler's true followers had to believe in "blood and soil" rather than in that tenuous and spiritual thing called decision.

Philosophical existentialism. According to Carl Schmitt's doctrine, the extreme or exceptional case was more revealing than the normal case. This idea, universalized into a first principle, became the spring that actuated the Kierkegaard renaissance of the 1920s in Germany and produced the philosophical current known as existentialism. The *extremus necessitatis casus* was conceived as the despair of the human person confronted with nothingness. The anguished awareness of this predicament might become the hour of the birth of man's true freedom. By an unpremeditated move, a "leap," he might recapture the lost contact with Being, thus miraculously winning the firm ground on which to build his life and an interpretation of the world. In a remarkable little book, *Die geistige Situation der Zeit* (1931), Karl Jaspers dramatized the present historical situation by interpreting it in the light of the Kierkegaardian concepts of despair and crisis. The physiognomy of the age, he wrote, "is characterized by the unsheltered man. . . . There is no god, is the clamor of the masses; and hence man is worthless, slaughtered in large numbers, because he is nothing" (p. 130). The writer of these words was filled with deep apprehension and horror at the approaching disaster, and he intended his book as an eleventh-hour appeal to what was noblest in man. But in the confusion of these years the existentialist appeal seemed an ambiguous message. The miraculous leap, the fruit of the existential crisis of despair, might land the patient anywhere. It might initiate a process of spiritual recuperation and finally give birth to true selfhood, as Jaspers devoutly hoped. But it might also complete the work of the evil charm that the false grandeur of national socialism cast upon the young—confused, disheartened, repelled by the sordid spectacle of the disintegrating republic and yearning for the extraordinary experience and the heroic deed. In its essence existentialism had nothing to .do with national socialism. But preaching the saving catastrophe was a dangerous thing at the moment when Hitler, the great beneficiary of catastrophes, was at the doorstep.

PHILOSOPHERS OF THE THIRD REICH

The moment Hitler became chancellor of the *Reich*, German philosophy lost its political significance. From then on, the party, and in the last analysis Hitler, determined what was true and what was erroneous in political thought. Intellectual life as a matter of public interest came to a standstill. But philosophy as an academic study was allowed to continue in a status of political neutrality. There was too little time between the seizure of power in 1933 and the outbreak of war in 1939 for the national socialists to remake philosophy and to secure a monopoly on the dogma of the racial superiority of the Aryans.

However, an attempt was made to integrate philosophy into the pattern of national socialist thought. Its outstanding document was "The Myth of the Twentieth Century" by Alfred Rosenberg, the chief ideologist of the party. According to Rosenberg, soul is race viewed from within, and it is the racial soul that moves world history. Thanks to the Germanic race, the soul achieved its final triumph in developing the ideas of honor and freedom, and the true mysticism, that of Meister Eckhart, which is Christian only in name and appearance, must be understood as the exaltation of the soul's freedom—the freedom even from God. But Rosenberg failed in spite of his elevated rank in the Nazi hierarchy. His sermons on the myth of blood embarrassed Hitler, who, though he hated Christianity, wished to avoid an open conflict with the Christian churches. His fellow Nazi leaders refused to take him seriously, and trained philosophers saw him as the man of little learning

and less intelligence that he actually was. Thus, the invasion of philosophy by the party miscarried.

The corresponding attempt of philosophy to gain a foothold in Nazism was likewise frustrated. Professors of philosophy, like their colleagues in other fields, yielded to the temptation of adapting themselves and their ideas to the victorious system. The antiliberalism and antirationalism of the pre-Hitler years were still alive in their minds and a great prize beckoned. Each aspired to be acclaimed the philosopher of the Third Reich. The temptation was greatest in the first years of the Hitler regime. Warning voices at that time were drowned by an oratory that celebrated the rebirth of the nation. Attuning their minds to the public mood, learned newcomers to the Nazi camp sat down to fabricate philosophies worthy of the occasion. The internationally known periodical *Logos* was rebaptized *Zeitschrift für deutsche Kulturphilosophie*, and its new editor, Hermann Glockner, confessed in the opening issue that two souls, alas, dwelled in his breast—the soul of a peasant and that of a soldier. Another soldier-philosopher, Hans Heyse, improvised a philosophy of history according to which the Third Reich achieved the long-delayed reconciliation of idea and existence, at war with one another throughout the course of previous history. Alfred Bäumler, appointed professor of political pedagogy in the University of Berlin by the Hitler government, went even further in asserting that philosophy, in order to attain full concreteness, must substitute for the cold abstraction *existence* the living person of Adolf Hitler. Kurt Hildebrandt, inspired by Stefan George's poetical conception of heroism, furnished a heroic portrait of Plato as the archenemy of democracy. Erich Rothacker, a pupil of Dilthey, improved upon his master's historicism by reinterpreting it in the light of the concept of race. And Ernst Krieck, to conclude this list, offered a philosophy of education for the new master race.

The real national socialists, meanwhile, deeply distrustful of all intellectuals and attending to more urgent business, had no time to listen to this chorus. Long before catastrophe overtook the Hitler *Reich*, the bankruptcy of the pseudo-philosophical enterprise became evident and many of the recent converts turned renegade. A memorandum of April 3, 1944, drawn up for Alfred Rosenberg by the staunchest national socialist among German academic philosophers, Alfred Bäumler, revealed a desperate situation—aloofness on the part of the respectable scholars existed everywhere, while ambitious incompetence was thriving under party protectorship. The game was up. The hope of bringing together philosophy and the party had proved an illusion.

Unfortunately, one real philosopher had taken part in this game by putting his existentialist ideas at the disposal of the masters of the day. Martin Heidegger, in an address he delivered as rector of the University of Freiburg, interpreted the Hitler state as the political actualization of true philosophy—that is, "questioning, unsheltered firmness amidst the uncertainty of Being" (*Die Selbstbehauptung der deutschen Universität*, Breslau, 1933, p. 13). The precariousness of Being, he affirmed, forced upon the nation three forms of labor and struggle: labor service, military service, and research service. This was a forceful but belated proclamation. The time for waxing eloquent over heroic fortitude in Nietzsche's style was gone. Naked brutality had won the day. The story of German philosophy and national socialism ended in an anticlimax.

Bibliography

ORIGINAL DOCUMENTS

Anger, Walter, ed., *Das Dritte Reich in Dokumenten*. Frankfurt am Main, 1957.

Goebbels, Josef, *Wesen und Gestalt des Nationalsozialismus*. Berlin, 1934.

Goebbels, Josef, *Goebbels Tagebücher*, Louis Lochner, ed. Zurich, 1948.

Hitler, Adolf, *Adolf Hitler spricht*. Leipzig, 1934.

Hitler, Adolf, *Mein Kampf*. Munich, 1934.

Hitler, Adolf, *Hitler's Secret Conversations 1941–1944*. New York, 1953.

Hofer, Walther, ed., *Der Nationalsozialismus Dokumente 1933–1945*. Hamburg, 1957.

Picker, Henry, *Hitlers Tischgespräche im Führerhauptquartier 1941–1942*, 2d ed., Percy Ernst Schramm, ed. Stuttgart, 1963.

Poliakow, Leon, and Wulf, Josef, *Das Dritte Reich und seine Denker. Dokumente*. Berlin-Grunewald, 1959.

Rosenberg, Alfred, *Kampf um die Macht, Aufsätze von 1921 bis 1932*. Thilo von Trutha, ed. Munich, before 1938.

Rosenberg, Alfred, *Weltanschauung und Glaubenslehre*. Halle, 1939.

Rosenberg, Alfred, *Der Mythus des Zwanzigsten Jahrhunderts*. Munich, 1943.

Rosenberg, Alfred, *Letzte Aufzeichnungen. Ideale und Idole der nationalsozialistischen Revolution*. Göttingen, 1955.

CONTEMPORARY LITERATURE

Bäumler, Alfred, *Weltdemokratie und Nationalsozialismus. Die neue Ordnung als geschichtsphilosophisches Probleme*. Berlin, 1943.

Beck, Friedrich Albert, *Idee und Wirklichkeit. Eine Untersuchung über den Nationalsozialismus als Einheit von Geist und Leben*. Würzburg, 1936.

Benn, Gottfried, *Der neue Staat un die Intellektuellen*. Stuttgart, 1933.

Brady, Robert K., *The Spirit and Structure of German Fascism*. London, 1937.

Dietrich, Otto, *A Revolution in Thought*. Berlin, 1939.

Gleichen, Konrad, *Adolf Hitler*, 2 vols. Zurich, 1936.

Grunsky, Hans Alfred, *Der Einbruch des Judentums in die Philosophie*. Berlin, 1937.

Heyse, Hans, *Die Idee der Wissenschaft und der deutschen Universität. Rede. Über Geschichte und Wesen der Idee des Reiche*. Königsberg, 1934.

Heyse, Hans, *Idee und Existenz*. Hamburg, 1935.

Jünger, Ernst, *Der Aufmarsch. Eine Reihe deutscher Schriften*. Leipzig, 1926.

Jünger, Ernst, *Die totale Mobilmachung*. Berlin, 1931.

Kneller, George F., *The Educational Philosophy of National Socialism*. New Haven, 1941.

Krieck, Ernst, *Die Erneuerung der deutschen Universität*. Marburg, 1933.

Krieck, Ernst, *Völkisch-politische Anthropologie*. Leipzig, 1936. Vol. I.

Krieck, Ernst, *Leben als Prinzip der Weltanschauung und Problem der Wissenschaft*. Leipzig, 1938.

Krieck, Ernst, *Weltanschauliche Entscheidung*. Vienna and Leipzig, 1939.

Krieck, Ernst, *Heil und Kraft. Ein Buch germanischer Weltweisheit*. Leipzig, 1943.

Kuhn, Helmut, "Über Carl Schmitt *Der Begriff des Politischen*." *Kant-Studien*, Vol. 38 (1933), 190–196.

Kuhn, Helmut, *Freedom Forgotten and Remembered*. Chapel Hill, N.C., 1943.

Moeller van den Bruck, Arthur, *Das Dritte Reich*. Berlin, 1923; 3d ed., Hans Schwarz, ed., Hamburg, 1931.

Neumann, Franz, *Behemoth. The Structure and Practice of National Socialism 1933–1944*. New York and Toronto, 1942.

Nicolai, Helmut, *Der Staat im nationalsozialistischen Weltbild*. Leipzig, 1934.

Rauschning, Hermann, *Die Revolution des Nihilismus*. Zurich, 1938; 2d ed., introduction by Golo Mann, Zurich, 1964. Translated by E. W. Dickes as *The Revolution of Nihilism*. New York, 1939.

Reventlow, Ernst Graf von, *Deutscher Sozialismus. Civitas Dei Germanica*. Weimar, 1930.

Viereck, Peter, *Metapolitics. From the Romantics to Hitler*. New York, 1941.

Wundt, Max, *Der ewige Jude. Ein Versuch über Sinn und Bedeutung des Judentums*. Munich, 1933.

Wundt, Max, *Die Wurzeln der deutschen Philosophie in Stamm und Rasse*. Berlin, 1944.

POSTWAR LITERATURE

Barraclough, Geoffrey, *The Origins of Modern Germany*. Oxford, 1949.

Broszat, Martin, *Der Nationalsozialismus*. Hanover, 1960.

Bullock, Alan, *Hitler. A Study in Tyranny*. New York, 1952; 2d rev. ed., New York, 1960.

Daluces, Jean, *Le Troisième Reich*. Paris, 1950.

Glum, Friedrich, *Philosophen im Spiegel und Zerrspiegel. Deutschlands Weg in den Nationalismus und Nationalsozialismus*. Heidelberg, 1946; 2d ed., Munich, 1954.

Grosse, Franz G., *Die falschen Götter. Vom Wesen des Nationalsozialismus*. Heidelberg, 1946.

Klemperer, Klemens von, *Germany's New Conservatism. Its History and Dilemma in the Twentieth Century*. Princeton, 1957.

Krockow, Christian Graf von, *Die Entscheidung. Eine Untersuchung über Ernst Jünger, Carl Schmitt, Martin Heidegger*. Stuttgart, 1958.

Mohler, Arnim, *Die konservative Revolution in Deutschland 1918–1932. Grundriss ihrer Weltanschauungen*. Stuttgart, 1950.

Neurohr, Jean F., *Der Mythos von Dritten Reich. Zur Geistesgeschichte des Nationalsozialismus*. Stuttgart, 1957.

Shirer, William L., *The Rise and Fall of the Third Reich*. New York, 1960.

Stern, Fritz, *The Politics of Cultural Despair. A Study in the Rise of Germanic Ideology*. Berkeley and Los Angeles, 1961.

Sontheimer, Kurt, *Antidemokratisches Denken in der Weimarer Republik. Die politischen Ideen des deutschen Nationalsozialismus zwischen 1918 und 1933*. Munich, 1962.

Weinreich, Max, *Hitler's Professors*. New York, 1946.

HELMUT KUHN

GERSHON, LEVI BEN. See GERSONIDES.

GERSON, JEAN DE (1363–1429), French religious reformer and writer on mysticism, was born at Gerson-les-Barbey in Champagne. He was educated at the University of Paris and was soon well known both as a teacher of theology and as a preacher. In 1395 he was elected chancellor of the university. Gerson played an important part in the attempts to heal the Great Schism, culminating in the Council of Constance (1414–1418). His last years were spent in comparative obscurity at Lyons.

Gerson's philosophical position was different from that of any of the main schools of his time. Although he had been brought up under the influence of nominalism, he made liberal use of Platonist ideas derived from Pseudo-Dionysius and Bonaventure, and he appears to have been sympathetic to Thomism, which became popular again during his period as a reforming chancellor at the university. He made use of nominalistic criticisms of Scotist theologians, who employed an array of technical terminology in constructing theories about the divine nature and whom Gerson held chiefly responsible for the existing state of aridity in theology. Nevertheless, he was dissatisfied with the divorce between revelation and metaphysical reasoning implied by nominalism. Thus, his chief concern was to provide the framework for a theology that would express personal piety and, at the same time, contain intellectual checks upon that piety. Part of his originality was that he lectured at Paris on the theory and practice of contemplation, instead of treating theology in a merely speculative fashion. Gerson's eclecticism was thus a consequence of his religious and reforming interests.

In theology Gerson criticized Jan van Ruysbroeck for some of his language in the third part of *The Spiritual Marriage*, which seemed to imply that in the beatific state the soul becomes essentially united with the divine Being. Gerson regarded Ruysbroeck's way of expressing himself as dangerous and unorthodox, since the transcendence of God requires that no finite being can be identified with him. John of Schoonhoven, from Ruysbroeck's monastery at Groenendaal, replied that Ruysbroeck had been misinterpreted and that it was unsuitable to discuss mystical doctrines in the atmosphere of the schools. This led to a counterreply from Gerson, because Schoonhoven's position was opposed to the rationale of the very reforms which Gerson was trying to effect, according to which theology would be more than a merely academic discipline.

Not surprisingly, Gerson's most important writings—for example, "The Mountain of Contemplation" and "Mystical Theology"—are centrally concerned with bringing practical religion into the schools. According to Gerson, the highest aspects of the soul are the pure intelligence and the synderesis, or that which inclines the soul toward the good. The cognitive and affective aspects of the soul are closely related; thus, the knowledge of an object involves a feeling toward it, and feeling involves an element of intellectual knowledge. This psychology provided a rationale for Gerson's strictures upon merely theoretical theology. His account of mystical theology likewise incorporated the thesis that the intellect and the synderesis attain their respective perfections through mutual cooperation.

Mystical theology, for Gerson, was not so much the study of mysticism as it was the way of contemplation itself. In the highest stage the soul attains union with God, but this union is a union of love, in which the human will is in total conformity with the divine will. Gerson resisted those interpretations which implied that there was a substantial identity with God or that the love uniting the soul and God could be identified with the Holy Spirit. Thus, Gerson stated a view of mysticism that was sympathetic, practical, and orthodox; and for this reason he was widely influential in the fifteenth century. Moreover, his other main concern, the healing of the Great Schism, expressed the nature of the reforms he wished to promote. He held that on the one hand, the external and institutional aspects of religion must be in good order; but on the other hand, theology and religion must be liberated from formalism. Gerson had some influence on Luther.

Bibliography

Gerson's works have been collected in the five-volume *Johannis Gersonii Opera Omnia*, M. L. Ellies du Pin, ed. (Antwerp, 1706).

Works on Gerson are James L. Connolly, *John Gerson, Reformer and Mystic* (Louvain, 1928); and John B. Morrall, *Gerson and the Great Schism* (Manchester, 1960).

NINIAN SMART

GERSONIDES, or Levi ben Gershon (1288–1344), also known by his acronym, "RaLBaG," French Jewish philosopher, Biblical exegete, mathematician, and astronomer, was born at Bagnols and died at Perpignan. He was the inventor of two astronomical instruments, the Jacob's staff ("baculus") and an improved camera obscura. Gersonides' literary contributions include Biblical commentaries of a philosophical and moral tone, supercommentaries to Averroes' treatises on Aristotle, and his philosophical masterwork, *Milḥamot Adonai* ("Wars of the Lord"). Because of his knowledge of Averroes, Gersonides was exposed to a more authentic version of Aristotle than was available to his predecessors and was thus motivated to re-examine certain problems that he felt had previously been treated inadequately or incorrectly. These problems, corresponding to the six sections of the "Wars," are (1) the nature and immortality of the soul, (2) prophecy, (3) the nature of God's knowledge, (4) divine providence, (5) miracles and the structure of the universe, and (6) the creation of the world. Methodologically, he recognized the authority of the four roots of knowledge (as first formulated by Saadia Gaon), namely, reason, sensory perception, divine revelation, and rabbinic tradition, in that order of priority, although he seldom cited the last specifically.

The work begins with a detailed analysis of Aristotle's doctrine of the soul according to the interpretations of Alexander of Aphrodisias, Themistius, and Averroes. In agreement with Alexander, Gersonides maintained that the material or hylic intellect is a capacity inherent in the sensitive soul. Under the agency of the Active Intellect, the last of the separate intelligences, the material intellect is transformed, through the acquisition of ideas, into an actual or acquired intellect. Opposing the nominalism of Alexander and Maimonides, Gersonides maintained the reality of the ideational content of the acquired intellect. It is this acquired intellect which survives independently after the death of the individual.

Gersonides' account of the nature of God's knowledge is related to his theory of divine attributes. Maimonides' theory of homonymy, according to which attributes in general and the term "knowing" in particular refer to entirely different concepts when applied to God and man, allowed Maimonides to maintain both God's absolute omniscience and man's free will. Rejecting this as absurd, Gersonides reaffirmed, in agreement with the Muslim philosophers Avicenna and Averroes, that attributes are to be treated as ambiguous terms, applied in a primary sense to God but in a derivative sense to man. Furthermore, the attributes imply no plurality in God' nature since they are subjects of discourse and not of essence, just as the terms "redness" and "color" imply no plurality in the concept "red."

Since God's knowledge is similar in nature to man's, he cannot know the contingent and consequently knows the particulars only insofar as they are ordered. This amounts to a virtual restriction of divine knowledge to the universals. Since men are endowed with free will, this restriction normally precludes special providence for individuals. However, some individuals enjoy special providence; this consists in a knowledge, received from the Active Intellect, of stellar configurations that determine events on earth. Modern scholarship has not generally noted that this explanation of special providence for the intellectual elite was foreshadowed in one of the two discussions of the problem in Maimonides' *Guide for the Perplexed* (III.51).

The communication of astrological information to the human intellect by the Active Intellect is known as prophecy. The prophet, to the extent of his ability, interprets the general information received, in the light of the particular circumstances with which he is concerned, Gersonides' tendency to deny God's direct involvement in terrestrial affairs is further illustrated by his theory that the capacity for miracles was implanted in nature so that miracles do not represent any specific divine concern.

In his discussion of the origin of the world, Gersonides agreed with Maimonides that it was indeed created but, in opposition to him, maintained that *ex nihilo nihil fit*. Rather, he posited an absolutely formless matter (not eternal in time since time did not exist before the creation of the world) out of which the world was formed. Gersonides found this dualism useful in ascribing the origin of evil to matter.

Bibliography

Gersonides' *Milḥamot Adonai* ("Wars of the Lord") was first printed at Riva di Trenta (1560) and reprinted at Leipzig (1866). The editions omit the rather technical astronomical treatise in the fifth book which is extant in manuscript and which was translated into Latin by order of Clement VI. The partial German translation by Benzion Kellerman, *Die Kämpfe Gottes von Lewi ben Gerson* (Berlin, 1914), should be read in conjunction with Isaac Husik's review, "Studies in Gersonides," in *Jewish Quarterly Review*, N.S. Vol. 8 (1917–1918), 113 ff. and 231 ff. For a complete bibliography, see *Encyclopedia Judaica* (Berlin, 1929), Vol. IV, p. 656; Vol. VII, pp. 328 ff. and 338, to which may be added H. Wolfson, "Maimonides and Gersonides on Divine Attributes as Ambiguous Terms," in M. Davis, ed., *Mordecai Kaplan Jubilee Volume* (New York, 1953), pp. 515–530.

Frank Talmage

GESTALT THEORY. The Gestalt movement in psychology began early in the twentieth century; its founders were the German psychologists Max Wertheimer, Wolfgang Köhler, and Kurt Koffka. A Gestalt is essentially an organized whole whose parts belong together, as opposed to being simply juxtaposed or randomly distributed. As Wertheimer put it, "What happens to a part of the whole is determined by intrinsic laws inherent in this whole." The Gestalt theorists believed this principle to be of wide application and to be relevant to the psychology of perception in particular.

History. As early as 1890 Christian von Ehrenfels had pointed out that to appreciate a melody we need to be aware not of single tones in isolation but of a succession of tones which combine in a particular way. If notes of the same pitch as those of the original melody are presented in a different temporal order, there will be a completely different effect, whereas the same melody played in a different key is immediately recognizable, even though the notes are different in pitch from the original ones. The melody as a whole was said by von Ehrenfels to have a *Gestaltqualität* independent of the qualities of the separate notes. Wertheimer, Köhler, and Koffka were concerned to apply the concept of Gestalt over a wide area and thus give a new direction to psychological research.

A central feature in their view was the doctrine of isomorphism, which asserts that our experiences have the same structure as the brain processes which underlie them. Thus, if the stimulus is a nearly complete circle which the subject sees as a complete circle, the doctrine of isomorphism would assert that there must be some pattern in the brain that is isomorphic with the complete circle, as opposed to the incomplete one. The detailed neurological hypotheses which they put forward are of questionable value, but the general principle is still of interest, as is Köhler's demonstration that there are Gestalten in physical nature, for example, the soap bubble, whose spherical shape is the necessary result of the total forces in operation at any one time (see Koffka, *Principles of Gestalt Psychology*, p. 14).

The following are some typical examples of the Gestalt principle as applied to vision: Figure 1 appears as a cross;

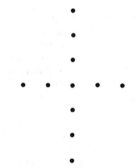

Figure 1

FROM "GESTALT PSYCHOLOGY" BY KURT KOFFKA, P. 77. BY PERMISSION OF HARCOURT, BRACE & WORLD, INC., N.Y.

if, however, we consider the effect on the retina of the eye of each of the dots in isolation, there is nothing to account for the way in which they are organized. Implicit in traditional thinking, according to Köhler and Koffka, is the so-called "constancy hypothesis"—the hypothesis that stimulation of a particular point on the retina has a constant effect regardless of the total pattern of stimulation. Yet if the constancy hypothesis were true, it would be hard to explain the obvious recognizability of the "4" in Figure 2a and its camouflage in Figure 2b, since the same retinal points are being stimulated in both cases. Similarly one cannot explain how a man who moves from twenty yards

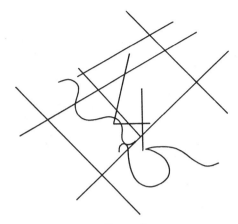

Figure 2a

FROM "GESTALT PSYCHOLOGY" BY WOLFGANG KÖHLER, P. 193. BY PERMISSION OF LIVE-RIGHT, PUBLISHERS, N.Y.

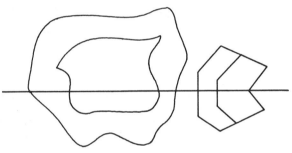

Figure 2b

FROM "GESTALT PSYCHOLOGY" BY WOLFGANG KÖHLER, P. 185. BY PERMISSION OF LIVE-RIGHT, PUBLISHERS, N.Y.

away to ten yards away continues to look approximately the same size, since the retinal stimulation must by the laws of optics be quite different. Indeed there are many characteristics of the perceived world (what Koffka terms the "behavioral," as opposed to the "geographical," environment) which do not bear a one–one relationship to anything in the pattern of stimulation. Thus, in Figure 3 we see the lines as four pairs, but the "togetherness" of each pair has no direct counterpart in the system of stimuli; and in Edgar Rubin's famous example (Figure 4), whether we see the white as "figure" and the black as

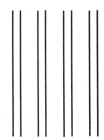

Figure 3

FROM "GESTALT PSYCHOLOGY" BY DAVID KATZ, P. 26. BY PERMISSION OF METHUEN AND COMPANY, LTD., LONDON.

Figure 4

FROM EDGAR RUBIN AS REPRODUCED IN "GESTALT PSYCHOLOGY" BY DAVID KATZ, P. 47. BY PERMISSION OF METHUEN COMPANY, LTD., LONDON.

"ground" or vice versa, there is no direct counterpart to the "thinglike" character of the figure and the absence of this character in the ground.

This thinglike character, the character of "productivity," which occurs in some causal transactions, the character of "being mine," which belongs to, say, my hand in contrast to an object on which my hand is resting, the character of anger present in someone's face—these are some of the many features which are present in the behavioral environment, even though they are necessarily absent from the world of physics because there is nothing in the stimulus situation directly corresponding to them. On the Gestalt view what is all-important is the way in which the immediate, or "proximal," stimuli (for example, light waves or sound waves) combine in space and time; when these combinations are of a certain kind, certain perceptual organizations will arise (for example, two parts of a diagram will be seen as belonging together), and laws can be framed in terms of which such organizations can be predicted. Details of these laws have been set out by David Katz; they include the law of proximity, which states that, other things being equal, in a total stimulus situation those elements which are closest to each other tend to form groups, and the law of closed forms, which states that, other things being equal, lines which enclose a surface tend to be seen as a unit.

A law of a more general kind is that of *Prägnanz*. As formulated by Koffka (*op. cit.*, p. 110), this law states: "Psychological organisation will always be as 'good' as the prevailing conditions allow. In this definition the term 'good' is undefined. It embraces such properties as regularity and symmetry, simplicity and others." In other words, when the stimuli are of a certain kind, there are forces within the organism which operate in the direction of maximum simplicity; hence, we tend to see "good" figures—squares and circles, for example—rather than less regular ones. The word *Prägnanz* is of course ultimately connected with the Latin *impregnare*. The suggestion here, however, is not that of something being fertilized or made pregnant but rather of something being stamped or pressed into a particular shape (compare the word *prägen*, which is used primarily to refer to the minting of coins). Certain types of configurations, one might say, are particularly impressive; they carry a certain stamp or they strike us in particular ways.

Contrary to what has sometimes been said, the Gestalt psychologists did not dispute that past experience can influence perception; this is made plain by Katz in *Gestalt Psychology* (pp. 28–29). Their criticism was directed against the view of perception which invoked past experience as a *deus ex machina* when observed results did not fit the constancy hypothesis. Thus a penny, unless its flat surface is directly in front of us, might be expected from the laws of optics to look elliptical. Since it does not, one can preserve the view that the "basic datum" is an ellipse by postulating a rapid process of inference based on past experience. On this view we *infer* that the penny is round because of our alleged previous experience of round pennies. According to the Gestalt psychologists, however, not only is there nothing in introspection to suggest such an inference; they would also have questioned whether in fact it is particularly common in ordinary life for pennies to have their flat surfaces directly in front of the observer—a condition which their opponents' theory seems to require. In contrast, their view was that when the proximal stimuli combine in a certain way a particular perceptual organization is forced upon us; thus a circle is a "good" figure, and hence the "internal forces" will operate in the direction of a circle rather than an ellipse.

Interesting experimental studies include those of Wertheimer ("Experimentelle Studien über das Sehen von Bewegung," in *Zeitschrift für Psychologie*) on the perception of movement, those of Köhler (*The Mentality of Apes*) on problem solving in apes, those of Wertheimer (*Productive Thinking*) and Duncker ("On Problem Solving") on problem solving in humans, that of Katz (*The World of Colour*) on the perception of color, that of Rubin (*Synsoplevede Figurer*) on the figure–ground distinction, those of Lewin (*Principles of Topological Psychology*), who has attempted to apply Gestalt principles to the study of social situations, and those of Michotte (*La Perception de la causalité*)—although he was not a member of the original group—on the conditions in which we receive an impression of causality. A recent interesting development is the attempt to relate figural goodness to the amount of information (in the mathematical sense) needed to specify a particular pattern or figure (see especially Attneave, *Applications of Information Theory to Psychology*, p. 82). The problem of perceptual Gestalten has arisen in an acute form in the programming of computers to carry out pattern recognition (see, for instance, Kirsch, "Computer Interpretation of English Text and Picture Patterns").

Science and common sense. The advance of science continually brings in its train a challenge to our common-sense beliefs about the world. At one time or another in the history of scientific thought it has been held, for example, that sense perception is unreliable, that the things around us are not really colored, that the floor on which we

walk is not really solid, and that no two events are ever exactly simultaneous. In contrast with many other scientific systems, Gestalt theory involves the attempt to call us away from such paradoxes back to common sense; it invites us to consider the world as we in fact experience it, not as we might expect to experience it in the light of the latest scientific developments.

It does not, of course, follow, that philosophical paradoxes can be disposed of simply by pointing out that experience is in fact of such-and-such a kind. Thus, it is no argument against Locke's account of substance or Hume's account of causality to point out that the behavioral environment is found by experience to consist of things in causal interaction, any more than it is an argument against the distinction between primary and secondary qualities to point out that we are aware of greenness as being in the grass and not in our heads. Similarly, a philosopher who wishes to defend the sense-datum terminology cannot be refuted simply by an appeal to Rubin's claim that what we perceive is organized into figure and ground and is not just "a mosaic of sense data." As a corrective against those who mistake the point of philosophical arguments, it may be helpful on occasions to make explicit exactly what we are aware of at the common-sense level, but this does not prove the philosophical arguments to be wrong.

Despite the emphasis on naive judgment, however, the Gestalt program does not involve an uncritical return to naive realism. Rather, its claim is that the gulf between what common sense tells us and what science tells us is not, after all, as great as might be supposed; the world of nature is *gestaltet* no less than are our experiences. Moreover, although in some of their discussions Köhler and Koffka speak in traditional terms about "the relation between mind and matter," their views do not fit easily into the traditional categories of interactionism, epiphenomenalism, and parallelism; indeed, like many modern philosophers, they are critical of a starting point which forces us to decide between theories couched in these terms.

Positivism and behaviorism. The prevailing scientific attitude of the time, which Koffka called "positivism," was mistaken, on the Gestalt view, because it allowed no place for the categories of meaning and value. The important fact for psychology is that the behavioral environment is organized—it is intelligible. Thus we are making *sense* out of a person's facial expression when we say that he is angry. Similarly, if a person listens to music, he is sometimes aware that a chord with the leading note (the seventh of the scale) at the top *requires* to be followed by the tonic chord of the original key; the cadence has its special meaning only if the second chord follows the first. This remains true even though such "requiredness," as Köhler terms it in *The Place of Value in a World of Facts*, can play no part in the world of physics. As physical science advances we are enabled to make continually more refined statements about the geographical environment; but in so doing, on the Gestalt view, we are in danger of losing sight of facts—those of the behavioral environment—which for the psychologist are of special interest. Koffka agreed that vitalism is "no solution but a mere re-naming of the problem"; but by taking seriously the concept of Gestalt one can, he held, be anti-mechanistic without being obscurantist.

There is also an attack on the allegedly "scientific"

creed of behaviorism, whose development was almost contemporary with that of Gestalt theory. The term "behaviorism," as Köhler understands it, implies a denial that there can be "a science of direct experience," either because there is no such thing as direct experience or because if it exists, it is not accessible to public scrutiny. In reply Köhler points out that no scientist can even begin to experiment unless he starts from his own experienced world. He also points out that one has as little or as much justification to be skeptical about the world of experience as one has to be skeptical about the world of physics; there is no good reason why the behaviorist should choose to ignore the world of experience while taking the world of physics on trust.

Isomorphism. It is far from clear whether the doctrine of isomorphism constitutes a radically new discovery, as the Gestalt theorists supposed, or whether it is a somewhat high-sounding way of asserting the obvious. Most twentieth-century psychologists, if asked, would doubtless express the hope that complete explanations of perception and learning will eventually be found in terms of brain processes. If, therefore, the contribution of Gestalt theory is to be distinctive, clearly some more far-reaching claim must be involved.

Koffka expressly pointed out that Gestalt theory does not stand or fall with the correctness of a particular theory about perceived movement. According to Koffka its more general objective is to contribute to "the integration of value, life, and mind. . . . The Gestalt concept . . . cuts across the division of realms of existence, being applicable in each of them." That is, there are Gestalten in nature (for example, the soap bubble); there are Gestalten in the living brain; and there are Gestalten in our conscious experience. In traditional discussions about the relation between mind and body, according to Köhler, it was "tacitly assumed that only *microscopic* events in the cortex can be the correlates of mental life." In contrast, the doctrine of isomorphism invites us, in Koffka's words, to "think of the physiological processes not as molecular but as molar phenomena. . . . If they are molar, their molar properties will be the same as those of the conscious processes which they are supposed to underlie." As has already been pointed out, this is not just an answer within the context of traditional mind–body dualism; it is an attempt to look at this whole family of problems afresh.

The distinction between the geographical and behavioral environments gives rise to difficulties of its own. One very reasonably asks, in the first place, what kind of duality is involved. Clearly, there are not two environments in the same sense that there are—or might be—two rooms in a country cottage. If a child specialist recommended a change of environment for a child, it would make no sense to reply "very well; we will change him from the geographical to the behavioral environment." One is reminded in this connection of Arthur Eddington's claim—which in fact involves the same kind of difficulty—that he is writing simultaneously at two tables. Second, if we take the idea of two environments at its face value, we are tempted to ascribe some kind of superior status or "reality" to one or the other. It is the geographical environment, according to Koffka, whose contents are "real": "The pen with which I am writing is a unit in my behavioural environment and so

is the *real* pen in the geographical" (italics added). What is "real," however, does not apparently coincide with what is "given"; ". . . every *datum* is a behavioural datum; physical reality is not a datum but a constructum." The suggestion that each of us somehow "constructs" a physical world out of his immediate experiences implies a phenomenalist view which in the last resort leads inevitably to solipsism. Clearly this was not Koffka's intention, but he gave no indication how such a conclusion can be avoided.

The important point, according to Köhler and Koffka, is that the concept of Gestalt cuts across these two different kinds of reality. In the words of Köhler, "Any actual consciousness is in every case not only blindly coupled to its corresponding psychophysical processes, but is akin to it in essential structural properties." The difficulty here is that *anything* can be regarded as "structurally akin" to anything else, provided enough rules are given. Many maps are structurally akin to landscapes in that they involve the same geometrical shapes; but if one is allowed sufficient rules for specifying what represents what, a map of England (as we now call it) could function without any misrepresentation as a map of France. What Köhler needs to argue for is some relatively clear-cut and uncomplicated structural relationship. Thus, it may well be that the shape of the areas stimulated in the cortex has something in common with the shape which we observe in an object, although it is hard to see how there can be any close parallel in the case of color, since, when X is looking at a green object, Y does not find anything green in X's cortex. One must suppose that the use of the term "psychophysical" (instead of "physical") to describe processes in the brain is intended to emphasize these relatively close structural similarities.

Knowledge of other minds. In reply to the charge of solipsism, Köhler and Koffka could point out that they both discuss the problem of knowledge of other minds at some length. The main feature of philosophical interest in these discussions is that structural similarities are pointed out between behavior which is noticed by others and so-called "inner states," which are discriminated only by the person himself. A person's wincing may have precisely the same temporal properties as his twinges of pain, and the sound of his rising voice may have the same movement properties as his inner feelings of rising anger. Koffka pointed out that a character in a Mickey Mouse cartoon can quite well look exuberant or dejected; and if we can directly observe such exuberance or dejection in these cases, there seems to be no reason why we should not directly observe it in our friends. Similarly, Michotte has argued that visual experiences of live movement are structurally similar to kinesthetic and other experiences that we have when we make an effort. These considerations are not, of course, sufficient to remove all possible skeptical doubts; but they at least make clear the conditions in which we can justifiably say of a person that, for example, he is angry, dejected, or making an effort.

"Seeing" and inference. Koffka suggested that the word "see" should be used in a "purely phenomenological" sense, that is, in such a way that the words which follow are a simple description of our experience. Thus, if we look at a table which is partly covered by a book, we are not aware of any gap or hole in the table in the area where the book is; and Koffka therefore wanted to say that what we *see* is a complete table. On his view it is necessary to describe our experience without being influenced by considerations of what we might expect to see on the basis of scientific knowledge—in this case, by our knowledge about the characteristics of the light waves striking the retina.

In ordinary usage, when we say that we or someone else saw something, this is normally not just the report of a visual experience; there is also an implicit claim to correctness. If the person is in fact deceived, then one is wrong to use the word "saw," just as one would be wrong to say that a person has "proved" something if his argument contains a fallacy. One might therefore express Koffka's difficulty by saying that, as our knowledge of physics increases, claims to *correctness* will force us further and further away from naive description. "Why, " he asked rhetorically, "are we so hopelessly stupid as to call the colour of our table-cloth on the candle-lit dinner table white, when Helmholtz told us that it was yellow?" According to Koffka's proposed usage we actually see a white tablecloth, the evidence of the physicists notwithstanding.

This "purely phenomenological" sense of "see," however, is unnecessary. We already possess the expression "seeing-as" for situations where we do not wish to make claims to correctness. On this usage, we *see* the tablecloth *as* white even though we might have expected to see it as yellow. Similarly, a person who is exposed to an ambiguous diagram may *see* it *as* two-dimensional, even though on another occasion he sees it as three-dimensional. Unless one is an extreme skeptic and asserts that claims to correctness are never appropriate when visual perception is involved, it is surely useful to have a terminology which enables us to make such claims on some occasions and to withhold them on others.

Moreover, Koffka's proposed usage, if adopted consistently, carries the paradoxical consequence that we can never be sure or unsure about what we see, nor can we be right or wrong. If we look more carefully at something, or if others give us a verbal description or point to a contour line, we may, of course, see something new; but we were still neither right nor wrong about what we saw before.

There is the further paradoxical consequence that no two people can ever see the same thing. Köhler is apparently prepared to accept this, since he expressly tells us that no two scientific investigators ever see the same galvanometer. Moreover, if everything that we see (in Koffka's sense) is, by definition, part of the behavioral environment, this has the effect of turning the behavioral environment into a home for every erroneous perception which has been made. It is as bad as having to postulate false facts to ensure that false propositions refer to something. In general, the distinction between the geographical and behavioral environments involves many points of interest, but in philosophizing in this area, Koffka in particular was not successful in avoiding paradoxical consequences.

As far as psychology is concerned, the work of the Gestalt theorists has led to the discovery of a large number of new facts, particularly in the sphere of perception, and to a reinterpretation of facts which were already known. On the basis of the laws of structural organization, predictions can be made about what will be perceived when the proximal stimuli are of a particular kind, and these predictions normally work. The neurological explanations are inadequate by present standards, but even in this area the Gestalt theorists have at least called attention to problems which require to be solved, and, in particular, they have taken seriously the challenge presented by our ability to perceive spatial and temporal relationships.

On the broader theoretical issues, traditionally the province of philosophy, their main contribution has been to indicate the need for a change of emphasis. In the light of advancing scientific knowledge, it appeared to be the case that what we thought we were perceiving was not what we were really perceiving at all ("the grass is not really green," "the white tablecloth seen in candlelight is really yellow," and so on). For the Gestalt theorists, however, as for some modern philosophers, such claims were paradoxical and confused. Whatever physics tells us, the starting point, on the Gestalt theorists' view, must necessarily be the world as perceived by common sense; this is the world to which organisms respond, and it is therefore of special importance for the psychologist; moreover, if we ourselves did not perceive it in certain ways, physics could not even begin. This is to say, in effect, that language descriptive of ordinary experience can never be reduced to the language of physics —a thesis which has been held in many forms but which has seldom been defended in such a sustained and systematic way.

Bibliography

Attneave, F., *Applications of Information Theory to Psychology.* New York, 1959. For the relevance of information theory to Gestalt theory, see especially p. 82.

Duncker, K., "On Problem Solving," translated by L. S. Lees, in *Psychological Monographs,* Vol. 58, No. 5 (1945). A short monograph with some interesting experiments on problem solving.

Ehrenfels, Christian von, "Über Gestaltqualitäten." *Vierteljarsschrift für wissenschaftliche Philosophie,* Vol. 14 (1890), 249–292. Of historical interest.

Ellis, W. D., *A Sourcebook of Gestalt Psychology.* London, 1938. A helpful collection of the writings of Gestalt psychologists in one volume; recommended as a standard textbook.

Hamlyn, D. W., "Psychological Explanation and the Gestalt Hypothesis." *Mind,* Vol. 60, No. 240 (1951), 506–520. A philosophical article in which, among other things, the concept of Gestalt is compared with that of substance.

Hamlyn, D. W., *The Psychology of Perception.* London, 1957. Contains a critical examination of some of the concepts of Gestalt theory in the light of recent British philosophy.

Hartmann, G. W., *Gestalt Psychology; A Survey of Facts and Principles.* New York, 1935. A readable account of the history of the movement and its discoveries up to 1935. Contains brief biographical details of Wertheimer, Köhler, and Koffka and a list of important dates. Recommended as a standard textbook.

Henle, M., ed., *Documents of Gestalt Psychology.* Berkeley, Calif., 1961. A collection of papers on Gestalt psychology by various authors, mostly dating from 1950 onward.

Katz, David, *Der Aufbau der Farbwelt.* Translated by R. B. Macleod and C. W. Fox as *The World of Colour.* London, 1935. Interesting discussions of the perception of color.

Katz, David, *Gestalt Psychology; Its Nature and Significance,* translated by Robert Tyson. New York, 1950. An excellent introductory textbook.

Kirsch, R. A., "Computer Interpretation of English Text and Picture Patterns." *Institute of Electrical and Electronic Engi-*

neering *Transactions on Electronic Computers, Electronic Devices* Vol. 13, No. 4 (1964). Illustrates some of the difficulties in programming computers to be aware of perceptual Gestalten.

Koffka, Kurt, *The Growth of the Mind*, translated by R. M. Ogden. London, 1924. An introduction to child psychology from the Gestalt viewpoint.

Koffka, Kurt, *Principles of Gestalt Psychology*. New York and London, 1935. A comprehensive survey of all the relevant experimental work up to 1935, accompanied by theoretical discussion of wide scope. Not easy reading, but a standard text. See pp. 655–661 for discussion of knowledge of other minds.

Köhler, Wolfgang, *The Mentality of Apes*, translated from the 2d rev. German ed. by Ella Winter. London, 1925; paperback ed., Harmondsworth, 1957. A classic work on problem solving. This work and his *Gestalt Psychology* (see below) are recommended as standard texts.

Köhler, Wolfgang, *The Place of Value in a World of Facts*. New York, 1938. William James lectures. A scholarly discussion of philosophical issues.

Köhler, Wolfgang, *Dynamics in Psychology*. London, 1942. An amplified version of lectures given at the University of Virginia in 1958.

Köhler, Wolfgang, *Gestalt Psychology; An Introduction to New Concepts in Modern Psychology*. New York and Toronto, 1947. An interesting although somewhat discursive discussion of general principles. See Ch. 17 for the problem of knowledge of other minds.

Lewin, Kurt, *Principles of Topological Psychology*, translated by Fritz Heider and Grace M. Heider. New York and London, 1936. An attempt to apply Gestalt principles to the study of social situations.

Madden, Edward H., *Philosophical Problems of Psychology*. New York, 1962. Contains a critical examination of some of the key concepts of Gestalt theory.

Michotte, Albert, *La Perception de la causalité*. Louvain, Belgium, 1946 and 1954. Translated by T. R. Miles and E. Miles as *The Perception of Causality*. London, 1963. A systematic study of moving Gestalten, with special reference to the conditions in which we receive an impression of causality. See Chs. 12–13 for the problem of knowledge of other minds.

Rubin, Edgar, *Synsoplevede Figurer; Studier i psykologisk Analyse*. Copenhagen and Oslo, 1915. Translated by Peter Collett as *Visuell wahrgenommene Figuren*. Copenhagen, Berlin, and London, 1921. An abridged version, translated by Michael Wertheimer, appears in D. C. Beardslee and Michael Wertheimer, eds., *Readings in Perception*. Princeton, N.J., 1958. Pp. 194–203. Interesting pioneer work.

Wertheimer, Max, "Experimentelle Studien über das Sehen von Bewegung." *Zeitschrift für Psychologie*, Part I, Vol. 71 (1912), 161–265. Of historical interest; commonly regarded as marking the beginning of the Gestalt movement.

Wertheimer, Max, *Productive Thinking*, S. E. Asch et al., eds. New York and London, 1945. An important contribution to the study of problem solving.

T. R. MILES

GEULINCX, ARNOLD or Aernout (1624–1669), Flemish metaphysician and moralist, was born in Antwerp. He studied philosophy and theology at Louvain and in 1646 was made professor of philosophy, a position he held for 12 years. Although information about his life at Louvain is limited and his important works date from a later period, it appears that as a student he was influenced by the Cartesian Guillaume Philippi, that in his teaching, as later, he attacked scholastic physics from a Cartesian point of view, and that he was also attracted by the doctrines of Cornelis Jansen.

In 1658, on charges that were not made public but that may have been prompted by his criticisms of scholasticism and accepted religious practices, he was deprived of his professorship and left Louvain for Leiden. At the same time, he renounced Roman Catholicism and became a Calvinist. Arriving in Leiden in distressed circumstances, he was assisted by the Cartesian Abraham van der Heyden (Heidanus) and set to work on a study of fevers, which he presented for the doctorate in medicine. Despite his precarious situation at first, Geulincx succeeded in publishing treatises on logic and method (*Logica Fundamentis Suis . . . Restituta*, Leiden, 1662, and *Methodus Inveniendi Argumenta*, Leiden, 1663) and the first part of his most accomplished work, the "Ethics" (*De Virtute et Primis Ejus Proprietatibus*, Leiden, 1665). He was appointed professor extraordinary of philosophy at the university in 1665 and remained in Leiden until his untimely death, in 1669. Six years later the complete "Ethics" was published, under the title Γνωθι σεαυτον, *Sive . . . Ethica* (Leiden, 1675). His "Physics," taken from manuscripts used in his classes, appeared in 1688 (*Physica Vera*, Leiden); commentaries on Descartes's *Principles of Philosophy* in 1690 and 1691 (*Annotata Praecurrentia, Annotata Majora*, Dordrecht); and the very important "Metaphysics," published apparently from a student's copy, in 1691 (*Metaphysica Vera et ad Mentem Peripateticam*, Amsterdam).

Occasionalism. Geulincx is best known for his occasionalist theory of causation and his denial of the substantiality of particular created things. Following Descartes's order of procedure in his "Metaphysics," he considered at the outset the possibility and the limits of doubt and found that our first knowledge is of the self as a thinking thing. Consideration of the various states of the self or mind led him to formulate a principle, which he took to be self-evident though obscured by prejudices, that expresses a necessary condition implicit in our conception of an action: that something cannot be done unless there is knowledge of how it is done, or, as specifically related to activities of the self, that a person does not do what he does not know how to do (*impossibile est, ut is faciat, qui nescit quomodo fiat; quod nescis quomodo fiat, id non facis*).

The principle had far-reaching consequences in Geulincx' moral philosophy as well as in his metaphysics. Concerning the self, he contended that actions involving movements of the body cannot in truth be attributed to the self and that the mind or soul is not, as it is often supposed to be, the true cause of movements of the body. Not only are we unaware of changes in the brain, nerves, and muscles requisite for, say, moving the arm, but even if we know of these changes from a study of physiology, our knowledge is based on ex post facto observation of sequences of volitions and physiological happenings, not on awareness of a supposed mental activity producing these movements. Though we have, Geulincx maintained, immediate knowledge and understanding of internal actions—that is, of acts not involving bodily movements and consisting solely of changes in a state of mind—we are not in like manner cognizant of how movements are initiated in the body or how external actions come about. Accordingly the influence of the human mind is limited to its own states, and the mind is not the master of—that is, the true cause of movements in—the body.

The principle was also invoked against the assumption

that bodies, or corporeal things, are capable of acting, either on minds or on other corporeal things. It is assumed, for instance, that a fire acts on a man's body and, affecting sense organs, nerves, and brain, produces sensations of light and heat in his mind. It is also assumed that in cases of impact one body striking another sets the second body in motion. But how, Geulincx asked, can a body produce these effects? To bring them about, according to his principle, it would have to know how. Yet admittedly a body is inanimate and, lacking consciousness, lacks the knowledge that on reflection we see is a necessary condition of acting. Bodies are *res brutae*. To suppose that they have the distinctively spiritual characteristic of acting is a signal instance of confusion involving the self-contradictory notion of corporeal action or causation. Arguing against the possibility of genuine corporeal causation as such, Geulincx, like the occasionalists Géraud de Cordemoy and Nicolas Malebranche, took it to be true a fortiori that bodies cannot act on minds. (There is no evidence that Geulincx was influenced by, or that he in turn influenced, the other occasionalists.)

Though the human mind does not act on the body and bodies do not act on the mind or on other bodies, changes obviously do take place, and in these changes we discern patterns or constant conjunctions of events. According to Geulincx, the agent responsible for these changes is God, and the patterns we observe are due to laws that God enacts and in accordance with which he operates. Explicating his theory of supernatural causation in the case of volitions and bodily movements, Geulincx iterated two analogies, the second of which was the subject of an important controversy among German historians in the nineteenth century. (1) When a child wants his cradle to move, it often happens that the cradle moves, not as a result of his willing it, but because the mother or nurse in attendance wills that it move. (2) Two clocks that are synchronized sound the hour in unison, not because one influences the other, but because they are fashioned in such a way that they keep the same time. The second illustration has been cited to show that Geulincx, like Leibniz, conceived of a pre-established harmony between mind and body and that he was the unacknowledged source of Leibniz' famous analogy of concurrent clocks and, by implication, of Leibniz' view of the relation between mind and body. Against this interpretation it can be argued convincingly (as was done by Eduard Zeller) that in Geulincx' view, God's actions, though in accordance with rules, are immediate or direct in the sense that there is nothing in mind or body comparable to the internal natures which, according to Leibniz, account for their successive states and mediate the will of God and the course of events. It is not the case, however, that the actions of Geulincx' God are *ad hoc* or, as Leibniz accused the occasionalists, that Geulincx' God is a *deus ex machina*. The rules of his action are fixed, and he simply applies them, with no special volitions required, in particular circumstances.

Substance. Geulincx' views about substance were roughly midway between Descartes's and Spinoza's. In the Synopsis of the *Meditations*, Descartes, drawing a distinction between body taken generally (*in genere sumptum*) and the human body, suggested that the former, like a person's mind, is a substance or pure substance (*puram . . . substantiam*), whereas the latter, insofar as it is a particular body differing from other bodies, is not. Following Descartes's lead, Geulincx contrasted body in itself (*corpus ipsum, corpus simpliciter dictum*), which he identified with extension, and particular bodies, which he claimed are modes of body (*aliquid ipsius corporis simpliciter dicti, modi corporis*). Body in itself is simple, unique, individual, infinite, and indivisible. Particular bodies are limitations of, or abstractions from, body in itself. They are not, he explained, constituent parts, nor are they figments of the mind (*entia rationis*); rather, they are related to body in itself as the superficies, or surface, of a particular body is related to that particular body. In another analogy, as the country is not a collection of fields, orchards, and meadows but the land on which these divisions are imposed, so corporeal nature is not an aggregate of particular bodies but the matter or extension common to them all and specified in various ways. The analogy also explains Geulincx' conception of mind. Like Spinoza (though independently), he held that individual minds are themselves not substances but modes of mind (*modi mentis*) or of infinite thinking substance, which he identified with God. We are, he said, both from God and in God (*ex Deo et in Deo*). To the extent to which we can transcend the distorting forms of our limited understandings and see the eternal truths in ourselves as they are in the mind of God, we lose our status as limited beings and are one with God. Geulincx' reflections on problems about substance paralleled Spinoza's. However, he preserved the Cartesian distinction between thinking substance and extended substance, or matter.

Ethics. In the letter prefaced to the first part of his "Ethics," Geulincx implied that his moral philosophy rounds out the system conceived by Descartes, who, though he proposed a provisional code of morality in the *Discourse*, did not bring this branch of the tree of knowledge to fruition. In Geulincx' view the subject matter of ethics is virtue, and virtue is located not in deeds but in a determination of the will—that is, in love of right reason or, since reason as prescriptive comprises laws imposed by God, in devotion to divine law. Though virtue is one and simple, there are four aspects, and these cardinal virtues are distinguished from and contrasted with the traditional cardinal virtues, which refer to actions or accomplishments, not to the locus of morality—namely, the condition of the will. (1) *Diligence* is attention to the voice of reason. Its issue is wisdom and prudence in conduct. (2) *Obedience* involves compliance with the dictates of reason. Though we are free to will in conformity to divine law or not, in the end we cannot but do what God wills. By obeying his prescriptions we attain freedom in the highest degree: we will what we can do and do not will what we cannot do, and our volitions are effective. (3) *Justice*, also, is a determination of the will: to will no more and no less than reason dictates. (4) *Humility* consists in knowledge, and denial, of self (*contemptio sui*) in the love of reason and of God. Contrasted with the virtuous man is the egoist, whose end in life is happiness. He is the slave of his passions and the creature of circumstance, whereas the virtuous man, not seeking happiness and resigned to what happens to him, is in a position to attain it.

Works by Geulincx

Arnoldi Geulincx Antverpiensis Opera Philosophica, Jan Pieter Nicolaas Land, ed., 3 vols. The Hague, 1891–1893. The standard edition.

Works on Geulincx

Grimm, Eduard, *Arnold Geulinx' Erkenntnisstheorie und Occasionalismus*. Jena, 1875.

Haeghen, Victor vander, *Geulincx: Étude sur sa vie, sa philosophie et ses ouvrages*. Ghent, 1886. A bibliography of Geulincx' works is on pp. 197–224.

Hausmann, Paul, *Das Freiheitsproblem in der Metaphysik und Ethik bei Arnold Geulincx*. Würzburg, 1934.

Hoffmann, Georg, *Das Gottesproblem bei Geulincx und Malebranche*. Düren, 1931.

Land, Jan Pieter Nicolaas, *Arnold Geulincx und seine Philosophie*. The Hague, 1895.

Nagel, Karl, *Das Substanzproblem bei Arnold Geulincx*. Cologne, 1930.

Terraillon, Eugène, *La Morale de Geulincx*. Paris, 1912.

Vleeschauwer, Hermann Jean de, "Three Centuries of Geulincx Research." *Mededelings van die Universiteit van Suid-Afrika*, Vol. 1 (1957), 1–72. Survey of writings on Geulincx.

ON GEULINCX AND LEIBNIZ

Eucken, Rudolf, "Leibniz und Geulinx." *Philosophische Monatshefte*, Vol. 19 (1883), 525–542.

Pfleiderer, Edmund, *Arnold Geulinx als Hauptvertreter der Okkasionalistischen Metaphysik und Ethik*. Tübingen, 1882.

Pfleiderer, Edmund, *Leibniz und Geulinx mit besonderer Beziehung auf ihr beiderseitiges Uhrengleichniss*. Tübingen, 1884. See also the review of this book by Rudolf Eucken in *Philosophische Monatshefte*, Vol. 20 (1884), 417–421.

Pfleiderer, Edmund, "Noch einmal Leibniz und Geulinx." *Philosophische Monatshefte*, Vol. 21 (1885), 20–39.

Zeller, Eduard, "Über die erste Ausgabe von Geulincx' Ethik und Leibniz' Verhältniss zu Geulincx' Occasionalismus." *Sitzungsberichte der Königlich Preussischen Akademie der Wissenschaften zu Berlin*, Vol. 29 (1884), 673–695.

ON EARLY EDITIONS OF GEULINCX' WORKS

Vleeschauwer, Hermann Jean de, "L'opera di Arnoldi Geulincx," in *Edizioni di filosofia*. Turin, 1958. Pp. 1–53.

WILLIS DONEY

GEYSER, JOSEPH (1869–1948), German critical realist philosopher, was born in Erkelenz, in the Rhineland. He received a doctorate in philosophy from the University of Bonn in 1898. He became an extraordinary professor at the University of Münster in 1904 and a full professor there in 1911. In 1917 Geyser was called to Freiburg, and in 1924 he succeeded Clemens Baeumker, the distinguished historian of ancient and medieval philosophy, at the University of Munich.

From his youth, Geyser opposed what he regarded as two basic tendencies in recent philosophy, an intellectualism strongly tinged with historical relativism and an overly abstract, idealistic Kantianism. He devoted himself to recalling philosophy to the asking of questions that are largely independent of any temporary situation and to the answering of these questions in an objective, critically realist manner. This attitude, but not Geyser's attachment to Thomistic tradition, was shared by the realist Oswald Külpe and the philosopher of nature Erich Becher. Above all, Geyser was totally devoted to the *philosophia perennis* (Leibniz), and through it he related himself to the older European intellectual traditions. Philosophy, he strongly believed, is not a constant new beginning. For Geyser, philosophy, in the words of the early Middle Ages, is like a dwarf perched on the shoulders of a great past in order to see farther. Classical philosophy, in the thought of Plato and Aristotle, was already approaching great truths, insights which have claims on the present as part of a constantly self-renewing stream of thought, a stream which has both enriched and been enriched by the Christian world view.

Geyser held that answers to philosophical questions must be based on direct contact with a real actuality, understood in the Aristotelian sense, as an entity independent of consciousness, and not on the creative activity of an idealistic, theoretical thought. Only thus can we stand on firm ground. Philosophy is in this view a kind of middle position between the reality of experience and the ideality of a creative reconstruction of the forms of existence. Geyser sensitively expounded this basic attitude in his short but deeply probing book, *Eidologie oder Philosophie als Formerkenntnis* ("Eidology, or Philosophy as Knowledge of Form," Münster, 1921). In this programmatic work, whose basic ideas were to guide Geyser's thought from then on, philosophy is presented as a progressive penetration into the realm of possible essences of being insofar as they offer themselves to experience.

Geyser's inclusive *Lehrbuch der allgemeinen Psychologie* ("Münster, 1908; 3d ed., 2 vols., Münster, 1920) had already been written from this point of view, which also formed the basis of Geyser's acute critique of Neo-Kantianism and Edmund Husserl's phenomenology in *Grundlegung der Logik und Erkenntnistheorie* ("Foundations of Logic and Epistemology," Münster, 1919) and *Auf dem Kampffeld der Logik* ("On the Battlefield of Logic," Freiburg, 1926), as well as of his later exposition of ontology and metaphysics. In all of these works we see Geyser as a relentless logician who was honest and strict with himself and an epistemologist capable of critical observations.

We can now examine how Geyser deals with modern problems. Geyser's *Psychologie* combined philosophical and modern empirical psychology, for he found it impossible to separate philosophy from psychology without damage to both disciplines. This open attitude permitted him to develop a method for recording mental life in all its unconscious, organic, and even ontological aspects. Nevertheless, Geyser fought against and tried to refute psychologism, the claim that even logical phenomena depend on psychological structures of experience. He developed an unambiguous distinction between actual psychological events and the logical, objective analysis of meaning (in the manner of Heinrich Rickert). With equal intellectual vigor he gave a firm basis to his logical objectivism bound to being and distinguished it from both epistemological idealism and the phenomenological theory of constitution.

Objectivism meant for Geyser that logical laws are not only inner relations of thought but that they also have a real ontological character and that they stand the test of analysis. According to Geyser, philosophy should therefore explain how man is capable of grasping the ideal logical order in reality itself. Here we come face to face with ultimate realities, which reveal themselves to the human intellect only after suitable deductive rational preparation. Nevertheless, Geyser attains a knowledge of essence akin to that of phenomenology. But one could say that his phenomenology is Aristotelian and realistic, and Geyser can be credited with showing a connection, through Bernhard Bolzano, between the thought of Husserl and that of Aristotle. Geyser's epistemology is logically rational and tied to reality, and it stresses discursive, genetic methods. Only as a last resort could Geyser justify to his intellectual conscience an encounter with pure immediate insights.

The same rational and empirically bound method is evident in Geyser's views on causation, which provoked a many-sided controversy. These views are of particular relevance to contemporary discussions of the bases of natural science. The principle of universal causation, further seen as the law of causation, has always been considered to be the solid foundation of any given truth which can be discovered by analysis. In this sense it was one of the most essential supports of one of the traditional proofs of the existence of God. It was assumed to be evident and analytically a priori provable that the contingent world must have a supercontingent cause in God. Geyser investigated the distinctions between the ground of knowledge, the principle of contradiction, and the principle of sufficient reason. In *Philosophia Perennis, Festgabe Joseph Geyser,* Kurt Huber gives an exact summary of Geyser's critical investigations. In the same book Aloys Wenzel points out that Geyser was the first philosopher to further develop Schopenhauer's investigation of the principle of sufficient reason. Geyser showed further, in *Das Prinzip vom zureichenden Grunde* ("The Principle of Sufficient Reason," Ratisbon, 1929) and *Das Gesetz der Ursache* ("The Law of Cause," Freiburg, 1933), that only through experience can we discover the meaning of causality. Everything has its sufficient reason, including being: "Everything that comes into being does so through a cause." Such a notion is originally given to us in the mental experience of causation in willing. The notion contains a synthetic feature, but it nevertheless remains completely unconditional although it is not given to intuition as an analytic law of thought. The questions of whether the principle of causation is a priori, and of how it is related to matters of experience, is significant for any possible further epistemological and metaphysical construction which is in accord with experience. Controversy with Thomistic philosophers resulted from this statement.

Geyser's position was also clearly expressed in his metaphysics. He was committed to an inductive metaphysics, not to a purely speculative metaphysics derived from intellectual immediacy. He thus distinguished his own thought from metaphysics as practiced by such Neo-Thomists as Gallus M. Manser and Antonin-Dalmace Sertillanges.

Similarly, when Geyser, like Francisco Suárez, ascribed a concrete, individual spiritual essence to human existence, he did not do so primarily in the Thomistic sense of a universal spiritual essence which achieves individuality by being united with matter. In the foreground of Geyser's thought is the empirically unique real event. It is thus not surprising to learn that Geyser, although he recognized a rational metaphysical knowledge of God by analogy, critically denied any intuitive insight into God's existence. (Here he differentiated his thought from Max Scheler's philosophy of religion, which he criticized in *Max Schelers Phänomenologie der Religion,* Freiburg, 1929). It also shows why Geyser rejected any ontological proof of God, that is, any knowledge of God reached by even the concept of the most perfect being discovered by an a priori encounter with essence. Rather, he felt that the existence of God is to be discovered a posteriori by an interpretation of the "united facts of experience." Geyser's thought found its completion in a rationally founded metaphysical knowledge of God.

Geyser was one of the most inclusive systematic thinkers of modern times. Nicolai Hartmann, another great systematizer, once said that he had learned more from Geyser's criticisms of his ontology than from those of any other contemporary. Few recent philosophers can call such a consistently thought-out and complete world view their own. Geyser's world view was developed within and into an inner unity with his Christian conviction; this firmness of attitude toward the world was also expressed in his whole steady personality, which endured the unhappy experience of his homeland during the last years of his life under the perspective of hope.

Additional Works by Geyser

Über Wahrheit und Evidenz. Münster, 1918.
Erkenntnistheorie. Münster, 1922.
Augustin und die phänomenologische Religionsphilosophie der Gegenwart. Münster, 1923.
Einige Hauptprobleme der Metaphysik. Freiburg, 1923.
"Selbstdarstellung," in Hermann Schwarz, ed., *Deutsche systematische Philosophie,* Vol. II. Berlin, 1934.

Works on Geyser

Baur, Ludwig, "Joseph Geyser als Metaphysiker," in F.-J. von Rintelen, ed., *Philosophia Perennis, Festgabe Joseph Geyser.* Ratisbon, 1930. Vol. II, pp. 1173–1196.
Ettlinger, Max, "Joseph Geyser als Psychologe," *ibid.* Pp. 1131–1140.
Gabel, Herbert, *Theistische Metaphysik im Ausgleich von Idealismus und Realismus bei Joseph Geyser.* Freiburg, 1957.
Huber, Kurt, "Geysers Stellung in Logik und Erkenntnistheorie," in F.-J. von Rintelen, ed., *op. cit.* Pp. 1141–1172.
Rössli, J., *Das Prinzip der Ursache und des Grundes bei Joseph Geyser.* Fribourg, Switzerland, 1940.
Wenzel, Aloys, "Der Gestalt- und Ganzheitebegriff," in F.-J. von Rintelen, ed., *op. cit.* Pp. 657–684.

Fritz-Joachim von Rintelen
Translated by *Tessa Byck*

GHAZĀLĪ, ABŪ ḤĀMID MUḤAMMAD (in Persian, "Ghazālī," in its Arabic form, "al-Ghazālī"), Islamic theologian known to medieval Scholastics as Algazel. Ghazālī was born in 450 or 451 H. (A.D. 1058 or 1059) in Ghazāleh, a village on the outskirts of Tūs, in Khorāsān, northeastern Iran. His name is the same as that of his birthplace, which should be transcribed as Ghazālī, not as Ghazzālī. He died at Tūs in 505 H. (A.D. 1111). He was undoubtedly one of the strongest spiritual personalities of Islam, one of those who strove most effectively for the establishment of an "orthodox" Sufism that would transcend the legalistic and superficial religion of the doctors of the Law. Ghazālī was well known to the medieval Scholastics through a Latin translation of an unfortunately truncated work, *Maqasid al-Falāsifa* ("The Intentions of Philosophers"). As a result the true meaning of his work was completely misunderstood, and he was thought to be a philosopher, whereas in fact he was the most ardent critic of philosophy.

At the age of 36, Ghazālī experienced a profound crisis, provoked by the problem of intellectual certitude. He abandoned his professorship and his position as rector of Niẓāmīya University of Baghdad. During a period of ten years, clothed in the characteristic wool garment of the Sufis and completely absorbed in spiritual practices, he made solitary pilgrimages throughout the Muslim world, to Syria, Egypt, Mecca, and Medina. What he conveyed in his doctrines cannot be separated from this pathetic experience. He solved the problem of knowledge and certitude by affirming a degree of comprehension that left the heart no room for doubt, a comprehension that is the essential apprehension of things. The thinking soul becomes the focus of the universal Soul's irradiations, the mirror of intelligible forms received from the universal Soul. This theme dominates certain characteristic short treatises (the *Monqidh,* or "Preservative From Error," the *Risālat al-Ladonīya,* etc.) as well as the great synthesis entitled *Ihyā' 'Ulūm ad-Dīn* ("Revival of the Religious Sciences"). But this theme had already been treated, undoubtedly without his knowledge, by the Imāms of Shī'ism, and it does not differ essentially from the *Ishrāq* of Sohrawardī. This very theme led Sohrawardī to advance philosophy on a new basis rather than destroy the efforts of philosophers as such.

It is principally this aspect of Ghazālī's work, developed in his *Tahāfut al-Falāsifa* ("Autodestruction of the Philosophers") that Westerners have been inclined to emphasize. An attempt has even been made to read into it a more incisive and decisive critique or metaphysics than that of Kant. In fact, Ghazālī strove vehemently to destroy the demonstrative range that philosophers, Avicennians as well as others, accorded to their arguments regarding the eternity of the world, the procession of the Intelligences, the existence of purely spiritual substances, and the idea of spiritual resurrection. In general Ghazālī strove to refute the idea of any causality, of any necessary connection. According to him all that can be experimentally affirmed is, for example, that combustion of cotton occurs *at the moment of* contact with fire; it cannot be shown that combustion takes place *because of* the contact between cotton and fire. Nor can it be shown that there is any cause whatsoever. From this bursts forth the paradox of a thinker who professes the inability of reason to attain certitude while maintaining the certitude of destroying, with massive doses of rational dialectic, the certitudes of the philosophers. Averroës clearly discerned this self-contradiction and replied to it with his celebrated *Tahāfut al-Tahāfut* ("Autodestruction of the Autodestruction").

The same paradox is apparent in Ghazālī's other polemical works; in the "Courteous Refutation of the Divinity of Jesus Christ According to the Gospel"; in his treatise in Persian against all sorts of "freethinkers," or heretical thinkers (*Ibāḥīya*); and, finally, in the treatise against the Ismā'īlites (the Bāṭinites, or "esoterics"). The last treatise was overly influenced by the fact that it had been commissioned for political reasons by the 'Abbāsid caliph al-Mostaẓhir, and the savage *dialectic,* deployed against an essentially *hermeneutic* Shī'ite thought, rings false. The Ismā'īlites met this attack in the twelfth century with a monumental response (a work of the fifth Yemenite Dā'ī, in 1,500 pages), which unfortunately, is still unedited.

In any case, these polemical works had but a limited echo; Ghazālī's influence made itself felt principally through the *Ihya.* Without doubt this influence was, and remains, considerable in Sunnite Islam. In Shī'ite Islam, notably in Iran, it was another matter. First of all, his effort did not respond to the same necessity, since the teaching of the Imāms of Shī'ism had already opened the way to spiritual Islam. But his effort was not ignored in Shī'ism, especially in the Ispahan School. Mohsen Fayz (died 1091 H./A.D. 1680), one of the most celebrated pupils of Mollā Ṣadrā Shīrāzī (died 1050 H./A.D. 1640), even went so far as to rewrite the whole *Ihya* with a Shī'ite interpretation. (Certain authors believe with him, assuming the authenticity of the book entitled *Sirr al-'Ālamayn,* "Secret of the Two Universes," that Ghazālī would finally have rallied to Shī'ism.) In any case, in Iran no one ever thought or heard it said, as in the West, that the Ghazalian critique might have rendered impossible the continuation of philosophy in Islam and that Islamic philosophy was perhaps obliged to transport itself to Andalusia, where its last flames glowed with Ibn Bājja, Ibn-Tufayl, and Averroës. Avicennianism, for example, enriched and modified by diverse contributions, continued to develop in Shī'ite Iran, not only during the Safavid epoch but also afterward, even to this day.

Ahmad Ghazālī. Aḥmad Ghazālī, brother of Abū Ḥāmid, died in Qazvin, Iran, in 520 H. (A.D. 1126). His existence should be noted here primarily because he is hardly known to Westerners. Second, he, too, was a strong personality; he exercised an influence on his brother but, despite his fiery nature, did not succeed in communicating to him the passion of "pure love" that was consuming him. Aḥmad Ghazālī occupies an important place among the Islamic Platonists, who elaborated the Platonic doctrine of love, as found in the *Symposium,* from the time of Dāwud Ispahānī (died 297 H./A.D. 909) to the time of Ruzbehan Baqlī Shīrāzī (died 606 H./A.D. 1209). Aḥmad Ghazālī's "Breviary of Love" (*Sawānih al-'Oshshāq,* "The Intuitions of Those Faithful to Love") is a jewel of Persian literature; in his doctrine, lover and beloved are transubstantiated into the unity of the pure substance of love.

Bibliography

For works by Ghazālī, see *Al-Ghazali's Tahafut al-Falasifah* (*Incoherence of the Philosophers*), translated by S. A. Kamali (Lahore, Pakistan, 1958); *Al-Ghazali's Ihya' 'Ulūm al-Dīn, Book XX,* translated and annotated by L. Zolondek (London, 1963); W. Montgomery Watt, *The Faith and Practice of al-Ghazali* (London, 1951), which contains translations of the *Monqidh* under the title "Deliverance From Error" and of "The Beginning of Guidance"; Ignaz Goldziher, *Streitschrift des Ghazālī gegen die Bāṭinijja-Sekte* (Leiden, 1916; Neudruck, 1956), an abbreviated edition with introduction and summary of the work against the Ismāʿīlites; and *Réfutation excellente de la divinité de Jésus-Christ d'après les Évangiles*, a translation and commentary on the "Courteous Refutation," by R. Chidiac (Paris, 1939). See also *Averroes' Tahafut al-Tahafut (The Incoherence of the Incoherence)*, translated by Simon van den Bergh, 2 vols. (London, 1954), which incorporates most of Ghazālī's *Tahāfut al-Falāsifah*.

For works on Ghazālī, see Henry Corbin, *Histoire de la philosophie islamique*, Vol. I (Paris, 1964), pp. 251–261, with a detailed bibliography on pp. 358–359. See pp. 278–283 for Ahmad Ghazālī. See also W. Montgomery Watt, *Islamic Philosophy and Theology*, pp. 114–124, which includes bibliography (Edinburgh, 1962); this is Vol. I of *Islamic Surveys*.

HENRY CORBIN

GHOSE, AUROBINDO. See AUROBINDO GHOSE.

GIBBON, EDWARD (1737–1794), English historian and man of letters, was born at Putney, Surrey, of a well-to-do family. Frail and constantly ill, the child owed the preservation of his life to an aunt, Miss Catherine Porten, who also acted as his teacher. After instruction by a series of tutors and much reading on his own, he entered Magdalen College, Oxford, at the age of 15, with, as he later confessed, "a stock of erudition which might have puzzled a doctor, and a degree of ignorance of which a schoolboy would have been ashamed." Fourteen months at college, "the most idle and unprofitable of my whole life," ended with self-conversion to Roman Catholicism. His irate father immediately packed him off to Lausanne, Switzerland, under the care of Daniel Pavillard, a Calvinist minister who soon led him back to Protestantism. Thereafter, he developed a decidedly skeptical bent. During his five years' stay in Switzerland, Gibbon learned French, Italian, and Greek, and read all the Latin classics. He also fell in love with Suzanne Curchod. When his father refused consent to their marriage, "I sighed as a lover, I obeyed as a son." Mlle. Curchod later married Jacques Necker, distinguished French financier and statesman, and became famous as a *salonnière*. Gibbon never married.

Gibbon's first publication was *Essai sur l'étude de la littérature* (1761). A later manuscript fragment of a "History of the Swiss Revolution," also in French, was shown to David Hume, who approved of the project but chided the author: "Why do you compose in French, and carry faggots into the wood?" Thereafter, Gibbon composed all his major works in English. For more than two years (1759–1762), Gibbon was a captain in the Hampshire militia, and a surprisingly good one. In 1763, with the end of the Seven Years' War, he returned to the Continent, visiting Paris, Lausanne, and finally Rome. He records that it was on October 15, 1764, while musing amid the ruins of the Capitol, that the idea of writing about the decline and fall of the city—later extended to the empire—first occurred to him.

Returning to England in 1765, he became a man of letters and man about town. In 1774 he was elected to Dr. Johnson's Literary Club, where he became the intimate friend of Adam Smith. In the same year he obtained a seat in parliament, where he earned the distinction of never making a speech. He was, however, hard at work on his great history, the first quarto volume of *The History of the Decline and Fall of the Roman Empire*, which appeared in 1776. A letter of congratulation from the dying Hume "overpaid the labour of ten years," but warned that a clamor would arise. It did, and Gibbon responded three years later with a *Vindication*. The sixth and last volume of the history was published in 1788. At least fifty British replies and refutations were published before Gibbon's death, and literally hundreds have been published in many languages since. At his death, Gibbon left behind six drafts of an autobiography, which were pieced together and published in his *Miscellaneous Works* in two volumes by Lord Sheffield (London, 1796).

The history of the "Decline and Fall of the Roman Empire." Received as a masterpiece on first publication, Gibbon's history is still regarded as such, and has never been superseded. Certain misinterpretations of facts, to be sure, have been detected and many additional facts have come to light; some prejudices have been revealed and some misjudgments have become apparent, "but in the main things he is still our master, above and beyond 'date'"—so acknowledged J. B. Bury in the modern standard edition of the work.

It is the famous fifteenth and sixteenth chapters of the first volume, however, that entitle Gibbon to an honored place in the history of philosophy. These are the two chapters that stirred up violent controversy in 1776, and they are still controversial. The problem that Gibbon set himself was to explain the progress of primitive Christianity and its influence upon the ultimate fall of the Roman empire. Writing *en philosophe*, Gibbon comes to the conclusion that the fall of Rome represents "the triumph of barbarism and religion." He ironically dismisses the most commonly accepted causes of the triumph of Christianity, namely, the convincing historical evidence of the doctrine itself and the ruling providence of its great Author. He notes that through the course of time prejudice and passion have distorted and rendered ambiguous the meaning of the doctrine, while the providence of Deity remains inscrutable to man. The former cause, therefore, is unhistorical, while the latter is unphilosophical. Ruling out supernaturalism as a cause, Gibbon consequently confines himself in the fifteenth chapter to an analysis and discussion of the secondary causes of the rapid growth of the Christian church—causes which can be tested both by historical fact and by philosophical and psychological analysis.

With cool detachment of philosophical and historical inquiry, he examines the early history of the church in the same spirit that he would examine any period of secular history in which no assertions of supernaturalism had been made. He discusses five secondary causes of the rise of Christianity: (1) The inflexible zeal of the Christians was inherited in part from the Jews, who alone had broken the religious harmony of the ancient world, which was based upon mutual toleration of all creeds, and had insisted that theirs was the one and only true religion. The Christians turned this defensive zeal into both the proselytizing of all ranks of people and the persecution of all varieties of idolatry. (2) Belief in immortality, uncertain and disputed among the ancient philosophers and not to be found in the law of Moses, gradually began to be accepted by the Jews after their servitude to Egyptians and Babylonians. Early Christians, contemptuous of their present existence and convinced of their immortality, believed in the near approach of the end of the world, which was to be preceded by the Second Coming of Christ. At this time, believers and unbelievers alike would receive judgment—the former, eternal bliss; the latter, eternal damnation. As for the tortures which awaited sinners and deluded philosophers, Gibbon finds it proper "to draw a veil over the rest of this infernal description." (3) The early history of the church is replete with claims to miraculous powers and to divine inspiration. Such forms of superstition and "enthusiasm" made constant progress, until they became part of church tradition. But it remains the scholarly duty of the historian to examine such claims and to reject all pretensions to inspiration that are unacceptable in the light of reason. If the age of miracles once existed, all reasonable men, in contrast to the credulous and the fanatical, agree that at some time it either suddenly or gradually terminated. (4) The pure and austere morals of the early Christians were enhanced by two laudable human motives: repentance for past sins and the desire for perfection. Converted sinners became saints, disdainfully rejecting the natural human propensities for pleasure and action in favor of the monkish virtues of humility, meekness, and patience. A state of celibacy came to be exalted as the nearest approach to divine perfection, and sensual pleasure was inexorably replaced by spiritual pride. Passive obedience to civil authority led to a refusal to partake in any form of civil administration or military defense of the empire, even when it became evident that such disregard of the public welfare guaranteed the triumph of barbarism. In sum, the morals, and the errors, of the primitive Christians were in reality the excess of their virtues. (5) Though immune to both the business and the pleasure of the world, the primitive Christians took keen interest in the government of the church, an enthusiasm which gave rise to much religious contention. At first, the bishops were regarded as the equals of the people, but gradually took upon themselves arbitrary power, ultimately proclaiming themselves vice-regents of Christ. Thence arose the rigid distinction between clergy and laity. The early communion of goods among the Christians was soon relaxed, and the clergy adopted the tithe from the original Jewish code. Further clerical controls included excommunication, which involved not only spiritual but also temporal punishment. As to the actual numbers of Christians, nothing definite can be concluded, the figures of the Fathers being at complete variance with those of the pagan historians, and neither providing accuracy. Seneca, the two Plinys, Tacitus, Plutarch, Galen, Epictetus, Marcus Antonius, great sages all, have little or nothing to say about the "perfection" of Christianity. Alleged miracles for the benefit of the church passed unnoticed.

In the sixteenth chapter, Gibbon examines the question of the persecutions of the primitive Christians by some of the Roman emperors. The blame, he indicates, rests chiefly upon the intolerant zeal of the Christians themselves, which drove the emperors reluctantly toward persecution. Even so, there were frequent peaceful intervals, and the detailed accounts of the sufferings of the "martyrs"

were largely the inventions of later ecclesiastical writers. Gibbon estimates that no more than 2,000 Christians were executed during the period of the most vigorous persecution, and suggests a comparison with the hundreds of thousands of Protestants executed during the relatively brief period of the Reformation, the latter figure far exceeding all martyrdoms over the course of many centuries of early Christian persecution.

Gibbon's sources. Among the many influences upon Gibbon's method and philosophy, the following should be mentioned: first, Locke's common-sense approach to philosophy and religion; second, the rationalism of the deists; third, the philosophy of history presented in Montesquieu's treatise *Considérations sur les causes de la grandeur et de la décadence des Romains* (1734); fourth, the philosophical skepticism of Hume. From Hume he also learned the necessity of investigating the causes of historical events, and from Hume and Voltaire, the importance of cultural, social, and political history. The *Decline and Fall* has gone through multitudinous complete editions and condensations, both in English and in translation, and will continue to be read, not only as a great history, but also as a great piece of literature.

Works by Gibbon

Gibbon's works include the *Autobiography*, Dero S. Saunders, ed. (Cleveland, 1961), a more faithful version than Lord Sheffield's; *The Decline and Fall*, J. B. Bury, ed., 7 vols. (London, 1896–1900; 2d ed., 1909–1913), the modern standard edition. See also *The Letters of Edward Gibbon*, J. E. Norton, ed., 3 vols. (London, 1956).

Works on Gibbon

For literature on Gibbon, see J. B. Black, *The Art of History: A Study of Four Great Historians of the Eighteenth Century* (London, 1926); Harold L. Bond, *The Literary Art of Edward Gibbon* (Oxford, 1960); D. M. Low, *Edward Gibbon: 1737–1794* (London, 1937); Shelby T. McCloy, *Gibbon's Antagonism to Christianity* (Chapel Hill, N.C., 1933); J. E. Norton, *A Bibliography of the Works of Edward Gibbon* (Oxford, 1940); George Sarton, "The Missing Factor in Gibbon's Concept of History," *Harvard Library Bulletin*, Vol. XI (1957), 277–295.

E RNEST C AMPBELL M OSSNER

GILBERT OF POITIERS (Gilbertus Porreta, Gilbert de la Porrée), twelfth-century theologian and metaphysician. He was born at Poitiers about 1076 and received his first schooling there. Next he went to study under Bernard of Chartres, and later (but before 1117) he devoted himself to theology under Anselm at Laon. He seems to have succeeded Bernard as chancellor at Chartres between 1126 and 1137 and, after a short period as a master in Paris, was elevated in 1142 to the bishopric of Poitiers. He died greatly esteemed in 1154, although in the 1140s he had been made to feel the hostility of other theologians, principally Bernard of Clairvaux, who brought him to trial to account for his opinions at Paris in 1147 and at Rheims in 1148.

Gilbert wrote much and acquired great fame for his scriptural and Boethian commentaries. The former were the fruit of his years at Laon and included major expositions of the Psalms and of the Epistles of St. Paul, as well as other Biblical commentaries which have, with greater or lesser certainty, been ascribed to him. But the commentaries upon Boethius' four *opuscula sacra* (and especially that upon the *De Trinitate*) proved controversial. Although Gilbert was never officially condemned for theological error, after his trial in 1148 he appended a new preface to these commentaries professing his orthodoxy. In addition, the treatise *De Discretione Animae, Spiritus et Mentis* is now confidently ascribed to Gilbert. Highly uncertain, however, is Gilbert's authorship of the *Liber Sex Principiorum*. The six *principia* are the last six Aristotelian categories (place, time, situation, habit, action, and passion), which the writer of this treatise considered to be accessory forms (*formae assistentes*) or extrinsic circumstances of a substance. The first four categories, on the other hand, are either substance itself or necessarily inherent forms of a substance. This work enjoyed great authority in the Middle Ages as a completion of Aristotle's own *Categoriae*.

An understanding of Gilbert's authentic philosophical teaching must be based principally upon his Boethian commentaries and upon the literature inspired by his trial. Gilbert's doctrine of being and of the process of knowledge departs from a key distinction between substance and subsistence. A substance is an actually existing individual being which supports (*substat*) a number of accidents. Some beings, however—genera and species, for example—have no need of accidents and are more accurately described as subsistences than as substances. Forms or Ideas in themselves are subsistences and do not come into contact with matter. Only copies (*exempla*) descend into matter. The human mind arrives at the knowledge of the eternal Ideas by first "collecting" from concrete, individual things their substantial similarity, that is, their created or "native" forms (*formae nativae*), to which Gilbert attributed universality. By perceiving the similarity of forms within a group, the mind arrives at the concept of species and then, by the same process, it arrives at the concept of genus. Finally, transcending all created forms, it attains the primary forms, which are in God. Thus, Gilbert inquired why concrete forms agree with one another, and he focused his attention upon the *intellectus* of the universal which is abstracted from singulars. He based his theory of knowledge upon the Platonic doctrine of Ideas but also employed the Boethian–Aristotelian doctrine of abstraction.

The divine work of creation involved the production of forms, which are images of the divine Ideas, and the uniting of these forms to matter. Gilbert described the created being as a compound of the *id quod est* ("what it is") and the *id quo est* ("that by which it is"). Socrates is a man (*id quod est*), but he is what he is by virtue of his humanity and corporeity (*id quo est*). The origin of this distinction is the grammatical rule that, *in naturalibus*, every name signifies both a substance and a quality. But whereas all created being is compound, the divine being is absolutely simple. In God, essence (*id quod est*) and divinity (*id quo est*) coincide. Nonetheless, Gilbert applied the distinction to God, describing divinity as the form in God by which he is God. Gilbert's opponents, such as Bernard of Clairvaux, would not accept this separation of God and his divinity; they maintained that divinity is God, and not that by which he is. Gilbert's position was a

difficult one to maintain, but he had no desire to compromise the divine simplicity or unity, and his writings support his claim that he had not established a real distinction between God and his divinity.

In a similar manner, Gilbert's application of logical and grammatical principles to the problem of the Incarnation of Christ aroused suspicions. Gilbert was reluctant to say that the divine nature became flesh, preferring to say that a person, Christ, took a human nature. Other logicians of the day were similarly concerned to test various traditional formulations of the divine Incarnation in the light of Boethian concepts. If Gilbert slipped in his analysis of the person and natures of Christ, he did not intend to deny Christ's divinity or his humanity.

Gilbert's school of disciples survived as a strong force in the twelfth century and included John of Salisbury, Otto of Freising, Alan of Lille, Nicholas of Amiens, Radulphus Ardens, and John Beleth. It blended at times with the dialectical tradition stemming from Abelard, and, by its investigation of the character of essences, the school of Gilbert perhaps helped to prepare the way for the influx of Avicennian philosophy.

Works by Gilbert

Liber de Sex Principiis Gilberto Porretano Ascriptus has appeared in two modern editions: that by A. Heysse (Münster-in-Westfalen, 1929) and that by D. van den Eynde (Münster-in-Westfalen, 1953). Commentaries on Boethius may be found in J. P. Migne, ed., *Patrologia Latina*, Vol. 64 (Paris, 1847), cols. 1255–1412. N. M. Häring has edited new editions of the commentaries on the *De Trinitate* and on the *De Praedicatione*, which are in J. R. O'Donnell, ed., *Nine Mediaeval Thinkers* (Toronto, 1955); on the *De Hebdomadibus*, which is in *Traditio*, Vol. 9 (1953), 177–211; and on the *Contra Eutychen et Nestorium*, which is in *Archives d'histoire doctrinale et littéraire du moyen âge*, Vol. 21 (1954), 241–357. Häring has also edited the *De Discretione Animae, Mentis et Spiritus*, which is in *Mediaeval Studies*, Vol. 22 (1960), 148–191, and "A Christmas Sermon by Gilbert of Poitiers," in *Mediaeval Studies*, Vol. 23 (1961), 126–135. Gilbert's Biblical commentaries are unprinted save for the prologue and commentary on Psalms 1 and 2, edited by M. Fontana, in *Logos*, Vol. 13 (1930), 283–301.

See also *Commentarius Porretanus Anonymus in Primam Epistolam ad Corinthios*, edited by A. M. Landgraf, in Vol. 117 of the series *Studi e testi* (Vatican City, 1945), and E. Rathbone, *Notae Super Iohannem Secundum Magistrum Gil[bertum]*, in Vol. 18 of the series *Recherches de théologie ancienne et médiévale* (Louvain, 1951), pp. 205–210.

Works on Gilbert

The following works contain information on Gilbert: Étienne Gilson, *History of Christian Philosophy in the Middle Ages* (London, 1955), pp. 140–144; A. M. Landgraf, "Untersuchungen zu den Eigenlehre Gilberts," in *Zeitschrift für katholische Theologie*, Vol. 54 (1930), 180–213; A. Forest, "Le Réalisme de Gilbert de la Porrée dans le commentaire du *De Hebdomadibus*," in *Revue néo-scholastique de philosophie*, Vol. 36 (1934), 101–110; A. Hayen, "Le Concile de Reims et l'erreur théologique de Gilbert," in *Archives d'histoire doctrinale et littéraire du moyen âge*, Vol. 10–11 (1935–1936), 29–102; M. H. Vicaire, "Les Porrétains et l'avicennisme avant 1215," in *Revue des sciences philosophiques et théologiques*, Vol. 26 (1937), 449–482; M. E. Williams, *The Teaching of Gilbert Porreta on the Trinity*, Vol. 56 in the series *Analecta Gregoriana* (Rome, 1951); M. A. Schmidt, *Gottheit und Trinität nach dem Kommentar des Gilbert Porreta zu Boethius, De Trinitate* (Basel, 1956); S. Gammersbach, *Gilbert von Poitiers und seine Prozesse im Urteil der Zeitgenossen* (Cologne, 1959); and N. M. Häring, "The Case of Gilbert," in *Mediaeval Studies*, Vol. 13

(1951), 1–40; "A Latin Dialogue on the Doctrine of Gilbert," in *Mediaeval Studies,* Vol. 15 (1953), 243–289; and "Sprachlogische und philosophische Voraussetzungen zum Verstandnis der Christologie Gilberts," in *Scholastik,* Vol. 32 (1957), 373–398.

DAVID LUSCOMBE

GILES OF ROME (c. 1247–1316), scholastic philosopher whose real name was Aegidius Colonna Romanus, was born in Rome. Giles entered the Augustinian order of hermits in 1265 and subsequently studied at the University of Paris, where from 1268 to 1272 he was probably the pupil of Thomas Aquinas, who was then lecturing at the university as Dominican regent master. In 1277 the bishop of Paris made his far-reaching condemnation of 219 theses, mainly of Aristotelian origin but also including a number of Thomist propositions. Among these were Aquinas' doctrine that each being contains only one substantial form, as opposed to the traditional Augustinian belief in a plurality of forms. Giles, a young scholar, joined in the ensuing controversy with the publication of a sharply worded defense of the Thomist view, the *Liber Contra Gradus et Pluralitatem Formarum.* He attacked the Augustinian doctrine as being contrary to both reason and faith. Upon his refusal of Bishop Tempier's demand for a retraction, Giles left Paris, perhaps for a cooling-off period, but returned in 1285 to take the first Augustinian chair in theology and to receive his license to teach. He remained a professor until 1292, when he was appointed prior general of his order. In 1295 Pope Boniface VIII appointed him archbishop of Bourges, in which office he remained until his death. In 1287 his teachings had become the official doctrine of the Augustinian order, although neither of the other great Augustinian thinkers of the fourteenth century, Thomas of Strasbourg and Gregory of Rimini (each a general of the order) followed his teachings.

Metaphysics. Giles's philosophical position still remains something of an enigma. The older view that he was strictly a disciple of Thomas Aquinas has gradually been modified. While it is true that he reached substantially the same conclusions as Aquinas on two of the burning issues of the day, the unity of the substantial form and the distinction between essence and existence, neither of these seems to have been from Thomist premises and, in the case of the second issue, the conclusion did not even lead to the same doctrine. In particular, Giles seems to have been influenced to a far greater degree than Aquinas by Neoplatonism, and especially Proclus, on whose *Liber de Causis* he commented in 1280. This affinity would explain his own treatment of the relation of essence to existence. Aquinas had never made a real distinction between the two but had regarded them rather as a composition in which *esse* is the actuality of *essentia,* which is itself the source of a being's actuality; or put another way, a being is what it is in virtue of the actuality (*esse*) that derives from its form (*essentia*). For Giles, on the other hand, *esse* and *essentia* were distinct things (*res*) from the outset. He therefore treated as real what for Aquinas were abstractions, an attitude confirmed in his Commentary on the *Liber de Causis,* where he thought in terms of a universe of intelligible beings. To attain intelligible knowledge, it suffices for the image of an object to act directly upon the possible intellect, which under the influence of the active intellect is able to conceive it as an intelligible species. This led Giles to the characteristically Platonic conclusion "that the same quiddity considered in things is particular, considered in the mind is universal."

Scientific contributions. Although knowledge of Giles's scientific outlook is even less comprehensive than that of his philosophical system, his treatment, often Neoplatonic, of time, movement, gravity, quantity, the intensification and remission of forms, and matter is known to us. Giles made his most original and important contribution to later scholastic scientific discussion concerning the nature of quantity. He posited a twofold quantity (*duplex quantitas*) that corresponds to the modern distinction between mass and volume. On the one hand, a body contains a constant quantity of matter, which limits its possibilities of development; for instance, a barleycorn cannot become a mountain. On the other hand, the same quantity of matter can undergo various changes in dimension, and according to its volume it will be denser or rarer in structure—as with, say, water or air. Giles took this distinction to infer that mass and volume were thus two independent quantities.

Giles also distinguished sharply between form and matter in the structure of a material substance—the so-called problem of the *mixtum.* This raised the question of what happened to the forms of the four material elements—fire, earth, air, and water—which composed any material substance when they were combined with form of that substance, for example, wood. Did they continue to exist separately, or were they absorbed into the substantial form? This was one of the earliest scientific problems to exercise the Scholastics, and while Giles based himself upon what Aquinas had already said, he also went further. He accepted Aquinas' solution that the forms of the material elements, once included in a material substance, no longer remained formally and actually in being but, rather, virtually as part of the qualities of the substance. To this, however, he added the distinction between the material and formal qualities. The former (*ex parte materiae*) remained the same through all changes in the substance; the forms, on the other hand, could not remain numerically the same. Another aspect of Giles's *mixtum* theory was of a hierarchy (*ordo realis*) among substantial forms, in which each higher form virtually contained the lower forms, the higher form being able to do more perfectly whatever the lower form could do.

Giles was also the first among the high Scholastics to state explicitly the problem of the increased speed of a falling body, namely, that this was not caused by the approach of its destination but rather by the growing distance from its starting point. Again, concerning a falling body in a vacuum, a problem which was to exercise successive generations of fourteenth-century thinkers, Giles was the first to pose it directly, taking a standpoint different from that of Aquinas. In his Commentary on Aristotle's *Physics,* Giles posed other original questions about movement: whether the sole cause of why movement took place in time, and not instantaneously, was resistance to the mover from the medium in which it moved, and whether in a vacuum movement itself would be composed of a succession of instants which in themselves did not constitute time. To both Giles answered in the affirmative. Thus the difference between movement in a medium and movement in a vacuum was that in the first case it was successive as opposed to instantaneous, owing to the resistance encountered; in a vacuum, on the other hand, it was *motus discretus in tempore discreto.* There can be little doubt from what is already known of his scientific speculation that Giles was the forerunner of the scientific inquiry so characteristic of the fourteenth century.

Political philosophy. Giles had been tutor to the future Philip IV (the Fair) of France, to whom he dedicated his *De Regimine Principium.* This work, stressing the Aristotelian view of a ruler, was based upon the *Ethics* and *Politics.* But with the outbreak of the struggle between Philip IV and Pope Boniface VIII in 1296, Giles took the pope's side. His *De Potestate Ecclesiastica* (probably written c. 1302) stated, in the most extreme form yet, the Augustinian view of society, in which the spiritual power is superior to the temporal and only the faithful can possess the just and righteous lordship derived from the universal lordship of the church. Lordship is a gift from God, and justice is submission to God through the church; hence, sin deprives the sinner of all right of lordship. Giles here sowed the seeds of the doctrine of dominion and grace that was to be developed by Richard FitzRalph and then turned against the church by Wyclyf.

Works by Giles

COMMENTARIES ON ARISTOTLE

Physics. Padua, 1483; Venice, 1492.
Posterior Analytics. Venice, 1488.
De Anima. Venice, 1496.
Prior Analytics. Venice, 1499.
Expositio in Artem Veterem. Venice, 1507.
Metaphysics. Venice, 1550.

OTHER WORKS

Quodlibeta. Venice, 1496.
"De Intellectu Possibili" and "De Gradibus Formarum," in *De Anima.* Venice, 1550.
Super Authorem Libri de Causis Alfarabium. Venice, 1550.
Commentary on the Sentences. Córdoba, 1707.
De Potestate Ecclesiastica, R. Scholz, ed. Weimar, 1929.
Aegidii Romani Theoremata de Esse et Essentia, Edgard Hocedez, ed. Louvain, 1930.

Works on Giles

PHILOSOPHY

Boffito, G., *Saggio di bibliografia egidiana.* Florence, 1911. A bibliography.
Egenter, R., *Die Erkenntnispsychologie des Aegidius Romanus.* Regensburg, 1926.
Hocedez, E., "Gilles de Rome et Henri de Gand sur la distinction réelle, 1276–87." *Gregorianum,* Vol. 8 (1927), 358–384.
Hocedez, E., "Gilles de Rome et saint Thomas," in P. Mandonnet, ed., *Mélanges Mandonnet,* 2 vols. Paris, 1930. Vol. I, pp. 385–409.
Makaay, S., *Der Traktat des Aegidius Romanus über die Einzigkeit der substantiellen Form.* Würzburg, 1924.
Mandonnet, P., "La Carriere seolaire de Gilles de Rome (1276–1291)." *Revue des sciences philosophiques,* Vol. 4 (1910), 480–499.
Nardi, B., "Egidio Romano e l'avverismo." *Rivista di storia della filosofia,* Vol. 3 (1947), 197–220; Vol. 4 (1948), 1–22.

Paulus, J., "Les Disputes d'Henri de Gand et Gilles de Rome sur la distinction de l'essence et de l'existence." *Archives d'histoire doctrinale et littéraire du moyen âge,* Vol. 15 (1940–1942), 323–358.

SCIENCE

Maier, A., *Die Vorläufer Galileis,* 2 vols. Rome, 1949.
Maier, A., *An der Grenze zwischen Scholastik und Naturwissenschaft im 14 Jahrhundert.* Rome, 1951.
Maier, A., *Zwei Grundprobleme der scholastische Naturphilosophie.* Rome, 1951.
Maier, A., *Metaphysische Hintergründe der spatscholastischen Philosophie.* Rome, 1956.
Maier, A., *Zwischen Philosophie und Mechanik.* Rome, 1958.

POLITICAL PHILOSOPHY

Gwynn, Aubrey, *The English Austin Friars in the Time of Wyclif.* Oxford, 1940.

BIBLIOGRAPHY

Gilson, Étienne, *Christian Philosophy in the Middle Ages.* London, 1955. Pp. 735–736. Complete bibliography.

GORDON LEFF

GILSON, ÉTIENNE HENRI, French Neo-Thomist philosopher, was born in 1884 at Paris. His higher education was acquired at the University of Paris. In 1907 he received his agrégé and in 1913, after several years of teaching, his doctorate, publishing both his minor and major theses, *Index scolastico-cartésien* and *La Liberté chez Descartes et la théologie.* The years 1914–1916 saw Gilson serving France as an officer on the battlefield. Captured at Verdun, he was a prisoner of war from 1916 to 1918. He spent two years as professor of philosophy at the University of Strasbourg and in 1921 became professor of the history of medieval philosophy at the Sorbonne, in which position he served until 1932, when he accepted the chair of the history of medieval philosophy at the Collège de France. Gilson cooperated with members of the Congregation of Priests of St. Basil of Toronto, at their invitation, to found, in 1929, the Institute of Mediaeval Studies, in association with Saint Michael's College in the University of Toronto. He has been a professor and director of studies at the institute since its foundation.

Numerous leading universities have conferred honorary degrees on Gilson, and many have invited him to deliver prominent lectureships, among them the Gifford lectures at the University of Aberdeen (1930–1931), published as *The Spirit of Medieval Philosophy;* the William James lectures at Harvard (1936–1937), since published as *The Unity of Philosophical Experience;* the Richard lectures at the University of Virginia (1937), published as *Reason and Revelation in the Middle Ages;* the Mahlon Powell lectures at the University of Indiana (1940), published as *God and Philosophy;* and the A. W. Mellon lectures in the fine arts (1955), published as *Painting and Reality.* Gilson founded and directs the famous *Études de philosophie médiévale* and the *Archives d'histoire doctrinale et littéraire du moyen âge* and is a director of *Mediaeval Studies,* the annual publication of the Pontifical Institute of Mediaeval Studies. Among the many academies and societies of which he is a member is the select French Academy, to which he was elected in 1947.

Philosophical position. Gilson's main thoughts may best be appreciated in company with two parts of his own intellectual history. (1) The great Jewish scholar Lucien Lévy-Bruhl advised Gilson to study the relation between Descartes and Scholasticism. From this research Gilson learned, he tells us, to read St. Thomas Aquinas and to recognize that the metaphysical conclusions of Descartes made sense only in the context of Thomas' metaphysics. (2) Further study of Thomas and other medieval thinkers from St. Augustine through Ockham proved for Gilson that there was no common philosophy employed within the theologies but, rather, there were different authentic philosophies.

To do the choosing, demonstrating, and judging that he considers one of the proper tasks of philosophy, Gilson gradually developed his personal philosophical position. The only philosopher, Gilson has maintained, who made him clearly realize the full metaphysical implications of the major problems was Thomas Aquinas, a fact that in no way lessened Gilson's intellectual freedom, for he always wanted to be free to agree with somebody when he thought that what was said was right. For him what characterizes Thomism is the decision to locate the act of existence in the heart of the real as an act that can be grasped only by or in the essence whose act it is, as an act, therefore, that has primacy not over and above being but within being. Thus, Thomism as an authentic existentialism is opposed equally to the "Thomistic" essentialists, who deposit a dead essence in the mind as a quiddity without preserving its contact with the act of being, and to such existentialisms as those of Kierkegaard, Heidegger, Jaspers, and Sartre, which, although divergent from one another, commonly deal with existence only as an object of a possible phenomenology of human existence and are phenomenologies still in search of ontologies.

Gilson's personal commitment to the existentialism of Thomism is related to one of his most central philosophical doctrines—namely, the reality and philosophical validity of what he terms Christian philosophy. In *The Spirit of Medieval Philosophy* and in many other books and articles Gilson has demonstrated that the Christian religion and its theologies have had the capacity to produce metaphysical conclusions and to transform philosophy itself. Several of its philosophical ideas the Greek philosophers never knew—for example, the existence of a unique God, the infinite, simple, supremely free Creator of the universe, as an all-powerful efficient cause, as well as the existence of man as a substantial composite of soul and body, free, made in God's image. Regarding the philosophical problem of how a speculation can be rational and philosophical if it is connected with religious beliefs, history as such is incompetent to answer, but philosophy provides the answer. History shows that the alliance of the two distinct orders of thought has produced positive philosophical results. Although Gilson recognizes, with Thomas and other medieval theologians, the *distinction* of philosophy and theology, he opposes their separation as practiced by Descartes and by numerous Neo-Scholastics from the sixteenth century to the present day, for whom philosophy became no more than temporary and successively different alliances with any sort of currently fashionable philosophical position that could be reconciled with revelation.

As Gilson sees it, in the medieval theologians what could be philosophically demonstrated received in theological works the full benefit of rational demonstration. Such philosophical demonstrations were part of sacred doctrine and were also philosophy because they were reached by the human intellect through its own light. In the case of Thomas, who represents for Gilson the best in Christian philosophy, the philosophy is that of a theologian with the order of development required for theological ends; hence, one cannot release Thomistic philosophy from its theological moorings without running the risk of not knowing its origin and end, of altering its nature, and even of not grasping its meaning. Apart from the historical fact of the nonseparation of philosophy and theology, Gilson is convinced that the very nature of philosophy does not demand that the philosophy of Thomas be extracted from the world of faith and the influence of revelation. Philosophy has been and can be authentically philosophy and Christian at one and the same time, for the orientation of Christian philosophy—to knowledge about God and man—entails no a priori exclusion of any area of philosophical research because nothing in the universe is irrelevant to knowledge about God and man.

This central theme in Gilson's philosophy—the nature and validity of Christian philosophy—has exasperated so-called Thomists seeking to develop a Thomism separate from theology; to rationalists it has seemed not to be philosophy at all. Gilson tirelessly re-presents the historical evidence and philosophical reasons to identify and justify Christian philosophy as the use that the Christian makes of philosophical reason when he associates religious faith and philosophical reflection. Rhetorically, Gilson asks why those who profess the Christian faith and its doctrines should see themselves excluded from philosophy simply because they prefer to philosophize about what they believe.

Other influential aspects of Gilson's philosophical doctrines concern education, social and political philosophy, the philosophy of art, and the history of modern and contemporary philosophy. In *Painting and Reality*, Gilson has interpreted the evolution of the art of painting, especially its most recent phases, in the light of his existential metaphysics. Because artistic beauty is made, not found, Gilson opposes mere imitation as artistic beauty; the function of any work of art *qua* art is solely to cause in us the contemplative pleasure of enjoying it. In a masterful defense Gilson analyzes the history of art from Leonardo da Vinci to the present, demonstrates that representation is not of the essence of art, and argues for the legitimacy of abstraction and the necessity to sacrifice all elements of reality that do not contribute to the plastic structure of a work.

Bibliography

The Christian Philosophy of St. Augustine, translated by Lawrence Lynch. New York, 1960.
    Elements of Christian Philosophy. Garden City, N.Y., 1960.
    The Philosopher and Theology. New York, 1962.
    Modern Philosophy, Descartes to Kant. New York, 1962. Written with Thomas Langan.

Introduction aux arts du beau. Paris, 1963.
The Spirit of Thomism. New York, 1964.
For works published before 1960, see Callistus James Edie, ed., *Mélanges offerts à Étienne Gilson* (Paris and Toronto, 1959), a bibliography of all articles, monographs, books, and translations of books by Gilson.

ROBERT G. MILLER, C.S.B.

GIOBERTI, VINCENZO (1801–1852), Italian philosopher, ecclesiastical polemicist, and statesman. Gioberti was born in Turin. As a statesman he upheld federalism as the goal of the movement for Italian unity. Gioberti's *Del primato morale e civile degli Italiani* (Brussels, 1843) is one of the great documents of the Risorgimento. His most famous polemical work is *Il gesuita moderno* (5 vols., Lausanne, 1846–1847), attacking the allegedly reactionary influence of the Jesuits on church policy. Throughout his intensely active career, philosophy remained his dominant interest. A long political exile (1833–1845) provided the occasion for the composition of his most important philosophical works: *Teorica del sovrannaturale* (Brussels, 1838), *Introduzione allo studio della filosofia* (Brussels, 1840), and *Degli errori filosofici di Antonio Rosmini* (Brussels, 1841; 2d enl. ed., 3 vols., 1843–1844).

"Protologia." In 1841 and 1842 Gioberti gave a course of lectures (published as *Cours de philosophie*, Milan, 1947). The second part of these lectures, "Protologie ou science première," was the first sketch of a subject of which many of Gioberti's works can be considered fragmentary studies. The term *protologia* may derive from the title of a work by Ermenegildo Pini (1739–1825) that was published in 1803. Gioberti envisaged *protologia* as "the science of the creative act and of the ideal formula which expresses it completely." Its complement is *deuterologia,* the theory of the sciences constructed by reflection on the basis of being as it is intuited. *Protologia* has three divisions: theology, logic, and cosmology, which includes psychology. The division arises out of the three elements of the ideal formula, "Being creates the existent." *Protologia* escapes the subject–object dichotomy; it studies neither the subject nor the object but the intelligible principle that relates the two.

Ontologism. Because of his constant affirmation that being-in-itself is constitutively present to the human intellect, Gioberti's philosophical position is generally described as ontologism. Being is present to the intellect as thought, not as a sensible property of mind itself; that is, the being which is present to the mind is not merely the being of the mind but being itself. Gioberti rejected what he called sensism, by which he meant the view that the being present to the human mind is simply its own being apprehended by the senses. Gioberti asserted that the activity of the human mind "concreates" its object in conjunction with the presence of being. The being constitutively present to the human mind is not merely possible being but real being, and indeed the most real being. This being is indeterminate, not in the sense that it lacks all distinction but in the sense that all distinctions are so related and fused that the human mind does not immediately succeed in discerning them. For this reason the original intuition of being can make known the existent only in conjunction with sensible experience. Sensible experience makes the existent present, but the existent is known by virtue of being. The existent is not, however, a part, determination, or moment of being but a creation of being. Existents are present in being as elements of its creative possibility, not as its modes or qualities (on this point Gioberti thought that he was in disagreement with Spinoza). The act of thought renders the existent present, and since this act is being and is act only insofar as it is being, it concreates the existent. The act of judgment, which is the pure form of knowledge, has a particular form for thus establishing any particular existent. Its ideal form, or "ideal formula," informs every judgment independently of its particular concern. This ideal formula, "Being creates the existent," is the presence of the pure form of the judgment in its pure possibility.

Language. Ontologism shows that thought is a creative act. The object of thought comes into being through the operation of thought in the word. In this view Gioberti was strongly influenced by Giambattista Vico, and like Vico he studied the problem of language as the general theory of the word. Language is the specific manner in which the concreative operation of thought and being is effected in the human matrix. The concreative act, to be actual and effective, must reflect the human condition—it must be psychologized, but not in the manner which Gioberti opposed as "sensism." Gioberti advocated a transcendent psychologism in which the transcendental operation is the transaction of a concrete existent subject. Language is transcendental in that it reflects the constitutive presence of being in accordance with the structure of the human mind while enabling the mind to transcend its own existential limits and achieve universal significance. In this process of transcendence the ideal formula is specified according to the form not only of the object but also of the subject. Language places knowledge beyond the subject–object split. It reduces the being mentioned in the ideal formula to the effective principle of concrete science.

The transcendental operation of language seems to be widely distributed throughout the numerical range of human subjectivity. Gioberti suggested that it is a transaction of particular groups and ultimately of the nation. This view was important in *Del primato morale e civile degli Italiani* and was given an aristocratic cast in the claim that within the nation the transcendental operation is the work only of an elite.

"Palingenesis." Language constitutes the first movement of the life of the spirit, a movement implicit in the ideal formula, "Being creates existence." It is thus at the focus of the genesis of existence and the real as object. The pure form of human thought moves from the immediate givenness of the existent to its ideal ground. In experience we encounter the end product of the movement expressed in the ideal formula. Thought must return the existent thus encountered to its ground in being. Its movement is therefore a *palingenesis*—a return of existence to being.

Mimesis is the mode of existence of that which is encountered in experience. It is a state, but not a radical or irremediable one, of alienation. *Methexis* is the state of the thinking subject, the intelligence whose constitutive principle is the intelligible, that is being. *Methexis* is the link which ends the alienation between being and existence in *palingenesis*.

Gioberti did not mean by *palingenesis* a dissolution of the distinctions of existence into the indeterminacy of ideal being. Rather, through *palingenesis* the being of the existent qua existent (that is, in its distinctness) is ideally grounded in being. Thus, being itself needs the movement of *mimesis* down into the world in order that it may come into its own actuality, or distinctness, through *methexis*. Hence, being is not absolutely transcendent. It reaches its actuality in the word and thus belongs inalienably to the region of culture and history. Gioberti's theory of language thus contains in germ a theory of culture and history. Culture and cultures are the historical forms of *palingenesis*.

Theology, politics, and ethics. The *palingenesis* of being is the central operation of the spirit and determines the actual form of the world. The fact that this one process can be studied from two points of view provided Gioberti with a basis for a correlative distinction and unity of theology and philosophy. Theology possesses a certain superiority deriving chiefly from its object, God. Supernatural theology does not, however, take possession of the internal, or constitutive, word of God; it must make use of analogies drawn from philosophy. Supernatural revelation makes use of the "natural revelation" of the word. Philosophy is therefore superior to theology in that it provides the interpretative categories of theology.

Palingenesis takes on deontological status as the supreme norm of action. In this aspect it is the axiological principle of both the moral and the political orders. In both morals and politics, in conscience and in law, the essential process is the return of existence to being. Similarly, Gioberti held that the church is the historical and institutional form of the *palingenesis* of being under the dispensation of revelation.

Gioberti's thought is still influential in two of the leading strands of contemporary Italian thought, Gentilean actual idealism and Christian spiritualism.

Works by Gioberti

Opere edite e inedite di Vincenzo Gioberti, Rome and Milan, 1938——. Edited by the Istituto di Studi Filosofici. 8 vols. of works and 11 vols of correspondence to date.
Della protologia, G. Massari, ed., 2 vols. Paris and Turin, 1857.
Nuova protologia, Giovanni Gentile, ed. Bari, 1912.
Scritti scelti di Vincenzo Gioberti, Augusto Guzzo, ed. Turin, 1954. Contains an important introduction.

Works on Gioberti

Bonafede, G., *Gioberti*. Palermo, 1942.
Bonafede, G., *Gioberti e la critica*. Palermo, 1950.
Bruers, A., *Gioberti*. Rome, 1924. Contains an excellent bibliography.
Giusso, L., *Gioberti*. Milan, 1948.
Stefanini, Luigi, *Gioberti*. Milan, 1947. The best modern treatment.

A. ROBERT CAPONIGRI

GIVEN, THE. See BASIC STATEMENTS.

GLANVILL, JOSEPH (1636–1680) was a skeptic, a prominent defender of the experimental research of the early Royal Society, a liberal rationalistic Anglican theologian and preacher, and a staunch and influential believer in witchcraft. His philosophical views contain in embryo many of the major elements of later British empirical thought. Glanvill studied at Oxford from 1652 to 1658, and subsequently gained his living as a relatively unsuccessful preacher. He wrote many works (often the same works in revised forms) and engaged in numerous controversies. He was early influenced by Henry More, and adopted some of the views of the Cambridge Platonists. He was also friendly with several of the leading figures in the Royal Society, especially Boyle, Hooke, Bishop Sprat, and the Society's founder, Bishop John Wilkins. As a result of his propagandistic efforts in behalf of the Society, Glanvill was elected a member in 1664 and made some minor scientific contributions.

Glanvill contended that his skepticism was intended to promote scientific endeavor by undermining confidence in uncertain and unreliable theories about knowledge and nature. Unwarranted dogmatism was the major enemy; once it had been overcome, by a demonstration of the limits of human knowledge, Nature and God could better be studied. Glanvill began his critique of human knowledge by comparing man's state before Adam's Fall with present conditions. Before the Fall, man had "knowledge of things in their *true, immediate, necessary* causes," through direct observation, in contrast to his present state of ignorance, in which there are many problems about the soul, the body, and nature that he cannot solve. Our present knowledge, except for mathematics and theology, derives from our senses. But we are unfortunately unable to perceive "the *hidden things of* Nature . . . the first springs and wheeles that set the rest agoing" (*Scepsis Scientifica*, London, 1885, p. 15). Our senses are deceptive, and are affected by our passions. Hence, all of our knowledge about the world is to some degree uncertain.

Glanvill's skepticism is presented most forcefully in his analysis of causality, in which he anticipates Hume in several respects. Perfect knowledge would be causal knowledge. But we cannot see causal connections; we only judge them from concomitancies, and "to argue from a concomitancy to a causality, is not infallibly conclusive" (*Vanity of Dogmatizing*, p. 190). To do so is to commit the fallacy of *post hoc, ergo propter hoc*. Further, the causal relation cannot be a deductive one, for if it were, we would be able to demonstrate that a contrary state of affairs is impossible, and that things cannot be otherwise. However, we do not know enough about nature to tell what is really impossible. We only measure the universe by "Principles of our own, not Universal Nature." As a result, we confuse what is inconceivable to us with what is really impossible, though "'tis not unlikely, but what's impossible to all *Humanity* may be possible in the *Metaphysicks* and *Physiologie* of Angels" (*Vanity of Dogmatizing*, p. 195; *Scepsis Scientifica*, p. 170). Thus, neither necessary nor immediate knowledge of causes is possible.

Having carried his skeptical analysis this far, Glanvill insists that he is not trying to destroy the possibility of scientific knowledge. His aim, he contends, is to destroy unwarranted dogmatism by showing "that Uncertainties *are not* Science." He then examines the degrees of certitude that may be possible, and shows how these may provide the basis for a useful and probabilistic science. Employing the distinction between "infallible" and "indubitable" certainty which Bishop Wilkins had employed in regard to religious knowledge, Glanvill contends that infallible certainty would amount to an absolute assurance that things cannot be otherwise than we conceive them. Such certitude cannot be attained, since our faculties "may be so contrived, as always to deceive us in the things we judge most certain and assured" ("Of Scepticism and Certainty," in *Essays on Several Important Subjects in Philosophy and Religion*, p. 50). Indubitable certitude exists when we have no reason to doubt, even though we may actually be wrong. This limited assurance is the basis for accepting basic logical and metaphysical principles, as well as the crucial premise of all human inquiry, *that our faculties are true*. (Glanvill classes the belief in this premise, however, as an act of faith.) This premise enables us to rely on our proof of God's existence, on our mathematical reasoning, on our senses when properly used, and on the uniform testimony of other disinterested persons. We can then have indubitable (though not infallible) knowledge in mathematics, theology, science, and history. The first two areas provide the most certain knowledge, since they deal with immediately known ideas and truths, and logical inferences from them. Glanvill considers mathematics to be constituted of unambiguous terms needing no sensory data, and religion of unchanging revealed truths. Science requires sense information, and depends on the reliability of our data and our faculties in given circumstances; hence, it is less certain than either mathematics or theology. History, involving other people's experiences, poses still more problems and doubts. The best we can do is to investigate nature and ourselves patiently and tentatively, in the manner of the Royal Society. This will yield the most reliable and useful information about the world that we are capable of obtaining, as evidenced by the tremendous achievements of modern science compared with those of the ancients. Glanvill believed that his favorite science, witchcraft, was also justified by this skeptical scientific method. First, he argued that like Hobbes, the anti-witch theorists were wrong in contending that it was impossible for witches to exist. We cannot tell that any factual claim is impossible, since to do so would require a demonstration that things cannot be otherwise. We can only appeal to the empirical evidence of testimony and observation, and such evidence, Glanvill insisted, was more in keeping with the witch theory than with a denial of it.

On the basis of his skepticism, empiricism, and his constructive theory of types of certitude, Glanvill provided one of the first rationales for the scientific work of the Royal Society. He espoused a view about the limitations of human knowledge and the bases for certitude which was developed in the Anglican theological tradition of William Chillingworth and Bishop Wilkins, and applied this to the "new science." In so doing, he preceded Locke, Newton, and Hume in suggesting some of the major features of later empiricism and skepticism, though he probably did not influence any of them directly.

Works by Glanvill

The Vanity of Dogmatizing. London, 1661; facsimile ed., New York, 1931.

Scepsis Scientifica or, Confest Ignorance, The Way to Science. A revised version of *The Vanity of Dogmatizing*, bound with a

defense of his views against Thomas White, an English Catholic philosopher. London, 1665; reprinted London, 1885, J. Owen, ed.

A Philosophical Endeavor towards the Defense of the Being of Witches and Apparitions. London, 1666.

Plus Ultra: or, the Progress and Advancement of Knowledge, Since the Days of Aristotle. London, 1668; facsimile ed., Gainesville, Fla., 1958.

Essays on Several Important Subjects in Philosophy and Religion. London, 1676.

Works on Glanvill

Cope, Jackson I., *Joseph Glanvill, Anglican Apologist.* St. Louis, 1956. Contains a complete list of Glanvill's writings.

Greenslet, Ferris, *Joseph Glanvill: A Study in English Thought and Letters in the 17th Century.* New York, 1900.

Popkin, Richard H., "Joseph Glanvill: Precursor of Hume." *Journal of the History of Ideas*, XIV (1953), 292–303.

Popkin, Richard H., "The Development of the Philosophical Reputation of Joseph Glanvill." *Journal of the History of Ideas*, XV (1954), 305–311.

Van Leeuwen, Henry G., *The Problem of Certainty in English Thought, 1630–1690.* The Hague, 1963.

Willey, Basil, *The Seventeenth Century Background.* New York, 1953. Ch. IX.

RICHARD H. POPKIN

GNOSTICISM (from the Greek *gnosis,* "knowledge") designates a broad variety of religious teachings that were rife in the Hellenized Near East of the first centuries A.D. and purported to offer knowledge of the otherwise hidden truth of total reality as the indispensable key to man's salvation. Most of the schools or sects in question were ostensibly Christian by the time our earliest witnesses, the Church Fathers, were familiar with them, and in consequence the whole movement was long regarded as essentially an aberration from Christian doctrine. However, although Gnosticism provided the first chapter in the history of Christian heresies, the Christian veneer of the systems playing that role is often thin to the point of transparency; and clearly non-Christian writings have come to light that by all criteria of content must be classed as Gnostic as well. The details of the literary evidence point to highly syncretistic origins, in which Jewish, Iranian, Babylonian, Egyptian, and other Oriental traditions were blended with one another and with Greek concepts in an extremely free manner. The results were as readily made to represent an alleged esoteric truth of the Christian message as to constitute a superior (Mani) or even hostile (Mandaeans) alternative to it.

This syncretism, pertaining mainly to the outer shell, does not preclude—in fact it tends to mask—a highly original inner unity of thought distinct from all the disparate historical elements employed in its representation. Massively mythological though this representation usually is, the substance thus expressed has philosophical significance as embodying a fundamental choice—the radical antithesis to the classical Greek choice—in the realms of universal theory and human practice at once. The powerful Gnostic impulse to elaborate its basic vision into grandly constructed, quasi-rational systems of thought where everything proceeds from an absolute beginning makes Gnosticism a landmark in the history of the speculative system as such; and it is the identity of that basic vision that defines what is Gnostic and alone justifies the classing of systems of such considerable diversity under one heading.

Gnostic teachers and schools. A number of gnostic teachers and writers are known by name (mainly those listed as heresiarchs in the patristic refutations), but much of the surviving literature is anonymous or pseudepigraphic, in keeping with the revelatory style in which it is cast. Historical individuals whose thought is documented by either critical accounts or direct fragments of their works include the Samaritan Simon Magus and his spiritual descendants Menander, Saturninus, Cerinthus, and Cerdon (first and second centuries); the Alexandrians Carpocrates, Basilides and his son Isidore, and, foremost, Valentinus with his illustrious disciples Ptolemaeus, Heracleon, Theodotus, and Marcus (second century); the Pontian Marcion and the Syrian Bardesanes (second century); and the Persian–Babylonian Mani (third century). Major sects whose doctrines are well documented but not identified by individual authors or founders are, in the Christian camp, the Barbeliotes, Sethites, and Ophites (the last actually a cluster of sects); in the Hellenistic–pagan camp, the Hermetic religion (perhaps merely a literature and not an actual sect); in the Semitic East, the anti-Christian Mandaeans. Towering over the known thinkers are Valentinus, Marcion, and Mani; and Valentinianism and Manichaeism respectively represent the culminations of the two main alternative types of Gnostic speculation. The last two are here considered merely for their part in and exemplification of the wider context (see MANI AND MANICHAEISM; VALENTINUS AND VALENTINIANISM).

Sources. With the exception of that of the Mandaeans, Gnostic literature was denied direct tradition under the dominion of Christianity and Islam after the eclipse of the Gnostic communities themselves. Thus, until fairly recently, information was supplied almost solely by the abundant indirect sources. These were, in the main, the anti-heretical works of the Church Fathers (Greek, Latin, and Syriac, from Irenaeus in the second century to Theodore bar Konai in the eighth century) with their diligent reports, summaries, and excerpts, and still later Islamic histories and compendia. However, for some time an impressive series of manuscript discoveries has been adding vastly to our store of original texts: Coptic–Gnostic papyrus codices from Egypt, belonging to the Christian branch of Gnosticism—the find in 1945 of a whole library at Nag Hammadi is revolutionizing the state of documentation in the area hitherto principally covered by the patristic testimony—Manichaean fragments in Persian, Turkish, and Chinese from Turfan in central Asia and in Coptic from Egypt, and the sacred writings of the Mandaeans of Iraq.

The Mandaeans are the one case of a Gnostic community surviving to the present with an unbroken written tradition of their voluminous Aramaic literature; it came to the attention of Western scholars in the nineteenth century, after it had escaped that of the Church Fathers in antiquity (probably because of the Fathers' predominantly Greek orientation). In all the other cases, the new original sources generally bear out, while greatly enriching, the testimony of the older indirect evidence. The following account, based on the entire, extremely varied material, is synoptic and selective, placing its emphases according to a conception of the whole as a system.

GNOSTIC DUALISM

A radically dualistic mood dominates the Gnostic attitude and unites its widely diversified expressions, whether doctrinal, poetical, or ethical. The dualism is between man and world, and between the world and God. In either case, it is a dualism of antithetical, not complementary, terms; and it is basically one: that of man and world mirrors on the plane of experience the primordial one of God and world and is, in Gnostic theory, deduced from it. The interpreter may hold conversely that the transcendent doctrine of a world–God opposition sprang from the immanent experience of a disunion of man and world, that is, it reflects a human condition of alienation. In the three-term configuration, man and God belong in essence together against the world but are in fact separated by the world, which in the Gnostic view is the alienating, divisive agency.

The object of Gnostic speculation is to derive these basic polarities—the existing state of things—by way of genetic myths from the first things and through such genealogy to point the way to their eventual resolution. The myth, a conscious symbolical construction, is thus predictive by being genetic, eschatological by being explanatory. Accordingly, the typical Gnostic system starts with a doctrine of divine transcendence in its original purity; traces the genesis of the world from some primordial disruption of this blessed state, a loss of divine integrity that leads to the emergence of lower powers who become the makers and rulers of this world; then, as a crucial episode in the drama, it recounts the creation and early fate of man, in whom the further conflict becomes centered; the final theme—in fact, the implied theme throughout—is man's salvation, which is more than man's, since it involves the overcoming and eventual dissolving of the cosmic system and is thus the instrument of reintegration for the impaired godhead itself, the self-saving of God.

God and the divine realm. The transcendence of the supreme deity is stressed to the utmost degree in all Gnostic theology. Topologically, he is transmundane, dwelling in his own realm entirely outside the physical universe, at immeasurable distance from man's terrestrial abode; ontologically, he is acosmic, even anticosmic: to this world and whatever belongs to it he is the essentially "other" and "alien" (Marcion), the "alien Life" (Mandaeans), the "depth" or "abyss" (Valentinians), even "the not-being" (Basilides); epistemologically, because of the transcendence and otherness of his being, and because nature neither reveals nor even indicates him, he is naturally unknown, ineffable, defying predication, surpassing comprehension, and strictly unknowable. Some positive attributes and metaphors do apply to him: Light, Life, Spirit, Father, the Good—but not Creator, Ruler, Judge. Significantly, in some systems one of his secret names is Man. Mainly, the discourse about him must move in negations, and historically Gnosticism is one of the fountainheads of negative theology.

However, the Absolute is not alone but is surrounded by

an aura of eternal, graded expressions of his infinitude, partial aspects of his perfection, hypostatized into quasi-personal beings (aeons) with highly abstract names (mostly of mental properties) and together forming the hierarchy of the divine realm, the pleroma (Plenitude). The emanation of this inner manifold from the primal ground, a kind of self-differentiation of the Absolute, is sometimes described in terms of subtle spiritual dialectics, more often in rather naturalistic (for instance, sexual), terms. Among the tenuously mythological entities that thus arise (such as Mind, Grace, Word, Knowledge, Life) are two more concrete ones with definite roles in the further evolution of the transcendental drama: Man as an eternal, divine, precosmic principle (sometimes even identified with the First Being himself) and Wisdom (Sophia), usually the last and youngest of the aeons. Extensive speculation about the diversity within the pleroma is the mark of advanced systems, but some degree of manifold on the upper reaches of being is requisite for all Gnostic metaphysics because it provides the condition for divine fallibility on which the movement into creation and alienation depends.

Lower powers and the Creator. In the genuine Gnostic systems the downward movement starts from an internal crisis in the divine realm itself, whereas in those under Iranian influence it is occasioned by the action of dark forces from without, thus presupposing the very dualism that the typical speculation lets evolve from the one monistic root. We shall mainly follow this latter, more prevalent type, which is free from Iranian influence. Here, the protagonist of crisis and fall is most often the female aeon Sophia (or such equivalents as Thought and Conception) who, from some overstepping of bounds—assertion of self-will, creative presumption, even excessive desire to know the unknowable Father—is drawn into a history of passion and error that leads her outside the blessed pleroma. (In another family of systems, Primal Man assumes the role of the sinking part of divinity.) Although the upper powers immediately set about healing this breach in the divine order, the downward trend set in motion by the original lapse must take its course, and the counterplay of these two trends henceforth governs the process. There ensues, in a development too complex and too variously elaborated to recount here, a train of ever lower hypostases descended from the erring Sophia, episodically broken by certain archetypal salvations.

The Demiurge. Early in the descending series—and marked with all the deforming effects of the Fall whose fruit he is—appears the Demiurge, the monstrous and benighted archon (lord) of the nether powers. This widespread Gnostic figure, telling symbol of the Gnostic hostility toward the world, is clearly a polemical caricature of the Old Testament God, and the identity is made explicit by frequent transference to him of well-known utterances and actions of God from the Biblical text. Pride, ignorance, and malevolence of the Creator are recurring themes in Gnostic tales, as are his humbling and outwitting by the higher powers bent on thwarting his designs. However, over the whole range of Gnostic mythologizing the archon's image varies, and there are milder versions in which he is more misguided than evil and thus open to correction and remorse, even to final redemption. He is always a problematical and never a venerable figure.

Finding himself in the void or chaos outside the pleroma, possessed of the power inherited from his mother but ignorant of the divine worlds above him, he believes himself to be the only God and engages in creations chiefly designed to satisfy his ambition, vanity, and lust for dominion. Prominent among the host of lower powers that issue from him are six further archons whom he installs in six successive heavens; he occupies the seventh above them. Thus originate the cosmic order and its system of rule, the universe of Babylonian astrology with its seven planetary spheres and the almighty planetary deities. An eighth region beyond them (corresponding to the sphere of the fixed stars) is occupied by the mother Sophia, still exiled from the pleroma, who has no part in the creation and government of the world but intervenes in both for the purposes of salvation. The Valentinian version, the subtlest of all, depicts the Demiurge as trying vainly to imitate the perfect order of the aeons with his physical one, and their eternity with the counterfeit substitute of time—thus adding to the parody of the Biblical Creator that of the Platonic Demiurge. However, the chief instance of illicit and bungling imitation is the creation of man.

The remaining part of creation is the joint work of the seven archons. Indeed, the early systems (such as that of Simon Magus) simply name the seven as the creators of the world; and the pre-eminence of one of them, growing into a kind of monotheism of cosmic (lower) divinity, seems to be characteristic of the mature stage of Gnostic speculation. There, an episode, told with almost identical words in the cosmogonies of many different schools, rings in the next act in the drama of creation: the First Archon (the Demiurge), exulting in his works with the Scriptural proclamation "I am God and there is none other than I," draws the retort from on high, "Thou art mistaken! Above thee is First Man."

Creation of earthly man. Some such divulgence of superior godhead (here meant as no more than a humbling of the Creator's pride, elsewhere serving some other purpose in the divine strategy), and especially the appearance of a divine form with it, inspire the archons with the audacious plan to equal the upper perfection in a work of their own—to create terrestrial man—an effect not foreseen in the divine move. Letting them say on this occasion, "Come, let us make a man after the image we have seen," the Gnostics turned to account the puzzling plural of Genesis 1.26, and the resulting *imago Dei* character of created man, far from being a straight metaphysical honor, assumes an ambiguous, if not sinister, meaning. The motive for the archons' resolve is either simple envy and ambition, or the more calculating one of entrapping divine substance in their lower world by the lure of a seemingly congenial receptacle that will become its most secure bond. The imitation, presumptuous and blundering, is nevertheless effective. Although the mere creature of the archons—the body and a natural soul compounded from their several psychic powers—is not viable by itself, it becomes so through the injection of a spiritual element from beyond.

For this presence of transcendent spirit (pneuma) in psychophysical man—in itself a paradoxical, unnatural fact and the fulcrum of the whole soteriological drama—Gnostic speculation offers various explanations, their chief difference being whether the presence marks a success of the nether powers or a stratagem of the upper ones. In the first alternative, the causality operative on the divine side admits in turn the several variations of being a victim of violence (Mani), of deception, or of its own downward inclination (Poimandres). In the other alternative (the Valentinians), the divine seed is secretly deposited in the creature of the unknowing Demiurge in order to turn his work into an unintended vehicle of salvation. However, this variant is no more optimistic than the first, since the soteriological stratagem merely makes the best of a basic evil, of these divine portions' having become divorced from their source in the first place. In any case, the pneuma's innerworldly existence is a state of exile, the result of primeval divine tragedy; and its immersion in soul and body is the terminal form of that exile. For the archons, on the other hand, the incorporation of this transcendent element into their system is a condition of the system's existence, and its retention therefore becomes to them a matter of survival—their work's and their own. Hence, they must resist at all cost the spirit's extrication from the cosmic involvement, which the upper powers seek for the regaining of divine wholeness. The means of this extrication is knowledge.

History of man. The process of conveying the saving knowledge to the world-imprisoned hostage of Light begins with Adam himself and runs through the history of mankind in a constant counterplay with the archontic powers. Human history is thus eschatological from the beginning. In the light of this scheme, the Scriptural account of early man, especially the Paradise story, is boldly recast, with all value signs reversed. The most significant of these reversals concerns the serpent, which, as the first bringer of knowledge in defiance of the Creator's mandate of ignorance, becomes the general symbol of the acosmic spiritual principle that works for the awakening of its captive kin in the world. The revelatory line thus started, and continued through the generations, ends in Christ (or may go beyond him to further revelations of the truth). Hence the cult of the serpent in a major group of Gnostic sects, the Ophites (from the Greek *ophis*, serpent). In the same spirit of reversal, Cain, Esau, and other rejected figures of the Old Testament became to certain sects (Cainites, Carpocratians, Perates) bearers of the pneumatic heritage, forming a secret lineage of gnosis and persecuted by the world god for this reason; their opposites, such as Abel and Jacob, his favorites, represent the unenlightened majority. Independently of the intention to scandalize that is evident here, the Gnostic scheme called for a prophetology in succession of the Adamitic revelation, for which Iranian tradition offered the idea of an eternal Messenger who moves through history in ever new incarnations. These messengers were variously identified with names from the religious past; in the final consolidation by Mani we find them reduced to four: Buddha, Zoroaster, Jesus, Mani. The significant omission of Moses from this list requires a comment on the anti-Judaism among the Gnostics.

The this-worldly spirit of the Hebrew religion combined with historical circumstance to make the Old Testament a prominent target of Gnostic dislike, to varying degrees. The extreme of hostility, even contempt, is found in Marcion, for whom this admittedly authentic revelation of the Creator and Lord of this world shares all the blemishes of its source: It is as opposed to the gospel of salvation as its divine author is to the God that saves and as this world, his work, is to the nonmundane realm beyond. Simon Magus and others are hardly less intransigent. A more qualified view is taken by the Valentinians: the law is at least partly prefigurative of the higher truth, and the prophets, although mainly inspired by the Demiurge, are sometimes (and unbeknown to him) used by his mother, Sophia, for her own messages, which thus are interspersed in the inferior bulk. There are other shades of opinion, but rejection of the whole body of Hebrew Scripture, joined with irreverent exegetical use, is by far the rule; and on this issue, and on the related one of the identity or nonidentity of the God of Moses with the Father of Jesus Christ, the main battle was fought between the church and the heretics.

Cosmos and human nature. The material universe, the domain of the archons, is like a vast prison whose innermost dungeon is the earth, the scene of man's life. Around and above it, the cosmic spheres are ranged like concentric enclosing shells. Their number is usually seven, with a surrounding eighth that does not belong to the archontic realm proper but is intermediate between the cosmos and the upper world of the pleroma. There was, however, a tendency to multiply structures and to make the scheme more and more extensive: Basilides counted no fewer than 365 heavens. The religious significance of this cosmic architecture lies in the idea that everything that intervenes between here and the beyond serves to separate man from God, not merely by spatial distance but through active demonic force. Thus, the vastness and multiplicity of the cosmic system express the degree to which man is removed from God.

The spheres are the seats of the archons, whose ruling set of seven are the planetary gods of the Babylonian pantheon, now significantly renamed with synonyms for the Hebrew God—another sign of the latter's degradation. The archons collectively rule the world that they (or their overlord) made, and each individually in his sphere is a warder of the cosmic prison. Their tyrannical world rule, called Fate (*heimarmene*), is physically the law of nature, morally the law of justice, as exemplified in the Mosaic law, which issued from the Demiurge or the angels and, with its threat of retribution, aims at the enslavement of man as much as the first does with its force of necessity. As guardian of his sphere, each archon bars the passage to the souls that seek to ascend after death, in order to prevent their escape from the world and their return to God.

Man, the main object of these vast dispositions, is composed of flesh, soul, and spirit. Reduced to ultimate principles, his origin is twofold: mundane and extramundane. Both the body and the soul are products of the cosmic powers, who shaped the body in the image of the divine Primal Man and animated it with their own psychical forces: these are the appetites and passions of natural man, each stemming from and corresponding to one of the cosmic spheres, and all together making up the astral soul of man, his psyche. Through his body and his soul man is a part of the world and is subjected to *heimarmene*. Enclosed in the soul is the spirit, or pneuma (also called the spark), a portion of the divine substance from beyond that has fallen into the world; the archons created man for the express purpose of keeping it captive here. Thus, as in the macrocosm man is enclosed by the seven spheres, so in the human microcosm the pneuma is enclosed by the seven soul vestments originating from them. These psychical envelopments are considered impairments and fetters of the transmundane spirit, and its incarnation in the outer, material body merely completes the complex imprisonment. The resulting human constitution is, then, comparable to an onion with so many layers, on the model of the cosmos itself but with the order reversed; what is outermost and uppermost in the cosmos is innermost in man, and the innermost or nethermost stratum of the cosmic order, the earth, is the outer bodily garment of man. Only the innermost or pneumatic man is the true man, and he is not of this world, as his original in the total order, the deity, is external to the cosmos as a whole. In its unredeemed state the spirit, so far from its source and immersed in soul and flesh, is unconscious of itself, benumbed, asleep, or intoxicated by the poison of the world—in brief, it is ignorant. Its awakening and liberation are effected through knowledge.

Eschatology: salvation through gnosis. The nature of Gnostic dualism determines the general concept of salvation, and the stratifications of cosmos and man condition its details. Its basic premise is that the transcendent God is as alien to this world as the pneumatic self is in the midst of it. The goal of Gnostic striving is the release of the inner man from the bonds of the world and his return to his native realm of light. The necessary condition for this is that he know about the transmundane God and about himself, that is, about his divine origin as well as his present situation, and hence, also about the nature of the world that determines his situation. Such knowledge is witheld from him by precisely the selfsame situation that requires it, for ignorance is the essence of mundane existence, just as it was the principle of the world's coming into being. In particular, the transcendent God is unknown in the world and cannot be discovered from it; therefore, revelation is needed. The necessity for revelation is inherent in the innercosmic condition; and its occurrence alters this condition in its decisive respect, that of ignorance. Revelation, or the "call," is thus already a part of salvation. Its bringer is a messenger from the world of Light who penetrates the barriers of the spheres, outwits the archons, awakens the spirit from its earthly slumber, and imparts to it the saving knowledge from without. The mission of this transcendent savior begins even before the creation of the world, since the fall of the divine element preceded creation, and the archetypal redemption indeed takes place in the precosmic stage. It is the incompleteness of this initial restoration, whether of Sophia or of Mani's Primal Man, that leads to the genesis of the world and the protraction of the saving process throughout its history. The fact that in the discharge of his task the eternal messenger must himself assume the lot of incarnation and cosmic exile, and the further fact that, at least in the Iranian variety of the myth, he is in a sense identical with those he calls—the once lost parts of his divine self—give rise to the moving idea of the "saved savior" (*salvator salvandus*).

The knowledge revealed by the messengers, for short "knowledge of God," comprises the whole content of the Gnostic myth, with everything it has to teach about God, man, and world, including the history of the beginnings which alone offers the key to the secrets of existence; that is, the revelation contains the elements of a theoretical system. On the practical side, however, it is more particularly "knowledge of the way"—of the soul's way out of the world—comprising the sacramental and magical preparations for its future ascent and the secret names and formulas that force the passage through each sphere. Equipped with this gnosis, the soul after death travels upward, leaving behind at each sphere the psychical vestments contributed by that sphere; thus the spirit, stripped of all foreign accretions, reaches the God beyond the world and reunites with the divine substance. (The most circumstantial description of this ascent is found in the "Poimandres," the first treatise of the Hermetic corpus.) On the scale of the total divine drama, the individual ascent is part of the restoration of the deity's own wholeness, impaired by the events of the beginning. Only through the loss suffered then did the deity become involved in the destiny of the world, and only to retrieve his own does he intervene, through his envoys, in cosmic history. With the completion of this ingathering, the cosmos, deprived of its elements of light, will come to an end.

Morality. In this life the pneumatics, as the possessors of gnosis called themselves, are set apart from the mass of mankind. The immediate illumination that makes the individual sovereign in the sphere of knowledge (hence the great variety of Gnostic doctrines) also inspires superior rules of conduct. Generally, the pneumatic morality is determined by hostility toward the world and contempt for all mundane ties. From this principle, however, two contrary conclusions could be drawn, and both found their extreme partisans: the ascetic and the libertine. The ascetic deduces from the possession of gnosis the obligation to avoid further contamination by the world and therefore to reduce the world's use to a minimum; the libertine derives from the same possession the privilege of unrestrained freedom. The libertine conclusion, more startling and more devious, is argued thus: The law, since it represents the will of the Demiurge and is one form of his tyranny, does not obligate the pneuma, which is "saved in its nature" and can be neither sullied by actions (which in themselves are morally neutral) nor frightened by the threat of archontic retribution which can affect only the body and the psyche). Thus the pneumatic, since he is free from the power of fate, is also free from the yoke of the moral law, and all things are permitted to him. This freedom, however, is more than merely permissive; its practice is bidden by metaphysical interest. Through intentional violation of the demiurgical norm (for which the mythological vilification of the Demiurge prepares) the pneumatic thwarts the design of the archons and thus paradoxically contributes to the work of salvation. From the motive of defiance it is then only one step further to the teaching of the Cainites and Carpocratians that there is a positive duty to perform every kind of action, to leave no deed undone, no possibility of freedom unrealized, in order to render nature its due and exhaust its powers; only in this way can final release from the cycle of reincarnations be obtained. Gnostic libertinism thus spans the whole scale from mere negative license to positive Faustian obligation—at which point it loses again some of the contrast to its ascetic alternative.

The latter alternative, too, betrays the common root in Gnosticism from which both opposites spring. Although more obvious in the libertine choice, the element of defiance shows in the ascetic one as well; as much as it may serve purification or other perfectionist ends normally associated with asceticism, it often has the declared purpose of obstructing the cause of the Creator, even just to spite him, by refusing to use his works (a kind of metaphysical strike). This obstructive aspect is especially clear in the abstention from sexual intercourse and marriage when, as in Marcion and Mani, its purpose is not to help replenish the world of the Demiurge and further disperse in it the captive light—thereby prolonging its exile and making its ingathering more difficult. Indeed, according to Mani, the reproductive scheme was instituted by the archons with precisely this end in view. Asceticism is thus a matter less of ethics than of metaphysical alignment, and its common ground with libertinism is the determination not to play the Creator's game. The one repudiates allegiance to nature through abstention; the other, through excess. Both are lives outside the mundane norm. Freedom by use and freedom by nonuse are thus alternative expressions of the same acosmism.

Acosmism. Acosmism, the real basis of the Gnostic position, contains the seeds of nihilism; the very extremism of divine transcendence has nihilistic implications. As the totally other, alien, and unknown, the Gnostic God has more of the *nihil* than of the *ens* in his concept. For all purposes of man's relation to the reality that surrounds him, this hidden God is a negative term; no law emanates from him—none for nature, and thus none for human action as a part of the natural order. His only relation to the world is the negative one of saving from the world. Antinomianism follows naturally, even if not inevitably, from these premises.

Two types of gnostic dualism. This article has kept mainly to the Syrian–Egyptian stream of Gnostic speculation, to which the majority of systems, especially the Christian ones, belong. There is, however, another, Iranian line of speculation that culminates in Mani.

Both types, being Gnostic, were evolved to explain the same facts of a dislocated metaphysical situation—both are dualistic concerning their common theme: the existing rift between God and world, world and man, spirit and flesh. The Iranian type, in a Gnostic adaptation of Zoroastrian doctrine, starts from a dualism of two opposed principles and then must explain how the original Darkness came to engulf elements of the Light—it describes the world drama as a war with changing fortunes; and the divine fate, of which man's fate is a part and the world an unwilled by-product, is explained in terms of mixing and unmixing, captivity and liberation. Here the knightly male figure of First Man, the warrior, assumes the role of the exposed and suffering part of divinity. The Syrian speculation, with the female Sophia in that role, undertakes the more ambitious task of deriving dualism itself, and the ensuing predicament of the divine in the system of creation, from the one and undivided source of being. It does this by means of a genealogy of personified divine states evolving from

one another that describes the progressive darkening of the original Light in categories of guilt, error, and failure. This devolution within the divine being ends in the decadence of complete self-alienation that is this world. Both dramas start with a disturbance in the heights; in both, the existence of the world marks a discomfiture of the divine and a necessary, in itself undesirable, means of its eventual restitution; in both, the salvation of man is that of the deity itself. The difference lies in whether the tragedy is forced upon the deity from without by the trespass of an independent Darkness, which thus has the first initiative (the deity itself being in perfect tranquillity), or is motivated from within itself, with Darkness and Matter the products of its passion, which they hypostatize in external terms. To divine defeat and sacrifice in the first case correspond divine gult and error in the second; to compassion for the victimized Light, spiritual contempt for demiurgical blindness; to eventual divine liberation, reformation through enlightenment.

The Manichaean and Valentinian systems respectively exemplify the two types. The Iranian type, with its high-minded story of battle, defeat, and recovery, lends itself to more concrete and gripping dramatization. However, only the subtler Syrian type, by according metaphysical status to knowledge and ignorance as modes of the divine life and therefore as universal, cosmogonic categories, can do full justice to the redemptional claim made on behalf of knowledge in all Gnostic religion. Valentinian speculation inferred that the human individual event of pneumatic knowledge reverses the precosmic universal event of divine ignorance and is in its redeeming effect of the same ontological order. Thus the actualization of knowledge in the person is at the same time an act in the general ground of being.

Bibliography

PRIMARY SOURCES

New Testament Apocrypha are translated in M. R. James, ed., *The Apocryphal New Testament* (Oxford, 1953), and in E. Hennecke and W. Schneemelcher, eds., *Neutestamentliche Apokryphen* (Tübingen, 1959–1964). Editions of the original texts are listed there. The following Apocrypha are noteworthy for their Gnostic contents: the "Acts of Thomas," containing the Hymn of the Pearl; the pseudo-Clementine "Homilies and Recognitions"; and the "Odes of Solomon." See also the section on Coptic sources.

Patristic sources, in standard editions and translations, include Irenaeus of Lyon, *Against the Heresies;* Clement of Alexandria, *Excerpts from Theodotus* and *Stromateis;* Tertullian of Carthage, *Against Marcion, Against the Valentinians, On the Plea of the Heretics,* and *On the Soul;* Hippolytus of Rome, *Philosophoumena;* Origen, *Against Celsus* and *Commentary on the Gospel of John* (containing the fragments of Heracleon); and Epiphanius of Salamis, *Panarion.* Collections of patristic texts (Greek and Latin) may be found in A. Hilgenfeld, *Die Ketzergeschichte des Urchristentums* (Leipzig, 1884), and W. Völker, ed., *Quellen zur Geschichte der christlichen Gnosis* (Tübingen, 1932).

Coptic sources include C. Schmidt, *Koptisch-gnostische Schriften* (Leipzig, 1905) and *Pistis Sophia,* Coptica II (Leipzig, 1925); W. Till, ed., *Die gnostischen Schriften des koptischen Papyrus Berolinensis 8502* (Berlin, 1955). The newly discovered Nag Hammadi texts, so far as published, include the following: M. Malinine, H. C. Puech, and G. Quispel, eds., *Evangelium Veritatis* (Zurich, 1956 and 1961), translated in K. Grobel, *The Gospel of Truth* (New York and Nashville, Tenn., 1960); H. M. Schenke,

"Das Wesen der Archonten," in *Theologische Literaturzeitung,* Vol. 83 (1958), 661–670; A. Guillaumont, H. C. Puech, and others, eds., *The Gospel According to Thomas* (Leiden, 1959), translated in R. M. Grant and D. N. Freedman, *The Secret Sayings of Jesus* (London and New York, 1960), and also translated by J. Leipoldt, J. Doresse, T. Säve-Söderbergh, H. Quecke, and R. McL. Wilson; M. Krause and P. Labib, *Die drei Versionen des Apokryphon des Johannes* (Wiesbaden, 1962), also translated by S. Giverson; A. Böhlig and P. Labib, eds., *Die koptisch-gnostische Schrift ohne Titel aus Codex II von Nag Hammadi* (Berlin, 1962), and *Koptisch-gnostische Apokalypsen aus Codex V von Nag Hammadi* (Halle, 1963); M. Malinine and others, eds., *De Resurrectione Epistula ad Reginum* (Zurich and Stuttgart, 1963); W. Till, *Das Evangelium nach Philippos,* Texte und Studien II (Berlin, 1963), also translated by R. McL. Wilson. See also H. C. Puech, "Gnostische Evangelien und verwandte Dokumente," in E. Hennecke and W. Schneemelcher, eds., *Neutestamentlich Apokryphen,* Vol. I (Tübingen, 1959), pp. 158–271.

Hermetica are collected in A. D. Nock, ed., *Hermès Trismégiste,* translated by A. J. Festugière, 4 vols. (Paris, 1945–1954), which contains text, translation, and notes and supersedes all earlier editions.

Writings of the Mandaeans are in the following editions and/or translations: M. Lidzbarski, *Das Johannesbuch der Mandäer* (Giessen, 1905 and 1915), *Mandäische Liturgien* (Berlin, 1920), and *Ginza. Der Schatz oder das grosse Buch der Mandäer* (Göttingen, 1925); and E. S. Drower, *The Book of the Zodiac* (London, 1949), *Diwan Abatur* (Vatican City, 1950, Studi e testi 151), *The Haran Gawaita* (Vatican City, 1953, Studi e testi 176), *The Canonical Prayerbook of the Manaeans* (Leiden, 1959), *The Thousand and Twelve Questions* (Berlin, 1960), *The Coronation of the Great Šišlam* (Leiden, 1962), and *A Pair of Naṣoraean Commentaries* (Leiden, 1963).

For writings of the Manichaeans, see bibliography to MANI AND MANICHAEISM.

A selection of materials from the first four sections of this bibliography can be found in R. M. Grant, *Gnosticism: A Sourcebook of Heretical Writings* (London and New York, 1961).

SECONDARY SOURCES

General studies include F. C. Baur, *Die christliche Gnosis* (Tübingen, 1835); C. W. King, *The Gnostics and Their Remains,* 2d ed. (London, 1887); W. Bousset, *Hauptprobleme der Gnosis* (Göttingen, 1907); A. Harnack, *Lehrbuch der Dogmengeschichte,* 4th ed. (Tübingen, 1909), Vol. I; H. Leisegang, *Die Gnosis* (Leipzig, 1924; 4th ed., Stuttgart, 1955); E. de Faye, *Gnostiques et gnosticisme* (Paris, 1925); F. C. Burkitt, *Church and Gnosis* (Cambridge, 1932); H. Jonas, *Gnosis und spätantiker Geist,* 2 vols. (Göttingen, 1934 and 1954; 3d ed., 1964), and *The Gnostic Religion* (Boston, 1958; 2d ed., 1963); J. Dupont, *Gnosis* (Louvain, 1949); G. Quispel, *Gnosis als Weltreligion* (Zurich, 1951); R. McL. Wilson, *The Gnostic Problem* (London, 1958); and R. M. Grant, *Gnosticism and Early Christianity* (New York, 1959).

Special studies include many important articles in periodicals, but for reasons of space, only books are listed here.

On the Valentinians, see bibliography to VALENTINUS AND VALENTINIANISM.

On Nag Hammadi, see F. L. Cross, ed., *The Jung Codex* (London and New York, 1955); H. M. Schenke, *Die Herkunft des sogenannten Evangelium Veritatis* (Göttingen, 1959); J. Doresse, *The Secret Books of the Egyptian Gnostics* (New York, 1960); and W. C. van Unnik, ed., *Evangelien aus dem Nilsand* (Frankfurt, 1960).

On Hermetism, see R. Reitzenstein, *Poimandres* (Leipzig, 1904); J. Kroll, *Die Lehren des Hermes Trismegistos* (Münster, 1914); W. Scott and A. S. Ferguson, eds., *Hermetica,* 4 vols. (Oxford, 1924–1936); W. Gundel, *Neue astrologische Texte des Hermes Trismegistos* (Munich, 1936); A. J. Festugière, *La Révélation d'Hermès Trismégiste,* 4 vols. (Paris, 1944–1954); and G. van Moorsel, *The Mysteries of Hermes Trismegistos* (Utrecht, 1955).

On the Mandaeans, see W. Brandt, *Die Mandäer* (Amsterdam, 1915); R. Reitzenstein, *Das mandäische Buch des Herrn der Grösse* (Heidelberg, 1919); H. Odeberg, *Die Mandäische Religionsanschauung* (Uppsala, 1930); E. S. Drower, *The Mandaeans of*

Iraq and Iran (Oxford, 1937), *Water Into Wine* (London, 1956), and *The Secret Adam* (Oxford, 1960); and K. Rudolph, *Die Mandäer,* 2 vols. (Göttingen, 1960–1961).

On other special aspects of Gnosticism, see R. Reitzenstein, *Das iranische Erlösungsmysterium* (Bonn, 1921), and *Die hellenistischen Mysterienreligionen,* 3d ed. (Leipzig, 1927); R. Reitzenstein and H. Schaeder, *Studien zum antiken Synkretismus* (Leipzig, 1926); A. Harnack, *Marcion,* 2d ed. (Leipzig, 1924); C. H. Kraeling, *Anthropos and Son of Man* (New York, 1927); W. Bauer, *Rechtgläubigkeit und Ketzerei im ältesten Christentum* (Tübingen, 1934); S. Pétrement, *Le Dualisme chez Platon, les gnostiques et les manichéens* (Paris, 1947); H. J. Schoeps, *Urgemeinde, Judenchristentum, Gnosis* (Tübingen, 1956); G. Scholem, *Jewish Gnosticism* (New York, 1960); A. Wlosok, *Laktanz und die philosophische Gnosis* (Heidelberg, 1960); J. Jervell, *Imago Dei* (Göttingen, 1961); and H. M. Schenke, *Der Gott 'Mensch' in der Gnosis* (Göttingen, 1962).

HANS JONAS

GOBINEAU, COMTE JOSEPH ARTHUR DE (1816–1882), French philosopher, historian, novelist, and diplomat. Gobineau's diplomatic duties during the Second Empire carried him to Switzerland, Persia, Greece, and Brazil, where he produced a number of historical and ethnographic works of considerable merit. He is best known for his *Essai sur l'inégalité des races humaines* (4 vols., Paris, 1853–1855; Vol. 1 translated into English by Adrian Collins as *The Inequality of Human Races,* London, 1915). This work is usually considered an important contribution to nineteenth-century racist thought; but Gobineau's racism was a by-product of his attempt to account for the decline of the European aristocracy in terms of the more general problem of the decline and fall of civilizations.

Gobineau presented his work as an essay in positivistic social theory; in the preface to the second edition (1884), he argued that Henry Thomas Buckle and Charles Darwin had merely proceeded along lines originally marked out by himself. Superficially, then, Gobineau's work resembled those positivistic theories of culture in which his century abounded. However, it differed from them in its categorical rejection of the doctrine of "progress." His work was profoundly pessimistic, and in the end Gobineau predicted the ineluctable decay, not only of Western civilization, but of the whole of humanity. Thus, Gobineau's racism differed from the later racism of the imperialist period. He was neither a nationalist nor a proponent of the idea of "the white man's burden." He was rather an apologist for a class that had come to feel that since it no longer had a genuine social role to fill, society itself was no longer possible.

Gobineau held that the human species was originally divided into three races as a result of environmental conditioning. The Negro race is dominated by "desire" and the need to gratify desire, and hence is the natural enemy of civilization. Driven by the need for sensual gratification alone, the Negro lacks both speculative and technical capability. The yellow race is the antitype of the Negroid, lacking in physical vigor but possessing a natural talent for technical accomplishment that allows it to create pseudo civilizations but prohibits it from developing any genuine science. The white race is superior to the other two because it combines energy and intelligence in just the right proportions. The white race has a genuine "love of life," but it is able to control and direct that love to culturally creative ends. The white man is a speculative thinker, which allows him to create both a science of nature and a science of politics. This makes of the white man the natural conqueror of the other two races. Whatever these other races have accomplished in the way of civilizational growth they owe to the superaddition of white blood, Gobineau held.

By the same token, however, racial intermixture results in the debilitation of the white race. Unlike the Darwinists, who saw survival itself as evidence of fitness, Gobineau held that in every racial mixture it is the weaker strain that predominates. In the long run, then, racial intermixture must result not so much in the elevation of inferior breeds as the mongrelization of the entire species. Thus envisaged, the white race is caught on the horns of a dilemma. Its inherent excellence drives it forth to world conquest, but that very conquest leads to its decline. Gobineau's theory of civilization, in short, was not so much an attempt to explain the facts of history as to justify his own overriding sense of *senescens saeculum*, a product of the breakdown of the social class to which he belonged.

Obviously, such a theory could not serve as a rationalization for imperialistic expansion, for if Gobineau were right, it would be better for the white race to cease expanding and seal itself off from contact with all other races. But Gobineau was valuable to the reactionary groups of his time even though he opposed imperialism, for he was an ardent enemy of liberalism. His theory explicitly designated the social egalitarianism of the radicals as an instrument of further mongrelization. The city of Paris, where the races mixed in perfect equality, proved his point, he wrote, because there "tradition is respected not at all."

As for nationalism, Gobineau regarded this phenomenon as another evidence of the breakdown of racial solidarity. He dreamed of an international aristocracy of blood to which the purest elements of all nations belong. His book *La Renaissance* (Paris, 1877; translated into English by P. V. Cohen as *The Renaissance*, New York, 1913) was intended to demonstrate that as long as the white race had retained its internationalist sense of caste and eschewed expansion and intermixture, it had remained creative and productive. Neither libertarian nor expansionist, the aristocracy of the Renaissance, as represented by such figures as Cesare Borgia, Michelangelo, and Raphael, was able to produce masterpieces of art and politics. The problem of race did not intrude itself into Gobineau's handling of the Renaissance, because in *La Renaissance* he was dealing with a preliberal, amoral, and creative example of the white race's power. But this book does contain an implicit criticism of his own age, dominated, in his opinion, by weak-willed liberals and traditionless mongrels.

Additional Works by Gobineau

Trois Ans en Asie. Paris, 1859.
Les Religions et les philosophies dans l'Asie centrale. Paris, 1865.
Histoire des Perses, 2 vols. Paris, 1869.
Correspondance d'Alexis de Tocqueville et d'Arthur de Gobineau. Paris, 1959. The correspondence is also available in an English translation by John Lukacs in Alexis de Tocqueville, *The European Revolution & Correspondence with Gobineau* (Garden City, N.Y., 1959), edited by Lukacs.

Works on Gobineau

Combris, Andrée, *La Philosophie des races de Gobineau*. Paris, 1937.
Falk, Reinhold, *Die weltanschauliche Problematik bei Gobineau*. Berlin, 1936.
Ferguson, W. J., *Renaissance in Historical Thought*. New York, 1948. On Gobineau as historian.
La Nouvelle Revue Française, Vol. 42 (February 1934). Issue dedicated to Gobineau and his work.
Schemann, Ludwig, *Gobineau und die deutsche Kultur*. Leipzig, 1910; 7th ed. Leipzig, 1934.
Sellière, Ernst, *Le Comte de Gobineau et l'aryanisme historique*. Paris, 1903.
Streidl, Rudolf, *Gobineau in der französichen Kritik*. Würzburg, 1935.

HAYDEN V. WHITE

GOBLOT, EDMOND (1858–1935), French philosopher and logician. Goblot was born at Mamers. He studied under Jules Lachelier and Étienne Boutroux and succeeded Arthur Hannequin to the chair in the history of philosophy and the sciences at the University of Lyons. In addition to *Vocabulaire philosophique* (Paris, 1901), he wrote numerous articles, of which the most notable are undoubtedly those he devoted to finality (1899–1904), which he conceived of somewhat in the Kantian manner as "complex fitness." He also dealt with epistemology both in his doctoral thesis, *Essai sur la classification des sciences* (Paris, 1898), and later in *Le Système des sciences* (Paris, 1922); he treated moral and social questions in *Justice et liberté* (Paris, 1904) and *La Barrière et le niveau, étude sociologique sur la bourgeoisie française* (Paris, 1925).

Goblot's most striking work, however, was his *Traité de logique* (Paris, 1918), which quickly became the breviary on this subject for a whole generation of French students. This is logic understood in a broad sense and includes chapters on induction and its foundation, on teleological reasoning, on the scientific mind, and on value judgments (this was subsequently developed into a book, *La Logique des jugements de valeur*, Paris, 1927). Formal logic itself is not at all formalized in the book.

The author stands aside from the developments in symbolic logic, and his work is in many respects behind the times. It is to be associated, rather, with that group of writings which, in the course of the nineteenth century, made apparent the inadequacies of traditional logic. Its criticisms bear, among other things, on the excessive importance accorded by traditional logic to the categorical syllogism, as against the hypothetical syllogism. The most original thesis consists in a conception of deductive reasoning that seeks to provide a solution for the classic problem which troubled Poincaré especially: How is it possible for a deduction to be rigorous and also to be a fruitful addition to our knowledge, at least in the case of the mathematical demonstration if not in the case of the syllogism?

To demonstrate, replies Goblot, is to construct. In order to demonstrate that a hypothesis entails a certain consequence, one constructs the consequence along with the hypothesis. The operations of construction are not logical operations; they are external operations that are executed purely mentally, and their result constitutes the object of a "logical statement" (*constatation logique*). These constructions, which display the creative activity of the mind, nevertheless have nothing of the arbitrary about them. What controls them is not the rules of logic, but the propositions previously accepted. Each constructed truth becomes an instrument with which to construct others. Hence deduction is not doomed, as is said, to pass "from the general to the particular"; on the contrary, it often relies on a special privileged case, to which it reduces the general case. In this manner it enlarges our knowledge.

Bibliography

See J. Kergomard, P. Salzi, and F. Goblot, *Edmond Goblot, la vie, l'oeuvre* (Paris, 1937), which includes a bibliography; and, on the *Traité de logique*, two critical studies: J. Nicod, *Revue de métaphysique et de morale* (1919), 375–385, and A. Lalande, *Revue philosophique*, Vol. 87 (1919), 131–154.

ROBERT BLANCHÉ
Translated by *Albert E. Blumberg*

GOD, ARGUMENTS FOR THE EXISTENCE OF.

See COMMON CONSENT ARGUMENTS FOR THE EXISTENCE OF GOD; COSMOLOGICAL ARGUMENT FOR THE EXISTENCE OF GOD; DEGREES OF PERFECTION, ARGUMENT FOR THE EXISTENCE OF GOD; MORAL ARGUMENTS FOR THE EXISTENCE OF GOD; ONTOLOGICAL ARGUMENT FOR THE EXISTENCE OF GOD; POPULAR ARGUMENTS FOR THE EXISTENCE OF GOD; RELIGIOUS EXPERIENCE, ARGUMENT FOR THE EXISTENCE OF GOD; TELEOLOGICAL ARGUMENT FOR THE EXISTENCE OF GOD.

GOD, CONCEPTS OF.

It is very difficult—perhaps impossible—to give a definition of God that will cover all usages of the word and of equivalent words in other languages. Even to define God generally as "a superhuman or supernatural being that controls the world" is inadequate. "Superhuman" is contradicted by the worship of divinized Roman emperors, "supernatural" by Spinoza's equation of God with Nature, and "control" by the Epicurean denial that the gods influence the lives of men. Therefore, while the above definition satisfies a wide range of usages, it is not universally applicable.

This article will deal with five problems: the transcendence and immanence of God, his relation to the world, his chief attributes, the extent to which he is "personal," and the ways by which he can be known. In discussing these problems it will be necessary to consult the data provided by both religion and philosophy. But purely religious data (in contrast with theological speculations based on them) will be mentioned only when they are relevant to philosophical understanding.

Transcendence and immanence. In Judaism and Christianity, God is unquestionably transcendent. He is "wholly other" than the world he made. In Judaism his transcendence was emphasized by, among other things, the prohibition of idols, the explicit teaching of Isaiah 40.12–26, the sacredness of the Tetragrammaton, and the speculations of Philo who, in a typical passage, speaks of God

Platonically as "the pure and unsullied Mind of the universe, transcending virtue, transcending knowledge, transcending the good itself." The New Testament, in confirming the Old Testament, repudiates the claims of Hellenistic *gnosis* by affirming that "no one has ever seen God" (John 1.18) and that all our knowledge of him is like a confused reflection in a mirror (1 Cor. 13.12). Among later Christian thinkers this Biblical attitude was reinforced partly by the influence of Neoplatonism and partly by the experience of the mystics (especially Dionysius the Pseudo-Areopagite). Hence, in the *Summa Contra Gentiles* (I, 14), Aquinas says that "the divine substance exceeds by its immensity every form which our intellect attains," so that while we can know *that* God is (*quod sit*) we cannot know his essence or *what* he is (*quid sit*). In recent times divine transcendence has been stressed by Kierkegaard and Barth, as opposed to Hegelian attempts to obtain a rational and synoptic understanding of ultimate reality. From a phenomenological point of view, Rudolf Otto, in his *Das Heilige* (Marburg, 1917), defined the object of worshp as a *mysterium tremendum et fascinans* that is revealed to a suprarational faculty of the soul.

Christian theologians claim that this transcendent God can be spoken of either negatively by the *via negativa* or *via remotionis* (the apophatic way) or positively (by the cataphatic way). According to the negative way, we deny qualities to God by the use of such adjectives as "*incorporeal*" and "*uncreated*." Thus we come to know him by knowing what he is not. But we also speak positively of God (for example, by predicating goodness or wisdom of him). Aquinas denied that positive predicates are definable in terms of negative ones. He also denied that they simply point to God as an indeterminate cause of finite properties. In his view, they refer to God in a positive manner through an "analogy of proportionality." Thus goodness exists in God in a "supereminent" form, proportionate to his infinite mode of being. Through this theory of analogical predication, Aquinas hoped to steer a middle course between the anthropomorphism of univocal predication, on the one hand, and the agnosticism of equivocal predication on the other.

According to the main tradition of Christian thought, God is also immanent. Augustine held that the light of God's presence in the human mind enables it to recognize eternal truth. Aquinas, while rejecting the Augustinian theory of illumination, affirmed God's omnipresence unambiguously. "God is in all things, not, indeed, as part of their essence, or as a quality, but in the manner that an efficient cause is present to that on which it acts. Hence God is in all things, and intimately" (*Summa Theologica* Ia, 8, 1). Similarly, the mystics affirm that the transcendent God is present (even when unrecognized) at the "ground" or "apex" of the soul. But some philosophers have *identified* God's substance either partly or wholly with the world. The clearest exponent of this concept in Western thought is Spinoza, whose identification of God with Nature a paradigm of pantheism. Such later philosophers as Edward Caird and Sir Henry Jones, who equated the Christian God with the Hegelian Absolute, approximated pantheism in varying degrees. Many modern theologians, such as Barth and Bultmann, who have followed Kierkegaard in reaffirming God's transcendence, have either denied or ignored his immanence. Paul Tillich is a notable exception. While he spoke of God "existentially" as the transcendent Object of our "ultimate concern," he also held that we could not know God without "participating" in him.

God and the world. The degree to which God is transcendent or immanent depends on the view that is taken of his relation to the world. At least five views are possible.

God as final cause. God can be viewed as a final, though not efficient, cause of the world. This view was held by Aristotle. According to him, God is the world's "prime mover." God "moves" the world in the sense that he educes form from its material structure by inspiring it, through a series of subordinate movers or "intelligences," to love him as its end or goal. Yet Aristotle expressly denied a creation of the world; he considered matter to be ungenerated and eternal.

World as emanation from God. The world may be regarded as in some way an emantion from, or self-expression of, God. This view has taken three main forms.

According to Plotinus, the One, or "first god," is beyond all thought and being. The One's simplicity would be violated if the world were a part of it. Its unchangeability would be violated if it were to create the world by an act of will. Therefore Plotinus propounded his theory of "emanation." Mind, Soul, and the material world flow from the One (as rays flow from the sun) without impairing its self-sufficiency.

According to Spinoza, the world *is* God (the only substance) under his attributes of thought and extension. Everything follows from his essence by a logical necessity. "Things could not have been produced by God in any other manner or order than that in which they were produced. All things must have followed of necessity from a given nature of God, and they were determined for existence or action in a certain way by the necessity of the divine nature" (*Ethics* I, prop. 33). Critics of Spinoza have continually pointed out that on these premises it is very hard to account for, first, the individuality which human persons *seem* to have; second, their apparent freedom, which Spinoza elsewhere attempts to analyze; and third, the fact of evil, especially in its moral forms.

The same type of relation between God and the world was posited by Hegel. Unlike Plotinus, he regarded God or the Absolute as in its essence a self-diversifying unity. Unlike Spinoza, he conceived of God's self-expression as a dynamic process that is discoverable in historical events. Hegel's thought is not free from ambiguity. He sometimes speaks of God as an independently existing entity. But his final and distinctive view is that the Absolute Spirit does not exist apart from the human spirits in which it is progressively evolved.

World as pre-existent matter set in order. The third way of relating God to the world was stated by Plato in his *Timaeus.* According to this dialogue (29E–30), God is bounded on the one hand by the world of Forms and on the other by pre-existent matter. His task is to impose the Forms on matter, and so construct a rationally ordered whole. Being wholly good, and therefore free from jealousy, he wished everything to be like himself. Since an

intelligent being is superior to an unintelligent one, and since intelligence cannot be present in anything that is devoid of soul, "he put intelligence in soul, and soul in body, that he might be the creator of a work which was by nature best." (In the *Republic* 597, Plato implies that God creates the Forms, but this was not his usual view.)

Creation "ex nihilo." In contrast with all the previous views, Christian theists since Augustine have held the doctrine of creation out of nothing. This phrase is meant to exclude both the idea that the world is a necessary emanation from God's nature and the idea that matter pre-exists his creative act. God brings the whole world into being by an undetermined choice. He does not need the world to complete his nature, for he is wholly self-sufficient. He is not confronted with an alien Necessity, for he is the efficient cause of all that is.

This conception of the relation between the Creator and the creature can be elucidated through the contrast between necessary and contingent being. God exists necessarily. In him essence and existence are identical. He is self-existent in a unique and incomprehensible way. Creatures, on the other hand, are contingent. Their essence, while pre-existing ideally in the mind of God, would not have achieved independent being if he had not chosen to grant it by a free act of love. Therefore, while they participate in him both by nature and by grace, they never lose their created status. They can be deified (as the Greek fathers taught) within their finite limits, but they cannot become divine in the sense of sharing God's aseity.

The full Christian doctrine does not restrict God's creative act to an initial moment in the cosmic process. All things owe their being continuously to his power. He is a first cause in the order of existence, not of time, for he himself is supratemporal. Hence it is irrelevant to theology whether the world did or did not have a temporal beginning. Aquinas held that while such a beginning was revealed through Scripture, it could not be rationally proved. All reason knows is that God is the eternal, ever-present, and creative source of anything that does (or can) exist. Creation and preservation are identical.

However, while no creature exists from itself (*a se*), every creature exists by itself (*per se*) or in itself (*in se*). Created substances have a relative independence, or derived autonomy. These paradoxical expressions are required in order to affirm the truth that while creatures owe their being to God as their first cause, they also act according to secondary causes that are appropriate to their natures. The distinction between these two types of cause is necessary for a true assessment of the relation between science and theology. Because finite things exist *per se,* their secondary causes are discoverable without the aid of faith. But the discovery of secondary causes does not, without a further, nonscientific, act of inference or intuition, either permit or prohibit belief in a first cause, God.

Yet God, as first cause, can suspend or transform secondary causes in order to perform his will. When he does so, his action is called a miracle. A miracle does not violate nature. It is a case of nature behaving in an abnormal way through a special act of the same creative power which is at work in the normal processes that can be subsumed under scientific laws. If the essence of finite being is to be dependent on God's will (and so to possess a *potentia obedientialis* in relation to it), miraculous acts are not less natural than nonmiraculous ones. But while the abnormal character of an event is empirically verifiable, its miraculous character as an act of God can be discerned by faith alone. (Many theologians readily admit that at least some of Hume's skeptical objections have considerable prima-facie force.)

The relation between divine causality and the human will has been extensively discussed by theologians. The doctrine of predestination, in its rigid Augustinian form, would seem to be obviously incompatible with human freedom. Yet even those theologians who reject the doctrine are obliged to face the problem of the manner in which God acts on men both by nature (through his general providence) and by grace (through the supernatural gift of the Holy Spirit). While various attempts have been made to separate divine and human action so that, for example, the human will is left wholly autonomous in a strictly moral choice, many theologians (recently, D. M. Baillie and A. M. Farrer) affirm, on grounds of Scripture and experience, that the divine and human wills act simultaneously throughout the Christian life, but that the manner of their interaction is a paradox, or mystery, that cannot be unraveled by the intellect.

God as final stage of cosmic process. Samuel Alexander held the eccentric view that God qua deity, so far from being the ground of the cosmic process, is (ideally) its final stage. The world evolves from space time through matter and life to mind. God exists wholly within the world, which is his "body," but he does not yet exist as deity (that is, as an infinite, transcendent, Being). Moreover, he will never so exist. Deity, as a state of infinite perfection, is a goal to which the world (or God considered as the world) continually strives but which is unattainable.

Some philosophers have combined two or more of these views. Thus A. N. Whitehead, while rejecting the idea that God is the world's efficient cause, held, as did Aristotle, that he is a final cause who (like Plato's God) brings order into the world by ensuring the ingredience of eternal objects (which, however, do not exist independently) in the realm of temporal flux. But Whitehead also shows his affinity with Alexander by asserting that it is as true to say that the world creates God as it is to say that God creates the world.

The divine attributes. In most systems of religion and philosophy, God is endowed with characteristics that distinguish him from other forms of being.

Infinity. The infinity of the Christian God was implied above in the accounts of his transcendence and creative power, and in most systems, God's infinity makes him free, in degree, if not in kind, from at least some human limitations. But he is not strictly infinite unless he is limitless throughout the whole range of his existence. He can be wholly limitless, however, only if he is self-existent and thereby self-sufficient. If (as Hegel thought) God needs the world as the sphere of his self-development, or if (as Plato thought) he copies an independent realm of Forms, he is *pro tanto* limited. He is strictly infinite only if his essence is identical with existence, as Aquinas held when he said

that the most appropriate name for God is the one disclosed to Moses according to the Vulgate text of Exodus— *Qui Est* ("He Who Is"). If God is thus infinite, he must possess all properties in a mode that is free from every limitation. He must be one, simple, incorporeal, immutable, impassible, eternal, good, omniscient, and omnipotent.

Unity. The Greek philosophers were apt to speak interchangeably of "god" and "the gods" (as may be seen, for example, from Plato's *Laws* 900–905 and the *Discourses* of Epictetus I,3,1). But in Judaism the belief that Yahweh is the only God became an unquestioned axiom that was inherited by Christians and defended by Aquinas on the grounds that if there were two gods, one would possess what the other lacked, so that neither would be absolutely perfect (*Summa Theologica* Ia, 11, 3). Similarly, Muslims hold as a primary article of faith that "there is no god but God." But Christians differ from Jews and Muslims in believing that the one God exists in a threefold form as Father, Son, and Holy Spirit. He is one substance (*substantia, ousia*) in three persons (*personae, hypostaseis*).

Simplicity. According to Christianity and Neoplatonism, God is one also in the sense that he is absolutely simple; for the distinctions (such as those between essence and existence, substance and accidents) which make a finite being composite are inapplicable to him. Plotinus interpreted this simplicity as a bare, characterless, self-identity. But Aquinas held both that God actually possesses the perfections we ascribe to him and that these coalesce in an unimaginable unity. Each of God's attributes is objectively distinct, but each expresses his whole being.

Incorporeality. Those philosophers who regard the world as an aspect of God or an unfolding of his essence are obliged to think of him materially. Thus the Stoics identified him with nature's basic elements, air and fire. Similarly, Augustine learned from Manichaeism that God is a bright and very subtle substance. But the immateriality of God has constantly been taught by Platonists and Christians on the ground that matter, being a principle of limitation, is incompatible with his perfection.

Immutability. That God's nature cannot change (for change implies imperfection) was affirmed by Plato and the Old Testament. It was reaffirmed by Christian theologians, especially Augustine.

Impassibility. Impassibility is equivalent to immutability, if it means that God cannot suffer change from either an external or an internal cause. But it has also been taken to mean that God cannot experience pain. While there is an apparent contradiction between this last meaning and Biblical descriptions of God's love, it has been maintained by some theologians (but denied by others) that, although Christ experienced pain in his *human* nature, God cannot experience it in himself, for, being wholly perfect, he is pure Joy.

Eternity. In the Bible, God's eternity signifies an everlasting, endless time. In later Christian thought (through the influence of Platonism) it was understood as "timelessness." It is, in the famous definition of Boethius, *interminabilis vitae tota simul et perfecta possessio* ("eternal life possessed perfectly and simultaneously," *De Consola-*

tione Philosophiae V, vi). God, it is said, would not be perfect unless he possessed his whole being in a simultaneous act.

Goodness. The moral order has sometimes been interpreted nontheistically through such abstract ideas as *Rita* (in India), *Tao* (in China), and *Dike* (in Greece). The gods of Graeco-Roman polytheism were notoriously immoral. But in Christian thought, Plato's affirmation that God is wholly good (*Republic* 379) was combined with the Hebraic vision of Yahweh's righteousness. Hence Aquinas considered it to be axiomatic that "God is sheer goodness, whereas other things are credited with the sort of goodness appropriate to their natures" (*In Boethium de Hebdomadibus* 5).

Omniscience. Omniscience is entailed by infinity. But a special problem is created by the view that God now knows future *freely chosen* human acts. Those who hold this view urge, first, that since God is timeless it is, strictly speaking, incorrect to say that he "foreknows" events, and second, that even if we say this (speaking from our finite standpoint), we need not assume that a human act, because it is foreknown, is predetermined—by either God or any other factor outside the agent's will. To say that a human act can in principle be predicted is not to say that the agent has no control over it or is not really active and responsible for what he does; this, at any rate, is a view of human action widely held by philosophers at the present time. But other theists (notably James Ward and F. R. Tennant) consider it contradictory to say that a free choice can be known in any sense until it has been made. They affirm that God is ignorant of future human choices and that his ignorance is a "self-limitation" he deliberately incurred in granting man free will.

Omnipotence. Omnipotence too is entailed by infinity. It is important to note that in the Creeds, *Pantocrator* and *omnipotens* imply that God is ruler of all things, rather than that he can do anything. He cannot act against either reason or morality. But it is extremely difficult to explain the existence of evil in a world created by a God who is both infinitely powerful and infinitely good. Various explanations have been given. Thus, evil has been traced to the fall of a first man or World Soul. Again, it is said that God permits (even if he does not inflict) unmerited suffering as a means of purifying the soul for eternal life. But many theologians would endorse Friedrich Von Hügel's frank admission that no explanation is fully satisfying. It is therefore not surprising that some philosophers (notably J. S. Mill) have tried to relieve God of apparent responsibility for evil by supposing that he is finite both in knowledge and in power. (Christians believe that God displays his omnipotence by *overcoming* evil through the ministry of Christ; but an exposition of this belief would involve a study in the doctrines of Incarnation and Atonement.)

Personality. In the preceding sections it has been assumed that God is personal. The assumption is justified by the fact that, while in the primitive stages of religion he has often been conceived subpersonally, philosophers (in the West, at any rate) have nearly always described his nature to some extent by analogy with the human self.

Thus, according to Plato, Aristotle, and Spinoza God has mental properties. But two conditions must be fulfilled if God is to be *fully* personal. First, it must be possible to speak of him as loving, or caring for, mankind. Second, it must be possible to speak of him truly through images drawn from human life. The Aristotelian and Spinozistic concepts of him fail to meet the first of these conditions. While Aristotle's First Mover contemplates himself, he does not have any knowledge of the world. Therefore, like Spinoza's God, he cannot return the love that he receives.

The second condition is not universally fulfilled either. Some thinkers have attempted to mediate between philosophy and religion by suggesting that concrete images of God are inadequate attempts to grasp a Reality that is suprapersonal. Thus Hegel held that Absolute Spirit can be adequately known only by the speculative intellect. Consequently, when he speaks of the Absolute as God he means (as Aristotle meant) self-thinking Thought. The personal God of theism is a prerational and imperfect representation (*Vorstellung*) of the Absolute. On the ascending scale of truth, religion occupies an intermediate place between art and philosophy.

This contrast between religion and philosophy becomes even more acute when the Absolute is equated with a suprarational Unity. Here there is a striking parallel between Indian monism and the thought of F. H. Bradley. Some Hindu scriptures (notably the *Bhagavad-Gita*) describe God as a personal being, the Lord of the universe, whose "grace" (*prasada*) requires the "loving devotion" (*bhakti*) of his worshipers. The *Gita* is especially significant. Through the theophany in the eleventh chapter, it declares that Krishna (the incarnate God, and friend of Arjuna) is "more to be prized even than Brahman." But Śankara, following the nondualistic strain in the Upanishads, held that the sole reality is the impersonal Absolute (Brahman) with which the soul is numerically identical. Personal concepts of the Absolute belong to the sphere of illusion (maya). They are forms under which the One appears to untutored minds. Likewise F. H. Bradley held that since Reality is nonrelational, a personal God is "but an aspect, and that must mean but an appearance, of the Absolute" (*Appearance and Reality*, Oxford, 1930, p. 397).

Christians, however, are obliged by revelation to identify the Absolute with a God who is fully personal, both in himself and in his dealings with mankind. Such primary images as Father, King, and Friend mediate a knowledge that cannot be surpassed by abstract speculation. During this century the personal nature of religious conviction has been stressed in varying terms by such writers as William Temple, John Oman, John Baillie, Karl Barth, Emil Brunner, Martin Buber, and the existentialists (especially Søren Kierkegaard, Rudolf Bultmann, and Gabriel Marcel). Buber's distinction between an "I-Thou" and an "I-It" relationship and Kierkegaard's contrast between subjectivity and objectivity have been widely used to express the difference between a personal and an impersonal attitude to God. At the same time, many theologians are aware that an unqualified application of personal categories to God results in anthropomorphism. Divine personality wholly transcends its finite counterpart. It is unique both because of the fact that essence and existence are identical in it and because of the mystery of its triune character.

The knowledge of God. There are three main routes to God: reason, revelation, and religious experience.

Both Plato and Aristotle claimed that reason can obtain a certain knowledge of God's existence and nature. This claim has been endorsed by many Christian theologians. Thus, St. Augustine, writing from within the Platonic tradition, affirmed that the human intellect by nature participates in eternal Truth. Furthermore, many theologians have held that God's existence can be proved. These proofs may be divided between those which take the form of a priori reasoning from God's essence and those which take the form of a posteriori reasoning from finite experience. The first type of proof is exemplified chiefly by the Ontological Argument, which was first formulated by St. Anselm and restated by Descartes. In its Anselmic form it runs as follows: the idea of God is the idea of that than which nothing greater can be conceived; a being that exists is greater than a being that does not exist; therefore God exists. In view of the criticisms to which this proof has been subjected (especially by Aquinas and Kant), it is widely considered to be invalid by both theologians and philosophers today. The main a posteriori arguments received their classical formulation from Aquinas.

He constructed five proofs based on the facts of motion, causality, contingency, relative perfection, and design. (The first, second, and third of these Five Ways are different forms of the Cosmological Argument—the argument that the world in all its aspects shows its dependence on self-existent Being.) Kant rejected *all* proofs based on the use of the "speculative reason." But he maintained that the "practical reason" is obliged to postulate both God and immortality. Since World War I, natural theology has been vigorously attacked, on the one hand by Karl Barth and, on the other, by those philosophers who deny the possibility of metaphysics. However, many twentieth-century philosophers (chiefly Roman Catholic Thomists—but also others, such as the late A. E. Taylor) have held that the main a posteriori proofs can be presented cogently.

Aquinas affirmed that in addition to a natural knowledge of God there is a supernatural knowledge revealed by Christ and received through faith. Thus, while reason can infer that God is the Creator, it cannot discover that he is Three-in-One. Locke reproduced this distinction in his *Essay Concerning Human Understanding* (Book 4, Ch. 18). But in his *Reasonableness of Christianity* he paved the way for the deists, who held that the Gospel merely "republishes" the basic truths of natural religion and morality. The supernatural character of revelation was also denied later by those Hegelians who regarded Christ as the highest instance of the Absolute's universal presence in humanity.

Religious philosophers from Plato onward have claimed that it is possible to have a *direct* knowledge of divine reality. Among Christian thinkers, some hold that this knowledge is available (even if in a confused form) to everyone; others restrict it to the recipients of Biblical revelation. Some regard it as the highest activity of ordinary mental powers; others assign it to a special faculty of the soul. Some describe it intellectually as an insight or intuition; others stress its volitional character by calling it a confrontation or encounter. Apart from these differences, it is necessary to distinguish between an experience that is mediated and one that is immediate. As many recent writers have stressed (notably, William Temple, John Oman, and H. D. Lewis), religious experience is normally mediated through secular experiences, including those which are formulated in the premises of the a posteriori proofs. Thus, we become aware of God as eternal through the contingency of finite things and as holy through the demands of the moral law. (Even the divinity of Christ is experienced, in the first place, through meditation on his human life and on the impact which it made on his disciples.) But there is also an immediate, purely spiritual experience that is called "mystical." While Christian and non-Christian mystics often use the same terminology, the former (when they are orthodox) differ from many of the latter at two points. First, they affirm that God is transcendent as well as immanent. Second, and as a consequence, they claim, not an absorption into the Godhead, but a union of love and will in which the distinction between the Creator and the creature is permanently retained.

Bibliography

A. E. Taylor's article on theism in J. Hastings, ed., *Encyclopedia of Religion and Ethics* (New York, 1908–1926), is still authoritative. The best single book on Greek thought about God up to and including Plato remains James Adam's *The Religious Teachers of Greece* (Edinburgh, 1908). On the period from Augustine to Scotus, there are admirable accounts by F. Copleston in Vol. 2 of his *A History of Philosophy* (London, 1954). This book also contains an excellent bibliography. Most of the relevant passages in Aquinas are assembled in the two anthologies, *Philosophical Texts* and *Theological Texts*, selected and translated by T. Gilby (Oxford, 1951 and 1955). On the modern period, there is much useful material in A. S. Pringle-Pattison's *The Idea of God* (Oxford, 1920) and in E. L. Mascall's *He Who Is* (London, 1943). The latter re-examines the essentials of theism, and contains a full bibliography. See also J. Collins' very comprehensive *God in Modern Philosophy* (London, 1960); Illtyd Trethowan's *The Basis of Belief* (London, 1960), a concise summary of recent work on natural theology; and F. Ferré's *Language, Logic and God* (London, 1962), a full account of recent writing on religious subjects from an empiricist point of view. The classical analysis of religious experience remains Rudolf Otto, *Das Heilige* (Marburg, 1917), translated by J. W. Harvey as *The Idea of the Holy* (1925). The best modern defense of the miraculous element in Christianity is C. S. Lewis, *Miracles* (London, 1960). A full survey of recent writing on revelation is contained in John Baillie, *The Idea of Revelation in Recent Thought* (Oxford, 1956).

H. P. OWEN

GÖDEL'S THEOREM. By Gödel's theorem the following statement is generally meant:

In any formal system adequate for number theory there exists an undecidable formula—that is, a formula that is not provable and whose negation is not provable. (This statement is occasionally referred to as Gödel's first theorem.)

It is sometimes added that the undecidable formula is true.

A corollary to the theorem is that the consistency of a formal system adequate for number theory cannot be proved within the system. (Sometimes it is this corollary that is referred to as Gödel's theorem; it is also referred to as Gödel's second theorem.)

These statements are somewhat vaguely formulated generalizations of results published in 1931 by Kurt Gödel, then in Vienna ("Über formal unentscheidbare Sätze der Principia Mathematica und verwandter Systeme I," received for publication on November 17, 1930; a summary of Gödel's results was presented in a communication to the Vienna Academy on October 23, 1930: "Einige metamathematische Resultate über Entscheidungsdefinitheit und Widerspruchsfreiheit").

HISTORICAL BACKGROUND

Axiomatization. Mathematicians long practiced mathematics before reflecting on its nature, its methods, and its results; critical investigation of the foundations of mathematics did not begin until the second half of the nineteenth century. Perhaps the main single impulse behind this investigation came from the discovery of non-Euclidean geometries, and for some time great efforts were exerted in revising and perfecting the foundations of geometry. These efforts culminated in David Hilbert's *Grundlagen der Geometrie* (Leipzig, 1899). Other fundamental concepts that mathematicians had used for a long time in a naive fashion were critically analyzed. Richard Dedekind examined the notions of natural number and real number. Mathematicians were engaged in a broad process of axiomatization.

Formalization. A trend from an altogether different direction began to shape the process of axiomatization. Logic was entering its modern renaissance and by the end of the century had become so bold as to undertake the reconstruction of parts of mathematics (Gottlob Frege, *Begriffsschrift*, Halle, 1879). Axiomatization was beginning to give way to formalization.

In an axiomatized theory the mathematician starts from undefined notions and axioms about these notions. He then proves theorems. But theorems and proofs are written in ordinary language (that is, the ordinary language of the mathematician, with its limited vocabulary and its standardized phrases), and the means of proceeding from axioms to theorems is ordinary logic, which permits the use of any argument that carries conviction (some of these arguments, such as mathematical induction, are specifically mathematical).

In a formalized theory signs are introduced for propositions, predicates, relations, individuals, logical connectives (such as negation, implication, and conjunction), and quantifiers. Statements are transformed into formulas within a clearly delimited system. Formulas are inferred from other formulas according to certain definite and explicit rules, and the application of these rules requires nothing but the physical recognition of the shapes of signs; meaning is not involved.

Formal systems. An important step toward formalization was A. N. Whitehead and Bertrand Russell's *Principia Mathematica* (3 vols., Cambridge, 1910–1913), although some haziness still clung to certain parts of their system. The notion of formal system, which had already been introduced by Frege, finally found wide acceptance in the 1920s.

In such a system signs are manipulated according to rules that ignore the interpretations of the signs and simply deal with marks written one after another. We have well-formed formulas (that is, strings of marks satisfying certain conditions as to their shapes and occurrences) and proofs (that is, sequences of well-formed formulas also satisfying certain perceptual conditions). Hilbert, in particular, insisted that mathematics reduces to an inventory of such formulas and proofs. These formulas and proofs, which are the subject of a new science, proof theory, or metamathematics, are studied by any method that carries intuitive, perceptual conviction: we recognize signs, we obtain a certain formula from a given formula through a certain substitution, we use induction on the length of formulas, and so forth. Hilbert hoped that these methods, which he said were finitary, would yield consistency proofs of formal systems.

Consistency. The problem of consistency became an explicit concern of mathematicians with the advent of non-Euclidean geometries. The axioms of Euclidean geometry seemed, somehow, to be objectively true, and as the methods of deduction were expected to lead from true propositions to true propositions, every theorem was considered true. Since of two contradictory propositions one is false, no theorem could be the negation of another theorem.

But if axioms are no longer accepted as true, if a proposition and its negation can alternatively be taken as axioms, then theorems are no longer necessarily true, and there is no guarantee that a deduction will not lead to a contradiction. In fact, prior to the creation of non-Euclidean geometry Gerolamo Saccheri (1667–1733) derived consequences from assumptions incompatible with Euclid's axiom of parallels in the hope of coming to a contradiction and thus obtaining an indirect proof of the axiom. He did not succeed, but the problem of the consistency of Lobachevskian geometry was not solved until 1868, by Eugenio Beltrami, who showed that a certain Euclidean model satisfies the Lobachevskian axioms and thus established that Lobachevskian geometry is consistent if Euclidean geometry is. This type of proof is now known as a relative consistency proof. Since Beltrami's, many relative consistency proofs have been given. An important one is the consistency proof of Euclidean geometry as axiomatized by Hilbert relative to the real number system through the introduction of Cartesian coordinates.

Frege was the first to stress the need of a consistency proof for arithmetic, in *Die Grundlagen der Arithmetik* (1884). According to Frege, we should ensure the consistency of arithmetic by exhibiting objects that could be regarded as forming the extension of the predicate "to be a natural number." Frege thought that he had found these objects in the domain of logic and that he had thus reduced arithmetic to logic. Numbers were identified with extensions of certain concepts. The number belonging to the concept F is the extension of the concept "to be equivalent to the concept F." Frege's attempt, which can be considered a relative consistency proof of arithmetic, was ruined when Russell discovered a contradiction in Frege's logic in 1901.

In an attempt to save Frege's enterprise, Russell introduced the theory of types, defining numbers as classes of equivalent classes. This definition yields a consistency proof of number theory relative to set theory. However, it is doubtful whether anything is gained. Sets themselves have to be defined. If they are taken naively, they are at the mercy of a paradox. If they are characterized by an axiomatic theory, the problems of consistency and categoricity will arise for that theory just as for arithmetic and will present difficulties of at least the same order (in fact, greater).

Relative consistency proofs have a limit: in the end there will be one or several theories whose consistency cannot be proved by such methods. For these theories we need a consistency proof of a different kind, an absolute consistency proof. Such a proof, like any proof, makes use of certain methods and tools, and it cannot be more trustworthy than the means on which it depends. Hence, in a sense, there is no absolute proof; every proof rests on something previously established or accepted. We can speak of a consistency proof as absolute, however, if, in contradistinction to a relative consistency proof, it is not a mere translation into another system. The first attempt at an absolute consistency proof of arithmetic was perhaps the one presented by Hilbert at the Heidelberg International Congress of Mathematicians in 1904 ("Über die Grundlagen der Logik und der Arithmetik"). It was a bare sketch, but it already contained the fundamental idea that recurred in Hilbert's subsequent attempts: to show, by mere considerations about signs, that a formula like $1 \neq 1$ is not derivable in the system.

Consistency of arithmetic. The search for an absolute consistency proof of arithmetic had become important because the consistency of other parts of mathematics (geometry and, with certain set-theoretic assumptions, the real number system) had been reduced to that of arithmetic, whereas the consistency of arithmetic did not seem to be reducible to that of any other branch of mathematics (if, as for very good reasons one might, one leaves out set theory). The search was a natural result of the emergence of the notion of a formal system, but the paradoxes discovered at the turn of the century gave it an added urgency (directly, and also indirectly by imposing the adoption of the notion of formal system). In the 1920s, Hilbert and his disciples made great efforts to secure a consistency proof of arithmetic. Results were published by Wilhelm Ackermann (1924), John von Neumann (1927), and Jacques Herbrand (1930 and 1931). But these results fell short of the goal. The arguments used in the proofs could establish consistency only if some restrictions were introduced in the axiom of mathematical induction. Consistency was proved only for subsystems of arithmetic. It was at this point that Gödel's paper was published.

PROOF OF GÖDEL'S RESULTS

To present Gödel's results and appraise their significance, a sketch of his proofs will now be given, not, however, for the system that he used, but for a simpler system, obtained by embedding the axioms necessary for number theory in a predicate calculus of first order.

The underlying logic is a predicate calculus of first order with identity. Its primitive symbols are $\sim$ (negation), $\supset$ (conditional), ((left parenthesis),) (right parenthesis), , (comma), $x, y, z, ,$ (lower stroke), and $=$. It has an indefinite supply of individual variables—$x, y, z, x_,, y_,, z_,, x_{,,} y_{,,} z_{,,} \cdots$ —and no predicate variables. The primitive symbols for number theory are 0 (zero), $'$ (prime, denotes the successor function), $+$ (addition sign), and $\cdot$ (multiplication sign). The natural numbers, $0, 1, 2, 3, \cdots$ (and these are meant, from now on, when numbers are mentioned), are represented in the system by the numerals $0, 0', 0'', 0''',$ $\cdots$ The symbol 0 followed by k primes (this represents the number k in the system) will be denoted by $0^{(k)}$. The axioms and rules of inference of the system are the customary logical axioms and rules for a predicate calculus of first order with identity, together with the following number-theoretic axioms:

$$(x)\sim(0=x'),$$
$$(x)(y)(x'=y' \supset x=y),$$
$$(x)(x+0=x),$$
$$(x)(y)(x+y' = (x+y)'),$$
$$(x)(x \cdot 0=0),$$
$$(x)(y)(x \cdot y' = (x \cdot y)+x).$$

The principle of mathematical induction is represented in the system by the following axiom schema:

$$A(0) \supset ((x)(A(x) \supset A(x')) \supset (x)A(x)),$$

where $A(x)$ stands for any well-formed formula of the system, and $A(0)$ and $A(x')$ are the results of the substitution of 0 and x', respectively, for x in $A(x)$. The schema yields an axiom whenever $A(x)$ is replaced by a well-formed formula of the system, and denumerably many axioms are thus obtained.

The system just presented will be called S. The system S provides a satisfactory formalization of that part of number theory which does not make use of the notion of limit.

Consider, for example, a system A that contains the individual constants of S but is somehow very deficient in its quantification theory. It may be that the formula

$$0+0'=0'+0$$

is provable in A; in fact, it may be that for any k the formula

$$0+0^{(k)}=0^{(k)}+0$$

is provable in A, while the formula

$$(x)(0+x=x+0)$$

is not. The system A would then be said to be ω-incomplete. A system of arithmetic in which the natural numbers are represented by individual constants is ω-complete if it contains no well-formed formula $B(x)$ such that $B(0^{(k)})$ is provable for every k whereas $(x)B(x)$ is not provable. An ω-incomplete system may even be such that while $B(0^{(k)})$ is provable for every k, not only is $(x)B(x)$ not provable, but $\sim(x)B(x)$ is provable. Such a system would be said to be ω-inconsistent. A system of arithmetic that contains a representation of the natural numbers is said to be ω-consistent if it contains no well-formed formula $B(x)$ such that $B(0^{(k)})$ is provable for every k and also $\sim(x)B(x)$ is provable. If a system is ω-consistent, it is consistent, but the converse does not hold, as will be shown later.

The formulas of system S are sequences of occurrences of the 14 primitive symbols. We now assign a number to each of these formulas. To each occurrence of a primitive symbol in a formula we assign a number according to the following code:

$$\sim \supset (\ ) \ , \ x \ y \ z \ , \ = \ 0 \ ' \ + \ \cdot$$
$$1 \ 2 \ 3 \ 4 \ 5 \ 6 \ 7 \ 8 \ 9 \ 10 \ 11 \ 12 \ 13 \ 14.$$

Thus, to a formula of S, say $(x)(x=x)$, there will correspond a sequence of numbers:

$$3, \ 6, \ 4, \ 3, \ 6, \ 10, \ 6, \ 4.$$

To this sequence we assign one number, namely,

$$2^3 \cdot 3^6 \cdot 5^4 \cdot 7^3 \cdot 11^6 \cdot 13^{10} \cdot 17^6 \cdot 19^4.$$

This is the Gödel number of the formula.

More generally, the Gödel number of a formula consisting of k occurrences of primitive symbols is

$$2^{s_1} \cdot 3^{s_2} \cdot 5^{s_3} \cdot \ \cdot \ \cdot \ \cdot \ p_k{}^{s_k},$$

where p_k is the kth prime number and $s_1, s_2, s_3, \cdot \cdot \cdot, s_k$ are the numbers assigned, in that order, to the occurrences of primitive symbols by the "dictionary" above.

A number of remarks can be made about the Gödel numbers of formulas:

(1) Every formula has exactly one Gödel number.

(2) Different formulas have different Gödel numbers.

(3) Given any formula, the method for obtaining its Gödel number is effective—that is, a well-determined result is arrived at through a finite number of well-determined steps.

(4) Given any number, there is an effective method for deciding whether or not the number is the Gödel number of a formula and, if it is, for actually writing down the formula.

Statements (1) to (4) hold, as can readily be seen, because every number has a unique prime factorization, and given any number, its factorization can be effectively obtained.

In the set of Gödel numbers of formulas we distinguish the subset of Gödel numbers of well-formed formulas and note that

(5) Given any number, there is an effective method for deciding whether or not the number is the Gödel number of a well-formed formula.

We now define the Gödel number of a sequence of formulas. If the formulas of the sequence have Gödel numbers $f_1, f_2, f_3, \cdot \cdot \cdot, f_k$, the Gödel number of the sequence is

$$2^{f_1} \cdot 3^{f_2} \cdot 5^{f_3} \cdot \cdot \cdot \cdot \cdot p_k{}^{f_k},$$

where p_k is the kth prime number.

We observe the following:

(6) Every sequence of formulas has exactly one Gödel number.

(7) Different sequences of formulas (differing either by formulas they contain or by the order in which these formulas occur) have different Gödel numbers.

(8) Given any sequence of formulas, the method for obtaining its Gödel number is effective.

(9) Given any number, there is an effective method for deciding whether or not the number is the Gödel number of a sequence of formulas and, if it is, for actually writing down the sequence.

A proof in S is a sequence of well-formed formulas satisfying certain conditions, and in the set of Gödel numbers of sequences of formulas we distinguish the subset of Gödel numbers of proofs. We observe that

(10) Given any number, there is an effective method for deciding whether or not the number is the Gödel number of a proof.

The reason for this will be apparent if one recalls what a proof in S is.

(It may be that a number is the Gödel number of a formula and the Gödel number of a sequence of formulas. There is no special reason to guard against this. The same typographical word may occur in English and in Hungarian, but this causes no confusion so long as we remember whether we are reading English or Hungarian. Note also that the Gödel number of a formula is not the Gödel number of the sequence consisting of just that formula.)

Consider now the predicate "u is a proof of v." This predicate holds for two numbers u and v if and only if u is the Gödel number of a sequence of formulas that is a proof of the formula whose Gödel number is v, or, more briefly, formula sequence number u is a proof of formula number v. The predicate is effectively decidable, in the sense that given any two numbers u and v, there is an effective method for deciding whether or not the predicate holds of u and v.

Consider also a function $w = f(s,t)$, where w is the Gödel number of the formula we obtain by replacing in the formula whose Gödel number is s each free occurrence of the variable y by $0^{(t)}$. (If y does not occur in formula number s, then clearly $w = s$.) This function is effectively calculable: given numbers s and t, we write down formula number s and the term $0^{(t)}$, perform the substitution, and compute the Gödel number of the formula thus obtained.

With a predicate $\Phi(u,v)$ we associate a function $\phi(u,v)$, the characteristic function of the predicate, such that $\phi(u,v) = 0$ if $\Phi(u,v)$ holds, and $\phi(u,v) = 1$ otherwise. The characteristic function of an effectively decidable predicate is effectively calculable. Observe also that if two functions $\phi(u,v)$ and $\psi(u,v)$ are effectively calculable, so is the compound function $\phi(u,\psi(u,v))$: from u and v the value of $\psi(u,v)$, say w, is found; then the value of $\phi(u,w)$ is found.

The term "effectively calculable," with regard to a function, has been used until now in a fairly clear, but intuitive and undefined, sense. There is a class of functions, the primitive recursive functions, that are effectively calculable. (Their exact definition is irrelevant to the present discussion.) We can also speak of primitive recursive predicates: a predicate is primitive recursive if its characteristic function is primitive recursive.

Gödel proved two crucial points in his 1931 paper:

(1) The predicate "u is a proof of v" and the function $w = f(s,t)$ are primitive recursive; so is the predicate "u is a proof of $f(t,t)$" obtained by substitution.

(2) Primitive recursive functions are numeralwise representable in Gödel's system (and would also be in our S) in the following sense: if the function $v = \phi(s)$ is primitive recursive, there is some well-formed formula $A(x,y)$ of the system such that $A(0^{(v)}, 0^{(s)})$ is provable if $v = \phi(s)$ and $\sim A(0^{(t)}, 0^{(x)})$ is provable if $v \neq \phi(s)$.

Being primitive recursive, the predicate "u is a proof of $f(t,t)$" is numeralwise representable in S and is represented by a formula $Q(x,y)$. Let i be the Gödel number of the formula $(x) \sim Q(x,y)$ and let G stand for the formula $(x) \sim Q(x, 0^{(i)})$.

Theorem 1, part 1. If S is consistent, G is not provable in S.

First, observe that the Gödel number of G is $f(i,i)$, because G was obtained when, in formula number i, we replaced y with $0^{(i)}$. If G were provable, the predicate "u is a proof of formula number $f(i,i)$" would hold for some u, and hence $Q(0^{(k)}, 0^{(i)})$ would be provable in S for some k. By the rules of quantification theory, $(\exists x)Q(x, 0^{(i)})$ would be provable, and hence so would $\sim(x) \sim Q(x, 0^{(i)})$. But this last formula is $\sim G$. Thus, G and $\sim G$ would be provable, and S would be inconsistent. By contraposition, if S is consistent, G is not provable.

Theorem 1, part 2. If S is ω-consistent, $\sim G$ is not provable in S.

Since S is ω-consistent, it is consistent; hence, by part 1 of Theorem 1, G is not provable, and the predicate "u is a proof of $f(i,i)$" does not hold for any u. Therefore, $Q(0^{(k)}, 0^{(i)})$ is disprovable for every k, or $\sim Q(0^{(k)}, 0^{(i)})$ is provable for every k. If S is ω-consistent, $\sim(x) \sim Q(x, 0^{(i)})$ is not provable; this last formula is nothing but $\sim G$.

Therefore, we have obtained a well-formed formula G of S such that neither G nor $\sim G$ is provable in S. The formula G is undecidable in S, and S is said to be incomplete.

By part 1 of Theorem 1, formula G, which is $(x) \sim Q(x, 0^{(i)})$, is not provable (if S is consistent, which is assumed in what follows). But the formulas $\sim Q(0^{(k)}, 0^{(i)})$, for $k = 0, 1, 2, \cdots$, are all provable. However, their generalization—namely, $(x) \sim Q(x, 0^{(i)})$—is not. Hence, S is ω-incomplete, according to the definition of this notion given above. We note that the undecidable formula G is of the form $(x)A(x)$ and that $A(0), A(0'), A(0''), \cdots, A(0^{(k)}), \cdots$ are provable for any k.

Before we proceed let us review the argument. Thus far, we have a well-formed formula G; its Gödel number is $f(i,i)$, where i is the Gödel number of another specific formula. When interpreted according to the metasystematic coding, G states that "formula number $f(i,i)$ is not provable," or, more vividly, "I am not provable."

Liar paradox. The analogy with the Liar paradox is obvious, but there are important limits to this analogy. If by any one of a number of known devices we make a sentence state "I am not true," we have a paradox: the sentence implies its negation; the negation implies the sentence. (The solution of this paradox will not be discussed here; it is generally solved by the introduction of a distinction between language and metalanguage.) But if we somehow make a sentence state "I am not provable," the paradox does not appear. Let g denote the sentence, and, insofar as the notion "provable" is concerned, assume merely that no false sentence is provable. If g were provable, it would be false, hence not provable; therefore, it is not provable (if P implies $\sim P$, then $\sim P$) and true (because of what it states). The negation of g, which states that g is provable, is false, hence also not provable. We skirt the paradox but never fall into it. The sentence g is unprovable and true; its negation is unprovable and false. The only point that may cause some surprise is that we have to introduce a distinction between "true" and "provable." If we refuse to do so, the paradox reappears.

Richard paradox. As Gödel noted in the introductory part of his 1931 paper, his argument is also related to the Richard paradox. Let us briefly review this paradox, in a form adapted to the present purpose. Consider infinite sequences of 0's and 1's. Such a sequence may or may not be definable in a finite number of words. List the finitely definable sequences in the lexicographical order of their definitions. A table is obtained that is infinite in two directions—for example,

(1)

$$\begin{array}{ccc} 1 & 0 & 0 & \cdots \\ 1 & 1 & 1 & \cdots \\ 0 & 1 & 0 & \cdots \end{array}$$

Now consider a sequence, to be called the antidiagonal sequence associated with the table, defined thus: "The kth term of the antidiagonal sequence is to be 0 or 1 according as the kth term of the kth sequence in table (1) is 1 or 0." With our example of table (1), the antidiagonal sequence would be $0\ 0\ 1\ \cdots$. The antidiagonal sequence has a finite definition, the sentence in quotation marks; hence, it should appear, at its lexicographical place, as a line in table (1). However, this sequence differs from any line of the table in at least one place: for any k, if the kth line has 0 as its kth term, the antidiagonal sequence has 1 as its kth term, and vice versa. This paradox, stated by Jules Richard in 1905, has been the object of much discussion. It shows, on the whole, that the notion "definable" lacks precision. By a suitable modification of Richard's argument it is possible to exhibit, in place of a not finitely definable sequence, an unprovable proposition and, at the same time, to avoid the paradox.

Consider the well-formed formulas of our system S that contain exactly the free variable x. These formulas can be ordered, say lexicographically. Let $F_i(x)$ be the ith such formula. We define a_{ij} and b_{ij} by

$$a_{ij} = \begin{cases} 1 & \text{if } F_i(0^{(j)}) \text{ is true,} \\ 0 & \text{if } F_i(0^{(j)}) \text{ is not true,} \end{cases}$$

$$b_{ij} = \begin{cases} 1 & \text{if } F_i(0^{(j)}) \text{ is provable,} \\ 0 & \text{if } F_i(0^{(j)}) \text{ is not provable.} \end{cases}$$

Using these definitions, we obtain the following tables:

$$
\begin{array}{cccc}
a_{00} & a_{01} & a_{02} & \cdots \\
a_{10} & a_{11} & a_{12} & \cdots \\
a_{20} & a_{21} & a_{22} & \cdots \\
\multicolumn{4}{c}{\cdots\cdots\cdots\cdots\cdots}
\end{array}
$$

(2)

and

(3)

$$
\begin{array}{cccc}
b_{00} & b_{01} & b_{02} & \cdots \\
b_{10} & b_{11} & b_{12} & \cdots \\
b_{20} & b_{21} & b_{22} & \cdots \\
\multicolumn{4}{c}{\cdots\cdots\cdots\cdots\cdots}
\end{array}
$$

The general term of the antidiagonal sequence associated with table (2) is $1-a_{jj}$, and the general term of the antidiagonal sequence associated with table (3) is $1-b_{jj}$. Now, if the antidiagonal sequence associated with table (2) appeared in table (2), there would be a k such that

(4)
$$a_{kj} = 1 - a_{jj}$$

for every j; the existence of such a k would lead to

(5)
$$a_{kk} = 1 - a_{kk},$$

which expresses the Richard paradox. But the antidiagonal sequence associated with table (2) may very well appear in table (3); that is, there may very well be a k such that

(6)
$$b_{kj} = 1 - a_{jj}$$

for every j. This is precisely Gödel's shift from "true" to "provable." The antidiagonal sequence is located not on a line of its own table, which would lead to the paradox, but on a line of some other table. (That a k satisfying (6) actually exists has to be proved, and a large part of Gödel's paper was devoted to the proof of just this statement, expressed in other terms.) By substitution, (6) yields

(7)
$$b_{kk} = 1 - a_{kk}.$$

If we assume that S is consistent and sound, no nontruth is provable; hence $a_{ij} \geq b_{ij}$, and (7) yields $a_{kk}=1$ and $b_{kk}=0$, that is, the existence of an unprovable true proposition.

Truth of an undecidable formula. In what sense is formula G, which was proved above to be undecidable in S, true?

The system S has an arithmetic interpretation that follows the customary rules for interpretations of applied predicate calculi of first order with identity. In particular, it is sound; that is, no provable formula is false under the interpretation. The rules are such that every closed well-formed formula takes the value *true* or the value *false* when certain values are assigned to its variables and constants. In the arithmetic interpretation, to an individual variable there corresponds a natural number, to the individual constant 0 the number 0, to x' the successor of the number corresponding to x, and to $x+y$ and $x \cdot y$ the sum and the product, respectively, of the numbers corresponding to x and y. The formulas $\sim Q(0^{(k)},0^{(i)})$, with $k=0, 1, 2, \cdots$, are fairly long when written out in full, and the statements of arithmetic that are their interpretations are fairly complex. How-

ever, since these formulas are provable and the interpretation is sound, the value *true* is assigned to each of them. By the rule of interpretation that governs the universal quantifier, $(x)\sim Q(x,0^{(i)})$ is true. Therefore, the undecidable formula G, when given its arithmetic interpretation, is a true statement of arithmetic, and $\sim G$ a false one.

The formula G is also true under the metasystematic coding: G is unprovable, and that is precisely what G states under that coding. The formula $\sim G$, which under the coding states that G is provable, is false.

Consistency of arithmetic. Theorem 1 has an important consequence for the consistency of S. The consistency of an axiom system such as S can be expressed in a variety of ways:

(1) There is no well-formed formula A such that both A and $\sim A$ are provable; or

(2) There is at least one well-formed formula A that is not provable; or

(3) $(0=0')$ is not provable.

Let us select any one of these statements, the last one, for instance. It can be written: "For every u, it is not the case that u is the Gödel number of a proof of $2^3 \cdot 3^{11} \cdot 5^{10} \cdot 7^{11} \cdot 11^{12} \cdot 13^4$." Let "$m$" denote this last number. There is a well-formed formula of S—namely, $(x)\sim P(x,0^{(m)})$—whose interpretation by the metasystematic coding is the statement in quotation marks. (The formula $P(x,y)$ is the well-formed formula of S by which the primitive recursive predicate "u is the Gödel number of a proof of formula number v" is numeralwise represented in S.) Let the formula $(x)\sim P(x,0^{(m)})$ be denoted by C.

Theorem 2. If S is consistent, C is not provable in S.

The well-formed formula $C \supset (x)\sim Q(x,0^{(i)})$ states, with our coding, that if S is consistent, formula G is not provable; hence, it expresses, in S, part 1 of Theorem 1. The proof of part 1 of Theorem 1, which makes use of relatively simple arguments, can be formalized in S, and we have the result that $C \supset G$ is provable in S. If C were provable, G would also be (by the rule of detachment), which would contradict part 1 of Theorem 1. Hence, if S is consistent, C is not provable in S.

In other words, the consistency of S is not provable by arguments that can be formalized in S. Theorem 2 gives to Gödel's results their full import. Theorem 1, in its strict syntactic formulation—that there exists an undecidable formula—remains of limited interest: even in the pure predicate calculus of first order there are undecidable formulas, namely, all satisfiable nonvalid formulas, such as $(\exists x)F(x) \supset (x)F(x)$. Theorem 1 acquires a new importance when its semantic aspect is considered, namely, when we recognize that the undecidable formula G is true (in the number-theoretic interpretation). The theorem then asserts that there exists an unprovable true proposition of arithmetic. The importance of Theorem 1 comes also from the fact that the undecidable formula has a special structure; it is of the form $(x)F(x)$, where $F(x)$ is primitive recursive. It is the specific form of the undecidable formula of Theorem 1 that leads to the proof of Theorem 2.

The proofs of Theorems 1 and 2 have been sketched for the system S, which is first-order arithmetic. Gödel proved the analogues of these theorems for a much stronger system, P, which includes the theory of types. Hence, his results are much stronger than our Theorems 1 and 2. However, Gödel proved that in P (or even in P enlarged by an additional ω-consistent decidable class of axioms) there exists an undecidable formula of first-order arithmetic. These powerful systems cannot decide all first-order arithmetic propositions. Moreover, the arguments remain quite similar, whether they are carried out in S or in P, and that is why S could be used in order to make the presentation simpler.

INFLUENCE OF GÖDEL'S RESULTS

Decidability and effectiveness. Gödel's results provoked immediate interest when they were published, and they were promptly accepted. The following years saw the appearance of a number of papers and works directly connected with these results. By dealing with an undecidable formula somewhat more complicated than the one considered by Gödel, J. B. Rosser ("Extensions of Some Theorems of Gödel and Church") was able to replace the assumption of ω-consistency made by Gödel in the proof of his analogue of part 2 of Theorem 1 by that of mere consistency. Once this modification has been made, parts 1 and 2 of our Theorem 1 can be combined into the following statement: if S is consistent, neither G' nor $\sim G'$ is provable in S (G' being the analogue of Rosser's formula in our S). In the proof of (his analogue of our) Theorem 2, Gödel had stated (and this is fairly clear) that the relatively simple arguments used in the proof of (his analogue of) part 1 of Theorem 1 can be carried out in his formal system P and hence that (his analogue of) $C \supset G$ is provable in P. In the second volume of their *Grundlagen der Mathematik* (1939), Hilbert and Bernays went through the painstaking details of the proof for two systems of arithmetic, Z_μ and Z (our system S is equivalent to Z). In 1934, Gödel gave a series of lectures at Princeton on his theorems; the notes of these lectures, prepared for publication by S. C. Kleene and J. B. Rosser, present the most important results of the 1931 paper in a more succinct form. These notes also codify the notion of recursive function (that is, general recursive, as opposed to primitive recursive), which had been proposed by Herbrand in his 1931 paper on the consistency of arithmetic and also in an unpublished, and presumably now lost, letter to Gödel. His purpose was to give a definition of what is intuitively meant by an effectively computable function, but his presentation suffered from several defects. Gödel, in the Princeton lectures, gave a complete and precise form to Herbrand's notion.

The next few years saw a rapid development of the theory of these functions, and Kleene, by means of them, was able to formulate undecidability results ("General Recursive Functions of Natural Numbers") of a somewhat different character from those of Gödel. Closely related to Gödel's results is Alonzo Church's theorem (1936) that there exists no decision procedure for deciding whether or not a formula of the pure predicate calculus of first order is provable. In 1937, Alan Turing published a long paper ("On Computable Numbers, With an Application to the Entscheidungsproblem") that gave the notion of formal system its full generality. Later, Alfred Tarski (*Undecidable Theories*) presented a general theory of undecidability.

Thus, Gödel's paper gave a strong impetus to the study of questions of effectiveness and decidability and marked the beginning of a new period in the history of logic. It was as important for the new methods it introduced as for the results it presented. The arithmetization of metamathematics—that is, the representation of metamathematical notions in the system S by means of Gödel numbers—became an everyday tool of the logician.

Nonstandard models of arithmetic. The undecidability of the formulas G and $\sim G$ entails that the formal systems S' and S'' that we obtain by adjoining G and $\sim G$, respectively, to the axioms of S are consistent (on the assumption that S is consistent). By the completeness theorem of first-order logic, S' has a model, M', and S'' has a model, M''. Both M' and M'' are models of S, but they differ: G is true in M', whereas it is false in M''. Hence, these two models are not isomorphic. Thus, Theorem 1 leads to the conclusion that there exist nonstandard models of arithmetic, that is, models in which the domain of individuals contains individuals other than $0, 0', 0'', \cdots$. As early as 1922, Skolem had stated that such models might exist ("Einige Bemerkungen zur axiomatischen Begründung der Mengenlehre," p. 224; see also *Über einige Grundlagenfragen der Mathematik*, pp. 45–47), and in 1933 he actually exhibited a nonstandard model of arithmetic (*Über die Unmöglichkeit einer vollständigen Charakterisierung der Zahlenreihe mittels eines endlichen Axiomensystems*). It can now be seen that the existence of such models is directly connected with the existence of propositions that are undecidable in S.

Consistency proofs of arithmetic. In 1936, Gerhard Gentzen published a consistency proof of arithmetic ("Die Widerspruchsfreiheit der reinen Zahlentheorie"; new, more readable version in "Neue Fassung des Widerspruchsfreiheitsbeweises für die reine Zahlentheorie"). The system that he considered is equivalent to our S, although formulated quite differently. Gentzen's method consists in transforming every proof in such a way that its last formula becomes a true numerical formula. He indicated the definite steps that must be taken to accomplish that end, and the essential part of his demonstration is to show that the reduction is accomplished after a finite number of steps. In order to show this, an ordinal is assigned to every proof and then use is made of transfinite induction up to a certain denumerable ordinal, namely, the first ordinal that is greater than all the ordinals of the infinite sequence $\omega, \omega^\omega, \omega^{\omega^\omega}, \cdots$ and was called ϵ_0 by Cantor. Transfinite induction up to an ordinal α is a method of proof that generalizes mathematical induction: if for any ordinal $\beta < \alpha$ a property holds of β whenever it holds of every ordinal $\gamma < \beta$, then the property holds of all ordinals less than α.

From Theorem 2 above we can infer that Gentzen's demonstration cannot be transcribed as a proof in S. In 1943, Gentzen presented a direct proof that the principle of transfinite induction up to ϵ_0 is not derivable in S, while transfinite induction up to any $\alpha < \epsilon_0$ is reducible to mathematical induction ("Beweisbarkeit und Unbeweisbarkeit von Anfangsfällen der transfiniten Induktion in der reinen Zahlentheorie"); hence, in a sense, his proof uses the minimum means that go beyond S. Transfinite induction up to ϵ_0 involves only a fragment of the denumerable ordinals, not the whole scale of Cantor's ordinals (where paradoxes may eventually appear); that fragment can, moreover, be introduced independently of Cantor's theory, by a process of "construction" that avoids the questionable parts of intuitive set theory. Whether one "sees" the ordinals up to ϵ_0, whether induction on these ordinals is more transparent than the original arithmetic axioms and logical rules that it is called to justify—all that seems to be a subjective question. The fact remains that the consistency of first-order arithmetic cannot be proved by any weaker means.

Other consistency proofs of arithmetic were presented by Wilhelm Ackermann (1940), P. S. Novikov (1943), Paul Lorenzen (1951), Kurt Schütte (1951; 1960), I. N. Khlodovskii (written 1946–1948, published 1959), Erik Stenius (1952), Gaisi Takeuti (1953; 1955), and Gödel (1958). Some of these proofs use methods similar to that of Gentzen, some follow different lines, but each of them at some point makes use of some argument that is not formalizable in S.

Theorem 2 also throws light on a number of consistency proofs of arithmetic that had been presented before the publication of Gödel's paper. As was mentioned earlier, the proofs of Ackermann, von Neumann, and Herbrand could not be carried out without the introduction of some restrictions on the axiom of mathematical induction. Since all these proofs employ means that are formalizable in S, Theorem 2 explains why they could not establish the consistency of the full system of arithmetic.

Systems with infinite proofs. As was noted above, S is ω-incomplete; that is, there is a well-formed formula—namely, $\sim Q(x,0^{(i)})$—such that $\sim Q(0,0^{(i)})$, $\sim Q(0',0^{(i)})$, $\sim Q(0'',0^{(i)})$, $\cdots$ are provable in S, whereas $(x)\sim Q(x,0^{(i)})$ is not. This is certainly a departure from intuition. It means either that the universalization of a proposition is unprovable while each of its instances is provable or that the proposition holds of objects other than $0, 0', 0'', \cdots$. (This shows again the connection between Gödel's results and the existence of nonstandard models of arithmetic.) To remedy the situation, one might propose adjoining to S the following rule: From $A(0)$, $A(0')$, $A(0'')$, $\cdots$, infer $(x)A(x)$. This rule, which we shall call the rule of infinite induction, was proposed by Hilbert at the end of 1930, soon after the publication of the abstract of Gödel's paper. It differs from the other rules of S (detachment, for example) in that it contains infinitely many premises. These premises have to be established by some metasystematic argument; that is, "for every k, the formula $A(0^{(k)})$ is provable" has to be established in the metasystem before we can infer "$(x)A(x)$ is provable in S." This means that the new system is not a formal system. (Schütte proposed calling such systems semiformal systems.) We are thus led to consider systems in which certain kinds of infinite proofs are admitted and to which Gödel's theorem does not apply. Such systems can be demonstrably ω-complete and consistent.

The question of infinite proofs had already been considered by L. E. J. Brouwer in 1927 ("Über Definitionsbereiche von Funktionen," p. 64, note 8) and by Ernst Zermelo in 1931 ("Über Stufen der Quantifikation und die Logik des Unendlichen"; see also "Grundlagen einer allgemeinen Theorie der mathematischen Satzsysteme"). While Brouwer's motives were quite remote from our present discussion, Zermelo wanted to avoid the consequences of the Löwenheim–Skolem theorem for set theory—that is, limitations that are inherent in formal systems and are not unrelated to those uncovered by Gödel. After the publication of Gödel's paper, Turing ("Systems of Logic Based on Ordinals") investigated logics that are not formal systems, and Rosser studied the effect of adjoining the rule of infinite induction to a formal system. Infinite proofs were already suggested by the assignment of ordinals to proofs in Gentzen's consistency proof, and in the 1950s such infinite proofs were investigated by Lorenzen, Schütte, and Ackermann. Since prior to one application of the rule of infinite induction the infinitely many premises have to be proved in a metasystem, a semiformal system can be regarded as an infinite sequence of formal systems, each of which contains all the preceding ones (the sequence may have an ordinal greater than ω). Hao Wang ("The Formalization of Mathematics") proposed a similar overlapping of formal systems to escape some of the consequences of Gödel's theorem.

Finitism. Gödel's analogue of our Theorem 2 marked the end of Hilbert's hopes of proving the consistency of arithmetic by means more restricted than those formalized in S. Hilbert's original idea had been that once mathematics was formalized, metamathematical investigations, such as those concerning consistency, could be reduced to perceptual considerations about strings of signs. In its extreme form this program is unrealizable. Consistency, the absence of contradiction, cannot be "seen." It has to be established by some argument—in fact, by an indirect argument: from the assumption that the system contains a contradiction, some refutable conclusion must be drawn. The supply of finitary means was therefore left somehow, and finitism had a fringe of vagueness. Thus, although it was hoped that this fringe would remain well within S, and although Gödel's result was undoubtedly unexpected from the finitist point of view, Bernays, Hilbert's collaborator ("Sur les Questions méthodologiques actuelles de la théorie hilbertienne de la démonstration" and "Zur Beurteilung der Situation in der beweistheoretischen Forschung"), was able to claim with some reason that this result imposed an extension, rather than total rejection, of Hilbert's conception, since finitism was already a compromise between the original intention and the necessities uncovered by investigations of the 1920s. Gödel himself stated in his 1931 paper that his result did not contradict Hilbert's conception since there might exist a consistency proof of arithmetic that would be finitist and could not be expressed in the formalism of Gödel's system P. After Gentzen's proof, which showed what specific means are necessary for a consistency proof of arithmetic, Gödel interpreted his own result as establishing that such a proof must involve more than perceptual (*anschauliche*) properties of concrete combinations of signs, that it requires abstract notions in which the meaning of these combinations of signs enters (see "Über eine bisher noch nicht benützte Erweiterung des finiten Standpunktes").

Intuitionism. Gödel's results can be regarded as having established that mathematics cannot be formalized in one formal system. Some hierarchy of systems is necessary. This conclusion is, in a sense, a limitation on the notion of formal system. Hence, it brings support to that school in the foundations of mathematics which considers such a notion to be of minor significance—namely, the school of intuitionism. Although intuitionism would certainly not recognize Gödel's proof as a meaningful part of intuitionistic mathematics, it regards the very existence of such a proof as one more argument showing that Hilbert's program of founding mathematics on a metamathematical consistency proof cannot be carried out. The increasing interest in intuitionism has not, however, led to a general adoption of Brouwer's ideas. The construction of non-Gödelian systems, although necessarily going beyond the notion of formal system, has retained much of the spirit and methods of the Hilbert school. The climate of the investigations into infinite proofs and semiformal systems remains much closer to that of the Hilbert school than to that of intuitionism. The effect of Gödel's theorem upon the foundations of mathematics has been not so much a direct adoption of intuitionistic ideas as a reinterpretation of some of these ideas in semiformalistic terms.

EPISTEMOLOGICAL SIGNIFICANCE

The publication of Gödel's paper in 1931 marked an important point in the history of logic. The notion of formal system, introduced by Frege in 1879, had become by then the accepted standard of precision in the foundations of mathematics. It seemed to embody the Aristotelian ideal of a perfect deduction from first principles. Gödel's results, by showing that mathematics cannot be completely and consistently formalized in one system, shattered this ideal. The bounds of mathematics cannot be those of one system. Since mathematics has often been regarded as the standard of rational knowledge that other sciences should strive to attain, Gödel's theorems seem to acquire significance for the whole body of human knowledge; they certainly establish that the old ideal of a deductive system cannot be maintained. However, all sciences other than mathematics are so remote from a complete formalization that this conclusion remains of little consequence outside mathematics.

Gödel's results raise questions about the role of formalization and its relation to intuition: the undecidable proposition is, after all, decided, and by a fairly simple argument. The natural numbers, which cannot be uniquely determined by any formal system, are quite stable and unambiguous objects of our thought. Because of this discrepancy between intuition and formalization, Gödel's results have been called on to buttress various solutions of epistemological problems. But what can actually be inferred from the discrepancy?

A common argument runs as follows: We obtain the natural numbers from 0 by repeatedly taking the successor: $0, 0', 0'', \cdots$. This mode of generation seems completely transparent to our minds. We are not in doubt about what is and what is not a natural number. We can use the natural numbers for counting, and we are never going to confuse any natural number with some other mathematical object, such as a polynomial, or with some nonmathematical object, such as the Eiffel Tower. If formalization does not succeed in uniquely characterizing the natural numbers,

there is something inherently wrong with it, since the unaided human mind succeeds in doing that.

There are several flaws in this argument. The repeated iteration of the successor operation seems—and perhaps is—very clear to our minds, but it either is circular (to obtain any number, we take the successor of 0 a certain number of times) or rests upon hidden and rather complex set-theoretic assumptions ("finitely many times"). The intuitive characterization is so clear because, in fact, no definition at all has been given. A few numbers have been exhibited, and intuition is assisted by words like "repeatedly" and "and so on" or by three dots. The procedure would be unobjectionable if we wanted to define finitely many numbers. For practical purposes of counting, numbers up to some very large N would suffice. Such numbers could, of course, be completely characterized in a fairly simple formal system. However, we would still be far from the general notion of number. One could immediately raise the question of the existence of $N + 1$. But—what is more important—counting, even indefinitely continued counting, is not the only use to which we put numbers. We state propositions about all numbers and pass judgment on these general propositions. This requires the use of the principle of mathematical induction, which involves the notion of property or of set. These notions are such that as soon as they are brought in, the crystalline transparency of the number sequence vanishes.

We can distinguish three levels of complexity in the notion of number. At the first level we simply consider the successor operation, applied once: from an object n we go to an object n', which is the unique successor of n and is different from n. This is fairly clear, but even here the question arises whether n' is different from *any* number smaller than n. At the second level the successor operation is repeated "finitely many times," and we either fall into circularity or hang on to an intuitive notion of finite set. At the third level we have to stipulate that the objects obtained from 0 by the repeated application of the successor operation are *all* the numbers. We are therefore not justified in claiming that intuition directly leads us to an understanding of natural numbers, and the situation is perhaps not so different from that in many other parts of mathematics. The intuition that an eighteenth-century mathematician had of a continuous curve was quite secure, and for any simple curve he could confidently tell whether the curve was continuous; however, general statements involving continuity could not be firmly established until the $\epsilon - \delta$ definition of continuity was adopted.

We are led to similar conclusions if we consider the question of the truth of Gödel's undecidable proposition. This proposition is of the form $(x)A(x)$, with decidable $A(x)$. The truth of $(x)A(x)$ in the customary arithmetic interpretation is established by two arguments: (1) for each k, the formula $A(0^{(k)})$ is provable in S, and hence true, because of the soundness of the interpretation; and (2) from the truth of $A(0^{(k)})$ for each k we infer the truth of $(x)A(x)$. These two arguments are not the product of some intuition transcending all formalization. They can be formalized quite easily—not in S, but in a metasystem that contains the predicate "true in S." This metasystem, if formalized, will in turn contain an undecidable proposition, and we are led, as we saw above, to a sequence of formal systems, but this is very different from an intuition that would immediately proffer us the truth of $(x)A(x)$. It must be added that arguments (1) and (2) above yield the truth of $(x)A(x)$ provided S is consistent, and this assumption cannot be discharged by sheer intuition.

The bearing of Gödel's results on epistemological problems remains uncertain. No doubt these results and other "limitation" results have revealed a new and somewhat unexpected situation insofar as formal systems are concerned. But beyond these precise and almost technical conclusions, they do not bear an unambiguous philosophical message. In particular, they should not be rashly called upon to establish the primacy of some act of intuition that would dispense with formalization.

Bibliography

Ackermann, Wilhelm, "Begründung des 'tertium non datur' mittels der Hilbertschen Theorie der Widerspruchsfreiheit." *Mathematische Annalen*, Vol. 93 (1924), 1–36.

Ackermann, Wilhelm, "Zur Widerspruchsfreiheit der Zahlentheorie." *Mathematische Annalen*, Vol. 117 (1940), 162–194.

Bernays, Paul, "Sur les Questions méthodologiques actuelles de la théorie hilbertienne de la démonstration," in F. Gonseth, ed., *Les Entretiens de Zurich sur les fondements et la méthode des sciences mathématiques, 6–9 décembre 1938, Exposés et discussions*. Zurich, 1941. Pp. 144–152; see also discussion on pp. 153–161.

Bernays, Paul, "Zur Beurteilung der Situation in der beweistheoretischen Forschung." *Revue internationale de philosophie*, Vol. 8 (1954), 9–13. Discussion on pp. 15–21.

Brouwer, L. E. J., "Über Definitionsbereiche von Funktionen." *Mathematische Annalen*, Vol. 97 (1927), 60–75.

Frege, Gottlob, *Die Grundlagen der Arithmetik, eine logisch-mathematische Untersuchung über den Begriff der Zahl*. Breslau, 1884. Translated by J. L. Austin as *The Foundations of Arithmetic, a Logico-mathematical Enquiry Into the Concept of Number*. Oxford and New York, 1950; 2d rev. ed., 1953.

Gentzen, Gerhard, "Die Widerspruchsfreiheit der reinen Zahlentheorie." *Mathematische Annalen*, Vol. 112 (1936), 493–565.

Gentzen, Gerhard, *Neue Fassung des Widerspruchsfreiheitsbeweises für die reine Zahlentheorie*. Forschungen zur Logik und zur Grundlegung der exakten Wissenschaften, N.S. No. 4 (1938).

Gentzen, Gerhard, "Beweisbarkeit und Unbeweisbarkeit von Anfangsfällen der transfiniten Induktion in der reinen Zahlentheorie." *Mathematische Annalen*, Vol. 119 (1943), 140–161.

Gödel, Kurt, "Einige metamathematische Resultate über Entscheidungsdefinitheit und Widerspruchsfreiheit." *Anzeiger der Akademie der Wissenschaften in Wien, mathematische-naturwissenschaftliche Klasse*, Vol. 67 (1930), 214–215.

Gödel, Kurt, "Über formal unentscheidbare Sätze der Principia Mathematica und verwandter Systeme I." *Monatshefte für Mathematik und Physik*, Vol. 38 (1931), 173–198. Authorized translation by John van Heijenoort in *From Frege to Gödel* (see below).

Gödel, Kurt, *On Undecidable Propositions of Formal Mathematical Systems*, lecture notes by S. C. Kleene and J. B. Rosser. Princeton, N.J., 1934.

Gödel, Kurt, "Über eine bisher noch nicht benützte Erweiterung des finiten Standpunktes." *Dialectica*, Vol. 12 (1958), 280–287.

Herbrand, Jacques, *Recherches sur la théorie de la démonstration*. Thesis, University of Paris, 1930. Published in *Prace Towarzystwa Naukowego Warszawskiego*, Wydział III, No. 33 (1930).

Herbrand, Jacques, "Sur la Non-contradiction de l'arithmétique." *Journal für die reine und angewandte Mathematik*, Vol. 166 (1931), 1–8.

Hilbert, David, "Über die Grundlagen der Logik und der Arithmetik," in *Verhandlungen des Dritten Internationalen Mathematiker-Kongresses in Heidelberg vom 8. bis 13. August 1904*. Leipzig, 1905. Pp. 174–185.

Hilbert, David, and Bernays, Paul, *Grundlagen der Mathematik*, 2 vols. Berlin, 1934–1939.

Khlodovskii, I. N., "Novoe dokazatelstvo neprotivorechivosti arifmetiki" ("A New Proof of the Consistency of Arithmetic"). *Uspekhi matematicheskikh nauk*, Vol. 14 (1959), 105–140.

Kleene, S. C., "General Recursive Functions of Natural Numbers." *Mathematische Annalen*, Vol. 112 (1936), 727–742.

Lorenzen, Paul, "Algebraische und Logistische Untersuchungen über freie Verbände." *Journal of Symbolic Logic*, Vol. 16 (1951), 81–106.

Novikov, P. S., "On the Consistency of Certain Logical Calculus." *Matematicheskii sbornik*, N.S., Vol. 12 (1943), 231–261.

Rosser, J. B., "Extensions of Some Theorems of Gödel and Church." *Journal of Symbolic Logic*, Vol. 1 (1936), 87–91.

Rosser, J. B., "Gödel Theorems for Non-constructive Logics." *Journal of Symbolic Logic*, Vol. 2 (1937), 129–137.

Schütte, Kurt, "Beweistheoretische Erfassung der unendlichen Induktion in der Zahlentheorie." *Mathematische Annalen*, Vol. 122 (1951), 369–389.

Schütte, Kurt, *Beweistheorie*. Berlin, Göttingen, and Heidelberg, 1960.

Skolem, Thoralf, "Einige Bemerkungen zur axiomatischen Begründung der Mengenlehre," in *Matematikerkongressen i Helsingfors den 4–7 Juli 1922, den Femte Skandinaviska Matematikerkongressen, Redogörelse*. Helsinki, 1923. Pp. 217–232.

Skolem, Thoralf, *Über einige Grundlagenfragen der Mathematik*. Skrifter Utgitt av det Norske Videnskaps-akademi i Oslo, I. Matematisk-naturvidenskapelig Klasse 1929, No. 4.

Skolem, Thoralf, *Über die Unmöglichkeit einer vollständigen Charakterisierung der Zahlenreihe mittels eines endlichen Axiomensystems*. Norsk Matematisk Forenings Skrifter, Series 2, No. 10 (1933). Pp. 73–82.

Stenius, Erik, "Das Interpretationsproblem der formalisierten Zahlentheorie und ihre formale Widerspruchsfreiheit." *Acta Academiae Aboensis, Mathematica et Physica*, Vol. 18, No. 3 (1952).

Takeuti, Gaisi, "On a Generalized Logic Calculus." *Japanese Journal of Mathematics*, Vol. 23 (1953), 39–96. Errata, Vol. 24 (1954), 149–156.

Takeuti, Gaisi, "On the Fundamental Conjecture of GLC." *Journal of the Mathematical Society of Japan*, Vol. 7 (1955), 249–275, 394–408.

Tarski, Alfred; Mostowski, Andrzej; and Robinson, R. M., *Undecidable Theories*. Amsterdam, 1953.

Turing, A. M., "On Computable Numbers, With an Application to the Entscheidungsproblem." *Proceedings of the London Mathematical Society*, 2d series, Vol. 42 (1936–1937), 230–265; Vol. 43 (1937), 544–546.

Turing, A. M., "Systems of Logic Based on Ordinals." *Proceedings of the London Mathematical Society*, Vol. 45 (1939), 161–228.

Van Heijenoort, John, *From Frege to Gödel, Source Book on Mathematical Logic, 1879–1931*. Cambridge, Mass., 1966.

Von Neumann, John, "Zur Hilbertschen Beweistheorie." *Mathematische Zeitschrift*, Vol. 26 (1927), 1–46.

Wang, Hao, "The Formalization of Mathematics." *Journal of Symbolic Logic*, Vol. 19 (1954), 241–266.

Zermelo, Ernst, "Über Stufen der Quantifikation und die Logik des Unendlichen." *Jahresbericht der Deutschen Mathematiker-Vereinigung*, Vol. 41 (1932), 2d sec, 85–88.

Zermelo, Ernst, "Grundlagen einer allgemeinen Theorie der mathematischen Satzsysteme (Erste Mitteilung)." *Fundamenta Mathematicae*, Vol. 25 (1935), 136–146.

J. VAN HEIJENOORT

GODFREY OF FONTAINES, scholastic philosopher and theologian, was a native of Fontaines-les-Hozémont in the principality of Liège. He was born of a noble family about the middle of the thirteenth century, the exact date unknown. About 1270 he began studies at the University of Paris and became a *magister regens* in the faculty of theology there in 1285, having studied under Henry of Ghent and Gervais of Mt. St. Elias. His regency lasted until 1297, and during this period he produced 14 of his *Quodlibets,* his most important works. There is evidence that he resumed teaching at Paris about 1303 or 1304, composing *Quodlibet* XV at this time. Canon of Liège, probably also of Paris, and provost of Cologne (1287–1298), Godfrey was chosen bishop of Tournai in 1300 but renounced his rights when the election was contested. He is cited among the senior members of the Sorbonne until 1306 and probably died about that time. The obituary at the Sorbonne dates his death October 29, but does not give the year.

Godfrey's doctrinal preferences generally favor the positions of St. Thomas Aquinas, but he manifests a marked independence of judgment on certain points and sometimes works out the logic of Aquinas' principles to different conclusions. Some historians (M. De Wulf, E. Gilson) see Godfrey as an opponent of St. Thomas' distinction between essence and existence in finite being, and attribute Godfrey's stand to a hard-and-fast Aristotelianism that refused to admit an act of the form. Others see Godfrey as opposing the realism of Giles of Rome rather than St. Thomas. Godfrey held that in the divine mind there is no proper idea of individuals distinct from their species. On the hotly debated issue of the oneness or plurality of substantial forms in composite beings, Godfrey always remained hesitant. He would have favored the doctrine of the unicity of form were it not for the fact that it seemed to contradict theological truths.

Godfrey showed particular acumen in his treatment of psychological problems. Under the influence of Averroës, probably through Siger of Brabant, he espoused an Aristotelianism stricter than that of most of his contemporaries. Godfrey criticized and rejected the so-called Augustinian theory on the genesis of ideas, insisting on the close dependence of human concepts on sense experience. He insisted strongly on the passive nature of the human intellect—the abstractive function of the agent intellect does not consist in the production of any positive disposition in the sensible image upon which it works, but in disregarding in a merely negative way the concrete particularizations characteristic of the image. This outlook is intimately connected with an Avicennan realism of abstract essence, so that Godfrey held that the intellect does not produce intelligibility or universality either in things or in images, but that the agent intellect places the images under an illumination such that the quiddity or essence of the object can appear alone and act on the possible intellect and become known to us.

In his explanation of human free will Godfrey adhered closely to the Thomistic doctrine, but he insisted more than St. Thomas upon the freedom of the intellect as its foundation. Against the voluntarism of Henry of Ghent, Godfrey stressed the formal influence of the intellect upon the will to the point of making it an efficient cause, whereas St. Thomas, in different historical circumstances against the Averroists, minimized the formal influence of the object upon the will. In other respects Godfrey did not break cleanly with the Augustinian tradition. For example, he made an interesting equivalence of the active and pas-

sive intellects with Augustine's "memory," the passive intellect inasmuch as it conserves species and is a *habitus,* the active intellect inasmuch as it contributes to actual knowledge.

Godfrey was a lively controversialist, combating at length the opinions of his contemporaries, particularly Henry of Ghent, Giles of Rome, and James of Viterbo. Not only did he engage in an active dialogue with his contemporaries, but he also occupied himself with pressing problems—moral, legal, social, and political—arising from daily life. Among his admirers can be listed John the Wise, Peter of Auvergne, and Gerard of Bologna; among his critics, Bernard of Auvergne, Gonsalvus of Spain, and John Duns Scotus. His influence was widespread and lasted well into the fourteenth century but waned thereafter.

Works by Godfrey

Les Philosophes Belges, Vols. 2–4 and 14, *Les Quodlibets de Godefroid de Fontaines,* M. De Wulf, A. Pelzer, J. Hoffmans, O. Lottin, eds. Louvain, 1904–1937.

Works on Godfrey

Arway, R., "A Half Century of Research on Godfrey of Fontaines." *The New Scholasticism,* Vol. 36, No. 2 (April 1962), 192–218.
De Wulf, M., *Un Théologien-philosophe du XIIIe siècle.* Brussels, 1904.
De Wulf, M., *Histoire de la philosophie médiévale.* Louvain, 1936. Vol. II, pp. 293–297, 308.
Gilson, E., *History of Christian Philosophy in the Middle Ages.* New York, 1955.
Gilson, E., *La Philosophie au moyen âge.* Paris, 1952.
Glorieux, P., "Un Recueil scolaire de Godefroid de Fontaines." *Recherches de théologie ancienne et médiévale,* Vol. 3 (1931), 37–53.
Glorieux, P., "Notations brèves sur Godefroid de Fontaines." *Recherches de théologie ancienne et médiévale,* Vol. 11 (1939), 168–173.
Lottin, O., *Psychologie et morale aux XIIe et XIIIe siècles.* Louvain, 1942–1954. Vol. I, pp. 304–339; Vol. II, pp. 267–269; Vol. IV, pp. 575–599, 682–683.
Lottin, O., "Le Libre Arbitre chez Godefroid de Fontaines." *Revue néoscolastique de philosophie,* Vol. 40 (1937), 213–241.
Lottin, O., "Le Thomisme de Godefroid de Fontaines en matière de libre arbitre." *Ibid.,* 554–573.
Überweg, F., *Grundriss der Geschichte der Philosophie,* 12th ed. Basel, 1951. Vol. II, pp. 502–504, 765.

ROBERT J. ARWAY, C.M.

GODWIN, WILLIAM (1756–1836), English political philosopher, novelist, and essayist, was born at Wisbech, in Cambridgeshire, where his father was a dissenting minister. He was educated at Hoxton, one of the dissenting colleges that had been founded because of the refusal of the established universities to admit nonconformists, and himself entered the ministry in 1778. By 1783, apparently as the result of reading Helvétius and Holbach, he had lost his faith, and instead took to literature as a means of livelihood. Much that he wrote at this time was hack work, including three novels, none of which have survived. He did, however, gain some reputation as a political journalist, contributing regularly to such Whig publications as *The Political Herald* and *The New Annual Register.*

In 1791 Godwin managed to free himself from hack work

by persuading a publisher to subsidize him while he settled down to a serious treatise on political theory. The *Enquiry concerning Political Justice* (London, 1793) was the kind of book the intellectual radicals of the day had been waiting for, and Godwin soon became a celebrity. In this work, he set down, with passionate sincerity and a complete absence of compromise, the radical beliefs that were emerging from the French Revolution and the intellectual ferment that had preceded it. The book went through three editions (2d ed., 1796; 3d ed., 1798).

For a few years Godwin was happy and successful. His novel *Things as They Are; or, the Adventures of Caleb Williams* (London, 1794) was widely acclaimed as a masterpiece. In the same year, his *Cursory Strictures on the charge delivered by Lord Chief Justice Eyre to the Grand Jury* (London, 1794) which protested against the committal on charges of treason of twelve leading radicals, may have been partly responsible for the acquittal of three of the defendants and the dropping of the charges against the others. He also published a volume of essays, *The Enquirer* (London, 1797).

In 1797 Godwin married Mary Wollstonecraft, the author of *A Vindication of the Rights of Woman*. She died in the same year, a few days after the birth of their daughter Mary, who was to become the wife of Shelley. In 1798 Godwin wrote a memoir of his wife (*Memoirs of the Author of A Vindication of the Rights of Woman*, London, 1798), and in the following year another novel, *St. Leon* (London, 1799).

From then on his fortunes declined. Radicalism came into disfavor, and Godwin was fiercely attacked, sometimes by his former friends. One of these preached a sermon against him, to which he replied in *Thoughts Occasioned by Dr. Parr's Spital Sermon* (London, 1801).

In the same year, 1801, he married a widow, Mary Jane Clairmont. His second marriage was less happy than his first. Before long he was back at hack work, and the last years of his life were spent in poverty.

Though he continued writing until his death, many of his later books were potboilers. The most important of these works (all of which, with one exception, were published in London) are his novels *Fleetwood* (1805), *Mandeville* (Edinburgh, 1817), *Cloudesley* (1830), and *Deloraine* (1833); his *Life of Chaucer* (1803); *An Essay on Sepulchres* (1809); *Of Population* (1820), a reply to Malthus; and *Thoughts on Man* (1821). He had expressed his views on religion in a book which he called *The Genius of Christianity Unveiled*, but it was not published until long after his death, when it appeared under the title of *Essays Never Before Published* (London, 1873).

ANARCHISM

Godwin's political theory is uncompromisingly anarchist. He was opposed to all kinds of coercion, including punishment, partly because of his determinism. "The assassin," he said in *Political Justice*, "can no more help the murder he commits than the knife in his hand." Such a view might be thought to lead to an authoritarianism based on the need to condition men rigidly so that their actions will not be antisocial. Godwin did indeed believe that it is

society that molds men's characters and actions. He was one of the earliest proponents of what is now called cultural determinism, but he combined this view with a quite extreme liberalism and individualism.

Types of society. Before Godwin, Montesquieu (and indeed Plato) had already maintained that each type of government developed not only its own characteristic type of institution, but also its own characteristic attitudes and value judgments within the minds of its citizens. Montesquieu distinguished three main types of government, each with its own characteristic "spirit": despotism, whose spirit is fear; monarchy (the aristocratic semifeudal type of society still current in most of eighteenth-century Europe), whose spirit is honor; and the republic (which for Montesquieu suggested Sparta, oddly idealized in the eighteenth century, as much as the actual contemporary example), whose spirit is virtue, used not quite in its modern sense but rather to mean public-spiritedness.

Where Godwin differed from the modern anthropologist and, to some extent at least, from Montesquieu, was that he saw all three types of society as corrupting their citizens—even monarchy, with its ideal of honor, so much admired in Godwin's time. Honor demands that one shall do what is fitting to one's rank; this was thought a sufficient motive to keep the wheels of society turning and to insure decent and at times even noble behavior. Falkland, in *Caleb Williams*, is a portrait of the Man of Honor. He is a thoroughly charming, accomplished, and benevolent man, but at the moment of crisis he is prepared to commit murder and further crime rather than see his good name disgraced. The moral is clear enough: honor is not enough to make men behave benevolently. Only benevolence will do that.

In some ways Godwin was more sympathetic to the republican ideal than to any other. Montesquieu's Republic is a state like Sparta, in which there is equality, frugality, and complete submission of the individual to the state. Godwin was strongly in favor of equality; he shared the republican objection to ostentation and luxury; and he agreed that it was the supreme duty of the individual to merge his own welfare with that of his neighbor. Nevertheless, Godwin rejected the republican ideal quite as decisively as the monarchic one—first, because it turns men's attention away from human beings toward a quite mythical entity called the State, and second, because it teaches men to merge their own judgment in that of the majority.

Corrupting influence of governments. Behind these objections, there is a quite general criticism which would apply to any type of government. Godwin believed that social institutions corrupt because they create prejudice; they prevent men from seeing things as they are. Men in society see themselves and one another through a mist of preconceived ideas—as members of this or that social class, as fellow countrymen or foreigners, but never as the unique individuals they really are. To some extent this is inevitable, in society or out of it: all generalizations, according to Godwin, distort the particulars which are subsumed under them; and yet it is impossible to think at all without generalizing. Nevertheless, to see things as they are, though difficult, is not impossible. However, it is peculiarly difficult to see ourselves and our fellow men as they are unless we can get close enough to them to sympathize with them and to realize the true complexity of their motives.

Government perverts our judgment in three main ways. First, it creates artificial barriers between men, as the result of social inequality and of the insincerity which results from the perpetual effort to keep up with the Joneses.

Second, it encourages us to do the right things for the wrong reasons. Patriotism and social prestige are both wrong reasons for treating other men benevolently. Punishment, which leads men to keep the law from fear and not because they understand the reasons for keeping it, acts in the same way. The objection to doing the right thing for the wrong reason is that, since it results in the muddling of men's minds, they will become quite incapable of adapting their actions intelligently to changed circumstances; and consequently the things they do will not for long be the right ones.

Third, government encourages us to acquiesce in the opinions of others, whether of the majority or some minority of rulers. This means that we accept conclusions without really understanding the evidence upon which they are based. Consequently we are acting from prejudice, without any real understanding. Once again, this can only make us unfit to cope with a complex and changing world. "The history of mankind," Godwin said, "is little else than a record of crimes" (*Political Justice*, I, ii), crimes which are caused ultimately by man's inability to see things as they are and to think clearly about them.

The ideal society. For these reasons, Godwin rejected all three of Montesquieu's forms of society. Godwin did not, however, merely want to put a fourth type of government in place of the other three. He believed not merely that all existing governments have corrupted society, but also that government as such is necessarily corrupting.

In what kind of society, then, can one hope to escape prejudice? Obviously not in a large society, because every individual is unique, and one can avoid prejudice only by an intimate and sympathetic understanding of one's fellows. Indeed, it is rare enough to know even one person well enough not to misjudge him. In this connection, it is worth noticing that Godwin had an almost morbid obsession with friendship. In all his novels the central figure complains of being without a friend, and is cut off from the rest of his fellows—usually as the result of his own prejudices. This loneliness is, for Godwin, the central tragedy of the human situation.

The ideal community, then, must not be large and must not be highly organized. The citizen must never be a cog in a machine, unable to see the significance of his everyday activities. There must be no class distinctions which prevent us from seeing individuals as individuals. And there must be no formal rules and regulations, because these are rules of thumb which demand the acquiescence of the individual in propositions he doesn't really understand. For the same reason, there is to be no punishment. For Godwin, the ideal society is one in which individuals cooperate without any kind of compulsion because they like and understand each other and wish each other well.

The need for gradual change. Godwin's ideal society is usually criticized as absurdly unpractical and utopian. The truth is that he was not really a political reformer in the ordinary sense. He was not very interested in blueprints for a "brave new world"; he did not believe in political organizations, and he had no program. He was primarily a moralist concerned with analyzing the causes of prejudice; once we understand these, according to him, the cure may very well be left to look after itself. We need to have some vague idea of the direction in which we wish to move, but we need have no more than that, because change can be brought about only very slowly and gradually. Godwin insisted again and again upon the folly of violent change. We can do nothing here and now but try to make a few small breaches in the wall of prejudice. If enough people can be brought to see what is wrong with society, society will right itself—but only by slow and gradual changes that will take generations. There is no question of a political program; political organizations are themselves a cause of prejudice. We are not even to point the way to the new society by setting an example of a better way of life. It is by reasoning and discussion that we must break down existing prejudice. The immediate task is to destroy the current ideals of honor and virtue. These ideologies have been created by existing institutions. They can be destroyed without destroying these institutions, however, because though prejudice is strong, it cannot entirely blind men to the facts. When supported by existing institutions, opinion can only be changed slowly—but it can be changed, and as it changes, the institutions will gradually be transformed.

MORAL THEORY

Society is to be transformed, then (even if only slowly and gradually), by means of a change in men's opinions—chief among them their opinions about what is desirable. But here a major difficulty presents itself. Even if men can be brought to see things as they are, how can their moral beliefs be changed thereby, since, as Hume had pointed out, it is impossible to derive any conclusion about what ought to be the case from knowledge about what is the case? Godwin knew of Hume's views and agreed with them, at least in part. In a certain sense, Godwin believed that virtue is knowledge; but he also insisted quite emphatically that "moral reasoning is nothing but the awakening of certain feelings" (*Political Justice*). It is in order to reconcile these two positions that he introduced his concept of natural goodness.

Godwin's utilitarianism. Godwin was a thoroughgoing utilitarian. For him, the right action is the one that makes for the greatest happiness of the greatest number. His utilitarianism, however, is unusual in two respects. First, it is not derived from egoism: the "greatest happiness" principle is ultimate, and cannot be derived from self-interest. Second, Godwin was quite prepared to push utilitarianism to its logical conclusion and openly embrace the consequences which many critics have regarded as fatal to it. He repudiated as immoral any obligations which cannot be derived from the general obligation to promote the general happiness—such obligations, for example, as promises and other contractual obligations, or the domestic obligation to prefer the happiness of one's friends and family to the greater happiness of others. He caused considerable scandal by the passage in *Political Justice* in which he said that one ought to save Fénelon from a burning building rather than his chambermaid (supposing that the archbishop has more to contribute to the general happiness), even if the chambermaid is one's own mother.

Knowledge and virtue. For Godwin, then, our belief that *X* is desirable is true only when *X* is something that will make for the general happiness. Since "moral reasoning is nothing but the awakening of certain feelings," the virtuous man is the one who does desire whatever makes for the general happiness. How will seeing things as they are awaken this desire? The following may serve as an example: If someone says that it is a bad thing that millions of people in a distant part of the world are starving, I may very well agree, but the chances are that I won't do anything about it. But now suppose that one of them comes and starves on my doorstep. Almost certainly I shall be moved to feed him. When I see a man starving before my eyes, the proposition "starvation ought to be relieved" takes on a new meaning for me. I can now see in detail precisely how and why starvation is evil; I can see exactly how the generalization applies to the particular instance. It is not a question of perfect knowledge being reinforced by emotion, since my knowledge before was imperfect. When it becomes perfect, it necessarily brings the emotion with it. Thus, if I *know* in this sense that *X* is desirable, and if I not only accept this as a rule of thumb but also fully understand the evidence on which it is based, then I cannot but desire it.

The causes of imperfection. Because he held that men are "perfectible" and "naturally good," Godwin has been accused of excessive optimism. He did not mean, however, that men are, or are likely to become, perfect. He was merely saying that imperfection has causes (usually social causes) which may be removed. To talk about original sin is to give up the search for the causes of sin. It is as if we were to say "disease is a natural phenomenon" and turn our backs on medicine. In general, no doubt, wickedness, like disease, is always with us; but any particular piece of wickedness, like any particular disease, has specific causes, and it may be possible to remove them. That the causes are far-reaching and difficult to remove, Godwin did not deny. He was even prepared to grant that there may be "something in the nature of man incompatible with absolute perfection." Men can never fully understand the principle of universal benevolence, simply because they cannot hope to know all their fellows intimately. But this is an ideal toward which we can strive and which, even if it can never be reached, can always be brought a little closer.

Rights. As a thoroughgoing utilitarian, Godwin, like Bentham, denied that there are any natural rights. The only right, which is also a duty, is to do whatever makes for the general happiness. He would not concede the rights to life and liberty. Nevertheless, the individual has one right—the right of private judgment. The reason for this is simply that, in the final analysis, nothing will be gained if

men do not understand the reasons for acting as we wish them to act. When men see things as they are, they will quite freely and without any kind of coercion do what makes for the general happiness. Any attempt to coerce them will hinder them from seeing things as they are and will therefore do more harm than good. In this way, Godwin was able to reconcile utilitarianism with the utmost insistence on individual freedom, and especially on freedom of thought and opinion.

The basis of Godwin's ethics. Godwin's basic beliefs may be summarized in three propositions—one about ethics, one about logic, and one about social psychology.

The nature of virtue. The ethical proposition is that to be virtuous is to feel the right emotions. The right emotions are those that men feel when they see all the facts clearly. When we analyze these emotions, we find that they are all consistent with the "greatest happiness" principle.

In the last analysis, statements about morals are expressions of feeling. But this does not mean that we cannot reason about morals. There are good and bad reasons for feeling frightened or angry. Fear is appropriate in a situation of danger. We do not doubt that if once we make a man see the full facts of the situation, the emotion of fear will come of its own accord. In the same way, if we want men to feel the appropriate emotions of benevolence, pity, affection, and so on, we can do it by making them realize the full facts about human beings. It is in this sense that men are naturally good.

Generalizations. The logical proposition is that true knowledge is of particulars and all generalizations are, if not false, at least seriously misleading. It is possible to know in a sense that a situation is dangerous without feeling the appropriate emotion. A man may ignore the danger out of bravado, but in that case we may say that he does not fully appreciate the danger. He knows, as a generalization, that the situation is dangerous, but he does not know the particulars which the generalization expresses—which is to say that he does not really know the generalization at all.

But we cannot, of course, do without generalizations. It is impossible to know every particular in all its particularity. Here, then, is an inescapable source of error. It is particularly likely to mislead us in our judgments of human beings and of human actions, for every human being is unique. Since we cannot know everyone intimately, we have to rely on generalizations, any one of which may be seriously misleading when applied to a given individual. Such generalizations form, as it were, a distorting glass through which we look at the world. And, since virtue depends on feeling the appropriate emotions toward other human beings, emotions which depend on a clear perception of all particulars, the logical proposition is an adequate explanation of human frailty. It also explains what Godwin meant by prejudice.

Political institutions influence beliefs. The proposition about social psychology is that the generalizations men believe depend on the political institutions under which they live. In practice, the particular distorting glasses we use are, so to speak, handed out to us by the governments under which we live. Our opinions about how human beings actually behave are influenced by concepts derived from legal institutions, like "thief" or "murderer," or concepts derived from social institutions, like "lord" or "pauper." These stereotypes come between us and the actual human beings around us. Our opinions about how human beings ought to behave are distorted by concepts like "honor" and "virtue," which stem directly from political institutions, as Montesquieu had clearly demonstrated. This is what Godwin meant by the corrupting effect of government.

Godwin's solution. Two main conclusions follow from these three basic beliefs: first, that if we want to improve human beings, we must help them to see things, and particularly each other, as they are; and second, that this can be done by simplifying society, by sweeping away social categories like rank and the legal categories that depend on punishment, and by encouraging individual judgment so that men will no longer trust to rules of thumb.

Bibliography

Godwin's books are out of print, except for *Political Justice*, of which there is a facsimile of the third edition, with variant readings from the other editions and a valuable introduction by F. E. L. Priestley (Toronto, 1946).

The most detailed biography is C. Kegan Paul, *William Godwin: His Friends and Contemporaries*, 2 vols. (London, 1876), which contains extracts from Godwin's letters and journals, not published elsewhere. More recent biographies are Ford K. Brown, *Life of William Godwin* (London, 1926); George Woodcock, *William Godwin* (London, 1946); and R. G. Grylls, *William Godwin and His World* (London, 1953).

There is a brief but useful analysis of his thought in H. N. Brailsford, *Shelley, Godwin, and Their Circle* (London, 1913) and a fuller one in David Fleisher, *William Godwin* (London, 1951). The philosophical issues are discussed in D. H. Monro, *Godwin's Moral Philosophy* (Oxford, 1953).

D. H. MONRO

GOEDEL'S THEOREM. See GÖDEL'S THEOREM.

GOETHE, JOHANN WOLFGANG VON (1749–1832), German poet, pantheist, novelist, and scientist. He was born in Frankfurt am Main and died in Weimar. Goethe's literary genius disclosed itself early. He wrote numerous lyric poems, invariably inspired by love affairs, while still in his teens. University studies in Leipzig and Strasbourg were less important to his development than were his extracurricular interests: occult philosophy, astrology, and religious mysticism while in Leipzig; and his friendship with Herder at Strasbourg, a friendship which evoked Goethe's passion for Shakespeare, nature, and German folk poetry. The historical drama *Götz von Berlichingen*, written while Goethe was a law student in Strasbourg, marks the start of his *Sturm und Drang* ("storm and stress") period. *Die Leiden des jungen Werthers* (*The Sorrows of Young Werther*, 1774), written to purge himself of the despair engendered by his love for Charlotte Buff, who married another man, marks the high point of this phase of Goethe's career. *Werther*, translated into numerous languages, made Goethe famous throughout Europe. Other works belonging to this period were the dramas *Stella*, *Egmont*, and the "Gretchen" episodes of *Faust*.

In 1775, at the invitation of Karl August, duke of Saxe-Weimar, Goethe moved to the court at Weimar. Here, in addition to his work as chief of state and his continued literary activity, Goethe's interest in the sciences developed. His official duties involved such diverse matters as horticulture, mining, road inspection, and later the management of the state theater. In Weimar, Goethe's involvement with Frau Charlotte von Stein, an intellectual lady of refined tastes in the arts, lasted for 12 years. His writings during those years included some of his greatest lyrics. It is said that Frau von Stein exercised a humanizing, moral influence on Goethe.

Goethe's trip to Italy in 1786 was to his own mind the climax of his life. In his thinking about art and literature, the classical ideal of calm beauty replaced the representation of tempestuous emotion and rebelliousness characteristic of the *Sturm und Drang* movement. *Iphigenie auf Tauris* (1787), a verse reworking of an earlier play, and *Torquato Tasso* (1789) exemplify the new style.

Returning to Weimar, Goethe took a new mistress, Christiane Vulpius, who bore him a son in 1789 and whom he married in 1806. Many of Goethe's scientific studies were published in this period: *Versuch, die Metamorphose der Pflanzen zu erklären* (*Essay on the Metamorphosis of Plants*, 1790), *Beiträge zur Optik* ("Contributions to Optics," 1791 and 1792). Earlier he had published his discovery that a part of the human jawbone is analogous to the intermaxillary bone in apes (1784). Goethe returned to Italy in 1790 but did not find the excitement and inspiration of his earlier travels. In 1792 he accompanied Karl August in a battle against the French revolutionaries. In 1794 began Goethe's friendship—more literary and intellectual than personal—with Schiller, which lasted until Schiller's death in 1805. Schiller was a sympathetic critic and he encouraged Goethe's work on *Faust*. It has been thought that Schiller's Kantian background stimulated Goethe's interest in Kant, but Goethe was familiar with Kant's writings even before 1794.

While the political and social tumult of the Napoleonic era dominated the minds of his contemporaries, Goethe calmly concentrated his attention on optics and plant morphology. Perhaps as a result of Goethe's indifference to the popular causes of nationalism and democracy, his reputation declined somewhat, but the appearance of *Faust* (Part I) in 1808 and the psychological novel *Die Wahlverwandtschaften* (*Elective Affinities*) in 1809 served to restore his stature. Some of Goethe's subsequent works were *Zur Farbenlehre* ("Toward the Theory of Colors," 1810), which contains an extended attack on Newton's theory of light; *Dichtung und Wahrheit* (*Poetry and Truth*, 1811, 1812, 1814, and, posthumously, 1833), a series of autobiographical essays; *Italienische Reise* (1816–1817), the record of his Italian travels; *Zur Morphologie* (1817–1824); and the second part of *Faust*, completed in 1831, just before his death. Goethe was buried in Weimar beside Schiller.

Philosophy. Although Goethe was not a systematic thinker and even asserted that philosophy only ruined him for poetry, he was aware of the philosophical and scientific tendencies and controversies of his time; and while he admitted his lack of a "proper organ for philosophy," he did not hesitate to express himself on numerous philosophical and scientific questions. In addition to specific essays and pronouncements, his poems and novels were often vehicles for expressing his intellectual convictions concerning God, man, and nature.

Spinoza and Goethe. The influence of Spinoza on Goethe's over-all *Weltanschauung* was considerable, although the importance of Kant, Leibniz, and Schelling is also evident. Goethe first became slightly acquainted with Spinoza's philosophy while in Strasbourg, but it was in 1774 that his acquaintance with Friedrich Jacobi (who regarded Spinoza's views as the only rational philosophy) drew his full attention to Spinoza. Goethe's commitment to pantheism is often cited to show his agreement with Spinoza. Yet when Goethe himself spoke of his relation to Spinoza, he emphasized the ethical as much as the metaphysical doctrines of Spinoza and Spinoza's "all-harmonizing peace," which contrasted with his own restlessness. Spinoza's rejection of final causes and his defense of determinism and of the view that praise, condemnation, and regret are attitudes reflecting an inadequate understanding of inexorable natural processes were accepted by Goethe and given expression in *Faust* (especially in the opening scene of Part II). Goethe said that Spinoza's mathematical method was the opposite of his own poetic way of feeling and expressing, and that Spinoza's orderly treatment of moral questions made Goethe his passionate disciple and convinced admirer. He defended Spinoza against the charge of atheism and claimed (without slavish regard for accuracy) that Spinoza was the most theistic and Christian of philosophers, since for him all existence is God and thus no proof of God's existence is needed.

The central thesis of Spinoza's system, Goethe thought, was that the universe contains and expresses a creative force which appears as a duality (*Zweiheit*) but is in fact a unity. God is not simply the cause but the indwelling spirit of the world, the all-embracing actuality. Goethe, however, questioned Spinoza's contention that reason can attain an adequate knowledge of God–nature. We cannot comprehend this infinite whole, and when we attempt to do so, even in a limited way, we must use imagination and intuition, not the method of mathematics.

Leibniz and Goethe. While Goethe's view of nature was, like Spinoza's, deterministic and nonteleological, his mystical feeling for nature was more akin to Schelling, and he resembled Leibniz in maintaining that everything in nature is in some sense animate (*Beseelt*). The universe consists of an infinite number of unique beings—Leibnizian monads—each alive and harmonious with all others. The essence of these individuals is activity and creativity. Goethe's knowledge of Leibniz was probably derived from Goethe's friend Johann Kaspar Lavater, the Swiss theologian who linked his theory of phrenology with the theory of Leibniz' monadology, and from Shaftesbury, whose presentation of Leibnizian optimism involved the belief, so congenial to Goethe, that nature's physical beauty expresses the divine harmony.

Kant and Goethe. Goethe was inclined to take from philosophers whatever elements or fragments fitted his intuitions and feelings. Thus, while he found Leibniz' confident optimism appealing, he also praised Kant for destroying the popular optimistic teleology of common-

sense philosophers who with Philistine wisdom sought to demonstrate that everything in nature exists to satisfy some human purpose. Goethe's enthusiasm for Kant was mainly based on Kant's *Critique of Judgment.* He was pleased with Kant's claim that nature and art both resemble purposive agents but pursue no external goal. He maintained also that art mediates between nature and freedom, since it is produced by the artist in conformity with principles that operate in nature as well.

Goethe, like many of Kant's contemporaries (including Mendelssohn and Herder), had little understanding of the *Critique of Pure Reason;* and while he praised Kant's ethics, he rejected most of Kant's central claims. In particular, he denied the opposition of duty and inclination, reason and sensuality, and regarded Kant's Calvinistic notion of a radical evil in human nature as a sad regression toward Christian orthodoxy. Goethe also took exception to Kant's view of knowledge. He insisted that imagination (*Phantasie*) was an avenue to knowledge distinct from and supplementary to Kant's faculties of reason, understanding, and sensibility. Furthermore, Goethe held, men are capable of intellectual intuitions, and with such nonsensuous insights they may hope to penetrate the heart of nature.

Scientific theories. Goethe thought his scientific theories were as important as his literary works. The concepts of primal phenomena (*Urphänomen*) and primal polarity (*Urpolarität*) were central to his conception of the world and were the foundations for both his scientific studies and his conception of man and existence.

Primal phenomena. Nature's secrets can only be understood by discovering, through intellectual intuitions, her ideal: ground phenomena. In optics the primal phenomenon is the opposition or antipathy of light and darkness. This *Urphänomen* (which in this instance is also an example of polarity) is the goal and limit of a scientific investigation of light. In mineralogy and geology the *Urphänomen* is granite, which Goethe believed to be the base of the earth's crust.

In the organic realm there are primal shapes and modes of development which nature repeatedly uses, like a theme and variations in music. The same organ is transformed manifoldly through metamorphosis. In plants the leaf is the organ which is varied to form all the parts of the plant. The study of the basic formations, morphology (*Gestalten*), would disclose the secret principles according to which nature operates. Seeking the primal image or idea by observing and comparing the metamorphosis of organisms, Goethe conjectured that a primal plant (*Urpflanze*), might be the basic model according to which all plants are patterned. This theory has sometimes been cited to show Goethe as a forerunner of the theory of evolution, but it is not at all clear that he believed in the historical evolution of species from a common ancestor. The doctrine of the *Urpflanze* is more Platonistic and, perhaps, mythical than Darwinian, Darwin's reference to Goethe as a "pathmaker" notwithstanding.

Polarity. Goethe's distrust of mathematics and experimental instruments (such as prisms) was, unfortunately, great. He believed that numbers and equations only distort our vision of nature. Newton's physics was repellent to him; Newton's theory that white light contained the spectrum seemed to him absurd because light was an elemental entity, an inscrutable attribute of the world that could not be analyzed. Goethe attempted to explain the origin of color phenomena out of an original polar opposition of light and dark. If light and dark are mixed directly, the result is gray; but a "murky medium" (such as a prism, according to Goethe) produces a cooperation of the polar opposites, and this cooperation produces colors. The activity of the eye in color perception is explained by the rule that brightness is "demanded" when the eye encounters darkness. The perception of every color produces a "demand" for the complementary color.

Goethe used extensively the idea of polarity, of attraction and repulsion as basic cosmic forces. He explained the metamorphosis of plants in terms of the periodic alternation of contraction and expansion. Contraction (*systole*) produces specific differentiation; expansion (*diastole*) produces an "advance into the infinite." The importance of polarity is seen also in magnetism—another *Urphänomen*—and in the activity of the heart, the rhythm of life, and in man's moral activity where the good is brought into play by its contrary, evil. Schelling had said that there is no life without opposites, and Kant had claimed attraction and repulsion to be the only essential forces of matter. Goethe adopted these principles in both his science and his art. The whole of existence is "an eternal parting and uniting."

Striving. Polarity is one of the driving wheels of nature, and while Goethe's use of this idea may suggest a cyclical view of life and history, his concept of gradation (*Steigerung*) is that of a constantly striving ascent. This upward striving Goethe believed to be a universal characteristic of nature. It discloses itself in the "higher intention" of every heavenly body and in the variations of similar organisms developing from a basic form. What Goethe meant by this is not very clear, but in *Faust* the idea is applied to man. Every man, said Goethe, innately feels an urge to strive upwards. This striving involves all his capacities, his creativity in every sort of action and experience. Faust's insatiable love of life and hunger for new experience are expressive of this natural longing.

Religion. Goethe early rejected positive religion. With Spinoza, he came to regard creeds and dogmas as irrelevant to the veneration of God-nature. Although Goethe was on friendly terms with many ardent Christians and although he even spoke at times of a providential God, he opposed the dogmatism of churches and theologians and regarded the idea of miracles as a "blasphemy against the great God and his revelation in nature." Since Goethe maintained that no set of concepts could be adequate to the unfathomable infinity of the divine, it is not surprising that his pronouncements concerning God are somewhat ambiguous and inconsistent. While the remark on miracles seems to imply a distinction between God and nature, this is, of course, not Goethe's usual position.

Goethe rejected asceticism and the tendency to devalue the physical in favor of a supernatural world. To Lavater he wrote that he could find a thousand pages of various books as lovely, useful, and indispensable to mankind as the Gospels. He claimed that he was unchristian rather than anti-Christian but declared the crucifix to be "the most repugnant thing under the sun." Although at one time he spoke of the Gospels as messages from God, he clearly did not intend this in the ordinary sense, since he held that God, being the inexorable order of nature, cannot have any personality or be in any sense outside the natural world. Thus God does not cause or control the world in the way that theists have believed. "What sort of God would it be, who only pushed from without?" (*Was wär' ein Gott, der nur von aussen stiesse?*, in *Weltanschauliche Gedichte*, 1815). The ambiguity (or richness) of Goethe's theology may be seen in what is perhaps his most famous remark on this topic: "We are pantheists when we study nature, polytheists when we poetize, monotheists in our morality" (*Wir sind naturforschend Pantheisten, dichtend Polytheisten, sittlich Monotheisten*, in *Maximen und Reflexionen*, No. 807).

Since every man is part of nature and, hence, of the divine, he shares the basic impulses of all natural things—specifically, as already noted, the urge to develop upward and outward, the striving for an ideal. Action and striving are not only means to some static goal but are also ends in themselves. Since there is no goal for man apart from his life, man struggles, like Faust, with the fear of life (*Lebensangst*) and is tempted by care (*Sorge*). Some have argued that Goethe saw man's fulfillment in activity itself, but perhaps it would be more accurate to say that there is no fulfillment—contentment means annihilation—so that man is destined to be dissatisfied, unfulfilled, no matter what he achieves.

Bibliography

Goethe's writings are available in many editions, one of the standard being K. Burdach and others, eds., *Jubiläums-Ausgabe*, 40 vols. (Stuttgart and Berlin, 1902–1907). Goethe's most important works, except *Zur Farbenlehre* and *Beiträge zur Optik*, have been translated into English. Goethe's *Botanical Writings* were translated by Bertha Mueller (Honolulu, 1952) and by Agnes Arber as *Goethe's Botany; the Metamorphosis of Plants* (Waltham, Mass., 1946). Of the dozens of English translations of *Faust*, recent versions by Bertram Jessup (London, 1958) and by Walter Kaufmann (New York, 1961) are sensitive. Kaufmann's version includes sections of Part II and has the German text facing the English.

For an account of *Zur Farbenlehre* and *Beiträge zur Optik*, see Rudolf Magnus, *Goethe als Naturforscher* (Leipzig, 1906), translated by Heinz Norden as *Goethe as a Scientist* (New York, 1949), a very sympathetic account. A more critical discussion of Goethe's contributions to science is found in C. S. Sherrington, *Goethe on Nature and on Science* (Cambridge, 1942).

Many philosophers have written on Goethe (Dilthey, Simmel, Max Wundt, Rickert, and von Rintelen, to name only a few), and some may be read in English: Ernst Cassirer, "Goethe and the Kantian Philosophy," in his *Rousseau, Kant, Goethe*, translated by James Guttmann and others (Princeton, N.J., 1945); Benedetto Croce, *Goethe* (Bari, 1909), translated by Emily Anderson (London, 1923); and the beautiful and perceptive chapter on *Faust* in George Santayana, *Three Philosophical Poets* (Cambridge, Mass., 1922). Thomas Mann's essays on Goethe, which include discussions of Goethe's political views, are in his *Freud, Goethe, Wagner*, translated by H. T. Lowe-Porter (New York, 1937) and in his *Essays of Three Decades* (New York, 1947). Karl Viëtor, *Goethe the Thinker*, translated by B. Q. Morgan (Cambridge, Mass., 1950), discusses Goethe's science and philosophy comprehensively. See also Fritz-Joachim von Rintelen, *Der Rang des Geistes* (Tübingen, 1955).

ARNULF ZWEIG

GOGARTEN, FRIEDRICH, German theologian, was born in 1887 at Dortmund. After serving as a pastor in Thuringia, in 1927 he became professor of systematic theology at Jena and in 1935 moved to the corresponding chair at Göttingen. He was early associated with the new dialectical theology and its revolt against liberalism and idealism. Within this movement he stands nearer to Rudolf Bultmann than to Karl Barth, but he has worked out a distinctive position of his own. His thought shows the influence of existentialist philosophy, but he claims that it also continues the insights of Luther, on whom Gogarten is a recognized authority.

Gogarten believes that Luther delivered Christian theology from the hold of metaphysics. This achievement was obscured in the period of Protestant orthodoxy following the Reformation, but it is now time to revive his insights, which can be restated in terms of current existentialist philosophy. According to Gogarten, the major Christian doctrines were formulated under the domination of metaphysical categories, in an age when history was understood as a process that takes place within a stationary metaphysical framework and when the course of history was supposed to be determined by metaphysical factors. Deliverance from metaphysics makes it possible to take history with a new seriousness. Man is responsible for history and creates it by his decisions. So far are we from having an obligation to interpret history in the light of metaphysics that we must rather view metaphysical systems themselves as products of history. Christianity is not dependent on any metaphysical system but is rather the summons to a historical self-understanding, in which we accept responsibility for our own historical existence under the word of God, which addresses us in Christ.

These emphases, which Gogarten relates as much to the *sola fide* of Luther as to modern existentialism, are developed into a secular interpretation of the Christian gospel. The Christian faith brings man to maturity and strips the world of every mythical or numinous property. The world is deprived of its religious power and is handed over to man as the son who has come of age, the heir to whom God has entrusted the creation. These views are related by Gogarten especially to the teaching of St. Paul in Galatians 4. 1–11.

Works by Gogarten

Ich glaube an den dreieinigen Gott. Jena, 1926.
Illusionen, eine Auseinandersetzung mit dem Kulturidealismus. Jena, 1926.
   Glaube und Wirklichkeit. Jena, 1928.
   Politische Ethik. Jena, 1932.
   Das Bekenntnis der Kirche. Jena, 1934.
   Die Kirche in der Welt. Heidelberg, 1948.
   Die Verkündigung Jesus Christi. Heidelberg, 1948.
   Verhängnis und Hoffnung der Neuzeit. Stuttgart, 1953.
   Entmythologisierung und die Kirche. Stuttgart, 1953. Translated as *Demythologizing and History.* London, 1955.
   Der Mensch zwischen Gott und Welt. Stuttgart, 1956.
   Die Wirklichkeit des Glaubens. Stuttgart, 1957. Translated by Carl Michalson and others as *The Reality of Faith.* Philadelphia, 1959.
   Gogarten has also edited various works of Luther and has contributed extensively to *Zwischen den Zeiten,* the journal of the dialectical theology group.

Works on Gogarten

Siegfried, T., *Die Theologie der Existenz bei Friedrich Gogarten und Rudolf Bultmann.* Gotha, 1933. The most satisfactory critical exposition of Gogarten's thought.

JOHN MACQUARRIE

GOLDEN RULE. One early use of the word "golden" in English is "most excellent, important, or precious." With reference to rules or precepts it was used to mean "of inestimable value," and the expression "the golden rule" was often specifically used with reference to the precept in Matthew: "Therefore all things whatsoever ye would that men should do to you, do ye even so to them: for this is the law and the prophets" (7.12). Thus, the principle that has come to be known as the golden rule has been so called presumably because it has been regarded as being of inestimable value or importance. This regard was not derived solely from the fact that it was set forth in the Sermon on the Mount. The golden rule has been widely accepted, in word if not in deed, by vast numbers of greatly differing peoples; it is a basic device of moral education; and it can be found at the core of innumerable moral, religious, and social codes. So far as can be determined from available records, it was probably first formulated by Confucius some five hundred years before Christ—"What you do not like when done to yourself do not do to others"—and the multitude of different formulations testify to its widespread acceptance and influence.

There is probably no principle which has been so widely accepted and remained so controversial. Nonetheless, the golden rule has been the subject of comparatively little philosophical discussion. It is usually mentioned, when it is mentioned at all, only in passing, and it has generally received more attention in theological and inspirational literature. However, there are signs of increasing philosophical interest in it.

One of its commonest formulations today is "Do unto others as you would have them do unto you." It is commonly supposed that there are significant differences between this, the positive formulation, and the negative formulation, "Do not do unto others what you would not have them do unto you," and that the positive formulation "marks a distinct advance" since it "prescribes positive services rather than mere abstinences" and "sets forth an ideal which is higher and therefore more difficult to realize." It can be argued, however, that this is an error resulting from faulty analysis and perhaps also from theological bias. In connection with a specific action or object of desire, there is a considerable difference between a positive desire, a desire to do it or have it done to oneself, and a negative desire, a desire not to do it or not to have it done to oneself. But in the abstract, so the argument runs, there is only a difference in formulation, and a want, wish, or desire formulated in negative terms can always be reformulated in positive terms. For example, there is no difference between not wanting others to lie to oneself and wanting them not to lie to oneself, wanting them to tell one the truth and wanting them not to fail to tell one the truth. In general, "A wants x to happen" is equivalent to "A does not want x not to happen," and "A does not want x to happen" is equivalent to "A wants x not to happen." Thus, according to this line of argument, every desire formulated negatively, which would come within the scope of the negative golden rule, can be reformulated positively and will then come within the scope of the positive golden rule. It would follow, then, that there is no logical or moral difference between the negative and positive formulations, only a psychological or rhetorical one.

On either account the negative formulation of the golden rule is to be distinguished from the denial of the golden rule: "Do not do unto others as you would have them do unto you." Obviously, this is not a formulation of the golden rule at all but is, rather, its total rejection. The denial of the golden rule is usually supported by the claim that the golden rule presupposes a uniformity of human nature, in the sense of a uniformity of tastes, interests, needs, and desires, and the attendant claim that there is no such uniformity. One way of meeting this objection is to deny that the golden rule involves any such presupposition. It has been argued that it is necessary to make a distinction between the particular interpretation and the general interpretation of the golden rule. The particular interpretation implies that whatever in particular one would have others do to or for him, he should do to or for them. It is in the particular interpretation that, to take some of the standard objections, the golden rule "authorizes the quarrelsome person who loves to be provoked, to go about provoking others, and the person who hates friendliness and sympathy to be cold and unsympathetic in his dealings with others" (L. J. Russell). But these consequences, it has been claimed, do not follow from the general interpretation. On this interpretation what one has to consider is not what in particular one would have others do to or for oneself but, rather, the general ways in which one would have others act in their treatment of oneself. If one abstracts his general wishes from his particular desires, what one would have others do is to take account of his interests, needs, and desires, which may be quite different from theirs, and either satisfy them or not wilfully frustrate them. What the golden rule requires a person to do, then, is to take account of the wishes of others and accord them the respect and consideration he would want them to accord to his. In other words, what the golden rule requires of each of us is that we should treat others in accordance with the same principles or standards that we would have others apply in their treatment of us. Thus, the golden rule, if this argument is sound, is compatible with differences in interests, needs, tastes, wishes, and desires and does not presuppose that human nature is uniform in the sense specified.

Another principle which should be distinguished from the golden rule is what might be called its inversion: "Do unto others as they would have you do unto them." The inversion of the golden rule has received some support, and it has even been urged that it replace the golden rule as a guide to conduct, mainly as a consequence of the same sort of objection as the distinction just outlined is intended to eliminate. It has been claimed that the inversion of the golden rule has "the merit of stressing the need for an understanding of other people as a basis of our behavior toward them" and does not presuppose any uniformity or identity of nature in the beings it is intended to govern.

One counterargument to this is that the implications of the inversion of the golden rule are more absurd than the alleged implications of the golden rule itself and that it is tantamount to a rule that would require everyone always to do whatever anyone else wants him to do, a rule it is impossible to follow in a world of conflicting interests. Once it is recognized, the argument runs, that the "uniformity of human nature," in the sense of an absolute identity of interests, needs, and desires, is not a presupposition of the golden rule, any temptation to substitute the inversion of the golden rule for the golden rule itself should disappear. For in its general interpretation the golden rule does require us to take account of and accord respect to the differing needs, interests, and desires of others, and it is just this that the inversion of the golden rule is intended to bring about. However, the question remains whether the inversion of the golden rule cannot be rescued from at least some of the more obvious objections to it by means of a distinction similar to that made between the particular and the general interpretation of the golden rule.

In the course of time a number of anomalous interpretations of the golden rule have found strong support. On the one hand, it has been said that the golden rule comprehends all the requirements of morality in a single formula; on the other, it has been said that the golden rule is only a guide, that it is far from complete, that it requires rules, a sense of justice, or even a whole system of morality for its proper interpretation and application. Again, the golden rule has been said to be not only consistent with but actually to comprehend all of utilitarianism; it has also been said to provide just that element, the requirement of justice or fairness, that is alleged to be most lacking in a utilitarian theory. On this interpretation the golden rule is regarded as being the basis of justice, sometimes also the basis or equivalent of Kant's categorical imperative. Finally, it has been claimed that the golden rule is a perfect guide to conduct and that the only thing needed to make the world perfect is for everyone to follow it; at the same time it has been claimed that the golden rule leads to paradoxes and is misleading, false, or absurd.

Each of the points and issues mentioned here is discussed, more or less adequately, in one or more of the sources listed in the Bibliography. But no one has yet dealt satisfactorily with the question of why this precept should have appeared in the codes and outlooks of so many diverse peoples and sages. The golden rule, in one version or another, has a prominent place in all the major religions and most minor ones; it has been enunciated by pagan philosophers both before and after Christ and by Sophists (Isocrates) and anti-Sophists (Aristotle). There are no detectable historical traces which could explain this, and the historical diffusion theory is worthless as an explanation here. The nearly universal acceptance of the golden rule and its promulgation by persons of considerable intelligence, though otherwise of divergent outlooks, would therefore seem to provide some evidence for the claim that it is a fundamental ethical truth.

Bibliography

Baier, Kurt, *The Moral Point of View*. Ithaca, N. Y., 1958. Pp. 202–211.

Browne, Lewis, *The World's Great Scriptures*. New York, 1946. P. xv.

Butler, Joseph, *Sermons*. Oxford, 1897. Sermon X, Sec. 18, pp. 154–155.

Cadoux, A. T., "The Implications of the Golden Rule." *The International Journal of Ethics*, Vol. 22 (1912), 272–287.

Dihle, Albrecht, *Die Goldene Regel, eine Einführung in die Geschichte der antiken und frühchristlichen Vulgärethik*. Göttingen, 1962. Vol. VII of *Studienhefte zur Altertumwissenschaft*.

Garnett, A. Campbell, *Ethics*. New York, 1960. Pp. 92, 126.

Goldstein, Morris, *Thus Religion Grows*. New York, 1936. Pp. 118, 127.

Gould, James A., "The Not-So-Golden Rule." *The Southern Journal of Philosophy*, Vol. 1 (1963), 10–14.

Hare, R. M., *Freedom and Reason*. Oxford, 1963. *Passim*.

Hertzler, J. O., "On Golden Rules." *The International Journal of Ethics*, Vol. 44 (1934), 418–436.

Hirsch, Emil R., "The Golden Rule," in *The Jewish Encyclopedia*. New York and London, 1904. Vol. VI, pp. 21–22.

Hume, Robert Ernest, *The World's Living Religions*. New York, 1927. Pp. 265–267.

MacIver, Robert M., "The Deep Beauty of the Golden Rule," in Ruth Nanda Anshen, ed., *Moral Principles of Action*. New York, 1952.

Ramsey, Paul, *Basic Christian Ethics*. New York, 1950. P. 61.

Russell, L. J., "Ideals and Practice." *Philosophy*, Vol. 17 (1942), 109–110.

Sharp, Frank Chapman, *Ethics*. New York, 1928. Pp. 140–141, 334–339.

Sidgwick, Henry, *The Methods of Ethics*, 7th ed. London, 1930. Pp. xvii, 379–380, 384–385.

Sidgwick, Henry, *Outlines of the History of Ethics*, 6th ed. London, 1931. P. 167, note.

Singer, M. G., "The Golden Rule." *Philosophy*, Vol. 38 (1963), 293–314.

Spooner, W. A., "Golden Rule," in James Hastings, ed., *The Encyclopedia of Religion and Ethics*. New York, 1914. Vol. VI, pp. 310–312.

Tasker, J. G., "Golden Rule," in James Hastings, ed., *A Dictionary of Christ and the Gospels*. New York, 1907. Vol. I, pp. 653–655.

Thomas, George F., *Christian Ethics and Moral Philosophy*. New York, 1955. Pp. 48, 55, 429–430.

Tsanoff, Radoslav A., *The Moral Ideals of Our Civilization*. New York, 1942. Pp. 171, 234, 414, 421, 496, 512.

Tsanoff, Radoslav A., *Ethics*, 2d ed. New York, 1955. Pp. 31–33.

Votaw, C. W., "Sermon on the Mount," in James Hastings, ed., *A Dictionary of the Bible*. New York, 1904. Vol. V, pp. 41–42.

Weiss, Paul, "The Golden Rule." *The Journal of Philosophy*, Vol. 38 (1941), 421–430.

Weiss, Paul, *Man's Freedom*. New Haven, 1950. Pp. 138–154.

Westermarck, Edward, *The Origin and the Development of the Moral Ideas*. London, 1906. Vol. I, pp. 102–103.

Whately, Richard, *Lessons on Morals*. Cambridge, Mass., 1857. Ch. 4.

Wheelwright, Philip, *A Critical Introduction to Ethics*. New York, 1949. Pp. 165, 207.

MARCUS G. SINGER

GOOD, THE. Following Aristotle, most philosophers have distinguished between intrinsic goods and nonintrinsic goods. An intrinsic good is something valuable in and of itself; a nonintrinsic good is something valuable by virtue of its relationship to an intrinsic good.

Nonintrinsic goods have been variously classified. That which is valuable as a means to the achievement of an intrinsic good is often called an instrumental good. If, for instance, health is considered an intrinsic good, then medicine and surgery would be instrumental goods. Something, such as a dissonant chord in a symphony, whose value depends upon being a part of a whole, is frequently called a contributory good. Finally, a number of philosophers who maintain that all intrinsic goods must be experiences of sentient beings employ the term inherent good, introduced by C. I. Lewis, to refer to the objective or material features of whatever serves as a more or less immediate condition of intrinsic good. If the pleasure experienced in contemplating a beautiful landscape is an intrinsic good, then the beautiful aspects of the landscape itself are inherent goods.

For the classification of intrinsic goods there is no clear and standard vocabulary. The terms "ultimate good" and *summum bonum* are often used for some allegedly superior intrinsic good, but these terms are ambiguous. Sometimes they mean the highest in a scale or hierarchy of values. This was no doubt Aristotle's meaning when he spoke of intellectual contemplation as the ultimate good and also St. Thomas' when he singled out beatitude as the *summum bonum*. Often, however, the terms are used to denote some feature or characteristic common to all concrete instances of intrinsic good and without which they would not be intrinsic goods. When Aristotle referred to the exercise of one's native capacities or activity in accordance with nature as the ultimate good and when hedonists speak of pleasure as the ultimate good, this second meaning is no doubt intended. In what follows, we shall use the term "highest good" to refer to the pre-eminent good in a scale of values and the term "good-making characteristic" to refer to any feature by virtue of which a concrete intrinsic good is said to be good.

A catalogue of the various good-making characteristics proposed by Western philosophers would consist of a large number of disparate items. Some (such as happiness and pleasure) are predicated of more or less extended subjective states. Others (such as the exercise of one's native capacities) are predicated of human behavior. Still others (such as being desirable or being an object of interest) are predicated of subjective experiences, human activities, and objective situations. Moreover, whereas some philosophers maintain that there is a unique good-making characteristic common to all instances of intrinsic good, others argue that that there exists a variety of distinct features by virtue of which concrete wholes may qualify as instances of intrinsic good.

Objectivism and subjectivism. Of what concrete wholes may goodness properly be predicated? The issues raised by this question have often been expressed in terms of an antithesis between "objectivism" and "subjectivism." Neither of these expressions has a single clearly defined meaning. For present purposes, however, a subjectivist may be regarded as someone who holds that no human activity or objective state of affairs is good unless it has a tendency to arouse a desirable subjective state in sentient beings. Alternatively, a subjectivist may be defined as someone who holds that "goodness" is primarily predicable of subjective states and only derivatively or secondarily predicable of other things. By an objectivist, on the other hand, we shall mean someone who holds that goodness may properly be predicated of at least some human activities or objective states of affairs independently of any tendency they may have to arouse desirable subjective states.

Lewis' distinction between intrinsic and inherent good presupposes subjectivism in the sense just defined, and it is probably safe to say that subjectivism is more common than objectivism both in the Western historical tradition and in popular contemporary thinking. The principal exceptions are Plato, for whom apparently the transcendent Idea of the Good was the primary meaning of "good," and ethical deontologists, who argue for the goodness of certain types of moral behavior regardless of their consequences for human well-being. Aristotle may also be an exception, but this is doubtful. He did define "good" as a kind of activity, but his definition was intended as an explication of the term "happiness," which would ordinarily be taken to denote a subjective state. It is, therefore, reasonable to suppose that he valued activity in accord with human nature only because of its tendency to produce a subjective sense of well-being. This interpretation is all the more likely because our vocabulary for subjective states is so impoverished that we are often obliged to describe them in terms of the physically observable conditions accompanying them, thus blurring the distinction between intrinsic and inherent good.

Although by definition all subjectivists hold that an activity or objective state of affairs is good only if it leads to some desirable subjective state, no one appears to have maintained the converse of this proposition. The fact that something produces a desirable subjective state does not of itself justify our calling it good. If, for instance, a drug produces a moderately euphoric state but at the same time severely damages health, either it would not be classified as a good at all or else it would be so classified only with qualifications.

All subjectivists agree that nothing is a proper object of choice unless there is reason to believe that its desirable consequences outweigh its negative consequences, if it has any. It would not, therefore, be correct to say that the subjectivist has no criterion other than personal feeling for evaluating proposed goods. To determine whether a proposed inherent good has on the whole more desirable than undesirable subjective consequences requires empirical knowledge of the properties and causal effects of the alleged inherent good. It is, however, true that decisions as to what subjective states qualify as intrinsically good are almost certainly conditioned by such factors as personal temperament, education, cultural conditioning, and historical circumstances. It is also true that any particular assignment of relative values to diverse subjective states is difficult to justify. It is, therefore, to be expected that the class of inherent goods which the subjectivist may reasonably pronounce to be universally and unqualifiedly good will be small in number or even nonexistent.

Good-making characteristics. Is there a single property by virtue of which all intrinsic or inherent goods are good? This question has often been answered affirmatively, but none of the affirmative answers has met with general favor. Aristotle and John Stuart Mill both said that all inherent goods must have the property of conducing to happiness and that only those things are inherently good which do conduce to happiness. Both of these authors recognized, however, that the term "happiness" is too vague to be of much use. Most persons would agree that all inherent goods are productive of happiness—but only because each person gives the term "happiness" a concrete meaning to his own liking. As soon as the several different concrete meanings are made explicit, general agreement vanishes. Besides, this answer to our question leaves untouched the problem of determining what specific inherent goods do in fact lead to happiness. Similar remarks apply with regard to "the desirable" or "object of interest" as names of a unique good-making property.

Aristotle explicated the concept of happiness, declaring that it consisted in activity in accordance with human nature. This formula was taken over by Thomas Aquinas and and is still espoused by most Catholic philosophers. It also played a role in Stoicism and in the thinking of many natural-law theorists. It presupposes, however, an essence or nature common to all members of the human species that disposes each of us to derive satisfaction from the exercise of certain innate desires, drives, or faculties. With the emergence of Darwinism, the collapse of the doctrine of fixed species, and the subsequent disrepute of the metaphysical doctrine of essences, the formula has lost much of its attractiveness. It has also suffered from a growing consciousness of the extent to which the ensemble of desires and dispositions constituting an individual human personality are shaped by individual temperament, culture, and historical circumstances.

The utilitarians, following the lead of the classical hedonists (especially the Epicureans), interpreted happiness as a life of many pleasures and few pains. For them the common feature of all concrete intrinsic goods is pleasure. It is generally felt, however, that pleasure cannot be common to all intrinsically good experiences unless the term is given an unconventionally wide meaning. Many philosophers believe, for instance, that the satisfaction often accompanying the performance of one's moral duty or the sense of achievement and self-esteem often accompanying creative work, though both intrinsic goods, ought not properly to be called pleasures. Either, therefore, the hedonists use the term "pleasure" conventionally, in which case the doctrine is inadequate, or else they use it in a wide and unconventional fashion, in which case the hedonist is proposing a near platitude of the same kind as that which consists in saying that happiness is the only intrinsic good.

G. E. Moore. The most interesting twentieth-century doctrine holding that a unique good-making characteristic exists was proposed by G. E. Moore. Moore distinguishes between what he terms "the good," by which he means concrete experiences that may be said to be instances of good, and "good" (used without article or other qualifier), by which he means a unique good-making property. The originality of his position consists in the affirmation of the nonnatural character of good. Good, he says, like yellow, is a simple and indefinable property; but, unlike yellow, its presence in any concrete experience must be determined by an act of intuition rather than by ordinary introspection or the use of the physical senses. The best-known of his arguments for the existence of this unique, nonnatural, and indefinable good-making property is called the open-question argument. If, he argued, the term "good" denotes a natural property or any set of natural properties, then there ought to be an acceptable definition of "good" having the form "Good is *X*," where *X* is replaced by the name of a natural property or set of properties. In fact, however, the argument continues, no definition of this form is satisfactory. No matter what natural property or set of properties one substitutes for *X*, one can always meaningfully ask: "But is something with these properties really good?"

Analytic philosophers. Most Anglo-American philosophers have been much influenced by Moore's views. This is especially true of the so-called analytic philosophers. Few, however, have accepted Moore's conclusion. In general they contend that "good" cannot be defined in terms of any single natural property or set of natural properties, not because it denotes a nonnatural property but rather because in different contexts it is used to refer to objects having different properties. Put somewhat differently, good cannot be defined because the traits or properties of things which justify our calling them good are not the same on all occasions of the term's use. The criteria by virtue of which we say that an association between human beings is good are not the same as those by virtue of which we declare that a work of art is good, nor is either set of criteria used in these two contexts identical with the criteria used in determining whether a meal is good. Good experiences have no common denominator. This view has been held by, among others, R. M. Hare and Paul Edwards.

Dewey. Although the analytic philosophers arrived at their position by a different route than the pragmatists did, their position accords with that of the pragmatists on this point. For John Dewey, as for the contemporary analysts, the search for an ultimate good in the sense of a property common to all good experiences is doomed to failure. Whereas, however, the analysts arrived at this conclusion by reflecting upon linguistic usage, Dewey's conclusion follows from metaphysical considerations, especially his views regarding the nature of human experience. Human nature, Dewey maintained, is highly plastic by virtue of its cultural and historical dimensions. What, therefore, is desirable in one culture or historical context may well be undesirable in another. The concept of an ultimate good is not only mistaken but nefarious. By implicitly denying the plasticity of human nature, it impedes both the enrichment of the individual human personality and social progress.

In his reaction against the classical tradition, Dewey even denied the validity of the distinction between intrinsic and nonintrinsic goods. It appears that in denying the validity of this distinction, however, he confounded the notion of intrinsic good defined simply as something desirable in and of itself with the notion of an ultimate good either in the sense of a unique good-making characteristic or in the sense of a single highest good common to all members of the human species. It is true, as Aristotle himself pointed out, that many things desirable in and of themselves are also desirable for the sake of their consequences. Health is desirable both in itself and as a condition of a number of pleasurable experiences. It is also

true that many goods which are originally or primarily instrumental come nonetheless to be valued for their own sakes. This is illustrated by the satisfaction one may take in possessing a large reserve of ready cash. Even so, it would be sheer folly to deny the soundess of the distinction between a concrete instrumental good such as surgery and a concrete intrinsic good such as health. Even if there were no purely instrumental or purely intrinsic goods, the distinction would still be conceptually sound.

The highest good. The concept of the highest good or *summum bonum* has been most notably present among those philosophers, like Aristotle and Thomas Aquinas, who hold that human beings share a common nature or essence. For Aristotle, man was essentially or by nature a rational animal, rationality being the one significant trait distinguishing him from the beasts. Consequently, man's highest good will consist in the exercise of his rational powers, or contemplation. For the Thomists, all men are endowed by their creator with a natural tendency to seek beatitude. This tendency may lie dormant or be perverted, but it cannot be eradicated. God, said Aquinas, draws us toward himself like a magnet. To resist this attraction is to pervert our nature. By allowing ourselves to be drawn to God, we fulfill our nature and experience the greatest satisfaction of which we are capable.

The loss of confidence in the metaphysical presuppositions underlying these views has already been noted. Even those who do not accept the idea of a supreme value for all human beings are, however, confronted with the problem of choice, which presupposes a relative ranking of values. It is clear that men are incapable of simultaneously realizing all of the goods they are capable of envisaging. Unless, therefore, one maintains that choices between incompatible goods are wholly arbitrary, the rejection of the classical notion of a *summum bonum* does not release the philosopher from the task of providing criteria in the light of which choices or preferences may be evaluated.

Bentham. The best-known effort to provide criteria for evaluating choices is that of the utilitarian Jeremy Bentham. To evaluate the relative merits of proposed inherent goods, Bentham proposed a number of criteria, including such things as the intensity and duration of the pleasures or pains which the alleged goods tend to produce and the number of persons capable of benefiting from them. The details of Bentham's "hedonistic calculus," as it is often called, have elicited considerable criticism, but the principal objections can be understood without a knowledge of these details.

One major objection is that Bentham's criteria are too mechanical or quantitative. Pleasures, satisfactions, goods, or whatever one chooses to call the possible objects of choice differ not only in quantity but also in quality; and a rational preference necessarily involves an estimate of these qualitative differences. John Stuart Mill suggested that by Bentham's criteria alone a contented pig would probably be better off than a discontented Socrates; but the intellectual satisfactions available even to an otherwise unhappy Socrates are qualitatively superior to the pig's pleasures and must be taken into account in any rationally chosen scale of values. Philosophers do not, of course, agree about which values are qualitatively superior to others, and very few have even attempted to provide a criterion for determining when one value is qualitatively superior to another. Mill proposed that the qualitatively superior of two goods would be that actually chosen by the person who had experience of both. This suggestion, however, presupposes that men are more alike in their capacity to derive satisfaction from similar concrete experiences than is probably the case.

A second major objection to Bentham's calculus is that pleasures are quantitatively incommensurable. There are standard techniques for determining degrees of temperature, density of air pressure, relative weight of physical objects, and so forth. But there is no standard measure for degree or intensity of pleasures. Sometimes this objection is offered only as a reminder of the practical difficulties in applying Bentham's criteria. At other times it is offered as an objection in principle, the idea being that the absence of a standard measure for intensity of pleasure renders the concept empty. The rejoinder here is that the concept of intensity of pleasure is widely accepted and often easily applied. It is difficult, for instance, to see on what grounds one could object to the judgment that the pleasure accompanying sexual orgasm is ordinarily more intense than the pleasure derived from slaking one's thirst. The absence of a clearly statable standard of measure may legitimately puzzle or disconcert us, but it would be unreasonable to hold judgments of the kind illustrated suspect for this reason alone.

Bibliography

This bibliography is limited to works by authors cited in the text. For further bibliographical references, see Ethics, History of, and Ethics, problems of.

Aristotle, *Nicomachean Ethics,* in *The Basic Works of Aristotle,* Richard McKeon, ed. New York, 1941.

Bentham, Jeremy, *The Principles of Morals and Legislation.* New York, 1948.

Dewey, John, *Human Nature and Conduct.* New York, 1922.

Dewey, John, *Theory of Valuation.* Chicago, 1939.

Edwards, Paul, *The Logic of Moral Discourse.* Glencoe, Ill., 1955.

Hare, R. M., *The Language of Morals.* Oxford, 1952.

Lewis, C. I., *An Analysis of Knowledge and Valuation.* La Salle, Ill., 1946.

Mill, John Stuart, *Utilitarianism.* London, 1861.

Moore, G. E., *Principia Ethica.* Cambridge, 1903.

Oates, W. I., *Stoic and Epicurean Philosophers.* New York, 1940.

Plato, *The Republic,* translated with an introduction by A. D. Lindsay. New York, 1957. Paperback edition.

Thomas Aquinas, *Summa Theologica,* translated by the Fathers of the English Dominican Province, 24 vols. London, 1920–1924; 3 vols. New York, 1947.

Robert G. Olson

GOODMAN, NELSON, distinguished American philosopher of science and language, was born in Massachusetts in 1906. Goodman received the Bachelor of Science degree from Harvard in 1928 and took his Ph.D. in philosophy there in 1941. After an instructorship at Tufts College (1945/1946), he was appointed associate professor at the University of Pennsylvania (1946–1951) and then professor (1951–1964). Since 1964 Goodman has been the Harry Austryn Wolfson professor of philosophy at Brandeis University.

Goodman's delineations of certain strategic problems in epistemology, philosophy of science and constructional methods, as well as the results of his own inquiries, are fundamental in the areas in which he has worked. Specifically, these include theories of inductive logic or confirmation, problems concerning the nature of causal or lawlike regularity, theories of the structural or logical simplicity of theories, and constructions of linguistic systems within which philosophical problems may be solved, as well as theories of the adequacy or accuracy of such systems. Because of his achievements any further significant contributions to these areas may be expected to rest, in some measure, upon his work.

In this brief compass no attempt will be made either to give a comprehensive account of Goodman's ramified views or to rehearse in full detail any one of his major achievements. Instead, we will give an account of a few aspects of his major contributions in just sufficient detail to make their general import intelligible and to show something of their interconnections.

Our order of presentation of topics is quite independent of their chronology in Goodman's philosophical development. We begin with those of his important studies with which there appears to be widest familiarity.

Inductive theory. One of Goodman's characterizations of the task of inductive theory is that it consists in "formulating rules that define the difference between valid and invalid inductive inferences." On this usage a set of rules for discriminating valid acceptances or nonacceptances of hypotheses from those which are invalid constitutes an inductive theory, or, alternatively, a theory of confirmation or a theory of projection.

Goodman's contribution to the provision of such inductive canons has been threefold. First, he has provided an analysis of the character of philosophical problems about induction. Second, he has furnished a critique of the problems still to be solved and of the versions of confirmation theory which have been at all fully elaborated (notably those of Carnap and Hempel; see *Fact, Fiction and Forecast,* especially pp. 24–34, 48–51, and 68–86, and also the published exchanges between Carnap and Goodman to which reference is made on p. 86). Third, he has made advances, explicitly in the form of a discussion of a *theory of projection,* toward the solution of some of the problems thus delineated. Where *induction* is construed narrowly as inference about future cases on the basis of examined cases, *projection* is, by contrast, inference about any unexamined cases on the basis of examined ones. We will consider each of these three aspects of his contribution in turn.

The "problem of induction." Goodman argues that the so-called problem of induction, when it is construed as the problem of *justifying* induction, is one that may be "dissolved" as soon as we see what is at issue. Moreover, this "dissolution" highlights all the more clearly the bona fide problem that he calls the new riddle of induction. As he sees it the problem is not to justify induction but to be able to distinguish valid from invalid inductions. On Goodman's view the dissolution of the *old* problem of induction, that is, of the problem of justifying induction, is accomplished when we come to understand that a genetic or descriptive account of our inductive behavior, such as the one that Hume *almost* brought off, furnishes the basis of such a justification. That this is a cogent view, he points out, can be seen when we raise the question of justifying *deduction*. How do we justify a deductive inference? By showing that it conforms to specific logical rules of deduction. By the same token, an inductive inference can be justified by showing that it conforms to a specific rule of induction.

One may immediately ask, however, what justification we have for adopting a set of rules of induction as valid. Of course, the same question might be asked concerning a set of deductive rules. The answer may be indicated by furnishing a parable.

Consider the situation of an imaginary philosopher to whom we may give the name "Aristotle." Aristotle has a keen interest in the area of deductive inference. In this area, he finds that although there is *already* an established practice among humans of making deductive inferences and although there is *already* a practice of discriminating, among ostensible inferences of this type, those which are correct from those which are not, nevertheless no one has yet made explicit or systematically codified the implicit rules upon which such discriminations appear to be based.

Our imaginary philosopher decides to undertake this task and eventually comes forward with such a codification. Using his codification people are enabled to make explicit their reasons for discriminating valid from invalid deductions by referring to the explicit rules which Aristotle has placed conveniently at hand. Of course no one would have paid any attention at all to these rules if they did not, with fair accuracy, reflect established practice—this is indeed what constitutes their validity as a set of rules. In the course of many years, however, other philosophers come forward to point out anomalies in Aristotle's set of rules. They point out that in certain cases some of his rules yield unacceptable inferences, and these philosophers suggest amendments which will remove the anomalies. When the amendments are incorporated they, in turn, have the effect of modifying practice. As Goodman puts it:

> [Deductive] inferences are justified by their conformity to valid general rules, and . . . general rules are justified by their conformity to valid inferences. But this circle is a virtuous one. The point is that rules and particular inferences alike are justified by being brought into agreement with each other. A rule is amended if it yields an inference we are unwilling to accept; an inference is rejected if it violates a rule we are unwilling to amend. The process of justification is the delicate one of making mutual adjustments between rules and accepted inferences. . . ." (*Fact, Fiction and Forecast*, p. 67)

If we return our attention to induction we see that an analogous situation obtains. Particular inductive inferences are justified by reference to rules of induction, and rules of induction are justified by reference to particular practices of inducing. Hume was on the right track in giving a descriptive account of inductive practice and in explicating rules of causal inference which he held to be in conformity with this practice. Those who have criticized him for this have been wrong.

We are thus quits with the old problem of induction, but the new, very formidable "riddle of induction" still remains. For although Hume was right in turning to description of actual practice, his description was insufficiently precise. He pointed out that observed regularities give rise to habits of expectation and that predictions based on such regularities are "normal or valid." But the defect in Hume's account, Goodman shows, lies in his failure to note "that some regularities do and some do not establish such habits; that predictions based on some regularities are valid while predictions based on other regularities are not. . . . To say that valid predictions are those based on past regularities is thus quite pointless" (*ibid.*, pp. 81–82). Accordingly, the new riddle of induction consists in finding a set of rules of inductive logic which will do for us what Hume failed to do. Thus, the problem is not to justify induction but adequately to codify it. An adequate codification would presumably stand to inductive practice very much as the codification of deduction, accomplished by our mythical Aristotle, stood to deductive practice as described in our parable above. In particular, it would presumably consist of a set of rules the appeal to which would serve to validate specific acceptances or rejections of scientific hypotheses or theories.

Critique of confirmation theory. In "The Problem of Counterfactual Conditionals" (reprinted without major change as Chapter 1 of *Fact, Fiction and Forecast*) Goodman was able to show that a solution to the problem of achieving an adequate interpretation of counterfactuals is intimately connected with many of the other crucial questions of the philosophy of science and that such a solution could be achieved only if various critical questions about the nature of scientific laws and of confirmation theory could be answered.

He shows, in particular, that the problem of furnishing adequate criteria for distinguishing true from false counterfactual conditionals has as a constituent the problem of adequately defining "scientific law," that this requires us to distinguish those hypotheses which are *confirmed* by their instances from those which are not, and that this, in turn, requires the fashioning of an adequate theory of confirmation. It is together the burden of the last part of "The Problem of Counterfactual Conditionals," of two brief articles on confirmation theory and of several passages in Chapter 3 of *Fact, Fiction and Forecast* that extant confirmation theories are defective, for they provide no means (except such as vitiate the theories through question-begging stipulations about what primitive predicates may be comprised in confirmable hypotheses) to distinguish the hypotheses to which such theories may be applied. Goodman, for example, points out that extant provisions of criteria for what constitutes a confirming instance in such defective theories either have the consequence that "any statement will confirm any statement" (*ibid.*, p. 81) or make question-begging assumptions, mentioned before, about the recognizability of "purely qualitative predicates" which are held to be the only permissible ones that may occur in (thus distinguishable) confirmable hypotheses. He shows, in short, that a desideratum of theories of confirmation is a definition of "confirmable hypothesis." In the final chapter of *Fact, Fiction and Forecast* he attempts to fill this need through advances on the problem of defining "projectible" as a predicate of hypotheses.

Theory of projection. In earlier discussions Goodman had shown that certain dispositional terms (other than "projectible") may be adequately defined by *projecting* them over the extensions of (that is, by defining them in terms of) certain carefully specified nondispositional or *manifest* predicates. Such earlier successes provide important paradigms. If on their model the meaning of the term "projectible" can be clarified, it will be feasible to decide to which hypotheses the term applies, and a crucial desideratum of heretofore defective theories of confirmation will have been taken care of.

Inasmuch as the term "projectible" is itself a dispositional predicate we may expect that among the manifest predicates which will occur in any candidate definiens will be the *corresponding* manifest predicate: "projected." However, defining "projectible" in terms of "projected" offers some very special difficulties which do not arise in the case of many dispositional predicates. The predicate "projectible" is like "desirable." It is not the case that every hypothesis which has been actually projected ought to have been or ought to be projected. (A hypothesis is characterized as having been *actually projected* if "it is adopted after some of its instances have been examined and determined to be true, and before the rest have been examined"; *ibid.*, p. 90).

Goodman, perhaps unlike Mill in confronting "desirable" is explicitly aware of the trap, and although his task is thereby enormously complicated, he avoids falling into it. He proposes, eventually, an explication of "projectibility" that provides criteria for discriminating projectible hypotheses based on past projections and certain other characteristics of our actual linguistic habits. In particular, attention to actual projections of hypotheses enables Goodman to explicate a relevant sense of *projected predicate* (a predicate occurring in an actually projected hypothesis). This, in turn, leads to his explication of a concept that becomes pivotal to his theory of projection: the concept of "entrenchment"—more specifically, the concept "is a much better entrenched predicate than."

One predicate, *P*, is said by Goodman to be much better entrenched than another predicate, *Q*, if *P* and all predicates coextensive with it have actually been projected much more often than *Q* and all predicates coextensive with it. Thus, take the predicate "grue" (which applies to any blue thing not examined before some time, *t*, and also to any thing examined before time *t* and found to be green). This "highly artificial" predicate, occurring in the hypothesis "The next emerald to be examined (after time *t*) will be grue" allows that hypothesis to be *equally highly evidenced* with the more usual "The next emerald to be examined (after time *t*) will be green." But hypotheses employing "grue" (or any term applicable to exactly the things "grue" is applicable to) have, nevertheless, been much less frequently projected (for example, used in making predictions) than have hypotheses using "green" (or any term applicable to exactly the things "green" is applicable to). This is part of the basis upon which "green"

is judged a much better-entrenched predicate than is "grue"; and Goodman's theory attempts to show how, although they are equally well evidenced, hypotheses containing much better-entrenched predicates are to be preferred to ones that contain much less well-entrenched predicates. Goodman points out that when we speak of the entrenchment of predicates we are really speaking of the entrenchment of habits of classification. This is to say that talk of the entrenchment of predicates is, in effect, talk of the entrenchment of their extensions. And, a little later on, still referring to his elucidation of entrenchment, he says:

> Like Hume, we are appealing here to past recurrences, but to recurrences in the explicit use of terms as well as to recurrent features of what is observed. Somewhat like Kant, we are saying that inductive validity depends not only upon what is presented but also upon how it is organized; but the organization we point to is effected by the use of language and is not attributed to anything inevitable or immutable in the nature of human cognition. To speak very loosely, I might say that in answer to the question what distinguishes those recurrent features of experience that underlie valid projections from those that do not, I am suggesting that the former are those features for which we have adopted predicates that we have habitually projected. (*Ibid.*, pp. 96–97)

The import of these considerations is that what constitutes a valid projection, and consequently what comes to constitute a projectible hypothesis, is a result of how we have, as a matter of fact, come to classify.

If Goodman's attempt to define "projectible" is successful, we have at hand the means of solving the problem of distinguishing confirmable from nonconfirmable hypotheses and thereby of surmounting a major obstacle in the way of providing a logic of induction.

These results of Goodman's—both the critique of extant theories and the positive proposals put forward in 1955 (*ibid.*)—are clearly still being digested by people in the field, if one may judge by the discussions of them that (ten years later) appear in print with increasing frequency.

Theory of structural simplicity. An early version of Goodman's calculus of simplicity (later extensively modified) occurs in Part I, "On the Theory of Systems," of his first book, *The Structure of Appearance*. There the calculus is exclusively connected with considerations somewhat more general than those involved in, for example, assessing the simplicity of scientific theories. In *The Structure of Appearance* interest in simplicity is interest in the simplicity of the primitive predicate basis of *any* constructional system; that is, any constructed linguistic system or axiomatic system which makes explicit what are the primitive (that is, the undefined) terms of the system. The main general problem which Goodman addresses is that of delineating criteria of adequacy for constructional systems generally, rather than for scientific theories in particular. For the constructor of such systems this problem is often posed—in part, at least—as the problem of choice among alternative primitive predicate bases. In choosing a primitive basis such considerations as antecedent clarity and "defining power" are obviously to be taken into account, but Goodman shows that the simplicity—the structural or logical simplicity—of such bases, is also an at least equally important consideration.

In his later writings on the subject (particularly in "The Test of Simplicity" and *Fact, Fiction and Forecast*) Goodman also makes clear the relationship of measures of simplicity to the philosophy of science. He maintains that simplicity is a primary consideration guiding choices among scientific theories or systems of hypotheses. It is a mistake to believe that simplicity becomes a factor only after we have first sought a true system and then turn to matters of elegance. He maintains that, on the contrary, our concern with simplicity is an inevitable concomitant of our concern with system. For, he points out, we achieve systematization only to the extent that the basic vocabulary and principles we employ in dealing with some subject matter come to be simplified. The important thing to note is that "when simplicity of basis vanishes to zero—that is, when no term or principle is derived from any of the others—system also vanishes to zero. Systematization is the same thing as simplification of basis" ("The Test of Simplicity," p. 1064).

Goodman finds the key to the problem of measuring the structural simplicity of predicate bases in a "meagre and negative" but highly plausible principle: "If every basis like a given one can always be replaced by some basis like a second, then the first is not more complex than the second" (*ibid.*, p. 1066). The relation "always replaceable by" between predicate bases holds in cases where the replacement is a matter of a purely routine procedure that can always be applied (presumably, for example, in case there is available some *decision procedure* for determining replaceability). Employing this key principle and some results in the theory of relations, Goodman provides a means of effecting the requisite measures. The *calculus of simplicity* is applicable only to theories that have been at least sufficiently formalized to enable discrimination of their primitive predicates. Its applicability (for example, as a factor in assessing the acceptability of some scientific theory) is thus severely limited for the present by the paucity of scientific theories that have reached this stage of formalization. On the other hand, this situation would be importantly alleviated if some means could be found either to bring more such theories to the requisite stage of formalization or to modify the calculus in such a way that useful applications of it may be made even to less fully formalized systems.

For the time being, applications of the simplicity measures may, however, be made to constructional systems devised for purposes of philosophical explication (for example, see Goodman's own system in *The Structure of Appearance*).

Constructionalism. Whatever its importance for both philosophy of science and constructional methods, furnishing a way of measuring the simplicity of bases of any constructed systems by no means represents Goodman's only contribution to constructional methods. The first three chapters of *The Structure of Appearance* (for example) provide also a discussion of the problem of assessing the adequacy and the accuracy of definitional systems. Here an especially significant discussion (for example, in Ch. 1)

provides both an illuminating critique of criteria which in the past have been adduced for assessing such systems and a newly developed criterion, *extensional isomorphism,* for assessing the *accuracy* of such systems. The development of this criterion throws new light on the entire program of philosophical or logical analysis.

Although full elucidation of the criterion is beyond the scope of the present article, some general inkling of its import may perhaps be conveyed by pointing out some of its differences from some of the criteria which have been previously offered for the adequacy of philosophical analyses. It has long been recognized that full synonymy of analysandum (the concept or term being subjected to philosophical analysis) and analysans (the concept or term constituting the product of the analysis) is too strong a requirement. Accordingly, weaker criteria (for example, *intensional identity* or *extensional identity* of analysandum and analysans) have been proposed. In *The Structure of Appearance* Goodman argues that even the weakest of these—extensional identity—is too strong a requirement to place on tasks of analysis, for none can totally fulfill such a condition. He proposes instead a criterion which does not "square" an analysandum with its analysans in any one-to-one fashion but rather tests the whole *system* of concepts to which the analysandum belongs against the whole newly constructed system to which the analysans belongs. The meeting of specified and relatively weak extensional correspondences between two such systems is sufficient—and indeed is the most that can cogently be required—to warrant the accuracy of the analysis.

The discussions of new constructional methods in the first chapter of *The Structure of Appearance* and the presentation of a version of the calculus of individuals which had been developed by H. S. Leonard and Goodman (in "The Calculus of Individuals and Its Uses") are well supplemented by the specific application of these and other devices to a detailed critique of Carnap's *Der logische Aufbau der Welt* (in Ch. 5). An important application is also provided by the construction (in Chs. 6–11) of his own systematic explication of phenomenal concepts or predicates.

Phenomenalism and nominalism. Goodman's actual work upon, and his defenses of work upon, phenomenalistic systems lead many observers to conclude that he subscribes to phenomenalism as a philosophical position. The fact is, however, that he has written in full and explicit detail about the relative unimportance and the opacity of questions about the epistemological priority of the phenomenal (and "rival," for example, physicalistic) systems, and there seems to be no good reason to doubt the sincerity of his disavowals of that kind of philosophical commitment. (See *The Structure of Appearance*, Ch. 4 and *passim*, and "The Revision of Philosophy.") All of this is notwithstanding the fact that he has made contributions to the solution of many very complex problems that are involved in the construction of a phenomenalistic system.

If phenomenalism represents, for him, no particular philosophical commitment, *nominalism*, on the other hand, surely does. His major writings on this topic (in his and Quine's "Steps Toward a Constructive Nominalism" and in his *The Structure of Appearance; Fact, Fiction and*

Forecast; and "A World of Individuals") obviously constitute a fundamental philosophical conviction. Although Goodman's and Quine's nominalism coincide importantly (for example, in their mutual rejection of classes, see "Steps Toward a Constructive Nominalism"—but note, however, that in later writings Quine appears no longer to embrace such views) it should nevertheless be observed that their nominalistic positions are quite disparate. Thus, Quine apparently rejects, so to speak, classes on account of their being abstract entities; whereas Goodman rejects, so to speak, classes not on account of their being abstract entities (his system in *Structure,* indeed, refers to abstract entities categorematically) but rather on account of their being *nonindividuals.* It is the notion of a *nonindividual* that Goodman finds unintelligible, and he is conscientious in avoiding any philosophical or logical method which presupposes or extorts the claim that there exist any nonindividuals. The consequent austerity in bases chosen and logical tools available to him have had, in fact, fruitful results in eliciting complex, ingenious, and far-reaching techniques or methods of constructional analysis.

We have indicated that there are differences between what might be called G-nominalism (Goodman's position)—the view, on the one hand, that there are no nonindividuals—and the position that might be called Q-nominalism—the view that there are no abstract entities, on the other. While it would, again, be beyond the scope of this article to give a detailed account of G-nominalism, it may yet be illuminating to remind the reader that Goodman himself has characterized his position as a sort of "superextensionalism." The usual or classical extensionalist position prohibited some otherwise indiscriminate multiplication of entities by imposing a principle to the effect that two entities (say, two classes) which have, so to speak, the same proximate constituents are identical. G-nominalism goes further; it imposes the condition that any two things which have the same systematically *ultimate* constituents are identical.

Thus, consider the systematic atoms (things not having anything else in the system as possible consituents) *a, b, c,* and *d.* Suppose in a (classically) extensional system *A* we discriminated the classes of pairs {*a,c*} and {*b,d*}, and suppose in system *B* we discriminated the classes {*a,b*} and {*c,d*}. For classical extensionalism, systems *A* and *B* would *not* be identical; that is, the proximate constituents—the two classes of pairs—are different, and hence the world's population on this account is increased by two more classes. The G-nominalist, however, has a stronger condition for diversity. For him there are not, say, the eight different entities consisting of the four atoms and the four classes of pairs of them. Rather, there are only four entities—the ultimate atoms of the system themselves. The cogency of this view is argued with great vigor and clarity in "A World of Individuals."

Work in progress. Goodman's current interest appears to be an analysis of representationalism in a very broad sense of this concept taken presystematically. Thus, the focus of his attention is not only upon representation as a phenomenon involving, for example, paintings in aesthetics but also upon the representational aspects or functions of maps, graphs, musical scores, and choreographic nota-

tions, and, in addition, theories and other descriptions. His deep and abiding interest in this topic is evidenced too as a recurrent thread in many of his works, from very early ones to the present. The articles in which this concern is most obviously expressed are "On Likeness of Meaning," "Sense and Certainty," "The Way the World Is," and "About." The concern is also dominantly present in his John Locke lectures (given at Oxford in 1962), soon to be published.

Works by Goodman

"The Calculus of Individuals and Its Uses." *Journal of Symbolic Logic,* Vol. 5 (1940), 45–55. In collaboration with H. S. Leonard.

"A Query on Confirmation." *Journal of Philosophy,* Vol. 43 (1946), 383–385.

"On Infirmities of Confirmation-theory." *Philosophy and Phenomenological Research,* Vol. 8 (1947), 149–151.

"Steps Toward a Constructive Nominalism." *Journal of Symbolic Logic,* Vol. 12 (1947), 105–122. In collaboration with W. V. Quine.

"On Likeness of Meaning." *Analysis,* Vol. 10 (1949), 1–7.

"An Improvement in the Theory of Simplicity." *Journal of Symbolic Logic,* Vol. 14 (1950), 228–229.

The Structure of Appearance. Cambridge, Mass., 1951.

"Sense and Certainty." *Philosophical Review,* Vol. 61 (1952), 160–167.

Fact, Fiction and Forecast. London, 1954; Cambridge, Mass., 1955.

"Axiomatic Measurement of Simplicity." *Journal of Philosophy,* Vol. 52 (1955), 709–722.

"The Revision of Philosophy," in Sidney Hook, ed., *American Philosophers at Work.* New York, 1956. Pp. 75–92.

"A World of Individuals," in *The Problem of Universals.* Notre Dame, Ind., 1956. Pp. 13–31.

"The Test of Simplicity." *Science,* Vol. 128 (1958), 1064–1069.

"Recent Developments in the Theory of Simplicity." *Philosophy and Phenomenological Research,* Vol. 19 (1959), 429–446.

"The Way the World Is." *Review of Metaphysics,* Vol. 14 (1960), 160–167.

"Positionality and Pictures." *The Philosophical Review,* Vol. 69 (1960), 523–525.

"About." *Mind,* Vol. 70 (1961), 1–24.

"Safety, Strength, Simplicity." *Philosophy of Science,* Vol. 28 (1961), 150–151.

RICHARD S. RUDNER

GORGIAS OF LEONTINI in Sicily, Greek Sophist and rhetorician, was probably born before 480 B.C. and is known to have been alive in 399 B.C. He came to Athens on a diplomatic mission in 427 B.C. to seek help for his native city and subsequently traveled widely, giving public lectures and private instruction in many Greek cities, especially in Thessaly. Among his numerous pupils were Isocrates and perhaps Thucydides.

Whether Gorgias should be classed as a Sophist has been much discussed. In Plato's *Gorgias* he is described as a teacher of rhetoric, not as a Sophist, and in *Meno* (95C) we are told he refused to claim that he could teach virtue, as other Sophists claimed. On the other hand, Plato recognized Gorgias, together with Prodicus and Hippias, as a professional educator of men (*Apology* 19E), and he certainly taught the art of persuasion as a means to political success. Whatever was the precise content of his teaching, he must in a general sense be regarded as belonging to the sophistic movement.

His writings comprised speeches, of which some specimens survive, clearly exhibiting the distinctive antithetic style for which he was famous; a technical treatise or treatises on rhetoric; the treatise "On That Which Is Not, or On Nature," of which two partially divergent summaries survive, one in Sextus Empiricus (*Adversus Mathematicos,* VII, 65–87) and one as the third part of the pseudo-Aristotelian treatise *On Melissus, Xenophanes, Gorgias,* usually referred to as *MXG.* Gorgias' claim to a place in the history of philosophical thought rests primarily upon the assessment of this last treatise. But it is clear, quite apart from this work, that he had a considerable interest in the physical sciences—Plato attributes to him an Empedoclean theory of perception by effluences and pores, thus implying an external world existing independently of our perceptions of it (*Meno,* 76C). The representation of Gorgias gazing at an astronomical sphere on the tomb of Isocrates is good evidence for his interests in that field, especially when we are also told that he held that the sun was a red-hot mass.

The treatise *On Nature* was divided into three parts. The first maintained that nothing is; the second, that even if it is, it cannot be comprehended by men; and the third, that even if it can be comprehended, it cannot be communicated to another person. This treatise has frequently been interpreted as involving a skeptical denial of all existence. It has also often been treated simply as a parody or joke against philosophers, or a purely rhetorical exercise. The detail and subtlety of the supporting arguments make it fairly certain that it had some serious intellectual purpose other than parody, and, while there are indications that Gorgias did not wish to propound a nihilism that would simply seek to sweep away everything, there are considerable difficulties in deciding just what he did have in mind. According to one view, he meant to deny both the existence of Eleatic Being and that of Not-Being, which the Eleatics themselves rejected. But it is fairly clear that in the two later parts of the treatise the interest centers on the status of objects of perception rather than on Being and Not-Being, and the version preserved in *MXG* suggests that this was what he was concerned with in the first part as well. In this case the discussion would not be about Being and Not-Being but, rather, about the question of whether "being" can be attributed or denied to anything without resultant contradiction. Gorgias maintains that we cannot say of a thing either that it is or is not, without absurd results. If it is, it must, for example, be either one or many; and in either case this implies, so Gorgias argues, that it also is not. If, on the other hand, it is not, this implies also that it is. We would say that these conclusions rest only on confusions between different senses of the verb "to be," but Gorgias appears to have believed in the conclusions he reached. It was probably no accident that his pupil Lycophron proposed to omit the verb "to be" in such sentences as "Socrates is white."

In the second part we are invited to infer, from the fact that we can think about nonexistent animals, that thoughts do not involve the existence of things thought and thus that thoughts as such do not possess existence. From this it is inferred that if anything is, it cannot be thought. This opens a gulf between things and thoughts about these things. In the third part, this gulf is found also to occur

between words and things and between the thoughts of two different people. Since external phenomena are distinct both from the words describing them and from thoughts about them, they cannot either be thought (or known) or communicated by one person to another. This seems to be the general trend of the obscure and often textually corrupt formulation of the arguments in the later part of the treatise. Although much will always be controversial, it seems clear that the arguments in the later part involve the recognition of the independent status of phenomena in relation to people's thoughts about them.

According to Plato, Gorgias regarded the art of rhetoric as superior to all other arts. Hermann Diels propounded the theory that he began with an interest in physical science, became skeptical in the period represented by the treatise *On Nature,* and finally abandoned science for rhetoric regarded simply as a part of the art of persuasion. There is no positive evidence for this sequence and no evidence that Gorgias ever lost interest in physical questions. But the position in the treatise does seem to be inconsistent with the full Empedoclean doctrine of effluences and pores, which does not seem to have envisaged a fundamental difference in nature between objects and thoughts about them; and to that extent Diels may have been right. The details of Gorgias' rhetorical theory were probably of great importance, but they can hardly be recovered in the present state of the evidence.

Bibliography

Fragments and testimonia may be found in H. Diels and W. Kranz, *Fragmente der Vorsokratiker,* 10th ed. (Berlin, 1961), Vol. II; commentary and text of *On Melissus, Xenophanes, Gorgias* is found in Mario Untersteiner, ed., *Sofisti, testimonianze e frammenti,* Fasc. II (Florence, 1949). Also see Untersteiner's *I sofisti* (Turin, 1949), translated by Kathleen Freeman as *The Sophists* (New York and Oxford, 1954), Chs. 4–9.

For works on Gorgias, see G. Calogero, *Studi sull'eleatismo* (Rome, 1932); G. B. Kerferd, "Gorgias on Nature or That Which Is Not," in *Phronesis,* Vol. 1 (1955–1956), 3–25; and Plato, *Gorgias,* E. R. Dodds, ed. (Oxford, 1959).

G. B. KERFERD

GRACIÁN Y MORALES, BALTASAR (1601–1658), Spanish Jesuit and author of several baroque, obscure, laboriously polished books in which he expounded and illustrated conceptism, or metaphysical wit. Conceptism (from *concepto,* thought) is the quest for fine, brilliant, subtle thoughts expressed in antitheses, ambiguities, new words, and elaborate conceits.

Gracián published only one book under his real name, *El Comulgatorio* ("Sanctuary Meditations for Priests and Frequent Communicants," 1655). A book of devotion, it enjoyed great success in several languages until the nineteenth century but is little used today. All his other books were published under pseudonyms without the permission of his superiors, for which offense he was disciplined because their subjects were thought too worldly for a priest, especially at a time when the Society of Jesus was struggling against Jansenism. The first was *El héroe* (1637), a portrait of a Christian political superman, similar to scores of books printed in Europe in the sixteenth and seventeenth centuries in answer to Machiavelli's *The Prince.*

Governance, then in the hands of absolutist rulers, was thought to be an art that could be taught in analytical character studies of the "exceptional man." Unfortunately, Gracián's model was Philip IV of Spain. However, in *El político* (1640) he took Ferdinand the Catholic as a more plausible subject for another panegyric on the Great Man. Such works fell from favor as government came to be conceived more democratically, but romanticism revived the cult of the hero, and Gracián's books were annotated by Napoleon and admired by Nietzsche.

In *El discreto* (1646) Gracián continued his portraits of perfect types, descending to the level of the man of the world to describe the perfect gentleman as seen by provincial Spanish society. This book is remembered for its formula for the ideal life: first converse with the dead, then with the living, finally with oneself. In other words, first book learning, then travel and worldly experience, and last, meditation and preparation for death. From these three books, and others like them that remained unpublished, Gracián extracted an anthology of three hundred aphorisms, published as *El Oráculo manual* (1647), or *Art of Worldly Wisdom*. These wise sayings have enjoyed constant success. La Rochefoucauld echoed many of them in his *Maximes*, and Schopenhauer translated them into German.

La agudeza y arte de ingenio (1642–1648) is a treatise on rhetoric and aesthetics that codifies the taste of the baroque age with its thirst for conceits, subtlety, eloquence, and artifice. Composed in a tortured hermetic style—the style Gracián praised as literary perfection—the book has never been translated into English. Literary historians consider it the beginning of the decadence of Spanish literature.

Gracián then wrote a quite unexpected book, for which his uneventful, sheltered existence offers no explanation but on which his fame rests. After extolling heroism, kingliness, *savoir-faire*, and poetic beauty in the works so far mentioned, he composed *El criticón* (1651–1657), a bitterly critical satire of the very society he had been exploring so complacently. It is a long philosophical novel, painstakingly allegorical and overadorned to the point of obscurity, that has been compared with the paintings of Bosch. A noble savage, Adrenio, is brought to Europe and shown all the inventions and refinements of civilization. Critilo, a man of the world, directs an "experiment" that becomes an inventory of human knowledge at that date, reviewing most of the questions that then interested moralists, scholars, and statesmen. The idea, later used by Pascal and Voltaire, was not new; such didactic allegories were already known in Spain, perhaps because Indians really had been taken on "conducted tours" of civilization there. What was striking was the extent to which Gracián's characters came to pessimistic conclusions; their judgments on civilization were uniformly unfavorable. Long before Rousseau, Gracián said that, although man was created pure in the state of nature and left God's hands perfect, civilization corrupted and debased him. Yet, he added, as man grows older, he can acquire wisdom to free himself from slavery to worldly illusions, to begin the hard apprenticeship of renunciation and preparation for death. Gracián's pessimism was redeemed by faith in salvation

beyond life. The world is not wholly bad; it is a mixture of true and false values, of misleading images and authentic shadows of eternal life. This world is a profoundly ambiguous tragicomic farce, with a concealed sense that is to be sought in another world of eternal being. This combination of extreme pessimism and a confident religious faith introduced a curious ambivalence into Gracián's view of the world, notably of the things that he most admired: social success, worldly glory, and political power. Perhaps on only one subject was he utterly pessimistic—woman, whom he called "a Satanic creature, vile, inferior." Schopenhauer agreed with him here, but on other matters the German misrepresented the Spanish Jesuit's pessimism by taking it out of its religious context. To be sure, some critics have argued that Gracián's piety was pretense, designed to get his work past the Inquisition's censorship. Voltaire knew *El criticón*, so resemblances to *Candide* might not be accidental; but Gracián's clearest philosophical influence was over Schopenhauer and Nietzsche.

Works by Gracián y Morales

Obras completas. Madrid, 1960.
The Heroe, translated by J. Skeffington. London, 1652.
The Complett Gentleman, translated by T. Saldkeld. London, 1726.
The Oracle: A Manual of the Art of Discretion, translated by L. B. Walton. London and New York, 1963.
The Art of Worldly Wisdom, translated by Joseph Jacobs. New York, 1943. Also translated by Otto Eisenschiml. New York, 1947.
The Critick, translated by Sir Paul Rycaut. London, 1681.

Works on Gracián y Morales

Bell, A., *Baltasar Gracián*. Oxford, 1921.
Correa-Calderón, E., *Baltasar Gracián*. Madrid, 1961. Includes a bibliography of the extensive literature on Gracián.
Romera-Navarro, M., *Estudios sobre Gracián*. Austin, Tex., 1950.

Neil McInnes

GRAMSCI, ANTONIO (1891–1937), Italian socialist born in Sardinia, founded the Italian Communist party in 1921. He turned from political action to philosophical study when the Fascists jailed him in 1926 in order, said the public prosecutor, "to stop that brain working for twenty years." That brain, one of the most gifted that communism has produced, could not be stopped even by the inhuman conditions of Mussolini's prisons: Gramsci filled three thousand pages with writing on a vast range of philosophical and political subjects. His frail health undermined by ill treatment, he died in Rome a week after his commuted term ended.

From the 32 prison notebooks, devoted editors have extracted "books" by grouping fragments on connected topics. In addition, *L'ordine nuovo* (1954) is a collection of articles from a socialist newspaper of that name, *Letteratura e vita nazionale* (1950) contains book and drama reviews, and *Lettere dal carcere* (1947) are his letters from jail. The heroic conditions under which he worked, and his founding role in Italian communism, may be responsible for overestimation of Gramsci's contribution to philosophy, but there is no doubt of his erudition and critical powers.

His philosophical notes (they seldom attain essay length) go beyond defense of Marxist doctrine; they mean to be a refutation of the idealism of two eminent ex-Marxists, Croce and Sorel. His criticism of them is seldom hostile, and in fact implies a disparaging opinion of orthodox Marxist–Leninist thought. Gramsci's central thesis is that Marx's "materialist" overturning of Hegel was not a once-for-all affair that left communism, in Engels' phrase, the secure "heir of the classical German philosophy." It had to be a continuing effort, to be repeated by each generation. Better, it was a Vico-style cycle in which the same work of philosophical synthesis recurred at ever higher levels. Gramsci saw that official Marxist thought in his day was in danger of relapsing into that vulgar materialism from which Marx's Hegelian training had rescued socialism a century before. Thus, it needed a new blood transfusion from speculative philosophy, a synthesis with Neo-Hegelian idealism, notably with Croce and Gentile.

This diagnosis entailed departure from the standard Marxist view on how philosophy "culminated" in revolutionary action. The last of Marx's Theses on Feuerbach—"the philosophers have only *interpreted* the world in various ways; the point however is to *change* it"—had been taken to mean that philosophy would be realized in, and replaced by, revolutionary action. The postrevolutionary world would have no room for mere speculation, and philosophy would become the ideological branch of the administration. Gramsci replied that philosophy could not be realized in, and even less supplanted by, political action. If the proletariat were to be "the heir of the classical German philosophy" (and if it were not, the revolution would be a cultural failure), it would have to pursue some recognizably philosophical activity. Specifically, it would be bound to go on reckoning with speculative idealism, putting it back on its feet as Marx did with Hegel and as Gramsci hoped to do with Croce.

Any one philosophy or system could indeed "culminate," or be realized. In fact, if it were a significant cultural product and not reverie, it surely would be. Yet that realization, the passage from speculation to action, from theory to practice, was not the "end" of philosophy foreseen by many Marxists. Rather, it was the transposition of private thinking into historically effective mass beliefs and a new ethic. Thus, Gramsci's program was to synthesize Lenin and Croce, to produce a reinvigorated Marxist philosophy that could be translated into a mass faith "like the Protestant Reform or the French Enlightenment."

The victory of such a new ethic was the essence of revolution, which meant above all "a moral and intellectual reform" and the "creation of a new integral culture." In all this, Gramsci explicitly followed Sorel but, against him, he denied that a "revolution of ideas" could do without politics, as Lenin practices it. His defense of Leninism, and of political organization generally, was a genuine contribution to political theory. Incidentally, it involved a fresh assessment of Machiavelli. Gramsci wanted to be "both Robespierre and Kant," and indeed he succeeded in combining—at least on paper and in jail—the tough-minded political practicality of communism with a liberal attachment to classical education and philosophical culture.

Works by Gramsci

Gramsci's *Opere* were published in six volumes in Turin (1947–1954). The works extracted from the prison notebooks are *Gli intellettuali e l'organizzazione della cultura* (1949); *Il risorgimento* (1949); *Note sul Machiavelli, sulla politica e sullo stato moderno* (1949); *Passato e presente* (1951); and *Il materialismo storico e la filosofia di Benedetto Croce* (1948).

English editions of Gramsci's work include *The Modern Prince and Other Writings*, translated by Louis Marks (London, 1957) and *The Open Marxism of Antonio Gramsci*, translated and edited by Carl Marzani (New York, 1957). Both works contain selections from the prison notebooks.

Works on Gramsci

For works on Gramsci, see J. McKay Gammett, *Antonio Gramsci and the Ordine Nuovo Movement* (Ann Arbor, Mich., 1960); N. Matteuci, *Antonio Gramsci e la filosofia della prassi* (Milan, 1951); L. Lombardo-Radice and G. Carbone, *Vita di Antonio Gramsci* (Rome, 1951); C. Ottino, *Concetti fondamentali nella teoria politica di Gramsci* (Milan, 1956).

NEIL McINNES

GRAY, ASA (1810–1888) was a leading American interpreter of Darwin's theory of evolution. Born in Sanquoit, in central New York, he became deeply interested in botany as a youth. Although he received a medical degree from Fairfield Medical School in 1831, he decided to devote his life to botanical studies, in which field he soon gained an international reputation. Harvard University appointed him Fisher professor of natural history in 1841, a post he held for over forty years. His writings both popularized the subject of botany and advanced it scientifically. Through his correspondence with Charles Darwin in 1856 and 1857, Gray obtained a preview of the theory of evolution by natural selection. When the *Origin of Species* was published, Gray wrote one of the first reviews, in the *American Journal of Science and Arts* (March, 1860). This review, with several other essays on evolution, was reprinted under the title *Darwiniana* (1876).

Gray's attitude to Darwin's theory was open-minded but cautious. He regarded it as a plausible scientific hypothesis, although far from conclusively proved. As an explanation of the diversification of species, it was markedly superior to the doctrine of special creation. However, it did not really explain the origin of species because it failed to give a satisfactory account of the cause of variations. Gray thought that Darwin was often rash in drawing conclusions that outran the evidence, as when he asserted that all species must have descended from "four or five primordial forms" and when he contended that man's mental powers must have had an evolutionary origin. This last contention "accumulates improbabilities beyond belief."

Against those who said that the Darwinian theory implied atheism, Gray argued that "it is neither atheistical in statement nor in intent." The theory could be given a nontheistic interpretation, but it could equally be given a theistic one. A central question was the presence or absence of design in nature as a whole, and this question was one for the natural theologian or the philosopher, not for the biologist. Gray himself favored a theistic interpretation, since the idea of a Designer of the universe "is most natural to the mind." It was not even true to say that Darwin's theory was mechanistic. It assumed that adaptations produced by natural selection are useful to organisms, enabling them to achieve certain ends, and this assumption clearly reintroduced purpose or teleology into natural history. "If purpose in this sense does not itself imply design, it is certainly compatible with it and suggestive of it."

Gray's cool analysis of Darwinism coupled with his espousal of theism irked some of Darwin's militantly agnostic supporters, though not Darwin himself, who valued Gray as a friend and searching critic.

Works by Gray

Darwiniana: Essays and Reviews Pertaining to Darwinism. Cambridge, Mass., 1876. New edition with an introduction by A. H. Dupree, Cambridge, Mass., 1963.
Scientific Papers. Boston and New York, 1888.
Natural Science and Religion. New York, 1880.
Letters of Asa Gray, Jane Loring Gray, ed., 2 vols. Boston and New York, 1893.

Works on Gray

Dupree, A. H., *Asa Gray: 1810–1888.* Cambridge, Mass., 1959.
Robinson, B. L., "Asa Gray." *Science*, Vol. 62 (1925), 45–46.

T. A. GOUDGE

GREAT MAN THEORY OF HISTORY. Any generalization that affirms the historical significance of outstanding human individuals can be termed a "great man theory of history." The expression has been most frequently used in reference to comprehensive claims to the effect that great men are the key to the intelligibility of history; it is also applied, however, to generalizations that merely state how great men, as one factor among others, are historically significant. After a brief survey of developments in great man theory, the following discussion will contain a description of great man theories, emphasizing principal characteristics and variant types, and a critical analysis of some sources of controversy regarding this topic.

Individuals figure prominently in most forms of early historical writing, and this characteristic applies generally to Western historiography until modern times. Even today, what has been called by E. H. Carr the "Good Queen Bess" and "Bad King John" view of history has not lost public favor, nor does it lack philosophical supporters. Prior to 1800, no theoretical justification of this feature of historical practice had been attempted. Beginning in the seventeenth and eighteenth centuries, however, a critical awareness developed that drew attention to the hitherto tacit assumption that great men are of paramount historical significance. In the nineteenth century we find the first explicitly formulated great man theories, notably those of Hegel and Carlyle. Together with the question as to the scientific status of history, the great man theory emerged as one of the central issues of the day in Europe, England, and America. Philosophers, historians, and social scientists joined in the debate; Tolstoy's *War and Peace* and Hardy's *The Dynasts* were among the literary repercussions.

History, said Thomas Carlyle in his influential lectures of 1840, is "the biography of great men." This conception appealed to those who contemplated with dismay the emergence of a powerful middle class threatening to infect politics, art, and morals with mediocrity and those who charged that nose-counting social science was blind to the inspirational quality of great leaders and to the mystery of creative genius. But self-conscious nationalism, together with a new historical awareness of cultural growth and continuity as social phenomena, tended to qualify the role attributed to the great man. The spectacle of revolutionary mobs, the imponderables of mass military operations, and the ephemeral Napoleonic empire strengthened the conviction that history was really the work of countless human beings or of powerful impersonal forces. In the latter half of the nineteenth century the most sensational attacks on the great man theory were carried out in the name of science by Herbert Spencer and Karl Marx, only to be met by vigorous reaffirmations of the heroic view in one form or other. These affirmations were crudely exploited in support of twentieth-century dictatorships but recent thought, on the whole, takes a dim view of sweeping historical generalizations, including both comprehensive great man theories and categorical denials of the great man's significance.

CHARACTERISTICS OF GREAT MAN THEORIES

Valuations and practical considerations permeate discussions pro and con of the historical significance of great men. The conscious endeavor toward a value-free social science (exemplified by Max Weber's theory of the charismatic leader or C. Wright Mills's analysis of the "power elite") and attempts (those of Mannheim and Dewey, for instance) at forcing valuational assumptions into the open for empirically grounded appraisal have only partially changed this situation.

Ethical overtones of "great." The terms "great" and "outstanding" are frequently used eulogistically. Nietzsche's term "superman" (Übermensch), has such a connotation. The praiseworthiness of greatness is apparent in Carlyle's and Hegel's identification of great men with heroes. For Carlyle, hero worship of the authentic hero is commendable because heroes are sent by Providence to enlighten, to lead, and to save us. In Hegel's views, "world-historical" individuals, individuals whose actions correspond to the requirements of a necessary stage in the history of the world, are properly called heroes because Reason, generative principle of world history, works through them and Reason is good; in doing what is necessary, they do what ought to be done. From a value-free standpoint, on the other hand, the judgment that Hitler was a great man would be altogether independent of a moral appraisal of his character or historical influence.

Great men as moral exemplars. The traditional and still influential idea that the purpose of history is moral instruction gives rise to a special form of the great man theory. From this standpoint, to assert that great men are historically significant is tantamount to asserting that it is beneficial for us to read about them—not that we thereby understand history any better, but that we become better persons. If history is essentially a means of forming good character, then indeed great men are the substance of history.

Freedom, moral responsibility, and historical inevitability are recurrent themes in discussions of the great man theory. The thesis of historical inevitability is not incompatible with some versions of the heroic view of history (for instance, that of Hegel and of some Marxist theorists), in which the hero is said to achieve freedom of action in the sense that he is able to do what he sets out to do, his objectives coinciding with historical necessity. But as usually conceived, the heroes of history are a living refutation of historical determinism. If great men determine history by deliberate actions based on anticipated consequences, that suffices to deliver mankind from inexorable fate. Because the influence of these men is so considerable, they are capable of achieving whatever they intend to do, whereas what the average agent intends to accomplish is distorted beyond recognition in the combined result of social behavior. Through exceptional persons, mankind has a measure of responsibility for and control over its historical destiny.

Freedom and creativity. Bergson and Nietzsche, who represent, respectively, philosophical vitalism and voluntarism, view historical determinism as at best a useful scientific fiction. They emphasize the creative achievements of exceptional men, the free spirits, who break with convention and orthodoxy, revealing new ways of life, new dimensions of human experience. The judgment that creativity is intrinsically valuable is an integral part of their theories of history. In a similar vein, William James argued that even if social determinism is theoretically admissible as an approach to historical understanding, the individual's opportunities for shaping his destiny, however meager, are of primary importance to us as human beings, so that the great man approach to history is more humanly appropriate.

In the writings of these philosophers, as in Emerson's *Representative Men*, moral counsel is unmistakably conjoined with the positive evaluation of creativity: we should be as self-reliant, heroic, free, and creative as possible. The effect of this advice (which contrasts with Carlyle's advocacy of a deferential hero worship) is to blur the distinction between the great man and the not so great; the great man theory of history becomes an appeal for creative endeavor addressed to all mankind. Some contemporary discussions, on the other hand, call particular attention to the pathological character of the fanatical leader and his worshipers, reflecting current concern with the political and moral implications of dictatorship and the cult of personality. Historical inevitability, it has been argued, threatens neither freedom nor moral responsibility; it is rather the heroic view of history that could vitiate the democratic principle of mutual responsibility for political decisions and actions.

Great men as keys to historical intelligibility. Although the historical significance of great men has been stressed for the purpose of moral education and has also been closely connected with other ethical and political issues, most persons nevertheless consider a great man theory of history as fundamentally a cognitive claim made with regard to a distinctively theoretical problem and most of the literature on the topic assumes that this problem can be treated separately. Pedagogical and moral issues and

insights aside, how is history intelligible?—that is the crux of the matter. Great man theories provide one answer. Are outstanding individuals ever, often, or always the key to historical knowledge? Constructive discussion of this problem requires an analysis of the conflicting views on this matter as well as an awareness of the assumptions underlying conflicting opinions.

The problem of standards. A frequent stumbling block has been disagreement as to the formal requirements and standards of verification apposite to a theory of history. In the judgment of the social scientist the very informality of the reflections of a Burckhardt on the subject of great men may disqualify the reflections as a theory, whereas a historian would take such informality for granted. Social scientists argue even among themselves, however, as to the precise formal and evidential requirements of a proper theory.

The historian's objective. The objectives of historical inquiry constitute another source of disagreement. Is the historian's objective a causal explanation or is it a characterization of some aspect of an historical period or people—for example, its distinctive style, "mind," or "spirit"? If the historian's objective is causal explanation, then if great men are among the causal factors in history, they will be judged historically significant. If the historian's objective is characterization, and if great men are especially representative of what is to be characterized, they will likewise be judged historically significant. An analysis of these two views of the great man theory of history, which may be called the causal and the representative theories, forms the substance of the remainder of this article.

TYPES OF GREAT MAN THEORIES

It is said, on the one hand, that great men are the principal, or are among, the principal causes of history. On the other hand, it is maintained that great men personify, typify, "sum up," or represent historical movements or periods, the implication being that only by familiarizing ourselves with these representative persons can we understand history. The two views are sometimes combined, as in Hegel's idea that the hero "actualizes his age," but the efficacy of the great man need not take the form of making others think, feel, and act as he does. The truth or falsity of either the causal or the representative thesis would appear to be logically independent of the truth or falsity of the other. It cannot be assumed that either causal explanation or representativeness is uniquely appropriate as an objective of historical inquiry or that one is subordinate to the other.

Representative theory. Up to the present, no empirical historical theory about great men as representative individuals has been carefully worked out. What are found instead are statements by historians or observers of the historical scene to the effect that so-and-so was a distinguished person and personified his times or social group and, together with these statements, some vague indication that this combination of circumstances is not surprising.

It would be a precarious undertaking to attempt a precise analysis of the implicit meaning of such assertions. It can plausibly be conjectured, however, that the historian, if pressed, might explain that he did not mean to claim that there is a universal, lawlike correlation between being great and being representative, but that he had been calling attention to the applicability of the great man theory. In the form referred to, the latter might be stated as follows: It is often the case that the abilities, interests, accomplishments, character traits, or style of life of individuals who emerge from anonymity in a society exemplify characteristics that, in less noteworthy form, are common to members of the group to which the exceptional individuals belong; therefore, it behooves the working historian to be on the lookout for this correlation. Thus, the so-called "theory" turns out to be a statement of occasional correlation functioning as a methodological principle.

It would appear, however, that the emphasis on the great man as the key to the understanding of history derives in part not from a thesis about history as such, but from considerations linked to the attainment—and, perhaps, retainment—of historical knowledge. The assumption is that we can more readily, and perhaps more adequately, grasp and retain in mind the characteristic traits of the human past when these are made available to us as personified in outstanding individuals. From this angle one can understand why the historian might prefer focusing upon a vivid personality, a Leonardo da Vinci, for example, to presenting a statistically fabricated composite, precise but colorless, of the typical man of the late Italian Renaissance.

Critics of the great-and-representative-man approach to historiography have argued plausibly that it leaves something to be desired as a disclosure of the life of the bulk of mankind, for even if the great man is representative, even if through the historian's descriptive account of him we become familiar with the traits of the times and of society at large, we still do not know what form these traits assumed in the concrete experience of the multitudes of ordinary men.

Causal theory. Theories of the causal type differ among themselves in their scope, in their concept of influence, and in their notion of the relevance to the theory of the origin of outstanding leader.

Scope. Their scope may depend upon how history is conceived—whether it is restricted, for instance, to political affairs, or embraces all that men have ever felt, thought, and done. Even when history is broadly conceived, a theory may be explicitly restricted to some particular area such as art history or the history of scientific discovery.

Influence. Sometimes it is assumed that influence must manifest itself as original or pioneering achievement, but it can also be more broadly conceived so as to include even the accomplishment of destruction. A distinction is sometimes made between the great man as originator or creator and the great man as merely the executor or instrumental agency. Moreover, in some theories a particular manner of exerting influence seems to be an integral part of such theory. Carlyle emphasized the personal magnetism of the hero, his ability to arouse the hero-worshiping propensity of the ordinary man; and Max Weber likewise stressed the charismatic quality mediating the effectiveness of the leader of men.

Origin of outstanding individuals. Herbert Spencer and his followers argued against the great man theory that since outstanding persons are themselves social products, their influence reduces to an instance of social determinism. William James countered that in historical theory the secondary question as to the origin of outstanding individual abilities must be distinguished from the primary question as to the historical influence of these persons, just as Darwin distinguished between the origin of biological differences and the effects of these differences.

THE MEANING OF "GREATNESS"

Even though the concept of greatness has come to be regarded with the caution due any term so rich in extra-theoretical associations, it is worth remarking on its use in great man theories of the causal type. Is greatness equivalent to being historically influential? Many discussions presuppose unusual ability, virtuous character, and valuable achievement as defining characteristics of the great man. Thus, assuming it to be a fact that Harry Truman, president of the United States toward the end of World War II, personally made a decision of "world-historical" consequence when he directed that the atomic bomb be utilized against Japan, this fact alone would not warrant the judgment that Truman was a great man. It does not suffice that he happened to dispose of certain constitutional powers at that moment of history. It would have to be shown besides that his influential decision resulted from exceptional abilities and strength of character and that it was beneficial in its effects.

But should all eulogistic connotations of greatness be scrupulously avoided? There seems to be no conclusive objection to a precisely formulated value criterion of greatness. A value judgment implicit in the concept of greatness would, in principle, not compromise the objectivity of a theoretical inquiry into the influence of any or all of the class of human beings defined by the concept. What does seem important is that the definition permit the following to be differentiated: (a) the extent of the influence of an Attila or an Einstein described in nonevaluative terms, (b) whether this influence was beneficial or not, and (c) whether these men were of good character.

ESTIMATING THE INFLUENCE OF GREAT MEN

At the center of controversy over the causal theory has been the matter of estimating influence. The principal considerations in this regard are the following. One may claim that a great man is only one of a set of conditions such that in the absence of any one of the set the event would never have occurred. This would be to claim that the great man is one of several necessary causes of the occurrence of the historical event. On the other hand, one may claim that a great man is a sufficient cause of the occurrence of an event; that, given the presence of a great man, the event would have occurred no matter what the other circumstances might have been. In its most sweeping form, the generalization contained in the great man theory utilizes this latter formula, claiming that a great man is the sufficient condition of every historical event. But even Carlyle did not consistently and unequivocally make this extreme claim.

Criteria for estimating influence. Yet if it is held that for each historical event there is a set of necessary causes, what warrant is there, assuming that the great man is only one among the necessary causes, for emphasizing his historical influence? Is he any more important, irreplaceable, fundamental, or influential than any of the other necessary causes? The only logical basis for a comparative judgment in his favor is a criterion that more narrowly determines the objective of the specific inquiry. For example, a causal factor might be judged important if the inquiry is directed toward ascertaining which causes were subject to human control or which were unusual or novel by comparison with more stable or normal features of a situation. No one such criterion can be justified by appealing to the historical process itself. In practice, historians and social scientists employ various criteria. Relative to one or another criterion of importance, the great man theory might find considerable empirical warrant; but unless there is unanimity as to criteria, there may be disagreement about the historical role of great men. This disagreement has nothing to do with what caused what; it stems from how causal factors are to be characterized and selected as pertinent to specific inquiries. Neither empirical evidence alone nor purely rational arguments can resolve such disagreements.

Levels of analysis. Is it the case, however, that great men are usually or always among the necessary causes of historical events? Whether they are judged to be so or not may depend, again, not only upon the facts but also upon the specific way in which the problem of historical explanation is posed. For example, a cause that would be judged necessary from a short-range point of view might be judged inconsequential from a long-range point of view. Indeed, it is frequently argued that the great man theory is myopic, that the influence of the great man dwindles proportionately as we extend our historical perspective. Also, the term history can be used restrictively to mean only a certain area of human experience (such as political events), only one type of occurrence (such as developmental sequences), or only one level of analysis (such as psychological). Even a well-substantiated claim as to the decisive influence wielded by great writers, composers, or religious leaders in their respective fields of cultural activity will not suffice to confirm the great man theory if it is presupposed that history, properly speaking, consists of political and economic events. Here, again, different presuppositions of inquiry can give rise to disagreements about the significance of great men that cannot be settled by appealing to the facts. The facts may warrant different conclusions depending on different presuppositions. For example, the Marxian definition of history in terms of class struggle logically requires a level of analysis in respect to which no individual, however outstanding in ability, exercises a decisive influence on events. But the supposition that this is *the* definition of history, that there is only one proper level of analysis, only one criterion for comparing causes, has proved to be a source of embarrassment to Marxist theoreticians and has provoked critics into dogmatic counterassertions.

Areas of agreement. It should be emphasized that the kind of relativity of historical theories, including great man theories, disclosed in the preceding analysis by no means summarily discredits those theories. By explicit statement it should be possible to achieve mutual understanding of different—but equally appropriate—definitions of greatness, criteria of causal comparison, levels of analysis, temporal perspectives, and conceptions of history. This is not to minimize the difficulties of empirical investigation, beginning with the formidable task of ascertaining in particular cases whether, from a certain point of view and level of analysis, a great man was among the necessary causes. Notwithstanding these difficulties, there is wide agreement among empirically oriented inquirers that outstanding persons have sometimes been "important" necessary causes of political and economic developments, and even more confident judgments are expressed as to the "decisive" influence of great artists, scientists, philosophers, and others upon developments in their own areas of competence. This unanimity attests not to the truth of the great man theory but to extensive *de facto* agreement on specific presuppositions of inquiry of the sort revealed by an analysis of disagreement.

Bibliography

RECENT WORKS

Ball, Margaret M., "The Leadership Principle in National Socialism." *Journal of the History of Ideas*, Vol. III (1942), 74–93. Includes references to Wagner, Nietzsche, Treitschke, and Spengler.

Carr, E. H., *What Is History?* London, 1961. A qualified appreciation of the great man view by a historian.

Dray, William, *Laws and Explanation in History*. London, 1957. Ch. IV. General discussion of the logic of causal analysis in history.

Hook, Sidney, *The Hero in History*. New York, 1943. An exceptionally wide-ranging study from the standpoint of scientific empiricism and democratic political philosophy.

Oman, Charles, *On the Writing of History*. New York, 1939. A historian defends the importance of great men.

EARLIER WORKS

Bergson, Henri, *Les Deux Sources de la morale et de la religion*. Paris, 1932. Translated by R. A. Audra and Cloudesley Brereton as *The Two Sources of Morality and Religion*. New York, 1935.

Burckhardt, Jacob, *Weltgeschichtliche Betrachtungen*. Stuttgart, 1905. Translated by J. H. Nichols as *Force and Freedom: Reflections on History*. New York, 1943.

Carlyle, Thomas, *On Heroes, Hero-Worship, and the Heroic in History*. London, 1840.

Emerson, Ralph Waldo, *Representative Men*. Boston, 1850.

Hegel, G. W. F., *Die Philosophie der Geschichte*. Berlin, 1837. Translated by J. Sibree as *The Philosophy of History*. London, 1861.

James, William, "Great Men and Their Environment" and "The Importance of Individuals," in *The Will to Believe*. New York, 1897.

Mill, John Stuart, *A System of Logic*. London, 1843; 8th ed., 1872. Especially Book VI, Ch. 11.

Plekhanov, Georgi, "The Role of the Individual in History." 1898 (under pseudonym of A. Kirsanov). Reprinted in *Osnovnye Voprosi Marksizma*. St. Petersburg, 1908; 2d ed., 1928. This second edition translated by Eden and Cedar Paul as *The Fundamental Problems of Marxism*. London and New York, 1929. Essay also separately published under same title. New York, 1940.

Spencer, Herbert, *The Study of Sociology*. New York, 1874.

SCIENTIFIC INVESTIGATIONS

Gouldner, Alvin W., ed., *Studies in Leadership*. New York, 1950.

Keller, Suzanne, *Beyond the Ruling Class.* New York, 1964. A study of various elites in modern society, with an extensive bibliography of major and minor works of all sorts dealing with elites: statistical analyses, illustrative material, theoretical discussions, and so on.

Mills, C. Wright, *The Power Elite.* New York, 1956.

ROBERT STOVER

GREEK ACADEMY. Academeca was the name of a public park, equipped with a gymnasium and lecture facilities, located about a mile northwest of the Dipylon Gate of ancient Athens. There, probably shortly after 387 B.C., Plato bought a house and estate and began to teach, so successfully that his school dominated the facilities of the area, was named after the park, and continued until Justinian's closure of the pagan schools of philosophy in 529.

Classification. The main philosophical contributions of the Academy had been made by the time of Antiochus' death (c. 68 B.C.); the different phases in this period were classified into Old Academy and New Academy or, by some ancients, as Old (Plato and his immediate successors), Middle (marked by Arcesilaus in the middle of the third century B.C.) and New (dominated by Carneades in the second century B.C.). To this were sometimes added a Fourth Academy (Philo of Larissa, head 110/109–80 B.C.) and a Fifth Academy (under his successor, Antiochus). Broadly speaking, the Old Academy was occupied with problems posed by Plato, Middle and New with aspects of skepticism, and the Fifth with the eclecticism introduced by Antiochus. The history of Middle Platonism and Neoplatonism is distinct from that of the Academy, which was, however, a notable Neoplatonic center under Proclus in the fifth century.

Evidence. Plato is the only leading Academic whose published works have survived, and they are not primarily internal documents of the school; our knowledge of the doctrines of his successors and of the functioning of the Academy is tantalizingly limited to fragmentary references, opponents' criticisms, and later summaries.

Organization. At first the organization may have been informal and fluid, with Plato's personality and interests forming the center of gravity. At some point this fused into a nonfee-paying (fees were instituted by Speusippus), nonresidential corporate society, possibly in the form of a religious guild (*thiasos*), joined in the common worship of the Muses and in pursuit of truth at their shrine of learning (*Mouseion*) which Plato built on his estate. There were regular dining and other formal ceremonies. Plato appointed his successor; thereafter, the members elected their head, who held the original estate for the society and who governed until his death.

Teaching. Apparently the teaching varied to some extent among the junior and senior members of the society. Plato's own writings indicated that he had a practical aim in training young men and inspiring them with his political ideals, but he also suggested that the process required much time and study; thus, we find that the most important members remained within the school, researching and teaching, for years or for a lifetime (for instance, Aristotle and Speusippus). Practical political contributions of the Academy therefore came from senior members who were advising rulers or drafting legal codes rather than from former students who had chosen political careers. See, for example, the details given by Plutarch in *Moralia* (1126 CD); however, the extent of Academic influence is in dispute (see E. Zeller, *Die Philosophie der Griechen* II, 420, n. 1). The *Republic* declares mathematics and dialectic to be the fundamental studies, thereby placing the Academy in opposition both to the literary education of the rival school of Isocrates and to the training in techniques characteristic of some professional sophists. These subjects were chosen not only because their object was real Being, as Plato thought, but also because their method forced students into a Socratic self-learning and willingness to follow a communal discussion wherever the rational argument led.

What is certain is that instruction did not consist in the propagation of orthodox doctrine. There is a hostility to the lecture system in Plato's dialogues, which, together with the notorious failure of his public lecture on the Good, suggests that the main activity of the Old Academy lay in discussions and seminars (of which there is also some contemporary evidence in a comic fragment of Epicrates). Aristotle's mention of unwritten tenets and ascription to Plato of certain doctrines which do not appear in the dialogues (such as the equation of Forms and Numbers, the principles of Unity and Indeterminate Duality, mathematical entities of intermediate status between Forms and phenomena) have led some scholars to posit an esoteric oral teaching of Plato's, and others to suggest that Plato did no oral teaching at all in the Academy.

Both extremes, however, run counter to evidence. Aristotle may be reflecting Plato's part in some exploratory debates with senior members, for while the young and inexperienced had to be nursed and stimulated along educational paths by Plato, it is clear that no consideration of orthodoxy froze research. For such stimulation Plato posed problems, such as accounting for the movements of the planets, which produced a variety of answers including, according to Simplicius, Eudoxus' famous hypothesis of concentric heavenly spheres. We have evidence of equally lively and uninhibited debate in the Old Academy on the theory of Forms, mathematical metaphysics, classification, soul, good, and pleasure. It was at this higher level that the Academy was most successful and influential; in the conflict of educational ideals for schooling the young, the literary education of Isocrates and the rhetorical schools completely defeated in the elementary and state schools the philosophical, scientifically based Academy. However, the latter throughout its history preserved the high ideals of a society dedicated to the disinterested and independent inquiry after knowledge, ideals that succeeding ages—from the Lyceum of Aristotle to the present day—have recognized as models and standards for their own institutes of advanced study.

OLD ACADEMY

The head of the society naturally influenced all members, so the history of the Old Academy is largely an account of Plato's pupils. The most brilliant was Aristotle, a member from his eighteenth year until Plato's death in 347 B.C.; his philosophy stems from the Academy, where his earliest works were written. There is some evidence that he was still being considered for the headship at Speusippus' death in 339 B.C. and that he finally broke away to found his own school four years later.

Mathematical research was particularly distinguished in the Old Academy. Theaetetus of Athens, tragically killed in battle in 369 B.C., succeeded in generalizing the theory of irrationals and in constructing and circumscribing the five regular solids, thereby laying the foundations of Euclid's solid geometry in Books 10 and 13. Still more important was Eudoxus of Cnidus, who with his pupils joined forces with Plato (c. 367 B.C.) for a few years. Apart from the influential astronomical theory of concentric spheres, he is credited with a general theory of proportion and a method of exhaustion fundamental to Greek geometry. He criticized Plato's theory of Forms, arguing that Form, to be a cause, must be immanent in phenomena, as white is the cause of whiteness of that in which it is mixed. He apparently regarded Form as a kind of substance. This seems to have drawn reactions from Plato and Aristotle. Eudoxus' championship of hedonism likewise produced opposing arguments from Plato and Speusippus. Another astronomer, Philippus of Opus, is reported to have edited Plato's *Laws* and to have written its appendix, the *Epinomis;* whether written by him or by Plato, the latter is an important document of a stage in the Academy at which mathematical astronomy advanced from a propaedeutic science to the central science of Being and theology.

Heraclides of Pontus (c. 390–c. 310 B.C.), temporary head of the Academy during Plato's third Sicilian journey, unsuccessful candidate in the election of 339 B.C., and later associated with the Lyceum, had a Pythagorean bias and was a prolific, learned, and elegant writer on a wide variety of subjects rather than an original thinker. He appears to have responded to the problem of the planets' motion, but it remains uncertain whether he partially anticipated Aristarchus' heliocentric system and posited the rotation of the earth on its axis, as was thought. He posited an atomic theory of irregular units of mass but attacked the mechanical atomic theory of his day, holding that matter was subject to a divine teleology.

Speusippus, who succeeded his uncle Plato in 347 B.C., may well have been the senior member or even a founder of the society. He and the third head, Xenocrates of Chalcedon (c. 396–314 B.C., head 339–314 B.C.), another pupil of Plato's from his earliest years, were thought by Aristotle and others to be concerned with similar problems. Although neither was a great philosopher, a study of fragments of their writings reveals a development of trends apparent in Plato's later work, some positions between Plato and Aristotle, and some foreshadowing of later Platonism. Both, but especially Speusippus, were strongly influenced by the current Pythagorean fashions in the Academy. In the school debate over the division of Being into the three spheres of Forms, Mathematicals, and Physicals, Speusippus replaced Plato's Forms with mathematical entities and Xenocrates identified Forms and Mathematicals. Both were preoccupied with the derivation of a hierarchy of substances from mathematical first principles—Speusippus disjointedly, according to Aristotle, in that he abandoned the uniform interdependence of the whole universe on one set of first principles and assumed different principles for different kinds of substance in series. Xenocrates posited the Platonic Unity and Indeterminate Dyad (or continuum of opposites such as great and small). Good, which was derivative for Speusippus (coming at the end of becoming), was distinguished from both Unity and Being. Soul fell into the mathematical classification—as self-moving number for Xenocrates and seemingly as a form of extension for Speusippus, a theory of great importance for the later Stoic, Posidonius. Another Pythagorean trait was the strong theological interpretation of their mathematical cosmology, also hierarchical in treatment, Xenocrates advocating the influential doctrine of *daimones,* animate beings between gods and men. In dealing with the Academic problem of real definition by *diaeresis* (division) and classification, Speusippus suggested in an important work, *Homoia* ("Resemblances"), that definition by division was impossible without knowing all existing things, the essential nature of any one concept being constituted solely in its relation of likeness and difference to every other concept. Xenocrates foreshadowed Aristotle by asserting the logical and ontological priority of species over genus. In epistemology both continued the trend of allowing more cognitive importance to perception; Xenocrates, who had a weakness for triadic systematization, worked out spheres of the universe corresponding to cognitive powers: the sphere within the heavens as perceptible, that outside the heavens as intelligible, the heavens themselves as a mixture of both and thus objects of opinion. Both men were prolific writers on practical ethics; they held that happiness can come into being from virtue alone but that virtue is not the only good. Speusippus campaigned against pleasure as being contrary to both pain and good.

The next head, Polemon of Athens (elected 314 B.C.), concentrated on conduct, elaborating Xenocrates' conception of happiness as life "in accordance with nature," a phrase which, especially through the Stoa, became the center of ethical debate. Polemon had more personal influence than philosophical originality, but he is of some importance for the Academy of the first century B.C. His friend, Crantor of Soli in Cilicia (c. 335–c. 275 B.C.), wrote a famous work, *Peri Penthous* ("On Grief"), a prototype of an ethical genre later popular, directed against the extreme views of the Stoics on pain and the affections.

MIDDLE AND NEW ACADEMIES

Crantor's reaction to the Stoa heralded a major change in the school. Until Crates of Athens (elected head 270 B.C.), the main topics of inquiry were Platonic questions and developments. The next head, Arcesilaus of Pitane (316–241 B.C.), is reputed to have concentrated on an attack on the Stoic theory of knowledge. He was probably reacting not only to an ontology and epistemology inimical to the Platonic tradition but even more to the dogmatic character of Stoicism, which he countered by an exaggerated form of Socratic skepticism: not only did he know, like Socrates, that he knew nothing, but he is also said to have doubted whether he could ever know that he knew the truth. He imitated Socrates in writing nothing and taught mainly in open debate, introducing to the school the system of arguing on both sides of a question. Nevertheless, he saw to it that Plato's works were studied; and in the controversy with the Stoa, the Academy maintained that by "suspension of judgment" (*epoche*) they were not inhibited in their main philosophic task of a continual search for truth, however unattainable, or from moral action, as a guide for which Arcesilaus recommended "the reasonable." The dialectical influence of Arcesilaus set the Academy firmly in the main stream of Greek skepticism, but it was an age of formalization through controversy. Arcesilaus helped to produce Chrysippus, the great fortifier of Stoicism; Chrysippus was in turn the whetstone of the most brilliant figure of the second century B.C., Carneades of Cyrene (214–129 B.C.), who systematized a comprehensive and devastating skeptical attack against the whole philosophy of the dogmatic schools. But while Carneades had penetrating observations on sense perception, probability, causation, fatalism, and anthropocentric theology, he seems, both in method and content, to have drifted some way from the original Socratic–Platonic tradition.

Reaction began with Philo of Larissa (160/159–80 B.C., head from 110/109), Cicero's teacher, who, while maintaining skepticism against Stoic epistemology, reclaimed his Platonic ancestry. It was completed with Philo's pupil and opponent, Antiochus of Ascalon (c. 130–c. 68 B.C., head from c. 79 B.C.), who came to think that the representatives of the New Academy had perverted the teaching of the Old Academy by maintaining that no truth could be grasped, thereby destroying any criterion of true and false and, in Antiochus' opinion, inhibiting action through denial of certainty. Antiochus reinstated a dogmatism whereby a criterion of truth arising from but not contained in the senses was grasped by the mind as self-evident. His reinterpretation of Platonism was marked by an eclecticism in ethics which enabled him to propose that the Stoa and Peripatos had merely followed the lead of the Old Academy, differing from it in terms rather than in substance.

In fact, the theories of morals of the three schools were all naturalist, and Antiochus' distorted arguments were facilitated by certain shared areas of discussion, covered by Polemo and the early Peripatos and Stoa, based on "the things according to nature" (*ta kata physin*) to which human beings had a natural affinity (*oikeiosis*). Doubtless there had been interchange of ideas, which was fostered even by the New Academy's insistence on arguing on both sides of the question, but Antiochus blurred the quite different approaches of the schools to a common area of dispute.

His thesis may have been further encouraged by the early "Platonic" works of Aristotle which were then popular, and influenced by the Stoic Panaetius, who had admired Plato and who gave greater prominence in his teaching than had earlier Stoics to the "intermediate natural things" (health, wealth, etc.), which, although the material of ethics, were held by Stoics to be in themselves of only relative value and morally neutral compared with the absolute value of the rational operation of virtue. Antiochus, however, maintained that the end of action, the happy life (*beata vita*), although possible through virtue alone, was completed (*beatissima*) by bodily and external goods. Thus Antiochus shared a graded axiology with the Old Academy and Peripatos; for him the difference between virtue and other goods was one of degree, for the Stoa there was a difference of kind. In a manner similar to some Stoic arguments, he held that the chief good was based on natural instincts for self-preservation and self-development, so that from the germ of virtues in the impulses of childhood man gradually attained knowledge of his own nature; but for Antiochus the perfection of human nature involved all parts of it, not only the highest, and also man's relationship to others and to the community.

This attempted dogmatic synthesis of the three great schools was of minor philosophical interest in itself, but of major importance for subsequent Greek thought. Apart from professional Academics, Antiochus profoundly influenced the popular expositor Cicero, some Stoics with doxographic interests like Arius Didymus, who taught at the court of Augustus, and Middle Platonists such as Albinus of Smyrna, whose lectures Galen attended in 151/152. Albinus' markedly eclectic epitome of Platonism (the *Didaskalikos*) still survives. Indeed, without the growth of syncretism initiated by Antiochus, the fusion that created the final explosion of ancient thought in Neoplatonism would not have been possible.

Throughout the long history of the Academy, the founder's works were studied and his birthday revered with celebrations. It is a remarkable tribute to his personality, philosophy, and educational ideals that through the very different phases of the school all members considered themselves his true heirs, so that one man's ideas stimulated his pupils over nine hundred years without in any way rigidifying their thought.

Bibliography

Some continuous texts are Diogenes Laërtius, *Lives*, Books III and IV; Aristotle, *Metaphysics*, Books A, M, and N; Cicero, *Academica* and *De Finibus*, Books IV and V; Sextus Empiricus, *Outlines of Pyrrhonism* and *Against the Dogmatists*; Siegfried Mekler, *Academicorum Philosophorum Index Herculanensis* (Berlin, 1902).

Fragments include P. L. Lang, *De Speusippi Academici Scriptis* (Bonn, 1911); Richard Heinze, *Xenocrates* (Leizpig, 1892); Fritz Wehrli, *Herakleides Pontikos* (Basel, 1953); Georg Luck, *Der Akademiker Antiochus* (Bern, 1953); and C. J. de Vogel, *Greek Philosophy*, Vol. II (Leiden, 1953; 2d ed., 1960) and Vol. III (Leiden, 1959).

A standard work is Eduard Zeller, *Die Philosophie der Griechen in ihrer geschichtlichen Entwicklung*, 6th ed. (Hildesheim, 1963), II.1.2 and III.1.1 and 2.

Introductory works on the Old Academy include G. C. Field, *Plato and His Contemporaries* (London, 1930; 2d ed., 1948); Werner Jaeger, *Aristotle* (Berlin, 1923), translated by Richard Robinson (Oxford, 1934); A. E. Taylor, *Plato, the Man and His Work* (London, 1926); Sir David Ross, the Introduction to Aristotle's *Metaphysics* (Oxford, 1924; 2d ed., 1953); Hans Herter, *Platons Akademie* (Bonn, 1952); and C. B. Armstrong, "Plato's Academy," in *Proceedings of the Leeds Philosophical Society* (1953), 89 ff.

Important works of detail include Léon Robin, *La Théorie platonicienne des idées et des nombres* (Paris, 1908); Julius Stenzel, *Zahl und Gestalt bei Platon und Aristoteles* (Leipzig and Berlin,

1933); H. F. Cherniss, *Aristotle's Criticism of Plato and the Academy* (Baltimore, 1944) and *The Riddle of the Early Academy* (Berkeley, 1945); Sir David Ross, *Plato's Theory of Ideas* (Oxford, 1953); Philip Merlan, *From Platonism to Neoplatonism* (The Hague, 1953) and "Zur Biographie des Speusippos," in *Philologus*, Vol. 103 (1959), 198 ff.; Paul Wilpert, *Zwei Aristotelische Frühschriften über die Ideenlehre* (Regensburg, 1949); and Shlomo Pines, *A New Fragment of Xenocrates and Its Implications* (Philadelphia, 1961).

See also H. J. Krämer, *Arete bei Platon und Aristoteles* (Heidelberg, 1959), and Konrad Gaisser, *Platons ungeschriebene Lehre* (Stuttgart, 1963). The latter contains a very convenient collection of *Testimonia Platonica: Quellentexte zur Schule und mündlichen Lehre Platons*, on pp. 441–557.

For works on the Middle and New academies, see Victor Brochard, *Les Sceptiques grecs* (Paris, 1887); Albert Goedeckemeyer, *Die Geschichte des griechischen Skeptizismus* (Leipzig, 1905); M. M. Patrick, *The Greek Skeptics* (New York, 1929); Léon Robin, *Pyrrhon et le scepticisme grec* (Paris, 1944); Olof Gigon, "Zur Geschichte der sogenannten Neuen Akademie," in *Museum Helveticum*, Vol. 1 (1944), 47 ff.; Max Pohlenz, *Die Stoa*, Vol. I (Göttingen, 1948) and Vol. II, 2d ed. (Göttingen, 1955); R. E. Witt, *Albinus and the History of Middle Platonism* (Cambridge, 1937); and A. Weische, *Cicero und die Neue Akademie* (Münster, 1961).

I. G. KIDD

GREEK DRAMA. When Plato spoke of an ancient quarrel between poetry and philosophy, and when Aristotle said that poetry is more serious and more philosophical than history, they were both thinking primarily of epic and dramatic poetry, especially of tragedy. The reason why the two great Greek philosophers paid so much attention to dramatic poetry is closely connected with the reasons why Greek tragedy continues to deserve the interest of philosophers today. An account of philosophical ideas in Greek drama can usefully begin with some consideration of ancient philosophical ideas about Greek drama.

Plato and Aristotle. It is well known that Plato was hostile to what he regarded as the inflated pretensions of the poets as moral and religious teachers and to the arrogant claims made on their behalf by rhapsodes and expositors. In numerous dialogues (notably in *Apology, Ion,* and *Republic*) he reiterated the complaint that poets lack the knowledge which, he believed, can be achieved only by rigorous philosophizing and which is necessary for the understanding of the human situation and the ordering of human life. The poets pronounce on life's problems without being able to "give an account" (λόγον διδόναι) of themselves and their ideas. Plato might ironically allow that, like conventional statesmen, they have some divinely inspired glimpses of moral and political truth, but he insisted that they lack the true knowledge that is achieved by the philosopher after strenuous dialectical thought.

Tragedy is essentially a kind of rhetoric (*Gorgias* 502D), and Plato reviled it with all the passion that he displayed in his attacks on forensic and political oratory. All these are the arts of mere persuasion, and they are customarily used to persuade men of what is false. Plato explicitly held that most orators, politicians, and poets are dishonest or ignorant, or both, and even the most famous of them would be refused admission to the ideal republic.

One of Plato's most important grounds for despising literature was based on the theory of Forms. The poet deals in the concrete and particular; dialectic, like its mathematical archetype, is concerned with the abstract

and universal. It follows that even an honest poet must inevitably fail to achieve and convey knowledge and understanding, since he is operating at entirely the wrong level. He presents images of images; he and his audience are at two removes from the world of reality and truth (*Republic* 597E).

Aristotle, the philosopher of the concrete particular substance, with his keen interest in the actual particular specimen, was more sympathetic to poetry and literature. Poetry is philosophical because it portrays the nature of man in general by presenting particular individual men in such a way that each portrait throws light on other individuals, just as the biologist studies the genus or the species by attending in detail to actual particular specimens. A chronicle of "what Alcibiades did or suffered" tells us only about Alcibiades. Oedipus or Agamemnon is Man as well as *a* man. Aristotle regarded the poets as contributors to thought, knowledge, and understanding, not as mere entertainers.

The opposite views of Plato and Aristotle on the value of literature must not be allowed to hide the importance of a point on which they agreed. Plato's attack on poetry, like Aristotle's more sympathetic treatment, presupposes that there is an overlapping of function between philosophy and literature. Plato thought that the poets gave wrong answers to the questions and problems that he dealt with in his dialogues, but the very form of his attack implies his recognition that the poets are also concerned with those questions and problems. The old battle between philosophy and poetry could not take place at all unless the two parties shared at least a battleground.

This point is confirmed, and its importance is underlined, by further knowledge of the history of ancient literature and philosophy. It was only in the time of Plato and Aristotle themselves that there began to appear any very clear distinctions between philosophy, history, science, and imaginative literature. Homer had fulfilled all the functions that were later divided among historians, tragic and comic poets, philosophers, theologians, moralists, and scientists. Parmenides and Empedocles were poets as well as philosophers; they did not write both poetry *and* philosophy—their poetry *was* their philosophy. Heraclitus wrote in prose but in an oracular, literary manner. Hesiod is part of the history of philosophical and cosmological speculation as well as of the history of literature. Plato himself wrote philosophy that is also literature and, in spite of his own strictures, imaginative and dramatic literature.

Modern views. Modern controversy about Greek tragedy has followed similar lines. Many scholars and critics have praised the Attic tragedians as religious and moral thinkers and prophets, thus accepting Plato's view of the nature of the aims and themes of the ancient plays while often strongly dissenting from his valuation of them. Others, by contrast, have denied that the tragedians either showed or meant to show any moral or religious depth or originality, and have presented them as "mere" poets and playwrights whose purpose was purely literary and dramatic and who used traditional mythological and religious material simply because it was traditional.

This dispute is misconceived and is based on a false

dichotomy. It not only ignores the artificiality of any attempt to draw a sharp distinction between literature and philosophy in Greek times but also involves drawing a distinction between them that is too sharp to be faithful to the nature and function of literature and philosophy in any age, including our own. Both parties to the dispute share Plato's mistaken assumption that nothing can count as philosophical, religious, or moral thought unless it is explicitly and formally general and systematic. Aristotle's recognition that fifth-century tragedy illuminated morality and religion by a dramatic presentation of particular events and characters needs to be extended to literature in general. The themes of Greek tragedy are the themes of literature: Man, God, Nature, Chance, Freedom, Will, Fate, Necessity, and Good and Evil. Most, if not all, of these themes are also themes of great and permanent philosophical interest, and philosophers should not despise the contributions of dramatists, poets, and novelists to our understanding of them.

Tragedy. Aeschylus, Sophocles, and Euripides had much in common: they all drew their characters and plots from a common stock of religious mythology and historical legend inherited from Homer, and they all used their plays as means of presenting the relations between men and gods. The stories of the Trojan War, of Agamemnon and the House of Tantalus, of Oedipus and the House of Cadmus recur in the works of all three. (A "history play," such as *The Persians* of Aeschylus, is exceptional, although commentators have found historical and political allusions in many of the plays that are based on mythical themes.)

Aeschylus and Sophocles were relatively orthodox in their treatment of the traditional themes. The *Oresteia* of Aeschylus presents, through the story of the working out of a family curse, a study of the conflict between man's efforts to choose and guide his own life and the almost irresistible weight of past events and external influences. Agamemnon "puts on the yoke of necessity" when he chose to sacrifice his daughter Iphigeneia rather than to risk the ruin of the Greek expedition against Troy. In that phrase and in that incident Aeschylus combines an awareness of the force of circumstance with a consciousness of the responsibility that a man bears for his own actions, however circumscribed they are by what lies outside his control. The yoke is a yoke of necessity; but it is Agamemnon who puts it on. In the same trilogy Aeschylus portrays the growth of revenge ("a kind of wild justice," as Bacon called it) into the cultivated plant of civil law. His *Prometheus Bound* is also concerned with conflict. The struggle between Prometheus and Zeus is also the struggle between man's aspiration after knowledge and power and the forces of nature and environment represented by the gods. Men pay in suffering for every step in understanding.

The *Oedipus Tyrannus* of Sophocles also shows the price that must be paid for knowledge and self-knowledge. The man who answered the riddle of the Sphinx finds, when he knows his own nature and his own circumstances, that not all knowledge is sweet, and blinds his eyes that have seen too much. And yet it was ignorance that led him to his tragic end. If he had known more and had known it sooner, he would have done better and fared better. In the *Antigone* we find the "conflict of right with right" that led to Hegel's definition of tragedy; the legitimate claims of Creon, the civil power, are set against Antigone's ardent loyalty to holy and unwritten laws.

Euripides used the same stock of mythical material but in a different spirit. He was a friend of Anaxagoras and a student of the sophists and orators, whose influence is seen in his set debates and rhetorical speeches. The sophistry of Hippolytus ("my tongue it was that swore; my heart is not forsworn") and the atheism of Bellerophon are only two examples of the "free thought" of some of his characters that shocked Aristophanes and other conventional Athenians. It was debated, and is still debated, whether Euripides was himself an atheist or a modernistic theologian. To the modern reader of the plays the question is of merely academic interest. In the *Hippolytus* and the *Bacchae* he vividly presents conflicts between Aphrodite and Artemis and between Dionysus and the forces of order and restraint. The impact of these conflicts on a modern reader is not much affected by questions about whether Euripides literally believed in the gods of the Greek pantheon or merely used them as personifications of forces in human nature that are as familiar to us as they were to his original audience.

In reading Greek tragedy, as in reading any work of imaginative literature, we must beware of attributing to the author the opinions and attitudes expressed by his characters. The best Greek tragedies are as dialectical as the works of Plato. The issues they deal with are too complex and subtle to allow a neat answer to be given to them in the speeches of any one character. The dramatist presents and portrays; he does not argue and declaim.

Comedy. Attic comedy is of little more than historical interest from the philosophical point of view. The *Clouds* of Aristophanes pillories and parodies a "Socrates" who is made to represent all that was new and disturbing in contemporary Greek thought. Aristophanes shows here and in several other plays (especially in the *parabasis,* or address of the chorus to the audience on current topics) that he was a conservative who looked back to the golden days of Aeschylus and the other "men of Marathon." His satirical purpose could best be served by ignoring the great diversity in the movements of thought that he disliked: Pythagorean and Orphic mysticism, natural speculation, sophistic attacks on conventional morality and religion, and the revolutionary theology of Euripides.

Comedy, like tragedy, was religious in its origin, and Aristophanes, if read with caution, can contribute to our knowledge of the history of Greek religious thought. But no comic writer can be trusted very far as a source of information on philosophical or scientific thought, and in particular Aristophanes' account of Socrates needs more delicate handling than it has received from scholars preoccupied with the "Socratic question." What the *Clouds* does show is that philosophical speculation was of some interest to the general public in Athens, even if only as a butt of jokes and gibes. Socrates testifies in Plato's *Apology* that attacks by comic poets helped to foster prejudice against him.

The contest between Aeschylus and Euripides in the

Frogs of Aristophanes is one of the earliest examples of literary criticism, and it preaches, as Plato did, that the poet's function is to edify and instruct his audience.

Bibliography

The Oxford Classical Dictionary. Oxford, 1949. See the articles on Aeschylus, Sophocles, Euripides, tragedy, Aristophanes, and comedy.
Adkins, A. W. H., *Merit and Responsibility: A Study in Greek Values.* Oxford, 1960.
Havelock, E. A., *Preface to Plato.* Oxford, 1963.
Kitto, H. D. F., *Greek Tragedy.* London, 1939.
Lloyd-Jones, P. H. J., *The Greeks.* London, 1962.
Lucas, D. W., *The Greek Tragic Poets,* 2d ed. London, 1959.
Verrall, A. W., *Euripides the Rationalist.* Cambridge, 1895.

RENFORD BAMBROUGH

GREEN, THOMAS HILL (1836–1882), English idealist philosopher, was born the fourth son of a Church of England clergyman at Birkin in Yorkshire. His mother died when he was only a year old. Green received his early education from his father before going at the age of 14 to Rugby School, which had been reorganized on distinctive lines by Thomas Arnold a few years earlier. The corporate side of life at Rugby had little appeal for Green, but his fellow scholars were already impressed by his seriousness and independence of mind. Academically, he was able but not outstanding. In 1855 he entered Balliol College, Oxford, where he was an undergraduate for the next four years. Green was only a moderate classical scholar, but he got first-class honors when he took the final examinations in *Literae Humaniores,* preparation for which gave him his first serious work in philosophy. He was elected a fellow of Balliol in November 1860 but did not get a regular teaching post there for several years. In 1863 he refused an offer of the editorship of *The Times of India,* then being started in Bombay; in 1864 he was an unsuccessful candidate for a philosophy chair at the University of St. Andrews. In 1865 and 1866 he served as assistant to a Royal Commission investigating school education in England and Wales, working mainly in and around Birmingham. From 1866 onward he was heavily engaged at Balliol, where he became the first nonclerical tutor; by 1870, the year in which Benjamin Jowett became master, much of the administration of the college had fallen on his shoulders. He continued to serve as a tutor until 1878, when he was elected Whyte's professor of moral philosophy at the university.

By this time Green had married Charlotte Symonds (1871) and had published his first major philosophical work, the long critique of empiricism which constitutes the introduction to the edition of Hume's works which he produced with T. H. Grose. He had also begun to take an active part in social work and in local politics. From 1872 on he was prominent in the temperance movement (one of his brothers was a hopeless drunkard), and in 1876 he became a member of the Oxford town council, being the first active teacher in the university to hold such an office. He also played a major part in a movement to found a new high school in Oxford. Unfortunately, however, his health deteriorated sharply during these years, and matters were not improved by the added lecturing duties of the professorship, which Green undertook with characteristic thoroughness, writing out his lectures in full. He had long planned a major work on moral philosophy, but his *Prolegomena to Ethics* was still incomplete when he died in 1882. It was published by A. C. Bradley the following year. Green's other philosophical and miscellaneous writings were collected in three volumes by R. L. Nettleship, who also wrote the long memoir printed in Volume III.

Green has recently been described as the first professional philosopher in the modern sense; he was certainly one of the first specialized teachers of the subject in Oxford. But he exercised influence in many spheres outside philosophy. His work as a Balliol tutor did much to produce a distinctive type of Oxford graduate, unknown in the mid-nineteenth century: hard-working, intensely serious, aware to a surprising degree of social problems and realities. In politics he was important not only because of what he did to ease relations between "town and gown" in Oxford but also for his pronounced radicalism: he was a strong supporter of Bright against Palmerston and of the cause of the North in the American Civil War. His essay "Liberal Legislation and Freedom of Contract" (1881) is important for its criticisms of pure laissez-faire liberalism and can be seen as anticipating the doctrine of the welfare state. Theologically, Green was not strikingly original, but the low value he set on dogma and historical tradition was certainly not without its effect. By insisting on the independent authority of philosophy he may well have persuaded many intending ordinands to take up other careers. Although very different in his philosophical views and immediate disciples from his contemporary Henry Sidgwick, he made much the same contribution to the secularization of Oxford as Sidgwick made to the secularization of Cambridge.

Critique of "popular philosophy." A useful point of entry into Green's philosophical thought is to be found in his early essay "Popular Philosophy in its Relation to Life," originally published in 1868. The "popular philosophy" of the title was that professed by the advanced thinkers of the time, whom Green explicitly compared with the ancient Sophists. Like the Sophists they were superficially clear and rhetorically persuasive; again like them, they owed their apparent success to a refusal to examine their basic notions. Yet these notions, when applied in the concrete, turned out to be wholly inadequate; they could not successfully be brought to bear on life, as understood in art or religion or moral practice. In "Popular Philosophy" Green set himself to demonstrate this conclusion only in the case of ethics, reviewing for this purpose the doctrines of Butler, Hume, and Rousseau, but it was obvious that he had wider considerations in mind. When he spoke of the need for an "adequate theory," of which the philosophy of Hegel might offer a foretaste, he was implying that the philosophers he was considering were wrong not only in their ethical distinctions but also in their whole method and metaphysical outlook. Following Locke, they assumed that truth could be arrived at by simple introspection; they had no notion of the difference between image and concept and hence no tenable theory of thinking. The statement of their theories presupposed a continuing self-identical subject, but the theories themselves had no room for any such thing. Nor, in practice, had they anything like an adequate grasp of the workings of the human mind, which they looked on as an isolated automaton mechanically pursuing pleasure and seeking to avoid pain, instead of as an active agent whose interest and welfare were intimately bound up with those of others.

The corrective to popular philosophy, Green said at this stage, was to be found in "the deeper views of life which the contemplative poets originated" and in the notions of "evangelical religion," as well as in some of the better insights of Rousseau. It was not "'within his own breast'" that Wordsworth had looked to "read what he was," but to "the open scroll of the world, of the world, however, as written within and without by a self-conscious and self-determining spirit" (*Works*, Vol. III, p. 119). Similarly, the evangelical insistence on the sense of sin showed the superficiality of the moral philosophy of the Enlightenment, which could represent vice as an object of regret or distaste but never as an object of abomination. Much of Green's mature philosophy becomes intelligible if we bear these remarks in mind. He took neither poetry nor religion to be a substitute for philosophy, but nonetheless he felt deeply that both had important lessons to teach the philosopher.

Critiques of Hume and naturalism. The more academic criticisms sketched in Green's early essay were elaborated in the introduction to his edition of Hume's works (1874). Green's view was that Hume was a major philosopher who had taken Locke's ill-thought-out assumptions to their logical conclusion and, in so doing, had revealed their absurdity. Hume's first principle was that nothing is real save feeling; Green attacked this view with the argument that to say that something is real is to relate it to other things and that relations are not given in feeling but are the work of the mind. Hume's attempt to ground "philosophical" in "natural" relations, that is, in what is given to sense, was a failure. So was his theory of the self as a succession of perceptions, for relating clearly demands an unchanging subject that relates. The argument of this passage was carried further in the first book of the *Prolegomena to Ethics,* where Green claimed that not only our consciousness of nature but also nature itself presuppose an "eternal," self-identical, and self-differentiating subject which is the source not only of the connections in thought but also of its material. A halfway position, such as Kant had taken, was not intellectually defensible: the thing-in-itself and its empiricist counterpart, the sheerly given, remain unintelligible on this type of view.

Green's object in metaphysics was plainly to state an alternative to materialism, which struck him as both insidiously attractive and intellectually preposterous. Much the same ambition informs his writings on ethics, in which field he again saw himself as developing an antinaturalist position. In his critique of moral sense theories, which forms part of his general criticism of Hume, he represented the supporters of those views as one and all hedonists, on the ground that they made the passions the only spring of action and thought of reason as practically inert. Hence, his own first aim in the *Prolegomena* was to establish that

human actions spring from *motives* and to show that motives are not "natural phenomena." He defined a motive (Sec. 87) as "an idea of an end, which a self-conscious subject presents to itself, and which it strives and tends to realise." The vital point here was the connection between motives and a continuing subject consciously pursuing good; human action, for Green, was entirely different from animal behavior, for although much of it had animal impulses as its basis, these impulses were transformed in being brought into consciousness and thought of in relation to long-term aims. As for the good with which action is concerned, Green said (*ibid.,* Sec. 92) that "anything conceived in such a way that the agent acts for the sake of it, must be conceived as *his own* good, though he may conceive it as his own good only on account of his interest in others, and in spite of any amount of suffering on his own part incidental in its attainment." But in practice he had little to say about the connection of good with the satisfaction of the agent: The moral ideal must be realized in persons, but one person's claims to moral self-expression were as good as those of another, and moral progress came about with the realization that more and more persons and types of person were entitled to have their claims considered. Green made much use of the phrase "the common good" in speaking of the ultimate aim of moral action, but his alternative description of the end as the attainment of "human perfection" is in some ways more appropriate, provided it is added that he wanted to see human perfection realized without distinction of persons.

Political philosophy. In ethics Green had clearly learned a lot from Hegel, although his general outlook remained more Kantian than Hegelian—both in theory and in practice he must be counted as a liberal moralist. His political philosophy also is in the liberal tradition, despite its rejection of such elements of older liberal political theory as the doctrine of the contract. The state, according to Green, is the product of will, not of force, insofar as the system of rights and duties it operates rests on a moral as opposed to a merely natural basis. Green was as emphatic in his political as in his ethical theory that rights cannot be created out of nothing, in the way Hobbes and Spinoza supposed. But although he thus saw the state as, in a sense, a moral organism, Green had no inclination to endow it with positive moral authority. The state might sometimes have to inhibit the freedom of particular men to enable others to be free at all, but the end of political action could only be to put citizens in a position to lead the good life. The liberalism he favored was thus in the end a negative liberalism, concerned with creating the minimum conditions in which people could exercise moral choice and, for the rest, leaving matters to their voluntary efforts.

Compared with that of his younger contemporary F. H. Bradley, Green's literary style was flat and uninteresting. The moral earnestness which is apparent in so much of his writing also has had much to do with its neglect by more recent philosophers. But however earnest he was, he was at the least estimate an influential thinker; to describe him, as C. D. Broad did, as "thoroughly second-rate" is to forget the extent to which his articulation of problems is still accepted, for example in political philosophy. Nor are his solutions entirely without interest, if only we can divest them of the stiff Victorian garments in which he chose to clothe them.

Bibliography

The Works of Thomas Hill Green, R. L. Nettleship, ed., 3 vols. (London, 1885–1888), contains all Green's surviving writings except his introductions to Hume (in Hume's *Works,* T. H. Green and T. H. Grose, eds., London, 1874) and the *Prolegomena to Ethics,* A. C. Bradley, ed. (Oxford, 1883).

For literature on Green, see J. Pucelle, *La Nature et l'esprit dans la philosophie de T. H. Green,* 2 vols. (Louvain, 1961–1965), which is the fullest commentary; see also Pucelle's *L'Idéalisme en Angleterre* (Neuchâtel, 1955).

For Green's ethics, see W. D. Lamont, *Introduction to Green's Moral Philosophy* (London, 1934). On his political views, compare A. J. M. Milne, *The Social Philosophy of English Idealism* (London, 1962), and M. Richter, *The Politics of Conscience: T. H. Green and His Times* (London, 1964), which also contains biographical details supplementing Nettleship's memoir in *Works,* Vol. III. Mrs. Humphry Ward's novel *Robert Elsmere* (1888) is dedicated to Green's memory, and one of its characters is said to portray him.

W. H. WALSH

GREGORY OF NAZIANZUS (329/330–c. 390), poet, theologian, and bishop, was born at Arianzum in Cappadocia. Although his parents were Christians, he enjoyed an excellent classical education at Caesarea in Palestine and at the universities of Alexandria and Athens. He was from his earliest years a close friend of the other two Cappadocians, Gregory of Nyssa and Basil the Great. Baptized at about the age of thirty, he was ordained by his father, the local bishop—apparently against his will—and immediately fled. After his penitent return, Basil appointed him bishop of the isolated town of Sasima. However, Gregory refused to go and remained with his father at Nazianzus, staying on after his father's death in 374. After a period of monastic living he was approved as bishop of Constantinople under Emperor Theodosius, but distrust of his own administrative ability once again forced him to resign after a year. After a few years at Nazianzus, he finally retired to his estate at Arianzum and devoted his last years to writing; it was here, between 384 and 390, that he wrote his greatest poems.

Adequate study of Gregory is still hampered by the lack of a full critical edition of his works. The bulk is poetic (more than 16,000 lines). There are also 44 orations, including the important dogmatic ones (numbers 27–31, delivered in 380), and 244 authentic letters.

Gregory Nazianzen is the most literate, self-conscious stylist of the three Cappadocian Fathers, although perhaps not as profound as Gregory of Nyssa nor so immersed in ecclesiastical affairs as Basil the Great. Although he once compared philosophy to "the plagues of Egypt," his poetry shows the wide influences of all the Greek schools, and especially of the Stoic–Cynic. In morals Gregory reflects a sharply critical view of contemporary worldliness and sensuality; and his introspective poetry (especially the autobiographical "De Vita Sua") marks a new era in Christian self-awareness and is comparable to Augustine's *Confessions*. However, the bulk of his verse is coldly classical and heavily didactic.

Gregory was fully aware (see *Oration* 20.17) of the role

of speculation in theology. He contributed to Trinitarian theology by clearly defining the relations and properties of the three Persons of the Trinity. In Christology he insisted on the two distinct natures in Christ bound by a "union according to essence," copresent to each other by "circumincession"—a term later applied to the Persons of the Trinity. In developing traditional dogma, Gregory's discussion is sometimes sharper than either Basil's or Gregory of Nyssa's, although he is vague on the doctrines of hell and original sin.

Works by Gregory

Works, C. Clemencet and A. B. Caillau, eds., 2 vols. Paris, 1778 and 1840. Reprinted in J. P. Migne, ed., *Patrologia Graeca*. Paris, 1857–1866. Vols. 35–38.

Nicene and Post-Nicene Christian Fathers, Series II. New York, 1887–1892; Oxford, 1890–1900. Vol. VII, pp. 185–498. A translation of selected orations and letters by J. E. Swallow, with an introduction by C. G. Browne.

Five Theological Orations, A. J. Mason, ed. Cambridge, 1899. Critical edition.

Works on Gregory

Campenhausen, Hans von, *The Fathers of the Greek Church,* translated by S. Godman. New York, 1959. Pp. 95–106.

Pellegrino, M., *La poesia di S. Gregorio Nazianzeno*. Milan, 1932.

Plagnieux, J., *S. Grégoire de Nazianze, Théologien*. Paris, 1951.

Quasten, Johannes, *Patrology,* Vol. III, *The Golden Age of Greek Patristic Literature*. Westminster, Md., 1961. Pp. 236–254.

Werhan, H. M., ed., *Lexikon für Theologie und Kirke,* 2d ed. Freiburg, 1960. Vol. IV, pp. 1210 ff.

HERBERT MUSURILLO, S.J.

GREGORY OF NYSSA (c. 330–c. 394), Christian theologian and Father of the Eastern church, was born in Cappadocia. Resisting the invitation of his brother, Basil the Great, to join his monastic community at Annesis, Gregory married and became a teacher of rhetoric. In 372 Basil, bishop of Caesarea, had Gregory appointed bishop of Nyssa; but Gregory was deposed in 374 by a local synod dominated by the Emperor Valens and the Arian party. Restored to his see in 377, Gregory began to grow closer to Basil's monastic and theological ideals. After Basil's death in 379, Gregory engaged more and more in writing and in the vigorous administration of his diocese; he was an important figure at the councils convoked at Constantinople in 381, 383, and, just before his death, in 394. An ardent defender of the orthodox Trinitarian doctrine of Nicaea against the Arians and semi-Arians, he was also popular in court circles at Constantinople. Toward the end of his life, when his influence began to wane, he devoted himself to the deepening of the traditional Christian heritage of mystical theology; during this period, from about 390 until his death, he composed some of his most profound works, the *Commentary on the Song of Songs* and the *Life of Moses,* which represent the culmination of the process inaugurated in his earliest work, the *Treatise on Virginity* (c. 370).

Gregory's originality lay chiefly in the depth and mystical awareness he brought to the problem of man's knowledge of the Transcendent. Many of his works, such as the *Life of Moses,* can be understood on three levels: Moses represents the life of the true believer, the Christian philosopher, and the mystic attempting to find God in the universe. In his exposition of the Trinity and his discussion of God's nature, Gregory penetrated deeper than any other Eastern Father. The core of his theology is the historical perfection of man through the restoration of the divine image, regained by the Atonement and communicated through the Church. In his doctrine of the *Apokatastasis*—the restoration of all men, even the damned, to the vision of God at the end of time—Gregory reveals his loyalty to Origen as well as his own attempt to create a harmonious structure of salvation history. Throughout his work we see the development of the doctrine of the spiritual or mystical senses (implying a direct intuition of God's presence) and an analysis of ecstasy that prepared the way for Dionysius the Areopagite, Maximus the Confessor, and later Byzantine mysticism.

In his epistemology Gregory is derivatively Neoplatonic, and his allegorical exegesis reflects the anthropology of Origen and Philo of Alexandria as well as the eclectic philosophy of Hellenistic Asia Minor. But Gregory never slavishly followed any master, and scholars like H. F. Cherniss go too far when they suggest that Gregory's theology was merely a question of giving Christian names to Plato's doctrines. Rather, the opposite view of Jean Daniélou and others seems closer to the truth: Gregory's theology represents a subtle transformation of Neoplatonism into authentic Christianity, whereby the intuitive vision and ethical achievement of the Christian mystic (in Daniélou's terminology, *epektasis*) was the culmination of the pagan philosopher's quest.

Bibliography

For works by Gregory of Nyssa, see Jean Daniélou and Herbert Musurillo, eds., *From Glory to Glory: Texts from Gregory of Nyssa's Mystical Writings* (New York, 1961).

A critical edition of Gregory's works is Werner Jaeger and others, *Gregorii Nysseni Opera* (Leiden, 1952——).

For works on Gregory, see H. F. Cherniss, *The Platonism of Gregory of Nyssa* (Berkeley, 1930); Berthold Altaner, *Patrology*, translated by Hilda C. Graef (New York, 1958), pp. 351–357; and Johannes Quasten, *Patrology* (Westminster, Md., 1960), Vol. III, pp. 254–296.

HERBERT MUSURILLO, S.J.

GREGORY OF RIMINI (c. 1300–1358), a member of the Augustinian friars and one of the foremost thinkers of the fourteenth century. He was born in Italy and died in Vienna, where he spent the last 18 months of his life as general of the Augustinian order. A large part of his active career was spent at Paris, where he studied from 1323 to 1329. After teaching in Italy, he returned to Paris in 1341 and remained there for ten years. During this second sojourn in Paris he wrote his main work, a *Commentary on the Sentences*. None of the other writings ascribed to him, ranging from Biblical commentaries to a treatise on the remission and intensification of forms, has survived.

Gregory's system was a reassertion of St. Augustine's teachings in fourteenth-century terms. He shared the contemporary awareness of the radical contingency of the created order and the unbridgeable gulf between God and his creatures that it entailed. He thereby followed Ockham and his confreres in rigorously confining natural knowledge to what could be verified and in excluding theological truths and evidence for God's existence from ratiocination. On the one hand, God was sovereignly free and man had no means of knowing what He might do; on the other, the knowledge accessible to man dealt only with contingencies and was ever liable to be superseded if God so willed. In consequence, there was no guarantee that the world was not infinite or eternal or that there was only one world; and even if its finiteness was accepted, God could still transform it. Gregory parted from the Ockhamists, however, in his refusal to allow this distinction between natural experience and God's will to undermine the traditional certainties. Even if natural knowledge was confined to practical experience, there still remained an inner realm of knowledge that was the source of all necessary truths and nonsensory principles. Similarly, although God was unconstrained and his ways inscrutable, he still acted in accordance with his perfections.

Thus Gregory rebutted the Ockhamist assertions that God could cause a man to sin, or mislead him, or command a man to hate him: God's freedom could not violate his own nature as revealed in the Scriptures. Although Gregory subscribed to the current distinction between God's ordained power (*potentia ordinata*) and his absolute power (*potentia absoluta*), by which he could do anything without qualification, he never—unlike the Ockhamists—employed the latter to override dogma. Gregory accordingly adhered to the accepted dogmatic tenets whether they concerned God's foreknowledge, man's fallen state, or the theological virtues. Only in the case of the physical world did he acknowledge the possibility, both on epistemological and theological grounds, that the world could be other than it was: that it might be infinite or eternal. Gregory joined in the current reversion to the earlier view that theology was *sapientia* (wisdom) rather than *scientia* (scientific knowledge). It was distinguished by its inaccessibility to the nonbeliever, and faith, far from being communicable, was the barrier that divided the Christian from the infidel. In this, as in other ways, Gregory shared in the changed outlook of the time, while remaining true to the tradition of St. Augustine.

Bibliography

The sole extant work of Gregory of Rimini, *Commentary on the Sentences*, was published in eight printed editions (Paris, 1482, 1487, 1520; Milan, 1494; Valencia, 1500; Venice, 1503, 1518, 1522). A photographic reprint of the 1522 Venice edition is No. 7 in the Franciscan Institute's text series (St. Bonaventure, N.Y., 1955).

For literature on Gregory of Rimini, see Gordon Leff, "Gregory of Rimini, A Fourteenth-century Augustinian," in *Revue des études augustiniennes*, Vol. VII, No. 2 (1961); Gordon Leff, *Gregory of Rimini* (Manchester, 1961); M. Schüler, *Prädestination, Sünde und Freiheit* (Stuttgart, 1934); D. Trapp, "Augustinian Theology in the Fourteenth Century," in *Augustiniana*, Vol. VI (1956); P. Vignaux, *Justification et prédestination au 14e siècle* (Paris, 1934); J. Würsdörfer, *Erkennen und Wissen nach Gregor von Rimini* (Münster in Westfalen, 1917).

GORDON LEFF

GROSSETESTE, PSEUDO-. See PSEUDO-GROSSETESTE.

GROSSETESTE, ROBERT (c. 1168–1253), was one of the most influential Englishmen of his day—initiator of the English scientific tradition, one of the first chancellors of Oxford University, a famous teacher and commentator on the newly discovered works of Aristotle, an important translator from the Greek, friend to the mendicant orders, first lecturer to the Oxford Franciscans, and zealous bishop of England's largest diocese. However, his life is imperfectly known and much of his work remains unpublished. He was born of humble parents in the county of Suffolk between 1168 and 1175 and by 1190 had become *magister in artibus* at either Oxford or Paris. Sometime between 1190 and 1198 he was a member of the household of William de Vere, bishop of Hereford, and may have taught in the Hereford schools. After the bishop's death in 1198, Grosseteste was a member of the arts faculty at Oxford or possibly at Cambridge. He probably studied theology at Paris during the *suspendium clericorum*, 1209–1214. At some time between 1214 and 1221 he became chancellor of Oxford University. In 1229 he became the first lecturer to the Oxford Franciscans, leaving this post only on his elevation to the see of Lincoln in 1235. He was bishop of Lincoln until his death 18 years later.

Grosseteste lived at a crucial period in intellectual history: the scientific and philosophical writings of the Muslims were just becoming known in Latin Europe and the works of the Hellenistic writers and the recently rediscovered works of Aristotle were being translated, disseminated, and lectured upon. As teacher, commentator, and translator, he took an active part in this movement. Basically Augustinian in outlook and relying heavily on the standard authors, he was nevertheless deeply influenced by Muslim learning, especially Avicenna and the astronomers, by the Jew Avicebrón, and by the newly found Aristotelian works. He never wrote a comprehensive philosophical work or devised a system, but he developed many characteristic views that have had a profound influence on the later development of both philosophy and science. The most important of his many philosophical works are *De Luce* ("Light"), *De Motu Corporali et Luce* ("Corporal Motion and Light"), *Hexameron*, and commentaries on Aristotle's *Posterior Analytics* and *Physics*.

Light metaphysics. Basic to Grosseteste's view of the universe is his metaphysics of light. He held that in the beginning God created the first corporeal form (*lux*), which had the property of instantaneously multiplying itself infinitely in every direction, and simple matter, an unextended substance. The original point of light was joined to unextended matter (since matter and form never exist separately) and in its expansion drew matter out into spatial dimensions. The resulting universe was a sphere extremely rare at the periphery but dense and opaque near the center. It was finite because a simple substance multiplied an infinite number of times would result in a finite quantity, and the matter of the periphery (the firmament) was completely actualized and capable of no further change.

When this perfect first body, containing only first matter and first form, had been created, it diffused its reflected light (*lumen*) back to the center, where the *lumen* gathered together the mass existing below the first body, again rare-fying the outermost parts and making the center more dense. The second sphere was thus formed, as were, by a similar process, all 13 spheres, including the four elements. On the outside of our universe, matter is completely actualized and capable of no further change, while at the center the degree of actualization is less and matter remains susceptible of taking on a variety of forms. From first form (light) every subsequent form is generated, both substantial and accidental, and every privation derives from the privation of light.

Since all things have in common first form and first matter, they are, in a sense, one. But each thing includes a hierarchy of form superadded to the original form of corporeity, making it the individual thing it is. Most of Grosseteste's other views were either derived from or imply his light metaphysics. He considered light the cause of local motion, the means by which the soul operates on the body (he denied that the soul is the form or perfection of the body), and the principle of intelligibility in the created universe.

Theories of knowledge. Grosseteste had two distinct theories of knowledge. The first, in the Augustinian tradition and strongly influenced by Avicenna, held that men may acquire knowledge by virtue of the intellect alone, without recourse to sense. The second held that certain knowledge may also be gained through sense perception. Although sense turns toward matter and is therefore unstable, imperfect, and subject to imaginative embellishments, it also follows reason, even though confusedly, and does not obscure the species it provides. Reason, which understands the principles of nature in a single manner, either corrects or completes whatever was lacking in the senses.

Both these ways of knowing involve another of Grosseteste's key concepts, the purgation of the mind. It is not until the desires of one's mind (*affectus mentis*) are purged of error that the gaze of one's mind (*aspectus mentis*) can be raised to the eternal and true and can overcome the delusions caused by corporeal phantasms. "Many men," Grosseteste said, "can prove by sure reasons that the Intelligences exist and that God exists but they do not understand the Divine Essence or the non-corporeity of the Intelligences. . . . Aristotle and others, who firmly knew by discursive reasoning that eternity was simple but saw it under the phantasms of temporal extension, have affirmed many improper things such as the perpetuity of time and motion and consequently the eternity of the world." In this quotation from the *Commentary on the Physics*, we see Grosseteste at once as one of the foremost critics of the dangers latent in the works of Aristotle and yet also among the leaders in introducing Aristotle's natural philosophy into western Europe.

Infinity. One of Grosseteste's most original and influential teachings concerns infinite aggregates. He believed that "one infinite number can be related in any proportion, numeral or non-numeral, to another infinite number." To God, infinite numbers are finite, and he determines the primary cubit (and every other measure) by a certain infinite number and a half-cubit by another infinite number half (to him) that of the cubit, and so on. But such a manner of measuring is possible only to one to whom the infinite is finite. Being finite, we must necessarily adopt a different manner of measuring, that is, by commensurable magnitudes as accidents of matter.

Scientific method. It is as a scientist and innovator in scientific method, however, that Grosseteste has attracted the interest of the twentieth century. In his most important scientific writings he progressively developed a characteristic method of investigating nature that employed analysis (*resolutio*) and synthesis (*compositio*) in physical inquiries, first breaking down a problem into its simplest parts, then framing a hypothesis that would show how these elements are to be combined in order to produce the phenomenon under investigation. He also held that an experimental universal of provisional truth might be obtained by observing that a given effect always results from a particular cause, if one controlled his observation by eliminating any other possible cause of the effect.

In addition to this framework, Grosseteste used experiments as an integral part of his investigation: as aids in accomplishing his analysis, as suggestions in framing his explanatory hypothesis, and most important, as tests of the truth or falsity of a hypothesis. He also employed mathematics in his researches, holding that since light is the cause of local motion and the means by which superior bodies act on inferior ones, and that since light behaves according to geometric rules, therefore all local motion can be described mathematically. He denied, however, that mathematical entities have any objective being and insisted that they are simply abstractions from physical bodies and exist only in the minds of mathematicians.

Another of his basic principles was that of the subordination of sciences. A superior science, he said, may provide the cause for which the inferior science provides the effect. In the study of heavenly bodies, for instance, the sciences of mathematics, astronomy, and physics are concerned. Mathematicians abstract magnitudes from motion and matter and demonstrate the accidents per se with respect to magnitudes. Physicists, on the other hand, demonstrate the figured magnitudes in the sense that they belong to physical bodies. Astronomers have much in common with physicists, but whereas they might both be studying the same body—for instance, the moon—the physicist demonstrates that the predicate belongs to the subject by nature, while the astronomer does not care whether it belongs to it by nature or not.

Grosseteste wrote four works on astronomy. His work *De Sphaera* ("On the Sphere") is a theoretical treatise. The other three works are primarily concerned with reforming the Julian calendar, which was nearly four days in error at that time. Using the works of Ptolemy, al-Battani, and Ibn Thebit, he worked out a program for calendar reform which continued to find supporters until it was largely incorporated into the Gregorian reform of 1582.

Grosseteste was in many ways the hinge between the early and late Middle Ages. He had at his disposal the standard late Roman authors and the recently introduced Greek and Arabic sources. His powerful, resourceful, and disciplined mind assimilated and transformed this material. He left many loose ends and sometimes failed to think through his positions; and in his scientific works, despite his methodological triumphs, he was not a notable experimenter. Still, so powerful was his thought that he

influenced an uninterrupted succession of philosophers and scientists throughout Europe for three hundred years after his death.

Bibliography

The basic bibliography of Grosseteste's works, printed and manuscript, is S. H. Thomson, *The Writings of Robert Grosseteste, Bishop of Lincon, 1235–1253* (Cambridge, 1940).

Grosseteste's most important scientific works are *De Generatione Stellarum* ("The Generation of the Stars"), *De Generatione Sonorum* ("The Generation of Sounds"), *De Impressionibus Elementorum* ("The Impressions of the Elements"), *De Fluxu et Refluxu Maris* ("The Tides"), *De Cometis* ("The Comets"), *De Colore* ("Color"), *De Calore Solis* ("The Heat of the Sun"), *De Iride* ("The Rainbow"), the astronomical work *De Sphaera* ("The Sphere"), and two *Computi*. His scientific method developed in these was further elaborated in his commentaries on the *Physics* and *Posterior Analytics* of Aristotle and in two short works, *De Lineis, Angulis, et Figuris* ("Lines, Angles, and Figures") and *De Natura Locorum* ("The Nature of Places").

Modern editions of Grosseteste include L. Baur, *Die philosophischen Werke des Robert Grosseteste, Bischoffs von Lincoln* (Münster, 1912); S. H. Thomson, "The Text of Grosseteste's *De Cometis*," in *Isis*, Vol. 19 (1933), 19–25, and "Grosseteste's *Questio de Calore, De Cometis, and De Operacionibus Solis*," in *Medievalia et Humanistica*, Vol. 11 (1957), 34–43; R. C. Dales, *Roberti Grosseteste Commentarius in VIII Libros Physicorum Aristotelis* (Boulder, Colo., 1963), and "Grosseteste's Treatise *De Finitate Motus et Temporis*," in *Traditio*, Vol. 19 (1963), 245–266; E. Franceschini, "Un inedito di Roberto Grossatesta," in *Rivista di filosofia neo-scolastica*, Vol. 44 (1952), 1–11.

Studies of Grosseteste's thought include L. Baur, *Die Philosophie des Robert Grosseteste* (Münster, 1917); D. E. Sharp, *Franciscan Philosophy at Oxford in the Thirteenth Century* (Oxford, 1930); L. E. Lynch, "The Doctrine of Divine Ideas and Illumination in Robert Grosseteste," in *Mediaeval Studies*, Vol. 3 (1941), 161–173; R. C. Dales, "Robert Grosseteste's *Commentarius in VIII Libros Physicorum Aristotelis*," in *Medievalia et Humanistica*, Vol. 11 (1957), 10–33, and "The Scientific Works of Robert Grosseteste," in *Isis*, Vol. 61 (1961), 381–402.

A. C. Crombie, *Robert Grosseteste and the Origins of Experimental Science* (Oxford, 1953), contains a comprehensive bibliography and list of manuscript sources. D. A. Callus, ed., *Robert Grosseteste, Scholar and Bishop* (Oxford, 1955), sums up recent scholarship on Grosseteste's life and thought and contains a select bibliography and guide to key manuscripts.

The standard biography is F. S. Stevenson, *Robert Grosseteste, Bishop of Lincoln* (London, 1899).

RICHARD C. DALES

GROTE, JOHN (1813–1866), English moral philosopher and epistemologist, was born at Beckenham in Kent. He was a younger brother of George Grote, the historian. Grote studied classics at Cambridge and became a fellow of Trinity College in 1837. He took orders in the Church of England and eventually obtained a church living at Trumpington, where he resided until his death. In 1855 he succeeded William Whewell as Knightbridge professor of moral philosophy at Cambridge. For a number of years an informal group, sometimes called the Grote Club, met regularly with him for philosophical discussion; Henry Sidgwick and John Venn were among its members.

Grote's writings were concerned primarily with ethics and theory of knowledge. He thought the former the more important study and intended the epistemological discussions in his *Exploratio Philosophica* to serve as prolegomena to his moral theory. Throughout his work he criticized the claim that only science or the "positive standpoint" could give us truth. Science treats perception simply as the action of one body on another, and it investigates the antecedents and concomitants of all thoughts and feelings indifferently. Hence it can give no adequate account of truth or falsity in thought. Philosophy, which is the study of thought and feelings as we are directly aware of them from within, can deal with truth and falsity, but it cannot give causal explanations. Hence the positive and the philosophical standpoints can lead us to truths which supplement each other. Grote argued with considerable acuteness that confusion of these standpoints was responsible for many of the difficulties of traditional theories of perception and knowledge, but he confessed himself unclear as to how they were related.

In ethics, Grote argued that utilitarianism overlooked the fact that man is essentially as active a creature as he is a sentient one. Concentrating only on human sentience, utilitarianism provides a theory of the good in feeling, but since it says little about right acting, it is unable to give an adequate account of the right distribution of good. The attempt to construct a positive science of morality is misguided and hopeless, since it omits the "ideal" element, or conception of what ought to be, which is central to morality. An ethical principle cannot be derived from facts alone, nor can it usefully be made true by definition; hence a basic intuition is required. There is, however, an important utilitarian element in morality, and that element provides a necessary check on possibly spurious intuitions. Grote suggested that the old conflict between utilitarianism and intuitionism should be seen as a conflict between partial views of a whole truth.

Grote held that the philosophical standpoint was more fundamental than the scientific. He gave a number of reasons for this. Underlying them is the view that the attempt to come to a rational understanding of the world implies the belief that the world is already rational, which implies in turn the belief that it is the creation of a mind. But mind, Grote held, can be understood as such only from the philosophical standpoint. The attempt to act morally in the world presupposes, similarly, a belief that the world is morally ordered, and this implies a belief in a moral governor. Grote interpreted these beliefs theistically. His development of them anticipated in many ways the absolute idealism of the generation after him. He argued that all truth is systematically interconnected; that truth is ultimately to be understood as coherence, rather than correspondence; and that the distinctions of perception and conception and of necessity and contingency are relative. In ethics he worked toward a view emphasizing self-development and man's duty in his station.

It has been said that Grote should be viewed as the first of the Cambridge analytic philosophers, and certainly his great respect for ordinary language and ordinary thought, his persistent attempts to find and remove logical confusions, his insistence on the importance of clarity, and his pursuit of it in detailed and painstaking criticism have obvious affinities with the work of that group. There is, however, little evidence to show that he had much direct influence on anyone, and his writing, which is difficult and prolix, has been very little studied despite its acuteness and considerable originality.

Bibliography

With the exception of *Exploratio Philosophica*, Vol. 1 (Cambridge, 1865), Grote's main writings were edited from his papers and published posthumously by his literary executor, J. B. Mayor. They are: *Examination of the Utilitarian Philosophy* (Cambridge, 1870); *Sermons* (Cambridge, 1872); *Treatise on the Moral Ideals* (Cambridge, 1876); and *Exploratio Philosophica*, Vol. 2 (Cambridge, 1900). There are also some papers, of which the most interesting is a series called "Glossology" in the *Journal of Philology*, 1872 and 1874. Further details may be found in Mayor's prefaces to the volumes he edited. There are no detailed secondary studies, but G. Watts Cunningham, *The Idealistic Argument* (New York, 1933) has a chapter on Grote.

J. B. SCHNEEWIND

GROTIUS, HUGO (1583–1645), or Huig de Groot, Dutch jurist and statesman, was born at Delft, of a distinguished Calvinist family. He entered the University of Leiden when he was 11, graduating with great distinction at the age of 14. At 15 he served as a member of a Dutch mission to France and obtained the degree of Doctor of Law at the University of Orléans. In 1601 Grotius was asked for a legal opinion by the Dutch East India Company in an international case, which appears to have spurred the writing of his pamphlet in defense of freedom of the seas (*Mare Liberum*, 1609) and generally stimulated his enduring interest in international law. In 1607 Grotius was appointed advocate general of the fisc of the provinces of Holland, Zeeland, and Friesland. In 1613 he became the pensionary for Rotterdam and went to England as a member of a Dutch diplomatic mission. A bitter theological dispute, in which Grotius sided with the estates of Holland against orthodox Calvinism (supported by Prince Maurice of Holland) led to a special trial and the condemnation of Grotius to life imprisonment. During his imprisonment he wrote the famous pamphlet, *De Veritate Religionis Christianae* (Leiden, 1627). In 1621 Grotius escaped from prison and fled to France, where he wrote his great work *De Jure Belli ac Pacis* (1620–1625), dedicated to Louis XIII. Grotius later returned to Holland. From 1634 to 1644 he was Swedish ambassador to France. He was recalled to Sweden in 1644 and died in Rostock on his way back from Sweden to Holland shortly after.

Grotius' enduring influence upon legal science and, in particular, on the science of international law may be attributed to qualities somewhat comparable to those of John Locke. Both men formulated, articulated, and systematized, at a critical point in history, certain ideas and principles that suited the needs of a changing society.

But whereas Locke articulated the rights of the individual in a rapidly expanding, acquisitive, and increasingly antiabsolutist society, Grotius understood that the international society of burgeoning sovereign states had to find and abide by certain rules of conduct in war and peace, formalizing diplomatic relations and mutual respect for sovereignty. Since modern international society is still dominated by the legal and political supremacy of the national state, Grotius' classical treatise, *De Jure Belli ac Pacis*, is still an essential foundation for international law. The international order of the Middle Ages, based on the twin foundations of the ecclesiastical authority of the Church of Rome and the political authority of the emperors, had crumbled together with the social, economic, and spiritual conditions on which it was based. New kingdoms, dukedoms, principalities, and cities had emerged from the debris. Europe was torn by wars, big and small, motivated by religious, dynastic, political, and social conflicts. While Grotius wrote his principal work, the Thirty Years' War was raging in much of Europe, demonstrating the destructive effects of the lawlessness of a society which had not yet developed new rules of intercourse appropriate to the emerging society of sovereign nations. There was no prospect of re-establishing the international authority exercised by popes and emperors. There was no hope of abolishing or outlawing war. But there was an urgent need to establish a new code of behavior, and, more than that, a need to humanize the conduct of war even within modest limits. To lay the foundations for such a development was a gigantic task, a task only for someone who could combine the qualities of philosopher, political scientist, jurist, humanist, and diplomat. That man was Hugo Grotius, a man of prodigious learning—theologian, philologist, historian, and poet, as well as jurist—who was also an active diplomat.

All his various interests are reflected in his great treatise, a rambling work ranging over many fields of human knowledge, studded with quotations and references to innumerable scholars and sources. *De Jure Belli ac Pacis* established a partially legalized system of international relations by blending certain general principles of political and moral philosophy with state practice. It is this combination that gives to Grotius' work the flexibility and durability that enabled subsequent generations to make use of it by emphasizing the one or the other aspect.

Natural law. Grotius was first a major exponent of the philosophy of natural law and of social contract. Second, he was an Aristotelian whose deepest and most abiding belief was in the power of reason and the rationality of man. Third, Grotius was a pragmatic diplomat who, through the observation and practice of diplomacy in a singularly disturbed and savage period, was fully aware of the practices of states in peace and war—and it was war that dominated both the life of the people and the thought of Grotius. But fourth, Grotius was a humanist in the spirit and tradition of his master, Erasmus of Rotterdam, a man who abhorred the brutality and lawlessness of war and violence, and whose principal purpose, therefore, was not only to civilize the conduct of war but also to place certain limitations upon its legality. He combined this last objective with his belief in reason and in natural order in the formulation of his famous theory of the *bellum iustum* ("the just war").

As a natural law philosopher, Grotius was much closer to the Stoics than to the Scholastics. Like the former, he derived the postulates of natural law from principles of reason rather than of divine order. Such reason was founded in the human intellect. "Natural law is so immutable that it cannot be changed by God himself."

The natural law doctrine provided Grotius with the theoretical foundation for certain overriding principles of order in the relations between states. It also gave him faith in the rationality of man and in man's potentialities for developing a better society in accordance with the needs of social and international life. Grotius was, of course, well aware that there was in his time no law-giving authority superior to the will of the states. It was, therefore, necessary for him to find some principle that could bind the nations to a common standard of behavior. He found this principle in *pacta sunt servanda*, the respect for promises given and treaties signed. In the absence of an international sovereign authority, modern international lawyers, such as Dionisio Anzilotti and Hans Kelsen, have reaffirmed the same principle as the meta-legal foundation of international law.

Grotius formulated a large number of other principles of natural law that inevitably share the weakness of all natural law teachings—that is, the sublimation of certain political postulates into immutable principles of order. Among Grotius' rules of natural law were respect for other people's property and the restitution of gain made from it, the reparation of any damage caused by a person's (or nation's) fault, as well as certain elementary principles of punishment. The political coloration of natural law is more evident in Grotius' postulate of the freedom of the seas. This postulate corresponded to the interests of the Netherlands as the world's leading maritime nation. It was opposed by the Englishman, John Selden (*Mare Clausum*, London, 1635), at a time when England was still struggling against stronger maritime nations.

Social contract. The other pillar of Grotius' legal philosophy was the theory of social contract, which also led him to emphasize the supremacy of the compact as the highest binding principle of law. Unlike later theorists of social contract, Grotius considered the contract as an actual fact of human history. In his view, the constitution of each state had been preceded by a social contract, by means of which each people had chosen the form of government they considered most suitable for themselves. While each people had the right to choose their own form of government, they forfeited the right to control or punish the ruler, however bad his government, once they had transferred their right of government to him. Generally, Grotius, like Hobbes, reflected not only the need of a disturbed society for strong governmental authority, but also the essentially absolutist and predemocratic character of government of that period. In his own official and diplomatic career Grotius represented autocratic governments.

International law. Aware of the insufficiency of natural law to supply more than certain general guiding principles, Grotius based the principal body of international law on *ius voluntarium* (the body of treaties and other engagements that form the bulk of international state practice). Although a realist, Grotius was not a cynic. He believed not only in the essential rationality of man and peoples, but also in the necessity of progress from war to peace, from international anarchy to international order. His principal contribution in this respect was his theory of the *bellum iustum*. A major part of the second book of his treatise was devoted to the problems of the legality of war. For a war to be just, there must exist a legal cause for it. Essentially, there are only three types of just wars: those which are conducted in defense against an actual or immediately threatening injury; those aimed at the recovery of what is legally due; and those inflicting punishment for a wrong done. Each of these categories allows for a great degree of latitude, especially in the absence of an impartial international judicial authority that can decide between conflicting claims. Nevertheless, this emphasis on the need to justify war, and the limitation of its justification to causes that even today would be regarded as essentially defensive against wrongful injury, was a remarkable contribution to international order. It became obscured and forgotten during subsequent centuries of absolute national sovereignty, particularly during the nineteenth century when the aggressive national state celebrated its greatest triumphs, in practice as in theory. In our own time, the League of Nations Covenant and the United Nations Charter have attempted once again to distinguish between just and unjust wars. The future of mankind may well depend on the elaboration of an authoritative method of finding reliable and enforceable criteria for distinguishing between wars of aggression and wars of defense and on the establishment of an impartial forum to decide on claims for the reparation of wrongs alleged to be inflicted by one state on another.

International law in our own day is still essentially based on state practice as recorded in custom, treaties, and other international agreements; but these practices allow for the evolution of international law, not so much in the terminology of natural law as in the similarly conceived evocation of "general principles of law recognized by civilized nations." Some of these principles were applied, with dubious theoretical justification, in the Nuremberg and Tokyo trials of German and Japanese war criminals.

Grotius' doctrines were inevitably a mixture of reactionary and progressive principles. On the one hand he felt compelled to justify many barbarous practices of war, subsequently condemned in modern rules of warfare (yet surpassed in cruelty by modern war). Again, Grotius concurred with the great majority of legal and political philosophers in denying to the individual the right of resistance to an oppressive sovereign, although he affirmed the right of passive resistance of an individual against unjust wars. On the other hand, Grotius anticipated by centuries some of the principles of the Nuremberg Charter by regarding as justified a war waged to prevent the maltreatment by a state of its own subjects. And Grotius' concern with the individual stands in noble contrast to subsequent absolutist political theories.

In working and thinking within the limitations of his time, Grotius did not differ from any other philosopher, jurist, or political scientist. What is remarkable is that, in the midst of a war that threatened to undermine the whole fabric of European society, he developed principles and standards that can still serve as the basic themes for the struggle for international order in our time.

Works by Grotius

De Jure Belli ac Pacis Libri Tres. Paris, 1625. Translated by F. W. Kelsey and others under the same title from the 1646 edition. Oxford, 1925.

Works on Grotius

Balogh, Elemér, "The Traditional Element in Grotius' Conception of International Law." *New York University Law Quarterly Review*, Vol. 7, No. 2 (1929), 261–292.
Basdevant, Jules, "Grotius," in A. Pillet, ed., *Les Fondateurs du droit international.* Paris, 1904. Pp. 125–267.
Gurvitch, George, "La Philosophie du droit de Grotius et la théorie moderne du droit international." *Revue de métaphysique et de morale*, Vol. 34, No. 2 (1927), 365–391.
Lauterpacht, Sir Hersch, "The Grotian Tradition in International Law." *British Year Book of International Law*, Vol. 23 (1946), 51.
Nussbaum, Arthur, *A Concise History of the Law of Nations.* New York, 1954. Pp. 96–112.
Ter Meulen, Jacob, and Diermanse, P. J. J., *Bibliographie des écrits imprimes de Hugo Grotius.* The Hague, 1950.
Van Eysinga, W. J. M., *Huigh de Groot, een Schets.* Haarlem, 1945.
Wolf, Eric, *Grotius, Pufendorf, Thomasius.* Tübingen, 1927.

WOLFGANG FRIEDMANN

GUILT. There are two main forms of the idea of guilt—moral guilt and legal or quasi-legal guilt. Originally these were not sharply distinguished, but enlightened thought requires that they should be. In outward substance the two often coincide. In committing a crime one is usually morally at fault, but the degree of one's guilt is not likely to be the same in the two respects in such instances. We may in any case be morally guilty and legally innocent—and vice versa. Few who consult this book have committed a crime, but who is there who has never done anything for which he may be morally reproached? Some of the most vicious things men do are well within the law. Nor would it be wise to legislate against all forms of moral evil—much of that would defeat the purpose of morality. One may also break the law and incur no moral blame. This might be because of unavoidable ignorance (of the law or of some matter of fact), but we could be blameless even in committing a crime deliberately. That would come about if we broke the law on conscientious grounds. Some of the people we admire most (religious or political martyrs, for example) have put religious or moral scruples before the claims of the law. They were not in all cases outwardly justified. The outward justification of resistance to the law is greatest under oppressive government. The duty to conform is very great when there are constitutional means of seeking redress or reform. Upholding constitutional procedure is normally much more important than righting a particular wrong. Resistance (but not of course normal opposition) is very extreme medicine in a democracy, and it is not always justified under tyranny. Persuasion is the best means of reform. But whether outwardly justified or not, a person is free from moral blame (and perhaps worthy of much praise) if he breaks the law in obedience to his own conscience.

Moral guilt and determinism. Legal responsibility means liability to punishment, and legal guilt thus means that one has merited some punishment. This may be understood in a retributive, reformative, or deterrent sense. On the latter view, the commonest today where strictly legal or social issues are concerned, absolute freedom of choice is not presupposed. It is of course pointless to seek by punishment to deter someone who in no sense controls what he does—or to make him an example for others. We restrain the insane or the delirious. We do not punish them, and it is absurd to punish people for what they do by accident. But punishment is not made pointless when we act in character and wittingly do certain things even though, being the persons we are, we could not help doing them. Punishment as deterrence is consistent with determinism, for our conduct on other occasions—and the conduct of other persons—could be affected by punishment or the threat of it. But in moral matters punishment is a secondary issue. To be morally guilty is to have incurred moral disvalue or to be morally blameworthy. This may call for punishment or some other outward censure, but that is a further question.

Moral guilt is a more basic notion than punishability. It is a unique moral concept not to be merged in associated social and legal notions. Moral guilt presupposes freedom of a more radical kind than legal guilt and is hard to reconcile with any form of determinism. The moral evil it involves must be distinguished sharply from nonmoral evils like sickness, pain, error, and stupidity. I am not to blame for being ill or for failing to win a race, compose a poem, or solve a mathematical problem. I am to blame for moral failure. I cannot help the former failures, provided I try, if it is my duty. But it is hard to see how there could be moral failure if there is any sense in which I could not help it.

The assumption of absolute freedom. But how strictly are these last words to be understood in the case of moral guilt? Is absolute freedom presupposed? If it is, are we ever guilty in the strictly moral sense? Is there not some continuity of character and conduct? Plainly there is such a continuity, and advocates of absolute freedom of choice as a moral requirement have therefore argued that moral praise or blame only apply on the occasions where there is a conflict between "duty and interest"—that is, between what we most want to do and what we think we ought to do. During much of one's life there is no such conflict, and we can therefore anticipate one another's actions with much confidence: we know what to expect of people we have come to know. But character and duty will sometimes draw apart. To that extent, it is maintained, nothing affects the outcome but the act of choice itself. If we fail to make the effort of will—an absolutely free one in this case—to overcome some weakness of character, and if we thus follow the line of least resistance rather than the call of duty, we incur moral guilt. The degree of the guilt depends not on the outward features of the situation and the magnitude of the ill we do, or at least not directly so, but on the effort of will that would have been required to do right. But it should be noted well that the more outwardly vicious an act may be, the less is the effort needed to resist a temptation to do it, for one can normally presuppose much natural resistance to the act in one's own character. The less the effort required, the more we are to blame for not making it; the greater the effort we do make, the greater our moral worth.

It follows from this view that while we may, for practical and kindred purposes, censure misdeeds in their outward form, we need to be very chary of passing strictly moral judgments on other persons. If we have reason to believe (as is often the case) that someone has acted contrary to his moral convictions, we can impute to him some measure of blame, but how much is much harder to assess than the outwardly objectionable features of a situation. It is also much harder to assess the positive moral worth of another person than to assess his moral guilt. For we know in the latter case that the effort required was not forthcoming; in the former case it is harder to know how much to ascribe to natural good qualities of character, a benevolent or naturally plucky nature, and so on, and how much to free effort. Only the agent himself and God can know the full inner story.

The feeling of guilt. We must, however, distinguish "guilt" in the strict moral meaning from the sense of guilt. The latter is the feeling that accompanies the consciousness of being guilty. It is appropriate that we should feel remorse for wrongdoing, the proper tone of the feeling being determined by its appropriateness to the situation of guilt. There are kindred feelings appropriate to the wrongdoing we encounter or suspect in others, feelings or attitudes of blame and indignation. The feelings we actually have are not always appropriate to the situation, and there may thus be a sense of guilt out of all proportion to the facts of the case. Some people seem even to enjoy the sense of guilt and to cultivate it. Psychologists have helped us a great deal today to understand these deviations and that other curious aberration by which some people feel guilty for things they have not done at all.

Psychological reasons. Some psychologists go further. They try to account for guilt entirely in terms of psychology. A common form of this attempt is that which ascribes guilt to an alleged "need for punishment." This need comes about through punishment or some other disapproval we suffer in infancy. Coming to expect punishment for certain acts, we feel distress when we wait for it without getting it over, and the strain and anxiety induced in this way is suppressed and operates subconsciously afterwards to produce the sense of guilt in mature experience. There is also the introjection into the "superego" of the relief experienced by those who punish us. These theories no doubt reflect states of mind which psychological investigation uncovers, and the layman can appreciate much of them from common experience. But they seem nonetheless to be mainly concerned with aberrations and an unhealthy assumption of guilt, or perverse ways of dealing with it. The core of guilt is an ethical one, which psychology does not explain away.

Collective versus individual guilt. If guilt, in the proper sense, turns on deliberate wrongdoing, it seems that no one can be guilty for the act of another person—there can be no shared or collective or universal guilt. Guilt is incurred by the free choice of the individual. But many have questioned this. Among them are some sociologists who misrepresent in this way the dependence of the individual on society. But the main location of the idea of collective guilt is religion. Many forms of the doctrines of original sin and universal sin regard guilt as a pervasive state of mankind as a whole. It is the guilt of "man," not of this or that person as a whole. Others qualify this and speak of original sin which does not include original guilt. Others hold that while there can be no "great sin" and "little sin," there is inequality of guilt. But it is hard to reconcile the notion of universal sin or guilt, in any form, with elementary ethical convictions. Such notions can also do great harm, both by leading to victimization of the innocent—as in the treatment of Jews by the Nazis—and in undermining the sense of responsibility; for collective guilt is not the guilt of anyone in particular.

Sources of doctrines of collective guilt. Why then do such doctrines of collective guilt seem plausible? Mainly through religious confusions like the following. (1) The sense of religious unworthiness, the awe felt in the presence of God, is mistaken for moral culpability. (2) Certain forms of religious experience are apt to be overwhelming, and the strain is eased at times by incapsulating the divine within the finite media or symbols by which it is known. This is the root of idolatry. The most grievous form of this is that by which the person himself becomes the idol—he aspires to make himself as God. But this distortion of religious experience tends to be conflated, in the heat of prophetic experience, with the expressly moral wickedness of putting one's own wishes before the proper claims of others. This encourages the notion of an unavoidable state of sin and guilt. (3) Guilt is what we seem most disposed to suppress, and at the unconscious level the confusions noted are apt to be intensified. (4) Religious doctrines have often been based on first-order religious utterances taken out of their full context and apart from the experience which prompted them. The figurative character of such utterances is also overlooked—for example, in interpretations of the metaphors of "bondage" or of "sin warring in all my members." (5) Wrongdoing has a cumulative influence which affects the state and the situation of persons irrespective of their own guilty actions; it thus tends to drive men in on themselves and hinder healthy relations with other persons—and with God. This also, or the misrepresentation of it, lies behind misleading doctrines of collective guilt. (6) The idea of universal guilt has often been made the pretext for evading the challenge of high ideals professed by religious people. This seems especially true of much Augustinian theology. (7) Religious confusions are deepened by confusions between the points of view of law—where the idea of corporated guilt has some place—and the point of view of morality.

Recent anthropology has thrown new light on the origin of the idea of guilt. There was at first little distinction between the points of view of law and of morality, both being merged in communal custom. Nor was heed adequately paid to whether the results of an act were those a person intended. The community was also more the bearer of guilt than the individual, and harsh judgments were thus passed on the innocent and bitter feuds perpetuated. But we should not allow this to determine for us how guilt must be understood in enlightened thought. Ethical notions are not jeopardized by having lowly and doubtful origins.

Religious thought today helps us to appreciate what is true and what is false in notions like collective guilt. But much recent sociology and some recent ethics go further and challenge the ultimacy of the ideas of guilt and responsibility. These are thought by some moralists and psychologists to be ideas we ought to have outgrown—"theological anachronisms." A sound ethical theory and better understanding of religion should correct these tendencies.

Bibliography

For a general discussion of the subject, see the symposium on "Guilt" by H. D. Lewis, J. W. Harvey, and G. A. Paul, in *Proceedings of the Aristotelian Society*, Supplementary Volume XXI. See also the papers on Free Will, Responsibility, and Guilt by C. A. Campbell, P. H. Nowell-Smith, and Erich Fromm in Milton K. Munitz, ed., *A Modern Introduction to Ethics* (New York, 1958), pp. 356–416. Sir Walter Moberly, *Responsibility* (Oxford, 1952) consists of three lectures dealing with the moral and religious aspects of guilt and sin. A classical discussion of the religious and Biblical side of the subject is F. R. Tennant, *The Concept of Sin* (Cambridge, 1912). N. H. G. Robinson, *Faith and Duty* (New York, 1950) is a first-rate survey of the subject in the work of representative recent theologians like Barth, Brunner, and Niebuhr. The liberal approach to this subject may be found in L. Harold DeWolf, *The Religious Revolt Against Reason* (New York, 1944) and in H. D. Lewis, *Morals and the New Theology* (New York, 1948), Chs. 5–7.

The Freudian view is well presented in J. C. Flügel, *Man, Morals, and Society* (New York, 1961). This should be considered along with Freud's *New Introductory Lectures on Psychoanalysis* (New York, 1933), pp. 78–106 and Susan Isaacs, *Social Development in Young Children* (New York, 1933). More recent psychoanalytic works are Melanie Klein and others, *Developments in Psychoanalysis* (New York, 1952); Melanie Klein, *Envy and Gratitude: A Study of Unconscious Sources* (New York, 1957); and E. Glover, *Technique of Psychoanalysis*, rev. ed. (New York, 1955). There are also helpful references to guilt in Walter J. H. Sprott, *Social Psychology* (London, 1952), p. 168 ff. The tradition of Pavlov is continued in B. F. Skinner, *Science and Human Behavior* (New York, 1953), in which the conditioning effect of early training is stressed.

There is a short discussion of guilt in T. R. Miles, *Religion and the Scientific Outlook* (New York, 1959), Ch. 12.

The sociological approach is well exemplified in Barbara Wootton, *Social Science and Social Pathology* (London and New York, 1959). Criticism of this approach will be found in H. D. Lewis, *Freedom and History* (New York, 1963), and there is further discussion of the religious implications of the sociological approach in Fred Berthold, *The Fear of God* (New York, 1959).

H. D. LEWIS

GUYAU, MARIE JEAN (1854–1888), French moral and religious philosopher, who in a short life produced several significant works that helped to reconcile positivism and vitalism. Guyau was born in Laval, France, but because of ill health, lived for a time in the French Sudan; he died at Menton in France.

In his philosophically most significant work, *Esquisse d'une morale sans obligation ni sanction* (Paris, 1885), Guyau showed first that all previous attempts to find a basis for morality were inadequate. He pointed out the infinite variability of moral judgments and the fact that strong feelings of obligation can apply to even apparently immoral acts, such as the most irrational vendettas. He claimed that a purely formal, moral requirement could hardly account for the feeling of obligation, which we experience not as a logical necessity but as a demand that may or may not be satisfied. Obligation is a sensed feeling of resistance to desire; it is not, as in Kant's view, nonnaturally transmitted from some intelligible and nontemporal realm. A person apprehends a duty as inseparable from a content and needs to believe in the goodness not only of his intention, but of his act itself. Thus duty is expressed through, and has its source in, empirical reality. Guyau made an interesting attempt to assimilate even Kantian formalism to a naturalistic ethics by pointing out that universality of the sort expressed in Kant's categorical imperative produces a logical satisfaction based on a natural instinct for order.

Guyau looked to life for the principle of morality, and because he found this principle in "life at its most intensive and extensive," his spring of action has been compared to Nietzsche's Will to Power, though Guyau's life force was creative and altruistic rather than self-centered and aggressive. He spoke of *fécondité morale*. Life seeks to expend itself in creation: sexuality brings selflessness, whereas natural or enforced celibates tend to be self-centered. Altruism thus has an instinctive basis; and unselfishness is not self-denial.

The impulse to creation is the natural equivalent of the categorical imperative; it precedes all philosophical reasoning concerning the nature of the good. There is no question of calculating what one must do; one is impelled to act. Inverting the accepted moral reasoning, Guyau held that "I can, therefore I must."

Elucidating further the notion of a vital moral impulse, he invoked the theory of *idées-forces* of his stepfather, Alfred Fouillée, according to which the idea of a higher action is a force tending to realize that action. The man who does not act according to his "highest" thought is guilty of self-betrayal, is a living lie. This notion of unity of being and consistency of outward behavior with inner vision anticipated the more recent conception of authenticity, the antithesis of which—Sartre's "bad faith"—corresponds to Guyau's "falsehood in action." Guyau's view involved, moreover, the same difficulty of being amoral and aesthetic rather than genuinely ethical.

Nevertheless, Guyau made every effort to link his vital drive to traditional moral values; he held that "by virtue of evolution" our satisfactions broaden and become more impersonal and altruistic. This is particularly true of intellectual and aesthetic pursuits, which aim at communication, at making insights and experiences more widely available.

Reflection runs counter to the vital impulse. The problem of morality is that of reconciling inhibiting consciousness with the principle of spontaneity. This is effected by a kind of sublimation of the readiness to take purely physical risks, which is a condition of survival in primitive man. Guyau extolled speculative originality and moral pioneering as *risques de la pensée*. As *idées-forces*, they lead on to action and may result in the ultimate expenditure of self-sacrifice for an ideal.

Aesthetics also is based on life. The beautiful is an expression of, and an addition to, our vitality; and art helps us to participate in universal life.

Just as, for Guyau, moral and aesthetic feelings dispensed with transcendent principles, similarly, religion in Guyau's conception was freed from dogma and became a feeling of dependence on the universe, which is the source of life. Guyau was an agnostic. He rejected the doctrine of vicarious redemption in favor of that of man as his own savior, and he had no sympathy with the attempt to retain religion as a useful lie for the better policing of an otherwise immoral populace. The future, as Guyau saw it, has no place for traditional religion, but only for a mankind that is autonomous in intellectual speculation, morality, and art. Yet all men will still be united by a social bond with each other and with all beings of the universe.

Works by Guyau

La Morale d'Épicure et ses rapports avec les doctrines contemporaines. Paris, 1878.
La Morale anglaise contemporaine. Paris, 1879.
Vers d'un philosophe. Paris, 1881.
Les Problèmes de l'esthétique contemporaine. Paris, 1884.
Esquisse d'une morale sans obligation ni sanction. Paris, 1885.
L'Irréligion de l'avenir. Paris, 1887. Translated as *The Non-Religion of the Future.* London, 1897. Reprinted with an introduction by N. M. Glatzer. New York, 1962.
L'Art au point de vue sociologique. Paris, 1889.
Education et hérédité. Paris, 1889. Translated by W. J. Greenstreet as *Education and Heredity.* London, 1891.
La Genèse de l'idée de temps. Paris, 1890.

Works on Guyau

Aslan, G., *La Morale selon Guyau.* Paris, 1906.
Fouillée, Alfred, *La Morale, l'art, et la réligion d'après Guyau.* Paris, 1889; 4th ed., augmented, 1901.
Jankélévitch, Vladimir, "Deux philosophes de la vie: Guyau et Bergson." *Revue philosophique,* Vol. 97 (1924), 402–449.
Royce, Josiah, "J. M. Guyau," in his *Studies of Good and Evil.* New York, 1925.

Colin Smith

H

HABIT. See Custom.

HAECKEL, ERNST HEINRICH (1834–1919), German zoologist and monist philosopher. Haeckel was born in Potsdam. He studied medicine and science at Würzburg, Berlin, and Vienna with such authorities as Johannes Müller, Rudolf Virchow, and R. A. Kölliker. After practicing medicine for a short time, he went to the University of Jena in 1862 to teach zoology.

Haeckel was the first noted German biologist to grant enthusiastic acceptance to organic evolution, and Darwin gave him credit for propagating the theory of evolution in Germany. His views were the source of considerable controversy in biology, philosophy, and religion. He battled with his colleagues about their early hostility to Darwin's theory and their reluctance to include man and his consciousness in the evolutionary process. His dislike of the power of the church in social and political matters and his liberal opposition to Bismarck and other political figures resulted in many controversies; his rejection of free will, immortality, and the personality of God also antagonized many. Haeckel's achievements in zoology brought him academic offers from famous institutions, but he chose to remain at Jena, partly because of the academic freedom he found there.

His interests were broad; he published travel works and illustrated some of his own scientific essays. He founded the Monistic League to propagate his religious views. He had considerable popular success in science and was prominent in the movement to enlighten mankind about scientific developments.

Scientific contributions. In biology Haeckel helped to publicize and promulgate what he called the "biogenetic law": "*Ontogenesis is a brief and rapid recapitulation of phylogenesis,* determined by the physiological functions of heredity (generation) and adaptation (maintenance)" (*The Riddle of the Universe,* New York, 1900, p. 81). He was a pioneer in drawing up genealogical schemata of the relationships between various orders of animals. Many of his major groupings are still accepted, although the finer divisions have undergone much revision. He was convinced of the essential unity of organic and inorganic nature, and argued that the simplest protoplasmic substances arose from inorganic carbonates through spontaneous generation. Individual primitive organisms, which Haeckel termed "monera," were differentiated out of these protoplasmic compounds. Haeckel believed that to reject this kind of spontaneous generation was tantamount to accepting a miraculous origin of life.

His theory of *gastraea* also received much attention. Haeckel argued that the entire animal world is made up of two groups: primitive unicellular animals, the protozoa, and multicellular animals with complex tissues, the metazoa. Haeckel believed that all the metazoa evolved, in accord with his biogenetic law, from one simple, long-extinct form, the *gastraea.* Although this theory of evolution from *gastraea* is no longer accepted, it influenced embryological research for nearly half a century.

Doctrine of substance. Haeckel's conviction on the great importance of organic evolution led him into many other fields. His *Die Welträthsel* (Bonn, 1899; English translation by Joseph McCabe, *The Riddle of the Universe*) became a best seller. The title derived from Emil Du Bois-Reymond's 1880 address to the Berlin Academy of Sciences on seven "world enigmas" (the nature of matter and force, the origin of motion, the origin of life, the order in nature, the origin of simple sensation and consciousness, rational thought and speech, and freedom of the will). Haeckel believed that his monistic outlook could resolve these problems, and others, leaving one "comprehensive riddle," the problem of substance. He insisted upon the essential unity of all substance, but also insisted that the "real character" of substance was as little understood as in the days of Anaximander and Empedocles. Indeed, it became "more mysterious and enigmatic" as more and more became known about its attributes and their evolutionary forms. Haeckel was especially opposed to theological dualism, but he also carefully distinguished his view from both materialistic and idealistic monisms.

Haeckel construed materialism as holding that atoms are "dead," and are moved only by external forces. He maintained instead that both matter and ether possess sensation and will in the lowest grade. They experience a dislike of strain, and struggle against it, and a liking of "condensation," for which they strive. Haeckel denied the existence of empty space and of action at a distance. Those parts of space not occupied with ponderable atoms are filled with ether; action is either the result of immediate contact or occurs through the mediation of ether.

On the other hand, Haeckel rejected any attempt to regard the world as immaterial or nonnatural. Infinitely extended matter and sensitive and thinking spirit, or energy, are two fundamental attributes of the all-embracing universal substance. Every living cell has psychic properties, and multicellular organisms have as their psychic functions the totality of the psychic properties of their parts. Although Haeckel insisted that his view of substance was Spinoza-like rather than materialistic, many of his specific views are similar to those of nineteenth-century materialism. His confidence that "consciousness, thought, and speculation" are "functions of the ganglionic cells of the cortex of the brain," his "hard" determinism, his mechanism, his complete rejection of the supernatural, and his enthusiasm for science all inclined his contemporaries to classify him as a materialist.

Haeckel, then, saw the world as an eternal evolution of substance, and man as part of that evolution. The "law of substance," a law of mechanical causality, established "the eternal persistence of matter and force, their unvarying constancy throughout the entire universe" (*The Riddle of the Universe*, p. 4). He regarded the laws of the conservation of energy and the conservation of matter as inseparable and as parts of his law of substance. Haeckel referred to "great eternal iron laws," and rejected all teleological views. The appearance of design in the world is a consequence of natural selection rather than of the action of a purposive agency.

Although Haeckel often emphasized the tentative nature of scientific conclusions and the necessity for the modification and improvement of hypotheses, on some issues he assumed the finality of certain scientific propositions, including many rejected today. He made this assumption most frequently in his polemics against the philosophic and religious views that he regarded as incompatible with science. Haeckel did not generally consider in detail the technical problems philosophers were debating, but tended rather to attack or to defend the conclusions of technical philosophers on the basis of the scientific results of his day and extrapolations from them.

Theory of knowledge. Despite his insistence that much of philosophy was far too speculative and a priori, Haeckel held that both empiricism and rationalism are necessary to develop satisfactory knowledge. Although he was hostile to "pure metaphysics," he was also critical of those who advocated a "pure empiricism." The opposition between experimental science and philosophy must and can be overcome.

Haeckel held that the thing-in-itself lying behind knowable phenomena is unknown. He suggested that we need not trouble about this situation; we have no means for investigating the thing-in-itself, and are not even certain it exists. The only genuine knowledge is knowledge of nature, and it consists of "presentations" (combinations of sense impressions in the knowing subject) corresponding to external things. Comparative and critical observation tells us that normally the impressions received by the brain and sense organs from the outer world are the same

for all rational people, and that normally the same presentations are formed. Those presentations are true which correspond to the knowable aspects of things, even though things-in-themselves" cannot be reached.

Haeckel's views on knowledge were closely connected to biological findings. He argued that man's sense activity, which forms the beginning of all knowledge, was slowly and gradually evolved from the other primates. The sense organs of all primates are structurally similar, and Haeckel insisted that these organs also function similarly, in a way describable by the same chemicophysical laws. The rod-shaped cells in the retina, the auditory cells in the ear, the olfactory cells in the nose, and the taste cells on the tongue were evolved from simple, undifferentiated cells of the skin. Invoking his biogenetic law, Haeckel concluded that man's higher sense organs were derived from the epidermis of lower animals. Our sense impressions are associated in the cortex of the brain so that isolated elements are united into integrated wholes. Haeckel called these integrated presentations "faith in the broad sense," because they go beyond our sense impressions. In this sense, science requires faith in the construction of both hypotheses and unifying theories. (In the main, Haeckel used "theory" to refer to hypotheses about a common cause for diverse phenomena.) However, he rejected religious faith, which he termed "faith in the narrower sense." He insisted that religious belief always means a belief in miracles and thus contradicts the "natural faith of reason." Even religious liberals, he contended, are forced into the acceptance of superstition, and their faith is no less irrational than the "crude spirit-faith of primitive fetishism."

Psychology. Haeckel attempted a scientific account of the soul. He regarded it as a natural phenomenon, so that psychology was a natural science, a part of physiology. Psychology was the "foundation and the postulate" of all the sciences, since knowledge of nature is "part of the life of the soul." The great difficulty in establishing a naturalistic psychology is that such a science presupposes a thorough knowledge of the human organism, especially the brain. Haeckel deplored the lack of biological training of the psychologists of his time. He insisted that psychic processes, like all others, are subject to the law of substance, and held that the prevalence of mind–body dualisms in psychology has led to a greater confusion of ideas there than in any other department of knowledge. Yet Haeckel did not insist on a nonintrospective psychology; he described the introspective method as "extremely valuable and indispensable." But it had to be supplemented by experimental methods.

Haeckel regarded consciousness as the "central mystery of psychology," and the citadel of all mystical and dualistic errors. He insisted that consciousness is a natural phenomenon, dependent upon a material substratum. He suggested that consciousness can perhaps best be conceived as "internal perception" and can be compared to the action of a mirror. The chief difficulty in the way of a scientific understanding of consciousness is that the subject and the object of knowledge are one and the same; our only source of knowledge of consciousness is consciousness itself. We can therefore only know the consciousness of others by comparing it with our own. This works rather well when the comparison is made between normal people, but the analogy may break down badly when a comparison is made between the normal and the abnormal, or between different evolutionary levels. However, the difference between the consciousness of man and of other animals is a difference of degree only, not of kind. Haeckel thought it probable that consciousness arises with the centralization of the nervous system, and that the lower classes of animals lack that faculty. The province of unconscious psychic actions, reflex action, for example, is more extensive than that of conscious ones, but the two areas are closely connected.

The consciousness of man and of other mammals biologically close to man is changeable and is modified by both internal and external causes. Consciousness is dependent upon the normal development of certain organs and gradually develops in the child as those organs develop. Despite Haeckel's use of a "faculties" terminology, his views on psychology are often similar to those of recent functionalists.

Attack on traditional religion. Haeckel's attack on supernatural religions had many facets. He unequivocally rejected revelation and theological faith. He was outspoken in combating the superstitions associated with the world's great religions. He scathingly attacked the influence of the church as an institution in politics and education. Indeed, he frequently coupled these problems, holding that the German government would not improve until it was free from church influence and its citizens received a better, more scientific, education. Haeckel even claimed that such questions as whether a monarchy is preferable to a republic and whether the constitution should be aristocratic or democratic are subordinate to the "supreme question": Shall the government be secular or dominated by the clergy? Haeckel was no respecter of religious heroes, prominent clerics, sacred myths, or widely held dogma. He tried to show that theological beliefs are incompatible with scientific data, unreasonable, or merely dogmatic.

Haeckel's admiration for the views of Spinoza and Goethe and his belief that mankind's ethical aspirations needed some support led him to advocate a monistic religion. "The ethical craving of our emotion is satisfied by monism no less than the logical demand for causality on the part of reason." He had great respect for the ethical values of primitive Christianity, and felt that Christianity had been so influential in the social and political movements of civilized history that "we must appeal as much as possible to its existing institutions in the establishment of our monistic religion" (*The Riddle of the Universe*, p. 336). He maintained, therefore, that he sought a rational reformation, rather than a revolution, in religion. However, the extent of his criticisms of Christianity appear to be revolutionary.

Haeckel wanted to give rational support to the true, the good, and the beautiful, and he considered the relation of that trinity to prevailing Christian notions. Truth is to be found in the study of nature by means of critical observation and reflection, and hence revelation must be rejected. However, what "we call virtue, in our monistic religion coincides for the most part with the Christian idea of virtue," especially the Christianity of the first three centuries.

Charity, toleration, compassion, and assistance are humanistic as well as Christian precepts, and are to be emphasized in the monistic religion.

On the other hand, Haeckel maintained that early Christianity preached the valuelessness of this-worldly things, because this life was merely a preparation for eternity. Hence the beautiful was of little consequence. Haeckel was especially interested in art forms in nature and believed that the microscope had newly aroused our aesthetic sense.

All forms of theism are to be opposed. A pantheism that identifies God and substance is necessarily "*the world-system of the modern scientist.*" All scientists who think theism can be reconciled with science are, in Haeckel's view, either dishonest, or confused, or victims of sophistry. If atheism is construed as a denial of the existence of a personal and extramundane god or gods, then Haeckel agreed with Schopenhauer's remark that pantheism is only a polite form of atheism. In short, Haeckel's criticism of traditional religions was that their doctrines are often intellectually wrong; that they generate unrealistic hopes; and that the social, political, and educational consequences of supernaturalism are malignant. Haeckel's criticisms, especially of Roman Catholicism, are often strongly worded. Thus he wrote that the obligatory celibacy of the clergy, auricular confession, and the sale of indulgences were designed for the purposes of strengthening the rule of the church over the "credulous masses and making as much material profit as possible out of them."

Ethics and social views. In ethics, Haeckel felt that traditional theories often either emphasize altruism too much (as in the case of many religious views) or emphasize egoism too much (hedonisms). He held that there should be an "equal emphasis" on self-love and love of one's neighbor. The "highest aim of all ethics" is to re-establish a "natural equality" of egoism and altruism. Along with this should go an emphasis on the body as well as the soul; an emphasis on fair treatment of animals as well as humans. Haeckel believed that a recognition of man's evolution would incline us to be more sympathetic to animals, and that Christian attitudes easily lead to cruelty toward animals. Haeckel regarded the family as the foundation of society and as a necessity for man as well as for the higher social animals, whereas Christianity, he believed, tends to disparage the family as a this-worldly phenomenon. Haeckel also opposed the tendency that he found in Christianity to make woman subordinate to man and to regard sexual intercourse as "unclean." He was especially hostile to the hypocrisy he believed is often found in the church toward sex.

Haeckel was much interested in social reform, holding that progress is a law of nature. He compared the rapid progress made in the natural sciences with the lack of progress in government, the administration of justice, education, and social and moral organization. He gave special attention to justice. He believed that students of jurisprudence need much more education in science than they usually receive, and that their knowledge of human nature is sadly deficient. Politicians too make practical decisions of great import with no scientific grounding in the appropriate areas. He also decried the many impediments to free inquiry, whether they stem from political reaction or from theological superstition. He was highly optimistic about the consequences of an improved system of education.

Many of Haeckel's views which caused violent disputes in the past are today widely accepted by educated people. Much of the antagonism toward him was centered on his insistence that man is a part of nature and in the evolutionary stream. Although large portions of the scientific part of Haeckel's world view have since been rejected, much is still regarded as sound. His views on religion would still be challenged by many; some, of course, find them mild.

Additional Works by Haeckel

Generelle Morphologie der Organismen, 2 vols. Berlin, 1866.
Natürliche Schöpfungsgeschichte. Berlin, 1868. Translated into English by E. R. Lankester as *The History of Creation*. London, 1876.
Anthropogenie. Leipzig, 1874. Translated into English by Joseph McCabe as *The Evolution of Man*. New York, 1910.
Der Monismus als Band zwischen Religion und Wissenschaft. Bonn, 1893. Translated into English by J. Gilchrist as *Monism as Connecting Religion and Science: The Confession of Faith of a Man of Science*. London, 1894.
Der Kampf um den Entwickelungs-Gedanken. Berlin, 1905. Translated into English by Joseph McCabe as *Last Words on Evolution*. London, 1906.
Die Lebenswunder. Stuttgart, 1904. Translated into English by Joseph McCabe as *The Wonders of Life*. New York. 1904.
Freie Wissenschaft und freie Lehre. Stuttgart, 1878. Translated into English as *Freedom in Science and Teaching*. New York, 1879.

Works on Haeckel

Bölsche, Wilhelm, *Ernst Haeckel: Ein Lebensbild*. Leipzig, 1900. Translated into English by Joseph McCabe as *Haeckel: His Life and Work*. London, 1906. Contains a useful bibliography up to 1900 as well as detailed accounts of Haeckel's life and work. McCabe added a supplementary chapter, "The Crowning Years," which gives an account of the controversies in which Haeckel engaged after the publication of *The Riddle of the Universe*.
Merz, J. T., *A History of European Thought in the Nineteenth Century*. Edinburgh, 1903. Treats Haeckel and his contemporaries in some detail.
Perry, R. B., *Present Philosophical Tendencies*. New York, 1912. Gives a brief account of Haeckel and his contemporaries and also discusses the leading issues that engaged their interest.
Schmidt, Heinrich, *Ernst Haeckel, Leben und Werke*. Berlin, 1926.

ROLLO HANDY

HÄGERSTRÖM, AXEL (1868–1939), Swedish philosopher, was the son of an orthodox minister of the Swedish Lutheran church and grew up in an intensely religious atmosphere. With the intention of following his father's profession, in 1886 he began theological studies at Uppsala University, which was to remain his academic home throughout his life. His interests, however, were soon diverted from theology to philosophy. From 1893 to 1911 he was docent (roughly, assistant professor), and from 1911 to 1933 professor, of "practical philosophy" (philosophy of morals, law, and religion). During his student days the idealistic metaphysics of C. J. Boström was still influential in Uppsala, although this mode of thought was soon to be swept away by a kind of Neo-Kantianism. Hägerström's publications around the turn of the century

mirror this situation. Under the influence of Kant, he came to regard metaphysics as impossible and, going further than Kant, rejected the hypothesis of the *Ding an sich* (especially in *Kants Ethik*, Uppsala, 1902). Like Kant, he considered the pure Ego, the same in all individual minds, as somehow the principle of the reality given to us, as the source of the laws of logic, and also as the source of certain synthetic propositions a priori, such as the principle of causality. Gradually the role played by this pure Ego was taken over, in his thought, by "the concept of reality," which he treated in *Das Prinzip der Wissenschaft* ("The Principle of Science," Uppsala, 1908) and *Botanisten och filosofen* ("The Botanist and the Philosopher," Uppsala, 1910).

Speculation about the concept of reality was to remain a fundamental ingredient in his mature philosophy, but it gradually lost most of its original Kantian flavor. In 1909 Hägerström wrote his *Social teleologi i marxismen* ("Social Teleology in Marxism," Uppsala). Although this study is a sharp criticism of the Marxist philosophy of history, it seems evident that he was influenced by, or at least in strong sympathy with, certain other aspects of Marxism—its materialism and its views on the functions of ideologies. In his lectures Hägerström soon characterized his own outlook as "enlightened materialism." To give an adequate characterization of his philosophy in a few key words is difficult, for he himself never presented his views in a systematic fashion. His many philosophical writings are mostly devoted to rather special questions, and much of their space is taken by polemics against authors with whom he disagrees. The influences that molded his thought were diverse and seemingly somewhat incompatible. His final philosophical positions were, on the whole, as far to the left as possible of religion and of any philosophical system, such as that of Boström, that was akin to or gave support to religion. As his motto Hägerström once chose the Catonian paraphrase: "Besides, I think that metaphysics ought to be destroyed."

Critique of metaphysics. Like so many antimetaphysicians, Hägerström was prone to label any view opposed to his own as metaphysical. The word "metaphysics" as he used it remains somewhat vague as to connotation as well as to denotation. He held, however, that all metaphysical doctrines suffer from a common fundamental fault, that of (implicitly or explicitly) assuming that "reality itself is something real" (or "being is something that there is"). This assumption is as "absurd" as, for example, the assumption that triangularity is something triangular. Hägerström thought it possible to prove positively (1) that the spatiotemporal world of experience exists and (2) that nothing may exist outside this world. In his proof of (1) he made use of an "analysis of the concept of reality" and also of ideas reminiscent of Descartes's *Cogito*. To deduce (2) from (1) he invoked the principle that two entities can not exist "outside each other" except as parts of a spatiotemporal context. His materialistic conception of the world of experience does not exclude the existence of consciousness, but consciousness, in his opinion, is a quality of certain material bodies (the psychophysical organisms).

Critique of "subjectivism." In an act of consciousness (awareness) we are always conscious of something. If *C* is a consciousness of *O*, then *C* and *O* are, according to

Hägerström, always two distinct entities; and further, the fact that a consciousness of *O* exists does not imply that *O* is endowed with any special intrinsic quality (such as being "mental," being a "perception," or being an "idea"). To overlook this is, in his opinion, the fundamental "subjectivist" mistake, which he thinks he can trace in the majority of philosophical epistemologies. This mistake gives rise to a secondary "subjectivist" mistake, the assumption that our knowledge about our own acts of consciousness is the immediate knowledge from which our knowledge of the external world must be derived.

Theory of value. Hägerström's first work in value theory was "Kritiska punkter i värdepsykologien" ("Critical Points in Value Psychology," in *Festskrift för E. O. Burman*, Uppsala, 1910), in which he raised objections to certain views of the Austrian school of value theory (Alexius Meinong, Christian von Ehrenfels, and others). He rejected especially their distinction between valuating emotive experiences and value judgments as theoretical judgments about the occurrence of such experiences. The value judgment, he claimed, is itself essentially emotive. By the time of his inaugural lecture, published as *Om Moraliska Föreställningars Sanning* ("On the Truth of Moral Ideas," Uppsala, 1911), Hägerström had arrived at the "value-nihilistic" doctrine that was to remain one of the most characteristic traits of his philosophic position. Statements of value, such as "To lie is bad," are neither true nor false: they lack truth value. Of the many arguments by which he tried to corroborate this view, the following is typical: A statement is true (or false) if, and only if, the judgment (as a mental phenomenon) expressed by the statement is true (or false); a statement of value, however, does not express any genuine judgment, but an "association" between an "idea" (for instance, the idea of lying) and an emotion. In his work *Till frågan om den objektiva rättens begrepp* ("On the Question of the Notion of Law," Uppsala, 1917), he elaborated this view also with respect to deontic statements. A statement such as "I ought not to lie," or "It is my duty not to lie," corresponds, not to a judgment with a truth value, but to an association between an "idea" and a "conative impulse." In this respect deontic statements are closely akin to imperatives. The persistent illusion that value statements and deontic statements have a truth value is caused by the relative stability of the underlying associations, which are built up and supported by the suggestive influence of a number of factors in the social system (such as early education by parents and teachers and the pressure of public opinion).

Hägerström nourished the hope that the spreading of his value-nihilism would contribute to the creation of a more tolerant, more humane, and less vindictive morality. Since he believed that the task of the moral philosopher is to analyze the mental phenomena expressed by, for example, statements of value, and since he took emotions to be an essential constituent in such phenomena, he became deeply interested in the nature of emotion. In order to substantiate his value-nihilism, he thought it important to demonstrate the subjective character of emotions; being "subjective," emotion can not be a source of knowledge—for instance, knowledge of values. Like all mental phenomena, an emotive experience is either an act of being conscious (aware) of something or some combination of such acts. What might commonly be called an emotive experience, such as enjoying the prospect of going to the cinema, is a combination of intellectual and purely emotive ingredients. The purely emotive experiences, such as a mere feeling of pleasure, consist in being conscious of a certain emotive quality (here a pleasure quality). In his earlier publications, Hägerström seems inclined to regard emotion as "subjective" because emotive qualities are qualities of the Ego. Later he experimented with a variety of explanations. According to one, emotion is "subjective" because the emotive qualities are experienced without "localization." Here, Hägerström invokes his principle that localization in the spatiotemporal context is essential to reality and objectivity, but the form of his argument remains somewhat vague. According to another of his somewhat puzzling explanations, emotion is "subjective" because the emotive qualities inhere in the psychophysical organism that has the emotion, and not in "external" objects.

In some of his works he assumed a "projection of emotive qualities onto external objects." When I look at a painting that pleases me, in his opinion, I project the quality of pleasure experienced by myself onto the painting: I perceive the painting as pleasant, just as I perceive it as square or as dark. On this view, the epistemological distinction that he wished to maintain between emotive qualities and, say, colors, becomes rather problematical. Some Swedish critics of his value theory have taken this view as starting point for their criticism—Einar Tegen, "The Basic Problem in the Theory of Value," in *Theoria*, Vol. 10 (1944), 28–52; and Sören Halldén, *Emotive Propositions* (Stockholm, 1952).

Legal philosophy. Hägerström began his mature work in legal philosophy with a criticism of a doctrine, common in nineteenth-century "legal positivism" (*Rechtspositivismus*), according to which "positive law" (as opposed to "natural law," *Naturrecht*) is somehow the expression of a will actually existing in society. His essay "Är gällande rätt uttryck av vilja?" ("Is Positive Law an Expression of Will?") in *Festskrift tillägnad Vitalis Norström* (Göteborg, 1916) and his previously mentioned book *On the Question of the Notion of Law* are largely devoted to a painstaking criticism of this doctrine in its many varieties. Hägerström devoted much energy to the attempt to clarify the nature of positive law and those factors in "the social machinery" that uphold the law. He maintained that our common view of legal phenomena is blurred by "magical ideas" that can be traced far back in history. In *Der römische Obligationsbegriff im Lichte der allgemeinen römischen Rechtsanschauung* ("The Roman Notion of Obligation in the Light of the General Roman View of Law," Vol. I, Uppsala, 1927; Vol. II, Uppsala, 1941), he tried to demonstrate the magical element in ancient Roman law. He believed that such Roman concepts as *ius, dominium,* and *possessio* are magical ideas and that the old Roman legal acts, such as *mancipatio* and *stipulatio* are acts through which magical powers over things or persons are established.

Critical history of ideas. In his lectures (some of which have been posthumously published) Hägerström discussed, with a wealth of learning, the history of religious, philosophical, political, and legal ideas. The history of ideas appeared to him largely as the history of confusions and errors flowing from certain inborn mechanisms of the human mind. To explain them he used to point especially to certain thought processes that, in his opinion, almost inevitably take place when the emotions and the projection of emotive qualities interfere with intellectual operations.

Influence. In Sweden, and also in the neighboring Scandinavian countries, Hägerström has exercised great influence. With his pupil and colleague Adolf Phalén he became the founder of the so-called Uppsala school of philosophy, which flourished in the 1920s and 1930s and has had a lasting effect on the whole academic philosophical atmosphere in Sweden. Common to the members of this school—most of whom disagreed with much of Hägerström's own philosophy—were a distrust of metaphysical speculation and of epistemological subjectivism, a realistic (sometimes almost naively realistic) conception of the external world, an interest in the phenomenological analysis of mental acts and their contents, an emotive theory of value (of some kind or another), and an insistence on conceptual analysis as a central task of philosophy. Some of the original members of the Uppsala school became strongly influenced by the Cambridge school of analysis in England and by logical empiricism. Outside philosophy proper, Hägerström gave rise to a school of jurisprudence (Vilhelm Lundstedt, Karl Olivecrona, Alf Ross).

Bibliography

ADDITIONAL PRIMARY SOURCES

"Axel Hägerström," in *Die Philosophie der Gegenwart in Selbstdarstellungen*. Leipzig, 1929. Vol. 7.
Socialfilosofiska uppsatser ("Essays in Social Philosophy"). Stockholm, 1939.
Religionsfilosofi ("Philosophy of Religion"). Stockholm, 1949.
Moralpsykologi ("Psychology of Morals"). Stockholm, 1952.
Inquiries into the Nature of Law and Morals, translated by C. D. Broad. Uppsala, 1953. Translation of some of Hägerström's works.
Filosofi och vetenskap ("Philosophy and Science"). Stockholm, 1957.
Rätten och staten ("The Law and the State"). Stockholm, 1963.

SECONDARY SOURCES IN GERMAN AND ENGLISH

Broad, C. D., "Hägerström's Account of Sense of Duty and Certain Allied Experiences." *Philosophy*, Vol. 26 (1951), 99–113.
Cassirer, Ernst, *Axel Hägerström*. Goteborg, 1939.
Ofstad, H., "Objectivity of Norms and Value-Judgments According to Recent Scandinavian Philosophy." *Philosophy and Phenomenological Research*, Vol. 12 (1951), 42–68.
Passmore, J., "Hägerström's Philosophy of Law." *Philosophy*, Vol. 36 (1961), 143–160.
Sandin, R. T., "The Founding of the Uppsala School." *Journal of the History of Ideas*, Vol. 23 (1962).

SECONDARY SOURCES IN SWEDISH

Hedenius, I., *Om rätt och moral* ("On Law and Morals"). Stockholm, 1941.
Marc-Wogau, K., "Axel Hägerströms verklighetsteori" (Axel Hägerström's Theory of Reality"). *Tiden* (1940), 286–299, 360–366.
Marc-Wogau, K., "Uppsalafilosofien och den logiska empirismen" ("The Uppsala Philosophy and Logical Empiricism"). *Ord och bild*, Vol. 53 (1944), 30–38.
Marc-Wogau, K., "Axel Hägerström och kritiken av subjektivismen" ("Axel Hägerström and the Critique of Subjectivism"), in *Harald Nordensson 60 år*. Stockholm, 1946.
Marc-Wogau, K., "Känsla och värde enligt Axel Hägerström och Hans Larsson" ("Emotion and Value According to Axel Hägerström and Hans Larsson"). *Ord och bild*, Vol. 55 (1946), 245–260.
Oxenstierna, G., *Vad är Uppsala-filosofien* ("What Is the Uppsala Philosophy?"). Stockholm, 1938.
Waller, M., *Axel Hägerström, Mannisker som fa Kände* ("Axel Hägerström, the Man Whom Few Knew"). Stockholm, 1961.

A. WEDBERG

HALEVI, YEHUDA (c.1075–1141), or Judah ha-Levi, philosopher of Judaism, was born in Toledo, Spain. In his youth he received an excellent grounding in Biblical and rabbinic literature, as well as in the secular, particularly philosophic, disciplines. Halevi early displayed a marked poetic gift, which culminated in a body of Hebrew poetry noted for its adaptation of Arabic poetic forms to the Hebrew idiom and for its religious profundity. He practiced the profession of medicine for most of his life, residing in both Christian and Muslim Spain, a fact that may account for his excellent knowledge of Judaism's two descendant religions. His decision to leave for a perilous pilgrimage to Palestine was the result of his intense longing to see the Holy Land, a longing that is reflected in both his poetry and his philosophic work. Legend has it that he was killed in 1141 by an Arab horseman as he kissed the soil of the Temple Mount in Jerusalem, but there is no historic confirmation of this, since he cannot be traced beyond Egypt on his way to Palestine.

Yehuda Halevi's philosophic work *Kuzari: The Book of Proof and Argument in Defense of the Despised Faith*, written shortly before his departure for Palestine, uses as its framework the historically verified conversion to Judaism of the Khazar King Bulan II and most of his people about the year 740. This event had assumed almost legendary proportions by Yehuda Halevi's time, serving as a source of great religious satisfaction to the otherwise badly suppressed Jewish masses. In his work Yehuda Halevi reconstructed imaginatively the discussions that led to the king's conversion. At the beginning we are told that an angel has appeared to the king in his sleep and has informed him that the Creator was pleased with his intentions but not with his way of acting. In the hope of learning a better way of life the king calls in representatives of Aristotelian philosophy, Christianity, and Islam, but they all fail to satisfy him. The king did not originally plan to call on a representative of Judaism, judging this religion unworthy of serious consideration because of the misery of its adherents, but his dissatisfaction with the other presentations causes him to alter his decision and to call for a rabbi. The discussion with the rabbi constitutes the rest of the volume.

The rabbi begins his presentation by asserting his belief in the God of Abraham, Isaac, and Jacob, who led the Israelites out of Egypt and whose intervention in the history of Israel has been continuous ever since. By beginning in this way, Yehuda Halevi broke sharply with the tradition of Aristotelian rationalism that characterized the bulk of medieval Jewish philosophy. He was very much aware of the profound abyss separating the God of the philosophers, who is self-contained, unmoved, and non-personal, from the personal and historic God of the Bible. For this reason he dispensed entirely with traditional proofs for the existence of God, the usual prolegomena of medieval Aristotelianism—whether Jewish, Christian, or Muslim—to the defense of the faith. For Yehuda Halevi it was history that was decisive. The God who reveals himself in the history of Israel could not have been reached by philosophical speculation but only by revelation. Similarly, Yehuda Halevi's interest in miracles reflected his view of history as the realm in which revelation takes place. The superiority of Judaism over its competitors follows, for Yehuda Halevi, from the public character of the Sinaitic revelation upon which Judaism is based. At Sinai, 600,000 men, women, and children were addressed by God, a mass revelation that no other religion can claim. This precludes the possibility of error or deception, a possibility that cannot be discounted in those instances where the revelation is restricted to one or to a few.

Yehuda Halevi's attitude to the knotty problem of anthropomorphism also reflected his anti-Aristotelian orientation. Although he was not in sympathy with a literal interpretation of many of the terms applied to God by the Biblical authors, realizing that this would lead to a humanization of God even to the extent of attributing corporeality to him, Yehuda Halevi was not willing to go the other extreme and strip God of all attributes, making it all but impossible to speak about him. There are events that can be experienced as proceeding from God directly. When Biblical authors, such as the prophets, applied a term like "merciful" to God, they were referring to those actions of God that are experienced by man as merciful and as coming from God. Although the term "merciful" is therefore applicable more to the effects of God's actions than to his essence, to the extent that his actions are *his* discourse about God becomes possible.

The religious particularism that is fundamental to Biblical religion was no source of embarrassment to Yehuda Halevi. The election of the people of Israel and of the land of Israel were fundamental concepts of his religious nationalism. This nationalism was based on the divine election of a people and a land for the proclamation to all mankind of those demands that God makes of all people, but for the special representation of which he has chosen one nation, whose suffering derives from its unfaithfulness to its mission. These themes permeate Yehuda Halevi's poetic works as much as they do his philosophical writings.

Works by Yehuda Halevi

The *Kuzari* is Yehuda Halevi's major philosophical work. The German translation, *Das Buch al-Chazari*, by Hartwig Hirschfeld (Leipzig, 1887), contains both the Arabic text and the Hebrew translation by Yehuda ibn-Tibbon. Hirschfeld also translated it into English, as *Book of the Kuzari* (New York, 1946), adding an Introduction and notes. There is an abridged edition of Hirschfeld's English translation, edited and with an Introduction by Isaac Heinemann, in *Three Jewish Philosophers* (Philo, Saadya Gaon, and Jehuda Halevi), edited by H. Lewy, A. Altman, and I. Heinemann (paperback, Cleveland and New York, 1960).

Works on Yehuda Halevi

See David Druck, *Yehuda Halevy: His Life and Works*, translated from the Yiddish by M. Z. R. Frank (New York, 1941); Rudolf

Kayser, *The Life and Time of Jehudah Halevi*, translated from the German by Frank Gaynor (New York, 1949); Isaac Husik, *History of Mediaeval Jewish Philosophy* (New York, 1958), pp. 150–183; and Julius Guttmann, *Philosophies of Judaism*, translated by D. W. Silverman (New York, 1964), pp. 120–133. That Yehuda Halevi was influenced by the Islamic philosopher al-Ghazali has been proved by David Kaufmann in *Geschichte der Attributenlehre in der jüdischen Religions philosophie des Mittelalters* (Gotha, 1877), pp. 119–140. See also J. Guttmann, *op. cit.*, p. 427, note 137, for other references on the subject of al-Ghazali's influence.

MICHAEL WYSCHOGROD

HALLER, ALBRECHT VON (1708–1777), Swiss medical scientist, poet, and journalist, also contributed to such varied subjects as botany, history, mathematics, philology, theology, and philosophy. Haller was born in Bern, Switzerland, and although he suffered from ill health as a child, he was an extraordinarily precocious student. In 1727 he completed medical training at Leiden under Boerhaave (whose *Institutiones* he later edited with elaborate commentaries) and then turned to writing poetry. His famous "Die Alpen" was original both in its feeling for the wild, sublime aspects of nature and in its defense of primitivist values against the vices of overcivilization. Of hardly less interest were such didactic philosophical poems as "Über den Ursprung des Übels," "Über Vernunft, Aberglauben und Unglauben," and "Über die Ewigkeit." His love of nature also inspired the patient researches into Swiss flora that were eventually to result in his botanical masterpiece *Historia Stirpium Indigenarium Helvetiae Inchoata* (1768).

Appointed in 1736 to the chair of medicine, surgery, and botany at the University of Göttingen, Haller took time from his multifarious academic and scientific activities to edit the monthly journal *Göttingische gelehrte Anzeigen*, to which he contributed innumerable articles on almost every branch of learning. Returning to Bern in 1753, he served in several public posts while continuing his scientific and literary pursuits. His monumental treatise on physiology, *Elementa Physiologiae Corporis Humani* (1757–1766), included the fruits of a lifetime of pioneering investigation. His principal work in anatomy was the *Iconum Anatomicarum* (1743–1756). Haller's compilation of a series of very useful critical bibliographies embracing the fields of botany, anatomy, surgery, and practical medicine reflected the amazing breadth of his reading. Finally interesting himself in political problems, he composed three philosophical novels—*Usong* (1771), *Alfred* (1773), and *Fabius und Cato* (1774)—in which he expressed theoretical views on government reminiscent of the Platonic ideal of a republic ruled by a natural aristocracy.

Haller's main contribution to the history of philosophy was perhaps an indirect one. His discoveries concerning the physiology of the central nervous system, particularly his epoch-making experimental clarification of the irritability principle, presented in *De Partibus Corporis Humani Sentientibus et Irritabilibus* (1752), aided the development of a materialistic and behavioristic psychology, especially by La Mettrie and Diderot. But his own philosophical opinions, deriving eclectically from Scholasticism, Descartes, and Leibniz, represented mostly an attempt to forestall the "radical" conclusions prompted by

his scientific thought. Against naturalistic and deterministic assertions, Haller defended the dualistic doctrine of
an immaterial, immortal soul in man and the freedom of
the will. Conceiving of the natural world in profoundly
teleological terms, he clung to preformationism in the
theory of generation. Of a markedly pious temperament,
Haller eventually came into conflict with various attitudes
typical of the Enlightenment. Against deism and incredulity
he argued for the authenticity of revelation, the reasonableness of Christian dogma, and the indispensability of
religion as the basis of social morality; for this point of
view see his *Briefe über die wichtigsten Wahrheiten der
Offenbarung* (1772). In this role he emerged as a critic of
such French *philosophes* as Voltaire, La Mettrie, Montesquieu, and Helvétius. Moreover, Haller was hostile toward
Rousseau not only for his deistic and antiprogessive views
but more particularly because of the doctrine of popular
sovereignty in the *Social Contract,* of which Haller offered
a refutation in *Fabius und Cato.*

Works by Haller

SCIENTIFIC WORKS

Opera Minora Emendata, 3 vols. (Lausanne, 1762–1768), is the
closest thing to a collected edition; these volumes contain various
anatomical, physiological, and medical studies.
   The classic *De Partibus Corporis Humani Sentientibus et Irritabilibus* appeared in English as *A Dissertation on the Sensible
and Irritable Parts of Animals* (London, 1755); a new edition with
the same title has an introduction by Oswei Temkin (Baltimore,
1936). The most important version of this work, however, is the
French translation, *Mémoires sur la nature sensible et irritable des
parties du corps animal,* 4 vols. (Lausanne, 1756–1760), which has
extensive supporting material.
   Haller's great eight-volume work on physiology, *Elementa
Physiologiae Corporis Humani,* has never been translated into
English. An earlier and much briefer treatise on physiology, however, *Primae Lineae Physiologiae* (1747; 1751; 1765), has had
several English editions: *Dr. Albert Haller's Physiology . . . ,*
2 vols., translated by Samuel Mihlis (London, 1754; 2d ed., 1772);
First Lines of Physiology . . . , translated from the correct Latin
edition printed under the inspection of W. Cullen (Edinburgh,
1786; Troy, N. Y., 1803).

OTHER WORKS

Briefe über die wichtigsten Wahrheiten der Offenbarung (Bern,
1772) has been translated as *Letters From Baron Haller to His
Daughter on the Truths of the Christian Religion* (London, 1780).
   Usong has appeared in two English versions, *Usong: An Eastern
Narrative, Written in German* (London, 1772) and *Usong: An
Oriental History in Four Books* (London, 1773). *Alfred* has been
translated by F. Steinitz as *The Moderate Monarchy or Principles
of the British Constitution, Described in a Narrative of the Life
and Maxims of Alfred the Great* (London, 1849).
   Mrs. Howorth translated *The Poems of Baron Haller* (London,
1794).

Works on Haller

Beer, Rüdiger, *Der grosse Haller,* Säckingen, Germany, 1947.
   Hochdoerfer, Margarete, *The Conflict Between the Religious
and Scientific Views of Haller.* Lincoln, Nebr., 1932.
   Irsay, Stephan d', *Albrecht von Haller: Eine Studie zur Geistes-
geschichte der Aufklärung.* Leipzig, 1930.
   Jenny, H. E., *Haller als Philosoph.* Basel, 1902.
   Schär, Rita, *Hallers neue anatomisch-physiologische Befunde
und ihre heutige Gültigkeit.* Bern, 1958.

Tonelli, Giorgio, *Poesia e pensiero in Albrecht von Haller.*
Turin, Italy, 1961.

ARAM VARTANIAN

HAMANN, JOHANN GEORG (1730–1788), German
Protestant thinker and critic of the Enlightenment, was
born in Königsberg. In no sense a professional philosopher, and largely self-educated, he made his living as a
secretary-translator and later as a government warehouse
manager in Königsberg.

Writings. Hamann's originality early caught the eye of
such diverse figures as Goethe, Hegel, and Kierkegaard,
but his famous "darkness"—his opaque style—has daunted
all but the most persistent investigators. Study of Hamann
has long been dominated by Hegel's picture of him as an
irrationalist and the paradigm of an individualist and also
impeded by discouraging delays in the publication of
complete editions of his works and letters. Following
World War I, Hamann's influence on Kierkegaard began to
be appreciated, but only recently have scholars been able
to expose enough of their subject so that the real dimensions of his thought could be guessed.

Meditations and occasional pieces. Hamann's simplest
writings were not intended for publication. These consist
of his reflections following financial and spiritual crises he
underwent on a business trip in 1758—*Biblische Betrachtungen* ("Biblical Meditations"; 1758), *Gedanken über
meinen Lebenslauf* ("Thoughts on the Course of My Life";
1758–1759), and *Brocken* ("Fragments"; 1758). The *Sok-
ratische Denkwürdigkeiten* ("Socratic Memorabilia"; 1759)
was his first public attack on the spirit of his century. A
meditation on Socrates and his relation to Christ, it adumbrates the central concern of Hamann's intellectual career,
the relation of philosophy to Christianity. Hamann saw himself as continuing the work of Luther, under the different
conditions of a later age. Whereas for Luther the problem
had been the relation of faith to the "law," the established
ecclesiastical and religious systems, the problem now concerned faith and philosophy.

Most of Hamann's writings were short occasional pieces.
Die Magi aus Morgenlande ("The Wise Men From the
East"; 1760), an essay on the symbolic meaning of eighteenth-century astronomical observations, earned him the
sobriquet of the "Wise Man of the North." His reputation
during his lifetime was largely based on such collections
of essays as the *Kreuzz üge des Philologen* ("Crusades of the
Philologian"; 1762), which contains the influential "Aes-
thetica in Nuce" ("Aesthetics in a Nutshell"), and on some
political satires—*Lettre néologique et provinciale* ("Neolog-
ical and Provincial Letter"; 1761), *Lettre perdue d'un
sauvage du nord à un financier de Pe-kim* ("Lost Letter of a
Savage of the North to a Financier at Peking"; 1773), and
Le Kermes du nord ("The Worm of the North"; 1774). The
sarcasm and irony characteristic of Hamann's style are
readily apparent from some of his titles.

Philosophy as criticism. In what sense was Hamann a
philosopher? Like Augustine, Anselm, Aquinas, Pascal,
and Kierkegaard, Hamann is difficult to classify. His relation to philosophy was ambivalent and paradoxical. His
thought moved between the twin figures of Socrates and

the "Philologian." The figure of Socrates, the philosophical hero of the Enlightenment, Hamann adopted for his own purposes, to turn the symbol of the Enlightenment against itself and to call for a philosophical confession of ignorance in place of philosophical pretensions to knowledge. The term "Philologian" was selected for its ambiguity, in that it suggests both a "lover of the word" and a "lover of reason."

Like Socrates, Hamann considered man to be the crucial problem. (Hamann's famous simile compares self-knowledge to a "descent into hell," suggesting later explorations, by existentialism and depth psychology, into the anxieties and subconscious turmoil of the human psyche.) Like Socrates, he called for and practiced a critical and questioning philosophy; he especially appreciated the acid analyses of Hume's reason. His answer to Kant's criticism of metaphysics was a higher level of criticism, not "metaphysics" but "metacriticism." But as the Philologian, Hamann saw Socrates as a forerunner and prophet (although an unwitting one) of the Christ and philosophy as a discipline seen in its true light only in the context of Christianity.

Criticism of the Enlightenment. Hamann's friends included many of the luminaries of the German Enlightenment, but personal relationships did not deter him from mounting the most severe criticism. (He believed friendship was like Mount Etna, "fire in the bowels" but "snow on the head.")

What were Hamann's objections to the philosophy of the Enlightenment? He viewed as "idealistic vanity" the attempts of leading Enlightenment thinkers to base philosophy upon undeniable rational truths (Moses Mendelssohn), to speak of "pure" reason (Kant), to discover a "natural religion" (the deists), to penetrate the mystery of man's constitution and isolate the origin of man's linguistic capacities (Herder and others), and to separate the knowledge of God from its provenance in historical revelation (Lessing). Hamann valued Hume's skepticism but insisted that it illustrated not the glory but the bankruptcy of reason. Skepticism is a paradigm of the ambiguity of all human powers—reason so conceived and directed is self-destructive. Hume, he felt, performed a service for philosophy in demonstrating what happens when reason is conceived as purely analytical, stripped of its functions of comprehension and intuition and removed from its orientation in religion and its foundations in historical experience.

Hamann's objections to Enlightenment philosophy can be illustrated by two sexual images he employed (such images were characteristic of his style). The rationalism of the age was trying to strip truth of her clothes, or, to change the figure, was trying to divorce what Nature had joined together, to attain reality by removing all excrescences, such as tradition, history, and experiential particulars. For Hamann truth appeared most authentically as "enfleshed" and therefore embodied in a unity of reason, faith, and sensual experience. He was skeptical of abstractions and saw language as the means by which the reason is confused as well as the means by which it expresses itself (the "seducer" as well as the "helpmeet" of man). He

insisted on the wisdom and religious depth inherent in the naïve vernacular, in imagery, and in myth. A "coincidence of opposites" was to be expected in the present world, even where the opposites seemed to be the most surprising and paradoxical—flesh and spirit, God and man, sensual language and transcendent conceptuality, history and reason. The most radical skepticism conceals a surreptitious credulity, and the most notorious agnosticism a covert religion.

Quarrels with other thinkers. Hamann's belief that the Enlightenment was sacrificing the concreteness, historicity, and earthiness of reality to the paramount desire of rationalism to systematize initiated his quarrel with such thinkers as Herder, Mendelssohn, Kant, and Lessing as well as obscure lesser lights. *Philologische Einfälle und Zweifel über eine akademische Preisschrift* ("Philological Ideas and Doubts About a Writing Which Received an Academic Prize"; 1772) attacks Herder's prize-winning essay on the origin of language; *Golgatha und Scheblimini* (1784) is a criticism of Moses Mendelssohn's theory of "natural religion" and its relation to church and state; *KONXOMPAX* (1779) contains a satire on Lessing's dichotomy between the knowledge of God and the knowledge of "accidents" of history.

Criticism of Kant. Hamann's evaluations of Kant's *Critique of Pure Reason* are found in his letters and in several essays, one of which is called "Metacritik über den Purismum der Vernunft" ("Metacritique of the Purism of the Reason"; 1784). The issue between these thinkers is the extent to which reason can be "pure" (that is, devoid of experience). Hamann objected not only to Kant's overvaluation of formal knowledge but also to the belief that Kant demonstrated that in some respects reason can be separated from sense experience.

Language. To Hamann, demonstration of a separation between reason and sense experience is impossible because it depends on language, or mental symbols, the "purity" of which is ambiguous. This ambiguity cannot be removed (and the old Platonic ideal of knowledge of forms refurbished) by the double maneuver of surrendering knowledge of reality itself and locating the forms of space and time in the knowing ego, known to be emptied of fallible sense experience. The mark of such an "emptiness" (absence of sense experience) would be a synthetic judgment a priori, and according to Kant this would be based on the pure forms of sensible intuition. However, to Hamann these forms of intuition, which he took to be types of *language*, cannot be demonstrated to be pure, because language contains the capacity to create what may be an illusion. "Not only does the entire capacity to think rest upon language . . . but language is also in the middle of the misunderstanding of reason with itself. . . ." The forms of intuition are not simply passive channels for the content of experience, but active forms of language (or of symbols) that have the power to deceive the mind and create the illusion that they are a priori and necessary.

In the new picture of being that Hamann offered as an alternative to his age, man is seen as a creature of flesh and blood ("the heart beats before the head thinks"), history as a living communication of the meaning of man's existence ("a continuing sign"), and the world as the "language" of God ("speech to the creature through the creation"). The metaphor of "language" points to the symbolic nature of the world, which is not to be exhausted in its material significance, deified in a pantheism, or transcended by reason in a Platonic dualism.

Influence. Scholarly interest in Hamann has focused upon his influence on the *Sturm und Drang* and romantic movements and on such figures as F. H. Jacobi, Schelling, Hegel, and Schleiermacher; upon his role as a forerunner of existentialism; upon his pioneering exploration of the nature of human sexuality (see his *Versuch einer Sibylle über die Ehe* ["Essay of a Sibyl on Marriage"; 1775] and *Schürze von Feigenblättern* ["Skirts of Fig Leaves"; 1777]); upon his influence on religious thought, such as the Movement of Awakening (*Erweckungsbewegung*, a revival of intellectual pietism) and neo-orthodoxy; upon his contributions to a philosophy of language; and upon his reconception of reason as essentially historical.

Works by Hamann

Werke, Josef Nadler, ed., 6 vols. Vienna, 1949–1957.
Briefwechsel, Walther Ziesemer and Arthur Henkel, eds., 8 vols. Wiesbaden, 1955——.

Works on Hamann

Blanke, Fritz, et al., *Hauptschriften erklärt*, 8 vols. Gütersloh, 1956——. Commentaries on Hamann's major works. Vol. I contains a comprehensive bibliography (pp. 145–176).
Leibrecht, Walter, *Gott und Mensch bei Johann Georg Hamann*. Gütersloh, 1958.
Metzke, Erwin, *J. G. Hamanns Stellung in der Philosophie des 18. Jahrhunderts*. Halle, 1934.
Nadler, Josef, *Johann Georg Hamann, der Zeuge des Corpus Mysticum*. Salzburg, 1949. Biography.
Salmony, H. A., *Johann Georg Hamanns metakritische Philosophie*. Zollikon, 1958.
Smith, Ronald Gregor, *J. G. Hamann, With Selections From His Writings*. London, 1960.

W. M. ALEXANDER

HAMELIN, OCTAVE (1856–1907), French idealist philosopher, carried further the neocriticism of Charles Renouvier and Jules Lachelier. Renouvier had criticized the categories of Kant, maintaining that the category of relation really included all the others. He had also criticized the fact that Kant had not included personality in the categories, though he should have, since the will determines thought no less than does speculative reason. Thought, according to Renouvier, manifests relation in two ways—in the relations of its elements to each other, and in the relation of judgment to consciousness. The latter relation is always unique because consciousness displays its spontaneity in the synthesis of the objects which it posits.

Hamelin started from a similar position; in fact, he always declared himself a disciple of Renouvier. However, Renouvier had taken account of contingency and discontinuity, and for him the pursuit of truth involved a recurrent dilemma, in which a free choice or wager was presented to the seeker. Hamelin, on the other hand, was much more intransigently rationalistic, and in this he was influenced by Lachelier. A priori thinking pervaded

Hamelin's system, and he envisaged a reality made entirely transparent and intelligible by a process of rational deduction. "Knowledge will no longer be seen as the invasion of the subject by alien elements, but as a putting into action by the subject of his potentialities."

Such an idealistic system requires some principle that accounts for change yet allows change to remain compatible with the necessity of rational deduction. In Hamelin's system this principle is correlation, and following Hegel, Hamelin pictured a dialectical evolution of reality through the synthesis of complementary opposites. This movement is from abstract elements toward the constitution of concrete reality—toward the constitution, indeed, of conscious personality—and not, as in Hegel, toward the indefinite pursuit of an Absolute. Hamelin's philosophy was a highly ingenious, if perhaps unsuccessful attempt to do away with the dilemma that dogged nineteenth-century French philosophy, the dilemma of a necessary realm of thought and a contingent domain of occurrences. Hamelin brought contingency, freedom, and personal consciousness within his dialectical system, making them the necessary outcome of incomplete, abstract categories that invoke them. They make their appearance, moreover, as the product of the dialectical process and as the coming to fruition of a hitherto inchoate reality.

Hamelin deduced the categories, or elements of representation, according to this dialectical principle. Relation is the synthesis of being and nonbeing, as that which consists in interdependence. The antithesis of relation is what is essentially independent, number. Number and relation are synthesized in time. Space stands in antithesis to time, since its parts, though separate, are also simultaneous and reversible. The space–time antithesis is transcended in motion, still a quantitative concept, which finds its opposite in what is unaffected by it, quality. Motion and quality are synthesized in modification (*altération*), which is the movement of quality. Modification is contrasted with a kind of resistance to change that tends to perpetuate the initial state, and this is specification, or the notion of class or species. Out of the interaction of modification and specification comes causality, or change brought about in beings through their sharing the world with other beings. Opposed to causality is a principle of persistence within the self, which is finality. The ultimate synthesis is in independence and self-sufficiency, which is expressed as free becoming and is an active system, or conscious self.

The characteristic of Hamelin's philosophy is its strictly a priori derivation of the concrete and individual consciousness from general and abstract elements. There is a kind of dynamism of incomplete abstraction working toward its own fulfillment and specification as successive logical demands are met. The element of contingency, which is inescapable in reality, finds its way into the system in the freedom of the individual consciousness: "What provides the explanation of consciousness is the need to choose."

Hamelin proceeded as far as anyone could in the idealistic direction. His no longer fashionable metaphysical deduction of the world through a series of necessary relations has met with some criticism from more recent French philosophers, whose tendency has been rather to see meaningful experiences as involving a compromise between a world of brute facts, which is prereflective, and a mind that almost necessarily orders them, albeit according to its own requirements and in the light of its own tasks.

Works by Hamelin

Essai sur les éléments principaux de la représentation. Paris, 1907.
Le Système de Descartes. Paris, 1910.
Le Système d'Aristote. Paris, 1920.
Le Système de Renouvier. Paris, 1927.

Works on Hamelin

Parodi, D., *La Philosophie contemporaine en France*, 3d ed. Paris, 1925.
Parodi, D., *Du Positivisme à l'idéalisme.* Paris, 1930.

COLIN SMITH

HAMILTON, WILLIAM (1788–1856), Scottish philosopher and logician. Hamilton was born in Glasgow and was educated at Glasgow, at Edinburgh, and at Balliol College, Oxford, where he took his B.A. in 1811. After leaving Oxford he studied law and in 1813 was admitted to the Scottish bar. He was appointed professor of civil history at the University of Edinburgh in 1821 and was elected to the chair of logic and metaphysics in 1836. Hamilton, a man of stupendous erudition, was strongly influenced by Thomas Reid and Immanuel Kant.

Psychology. Hamilton divided "mental modifications, or phenomena" into three classes—the phenomena of knowledge or cognition; the phenomena of feeling, of pleasure and pain; and the phenomena of will or desire, the exertive or connative powers. Knowledge, feeling, and will or desire cannot exist independently of one another. Every state of mind is a combination of all three, although proportions may vary. We can conceive of a being who knows some one thing or another but is totally devoid of feeling, desire, and volition; or of a being capable of knowledge and feeling only; but not of a being having the capacity for pleasure and pain and the capacity to will, but lacking the faculty of knowledge.

Mental phenomena are included under the phenomenon of consciousness. When one knows, he knows or is conscious that he knows; when one feels, he knows or is conscious that he feels; and when one desires, he knows or is conscious that he desires. Consciousness is not something in addition to knowledge, feeling, and desire, but the general condition of their existence. It is a relation between a knowing (or conscious, or intelligent) subject and an object of knowledge, in this case a modification of the mind. Although Hamilton sometimes denied the possibility of unconscious mental states, at other times he argued that "the mind exerts energies, and is the subject of modifications, of neither of which it is conscious" (*Lectures on Metaphysics*, Lecture 18).

Perception. In perception, according to Hamilton, we have an immediate or presentative rather than a mediate or representative knowledge of the object. In presentative cognition a thing is known in itself rather than via something other than itself. When I see a cat I come to know the animal in itself as contrasted with, for example, my

knowledge of a past event, which is acquired through testimonials and other means distinct from the event thus cognized. I may have representative knowledge of the past, the future, and the merely possible, as in imagination. Immediate presentative knowledge is of that which exists here and now. Perception is the faculty presentative of the phenomena of the nonego (matter), and self-consciousness is the faculty presentative of the phenomena of the ego (mind). A thing is known in itself only if it be known as actually existing in its when (now) and its where (here). Perception has for its objects the primary qualities of bodies. Knowledge of secondary qualities is never immediate, in that all we can know of them is that some unknown external cause is responsible for the "present affections of the conscious subject." Thus Hamilton agreed with Thomas Reid that we have a "direct notion" of primary qualities but only relative notions of the secondary qualities of things.

In perception we are intuitively aware of the duality of ego and nonego. This is an immediate, primitive datum of consciousness, to whose existence the natural realist (or natural dualist—both terms were used by Hamilton to designate holders of views like his own) is implicitly committed. Perception is not inference. We do not first become aware of some mode of consciousness and then infer from this awareness the present existence of a physical object as cause of that modification. Nor are we aware of an inner representation or referent from which we conclude the existence of an object referred to or represented. Representative theories of perception presuppose what on their own terms could not be the case. In order to know that *A* refers to or represents or is a sign of *B*, it must be possible to gain knowledge of the existence and nature of *B* independently of our knowledge of the existence and nature of *A*.

Relativity of knowledge. Granting that our senses inform us of the existence and the nature of physical objects, just what information do they provide us with? Hamilton held that our knowledge of mind and of matter is relative and conditioned and that "of existence absolutely and in itself, we know nothing" (*Lectures on Metaphysics*, Lecture 8). Our knowledge of the ego as well as of the nonego is purely phenomenal. The self is known to us only via the phenomena of the immediate introspective awareness of the flow of experience. In external perception we come to know about physical objects only as they appear to us through the senses. A physical object as known is that which appears to us as extended, solid, divisible, figured, colored, hot or cold. Thus, "matter" or "body" is a name for a certain set of appearances or phenomena, but these must be regarded as appearances *of* something. This something, however, is inconceivable apart from its phenomena, absolutely and in itself, out of relation to a knower. By virtue of a "law of thought" we are compelled to think of something absolute, unknown, and unknowable as the subject, substance, or substratum of the relative, the phenomenal, the known. The same reasoning applies to mind.

That a thing or a quality of a thing is known in itself does not mean that it is known in its "absolute existence" out of relation to the knower, for this is impossible. Hamilton meant, presumably, only that it is not known through a process of inference from signs or representations. All knowledge is relative in that in order to be known a thing must be related to the knower, the relation being precisely that of the knower to the known. But this is trivial. Hamilton pointed out that the way a thing appears to us in perception is relative in another sense—it is a function not only of the objective qualities of the thing, but of the medium and the sense organs as well. When I perceive a book, the phenomena or appearances of the external object are a resultant of the contributions of the book, of the intervening medium, and of the sense organs. Consequently my knowledge of the book is modified through certain intermediate agencies and must be relative. But, as Mill pointed out in *An Examination,* this conclusion does not follow; rather than entailing the relativity of all knowledge of physical objects, the considerations adduced show at most that that part of the knowledge that is not contributed by the book itself is relative.

Philosophy of the conditioned. To think of a thing is necessarily to think of it as a thing of a certain sort, to classify it, to subsume it under a concept. Thought imposes conditions on its object. Therefore the conditioned is the only possible object of knowledge. The absolute, the non-relative, the unconditioned is inconceivable; all we can know is *that* it is, not *what* it is. Although many things are inconceivable to us, nonetheless we know that some of them must be true. Hamilton claimed that, given the principles of contradiction and excluded middle, all actual thought lies between two extremes, each of which is inconceivable. The extremes represent that which is absolute or unconditioned. One of these absolutes we know must be true because they are mutually contradictory; but since both are inconceivable we cannot know which is true. "The Conditioned is the mean between two extremes—two unconditionates, exclusive of each other neither of which can be conceived as possible, but of which . . . one must be admitted as necessary" (*Discussions,* p. 22). The weakness of the human mind thus restricts its objects of positive thought to the mean. As illustration Hamilton argued that space must either be bounded or unbounded. One alternative must be true, but both cannot be, even though we cannot positively conceive of either one. Similarly we cannot conceive of an absolute beginning of time or of an infinite regress. We cannot conceive of an absolute end of time or of an infinite prolongation, although one or the other must be admitted to be true.

Logic. Hamilton regarded his doctrine of the quantification of the predicate as his most important contribution to logic. The doctrine is based on the self-evident truth that we can operate rationally only with what we already understand. This in turn leads to the postulate that we ought to be able to state explicitly what is thought implicitly. When we make a judgment we always implicitly understand the quantity of the predicate as well as the quantity of the subject. Since the predicate is always quantified in thought, and since every quantity is either all or some or none, we always regard the predicate of a judgment as denoting all, some, or none of the objects in its extension. The proposition "All men are animals" must mean either that all men are all animals (all men and only men are animals), or that all men are some animals (all

men, but not men only, are animals) "Some animals are carnivorous" becomes "Some animals are some carnivorous," which is to be understood as some and some only, that is, some animals are carnivorous and some are not. Among the advantages of this innovation, according to Hamilton, are the reduction of propositions to equations, the simplification of the doctrine of conversion, the abolition of the figured syllogism and the consequent manifestation of the absurdity of reducing syllogisms of other figures to the first.

Since in Hamilton's view logic is the science of the laws that of necessity govern all valid thought, criticisms of him drawn from psychological considerations are relevant. It comes as something of a surprise to the beginner in logic that conversion of the universal affirmative "All *S* is *P*" is only by limitation to "Some *P* is *S*." But in Hamilton's view this should be obvious to all and should not represent a new idea as in fact it does.

Works by Hamilton

ORIGINAL PHILOSOPHY

"On the Philosophy of the Unconditioned." *Edinburgh Review,* Vol. 1 (1829), 194–221.

Discussions on Philosophy and Literature, Education and University Reform. London, 1852.

Lectures on Metaphysics and Logic, H. L. Mansel and John Veitch, eds., 4 vols. Edinburgh and Boston, 1859–1860.

EDITING AND COMMENTARY

The Works of Thomas Reid, 2 vols. Edinburgh, 1846. Hamilton edited this work and added important commentaries.

The Works of Dugald Stewart, 11 vols. Edinburgh, 1854–1856. Hamilton edited this work.

Works on Hamilton

Grave, S. A., *The Scottish Philosophy of Common Sense.* Oxford, 1960.

Mill, John Stuart, *An Examination of Sir William Hamilton's Philosophy,* 2 vols. London, 1865.

Rasmussen, S. V., *The Philosophy of Sir William Hamilton.* Copenhagen, 1925.

Stirling, J. H., *Sir William Hamilton.* London, 1865.

Veitch, John, *Hamilton.* Philadelphia and Edinburgh, 1882.

Wight, O. W., *Philosophy of Sir William Hamilton.* New York, 1854.

TIMOTHY J. DUGGAN

HAMPSHIRE, STUART NEWTON, born in 1914 in Lincolnshire, England, was formerly a fellow of All Souls College and of New College, Oxford, and then Grote professor of mind and logic at University College, London (1960–1963). He is now professor of philosophy at Princeton University. Hampshire's contribution to philosophy, while clearly belonging to the main current of contemporary work in the English language, is highly individual. His work displays a broad and systematic outlook, concerned with bringing together views in the theory of knowledge, metaphysics, the philosophy of mind, ethics, and aesthetics. Among influences outside philosophy itself, it shows a particular awareness of psychoanalysis and of the history and criticism of literature and painting. His philosophical style is distinctive, a sensitive blend of the argumentative and the exploratory, which can be seen as the product of two contrasting influences: a sympathy with the outlook of Friedrich Waismann (himself influenced by Wittgenstein) that there can be no proofs in philosophy, together with a respect for the aim of J. L. Austin and other recent philosophers to reach definite results by definite methods.

Hampshire has shown a constant interest in the connections between meaning and confirmation. To this extent, there are links between his concerns and those of logical positivism, and a relatively early paper, "Logical Form," shows a recognizably positivist spirit in explaining differences of form in terms of differences in methods of confirmation. However, Hampshire's views have never in fact been positivist. In particular, he has been not so much concerned to assign a privileged possibility of certainty to some special class of statements but rather to explore the various certainty conditions of different classes of statement.

The connections between meaning and certainty conditions have been particularly explored with reference to psychological statements. Hampshire rejects the possibility of Cartesian statements of immediate experience, independent of any bodily conditions. He emphasizes both the need of communication with other persons for self-knowledge ("The Analogy of Feeling") and the dependence of the subject's sense of his identity on his being a physical agent in a physical environment. This idea is treated in detail in *Thought and Action*, where some influence of Jean-Paul Sartre and of Maurice Merleau-Ponty can be seen. While stressing the connections between mental concepts and physical agency, Hampshire has sought at the same time to give an intelligible place to introspection and to the possibility of incorrigible declarations by a speaker of his own mental states, particularly in the case of intentions: besides *Thought and Action*, see "*Self-knowledge and the Will*" and the important article "On Referring and Intending." In line with this is his rejection of any thoroughgoing behaviorist analyses of psychological concepts (review of Gilbert Ryle's *Concept of Mind*) and his interesting account of the notion of a *disposition* as applied to human character ("Dispositions"), an account more recently elaborated in psychoanalytical terms (in "Disposition and Memory"). Human dispositions must be distinguished logically from merely "dispositional properties," such as are possessed by material objects; dispositional properties can exist without having been manifested, but ascription of human dispositions implies some actual manifestations of them in the life of the individual. Moreover, the *understanding* of a human disposition is of a different character, being basically historical or genetical. Psychoanalysis is taken to reveal a basic way of understanding the individual's disposition, as rooted in his early experiences and consisting in the generalization to a class of situations of primitive responses; the influence of the primitive situations is to be seen in terms of unconscious memory. These ideas provide a link between the concept of a disposition and those of rationality and freedom; control over one's dispositions may be increased by self-knowledge, the understanding of how they have come about.

The emphasis on the psychoanalytical type of account of dispositions—that is, a genetical account—is a particular application of the wider view that human activities must be understood historically. This view has had an important influence on Hampshire's outlook on ethics, which rests on two points—that any comprehensible system of ethics must be grounded in a view of human nature and that all views of human nature are historically conditioned and essentially revisable. However, the historical changes in views of human nature or "the powers of the mind" are comprehensible only against a background of something identified, under any view, as essential to human nature, and this Hampshire finds in the possibility of self-conscious intentional action. From this point of view, Hampshire seeks to illuminate two basic (and, he would hold, permanent) distinctions: that between art and other human activities and that between human actions and mere events. Art is connected with the absence of an intentional project (see "Logic and Appreciation"); the appreciation of art is a process of free exploration. The distinction between actions and mere events involves his theory of freedom, which turns on a basic distinction between decision and prediction, and on the claim that there is an ineliminable human power of "standing back" from any prediction of one's future actions, the situation thus being changed (see *Thought and Action* and "Decision, Intention and Certainty"). Whether this has the consequence that determinism is impossible is perhaps not entirely clear; it is notable that Hampshire treated these questions in an illuminating book on Spinoza, and his sympathy for a Spinozist connection of freedom and knowledge, rather than a supposed freedom of the will, certainly continues (see "Spinoza and the Idea of Freedom").

Bibliography

The following are works by Hampshire:

"Logical Form." *PAS*, Vol. 48 (1947–1948), 37–58.

"Fallacies in Moral Philosophy." *Mind*, Vol. 58 (1949), 466–482.

Critical notice of Ryle's *Concept of Mind*. *Mind*, Vol. 59 (1950), 237–255.

"Freedom of the Will." *PAS*, Supp. Vol. 25 (1951), 161–215.

Spinoza. Harmondsworth, England, 1951; London, 1956.

"The Analogy of Feeling." *Mind*, Vol. 61 (1952), 1–12.

"Logic and Appreciation." *World Review* (1952). Reprinted in William Elton, ed., *Aesthetics and Language*. Oxford, 1959.

"Self-knowledge and the Will." *Revue internationale de philosophie*, Vol. 7, No. 25 (1953), 230–245.

"Dispositions." *Analysis*, Vol. 14 (1953), 5–11.

"On Referring and Intending." *Philosophical Review*, Vol. 65 (1956), 1–13.

"Identification and Existence," in H. D. Lewis, ed., *Contemporary British Philosophy*, Third Series. London, 1956. Pp. 189–208.

"Decision, Intention and Certainty." *Mind*, Vol. 67 (1958), 1–12. Written with H. L. A. Hart.

Thought and Action. London, 1959.

Feeling and Expression. London, 1960. Inaugural lecture.

"Spinoza and the Idea of Freedom." *Proceedings of the British Academy* (1960), 195–215.

"J. L. Austin." *PAS*, Supp. Vol. 34 (1960), 1–14.

"Friedrich Waismann." *Proceedings of the British Academy* (1960).

"Disposition and Memory." *International Journal of Psychoanalysis*, Vol. 43 (1962), 59–68.

Freedom of the Individual. London, 1965.

For a discussion of Hampshire's views on freedom, see D. F. Pears, ed., *Freedom of the Will* (London, 1963), Chs. 6 and 7.

BERNARD WILLIAMS

HAN FEI TZU (c. 280?–233 B.C.), the outstanding authority of the Legalist school of Chinese philosophy during the Warring States Period (403–221 B.C.), lived some two centuries or more later than Confucius, Lao Tzu, and Mo Tzu. His works consist of 55 treatises. He was an aristocrat of the state of Han, in the northwest, where a movement of political reform had arisen. In the rest of the Chinese kingdom, Confucianism, Moism, and Taoism still maintained the theory of government by customary morality, religious sanctions, and personal virtuous example or even "inaction" (or "nonaction") by the ruler. Since the traditional feudal system had collapsed generally throughout China, new thinkers spoke of government by positive law, exaltation of the state at the expense of the individual, and possession of supreme power by the ruler. Out of these thoughts of his predecessors, Han Fei made a comprehensive synthesis and formed his unique doctrine of legalism. This doctrine was greatly admired by the ruler of the state of Ch'in, who by its adoption eventually became the first emperor of the unified Ch'in Empire. Han Fei had been invited to the court of Ch'in, but he was forced to commit suicide by Li Ssu, chief minister of Ch'in and former associate of Han Fei. Although they had studied together under Hsün Tzu, the exponent of a reformed Confucianism, political jealousy overcame Li Ssu.

Han Fei accepted only one point of Hsün Tzu's philosophy, that human nature is originally evil. He then insisted that all men act from selfish motives and that a system of rewards and punishments can provide an effective control for the government, for there is no one who does not fear punishment and welcome rewards. The ruler can then rule the state through a set of severe laws without his own interference. In economics, too, the government should adopt a laissez-faire policy, leaving people alone to carry on free competition; this will cause them to be more active and frugal, with the result that production will increase. Thus, Han Fei reinterpreted the inaction principle of Lao Tzu in such a way that the sovereign, like the helmsman of a great ship, simply makes slight movements with the "two handles" of reward and punishment, and the whole state follows his desires and dictates.

While "statecraft" serves to keep the sovereign in power, laws are to be obeyed by the people. Han Fei said: "The intelligent ruler sees to it that his subjects do not allow their minds to wander beyond the scope of law; nor perform acts of favoritism within it" (*Works*, Treatise II). He also observed: "In the state of the intelligent ruler there is no literature of books and records, but the laws serve as teachings. There are no sayings of the early kings, but the officials act as teachers." Once laws have been established everyone should obey them; no heterodox doctrines of private individuals and traditional authorities should prevail. This led the first emperor to practice totalitarian regimentation, "burning the books and burying the literati" (*Works*, Treatise XIX).

It was Han Fei who supplied a rational explanation for revolutionary changes from the old order. He asserted: "Affairs go according to their time and preparations are made in accordance with affairs. . . . The sage does not aim at practising antiquity and does not model himself upon what is considered to be permanently correct" (*ibid.*). Indeed, history does not repeat itself. Politics, therefore, must look always to the present and to changing circumstances rather than to any static idea or ideal. In a word, Han Fei can be regarded as a radical positivist or perhaps as the extreme realist of ancient China.

Bibliography

For works by Han Fei Tzu, see *The Complete Works of Han Fei Tzu*, translated by W. K. Liao, 2 vols. (Vol. I, London, 1939; Vol. II, London, 1959); Wing-tsit Chan, *A Source Book in Chinese Philosophy* (Princeton, N.J., 1963), pp. 251–261, which contains selections from Han Fei's writings in translation with an introduction; *Han Fei Tzu; Basic Writings*, translated by Burton Watson (New York, 1964), in paperback; and W. T. de Bary, Wing-tsit Chan, and Burton Watson, *Sources of Chinese Tradition* (New York, 1960), pp. 136–150, which contains selections with an introduction.

See also Fun Yu-lan, *A History of Chinese Philosophy*, translated by Derk Bodde, Vol. I (Princeton, N.J., 1952); and Arthur Waley, *Three Ways of Thought in Ancient China* (London, 1939).

NAI Z. ZIA

HANNEQUIN, ARTHUR (1856–1905), French philosopher, born at Parny-sur-Saulx (Marne), served as professor of the history of philosophy and the sciences at the University of Lyons. This was the first official instruction in the history of science offered at a French university. Hannequin took a very broad view of his subject, conceiving of it not as a dry chronicle recounting a sequence of isolated discoveries but as the inward study of a system of concepts in a perpetual process of reorganization. This is what justifies the connection of the history of science with the history of philosophy.

The connection between science and metaphysics is made manifest in Hannequin's authoritative doctoral thesis, *Essai critique sur l'hypothèse des atomes dans la science contemporaine* (Paris, 1895). There he argued (1) that atomism is a necessary condition for science because our understanding conceives only number clearly and distinctly and imposes the discontinuity of number upon the perceptible continuity of extension and motion; (2) that from this fundamental conflict between number and the continuous, between the demands of the understanding and the data of perception, there inevitably result contradictions in the scientific concepts of the atom; (3) that these contradictions can be overcome only by ascending from physical atomism, which remains on the plane of phenomena, to a metaphysical atomism in which the subjective character of the forms of our representation is recognized. "Atoms disappear along with the continuous in proportion as one ascends toward the activities and the true unities of which they are but the reflection, toward the monads and the minds." These monads, however, are far from being sealed off from one another and are constantly interacting.

In 1890, Hannequin was warned by his doctors that he had little time to live. But with a fierce yet serene energy, he fought, week after week for 15 years, an ever imminent death, which finally struck him down before he had reached his fiftieth year. Thus, he was unable to realize the great works which he planned, the first fruits of which his students alone received. In general, he was interested only in philosophers of the very first rank—Descartes,

Spinoza, Leibniz, Kant. Above all was Kant, whose profound inspiration he sought to defend by resolutely maintaining, against some of the subsequent developments of critical philosophy, the radical heterogeneity of perception and the understanding and the existence of the things-in-themselves.

Bibliography

The relatively brief writings, published or unpublished, that Hannequin was able to complete were collected after his death, together with a French translation of his Latin thesis on the early philosophy of Leibniz, and appeared in two volumes under the title *Études d'histoire des sciences et d'histoire de la philosophie* (Paris, 1908).

See also the long critical study by Louis Couturat of Hannequin's *L'Hypothèse des atomes* in *Revue de métaphysique et de morale*, Vol. 4 (1896), 778–797, and Vol. 5 (1897), 87–113, 221–247. On Hannequin's work as a whole see the account by J. Grosjean in *Revue de métaphysique et de morale*, Vol. 15 (1907), 217–255, and in the Introduction to the posthumous *Études* (above), Vol. I, pp. xxi–ci.

ROBERT BLANCHÉ
Translated by *Albert E. Blumberg*

HAPPINESS. The terms "happiness" and "happy" have been conspicuous in the literature of moral philosophy. Utilitarians have claimed that the measure of right action is whether it makes for the greatest happiness of the greatest number, while hedonists and eudaemonists have affirmed that happiness (somewhat differently conceived by each) is the only thing that is worthwhile in itself. Indeed, almost everyone thinks that happiness is one of the most important goals, if not the supreme goal, of life.

In determining what the terms "happiness" and "happy" mean, it is convenient to concentrate on "happy," on the assumption that any sentence containing "happiness" can be rephrased in a synonymous sentence containing "happy." For instance, "He found happiness in marriage" means approximately the same thing as "He was made happy by his marriage." "Happy" has some uses that are not closely related to happiness—for example, "by happy coincidence." We may properly confine ourselves to the uses of "happy" in which the term is applied to a person or to a span of life ("He is very happy"; "That was the happiest time of my life").

Any correct definition of "happy" must take into account certain facts of English usage as well as the fact that we know that certain statements referring to happiness are true, namely, the following. (1) Whatever "happy" means, at least it is possible to be happy in different degrees: one man can be happier than another, and one year of one's life can be happier than some other year. (2) We know that a state of being happy can change, either to a state of being unhappy or to one of a different degree of happiness. It has sometimes been said that a man is not properly called happy unless his life is happy as a whole (see Aristotle, *Nicomachaean Ethics* 1100a); but it is clearly possible, in accordance with the way in which the word "happy" is used in English, for a person to be happy for a period of time irrespective of what happens to him afterward. (3) "Happy" is sometimes used with prepositions, such as "about," "with," and "at." Obviously a person can be happy when he is not happy with certain things, although we would not say that a man was happy if he were not happy with anything in his life. (4) Contrary to what has sometimes been suggested, a person can be happy even though he does not have everything he wants, but John Stuart Mill was right in suggesting that gratification of certain desires (he thought, those associated with the higher faculties) is necessary for happiness. Mill's particular identification of what must be done for happiness may be mistaken, but it is true that a person is not happy unless the desires he regards as being important are satisfied, or unless he thinks they probably will be satisfied. What is not necessary for happiness is gratification of peripheral desires, such as, perhaps, the desire for a new car. In view of this, William McDougall connected happiness with the important "sentiments" or systems of desires. (5) Doubtless there is a connection between the preceding point and the fact that "happy" seems to refer to a deeper level of experience than terms like "gay," "comfortable," "amused," "gratified," "pleased," and "enjoying oneself." If we say that a man "gets pleasure" from playing his violin, we mean something very different from what we mean if we say he "finds happiness" in his music-making; we would say the latter only when we thought his playing served to improve his perspective on or relieve his anxieties about his problems, thus perhaps enhancing his enthusiasm for living, or something of this sort. (6) Although we would not say that a person was a happy man if we thought he never enjoyed himself, we can say he is a happy man when he is not enjoying himself at the moment—for example, when he is in the dentist's chair. Also, we think that a person can be happy over a stretch of time even if he has very few sensory enjoyments—no wine, women, or song—during that time; we certainly think this if we know that he enjoys his work. Moreover, a man's having numerous sensory pleasures does not guarantee that he is happy: a person can divert himself with many hours of pleasure, yet still be quite unhappy and think he has nothing to live for.

Bearing the foregoing points in mind, the following proposal for a definition of "happy" may be suggested. There are two components of being happy. The first is dispositional: in order to be happy it is necessary that one like (which means very much the same as "be happy with," the prepositional use of the word) those parts of one's total life pattern and circumstances that one thinks are important. To say that one likes them is in part to say that one is "satisfied" with them—that one does not wish them to be substantially different, and that they measure up, at least roughly, to the life ideal one had hoped to attain; but it also implies, to some degree at least, a positively favorable attitude. The "total pattern" of one's life includes one's prospects: one may be happy in conditions one could not tolerate if one did not see them as stages leading to something else.

The second component of happiness is the occurrence (or nonoccurrence) of certain feelings or emotions. Happiness is sometimes said to be a species of joy in regard to one's total situation. This goes too far: a real emotion of joy occurs only when there has been some markedly favorable turn of circumstances—for example, when something has happened that one wanted to happen but was not sure would occur. And clearly we can say that a person is happy even if he is not feeling joy at good fortune all the time. But if a man is happy, he will not be subject (except briefly—for example, in connection with disappointments about noncentral things) to gloom, anxiety, restlessness, depression, discouragement, and shame, for these feelings will not occur if he likes the total pattern of his life insofar as the parts he deems important are concerned. But are no positive feelings required? It seems we would not call a man happy if he did not frequently feel joy or enthusiasm or enjoy what he was doing or experiencing. Exactly how much of this there must be one cannot definitely say. It is clear, however, that one could not like the total pattern of one's life unless some of these things occurred, although whether the connection between the two is logical or causal is a question we may leave open.

Thus far we have spoken about happiness as if it were an all-or-nothing affair. This is an oversimplification: a man can be happy in his job but unhappy in his marriage. Thus, there may be some aspects of his life that he considers important, that he does not like—or at least that he may not like very much. One person is happier than another person if he likes a larger proportion of the aspects of his life pattern or circumstances that he deems important, or if he likes them better than the other person.

The introduction of this comparative notion points to a vagueness in our definition of "is happy." In order to be happy, must one be satisfied with *all* features of one's life that one considers important? (There need not be a sharp line between what one thinks important and what one doesn't.) And how well must one like them? The term "happy" itself seems vague on this point: one person can demand more reasons than another for classifying someone as happy, without straying beyond the boundaries laid down by correct English. One possible way of sharpening the definition would be to say that a man is happy if it is false that most people are happier than he is.

A period of a person's life may be said to be happy if the person was happy during most of it. Ways of explaining "that year was happier than this year" will be obvious.

We often speak of "feeling happy." This means feeling the way one typically or ideally does if one *is* happy—that is, being neither depressed nor anxious and moreover having at least one of the positive feelings characteristic of being happy, such as enjoying what one is doing, feeling joy, and so forth. One can be happy, of course, without actually feeling happy at the time.

Thus, the creed of utilitarianism is mistaken if it holds, as J. S. Mill claimed, that "By happiness is intended pleasure, and the absence of pain; by unhappiness, pain, and the privation of pleasure." Even further from the truth was Jeremy Bentham's statement: "By utility is meant that property in any object, whereby it tends to produce benefit, advantage, pleasure, good, or happiness (*all this in the present case comes to the same thing*) . . ." (italics added).

Happiness is not identical with welfare or well-being. A person can be quite happy in a situation which is harmful to him if he does not know it is, and perhaps even if he does. Thus, a person's fortune may be dwindling if it is invested in bonds during a time of inflation, but he may be quite happy if he is ignorant of economics or even if he

sees what is happening (perhaps he is a poet). Furthermore, we may contribute to a person's welfare without affecting his happiness: for instance, we may improve his standard of living but not make him happier if he was quite content with the pattern of his life before, or if he regards the change as unimportant.

Philosophers who have written about happiness have largely agreed about the kind of life which is favorable to it—a life of uprightness, not given to excesses, and infused with understanding of the world and man's place in it. Some recent writers in psychology have added that it should include interests in other people and in causes, and acceptance of an objective picture of oneself. Other writers have pointed to evidence which shows that people can tolerate major areas of dissatisfaction (that is, discount their "importance") if they have many positive enjoyments in life, such as social contacts, opportunities for entertainment, and so forth. The question of what conditions are necessary for happiness is manifestly a question for scientific psychology.

Bibliography

Aristotle, *Nicomachaean Ethics*, Books I and X.
Duncker, K., "On Pleasure, Emotion, and Striving." *Philosophy and Phenomenological Research,* Vol. 1 (1941), 391–430.
Hare, R. M., *Freedom and Reason.* Oxford, 1963. Pp. 125–129.
Mill, J. S., *Utilitarianism.* Indianapolis and New York, 1957. Ch. 2.
Reuning, Karl, *Joy and Freude.* Swarthmore, Pa., 1941.
Stace, W. T., *The Concept of Morals.* New York, 1937. Ch. 6.
Wright, G. H. von, *The Varieties of Goodness.* New York, 1963. Ch. 5.

RICHARD B. BRANDT

HARNACK, CARL GUSTAV ADOLF VON (1851–1930), German church historian and theologian. He was born at Dorpat (now Tartu) in Estonia, where his father, Theodosius Harnack, was a professor of practical theology at the German-dominated university. Carl Harnack studied at Dorpat and then at Leipzig, becoming a *Privatdozent* there in 1876. He held chairs at Giessen from 1879 and Marburg from 1886 before going, in 1888, to Berlin, where he was a professor until his retirement, in 1924. He died at Heidelberg.

Harnack has come to be regarded as the typical representative of liberal theology. Following Albrecht Ritschl and the members of his school, Harnack stressed the ethical teaching of Christianity and avoided the more speculative flights of theology, but he went further than his predecessors in the direction of an undogmatic, practical statement of the Christian faith. Harnack's appointment to the chair at Berlin was opposed by conservative elements in the Lutheran church, but by the time he retired he had trained a whole generation of students in the ways of liberal theology and in what he believed to be the unprejudiced pursuit of theological truth. His last years were spent in opposing the nascent "dialectical theology" of the school of Karl Barth, which he saw as threatening the scientific character of the discipline.

The problem of dogma. The vigor with which Harnack advocated the cause of liberal theology was matched by his vast erudition. Few Protestant scholars have equaled his knowledge of early Christian history and literature. One of

Harnack's major works, the monumental *Lehrbuch der Dogmengeschichte* (3 vols., Freiburg, 1886–1889; many subsequent eds. published at Tübingen; 3d ed. translated as *History of Dogma*, 7 vols., London, 1894–1899), not only gives a detailed account of the history of Christian dogma, especially in the early formative centuries, but also expounds a definite thesis concerning the nature and development of this dogma.

As Harnack understood it, religion is primarily a practical affair and aims at the right ordering of life. In Christianity, the power of achieving a well-ordered or blessed life had its origin in Jesus Christ and the revelation of God that he brought. But although religion has this practical character, it also implies certain beliefs concerning God, man, and the world; the religious man seeks to make his beliefs explicit and to formulate them in propositions. This happens especially when a religious community comes into being and subscription to the basic beliefs of the community is made the condition of membership—hence the rise of dogma in the early church.

However, Harnack regarded this development as a perversion of the original teaching of Jesus, obscuring its essentially practical character and destroying its spontaneity. On the whole, he saw the history of Christian thought as one of deterioration, a falling away from the original truth rather than an unfolding of it. The process began when the primitive preachers made Jesus himself, as the supernatural Christ, the center of their message, rather than simply repeating Jesus' teaching about the kingdom of God, which Harnack understood as an ethical ideal. The transformation of Christianity into dogma accelerated in the Hellenistic world; the extreme case can be seen in the Gnostic sects, where the supposedly original gospel of Jesus was altogether absorbed into Hellenistic philosophy. With the Reformation an attempt was made to emancipate Christianity from dogma, but it was only partially successful, and dogma persisted into Protestantism.

The essentials of Christianity. In a series of popular lectures, which attracted huge audiences at the university of Berlin in the winter of 1899/1900 and was subsequently published as *Das Wesen des Christentums* (Leipzig, 1900; translated as *What Is Christianity?*, London, 1901), Harnack expounded what he believed to be the core of the Christian religion, set free from the encrustations of dogma that had been laid down through the centuries. The core is to be reached by penetrating back to the teaching of Jesus himself, and Harnack represented this teaching as proclaiming the fatherhood of God, the infinite worth of the human soul, and the ethical ideal of the kingdom of God. The supposedly original gospel of Jesus is also claimed to be the only version of Christianity that can make sense for modern minds, since it is free from theological and metaphysical mystifications.

Harnack's views once commanded a wide following, but this, however, has declined sharply in recent times, owing to the criticism of such scholars as Alfred Loisy, Albert Schweitzer, and Karl Barth.

Additional Works by Harnack

Harnack's literary output was immense, consisting not only of books and articles but also of critical editions of many early reli-

gious documents. In addition to the two books mentioned in this article, the following are important:

Das apostolische Glaubensbekenntnis. Berlin, 1892. Translated as *The Apostles' Creed.* London, 1901.

Die Geschichte der altchristlichen Literatur bis Eusebius, 2 vols. Leipzig, 1893–1904.

Beiträge zur Einleitung in das Neue Testament, 4 vols. Leipzig, 1906–1911. Translations of parts of this work: *Luke the Physician.* London, 1907. *The Sayings of Jesus.* London, 1908. *The Acts of the Apostles.* London, 1909.

Entstehung und Entwicklung der Kirchenverfassung und des Kirchenrechts in den zwei ersten Jahrhunderten. Leipzig, 1910. Translated as *The Constitution and Law of the Church in the First Two Centuries.* London, 1910.

Marcion. Leipzig, 1921.

Ausgewählte Reden und Aufsätze. Berlin, 1951.

Works on Harnack

Zahn-Harnack, Agnes von, *Adolf von Harnack.* Berlin, 1936. The standard biography of Harnack. See also her article on Harnack in *Die grossen Deutschen*, Vol. IV, pp. 255–266. Berlin, 1957.

JOHN MACQUARRIE

HARRINGTON, JAMES (1611–1677), English political philosopher and publicist. As the eldest son of Sir Sapcote Harrington, of Rand, Lincolnshire, he belonged to a junior branch of a family which had been prominent from the days of Richard I. An erudite man, Harrington must have acquired his great knowledge of languages, literature, and history largely independently, since he spent only two or three years at Oxford and in the Middle Temple and took no degree. During the 1630s he traveled extensively on the Continent and served in an English volunteer regiment in the forces of one of the palatine electors. From these experiences, and especially from a visit to Venice, he gathered much of the data which later formed the raw material for his political theory.

When civil war broke out in England, Harrington took a neutral position, despite his republican sympathies, because of his personal regard for the king, and at one point attempted the role of mediator between royal and parliamentary interests. But after Charles I's execution in 1649 he devoted himself to the construction of a republican political theory, which culminated in 1656 in the publication of his major work, *The Commonwealth of Oceana,* a blueprint for a perfect republic.

He was imprisoned by Charles II in 1661 on a false charge of treason. His mind became deranged while he was in prison, and he never fully recovered his faculties after his release. He died at his Westminster home in 1677.

Although *Oceana* has the form of a utopia, Harrington stands squarely in the British empiricist tradition. Even Machiavelli, whom he admired as "the only Polititian of later Ages," he criticized for violating the canons of empiricism by using such concepts as "virtue" and "corruption," which Harrington held to be meaningless as analytical tools.

Harrington's own concepts are sociological, rather than psychological or ethical. A stable governmental system always represents the dominant property-owning groups of a society. Where political and economic power are held by the same hands, and a single person controls three-fourths of all the property, the political system will be an absolute monarchy. If a few hold three-fourths of the property, it will be a mixed monarchy. If property is so dispersed that no monopoly vests in a single social interest, the system will be a republic, or "common-wealth."

Harrington made no moral ranking of the forms of government. Words like "tyranny," "oligarchy," "anarchy" he used descriptively rather than evaluatively, to signify unstable governmental forms which do not match their foundations, those in which power is held incommensurately to the distribution of property. The theoretical question which preoccupied him was stability, and the chief cause of revolution and civil war he identified as an incongruence between social balance and form of government. Conflict he viewed as a mechanism for bringing the two into close proportion. He was not an economic determinist, however, for he thought it just as possible to "frame the foundation unto the Government" as the reverse.

Like Machiavelli, Harrington preferred the republican system to all others. He wrote of "that *Reason* which is the interest of mankind, or of the whole," as "a Law of Nature," and described "the publick interest of a commonwealth" as "nearest that of mankind." Since he espoused a radically hedonic view of human motivation, this must mean he preferred republics because in them the things men enjoy are more widely distributed than in systems with a narrower property base. Not absolute equality but a middle-class order is implied, however. For "leveling" impedes economic growth and the social accumulation of the riches mankind desire.

More sanguine than Machiavelli, Harrington thought it possible to create a perfectly stable and unchanging republic. It could be maintained by an "equal Agrarian" law, fixing forever a middle-class distribution of property, and by arranging a suitable balance of interests in the organization of the government through such devices as separation of powers, division of the legislature, and rotation in office.

Bibliography

The latest edition of Harrington's collected works is John Toland's *The Oceana of James Harrington and His Other Works*, 4th ed. (London, 1771), and of *Oceana*, the edition of S. B. Liljegren (Heidelberg, 1924). See also Charles Blitzer's volume of excerpts, *Political Writings of James Harrington* (New York, 1955).

Among the works on Harrington, consult Charles Blitzer, *An Immortal Commonwealth: The Political Thought of James Harrington* (New Haven, Conn., 1960); H. F. Russell-Smith, *Harrington and His Oceana* (Cambridge, 1914); Christian Wershofen, *James Harrington und sein Wunschbild vom germanischen Staate* (Bonn, 1935); Zera S. Fink, *The Classical Republicans* (Evanston, Ill., 1945), Ch. 3.

WILLIAM T. BLUHM

HARRIS, WILLIAM TORREY (1835–1909), American philosopher and educator, was born in North Killingly (now part of Putnam), Connecticut. He attended preparatory schools in his native state and entered Yale College. There he was led to philosophy by Bronson Alcott's "Conversations" on Platonism, which convinced him of "the ideality of the material world" through "insight and reliance on reason." He left Yale in his junior year, dissatisfied with the deficiency of modern science and literature in the curriculum, and went to St. Louis.

In St. Louis, where Harris taught school for 8 years and was an administrator for 14, he met Henry C. Brokmeyer, a Prussian immigrant who had acquired an enthusiasm for Hegel from reading F. H. Hedge's *Prose Writers of Germany* (1847) during some disputatious months at Brown University. In 1858, Harris, Brokmeyer, and a few friends began meeting informally as a Kant Club to find the root of Hegel's thought. Harris imported a copy of Hegel's larger *Logic* and encouraged Brokmeyer to undertake a translation, which was never satisfactorily finished but was circulated in manuscript. After the Civil War, adherents of the Kant Club joined the St. Louis Philosophical Society, organized in 1866 with Brokmeyer as president, Harris as secretary, and Denton Snider, G. H. Howison, A. E. Kroeger, and Thomas Davidson among the leading members.

When the editor of *The North American Review* rejected one of Harris' articles as "the mere dry husk of Hegelianism," Harris and the St. Louis Society founded *The Journal of Speculative Philosophy*. Edited by Harris from 1867 to 1893, the *Journal* published numerous translations of German philosophers, particularly Hegel, and original essays by Emerson, J. H. Stirling, James Ward, William James, John Dewey, and C. S. Peirce. In defending Hegel's views in America, Harris and Brokmeyer had been preceded by a group of Ohioans that included J. B. Stallo and August Willich, who became "auxiliaries" of the St. Louis Society, as did Emerson, Henry James, Sr., Karl Rosenkranz, and Ludwig Feuerbach. But Harris was outstanding among American philosophers up to 1900 as an active public lecturer, a leader of the St. Louis movement and of the Concord School of Philosophy from 1879 to 1887, U.S. commissioner of education from 1889 to 1906, editor of America's first regular journal devoted to philosophy, and author of some five hundred articles and of a book on Hegel's *Phenomenology* and *Logic*.

Like Hegel, Harris saw philosophy as a science concerned with necessary factors in experience related systematically to a first principle. Reflection on sensible objects and their changes, he believed, immediately reveals two necessary factors with which philosophy is concerned, space and time. Both are "infinites" in that they are conditions of all experience. From a parallel analysis he concluded that there are three grades or stages of knowing. The first concentrates on the object and the surface of things as isolated and independent. The second sees how things exist only in relation to other things and thus concentrates on their dependence, on what they are not when taken by themselves as separate and isolated. The third "discovers the independence and self-relation underlying all dependence and relativity"; in discovering what is self-related it discovers "the infinite." These mutually related stages are to be found in every aspect of experience, and since there are no things-in-themselves behind experience, they characterize all aspects of our world. Harris thus attempted to put into plain English the main features of Hegel's dialectic. Through Brokmeyer, Harris came to believe that such dialectic illuminated the Civil War (legal right would be unified with moral right), American politics, and even problems of school administration—a use of philosophy that pleased the practical, institution-minded members of the St. Louis movement.

Proceeding dialectically from "seeming" to "truth," Harris analyzed causality and concluded that it incorporates space and time in a higher unity but also implies a "self-separation" of energy whereby a cause sends a stream of influence to other things. Without such self-separation a cause could not act upon something to bring about an effect. So conceived, causality must be grounded in "self-activity," which is necessarily self-related and thus independent, free, and creative. Ultimately, in Harris' view, the only authentic self-activity is God, conceived by Harris, following Aristotle and Hegel, as the unmoved motion and self-contained existence of Reason, which, as Reason, is also personal. Like Hegel, Harris believed that philosophy approaches Absolute Reason through conceptual analysis to first principles, whereas religion receives the Absolute "into the heart" through symbols.

As a corollary to the presupposition of relatedness in self-activity, Harris saw education as the self-development of the individual mediated through the salient traditions of civilization. With the self-development of the individual in view, he linked public schools with democracy, conceived of as self-government involving woman's suffrage and separation of religion from the state. With the traditions of civilization in mind, he criticized excessive vocationalism. Along similar lines, his social philosophy viewed civilized freedom as the will of the individual effectuated in such institutions as family, civil society, state, and the Invisible Church, the "absolute institution" uniting all men of all time. In spite of his stress on institutions, Harris apparently gave some kind of precedence to "self-activity" *simpliciter;* he admired the ruthless individualism of the "gilded age" and condemned socialism in all its aspects.

Works by Harris

Hegel's Logic, a Book on the Genesis of the Categories of the Mind. Chicago, 1890. The preface outlines the genesis of the author's views in relation to Kant and Brokmeyer.
Introduction to the Study of Philosophy, Marietta Kies, ed. New York, 1890. Topically arranged selections from Harris' numerous articles.

Works on Harris

Leidecker, Kurt, *Yankee Teacher, the Life of William Torrey Harris.* New York, 1946. The most complete biography.
Pochmann, Henry A., *German Culture in America, Philosophical and Literary Influences.* Madison, Wis., 1957. Pp. 257–304. Details on the St. Louis movement and the Concord School of Philosophy.
Schaub, Edward L., ed., *William Torrey Harris.* Chicago, 1936. Essays by American philosophers on major aspects of Harris' life and thought.

LOYD D. EASTON

HART, HERBERT LIONEL ADOLPHUS, professor of jurisprudence at Oxford, was born in 1907. Hart emerged in the 1950s as the most important writer on jurisprudence since Hans Kelsen. His writings display the influence of the English school of Jeremy Bentham and John Austin, but he is also indebted to such legal writers as Kelsen and Wesley Hohfeld. If, as Hart thinks, the main task of jurisprudence is the analysis of legal concepts, he has the special advantage of being not only a lawyer but

also a philosopher in command of the methods of conceptual and linguistic analysis developed by Gottlob Frege and Ludwig Wittgenstein, G. E. Moore, and Hart's Oxford colleague, J. L. Austin. It is to this form of analytical philosophy that one can trace many of Hart's characteristic doctrines, for instance, his insistence, in "The Ascription of Responsibility and Rights," that a legal concept such as contract is defeasible. By this claim Hart means to deny the traditional assumption that the concept can be defined by specifying the necessary and sufficient conditions of its application. In fact, he thinks, the sufficiency of the conditions may be defeated by certain defenses. In the case of contract fraudulent misrepresentation or duress would constitute such defenses or exceptions. Again, in his inaugural lecture, "Definition and Theory in Jurisprudence," Hart argues that the traditional attempt to define such legal terms as "right" and "corporation" *per genus et differentiam* suggests that these words stand for or describe things or persons or events. It is then falsely concluded by traditional theorists that the term "right" stands for some superempirical entity, or by the American realists that it describes our prophecies of the behavior of courts, or by the Scandinavian realists that it stands for some fictitious power. An illuminating analysis of such concepts will not assume that legal terms "stand for" anything. Rather, it will specify the conditions under which statements that employ these terms are true, and it will specify the manner or purpose of their use. Such statements may, in fact, be "performative," to appropriate a term of J. L. Austin's; they may be employed not merely to describe rights but to ascribe them, or to confer or transfer them.

Hart's most elaborate analyses are of the notions of legal causation and of the concept of the law itself. In *Causation in the Law,* written with A. M. Honoré, Hart argues that the plain man's notion of causation is fundamental to our thinking about the occasions on which it is just or fair to punish or to exact compensation. Traditional philosophical analyses of causation do not explicate the common-sense view. Hume denied the validity of the plain man's distinction between cause and condition, and even Mill, who allowed it, failed to see that our judgment of what is abnormal in a situation, or our sense of what is attributable to a deliberate human action, governs our "selection" of the cause of an event. Once the ordinary man's notion is understood, it will be seen that the causal judgments of courts are not necessarily obscure and that they are not simply judgments of expediency, justice, or policy disguised as judgments of causal fact. Hart and Honoré conclude that in the present state of Anglo-American law, judgments of causality cannot, as modern critics contend, be replaced by large-scale principles such as foreseeability or risk, or by the case-to-case intuitions favored by such a rule-skeptic as Leon Green.

In *The Concept of Law* Hart rejects the Austinian analysis of law as the sovereign's coercive orders. This model cannot account for primary rules, such as those of the criminal law, that impose duties; but it is even less capable of analyzing the secondary rules, of either private or public law, that create powers. Indeed, the Austinian theory cannot account for the notion of a rule at all, and it is precisely in the union of primary and secondary rules that Hart finds the key to jurisprudence. The presence of secondary rules is crucial to the existence of a legal system, for a rule of recognition is required to identify primary rules, a rule of change is required to alter them, and a rule of adjudication is required for determining when they have been broken. Hart necessarily rejects rule-skepticism (for it misunderstands or denies the importance of rules in the operation of a legal system), but he also rejects the formalism, or "mechanical" jurisprudence, that American legal realists and rule-skeptics set themselves against.

Although Hart allows that the mere following of rules imports features closely related to the requirements of justice into a legal system, and although he concedes to advocates of natural-law doctrines that the mere requirement of human survival makes a certain specific content of law a natural necessity, he nevertheless upholds the positivistic tradition of Bentham and Austin and denies any logically necessary connection between the concepts of law and morality. As he observes in his Oliver Wendell Holmes lecture, "Positivism and the Separation of Law and Morals," it cannot follow from the mere fact that a rule violates the standards of morality that it is not a rule of law, and, conversely, it cannot follow from the mere fact that a rule is morally desirable that it is a rule of law. In his *Law, Liberty and Morality* Hart argues that it is not the proper role of criminal law to enforce morality *as such*, and he rejects what he calls legal moralism, both in the moderate form (urged by Lord Devlin), which claims the enforcement of morals to be necessary for society's existence, and in the more extreme form (urged by J. F. Stephen), which argues it to be valuable in itself.

In a series of important articles Hart discusses the fundamental requirements of criminal liability, and in his presidential address to the Aristotelian Society he offers a "Prolegomenon to the Principles of Punishment" that transcends the traditional debate between retributionists and utilitarians. Indeed, Hart may be regarded as the outstanding contemporary representative of the tradition of English analytical jurisprudence and as one of the leading spokesmen of English liberalism.

Bibliography

"The Ascription of Responsibility and Rights." *PAS*, Vol. 49 (1948–1949), 179–194.

"Definition and Theory in Jurisprudence." *Law Quarterly Review*, Vol. 70 (1954), 37–60.

"Legal and Moral Obligation," in A. I. Melden, ed., *Essays in Moral Philosophy*. Seattle, 1958. Pp. 82–107.

"Positivism and the Separation of Law and Morals." *Harvard Law Review*, Vol. 71 (1958), 593–629.

Causation in the Law. Oxford, 1959. In collaboration with A. M. Honoré.

"Prolegomenon to the Principles of Punishment." *PAS*, Vol. 60 (1959–1960), 1–26.

The Concept of Law. Oxford, 1961.

Law, Liberty and Morality. Stanford, 1963.

MARSHALL COHEN

HARTLEY, DAVID (1705–1757), association psychologist and moral philosopher, was born in Luddenden, Halifax, England, and was educated at the Bradford grammar school and Jesus College, Cambridge. He was elected a fellow of Jesus but lost his fellowship when he married. He did not take holy orders, probably because of doctrinal scruples. Although he never received a medical degree either, he became a physician and practiced medicine in, successively, Newark, Bury St. Edmunds, London, and Bath. He was a friend of bishops Butler, Law, and Warburton.

Hartley's contribution to philosophy is his treatise *Observations on Man, His Frame, His Duty and His Expectations* (London, 1749). The first part, called "Observations on the Frame of the Human Body and Mind," is Hartley's exposition of the doctrines of vibration, association, and the seven classes of intellectual pleasures and pains. The second part, called "Observations on the Duty and Expectations of Mankind," consists of arguments for the existence of God, a defense of the truth of Christianity, a set of rules of conduct, and an estimate of our legitimate expectations in this life and hereafter.

Hartley's merit lies not in innovation but in consolidation. Borrowing several doctrines from his predecessors, he offers a comprehensive account of human nature. He treats mind and body as parts of a coordinate system capable of influencing each other. Thus, his work is a mixture of speculative physiology and psychology. While his conclusions may be criticized for their lack of an experimental basis (although he appeals frequently to experience), he nonetheless deserves credit for supporting the conceptual ideal of a unitary system of mind and body. Hartley's theory of knowledge is Locke's, offered in a context of religious sentiment. Despite the role which association plays in Hartley's philosophy, there is no mention of Hume in his pages. By freeing the doctrines of learning by experience and of psychological association from skeptical associations, Hartley gave them a respectability that assured them a general currency.

The three aspects of human nature that Hartley wished to explain are sensation, motion, and the generation of ideas. With regard to sensation, he wanted to account for the way in which impressions on the senses register perceptions in the mind. He postulated, first, that the "white medullary substance" of the brain, the spinal marrow, and nerves is the immediate instrument of sensation. He then claimed that when an external object is impressed on the senses, it occasions, first in the nerves linking the senses and the brain and then in the brain, vibrations of the infinitesimal medullary particles. These vibrations are the means of conveying the sensation to the brain.

From this account of sensation, Hartley moved on to his account of the origin of ideas. Sensations may remain in the mind for a short time after the sensible object has been removed from the vicinity of the senses. By being often repeated, sensations leave in the mind certain vestiges, types, or images of themselves. These images are the simple ideas of sensation, the materials from which complex ideas are made. Once the mind is supplied with simple ideas, the association of sensations and ideas may come into play. The first requirement is that we must have a given set of sensations "a sufficient number of times." These sensations then acquire such a power over their corresponding ideas that when any member of the set is impressed on the senses, it is able to excite in the mind the rest of the corresponding ideas that belong to the set. In this way simple ideas collect and become a complex idea.

In addition to arguing for an association of sensations and corresponding sets of ideas, Hartley also argued for a kind of association that depends on the sensory vibrations. Regularly occurring sensory vibrations leave behind in the nerves miniatures of themselves which he calls "vibratiuncles"; and even as a general sensation is able to call up a corresponding set of ideas in the mind, so a sensory vibration is able to call up a corresponding set of vibratiuncles in the nerves. Similarly, a complex idea may call into being the set of vibratiuncles appropriate to the complex of sensations with which the idea corresponds. Hartley claimed that some of the vibratiuncles attending upon complex ideas may be as vivid as any of the sensory vibrations excited by the direct action of objects.

In his account of human motion, Hartley again made use of the "white medullary substance" of the brain, spinal marrow, and nerves. He postulated this substance as the immediate instrument of motion. The motor nerves link brain and muscles; motion results as vibrations pass from the brain along the motor nerves and issue in muscular action. Briefly stated, then, Hartley's general theory of motion is that when objects are impressed in the senses, the vibrations excited in the sensory nerves spill over to the motor nerves by way of the brain and the higher ganglia; this process has a consequent effect on the muscles, and a motion results. According to Hartley, there are two sorts of motion, automatic and voluntary. They are distinguished by the fact that automatic motion depends on sensation, and voluntary motion depends on ideas. Hartley makes "automatic motion" cover a varied class, which includes such motions as the heart's beating, crying, and voluntary actions that have become habitual through repetition. Heartbeats can be fitted into his theory only by the vaguest references to the spill-over effect of the vibrations occasioned by sensation and by the additional suggestion that the circulation of the blood may also cause the heart to beat. The "motion" that best conforms to the theory is a fit of crying which results from a frightening experience or from the pain of being injured. In his theory of motion, Hartley did not intend "sensation" always to be the equivalent of "perception." For instance, the motion of breathing is excited in a newborn infant by cold air and the rough handling of the midwife, sensations which, for the infant, are not perceptions of anything.

In contrast to the automatic motions which depend on sensation, there are the voluntary motions which depend on ideas. A person's will consists of one of his ideas associated with sensory and motor vibratiuncles that are strong enough to excite the motor vibrations which, in turn, issue in muscular action. A voluntary action, for Hartley, is one that follows after an idea in the mind and not as a consequence of some outside force. He made it clear that "voluntary" must not mean "uncaused," and he argued that we have no "power of doing different things, the previous circumstances remaining the same." Indeed, he stigmatizes such an account of freedom as "philosophical freedom." He freely acknowledged that he was a mechanist, but he held that practical freedom does exist, in the sense that the causes of actions may sometimes originate within a person. Nevertheless, he staunchly maintained that human action cannot be exempted from the reasonable and useful belief that everything has a cause. Indeed, he subscribed to this belief even though he knew that many of his readers would think him a greater friend to religion if he had not stated it explicitly.

Hartley distinguished seven different classes of pleasures and pains which may accompany our sensations (and consequently our ideas), and thus reinforce their affective power, namely the following: (1) those of Sensation, as they arise from impressions made on our external senses; (2) those of Imagination, as they arise from natural beauty and deformity; (3) those of Ambition, as they arise from the opinions of others concerning ourselves; (4) those of Self-Interest, as they arise from our possession (or want) of the means of happiness; (5) those of Sympathy, as they arise from the pleasures and pains of our fellow creatures; (6) those of Theopathy, as they arise from affections excited by our contemplation of Deity; and (7) those of the Moral Sense, as they arise from our awareness of moral beauty and deformity.

The classes of pleasures and pains are here arranged in an ascending order of value, from least to most valuable; and from this scale, Hartley derived the rule of life. The pleasures of sensation, imagination, ambition, and self-interest are not in themselves worthy of pursuit. But the pleasures of sympathy are worthy of pursuit in themselves and set a proper limit to our interest in the first four classes of pleasure. Moreover, the pleasures of sympathy are consistent with those of theopathy and the moral sense. Together, these last three classes of pleasure constitute, as a whole, the worthiest object of human pursuit that can be found.

Bibliography

The dissemination of Hartley's doctrines was aided by his enthusiastic admirer and younger contemporary, the scientist Joseph Priestley. Priestley published an abridged version of the *Observations* under the title *Hartley's Theory of the Human Mind on the Principle of Association of Ideas* (London, 1775). While Priestley omitted the theory of vibrations, it is said that he was inclined to believe in it. Hartley is also the author of an *Enquiry into the Origin of the Human Appetites and Affections* (Lincoln, England, 1747). See also G. S. Brett, *A History of Psychology*, 3 vols. (London, 1912–1921), Vol. II, pp. 278–286, and Howard C. Warren, *A History of Association Psychology* (New York, 1921), pp. 50–64.

ELMER SPRAGUE

HARTMANN, EDUARD VON (1842–1906), German pessimistic philosopher. Karl Robert Eduard von Hartmann was born in Berlin, the son of a Prussian artillery officer. Von Hartmann entered a school for artillery officers, but a knee injury in 1861 that aggravated older rheumatic ailments barred him from a military career and left him a lifelong semi-invalid. After two years devoted to musical composition and painting, he turned to an intensive study of philosophy. By 1867 von Hartmann had nearly finished his *Die Philosophie des Unbewussten* (Berlin, 1869; 9th ed. translated by W. C. Coupland as *The Philosophy of the Unconscious*, 3 vols., London, 1884). This work brought him prompt and widespread recognition, and the rest of his professional life was devoted to a long series of books that amplified and in some details modified its views, and applied them to various fields of philosophy and problems of contemporary culture. Before his death he had published the first volume of an eight-volume *System of Philosophy* (*System der Philosophie im Grundriss*, Bad Sachsa, 1907–1909). Unlike Schopenhauer's, von Hartmann's pessimism did not keep him from two happy and fruitful marriages.

Influences on von Hartmann. Although he is generally regarded as a follower of Schopenhauer, von Hartmann found Schopenhauer's intense morbidity and his intuitive procedure temperamentally alien, and he corrected a basic incompatibility between Schopenhauer's Kantian phenomenalism and his Platonism by imposing upon the doctrine of the "will to live" a Hegelian but nondialectical doctrine of an intelligible categorial structure. Von Hartmann also acknowledged an indebtedness to the early Schelling for his theory of the unconscious, to the later Schelling for the process in which nature and consciousness emerge from unconscious potencies, and to Leibniz for the synthesis of individualism and monism. In *Die Philosophie des Unbewussten* von Hartmann built these influences into a system inductively grounded upon the data provided by the natural and historical sciences.

Will and Ideas. Although Schopenhauer's concept of Will is needed to explain the dynamism of the world process, it cannot, according to von Hartmann, explain the world order. Hegel's dialectic is absurd, but his concept of the notion is required to explain world order, even though it cannot account for the process by which, according to both Schopenhauer and Hegel, self-consciousness comes into being out of the unconscious. Ideas define the "what" of the world; Will determines its "that." The opposition of Will to the ordering of the Ideas brings about the emergence of consciousness and individuals.

Individuation results from the conflict of purposes into which the universal Will is driven through its resistance to its logical counterpart, the Ideas. Consciousness is required to emancipate the Ideas from bondage to the Will and its torments. Since space and time are the "sole principium individuationis known to us" (*Philosophy of the Unconscious*, Vol. II, p. 230), the result is a phenomenal but real evolutionary process of nature involving the greatest possible emergence of purposes. Consciousness, when it attains its maturity, will "suffice to hurl back the total actual volition into nothingness, by which the *process* and the *world ceases* . . . without any residuum whatever." (Von Hartmann suggested later, in Volume III, that the undifferentiated, substantial Will might continue to proliferate other orders of consciousness after this destruction.)

In this differentiation between the Unconscious Will and the Ideas, three orders of being must therefore be distinguished: (*a*) the metaphysical order of the unconscious; (*b*) the objective phenomenal-real order of nature; and (*c*) the subjective-ideal order of consciousness. The physiological unconscious in the second order ("the resting molecular predispositions of the central organs of the nervous system," *Die moderne Psychologie*, Bad Sachsa, 1901, p. 76), provides an unconscious ground for the total consciousness of an organism; conscious perception, in turn, is the bond by which knowledge of the transcendent but phenomenal-real order becomes possible.

Categories. In his *Kategorienlehre* (Berlin, 1896) von Hartmann distinguished between categorial concepts and the categorial functions of which they are the conscious representations. These unconscious rational functions assure that the concepts establish a relationship between phenomena and the thing-in-itself. There are innumerable categories, distinguishable as categories of sense and thought. There are two kinds of sense categories: sensations, which include quality, intensive quantity, extensive quantity (for example, temporality), and perceptions (that is, spatiality). The categories of thought include the primary category of relation, the categories of reflective thought (comparing, distinguishing, measuring, modality, etc.), and the categories of speculative thought (causality, finality, substantiality).

Teleology. Von Hartmann rejected both the irrational intuitionism of Schopenhauer and the mechanistic and materialistic assumptions of much of the science of his day. His own view of nature was teleological, an interpretation he undertook to demonstrate mathematically by a calculation of probabilities (he estimated the probability of eyesight being produced by mere mechanical processes as less than $15/10^7$) and also by analogies with alleged facts of experience. Instincts are unconsciously purposive, for example, and unconscious ideation in the nerve endings must be assumed to explain the slightest voluntary bodily movements. It is noteworthy that von Hartmann was one of the first to criticize Darwinism, arguing that evolution requires a vitalism and a "heterogeneous generation" of new variations within the germ cells of existing forms of life.

Pessimism. Among the factors that account for the great popularity of *The Philosophy of the Unconscious*, the most important is von Hartmann's restatement and justification of philosophical pessimism in the third volume. He regarded Kant, not Schopenhauer, as the father of his pessimism: this is not the worst of all possible worlds; indeed, the infinite purposiveness of the particulars in it makes it the best of all possible worlds. Nevertheless, it can be shown that it would be better if there were no world at all, and, paradoxically, the purposiveness of this world is moving to that end.

The argument for pessimism in *The Philosophy of the Unconscious* consists of a remarkable combination of neurological and psychological considerations with commonsense considerations about the misery in the world. Pessimism results from the successive dispelling of three stages of optimistic illusion. The first stage is that happiness has already actually been attained in the present stage of the world; the second is that happiness can be attained in a transcendent life after death; and the third is that happiness will be attained in a future state of this world.

In a later historical and critical essay on pessimism, *Zur Geschichte und Begrundung der Pessimismus* (Berlin, 1888), von Hartmann modified this sweeping argument for the misery of the world by setting up five criteria of value (*Wertmassstäbe*): pleasure, purposiveness, beauty, morality, and religiosity. His pessimistic theory of the *Weltlustbilanz*, he now claimed, was based on only the first criterion, and he described his theory as a "eudaemonological pessimism" but a "teleological-evolutionary optimism" in the nonhedonistic fields of value. He still held that efforts to assess values always involve the subjective, hedonistic component, and therefore involve a balance of misery.

Von Hartmann was concerned with showing that, far from making ethics and religion impossible, pessimism is the only foundation for a tenable ethical system and that it provides as well the wider teleological perspective from which religion, including contemporary Christianity, can be evaluated. In his *Phänomenologie des sittlichen Bewusstseins* (Berlin, 1879) he tried to show that all previous efforts to provide 'a philosophical basis for ethics, whether hedonistic, or built upon formal principles (which, he held, inevitably collapse into an ethics of ends), or socially oriented like utilitarianism and social democracy, had failed because they are untrue of man and the universe. The proper goal, which unites all lesser ethical ends, can only be a cooperative participation in the cultural process contributing to the satisfaction of all particular wills and, therefore, contributing *ipso facto* to the termination of the universe.

This conclusion anticipates von Hartmann's religious thought. The ethics of pessimism becomes a cosmic drama of redemption. The goal of the absolute religion of the future must be to save God, as Will, from the agony involved in his own inevitable creativity. The essence of vital Christianity, according to von Hartmann, lies in its pessimism about the present world, and liberal Protestantism is the last dying phase of Christian ethics because, by adhering to a faith in social progress, it has lapsed into the first stage of optimism.

Although the unorthodox nature and clear forcefulness of von Hartmann's thought drew a popular following, much critical comment was directed at his paradoxical theory of the unconscious, his criticism of religion, and the incompatibility between his pessimism and his idealistic ethics and philosophy of religion.

Except for a brief attempt to revive interest in von Hartmann's work during the years after his death, it has been largely neglected. He has been hailed as the last of the great speculative idealists, as a philosopher of science who opposed the mechanistic materialism of his time and anticipated the vitalism of the twentieth century, and as a psychologist who introduced the unconscious as a decisive mental factor. His criticism of the human predicament, along with Schopenhauer's, prepared the way for more complete, intensified forms of pessimism and nihilism in the twentieth century.

Bibliography

Additional works by von Hartmann include *Ausgewählte Werke*, 13 vols. (Leipzig, 1885–1901); *Das Unbewusste vom Standpunkte der Physiologie und Descendenztheorie* (Berlin, 1872); *Die Selbsterzetzung des Christentums und die Religion der Zukunft* (Berlin, 1874); *Wahrheit und Irrthum im Darwinismus: eine kritische Darstellung der organischen Entwickelungstheorie* (Berlin, 1875), translated by H. J. Darcy as "The True and the False in Darwinism," in *Journal of Speculative Philosophy*, Vol. 11 (1877), 244–249 and 392–399; *Kritische Grundlegung des transcendentalen Realismus* (Berlin, 1875); *Die Religion des Geistes* (Berlin, 1882), translated by Ernest Dare as *The Religion of the Spirit* (London, 1886), Part III separately translated by Thomas Hitchcock as *Religious Metaphysics* (New York, 1883); *Philosophie des Schönen* (Leipzig, 1882); *Das Grundproblem der Erkenntnistheorie* (Leipzig, 1889); *Geschichte der Metaphysik*, 2 vols. (Leipzig, 1889–1890); and *Das Problem des Lebens* (Bad Sachsa, 1906).

A chronological bibliography of von Hartmann's writings, prepared by Alma von Hartmann, appeared in *Kantstudien*, Vol. 17 (1912), 501–520. See also Hans Stäglich, *Verzeichnis der Eduard von Hartmann-Literatur* (Leipzig, 1932).

For interpretation and criticism, see Arthur Drews, *Eduard von Hartmanns philosophisches System in Grundriss* (Heidelberg, 1902); Otto Braun, *Eduard von Hartmann* (Stuttgart, 1909); Leopold Ziegler, *Das Weltbild Hartmanns* (Leipzig, 1910); E. H. di Carlo, *La filosofia della storia de Eduard von Hartmann* (Palermo, 1906); R. O. Petraschek, *Die Logik des Unbewussten*, 2 vols. (Munich, 1926); and W. Rauschenburger, *Eduard von Hartmann* (Heidelberg, 1942).

In English, J. W. Caldwell, "The Epistemology of Eduard von Hartmann," in *Mind*, n. s. Vol. 2 (1893), 185–207, and "Hartmann's Moral and Social Philosophy," in *Philosophical Review*, Vol. 8 (1899), 465–483 and 589–603, are noteworthy.

Two popular but accurate accounts of von Hartmann's thought and influence are contained in G. Stanley Hall, *Founders of Modern Psychology* (New York, 1912), pp. 181–246, and Radoslav Tsanoff, *The Problem of Evil* (New York, 1931), Ch. 12.

L. E. LOEMKER

HARTMANN, NICOLAI (1882–1950), German realist philosopher, was born in Riga, Latvia, and educated at St. Petersburg, Dorpat, and Marburg. He was a professor at Marburg from 1920 to 1925, at Cologne from 1925 to 1931, at Berlin from 1931 to 1945, and at Göttingen from 1945 until his death.

THE WORK AND THE MAN

The typical German philosopher of the past hundred years gives generous assistance to anyone wishing to become acquainted with his main ideas. He will have published at least one work on a philosopher of the past, who, with the regrettable exception of a few Greeks, turns out to be either German himself or mediocre and, with no exception at all, proves to be someone who could have been the professor's disciple or apostate. By simply observing what the author lauds and damns, stresses and omits, one may gather in concentrated form the materials for a portrait, not of the sitter, to be sure, but of the artist himself. This is true of even so eminently fair a German philosopher as Nicolai Hartmann. In his essays on the history of philosophy, "Zur Methode der Philosophiegeschichte" (1910) and "Der philosophische Gedanke und seine Geschichte" (1936), Hartmann advocated an approach to the history of philosophy in line with that to the history of science (these essays, as well as all others referred to, are reprinted in *Kleinere Schriften*). The history of philosophy is to be presented not as the coming to be and passing away of personal systems but as the progressive accumulation of impersonal insights. Yet many of Hartmann's numerous studies in the history of philosophy show that what he valued as impersonal, objective clarifications and solutions of the past more often than not anticipated views of his own.

In writing his first historical work, *Platos Logik des Seins·* ("Plato's Logic of Being," Giessen, 1909), which was his earliest publication as well, Hartmann was so immersed in the Neo-Kantianism of Hermann Cohen and Paul Natorp that he viewed Plato's ideas as absolute hypotheses in the Neo-Kantian sense of foundational positions taken by thought in its work of constituting reality. His two-volume work on German idealism, on the other hand, particularly the volume on Hegel (1929), bears witness to his accomplished liberation from idealism and the emergence of his main anti-Neo-Kantian positions. What he valued in Hegel's philosophy was not its systematic character but its aporetics; not its speculative idealist position but its being, as aporetics, prior to any position; not the Absolute and its self-realization—not even its dialectic, though Hartmann was fascinated and irritated by it, like a skilled craftsman in the presence of genius—but a sort of theory of emergence, describing and exploring, rather than constructing and deducing, basic strata and modes of Being and their interrelations; not the theological and teleological monism of the Spirit, with a capital S, but the discovery—or, rather, rediscovery, since Vico had been forgotten—of the objective spirit, with a small s, that is, superindividual powers such as languages, moral customs, legal systems, into which individual consciousnesses are born and within which they carve their little niches.

Thus, in the end the Hartmannian Hegel is, in method, an aporetician who prefers careful analyses of problems to traditional solutions and, in subject matter, an ontologist engaged in describing a multitude of modes and strata of Being. In brief, what is alive in Hegel is Hartmann, for aporetics, particularly an aporetic epistemology "this side of realism and idealism," an ontological pluralism, and the categorial exploration of the real world, including the spirit as its highest stratum, describe all but one of the major commitments of Hartmann. The exception is his axiology, an exploration of the realm of values, a program that Max Scheler had designed in open battle against the Kantian formalism in ethics but whose execution had to wait for Hartmann's *Ethics,* the only major work of his translated into English.

In his *Grundzüge einer Metaphysik der Erkenntnis* ("Outlines of a Metaphysic of Knowledge," Berlin, 1921), Hartmann presented in book form, for the first time, his aporetic and ontological epistemology. The book, published six years before Heidegger's *Sein und Zeit,* caused quite a stir precisely because it heralded the Continental renascence of ontology by asserting that epistemology is based on ontology and not the other way around. Almost all of Hartmann's subsequent books are in ontology, with his trilogy *Zur Grundlegung der Ontologie* ("Foundations of Ontology," Berlin, 1935), *Möglichkeit und Wirklichkeit* ("Possibility and Reality," Berlin, 1938), and *Der Aufbau der realen Welt* ("The Structure of the Real World," Berlin, 1940) forming his ontological *opus maximum.* To these might be added his *Philosophie der Natur, Abriss der speziellen Kategorienlehre* ("Philosophy of Nature, Outlines of the Special Doctrine of Categories"), which he began in 1927 but did not publish until 1950 (Berlin). In fact, his own philosophical work follows the plan he wished the history of philosophy to follow; there is much steady progress and expansion. The germs of his central ideas—many of them images rather than concepts—can be seen even in his early Neo-Kantian writings. For example,

so typical an image as that of "the strata" and their hierarchy, basic to his later ontology, is already germinally active in his early *Zur Methode der Philosophiegeschichte* of 1909.

There was only one revolution in Hartmann's thinking. This was the revolution against the Neo-Kantian idealism of his philosophical youth. It must have been a matter of profound travail for him, even though he was undoubtedly helped by certain select aspects of Husserl's phenomenology, in particular its Platonizing intuition of essences and its program for a merely descriptive reappropriation of experience. Whatever one may think of Hartmann's ontology philosophically, one cannot help being awed by his self-liberation from the grand German tradition of transcendental idealism, a liberation much more strenuous to a German than to Anglo-Saxons like Russell and Moore or Americans like Dewey, all of whom, to be sure, had somewhat similar conversions. These other conversions, however, were returns to the main current of their national philosophical traditions, whereas Hartmann's went counter to the main current of his. Indeed, even the severest critic of Hartmann's philosophy will respect the man himself. His philosophy reveals him to have been a careful, disciplined, honest, and sober conservative, kept by his common sense from philosophical extravaganza, but kept also from asking or appreciating radically revolutionary questions of either the existentialist or the new empiricist kind. Though as a person he was unmistakably German, his way of doing and writing philosophy was not at all typical of recent German philosophers. He cherished discussions and admitted to having learned from his students. He wrote not in the attitude of "the reader be damned" but with true courtesy toward his public, not to awe with profundity of learning but to guide with lucidity and thoroughness.

PHILOSOPHICAL POSITIONS

In presenting Hartmann's major positions it is advisable to begin with his conception of aporetics as philosophical method, not only because Hartmann himself put it at the beginning of his "Systematische Selbstdarstellung" (in Hermann Schwarz, ed., *Deutsche systematische Philosophie nach ihren Gestaltern,* Vol. I, Berlin, 1933; reprinted in *Kleinere Schriften,* Vol. I), but also because it is that part of Hartmann's philosophy which philosophers of the English tradition should find the most congenial.

Aporetics and epistemology. Aporetics is the unraveling of problems (aporia) into their strands; their presentation as clear-cut issues, preferably in the form of antinomies; and the weighing of the pros and cons of apparent solutions. There are some philosophical problems—the metaphysical problems—that will turn out to be in principle insoluble. Yet their unraveling is still useful, for as some part of the issues may turn out to be soluble, their discussion will contribute to the location and diagnosis of the unmanageable remainder. Aporetics is the central business of philosophy, all too often abandoned in favor of system building. Hartmann did not tire of pointing out that aporetics is what the Platonic dialogues and the best pages of Aristotle exemplify. However, this will hardly suffice in the age of science, when the nature of philosophy and philosophical problems is itself an aporia. Rather, one would wish to know what, if anything, distinguishes philosophical from logical or scientific problems. One would wish to know, besides, what it is that makes some philosophical issues insoluble and what the criteria are in terms of which some answers are solutions and some are not. Hartmann saw philosophical problems as arising from what he took to be the facts and from the contradictions they appear to harbor. His philosophical method, then, consisted really of two parts, a phenomenological presentation of the facts and an aporetic discussion of their implicit contradictions.

A typical example of Hartmann's descriptive–phenomenological and aporetic method may be found in his *Grundzüge einer Metaphysik der Erkenntnis*. No merely descriptive account of experience can plausibly deny that the objects known by a consciousness are experienced as existing independently of their being known. This fact, however, harbors in itself riddles in the form of flagrant contradictions: consciousness, in knowing an object, transcends itself, yet anything known to consciousness is thereby a content of consciousness—that is, is immanent—and consciousness never transcends itself. The same riddle, but formulated from the side of the object, concerns the influence of the object on the subject. On the one hand, the object must break into a consciousness and produce an image of itself; on the other, the object must remain outside the subject, for it is, as object, something transcendent and indifferent to its being known by a subject.

Hartmann neither questioned the nature of the facts he supposed himself to be describing nor entertained any suspicion that the antinomies he found in those facts might be due to the sort of language he used in describing them. Instead, he proceeded from knowing to being. The epistemic aporias are essentially ontic aporias, for both the object and the subject are beings (*Ansichseiendes*). The object is not exhausted in its being an object of a subject. Like a nocturnal thief caught in a sudden glare of light, it emerges out of an unredeemably transobjective and metarational background, a background that is in part beyond any human cognition, even beyond any possible sort of cognition. In knowing an object the subject knows "a thing that is," a being. In turn, the consciousness that knows the object is itself something not exhausted by its being a subject. It emerges out of a transsubjective and metarational medium; it is itself "a thing that is, a mode of Being." Hence, the epistemic relation between knower and known is really an ontic relation holding between one being and another, and the problems in epistemology are, or issue in, problems in ontology. As beings, both subject and object are ontologically homogeneous and are members of a context of Being (*Seinszusammenhang*). Within this context their relationship, so puzzling when taken in epistemological abstraction, becomes conceptually manageable, though an insoluble, and hence metaphysical, problem remains. This problem, however, concerns not the fact *that*, but rather how, subject and object stand in relation to each other.

In short, by seeing both subject and object as *Ansichseiendes*, Hartmann believed himself to have discovered that they are ultimately members of one matrix and context of Being. This is supposed to explain that they are related, though the how of their relation remains mysterious. Thus, the Hartmannian turn from epistemology to ontology looks suspiciously like a piece of verbal magic, as if a biologist, puzzled by the relation between males and females, proposed to solve the puzzle by calling both males and females "sexuals" and hence members of the sex context, thus "explaining" that they have sexual relations, though still wondering how they have them. Hartmann's reduction of epistemology to ontology *is* a piece of philosophical verbal magic if "subject" and "object" have empirical meaning, as "male" and "female" do. But if "subject" and "object" have no empirical meaning, what sort of meaning do they have? This basic question is unasked, and one cannot help wondering if the main use of the terms is not to engender the antinomies without which epistemologists would be out of work. In sum, Hartmann's phenomenological emphasis on descriptive facts seems to bring philosophical problems closer to empirical ones, whereas his aporetic emphasis on antinomies seems to bring them closer to logical ones. It is this basic ambivalence in his conception of philosophical method that cannot but be reflected in his conception of ontology.

Ontology. If there is anything twentieth-century ontologists have had in common it is their unquestioning belief that the term "Being" is the name of something or other. What is debated is rather what "Being" is a name *of*: a quality or feature shared by all beings (and if so, whether this class, as *summum genus*, is distinguished from other classes merely by its higher degree of universality); some relation that any *x*, in order "to be a being," must have to be a subject, or man, or God; or an individual being who is the ground of all beings. Since they have not questioned that "Being" is a name, these ontologists, like their predecessors, have a problem concerning the unity of Being. Protons and principles, nations and numbers, salads and sentences are all said to have some sort of Being, and yet, because they *are* so differently, the ontologist is compelled to admit different kinds of Being. But this would make Being itself the genus of these kinds, just another class concept, albeit more abstract or universal, depriving ontology, in the process, of its metaphysical weight and attraction. In this predicament ontologists have chosen a linguistic escape. Instead of talking of kinds of Being, they prefer to talk of modes of Being. They thus believe themselves to be preserving the unity of Being in the variety of beings without prostituting Being to a mere class name—and a name, of course, it must be.

To a degree, Hartmann shared with the most outspoken ontologists of the mid-twentieth century, the existentialists, both the referential use of "Being" and the preservation of the unity of Being via modes. However, he was at once simpler and more confused than they. Heidegger, for example, made the most of the distinction between Being and beings, between *das Sein* and *das Seiende*, and, correspondingly, between ontological and ontic investigations. But Hartmann, at least in his pre-Heideggerian writings (such as *Grundzüge einer Metaphysik der Erkenntnis*), seems to have been rather uncertain about this difference and to have used the term "ontological" for any investigation concerned with beings. This makes the concept of ontology simpler, as it keeps the white whale of Being from perturbing the Ahab of beings, but it also makes the concept more confused, as one is now at a loss to distinguish between ontology and science, both of which have to do with beings. In his pre-Heideggerian *Grundzüge,* Hartmann was similarly apt to be very cavalier about the problem of the unity of Being, and he spoke of modes and strata of Being as if they were merely basic kinds of beings. Even though in his later works all this appears to have changed, presumably under the influence of Heidegger's *Sein und Zeit,* and Hartmann no longer slid *terminologically* from "beings" to "Being" as he had in the *Grundzüge* (p. 182), *conceptually* the distinction between Being and beings and the problem of the unity of Being remain rather vague and were for him hardly the matter of primary philosophical concern they were for Heidegger.

Hartmann distinguished between two basic modes of Being (*Seinsweisen*), very much as the American new realists distinguished between existence and subsistence twenty years before him. One mode of Being consists of particulars, localizable in time and space, the other of universals—for example, essences, values, numbers. The former are real, the latter ideal; both are equally objective and independent of the subject. The ideals are logically prior to the reals, for a real is what it is only by virtue of an essence present in it (or valuable only by virtue of a value present in it). This apriority of ideal entities, however, does not exclude their being possible objects of experience, ideals being given in intuition just as reals are in perception. (Here "perception" and, it would seem, "intuition" must be used generously enough to include the emotional, for, following Max Scheler, Hartmann asserted valuables, if not values themselves, to be experienced emotionally rather than cognitionally.) Nor does the apriority of ideal entities exclude the possibility that the intuitional acts in which they are experienced are, *in ordo essendi,* grounded on the perceptual acts in which reals are experienced. As in Husserl, then, the a priori is not opposed to, but is rather part of, the empirical.

Within each of the two basic modes of Being, Hartmann distinguished between several strata of Being (*Seinsschichten*). The strata of reality correspond to the distinctions between inorganic nature, organic nature, consciousness, and superindividual culture (*Geist*)—all of them reals, but the last two also agents and carriers of ideals. Each stratum has basic, so-called categorial features, which it is the task of regional ontologies to lay bare. The strata form a hierarchy in which one stratum's dependence on the existence of another and partial freedom (autonomy) from the other's laws mark the higher from the lower. The working out of these regional ontologies through categorial analyses was one of Hartmann's central preoccupations, especially in *Der Aufbau der realen Welt.*

The distinctions between the two modes of Being and between the several strata within each mode were related by Hartmann to the traditional three modalities of possibility, reality, and necessity. Originally these are ontological modalities: it is beings that are possible, real, or necessary (*Seinkönnen, Sein, Seinmüssen*). Only derivatively are

they distinctions concerning validity or certainty of knowledge. The many-dimensional relations of the ontological modalities to the modes and strata of Being, on the one hand, and to judgment and knowledge, on the other, are explored in *Möglichkeit und Wirklichkeit,* the most complex and difficult of Hartmann's works.

The revolution of the *Grundzüge einer Metaphysik der Erkenntnis,* making epistemology ontological, revenges itself upon Hartmann's ontology, making it epistemological. A being is primarily understood as that which is *an sich* (in itself), and this *an sich,* the traditional substance of ontology, is defined epistemologically as that which is indifferent to its being known by a subject. Moreover, this *an sich* is either that of reals or that of ideals. Reality and ideality, the two basic modes of Being, become two basic classes of beings. The genus common to both is the *an sich.* Thus, Hartmann appears to have slipped back into class concepts and some sort of taxonomy, half epistemological, half empirical. As with the modes, so with the strata: it is not at all clear what distinguishes strata of Being from kinds of beings. The several strata of reality seem to be related to reality as so many classes are to a genus. Finally, it is not at all clear what distinguishes the concept of a stratum from that of a mode. The two modes of Being, reality and ideality, are themselves related to each other in a multidimensional hierarchical order, very much like the strata, and it would therefore seem that the main difference between mode of Being and stratum of Being is, as with class concepts, the degree of abstractness or universality. In fact, in his *Ethics* Hartmann dealt with ideality as if it were just another stratum and not a mode. If the modes and strata of Being were just kinds of beings, it would follow that ontology is empirical and that the categories are concepts, like any other class concept but more universal. Here lies, as was hinted before, a crucial difficulty of Hartmann's ontology, a difficulty that is shared, *mutatis mutandis,* by Samuel Alexander's and Alfred North Whitehead's conceptions of categories and that reflects some really basic indecision on their respective conceptions of philosophy. Categories, as Hartmann conceived them, are descriptive of the behavior of different kinds of beings, yet are supposed to be different in kind, not just in the degree of universality, from both the class concepts of ordinary experience—such as "tree" or "rodent"—and the functional concepts of science. At the same time, categories are supposed to be related—and it seems, in some sense, necessarily related—to both. But neither difference nor relation is clearly worked out, and Hartmann's ontology, like Alexander's and Whitehead's cosmologies, continues to hover between the empirical and the a priori as well as between science and ordinary experience.

Ethics. Indecision of this and other sorts haunts Hartmann's *Ethics.* Moral philosophy must not be casuistry; it must not try to teach what one ought to do in a particular situation. Rather, it should give the general criteria for a universal ethic. This sounds Kantian enough. But whereas Kant used it as a steppingstone to philosophically central investigations concerning the logical nature and the transcendental foundation, if any, of these principles, Hartmann veered off in a very different direction. Somewhat like a course in art appreciation, ethics is supposed to make men sensitive to the wealth of values present in the world. This, however, makes Hartmann uncomfortable; it is not academically respectable. The task of moral philosophy is, rather, to present clearly, force into consciousness, and "establish" values, raising to the plane of science what was a mere affair of feeling. How are the two conceptions of moral philosophy—that of making explicit universal principles of what ought to be done and that of raising value feelings to the plane of science—to be united? What one ought to do can be gauged only if one has an insight into what is valuable in life.

In fact, however, this synthesis of the Kantian apriority of moral principles with the manifoldness of values, "which Nietzsche had discerned only to let it melt away in historical relativism," is only a secondary aim of Hartmann's *Ethics*. Its central task is an analysis of the content of values, an elaborate axiology exploring the multitude of values and their relations to each other, to the ought, and to the real. This is the main body and the core of Hartmann's work in moral philosophy. It fills the second volume of the *Ethics;* the third is devoted to the problem of the freedom of the will. The first volume, besides developing his conception of moral philosophy, is a phenomenology of morality. Typical moral philosophies of the past are discussed with the aim of discovering in each of them a sound insight into some partial aspect of the moral phenomenon. Kant, for example, is said to have seen very clearly that ethical principles do not have the empirical sort of universality. They are a priori. Yet Kant's uncritical use of the Aristotelian form–matter dualism made him equate the a priori with the formal, and his epistemology made him equate the formal with the (transcendentally) subjective. Against this Kantian formalism and subjectivism Hartmann's axiology asserts an a priori of objective content—that is, of values as ideal entities that are intuitable.

It may, of course, be argued against this value objectivism that a judgment like "*x* is valuable" or "*x* is more valuable than *y*" will at some time and by some people be considered true and at some other time and by some other people false without there appearing to be any universal criteria of distinguishing, or any method of testing, the truth or falsity of these rival claims. But Hartmann answers this and other relativistic arguments by comparing the intuitional sense of values with a source of light. Light will penetrate darkness and illumine objects according to the strength of its source and will reveal the below and above of objects according to the position of its source, none of this preventing the objects and their spatial relations from being objective and knowable. This comparison assumes what was to be proved. It assumes that any particular sense of values is able to determine its own weaknesses with respect to all other possible senses of values, quite unlike a particular source of light, whose characteristics could not be objectively determined were it not for the sun and the light of day and the knowledge thus made possible. Hartmann's methodological reliance on an intuitional sense of values leaves his readers without a theoretical basis upon which to check and argue the truth or falsity of his observations in the realm of values. One cannot help being

pleased with them as one might be with the descriptions of a foreign though somewhat familiar country, but since the recommended means of transportation is in no public domain, the country might as well be Cockaigne. There is no use arguing with the Baedeker of Cockaigne: anyone may write his own. However, Hartmann's actual work in describing values is far superior to the account he gives of its method, and it is likely that this second volume of his *Ethics* will be found not only enjoyable but also useful.

Hartmann defined freedom of the will as independence from any determination that is constraint without this independence becoming indetermination. Indetermination is not only ontologically impossible; above all, it has once and for all been overcome in the Kantian conception of freedom as autonomy. Indeed, to Hartmann any determination that is not autonomy is constraint, and therefore autonomy fulfills the requirements of a definition of freedom of will. It is logically impossible for a will, insofar as it determines itself, to be either constrained or undetermined. If this is what freedom of will is, how can there be such a thing?

Hartmann's answer has two parts. The first is general, in terms of the hierarchy of ontological strata. Hartmann had asserted that the mark of a stratum's being higher than another is, in part, its autonomy—that is, the emergence of a new sort of determination or law. Autonomy is, then, a general ontological feature to be found, by definition, in any stratum but the lowest, and the autonomy called freedom of will is only a particular type of this general feature. Very much like theories of emergence, such as these of Alexander and Whitehead, which assume the miracle of emergence to be less miraculous if it is repeated, Hartmann's theory explains freedom of will as moral autonomy by making autonomy a universal ontological feature and then describing moral autonomy as a species of it.

The second part of his answer is concerned with this specific nature of moral autonomy. The will, in order to be free, must not be determined by the causal apparatus of nature, nor must it be determined finalistically by values and the corresponding oughts they confront us with. In either case the will would be determined by something outside it; that is, it would be constrained. However, if there were only these two kinds of determination, the causal determination of nature and the finalistic determination of values, then a will independent of nature would be one determined by the ought, and a will independent of the ought would be one determined by nature (indetermination being ontologically impossible); in either case the will would not be free. This is the most basic of Hartmann's aporias connected with the freedom of will. Hartmann proposed to solve it by positing a third kind of determination, whose nature he admitted to be completely inscrutable and metaphysical, a determination that belongs to the person itself, a self-determination through which an agent commits himself to the realization of value. Only such a third kind of determination, above both nature and value, explains the possibility of freedom of will.

Quite apart from the mistaken identification of determination and constraint, what seems particularly objectionable is Hartmann's suggestion of a kind of determination that is in principle inscrutable as a solution to the basic aporia of free will. Postulating an unknowable *x* as the solution to a problem is like shouting "victory" to undo defeat. In his escape from Kant's conception of autonomy as self-legislation of rational beings Hartmann fell under the spell of a supposed metaphysical ground in which a person and his decision making are taken to be rooted—a romanticism somewhat like Sartre's "dreadful freedom," which on closer inspection turns out to be mere whim.

The absence of religious thought in Hartmann's philosophy is conspicuous. Value realism offers logical difficulties to theology, and it is, besides, more naturally connected with a life attitude whose religiosity—if this word can here be used—lies in value commitments and not in a personal relation to God. Thus, Hartmann's value realism, as well as his pro-scientific persuasions and his empirically colored ontology, makes his proximity to atheism quite understandable. Very much unlike his beloved German idealists, who expressed the main existential spring of their philosophical energy in the problem of the "relation of the infinite and the finite," Hartmann was energized by no such preoccupations. His were intellectual aporias, not existential quandaries.

Hartmann's influence on German philosophy, though for a while considerable, was unable to stem the tide of existentialism. With the mid-twentieth-century return of German philosophy to a more sober and rational style, a new esteem for Hartmann began to develop in Germany. In the English-speaking world in the same period his *Ethics* was greeted with respect and then allowed to disappear, leaving hardly a trace. His only notable influence in fields other than ethics seems to have been on W. M. Urban, but as Urban's books have been ignored, Hartmann's effect in English-speaking countries has been limited to such indirect sources as Mario Bunge's somewhat Hartmannian books. Perhaps the sobriety, carefulness, and common sense of his general philosophical style are too much in the English and American tradition to attract our interest, and his logical and analytic naïvetes too numerous to hold it. It will take some time before these naïvetes are overlooked for the sake of his insights in the realm of values.

Additional Works by Hartmann

Philosophische Grundfragen der Biologie. Göttingen, 1912.
Die Philosophie des deutschen Idealismus, 2 vols. Berlin, 1923–1929. Vol. I, *Fichte, Schelling und die Romantik;* Vol. II, *Hegel.* Related are "Aristoteles und Hegel," in *Beiträge zur Philosophie des deutschen Idealismus,* Vol. 3 (1923); and "Hegel und das Problem der Realdialektik," in *Blätter fur deutsche Philosophie,* Vol. 9 (1935). Both are reprinted in *Kleinere Schriften* (see below).
Ethik. Berlin, 1926. Translated by Stanton Coit as *Ethics,* 3 vols. London, 1932.
Das Problem des geistigen Seins. Untersuchungen zur Grundlegung der Geschichtsphilosophie und Geschichtswissenschaften. Berlin, 1933.
"Neue Wege der Ontologie," in *Systematische Philosophie.* Stuttgart, 1943. Translated by R. C. Kuhn as *New Ways of Ontology.* Chicago, 1953. This summarizes *Der Aufbau der realen Welt* (Berlin, 1940).
Teleologisches Denken. Berlin, 1951.
Ästhetik. Berlin, 1953.
Kleinere Schriften, 3 vols. Berlin, 1955–1958. Vol. I, *Abhandlungen zur systematischen Philosophie;* Vol. II, *Abhandlungen*
zur Philosophiegeschichte; Vol. III, *Vom Neukantianismus zur Ontologie.* This collection reprints many articles originally published in journals.

Works on Hartmann

Baumgartner, H. M., *Die Unbedingtheit des Sittlichen; Eine Auseinandersetzung mit Nikolai Hartmann.* Berlin, 1962.
Feyerabend, P. K., "Professor Hartmann's Philosophy of Nature." *Ratio,* Vol. 5, No. 1 (June 1963).
Heimsoeth, Heinz, and Heiss, Robert, eds., *Nicolai Hartmann. Der Denker und sein Werk.* Göttingen, 1952. Fifteen essays, with bibliography.
Kanthack, Katharina, *Nikolai.Hartmann und das Ende der Ontologie.* Berlin, 1962. A critique of Hartmann's ontology from the viewpoint of what the author believes to be the new, Heideggerian era of philosophy.
Tymieniecka, Anna-Teresa, *Essence et existence; Étude à propos de la philosophie de Roman Ingarden et Nicolai Hartmann.* Paris, 1957.
Wirth, Ingeborg, *Realismus und Apriorismus in Nicolai Hartmanns Erkenntnistheorie.* 1965.

WALTER CERF

HARVEY, WILLIAM (1578–1657), English doctor and anatomist, demonstrator of the principle of the circulation of the blood. He was born at Folkstone, Kent, and educated at King's School, Canterbury, and Gonville and Caius College, Cambridge. After taking his B.A. in 1597, he left Cambridge for Padua, where he worked with the anatomist Fabrizzi d'Acquapendente (often Latinized as Fabrizio of Aquapendente). Fabrizzi had observed the valves in the veins, although he had not understood their function; Harvey told Robert Boyle that he had developed his theory of the circulation of the blood by reflecting on the operation of these valves, perhaps while still at Padua. In 1602 Harvey graduated from Padua with a medical degree and incorporated as an M.D. of Cambridge. Taking up practice in London, he was married in 1604 to Elizabeth Browne, daughter of the Physician to James I. He was elected fellow of the Royal College of Physicians in 1607, and two years later was appointed physician to St. Bartholomew's College, a position he held for 34 years. In 1616, when he began to lecture as Lumleian lecturer in surgery of the Royal College of Physicians (a post he assumed in 1615), he was already expounding his theory of the circulation of the blood, although he did not publish his *Exercitatio Anatomica de Motu Cordis et Sanguinis in Animalibus* ("An Anatomical Exercise concerning the Motion of the Heart and the Blood") until 1628. Appointed Physician Extraordinary to James I in 1618, and in 1631 to Charles I, Harvey was identified with the royalist cause during the Civil War. In 1642 his London house was ransacked by Parliamentary troops who destroyed notes and specimens. Charles I appointed him warden of Merton College, Oxford, in 1645.

After the Civil War Harvey lived a secluded life, retiring from practice and devoting himself to embryological research. Pleading age, he declined the presidency of the Royal College of Physicians in 1654, and in 1656 resigned from his Lumleian lectureship. He died at Roehampton.

There has been considerable dispute whether the discovery of the circulation of the blood can properly be ascribed to Harvey. As early as 1543, Andreas Vesalius had expressed doubts about the traditional Galenic account, according to which blood was made in the liver, flowed through the veins, and was then excreted, except for a small part which passed through minute channels in the septum to the right ventricle and so into the arteries. Vesalius complained that he could not find the channels through the septum. Michael Servetus (1511–1553), Andrea Cesalpino (1519–1603), and especially Matteo Realdo Colombo (1516–1559) all gave a reasonably accurate picture of the flow of blood through the lungs—the so-called "lesser circulation." But none of them recognized that the entire blood supply circulated through the body.

Harvey used the comparative method. Confused by the rapidity of movements within a living human body, he dissected such cold-blooded animals as toads and shrimps, in which movement is slower. Many of his contemporaries criticized him on the ground that what was true of the lower animals had no application to man. But for Harvey, as for Aristotle, man formed part of the animal kingdom.

Harvey's great importance lies in the fact that he used the concepts of mechanics in his analysis of physiological processes. He described the working of the heart in the language of pumps; he applied mathematical calculations to show that the body could not possibly manufacture the quantity of blood which, according to Galen's theory, would have to flow through it. The fact that blood still had a quasi-mystical significance made his matter-of-fact approach particularly significant.

Harvey's work greatly influenced many early modern philosophers, including Descartes and Hobbes (otherwise so different), who both put Harvey on a level with Galileo. They saw that Harvey had broken down the barrier between the animal and the human body, and between the processes of the body and the processes of mechanics. Thus Harvey's discovery gave empirical support to their mechanistic hypotheses. Descartes objected, however, that Harvey had not shown from first principles that the blood must necessarily circulate; he had been content to say that the heart is in fact a pump and that the blood does in fact circulate. Harvey replied to Descartes in his letters to the French anatomist Jean Riolan, who had rejected Harvey's theory. These letters were included in *Exercitationes Duae Anatomicae de Circulatione Sanguinis, ad Johannem Riolanum Filium Parisiensem* (1649) ("Two Anatomical Exercises Concerning the Circulation of the Blood, Addressed to Jean Riolan, Jr., of Paris"). Scientific truth, Harvey argued, is to be discovered by direct observation. "No more certain demonstration or means of gaining faith can be adduced than examination by the senses, than ocular demonstration." In this respect, Harvey compares biology favorably with astronomy. The astronomer, he suggests, argues from appearances. He cannot see what happens in an eclipse; all he actually sees is one disc sliding across another, whereas the biologist can see the heart beating in a shrimp. Observation shows us that the blood circulates, and that is enough for the biologist. This is a classic statement of the attitude of the observational biologist, in opposition to the Cartesian mathematico-physical conception of science. The *Letters to Riolan* also contain Harvey's criticisms of the attempt to explain physiological functioning in terms of "spirits." "Persons of limited in-

formation when they are at a loss to assign a cause for anything, very commonly reply that it is done by the spirits."

Harvey's other major work is contained in his *Exercitationes Duae Anatomicae de Generatione Animalium* ("Two Anatomical Exercises Concerning the Generation of Animals," 1651). Although this work was important in developing the view that each living thing is produced from an egg, as opposed to the doctrine of spontaneous generation, it lacks the scientific assurance of the *De Motu Cordis*. The fact that Harvey had to rely upon the unaided eye very much limited his achievement in this area. The first work of any consequence carried out with a microscope was done in 1660 by Marcello Malpighi, who took Harvey's theory as his point of departure.

Works by Harvey

The collected Latin works of William Harvey were published in London as *Opera Omnia* in 1766; the earliest English texts, dating from 1653, have been reprinted, edited by Geoffrey L. Keynes (London, 1928); a complete English translation was prepared by Robert Willis for the Sydenham Society, London, in 1847. The notes Harvey prepared in 1615 for his Lumleian lectures were published in facsimile as *Praelectiones Anatomiae Universalis* (London, 1886) and translated by C. D. O'Malley, F. N. L. Paynter, and K. F. Russell as *Lectures in the Whole of Anatomy* (Berkeley, 1961). The manuscript *De Motu Locali Animalium* (1627) was first published in Cambridge, England, in 1959, edited by Gweneth Whitteridge. See also *De Motu Cordis*, edited and translated by Kenneth James Franklin as *Movement of the Heart and Blood in Animals* (Oxford, 1957); *The Circulation of the Blood*, containing Harvey's reply to Jean Riolan, edited and translated by Kenneth James Franklin (Oxford and Springfield, 1958).

Works on Harvey

For literature on Harvey, see Geoffrey L. Keynes, *A Bibliography of the Work of William Harvey* (London, 1928; 2d ed., Cambridge, 1953), and *The Personality of William Harvey* (London, 1949); Henry P. Bayon, "William Harvey," in *Annals of Science*, Vol. 3 (1938), 59–118, 435–456; Vol. 4 (1939), 65–106, 329–389; Étienne Gilson, *Études sur la rôle de la pensée médiévale dans la formation du système cartésien* (Paris, 1951), Ch. 2; A. Rupert Hall, *The Scientific Revolution 1500–1800* (London, 1954); Louis Chauvois, *William Harvey* (New York, 1957); *Proceedings of the Harvey Tercentenary Congress*, John McMichael, ed. (London, 1958); John Arthur Passmore, "William Harvey and the Philosophy of Science," *Australian Journal of Philosophy*, Vol. 36, No. 2 (1958), 85–94.

JOHN PASSMORE

HATANO SEIICHI (1877–1950), Japanese historian of philosophy and philosopher of religion. Hatano was born in Nagano and died in Tokyo. He studied at Tokyo University, where his thinking was formed by Raphael von Koeber, a pupil of Eduard von Hartmann. He wrote his doctoral thesis, "A Study of Spinoza" (1904), in German. In 1901 he had published *Seiyo tetsugaku shiyo* ("Outline of the History of Western Philosophy"; Tokyo), a book whose scholarship established his reputation. He went to Germany in 1904 and studied under Adolf Harnack and Otto Pfleiderer at Berlin for two years, then under Windelband at Heidelberg. He also developed his studies of Protestant theology (he had been baptized in 1902) under J. Weiss, E. Troeltsch, and A. Deissmann. Their lectures prepared him to be a temporary replacement for Anesaki

Masaharu, Tokyo University's well-known historian of religion. From his lecture notes he published *Kirisutokyō no kigen* ("The Origin of Christianity"; Tokyo, 1908). In a much later book, *Genshi kirisutokyō* ("Primitive Christianity"; Tokyo, 1950), he rose above the historicotextual criticism of his early days to present a more thorough study of the essence of Christianity. But at the beginning of the century this type of work was a novelty in Japan.

In 1917 he resigned from Waseda University, where he had taught for many years, and at the invitation of Nishida Kitarō, the leading philosopher of Japan, he joined the staff of Kyoto University; he taught there until he retired in 1947. Subsequently he became the president of Tamagawa University in Tokyo. At Kyoto he had the chair of science of religion, and from 1922 he held the chair of Christianity. Hatano developed his philosophy of religion in four books (all published in Japanese, in Tokyo): "The Essence and Fundamental Problem of Philosophy of Religion" (1920); "Philosophy of Religion" (1935); "Introduction to Philosophy of Religion" (1940); *Time and Eternity* (Japanese edition, 1943; English edition, 1963). His main idea is that the comparative study of religion presupposes a philosophy of religion because values are a necessary element of that science. As philosophy, religion must start from the reality of the religious experience of God; this experience is first an experience of the God of power, then a quest for the God of truth, and finally an experience of the God of love. Hatano distinguishes three kinds of time: the natural, encompassing the realm of nature; the cultural, characterized by eros; and the eternal, in which agape, or Christian love, triumphs. Original, too, are his observations on the "about-to-come" future (*shōrai*) and the distant future (*mirai*). The first is implicitly part of our present; it is the future we are making, the supplier of being. The second is time which will never be experienced by the subject. Clearly Hatano is much influenced by Christian ideas and takes almost nothing from the Oriental climate of thought; even so this type of philosophy of religion was and still is very influential in Japanese thought.

Bibliography

Hatano's works have been published in Japanese as *Hatano Seiichi zenshū* ("The Complete Works of Hatano Seiichi"), 5 vols. (Tokyo, 1949). Vols. III–V include Hatano's works on the philosophy of religion. One of his works on that subject, *Toki to eien* (Tokyo, 1943), has been translated by Ichiro Suzuki as *Time and Eternity* (Tokyo, 1963). For a discussion of Hatano's thought see G. K. Piovesana's *Recent Japanese Philosophical Thought, 1862–1962* (Tokyo, 1963), pp. 123–131.

GINO K. PIOVESANA, S.J.

HAYASHI RAZAN (1583–1657), Japanese Confucianist, helped establish the Chu Hsi (Japanese: Shushi) school as the state doctrine of the Tokugawa government (1603–1867), which played an important role in shaping the national character. Hayashi, who was born in Kyoto, began studying Confucianism at the age of 22, under Fujiwara Seika (1561–1619) and like his teacher abandoned Buddhism for the Neo-Confucianism of the twelfth-century Chinese philosopher Chu Hsi. Fujiwara recommended his talented pupil to Tokugawa Ieyasu as official adviser, a

post Hayashi continued to fill under Ieyasu's successors. Through his son Gahō (1618–1680) and grandson Hōkō (1644–1732), both erudite Neo-Confucianists, Hayashi's influence spread. Gahō and Hōkō became hereditary heads of the Confucianist college (Shōheikō) of Edo (Tokyo), center of Japan's orthodox Chu Hsi-ism. Hayashi is credited with an important role in the various codes promulgated by the Tokugawa to reorganize the country under strict military rule. That he also determined educational policy is beyond dispute.

Hayashi, in contrast to his master Fujiwara, was very intolerant toward other doctrines—specifically, Wang Yang-ming Confucianism, Lao Tzu, Buddhism, Christianity. Thus he is noted more for his negative polemics than for developing Chu Hsi's ideas, which he followed rather faithfully. An instance of deviation from Chu Hsi is Hayashi's almost monistic conception of *ri*, the principle, together with *ki*, the material-force. He came near to identifying these two basic concepts, thus approaching the rival school of Wang Yang-ming. Nevertheless, he sharply criticized Wang Yang-ming's "intuitive knowledge" and Kaibara Ekken's views. Hayashi disapproved of Lao Tzu's emphasis on the "Nameless," or the Way understood as the indescribable Great One, intent as he was on stressing social relationships. For Buddhism's escape from society and neglect of loyalty and filial piety he had nothing but scorn, fighting until his death against influential Buddhist monks. His strictures on Christianity were many (Christians were then being persecuted and banished from Japan). He focused, however, on ethical questions and social differences neglelected by Christianity. Only with Shintoism did he desire compromise and amalgamation.

Bibliography

See W. T. de Bary, Ryusaku Tsunoda, and Donald Keene, eds., *Sources of Japanese Tradition* (New York, 1958), pp. 350–361, and Kyoto Shisekikai, ed., *Razan Sensei Shibunshū* ("A Collection of Poems and Essays by Master Razan"), 4 vols. (Kyoto, 1918–1921). A biography in Japanese is Hori Isao, *Hayashi Razan* (Tokyo, 1964); this work has a good bibliography of Japanese references. For further bibliography see JAPANESE PHILOSOPHY.

GINO K. PIOVESANA, S.J.

HAZLITT, WILLIAM (1778–1830), English essayist, journalist, and critic, began his literary career as a "metaphysician," and the principles of his youthful philosophical writing survived to govern his thought during the years when a more brilliant prose style won him fame. Born at Maidstone, Kent, the son of a Dissenting minister, Hazlitt kept faith politically with his Unitarian heritage, but at an early age revolted against his father's rationalistic theology. After trying unsuccessfully to become a painter, he turned in his thirties to journalism and to popular lecturing, and until his death made his living in London as a writer for periodicals. Twice unhappily married, always the fierce defender of both the French Revolution and Napoleon, Hazlitt succeeded in alienating most of his friends and much of his public, although his critical influence on the literature of his time was perhaps second only to Coleridge's. Unlike Coleridge, his erstwhile friend and mentor, Hazlitt did not ground his thought in a version of the new Idealism; he stands alone in his age as a romantic thinker who developed a critique of empiricism that nonetheless supported the values and methods of the empiricist tradition.

Hazlitt continued the redefinition of the individual begun by Godwin in *Political Justice* (1793). Four years before his first meeting with Coleridge in 1798, and while still a student at Hackney College in London, Hazlitt conceived his "metaphysical discovery"—a refutation of necessary egoism. Actually, his position had been anticipated by Joseph Butler and Hume, but his arguments were original in his insistence on imagination—a power inseparable yet distinct from present sensation and past feeling—as the source of voluntary action, and even of self-consciousness.

His first book—*An Essay on the Principles of Human Action,* to which was added *Some Remarks on the Systems of Hartley and Helvétius* (1805)—argued that ideas of good determine conscious pleasure and self-interest, not the reverse, and that the same "reasoning imagination," which alone can unify sensations from moment to moment, is responsible for all the mind's "associations" except those arising from mere contiguity in experience. In his lectures at the Russell Institution in 1812 on the "Rise and Progress of Modern Philosophy," this line of thought inevitably led Hazlitt to challenge all epistemology, including Berkeley's and Hume's, that relied on the Lockean premise of "simple" impressions in perception. To perceive the simplest object requires a "general idea," or some act of mind to "comprehend" objects in their sameness or wholeness before qualities can be differentiated. Failure to recognize an activity of mind inhering in sense perception itself had led, he believed, to the vain war between philosophies of "Necessity" and of "Liberty"—between a mechanism or materialism that reduced mind to sensation and an idealism like Kant's that mistook man's formative consciousness for a power of will essentially free of sensory experience.

Hazlitt also came to oppose, then, the transcendentalism that Coleridge introduced from Germany. As is clear from a *Prospectus* (1809) for his projected history of English philosophy, Hazlitt saw himself as a loyal reformer of empiricism, although he admittedly left unresolved the central problem of the degree to which ideas are determined by the mind itself, on the one hand, and by "nature" on the other. In part, it was his belief that this dualism must remain intractable to reason which made him forsake formal analysis for the "familiar style" of his literary journalism. Averse to system and always more concerned with the cultural impact of ideas, he began, after 1812, to turn from an analysis of the formal problem to an exploration of the interaction of mind and world in experience as it is known by the self in life or realized by "genius" in the arts. Still affirming that "the mind is one," he made his theme the "everlasting contradiction" of man's nature—the "action and reaction" between the mind and the passional self as dialectical functions of the same unity of consciousness.

From his awareness of this conflict in consciousness Hazlitt forged no metaphysic of his own beyond a vague vitalist belief that "the spirit of life and motion" gave the mind a radical "sympathy" with the physical world. In religion he seems to have remained a modest agnostic,

certain only that God is intellectually unknowable. Hazlitt thought that only in the aesthetic mode of imagination could the mind transcend experience, and even then it could attain to no intuition beyond "the soul of nature." The insistence that "passion" is the source both of man's freedom and of his bondage—a bondage to individual "character" that nonetheless implies the freedom of the self to sympathize with other selfhood—underlies Hazlitt's polemic on all fronts; it links his criticism of Malthus and the utilitarians to his aesthetic theory that organic particularity is the basis of value in the arts.

In the England of 1830, when Hazlitt died impoverished in London, a humanism so darkly paradoxical found little favor; but his powers as a thinker have been increasingly recognized, and he appears today as the versatile Montaigne of his age, often prefiguring in his essays the dynamicist philosophies of Nietzsche, Bergson, William James, and Freud.

Bibliography

Hazlitt's philosophical writings are to be found mainly in *Complete Works*, P. P. Howe, ed., 21 vols. (London, 1930–1934), Vols. I, II (which includes the 1812 lectures), and XX. For studies on Hazlitt, see Elisabeth Schneider, *The Aesthetics of William Hazlitt* (Philadelphia, 1933); Herschel Baker, *William Hazlitt* (Cambridge, Mass., 1962); James Noxon, "Hazlitt as Moral Philosopher," in *Ethics*, Vol. 72 (1963), 279–283. For further bibliography, see Elisabeth Schneider, "William Hazlitt," in C. W. and L. H. Houtchens, eds., *The English Romantic Poets and Essayists: A Review of Research and Criticism* (New York, 1957).

JOHN KINNAIRD

HEAT, SENSATIONS OF. Descartes, in the *Sixth Meditation,* argued: "I have a sensation of heat as I approach the fire; but when I approach the same fire too closely, I have a sensation of pain; so there is nothing to convince me that something in the fire resembles heat, any more than the pain; it is just that there must be something in it (whatever this may turn out to be) that produces the sensations of heat or pain." Locke and Berkeley took similar positions. Berkeley's main arguments, in his *First Dialogue,* are (1) that intense heat is not distinct from a very great pain, and that since pain exists only in the mind, so must intense heat; (2) that the possibility of the same thing's feeling warm to one hand and cold to the other disproves the principle that "whatever degree of heat we perceive by sense we may be sure the same exists in the object that occasions it"; and (3) that since the pain occasioned by a pin is not judged to be in the pin, so the sensation occasioned by the fire, or anything like it, should not be judged to be in the fire. When discussing the method of arguing employed in the second of these arguments, as it applied to extension and color, Berkeley remarked that it "doth not so much prove that there is no extension or colour in an outward object, as that we do not know by sense which is the true extension or colour of the object" (*The Principles of Human Knowledge,* Sec. XV). One way of meeting the first and third of the arguments would be to distinguish between two senses of the term "sensation." Such a distinction would be exhibited in the proposition: "One can feel hot without feeling the heat of anything, and one can feel the heat of something without feeling hot."

Feeling hot could be termed a "bodily sensation"; feeling the heat of something, a "perceiving sensation." In reply to the first of Berkeley's arguments, it could then be admitted that to have the bodily sensation of feeling intensely hot is to be in pain and that bodily sensations, like pains, are in the mind; but it could be denied that therefore those qualities, like intense heat, of which we have perceiving sensations, are in the mind also. In reply to the third argument, it could be admitted that neither bodily sensations nor anything like them should be judged to be in material (that is, nonsentient) things, but it could still be maintained that those qualities of which we have perceiving sensations are in material things. What justifies us in judging material things to be hot or cold is our having perceiving sensations of their being so, provided we have no reason to think we are misperceiving.

C. Strang, in "The Perception of Heat," acknowledged that in calling a material object warm or cold "we feel we are saying something about the object as it is in itself and not merely as it is in relation to ourselves"; but Strang denies that warmth and coldness are in fact intrinsic properties of objects. His argument seems to be that objects have *one* determinable property (temperature); that there are *two* distinct sensations (hotness and coldness); that what is unitary cannot correspond to what is not unitary; and, therefore, that anyone who supposes that objects "are capable of having two distinct properties corresponding to the two distinct sensations" must be mistaken. The basis for a linguistic philosopher's reply to this argument is provided by the *Concise Oxford Dictionary* definition of "temperature": "degree or intensity of sensible heat of a body or of the atmosphere especially as shown by thermometer." An object cannot be said both to lack a certain property and to have a certain degree or intensity of that property. That a hot object feels distinctly different from a cold one is of no more significance than that a rough object feels distinctly different from a smooth one.

Meeting Berkeley's arguments by distinguishing between bodily sensations and perceiving sensations raises a problem: Why do we use the same "thermal" words both to report bodily sensations and to describe material things if it is not because we can, somehow, see a resemblance between some of our bodily sensations and some of the qualities of material things? G. N. A. Vesey, in "Berkeley and Sensations of Heat," suggested that we call the bodily sensations that we normally have when our bodies, as material things, are hot or cold, sensations of "feeling hot" or of "feeling cold" because (causal *because*) they are the sensations we normally have when our bodies, as material things, are hot or cold. For purposes of communication we have to describe our bodily sensations somehow, and the use of thermal words comes naturally to us for the (causal) reason mentioned. D. M. Armstrong objected to this kind of explanation because if "there is a mere *contingent connection* between sensations of heat and the heat of a limb . . . it is very mysterious that we have no vocabulary to describe the sensations as they are, in their own nature, apart from the conditions in which they are normally produced" (*Bodily Sensations,* Ch. 7). Vesey replied to this objection that (1) in order for us to tell other people what our sensations are, it is essential that we characterize them

in a manner which relates them, in one way or another, to public phenomena; that (2) the "nature" of "sensations as they are in their own nature" is the nature we apprehend them as having when a certain way of describing them comes to us naturally; and that (3) the reason why a certain way of describing sensations comes to us naturally need not be a reason of which we are conscious.

Armstrong's own view, like that of Gilbert Ryle, is that "to have a sensation of heat is to feel that a portion of our body is hot." According to this view, there is one material thing—namely, one's own body—the heat of which one can feel without touching it. But to talk of "feeling" the heat of one's hand without touching it would be like talking of "feeling" the roughness of the back of one's hand without touching it. Armstrong replied to this that it is an empirical fact about our proprioceptive powers that we are able to perceive the heat of our hand directly but not the roughness of its surface.

One's own body, in Armstrong's view, is, moreover, the *only* material thing the heat of which one can be aware of immediately. In the case of other material things, it is only the "*difference* in the heat of the surface of our body and the surface of the object touched" of which one is immediately aware (*Bodily Sensations,* p. 16). (By this Armstrong does not mean merely that whether something feels hot or cold to our touch depends on whether the part of our body with which we touch it is relatively hotter or colder than the object touched.) To the objection that my telling that water is hot by putting my hand in it "normally involves little or no consciousness of the heat of my hand, or of the surface of my hand," Armstrong replies that "we very often perceive relations between things without any clear perception of the nature of the related things taken by themselves." However, to perceive relations between things, we must perceive the things themselves; it is not sufficient that one of the things is that *with which* we perceive. Armstrong's view, that what we perceive is a heat difference, is part of his general theory that all immediate tactual perception is perception of a relation between one's body and something in contact with it.

Bibliography

BACKGROUND

Berkeley, George, *First Dialogue* and *Principles of Human Knowledge,* in *Works,* Vol. II, A. A. Luce and T. E. Jessop, eds. Edinburgh, 1949. Pp. 47, 175–179.

Descartes, René, *Philosophical Writings,* translated and edited by G. E. M. Anscombe and P. T. Geach. Edinburgh, 1954; pp. 118–119.

Locke, John, *Essay Concerning Human Understanding,* A. S. Pringle-Pattison, ed. Oxford, 1924. Book II, Ch. 8, Sec. 16.

APPLICATIONS AND CRITICAL DISCUSSIONS

Armstrong, D. M., *Bodily Sensations.* London, 1962. Chs. 4 and 7.

Armstrong, D. M., "Vesey on Sensations of Heat." *Australasian Journal of Philosophy,* Vol. 41, No. 3 (December 1963), 359–362.

Findlay, J. N., "Recommendations Regarding the Language of Introspection." *Philosophy and Phenomenological Research,* Vol. 9, No. 2 (1948), 212–236.

Ryle, Gilbert, "Sensations," in H. D. Lewis, ed., *Contemporary British Philosophy,* 3d series. London, 1956.

Strang, C., "The Perception of Heat." *PAS,* Vol. 60 (1960–1961), 239–252.

Vesey, G. N. A., "Armstrong on Sensations of Heat." *Australasian Journal of Philosophy*, Vol. 41, No. 2 (August 1963), 250–254.

Vesey, G. N. A., "Berkeley and Sensations of Heat." *Philosophical Review*, Vol. 79, No. 2 (April 1960), 201–210.

G. N. A. Vesey

HEBBEL, CHRISTIAN FRIEDRICH (1813–1863), German poet and playwright, was born in Wesselburen in the duchy of Holstein and died in Vienna. His father, an impoverished bricklayer who became destitute as a result of having guaranteed a loan that was defaulted, hated this son who showed no aptitude for earning a living. The boy's mother was more indulgent and protected him from the brutality of the father. It was thus possible for young Hebbel to keep alive his consuming passion for learning. At the age of 14 he was employed as a clerk by a parish official named Mohr, who allowed him to use his library. Mohr treated Hebbel as a common servant, however, and for this Hebbel never forgave him.

Through the good offices of Amalie Schoppe, the editor of a popular magazine, Hebbel received enough money to go to Hamburg in order to try to complete his fragmentary education. There he met Elise Lensing, a seamstress ten years his senior who cherished an abiding love for him; over the years she gave him clothes, lodging, money, and two sons, both of whom died young. Hebbel, who was ridden by his demon to acquire learning and develop himself as a writer, refused to marry Elise. Instead, he went on to study at the universities of Heidelberg and Munich. In the late winter of 1839, he made the arduous trip from Munich back to Hamburg on foot. In the same year he completed his first play, *Judith*, which he cited as his chief accomplishment when he applied for a travel stipend to King Christian VIII of Denmark. The king granted the stipend, and Hebbel went to Paris and from there to Rome. Because his resources were dwindling, he struck out for Germany by way of Vienna, where he met the talented actress Christine Enghaus, to whom he became engaged after three months. Whether or not Hebbel was largely influenced in this decision by the prospect of financial and social security, the marriage was a happy one and enabled Hebbel to take a place of honor in artistic and intellectual circles. His early death must be attributed in large measure to the hardships he had endured in order to realize his genius.

With the desperate seriousness of the self-educated man, Hebbel dedicated himself to presenting in artistic form his solution, sometimes characterized as "pantragic," of what he considered the ultimate philosophical problem, the incomprehensible escape of the individual from the Absolute or Idea, man's freedom in relation to God.

In Hebbel's dualism individual forms exist only by virtue of having differentiated themselves from the Absolute. Their struggle to maintain themselves as separate entities is a rebellion, the primeval sin of individuation. The sinfulness of the individual consists merely in the fact that he exists, and it is in no way dependent upon the nature or direction of his individual will. For his sinfulness the individual must be punished; he will have to submerge his particular being in the undifferentiated whole. The more splendid, vigorous, and powerful he is, the greater is the threat he poses to the Absolute and the more tragic is the struggle, which can end in only one way. There is only one necessity—that the Absolute maintain itself. However, although the existence of individual forms threatens the Whole, it is precisely the process of individuation that gives life to this closed system. If it were not for the mysterious freedom of the individual forms, the Absolute would become rigid and lifeless. The total life process is dependent on the metabolic flow of individual forms, which may appear at one point in time; may be submerged forever; or may, whether they retain their identities or their elements enter into new combinations, reappear at another point only to lose individuality again in the never-ending compact flux of history, compact because nothing new enters the universe and nothing leaves it.

It is the common task of philosophy and art, particularly drama and more specifically Hebbel's drama, to describe and make understandable this supreme philosophical problem. Philosophy must fail in its part of the common task, to determine the original cause of individuation, because this ultimate cause is unfathomable. But the drama is not concerned with this question. It accepts individuation as the prime condition of life and presents the tragic struggle of the All and the one in a way that makes it comprehensible to aesthetic intuition. In the drama the metaphysical breach is closed; the defeat of the tragic hero mirrors the cosmic process.

In order to achieve his aim, Hebbel sets the action of his plays at critical times in history, for at such times the relation of the individual to the Whole is most poignantly manifested. In some plays—for example, *Judith, Maria Magdalene, Herodes und Mariamne*—the prevailing form of the Idea is shown to be on the verge of breaking up. In others—*Genoveva, Agnes Bernauer, Gyges und sein Ring*—the prevailing form of the Idea, although threatened, affirms itself and persists. In both instances, whether the individual is opposed to the Idea or is an instrument of it, the end is tragic, and all individuals meet the same fate—they are crushed and absorbed by the Whole.

Hebbel always insisted that despite obvious parallels he had evolved his metaphysical truths independently of the romantic nature philosophy of German idealism. For a long time, in the absence of specific evidence to the contrary, many literary historians accepted this assertion. Recent research, however, has shown that Hebbel had early steeped himself in certain writings of Gotthilf Heinrich von Schubert, the natural scientist and philosopher, and Ludwig Feuerbach. The ideas he found there he experienced with such intensity that he incorporated them into his own psychic structure although his pride as a self-taught man did not allow him to acknowledge his debt.

Works by Hebbel

Sämtliche Werke, historisch-kritische Ausgabe, R. M. Werner, ed. Berlin, 1904–1907. The major sources for Hebbel's theories are *Mein Wort über das Drama* and *Vorwort zu Maria Magdalene*, both in Part I of this edition. Equally important are various passages in the diaries (Part II) and letters (Part II).

Works on Hebbel

Campbell, T. M., *The Life and Works of Friedrich Hebbel*. Boston, 1919.

Flygt, Sten G., *Friedrich Hebbel's Conception of Movement in the Absolute and in History.* Chapel Hill, N.C., 1952.

Kreuzer, Helmut, ed., *Hebbel in neuer Sicht.* Stuttgart, 1963.

Kuh, Emil, *Biographie Friedrich Hebbels.* Vienna and Leipzig, 1907.

Liepe, Wolfgang, *Beiträge zur Literatur und Geistesgeschichte.* Neumünster, Germany, 1963. Contains several essays illuminating the relationships between Hebbel's thought and the thought of Friedrich Wilhelm Joseph von Schelling, Ludwig Feuerbach, and Gotthilf Heinrich von Schubert.

Meetz, Anni, *Friedrich Hebbel.* Stuttgart, 1962.

Purdie, Edna, *Friedrich Hebbel: A Study of His Life and Work.* Oxford, 1932.

Scheunert, Arno, *Der Pantragismus als System der Weltanschauung und Aesthetik Hebbels.* Leipzig, 1930.

STEN G. FLYGT

HEDONISM (Greek, ἡδονή, "pleasure") is a term which refers to either of two distinct but related views, one a thesis in normative ethics, the other a generalization about human psychology.

Ethical hedonism. The first view, called "ethical hedonism," affirms that only pleasure is intrinsically desirable and that only displeasure (or pain) is intrinsically undesirable. More fully stated, it is the thesis that only pleasant states of mind are desirable in themselves; that only unpleasant states of mind are undesirable in themselves; and that one state of affairs is more desirable in itself than another state of affairs if and only if it contains more (in some sense) pleasant states of mind than the other (the quantity of value in a state of affairs being measured by the quantity of pleasure in it).

This thesis has been defended by a distinguished line of philosophers from the early Greeks to the present, including Aristippus, Epicurus, Locke, Hobbes, Hume, Bentham, Mill, and Sidgwick. Other philosophers have thought that happiness is the only thing that is intrinsically desirable; and if saying that a man is happy at a given time is the same as saying that he is experiencing pleasure at the time, then their names could be added to this roster. Many philosophers, however, have thought that happiness is different from pleasure, and there has been disagreement and confusion about what "happy" and "pleasant" mean.

The hedonist thesis was a part of traditional utilitarianism, as represented, for instance, by Bentham and Mill, with their "greatest happiness principle." These writers combined the generic principle of utilitarianism—namely, that an act is morally right if performing it would produce, or could reasonably be expected by the agent to produce, at least as much intrinsic goodness in the world as any other act the agent could perform at the time—with the thesis of hedonism about what is intrinsically good. Traditional utilitarianism is thus a species of utilitarianism that is defined as asserting just the "generic thesis"; other kinds of utilitarianism (for example, that of G. E. Moore) reject hedonism. Unlike utilitarianism, ethical hedonism is not at all a proposal about which acts are morally right; it is only an affirmation about which states of affairs are intrinsically good or desirable.

What is meant by saying that a state of affairs is intrinsically desirable, as opposed to simply desirable, is that it is desirable, good, worthwhile, worthy of choice, when *taken by itself*, viewed abstractly, and in particular considered without reference to consequences. Many things (for example, a visit to the dentist) are worthwhile in view of their consequences, which nobody would say are intrinsically desirable. The hedonist does not deny that other things are desirable; he denies only that they are intrinsically worthwhile. He agrees that something can be desirable instrumentally—as a means to an end—even when it is not intrinsically desirable. (A thing can, of course, be both intrinsically and instrumentally desirable: pleasant experiences can be good in themselves and also instrumentally good, if, for example, they are relaxing and enable one to work better on the following day.) He does add, however, that something is instrumentally desirable only to the extent that it is a means to later pleasure, since a thing can be instrumentally desirable only if it is a means to attaining the intrinsically desirable.

When consequences are taken into account, the hedonist's view about what states of affairs are desirable is apt to differ very little from the view of the nonhedonist. In fact, if one reads various writers' accounts of the "good life," one finds that they are pretty much alike, whether the author professes to be a hedonist or a nonhedonist. Thus, Epicurus, for instance, advocated a simple life devoted to philosophical reflection, with a diet of bread, cheese, and milk, and with its tranquillity unendangered by surging bodily passions. And J. S. Mill affirmed that having a good character is "part" of a person's happiness, so that according to him, character is intrinsically good after all by virtue of the fact that it is a part of happiness. Some hedonists, however, have advocated a more distinctive ideal for living: the Greek Aristippus thought that physical enjoyments are the richest source of pleasure and should be fully cultivated.

The meaning of the hedonist's thesis, of course, depends on what is meant by "pleasure." It is true that the associations of the word "pleasure" are such that if an English-speaking person says he favors a "life of pleasure," he is naturally taken to be advocating a life dedicated to the sensory enjoyments—wine, women, and song. Hedonists have not intended the term to carry this implication, however, and the strict meaning of the term does not. It is perfectly correct for a student to say, "I got a great deal of pleasure out of writing that paper." To say that an experience is pleasant (for example, "a pleasant evening"), is, in a strict sense, simply to say that one enjoyed it, or that one enjoyed himself during it. Thus, hedonism is done least injustice if it is taken as simply saying that an intrinsically desirable state of affairs is always a state of consciousness in which the person is enjoying himself in one way or another. Since reflection, reading, and creation are activities that people often enjoy, the hedonist means to include these activities, or states of mind, in the category of "pleasures," just as much as the so-called "passive" enjoyments, such as eating, drinking, and sex.

Hedonists have often disagreed about the proper analysis of "pleasure" or "enjoyment." Epicurus, for instance, said that pleasure is simply the absence of painful want or longing. Moreover, during the past fifty years, psychologists have also disagreed substantially on this point, some holding that pleasure is a special kind of sensation, others that it is a quality of certain kinds of feeling, and so forth. In recent years a considerable body of philosophical literature has accumulated on the subject of the analysis of "pleasant." (See PLEASURE.) While a generally accepted conclusion has not yet been reached, it is plausible to say that a person is enjoying himself (that is, his state of mind is pleasant) if and only if at the time he likes his experience or activity *for itself*, in the sense that, aside from moral considerations or considerations of consequences or of the possibility that something he likes even better could be substituted, he does not wish to change it and in fact would wish to avoid changing it if such a change impended. If this interpretation is accepted, the thesis of hedonism becomes the affirmation that a state of affairs is intrinsically desirable if and only if it is, or contains, an activity or experience which, at the time, the person likes for itself; and one state of affairs is more desirable intrinsically than another if it is, or contains, an experience or activity which, at the time, is liked better for itself. States of affairs which the hedonist thesis apparently rules as being only instrumentally rather than intrinsically desirable, from the point of view of a particular person, are such things as fame after his death and states of knowledge and character (since the latter are not experiences or activities at all, but capacities or dispositions).

Psychological hedonism. Many (but not all) ethical hedonists have supported their ethical affirmation of hedonism by an appeal to a psychological doctrine known as "psychological hedonism." This theory historically has taken rather different forms; the significance of each for ethical hedonism must be assessed separately. The element common to them is the assertion that actions or desires are determined by pleasures or displeasures, whether prospective, actual, or past. The importance of the theory, however, transcends its relation to ethical hedonism: certain psychologists today are inclined to accept some form of it as a correct account of human motivation.

Goal is pleasure. The first and historically most important form of the theory of psychological hedonism may be called the "goal is pleasure" theory, according to which a person is motivated to produce one state of affairs in preference to another if and only if he thinks it will be more pleasant, or less unpleasant, for himself. This thesis, of course, is not intended to be a generalization about simple reflex or habitual behavior. The "belief" in question need not be explicit in the sense of having been verbally formulated before action; it may be an unformulated assumption. The theory is not simply about purposive action; it is also a theory about desire: a person is asserted to want one thing more than another if and only if he thinks its occurrence will be more pleasant for him.

The relation of this form of psychological hedonism to ethical hedonism may be explained by the following argument, often used by ethical hedonists. It is assumed as a major premise that something is intrinsically desirable if and only if it is something that people desire for itself. The minor premise is the "goal is pleasure" theory—namely, that people want only pleasure for itself. It is therefore concluded that pleasure is the only thing that is intrinsically desirable. The third-century writer Diogenes Laërtius said of Epicurus that "as proof that pleasure is the end he ad-

duces the fact that living things, so soon as they are born, are well content with pleasure and are at enmity with pain, by the prompting of nature and apart from reason."

Contemporary ethical hedonists seldom appeal to the "goal is pleasure" theory to support their views, partly because the theory seems incompatible with obvious facts. For instance, political figures seem to take a strong interest in securing favorable notice in books on history that will appear after their death. This motivation obviously does not depend on the belief that the future event will be pleasant for them personally. Again, individuals often appear to risk personal loss for some moral principle or in order not to forsake a friend (this is illustrated by Dean Acheson's famous remark, "I will never turn my back on Alger Hiss"). Adherents of the "goal is pleasure" theory tend to explain such facts by saying that the individual would be unhappy in the future—and knows he would be—if he failed to live by his principle or forsook his friend; hence, the action is motivated by a calculation of personal pleasure after all. What the theory must hold, though, is that a belief to this effect, at least vaguely espoused by the agent, is a necessary condition of the motivation; and this seems implausible. Adherents of the theory may be confusing two things: the agent's belief that a certain future situation will be relatively more pleasant for him, and the agent's thought of that future situation being attractive or repugnant now. A person may say, "I *am unhappy with the idea* of dropping my friendship with X, in whose integrity I believe." This statement may be true and also an important clue to understanding his behavior. But this is very different from saying, "I'll continue my friendship with Mr. X *because I think I'll be less happy if I don't,*" a kind of statement that would ordinarily be taken as proof that the person did not care about his friend. Adherents of the theory may always argue that the reasoning required by their theory takes place unconsciously, but the postulation of this is *ad hoc,* the only reason for it being that it saves the theory from conflict with observation.

Motivation by pleasant thoughts. As suggested above, adherents of the "goal is pleasure" form of psychological hedonism sometimes confuse it with a different thesis which we may call the "motivation by pleasant thoughts" theory. This theory is the assertion that a person will choose to do A rather than B or will prefer A to B (whether an action or a situation), if and only if the thought of A (with its expected consequences) is more attractive, or less repugnant, than the thought of B (with its expected consequences). This theory is not obviously false: indeed, as a proposal about preference it could be an analytic proposition which sets forth one test we use to decide whether a person prefers one thing to another. As a proposal about action it is clearly a synthetic proposition. As such, it may not be able to explain the fact (if it is a fact) that sometimes the thought of doing A is not more attractive or less repugnant than the thought of doing B, but the agent simply decides to do A (perhaps he is required to make up his mind between the two).

Even if this form of psychological hedonism is true, however, it gives no support to ethical hedonism, since it sets no restrictions on the *kind* of goal which may be attractive or repulsive to a person. If support of ethical hedonism requires a demonstration that people desire only pleasure, then the present theory does not provide such support. For assuming that desiring a thing *means* finding the idea of it pleasant or attractive, it does not follow that only the idea of pleasure itself is attractive. Hence, it does not follow that only pleasure is desired, and it is therefore no part of the "motivation by pleasant thoughts" theory to assert that only pleasure is desired.

Conditioning by pleasant experiences. The third form of psychological hedonism, the "conditioning by pleasant experiences" theory, is a theory about the causal conditions of a person's wants or values. Roughly, it asserts that at least one's fundamental values can be correlated with past enjoyments or rewards, that these enjoyments are at least part of the causal explanation of the values, and that a person's values can be controlled by manipulating his enjoyments. If a person values ice cream, it is because in the past he has enjoyed ice cream (and not been made sick by it). The truth of this theory is hardly open to question insofar as it merely affirms that past enjoyments have some influence on likes and values; but its truth can be widely questioned if the theory is claimed to give a complete account of likes and values, which, according to experimental evidence, seem to be influenced by numerous factors. Acceptance of the theory, however, does not commit one to assert that persons desire only pleasure. The theory is consistent with saying that people want and value things such as posthumous fame or being a generous or courageous person. All the theory claims is that *whatever* values one has have been acquired because of past enjoyments or punishments of one sort or another—perhaps the enjoyment of parental praise or the punishment of parental reproaches.

Further arguments in support of ethical hedonism. Acceptable psychological theory, as we have seen, does not indicate that people desire only pleasure or things they think will be pleasant for them, or that people prefer *A* to *B* if and only if they think *A* will be more pleasant to them than *B*. Ethical hedonism, therefore, cannot appeal to psychological theory in support of its thesis.

Ethical hedonists sometimes rely on one or more of three other lines of argument in support of their view. The first line of reasoning is simply that ethical hedonism is an analytic truth that is true by definition. John Locke, for instance, defined "good" as that "which is apt to cause or increase pleasure," and Spinoza defined it as "every kind of pleasure, and all that conduces thereto." The flaw in this contention, however, is that many people have at least thought either that some things other than pleasure are intrinsically good or that some kinds of pleasure are intrinsically bad. In the face of this, it is not easily claimed that "intrinsically good" simply *means* pleasant.

The second line of reasoning, which is more substantial, starts from the premise that it is usually agreed that at least some forms of pleasure are intrinsically good and proceeds by contesting the claim that anything else is intrinsically good. If the claims on behalf of other things are successfully refuted, it is concluded that ethical hedonism is left holding the field. The assessment of this line of reasoning

is obviously a complex matter, since it presupposes conclusions about how to adjudicate ethical disputes. There is space here only to mention some examples frequently debated by hedonists and their opponents.

Critics of hedonism often urge that some kinds of pleasure are intrinsically bad—for example, malicious pleasure in the suffering of another person. And, they say, some unpleasant experiences are intrinsically good—for example, the punishment of one who has been cruel to another. Furthermore, it may be claimed that various things in addition to pleasure are intrinsically good: knowledge, certain traits of character, kindly or courageous deeds, life itself (at least the survival of mind with memory) even if it is not positively pleasant, being the object of respect or love on the part of other persons, being remembered after death, achievement, whether intellectual or aesthetic. Anyone who accepts any of these points cannot, strictly speaking, be an ethical hedonist.

A third, more practical, line of reasoning by hedonists has been the contention that their view makes possible scientific and objective evaluations of social planning which other views do not. For instance, if the question arises whether a certain tariff should be raised, the hedonist may say that his theory enables us (in principle at least) to decide objectively whether the tariff will do good, for we have only to decide whether a greater net sum of pleasures will be produced with or without the tariff.

This conception has come in for a great deal of criticism in recent decades, some of it unfair. One criticism, which appears repeatedly in the writings of economists, makes the point that we can know nothing about the mental states of other persons, since there is no way of observing them directly; hence, the whole idea that theoretically an individual could determine the effects of a tariff on the happiness of anyone but himself is absurd. This criticism probably goes too far, but questions concerning other minds cannot be evaluated here. A more forcible objection is the following. If "is pleasant" is analyzed as meaning "is an experience liked at the time by the person, for itself," then presumably *A*'s experience can be said to be pleasanter than *B*'s, if *A* likes his experience more intensely. In theory, then, we might show that a tariff on bicycles would do more harm than good, if we could match every pleasant experience it would produce with an experience at least equally pleasant (one liked at least equally as intensely) and of at least equal duration, which the tariff prevents, *and* if in addition it costs us pleasures that are not matched with those it produces, or if some of the pleasures it costs us are more intense than the matching pleasures it produces, and the reverse is not the case. So far a decision could be reached, in principle at least. But it is possible that things might be too complex to permit such a simple matching. It might be that we would be forced to compare a more intense but brief pleasure with a less intense pleasure of greater duration; and it is not clear what would be meant by saying that one such experience "contains more pleasure" than the other. Thus, it is not clear that in principle the comparison could be made, except in special favorable situations. In this respect, however, the hedonist seems correct on one point: there is no other theory of the intrinsically desirable which makes such evaluations more scientific or more objective.

Bibliography

PSYCHOLOGICAL HEDONISM

Duncker, K., "Pleasure, Emotion, and Striving," in *Philosophy and Phenomenological Research*, Vol. 1 (1940), 391–430.
Troland, L. T., *Fundamentals of Human Motivation*. New York, 1928. Ch. 16.
Young, P. T., "The Role of Hedonic Processes in the Organization of Behavior," in *Psychological Review*, Vol. 59 (1952), 249–262.

ETHICAL HEDONISM

Bentham, Jeremy, *Principles of Morals and Legislation*. Many editions.
Diogenes Laërtius, *Lives of Eminent Philosophers*. London, 1925. Bk. II (Aristippus) and X (Epicurus).
Ewing, A. C., *Ethics*. London, 1953. Ch. 3.
Mill, J. S., *Utilitarianism*. Many editions.
Moore, G. E., *Ethics*. Oxford, 1949. Chs. 1–2.
Sharp, F. C., *Ethics*. New York, 1928. Ch. 19.
Sidgwick, Henry, *Methods of Ethics*. London, 1922. Bk. III, Ch. 14.

MEASUREMENT OF PLEASURES

Alchian, A. A., "The Meaning of Utility Measurement," in *American Economic Review*, Vol. 43 (1953), 26–50.
Bentham, Jeremy, *Principles of Morals and Legislation*. Ch. 4. Many editions.
Cohen, Morris, and Nagel, Ernest, *Introduction to Logic and Scientific Method*. New York, 1936. Pp. 293–298.
McNaughton, R., "A Metrical Conception of Happiness," in *Philosophy and Phenomenological Research*, Vol. 14 (1954), 172–183.

RICHARD B. BRANDT

HEGEL, GEORG WILHELM FRIEDRICH (1770–1831), German idealist philosopher, was born at Stuttgart and entered the theological seminary at the University of Tübingen in 1788. Among his fellow students were Schelling and the poet Friedrich Hölderlin. After graduating he became, in 1793, a resident tutor in the home of an aristocratic family at Bern, and in 1796 he took a similar post in Frankfurt. In 1800 he went to Jena, where Schelling had succeeded Fichte as professor of philosophy and was developing an idealist philosophy of nature and metaphysics. Having been accepted as a teacher at Jena on the strength of his dissertation, *De Orbitis Planetarum* (1801), Hegel collaborated with Schelling in editing the philosophical journal *Kritisches Journal der Philosophie* and published his first book, *Differenz des Fichte'schen und Schelling'schen Systems der Philosophie* (1801). Notable articles by Hegel in the *Kritisches Journal* were "Glauben und Wissen" (1802) and "Über die wissenschaftlichen Behandlungsarten des Naturrechts" (1802–1803). At Jena, Hegel wrote his first major work, *Phänomenologie des Geistes* (*Phenomenology of Mind*, Würzburg and Bamberg, 1807). Completed about the time of Napoleon's victory over the Prussians at Jena in 1806, it was not published until 1807, after Hegel had left Jena to become editor of a daily paper at Bamberg in Bavaria.

In 1808, Hegel was appointed headmaster of a school in Nuremberg, a post he held until 1816. While at Nuremberg, Hegel published his *Wissenschaft der Logik* (*Science of Logic*)—Vol. I, *Die objective Logik* (2 vols., Nuremberg, 1812–1813, and Vol. II, *Die subjective Logik oder Lehre vom Begriff* (Nuremberg, 1816). From 1816 to 1818, Hegel was professor of philosophy at Heidelberg. There he published *Encyklopädie der philosophischen Wissenschaften im Grundrisse* (*Encyclopedia of the Philosophical Sciences in Outline*) in 1817. In 1818, Hegel was appointed professor at the University of Berlin, where he became famous and influential. *Naturrecht und Staatswissenschaft im Grundrisse* (*Philosophy of Right*) appeared there in 1821; a second edition, edited by E. Gans as *Grundlinien der Philosophie des Rechts*, was published in Berlin in 1833. In 1827 a second, much enlarged edition of the *Encyclopedia* appeared.

Hegel died during a cholera epidemic in 1831. After his death a group of his friends compiled an edition of his works in 18 volumes (Berlin, 1832–1840). Several of Hegel's works were published for the first time in this edition: *Vorlesungen über die Aesthetik* ("Lectures on Aesthetics," translated as *The Philosophy of Fine Art*, H. G. Hotho, ed., 2 vols., 1835–1838); *Vorlesungen über die Philosophie der Geschichte* (*Lectures on the Philosophy of History*, E. Gans, ed., 1837); *Vorlesungen über die Philosophie der Religion* (*Lectures on the Philosophy of Religion*, Philipp Marheineke, ed., 2 vols., 1832); and *Vorlesungen über die Geschichte der Philosophie* (*Lectures on the History of Philosophy*, K. L. Michelet, ed., 2 vols., 1833–1836). This edition also contains notes taken by students of Hegel's comments on the *Encyclopedia* and on *Philosophy of Right*, which he was in the habit of using as textbooks.

In his biography, *Georg Wilhelm Friedrich Hegels Leben* (Berlin, 1844), Karl Rosenkranz referred to and quoted from the manuscripts of works written by Hegel prior to the publication of the *Phenomenology of Mind*. Not all the manuscripts known to Rosenkranz have survived, but toward the end of the nineteenth century Wilhelm Dilthey made a study of those that have and published an account and discussion of them in the *Proceedings of the Berlin Academy* in 1905. This has since received the title *Die Jugendgeschichte Hegels* and is reprinted in the fourth volume of Dilthey's collected works. Dilthey's pupil and editor, Herman Nohl, then published, under the title *Hegels theologische Jugendschriften*, the text of a great part of what Hegel had written while he was at Bern and Frankfurt. The chief of the writings unpublished during Hegel's lifetime are the essay "Das Leben Jesu" ("Life of Jesus," 1795), *Die Positivität der christlichen Religion* (*The Positivity of the Christian Religion*, 1796), and *Der Geist des Christentums und sein Schicksal* (*Spirit of Christianity and Its Destiny*, 1799). In 1915, Hans Ehrenberg and Herbert Link published, under the title *Hegels erstes System* (Heidelberg, 1915), an early version, written at Jena but never published by Hegel, of what later became the system sketched in the *Encyclopedia*. Since then Georg Lasson (*Hegels Jenenser Logik*, Leipzig, 1923) and Johannes Hoffmeister (*Hegels Jenenser Realphilosophie*, 2 vols., Leipzig, 1932) have published still other writings that

Hegel had left unpublished. Thus, much more is now known about Hegel's writings and philosophical development than was generally known in the nineteenth century.

MAIN THEMES OF HEGEL'S PHILOSOPHY

Mind. In the Preface to the *Phenomenology,* Hegel wrote that only mind (*Geist*) is real, and he constantly reiterated this view. (I have translated Hegel's *Geist* as "mind," in agreement with Wallace's view that "to average English ears the word Spiritual would carry us over the medium line into the proper land of religiosity"—*Hegel's Philosophy of Mind,* Oxford, 1894, p. l.) Thus, he must be regarded as a philosophical idealist. He wrote rather slightingly of Berkeley, however, whose works he does not seem to have studied closely, and is sometimes described as an objective idealist in order to absolve him from suspicion of the subjective idealism that has often been attributed to Berkeley. Hegel's idealism presupposed the work of Kant and was influenced by Fichte and Schelling, but his early unpublished writings show that he had preoccupations of his own, independent of his famous German predecessors.

When Hegel said that only mind is real, he did not mean that material things do not exist and that only minds do. Mind was not, in Hegel's view, a plurality of immaterial substances but a system of individuals actively developing their potentialities by embodying them in increasingly complex forms. A fundamental feature of mind, according to Hegel, is freedom, and nothing that is partial or finite can be wholly free. The mind that is the only reality is therefore infinite. Furthermore, no one is free unless he is conscious of what he is doing, and infinite mind is therefore self-conscious mind. Artists and statesmen, merchants and saints, all busy themselves with their more or less partial tasks without necessarily concerning themselves with what it is that they are doing. According to Hegel, it is the function of the philosopher to make men conscious of what art and politics, commerce and religion, are, so that mind can exert itself to its utmost range and thus become absolute. Like Pythagoras, Plotinus, and Spinoza, Hegel was a philosopher who held that philosophy is an activity which purifies and frees the mind.

Dialectic. Hegel is, of course, famous for his dialectical method, but it is enormously difficult to explain this in a brief compass. It should first be noted that Hegel set out his systematic writings in dialectical triads comprising a thesis, antithesis, and synthesis. Thus, he divided his *Encyclopedia,* in which he expounded his system as a whole, into three fundamental division sections—"Logic," "Philosophy of Nature," and "Philosophy of Mind." In the first he expounded the categories as developing forms of thought; in the second, he said "the Idea" is considered in its "otherness" (*Anderssein*) or externality; and in the third, mind is considered as existing "for itself," as conscious of itself and of the institutions it has given rise to. Within these main divisions there are further triadic subdivisions, although a very large number of subdivisions are not of this nature. It is therefore clear that Hegel himself regarded his whole work as a dialectical construction, with thought and nature as opposites united in mind and society, in the artistic and religious products of man, and, ultimately, in the activity of philosophical self-consciousness.

Hegel's system, then, has a dialectical structure, but what is his dialectical method? Hegel, like Spinoza, held that error resides in incompleteness and abstraction, but, unlike Spinoza, he held that the incompleteness and abstraction can be recognized by the contradictions they generate. It is the business of the philosopher, he held, to bring out the contradictions latent in partial or abstract views and to emphasize and elaborate them in such a way that less partial and less abstract views can be constructed that nevertheless retain in themselves what there was of truth in the original views. The same method is to be brought to bear on the less partial and less abstract views in their turn and to be pressed as thoroughly as it can be. This method of pressing and accentuating contradictions is not to be used merely to discard error but also to preserve truth. Because of the happy circumstance that in German *aufheben* means both "to cancel" and "to preserve"—its literal meaning is "to lift up"—Hegel was able to express this aspect of his view with brevity and acuity. The concept or view that is *aufgehoben* is transcended without being wholly discarded. Hegel's *Phenomenology of Mind* was an account of how various human attitudes—reliance on sense experience, the belief in substance, otherworldliness, strenuous moralism, and so on—all have some point and are yet contradictory, leading to the conclusion that "truth is a bacchanalian revel where not a member is sober," as Hegel put it in the Preface. His *Logic* gave an account of how the categories are related in this way. In his *Lectures on the History of Philosophy* he sought to show that the major philosophical outlooks from that of the Ionians on are, on the one hand, positive contributions that we could not do without and, on the other hand, contradictions that we have to overcome.

History. Another feature of Hegel's philosophy is its concern with history. Much as Hegel admired Plato's philosophy, he held that it was impossible to be a Platonist in the nineteenth century, when the philosophical context differed so greatly from that of Plato's day. In his *Lectures on the Philosophy of History,* Hegel argued that the history of man in the concrete was as much a progression as the history of his thought. This he deduced from the thesis that mind is of its very nature free. Thus, each historical epoch, according to Hegel, embodied some aspect of or stage in the development of man's free mind, and it would be absurd for an individual to go counter to his time except insofar as he was preparing the way for future epochs. Hegel borrowed this "progressivism," as it may be called, from the philosophers of the Enlightenment. It has greatly influenced Marxism.

Christianity. Hegel thought his system provided a defense of Christianity, and both supporters and opponents of his system have taken this view of it. Those known as right Hegelians considered Hegel's apologetic successful, whereas the left Hegelians argued that his Christianity had been only superficial and his Christian terminology a disguise for something very different. In his system Hegel placed philosophy above religion in the dialectical scale, and this may give some support for the interpretations of the left. Yet there is ambiguity in Hegel's view on this, as on other important matters. On one hand, he held that only infinite mind is real; on the other hand, he held that infinite mind cannot be distinct from or beyond the finite and partial. He thought that these views were not incompatible, but it has been argued that the second is a denial of the first and, hence, a denial of any form of theism.

This article will briefly describe Hegel's early works that were posthumously published in *Hegels theologische Jugendschriften*. It will continue with an account of the *Phenomenology of Mind,* Hegel's first important book, and conclude with a brief discussion of the Hegelian system based chiefly on the *Encyclopedia.*

EARLY UNPUBLISHED WRITINGS

"Life of Jesus." Even before he wrote his "Life of Jesus," Hegel had written some comments on Christianity in which he criticized it for its belief in the efficacy of prayer and had contrasted it, to its detriment, with the this-worldly, social religion of the Greeks. Jesus, he held, was obscurantist and narrow-minded in comparison with Socrates. In the "Life of Jesus" it almost seems as if Hegel had decided to rewrite the Gospels in the form of a Kantian manifesto. He began by claiming that God is pure reason. He described Jesus as the son of Joseph and Mary. The only miracles Hegel mentioned he interpreted naturalistically, bringing the work to an end with the death and burial of Jesus. The central theme is the conflict between the virtuous Jesus acting dutifully for the sake of the moral law and the Jewish priesthood calling for the meticulous observance of a set of irrational rules said to be commanded by God. Jesus is depicted as saying to the Pharisees, "When you regard your ecclesiastical statutes and positive commands as the supreme law given to mankind, you fail to understand the dignity of man and the power he has of creating out of himself the idea of the divinity and knowledge of his will." This improbable allocution is typical of the way in which this work denudes the Gospel narrative of what is individual and poetical.

"The Positivity of the Christian Religion." The theme of *The Positivity of the Christian Religion*—the place in the Christian religion of the rational, on the one hand, and of the merely factual and historical, on the other—was already raised in the "Life of Jesus." Developing the implications of the then current distinctions between natural law and positive law and between natural religion and positive religion, Hegel argued that the positive element rested on authority and was not wholly based on the dignity of man. In Christianity, according to Hegel, the main positive element was provided by Judaism, a highly authoritarian religion. But Jesus himself brought elements of positivity into the rational morality that it was his prime aim to teach; he could not have obtained a hearing from the Jews of his day if he had not claimed God's authority for his teachings. "Jesus therefore demands attention for his teachings, not because they are adapted to the moral needs of our spirit, but because they are God's will" (*Early Theological Writings,* p. 76). In claiming to be the Messiah, Jesus was using the language his listeners would understand. His followers, from a natural interest in the details of his life, developed these positive elements into

Christianity. They appealed to miracles as proofs of Jesus' divinity and virtue, and instead of revering him for his teaching about virtue, they revered his teaching about virtue because of the miracles he was supposed to have performed.

Hegel asked how it happened that the pagan religion of the Greeks and Romans was overcome by Christianity. His answer was that at the periods of their greatness the Greeks and Romans were free peoples each individual of which regarded his own good as inseparable from the good of his community. When they lost their freedom, they lost the motives that bound them to their fellows; government and authority were now imposed from without, weighing down upon isolated individuals who came to regard their lives as individual possessions to be preserved irrespective of the social whole that alone gave them meaning.

> Thus the despotism of the Roman emperors had chased the human spirit from the earth and spread a misery which compelled men to seek and expect happiness in heaven; robbed of freedom, their spirit, their eternal and absolute element, was forced to take flight to the deity. [The doctrine of] God's objectivity is a counterpart to the corruption and slavery of man. (*Ibid.,* pp. 162–163)

"The Spirit of Christianity." In *The Spirit of Christianity* Hegel continued and sharpened his attack on Judaism, which he regarded as a religion of domination. He now criticized Kantian ethics as well, however, finding in it elements of the same positivity he had criticized in the Jewish religion and had seen as a contamination in the teachings of Jesus. Kant had contrasted his rational religion with the religion of the Siberian shamans on the ground that these primitive men, as well as some civilized prelates and puritans, irrationally worshiped alien forces that they regarded as exerting domination over men. But according to Hegel, the difference between the believers in these positive creeds and the follower of the religion approved by Kant is "not that the former make themselves slaves, while the latter is free, but that the former have their lord outside themselves, while the latter carries his lord in himself, yet at the same time is his own slave" (*ibid.,* p. 211). Hegel here first used the word "morality" (*Moralität*) as a pejorative description of the Kantian morality, which he now considered to be a submission of man's inclinations, including his impulses and his feelings of love, to a universal reason held to be free from and above all passion. He held that virtue demands more than this and that in the Sermon on the Mount Jesus made higher demands. "The Sermon does not teach reverance for the laws; on the contrary, it exhibits that which fulfils the law but annuls it as law and so is something higher than obedience to law and makes law superfluous" (*ibid.,* p. 212). Thus, duty takes a lower place than love. ". . . Jesus makes a general demand on his hearers to surrender their rights, to lift themselves above the whole sphere of justice or injustice by love, for in love there vanish not only rights but also the feeling of inequality and the hatred of enemies which this feeling's imperative demand for equality implies" (*ibid.,* p. 218). Hegel here saw in the ethics of the Sermon on the Mount and in the conduct of

Jesus something of the "beautiful soul" described by Goethe in *Wilhelm Meister*. Jesus retained his dignity by refusing to defend himself or to uphold his rights.

Hegel went on to discuss with subtlety the possible consequences for the individual and for other men of resistance to evil, on the one hand, and of withdrawal from conflict, on the other. In this part of the work the beginnings of dialectical method as it was used a few years later in *Phenomenology of Mind* may already be discerned.

"PHENOMENOLOGY OF MIND"

The *Phenomenology* is the most obscure and the most interesting of Hegel's works. On the title page it is described as a "System of Science, Part I. The Phenomenology of Mind," but this arrangement of Hegel's system was not continued in the *Encyclopedia*, where the section headed "Phenomenology of Mind" is contained in the third part and deals with only some of the topics of the original *Phenomenology*. Hegel put the *Phenomenology* together rather hastily and was uncertain what to call it. Different copies of the first edition have slightly differing titles, and what seems like a new title, "Science of the Experience of Consciousness," is placed after the Preface and before the Introduction. Insofar as there is a central theme, it consists of an account of the various stages of human consciousness from mere sense awareness to absolute knowledge, but there are many digressions into topics of current interest, such as Goethe's description of the "beautiful soul," the Reign of Terror, and F. J. Gall's phrenology. The difference between the dialectical progression of the *Phenomenology* and of the *Encyclopedia* was cited soon after Hegel's death as evidence of the inadequacy of the dialectical method (C. F. Bachmann, *Über Hegels System und die Nothwendigkeit einer nochmaligen Umgestaltung der Philosophie*, Leipzig, 1833). In the twentieth century Marxists have preferred the *Phenomenology* to Hegel's other writings because Marx himself admired it and because of its account of how man develops by transforming the natural world through his labor. Existentialists have preferred it to the later system because of its account of man as maker of himself; no doubt they are also impressed by Hegel's references to death and the fear of death.

The *Phenomenology* begins with a dialectical discussion of sense perception in which it is argued that knowledge of physical things presupposes the view that the physical world consists of forces interacting according to laws. Hegel maintained that knowledge of such a world is really a type of self-knowledge, since in penetrating to the forces behind phenomena we become aware of what we ourselves have devised and put there. "Behind the so-called curtain which is to hide the internal constitution of things, there is nothing to be seen unless *we ourselves* go behind." The physical world of scientific theory presupposes self-conscious beings. When he analyzed self-consciousness, Hegel argued that it presupposed a plurality of living and desiring beings each of whom seeks to subdue the world to his own wishes, to make it part of himself.

Master and slave. No individual will rest satisfied with a conquest that fails to secure the conscious acknowledg-

ment of other men. Hence, there is a struggle for both power and recognition. In this struggle some will take greater risks than their competitors; those who risk the least will become the slaves or bondsmen of those who face death by risking their lives. In order to preserve his life, the slave submits to the master, who regards the slave as nothing but a means to his own designs. The slave is forced to work, whereas the master can enjoy leisure in the knowledge that the slave is reshaping the natural world to provide the products of his labor for the master to consume. Thus, the master's leisure protects him from experience of the negativity of nature, whereas the slave, in struggling with nature's recalcitrance, learns its secrets and puts mind into it. The master, in consuming, destroys; the slave, in working, creates. But the master's consumption depends upon the slave's work and is thus impermanent, whereas the slave's labor passes into things that have a permanent existence. Hegel argued, too, that the slave's work in transforming the natural world is a consequence of his fear of the master, who can kill him. Death is overcome by the works of civilization. The man who risks his life and becomes the first master breaks the bonds of nature and starts the process that will incorporate mind into it.

It is not surprising that this section in the *Phenomenology* has greatly interested Marxists. Both Georg Lukács, in *Der junge Hegel*, and Herbert Marcuse, in *Reason and Revolution* (2d ed., London and New York, 1955), contrived to discuss it without mentioning Hegel's emphasis on the fear of death. In *Introduction à la lecture de Hegel*, Alexandre Kojève brought out the importance of the fear of death and showed, too, that Hegel was here concerned with the transition from nature to history, from mere life to thought, from animality to freedom.

The unhappy consciousness. The next dialectical transition is from mind that is attempting to master nature to mind that seeks freedom and independence in itself, that says, "It is in thinking that I am free because I am not in another but remain completely with myself alone," an attitude exemplified in stoicism. But stoicism passes over into skepticism, for the stoic finds freedom in himself as a rational, thinking being, whereas the skeptic, pushing freedom still further, uses thought to dissipate its own categories. This, according to Hegel, was the state of mind that prevailed when the Roman Empire was dissolving. Christianity was an attempt on the part of men in intellectual despair to find stability in an eternal and infinite God.

Hegel called this frame of mind the unhappy consciousness. The individual is divided within himself, conscious of his own isolation, attributing all that is good to the activity of God. What Hegel said here was elaborated from a passage in *The Positivity of the Christian Religion* describing how the eternal and absolute in man had been "forced to take flight to the Deity." The unhappy consciousness was regarded by Hegel as a characteristic of both Judaism and Christianity and as the condition of all men at all times who believe in a transcendent God before whom they are as nothing. It is a stage on the way to higher forms of self-mastery.

It will be noted that in this part of the *Phenomenology* Hegel passed from epistemology through a sort of speculative sociology to an account of historical stages in human consciousness. According to Rosenkranz, Hegel, in his last years, used to refer to the *Phenomenology* as his philosophical "voyage of discovery," and it does seem that the course of the argument, although arresting, was not altogether foreseen. Royce was right when he said that in this book Hegel described "in serial order, some varieties of experience which . . . are at once characteristic of the general evolution of the higher intellectual life, and are examples of the transition from common sense naiveté to philosophical reflection and to the threshold of an idealistic system" (*Lectures on Modern Idealism*, J. Loewenberg, ed., New Haven, 1919, p. 139).

Reason as "objectivity." After discussing certain scientific theories of his time under the heading "Reason as Observer," Hegel went on to consider some of the ways in which reason becomes practical. He depicted the man who, like Faust, tries to make the passing moment stay. When this attempt fails, as inevitably it must, ideals are sought in a spirit of sentimental disillusionment, but such romantic crusades are never really serious. In reaction to this frivolity there develops a taste for the hard intellectual pursuits of disinterested scholarship, the concern for "objectivity," for facts, for "the thing itself." But these allegedly disinterested researchers actually go into a sort of intellectual jungle (*das geistige Thierreich*) where, deceiving one another and themselves, they tear one another to pieces in the service of truth. It soon emerges that it is not the facts that matter but a certain proprietorship that scholars working in their special fields claim over the facts.

The dialectic of morality. In the next part of the *Phenomenology*, entitled "Mind," Hegel considered how the mind of man is embodied in his rules and institutions. This part constitutes both an account of the main types of moral attitude and a philosophy of history. These two lines of thought come together insofar as Hegel regarded the historical development from the Greek and Roman civilizations through early and medieval Christianity to Protestantism and the French Revolution as an unfolding of the main aspects and stages of freedom and, hence, as a dialectical actualization of what was merely latent and implicit in the morality of the ancient world. This unfolding is dialectical because it proceeds by oscillations and because it is made possible by conflict, in the ancient world by the conflict between the gods of the family and the laws of the city and in the modern world by the conflict between the claims of the individual and the demands of society.

In this part Hegel gave indications of the doctrine of alienation that attracted Marx in the 1840s. In building his civilization, man creates institutions and rules that are simultaneously his own products and alien constraints upon him. He may not even understand them, so that they appear strange to him. It was Hegel's view, of course, that without these institutions and rules and without the restrictions upon willfulness that they impose, mind could not reach its higher levels.

Religion and absolute knowledge. In the last two parts of the *Phenomenology*, Hegel presented the dialectic of religion and the passage to absolute knowledge. In the earlier developments of mind the individual has to find his place in the natural world and in society, but in religion he gains consciousness of the Absolute Being. This is first approached in the primitive religions of nature, in which men worship trees, streams, or animals. Next come those forms of religion in which the Absolute Being is approached through such works of art as temples and statues. This type of religion reached a high level in ancient Greece, but when God was represented in human form, he came to be regarded as merely human and hence was lost sight of in the tragic heroes of Greek drama. As the religious element was discarded from tragedy, it gave way to comedy, in which the contingencies of human life were paraded and criticized, and God was completely ignored in favor of human self-knowledge. "The individual self is the negative force through and in which the gods . . . disappear."

This skeptical and sophisticated humanism is succeeded by Christianity, in which God is revealed to man in Christ. Here the human and the divine are no longer sundered, and God is seen to be present in the world. But it is easy to overemphasize the historical features of Christianity and, as Hegel put it, to neglect the spiritual revelation in the attempt to uncover the often commonplace ideas of the early Christians and to gain knowledge of the mere externality and particularity of Jesus. Thus, no religious experience, not even that of Christianity, can bring absolute knowledge. The historical element in Christianity, although necessary in order to avoid regarding the Absolute Being as apart from the world, is nevertheless inseparable from perception and imagination. The events of the Gospels are, so to speak, pictured or represented. Religion therefore leads on but is subordinate to the supreme form of knowledge, the philosophical, in which human history is "conceived history, the recollection of the Absolute Mind and its graveyard, the actuality, truth and certainty of its throne, without which it would be for ever alone and devoid of life." In these last words of the *Phenomenology*, Hegel made it clear that the course of history, philosophically conceived, was in his view the incarnation of the Absolute Mind. Apart from the history of man God would be alone and lifeless (*das leblose Einsame*). It would seem, indeed, that without the historical development of man and his freedom there would be no God.

THE HEGELIAN SYSTEM

It has already been mentioned that before writing the *Phenomenology*, Hegel had written but had left unpublished some attempts at a complete system of philosophy and that the *Phenomenology* was described on its title page as the first part of a system of science. It turned out that the *Science of Logic* (1812–1816) became the first part of Hegel's final system. A shortened and revised version of the *Science of Logic* appeared in 1817 as the first part of the *Encyclopedia*, a book intended for use at his lectures. A second, very much elaborated edition of the *Encyclopedia* appeared in 1827, and a third in 1830. This last edition was reprinted in the edition of Hegel's collected works published soon after his death, with inserted "additions" taken from the notebooks of students who had attended Hegel's lectures. These additions, which are most frequent in the first and second parts of the *Encyclopedia*, help greatly in the understanding of Hegel's argument but do not have quite the authority of the main text. Such additions are less frequent at the end, since the editors considered that the *Philosophy of Right*, first published in 1821, and some of the sets of lectures, provide commentary of this sort.

The "Encyclopedia." The *Encyclopedia* starts with a discussion of "Logic"—a revision of *Science of Logic*—and proceeds to the sections "Philosophy of Nature" and "Philosophy of Mind." The transition from the "Logic" to the "Philosophy of Nature" is not easy to understand. There are statements which say that the idea decides to allow nature to go forth freely from itself (Sec. 244), that "Nature has come to pass as the Idea in the form of otherness" (Sec. 247), and that nature is "the unresolved contradiction" (Sec. 248). The last main heading in the "Philosophy of Nature" is "The Aniamal Organism." Toward the end of this section there is an account of the individual animal as having "an original sickness" and "an innate germ of death" (Sec. 375), which leads to the assertion that with the subjectivity of living organisms the "outside-itself-ness" (*Aussersichsein*) of nature is transcended by the "interiority" (*Insichsein*) of actuality (Sec. 376). Hegel later claimed (Sec. 381) that mind presupposes nature but is "the truth [of nature] and its absolute ground [*deren absolut Erstes*]." He also stated that the essence of mind is freedom (Sec. 382). A fundamental comment on the dominating triadic division must be made before going further into the details of the system. The revised "Science of Logic" that appeared in the *Encyclopedia* was concerned with the categories of thought, proceeding from the most inadequate and abstract to the most concrete and adequate, from being to the Absolute Idea. The inadequacies of the abstract categories show themselves through the contradictions they give rise to. Being is more abstract than becoming; becoming, more abstract than being-for-self; these early categories, more abstract than the latter categories of life, and so on. But Hegel was always concerned with the categories of thought and their relations to one another. When he wrote that the idea decided to allow nature to go forth freely from itself, was he saying that thought is the Divine Being that created nature? The religious overtones that accompany Hegel's major transitions cannot be ignored, but those who wish to interpret him naturalistically—an interpretation his early writings and the *Phenomenology* may well justify—can take the view that the decision and the free going forth are meant to indicate that nature is not deducible from the categories of thought, that there is a contingency about it that no system of logic and no elaboration of concepts can eliminate. In *Subjekt–Objekt* (Berlin, 1951) Ernst Bloch suggested that the free decision of the Absolute Idea is reminiscent of the arbitrary act of an absolute monarch, and he quoted a passage from Schelling's *Philosophie und Religion* (Tübingen, 1804) which held that "the descent of finite things from the Absolute" is a "primal accident [*Urzufall*]." In the third part of the *Encyclopedia*, Hegel described mind as it develops in the natural world, mind as it transforms the natural world in creating the works of civilization, and mind fully aware of itself in the complete self-consciousness of philosophical thought. The "Logic" culminates in the Absolute Idea, the most adequate category but still a category. In the "Philosophy of Nature," where there is no Absolute, the culminating point consists of mortal individuals belonging to persisting animal species. The "Philosophy of Mind" culminates in Absolute Mind, the consciousness man gains of himself through understanding his own history in a civilization that he has imposed upon the contingencies of nature.

"Logic." Like the Hegelian system as a whole, each of its three main sections—"Logic," "Philosophy of Nature," and "Philosophy of Mind"—is again divided into three. The "Logic" is divided into the "Doctrine of Being," the "Doctrine of Essence," and the "Doctrine of the Concept [*Begriff*]." "The difficulties in presenting a comprehensible summary of Hegel's views are at their greatest in relation to the "Logic," and all that will be attempted is an indication of a few of Hegel's most characteristic views.

"Doctrine of Being." In the "Doctrine of Being" Hegel was concerned with the most abstract categories. Being itself, the most abstract of all, amounts to the same as nothing. Like Russell in his theory of descriptions, Hegel held that nothing can be said to be unless some characteristic is attributed to it; hence, in Hegel's terminology being leads on to determinate being, which involves the notion of quality. On the ground that a quality is something distinct from other qualities, Hegel argued that quality implies the category of a unit (*das Eins*) and that this in turn leads on to quantity. This part of the "Logic" was completed by transitions to degree and measure.

Hegel's object in the "Doctrine of Being" was to show that these categories are not independent of one another but develop from one to the other in an ascending order of adequacy. We know more about something when we know the proportions of its parts than when we know only how many parts it has, that it is, or that it is something or other. An important element in this part of the "Logic" is Hegel's criticism of infinite numerical series as the false infinite and his contrast between the false and the true infinite, which is not an incompletable progression of similar items but a completed, complex whole of supplementary parts. The true infinite is not to be reached by attempting the impossible task of moving from one finite to the next but must comprise the finite.

"Doctrine of Essence." The "Doctrine of Essence" is concerned with such distinctions as that between a thing's nature and its appearances, forces and their manifestations, form and matter. Hegel exploited the difficulties ("contradictions") that arise when these oppositions are so accentuated that we are left with featureless essences, on the one hand, and unattached appearances, on the other. Typical of his treatment of these topics is his claim that "the explanation of an appearance in terms of a force is an empty tautology" (Sec. 136) and his assertion that as a man's outward actions are, so his inner aims and intentions must be (Sec. 140).

"Doctrine of the Concept." A prominent feature in the "Doctrine of the Concept" is Hegel's critical treatment and reorganization of the traditional formal logic. Thus, he classified judgments in terms of his own division of "Logic" into being, essence, and concept. The classification progresses from the mere factual attribution

of a quality, through disjunctive and necessary judgments in which the predicate belongs essentially to the subject, to judgments of value which assert that a thing is good or bad just because it is that individual thing. Judgments gain in adequacy as they advance from mere factual attribution to attribution for reasons contained in the subject. Hence, the more developed forms of judgment are indistinguishable from inferences. In his account of the syllogism Hegel placed inferences in which the terms are only contingently connected at the bottom of a scale leading up to the disjunctive syllogism, in which a genus is exhaustively specified.

Although Hegel retained the terms and distinctions of the traditional formal logic, the use he made of them was highly original. Instead of setting out the types of judgment and the figures and moods of the syllogism as equally valid forms, he regarded judgment as implicit inference and inference as ordered in a scale of ascending rationality. This conception of logic influenced such later writers as Christoff Sigwart and R. H. Lotze and was developed in both F. H. Bradley's *Principles of Logic* (London, 1883) and Bernard Bosanquet's *Logic: The Morphology of Knowledge* (2 vols., Oxford, 1888).

The argument of Hegel's "Logic" can be very briefly summarized. The least that can be said about anything is that it is. More is said about it when it is qualified, numbered, or measured; still more is said about it when it is explained in terms of essences, grounds, or causes. Most is said about it when it is placed in the context of life, purpose, will, and value.

"Philosophy of Nature." At the end of the eighteenth and the beginning of the nineteenth century there was a great deal of philosophizing about nature. Electricity was held to have cosmic significance, and Schelling made much of the opposition between positive and negative poles. Poets as dissimilar as Blake and Goethe rejected what they regarded as the unduly quantitative physics of Newton. Spinoza was revived, and among German poets and philosophers much was said about the ἐν καὶ πᾶν, the one and the all. It is not surprising, therefore, that Hegel's dissertation of 1801, *De Orbitis Planetarum*, was critical of Newton and sought to provide an a priori justification of Kepler's laws. At the end of the dissertation Hegel mentioned some numerological accounts of the distances and number of the planets and expressed the opinion that if Plato was right in the *Timaeus*, there could be no planet between Mars and Jupiter. Hegel did not then know that Ceres, an asteroid between these two planets, had been discovered at the beginning of the year. However, even after he had heard of this discovery and of the discovery of several other asteroids soon after, he continued to hope that philosophical reasons could be given for the positions of the heavenly bodies. In an addition to Section 270 of the *Encyclopedia*, Hegel tried to show that these asteroids filled a gap that would otherwise have been unreasonable. The addition ends with the words: "Specialists do not think about such matters. But a time will come when in this science there will be a demand for concepts of the Reason."

It should be mentioned here that Hegel accepted and developed Kant's distinction between the reason and the understanding. According to Hegel, the understanding, although a necessary stage of thought, is less philosophical than the reason. To think in terms of the understanding, as is done in mathematics, the natural sciences, and traditional metaphysics, is to think in terms of fixed and uncriticized categories, to think undialectically or in prephilosophical terms. The reason moves dialectically toward completeness in terms of fluid categories that constantly amend themselves. Thus, when Hegel wanted astronomers to pay attention to "concepts of Reason," he wanted astronomy to take its place within a system of philosophy. This place must be a subordinate one, for Hegel wrote in the Introduction to the "Philosophy of Nature" (Sec. 248): "Even if arbitrary will, the contingency of mind, leads on to wickedness, this is nevertheless something infinitely higher than the regular movements of the planets or than the innocence of the plants: for what goes wrong in that way is nevertheless mind." Here Hegel was emphasizing the gulf between mind and nature, even though he held that the understanding does not give a complete knowledge of nature.

Mechanics. The three main divisions of the "Philosophy of Nature" are concerned with mechanics, physics, and organic nature. The astronomical theories expounded in the first part have already been touched upon. This part also contains a brief discussion of space and time. Following Kant, Hegel regarded them both as "forms of sensibility," or, more strikingly, as "the non-sensible sensible." Although he regarded arithmetic and geometry as sciences of the understanding, he considered the possibility of a philosophical mathematics at the level of measure or proportion (mass).

Physics. The second part of the "Philosophy of Nature" moves through various triads from light, the elements, sound, heat, to electricity and chemical combination. Hegel commented upon the philosophical significance of each form of matter. The comment on heat is characteristic:

Heat is the re-establishment of matter in its formlessness, its fluidity, the triumph of its abstract homogeneity over its specific determinations. . . . Formally, that is in relation to spatial determinations in general, heat therefore appears expansive, as cancelling the limitations which the specification of the indifferent occupation of space is. (Sec. 303)

That is, when heat spreads out from a heated thing, that thing is not confined to one place, as it would be if it were not heated. Or as Hegel put it in the next section, heat is the "real negation of what is specific and exclusive in body."

Organic nature. In the last main triad of the "Philosophy of Nature," Hegel passed from geological nature through vegetable nature to the animal organism. The most interesting part of this triad is the last, in which Hegel discussed animal species and their relationships. He seems to have thought that violent death is, in the animal world, "the natural fate of the individual" and that because of the contingency of nature animal life is "uncertain, anxious, and unhappy" (Sec. 369). But other members of the same species are not only hostile to the individual; they are also, like him, continuations of the species, and, hence, the individual feels a need to unite himself to the species (*Gattung*) and to continue it by copulation (*Begattung*)—the play on words is, of course, deliberate. Thus, Hegel seems to have held that animal sexual union is not merely a contingent affair. On the other hand, since the new individuals produced in this way only repeat the features of their parents and other ancestors, their constant reproduction is an instance of the false infinite, not of the true infinite in which completeness and perfection are achieved.

"Philosophy of Mind." The major triad in the "Philosophy of Mind" consists of "Subjective Mind," "Objective Mind," and "Absolute Mind."

"Subjective Mind." Under the heading "Subjective Mind" and the subheading "Anthropology," Hegel dealt with the soul as a natural entity in the physical world; the soul as a sensitive, feeling being; and the soul as a being that can express itself and act upon the world through its body. The upright body, the hand "as the absolute tool" (Sec. 411), the mouth, and the power of weeping and laughing all enable man to express in nature—to externalize—his thoughts and feelings. Furthermore, the world has effects upon man's body that are internalized by him—Hegel here made a play on the word *Erinnerung*, which means "recollection" but, if taken in the literal sense of its German etymology, can be taken to mean "internalization." When the organism reacts to immediate stimuli in the light of its own experience, mind has evolved beyond the mere animal level and has reached the stage of consciousness.

Hegel discussed the next moment of subjective mind under the heading of the "Phenomenology of Mind," going through the main phases distinguished in the earlier chapters of his book with that title—namely, sense experience, perception, understanding, desire, the self-consciousness that recognizes others (containing the discussion of master and slave), reason.

The third triad of subjective mind, which is headed "Psychology," contains descriptions of such intellectual functions as intention, representation, recollection, imagination, memory, and thought and descriptions of the practical drives, impulses, and seekings after satisfaction.

This part ends with a brief section headed "Free Mind." Here it is asserted that the unity of theoretical and practical mind is free will. Hegel meant that human freedom is possible only on the dual basis of thought and impulse and consists of the rationalizing and systematizing of the impulses and passions. "This will to freedom," he said, "is no longer an impulse that demands satisfaction, but the character—the mind's consciousness grown into something non-impulsive" (Sec. 482).

"Objective Mind." At the very end of his discussion of subjective mind Hegel wrote that the freedom which is the culmination of subjective mind is only a concept, "a principle of mind and heart destined to develop into the objective phase, into legal, moral, religious and scientific actuality" (Sec. 482). The rest of the system is therefore concerned with the ways in which the human will, in which thought and impulse ("mind and heart") are combined in freedom, becomes effective (this is the idea behind the word "actuality," which translates *Wirklichkeit*)

in the public world, the world in which men act and in which their thoughts and deeds give rise to rules, institutions, and organizations. These rules, institutions, and organizations are independent of each man and thus may be regarded as kinds of objects, though not as physical objects. Men build up in the natural world a world other than the natural world by working on nature and transforming it and by creating systems of property, economic organizations, class differentiations, and the like. The triad that makes up objective mind comprises law (*Recht*), subjective morality (as Wallace translated *Moralität*), and social morality (as Wallace translated *Sittlichkeit;* Knox translated it as "ethical life"). The first part covers legal rights and duties as exemplified in property, contract, and punishment. The second is concerned largely with the morality of intention and conscience—the term *Moralität* was used by Hegel somewhat pejoratively to mean a sort of ethics (of which Kant was, in his view, the chief exponent) in which the agent is unduly governed by the subjective and internal aspects of decision and action.

The third part is itself a triad. The first stage of social morality is the family, "the natural or immediate phase" of objective mind (*Philosophy of Right*, Sec. 152). When members of the family have matured, they detach themselves from it and enter the world of independent men who compete in an economic arena free from tribal allegiances. This phase of social life Hegel called "civil society." It is the world of intelligent, responsible individuals in their business relationships, free from irrational tribal loyalties, allowing their connections with one another to be formed by the coincidence of wants in a market of wide extent. Indeed, it is the aspect of human society that the classical economists, whom Hegel admired, had analyzed and justified. But civil society cannot exist as a mere market, for markets need to be policed, whereas trades and industries themselves find common concerns that unite the individuals in corporations of various kinds.

There is thus a double necessity for the state—as the upholder of fair dealing and as the ultimate curb on the selfishness of corporations within civil society. In the *Encyclopedia*, Hegel wrote of "the unification of the family principle with that of Civil Society" and described it as a unification of the love that is essential to the family with the conscious universality that is the mark of civil society (Sec. 535). In the *Philosophy of Right* (Sec. 257) the state was described as "the actuality [*Wirklichkeit*] of the ethical Idea"—that is, as its effective embodiment. In the same section of the *Philosophy of Right*, Hegel wrote that "the mind of a nation (Athene for instance) is the divine, knowing and willing itself," and in an addition to Section 258 is the famous phrase "The march of God in the world, that is what the State is." But this section has been misunderstood. In the sentence before that in which he had written that the state is divine, Hegel had said, with the family in mind, "The *Penates* are inward gods, gods of the underworld," so that it is not only to the state that he attributed divinity. Furthermore, in the same addition as that in which he claimed that the state is "the march of God in the world," he said that the state "stands on earth and so in the sphere of caprice, chance and error, and bad behaviour may disfigure it in many respects." Hegel's main concern was, as he stated, to analyze the state at its best. Although, like Aristotle, he regarded the state as the highest social achievement of man, he also held, again like Aristotle, that within the state there should be guarantees against arbitrariness and despotism. He did not take a favorable view of "popular suffrage" on the grounds that "in large states it leads inevitably to electoral indifference" and that "election falls into the power of a few, of a caucus" (*Philosophy of Right*, Sec. 311). He strongly believed that all important interests should be represented and thought that there should be a constitutional monarchy with considerable powers advised by an upper and a lower house.

This brings us to the most controversial part of Hegel's account of objective mind, his philosophy of history. Whatever else is involved in his view that the state is man's highest social achievement, it undoubtedly implies that there is no superior body or group by which its claims may be assessed. States are necessarily independent beings. Their relations are regulated to some degree by custom, and there is an international law that regulates dealings between subjects of different states and requires adherence to treaties, as if they were a sort of contract. When the vital interests of states clash, however, there is no alternative except war. War between states, Hegel had said in his "Die Verfassung Deutschlands" ("Constitution of Germany," 1802; first published in Georg Lasson, ed., *Schriften zur Politik und Rechtsphilosophie*, 2d ed., Leipzig, 1923), does not decide which of the rights of the conflicting states is the true right—for both are—"but which right has to give way to the other." Hegel believed that war performs the function of keeping before the minds of men the realities of death and destruction. He held that states are individuals and that all individuals persist in their existence by ensuring that other individuals recognize them as they recognize the others. The very concept of a state therefore requires that there be a plurality of them, and this makes war a part of the system of states even though war is not their natural condition but an interruption of the normal state of peace. Hegel argued that since war is a relation between states and not a relation of individual men to one another, the rights and interests of noncombatants should be maintained to the utmost. For the same reason he was in favor of professional armies and against conscription or any form of levy en masse.

Each nation is limited by geographical and other accidental features and hence can build up only a particular culture and can have only a particular, not a universal, history. Thus, nations, when they reach the level of statehood, make their contribution to the whole in the part they play in world history (*Encyclopedia*, Sec. 548). World history is not wholly an affair of chance or contingency; as the work of mind it could not be. Therefore, the history of the world has a rational structure, and any historical writing that ignored this "would be only an imbecile mental divagation, not as good as a fairy-tale" (Sec. 549). This rational structure, according to Hegel, is the development of freedom.

"Absolute Mind." The triad which completes the Hegelian system is composed of art, revealed religion, and philosophy. It will be remembered that at the end of the *Phenomenology* Hegel proceeded from the religion of nature to the religion of art and then to the philosophical knowledge of the history of the world. In the *Encyclopedia* art is given what seems to be a more independent status, but the details of the argument hardly bear out the general scheme, since the transitional sections describe a transition from objective mind to religion, as in the *Phenomenology*. Thus, in the concluding sections of the *Encyclopedia* art is regarded as an inadequate form of religion, religion as a more adequate form of art, philosophy as religion freed from picture thinking and wholly rationalized, and all three as manifestations of Absolute Mind. Art is the embodiment of Absolute Mind in material things fashioned by the artist, who, in a sense, is thus "the master of the God" (*Encyclopedia*, Sec. 560). In classical art the embodiment takes place without any antithesis between the embodiment and the mind that is embodied. In the art of the sublime, which preceded classical art, the Absolute Mind is regarded as something that defies embodiment and remains forever beyond and behind the sensible forms that succeed only in symbolizing it. The defect of artistic representation is that the sensible symbols may be taken to refer to another world beyond, which is as limited as this world is falsely taken to be. Thus, men worship idols or even bones, "which point to the unspiritual objectivity of that other world" (*ibid.*, Sec. 562).

God is therefore not something grander and more powerful than the natural world yet fundamentally like it, nor is he something beyond the world that must remain forever inaccessible to man. God is manifested in the world, and this is the truth that revealed religion has expressed most adequately in the Christian doctrine of the Incarnation. Without this doctrine God would still be regarded as beyond the world and, thus, as incomplete and finite. Even with this doctrine he is conceived of through the medium of particular historical events that introduce an element of contingency and irrelevance into our conception of him. In philosophy the artist's external vision and the mystic's internal vision are united in a mode of thought in which there is no further conflict. The philosopher who achieves ultimate self-knowledge is freed from the conflicts that inevitably disturb the inferior levels of knowledge. By philosophizing to the end, he has made himself free (*ibid.*, Sec. 576).

THE DIALECTICAL METHOD

Contradiction. It is now necessary to give more detailed attention to Hegel's dialectical method. There are interpreters of Hegel who say that Hegel denied the principle of contradiction in that he held that contradictories can both exist and that contradictory propositions can therefore both be true. Others deny this interpretation, maintaining, instead, that, according to Hegel, since contradiction is a mark of inadequacy and falsehood, contradictions are to be found in the lower categories but are absent from or resolved in the Absolute Idea. This view is summed up in Michael Oakeshott's reference to "the element of self-contradiction inherent in all abstraction" (*Experience and Its Modes*, Cambridge, 1933, p. 328). Those who take the first view can quote some convincing passages from Hegel's *Science of Logic*. For example, there he wrote that "all things are in themselves contradictory," that "movement is existing contradiction itself," and that "only insofar as something has contradiction in itself does it move, have impulse or activity."

If Hegel had rejected the principle of contradiction in the sense that that principle is understood by formal logicians, his case would indeed be serious, for it follows from the rejection of this principle that any proposition can be true and false and that there is thus no means of distinguishing truth from falsehood. It is important, therefore, to see whether Hegel did reject the principle of contradiction in this sense and whether its rejection is part of his dialectical method. That these questions are not easy to answer becomes apparent if we consult some of the commentators on the passages I have just quoted. J. M. E. McTaggart, in his *Commentary on Hegel's Logic*, was dissatisfied with the whole section and claimed that in it Hegel had allowed himself to be too much influenced by Schelling's view on polarity and opposition. "The whole point of the dialectic," McTaggart protested, "is that the perception of a contradiction is a reason for abandoning the category which we find contradictory." Indeed, he found this part of the *Logic* so unsatisfactory that he proposed to amend the sequence of categories by leaving out contradiction altogether.

McTaggart said nothing, however, about Hegel's statement that there are existing contradictions. G. R. G. Mure, in his *A Study of Hegel's Logic*, did not evade this difficulty. Examining Hegel's text more closely than McTaggart had done, he pointed out that on the ground that "the contradictory cannot be imagined or thought" Hegel rejected the common-sense view that things cannot be self-contradictory but that thought can be. Mure called attention, too, to Hegel's statement that self-contradiction is not a mere disease of thought but something which it must pass through on its way to truth. Furthermore, according to Hegel, it is finite things that are self-contradictory, and they are contradictory not in relation to one another but by virtue of their relation to what is infinite; Hegel "is not suggesting that Big Ben can now read both 9 P.M. and not 9 P.M." (p.105). Although this is an improvement on McTaggart, it left out of account Hegel's statement that for something to move, it must be both here and not here at the same time. What Hegel said about movement is not altogether unlike Mure's example of Big Ben. So the difficulty remains.

In the "Logic" sections of the *Encyclopedia* which was written later than the *Science of Logic* contradiction is not a separate category at all. Perhaps the reason for this difference is that Hegel had second thoughts and gave up the idea of contradiction in the nature of things. But although contradiction is no longer a category in the *Encyclopedia*, Hegel still sometimes wrote as if there were contradictions in the nature of things. For example, he stated that although such concepts as "square circle," "many-sided circle," and "straight curve" are self-contradictory, geometers nevertheless regard circles as polygons composed of very short sides and "the center and circumference of a circle as opposite and contradictory to one another" (*Encyclopedia*, Sec. 119). Hegel also suggested that polarity in physics goes against the ordinary logic—

but he used the word "opposition" (*Entgegensetzung*) rather than "contradiction" (*Widerspruch*).

In *Geschichte der neueren Philosophie* (Heidelberg, 1901, Vol. VIII, Part 2) Kuno Fischer tried to overcome the difficulty by distinguishing between two sorts of contradiction, "necessary contradiction" and "impossible contradiction." The example of a square circle illustrates the notion of an impossible contradiction, a *contradictio in adjecto*, for it is impossible for the same thing to be both circular and square. When a circle is regarded as a many-sided polygon, however, the contradiction is not *in adjecto* but in *subjecto*, for the circle is then being regarded as in the process of being formed or generated from these many sides. This, Fischer held, is the contradiction involved in all becoming (the first concrete category of the "Logic," the synthesis of being and nothing). Fischer's suggestion is therefore that there is not a vicious or stultifying contradiction involved in becoming or in movement, contradictory though they must in some sense be. But although this may be a correct exposition of Hegel's view, it is hardly a defense of it, since it merely repeats without explaining his claim that there are contradictions in the objective world.

By drawing this distinction, Fischer has nevertheless raised the question of whether Hegel intended the word "contradiction" to be used in the way it is used in formal logic. The answer is clear enough. Hegel did not regard formal logic as a philosophical science, and he therefore rejected any idea that its categories should dominate philosophical thought. Thus, the fact that the word "contradiction" is used in a certain way by formal logicians was not for him a reason for confining himself to that meaning. When Hegel was advocating the dialectical method, he had in mind a method in which oppositions, conflicts, tensions, and refutations were courted rather than avoided or evaded. Hegel was a student of the classical, laissez-faire economists who held that wealth would be maximized by the free play of competition. In this view if traders and producers ceased to compete with one another, the whole level of economic life would be lowered. General prosperity could be reached only at the expense of labor and anxiety. So it is, Hegel believed, with the categories of our thought, the systems of philosophers, and the forms of life and society. There is no tranquillity to be had by withdrawal and isolation. Our categories compete with one another, and out of their competition emerges something better than either of them could have accomplished alone. But it is not possible for the superior category to go into retirement, for without the spur of competition it would fall into decay. Furthermore, just as competition requires the competitors to continue in business—for if one destroys the others, there is monopoly and stagnation—so the competing categories cannot be swallowed up and lost in the Absolute Idea but must all play their part in maintaining its life and stability. There is nothing fanciful in this comparison. Indeed, it gains support from Hegel's "System der Sittlichkeit" of 1802 ("System of Morality"; in *Schriften zur Politik und Rechtsphilosophie*, Georg Lasson, ed., 2d ed., Leipzig, 1923), in which it is quite clear that Hegel's systematic thinking was influenced by his understanding of economic theory. For example, in this essay he developed the triad need – labor – enjoyment and described labor as "the destruction of the object . . . but in such a way that another is put in its place." Here Hegel compared labor with knowledge and undoubtedly had in mind (in accord with his tendency to take German words in the sense of their roots) the element of negation (*nicht*) in the word for destruction (*Vernichtung*). The destruction of the natural object is the creation of an artificial one.

Negation. Negation, indeed, is the vital notion in Hegel's account of the dialectic. In the Preface to the *Phenomenology* Hegel wrote, "The life of God and divine knowledge may, if we wish, be described as love disporting with itself; but this idea is degraded into mere edification and insipidity if it lacks the seriousness, the pain, the patience and the labour of the negative." "Seriousness," "pain," "patience," and "labor" would be strange words to use of the negative symbol of formal logic. Expressed in theological – economic terms Hegel's view is that God cannot be a mere consumer, for there is no consumption without labor, and labor has to face a recalcitrant nature that has to be understood and humored. Thus, there is no God apart from nature. In moral terms there is no good without evil, and in logical terms there is no truth without error. These, according to Hegel, are central truths of dialectics.

But surely, it will be said, this conflicts with such obvious facts as that there are some who consume without working, that in mathematics there are sequences of necessarily true propositions with no admixture of falsity, and that some things—for example, conscientious action—are good without qualification. As to the first point, Hegel argued in the *Phenomenology* that the master who consumes what his slave produces for him destroys what he consumes, whereas the slave shapes the external world in such a way that mind is embodied in it. Hence, the slave is on the road to freedom, whereas the master, who does not work, destroys without creating. As to mathematics, Hegel was inclined to hold it in contempt. There is no space here to consider the strange things he said about it, and it need only be remarked that he held that philosophical truth is utterly different from mathematical truth in that false philosophical views are taken up into true philosophy whereas false mathematics is not taken up into true mathematics. As to the alleged unmixed goodness of conscientious action (the Kantian "good will"), Hegel held that the morality of conscience contained in itself the seeds of willfulness and arbitrariness, for the most atrocious deeds can be defended on the ground that the man who committed them genuinely thought them right. Obedience to one's own conscience, Hegel thought, is an advance over obedience to the commands of an external lord but is nevertheless an unstable basis for morality.

Several ways in which the negative element is important in Hegel's method have been discussed. There is the conceptual competition without which thought must decay. Then, there is the polar character of certain fundamental notions which makes the one unthinkable without its opposite. At the prephilosophical level Hegel gave above and below, right and left, father and son, as examples. At the

philosophical level his examples, were good and bad, master and slave, thought and nature. But not only do these opposites require each other; they also pass into each other. Good will can pass over into atrocity; philosophical truth is the result of errors that supplement each other; the master satisfies his desires but becomes dependent upon the labor of the slave in order to do so; and the slave, by work, controls his desires and develops a rational will. The life of thought in conceptual conflict, the mutual dependence of polar opposites, and the instability or oscillations of philosophical and moral attitudes are different sorts of dialectic which Hegel emphasized on different occasions. If they have anything in common, it is the activity of negation.

There are two other aspects of the dialectic to discuss, the role of reason and understanding and the role of skepticism.

Reason and understanding. First, Hegel, following Kant, contrasted the reason, the source of dialectical thinking, with the understanding, the predialectical mode of thought. The understanding, as Hegel saw it, is the type of thinking that prevails in common sense, in the natural sciences, and in mathematics and those types of philosophy that are argued in quasi-scientific or quasi-mathematical ways. Fixed categories are uncritically adhered to, demonstrations are produced (only to be demolished), analyses are made, and distinctions are drawn. Analyzing and distinguishing are necessary foundations of philosophical activity but only to prepare the way for the more sinuous and subtle method of the dialectic. Once an analysis has been made, the elements of it are seen to conflict and collide as well as to cohere. First, the understanding isolates, then comes the Reason's negative moment of criticism or conflict, and after that its speculative moment of synthesis. It should be mentioned that distinctions somewhat similar to the distinction between the understanding and the reason had already been made by Plato when he distinguished between the highest knowledge and knowledge in the various sciences, by Spinoza in his second and third kinds of knowledge, by Pascal with his *esprit de géometrie* and *esprit de finesse,* by Hume with his reason and imagination, and by Burke when he contrasted the abstract rationalism of the Enlightenment with the organic, evolutionary view of society that he preferred. These distinctions are not all quite like that drawn by Hegel, but in his theory there is something corresponding to each of them.

Skepticism. Second, Hegel thought that skepticism was an important forerunner and essential ingredient of the dialectical method. In a review of a book by G. E. Schulze that appeared in 1802, Hegel wrote appreciatively of the skepticism of Sextus Empiricus and of the skeptical features in the philosophy of Parmenides, of whom he wrote, "This skepticism, which in its pure *explicit* form comes forward in Parmenides, is to be found *implicit* in every genuinely philosophical system, for it is the free aspect [*die freie Seite*] of every philosophy" ("Verhältnis des Skeptizismus zur Philosophie," in *Kritisches Journal der Philosophie,* Vol. 2 (1802), 1–74; quoted from *Sämtliche Werke,* Georg Lasson, ed., Vol. I, pp. 174–175). In the same essay Hegel wrote that when Spinoza held that God is the immanent but not the transcendent cause of the world, he was equating the cause with the effect, even though the very notion of an effect implies that it is distinct from the cause. Hegel agreed with Spinoza's equation but concluded that it shows that the reason can accept the principle of contradiction only as a formal principle. In "genuine" philosophy cause and effect are seen as both distinct and identical.

Hegel illustrated his comment that skepticism is "the free aspect" of philosophy in the following way. Dogmatists, he said, regard individual men as objects in the power of rules, laws, and customs. The more the dogmatists study man, the more they show him in subjection to these forces. When, however, the skeptics attack dogmatism, "they raise the freedom of Reason above this necessity of nature." An example of this is the way in which Europeans came to question their own concepts of law and morals when they were brought face to face with cultures very different from their own. When such skeptics as Montaigne mockingly insisted on these differences, men became more conscious of their own institutions and recognized the possibility of changing them. In theoretically breaking down men's traditional views and institutions, the skeptic frees men from the unconscious power of these views and institutions. Hegel repeated his general assessment of skepticism in the *Encyclopedia* (Sec. 81, addition 2) and in his *Lectures on the History of Philosophy*. In these lectures Hegel said that skepticism is "the demonstration that all that is determinate and finite is unstable." Hegel went on to say that "positive philosophy," by which he meant philosophy that is not content to remain in total skepticism, "has the negative to Scepticism in itself; thus it does not oppose, nor is it outside of it, for Scepticism is a moment in it" (Haldane and Simpson, 1955, Vol. II, p. 330).

FREEDOM

From what has just been said, it is clear that Hegel's account of dialectic and of reason is closely linked with his view of freedom. The exercise of thought in its most developed forms involves the negation of what had seemed firm and certain and the opening up of new possibilities. That mind is freedom applies both to the understanding and the reason, since both are spontaneous activities that interpret and arrange. But because the understanding is confined to a fixed system of categories, it is less free than the reason that criticizes, stretches, and transforms the categories of the understanding.

Freedom is, of course, logically connected with will, and according to Hegel, will is as essential to mind as intellect is. Reference has already been made to Section 482 of the *Encyclopedia*, in which Hegel asserted that the unity of theoretical and practical mind is free will. In the preceding sections he had argued that thought presupposes mind as practical, since classifying and explaining are activities through which the world is, so to speak, appropriated by the mind. In the sections of the *Encyclopedia* in which he expounded the categories of cognition and of will, Hegel endeavored to show that mere cognition is at a lower stage than will and that will is thus the actuality of what is only

potential in knowledge. He also argued that the freedom and necessity that are opposed to each other are abstractions and that what is concrete must combine both. The very nature of necessity, he continued, presupposes a will on which it is a constraint.

At the logical–metaphysical level, therefore, Hegel held a view which implied that freedom is essential to mind, both the presupposition and outcome of intelligence, and in its concrete form inseparable from constraint and necessity. This view of the matter pervaded his account of freedom in the social and political sphere. Freedom is not something merely opposed to constraint; on the contrary, it presupposes and requires restraint. This is true of concrete freedom. However, abstract or negative freedom, when it is more than a moment in actual or positive freedom, is a purely destructive force. Hegel considered that this negative freedom played a large part in the French Revolution. The old corporations and institutions were destroyed in such a frenzy of annihilation that it took several years for new institutions to be created and recognized as authoritative. Furthermore, when the conflicting interests in society are overcome, individuals come to be treated as equal, undifferentiated, replaceable, and expendable units. The events of the Reign of Terror thus led Hegel to hold that purely negative freedom was associated with force and death. The logical connections are not altogether clear, but it may well be that the links between egalitarianism, antinomianism, violence, and contempt for human life are not wholly accidental.

Freedom, according to Hegel, is something that has to be achieved, and it therefore would be impossible in the absence of opposition and negation. Hence, although negative freedom in its abstract form is a "fury of destruction," it is a necessary element in concrete freedom. Free will is not the liberty of indifference but the rational organization of the feelings and impulses.

Rationality is not a power that could reside in an isolated individual, however. To be rational, the individual must draw upon the resources of an organized and differentiated society and must be "formed" and educated to do this. His will is then in harmony with the ends of the various social groups by which he has been influenced and, in civilized societies, with the more complex ends of the state. In conforming to these pressures and in obeying the laws of the state, the individual is achieving his own rational ends and in so doing is free.

Hegel, like Rousseau, also held that an individual might be free even when he was being coerced, for although he might dislike the force applied against him, this dislike would be an expression of his particular whims, not of his rational insight, as can be seen when he approves of the imposition of a like force upon other people in like circumstances. Insofar as the criminal who is being punished would wish others to be punished who committed a like crime against him, he wills his own punishment.

Freedom in history. Hegel considered that the history of the human race is a development from less to greater freedom and from less adequate forms of freedom to freedom in its perfection. Thus, his philosophy of history can be understood only in terms of his conception of freedom. In the Oriental world there was no freedom for the subjects and only an arbitrary, irrational freedom for the despot who ruled over them. In the classical world of Greece and Rome there was a more adequate conception of freedom, and more men achieved freedom than in the Oriental despotisms. In the Greek city-state the citizens often regarded themselves as finding their fulfillment in the achievements of their city, apart from which they conceived of no life for themselves. Indeed, they might accept personal defeat and misfortune and submit to what they called destiny and still regard themselves as free in so doing. Of course, there were slaves who had no part in this activity and had no freedom.

Christianity offered the prospect of freedom to all men, a freedom, furthermore, that transcended the given social order. In what Hegel called the Germanic world—that is, the Christian civilization that grew out of Protestantism— this latest form of freedom was being realized in the manifold institutions of Europe and America and in the states in which these institutions flourished and by which they were regulated and protected. In Christianity the individual is regarded as of infinite value, as a candidate for eternal salvation, and although the emphasis on subjective freedom can lead, as it did in the French Revolution, to contempt for social institutions, it comprises the form and aspect of freedom that gives its special quality to modern civilization, with its romantic art, romantic love, and support for the rights of conscience (*Philosophy of Right*, Sec. 124).

It is apparent from the foregoing that Hegel rejected the liberal view that man is free to the extent that he is guaranteed a sphere within which he can do what he wishes without interference from others who are guaranteed a like position. Such freedom he stigmatized as negative, abstract, or merely willful. Men enjoy concrete freedom when the various orders and groups of civilized life are maintained in and by the state. In this passage of the *Lectures on the Philosophy of History* (Hoffmeister, Vol. XVIIIA, p.111) Hegel also emphasized that in submitting their private wills to the laws of the state and to the rules of its subordinate but free institutions, men were submitting their passions to the control of reason. Thus, the argument comes full circle. The theoretical reason is inseparable from will and from freedom; necessity and negative freedom are only abstractions; in concrete freedom the negative, destructive element is held in check and rendered fruitful by being realized in institutions; the individual enjoys concrete freedom when he is educated to live in a civilized state and to be guided by the reason that permeates it.

There is no space here to criticize this view in any detail, for in a way it is a cross section of the whole Hegelian metaphysic. It should be noted, however, that when a critic maintains that real freedom is what Hegel called negative or abstract freedom and when he goes on to maintain that "concrete freedom" is not freedom but indoctrinated submission, then he is criticizing Hegel's terminology rather than the substance of his view. To say that freedom consists of a willing acceptance of the tasks imposed by a civilized state is certainly to extend and perhaps to distort the ordinary senses of the term and to capture a word from the liberal vocabulary for use in a far from liberal scheme of concepts. It was Hegel's view,

however, that the thoughts that the liberal phraseology expressed necessarily move in the directions he described and that societies themselves, the embodiments of men's thoughts and aims, move in these directions, too.

AESTHETIC THEORY

We have already seen that Hegel discussed the nature of art and of beauty toward the end of both the *Phenomenology* and the *Encyclopedia*. Art, according to Hegel, is one of the manifestations of Absolute Mind, of which religion and philosophy are the other two. Thus, although art presupposes the civilized life of the state, it also transcends it. In his lengthy *Vorlesungen über die Aesthetik* ("Lectures on Aesthetics") Hegel developed his theories of art and beauty in great detail. The lectures possess great power and attraction, and so much of their value resides in the details that a summary treatment is bound to be difficult.

Three styles of art. Hegel's account of beauty is a modification of Schiller's view, in his *Letters on the Aesthetic Education of Mankind* (1795), that beauty is the mediation between the sensible and the rational. According to Hegel, beauty is the rational rendered sensible, the sensible appearance being the form in which the rational content is made manifest. This sensible embodiment of the rational, he held, can take place in three principal ways, symbolic art, classical art, and romantic art.

Symbolic art. In the first and least adequate form, symbolic art, the sensible shape merely symbolizes the rational content without penetrating and transforming it. A lion may symbolize courage; a bird, the soul; or a temple, the presence of a god who nevertheless remains a mystery. Thus, in symbolic art the sensible object refers away from itself to a rationality that is enigmatically and mysteriously beyond it. In thus referring away from the sensible symbol to something vast and merely adumbrated, symbolic art sometimes achieves the sublime.

Classical art. In classical art, the second form of sensible embodiment, the sensible expression is adequate to the idea that it gives expression to and does not point vaguely beyond itself. This is typified in sculptures of the human body so formed that the divine ideal is realized in the stone, not merely hinted at. A temple makes us think of the god but is not the god. In a statue of Apollo the god is visible and tangible in the stone. Hegel pointed out that works of classical art have independence and completeness, so that when they have been created, it seems that there is nothing more left to do done. "Nothing more beautiful," he wrote, "can be or become."

Romantic art. Christianity, however, with its emphasis on the infinite value of the individual and upon subjective freedom, made classical art seem somewhat unsatisfactory. More is required than works of art in which reason, as Hegel put it, "stands in quiet and blessedness in bodily form." When the self and its inner life are regarded as of infinite value, the forms of art must move on from balance and harmony to the storm and turmoil of the subjective. According to Hegel, it is in romantic art that this progress to subjectivity and self-consciousness is achieved. Romantic art turns its back on the quiet and balanced beauty of the classical and "weaves the inner life of beauty into the contingency of the external form, and allows full scope to the emphatic features of the unbeautiful." In romantic art, as in symbolic art, there is much that is bizarre and even grotesque, but romantic art is on a higher level than symbolic art because the mind expressed in it is more complex and sophisticated. And in romantic art the mind has achieved a greater measure of freedom than in classical art because romantic art is less involved in and hampered by the sensible embodiment.

Products of art. Hegel's view of the three main types of beauty is closely linked with his view of the main types of artistic product. Hegel divided the arts into architecture, sculpture, painting, music, and poetry. Works in any of these mediums may be produced in the symbolic, classical, or romantic styles, but, according to Hegel, architecture is particularly appropriate to symbolic art, sculpture to classical art, and painting, music, and poetry to romantic art.

Architecture. Architecture, Hegel held, is the basic art, the art that men first practice, for its material is mindless and its forms depend upon the weight and physical properties of this mindless medium. The architecture of early men, by bringing them together to worship the gods in temples, served to bring unity into their societies. Hegel imagined the men who built the first temples as they cleared the ground on which to build them, and he described this as "clearing the undergrowth of finitude."

Sculpture. In architecture a house is provided for the god, and the god is prepared for and expected. He is not, however, embodied or manifested in the stones of a mere building. In classical sculpture the god is embodied in the stone in such a way that all the parts of the statue combine in expressing and proclaiming him. Hence, it is not a mindless symbol of the mind beyond but a unified expression of it. Hegel contrasted the stiff regularity of Egyptian sculpture with the harmonious independence of the Greek, the acme of classical art. In Christian sculpture this Greek ideal does not predominate, and even when, as with Michelangelo, it is fully understood and mastered, it is associated with "the kind of inspiration that is found in romantic art."

Painting, music, and poetry. The three romantic arts of painting, music, and poetry differ from the arts of sculpture and architecture, according to Hegel, by being more "ideal." One thing he seems to have meant was that the productions of these arts are not three-dimensional like the productions of architecture and sculpture. Painting, of course, is two-dimensional, and Hegel thought it is more ideal than sculpture because it is further removed from the solid substance of material things. He appears to have argued that the painter transforms to an extent that the sculptor has no need to do. In reducing the three dimensions to two, space is somehow rendered more "inward" and "subjective," and the first step has been taken on the road to poetry.

The next step toward subjectivity is taken by music, which abandons all the dimensions of space as well as the senses of sight and touch. Hearing, according to Hegel, is a "more subjective" sense than sight because it is less practical and more contemplative.

In poetry the sensible elements of music, the notes or tones, are replaced by words that stand for thoughts. "The art of poetry," Hegel wrote, "is the universal art of mind that has become free and is no longer dependent upon external sensible material for its realization." Within poetry as a whole he distinguished epic, lyric, and dramatic poetry. Hegel's account of dramatic poetry is particularly interesting. "In tragedy," he wrote, "individuals destroy themselves through the onesidedness of their upright will and character, or they are forced to resign themselves and identify themselves with a course of action to which they are fundamentally opposed." In comedy, on the other hand, there is no such reconciliation, the characters pursue courses of action that have only subjective significance. Indeed, in comedy, according to Hegel, the subjectivity characteristic of romantic art is taken to such an extreme that all unity is dissolved; with it goes beauty, too. In comedy there is merely a series of subjective interests playing against one another, as opposed to the aim of all art, which is the revelation of the eternal and divine in sensible form.

Natural beauty. The discussion has thus far been confined to the beauty of works of art (*das Kunstschöne*). It is with this that by far the greater part of the "Lectures on Aesthetics" is concerned. In the second chapter, however, Hegel did say something about natural beauty (*das Naturschöne*). He discussed the notions of regularity, symmetry, harmony, and conformity to law and also the beauty claimed for plants, animals, and human beings. He concluded his discussion of the subject with some comments on how natural beauty falls short of artistic beauty. Plants and animals, he granted, are more beautiful than inanimate natural objects, but what we see of them is their outward coverings, not the soul that works within, for that is concealed by the visible feathers, hair, scales, fur, and the like that cover them. Hegel referred to natural beauty as the "prose of the world." Although Hegel did not altogether deny the beauty of nature, it is clear that he ranked it very low. Indeed, the structure of his system made this inevitable, for it is the self-conscious achievements of man that form its culmination.

It would seem that the triadic divisions of the "Lectures on Aesthetics" constrained and even corrupted Hegel's argument. An example of this occurs in his account of dramatic poetry, into which he introduced a species called "drama," the function of which was to add one species to tragedy and comedy and thus make three species of dramatic poetry.

Hegel also tended to confuse conceptual and historical relationships. For example, the distinction between symbolic, classical, and romantic art was intended to be made on conceptual grounds, but, on the other hand, Hegel had in mind historical progression. Here, as elsewhere, Hegel confused historical types, such as romanticism, with conceptual types, such as tragedy, which have no necessary temporal sequence. Perhaps the most interesting case of this is Hegel's suggestion that art comes to an end with the highest flights of romanticism. We have already seen that Hegel brought his account of dramatic poetry to an end with comedy, the most subjective of all art forms. At the very end of the "Lectures on Aesthetics" he said that "in this culmination comedy is leading straight to the dissolution of art in general." It is unlikely that Hegel believed that art was coming to an end, any more than he believed that with the Prussian state, history was coming to an end. Yet in each case he argued in such a way as to suggest that the culmination of a conceptual sequence must also be the conclusion of a historical progress. Insofar as he held that history was the movement of the Divine in the world, it was natural to make this identification, extravagant as it is. Bosanquet, who denied that Hegel believed that art was on the point of final dissolution, held that he did foresee that it was about to suffer an eclipse in the new form of society. "But we must claim extraordinary insight for him, who, still under the spell of Schiller and Goethe, described the present exhaustion of the art-impulse and the conditions hostile to it in language approaching that of Ruskin and William Morris" (*A History of Aesthetic*, 4th ed., London, 1917, p. 361).

PHILOSOPHY OF RELIGION

A few commentators have regarded Hegel's philosophy as atheistic, but most have considered it to be either theistic or pantheistic. Certainly religious expressions abound in his writings, even in the *Logic*. It has been shown how closely he associated art with religion and how he applied religious epithets to the state. It was also pointed out that the *Phenomenology* might with some justification be interpreted in atheistic terms. It would be obviously overstraining the evidence, however, to interpret Hegel's mature system in this way, for in the system religion is a form of Absolute Mind, along with art and philosophy, which is the supreme expression of the Absolute Mind. According to Hegel, religion represents or pictures the Absolute, whereas philosophy conceives or thinks it. The same truth, that is, expressed in quasi-imaginative form in one and in conceptual form in the other.

Christianity. Since the concept is supreme and ultimate, philosophy surpasses religion to this extent, but in doing this, it finally and fully justifies Christianity, which is the absolute religion. The doctrine that elevates Christianity above all other religions is the doctrine of the Incarnation, which, according to Hegel, is the religious expression of the philosophical truth that the Infinite Being is not distinct from what is finite but is necessarily manifested in it. Hegel also interpreted the doctrine of the Trinity in philosophical terms. In the "Science of Logic" God is revealed as he is before the creation of the world; in the "Philosophy of Nature," in his material embodiment; and in the "Philosophy of Mind," as reconciling the finite and the Infinite. In this way the Father, the Son, and the Holy Spirit are explained in terms of the main themes of the Hegelian system. Again, Hegel interpreted the doctrine that God is love to mean that although the Infinite Being cannot exist without negation and opposition, the negation and opposition are finally reconciled. Finally, it should be mentioned that Hegel gave a series of lectures on the traditional proofs for the existence of God. He admitted the force of Kant's criticisms of these proofs but claimed to have reformulated the arguments so as to meet the criticisms. In particular, he held that the Ontological Argument, which Kant had regarded as vital but unsound, was valid when properly understood.

Undoubtedly, Hegel's later writings are much closer to orthodox Christianity than his earlier ones. The early "Life of Jesus" had nothing to say about the Resurrection, whereas in the *Lectures on the Philosophy of Religion* this doctrine was stated and defended. Hegel here wrote of "the death of death," of "the triumph over the negative," of mind as "the negative of this negative which thus contains the negative in itself," and of "the division of the divine idea and its reunion" that is "the whole of history." Although Hegel said that God appeared in the flesh at a particular time and in a particular individual, his account of the matter seems to be extremely general. In the Christian doctrine of the Incarnation, God became man in Jesus Christ at a particular time and place, whereas Hegel's God is incorporated in the finite world. It would seem that a highly specific historical view is replaced by a highly general metaphysical one. Hegel himself did not take this view of his own work, nor did a younger contemporary of his, Karl Friedrich Göschel, in his *Aphorismen über Nichtwissen und absolutes Wissen im Verhälnisse zur christlichen Glaubenserkenntnis* (Berlin, 1829). In the *Encyclopedia* (Sec. 564) Hegel recommended this book, which is generally regarded as giving a theistic account of the Absolute. Just before referring to Göschel's book, Hegel had written, "God is only God in so far as he knows himself; his self-knowledge is moreover his consciousness of himself in man and man's knowledge *of* God, a knowledge that extends itself into the self-knowledge of man *in* God."

What cannot be doubted is that Hegel's philosophy of religion contained elements that could easily be developed in ways that go counter to orthodox Christianity. Thus, when D. F. Strauss argued, in his *Life of Jesus* (1835), that the Gospel story was a set of myths, he was consciously working out what he thought was the consequence of Hegel's view that in religion the truth about God is understood in representative or pictorial terms. Again, Ludwig Feuerbach, in his *The Essence of Christianity* (1841), endeavored to interpret the Christian doctrines in human and psychological terms as the imaginary fulfillment of wishes that cannot be satisfied here on earth. We have already referred to the passage in Hegel's *The Positivity of the Christian Religion*, in which he said that in the days of imperial Rome men who had been robbed of their freedom in this world sought for it in a heaven beyond. Feuerbach, who, of course, had not seen this work, could have read something similar in the *Phenomenology*. It is a very short step from Hegel's view that the infinite is manifested in the finite to the view that it is a projection of it. Perhaps the truth of the matter is that the Christian religion, according to Hegel, is adequate in its own sphere and that the philosophy of religion is required to counteract false religious views and false views about religion but is not a substitute for it. This is the interpretation given by Lasson in the Introduction to Hegel's philosophy of religion printed at the end of his edition of Hegel's *Lectures on the Philosophy of Religion*.

Works by Hegel

The edition of Hegel's collected works, *Werke. Vollständige Ausgabe*, published soon after his death has already been mentioned. This was republished in 26 volumes under the editorship of Hermann Glockner (Stuttgart, 1927–1940) as the jubilee edition. Volumes 23–26 of this edition are an invaluable *Hegel-Lexikon* (1st ed., 1935; rev. ed., 2 vols., 1957). Mention must be made of Georg Lasson's edition, *Georg Wilhelm Friedrich Hegels Sämtliche Werke* (Leipzig, 1905——); this was to have been revised and re-edited by Lasson and Johannes Hoffmeister, and some volumes were published (Hamburg, 1949——). As a result of the death of Lasson and of Hoffmeister, the plan was altered. The *Sämtliche Werke, neue kritische Ausgabe*, which Hoffmeister started to edit, will continue under the editorship of various scholars. This edition contains Hegel's letters in *Briefe von und an Hegel*, 4 vols. (1952–1960). The unpublished writings prior to 1800 will appear in this new critical edition under the editorship of Gisela Schüler. Another collection with still earlier documents is *Dokumente zu Hegels Entwicklung*, edited by Hoffmeister (Stuttgart, 1936).

Some of Hegel's early writings were translated from Herman Nohl, ed., *Hegels theologische Jugendschriften* (Tübingen, 1907) by T. M. Knox as *Early Theological Writings* (Chicago, 1948). There is a translation of the *Phenomenology of Mind* by J. B. Baillie (London, 1910; 2d ed., 1931). William Wallace translated the Encyclopedia "Logic," with excellent Prolegomena in *The Logic of Hegel* (Oxford, 1873); there are subsequent editions. He also translated the last part of the *Encyclopedia* (in *Hegel's Philosophy of Mind*, Oxford, 1894). See also *The Science of Logic*, translated by W. H. Johnston and L. G. Struthers, 2 vols. (London, 1929); *The Philosophy of Right*, translated and edited by T. M. Knox (Oxford, 1942), a very fine work of scholarship; *The Philosophy of Fine Art*, translated by F. P. B. Osmaston, 4 vols. (London, 1920); *Lectures on the Philosophy of Religion*, translated by E. B. Speirs and J. B. Sanderson, 3 vols. (London, 1895); and *Lectures on the History of Philosophy*, translated by E. S. Haldane and F. H. Simson, 3 vols. (London 1892–1896; reprint, 1955). J. Sibree's translation of the *Lectures on the Philosophy of History* (London, 1857) has been reprinted several times. See also *Hegel's Political Writings*, translated by T. M. Knox with an introductory essay by Z. A. Pelczynski (Oxford, 1964). There is a translation of the *Encyclopedia* with notes by Gustav E. Mueller (New York, 1959). There are two useful books of selections, *Hegel: Selections*, edited by Jacob Loewenberg (London and New York, 1929), and *The Philosophy of Hegel*, edited by C. J. Friedrich (New York, 1953).

Works on Hegel

THE SYSTEM

Caird, Edward, *Hegel*. London and Edinburgh, 1883.

Copleston, Frederick, *A History of Philosophy*, Vol. VII, *From Fichte to Nietzsche*. London, 1963. Chs. 9–11.

Croce, Benedetto, *Ciò che è vivo e ciò che è morto della filosofia di Hegel*. Bari, Italy, 1907. Translated by Douglas Ainslie as *What Is Living and What Is Dead in the Philosophy of Hegel*. London, 1915.

Findlay, J. N., *Hegel: A Re-examination*. London, 1958. Emphasizes the *Logic* and interprets Hegel in somewhat nonmetaphysical terms.

Glockner, Hermann, *Hegel*, 2 vols. Stuttgart, 1929. These are Vols. XXI–XXII of the jubilee edition of Hegel mentioned above.

Grégoire, Franz, *Études hégéliennes*. Louvain, Belgium, and Paris, 1958. Contains detailed and fruitful discussions of the central issues.

Haering, T. L., *Hegel: Sein Wollen und Sein Werk*, 2 vols. Leipzig, 1929. A leading authority.

Hartmann, Nicolai, *Die Philosophie des deutschen Idealismus*, Vol. II, *Hegel*. Berlin and Leipzig, 1929.

Kaufmann, Walter, *Hegel: Reinterpretation, Texts and Commentaries*. New York, 1965.

Kline, George L., "Some Recent Re-interpretations of Hegel's Philosophy." *The Monist*, Vol. 48 (1964), 34–73.

McTaggart, J. M. E., *Studies in Hegelian Cosmology*. Cambridge, 1901. Stimulating and idiosyncratic.

Mure, G. R. G., *An Introduction to Hegel*. Oxford, 1940. Emphasizes Hegel's debt to Greek philosophy, Aristotle in particular.

Pringle-Pattison, A. S., *Hegelianism and Personality*, 2d ed.

London and Edinburgh, 1887. The first edition was published under the name Andrew Seth. See the article "The Absolute."

Seeberger, Wilhelm, *Hegel: Oder die Entwicklung des Geistes zur Freiheit*. Stuttgart, 1961. A new statement of the "orthodox" interpretation.

Stace, W. T., *The Philosophy of Hegel*. London, 1924; New York, 1955. A detailed account based on the *Encyclopedia*.

Serreau, René, *Hegel et l'hégélianism*. Paris, 1962. Brief but informative book with good introductory account of the various Hegelian schools.

EARLY WRITINGS

Asveld, P., *La Pensée religieuse du jeune Hegel*. Louvain, Belgium, 1953.

Dilthey, Wilhelm, *Die Jugendgeschichte Hegels*. Berlin, 1906. It is included as Vol. IV of Dilthey's *Gesammelte Schriften* (Berlin and Leipzig, 1921).

Hyppolite, Jean, *Introduction à la philosophie de l'histoire de Hegel*. Paris, 1948. A valuable account of Hegel's early views on history and politics.

Kaufmann, Walter, "The Young Hegel and Religion," in his *From Shakespeare to Existentialism*. Boston, 1959. Ch. 8.

Lukács, Georg, *Der junge Hegel*. Berlin, 1948. An interesting Marxist interpretation.

Peperzak, A. T. P., *Le Jeune Hegel et la vision morale du monde*. The Hague, 1960.

Walsh, W. H., "The Origins of Hegelianism," in his *Metaphysics*. London, 1963. Ch. 9.

"PHENOMENOLOGY OF MIND"

Hyppolite, Jean, *Genèse et structure de la Phénomenologie de l'Esprit de Hegel*. Paris, 1946.

Kojève, Alexandre, *Introduction à la lecture de Hegel*. Paris, 1947. Gives the "atheistic" interpretation.

Loewenberg, Jacob, "The Exoteric Approach to Hegel's Phenomenology. I." *Mind*, N.S. Vol. 43 (1934), 424 ff.

Loewenberg, Jacob, "The Comedy of Immediacy in Hegel's Phenomenology. II." *Mind*, N.S. Vol. 44 (1935), 21 ff.

Wahl, Jean, *Le Malheur de la conscience dans la philosophie de Hegel*. Paris, 1929; 2d ed., 1951.

"LOGIC"

Hyppolite, Jean, *Logique et existence*. Paris, 1953.

McTaggart, J. M. E., *Commentary on Hegel's Logic*. Cambridge, 1910.

Mure, G. R. G., *A Study of Hegel's Logic*. Oxford, 1950.

DIALECTIC

Coreth, E., *Das dialektische Sein in Hegels Logik*. Vienna, 1952.

Grégoire, Franz, *Études hégéliennes*. Louvain, Belgium, and Paris, 1958. See Study II.

McTaggart, J. M. E., *Studies in the Hegelian Dialectic*. Cambridge, 1896; 2d ed., 1922.

Mueller, Gustav E., "The Hegel Legend of Thesis, Antithesis and Synthesis." *Journal of the History of Ideas*, Vol. 19 (1958), 411–414.

Popper, Karl, "What Is Dialectic?" *Mind*, N.S. Vol. 49 (1940), 403–426, Revised and reprinted in his *Conjectures and Refutations* (London, 1963), Ch. 15.

SOCIAL AND POLITICAL PHILOSOPHY

Foster, M. B., *The Political Philosophies of Plato and Hegel*. Oxford, 1935. An original and valuable discussion.

Grégoire, Franz, *Études hégéliennes*. Louvain, Belgium, and Paris, 1958. See Study IV.

Haym, Rudolf, *Hegel und seine Zeit*. Berlin, 1857; reprinted, Hildesheim, 1962.

Kaufmann, Walter, "The Hegel Myth and Its Methods," in his *From Shakespeare to Existentialism*. Boston, 1959. Ch. 7 is a criticism of Ch. 12 of Popper's *The Open Society and Its Enemies.*

Knox, T. M., "Hegel and Prussianism." *Philosophy,* Vol. 15 (1940), 51–63.

Plamenatz, John, *Man and Society,* 2 vols. London and New York, 1963. Vol. II, Chs. 3–4, "The Social and Political Philosophy of Hegel."

Popper, Karl, *The Open Society and Its Enemies,* 2 vols. London, 1945. See Vol. II, Ch. 12.

Rosenzweig, Franz, *Hegel und der Staat,* 2 vols. Oldenburg, Germany, 1920.

Weil, Eric, *Hegel et l'état.* Paris, 1950.

AESTHETICS

Bosanquet, B. *History of Aesthetic.* London, 1892. Chs. 2, 12.

Teyssèdre, B., *L'Esthétique de Hegel.* Paris, 1958.

PHILOSOPHY OF RELIGION

Chapelle, A., *Hegel et la religion,* Vol. I, *La Problématique.* Paris, 1964——. The first of four projected volumes on the subject.

Grégoire, Franz, *Études hégéliennes.* Louvain, Belgium, and Paris, 1958. Study III.

Iljin, I., *Die Philosophie Hegels als kontemplative Gotteslehre.* Bern, 1946.

McTaggart, J. M. E., *Studies in Hegelian Cosmology.* Cambridge, 1901. Especially Chs. 2, 3, 6 ("Sin"), and 8 ("Hegelianism and Christianity").

Mueller, Gustav E., "Hegel's Absolute and the Crisis of Christianity," in D. C. Travis, ed., *A Hegel Symposium.* Austin, Tex., 1962.

For further discussion see *Hegel-Studien,* Vol. I (Bonn, 1961), Vol. II (Bonn, 1963), and Supp. Vol. I (Bonn, 1964). This is edited by F. Nicolin and O. Pöggeler and contains articles, reviews, and bibliography. See also *Études hégéliennes* (Neuchâtel, 1955), containing articles by Alexandre Kojève, Georges Bataille, R. Queneau, Jean Wahl, and Eric Weil, and *A Hegel Symposium* (Austin, Texas, 1962), with articles by C. J. Friedrich, Sidney Hook, Helmut Motekat, Gustav E. Mueller, and Helmut Rehder.

H. B. ACTON

HEGELIANISM. The influence of Hegel has been felt not only in systematic metaphysical thinking but also in aesthetics, political and social theory, Protestant theology and philosophy of religion, and historiography, particularly the interpretation of intellectual history. But Hegel's influence has functioned differently in different fields, and movements which have been influenced by one aspect of his thinking have generally been very critical of other aspects.

Different but recognizably Hegelian movements have often reached nearly opposite conclusions among themselves. This great diversity within Hegelianism is due not only to historical contingencies but also to contradictory tendencies within Hegel's system. Hegel himself treated all contradictions as dialectical moments in the life of Absolute Spirit, unified in a single comprehensive system of philosophy. But to call this synthesis dialectical is to say that it contains tremendous tension. In Hegel's own philosophy the idealistic first moment of the dialectic always finally triumphs over the historical concreteness of the second. Yet the tension remains, producing violent disputes over what Hegelianism really teaches. And those who followed Hegel were not often willing or able to maintain this tension.

OLD HEGELIANISM

Hegelianism as a philosophical school came into its own during the 1820s, when Hegel exercised a tremendous influence, largely in person, through his great courses of lectures at the University of Berlin. There soon grew up a talented circle of loyal disciples composed largely of colleagues and former students. Hegelianism, however, was not only a system but a method of thinking, which the disciples were encouraged by the master's own example to apply to diverse fields. Some, such as Georg Gabler (1786–1853), Leopold von Henning (1791–1866), and Julius Schaller (1807–1868), were primarily systematic philosophers. Theologians, such as Hegel's colleague in Heidelberg, Karl Daub (1765–1836), and Philipp Karl Marheineke (1780–1846) in Berlin, developed Protestant dogmatics on the basis of the dialectical method, in opposition to both theological rationalism and supernaturalism. The jurist Eduard Gans (1798–1839) treated the development of law, historically and systematically, as a dialectical progression of concepts. In the mid-1820s Karl Michelet (1801–1893) began a long career as a Hegelian philosopher by producing works on ethics and philosophy of law. Hegel's influence was particularly strong in aesthetics, inspiring a number of special dialectical studies of movements in art and literature by Heinrich Rötscher (1803–1871), Heinrich Hotho (1802–1873), and Karl Rosenkranz (1805–1879), among others. Rosenkranz and Hermann Hinrichs (1794–1861) produced early works in theology and political philosophy as well as in aesthetics. Karl Heinrich Schultz (or von Schulzenstein; 1798–1871) even attempted to mediate the development of physiological knowledge through the dialectical logic.

This circle of disciples defended the Hegelian synthesis as a whole against all critics. In July 1826 it formed, in Hegel's home, a "society for scientific criticism" with three divisions—philosophical, natural scientific, and philosophical–historical. This society founded the *Jahrbücher für wissenschaftliche Kritik* as the official Hegelian journal. Its members constituted the original "old Hegelians," though this term was later used more broadly, as the virtual equivalent of the Hegelian right wing. The group's greatest contribution to the propagation of orthodox Hegelianism was the editing of Hegel's *Collected Works,* including the lectures compiled from the combined notes of many persons who had heard them; the works began to appear in 1832, immediately after the death of Hegel.

THEOLOGICAL CONFLICT FROM 1830 TO 1841

Although Hegelianism was always vigorously attacked from other philosophical standpoints and by such orthodox theologians as E. W. Hengstenberg (1802–1869), there were no notable conflicts within the Hegelian school itself until nearly the end of Hegel's life. The first serious conflicts developed over theological issues. Old Hegelians had generally been defenders of Christianity, and some were inclined to interpret Hegel in a highly theistic way. Karl Göschel (1781–1861) even attempted to reconcile Hegelianism with supernaturalistic beliefs in a personal God and in personal immortality. Christian Weisse (1801–1866) and I. H. Fichte (1796–1879), both of whom later renounced Hegelianism, limited the applicability of the dialectical method in the interests of speculative theism.

Immortality. The first decisive step away from theism was taken by Ludwig Feuerbach (1804–1872) in an anonymous work entitled *Thoughts Regarding Death and Immortality* (1830). He denied on Hegelian grounds any personal survival of death and argued that the true religious implication of Hegelianism was pantheistic. Belief in personal immortality is an act of egoistic vanity which merely accentuates man's finitude; the acceptance of the fact of death is necessary if men are to begin the true religious task, which is the liberation from a standpoint of limited particularity to that of Infinite Spirit. More influential than Feuerbach's work but defending essentially the same position were Friedrich Richter's *The Doctrine of Last Things* (2 vols., 1833–1844) and *The New Doctrine of Immortality* (1833). Weisse admitted that Hegel's own view implied a denial of personal immortality but argued that the Absolute, as subject, could legitimately be given a more personalistic interpretation which would allow for immortality. Göschel, joined by Hinrichs, rejected the pantheistic reduction of Hegelianism and offered speculative proofs for immortality on the grounds of the superiority of Spirit over nature and the transcendence of individuality over the abstract opposition of universal and particular.

Christology. The conflict over immortality was soon eclipsed by the more basic conflict over Christology launched by D. F. Strauss's *Life of Jesus* (1835–1836). Carrying the critical–historical methods developed by F. C. Baur and Wilhelm Vatke to more radical conclusions, Strauss (1808–1874) denied the historicity of the supernatural acts and attributes ascribed to Jesus in the New Testament. What the early church saw in Jesus was really the unconscious projection of its own mythological conceptions. But there was a hidden truth in the myth—the truth that the divine nature is incarnate in the human; however, the Incarnation occurs not in one man but in the race as a whole. This, Strauss argued, is the authentic implication of Hegel's philosophy of religion, though Hegel himself was prevented from drawing it because of his romantic attitude toward historic individuals. Speculative truth, which for Strauss assumed an increasingly pantheistic form, must be sharply separated from the alleged events of the Gospel.

In the controversy which followed the Hegelian school fell into fairly clear divisions, which Strauss himself designated, on the model of the French parliament—left, center, and right. This division originally turned on the attitude toward the relation between speculative Idea and Gospel history. On the right Göschel, Gabler, and Bruno Bauer (1809–1882) attempted a complete reconciliation of the two, supposing that the divine comes to complete expression in particular individuals and events. Rosenkranz, at the center, was skeptical of many of the signs and wonders in the Gospel story but argued that the Absolute must manifest itself as an individual. The left signified Strauss's own position.

God. Bauer, however, soon adopted a position more radical than that of Strauss himself. Rejecting not only the historicity of the Gospel story but also the mythological interpretation, Bauer argued that the story was the conscious invention of a single author. Moreover, he soon declared that the true outcome of the Hegelian view was neither theism nor pantheism but atheism, for by the 1840s the controversy had moved from Christology to the doctrine of God. The most influential left view on this subject, however, was not Bauer's but Feuerbach's, which attained classic expression in *The Essence of Christianity* (1841). According to Feuerbach, humanity is not only the true subject of Christology (Strauss) but of theology in general. The theistic view, which ascribed quasi-human predicates to a divine subject, must be reversed: Mankind is the absolute subject, to which divine attributes are to be ascribed. This reversal, according to Feuerbach, reaches to the heart not only of theology but of philosophical idealism as well, which is merely disguised theology. Feuerbach employed a genetic–psychological explanation to set right what philosophy has confused. The idea is not the truth of human existence, but human existence is the source and truth of the idea. The senses, not the transcendent consciousness, are the primary mediums of knowledge. Concrete human relationship, not Spirit, is the basis of human community. Love between man and man, not faith in a transcendent God, is the truth of Christianity. The confusion of these is not, for Feuerbach, simply a logical or factual error but the result of an existential condition of human self-alienation. God is the creation of man, a creation onto which man has projected his own highest potentialities; he has not only divested himself of what is properly his own but has also placed himself in subjection to it. Man is divided against himself, and Feuerbach saw his own humanistic view, his religious atheism, as the negation of the negation of man, man's joyous return to himself.

LEFT-WING HEGELIANISM

The distinction between right- and left-wing Hegelianism was soon construed much more broadly than in Strauss's original theological formulation. Karl Löwith (*Von Hegel zu Nietzsche*, p. 83) has made the distinction in a suggestive way. In Hegel's formula that the rational is the real and the real is the rational is epitomized the tension between the revolutionary and conservative implications of his dialectic. The division of Hegelianism into a right and left wing is a breaking of this tension. The right wing maintains that the real is, as such, rational; the result is accommodation. The left insists that only what is rational is substantial, that an unperfected, alienated state of existence must give way by its own inner necessity. Hegel's system had synthesized philosophical idealism, the Christian religion, the politics of monarchy, and bourgeois culture. The left wing, or "young Hegelians," seized the critical implications of Hegel's dialectic to dissolve the synthesis and attack all four of its parts. The present order is not to be defended rationally but assaulted on behalf of the future, in political act as well as in philosophical theory.

Ruge. The *Hallischen Jahrbücher für deutsche Wissenschaft und Kunst* of Arnold Ruge (1803–1880) mirrors in its development the rise of the Hegelian left, whose central organ it became. At its founding in 1838 the journal was of such orthodox Hegelian coloring that it praised

Göschel, declared that philosophy and dogma differ only in form, and permitted Strauss and his friend F. T. Vischer to contribute articles only on condition that they withheld their radical theological views. Its politics were stanchly Prussian, its religion stanchly Lutheran; Ruge challenged anyone to show that he had departed from Hegel's views at a single point. By the next year, however, the journal was not only publishing attacks on Göschel and theological salvos by Strauss but also ridiculing the Prussian government and carrying Feuerbach's critique of the Hegelian system. Feuerbach and Bauer soon became frequent contributors. Although the Prussian state was praised for having annihilated the church, it was otherwise sharply criticized in the name of liberalism and reason.

After moving from Prussia to Saxony in 1841 and being renamed the *Deutsche Jahrbücher,* the journal adopted a still sharper tone. The right Hegelians were reproached for their philosophical, theological, and political orthodoxy; Christianity was renounced; and war was declared against political servitude. The authentic result of Hegelianism was held to be the discovery of the spirit of history, expressed in the *Zeitgeist* of an age, both in the events of the age and in its philosophical standpoint. Timeliness, adequacy to the spirit of the age, was the ultimate measure of a philosophy. Indeed, Hegel had said that every individual is a child of his time and philosophy is the grasp of the spirit of an age in thought. But whereas for Hegel philosophy was therefore primarily retrospective, for Ruge and his associates it was prophetic, the formulation of the forward movement of the age into the future.

When his journal was banned in Saxony, Ruge moved to Paris, where, with Karl Marx (1818–1883), he founded the short-lived *Deutsch–französischen Jahrbücher* in 1844. The journal now held that the age demanded not mere constitutional monarchy or even liberal democracy, but socialism. Yet Hegelian philosophy still had a decisive role. As Ruge explained in the opening issue, since the Hegelian system has "constituted the whole transcendent world of all previous metaphysics as the realm of reason, it remains to us only to overcome the transcendence of reason in order to enjoy the advantage of its logical certainty and consequence." Although reason must move from the Hegelian heaven to the earth, it has in the Hegelian logic a "celestial map" by which to navigate in its earthly, political pursuits. Philosophy will indeed be turned to the attainment of freedom, but "by freedom we mean real human, i.e. political freedom, not any sort of blue metaphysical vapor."

Marx. Self-alienation, as the opposite of freedom, was given fresh significance, especially in Marx's contributions to the *Deutsch–französischen Jahrbücher.* Feuerbach's analysis of self-alienation in religion furnished the paradigm, even when Marx went beyond Feuerbach in his attempt to grasp the root of religious alienation itself. Marx argued that the social, economic, and political structures which men have created had become alien powers which tyrannize them. By investing these structures with authority over them, men have divested themselves of their own humanity. This acute social alienation is the basis of religious alienation. Although, therefore, "the critique of religion is the presupposition of all criticism," it is not enough, with Bauer and Feuerbach, to call for the end of

religion, since religion is not the cause, but the expression, of self-alienated man. One must attack the real conditions which have placed men in this bondage. As he further developed his theory, Marx gave a decisive place to the dialectic of history lacking in other forms of left-wing Hegelianism. One attacks existing conditions not in the hope of realizing an abstract ethical ideal but in the confidence that there is in the existing conditions themselves an essential instability, that these conditions contain the seeds of their own overthrow and of the establishment of the socialistic order in which men can appropriate their free humanity for the first time.

Marx found these seeds of revolution in the position of the proletariat in bourgeois society, and he later translated his historical dialectic into economic and social theory (see HISTORICAL MATERIALISM), but even in the Preface to the second edition of *Capital,* written when the influence of Hegel was generally considered dead (1873), Marx declared himself "the pupil of that mighty thinker." Hegel had simply stood his dialectic on its head; turned right side up—that is, oriented to actual material conditions—one discovers "the rational kernel within the mystical shell." Then, far from glorifying the *status quo,* the dialectic may be used to recognize both "the existing state of things" and "the negation of that state, . . . its inevitable breaking up; because it regards every historically developed social form as in fluid movement." It "lets nothing impose upon it, and is in its essence critical and revolutionary." Partly under the influence of Marx, other left-wing Hegelians—notably, Moses Hess (1812–1875) and Ferdinand Lasalle (1825–1864), as well as Ruge and Marx's alter ego, Friedrich Engels (1820–1895)—saw socialism as the consequence of the historical dialectic, though all but Engels later broke with Marx.

Others on the left, skeptical of the historical dialectic, developed the variations in the dialectic of self-alienation. The diagnosis of estrangement depended upon the view of the true estate from which men were estranged. For Feuerbach the absolute was humanity, made concrete in interpersonal relations. For Bauer it was the critical consciousness of the pure ego. Max Stirner (pseudonym for Johann Caspar Schmidt, 1806–1856), in *The Single One and His Property* (1845), argued—as Bauer had done with self-consciousness, Feuerbach with humanity, and the communists with society—that the absolutizing of anything except the individual ego was still "religious," still a self-alienated viewpoint. Feuerbach himself, in his *Lectures on the Essence of Religion* (1848), unveiled a religion of nature and declared that whatever is needed for the self-preservation of the individual is the highest good. He later held that the human state is constituted by its material sustenance—"Man is what he eats."

After the disappointment of revolutionary hopes in the revolution of 1848 the Hegelian left-wing movement largely dissolved as such.

RIGHT-WING HEGELIANISM

Partly because their views made them unacceptable to the conservative governments which controlled the German universities, the left-wing Hegelians were nonacademic and antiprofessorial. Several young Hegelians had been dismissed from academic posts, and they largely turned to pamphleteering and active social agitation. Those on the right were all professors who expressed themselves with speculative precision and calm in massive scholarly volumes. Yet many were active in politics, and some, like Rosenkranz and Vischer, were influential members of the parliamentary assemblies in Berlin and Frankfurt during the late 1840s. Their politics were generally liberal rather than revolutionary; they were certainly not reactionaries, as some left-wing Hegelians became (for example, Strauss but also, at least in practical result, Bauer and Feuerbach, who opposed any partial reforms which would not usher in a new humanity). The right Hegelians tended to regard the more revolutionary programs of the left as an attempt to impose abstract ideals on the substantial reality of the existing order, an attempt that manifested a disrespect not only for this reality but also for the rational–historical Spirit immanent in it. If the historical dialectic seemed to the right-wing Hegelians to justify the maintenance of the existing order rather than its overthrow, they generally favored constitutional monarchy with a representative legislature, the end of feudalistic oppression in labor relations, and religious, academic, and journalistic freedom. But the results of the revolution of 1848 were almost as disappointing to the liberals as to the revolutionaries, and the active political involvement of the Hegelian right generally abated thereafter.

The effects of criticism, diffusion, and the influence of other philosophical schools left a fairly small circle of important figures, all academicians, who were still self-confessed Hegelians in the mid-1840s. Prominent in this circle were Rosenkranz, Johann Erdmann (1805–1892), Vischer, Rudolf Haym (1821–1901), Eduard Zeller (1814–1908), Michelet, and Kuno Fischer (1824–1907). Each of these men criticized, sometimes very sharply, important aspects of Hegel's system and made original contributions of their own. In systematic thought as in politics they were conservative only in comparison to the left-wing Hegelians. They generally remained disciples of Hegel, however, in the systematic form of their thought; in their resistance to materialism, naturalism, and empiricism; in their metaphysical idealism; in their historical orientation; and in their continuing preoccupation with Hegel's own central themes. Yet there are exceptions to these generalizations—for example, in the treatment of the dialectic of history by Zeller, Fischer, Haym, and Michelet independent of absolute idealist metaphysical presuppositions. Vischer, on the other hand, constructed his massive *Aesthetik* (1846–1857) on an idealistic basis independent of historical development; he no sooner completed this work, moreover, than he repudiated Hegelian idealism altogether. Rosenkranz and Erdmann were the only major figures who continued to defend the main substance of the Hegelian synthesis, with many corrections in detail to be sure, well into the second half of the nineteenth century. Rosenkranz composed substantial works on practically every major field included in Hegel's system. He treated the Hegelian philosophy as the fulfillment of Kantian idealism and of German idealism in general—in fact, as the fullest philosophical projection of the German spirit. His clearest exposition of this thesis appeared in his work

prepared for the centennial of Hegel's birth, in 1869, entitled *Hegel as the National Philosopher of Germany* (abridged English translation by G. Hall, St. Louis, 1874).

Erdmann, like Rosenkranz, produced wide-ranging systematic treatises, but his outstanding contribution was his work in the history of philosophy—notably, his *Outline of the History of Philosophy* in two volumes (Berlin, 1866), to which he added an excellent appendix, *German Philosophy Since Hegel*, in 1870, defending Hegelianism in the course of an unusually full treatment of its historical proliferation and dissolution. In general, the most important achievement of right-wing Hegelianism was probably its distinctively philosophical treatment of the history of philosophy. In addition to Erdmann's work there may be mentioned F. K. A. Schwegler's *Outlines of the History of Philosophy in Epitome* (Stuttgart, 1848; translated by J. Seelye, New York and London, 1856) and *History of Greek Philosophy* (Tübingen, 1859); Michelet's *History of the Last Systems of Philosophy in Germany From Kant to Hegel* (2 vols., Berlin, 1837–1838) and *The History of Mankind in Its Course of Development From 1775 to the Most Recent Times* (2 vols., Berlin, 1859–1860); various studies in Greek philosophy by Zeller; and Fischer's *History of Modern Philosophy* (8 vols., Mannheim and Heidelberg, 1852–1893; Vol. I translated by J. P. Gordy, New York, 1887). Even those who did not share Hegel's view that the history of philosophy reflects the systematic unfolding of the Absolute Spirit nevertheless insisted that this history is no mere adjunct to or preparation for philosophical thinking but part of its essential content. Fischer, for example, understood "spirit" in a humanistic sense, acknowledged no final absolute system, and regarded Hegel primarily as the philosopher of evolution. But in the Preface to the first volume of his celebrated *History* he argued against any separation of constructive philosophy from the history of philosophy. Philosophy is the self-understanding of the human spirit; all understanding of the world is included in man's self-understanding. But because man, unlike a stone, is an essentially historical being, philosophy can approach its proper object only by engagement in its own history. This understanding of the historicity of philosophy directly foreshadowed Wilhelm Dilthey's concept of *Geistesgeschichte* and more recent existentialist anthropology.

OTHER NINETEENTH-CENTURY DEVELOPMENTS

German idealism had already had considerable impact abroad by the 1820s, and as Hegel came to be known as the successor of Kant, Fichte, and Schelling, foreign students came to Berlin in great numbers to hear him. Visiting professors also were influenced by Hegel—for example, Victor Cousin from France, whose close association with Hegel began in 1817, when Hegel was still at Heidelberg.

Northern Europe. The Danish man of letters J. L. Heiberg (1791–1860) introduced Hegelianism into Denmark, where it became the predominant school of thought during the 1830s and 1840s. Heiberg claimed that Hegel had freed him for the vocation of comic dramatist by refining his strong pantheistic bent to the extent that he could take seriously the finite and even farcical aspects of existence in their dialectical relation to the infinite. Other Danes adapted Hegelianism to different purposes. H. L. Martensen (1808–1884), for example, developed an influential Protestant dogmatic. Such Hegelian interpretations of Christianity were the target of Soren Kierkegaard's vigorous polemic against Hegelianism in the 1840s and early 1850s, developed most carefully in his *Concept of Dread* (Copenhagen, 1844) and *Concluding Unscientific Postscript* (Copenhagen, 1846). Although of little immediate influence, these were seminal works in the development of twentieth-century existentialism. They epitomize the ambivalent relationship of existentialism to Hegelianism: Kierkegaard found in Hegelianism the ultimate philosophical expression of what he was protesting against—the point of view of the observer for whom a "system" of reality is possible. Against the standpoint of this observer he set that of the maker of ethical and religious decisions. But in attempting to reflect on the situation of this agent, Kierkegaard was obliged to draw heavily on Hegelian categories and dialectical methods. His existential dialectic is unthinkable apart from his Hegelian background.

Hegelianism also dominated the other northern countries for some decades. An outstanding center of the school was at Kristiania (Oslo) in Norway, devoted particularly to problems in metaphysics and philosophy of religion. M. J. Monrad (1816–1897) was a powerful Hegelian there. In Holland, P. G. van Ghert (died 1852), who was a student of Hegel's during his Jena years and later his close friend and follower, influenced Dutch education as minister of culture. A more important Hegelian was G. J. P. J. Bolland (1854–1922), professor of philosophy at Leiden.

France and Italy. Hegelianism had a substantial impact on French thought in the 1840s. In 1844 two important studies in Hegel's thought appeared—Adolph Ott's *Hegel et la philosophie allemande* and Louis Prevost's *Hegel, exposition de sa doctrine.* The Hegelian left, represented by Marx and Ruge in Paris, also gave a spur to revolutionary sentiment and deeply affected such figures as Proudhon. The Italian Augusto Vera was an enthusiastic academic proponent of Hegelianism in both France and Italy. In France he produced an *Introduction à la philosophie de Hegel* in 1855 and in 1859 a French translation of Hegel's *Logic,* with extensive introduction and commentary. Returning to Italy, Vera helped to make Naples a Hegelian center, meanwhile producing another French translation and commentary, *Philosophie de la nature de Hegel* (1863–1866). The Italian school produced a number of important Hegelian thinkers, including Bertrando Spaventa (1817–1883), Raffaele Mariano (1840–1912), and Pasquale d'Ercole (1831–1917).

Eastern Europe. Hegel was the inheritor of a longstanding eastern European interest in German idealism and, still earlier, in German mysticism. But the students from Russia, Poland, and the Slavic countries who came to Berlin were not only interested in Hegel's religious and metaphysical thought. He also represented to them the philosophical epitome of Westernism and a vision of the nation-state that gave form to their own stirrings toward nationalism (and Pan-Slavism) and Westernization. The eastern Europeans, however, rejected any suggestion that

history had reached its fulfillment in Germanic culture. Count August Cieszkowski (1814–1894) of Poland, for example, in his *Prolegomena to Historiosophy* (Berlin, 1838), argued that Hegel's philosophy of history contained only two essential moments—the world of classical antiquity and the Christian–Germanic world. The unresolved conflicts demanded an age of synthesis, then dawning, which would relate dialectically to the other two as organism to mechanism and chemism, will to feeling and knowledge, the ethical state to law and morality. Cieszkowski was also characteristic of the easterners in giving Hegelianism a strong practical orientation, toward a philosophy of life and action. Speculative reason does indeed carry man beyond mere blind, instinctive action, but the Absolute, the life of freedom, lies beyond theory or contemplation, in fully conscious action. Its ultimate end lies not in theoretical comprehension but in the practical realization of humanity as a family of nations. God stands above the world, as its judge, to whom men are authentically related neither in pictorial representation nor in speculative abstraction but in active intuition (*God and Palingenesis,* Berlin, 1842).

Another Pole, S. F. Trentowski, who lectured in Freiburg during the 1830s and 1840s, also revised the Hegelian system. His educational works in particular had a great influence on his native land. Other prominent figures were Józef Kremer (1806–1877), also Polish, and the Czechs H. J. Hanuš (1812–1869) and Augustin Smetana (1814–1851). An important Russian thinker, I. V. Kireyevski (1806–1856), was closely associated with Hegel even before his Berlin years. Another conservative Russian Hegelian, N. V. Stankevich (1813–1840), was the leader of an influential philosophical circle in Moscow which included Michael Bakunin (1814–1876) and Vissarion Belinski (1811–1848). However, Belinski and Bakunin took a sharp turn to the left, Belinski as a socially radical literary critic, Bakunin finally as an active revolutionary leader. Bakunin was associated with Ruge's circle in Berlin and Paris in the 1840s and later became Marx's bitter rival for the leadership of the First International. Other Russians who developed the social revolutionary implications of the Hegelian dialectic were Alexander Herzen (1812–1870), who spoke of it as "the algebra of revolution," and N. G. Chernyshevski (1828–1889). Such men helped to prepare the Russian soil for Lenin.

America. Hegelian thought played a colorful role in German settlements in the United States during the second half of the nineteenth century. Many of the recent arrivals were literate, liberal, and passionate men, some exiled by the revolutions of 1848. They had been schooled in German idealism and its literary counterparts, and they transferred their disappointed hopes for human, cultural fulfillment in a free society to their new homeland. Native Americans as well as the new immigrants in these German settlements found in Hegel a philosophy of progress and cultural synthesis, practical idealism and openness to novelty and experiment. St. Louis and Cincinnati were the creative centers of Hegelian thought in America.

St. Louis school. The St. Louis school in particular carried the Hegelian theory of the westward movement of the Absolute Spirit to exalted conclusions regarding the destiny of the American frontier. Leaders of the St. Louis school were Henry Conrad Brokmeyer (1826–1906) and William Torrey Harris (1835–1909). Brokmeyer, a German Jewish immigrant, had roamed the United States as a jack-of-all-trades and had lived in the wilderness of Missouri as a hermit. He met Harris, a native New Englander, in St. Louis in 1858, and the two men founded the informal Kant Club; both had come to German idealism by way of New England transcendentalism, but they were already enough committed to Hegel that they saw Kantian studies and transcendentalism as preparation for a proper study of the master. After the Civil War, in which Brokmeyer served as a colonel and raised a German regiment, they founded the St. Louis Philosophical Society. The society studied and discussed Hegelian texts, including an English translation of Hegel's *Science of Logic* on which Brokmeyer worked for years without completing, and published *The Journal of Speculative Philosophy* under Harris' editorship. This distinguished journal published studies that ranged through the whole tradition of classical philosophy, particularly Greek and German, and included translations of German Philosophical works as well as original essays by the leading American thinkers, from the aging transcendentalists to the new wave of pragmatists. Throughout the society's activities there was a consistent effort to interpret the American destiny through Hegelian dialectics. The Civil War, for example, was seen as a tragic necessity, the collision between the abstract right of the South and the abstract morality of the North, out of which a new ethically concrete national consciousness would emerge. St. Louis, as the fulcrum on which North versus South as well as East versus West was balanced, would bring the new order into existence. Recognizing a close relation between politics, education, and culture, the St. Louis circle concentrated in particular on the dialectical analysis of issues within and between these areas. The circle was devoted to action as well as analysis, a number of its members rising to prominence in practical capacities. Brokmeyer, for example, was elected to a term as lieutenant governor of Missouri. Harris devoted himself to educational theory and practice and as U.S. commissioner of education for 17 years exerted great influence on the development of public education in America.

Cincinnati. Cincinnati contained no cohesive Hegelian circle like that in St. Louis, and although the Cincinnati Hegelians were in close communication with the St. Louis circle, their interests and commitments differed. The St. Louis group had little traffic with the Hegelian left and rigorously excluded socialistic radicals from membership. Although by no means religiously orthodox, Harris and Brokmeyer were eloquent foes of all tendencies leading to pantheism, atheism, or materialism. By contrast, August Willich (1810–1878), a prominent Ohioan and editor of the *Cincinnati Republikaner* from 1858 to 1861, was an unabashed left-wing Hegelian who vigorously attacked Christianity on Feuerbachian and Marxist grounds. He had resigned his commission in the Prussian Army and had been active in the revolution of 1848 as president of the Cologne Communist League. He had been a close associate of Marx and Engels and a member of the Communist League during his brief exile in London. He wrote a fa-

vorable review of Marx's *Contribution to the Critique of Political Economy* for the *Cincinnati Republikaner.* Unlike Marx, he insisted on linking socialism closely with the rights of man and republican principles of government and saw the aim of government as the actualization of "humanity" in Feuerbach's sense. But he praised Marx's understanding of the historical dialectic and agreed that economic conditions must provide the soil from which socialism can grow. Willich, however, thought that the road to the future lay in bringing the workers to political power through labor unions. He organized four companies of workers for service in the Civil War, and although he distinguished himself as a major general, he never ceased lecturing the "citizens"—his troops—on socialism.

Willich had been brought to Cincinnati by John Bernard Stallo (1823–1900), his close friend and the most important philosopher among the Cincinnati Hegelians. Like Willich, Stallo was active in politics and an early organizer of the Republican Party. As a political philosopher he attempted to translate Hegel's view of the state into democratic terms. The individuality of the state is based not on a monarch but on the community as a whole, whose will is revealed through the majority vote. For, as Stallo argued in *State Creeds and Their Modern Apostles* (1872), the vote is "a trial of strength" in which the partial claims of each segment of the community are registered and reconciled to the good of the whole. "Take the whole result, and it looks much like the regular outcome of a dialectic process—like the deliberate result of reasoning" (p. 34). Seeing eternal reason in the inner development of the state itself, Stallo argued for the strict secularity of the state, fully separated from the church, and campaigned against Sabbath laws and Bible reading in the public schools. Stallo's most original contributions were in the philosophy of science, but after publication of his early *General Principles of the Philosophy of Nature* (1848) he largely outgrew the direct influence of Hegel in this field.

Deeply influenced by the Hegelian left in theology and a close friend of Stallo and Willich was the pastor of the liberal First Congregational Church from 1856 to 1862, Moncure D. Conway (1832–1907). A Virginian by birth, Conway was trained in German thought and was especially influenced by D. F. Strauss. Throughout his career (later pursued in London and New York, though he remained in touch with Cincinnati) Conway developed a naturalistic, socially liberal philosophy of religion "founded on the rock of natural science" and replacing the supernatural deity with Strauss's "law-governed Cosmos, full of life and reason." On the other side was William Nast (died 1899), "the father of German Methodism" and a scholarly defender of evangelical Christianity in Cincinnati who was editor of *Der christliche Apologete* from 1839 to 1894. Nast, a former roommate of Strauss, was conversant with German thought and in a position to attack Strauss on his own terms. He also blamed godlessness, materialism, and communism for the failure of the German revolution and was a sharp critic of left-wing Hegelian theorists and organizers in Cincinnati, including Willich, Stallo, and Conway.

Great Britain. The influence of Hegelianism in British thought can be dated precisely. It began with the publication of *The Secret of Hegel* by J. H. Stirling in 1865. Hegelianism had previously been excluded from British philosophy by the overwhelming dominance of the native tradition—empiricist, utilitarian, ahistorical, skeptical of metaphysical and theological speculation. To be sure, the novelist George Eliot had translated two important works from the Hegelian left. However, although publications of her translation of Strauss's *The Life of Jesus* (1846) and Feuerbach's *The Essence of Christianity* (1854) were sensational events in the nineteenth-century crisis of faith among British intellectuals, their criticisms of traditional belief were more influential than their Hegelian reconstructions. Hegel's own thought was regarded, even by those who had some acquaintance with it, as the most egregious example of German speculative lunacy. According to J. S. Mill, Hegel "has fairly earned the honour which will probably be awarded him by posterity, of having logically extinguished transcendental metaphysics by a series of *reductiones ad absurdissimum*" (*Examination of Sir William Hamilton's Philosophy*, p. 60). Stirling's *The Secret of Hegel* did not change the minds of thinkers of Mill's persuasion; Mill, in fact, opposed Stirling's appointment to the chair of moral philosophy at the University of Edinburgh in 1868 on the ground that the immature minds of university students should not be exposed to the study of Hegel. But Stirling's knowledgeable and spirited advocacy of Hegel attracted many for whom the native philosophical tradition had become sterile.

Green and Caird. Some gifted thinkers—notably, T. H. Green (1836–1882) and Edward Caird (1835–1908)—had already embarked on the study of Kant and Hegel at the time Stirling's book appeared and soon joined Stirling in a vigorous polemic against the dominant British school. Green in particular, a powerful personality and a constructive thinker in his own right, became the great opponent of Mill at Oxford. Stirling had hailed Hegel as the new Aristotle; what Aristotle had done for ancient Greece, Hegel had done for modern Europe—synthesized all that was of permanent intellectual and spiritual value into a single vision of the whole of things. Green was more typical of Neo-Hegelianism in regarding Hegel as a point of departure for his own constructive thinking. He was very suspicious of the dialectical method and made virtually no use of it himself, nor was his thinking intrinsically oriented to history as Hegel's was. He found in Hegel the key to the completion of the critical philosophy of Kant by which its epistemological, ethical, and religious difficulties could be resolved. If there are no isolated sense impressions in our experience, it is because there are no isolated facts in the world. Our ordering of experience, fallible as it is, is possible only because reality itself is a system of ordered mutual relations and because the existence of this system implies the existence of an eternally complete consciousness, an absolute mind. Green did not, like some of his successors, teach the identity of finite minds in the infinite; he taught that the manifestation of the infinite in the finite constitutes an ontological bond among men. The self is essentially social, and in Green's ethic of self-realization its own good is realized only in relations with others in a community having common laws, customs, and institutions. The eternal self, in which all the possibilities of the finite self are already actualized, is mediated to the finite self through society. Kant's abstract "ought" and ethical commonwealth of humanity were thus to be given a concrete locus in actual social existence. Caird and Stirling also stressed Hegel's continuity with Kant. Hegel was also important for Caird, Stirling, and Green because in him they found the possibility of bridging the gulf between faith and reason by revealing the rational kernel in the mythical and outwardly historical husk of the religious tradition. Caird and his brother John Caird (1820–1898), a theologian, especially devoted themselves to this task.

Neo-Hegelianism. By the time of Green's death there was a flourishing Neo-Hegelian school, whose younger members a year later (1883) published as a manifesto a collection called *Essays in Philosophical Criticism.* Among the contributors were Lord Haldane, J. S. Haldane, Andrew Seth Pringle-Pattison, D. G. Ritchie, Sir Henry Jones, W. R. Sorley, and Bernard Bosanquet, all of whom were important in the movement. The same year F. H. Bradley (1846–1924) published his *Principles of Logic;* his *Ethical Studies* (1876) had preceded, and *Appearance and Reality* (1893) was to follow a decade later. Bradley, an original philosopher of the first rank, was more independent of Hegelianism than Bosanquet, the other outstanding constructive thinker of the group; the two had occasion to criticize each other, but together they were primarily responsible for the fact that the school dominated British philosophy for three decades. J. M. E. McTaggart (1866–1925) also deserves mention as a metaphysician and as a commentator on the works of Hegel.

Some Americans have also been noted for philosophical thinking akin to this movement—most prominently, Josiah Royce of Harvard (1855–1916), whose career was contemporary with it, and Brand Blanshard of Yale, a respected constructive thinker still firmly proceeding against the current streams. These men were professional academic philosophers for the most part, creators of learned, substantial, and original works on classical problems in logic, metaphysics, aesthetics, epistemology, philosophy of religion, politics, and ethics. They were Hegelians only in a tenuous sense; perhaps "absolute idealism" would be a less misleading title for the movement than "Neo-Hegelianism," since they were interested in Hegel primarily as the builder of an idealistic metaphysical system. They probed deeply into the relation of time to eternity, the many to the one, matter to mind, the individual to the collective. Hardly a hint of Hegel's historical dialectic appears in their work, except under a primarily evolutionist aspect. Yet interest in Hegel in English-speaking countries developed through their work; that it so developed has had a good deal to do with the one-sidedness and, sometimes, distortion in the understanding of Hegel in England and the United States.

British Neo-Hegelianism was eclipsed almost as abruptly as it had appeared. The British empiricist tradition reasserted itself in new forms around the turn of the twentieth century. G. E. Moore and Bertrand Russell led the attack, primarily against Bradley but more broadly against the basic methods and presuppositions of Neo-Hegelianism. William James and John Dewey in America also launched a new direction—empirical, pragmatic, and pluralistic. By the start of World War I the complexion of Anglo-American thought had changed dramatically. The process was doubtless accelerated by the widespread tendency to identify Prussian statism with Hegelian political theory. In the dedication to *The Metaphysical Theory of the State* (1918), directed primarily against Hegel and Bosanquet, L. T. Hobhouse declared: "In the bombing of London I had just witnessed the visible and tangible outcome of a false and wicked doctrine, the foundations of which lay, as I believe, in the book before me [Hegel's *Phenomenology*]." In what Hobhouse took to be its "theory of the God-state all that I had witnessed lay implicit." Such caricatures were protested, but in any case the future lay with logical empiricism and linguistic analysis.

TWENTIETH-CENTURY HEGELIANISM

Hegel had a more pervasive but more diffuse impact on the twentieth century than on the nineteenth. Hegelian ideas and methods have profoundly affected movements as diverse as Marxism–Leninism, pragmatism, and existentialism, but these movements have also included Hegel's sharpest modern critics, and the Hegelian features have in each case been reshaped by other influences and by original developments. The figure who has so deeply affected twentieth-century thought is, so to speak, a new Hegel. Hegel's many-sidedness has always led to his work's being put to radically different uses. Royce, for example, writing in 1885, spoke of "two Hegels: one the uncompromising idealist, with his general and fruitful insistence upon the great fundamental truths of idealism; the other the technical Hegel of the *Logic*, whose dialectic method seems destined to remain, not a philosophy, but the idea of a philosophy" (Preface to *The Religious Aspect of Philosophy*). For Royce the living Hegel was clearly the former. Some hint of the change that has taken place is revealed by comparing the comment of another American, William Barrett, from the Foreword to *What Is Existentialism?* (1964). Barrett also speaks of two Hegels—"the last audacious representative of classical rationalism, and the first pioneer of a new historical mode of thought." In his treatment of Spirit, Hegel "immerses man within history with a completeness beyond any previous thinker." It is only a short step "from this Hegelian insistence on the essentially historical character of the human spirit to the existentialist slogan: 'Man has no nature, but only a history.'" From this point of view the dialectic is no arbitrary or fruitless technical exercise but an attempt to understand historical existence as it actually presents itself in its concreteness, its tensions and conflicts, its continual novelty.

German Neo-Hegelianism. There have been two major Neo-Hegelian movements besides the British—the German and the Italian. The Hegel renaissance in Germany began around the turn of the century; during the preceding decades Hegel's influence was so dead in his homeland that Erdmann could describe himself in 1870 as "the last of the Mohicans." This renaissance was given impetus from an unexpected quarter, the school of Wilhelm Dilthey (1833–1911), whose monograph *Der junge Hegel* (1905) helped to cast Hegel's later work into a new light more congenial to Dilthey's "philosophy of life." By rejecting

Hegel's system as such, Dilthey's school brought to light the relativistic, positive, irrational moments in his thought. At the same time the Neo-Kantian school was led to Hegel, discovering in the dialectic and philosophy of Spirit keys to the unity of classical German philosophy. Among figures prominent in this Hegel renaissance were Wilhelm Windelband (1848–1915), Hermann Cohen (1842–1918), Paul Natorp (1854–1924), Ernst Troeltsch (1865–1923), Georg Lasson (1862–1932), who edited the modern critical edition of Hegel's works, Ernst Cassirer (1874–1945), Nicolai Hartmann (1882–1950), Theodor Haering (born 1884), Hermann Glockner (born 1896), and Richard Kroner (born 1884).

Italian Neo-Hegelianism. Italian Neo-Hegelianism had a still more historicist orientation than the German. Benedetto Croce (1866–1952) and Giovanni Gentile (1875–1944) were its leading representatives. Gentile even offered a rationale for the fascist state on the basis of the brute givenness of political fact, beyond which there was no court of appeal. By contrast with Nazi theorists, whose racist ideology of blood and soil led them explicitly to reject the Hegelian view of the ethical state, Italian fascists were happy to accept Gentile's "Hegelian" justification. Croce, a passionate antifascist, broke with Gentile on this issue. A prolific and original writer, Croce has had a wide influence in aesthetics and philosophy of history. His friend, the Englishman R. G. Collingwood (1889–1943), exhibited a close affinity with the thought of Croce, particularly in his influential work *The Idea of History* (1946).

Recent Hegelian studies. Since World War II there has been a torrent of Hegel scholarship in eastern Europe (see especially the works of Ernst Bloch and Georg Lukács) and in France, Germany, and the United States. The Hegelian insight that opposing views become reconciled in the subsequent history of thought has been illustrated again. Just as an earlier generation discovered the essential affinity of Kant and Hegel, so now much of the interest in Hegel has developed among Marxists, on the one hand, and, on the other, among existentialists and phenomenologists, particularly of the school of Heidegger. Even some Thomists and linguistic analysts have shown a recent interest in Hegelian thought.

Bibliography

Easton, Loyd D., "German Philosophy in Nineteenth-century Cincinnati—Stallo, Conway, Nast and Willich." *Historical and Philosophical Society of Ohio Bulletin*, Vol. 20, No. 1 (1962), 15–28.

Easton, Loyd D., "Hegelianism in Nineteenth-century Ohio." *Journal of the History of Ideas*, Vol. 23, No. 3 (1962), 355–378.

Erdmann, Johann E., *A History of Philosophy*, Vol. III, *German Philosophy Since Hegel*, translated by W. S. Hough. London and New York, 1890.

Haldar, Hiralal, *Neo-Hegelianism*. London, 1927. A survey of the British school.

Hook, Sidney, *From Hegel to Marx: Studies in the Intellectual Development of Karl Marx*. New York, 1950.

Jakowenko, Boris, *Ein Beitrag zur Geschichte des Hegelianismus in Russland*. Prague, 1934.

Kline, George L., "Some Recent Reinterpretations of Hegel's Philosophy." *The Monist*, Vol. 48, No. 1 (1964). This entire issue of *The Monist* is on the general topic "Hegel Today."

Lasson, Georg, *Was heisst Hegelianismus?* Berlin, 1916.

Levy, Heinrich, *Die Hegel-Renaissance in der deutschen Philosophie.* Charlottenburg, Germany, 1927.

Löwith, Karl, *Von Hegel zu Nietzsche.* 4th ed. Stuttgart, 1958. Translated by David E. Green as *From Hegel to Nietzsche.* New York, 1964.

Löwith, Karl, ed., *Die Hegelsche Linke.* Stuttgart and Bad Cannstatt, 1962.

Lübbe, Hermann, ed., *Die Hegelsche Rechte.* Stuttgart and Bad Cannstatt, 1962.

Lukács, Georg, *Die Zerstörung der Vernunft.* Berlin, 1954.

Marcuse, Herbert, *Reason and Revolution: Hegel and the Rise of Social Theory,* 2d ed. New York, 1954.

Moog, Willy, *Hegel und die Hegelsche Schule.* Munich, 1930.

Pochmann, Henry A., *German Culture in America: Philosophical and Literary Influences 1600–1900.* Madison, Wis., 1957. St. Louis movement, pp. 257–294.

Tschiżewskij, Dmitrij, ed., *Hegel bei den Slaven.* 2d ed. Bad Homburg, 1961. Essays on Hegelianism in Russia, Poland, Czechoslovakia, and the Balkans.

STEPHEN D. CRITES

HEIDEGGER, MARTIN, German philosopher, is widely considered the central figure in contemporary existentialist thought. According to Heidegger, it is the nature, the vocation of man, to ask the all-important question, What is it, to be? And yet we fail to ask it, and it is our nature equally, our responsibility and our guilt, that we fail to do so. To summon us to our vocation, to warn us of our failure, has been, he avows, his single aim. Heidegger's lectures on the "law of sufficient reason" (*Der Satz vom Grund,* 1957) conclude with the exhortation, "Does not the essence of man, does not his belonging to Being, does not the essence of Being itself remain ever yet and ever more overwhelmingly what befits thought? . . . That is the question. That is the world question of thought. Its answer will decide what becomes of the earth and of the existence of man on this earth." On this same note, thirty years earlier, he had opened his greatest and most influential work, *Sein und Zeit* (*Being and Time*): "Do we have an answer today to the question, what we really mean by the word "being" [*seiend*]? By no means, and so it behooves us to pose anew the question of the sense of Being [*die Frage nach dem Sinn von Sein*]."

Born in 1889 in Baden, Heidegger became *Privatdozent* at the University of Freiburg in 1915, professor at Marburg in 1923, and professor at Freiburg in 1928. As a student at Freiburg he had been trained in the phenomenological method of Edmund Husserl; *Being and Time,* first published as a volume of the *Jahrbuch für Philosophie und phänomenologische Forschung,* was dedicated to Husserl. In 1933 Heidegger became the first National Socialist rector of the University of Freiburg, and in a public lecture, "Role of the University in the New Reich," celebrated the advent of a new and glorious Germany. During this time he publicly renounced any allegiance to Husserl, but in at least one recent work he appears to have reinstated him. Whatever his particular politics, however (and despite the unquestioned events of 1933, these have been a matter of some dispute), a strand of extreme nationalism certainly runs through his work. Holding as he does a mystical view of language, he subscribes with zeal to the widespread opinion that philosophizing is possible, if not only in German, then only in German and Greek. In a work published as late as 1953, the *Einführung in die Metaphysik* (*Intro-*

duction to Metaphysics), he summons his people as the people of the center, caught in the giant pincers between those two barbarian mass societies, America and Russia, to renew, as they alone can, the great "beginning" of Western thought—to save man fron nihilism and gadgetry, and Being itself from the "mist and vapor" man's destiny has made of it.

The significance of Heidegger's thought, however, cannot be assessed solely, or even principally, in terms of his politics or national enthusiasm; his influence, particularly the influence of *Being and Time,* ranges as far as the theology of Rudolf Bultmann and Paul Tillich and the extensive movement of existential psychoanalysis in which, for example, the Swiss psychiatrist Ludwig Binswanger was a pioneer. This article will summarize the principal arguments of *Being and Time* and describe the central theme of Heidegger's later work. It will then compare the earlier and later publications.

"Being and Time": Part One. *Being and Time,* though directed, like all of Heidegger's thought, to the Quest for Being, consists principally of a massive analysis, in the phenomenological tradition, of man—*Dasein,* or human being. Since it is man who alone among beings seeks Being, this is the necessary preliminary to the search for Being itself. Part One describes man's inauthentic or everyday existence. Human being, Heidegger finds, displays three fundamental aspects, all, however, constituting one internally unified structure. These aspects are facticity, existentiality, and forfeiture (*Verfallen*).

Facticity. Facticity means that human being is always already in a world—a world into which, beyond its willing, it has been cast (*geworfen*). "World" in this instance is not used in the sense of the immense, indefinitely extended cosmos of astrophysics, but rather in the sense in which one speaks of the "world of sports" (a common sphere of activity or interest), the "world of Shakespeare" (the time and the society which affects and is affected by a personality), or most typically perhaps, of two people as "worlds apart" (the mental universe, the perspective through which one's physical, geographical, and historical environment becomes one's very own). I am always already in a world, in the sense in which my world is *my* world: it could no more be a world without me than I could be myself without it. Heidegger's concept of world, or of things-in-the-world, has sometimes been compared with that of John Dewey. Certainly, in its interpretation of objects, Heidegger's theory is markedly pragmatic. Things are for him no Cartesian *res extensae,* existing independently of us; they are "stuff" (*Zeug*) for "use" (*Gebrauch*), which are at "hand" (*zuhanden*) for our "handling" (*hantieren*). For Heidegger, as for Bergson, man is a maker, *Homo faber,* before he is *Homo sapiens*: it is materials, tools, opportunities, by which he finds himself surrounded. Yet this is only to say that Heidegger, Dewey, and Bergson all participate in a twentieth-century revolt against the simple world picture of Descartes or Newton. Within this common trend, Heidegger's concept of facticity, in its deeper sense, points in a direction different from Dewey's. It is not the New World buoyancy of pragmatism, able to remake our lives by the sheer force of common sense, that supports it, but a deeply European sense of historical dependence and entanglement. I am cast into a world not of my making, although it is mine to appropriate and assimilate, freely, yet within the inescapable limits of contingency.

Existentiality. The act of appropriation, of making my world mine, constitutes the second of the three inseparable characteristics of human being: existentiality, or transcendence. The term "existentiality" refers again, not to existence in the sense in which sticks and stones exist, but to the inner personal existence for the designation of which it has become, through Kierkegaard, a quasi-technical term. Human being exists as anticipation of its own possibilities: it exists in advance of itself and grasps its situation as challenge to its own power of becoming what it may, rather than being what it must be. Human being is always reaching out beyond itself; its very being consists in aiming at what it is not yet. Yet such projection of itself never outruns the boundaries of the world it has been given: it is projection *in* and *of* and *with* the world. Existentiality is the anticipation of human being by itself and therewith of its world: it is understanding of the world. Once more, self and world are inseparable.

Forfeiture. In its own self-projection and self-transcendence, then, human being at once understands its world and becomes itself. Yet if the world is material for our creative energy, it is also the agent by which we are seduced from the essential drive to understand and to create. Human being is not only *in* the world and shapes its world; in this creative endeavor it becomes forfeit to the world. Forfeiture, the third fundamental attribute of human being, means "ontologically" that we forget "Being" for particular beings. In a human sense, it means the scattering of the essential forward drive through attention to the distracting and disturbing cares of everyday and of the things and people that surround us everyday. Thus, inevitably and continuously, the forward driving "I" is sacrificed to the persistent and pressing "they." To the question "Who is human being?" we must answer, "The indifferent and anonymous crowd—*das Man.*" Human being in its everyday mode is promiscuously public; it is life with others and for others in alienation from the central task of becoming itself.

Human being. What, then, is the upshot of this preliminary analysis? Its most important theme is the double tension which it describes as constituting human being. Man is determined yet free, free yet enslaved. If I am here, now, what heredity and environment have made me, so are these, conversely, what *I* make of them. But that is not all. This driving, integral, all-essential I is hidden, almost all my life, by the daily round, the daily crises, the daily moods, which could not add up to an I, to a life, to a person, unless they were somehow bound to the center they circumnavigate, unless they expressed somehow the very being they betray. Spinoza, Leibniz, and Kant all have described man as bound yet free. But it is the double nature of this bondage which Heidegger has shown. Freedom lives in the tension of history, in the challenge of my situation, my body, my family, my city, my country. But freedom lives equally in the tension of the unhistorical, the purely present—the passing mood, the gossiping neighbor, the chores of office or kitchen, the escape of travel or television, the flight of the self from itself.

"Being and Time": Part Two. Against the scattering of everyday or inauthentic existence, the second part of *Being and Time* seeks to single out an authentic being. It is here that Heidegger develops his concept of existential or historical time. This somewhat tortuous argument can be elucidated by considering three concepts developed in the course of it: dread, conscience, and destiny.

Dread. We have seen that human being is distracted in the petty concerns of everyday life. The question arises, Is there any emergence from forfeiture? If the self is in flight from itself, can it in any way turn back to itself, facing its own being with honesty and directness? This, as Heidegger puts it, is equivalent to the question, Is there any wholeness of human being—any way to grasp it entirely rather than in stray and scattered bits? The answer is found through looking at the moods, the states of mind, that mark the momentary condition of the individual. There *is* one mood which is unique, which does recall human being from self-betrayal to self-knowledge; that mood is dread. Other moods and passions have everyday objects *in* the world; dread (*Angst*) has no such nameable, isolated object. It is a sense of the loss of objects, of nothingness, which lays hold of me when I face, not this or that thing or person, but the whole structure of being-in-the-world itself. For when I see my life, which is my world, in its entirety, I see its ending, death. Dread is of life as a whole—that is, of death as end, ground, and boundary of life. Life in its entirety is life facing death. Of all moods, dread only brings this knowledge, lifts human being out of its scurrying self-forgetfulness to the vision of its wholeness—the knowledge of itself as "being-to-death." Dread alone brings to human being its proper freedom, transforms the alien absurdities of stubborn fact into an essential possibility of being itself, in Heidegger's words, "set free from the illusions of the 'they,'" in passionate, self-assured, anxious freedom to death" (*Sein und Zeit*, p. 266).

Human being, then, in its totality, its authentic being, is being-to-death. Heidegger has reached this conclusion, however, not simply by looking at dread as a uniquely revealing mood, but at the same time by an abstract argument—by discovering being-to-death as, in his words, an "ontological possibility." There are two sides to the argument, which so far point to the same conclusion. If human being is to be a unity, it can be so only as a whole, that is, in relation to its ending, death. If human being is to rise from forfeiture to authenticity, it can do so only in isolation from the seductive "they." Only death, or the relation to death, brings such isolation, for my death is the only event in my life, Heidegger says, which is uniquely mine: it is *eigentlich* ("authentic") because it is *eigen* ("my own").

Conscience. Now there arises the question of whether any phenomenon in human existence actually realizes this possibility—that is, whether this "ontological" conclusion is fulfilled in fact. Heidegger's answer is that there is such a phenomenon—namely, conscience. (Dread, presumably, is the mood in which human being is open to the voice of conscience, and conscience itself is the fuller structure which is expressed in and through dread.) Conscience exemplifies in its occurrence all three aspects of human being. It is the voice by which human being, speaking in secrecy and silence, calls itself out of the distraction of self-forgetfulness to the lonely avowal of its own responsibility for being itself. Thus conscience is the call of the self to itself, out of forfeiture to authenticity. Such an avowal, however, takes place only through the acknowledgment that this self which I ought to become is *given* me—that I am thrown into a world not of my choosing and that precisely this contingent character of my situation *is*, despite myself, the self I have the task of choosing.

Thus, in conscience the self bids itself transcend the facticity which it yet inalienably is. The phenomenon of conscience, in other words, reveals once more the double tension which appeared earlier to be characteristic of human being. It challenges human being to escape from enslavement into freedom and by the same act to transform historical necessity into resolution. This tension is on each side a lack. I never escape forfeiture; facticity is inalienably the alien ground of my existence. On each side it is equally an obligation. Conscience tells me I *ought* resolutely to face my own inner capability instead of forgetting myself in this and that. I *ought* to make my situation vitally mine, rather that let it inflict itself upon me. But despite—or in—this "ought," the lack persists: the self owes to itself a debt it cannot discharge. And yet the very recognition of this debt, of this "not," *is* its resolve to become itself. In recognizing itself as essentially in debt, it knows itself, not in distraction, but in its inmost capability. It knows itself as guilty, for the German *Schuld* carries what for us are two meanings—debt or obligation in the legal sense and guilt in the full stigmatizing sense of the word. Heidegger insists, however, that this assertion has nothing to do, one way or another, with the theological concept of sin; it is, he insists, the outcome of a purely phenomenological analysis of human being as such. And it is certainly very different, in its egocentricity, from the traditional ethical concept.

Destiny. But what of the other thread of the argument? How does human being become a whole? It is here, finally, that the meaning and structure of existential time emerge and that human being is found to be primarily historical—that is, to possess a destiny. What is existential time? In the first place, it is not just time, but my time; it is the span of my life. Time in this sense is the "ontological" ground of human being, what human being most truly and deeply *is*. Second, the basic tense of existential time is future. It moves not from past through present to future, but out of the future through the past to the present. Reaching out to the future, it turns back to assimilate the past which has made the present. Third, it is finite. My time will be finished. If I face the future, *that* is the ultimate future I have to face. So time future must be time finite: human being, as time, is being to death. But there is still another point. Personal time is finite in two directions: if it will end, it also had a beginning. In looking forward to its end, in seeing as an entirety the span of its life, human being assumes also an essential relation, a relation of understanding and assimilation, to its beginning. Turning back from the anticipation of its own nonbeing—that is, from the face of death—it also faces freely, as its own, the history that has been given it by its beginning—given it not *by* its own responsibility, but nevertheless *for* its own responsibility.

True responsibility is grounded in the structure of personal time. Once we see human being as time, we see conscience, the voice which calls human being to its freedom, as rooted in time and the finitude of time—in being-to-death. And guilt, the burden which conscience shows human being it must bear, also has the same root: it is the sense of the discrepancy between the given past and the whole I ought to, but never can, create of it.

It is in the same context, finally, that we discover destiny. In this relation to future and past, to death and birth, the present itself is raised out of forfeiture to an authentic present, which *is* my destiny—that is, to play freely, in my time and for my time, the role into which, by no choice of mine, I have been cast; to play for no audience and no applause, but solely for the sake of the performance itself which I am and beyond which I am nothing. Destiny is possible, Heidegger says, only when "in the Being of a being death, guilt, conscience, freedom and finitude dwell together at its very source." Only such a being is "properly historical"; only such a being has a destiny. For not everyone has a destiny: destiny is a pattern achieved only by the rare individual who in dread and silence has come face to face with his own nothingness and has shaped his life in the light, or the darkness, of that encounter.

To live in the mode of destiny, Heidegger says, is to live historically. But when we come to history, surely we have passed beyond the horizon of the single, death-dreading individual. Indeed, Heidegger does distinguish between *Schicksal,* individual destiny, and *Geschick,* a collective destiny "by which we understand the story of human being in togetherness with others" (*Sein und Zeit,* p. 386). Moreover, he pays tribute to the historical theories of Wilhelm Dilthey, Paul Yorck von Wartenburg, and Nietzsche, even to the point of declaring that the whole aim of his work was to subserve Yorck's distinction between the "historic" and the merely "ontic." Yet in *Being and Time* as a whole, any comprehensive conception of history, of the rootedness of the single person among and along with his contemporaries, seems quite lacking. The dominant theme of *Being and Time* remains the vision of the lonely will driven by dread to face the prospect of its own dissolution, in retrospect its guilt, and yet to realize in this twin terror its proper freedom.

Heidegger's later work. Although it is on the "existential" analysis of *Being and Time* that Heidegger's influence chiefly depends, he himself is an ontologist. He has, on his own account, but one theme—the quest for Being. Within this one search, *Being and Time* was only trying, in the words of a disciple, Max Müller, "to clear a space in order to face the infinite question of Being with the finite powers of man" (*Existenzphilosophie im geistigen Leben der Gegenwart,* p. 52). If we are to assess Heidegger's philosophy in general, therefore, we must look at some of the themes characteristic of his later publications and connected with this broader search.

History. "History" recurs here, but with a peculiar metaphysical slant. Thus, for example, in the *Introduction to Metaphysics,* when Heidegger asks, "How is it with Being?" he finds this question rooted in the intellectual history of the West, and in particular, in the phenomenon of nihilism. When we try to look Being in the face, to consider what it is that is, we can find nothing to say. Being, as distinct from any particular thing, is almost nothing. Nietzsche, who expressed tragically the crisis of our time, called it a haze, and its designation, he said, was "only the name for a great error." Can this be so? Or is it we ourselves, Heidegger asks, that are at fault: Is it our history in which the "nothingness" of Being lies? Being, he argues, has come to seem as nothing because we have "fallen out of Being"—we have lost the "nearness and shelter of Being." Running foolishly after this thing and that, we have betrayed our true vocation, which is to seek the Ground through which all things are—the Holy, Being itself. This is our history and at the same time our forgetfulness of history. We live in a world darkened by our forgetfulness of what we are and of what Being is. And it is the history of Being, too, that we should so betray it and ourselves.

"Darkening of the world." The "darkening of the world" is Heidegger's constant theme. So, for example, in *Holzwege* ("Woodpaths," 1950), he tells us that we live in the age of research, of the planned, systematic coordination of intellectual tasks. And what sort of tasks can be planned and coordinated? Neat, limited, manageable tasks—tasks, primarily, that demand inventiveness rather than understanding, tasks for engineering know-how rather than theoretical insight. Heidegger draws no line between pure and applied science. Science for him is research, and research is a procedure for solving well-packaged problems. Such problems are, in general, those of manufacture, of inventing new and better gadgets. According to Heidegger, *das Herstellbare,* the collection of gadgets, is what we are after; that is what specialization, the rigid departmental structure of expertise in our society, amounts to. And all this vast proliferation of technical skills nevertheless has its inner unity—that is, its historical and metaphysical unity. It *had* to happen this way. It had to happen this way *because* we are fallen out of Being. We are more concerned with beings, from genes to space ships, than with our true calling, which is to be shepherds and watchers of Being. So it is that we are lost, and Being itself has become a haze and an error—nothing.

Greek philosophy. Heidegger is, of course, by no means alone in his critique of our "needy time." What distinguishes his view of modern decadence, however, is the notion (to which he returns again and again) that the whole story has already been told, essentially, in Greek, and even in pre-Socratic, philosophy. For him, a reflective reaffirmation of liberalism would be meaningless: the liberal conception of a free society, with its "culture," its "values," its "ideals," is a helpless gesturing, a last foolish gasp before the total negativity of Marxism engulfs us. And an older authoritarianism would be just as impotent. The damage was done completely very long ago. As Nietzsche saw, Christianity, too, was at its very start doomed not to redeem but to destroy. What happened, then, between the time of Parmenides and Aristotle? Much of Heidegger's answer is tied to a play on Greek and German phrases (his fantasies in translation and etymology are notorious), but the gist of it is, again, the loss of Being. One section of the *Introduction to Metaphysics* is called "Being and Thought," a dichotomy, Heidegger explains, which did not

exist for the first and greatest thinkers of the West. For Parmenides, *einai* (Being) and *noein* (Thought), which Heidegger calls *Vernehmen* (in a very general sense, "awareness"), were one. Human existence, according to Heidegger, was rooted in this oneness. Man was deep in Being and drew his life from the appearance of Being—which was truly appearance, not illusion—as well as from the becoming of Being, which again was at one with Being, not the mere flux which the misinterpretation of Heraclitus has led us to think it was. Logos, which is the same as Being, held man, rooted and at home. But by the time of Aristotle, man had broken loose from this first great anchorage and floated out upon that tide of nihilism on which we are still adrift. Man had become "a rational animal," the animal that *"has"* logos," can calculate, knows its way about—the most successful animal, but the animal, torn from its ground in Being, whose very being is *unheimlich,* uncanny, literally "unhomely," "not-at-home." Heidegger's theory of truth tells the same story. For the pre-Socratics truth was *aletheia,* the unhiddenness of being. By the time of Aristotle truth had become a property of propositions—their "correspondence" with "facts." And this loosening of truth from Being led directly to nihilism and to Nietzsche's dictum that Being is a "haze."

Poetry and language. It is Heidegger's mission to recall us from this nihilistic destiny—or at least to recall those of his German-speaking fellows who will heed his call. His philosophical appeal to poetry, which is another recurrent theme in his work, has the same root. Language, in Heidegger's use, is magical—hence the preponderance of wordplay in his argument. But language is magical because, as he says, "Language is not simply one tool which man possesses along with many others; it is only language that makes possible our standing within openness to what is" (*Erläuterung zu Hölderlins Dichtung,* p. 35). This does not hold, to be sure, of our trivial gossip or of our hard and empty scientific or pseudoscientific terminology. Such talk, like the "culture" it expresses, has lost its hold on Being. It is rootless, like the *Massenmensch* (mass-man) whose complacent mediocrity it conveys. But in its true origin language is different: in its true origin language is poetry, and poetry is "the primal language of an historical people" in which it "founds Being." And conversely, therefore, the great poets are the ones who can restore language to its primal power.

Thus, Heidegger grounds his own ontological grounding of language—language conceived as the house of Being, even the foundation of Being—in the interpretation of such lines of Hölderlin as *dichterisch wohnet der Mensch* ("man dwells poetically") or *seit ein Gespräch wir sind* ("since we are discourse"). Our nihilistic destiny, as well as our hope of redemption, is tied to the question "Why be a poet in a needy time?" (*Wozu Dichter in dürftiger Zeit?*). And the appeal to poetry is also an appeal to prophecy: "The poet names the Holy. The poet speaks Being." It is the poet, Heidegger says in his essay on Rilke, "Woodpaths," who brings a trace of the vanished gods into the cosmic night. Man as such, as Nietzsche said, is a venture. The poets are those who venture more; they are "the more daring" who are on "the track of the holy" (*die Spur des Heiligen*)—that which "heals" and is at the same time "whole." They are *auf der Spur zum Heilen*—"on the track to healing," which is equivalent to wholeness. Through them we may hope, perhaps, to recover that "illumination of Being" from which we have so long gone astray. And it is first and foremost through Hölderlin, the poet who himself felt so keenly the tie with classical antiquity, that we may sense something of the god who is "near yet hard to grasp"—a god remote from theology or piety or any of the ordinary avenues of religious custom or feeling, but who presides over that long-lost Being of which the "quest for Being" is in search.

Earlier and later works compared. Every great thinker, Heidegger declared, thinks but one thought, and one cannot help believing that he means this maxim to apply to himself. In his devotion to the search for Being, Heidegger and his disciples constantly tell us, his lifework constitutes a seamless whole. Yet there are striking differences between *Being and Time* and the long list of titles that followed it. First of all, there is a marked contrast in style. The earlier book is written as though with a sledge hammer: repetitive though its blows are, they are heavy, and the syntax is notoriously twisted and obscure. The later works flow much more easily; the attacks on our decadence pour out in practiced periods. Even the word magic—though puns are Heidegger's stock in trade from start to finish—has a new slickness that results from a kind of special Heideggerian technique (as he himself derisively remarked), so that one almost comes to anticipate such (untranslatable) neologisms as *Gestell* (literally, "frame"), or *Geviert* ("foursome"), or puns like that on *heilig* ("holy") and *heilen* ("to heal"). With this smoother technique, the proportion of wordplay to truth seems likewise to have altered: for *Being and Time,* for all its absurdities, has a core of truth. We can support this very general statement by observing what, despite the avowed harmony of Heidegger's earlier conceptions, has happened to some of them in his later works, particularly in the most imposing and systematic of these, the *Introduction to Metaphysics.* Three such concepts—nothingness, history, and world—will be examined here.

Nothingness. In *Being and Time* we have seen the role played by dread and by its object, which is nothing. It is the sharp edge of the conception of Being to death, of man facing nothingness, that gives drive and aim to the whole book. Dread—the dread of our own nonbeing—is the bridge from forfeiture to authenticity, the support of conscience and resolve. What makes me human and gives form and design to my truly, inwardly finite life is not the colorless abstract consciousness of Locke or Leibniz, but the dramatic, nauseating awareness of my impending nonexistence. In the *Introduction to Metaphysics,* Heidegger is careful to maintain this concept of the dread of death in a reduced and minimal role. He finds this dread (by a beautifully simple mistranslation) in Sophocles' *Antigone:* man who "comes resourceless to nothing" is said to "come, resourceless, to—Nothing." That death vanquishes man, Sophocles does indeed say; but the equating of death with the Heideggerian "nothing" is a purely Heideggerian insertion. Apart from this passage, moreover, the Nothingness of *Being and Time* plays very little part in the later publications. In the later works, however, "Nothing" is

important in two other and very different senses, to which Heidegger moves without excuse or argument as if they *were* the "nothing" of *Being and Time*. One is the conception of nihilism—that is, the conception of the forgetfulness of Being in which we live. This, it is true, was the formal definition of *Verfallen*, or forfeiture, which meant forgetting Being for beings; and to this extent there is, once more, a formal unity between the earlier and later works. Yet it was the human, not the intended, ontological meaning that was significant in *Being and Time*. And besides, if we consider more closely the unifying formal definition, we can see how confused the situation is. Nihilism is a kind of general forfeiture, the decline (*Verfall*) of the West, the nothingness of forgetting Being. But dread is the mood which awakens human being to conscience, to resolve, to authenticity. To face nothingness, to be "in nothing," before nothing, is to overcome the forgetfulness of Being—that is, to overcome nihilism. The "nothing" of dread, therefore, is the very opposite of that nothingness, or alienation from Being, which Nietzsche, according to Heidegger, tragically personified. Again, there is ostensibly a bridge between the two conceptions: for Being itself, we are told, must be held down into Nothingness, it must appear as nothing, in order to be.

Thus, Heidegger puts the question of Being in the form, "Why is there anything at all and not rather nothing?" And this second new meaning of nothingness may then be said to be the ontological offshoot of dread, since, like human being, Being itself must confront nothing. So it is that the neologistic catch phrase of *What Is Metaphysics?*, *Das Nichts nichtet* ("Nothing nots"), appears as a true dictum of ontology. But once more, this formal unification removes the human meaning, the truth, of the concept of dread, and at the same time makes nonsense of the historical theory of nihilism. For if Being must be held down into nothing, then those who live in "nothing" are those who live truly in Being. They are not, after all, the lost souls, but the saved.

In short, we are presented here with a purely sophistical intermingling of three concepts. First, there is the concept of the dread of death, which Heidegger had made distinguished use of in *Being and Time*. Second, there is the concept of nihilism, about which Heidegger indeed has something to say, but which has been treated with more accuracy and cogency by other writers. And third, there is the concept of Nothing in union with Being, which again might be a meaningful conception, as it almost miraculously becomes when it is translated into theological terms by Paul Tillich or Rudolf Bultmann. Heidegger himself, however, gives it no such basis in reason or worship. The concept appears, rather, as a device designed to let him move, without seeming to move, from the human concept of dread to the ontological horizon of pure Being.

History. Heidegger was acclaimed as a prophet of *Geschichtlichkeit* ("historicity") and as one who carried on the message of Dilthey concerning the unique and living nature of history. Yet, as has been indicated, he failed to show how the historical character of the individual's life bears on the broader problems of the history of nations. His *Geschichtlichkeit* remains that of the individual person; his *Geschick* (fitness), the destiny of peoples, is tied to *Geschichtlichkeit* by a mere pun, not by any solid argument. In this regard, *Being and Time* leaves its reader with an open question, the answer to which we may search the later works in vain. "History" is omnipresent, yet its meaning, like that of dread, has lost its old force and gained nothing new to take its place. The concept occurs in three different contexts, all of which are exemplified in the *Introduction.*

First, at the farthest remove from the conception of given, contingent, personal history, there is the history of Being. In itself, this seems to be an empty conception. Second, insofar as the phrase "history of Being" acquires content, it becomes history in a different sense, or at least in a different context. It becomes the story not of Being, but of our understanding of Being. This, of course, is the history of Greek philosophy as Heidegger tells it. What sort of "history" is this? It starts, reasonably enough, from Heidegger's objection to the methods of nineteenth-century *Geistesgeschichte* (intellectual history), which made of Parmenides a "materialist" or an "idealist," or of Anaximander, with his *dikē* and *adikia,* a solid Christian moralist. It is true that this account of pre-Socratic thought was narrow and superficial. But if historians are often dry and foolish that does not justify our throwing away all sober canons of scholarship and reading our own thoughts into ancient texts. To mention but one example, Heidegger's exposition of Being as *Ständigkeit* ("permanency") is full of inferences from the verb "to stand" (*stehen*), "stance or attitude" (*Stand*), and so forth, which are matters of German linguistics entirely unrelated to the Greek words *einai* or *ousia.* Once he gives this exposition of Being, moreover, Heidegger can then proceed to identify *ousia* (being or entity), now understood as *Ständigkeit,* with *physis* (nature or growth), through the fortunate circumstance that "originate" or "come into being" in German is *ent stehen.* This is again a play on the German root, since the Greek carries no connotation of "standing." Heidegger's rhetoric about perspectives notwithstanding, such illegitimate procedures must surely be taken as the mark of an unhistorical approach. In the broader sweep of Heidegger's history of the West, it is also strikingly unhistorical and antihistorical, as other critics have rightly shown, to make no distinction between ancient and modern—to write as if the whole story of the Western mind had been finished by the time of Aristotle and as if neither Rome nor Christianity had played any substantive part in our tradition. Nor is it the mark of a just historical sense to equate the spiritual history of the West (even if one saw it whole) with the spiritual history of mankind.

Finally, there is a third context in which Heidegger refers to "history," "historical calling," and the like. (Of this, one example has already been mentioned—namely, Heidegger's exhortation to the German people. The Parmenides–Aristotle story leads, in its outcome, to the same appeal.) In this context, history is, as Heidegger calls it, "history as present," destiny in the sense of a present task. In terms of the account of history in *Being and Time,* it seems to resemble more closely history as future; it is a shadow of Nietzsche's conception of monumental history. But again, this borrowed notion fails to resolve the puzzle left at the close of *Being and Time.* The contrast between true and false, depth and surface history, is put to shrewd rhetorical use, but beyond this we are given no further understanding of what "history" means. The limited but genuine "historicity" of human being is forgotten, and nothing of substance is put in its place.

World. The conception of Being-in-a-world forms both the all-inclusive horizon of *Being and Time* and the limit to which its argument proceeds. Heidegger's analysis of human being, like human being itself, includes a complex and mutually related manifold (i.e., everyday existence with its three aspects—contingency, forfeiture, transcendence—and authentic existence, with its resolve), all of which are germane to the concept "world." Because the world in this sense is limited, the analysis is also held within definite and intelligible bounds. However obscure and entangled its thought, our finitude, reflecting on itself, cannot stray off into infinity. It remains within the circle of responsible self-criticism and self-appraisal—a circle which, far from being vicious, is in one form or another the only valid method of philosophy. What has happened to this horizon of "world," which confines and controls the finite appreciation of finitude? Again, the concept "world" is inserted in the *Introduction,* presumably as a kind of safeguard, to make sure that the old and the new shall seem to coincide. But it no longer has the central position that it had, either in content or in method. It is no longer my Being-in-a-world, but Being, which presides over this and all being, that is our goal and our guide. Being, however, is elusive; we not only do not know it, we do not even yet know how to ask for it. Hence, this change of course is a loss of direction, a total loss of guidance. We may reach here, there, and everywhere, yet no familiar landmark helps us on our way, no Hobbesian canon can guide or check our wanderings with an inward "aye" or "nay." The analysis of human being as Being-in-a-world had shape and direction; beside it, the search for Being itself is formless and blurred.

This is not to say that no finite creature can reflect upon infinity. Existentialism itself had its beginning in the work and person of Kierkegaard, for whom the one pressing, tragic dilemma was precisely that of the finite creature face to face with an infinite God—face to face, yet an abyss away. And it may be that Heidegger, in turning away from finitude, is turning again to religion of a sort. The first step toward nihilism, he says, is the disappearance of the gods, and the vanished gods, the Immortals, the Holy, are often before us in his later work. But again, one can only record, in conclusion, a subjective impression: if he is a prophet, he is a very dubious prophet. Despite the fact that Heidegger's scathing rhetoric has been widely accepted and admired, the verbal effects come too easily to be profound. Even if he is a seeker after dim and distant goals, he is at best a not quite convincing seeker.

Works by Heidegger

Die Kategorien- und Bedeutungslehre des Duns Scotus. Tübingen, 1916.

Sein und Zeit, I. Halle, 1927. Translated into English by J. Macquarrie and E. S. Robinson as *Being and Time.* New York, 1962.

Kant und das Problem der Metaphysik. Bonn, 1929. Translated into English by J. S. Churchill as *Kant and the Problem of Metaphysics*. Bloomington, Ind., 1962.

"Vom Wesen des Grundes," in *Festschrift für E. Husserl, Jahrbuch für Philosophie und Phänomenologische Forschung* (Halle, 1929); published separately, Frankfurt, 1949.

Was ist Metaphysik? Bonn, 1929; 5th ed., with introduction and postscript added, Frankfurt, 1951. Translated into English by R. F. C. Hull and Alan Crick as "What Is Metaphysics?" in *Existence and Being*, W. Brock, ed. Chicago, 1949. Introduction to 5th ed. translated into English by Walter Kaufmann as "The Way Back Into the Ground of Metaphysics," in his *Existentialism From Dostoevsky to Sartre*. New York, 1956.

Die Selbstbehauptung der deutschen Universität. Breslau, 1933.

Hölderlin und das Wesen der Dichtung. Pfullingen, 1936. Translated into English by Douglas Scott as "Hölderlin and the Essence of Poetry," in *Existence and Being*, W. Brock, ed. Chicago, 1949.

Hölderlins Hymne: "Wie wenn am Feiertage. . . ." Halle, 1941.

Platons Lehre von der Wahrheit. Berne, 1942; 2d ed., with *Brief über den Humanismus*, Berne, 1947.

Vom Wesen der Wahrheit. Frankfurt, 1943. Translated into English by R. F. C. Hull and Alan Crick as "On the Essence of Truth," in W. Brock, ed., *Existence and Being*. Chicago, 1949.

Erläuterung zu Hölderlins Dichtung. Frankfurt, 1944; expanded ed., Frankfurt, 1950, 1951.

Brief über den Humanismus. Frankfurt, 1949.

Holzwege. Frankfurt, 1950. Translation of the second essay, "The Age of the World View," by M. Grene in *Measure* (1951), 269–284.

Der Feldweg. Frankfurt, 1950.

Einführung in die Metaphysik. Tübingen, 1953. Translated into English by R. Manheim as *An Introduction to Metaphysics*. New Haven, 1959; New York, 1961.

Aus der Erfahrung des Denkens. Pfullingen, 1954.

Was heisst Denken? Tübingen, 1954.

Vorträge und Aufsatze. Pfullingen, 1954.

Zur Seinsfrage. Frankfurt, 1955. Reprint of *Über 'die Linie'* from *Festschrift für Ernst Jünger*. Translated into English as *Question of Being*, W. Kluback and J. T. Wilde, eds. New York, 1958.

Was ist das—die Philosophie? Pfullingen, 1956. Translated into English by W. Kluback and J. T. Wilde as *What Is Philosophy?* London, 1958.

Der Satz vom Grund. Pfullingen, 1957.

Identität und Differenz. Pfullingen, 1957. Translated by K. F. Leidecker as *Essays in Metaphysics: Identity and Difference*. New York, 1960.

Gelassenheit. Pfullingen, 1959.

Unterwegs zur Sprache. Pfullingen, 1959.

Die Frage nach dem Ding. Tübingen, 1962.

Works on Heidegger

Carnap, R., "Überwindung der Metaphysik durch logische Analyse der Sprache." *Erkenntnis*, Vol. 2 (1932), 219–241. Translated by A. Pap as "The Elimination of Metaphysics Through Logical Analysis of Language," in A. J. Ayer, ed., *Logical Positivism*. Glencoe, Ill., 1959.

Grene, M., *Heidegger*. New York, 1957.

Kaufmann, W., *From Shakespeare to Existentialism*. Boston, 1959. Ch. 17.

Kockelmans, A., *Martin Heidegger, een inleiding in zijn denken*. Tielt, Belgium, 1962.

Kraft, Julius, *Von Husserl zu Heidegger*, 2d ed. Frankfurt, 1957.

Langan, T., *The Meaning of Heidegger*. New York, 1959. A sympathetic but unilluminating account.

Lukács, G., "Heidegger redivivus." *Studi filosofici*, No. 3 (1948).

Löwith, K., *Denker in dürftiger Zerit*. Frankfurt, 1953.

Marx, Werner, *Heidegger und die Tradition*. Stuttgart, 1961.

Müller, M., *Existenzphilosophie im geistigen Leben der Gegenwart*. Heidelberg, 1949.

Stegmüller, Wolfgang, *Die Hauptströmungen der Gegenwarts-philosophie*, 2d ed. Stuttgart, 1961. Pp. 135–194, "Existential-ontologie: Martin Heidegger."

Vycinas, V., *Earth and Gods*. The Hague, 1961.

Wyschogrod, M., *Kierkegaard and Heidegger*. New York, 1954.

MARJORIE GRENE

HEIDELBERG SCHOOL. See NEO-KANTIANISM.

HEIM, KARL (1874–1958), German theologian, was born at Frauenzimmern in Württemberg. He studied at Tübingen and was professor of theology at Münster (1914) and at Tübingen from 1920 until his death.

Heim's work has philosophical interest insofar as he was concerned all of his life with the problem of restating Christianity in a form that would be credible in the scientific age. His early work explored the epistemology of religious faith, and his developed account draws on the I–thou philosophy of Buber and also on some of the concepts of modern science. Heim's fundamental point was that the experiencing subject cannot itself become an object and so cannot be brought under the objectifying categories of scientific thought. Thus we have a way of breaking out of, or transcending, the objective world of science, for there is open to us also a nonobjectifiable, interpersonal world. Heim spoke of this as a further dimension of experience, analogous to a dimension of space. This suggests a new way in which we may try to think about the transcendent God; and belief in such a God seemed to Heim the most important point calling for defense and restatement in the Christian tradition. Modern cosmology has made it senseless to talk of such a God as "up there" or "out there" or "beyond." But this God is not an object in the world any more than the experiencing subject is, and God too must be sought in the nonobjectifiable dimensions of experience, not in the realm of I–it. Just as the situation is revolutionized if we add a third dimension to a two-dimensional manifold, and what was hitherto impossible in two dimensions may be possible in three, so Heim believed that the conflicting attitudes of religion and science may be reconciled by admitting the multidimensional character of experience. We are familiar today with the notion of geometries of more than three dimensions, and we can think of an interpersonal space as having a different order and structure from physical space. Both kinds of space are embraced in an archetypal space, which is also a suprapolar space because it resolves the polarities of both the interpersonal and the physical spaces. This suprapolar space is the abode of God; it cannot be proved, but it is disclosed in the experiences of faith which may be likened to opening up new dimensions of a fuller life. Heim also taught a doctrine of panpsychism, which suggested that the further dimensions opened up in man's encounter with other persons and with God are at least potentially present at all levels of being.

Principal Works by Heim

Glaubensgewissheit. Leipzig, 1916.

Glaube und Denken. Berlin, 1931. Translated as *God Transcendent*. Edinburgh, 1935.

Jesus der Herr. Berlin, 1935. Translated as *Jesus the Lord*. Edinburgh, 1959.

Der christliche Gottesglaube und die Naturwissenschaft. Tübingen, 1949. Translated as *Christian Faith and Natural Science.* London, 1953; New York, 1957.

Die Wandlung im naturwissenschaftlichen Weltbild. Hamburg, 1952. Translated as *The Transformation of the Scientific World View.* London, 1953; New York, 1954.

Weltschöpfung und Weltende. Hamburg, 1958. Translated as *The World: its Creation and Consummation.* Philadelphia, 1962.

Works on Heim

Eisenhuth, H. E., "Im Gedenken und Karl Heim," in *Theologische Literaturzeitung,* Vol. 83 (Leipzig, 1958), 657–662.

Spemann, F., *Karl Heim und die Theologie seiner Zeit.* Tübingen, 1932.

JOHN MACQUARRIE

HEISENBERG, WERNER, German physicist, was born in Würzburg in 1901. Heisenberg studied physics in Munich under Arnold Sommerfeld and received his doctorate from Munich in 1923. He became a lecturer and assistant to Max Born at Göttingen in 1924. He continued his studies at the University of Copenhagen, where he collaborated with H. A. Kramers. He succeeded Kramers in 1926 as lecturer in physics there. Heisenberg was professor of physics at Leipzig from 1927 to 1941 and professor at Berlin and director of the Kaiser Wilhelm Institute for Physics from 1941 to 1945. He was named honorary professor and director of the Max Planck Institute for Physics at Göttingen in 1946 and has been honorary professor and administrative director of the Max Planck Institute for Physics and Astrophysics in Munich since 1958. He was awarded the Nobel prize for physics in 1932.

Heisenberg's contributions to physics are contained in over 120 papers covering a great variety of topics. We shall here deal with two topics only, with the invention of matrix mechanics and with Heisenberg's more recent theory of elementary particles.

Matrix mechanics. The *older quantum theory* of Bohr and Sommerfeld had tried to combine classical physics with the new quantum laws and to utilize the predictive power of both. The resulting theory was a mixture of classical notions—some useful, others apparently redundant—of new ideas and of *ad hoc* adaptations. Thus, for example, transition probabilities and selection rules were calculated, or guessed at, by examining the Fourier coefficients of the motions

$$\Phi_i(t) = \sum_{n=-\infty}^{+\infty} X_i(n,\omega_i) \exp(in\omega_i t)$$

of the independently vibrating parts of the atom, while the motion Φ_i itself had to be denied any physical significance. In addition, the theory had failed in important respects. It clearly was but an intermediate step on the way to a satisfactory mechanics of the atom. The final theory is essentially due to the efforts and the very different philosophies of two men, Heisenberg and Schrödinger.

According to Heisenberg we must abandon all attempts to give a detailed description of the unobservable internal motions of the atom. Such motions are but the result of the continued use of classical ideas in a domain that is inaccessible to direct experimental examination. Considering that these ideas may be in need of revision it would seem

to be wise to construct a theory that is expressed solely in terms of such "outer" magnitudes as frequencies and intensities of spectral lines. Speaking formally this means that we want to predict by using the X_i *directly* and without appeal to the Φ_i. Now Bohr's investigations had already gone a long way toward determining the required properties of the X. His idea of a rational generalization corresponds exactly to what Heisenberg had in mind. Heisenberg himself provided additional rules of calculation which were sufficient for solving some simple problems, such as the problem of the harmonic oscillator. It was not known to him at the time that the rules were those of an algebra of noncommuting matrices; this was soon recognized by Born, who, together with Pascual Jordan and Heisenberg, completed the formalism a few months after Heisenberg's first paper had appeared. A new atomic mechanics was at last in sight. Its meaning, however, was far from clear. Macroscopic objects whose positions and momenta could be ascertained with a higher degree of precision were represented by infinite arrays of complex numbers, none of them corresponding in a simple way to visible properties. "Can you imagine," objected H. A. Lorentz at this stage, "me to be nothing but a matrix?" It was again Heisenberg who, after the theory had been completed in a somewhat unexpected fashion by Schrödinger, made an essential contribution here by showing, in his *uncertainty relations,* to what extent classical notions could still be used in the interpretation of microphysical theories.

Heisenberg was to use the principle to rebuild a theory by working "from the outside in" once more in 1943, in order to eliminate certain difficulties in the quantum theory of fields. Believing these difficulties to be due to the disappearance of the ordinary space-time relations below 10^{-13} cm., he tried to replace field theory by a formalism which for any interaction transforms asymptotic anterior states into asymptotic posterior states without dealing with the details of the interaction. This so-called *S-matrix theory* was taken up by Geoffrey Chew and others for the calculation of the properties of strongly interacting particles. This has led to what some physicists regard as the beginning of a "third revolution" of twentieth-century physics, to the idea that particles are composites and that the properties of all of them can be obtained in a step by step procedure, starting with the interaction of any small subset ("bootstrap hypothesis"). Spatiotemporal relations are alien to this scheme, which therefore cannot develop a theory of measurement. Nor does there seem to be any possibility of extending it to other types of interaction.

Elementary particle theory. Heisenberg, who had been the first to stress the nonexistence of a criterion for distinguishing "elementary" particles from composites, has in the meantime developed a different theory in which elementary particles are stationary states of a single physical system, "matter." The field operators refer no longer to particles but to this basic matter (which Heisenberg sometimes compares to Anaximander's *apeiron*). The masses of the particles arise wholly from the interactions due to the nonlinearity of the basic field equation. There are no "bare particles." Other properties are supposed to follow from the symmetries of the field equation. Strange particles of spin 0 and 1/2 have been dealt with, to a certain extent, on the basis of approximation methods (this refers to 1962). There are only programs, no exact predictions, for weak interactions.

Heisenberg's philosophical speculations have always been intimately connected with his physics. They have been original and exciting. The same cannot be said about his more general observations on philosophical matters. However, he should not be blamed for this disparity, as it is at any rate only in close connection with reality that philosophy can be both interesting and fruitful. (For a discussion of Heisenberg's contributions to quantum theory, see QUANTUM MECHANICS, PHILOSOPHICAL IMPLICATIONS OF.)

Bibliography

Heisenberg's early work and its relation to wave mechanics and to experiment is described in *Die physikalischen Prinzipien der Quantentheorie* (Leipzig, 1930), translated by Carl Eckart and Frank C. Hoyt as *The Physical Principles of the Quantum Theory* (Chicago, 1930). The theory of the S-matrix is explained in "Die 'beobachtbaren Grössen' in die Theorie der Elementarteilchen," in *Zeitschrift für Physik*, Vol. 120 (1943), 513–538 and 673–702. For a survey of Heisenberg's new field theory, see "Quantum Theory of Fields and Elementary Particles," in *Reviews of Modern Physics*, Vol. 29 (1957), 269–278, and "Die Entwicklung der einheitlichen Feldtheorie der Elementarteilchen," in *Naturwissenschaften*, Vol. 50 (1963), 3–7. *Die Physik der Atomkerne* (Braunschweig, 1943) explains nuclear physics and Heisenberg's contributions to it. *Wandlungen in den Grundlagen der Naturwissenschaften* (Leipzig, 1935) is a survey of advances and discoveries from 1900 to 1930. *Physics and Philosophy* (New York, 1959), which contains the Gifford lectures given in 1955/1956, deals with the same subject on a broader historical and philosophical basis and also discusses current objections to the Copenhagen interpretation of quantum theory.

For the atmosphere at Göttingen in the "golden twenties," see F. Hundt, "Göttingen, Kopenhagen, Leipzig im Rückblick," in Fritz Bopp, ed., *Werner Heisenberg und die Physik unserer Zeit* (Braunschweig, 1961), pp. 1–7, and Robert Jungk, *Brighter Than a Thousand Suns* (New York, 1958).

PAUL K. FEYERABEND

HELLENISTIC THOUGHT. The word "Hellenistic" denotes that period of Greek history which can be defined in political terms as extending from the conquests of Alexander (d. 323 B.C.) to the extinction by the Romans of the kingdoms that his successors established, a process virtually completed by the subjugation of Cleopatra's Egypt (30 B.C.). The end of the fourth century saw the making of two positive philosophies, Zeno's Stoicism and Epicurus' materialist hedonism, which were to win adherents for five centuries and to exert an intermittently powerful influence in more modern times. There was a critical reaction to them, particularly to Stoicism, in what was called the Middle and New Academy under the leadership of the skeptical Arcesilaus and Carneades. This article presents a general picture of intellectual trends in the Hellenistic era.

Landmarks in the history of thought tend to be less clear than those in political history, with which they do not necessarily coincide. There is, however, reason for recognizing a period of Hellenistic thought that corresponds with the political period. It ends with a return to classicism, with a rediscovery of the fourth and fifth centuries, which took many forms: in literature and rhetoric there was Atticism, the study and imitation of classical Athenian models, in sculpture the archaizing movement, in philosophy a revival of interest in Plato and Aristotle. As early as the late second century, Panaetius tried to give Stoicism a new look by an infusion of Platonism, and he was followed in this by Posidonius; Antiochus of Ascalon began to recall the Academy to the heritage of its founder; and a little later the writings of Aristotle began to occupy a long line of commentators. In the Greco-Roman period the Greeks compensated for their political submission by remembering their past glories. By contrast the Hellenistic age, although ready enough to adapt its predecessors, was at first one of self-confident independence and conscious originality, which matched the political expansion of the Greek world. Unfortunately, little remains of its prose literature; our knowledge is derived mainly from later writers, who chose to report what suited their interests. Generalizations are thus more than usually dangerous.

Specialization. The Hellenistic age was pre-eminent in its vigorous development of the sciences, particularly mathematics, astronomy, and medicine, and these subjects lost their old association with philosophy. Although experiment was not unknown, the vogue was for observation and the collection of facts; and many scholars made language, literature, and history the objects of such factual research. Thus topics that had been peripheral, but perhaps stimulating, to earlier philosophers became the business of specialists.

Moreover, there grew up a geographical separation: the sciences flourished in Alexandria and Pergamum, whereas philosophers were increasingly drawn to Athens. Early in the period there were logicians at Megara and hedonists in Cyrene; Epicurus made his debut in Asia Minor, and Zeno sent men out to foreign countries. But later all the philosophers of whom anything is known worked in Athens, although many of them were not Athenian by birth; of the famous heads of the Academy, Arcesilaus came from Aeolia, Carneades from Cyrene, Clitomachus from Carthage, Philo from Thessaly, and Antiochus from Syria. Only at the end of the period did Rhodes enjoy a brief distinction, when Panaetius and Posidonius were at work there.

Posidonius indeed attempted to integrate philosophy and some of the specialist studies—history, anthropology, geography, and astronomy; but Stoic dogma was by then so firmly established that his unorthodoxy reduced the influence that his originality deserved. The intellectual energy that marked the opening of the period was diminished along with declining material prosperity, and the hostility of the later Ptolemies to Greek learning accelerated the decay of scientific inquiry.

Philosophy suffered by reason of its separation from science. Epicureans were obliged by their principles to give a mechanical account of celestial, as of other, phenomena, but shut their eyes to the relevant discoveries of the astronomers. Chrysippus grudgingly mentioned the anatomists who had shown the derivation of the nervous system from the brain, but clung to the view that the heart was the command-station of the soul. Psychology, in fact, stagnated because it continued to be the subject of a priori philosophizing, aided by a few random observations; it was not a subject of systematic inquiry.

Narrowed scope of philosophy. Hellenistic philosophy has not the range of Plato's Academy or Aristotle's Lyceum. It is often said that there was a concentration on ethics; this is explained by the deteriorated status of the city-state and the insecurity of times made hideous by the meaningless and destructive wars of the Hellenistic monarchs. Traditional guides to conduct were lost, and philosophy was called in to give the individual a road to follow and an assurance that it would lead him to happiness. It is certainly true that all the schools set up the attainment of happiness as the ultimate aim of their teaching; but this was nothing new, as is shown by Aristotle's *Nicomachean Ethics* and it must be remembered that for Plato, as for Socrates, the most important thing in life was care for the welfare of the soul. Hellenistic concentration on ethics has been exaggerated because practical morality was the chief concern of the Greco-Roman world, from which so much of our information derives. Thus so little survives of Chrysippus' work on logic that its originality was long ignored, yet it comprised about a third of his immense literary output. Similarly there are only tantalizing fragments of Epicurus' 37-book *On Nature*. In theory the only use of science was to free man from fear, but in practice he must have found many problems interesting per se, however much he might at times refuse to pursue questions beyond the point of usefulness.

Universal humanity. The life of the city-state came to no sudden end with Alexander. For two generations Athens still knew foreign wars and civil revolutions. In all cities there was great activity in building, in mounting festivals, in public education and welfare; and the law courts remained busy. Many men might be content with the life of the city, but there were others whose horizons were wider; there was more mobility, which led to the growth of a common Greek speech. That all men had something in common, that all had Zeus as a father, were ideas familiar to the classical Greeks, but the thought that a universal humanity united all became more prominent in the Hellenistic period. When the Cynic Diogenes called himself "a citizen of the world," he intended primarily the negative meaning that he owed no local allegiance. To the Stoics the world was a city with laws made by God, and its citizens realized, however imperfectly, that they belonged to one another, were like one another, and had duties to one another. Among these duties was one based on a natural inclination, that of instructing the ignorant. The desire to preach the truth and communicate the secret of happiness seems to have been even stronger among the Epicureans. "Friendship," said Epicurus, "goes dancing round the world, summoning us all to awake to felicity."

In the Greco-Roman world some knowledge of philosophical doctrines was widespread, even to be expected, among educated circles. The Hellenistic age must have seen the beginning of the change by which philosophy ceased to be the interest of a small minority and gained a recognized position; it is significant that in 156 B.C. the Athenians chose the heads of the three chief philosophic schools to represent them on an embassy to Rome. At the same time there was a spread of a popular simplified moral

teaching, of which Bion and Menippus are the best-known representatives; "philosopher" as applied to them would be a misnomer, but they passed on (or ridiculed) ideas that had originated with philosophers.

Importance of the individual. With the recognition of a common humanity went an increasing awareness of individuality. In art, above all in literature, character is depicted and analyzed. With this knowledge of man came a readiness to find in his nature a norm for action; he could discover within himself the laws he should obey, not seek them in social custom or the will of the gods or an objective self-existing Right. For the Epicurean, human "nature," arbitrarily limited to the physical, was the sole test. The Stoic recognized a "universal nature" too, but as something of which he was a part: his own impulses and his own reason would carry him along the right road. Even the skeptic from the Academy relied upon his reason as the only light available to guide him to the probabilities that governed his actions. At no other time in antiquity were philosophers so confident of man's self-sufficiency, even though the Stoics could simultaneously regard him as controlled by Fate. And for the dogmatic schools self-sufficiency meant not only that man was his own arbiter, but also that he could by his own effort secure what to Aristotle seemed impossible, an impregnable happiness untouched by external events.

This humanism had no need of the otherworldliness that is so prominent in Plato. Otherworldliness played no part in Hellenistic philosophy until toward the close of the period a revived Pythagoreanism heralded the new age. A transcendent God and a human soul exiled in this world are conceptions as alien to the Stoics as to Epicurus. Both ideas were rejected for the philosophical reason that it could not be understood how the immaterial could either affect or be affected by the material.

Dogmatism. A characteristic feature of the Hellenistic age is the "school" of philosophy, that is, a succession of men concerned with maintaining in essentials the views of a founder. The followers of Epicurus regarded him as a man of superhuman wisdom and never seriously modified his teaching. Among the Stoics there was more change, but much of it consisted of a shift of emphasis, or the use of new formulas—the better to express old ideas. The novelty is sometimes exaggerated by modern writers, whereas the Stoics themselves were more conscious of the continuity. Chrysippus is said to have declared that if only he were shown the doctrines he would find the proofs; although he differed from Zeno on points of substance, the anecdote shows how his work was regarded. This ossification was promoted by a general fondness for the invention of technical terms, which tend to determine thought, and was also encouraged by the polemics of the New Academy. In the face of external attack it is natural to close ranks. But orthodoxy is more often associated with religion than with philosophy, and for some men philosophers were now meeting the craving for a creed that contemporary religion could not satisfy.

Religion. The inadequacy of the traditional gods appears from the Hellenistic fascination with the idea of chance or luck (*Tyche*) as the determining factor in human affairs. Some might robustly deny its importance, and the Stoics saw in it only a name for causation that lay outside human ken. But to the popular mind it was such a powerful thing that it must be a "god," so that it came to be worshiped and propitiated, and to some extent this empty negation of rationality took the place of the personal gods of tradition. Often hardly less negative is the common assignment of events to an anonymous "supernatural influence" (*daimonion*). But though many men found the traditional gods insufficient, that is not to say that all did so, or even that all the dissatisfied also disbelieved. The third century was a great era of temple-building; it would be absurd to see in this nothing but evidence of secular ostentation. The numerous religious associations were effectively social clubs, but their divine presidents may yet have had a meaning for the members. Zeno and Epicurus both found it worthwhile to accommodate the gods in their systems. And when in the end the Hellenistic skepticism, atheism, euhemerism, and rationalism receded, some of the old figures still survived and became objects of the new devoutness and religious feeling.

Bibliography

Among standard histories of philosophy, E. Zeller, *Die Philosophie der Griechen*, Vol. III, E. Wellmann, ed., 5th ed. (Leipzig, 1923), and F. Ueberweg, *Grundriss der Geschichte der Philosophie*, Vol. I, K. Praechter, ed., 12th ed. (Berlin, 1926), give a good introduction to the period. W. W. Tarn, *Hellenistic Civilisation*, 3d ed., revised by G. T. Griffith (London, 1952), provides a cultural survey. P. Wendland, *Die hellenistische-römische Kultur* (Tübingen, 1912) was an influential work, with emphasis on religion and on interactions between Greek and oriental thought (see, for instance, his treatment of Philo). The excellent sketch in E. R. Dodds, *The Greeks and the Irrational* (Berkeley, Calif., 1951), pp. 236–250, balances religion and philosophy. B. Farrington, *Greek Science*, Vol. II, *Theophrastus to Galen* (Baltimore, Md., 1949), relates science and philosophy in a somewhat controversial way. The most recent guide to religion is N. M. P. Nilsson, *Geschichte der griechischen Religion*, 2d ed., Vol. II (Munich, 1961).

FRANCIS HENRY SANDBACH

HELMHOLTZ, HERMANN LUDWIG VON (1821–1894), German physiologist and physicist. He was born in Potsdam and educated at the Potsdam Gymnasium, where his father taught philology and classical literature, and at the Royal Friedrich-Wilhelm Institute of Medicine and Surgery in Berlin, from which he graduated as a doctor of medicine at the age of 21. Helmholtz' outstanding scientific talent led to the curtailment of his required ten-year service as a Prussian army physician and surgeon. After the presentation and publication of his famous paper *Über die Erhaltung der Kraft* ("On the Conservation of Energy") in 1847, he held only academic posts. He was instructor in anatomy at the Academy of Arts in Berlin (1847–1848), professor of pathology and physiology at Königsberg (1848–1855), professor of physiology and anatomy at Bonn (1855–1858), professor of physiology at Heidelberg (1858–1871), professor of physics at Berlin (1871–1888), and the first president and director of the Physico-Technical Institute in Berlin from 1888 until his death.

Helmholtz contributed over two hundred papers and books of outstanding importance in medicine, anatomy, physiology, psychology, and physics. He also published papers in mathematics and in philosophy, and delivered many popular lectures to publicize significant scientific investigations and to point out their philosophical implications. He was the first to measure the speed of nerve impulses, and he invented the ophthalmoscope. His paper "On the Conservation of Energy" became the cornerstone of the science of thermodynamics and set the direction of much of physics for the next half century. His monumental three-volume *Handbuch der physiologischen Optik* (*Handbook of Physiological Optics*, 1856–1866), frequently called the principia in its field, was matched in 1863 by a work equally basic to physiological acoustics, *Die Lehre von dem Tonempfindung* (*On the Sensations of Tone as a Physiological Basis for the Theory of Music*). In mathematics he was a pioneer in the field of non-Euclidean geometry, arriving independently at conclusions similar to those of Bernhard Riemann and seeing more quickly than others the philosophical importance of these new developments. In physics he contributed substantially to the establishment of the Faraday–Maxwell conception of electrical phenomena, both by his own theoretical investigations and through his encouragement of his most famous student, Heinrich Hertz. Helmholtz greatly influenced the intellectual climate in many German universities, and he may rightly be considered one of the fathers of the philosophy of science.

Empiricism and opposition to metaphysics. Helmholtz wrote only one long essay, *Die Tatsachen in der Wahrnehmung* ("The Facts of Perception," 1878), that he explicitly considered to be in the field of philosophy. Most of his philosophy is contained in a number of short, popular essays and in the body of his various scientific works. The scientific works, however, contain frequent passages of philosophical importance and always show a clear awareness of philosophical issues. Furthermore, many of his papers on science and mathematics, such as those on the foundations of physics and mathematics, would now be included in the philosophy of science.

Helmholtz' philosophy was at all times closely related with his scientific investigations. One of the motives for the work that led to the paper "On the Conservation of Energy" was his desire to discredit vitalism as a scientific hypothesis and as a metaphysical position. Indeed, from the beginning of his career he was opposed in general to metaphysical speculation, feeling that the idealists, Schelling and Hegel in particular, and a number of materialists had perverted philosophy and turned it from its main function, which was the study of human knowledge. Helmholtz was close to Kant in his philosophy; he believed that in *The Critique of Pure Reason* Kant had asked the right questions and had moved part of the way toward answering them. He was also close to the classical British empiricists, believing that a scientifically and mathematically sophisticated empiricism along the lines initiated by Locke would provide highly reliable answers to a number of the basic questions of philosophy.

Knowledge and perception. For Helmholtz the central questions in philosophy were "In what ways do our ideas correspond to reality?" and "What is true in our sense perception and thought?" Answering these questions was the common task of both philosophy and the sciences, the two disciplines approaching them from opposite directions. The task of philosophy is to study the formal aspects of knowledge, our forms of intuition and representation, and the general categories in terms of which we order knowledge. The task of the sciences is to study the world of reality and to find the laws of nature that cause or determine both objective sequences of events and the sensations we experience. The formal aspects of knowledge, our forms of intuition and representation, and our intellectual categories, condition the ways in which we should and do formulate scientific knowledge. Scientific investigations, specifically the findings of physiological optics and acoustics, help us to understand our forms of intuition and the mental operations involved in knowing.

Although Helmholtz' position was basically Kantian, it was markedly different from Kant's on certain important points because of Helmholtz' study of physiological optics, physiological acoustics, and non-Euclidean geometry. His answer to the question "In what ways do our ideas correspond to reality?" was based upon certain discoveries in the physiology of sensation and, in particular, upon the principle of specific nerve energies. This principle was implicit in the psychological theories of a number of British empiricists; it was made explicit by Johannes Müller and was extended significantly by Helmholtz. Fundamental to this view is the theory that all we know about the external world is brought to consciousness as the result of certain changes produced in our sense organs by external causes. These changes are transmitted by the nerves to the brain, where they first become conscious sensations. In the brain they are interpreted and combined to produce our perceptions of external objects by mental processes that Helmholtz called unconscious inferences—processes he considered to be the same as those that are operative when a child learns his native language. Thus, in the case of vision, excitations of the nerves of the retina are transmitted by the optic nerve to the brain, where they are experienced as sensations and where they are unconsciously interpreted and combined to form visual perceptions of objects and their properties.

According to the principle of specific nerve energies, there is no one-to-one correspondence between a sensation experienced and a specific property of the object causing that sensation. It is perfectly possible for similar or identical sensations to be the effects of diverse causes or for a single cause, because it affects more than one kind of nerve, to result in qualitatively distinct sensations. As a result, the most that can be claimed is that sensations are caused by external objects, that they are the subjective signs of these objects and their properties but are in no way images of them. The relation is one of sign to object signified, and even so, as such it is not an invariant relation. The only exception—an important one—is the correspondence in temporal sequence between external events and subjective sensations. Indeed, it is this correspondence that enables the scientist to determine the order of external events—that is, to determine the invariant laws of nature.

Because, with the notable exception of temporal sequences, there are no invariant, but only fairly uniform, relations between the sensations we experience and the objective world, Helmholtz felt that we can speak of our ideas as true only in a practical sense. Sensations are signs that we learn to use in order to regulate our movements and actions. When we have learned to interpret these signs, we are able to control our actions and are able to bring about results we desire or to avoid dangers.

> [However, to ask] whether the idea I have of a table, its form, strength, colour, weight, etc., is true *per se*, apart from any practical use I can make of this idea, and whether it corresponds with the real thing, or is false and due to an illusion, has just as much sense as to ask whether a certain musical note is red, yellow, or blue. Idea and thing conceived evidently belong to two entirely different worlds, which no more admit of being compared with each other than colours and musical tones or than the letters of a book and the sounds of the words they form. (*Handbook of Physiological Optics*, Vol. III, p. 19)

Space and geometry. Helmholtz' study of perceptions of space and of spatially oriented objects led him into the field of non-Euclidean geometry. His interest in general problems of spatial perception led to the investigation of the analytic properties that any space must have in order to permit the establishment of congruence relations between bodies and surfaces. As he saw it, congruence can be established only if rigid bodies or systems of bodies can be moved toward one another with unaltered form—that is, only if the congruence of geometrical figures is a relation independent of all movements in space. Thus, he took the actual fact of spatial measurements through the establishment of congruence as a starting point and investigated the most general analytical properties of any space in which the movements necessary for this measurement can occur. He found that such movements and measurements were possible not only in Euclidean space but also in the spaces investigated by Riemann and Nikolai Ivanovich Lobachevski or in any space with a constant measure of curvature. Helmholtz concluded that Kant was mistaken in claiming that the axioms of Euclidean geometry were synthetic a priori principles necessarily true of space. Spaces that are not Euclidean can be conceived; the geometries of these spaces can be formulated; models or interpretations of them can be given, and on the basis of experience, it is impossible to determine which of these geometries is that of real space. Kant was correct in considering space to be a form of intuition but wrong in claiming that space must necessarily possess Euclidean characteristics.

Philosophy of physics. Helmholtz' philosophy of physics was a classic formulation of nineteenth-century mechanism. He felt that the primary function of the physical sciences was to search for laws that express observed particular processes in general terms, so that from these laws other particular processes could be deduced. The discovery of these laws is the task of experimental physical science.

> The theoretical part . . . endeavors to ascertain the unknown causes of processes from their visible effects; it seeks to comprehend them according to the law of causality. . . . Thus, the final goal of the theoretical

natural sciences is to discover the ultimate invariable causes of natural processes. ("On the Conservation of Energy," Introduction)

According to Helmholtz, these ultimate causes are simple Newtonian forces, so that a causal explanation in physics is at the same time an explanation in terms of forces.

Theoretical natural science must, therefore, if it is not to rest content with a partial view of the nature of things, take a position in harmony with the present conception of the nature of simple forces and the consequences of this conception. Its task will be completed when the reduction of phenomena to simple forces is completed, and when it can at the same time be proved that the reduction given is the only one possible which the phenomena will permit. This will then be established as the necessary conceptual form for comprehending nature, and we will then be able to ascribe objective truth to it. (*ibid.*)

These statements always represented the ultimate aim of scientific explanation for Helmholtz. It was a goal that grew more distant as the nineteenth century advanced.

Works by Helmholtz

Über die Erhaltung der Kraft. Berlin, 1847.
Handbuch der physiologischen Optik, 3 vols. Leipzig, 1856–1866. Edited and translated by J. P. C. Southall as *Handbook of Physiological Optics.* New York, 1924–1925.
Die Lehre von dem Tonempfindung. Leipzig, 1863. Translated by A. J. Ellis as *On the Sensations of Tone as a Physiological Basis for the Theory of Music.* New York, 1948.
Populäre wissenschaftliche Vorträge, 2 vols. Leipzig, 1865–1871. Translated as *Popular Lectures on Scientific Subjects, First and Second Series,* New York, 1873–1891.
Die Tatsachen in der Wahrnehmung ("The Facts of Perception"). Berlin, 1878.
Schriften zur Erkenntnistheorie, Paul Hertz and Moritz Schlick, eds. Berlin, 1921.

Works on Helmholtz

Crombie, A. C., "Helmholtz." *Scientific American,* Vol. 198, No. 3 (1958), 94–102.
Koenigsberger, Leo, *Hermann von Helmholtz,* 3 vols. Berlin, 1902–1903. Translated by F. A. Welby. Oxford, 1906.
McKendrick, John Gray, *Hermann Ludwig Ferdinand von Helmholtz.* London, 1899.

RUSSELL KAHL

HELMONT, JAN BAPTISTA VAN (1577–1644), Flemish physician and chemist, was born in Brussels, studied philosophy and medicine at Louvain University, and became a doctor of medicine in 1594. From 1600 to 1605 he traveled in Switzerland, Italy, Germany, and England in order to enrich his medical knowledge, but he was deeply dissatisfied by the dominance of Galenism in the medical schools he visited. In 1609 he left Brussels for Vilvorde, where he lived in retirement and meditation until 1616. Returning to Brussels, he published his *De Magica Vulnerum Curatione* (Paris, 1621), but the work was suspected of heresy, and van Helmont was subjected to a long inquisitorial process. He was imprisoned for a short time in 1634, and prosecutions lasted until 1636.

Van Helmont's main importance lies in his contributions to medicine and chemistry, but his philosophical views do not lack interest. For a time he was a supporter of the Hippocratic empirical approach to medicine that opposed the Aristotelian and Galenic doctrines which prevailed in the medical schools. During his retirement in Vilvorde, he came under the influence of Paracelsus and the hermetic writings. He suggested often in his writings that he was an adept, and boasted of being able to make gold and produce the panacea. Even after accepting the hermetic theory of knowledge, van Helmont did not give up the experimental approach to scientific practice, which led him to important discoveries in chemistry (he founded the chemistry of gases and physiological chemistry) and in medicine (particularly concerning catarrh and asthma). This is generally considered a contradiction by commentators; but the hermetic school traditionally coupled a pronounced empirical bent to its stress on an inner light and on revelation, or the wisdom of the ancients, as genuine sources of knowledge.

Van Helmont held that the intellect constitutes the human soul. It is the true image of God and the source of knowledge, which is attained by immediate intuition of an inner illumination caused by God, evoked by introspection and prayer, and conditioned by faith. Reason, the discursive power, contrary to Aristotle, is only a connecting link between intellect and the senses, and leads only to error.

In natural philosophy van Helmont held that the world was composed of matter (either water or air), and an efficient cause, which was the "original ferment" or *initium seminale*—his own version of the "soul of the world" (the active principle of hermetic philosophy). In biology and physiology van Helmont was an iatrochemist. Life results from a vegetative soul (*archaeus influus*), and every organ of a living body has its own *archaeus insitus* that determines its special function. Diseases arise from disorder in these *archaei*; a disease is an error deriving from an *idea morbosa*. These doctrines originated in the Stoic and Neoplatonic traditions of the hermetic school.

Works by van Helmont

Ortus medicinae, ed. by Mercurius van Helmont. Amsterdam, 1648.
Opera. Lyons, 1667.

Works on van Helmont

Nève de Mévergnies, P., *J. B. van Helmont philosophe par le feu.* Liège and Paris, 1935.
Pagel, W., "J. B. van Helmont," in *Einführung in die philosophische Medizin des Barok.* Berlin, 1930.
Redgrove, H. S., and Redgrove, J. M. L., *J. B. van Helmont, Alchemist, Physician, and Philosopher.* London, 1922.
Strunz, F., *J. B. van Helmont.* Leipzig and Vienna, 1907.
Waele, H. de, *J. B. van Helmont.* Brussels, 1948.

GIORGIO TONELLI

HELVÉTIUS, CLAUDE-ADRIEN (1715–1771), was born into a highly respected medical family; his father was first physician to the queen of France. After his education at the College Louis-le-Grand and at the age of only 23, Helvétius obtained, through influence at court, the lucrative post of *fermier-général*, in which he soon grew rich. He became known, however, for the philanthropic and enlightened uses he made of his great wealth, particularly as a patron of philosophers and men of letters. For a time Helvétius turned to poetry and, in a piece entitled *Le Bonheur*, extolled the supreme pleasures of the intellectual life. Taking his own advice, he resigned in 1751 from tax-farming, married, and retired to his country estate, thenceforth devoting himself primarily to philosophical and literary pursuits. The publication in 1758 of his principal work, *De l'Esprit*, proved to be one of the ideological *causes célèbres* of the eighteenth century. Appearing at a moment of political reaction, *De l'Esprit* was noisily condemned by the authorities, both ecclesiastical and ministerial, for its dangerously heretical and subversive opinions. Suppression of the book signaled a grave—but fortunately temporary—setback for the party of *philosophes* and Encyclopedists. Despite the recantations that Helvétius was forced to make regarding *De l'Esprit*, he reaffirmed his ideas even more strongly in *De l'Homme, de ses facultés intellectuelles, et de son éducation,* published posthumously in 1772.

The thought of Helvétius sprang mainly from the predominant current of sensualism in the Enlightenment, which he fashioned with marked originality into what may be described as a thoroughgoing doctrine of "environmental behaviorism." Like Locke, he held that the primary function of the mind was the registering of sense impressions arising from the external world. Calling this faculty *sensibilité physique,* he held it to be the exclusive source not only of all ideas and judgments (which, he said, resulted from the mental comparison of sensations) and of memory (which is simply a weakened sensation), but of all the emotions as well; he described emotions as variations of the two root-sensations of pleasure and pain that usually accompany sensory experience. Diverging, however, from the mainstream of Lockeanism represented in France at the time chiefly by Étienne Bonnot de Condillac, Helvétius was concerned with deriving from sensationist premises a psychological, rather than epistemological, theory. His basic contention was that the intellectual and moral capabilities, no less than the entire complex of values and motivations peculiar to any individual, are to be explained solely as the product of education—that is, of the total cumulative environment from the moment of birth. The biological or hereditary influences on the individual are considered, by contrast, to be uniform in all who are "normally constituted"; moreover, it is deemed unnecessary to include such "constants" in the causal investigation of behavior. Whereas Locke had rejected innate ideas, Helvétius proceeded to the rejection of innate abilities, or, more exactly, of innate inequalities in the apparatus of natural talents and inclinations with which every normal person is endowed. In expounding this radically environmentalist psychology, he did not feel obliged to assume any metaphysical position concerning the substantive nature of mind. Nevertheless, it is clear enough, as the concept of *sensibilité physique* implies, that Helvétius, swayed perhaps by contemporary materialists such as Diderot and La Mettrie, had in fact adopted a naturalistic view of man as logically the most suitable context in which to develop his behaviorist thesis.

In the mass of empirical evidence, often valuable and

sometimes penetrating, adduced in support of the absolute case for environment versus heredity, two arguments stand out. Aware that exceptional talents do not always result from equally exceptional educations, Helvétius attempted to justify environmentalism by introducing the notion of *hasard*. According to this, a trivial and chance occurrence—such as Newton's observation of an apple falling to the ground—could, under certain conditions, have the most far-reaching consequences—such as the discovery of universal gravitation. Helvétius reached the reassuring, if tenuous, conclusion that genius is common to all persons, but the special sequence of events needed to actualize it is exceedingly rare. His other and much more plausible line of reasoning affirms that the development of intelligence, talent, or any ability whatever is proportional to the degree of *passion*, or emotional motivation, felt by the individual. Having thus translated the problem of inborn inequalities of mental capability into one of inborn emotive potential, Helvétius ended by finding that anyone may, by the appropriate stimulation of his passions, be rendered superior in any field of endeavor.

Throughout his writings, Helvétius emphasized the ethical and social implications of his psychology. The conception of the human being as a sort of behavioral *tabula rasa,* uniformly malleable by external controls into whatever forms might be judged desirable, favors obviously the practical ideal of reforming man and society on a grand scale. It devolves upon the "legislator–philosopher" to achieve this goal by a system of reeducation based on the scientific knowledge of the mechanics of behavior in relation to environment—an ambition aptly summarized by the sanguine dictum *l'éducation peut tout.* The supreme ethical criterion is, in turn, described as "public utility" (or such equivalents as *intérêt général, bonheur général*), which Helvétius further defined, in keeping with the pleasure–pain principle, as the maximum of pleasure compatible with a minimum of pain in the whole of a given society. But individual conduct in any environment is already determined by the pleasure principle, or self-interest, and Helvétius tried to show that, in addition, the multiplicity of pleasurable ends that men automatically seek, however "nonmaterial" in appearance, are all ultimately reducible to *sensibilité physique.* It is futile, therefore, to try to inculcate the social virtues by mere moralizing and even more so by condemning pleasure. Men can be changed for the better only through the manipulation of their passions. The key idea, to which all of Helvétius' thinking leads, is that the moral improvement and happiness of mankind can result only from political reforms having as their object the establishment of a system of public education (in both the narrow and the broad sense), by means of which the closest possible linkage would be effected between any individual's socially beneficial acts and his rewards in the form of gratified *sensibilité physique.* For example, Helvétius suggested that society methodically offer the choicest sexual enjoyments to its most virtuous and useful members. More generally and especially in the long polemical sections of *De l'Homme,* he inveighed against what he regarded as the two major obstacles to the triumph of a hedonistic ethics founded on the standard of public utility—namely, Christianity with its irrational dogmas and ascetic, otherworldly morality and the feudal structure, economic inequities, and autocratic practices of the *ancien régime*. An aura of agnosticism, no less than a revolutionary fervor, surrounds the writings of Helvétius; while he does not argue the philosophical case for atheism, he patently assigns no positive value to a belief in God and even finds it pernicious to the *bonheur général* that he envisions.

The principal weakness of Helvétius' philosophy is its one-sided, reductive use of the factor of environment, at the expense of physiological predisposition—a defect which provoked a solid refutation from Diderot. Stated in absolute form, environmental behaviorism is paradoxical. Because no two educations, as Helvétius himself admitted, can ever be even remotely similar, it is impossible either to prove or to disprove his basic supposition that the same environmental causes will invariably produce the same behavioral effects. The representation of the mind as essentially passive sets up, moreover, a false dichotomy between it and the natural as well as social environment in which, from a more realistic standpoint, the individual is perceived to be a peculiarly dynamic and, indeed, creative participant. Finally, the ideal of public utility, when considered positively, remains rather vague and elusive, despite the abuses of the *ancien régime* attacked in its name. But historically the many valid elements of Helvétius' thought exerted considerable influence in several directions; on the Encyclopedist movement, especially Baron d'Holbach; on Pierre Cabanis and the *idéologues;* on the British utilitarians, particularly Jeremy Bentham; and, in a general long-range sense, on the rise of both democratic and socialistic doctrines and on the growth in modern societies of the comprehensive role given to public education.

Principal Works by Helvétius

Oeuvres complètes, 3 vols. Paris, 1818.
De l'Esprit; or Essays on the Mind and Its Several Faculties. London, 1759.
A Treatise on Man; His Intellectual Faculties and His Education, translated by William Hooper. London, 1777.
Notes de la main d'Helvétius, Albert Keim, ed. Paris, 1907.

Works on Helvétius

Cumming, Ian, *Helvétius: His Life and Place in the History of Educational Thought.* London, 1955.
Horowitz, Irving, *Claude Helvétius: Philosopher of Democracy and Enlightenment.* New York, 1954.
Keim, Albert, *Helvétius, sa vie et son oeuvre.* Paris, 1907.
Momdjian, K., *La Philosophie d'Helvétius,* translated from the Russian by M. Katsovitch. Moscow, 1959.

ARAM VARTANIAN

HEMPEL, CARL GUSTAV, German-American philosopher, was born on January 8, 1905 in Oranienburg, Germany, and studied at the universities of Göttingen, Heidelberg, and Berlin, receiving his Ph.D. from Berlin in 1934. Trained originally in physics and mathematics, Hempel turned to philosophy and came under the influence of Hans Reichenbach, Moritz Schlick, and Rudolf Carnap. He was a member of the so-called Berlin group, which was allied with the Vienna Circle. Hempel left Germany in 1934, did research in Brussels until 1937, and then came to the United States, where he was naturalized in 1944. He taught at Yale from 1948 to 1955 and at Princeton from 1955 on, and served as president of the American Philosophical Association, Eastern Division, in 1961. He is a member of the American Academy of Arts and Sciences.

Hempel has made contributions in logic, philosophy of mathematics, and methodology and philosophy of science. Although he has not deviated far from the basic viewpoints of logical positivism, he has been one of its most astute internal critics, and his views have become progressively more liberal than the earlier restrictive tenets of positivism.

Criteria of meaning. In "Problems and Changes in the Empiricist Criterion of Meaning" (1950), Hempel gave an exhaustive critique of the various versions of the verifiability criterion of meaning and suggested "the translatability criterion," according to which a statement is meaningful if translatable into "an empiricist language." His more recent views are that the sharp dichotomy between cognitive significance and nonsense should be replaced by a graduated differentiation that admits of degrees, and that systems of statements, not isolated statements, should be taken as ultimate units of significance.

Theoretical and observational terms. A related problem studied by Hempel, in *Fundamentals of Concept Formation in Empirical Science* (1952) and elsewhere, is that of articulating the link between "theoretical terms" and "observational terms"—that is, the problem of clarifying how scientific terms (for example, "electron" or "id"), ostensibly referring to unobservable entities and properties, can have observational significance. Rejecting as too restrictive the earlier positivist thesis of physicalism and P. W. Bridgman's operationism, Hempel introduced the notion of "an interpretative system." Such a system, consisting of statements using both theoretical and observational terms, is to effect "a partial interpretation" of a theoretical system so that the complex of the theory plus its interpretative system yields testable observational consequences.

Confirmation. Hempel was one of the first to attempt a precise definition of the concept of confirmation. In "A Purely Syntactical Definition of Confirmation" (1943) and "Studies in the Logic of Confirmation" (1945), he offered a definition of "observation report O confirms hypothesis H" for languages of simple structure; in "A Definition of 'Degree of Confirmation'" (1945, with P. Oppenheim), he proposed a definition of the quantitative concept, "evidence E confirms hypothesis H to the degree r." Better known than these technical definitions is Hempel's discovery and discussion of "the raven paradoxes" of confirmation in the first two studies cited above.

Explanation. In "Studies in the Logic of Explanation" (1948, with P. Oppenheim) and other works, Hempel gave a rigorous analysis of scientific explanation on the basis of a model—now commonly known as "the deductive model" or "the covering-law model." On this model, the occurrence of an event is explained when a statement describing that event is deduced from general laws and statements of antecedent conditions; a general law is explained when it is deduced from more comprehensive laws. This view of explanation, and particularly its application to historical explanation and explanation of human actions, has aroused acute controversy. In "Deductive-Nomological vs. Statistical Explanation" (1962), Hempel generalized the covering-law model to include statistical or probabilistic explanation. He also proposed the concept of "epistemic utility" to explicate the notion of "accepting a hypothesis" on the model of decision making under uncertainty.

Works by Hempel

(1) *Der Typusbegriff im Lichte der Neuen Logik.* Leiden, 1936. Written with Paul Oppenheim.
(2) "The Function of General Laws in History." *The Journal of Philosophy,* Vol. 39 (1942), 35–48.
(3) "A Purely Syntactical Definition of Confirmation." *The Journal of Symbolic Logic,* Vol. 8 (1943), 122–143.
(4) "Studies in the Logic of Confirmation." *Mind,* Vol. 54, (1945), 1–26, 97–121.
(5) "A Definition of 'Degree of Confirmation.'" *Philosophy of Science,* Vol. 12 (1945), 98–115. Written with Paul Oppenheim.
(6) "On the Nature of Mathematical Truth." *The American Mathematical Monthly,* Vol. 52 (1945), 543–556.
(7) "Studies in the Logic of Explanation." *Philosophy of Science,* Vol. 15 (1948), 135–175. Written with Paul Oppenheim.
(8) "Problems and Changes in the Empiricist Criterion of Meaning." *Revue internationale de philosophie,* Vol. 4 (1950), 41–63.
(9) *Fundamentals of Concept Formation in Empirical Science.* Chicago, 1952.
(10) "The Theoretician's Dilemma," in Herbert Feigl, Michael Scriven, and Grover Maxwell, eds., *Minnesota Studies in the Philosophy of Science,* Vol. 2 (Minneapolis, 1958), 37–98.
(11) "Deductive-Nomological vs. Statistical Explanation," in Herbert Feigl and Grover Maxwell, eds., *Minnesota Studies in the Philosophy of Science,* Vol. 3 (Minneapolis, 1962), 98–169.
(12) *Aspects of Scientific Explanation.* New York, 1965. The title essay is a new work by Hempel. In addition, 11 important earlier articles are reprinted, including the following articles cited above: (2), (4) and (7) with new postscripts, (8) with changes and revisions and in combination with another article, and (10).

Works on Hempel

Carnap, Rudolf, *Logical Foundations of Probability.* Chicago, 1950. See Secs. 87 and 88 for discussion of Hempel's analysis of confirmation.
Dray, William, *Laws and Explanation in History.* London, 1957. Critical discussion of Hempel's views on historical explanation.
Scheffler, Israel, *The Anatomy of Inquiry.* New York, 1963. Contains critical but sympathetic discussions of Hempel's views on explanation, confirmation, and cognitive significance.

JAEGWON KIM

HEMSTERHUIS, FRANS (1721–1790), Dutch philosopher, was born at Franeker, the son of the famous Greek scholar Tiberius Hemsterhuis. Hemsterhuis was a clerk of the State Council and devoted his free hours to his favorite studies—numismatics, fine arts, and philosophy. In his last years his philosophy was very much influenced by his friendship with the Princess von Gallitzin, the wife of the Russian ambassador at The Hague. Thus, his life and work may be divided into two periods.

In the first period Hemsterhuis' *Lettre sur l'homme et ses rapports* (1772) was his principal work, preceded by two small, closely connected treatises, *Lettre sur la sculp-* ture (1765) and *Lettre sur les désirs* (1769). In *Lettre sur la sculpture* Hemsterhuis argued that the essence of the aesthetic experience is a longing to unite oneself with the art object. This concept became part of his theory of ethics, which is set out in *Lettre sur les désirs.* The most perfect happiness for the soul is the union with the beloved object irrespective of whether it is an object of art, a person, or God. This Platonic Eros is for Hemsterhuis analogous to the power of attraction in the physical world. This theory is further developed in *Lettre sur l'homme,* on which the Platonic dialogues of his second period are based. On the subject of the nature of man Hemsterhuis thought in terms of a dualistic philosophy like Descartes's, but Hemsterhuis' dualism was combined with an empiristic-sensationalistic theory that he probably derived from Locke and Condillac. Through sensory perception man receives an image of what exists in reality. This image, however, is incomplete, and if man had other organs, he could perhaps see other aspects of reality. Through what Hemsterhuis calls the "moral organ" man is aware of an immediate feeling of his relationship with God. The moral organ is also responsible for the feeling of relation, rapport, that man has with thousands of other men, and the development of such relations is dependent on the perfection of the moral organ. This theory leads to an individualistic concept of man's moral duties, which is one of the reasons for Hemsterhuis' influence on the German philosophy of *Sturm und Drang* and romanticism.

In the second period of Hemsterhuis' life he wrote four Platonic dialogues the most important of which are *Aristée ou de la divinité* (1779) and *Alexis ou de l'âge d'or* (1783 but published in 1787). In *Aristée* Hemsterhuis, who originally believed in a personal God, is converted to a clear pantheism. God's omnipresence is the basis of man's relation to him, and it is mainly thanks to the moral principle, as the "moral organ" is called in later years, that man is able to come nearer to God. In *Alexis* Hemsterhuis, perhaps influenced by contemporary German philosophy, presented for the first time his concept of the golden age and the harmonious development of the individual. He also introduced the notion of the value of poetical truth (truth discovered by the poet in moments of enthusiasm). With these ideas Hemsterhuis had moved far from his earlier rationalism, and his thought was received with admiration and approval by representatives of the *Sturm und Drang* and romantic movements in philosophy.

In the first period F. H. Jacobi and J. G. Herder were among Hemsterhuis' admirers; in the second period he was very popular with and influenced the two Schlegels and Novalis.

Works by Hemsterhuis

During his lifetime most of Hemsterhuis' works were printed for private circulation in small and anonymous editions. Some of his early treatises are still in manuscript form in public collections. The latest complete, but rather inaccurate, edition is François Hemsterhuis, *Oeuvres philosophiques,* Louis Susan Pedro Meijboom, ed. (Leeuwarden, Netherlands, 1846). A German translation edited by Julius Hilsz was published at Leipzig (1912). A very recent edition of one of his works is François Hemsterhuis, *Lettre sur l'homme et ses rapports. Avec le commentaire inédit de Diderot,* George May, ed. (New Haven, 1964).

Works on Hemsterhuis

Brummel, Leendert, *Frans Hemsterhuis. Een philosophenleven.* Haarlem, 1925.

Brummel, Leendert, "Frans Hemsterhuis." *Algemeen Nederlands Tijdschrift Voor Wijsbegeerte en Psychologie,* Vol. 34 (1940), 17–26.

Brachin, Pierre, *Le Cercle de Munster (1779–1806) et la pensée religieuse de F. L. Stolberg.* Lyon and Paris, 1952.

Brachin, Pierre, "Hemsterhuis' Beziehungen zum Gallitzinkreis," in *Pariser Universitätswoche an der Ludwig-Maximilians-Universität zu München vom 14. bis 19. Februar 1955.* Munich, 1955. Pp. 203–216.

Loos, Waltrand, "Der Briefwechsel des Philosophen Hemsterhuis mit der Fürstin Gallitzin, mit einem Schlüssel zu seiner Geheimschrift." *Westfalen,* Vol. 39 (1961), 119–127.

LEENDERT BRUMMEL

HEN/POLLA. In one form or another the problem known as that of the One (*Hen*) and the Many (*Polla*) pervades the whole history of Greek philosophy. According to Aristotle (*Physics* I, 2–3), it arose first in the pre-Socratic inquiry into whether there is one first principle or source—for example, water alone, or air alone—for things, or whether there is more than one first principle. If we are to avoid "coming into being out of nothing," we must either deny with Parmenides that there is any multiplicity arising from the first principle, or else we must suppose that somehow or other multiplicity is already present within the unitary first principle. If we choose the second supposition, we are faced with a problem that is no longer purely physical, namely, how one thing can also be many.

In the period after Parmenides it became clear that this problem arose at a number of different levels of thought, though it usually seemed natural to suppose that a solution at one level would solve the problem at other levels as well. It arose in relation to the phenomenal world in three ways: how one thing can possess a number of different characteristics, how one thing can change into another, and how one thing can have many parts. It arose, above all for Plato, as a problem concerning metaphysical entities such as forms—how unitary forms can be split up among many particulars, and how one form can possess a number of attributes. It arose in the theory of predication as the question of how a number of predicates can be applied to a singular subject. It arose in logic especially as the problem of how classification of many things under one head can be justified. It was also discussed (by Aristotle in the *Physics*) in terms of the number of first principles, even when the question of their number was no longer seen from within a purely physical framework.

Only some of the more important treatments can be mentioned here. The earlier Pythagoreans subordinated One and Many to Limit and Unlimited in their table of opposites (see APEIRON/PERAS). It remained a standard problem for the Eleatics after Parmenides, and Zeno leveled some forty arguments against plurality, of which one or two survive. The Sophist Protagoras tackled the problem at the level of perception, and Gorgias' pupil Lycophron dealt with it as a problem of predication by banishing the word "is" in statements such as "Socrates is white"; Antisthenes, the Megarians, and the Eretrians, according to some, followed the same path. Plato discussed the question repeatedly, most explicitly in Part Two of the *Parmenides* and in the *Philebus,* but of vital importance is his approach to predication in the *Sophist.* His discussion was continued by Speusippus, and by Aristotle in the *Metaphysics* (I, 6) and in the *Physics,* where he propounded a solution in terms of "substrate," "privation," and "form." The Neoplatonists saw it as the problem of how the multiplicity of the world order can proceed from the ultimate absolute unity.

Bibliography

Virtually the whole of F. M. Cornford's *Plato and Parmenides* (London, 1939) is concerned with the Hen/Polla problem in one way or another.

G. B. KERFERD

HENRY OF GHENT, Augustinian secular theologian, traditionally known as *Doctor Solemnis,* was born at Ghent or Tournai, probably in the second quarter of the thirteenth century. In addition to holding high ecclesiastical office at Bruges and Tournai, he taught both arts and theology at the University of Paris. In 1277 he served on the theological commission which prepared the condemnation issued by Stephen Tempier, bishop of Paris, against the Averroism of Siger of Brabant and Boethius of Dacia. He died in 1293.

Henry's principal writings are a *Summa Theologica* and fifteen *Quodlibeta* (occasional disputations). The extended criticism of his ideas by Scotus, Ockham, and others is a sign of his considerable influence in his own age. In the sixteenth century the Servite friars chose him as their official theologian, although he had never belonged to their order.

As a philosopher, Henry of Ghent stood in the main line of development of medieval Platonism. The Augustinian tradition, already brilliantly represented in the thirteenth century by Bonaventure and Matthew of Acquasparta, was unmistakably the weightiest element in his thought, and the Platonic orientation thus established was further strengthened by the influence of Avicenna. At the same time, following Bonaventure and other earlier Augustinians, he incorporated a number of Aristotelian ideas into his synthesis. Furthermore, in adapting the Neoplatonic metaphysics of Avicenna to the requirements of the Christian view of God and creation, he anticipated certain critical tendencies of the fourteenth century, by which the whole structure of medieval realism was to be undermined. It is fair to say that Henry failed to blend these diverse elements into a fully coherent system. Nonetheless, in inspiration and aim he was the true precursor of John Duns Scotus, the last great constructive philosopher of the Middle Ages.

Being. For Henry of Ghent the starting point of metaphysical thinking was the idea of being (*ens* or *res* or *aliquid*), out of which the metaphysician draws the intelligible essences virtually contained in it. Analysis shows that being is an analogical idea. Taken in its widest sense, it includes both imaginary entities (*res secundum opinionem*), which exist only in the mind, and genuine beings (*res secundum veritatem*), which exist, or at any rate can exist, outside the mind. Genuine being, which is the proper object of metaphysics (*ens metaphysicum*), is further divided into Being Itself (*ipsum esse*), or God, and contingent beings, or creatures. Finally, creaturely being is divided into that which exists in itself (substance) and that which exists in another (accident).

Genuine beings, actual or possible, are distinguished from imaginary entities by their possession of "essential being" (*esse essentiae*). This essential being is not a rudimentary mode of existence. It is best described as an intrinsic possibility or intelligibility which pertains to definable essences as reflections of the divine ideas. It is to be contrasted with the intrinsic impossibility and incoherence of *res secundum opinionem*.

Actual beings are distinguished from merely possible beings by their possession of "existential being" (*esse existentiae*). This existential being is not a principle or act within actually existing things; Henry refused to accept the real distinction between essence and existence as formulated either by Giles of Rome or by Thomas Aquinas. The difference between essential and existential being is to be found not in things themselves but in the relation of essences to God. Essential being consists in being thought by God, while existential being consists in actually depending on God as creative Cause.

Apart from the fact that each actual being, as a product of divine creativity, is individually related to God, individual things, in which specific essences are multiplied, require no explanation of their individuality. Individuation involves no addition, whether of matter or of act of existence, to the intelligible essence. In analyzing the individual as such it is sufficient to say that it is internally undivided and is not identical in existence—that is, in its relation to the Creator—with any other individual.

Divine freedom. The transition from essential to existential being, or the act of creation, is an act of divine freedom. Individual beings come into existence not from any intrinsic necessity but because God freely wills to create. Here the Christian and Augustinian conception of God's transcendent liberty excludes the Avicennian idea of the divine will as subject, equally with the divine intellect, to necessity. In his fear of compromising God's freedom in creation, Henry further minimized the intelligibility of individual beings. There are no divine ideas of singular things as such; God knows them only through their essences considered as multipliable in numerically distinct beings. Consequently, the existence of creatures can in no way be deduced from God's eternal ideas.

Necessary and contingent being. The fundamental metaphysical notion of being is neither simply derived from sense experience nor strictly innate in the human mind. It is indeed formed by the mind from within, but on the occasion of sense experience. It would actually be more correct to say that two fundamental notions of being are formed by the mind, since the concepts of necessary or divine Being and contingent or creaturely being are radically distinct and cannot be deduced from a more general notion. When we conceive being unconfusedly, we always conceive either necessary Being or contingent being—never some undifferentiated, neutral being.

In thus asserting the irreducible duality of the notion of being, Henry was again trying to exclude any suggestion that God necessarily creates. If neither divine Being nor creaturely being can be deduced from a universal concept of being, one argument for necessitarianism is effectively undermined. The further consequences of Henry's principle, however, were disastrous for his own metaphysical enterprise. His insistence that there is no positive content common to the two fundamental notions of being leaves a gap between divine Being and creaturely being which no mere affirmation of analogy between the two concepts can bridge. But if, as Henry claimed, there is some empirical factor in the formation of our notions of being, it is hard to see how necessary Being can be conceived, let alone demonstrated, as long as the gap remains. It is true that an a posteriori or "physical" proof of God's existence, based on experience of individual objects rather than on metaphysical principles, is possible, but such a proof can attain only to a supreme Being, not to a necessary Being. An appeal to divine illumination—the obvious remaining alternative—was excluded for Henry because he did not conceive of the divine light as a power impressing ideas upon the human mind. Although Henry refused to draw it, the conclusion seems inevitable that no firm basis can be found for a metaphysical theology.

With Henry of Ghent, medieval Platonism was clearly entering its final phase. In his thought, for all its predominantly Augustinian and Avicennian character, more or less novel concerns—a new stress on divine freedom, a fresh interest in sense experience, a new emphasis on sheer particularity—already modified the Platonic view of reality. Henry is thus a significant symbol of the transition from the constructive to the critical period of medieval thought.

Bibliography

Henry of Ghent's major works are his *Summa* (Paris, 1520; reprinted, St. Bonaventure, N.Y., 1953) and his *Quodlibet* (Paris, 1518).

For a discussion of Henry of Ghent and his works, see Jean Paulus, *Henri de Gand: Essai sur les tendances de sa métaphysique* (Paris, 1938).

EUGENE R. FAIRWEATHER

HENRY OF HARCLAY (c. 1270–1317), English scholastic theologian and philosopher, was born in the diocese of Carlisle. After studying at Oxford and Paris, he was ordained a priest in 1297 and obtained his master of theology about 1310. He taught at Oxford, becoming chancellor of the university in 1312. He wrote an unedited "Commentary on the *Sentences*," and "Disputed Questions," most of which are unpublished. He died at Avignon.

Early in his career, while commenting on the *Sentences,* Henry defended the main theses of Duns Scotus. Later, he criticized Scotism, teaching a doctrine of universals close to that of Ockham. He held that there are no common natures or essences in reality; there are only individuals, each of which has its own nature. Since there are no common natures, there is no need of the Scotist haecceity to render them individual. As Ockham later said, realities are individual not by an added "thisness" but by themselves.

Henry's doctrine of universals is based on this notion of

reality. According to him, an individual can be conceived of either distinctly or indistinctly. When distinctly conceived, it is known through a particular concept; when indistinctly conceived, it is known through a universal concept. A universal is a confused concept by which the mind knows one individual without distinguishing it from others in the same genus or species. Inasmuch as an individual can be known through general concepts, Henry called it universal. For example, Socrates indistinctly conceived is man, animal, and body. Ockham criticized Henry's conceptualism because it ascribed some universality to things outside the mind.

Henry rejected the Scotist doctrine of the divine ideas as essences of creatures existing in God with cognitional being. He adopted a variation of the theory that the ideas are really the same as the divine essence itself known by God as imitable by creatures. God is known through concepts univocal to Him and creatures.

Henry stressed the omnipotence of God and the radical contingency of creatures. He claimed that no creature is naturally indestructible; the human soul is immortal not by nature but by divine grace. According to Henry, St. Thomas betrayed Christianity by teaching the natural immortality of the soul.

Bibliography

Balić, Carlum, "Henricus de Harcley et Ioannes Duns Scotus," in *Mélanges offerts à Étienne Gilson*. Paris and Toronto, 1959. Pp. 93–121.

Gilson, Étienne, *History of Christian Philosophy in the Middle Ages*. New York, 1955. Pp. 480–483, 779.

Kraus, Johannes, "Die Universalienlehre des Oxforder Kanzlers Heinrich von Harclay." *Divus Thomas,* Vol. 10 (1932), 36–58, 475–508; Vol. 11 (1933), 76–96, 288–314.

Maurer, Armand, "Henry of Harclay's Question on the Univocity of Being." *Mediaeval Studies,* Vol. 16 (1954), 1–18.

Maurer, Armand, "Henry of Harclay's Questions on Immortality." *Mediaeval Studies,* Vol. 19 (1957), 79–107.

Maurer, Armand, "Henry of Harclay's Questions on the Divine Ideas." *Mediaeval Studies,* Vol. 23 (1961), 163–193.

Pelster, Franz, "Heinrich von Harclay, Kanzler von Oxford, und seine Quästionen." *Miscellanea Francesco Ehrle,* Vol. 1 (1924), 307–356.

ARMAND A. MAURER

HERACLITUS OF EPHESUS, pre-Socratic philosopher. Exact dating of Heraclitus' life is impossible, since the two different ancient chronologies are probably worthless; the more plausible of the two connects him with Darius of Persia (d. 486 B.C.). References by Heraclitus to other writers make it impossible to date his work much before 500 B.C.; references to him (not by name) in Parmenides and the Sicilian poet Epicharmus are uncertain. Since Heraclitus ignores Parmenides, one can scarcely date his work after 460 B.C. Little is certain, about his life, except for his domicile in Ephesus, an Ionian city of Asia Minor. Hellenistic biographers invented biographical facts, either to fill the void or to take the only revenge open to them for Heraclitus' insults to mankind. The story most often believed—that he gave up his (not necessarily exclusive) kingship to his younger brother—could be based on the traditional motif of philosophers' unworldliness coupled with his own statement from another context,

"The kingdom is a child's." The legend of the "weeping philosopher" is late and based on a combination of a Platonic joke, Heraclitus' theory of flux, and a misunderstanding of Theophrastus' word "melancholia," which originally meant "impulsiveness."

Work. The nine "Letters of Heraclitus" are spurious, having been produced by Cynic or Stoic rhetoricians of the first century A.D. Heraclitus wrote one book, title (if any) unknown. The fact that it was a connected exposition and not merely a collection of sayings is suggested by the elaborate introductory sentence still extant. The book itself is now lost, and how long it survived is uncertain. Several ancient commentaries and metrical "versions," mostly Stoic, are also lost. Fortunately, many ancient authors from Plato on quoted Heraclitus; but citations may often come from anthologies or metrical versions, are often torn from context, and are seldom verbally reliable. Heraclitus must be pieced together, a process hindered by ancient misunderstandings.

Style. Ancient opinion, generally unfavorable, nicknamed Heraclitus "the obscure," mentioning ambiguities of word order and division. The problems of interpreting fragments are deepened by frequent metaphors and pregnant utterances; Heraclitus probably compared his own style to that of the Sibylline oracles. The fragments offer more instances of illustration than of argument, almost confirming Aristotle's imputation that Heraclitus was guilty of not reasoning. Connection between topics was probably more verbal (in the Archaic manner) than logical. Accustomed to poetic vocabulary, Heraclitus used few technical terms or verbal abstracts, and those he did use were for cognitive rather than external processes. Personal knowledge of his homely illustrations adds force to his statements. But he polished his sentences, anticipating such devices of rhetoric as alliteration, homoeoteleuton, and rhythmic balance. His doctrine of the unity of opposites invited antithesis and juxtaposition of contrasting descriptions at the expense of normal word order. His style was thus appropriate to his matter, as in his numerous puns, which were not intended to amuse but reflected the untutored assumption that a word's form resembles the thing it signifies. Heraclitus' style is biting, earnest, and prophetic.

Physical views. Heraclitus abandoned genetic explanations of the world, believing it uncreated. In his view, all events take place according to a "Logos," a term he left undefined. Since the Logos can be heard, it must be expressible in words; but it would appear that "Logos" signifies far more than Heraclitus' book, since the philosopher reproaches men for not understanding the Logos before they hear it and advises listening to the Logos, not to himself. Logos is both discourse and contents, both the truth about things and the principle on which they function. Being common to all things, the Logos would be accessible to men if it were not for their folly. In this objective sense, there is also a Logos of the soul, although deeply hidden. The Greek word *logos* can mean "proportion," and for Heraclitus one change takes place in the same proportion as the reverse change. The English word that best covers Heraclitus' philosophical uses of "Logos" is "formula." But this Logos has a material aspect in the form of Fire. We find it difficult to conceive of a "formula" as being material, but the concept of incorporeal existence was not available to Heraclitus. His idea that an abstract "formula" was the world's ruling stuff was a significant step toward the availability of such a concept, not its attainment. Symbolized by "thunderbolt" in its function of "steering all things," Fire is also associated with human wisdom and doubtless governed the world intelligently. The truth expressed in the Logos is principally the unity of opposites. These opposites, however, are engaged in perpetual strife, and Strife is not only right and normal, but is also, like the Logos, "common," and everything happens according to it. It is tempting simply to identify Fire, Logos, and Strife, but that is an oversimplification; we have not so much a formally coherent system as several lines of thought closely associated but not fully integrated. The unity of the opposites struck Heraclitus so forcibly that he leaped to the conclusion that all things are one.

Unity of opposites. Pairs of opposites exemplify the unity of all things by standing in several different relationships to each other. First, they may be logically indistinguishable, as in "Beginning and end are 'common' on the circle." Second, they may be in unvarying mutual succession: thus, day and night are one, because, in modern terms, they are "temporally continuous"—a possible sense for "one" Greek. Other examples of this type, harder to interpret, are living–dead, awake–asleep, and young–old. Hot–cold and wet–dry should perhaps be included here: of each pair, one member changes invariably and solely into the other, without significant temporal discontinuity. The remaining types are liable to give the impression of relativism; but it should be stressed that Heraclitus was insufficiently aware of epistemological problems to ask himself the relevant questions, and also that strife (and therefore opposition) was fundamental to his natural philosophy. When Heraclitus says "the road up and down is one and the same," he does not mean that "up" and "down" are relative terms, but that their unity in opposition results from their predicability of the same object. The same holds for another saying, "In writing, the course taken, straight and crooked, is one and the same"; one is tempted to say that curvature and straightness "inhere" in the movement, but the word "inhere" and the distinction between qualities and objects are anachronistic. Also, only superficially relativistic is the following type of assertion: "The sea is both purest and foulest; drinkable and salutary for fish, to men undrinkable and poisonous." Here Heraclitus deduces the unity of opposites from the opposite effects of one thing on different creatures; but he does not deduce the absence of opposition. Lastly, one opposite may be a necessary condition for the perception of another: "Disease makes health pleasant and good, hunger satiety, weariness rest." Opposition remains, but the impossibility of experiencing one fully without the other connects the opposites. The tempting word "connection" is justified by Heraclitus' use of a similar word: "Men do not understand how what is being borne apart is being brought together with itself; a backward-stretching *harmonia* as of bow and lyre." "Harmonia" here cannot be purely musical, nor does it mean "concord"; "connection" seems the best proposed rendering, referring to the strings connecting the arms of bow and lyre. For Heraclitus, such a connection proved opposites the same. Those who find difficulty in understanding this mode of thought may recall that to distinguish between different senses of one word was (except for obvious homonyms) an unknown logical venture. If opposites were one in the sense (in our terms) of "connected" or "continuous," they were also one in the sense of being "identical"; Heraclitus could not make the Aristotelian distinction between unity as continuity and as identity. Furthermore, beginning and end *are* indistinguishable on the circle, and the road up and down *is* physically the same; Heraclitus can hardly have made the distinctions offered here between types of opposition. Heraclitus believed both connection and difference between opposites to be valid, but considered the unity more important and valuable, because less obvious. This valuation reappears in the combined statements: "The human character does not have insights, but the divine does," and "To the god all things are beautiful and good and just, but men opine that some are just and some unjust." The same valuation, taken together with the status of Logos and Fire, probably evoked the remark, "God is day, night; winter, summer; war, peace; satiety, hunger," adding "He changes as fire (?) does when mixed with things sacrificed and called by the name appropriate to the taste of each." Here Heraclitus apparently implies that each pair of opposites is united in the deity, that each is of equal standing, and that all are somehow divine. The relation of this deity to the Logos must be close, but is undefined.

Change and measure. For Heraclitus change takes place between opposites, but like his predecessors and successors he also talked of change between cosmic masses (a better term than "elements," since Heraclitus hardly analyzed the composition of particulars). He thought these masses to be three in number; fragments that name four are suspected to be Stoic perversions. The three are fire (associated particularly with the bright sky), sea, and earth, and they correspond to our gaseous, liquid, and solid states of matter; but other philosophers ignored Heraclitus' hint, and four became the canonical number. Heraclitus wrote, "The turnings of fire are: first sea, of sea half earth and half 'prester,'" and "Earth is fused as sea and is measured in the same proportion as before (? before it became earth)." "Prester" is a meteorological phenomenon, possibly lightning, representing fire or a way of changing into fire. Either the sea *is* half fire, half earth, or it *is turning* half to fire and half to earth. Heraclitus' statement, which is not cosmogonical, describes the course of changes in the existing world. Theophrastus applied the saying about the "way up and down" to this course—an application of doubtful correctness. Details of the proportions are obscure, and so is the integration of opposites with cosmic masses. This fact is not surprising, for the assignment of opposites to "elements" remained a standing problem of Greek thought. The importance of proportion in change is clear, however; without its maintenance, the balance of the opposites would be destroyed, and Strife would cease. The world's stability depends on balanced strife between opposites, and compensation of local or temporary imbalance. Nevertheless, Fire has some pre-eminence: "All things are an equal exchange for fire, and fire for all things, as goods for gold and gold for goods." In this instance, Fire is set against all things, as in the statement about "turnings." Again, "No god or man created this world order, but it always was and is and will be: an ever-living fire, being kindled in measures and extinguished in measures." These fragments do not justify the Stoic interpretation of Heraclitus' Fire as an ultimate universal conflagration; the emphasis on balance and measure is strong enough to refute that interpretation. The probably Heraclitean notion of a Great Year need not imply the conflagration either. This period of 10,800 years (360 thirty-year generations) may represent either an eschatological cycle for souls or a physical cycle in which a given piece of matter returns to its original position. The "exchange" of all things for fire is the part extinction and part rekindling of the fire which is the world order; perhaps each thing has an exchange value in terms of fire. This extinction and rekindling show that changes really take place from and into fire and that individual nonfiery objects are not fire; fire is not a substratum. The reasons for Fire's primacy in Heraclitus' thought were, doubtless, complex. In the first place, the ebb and flow of flame afforded an apt symbol for constant balanced change; second, Anaximander had written of one stuff "holding the helm" of all things; and furthermore, heat was associated with life, and early Greek thinkers often transferrred animate states and processes to inanimate Nature.

In details also measure was important; Heraclitus wrote of the sun's measures, which were not to be overstepped without punishment. But little is known of his detailed astronomical and meteorological views. He cannot have meant that the sun is literally "only a foot wide." Doxographical tradition records his interpretation of the heavenly bodies as bowls containing fire; he explained the moon's phases by the gradual turning of its bowl and apparently asked no further questions. He thought the sun new every day, probably as being extinguished each sunset and rekindled when fire gathered in the bowl each morning. The sun's fire was nourished by a bright exhalation from earth or sea. Theoretically, absence of sunlight should suffice to cause darkness, and Heraclitus even said, "If there were no sun it would be night." Doxographical evidence suggests, however, that he postulated a second, dark exhalation to quench the sun's fire. The stars, more distant, were beyond reach of this exhalation. Doxographers allege this exhalation in explanation of seasons, months, years, rains, winds, and so forth; the extent and manner of its operation are uncertain, and in this report some have suspected Peripatetic "interpretation." To integrate the exhalations with opposites and cosmic masses is difficult. Theophrastus' reproach of "incompleteness" perhaps indicates the absence of a systematic astronomy or meteorology. Heraclitus' naïveté in such matters may reasonably be attributed to his being less interested in them than in his logical discovery about opposites and its physical implications.

Flux. One elaboration of that discovery, was of immediate physical importance, namely, the theory of flux. Although this theory has often been exaggerated, it did not signify that everything, without physical or logical exception, was continually changing and therefore inaccessible to knowledge, for such was the theory of Cratylus, sharply distinguished by good evidence from Heraclitus' theory. One explanation of the latter's theory is that Heraclitus, comparing all things to a river, meant that they all changed all the time; applied to natural objects, this means that even apparently stable things are changing, although total balance is always maintained. This view is sometimes rejected as being precluded by common sense and Heraclitus' acceptance of sense evidence. It is then maintained that the river illustrates not perpetual, but measured, change. But in the various "river statements" extant, there is nothing explicit about measures; the concept of the river's remaining the same amid the flow of different waters is consistent with either interpretation. Heraclitus valued the senses highly, but emphasized their need of an understanding mind as interpreter, and the probably Heraclitean remark that one cannot step twice into the same river sounds more like an emphatic parable of continuous change.

Psychology. Although skeptical of final knowledge of the soul, Heraclitus arrived, partly by introspection, at a psychology that neatly dovetailed into his cosmology. Souls fit into the cosmic flux, apparently occupying the same place as Fire: "It is death for souls to become water." Total wateriness means death, but in life the fiery soul is wisest and best when kept dry. A drunkard, having a wet soul, does not know where he is going, but is led by a child. This implies that a dry soul guides the body just as Fire steers all things. Partial extinction and rekindling obtains in man as in Nature, for sleep extinguishes certain senses. The afterlife in Heraclitus is obscure; we know that "there await mankind after death things they do not expect," and that at least "souls smell in Hades"—whatever Heraclitus meant by "Hades." Perhaps some special fate awaited the dead in battle, whom "gods and men honor," for "Greater deaths are allotted greater portions"; but if everything joins the cosmic flux anyway, this statement is difficult to understand; these fragments, out of context, constitute an uncertain foundation for theory. Life and death, as alternate states, are the same. This concept need not imply metempsychosis and more probably reflects either the tradition of a grandfather's rebirth in his grandson or the alternate dissolution of the body and formation of another from similar materials; either view would also explain the mutual succession of young and old. The living and dead are also somehow continuous: in an epistemological context, "The living touches the dead in sleep, the waking touches the sleeping." In sleep, the Greek Skeptic Sextus Empiricus records, the soul is cut off from the outside world by the blocking of passages used by the senses. Thus, the soul loses memory, but recovers it on awakening. The soul in sleep maintains residual contact with externals by breathing; to this contact (obviously lost in death) the soul owes some of its intelligence.

The senses. Heraclitus was perhaps the first Greek speculative philosopher to raise the question of the validity of sense perception. So far as the senses go, he did not believe that they actually deceive: "I prefer things of which there is sight, hearing, learning." He called the eyes more accurate witnesses than the ears—perhaps intending a warning against hearsay. An injunction to independent inquiry, "Lovers of wisdom must be good inquirers into many things," is not contradicted by "Learning of many things does not teach insight"; Heraclitus distinguishes true philosophical insight from indiscriminate gathering of facts, believing facts to be necessary but not sufficient for insight. The soul is both agent and interpreter of sensations; its relation to the body is that of spider to web. The soul, being firmly and "proportionally" joined to the body, rushes to any injured part of it. If the soul interpreter is barbarous—that is, if it does not understand the language—insight will not result. Heraclitus frequently abuses men for their lack of understanding; he compares their opinions to children's playthings, denounces them as deaf to what they hear and as asleep even when awake, and rebukes them for relying on individual, rather than on "common," thought, which he associates with insight. The object of insight is the way in which the world functions—"how all things are steered through all things." Thus, the intelligent Fire and Logos are objects of knowledge by the fiery human soul at its most intelligent.

Theology. The comparison with children is developed theologically: man is to god as child to man; similarly, compared with a god, man resembles an ape. Divine insight contrasts with human lack of it. Heraclitus disapproved of many popular cults: he compares purification of blood guilt by blood sacrifice to washing off mud with mud and compares praying to statues with talking to walls. He condemns the mystery cults, perhaps for a similar lack of spirituality, as "conducted in an unholy manner." The best that can be said for oracles is that their style, by which they "neither speak nor conceal but give a sign," deserves approving imitation. All that can be said for the procession and the hymn to Dionysus (otherwise a shameful phallic rite) is that they imply the identification of Dionysus with Hades, here possibly representing life and death, respectively. But there is a wide gulf between disapproval of polytheist cults and espousal of monotheism, and there is insufficient evidence that Heraclitus crossed it. The question of monotheism versus polytheism was not raised in Archaic Greece. In referring to "the one wise thing" which "is willing and unwilling to be called Zeus," he doubtlessly means that Fire or Logos is supreme but lacks the personal attributes attached to Zeus in cult and myth. But even though a tendency toward monotheism is observable, we cannot credit Heraclitus with solving a problem he probably never considered. He attacked myth when it conflicted with his theories; he criticized Hesiod for distinguishing Day and Night, and Homer for recounting a prayer for an end to strife.

Ethics. In the statement "Character is *daemon* to man," theology merges with ethics. According to traditional belief, a divine being, or *daemon*, accompanied man through life, bringing him good fortune or bad: Heraclitus ascribed men's fortunes to internal forces. Although he implies the possibility of action in accordance with the Logos, he gives little detail. One should not get drunk or reveal ignorance; what men want is not good for them; punishment awaits liars—there is little system here. From contemptuous words about "the many" it appears that Heraclitus considered glory more permanent and valuable than sensual gratification. It is unlikely that he abolished ethics by completely identifying good and evil. Theology merges with politics in the doctrine of the one divine law that nourishes and gives strength to all human laws. Anaximander had projected justice into the world, but Heraclitus introduced the first extant connection of divine (unwritten) law with the laws of states, which was the origination of the theory of "natural law." Other political views of Heraclitus, expressing mainly typical antidemocratic sentiments, are less significant.

Influence. Heraclitus' doctrine of simultaneously converging and diverging opposites generated only faint echoes. It supplied some minor Hippocratic writers with an excuse for thoughtless paradox and may be said to reappear in Anaxagoras' refusal to separate the opposites in "the one cosmos," and again in Diogenes of Apollonia's argument that action of one thing on another implies their constitution from one substance. Possibly Empedocles' theory of alternate states of unity (under Love, or *Harmonia*) and diversity (under Strife) owes something to Heraclitus' theory of opposition, as well as to Eleaticism. Later, more emphasis was laid on flux. Plato's "Heracliteans . . . around Ephesus" may be jocular, but the Athenian Cratylus adopted the concept of flux and also made explicit the "natural" resemblance between name and object. In Plato's *Cratylus*, Socrates demonstrates the difficulties in this combination, and Cratylus was later driven to abandoning language and communicating by gesture. Exaggerating Heraclitus' river statement, Cratylus said that you could not step into the same river once. His importance derives from Aristotle's statement that he introduced Heraclitean flux to the young Plato, who was (partly) thereby persuaded to deny knowability and reality to particulars. Aristotle not only depreciated Heraclitus, but vitiated later understanding of him by assimilation to his Milesian predecessors and by propagation of the world conflagration interpretation appropriated by the Stoics. Many aspects of genuinely Heraclitean doctrine appealed to the Stoics: Heraclitus' psychology gave them the image of spider and web; Cleanthes drew on the concept of the primacy of fire as well as the Heraclitean ideas of unity, harmony, war, and insight, but gave them a deeper religious import. For Stoics too the soul was material and the Logos common to mind and external world; for both the Heracliteans and the Stoics, the Logos was divine, eternal, all-pervading. The Stoics added a creative power whereby the Logos informed objects, creatures, and thoughts. Philo's connection of this Logos with the Divine Wisdom prepared for the transcendent yet incarnate Logos of Christianity. Later Christian writers either, like Clement of Alexandria, found in Heraclitus one middle way between pagan rationalism and Christian anti-intellectualism or, like Hippolytus, rebutted heresies by assimilation to Heraclitean paganism.

Bibliography

TEXTS

Volume I of H. Diels and W. Kranz, *Die Fragmente der Vorsokratiker*, 10th ed. (Berlin, 1961) contains the standard critical text with a competent German translation, but is over-optimistic in attribution to Heraclitus. R. Walzer, *Eraclito* (Florence, 1939) prints contexts of ancient citations more fully.

INTRODUCTIONS

W. K. C. Guthrie, *History of Greek Philosophy*, Vol. I (Cambridge, 1962) has a sober, impartial survey. G. S. Kirk and J. E. Raven, *The Presocratic Philosophers*, 2d ed. (Cambridge, 1960) contains a critical account and selected texts and translations. H. Fränkel, *Dichtung und Philosophie des frühen Griechentums*, 2d ed. (Munich, 1962) sets Heraclitus in both literary and philosophical context.

BIBLIOGRAPHY

E. Zeller and R. Mondolfo, *La filosofia dei Greci*, Part I, Vol. IV (Florence, 1961) is a monumental survey, with copious ancient and modern references.

ADDITIONAL BACKGROUND

K. Reinhardt, *Parmenides und die Geschichte der griechischen Philosophie* (Bonn, 1916) is fundamental, but unsound on chronology and Orphic influence. O. Gigon, *Untersuchungen zu Heraklit* (Leipzig, 1936) is a stimulating work, more incisive on psychology than cosmology. G. S. Kirk, *Heraclitus, the Cosmic Fragments* (Cambridge, 1954) is exemplary in its field for thoroughness in study of text and interpretation. It is well criticized by G. Vlastos, "On Heraclitus," in *American Journal of Philology*, Vol. 76 (1955), 337–368.

MICHAEL C. STOKES

HERBART, JOHANN FRIEDRICH (1776–1841), German philosopher, psychologist, and educational theorist, was born in Oldenburg; he entered the University of Jena in 1794. Although he studied under Johann Gottlieb Fichte, Herbart was unable to accept Fichte's view of the ego and its psychology, and in reaction he laid the basis for his own metaphysical and psychological views. In 1797 Herbart took a post in Switzerland as tutor. He held the position for three years and, during this period, worked out to a large extent the views which he was to refine and elaborate for the rest of his life.

After he took his doctorate at Göttingen in 1802, Herbart remained there for the next seven years. *Allgemeine Pädagogik* ("General Theory of Education") and *Hauptpunkte der Metaphysik* ("Main Points of Metaphysics"), both of which appeared in Göttingen in 1806, and his *Allgemeine praktische Philosophie* ("General Practical Philosophy," Göttingen, 1808) were major fruits of this period. In 1809 Herbart moved to Königsberg to occupy Kant's former chair, and there he published his *Lehrbuch zur Psychologie* ("Compendium of Psychology," 1816), *Psychologie als Wissenschaft* ("Psychology as a Science," 1824–1825), and *Allgemeine Metaphysik* ("General Metaphysics," 1828–1829). When the political situation rendered Königsberg continually less attractive and Herbart failed to secure Hegel's chair at the University of Berlin, he returned to Göttingen in 1833 and remained there until his death.

The parts of philosophy. Philosophy, according to Herbart, cannot be characterized by its subject matter but only by its method, which is the reworking (*Bearbeitung*) of concepts; and the possible kinds of such elaboration determine the major divisions of philosophy.

The first kind of reworking renders concepts clear and distinct. Distinct concepts can be formed into judgments and these judgments can be organized into inferences.

This process of distinguishing and ordering concepts is logic.

But experience gives rise to many concepts which, the more distinct they become, the more contradictory they appear, a sure sign that we are missing both being and truth. Our ideas must, therefore, undergo an "enlargement" (*Ergänzung*), which will remove the contradiction. This second kind of reworking of concepts gives us the second great division of philosophy, metaphysics.

Concepts in the third class are like the metaphysical concepts in that they cannot remain merely at the level of clarity and distinctness, as do the logical concepts. But while the metaphysical concepts involve only enlargement, this third class involves in addition an intuitive judgment of approval or disapproval. Thus we get the last great division, aesthetics. Aesthetics includes a series of doctrines of art or practical sciences. One of these, ethics, issues necessary (and not merely conditional) prescriptions because we continuously and necessarily concern ourselves with its object, ourselves.

Metaphysics. Metaphysics consists of four parts: (1) method, the general principles of the proper method and order of procedure; (2) ontology, the study of the real; (3) synechiology, the study of those forms of experience which have continuity (such as space, time, and motion), and (4) eidolology, the examination of the possibility of knowledge.

Method. The first task of metaphysics is to define "the given" in experience. Common sense says that it is "things with multiple and changing characteristics." But this concept violates the law of identity. For any single thing dissolves into a multiplicity of qualities when we describe it; it is at once both a unity and not a unity. Substance, cause, ego, time, and space are also contradictory. Yet they must be "given" in some sense, since we cannot change them at will. In moving to metaphysical concepts freed from contradiction, we use as our chief tool the "method of relations." A contradictory concept of experience, A, unites the contradictory terms M and N. M is thus both identical and nonidentical with N. If one further divides M into M' and M'', one element will still be identical with N, the other not; this contradiction disappears only when we admit that, although each of the parts of M is not identical with N, they mutually modify each other so that together they become so. Thus, in the syllogism, the conclusion must be contained in the premises; and thus the premises must change into or cause the conclusion. But M' and M'', the premises or cause, are not individually the same as N, the conclusion or effect. Hence M' and M'', the premises, must mutually modify each other so as to become identical with the conclusion.

Ontology. Ontology deals with being. Since being is not directly given in experience, it is easy to say that there is no being. But it is hard to live with this judgment, for things continue to appear. What, then, is it that appears? Appearances or phenomena cannot be taken as the only reality, for the concept of absolute position (being in absolutely no relation whatever to anything) cannot be applied to them; they are always related to something else. Nor can phenomena be reduced to our sensations of them and then located in an ego, for our sensations are not just sensations of sensations, and the concept of the ego is itself contradictory.

We are thus led to posit "being" as a plurality of beings or reals (*Realen*), with the essence of each real a single quality, absolutely simple, without parts, degree, or negation, always immutably identical with itself. But how can this concept of being be reconciled with our experience, which is both the basis of metaphysics and its test? The absolute position of reals seems to contradict the multiple relations in which things appear to us. But being can be conceived by mind; and in mind a being is only an image (*Bild*). Mind also can simultaneously represent several beings, which, as images, can stand in many different relations to the first one. These relations are "contingent viewpoints" (*zufällige Ansichten*), which exist in thought, not in things-in-themselves. Just as in analytic geometry the same point can be part of an infinite number of curves, so a single real may enter many contingent viewpoints.

Experience presents us with complex aggregates which we call things. Yet we cannot say that the aggregate exists, for colors, sounds, and such exist only in the perceiving subject. Nor can we say that something having those qualities—that is, substance—exists, for substance cannot be being if being is simple, since substance appears as endowed with manifold and varying qualities. How, then, can attributes and modes inhere in substance? By the method of relations. If *A* is a substance and *a* an attribute, analysis of *A* into multiple elements (*A'*, *A''*, and so on) will not resolve the contradiction unless we say that *a* is not identical with any one of the *A*'s but with the totality of them, the number of which remains undetermined but which must be at least two if mutual modification between them is to occur. Substance, then, is explainable as multiple beings in conjunction (*zusammen*) with each other, many reals grouped about one real. This conjunction explains that unity which we attribute to substance, although the essential unchanging quality of that central real is unknown to us; and the other reals in conjunction with it account for the varied and varying attributes we experience, although those attributes are not the essential qualities of those various reals.

The conjunction and the separation of the reals explain those sensible appearances which led to their postulation. Such mutual interaction would seem to lead to mutual destruction, but, just as in an equilibrium of forces both forces remain constantly what each is, though balanced, so in the concatenation of reals, the mutual perturbations (*Störungen*) which would lead to mutual destruction are counterbalanced by individual acts of self-preservation through which each real strives to remain what it is.

These acts of perturbation and self-preservation constitute real phenomena (*das wirkliche Geschehen*), as distinct from sensible phenomena or appearances (*Erscheinung*), of which the real ones are the basis and explanation. To what or to whom do they appear? This is the problem of the ego, self, or soul-substance.

The ego, or self, poses the same problems as do the other substances, and the solution is the same. The unity and diversity of the ego are explained by the coming and going of reals. The soul, which is not the ego of consciousness, is a real, but one endowed with mind which is the seismograph that records, in the form of presentations or ideas (*Vorstellungen*), the acts of self-preservation of the soul vis-à-vis the other reals. These presentations are the sensible phenomena given in experience. With metaphysics thus having shown the origin of our ideas, psychology will show their development and combination.

Synechiology. Synechiology concerns that which is continuous (*das Stetige*)—notably space, time, and motion. Continuity, as union in separation and separation in unity, is a contradictory concept (though undoubtedly given in experience), which must be explained by metaphysics. As far as being is concerned, space and time are "obviously nothing." They, like the continuity which we attribute to them, are merely natural and necessary products of the psychic mechanism. What essentially characterizes space and time is the mutual exteriority (*Auseinander*) of the parts. But between points of space or time it is always possible to *conceive* additional parts, and this further functioning of the psychic mechanism makes space and time seem to flow uninterruptedly.

But the comings and goings of the reals imply some sort of space, time, and motion, even though these are distinct from their sensible counterparts, such as "intelligible space." Although two reals, *A* and *B*, are actually apart, we can conceive the possibility of *B*'s being with *A* and *A*'s being with *B*. Thus space is the simple possibility *in mind* for one real to be together with another from which it is separated in reality, an "image" without reality. Space thus being completely accidental for reals, we can, by putting *A* in the place of *B* and *B* in the place of *A* and further continuing to add more reals and more dimensions, generate lines infinite in all directions, even though each line is "fixed" (*starre*) with a determinate number of points rather than continuous (*stetige*) with mutual interpenetration (and hence indefiniteness in number) of the parts. The psychic mechanism then conceives of these "fixed" lines as continuous by interpolation. Intelligible space, as thus generated, corresponds to the sensible space of phenomena and shares its contradictions, but these need not trouble us since they have nothing to do with being. Intelligible space is a purely conceptual artifact (*Gedankending*), not imposed by mind on things but generated by mind as a necessary aid to thought. Once intelligible space has been generated, the explanation of matter becomes possible. It is a question of asking what situation the images of reals should occupy with respect to intelligible space in order to account for matter. The answer is "incomplete interpenetration."

Eidolology. Eidolology examines the possibility of knowledge and its limits. In all knowledge, matter and form can be distinguished. The matter is simple presentations or sensations. They do not enable us to know what is, but they do oblige us to believe that something is. But the given has form as well as matter. Sensations are not given us in isolation but formed into groups, which cannot be separated at will and which constitute things. Doubtless, in the form in which they appear to us, things exist only in and for mind. But the constancy and the modifications of these groups of sensations have their basis in the conjunction and separation of the reals. Thus mind, though it cannot know the qualities of the reals through sensation, does know their relations; and even were our sensations wholly different from what they are, their forms would be the same, arising as they do from the objective separations and connections of the reals. Knowledge through concepts is likewise valid knowledge, although it too is knowledge only of relations. "We live amid relations and need nothing more."

Psychology. Everything in mind arises in some fashion out of presentations. There are no faculties, no innate ideas, no concepts a priori. The soul is a real in which countless acts of self-preservation are provoked through its contacts with other reals, and these efforts in turn produce in mind the presentations, some of which oppose, some of which reinforce, each other. Although reals and presentations are not forces, they can best be understood by analogy with forces, and hence the synthetic part of psychology consists of the statics and mechanics of mind. Complex mathematical formulas, corresponding to those of the statics and mechanics of physics, describe the interplay of presentations.

Presentations of different sorts do not oppose each other (for instance, colors do not oppose sounds); but presentations of the same sort do (for instance, red opposes blue). In the latter case, what remains after arrest is an equilibrium, a weakening or obscuring of the original presentations that is reached progressively by a process of sinking (*Senkung*). A presentation, if it has not undergone arrest, is present in consciousness. Sinking under arrest, it may be forced below the threshold of consciousness. Yet a presentation below the threshold of consciousness is subject to recall or rising (*Hebung*) by the appearance of a new presentation similar to it, and the speed of this rising depends on the degree of similarity between the two presentations. This new presentation also produces a vaulting (*Wölbung*) or "arching" of all other arrested presentations similar to it. The coming of a new presentation, *B*, produces the rising (*Hebung*) of the similar older presentation *A*. But as *A* is pulled up, other older presentations similar to *A* but less similar to *B* are also pulled up in a *Wölbung*, or arching. The analogy to a beater being pulled out of stiff whipped cream is exact. The surface of the cream closest to the beater is pulled up most (*Hebung*), but the whole center surface arches somewhat (*Wölbung*).

The feelings, the desires, and the will have their origin in presentations. Some feelings arise out of the fusion of opposed presentations, and the pleasantness or unpleasantness depends on the amount of opposition. Other feelings originate in the strain which the rising, produced by a new presentation, puts on ties which an old presentation already has with one or more others. Thus the sight of an object belonging to a dead friend evokes the memory of him, but the thought of his death tends to repress the memory and thus to produce a painful feeling. Pleasant feelings arise in the contrary situation, when the other associated presentations all facilitate the recall of the original one. The desires are closely connected with the feelings. In a situation giving a painful feeling, where *A* is lifted toward consciousness by the appearance of *C* and is simultaneously depressed by its earlier relation to *B*, the feeling of effort by which the resistance is overcome will be a desire and *A* will appear as the object of desire. The will, in turn, is only a particular form of desire, the realization of which is seen as possible.

Concepts, also, have their origin in the fact that each new presentation produces the vaulting of the images of similar previous presentations already in mind, in which process the similarities are reinforced and the differences between them are repressed, as in a composite portrait. (For Herbart's theory of the assimilation of new impressions, see APPERCEPTION.)

Ethics. Ethical judgments are aesthetic judgments involving pleasure and displeasure. Since the completely simple cannot be pleasing or displeasing, these judgments must be directed to something complex, to relations. Since Herbart, like Kant, sought the basis of ethics in the good will, the five possible relations of the will suggest five corresponding fundamental ethical ideas.

The idea of "inner freedom" is the correspondence between a single act of a single will and the judgment passed on it. Harmony between the "objective" will (the inclinations) and the "subjective" will (the intuitive ethical judgment) is absolutely pleasing; its contrary, displeasing.

"Perfection" relates the varied acts of a single will. To this multiplicity, three quantitative concepts may be applied: the strength of any single effort (intensity), the multiplicity of the objects encompassed by the will (extension), and the concentration of this manifold into a total power (a new intensity developing out of extension). There is no absolute standard, but the stronger and more concentrated will is more pleasing than the weaker.

The idea of "benevolence" arises when one will comes to terms with the will of another. Yet this relation is internal to the first will in that it takes the will of the other person as an object.

The idea of "law" concerns the relations between the wills of two persons who desire some one thing. The ensuing strife is not, however, merely the contrary of the idea of benevolence, since both wills are turned directly toward the object and only indirectly toward each other.

The idea of "equity" arises from the intentional doing of an act of ill or good, a displeasing imbalance between two wills which can be rectified only by some appropriate requital through reward and punishment.

These five basic ethical ideas cannot be isolated in estimating character or in organizing social or political life; each must be tempered by all the others. Together, they exhaust the possible relations of the will, since the addition of more wills repeats in more complicated fashion those already covered by law and equity. But extension is possible if the many wills of a group can be analogized to that of a single rational being. Then five analogous social ideas appear in the reverse order. Members of this society will seek to avoid strife through a "system of law." But transgressions lead to a "system of requital." The benevolent spectator would wish for the greatest possible sum of well-being attained through the rational distribution of the available goods according to a "system of administration." Then increased well-being would produce an intensity and range of strivings reconciled under a "system of culture." With the obedience of each to the moral insight of all, the many would become one in an "ideal society."

Education. Education takes its aim from ethics; psychology then shows it the means and hindrances to this end. The aim is moral strength of character, a will with inner freedom whose volitions are always in accord with the moral law. The three major divisions of education are instruction (*Unterricht*), discipline (*Regierung*), and training (*Zucht*). Since psychology shows that the entire mental life (including the desires and the will) is built out of presentations, instruction (with its four steps of clarity, association, system, and method) is directed toward enlarging the child's circle of thought and developing in him a many-sided interest by efficiently introducing the proper presentations into his apperceptive mass. Discipline keeps the child obedient and attentive so that instruction and training can do their work before the child has developed a proper will of his own. Training works constantly with instruction and discipline to form the will directly through such means as environment, examples, and ideals. Under discipline, the child acts rightly because he must; under proper instruction and training, he acts rightly because he wills to do so.

Bibliography

The writings of Herbart were published in *Collected Works*, G. Hartenstein, ed., 2d ed., 13 vols. (Hamburg, 1883–1893), and *Collected Works*, K. Kehrbach and O. Fluegel, eds., 19 vols. (Leipzig, 1887–1912; reprinted 1963).

An introduction to Herbart's philosophical psychology is G. F. Stout's essay (1888), reprinted in his *Studies in Philosophy and Psychology* (New York, 1930). Works on Herbart include G. Weiss, *Herbart und seine Schule* (Munich, 1928); T. Fritzsch, *J. F. Herbarts Leben und Lehre* (Leipzig, 1921); and M. Mauxion, *La Métaphysique de Herbart* (Paris, 1894).

HAROLD B. DUNKEL

HERBERT OF CHERBURY (1583–1648), English deist, metaphysician, soldier, duelist, philanderer, diplomat, historian, and poet. Edward Herbert, first Baron Herbert of Cherbury, was born at Eyton, Shropshire, and studied at University College, Oxford. His poetry, in English and Latin, long eclipsed by that of his pious younger brother, George Herbert, has won increasing recognition in the present century. Both brothers were disciples of John Donne.

Herbert's historical works are *Expeditio in Ream Insulam* (1656; in English, 1860) and *The Life and Raigne of King Henry the Eighth* (1649), both inspired more by the desire to flatter Charles I than by genuine historical aspiration. A *Dialogue between a Tutor and his Pupil* (anonymous but undoubtedly by Herbert), chiefly concerned with the reformation of religious instruction, appeared only in 1768; it was published, apparently, because of the popularity of *The Life of Edward Lord Herbert of Cherbury, Written by Himself*, which had been printed by Horace Walpole four years earlier. Ending abruptly with Herbert's recall in 1624 as ambassador to France, the autobiography, however interesting and amusing because of its chitchat and devotion to pomp and circumstance, is disappointing to the student of ideas.

Herbert has been called the father of English deism and the first English author of a purely metaphysical treatise. His unchallenged right to both titles rests upon three publications: *De Veritate, Prout distinguitur a Revelatione, a*

Verisimili, a Possibili, et a Falso (Paris, 1624; in French, 1639; London, 1633; enlarged, 1645; in English, Bristol, 1937); *De Causis Errorum*, including *De Religione Laici* and *Appendix ad Sacerdotes* (London, 1645); and *De Religione Gentilium Errorumque apud Eos Câusis* (Amsterdam, 1663; in English, London, 1705).

Herbert was not given to acknowledge his sources (Aristotle and Cicero are the sole authors specifically alluded to in *De Veritate*), but his thought derives in general from Neoplatonism, Neo-Stocism, and skepticism, with some enigmatic references to certain "recent writers" and "the medical authorities"; although it must be added that Herbert himself possessed considerable originality. He stood apart from the general flow of new scientific ideas which were fostered by Bacon and the practicing scientists of the seventeenth century.

The problem of truth. The first eight sections of *De Veritate*, a work dedicated to "every sane and unprejudiced reader," deal with the meaning and the attainment of truth. Eschewing those who maintained that truth is unobtainable, those who maintained that all truth is obtainable, and those who relied solely on implicit faith, Herbert sought to derive truth from what is universal. According to his theory truth is eternal and universal and, within limits, is recognizable by man. Four varieties of truth exist: truth of thing or object, of appearance, of concept, and of intellect. Herbert had the unusual idea that human natural instincts, or faculties, were infinite in number to coincide with the infinity of things; but that they too could be grouped under four heads—natural instinct (light of nature), which dominates the other faculties; internal apprehension (conscience and will); external apprehension (sensation); and discursive thought (reason). These faculties, which Divine Providence has given to every mind, will, if properly exercised, infallibly provide man with the "Common Notions." Herbert maintained that religion and law, about which in a general sense all peoples agree, are examples of Common Notions. The mind is not a *tabula rasa* to be written upon by the objects of experience; rather it is at birth in possession of the innate truths that give meaning to experience.

Of the four categories of instincts, or faculties, reason is the weakest and the last to be resorted to; its special task is the examination of the analogy between things. At its best, reason becomes genuine logic. The key to Herbert's ostensible derogation of reason is that he restricts the term to logic or method, giving other names to the intellectual faculties; actually he was a firm rationalist.

The problem of truth is taken up again by Herbert in the last three sections of *De Veritate*. Here he argues that certainty results only from the Common Notions, and that history and tradition can never provide more than probability. Possibility, which refers to the future, is on even more tenuous ground (yet immortality is to be believed in because of the transcendent goodness of God). Falsity is that which is neither true, nor probable, nor possible. Error cannot exist in the thing itself, nor in the intellect (except through failure to employ the Common Notions).

In all of his somewhat confused theorizing about harmony, uniformity, and universality, which constitute the final tests of truth, Herbert, safeguarded his theories against actual matters of fact by ruling out madmen; persons bereft of their senses; those who are headstrong, foolish, weak-minded, imprudent; those who deliberately prevent themselves from receiving the Common Notions; the wretched, half-educated crowd; the popular windbags or enthusiasts—in brief, it would seem, all those who disagree with him.

Despite his somewhat immodest pretension to innovation—"I believe myself to be the first to describe the sphere of all the faculties of man"—there are some insights in his a priori psychologizing that sound surprisingly modern. Although adhering to the ancient dogma that there are four humors in man to correspond to the four elements in nature, Herbert found it absurd to suppose that there are only five senses in man. Licentiousness, lust, apathy, depression, insanity, for instance, are not consonant with the ordained nature of man. Such feelings and passions are to be attributed not to sin but to physical disease, and are to be alleviated by physical, rather than by spiritual, means. In sum, the first eight sections of *De Veritate* comprise a curious mixture of metaphysics and introspective psychology, both obsolete and modern.

The problem of religion. Had Herbert stopped short at this juncture—as he did until the expanded London edition of 1645—he would hardly have attained the position, and the notoriety, that he holds in the history of thought. The added section IX deals with the Common Notions concerning religion, and section X, with revelation. (The remaining three sections, XI–XIII, as mentioned earlier, deal with probability, possibility, and falsity.) In the 1645 edition are to be found Herbert's first fully expressed deistic notions, which were to be repeated and strengthened in later publications.

Curtly dismissing implicit faith, an infallible church, and the sacred authority of priests and preachers, Herbert argued that such bases may support false religion equally with true. Therefore, the origins of all religions must first be investigated historically and then, and more importantly, be tested by the Common Notions. It is only through the Common Notions that the true Catholic church can be acknowledged. These religious Common Notions or universals known to all men in all times and in all places are few in number.

Stated more succinctly in *Ancient Religion of the Gentiles*, the English translation of *De Religione Gentilium*, these religious truths are: (1) that there is one supreme God; (2) that He ought to be worshipped; (3) that virtue and piety are the chief part of divine worship; (4) that we ought to be sorry for our sins and repent them; and (5) that divine goodness dispenses rewards and punishments both in this life and after it. By the discovery of these five principles, Herbert acknowledged that he thought himself "far more happy than Archimedes."

The emphasis in *De Veritate* is thus on natural religion. Revelation is not wholly excised, but it is not granted to privileged groups; it is given as a message to all mankind, or reserved for the individual mind. (Herbert relates in his autobiography how he prayed for a sign from heaven granting permission to publish his book; the sign came immediately in the form of "a loud yet gentle noise," and the book was accordingly published.)

Of all revelations Christianity is acknowledged to be the best because it is closest to the five religious Common Notions. The precepts of the Decalogue are examined in *De Veritate* and declared to be true and universally known; the Decalogue constitutes God's gracious reminder to the hearts of corrupt men. Nevertheless, the tone of the book is in direct opposition to the rigid bibliolatry of Puritanism. Priests are advised to abandon mysteries and prophecies, and miracles which establish or support unworthy beliefs—that is, not religious Common Notions—are declared fraudulent.

The further works promised in *De Veritate* added little to Herbert's basic views, but were considerably more outspoken.

De Causis Errorum is a fragment expanding but not particularly edifying the treatment of logical fallacies—that is, of error—in *De Veritate*. *De Religione Gentilium*, derived largely from Gerardus Vossius' *De Theologia Gentili* (Amsterdam, 1641), is one of the earliest treatises on comparative religion and is, in a sense, a forerunner of Hume's *The Natural History of Religion* (1757). It argues that the ancient pagans were cognizant of the five religious Common Notions, which can be found in their multitudinous religions. These religions, therefore, are fundamentally the same—as are all natural religions, including Christianity. However, none of these religions is perfect; all, like Christianity, have been somewhat defiled by the machinations of priests. Herbert's thesis that the Common Notions are basic to all religions is further developed in the posthumous *Dialogue between a Tutor and his Pupil*. In this discursive work of some 272 pages, the pupil is advised to start with reason before proceeding to a faith that is clear and evident to all mankind. What proceeds from reason leads to truth, but what proceeds from faith leads only to belief. Virtue is extolled as the fundamental part of worship, along with contrition for sins committed.

De Religione Laici, published in the same volume as *De Causis Errorum*, presents Herbert at his best in religious thinking; it is concise, direct, and cogently reasoned. The complex metaphysical psychology of *De Veritate* is gone and so is the tedious survey of the early history of religions in *De Religione Gentilium*. The layman's problem is how to distinguish the best religion from among the many offered. The answer, of course, lies in universality—specifically, in the five religious Common Notions. In *De Religione Laici*, Herbert states that the Bible should be conceived of as history and tested accordingly; what is universal in it is to be accepted as the word of God; what is not, is simply human, sometimes obscure and sometimes meaningless. The layman is warned that many priests have a way of introducing nonuniversal attributes into their characterization of God and of restricting religion to their own cult. Yet, since not all priests are guilty, that layman is most unwise who abandons all religion because some priests are corrupt.

In view of the fact that Herbert was frequently both refuted and accepted during the century after his death, it is difficult to accept the verdict of several historians of deism that he was ignored and had little or no influence. In England, his thought was propagated by his disciple Charles Blount (1654–1693); on the Continent, his work was seriously received, although not accepted, by Gassendi and Descartes.

The first specific attack on Herbert's system of religion seems to be that by Nathanael Culverwel in *Light of Nature* (1652). This was followed by attacks by Peter Musäus, Richard Baxter, Johan Musäus, Georgius Nicolaus Seerup, Christian Kortholt the Elder, and Michael Berns—the last two linking Herbert with the other notorious "atheists," Hobbes and Spinoza. In that same year Jenkin Thomasins linked Herbert with Bodin, another "atheist." John Locke attacked Herbert's theory of innate ideas in the *Essay Concerning Human Understanding* (1690), but accepted some aspects of his religious liberalism in the *Reasonableness of Christianity* (1695). In the eighteenth century the controversy was continued by Thomas Halyburton (1714), Ezechiel von Spanheim (1745), John Leland (1754), Johann Trinius (1759), and, as late as 1783, by John Ogilvie.

Although Charles Blount was Herbert's only acknowledged disciple, his religious Common Notions are characteristic of the deists of the eighteenth century, as are also his strictures on priestcraft, his naturalistic interpretations of parts of Scripture, and his disavowal of faith as a sound foundation for religion.

Works by Herbert

Lord Herbert of Cherbury's De Religione Laici, Harold R. Hutcheson, ed. and trans. New Haven, 1944.
    De Veritate. English ed., Bristol, 1937.
    Wright, Herbert G., "An Unpublished Manuscript by Lord Herbert of Cherbury entitled *Religio Laici*." *Modern Language Review*, Vol. XXVIII (1933), 295–307.

Works on Herbert

Hucheson, Harold R., "Lord Herbert and the Deists," *Journal of Philosophy*, Vol. 43 (1946), 219–221.
    Rémusat, Charles F. M. de, *Lord Herbert of Cherbury; sa vie et ses oeuvres: ou les Origines de la philosophie du sens commun et de la théologie naturelle en Angleterre*. Paris, 1874.
    Webb, Clement C. J., *Studies in the History of Natural Theology*. Oxford, 1915.
    (See also the general bibliography under DEISM.)

ERNEST CAMPBELL MOSSNER

HERDER, JOHANN GOTTFRIED (1744–1803), German philosopher and critic was born the son of a schoolmaster in Mohrungen, a small town in East Prussia. After an early education largely devoted to the study of Latin, he enrolled as a medical student at the University of Königsberg in 1762. He found, however, that he had an inconvenient tendency to faint during dissections and operations, which prompted him to change to theology. This shift of subject and interest led to an acquaintance with Kant, who in order to encourage Herder, remitted the fees customarily paid for attendance at his lectures. Kant also allowed him to read some of his unpublished manuscripts and introduced him to the writings of Montesquieu, Hume, and Rousseau. Another thinker who played an important part in Herder's intellectual development at this formative period was the antirationalist philosopher J. G. Hamann ("the Magus of the North"), who became a lifelong friend and correspondent and was to exercise a considerable influence upon the direction subsequently taken by Herder's thought.

When he left Königsberg in 1764 Herder took up a teaching post at the cathedral school in Riga, contributing to various periodicals and establishing a reputation as an enlightened theologian (he was ordained in 1765): it was in Riga that he wrote and published his first important work, *Über die neuere deutsche Literatur: Fragmente* ("Fragments concerning Recent German Literature," Riga, 1767), in which problems of language and linguistic development were discussed and given prominence. "Language," he affirmed, "is a tool of the arts and sciences and a part of them; whoever writes about the literature of a country must not neglect its language." In 1769, the year of the publication of another book entitled *Kritische Wälder* ("Critical Forests," Riga), Herder resigned from his position at Riga, and after a period of travel that included a visit to Paris, he finally settled for a time in Strasbourg. There he met Goethe, upon whom Herder's ideas regarding poetry and its role in human life appear to have produced an immediate and powerful impression. Herder also won a prize offered by the Berlin Academy for an essay on the origin of language, *Abhandlung über den Ursprung der Sprache* (Berlin, 1772) in which he clearly adumbrated a number of themes that were to recur in his subsequent work. The same year (1771) saw his appointment as court preacher to the count of Schaumburg-Lippe at Bückeburg. Three years later his *Auch eine Philosophie der Geschichte* ("Another Philosophy of History," Riga, 1774) appeared. In 1776, Herder left Bückeburg to take up the post in which he was to remain for the rest of his life; he became *Generalsuperintendent* of the Lutheran clergy at Weimar. Because of doubts (not altogether unfounded) concerning Herder's orthodoxy, the appointment ran into certain difficulties. Herder finally received it, partly as a result of Goethe's influence with Duke Karl August of Weimar.

Herder's career at Weimar was burdened with heavy administrative responsibilities and duties, and he also suffered from financial anxieties because of his large family. This did not, however, prevent him from continuing with his own writing and researches. In 1778 he published at Riga an essay concerned with psychological topics entitled *Vom Erkennen und Empfinden der menschlichen Seele* ("Of the Cognition and Sensation of the Human Soul"). Between 1784 and 1791 his famous *Ideen zur Philosophie der Geschichte der Menschheit* ("Ideas for the Philosophy of the History of Mankind")—a massive work in four parts—also appeared there. From 1793 to 1798 his publications included, among others, *Briefe zur Beförderung der Humanität* ("Letters for the Advancement of Humanity," 10 vols., Riga, 1793–1797) and *Christliche Schriften* ("Christian Writings," Vols. 1–3, Riga, 1794–1797; Vols. 4, 5, Leipzig, 1798). Finally, during the last few years of his life, he wrote two books attacking Kant's philosophy as dangerously muddled and perverse. a *"Metakritik"* of the *Critique of Pure Reason* (2 vols., Leipzig, 1799) and *Kalligone* (3 vols., Leipzig, 1800), the latter being a criticism of the aesthetic doctrines advanced by Kant in his *Critique of Judgment*. These works aroused considerable controversy and were regarded by Kant's followers as containing radical misinterpretations and misrepresentations of Kantian ideas. It may be true that Herder did not always do Kant justice; nonetheless, some of his objections can be seen in retrospect to have been acute and forceful. He rejected, for example, the Kantian view that mathematical propositions were synthetic a priori as an error deriving from a failure to recognize the ultimately tautological character of arithmetic and geometry: "The proposition $7 + 5 = 12$ is . . . identical: $1 = 1$." He drew attention to some of the difficulties surrounding Kant's conception of space and time as "forms of intuition"; and he made some sharp comments on Kant's tendency toward reification and artificial abstraction when describing the operations of the human intellect.

Besides being a most prolific and fertile writer, Herder was also a far-ranging and voracious reader, with an immense capacity for concentrated study and a wide knowledge of European languages. The great variety of his interests—psychological, historical, aesthetic, linguistic, religious, and philosophical—and the originality he displayed in his exploration of these diverse fields make him a figure of outstanding interest and significance. At the same time, the very complexity of his achievement renders it difficult to summarize. He cannot be said to have produced an over-all "system" in the classical manner, nor can his numerous and influential contributions to thought and speculation be appropriately represented as interrelated elements in a single grand design. This applies even to his most ambitious and comprehensive book, the *Ideen*, of which he himself wrote that it was made up of "stones for a building which only centuries can finish" and which (as Kant indicated in a somewhat heavily ironical review) was certainly not a model of consistency or precise expression. Herder's peculiar genius lay in quite other directions, above all, in his capacity for seeing beyond the boundaries within which the intellectual life of his age was largely enclosed and in his ability to envisage fresh and fruitful ways of interpreting the products of human culture and history. In these respects, despite there being little evidence to suggest any direct influence, Herder's true ancestor was Giambattista Vico. Unlike the neglected Italian philosopher, however, Herder's ideas were not overlooked or treated as merely eccentric aberrations; on the contrary, they had immediate repercussions upon the thought of his time and were destined during the early nineteenth century to play a formative role in the development of the romantic movement.

Herder may be said to have attacked the assumptions underlying the outlook of the eighteenth-century Enlightenment, or *Aufklärung*, at four main points: its conception of the human mind and personality, its theory of language, its attitude toward poetry and the arts, and its approach to history and to historical development. Although what Herder had to say on these different topics overflows tidy classification and division, it will be useful for present purposes to consider them separately.

Psychology. Herder was from the start wholly opposed to "faculty psychology" of the kind formulated in the eighteenth century by rationalists like Christian Wolff. The human mind was not, according to Herder, split up into a number of compartments, nor was it an assemblage of inner personages with names like "reason," "will," "desire," and so forth, each of whom performed a particular function. Such views were relics of outdated medievalism, "philosophical nonsense" resulting from false abstraction

and hypostatization and leading to disastrously artificial and static conceptions of human nature. Reasoning, perceiving, wanting, feeling, and the rest were one and all activities or attributes of the human being considered as a total, unitary personality; they could not be traced back to a set of independent sources mysteriously located in different areas of the mind. In the last analysis "the inner man, with all his dark forces, stimuli, and impulses, is simply one" (*Sämtliche Werke*, Vol. 8, p. 179). Moreover, not only was it wrong to divide up the mind itself: the traditional division between mind on one side and body on the other was also misconceived. Herder suggested on a number of occasions that the psychological and physiological aspects of a man were inseparably bound up with one another; psychology truly understood was "physiology at every step" (*ibid.*, p. 180).

From some of the things he said Herder might, indeed, be considered as anticipating by more than a century modern behaviorist and physicalist doctrines. Nevertheless, there is an important difference—all Herder's writings on psychological subjects were ultimately based upon an explicitly metaphysical conception, the notion of *Kraft*. He did not think that *Kraft* was rationally explicable. Though not itself rationally explicable or susceptible to observational or scientific analysis, *Kraft* nevertheless represented something whose existence must be presupposed in philosophy. It signified for Herder a kind of primitive force or energy that had to be assumed in any adequate interpretation of existence. Thus it found embodiment in every department of human life and conduct, giving a dynamic unity to the variety of ways in which men act and express themselves; at the same time it was treated by Herder as in some sense informing the nonhuman or "natural" realm of phenomena as well. There are clear affinities between this doctrine and vitalistic philosophies of the type propounded by Schopenhauer and Bergson in the nineteenth century.

Language. Herder's criticisms of faculty psychology and, in particular, of the conception of reason as a superior agency intent upon subordinating other spheres of mental activity to its control were connected with his views on language. In the first place, and in line with what has already been said, man's reasoning power does not operate in isolation from his other capacities and propensities. "It is one and the same mind that thinks and wills, understands and perceives, exercises reason and has desire" (*Sämtliche Werke*, Vol. 21, p. 18). Second, and here he owed much to Hamann, the use of reason and the use of language cannot be considered in abstraction from one another. An examination of human reasoning is *ipso facto* an inquiry into some of the ways in which human beings characteristically express themselves in language; for thinking essentially involves language, whether employed silently "in the head" or in overt vocal utterance—thinking is "inward speaking" (*ibid.*, p. 88). It follows that speech is not a dispensable instrument of reason, nor reason something we are born with and which we possess before we have any conception of language and communication. On the contrary, the development of reason in the child is the result of training—training in the use of significant signs (*Merkmale*), the mastery of which is a prerequisite of all logical thought.

It must not be supposed that Herder wished to confine language to one valid form, one particular type of employment. He attacked the view that the "philosophical," or scientific, mode of discourse familiar to writers of his own time should be accorded a pre-eminent status, and he sharply distinguished that mode from what he called "poetic" speech and communication, with its vivid and pregnant symbolization. This distinction was conceived in historical terms. The earliest forms taken by language are to be found in primitive periods, when the use of cries or expressive gestures to indicate passions and emotions is paramount. These periods gradually give way to ages in which men naturally communicate through the rich metaphors and sensuous imagery of poetry. It is only in later and more sophisticated stages of social development that prosaic and literal forms characteristic of scientific discourse become customary—periods when, Herder sometimes implied, the vitality of culture is on the wane, with uncreative reflection superseding spontaneous and imaginative invention. But whatever the historical period, language of some description occurs, language being intrinsic to the very idea of what it is to be a man. Herder had no patience with the opinion, which he attributed to Rousseau and Condillac, that language was something men had deliberately constructed at a particular time in order to facilitate the achievement of social and individual objectives. Indeed, the entire question of the actual "origin" of language seemed to Herder an idle one that should be put aside in favor of the more fruitful problem of determining language's varying roles and functions in different cultural and historical settings.

Art. The same insistence upon a historical approach that marked Herder's attitude toward language underlay his treatment of the problems of aesthetics. From the first he criticized the notion that there is an innate and constant faculty of taste which, like the other mental faculties, remains invariant from age to age; he also challenged the accompanying belief that there is a uniform standard of beauty that is acceptable to all men at all times. In particular, he objected to the dictum propounded by F. J. Riedel in his *Theorie der schönen Künste und Wissenschaften* ("Theory of the Arts and Sciences," Jena, 1767) that "whatever must please everyone is beautiful." Apart from the fact that such a view completely failed to take into account the environmental and psychological factors that influence artistic creation and appreciation at different periods, it was plain that the dictum in question made nonsense of the whole conception of serious criticism.

In place of such ideas Herder emphasized the degree to which historical conditions mold aesthetic conceptions. He pointed out, too, that the products of artistic genius are of immense significance in the interpretation of the human past and the development of the human mind. In this sense aesthetics can be said to be an important part of anthropology, for the works of art men create are expressions of the whole human personality as it emerges in the context of particular times and places. Previous theorists had ignored these considerations, overlooking the empirical data with all their profound implications and preferring instead to be guided by a priori assumptions that made it impossible for them to respond sympathetically to the art

forms of ages dissimilar in character to their own. Blinded by scholastic dogmatism, insistent upon the universal validity of certain "classical" canons and standards, they seemed not to perceive that, far from being something artificial and contrived, poetry was a natural and primary expression of the human psyche, as the popular ballads and songs of folk poetry sufficiently demonstrated. Even Homer and much of the Bible had to be read and understood in this "human way" if they were not to be totally misinterpreted and their real meaning lost in the morass of "unhistorical philosophizing" which contemporary exegesis was so lamentably prone to offer.

History. Notwithstanding his important contributions to other fields, it is for his philosophy of history that Herder is chiefly known and remembered today. His *Ideen zur Philosophie der Geschichte der Menschheit* is a curious and in some ways contradictory work. On the one hand, it reflects certain dominant Enlightenment interests; teleological and progressivist notions of historical development appear in it, and Herder showed respect for such humanistic ideals as freedom and social improvement. At the same time its chief interest lies precisely in the manner in which it departs from various prevailing trends of Enlightenment thought. Not only does it exhibit a range and erudition that, considering the period of writing, is astonishing (Herder did not confine himself to European history and sources but insisted upon the importance of such other cultures as China, India, and the Middle East); it is also packed with original and imaginative suggestions for the reinterpretation of the human past and contains a great deal of trenchant criticism of the historiography of the time. These methodological theses and proposals Herder propounded through the medium of a gigantic survey. He began with a discussion of man's place in the realm of physical nature and of the links that connect him with other forms of organic life, passed on to a consideration of the primitive or prehistoric phases of human society, and concluded with an examination of recorded history up to the beginning of the sixteenth century.

In Herder's philosophy of history some of the themes already referred to recur. He specifically rejected the idea, common among historians of his time, that there exist certain invariant laws or standards of consciousness and behavior that are applicable to all men at all periods and in terms of which everything that has happened in the human past must ultimately be understood and judged. Other writers had admittedly recognized that the actual data often enough seemed to clash with this conception. They had, however, tried to explain away such deviations from the accepted norms by appealing to the operation of factors like irrational passions or "prejudices" that unfortunately interfered with the natural, reasonable, or proper course of things and led men to act in eccentric or foolish ways. From this view, an important part of the value of history as a study lay in the lessons it can teach us: to be acquainted with the aberrations of the past is to be equipped with knowledge that will help us to avoid committing similar errors ourselves. Herder's position was quite different. It was absurd, he thought, to seek to impose upon the historical material, in all its manifest richness and variety, a single uniform pattern of interpretation. Such a procedure, if followed, could have the effect only of turning the historian into a kind of dogmatic schoolmaster, intent upon treating as ridiculous mistakes and blunders activities that are wholly intelligible and appropriate when considered in relation to their own historical period and cultural milieu. Here, indeed, was the basic tenet of Herder's methodology: every historical age and culture has its own character and its own value, and it follows that "the historian of mankind must, like the Creator of our race or like the genius of the earth, view without partiality and judge without passion" (*Ideen*, Bk. 11, Ch. 6). For humanity has not one form, but many, and these forms find expression in the host of different societies and nations that populate the historical scene.

Herder in general maintained that every known society—Chinese, Indian, Egyptian, Greek, Roman, and so on—had grown and developed in a distinctive manner and in response to the combination of environmental conditions presented by its particular time and place. The analogy that constantly recurred in his writings was that of a biological organism. Like an organism, a society should be considered in and for itself, "without foisting any set pattern upon it" (*Ideen*, Bk. 14, Ch. 6). What, in effect, this means so far as historical practice is concerned is that the historian should aim at achieving a sympathetic understanding of cultures other than his own, an understanding founded in the realization that the modes of life, thought, and art characteristic of one society or period will not be found in another—each has its own individual contribution to make, and this is necessarily unrepeatable and unique. Thus, human achievements must be interpreted and assessed in relation to the cultural milieu to which they essentially belong. To attempt to prize them out of the contexts in which they are embedded and to compare and judge them according to some external and supposedly superior standpoint that mysteriously transcends the conditions of time, place, and circumstance, setting determinate limits to all human activity of whatever kind, is to display a complete misunderstanding of history and its subject matter. In brief, "Shakespeare was no Sophocles, Milton no Homer, Bolingbroke no Pericles" (*Ideen*, Bk. 13, Ch. 7). The most that can be said is that "they were in their kind, and in their situation, what those were in theirs."

Herder's conception of history exercised an important influence upon the course taken by subsequent historiography. Furthermore, some of his ideas are to be found, reformulated and elaborated, in later speculative systems and theories of the kind propounded by Hegel and Oswald Spengler. Partly as a result of this, views have been attributed to Herder that he did not hold. In particular, he is sometimes said to have anticipated the extreme nationalist and racist doctrines of Hitler and Alfred Rosenberg. In fact there is no justification for treating him as a forerunner of Nazism. The moral to be drawn from his writings is that each nation should respect the culture of other societies while remaining true to its own, not that it should arrogate to itself a position of privilege that entitles it to dominate its neighbors. Herder was in no sense a militarist, and he remained throughout his life a consistent opponent of absolutist and illiberal governments.

Works by Herder

Sämtliche Werke, Bernhard Suphan, ed., 33 vols. Berlin, 1877–1913.

Abhandlung über den Ursprung der Sprache. Berlin, 1772. Translated anonymously as *Treatise upon the Origin of Language*. London, 1827.

Ideen zur Philosophie der Geschichte der Menschheit, 4 vols. Riga, 1784–1791. Translated by T. O. Churchill as *Outlines of a Philosophy of the History of Man*. London, 1800. 2d ed., 2 vols., London, 1803.

Gott: einige Gespräche. Gotha, 1787. Translated by F. H. Burkhardt as *God; Some Conversations*. New York, 1940.

Works on Herder

Barnard, F. M., *Between Enlightenment and Political Romanticism*. Oxford, 1964.

Clark, R. T., *Herder: His Life and Thought*. Berkeley and Los Angeles, 1955. The fullest recent study. Includes useful discussions of all Herder's principal works.

Dobbek, Wilhelm, *J. G. Herders Humanitätsidee*. Brunswick, 1949.

Gillies, Alexander, *Herder*. Oxford, 1945. Very brief, but recommended.

Haym, R., *Herder nach seinem Leben und seinen Werken*, 2 vols. Berlin, 1877–1885.

Knorr, F., *Das Problem der menschlichen Philosophie bei J. G. Herder*. Coburg, 1930.

Kronenberg, M., *Herders Philosophie, nach ihrem Entwicklungsgang und ihrer historischen Stellung*. Heidelberg, 1889.

Lovejoy, A. O., *Essays in the History of Ideas*. New York, 1960. Pp. 166–182. A helpful discussion of Herder's ideas on history in relation to Enlightenment preconceptions.

McEachran, Frank, *The Life and Philosophy of Johann Gottfried Herder*. Oxford, 1939.

Rouche, M., *La Philosophie de l'histoire de Herder*. Paris, 1940.

PATRICK GARDINER

HERMETICISM is the outlook associated with the Hermetic writings, a literature in Greek which developed in the early centuries after Christ under the name "Hermes Trismegistus." Much of it is concerned with astrology, alchemy, and other occult sciences, but there is also a philosophical Hermetic literature. The treatise known as the *Asclepius* and the collection of treatises grouped as the *Corpus Hermeticum* are the most important of the philosophical Hermetica, though some other fragments are preserved in the anthology of Stobaeus. These writings are probably to be dated between A.D. 100 and 300. They are an amalgam of Greek philosophy, particularly Platonic, with other elements from the heterogeneous late antique culture. The *Pimander*, the first treatise in the *Corpus Hermeticum*, has obvious affinities with Genesis, suggesting an influence of Hellenistic Judaism. There may also be Persian influences, and the possibility of some contact with Christianity cannot be excluded. The ascription of their authorship to "Hermes Trismegistus," supposed to be an Egyptian priest, encouraged the belief that these writings transmitted ancient Egyptian wisdom; the *Asclepius* in particular has a strong pseudo-Egyptian coloring.

There is much difference of opinion among scholars as to the various elements which make up the Hermetica, which are the work of an unknown number of unknown authors; even individual treatises may often be a fusion of fragments. They have a certain unity of tone, however, since they all exhibit a similar type of philosophical–religious approach to the cosmos, involving regenerative experiences and outbursts of religious ecstasy. It has been suggested that they may be the literature of a gnostic sect. The philosophical Hermetica, with their lofty aspirations, cannot be altogether isolated from the magical and occult type of literature which also goes under the name of "Hermes Trismegistus," for the experiences of the Hermeticist, as described in the philosophical–religious treatises, take place within an astrological framework and imply, particularly in the *Asclepius*, a religious use of magic.

History. Although much is in debate concerning the Hermetica themselves, we are on firmer ground when we come to the history of their legend. In the fourth century Lactantius taught that these writings were the work of an Egyptian seer who lived not long after the time of Moses, whose account of creation he confirmed and, indeed, improved and whose mentions of a "son of God" were prophetic of Christianity and to be compared with passages in the Gospel according to St. John. Augustine also believed in the extreme antiquity of "Hermes Trismegistus," but he disapproved of the magical cult described in the *Asclepius*. Nevertheless, there was ample authority in Christian writers for an attitude of respect for Hermes. Lactantius places him with the sibyls as a gentile prophet of Christianity. The myth of "Hermes Trismegistus," the Egyptian sage who was the actual author of all the writings assigned to him and who lived long before the Incarnation, which he prophetically foresaw, was to give great authority to the Hermetica.

The *Asclepius* was known in the Middle Ages in the Latin translation wrongly attributed to Apuleius of Madaura; certain pseudo-Hermetic writings were also known. The collection of treatises grouped as the *Corpus Hermeticum* seems to have been already known in this form to Psellus in the eleventh century but did not reach the West until the Renaissance.

Influence on Renaissance. The Hermetica made an impact on the Renaissance the importance of which has begun to be realized only in recent years. About 1460 a manuscript containing an incomplete Greek text of the *Corpus Hermeticum* was brought to Florence. Cosimo de' Medici ordered Marsilio Ficino to translate this at once into Latin, before beginning his translation of the works of Plato. This illustrates the Renaissance attitude, which treated the Hermetica as texts much more ancient than the Platonic writings and as the "Egyptian wisdom" believed to be one of the founts of *prisca theologia* which descended in an unbroken line to Plato and the Neoplatonists. When Ficino found scraps of Platonic philosophy in the late antique Hermetica, he assumed that he was dealing with the ancient Egyptian source of Greek wisdom. Like the interpretation of "Hermes Trismegistus" as a gentile prophet, in which Ficino also firmly believed, this view of the Hermetic writings as a source of Plato and the Platonists depended on the misdating of those writings. To this most influential error is due the fact that there is a Hermetic core to Renaissance Neoplatonism. Ficino's work on astral magic is based on the magical passages in the *Asclepius*. Pico della Mirandola opened his *Oration on the Dignity of Man* with a quotation from the *Asclepius*.

Throughout the sixteenth century the Hermetic writings were eagerly read in the many editions of Ficino's translation, and new editions and commentaries were published by Lefèvre d'Étaples, Symphorien Champier, Foix de Candale, Francesco Patrizi, and others. The first edition of the Greek text of the *Corpus Hermeticum* appeared in 1554.

The influence of this intensive study of the Hermetica can be traced throughout the Renaissance. It penetrated some types of Renaissance theology. Christian Hermeticists who wished to avoid the magic excluded the magical passages in the *Asclepius* from their canon. On the other hand, for Renaissance magicians and philosophers the animist and magical view of nature which they extracted from the Hermetic writings was the most attractive feature. A striking instance of Hermetic influence on a Renaissance philosopher is Giordano Bruno, who rejected the Christian interpretation of the Hermetica and regarded Hermeticism as a pure Egyptian religion and philosophy which he made the basis of his animist interpretation of nature.

In 1614 the great Greek scholar Isaac Casaubon dated the Hermetica as written in post-Christian times, thus shattering the myth of their ancient Egyptian authorship on which Renaissance Hermeticism had rested. With the rise of seventeenth-century thought the influence of Hermeticism receded, though there were many survivals of the Renaissance attitudes to the Hermetic writings. The part played in the immediately premodern period by Renaissance Hermeticism in the directing religious attention toward the cosmos and toward operating with cosmic powers has yet to be assessed.

Bibliography

TEXT

Festugière, A.-J., and Nock, A. D., eds., *Corpus Hermeticum*, 4 vols. Paris, 1945–1954. Text and French translations of *Corpus Hermeticum, Asclepius*, and fragments.

STUDIES

Dodd, C. H., *The Bible and the Greeks*. London, 1935.
Dodd, C. H., *The Interpretation of the Fourth Gospel*. Cambridge, 1963.
Festugière, A.-J., *La Révélation d'Hermès Trismégiste*, 4 vols. Paris, 1950–1954.
Nock, A. D., *Conversion*. Oxford, 1933.
Reitzenstein, R., *Poimandres*. Leipzig, 1904.
Wilson, R. McL., *The Gnostic Problem*. London, 1958.

INFLUENCE ON THE RENAISSANCE

Garin, E., and others, eds., *Testi umanistici su l'ermetismo*. Rome, 1955.
Kristeller, P. O., *Supplementum Ficinianum*. Florence, 1937. Bibliographic.
Walker, D. P., *Spiritual and Demonic Magic From Ficino to Campanella*. London, 1958.
Yates, Frances A., *Giordano Bruno and the Hermetic Tradition*. Chicago, 1964.

FRANCES A. YATES

HERSCHEL, JOHN (1792–1871), son of the astronomer William Herschel, worked in mathematics, chemistry, optics, and solid-state physics; pioneered in photography and instigated the regular use of photography in astronomy; invented blueprints; initiated simultaneous world-wide meteorological observations; introduced the theory of isostasy in geology; and was the world's leading observer-theoretician of double stars and nebulae. His *Treatise on Astronomy* (1833), continued as *Outlines of Astronomy* (1849), although deliberately common sense in treatment, was authoritative in content even for professionals until the 1860s. He was England's most famous scientist from 1830 to about 1860.

Herschel's *Preliminary Discourse on the Study of Natural Philosophy* (1831) was a starting point for his philosophic contemporaries, the more radical (post-Kantian) Whewell and the more conservative (Humean) Mill; in fact, many errors were deleted from Mill's *Logic* in its second edition because Herschel supplied detailed criticisms of the scientific passages in the first edition. Herschel's full position was expressed later, in papers collected as *Essays from the Edinburgh and Quarterly Reviews* (1857) and *Familiar Lectures on Scientific Subjects* (1867) and in remarks in his scientific books. His best-known philosophic followers were William Stanley Jevons and James Clerk Maxwell.

In theory of knowledge, Herschel's basic concept was the law of continuity, which for him defined the rationality of a system. In his version of the law, he asserted that scientists *observe* not continuous phenomena (not even simple extension), but "dotted outlines which the mind . . . fills up." Thus *"we assume continuity where we find none."* Herschel refused any philosophic solution of this disparity between observation and thought and accepted the harmony of mind with external nature as an ultimate fact, pre-established by God.

Next, he was a "decided disciple of old Boscovich"; matter is "a collection of mathematical points—mere *localization of forces*"; and therefore it is foolish to picture kinetic-molecular processes as "the 'clashing together' of 'atoms' " or as the "knocking about of billiard balls." Force as hitherto understood, he pointed out, was always associated with matter, that is, inertia; but in electricity and in the "quasi-undulatory propagation of qualities" we see noninertial agents. So the kind of force presented in theories of mechanics is not primary. More basic physical powers exist, he asserted, but are not yet (1840) understood.

Science should uncover not only laws (formal relations among parameters) but also causes. Causation is not Humean succession but (as in the Scottish common-sense school) is known from our consciousness of effort when we exert force. Causes are *not* will, however, but the physical intermediaries between will and muscular contraction. These may also exist in connection with inanimate bodies.

This general position is well beyond Boscovich and Thomas Reid but is not idealistic. It points toward the theory of the conservation of energy, which, however, Herschel did not approve in its 1860 form. He felt that "potential energy" was not a physical reality, but a mere mathematical expression introduced into the theory *"to save the truth of its verbal enunciation."*

In methodology Herschel was interested in discovery, not in a justification of the process of induction. (Mill's "methods" were derived directly from Herschel's *Dis-*

course.) Thus one Herschelian method was "at once to form a bold hypothesis," that is, to guess. Herschel emphasized the central importance of rigorous deduction to confirm hypotheses; it is this which makes science not a craft. One should at all costs avoid specialties of investigation (e.g., chemistry vs. physics), for no actual phenomenon is so divided. Herschel thought that contingency is the most obvious aspect of the universe. Science must grapple with the apparently arbitrary complexities of the actual world, such as sun-spot changes, the shapes of nebulae, the variations in terrestrial magnetism, trade winds, etc., and try to reduce them to scientific laws. It should not content itself with simple general laws concerning force and matter considered in abstraction.

Herschel's contemporary influence was perhaps greatest among working scientists. He gave a reasoned basis for the shift from a purely abstract treatment of physical parameters (as in Lagrange) to a belief in the actual existence of the entities used in scientific theories (e.g., the fields of force of his friend Faraday and his admirer Clerk Maxwell, which were felt to be actually present in space, not merely mathematical symbols). He upheld the importance of the scientist's feeling for the reality of his constructs. Sheltered by his great authority, scientists pursued their intuitional ideas without worrying about attacks from Humean or other philosophers, or from Evangelical preachers. Herschel, for example, authoritatively established the naturalistic origin of species as a proper subject of investigation for Victorian Englishmen. Young scientists of the period, such as Charles Darwin and Thomas Andrews, admired him extravagantly.

Bibliography

There are no modern editions of Herschel's works. Recent partial treatments are C. J. Ducasse, "John Herschel's Philosophy of Science," in the American Council of Learned Societies collection, *Studies in the History of Culture* (Menasha, Wis., 1942), reprinted in E. H. Madden, ed., *Theories of Scientific Method* (Seattle, 1960); W. F. Cannon, "The Impact of Uniformitarianism," *Proceedings of the American Philosophical Society*, Vol. 105 (1961), 301–314; and W. F. Cannon, "John Herschel and the Idea of Science," *Journal of the History of Ideas*, Vol. 22 (1961), 215–239, containing an error on "will" that has been corrected in the present article.

WALTER F. CANNON

HERTZ, HEINRICH RUDOLF (1857–1894), German physicist and philosopher of science, was born in Hamburg. Early in his student days he showed an interest in engineering but soon took up the study of physics, to which he quickly made important contributions, mainly in the study of magnetism and electricity. He studied in Berlin under Hermann von Helmholtz and Gustav Kirchhoff and inherited their interest in the philosophy of science. In 1883 he began teaching in Kiel, where he worked on Maxwell's electromagnetic theory. He became professor of physics at the technological institute at Karlsruhe in 1885, where he produced his most celebrated work on electromagnetic waves. In 1889 he was appointed professor of physics to succeed Clausius at Bonn. He was in failing health, however, and he died five years later.

Hertz's most important book for philosophy is his *Prin-*

ciples of Mechanics, written during his last illness and published in 1894. This is an attempt to rewrite classical mechanics in such a way as to exhibit its systematic nature, increasing its rigor, reducing its assumptions to a minimum, and keeping it as empirical and nonmetaphysical as possible. His aims were firmly in the spirit of his teachers and of Ernst Mach, who expressed his admiration for Hertz's work. The Preface to the *Principles of Mechanics* is a classic in the philosophy of science and deserves to be better known.

Hertz was prepared to admit that various logical categories of statement figure necessarily in the sciences; he even thought, unfashionably, that metaphysical statements could be of considerable value to the scientist. But, he held, it is of the utmost importance for anyone who would understand the methods of the sciences, and for the scientist himself, to distinguish clearly the different categories of statement and not to suppose that, for example, a nonempirical statement is empirical. In his reconstruction of mechanics he wanted especially to ensure, among other things, that such distinctions are made.

Rather in the manner of Kant, who greatly influenced the philosopher-scientists of this period, he begins by dividing mechanics into two parts, one depending upon the formal necessities of our thought and the other depending upon our experience. Moreover, as Poincaré was to argue later, certain features of mechanics depend upon our arbitrary choice. The structure of scientific theories in general exhibits these features, and understanding this structure involves disentangling them.

Further, very much in the modern manner, Hertz holds that a scientific theory is a deductive system that, according to whether it is correct or incorrect, corresponds or fails to correspond to the observable world. *The Principles of Mechanics* shows how one such theory can be set out as an axiom system in which we may deduce conclusions that are testable against reports of our observations.

However, Hertz's aim in this was not merely theoretical and academic, for he seems to have thought that the progress of science might be impeded if scientists do not fully and clearly understand the logic of the concepts they use. He holds, and regards it as generally held by scientists, that the laws of mechanics are fundamental in the solution of all problems in physics; yet there are concepts used in mechanics that are by no means clear and upon which physicists do not even agree. The outstanding example of such a concept—and here Hertz agrees with Mach—is "force." In fact, Hertz fiercely criticizes physicists for relying on this concept without having any very clear notion of what it entails.

The way to understand the concept of force is to see how it functions in the theories in which it is used. But when we look at classical mechanics, we find that force is not used in the way physicists think it is; the usual method of expounding mechanics obscures this and, in general, obscures the very nature of the concept of force. The understanding of scientific concepts is inextricably bound up with the understanding of the theories in which they figure.

Hertz's approach to mechanics is largely determined by his views about explanation in general; mechanics explains the motions of bodies by bringing them under laws, but these laws cannot be in terms only of what is directly observable. Hertz seemingly holds that it has been found that this is so, although he also shows signs of thinking that it must be so—that it is a necessity of explanation. At any rate, he points to many of the explanations accepted in the sciences and shows that they rely upon concealed mechanisms or, as he says, " 'confederates' concealed beyond observed masses and motions."

Representations of mechanics. There are two existing interpretations of mechanics that rely upon force and energy, respectively, as the nonempirical concepts to be used in explanation. Here a further presupposition of Hertz's enters: We will understand our explanations best if all the concepts we use are as similar as possible to concepts of what we experience, that is, to empirical concepts. Force and energy are quite unlike anything we experience, so Hertz seeks to replace them, in his rewriting of mechanics, by motion and mass, which are exactly like observed motion and mass except that they are unobserved (concealed). Or, rather, force and energy are given minor and subordinate roles in his mechanics; all the important roles go to mass and motion. This, he believed, fitted in with the physical theorizing of his time. For example, Maxwell gave an account of electromagnetic forces in terms of concealed masses and motions.

Although force and energy are not empirical concepts, space, time, and mass are. Hertz therefore reconstructs mechanics using only space, time, and mass as primitive concepts. This means that they are not defined in any verbal or symbolic way, although we understand them through our experience of observable masses in motion. Force and energy must not figure in mechanics—as they have tended to do—as basic terms, *as if* they were empirical concepts. They may be introduced at some later stage, but only by defining them—ultimately, at least—in terms of the primitives.

Hertz outlines the two existing "representations" or "images" of mechanics, criticizes them, and then develops his own alternative, which forms the bulk of *The Principles of Mechanics.* He puts forward, as tools of criticism for theories or their representations, three conditions that they must fulfill. They must be *logically permissible* (sometimes abbreviated to *permissible*), that is, consistent with the laws of our thought; they must be *correct,* that is, their structure must not conflict with the structure of observable things; they must be *appropriate,* that is, they must be simple in the sense of containing the fewest possible superfluous or empty relations. Appropriateness is merely relative: we should, where there are alternatives, accept the more appropriate rather than the less appropriate. These requirements concern the three features of theories mentioned above—one depending upon the nature of our minds, one depending upon our external experiences, and one depending upon our conventional systems of notation.

The first representation Hertz considers is the one then current in most textbooks, taking space, time, force, and mass as its fundamental concepts. It is, among other things, too much influenced by the historical development of mechanics, the order of which may have little to do with its logical structure. It takes force as an independent concept and regards force as the cause of motion. However, the weakness of this representation is that the idea of force is not clear. This affects both the permissibility and the appropriateness of this version: because our notion of force is vague, it cannot help us to reason precisely, and because we associate with it certain nonessential anthropomorphic ideas, it imports superfluous elements into mechanics. This latter point also seems, for Hertz, to include the idea that too much which is not directly perceptible is thus brought into mechanics. He looks askance at forces that "cancel out in the calculations" as robbing an explanation of its simplicity, or what Mach calls its economy. Apart from this, the first representation satisfies the condition of correctness; if we are merely considering alternative ways of expressing mechanics, we should indeed expect something to be satisfactory in each. What is satisfactory here is that the structure of this way corresponds to, or at least does not conflict with, the structure of observable phenomena.

The second representation is one that was favored in Hertz's day by the more advanced physicists, including Helmholtz. This representation attempts to sidestep the difficulties involved in the concept of force by taking as fundamental the concepts of space, time, mass, and energy. It is then possible to introduce force by definition and merely as an aid to calculation. The advantage of energy over force, it was claimed, was that energy depends upon direct experience because it depends only upon positions or velocities, both of which are directly experienced. This insures that the second representation is more appropriate than the first. If we consider only motions that occur in nature, Hertz argues, it lacks nothing in correctness. Its weakness lies in its permissibility, as is seen when we try to define energy, as it is here used, in terms of "simple, direct experiences." A substantial view of energy tended to be associated with this representation, but it is difficult to treat potential energy as a substance, especially when, as is sometimes necessary, we must ascribe negative potential energy to a system or must regard the potential energy of a finite quantity of matter as infinite. This version is superior to the first, but it still contains serious difficulties.

Hertz's representation. Since force and energy, respectively, appear to be responsible for the problems arising over these two representations, Hertz attempts to do without them, at least as primitive concepts for his representation. He begins with space, time, and mass. That is, he begins with kinematics, the abstract study of motion, and sets out to derive the whole of mechanics from it without using force and energy except as devices for calculation. Kirchhoff had already asserted that three independent concepts are necessary and sufficient for mechanics.

Time, space, and mass are primitive terms for Hertz's system, but they are not mere abstract counters like the uninterpreted symbols of the logicians. They are understood through experience, and the particular experiences that are to count for the purposes of mechanics can be specified. Moreover, these concepts are, as we also discover in experience, permanently related in various ways. Hertz puts forward a "Fundamental Law" that has similarities to the law of inertia and that summarizes the connection between the three basic concepts taken together: "Every natural motion of an independent material system consists herein, that the system follows with uniform velocity one of its straightest paths." This law, together with the concepts of space, time, and mass and the hypothesis of concealed masses, allows us, by purely deductive reasoning, to derive the whole of mechanics and so to explain mechanical phenomena.

Other concepts, such as force and energy, are introduced into the system later by definition and so are regarded merely as aids to deduction. They are defined ultimately in terms of the primitive concepts.

The Principles of Mechanics is divided into two parts to emphasize the independence of the mathematical form and the physical content of mechanics. The equation "2 horses + 2 horses = 4 horses" has a mathematical form, expressed by "$2 + 2 = 4$," that is independent of its application to horses. In the same way, mechanics as a whole can be regarded as having these two aspects. Book I of the *Principles* draws out the implications of the fundamental ideas: space, time, and mass. At this stage these concepts are intuitive and independent of experience except insofar as all our intuitions and modes of reasoning depend upon experience. Book II contains the application of these concepts to experience through the Fundamental Law and the derivation of testable assertions about observable phenomena. The apparently equivocal nature of Hertz's basic concepts can best be understood in relation to Kantian philosophy: our intuitions, peculiarly adapted to fit the general form of what we experience, are analogous to colored spectacles which determine our seeing the world as colored. Nevertheless, the details of our pictures of the world have the nature of hypotheses and are open to empirical testing.

Hertz's account of mechanics is important from the standpoint of the philosophy of science because it represents an early attempt to see a scientific theory as a system and to bring out its logical structure accordingly. It was influential in connection with the conventionalism later championed by Henri Poincaré and attempted to do justice to, on the one hand, the undoubted empirical nature of science and, on the other, the apparent claims of scientific laws to embody natural necessities. Hertz's view that mechanics is the foundation of all physical explanation was the most backward-looking element in his work and was strangely belied by both his scientific work, which was largely influential in breaking down that view, and his work in the philosophy of science, which contained the seeds of a far more flexible view of explanation.

Works by Hertz

Gesammelte Werke ("Collected Works"), Philipp Lenard, ed. Leipzig, 1894–1895.

Untersuchungen über die Austreitung der elektrischen Kraft. Leipzig, 1892. Translated by D. E. Jones as *Electric Waves.* London, 1893. This volume contains Hertz's most important papers on Maxwell's theory and a preface by Kelvin (in the English edition). Hertz approved the translation.

Die Prinzipien der Mechanik. Leipzig, 1894. Translated by D. E. Jones and T. E. Walley as *The Principles of Mechanics.* London, 1899. This is the most important source for Hertz's ideas on the philosophy of science.

Schriften Vermischten Inhalts. Leipzig, 1895. Translated by D. E. Jones and G. A. Schott as *Miscellaneous Papers.* London, 1896.

Works on Hertz

Braithwaite, R. B., *Scientific Explanation.* Cambridge, 1953. See especially Chs. 3 and 4.

Brill, Alexander von, "Über die Mechanik von Hertz." *Mathematisch-Naturwissenschaftliche Mitteilungen,* Vol. 2 (1900), 1–16.

Fitzgerald, G. F., "The Foundations of Dynamics." *Nature,* Vol. 51 (1895), 283–285.

Foulkes, P., "The Concept of Force." *Australasian Journal of Philosophy,* Vol. 29 (1951), 175–180 and Vol. 30 (1952), 130–132. Reply to Smart.

Hesse, Mary B., *Forces and Fields.* London, 1961. See especially pp. 212 ff.

Hempel, C. G., *Fundamentals of Concept Formation in Empirical Science.* Chicago, 1952. This is Vol. II, No. 7, of *International Encyclopedia of Unified Science.*

Jammer, Max, *Concepts of Force.* Cambridge, Mass., 1957.

Lindsay, R. B., and Margenau, Henry, *Foundations of Physics.* New York, 1936. See especially Ch. 3.

Mach, Ernst, *Die Mechanik in ihrer Entwickelung historische-kritisch dargestellt.* Leipzig, 1883. Translated by T. J. McCormack as *The Science of Mechanics.* 4th ed., Chicago, 1919; taken from the fourth German edition of 1901.

Maxwell, J. C., "Ether," in *Encyclopaedia Britannica,* 9th ed. Edinburgh, 1875–1889. Vol. VIII, pp. 568–572.

Poincaré, Henri, "Les Idées de Hertz sur la mécanique," in *Oeuvres de Henri Poincaré.* Paris, 1916–1956. Vol. VII, pp. 231–250. This has been partially translated by A. Miller in Arthur Danto and Sidney Morgenbesser, eds., *Philosophy of Science.* New York, 1960. Pp. 366–373. Both versions give an account of the reasons for dissatisfaction with the concept of force.

Russell, Bertrand, *The Principles of Mathematics.* Cambridge, 1903. Ch. 59.

Schilpp, P. A., ed., *Albert Einstein, Philosopher-Scientist.* Evanston, Ill., 1949. Contains an assessment of both the scientific and the philosophical works of Hertz. See especially Section I and Section II, Parts 2 and 19.

Smart, J. J. C., "Heinrich Hertz and the Concept of Force." *Australasian Journal of Philosophy,* Vol. 29 (1951), 36–54.

Smart, J. J. C., "The Concept of Force." *Australasian Journal of Philosophy,* Vol. 30 (1952), 124–130.

Watson, W. H., *On Understanding Physics.* Cambridge, 1938.

PETER ALEXANDER

HERZEN, ALEXANDER IVANOVICH (1812–1870), Russian editor, essayist, and social philosopher. Herzen, the illegitimate son of I. A. Yakovlev, was graduated from the faculty of physics and mathematics of Moscow University in 1834 and was promptly exiled to the provinces for radicalism (1835–1840, 1841–1843). He emigrated from Russia in 1847 and spent the remainder of his life in western Europe. In London he founded the first "free Russian journal," *Kolokol* ("The Bell"), in 1852. There, during the 1850s he published, in eight parts, his *Byloye i Dumy (My Past and Thoughts),* a brilliant personal memoir and history of nineteenth-century ideas.

Herzen's first essay in metaphilosophy, "Diletantizm v Nauke" ("Dilettantism in Science"), was published as a series of four articles in *Otechestvennyie Zapiski* in 1843. Herzen used the term "science" (*nauka*) in the broad sense of Hegel's *Wissenschaft* and focused his critique on four kinds of scientific dilettantes: naive dabblers; romanticizers of the past without interest in the problems of today; pedantic specialists who in their ivory towers write erudite books about erudite books; and the "Buddhists of science," or right Hegelians, who offer a purely speculative

account of historical reality and make no effort to change it. Herzen opposed to all four kinds of dilettantism a "committed" philosophy of the act (*filosofiya dela*) which seeks to reconcile abstract speculation with vital human needs. (Later, Herzen spoke of Hegel's dialectic as an "algebra of revolution.")

In "Pisma ob Izuchenii Prirody" ("Letters on the Study of Nature"), published as a series of eight articles in *Otechestvennyie Zapiski* in 1845–1846, Herzen attempted to reconcile the opposed interests of natural science, which tends toward empiricism, and philosophy, which tends toward idealism. But empiricism and idealism are Hegelian "moments," incomplete and one-sided dialectical phases, each requiring the other. In the end Herzen stressed the rights of empiricism as closer than those of idealism to the real needs of living individuals.

In works written after 1847 Herzen outlined his defense of the existing individual against the collective encroachments of society, history, and progress. Nonhuman individuals are constantly sacrificed to supraindividual ends, as in the slow formation of a coral reef from the skeletons of millions of tiny sea creatures. "The polyps die," Herzen wrote, "not suspecting that they have served the progress of the reef" (*Byloye i Dumy,* in *Sobraniye Sochinenii,* Vol. X, p. 123). But men are not polyps; human individuals should not be sacrificed to build any coral reef of historical progress, however grandiose.

Herzen developed, in *S Tovo Berega (From the Other Shore;* Paris, 1850) and later works, a philosophy of contingency, emphasizing the "tousled improvisation" of history. Historical development does not exhibit the rational, purposive structure which Hegelians see in it; therefore, men are free to impose their own purposes on its "whirlwind of chances." "Outside us everything changes, everything vacillates. We are standing on the edge of a precipice and we see it crumbling. . . . We shall find no haven but in ourselves, in the consciousness of our unlimited freedom, of our autocratic independence" (*From the Other Shore,* p. 128).

Herzen stressed the lived sense of freedom and attempted to reconcile this psychological fact with a deterministic theory. In a letter (written in French in 1868) to his son, who had defended a fashionable physiological reductionism, he called the idea of freedom a "phenomenological necessity," adding, "the conscious self cannot move or act without positing itself as free, that is to say as to having within certain limits the power to do or not to do. Without this belief, individuality dissolves and is lost . . ." (*Sobraniye Sochinenii,* Vol. XX, pt. 1, p. 436).

Anticipating Dostoyevsky's "Legend of the Grand Inquisitor" (1880), Herzen in 1847 stated the theme of escape from freedom and the burden of moral responsibility. The love of moral freedom, in Herzen's words, is "purely Platonic and ideal," whereas the love of intellectual authority is a solid *mariage de raison* in which "dreams and poetry are sacrificed for domestic comfort [and] order" (*ibid.,* Vol. II, p. 90).

Herzen formulated not only an extreme moral relativism—"What was admirable behavior yesterday may be abominable today" (*From the Other Shore,* p. 141)—but also an embryonic emotivism in ethics. Moral judgments are expressions of taste or preference on the model of "I like lobster"; there is no point in my arguing with someone who does not like lobster. According to Herzen, "there are no general rules, but [only] an improvisation of conduct, . . . a tact, an aesthetics of human actions" (*Sobraniye Sochinenii*, Vol. XXIX, pt. 1, p. 148). On this, as on other points, Herzen anticipated Nietzsche — who may have read some of Herzen's works in translation.

Works by Herzen

Sobraniye Sochinenii v Tridtsati Tomakh ("Collected Works in Thirty Volumes"). Moscow, 1954–1964.
My Past and Thoughts, translated by Constance Garnett, 6 vols. New York, 1924–1927.
From the Other Shore and *The Russian People and Socialism*, Isaiah Berlin, ed. London and New York, 1956. Introduction by the editor.
Selected Philosophical Works, translated by L. Navrozov. Moscow, 1956.

Works on Herzen

Malia, Martin, *Alexander Herzen and the Birth of Russian Socialism: 1812–1855*. Cambridge, Mass., 1961.
Zenkovsky, V. V., *Istoriya Russkoi Filosofii*, 2 vols. Paris, 1948–1950. Translated by George L. Kline as *A History of Russian Philosophy*, 2 vols. London and New York, 1953. See pp. 271–298.

GEORGE L. KLINE

HESS, MOSES (1812–1877), socialist journalist and organizer, intellectual precursor of Zionism, and often called the father of German socialism. Hess was born in Bonn of Jewish parents. A left-Hegelian, he was a mentor and co-worker of Engels, Marx, and Ferdinand Lassalle. He led radical workers' groups in Paris and Belgium, edited the famous *Rheinische Zeitung,* and was the leader of the "true," or "philosophical," German socialists of the 1840s. Later he became Lassalle's chief organizer in the Rhineland and a foreign correspondent for European and American newspapers. His published books and countless essays include works on the philosophy of history and on socialism, a famous call for a Jewish state, and a comprehensive theory of the laws of science, society, and socialism.

Hess used the principles of Spinoza, Hegel, and Fichte to demonstrate the inevitability and justice of a society lacking distinctions of class and wealth, without "contradictions" between private passion and public law, and without external compulsion. Hess took this to be both the social expression of pantheism and the inevitable result of the dialectical development of the self-realization of the Absolute Spirit in history. This was the theme of his early work, *Die Heilige Geschichte der Menschheit* (Stuttgart, 1837). Later, under the influence of Feuerbach, Hess rejected Hegelian transcendentalism. He then created a "philosophy of the deed," based on a belief in the human spirit as the unconditioned ultimate reality. He stressed the creative power of man and man's historical "alienation" of that power to various mythical transcendent powers—God, the state, fate, or, in Hess's day, the laws of history and economics. Hess insisted that there are no objective limits to man's power to create a society free from exploitation and compulsion.

Marx and Engels attacked this kind of moralistic and philosophical socialism (and later Hess himself) as inade-

quate to the harsh realities of economic determinism and the class struggle. The influence of Marx and the failure of romantic idealism in the widespread revolutions of 1848 helped to convert Hess from idealism to materialism. He now spoke of ideas as the "reflex" of material conditions and the class struggle, and he predicted the inevitable termination of the economic "contradictions of capitalism" in overproduction, proletarian misery, depression, revolution, and finally, socialism.

In the end, however, Hess became pragmatic. He rejected dialectical materialism as he had rejected dialectical idealism. He worked with Ferdinand Lassalle to found German social democracy, and like Lassalle he hoped for radical social reform through universal suffrage and the nationalization of the means of production. And it was in this spirit, not Marx's, that the German Social Democratic party started its career. In the 1860s, fearful of the future of the Jews of Europe, Hess worked for a Jewish and socialist state in Palestine.

Works by Hess

Die europäische Triarchie. Leipzig, 1841.
Jüdische Schriften, Theodor Zlocisti, ed. Berlin, 1905.
Rom und Jerusalem. Leipzig, 1862. Translated by M. Waxman as *Rome and Jerusalem*, New York, 1918.
Sozialistische Aufsätze, 1841–1847, Theodor Zlocisti, ed. Berlin, 1920.
Moses Hess Briefwechsel, Edmund Silberner, ed. The Hague, 1959.

Works on Hess

Berlin, Isaiah, *The Life and Thought of Moses Hess*. London, 1959.
Lukács, Georg, "Moses Hess und die Probleme der idealistischen Dialectik." *Archiv für die Geschichte des Sozialismus und der Arbeiterbewegung*, Vol. 12 (1926), 105–155.
Weiss, John, *Moses Hess: Utopian Socialist*. Detroit, 1960.
Zlocisti, Theodor, *Moses Hess, Der Vorkämpfer des Sozialismus und Zionismus*, 2d ed. Berlin, 1921.

JOHN WEISS

HICKOK, LAURENS PERSEUS (1798–1888), was America's first systematic philosopher and also won distinction as a theologian and educational administrator. He was born in Bethel, Connecticut, and was educated at Union College. He trained for the ministry under William Andrews and Bennett Tyler, who was a major spokesman for "old school" Calvinism. Hickok served well as pastor at Kent, Connecticut (1823–1829), and Litchfield, Connecticut (1829–1836). He then became professor of theology at Western Reserve College (1836–1844) and Auburn Theological Seminary (1844–1855). His alma mater, Union College, called him to serve as vice-president and professor of mental and moral philosophy (1855–1866) and president (1866–1868). In 1868 he retired to Amherst, Massachusetts, where he wrote several books over the next twenty years.

The core of Hickok's philosophic enterprise was the attempt to allow adequate weight to the claims of reason and experience in all domains of intellectual life. Ultimately, he was convinced, the rational and the empirical modes of thinking could not lead to contradictory conclusions; human intelligence might begin with general principles and rationally deduce facts or might begin with observed facts and gradually uncover general principles. In either case the facts were the same, and the principles were the same. Rational science is science as known by God; empirical science is science as learned by men. Different criteria of validity are to be applied to man's ideas in these two types of scientific thinking. In the empirical area ideas are tested by their experimental consequences; in the rational area ideas are tested by their congruence within a systematic pattern. Each type of thinking has, however, its proper place; the speculative mode should not be used when the investigative mode is in order, but neither should men become so enamored of empirical investigation that they neglect rational speculation.

Despite this careful balancing of empirical and rational method, Hickok did not regard the discoveries of empirical science as part of philosophy. His own work *Empirical Psychology; or, The Human Mind as Given in Consciousness* (1854) was an introspective study of the workings of the human mind. Hickok thought of this study as prephilosophic. He also published a philosophic work in the same field—*Rational Psychology; or, The Subjective Idea and the Objective Law of All Intelligence* (1849). Here no attention was given to the data of introspection; hence, this work was properly "philosophy." In all the other fields to which he gave consideration, Hickok's work was completely dominated by rational, speculative system building.

Although there was some trace of the ideas of Kant in American philosophy before Hickok, he was the first professor of philosophy in the United States to attempt to make systematic use of Kant and the post-Kantian German rationalists. Thus, he was an important figure in the transition from the orthodox academic teaching of Scottish realism in the first half of the nineteenth century to the dominance of idealism in the latter part of the century.

Works by Hickok

Rational Psychology; or, The Subjective Idea and the Objective Law of All Intelligence. Auburn, 1849; rev. ed., New York, 1870.

A System of Moral Science. Schenectady, 1853; rev. ed., with the cooperation of Julius H. Seelye, Boston, 1880.

Empirical Psychology; or, The Human Mind as Given in Consciousness. Schenectady, 1854; rev. ed., with the cooperation of Julius H. Seelye, Boston, 1882.

Rational Cosmology; or, The Eternal Principles and the Necessary Laws of the Universe. New York, 1858.

Creator and Creation; or, The Knowledge in the Reason of God and His Work. New York, 1872.

Humanity Immortal; or, Man Tried, Fallen and Redeemed. Boston, 1872.

The Logic of Reason, Universal and Eternal. Boston, 1875.

Works on Hickok

Union Worthies, Number Two; Laurens Perseus Hickok, Class of 1820, published by Union College in 1947, contains three appreciations of Hickok by Harold A. Larrabee, Herbert W. Schneider, and Julius Seelye Bixler, as well as a bibliography of Hickok's chief writings. Other discussions are in H. W. Schneider, *A History of American Philosophy* (New York, 1946; 2d ed., 1964), and in Joseph L. Blau, *Men and Movements in American Philosophy* (Englewood Cliffs, N.J., 1952).

J. L. BLAU

HILBERT, DAVID (1862–1943), German mathematician, was born in Königsberg and, except for a semester at Heidelberg, did his university studies there. His dissertation, presented in 1884, was on a problem in the theory of algebraic invariants, and it was to this theory that Hilbert devoted his mathematical researches until 1892. Through these penetrating investigations Hilbert obtained many pregnant results, some of them (*Hilbertscher Nullstellensatz, Hilbertscher Irreduzibilitätssatz*) still known by his name. The methods he used in these investigations inaugurated a trend toward treating algebra more conceptually and have since become dominant in the field.

In 1886 Hilbert became a *Privatdozent* and in 1892 an extraordinary professor at the University of Königsberg. In 1893 he was named by the minister of culture Friedrich Althoff to succeed his teacher, Felix Lindemann, as an ordinary professor at Königsberg. In 1895 Hilbert accepted an invitation initiated by Felix Klein, to the University of Göttingen to succeed Heinrich Weber. Hilbert remained at Göttingen, despite many offers of other chairs, notably from Leipzig in 1898, Berlin in 1902, and Heidelberg in 1904. The invitation from Berlin led to Hilbert's obtaining, through the help of Althoff, a chair at Göttingen for Hermann Minkowski, whom Hilbert had known since they were students at Königsberg. The personal intercourse between the two investigators was highly stimulating to both men but was prematurely ended, to Hilbert's grief, by Minkowski's death in 1909.

Hilbert's most important mathematical investigations were carried out between 1892 and 1909. He simplified the existing transcendence proofs for the numbers e and π. His investigations in the theory of algebraic number fields, in particular his monumental report "Die Theorie der algebraischen Zahlkörper" (1897), greatly amplified existing theory and directed further research in the field. His famous *Grundlagen der Geometrie* is discussed below. He showed the possibility of directly supporting the Dirichlet principle, that the existence of a conformal mapping may be inferred from the presumed existence of a minimum of a certain integral (which Bernhard Riemann had taken as the basis for his general theorems concerning conformal mappings), by means of an existence proof. This method for giving an existence proof, when worked out by Richard Courant and Hermann Weyl, proved very successful. Hilbert's contributions to the calculus of variations, in particular his statement of the *Unabhängigkeitssatz* ("independence axiom"), constituted an illuminating commentary on Adolf Kneser's textbook in the field. He continued the theory of Ivar Fredholm concerning integral equations. In particular, he introduced the analysis of infinitely many variables and generalized the transformation to principal axes. The theory thus established has proved highly fruitful in topology and in physics, particularly in quantum mechanics. Utilizing a result of Adolf Hurwitz, Hilbert solved the Waring problem concerning the representation of natural numbers by sums of nth powers.

Hilbert's familiarity with the various domains of mathematics was impressively demonstrated by the address "Mathematische Probleme," which he presented at the Second International Congress of Mathematicians in Paris in 1900. In this address Hilbert surveyed the situation then existing in mathematics, at the same time formulating 23 problems which have much occupied mathematicians since then. A great many of these problems have been solved in the meantime.

After Minkowski's death Hilbert turned to problems of theoretical physics. He first applied the theory of integral equations to the kinetic theory of gases and to the theory of radiation. Immediately after the appearance of Einstein's general theory of relativity, Hilbert published "Die Grundlagen der Physik" (1915–1916), which offered the first proposal of a way to unify gravitational theory and electrodynamics.

After 1916 Hilbert returned to the problems of the foundations of mathematics. These investigations led to the development of proof theory, which will be discussed below.

In his later years Hilbert gave lectures providing careful general surveys of mathematics, such as "Anschauliche Geometrie" (on intuitive geometry), as well as popular philosophical lectures. The spirit of these philosophical lectures can be seen in the speech "Naturerkennen und Logik," which he gave at the congress of natural scientists in Königsberg in 1930. At this congress his native city named him an honorary citizen.

Hilbert's character was not that of a specialized scientist. He took pleasure in the joy of life, especially in sociability, and also took a vivid interest in political events. He enjoyed the exchange of ideas both in science and in general thought; in discussions he had a predilection for pregnant, sometimes paradoxical, formulations.

Hilbert had a great many pupils, and he was the adviser on many famous dissertations whose themes were suggested by his investigations. He had the satisfaction of seeing his work highly appreciated in his own lifetime.

The memory of Hilbert's personality is vivid in all those who knew him, and the impulses he gave to science are still effective in the research of today.

THE FOUNDATIONS OF GEOMETRY

In Hilbert's scientific work, his studies in the foundations of mathematics constitute an important part. These investigations fall into two stages separated by an interval of nearly 13 years. The first period, which extends from about 1893 to 1904, embraces Hilbert's inquiries into geometric axiomatics and is highlighted by the publication of the *Grundlagen der Geometrie* (1899), the work that made Hilbert's name familiar to a wide public of scientists and philosophers. The second period, which began with the publication in 1917 of "Axiomatisches Denken," centers on the foundations of arithmetic and the development of Hilbert's program for proof theory.

Abstract axiomatics. A main feature of Hilbert's axiomatization of geometry is that the axiomatic method is presented and practiced in the spirit of the abstract conception of axiomatics that arose at the end of the nineteenth century and which has been generally adopted in modern mathematics. It consists in abstracting from the intuitive meaning of the terms for the kinds of primitive objects (individuals) and for the fundamental relations and in understanding the assertions (theorems) of the axioma-

tized theory in a hypothetical sense, that is, as holding true for any interpretation or determination of the kinds of individuals and of the fundamental relations for which the axioms are satisfied. Thus, an axiom system is regarded not as a system of statements about a subject matter but as a system of conditions for what might be called a relational structure. Such a relational structure is taken as the immediate object of the axiomatic theory; its application to a kind of intuitive object or to a domain of natural science is to be made by means of an interpretation of the individuals and relations in accordance with which the axioms are found to be satisfied.

This conception of axiomatics, of which Hilbert was one of the first advocates (and certainly the most influential), has its roots in Euclid's *Elements,* in which logical reasoning on the basis of axioms is used not merely as a means of assisting intuition in the study of spatial figures; rather, logical dependencies are considered for their own sake, and it is insisted that in reasoning we should rely only on those properties of a figure that either are explicitly assumed or follow logically from the assumptions and axioms. This program was not strictly adhered to in all parts of the *Elements,* nor could it have been, for its system of axioms was not sufficient for the purpose. The first axiom system meeting the requirements of the program was given by Moritz Pasch in his *Vorlesungen über neuere Geometrie* (Leipzig, 1882).

This abstract kind of axiomatics, which consists in separating out the purely mathematical aspects of a theory, is not the only possible one. Hilbert himself knew that it can be applied advantageously only in domains of science whose theoretical development is sufficiently advanced. But abstract axiomatics is useful wherever the logical dependence or independence of theoretical assumptions is under investigation.

The distinguishing property of Hilbert's axiomatics is frequently described by saying that in it the terms for the kinds of elements (points, straight lines) and for the relations (incidence, betweenness, congruence) are *implicitly defined* by the axioms. This expression, first introduced in 1818 by J. D. Gergonne (Hilbert did not employ it), is often used in a misleading way. The axioms generally impose conditions on the relations and on the kinds of elements of the system; some of these conditions are partial characterizations of the relations or the kinds of elements, others characterize the system with respect to the elements and relations. The entire axiom system—as Hilbert observed in a letter to Gottlob Frege—can be regarded as a single definition. But this is an *explicit* definition of a term denoting the relational structure in question. The defined concept is a predicate of the second type (*zweiter Stufe,* as Frege called it), applying to domains of things and to certain relations between them.

Non-Archimedean systems. Another main feature of Hilbert's *Grundlagen der Geometrie* is the development of geometry, and, in particular, of plane geometry, independently of the Archimedean axiom. This axiom states that given any two line segments, either may be exceeded by an entire multiple of the other. Thus, it partly compensates for the absence of general commensurability of line segments. It was with the help of this axiom that the theory of proportions was established in Book V of Euclid's *Elements* (attributed to Eudoxus). It is also a consequence of this axiom that, once a unit segment is chosen, there corresponds to any line segment a real number (in Richard Dedekind's sense of the term) that is its measure (ratio number); therefore, Hilbert also called the Archimedean axiom the axiom of measurement.

Recourse to the Archimedean axiom introduced an arithmetical element into reasoning, and hence avoidance of it in geometrical proofs amounts to an emancipation from a nongeometrical type of reasoning. The avoidance of nongeometrical reasoning does not preclude an analytic geometry. In fact, Hilbert was able to construct a calculus of line segments, independent of the Archimedean axiom, in two different ways.

One method operates within the framework of metric plane geometry. It is based on the axioms of incidence (for the plane), those of order, those of congruence, and the parallel axiom. Hilbert defines the sum of segments in the usual way and the product of segments, after establishing a unit segment, by a parallel construction; he then shows that by these definitions the usual computation laws for sum and product are satisfied.

By this segment calculus an elementary foundation of the theory of proportions and thereby also of analytic geometry is obtained. Hilbert further showed how with the aid of the segment calculus the theory of the areas of polygons can be set up without supposing, as is assumed in Euclid, that to any polygon there corresponds its area as a quantity, i.e., in agreement with Euclid's axioms of quantities. Thus he showed that no accessory reliance on intuition is required for the theory of areas of polygons.

Hilbert conjectured that the theory of the volumes of polyhedrons is not fully analogous to the theory of the areas of polygons. He posed the problem of showing that tetrahedrons of equal volume cannot always be obtained from one another by a series of processes of pairwise additions and subtractions of congruent polyhedrons, a problem solved by Max Dehn ("Über raumgleiche Polyeder" and "Über den Rauminhalt"). Various investigations have derived from this problem.

Hilbert's second calculus of line segments independent of the Archimedean axiom is for *affine* geometry of the plane. A difficulty here is that the axioms of plane affine geometry do not suffice for the foundation of this geometry. The same holds for plane projective geometry.

Hans Wiener stated at the Naturforscherversammlung in Halle (1891) that it is impossible to give autonomous foundations to both plane projective geometry and plane affine geometry by adjoining to the axioms of incidence the Desargues theorem and a specialized form of the Pascal theorem on conic sections (with the conic section degenerated to a pair of straight lines). Hilbert was impressed by these statements and gave a proof of them for affine geometry by means of a calculus of segments. Here sum and product of segments are defined by elementary parallel constructions, and, with the aid of the Desargues theorem, the computation laws, with the exception of the commutative law for the product, are proved to be satisfied. These proofs were simplified by Arnold Schmidt in the seventh edition of the *Grundlagen.*

This calculus of segments leads to an analytic geometry over a skewfield—as it is called today—for the plane. This geometry can be extended, as Hilbert showed, to an analytic geometry of three-dimensional space satisfying the incidence axioms and the parallel axiom for the space. This is the extent of the role of the Desargues theorem. The specialized Pascal theorem is needed to prove that the segment calculus satisfies the commutative law for multiplication. This law, as Hilbert showed, can be inferred from the other computation laws and the laws of order with the aid of the Archimedean axiom, but not without it. (Gerhard Hessenberg proved, somewhat later, that the Desargues theorem is a consequence of the specialized Pascal theorem.)

Hilbert's positive treatment of the Archimedean axiom and, in particular, the question of its independence complemented his elimination of it from the foundations of geometry. The possibility of a non-Archimedean geometry was first considered in detail by Giuseppe Veronese in his *Fondamenti di Geometria* (Padua, 1891). This possibility can be inferred, by the methods of analytic geometry, from the existence of a (generalized) number system for which the operations of sum and product and their inverses, as well as the operation $\sqrt{1+a^2}$ and the relation "smaller than," can be defined in such a way that the familiar computation laws, but not the Archimedean axiom, are satisfied.

Hilbert gave as an instance of such a non-Archimedean system a system whose elements are algebraic functions of an argument t. But the instance he presented in "Über den Satz von der Gleichheit der Basiswinkel im gleichschenkligen Dreieck" is easier to operate with. (This essay is one of a series of studies closely connected with the *Grundlagen* and added to it as appendixes in the second and later editions; this essay forms Appendix II.) It deals with the possibility of restricting, in plane geometry, the last congruence axiom concerning triangles to the case of triangles assigned to one another in equal orientation. The effect of this restriction is to admit as congruences only those transformations obtained by translations and plane rotations, thus excluding symmetry from the notion of congruence. Two kinds of questions arise, those concerning the anomalies which can occur in a model of the restricted axiom system and those relating to the ways of compensating for the weakening of the triangle congruence axiom. Many anomalies are stated by Hilbert to occur in two models which he ingeniously constructed. Concerning different methods of compensating for the restriction of the triangle congruence axiom, see Supplement V2 of the ninth edition of the *Grundlagen* (pp. 264–268) and the literature mentioned there in the footnote on p. 265.

Characterization of the plane. As Blumenthal's biography indicates, Hilbert was led to the problems of Appendix II by investigations (reprinted in Appendix IV) in which he gave a very different foundation for plane geometry from that presented in the main part of the book. The problem here is to characterize the plane by means of the properties of the manifold of congruent motions. It was first treated by Hermann von Helmholtz and soon after by Sophus Lie, who emphasized its group-theoretic aspects. Both Helmholtz and Lie proceeded by the methods of the differential calculus. Hilbert sought to avoid any assumption concerning differentiability. His arguments in Appendix IV are within the framework of the theory of point sets. They rely especially on Camille Jordan's theorem concerning simply closed continuous curves (Jordan curves) in the "number plane," which generalizes the theorem on the decomposition of the plane by a simple polygon. Hilbert starts from a characterization of the geometric plane as a two-dimensional manifold by means of the concept of neighborhoods introduced in an axiomatic way—this is now a familiar method in topology, but at that time it was scarcely known at all.

Two characterizations of the "plane" are offered. According to the narrower definition the plane is topologically equivalent to a connected domain in the number plane; according to the wider definition it is locally equivalent (homeomorphic) to the interior of a Jordan curve and is globally connected. Hilbert chose the narrower characterization for simplicity.

The concept of continuous transformation can be defined by means of the representation of the geometric plane in the number plane. The motions are then taken as special continuous one-to-one transformations of the geometric plane onto itself such that in the representation each Jordan curve preserves its orientation. This provisional characterization of the geometric plane is then completed by three axioms on motions: (1) The motions constitute a group with respect to their composition; (2) given two different points, A and B, there are infinitely many points into which B can be transformed by a motion keeping A fixed; (3) if A, B, C and A', B', C' are triples of points in the geometric plane (the members of a triple not necessarily being different) and if in an arbitrary proximity of A, B, C there exist triples P, Q, R and in an arbitrary proximity of A', B', C' there exist triples P', Q', R' such that P, Q, R is transformed by a motion into P', Q', R', then A, B, C is transformed by a motion into A', B', C'.

In a valuable discussion that made use of set-theoretic, topological, and group-theoretic arguments, Hilbert proved that from these axioms, with the obvious definition of congruence by means of the concept of motion and a suitable set-theoretic definition of straight line, it follows that the geometric plane under consideration satisfies the axioms of plane geometry as stated in the main part of the *Grundlagen*, with two exceptions: (1) the triangle congruence axiom is obtained only in the restricted form relating to motions, and (2) the parallel axiom does not result. Two possibilities then remain: the plane satisfies either Euclidean geometry or Bolyai–Lobachevski geometry.

Hilbert's handling of these problems disclosed a new direction of investigation, which is still being pursued. His results have been extended in three ways: (1) by weakening the topological assumptions through the adoption of the wider characterization, mentioned above, of a two-dimensional manifold, (2) by generalizing the discussion to higher dimensions, and (3) by modifying the axioms on the motions. (See the surveys of these researches in the introduction to Freudenthal's "Neuere Fassung des Riemann–Helmholtz–Lieschen Raumproblems" and his "Im Urkreis der sogenannten Raumprobleme.")

Continuity. A final aspect of Hilbert's axiomatization of geometry in the *Grundlagen* is his treatment of continuity.

The Archimedean axiom is stated as an axiom of continuity, yet it excludes only a particular kind of discontinuity. In fact, if this axiom alone is added to the Hilbert axioms of incidence, order, and congruence (including the parallel axiom), then the axiom system is satisfied by an analytic geometry constructed over a *restricted* number system consisting only of algebraic numbers and not including the square root of each positive number.

In this respect Hilbert's axioms differ from those of Euclid's *Elements*. Euclid explicitly postulated the construction of a circle around a given point with a given radius (and implicitly made assumptions about the intersection of circles and of circles with straight lines). However, in order to realize by constructions the existence statements of Hilbert's axioms, it is sufficient to have, in addition to a ruler, not a compass but an *"Eichmass"*—that is, an instrument for determining a given distance on a given straight line from a given point in a prescribed direction. Hilbert showed, in Chapter 7 of the *Grundlagen*, that the *Eichmass* and the ruler allow us to perform all the constructions corresponding to the existence axioms.

Chapter 7 also discusses the question of the analytical representation of the constructions with ruler and *Eichmass*. It turns out that the ratio numbers of line segments constructible from a given unit length with ruler and *Eichmass* are the real numbers obtainable by the elementary arithmetical operations together with the operation $\sqrt{1+c^2}$. This domain of numbers is narrower than that obtained when the operation $\sqrt{1+c^2}$ is replaced by that of extracting the square root of an arbitrary positive number. The latter domain is the one composed of the ratio numbers of the lengths constructible by ruler and compass, but by no means does it contain all algebraic numbers. Yet, whereas the set of all algebraic numbers is denumerable, the set of all ratio numbers has a higher infinity. Hence, in order to characterize the geometric continuum a further axiom is required. It then becomes apparent that geometric continuity is related to continuity in the theory of real numbers.

When Hilbert wrote the *Grundlagen* the question of conceptually formulating the continuity property of an ordered set had been settled by the Dedekind axiom of *Lückenlosigkeit* and its equivalent, the principle of the least upper bound. For a metrical set, each of these axioms implies the Archimedean property.

Completeness. In direct connection with his work on the foundations of geometry, Hilbert undertook an axiomatization of theory of real numbers. In the paper "Über den Zahlbegriff" (published in 1900 and reprinted as Appendix VI of the *Grundlagen*), he presents an axiom system characterizing the system of real numbers as an ordered Archimedean field that cannot be extended to a wider ordered Archimedean field. He thus replaced the continuity axiom by (1) the Archimedean axiom and (2) a condition of maximality which he called the axiom of completeness.

Hilbert introduced into geometry a corresponding axiom of completeness (which first appears in the second edition of the *Grundlagen*) stating that the space characterized by the axiom system including the axiom of completeness constitutes a maximal (that is, not extensible) model of the other axioms. The connection between the geometrical and the arithmetical completeness axiom is given by the circumstance that any model of the axioms of incidence, order, and congruence and of the parallel and the Archimedean axiom can be represented by an analytic geometry over an ordered Archimedean number field, which again is isomorphic with respect to sum, product, and order to a subfield of the field of all real numbers.

The statement of the completeness axiom is very suggestive, and it was with Hilbert's introduction of this axiom that the notion of a maximal model was first conceived. Yet, because of its reference to other axioms, the completeness axiom offers difficulties, particularly with respect to questions of independence. The possibility of decomposing the full continuity axiom into the Archimedean axiom and another axiom which does not entail it is given by Cantor's continuity axiom. (See Federigo Enriques, "Prinzipien der Geometrie," and Richard Baldus, "Zur Axiomatik der Geometrie III: Über das Archimedische und das Cantorsche Axiom.")

Consistency. In "Über den Zahlbegriff" Hilbert recommended substituting an axiomatic presentation of the theory of real numbers for the "genetic" method of treating them. Despite the great pedagogical value of the genetic method, he said, the axiomatic method is to be preferred for the definitive formulation and logical precision of the theory.

This point of view has decisive consequences for the problem of consistency. Hilbert proved the consistency of the geometrical axiom system by using the arithmetical model provided by analytic geometry. But if arithmetic is set up as an axiomatic theory, then Hilbert's proof establishes only a relative consistency. This, of course, is a valuable result, since the structure described by the axioms for the arithmetical continuum is much simpler than that of Euclidean space. The reduction to arithmetic, however, cannot then be regarded as a kind of direct verification by intuitive evidence, for the task of proving the consistency of the axiomatic theory of real numbers remains. This problem was one of those Hilbert posed in "Mathematische Probleme" (*Gesammelte Abhandlungen*, Vol. III, pp. 290–329).

At that time Hilbert thought that a suitable modification of the methods of Dedekind and Weierstrass in the theory of irrational numbers would suffice to obtain the desired proof of consistency. Not long after, however, in the address "Über die Grundlagen der Logik und der Arithmetik" to the Heidelberg Congress of Mathematicians, Hilbert presented an essentially altered view. This alteration was no doubt brought about through the discovery by Russell and Zermelo of very significant forms of the logical paradoxes which gave a more fundamental aspect to the difficulties that Cantor had earlier found with respect to "inconsistent sets." These difficulties showed that in set theory we cannot in general assign to a predicate P "the set of all those things for which P holds" as an object belonging to the universe of discourse.

Hilbert stated that these paradoxes seemed to show that the views and methods of logic "conceived in the traditional sense" ("*im hergebrachten Sinne aufgefasst*") are not equal to the strong requirements of set theory. And, although he strongly opposed Leopold Kronecker's tend-ency to restrict mathematical methods, he nevertheless admitted that Kronecker's criticism of the usual way of dealing with the infinite was partly justified.

The resulting point of view was not yet explicitly developed in Hilbert's Heidelberg address. However, Hilbert presented there the following programmatic ideas: (1) One must include in the arithmetical theory whose consistency is to be demonstrated the methods of logical reasoning used in the theory; (2) the methods of symbolic logic for representing mathematical sentences by formulas are to be applied; (3) the sequences of formulas representing mathematical proofs can be made the object of intuitive elementary reasoning regarding their structural properties and relations, and in this way proofs of consistency can be carried out. Various devices for proving consistency were also exhibited.

Hilbert's investigations of the foundations of arithmetic remained in this provisional state for a long time. During the interval major developments took place in the foundations of mathematics and in mathematical logic. Zermelo proved the well-ordering theorem and published his axiom system for set theory in 1908. Two years later the first volume of Russell and Whitehead's *Principia Mathematica* appeared. Julius König attempted to carry out Hilbert's plan, but his work was interrupted by his premature death and appeared only in fragmentary form, edited by his son, in 1914 (*Neue Grundlagen der Logik, Arithmetik und Mengenlehre*, Leipzig, 1914). In this work some steps of the later Hilbert proof theory are already carried out, but Hilbert did not know of it when he again took up his investigation of the foundations of arithmetic.

PROOF THEORY

Hilbert's return to the problem of the foundations of arithmetic was announced by his delivery at Zurich in 1917 of the lecture "Axiomatisches Denken." In the latter part of this lecture he pointed out several epistemological questions which, as he said, are connected with that of the consistency of number theory and set theory: the problem of the solubility in principle of every mathematical question; that of finding a standard of simplicity for mathematical proofs; that of the relation of contents and formalism in mathematics; and that of the decidability of a mathematical question by a finite procedure. Questions of this kind, he observed, seem to constitute a domain that should be investigated, and to carry out this investigation it will be necessary to inquire into the concept of mathematical proof. The general idea and the aims of proof theory were thus proclaimed, but the means of investigation were not thereby fixed, for indeed the theory was not to rely on the current mathematical methods.

At the time of his Zurich lecture Hilbert tended to restrict the methods of proof-theoretic reasoning to the most primitive evidence. The apparent needs of proof theory induced him to adopt successively those suppositions which constitute what he then called the "*finite Einstellung*."

Consistency. In his first publication on proof theory, "Neubegründung der Mathematik, Erste Mitteilung," Hilbert explains how number theory can be treated in a finitist way, whereas mathematics in general transcends finitist methods. But, Hilbert argues, we can regain an elementary kind of mathematical objectivity by formalizing the statements and proofs, using the methods of symbolic logic, and by taking the representing formulas and proofs directly as objects. In the same paper Hilbert also gives indications of the nature of formalization and presents an instance of a proof of consistency—as yet for only a very restricted system.

A more advanced stage is reached in Hilbert's lecture at the Leipzig congress of the Deutsche Naturforscher Gesellschaft in 1922, "Die logische Grundlagen der Mathematik."

In this speech the method is presented of dealing in proof theory with the logical forms of generality and existence (quantifiers) by means of a logical choice function which assigns to any predicate A an object τA for which A holds only if it is generally satisfied. This idea is formally expressed by the "transfinite axiom," $A(\tau A) \rightarrow A(a)$, in which a predicate expression can be substituted for A and any term representing an individual can be substituted for a. A slight modification, soon applied, replaced the function τA by the function ϵA, dual to it, whose axiom is $A(a) \rightarrow A(\epsilon A)$.

By means of the choice function the quantifiers can be eliminated from a formalized proof in such a way that the rules for the use of "all" and "exists" are reduced to applications of the transfinite axiom, so that the explicit logical structure of the proof becomes transformed into an elementary one, consisting only in applications of the propositional calculus and substitutions.

The task of proving the consistency of a formalized domain of arithmetic is thus essentially reduced. This task—in virtue of the law "ex falso quodlibet"—amounts to showing that the formula $0 \neq 0$ cannot be derived in the domain; in other words, to showing that in any formal derivation of the formalized domain having a numerical end formula, this end formula differs from the formula $0 \neq 0$. Consideration of formalized proofs can now be restricted to those obtained by the transformation using the function ϵA. The main problem is then to eliminate the formulas resulting from the transfinite axiom by substitution (the "critical formulas").

The method that Hilbert indicates for attacking this problem consists—after first removing the free variables, which is possible—of a sequence of steps. In each step the terms that occur are replaced by numerical values. Then, either all critical formulas turn into true numerical formulas, and the attempted elimination is effected, or the result of the step determines a next step. It must still be shown that the process has an end, and this, at least in the simple cases, can be seen to hold.

This method is not in principle restricted to cases where the predicates to which the logical choice function applies are number predicates and where the individuals are therefore natural numbers; it can also be used for individuals of higher types. The particular case in which number functions are taken as individuals is essential to the formalization of the theory of real numbers. In the Leipzig lecture, Hilbert gave several indications of how this formalization can be performed; in particular, he showed how

some form of the Zermelo choice principle (used in the theory of functions of real numbers) can be derived from the transfinite axiom related to the type of real numbers (as individuals).

Thus, it seemed that carrying out proof theory was only a question of mathematical technique. Such an expectation, however, turned out to be illusory. An indication was that the first substantial consistency proof following Hilbert's scheme of reasoning by Wilhelm Ackermann (in his thesis, "Begründung des 'tertium non datur' mittels der Hilbertschen Theorie der Widerspruchsfreiheit") required an essential restriction of the formal system not envisaged in the original plan. Similarly, in John von Neumann's inquiry "Zur Hilbertschen Beweistheorie," where a formal system for the logic of first and second order (including the first four Peano axioms) was set up and a consistency proof using Hilbert's method was given, the consistency proof did not apply to the full system but excluded the comprehension axiom, which provides the manipulation of substitutions for variables of second type. Thus, two highly able investigators did not succeed in obtaining a consistency proof for a formal system of the theory of real numbers by means of the above-mentioned Hilbert method (connected with the logical choice function) of eliminating the critical formulas.

A second method of eliminating the critical formulas, devised by Hilbert and elaborated by Ackermann, yields the proof of a general theorem which states that any axiomatic system, formalized within the frame of standard logic (that is, propositional logic and the rules governing quantifiers), whose axioms have a finitist interpretation is consistent (see Hilbert and Bernays, *Grundlagen der Mathematik*, Vol. II, Sec. 1, esp. pp. 18–38). The method is one of the easiest for proving an important theorem of mathematical logic (first stated by Jacques Herbrand in his doctoral dissertation) which yields a kind of normal form for derivations in pure logic and which also can be applied to decision problems. But this method is not sufficient to demonstrate the consistency of the proper formal system of number theory and therefore is the less sufficient for the systems of infinitesimal analysis.

Completeness. Ackermann revised and simplified the proof presented in his thesis. It was thought that by this modified proof and by that of von Neumann the consistency of formalized number theory, at least, had been proved. Such was the situation when Hilbert presented, at the International Congress of Mathematicians in Bologna in 1928, his "Probleme der Grundlegung der Mathematik." To the problem of proving consistency he here added two problems of completeness: the problem of showing that every universally valid logical schema is derivable by the rules of the predicate calculus and the problem of showing the completeness of formalized number theory, in the sense that the formal system of number theory contains no formula which, together with its negation, can be shown to be underivable in the system.

Gödel's results. Kurt Gödel soon took up both these problems of completeness, but he stated completeness only for the case of the predicate calculus (first-order functional calculus), whereas he proved the incompleteness of formalized number theory even in the strong sense that no strictly formal system is possible in which each true number-theoretic proposition is derivable. At the same time Gödel proved a theorem from which it follows that a finitist proof of consistency for a formal system strong enough to formalize all finitist reasonings is impossible ("Über formale unentscheidbare Sätze der Principia Mathematica und verwandte Systeme I"). Von Neumann was convinced that this last condition holds for the formal system of number theory, and hence he inferred that Gödel's result implies the impossibility of a finitist consistency proof not only for the broader systems discussed by Gödel but even for the formal system of number theory.

To corroborate this inference he was able to show that in the proof of consistency of the formal system of number theory by the elimination of critical formulas, the demonstration that the process of elimination has an end did not apply in full generality (see Hilbert and Bernays, *Grundlagen*, Vol. II, pp. 123–125). It thus became clear that in two respects Hilbert's program demanded more than can be fulfilled: mathematical theories cannot be formalized with full adequacy, and consistency proofs cannot be strictly finitist in the essential cases.

Broadening of proof theory. It soon became apparent that proof theory could be fruitfully developed without fully keeping to the original program. It was discovered that a proof of consistency for the formal system of number theory, although not a finitist one, is possible by methods of proof admitted by L. E. J. Brouwer's intuitionism.

Arend Heyting, in two papers of 1930, set up a formal system of intuitionistic number theory. And, as Gödel and Gerhard Gentzen independently observed, there is a relatively simple method of showing that any contradiction derivable in the formal system of classical number theory would entail a contradiction in Heyting's system. Hence, from the consistency of Heyting's system the consistency of the classical system follows (Kurt Gödel, "Zur intuitionistischen Arithmetik und Zahlentheorie"—Gentzen withdrew his own paper, already in print, because of the appearance of Gödel's paper).

In this way it appeared that intuitionistic reasoning is not identical with finitist reasoning, contrary to the prevailing views at that time. In particular, intuitionistic reasoning deals with concepts not admitted as methods in finitist proofs, such as the quite general concept of consequence when it is not delimited by any rules of proof. It thus became apparent that the *"finite Standpunkt"* is not the only alternative to classical ways of reasoning and is not necessarily implied by the idea of proof theory. An enlarging of the methods of proof theory was therefore suggested: instead of a restriction to finitist methods of reasoning, it was required only that the arguments be of a constructive character, allowing us to deal with more general forms of inference.

By this modification of the program, various proofs of consistency for the formal system of number theory were obtained, the first by Gentzen ("Die Widerspruchsfreiheit der reinen Zahlentheorie," "Die gegenwärtige Lage in der mathematischen Grundlagenforschung," and "Neue Fassung des Widerspruchsfreiheitsbeweises für die reine Zahlentheorie"). Ackermann was then able to complete the consistency proof proceeding by the method of eliminating the critical formulas ("Zur Widerspruchsfreiheit der Zahlentheorie"). The broadened methods also permitted a loosening of the requirements of formalizing. One step in this direction, made by Hilbert himself, was to replace the schema of complete induction by the stronger rule later called infinite induction ("Die Grundlegung der elementaren Zahlenlehre" and "Beweis des Tertium non datur").

However, going beyond finitist methods is not generally required in proof theory; many important results have been obtained by finitist methods, results concerning the following topics: pure logic, the combinatorial calculus, completeness (the completeness of a system of real algebra), undecidability, and relative consistency.

One main result concerning relative consistency is connected with Hilbert's attempt at a positive solution of Cantor's continuum problem in the paper "Über das Unendliche." The sketch of a proof given in this work contains many detailed arguments, and it stimulated the study of recursive definitions. As a whole, however, the sketch was fragmentary, and there were in principle hindrances to its completion. Twelve years later Gödel connected the ideas of Hilbert's paper with the concepts of axiomatic set theory and proved the consistency of Cantor's continuum hypothesis in its generalized form on the assumption that axiomatic set theory (without the axiom of choice) is consistent. (Nevertheless, this result, which is obtained by a powerful method of proof, does not settle the continuum problem. In fact, from results obtained by Paul Cohen it appears that axiomatic set theory, at least in its formal delimitation, leaves this problem fully undecided.)

On the whole, Hilbert's idea of making mathematical proof an object of mathematical research by means of formalization has proved to be very fruitful. And although Hilbert's work in the foundations of arithmetic has not had the effect he sought, "to remove once and for all the questions of foundations in mathematics" ("die Grundlagenfragen in der Mathematik als solche endgültig aus der Welt zu schaffen"—"Die Grundlagen der Mathematik," p. 65, and "Die Grundlagen der elementaren Zahlenlehre," p. 489), he did establish proof theory as a valuable domain of mathematical investigation, and thus Hilbert was a pioneer in the newer mathematical foundation theory, as he was in many other fields of mathematics.

Works by Hilbert

ON THE FOUNDATIONS OF GEOMETRY

Die Grundlagen der Geometrie. Leipzig, 1899; 9th ed., Stuttgart, 1961. The first edition was published as a *Festschrift* for the unveiling of the Gauss–Weber memorial. The second and later editions were published as textbooks. Most incorporate modifications and additions. Translated by E. J. Townsend as *Foundations of Geometry.* La Salle, Ill., 1902.

"Über den Satz von der Gleichheit der Basiswinkel im gleichschenkligen Dreieck." *Proceedings of the London Mathematical Society,* Vol. 35 (1903), 50–68. Reprinted as Appendix II to the *Grundlagen,* 9th ed. Pp. 133–158.

"Über die Grundlagen der Geometrie." *Mathematische Annalen,* Vol. 56 (1902), 381–422. Reprinted as Appendix IV to the *Grundlagen,* 9th ed. Pp. 178–230.

"Neue Begründung der Bolyai–Lobatschefskyschen Geometrie." *Mathematische Annalen,* Vol. 57 (1903), 137–150. Reprinted as Appendix III to the *Grundlagen,* 9th ed. Pp. 159–177.

ON THE FOUNDATIONS OF ARITHMETIC

"Die Theorie der algebraischen Zahlkörper." *Jahresbericht der Deutschen Mathematikervereinigung,* Vol. 4 (1897), I–XVIII, 175–546.

"Über den Zahlbegriff." *Jahresbericht der Deutschen Mathematikervereinigung,* Vol. 8 (1900), 180–184. Reprinted as Appendix VI to the *Grundlagen,* 7th ed. Leipzig, 1930. Pp. 241–246.

"Über die Grundlagen der Logik und Arithmetik," in *Verhandlungen des Dritten Internationalen Mathematiker-Kongresses in Heidelberg vom 8. bis 13. August 1904.* Leipzig, 1905. Pp. 174–185. Reprinted as Appendix VII to the *Grundlagen,* 7th ed. Pp. 247–261.

"Axiomatisches Denken." *Mathematische Annalen,* Vol. 78 (1918); 405–415.

"Neubegründung der Mathematik. Erste Mitteilung." *Abhandlungen aus dem mathematische Seminar der Hamburgischen Universität,* Vol. 1 (1922), 157–177.

"Die logischen Grundlagen der Mathematik." *Mathematische Annalen,* Vol. 88 (1923), 151–165.

"Über das Unendliche." *Mathematische Annalen,* Vol. 95 (1926), 161–190.

"Die Grundlagen der Mathematik." *Abhandlungen aus dem mathematische Seminar der Hamburgischen Universität,* Vol. 6 (1928), 65–85.

"Probleme der Grundlegung der Mathematik." *Mathematische Annalen,* Vol. 103 (1929), 1–9.

"Die Grundlegung der elementaren Zahlenlehre." *Mathematische Annalen,* Vol. 104 (1931), 485–494.

"Beweis des Tertium non datur." *Nachrichten des Gesellschaft der Wissenschaft zu Göttingen* (1931), 120–125.

TEXTBOOKS

Grundzüge der theoretischen Logik, Berlin, 1928; 3d ed., 1949. By D. Hilbert and W. Ackermann. Translated by Lewis M. Hammond and others as *Principles of Mathematical Logic.* New York, 1950.

Grundlagen der Mathematik, 2 vols. Berlin, 1934–1939. By D. Hilbert and P. Bernays.

COLLECTED WORKS

Gesammelte Abhandlungen, 3 vols. Berlin, 1932–1935.

Studies Related to Hilbert's Work

Bernays, Paul, "Über Hilberts Gedanken zur Grundlegung der Arithmetik." *Jahresbericht der Deutschen Mathematikervereinigung,* Vol. 31 (1922), 10–19.

Bernays, Paul. "Die Bedeutung Hilberts für die Philosophie der Mathematik." *Die Naturwissenschaften,* 10th year (1922), No. 1. This number was devoted to Hilbert on his sixtieth birthday. It contains the following papers: Otto Blumenthal, "David Hilbert"; Otto Toeplitz, "Der Algebraiker Hilbert"; Max Dehn, "Hilberts geometrisches Werk"; Richard Courant, "Hilbert als Analytiker"; Max Born, "Hilbert und die Physik"; and a list of Hilbert's publications up to 1921 compiled by Karl Siegel.

Bernays, Paul, "Die Philosophie der Mathematik und die Hilbertsche Beweistheorie." *Blätter für deutsche Philosophie. Zeitschrift der Deutschen Philosophischen Gesellschaft,* Vol. 4, Nos. 3–4 (Berlin, 1930), 326–367. This number also contains articles on the foundations of mathematics by Heinrich Scholz, A. Fraenkel, Rudolf Carnap, Carl Menger, and Walter Dubislav.

Bernays, Paul, "Sur le platonisme dans les mathématiques." *L'Enseignement mathématique,* Vol. 34 (1935), 52–60.

Bernays, Paul, "Hilberts Untersuchungen über die Grundlagen der Arithmetik," in David Hilbert, *Gesammelte Abhandlungen,* Vol. III. Berlin, 1935. Pp. 191–216.

Blumenthal, Otto, "Lebensgeschichte," in David Hilbert, *Gesammelte Abhandlungen* (see above), Vol. III, pp. 388–429.

Kreisel, Georg, "Hilbert's Programme." *Dialectica,* Vol. 88 (1923), 151–165. Reprinted in Paul Benacerraf and Hilary Putnam, eds., *Philosophy of Mathematics.* Englewood Cliffs, N.J., 1964. Pp. 157–180.

ON THE FOUNDATIONS OF GEOMETRY

Baldus, Richard, "Zur Axiomatik der Geometrie III. Über das Archimedische und das Cantorsche Axiom," in *Sitzungsbericht des Heidelberger Akademie des Wissenschaft,* 5. Abhandlung. Leipzig, 1930. Pp. 3–12.

Bernays, Paul, "Bemerkungen zu den Grundlagen der Geometrie," in *Studies and Essays Presented to R. Courant on His 60th Birthday.* New York, 1948. Pp. 29–44.

Dehn, Max, "Über raumgleiche Polyeder." *Göttinger Nachrichten* (1900).

Dehn, Max, "Über den Rauminhalt." *Mathematische Annalen,* Vol. 55 (1902), 465–478.

Enriques, Federigo, "Prinzipien der Geometrie," in *Enzyclopädie des mathematischen Wissenschaften,* Vol. III, Pt. I. 1907–1910. Pp. 34 ff. See especially p. 36.

Freudenthal, Hans, "Neuere Fassung des Riemann–Helmholtz–Lieschen Raumproblems." *Mathematische Zeitschrift,* Vol. 63 (1955–1956), 374–405. See in particular the Introduction.

Freudenthal, Hans, "Zur Geschichte der Grundlagen der Geometrie." *Nieue Archief voor Wiskunde,* Vol. 4 (1957), 105–142. Includes a review of the 8th edition of Hilbert's *Grundlagen der Geometrie.*

Freudenthal, Hans, "Die Grundlagen der Geometrie um die Wende des 19. Jahrhunderts." *Mathematisch-Physikalische Semesterberichte,* Vol. 7, No. 1 (Göttingen, 1960), 2–25. A translated extract of this article appeared as "The Main Trends of the Foundations of Geometry in the 19th Century," in Ernest Nagel et al., eds., *Logic, Methodology and Philosophy of Science.* Stanford, Calif., 1962.

Freudenthal, Hans, "Im Urkreis der sogennannten Raumprobeme," in Yehoshua Bar-Hillel, ed., *Essays on the Foundation of Mathematics.* Jerusalem, 1961. Pp. 322–327.

Hessenberg, Gerhard, "Beweis des Desargueschen Satzes aus dem Pascalschen." *Mathematische Annalen,* Vol. 61, 161–172.

Kagan, B., "Über die Transformation der Polyeder." *Mathematische Annalen,* Vol. 57 (1903), 421–424.

Schatunowski, S. O., "Über den Rauminhalt der Polyeder." *Mathematische Annalen,* Vol. 57 (1903), 496–508.

Schmidt, Arnold, "Die Herleitung der Spiegelung aus der ebenen Bewegung." *Mathematische Annalen,* Vol. 109 (1934), 538–571.

Wiener, Hans, "Grundlagen und Aufbau der Geometrie." *Jahresberichte der Deutschen Mathematikervereinigung,* Vol. 1 (1892), 45–48.

IMPORTANT PAPERS ON PROOF THEORY

Ackermann, Wilhelm, "Begründung des 'tertium non datur' mittels der Hilbertschen Theorie der Widerspruchsfreiheit." *Mathematische Annalen,* Vol. 93 (1924–1925), 1–36.

Ackermann, Wilhelm, "Zur Widerspruchsfreiheit der Zahlentheorie." *Mathematische Annalen,* Vol. 117 (1940), 162–194.

Cohen, Paul J., "The Independence of the Continuum Hypothesis," I and II. *Proceedings of the National Academy of Sciences,* Vol. 50 (1963), 1143–1148, and Vol. 51 (1964), 105–110.

Gentzen, Gerhard, "Untersuchungen über das logische Schliessen," I and II. *Mathematische Zeitschrift,* Vol. 39 (1934), 176–210, 405–431.

Gentzen, Gerhard, "Die Widerspruchsfreiheit der reinen Zahlentheorie." *Mathematische Annalen,* Vol. 112 (1936), 493–565.

Gentzen, Gerhard, "Die gegenwärtige Lage in der mathematischen Grundlagenforschung" and "Neue Fassung des Widerspruchsfreiheitsbeweises für die reine Zahlentheorie." *Forschungen zur Logik zur Grundlegung der exakten Wissenschaften,* N.S. No. 4 (1938), 5–18, 19–44.

Gödel, Kurt, "Über formal unentscheidbare Sätze der Principia Mathematica und verwandter Systeme I." *Monatschefte für Mathematik und Physik,* Vol. 38 (1931), 173–198.

Gödel, Kurt, "Zur intuitionistischen Arithmetik und Zahlentheorie." *Ergebnisse eines mathematische Kolloquiums, 52 Kolloquium* (June 1932), Vol. 4 (1933), 34–38.

Gödel, Kurt, *The Consistency of the Axiom of Choice and of the*

Generalized Continuum-hypothesis With the Axioms of Set Theory. Princeton, N.J., 1940.

Herbrand, Jacques, "Recherches sur la théorie de la démonstration." *Travaux de la Société des Sciences et des Lettres de Varsovie,* Classe III, No. 33 (1930), 33–160. Thesis, University of Paris.

Heyting, Arend. "Die formalen Regeln der intuitionistischen Logik." *Sitzungsberichte der Preussischen Akademie der Wissenschaften,* Physical-mathematical section, 1930 II. Berlin, 1930.

Heyting, Arend, "Die formalen Regeln der intuitionistischen Mathematik." *Sitzungsberichte der Preussischen Akademie der Wissenschaften,* Physical-mathematical section, 1930 II. Berlin, 1930.

Neumann, John von, "Zur Hilbertschen Beweistheorie." *Mathematische Zeitschrift,* Vol. 26 (1927), 1–46.

PAUL BERNAYS

The Encyclopedia of Philosophy

The
ENCYCLOPEDIA
of
PHILOSOPHY

PAUL EDWARDS, *Editor in Chief*

VOLUME FOUR

Macmillan Publishing Co., Inc. & The Free Press

NEW YORK

COLLIER MACMILLAN PUBLISHERS

LONDON

The Encyclopedia of Philosophy

H

[CONTINUED]

HINDUISM is the dominant religion of India; it has also been long established in Nepal and Ceylon and is found in other areas among emigrant Indians. It has over 400 million adherents in Asia. In addition, the Hindu doctrines known as Vedānta have made some converts in the West.

Because of the diverse elements absorbed into Hinduism during its long evolution, and because of the latitude allowed in the interpretation of scripture, there is no single system of belief which can be said to represent Hinduism. There are, however, two main marks of Hindu orthodoxy: acceptance of the Vedic scriptures as revelation (śruti, literally "what is heard") and participation in the Hindu social structure. Thus Jainism and Buddhism, which doctrinally are not very far removed from some Hindu patterns of belief, are considered unorthodox because they do not acknowledge the Veda. Although belief in reincarnation and in the eternity of the soul or self (puruṣa, ātman) is nearly universal among Hindus, Hindu theology and metaphysics range from belief in a divine Absolute to atheism. Likewise, there is a great range of religious practices and of alternative and overlapping mythologies.

The Vedic period. The two main elements which gave rise to Hinduism were the religion of the Aryans, who invaded India from the northwest during the second millennium B.C., and the beliefs of the conquered population. The literary expression of the Aryan religion is found in a substantial number of hymns, probably dating, in more or less their present form, from 1400 B.C. to 800 B.C. These were arranged in three collections, to which a fourth was later added, and of which the most important is the Ṛg-veda ("Royal Knowledge"). In the latter part of the Vedic period there were appended ritual works, known as the Brāhmaṇas, and out of these in turn grew the Upaniṣads, dating from 800 B.C. onward and containing religious and philosphical speculations. All these writings came to constitute the sacred scriptures of Hinduism and are collectively known as the Veda. The canon is somewhat fluid, however, and certain other writings, notably the Bhagavad Gītā (c. 200 B.C.—there is considerable controversy about the date), are included as a "fifth Veda."

The Vedic hymns are addressed to a variety of gods, some of whom have counterparts in Roman and Greek religion (for example: Dyauspitṛ, Jupiter; Varuṇa, Oura-

nos). They are mainly connected with, or are partial personifications of, natural forces (Agni is Fire, Vāyu is Wind, Indra controls thunderbolts, and so on), but the polytheism is modified by two factors. First, there is the tendency (known as henotheism) to regard the god addressed as being supreme; while worshiping one deity, the hymn writer ignores or discounts the other gods, transferring their epithets to the god addressed. This tendency has its counterpart in modern Hinduism, where Viṣṇu and Śiva are treated as alternative manifestations of the Godhead. Second, in the hymns there is speculation leading to the view that there is only one divine Reality, although it is called by different names. Again, this represents an attitude carried over into modern Hinduism: it is now common to regard the great religions of the world as so many different ways of representing, and reaching out to, the one Truth.

The Upaniṣads. The Brāhmaṇas show that, in the settled period after the Aryan invasions, there was increasing elaboration of ritual. The sacrificial rites, administered by the priestly class (Brahmins), needed to be described and explained. From this preoccupation with ritual there emerged a desire to explain its inner meaning, and this is one main concern of the Upaniṣads. They try to answer in various ways the question "What is Brahman?" (the sacred power implicit in ritual performances). Brahman came to be thought of as the power sustaining the whole cosmos, and thus the question prompted an inquiry to find a single principle that underlies the multiplicity of phenomena. The monotheistic tendencies of the period of the Vedic hymns were reinforced by this new direction of thought, although a tension between belief in a personal God and speculation about the rather impersonally conceived Brahman (the word is neuter) is indicated in the Upaniṣads and is found frequently in later Indian metaphysical theology.

At the same time, the Upaniṣads were moving away from the older Brahmanic religion, partly because they incorporated pre-Aryan elements. A sign of this is the prominent part played in some passages by the kṣatriyas, members of the warrior or noble class—the Brahmins were the traditional controllers of sacred knowledge. Further, there is, in line with the search for the inner meaning of the sacrifices, a certain hostility to ritualism conceived as merely outward observance.

1

Little is definitely known about pre-Aryan religion. The archaeological remains of the Indus valley civilization of the third millennium B.C. (which showed a remarkable degree of urban development) indicate that the cult of Śiva, which was to loom so large in later Hinduism, probably originated there. It is probable, too, that yogic techniques, such as are characteristic of Jainism, Buddhism and classical Yoga, are of pre-Aryan origin, although the practice of austerity (*tapas*) was central to the *soma* sacrifice of the early Vedic period. (This cult involved the ritual use of an intoxicating liquor made from the *soma* plant.) Also pre-Aryan is the belief, characteristic of all religions of Indian origin, in reincarnation. It is not found in the Vedic hymns, but appears in the *Upaniṣads*.

The increased religious interest in contemplative techniques and in concentration upon the inner self blended with the Brahmanic tendency to equate the macrocosm with the microcosm. The whole world process was seen as a sacrificial rite, and the sacred power implicit in the cosmos was seen as somehow also implicit in the individual. The knowledge of the essential meaning of ritual was identified with knowledge of the self. These strands of thought were intertwined in the famous equation which forms the most influential point of Upaniṣadic teaching—*Brahman* is the Self (*ātman*). In the *Chāndogya Upaniṣad* (VI viii 7) the old Brahmin Uddālaka teaches his son Śvetaketu the true meaning of the *Veda*: the finest essence of the world is the Self, and "That thou art" (*tat tvam asi*). In brief, the eternal element within man is identical with *Brahman*, the sacred power pervading and sustaining the cosmos.

Much of later Indian theology turns on the interpretation of this famous saying and its analogues. If it is taken to assert strict numerical identity, then the highest spiritual goal is the realization of one's inner identity with the divine Absolute. (This is the basis of the system of Śankara, the eighth-century Hindu theologian.) Thus, theistic religion, involving personal devotion to a Being conceived as distinct from the worshiper, has only secondary significance. Nevertheless, while the identity teaching is centrally important in the Upaniṣadic writings, a theistic strand of thought is not wanting, notably in the brief *Īśa Upaniṣad* and the more extensive *Kaṭha Upaniṣad*. Also, in line with a general trend throughout Indian religion, the existence of the many Vedic gods is not denied, although they retain only an inferior status. In the *Kena Upaniṣad*, for instance, Agni, Vāyu, and Indra are represented as under the control of *Brahman;* and in the *Bṛhadāraṇyaka Upaniṣad* they are regarded as partial manifestations of *Brahman* (III ix 1). Hence the *Upaniṣads* represent a transcending of the older Vedic religion and an attempt to point the way to a contemplative knowledge of the spiritual principle underlying the world. Still, the Upaniṣadic revolution was a revolution from within the Vedic tradition, even though it made use of pre-Aryan elements.

Meanwhile, during the same period (800–500 B.C.) other teachings were challenging Brahmanic religion from without, notably those of Vardhamāna (Mahāvīra), the Jain teacher, and of the Buddha (later sixth and early fifth centuries B.C.). Although Jainism and Buddhism remained unorthodox, the tendencies upon which they were based were represented within orthodoxy, notably in the Sāmkhya–Yoga philosophical system, which propounded a doctrine of the plurality of eternal souls and was basically atheistic. Though given its classical formulation in a later period, Sāmkhya–Yoga had roots going back to these early centuries. (For a discussion of Sāmkhya, see INDIAN PHILOSOPHY.)

The Gītā. In the three centuries or so after the composition of the classical *Upaniṣads*, there was considerable development of theistic ideas, and these were synthesized with Brahmanic and yogic concepts in the most famous religious writing of the Indian tradition—the *Bhagavad Gītā* ("Song of the Lord"). It is one book of the immense poem the *Mahābhārata*, which together with the *Rāmāyāna*, the other great Hindu epic, has had enormous influence on popular religion and thought.

The *Gītā* opens with the hero Arjuna awaiting the start of a great battle. He is troubled by the thought of the destruction to come, especially since he has friends and relatives among the enemy. Kṛṣṇa (Krishna), an incarnation of Viṣṇu, is acting as Arjuna's charioteer, and conveys the teachings of God relevant to Arjuna's situation. Briefly, the ethical point is that as a warrior Arjuna has a duty to fight, a duty that must be performed without regard of its results to him and in a spirit of faithfulness to God. As such, the *Gītā* is a defense of the social order, where each person has his allotted duty. However, behind the rather conventional ethics lies a fervent expression of the majesty and compassion of God, and it is to this that the *Gītā* owes its wide religious influence. The theophany in Chapter 11, where Kṛṣṇa no longer appears in human disguise but in all his terrible glory, is one of the most stunning visionary passages in religious literature.

In line with the personal description of God, the *Gītā* stresses grace. One must do one's duty, but this is not what brings salvation—rather, "Abandoning all duties, come unto Me alone for shelter. Be not grieved, for I shall release you from all evils" (xviii 66). This valuation of the personality and gracious mercy of God means that the *Gītā*, while not repudiating the Upaniṣadic concept of *Brahman*, relegates it to second place. Thus, as S. N. Dasgupta remarks in *A History of Indian Philosophy* (Vol. II, p. 476, "For I am the abode of *Brahman*" (xiv 27); *Brahman* is "upheld in the superpersonality of God." At the same time, the *Gītā* makes use of Sāmkhya ideas: nature (*prakṛti*) is distinguished from the innumerable eternal souls, but it is a projection of the supreme Being and not (as in Sāmkhya) a self-subsistent entity. Since it is a religious poem, rather than a systematic exposition, the relation between the varied theological and metaphysical elements in the *Gītā* is not always clear and consistent; this is one reason why different commentators have given it rather different interpretations. Thus Śankara managed to interpret it in line with his nondualistic doctrines.

Viṣṇu, Śiva, and mythological cosmology. The *Gītā* expresses the religion centering on Viṣṇu, but it also refers to the rival cult of Śiva. These two great gods have come to be treated as different manifestations of the one Being, and are iconographically linked with Brahmā, the creator God, as a three-headed trinity, the *Trimūrti*. Viṣṇu is associated with ten *avatars* (incarnations), the most notable of whom are Rāma, the benevolent king of Ayodhyā and hero of the *Rāmāyaṇa*; Kṛṣṇa, whose legend combines pastoral eroticism, military exploits, and a dying god; and the Buddha, thereby adopted into the Hindu pantheon. Śiva is a fiercer figure and symbolizes both the creative and the destructive aspects of deity. The creative side is seen in the chief symbol through which he is worshiped, the *lingam*, or (rather abstractly carved) phallus. One of the best-known representations of Śiva is as lord of the dance—creation being seen as an exuberant mode of self-expression, rather than as a deliberate act with an ulterior purpose. At the same time, Śiva is the great yogin, wrapped in meditation, and so there is considerable emphasis on ascetic and introspective mysticism in Śaivism; Vaiṣṇavism stresses *bhakti*, the loving adoration of God. This is only a matter of relative emphasis, however, since both elements appear with varying strength in several phases of both cults.

These two supreme figures do not exclude lesser cults, and Hindu mythology and religious practice are luxuriant and complex. From the theological point of view, however, the gods are normally synthesized as so many manifestations of the one Being which have been adapted to the level and situation of the adherents.

The backdrop against which the lesser deities act is provided by a grandiose cosmology. Generally the universe is conceived as "pulsating"—recurrently being destroyed and recreated, each period (*kalpa*) being calculated as over 4,300 million years. The world is an immense series of virtually repetitive cycles and is often depicted as being periodically absorbed into and emanated from the divine Being.

The medieval renaissance. During the period from the *Gītā* to the theologian Śankara (eighth century), Buddhism was powerful in most parts of India, and Jainism also flourished. The revival of orthodoxy, in addition to being a factor in the ultimate disappearance of Buddhism from India, also found expression in the teachings of the greatest theologians of the Indian tradition—Śankara, Rāmānuja (twelfth century) and Madhva (thirteenth century). They were exponents of Vedānta (literally, "the end of the Veda"), which was an attempt to systematize the teachings of revelation. (In modern Western usage, "Vedānta" often refers exclusively to a system derived from that of Śankara.) Śankara, a Śaivite, systematized and restored the central Upaniṣadic teachings in Advaita Vedānta (Nondualistic Vedānta), and gave a strictly monistic interpretation to the *Brahman-Ātman* equation. Rāmānuja, a Vaiṣnavite, gave a metaphysical rationale to the devotionalist movement in south India, which was associated with the Āḷvārs, the Tamil poets whose hymns expressed a fervent love of and reliance upon a personal Lord. Rāmānuja, in his Qualified Nondualism (*Viśiṣṭādvaita*), a doctrine which, unlike Śankara's, made some distinction between the soul and God, stressed the *bhaktimārga* (way of devotion) and the need of God's grace. His followers became divided on this issue between the "monkey" school and the "cat" school: the mother monkey leads her young by the hand, but the young one has to walk; the cat takes her kitten by the scruff of the neck. These are analogies of the relation between God as savior and the soul.

Madhva further developed a dualistic theology, making an unequivocal distinction between selves (and the world) and God. Devotional theology likewise developed within Śaivism in the *Śaivasiddhānta* (Śaivite doctrine), which subscribes to a collection of Tamil sacred texts. It is based on the distinction between God, souls, and matter. The last binds souls through karma; but Śiva is lord of karma, and faith in him can bring release in which the soul is united with, but not merged in, God.

Islam and the Indian response. In the eleventh century Muslim forces began to invade India, and by the fourteenth century Muslim rulers controlled most of northern and central India and were penetrating southern India. The Muslim condemnation of idolatry and success in conversions had a severe impact on Hinduism. However, there were many who wished to establish a synthesis between the two faiths. The Emperor Akbar (1542–1605) attempted to found such a syncretistic religion, but without success. Kabīr (1440–1518), a Muslim by birth, preached against the religious externals dividing men and affirmed the unity of the God whom both Muslims and Hindus worshiped. Nānak (1469–1538), who was originally Hindu, continued this movement and founded the Sikh religion (which received some encouragement under Akbar). Although it started as an attempt to bring the two faiths together, Sikh developed into a third and idiosyncratic religion with its own scriptures. The later *Gurus* (Teachers, and successors of Nānak) instituted military obligations, a special form of dress, and other customs.

The modern period. The British conquest of India had a great effect on the social and religious situation. The abolition of *satī* (suttee) and other measures cut at traditional orthodoxy, and modern communication and education had some influence on breaking taboos associated with the caste system. But more important, the influx of Christian missionaries presented a new challenge to orthodoxy. Hinduism, in responding, acquired a new vitality.

Important among reforming and revivalist movements was the Brahmo-Samāj (Society of Believers in God), founded by Raja Ram Mohan Roy (1772–1833), whose remarkable gifts were directed toward interreligious cooperation and the establishment of a Hindu unitarianism set against idolatry. Influenced by this movement were the Tagores, notably Rabindranāth (1861–1941), who reinterpreted the *Upaniṣads* in a life-affirming sense, so that the inner life can be reconciled with active service of the divine Being in the world. More conservative was Dayananda Sarasvati (1824–1883), founder of the Arya-Samaj (Aryan Society), who looked back to the *Vedas* as the purest expression of monotheism.

The most striking nineteenth-century development was that stemming from the life and teachings of the Bengali saint Ramakrishna (1836–1886). He was not an intellectual, but his life was an expression of the ideas of Vedāntism. Ramakrishna tested the teachings of the various great faiths by practicing each of them and experiencing the appropriate religious vision in every case. Thus, he laid the base for a universal message; namely, that different religions could provide contexts for the pursuit of the contemplative life. Since Hinduism was claimed to embrace a variety of cults and ideas, its theology could provide a rationale for this "inclusive" view of religions.

Ramakrishna's disciple Vivekananda (1863–1902) was chiefly responsible for conveying this message both in India and in the West and for organizing the Ramakrishna Mission, devoted to education and good works. This remains a powerful and impressive element in contemporary Hinduism. Another important modern movement stems from the life and writings of Aurobindo Ghose (known by his first name; 1872–1950), who interpreted Hinduism in a world-affirming sense and human history as part of an evolutionary process toward a higher spiritual life.

Throughout the modern period, moreover, classical Hinduism has developed a strong apologetic against other faiths, mainly by claiming that all religions are at least partially true and that Hinduism can provide the best synthesis. A well-known representative of this trend is Sarvepalli Radhakrishnan. However, the chief figure of modern Hinduism was Mahatma Gandhi (1869–1948), who did much as a reformer, breaking down traditional attitudes about untouchability and communal hatred. He exemplified in his life his teaching of nonviolence, which contributed a political and social interpretation to the ancient Indian concept of *ahimsā* ("non-injury"; that is, to living beings).

Hindu rites and social institutions. Generally, ceremonial worship in Hinduism is not congregational, but is performed individually in temple and home. Domestic rites, especially for the Brahmin, are complex, involving ablutions, the cult of consecrated images and of other holy objects, such as the *tulasi* or basil plant, and offerings to the fire god. Personal prayers center on the recitation of sacred verses, notably the *gāyatrī* (a verse from the *Ṛg-veda*), calling on the light of the divine Creator for guidance. Temple rites are performed by priests, often with laymen as spectators; and some of the ceremonies concerned with the images of the gods are most elaborate (washing and dressing the god, putting him to sleep, and so on). Laymen also visit temples to make their own obeisances and offerings to the gods. For example, pilgrimages to the holy city of Banaras are an important part of popular Hinduism. Bathing in the Ganges at Banaras brings especial merit and heavenly rewards, and many pious Hindus spend their last days there in the hope of a holy death.

The caste system is the framework of moral and religious obligations. It is an elaboration of what in Vedic religion was the scheme of *varṇas* (literally "colors"), wherein society was divided into four classes—Brahmin (priests), *kṣatriya* (nobles, warriors), *vaiśya* (merchants), and *śūdra* (laborers, artisans). Those who belonged to the first three *varṇas* were called *dvija* ("twice-born"), and knowledge of the *Veda* was restricted to them. Below the four classes came a substratum of outsiders, or outcastes; no doubt many among the lowest class and these outsiders were members of the conquered population whom the Aryans had come to dominate. In the course of time these divisions became more rigid, and there was also a proliferation of subclasses (*jāti*) based on occupation, religious affiliation, geographical divisions, tribal assimilation, and other factors. There were religious sanctions against intermarriage, commensality, and so on, and the observances required of an individual were largely determined by his social status. In recent times, through the social changes enforced by modern communications, industrial life, and business life, and through the reforming activity of Gandhi and others, there has been some modification of the caste system; outcastes are no longer excluded from temple worship and educational opportunities.

Important to religion was the theory of the four *āshramas*, or stages of life. In principle, the high-caste Hindu's life is divided into four periods. First, he is a pupil or student; second, a householder and family man; third, he begins to relinquish his family ties, to become a *vāna-prastha* (literally, "forest dweller"); finally, he becomes a *samnyāsin*, devoting himself entirely to the spiritual quest. In the last stage he is beyond *dharma*—beyond the structure of moral and social obligations. Reflecting this is the frequent doctrine that the divine Being is "beyond good and evil," not tied down to any particular duties, for duties essentially arise within the society. The four stages of life held up the ideal of renunciation in a way that could be practical for a man who played his part in society, and was a means of combating the entry of young men and women into the Buddhist monastic order. The ideal is reflected in contemporary India by the large number of wandering holy men and recluses, as well as by monastic recluses.

The complexities of the Hindu social order form a substratum for the varieties of cults, mythologies, and doctrines which make up Hinduism, and in some degree they explain its diversity. The compromise implicit in this situation is the basis of Hinduism's contemporary claims to fulfill and comprehend other faiths; but while such a compromise is in part rational, other faiths do not necessarily recognize that the desirability of religious coexistence determines issues of truth and falsity.

Bibliography

GENERAL

Basham, A. L., *The Wonder That Was India*. London, 1954. A most excellent general survey of Indian culture.

Bouquet, A. C., *Hinduism*. London, 1948. A less satisfactory general introduction.

Farquhar, J. N., *A Primer of Hinduism*. London, 1912. A good brief reference book.

Renou, L., *Religions of Ancient India*. London, 1953. A more technical work.

Zaehner, R. C., *Hinduism*. London, 1962. The best brief introduction.

See also the bibliographies to YOGA and INDIAN PHILOSOPHY.

VEDIC PERIOD

Keith, A. B., *The Religion and Philosophy of the Veda and Upanishads*, 2 vols. Cambridge, Mass., 1925.

Macdonell, A. A., *Vedic Mythology*. Strasbourg, 1897.

Der Rig-veda, translated by F. Geldner, 3 vols. Cambridge, Mass., 1951.

Vedic Hymns, translated by F. Max Müller and H. Oldenberg, 2 vols. Sacred Books of the East. Oxford, 1891 and 1897.

Whitney, W. D., *The Atharva Veda*. Cambridge, Mass., 1905.

UPANIṢADS

Eggeling, J., *The Śatapatha Brāhmaṇa*, 5 vols. Sacred Books of the East. Oxford, 1882–1900.
Hume, R. E., *Thirteen Principal Upanishads*. Oxford, 1921.
Macnicol, N., *Hindu Scriptures*. London, 1938.
Mehta, P. D., *Early Indian Religious Thought*. London, 1956. On the *Brahman–Ātman* identification.
Piggott, S., *Prehistoric India*. London, 1951. On pre-Aryan religion.
Radhakrishnan, Sarvepalli, *The Principal Upaniṣads*. London, 1953.
Smart, Ninian, *Reasons and Faiths*. London, 1958. On the *Brahman–Ātman* identification.
Zimmer, H., *Philosophies of India*. New York, 1957. On pre-Aryan religion.

GĪTĀ

Edgerton, F., *The Bhagavad Gītā Translated and Interpreted*, 2 vols. Cambridge, Mass., 1952. The best treatment and translation of the *Gītā*.
Hopkins, E. W., *Epic Mythology*. Strasbourg, 1915.

VIṢṆU, ŚIVA, AND MYTHOLOGICAL COSMOLOGY

Bhandarkar, R. G., *Vaishnavism, Śaivism and Minor Religious Sects*. Strasbourg, 1913.
Carpenter, J. Estlin, *Theism in Medieval India*. London, 1921.

MEDIEVAL RENAISSANCE

Banerjea, J. N., *Development of Indian Iconography*. Calcutta, India, 1946.
Paranjoti, V., *Śaiva Siddhānta*, 2d ed., rev. London, 1954.
Radhakrishnan, Sarvepalli, *The Brahma Sūtra*. London, 1960.

ISLAM AND THE INDIAN RESPONSE

MacAuliffe, M. A., *The Sikh Religion*, 6 vols. Oxford, 1909.

MODERN PERIOD

Farquhar, J. N., *Modern Religious Movements in India*. New York, 1919.
Fischer, L., *The Life of Mahatma Gandhi*. New York, 1951.
Hindu Dharma. Ahmedabad, 1950. A selection of Gandhi's writings.
Sharma, D. S., *The Renaissance of Hinduism*. Banaras, 1944.
Vivekananda, *The Gospel of Sri Ramakrishna*, 2d ed. Madras, India, 1947.

HINDU RITES AND SOCIAL INSTITUTIONS

Carstairs, G. M., *The Twice-Born*. London, 1961.
Dubois, Abbé, *Hindu Manners, Customs and Ceremonies*, 3d ed. Oxford, 1906.
Hopkins, E. W., *Ethics of India*. New Haven, 1924.
Hutton, J. H., *Caste in India*. Cambridge, 1946.
O'Malley, L. S. S., *Popular Hinduism*. Cambridge, 1935.

NINIAN SMART

HIPPIAS OF ELIS, Greek Sophist and polymath, was probably born before 460 B.C. The date of his death is not known, but Plato speaks of him as one of the leading sophists at the time of the death of Socrates in 399 B.C. On a number of occasions he acted as ambassador for his native city and also traveled widely, earning very large sums of money. He claimed to be a master of all the learning of his day, and his teaching and writings included elegies, tragedies, dithyrambs, historical works, literary discourses, epideictic speeches, discussions of astronomy, geometry, arithmetic, music, painting, sculpture, and ethics, and a technical system of mnemonics. None of his writings survives, but a reference in a papyrus book list of the third century suggests that at least one of his works survived until that date. Our knowledge of his teaching rests above all upon the picture of him given in Plato's dialogues, the *Hippias Major* (now generally accepted as written by Plato), the *Hippias Minor,* and the brief sketch in the *Protagoras.*

His polymathy invites comparison with Plato's more philosophic approach to reality; and Hippias has often been presented as standing for a superficial encyclopedic approach to knowledge, in contrast with the more profound penetration of the genuinely philosophic search for truth. This is the way Plato came to view all the sophists, but it is probably unfair to Hippias, who in some ways anticipated Aristotle's approach to the whole range of human knowledge. Mathematics and astronomy in the sophistic period were certainly not studied for their practical application in everyday life but, rather, in the pursuit of knowledge for its own sake. Hippias made a really important contribution to mathematical development through his discovery of the curve known as the quadratrix, used for the trisection of an angle and later in attempts to square the circle. He was also used by Eudemus as a source for the early history of geometry, which would suggest that he himself may have written a history of mathematics. He was fairly certainly the source of Aristotle's information about the doctrines of Thales, and he may also have been responsible for the main lines of the schematized picture of the history of the pre-Socratics found in Plato's *Sophist* (242D).

Whether he had any general theory of the nature of reality is not certain, but it is probable that he did. In the *Hippias Major,* Plato attributes to him a "continuous doctrine of being," which implies that some particular doctrine was regularly attributed to him. This doctrine dealt with "continuous physical objects that spring from being" (301B), and was opposed to Socrates' attempt to distinguish "the beautiful" from "beautiful objects." While the details of the doctrine are not given, it seems clear that Hippias objected to attempts to explain phenomena in terms of qualities or entities whose existence does not lie wholly within the phenomena that exemplify them. If this is so, then he held to the standard sophistic rejection of the position of Parmenides—for Hippias, phenomenal reality was the whole of reality. If Plato presents the matter correctly, Hippias regarded reality as composed of concrete physical objects such that all qualities applicable to any group will also apply individually to each member of the group, and all qualities found in each of the individual objects will also apply to the group as a whole.

In ethics Hippias propounded an ideal of individual self-sufficiency. Plato's evidence in the *Protagoras,* together with that of Xenophon in the *Memorabilia* (Book IV, Ch. 4, Sec. 5), shows that Hippias made free use of the opposition between nature and convention and that he accepted the overriding claim of Nature in cases of conflict. That he originated this antithesis has often been asserted, but no ancient source suggests this; and there is good evidence that the origins of the doctrine are earlier than Hippias. In the *Protagoras*, Hippias declares that his listeners are kinsmen, friends, and fellow citizens by Nature because the friendship of like to like comes by Nature, not by convention. While this clearly contains the seeds of a doctrine of cosmopolitanism, it should be remembered that Hippias' listeners in the dialogue are all Greeks and are all alike in their interest in sophistic discussion.

Bibliography

Fragments and testimonia are found in H. Diels and W. Kranz, *Fragmente der Vorsokratiker*, 10th ed. (Berlin, 1961), Vol. II. Mario Untersteiner, *The Sophists*, translated by Kathleen Freeman (Oxford, 1954), presents a picture of Hippias that rests on the speculative attribution to him of much anonymous material unlikely to be his. Thomas Heath, *A History of Greek Mathematics* (Oxford, 1921), Vol. I, discusses the mathematical contribution of Hippias.

G. B. KERFERD

HIPPOCRATES OF COS (c. 460–c. 380 B.C.), the patron saint of scientific medicine, taught, according to Plato, that it is impossible to treat any part of the body without taking account of the whole body (*Phaedrus* 270A); according to the history of medicine written by Aristotle's pupil Meno, he explained illness as being brought about by air secreted by undigested food. This is all that is known about Hippocrates from testimonies of the classical age. It is, however, a method of treatment and a theory of disease that are not basic to any of the so-called Hippocratic writings. In the Hellenistic age, Hippocrates was most often hailed as an empiricist, and various books of the *Corpus Hippocraticum* are quoted as his, whether they are books on prognosis, on surgery, or on the etiology and cure of diseases along the lines of both empirical and rational medicine. In the second century Galen, a Platonist by persuasion, saw in Hippocrates the philosophical doctor who, before Plato, had taught much of what Plato was to teach. His interpretation of the Hippocratic doctrine and the Hippocratic work became canonical by the end of antiquity, although Galen himself was quite aware that he was merely interpreting the evidence available and that the genuineness of any Hippocratic treatise had to be demonstrated. From then on, through the Middle Ages and the Renaissance, and until the beginning of the nineteenth century, Hippocrates' name stood as the symbol of a medical wisdom that understands the nature of the human body as dependent on the nature of the universe, and the Hippocratic treatises were studied as the incunabula as well as the perfection of medical insight.

In the course of the nineteenth century, Hippocrates was dethroned as the scientific authority. For historical scholarship only the earliest evidence was acceptable as a basis on which to judge the achievement of Hippocrates, and one tried to account for the change in the ancients' evaluation of his teaching, especially for the attribution of the so-called Hippocratic treatises to him. The most likely hypothesis is that the medical writings of the fifth and fourth centuries B.C. circulated without the names of their authors and that from early Alexandrian times on, literary critics and medical scholars had attempted to find among them works of Hippocrates, in whom they were interested. This interest stemmed from the fact that Plato and Aristotle spoke of Hippocrates and quoted him. He may also have been remembered as an unusually successful physician, for a doctor gains renown not only as a writer and theoretician but also, if not above all, as a practitioner. One of the great Hellenistic schools of medicine traced its origins to the Coan medical tradition. In the eyes of Galen and his contemporaries, it was in Hippocrates' favor that he lived in the classical era, in which the archaism of the second century discovered the beginnings of all things.

Whether or not this is the right explanation for the ascendancy of Hippocrates, it is certain that no more can be said about his achievement than what is told by Plato, and by Aristotle and his school. For the historian, his "writings," with the exception of a few books that are probably of a later date, represent medicine as it was practiced at the turn of the fifth to the fourth century B.C. and are, for that reason, of great interest. They show, first of all, that by that time Greek medicine had learned not only to describe the details of a disease, as had Oriental medicine, but also to grasp its whole course, to give a picture of disease entities. Etiologies varied from a one-humor theory to a four-humor theory; explanations of the causes of illness ranged from the air inhaled to the food and drink taken in. Treatment consisted predominantly in changes in regimen; the use of drugs was relatively restricted and of secondary importance. Outstanding surgery was performed on fractures, dislocations, and wounds of the head but was almost never undertaken in cases of an affliction of the internal organs. (Anatomy was animal anatomy, not human anatomy.) Prognosis was as highly developed as diagnosis and included, in addition to a prediction of the outcome of an illness, a "foretelling" of the present condition of the patient—without gathering information from him—and even of previous stages of his sickness. As early as the classical age, Greek medicine concerned itself with the healthy as well as with the sick, prescribing for the rich a very rigorous regimen that hardly left the individual free to do as he pleased at any given moment, and for the poor, at least a set of precautionary measures meant to avert the worst dangers of haphazard living.

Since the *Corpus Hippocraticum* is a collection of treatises by diverse authors, one can find in it support for a variety of principles. Bacon and Galileo quoted "Hippocrates" as the protagonist of experiment and observation; Voltaire admired his renunciation of an empty metaphysics. (The *facies Hippocratica* was famous as the embodiment of cool and detached observation; the first aphorism—life is short; art, long—was the proverbial slogan of skepticism.) Leibniz invoked Hippocrates' endorsement of the harmony and interconnection of all things; Berkeley compared Newton's physics to his teaching. The multiplication of disease entities was defended by reference to his authority, as was the insistence on including the various forms of an illness under one name. Treatment based on the dogma of *contraria contrariis* (cure opposites with opposites)—no less than that based on the dogma of *similia similibus* (cure like with like)—was called Hippocratic.

Two features can perhaps be called characteristic of all the medical treatises of the classical age. Whatever the explanation of diseases, whatever their cure, the individuality of the patient was never lost sight of. The art of the physician lay in his ability to strike a balance between knowledge that abstracts from particular conditions and that is, of necessity, general, and the specific requirements of the situation at hand. Moreover, medical treatment was not divorced from ethical considerations. In most of the Hippocratic writings, medical ethics is, to be sure, an ethics of performance. Since he is a craftsman, by ancient social standards, the physician wants to do his job well, that is, as a competent and responsible craftsman should. But some of the treatises infuse philosophical morality into medical craft. The *Hippocratic Oath*, probably of Pythagorean origin, was the document that for the Middle Ages and later centuries embodied the highest aspirations of the doctor, who is here "not to harm but to help." It has kept the name of Hippocrates alive even in a world in which the knowledge of the Greece of old has become obsolete and the past of medicine mere history.

Bibliography

The complete works of "Hippocrates" must still be read in E. Littré, ed., *Oeuvres complètes d'Hippocrate*, 10 vols. (Paris, 1839–1861).

In the four-volume Loeb edition of Hippocrates (Cambridge, Mass., 1948–1953), Vol. III, W. H. S. Jones and E. T. Withington, eds., is a selection of the most important treatises and is valuable for the introduction to the various essays.

The interpretation of Hippocrates given here is set forth in detail in Ludwig Edelstein, ΠΕΡΙ ΑΕΡΩΝ *und die Sammlung der Hippokratischen Schriften* (Berlin, 1931), and in A. Pauly and G. Wissowa, eds., *Realencyclopädie der classischen Altertumswissenschaft*, Supp. VI (Stuttgart, 1935), Cols. 1290 ff. For survival in the Middle Ages and later centuries, see Pauly and Wissowa, Cols. 1335 ff.

Concerning later literature, see Ludwig Edelstein's "The Genuine Works of Hippocrates," in *Bulletin of the History of Medicine*, Vol. 7 (1939), 236 ff. Also see his paper "The Hippocratic Oath," which is *Supplement to the Bulletin of the History of Medicine*, Vol. 1 (1943).

LUDWIG EDELSTEIN

HISTORICAL EXPLANATION. One of the tasks historians set themselves is to explain why the events in which they are interested have occurred. Why were the Athenians disastrously defeated in Sicily? Why did the nation-state emerge out of the feudalism of western Europe? Why did the American colonies rebel against the England of George III? Why did Soviet Russia sign a nonaggression pact with Nazi Germany? Philosophers and philosophically minded historians are concerned with the structure which such explanations have, or should have. Does a historical explanation differ from explanation in science, or is there but a single type of explanation? What logical criteria must a historical explanation meet if it is to be an adequate one?

The problem of the nature of historical explanation posed in this specific way is a relatively new one. To begin with, methodological problems of this sort—whether in history or science—were not investigated until the nineteenth century. But more specifically, until the post-Enlightenment period, few would have thought that there could be a special problem about historical explanation; that is, about the explanation of events involving human participants. During the eighteenth century many believed that the time was near when all things would be explained by means of a universal physics. The methods of Newton were seen as applicable to all of nature.

EXPLANATION IN HISTORY AND IN NATURAL SCIENCE

By the latter half of the nineteenth century, the philosophy of science and the philosophic analysis of the methods of history had become specialized pursuits. The question of the logical structure of a historical explanation was raised for the first time. Philosophers had to contend not only with the theories of Newton and his followers, but also with the philosophies of Kant and Hegel. Writers such as Helvétius, who had anticipated that a complete mechanics of human nature would soon be achieved, now seemed to belong to an era of overconfident simplification. With the Kantian distinction between noumenon and phenomenon and the Hegelian distinction between Spirit and Nature in the background, influential philosophers such as Wilhelm Dilthey and Heinrich Rickert felt impelled to make a sharp distinction between those sciences which take as their subject matter the physical, nonhuman world (*Naturwissenschaften*), and those which study man as a being with a mind (*Geisteswissenschaften*). There were two scientific methodologies, instead of one, to be worked out: the logical structure of historical explanation, which belonged to the human sciences, was taken to be essentially different from the explanation of physical phenomena.

The dualism of explanation. Three major reasons were usually cited in support of this dualism of explanation. (1) The nature of human beings is not like that of purely physical or even mindless biological entities. Man's nature is not fixed once and for all, but is essentially modified by the culture in which he lives. In the words of a later follower of Dilthey, Ortega y Gasset, man has no nature; he has only a history. But if this is so, there can be no universal laws about human beings. Hence, if there *are* explanations of human acts, they cannot be based on causal laws analogous to those of the natural sciences.

(2) The second reason prescinds from the first. When we seek an explanation of a purely physical event, we may well be satisfied if it is explained in terms of antecedent causal conditions. However, even if we suppose such an explanation to be possible, it is said to miss the point when a human act is under consideration. Men have purposes when they act; they have motives and intentions; they make plans, and thus their actions are in part determined by some goal they seek to achieve in the future. If a human act is to be explained satisfactorily, we must above all understand that act, by seeing the motives and purposes which entered into its performance, as well as the particular character of the man whose motives and purposes they are. In history it is explanation by the method of empathic understanding (*Verstehen*) that is sought.

(3) Finally, it was pointed out that historians are interested, not in a nature which repeats itself (whether in the revolution of the planets or the cycle of life), but in hap-

penings that occur only once. Historians are concerned not with revolution in general, but with particular revolutions and their particular concatenations of circumstances and personalities. Because historical events are unique they cannot be explained in terms of general laws.

Implications of dualism in explanation. The implications of this view are far-reaching. There must be two logics of science, two methods of inquiry, two standards of adequacy. The human sciences cannot be modeled on the pattern of the natural sciences; they cannot aspire to the predictive powers of the sciences of the physical universe. Indeed, historical explanation is radically different from explanation in natural science. It requires a reconstruction in the historian's mind of the character of those who acted in the past and of the circumstances under which they acted; the explanation is said to be successful when the historian gets the sense of reliving the past he seeks to explain.

THE COVERING LAW MODEL

Throughout the first three or four decades of this century, the view of historical explanation outlined above remained the most influential. There were dissenters (for example, Morris Cohen, Karl Popper, and Maurice Mandelbaum), but the dissent did not coalesce into a dominant position until the appearance, in 1942, of an article by Carl G. Hempel, "The Function of General Laws in History." The basic claim of this paper is that historians explain the events of human history precisely in the same way that natural scientists explain the events of the physical world. The article begins, therefore, with an outline of the logical structure of explanation in the natural sciences.

An event is explained if, and only if, the statement asserting its occurrences (*E*) can be logically deduced from premises consisting of (1) a set of well-confirmed statements expressing instantial or determining conditions, and (2) a set of well-confirmed universal hypotheses, that is, general laws. *E* is the explanandum, and the two sets of statements (of conditions and laws) are the explanans, whenever *E* is deducible from these two sets of premises.

It should be noted that the structure of an explanation is seen here to be identical with that of a prediction. If one has the information contained in the two sets of premises prior to the occurrence of the event mentioned in the explanandum, then the deduction of *E* is the deduction of a statement about a future event, and the event is thus predicted. (For a detailed discussion of the covering law model see EXPLANATION IN SCIENCE.)

Covering law model in historical explanation. The covering law model is the logical structure of an explanation in science; but is it also the model of historical explanation? In one sense, this question must be answered in the negative. Seldom, if ever, does one *actually* find in history books a set of statements which have the form of this model. Explanations found in works of history (past or contemporary) rarely state instantial conditions with the requisite completeness and accuracy. Even less frequently do historians offer explanations which mention the general law or laws in virtue of which the explanandum is deducible. But the gap between the covering law model and actual historical explanations is even wider than these points would indicate. When one considers the immense complexity of the events historians seek to explain, one quickly comes to recognize that with respect to the vast majority of such events, historians are extremely unlikely ever to come into possession of all the relevant instantial conditions that must be part of the explanans. Still less can it be expected that there will ever be a body of the requisite well-confirmed laws to "cover" such events as revolutions, losses of battles, legal decisions, or religious reforms.

And yet, the proponents of the covering law model affirm that the structure of historical explanation is the same as that of science. The explanations historians offer in their writings are, in various ways, approximations to that model. They are what Hempel calls explanation "sketches" which require "filling out" if they are ever to become full-fledged explanations. Incomplete and imprecise statements of initial conditions will have to be made progressively more complete and more precise. Universal hypotheses connecting these conditions with the event to be explained will have to be made explicit; they must then be refined in the light of evidence that can be cited in their support, until they achieve the status of bona fide laws and the explanandum is deducible from the premises.

Answers to the dualists. According to those who hold that the covering law model applies to history, there is, then, no basic methodological difference between the natural and the human sciences. They will agree with those who see such a difference that historical events are unique. But they will also point out that, strictly speaking, so is any event, at least in its spatial and temporal locus. In the first place, historical explanation, like explanation in any other domain, is never an explanation of an event simply and as such, but always of an event considered to be of a certain type. An event taken as unique can only be experienced; if it is in some way to be known, it must be known as belonging to a certain class. The statement of the explanandum specifies that the event is to be explained as an event of a certain kind, and the law connects an event considered as being of that kind with the initial conditions.

Second, there is no doubt that human motives and intentions are relevant to the explanation of human events. But if this is so, it would seem to be equally true that there must be evidence as to the character of the motives, intentions, beliefs, and attitudes of the participants in the event to be explained, and that there must be grounds for supposing that these psychological facts were indeed causally efficacious in bringing about the event in question. And these grounds are seen by the covering law theorist to be general statements which connect such psychological facts with actions of the sort to be explained. The sense of identification with a historical figure, however desirable, is not enough. A covering law is needed to assure that what is felt to be the case is actually so.

There is, finally, the dualist's view that general causal laws about human behavior are impossible of attainment. Adherents to the covering law theory do not deny that at different times and places men have thought, felt, and acted in very different ways. But it need not be concluded from this that it is impossible to establish laws governing human behavior. It follows, rather, that most of the psychological and sociological laws which are likely to be relevant to historical events will not be applicable to all human beings, but only to those with a certain set of specified characteristics. Such laws, then, will not take the simple form, "If *x* is a man, then, given conditions *c,* he will do *a.*" Instead, they will be of a much more restrictive sort: "If *x* is a man who is *l* and who is *m* and who is *n,* then, given *c,* he will do *a.*" Thus, while agreeing with some of the insights of the dualists, the proponents of the covering law model see in them no obstacle to the view that there is a single logic of explanation, whether historical or scientific.

ALTERNATIVES TO COVERING LAW MODEL

The covering law model is the starting point of much of the contemporary discussion of historical explanation. It has adherents among philosophers and among those relatively few historians who are interested in applying social science techniques to the study of history. Not all of those who support this model for history accept it in precisely the form outlined above. But suggestions for one or another modification of the covering law model can be discussed further on. The covering law model has provoked numerous more basic disagreements; indeed, the alternative analyses of historical explanation may be conveniently divided into three groups, the first being closest to, and the third furthest from, the covering law model.

Universal hypotheses not a requirement. There are those who agree with the proponents of the covering law model that the explanans of a historical explanation must contain not only a set of instantial conditions, but also general statements of some kind. According to these writers, however, a historical explanation may be complete and emphatically not a mere sketch that requires further "filling out," even when its generalization or generalizations fall short of being universal hypotheses in various degrees and ways.

When the requirement of a law is relaxed in this way, it no longer makes sense to speak of deducibility. For example, according to Patrick Gardiner in *The Nature of Historical Explanation,* historians employ generalizations that make imprecise correlations, to which exceptions may be granted and whose terms may be "open." Such statements (Gardiner prefers to call them "assessments" or "judgments") fashion some sort of link between the details of the instantial conditions and the event to be explained: they serve as "guiding threads." In fulfilling this function, they do all that is needed for a complete historical explanation. Statements of this kind are not made provisionally, because nothing better is available at the moment, but they are explicitly said to constitute the end of historical inquiry.

Sufficient condition model. A proposal by T. A. Goudge will serve to exemplify a second alternative to the covering law model. According to him, historical explanation cannot be expected to achieve more than the following pattern: The explanation indicates conditions, temporally prior to or simultaneous with the event to be explained, which are jointly sufficient but not independently necessary for the occurrence of the event. A historical explanation would be complete if the conditions specified were independently necessary for the occurrence of the event to be explained.

In this sufficient condition model of historical explanation, laws or law-like statements are explicitly said not to play a role. The event to be explained is fully explained by virtue of the fact that it "falls into place" as the terminal phase of a sequence which, in its entirety, constitutes the sufficient condition for the occurrence of the event. The logical relation between the explanans and the explanandum is said to be not implicative, but conjunctive. The deductive model is "the wrong model to have in mind." Instead, coherent narrative is taken to be the model of explanation.

Necessary condition model. For a narrative to be coherent does not, of course, require that the conditions said to bring about the events of the story be sufficient conditions. Accordingly, there are writers who depart still further from the covering law model by claiming that an event may be adequately explained by citing merely necessary conditions for its occurrence. W. B. Gallie, for example, sets forth the following requirements for what he calls a "characteristically genetic explanation" of an event: it must first mention a number of temporally prior necessary conditions of the event, and then indicate that the event is of such a kind that for its occurrence some one of a disjunction of describable conditions is necessary. Finally, the event is explained when the writer points out which of the disjunctive set of conditions was in fact necessary for the occurrence of the event to be explained. If some particular historical explanation (following this pattern) were to be held inadequate, Gallie would consider it irrelevant and of no help at all to mention general laws in an attempt to improve the explanation. Improvement of an inadequate explanation would require the specification of different or additional necessary conditions.

Essentially the same position is held by both Arthur C. Danto and William Dray. For both of them, an event is explained when the necessary conditions for its occurrence have been indicated. But both of them go further than Gallie in regarding coherent narrative as a model of explanation. No general statements are required. In Dray's words, an event is explained when we "can trace the course of events by which it came about."

CRITIQUE OF THE COVERING LAW MODEL

Almost all the writers who reject the covering law model of historical explanation and propose one or another alternative analysis include among their objections to the deductive model the fact that no explanations actually conforming to the model are to be found in the works produced by professional historians. Moreover, historians do consider themselves to be offering genuine explanations. At least on some occasions, members of the profession are satisfied that an explanation—not at all in conformity with the covering law model—is entirely successful and not in need of further modification. Finally, when historians are not content with a given proffered explanation, the direction of criticism and of subsequent improvement is never that which the perspective of the deductive model would dictate. Historians do not seem to support the covering law model, even as an ideal.

Philosophy, in the view of these opponents of the covering law model, has the job of explicating what historians actually think and do when they explain, and not of legislating what they ought to do. Since the vast majority of historians neither do, nor think they ought to, explain by means of the deductive model, that model cannot constitute the correct account of historical explanation. Given this as the basis for rejecting the covering law analysis, it is not hard to see the grounds upon which the various alternative proposals rest. They are typically supported by numerous examples which are chosen to show that the proposal being defended actually conforms, in the widest sense, to the practice of historians. This is what historians say and think and this, too, is what satisfies (as explanatory) the audience historians address; therefore, this is what consitutes a historical explanation.

Not all objections to the deductive model are based upon the claim that the practice of historians fails to conform to it. Various arguments have been proposed to show that the covering law model cannot even be held as an ideal and that, in principle, no explanation of a historical event can conform to it.

One such argument, advanced in large part by William Dray in *Laws and Explanation in History,* can be stated in the form of a trilemma. What must the law be like which will "cover" the event to be explained, so that given the instantial conditions, the explanandum is deducible from it together with instantial conditions? (1) The general statement may be well confirmed, but so safely stated that, even though the explanandum is subsumable under it, it has no explanatory force. Popper's "law of the sociology of military power" is a good example: "If of two armies which are about equally well armed and led, one has a tremendous superiority in men, the other army never wins." Not only will few be satisfied with an explanation utilizing so trivial a law, but, as Dray points out, such statements readily become so general that their truth rules out nothing whatsoever.

(2) One may descend from these great heights of generality and state a covering law in a less trivial fashion. To explain why Louis XIV became unpopular, to take an example discussed by both Gardiner and Dray, one might utilize the general statement, "Rulers who pursue policies detrimental to their subjects' interest become unpopular." But surely this is no law, in the simple sense that the statement is flatly false. There have been rulers who have pursued such policies who nevertheless remained popular. To save the statement, one must qualify it by a phrase such as "usually" or "often" or "for the most part." But as soon as this is done and it becomes more plausible to suppose that the resulting general statement is true, the explanandum is no longer deducible from it conjoined with appropriate initial conditions. Modified in this way, the covering law no longer covers.

(3) Faced with such alternatives, one may well attempt to render the general statement so specific that it is neither trivial nor in need of a qualification that makes it impossible to deduce the explanandum. One may thus be easily led to state a covering law that approximates the following form: "Whenever there is a condition exactly like this one, an event happens exactly like that one," where the "this" and the "that" stand for detailed and specific descriptions of the instantial conditions and the event to be explained, respectively. Now the explanandum is surely deducible and the general statement is certainly not trivial in the fashion of the law of military power. However, if "this" and "that" are replaced by descriptions of complete specificity (by utilizing definite descriptions), then it is hard to see in what way the statement is general or in what way it can be said to be a law. If, on the other hand, both the antecedent and the consequent fall at least somewhat short of being definite descriptions, the number of instances for which the "law" can be expected to hold would still be far too small to enable it to be established as a law.

DEFENSE OF THE COVERING LAW MODEL

The debate about the nature of historical explanation has not been brought to a halt with these criticisms of the covering law model. Indeed, the proponents of the model make replies to both types of criticism leveled against them—first, that the model is inappropriate for history, and second, that it is not a possible one for history.

(1) The fact that historians do not state general laws when they explain and that very few historians think they ought to is not sufficient evidence to show that the logic of a historical explanation does not require such general statements. To explain why an event has occurred is to state the cause or causes which brought it about. If, as many of those who oppose the covering law model maintain, an explanation is complete without including such a law, then there is no way of knowing that the alleged causes of the event actually are causes. Only when we have evidence that events like C are regularly followed by events like E are we entitled to make the claim that this C is the cause of that E. A general statement is implicit in a historical explanation not because of the thinking and doing of historians, but because of the logic of our knowledge about causes. What distinguishes "The bottle broke because the light was turned on," from "The bottle broke because it fell to the floor," is that the first alleged explanation cannot and the second can be subsumed under a proposition stating a regularity. The charge of inappropriateness is thus bypassed: the analysis of historical explanation rests not simply on the practice of historians but on attempts to meet broader philosophic requirements as well. The insistence upon the inclusion of a statement of a regularity in a historical explanation is testimony to the fact that the proponents of the covering law model hold a Humean position on causality.

(2) As a response to the second class of arguments—that the covering law model is not a possible one—there are signs that the proponents of the model are prepared to modify their position. To begin with, some leading proponents of the covering law model (particularly Ernest Nagel and Carl Hempel) are now ready to accept probabilistic and statistical laws in place of perfectly universal hypoth-

eses. Needless to say, they thereby also accept the fact that the explanandum is no longer deducible from the explanans; given the premises, one may infer only that the event probably occurs.

But there are also signs that in other respects the covering law model is due for a restatement. The arguments of the opponents of the model have shown that there is a problem about the nature of the covering law. To put it in an extreme fashion, there are no laws which directly connect typical historical events with their antecedent conditions. If one looks at gross historical events—the start of a war, the beginning of a counterrevolution, the reformation of a religious institution, the migration of a tribe of people—it would seem to be true that the laws covering such events must either be loose and trivial or so specific as to lose their character as laws. In a recent article on historical explanation and covering laws, Maurice Mandelbaum points out that such events need to be analyzed into component events about which genuine laws are or may become available.

> When I ask what caused a man to fall off a ladder, . . . I do not expect to be given an answer which states a regular conjunction between any other type of event and the type of event which constitutes a falling off a ladder. . . . In order to account for the man's fall I must know that unsupported bodies do fall. If the man's fall was connected with the fact that he fainted, I must also know that when fainting occurs one's muscles relax, since this will account for the fact that he lost his grip.   ("Historical Explanation")

Hempel's formulation of the covering law model provides for a plurality of initial conditions and laws. This plurality must be taken more seriously than the adherents of the model have heretofore taken it. Explanation does require the citing of laws, but it does not follow that there are laws for every type of event that occurs, no matter how the historian formulates the explanandum. Laws are applicable to many components of the event to be explained, and it is part of the historian's task to analyze the event into these explicable components. On this account, then, the explanation of a historical event is a conjunction of explanations (each of which follows the covering law model) of the component events into which the historical event is analyzed. Such an explanation escapes the charge of making use of laws that are either trivial or no laws at all, while at the same time it meets the requirements placed upon it by an adequate theory of causality and, more generally, by an acceptable theory of knowledge.

Bibliography

ANTHOLOGIES OF CONTEMPORARY DISCUSSIONS

Feigl, Herbert, and Sellars, Wilfrid, eds., *Readings in Philosophical Analysis* (RPA). New York, 1949.

Feigl, Herbert, and Brodbeck, May, eds., *Readings in the Philosophy of Science* (RPS). New York, 1953.

Gardiner, Patrick, ed., *Theories of History* (TH). Glencoe, Ill., 1959.

Hook, Sidney, ed., *Philosophy and History: A Symposium.* New York, 1963.

EXPLANATORY DUALISTS

Collingwood, R. G., *The Idea of History.* Oxford, 1946.

Dilthey, Wilhelm, *Gesammelte Schriften.* Stuttgart, 1957–1960. See especially Vol. VII.

Mandelbaum, Maurice, *The Problem of Historical Knowledge.* New York, 1938. Discussion and bibliography.

Rickert, Heinrich, *Die Probleme der Geschichtsphilosophie.* Heidelberg, 1924.

Rickert, Heinrich, *Die Grenzen der naturwissenschaftlichen Begriffsbildung.* Tübingen, 1929.

PROPONENTS OF THE COVERING LAW MODEL

Cohen, Morris R., *Reason and Nature.* New York, 1931; 2d rev. ed., Glencoe, Ill., 1953. See portion reprinted in RPS.

Donagan, Alan, "Explanation in History." *Mind,* Vol. 66 (1957); reprinted in TH.

Frankel, Charles, "Explanation and Interpretation in History." *Philosophy of Science,* Vol. 24 (1957); reprinted in TH.

Hempel, Carl G., "Deductive-nomological vs. Statistical Explanation," in Herbert Feigl and Grover Maxwell, eds., *Minnesota Studies in the Philosophy of Science,* Vol. III, *Scientific Explanation, Space, and Time.* Minneapolis, 1962.

Hempel, Carl G., "The Function of General Laws in History." *The Journal of Philosophy,* Vol. 39 (1942); reprinted in RPA and TH.

Hempel, Carl G., and Oppenheim, Paul, "The Logic of Explanation." *Philosophy of Science,* Vol. 15 (1948); reprinted in RPS.

Mandelbaum, Maurice, "Historical Explanation: The Problem of 'Covering Laws.'" *History and Theory,* Vol. I (1961).

Nagel, Ernest, "Some Issues in the Logic of Historical Analysis." *The Scientific Monthly,* Vol. 74 (1952); reprinted in RPS and TH.

Nagel, Ernest, "Determinism in History." *Philosophy and Phenomenological Research,* Vol. 20 (1960).

Nagel, Ernest, *The Structure of Science.* New York, 1961.

Pitt, Jack, "Generalizations in Historical Explanation." *The Journal of Philosophy,* Vol. 56 (1959).

Popper, Karl R., *The Logic of Scientific Discovery.* New York, 1959; original German ed., 1935.

Popper, Karl R., *The Open Society and Its Enemies,* rev. ed. Princeton, N.J., 1950.

Weingartner, Rudolph H., "Explanations and Their Justifications." *Philosophy of Science,* Vol. 28 (1961).

Weingartner, Rudolph H., "The Quarrel About Historical Explanation." *The Journal of Philosophy,* Vol. 58 (1961).

White, Morton, "Historical Explanation." *Mind,* Vol. 52 (1943).

CRITIQUES AND ALTERNATIVES TO THE COVERING LAW MODEL

Berlin, Isaiah, *Historical Inevitability.* Oxford, 1954.

Danto, Arthur C., "Laws and Explanations in History." *Philosophy of Science,* Vol. 23 (1956).

Danto, Arthur C., "On History and Theoretical Science." *Studium Generale,* Vol. 11 (1958).

Dray, William, "'Explaining What' in History," in TH.

Dray, William, *Laws and Explanations in History.* Oxford, 1957.

Gallie, W. B., "Explanations in History and the Genetic Sciences." *Mind,* Vol. 64 (1955); reprinted in TH.

Gardiner, Patrick, *The Nature of Historical Explanation.* Oxford, 1952.

Goudge, T. A., "Causal Explanation in Natural History." *The British Journal for the Philosophy of Science,* Vol. 9 (1958).

Scriven, Michael, "Explanation and Prediction in Evolutionary Theory." *Science,* Vol. 130 (1959).

Scriven, Michael, "Truisms as the Grounds for Historical Explanations," in TH.

Walsh, W. H., *An Introduction to Philosophy of History.* London, 1951; rev. ed., London, 1958.

Symposium on Explanations in History. *PAS,* Supp. Vol. 30 (1956).

BIBLIOGRAPHIES

Gardiner, Patrick, *Theories of History*. Glencoe, Ill., 1959.
Mandelbaum, Maurice, *The Problem of Historical Knowledge*. New York, 1938. Includes older literature.
Rule, John C., "Bibliography of Works in the Philosophy of History 1945–1957." *History and Theory*, Supplement I (1961).
Theory and Practice in Historical Study: A Report of the Committee on Historiography. Social Science Research Council Bulletin 54. New York, 1946.

RUDOLPH H. WEINGARTNER

HISTORICAL MATERIALISM. The materialist conception of history was put forward by Karl Marx and Friedrich Engels and subsequently adopted by their followers and incorporated in the doctrine of Marxism–Leninism. According to historical materialism, the structure of society and its historical development are determined by "the material conditions of life" or "the mode of production of the material means of existence." These last two phrases are quoted from Marx's Preface to his *Critique of Political Economy* (1859), in which he gave a brief presentation of the view. Marx and Engels had formulated it, however, in their *The German Ideology*, written in 1845–1846 but not published until 1932. Marx himself gave a brief account in his *Poverty of Philosophy* (1847) and more concisely perhaps in a letter to Paul Annenkov, written in December 1846, while Marx was working on the *Poverty of Philosophy*. A vigorous sketch is given in the *Communist Manifesto* of 1848. Marx's chief work, *Capital* (the first volume of which was published by Marx in 1867 and the other two by Engels after Marx's death) is an application of the historical-materialist view to the capitalist form of society.

ORIGIN OF THE THEORY

Marx wrote in the Preface to the first edition of *Capital* that he conceived "the development of the economic structure of society to be a natural process." This is the main force of the adjective "materialist" in the phrase "materialist conception of history." Marx used the word "materialist" to make a contrast with what is obviously or implicitly supernatural, metaphysical, or speculative. He believed that a general science of human society could be worked out only by describing and explaining society in empirical terms. He admired those English and French writers who, by writing "histories of civil society, of commerce and industry," gave the writing of history "a materialist basis" (*The German Ideology*, p. 16). He and Engels regarded industry and commerce as "material" by contrast with religion and morals, and even by contrast with politics and law. Thus the materialist conception of history is intended to be a naturalistic, empirical, scientific account and explanation of historical events, which takes industrial and economic factors as basic. It would seem that nothing could be more consonant with scientific common sense, nothing less metaphysical or speculative.

In some of Marx's writings of an earlier date than *The German Ideology*, however, it becomes evident that the later, would-be scientific view arose out of a metaphysical

prototype, a sort of "Ur-Marxismus," which continued to exert an influence on all of Marx's systematic work. Prior to his collaboration with Engels, which began in 1844, Marx had justified his radical views by philosophical and moral, rather than economic, considerations. In 1844, however, Engels encouraged Marx to make an intensive study of economics, which resulted in an uncompleted and unpublished critique of political economy combined with a critique of the Hegelian philosophy. These so-called *Economic and Philosophical Manuscripts of 1844,* or "Paris manuscripts," are the first draft of the comprehensive treatise that Marx was engaged in writing all his life, and of which *The German Ideology*, the only recently published *Grundrisse der Kritik der politischen Ökonomie* ("Outline of a Critique of Political Economy," 1857–1858), the *Critique of Political Economy* itself (1859), and *Capital* are successive, but incomplete stages.

While writing the *Economic and Philosophical Manuscripts,* then, Marx was bringing his newly acquired economic knowledge to bear upon views he had reached in criticizing certain of Hegel's writings. Marx had noticed how Hegel described the development of the human mind as a process of externalizing its ideas in order to transform the material world and to "humanize" it. According to Hegel, the labor of men's hands was not, in general, an obstacle to human development but, rather, the very process by which it took place. Hegel recognized, of course, that when labor was greatly subdivided, some jobs became trivial and even degrading. But this, he thought, made possible, through the differentiation of society into orders or classes, the production of works of mind that would have been beyond the power of less differentiated societies. The word that Hegel had used for the process of externalizing ideas into the natural world was "alienation" (*Entäusserung*). Now Marx thought that in the capitalist social order the labor of individual men did not serve to develop the human mind and to humanize the natural world. Labor had become the production of commodities for sale and was itself a commodity bought and sold in the market, so that it served not to unfold the capacities of the laborer but to subject him to impersonal market forces over which he had no control. A worker's labor, and hence he himself, were alienated in the sense of being sold to someone else. His work resulted in the creation of a social system whose operations were hidden from him. The wage system perverted his labor so that the natural world was not transformed by that labor into a manifestation of human power but was rendered strange and even hostile to the workers.

"Estrangement" (*Entfremdung*) was another word used by Hegel that Marx took over in this context. A truly human existence would be possible only when money and private property, and hence wages too, had been abolished through the establishment of a communist social order. A communist society, Marx wrote, is "the solution to the riddle of history."

It is important to notice that in these early writings Marx was criticizing capitalism in metaphysical and moral terms. But for the perverting influence of capitalism, human labor would be what it ought to be, the self-development of the individual worker. It should be noted, too, that Marx, like Hegel, thought that the human mind could develop its powers only by working on, and transforming, the natural world. This conception is a metaphysical predecessor of the view that the "mode of production of the material means of existence" is what determines the development of society. Again, the view that capitalism distorts the efforts of the worker and is hence unnatural and impermanent is the metaphysical predecessor of the view that capitalism contains the seeds of its own destruction. Finally, the idea that communism would solve the riddle of history by releasing men from their own unwilled, unwanted productions is the metaphysical predecessor of the planned but noncoercive communism that Marx afterward believed must result from the dissolution of capitalism.

OUTLINE OF THE THEORY

Historical materialism consists, in the first place, of a sociological analysis thought to be applicable to all but the most primitive human societies. On the basis of this analysis an account is given of the rise and fall of various social systems. Marx's main work, of course, was his analysis of capitalism—indeed, the very use of the word "capitalism" for a form of society suggests that its characteristics depend upon its economy. Finally, on the basis of the sociological analysis, the prediction is made that capitalism will collapse and ultimately be succeeded by a communist society, in which there will be no wages, no money, no class distinctions, and no state.

Marx, who was greatly interested in the social structure of primitive societies, would doubtless have agreed with Engels' description, in his *Origin of the Family, Private Property, and the State* (1884), of the most primitive societies as being without private property or political institutions. Within the more developed societies, with which he was principally concerned, Marx distinguished several elements: (1) "the productive forces," which consist of the tools, skills, and techniques by which men obtain the wherewithal for life; (2) "the relations of production," which are the ways in which the producers are related to one another in production and which form "the economic structure of society"; (3) the political and legal institutions of the society; and (4) the ideas, habits of thought, ideals, and systems of justification, in terms of which the members of the society think of themselves and of their relations to one another. Marx thought that these ideas were distorted pictures of, and relatively ineffective agents in, the social reality, and he therefore referred to them as "ideologies." Marx gave various lists of ideologies that, when combined, yield the following: religion, theology, speculative philosophy or metaphysics, philosophy, morality, ethics, art, and "political ideology," such as contrasting views on democracy, aristocracy, and the struggle for the franchise.

Analysis of social structure. Marx called the productive forces and the relations of production together "the material conditions of life." In the Preface to the *Critique of Political Economy* he wrote that they are "the real basis on which a juridical and political superstructure arises and to which definite forms of social consciousness correspond."

The primary social activity is production, which always involves relations with other men, both in the work itself and in the distribution of the product. It is upon these relationships that the political and legal superstructure and the ideological superstructure are formed. To understand the religion, morality, art, or philosophy of a society, and to understand its politics and law, it is necessary to ascertain the nature of its productive forces and economic structure. Whereas in the *Economic and Philosophical Manuscripts* Marx had deplored the way in which men's labor enslaves them to the production of commodities, in the *Critique of Political Economy* he explained or sought to explain, how the productive forces determine certain social structures into which men are forced to fit their activities. Thus Marx laid great stress upon the fact that the structure of society is something that individuals find waiting for them and are powerless to alter.

Division of labor. According to Marx, a vitally important connection between the productive forces and the productive relationships is the nature of the division of labor that has been achieved and the degree to which it has been developed. In *The German Ideology*, Marx and Engels wrote that "division of labor and private property are, moreover, identical expressions." This probably means that when products are made by specialists who do not themselves use them, then they must be exchanged by, or sold to, those who do and so must be owned by the original maker. An associated idea is that the division of labor fosters the production of goods for sale, thus encouraging the production of commodities and enhancing the power of money. Marx and Engels did not think, however, that property was all of one type, and in *The German Ideology* they distinguished four main types that play an important role in their theory of history and society: tribal property, which is characteristic of a low level of the division of labor; state property, such as the roads, public buildings, and stores of grain under the ancient forms of despotism; feudal property, consisting of lands and services controlled by military landowners whose needs are supplied by serfs; and capital, which rests on the separation between production and commerce and results in the employment of men who work for wages and produce goods that are sold in wider and wider markets to make profits for the capitalist.

Property and power. The next step in the Marxian analysis is the claim that the main power or influence in a society belongs to those who own and control the main type of property in it. In tribal society the property is jointly owned; hence power is diffused throughout the society and there is no dominant class. The other types of property involve a distinction between those who control property and those who do not. Those who control a predominant type of property are the predominant power in society and are able to make arrangements benefiting themselves at the expense of the rest of the population. In feudal society, for example, the feudal lords are the ruling class. They are able to get what they want from the serfs who work for them, and even from rich merchants, whose type of wealth is subordinated to the landed interests. The interests of serf, merchant, and lord are not the same; indeed, they necessarily conflict at certain points. But while the productive forces and type of property are predominantly feudal, the feudal lords are able to settle these conflicts in their own favor. While the feudal system operates, any frictions and tensions are dealt with within its terms. The political movements in a feudal society express, or "reflect," these conflicts of interest between classes.

Economics, politics, and culture. If the political activities of men are regarded as merely phenomenal in comparison to their productive and economic activities, then their moral beliefs, religious and artistic achievements, and philosophical theories must be regarded as even less real, as epiphenomenal. The writers of books on political philosophy, for example, are taking part, but in a rarefied or ghostly form, in the phenomenal political activities and the real industrial ones. The predominant mode of the material conditions of life will have the cultural forms appropriate to it, in which the religion, art, and philosophy are what they are because of the nature of the technology and economy. The controversies between "schools" of philosophy, the movements for the reform and renovation of religious belief, the revolutions of morality, and even changes in artistic style, are merely the shadows cast by the "real" business of human living, which is production and exchange.

Historical epochs. Thus far an outline has been given of what, in Auguste Comte's language, might be called "the social statics" of historical materialism. It is now necessary to describe "the social dynamics" of the view: its account of historical change and development. In outline, this is the assertion that, just as "the material conditions of life" are fundamental in the structure of a society, important changes in the material conditions of life sooner or later bring with them important changes in the legal and political superstructure and in the ideological superstructure. It is also held that important changes in the superstructures can be brought about only by changes in the basis, that politics, law, and ideology are incapable in themselves of any fundamental influence on social development. All important social changes, it is held, must originate in productive activities and the organizations in which they take place. This is the central element of the theory of historical materialism.

This theory is also a theory of historical epochs. The original state of primitive communism was succeeded, according to the Marxist view, by the ancient forms of slave-owning society; these were succeeded by feudalism, and feudalism by capitalism. According to *The Origin of the Family*, the transition from primitive communism to the next phase was due to the introduction of private property. It is clear, of course, that the introduction of private property would bring with it very important social changes, but how is private property itself introduced? We have already seen that one idea is that it is brought about by the division of labor. In *The Origin of the Family* Engels also suggested that it was furthered by changes in the structure of the family and by the discovery of iron and bronze. The former would hardly be a technological invention, although the latter was. Engels' doubts on the matter may be seen from the fact that when he discussed the question of how the common ownership of herds was succeeded by private ownership he vaguely said that "the

herds drifted into the hands of private individuals." However private property is held to have arisen, the division of labor brought with it the transformation of goods into commodities and their sale for money.

The next epoch after the period of primitive communism was that of ancient slave society. Marx and Engels held that it was the labor of slaves that made possible the art and science of ancient Greece and the cities, commerce, and bureaucracy of ancient Rome. The slave system broke down largely because of its wastefulness and was replaced by the feudal system, in which features borrowed from the social system of the barbarian invaders were utilized. The basis of the feudal system was the ownership of land by feudal lords, whose dependents had to render them services of various kinds.

The feudal system was fundamentally an agricultural society, but in the towns some men managed to become wealthy by means of trade and by organizing the production of goods in large workshops where they employed considerable numbers of men for wages. These bourgeois, as they were called, were the forerunners of the capitalist system. They attracted men from the countryside to work for them in producing goods sold in widely expanding markets. In this and other ways they acted in opposition to the predominant feudal arrangements that confined serfs to the areas of their birth. Finding themselves hampered by the feudal laws, the bourgeois endeavored to change them and thus entered upon a political struggle with the aristocracy. They justified their actions by appealing to a new ideology according to which aristocratic distinctions based on family connections, and control over the movements of men and over trade, were in opposition to the "natural" order of individual freedom and equality. As the new methods of production and the new modes of life that went with them were extended, a new order of society was gradually formed within the old. New types of production and trade had been adopted that could come to fruition only if the laws and customs that hampered them were abolished. When, therefore, the bourgeoisie were strong enough, they took political action to achieve this and gained political power by a series of revolutions, of which the French Revolution of 1789 was the culmination. From being a progressive class they became the ruling class, and their landowning opponents declined from being the ruling class into being a reactionary class, which, however, could not return society to its earlier state, because the new productive forces were superior to the old ones.

This interpretation of the change from feudalism to capitalism illustrates the Marxist analysis of political revolutions. Marx and Engels regarded such revolutions as the means by which a progressive class, that is, the class that controls some newly emerging productive force, brings about those changes in the productive relationships that enable the new productive forces to become effective. Feudal institutions and, in particular, feudal laws of property would have stifled the development of the capitalist modes of production. By their seizure of political power, the bourgeoisie made laws that enabled capitalism to become a going and growing concern.

Social prediction. Historical materialism makes two main predictions. The first is that the capitalist system will break down as a result of its internal contradictions. The second is that, after a period of proletarian dictatorship, it will be succeeded by a communist society.

Breakdown of capitalism. In *Capital*, Marx was largely concerned with an analysis of the capitalist order, but he also briefly considered the future of capitalism. He held that the capitalist economy was so far out of human control that economic crises were inevitable features of it. He held, too, that in competing with one another to sell their goods at a profit the capitalists would find it necessary to push down the wages of their employees to the lowest level consistent with their being able to produce at all. Furthermore, the advantages of large-scale production would be such that the larger capitalists would drive their weaker rivals out of business and into the ranks of the proletariat. As a few capitalists became richer, the mass of workers would become poorer. At the same time the growth of scientific knowledge would enable the larger capitalist concerns to improve their technology, so that nature would be brought under human control as never before. Thus, the subdivision of labor is increased, and great numbers of men, organized in manifold ways, cooperate, often in ways unknown to one another, in the manufacture of a single article. But although production is thus highly socialized, ownership of the means of production and of the commodities produced is still an individual matter. Engels expressed this by saying that there is a contradiction between capitalist appropriation and social production that must result in the elimination of the former. The conditions of life imposed on workers in capitalist production teach them how to cooperate against their employers. The capitalist mode of ownership stands in the way of the fullest development of planned production. "The centralization of the means of production and the socialization of labor reach a point where they prove incompatible with their capitalist husk. This bursts asunder. The knell of capitalist property sounds. The expropriators are expropriated" (*Capital*, Vol. I, Ch. 24).

Arrival of communism. Just as the bourgeoisie found it necessary to achieve control of the state in order to bring the feudal system to an end, so the proletariat will find it necessary to wrest the state from capitalist control in order to bring capitalism to an end. Thus while the proletariat, or their spokesmen, are criticizing the bourgeoisie, they constitute the rising, progressive class, and when they have overcome the bourgeoisie, they will become the ruling class. But once the bourgeoisie are ousted, there will be no other class for the proletariat to oppose. The proletariat will be the only class, or rather, the class that will bring class divisions to an end. In the absence of class conflicts, politics and the state will become redundant, and a social order will arise in which production will be carried out in accordance with plans devised without coercion for the good of all. According to *The German Ideology*, the outcome will be "the control and conscious mastery of those powers which . . . have till now overawed and governed men as powers completely alien to them." Twenty years later Marx wrote of "a process carried on by a free association of producers, under their conscious and purposive control," adding: "For this, however, an indispensable requisite is that there should exist a specific material groundwork (or a series of material conditions of existence) which can only come into being as the spontaneous outcome of a long and painful process of evolution" (*Capital*, Vol. I, Ch. 1).

PROBLEMS OF INTERPRETATION

In the course of the many discussions of historical materialism since Marx's day, among Marxists as well as between Marxists and their critics, various problems of interpretation have come to light. Questions arise about the nature and status of the theory itself. There is the question whether the theory is to be interpreted as asserting the primacy of technology both in the structure of society and in the promotion of social change or whether the prime element is wider in scope and is intended to embrace economic as well as technological relationships. A third problem concerns the connection or lack of connection between historical materialism as a value-free sociological theory and as an element in the socialist outlook and an ethical justification of socialist expectations.

Nature and status of the theory. Is historical materialism the statement of an established sociological or historical law? Is it an extremely wide-ranging and complex hypothesis liable to refutation as research advances? Or is it, as some have suggested, not so much a hypothesis as a method, or recipe, or set of hints for framing one? The Marxist–Leninist tradition of the Russian and Chinese Communist parties undoubtedly adopts the view that it is an established law, as reference to Marxist–Leninist textbooks shows. It is sometimes said that Marx himself held the methodological view about his own theory. This is supported by a phrase in the preamble to his famous account of historical materialism in the Preface to the *Critique of Political Economy*: "The general conclusion I arrived at—and once reached it served as the guiding thread in my studies. . . ." But in this passage Marx is describing how he came to adopt the view, so that the expression "guiding thread" relates to the use he made of the idea in its early stages rather than to the theory once it was established. It seems fair to say that historical materialism was a view that Marx was constantly trying to support but never to refute. Furthermore, as will be shown, the theory contains features suggesting that Marx held it to be a necessary truth. Lenin, in an early pamphlet entitled *What the "Friends of the People" Are* (1894), said that historical materialism was "no longer an hypothesis, but a scientifically proven proposition," but he admitted at least the possibility of its being upset. In *Materialism and Empirio-Criticism* (1909), however, he considered that historical materialism was a consequence of dialectical materialism and thus to be proved in quite a different way.

The prime social determinant. Was the prime social determinant, in Marx's view, the productive forces, or was it the whole composed by the productive forces and the productive relationships? Was it, that is, technology alone, or technology plus economy? The Marxist–Leninist tradition favors the first interpretation, and there are many passages in Marx's writings to support it. For example, Marx wrote in *The Poverty of Philosophy*: "In acquiring new productive forces men change their mode of production, and in changing their mode of production, their manner of gaining a living, they change all their social relations. The windmill gives you society with the feudal lord; the steam mill, society with the industrial capitalist." A similar point of view is indicated in the *Communist Manifesto*, in which Marx wrote: "The bourgeoisie cannot exist without constantly revolutionizing the instruments of production, and thereby the relations of production, and with them the whole relations of society." In a footnote to Chapter 13 of Volume I of *Capital* he said that "the only materialist method" is to show how technology "uncovers man's active dealings with nature, the direct productive process of his life, and, at the same time, of his social relationships (*seiner gesellschaftlichen Lebensverhältnisse*) and the mental conceptions that arise from them." In the same passage he talked about those who uncritically abstract from "this material basis," and he advocated tracing the development of "the celestial forms" of these real relationships (*wirklichen Lebensverhältnisse*) from the real relationships themselves. It is clear that Marx was here arguing that religious ideology should be explained in terms of real social relationships and that these, in their turn, should be explained by reference to technology. But the language he used does not suggest that he was making sharp distinctions. Indeed, what he criticized is the attempt to consider other forms of life in abstraction from technology, so that he could be regarded as upholding what Benedetto Croce in 1896 called the "realistic view of history."

Certainly Marx said a number of things that contradict a merely technological theory of history. Perhaps the most compelling evidence for the view that Marx regarded the basic social determinant as comprising more than technology is his account in *Capital* of the rise of modern capitalism. According to Marx, modern capitalism began with the setting up of large workshops in which men worked for wages in producing goods that the capitalist employer sold for profit. These workshops or factories were new forms of organization, not new methods of production. If they are to be regarded as productive forces, then organization is a productive force. How far is this to be taken? These early capitalists were trying to supply a wider market than had hitherto been possible, and thus considerations of demand and of economic efficiency enter into the notion of a productive force. This notion, indeed, can be extended to include commerce, piracy, and war, and Marx and Engels did so in the early pages of *The German Ideology*. But if commerce is a productive force, then the distinction between productive forces and productive relations is blurred, if not abolished altogether. And if war is a productive force, then it would seem that politics is also a productive force, and in this way the distinction between basis and superstructure disappears.

That Marx and Engels were not clear about all this may be seen in two letters from Marx to Engels on the subject of armies and armaments. In a letter to Engels dated September 25, 1857, Marx wrote: "The history of the army brings out more clearly than anything else the correctness of our view about the connection of the productive forces and social relations. The army is particularly important for economic development, *e.g.* wage payments first fully developed in the army among the ancients. Thus the *pecu-*

lium castrense was among the Romans the first legal form in which the chattels of those who were not fathers of families were recognized. . . ." In a letter dated July 7, 1866, Marx referred to the new types of weapons that the manufacturers were trying to sell to Louis Napoleon and commented: "Where does our theory about the determination of the organization of labor by the means of production get more brilliant support than from the human slaughter industry?" In the first of these letters the idea is that the waging and winning of war depend upon the refinements of armament manufacture, which, in their turn, depend upon the level of technology achieved in the society. Here the armaments industry seems to be regarded as a means of production, and the waging of war as the organization of labor. It should be noted, too, that in the first letter the distinction is between productive forces and social relations, where the social relations referred to are working for wages and owning chattels. In the second letter, however, the distinction is between the means of production and the organization of labor. It is possible that by "productive forces" and "means of production" Marx meant much the same thing, but "social relations" is clearly a much wider notion than "organization of labor." In the light of such examples, it can hardly be denied that Marx had no precise view of the theory that he was putting forward.

The place of values in the theory. The third problem of interpretation concerns the connection between historical materialism as an alleged scientific theory and the advocacy of an eventual classless society apparently involved in it. On the one hand, there is the claim that historical materialism is scientifically established and explains how things are and predicts what they will be. On the other hand, there is the promise that out of the contradictions of capitalism a superior form of society will arise in which there will be no more coercion or exploitation. By a happy conjunction a moral millennium is held to be predictable on scientific grounds. As was said at the beginning of this article, the doctrine of historical materialism arose out of an earlier metaphysicomoral view in which scientific objectivity played no part. Some critics therefore take the view that Marx was at the same time a moralist and a sociologist and that he never succeeded in reconciling these roles. Others go still further and suggest that the scientific works are nothing but a vehicle for his moral aims. On the other hand, defenders of Marx argue that he rightly refused to make the distinction between fact and value that is implicit in the claim that social science should be "value-free." They argue that Marx considered that theory and practice are inextricably mingled, so that it is impossible to understand the working of social processes without at the same time obtaining control over them. Marx very probably believed that capitalist society develops in ways that are not intended by anyone and that it would be succeeded by a form of society in which men's aims and intentions would find scope for fulfillment. Thus, in his view, the processes of capitalist society can be observed and explained as if they were the workings of some alien, nonhuman entity in which individuals are caught up as in some monstrous mechanism. Nevertheless, he also held that the machine would break down and be destroyed and that the activities of men, thus released, would be explicable not in impersonal terms but in terms of their collective aims.

THE VALIDITY OF HISTORICAL MATERIALISM

It has already been pointed out that historical materialism has been supported on grounds of very different sorts. It has been regarded as a method of investigating the facts of history, as an established historical hypothesis of great generality, and as a deduction from materialism, or, more specifically, from dialectical materialism. It has also been said that Marx regarded his view as more than a method and that if he regarded it as a hypothesis, he hardly considered the possibility of its being upset. We shall consider the various reasons put forward in its support, so that we can get a clearer understanding of the theory.

Deduction from dialectical materialism. The view that historical materialism is a deduction from dialectical materialism was apparently not put forward by Marx himself. Dialectical materialism may be implicit in Marx's writings but it is not explicit there, and when Marx wrote of materialism, he frequently meant nothing but a scientific, this-worldly view of things. In the Marxist–Leninist tradition, however, the argument has been used that if dialectical materialism is true, then historical materialism is true also. Thus in his *History of the Communist Party of the Soviet Union* (1938) Stalin wrote: "Further, if nature, being, the material world, is primary, and mind, thought, is secondary, derivative: if the material world represents objective reality, existing independently of the mind of men, while the mind is a reflection of this objective reality, it follows that the material life of society, its being, is also primary, and its spiritual life is secondary, derivative, and that the material life of society is an objective reality existing independently of the will of man, while the spiritual life of society is a reflection of this objective reality, a reflection of being." A somewhat similar argument is to be found in section 2 of Chapter 6 of Lenin's *Materialism and Empirio-Criticism* (English translation, Moscow, 1939, p. 115). Both Lenin and Stalin supported this view by reference to Marx's statement in the *Critique of Political Economy* that "it is not the consciousness of men that determines their being but, on the contrary, their social being that determines their consciousness." But Marx, in this passage, was not referring to materialism as a philosophy of nature, but to the ideologies that are formed in specific social circumstances. Furthermore, it does not follow from the fact (if fact it be) that there is nothing but matter and its forms of being, that the productive and economic activities of man provide the key to his politics, law, religion, philosophy, art, and morals. The adjective "material" does not have the same meaning in Marx's usage as it has when used in the phrase "material world" or "material object." The general acceptance of materialism does not entail any particular view about which features of human life can be used to provide an explanation for the rest.

It might be argued, of course, that if materialism is true, all social facts are reducible to physical facts or that all social laws are reducible to laws of physics. Marx and Engels, however, did not believe this. In an interesting letter, one of the last to pass between them, Engels maintained that "labor" is a social term that cannot be reduced to "work" in its physical or mechanical sense.

Historical materialism as obviously true. It is an exaggeration to say, as some have, that Marx gave no reasons at all for the doctrine of historical materialism. It is clear, however, that both he and Engels regarded it as obviously true. Thus, in the *Communist Manifesto* occurs the following question: "Does it require deep intuition to comprehend that man's ideas, views and conceptions, in one word, man's consciousness, changes with every change in the conditions of his material existence, in his social relations and in his social life?" Engels, in his speech at the graveside of Marx, referred to Marx's "discovery" as the discovery of "a simple fact." This "simple fact" is clearly neither a deduction from dialectical materialism nor a complex hypothesis based on a mass of historical information. It would seem to be the fact that men could not engage in politics, religion, philosophy, and art unless they were alive, with the wherewithal to do so. No one could reasonably deny this, but is every reasonable man therefore an implicit upholder of historical materialism? For this to be so, it would be necessary to show that the theory that the material conditions of life must provide the explanation for all other human activities is deducible from the fact that men must get the wherewithal to live in order to be in a position to engage in political, religious, philosophical, and artistic pursuits. But from the fact that obtaining the wherewithal to live is a *sine qua non* of politics, religion, and philosophy, it does not follow that these latter activities can be explained only in terms of the former. It seems that a mistake has been made not unlike the failure to distinguish between necessary and sufficient conditions. From the fact that men could not engage in these activities unless they kept themselves alive, it does not follow that how they keep themselves alive explains or "determines" these activities. Engels' statement could be denied only by someone who held that politics, religion, and philosophy were the pursuits of disembodied spirits. His simple fact is too simple to be of any theoretical value.

Argument from the essence of man. Marx himself had another argument suggesting that there is something obvious in the view that the productive forces are the determining factors in human society and human history. He wrote in *Capital*, Volume I, that toolmaking is what distinguishes man from other animals. He and Engels had argued in a similar way in *The German Ideology* that men "begin to distinguish themselves from animals as soon as they begin to *produce* their means of subsistence . . . ." Of course, beavers and bees do this too, but their hives and dams (Marx and Engels would probably have argued) are never improved upon and never serve as the starting points for other devices. Whatever the difference, Marx and Engels held that what is peculiar to human beings is that they make (and presumably improve) their means of life and that, therefore, this fact must be the key fact in sustaining human society and in explaining the course of human history as distinct from natural history.

This is to adopt an Aristotelian method of explanation in terms of essences. What men do, it is supposed, depends upon what men essentially are. It is assumed that there is some central feature common to all human beings and to them alone upon which all their other specifically human activities depend and in terms of which they must be explained. To this it may be objected, in the first place, that human beings are not the sort of beings to which essences may be attributed. Beings with essences are those that can be classified in some definite way in a well-defined system of classification. The Aristotelian scheme presupposed a world of things that can be so classified, and it was found necessary to abandon the scheme when it was realized that the world was too complex. Essences may be defined for artifacts with definite functions, such as chairs and knives. A knife is an instrument for cutting, a chair an article of furniture for seating one person. But human beings cannot be fitted into any single system of aims or functions. The Aristotelian definition of man as a rational animal sums up a view of man's place and purpose in the cosmos. It is absurd to suppose that there is any single thing that constitutes the humanity of man, as cutting constitutes the nature of knives. The choice of a single word such as "reason" or "political" or "toolmaking" gives the appearance of such an essence, but it is an appearance only, since each of these words expresses a highly complex notion that cannot be caught up as a definition with a single classificatory scheme. It has already been noted that man is not the only animal that makes its means of life, but that bees and beavers—to mention only two—do so as well. What differentiates human productions is that they are constantly improved on and form the basis for new ones that become progressively less and less like those from which they originated. To say that toolmaking is the essence of man is to refer to his inventiveness in one of its most concrete forms. If man has an essence, it is that he has none.

Why did Marx and Engels pick on toolmaking as the feature that differentiates man from the other animals. There does not seem to be any single answer. Marx, at any rate, was influenced by the archeological classifications of the periods of prehistory into the Stone Age, Bronze Age, and Iron Age. But of course he was wrong if he supposed that because prehistory has to be reconstructed from the material things left behind, these material things are the basic explanatory factors in all human society. (In any case, some of the archeological remains are not tools at all.) Insofar as archeologists adopt the hypothesis or method of historical materialism, they do so *faute de mieux,* for by the very nature of their business there is nothing else they can do.

A more fundamental reason for the view of Marx and Engels that toolmaking is the human essence is their acceptance, not perhaps altogether conscious in their later years, of the Hegelian view that men create their lives through labor. Technology is thus regarded as the concrete embodiment of the process by which nature is controlled and humanized.

Again, Marx and Engels lived at a time when men were becoming aware of the social effects of important industrial inventions. They saw that a new form of society was coming into being as a result of the invention of steam power and that a society with cotton mills and railroads required very different institutions from those of a society with cottage looms and stage coaches. In our own day the social influence of technological invention has become obvious, at any rate in a general way, even though the specific effects of particular inventions may sometimes be difficult to ascertain. But Marx and Engels noted this at a time when not everyone was aware of what was occurring. But it should be noted that this does not establish historical materialism. From the fact that important technological changes often make it necessary to change laws and to adopt new modes of life and thought, it does not follow that law and modes of life and thought can be decisively altered only as a result of technological change. Furthermore, from the great social importance of technological invention nothing follows as to the causes and conditions of technological invention itself.

Linkage of productive forces and relations. In saying that Marx regarded historical materialism as obviously true we are saying that he regarded it as obvious that the productive forces "determine" the productive relationships. There is a sense in which productive relationships are necessarily linked with productive forces. For in inventing a new tool or machine it may well happen that the inventor is requiring so many men to work together such and such ways. A man might, for example, invent or design a sailing ship that required five men to sail it and each member of the crew to occupy a certain position in the vessel. Again, when it was discovered how to equip ships with steam or gasoline engines, the work demanded of seamen was altered and new relationships created among them. Controlling boilers and engines is quite different from handling lines and sails. The jobs are different, and the relationships of those who do the jobs are different too. The point therefore may be expressed by saying that sometimes the introduction of a new type of tool or machine necessarily involves the introduction of new job relationships. It would be natural enough to call these job relationships productive relationships in contrast with the tools or machines themselves, which might be called productive forces or means of production. With the terms understood in this way, then, it can happen that a change in productive forces necessarily brings with it a change in productive relationships, since the productive forces and the productive relationships may be different aspects of the same thing.

How far does this sort of productive relationship extend? We may take the example of the invention of the airplane to elucidate this question. An airplane at first was flown by one man; later models require several operators. Hence there are certain job relationships for the actual operation of the machine. In addition, however, an airport is required and, if journeys are to be undertaken, other places for landing and refueling. If an airplane is regarded as a machine for flying considerable distances from its base, then the provision of airfields with men to supervise take-offs and landings and to help in refueling is necessarily involved in the invention too. Thus there are rather extensive job relationships implicit in the invention of a machine for flying from one place to another. Now there is a principle of Roman law according to which the owner of land owns the whole volume of earth and air below and above it, *de caelo usque ad inferas* ("from heaven above to hell beneath"). If this principle were insisted on, those who fly airplanes would find it necessary to obtain permission from, or even make payments to, the intervening landowners before they could fly from their own territory. Actually, a system of permissions and exclusions has arisen according to which landowners within a country generally cannot prevent airplanes from flying over their land, whereas governments have certain powers of control over flights crossing their boundaries. Someone might argue that in inventing a machine for flying considerable distances from its base, the inventor was providing not only for the piloting of the aircraft and for its landing and refueling but also for the rules by which it would be controlled as it went from place to place. But this would be to extend the notion of job relationships much too far. Whereas piloting and landing and refueling may be regarded as aspects of flying the machine, and hence as necessary features of the invention, the rules under which the flights may be allowed are a different matter. An injunction to prevent the flight might have been issued after arrangements had been made for it to take place. Thus the third set of relationships is connected with the invention in a contingent way. It might be convenient to call these last relationships productive relationships as distinct from job relationships, even though use of the adjective "productive" exaggerates the connection with the actual operation of the machine. Thus it is clear that whereas a given invention may necessitate certain job relationships, it will be inconsistent with certain wider relationships and consistent with a variety of others. Use of the word "determine" both for the job relationships and the wider ones obscures this difference and encourages the idea that technology sets bonds of necessity upon the social system.

Argument from the history of capitalism. By far the greater part of Marx's historical work was concerned with the origins and development of capitalism, and it is therefore reasonable to regard this part of his work as an example and as a vindication of the doctrine of historical materialism. However, *Capital* deals mainly with the economic and industrial aspects of capitalism and all too briefly with political and ideological matters. It is not surprising that economic and industrial matters should play a large part in an analysis and history of economic and industrial developments. But *Capital* gives only minute and incidental support to the main thesis of historical materialism: the thesis of the dependence of other social institutions upon the technical and economic ones and the thesis of the primary historical influence of technology and economics. After Marx's death Max Weber put forward the view that the growth of capitalism in Europe was fostered by certain aspects of Protestant religious belief. Marx, of course, thought that religious belief is ideological and epiphenomenal, an ineffectual shadow of social reality. He would have found it necessary to reject Weber's view on grounds of principle, in spite of the concomitances and assimilations to which Weber called attention. This shows that Marx's view is not a hypothesis but part of a system of interpretation of very wide scope; part, indeed, of a philosophical outlook.

DIALECTICAL ASPECTS OF THE THEORY

The fundamental thesis of Marxist dialectics is that everything is in movement, and Marx and his followers have proclaimed the mutability of all existing social forms. This in itself, of course, would not distinguish historical materialism from, for example, Hegelianism or some types of liberalism. Another feature of Marxist dialectics, however, is the belief that although gradual changes are occurring all the time, there are also on occasion sudden changes of great scope in which existing types of being are succeeded by utterly new ones. This means that Marxists consider the emergence of new social forms to be as natural as evolutionary adaptation. One might say that their view of change is such as to make them expect the unexpected. A further tenet of Marxist dialectics is that development takes place through the clash of opposites. Thus the doctrine of the class struggle is regarded by Marxists as a vital feature of historical materialism. Changes in the means of production provide the clue to class struggles and social revolutions out of which new forms of life and thought are born. Philosophers of the Marxist–Leninist tradition hold that in communist society contradictions and oppositions would continue but that, in the absence of class differences, they would be "nonantagonistic."

The foregoing might be called the metaphysics of Marxist dialectics. (For a fuller discussion see DIALECTICAL MATERIALISM.) Marx himself, however, was much more concerned with dialectics as a method. Perhaps the most fundamental feature of the dialectical method as understood by Marx is its distrust of abstraction. This, too, is a Hegelian legacy, but whereas Hegel regarded the Absolute Spirit as the concrete reality, for Marx reality was the material world, along with embodied human beings organized together in various social orders. Philosophers who talk of spirit, or economists who talk of land, labor, and capital, according to Marx, obscure the physical basis of human life and action and substitute abstract categories for the concrete realities of human work and association. Abstraction, in this view of the matter, is a form of mystification. The only way to avoid mystification is to relate the things that people say and do to the material circumstances in which they live. But the abstract is contrasted not only with the concrete but also with what is whole or complete. Marx, like Hegel, thought that the parts of any whole were not indifferent to one another but were, on the contrary, linked closely together. This linkage was particularly close between the individuals and groups of human society. According to Marx, the institutions of work and production were the primary ones, but through their connection with these institutions, men's laws and politics, their philosophy, morals, art, and religion are interrelated and interdependent and cannot be understood in isolation from one another or from their material basis.

A further form of abstraction that Marx objected to was the claim that there are economic laws that apply to all human societies equally. Marx held (Preface to *Capital*, Vol. I, 2d ed.) that each main type of social order develops and functions in its own special ways, so that we cannot conclude from what happens in one type of society that anything similar will happen in another. Indeed, he said that to trace the laws of development of different types of society in this way, keeping the particular and peculiar in view, is the dialectical method. It should be noted, too, that Marx sometimes thought that the various social categories, such as productive forces and productive relations, could not be abstracted from one another, but collapsed one into the other, as Hegelian theories do. We have already seen that Marx treated forms of organization as means of production, thus blurring the distinction between productive forces and productive relationships. In the recently published *Outlines of a Critique of Political Economy* (1857) appears the following note: "Dialectic of the concepts productive force (means of production) and productive relationship, a dialectic to determine their limits, and which does not cancel their real distinction" (p. 29). It seems that Marx hoped to settle the problem by means of a dialectical *coup de main*.

RELATION TO OTHER ENDEAVORS

Marx was not the first to inquire into the history of technology and of industry and commerce, but undoubtedly his work greatly influenced the direction taken by historical research. Marxist historians have been particularly anxious to show how knowledge has been hindered or promoted by the prevailing productive forces and productive relationships. Thus, Benjamin Farrington, in his *Greek Science* (2 vols., London, 1944–1949), argued that the predominantly speculative and unpractical character of Greek science was due to the institution of slavery and the aristocratic contempt for manual work that went with it. George Thomson, in his *Studies in Ancient Greek Society*, I: *The Prehistoric Aegean* (London, 1949), presented evidence in favor of Engels' views on primitive communism. In Volume II of the same work, subtitled *The First Philosophers* (London, 1955), Thomson linked the categories employed by the pre-Socratic philosophers with economic and class factors and with Marx's notion of a commodity as "the uniform socially recognized" incarnation of human labor, concluding that "the Parmenidean One, together with the later idea of 'substance,' may therefore be described as a reflex or projection of the substance of exchange value" (p. 103). B. Hessen, in an essay entitled "The Social and Economic Roots of Newton's *Principia*" (*Science at the Crossroads*, 1931), argued that Newton was the typical representative of the rising bourgeoisie, and in his philosophy he embodies the characteristic features of his class" (p. 33). This type of view illustrates the more general inquiry into the connections between class and knowledge known as the sociology of knowledge. Karl Mannheim's *Ideology and Utopia* (*Ideologie und Utopie*, Bonn, 1929; translated by Louis Wirth and Edward Shils, London, 1936) shows how Marxism influenced this subject, but Max Scheler, who was not a Marxist, also helped develop it (*Die Wissenformen und die Gesellschaft*, Leipzig, 1926).

It should be emphasized that a materialist view of history is not necessarily linked with Marxist socialism, for it is possible to recognize the historical importance of the means of production and of economic and class interests without concluding that a classless, communist society must emerge. (This was done, for instance, by E. R. A. Seligman in *The Economic Interpretation of History*, New York, 1902). Furthermore, some historians and economists have adopted an economic interpretation of history without committing themselves to the Marxist views about the dominating influence of technology, of the means of production. Thus, Thorold Rogers, an undogmatic free trader, called attention to such influences as the shortage of labor created by the Black Death or the interference with trade routes by the Mongol invaders, but said: "You cannot, of course, separate, except in thought, and then only with no little risk of confusion, economical from social and political facts" (*The Economic Interpretation of History*, London, 1888, p. 281). Marxists have often gone to considerable lengths to distinguish the economic from the materialist conception of history. Thus, the Russian Marxist historian M. N. Pokrovsky has been criticized by orthodox Marxists for placing too much emphasis on market considerations and too little on the influence of the means of production.

Historical Materialist Works

MARX

"Oekonomische–philosophische Manuskripte," in D. Riazanov and V. Adoratski, eds., *Marx–Engels Gesamtausgabe*. Berlin, 1932. Division 1, Vol. III. Translated by Martin Milligan as *Economic and Philosophical Manuscripts of 1844*. Moscow and London, 1959.

Misère de la philosophie. Brussels and Paris, 1847. Translated by H. Quelch as *The Poverty of Philosophy*. Chicago, 1910.

Grundrisse der Kritik der politischen Ökonomie (Rohentwurf). Berlin, 1953. One section has been translated by J. Cohen as *Pre-Capitalist Economic Formations*, E. J. Hobsbawn, ed. London, 1964.

Zur Kritik der politischen Ökonomie. Berlin, 1859. Translated by N. I. Stone as *A Contribution to the Critique of Political Economy*. Chicago, 1904.

Das Kapital, 3 vols. Hamburg, 1867–1894. Vols. II and III edited by Friedrich Engels; Vol. III in two parts. English translation, Chicago, 1915. Vol. I translated by Samuel Moore and Edward Aveling, revised and amplified according to the fourth German edition by Ernest Untermann; Vol. II translated from the second German edition by Ernest Untermann; Vol. III translated from the first German edition by Ernest Untermann.

Karl Marx. Selected Writings in Sociology and Social Philosophy, T. B. Bottomore and Maximilien Rubel, eds. London, 1956.

MARX AND ENGELS

Die deutsche Ideologie, V. Adoratski, ed. Vienna, 1932. Translated as *The German Ideology*, R. Pascal, ed. London, 1938.

Manifest der kommunistischen Partei. London, 1848. Many English editions as *The Communist Manifesto*. See especially edition with an introduction by Harold Laski. London, 1948.

Selected Correspondence (1846–1895), Dona Torr, ed. New York, 1942. Contains Marx's 1846 letter to Paul Annenkov and important letters written by Engels after Marx's death.

ENGELS

Umrisse zu Kritik der Nationalökonomie (1844). Translated by Martin Milligan as "Outlines of a Critique of Political Economy," in Karl Marx, *Economic and Philosophical Manuscripts of 1844* (*op. cit.*).

Herr Eugen Dührings Umwälzung der Wissenschaft. Leipzig, 1878. Translated by E. Burns as *Herr Eugen Dühring's Revolution in Science*. London, 1934.

Die Entwicklung des Sozialismus von der Utopie zur Wissen-

schaft. Zurich, 1883. Translated by E. Aveling as *Socialism: Utopian and Scientific.* London, 1892.

Der Ursprung der Familie, des Privateigentums und des Staats. Zurich, 1884. Translated by E. Untermann as *The Origin of the Family, Private Property, and the State.* Chicago, 1902.

LENIN

What the "Friends of the People" Are (1894), in his *Collected Works,* Moscow and London, 1960——. Vol. I, 1960.

"Karl Marx," in his *Collected Works.* Moscow and London, 1960——. Vol. 21, 1964.

PLEKHANOV

K Voprosu o Razvitii Monisticheskago Vzglyada na Istoriyu. St. Petersburg, 1895. Translated by Andrew Rothstein as *In Defense of Materialism: The Development of the Monist View of History.* London, 1947.

Osnovnye Problemy Marksizma. 1908. Translated by E. Paul and C. Paul as *Fundamental Problems of Marxism.* London, 1929.

Works on Historical Materialism

Acton, H. B., *The Illusion of the Epoch: Marxism – Leninism as a Philosophical Creed.* London, 1955.

Adler, Max, *Lehrbuch der materialistischen Geschichtsauffassung,* 2 vols. Vienna, 1930.

Barth, P., *Die Philosophie der Geschichte als Soziologie,* 3d and 4th eds. Leipzig, 1922.

Berlin, Isaiah, *Karl Marx.* London, 1948.

Bober, M. M., *Marx's Interpretation of History,* 2d ed. Cambridge, Mass., 1950.

Clark, G. N., *Science and Social Welfare in the Age of Newton.* London, 1937.

Croce, Benedetto, *Materialismo storico ed economica marxista.* Palermo, 1900. Translated by C. M. Meredith as *Historical Materialism and the Economics of Karl Marx.* London, 1914.

Federn, Karl, *The Materialist Conception of History. A Critical Analysis.* London, 1939.

Goldmann, Lucien, *Recherches dialectiques.* Paris, 1959.

Hexter, J. H., *Reappraisals in History.* London, 1961.

Hook, Sidney, *Towards the Understanding of Karl Marx.* New York, 1933.

Hook, Sidney, *From Hegel to Marx.* New York, 1935.

Masaryk, T. G., *Die philosophische und soziologische Grundlagen des Marxismus.* Vienna, 1899.

Plamenatz, John, *German Marxism and Russian Communism.* London, 1954.

Pokrovsky, M. N., *History of Russia from the Earliest Times to the Rise of Commercial Capitalism.* London, 1932.

Pokrovsky, M. N., *A Brief History of Russia,* 2 vols. London, 1933.

Popper, K. R., *The Open Society and Its Enemies,* Vol. II, *The High Tide of Prophecy.* London, 1945,

Rubel, Maximilien, *Karl Marx. Essai de biographie intellectuelle.* Paris, 1957.

Tucker, Robert, *Philosophy and Myth in Karl Marx.* Cambridge, 1961.

Venable, Vernon, *Human Nature. The Marxist View.* London, 1946.

H. B. Acton

HISTORICAL SCHOOL OF JURISPRUDENCE.

The historical school of jurists was founded by Friedrich Karl von Savigny (1779– 1861). Its central idea was that a nation's customary law is its truly living law and that the task of jurisprudence is to uncover this law and describe in historical studies its social provenience. As in other schools of thought, acceptance of this approach did not necessarily mean agreement on its theoretical or practical consequences.

Germany. To followers of Savigny the identification of law with custom and tradition and the *Volksgeist,* or genius peculiar to a nation or folk, generally meant a rejection of rationalism and natural law; a rejection of the notion of law as the command of the state or sovereign, and therefore a disparagement of legislation and codification; and a denial of the possibility of universally valid rights and duties and of the individual's possession of nonderivable and inalienable rights. In positive terms, historical jurisprudence identified law with the consciousness, or spirit, of a specific people. Law is "found" by the jurist and not "made" by the state or its organs. Law is a national or folk and not a political phenomenon; it is a social and not an individual production; like language, it cannot be abstracted from a particular people and its genius; it is a historical necessity and not an expression of will or reason, and therefore it cannot be transplanted.

In addition to Savigny, the historical school was probably influenced by Johann Gottfried von Herder (1744– 1803) and the romantic notions of folk culture, by the emphasis on tradition in the work of Edmund Burke (1729– 1797), by the stress on historical continuity in the work of Gustav Hugo (1764– 1844), and by the Hegelian conception of Spirit. In Germany, the main proponents of historical jurisprudence were G. F. Puchta, Karl Friedrich Eichhorn, Rudolph von Sohm, and Otto von Gierke.

England. In England Henry Maine (1822– 1888) was closely identified with the historical school, although there is no evidence that he was directly influenced by the German thinkers. Modern historical jurisprudence in England was born with the publication in London of Maine's *Ancient Law* in 1861, the year of Savigny's death. Until then historical research in law had been neglected, but from that time on, the field was assiduously cultivated. In reaction against natural law and under the influence of Hobbes, the tendency in England had been to regard law as the command of the state, and the task of the jurist was conceived as a concern with the analysis of positive law without regard to historical or ethical considerations. Maine broke with these traditional attitudes. Probably influenced by Rudolf von Ihering (*Der Geist des römischen Recht,* 3 vols., Leipzig, 1852– 1865), Maine was stimulated to apply the historical method to jurisprudence. Darwin's *Origin of Species,* published two years before *Ancient Law,* also probably influenced Maine.

Maine rejected the natural law, rationalistic, and a priori approaches to the nature of law. In his *Early History of Institutions* (London, 1875) he saw a people's law as compounded of opinions, beliefs, and superstitions produced by institutions and human nature as they affected one another. Indeed, English common law seemed better to exemplify Savigny's views than did the law of Germany, which drew heavily on Roman law. But as an Englishman, Maine saw in law more than a people's customs; he observed and took into account the creative and reforming work of Parliament, and so he was led to recognize legislation as an instrument of legal growth. And he found that equity and legal fictions played creative roles in the common law. In these respects he departed radically from Savigny's monistic approach to law and its sources.

Maine's comparative historical studies, which took into

account diverse legal systems, kept him from a belief in the mystical uniqueness of a people and its genius and its law; he observed uniformities as well as differences in different legal orders, and so he was led to suggest that similar stages of social development may be correlated with similar stages of legal development in different nations. Maine differed from Savigny also in believing that custom might historically follow an act of judgment, so that the jurist could be seen to have had a creative role in making the law, even though he claimed only to have found it. Maine also noted the part played in early societies by the codification of customary law. In revealing the ideals operative in a society at a particular stage of its development and in relating them to social conditions, Maine stimulated the development of the use of the sociological method in jurisprudence. It thus became apparent that just as law cannot be divorced from history, so, too, it cannot be divorced from philosophy and sociology. Thus, if Savigny's historical jurisprudence was mainly conservative in import, Maine's work had a predominantly liberalizing effect. Then too, Maine's work influenced the development of comparative legal studies.

Other English scholars associated in varying degree with the historical school of jurisprudence are James Bryce (1838–1922), Frederic W. Maitland (1850–1906), Frederick Pollock (1845–1937), and Paul Vinogradoff (1854–1925).

Perhaps the greatness of historical jurisprudence lay in the fact that it provided its own seed of dissolution; for once it is admitted that law is historically conditioned, it is as impossible to limit the conception of law to a *Volksgeist* as to the commands of the sovereign; all forms of social control and all sources of law emerge as subjects for legitimate consideration and study.

Bibliography

WORKS OF HISTORICAL JURISPRUDENCE

Eichhorn, Karl Friedrich, *Deutsche Staats- und Rechtsgeschichte*, 4 vols. Göttingen, 1808–1823.
Gierke, Otto von, *Das deutsche Genossenschaftsrecht*, 4 vols. Berlin, 1868–1913. Partially translated by Ernest Barker as *Natural Law and the Theory of Society*. Oxford, 1934.
Puchta, G. F., *Das Gewohnheitsrecht*, 2 vols. Erlangen, 1828–1837.
Sohm, Rudolf von, *Institutionen des römischen Rechts*. Leipzig, 1883. Translated by J. C. Ledlie as *Institutes of Roman Law*. Oxford, 1892; 3d ed., Oxford, 1907.

COMMENTARIES

Allen, C. K., *Law in the Making*, 7th ed. Oxford, 1964. Ch. 2.
Friedmann, Wolfgang, *Legal Theory*, 3d ed. London, 1953. Ch. 14, with bibliography.
Friedrich, C. J., *The Philosophy of Law in Historical Perspective*, 2d ed. Chicago, 1963. Ch. 15.
Jones, J. W., *Historical Introduction to Theory of Law*. Oxford, 1940. Ch. 2.
Pound, Roscoe, *Interpretations of Legal History*. New York, 1923.
Pound, Roscoe, *Jurisprudence*. St. Paul, Minn., 1959. Vol. I.
Stammler, Rudolf, "Fundamental Tendencies in Modern Jurisprudence." *Michigan Law Review*, Vol. 21 (1923), 623 ff.
Stone, Julius, *The Province and Function of Law*. Cambridge, Mass., 1950. Ch. 18.
Vinogradoff, Paul, *Historical Jurisprudence*. London, 1920. Vol. I.

Walton, F. P., "Historical School of Jurisprudence and Transplantations of Law." *Journal of Comparative Legislation & International Law*, Vol. 183 (3d series, 1927).

MILTON R. KONVITZ

HISTORICISM. The early history of the term "Historicism" (*Historismus*) has not been sufficiently explored, as Erich Rothacker has pointed out. However, one clear case in which it was used in a sense closely allied to all of the senses which it has subsequently assumed is to be found in Carl Prantl's *Die gegenwärtige Aufgabe der Philosophie* (1852). Although the term was later employed as a means of characterizing the thought of Vico, its first widespread use probably dates from methodological debates among German-speaking political economists. In these debates, Carl Menger criticized Gustav Schmoller and his school for making economic theory unduly dependent upon economic history; this he characterized as *Historismus*. Thus, the term took on a depreciatory sense; it suggested an inappropriate use of historical knowledge and a confusion regarding the sorts of questions which could be answered by means of such knowledge. One may conjecture that the extension of its use during the first decades of the twentieth century was fostered by the currency of its depreciatory analogue, "psychologism" (*Psychologismus*): both terms were used in reference to attempts to extend the methods and results of a particular discipline into provinces in which that discipline was claimed to lack legitimate authority.

It was not until the period immediately following World War I, however, that *Historismus* came to be widely used. The impact of the war and the consequences of the German defeat led to attempts to reappraise the cultural and political traditions of the past, and in this reappraisal a central issue was whether a purely historical approach to human culture provided an adequate basis for the judgment of cultural values. This was not, of course, a new problem for theologians or for philosophers; it was one which had been forced upon their attention by dominant strains in nineteenth-century thought (for example, by Hegelianism, the results of historical Biblical criticism, and evolutionism). However, for those in Germany who had been reared in the tradition of historical studies and who were encountering the violent upheaval of the times, the question of the relations of cultural standards to historical change took on great immediacy. It was at this point that Ernst Troeltsch attempted to characterize historicism in a nonpolemical way, to examine its origins, and to assess its merits and limitations.

Troeltsch. In *Der Historismus und Seine Probleme*, Troeltsch used "historicism" to mean a tendency to view all knowledge and all forms of experience in a context of historical change. He regarded this tendency as one of the two fundamental discoveries of the modern mind: the other, with which he compared it, was the generalizing, quantitative approach to nature which he termed *Naturalismus*. Thus, like Wilhelm Dilthey, Wilhelm Windelband, Heinrich Rickert, and others, Troeltsch drew a distinction between the forms of understanding characteristic of the natural sciences and those which are appropriate to what one may perhaps best term the "historical sciences" (*die*

Geisteswissenschaften). What was of prime importance to him, however, was not the differences between the methodologies of the natural and the historical sciences, but the fact that each was a fundamentally different way of looking at the world, that is, each constituted a different *Weltanschauung*. Troeltsch documented the scope and the depth of historicism as a *Weltanschauung* by tracing its presence in the thought of a host of philosophers and sociologists of the nineteenth and twentieth centuries. He himself accepted the view that all knowledge and all forms of human experience are caught up in a process of change; however, he believed that this view tended to lead to an unmitigated moral and intellectual skepticism. It was this that constituted the crisis of historicism, and it was this that he sought to overcome. Unlike Rickert and others among his contemporaries, he believed that the skeptical consequences of historicism could be overcome only through history itself and could not be avoided by any appeal to transhistorical values. However, his own positive, religiously based views received only partial expression, for he died before he was able to complete the work which he had projected.

Mannheim. In 1924, almost immediately after the appearance of Troeltsch's work, Karl Mannheim wrote an essay, "Historismus," in which he too characterized historicism as a basic *Weltanschauung*. According to him, the static, theologically oriented conception of the world which characterized the Middle Ages had been retained in secularized form in the Enlightenment, because both cultures held to the doctrine of the atemporal character of the judgments of reason. According to Mannheim, this static conception had at last been abandoned, and all social and cultural reality was seen as being dominated by change. It was this radically temporalistic view of the world that he designated as historicism. Unlike Troeltsch, to whose work he devoted a portion of his essay, Mannheim did not recoil from the relativism of values which he saw that historicism entailed; rather, he was concerned to affirm it. However, on the basis of his own views regarding the intimate connections between theory and practice, he did not believe that either moral or intellectual skepticism was a necessary consequence of temporalistic relativism. Moral skepticism would not necessarily follow, since Mannheim believed that all values are rooted in the conditions of actual social existence and their discovery is not dependent upon our possession of some unchanging capacity for moral insight; furthermore, intellectual skepticism could be avoided through a recognition of the perspectival character of knowledge, and by means of the capacity of a sociology of knowledge to uncover the nature of divergent perspectives and reconcile them with one another. Thus, in Mannheim's use of "historicism," unlike Troeltsch's, there remained no vestige of the original depreciatory significance of the term.

Meinecke. In 1936 Friedrich Meinecke published a historical study entitled *Die Entstehung des Historismus* in which the term assumed a markedly different connotation. To be sure, Meinecke shared Troeltsch's view that historicism represented a break with those modes of thought which both characterized as naturalism. Furthermore, like Mannheim and others, he believed that there

was a fundamental opposition between the modern historical sense and earlier political philosophies which had relied upon the conception of a universal and unchanging natural law as the basis for moral and political judgment. Thus Meinecke regarded historicism as opposed to a static view of the world, and in this he was in agreement with Troeltsch and Mannheim. However, he proceeded to characterize this new world view in terms of an interest in that which is concrete, unique, and individual; he found the clue to the new view expressed in Goethe's use of the dictum *"Individuum est ineffabile."* This characterization of historicism was undoubtedly related to the fact that Troeltsch (among others) had viewed historical inquiry as concerned with the concrete, the unique, and the individual, and had contrasted this interest with the methods used in the natural sciences. However, in translating this particular methodological doctrine into a world view, Meinecke departed radically from the characterizations offered by Troeltsch and Mannheim. For them it was not the concept of individuality but the concepts of change and development which were fundamental to what they had termed "historicism." As a consequence of this difference in the meaning of the terms, some of the eighteenth-century historians who played dominant roles in Meinecke's account would not have been considered proponents of historicism by Troeltsch or by Mannheim. The difference emerges most strongly in the fact that Meinecke believed the culmination of modern historicism was to be found in the world views of Goethe and Leopold von Ranke, whereas one would expect such a high point to be identified with Hegel, with Marx, or perhaps with later evolutionary thought, were one to take the term in the meaning ascribed to it by Troeltsch and Mannheim. As a consequence of this shift in the meaning of the term, Meinecke naturally did not regard historicism as a force which threatened human values or which could lead to a radical transvaluation of values; thus, for him there was no crisis of historicism as there had been for Troeltsch.

Croce. The view with which Meinecke's characterization of historicism can best be compared is that of Benedetto Croce, even though Croce criticized Meinecke's work for its failure to emphasize nineteenth-century thought, and in particular because of its failure to appreciate Hegel's importance. Croce's own philosophic views had grown out of a reaction against positivism and materialism, in favor of idealism: in particular, he concerned himself with combatting positivist and materialist philosophies of history. What he rejected in these views was not the historicism which Troeltsch and Mannheim correctly discerned in them, but the fact that they attempted to interpret history naturalistically, that is; in ways similar to those used by the sciences in dealing with the nonhuman world. Like Vico and Hegel, with whose thought his own was directly affiliated, Croce regarded history as the self-development of the human spirit. Furthermore, since Croce, as an idealist, wished to deny that there was any realm of existence external to the human spirit, he interpreted the whole of reality as being encompassed within history: life and reality were nothing but the ever changing manifestations of the spirit. It was primarily with reference to this radical metaphysical idealism, rather than with reference to any more general currents in Western intellectual history, that Croce used the term "historicism" (*storicismo*). While Croce's own emphasis on the pervasiveness of change did in fact provide an example of what Troeltsch and Mannheim considered to be the basic feature of historicism, it was not with their thought, but with that of Meinecke, that his views had the greater affinity. Like Meinecke, Croce held that the means by which a naturalistic world view seeks to envision and grasp reality are totally inadequate because of the uniqueness and individuality of that which is historical. He therefore held—as did Meinecke—that genuine knowledge, as opposed to merely practical or pseudo-knowledge, comes only through an understanding of history. Croce endeavored to establish this antinaturalistic position throughout his philosophical writings; for Meinecke, the acceptance of this form of historicism was intimately connected with a religious sense of mystery.

England and the United States. The term "historicism" was adopted into the English language in the late 1930s and the 1940s both in the United States and in England. In neither country, however, was it used to refer primarily to a *Weltanschauung*; rather, what was of concern were questions regarding principles of explanation and of evaluation. In the United States, attention was directed to these issues through works by Morris R. Cohen, Maurice Mandelbaum, and Morton White, among others. In England, fuller discussions were to be found in articles by F. A. Hayek and Karl Popper.

One may plausibly infer from Hayek's discussion of historicism that the sense in which he and Popper conceived the notion probably derived from Menger's original contrast between scientific theory-construction and a primarily historical approach to problems in the social sciences. However, the specific form of historicism which both Hayek and Popper especially attacked was the nineteenth-century doctrine that there are laws of development which characterize social wholes and that it is possible, on the basis of a knowledge of such laws, to make scientific predictions about the future. Thus, the notion of "holism," which had not previously been directly associated with the definition of historicism, was injected into the discussion, and the chief protagonists of historicism were identified as Hegel, Comte, and Marx. When taken in this sense, three theses were common to historicist doctrines: (1) a rejection of "methodological individualism" in favor of the view that there are social wholes which are not reducible to the activities of individuals; (2) the doctrine that there are laws of development of these wholes, considered as wholes; (3) the belief that such laws permit predictions as to the course which the future will take. While these three theses were intimately connected with some of the doctrines previously characterized as examples of historicism, there seems to be no necessity for identifying historicism with holistic thought and with a belief in the possibility of prediction, as Popper and Hayek tend to do.

Definition of "historicism." Considering the very great diversity in usage which we have now traced, one may ask whether there is any characterization of historicism which can serve to connect the various ways in which the term has been used and which at the same time can give it a relatively clear meaning. Without suggesting that all problems concerning the deviant meanings of historicism can be solved in this way, the following definition may be proposed as an approximation of that goal: Historicism is the belief that an adequate understanding of the nature of anything and an adequate assessment of its value are to be gained by considering it in terms of the place it occupied and the role it played within a process of development.

It will be noted that this definition does not characterize historicism as a particular *Weltanschauung* but as a methodological belief concerning explanation and evaluation. As Popper's discussion makes clear, in the late eighteenth and nineteenth centuries, forms of what has been termed "naturalism" have closely resembled antinaturalistic theories, with respect to their presuppositions about the relation of historical change to the explanation and evaluation of events. Since it is misleading to regard positions as divergent as those of, say, Hegel, Comte, Marx, and Spencer as representative of one and the same *Weltanschauung,* it is preferable to conceive of historicism as a methodological principle.

Troeltsch and Mannheim were in agreement with Meinecke and Croce in holding that this new methodological principle was based upon the rise of a new concept of change and of history. Its original challenge to older modes of thought lay partly in its tendency to link evaluation with genetic explanation. It was this tendency which was fundamental to the so-called crisis of historicism, and it has also been against this tendency that Hayek and Popper, among others, have subsequently rebelled. However, the most radical aspect of historicism as a methodological principle has been its conception of what is presupposed in all explanations and evaluations of past events: that each event is to be understood by viewing it in terms of a larger process of which it was a phase, or in which it played a part; and that only through understanding the nature of this process can one fully understand or evaluate concrete events. It is partly because of this emphasis upon relating each event to some larger developmental process that historicism has come to be identified with holism and a belief in historical prediction. Important as this connection has undoubtedly been, a definition in terms of it fails to stress the more fundamental fact that historicism involves a genetic model of explanation and an attempt to base all evaluation upon the nature of the historical process itself. Popper, in his characterization of the position, therefore tends to separate his own use of the term "historicism" from its other, more frequent uses. The definition suggested here constitutes an attempt to epitomize many of these uses and to connect them with one another even where they are found to diverge.

Bibliography

The following bibliography is highly selective and deals only with those works in which historicism is the central topic of discussion and with works specifically mentioned in the article. The order is chronological, except that all works by the same author or concerned primarily with that author are placed together.

Prantl, Carl, *Die gegenwärtige Aufgabe der Philosophie* (Munich, 1852). A speech given before the (Bavarian) Akademie der Wissenschaften on March 27, 1852. In it, the term *Historismus* is used to designate a concrete, historically oriented method by means of which the impasses in the philosophy of the day could be avoided.

Menger, Carl, *Untersuchungen über die Methode der Socialwissenschaften* (Leipzig, 1883); reprinted as Volume II (London, 1933) of the *Collected Works*. These four volumes constitute numbers 17–20 of "Reprints of Scarce Tracts in Economics and Political Science," published by the London School of Economics and Political Science.

Menger, Carl, *Die Irrthümer des Historismus in der deutschen Nationalökonomie* (Vienna, 1884); reprinted in Volume III (London, 1935) of the *Collected Works*, 4 vols. A polemic against Schmoller's methodological views. This and the preceding item represent the first influential introduction of the term "historicism" into the literature of the social sciences.

Ritzel, Gerhard, *Schmoller versus Menger: Eine Analyse des Methodenstreits im Hinblick auf den Historismus in der Nationalökonomie* (Frankfurt am Main, 1950). A helpful doctoral dissertation concerned with the issues involved in the quarrel over method in political economy.

Troeltsch, Ernst, *Der Historismus und seine Probleme* (Tübingen, 1922). Only the first volume of this work was completed. It takes its point of departure from the "crisis of historicism" in postwar German intellectual life and treats fundamental problems of both formal and material philosophies of history through detailed discussion of almost all important nineteenth- and twentieth-century figures in these fields. Unfortunately, the structure of the discussion is not clear, largely because Troeltsch used the concept of "value" in discussing both the formal problems of a philosophy of history and the problem of meaning in history. His own solution of the latter problem, which was to have been the theme of his second volume, is briefly adumbrated in posthumously published lectures which he was to have given at Oxford. They were originally published as *Christian Thought, Its History and Application* (London, 1923; reprinted, New York, 1957), but they have been better known under the title *Der Historismus und seine Ueberwindung* (Berlin, 1924).

Troeltsch, Ernst, "Die Krisis des Historismus." *Die Neue Rundschau*, Vol. 33 (1922), 572–590. An excellent, brief, untechnical statement of the central theme of Troeltsch's classic work.

Hintze, Otto, "Troeltsch und die Probleme des Historismus." *Historische Zeitschrift*, Vol. 135 (1927), 188–239. Also to be found in Hintze's collected essays, *Zur Theorie der Geschichte* (Leipzig, 1942). A masterful analytical and critical exposition of Troeltsch's approach to historicism. It is also suggestive in the way in which it provides a rich historiographical background against which the work of Troeltsch and Meinecke can be viewed.

Mannheim, Karl, "Historismus." *Archiv für Sozialwissenschaft und Sozialpolitik*, Vol. 52 (1924), translated and edited by Paul Kecskemeti and reprinted in *Essays on the Sociology of Knowledge* (London, 1952). An important treatment of historicism as the dominant *Weltanschauung* of the post-Enlightenment period, and an attempt to work out its cultural and philosophic implications.

Croce, Benedetto, "Antistoricismo." *Proceedings of the Seventh International Congress of Philosophy* (Oxford, 1930); translated into German by K. Vossler, and published in *Historische Zeitschrift*, Vol. 143 (1931), 457–466. An attack upon what Croce regarded as two antihistorical tendencies in thought: "futurism" and the attempt to escape from historicity to fixed and absolute standards.

Croce, Benedetto, *La storia come pensiero e come azione* (Bari, 1938); English translation by Sylvia Sprigge, *History as the Story of Liberty* (New York, 1941). A series of studies representing Croce's most mature reflections on history, historiography, and historicism.

Cohen, Morris R., "History Versus Value," in *Reason and Nature* (New York, 1931), pp. 369–385. This essay was originally published in *Journal of Philosophy*, Vol. 11 (1914), 704–716, but its influence on Morton White and others probably dates from its inclusion in this volume.

Heussi, Karl, *Die Krisis des Historismus* (Tübingen, 1932). Contains a useful summary of early uses of the term and helpful references. Heussi's analysis of the concept should be consulted, but lacks an appreciation of the connection between the main currents of nineteenth-century thought and the ways in which the term has been used in the twentieth century.

Meinecke, Friedrich, *Die Entstehung des Historismus*, 2 vols. (Munich and Berlin, 1936). The classic account of the development of historicism interpreted as a new view of life and of historical experience. Its course is traced by means of a series of individual essays from seventeenth-century forerunners through Goethe and Ranke.

Meinecke, Friedrich, *Zur Theorie und Philosophie der Geschichte*, Vol. 4 of *Werke*, 6 vols. (Stuttgart, 1957–1962). Collected essays and reviews, including discussions of Heussi and Troeltsch, and additional materials concerning the theme of his own book.

Hofer, Walther, *Geschichtschreibung und Weltanschauung* (Munich, 1950). A study of Meinecke's thought, with special reference to historicism.

Rothacker, Erich, "Historismus." *Schmollers Jahrbuch*, Vol. 62 (1938), 388–399. A noted theorist of the *Geisteswissenschaften* offers an interpretation of the characteristic nature of historicism. Rothacker's "Das Wort 'Historismus,'" *Zeitschrift für Deutsche Wortforschung*, Vol. 16 (1960), 3–6, is a criticism of those who failed to trace early uses of the term.

Mandelbaum, Maurice, *The Problem of Historical Knowledge* (New York, 1938). A brief discussion of historicism is included.

Hayek, F. A., "Scientism and the Study of Society: The Historicism of the Scientistic Approach," in *The Counter-revolution of Science* (Glencoe, Ill., 1952), Part I, Ch. 7. First published in *Economica*, Vol. 10 (1943), 50–63. The above study first appeared as a whole in *Economica*, Vol. 9 (1942), Vol. 10 (1943), Vol. 11 (1944).

Popper, Karl R., *The Poverty of Historicism* (London and Boston, 1957). First published in *Economica*, Vol. 11 (1944), Vol. 12 (1945). (For remarks on its earlier composition, see Popper's "Historical Note" prefixed to the printed volume.) The exposition and attack upon historicism are intimately connected with Popper's theories concerning methodology in the social sciences. With respect to all of these topics, see also Karl Popper, *The Open Society and Its Enemies* (London, 1945).

Engel-Janosi, Friedrich, "The Growth of German Historicism." *Johns Hopkins University Studies in History and Political Science*, Series 62 (1944), No. 2. Offers a brief survey of a number of leading German-speaking historians, emphasizing the historicist elements in their work.

White, Morton G., "The Attack on Historical Method." *Journal of Philosophy*, Vol. 42 (1945), 314–331. A reply to some aspects of the attack on historicism.

White, Morton G., *Social Thought in America: The Revolt Against Formalism* (New York, 1949). Includes a characterization of historicism and an estimate of its role in the thought of selected social theorists.

Lee, Dwight E., and Beck, Robert N., "The Meaning of 'Historicism.'" *American Historical Review*, Vol. 59 (1953–1954), 568–577. A compilation and critical classification of the various ways in which the term "historicism" has been used; it proposes a pair of definitions to cover the most widely established usages.

Antoni, Carlo, *Lo storicismo* (Rome, 1957). Adds some information to that supplied by Heussi on the early uses of the term; offers a brief survey of the development of historicism (in its broadest sense) from the eighteenth century to Croce.

White, Hayden V., "On History and Historicisms," in Carlo Antoni, *From History to Sociology* (Detroit, 1959). English translation by Hayden V. White. The translator's introduction is a brief, useful historical sketch of types of historicism.

Rand, Calvin G., "Two Meanings of Historicism in the Writings of Dilthey, Troeltsch, and Meinecke," in *Journal of the History of Ideas*, Vol. 25 (1964), 503–518. A further attempt to elucidate the varied meanings of the term.

MAURICE MANDELBAUM

HISTORIOGRAPHY OF PHILOSOPHY. See PHILOSOPHY, HISTORIOGRAPHY OF.

HISTORY. See DETERMINISM IN HISTORY; GREAT MAN THEORY OF HISTORY; HISTORICAL EXPLANATION; HISTORY AND VALUE JUDGMENTS; HOLISM AND INDIVIDUALISM IN HISTORY AND SOCIAL SCIENCE; PHILOSOPHY OF HISTORY; SPECULATIVE SYSTEMS OF HISTORY.

HISTORY, PHILOSOPHY OF. In addition to the survey article PHILOSOPHY OF HISTORY, the Encyclopedia features articles on the following topics: DETERMINISM IN HISTORY; GEISTESWISSENSCHAFTEN; GREAT MAN THEORY OF HISTORY; HISTORICAL EXPLANATION; HISTORICAL MATERIALISM; HISTORICISM; HISTORY AND VALUE JUDGMENTS; HOLISM AND INDIVIDUALISM IN HISTORY AND SOCIAL SCIENCE; PROGRESS, THE IDEA OF; SOCIOLOGY OF KNOWLEDGE; and SPECULATIVE SYSTEMS OF HISTORY. See History, Philosophy of, in Index for articles on thinkers who devoted special attention to problems arising from the study and methodology of history.

HISTORY AND VALUE JUDGMENTS. The question whether history as a discipline or type of inquiry involves the making of value judgments typically arises when its claim to be classed as a "science" comes into question. For it is generally assumed to be central to the idea of scientific inquiry that conclusions should not incorporate or depend upon the value judgments of the investigator, whereas the accounts we find in history books generally seem to be thoroughly value-impregnated.

The philosophical analysis of history, however, cannot simply note this as a fact. What must be asked is whether value judgments *necessarily* enter into historical inquiry. Historians themselves often argue that they do. Thus Carl Becker has stated categorically that "the historian cannot eliminate the personal equation" ("What Are Historical Facts?"). And Charles Beard has declared: "No amount of renunciation could have made Andrew D. White into a Frederick Jackson Turner, or either of them into a neutral mirror" ("That Noble Dream"). But what these so-called "relativists" among historians have in mind seems to be chiefly the psychological difficulty of eliminating bias or prejudice from historical conclusions, human nature being what it is. What the philosopher of history wants to know is whether value judgments enter into the very structure of historical inquiry—whether their elimination is *logically* possible, the idea of history being what it is. An affirmative answer to this question, of course, would completely undermine the observations of a Becker or a Beard. For if historians' value judgments are a consequence of the nature of their inquiry, it would make no sense for them even to try to be "neutral mirrors."

Rather surprisingly, it is philosophers, not historians defending the scientific status of their discipline, who have generally made the most confident assertions of the potential value-freedom of history. These assertions have come especially from philosophers whose objectivism might be categorized broadly as "positivistic," and who approach the analysis of historical work assuming the basic logical and conceptual unity of the natural and the social sciences. Representing the task of history as the application of scientific method to the problem of establishing and explaining past societal facts, they argue that there is no possible role in such inquiry for the value judgments of the historian. Dependent as he is upon an imperfect knowledge of human nature, an exercise of judgment will doubtless often be required of a historian in reaching conclusions about the past. But this judgment will take the form of an estimate of probability, not of value. If value judgments do enter into the historian's final account, they can only be regarded as an excrescence upon his work as inquiry. At best they represent an intrusion of literary interests into the presentation of historical findings; at worst, a descent into propaganda—not history itself, but only a certain use of it.

The case for a contrary view has frequently rested upon two arguments. The first centers on the claim that the detailed facts of history, unlike those of the natural sciences, are in themselves value-charged, so that no mere appeal to general principles of scientific method will warrant the conclusion that value judgments play no essential part in the historian's work. The second contends that even if the historian's basic facts are in themselves value-free, the selection that he makes from them when he constructs a history will necessarily be value-guided. As will appear below, there are reasons for doubting that the first of these arguments will bear the weight usually placed upon it. The second, however, which Maurice Mandelbaum, in *The Problem of Historical Knowledge*, has called "the fountain-head of relativism," requires more serious consideration. It directs attention to crucial and distinctive features of historical investigation.

A VALUE-CHARGED SUBJECT MATTER?

The first argument has been reiterated in Isaiah Berlin's *Historical Inevitability*. The historian, Berlin maintains, cannot escape "that minimum degree of moral or psychological evaluation which is necessarily involved in viewing human beings as creatures with purposes and motives (and not merely as causal factors in the procession of events)."

Two considerations are invoked to reinforce such a claim. The first is that if the historian attempts any such escape, the language of historical description will certainly frustrate his intention. For unlike sciences that are properly so called, history has contrived no technical vocabulary capable of evaluatively aseptic pronouncement. Historians use "ordinary language," the instrument of plain men and women seeking to communicate the total experience of their daily lives; and the most casual inspection shows this language to be far from purely descriptive. The second consideration is that the objects of historical study—religious persecutions, displays of military genius, political partisanship, and the like—cannot even be properly conceived of if we do not recognize them as partly value-constituted. To strain out the value judgments from the historian's account of them would thus amount to a refusal to depict things as they really are. Leo Strauss, in *Natural Right and History*, pursuing a similar line of argument, directs attention especially to the history of art. Simply by including reference to a certain item in a history of painting, Strauss remarks, the historian commits himself to an aesthetic judgment. He must hold, for example, that it is not "trash."

The basic positivist objection to all such argument is that we cannot evaluate what we do not independently know. As Mandelbaum put it, what is evaluated must first be known as "object." If this is so, then a historian who offers a value-charged report ought always to be able to specify those features of what occurred which justify his value judgment. And this specification—which would itself be value-free—could be interpreted as describing what happened "objectively." As for the linguistic difficulty, this is to be regarded as no more than a practical problem, although one which, if historians are concerned about the place of their discipline among the sciences, points the way to desirable methodological reform. Not that it would be a simple matter for historians to implement a decision to avoid all value-reference in their narratives. For historical accounts are even more evaluative than they sometimes appear; their judgments may often be covert, as when G. M. Trevelyan observes that England in the eighteenth century was "wanting in public organization" rather than saying, for example, that it was "free" of it. The philosophically interesting question, however, is not how difficult and far-reaching an "objectivist" reform of current practice would have to be. It is whether it would be consistent with the idea of history even to recommend it.

Relativists have sometimes objected that to achieve a completely value-free historical narrative it would be necessary (as Berlin puts it) to "deal with human beings purely as material objects in space." If this were so, then there would be a good case for saying that we could disallow the proposed reform of history on conceptual or logical grounds alone. For the subject matter of history is human actions. And since a physical movement is not such an action apart from its expressing some purpose of the agent, the historian's account must clearly go beyond sheer physical description.

But attributing purposes to agents surely does not require the historian's evaluation of the actions which express the purposes. It is true that what we sometimes have in mind when we raise questions about the "nature" of a historical action is the appropriateness of a value judgment. Felton's assault on Buckingham, we may say, was "murder"; that is what he *did*. But if we wished, we could surely restrict our attention to those aspects of what he did that could be subsumed under the value-neutral term "killing"; and in doing so, contrary to Berlin's contention, we should not cease to view the agent as "a creature with purposes and motives." Even the history of art does not seem to require a value judgment by the historian simply to bring its objects of study into view. Artistic trash is still presumably art, provided it has artistic intent. It can be distinguished from other kinds of trash.

THE PROBLEM OF SELECTION

The distinction between art and trash, however, could be interpreted as making a quite different point: that historical narratives, besides being concerned with past human actions of specifiable kinds, limit themselves also to what is important or significant within this range. This leads to the second relativist argument, which Beard states thus: "Every written history . . . is a selection and arrangement of facts . . . an act of choice, conviction and interpretation respecting values." Almost everyone would accept at least the first part of what Beard claims here. It is a commonplace of historical inquiry that a historian cannot include all he knows about his subject matter in his finished account. It is clear also that when faced with the

need to select, what he generally tells us is in fact what he judges to be important. It may appear less obvious, however, that the historian must do this, or fail to write history at all; that is, that it follows from the idea of history that he should do so. For it may appear logically possible, at least, that he should simply select at random, or in accordance with some personal whim.

Against this—and surely with plausibility—relativists generally contend that a historian who merely conjoined true statements about the past, or some object of study in it, would not be constructing "a history" at all as we ordinarily understand this term. But how do we understand it? An ambiguity in our ordinary use of "history" is of some interest in this connection. Historical theorists have often remarked on the confusions that may arise out of the term's being used to designate both the course of events and the historian's account of it. But there is another and quite different distinction implicit in ordinary usage. In one sense, "history" seems to include the total human past, so that everything we do, significant or not, "passes into history." In a more restricted but equally common sense, however, we should not say that an entirely insignificant action "made history." It is in this sense that "history" is confined by Marx to the history of class struggle, and Spengler describes the intervals between periodic cultural cycles as "historyless." Relativists will want to argue that it is history in such a quasi-evaluative sense that guides the construction of a historical narrative. As Jacques Barzun put it in "Cultural History: A Synthesis," the phrase "exist in history" can be translated "are memorable." That "memorability" is an indispensable ingredient in the idea of history the Father of History himself would seem to have agreed. It was one of the chief aims of his work, Herodotus wrote, to "preserve from decay the remembrance of what men have done," and to "prevent the great and wonderful actions of the Greeks and Barbarians from losing their due meed of glory."

The point is not that to write history it is necessary to make selections in accordance with the value scheme of Herodotus or of some other specifiable authority. It is rather that the offering of a narrative *as* a history carries with it the implication that an appropriate and responsible standard of importance has been applied. This has the crucial consequence that the historian's "account," the answer he gives to the historical question he sets himself, can be challenged not only on the ground that some of its statements are false, but also on the ground that some of them, although true, report the "wrong" truths.

To some extent the selection of the "right" truths is to be determined not by reference to a standard of historical importance but by reference to the specific question the historian proposes to answer. If he is writing a history of the Jeffersonian era in the United States, for example, he can probably neglect what went on in China at the time; if he is writing an economic history, he need not refer, say, to a religious revival unless he regards it as a condition of an economic development independently selected. Considerations of "scale" also legitimately enter into the decision as to what shall be included. But mere exclusions in accordance with such criteria do not leave history as a kind of residue; the selection of what is significant must still be made from what is not ruled out in such obvious ways. So seriously, in fact, is the selective task regarded by historians themselves that they are often prepared to extend the very notion of historical truth beyond appraisals of a narrative's constituent assertions to appraisals of the choice of assertions made. And so are their readers. Would a history of Victorian England, for example, that neglected to mention the working-class movement be accepted as presenting a "true picture"? Or a history of Nazi Germany that completely ignored the mass murder of the Jews? Macaulay may be dated as a historian; but as a theorist of the discipline he still throws light on the idea of history. In his article "History" (1828) he wrote: "He who is deficient in the art of selection may, by showing nothing but the truth, produce all the effects of the grossest falsehood."

If the idea of history is the idea of an account, not just of the past, but of what is judged significant in the past, perhaps something further ought to be said about the first relativist argument, previously considered and dismissed. For if the justification of including each action or event in a historical narrative requires a judgment of relative importance, then, as Strauss held, although not quite for the reason he gave, the historian cannot avoid considering his subject matter evaluatively. And if the reason a certain action finds a place in the historian's account is that it was, say, a murder rather than mere killing, then it is surely reasonable to expect his language to show this, as Berlin said it should. The suggestion that historiography would somehow be improved—made more "scientific"—if only its evaluative content could be eliminated thus seems to rest on a misconception. At any rate, if "constructing a history" is at least part of the historian's proper task, it is plain that the elimination of value judgments from historical *language* would do nothing to eliminate them from historical inquiry.

What has been said, however, in qualified support of the argument from selection has made a large assumption: that the determination of the historical *importance* of a human action may require a moral, aesthetic, or some other kind of value judgment on the part of the historian. In fact, this is an assumption that many historical objectivists would question. Although granting the historian his obligation to select what is important, they would hold that, in the context of historical inquiry, "importance" is a causal notion. The "placing" of an event or action thus requires reference not to the historian's standard of evaluation but to causal connections with other events or actions. As Morton White put it in "Toward an Analytic Philosophy of History," the criterion of historical importance is "causal fertility," not moral and aesthetic considerations. Two lines of argument sketched below tend to bring into question the adequacy of any such attempt to show the dispensability of value judgments in historical selection. The first involves the denial that all history is explanatory in intent, the antirelativist case being much less plausible for descriptive than for explanatory history. The second draws attention to the role value judgments characteristically play in causal diagnosis itself.

Evaluation in descriptive history. By "explanatory" history is not meant history that only explains and never describes anything; it is rather history whose principle of organization arises out of aiming chiefly to answer the question, "Why or how did such-and-such happen or come to happen?" Similarly, by descriptive history is not meant history that contains no explanations, but rather history that aims chiefly to show within certain limits "what happened." Cecil Woodham-Smith's *The Reason Why*, which probes the circumstances of the charge of the Light Brigade, would be explanatory in our sense; G. M. Young's *Victorian England*, which offers a "portrait" of the age, would be descriptive. The distinction finds expression in the declaration of H. E. Barnes, in his *History of Historical Writing* (Norman, Okla., 1937), that the historian's responsibility is twofold: to "trace the genesis of contemporary culture and institutions," and to "reconstruct as a totality the civilizations of the leading eras of the past."

Even in the case of explanatory histories, it has appeared questionable to some philosophers that causal connection is the organizing principle of the narrative. A theory of historical explanation like that of Michael Oakeshott in *Experience and Its Modes* (Cambridge, 1933), for example, explicitly repudiates causality as a category of historical thinking, holding that the only explanation appropriate or possible in history is "a complete account of change. . . . in which no *lacuna* is tolerated" (p. 143). But even if all explanatory histories were causal—the selection of their every item being determined by the judgment that it formed a necessary link in a causal chain that culminates in some event or condition to be explained—there appears to be no parallel to this in the case of descriptive histories. Even in the latter, of course, events are often judged to be important because of what they lead to; but this is not the only principle of selection in them. In a history of Victorian England, for example, reference may well be made to the working-class movement because of its influence on the eventual development of the Liberal party; but its claim to be included may equally rest on its intrinsic interest as a powerful human response to industrialism. In a history of modern Germany, reference may similarly be made to the mass murder of Jews because of its effect on the outlook of the subsequently created Federal Republic; but even if it had had no effect, its intrinsic importance as an erruption of the demonic into twentieth-century life could hardly be ignored. Methodologists of history have often argued that all selection should be "relative to a problem"—as if this would insure the extrusion of such considerations. But part of the problem in descriptive history is to find out what is "memorable." And this is not necessarily a matter of discerning "causal fertility."

The claim that judgments of intrinsic, as well as instrumental, importance are required for the construction of a history is perhaps at its most plausible for the kind of descriptive history exemplified by Carlton Hayes's *A Generation of Materialism*, which offers a general survey of European history in the last quarter of the nineteenth century. The contrast is with a "theme" history like G. M. Trevelyan's *The English Revolution*, whose problem of selection is simplified, and to a degree "objectified," by its having a specified subject to characterize. Hayes's title may, of course, arouse the expectation that, like Trevelyan's, his work also has a theme: the "materialism" of the last generation of the century. In fact the title does not declare the subject of Hayes's inquiry, but formulates in briefest compass his conclusions about it. Unlike Trevelyan, he set himself the historical task not of describing something that stands out antecedently as a unity but of making clear the "main movements" within his period—whatever they may have been. It is true that he looked for (and found) unity in what he judged to be intrinsically important in the experience of the selected generation. But if he had found instead that it lacked such unity, he would in no way have disqualified himself from writing its history, although he might have had to take as a title something more like "Europe in the Late Nineteenth Century."

Given Hayes's problem, there is nothing for causally oriented selection to do until prior selections on grounds of intrinsic importance have been made. It might be added that if we accept the view of Henri Pirenne, in "What Are Historians Trying to Do?," that all histories are to be conceived as contributions to universal history, then period history must be judged a more fundamental type than theme history. For universal history is the ultimate case of period history.

Evaluation in causal analysis. One way of evading the conclusions of the argument is to deny the legitimacy, or even the possibility, of descriptive history. Something close to this appears to be implied by the oft-quoted dictum of John Dewey: "There is no history except in terms of movement toward some outcome. . . . The selection of outcome . . . determines the selection and organization of subject matter" (*Logic: The Theory of Inquiry*). Taken in support of the causal interpretation of importance, such a claim converts any apparently descriptive history into a covertly explanatory one.

Yet insofar as what explanatory history seeks is the causes of historical events, it may be doubted that even this is value-free in nature. For as philosophers like R. G. Collingwood and, more recently, H. L. A. Hart and A. M. Honoré (in *Causation in the Law*, Oxford, 1959) have emphasized, causal diagnosis is not simply a matter of determining a set of sufficient conditions for an event or action to be explained. The determination of cause requires the contrast of one or a few members of such a set with others that themselves lack causal status, even though they may be equally necessary for what ensued. Although relevant to the complete explanation of what occurred, the latter are regarded as "mere" conditions, a background against which the cause operates. No theory of how the necessity or sufficiency of the various explanatory factors can be objectively established—for example, by appeal to suitable empirical laws—will shed light on the criterion to be employed in singling out the specifically causal conditions. If we ask on what principle these conditions are actually selected in historical inquiry, we find value judgments characteristically playing an essential role.

Ample support for such a contention can be found in the kinds of disagreements historians often express about the causes of controversial events. The historiography of the American Civil War provides a case in point. Doubtless some of the disagreements historians have had about the causes of that event can be traced to differences in inductive judgments: differences about what the necessary conditions of the war actually were. Some may be traced

also to sheer confusion—the failure, for example, to specify exactly what was to be explained: the antagonism between the two sides, the outbreak of actual fighting, the outbreak at a precise time, and so on. But through more than a century of controversy there has always been a considerable overlap in the explanatory conditions cited by historians who do not seem to be talking at cross-purposes in any of these ways, yet differ vigorously on the conditions that properly constituted the cause.

Thus in the earliest period historians tended to split along sectional lines. Southerners, although agreeing that the resistance of the South to what was regarded as Northern aggression was one of the necessary conditions of the outbreak, nevertheless thought it obvious that the aggression, rather than the resistance, should be selected as cause. Northern historians, by contrast, selected what they regarded as Southern intransigence, although they were willing to concede that this intransigence was simply one of the many conditions without which war would not have occurred. The causal judgments of both were clearly guided by conceptions of what is reasonable and what is reprehensible in the behavior of the men of the two sides.

Following the first partisan outburst, historians generally recoiled from seeming to blame one side or the other, and sought objectivity and agreement by designating various social and economic conditions as the cause of the war. In the simplest case this was taken to be the unfortunate existence of the slave system itself. Seeking to avoid partisanship, these historians shifted the blame away from the protagonists altogether; and by blaming the predicament, as it were, rather than the protagonists' various responses to it, provided themselves with a causal conclusion.

That selection of causes really does involve an exercise of moral judgment on the historian's part may perhaps appear questionable to some philosophers. It was evident enough, however, to a third school of Civil War interpreters, the so-called revisionists. These historians, who arose shortly after World War I, tended to find the cause of the war in the actions of Northern and Southern extremists: shortsighted politicians, overzealous editors, and irresponsible agitators. Revisionist historians often make it quite plain that what they are challenging is the moral insensitivity of their predecessors; they are reasserting human responsibility for what occurred. To the revisionists the war appeared to be a "needless" evil; it could have been avoided and should have been. Because it nevertheless took place, its causes are to be sought in the actions of those who failed to prevent it.

The point of immediate philosophical interest is not that the moral judgments of any of these groups of historians are right or wrong. It is rather that none of them was able to reach a causal conclusion without *making* a value judgment; in these particular cases, a moral judgment. That causal inquiry, where human actions are involved, is linked to the task of assigning responsibility and blame is, of course, a perfectly familiar notion. But it is usually assumed that the causal question is logically prior to the moral one. In the cases just cited, it is quite otherwise: The causal diagnosis depends upon the value judgment, and incorporates it. The rationale for this conceptual state of affairs can be no more than suggested in the present compass. At least partly it is to be sought in the basic notion of a cause as that which "forces" or "makes" things happen, the notion of being "forced," when applied to human actions, bearing a sense that makes relevant such questions as the reasonableness of regarding one man's action as a threat to the legitimate interests of another. Who forced whom to act, in historical as well as everyday contexts, is a question that often cannot be decided without reference to appropriate standards of conduct. The historian's concept of cause, in other words, is a humanistic, not a physical, one.

What has been emphasized in this account is ways in which value judgments enter the historian's work, not casually or gratuitously (although they often in fact do so), but structurally and functionally. Value judgments enter history, it might be said, because the historian's conceptual scheme, and the questions he consequently asks, require them to be made. Whether history is nevertheless to be called a science is not a matter of great moment. What matters is that preconceptions about how a science must proceed, together with a desire to award this honorific title to historical work, not be allowed to lead to the philosophical misdescription of history. To suggest that value judgment is a literary excrescence upon historical inquiry proper, something superimposed upon answers given to genuinely historical questions, comes dangerously close to this. Not all the problems of "literary" history are literary, if by this is meant problems concerning the presentation of results. But neither are all nonliterary problems "scientific" in a sense that excludes the historian's value judgments.

Bibliography

For denials of the value-free nature of history by contemporary philosophers, see W. H. Walsh, "The Limits of Scientific History," in *Historical Studies III*, James Hogan, ed. (London, 1961); Peter Winch, *The Idea of a Social Science* (London, 1958); Leo Strauss, *Natural Right and History* (Chicago, 1953); Isaiah Berlin, "The Concept of Scientific History," in *History and Theory*, Vol. 1, No. 1 (1960), 1–31, and Berlin's *Historical Inevitability* (Oxford, 1954).

For a contrary view see Ernest Nagel, "Some Issues in the Logic of Historical Analysis," *Scientific Monthly*, Vol. 74 (March 1952), 162–169; A. O. Lovejoy, "Present Standpoints and Past History," *Journal of Philosophy*, Vol. 36 (1939) 477–489; J. H. Randall, Jr., *Nature and Historical Experience* (New York, 1958); Maurice Mandelbaum, *The Problem of Historical Knowledge* (New York, 1938). The Mandelbaum work offers a historical survey of the relativist view, with bibliographic references to the more important works by continental philosophers.

Useful works by historians are Herbert Butterfield, *The Whig Interpretation of History* (London, 1931); C. A. Beard, "That Noble Dream," in *American Historical Review*, Vol. 41 (1935), 74–87; G. M. Trevelyan, "Bias in History," in *An Autobiography and Other Essays* (London, 1949), pp. 68–81; Carl Becker, "What Are Historical Facts?," *Western Political Quarterly*, Vol. 8 (1955), 327–340; Jacques Barzun, "Cultural History: A Synthesis," in *The Varieties of History*, Fritz Stern, ed. (New York, 1956), pp. 387–402; Thomas Macaulay, "History," reprinted in Stern, *op. cit.*, pp. 72–89. Henri Pirenne, "What Are Historians Trying to Do?," in *Methods in Social Science*, S. A. Rice, ed. (Chicago, 1931), pp. 435–445.

W. H. DRAY

HOBART, R. E. See MILLER, DICKINSON S.

HOBBES, THOMAS (1588–1679), often called the father of modern analytic philosophy, was born in Malmesbury, Wiltshire, England. Hobbes later enjoyed jesting about the significance of his manner of entry into the world. (He was born prematurely when his mother heard of the approach of the Spanish Armada.) "Fear and I were born twins," he would say, adding color to his conviction that the fear of death and the need for security are the psychological foundations both of worldly prudence and of civilization itself. He died at the age of 91 in Hardwick, Derbyshire, after a life of travel, study, polemical controversy, and philosophical and literary activity that in his later years had virtually established him as an English institution.

Early years. Hobbes's father, Thomas Hobbes, was vicar of Westport, an adjunct of Malmesbury, but his conduct reflected little credit on his cloth. After being involved in a brawl outside his own church, he had to flee to London, leaving Thomas to be brought up by a wealthy uncle, who took the matter of his education very seriously. When he was only 14, Hobbes was sent to Magdalen Hall, Oxford, where he remained for five years before taking his bachelor's degree. He seems to have been bored by his Aristotelian tutors, although he acquired considerable proficiency in logic. The strong Puritan tradition of his college impressed Hobbes, but the drunkenness, gaming, and other vices that were prevalent equally impressed him. On leaving Oxford in 1608, Hobbes had the good fortune to become tutor to the young son of William Cavendish, earl of Devonshire. This circumstance introduced him to influential people, to a first-class library, and to foreign travel.

In 1610, on the first of Hobbes's visits to the Continent, he discovered the disrepute into which the Aristotelian system of thought was beginning to fall. Kepler had recently published his *Astronomia Nova*, and Galileo had just discovered the satellites of Jupiter through his telescope. Hobbes returned to England determined to devote himself to the pursuit of learning, a resolve that was probably strengthened by his meetings with Francis Bacon. Hobbes, however, thought little of Bacon's so-called method of induction, with its stress on observation and experiment, which was later to become the inspiration of the Royal Society. Nevertheless, he agreed with Bacon in his contempt for Aristotelianism, in his conviction that knowledge means power to be used for the improvement of man's estate, and in his advocacy of clear and concrete speech instead of the vague abstractions of the schools.

At this period of his life Hobbes had turned to the classics to gain an understanding of life and of philosophy, which, he thought, could not be found in the schools. After a period of reading and reflection, he decided to translate Thucydides into English, a significant choice. Like Thucydides, Hobbes believed that history was written for instruction, and he wished to instruct his countrymen on the dangers of democracy. In 1628, when Hobbes published his translation, Charles I had been on the throne for three years and was already at loggerheads with Sir John Eliot and John Pym. Hobbes's translation was the first of his many attempts to bring his countrymen to their senses and to make them aware of the tragedy that they courted: that of civil war, from which proceed "slaughter, solitude, and the want of all things."

Philosophical awakening. It was not until the time of his second journey to the Continent that Hobbes's career as a philosopher began. His patron had died, and as a temporary economy, Catherine, the countess of Devonshire, had dispensed with Hobbes's services. Hobbes took similar employment with Sir Gervase Clinton and, in 1629, accompanied Clinton's son on a journey to the Continent. There Hobbes developed a passionate interest in geometry, which impressed him as a method for reaching indubitable conclusions. Could not his convictions about the dangers of democracy be demonstrated? Could not his opinions about man, gleaned from his observation of the contemporary scene, from his insight into his own nature, and from his perusal of the pages of Thucydides and Machiavelli, be postulated as axioms from which theorems about the conditions of a commonwealth might be generated?

Hobbes's discovery of geometry gave him a method of analysis and a conception of scientific method, but he still lacked a conceptual scheme to give content to his demonstrations about man and society. In Paris, during his third journey to the Continent (1634–1637), again in the service of the Devonshires as tutor to William, the succeeding earl, he became a member of the intellectual circle of the Abbé Mersenne, who patronized Descartes and Gassendi. (Gassendi later became one of Hobbes's firmest friends.) Hobbes also made a pilgrimage to Italy in 1636 to visit Galileo, the leading exponent of the new natural philosophy. By the time of his return to England in 1637, he had conceived, perhaps at Galileo's suggestion, the main outlines of his philosophical system, in which the method of geometry and the concepts of the new science of motion were to be applied to man in society.

It is a mistake to think of Hobbes's interests as purely political. Hobbes claimed originality for his optics as well as for his civil philosophy, and at some point between his discovery of geometry and his return from his third journey to the Continent, he wrote his first philosophical work, the *Little Treatise*, in geometrical form, in which he sketched an explanation of sensation in terms of the new science of motion. His interest in sensation, according to his prose autobiography, arose from an encounter with some learned men who were discussing the cause of sensation. One of them asked derisively what sensation was, and Hobbes was astonished to find that none of them could say. From then on, he was haunted by the problem of the nature and cause of sense. He began to think he was near an explanation after it struck him that if bodies were always at rest or always moved at a constant rate, the ability to make discriminations would vanish, and with it all sensation. He concluded that the cause of everything, including that of sensation itself, must be in variations of motion.

In his verse autobiography, Hobbes graphically related how, on his third journey, he was obsessed by the omnipresence of motion. He was acclimating himself to Galileo's audacious suggestion that motion is the natural state of bodies and that they continue in motion to infinity unless they are impeded. This went against the crude evidence of the senses as well as against the established Aristotelian world view, in which rest was regarded as the natural state. But if Galileo's supposition could be entertained, Hobbes thought, even apparition itself could be explained as a meeting place of motions, and from Galileo's law of inertia the phenomena of sense and imagination could be deduced.

The state of turmoil in England on his return drove Hobbes to make his first systematic attempt to employ his geometrical approach and mechanistic psychology to present the realities beneath the appearances of the contemporary issues. His *Elements of Law*, circulated in 1640 in manuscript form during the session of Parliament, was the result. This work, which demonstrated the need for undivided sovereignty, was published in 1650 in two parts, *Human Nature* and *De Corpore Politico*. However, its arguments were taken from general principles of psychology and ethics, rather than from appeals to divine right. Many regard Hobbes's *Human Nature* as one of his best works. It consists largely of traditional psychology coordinated and underpinned by the conceptual scheme he had learned from Galileo.

Exile in France. Hobbes claimed later that his life would have been in danger because of the views expressed in *Elements of Law*, had not the king dissolved Parliament in May 1640. Six months later, when the Long Parliament impeached Thomas Wentworth, earl of Strafford, Hobbes fled to the Continent in fear for his life, later priding himself on being "the first of all that fled." A warm welcome awaited him in Mersenne's circle, and he settled down in Paris to his most productive philosophical period.

His first work was the composition of some 16 objections to Descartes's *Meditations*, which Mersenne submitted to Descartes in advance of its publication. This led to a rather acrimonious exchange between Descartes and Hobbes. In 1642 Hobbes published his *De Cive*, an expanded version in Latin of Part 2 of his *Elements of Law* (later to appear as *De Corpore Politico*). The additional sections dealt largely with a more detailed treatment of the relationship between the church and the civil power. During the period from 1642 to 1646, Hobbes published his *Minute or First Draught of the Optiques*, which he considered one of his most important and original works. He also started work on his most ambitious scheme—the construction of a trilogy on body, man, and citizen, in which everything in the world of nature and man was to be included in a conceptual scheme provided by the new science of mechanics. Hobbes made a beginning with *De Corpore*, which was to be the first work in the trilogy.

In 1646, however, political events again interfered with Hobbes's more abstract speculations. He was on the verge of accepting an invitation to retire in peace to a friend's house in Languedoc, in the south of France, when he was requested to act as tutor in mathematics to the future Charles II, who had just fled to Paris. Hobbes's tutorship, however, was interrupted, if not terminated, by a severe illness in 1647. He recovered after having consented to receive the sacrament on what he took to be his deathbed, and he was drawn again into political controversy by the presence of so many Royalist *émigrés*. A second edition of *De Cive* was published in 1647, but this was in Latin and had only a limited circulation. Hobbes therefore decided to blazon abroad his views on man and citizen for all to read, in English, with the arresting title of *Leviathan*. With Mersenne's unfortunate death in 1648, Hobbes began to feel increasingly isolated, for he was suspected of atheism and was an outspoken enemy of the Catholic church.

Political events in England provided a fitting prelude to the publication of *Leviathan*. Charles I was executed in 1649 and, until 1653, when Cromwell was made Protector, there was constant discussion and experimentation to find an appropriate form of government. *Leviathan*, published in 1651, was therefore very topical. It came out strongly in favor of absolute and undivided sovereignty, without the usual arguments from divine right. Indeed, Hobbes conceded popular representation but, by an ingenious twisting of the social contract theory, showed that it logically implied the acceptance of undivided sovereignty.

Return to England. Hobbes returned to England in 1651 after a severe illness and soon became embroiled in a heated debate with John Bramhall, bishop of Derry, Ulster, on the subject of free will. In 1645, in Paris, Hobbes had discussed the problem of free will with the bishop, and they both wrote their views on the matter soon afterward. A young disciple of Hobbes published his contribution in 1654, without Hobbes's consent, under the title *Of Liberty and Necessity*. Bramhall was understandably indignant and, in 1655, he published the whole controversy under the title *A Defence of True Liberty from Antecedent and Extrinsical Necessity*. In 1656 Hobbes replied by printing Bramhall's book, together with his own observations on it, which he called *The Questions Concerning Liberty, Necessity, and Chance*. Bramhall replied in 1658 with *Castigations of Hobbes his Last Animadversions*, which carried an appendix called "The Catching of Leviathan the Great Whale." Bramhall died in 1663, and Hobbes had the last word a few years later.

There was another controversy in which Hobbes was caught up for the major part of the twenty years that were left to him. This one involved John Wallis, professor of geometry at Oxford, who mercilessly exposed Hobbes's attempt in *De Corpore* (1665) to square the circle—not then such a ridiculous enterprise as it now seems—and Seth Ward, professor of astronomy, who launched a polemic against Hobbes's general philosophy. These two men were members of the "invisible college" that the king had recognized as the Royal Society in 1663. They were Puritans in religion and Baconians in their approach to science. Hobbes had annoyed them not simply by his attack on their religion and his contempt for the method of induction, but also by his diatribes on the universities as hotbeds of vice and sedition. Hobbes replied to their published criticisms with an emended English version of *De Corpore* with "Six Lessons" appended for Wallis. This was in turn attacked by Wallis, and the controversy dragged on for many years, often descending into personal vituperation on both sides.

Not all of Hobbes's remaining years, however, were spent on this abortive controversy. *De Homine*, the second part of his trilogy, was published in 1657. This dealt with optics and human nature, matters on which Hobbes's opinions were already well known; accordingly, it attracted little attention and was not translated.

After the Restoration, Hobbes was granted a pension and "free accesse to his Majesty, who was always much delighted in his witt and smart repartees" (John Aubrey, *Brief Lives*, pp. 152–153). Only once again did he fear for his life. After the Great Plague (1665) and the Great Fire of London (1666), some reason was sought for God's displeasure, and a spasm of witch-hunting shook Parliament. A bill was passed by Parliament for the suppression of atheism, and a committee was set up to investigate *Leviathan*. The matter was eventually dropped, probably through the king's intervention, but Hobbes was forbidden to publish his opinions thereafter.

In 1668 Hobbes finished his *Behemoth*—a history of the period from 1640 to 1660, interpreted in the light of his beliefs about man and society. He submitted it to King Charles, who advised against its publication (it was published posthumously in 1682).

Even at this advanced age Hobbes was still capable of exerting himself both physically (he played tennis until he was 75) and philosophically. John Aubrey, later his biographer, sent him Bacon's *Elements of Common Law* for his comments; and Hobbes, after protesting his age, managed to produce his unfinished *Dialogue between a Philosopher and a Student of the Common Laws of England* (published posthumously in 1681). This minor work was interesting in that Hobbes anticipated in it the analytical school of jurisprudence of the nineteenth century and came out unequivocally in favor of what has been called the command theory of law. At the age of 84 Hobbes wrote his autobiography in Latin verse after completing one in prose. At 86, for want of something better to do, he published a verse translation of the *Iliad* and the *Odyssey*.

LOGIC AND METHODOLOGY

Hobbes lived during the emergence of men who challenged not only traditional tenets about political and religious authority but also the wisdom of the past, especially that of Aristotle. Men were exhorted to find out things for themselves, to consult their own consciences, and to communicate with God directly, instead of through the established religious hierarchy. It was widely believed that all men have the gift of reason but that they make poor use of it through lack of a proper method. Books such as Bacon's *Novum Organum*, Descartes's *Regulae* and *Discourse on Method*, and Spinoza's *Ethics* were written to remedy this defect. Thus, Hobbes was not exceptional in believing that knowledge, which meant power, could be obtained only by adopting a certain kind of method.

According to Hobbes, the knowledge whereby most men live is the knowledge gleaned from experience, culminating in prudence and history—"the register of knowledge of fact." Hobbes described experience as "nothing but remembrance of what antecedents have been followed by what consequents." Bacon had tried to set out this sort of knowledge explicitly in his *Novum Organum*, and it was taken by the Royal Society to be the paradigm of science.

Doctrine of names. Hobbes, however, was very contemptuous of such grubbing around and peering at nature, not only in natural philosophy but also in civil philosophy. Had Galileo or Harvey, the pioneers of the new philosophy, made a laborious summary of their experience? And in civil philosophy, what store is to be placed on the dreary saws of practical politicians or the ossified ignorance and superstitions of the common lawyers? Mere prudence, which is the product of experience, should not be mistaken for wisdom. Wisdom is the product of reason, which alone gives knowledge of "general, eternal, and immutable truths," as in geometry.

In geometry, definitions are of paramount importance. Therefore, claimed Hobbes: "The only way to know is by definition." Thus, science is "knowledge of all the consequences of names appertaining to the subject in hand." It gives knowledge not of the nature of things but of the names of things. We start with certain terms or names about whose definition we agree. We connect these into such statements as "A man is a rational, animated body," just as we add items in an account. We then find that if we follow certain methods of combining the statements so created, conclusions can be drawn that are contained in the premises but of which we were ignorant before we started reckoning. "For REASON, in this sense, is nothing but reckoning, that is adding and subtracting, of the consequences of general names agreed upon for the marking and signifying of our thoughts."

Obvious objections to such an account of scientific knowledge immediately come to mind. How, for instance, can we be sure that such a train of reasoning applies to anything? How are the meanings of Hobbes's names fixed, and how are the rules for their combinations determined?

Hobbes supposed that "names are signs not of things, but of our cogitations." Words are not the only things that can be signs; for instance, a heavy cloud can be a sign of rain. This means that from the cloud we can infer rain. This is an example of a natural sign; other examples are animal warnings of danger and summonses to food. These natural signs are to be distinguished from language proper, which consists of sounds, marks, and other such significations determined—as are the ruler of civil society—by decision. Animal noises come about by necessity, not by decision, as human speech does. That is why, on Hobbes's view, animals, though capable of imagery, cannot reason; for reasoning presupposes words with meanings fixed by decision.

Hobbes thought that every man has his own private world of phantasms or conceptions, for which words are signs that function for him like a private system of mnemonics. These words act as signs to others of what a man thinks and feels. Although some words signify conceptions, they are not names of conceptions; for Hobbes seemed to use the word "name" for the relation of reference between names and things, and words like "signify" for the relationship between particular occurrences of a name and the idea in a person's mind. Some names are names of things themselves, such as "a man," "a tree," or "a stone," whereas others, such as "future," do not stand for or name things that as yet have any being. Such words signify the knitting together of things past and things present. In a similar way there are names, such as "impossible" and "nothing," that are not names of anything. Such names are signs of our conceptions, but they name or stand for "things" that do not exist.

Hobbes's doctrine was not altogether clear. He seemed to mean that all names serve as mnemonics to us of our conceptions and as signs to others of what we have in mind, but that only some names actually denote things in a strict sense. This leads to the distinctions that Hobbes introduced in relation to the logical function of names. Names can be either concrete or abstract. Concrete names can denote bodies, their accidents, or their names. Abstract names come into being only with propositions and denote "the cause of concrete names."

Universals. There are two classes of concrete names: proper names and universal names. A proper name, such as "Peter," is singular to one thing only; a universal name, such as "man," denotes each member of a class of things. A universal name, "though but one name, is nevertheless the name of diverse particular things; in respect of which together, it is called a universal; there being nothing in the world universal but names; for the things named are every one of them individual and singular."

Hobbes's doctrine of universal names was crucial to his attack on the scholastic belief in essences. The world, Hobbes maintained, contains no such essences for universal names to designate. "Universal" is the name of a class of names, not of a diaphanous type of entity designated by a name. The error of those who believe in essences derives from their tendency to treat a universal name as if it were a peculiar kind of proper name. It is the *use* of a name that makes it universal, not the status of the thing that the name designates.

Hobbes's doctrine of abstract names was more obscure but of cardinal importance in his account of scientific knowledge. Abstract names come into being when names are joined in propositions. A proposition is "a speech consisting of two names copulated, by which he that speaketh signifieth the latter name to be the name of the same thing whereof the former is the name." For instance, in saying "man is a living creature," the speaker conceives "living creature" and "man" to be names of the same thing, the name "man" being comprehended by the name "living creature." This relation of "comprehension" can be brought out in some languages by the order of words without employing the verb "to be." The copulation of the two names "makes us think of the cause for which these names were imposed on that thing," and this search for the causes of names gives rise to such abstract names as "corporeity," "motion," "figure," "quantity," and "likeness." But these denote only the *causes* of concrete names and not the things themselves. For instance, we see something that is extended and fills space, and we call it by the concrete name "body." The cause of the concrete name is that the thing is extended, "or the extension or corporeity of it." These causes are the same as the causes of our conceptions, "namely, some power of action, or affection of the thing conceived, which some call the manner by which anything works upon our senses, but by most men they are called accidents." Accidents are neither the things themselves nor parts of them, but "do nevertheless accompany the things in such manner, that (saving extension) they may all perish, and be destroyed, but can never be abstracted." Among such accidents some are of particular importance for science, those which Hobbes sometimes referred to as "universal things" or "such accidents as are common to all bodies." These are the abstract concepts by means of which a theory is developed about the underlying structure of nature. The endeavor of the scientist is to understand, by means of the resoluto-compositive method of Galilean mechanics, the universal cause—motion—without knowledge of which such fundamental theories could not be developed.

Misuses of words. Hobbes has often been called the precursor of modern analytical philosophy because he was particularly sensitive to the manner in which ridiculous (and dangerous) doctrines can be generated through confusion about how words have meaning. One class of absurdities is generated by failure to understand the different ways in which the copula "is" can function. Such terms as essence, reality, and quiddity, beloved by the schools, "could never have been heard among such nations as do not copulate their names by the verb 'is,' but by adjective verbs as runneth, readeth . . . ." The word "is" in a proposition such as "Man is a living body" has the function of "comprehension" or class inclusion. Something of the form "If x is a man, then x is a living body" is being stated. There is no commitment to the existence of men that is implied when "is" occurs in such statements as "Here is Thomas Hobbes."

Absurdities also arise if names of accidents are assimilated to names of bodies. For instance, those who say that faith is "infused" or "inspired" into a person treat faith as if it were the name of a body, for only bodies can be poured or breathed into anything. An accident is not in a body in the same sort of way that a body can be in a body—"as if, for example, redness were in blood, in the same manner, as blood is in a bloody cloth." Hobbes was also eloquent on the subject of names that name nothing.

Scientific truth. Hobbes's theory of scientific truth was not altogether consistent. He started with the important insight that "true" and "false" are attributes of speech, not of things. Truth, then, "consisteth in the right ordering of names in our affirmations." It characterizes propositions in which names of limited generality are "comprehended" by those of wider generality: for example, "Charity is a virtue." Hobbes held, it therefore seems, that all true propositions are analytically true, which is a plausible enough view if only geometrical truths are at issue. But Hobbes often spoke as if all truth must conform to this model. He saw that this raises the question of how the initial definitions are to be fixed, and about these definitions he often seemed to take a conventionist view by suggesting that "truth therefore depends upon the compacts and consents of men." He often linked the contract theory of the origin of civil society with a theory about agreement on definitions. When he was speaking about natural science, however, his position was not so clearly conventionist. The difference was caused by his assumption that men construct states just as they construct circles or triangles. But since they do not construct natural bodies in the same way, the problem therefore arises as to how Hobbes thought

that propositions of natural science, which did not come into being through decisions of men, say what is true about the natural world.

Hobbes thought that all the propositions of natural science are deductions from the basic theory of motion, in which there are primary propositions containing such simple unanalyzable concepts as motion, extension, and straightness. These are "well enough defined, when, by speech as short as may be, we raise in the mind of the hearer perfect and clear ideas of the thing named" (*De Corpore*). Such conceptions are featured in Hobbes's account of evidence, which is "the concomitance of a man's *conception* with the *words* that signify such conception in the act of ratiocination" (*Human Nature*). A parrot could speak truth but could not know it, for it would lack the conceptions that accompany the speaking of truth by a man who knows truth. "Evidence is to truth, as the sap to the tree . . . for this evidence, which is meaning with our words, is the life of truth. Knowledge thereof, which we call *science*, I define to be *evidence of truth*, from some beginning or principle of *sense* . . . ."

Conceptions, in Hobbes's view, are explained causally in terms of motions that arise in the head and persist after the stimulation of sense organs by external bodies. Names, which are joined together in true propositions, are signs of these conceptions in that they mark them for the individual and enable other people to make inferences about what he thinks. Thus, Hobbes must have thought that when a man knows (as distinct from when he merely speaks) what is true, his conceptions, as it were, keep pace with what he is saying. Some of these conceptions, those involved in understanding primary propositions, are clear and distinct ideas of things named. Thus, scientific systems are somehow anchored to the world of nature by means of names that refer to attributes of bodies of which we have a clear and distinct idea.

This theory resembles, in certain respects, the self-evidence theory of the Cartesians. However, it seems inconsistent with the conventionalism of Hobbes's other remarks about basic definitions and is a very confused account in itself, not very helpful in elucidating what makes scientific propositions true. In the empirical sciences the clarity of the ideas in the initial postulates is neither here nor there. What matters is whether statements deduced from them can be observationally confirmed.

Scientific inquiry. The ambiguity in Hobbes's account of truth is paralleled by the ambiguity in his account of scientific method, which he equated with the search for causes. One of his most famous definitions of philosophy or scientific knowledge (he did not distinguish between the two) occurs at the start of *De Corpore* (Molesworth ed.): "PHILOSOPHY is such knowledge of effects or appearances, as we acquire by true ratiocination from the knowledge we have first of their causes or generation: And again, of such causes or generations as may be from knowing first their effects." By "cause" Hobbes meant, of course, antecedent motion, and he was unusual in thinking that even geometrical figures are to be explained in terms of motion because of the movements involved in constructing them.

Hobbes's distinction between these two forms of philosophical knowledge is important. In the case of acquiring knowledge of effects from knowledge of causes or generation, his conventionist account of truth holds good. For instance, in the case of deciding that a figure must be a circle from our knowledge of the motions from which it was produced, "the truth of the first principles of our ratiocination, namely definitions, is made and constituted by ourselves, whilst we consent and agree upon the appellation of things." He used this method in *De Corpore* to explain parallel lines, refraction and reflection, circular and other forms of motion, angles, and similar concepts. It also seems that he had this model in mind when he thought about the generation of the artificial machine of the commonwealth.

When dealing with knowledge of causes from effects, however, Hobbes's account is far less clear-cut and conventionist. At the beginning of Part 4 of *De Corpore*, for instance, he said: "The principles, therefore, upon which the following discourse depends, are not such as we ourselves make and pronounce in general terms, as definitions: but such, as being placed in the things themselves by the Author of Nature, are by us observed in them . . . ." The explanations that we give in the natural sciences may be true, but it is impossible to demonstrate that they are necessarily true, for the phenomena are not generated by human contrivance, as are the phenomena of geometry and politics.

The method on which Hobbes was relying in both these types of scientific inquiry was, of course, the resoluto-compositive method of Galilean mechanics. In this method a typical phenomenon, such as the rolling of a stone down a slope, was taken. Such properties as color and smell, which were regarded as scientifically irrelevant, were disregarded, and the situation was resolved into simple elements that could be quantified—the length and angle of the slope, the weight of the stone, the time the stone takes to fall. The mathematical relations disclosed were then manipulated until functional relations between the variables were established. The situation was then synthesized or "composed" in a rational structure of mathematical relations. This is what Hobbes called analysis—the search for causes, given the effects. "Synthesis" consisted in starting from the known causes and deducing effects from them. In Galileo's hands this method was highly successful because he tested such deductions by observation. In Hobbes's hands the method was not so fruitful because it always remained an imaginary experiment.

Similar ambiguities in Hobbes's methodology complicate our effort to understand his conception of his trilogy on body, man, and citizen. He thought of geometry as the science of simple motions that could demonstrate how figures are generated by varieties of motion. Second came the philosophy of motion, as usually understood in the Galilean system, in which the effects of the palpable motions of one body on another were considered. Third came physics, the investigation of the internal and invisible motions that explain why "things when they are the same, yet seem not to be the same, but changed." Sensible qualities, such as light, color, heat, and sound, were to be explained, together with the nature of sensation itself. After physics came moral philosophy, the study of the motions of the mind—appetites and aversions. Such motions of the mind had their causes in sense and imagination. Finally, there was civil philosophy, the study of how states are generated from the qualities of human nature.

It is probable that Hobbes did not view the hierarchy of sciences as a rigorous deductive system. To start with, he never worked out the deductions in any detail—for instance, in the transition from what he called physics to moral philosophy, or psychology. Furthermore, what he said about the possibility of a self-contained science of politics contradicts his suggestion that it must be deduced from the fundamental theory of motion and that it supports the conventionist account of truth in politics. Hobbes said that even those who are ignorant of the principles of physics and geometry might attain knowledge of the principles of politics by the analytical method. They could start, for instance, with the question of whether an action is just or unjust; "unjust" could be resolved into "fact against law," and "law" into "command of him or them that have coercive power"; "power" could in its turn be derived from the wills of men who established such power so that they might live in peace.

This line of argument, developed in *De Corpore* after admitting the possibility of using the synthetic method to start from the first principles of philosophy and deduce from them the causes and necessity of constituting commonwealths, is confirmed by Hobbes's injunction in the Introduction to *Leviathan* that a man who is to govern a whole nation must "read in himself, not this or that particular man; but mankind: which though it be hard to do, harder than to learn any language of science; yet when I shall have set down my own reading, orderly and perspicuously, the pains left another, will be only to consider, if he find not the same in himself. For this kind of doctrine admitteth no other demonstration." It appears that Hobbes envisaged a relatively self-contained doctrine of politics based on introspection. His trilogy was, therefore, probably not conceived as forming a strictly deductive system. Its various elements were to be more loosely bound together by the fact that all three were sciences of motion.

PHILOSOPHY OF NATURE

Hobbes's natural philosophy seems to have been stimulated largely by the problem of the nature and cause of sensation that had so long haunted him. His theory was that the cause of everything, including sensation itself, lies in the varieties of motion. His first sketches of such a theory were in his *Little Treatise* and his early optical treatises, and his *De Corpore* was an ambitious development of this fundamental idea. Geometry, physics, physiology, and animal psychology were all incorporated within the theory of motion. Sensation occupied a shadowy middle position between the gross motions of the external world and the minute motions of the bodily organs.

The strange thing about Hobbes's preoccupation with sensation is that he seems to have been little troubled by the problems that are almost the stock in trade of philosophers—the problems of epistemology. He assumed that things exist independently of our perceptions of them and was convinced that "conceptions and apparitions are nothing really but motions in some internal substance of the head." The "nothing but" is very hard to accept, for obviously when we speak of "thoughts" and "conceptions," we do not *mean* the same as when we talk of motions in the brain.

Motion and qualities. On the status of the various sense qualities, Hobbes held, as did such natural philosophers as Kepler and Galileo, that secondary qualities—such as smells, colors, and sounds—are only appearances of bodies, whose real properties are those of extension, figure, and motion. Such secondary qualities are phantasms in the head, caused by the primary properties of external objects interacting with the sense organs, but the secondary qualities represent nothing outside. Hobbes argued that images and colors are "inherent in the sentient" because of illusions and because of images produced in other ways—for example, by blows on the optic nerve. But this proved too much, for representations of primary qualities are equally liable to deceive. Hobbes also proved too little, for he argued that secondary qualities represent no qualities of external objects because tastes, smells, and sounds seem different to different sentients. But there are standard tests for establishing the fact, for example, that a man is colorblind; and, as Berkeley later showed, the perception of primary qualities is infected with a similar relativity owing to the point of view and peculiarities of the percipient. Hobbes, in fact, gave but a halting philosophical patter to justify a distinction deeply embedded in the thought and practice of the new natural philosophers, for the basic tenet of these thinkers was that bodies in motion exist independently of our perception of them and that mathematical thinking about them discloses their real properties.

Hobbes regarded sensation and apparition as a meeting place of motions. Sense organs, he thought, are agitated by external movements without which there would be no discrimination and, hence, no sensation. Therefore, to give the entire cause of sense, an analysis is required of all movements in external bodies, which are transmitted to the sense through a medium. But sensation is not simply the end product of external motions; it also functions as an efficient cause of actions of sentient beings. Actions, in Hobbes's view, are really reactions to stimuli that are passed on by means of the sense organs. Sensation acts as a bridge between movements in the external world and the behavior of animals and men.

Hobbes's mechanical theory was distinctive in that he extended the Galilean system in two directions: into geometry at one end, and into psychology and politics at the other. He thought that no one could understand the definitions of geometry without grasping how motion is involved in the construction of lines, superficies, and circles. Geometry is the science of simple motions. It paves the way for mechanics, which explains the effects of the motions of one body on another, and for physics, which deals with the generation of sensible qualities from the insensible parts of a body in contact with other moving bodies.

Causation. All causation, in Hobbes's view, consists in motion. "There can be no cause of motion except in a body contiguous and moved." If bodies are not contiguous and yet influence one another, this influence has to be conveyed either by a medium or by emanations of minute bodies that impinge on others (the theory of effluxes). There can be no action at a distance. Hobbes combined this principle with his rendering of Galileo's law of inertia.

Hobbes extended this conception of causation to human actions: "A final cause has no place but in such things as have sense and will; and this also I shall prove hereafter to be an efficient cause." To bring about this transition from mechanics to physiology and psychology, Hobbes introduced the concept of "endeavour," which he defined as "motion made in less space and time than can be given . . . that is, motion made through the length of a point, and in an instant or point of time." In other words, he used the term to postulate infinitely small motions, and by means of this notion he tried to bridge the gap between mechanics and psychology. He thought that external objects, working on the sense organs, produce not only phantasms but also minute motions that proceed to the heart and make some alteration in the vital motions of the circulation of the blood. When these vital motions are thereby helped, we experience pleasure; when they are hindered, we experience pain. The body will be regulated in such a way that it will preserve the motions that help the vital motions and get rid of or shun those that hinder. This brings about animal motion. Even habits are nothing but motions made more easy by repeated endeavors; they are comparable to the bend of a crossbow.

Hobbes has often been called a materialist, but it is more appropriate to regard him as a great metaphysician of motion. He took concepts that have an obvious application to one realm of phenomena (mechanics) and developed a conceptual scheme that, he thought, could be applied to all phenomena. The plausibility of such a scheme derives from stressing tenuous similarities and ignoring palpable differences. There is a sense in which social life is a matter of bodies moving toward and away from other bodies, just as there is a sense in which work is moving lumps of matter about. But such descriptions are either unilluminating truisms, or, if they carry the "nothing but" implication, they are misleading. Habits, for example, may be formed in part by a variety of movements, but to suggest that by "habit" we mean nothing but a build-up of movements is ridiculous. This either confuses a question of meaning with a question of genetic explanation or it demonstrates the length to which Hobbes was prepared to go in rigging appearances to suit his metaphysical redescription.

Substance and accident. In his *De Corpore* Hobbes defined "body" as "that which having no dependence upon our thought, is coincident and coextended with some part of space." Bodies need not be visible. Indeed, "endeavours," which featured so widely in his system, are movements of minute unobservable bodies. Hobbes held that there is nothing else in the world but bodies, and he therefore did not flinch from the conclusion that "substance incorporeal" is a contradiction in terms. He argued that God cannot be such a substance. To Bishop Bramhall's question of what he took God to be, Hobbes replied, "I answer, I leave him to be a most pure, simple, invisible, spirit corporeal."

By "accident" Hobbes meant a property or characteristic that is not a part of a thing but "the manner by which any body is conceived." Most accidents, with the exception of figure and extension, can be absent without destruction of the body. But Hobbes was not altogether clear about the grounds for such an exception. If the grounds are the inconceivability of a body without figure and extension, why should not color be in the same category as figure? Hobbes regarded color as a subjective appearance brought about by the interaction of sense organs with the primary qualities of external objects; but if the criterion is one of conceivability, as Berkeley pointed out, it is as difficult to conceive of a body without color as it is to conceive of one without figure. Hobbes in fact defined "body" in terms of accidents that are mathematically tractable in mechanics and geometry. He tried to provide some kind of rationale for this basic assumption of the new natural philosophy by introducing the criterion of conceivability, which will not really do the work required of it.

Hobbes defined space as "the phantasm of a thing existing without the mind simply." By this he meant that what is called space is the appearance of externality. If the world were to be destroyed, and a man were left alone with his imagination and memories, some of these would appear external to him, or located in space, for the system of coordinates used to describe the relative position of bodies is a subjective framework. "Place is nothing out of the mind nor magnitude anything within it." A body always keeps the same magnitude, whether in motion or at rest, but it does not keep the same place when it moves. Place cannot, therefore, be an accident of bodies; place is feigned extension—an order of position constructed from experience of real extended things to provide a framework for their externality. Similarly, time is "the phantasm of before and after in motion." Time systems are constructed from the experience of succession.

Hobbes never made clear the relationship between any particular temporal or spatial system that an individual may devise and the system of coordinates adopted by the natural philosophers. Here again, Hobbes typically took for granted the system used by the scientists and tacked on a very brief philosophical story about its relation to the "phantasms" of the individual.

PSYCHOLOGY

Hobbes's psychology was not behavioristic, as it has sometimes been said to be, except insofar as behaviorism has often been associated with a materialistic metaphysical theory or with mechanical modes of explanation. Hobbes stressed the indispensability of introspection in the analysis and explanation of human behavior.

When Hobbes looked into himself he found, of course, motions that were in conformity with Galilean principles. He boldly proclaimed in *De Corpore* that "we have discovered the nature of sense, namely, that it is some internal motion in the sentient." The external body, either directly or via a medium, presses on the organ of sense, "which pressure, by the mediation of the nerves, and other strings and membranes of the body, continues inwards to the brain and heart, causeth there a resistance, or counterpressure, or endeavour of the heart to deliver itself, which endeavour, because outward, seemeth to be some matter without." Sensations are thus nothing but motions.

They have the character of externality because of the "outward endeavor" of the heart.

Perception. Having provided a mechanical starting point for his psychology, Hobbes then tried to describe what was known about psychological phenomena in terms compatible with a mechanical theory. One of the most obvious features of perception is that it involves seeing something as something, some sort of discrimination or recognition. Hobbes's way of saying this was that sense always has "some memory adhering to it." This was to be explained by the sense organs' property of acting as retainers of the movements of external bodies impinging on them. Without this retention of motions, what we call sense would be impossible, for "by sense we commonly understand the judgment we make of objects by their phantasms; namely, by comparing and distinguishing those phantasms; which we could never do, if that motion in the organ, by which the phantasm is made, did not remain there for some time, and make the same phantasm return."

The selectivity of perception raised a further problem. Why is it that men do not see many things at once? Hobbes again suggested a mechanical explanation: "For seeing the nature of sense consists in motion; as long as the organs are employed about one object, they cannot be so moved by another at the same time, as to make by both their motions one sincere phantasm of each of them at once." But this does nothing to explain why one object rather than another is selected. Hobbes's ideomotor theory made it hard to give a plausible account of the influence of interests, attitudes, and sets on what is selected in perception.

Hobbes also attempted a mechanical explanation of the phenomena of attention and concentration. When a strong motion impinges on the sense organ, the motion from the root of the sense organ's nerves to the heart persists contumaciously and makes the sense organ "stupid" to the registering of other motions.

Imagination and memory. Hobbes's account of imagination was explicitly a deduction from the law of inertia. "When a body is once in motion, it moveth, unless something else hinder it, eternally . . . so also it happeneth in that motion, which is made in the internal parts of a man when he sees, dreams, etc. For after the object is removed, or the eye shut, we still retain an image of the thing seen, though more obscure than when we see it . . . ." Imagination, therefore, is "nothing but decaying sense." This decay is not a decay in motion, for that would be contrary to the law of inertia. Rather, it comes about because the sense organs are moved by other objects, and subsequent movements obscure previous ones "in such manner as the light of the sun obscureth the light of the stars."

Memory, Hobbes claimed, differs from imagination only in that the fading image is accompanied by a feeling of familiarity. "For he that perceives that he hath perceived remembers," and memory "supposeth the time past." Hobbes thus seems to have more or less equated what is past with what is familiar, which is most implausible even if familiarity is often a hallmark of what is past. It is also difficult to see how, in his view, remembering something could be distinguished from seeing it for a second time, if the second impression of the thing is not very vivid.

Hobbes's fundamental mistake in all such descriptions

and explanations was to attempt to distinguish perform-ances, such as perceiving and remembering, by reference to subjective hallmarks vaguely consistent with his me-chanical theory, rather than by reference to the epistemo-logical criteria written into them. The fundamental dif-ference between perception and imagination, for instance, is not one of vividness or any other such accidental prop-erty; it is an epistemological difference. To say that a person imagines a tree rather than perceives it is to say something about the status of what is claimed. To perceive is to see something that really is before one's eyes; to imagine is to think one sees something that is not there. Similarly, to remember is to be right in a claim one makes about something in the past that one was in a position to witness, whereas to imagine is to be mistaken in what one claims. There are, of course, further questions about the mechanisms by means of which people perceive, imagine, and remember; and it could be that some such mechanical story as told by Hobbes might be true about such mecha-nisms. But in the language of such a story the basic episte-mological differences between these mental performances could never be made, and although the mechanical story might give an account of some of the necessary conditions of such performances, it is difficult to see how it could ever serve as a sufficient explanation of them.

Thought. The same general critique concerning neglect of epistemological criteria must be made of Hobbes's treatment of thought, which he equated with movements of some substance in the head. There may be movements in the brain that are necessary conditions of thought, but no description of such conditions should be confused with what is meant by "thought." We do speak of "the move-ment of thought," but this is a description of transitions, as from premises to conclusions or from problems to solu-tions, not of movements explicable in terms of mechanical laws.

Even though Hobbes's general account of thought was rather hamstrung by his obsession with mechanics, he nevertheless had some quite illuminating things to say about trains of thought, an account that owed more to Aris-totle than to Galileo. Hobbes distinguished "unguided" thought from that directed by a passionate thought or plan. Unguided thought followed principles that later came to be called principles of association—for example, spatiotem-poral contiguity and similarity. Hobbes, however, made no attempt to formulate principles of this kind. He was much more interested in, and attached much more importance to, guided thought, in which desire for an end holds the train of thought together and determines the relevance of its content.

Hobbes distinguished two main types of regulated thinking. The first was the classic Aristotelian case of de-liberation, where desire provides the end, and the means to this end are traced back until something is reached that is in a person's power to do. This faculty of invention is shared by the animals, but they do not share the other sort of guided thinking that Hobbes called prudence. In pru-dence the starting place is an action that is in a person's power to perform, and the store of past experience is used to speculate on its probable effects. In this case, delibera-tion leads forward to an end that is either desired or

feared. Hobbes seemed to think that people's prudence is in proportion to the amount of past experience on which they can draw. This sounds improbable, for although chil-dren cannot be prudent, many old people miss the rele-vance of their past experience.

Dreams. Dreams fascinated Hobbes. He attempted to determine what distinguishes them from waking thoughts and to develop a mechanical theory to explain them. He claimed that they lack coherence because they lack the thought of an end to guide them. Dreams consist of com-pounded phantasms of past sensations, for "in the silence of sense there is no new motion from the objects, and therefore no new phantasm." Dreams are clearer than the imaginations of waking men because of the predominance of internal motion in the absence of external stimulation. There is no sense of time in dreams, and nothing appears surprising or absurd.

There is an intimate connection between dreams and bodily states. Lying cold, for instance, produces dreams of fear and raises the image of a fearful object. The motions pass both from the brain to the inner parts and from the inner parts to the brain. So, just as anger causes overheat-ing in some parts of the body, overheating of the same parts can cause anger and, with it, the picture of an enemy. Dreams are thus the reverse of waking imaginations. Mo-tion begins at one end during waking life and at the other end during sleep. This tendency to project images pro-duced by bodily states gives rise to belief in apparitions and visions. Hobbes's treatment of dreams typified his approach to such matters. He seemed uninterested in the epistemological questions to which they give rise, as, for instance, in the thought of his contemporary, Descartes.

Passions. Hobbes's mechanical theory of human action hinged on his concept of "endeavour," by means of which he tried to show how the gross movements of the body in desire and aversion could be explained in terms of minute unobservable motions in the body. He postulated two sorts of motion in the body. The first is its vital motion, manifest in such functions as circulation of the blood, breathing, and nutrition, which proceeds without external stimulation or the help of the imagination. The second is animal mo-tion, which is equivalent to such voluntary movements as walking and speaking. This is always "first fancied in our minds" and is produced by the impact of external stimuli on the sense organs, an impact that gives rise both to phantasms in the brain and to internal motions that im-pinge on the vital motions of the heart. If the motion of the blood is helped, this is felt as pleasure; if it is impeded, as pain. Pleasure, Hobbes said, is "nothing really but motion about the heart, as conception is nothing but motion in the head." In the case of pleasure, the spirits—which were thought of as vaporous substances flowing through the tubes of the nerves—are guided, by the help of the nerves, to preserve and augment the motion. When this endeavor tends toward things known by experience to be pleasant, it is called appetite; when it shuns what is painful, it is called aversion. Appetite and aversion are thus the first endeavors of animal motion. We talk about "will" when there is deliberation before acting, for will is "the last appetite in deliberating."

Hobbes's theory of the passions was an attempt to graft

the traditional Aristotelian account of them onto his crude mechanical base. Love and hate are more or less the same as appetite and aversion, the only difference being that they require the actual presence of the object, whereas appetite and aversion presuppose its absence. These, together with joy and grief, which both involve foresight of an end rather than just an immediately perceived object, are the simple passions out of which others are compounded. Social life is a race for precedence that has no final termination save death. "So that in the first place, I put for a general inclination of all mankind, a perpetual and restless striving of power after power, that ceaseth only in death." To endure in the race requires foresight and scheming; to fail to compete is to die. A man who is convinced that his own power is greater than that of others is subject to what Hobbes called glory; its opposite is humility or dejection. Pity is grief for the calamity of another, arising from imagination that a like calamity may befall ourselves. Laughter is the expression of sudden glory caused by something new and unexpected in which we discover some superiority to others in ourselves.

Hobbes also introduced motion into his theory of individual differences. He thought that such differences are derivative from differences in passions and in the ends to which men are led by appetite, as well as to the sluggishness or agility of the animal spirits involved in the vital motions of their respective bodies.

The basic difficulty in understanding Hobbes's theory of motivation arises from his attempt to underpin a psychology derived from introspection, from the shrewd observation of others, and from the tradition going back to Aristotle with a mechanical theory whose outline was only very briefly sketched. Perhaps the essential criticism of any such theory is that actions cannot be analyzed into mere movements because, in any action proper—as distinct from a nervous tic or a reflex—the movements take place because of an end that the person has in mind. This end is what makes the action one of a certain sort, and, provided that the movements are directed toward this end, an almost indefinite range of movements can form part of the same action. Similarly, the movements involved in raising one's hand can form part of quite different actions, depending on the purpose for which the hand is raised—for example, to signal, to test the direction of the wind, to stretch the muscles, and so on.

Having something in mind—which is part of the concept of "action"—is not a movement, still less a movement of some internal substance of the head, if this is what Hobbes really believed. But Hobbes was not at all clear on the relationship between movements, whether observable or unobservable, and the cognitive components of appetites, aversions, and the various passions. Indeed, he seems to have held an extremely paradoxical and overintellectualistic view about the cognitive component of the passions. For he saw that passions are to be distinguished by their objects and by the judgment of the possibility of attaining such objects, yet he injected into his account a bizarre kind of egocentricity. For Hobbes, in all cases of passions the notion of "self" was part of the content of cognition. He seemed to think that all such "phantasms" of objects, by reference to which the passions are to be distinguished,

involve the thought of ourselves doing something or of our power to do something. Pity is thus seen as grief arising from our imagining ourselves in the same predicament as that of the one pitied. Hobbes's analysis of laughter palpably suffered from the same injection of egocentricity. Furthermore, how the highly sophisticated and narcissistic type of appraisal involved in the passions is to be reconciled with any attempt to represent them all as movements of the body and of some internal substance in the head is very difficult to determine.

For all its ambiguities, oversights, and obvious defects, Hobbes's psychology was remarkable, for he attempted to establish it as an objective study untrammeled by theological assumptions. To suggest that man is a machine was a great step forward in thought. Even though the hypothesis is probably untenable, it marked the beginning of the effort to use scientific methods and objective concepts in the sphere of human behavior. In the seventeenth century this was a novel undertaking, as well as a dangerous one.

ETHICS

Hobbes thought that, by employing the resolutive method, he could demonstrate the absolute necessity of leagues and covenants and the rudiments of moral and civil prudence from his two principles of human nature— "the one arising from the concupiscible part, which desires to appropriate to itself the use of those things in which all others have a joint interest; the other proceeding from the rational which teaches every man to fly a contranatural dissolution, as the greatest mischief that can arrive to nature." These two principles underlie Hobbes's account of the personal good, as well as his account of civil duty.

Hobbes was scornful of the notion that "good" and "evil" name any metaphysical essence. These words are "ever used with relation to the person that useth them: there being nothing simply and absolutely so; nor any common rule of good and evil, to be taken from the nature of the objects themselves." They name objects of our desires and aversions. We call a horse "good," for instance, because it is "gentle, strong, and carrieth a man easily." The desires of the individual determine what qualities are selected to furnish the ground for saying that an object is good.

Hobbes introduced a further refinement of this theory when he contrasted short-term goods with long-term goods. "Reason," he said, "declaring peace to be good, it follows by the same reason, that all the necessary means to peace be good also." This he contrasted with the sway of irrational appetite, whereby men "greedily prefer the present good." He thought that a man might not desire peace at a particular moment when influenced by some insistent desire; but when he sat down soberly in a cool hour, he would see that peace is a necessary condition of satisfying most of his desires in the long run. Thus, peace is something that he must desire both because of his fear of death and because of the other things he desires to do that a state of war would make impossible.

Hobbes was a nominalist, and he thought that all words have meaning, as if they were some kind of name. He did not see, as Berkeley seems to have seen a little later, that words like "good" have a prescriptive function and cannot be treated merely as if they were names. To say that something is good is to say that it is what it ought to be; it is to commend it. But also it implies that there are grounds for such commendation. It is to guide a person by suggesting grounds for his choice; it is not to order him or goad him. Hobbes saw that "good" is always thus connected with reasons, but he gave a very circumscribed account of what such reasons must be like, that is, characteristics of things desired. This was modified somewhat by what he said a man desires insofar as he uses his reason, that is, insofar as his "rational" as well as his "concupiscible" nature is involved. Hobbes's account of what a man desires would not be implausible if his account of human nature were acceptable, for then what men *must* desire could be predicted. But, if his account of human nature is rejected as oversimple, there cannot be quite such a tight connection as Hobbes suggested between "good" and what is, or will be, desired.

The connection is probably looser; given that words such as "good" have the practical function of guiding people's choices, it would be impossible to explain their effectiveness in this function if it were not generally the case that what was held up as good was something that people in general wanted. But it does not follow from this that any particular individual desires, or must desire, what is held up to him as good. Indeed, half the business of moral education consists in drawing people's attention to characteristics of things that they ought to desire but do not in fact desire.

State of nature and laws of nature. Morality is not concerned simply with the pursuit of personal good; it is also concerned with the acceptance of rules that limit the pursuit of good when it affects that of others. A tradition going back to the Stoics held that there was a small corpus of such rules, called the law of nature; these rules, which were universal preconditions of social life, did not depend, as do custom and law, on local circumstances. The Dutch jurist Grotius regarded this law of nature as a self-evident set of principles binding on all men (on kings as well as on their subjects) that would provide a rational basis for a system of international law; it was, he claimed, fundamental in the sphere of social rules in the same sort of way that Galileo's postulates were fundamental in the realm of nature. Morals could be brought within the expanding empire of the mathematical sciences.

Hobbes, therefore, was not original in his claim that "the true doctrine of the laws of nature is the true moral philosophy," nor was he original in likening its precepts to axioms. What was original was his claim that its precepts were axioms of prudence, insofar as "prudence" implies considerations limited to those that affect only the agent. For Grotius, the maintenance of society was a major need of man as a *social* animal, irrespective of purely private benefits. Hobbes, however, maintained that more or less the same set of rules that Grotius regarded as binding (such as keeping faith and fair dealing) could be shown to be axioms that must be accepted by any man who is both rational and afraid of death. "All society, therefore, is either for gain or for glory; that is, not so much for love of our fellows as for love of ourselves."

Man, Hobbes argued, shuns death "by a certain impulsion of nature, no less than that whereby a stone moves downward." This is what saves man from anarchy and civilizes him, for if man were driven merely by his "concupiscible" part, there would be no society, and the life of man would be "solitary, poor, nasty, brutish, and short." Men are equal enough in body and mind to render negligible any palpable claims to superior benefits, and even the weakest is able to kill the strongest. But man's fear of death brings him up short in his pursuit of power and leads him to reflect upon the predicament of a state of nature. His reason tells him that peace is necessary for survival and also "suggesteth certain articles of peace, upon which men may be drawn to agreement. These articles are they, which otherwise are called the Laws of Nature." One of these laws is that "men perform their covenants made." In this way Hobbes claimed to demonstrate "the absolute necessity of leagues and covenants, and thence the rudiments both of moral and of civil prudence."

Hobbes's demonstration gave only the semblance of validity because he isolated the concupiscible and rational aspects of man's nature from each other and, as in a Galilean imaginary experiment, explored the consequences of each independently. Given only man's self-assertion, then there must be a state of nature; given only his overwhelming aversion to death, then he must accept the conditions necessary for avoiding death. These axioms of prudence are hypothetical in relation to man's assumed fear of death. They are rules that a rational man must accept insofar as he wants to avoid death. But men are only partly rational and, although they have an overwhelming fear of death, they also want other things, such as power and glory. Presumably Hobbes, like Machiavelli, could also have laid down rules for obtaining power and glory that would have borne no resemblance to the laws of nature. Thus, Hobbes could not have been trying to show that virtue, as defined by adherence to the laws of nature, is natural to man or a deduction from his nature, as have many thinkers who have adopted a psychological starting point. Indeed, the general relationship between Hobbes's psychology and his ethics is too obscure for us to know quite what he was doing.

The key to Hobbes's "demonstration" really lies in what he did with it, for he went on to point out that the laws of nature are only theorems that any rational man would accept. Since these laws need the backing of the sword to insure peace, men have need of a "common power to keep them in awe, and to direct their actions to the common benefit." The rationale of Hobbes's demonstration can now be seen, for at the time that Hobbes was writing, England was precariously poised between anarchy and civil disorder. Hobbes's analysis was a Galilean "resolution" of such a situation into the simple components of human nature that formed its basis. He pointed out that, insofar as men want peace and security (and all men do want this, although they want other things as well), then they must see that, human nature being what it is, there are certain means that they must accept if they are to have what they want. It is irrational to want something and yet to refuse to take the only means that will ensure that what is wanted is obtained. Since the acceptance of social rules is based only on the fear of death, it is only the fear of death that will ensure that these rules are obeyed. Men therefore cannot have the peace they all desire unless they accept the sword of the sovereign that will make death the consequence of breaking the rules that are a necessary condition of peace.

Determinism and free will. The indeterminate position of Hobbes's psychology in relation to his ethics was encouraged by his belief in determinism—or "necessitation," as he usually called it—which he outlined in his controversy with Bishop Bramhall. Hobbes denied that there is any power in men to which the term "will" refers; what is commonly called will is but the last desire in deliberating. Furthermore, he argued, only a man is properly called free, not his desires, will, or inclinations. The liberty of a man "consisteth in this, that he finds no stop, in doing what he has the will, desire, or inclination to do." Liberty is "the absence of all the impediments to action that are not contained in the nature and intrinsical quality of the agent." To speak of liberty is not to make any suggestions about the determinants or absence of determinants of man's deliberations or decisions; it is to suggest that man is not externally constrained in his actions. There is, therefore, no contradiction in saying that a man acts freely and that his actions are also determined. Since all actions have causes and thus are necessitated, it is pointless to use "free" in the sense of "free from necessitation," as distinct from "free from compulsion." There are no such actions, although we may think that there are because we are ignorant of the causes of actions.

There is much to be said for Hobbes's recommendation on the use of the word "free"; many others, such as Locke and Hume, have followed him in confining it to the absence of constraint on a man's actions. But Hobbes's claim that all actions are necessitated is not so straightforward. Certainly he was right in suggesting that all actions are explicable—if that is what is meant by saying that they have causes—but so many different things can count as causes, ranging from deliberation and understanding to a stab of pain or a crack on the skull. Since Hobbes thought of man as a natural machine, he therefore viewed all causes as mechanical pushes. His doctrine carried the suggestion that the behavior of men is not only explicable but also somehow unavoidable because men's decisions and choices are simply manifestations of internal pushes.

Significantly enough, Bramhall did not object to Hobbes's doctrine insofar as it related to actions shared with animals or to spontaneous actions. What he could not allow was that voluntary actions, which follow on election and deliberation, should also be "necessitated." Bramhall pointed out the difficulties of likening actions and the grasp of objects and of means of obtaining them, which are inseparable from the concept of "action," to processes in nature explicable in terms of antecedent motions. In this contention Bramhall was substantially right, for although actions may involve movements, they are not reducible to movements.

Hobbes also disagreed with Bramhall on the implications of his doctrine of "necessitation" for moral judgments and for the operation of the law. Bramhall argued that if human actions are necessitated, then praise and blame, reward and punishment, are both unjust and vain. To the charge that they are vain, Hobbes replied that they are to be viewed as further determinants of choice. Praise and blame, reward and punishment "do by example make and conform the will to good and evil." To the charge of injustice, Hobbes argued that "the law regardeth the will and no other precedent causes of action"; also that punishments annexed to breaches of the law function as deterrents and necessitate justice. He went out of his way to distinguish punishment from acts of revenge or hostility and to stress its deterrent purpose, which is a sound position. Hobbes saw clearly that retribution is part of the meaning of punishment, but that it is the connection with authority that distinguishes it from other sorts of retributive acts. He also saw that, although retribution may be written into the meaning of punishment, its justification is not therefore necessarily retributive. Rather, it is to be justified for its preventive and deterrent function.

POLITICAL PHILOSOPHY

In his political philosophy Hobbes tried to conceptualize the relationship between the new nation-state, which had been emerging under the Tudors, and the individual citizen, who could no longer be regarded simply as having a set place in a divinely instituted order. In the old medieval society a man was bound by ties attaching to his status and by duties prescribed for him by the church. Tradition was the main form of social control, and traditions stretching back into the distant past assigned to a man his relatively fixed place in society. Aristotle's doctrine of natural kinds and natural places and his account of man as a social animal provided a fitting naturalistic foundation for the theological world view that was accepted by rulers and ruled alike. But with the rise of individualism and the social mobility that accompanied the rise of commerce and capitalism, this old conception of man in society no longer applied. Men had shaken off the ties of their guilds and local communities, and the new natural philosophy was beginning to render the naturalistic foundations of the former world view untenable.

Hobbes's picture of life as a race, in which we "must suppose to have no other good, nor other garland, but being foremost," was a gruesome caricature of an age of individualism, restless competition, and social mobility. But if the fetters of tradition were being cast away, what other form of social control could take its place to prevent the anarchy of a state of nature? The answer was to be found, of course, in the increasing executive power of the state and in the growth of statute law, together with the development of the individual conscience, whereby regulation from within replaced the external authority of the Catholic church. Hobbes distrusted the anarchic tendencies of the individual conscience as much as he loathed the extramundane authority of the Church of Rome. Both were to be banished, along with traditional ties; civil society could be reconstructed as a simple mechanical system.

Social contract. Hobbes had a model ready at hand by means of which he might present his Galilean analysis of the rationale of civil society—the social contract theory. The social contract theory, despite its obvious flaws, was an attempt to rationalize political obligation, to substitute an intelligible bargain for mystifying appeals to tradition and divine right.

The contract theory was resorted to mainly by those who wanted to challenge the absolutist claims of monarchs, to uphold the claims of the common law, or to lay down some sort of moral limits on control and interference by the central executive. Hobbes's feat was to employ this model to demonstrate that absolutism is the only possible logical outcome of consistent concern for individual interests. Indeed, he prided himself on grounding the authority of sovereigns, as well as the liberty and duty of subjects, upon axioms of human nature rather than on tradition and supernatural authority. In his attitude toward tradition and divine right, he was at one with the defenders of government by consent. But because of his overriding concern for security, and because of his rather depressing estimate of human nature, he came to the somewhat gleeful conclusion—highly displeasing to those who believed in government by consent—that absolutism could be the only rationally defensible form of government.

Hobbes did not seriously consider the social contract, as some did, as a quasi-historical hypothesis on how civil society might have come into existence. In his account the contract was featured as a framework for a Galilean resolution of civil society into its simple elements. Hobbes imagined the individual in a state of nature as having an unlimited right to "protect his life and members" and "to use all the means, and do all the actions, without which he cannot preserve himself." But he also has a right to all things "to do what he would, and against whom he thought fit, and to possess, use, and enjoy all that he would, or could get." Hobbes here was employing a very strange concept of right, for usually, when we talk about a right, we are indicating a rule that protects or should protect a person from interference in the doing of something that he might want to do. Hobbes, however, used the term in this way to talk about both what a person is entitled to do (when it is correlative with duties of noninterference on the part of others) and what a person cannot be obliged to renounce. When Hobbes declared that men have a "right of self-preservation," he meant not that an individual is entitled by some rule (of law, tradition, or morals) to life but that he cannot be obliged to renounce it because it is psychologically impossible for him to do so. "Natural rights" therefore have a quite different meaning in Hobbes's writing than in the works of Locke, Pufendorf, and other such defenders of natural rights. In these classical theories, natural rights are interests protected by natural law against the interference of others. Hobbes's natural-law theory is not connected in this way with his rather bizarre concept of natural rights.

Hobbes's "rights" of nature are derivative from man's tendency to assert himself and to seek power. But, as already shown, Hobbes held that man would also be driven by his fear of death to accept certain laws of nature, the second of which prescribed that every man should lay down his right to all things and "be contented with so much liberty against other men, as he would allow other men against himself." This could be done either by not interfering with others' enjoyment of their rights or by transferring one's right to another, in which case the transferrer is obliged not to hinder the recipient. Injustice consists in hindering a person whom it is a duty not to hinder. The mutual transferring of such rights is called a contract, and the third law of nature is "that men perform their covenants made."

Commonwealth. Hobbes deduced a mutual transfer of rights from his postulate of rational action under the impetus of fear. But men are not yet safe, for there may be danger in keeping covenants and it may be, on occasion, in people's interest to break them. "And covenants, without the sword, are but words, and of no strength to secure a man at all." Matters must be arranged so that it will never be in anyone's interest to break covenants, which cannot exist where there is no "common power" to enforce them. Thus, a social contract must be presumed in which it is *as if* every man should say to every other man, "I authorize and give up my right of governing myself, to this man, or to this assembly of men, on this condition, that thou give up thy right to him, and authorize all his actions in like manner." This contract unites the multitude into one people and marks the generation of "that great LEVIATHAN, or rather, to speak more reverently, of that mortal God, to which we owe under the immortal God, our peace and defence." The definition of commonwealth is, therefore, "one person, of whose acts a great multitude, by mutual covenants one with another, have made themselves every one the author, to the end he may use the strength and means of them all, as he shall think expedient, for their peace and common defence." The person that results is called sovereign, and everyone else is his subject. The sovereign is created by the contract but is not party to it. Thus, the people rule even in monarchies; a multitude becomes a people by having some device, such as that of representation, by means of which decisions binding on all are made on behalf of all. Some such "covenant" is implicit in speaking of a commonwealth as a people, as distinct from a multitude of men.

Up to this point there is much to be said for the sort of analysis that Hobbes gave, although some of its details are peculiar. He had considerable insight into the sort of thing we mean when we speak of a civil society, as distinct from a mere multitude of men. He saw clearly that societies are not natural wholes like toads, turnips, or colonies of termites. They exist because individuals act in accordance with rules that can be rejected, broken, or altered; they are artificial wholes. Therefore, if we are to speak of the "will" or "decision" of such an entity, there must be some higher-order rules of procedure, such as that of representation, by reference to which what is to count as a corporate decision is constituted. Individuals or groups of individuals are put in authority for such a purpose.

When Hobbes proceeded to the more concrete details of what must constitute the duties of rulers and subjects, however, he was not equally convincing, for this next step depended on his questionable account of human nature. The basic principle of human nature revealed by his Galilean resolution was "that the dispositions of men are naturally such that, except they be restrained through fear of some coercive power, every man will dread and distrust each other." No motive in human nature, except the fear of death, is strong enough to counteract the disruptive force of man's self-assertion. The fear of death must, therefore, be the explanation of the existence of civil society (insofar as there is a social order and not anarchy), and security must be the sole reason for the institution of the social order; there is simply no other reason for which men could be induced to give up their natural right to self-assertion. Since this is the sole reason for having a commonwealth, it follows logically that a commonwealth must be devised that will accomplish the end for which it exists. Sovereignty must be perpetual, undivided, and absolute, for to divide or limit sovereignty would be to risk anarchy; and such limitation would be illogical because it would be inconsistent with the *raison d'être* of sovereignty. *Salus populi suprema lex* ("The safety of the people is the supreme law"). Moreover, complete safety entails complete submission to an absolute sovereign. Thus, absolutism is the logical consequence of government by consent, once the real interest of individuals, which is the presupposition of the institution of commonwealth, has been clearly understood.

There are two obvious flaws in this stage of Hobbes's argument. The first is the assumption that the desire for security, deriving from the fear of death, is the sole reason for the institution of commonwealth, a reason that Hobbes more or less wrote into the meaning of "commonwealth." It is obviously a very important reason, but that it should be the only reason is plausible only if Hobbes's psychology were to be accepted. Even so, Hobbes should not have written the reason for instituting a commonwealth into what is *meant* by "commonwealth." The second flaw was well brought out by Locke, who argued that, even if security were the sole reason for the institution of commonwealth, absolute authority is a dangerous expedient from the point of view of individual interest. For the hypothesis is that the timid individual would exchange the possible threat to life presented by 100,000 men, all of whom individually might attack him, for the threat to his life made possible by the arbitrary authority of one man who has 100,000 men under his command. "Are men so foolish that they take care to avoid what mischiefs may be done them by polecats or foxes, but are content, nay think it safety, to be devoured by lions?"

Hobbes was led to his advocacy of undivided sovereignty by his interest in constitutional and legal matters. When Hobbes was writing, there was a clash between the higher-order principles of common law and of statute law. The common-law principle that custom, as interpreted by the judges, is to be consulted in declaring what the law is, existed alongside the principle of statute law, that rules laid down by a determinate body or person (for example, Parliament or the king) determine what the courts must recognize as valid law. Statute law was on the increase during this period, and it was intolerable to any clearheaded man that these two principles should operate side by side. Hobbes advocated the unambiguous supremacy of the principle of statute law and the abolition of common law. The need to introduce clarity and coherence into the confused constitutional situation that prevailed in Hobbes's time was obvious enough. But for Hobbes to suggest that it was a logical truth that there must be an

absolute sovereign in any commonwealth was to introduce dubious logical deductions into a field where a solution was more likely to be found by practical adjustments and compromises that reflected the strength of competing interests and were consonant with deep-seated traditions.

One of the traditions that Hobbes's geometric solution ignored was that of the liberty of the subject. In Hobbes's view, civil liberty lay "only in those things, which in regulating their actions, the sovereign hath praetermitted." It is unlikely, Hobbes suggested, that laws would be necessary to regulate buying and selling, and choice of abode, diet, a wife, a trade, and education. But whether such laws are necessary is entirely up to the sovereign. The liberty of the subject also consists in the lack of proscription of such acts that it would be vain to forbid because they are psychologically impossible for the subject to refrain from committing. These acts involve the right of the subject to preserve himself and to resist imprisonment. Hobbes also suggested that "in the act of submission consisteth both our obligation, and our liberty." Both the obligation and the liberty are to derive from the words "I authorize all his actions," which the subject is imagined to have expressed in instituting a commonwealth. The subject is released from his obligation only if the sovereign fails to do what he is there to do, namely, to guarantee security. This marks the extent of the subject's much-lauded "right to resist." Presumably Hobbes meant to stress that subjects submit voluntarily to authority. This is true enough, but what it has to do with the liberty of the subject, in any straightforward sense of "liberty," is difficult to grasp.

Law. Hobbes's concept of the role of natural law, once the law of the state had been established, was not altogether clear. He maintained that the laws of nature were "but conclusions, or theorems concerning what conduceth to the conservation and defence of themselves; whereas law, properly, is the word of him that by right hath command over others. But yet, if we consider the same theorems, as delivered in the word of God, that by right commandeth all things; then they are properly called laws." These "laws" always obligate *in foro interno*—that is, in matters of private conscience—in prescribing a general readiness of mind; but *in foro externo*, that is, in actions, the laws may not be obligatory if certain conditions, such as peace and security, are absent. Such conditions, when present, will in fact render it to the interest of the subject that he follow the laws of nature. A law properly so called always obligates *in foro externo* because of its source in the command of the sovereign, as well as because civil society, by definition, provides the conditions of security and the sanction that will make it always against a man's interest to disobey it. But do the laws of nature oblige *in foro externo*, if not incorporated in the civil law, when the security of civil society prevails? This depends on how seriously Hobbes meant his reference to theorems as authoritative edicts from God, for such derivation would give them a determinate source, as in the case of laws properly so called. Some take Hobbes seriously and claim that he really thought that the laws of nature oblige *in foro externo* as well as *in foro interno* whenever conditions of security prevail. Others hold that Hobbes never really thought that laws of nature oblige in a full sense *in foro externo* because his reference to their authoritative source is but a tactful concession to piety. He really thought of them merely as axioms of reason that oblige in a full sense only when they are issued by a temporal sovereign as commands and when conditions of security, together with sanctions, prevail in civil society.

Hobbes took this somewhat ambiguous view about the status of natural laws (or moral precepts) because of his extreme hardheadedness about laws properly so called. Law, he held, is the *command* of the sovereign, "the word of him that by right hath command over others." It is authority, not conformity with custom or reason, that makes a law. In this forthright view he was attacking the fiction of the common law that the law was there to be discovered, immanent in the customs of the people.

Whatever the merits of Hobbes's view—later adopted by the analytic school of John Austin—that laws are commands, Hobbes made a valuable contribution in helping to distinguish questions about law that are often confused. The question "What is a law?" should be distinguished from such other questions as "Is the law equitable or reasonable?" and "What makes a law valid?" Hobbes argued that a law is simply a rule issued by someone in authority. Whether it is reasonable or equitable is a further question, as are the questions of its validity, of its conformity with custom, and of the grounds on which a man could be obliged to obey it.

To claim that laws are *commands* was an oversimple and misleading way to bring out the prescriptive force of laws. But it was useful insofar as it connected law with authority, for laws, like commands, are utterances issuing from people in authority. In stressing the necessary connection between law and authority, Hobbes made an important contribution to political philosophy, for there is no necessary connection between authority and moral precepts or "laws of nature."

On the question of the person or body of men by whose authority laws should be made, Hobbes was more openminded than is often realized. He thought that this was not a matter that could be demonstrated; it was a matter of factual argument. He believed that the relative advantages of each form of government had to be considered in the light of the sole end of security. It was a factual matter which type of government was most likely to promote such an end. On the whole, he argued, monarchy is preferable because it is more likely to be undivided, strong, and wise.

RELIGION

At the time Hobbes wrote, ethics and politics were inseparable from religion. Even the Royal Society was founded by men who believed that science would reveal more of the details of God's creation and thus enhance his worship. Hobbes was one of the pioneers in the process of distinguishing religious questions from other sorts. He rigorously excluded theology from philosophy and tried to map the proper domains of faith and knowledge. He outlined a theory of the causes of religion and superstition and discussed the grounds of religious belief, and he conducted an elaborate inquiry into the use of various terms in the Scriptures. But all this analysis and theorizing was subordinate to his main interest in religion as a possible source of civil discord. It is seldom realized that more than half of *Leviathan* is concerned with religious matters, with Hobbes trying to defend the "true religion" from both Catholicism and the priesthood of all believers. He saw clearly that these doctrines were two of the main obstacles in the way of the absolutism that he advocated.

Hobbes made some interesting speculations about the natural causes of religion, which he said were "these four things, opinion of ghosts, ignorance of second causes, devotion toward what men fear, and taking of things casual for prognostics . . . ." These seeds of religion could be cultivated according to natural invention, which leads to superstition and nature worship, or according to God's commandments. "Fear of power invisible, feigned by the mind, or imagined from tales publicly allowed, RELIGION; not allowed, SUPERSTITION. And when the power imagined is truly such as we imagine, TRUE RELIGION."

Notion of God. What, then, constituted true religion for Hobbes? To reasonable men, God's commands amounted to the laws of nature. God's nature, however, was a much more baffling matter, even for a rational man. Certainly God must have "existence," which Hobbes took to be an attribute of God, in spite of his remarks elsewhere about the ambiguities of the verb "to be." In *Leviathan* Hobbes held that God is the cause of the world, "that is, a first and an eternal cause of all things; which is that which men mean by the name of God." In his later *De Corpore*, however, he indicated the difficulties in the notion of an unmoved mover. This was a difficult question for philosophers to determine and had better be handed over for decision to the lawful authorities. Hobbes also stressed God's irresistible power and maintained that the only solution to the problem of evil was to be found in this power. Did not God reply to Job: "Where wast thou, when I laid the foundations of the earth?" Job had not sinned; his suffering was an unfortunate consequence of God's manifestation of power.

The main function of reason, however, is to show what God cannot be—at ease, finite, figured, having parts, occupying a place, moved or at rest, plural, and having passions, rational appetite, sight, knowledge, and understanding. If we rely on natural reason, we must either qualify God in a negative way by adjectives, such as "infinite" and "incomprehensible," or by a superlative, such as "most high," and an indefinite, such as "holy," which are not really descriptions of his nature but expressions of our admiration. Thus, rational disputations about the nature of God are pointless and a dishonor to him, "for in the attributes which we give to God, we are not to consider the signification of philosophical truth; but the signification of pious intention, to do him the greatest honour we are able." The sovereign, therefore, must decide on God's attributes; and public, uniform worship must be instituted.

Reason and revelation. Reason, however, should not be "folded up in the napkin of an implicit faith, but employed in the purchase of justice, peace, and true religion." There is nothing in God's word contrary to reason. We must, however, be prepared in this world "to captivate our understanding to the words; and not to labour in sifting out a philosophical truth by logic, of such mysteries as are not comprehensible, nor fall under any rule of natural science." Reason should be kept very much to the fore when one is confronted with those who claim revelation, for if a man says that God spoke to him in a dream, this "is no more than to say he dreamed that God spoke to him." There are psychological explanations of such phenomena that cast doubt on their reliability as valid communications with God.

Dreams, visions, and inspiration, however, should not be dismissed altogether, for it is by such means that prophets have been informed of the will of God. What is needed are criteria for detecting true prophets. Hobbes suggested two necessary criteria: the working of miracles and the teaching of doctrines not at variance with those already established. Since miracles had by then ceased, there was no sign left to single out true prophets. And, in any case, the Scriptures, since the time of Jesus, had taken the place of prophecy.

Reliance on the Scriptures, Hobbes realized, is not altogether straightforward. Even supposing that it could be decided which books are authentic, and that the sovereign, by his authority, could make their teaching law, there is still the problem of what many of the terms used in the Scriptures mean. Hobbes went through most of the key terms in the Scriptures, giving meaning to them in a way consistent with his mechanical theory. He argued, for instance, that God must have a body and that the proper signification of "spirit" in common speech is either a subtle, fluid, and invisible body or a ghost or other idol or phantasm of the imagination; it may also have a figurative use in such a phrase as "spirit of wisdom." "Angels" signify images raised in the mind to indicate the presence of God. Hobbes made acute remarks about the nature of miracles that mingled radical probing with subtle irony (indeed, one often wonders whether his whole treatment of "the true religion" is not a colossal piece of irony).

On the relationship between church and state, Hobbes of course adopted an uncompromising Erastian position. A church he defined as "a company of men professing Christian religion, united in the person of one sovereign, at whose command they ought to assemble, and without whose authority they ought not to assemble." There is, therefore, no universal church to which all Christians owe allegiance, for there is no supreme sovereign over all nations.

Hobbes concluded *Leviathan* with his famous section on the Kingdom of Darkness, in which he castigated superstition and Catholicism as enemies of the true religion. The papacy, he remarked "is no other than the ghost of the deceased Roman empire, sitting crowned upon the grave thereof." The papacy ruthlessly exploits the fears of ignorant men to perpetuate the power of unscrupulous priests as a rival to the secular power.

Hobbes held that there is only one article of faith necessary for salvation: that Jesus is the Christ. On what authority did such a belief rest? Hobbes had some interesting things to say about the difference between knowledge and faith. The object of both is propositions, but in the case of knowledge we consider the proposition and call to mind what its terms signify. Truth here is a matter largely of following the consequences of our definitions. But when reasons for assent derive "not from the proposition itself but from the person propounding, whom we esteem so learned that he is not deceived, and we see no reason why he should deceive us; our assent, because it grows not from any confidence of our own, but from another man's knowledge, is called faith." Faith, therefore, depends on our trust in a man rather than on our grasp of truth. The faith that Jesus is the Christ must therefore come from the Scriptures and our trust in those who wrote them. But who is to interpret them? "Christian men do not know, but only believe the Scripture to be the word of God." St. Paul said, "Faith cometh by hearing," and that, according to Hobbes, means listening to our lawful pastors, who are appointed by the sovereign to interpret the Scriptures for us. Charles II and Cromwell must have been flattered by the magnitude of the problems on which they were required to issue authoritative edicts: the creation of the world, God's attributes, the authenticity of miracles, and the proper interpretation of the Scriptures. Hobbes regarded religion more as a matter of law than of truth.

Hobbes's treatment of religion leaves obscure exactly what he himself thought about such matters. His technique was always to push radical probing to the limit, and when the basis for the traditional doctrines seemed about to be cut away, the sovereign was summoned as a sort of *deus ex machina* to put everything in its orthodox place. Hobbes was obviously extremely skeptical about what could be demonstrated in the sphere of religion, but it is difficult to say whether his suggestion that the sovereign should pronounce on such matters as the creation of the world and the attributes of God was a subtle piece of irony, a pious protestation to protect himself against the charge of atheism, or yet another manifestation of his overwhelming conviction that there must be nothing touching the peace of the realm that the sovereign should not decide.

Works by Hobbes

English Works of Thomas Hobbes, 11 vols., and *Opera Philosophica* (Latin works), 5 vols., Sir William Molesworth, ed. London, 1839–1845; reprinted Oxford, 1961. All quotations in the text of this article are from this edition of the English works.

The Elements of Law, Natural and Political, Ferdinand Tönnies, ed. London, 1928. This also includes extracts from the *Little Treatise, or A Short Tract on First Principles* and *Excerpta de Tractatu Optico*.

Leviathan, Michael Oakeshott, ed. Oxford, 1947; New York, 1962. Latter is paperback with introduction by Richard S. Peters.

Body, Mind, and Citizen, Richard S. Peters, ed. New York, 1962. Paperback, with introduction by Peters, that contains selections from the Molesworth and Tönnies editions.

Works on Hobbes

Aubrey, John, *Brief Lives*, E. O. Dick, ed. London, 1950. Contains biography of Hobbes.

Brandt, Frithiof, *Thomas Hobbes' Mechanical Conception of Nature*, translated by Vaughan Maxwell and Annie I. Fausbøll. London, 1928.

Laird, John, *Hobbes*. New York and London, 1934.

Peters, Richard S., *Hobbes*. Harmondsworth, England, 1956. Paperback.

Robertson, G. C., *Hobbes*. London and Edinburgh, 1886.

Stephen, Leslie, *Hobbes*. London, 1904.

Strauss, Leo, *The Political Philosophy of Thomas Hobbes*. New

York and London, 1936; Chicago, 1963. The 1963 edition is paperback.

Warrender, J. H., *The Political Philosophy of Thomas Hobbes.* New York and London, 1957.

Watkins, John W. N., *Hobbes's System of Ideas.* London, 1965.

R. S. Peters

HOBHOUSE, LEONARD TRELAWNEY (1864–1929), British sociologist and philosopher, was born in a small village near Liskeard, in Cornwall. He was educated at Marlborough School and Corpus Christi College, Oxford, where he took firsts in classical moderations and "greats." During his undergraduate years he engaged in the study of current problems in politics and economics, along with other radically minded students such as Gilbert Murray and Arthur Acland. He was elected to a prize fellowship at Merton College in 1887 and to a fellowship at Corpus Christi in 1894.

Hobhouse's main interest was the study of the evolution of mind as the central factor in historical development. This, combined with an innate humanitarianism, made him dissatisfied with the passive role of an Oxford don, although even at Oxford he was active in the Labour movement, especially in such causes as trade unionism, the cooperative movement, and adult education. After leaving Oxford, Hobhouse became influential among the "New Liberals," who sought to combine Liberalism with a measure of organized collective action. He was very sympathetic to the Labour party, although he never joined it. Toward the end of his life Hobhouse grew disillusioned with party politics, and by 1927 he had ceased to belong to any party.

On leaving Oxford in 1897, Hobhouse joined the staff of the *Manchester Guardian*, with which he was associated for most of the rest of his life in one capacity or another. Sociology and philosophy, however, were always his main interests. His *Mind in Evolution* (1901) and *Morals in Evolution* (1906)—a remarkable synthesis of anthropology, ethics, and the history of religious and social institutions—led to his appointment to the new Martin White part-time chair of sociology in the University of London, converted in 1925 to a full-time chair. Hobhouse first opposed Britian's entry into World War I, but he came to support the Allied cause wholeheartedly. He saw the war as the direct outcome of Hegelian teaching, and his own contribution to the war effort was *The Metaphysical Theory of the State*, an extreme attack on Hegelian political theory, especially as found in Bernard Bosanquet's *Philosophical Theory of the State*.

Hobhouse, besides being a philosopher of distinction, made important contributions to anthropological techniques and was a pioneer in comparative and social psychology and one of the founders of sociology as a synthesizing science. The encyclopedic scope of his work and the reluctance of English universities to accept the new subject of sociology contributed to an underestimation of his work in any one field. In philosophy his concern with the reconciliation of different schools meant that he did not himself belong to any one school, and this militated against his due recognition by philosophers.

It is impossible to separate Hobhouse's philosophy from the rest of his work, since his achievement lay in interpreting philosophically a wealth of general and detailed knowledge. There was, however, no question of fitting everything into a fixed scheme. His procedure was empirical and undogmatic, leaving a place for new facts from science and life. His comprehensive studies began with epistemology; went on to an evolutionary interpretation, first of mind in animals and mankind and then of moral and religious ideas; turned next to values in man and society; and ended with a grand synthesis of his philosophical and scientific theories.

The strongest influences on Hobhouse were Herbert Spencer's evolutionary philosophy, Auguste Comte's Positivism, and the social philosophy of John Stuart Mill and T. H. Green. He parted company with Spencer in regarding the appearance of minds as a turning point in the evolutionary process and in accepting the idealists' organic view of society. At the same time he rejected the idealists' reduction of all things to the spiritual. His theory of knowledge was realist and empirical; knowledge cannot make its own object, for it is based on experience and is of reality, not appearance. All knowledge is sociologically conditoned, but a positivist philosophy, applying our knowledge of these conditions, provides safeguards against error. The object of the physical sciences ("matter"), subject to mechanical laws, is only one aspect of reality; there is another aspect ("mind"), subject to teleological laws. Hobhouse traced the close relation of the two aspects in the developing world order.

Works by Hobhouse

The Theory of Knowledge. London, 1896.
Mind in Evolution. London, 1901.
Morals in Evolution. London, 1906.
Social Evolution and Political Theory. London, 1911.
Development and Purpose. London, 1913; rev. ed., 1927. The revised edition is largely rewritten.
The Metaphysical Theory of the State. London, 1918.
The Rational Good. London, 1921.
The Elements of Social Justice. London, 1922.
Social Development. London, 1924.

Works on Hobhouse

Barker, Ernest, "Leonard Trelawney Hobhouse." *Proceedings of the British Academy,* Vol. 14 (1929), 536–554.

Carter, Hugh, *The Social Theories of L. T. Hobhouse.* Chapel Hill, N.C., 1927.

Ginsberg, Morris, "The Contribution of Professor Hobhouse to Philosophy and Sociology." *Economica,* Vol. 9 (1929), 251–266.

Ginsberg, Morris, "Leonard Trelawney Hobhouse." *The Journal of Philosophical Studies,* Vol. 4 (1929), 442–452.

Hobson, J. A., and Ginsberg, Morris, *L. T. Hobhouse, His Life and Work.* London, 1931.

Nicholson, J. A., *Some Aspects of the Philosophy of L. T. Hobhouse.* Urbana, Ill., 1928.

A. K. Stout

HOCKING, WILLIAM ERNEST, American idealist and philosopher of religion. Born in Cleveland, Ohio, in 1873, Hocking spent his early years in the Middle West and studied civil engineering at Iowa State University. Private reading stimulated an interest in philosophy and led him to study at Harvard, where he was influenced chiefly by William James and Josiah Royce. He completed his undergraduate and graduate studies at Harvard University and spent most of his long teaching career there, retiring in 1943.

Although his philosophical system embodies elements of pragmatism and realism, it is primarily an affirmation of Other Mind, or God, as ultimate reality known directly and intuitively. Hocking thus stands in the idealist tradition in modern philosophy and refers to his own position most commonly as "Objective Idealism." Primitive experience, involving the knowledge of other selves and the world, is conditioned by an immediate awareness of Other Mind, standing in an I–Thou relationship to the self. Both sensory and emotive experience have cognitive connections that point beyond self to Other Mind. Hocking's emphasis is on feeling linked inextricably with idea, so that the two are joined in immediate consciousness as an "idea–feeling couple." This concept of the union of idea and feeling is the source of the strong strain of mysticism in Hocking's philosophy, but it is a mysticism which does not abandon the role of intellect in clarifying and correcting intuition. He advances the "principle of alternation" between intuition and intellect as fundamental to the appropriation of metaphysical truth.

In his first book, *The Meaning of God in Human Experience* (1912), Hocking developed an empirical philosophy of religion, grounded in the tradition of classical idealism and at the same time drawing heavily on the mystical experience. In so doing, he sought primarily to defend idealism against arguments of the pragmatists and realists, and he has continued this defense over the years. His as yet unpublished Gifford Lectures of 1938–1939 and other more recent works show a continuing concern with the problem of "meaning in experience," of "fact and destiny," which challenges man to go beyond his day-to-day existence and seek understanding in the wholeness of things. Thus, as a philosopher Hocking has dealt primarily with metaphysical and epistemological questions in a manner in which religious sensitivity has played a prominent part.

At no point in his long career has Hocking devoted himself exclusively to intellectual issues. He played an active role in seeking United States acceptance of the League of Nations and in the 1920s and 1930s he was especially interested in social and political problems of the Middle East. More recently he has participated in a study of freedom of the press in the United States and has been active in support of the United Nations and other political and ethical causes. These active concerns have found expression in at least ten books and scores of articles and have extended his influence far beyond the realm of academic philosophy.

Bibliography

Hocking's major work is *The Meaning of God* (New Haven, 1912). Among other works that develop his philosophical and religious views are *Human Nature and Its Remaking* (New Haven, 1923); *The Self: Its Body and Freedom* (New Haven, 1928); *Types of Philosophy* (New York, 1929; rev. eds., 1939, 1959); *Living Religions and a World Faith* (New York and Toronto; 1940); and *Science and the Idea of God* (Chapel Hill, N.C., 1944).

RICHARD C. GILMAN

HODGSON, SHADWORTH HOLLOWAY (1832–1912), English metaphysician and epistemologist, was educated at Rugby and Oxford. Although he worked outside the universities, Hodgson was widely respected among English philosophers; he was elected president of the Aristotelian Society at its founding in 1880 and was re-elected for thirteen successive years. In the United States, William James recognized the similarity of many of his own doctrines to those of Hodgson, and acknowledged Hodgson's priority despite their profound differences on fundamental points of metaphysics.

Independent and workmanlike, Hodgson was remarkably free from the characteristics and fashions of late Victorian philosophy. He remained steadfast in a central position, attacking the superficial clarities of the associationists on the one side and the vague generalizations of the Germanizing idealists on the other. His primary achievement was to keep alive the firmness of intellectual analysis peculiar to the epoch of Sir William Hamilton and H. L. Mansel. In particular he carried out the line of investigation begun in J. F. Ferrier's *Institutes of Metaphysics*. J. C. Shairp, principal of St. Andrews University and Hodgson's friend and mentor, was his link with Ferrier. Hodgson got from Ferrier a sense of the importance of the relationship of being empirically distinguishable but inseparable, in the way, for example, that color is visually inseparable from shape but nevertheless distinguishable from it. As developed by Hodgson, this principle meant that the notion of logical independence is much more complex than most philosophers have realized. Color, for example, although it is not isolable from shape, does vary independently of shape. From this point of view, Hodgson was able to repudiate the crude logical atomism then prevalent among the associationists without running to the extreme of the sort of logical monism which denies outright the reality of independence.

At a deeper level still, Hodgson applied this same principle of distinguishability with inseparability to elucidate the relationship of consciousness to its objects, that is, of the subjective to the objective. This relationship was basic for Hodgson, and he felt it was disclosed by the kind of reflective analysis that Descartes used in establishing his *cogito*. Indeed, one might say that Hodgson's starting point was the distinction between this reflective consciousness and a prereflective consciousness in which the distinction between subject and object has not yet emerged.

Although he lacked Ferrier's striking originality, Hodgson was a thinker of great intellectual honesty and thoroughness. What gives his work its special value is the modern manner in which his untiring examination of the fashionable nineteenth-century problems combined technical competence with clarity. The long discussion of Hegel in *The Philosophy of Reflection* is still of interest. So too is Hodgson's treatment of the relationships between particulars and universals and between perception and conception. His careful reconsideration of the problem of free will in *The Metaphysic of Experience* can also be profitably consulted. We are free in the sense that we determine our own actions, but that which does the determining in each case is a set of neurocerebral conditions which is not self-determined, accompanied by consciousness. In this way, he held, free will and determinism are compatible. He explained our awareness of being free as simply our awareness of the uncertainty of the outcome of our acts of volition.

Hodgson held that consciousness gives us knowledge of a reality which is independent of consciousness and which is its condition, even though consciousness is our only evidence for that reality. The material object revealed by consciousness causes sensations in consciousness. It is material, but it is composed of elements which apart from the object would not be material. Consciousness is an epiphenomenon. It is always conditioned by organic and interorganic interaction and never conditions such interactions. The proximate causes of all psychical events lie in the neurocerebral system. There might be immaterial causes of such events, but experience reveals none.

Hodgson resembles Edmund Husserl among later philosophers, rather than Bertrand Russell, G. E. Moore, and their followers. Hodgson's doctrine that things are what they are "known as" anticipated in a way Husserl's phenomenological reduction, and his technique of distinguishing between inseparables approximates to Husserl's reduction to essences. Hodgson's ethics, though perhaps less interesting than his metaphysics, nevertheless shows the same conscientious struggle to clarify basic distinctions and can be as profitably studied as some other, better-known systems.

Works by Hodgson

Time and Space. London, 1865.
The Theory of Practice, 2 vols. London, 1870.
The Philosophy of Reflection, 2 vols. London, 1878.
The Metaphysic of Experience, 4 vols. London, 1898.

Works on Hodgson

Carr, H. W., "Shadworth Holloway Hodgson." *Mind,* N.S., Vol. 21 (1912).
Hicks, G. Dawes, "Shadworth Holloway Hodgson." *Proceedings of the British Academy,* Vol. 6 (1913).
Stout, C. F., "The Philosophy of Mr. Shadworth Hodgson." *PAS,* Vol. 1 (1892).

GEORGE E. DAVIE

HØFFDING, HARALD (1843–1931), Danish philosopher and historian of philosophy. Høffding was born in Copenhagen and lived there throughout his life. From 1883 to 1915 he was professor of philosophy at the University of Copenhagen. Høffding received a degree in divinity in 1865, but he had already decided not to take orders. A study of Søren Kierkegaard's works, and especially of his views on Christianity, had led to an intense religious crisis ending in a radical break with Christianity. Høffding sought in philosophy a new personal orientation and gradually developed into an extraordinarily many-sided liberal humanist. His philosophical development was influenced during a stay in Paris (1868/1869) by the study of French and English positivism, especially that of Auguste Comte and Herbert Spencer. Høffding always worked hard, and his activity as a scholar ranged over every branch of philosophy, including psychology. His works display a vast knowledge, a keen eye for essentials,

and a critically balanced judgment. They were translated into many languages and widely used as textbooks. By the turn of the century Høffding's reputation was world-wide and he knew personally many leading thinkers. He was the outstanding Danish philosopher of his day, and in 1914 the Royal Danish Academy of Sciences and Letters assigned him the honorary residence of Gammel Carlsberg, where he lived to the end of his life. The residence later passed to the physicist Niels Bohr, a younger friend of Høffding.

Of Høffding's many works only five can be discussed here. *Psykologi i Omrids på Grundlag af Erfaring* (Copenhagen, 1881; translated by M. E. Loundes as *Outlines of Psychology,* London) is based on the traditional tripartite division of the mind into knowledge, feeling, and will but puts primary stress on the will in the widest sense of the term. In this sense the will includes conation, urge, endeavor, need, demand, and desire. The will is seen as primary, knowledge as guiding the will, and feeling as a symptom of need or desire, which are themselves elements of the will. Høffding's view anticipated modern need and dynamic psychology.

In *Etik, en Fremstilling af de etiske Principper og deres Anvendelse på de vigtigste Livsforhold* ("Ethics: An Account of Ethical Principles and Their Application to the Chief Conditions of Life," Copenhagen, 1887) Høffding associated himself with British utilitarianism, which he called welfare ethics. The greatest happiness of the greatest number is the fundamental value. In the conflict between individual and social ethics, Høffding took the liberal view. The psychological basis of ethical valuation is a sympathetic feeling which at its highest development takes on the character of a universal and disinterested sympathy.

Den nyere Filosofis Historie, en Fremstilling af Filosofiens Historie fra Renaissancens Slutning til vore Dage (2 vols., Copenhagen, 1894–1895; translated by B. E. Meyer as *History of Modern Philosophy,* 2 vols., London, 1900; reprinted, 2 vols., New York, 1955) is a concentrated account of the various modern philosophers and philosophical schools marked by a fine balance between exposition and criticism. It is of special interest as the first study of modern philosophy to put the primary stress on the mathematicomechanical science and methods of Galileo and Newton in presenting the development of epistemology. Among the philosophers treated, Høffding found Spinoza, Hume, and Kant especially congenial.

Religionsfilosofi (Copenhagen, 1901; translated by B. E. Meyer as *Philosophy of Religion,* New York, 1906), in three parts, treats religious experience from the standpoints of epistemology, psychology, and ethics. Høffding claimed that the basis of all religion is a desire for belief in the existence of values, and that the various religions may be characterized by the kinds of values which they claim exist. The presentation is distinguished by its reasoned objectivity and its respect for religion. Høffding himself was an agnostic.

In *Den menneskelige Tanke, dens Former og dens Opgave* ("Human Thought: Its Forms and Its Problems," Copenhagen, 1910) Høffding set forth his theory of knowledge, including an outline for a doctrine of categories whose usefulness has been reduced by the development of modern logic. Høffding's interest in epistemology was psychological rather than strictly logical, and his interest in the psychological basis of knowledge was constructive rather than phenomenological. In general, Høffding followed Hume and Kant in regarding the forms and principles of human knowledge as being peculiar to human beings and their absolute ontological validity as being incapable of proof. The result is a compromise between empiricism and the Kantian critical philosophy.

Bibliography

There is a brief autobiography containing an account of Høffding's fundamental views in Raymund Schmidt, ed., *Die Philosophie der Gegenwart in Selbstdarstellungen,* Vol. IV (Leipzig, 1923). Kalle Sandelin, ed., *Harald Høffding in Memoriam* (Copenhagen, 1932), contains an excellent bibliography which lists 393 publications by Høffding as well as 425 papers and reviews concerning his works.

Frithiof Brandt

HOLBACH, PAUL-HENRI THIRY, BARON D'

(1723–1789), the foremost exponent of atheistic materialism and the most intransigent polemicist against religion in the Enlightenment. Holbach was born of honorable but obscure German parents in Edesheim, a small town in the Palatinate; his name was originally Paul Heinrich Dietrich. His upbringing and education were directed by his maternal uncle, Franciscus Adam d'Holbach, who had made a fortune in Paris and assumed French nationality. After studying at the University of Leiden, Holbach came to Paris, in 1749, married his second cousin Basile-Geneviève d'Aine, and soon became a French subject. On his uncle's death in 1753, he inherited the title of Baron d'Holbach, with properties yielding a handsome income of 60,000 livres. The following year his wife died, and in 1756 Holbach married her younger sister, Charlotte Suzanne d'Aine.

On settling in Paris, Holbach had associated with the younger *philosophes* who, with Diderot, d'Alembert, and Rousseau, were grouping around the *Encyclopédie,* to which he also became a major contributor. His *salon* soon became the main social center, and a sort of intellectual headquarters, for the Encyclopedist movement. The gatherings on Thursdays and Sundays, during more than three decades, at Holbach's house in Rue Royale-Saint-Roch were famous not only for his excellent dinners but also as a unique "clearinghouse" for radical ideas of every type. The more intimate meetings at his country estate of Grandval, near Paris, have been described in fascinating detail in Diderot's letters. The members of Holbach's circle, besides the assiduous Diderot, included Melchior von Grimm, Claude Helvétius, d'Alembert, Rousseau, Nicolas-Antoine Boulanger, Étienne Condillac, Jacques-André Naigeon, Turgot, and Condorcet. The baron also counted among his acquaintances many foreigners, notably David Hume, Edward Gibbon, Adam Smith, Joseph Priestley, Horace Walpole, David Garrick, Laurence Sterne, Cesare Beccaria, and Benjamin Franklin.

Because he left neither a body of correspondence nor personal papers, Holbach's character must be pieced together from contemporary accounts. The composite picture credits him with an impressive erudition, an extremely methodical mind, a collector's interest in art, and with the qualities of affability, discreet generosity, modesty, loyalty to friends, and a taste for virtuous simplicity. Diderot's more private remarks diverge somewhat from this public image, disclosing that the baron, at least with those nearest him, had moments of moodiness, petulance, and gruffness. But these traits just provide a touch of humanity without essentially altering the picture of him as the virtuous atheist. Even Rousseau, despite growing hostility, used him as the model for Monsieur de Wolmar, the altruistic unbeliever of *La Nouvelle Héloïse.* Indeed, Holbach's comportment as a social being evidently conformed to his deep desire to illustrate, by his own life and personality, the truth of a most cherished philosophical opinion, that atheism and morality are as plausibly bound together as religiosity and true virtue are not.

Although Holbach, until some years after his death, was publicly known merely as *le premier maître d'hôtel de la philosophie,* he had surreptitiously played a far greater role, known only to a few. Almost everything he wrote—whether because it expounded atheism and materialism, attacked Christianity, or castigated absolute monarchy, the state church, and feudal privilege—was highly subversive under the *ancien régime* and could have exposed him to the severest penalties. Consequently, his innumerable manuscripts were usually forwarded through secret channels to Holland for publication, after which the books were smuggled back into France. Owing to the strict anonymity that Holbach maintained, bibliographers have since been faced with insoluble problems of exact attribution concerning many texts linked to him.

Philosophical orientation. Holbach's literary career falls conveniently into three phases. A competent although uncreative student of chemistry, metallurgy, mineralogy, and geology, he translated into French, mainly during the 1750s, a number of works (mostly German) from these fields. He also contributed to the *Encyclopédie,* beginning in 1752, almost four hundred articles dealing with the same sciences. These interests shaped Holbach's philosophical outlook, for his materialism corresponded to the methodology and scope of a rigorously scientific explanation of things. In particular, the new evidence offered by geology concerning the earth's history negated, in his view, the doctrine of creation, and with it the existence of God.

The second phase of Holbach's activity, coinciding with the 1760s, consisted of a relentless militancy against organized religion in general and the Catholic church in particular. Not content with the repeated broadsides of his own composition, he also translated anticlerical, deistic, or materialistic works by various British authors (among them Peter Annet, Anthony Collins, Thomas Woolston, John Toland, and Thomas Hobbes), and he published, with the collaboration of Naigeon, a number of French antireligious texts that had long been circulating clandestinely in manuscript copies. Among Holbach's own tracts, the most important were *Le Christianisme dévoilé, ou Examen des principes et des effets de la religion chrétienne* (1761); *Théologie portative, ou Dictionnaire abrégé de la religion chrétienne* (1767); *La Contagion sacrée, ou Histoire naturelle de la superstition* (1768); *Lettres à Eugénie, ou Préservatif contre les préjugés* (1768); and *Histoire critique de Jésus-Christ, ou Analyse raisonnée des Évangiles* (1770). The themes recurring throughout these and similar books represent a vehement restatement of almost all the arguments for unbelief current in eighteenth-century France. The most characteristic are the following: The idea and cult of God sprang from the ignorant terror of primitive man seeking to placate the destructive powers of nature, and they have survived ever since through superstition; religious history is a catalogue of senseless disputes, intolerance, prejudice, persecution, and crime; the clergy is ordinarily engaged in exploiting the gullibility of the people for its own profit; religions have invariably supported tyrannical governments to further their own ambitions of domination; Scriptural "proofs" of Christianity are worthless as objective historical evidence; theological dogmas are a maze of delusion and mystification on which no rational, just, or useful social institution can be built.

Atheistic materialism. The third and properly philosophical stage of Holbach's output began in 1770 with the *Système de la nature, ou des Lois du monde physique et du monde moral.* This first—and only—example in the Enlightenment of a comprehensive, unmitigated defense of atheistic materialism was the culmination of a whole trend of ideas already expressed in varying degrees by La Mettrie, Helvétius, Diderot, and others. It caused much consternation in France, not only among spokesmen for the official faith but among the deistic *philosophes* as well. It was suppressed by judicial decree, and among the flood of refutations it provoked were those of Voltaire (the article "God" in the *Philosophical Dictionary*) and Frederick the Great (*Examen critique du Système de la nature*).

The *Système de la nature* defines man as a product entirely of nature, subject to the laws governing the physical universe which, in turn, constitutes the whole of reality. The soul, or spiritual substance, is an illusion; the moral and intellectual attributes of man are simply his organic machine considered in certain of its special, less visible operations. Since sensibility is a primary function of the animal organism, all our higher faculties are derived ultimately from the different forms that sensation takes. The only means of knowing man in nature is through the empirical and rational investigation of matter.

Nature is the sum of matter and motion. All matter is actually or latently in motion, since energy, or force, is among its inherent properties. The material universe is self-created and eternal. All change in nature represents a communication of motion, a redistribution of energy, which modifies the corresponding combination or disposition of material particles, elements, or aggregates. The totality of matter and motion are eternal and constant, but the specific forms they exhibit—rocks, plants, animals, oceans, heavenly bodies, and so forth—are forever changing. Each thing or being tends, by the laws of attraction and repulsion, to persist in its essence, until it is finally transformed into something else. Man is no exception: the ephemeral life of his species depends on the stability of the physical environment.

There is neither chance nor disorder in nature: all is necessity and order, an irreversible chain of causes and effects. Freedom is objectively meaningless when applied to human behavior, which, controlled by such factors as temperament, education, and environment, takes part in the universal determinism of nature. Virtue and vice, moreover, need not depend on free will; they simply describe actions favoring or hindering the mutual happiness of society and the individual.

Ethics. Holbach's principal aim was to construct a system of ethical and political values on materialistic grounds. The supreme natural goal of human existence is happiness, but no one can be happy without the services of others. Ethics, therefore, is the science of human cooperation to promote the well-being of the individual through that of society, and it is based on the positive knowledge of men's reciprocal social needs. If mankind has always been morally corrupt and unhappy, religion has been mainly to blame. Supernatural theology, by falsifying man's nature and linking his salvation to the illusory notions of God and immortality, has entirely subverted ethical truth. Holbach takes pains to show that, all attempted definitions of God being hopelessly self-contradictory, "God" is logically a meaningless term. It is understandable, then, that belief in God should have been historically of no moral utility. For religious morality, founded on dogmatic obscurantism and ritualistic futilities rather than on natural and social realities, has prevented human beings from perceiving and correcting the actual conditions productive of vice and misery. Atheism is thus the prerequisite of all valid ethical teaching. In place of the condemnation of sin, Holbach's exposition of secular and utilitarian ethics is typically accompanied by vibrant appeals to humanitarianism and moving exhortations to civic virtue—all in the name of "nature" and "happiness."

Political theory. In *Le Bon-Sens, ou Idées naturelles opposées aux idées surnaturelles* (1772), the most widely read of his books, Holbach offered a popular, unsystematic version of his philosophy. Thereafter, with the growing troubles of the Bourbon regime, he focused his attention on national problems and developed at great length the ethical and political sections of the *Système de la nature* in a new series of works: *Politique naturelle, ou Discours sur les vrais principes du gouvernement* (1773); *Système social, ou Principes naturels de la morale et de la politique* (1773); *Éthocratie, ou le Gouvernement fondé sur la morale* (1776); and *La Morale universelle, ou les Devoirs de l'homme fondés sur sa nature* (1776).

His own term "ethocracy" describes the gist of Holbachian political thought. The state, whose role is simply an extension of the social ethics of enlightened self-love, ought to nurture, in every possible way, the virtues of cooperation on which the good of society and the felicity of each of its members depend. The social pact itself is based on the useful services that the individual and society are able to render to one another, and it remains valid only to the extent that its mutually beneficial aims are fulfilled. Since, therefore, the legitimacy of any government varies directly with the happiness of one and all living under it, Holbach proclaimed with courageous logic the people's right, if there were no other hope of assuring their welfare, to overthrow and replace their rulers. Where the happiness of a society was at stake, it was the sovereign; governments, which were merely means to an end, had no absolute or divine authority.

More specifically, Holbach proposed radical political and economic reforms for France in keeping with the ethocratic ideal. He advocated, as against the extremes of republicanism and enlightened despotism, a limited, constitutional monarchy, in which intermediate parliamentary bodies would represent the interests of society and would maintain a balance between the opposing dangers of either popular or autocratic tyranny. He called for the abolition of hereditary class privileges and for their replacement by a hierarchy of status based on the degree of socially useful service actually rendered by its members. He defended the principle of progressive taxation according to wealth and wanted individual ownership of property to be as proportionate as possible to the value of work performed, thus eliminating the extremes of opulence and poverty. He insisted on the complete separation of church and state and on the toleration of all religious sects, with the government as a neutral preserving peace among them. Freedom of thought and of the press were to be inviolable; and government had the duty of providing a system of secular public education, with its main objective the inculcation of the social and civic virtues.

Sources and influence. Among the sources of Holbach's philosophy were classical and modern Epicureanism, the Cartesian universe of matter and motion in perpetual flux, the logical and metaphysical materialism of Hobbes, the determinism and "atheism" of Spinoza, the sensationalism of Locke, and Leibnizian dynamics. Nearer in time, Holbach was indebted to Helvétius for the utilitarian conception; to La Mettrie for the physiological psychology of the *homme machine;* and to the experimentalist, evolutionary materialism of Diderot, with whom he had the closest personal and ideological ties.

Despite serious shortcomings, Holbach's ideas are still of considerable interest. Although the value of his critique of Christianity is today limited by the onesidedness and unimaginativeness resulting from his polemical stance and propagandist aims, historically it led toward the objective and psychological study of religion as a distinctly human invention. The *Système de la nature* suffers, no doubt, from too much reliance on outmoded scientific theories; from an excessive generalization and simplification of the concrete complexities of nature; and from a tiresome combination of doctrinaire tone and humorless prolixity which were, unfortunately, peculiar to the author. Nonetheless, it remains a classic text in the development of atheistic materialism as the philosophical expression par excellence of modern science. The main weakness of Holbach's political thought is that it exaggerated a rationalist, moralistic, and prescriptive approach to the subject at the expense of the perhaps more important role of economic, sociological, and historical laws of development on which political institutions, and the changes to be made in them, must depend. Nevertheless, it served significantly to prepare for the French Revolution and contributed subsequently to the progress of democratic and utilitarian doctrines.

Works by Holbach

Holbach's works, despite innumerable editions, have never been published in collected form, and few of them have been reprinted since the first half of the nineteenth century. The following are English translations:

Christianity Unveiled; Being an Examination of the Principles and Effects of the Christian Religion. New York, 1795; London, 1819.

Common Sense: or Natural Ideas Opposed to Supernatural. New York, 1795, 1833, 1836. Also published as *Superstition in All Ages.* New York, 1878, 1890, 1920; Chicago, 1910.

The System of Nature; or, The Laws of the Moral and Physical World. London, 1795–1796; 1797, 1816, 1820, 1834, 1839, 1840, 1863, 1884; Philadelphia, 1808; New York, 1835; Boston, 1853.

Ecce Homo! or, A Critical Inquiry Into the History of Jesus of Nazareth. Edinburgh, 1799; London, 1813, 1823; New York, 1827.

Letters to Eugenia, on the Absurd, Contradictory, and Demoralizing Dogmas and Mysteries of the Christian Religion. London, 1819; New York, 1833; Boston, 1857.

Works on Holbach

Charbonnel, Paulette, ed., *Textes choisis; Préface, commentaire et notes.* Paris, 1957.

Cushing, Max Pearson, *Baron d'Holbach; A Study of Eighteenth-century Radicalism in France.* New York, 1914.

Hubert, René, *D'Holbach et ses amis.* Paris, 1928.

Lange, Friedrich Albert, *The History of Materialism,* translated by E. C. Thomas. New York, 1950. Bk. I, Sec. iv, Ch. 3.

Mauthner, Fritz, *Der Atheismus und seine Geschichte im Abendlande,* 4 vols. Stuttgart and Berlin, 1920–1923. Vol. III. Ch. 5.

Naville, Pierre, *Paul Thiry d'Holbach et la philosophie scientifique au XVIIIᵉ siècle.* Paris, 1943.

Topazio, Virgil, *D'Holbach's Moral Philosophy; Its Background and Development.* Geneva, 1956.

Wickwar, W. H., *Baron d'Holbach; A Prelude to the French Revolution.* London, 1935.

ARAM VARTANIAN

HÖLDERLIN, JOHANN CHRISTIAN FRIEDRICH

(1770–1843), German poet, novelist, and dramatist, was born at Lauffen, Württemberg. His father died when he was two, and his mother, who expected him to become a minister, had him raised in the evangelical monastery schools at Denkendorf and Maulbronn. In 1788 he entered the theological seminary of the University of Tübingen, where he received his master's degree in 1793. With his close friends and fellow students Hegel and Schelling he shared an enthusiasm for the French Revolution, a love of Spinoza, Plato, and Rousseau, and a distaste for the ministry. The example of his fellow Württembergian, Friedrich Schiller, proved of decisive importance. Emulating Schiller, Hölderlin composed moralistic hymns celebrating friendship, freedom, and love, which were published in 1792 as *Hymnen an die Ideale der Menschheit.* Schiller helped to get his first position as a tutor at Waltershausen near Jena in 1793, but Hölderlin soon left this post for Jena because of his desire to be nearer to Fichte and Schiller and also in the hope of establishing himself as a lecturer in philosophy. However, his attempt to enter into the Weimar–Jena circle failed: the relationship between Hölderlin and Schiller soon cooled, and in 1795 Hölderlin left Jena and its "airy spirits with metaphysical wings" in despair and returned to his mother in Nürtingen.

In 1796 Hölderlin became tutor to the son of the banker J. F. Gontard in Frankfurt, where Hegel, whom he had helped to find a tutoring position, soon joined him. In Gontard's wife Susette, Hölderlin found his Diotima, who introduced him to the mysteries. His poetry of this period, in which he celebrated Diotima and Greece in classical meters, shows that Hölderlin had emancipated himself from Schiller. An atmosphere similar to that in his neo-classical poetry pervades his lyric novel *Hyperion* (2 vols., 1797–1799), an idealization of the Greek struggle for independence. It is characteristic of Hölderlin that in this novel the attempt to establish an ideal society on earth collapses before the reality of battle. Forced to leave his position in Frankfurt in 1798, Hölderlin found refuge with his friend Isaak von Sinclair in Homburg, where he worked on his tragedy *Der Tod des Empedokles,* in which the Greek philosopher, priest, and statesman Empedocles atones for the sin of individuation by plunging into Mount Etna. In 1801, after short periods as a tutor in Stuttgart and in Hauptwyl, Switzerland, Hölderlin left for Bordeaux to assume another tutoring position. Sensing impending disaster, he likened himself to Tantalus, to whom the gods had given more than he could digest. Upon his return to Nürtingen in 1802, the year in which Susette Gontard died, the first signs of insanity were apparent. In 1804 Sinclair helped Hölderlin obtain a position as librarian in Homburg, and in the same year the poet's translations of *Oedipus* and *Antigone* were published. Although Hölderlin's illness continued to progress, the hymns he wrote at this time were of a power unsurpassed by his earlier work. In these hymns hexameter gave way to free rhythms; continuity and structure threatened to disappear; individual phrases and words assumed a significance that eludes—and therefore invites—analysis. After 1806 Hölderlin became all but silent. His remaining years were spent in insanity at Tübingen.

Hölderlin cannot be grouped with such romantics as his contemporaries Novalis or Friedrich Schlegel. The antinaturalistic moralism of Kant and Schiller, the subjectivism of Fichte, and in general the romantics' emphasis on artistic imagination and irony, which seems to reduce the world to a collection of mere occasions to be manipulated by the artist, ran counter to Hölderlin's almost religious veneration of nature. For him, nature possessed a value of its own; it did not depend on man for its value. Hölderlin's writings lack the lightness that characterizes German romanticism and that to him was a sign of the victory of the abstract spirit and artistic imagination over reality. His friend Hegel, and later Kierkegaard, were to state this criticism of romanticism with greater philosophic rigor. In a letter to Schiller of September 4, 1795, Hölderlin likened philosophy to an attempt to square the circle. According to him, philosophy is part of an infinite process of approximation. At each stage its results are inadequate; to forget this inadequacy is to forget the fate of finite man and to run the risk of substituting system for reality. But what is theoretically impossible is possible to the artist. The artist reveals reality with an adequacy that philosophy lacks.

Like the romantics, Hölderlin found that the meaning of reality is concealed by man's overinvolvement in the finite. Man's own interests prevent him from listening to the voices of nature. Therefore, the poet must mediate between gods and men. The poet senses the divine presence in the world, and this gives him the strength to name the gods, the appearances of the infinite in the finite. But this privilege is bought at a price: to be ready for the call of the gods, the poet must estrange himself from his fellow human beings. Hölderlin sensed the hubris in the poet's

claim to be the chosen spokesman of the gods. Thus, he accused himself of having sinned against his fellow men: since as a poet he neither loved nor served them in human fashion, they did not show themselves to him as human. Having been "raised in the arms of the Gods," the poet is necessarily alone. But is not this thought itself a presumption? In the last years before his insanity, Hölderlin, who referred to himself as "the false priest," repeatedly described his approaching illness as a punishment visited upon him by the gods as a warning to others.

The predicament in which Hölderlin thought he found himself, and to which he discovered no solution, is that the poet (and indeed every human being) stands between two claims—that of the everyday world and that of the gods. Between the two there seems to be no mediation. Hölderlin wanted to live what most romantics were content to imagine—a life dedicated to divine reality. The poet who takes his vocation seriously and is unwilling to seek refuge in the everyday is left with only one choice—that between insanity or death. Both Hölderlin's life and his work, which illustrate the power as well as the danger of such a view, have drawn the attention of such important modern thinkers as Wilhelm Dilthey, Karl Jaspers, Martin Heidegger, Ernst Cassirer, and Romano Guardini.

Works by Hölderlin

Historische kritische Ausgabe, N. Hellingrath, F. Sebass, and V. Pigenot, eds., 6 vols. Berlin, 1922–1923.

Some Poems of Friedrich Hölderlin, translated by Frederic Prokosch. Norfolk, Conn., 1943.

Stuttgarter Hölderlin Ausgabe, F. Beissner, ed. Stuttgart, 1946 ff.

Poems of Hölderlin, translated by Michael Hamburger. London, 1943. 2d ed. published as *Hölderlin, His Poems.* New York, 1952.

Selected Poems, 2d ed., translated by J. B. Leishman. London, 1954.

Works on Hölderlin

Allemann, B., *Hölderlin und Heidegger.* Zurich, 1954.

Böckmann, P., *Hölderlin und seine Götter.* Munich, 1935.

Böhm, W., "Hölderlin als Verfasser der ältesten. Systemprogrammes des deutschen Idealismus." *Deutsche Vierteljahrsschrift,* Vol. 11 (1927).

Böhm, W., *Hölderlin,* 2 vols. Halle, 1928–1936.

Butler, E. M., *The Tyranny of Greece over Germany.* Boston, 1958.

Cassirer, Ernst, *Idee und Gestalt. Goethe, Schiller, Hölderlin, Kleist.* Berlin, 1921.

Croce, Benedetto, "Intorno allo Hölderlin e ai suoi critici." *La Critica,* Vol. 4 (1941).

Dilthey, Wilhelm, *Das Erlebnis und die Dichtung. Lessing, Goethe, Novalis, Hölderlin,* 3d ed. Leipzig, 1910.

Guardini, Romano, *Hölderlin.* Munich, 1939.

Hamburger, Michael, *Reason and Energy.* New York, 1957.

Heidegger, Martin, *Hölderlin und das Wesen der Dichtung.* Pfüllingen, 1936. Translated in his *Existence and Being.* Chicago, 1949.

Heidegger, Martin, *Erläuterungen zu Hölderlins Dichtung.* Frankfurt, 1944; expanded ed., 1950, 1951.

Hildebrandt, K., *Hölderlin, Philosophie und Dichtung.* Stuttgart, 1943.

Hölderlin Jahrbuch. Tübingen, 1944 ff.; 22 vols. to date.

Jaspers, Karl, *Strindberg und Van Gogh. Versuch einer pathographischen Analyse unter vergleichender Heranziehung von Swedenborg und Hölderlin.* Bremen, 1949.

Michel, Wilhelm, *Das Leben Friedrich Hölderlins.* Bremen, 1949.

Peacock, R., *Hölderlin.* London, 1938.

Salzberger, L. S., *Hölderlin*. Cambridge, England, 1952.
Wahl, Jean, *La Pensée de Heidegger et la pensée de Hölderlin*. Paris, 1952.

KARSTEN HARRIES

HOLISM AND INDIVIDUALISM IN HISTORY AND SOCIAL SCIENCE. In most recent philosophical discussion, the contrast between holism and individualism in history and the social sciences has been presented as a methodological issue. Stated generally, the question is whether we should treat large-scale social events and conditions as mere aggregates or configurations of the actions, attitudes, relations, and circumstances of the individual men and women who participated in, enjoyed, or suffered them. Methodological individualists say we should. Methodological holists (or collectivists, as some prefer to be called) claim, rather, that social phenomena may be studied at their own autonomous, macroscopic level of analysis. Social "wholes," they say, not their human elements, are the true historical individuals.

This issue obviously bears directly upon the way we are to conceive the relations between such social sciences as psychology and sociology, and between these and historical inquiry. But it is commonly thought also to involve us in wide-ranging metaphysical problems—those of historicism and organicism, for example—and to have grave ethical and political implications as well. Sir Isaiah Berlin, in *Historical Inevitability* (Oxford, 1954), moves quickly from methodological to metaphysical issues when he represents holists as believing in "invisible powers and dominions," conceived as "impersonal entities at once patterns and realities, in terms of which . . . men and institutions must behave as they do." And May Brodbeck, in "Methodological Individualisms: Definition and Reduction," expresses a common opinion when she writes: "Culturally, holism is intimately connected with hostility toward the liberal political individualism of the Western tradition." Individualists, in their turn, have been castigated by their opponents for encouraging laissez-faire in economics and anarchy in politics, the alleged natural consequences of adopting an "atomistic" view of social life. Indeed, the threat of appropriate social consequences seems to have been regarded by some as a reason for accepting one or the other of these methodological positions. F. A. Hayek and K. R. Popper are well-known champions of the principle of methodological individualism as a bulwark against the supposed horrors of the "planned society"—or at any rate, against anything worse than "piecemeal social engineering."

It is not, in fact, entirely accurate to say that the methodological, metaphysical, and political doctrines have invariably gone together. Thomas Hobbes, for example, was in effect a methodological individualist who advocated something close to political absolutism; and Maurice Mandelbaum, as will appear below, is a contemporary methodological holist who would certainly repudiate "invisible powers" and "impersonal entities." But political or ethical argument has, in any case, a dubious place in an examination of holism and individualism as methodological prescriptions for social and historical research. Even if metaphysical questions cannot ultimately be ignored, it is

worthwhile, at least at the outset, to try to consider the contending methodological doctrines in their own terms. The discussion that follows makes no attempt to trace the considerable history of the problem in Western philosophy; rather, it is a report on what some contemporary philosophers have said by way of exposition and defense of the two positions. Since it has generally been the individualists who have taken the initiative in controversy, it will be convenient to set forth their position first.

Methodological individualism. J. W. N. Watkins, one of the most prominent recent advocates of methodological individualism, has presented it as primarily a theory of sociological or historical explanation. In his "Ideal Types and Historical Explanation," Watkins stated its requirements thus: "Social processes and events should be explained by being deduced from (*a*) principles governing the behaviour of the participating individuals and (*b*) descriptions of their situations." The elaboration of criteria for acceptable explanation is, of course, an activity characteristic of philosophers. What has most often concerned them, however, has been the formal or structural features of explanation, that is, the logical relation that must hold between an explanans and explanandum. Watkins' criterion, by contrast, is a material one. It makes a stipulation about the content of a social or historical explanans, holding that it must be "psychological," at least in the sense of being, in Watkins' words, about "the situations, dispositions and beliefs of individuals."

In formulating their material requirement, individualists often have in mind successful patterns of explanation in other branches of science. According to Watkins, the principle of methodological individualism is a correlate of the principle of mechanism in physics, which held triumphant sway from the seventeenth to the nineteenth centuries. An especially prestigious example of the application of the mechanistic principle is the explanation of the solar system by reference to Newton's laws and the positions, masses, and momenta of its component "individuals." Another example, often cited, is the explanation of the macro properties of a gas—its temperature, for example—as a resultant of the micro properties of its molecules. The best illustration of the same explanatory procedure in social science is afforded by classical economics, which regards macro states of the market as resultants of the dispositions and consequent activities of individual producers and consumers. There are differences (some will be discussed later) between the way particles in a mechanistic system are linked with what they explain and the way psychological facts about individuals are linked with social events. Methodological individualists, however, regard the likenesses as more instructive than the differences.

Methodological holism. The rival thesis of methodological holism is that explanations in history and social science may (some would say "must") employ holistic societal laws or dispositions. Social dispositions are envisaged as being holistic, not only in the sense of being macroscopic relative to individual behavior but as being irreducibly so. Except in extreme versions of the theory (usually framed by opponents for polemical purposes), psychological elements are not actually excluded from a social explanans; they are merely regarded as insufficient.

Thus, in their most usual form, the two methodological doctrines are not contraries but contradictories.

In elaborating their position, holists often match paradigm cases with the individualists. In economics, for example, they point to the Keynesian theory, which relates such variables as national income and savings, as showing the need to supplement the classical approach with a macroscopic one. In physics they note the decline of mechanism with the development of wave and field notions. And methodological holists do not limit their claims to cases in which social phenomena are explained by other societal factors. The explanation of individual actions themselves, they insist, may often have to be given partly in societal terms, employing laws that link individual behavior with types of social conditions. They deny, however, that this commits them either to organicism or to historicism. For *sui generis* societal laws can be of various logical types. They need not be organic, in the sense of relating the parts of the social system in a way that makes society self-regulating or self-maintaining, nor need they be developmental. There is thus no necessary connection between methodological holism and the dismal conclusion that men are caught up in some inexorable process that possesses something like a life of its own.

REFINEMENTS OF INDIVIDUALISM

The basic response of methodological holism to the individualist claim is that the procedures of history and social science are in fact largely holistic, and that attempts to apply the principle of individualism do not work. The theory of the social sciences should accept the consequences. To methodological individualists, on the other hand, failures of application simply indicate a need for further analysis and research. Yet the discrepancy between fact and theory has induced individualists to make a few concessions, which are often represented as "refinements" or "clarifications" of the original thesis. A brief look at four of these may help to sharpen the issue.

Levels of explanation. Individualists generally concede, first, that macro explanations may sometimes be both true and informative. The temperature of a gas, for example, may be explained by referring to a heat source that was applied to it, or to such simultaneous macro conditions as its volume and pressure; the outbreak of a revolution may be similarly explained by referring to economic or social trends in the society as a whole. According to Watkins, all the methodological individualist claims is that until we manage to reduce such explanations to terms of the molecular theory of gases or the psychology of individuals, we fail to achieve a full understanding of what has occurred. Thus, what the individualist seems to offer is not a criterion of being an explanation at all (for this, the satisfaction of formal criteria may be enough), but of being an ultimately satisfactory one. Yet the acceptability of "half-way explanations" (to use Watkins' term) is said to depend on the possibility of eventually reducing them to "rock-bottom explanations." The concession, in other words, is only with regard to "practice"; nothing is yielded at the level of "principle."

Anonymous individuals. A second refinement arises out of the suspicion that what is actually possible in social science, even "in principle," is seldom an explanation in terms of the dispositions of the specific individuals involved. We might explain the rise in a stock's value, for example, by pointing out that the individual dispositions that most stockholders may be presumed to share lead them to be willing to pay a higher price under the circumstances; but we could hardly hope to ground our conclusion in knowledge of the detailed motives and beliefs of all the individuals involved. Methodological individualists consequently limit their prescription, even for "rock-bottom explanations," to typical dispositions of anonymous individuals. Such explanations, they will point out, still follow the model of mechanistic physics, in which information about specific particles is not required. Unlike physical particles, it cannot, of course, be presumed that human beings are all alike, or even that they are similar in all respects relevant to the social resultant that is being studied. This is particularly the case in historical inquiry, with its concern for unique rather than recurring circumstances and events. Thus, it will often be impossible to give adequate historical explanations without taking at least some named individuals into account. Even in the field of history, however, there is considerable scope for the anonymous.

Unintended results. Advocates of individualism often emphasize that if explanation need not be in terms of the actions and dispositions of specific human beings, still less need it show that social phenomena are brought about deliberately, or even knowingly, by individuals. Methodological individualists do not question the contention, constantly reiterated by holists, that social phenomena are largely the *unintended* results of the behavior of hosts of interacting human beings. The individualist principle is thus to be distinguished from what K. R. Popper, in *The Open Society and Its Enemies* (London, 1945), has called the "conspiracy theory of society": the view that for every social effect there is a manipulator (hero or villain) to be found. Not that individualists doubt that public affairs are controllable through the knowledgeable intervention of people; they hold, rather, that even when events are not so controlled, they can be explained individualistically. The individualist principle is also to be distinguished from a second doctrine with which Watkins felt it is sometimes confused, namely, the view that social phenomena "reflect" the dispositions of component individuals. Social characteristics are often, in fact, quite different qualitatively from the characteristics of the individuals referred to in explaining them. But there is likewise no qualitative similarity between the thermodynamic properties of a gas and the mechanical properties of its elements.

Exceptions. Some individualists are willing to make a concession that leads to still a fourth refinement of the original doctrine. They allow that there are some social phenomena, at least, that may not be open to individualistic explanation at all, although they usually add that these exceptions are not very important for the theory of the social sciences—certainly not important enough to justify the acceptance of methodological holism as a general principle for explanation in these fields. The exceptions fall into two classes. The first contains phenomena that can be treated only statistically. The second consists of occasional instances of what may be genuinely organic "social" behavior: Watkins mentioned the physical union of mating couples, the ecstatic singing of revival meetings, the rioting of panicking crowds. But, individualists argue, we cannot extrapolate from such cases to the nature of "higher-grade" forms of social organization. The latter, even when unplanned, are related by "ideas" and involve people widely separated in space and time.

ARGUMENTS FOR METHODOLOGICAL INDIVIDUALISM

Clarified and refined, then, the principle of methodological individualism asserts that *ultimate* or *final* explanation of the more *significant* social phenomena must be given in terms of at least *typical* dispositions (including beliefs, attitudes, and volitions) of *anonymous* individuals involved. Individualists often seem to present this principle as self-evident. Yet arguments for it have been offered, among the most characteristic in contemporary literature being the five which are considered below. No separate presentation of the case for methodological holism will be given, since holists are generally content to offer rebuttals of what their opponents claim.

Metaphysical arguments. One common argument appeals directly to ontological considerations. According to Watkins, "the ontological basis of methodological individualism is the assumption that society . . . really consists only of people." Social "things" may even be said to be "created" by individuals, by their attitudes as well as by their actions. "Remove the attitudes of food officials, shop-keepers, housewives, etc., towards ration books," Watkins observed, "and they shrivel into bits of cardboard." To a methodological individualist it seems paradoxical to suggest that social objects, thus constituted, could be explained other than individualistically. To try to explain individual actions in social terms seems to involve referring what really exists to a mere "construction." Yet although ontological individualism offers the methodological doctrine a "basis," Watkins conceded that the former does not actually entail the latter. It might still be true that what is constituted by individual actions and attitudes is governed by autonomous social law, although the ontology of individualism makes this difficult to believe.

Today, few holists would argue directly from a corresponding ontological thesis, which would rest upon some such principle as "a whole is not equal to the sum of its parts," the social whole thus being conceived as free to operate in accordance with laws which hold true at its own "level of existence." Typical of objections to this are Ernest Nagel's observation, in *The Structure of Science*, that wholes are recognized in physical science, too, apparently without presenting special problems for individualistic explanation; and Popper's jibe, in *The Poverty of Historicism*, that the metaphysical principle of holism, although "trivially true," applies even to three apples on a plate. However, most methodological holists (for example, Mau-

rice Mandelbaum in "Societal Facts") prefer to argue that although social phenomena can be said to be ontologically dependent upon the actions and attitudes of individuals, the two are not simply identical. They point out, too, that their doctrine does not commit them to claiming that societies could exist without people, this being an absurdity eschewed even by full-blooded ontological holists like Hegel. The frequent use, in this connection, of the epiphenomenalist account of the mind–brain relation to show what might be meant by ontological dependence without identity is rather unfortunate. For, whereas a mind with no brain may be conceivable, few, if any, methodological holists would allow that society was conceivable without individuals. Many methodological holists, in fact, profess complete ontological individualism. What they demand of individualists is a willingness to try to *find out* whether there are any irreducible societal laws.

This takes us within range of a second metaphysical argument. According to Watkins, it is a "metaphysical commonplace that social events are brought about by people." He interpreted this "commonplace" to imply that individual men and women "together with their material resources" are the "only moving agents," indeed the "only causal factors," in history. Social wholes, whether or not they can be said really to exist, cannot *do* anything; in particular, they cannot affect the behavior of the concrete human beings who constitute them. Methodological individualists therefore disagree with economists who regard long-term cyclical waves in economic activity as, in Watkins' words, "self-propelling, uncontrollable and inexplicable in terms of human activities." They similarly oppose historical materialism, which, in its more uncompromising forms, at any rate, asserts a one-way causal relation between certain social conditions (the economic substructure) and the thoughts and actions of those who live under them. It is a "central assumption of the individualist position," Watkins declared, that "no social tendency is somehow imposed on human beings 'from above' (or 'from below')." Actually, even the more modest (and more usual) thesis of "interaction" between the social and the individual spheres is often deemed unacceptable by individualists.

The usual response of the holists to this line of argument is to ridicule the implied denial of social conditioning—as if men were not born into social situations in the first place. The "real oddity" of methodological individualism, wrote Ernest Gellner in "Explanations in History," is that "it seems to preclude *a priori* the possibility of human dispositions being the dependent variable in an historical explanation—when in fact this is what they often or always are." An associated peculiarity is that it precludes "the possibility of causes . . . being a complex fact which is not describable in terms of the characteristics of its constituent parts alone—which again seems often to be the case." Individualists, of course, would regard this charge as a misunderstanding of their doctrine. They would hold that the social conditioning of individuals, although real, is simply their conditioning by other individuals, referred to compendiously by holistic terms. And they would accept this claim that causes may be complex facts as long as the complexity of the cause is regarded as "resultant" from individual actions in the way indicated by the ontological argument. (Some individualists, however, would find it less easy to counter the argument that to speak of causes as "moving agents" at all is tacitly to accept an "activity" view of causation that has been suspect since Hume.)

Alan Donagan, in *The Later Philosophy of R. G. Collingwood*, provided a version of the individualist's causal argument which turns on a conception of human action made familiar by idealist philosophers. The only way men's actions can be explained, Donagan maintained, is through their "thoughts"; it is not men's actual situations which explain what they do, but their conception of the situations (although it may be necessary to refer to the actual situation in explaining a man's success or failure in translating his intentions into action). Thus, if physical causes, like climate, operate in history, they must operate indirectly; and the same is true of such social events and conditions as an economic depression or a military victory. Unless we are to challenge the common assumption that the causal relation is transitive, however, methodological holists may well feel that such considerations, even if they are acceptable in themselves, do little to establish Watkins' original contention. For to say that social causes require the mediation of individual thoughts and responses is not to establish the latter as the only "moving forces" in history. On the contrary, to cause individuals to cause is still to cause.

Epistemological arguments. The theory of action thus indicated has a bearing on a third general argument that is sometimes used by methodological individualists. This argument develops Watkins' contention that even if we learned to describe, predict, and control social events and conditions holistically, we still could not properly claim to *understand* them without treating them as a collection of individual responses. For "understanding," Watkins seemed to insist, requires the explanation of what happened in terms of *intelligible* human dispositions. What he appears to have had in mind is the discerning of the participants' reasons for doing what they did, which allows us the intellectual satisfaction of seeing why they thought their responses were appropriate. As Gellner has pointed out, there is a dual thesis here: first, that social or historical explanation must be couched in terms of the dispositions of individual human beings; second, that these dispositions must be of a special kind. For those who would claim, on general philosophical grounds, that explanation by reference to an agent's reason or motive is logically different from subsuming an occurrence under a law (or even under a "disposition" properly so called), the present claim opens up the possibility of giving individualistic explanations of social phenomena without reference even to psychological laws.

Many methodological holists would agree that to accept the additional thesis would make their position quite untenable, for it might be claimed that "intelligible" dispositions could be sought at the level of social wholes only on the assumption either of an immanent group mind or of an external historical providence: in other words, methodological holism now *would* require ontological holism. Something just short of this nevertheless sometimes appears to be entertained. Thus Morris Ginsberg, in *On The Diversity of Morals* (London, 1956), while denying for ontological reasons that society is itself a mind, conceded that it has a "mental organization" or "inner side" that is not identical with the mentality of any of its component individuals. Most methodological holists, however, simply deny the necessity of the additional criterion of explanation. They would hold that the essential claim of methodological individualism could be achieved without reference to intelligible dispositions if appropriate psychological laws could be found. And they would similarly claim for their own position that subsumption under autonomous societal laws (if such laws could be found) would yield understanding in the only sense significant to "scientific" inquiry.

A fourth argument makes the even more basic epistemological claim that whereas we can observe human individuals, we cannot similarly obtain knowledge of the macro features of social groups. As Watkins put it: "The social scientist and historian have no 'direct access' to the overall structure and behaviour of a system of interacting individuals (in the sense that a chemist does have 'direct access' to such overall properties of a gas as its volume and pressure and temperature, which he can measure and relate without any knowledge of gas molecules)." Since reliable knowledge of the dispositions and situations of individuals is readily available, Watkins continued, and since these individuals constitute the group, "a theoretical understanding of an abstract social structure should be derived from more empirical beliefs about concrete individuals." How else can what is said about social wholes be verified? Such an appeal to "hardheaded" empiricism is a shrewd blow. For the contenders here are (with a caveat, perhaps, about history) two theories of "scientific" inquiry. It would be odd if they did not both claim to be "empiricist."

Faced with this argument, many methodological holists insist that *some* social phenomena, at least—for example, parades, trials at law, battles—are directly observable. It is true that no one will notice such things if he lacks certain interpretative ideas or concepts. But this is not a peculiarity of social observation. Individual human actions themselves will not be "observed" unless we are able to discern the intentions and motives of the actors; and it may be questioned whether these can be known "directly" in a sense in which group phenomena cannot. The epistemological criterion of the individualists, in other words, either allows some social phenomena to be counted as observable or excludes the most interesting individual phenomena. Many holists nevertheless concede that the social wholes of most significance for history and social science cannot, in any ordinary sense, be directly observed. They reject instead the implication that this puts them at odds with accepted procedures in natural science. Not all physical theorizing proceeds, as in chemistry, from observables to what explains them: astronomy, for example, "constructs" its wholes as surely as sociology does. They admit, too, that assertions about societies must be verified by discovery of what individuals do. But they deny that this undermines their claim to possess knowledge, not just of the individuals but of the social wholes of which they are elements.

Linguistic argument. The fifth argument for methodological individualism, although it obviously has some affinity with both ontological and epistemological ones, is presented as a point of logic or semantics. As L. J. Goldstein stated it, in his "The Two Theses of Methodological Individualism," individualists require, as a condition of their being meaningful, "that all of the concepts used in social science theory be exhaustively analyzable in terms of the interests, activities, volitions and so forth of individual human beings." If this condition were met, the apparent holism of explanations employing societal laws would be tolerable, because it would be eliminable "by translation." Watkins himself denied that this conceptual thesis actually belongs to the central position of methodological individualism. The latter, he maintained, is a theory of explanation, not of concept-formation or description. Yet in arguing for the explanatory thesis, he characteristically slipped into the conceptual one. He maintained, for example, that to an individualist, the statement "The Jewish race is cohesive," if it is to be empirically meaningful, must mean such things as "Jews usually marry Jews"—a statement about anonymous individuals. And he commended Max Weber for insisting that the only way to make the meaning of social terms precise is to *define* them individualistically—as if such concepts appear holistic only when they remain vague or undefined.

Methodological holists have denied both that such analysis, definition, or translation is possible and that the conceptual thesis, even if sound, would establish the explanatory one. In arguing for the first of these positions in "Methodological Individualisms: Definition and Reduction," May Brodbeck allowed that there are no insuperable problems for conceptual individualism so long as we are dealing with group concepts that are basically statistical—as in "He got his votes from the poor." Less straightforwardly statistical locutions like "Boom follows slump" might present problems for individualistic translation only because their implied statistical reference is vague. The real difficulty arises over terms like "renaissance" or "the government." There seems to be no finite list of individual actions and attitudes that would count as their exemplifications; yet the problem does not seem to be one simply of vagueness. Appropriate exemplifications, furthermore, seem to vary from culture to culture, without our being able to say that the relevant terms are ambiguous—which suggests, perhaps, an evaluative element in their meanings. Terms within this range of social description appear to be *logically* holistic. As Mandelbaum has observed, the problem here is analogous to one which phenomenalists have paid great attention to in contemporary theory of perception. The full meaning of a material object statement, it is generally agreed, cannot be given by any finite set of sensation reports alone; we always need reference to "conditions of appearance," which are stated in the material object language. Attempts to translate societal statements into psychological terms founder on the similar need to specify the social conditions under which an action must be performed in order for it to count as an exemplification.

Mandelbaum himself actually wavered on this point. He conceded that partial translatability, at least, is required; otherwise there would be no way of verifying societal statements (an echo of the epistemological argument). He was sufficiently moved, too, by metaphysical considerations (both ontological and causal) to believe that full translation may be possible "in principle," even if this cannot be made the basis for a "practical" methodology. Many methodological holists have claimed, however, that full translatability would still not warrant the acceptance of the individualist thesis as it is most commonly understood, namely, that explanations should be (or should be capable of being) limited to psychological terms, with psychological laws as the only permissible kind of connecting generalizations.

SOME OBSCURITIES

Consideration of the claim that full translatability would not warrant acceptance of the individualist thesis calls attention to three important obscurities which have dogged much contemporary discussion. The first concerns the sense of "explain" in which a methodological individualist asserts that ultimately all explanations must be individualistic. The conceptual claim, it should be noted, has been stated not only as an argument for the explanatory one but also as though it were itself a theory of explanation—and so it is, in one important sense of the term. According to Watkins, every complex social situation or event is "the result of a particular configuration of individuals, their dispositions, beliefs, and physical resources and environments." This is often, and plausibly, read as meaning that we must be able to explain large-scale social phenomena as configurations or resultants of individual ones. But to explain something *as* something else is to explicate its nature: it is to explain it in the sense of showing *what it really is*. Although this kind of explanation is common in history and social science, however, it does not seem to be what methodological individualists have usually had in mind when advancing their explanatory thesis. What they envisage is explanation in the sense of showing how or why something *came to be* what it is: explanation that goes on to give causes, for example. It remains to be seen whether the conceptual thesis has any bearing on individualist claims about such explanations.

It may be objected that this ambiguity underlying the notion of being a "resultant" need not destroy the support given by the conceptual thesis to the full explanatory thesis, since what is specified in the productive sense may itself be treated, in its turn, as a resultant in the constitutive sense, thus achieving full "reduction." But this directs attention to a second obscurity in the individualist thesis, the question whether a "why" or "how" explanation in which all societal terms were replaced by psychological ones would involve the reduction of societal to psychological *laws*. Holists like Nagel and Brodbeck have contended that it would not, at any rate, achieve reduction in the sense most familiar to the philosophy of science. For the derivability of macro laws from micro laws, no matter what the field of inquiry, is at least partly an empirical matter. Even in such exemplary cases as the reduction of chemistry to physics, they have pointed out, composition laws, which specify the way individual behavior changes as groups increase in size, must be added to the ordinary laws of the micro discipline; and these, however "self-evident" they often seem, have an empirical status. If laws of individual psychology are to be related "reductively" to laws of group phenomena, empirical composition laws would similarly have to be found. The reduction could never be just a matter of definition.

Individualists may complain that this involves too restricted an interpretation of their demand that sociological and historical explanations be reduced to "psychological" terms. Thus, when Mandelbaum, a methodological holist, attacked the conceptual thesis on the assumption that no statement will be counted as psychological if it employs any societal term, his argument was rebutted by Donagan, an individualist, on the ground that hardly any human dispositions would be psychological on such a criterion. Watkins made it clear that, for him, a psychological disposition is simply one which specifies a way of acting and thinking that is open to an individual. Thus, he argued against an anthropological holist that marriage rules are widespread dispositions of anonymous individuals in a society to behave in a certain way, and against a historical holist that the "Calvinistic outlook" of seventeenth-century Huguenot traders was similarly individualistic. Behind the uncertainty about what is to count as "psychological," there in fact appear to lie two different interpretations of the conceptual thesis itself. The first, which imposes a limitation upon the *ways of behaving* that may be cited in a "rock-bottom" explanans, is the translatability thesis. The second, to which many methodological individualists appear to retreat under pressure, is the much weaker demand that an acceptable explanation employ concepts which can be *attributed* to an individual, or jointly to a group of them.

Willingness to move in the latter direction suggests that contemporary methodological individualists and holists are not really as far apart as they often seem. In spite of their insistence that what they put forward is a *methodological* doctrine which is merely supported by metaphysical considerations, it seems clear that what interests methodological individualists most is the related ontological claim that human beings are the "ultimate constituents" of the social world. By contrast, although methodological holists find themselves continually under fire for allegedly flirting with dangerous metaphysical notions, it appears that what they are most concerned to uphold is the *logical* respectability of using holistic collective concepts and macroscopic laws, if need be. As was indicated, many methodological holists protest their allegiance to ontological individualism, and this appears to be a perfectly coherent claim. Some would even accord the corresponding methodological principle of individualism "regulative status" as formulating an ideal to be striven for. What they resist is the conclusion a priori that we can realize the ideal, and the associated temptation to refuse anything less.

Bibliography

Brodbeck, May, "Methodological Individualisms: Definition and Reduction." *Philosophy of Science*, Vol. 25, No. 1 (1958), 1–22.

Danto, A. C., "Methodological Individualism and Methodological Socialism." *Filosofia*, Vol. 13, No. 1 (1962), 3–24.

Donagan, Alan, *The Later Philosophy of R. G. Collingwood.* Oxford, 1962.

Gellner, Ernest, "Explanations in History." *PAS* Supp. Vol. 30 (1956), 157–176. Reprinted under the title "Holism versus Individualism in History and Sociology," in Patrick Gardiner, ed., *Theories of History.* Glencoe, Ill., 1959. Pp. 489–503.

Goldstein, Leon J., "The Two Theses of Methodological Individualism." *British Journal for the Philosophy of Science*, Vol. 9, No. 33 (1958), 1–11.

Hayek, F. A., *The Counter-Revolution of Science.* Glencoe, Ill., 1952.

Mandelbaum, Maurice, "Societal Facts." *British Journal of Sociology*, Vol. 6, No. 4 (1955), 305–317. Reprinted in Patrick Gardiner, ed., *Theories of History.* Glencoe, Ill., 1959. Pp. 476–488.

Mandelbaum, Maurice, "Societal Laws." *British Journal for the Philosophy of Science*, Vol. 8, No. 31 (1957), 211–224. Has full bibliographical reference to much of the current literature.

Nagel, Ernest, *The Structure of Science.* New York, 1961. Pp. 336–397, 536–546. Like Donagan, he treats the problem of holism versus individualism in the context of a broader discussion of science.

Popper, K. R., *The Poverty of Historicism.* London, 1957.

Watkins, J. W. N., "Ideal Types and Historical Explanations," in Herbert Feigl and May Brodbeck, eds., *Readings in the Philosophy of Science.* New York, 1953. Pp. 723–743.

Watkins, J. W. N., "Historical Explanation in the Social Sciences." *British Journal for the Philosophy of Science*, Vol. 8, No. 30 (1957), 104–117. Reprinted in Patrick Gardiner, ed., *Theories of History.* Glencoe, Ill., 1959. Pp. 503–514.

W. H. DRAY

HOLT, EDWIN BISSELL (1873–1946), an American psychologist and philosopher, was noted for his innovations in philosophical psychology. His influence was greater in psychology than in philosophy. In his time he was the American psychologist best known and most respected by the British. Holt completed his undergraduate and graduate work at Harvard and taught there from 1901 to 1918, first as an instructor and then as assistant professor of psychology. In 1926 he returned from retirement to become visiting professor of social psychology at Princeton, but he retired permanently in 1936.

New Realism. Holt was one of the original six American New Realists who banded together in the first decade of the twentieth century in a polemic against idealism and representational realism. Holt was the only one, however, to attempt a systematic development of New Realism, first in a neutral monism, then, after giving that up, in a behaviorist theory of consciousness. In this attempt, Holt uncovered the fatal problems that were in New Realism from its beginning.

The New Realists took their start from the theory of consciousness of William James. James argued that consciousness was an external relation between a sentient organism and its objects, not a substance or entity. The latter view was the basis of the doctrine of the dualism of psychic and physical substances, and of an idealism that defined objects in terms of psychic or subjective substance, thereby giving them a mental or ideal status.

Holt replaced the dualism and psychic monism with a monism that was neutral, defining Being, or reality, neither in terms of mind (idealism) nor in terms of matter (materialism). The basic category of this neutral monism was "Being," which connoted nothing and denoted everything. This neutral Being could most readily be found in the concepts of logic and mathematics, the simplest known elements of Being. But in thus identifying Being with logical and mathematical terms and propositions, Holt gave it a distinctly mental or conceptual character. He admitted borrowing this approach from the idealist Josiah Royce, but he claimed that rather than arguing for idealism, his neutral monism reaffirmed the "sadly neglected truism" of New Realism: "everything is precisely what it is, and is not to be explained away as something else."

Yet Holt's analysis had an inescapable reductivist outcome. All things turn out to be "really" the same. That is, they turn out to be neutral entities (logical and mathematical terms) and the complexes made out of them (propositions), not the material things of common sense or the particles and elements of science. As one critic pointed out, this meant that it is the mathematical logician, not the physicist, who tells us what things are. By failing to keep clear the difference between the simplest elements of Being and the simplest known elements of Being, Holt threw doubt on the neutrality of his monism. The supposedly neutral logical and mathematical entities, he said, generate the further terms and propositions that make up all systems of being, or universes of discourse, through a "motion" of their own. Though Holt denied that this motion was a mental process, he did term it a "deduction," an intrinsic activity at work in the universe. Like any other object or aggregate, consciousness thus can be "deduced" from Being, and since Being is neutral, consciousness too is neutral; for all the complex constructions in experience are basically composed of neutral entities that maintain their identity despite the constructions they go into.

It is to these propositions, then, generated by the neutral entities of logic and mathematics through a "motion" of their own, that the nervous system responds. Although he admitted this might be considered fantastic, Holt stood by his position. James had said that the content of knowledge is the object of knowledge; content and object are not two separate things but are numerically one. Holt modified this only by noting that since our knowledge of an object is never complete, our ideas are never completely identical with their objects. When we say "My thought is of an object," we should say "My thought is a portion of the object; a portion of the object is my thought." Holt thought the representationalists had failed to see that an idea can represent an object only to the extent that it is identical with that object. An idea cannot represent space, then, without itself being spatial; the only adequate idea of a minute or an hour is just a minute or an hour. Holt thus passed from a partial qualitative identity of knowledge or consciousness and its objects to a numerical or existential identity. He had forgotten that he had begun with James's idea of consciousness as a relation.

No other New Realist developed monism in this thoroughgoing fashion. Holt carried it to its furthest conclusion. If consciousness and its object are numerically identical, do objects then have the character of consciousness (panpsychism), or does the content of consciousness have the character of objects (an inverted panpsychism, or "panobjectism")? Holt's anti-idealism ruled out panpsychism; consequently the elements of consciousness became objects themselves among all other objects, and the world for

Holt is populated with all those entities usually placed in consciousness: error, hallucination, delusion, secondary qualities, even volitions. The objective world contains physical counterparts to the errors of ordinary sense experience. Errors of thought, always cases of contradictory propositions, are equally objective. The "real," or objective, world is contradictory through and through; nature is a "seething chaos of contradiction."

Holt, in a later paper on the locus of concepts, confessed that his neutral monism had led him to write a mistaken book, an "absurd hocus-pocus" conjured up because he did not know at the time the true locus of these neutral "timeless and changeless entities." His failure to maintain their neutrality is admitted: these entities have no objective existence in nature. Although he promised to return to the subject, Holt never did. Nor did he produce the planned second volume that was to carry out the epistemological implications of his neutral monism. Instead, he turned to the development of a behaviorist theory of consciousness.

Behaviorist theory of consciousness. Holt saw that an extreme behaviorism would make the materialist's mistake of denying the facts, as well as the theory, of consciousness. While he described his own behaviorism as part of the "objective tendency" to abolish the subjective and to interpret mental phenomena in an "objective relational manner," he consciously sought to avoid slurring over or repudiating the "facts" of consciousness, and he modified his behaviorism accordingly.

Increasingly, ideas suggestive of subjectivity, if not dualism, such as integration of behavior, capacity to respond, suppression, and split personality, appeared in Holt's writings. The result was an oscillation between his objectivist, behaviorist ideas and the subjectivist ideas that he needed in order to do justice to the facts of consciousness.

In *The Freudian Wish*, he described behavior by examining the way in which reflexes are combined and integrated to produce that organized "synthetic novelty" which is the specific response, or behavior, and which is also the point at which awareness is born. He identified this reponse with Freud's "wish," including in it purpose, tendency, desire, impulse, and attitude. It was the replacement, Holt claimed, for sensation as the unifying factor of psychology. But he denied that this view meant he was falling back on the psychic or subjective; the basis for the view was objectively observable in what an organism does. While he did not deny that we have unobservable thoughts, he argued that they are often an "embroidery, a mere irrelevance to action," and eventually they too can be observed if one looks to behavior that is yet to come.

Holt thought the Freudian wish was the first key that psychology had discovered for an explanation of mind. It meant psychology "with a soul," not the "ghost-soul" but the "wishes" which are the soul. Like Aristotle, he identified the soul with the dynamic form of a body endowed with the capacity of life: it is what it can do. The behavior of such a body is distinguished from its random movements by its purposiveness, an objective reference that is found in every reflex. Behavior occurs when more than one reflex is set off by a stimulus. As the number of reflexes increases, the immediate stimulus "recedes" as the inciting and controlling factor. This recession of the stimulus is part of intelligence and deliberation. Holt also used it to give an account of consciousness and knowledge of spatially and temporally remote objects. Still, Holt could not avoid a basic monism. The "objective" world is the only world. What has been called the "subjective" world is the subtler workings of integrated objective mechanisms. It is the body that is the knower; the environing objects to which it responds are the known. And Holt revived his claim that the mind is the thing of which it is thinking.

By the end of his career, despite his lifelong objectivist–subjectivist oscillations, Holt was committed to an objectivist position. He described his last published book (on the learning process) as an essay toward radical empiricism, and it was supppsed to complete James's work of ridding philosophy and psychology of the absurdities of subjectivism and any form of psychophysical parallelism. There is only a sketchy idea at the end as to what direction Holt's epistemology might have taken. He thought at that point that he was but one short step away from a definition of awareness and consciousness in physiological terms. His "objectism" was reaffirmed: he sought to formulate a wholly physical and physiological psychology as a basis for the solution of any psychological problem. But he admitted that such a psychology had not yet given the slightest clue to the problem of secondary qualities.

Holt's last published writing set forth a materialism without apologies. Mind and cognition are neither mental nor cognitive, but physical—a matter of nerves and muscles. The active self is the physical body, that and nothing else. An experience of "self" is an experience of parts of one's body. Anything other than that, whether a self, ego, soul, or knower, does not exist.

Still, Holt modified this objectivism. He admitted that our physiological apparatus of perception and thought habitually distorts, mutilates, and disguises what it is perceiving. It subtracts from "the objective reality," and with the remainder it fuses inseparably "a vast amount of unreality of its own motor creating (subjective reality)." In a mistaken but significant interpretation of Kant, Holt claimed that these distortions are strikingly analogous to the Kantian categories in their distortion of things-in-themselves in intuition and understanding.

The ghost of subjectivism remained. Holt and the New Realists may have exorcised its idealist form, but the need for its inclusion was a constant embarrassment to them and was eventually the reason for the failure of New Realism to be anything more than an anti-idealist polemic.

Bibliography

Works by Holt are *The Concept of Consciousness* (London, 1914; manuscript completed in 1908), which presents his doctrine of neutral monism; "The Place of Illusory Experience in a Realistic World," in E. B. Holt and others, *The New Realism* (New York, 1912), pp. 313–376—the book contains essays by the six New Realists elaborating their 1910 platform statement; "Response and Cognition," in *Journal of Philosophy*, Vol. 12 (1915), 365–373, 393–409, reprinted in *The Freudian Wish; The Freudian Wish and Its Place in Ethics* (New York, 1915), his most popular and widely read book and one of the first introductions of Freud to a large American audience; "Prof. Henderson's 'Fitness' and the Locus of Concepts," in *Journal of Philosophy*, Vol. 17 (1920), 365–381;

Animal Drive and the Learning Process: An Essay Towards Radical Empiricism (New York, 1931), Vol. I, probably Holt's most significant publication in psychology; "The Whimsical Condition of Social Psychology and of Mankind," in Horace M. Kallen and Sidney Hook, eds., *American Philosophy, Today and Tomorrow* (New York, 1935); and "Materialism and the Criterion of the Psychic," in *Psychological Review*, Vol. 44 (1937), 33–53.

A secondary source is Syed Zafarul Hasan, *Realism; an Attempt to Trace Its Origin and Development in Its Chief Representations* (Cambridge, 1928), an extensive consideration of American philosophic realism in all its variations, including a critical exposition of Holt's philosophy.

THOMAS ROBISCHON

HOME, HENRY (Lord Kames, 1696–1782), aesthetician and moral philosopher, was born at Kames, Berwickshire, Scotland. He was educated at home and indentured to a writer of the signet in Edinburgh, but he resolved to become an advocate and was admitted to the Scottish bar in 1724. He became a judge of the Court of Session in 1752 and assumed the judicial title of Lord Kames. He was advanced to the High Court of Justiciary in 1763 and was still serving at the time of his death.

Kames wrote a number of books, several of them on legal subjects. His *Sketches of the History of Man* (2 vols., Edinburgh, 1774) bridged his interests in history and philosophy, and he frequently referred to the *Sketches* in his *Essays on the Principles of Morality and Natural Religion* (3d ed., Edinburgh, 1779). His other philosophical work is *Elements of Criticism* (2d ed., Edinburgh, 1763), a discussion of aesthetic principles.

Kames argued that the fundamental principles of the fine arts, or the elements of criticism, must be drawn from human nature. The fine arts are suited to human nature because man, as a sensitive being, is capable of pleasure; and the fine arts are calculated to give pleasure to eye or ear. Kames devoted the opening chapters of the *Elements* to an account of human emotions and passions. These chapters form the psychological prolegomena that he believed aesthetics requires. Perceptions and ideas occur independently of our wills, though we can sometimes will the cessation of a train of ideas. Ideas follow our perceptions and each other in accordance with the laws of association (resemblance, contiguity in time or place, and cause and effect). Emotions and passions occur in relation to our train of perceptions and ideas. A passion is an emotion that is accompanied by a desire. The general rule for the occurrence of emotions is that we love what is agreeable and hate what is disagreeable. Kames's basic principle of criticism is that every work of art that is conformable to the natural course of our ideas is so far agreeable, and every work of art that reverses that course is so far disagreeable. On the one hand, Kames wanted to establish that the agreeableness or disagreeableness of things is prior to our love or hatred; but on the other, he accounted for our emotional reactions to certain things by saying that the nature of man is originally framed with a relish for regularity, uniformity, proportion, order, and simplicity.

The fine arts that Kames had in mind are painting, sculpture, music, poetry, gardening, and architecture; but the first three are not discussed systematically in the *Elements*. Poetry is given the most extended criticism. Kames was especially interested in plays, and gardening and architecture share a chapter. He divided aesthetic qualities into two sorts: those which an object may possess in itself and those which it has in relation to other objects. Qualities of the first sort are grandeur, sublimity, motion, force, novelty, "laughableness," and beauty, which he conceded are both intrinsic and relational. The relational qualities which Kames discussed are resemblance and dissimilitude, uniformity and variety.

Kames argued that it should be possible to establish a standard of taste against which productions in the fine arts might be judged. We believe that things of a certain kind have a common nature, and individuals are perfect or right insofar as they conform to the common nature of their kind. Thus, it should be possible to determine the common nature that works of art of a certain kind ought to share and to assess the success with which a given work of art meets the ideal of its kind. Kames noted that every person is not fit to become a judge of the fine arts, since not everyone is capable of the refinement of taste that is required. This is no great hardship on the bulk of mankind. The fine arts only contribute to our pleasure and amusement, and it is not as necessary for everyone to have an authoritative sense of right and wrong in the fine arts as it is for everyone to have an authoritative moral sense.

In *Essays on the Principles of Morality and Natural Religion,* Kames discussed a wide range of philosophical topics, including liberty and necessity, personal identity, belief, external senses, and cause and effect. His thinking is influenced by Hume, either in quiet concurrence or by vigorous reaction. The two longest and most important essays are Essay II, "The Foundation of Morality," and Essay VIII, "Knowledge of the Deity."

For Kames, the foundation of morality is to be found in human nature. Looking there, he finds the moral sense that approves certain natural principles, which are enforced by natural rewards or punishments of pleasure or pain. These principles bind us to refrain from harming others, to tell the truth, to keep our promises, to act faithfully toward those who rely on us, to be grateful, and to be benevolent. While the moral sense is rooted in the nature of man, it admits of great refinements by culture and education.

A hasty reader might conclude that whenever Kames needed to solve a new perplexity in the foundation of morals, he discovered a new sense in mankind. For instance, he resolved the long-standing dispute over the artificiality of justice by declaring that justice is natural because it is founded on a natural sense of property. He claimed that this sense is necessarily antecedent to any social agreement; and indeed that any agreement to organize a society presupposes the existence in men of a sense of property.

In natural religion, Kames believed that he had brought to light a new argument to prove the existence of a god. In D. Cranz's *The History of Greenland* (London, 1767) Kames found an account of a Greenlander who argued in the following way for the existence of an artisan superior in power to man: A kayak is a work of art that can be made only by the most skilled of men, but a bird is an even greater work of art than a kayak; thus there must be an artisan to make birds who is even greater than man. Kames was most impressed by the fact that this argument came

from a savage and concluded that "the perception we have of Deity must proceed from an internal cause, which may be termed the Sense of Deity."

In the *Essays,* Kames generalized the Greenlander argument, contending, "We are so accustomed to human arts, that every work of design and use will be attributed to man, if it exceed not his known powers. *Nor do effects above the powers of man unhinge our notion of a cause: They only lead the mind to a more powerful cause.*" The italicized words in the passage above are especially interesting, because in an addendum to the third edition of the *Essays* (1779), Kames complained that Hume ignored the Greenlander argument in his *Dialogues Concerning Natural Religion;* and Kames believed that argument immune from any strictures on natural religion was found in Hume's *Dialogues.*

Bibliography

L. A. Selby-Bigge, ed., *British Moralists* (Oxford, 1897), Vol. II, contains a representative selection of passages from the essay on the foundation of morals (Essay II) in *Essays on the Principles of Morality and Natural Religion.*

ELMER SPRAGUE

HOMER. The Homeric poems, *Iliad* and *Odyssey* (probably eighth century B.C.), are of interest to the historian of philosophy because they provide the background, in language and to some extent in thought, from which Greek philosophy emerged. The hexameters of Parmenides and Empedocles follow the Homeric pattern closely, and they both use Homeric words and coin words for themselves after the Homeric model. They also sometimes use the same thought forms. For instance, a comparison may be drawn between Parmenides' journey (see Fr. 1) and Odysseus' journey to the underworld (*Odyssey,* Book 11). The Homeric simile is the forerunner of the natural philosopher's "working model," by which an unfamiliar process is explained by comparison with a more familiar one. For example, to illuminate his description of an evenly poised battle Homer introduced a "careful working woman" weighing wool in her scales; Empedocles compared the breathing process in animals with operations performed with a household instrument, the *clepsydra.*

Apart from these questions of language and style, the *Iliad* and the *Odyssey* influenced the content of later philosophical thought in various ways.

The world. The Homeric world picture was of a flat, disc-shaped earth, with the sky set over the top like an inverted metal bowl and Hades underneath the earth in a more or less symmetrical relation to the sky. The sun, moon, and stars were taken to move across the fixed heaven from east to west, but the manner of their return journey was not clear. The space between the earth and the sky contained *aer* (mist), and above that was *aether* (the bright air of the upper heavens). The earth was completely surrounded by the river of Ocean, personified and deified as Okeanos. In one exceptional passage (*Iliad,* Book 14, 200–248) Okeanos is called "the begetter of gods" and "the begetter of all things." Aristotle (*Metaphysics* A 3, 982b27) half seriously suggested that Homer's Okeanos was the forerunner of Thales' cosmogonical water. Plato, even less seriously, suggested (*Theaetetus* 152E) that Okeanos provided the origin of Heraclitus' flux theory. These are far-fetched ideas; the cosmology of Homer, such as it was, can hardly be seen as anything but a contrast with Ionian theories (see G. S. Kirk in *The Presocratic Philosophers*, Ch 1). But connections can be traced between some details of Homer's descriptions of the natural world and the speculations of later Greek philosophers of nature (see Charles Mugler, *Les Origines de la science grecque chez Homère*).

The gods. The historian Herodotus observed that Homer and Hesiod together had determined for all the Greeks what their gods were like, and this is probably the greatest significance of the Homeric poems for the history of philosophy (*History* II, 53). There is one general feature about the Homeric gods which is of much importance: they were not dark gods, accessible only to mystics and appeasable by magic, but on the whole very human and rational. They had powers over the world of human experience, and their powers were defined and hierarchical; in this we can see a hint of the orderly cosmos of later theory.

Some philosophers objected to the Homeric gods. Xenophanes launched the first attack: the gods behaved immorally; moreover, the conception of them was relative to the believer (see Fr. 16: "Ethiopians imagine their gods as black and snub-nosed . . ."). Heraclitus' objections were not explicitly against gods but against Homer as the educator of Greece; the Olympian gods were, however, near the center of his target. Plato's onslaught in the *Republic* (376E ff.) is well known; he wished to censor everything in the Homeric poems that was discreditable to the gods before the poems could be used in the education of the "Guardians" (it was general practice in Greece both before and after Plato's time to use Homer as the basis for moral and religious education).

Man. The Homeric view of man shows interesting differences from later theories. There was no unified soul, contrasted with body, as in the Pythagorean–Platonic tradition; instead, the psychic functions were distributed without much consistency over a number of entities. The *psyche*, which held the position of greatest importance from the time of Pythagoras, was merely a life-soul in Homer; it played no part in the thoughts, emotions, and actions of the living man. The *psyche* survived after death; it did not, however, retain the complete moral personality, as in the Platonic eschatology, but was a bloodless, helpless shadow. The thoughts and feelings of the living man were attributed to the *phrenes* (roughly speaking, the organs of the chest, although in later Greek the word means "diaphragm"), the heart, and the *thymos* (a mysterious entity probably connected, like *psyche*, with breath). *Nous* (mind), which became the most important part of the *psyche* in the psychology of Plato and Aristotle, was generally restricted in Homer to the intuitive understanding of a situation (like the English "to see" in its metaphorical sense); consequently, it was often connected with sense perception, not contrasted with it as in Plato. Unlike *phrenes*, *nous* was not a physical thing for Homer but a function.

Human action. The actions of the human characters in the *Iliad* and *Odyssey* are represented as being influenced or manipulated more or less constantly by the gods. Actions that might be otherwise difficult to explain, such as a sudden access of superhuman courage, are especially attributed to the intervention of a god. But it is not only the inexplicable or the uncharacteristic that is described thus; a successful shot with the spear or an unsuccessful one, a plan adopted, a fit of anger, a bad bargain, an untimely sleep—these and many other unremarkable events are described as caused by a god. The gods handle the heroes as arbitrarily as a mortal king might treat his subjects, although not, as a rule, with savagery.

The fact that so much of human action is attributed to the gods has led modern interpreters to say that Homeric man is "an open field," that Homer denies free will, and that he has no concept of the human personality. This is true in a sense, but it is misleading. Homer was not a philosopher who had confronted the free-will problem and decided upon determinism; apart from an occasional exception he offered no theories about motivation and responsibility. From the point of view of the responsibility of human characters, there is no opposition between "caused by a god" and "due to a human agent"; for example, one and the same attack by Sarpedon is described as due to Zeus and a few lines later as due to Sarpedon's *thymos* (*Iliad*, Book 11, 292 and 307). The moral relations between human beings are on the whole, although not entirely, unaffected by the interventions of the gods; a god may stir a man to excessive anger, but it is still felt appropriate to blame the man for his anger. The individual characters of the heroes remain fairly stable; the activity of the gods is not such as to make human beings unpredictable. But the Homeric poems generally show a limited sense of moral responsibility. They were composed at a time when shame still predominated over guilt as a motivating force, and the intention of the agent and his knowledge of the circumstances of his act (the two factors which of course played the chief part in later legal and philosophical theories of responsibility) receive little attention.

Homer provided the material for much of later Greek literature, which examined the relation of Homeric gods and men in a new way. The problem of individual human responsibility for actions in which gods were said to be involved, though hardly seen by Homer, was much discussed by the fifth-century tragedians and Sophists (see, for example, Aeschylus, *Agamemnon* 1497 ff.; Euripides, *Troades* 914 ff.; Gorgias, *Helen*).

Bibliography

Texts, edited by Thomas W. Allen, may be found in the Oxford Classical Texts (n.d.). Translations include *The Iliad*, translated by Richmond Lattimore (Chicago, 1962), and *The Odyssey*, translated by Robert Fitzgerald (New York, 1961). Relevant texts with translation and commentary are in G. S. Kirk and J. E. Raven, *The Presocratic Philosophers* (Cambridge, 1957), Ch. 1, Secs. 1 and 2.

Secondary sources include J. Böhme, *Die Seele und das Ich im Homerischen Epos* (Leipzig, 1929); E. R. Dodds, *The Greeks and the Irrational* (Berkeley, 1951); F. M. Cornford, *From Religion to Philosophy* (London, 1912); R. B. Onians, *The Origins of European Thought* (Cambridge, 1951); Bruno Snell, *The Discovery of the Mind*, translated by Thomas Rosenmeyer (Oxford, 1953), Chs. 1 and 2; Arthur W. H. Adkins, *Merit and Responsibility: A Study in Greek Values* (Oxford, 1960), Chs. 2–5; Charles Mugler, *Les*

Origines de la science grecque chez Homère (Paris, 1963); and Charles H. Kahn, *Anaximander and the Origins of Greek Cosmology* (New York, 1960), pp. 133 ff.

DAVID J. FURLEY

HÖNIGSWALD, RICHARD (1875–1947), German philosopher, was born in Magyarovar, a small Hungarian town near the Austrian border. He received a degree in medicine from the University of Vienna in 1902 and then studied philosophy under Alexius Meinong at Graz and Alois Riehl at Halle, receiving a doctorate in philosophy in 1904. He taught at the University of Breslau from 1906 until 1930, when he accepted a chair in philosophy at the University of Munich. Because he was a Jew, Hönigswald was deprived of his academic position in 1933. After the pogrom of 1938 he was sent to Dachau, but in 1939 he managed to immigrate to the United States. He lived in New York and engaged in research and writing until his death.

Hönigswald remained closer to the original doctrine of Kant, as exemplified in the Transcendental Aesthetic, the *Critique of Practical Reason*, and the *Critique of Judgment*, than did such Neo-Kantians as Hermann Cohen, Paul Natorp, and Heinrich Rickert. However, he emphasized the insufficient consideration Kant had devoted to the importance of the concrete subject as a historical and empirical entity. Out of this criticism of Kant, Hönigswald developed his own influential theory of concrete subjectivity, the psychology of thinking (*Denkpsychologie*). According to Hönigswald, the concrete subject, an individual monad, is both fact (*Tatsache*) and principle (*Prinzip*)—that is, it is both a constituent of the world and an entity that recognizes itself as the correlate of the world, confronting it in cognition, volition, and artistic productivity. In the concrete subject, ground and grounded, objectivity and object, coincide; in a natural object they are separated. This doctrine forms the basis of Hönigswald's cosmology. In its attempt to determine the concrete subject's position in the world and its specific temporal structure in terms of a regional ontology, Hönigswald's philosophy exhibits similarities to Husserl's *Konstitutionslehre*, Heidegger's analysis of *Dasein*, and Nicolai Hartmann's theory of stratified being. Hönigswald's approach differs from these in that he adhered to classical principles of validity (*Geltungsprinzipien*) in epistemology, ethics, legal and political philosophy, aesthetics, and the philosophy of religion. He found the key to the differentiation of the corresponding judgments and cultural realms in the constitutive features of the subject (thereby departing from Marburg and southwest German Neo-Kantianism), which he classed as intentionality, self-determination, reference to nature, and unlimitedness.

Hönigswald's philosophy of language made a considerable impact on Continental linguistics. Just as fact and principle coincide in the individual monad, Hönigswald claimed, the intermonadic reference of language constitutes the one other instance of the coincidence of fact and principle. Hönigswald's educational thought influenced such philosophers as Moritz Löwi and Alfred Petzelt, who, like him, emphasized the notions of tradition, concentration, and projection into the future. A number of thinkers, including Bruno Bauch, Theodor Litt, Wolfgang Cramer, and Hans Wagner, have engaged in evaluating Hönigswald's teachings for the study of fundamental problems in philosophy.

Works by Hönigswald

Über die Lehre Hume's von der Realität der Aussendinge. Berlin, 1904.
Hobbes und die Staatsphilosophie. Munich, 1924.
Immanuel Kant. Breslau, 1924.
Die Philosophie des Altertums, 2d ed. Leipzig and Berlin, 1924.
Die Grundlagen der Denkpsychologie, 2d ed. Leipzig and Berlin, 1925.
Über die Grundlagen der Pädagogik, 2d ed. Munich, 1927.
Grundfragen der Erkenntnistheorie. Tübingen, 1931.
Geschichte der Erkenntnistheorie. Berlin, 1933.
Philosophie und Sprache. Basel, 1937.
Schriften aus dem Nachlass. Vols. I-IV, Stuttgart, 1957–1961; Vol. V, Bonn, 1965; Vols. VI–X in preparation.

A fuller but incomplete bibliography may be found in Werner Ziegenfuss, *Philosophen-Lexikon.* Berlin, 1949. Vol. I, pp 553–554.

Posthumous papers are available in Hönigswald-Archiv, University of Bonn.

Works on Hönigswald

Opahle, Oswald, "Richard Hönigswald und seine Stellung zum Ganzheitsproblem." *Die Ganzheitsschule*, Vol. 10 (1961), 1–9.
Ueberweg, Friedrich, *Grundriss der Geschichte der Philosophie*, 13th ed., Vol. IV. Tübingen, 1951. P. 432.
Wolandt, Gerd, "Problemgeschichte, Weltentstehungsmythos und Glaube in der Philosophie Richard Hönigswalds." *Zeitschrift für philosophische Forschung*, Vol. 12 (1958), 188–217.
Wolandt, Gerd, *Gegenständlichkeit und Gliederung. Untersuchungen zur Prinzipientheorie Richard Hönigswalds.* Cologne, 1964.

GERD WOLANDT
Translated by *Eva Schaper*

HOOKER, RICHARD (1553–1600), English theologian and social and political philosopher. Hooker was born at Heavitree, near Exeter. His family was poor but well connected, and in 1568 Bishop John Jewel secured for Hooker a clerk's place at Corpus Christi College, Oxford. He became a fellow in 1577 and upon his marriage in 1581 was presented with the living of Drayton-Beauchamp and a few months later with the mastership of the Temple in London. At the Temple, Hooker came into violent conflict with William Travers, a Calvinist who lectured there in the evenings. Although Hooker always retained a high regard for Travers' intellect and integrity, he was forced by his own convictions to oppose the views of Travers. It was during this controversy that Hooker seems to have conceived the idea of writing a systematic treatise to uphold the establishment of church and state as represented by Queen Elizabeth's policies. In order to carry out this plan, he requested a transfer from the unquiet position in London to a country rectory. Thus he went to Boscombe near Salisbury, where he was able to write and complete the first four books of his projected treatise, *The Laws of Ecclesiastical Polity*, by 1593 or 1594. In 1595 he was promoted to the rectory of Bishopsbourne near Canterbury, where he completed the fifth, purely theological part of his treatise by 1597. During the following three years he wrote another three books for the *Laws*, but he did not live to see them published. He died toward the end of 1600.

Hooker's importance. Hooker was not an original thinker. His importance lies in the fact that he drew upon the various currents of medieval thought in order to explain the ecclesiastical and political institutions of Elizabethan England. Together with Francisco Suárez and Cardinal Bellarmine he belonged to the first Counter Reformation generation, and like the two Jesuits he elaborated the final implications of Aristotelianism and of Thomism in social and political philosophy. But unlike his two Jesuit contemporaries, he did not live in the orbit of the Roman Catholic revival. To both Suárez and Bellarmine the Renaissance, the Protestant Reformation, and the Erastian state were merely threats they had heard of—threats from the outside. But Hooker was an Englishman who had grown up and lived through the turmoil occasioned by the attempt of radical Protestantism to force Queen Elizabeth from her conciliatory path. As a result he had to parry the practical attack of the extreme Protestant wing, and he finally came face to face with the secular state's opposition to that wing. This confrontation lends Hooker's thought an air of real drama; and if he was less systematic in his exposition than Suárez, his writings have the advantage of revealing a genuine intellect at work, wrestling with problems, not merely teaching what is imagined to be the truth.

The source of authority. Hooker's analysis of the Puritan attack on the Elizabethan settlement in church and state had revealed to him the essential similarity of that case with a line of argument that had a long and distinguished medieval ancestry and in some ways went back as far as St. Augustine. The attack the Puritans mounted against the Elizabethan settlement drew heavily on Calvin and to a lesser extent on Wyclyf, and was ultimately analogous to all those medieval arguments that had denied the validity of natural law and therefore of the justification of secular authority in terms of natural law. Lacking a justification in natural law, the secular state, if it was to have any legal and moral basis at all, had to be subject to divine authority. To medieval writers this divine authority was represented on earth by the papacy; to the sixteenth-century Calvinists, it resided in the presbyteries of the godly and the elect. In order to combat the view that men have no natural reason with which to discover a natural law, and the view that any law discovered or made by men is incompatible with divine law, Hooker fell back upon the philosophy of St. Thomas. That philosophy had been developed during the thirteenth century to establish a doctrine of natural law and natural reason and to show how the rules thus discovered were fully compatible with those supernaturally revealed by God. The first book of Hooker's treatise is therefore a readable sixteenth-century compendium of Thomistic philosophy.

Natural and revealed law. Like St. Thomas, Hooker believed that man is by nature a social animal and that both the impulse to live in society and the need for some kind of government is inherent in human nature. Man is therefore created by God with the rational endowments necessary for the conduct of society and government. All social and political arrangements are hence subject to natural law, which is immutable. But since conditions of life vary from time to time and place to place, it is necessary to supplement the dictates of natural law with positive or "human" rules. All this was taken from Aristotle, but translated by both St. Thomas and Hooker into the context of Christian thought. Men desire not only to live, however, but also to live well. This further desire implies that they must find their ultimate happiness. Such ultimate happiness cannot be found in the attainment of a temporal, and therefore temporary, good, but only in the ultimate perfection that is God. Owing to the Fall, man cannot know by natural reason what he must do to obtain this final supernatural end. God has therefore revealed to man certain rules to supplement natural law. Hence it becomes clear that in order to achieve full human stature, man needs both natural law, for social and political purposes, and revealed law, for everlasting felicity. Revealed law is contained in the Bible and the traditions of the church. Natural law and revealed law are jointly, and not separately, the correct guide.

The "lex aeterna." In order to establish his point that the two sets of laws must be brought into operation jointly, Hooker delved into cosmology. God, he wrote, is the author of everything. He is a law unto himself, and that law is the *lex aeterna,* which is both the source of all other law and itself manifested in all other laws. In the divinely revealed law, it is manifested directly, so to speak; in natural law, indirectly. For natural law is discovered by human reason, and human reason is created by God according to the *lex aeterna;* therefore the dictates of natural law, and even the positive rules of human law, spring from the *lex aeterna.* God has given reason to every man. He has "illuminated" him. Although there is no explicit reference to St. Thomas in Hooker's text, this argument is a transcription of one of the central tenets of Thomism: *signatum est super nos lumen vultus tui, domine* ("the light of thy countenance is signed upon us, Lord"; Psalms iv. 6–7). Hence we learn the will of God by using our reason.

Other Thomist doctrines. Hooker identified himself with all the more salient doctrines of St. Thomas. He argued that God is pure act and that in him existence and essence coincide; that angels are immaterial and that they differ from all natural, not purely intellectual creatures in that they behold the face of God directly; that the soul is the form of man, and not a separate substance as St. Thomas' opponents had argued.

The will of man, Hooker wrote, is free. Everything good that reason sees as such has something unpleasant annexed to it. And everything evil that reason sees as such has something pleasant attached to it. For reason cannot see the absolutely good. Hence, although we always will the good, we can never will the absolutely good; as a result the will is always free to choose between several relative goods. Hooker believed that the two springs of human action are knowledge (reason) and will. The will always wills the good; and the good is apprehended by reason. Sin results from the imperfect operation of reason, which can never apprehend the absolutely good. Sin is therefore intimately linked with both the freedom of the will and the imperfection of reason. It is never committed as a positive action or desired for its own sake, but is the result of a loss. Evil, by implication, is a privation.

These subsidiary arguments were important to Hooker

not only because they enable the reader to identify the main lines of Thomism but also because they help to lead to the goal of the main argument. To avoid evil, it is necessary to supplement the law of nature. And since the law of nature is embodied in secular government, the revealed law is embodied in the church. Thus Hooker arrived at his main objective, the proof that church and state are intimately connected.

Ecclesiastical and secular society. As long as the argument remained confined to a high level of generality, it was easy to take for granted that this philosophy amounted in fact to a defense of the Elizabethan establishment, in which church and state were closely identified. Such reforms as Henry VIII and Elizabeth introduced into the church never really severed the visible continuity of ecclesiastical institutions and of canon law in England. The Elizabethan settlement, like Henry's acts of law, had been made by Parliament; in a very general sense, Parliament appeared to Hooker not as a purely secular institution. The bishops were part of it; and the electors themselves, being members of the church as well as members of a secular society, could easily be deemed to constitute in fact an ecclesiastical polity.

Hooker was explicit on the importance to his argument of the identity of the people who were the church with the people who were the commonwealth. He admitted that in countries where no such identity could be presumed, the natural society (being hierarchically lower than the ecclesiastical society) could not be deemed capable of making laws for the church. But in England, he was confident, complete identity obtained.

Thus Hooker was able to establish his initial point that the Puritan attack upon the Elizabethan settlement and the Puritan demand for the establishment of presbyteries and congregations was based on a false estimate of human nature. For it assumed that there was no natural law to justify the existence of secular society and of secular government, that all authority would ultimately have to be vested in the congregations representing the godly and the elect who embodied the only law there was, the divine law.

Naturalism and anti-Platonism. When Hooker turned to writing about the more particular arrangements of the Elizabethan settlement, he had difficulty squaring his Thomist theory with political practice, which was Erastian and naturalistic in the extreme. In an attempt to do so he drew heavily upon the ideas of Marsilius of Padua, who had completely subjected the church to the state. Hooker had begun as a confident Thomist; with the discovery that Thomism did not suffice to account for the intricacies of late Tudor politics, he found himself in a tangle once he began drawing upon ideas from the naturalistic thought of Marsilius, which was completely incompatible with Thomism.

The crux of the tangle was Hooker's unflinching Aristotelianism, probably absorbed when he was a student at Oxford. It was his Aristotelianism that prompted the experiment of bringing together the two great Aristotelian strands, that of St. Thomas and that of Marsilius, and yoking them to the defense of the Tudor state as Tudor ecclesiastical polity. If Hooker had been more observant and less wedded to Aristotle, he would have found another growing tradition of thought—Platonism—ready to hand.

Basically, Hooker was a Christian humanist, tolerant and fairly latitudinarian in theology. In the fifth book, which was devoted entirely to theology, he went out of his way to provide theological formulations that embraced to the point of ambiguity all the most controversial issues of the sixteenth century, so that as many disputants as possible would feel at home in his ecclesiastical polity. He was convinced that man was not wholly depraved and that the judicious exercise of human reason was absolutely essential to a Christian life. He saw no great and insurmountable chasm between nature and the supernatural and held that the mark of the Divine Creator can be detected in every creature.

Christian humanism had in a way been the mainstay of medieval Thomism. But in the sixteenth century, with Ficino and Erasmus, it had severed its connections with Aristotle and had been poured instead into the mold of Plato. Hooker was not only completely unaware of this revolution in thought; he actually went out of his way to attack one of the most popular Platonist teachers of his day, Petrus Ramus. It is true that Ramus' variety of Platonism was a vulgar one and that one cannot blame Hooker for taking up cudgels against him. But viewed in perspective, Hooker's stubborn Aristotelianism acquired an unnecessarily aggressive edge when it was led into the fray against the Ramists, who were conspicuously active at Cambridge at that time. Against their nimble handling of Ramus' theories of rhetoric, Hooker reiterated all the old stock in trade of Aristotelianism and thought that he had vanquished his opponents simply by his demonstration that they differed from Aristotle. In this respect Hooker showed himself to be much more medieval than one is led to expect from his high baroque prose style and his freely discursive and informal way of arguing.

Through his conviction that Aristotelianism was the only satisfactory vehicle of Christian humanism, Hooker weakened his own case. For it was this conviction that deprived him of the opportunity of becoming the link between the humanism of Colet, Erasmus, and More at the beginning of the sixteenth century and the Platonism of the Cambridge Platonists of the early seventeenth century. Platonism was fashionable enough in the England of Hooker: Edmund Spenser, William Harvey, Roger Ascham, Sir Philip Sidney were all Platonists in one way or another. But their Platonism was purely literary and emotional. Hooker was perhaps the only Elizabethan who could have deepened it. His Aristotelianism kept him aloof from these currents of thought, and thus he missed the unique opportunity that his great learning and the lucidity of his thought afforded him: injecting systematic philosophy into the Platonist current.

Natural law after Hooker. Although it may seem that Hooker's grand vindication of natural law helped to prepare the way for the revival of natural law in the seventeenth century, his arguments bear no relation to those of Grotius or of Locke. To Hooker natural law was the dictate of reason; and reason was a discursive power of sensibility, capable of intuiting the good. It can therefore provide premises as well as help to draw out conclusions and dictate right conduct. To Grotius, on the other hand, the dictates of right reason were mere calculations of enlightened self-interest. In his theory of natural law, reason merely provided the long-term views necessary for survival, and natural law ceased to be identified with the rules set down, indirectly, by God. They were, on the contrary, made out to be completely independent of God.

Works by Hooker

The best text for Hooker's works is J. Keble, ed., *Works,* 3 vols., in the 7th ed. re-edited by R. W. Church and F. Paget (Oxford, 1888). The most easily accessible edition is that of the Everyman Library, Nos. 101 and 102 (London and New York); it does not include Books VI–VIII. See also *Book I, Laws of Ecclesiastical Polity,* edited by R. W. Church (Oxford, 1882); *Book V, Laws of Ecclesiastical Polity,* edited by R. Bayne (London, 1902); and *Hooker's Ecclesiastical Polity: Book VIII,* edited with an introduction by R. A. Houk (New York, 1931).

Works on Hooker

Entréves, A. P., d', *The Medieval Contribution to Political Thought.* Oxford, 1939. Ch. 6.
Munz, Peter, *The Place of Hooker in the History of Thought.* London, 1952.
Paget, F., *Introduction to the Fifth Book of Hooker's Treatise of the Laws of Ecclesiastical Polity.* Oxford, 1899.
Shirley, F. J., *Richard Hooker and Contemporary Political Ideas.* London, 1949.
Sisson, C. J., *The Judicious Marriage of Mr. Hooker and the Birth of the Laws of Ecclesiastical Polity.* Cambridge, 1940.

PETER MUNZ

HOW AND WHY. See WHY.

HOWISON, GEORGE HOLMES (1834–1916), American personalist philosopher and mathematician. Howison was a graduate of Marietta College in Ohio and professor of mathematics at Washington University, where he became a member of the St. Louis Philosophical Society. He taught philosophy at the Massachusetts Institute of Technology, at the Harvard Divinity School, and at the Concord School of Philosophy before moving in 1884 to the University of California, where he organized what was to become an influential department of philosophy.

Howison, calling his system "Personal Idealism," maintained that both impersonal, monistic idealism and materialism run contrary to the moral freedom experienced by persons. To deny the freedom to pursue the ideals of truth, beauty, and "benignant love" is to undermine every profound human venture, including science, morality, and philosophy. Thus, even Personalistic Idealism (B. P. Bowne and E. S. Brightman) and Realistic Personal Theism (Aquinas) are inadequate, for they make finite persons dependent for their existence upon an infinite Person and support this view by an unintelligible doctrine of *creatio ex nihilo.*

Howison's Personal Idealism, therefore, is founded on what he believed to be an undeniable fact: the freedom crucial to human existence is untenable if the individual is dependent for his existence upon any other being, including a Creator–God or an Absolute One. Therefore, self-determining beings must be uncreated and eternal; yet the unique quality of human freedom presupposes that each person stands in an individual relationship to other persons, subpersonal beings, and God.

How, then, does this plurality of uncreated beings compose a universe and not a mere collection of beings, a pluriverse? Howison answers that it is the very nature of undeniable, self-active, unified, thinking beings to define themselves and to fulfill themselves as individuals. In this very act of self-definition and self-fulfillment they find themselves related to other beings. "Thus, in thinking itself as eternally real, each spirit thinks the reality of other spirits."

Is there a God to unify the many grades of self-active beings? Yes, but any unification must not infringe upon individual growth to moral perfection. Creation as efficient cause must give way to creation in accordance with an Ideal present in each being. The fulfillment of this Ideal calls for a world composed of "*all* the individual differences compatible with the mutual reality of all." Thus, basic harmony is possible because, as each individual defines himself, he finds the Ideal of self-definition by which to measure himself. And God, who is "defined as self-existent by every other self-defining being," is the indispensable standard for measuring reality.

In this Personal Idealism there is, then, no one Prime Mover or Creator. Reality is a republic of self-active, self-defining spirits, each moving toward the Ideal exemplified by God, "changelessly attentive to every other mind, rationally sympathetic with all experiences, and bent on its spiritual success. . . ." Nor are the vast number and the gradation of minds that compose the different levels of matter, life, and mind the product of evolution; what we know as nature and evolution is the product of the various kinds of self-active beings, moved ultimately by the final causes of their inner beings toward a common goal.

Bibliography

Buckingham, J. W., and Stratton, G. W., *George Holmes Howison, Philosopher and Teacher.* Berkeley, 1934. Includes a bibliography and complete reprint of *The Limits of Evolution and Other Essays Illustrating the Metaphysical Theory of Personal Idealism* (1901).
Cunningham, G. W., *The Idealistic Argument in Recent British and American Philosophy.* 1933. Ch. 12.

PETER A. BERTOCCI

HSÜN TZU (c. 298–c. 212 B.C.), also called Hsün Ch'ing or Hsün Ku'ang, was an ancient Chinese philosopher representing an unorthodox wing of Confucianism. Active in the concluding phase of the age of classical philosophy, he witnessed the climax of the Period of Warring States (403–422 B.C.). Hsün Tzu had a brief career as an official in the states of Ch'i and Ch'u, but he was best known as a leading scholar of his day. He left a work known as *The Hsün Tzu,* consisting of 32 chapters or essays that covered a wide range of subjects, such as nature, man, government, education, psychology, and logic. The broad interest and matter-of-fact approach of Hsün Tzu readily remind one of Aristotle, his older contemporary on the other side of the globe.

Hsün Tzu called himself a Confucianist, but, having had the benefit of the assorted schools of philosophy of the classical age, his teachings tended to deviate from the Confucian orthodoxy. His views on such fundamental notions as those of nature and man were at once distinctive and refreshing. Whereas Heaven (*T'ien*) was regarded in the traditional view sometimes as a moral principle and sometimes as a divine presence, Hsün Tzu proclaimed, "Heaven conducts itself with constant regularity." Listeners were exhorted to conceive of Heaven not as an object of worship or a source of blessing but as the totality of nature pursuing its own course unconcerned and unaffected by human conduct. The part of wisdom for man lay therefore in everyone attending to his own affairs without relying on divine assistance. The chapter "On Heaven" (Bk. 17) in *The Hsün Tzu* actually suggested the employment and harnessing of heaven for the advancement of human welfare, a Baconian note anticipating Francis Bacon by some eighteen centuries.

On the subject of human nature Hsün Tzu ran into even more open conflict with Mencius, who had maintained that human nature was good. The chapter "Human Nature is Evil" (Bk. 23) opened with the declaration "The nature of man is evil; his goodness is acquired." For the acquisition of goodness the most effective means was to be found in the authority of the sage-kings and the usage of ceremonials, according to Hsün Tzu, and "accumulation" was said to be the key to this educational process. Hsün Tzu said, for instance, "When enough good deeds are accumulated to constitute a high virtue, spiritual enlightenment naturally arrives and the heart of the sage is there at hand" (*The Hsün Tzu*, Bk. 1).

Hsün Tzu's departure from the moralistic and idealistic trends of orthodox Confucianism in favor of a more realistic standpoint might be partly attributable to the hopelessly chaotic condition of his day. It is further noteworthy that Hsün Tzu's two leading disciples, Han Fei and Li Ssu, became, respectively, the representative thinker and the practitioner of the Machiavellian type of philosophy known as Legalism. Hsün Tzu himself maintained, however, that he was a Confucianist. In spite of the notable deviations, he was in complete agreement with Confucius and Mencius—but in contradiction to the Legalists—with regard to the final objective of all teaching, the importance of the individual and his achievement of perfection. To Hsün Tzu, as to all other Confucianists, every man on the street had the potentiality of becoming a sage.

Bibliography

Hsün Tzu's works were translated in part by Homer H. Dubs as *The Works of Hsüntze* (London, 1928). The Chinese text of Book XXII of *The Hsün Tzu*, together with an English translation by Y. P. Mei, was published as "Hsün Tzu on Terminology," in *Philosophy East and West*, Vol. 1, No. 2 (1951), 51–60.

For literature on Hsün Tzu, see also Y. P. Mei, "Hsün Tzu's Theory of Education," which contains an English translation of Book I of *The Hsün Tzu*, "An Exhortation to Learning," together with the Chinese text, in *Tsing Hua Journal of Chinese Studies*, Vol. 2, No. 2 (1961), 361–379.

Y. P. Mei

HUET, PIERRE-DANIEL (1630–1721), the last Christian skeptic in the line of Montaigne and Charron, was born in Caen, Normandy. His father had been converted from Calvinism. Young Huet studied with the Jesuits and, after taking a degree in mathematics, went in 1652 with the Protestant scholar Samuel Bochart to the court of Queen Christina of Sweden. There he discovered a manuscript of Origen, which later led him to write his *Origenis Commentaria in Sacrum Scripturam* (Rouen, France, 1668). En route home in 1653 he stopped in the Netherlands, where he met many savants. A discussion with one of them, Rabbi Menasseh ben Israel, led Huet to write his *Demonstratio Evangelica* (1679). From the Netherlands Huet returned to Caen, where he founded the Academy of Sciences, corresponded with learned men throughout the world, and worked on his studies on Origen. He often traveled to Paris and entered several of the learned literary salons. His reputation as a man of letters and science grew, and in 1670 Louis XIV appointed him to be Bossuet's assistant as the dauphin's teacher. While holding this post, Huet started a famous set of editions of classical authors, *Ad Usum Delphini*. After several years Huet decided to become a priest and was appointed abbot of Aunay and afterward bishop of Soissons. He did not like that post and exchanged it for the bishopric of Avranches. In 1699 he retired to a Jesuit institution in Paris, to which he had donated his enormous library (transferred after the suppression of the Jesuit order to the Bibliothèque Nationale, where they constitute a basic part of the collection).

Huet wrote many works on history, philosophy, theology, and literature and was regarded by figures like Leibniz as the most learned man of his age and as an excellent Latin poet. His most philosophically interesting works are the *Demonstratio Evangelica, Censura Philosophiae Cartesianae* (1689), *Nouveaux mémoires pour servir à l'histoire du cartésianisme* (1692), *Questiones Alnetae de Concordia Rationis et Fidei* (1692), and its notorious concluding section, the *Traité philosophique de la foiblesse humain*, published posthumously in 1723.

The *Demonstratio Evangelica* showed signs of philosophical skepticism and empirical and liberal views. After arguing that no absolute certainty could be attained in mathematics or theology, Huet tried to establish religious truth inductively, by showing the common elements in all religions, ancient and modern. The privileged position of Christianity was primarily because of its expressing best the features of natural revelation. (Doctrinal differences within Christianity had little interest for Huet. Hence, he could join his friend Leibniz in trying to reunite all the churches.)

Huet's writings against Cartesianism showed a much more developed epistemological skepticism. He utilized all of Sextus Empiricus' weapons to attack Descartes's claims that the *cogito* was the fundamental, indubitable truth and that whatever was clearly and distinctly conceived was true. Joining the previous critics Gassendi, Hobbes, and Simon Foucher, Huet, in an intensive examination of the Cartesian theory of knowledge, contended that "I think, therefore I am" was a dubious claim and that no certain knowledge about the world could be attained by Descartes's "way of ideas." In his *Censura* and an unpublished defense of it, Huet argued that not only is "I think, therefore I am" an inference but also that it involves a time sequence from the moment when thinking is occurring to the moment when one realizes that he thought and that memory may be inaccurate. If one is immediately conscious of thinking, the realization about existence is a possible future event. Hence, one cannot be simultaneously aware and certain of the ingredients of the *cogito* and, thus, of its indubitability.

Besides analyzing the Cartesian arguments, Huet ridiculed both the theory and its founder. The *Nouveaux mémoires* is a spoof about Descartes's life after his supposed death in Stockholm, when Descartes tried to expound his philosophy in Lapland. Huet also joined the Jesuit anti-Cartesians in accusing Cartesianism of irreligion and incoherence, advocating, instead, a type of probabilistic nonmetaphysical view of the world.

The full presentation of Huet's skepticism appears in the posthumous *Traité philosophique*, which the Jesuits denounced as a forgery written to embarass the church. (The manuscript, which is in Huet's handwriting, and discussions in his correspondence eliminate any doubts about Huet's authorship.) The traditional Pyrrhonian position is set forth, criticisms of skepticism considered and refuted, and a modern skepticism advocated in opposition to Cartesianism. Huet's skepticism consisted of doubting that any genuine knowledge about reality can be attained by human means while offering experimental science and pure fideism as the means for finding out something about nature, God, and man. In the *Traité*, in his correspondence, and in his marginalia, especially to his copy of Pascal's *Pensées*, an extreme fideism appears, in which it is denied that there can be any rational defense of religion. Huet thought Pascal too rationalistic because of his wager argument. Faith, and faith alone, could lead to any religious views. It is difficult to determine what or how much Huet himself actually believed. As a prelate and theologian, he was extremely latitudinarian and was in friendly contact with scholars everywhere, regardless of their religious or nonreligious affiliations.

In his day Huet was quite influential and was taken seriously by Leibniz, Bayle, and others (Spinoza even feared that Huet was writing a refutation of his views). A major transitional figure, he helped to destroy Cartesianism and to further empirical science. His immense erudition provided some of the basic materials for the Enlightenment. His pioneer work in comparative religion was taken by later scholars as ammunition against traditional religion. However, his skeptical argumentation was taken less seriously than that of Bayle or Hume. A vast amount of unpublished material may provide a clearer picture of Huet's views and his role in the intellectual world.

Works by Huet

Demonstratio Evangelica. Paris, 1679.
Censura Philosophiae Cartesianae. Paris, 1689.
Traité philosophique de la foiblesse de l'esprit humain. Amsterdam, 1723. Translated by E. Combe as *An Essay Concerning the Weakness of the Human Understanding.* London, 1725.

Works on Huet

Barthomèss, Christian, *Huet évêque d'Avranches ou le scepticisme théologique.* Paris, 1850.
Dupront, A., *P.-D. Huet et l'exégèse comparatiste au XVIIe siècle.* Paris, 1930.
Popkin, Richard H., "The Manuscript Papers of Bishop Pierre-Daniel Huet," in *Year Book of the American Philosophical Society, 1959.* Philadelphia, 1959. Pp. 449–453.
Popkin, Richard H., "The High Road to Pyrrhonism." *American Philosophical Quarterly*, Vol. II (1965), 1–5.
Tolmer, Léon, *Pierre-Daniel Huet (1630–1721), humaniste-physicien.* Bayeux, France, 1949.

RICHARD H. POPKIN

HÜGEL, BARON FRIEDRICH VON (1852–1925), Roman Catholic philosopher of religion and writer on mysticism. He was born in Florence, Italy, and succeeded to his father's (Austrian) title in 1870. Most of his life was spent in England. His most important writings were *The Mystical Element of Religion as Studied in St. Catherine of Genoa and Her Friends* (London, 1908), *Essays and Addresses on the Philosophy of Religion* (London, 1921 and 1926), and *The Reality of God* (published posthumously; London, 1931).

Von Hügel's philosophical position was opposed both to idealism and to what he called positivism. By positivism he meant the doctrine that knowledge is exclusively confined to sense perceptions and to the laws that connect them. He rejected this position on the grounds that sense experience is accompanied by a strong "pressure on our minds" to credit it with "trans-subjective validity" (that is, to accept that it tells us something about an external world existing independently of our experience of it) and that refusal to assent to this pressure would mean that positivism collapses into skepticism, which is self-defeating. Moreover, since it is our own minds that we are immediately aware of, our apprehension of reality will be more certain if there is no phenomenal content. This idea paves the way for von Hügel's justification of the epistemological importance of mystical experience. He criticized idealism for a subjectivism similar to that implicit in positivism.

Von Hügel distinguished between knowledge of abstract ideas and of numerical and spatial relations, on the one hand, and knowledge of real existences on the other. The former is clear and readily intelligible; the latter is never totally clear, since any statement or set of statements about a real object will fail to exhaust what is to be discovered in it. The "higher," or more complex, the entity, the less clear is one's apprehension of it. Von Hügel was therefore concerned with opposing philosophical theories that claimed to give a clear and exhaustive analysis of types of existence (for example, he criticized Hume's account of the individual). Reality, according to von Hügel, is indefinitely apprehensible, a fact which serves to explain both the revisionism of science and the gropings of religion. The obscurity involved in religion is an index of the richness of its subject matter. "Religion," he said, "can't be clear if it is worth anything."

The concept of the Infinite occupies a central position in von Hügel's philosophy. He held that there was no good reason for neglecting or doubting the validity of man's sense of the Infinite, which should be taken quite as seriously as sense experience; in this, he in effect conjoined a critique of religious experience and traditional Catholic natural theology. The critique of religious experience involved the examination of the claims of great religious figures of all ages. He was opposed to simply accepting the testimony of the individual; rather, he pointed to the errors and excesses of many individual interpretations of religion, some of which involved the denial of plain facts. At the same time, he was sympathetic to the insights claimed by non-Christian religions. His doctrine of religious knowledge was not exclusive to any one tradition, although he was opposed to relativism. Von Hügel also argued against various theories arising from religious experience, such as the extreme dualism of Kierkegaard and the monism of some mystics (for instance, the doctrine of the identification of the soul with God). He maintained that Kierkegaard differentiated to such an extent between God and man that intercourse between the two became incomprehensible. A crucial argument of von Hügel's was that the impinging of the Infinite on man's experience, emotions, and will implies the spiritual nature of the Infinite; for otherwise it would be hard to account for its inspiring power.

According to von Hügel's theory of knowledge, it is artificial to divorce the cognitive aspects of experience from the affective and volitional aspects; and therefore the religious apprehension of the Infinite is not limited to grasping a theoretical concept but includes a vital response. For this and other reasons, von Hügel defended a sacramental and institutional faith—namely, that of Catholicism. But in his openness to and sympathy with the critical evaluation of the Biblical tradition by the methods of scientific history, von Hügel belonged to the Catholic Modernist movement.

Bibliography

Additional works by von Hügel are *Eternal Life* (Edinburgh, 1912); *The German Soul* (London, 1916); *Readings from von Hügel,* Algar Thorold, ed. (London, 1928); and *Letters to a Niece* (New York, 1950).

A work on von Hügel is L. V. Lester-Garland, *The Religious Philosophy of Baron Friedrich von Hügel* (London, 1938).

NINIAN SMART

HUGH OF SAINT VICTOR. See SAINT VICTOR, SCHOOL OF.

HUI SHIH (370?–310? B.C. or a few years earlier) was a logician in ancient China. He was a friend of Chuang Tzu and served as prime minister of the state of Wei. He taught his logical doctrines to the Dialecticians, through whom his influence was felt by Huan T'uan and Kung-sun Lung. Of the five carloads of books he was reported to have written, only ten paradoxes and a few fragmentary statements have survived. Since the arguments leading to these paradoxes are missing, it is difficult to ascertain their original meaning. Attempts have been made to relate them to earlier or contemporary philosophies, such as later Moist logical works or the *Chuang Tzu*. All that can be established, however, is that during Hui Shih's time certain physical, logical, and mathematical concepts were common subjects of debates and discussions among thinkers. Hui Shih's paradoxes and statements seem to be the result of such debates and discussions. The following are his paradoxes and statements, to each of which is added a brief explanatory note:

(1) "The greatest has nothing beyond it, and is called the Great Unit; the smallest has nothing within it, and is called the Little Unit." (Here an attempt has been made to express the mathematical concepts of infinity and dimensionless point.)

(2) "It has no thickness, and cannot be increased in thickness; it extends over one thousand *li.*" (This is an attempt to grasp the notion of the two-dimensional plane.)

(3) "The heaven is as low as the earth; and mountains are as level as marshes." (This expresses the relative nature of things; how things are perceived depends on the moment of time or on one's viewpoint.)

(4) "The moment the sun reaches the zenith it declines; and the moment a thing is born it dies." (All things are in a process of change.)

(5) "A great similarity differs from a little similarity. This is called the little similarity-and-difference. All things are both similar and different. This is called the great similarity-and-difference." (The common-sense idea of similarity and difference is contrasted with a philosophic recognition that similarity and difference depend on viewpoints: viewed from the standpoint of similarity, all things are similar, and viewed from the standpoint of difference all things are different.)

(6) "The south has no limit and has a limit." (Viewed from the standpoint of infinity, the south has no limit, but viewed from the standpoint of the finite, it has a limit.)

(7) "I go to Yüeh today and arrived there yesterday." (In (6) spatial relativity is expressed; what is expressed here is temporal relativity.)

(8) "Connected rings can be separated." (The separation may be effected either by smashing the rings in the manner of cutting a Gordian knot or by considering the relative nature of connection and separation, according to which the selfsame phenomenon may be viewed as connection or separation, depending on the point of view.)

(9) "I know the center of the earth; it lies north of Yen and south of Yüeh." (It is tempting to think that Hui Shih might have entertained the notion that the earth was round; hence any point could be the center.)

(10) "Love all things equally; the universe is one." (Viewed from the standpoint of similarity, all differences fade away, leaving a homogeneous whole; hence the universe may be said to be one. This implies a solidarity of all things, which, when made the object of one's affection, should be loved equally.)

Bibliography

Hui Shih's "The Ten Paradoxes" are in Chapter 33 of the *Chuang Tzu.* The translation is given in this article.

For literature on Hui Shih, see Vol. I, pp. 194–203, of Fung Yu-lan, *A History of Chinese Philosophy,* translated by Derk Bodde, 2 vols. (Princeton, N.J., 1952–1953); and Joseph Needham, *Science and Civilization in China,* Vol. II (Cambridge, 1956).

VINCENT Y. C. SHIH

HUMANISM is the philosophical and literary movement which originated in Italy in the second half of the fourteenth century and diffused into the other countries of Europe, coming to constitute one of the factors of modern culture. Humanism is also any philosophy which recognizes the value or dignity of man and makes him the measure of all things or somehow takes human nature, its limits, or its interests as its theme.

In the first meaning, which is historical, humanism is a basic aspect of the Renaissance and precisely that aspect through which Renaissance thinkers sought to reintegrate man into the world of nature and history and to interpret him in this perspective. The term "humanism" in this sense derives from *humanitas,* which at the time of Cicero and Varro meant the education of man as such, and what the Greeks called *paideia:* the education favored by those who considered the liberal arts to be instruments, that is, disciplines proper to man which differentiate him from the other animals (see Aulus Gellius, *Noctes Atticae* XIII, 17). The humanists held that through classical letters the "rebirth" of a spirit that man had possessed in the classical age and had lost in the Middle Ages could be realized, a spirit of freedom that provided justification for man's claim of rational autonomy, allowing him to see himself involved in nature and history and capable of making them his realm. Humanism as "return to antiquity" did not consist in a simple repetition of the ancient past but in the revival and a development of capacities and powers that the ancients possessed and exercised but which had been lost in the Middle Ages (as they believed). In speaking of such a return the humanists rejected the medieval heritage and chose that of the classical world instead. The privilege that they accorded to the humanities—poetry, rhetoric, history, ethics, and politics—was founded on the conviction that these disciplines alone educate man as such and put him in a position effectively to exercise his freedom.

Freedom. The exaltation of freedom was, in fact, one of the major themes of the humanists; but the freedom of which they spoke is that which man can and should exercise in nature and in society. The fundamental institutions of the medieval world—the empire, the church, and feudalism—seemed to be the guardians of a cosmic order which man had to accept but which he could not modify to the slightest degree. They worked primarily to show that all the material and spiritual goods to which man can aspire (from daily bread to truth) derive from the order to which he belongs, that is, the hierarchies which are the interpreters and custodians of the cosmic order. Humanism, which was born in the cities and the communes that had fought and were fighting for their autonomy and that saw in traditional hierarchical orders an obstacle rather than an aid to the goods indispensable to man, defended man's freedom to project his life in the world in an autonomous way. Gianozzo Manetti (1396–1459), Marsilio Ficino (1433–1499), and Pico della Mirandola (1463–1494), in exalting freedom, exalted man's capacity to form his world, to vary it, and to better it absolutely. Pico, above all, expressed this faith in man with the famous words he attributes to God in the *Oration on the Dignity of Man:*

I have given you, Adam, neither a predetermined place nor a particular aspect nor any special prerogatives in order that you may take and possess these through your own decision and choice. The limitations on the nature of other creatures are contained within my prescribed laws. You shall determine your own

nature without constraint from any barrier, by means of the freedom to whose power I have entrusted you. I have placed you at the center of the world so that from that point you might see better what is in the world. I have made you neither heavenly nor earthly, neither mortal nor immortal so that, like a free and sovereign artificer, you might mold and fashion yourself into that form you yourself shall have chosen.

The same theme was treated later by the French humanist Charles Bouillé (Carolus Bovillus, 1475–c. 1553) in his *De Sapiente,* where the wise man is compared to Prometheus, in that wisdom confers on man powers which perfect his nature. One deals here (as is evident today) with speculations influenced by an excessive confidence in man's capacity to shape his life in the world, a confidence which was tempered by the skeptical developments that humanism underwent outside of Italy in the following century in the work of Michel de Montaigne (1533–1592), of Pierre Charron (1541–1603), and of Francisco Sánchez (1552–1581). This confidence, however, constituted the new doctrine of humanism in contrast with the medieval mentality.

Naturalism. If by naturalism one means the conviction that man is a part of nature—that nature is his realm, that the features which tie him to nature (his body, his needs, his sensations) are essential to him to the point that he cannot abstract from them or ignore them—then one can speak of a naturalism in humanism. Though the humanists exalted the soul of man for its powers of freedom, they did not forget the body and that which pertains to it. The widespread recognition of the value of pleasure among the humanists and their aversion to medieval asceticism clearly show the new evaluation of man's natural aspects. The *De Voluptate* of Lorenzo Valla (1407–1457) is the major document of this evaluation. The thesis of the dialogue is that pleasure is the sole good for man, that is, the sole end of human activities. The laws that regulate the cities have been made for utility, which in turn generates pleasure. Every government is directed to this same end. Virtue is none other than the calculus of pleasure; and pleasure, or at least utility, is the end of the liberal arts, like medicine, jurisprudence, poetry, and oratory, which attempt to satisfy the needs of life. In the *De Professione Religiosorum,* Valla denies any religious superiority to monastic life. The life of Christ, he says, is not followed only by those who belong to religious orders but by all those who, inside and outside of clerical circles, dedicate their activities to God. With Valla, Coluccio Salutati (1331–1406), Gianozzo Manetti, and Poggio Bracciolini (1380–1459) carried on the debate against asceticism and against monastic life which took it as the ideal.

The recognition of the place of pleasure in the moral life brought the humanists to the defense of Epicurus, whom the Middle Ages had considered the philosopher of impiety. In their eyes Epicurus was the master of human wisdom, the philosopher who saw man in his true nature.

As well as the naturality of man, the humanists recognized his social and political character and insisted, therefore, on the superiority of the active life to the contemplative, of moral philosophy to physics and metaphysics. Leonardo Bruni (c. 1370–1444) affirms in the *Isagogicon*

Moralis Disciplinae: "Moral philosophy is, so to speak, our territory. Those who betray it, and give themselves over to physics, seem in a way to occupy themselves with foreign affairs and to neglect their own." These words do not express, as it has sometimes been held, the humanists' aversion to the investigation of nature but rather their insistence on an aspect of human life that medieval philosophy seemed unjustly to have neglected. Matteo Palmieri's (1406–1475) essay *Della vita civile* and Bartolomeo de' Sacchi's (1421–1481) *De Optime Cive* express the same idea. Bruni, in fact, translated Aristotle's *Nicomachean Ethics* and *Politics* and his books on economics. All of the humanists tended to contrast the "moral" Aristotle, the ancient master of wisdom who described the virtues and vices of man as a political animal and determined the conditions and forms of civil society, with Aristotle the "physicist" and "metaphysician" of the medieval tradition. They gave the "moral" Aristotle the credit for recognizing the value of money as an indispensable item for the well-being of the individual and for the life of the society, and they considered contempt for money a manifestation of the medieval asceticism which was based on ignorance of human nature. Humanism thus opened the way for the work of Machiavelli (who also in many ways was a humanist), which cleared the world of politics of any metaphysical or theological suggestion and was dedicated to showing, without prejudice, the choices offered to the political man in various circumstances, based on the conviction that the limit of political activity is to be found within politics alone.

Historical perspective. The "return to antiquity," which was the watchword of humanism, was responsible for one of its most important realizations, that of the historical perspective of events. The Middle Ages knew (in great part) and utilized classical culture but utilized it by assimilating it and making it contemporary. Facts, figures, and doctrines did not have for the writers of the Middle Ages a precise and individuated aspect but were considered only for the value they could have in the universe of discourse in which these writers moved. Geography and chronology were useless from this point of view. Humanism made clear for the first time the perspective of historiographic distance. Platonists and Aristotelians argued with each other in the Renaissance, but their common interest was the discovery of the true Plato and the true Aristotle—that is, of the genuine doctrine of their founders, undeformed and uncamouflaged by the medieval "barbarians." Philological demands were not accidental to humanism but essential to it. The defense of classical eloquence was a defense of the genuine language of the classical age against the deformations that it had undergone in the Middle Ages, and there was an attempt to revive it in its original form. The discovery of documentary falsifications and false attributions, the need to discover texts and revive them in authentic form by studying and collating codices, and the attempt to understand the personalities of the literary men and the philosophers of the past in their own worlds are all the indications of humanism's fundamental concern for historicity. Doubtless in its results it realized the task of historical restoration only partially and imperfectly, but the task is never exhausted and is repeatedly

proposed to historiographic endeavor. The humanists were aware of the value of this task, and they initiated it and insured its continuance by leaving it as a legacy to modern culture.

The discovery of historical perspective was, with respect to time, what the discovery of optic perspective in Renaissance painting was with respect to space: the capacity to realize the distance of the objects from each other and from the viewer and therefore the capacity to understand them in their actual place and time and in their distinction from each other—in their individuality. The significance of human personality as an original and autonomous center organizing the various aspects of life was conditioned by perspective in this sense. The importance that the modern world attaches to human personality is the consequence of an attitude made possible by Renaissance humanism.

Religion. For all its antipathy toward asceticism and theology, humanism did not have an antireligious or anti-Christian character. Its interest in defending the value and freedom of man drew it into discussing the traditional problems of God and providence and of the soul, its immortality, and its freedom—discussions that were frequently concluded in much the same form as that accepted by the medieval tradition. However, in the context of humanism these discussions assumed a new significance because they had the purpose of understanding and justifying the capacity for initiative of man in the world. This capacity was defended even in the religious sphere, for the religious discussions of the humanists had two principal themes: the civil function of religion and religious tolerance.

The civil function of religion was recognized on the basis of the correspondence between the heavenly and earthly city. The heavenly city was the norm or the ideal of man's civil life; but precisely because it was such, its recognition meant the commitment of man to realize, as much as possible, its characteristics in the earthly city. Gianozzo Manetti in his *De Dignitate et Excellentia Hominis* saw in the Bible not only the proclamation of superterrestrial happiness but also of earthly happiness. Religion, according to Manetti, was the confidence in the value of man's work, in the success of this work, and in the reward that man will find in the future life. For Manetti, as for Lorenzo Valla and many others, the fundamental function of religion was to support man in the work of civil life, in political work and activity.

Tolerance. The religious views of humanism were profoundly permeated by the spirit of tolerance. The concept of tolerance which has come to be affirmed in the modern world as an effect of the wars of religion in the sixteenth and seventeenth centuries implies the possibility of peaceful coexistence between the various religious confessions which remain different from each other and are not reducible to a single confession. For the humanists instead, the attitude of tolerance derived from their conviction of the fundamental unity of all the religious beliefs of mankind and therefore of the possibility of a universal religious peace. Moreover, according to the humanists, religious peace implies the essential identity between philosophy and religion. "Does St. Paul teach something more than Plato taught?" asked Leonardo Bruni. According to the point of view of the Fathers of the church, which was shared by all the humanists, Christianity simply brought to fulfillment the wisdom that ancient philosophy had elaborated, because reason, which had supported and guided this philosophy, is the same which became incarnate in the Word. These concepts were clearly expressed in Marsilio Ficino's *De Christiana Religione* (1474).

Pico della Mirandola was, on the other hand, the most inspired proclaimer and prophet of a regenerate peace which would conciliate all the religions and all the philosophies of the world. The *Oration on the Dignity of Man* (which originally was to be called the *Hymn of Peace*) proposed to lay the foundation of the universal peace by showing the accord between Platonism and Aristotelianism; between these two doctrines and the other philosophies of antiquity, the cabala, magic, patristics, and Scholasticism; and between the entire world of philosophy and Christianity and religious revelation. With Pico, many humanists held that this diversity of belief came from a single source, from a primordial revelation that these beliefs express in a partial but not contradictory way. The "return to origins" would be a return to the religious peace of the happy ancestors of the human race and the end of theological hatred and intolerance. Later, in the first decades of the sixteenth century, religious tolerance was defended in a modern and effective way by the great Dutch humanist Desiderius Erasmus (1466–1536) and by the Englishman Thomas More (1478–1535) in his famous *Utopia* (1516).

Science. Renaissance humanism can be considered one of the conditions that contributed to the birth of modern science. The "return to antiquity" revived doctrines and texts that had been neglected for centuries: the heliocentric doctrines of the Pythagoreans and the works of Archimedes, Hippocrates, and the other physicians of antiquity. From the Platonism and Pythagoreanism revived by the humanists the thesis maintained by Leonardo, Copernicus, and Galileo was derived: that nature is written in mathematical characters and that to understand it, one must know the language of mathematics. Moreover, so that men would decide to interrogate the "book of nature" directly through experimentation, and refuse to follow Aristotle's works blindly, the trust in Aristotle's authority had to be weakened. On the other hand, the conviction was affirmed that man is a natural being, that he is interested in making nature his domain and that he can question and understand nature with the tools that nature supplies to him, that is, with the senses.

Both of these conditions were realized in the work of the humanists. The criticism that the Scholastics of the fourteenth century (Ockham, Buridan, Albert of Saxony, Nicholas of Oresme, and others) leveled against some points of Aristotelian physics (criticisms today rightly recognized as antecedents of modern science) do not authorize making medieval Aristotelianism the matrix of this science. These criticisms were a manifestation of the rebellion against Aristotelianism that in the fourteenth and fifteenth centuries gave rise to humanism. They therefore did not constitute the link between Aristotelianism and science; on the contrary, they constituted the first break in the traditional Aristotelian front. The definitive break was accomplished by humanism.

In the sixteenth century this break extended even into the field which traditionally had been the uncontested domain of Aristotle, the field of logic. The Italian Mario Nizolio (1498–1576), the Frenchman Peter Ramus (1515–1572), and the Spaniard Juan Luis Vives (1492–1540) criticized the formalism and the artificial character of Aristotelian logic, as had the German Rudolf Agricola (1442–1485), and all demanded a logic better suited to the needs of natural experience and nearer to the forms of ordinary language.

"Humanism" has also been used to designate the following doctrines:

(1) Communism, in that it would abolish man's alienation from himself, which is a product of private property and capitalistic society.

(2) Pragmatism, because of its anthropocentric view which, as Protagoras did, makes man "the measure of all things."

(3) Personalism (also called spiritualism), which affirms man's capacity to contemplate the eternal truths or, in general, to enter into a relationship with transcendent reality.

(4) Existentialism, which affirms that "there is no other universe than the human universe, the universe of human subjectivity."

Bibliography

RENAISSANCE HUMANISM

On the Renaissance, only those recent works which can serve as documentation and justification for this presentation are cited.

Abbagnano, Nicola, *Storia della filosofia.* Turin, 1964. Vol. II, Part 4.

Cassirer, Ernst, *Individuum und Kosmos in der Philosophie der Renaissance.* Leipzig and Berlin, 1927. Translated by Mario Domandi as *Individual and Cosmos in Renaissance Philosophy.* New York, 1963.

Garin, Eugenio, *L'umanesimo italiano.* Bari, 1952.

Garin, Eugenio, *Medioevo e rinascimento.* Bari, 1954.

Garin, Eugenio, *La cultura filosofica del rinascimento italiano.* Florence, 1961.

Toffanin, G., *Storia dell'umanesimo,* 3 vols. Bologna, 1950.

HUMANISM IN GENERAL

Jaeger, Werner, *Humanism and Theology.* Milwaukee, Wis., 1943. Personalism as humanism.

Maritain, Jacques, *Humanisme intégral.* Paris, 1936. Personalism as humanism.

Marx, Karl, *Economic and Philosophical Manuscripts of 1844,* translated by Martin Milligan. Moscow and London, 1959. Part III. Communism as humanism.

Sartre, Jean-Paul, *L'Existentialisme est un humanisme.* Paris, 1946. Existentialism as humanism.

Schiller, F. C. S., *Humanism.* London, 1903. Pragmatism as humanism.

Schiller, F. C. S., *Studies in Humanism.* London, 1907. Pragmatism as humanism.

NICOLA ABBAGNANO
Translated by *Nino Langiulli*

HUMBOLDT, WILHELM VON (1767–1835), Prussian statesman, humanist, and linguistic scholar, was born in Potsdam; a younger brother was the scientist and explorer Alexander von Humboldt. Humboldt's early education was placed in the hands of private tutors and was augmented by private instruction in Greek, philosophy, natural law, and political economy from distinguished men of Germany's Enlightenment. From these youthful studies Plato's idea of the soul and Leibniz' concept of force left lasting impressions on his thought.

During and after his university years at Frankfurt an der Oder (1787) and at Göttingen (1788–1789), Humboldt began to question the rationalistic presuppositions of the Enlightenment. Like Herder, he viewed human society as a manifold of organic forces, closer to nature than to reason, and came to believe that true knowledge of humanity depended on the cultivation not of pure analytical reason but of deep-lying intuitive faculties.

Humboldt's political philosophy was outlined in a long essay, *Ideen zu einem Versuch die Grenzen der Wirksamkeit des Staats zu bestimmen*, written in 1791. Focused on the central theme of his thought—the inalienable value of the individual—this work propounds the humanistic creed that man's goal is "the highest and most proportional development of his powers to a complete and consistent whole." Reason must guide this development, but reason for Humboldt was a formative rather than a generative faculty. He criticized state control of education and religion for inflicting an arbitrary framework on diverse, organically developing human forces, whose unity could not be imposed from without but sought only from within.

In the last decade of the eighteenth century Humboldt was occupied with various scholarly projects, none of which he completed; at the same time his growing friendship with Schiller and Goethe brought him into contact with contemporary aesthetic problems. From 1802 to 1807 he was Prussian ambassador to the Vatican, and in 1808 he was appointed to the ministry of religious and educational affairs in Berlin, in which position he drafted several papers on education and was chiefly responsible for the foundation of the University of Berlin. Thereafter, he served as Prussian diplomatic representative in Vienna (1810–1813), at the peace negotiations before and after Napoleon's downfall (1814–1815), and in London (1817–1818). Defeated in his effort to achieve a constitutional monarchy for Prussia in 1819, he retired from public service and devoted the remainder of his life to study.

History. Humboldt's humanism was based on his idea of historical experience. "The broadening of our existence and of our knowledge," he wrote in a letter of 1823, "is possible historically only through the contemplation of previous existence." Searching for a discipline by which man's accumulated historical experience could become the foundation for a philosophy of man, Humboldt had already written several essays and drafts outlining principles for the study of Greek antiquity (*Über das Studium des Altertums und des griechischen insbesondere*, 1793), for a comparative anthropology (*Plan einer vergleichenden Anthropologie*, 1795), and finally for the historian's profession (*Die Aufgabe des Geschichtschreibers*, 1821). Sharing his generation's enthusiasm for ancient Greece, Humboldt believed that the study of Greek culture in its broadest aspects would promote a true philosophical knowledge of men, including "the knowledge of the manifold intellectual, sentient, and moral human powers." For Humboldt the Hellenic world was a unity of diverse forces, a cultural unity which his own times lacked but might regain through a comprehensive study of the Greeks. His plan for

a comparative anthropology was to study the moral character of different human types; a great variety of sources would provide the data for establishing an ideal norm, which was not adequately represented by any specific individuality. To comprehend the wholeness in the diversity of human types required aesthetic insight, which was fundamental to the art of the historian. In an essay on Goethe's *Hermann und Dorothea*, he concluded that epic poetry, of which Goethe's drama was an example, could be compared to history. "The condition of the soul which gives rise to the necessity of history (in the truest and highest sense of the word) is similar to that out of which an epic is produced with the help of imagination and art." In Humboldt's essay *Die Aufgabe des Geschichtschreibers*, in which the affinity of his thought to Schelling's philosophy is clearly manifested, the historian's imagination is likened to the poet's. It differs from the free fantasy of the poet's in that it is more strictly subordinated to the historian's experience and feeling for reality; it is actually a "divining faculty" (*Ahndungsvermögen*) and a "connecting ability" (*Verknüpfungsgabe*).

The most notable feature of this essay is Humboldt's attempt to elucidate the role of ideas in history. "Everything that is active in world history," he declared, "is also stirring in the inner being of man." The ideas in history have preserved human experience in the mind. "The eternal original ideas of everything conceivable provide existence and value, the beauty of all physical and spiritual forms, the truth in the unalterable working of every force according to its indwelling law, the justice in the inexorable course of events which are eternally regulated and meted their just reward." For Humboldt the goal of history is "the realization of the idea representing itself through humanity from all sides and in all forms in which the finite forms can be connected with the idea." The task of the historian is therefore to represent this process of ideas being actualized in history.

Language. Humboldt's language studies represent his chief legacy to posterity and marked, according to Ernst Cassirer, a new epoch in the history of the philosophy of language. Humboldt saw in the origin of language that crucial moment when man emerged from nature and, thus, the moment of connection between nature and idea. Language is for Humboldt the faculty by which man is identified as man. Speech and understanding are only different products of the power of language. The formation of languages depends on the spiritual forces of humanity, and languages are thus not merely an intermediary between individuals but "the most radiant sign and certain proof that man does not possess intrinsically separate individuality." Languages delineate the cultural characteristics of nations, each of which has its own individuality and arouses a sense of unity in men.

Humboldt's chief contribution to the study of linguistics was his concept of the "inner form" of languages (*innere Sprachform*), which consists of more than just external grammatical principles; it implies a deep-rooted subjective view of the world, a spiritual attitude, that controls the formation of concepts. "Because of the mutual dependency of thought and word," he wrote, "it is evident that the languages are not really means of representing the truth that has already been ascertained, but far more, means of discovering a truth not previously known. Their diversity is not a diversity of sounds, but of world outlook."

Humboldt's idea that each language has its own characteristic outlook, or inner form, found support in the linguistic studies of A. F. Pott and Heymann Steinthal in the nineteenth century and was suggested anew in the twentieth in the works of Benjamin Lee Whorf and Edward Sapir. His influence can also be traced in other areas of nineteenth-century thought—a passage from his political treatise provided the motto for J. S. Mill's essay *On Liberty;* his notion of the idea in history is closely related to Leopold von Ranke's doctrine of ideas; and his notion of historical experience is basic to the philosophy of Wilhelm Dilthey. In the twentieth century Ernst Cassirer, in the first volume of *The Philosophy of Symbolic Forms,* provided a penetrating evaluation of Humboldt's linguistic insights and a general philosophical context for the unmethodical profusion of his thought.

Works by Humboldt

Gesammelte Werke, Karl Brandes, ed., 7 vols. Berlin, 1841–1852.

Gesammelte Schriften, Royal Prussian Academy, ed., 17 vols. Berlin, 1903–1936.

Werke, A. Flitner and K. Giel, eds. Darmstadt, 1960——. Four of the projected five volumes are completed.

Humanist Without Portfolio: An Anthology, Marianne Cowan, ed. Detroit, Mich., 1963. Translated by the editor.

Works on Humboldt

BIOGRAPHIES

Haym, Rudolf, *Wilhelm von Humboldt. Lebensbild und Charakteristik.* Berlin, 1856.

Kaehler, Siegfried, *Humboldt und der Staat.* Munich and Berlin, 1927.

Leroux, Robert, *Guillaume de Humboldt: La Formation de sa pensée jusqu'en 1794.* Paris, 1932.

Spranger, Eduard, *Wilhelm von Humboldt und die Humanitätsidee.* Berlin, 1909.

STUDIES

Adler, G. J., *Wilhelm von Humboldt's Linguistical Studies.* New York, 1866.

Arens, Hans, *Sprachwissenschaft.* Munich, 1955.

Goldfriedrich, J., *Die historische Ideenlehre in Deutschland.* Berlin, 1902.

Kittel, Otto, *Wilhelm von Humboldts geschichtliche Weltanschauung im Lichte des klassischen Subjektivismus der Denker und Dichter von Königsberg, Jena und Weimar.* Leipzig, 1901.

Leroux, Robert, *L'Anthropologie comparée de Guillaume de Humboldt.* Publications de l'Université de Strasbourg, Fasc. 135. Strasbourg, 1958.

Wach, Joachim, *Das Verstehen,* Vol. I. Tübingen, 1926.

HOWARD ISHAM

HUME, DAVID (1711–1776), Scottish philosopher and historian, was born in Edinburgh. His father owned a small estate called "Ninewells" near Berwick and was a distant cousin of the earl of Home. His mother, Katherine Falconer, came from a family of lawyers, and young Hume was steered toward this profession. But soon after leaving Edinburgh University at the age of 15, he conceived a dislike for the law and embarked on a course of intense study of his own devising, which eventually led to the formulation of a complete philosophical system, published anonymously in 1739 as *A Treatise of Human Nature.*

Hume was deeply disappointed at the reception of his revolutionary book. He expected fury and learned controversy; he received neglect, mockery, and incomprehension. Indeed, Immanuel Kant and Thomas Reid were probably the only contemporary philosophers capable of understanding Hume. Blaming his own literary inexperience, Hume published anonymously in 1740 *An Abstract of a Treatise of Human Nature* and in 1748 and 1751 respectively *Philosophical Essays concerning the Human Understanding* and *An Enquiry concerning the Principles of Morals. Philosophical Essays* was retitled *An Enquiry concerning the Human Understanding* in a 1758 edition. From 1748 on, Hume acknowledged authorship of all major works except the *Treatise* and the *Abstract.* In his advertisement to a later edition of the two *Enquiries,* Hume expressly desired that they and not the *Treatise* should be "regarded as containing his philosophical sentiments and principles."

The *Enquiries* differ from the *Treatise* in style, in the omission of a number of elaborate psychological speculations, particularly concerning space, time, and sense perception, and in the inclusion of chapters on miracles, providence, and the theological implications of the free-will problem, all of which Hume had omitted from the *Treatise* because of their openly antireligious tendency.

Hume made no further important contributions to philosophical literature, except the *Dialogues concerning Natural Religion,* published posthumously and probably written in the 1750s. The reasons for this were, first, the lack of contemporary minds capable of understanding Hume and stimulating him to further researches and, second, the fact that Hume's dominant passion was not scientific curiosity but, in his own words, "love of literary fame."

Having restated his philosophy to his own satisfaction, Hume sought literary fame in other fields, principally in history and secondarily in moral and political thought, including economics, in which he won a reputation during his lifetime comparable to that of his great friend Adam Smith.

Hume was never an academic, though he made two unsuccessful applications for chairs of philosophy, at Edinburgh and at Glasgow. He was a man of letters and to a lesser extent a man of affairs. His principal appointments were as secretary to General St. Clair from 1746 to 1749 on a military expedition to Brittany and a diplomatic mission to Turin; as keeper of the Advocates Library, Edinburgh, where he wrote his *History of Great Britain,* from 1752 to 1757; as private secretary to Lord Hertford, British ambassador in Paris, from 1763 to 1766, where for a time Hume was *chargé d'affaires;* and as undersecretary of state, Northern Department, from 1767 to 1768.

Hume was a deservedly popular figure in the literary world of the period. Sociable, witty, kind, ingenuous in his friendships, innocently vain, and devoid of envy, he was known to French friends as "le bon David," and in Scotland as "Saint David." He never married, though he had many women friends, and the manner in which he faced his death from cancer was a paradigm of cheerful philosophic acceptance of annihilation, in the ancient Epicurean tradition.

THE ORIGINS OF THE "TREATISE"

Though one may, as Hume desired, judge his philosophy by the *Enquiries*, it is to the *Treatise* that one must look first in order to understand him. This work seems to have been conceived in a moment of inspiration when Hume was about eighteen. In a letter to a physician, dated 1734, Hume related that after long and unsatisfactory study of the various systems of philosophy, he felt a growing boldness of temper and sought for himself a "new medium by which truth might be established." At last "there seemed to be opened up to me a new scene of thought, which transported me beyond measure and made me, with an ardor natural to young men, throw up every other pleasure or business to apply entirely to it." After five years of this exertion, Hume was a sick young man—hence the letter to the physician. A change of occupation in a Bristol merchant's office helped him; and in a quiet retreat at La Flèche, in Anjou, where Hume stayed for three years, the book was finally completed, a long book, a young man's book, the outcome of eight years' intense intellectual labor.

We shall never know what the "new scene of thought" was. But we can identify the main currents in contemporary thought with which Hume was concerned and describe his response to them as presented in his completed work.

First, there was the influence of the great seventeenth-century rationalistic metaphysical systems of Hobbes, Descartes, Leibniz, Spinoza, and Malebranche. These thinkers all argued deductively, most of them professedly in the manner of Euclid, to prove the truth of sweeping propositions about the nature of the universe, God, and the human soul.

Second, there was the influence of Sir Isaac Newton, who by confining himself to hypotheses capable of being tested experimentally had shed immense light on the phenomena of nature. Newton's doctrines were taught in Edinburgh, around the time when Hume was a student, by two successive professors of mathematics, James Gregory and Colin Maclaurin.

Third, there was the influence of the British empiricist school of philosophy of Locke, Shaftesbury, Mandeville, Hutcheson, and Joseph Butler, in whose footsteps Hume professed to be following. These thinkers viewed with suspicion the grandiose systems of the Continental rationalists and sought by an unprejudiced examination of the faculties and principles of the human mind to establish the limits of our knowledge and the foundations of our duties.

Fourth, there was the influence of rationalistic systems of ethics, of which Samuel Clarke's provides the best example. Clarke combined an admiration for Newton with a completely a priori system of ethics, in which the principles of right and wrong that oblige not only men but God were held to be as self-evident or demonstrable as the propositions of Euclid.

Fifth, there were the great religious controversies of the preceding centuries, between Catholics and Protestants and, later, between theists and deists.

Finally, and closely connected with the religious controversies, there was the intense preoccupation of French thinkers with skepticism. This ancient discipline, rediscovered during the Renaissance in the text of Sextus Empiricus, aimed at the complete suspension of judgment, to be achieved by posing a counterargument to any argument that might be produced. Since the time of Montaigne, skepticism had been employed by Catholics and Reformers against one another, and since Descartes's unsuccessful attempt to silence it once and for all, its chief protagonist had been Pierre Bayle, one of Hume's favorite authors. Berkeley, generally regarded as a British empiricist, was not classed as such by Hume, but as a skeptic and a very powerful one.

Hume's policy, both in the *Treatise* and in the *Enquiries*, was to apply the Newtonian experimental method to the British empiricists' investigations into the powers and principles of the human mind. The intended result was to be a truly experimental science of human nature. The findings of this science were to provide a touchstone by which the arbitrary hypotheses of the rationalist metaphysicians could be tested. In the youthful ardor of his introduction to the *Treatise*, Hume even promised "a complete system of the sciences, built on a foundation almost entirely new." But in Part IV of Book I of the *Treatise*, a new force appeared—skepticism. Hume first used skepticism to discomfort his enemies and then drew its fangs in order to live with it himself. But in the *Treatise* this approach was only hinted at; and in the final chapter of Book I Hume seemed distinctly frightened of his new tool. In the first *Enquiry* and the *Dialogues concerning Natural Religion* the policy is clearer. The main enemy in the *Enquiry* is not metaphysics but religion. The metaphysical jungle must be cleared, because it is a dangerous lurking place for superstition. Skeptical arguments are logically unanswerable but powerless against the natural sentiments and convictions that govern our judgment in daily life. They can, therefore, safely be used to tease the theologians and set them quarreling with one another ("Natural History of Religion") and to serve as an antidote to dogmatism and overcertainty of every kind. They offer no threat to common sense, to mathematics, to morals, or to the experimental sciences, all of which, unlike metaphysics, are protected by the force of the natural sentiments and convictions. Naturalism deprives the skeptic of his sting, and reconciles him with the experimental scientist.

HUME'S LOGIC

Plan of the "Treatise." According to Hume, the four main divisions of the science of man are "logic, morals, criticism, and politics." Logic, whose end is said to be to "explain the principles and operations of our reasoning faculty and the nature of our ideas," occupies Book I of the *Treatise* and the whole of the first *Enquiry*. Morals and politics occupy Book III of the *Treatise* and the second *Enquiry*. Criticism, by which Hume meant roughly what we should call aesthetics, is supposed to be covered in Book II of the *Treatise* ("Of the Passions") and in the dissertation "*On the Passions*."

The main purpose of Book I of the *Treatise* is to establish empiricism as an empirical fact and thereafter to examine several metaphysical systems and philosophical problems. Hume's empiricism may be summed up in two propositions.

(1) All our ideas are derived from impressions of sense or inner feeling. That is, we cannot even conceive of things different in kind from everything in our experience.

(2) A matter of fact can never be proved by reasoning a priori. It must be discovered in, or inferred from, experience.

From these two propositions it follows that metaphysical systems telling us of the existence of God, the origin of the world, and other matters transcending human experience, have no meaning, and even if they had, could not be shown to be true.

There were two principal groups of concepts by means of which metaphysicians had claimed to transcend the limits of experience: space, time, number, geometry, and arithmetic, on the one hand; and cause and effect, force, energy, and necessity, on the other. Plato had argued from the unalterable exactitude of geometrical and arithmetical truths to the existence of intelligible forms more perfect than their approximations in the shifting world of sense. Leibniz argued from the infinite divisibility of space, and therefore of matter, to the unreality of both; for if infinitely divisible, they have no constituent parts, and the whole cannot exist without its parts. Only if the universe consists of an infinite number of indivisible souls, distinguished from one another solely by the differences in their ideas, and each mirroring the whole from a different point of view, can infinite divisibility and individuality be reconciled. The arguments based on causality were many and varied. Material things are plainly inert and inactive and therefore cannot cause anything, said Malebranche and Berkeley; therefore, the only true causes are spirits, finite and infinite. The cause, said Descartes, must possess at least as much reality as the effect. The cause of my idea of a Perfect Being is therefore a Perfect Being.

For this reason we find that Book I, Part II of the *Treatise* is devoted to our ideas of space, time, and number, and much of Part III to cause and effect.

The plan of Book I is as follows: Part I, evidence for the general proposition that ideas are derived from impressions; Part II, evidence for the empirical origin and application of our ideas of space, time, number, and existence; Part III, evidence for the purely conceptual character of questions decidable by reason a priori, for the empirical character of all questions of fact, and for the part played by the cause–effect relation in deciding such questions; Part IV, various metaphysical systems and problems considered.

The origin of ideas. For the professed founder of a new experimental science, Hume began in a distressingly dogmatic and a priori manner. "All the perceptions of the human mind resolve themselves into two distinct kinds, which I shall call impressions and ideas." Exhaustive dichotomies always merit suspicion, and this one is no exception. Hume did not in fact succeed in maintaining it. Impressions are supposed to be either sensations, passions, or emotions, but he soon introduced a number of familiar experiences which are none of these, for instance: the order in time of the five notes of a tune is not a *sixth* impression, but a *manner* in which the five impressions occur; an "idea of an idea" is distinguished, not by the impressions which it represents, but by the representation

of a certain indefinable "je-ne-sais-quoi"; belief is said to be neither part of the idea believed nor a distinct impression produced by that idea, but a special *manner* in which the idea is conceived.

Hume came to accept this cramping dichotomy because he was unable entirely to throw off a picture of the mind that, with slight variations, had dominated philosophical thinking for over a century. The mind was pictured as an immaterial thing with the powers of receiving representations of things in the world which it inhabits, of reasoning about these representations, and of making decisions that are somehow translated into physical action by the body to which the mind is temporarily attached. These representations were usually called "ideas." This word, now so familiar, but not to be found in the Authorized Version of the Bible or in Shakespeare, was a technical term of the Platonic philosophy, originally signifying those perfect intelligible archetypes which were the only objects of true knowledge, which the soul had seen before incarnation, and of which the soul is now sometimes reminded by sensible things, such memories appearing as a priori knowledge. The Christian Platonists, disbelieving in the prenatal existence of the soul, substituted for the inborn memories of the archetypes, inborn representations of them, which they called "innate ideas." It was from the possession of and by reflection on these innate ideas that we came by the knowledge of such necessary truths of metaphysics, mathematics, and morals as our Maker had thought it necessary for us to have and which could not be discovered from experience.

Empiricists—for instance, Locke—denied the existence of these innate ideas; but in doing so, they accepted the accompanying general picture of mind informed about the world around it by means of the ideas it possesses. Not being innate, these ideas must come from experience, which Locke defined as "sensation and reflection." Ideas of sensation come from our sense organs, ideas of reflection from our consciousness of our mental processes. The former are representations of things outside us and entirely sensuous in character; the latter, entirely subjective, representing in some mysterious way such processes as perceiving, combining, comparing, and abstracting. Memory somehow stores these representations, or copies of them, and has them handy when required for thinking. From this it was an obvious and inevitable step to treat the "ideas," which were supposed to provide the means of thinking, as mental images. Locke sometimes seems to have done so; Hume did so openly and consistently.

Hume's first departure from Locke's position was purely terminological. He called Locke's ideas of sense and reflection "impressions" and reserved the term "idea" for representations of imagination and memory. But Hume saw very clearly that if our primary information consists of nothing but representations and our thoughts of nothing but copies of those representations, then we can never find out how accurate the representations of sense may be, nor can we form any ideas of the real world, as distinct from our impressions of it. Hume also rejected the immaterial substance that supposedly possesses the ideas, professing to be unable to discover any such thing. These moves are not made until Book I, Part IV of the *Treatise*, but their logical effect is to vitiate Book I, Part I altogether. For with no mind to have the ideas and no hope of the ideas representing the world to us, the notion of ideas should have been abandoned altogether. But so persuasive was the prevailing picture of the mind and its ideas that Hume kept them in his scheme even when they had nothing to represent or belong to, and he still endeavored to construct his world picture entirely out of them. So, for that matter, did several great philosophers who succeeded him.

In Book I, Part I, Hume was content to remain silent about the material world, from which our impressions are thought to come and which they are supposed to represent, and also about the mind, which has the impressions. Impressions of sense "arise in the soul from unknown causes," and impressions of reflection stem from ideas of impressions of sense; fear, for instance, is an impression of reflection resulting from an idea of pain, and pain in turn is an impression of sense. Hume's concern was with the relation between impressions and ideas, in terms of which he found a deceptively simple way of stating the first of the two basic propositions of empiricism: "Every simple idea is derived from a corresponding impression." Thinking is a matter of mental imagery, and the constituents of all our mental pictures, however varied and fanciful, are representations of impressions of sense. This doctrine effectively restrained the human mind within the limits of experience and provided Hume with the first two of his three principal tools of philosophical inquiry—his microscope, his razor, and his fork.

The "microscope" is described in the *Treatise*, Book I, Part III, Section II, and more fully in the first *Enquiry*, Section VII, Part I, where it is actually called a microscope. Its use is as follows. To examine and understand an idea, first reduce it to its simple constituent ideas. Then, if any one of these is still obscure, produce the impression from which it is derived. By "producing" the impression, as opposed to the idea, Hume should have meant arranging for the actual occurrence of the impression. Anything short of this can only be considering the idea in a different way. The use of the microscope, therefore, ought to be a genuine psychological experiment. It is doubtful whether Hume fully realized this implication, and how often he made genuine experiments is not known. The only clear case is the experiment with a spot of ink on paper (*Treatise*, Bk. I, Pt. II, Secs. I, IV). Probably Hume did not distinguish between the literal "production of the impression" and a quite different procedure, the illustration of a general idea, whether simple or complex, by concrete particular cases, imaginary or recorded. This confusion was assisted by the fact that certain impressions of reflection in which Hume was greatly interested, such as moral approval, can be actually produced in the mind by considering imaginary cases. (For an example of the use of imaginary cases under the title of "experiments," see the *Treatise*, Bk. II., Pt. II, Sec. II.)

The use of concrete cases to clarify conceptual problems in general and philosophical problems in particular is a method by which Hume and many others have achieved valuable results. But giving oneself impressions is likely to be of interest only to the physiologist, if to anyone.

Hume's "razor" is closely associated with his "micro-scope." If a term cannot be shown to evoke an idea that can be analyzed into simple constituents for which impressions can be produced, then it has no meaning. There is an affinity between Hume's "razor" and the verification principle of the logical positivists. Both attempt to formulate precisely the general principle that to understand a word or expression one must know how one would use it in relation to concrete cases one has met or might meet in experience. Assuming that this was the principle Hume in fact often employed, one can understand how he came to make so many important contributions to philosophy, in spite of his mistaken doctrine of impressions and ideas. Hume's "fork" will be considered later, when his skepticism is treated.

Abstract ideas. Empiricists who maintained that all our ideas are derived from experience had found difficulty in accounting for general ideas, for which general terms such as "man," "triangle," "red," or "motion" were supposed to stand. For we see only particular men, triangles, shades of red, and bodies moving. Locke had supposed that we have a power of abstraction, by which from the particular ideas of sense we manufacture general ideas, which represent only the features common to all individuals of the same sort and omit what is peculiar to each. But Berkeley had pointed out that if you eliminate from your idea, or image, of a particular man all the features peculiar to him and not shared by all other men, you have no image left. This was particularly clear in the case of an idea like "red." There is no imaginable feature common to all shades of red. My general idea of red must either be no shade of red at all, which is absurd; or all shades at once, which is impossible because they are mutually exclusive; or none and all at once, which is self-contradictory. Berkeley maintained that the idea in the mind answering to a general term is always particular and specific but that the use made of it is general. It is used to stand for all other particular ideas of the same sort or similar to it in some respect. Hume followed Berkeley, acclaiming this view as a great discovery, but went further in attempting to explain what is meant by the particular idea "standing for" all others of the same sort. To do so he invoked the doctrine of association of ideas. Ideas whose impressions are alike or contiguous in space or time become associated in the mind; that is to say the mind has a tendency to pass from one to another. A general term is associated by contiguity—that is, by the times and places of its use—with the several particular things to which it is applied; the ideas of these are associated by resemblance with one another and with any others like them in the same way. So the term "stands for" the general idea, in that it tends to evoke by association particular members of a family of ideas associated by resemblance and unlimited in number.

The merit of this theory is that it explains how I, for instance, can understand a general term without either forming "a general abstract idea" or conceiving an infinite number of particular ones. My understanding consists in nothing that I actually do, but in what I am prone to do if necessary, that is, to go on visualizing other instances. This was the first of many uses Hume made of the principle of association of ideas. This principle was not his own discovery, but he did claim in the *Abstract* that the use he made of the principle was the most original part of his work, and in the *Treatise* he compared its importance in the mental world with that of attraction in the physical world. There is an element of truth in Hume's theory of abstract ideas. One way in which understanding of a general term can show itself is in the ability to visualize particular instances. But he failed to see, first, that there are many other abilities in which understanding of a general term can be shown, such as the abilities to recognize, depict, and make instances, to carry out instructions, and to construct significant sentences in which the term occurs; second, what is required for understanding of a general term is not merely a tendency to continue in a certain direction, such as association might account for, but an ability to avoid and correct mistakes in its use.

Space, time, and existence. In the *Treatise*, Book I, Part II, Hume tried to explain the nature of those ideas which provide the framework and outline of our world. He wanted to show that they are such as to provide no basis for metaphysical arguments about the nature of the universe.

Space and time. Space and time are nothing but the manners in which our impressions occur—alongside one another if they are impressions of sight and touch, and one after the other in all cases. Following Berkeley, though without acknowledgment, Hume maintained that neither our impressions nor our ideas are infinitely divisible, but rather reach a minimum beyond which we can neither see, feel, nor imagine anything smaller in size or shorter in duration. These minima Hume called visible and tangible points. Their existence was said to be an empirical fact, and the experiment with the spot of ink was adduced to support it. Hume then, by a dubious application of the doctrine of impressions and ideas, argued that since none of our ideas are infinitely divisible, we have no idea of infinite divisibility, and the expression is therefore meaningless.

Considering the objections of mathematicians to such a view, Hume maintained first that his perceptible points were proof against the objections which mathematicians bring against the traditional conception of an indivisible point; second, that the geometers' definitions of surface, line, and point were unintelligible unless we suppose indivisibles, so that they cannot without self-contradiction base arguments against indivisibles on these concepts; and finally, that no geometrical arguments can be decisive with regard to minute quantities, because the ideas of geometry are derived from the imprecise appearances of sense, and the "maxims" concerning them are therefore "not precisely true." He illustrated this lack of precision by asking whether geometers have any more exact standard of equality or of flatness or of straightness than the sensible proportions of bodies and by what right they maintain that two straight lines have no common segment when they meet at a very small angle or that a tangent only touches the circle at a single point when the circle is very large.

Finally, Hume explained how we can talk intelligently about a vacuum, even though our idea of space is derived entirely from the order of sensible points and we consequently have no idea of empty space. The idea of a vacuum is derived from such impressions as those of two points of light in complete darkness, which, though nothing lies between them, are visibly related to one another in

the same way as pairs of impressions which have others between them.

Hume apparently gave considerable further thought to the philosophy of mathematics. In the first *Enquiry* (Sec. XII, Pt. II) the equally convincing arguments for and against indivisible minima are represented as the main source of skepticism with regard to reason. Hume held, however, that we cannot be content with skepticism on this point. For he held that mathematics is one of the two kinds of valid reasoning. In a footnote he suggested that it might be possible to resolve the contradictions concerning infinite divisibility by recourse to Berkeley's theory of abstract ideas. He wrote, "It is sufficient to have dropped this hint at present, without prosecuting it any further." It is clear, therefore, that Hume either had not read or did not accept Berkeley's own resolution of this problem in his *Principles of Human Knowledge*, sections CXVIII–CXXXIV. Hume's letters reveal that he later wrote a dissertation on geometry to be included with the *Four Dissertations* published in 1757 but suppressed it after receiving decisive criticisms from the second earl of Stanhope.

Existence. Hume's account of the idea of existence is of greater philosophical interest. In the *Treatise* (Bk. I, Pt. II, Sec. VI) Hume argued that every idea is the idea of a being. Existence must therefore be either a separate idea that accompanies every other idea or the very same with the idea of the object we think of. The former suggestion being plainly false, Hume chose the latter. Therefore, he concluded, "Any idea we please to form is the idea of a being; and the idea of a being is any idea we please to form." Several important consequences follow. First, we cannot form an idea of anything specifically different from ideas and impressions. The representative theory of perception is therefore nonsensical, for it maintains that the ideas in the mind represent material substances specifically different from them. Second, since to conceive of God or any other being and to conceive of the existence of that being are the same thing, it is nonsense to say that the idea of God has the peculiar characteristic of also entailing the idea of existence. Though Hume did not explicitly draw this conclusion or mention the Ontological Argument, he probably had the argument in mind and certainly anticipated Kant's reason for rejecting it, i.e., that existence is not a predicate. Third, the traditional account of judgment as the uniting of ideas is false, for in the judgment "God exists," there is only one idea present.

Farhang Zabech, in his *Hume: Precursor of Modern Empiricism*, and John Passmore, in *Hume's Intentions*, have maintained that Hume was unable on this basis to explain the idea of nonexistence. Hume did in fact offer an account of this idea (*Treatise*, Bk. I, Pt. I, Sec. V). The idea of nonexistence, he claimed, is the idea of the object together with the exclusion of the object from all times and places in which it is supposed not to exist. If I think of mermaids as nonexistent, I think of mermaids and the seas of this planet and "exclude" the former from the latter. It will be considered later whether there is any intelligible interpretation of "exclusion," as used in this context.

A priori and empirical knowledge. Both the *Treatise* (Bk. I, Pt. III) and the first *Enquiry* (Sec. IV, Pt. I) begin by drawing a distinction of the greatest importance. In the

Treatise it is between "knowledge" and "probability"; in the *Enquiry,* between "relations of ideas" and "matters of fact." Hume claimed that these two classes exhaust the field of discoverable truth. The distinction, often referred to as "Hume's fork," corresponds roughly to the traditional one between necessary and contingent truths but not as closely as some have thought to the later distinction between analytic and synthetic propositions.

The essence of the distinction is the same in both works. Some truths depend on our ideas. They state relations between our ideas that cannot be altered without altering the ideas, because any attempt to do so results in a "contradiction." These are relations of ideas, the subject matter of knowledge and science. Other truths do not depend on the ideas concerned. They can be conceived to be false without any contradiction. Relations of ideas can be discovered in two ways, by intuition and by demonstration. I may consider two ideas and perceive a relation between them, for example, that two is half four; or I may discover a relation by the interposition of other ideas, as in Euclid's demonstration that the internal angles of a triangle are equal to two right angles. Matters of fact can also be discovered in two ways, by observation and by inference. The validity of observation was, for the purposes of this argument, taken for granted, as Hume elsewhere said it always must be.

The question Hume considered here was the nature of nondemonstrative inference. He stated that such inferences always rest on the relation of cause and effect. If I observe *A* and infer *B*, it can only be because I believe *A* and *B* to be causally connected. This is true in the rather odd sense that Hume chose to give to the word "cause." The man who sees the feet of the passers-by from a basement window and infers the presence of their bodies and heads, would not ordinarily be said to argue from effects to causes or vice versa. But Hume would say that such an inference was based on knowledge of causes and effects, simply because it is based on knowledge of what usually does and does not happen.

The importance of Hume's doctrine lies not in his definition of an effect as an unvaried and expected sequel, but in his insistence that there is no other way of anticipating or supplementing our observations than by inferences based on our experience of what always or usually happens. It does not matter whether we use the term "cause" to refer to any kind of regular conjunction or keep it for some special sort. Hume's point is that there are no cause and effect relationships that provide a way of bypassing the appeal to experience on questions of fact. For the question whether *A* causes *B* depends on, even if it is not identical with, the question whether *A* in fact happens without *B*, which only experience can decide.

There is a second important contention that Hume based on the distinction between relations of ideas and matters of fact. In the *Treatise* it remains unstated, though often implied. In the first *Enquiry* (Sec. XII, Pt. III) it is stated explicitly, "Whatever *is* may *not be.* . . . The non-existence of any being, without exception, is as clear and distinct an idea as its existence." Every existential proposition states a matter of fact. Its truth must be determined empirically. So God's existence cannot be proved a priori.

What exactly is the nature of the distinction between relations of ideas and matters of fact? One solution Hume would not accept was the view that a proposition expressing a relation of ideas is true by definition. Following Locke, who called propositions true by definition "trifling propositions," Hume poured scorn on such a truth as "that where there is no property there can be no injustice," which is supposed to rest on the definition of injustice as the violation of property. He contrasted this proposition with the Pythagorean theorem, which, he said, cannot be known without thinking it out, "let the terms be ever so exactly defined" (first *Enquiry,* Sec. XII, Pt. III). The ensuing denunciation of all "syllogistic reasoning" must be taken to apply to deductions from premises which are "trifling." Hume himself did plenty of syllogistic reasoning, but his premises, he would have said, were matters of empirical fact or, occasionally, relations of ideas.

If one remembers that Hume thought of ideas as images, and primarily as visual images, it is easier to understand what he meant by "relations of ideas." He said in the *Treatise* (Bk. I, Pt. III, Sec. I) that the relations which depend on ideas are "resemblance, contrariety, degrees in quality, and proportions in quality and number." Causation, identity, and spatiotemporal relations are not relations of ideas.

As an analogue to "ideas," consider a typically graphic representation, a map of the world. Cornwall and Italy resemble each other in shape. How would you remove this resemblance from the map except by altering the shape of one or both countries? Consider another map, representing the international date line as passing to the east of a certain island, whereas the first map makes it pass to the west of the island. This contrariety cannot be removed except by altering one of the maps (although it can, of course, be explained in other ways). The central Atlantic is bluer than the North Sea; Iceland is bigger than the Isle of Wight; there are more islands in the Swedish archipelago than in the Hebrides. None of these relations can be altered without changing the graphic representation of the terms.

By contrast, consider causation, identity, and position. The whole map might be produced by a different process and look the same. The representation of any island could be moved toward or away from any other, without altering the appearance of either. Is this Pacific island that is on the right-hand edge of the map the same as that Pacific island on the left hand edge, or is it another island of the same shape? The appearance on the map would be the same in either case.

Hume used three other formulas, with variants, to express the nature of a necessary truth. The first is that "whatever objects are different are distinguishable, and whatever objects are distinguishable are separable by the thought and imagination" and conversely that "whatever objects are separable are also distinguishable and whatever objects are distinguishable are also different" (*Treatise,* Bk. I, Pt I, Sec. VII). The second is that it is impossible "for the imagination to conceive anything contrary to a demonstration" (*Treatise,* Bk. I, Pt. III, Sec. VII). The third is that if a proposition were demonstrably false, it would imply a contradiction (*Enquiry,* Sec. IV, Pt. I).

All three principles apply to the examples considered above: the first draws our attention to the objects (the impressions corresponding to the ideas), the second to the ideas, and the third to the "proposition" (the sentence) expressing the relation of ideas or its denial.

The resemblance between Cornwall and Italy is nothing different or distinguishable or separable from the shapes of the two peninsulas. The contrariety between the two maps is nothing distinct from what is represented in each. Nor are the differences in degree of blueness, in size, or in number different and distinct from either the degrees of blueness of the two seas, or the sizes of the two islands, or the numbers of the two archipelagoes.

We cannot imagine a change in resemblance without a change in the resembling objects, a removal of contrariety without a change of the contrary representations, a change of relation in degree, size, or number without imagining a change in the qualities, sizes, or numbers of the related terms.

Finally, if we try to understand a sentence that denies an actual relation of ideas, that is, if we try to "conceive the ideas according to the proposition," we find the ideas display a contradiction. If it is said that the shape of Cornwall is not like the shape of Italy, one must first visualize the shapes of the two peninsulas as they are, then alter them so that they are no longer alike, but at the same time keep them as they are. Thus the denial of a relation of ideas is a self-canceling cue for visualization. This is clearest in the case of numerical proportion: "Jones has six children, two sons and three daughters"; visualize this family according to the meaning (the customary associations) of the words, and you will find yourself alternately including and excluding a sixth child.

The above is only a suggested interpretation of Hume. What light it throws on the problem of necessary truths is another matter.

An interpretation of Hume's theory of nonexistence can now be given. "There are no mermaids" is a proposition instructing us to visualize seas and mermaids, but forbidding us to visualize the latter in the former. In this view, a negative existential statement presupposes a field or spatiotemporal region, suggests the idea of an object, and by the use of the negated verb, activates a disposition to inhibit or cancel the visualization of the object in the field.

Cause and effect. Hume found that all inferences from the existence of one object to that of another are nondemonstrative and based on the relation of cause and effect. He then showed that they are not even indirectly demonstrative, for neither any specific causal relation, nor the proposition that every event has a cause, nor even the claim that the unobserved resembles the observed can be known either by intuition or demonstration. An exception to any causal connection is clearly imaginable; so is a pure fluke or a sudden change in the course of nature. Only by experience can we know whether any of these occur.

Hume therefore had to answer two questions: What is our idea of cause and effect? How does experience enable us to discover causes and make inferences?

Hume maintained that the terms "cause" and "effect" do not stand for any features, observed or inferred, in the objects to which they are applied; aside from their contiguity in space, succession in time, and the constant conjunction of like objects in past experience. There are no other features to observe; and if there were concealed "powers" that we infer from the conjunction, we should not be able to explain or predict the phenomena any better than we can without them. For we should not know why, but only that, certain objects have certain powers, and the persistence of the powers and the nature of their effects would be predictable only from the same empirical data and with the same degree of accuracy as they are at present. A similar criticism is leveled at the power of providence, as it is supposed to be inferred from its effects.

But over and above contiguity, succession, and constant conjunction, there is, Hume said, another element in our idea of cause, the idea of necessary connection, although as we have seen, Hume's microscope can find no impression corresponding to it. Therefore, Hume examined the way in which we actually discover causal relations and base inferences on them. It is, he said, a simple matter of association of ideas. Experience shows A to have been frequently followed by B and never to have occurred without B. The idea of B is therefore associated with A in a way in which no other idea is. As a result, when the idea of A occurs, the mind is determined to pass to the idea of B, and when the impression of A occurs, it is determined not only to form the idea of B but to transfer to that idea a share of the "vivacity" of the impression of A.

In terms of this account Hume could explain four things. The inference is the transition from the impression of A to the lively idea of B. The lively idea of B, associated with the present impression of A, is belief in B; and the feeling we have of being determined to pass from the idea of A to that of B, or from the impression of A to the belief in B, is the origin of our idea of necessary connection. Finally, since this "determination" of the mind depends solely on repetition (of past conjunctions) and not on any reasoning, it is due to custom or habit. By a customary association Hume meant an association reinforced by repetition. This identification of the impression of necessary connection was supported by the following argument: "The necessary connection betwixt causes and effects is the foundation of our inference from one to the other. The foundation of our inference is the transition arising from the accustomed union. These are, therefore, the same" (*Treatise*, Bk. I, Pt. III, Sec. XIV).

Consequently, any talk of power, efficacy, energy, force, or necessity which implies that it is something existing in the cause, whether material or spiritual, natural or supernatural, is pronounced meaningless.

Finally Hume offered two definitions of cause: (1) "an object precedent and contiguous to another, and where all objects resembling the former are placed in like relations of precedency and contiguity to those objects that resemble the latter"; and (2) "an object precedent and contiguous to another and so united with it that the idea of the one determines the mind to form the idea of the other, and the impression of the one to form a more lively idea of the latter."

In the first *Enquiry* (Sec. VII, Pt. II) Hume added to the former of the two definitions the following alleged equivalent: "Or in other words where, if the first object had not been, the second had never existed." In fact this proposition is neither entailed by nor equivalent to the first definition.

Belief. Could Hume reconcile his definition of belief as a "lively idea associated with a present impression" with his thesis that all beliefs about matters of fact rest on causal inference? If other associations, for instance, resemblance or contiguity, do not enliven ideas, why does constant conjunction? If they do, why do they not produce belief?

Hume first replied that the other relations do enliven ideas already believed in as realities. But if an idea is only "feigned," such as the idea of someone resembling an illustration in a fairy story, the other relations make little difference to its liveliness. But Hume did not feel satisfied with this reply and went on to describe a difference between a "feigned" idea resembling a present impression and an idea customarily associated with one. The former is arbitrary, variable at will, capricious, inconstant. The latter is involuntary, fixed by the unalterable past, and a member of a whole system of ideas similarly enlivened, which together with our impressions and our memories form a stable and coherent world picture, which we please to call "reality." But the essence of belief was no longer the vivacity of the picture; it was also its coherence with a general picture, its constancy, its involuntariness.

The same criteria were invoked to deal with the problem of beliefs resulting from education. Education, by repeated conjunction of ideas, sets up habits of association. Most of our beliefs result from education and endure in the face of experience to the contrary, so firmly does repetition infix ideas in our minds. But when we reflect on such beliefs and remember that educators can say what they please and when we find that they contradict both one another and our experience, we form a general distrust of such beliefs.

By the time Hume came to write the "Appendix" to the *Treatise* he saw the need to give a revised account of belief, which would connect it with the features characteristic of inferences from experience and differentiate it from those characteristic of the fancies of superstition, propaganda, and poetical imagination. Accordingly, he added to "vivacity" a range of other terms, "force," "solidity," "firmness," and "steadiness." Belief was "something felt by the mind, which distinguishes the ideas of the judgment from the fictions of the imagination. It gives them more force and influence; it makes them appear of greater importance; infixes them in the mind; and renders them the governing principles of all our actions." In the final clause of the above quotation Hume at last grasped the central characteristic of belief, that it manifests itself in conduct. Compared with this, its effects on our mental imagery are of secondary importance.

Determination of the mind. The feeling of "determination," to which Hume traced the idea of necessary connection, is not the same as the feeling of belief. For determination carries the mind from the idea of the cause to that of the effect, as well as from the impression of the cause to a lively idea of—that is, to a belief in—the effect. The term "determination" expresses the relation of precise dependence, with none of the metaphysical overtones of "force," "energy," "agency," or "power." A modern psychologist might say, "What we expect is determined by our past experience and our present percepts," and mean exactly what Hume meant.

The feeling of determination was postulated to distinguish between a transition of thought that is determined by imposed factors and one that is arbitrary and alterable at will. There are some things that I cannot help thinking and others that I only choose to suppose; but the presence or absence of a feeling of determination surely cannot be a decisive mark of the distinction between the two classes.

Many critics have thought that Hume's use of the determiniation of the mind in his account of causality and necessary connection made that account circular, and in his second definition of a cause there is a kind of circularity. He did not define cause in general in terms of itself under the same or another name. The circularity is not like that of defining pain as the anticipation of an increase in suffering. But he did define the causal relation between A and B as their regular conjunction, plus their effect on the mind. So A is the cause of B partly in virtue of the fact that their regular conjunction is the cause of something else. The worst kind of circular definition leaves the problem untouched. This kind shifts the problem but does not solve it.

Hume should have eschewed the method of formal definition. Instead of offering a paraphrase of "A caused B," he should have told us what a man is doing who says that A is the cause of B. Such a man is not, as Hume's definition suggests, conjoining two assertions, one about the objects, the other about his mind; he is making one assertion, that A without B would be unprecedented, and also, by the (causal) terms which he uses, expressing the "determination of his mind," or whatever we choose to call it. This feeling of determination is caused; but then so is everything.

Some have felt that Hume's account is circular in an even simpler way, that he was saying, "The necessity of natural processes is only the necessity of our thoughts projected onto things." This is clearly not what Hume meant and he was at pains to say so (*Treatise*, Bk. I, Pt. III, Sec. XIV). He opened the door to such misunderstandings when he said that "upon the whole, necessity is something that exists in the mind, not in the objects." But this idiom is similar to "beauty is in the eye of the beholder." And no one would take this to mean that pictures and sunsets are not really beautiful but that the eyes of the people who look at them are so.

A final difficulty concerning the feeling of determination is the question whether we have an impression of causation when we have this feeling, that is, whether the customarily associated ideas, as they succeed one another in the mind, seem connected and not merely conjoined? If they do not, it is not clear how the feeling can be the source of the idea of necessary connection. If they do, then Hume's unrestricted statement that events seem conjoined but not connected (first *Enquiry*, Sec. VII, Pt. II) must be qualified: We have a wide variety of feelings—feeling sick, hungry, sleepy, inclined to do this, unable to do that, obliged to do the other—feelings which seem connected with the states of which they are symptoms. Nor does it seem plausible to say that we have to learn by experience what to expect when we have one of these feelings. It seems clear that Hume should have spoken only of external events as never seeming to be connected.

Albert Edouard Michotte in *The Perception of Causality* claimed to have shown experimentally that even some external events seem causally connected; he held that under certain precisely specifiable stimulus conditions we experience definite impressions of mechanical causality of two main types, which he called "the launching effect" and "the entraining effect." The former would apply precisely to Hume's favorite case of the impact of the billiard balls. Michotte differed from Hume on another point, the role of experience in the discovery of causes. He denied that we need a build-up of repeated conjunctions to give belief in causality. A single case often suffices, even without a background of scientific knowledge. A child needs to be scratched only once by a cat to connect the cat, the injury, and the pain. The function of experience, Michotte claimed, is to show which of the seemingly necessary conjunctions are not really so. A somewhat similar view was elaborated by Karl Popper in *The Logic of Scientific Discovery*. According to him, the function of experiments in science is only to disprove the hypotheses that seem to be worth testing. Induction plays no part in scientific method.

Hume would undoubtedly answer that, nevertheless, the man of sense trusts and employs a theory, a machine, or an institution with a confidence proportionate to the number and variety of the tests it has survived. The more it has survived, the more it is likely to survive. There would seem to be room, in science and in ordinary life, for both methods: confirmation and disproof.

Probability. The teaching of experience is not always unequivocal. A die always falls flat on one of its sides, but there are six of them, and experience does not tell us on which of them it will settle on a given occasion. Four out of every five men recover from a certain disease, but we do not know if a given patient will be one of the unlucky ones.

Hume would have called the first example a case of the probability of chances, the second a case of the probability of causes (*Treatise*, Bk. I, Pt. III, Secs. XI and XII). Reason, said Hume, is powerless in either case. Although four of the six sides of the die are marked with a cross and only two with a circle, there is no reason why the event should fall on that side where there is a superior number of chances. Similarly, four out of the next five patients will recover, but reason cannot tell us which.

Hume's criticism of the logic of chance is admirable. His psychological solution is dubious. He said that in both types of case the force of custom, which determines us to expect what we have experienced before, is split up into as many parts as there are chances; so we have six lively ideas of the fall of the die, four representing it with a cross uppermost, two with a circle; four lively pictures of the patient recovering, one of his dying. The similar images reunite, forming two ideas in each case, one of which is stronger and livelier than the other in proportion to the greater number of constituent images that concur in it. A probability is a stronger belief opposed by a weaker and incompatible one.

MIND AND MATTER

In the *Treatise*, Book I, Part IV, and in the first *Enquiry*, Section XII, Hume considered two perennial problems of philosophy, our knowledge of the external world and the relations of mind and matter. His semantic and epistemological principles made his solution almost inevitable.

To conceive, to know, or to believe are nothing but to have ideas, to have ideas unalterably related, or to have vivid and steady ideas. Ideas are merely copies of impressions. Therefore, we can not conceive of, know of, or believe in, anything of which we have no impression. We have no impression of the mind, save as an assemblage or "bundle" of impressions and ideas. We have no impression of a physical thing distinct from our impressions of it. "Spiritual substances" and "corporeal substances" are therefore meaningless metaphysical jargon.

But Hume saw that we do talk quite significantly about and believe in both ourselves and the things around us. The problem was to describe the nature of these two beliefs and discover their causes. Hume admitted breakdowns in his answers to both problems but affected to welcome his failures as additional support for his skepticism.

Both accounts start from the initial assumption, mistaken by Hume for an empirical fact, that our primary data are nothing but sensations, feelings, and images. So Hume had to conclude that the mind is nothing but a bundle of perceptions related by resemblance, succession, and causation, to which we ascribe an identity by a kind of fiction. A succession of related perceptions feels to the mind very like an identical, that is, an uninterrupted and unvaried, perception. We are apt to confuse things that feel alike, so we mistake the series of related but different perceptions that make up the mind for a single unvarying perception; hence the illusion of a permanent self. But this account, Hume recognized, in his "Appendix" to the *Treatise*, failed to explain how the successive perceptions are united in consciousness. Hume pleaded the privilege of a skeptic" and left the question unresolved.

The bundle theory of the self helped Hume explain the external world. Perceptions are distinct, independent, self-sufficient entities; they occur in bundles, so far as we know. But the idea of a perception that is not a member of any bundle is not self-contradictory, as Berkeley had supposed. So if I think of a set of impressions that are related to one another (as are those which I call a shoe) but are not part of any bundle or person, I am thinking of a shoe which nobody is seeing. And if such a set of ideas were enlivened, I should be believing in the existence of an unseen shoe.

It remained for Hume to explain what suggests and enlivens such ideas to our minds. Two features of our impressions, he said, suggest to us the idea of unperceived perceptions—"constancy" and "coherence."

My impressions of a mountain are like one another. It looks much the same each time. The impressions form a constant series. Since they are very similar but interrupted, they feel to the mind like an uninterrupted and unvarying series and are mistaken for one. So I come to think of the mountain as a continuous object. When I notice the interruptions in my impressions of it, I resolve the contradiction by supposing unperceived perceptions to fill up the gaps in the series. These ideas are enlivened by their association with the impressions I have. So I have a vivid picture of, a belief in, a mountain existing continuously and therefore independently of my interrupted perceptions.

Changing objects are believed to exist independently if the impressions of them display *coherence*. If I sit and watch my fire die slowly down, I get an uninterrupted series of varying impressions. If I leave the room and then return, I get an interrupted series; but it matches the uninterrupted series, allowing for the gaps. Moreover, the effects of the two series are the same. In both cases the room gets colder; the effects seem to be independent of the gaps. The supposition of unperceived perceptions to fill the gaps restores to me a regular picture of the behavior of fires and their effects on room temperature. The ideas of the unseen dying coals are enlivened by association with all my experiences of watched fires.

But again Hume's thought takes a skeptical turn. This everyday world-picture provides the field in which we investigate causes and effects, including the causes of our impressions. We find our impressions to be wholly dependent on our sense organs and nervous system. It is therefore empirically impossible that perceptions should exist in the absence of a percipient, that there should be perceptions that are unperceived. Common sense presupposes unperceived perceptions; science is founded on common sense, but science disproves the existence of unperceived perceptions.

The scientist has an answer. He distinguishes between objects and our perceptions of them. The former are independent and continuous, the latter fleeting and subjective. But the sensible qualities of objects, their color, temperature, sound, smell, taste, depend on our nerves and sense organs; they must be merely apparent. The objects, the scientist says, have only the "primary" qualities of extension, that is, size and figure, motion, and solidity. Hume followed Berkeley in denying that we can form any idea of a thing having only these qualities. Hume argued that motion presupposes a body moved; a body presupposes something extended and solid. The idea of extension is that of juxtaposed colored and/or solid minimal parts. Color being merely apparent, all depends on solidity. But solidity means impenetrability; impenetrability involves two bodies which will not unite. And we have no qualities left in terms of which to conceive these bodies. "Our modern philosophy leaves us no just or satisfactory idea of matter." "There is a direct and total opposition betwixt our reason and our senses" (*Treatise*, Bk. I, Pt. IV, Sec. IV).

Hume next examined the traditional arguments about the conjunction and interaction of mind and body (*Treatise*, Bk. I, Pt. IV, Sec. V). Spiritual substance and material substance are equally inconceivable. The distinction between unextended and extended lies elsewhere, between the impressions of sight and touch, which alone provide us with an idea of extension, and those of smell, taste, sound, feeling, and passion, which do not. The idea of local conjunction is simply inapplicable to the latter variety of impressions. They exist, but exist nowhere. There is no mystery about motion causing thought, for no causal relation is intelligible. Anything may cause anything, and cause and effect are always distinct. Motion and thought are in no way peculiar: reflection shows them to be distinct; experience shows them to be constantly conjoined.

SKEPTICISM

Hume outlined his general position with regard to skepticism in the *Treatise*, Book I, Parts IV and VII, and in the first *Enquiry*, Section XII. Apart from differences in emphasis and tone, the position is the same in both works. He distinguished two main forms of skepticism, "antecedent" and "consequent." Each may take either an extreme, "Pyrrhonian" form or a mitigated and moderate form.

By "antecedent" skepticism Hume meant a procedure like that of Descartes's method of doubt, by which, before any sort of examination of our faculties or methods of reasoning, we doubt them all and demand some antecedent, infallible criterion for deciding which faculties, if any, to trust. Such a skepticism, Hume held, is in fact unattainable and would be quite incurable if it were attained. But in a mitigated form, as a general counsel of diffidence and caution, it has its use.

Consequent skepticism is the method Hume himself practiced. That is, he based his doubts as to the certainty and extent of our knowledge on an examination of our faculties. That is why, in the *Treatise*, skepticism was not introduced until Book I, Part IV, *after* the discussion of knowledge and probability, and in the *Enquiry* the discussion of those same topics in Section IV, is headed "Skeptical Doubts concerning the Operations of the Understanding." Consequent skepticism, again, may take a Pyrrhonian form, appearing in the *Treatise* as the first attack of utter despair. Belief has been shown to be nothing but a feeling, its causes to lie in the imagination. Moreover, the processes which give rise to belief, if allowed to continue, eventually destroy it. Belief in our reason, senses, and memory is nothing but a natural instinct, safeguarded by natural defense mechanisms, which alone save it from self-destruction.

Even the most extreme ancient skeptics admitted that we must live; and since reason cannot tell us how to live, they recommended that we follow nature, under which they included natural appetites and instincts, the sensible appearances of things, and the traditions of one's city. Hume, who regarded both mathematical and empirical reasoning as natural, since each follows a natural "determination" of the mind, found that he could maintain his skepticism and still perceive, remember, calculate, and infer, provided he confined himself to "common life," whose problems natural reasoning is adapted to meet. Since "nature by an absolute and uncontrollable necessity has determined us to judge as well as to breathe and feel," Hume would be as unorthodox a skeptic if he stopped judging as an ancient skeptic would have been had he stopped breathing.

Hume thus reached his final stage of mitigated consequent skepticism. Its two main characteristics are an undogmatic moderation and a refusal to go beyond common life. Nevertheless, it permitted rich intellectual life. The science of man, on which it was founded, was also permitted by it, for its conclusions are only "those of common life, methodized and corrected." Metaphysics, if it consists in the empirical study of our "sublimer" ideas, is also natural—for curiosity is as natural a motive as any and its gratification a natural pleasure. Further, if we do not prosecute such studies, the theologians will, and will take advantage of our ignorance to give metaphysical coverage to their dangerous dogmas.

Mathematics, though at first sight a source of unanswerable skeptical arguments, had been restored to the fold of natural activities by Hume's demolishment of the dogma of infinite divisibility. And all the experimental sciences, as well as history and geography, are merely extensions of the natural ways of thinking, which we cannot help using in common life. Hume's "fork," his third implement, was now completed, and he could use it to stoke the bonfire of unprofitable books described in the famous peroration to the first *Enquiry*: of every piece of pretended reasoning he demanded, "Is it abstract reasoning concerning quantity and number?" or "Is it experimental reasoning concerning matters of fact?" If the answer was "neither," he consigned it to the flames.

The attitude of mitigated skepticism was supposed to follow from a proper understanding of "the force of the Pyrrhonian doubt, and of the impossibility that anything but the strong power of natural instinct, could free us from it." No doubt nature would save us from Pyrrhonism; but is it not possible that there are some holes in the skeptics' arguments, quite apart from the fact that in undermining all arguments they undermine themselves?

The Pyrrhonian arguments that Hume presented are as follows: (1) his own argument about the nature of causal inference; (2) the mathematical arguments about infinite divisibility, which he thought could be met; (3) the argument from the unavoidability and incoherence of the representative theory of sense perception; and (4) a peculiar argument, apparently of Hume's own invention, used in the *Treatise*, Book I, Part IV, Section I, and not repeated in the *Enquiry*. The first and third of these correspond to perennial problems in the theory of knowledge that have seemed to most philosophers to demand and to defy solution, the problem of induction and the problem of perception. The former problem was given its classical statement by Hume in the *Treatise*, Book I, Part III; the latter he stated very well in Book I, Part IV, Section II.

The skeptic tries in both these contexts to make it appear that when he asks "How do you know?" or "What right have you to be sure?" the only possible sort of answer is to produce direct observations and inferences from them. The only alternative is supposed to be a blind reliance on instinct. Intelligent anticipation must, therefore, be composed of past observations plus an inference—but what sort of inference? Sense perceptions must be awareness of sensations (or impressions or sense data) plus an inference—but what sort of inference? Hume showed quite clearly that no sort of inference known to logicians would fill the bill in either case.

The answer is that between the formal procedures of observation and deduction and the mechanical operation of instinct lies the whole field of acquired abilities, of which observation and deduction are themselves rather advanced instances. Knowledge comes from having learned to use our eyes and our memories, as well as from having learned how to talk, to record, to tabulate, and to deduce.

The skeptic makes it appear that induction (commonly known as intelligent anticipation) is peculiar in that it will only work if things behave regularly. In fact, every sort of ability is in the same position. In an irregular world there could be neither learned nor unlearned abilities of any kind whatever. The verb "can" would have no application. In fact, all language would be impossible.

The mathematical arguments need no further discussion. There are still unsolved problems in mathematical philosophy, but they are not the same as Hume's.

The last argument, peculiar to Hume, is introduced by a harmless truth: however "certain and infallible" the rules of a demonstrative science may be, I may always make a mistake in applying them. Whether I have done so is a question of fact, that is, of probability. So all demonstrations degenerate into probability, the probability of there having been no mistake. But in any probable judgment I may have misassessed the evidence; so I must review my past form to determine the likelihood of error; in this review too I may have made mistakes, and so the argument may be repeated to infinity. Each judgment, "however favorable to the preceding one," raises a new doubt; each doubt detracts a little from the probability of the original judgment, which, unless the process is arbitrarily stopped, must eventually wither away altogether.

Thus, Hume concluded, the natural and proper procedures of probable reasoning, as employed by every prudent man, would totally destroy our belief in everything if allowed to proceed unchecked. Nature usually saves us by forcing us to make up our mind and stop bothering. If we do continue the process, she prevents it having any considerable effect on our beliefs. Hume clearly regarded this argument as unanswerable, but unconvincing. He said that his intention in producing it was to show that "belief is more properly an act of the sensitive, than of the cogitative part of our nature." If belief were a voluntary act, owing allegiance to logic alone, it would on every occasion destroy itself.

The argument is plainly sophistical but phrased in such vague terms that it would be a lengthy task to set out all the various possible cases covered and explain the fallacy in each. Take one case. I judge (1) that Bucephalus will probably win the 2:30. But then I reflect (2) that I am not a good judge of form. Then I reflect (3) that I am not a very good critic of my own performances in these matters. The force of (3) is to counteract (2) and leave (1) unchanged but subject—as it always should have been—to the proviso "unless I am mistaken." And how am I supposed to proceed further in this regress? Where shall I find evidence of my powers of criticizing my own criticisms of my judgments, distinct from the evidence of my powers of criticizing my own judgments? I have reached an assessment of my powers of picking up my own mistakes, and beyond this it is not possible to go. Every further step is the same step repeated.

To conclude, Hume was right to remind us that in no species of reasoning whatever are we immune from error; in the end, after the most careful possible use of analytical and experimental techniques, we must pronounce what *seems* to us the probable or inevitable conclusion and await the judgment of others. But to appreciate the merits of this procedure it is not necessary, as Hume supposed, to be baffled by Pyrrhonian sophistries.

MORAL PHILOSOPHY

Hume's theory of moral judgments is that to consider a character trait or an act which springs from it as virtuous or vicious is to have a special sort of feeling of pleasure or displeasure toward it. The distinctive character of this feeling is that it is aroused only by human characters and actions, that it is aroused only when the type of the character or action is considered in general, neglecting any individuating features of a particular case, and that the feeling is affected by no features of the character or action other than its pleasantness or unpleasantness, its usefulness or harmfulness, either to its possessor or to others affected by it.

This theory of moral judgments bears a very close analogy to Hume's theory of beliefs about questions of fact. In neither case is the judgment a voluntary act in accordance with a priori principles of logic or of natural law. In both cases it is a kind of feeling that arises irresistibly, given the appropriate conditions of past experience and present perception. Both can be "regulated," or indirectly controlled, in accordance with general rules, by reflecting on certain aspects of our experience and neglecting others. Such regulation is itself a propensity natural to the more intelligent mind, motivated by a desire for consistency with oneself and agreement and cooperation with others.

So close is this analogy that Norman Kemp Smith, in *The Philosophy of David Hume*, argued that Hume's theory of belief was modeled on his theory of moral approval, which was substantially derived from Francis Hutcheson. According to Kemp Smith the discovery that this account of judgment could be extended from value judgments to judgments of fact was the "new scene of thought" which so transported Hume at the age of 18.

Though Hume's theory of morals is derived from Hutcheson, Hume would surely have been more explicit about it had he been consciously extending his theory of moral judgment to other judgments. Probably no one, not even Hume himself, quite realized that this is what he had in fact done until Kemp Smith pointed it out.

In spite of this close analogy, there are important differences, according to Hume, between judgments of fact and judgments of value. Judgments of fact, like judgments concerning relations of ideas, can be true or false. Judgments of taste and of morals cannot. On the strength of this distinction, Hume introduced a definition of "reason" as "the discovery of truth or falsehood," a definition according to which moral distinctions cannot be "the offspring of reason." Judgments of fact, like judgments concerning relations of ideas, are "inactive." They can never by themselves produce or prevent any action. Judgments of value can do so. Judgments of value form a class that is logically isolated from relations of ideas and matters of fact, as the latter two classes are logically isolated from one another. No probable or demonstrative inference can be made from a relation of ideas to a matter of fact, from either to a judg-

ment of value, from a value judgment to a relation of ideas or to a matter of fact, or from a matter of fact to a relation of ideas.

Hume's theory of morals may be considered under three heads: his contention that reason alone cannot decide moral questions, his contention that a "moral sentiment" decides such questions, and his contention that the moral sentiment is actuated only by what is either pleasant or useful. In the first two contentions can be seen the beginnings of modern subjectivism and a strong resemblance to the views of C. L. Stevenson in his *Ethics and Language*. In the third can be seen one of the origins of the utilitarianism of Bentham and Mill.

Antirationalist arguments. Moral decisions sometimes produce and prevent actions; decisions of reason have no such power. Therefore moral decisions are not decisions of reason. The second premise is the conclusion of arguments offered in the *Treatise* (Bk. II, Pt. III, Sec. III). These run as follows: abstract reasoning concerning relations of ideas can never affect action, which is concerned with "realities," not ideas. The only practical employment of mathematics is to "direct," or quantify, our judgments concerning causes and effects, as in engineering and accountancy. Knowledge of causes and effects, whether purely qualitative or refined by measurement and calculation, only affects our actions if the objects so connected are of some interest to us. Nothing can make them of interest to us but the pleasure or pain we expect from them. It is not the reasoning concerning causes and effects which moves us to action, but the desire of the pleasures and fear of the pains which we foresee by this reasoning.

Nor can a rationalist escape by admitting that actions are always due to passion and then distinguishing between reasonable and unreasonable passions. Passions, since they neither represent nor assert anything, cannot be untrue to facts or incompatible with propositions. They may be excited by false or unreasonable judgments concerning the existence of desirable or undesirable objects or concerning the means of achieving or avoiding them. It is the judgments which are reasonable or unreasonable, and not the passions. It is in this context that Hume produced that notoriously provocative overstatement, "Reason is, and ought only to be, the slave of the passions." An error of reasoning is a mistake. If the rationalists are correct, wrongdoing must be some kind of mistake. But mistakes of fact and miscalculations are not blameworthy; and if wrongdoing were defined as a mistake about right and wrong, the definition would be circular.

If right and wrong are discoverable by intuition or demonstration, they must depend on some relation of ideas. The relations concerned in other abstract reasoning are resemblance, contrariety, degrees in quality, and proportions in quantity and number. Morality cannot consist in any of these, since they apply equally to irrational and inanimate objects, whereas morality does not. If morality consists in some other relation, it must satisfy two requirements. First, it must hold only between an action of the mind and an external object. If it can hold between states of mind, we may be guilty of crimes without doing anything to, or even thinking about, any object in the world. If it can hold between external objects, then they, as well as persons, can be guilty or praiseworthy. Second, the relation must be such as to be intuitively or demonstrably obligatory on the will of every rational being. Hume, oddly regarding obligation as a causal relationship, concluded from his account of causation that this requirement cannot be met.

Morality does not consist in any matter of fact inferable from experience. Consider willful murder. "Examine it in all lights, and see if you can find that matter of fact . . . which you call *vice*. The vice entirely escapes you as long as you consider the object." All you can find is a sentiment of disapprobation in your own breast. This sentiment in you is the vice of the action, just as a certain sensation in you is, "according to modern philosophy," the color of an object.

Hume's two main arguments against rationalism appear to be valid against views of the type he had in mind, which assimilated moral reasoning either to mathematical or to empirical reasoning. Hume's paradigm of practical unreason, the man who prefers the destruction of the entire world to the scratching of his finger, is guilty of no miscalculation or faulty inference from the available evidence. Nevertheless, most readers feel dissatisfied with Hume's arguments: first, because many types of wrong conduct, like the preference above cited, do seem to be, in an ordinary sense of the word, unreasonable; and second, because Hume depicted an unreal separation between the "idle judgments" of "inactive" understanding and the busy "passions" which push us into or hold us back from action.

The reasons by which I justify doing or approving something must resemble the reasons by which I justify believing something, in the sense that if they are good reasons, they must be equally good for anyone else in a similar situation doing or approving the same action, just as what is good reason for my believing any proposition is good reason for anyone else's believing it. But no such reasons can be given for the preference above cited. No one else would accept any reason for this preference or this preference as a reason for the corresponding action, nor would the man himself approve of similar preferences and actions in others. To select one's own fingers, out of all the fingers in the world, to be preserved at any cost is arbitrary, and the arbitrary is commonly opposed to the rational.

Both Hume and Kant were aware that this principle of justification by general and universally applicable criteria is central to the moral judgment. Hume imputed our observance of it to a "calm passion," dislike of muddle and controversy; this dislike makes use of another calm passion, "sympathy," in order to provide itself with a common and impartial standard for judging human character. Calm passions are often confused with reason, because their tranquil (but often efficacious) working feels very similar. Therefore, he said, this sense of "reason" and "reasonable" is an improper one.

But if Hume downgraded the universalization principle to the level of a mere matter of minor conveneince, Kant upgraded it to too high a level, making it not only the sole source of moral distinctions but also the essence of that rationality which is the essential nature of man's "noume-

nal self." Kant's most valuable countermove to Hume was to regard moral judgments as imperatives, not expressions of feeling; and imperatives (instructions, advice, and commands, for example), unlike feelings, can be logically related to one another and, thus, are subject to appraisal as self-contradictory or coherent, as arbitrary or capable of being subsumed under a principle—that is, as rational or irrational.

Hume exaggerated the gulf between the "idle" judgments of understanding and the motivating passions. Acting, believing, and wanting are not distinct processes causally related; the concepts are logically dependent on one another. The character of an action, as distinct from a mere bodily response like vomiting, is determined by its intention, that is, by what the agent wants and how he thinks his voluntary movements will bring it about. The reality of a belief is determined by the agent's readiness to do what will satisfy his wants if the proposition believed is true. The reality of his want is determined by his readiness to do what he thinks will realize its object. Hume represented believing and wanting as "distinct objects" inexplicably causally related; they are really two logically interdependent aspects of intelligent behavior. This mistake gives many of his arguments an air of unreality.

Hume concluded the *Treatise*, Book III, Part I, Section I, with an "observation" which he could not "forbear adding, . . . which may be found of some importance." It has in fact enjoyed endless discussion and been canonized as the principle, "No *ought* from an *is*." Hume said that in all "systems of morality" he had met, the author would start in "the ordinary way of reasoning," proving, for example, the existence of God or describing human society, then suddenly would switch from "is" and "is not" to "ought" and "ought not," for example, from "God *is* our creator" to "We *ought* to obey him." No explanation was ever given of this "new relation" or of how it could be a deduction from others which were entirely different from it; let the reader try to give this explanation, and all "the vulgar systems of morality" would be overthrown, for he would see that moral distinctions are not "founded merely on the relation of objects, nor perceived by reason."

It has been claimed by Geoffrey Hunter in "Hume on 'Is' and 'Ought' " (*Philosophy*, Vol. 37, 1962, and Vol. 38, 1963) that Hume did not say that "ought" is deducible from "is" but that if we try to explain how "ought" is deducible from "is," we shall see that the rationalists' explanations were wrong. Hunter suggested that Hume meant that his system and no other could explain the inference from "is" to "ought"; it is an inference from a cause, the agreeable or useful character, to its effect, the sentiment of approbation.

This cannot have been what Hume meant. The whole of Section I of the *Treatise*, Book III, Part I, is directed to prove that moral decisions, which must include an "ought" judgment, are not discoverable by any kind of inference. Is Hunter's suggestion what Hume ought to have meant? If virtue is approval and approval is an effect, why can virtue not be inferred from its cause, like any other effect? Hume's probable answer can be extracted from the following passage of the same section. "You can never find it [the viciousness of willful murder] until you turn your reflection into your own breast, and find a sentiment of disapprobation, which arises in you, towards this action. Here is a matter of fact; but it is the object of feeling, not of reason. It lies in yourself, not in the object." You must look into your *own* breast; the vice lies in *yourself.* What all or most other people feel is irrelevant except insofar as the thought of it affects *your* feelings. Your sentiment is "the object of feeling, not of reason." I think Hume would have said that there is no such thing as inferring one's own present feelings. If there were, they would be subconscious ones, and nobody decides between right and wrong by what he infers his subconscious approvals and disapprovals to be. Other people's feelings are no doubt a matter of inference; but what would we think of someone who said, "It looks as if most people disapprove of corporal punishment, so it must be wrong, though I personally feel no disapproval at all?" Several critics (for example, C. D. Broad in *Five Types of Ethical Theory*) have thought Hume maintained virtue to be what all or most men approve of. Their mistake may arise from confusing the procedure Hume recommended for the moral philosopher (in Appendix I of the *Enquiry concerning the Principles of Morals*) with that which he claimed underlies the making of moral judgments in ordinary life.

In the second *Enquiry* Hume postponed discussion of the rationalist versus sentimentalist controversy until he had shown that utility and nothing but utility is the determinant of our approval and disapproval. He then dealt more sympathetically with reason, emphasizing the richness and diversity of the preparatory work it has to do before a moral judgment can be made. But from these concessions he derived a new antirationalist argument. The moral judgment cannot be finally made until reason has done all that it can do in analyzing the facts and implications of the case. If anything relevant still remains to be discovered by reason, it is too soon to pass a moral judgment; if nothing relevant still remains to be discovered, "the understanding has no further room to operate," and the moral judgment must be executed by some other faculty (*Enquiry concerning the Principles of Morals*, Appendix I).

The moral sentiment. Hume ascribed moral decisions to sentiment for several reasons: because that seemed the only alternative to reason, which he had rejected; because sentiment was the only impression he could find for the idea of vice, and because moral decisions influence action, something which only feelings and passions can do. The view was thus partly dictated to him by his philosophy of mind.

The moral sentiment is pleasant if it is a feeling of approval, unpleasant if one of disapproval. Its object is always a human character or quality; actions are only concerned insofar as they indicate character. The sentiment therefore contains an element of love or hatred if its object is another's character and of pride or humility (or shame) if it is one's own. This differentiates it from our favorable or unfavorable feelings toward inanimate objects. The moral sentiment arises only when a character or quality is considered generally. This differentiates the feeling of moral sentiment from all partial and interested feelings and frees it from fluctuations due to variations in temporal or spatial

distance from the observer. Finally, no feature of a character, when so considered, influences this sentiment except the tendency of that character to be pleasant and useful, or unpleasant and harmful, either to its possessor or to others.

This is a very plausible account of moral approval and disapproval in regard to their objects, the associated feelings (such as shame), and the conditions under which they are properly felt. It should be noted that Hume was not talking about deciding whether actions are right or wrong, that is, forbidden or permitted by existing rules. He was talking about goodness and badness, virtue and vice, which are qualities from which actions spring. He often called disapprobation a "sentiment of blame." Blaming someone is imputing his error to a fault in his character.

What is doubtful is the categorization of moral approval as a "sentiment" or "feeling." If disapprobation is blame, presumably approval is praise; blame and praise are not "feelings." Is the degree of disapprobation really commensurate with the strength of feeling? How "calm" can a passion be and still be a passion? If it is calm, what is the measure of its strength? What common quality do the pleasure of moral approval, the pleasure of sweet music, and the pleasure of struggling to the summit of a mountain share? Do they *feel* at all alike?

These considerations have led modern philosophers to class approval and similar states as dispositions, tendencies to act in certain ways, dispositions which may intimate their existence to their possessor by a feeling (as tiredness does) but are not themselves feelings. But several who take this view, C. L. Stevenson (*Ethics and Language*), P. H. Nowell Smith (*Ethics*), and the present writer (*David Hume, His Theory of Knowledge and Morality*), have made a miscategorization as bad as Hume's in calling these dispositions "attitudes." Attitudes are assumed, taken up, or adopted voluntarily and usually disingenuously; approval and disapproval are not assumed at will, any more than beliefs are. We experience them involuntarily (if we are honest men). That was Hume's reason for calling them both feelings.

Finally, Hume considered how the general tendency of a character to promote happiness arouses this sentiment of approbation, either through a psychological mechanism of sympathy or through an original instinct of benevolence or humanity. The former explanation prevailed in the *Treatise* and the second *Enquiry* (Sec. V). The latter replaced it in Appendix II to the second *Enquiry*. Sympathy is a general psychological process whereby a lively idea of any passion tends to become that passion itself in a mild form. In this way the supposed pleasures of others become my pleasures. Humanity is a special original instinct prompting me, *ceteris paribus*, to prefer pleasure to pain, no matter whose.

Justice and utility. Justice is commonly opposed both to expedience and to sentiment; it seems, therefore, a stumbling block to Hume's theory and a potential stronghold for the rationalist. Hume therefore devoted much space both in the *Treatise* and the second *Enquiry* to proving that principles of justice depend entirely on the inventions and traditions of men and that the obligation to observe and enforce them arises solely from their utility.

In the *Treatise* Hume first proved the artificiality of

justice, then proceeded to show that such artifices are devised only for their usefulness. In the second *Enquiry*, he first proved their usefulness, then showed their artificial character, though he tactfully avoided labeling justice an "artificial virtue," as he had in the *Treatise*.

The argument for the artificiality of justice in the *Treatise* is that justice is a virtue; a virtue is a praiseworthy motive to action; and the praiseworthy motive to just acts cannot be merely the desire to be just, on pain of vicious circularity. There is no natural motive which always points to the just act. Justice does not necessarily conform to either the agent's private interest, his personal friendships, or the public interest. It must therefore arise from some artifice whose merits we learn. In the *Enquiry* Hume stressed the complicated procedures by which jurists work out a vast variety of different criteria for the determination of rights in varying circumstances; he pointed out that what is just depends, in particular contexts, on such various and plainly artificial conventions as the prohibited degrees of marriage, the rules of courtly love, the rules of war, of games, of the road.

Hume's arguments for the utilitarian foundation of justice consist, in both works, in inviting us to consider real or imaginary situations in which justice would be useless and admit that in these cases it either ceases or would cease to be a virtue. These situations are unlimited abundance of transferable goods, unlimited benevolence in the hearts of men, extreme dearth of necessities in famines and sieges, transactions with animals and savages, who are incapable of or ignorant of the rules. Hume added that perfect equality is not considered a requirement of justice, simply because the attempt to preserve it would be impracticable and pernicious.

On what kind of artifice does justice depend? Not, as many philosophers have supposed, on a contract, for contracts are themselves artifices of the kind in question. It depends on conventions. By a convention or agreement, Hume meant the manifestation to one another by two or more persons of the intention each has to behave, so long as others do likewise, in a certain way that is beneficial to all if followed by all. The longer such intentions are normally fulfilled, the more trustworthy and useful are such agreements. Hume's paradigm case is that of two men pulling the oars of a boat. It is, he maintained, simply because the use of such words as "I promise" or "I give" are governed by conventions that we are able by their use to undertake contractual obligations and transfer proprietary rights. Contracts and promises are not the foundation of human cooperation, but a special case of it. A footnote on this subject (second *Enquiry*, Sec. III, Pt. II) is a remarkable anticipation of J. L. Austin's discoveries concerning the performatory use of language.

In the *Treatise* Hume pointed out that the use of such agreements to regulate the conjunction of forces, partition of tasks, and distribution of products is a lesson men learn in the natural society of the family and is a biological necessity for the survival and prevalence of the human species. Hume's views on politics follow from his theory of justice. Governments, laws, and institutions are useful to human society. Their justification is in their utility, which depends largely on the habitual trust men have in one another's allegiance to them. Consequently, an established trusted government should never be overthrown on grounds of religion or hereditary claims to thrones or in order to experiment with utopian theories. Nor does the authority of governments rest on a contract. Rather the authority of both governments and contracts rests on their utility ("of the Original Contract"). Hume was a conservative. Unlike later utilitarians, he hoped to overthrow nothing and would have liked to overthrow nothing except the Church.

Hume was probably wrong in thinking justice an artificial virtue esteemed for its utility alone. His arguments only prove that property, promises, governments, laws, rules of games, and the like are useful devices, which no man is obliged to respect unless others do likewise. These, or the respect for them, he equated with justice. But there is another, more usual sense of "justice," in which laws and the systems of property can themselves be unjust, in which a mother even in the golden age could be unjust to one child in favor of another. The idea of justice seems, as both Hume and Plato saw, to be somehow connected with the fact that mankind lives by cooperation, by sharing tasks and exchanging products. The man who, or system which, allocates to one man fewer of the tasks or more of the products than it does to another—unless for some reason equally valid for and acceptable to all—is unjust, or as we more usually say, "unfair." The willingness to be fair, the lack of which makes a man unfit to participate in any form of cooperation and distribution, whether instinctive or devised, is no more an "artificial" virtue than courage. And being essentially concerned with distribution, not with aggregation, it cannot be justified by its utility, unless equality, as well as "happiness," be admitted as an ultimate end.

GOD, FREEDOM, AND MIRACLES

A believer in God might justify his belief, if asked to, in several ways. He might offer an a priori argument—for instance, the Ontological Argument; he might offer a posteriori arguments, from the marvels of creation to a designing Mind; he might appeal to revelation and cite the miracles recorded in Scripture; he might say that, without an all-powerful Providence, human choices and endeavors are pointless; he might appeal to anthropology to show that it was unnatural for man to live without a religion and attempt to find some converging direction in the developments of particular faiths.

Hume had an answer to each such move. The first two are considered in the *Dialogues concerning Natural Religion*. The existence of God is a matter of fact. Therefore, as already shown in the *Treatise* and first *Enquiry* it cannot be proved a priori, but only from experience by an argument from effect to cause. But we have no experience of the origins of worlds. We must therefore rely on analogy, comparing the world to things of whose origin we have experience. But the world is as like an animal or a vegetable as it is like a machine. So it arose as likely from insemination as from design. Moreover, if God is known only as the cause of the world, we can know nothing of him except that he is such as to create the world we find. We can draw no inferences from his existence except such as are already warranted by our knowledge of the world. He is an empty hypothesis (first *Enquiry*, Sec. XI).

The third move is dealt with in the essay "On Miracles" (first *Enquiry*, Sec. X). Since a miracle is by definition a breach of a law of nature, a known miracle must be a breach of a known law. But a known law of nature by definition carries the highest possible degree of probability, derived from extensive and uniform experience. A miracle can therefore only be accepted if the falsity of the testimony for it would be an even greater miracle, that is, a more glaring improbability than the miracle first alleged. Hume did not deny that this could ever happen. Laws of nature do have to be amended in the light of startling new experiments. He did deny that a miracle can ever be proved as a justifiable foundation for a system of religion. His reason is that the record of known fabrications of marvels of this sort is so black that it is always more probable that a story of a miracle imputed to the action of a god has been made up than that it happened. Moreover, if not all religions are true and if all religions produce miracles, most miracles must be deceptions. All religions do produce miracles. There is, therefore, always a high probability that any one of them is a deception.

The fourth move is met by Hume's section "On Liberty and Necessity" (first *Enquiry*, Sec. VIII; *Treatise*, Bk. II, Pt. III, Secs. I, II). An event, Hume said, is either caused or it is not; in the former case it is causally determined, or necessary. In the latter case it is a pure fluke, or happens by chance. Nobody believes that human actions are of the latter kind, least of all moralists and theologians. How then can they scruple to admit that they are of the former kind? Because, Hume said, they confuse the liberty of indifference with the liberty of spontaneity. It is one thing to perform an uncaused action (if one can conceive such a thing), another to do what you want. Conversely, it is one thing to act from intelligible and natural motives, quite another thing to be compelled to do what you do not want or prevented from doing what you want. Everyone really agrees that, except for prisoners, men enjoy the liberty of spontaneity but not that of indifference, that they are subject to the necessity of causes but not that of constraint.

Three factors assist this confusion: Imagining that we find an objective necessity in physical causation and not finding it in the will, we conclude that there is no causality in the will. Finding that I can first raise and then lower my hand without any alteration of the conditions, I suppose there must be a total indifference between these movements—failing to notice that the cause of the difference on the second occasion was my desire to demonstrate my liberty. Theology confuses the question of freedom with its own problem of the origin of evil. In the *Treatise* Hume said that "religion has been very unnecessarily interested in the question"; he insisted that a causal connection between actions and motives is essential to the concepts of praise and blame, reward and punishment, whether human or divine. In the *Enquiry* Hume proceeded more archly. His argument was quite intricate; the following interpretation of the logical structure behind Hume's camouflage of irony was made by Antony Flew (*Hume's Philosophy of Belief*, Ch. 7).

Hume's causal determinism combined with theism entails that God is the originator of our actions. (All events with causes trace their causal ancestry to him, and our actions have causes.) Hence it follows that either no actions are evil, being due to God, or that God is responsible for our sins. Hume pretended to regard this as an objection to causal determinism; he really meant it as an objection to theism, for he had already shown that there is no alternative to causal necessity except chance, which is unacceptable to all parties.

Hume then examined the objection. The first alternative, that no actions are evil, can be avoided; even if our actions are precontrived by God, and the "bad" ones are as necessary as the good to the goodness of the whole, their badness consists in the sentiments they naturally arouse in the human breast, which are unaffected by such remote considerations. We are left with the second alternative, real moral evil for which God is responsible. Hume saw no way to meet this difficulty. With tongue in cheek, he concluded that such "sublime mysteries" are beyond the reach of unassisted reason and, therefore, of philosophy.

Finally, he argued that no one should suppose that a belief in theism is natural to mankind. In "The Natural History of Religion," an entertaining exercise in armchair anthropology from secondary sources, Hume maintained that there is no evidence of any specific instinct for religious belief. Some races have no religion. In all known cases the earliest religions were polytheistic and idolatrous, with no notion whatever of an intelligent cause of the whole frame of nature. They were as truly atheistic as would be the beliefs of a contemporary person who acknowledged elves and fairies but denied the existence of God. The polytheistic systems were not, according to Hume, primitive systems of science. Primitive man was not interested in accounting for the regular phenomena of nature; he took the familiar for granted, however marvelous. It was the bewildering successions of floods and droughts, sickness and health, calm and tempest, victory and defeat, birth and death, that alternately terrified and comforted, nourished and destroyed him; it was these contrary and diverse events which, by a natural tendency to see external things in his own likeness, he ascribed to diverse and warring invisible persons, amenable to flattery and bribes and even to threats and force of arms.

In short, it was not God as the author of nature but God as a particular providence for which primitive religions were an origin and prototype. The only original instincts involved were the fear of death and pain and the desire for security and pleasure, together with a tendency to personify inanimate things.

Hume constantly pretended, how sincerely it is difficult to say, to distinguish "true" or "philosophical" religion from superstition as above described. But the concession is in the end an empty one, for all that Hume's philosophical theism amounted to was that probably, and not in any scientifically respectable sense of "probably," the universe was due to something remotely analogous to a designing mind (*Dialogues concerning Natural Religion*, Pt. XII). But the moral attributes of God, providence, immortality, and the whole Christian story from the Fall to the Day of Judgment he regarded as superstition.

Works by Hume

A Treatise of Human Nature, Bks. I and II, 2 vols. London, 1739. Bk. III, London, 1740. Modern editions are by L. A. Selby Bigge (Oxford, 1888 and 1896) and by A. D. Lindsay (London and New York, 1911, 2 vols.). A recent edition of Book I only, by D. G. C. Macnabb (New York, 1962), also includes the *Abstract*.

An Abstract of a Treatise of Human Nature. London, 1740. Modern edition by J. M. Keynes and Piero Sraffa, eds. Cambridge, 1938.

Essays, Moral and Political, 2 vols. Edinburgh, 1741–1742.

Three Essays ("Of Natural Character," "Of the Original Contract," and "Of Passive Obedience"). London, 1748.

Enquiry concerning Human Understanding. London, 1748. Published as *Philosophical Essays concerning Human Understanding* as were all the early editions prior to that of 1758. Modern edition by C. W. Hendel. New York, 1955.

Enquiry concerning the Principles of Morals. London, 1751. Modern edition by C. W. Hendel. New York, 1957.

Hume's Enquiries, L. A. Selby Bigge, ed. Oxford, 1894. Contains both *Enquiries*.

Political Discourses. London, 1752.

Four Dissertations ("The Natural History of Religion," "Of the Passions," "Of Tragedy," and "Of the Standard of Taste"). London, 1757.

Two Essays ("Of Suicide" and "Of the Immortality of the Soul"). London, 1777.

The Life of David Hume, Esq., Written by Himself, Adam Smith, ed. London, 1777. Reprinted in Mossner, E. C., *The Life of David Hume* and in Greig, J. Y. T., *The Letters of David Hume*. Often found under its original manuscript title, *My Own Life*.

Dialogues concerning Natural Religion. London, 1779. Recent edition by Norman Kemp Smith. Oxford, 1935; Edinburgh, 1947; New York, 1962.

History of Great Britain from the Invasion of Julius Caesar to the Revolution of 1688, 6 vols. London, 1754–1762. More recent edition by R. Worthington. New York, 1880.

Hume's Philosophical Works, T. H. Green and T. H. Grose, eds. 4 vols. London, 1874–1875. Includes all works listed above except the *Abstract* and the *History*.

Works on Hume

LIFE AND LETTERS

Greig, J. Y. T., *David Hume*. London, 1931.

Greig, J. Y. T., ed., *The Letters of David Hume*, 2 vols. Oxford, 1932.

Klibansky, Raymond, and Mossner, E. C., eds. *New Letters of David Hume*. Oxford, 1954.

Mossner, E. C., *The Life of David Hume*. Austin, Texas, London, and Edinburgh, 1954.

CRITICAL WORKS

Church, R. W., *Hume's Theory of the Understanding*. Ithaca, N.Y., 1935. The author contends that the constructive side of Hume's philosophy, particularly his theory of belief, is independent of his doctrine of impressions and ideas.

Flew, Antony, *Hume's Philosophy of Belief*. London and New York, 1961. A serious attempt to meet Hume's request to be judged by his *Enquiries* and not the *Treatise*, with special emphasis on his philosophy of religion.

Green, T. H., *General Introduction to Hume's Treatise*. London, 1874. A classical exposition from the idealist point of view of the traditional account of Hume's philosophy as a negative and untenable subjectivism.

Hendel, C. W., *Studies in the Philosophy of David Hume*. Princeton, N.J., 1925. Revised edition, New York, 1963. A sympathetic and scholarly interpretation of Hume's contribution to philosophy.

Kemp Smith, Norman, *The Philosophy of David Hume*. London, 1941. An authoritative assessment of Hume, stressing the parallelism between his ethics and his epistemology and the priority of the former.

Laing, B. M., *David Hume*. London, 1932. An attack on the traditional view of Hume's philosophy as a bankrupt atomistic sensationalism.

Laird, John, *Hume's Philosophy of Human Nature*. London, 1932. An acute and learned analysis of Hume's arguments and their relations to earlier and contemporary philosophers.

Leroy, André-Louis, *David Hume*. Paris, 1953. A lively discussion of Hume as seen through the eyes of a modern Continental.

Macnabb, D. G. C., *David Hume, His Theory of Knowledge and Morality*. London, 1951. An attempt to clarify Hume's arguments to the modern reader.

Michotte, Albert Edouard, *La Perception de la causalité*. Louvain, Belgium, 1954. Translated by T. R. Miles and E. Miles as *The Perception of Causality*. London, 1962. An account and discussion of experiments at the University of Louvain, claimed to prove the existence of an unlearned visual impression of mechanical causality.

Passmore, J. A., *Hume's Intentions*. Cambridge, 1952. A brief but acute analysis of the distinct but related trends in Hume's thought.

Price, H. H., *Hume's Theory of the External World*. Oxford, 1940. An original attempt to extract the elements of truth in Hume's account of sense perception.

Stewart, J. B., *The Moral and Political Philosophy of David Hume*. New York, 1963.

Taylor, A. E., "David Hume and the Miraculous," in his *Philosophical Studies*. London, 1934.

Zabech, Farhang, *Hume: Precursor of Modern Empiricism*. The Hague, 1960. An analysis of Hume's opinions on meaning, metaphysics, logic, and mathematics in relation to later philosophy.

D. G. C. MacNabb

HUMOR. Although the laughable is not usually thought of as a subclass of the beautiful (Aristotle, indeed, said that it was a subclass of the ugly), the problem of humor is a special case of the central problem of aesthetic theory. To find something laughable is to have a special kind of aesthetic emotion, but it is not at all easy to say just what features of the laughable situation evoke this emotion. Theories of humor attempt to answer this question.

Types of humor. The only way to evaluate theories of humor is to see how well they apply to different types of jokes or humorous situations. For this we need a list of the main types of humor. The attempt to provide one may, however, prejudge the issue, since the basis of classification may itself presuppose a theory of humor. Moreover, if any one theory is right, then in the final analysis jokes will be of only one type: they will all turn on release of inhibitions, or superiority to the misfortune of others, or whatever it may be.

With these reservations, the following may be regarded as the main types of humorous situations: (*a*) Any breach of the usual order of events, as wearing an unusual costume or eating with chopsticks when one is used to knife and fork (or with knife and fork when one is used to chopsticks). (*b*) Any breach of the usual order of events that is also felt to break a rule, whether of morality or etiquette. The drunkard, the glutton, the hypocrite, the miser are all stock figures of comedy, on the stage and elsewhere. (*c*) A special case of the second type is indecency, as in Restoration comedy or any smoking-room story. This has a different flavor from comic vice, just as comic vice has a different flavor from mere novelty and oddity. (*d*) Introduction into one situation of what is felt to belong to another, as Bernard Shaw's reference to conventional sexual morality as "the trade unionism of married women" or Mark Twain's introduction of a Connecticut Yankee into the Court of King Arthur. Finding connections between things we usually keep in separate compartments of our minds is, according to one version of the incongruity theory, the ultimate source of all humor. Whether this is correct or not, it is certainly one source that needs to be noted. (e) Anything masquerading as something it is not. This has been a favorite stage device, from *Twelfth Night* to *Charley's Aunt*, and is common enough in other forms of comedy. (f) Wordplay, of which puns are the most obvious, but not of course the only, example. (g) Nonsense, especially of the Edward Lear or Lewis Carroll type, which often turns on wordplay but is distinct from it. (h) Small misfortunes, like those provided by the banana skin, the custard pie, the thumb beneath the hammer. (i) Want of knowledge and skill, as in the schoolboy howler or the circus clown clumsily attempting to imitate the acrobat. (j) Veiled insults, as in the catty remarks in *The School for Scandal*.

Theories of humor. Most theories find the essence of humor in one or another of the following: superiority, incongruity, and relief from restraint. It has also been suggested that humor derives from ambivalent feelings, in which attraction and repulsion are both present.

Superiority theories. If we laugh at the miser, the drunkard, the glutton, the henpecked husband, the man who gets hit by the custard pie, the schoolboy howler, the person with faulty pronunciation, may it not be because we feel superior to all of these? This could account for our pleasure in humor. Accordingly, Hobbes regarded laughter as the result of a sudden access of self-esteem ("sudden glory") when we realize that our own situations compare favorably with the misfortunes or infirmities of others. We also laugh, he said, at our own past follies—provided we are conscious of having surmounted them—or at unexpected successes.

In support of Hobbes, or perhaps as a modification of his view, it may be said that in humor at its best we are conscious of surveying the whole human scene from some godlike level at which all men and women look pretty much alike: all weak, all lovable, all transparently obvious in their petty pretenses. If "superiority" is interpreted as this god's-eye view rather than as simply a sneering contempt for some failing we do not have, it is possible to account for laughter not merely at comic vice but also at comic virtue, as in Mr. Pickwick or Don Quixote. It may even explain why we often laugh with comic vice rather than at it. No one feels superior to Falstaff, but we may feel pleasantly conscious of "seeing through" him, and perhaps, in sympathizing with him, we feel superior, if only for the time being, to the conventional morality he flouts.

By extending Hobbes's theory in this way, it is possible to account for many of our classes of humor: indecency and masquerade as well as comic vice, small misfortunes, and ignorance. Alexander Bain extended Hobbes in two directions. Sometimes, Bain suggested, our laughter may be a manifestation not of our own feeling of superiority but of our sympathy with someone else who has triumphed in some way. This would account for laughter at veiled insults. Second, the triumph need not be over a person; it can be over anything at all that is conventionally treated

with respect. Mark Twain's debunking of feudal values was not directed at any individual, and Samuel Butler degraded a sunrise by comparing it to a boiled lobster. According to Bain, the essential feature of humor is degradation. Some writers have argued, not very plausibly, that in wordplay we triumph over the degradation of words. More credibly, nonsense may be regarded as the degradation of what Schopenhauer called "that strict, untiring, troublesome governess, the reason." Even incongruity, it is argued, always involves degradation. Typically, the incongruous effect is obtained by the bringing of something exalted into contact with something trivial or disreputable. Shaw's phrase has its force because trade unionism is much lower on the conventional scale of values than is chastity: the pleasure in seeing them linked is, at least in part, malicious.

Henri Bergson maintained that the particular characteristic exciting dirision is inflexibility, the inability to adapt oneself to the ever-changing demands of life. Laughter is always at "something mechanical encrusted upon the living." With Molière in mind, Bergson claimed that the comic character is usually a man with a fixed idea. This fits in with early stage comedy and with the etymology of the word "humor": a humor was originally a quirk, a kink, a mental (and primarily a physiological) oddity that throws a man off balance and twists his view of life. Hence, the comic character is simply a man with an obsession. The joke is to see how this obsession crops up again and again in the most varied situations, so that he always behaves in a manner wildly inappropriate to the circumstances as others see them but entirely appropriate to his own ruling passion.

With more ingenuity than plausibility, Bergson attempted to apply his formula to wordplay, which consists, he claimed, in showing that language is too rigid to be an accurate mirror of an infinitely fluid universe. His main emphasis, however, was on the social function of laughter; it is leveled, according to him, at the eccentric or nonconformist. This seems an unduly restricted view: the most penetrating humor is often aimed at the social code itself. There is nothing in Bergson's theory of humor that need have prevented him from conceding this: the conventions of society may often enough be characterized as "something mechanical encrusted upon the living."

Incongruity theories. It can be doubted whether the concepts of "superiority" or "degradation" or even "inelasticity" do justice to the very large element of humor that consists in the intellectual and emotional pleasure of finding connections where none were thought to exist. It is true that if this were the whole of humor, humor would be indistinguishable from fancy or imagination; but then, if "degradation" were the whole of humor, humor would be indistinguishable from malice.

Kant asserted that humor arises "from the sudden transformation of a strained expectation into nothing," and since his time incongruity has often been identified with "frustrated expectation." But there is more to incongruity than mere surprise, or even anticlimax; we must be, as it were, jolted out of one mental attitude into another completely and violently opposed to it. Usually this results from bringing together two things normally kept in separate compartments of our minds. Shaw's aphorism about the trade unionism of married women may once again serve as an example. Another is Samuel Butler's "God and the Devil are an effort after specialisation and division of labour." In Kant's view, the "degradation" of one of the two disparate ideas is quite incidental. What is important is that they normally evoke very different attitudes and that the connection between them appears to be genuine, not artificially contrived. It is on these two features that the neatness of a joke depends.

Kant's formula may be regarded as defective in that by putting the emphasis on surprise it ignores the logical connection between the two ideas that are linked. This is Schopenhauer's criticism. He claimed that all humor can be "traced to syllogism in the first figure with an undisputed major and an unexpected minor, which to a certain extent is only sophistically valid."

This formula applies most obviously to the mock-heroic or to certain types of satire. The point of Fielding's *Jonathan Wild*, for example, might be summarized syllogistically as: All generals and those who behave like generals are heroes; highwaymen behave like generals; therefore, highwaymen are heroes. Here the major premise is, conventionally, undisputed. The minor is, no doubt, "only sophistically valid," but only "to a certain extent"; there is enough resemblance in behavior to give the satire sting.

The formula applies, however, to other types of humor as well. Oscar Wilde is reported to have said, when he was in prison, "If this is the way the Queen treats her convicts, she doesn't deserve to have any." Here the major premise is: "Those who ill-treat their dependents deserve to lose them." This generalization is then made to apply to a case in which losing them would be no hardship and deserving to lose them no demerit. What is sophistical about the minor premise is the assumption that a convict is, along with a servant, a child, and the like, the kind of dependent to whom the generalization applies.

The objection to Schopenhauer's analysis is that it stresses the formal side of a joke to the exclusion of the content. For him, humor was purely a matter of finding connections where (except in a "sophistical" sense) none exist. By this view, all humor is of the type of Richard Whately's *Historic Doubts Relative to Napoleon Bonaparte*. The essence of it lies in the ingenuity of the argument, underlined by the absurdity of the conclusion. If any derision creeps in, it is at the expense of the reasoning, or perhaps of the governess Reason herself.

What this overlooks is the part that the abrupt dissolution of an attitude plays in our emotional lives. Kant's phrase "strained expectation" hints at this but does not characterize it adequately. *Jonathan Wild* would not be funny if it were not for the whole complex of emotions that cluster round the concepts of patriotism and national glory. To take another example, Gerald Bullett's adaptation of Tennyson, "Wearing the white feather of a blameless life," is funny, not merely because of its close resemblance to the wording of the original ("the white *flower* of a blameless life") but because of the startling difference in attitude that results from the alteration of a single word.

So far as superiority theories call attention to the emo-

tional element in humor, they do something to correct this inadequacy. It is doubtful, however, whether the emotion involved is either self-congratulation or malice. In any community certain attitudes are felt to be appropriate to some things and not to others, and there develop "stereotypes" of such figures as the typical politician, poet, businessman. The humorist drags into light the inconvenient facts that shatter these attitudes and puncture these stereotypes. Sometimes, as Bergson pointed out, the humor is at the expense of the person who is unable to live up to the conventional requirements, and here malice may creep in, but often enough the effect is to cast doubt on the conventional attitudes and values. Sometimes it is not clear which effect is intended. Wilde's witticism "Work is the curse of the drinking classes" may be taken either as a gibe at the working classes or as a questioning of the conventional Victorian attitudes to work and to drink. In either case one element in our enjoyment is certainly the sense of enlarged horizons that comes from seeing unexpected connections. This is in part an intellectual pleasure. So far as it is a conventional attitude that has been convicted of inadequacy, the accompanying emotion may be not malice or superiority but a feeling of liberation at the removal of intellectual blinkers.

Relief theories. Liberation, or relief from restraint, is regarded in a third type of theory as the central element in humor.

It is well known that people who have been undergoing a strain will sometimes burst into laughter if the strain is suddenly removed. It has been argued that all laughter is of this type and that any joke will be found, in one way or another, to remove the restraints which society imposes on our natural impulses. It is the liberation of our impulses from social constraints, not of our intellects from too narrow a point of view, that is emphasized by this type of theory.

What are these impulses that need liberating? One obvious one is the sexual impulse. Since the mention of the (conventionally) unmentionable is in itself a sufficient cause of laughter, it seems reasonable to say that at least one important type of humor depends on our being able to give vent to forbidden thoughts and feelings.

But thoughts about sex are not the only ones that society calls on us to suppress. Our aggressive impulses are also repressed. Children are taught that it is "rude" both to expose their bodies and to speak insultingly to others. Consequently, the relief theory can account, plausibly enough, for the malicious element in humor and, in general, for most of the aspects of humor that have given rise to superiority theories. Even nonsense can be explained, if it is conceded that trying to be rational all the time is a strain for most of us.

Relief theories have been given considerable impetus by the rise of psychoanalysis. Freud himself wrote a book on humor, in which he suggested that there is a basic resemblance between jokes and dreams. Both are essentially means of outwitting the "censor," the name by means of which Freud personified our internal inhibitions. In dreams forbidden thoughts are distorted and disguised; in humor insults are veiled, masquerading perhaps as compliments, and sexual references lurk behind apparently innocent remarks.

Freud did not, however, regard all humor as the release of inhibition. He distinguished between "harmless wit," indulged in for its own sake, and "tendency wit," which gives us the additional gratification of giving rein to repressed sexual or aggressive impulses. Harmless wit delights us because it provides us with "infantile play-pleasure." In learning to use words, Freud pointed out, children "experience pleasurable effects which originate from the repetition of similarities, the rediscovery of the familiar, sound-associations," and the like. In other words, the pleasure of playing with words and ideas, on which incongruity theories place so much stress, is admitted by Freud to be enjoyable for its own sake, not just as a means of seeking relief from restraint. It is, indeed, because this intellectual play is enjoyable in itself that we can use it to beguile the censor. When Oscar Wilde, for example, complained that "the youth of to-day are quite monstrous; they have absolutely no respect for dyed hair," we must suppose that the censor is so diverted by the discovery that this remark differs only in one word from the conventional head-shaking of the stuffier kind of matron that the malice in the remark (its complete exposure of the matron's pretensions and its revelation of her envy of youth) is allowed to go unchecked.

Freud explained "infantile play-pleasure" by invoking the concept of "psychic economy." In this he was influenced by Herbert Spencer. Spencer thought that humor consists essentially in the abrupt transition of thought from a noble or elevated idea to a trivial or degrading one, leaving the psyche with an unexpended fund of nervous energy that overflows into laughter, which is, according to him, a physical release of energy. Freud adapted this notion for his own purposes, identifying "psychic economy" first with the line of least resistance and then with the brevity and neatness that is the soul of wit.

Neither Spencer's nor Freud's use of the concept is very satisfactory. It may be pointed out against Spencer that when, for example, an innocent remark is transformed into a sexual reference, the second might be expected to call forth more emotional energy than the first. Against Freud it may be said that the lazy pleasure of following the path of least resistance is very different from our appreciation of the skill with which a master of humor links disparate ideas. When writers like Rabelais, Chesterton, Christopher Fry, James Joyce, and even Laurence Sterne play with words and ideas, it is exuberance rather than economy that they display.

Relation of the theories to the types. If the theories are evaluated by their ability to explain the main types of humor listed earlier, it would seem that none is completely adequate by itself. Each of them relies mainly on particular kinds of humor, either ignoring the rest or giving relatively lame accounts of them. Satire and laughter at small misfortunes are very well explained by superiority theories. Incongruity theories find difficulty in dealing with these but are much more satisfactory than superiority theories in dealing with wordplay, nonsense, and in-

decency. Relief theories can explain malice and indecency, and perhaps nonsense, but are driven to admit that wordplay and the finding of unexpected connections have an intrinsic appeal that cannot be reduced to relief from restraint.

Bibliography

GENERAL

Monro, D. H., *Argument of Laughter*. Melbourne and Cambridge, 1951; Notre Dame, Ind., 1963.

Sully, J., *Essay on Laughter*. London, 1903.

SUPERIORITY THEORIES

Bain, Alexander, *The Emotions and the Will*, 3d ed. London, 1888.

Bergson, Henri, *Le Rire*. Paris, 1900. Translated by Cloudesley Brereton and Fred Rothwell as *Laughter*. London, 1911.

Leacock, Stephen, *Humour: Its Theory and Techniques*. London, 1935.

INCONGRUITY THEORIES

Eastman, Max, *Enjoyment of Laughter*. New York, 1937.

Schopenhauer, Arthur, *Die Welt als Wille und Vorstellung*, 2d ed., 2 vols. Leipzig, 1844. Translated by E. F. J. Payne as *The World as Will and Representation*, 2 vols. Indian Hills, Colo., 1958.

RELIEF THEORIES

Freud, Sigmund, *Der Witz und seine Beziehungen zum Unbewussten*. Leipzig and Vienna, 1905. Translated by James Strachey as *Jokes and Their Relation to the Unconscious*. New York and London, 1960.

D. H. MONRO

HUNGARIAN PHILOSOPHY. Some authorities claim that the history of Hungarian philosophy begins with the thirteenth-century Averroist Boethius of Dacia, on the assumption that Dacia is Transylvania. But it is now certain that in his day Dacia referred to Denmark, or to the Scandinavian province of the Dominicans, and Boethius was born in Sweden. Now that he can no longer plausibly be claimed for Hungary, most Hungarian philosophers would scarcely be mentioned in the history of European philosophy. This is not because of lack of talent, but because of the tragic history of the nation. Philosophers spent their energies assimilating the philosophical ideas of Europe to prepare for a more creative environment at home, only to have that environment repeatedly destroyed by national disasters. Matyas Corvinus' court was an outstanding center of Italian humanism, and the nobility who died shortly afterward on the field of Mohács during the fighting against the Turks had assimilated the humanism of Erasmus as well. But their work perished with them.

The Reformation provided a new intellectual stimulus and gave a permanent pattern to Hungarian culture. Externally the Protestants cultivated ties with German and Dutch universities, while Catholics turned toward Austria and Rome. Internally Transylvania became the center of Protestant culture, and western Hungary, where the Jesuit Cardinal Péter Pázmány (1570–1637) founded the University of Nagyszombat, was dominated by scholastic philosophy. At the end of the eighteenth century, this university moved to Budapest and took Pázmány's name. Equally important in the history of Hungarian philosophy is the University of Kolozsvár in Transylvania.

Pázmány is best known in Hungary for his eminent apologetic work *Kalauz* ("The Guide," Bratislava, 1613), but he was an outstanding philosopher who was associated with the Italian prelate and controversialist Cardinal Bellarmine in Rome. His *Dialectica* is on universals and categories; his *Physica* seems to be on his main interest, physics in the Aristotelian sense. He wrote a now-lost *Metaphysica* and *De Anima,* and he also wrote on Aristotle's *De Caelo, De Generatione,* and *Meteorology.* Two other Jesuit professors at Nagyszombat were Martin Szentiványi (1633–1705), who tried to reconcile scholasticism with the empirical sciences, and János Keresztelo-Horváth (1732–1799), whose main interest was physics, but who wrote a Latin critique of Kant, *Declaratio Infirmitatis Fundamentorum Operis Kantiani Kritik des Reinen Vernunft* (Buda, 1797).

Two early Protestant philosophers were Pétar Laskai Csókás Monendulatus (?–1587) and János Apácai Csere (1625–1659). In 1585 the former published at Wittemberg a book on Nicholas of Cusa, *De Homine, Magno Illo in Rerum Natura Miraculo et Patribus Essentialibus.* Csere's career is an example of what a potential philosopher was expected to do at that time. He was the first to receive a doctorate from the new Dutch university of Hardwijk, and there are indications that he was offered a post at the University of Utrecht, but he returned home to become a schoolteacher. He wrote a "Little Hungarian Logic" (*Magyar Logikatska*, Fejervaratt, 1654) and published a general encyclopedia, *Magyar Encyclopedia*, in Utrecht in 1653. Some of its information was centuries out of date, but Csere's main concern was to provide reading matter in Hungarian.

The first modern Hungarian philosopher was a Kantian, István Márton (1760–1831), who taught at Papa and had to contend with strong official opposition to Kantianism. It is typical of Hungarian philosophy during this period that he expounded Kant in Latin in *Systema Philosophiae Criticae* (1820). But nationalistic ferment soon demanded not only the use of the Hungarian language but the development of what was claimed to be a national philosophy, the so-called "philosophy of harmony" (*egyezményes rendszer*). This was in fact a version of the Kantian philosophy of Wilhelm Traugott Krug, (1770–1842) and is best understood in Krug's own work. Because of its nationalist connections, the philosophy of harmony is more of sociological than of philosophical interest. The first philosopher of harmony was János Hetényi (1786–1853), the author of *Az Egyezményes Rendszer* (Pest, 1841). Others were Gusztáv Szontágh (1793–1853), who further systematized Hetényi's thought, and Samuel Köteles (1790–1831). All emphasized the practical value of philosophy. The harmony they stressed was not just a theoretical correspondence between our thoughts and the world, but also a correspondence that we should establish between our acts and moral laws and between men and God. János Erdélyi (1814–1868) criticized this movement and the idea of a

national philosophy, although he thought that Hegel suited the Hungarian mentality. His *Bölcselet Magyarországon* (Budapest, 1885) is a partisan but critical work on Hungarian philosophy. Károly Kerkápoly (1824–1891) was a Hegelian and a follower of Erdélyi, who studied under Johann Erdmann. He tried to substantiate Hegel in the details of history, which was his main interest. German philosophy, particularly that of Kant and Hegel, dominated Hungarian thought in the nineteenth century. A strong but short-lived enthusiasm for Comte toward the end of the century was soon followed by interest in Husserl and phenomenology.

Cyrill Horváth (1804–1888) was a Catholic Hegelian who tried to avoid a monism that would deny the transcendence of God. A revival of Thomism was due chiefly to János Kiss (1857–1930), who was the founding editor of the Neo-Scholastic *Bölcseleti Folyóirat* (1886–1906), founded the Aquinas Society and improved the style of the Hungarian language. The Neo-Scholastics were mainly interested in the history of philosophy, but since they also combated the most influential philosophical currents of their time, their writings are a useful index to the philosophical environment. Thus, Gyula Kozáry wrote on Comte, Wilhelm Wundt, and Descartes; József Trikál (1873–1950) argued against positivism, worked in the history of philosophy (especially the development of Augustinian and Franciscan thought), and wrote on anthropology and the theory of relativity; and Hildebrand Várkonyi, born in 1888, criticized Neo-Kantians.

Bölcselet Elemei ("Elements of Philosophy," Budapest, 1933) by Antal Schütz (1880–1953) deservedly became the standard Neo-Scholastic text. Schütz also tried to assimilate Neo-Kantian views, especially in ethics, and wrote a much discussed work on the theology of history, *Isten a Történelemben* ("God in History," Budapest, 1932). József Jánosi, born in 1898, wrote on the theory of knowledge (*Bölcselet és Valóság*, Budapest, 1940), and ethics (*Az Erkölcs Metafizikai Gyökererei*, Budapest, 1943), and is perhaps the most readable writer not only among scholastic but among Hungarian philosophers.

Just as Kiss revived scholasticism through his journal, his positivist contemporary Imve Pauer (1854–1950), professor at Budapest and editor of the rival journal *Atheneum* from 1891 to 1914, initiated a development which, although no more original, was more eclectic and hence more versatile. Károly Böhm (1846–1911), professor at Kolozsvár, was an independent system builder who incorporated elements from both Comte and Kant. Akos Pauler (1876–1933), was the greatest philosopher of this period. His thought reflects both the eclecticism of the time and the struggle between the scholastics and the moderns. Menyhért Palágyi (1859–1924) spent most of his time in Germany. Gyula Kornis, born in 1885, was professor at the University of Budapest until after World War II; his philosophy is best expressed in *Az Államférfi* ("The Statesman," Budapest, 1933).

Many contemporary Hungarian philosophers now live and work outside the country. Wilhelm Szilasi, born in 1889, has been at Fribourg since 1937. In his *Wissenschaft als Philosophie* (Zurich and New York, 1945) he attempted a synthesis of Husserl, Heidegger, and Kant. He is interested in the philosophy of language, particularly in connection with his interpretation of Plato and Aristotle. For him philosophy has practical implications as a means to eudaemonia. Károly Kerényi, born in 1897, is a classical scholar and student of Greek philosophy who also works in Switzerland. Sándor Varga von Kibed, born in 1902, moved from the ideas of Kant toward those of Bruno Bauch and Heinrich Rickert; he is a professor at Munich. Baron Béla von Brandenstein, born in 1901, is a professor at Saarbrücken, Germany, where his *Der Aufbau der Seins* ("The Structure of Being") was published in 1950 and his *Platon* in 1951.

György (Georg) Lukács, born in 1885, is the most original and influential of contemporary Marxist philosophers. Although he returned to Hungary after World War II, he could not single-handedly replace the activity of those who had left, and his own activities were handicapped by a struggle with the bureaucracy. The Hungarian Philosophical Society, founded in 1901, was dissolved in 1948, along with the societies for psychology and the social sciences. The two philosophical reviews *Atheneum* and *Pantheon* also ceased publication. In 1952, 2 out of 21 publications in philosophy were by Hungarians and 12 were by Russians. In 1957 an Institute of Philosophy was established, followed by the publication of the *Hungarian Review of Philosophy*. Of 41 philosophical works discussed in the *Review* between 1958 and 1960, 20 were by Russians and only 4 were by Hungarian authors. However, in 1957 the Hungarian Academy published Laszlo Erdei's dissertation *A Megismerés Kezdete* ("Foundations of Knowledge"), which was a philosophical study of Hegel and not a Marxist textbook. Lukács was one of two examiners. Nevertheless, a century-long effort to create an environment in Hungary for what is generally understood to be the philosophical life has been largely aborted.

(See Hungarian Philosophy in Index for articles on Hungarian philosophers.)

Bibliography

Alexander, Bernát, *Magyar Filozofia Története: Pallas Lexikon XII*. Budapest, 1896.

Bod, Péter, *Magyar Athenas*. Nagy-Szeben, 1766.

Erdélyi, János, *A Bölcsészet Magyarországon*, 2d ed. Budapest, 1885.

Hajos, József, *A Bölcselet Hazánkban: "A Bölcselet Története" Cimü Müvehen*. Székesfehérvár, 1941.

Hetényi, János, *A Magyar Philosophia Történetirásának Alaprajza*. Buda, 1837.

Hidasy, Kornél, *A Bölcsészet Hazánkbani Elöhaladásának Történelmi Vázlata*. Nagyszombat, 1855.

Kecskés, Pál, *A Magyar Bölcselet Multja: A Bölcselet Története Föbb Vonásaiban Cimü Müvében*. Budapest, 1933. 2d ed., Budapest, 1943.

Martai, László, *Régi Magyar Filozofusok*. Budapest, 1961.

Medveczky, Frigyes, "Zur Geschichte der philosophischen Besterbungen in Ungarn." *Ungarische Revue* (1886).

Mitrovics, Gyula, *A Magyar Bölcséleti Irodalom Vázlata. Függelék Schwegler Albert: "A Böcselet Története" Magyar Forditásához*. Budapest, 1914.

Ompolyi, Mátrai Ernö, *A Bölcsészet Magyarországon a Scholasztica Korában*. Budapest, 1878.

Sándor, Pál, *Filozofiai Lexikon*. Budapest, 1941.

Szlavik, Mátyás, "Zur Geschichte und Litteratur der Philosophie in Ungarn." *Zeitschrift für Philosophie und philosophische Kritik*, Vol. 107 (1895), 216–232.

Tankó, Béla, *Hungarian Philosophy*. Szeged, 1934. In English.

Torcsányi, Dezsö, *Bölcselet Történelem*. Papa, 1939.

Tordai, Z., *Esquisse de l'histoire du cartesianisme en Hongrie*. Budapest, 1965.

Ueberweg, Friedrich, *Grundriss der Geschichte der Philosophie*, 12th ed. Berlin, 1928. Vol. V, pp. 348–356.

JULIUS KOVESI

HUS, JOHN (c. 1369–1415), Czech church reformer and national hero. Born at Husinec in southern Bohemia, he made his way through the University of Prague, receiving his A.B. in 1393, his M.A. in 1396, and his B.D. in 1404. Some of the logical works of John Wyclyf were known in Prague in the early 1390s, and there is still extant a copy of a half dozen of Wyclyf's philosophical works in Hus's hand, made in 1398. Wyclyf's realism (*universalia ante rem*) found a warm welcome among Czech professors and students, not least because the German community at the university was strongly Ockhamist and Wyclyf's vigorous defense of universals (prior to individuals) fortified the Czechs' position. He was deeply influenced by the Augustinianism of the Victorine school of the twelfth century.

Hus became well known and popular, partly for his teaching and partly for his preaching in the vernacular. In 1402 Hus was named stated preacher in the Bethlehem Chapel, and his sermons in Czech were well attended by Czechs of all classes. In October 1401 Hus was elected dean of the arts faculty and in 1403 rector of the university (though there is some uncertainty as to this first rectorate). By this time disputes over Wyclyf's teachings had become acrimonious, and Hus with some of his friends undertook to defend Wyclyf from charges of heresy against a party largely of German professors, who demanded strict condemnation of Wyclyf's teachings. Hus continued his preaching and writing in the interest of reform, but in 1408 the Prague conservative hierarchy (mainly German) lodged specific charges of heresy against him. Soon thereafter the struggle for predominance in the university broke out between Czech and German. The Germans had three votes, the Czechs only one. Hus led the fight for a reversal of the proportion, and King Wenceslaus decided in the Kutná Hora decree of 1409 that the Czech professors and students should have three votes and all others combined, one vote. The Germans left in a body to form the University of Leipzig. Hus, as leader of the national Czech party, was elected rector of the university.

Opposition to Hus on the part of the conservative Czech clergy remained, and the serious charges of 1408 were renewed in 1409 and 1410. He disobeyed a summons to Rome and was excommunicated in 1411. Hus had formed his opinions clearly by then and was prepared to defend them under any conditions. He believed firmly in predestination and the unity of the church under the headship of Christ. He was deeply influenced by the teaching of Wyclyf but in one important matter he categorically disagreed. He rejected Wyclyf's teaching on the Eucharist, accepting completely the church's doctrine of transubstantiation. Realist philosophy was important in the formulation of his theological positions, and his competence in Scholastic exposition is evident in all his writings. From the excommunication of 1411 to his death four years later it was clear that his position and that of the established hierarchy were irreconcilable. In 1412 King Wenceslaus reluctantly had to withdraw his protection, and Hus went into exile to relieve the city of Prague from the interdict. It was during his exile that he finished his most important work, the *De Ecclesia,* very similar to a book under the same title by Wyclyf. He argued against the authority of the pope and the cardinalate over the church and their control of the means of salvation, basing his conclusions on the doctrine of predestination. "The church is the body of the predestinate." Inasmuch as only God knows who is predestinate, the pope's function and power are readily dispensable. The hierarchy could not tolerate so basic an attack on its existence. Hus appealed to the general council called for November 1414 at Constance and, receiving a safe-conduct from Emperor Sigismund, arrived in Constance on November 3. However, the safe-conduct was soon disregarded; Hus was imprisoned and interrogated at length. He asked simply to be shown from Scriptures or the Fathers where he was in error. The council demanded that he make a blanket recantation. No compromise was possible. Hus's concept of the church as the body of the predestinate, regardless of the decision of the pope and the hierarchy, was declared pure heresy. He was "relaxed to the secular arm" on July 6, 1415, and burned at the stake that morning. His martyrdom set off the Hussite Wars (1419–1434), which in turn isolated Bohemia from the rest of Europe for several generations. Hussitism, as it developed, took forms which Hus might not have approved.

Hus may not have been one of the leading minds of his century. On the other hand his commentary on the *Sententiae* of Peter Lombard, composed in 1407–1409, is a very impressive work and shows complete familiarity with the dominant currents of philosophical thought in the fourteenth and fifteenth centuries and an easy ability in the handling of contradictory arguments. His realism is confident and precise.

Works by Hus

The early edition of his collected works (1558; reprinted in 1715) is still indispensable. Some of his works have been published in modern critical editions: *Opera,* V. Flajšhans, ed. (Prague, 1903–1912), and *De Ecclesia,* S. H. Thomson, ed. (Boulder, Col., 1956). Also indispensable is *Documenta . . . Mag. Joannis Hus,* Francis Palacký, ed. (1869) containing his correspondence and salient documents of his career.

Works on Hus

There are several useful biographies in English: D. S. Schaff, *John Huss* (New York, 1915); Francis Lützow, *Life and Times of Master John Hus* (London, 1909). Johann Loserth, *Hus and Wiclif* (London, 1882), is bitterly anti-Hus, arguing that Hus borrowed all his ideas from Wyclyf. The classic study in Czech is by V. Novotný and V. Kybal, *M. J. Hus, Život a Učení,* 5 vols. (Prague, 1919–1931). See also two recent and important studies by P. de Vooght, *L'Hérésie de Jean Huss* (Louvain, 1960) and *Hussiana* (Louvain, 1960).

S. Harrison Thomson

HU SHIH (1891–1962), Chinese pragmatist, was educated in China, at Cornell University, and at Columbia University under Dewey. He was successively professor, chancellor of Peking National University, ambassador to the United States, and president of Academia Sinica in Taipei, Taiwan.

In 1916 he inaugurated the Literary Revolution in China by advocating the use of the vernacular style for writing instead of the formal, classical style, which, radically different from the spoken language, had become rigid and decadent. He succeeded in spite of strong opposition and thus set Chinese literature free. Since freedom of expression means also freedom of thought, the new literature led to the Intellectual Renaissance in China in 1917.

Hu did not claim to be a philosopher, but his own credo represented a new philosophy in China at the time. According to Hu Shih the universe, infinite in space and time, was not supernaturally created but is naturalistic and is governed by natural laws. All things, including psychological phenomena, have a scientific basis and can therefore be scientifically understood. Immortality is not personal but the sum total of individual achievement living on in the Larger Self. Truth must be historically and scientifically tested and is best expressed in democracy, freedom, progress, and social action.

His contributions to Chinese philosophy are important. As the leading disciple of Dewey in China, in 1919 he introduced pragmatism, which exerted tremendous influence and became the first concerted philosophical movement in twentieth-century China. Although the philosophy declined in influence in the later 1920s, its spirit of practical application, emphasis on problems instead of theories, the insistence on results, the critical approach, and the scientific method had become the generally accepted outlook in China.

In his writings on Chinese philosophy Hu Shih was the first to give it a clear outline, free from religious beliefs and legendary philosophy. He provided it with a historical and social environment. Lao Tzu, for example, was presented as a rebel against oppressive government and hypocritical society. Hu Shih discovered the methodology in Chinese philosophy, notably the "rectification of names" in Confucianism, the "three standards" or "laws of reasoning" in Moism, and the method of "names and actuality" in other philosophers. He removed the mysticism of Lao Tzu and Chuang Tzu, whom he regarded as realists championing the cause of complete individual freedom. While these views are extreme, he created an entirely new atmosphere in Chinese philosophy.

Bibliography

Hu Shih wrote two books in English, *The Development of the Logical Method in Ancient China* (Shanghai, 1922) and *The Chinese Renaissance* (Chicago, 1934). *Hu Shih Wen-ts'un,* 4 vols. (Taipei, Taiwan, 1953), is a collection of his works in Chinese. For a complete listing of his works in both Chinese and English, see *Bulletin of the Institute of History and Philology Academia Sinica,* Vol. 28 (Taipei, Taiwan, 1957), 889–914, which includes 83 items in English.

For literature on Hu Shih, see Wing-tsit Chan, "Hu Shih and Chinese Philosophy," in *Philosophy East and West,* Vol. 6, No. 1 (April 1956), 3–12.

Wing-tsit Chan

HUSSERL, EDMUND (1859–1938), German philosopher and the central figure in the phenomenological movement, began his career in mathematics, receiving his Ph.D. in 1881. After a brief assistantship to the noted mathematician Karl Theodor Weierstrass, he moved to

Vienna, where he attended the lectures of the philosopher Franz Brentano from 1884 to 1886, and decided to devote himself to philosophy (see PHENOMENOLOGY for a full critical account). He taught in Halle (1887–1901), Göttingen (1901–1916), and Freiburg (1916–1929), where he spent the remainder of his life, during the last few years exposed to various social and political pressures because of his Jewish ancestry.

Philosophy, for Husserl, was not just his occupation; it was of the utmost seriousness to him. He spoke of it as some men speak of their call to the priesthood or others of their most sacred moral duties. Were he to waver in his devotion, he would be untrue to himself; were he to lose faith in philosophy, he would lose faith in himself.

Philosophy, as he committed himself to it, was first and foremost a science. His conception of this philosophical science changed more than once, but he never wavered in his conviction that only a body of indubitable and objective truths deserves to be called "science." The truths he sought do not concern this or that particular subject matter. He sought the truths on which all other human knowledge rests.

Devoted to his pursuit with a moral fervor, he worked steadily throughout most of his long life, publishing eight books or long articles and writing 45,000 manuscript pages in shorthand, some of it practically ready for publication, the rest in less finished form. His search was for the unshakable foundation of human knowledge, which he often referred to as the "Archimedean point." More than once he was led to abandon earlier views, for it was all-important that the beginning should be made correctly. He spoke of himself with pride, mixed with sadness, as "a perpetual beginner." His writings, both the published and unpublished ones, are best regarded as more or less polished working papers. There is no Husserlian "system"; there are no incontestable phenomenological truths; there is no unambiguous and incontrovertible description of the phenomenological method.

The requirement that philosophy be scientific is specified in several imperatives for philosophers. The philosopher must seek complete clarity. He must seek apodictic certainty, at least for the starting points of his inquiry. He must be "radical" in the sense that he must take nothing for granted. Ideally, at least, philosophy is presuppositionless; no statement is to be admitted as true without scrutiny, no conception to be used without examination.

The search for clarity and understanding prompted Husserl's first philosophical inquiries. He was not satisfied with doing mathematics without complete clarity about the meaning of basic mathematical concepts. Encouraged by Brentano, he turned to the philosophy of mathematics, and in 1891 he published the first volume of his *Philosophie der Arithmetik*. In this book he attempted a psychological analysis of certain basic logical and mathematical notions. The concept of number, for instance, was to be elucidated by talking about the activity of counting. In his review of this book, the mathematician Gottlob Frege argued that logical and mathematical concepts differ from the psychological acts in which they may occur and that, therefore, the discussion of the latter does not serve to explicate the former. He accused Husserl of confusing psychology and logic.

Critique of psychologism. Husserl was impressed by Frege's objections. The promised second volume of the *Philosophie der Arithmetik* never appeared. Instead, he brought out his *Logische Untersuchungen*, in two volumes (1900–1901). The first of these volumes contains a thorough critique of the assumption underlying the earlier book, the assimilation of logic and psychology, a view which he called "psychologism." Psychologism is now rejected; the foundations of logic and mathematics are not to be found in psychology, for psychology is an empirical science. Logic and mathematics are a priori sciences. Philosophy, too, is a priori, dealing with rational concepts and necessary truths. Later, in an essay called "Philosophie als strenge Wissenschaft" (1910), Husserl generalized this new conception of philosophy by attacking "naturalism"—the claim that statements in the existing sciences are premises in philosophic argument—and "historicism"—the view that philosophic truths are not eternal truths but are relative to historical epochs. The second view had been defended by Dilthey and his followers.

The concept of philosophy as a science thus changes from philosophy as a part of empirical natural science to philosophy as an a priori, autonomous science. This science Husserl called "phenomenology" without knowing very clearly, at first, what that term meant to him. In the first edition of the *Logische Untersuchungen*, Husserl identified it with "descriptive psychology" in spite of his earlier polemic against psychologism. He soon realized that it was a mistake to use the word "psychology" to describe what he was doing and argued at length in "Philosophie als strenge Wissenschaft" that phenomenology and psychology must be distinguished. But he continued to insist that phenomenology is descriptive. This distinguishes the method of phenomenology, he thought, from the established practice of philosophy, which deduces what must be true of the world from prior assumptions instead of looking at the world and discovering what it is like. It is not altogether clear which other philosophers are genuinely open to this criticism; Husserl may well have been unfair to his predecessors. But his insistence that phenomenology is descriptive is another expression of the imperative that we must philosophize without presuppositions.

The second volume of the *Logische Untersuchungen* contained six separate essays concerned with concepts important in logic, such as "meaning" and "judgment." In these essays Husserl first discussed the concept of intentionality in detail. Following Brentano, he held that all mental acts are intentional. This means that a true description of a mental act—for example, "Husserl thought that all mental acts are intentional"—does not entail the existence or the truth of the intentional object, in this example, "mental acts are intentional." The doctrine of intentionality recognizes that all mental acts are, in principle, fallible.

Transcendental phenomenology. In the fifth essay of the *Logische Untersuchungen*, Husserl provided a description of the several elements of intentional acts. But what sort of descriptions are these? How are we to distinguish these phenomenological descriptions from ordinary psychological ones? In answer to this question, he introduced the "transcendental–phenomenological reduction" in a series of lectures entitled *Die Idee der Phänomenologie*

(1907). These lectures were not published, however, until after his death. The "reduction" first appeared in print in his lifetime in his *Ideen zu einer reinen Phänomenologie und phänomenologischen Philosophie* (1913). The transcendental-phenomenological reduction is a methodological device, required before one can begin to do phenomenology. Roughly, it is the transition from an ordinary, straightforward attitude toward the world and the objects in it to a reflective attitude. However, the precise nature of this device always remained an acute problem for Husserl.

Once we perform the reduction, Husserl claimed, we discover what he called the "transcendental ego," or "pure consciousness," for which everything that exists is an object. We discover that whatever is in the world is only as object for our pure consciousness. The task of describing the workings of this pure consciousness falls to the phenomenologist. Phenomenology is now characterized as the exploration and description of a realm of being, previously unsuspected, which is the absolute foundation of the experienced world, a realm of being, moreover, which is not accessible to empirical observation but only to phenomenological description and to something Husserl called "eidetic intuition."

Because the existence of the transcendental ego is indubitable, its discovery serves both to distinguish phenomenology from the empirical sciences and to provide the Archimedean point at which to begin our studies. These doctrines caused considerable stir, particularly among the members of the phenomenological movement, many of whom regarded them as regrettable lapses into metaphysics, a straying away from the primrose path of descriptive phenomenology.

For the next 10 or 15 years, Husserl held some rather extreme views on the transcendental ego. He said more than once that this ego would remain in existence even if the entire world were destroyed and that this ego is an individual entity, distinct from the self which is the object of my empirical self-observations or the observations of the psychologist. It sounds very much as if I had two selves, one of them the familiar empirical one, the other a transcendental and generally unknown one which would remain in existence even if my empirical self were destroyed together with the destruction of the world. One may well doubt that such a claim is supported by the description of phenomena.

True to his methodological maxims, Husserl refused to be discouraged by this sort of doubt. He was perfectly well aware of them; he continued to raise them himself, both in his later publications and in his unpublished notes. But true to the maxim that phenomenology describes and does not argue, he saw in these objections only a sign that the descriptions given of the transcendental ego so far were not adequate, and he tried to give better ones.

In the *Formale und transcendentale Logik* (1929) he still held that the transcendental ego exists "absolutely" and that all other things exist "relative" to it. But in his lectures given in 1935 and published under the title *Die Krisis der europäischen Wissenschaften und die transcendentale Phänomenologie* (Belgrade, 1936), the transcendental ego was said to be "correlative" to the world; it had lost its absolute status. Equally important is another change. The world is no longer said to be what it is for any transcendental individual but for an intersubjective community of individuals. The problem of the intersubjectivity of transcendental egos was first discussed in the *Cartesianische Meditationen*, which originated in a series of lectures given in Paris in 1929.

The concept of phenomenology now changed once again. Phenomenology was no longer the description of a separate realm of being but, rather, the reflection on and description of the ways in which our communal experience comes to be, what are the criteria for the coherence of different sorts of experiences and for their adequacy. Phenomenology no longer differed from the empirical sciences because it had a different subject from them but because it dealt with the world in a different way, the reflective, and reflected not on matters of fact but on the necessary conditions for coherence and adequacy of experience.

One other major change in the conception of phenomenology had occurred. Earlier, phenomenological reflection was to have provided the foundations of scientific knowledge (in a large sense of "scientific") by reflecting about scientific knowledge. Now Husserl distinguished sharply between the world as known to science and the world in which we live, the *Lebenswelt*. Scientific knowledge, he now believed, can be understood only if we first understand the *Lebenswelt*. The study of that lived world and of our experience of it becomes the first task of phenomenology.

Works by Husserl

Husserliana, Edmund Husserl, Gesammelte Werke. The Hague, 1950——. Nine volumes have been published thus far, and other volumes are in preparation. Vols. I–IX primarily contain unpublished writings and relevant working notes.

Philosophie der Arithmetik. Halle, Germany, 1891.

Logische Untersuchungen, 2 vols. Halle, Germany, 1900–1901. Translated by Hubert Elie as *Recherches logiques.* Paris, 1959–1963.

"Philosophie als strenge Wissenschaft." *Logos,* Vol. 1 (1910), 289–314. Translated by Quentin Lauer as "Philosophy as Rigorous Science," in Edmund Husserl, *Phenomenology and the Crisis of Philosophy.* New York, 1965.

Ideen zu einer reinen Phänomenologie und phänomenologischen Philosophie, Vol. I. Halle, Germany, 1913. Translated by W. R. Boyce Gibson as *Ideas—General Introduction to Pure Phenomenology.* London, 1931. The second and third volumes were published posthumously in *Husserliana, op. cit.,* Vols. IV–V (1952).

"Phenomenology," translated by C. V. Salmon in *Encyclopaedia Britannica,* 14th ed. Chicago, 1929. Vol. XVII, pp. 700–702.

Formale und transcendentale Logik. Halle, 1929. Translated by Suzanne Bachelard as *Logique formelle et logique transcendantale.* Paris, 1957.

Cartesianische Meditationen, in *Husserliana, op. cit.,* Vol. I (1950). Translated by Dorion Cairns as *Cartesian Meditations.* The Hague, 1960.

Die Krisis der europäischen Wissenschaften und die transcendentale Phänomenologie, in *Husserliana, op. cit.,* Vol. VI (1954).

Works on Husserl

Bachelard, Suzanne, *La Logique de Husserl.* Paris, 1957. An insightful and instructive commentary on Husserl's *Formale und transcendentale Logik* that contains some of the most intelligible statements about transcendental phenomenology.

Diemer, Alwin, *Edmund Husserl, Versuch einer systematischen Zusammenstellung seiner Phänomenologie.* Meisenheim am Glan, Germany, 1956.

Fink, Eugen, "Die phänomenologische Philosophie Edmund

Husserls in der gegenwärtigen Kritik." *Kantstudien,* Vol. 38 (1933), 319–383. A defense of Husserl against Neo-Kantian critics by Husserl's assistant. The article has Husserl's official approval.

Spiegelberg, Herbert, *The Phenomenological Movement,* 2 vols. The Hague, 1960. Discusses Husserl in Vol. I, pp. 73–167. Bibliography.

Szilasi, Wilhelm, *Einführung in die Phänomenologie Edmund Husserls.* Tübingen, Germany, 1959.

RICHARD SCHMITT

HUTCHESON, FRANCIS (1694–1746), moral-sense theorist, was born at Drumalig in County Down, Ulster. His father and grandfather were Presbyterian ministers. In 1711 he entered the University of Glasgow, taking both the arts and theological courses and probably finishing in 1717. He was licensed as a probationer preacher by the Ulster Presbyterians in 1719. Not long after, he was invited by the Presbyterians of Dublin to found a dissenting academy for their youth, and he remained in Dublin for the next ten years as head of the academy. His stay there was a turning point in the development of his thought, for he came under the influence of admirers of Shaftesbury's philosophy. Hutcheson's first two, and perhaps most important, books were published during this period. The University of Glasgow elected Hutcheson to its professorship of moral philosophy in 1730, a position which he held until his death. In 1746, while visiting Dublin, he contracted a fever and died.

At Glasgow, Hutcheson devoted himself to enriching the culture and softening the Calvinism of his fellow Presbyterians. The Presbytery of Glasgow tried him for teaching, in contravention to the Westminster Confession, the following "false and dangerous" doctrines: (*a*) that the standard of moral goodness is the promotion of the happiness of others and (*b*) that it is possible to have a knowledge of good and evil without, and prior to, a knowledge of God. Afterward, Hutcheson was able to speak of the matter as the "whimsical buffoonery" about his heresy, but the fact that the charges were brought is doubtless a measure of the effectiveness of his teaching. Hume sent a draft of Part III of *The Treatise of Human Nature,* "Of Morals," to Hutcheson for his comments prior to publication. Some indication of the spirit in which Hutcheson wrote his own work can be gathered from his rebuking Hume for a lack of warmth in the cause of virtue, which "all good men would relish, and could not displease among abstract enquiries."

The moral sense. Hutcheson's contributions to philosophy lie in aesthetics and moral philosophy. In the one he offers a theory of an internal sense by which we perceive beauty, and in the other he offers a theory of a moral sense by which we perceive and approve virtue and perceive and condemn vice. Hutcheson meant his theory of the moral sense to be a contribution to the contemporary discussion of how to analyze man's moral knowledge. There were two sides in the discussion. Clarke and his followers held that moral distinctions are made by reason on the basis of our knowledge of the unchanging and unchangeable fitness of things. The other side, owing its original allegiance to Shaftesbury, held that moral distinctions are the deliverances of a moral sense.

Both sides held two points in common. First, moral knowledge must be accounted for by showing how it can be acquired by the exercise of some human faculty. In this respect they were all Lockeans: if something is knowable, you must show how it can be perceived. Second, moral knowledge cannot be simply a revelation from God, though of course God may enter the picture indirectly by having endowed us with our moral faculty. And when it came to picking out actual instances of virtue and vice, both sides were in agreement about the value of benevolence and the wrongness of acts of violence against other persons. Their debate, then, was over the character of the moral faculty.

Perception and approval of virtue. Hutcheson plucked from Shaftesbury's rhapsodies the notion of a moral sense and endeavored to give a systematic account of it as the moral faculty of mankind. To see what Hutcheson's claim means, we must first of all consider what led him to make it. When you see someone doing something that is helpful to another, you say that his action is a virtuous one. But why is a helpful action counted as virtuous? It might be said that a helpful action is virtuous because it exhibits benevolence. But this does not take us very far, for we may still ask why benevolence is a criterion of virtue. Hutcheson knew the answer which some moral writers had given to this question: Helpfulness or benevolence is a possible relation between two human beings, and it is a fitting one. Therefore, it is virtuous. But how do you tell what is fitting and what is not? Your reason tells you. At this point, however, Hutcheson asked whether fittingness could be discovered by reason. After all, reason can tell us only that a certain relation does or does not exist; the moral quality of the relation, if any, remains to be apprehended. But by what? Certainly not by reason, Hutcheson argued, because the moral quality is not a relation. And if not by reason, then the only thing left is a sense: the moral sense.

Hutcheson's task was to offer an account of how the moral sense works. He located the moral sense on the map of Lockean psychology. Its deliverances are ideas of reflection which arise from our original perceptions of human actions. As he first described the moral sense, it is a determination of our minds "to receive amiable or disagreeable ideas of actions." The "amiable idea" or, as he sometimes spoke of it, "our determination to be pleased," has two jobs. It is both our perception of the virtue of an action and our approval of it. It so happens that those actions which we discern to be virtuous are always benevolent actions, and we are necessarily determined to discern their virtue as soon as we observe them. Hutcheson attributed both the connection between virtue and benevolence and our necessary perception of the virtuousness of benevolence to arrangements superintended by God. Like sight, the moral sense is universal in mankind. But just as some men are born blind, and others have defective sight, some men have no moral sense at all and others have defective moral senses.

The strength of Hutcheson's theory of the moral sense lies in his having given an account of how we know that benevolent actions are virtuous: they are virtuous because they please. He was careful to point out that they please irrespective of any advantage they may have to ourselves. He noticed that we may indeed perceive as virtuous an action that displeases us because it goes against our selfish interest, and we may desire that someone act in a certain way even though we should call it vicious. He also argued that in the first instance the moral sense works independently of education, custom, and example. These factors may strengthen the moral sense but cannot create it, for they really presuppose a moral sense. In order for a person to be given an education in morality, he must already be able to discern moral qualities. Similarly, in order for customs to be moral customs and for examples to be moral examples, morality must already have been discovered in order to give these factors a moral character.

In saying that virtue is what it is because it pleases, Hutcheson thought that he had given a completely satisfactory account of the nature of virtue. By means of the moral sense, virtue is perceived for what it is. It is an end to be sought for itself, and no further characterization of it is required. Hutcheson's critics, however, found that he had paid a disastrous price for making virtue comprehensible by the human understanding. If virtue is that which pleases, then must any action which pleases by virtuous? Why are the actions which exhibit benevolence the only ones that are counted as virtuous? These questions seem bound to be asked despite the stipulations with which Hutcheson hedged his account of our knowledge of virtue.

Both his theory and its difficulties stem from Hutcheson's tacit assumption of the Lockean guide that a piece of knowledge must be accounted for through an appeal to the faculty by which it is known. It was not open to Hutcheson to try the gambit that it would be logically odd to call an act of highway robbery, for example, virtuous. His first line of defense was to insist that the deliverances of the moral sense with respect to virtue are a distinctive kind of pleasure. But in later editions of his *Inquiry Concerning Moral Good and Evil,* Hutcheson played down the perceptual function and stressed approving and disapproving. Thus, the moral sense becomes a "determination of our minds to receive the simple ideas of approbation or condemnation, from actions observed . . . ." To call these ideas simple is to claim that they are not subject to further analysis and, hence, to further characterization. But this new position is not without its own difficulties. Approbation and condemnation are dispositions, not sensations; and only a most slavish allegiance to Locke's model of the mind could lead one to construe all mental acts as perceptions.

Motivation to virtuous action. Hutcheson's theory of the moral sense has yet a third part. As well as using it to account for the perception and approbation of virtue, he also used it to account for a person's motivation to behave in a virtuous way. A person pursues virtue because virtuous acts are pleasing to him and avoids vicious acts because they pain him. This account of moral motivation is perhaps the most convincing part of Hutcheson's theory. It enabled him to close the gap between someone's knowing what ways of acting are virtuous and his being inclined to act virtuously. Yet even here the theory gives us less than we might hope, for someone will be motivated to act benevolently only if benevolence pleases. And if other ways of acting please, even malevolence, perhaps, what then? Once more Hutcheson entered a stipulation too pat to be absolutely convincing: God has determined most men to be benevolent. Once again we must admit that he took this position for the best of reasons, for he was opposing those who would reduce all human motives to self-interest—and the many disinterested actions which people perform show the absurdity of this contention. But what Hutcheson's account of moral motivation requires is not the sensation of being pleased with benevolence but a disposition to be benevolent. Unfortunately, the psychological theory on which Hutcheson relied required him to reduce all mental phenomena to some sort of perception. Thus, his account of motives lacks an effective analysis of dispositions.

Aesthetics. Hutcheson's aesthetics closely parallels his theory of the moral sense. He found that we have an internal sense of beauty, a determination to be pleased by regular, harmonious, uniform objects, by grandeur, or by novelty. These perceptions occur necessarily and independently of our wills, but there is no corresponding "pain or disgust, any farther than what arises from disappointment." This limitation seems to have the curious consequence of leaving Hutcheson no room to account for perceptions of the ugly. The task of approving of the beautiful is not assigned to our sense of beauty. Presumably Hutcheson thought indifference to beauty allowable but indifference to virtue never so.

Role of passions and reason in moral life. Hutcheson's *Essay on the Nature and Conduct of the Passions and Affections* and *Illustrations Upon the Moral Sense* (published jointly in London, 1728) supplement the part of the *Inquiry* devoted to morals. In the essay on the passions, Hutcheson defined *sense* as every determination of the mind either to receive ideas independently of the will or to have perceptions of pleasure or pain. This definition led to the introduction of several new senses into Hutcheson's system. For instance, there is a public sense, which is our determination to be pleased by the happiness of others and to be uneasy at their misery. There is also the sense of honor, which makes the approbation or gratitude of others for any actions we have done the necessary occasion of pleasure.

In the *Illustrations Upon the Moral Sense,* Hutcheson's general aim was to characterize the role of reason in the moral life. With regard to actions, Hutcheson said that we may reason either to account for what excites someone to act as he does or to account for what justifies our approbation of an act. For example, we give the "exciting" reason when we account for a luxury-loving man's pursuit of money by pointing out that money may be used to purchase pleasures. We give the "justifying" reason when we account for our approving of a man's risking his life in war by pointing out that his conduct evidences public spirit. But it is never true that reasons are to be found independently of feelings, for "exciting" reasons presuppose instincts and affections, and "justifying" reasons presuppose the moral sense.

Supposing that we get our ideas of virtue and vice through a moral sense, Hutcheson acknowledged that there are certain truths which might be proved by reason. These are (1) what actions or affections obtain the approbation of any observer, and what actions or affections obtain condemnation; (2) what quality of actions gains approbation; (3) what actions really evidence kind affections and tend to the greatest public good; and (4) what motives excite men to publicly useful actions.

Bibliography

Hutcheson first presented his philosophy in the *Inquiry into the Original of Our Ideas of Beauty and Virtue* (London, 1725). The *Inquiry* is divided into two parts: "Concerning Beauty, Order, Harmony, Design" and "Concerning Moral Good and Evil." It is a much-revised work, the most notable changes occurring in the fourth edition (Glasgow, 1738). L. A. Selby-Bigge, ed., *The British Moralists* (Oxford, 1897), Vol. I, reproduces a substantial part of the second edition of the "Inquiry Concerning Moral Good and Evil," which taken by itself is an incomplete representation of Hutcheson's thought. In *A Short Introduction to Moral Philosophy* (Glasgow, 1747), an English version of the *Philosophiae Moralis Institutio Compendiaria* (Glasgow, 1742), Hutcheson uses "conscience" interchangeably with "moral sense," a possible sign of Butler's influence. Hutcheson is also the author of *A System of Moral Philosophy*, published posthumously in two volumes (London, 1755) by his son Francis. The *System* contains a biography by William Leechman. Other works by Hutcheson are *Metaphysical Synopsis* (Glasgow, 1742) and *Logical Compendium* (Glasgow, 1756).

For Hume's letters to Hutcheson, see J. Y. T. Greig, ed., *The Letters of David Hume* (Oxford, 1932), Vol. I.

Contemporary criticism may be found in *Letters Concerning the True Foundation of Virtue or Moral Goodness, wrote in Correspondence between Mr. Gilbert Burnet and Mr. Francis Hutcheson*, edited by Hutcheson (Glasgow, 1772), first published in the *London Journal* (1728).

Biographical and analytical material is contained in W. R. Scott, *Francis Hutcheson* (Cambridge, 1900); Ernest Albee, *History of English Utilitarianism* (London, 1902); and T. Fowler, *Shaftesbury and Hutcheson* (London, 1882).

For critical discussions, see James Bonar, *Moral Sense* (London, 1930), and D. D. Raphael, *The Moral Sense* (Oxford, 1947).

ELMER SPRAGUE

HUXLEY, THOMAS HENRY (1825–1895), biologist and the most versatile man of science of nineteenth-century England. He was born at Ealing, near London. Like many eminent Victorians, Huxley was self-educated. While still an adolescent he read extensively in history and philosophy, learned several foreign languages, and began a medical apprenticeship. In 1842 he entered Charing Cross Hospital, where he distinguished himself by winning prizes in chemistry, anatomy, and physiology, and by publishing his first research paper. From 1846 to 1850 he was assistant surgeon on H.M.S. *Rattlesnake* while it conducted surveying operations in Australian waters. Huxley made capital out of this voyage, as Darwin had done on the voyage of the *Beagle*, and sent home a number of scientific papers dealing with marine animals. These papers established his reputation as a first-rate biologist, and in 1851 he was elected a fellow of the Royal Society. After leaving the navy he settled in London, where he eventually obtained several small appointments, the chief one being that of naturalist at the Government School of Mines. Here he began his paleontological investigations, which resulted in more than twenty memoirs on the anatomy and classification of fossils. During the next four decades Huxley became one of the intellectual leaders of England. His strong, skeptical, earnest mind was enlisted on behalf of a great variety of causes. He championed Darwin's theory of evolution, disputed with churchmen about the Bible, worked for educational reforms, served on eight royal commissions, and refused a professorship at Oxford. As a public lecturer he was brilliant at clarifying abstruse subjects and developing polemical arguments. He also wrote copiously in forceful, eloquent prose. Yet he produced no really seminal ideas or *magnum opus*, partly because his efforts were so dispersed. In the following discussion, attention will be limited his views on the nature of science, metaphysics, ethics, and religion.

The nature of science. For Huxley, two aspects of the sciences were of special importance. One was their historical continuity with modes of thought used by men in the ordinary commerce of life. "Science," he once said, "is nothing but trained and organized common sense, differing from the latter only as a veteran may differ from a raw recruit . . . . The man of science, in fact, simply uses with scrupulous exactness the methods which we all habitually use carelessly" (*Collected Essays*, Vol. III, pp. 45–46). Hence there is a unity of procedure in all the sciences. This was the other aspect of the sciences which he deemed important, because it allowed a specification to be given of the steps that must be taken if the procedure is to be properly carried out. In an essay of 1854, "On the Educational Value of the Natural History Sciences" (*Collected Essays*, Vol. III), Huxley listed the steps as: (1) observation of the facts, including those elicited by experiment; (2) comparison and classification, leading to general propositions; (3) deduction from the general propositions to the facts again; and (4) verification. Later he came to see that hypotheses are essential to the procedure of science, especially as devices for "anticipating nature." But he did not sufficiently stress the connection between a hypothesis and the scientific problem that initiates an inquiry, or the role of the hypothesis in determining what facts are to be observed.

Evolution. It was the effective use of scientific method in Darwin's *Origin of Species* that helped to convert Huxley to the doctrine of evolution by natural selection. As a young man he had held antievolutionary views, not because he believed in the special creation of species, but because he failed to find a scientific explanation of how their transmutation could have been effected. Darwin's book proved to be "a flash of light which, to a man who has lost himself in a dark night, suddenly reveals a road that, whether it takes him straight home or not, certainly goes his way" (*Life and Letters of T. H. Huxley*, Vol. I, pp. 245–246). His reflection on having mastered Darwin's central thesis was, "How exceedingly stupid not to have thought of that."

Huxley espoused Darwinism not as a dogma, however, but as a "most ingenious hypothesis" which offered a rational account of how the organic world came to be what it is. The hypothesis was not contradicted by any known evidence, nor was it seriously rivaled; yet it was not established beyond a shadow of doubt. For instance, certain physiological peculiarities of organisms, such as hybrid sterility, had still to be explained in terms of natural selection. To Huxley, some of Darwin's formulations seemed quite unsatisfactory. To speak of variations "arising spontaneously" was to employ "a conveniently erroneous phrase." To commit oneself to the principle *natura non facit saltum* ("nature makes no leap") was to invite needless trouble. For in fact, Huxley declared, "Nature does make jumps now and then, and a recognition of this is of no small importance in disposing of many minor objections to the doctrine of transmutation" (*Collected Essays*, Vol. II, p. 77). But even if it remained to be shown that natural selection sufficed for the production of species, "few can doubt that it is a very important factor in this operation." To that extent Darwinism was certainly here to stay.

Huxley was sensitive to a number of philosophical questions generated by the theory of evolution. The questions which particularly interested him arose when three considerations were taken seriously. First, like all scientific theories, Darwinism "starts with certain postulates . . . and the validity of these postulates is a problem of metaphysics." Second, the theory of evolution had to be extended to the cosmos as a whole, if its scope was not to be arbitrarily restricted. But at that point philosophical issues had to be faced. Did the cosmos evolve from some "epicurean chance-world," or had its order been eternally the same? Finally, the study of organisms pointed to the conclusion that they began as, and are now, physicochemical systems. It could therefore be assumed that molecular motions are the basis of all vital processes, including so-called "conscious" ones. But if this was so, metaphysical materialism gained strong support.

Metaphysics and epistemology. The philosophical standpoint most congenial to Huxley was derived from his reading of Descartes, Berkeley, and Hume. Of prime importance was the contention "that our certain knowledge does not extend beyond states of consciousness, or the phenomena of mind. . . . Our sensations, our pleasures, our pains, and the relations of these, make up the sum total of the elements of positive, unquestionable knowledge" (*Collected Essays*, Vol. VI, pp. 317–318). Beyond this we have only uncertain inferences or beliefs. Hence, when we talk about "matter" and "the physical world," we are interpreting some mental phenomena, just as we are interpreting other phenomena when we talk about "mind" and "the self." For matter is only a postulated cause of certain conscious states, in the same way that mind is a postulated substratum of those same states. This is all that criticism leaves of "the idols set up by the spurious metaphysics of vulgar common sense."

Huxley expressed many of his philosophical ideas in a book on Hume that he wrote for the English Men of Letters series in 1878. He agreed with Hume's account of perception as a process which yields only sense impressions, but he held that Hume had failed "to recognize the elementary character of impressions of relation" and also had failed to make clear that having a sense impression is a case of knowing. Hume had correctly represented the order of nature as an unbroken succession of causes and effects, so that there can be no uncaused volitions such as proponents of "free will" postulate. But determinism, Huxley affirmed, is entirely compatible with ascribing responsibility to human beings for their deliberate actions. As Hume had rightly understood, "the very idea of responsibility implies the belief in the necessary connexion of certain actions with certain states of mind" (*Collected Essays*, Vol. VI, p. 222).

Metaphysical presuppositions of science. From this philosophical standpoint, Huxley dealt with questions which fall under the three considerations mentioned above. Science, he affirmed, postulates a rational order of nature, the operation of material forces, the universality of causation, and the immutable necessity of laws. All these factors need to be properly interpreted. Thus, "nature" is simply the totality of phenomena, whose regular occurrence constitutes nature's "rational order." Material forces are at best hypothetical entities which Huxley said he could not conceive clearly. As Hume had insisted, "causation" refers to the relation of invariable succession among phenomena. "Necessity" is a term which should be limited to logic and has no warranted application to the physical world. For the laws which science formulates are records of observed regularities, not agents which "force" things to happen as they do. Hence, "our highest and surest generalizations remain on the level of justifiable expectations, that is, very high probabilities." The quest for certainty in science is an irrational pursuit.

Agnosticism. It is also irrational to hope that we can ever know anything about the ultimate origin or ultimate nature of the universe. Speculation about such matters is fruitless, for they lie outside the limits of philosophical inquiry. To identify his position on this issue, Huxley coined the name "agnostic" about 1869. "It came into my head," he said, "as suggestively antithetical to the 'gnostic' of Church history, who professed to know so much about the very things of which I was ignorant" (*Life and Letters of T. H. Huxley*, Vol. I, p. 462). Agnosticism, however, is not another creed; it is an outlook which results from the adoption of a principle, at once intellectual and moral, which states that a man ought not to assert that he knows a proposition to be true unless he can produce adequate evidence to support it. Conversely, an agnostic repudiates as immoral "the doctrine that there are propositions which men ought to believe without logically satisfactory evidence." The justification of this principle lies in the success which follows upon its application, whether in the field of natural or of human history.

Because of an agnostic's outlook, he cannot accept the tenets of metaphysical materialism, according to which nothing exists in the world save matter, force, and necessity. For these three concepts are intelligible only insofar as they are related to the phenomena of mind. Hence, "Materialism is as utterly devoid of justification as the most baseless of theological dogmas." Yet to reject materialism is by no means to espouse idealism or spiritualism. "Spiritualism is, after all, little better than Materialism turned upside down" (*Collected Essays,* Vol. IX, p. 133). Nor does it follow that the sciences must eschew materialistic language. On the contrary, such language is often useful in investigating the order of nature, as Huxley himself showed in more than one paper. But to use materialistic language for scientific purposes is quite different from accepting a metaphysics based on materialism.

Epiphenomenalism. As a biologist, Huxley took the view that the bodies of animals, including man, are best regarded as mechanical systems. Yet the mind and states of consciousness undeniably exist, and their relation to the working of the physical body has to be explained. This was the question Huxley discussed in a well-known paper of 1874, "On the Hypothesis that Animals are Automata." States of consciousness are represented as being no more than effects of bodily processes—chiefly, the molecular changes in brain substance that has attained a certain degree of organization. Furthermore, no evidence can be found for supposing "that any state of consciousness is the cause of change in the motion of the matter of the organism." Animals, then, are conscious automata. The working of their bodily mechanism is unaffected by their mental activity. "The mind stands related to the body as the bell of the clock to the works, and consciousness answers to the sound which the bell gives out when it is struck." This is Huxley's version of epiphenomenalism. The doctrine did not purport to give an ultimate explanation of the mind–body relationship. It did not even purport to explain how the passage from molecular movement to conscious states is effected. Concerning the details of this passage, he declared, "I really know nothing and never hope to know anything."

Religion. The greatest impact of Huxley's agnosticism was on the religious dogmas of his time. As a young man he accepted a form of theism. In a paper of 1856, "On Natural History as Knowledge, Discipline, and Power" (*Royal Institution Proceedings*, London, Vol. II, 1854–1858, pp. 187–195), he contended that the design revealed by nature pointed to the existence of an Infinite Mind as its author. But he discarded this view when he became a Darwinian, on the ground that the argument from design had received its deathblow. Thenceforth, he attacked those who claimed to prove that a supernatural God exists, or who affirmed that Biblical and Christian doctrines are rationally credible. His most dramatic clash was with Bishop Wilberforce at the Oxford meeting of the British Association in June 1860, and his most protracted controversy was with W. E. Gladstone in the pages of the *Nineteenth Century*, from 1885 to 1891. Neither of these defenders of the faith was a match for Huxley.

Miracles. Huxley hammered away at the inconsistencies in, and the lack of evidence for, the Biblical cosmology, the creation stories, and the belief in demons, spirits, and miraculous occurrences which Christianity requires. The subject of miracles was of deep interest to him; miracles could not be rejected as impossible, he thought, because they are logically conceivable. Hence Hume's a priori reasoning against them was mistaken. Yet one can say that the occurrence of an alleged miracle, being antecedently a most improbable event, needs strong supporting evidence. But in each recorded case, evidence of this kind was lacking. In several essays Huxley discussed particular Biblical reports of miracles and found them unconvincing.

God. Although he rejected supernaturalism, Huxley was prepared to accept a Spinozistic conception of God as being identical with nature in its infinite complexity. "The God so conceived is one that only a very great fool would deny, even in his heart. Physical science is as little Atheistic as it is Materialistic" (*Collected Essays*, Vol. IX, p. 140). Once, in a letter to Kingsley, he said that he believed in "the Divine Government" of the universe. The phrase expressed his conviction that the cosmic process is rational rather than random, that the reign of law is universal, and that the order of nature has existed "throughout all duration." Yet the governing principles of the universe appear to be amoral, since what happens to men is "accompanied by pleasures and pains, the incidence of which, in the majority of cases, has not the slightest reference to moral desert" (*Collected Essays*, Vol. IX, p. 202).

Ethics. Toward the close of his life Huxley thought a good deal about the foundations of morality. He was dissatisfied with the attempts of Darwin and Spencer to harmonize man's moral sentiments and the theory of evolution. It was not that he doubted the evolutionary origin of those sentiments; what he doubted was whether Darwin or Spencer had appreciated the extent to which morality and nature are at war with each other. This was the theme with which he startled the Victorian world in his famous Romanes lecture, "Evolution and Ethics" (*Collected Essays*, Vol. IX, pp. 46–116), on May 18, 1893.

Its central contention is that "ethical nature, while born of cosmic nature, is necessarily at enmity with its parent." For a dominant feature of the natural world is "the intense and unceasing competition of the struggle for existence." Hobbes's depiction of nature as the war of all against all is correct. In this world, ruthless and predatory action is "best" for the individual. But in human society, "ape and tiger methods" are precisely what man's moral sense condemns. Hence, the practice of that which is *morally* best involves a repudiation of "the gladiatorial theory of existence" portrayed by Darwinism: "Let us understand, once for all, that the ethical progress of society depends, not on imitating the cosmic process, still less in running away from it, but in combating it." Accordingly, man although himself a product of evolution, has an obligation to subjugate the amoral or immoral aspects of evolution to moral ends. Yet Huxley's grounds for this conclusion are by no means clear. His only recourse was to fall back on a kind of ethical intuitionism which is hardly compatible with his other views.

The philosophical garment that Huxley wove is coarsely textured and has a number of loose ends. Thus his radical phenomenalism is not carefully interwoven with his evolutionism, and his agnosticism seems unconnected with his Spinozistic affirmations. Yet his grasp of philosophical issues was remarkable for a man who was also a leading scientist, educator, and public figure of his time.

Works by Huxley

Man's Place in Nature. London, 1864.
Hume. London, 1879.
Collected Essays, 9 vols. London, 1893–1894.
Scientific Memoirs, 5 vols. London, 1898–1903.
Life and Letters of Thomas Henry Huxley, 2d ed., 3 vols. Leonard Huxley, ed. London, 1903.

Works on Huxley

Mitchell, P. Chalmers, *Thomas Henry Huxley*. New York, 1900.
Davis, J. R. A., *Thomas Henry Huxley*. London and New York, 1907.
Peterson, Houston, *Huxley, Prophet of Science*. New York, 1932.
Bibby, Cyril. *T. H. Huxley: Scientist, Humanist, Educator*. London and New York, 1959.
Irvine, William, *Thomas Henry Huxley*. London, 1960.

T. A. Goudge

HYLOZOISM. See Panpsychism.

I

IAMBLICHUS (born in mid-third century, died within last ten years of Constantine's reign, 312–337) taught philosophy, apparently in Syria. Only short extracts of his more substantial philosophical works have survived. Although in general he maintained the system of Plotinus and Porphyry, his character and environment drew him with less detachment than they to various gnostic and magical practices which, like Platonic philosophy, were supposed to achieve salvation (see *De Mysteriis*, almost certainly authentic). Describing these practices as theurgic virtues, he placed them above the virtues of the intellect, which had been highest in the scale for Porphyry. For more than two centuries an authority for all Neoplatonists, Iamblichus was known by them as "the divine," in the sense of "inspired." It is quite wrong to think of him, however, as the man who betrayed philosophy to Oriental superstition and mysticism.

The beginnings of the extraordinary systematization of Neoplatonism that characterizes the Athenian school of Proclus can be traced to Iamblichus. He divided the second hypostasis (in this order) as Intellect qua intelligible—that is, objects of thought or Being—and qua intellectual—that is, acts of thought or Intelligence. More fundamentally, he introduced or made explicit the so-called imparticipables: everything substantial, whether an ordinary genus or species or one of the hypostases themselves, existed, according to him, not merely as "participated" (a Platonic form as commonly represented in the dialogues) and as "participant" (a particular instance of some property) but as "unparticipated" or "imparticipable"; participated forms were related to their imparticipables only as "proceeding" from them or "illuminated" ("irradiated") by them. He was combining Plato's account of universals, in which "participation" conflicts with the substantiality of the forms, and the Pythagoreans' assimilation of the genus–species relation to the generation of a number series from some first term.

All this helped to make room for the self-subsistent levels of reality by which Iamblichus hoped to resist Porphyry's overly monistic version of Plotinus. He insisted particularly that soul was distinct from intellect and human souls from pure souls. In his influential commentary (now lost) on the *De Anima* he maintained that Aristotle's work could be accepted by Platonists because its subject, the soul which was inseparable from a body, was only the "proceeding" soul. This was an important step in the separation of psychology from metaphysics.

Bibliography

De Mysteriis is edited by G. Parthey (Berlin, 1857); there is an English translation by A. Wilder (Greenwich, Conn., 1911, 1915) and a German translation, with notes by T. Hopfner (Leipzig, 1922). The minor works are in the Teubner classics, and further extracts are in Stobaeus, *Florilegium*, edited by C. Wachsmuth and O. Hense (Berlin, 1884–1912). See also Eunapius, *Lives of the Sophists* (London and New York, 1922); Proclus, *Elements of Theology*, edited and translated by E. R. Dodds, 2d ed. (Oxford, 1963); and E. Zeller, *Philosophie der Griechen*, 3d ed. (Leipzig, 1882) or a later edition, Part III, Sec. 2.

A. C. LLOYD

IBN BĀJJA, Abū-Bakr Muḥammad ibn Yaḥyā ibn al-Sāyigh, Islamic philosopher, known to the medieval Scholastics as Avempace, was born in Saragossa at the end of the fifth century H., eleventh century A.D., and died in Fez, Morocco, in 533 H./A.D. 1138. During his brief life he endured the tribulations occasioned by the Christian "reconquest" of Andalusia. It is known that he wrote several commentaries on Aristotle's treatises and that he was very learned in medicine, mathematics, and astronomy. He was involved in the quarrel initiated by the Peripatetics, during which al-Bīṭrogī, whom the Scholastics called Alpetragius, distinguished himself. Ibn Bājja opposed his own hypotheses to Ptolemy's system.

Ibn Bājja's philosophical works have remained incomplete, notably the treatise that gained him his reputation, *Tadbīr al-motawaḥḥid* ("The Rule of the Solitary"). For a considerable length of time this treatise was known only through a detailed analysis of it in Hebrew by Moses of Narbonne (fourteenth century) in his commentary on the *Ḥayy ibn Yaqzān* of Ibn Ṭufayl, the pupil of Ibn Bājja. Salomon Munk based his account of Ibn Bājja on this analysis. The Arabic original (now in the Bodleian Library at Oxford) was rediscovered by Miguel Asin Palacios.

The work's central theme is that of an *itinerarium* leading the man-spirit to unite itself with the Active Intellect ('*Aql fa"al, Intellegentia agens*). He who speaks of a "rule" or "discipline" assumes a mode of life regulated by actions demanding reflection, and this can be found only in the solitary man. This is why the solitary man's discipline should be the model for a member of the perfect City and the ideal State. The ideal State, it must be noted, is not the result of a priori conceptions, nor can it come into being by a political *coup d'état*; much more than a mere "social" reform, it is the fruit of a reform of customs that seeks to realize the fullness of human existence in each individual. For the time being, the solitary individuals live in imperfect states, with neither judge nor doctor except God. Their task is to become members of the perfect City. In order to found the regime of these individuals it is necessary at first to analyze and classify human actions, using the forms that they strive to fulfill as the point of departure.

For this reason the treatise is presented essentially as a "theory of spiritual forms," a sketch of the phenomenology of the spirit. The spirit progressively evolves from forms engaged in matter to forms that have been abstracted from it. Having then become intelligible in act, these forms thereby attain the level of intellect in act, reaching the level of pure spiritual forms, those forms that, inasmuch as they exist for the Active Intellect, have not had to pass from power to act.

Ibn Bājja imposed upon Islamic philosophy in Spain a completely different orientation than did Ghazālī. The motives of the solitary individual, of the stranger, and of the *allogène*, however, merge with the motives typical of the mystical gnosis in Islam. The same type of spiritual man is realized in these individuals, although their perception of the common goal differs and thereby the choice that determines their course. One of these courses in Spain was that of Ibn Masarra, which was continued by Ibn 'Arabi. Another was that of Ibn Bājja, later continued by Averroës.

Bibliography

Ibn Bājja's *Tadbīr al-motawahhid* has been edited and translated into Spanish by Miguel Asín Palacios as *Avempace, El régimen del solitario* (Madrid and Granada, 1946); the first section has been translated into English by D. M. Dunlop in *Journal of the Royal Asiatic Society* (1945), 61–81.

For discussions of Ibn-Bājja's philosophy, see Henry Corbin, *Histoire de la philosophie islamique*, Vol. I (paperback, Paris, 1964), pp. 317–325; S. H. Masumi, *Ibn Bajjah's 'Ilm al-Nafs* (Karachi, 1961); and Salomon Munk, *Mélanges de philosophie juive et arabe* (Paris, 1859; new ed., Paris, 1955).

HENRY CORBIN

IBN-GABIROL, SOLOMON BEN JUDAH (c. 1021–1058 or 1070), was first mentioned by Sā'd the Qadi of Toledo (c. 1029–1070), who claimed that ibn-Gabirol lived in Saragossa, was a keen student of philosophy, especially logic, and died sometime around A.D. 1058, after he had passed the age of 30. The Andalusian Jewish poet Moses ibn-Ezra (c. 1060–1139) claimed that ibn-Gabirol was born in Malaga and reared in Saragossa and spent a short but fruitful life in the service of philosophy and poetry. The Jewish philosopher Abraham ibn-Daud (c. 1110–1180) said that ibn-Gabirol died in 1070, but 1058 is more generally accepted.

The tone of some of ibn-Gabirol's secular songs, gloomy and bitter, is sometimes considered an indication of his unhappy lot—orphaned at an early age, poor, and ostracized by many of his contemporaries because of his irasci-

ble disposition and unorthodox philosophy. He did find some favor with Yequtiel ben Ishaq ibn-Hasan, a veritable Maecenas, at the court in Saragossa, and later with his patron, Samuel ibn-Nagrella, at the court of Zirid in Granada. Most, if not all, of this patronage seems to have resulted from his reputation as the greatest Jewish poet of his time in the West.

There are some four hundred extant secular and religious poems attributed to ibn-Gabirol. One, *The Kingly Crown*, has become a part of the Sephardic Jewish liturgy for the Day of Atonement. Its rhythmical, rhymed simplicity gives it a distinct Biblical flavor. In this poem of forty stanzas, ibn-Gabirol celebrated the divine attributes, the last of which is Will, so prominent in his philosophical work *The Fountain of Life*, and the wonders of creation, reminiscent of an Aristotelian–Ptolemaic world view. He concluded with an Augustinian self-analysis, marked by confession, penitence, and supplication.

In addition to his work in poetry, an anthology of ethical and sapiential sayings, *Choice of Pearls*, is attributed to him, but its authenticity is doubted by some.

Ibn-Gabirol's *The Improvement of the Moral Qualities* exists in one known Arabic text and four Hebrew versions, as well as in translations into other languages. The ethical aspect of ibn-Gabirol's philosophy is interesting because it appears to be an early, if not the first, attempt to systematize the basic principles of medieval Jewish ethics independently of religious dogma, ritual, or belief. The impulses of the human soul and how they can be trained to virtue or permitted to fall into vice are explained in relation to the five external senses, which are in turn explained by the four-element, or simple-body, theory of Aristotle. Stephen S. Wise claimed that "Gabirol's object is to establish a system of purely physio-psychological ethics." Certainly it is true that his interest was mainly in the animal rather than the rational soul. He emphasized the virtuous order that can be achieved *in* the external senses under the direction of the rational soul. In his treatment of the virtues and vices, ibn-Gabirol did refer to Biblical writings, but in a superficial and summary way, as a support of his own allegorical–poetic viewpoint.

It was not until nearly the end of the first half of the nineteenth century that Salomon Munk showed conclusively that ibn-Gabirol, the great Jewish poet, was the same man as Avicebrol, the recognized author of *The Fountain of Life*. An examination of the abstracts translated into Hebrew from the original Arabic by Shem Tob Falaquera in the thirteenth century and attributed to ibn-Gabirol showed substantial agreement with related passages of the *Fons Vitae* attributed to Avicebrol by the twelfth-century translators John of Spain (ibn-Daud, Avendehut) and Dominic Gundissalin. In the text of *The Fountain of Life* are found references to two other works by ibn-Gabirol, "The Treatise on *Esse*," Book 5.8, and the book of the Will, which is entitled "*Origo Largitatis et Causa Essendi*," Book 5.40. Unfortunately, these works cannot be found or identified. They may constitute, with *The Fountain*, the three parts of Wisdom: knowledge of matter and form (*The Fountain*), knowledge of Will (*The Origo*), and knowledge of the First Essence (*De Esse*). *The Fountain* is like the ethical work in its purely rational approach but differs in its complete lack of references to the Bible, the Talmud, or the Midrash. It is a treatise in the strict philosophical area of Neoplatonism as related to an eleventh-century Jewish mind. In it we find a Neoplatonic universe dependent on the Will of the First Author, supreme and holy.

The Fountain of Life, though composed in a dialogue form involving master and pupil, has none of the beauty and charm of the dramatic dialogues of Plato, the only other person mentioned by name in the work. The pupil seems to be a fictitious straight man, asking the proper questions at the proper time and giving a verbal nod of the head when appropriate. The opening section tells us that the discussion concerns the first part of Wisdom, the science of universal matter and universal form. Because of the nature of the topics involved, the work falls neatly into five parts:

(1) What we must presuppose in order to assign universal matter and form and predicate them of composite substances.

(2) The substance upholding the corporeity of the world.

(3) The acceptance of simple substances, such as the separated intelligences (i.e., angels).

(4) The science of understanding matter and form in simple substances.

(5) Universal matter and universal form in themselves.

The general method followed in this dialectical investigation is a search for the nature and existence of certain properties, which when found reveal the existence of the being that has these properties. In things we find there is something that "exists in itself," "is of one nature," is the "vehicle of diversity," and "gives everything its essence and name." These are the properties of universal matter. If one abstracts every sensible and intelligible form from things, the remainder is the common denominator called universal matter. Universal form is found "to subsist in another," "to perfect the essence of that in which it is," and "to give it being." By inspecting universal and particular sensible things, one finds four grades of matter and form: artificial-particular matter and its appropriate form, natural-particular matter (the matter of art products) and its form, natural-universal matter and its form, and celestial matter (the matter of the simple intelligences) and its form. Hence, there are common denominators for both matter and form: universal matter and universal form.

Every reality, except the First Essence, when viewed with its form is called a substance; when one conceives of something as receptive of form, then it is called matter, or hyle. Sensible forms require an extended substrate or body. The corporeal body is formed out of matter (which is itself incorporeal) and the corporeity-form, quantity. The first and simplest form and the highest matter are those that when united constitute the Intelligence. The Intelligence is the highest existence next to the First Essence. Below this are the rest of the hylomorphically composed souls—rational, sensitive, and vegetative—and then nature, the foundation of all inorganic things. Nature serves as the matter for the corporeity-form, quantity; the resulting substance is the matter of sensible qualities, like color.

One might say that ibn-Gabirol's universal hylomorphism represents an intermediate between the universal formlessness of Augustine and the later Franciscan variations. There are many differences from, as well as similarities to, scholastic thought, but the influence of Jewish religious ideas provides a basis for creation in his Neoplatonic universe. It seems that the Neoplatonic element in his thinking led ibn-Gabirol to consider the origin of all things as a necessary emanation from the First Author. But the Jewish element may have rebelled against this, as a necessary emanation would be in conflict with the absolute transcendence of God. The solution results in an intuitive view of the relation of all things to the First Author. This relation is necessary because matter is an expression of the essence of God, who is himself necessary. However, the dynamism of the Will of God leads to the need for a variety of forms that are initiated by God. Hence, the relation is voluntary and therefore free. In *The Fountain of Life* we have at times a strange mixture of Jewish religious ideas, Arabian Aristotelianism, and Alexandrine Neoplatonism, though we cannot be absolutely sure of the source of the ingredients because of the absence of definite historical information.

Solomon ibn-Gabirol's direct influence in philosophy seems to have been confined to certain Franciscans of the Augustinian tradition in the thirteenth and fourteenth centuries. They thought that ibn-Gabirol's universal hylomorphism supplied them with a suitable philosophical way of expressing the difference between creatures and God. The universal principle of limitation—namely, matter—becomes spiritual matter in all other creatures.

Works by ibn-Gabirol

Choice of Pearls, translated by A. Cohen. Library of Jewish Classics, IV. New York, 1925.

"'Fons Vitae' ex Arabico in Latinum Translatus ab Johanne Hispano et Dominico Gundissalino. Ex Codicibus Parisinis, Amploniano, Columbino," Clemens Bäumker, ed., in *Beiträge zur Geschichte der Philosophie des Mittelalters*, Band I, Hefte 2–4. Münster, 1892–1895.

The Fountain of Life, translated by H. E. Wedeck, Introduction by T. E. James. New York, 1962.

The Improvement of the Moral Qualities, translated by Stephen S. Wise. Columbia University Oriental Studies Publications, 1. New York, 1902.

The Kingly Crown, translated by Bernard Lewis. London, 1961.

Munk, S., *Mélanges de philosophie juive et arabe*. Paris, 1859. Includes French translation of *Fons Vitae*.

Works on ibn-Gabirol

Brunner, Fernand, *La Source de vie*, Book III. Paris, 1950.

Guttmann, Jacob, *Die Philosophie des Salomon ibn Gabirol*. Göttingen, 1889.

Kaufmann, David, *Studien über Salomon ibn Gabirol*. Budapest, 1899.

Gilson, Étienne, *History of Christian Philosophy in the Middle Ages*. New York, 1955.

Ueberweg, Friedrich, *Grundriss der Geschichte der Philosophie*, Vol. II, 11th ed., B. Geyer, ed. Berlin, 1928.

THEODORE E. JAMES

IBN-KHALDŪN, AB-AR-RAHMAN (1332–1406), Muslim statesman, historian, philosopher of history, sociologist, and political thinker of the fourteenth century, is probably the greatest creative genius produced by Muslim civilization. To Toynbee, ibn-Khaldūn's philosophy of history "is undoubtedly the greatest work of its kind that has ever yet been created by any mind in any time or place."

Ibn-Khaldūn was born in Tunis into a family of southern Arabian origin that had immigrated to Andalusia in the eighth century. With the decline of Muslim rule in Spain the family immigrated to northwest Africa, establishing itself first in Morocco and then in Tunisia. Muslim emigrants from Spain constituted an aristocracy in the Maghreb, and the Khaldūn family won fame in scholarship and statesmanship.

Ibn-Khaldūn surpassed the achievements of all the members of his family. Brought up in the traditional religious sciences and the philosophical–rational sciences which formed the two major streams of Islamic culture, he studied the Qur'ān, Arabic, traditions, jurisprudence, logic, and philosophy under several of the best scholars of his time and studied, taught, and occupied high positions in Tunis, Algeria, Morocco, southern Spain, and Egypt.

Medieval Muslim rulers were eager to enlist scholars either for government service or for the prestige that goes with their presence in the court. Ibn-Khaldūn enjoyed all the privileges of princely positions and suffered the odds of their fluctuations in medieval courts. He shared in the political maneuvers and conspiracies which accompanied the rise and fall of different rulers, and in trying periods, when he was in prison or was forced into exile, he devoted himself to the study of power and meditated on its historic laws and social dynamics.

Ibn-Khaldūn's greatest work, *Al-Muqaddimah* ("The Prolegomena"), was the first of seven volumes, written mostly from 1315 to 1318, of his universal history of the Arabs and Berbers, *Kitab al-'Ibar*. Although the last two volumes are of special value to historians as the best source for the history of northwest Africa, especially for the history of the Berbers, the introduction which outlines ibn-Khaldūn's philosophy of history overshadowed the narrative. The philosophic originality of this introduction was so great that ibn-Khaldūn became known as the author of *Al-Muqaddimah.*

Prior to ibn-Khaldūn, Muslim philosophers had concerned themselves with the reconciliation of Qur'ānic truth and rational truth, but this had led to an assimilation of Greek rationalism by Muslim theology rather than to the emergence of Muslim rationalism. The concern with religion and philosophy penetrated all Muslim disciplines— law, history, and the like. By the fourteenth century this method, which had its religious origins in the Qur'ān and the traditions of the Prophet and its philosophic origins in Greek rationalism, had reached its height.

Ibn-Khaldūn was an accomplished student of Muslim learning, but witnessing the decline of Muslim power and metaphysics, he decided to seek the concrete causes of this decline. History rather than metaphysics gave the answers to his questions about the changes in Islam's fortunes.

Ibn-Khaldūn sought not only historic truth but history as the way to truth. The Preface of his *Muqaddimah* reveals him to be a forerunner of all modern historicists. His Muslim predecessors had narrated the train of historic events; as he said, they saw history on the surface as no more "than information about political events. . . . They overlooked its inner meaning," which "involves specula-

tion and an attempt to get at the truth, subtle explanation of the causes and origins of existing things, and deep knowledge of the how and why of events." For ibn-Khaldūn history is therefore firmly rooted in philosophy and deserves to be accounted a branch of philosophy.

Traditional Muslim theologians, who were best represented by al-Ghazālī, rejected the Aristotelian notion of natural causality. They conceived of God as the first and only cause of all that is. Ibn-Khaldūn, as a Muslim believer, agreed with their ontology but introduced natural causality into history. Reason can see historic causes, not ontological causes. God in revelation is the teacher of ontological causes. Reason can grasp the limited phenomenon, but revelation introduces the limitless.

Ibn-Khaldūn's concern with historic methodology led him to historicism. For historic accuracy Muslim historiography had relied on the criticism of the sources. It elaborated on the method of *hadith,* the study of the traditions and sayings of the Prophet. Ibn-Khaldūn criticized this method and called for philosophical and rational methodology. The test of the accuracy of an event is not the reliability of the source but its conformity to the natural character or the natural law which the event should manifest.

To attain accuracy, the historian should therefore be a student of sociological and political causes and laws. He ought to be a philosopher of history.

[If the historian] trusts historical information in its plain transmitted form and has no clear knowledge of the principles resulting from custom, the fundamental facts of politics, the nature of civilization, or the conditions governing social organization, and if, furthermore, he does not evaluate remote or ancient material through comparison with near or contemporary material, he often cannot avoid . . . deviating from the high road of truth.

Ibn-Khaldūn called this introductory science to the study of history the science of *'umran,* or the science of civilization, and claimed to be its originator.

Civilization is the beginning and end of social development and political organization. Man is born naturally sociable. Society rises through man's ability to cooperate with other men for the satisfaction of his natural needs. Countrymen or nomads in primitive or tribal societies seek the satisfaction of their elementary need for food; townsmen in urban and more complex societies pursue higher economic, intellectual, and spiritual needs. Political organization, or the state, arises from individual and social needs for restraint, arbitrage, defense, and prosperity.

Asabyia, or group feeling, is the way to achieve leadership, enforce authority, and expand. Political organization or statehood leads to power and prosperity. The state is the form of civilization.

Arts and sciences can prosper only within a state. Resulting luxury is conducive to social and political disintegration. Like individual human beings, all societies, states, and civilizations go through cyclical states of emergence, growth, and decay. Civilizations, however, live longer than states, for the cultural faculties acquired by individuals and societies enable civilizations to survive political disintegration. The systematic formulation of this organistic theory of civilization is full of original observations about the influence of climate on social organization, the forms of society, the economic forces, the relation between labor and value, the psychological, social, and economic foundations of power, the forms of the state, the relation of state and religion, the role of education in society, the interdependence of prosperity and culture, and many other subjects.

Because these observations were formulated as natural laws, ibn-Khaldūn has been studied not only as a philosopher of history but also as a sociologist, political thinker, economist, educator, epistemologist, and historian of Muslim sciences. Guided by their own disciplines or convictions, different scholars have proclaimed him a forerunner of Machiavelli, Vico, Montesquieu, Hegel, Darwin, Spencer, Marx, Toynbee, and others. In his methodology and style ibn-Khaldūn is more a modernist than a medievalist. This partially explains his limited influence in medieval times and growing influence in modern times.

Al-Muqaddimah was written at a time when translation from Arabic into Latin had waned. Rediscovered by modern scholars and orientalists in the nineteenth century, excerpts of the book have been translated into French, German, Italian, English, and Japanese.

Ibn-Khaldūn has also been rediscovered by modern Muslim and Arab authors. More books in Arabic have been written about him than about any other medieval Muslim thinker. He has influenced historic, sociological, and political writings.

Bibliography

Ibn-Khaldūn's *Kitab al-'Ibar* was published in seven volumes (Būlāq, 1867) and translated into French by M'G. de Slane as *Histoire des Berbères* (Algiers, 1852–1856). *Al-Muqaddimah* has been translated by Franz Rosenthal as *The Muqaddimah: An Introduction to History*, 3 vols. (New York, 1958); it has also been translated into French by M'G. de Slane, 3 vols. (Algiers, 1862–1868).

Most of the biographical data covering ibn-Khaldūn's long and interesting career can be found in his autobiography, *At-Ta-rif bi-Ibn Khaldoun wa rihlatuhu gharban wa-Sharqan,* translated by Muhammad Tawit at-Tanji as *Biography of Ibn Khaldoun and Report on His Travels in the West and in the East* (Cairo, 1951).

Drawing from the autobiography and other sources, Walter J. Fischel wrote the story of ibn-Khaldūn's meeting and peace negotiations with Tamerlane in *Ibn Khaldūn and Tamerlane* (Berkeley and Los Angeles, 1952) and *Ibn Khaldūn's Activities in Mameluk Egypt 1382–1406* (Berkeley, 1951).

For works on ibn-Khaldūn see Gaston Bouthoul, *Ibn Khaldoun, sa philosophie sociale* (Paris, 1930); Muhammad Abdullah Enan, *Ibn Khaldoun: His Life and Work,* translated by Ashraf (Lahore, 1946); Abd el-Aziz Ezzat, *Ibn-Khaldoun et sa science sociale* (Cairo, 1947); Muhsin Mahdi, *Ibn Khaldūn's Philosophy of History: A Study in the Philosophic Foundation of the Science of Culture* (New York and London, 1957; paperback ed., Chicago, 1964); Sobhi Mahmassani, *Les Idées économiques d'Ibn Khaldoun* (Lyon, 1932); and Hussein Taha, *La Philosophie sociale d'Ibn Khaldoun* (Paris, 1925).

HASSAN SAAB

IBN PAQUDA, BAHYA BEN JOSEPH. See BAHYA BEN JOSEPH IBN PAQUDA.

IBN-RUSHD. See AVERROËS.

IBN-SĪNĀ. See AVICENNA.

IBN ṬUFAYL, Abū Bakr Muḥammad ibn 'Abd al-Malik (d. 580 H./A.D. 1185), Islamic philosopher, known to medieval Scholastics as Abubacer. Few details are known about the life of Ibn Ṭufayl, who was born at Guadix in the province of Granada and died in Morocco. Like all his colleagues, he was a scholar whose knowledge was encyclopedic; he was a mathematician, astronomer, philosopher, and poet. He served as vizier for and was a friend of the Almohad sovereign Abū Ya'qūb Yūsuf, and it was he who recommended that his friend Averroës be assigned the task of analyzing the works of Aristotle. Ibn Ṭufayl became known to medieval Scholastics (Abū Bakr having become Abubacer) through Averroës' translation of *De Anima,* which contained a brief criticism of Ibn Ṭufayl's doctrine identifying the possible (or passive) intellect with the imagination.

It was, however, because of his "philosophical novel," *Ḥayy ibn Yaqẓān,* a work that remained unknown to the Scholastics, that Ibn Ṭufayl later gained fame. It is worth noting that in the same era in the East Sohrawardī composed his own tales of symbolic initiations, in which he introduced, by extending the cycle of Avicennian tales, the "oriental philosophy" that Avicenna had already opposed to Peripatetic philosophy, but with only partial success. Ibn Ṭufayl referred to the Avicennian tales in the prologue to his philosophical novel, because he knew that the secret of Avicenna's "oriental philosophy" was partially contained therein.

Ibn Ṭufayl's work, however, is completely original and not in the least a mere amplification of an Avicennian tale. All it owes to Avicenna are the names of the *dramatis personae*: Ḥayy ibn Yaqẓān (*Vivens filius Vigilantis*), and Salamān and Absāl (a spelling certainly preferable to the mutilated form "Asāl," which figures in certain manuscripts).

In the works of Avicenna the name Ḥayy ibn Yaqẓān typified the Active Intellect, the central figure of Islamic Neoplatonism, simultaneously angel of knowledge and angel of revelation (the Holy Ghost and the angel Gabriel). For Ibn Ṭufayl this name is also that of the absolute hermit, mysteriously abandoned or spontaneously born on a desert island; in the absence of any human master and of all social falsification, the hermit becomes the perfect Sage. The superior pedagogy of the Active Intellect alone develops in him its natural faculties through a slow, rhythmic process evolving over the years. On a neighboring, inhabited island live two friends, Salamān, who typifies the practical and social spirit, and Absāl, contemplative and mystical, who lives like one in exile in his own country and finally decides to immigrate to the hermit's island, where he meets Ḥayy ibn Yaqẓān. In the course of their long conversations Absāl discovers that all that had been taught to him in matters of religion Ḥayy ibn Yaqẓān, the solitary, philosophical wise man, already knows, but in a purer form. Absāl discovers that religion is the *symbol* of a truth otherwise inaccessible to the common run of men. Together they attempt to deliver their spiritual message to the men on the island opposite them. Alas! in the face of the growing hostility that they encounter, they must accept an inescapable truth: the ordinary man is not able to understand.

Ibn Ṭufayl's novel is not an anticipation of Robinson Crusoe; each external episode must be understood on a spiritual level. On the other hand, in spite of its pessimistic ending it should not be concluded that the conflict Ibn Ṭufayl set forth (that between religion and philosophy) attained desperate proportions in the Muslim faith. In fact, another position and solution to the problem are sought in the "prophetic philosophy" of Shī'ism.

Bibliography

Ibn Ṭufayl's *Ḥayy ibn Yaqzān* has been translated by S. Ockley as *The Improvement of Reason* (London, 1708) and revised by A. S. Fulton (London, 1929).

For literature on Ibn Ṭufayl, see Henry Corbin, *Histoire de la philosophie islamique*, Vol. I (paperback, Paris, 1964), pp. 327–337 and the bibliography on p. 362.

See also Henry Corbin, *Avicenna and the Visionary Recital*, translated from the French by Willard R. Trask (New York, 1960).

HENRY CORBIN

IBN-ZADDIK, JOSEPH BEN JACOB (d. 1149), like other Jewish philosophers of a Neoplatonic cast, such as Yehudah Halevi and Abraham ibn-Ezra, was a poet as well as a philosopher and legist. Very few of his poems survive, and although he was highly praised as a Talmudist and served for the last 11 years of his life (1138–1149) as judge (*dayyan*) of the Jewish community of Córdoba, he does not seem to have written any systematic legal work. His philosophic work, on which his chief reputation rests, was originally written in Arabic, but the original no longer survives; a Hebrew translation, under the title *Olam Katon* ("The Microcosm"), was circulated in manuscript during the Middle Ages but was not printed until the mid-nineteenth century.

The general thesis of Joseph ibn-Zaddik's work is that since man's nature duplicates in reduced form the nature of the universe, knowledge of the self provides a key to all knowledge. It is unnecessary to study the special sciences. The study of man, the microcosm, will lead to the understanding of the universe, the macrocosm.

Ibn-Zaddik's *Olam Katon*, in fulfillment of this program, develops in its first part a metaphysical basis for the theory of man as the microcosm. Here the author showed acquaintance with both the Platonic and the Aristotelian traditions in the form in which they were maintained by Muslim philosophers. The second part of the work discusses both the physical and the psychological natures of man; it asserts a point-for-point correspondence between human nature and the physics of the universe. In the third part ibn-Zaddik turned to theological questions, particularly the question of divine unity. His theological discussion includes a proof of creation from the finiteness of the world: where there is creation, there must be a Creator; hence God exists. The philosopher was aware of the difficulties presented by a naive doctrine of divine attributes and resolved these difficulties by denying to the attributes a positive character. The fourth and final division of the work, continuing the pattern established by the Muslim philosophers, is devoted to God's justice and the implications of the divine government of the universe for man's duties. Ibn-Zaddik was firmly committed to a belief in human free will; he believed that a man must use his freedom to imitate the goodness of God and to seek knowledge of him. Success or failure in so doing leads to reward or punishment in the future life, but apparent rewards and punishments in this world are merely natural happenings and should not be understood as indications of divine favor or disfavor.

Bibliography

An unpublished English translation of ibn-Zaddik's *Olam Katon*, by Jacob Haberman (1954), is available in the library of Columbia University, New York. See also the discussion in the introduction to Haberman's translation; Isaac Husik, *History of Medieval Jewish Philosophy* (New York, 1916); Georges Vajda, *Introduction à la pensée juive du moyen âge* (Paris, 1947); and Joseph L. Blau, *The Story of Jewish Philosophy* (New York, 1962).

J. L. BLAU

IDEALISM, in its philosophical sense, is the view that mind and spiritual values are fundamental in the world as a whole. Thus, idealism is opposed to naturalism, that is, to the view that mind and spiritual values have emerged from or are reducible to material things and processes. Philosophical idealism is also opposed to realism (see REALISM) and is thus the denial of the common-sense realist view that material things exist independently of being perceived. Some philosophers who have held the idealist view in its antinaturalist form have not opposed common-sense realism, and thus it is possible to be a metaphysical idealist and an epistemological realist. More often, however, arguments against common-sense realism have been used in order to establish metaphysical idealism. The description "subjective idealism" is sometimes used for idealism based on antirealist epistemological arguments, and the description "objective idealism" for idealism that is antinaturalist without being antirealist.

In terms of these definitions, philosophical theism is an idealist view, for according to theism God is a perfect, uncreated spirit who has created everything else and is hence more fundamental in the world than any material things he has created. Marxist philosophers have therefore held that there are in principle only two main philosophical systems: idealism, according to which mind or spirit is primary in the universe, and materialism, according to which matter is primary in the universe (see DIALECTICAL MATERIALISM). If "primary" is taken not to mean "earlier in time" but rather to mean "fundamental" or "basic," then these Marxist definitions agree with those given above. The only objection to them is that many philosophers who accept theism would be unwilling to be labeled idealists, since they would take the view that idealists belittle the material world and regard it as illusory by comparison with mind or even as less real than mind, whereas theists do not belittle matter or regard it as in any way less real than mind. Certainly this is a difference between theism and some forms of idealism, but there is force in the argument that theism and both subjective and objective idealism may be classed together as opposed to materialism. Pantheism may be regarded as a more thoroughly idealist view than theism, since pantheism is the view that nothing exists except God and his modes and attributes, so that the material world must be an aspect or appearance of God. Theism, in contrast, is the view that God has created a world beyond or outside himself so that the material world, although dependent on him, is not an aspect or appearance of him. What unites idealism both with theism and with pantheism is the rejection of materialism and the assertion of a metaphysic that is favorable to religious belief.

HISTORY AND ORIGIN OF THE TERM

The word "idealism" came to be used as a philosophical term in the eighteenth century. Leibniz, in his *Réponse aux réflexions de Bayle* (written 1702; published in *Philosophischen Schriften*, C. I. Gerhardt, ed., 7 vols. Berlin, 1875–1890), criticized "those who like Epicurus and Hobbes, believe that the soul is material" and held that in his own system "whatever of good there is in the hypotheses of Epicurus and of Plato, of the greatest materialists and the greatest idealists, is combined here" (Vol. IV, pp. 559–560). In this passage Leibniz clearly means by "idealists" philosophers who uphold an antimaterialist metaphysic like that of Plato and himself. When, later in the century, Berkeley's views came to be discussed, the word "idealism" was applied, however, to the view that nothing could be known to exist or did exist except the ideas in the mind of the percipient. (Berkeley called his own view "immaterialism," not "idealism.") Thus, Christian Wolff (1679–1754), a follower of Leibniz, included idealists, along with materialists and skeptics, among "three bad sects" which he reprobated, and Diderot (1713–1784) wrote in 1749: "We call *idealists* those philosophers who, knowing only their own existence and that of the sensations that follow one another within them, do not grant anything else . . . " (*Lettre sur les aveugles*, London, 1749). The term "egoists" was also applied to holders of this view, as can be seen from the article entitled "Égoistes" in the *Encyclopédie*, edited by d'Alembert and Diderot, which started publication in 1750. Today the word "solipsists" is applied to what were then called "egoists" or "idealists." In the *Critique of Pure Reason* (Riga, 1781) Kant referred to his own view as "transcendental idealism," and in his *Prolegomena to any Future Metaphysics* (Riga, 1783) he called it "critical idealism." Thus, by this time the word "idealism" was beginning to lose the pejorative meaning that had linked it with extreme subjectivism.

The word "idealism" is derived from the Greek word ἰδέα, which simply means something seen, or the look of something. Plato used the word as a technical term of his philosophy to mean a universal (such as whiteness) in contrast to a particular (such as something white) or to mean an ideal limit or standard (such as absolute beauty) in contrast to the things that approximate or conform to it (such as the more or less beautiful things). According to Plato an Idea, or Form, is apprehended by the intellect, does not exist in time, and cannot come into existence or cease to exist as temporal things do and is hence more real than they are. In medieval philosophy Ideas or Forms were regarded as the patterns in accordance with which God conceived of things and created them, and hence they were thought of as existing in the mind of God. Descartes used the word "idea" for thoughts existing in the minds of men, sometimes retaining, however, the intellectual and objective character of ideas as understood in the Platonic tradition. But he also used the word "idea" for the effects

in embodied minds of external objects acting on the sense organs, and hence the word came to stand for changing sense perceptions as well as for unchanging objects of the intellect. Descartes also used the word "idea" for a shape or form stamped upon a soft material, as when he said in Section XII of his *Rules for the Direction of the Mind* (1628) that "shapes or ideas" are formed *in the brain* by things outside the body acting upon it. Locke, in *An Essay concerning Human Understanding* (London, 1690), used the word "idea" for perceptions of "sensible qualities" conveyed into the mind by the senses and for "the perception of the operations of our own mind within us, as it is employed about the ideas it has got . . . " (Bk. II, Ch. I, Sec. 4). The mind, he held, "stirs not one jot beyond those ideas which *sense* or *reflection* have offered for its contemplation" (*ibid.*, Sec. 24). Berkeley adopted Locke's terminology and held that by our senses "we have the knowledge *only of our sensations*, ideas, or those things that are immediately perceived by sense" (*Principles of Human Knowledge*, Dublin, 1710, Sec. XVIII). Thus, Berkeley here repeats a view already held by Locke.

Thus, the word "idea" was used variously to mean a Form in the Platonic sense, a Form as apprehended in the mind of God or by the human mind, a shape impressed on soft, yielding material, and, apparently by analogy with this last sense, a modification produced in a mind by the influence on it of external things that affect the sense organs. Neither a Platonic Form nor a shape is a mental entity. "Operations of the mind" clearly are, and so would be the effects in minds of material objects that produce "impressions" in them. Ideas in this last sense would seem to be like mental images, but mental images produced not by imagining but by the operation of external objects. This variation in meanings can be seen in Berkeley's *A New Theory of Vision* (Dublin, 1709), where he writes (Sec. XLI): " . . . a man born blind being made to see, would, at first, have no idea of distance by sight; the sun and stars, the remotest objects as well as the hearer, would all seem to be in his eye, or rather in his mind. The objects intromitted by sight, would seem to him (as in truth they are) no other than a new set of thoughts or sensations, each whereof is as near to him as the perceptions of pain or pleasure, or the most inward passions of his soul." It will be noticed that in his passage Berkeley comes close to assimilating "in his eye," a physical condition, to "in his mind," meant presumably to be a mental condition. Again, he puts "sensations" in apposition with "thoughts," although sensations and thoughts would seem to be as different as pains and concepts. There is also the suggestion that what is near to us is "in the mind," so that if colors and shapes are not, as they seem to be, at a distance from us, they must be in our minds. The passage is an important one for indicating the conflicts and confusions involved in the word "idea" and carried over into some of the arguments for idealism.

IMMATERIALISM

Berkeley gave the name "immaterialism" to the central thesis of his philosophy, the thesis that there is no such thing as material substance. Immaterialism has been prominent in idealist theories just because to prove that there is no material substance would be the most effective and spectacular way of disproving materialism. If there is no material substance, then matter cannot be the basis of what is or all that there is. Immaterialism has been supported by two main lines of argument. Along one line it has been argued that it is impossible that matter could be independently real. The arguments to this effect may be called the metaphysical arguments for immaterialism. Along the other line it has been argued that the colors, shapes, and sounds that are naturally taken to belong to independently existing material objects are in fact sensible qualities that cannot exist apart from being perceived. The arguments to establish this may be called the epistemological arguments for immaterialism. Although he did not call himself an immaterialist, Leibniz, on the evidence of the passage we have quoted, would have regarded himself as an idealist, and his arguments were metaphysical rather than epistemological. Berkeley, of course, is best known for his epistemological arguments, even though his argument that the very notion of something existing totally unperceived is self-contradictory may be classed as metaphysical. Arthur Collier, in his *Clavis Universalis* (London, 1713), used both epistemological and metaphysical arguments; the subtitle of his book, "a Demonstration of the Non-existence or Impossibility of an External World," allowed for both types of approach.

Leibniz. Leibniz' metaphysical idealism consisted of two main theses: (1) that matter is necessarily composite and hence cannot be substantially or independently real, and (2) that simple (that is, noncomposite) substances must be perceiving and appetitive beings even though they are not necessarily conscious or self-conscious. He gave the name "monad" to these independently real and essentially active substances, and he argued that space and time cannot be real containers in which substances exist but must be the order in which monads are related to one another. Thus, he held that space and time are not absolute existences but relations of coexistence and succession among created monads. He did not conclude from this, however, that space and time and material objects are mere illusions or delusions; delusions and dreams, he held, are by their very nature inconsistent and unpredictable, whereas the material world in space and time is regular and in part predictable. Leibniz was not quite explicit on the matter, but he seems to have believed that space and time were a sort of mental construction or *ens rationis* and that material things are regular appearances rather than real substances. Sometimes, however, he used the expression *phenomena bene fundata* for space and time. However this may be, Leibniz argued for an idealist system in which there is a series of realms of being with God as the supreme, uncreated spiritual substance. In the realm of created substances all the members are active and immaterial and some are self-conscious substances created in God's image. In the realm of appearances the elements are "well-founded" in the substantial realities, and in consequence they show a rational order even though, like the rainbow, they disappear when closely examined. Finally, there are isolated realms of mere illusion and delusion which, however, have their place in the total scheme of things. Leibniz believed that this metaphysical system could be proved by reason. He held, too, that sense experience is not an independent source of knowledge but is reason in a state of obscurity and indistinctness. Thus, he held that "we use the external senses as . . . a blind man does a stick" and that the world is revealed as it is by means of reason, not by means of the senses (*Letter to Queen Charlotte of Prussia*, 1702). Thus, he denied not only the substantial reality of matter but also the efficacy and even the possibility of mere sense experience. This is a theme which many later idealists have developed. It runs counter, however, to the empiricist immaterialism of Berkeley.

Berkeley. Berkeley is the best-known exponent of immaterialism on epistemological grounds. His basic argument is that what we immediately perceive are sensations or ideas, that sensations or ideas are necessarily objects of perception (their *esse*, as he put it, is *percipi*, their essence is to be perceived), and that what we call physical things, such as trees and rocks and tables, are orderly groups or collections of sensations or ideas and are hence mind-dependent like the sensations or ideas which compose them. This argument proceeds on the assumption that sense experience is basic and reliable. Matter is rejected on the ground that the senses inform us of ideas but not of material substances to which these ideas belong. The very notion of a material substance distinct from sensible qualities or ideas is, according to Berkeley, unimaginable and inconceivable.

Berkeley made the surprising claim that this view is in full accordance with common sense. According to common sense, he argued, trees and rocks and tables are immediately perceived and have the characteristics they are immediately perceived to have. But according to those who believe in material substance, what is immediately perceived are the ideas produced in the mind by material substances of which we can only have mediate or indirect knowledge. Furthermore, these indirectly perceived material substances do not have the characteristics of color, hardness, etc., which common sense says they have. Hence, Berkeley thought that material substances, even if they were conceivable, would be problematic existents, so that the theory in which they figured would give rise to skepticism about the existence of familiar things like trees and rocks and tables. Immaterialism, in contrast, with its claim that such things, being ideas, are immediately perceived, does not lead to skepticism about them.

In its reliance on sense experience, then, and in its acceptance of the view that trees and rocks and tables are immediately perceived and are as they seem to be, Berkeley's immaterialism is very different from that of Leibniz. On the other hand, there is an important point of similarity between their views which is often overlooked. Leibniz held that substances, or monads, that is, the basically real things that make up the world, must be active, perceiving beings. Berkeley held this too, for he argued that sensible qualities or ideas are dependent and passive existences that depend on independent and active beings. These independent and active beings, according to Berkeley, are selves. The difference between Berkeley and Leibniz is that Berkeley held that only selves are active, whereas Leibniz held that activity is possible at a lower level than that of selves. However, this view that what is real is active is an element in a number of idealist theories.

Berkeley also supported immaterialism with the argument that it is not possible even to conceive of anything existing apart from being thought of, for it must be thought of in the very act of being conceived. This argument was not used by Leibniz, but it has played an important part in the arguments of many idealists since Berkeley.

Collier. Arthur Collier's *Clavis Universalis,* which appeared posthumously in 1713, was possibly written before Berkeley's *Principles of Human Knowledge* (1710), in which Berkeley's immaterialist philosophy was first published. Collier used epistemological arguments to prove immaterialism, but, unlike Berkeley, he made no attempt to reconcile immaterialism with common sense. On the contrary, he said that in denying the existence of the material world he meant that bodies are as delusory as the visions of lunatics. Collier also produced metaphysical arguments for immaterialism, maintaining, for example, that matter can be proved to be both infinite in extent and not infinite in extent, infinitely divisible and not infinitely divisible, and since nothing can in fact have contradictory characteristics, matter cannot exist.

Knowledge of immaterialism was spread in Germany by the publication of a book that contained German translations of Berkeley's *Three Dialogues between Hylas and Philonous* (London, 1713) and Collier's *Clavis Universalis* and whose title was *Sammlung der vornehmsten Schriftsteller die die Wirklichkeit ihren eigenen Körper und der ganzen Körperwelt leugnen* (Rostock, 1756). The translator and editor, Johann C. Eschenbach, set out to refute as well as to translate the two books.

TRANSCENDENTAL IDEALISM

Kant, in his *Critique of Pure Reason,* described his own view as formal, critical, or transcendental idealism. Nevertheless, a famous passage of that book (B 274) is headed "Refutation of Idealism." Kant called the types of idealism he claimed to be refuting problematic idealism and dogmatic idealism, respectively. By problematic idealism he meant the view, which he attributed to Descartes, that the existence of objects in space outside us is doubtful. By dogmatic idealism he meant the view, which he attributed to Berkeley, that "space and all the things to which it belongs as an inseparable condition" is "something impossible in itself and hence looks upon things in space as mere imaginations" (B 274). Kant's interpretation of Descartes is not quite adequate, but his interpretation of Berkeley is so completely at fault that it seems possible that he had made use of Eschenbach's book and confused Collier's arguments with those of Berkeley. In any case, Kant's transcendental idealism is very different from the types of idealism we have so far considered. Kant held that it is not possible to gain knowledge of the world by rational thought alone, and thus he rejected all attempts such as those of Leibniz and Wolff to do so. On the other hand, he also held that mere sense experience does not give knowledge of the world either, since in the absence of interpretation, sense experience is "blind." Thus, Kant argued that unless our perceptions were organized within what he called the pure

a priori intuitions of space and time in terms of rational principles such as the requirement that our perceptions refer to things in causal relation with one another, knowledge of an objective world would be impossible. Without the a priori intuitions of space and time and the categories of the understanding, there would be a manifold of fluctuating sensations but no knowledge of the natural world. When Kant refuted the two types of idealism mentioned above, he argued that no one could become aware of himself unless there were enduring material substances with which he could contrast his own fleeting experiences. We should not be aware of selves unless we were also aware of material things. This line of argument disposes of the view that we could be certain of our own existence but doubtful about the material world and also of the view that material things are "mere imaginations." Unless there were material things in space, we should not know of our own existence or of our own imaginations.

Kant's transcendental idealism, therefore, is his view that space and time and the categories are conditions of the possibility of experience rather than features of things as they are in themselves. Whether things-in-themselves are in space and time and whether they form a causally interacting system we do not know, but unless we were so constituted as to place everything in spatiotemporal contexts and to synthesize our sensations according to the categories of the understanding, we should not have knowledge of an objective world. Kant did not think that this synthesizing was carried out by the empirical selves we are aware of in ourselves and others. He thought, rather, that a transcendental self had to be postulated as doing this, but of this transcendental self nothing could be known, since it was a condition of knowledge and not an object of knowledge. The natural world, or the world of appearances, as he calls it, somehow depends on a transcendental self of which we can know nothing except that it is. Whereas at the empirical level selves and material things are equally real, the knowledge we have at this level presupposes the synthesizing activities of a transcendental self of which we can know nothing.

Kant was regarded in his own day as a destroyer not only because he maintained that there was no basis for the rationalist, metaphysical constructions of Leibniz and Wolff but also because he held that no single one of the traditionally accepted arguments for the existence of God was valid and that it is impossible to prove the immateriality and immortality of the soul. Idealists such as Leibniz and Berkeley and Collier had considered that they had framed philosophical arguments that favored religious belief. Berkeley, for example, emphasized that his conclusions made atheism and skepticism untenable. He also claimed to have provided a new and cogent argument for the existence of God. According to Kant, however, sense experience cannot lead us beyond the natural world, and the categories of the understanding can be validly applied only where there are sense experiences and if applied beyond them can lead only to insoluble antinomies. For example, if the category of cause is used to transcend sense experience, then equally valid proofs can be made to show that there must be a first cause and that there cannot be a first cause. In the appendix to the *Prolegomena* Kant says that "idealism proper always has a mystical tendency" but that his form of idealism was not intended for such purposes but only as a solution of certain problems of philosophy. All this seems to place Kant outside the main idealist tradition and to indicate that he was developing a positivistic view. Nevertheless, at the end of the eighteenth century a group of philosophers who are known as Absolute idealists claimed to have been inspired by him. What, then, are the features of Kant's idealism which gave rise to views so different from his?

One is that Kant called specific attention to the elements of activity and spontaneity in knowledge. His view that knowledge of nature would be impossible apart from the activity of the understanding in synthesizing sensations in accordance with the categories led some of his successors to regard knowledge as analogous to construction or making. Another feature of Kant's philosophy that pointed in the direction of Absolute idealism was the thesis that synthesizing in terms of the categories presupposed a unitary transcendental self. It is true that Kant himself said that as a presupposition of experience the transcendental self could not be an object of knowledge, but some of his successors claimed to be rather more familiar with it. Some of Kant's views on morality and on freedom of the will also gave scope for development in an idealist direction. Kant held that the free will problem is insoluble by metaphysical argumentation, for it can be proved both that there must be a freedom of spontaneity and that there is no freedom and everything takes place according to laws of nature. But in his ethical writings that followed the *Critique of Pure Reason,* Kant argued that our knowledge of and respect for the moral law presupposed freedom of the will. He emphasized that this was not a metaphysical or speculative proof; his point was that metaphysics could not disprove freedom of the will, so that we are justified in accepting what morality presupposes. He argued, furthermore, that the existence of God and the immortality of the soul might also be accepted as practical concomitants of morality, as long as the fundamental impossibility of their being theoretically proved was recognized. Again, Kant introduced into his account of knowledge a faculty of reason (*Vernunft*), which, remaining dissatisfied with the understanding's confinement to the ordering of sense experiences, constantly strove for completeness and totality. Kant thought that the reason might in practice advance our knowledge by seeking for a completeness that is not in fact to be found—Kant used the expression *focus imaginarius* in this connection. Some of his successors transformed this suggestion into the claim that reason reveals a real, not an imaginary or merely methodological, totality.

ABSOLUTE IDEALISM

Fichte. The development from Kant's idealism to Absolute idealism can be most readily seen in the writings of Johann Gottlieb Fichte (1762–1814). Like Kant, Fichte believed that strict determinism is incompatible with morality and that our knowledge of the moral law presupposes the freedom of the will. Therefore, the philosopher is faced with choosing between two systems of thought, the deterministic system which Fichte called "dogma-

tism," of which Spinoza is the chief representative, and "critical idealism." Fichte recognized that the philosophy a man chooses depends on the sort of man he is, but he also thought that reasons could be given for preferring the idealist course. A reason on which Fichte placed great weight is that thought and intelligence cannot be accounted for within a system of causes and effects, for, in comprehending causal determination, they necessarily go beyond it. If, therefore, there is to be a fundamental account of things, it must start from the intellect. Fichte was here developing a suggestion by Kant in the *Groundwork of the Metaphysic of Morals* that the operations of the intellect transcend the phenomenal series of causes and effects. Thus, according to Fichte a free, intelligent ego (*Ich*) must be the starting point of philosophy, and everything else must somehow be "deduced" from this ego. Fichte, therefore, endeavored to go beyond Kant by showing that space and time and the categories are not just facts that must be accepted as they are but necessary conditions of intelligence. Even the material world is not merely matter of fact but is presented as a series of obstacles which must be overcome in the performance of our duties.

Schelling. Friedrich Wilhelm Joseph von Schelling (1775–1854) began his philosophical career as a supporter of Fichte—as the titles of two of his early works show: *Vom Ich als Prinzip der Philosophie* (Tübingen, 1795) and "Philosophische Briefe über Dogmatismus und Kritizismus" (in *Philosophische Journal*, 1796). Schelling's first account of his distinctive views was entitled *System des transzendentalen Idealismus* (Tübingen, 1800), but he later described his view as "absolute idealism," explaining that things are always conditioned by other things, whereas mind is undetermined and absolute. Fichte's idealism has sometimes been called a "moral idealism," since its basis is a system of active moral beings. Schelling's has sometimes been called an "aesthetic idealism," since Schelling argued that it is the artist who makes men aware of the Absolute. Although, like Fichte, he believed that free activity is basic in the world, he placed less emphasis on the distinction between individuals and came nearer to pantheism.

Hegel. Georg Wilhelm Friedrich Hegel (1770–1831) is too individual a philosopher to be readily classifiable, but he was undoubtedly the most comprehensive and the most influential of the Absolute idealists. In his *Encyclopedia* (Sec. 95) he writes of "the ideality of the finite," which he says is "the main principle of philosophy," and says that "every genuine philosophy is on that account idealism." Like much that Hegel wrote, this is somewhat cryptic, but it appears to mean that what is finite is not real and that the true philosophy, idealism, recognizes this. The matter is more fully discussed in the *Science of Logic* (Bk. 1, Sec. 1, Ch. 2), where Hegel says that philosophical idealism is the view that "the finite is not genuinely real." Here he also contrasts his form of idealism with subjective idealism and says that in denying the reality of the finite, idealist philosophy is at one with religion, "for religion no more admits finitude to be a genuine reality, than it admits finitude to be ultimate, absolute, or as basic (*ein Nicht-Gesetztes*), uncreated, eternal."

We need not linger over Hegel's rejection of subjective idealism, except to refer to what he says about Berkeley's immaterialism in the *Lectures on the History of Philosophy*. Hegel there argues that Berkeley says very little when he says that things are ideas, for this only amounts to recommending a change of nomenclature and calling things ideas, and this throws no new light on the status of things and ideas. Hegel's arguments are metaphysical rather than epistemological. He thought that Fichte was right when he tried to deduce or give reasons for the categories, and Hegel's *Science of Logic* may be regarded as his view of how the deduction should be carried out. Insofar as such a compact work can be summarized, its argument is that we say very little about the world when we say that it is, rather more when we say that it is measurable, or that it is a series of interacting things, more again when we think of it in terms of chemical combinations, still more when we apply the categories of life, more again when we apply the categories of theoretical reason, and most of all when we come to the categories of will and the pursuit of the good. What remains of the older metaphysical arguments is his view that the incomplete and inadequate categories lead to contradictions. These contradictions, Hegel held, are resolved as the higher categories are reached, in particular the category of the Absolute idea.

Hegel also tried to show that rudimentary mind operates in the natural world. But what most concerned him was the working of mind in human society. He set out a series of stages of human achievement proceeding from the family organization to "civil society" (what today we call the market economy), from civil society to the state, and then, at the highest levels, to art, religion, and philosophy. The idealist character of this construction may be seen from the fact that when Marx wished to set out a materialist view of society he took the economy as basic, the state as dependent on it, and regarded art, religion, and philosophy as ideologies which had no real influence.

Hegel's philosophy was elaborated after his death by a series of able successors and criticized from many points of view (see HEGELIANISM). It came to be known in England about the middle of the century, and Benjamin Jowett translated some passages (which he never published) for the use of his students. Absolute idealism was made known to a larger British public by James Hutchinson Stirling's *The Secret of Hegel* (2 vols., London, 1865), (Fichte's moral idealism had earlier influenced Thomas Carlyle, and Coleridge had been influenced by his reading of Schelling, although he had not accepted all of Schelling's views. Wordsworth's definition of poetry as "emotion recollected in tranquillity" seems to be a translation of a phrase of Schelling's which Coleridge noticed and copied into his notebook).

NEO-HEGELIANISM

About the time when German Absolute idealism was becoming known in England through the writings of Coleridge and Carlyle, it was also becoming known in the United States through a group of writers (mostly Unitarians) who came to be called the transcendentalists. Later, in the 1860s, idealist philosophy received more detailed and professional attention on both sides of the Atlantic. In 1867 at St. Louis, William Torrey Harris founded *The Journal of Speculative Philosophy,* in the first issue of which he referred disparagingly to the prevailing "brittle individualism" which he considered should be replaced by a philosophy in which the state was properly comprehended as a support for freedom. In the same period Thomas Hill Green was teaching philosophy at Oxford with the support of Benjamin Jowett. The nature of Green's influence may be seen from a letter sent to Green in 1872 asking him to speak to an essay society whose members felt the need for "earnest effort to bring speculation into relation with modern life instead of making it an intellectual luxury, and to deal with various branches of science, physical, social, political, metaphysical, theological, aesthetic, as part of a whole instead of in abstract separation," and sought for "co-operation instead of the present suspicious isolation." This letter was signed by, among others, F. H. Bradley, who had recently become a fellow of Merton College (Melvin Richter, *The Politics of Conscience. T. H. Green and His Age,* London, 1964, pp. 159–160). Both Harris and his circle and Green and his were critical of social individualism as well as of positivism and materialism. They aimed to provide an alternative to utilitarianism, which they thought was based on an inadequate pluralistic metaphysics.

Green's form of idealism was rather closer to that of Kant than to that of Hegel. It was built around two main themes, that the natural world cannot be self-contained and ultimate, and that there is no merely given experience. The first theme is an extension of Kant's theory of the transcendental ego, which Green held implied that nature presupposes "a principle which is not natural," a "spiritual principle" (*Prolegomena to Ethics,* Oxford, 1883, Sec. 54). The second theme, on the other hand, goes well beyond Kant, who believed that there was a "manifold of sense" which the understanding synthesized. Green's view that there is no merely given sense experience, and that all experience implies some sort of intelligent organization, was a central theme of subsequent idealist argument. It has a certain kinship with Leibniz' theory that ideas of sense are confused ideas of reason.

Green died in 1882, and the leading English idealist philosophers after that were F. H. Bradley and Bernard Bosanquet. In Scotland, where idealism very soon prevailed in the universities, Edward Caird's *A Critical Account of the Philosophy of Kant* (Glasgow, 1877) and Andrew Seth's (later Pringle-Pattison's) *Hegelianism and Personality* (London and Edinburgh, 1887) were notable contributions. But from the 1880s to the 1920s Bradley and Bosanquet dominated the philosophical scene in Great Britain. Bradley attempted to discredit the common-sense view of the world by bringing to bear a multitude of arguments to show that it involved self-contradictions, and he argued that these contradictions could be eliminated only if the world is shown to be a single, harmonious experience. The central theme of Bosanquet's idealism was that every finite existence necessarily transcends itself and points toward other existences and finally to the whole. Thus, he advocated a system very close to that in which Hegel had argued for the ideality of the finite. Bradley and

Bosanquet influenced one another a great deal. For example, Bradley's *Ethical Studies* (London and Edinburgh, 1876) influenced Bosanquet's account of society, and Bosanquet's *Knowledge and Reality* (London, 1885) led Bradley to modify very considerably the views he had set out in his *Principles of Logic* (London, 1883).

In the United States the most impressive contribution to the philosophy of idealism is Josiah Royce's *The World and the Individual* (First Series, New York, 1900; Second Series, New York, 1902). Royce was extremely learned in the literature of idealism, both German and British, and *The World and the Individual* was written in the light of his study of Kant, Fichte, Schelling, and Hegel and of his reading of Bradley's *Appearance and Reality* (London, 1893). Furthermore, Royce was acquainted with the empiricism and pragmatism of C. S. Peirce and William James and with Peirce's work in formal logic. Like Pringle-Pattison, Royce considered that Bradley went too far in regarding the individual mind as "fused" or "transformed" in the Absolute. The mystic who regards finite experience as mere illusion, Royce held, is an improvement on the realist who uncritically accepts it just as it is, but nevertheless the very point of idealism would be lost if the individual self is deprived of all cosmic significance. Royce believed he could show that the "world . . . is a realm of individuals, self-possessed, morally free, and sufficiently independent of one another to make their freedom of action possible and finally significant" (*The World and the Individual*, First Series, p. 395). Like Fichte, Royce endeavored to support this view by an analysis of the moral, rational will.

By the beginning of the twentieth century idealism had become a powerful force in the universities of the English-speaking world. Empiricism and realism were held to have been finally discredited, along with the utilitarianism and individualism that had so often accompanied them. Philosophical truth was thought to be a unity, so that similar principles animated idealist works on aesthetics, ethics, religion, and politics. Such leading British statesmen as Arthur J. Balfour and Richard B. Haldane and the South African prime minister Jan C. Smuts wrote books defending the idealist point of view. When the new provincial universities were being founded in Great Britain at that time, Haldane used his influence to foster the study of philosophy in them, as a central, unifying subject.

At the same time, however, points of view opposed to idealism were being vigorously developed. An example is G. E. Moore's "The Refutation of Idealism," which appeared in *Mind* (N.S. Vol. 12, 1903, 433–453). Another example is *The New Realism,* a collection of articles by American philosophers critical of idealism which was published in New York in 1912. Bertrand Russell urged that idealists were ignorant of new developments in logic and that this rendered their theories untenable. Ludwig Wittgenstein's *Tractatus Logico-philosophicus* (London, 1922) was symptomatic of a new, pluralist, antispeculative approach to philosophical problems. Moore's "The Conception of Reality" (*PAS*, 1913–1914) attempted to show that one of Bradley's theses was nothing but a consequence of his not realizing that the proposition "Unicorns are thought of" is of quite a different logical form from the proposition "Lions are hunted." In the 1920s the very possibility of speculative metaphysics was denied on the basis of the allegedly empiricist principle of verifiability. Furthermore, the idealist theses about the "unreality" of finite individuals and the "reality" of society or the state were held to be evil as well as meaningless.

But during this period when the idealist movement was under increasing attack, three important treatises appeared in which comprehensive idealist theories were developed. John M. E. McTaggart's *The Nature of Existence* (Cambridge, 2 vols., 1921–1927) defended a pluralistic idealism by means of metaphysical arguments designed to show that space, time, and matter cannot possibly be real. Michael Oakeshott's *Experience and Its Modes* (Cambridge, 1933), unlike McTaggart's work, seems to have been completely unaffected by the realist and empiricist arguments so widely accepted at that time. Brand Blanshard's *The Nature of Thought* (2 vols., London, 1939), on the other hand, maintains a constant and detailed criticism of behaviorist and empiricist arguments. It is noteworthy that in none of these elegantly written idealist works is there any attempt to defend a theistic position. Indeed, *The Nature of Existence* concludes its discussion of God by saying that "there can be no being who is a God, or who is anything so resembling a God that the name would not be very deceptive" (Sec. 500).

IDEALIST SOCIAL THEORY

Most nineteenth-century and twentieth-century idealist philosophers were agreed that utilitarians and individualists had a false view of what constitutes an individual person. They believed that since individuals are constituted by their relations to one another, the idea that society is an association of independently existing individuals is absurd. They thought, too, that it follows from this that freedom is something more positive than just being left alone by the government. Insofar as government is concerned with the common aims of individuals, it is not merely a constraint on them but a manifestation of their most rational purposes. Some idealist writers, therefore, saw no serious harm in Rousseau's claim that men can be forced to be free. T. H. Green was thus able to support temperance legislation on the ground that it enabled those protected by it to fulfill their abiding aims rather than their passing whims. Even so, Green had no doubts about the ultimate reality of individual persons, whereas Bosanquet, in his *Philosophical Theory of the State* (London, 1899) argued that the state is the real individual and that individual persons are unreal by comparison with it. But Bosanquet did not think that this justified socialist control. On the contrary, he believed that if society is organic and individual, then its elements can cooperate apart from a centralized organ of control, the need for which presupposes that harmony has to be imposed upon something that is naturally unharmonious. McTaggart was the one leading idealist who denied the relevance of metaphysics to social and political action. He was a Hegelian scholar who was in general agreement with Hegel's views, but he thought that Hegel was wrong in supposing that metaphysics could show that the state is more than a means to the good of the individuals who compose it. McTaggart concluded that "philosophy can give us very little, if any guidance in action. . . . Why should a Hegelian citizen be surprised that his belief as to the organic nature of the Absolute does not help him in deciding how to vote? Would a Hegelian engineer be reasonable in expecting that his belief that all matter is spirit should help him in planning a bridge?" (*Studies in Hegelian Cosmology,* Cambridge, 1901, p. 196).

SOME COMMENTS ON IDEALISM

Act and object. Moore, Russell, and other realist philosophers at the beginning of the twentieth century objected to idealism that its exponents failed to distinguish between the act of perception and the object of the act. It was rightly argued that the words "idea" and "sensation" were used vaguely and thus encouraged the confusion. According to the realist argument, colors and shapes are objects of the mind, whereas pains and feelings are states of mind, and what the idealists do is to say of the former that they are essentially mental, when this is true only of the latter. It may be questioned, however, whether the idealists were thus confused. Certainly Berkeley was not, since in the first of the *Three Dialogues Between Hylas and Philonous* he himself made this objection only to reject it on the ground that the only acts of mind are acts of will, and in perceiving we are passive and do not exert acts of will. In any case it is not easy to be sure that we can recognize or identify acts of perception. William James, for example, said he could distinguish no such thing (*Essays in Radical Empiricism,* New York, 1912), and Russell later took this view as well (*The Analysis of Mind,* London, 1921). Furthermore, even if the distinction is acceptable, what the object of perception still remains to be determined. It is hard to maintain that what is immediately perceived is a physical object, since this seems to be inconsistent with the physiology of perception. If the immediate object is a sense datum, as Moore and Russell argued, then this suggests a representative theory of perception. But representative theories of perception are liable to the objection that they make our knowledge of physical objects problematical. If, on the other hand, sense data are not intended to play their part in a representative theory of perception but are meant to be all that can be perceived, then common-sense realism has been abandoned and Berkeley is vindicated. Apart from this, the very notion of a sense datum is dubious, since it is impossible to specify what a sense datum is without reference to physical objects. The distinction between act and object does not, therefore, lead to any effective arguments against idealism.

Existence apart from mind. We have seen that Berkeley supported his immaterialist theory with the argument that nothing could exist apart from mind, since if we try to think of something existing unthought of we have to think of it, so that there is a contradiction in the very notion of thinking of something unthought of. Berkeley was by no means the only idealist who used this argument. It seems to have been accepted by Bradley, for example, when he wrote in Chapter 14 of *Appearance and Reality:*

We perceive, on reflection, that to be real, or even barely to exist, must be to fall within sentience . . . . Find any piece of existence, take up anything that any

one could possibly call a fact, or could in any sense assert to have being, and then judge if it does not consist in sentient experience. Try to discover any sense in which you can still continue to speak of it, when all perception and feeling have been removed; or point out any fragment of its matter, any aspect of its being, which is not derived from and is not still relative to this source. When the experiment is made strictly, I can myself conceive of nothing else than the experienced.

This general line of argument came under attack in *The New Realism,* where the objection to it was that it falsely concludes that whatever is must be experienced from the evident tautology that whatever is experienced is experienced. From the fact that nothing can be experienced without being experienced it does not follow that everything must be experienced. Another way of stating this objection is to distinguish (*a*) it is impossible to-think-of-something-existing-unthought-of and (*b*) it is impossible to think of something-existing-unthought-of. Berkeley and Bradley are accused of denying the possibility of (*b*) because of the obvious impossibility of (*a*) (G. Dawes Hicks, *Berkeley,* London, 1932).

Idealist metaphysics. Idealism involves the existence of some ultimate spiritual reality beyond what appears to common sense and ordinary sense experience. If it could be proved, therefore, that it does not make sense to speak of something that transcends sense experience, then idealism, like all other metaphysical systems, would be meaningless, as is claimed by logical positivism. Logical positivism, however, has been subjected to serious criticism and is by no means the chief alternative to idealism. It is linguistic philosophy, the philosophy that seeks to solve or to dissolve philosophical problems by showing that they arise out of linguistic misunderstandings, that today is the strongest opponent of idealism. Moore's insistence on the act–object distinction was not, as we have seen, a successful mode of attack on idealism. But when he criticized Bradley for misunderstanding the logic of propositions in which something is said to be real, he was starting a sort of philosophizing which has proved most inhospitable to idealist theories. Moore saw that when Bradley said that time is unreal he had no wish to deny such things as that people are sometimes late for their trains. Yet if there were no temporal facts, there would be no trains and no people to catch or to lose them. Moore felt that something had gone wrong with Bradley's argument, and he tried to locate the fault. He thought that Bradley believed that even though time is unreal, if it can be thought of then it must have some sort of existence. Moore thought he could show that this belief is groundless and arises from a misunderstanding of what is being said when something is said to be real. But Moore also came to believe that we know for certain such things as that there are trains and people and that in consequence we are justified in denying out of hand those philosophical views which would require trains and people and space and time and matter to be mere appearances or not to be real at all. It was through his attempts to understand the prevailing idealist metaphysics that Moore came to adopt his philosophy of common sense. This philosophy and the linguistic philosophy which grew out of it regard our prephilosophical beliefs and concepts as in a certain sense unassailable. If this view is correct, then idealism is based on misunderstandings. If it is not correct, then the idealist criticisms of our prephilosophical beliefs have to be taken seriously.

Idealism and the nature of thought. The idealist movement is important in the history of philosophy quite apart from the success or failure of idealist metaphysics. Idealists have insisted from Kant onward that thinking is an activity. This view of thinking was Kant's particular contribution to philosophy and is opposed to the Cartesian theory of knowledge. According to Descartes knowledge consists in the intuition of clear and distinct natures. What keeps us from obtaining knowledge, Descartes held, is the existence of prejudices which keep us from getting face to face with the ultimate clarities; once the prejudices are removed, the world shows itself as it really is. On this view the human mind is like a mirror which reflects what is there when it has been wiped clean. According to Kant, however, the mind approaches the world with concepts and presuppositions of its own. It does not reflect the world but tries to understand and interpret it. The activity of synthesizing is an activity of interpreting, and this can be done only by means of concepts which we already possess. According to Descartes we must wipe the mirror clean to be ready for undistorted visions; inquiry ends in revelation. According to Kant we gain knowledge as we improve and test our theories. Apart from natural science, nature is nothing but what men have to contend with in their daily concerns. This view was metaphysically elaborated by Kant's idealist successors, but they did not lose sight of an important implication of it which Kant had seen, the implication that the pursuit of knowledge was a spontaneous activity. They argued that knowledge and freedom go together and that therefore determinism and reductive materialism cannot be true. This would appear to be the essence of the idealist argument.

(See also the following articles in which theories associated with philosophical idealism are discussed: ABSOLUTE, THE; COHERENCE THEORY OF TRUTH; HEGELIANISM; IDEAS; NEO-KANTIANISM; NEW ENGLAND TRANSCENDENTALISM; PANPSYCHISM; PERSONALISM; RELATIONS, INTERNAL AND EXTERNAL; and SOLIPSISM. See Idealism in Index for articles on philosophers who are usually classified as idealists.)

Bibliography

A number of idealist texts are available in A. C. Ewing, ed., *The Idealist Tradition: From Berkeley to Blanshard* (Glencoe, Ill., 1957).

The meaning of the term "idealism" is discussed in Norman Kemp Smith, *Prolegomena to an Idealist Theory of Knowledge* (London, 1924).

On the history of idealism, see G. Watts Cunningham, *The Idealistic Argument in Recent British and American Philosophy* (New York, 1933); Nikolai Hartmann, *Die Philosophie des Deutschen Idealismus,* 2 vols., Vol. I, *Fichte, Schelling und die Romantik* (Berlin and Leipzig, 1923), Vol. II, *Hegel* (Berlin and Leipzig, 1929), 2d ed., 1 vol. (Berlin, 1960); J. H. Muirhead, *The Platonic Tradition in Anglo-Saxon Philosophy. Studies in the History of Idealism in England and America* (London, 1931); and Josiah Royce, *Lectures on Modern Idealism* (New Haven, Conn., 1919).

On idealist social theory, see A. J. M. Milne, *The Social Philos-*

ophy of English Idealism, which, in spite of its title, has a chapter on Royce.

For an analysis and criticism of idealism, see A. C. Ewing, *Idealism: A Critical Survey* (London, 1933).

H. B. ACTON

IDEAL OBSERVER THEORIES. See ETHICAL OBJECTIVISM.

IDEAS. The word "idea" is a transliteration of a Greek word of which the root meaning is "see." In classical Greek it never lost the possible meaning "visual aspect"; thus Plato writes of a person as being "very beautiful in idea," meaning "beautiful in visual aspect" or "good-looking" (*Protagoras* 315E). Very often visual shape is primarily involved, as when Plato refers to the "idea of the earth," meaning "the visible shape of the earth" (*Phaedo* 108D). The transferred sense of "type" or "kind" springs quite naturally from this use. Thus Thucydides writes of "many ideas [kinds] of warfare" (*Histories* I, 109).

In Plato's more technical use, the Ideas or Forms are always spoken of as (1) the objects of intelligence, in contrast with the objects of perception; (2) things which truly *are,* in contrast with changing objects of perception, which are in a state of *becoming;* (3) eternal, in contrast with the perishable world of change. But there are at least two irreconcilable strands in Plato's thought about Ideas. Sometimes he seems to have thought of Ideas much as later philosophers have thought of universals, as when he says that "we are accustomed to posit a single form for each group of many things to which we give the same name" (*Republic* 596A); consistent with this he speaks sometimes of the *presence* of the form in the particular or of the particulars as participating in the form (*Phaedo* 100D). But sometimes Plato writes as if his Forms were, rather, perfect exemplars or paradigms of which the sensible world is an imperfect copy or imitation; thus in the *Parmenides* Socrates says that the Forms are "as it were paradigms" and that "other things are like them and are copies of them" (132D). When the Forms are thus described, we also find Plato insisting that they are "separate," a doctrine in conflict with the language of "presence" and "participation" noted above. It is plausible to suggest that there is here a tension between the theory of universals and the theory of resemblance to standard objects as explanations of common names.

But it is the theory of Ideas as separate and eternal paradigms that appears in the *Timaeus,* the dialogue that had incomparably the greatest influence on later antiquity and the Middle Ages; there the divine demiurge is depicted as forming the world on the pattern of the eternal Forms. It will therefore be the aspect of Forms as paradigms, perfect exemplars, blueprints, particularly as patterns used by a divine agent in creation, which will be important in the development of the philosophical notion of an idea.

In the *Timaeus* the Forms, or Ideas, are eternal and independent objects to which the demiurge looks as patterns. But one of the most important and early modifications of this Platonic view is the religious conception of the Ideas as the thoughts of God. This is the view of Plotinus (*Ennead* III, 9, i), of Philo (*De Opificio Mundi* 4) and of Augustine (*De Diversis Quaestionibus LXXXIII,* Question 46). Clement of Alexandria simply defines an idea as a "thought of God" (*Stromateis* V, iii, 16.3). The ideas are still perfect and eternal exemplars, but now they are in the mind of God.

It is not a very long step to extend the term "idea" to cover patterns, blueprints, or plans in anybody's mind, not only in God's. Thus we find Aquinas saying that "the word 'idea' signifies a certain form thought of by an agent in the likeness of which he intends to produce an external work" (*Quaestiones Quodlibetales* IV, I, 1c); similarly Goclenius says that "in general an idea is a form or exemplar of a thing with an eye on which a workman makes what he has planned in his mind" (*Lexicon Philosophicum* 208A).

When the word "idea" was taken over into the French and English vernacular by learned men in the sixteenth century, there were thus two elements in the concept of an idea—that it was an exemplar or pattern and that it was a thought in a mind. Using the pattern element alone, Rabelais could speak of Pantagruel as being the "idea and exemplar of every joyous perfection" (*Pantagruel*, Book III, Ch. 51); but a pattern and its copy could be easily muddled so that Rabelais also could say, "En leur mariage semble reluire quelque idée et représentation des joyes de paradis" ("In their marriage some idea and representation of the joys of paradise seems to be reflected"; *Pantagruel*, Book III, Ch. 10). When the other, mental element is introduced, the meaning of "idea" quickly becomes "mental representation"; this is a very common meaning in sixteenth-century French and English, and the phrase of Montaigne, "Ayant par longue conversation planté vivement dans son âme une générale idée de celle de Plutarque" ("Having by long communion vividly emplanted in his own a general idea of the mind of Plutarch"; *Essays*, II, 4), could be paralleled many times.

Descartes. Thus when Descartes first began to write, the meaning "image or representation," often but not necessarily "in the mind," was already well known in the vernacular. In spite of the fact that Descartes is usually credited with the invention of the non-Platonic use of the term, we find him at first following this vernacular use. In his first Latin work, the *Regulae*, the word "idea" appears infrequently, but Descartes always uses it to mean an image or representation; when he first introduces it in the *Meditations*, he at once says, "Quelques-unes [de mes pensées] sont comme les images des choses, et c'est à celles-là seules que convient proprement le nom d'idée" ("Some [of my thoughts] are like images of things, and it is to these alone that the name 'idea' properly belongs"). It is only under the pressure of philosophical difficulties that he extends the term "idea" to cover the unimaginable, for which Hobbes duly reprimanded him: "When I think of a man I represent to myself an idea or image composed of colour and shape. . . . of God we have no image or idea" (*The Third Set of Objections*, Objection 5). There is therefore no need for any explanation why the word "idea" tends to mean "mental image" to seventeenth-century philosophers; this is what the word ordinarily meant in their time.

What does need explanation is why, if Descartes found the word "idea" to mean "properly" only "an image of a thing," he and other philosophers could use "having an idea" as a proper designation of all thought and could define an idea as the object of a mind when it thinks, in a liberal sense of "think" that includes sense perception. Part of the explanation is to be found in the representative theory of perception, held in some form by all the philosophers of the period; there was no extension of meaning in using "idea" of sense perception because it was believed that what was directly perceived was not things, but images of things—the images caused by and more or less resembling the things themselves. Another part of the explanation is the "image theory" of thinking: To think of something is or includes having either a mental image of that thing or, as some believed, a physical image on that part of the brain termed the "corporeal phantasy." Such a view was in the air at the beginning of the seventeenth century and was accepted by Pierre Gassendi and Hobbes without reservation. Descartes never doubted that many of our thoughts are images of things; his extension of the term arises from his gradual realization of the inadequacy of the image theory to account for all our thought even while he persevered in the use of its terminology. His use of the term to denote any object of thought became the standard one in philosophy, via such influential writings as the *Port-Royal Logic* and Locke's *Essay*. Only a few scholastically trained philosophers, such as Kant, have stood out for a more Platonic usage; thus Kant in the *Critique of Pure Reason* holds to the terminology of the transcendental ideas of reason to which no corresponding object can be perceptually given, as distinct from the concepts of the understanding ("Transcendental Dialectic," I, 2).

Most of the confusions in the "way of ideas" arise at least in part from the use of the term "idea" to cover both the representative percept and the object of conceptual thought. This can be illustrated in terms of the doctrines of innate ideas, concrete and abstract ideas, and simple and complex ideas.

Innate ideas. The mature Leibniz always maintained, and Descartes sometimes maintained, that all our ideas are innate. Thus Leibniz said that "all the thoughts and acts of the soul come from its own depths, with no possibility of their being given to it by the senses" (*New Essays Concerning Human Understanding*, Book I, Ch. i, 1). But this is a theory of *perception,* as is made clear by Descartes in his *Notes Directed Against a Certain Program,* his defense of the view:

Nothing comes from external objects to our mind through the organs of sense save certain corporeal motions . . . but not even these motions, and the configurations to which they give rise, are conceived by us as they occur in the sense-organs. . . . Whence it follows that the very ideas of motions and configurations are innate in us. So much more must the ideas of pain, colours, sounds, and the like be innate, so that our mind can, on the occasion of certain corporeal motions, display them to itself; for they have no similarity to the corporeal motions.

There is nothing here from which Locke would dissent, except verbally; no wonder that Leibniz said, in the Preface to his *New Essays*, "I am led to believe that at bottom his [Locke's] view upon this point is not different from mine. "The true controversy with Locke is, rather, exhibited by Descartes's view of concepts, expressed in the same terms as and never distinguished from the perceptual theory by philosophers of the time. According to this theory, some ideas are innate—for example, those of God, mind, body; others are adventitious—one's ordinary idea of the sun; still others are made (*factae*) or factitious—the ideas of the sun astronomers construct by reasoning. It is those innate and factitious ideas—which Descartes could as little say were *occasioned* by "corporeal motions" as Locke could say they were *caused* by "corporeal motions"—which raised a still-pressing difficulty.

Abstract and concrete ideas. The distinction between abstract and concrete ideas is virtually the distinction, misleadingly put, of concepts and percepts. The doctrine of abstract ideas was held by the Cartesians, and the best statement of it is to be found in *Port-Royal Logic*, Book I, Ch. 6. To have an abstract idea is to think of some feature or features of the perceptible without attending to other features which it has and which are as inseparable from it (except in thought) as are the length and breadth of a road. Locke took over the Port-Royal account of what abstraction was without change, even echoing its language, but tried to give a more thorough account of what it involved. He tried to give an account of abstraction in terms of a doctrine of simple and complex ideas, but by failing to distinguish thought and perception, he gives two incompatible accounts of this distinction. In Book III of the *Essay* he tells us that all ideas save those denoted by proper nouns are abstract. Of these some are indefinable; they are simple ideas. Others are definable; these are complex ideas. "The ideas first in the mind, it is evident, are those of particular things" (*Essay*, Book IV, Ch. vii, Sec. 9)—that is, we first perceive particular things; in thinking about them, we may come to form some very general ideas by omitting less interesting features and concentrating on those common to a whole group, which taken together form a complex idea; by further abstraction we can get to less and less complex ideas. It is clear that according to this view simple ideas involve the highest degree of abstraction. But in Book II we are told that the simple ideas enter the mind in perception simple and unmixed; they are objects of perception. Thus a theoretical analysis of the construction of concepts is inextricably confused with an atomistic doctrine of perception. If simple ideas are objects of perception and complex ideas are formed from them, then all abstract ideas ought to be imaginable, and Berkeley's famous sneers about the abstract idea of a triangle have some justification. But neither Berkeley nor Hume could emancipate himself from the basic confusion; this is true of Hume in spite of his famous distinction between ideas and impressions.

Thus the classical theory of ideas, which had held virtually undisputed sway in the seventeenth and eighteenth centuries among rationalists and empiricists, was based on the theories of representative perception and image-thinking. To continue to use the terminology after these theories had been abandoned as inadequate could lead only to confusion and a skepticism which, consistently developed, would be even more extreme than Hume's.

Reasonably, therefore, outside the empiricist tradition

the term "idea," as employed in the seventeenth and eighteenth centuries, soon ceased to appear in philosophical writings. Kant's representations have, indeed, some resemblance to ideas of sensation, and the thing-in-itself plays a part somewhat analogous to Locke's substratum. But there are important differences, and his concepts of the understanding are very far from being copies of representations. He does, indeed, use the term "idea" technically, but with a yet further removed significance. In the *Critique of Pure Reason*, he says: "I understand by 'Idea' a necessary concept of reason to which no corresponding object can be given in sensation" ("Transcendental Dialectic," I, 2). These ideas, such as that of the absolute unity of the subject, have, Kant holds, a valid regulative employment, but if we try to apply them to experience we become involved in metaphysical paralogisms. Insofar as the term continued to be used in Continental philosophy it was used, as by Hegel, in senses far removed from that in pre-Kantian philosophy.

But in British philosophy the terminology did not die an easy death. The empiricists could not abandon it, especially in their philosophical psychology in which the doctrine of the association of ideas continued to play the dominant role given to it by Hume. It was largely Bradley's polemic against psychologistic logic that finally led to the abandonment of the "way of ideas." But even Bradley, in the first chapter of his *Logic,* which is a *locus classicus* for the attack on psychologism, showed that he had not completely emancipated himself. He could still write that "the idea, in the sense of mental-image, is a sign of the idea in the sense of meaning," and added "without ideas no judgment," though in a note of 1922 he rejected these statements. By 1922 his own work and that of Moore had led to the elimination of the term "idea" from British philosophy, except as a part of nontechnical idiom.

In the United States, also, the term "idea" continued to have considerable currency. It was a key term in the pragmatism of Peirce, James, and Dewey, reflecting the fact that they, too, were heirs to the empiricist tradition though not to Humean skepticism. They avoided this skepticism in part by wholly abandoning the image theory of thinking with which the terminology of ideas was traditionally linked. In Dewey's instrumentalism, ideas became tools for directing our activities, responses to sensation rather than sensations. They were tied to practical transactions. In calling the idea a law of action, Dewey reminds us rather of the definition given by Aquinas quoted earlier in this article than of the traditional empiricist position. But Peirce could still think, like Bradley, of ideas as psychological entities, as well as in terms of pragmatic epistemology; and in James also the pragmatic doctrine that our ideas of an object have to be explained in terms of the sensations we expect from it and the reactions we make toward it had still not been completely disentangled from a more traditional empiricism.

Bibliography

For critical and historical discussions, see A. G. A. Balz, *Idea and Essence in the Philosophy of Hobbes and Spinoza* (New York, 1918); M. H. Carré, *Realists and Nominalists* (Oxford, 1946); E. Garin, *La Théorie de l'idée suivant l'école thomiste* (Paris, 1932); Paul Natorp, *Platons Ideenlehre* (Leipzig, 1930); W. D. Ross, *Plato's*

Theory of Ideas (Oxford, 1951); G. J. Warnock, *Berkeley* (Harmondsworth, 1953); John W. Yolton, *John Locke and the Way of Ideas* (Oxford, 1956).

For the nontechnical use of the term "idea" (*idée*) in the sixteenth and seventeenth centuries, see *The New English Dictionary* and Huguet's *Dictionnaire de la langue française du seizième siècle*.

See also the bibliographies to CONCEPT; INNATE IDEAS; RATIONALISM; and THINKING.

J. O. URMSON

IDENTITY. People age, some trees regularly shed their leaves, ice melts with the coming of spring, and wood, when burned, gives way to fire and ash. The world seems to be in perpetual flux, undergoing ceaseless transformation. Yet in spite of the alterations we notice, we want to say that this is the same tree which shed its leaves last month, that this adult is the same person we knew as a child, and that this pool of water is made up of the same "stuff" as the piece of ice which melted there. Philosophical reflection about the nature of change, about the problem of identifying or reidentifying something or someone, gives rise to a set of issues which cluster under the name "the problem of identity." In its simplest form, this problem may be thought of as the problem of trying to give a true explanation of those features of the world which account for its sameness, on the one hand, and for its diversity and change, on the other. Put in modern terminology, the problem is that of trying to give a true account of the use (or uses) of such words as "same," "identity," "change," and "diversity," and for such related expressions as "similar," "like," and "different," in order to delineate those features of the world which the use, or uses, of these terms is intended to mark out.

The outlook suggested by our unreflective apprehension of the world—that at any given moment it exhibits features of both permanence and change, of both sameness and difference—is sometimes called the common-sense view of the world. This view seems supported by logical considerations, as well as by those based upon observation. For it seems a matter of logic that when someone truly asserts of something that it is changing, he thereby implies that there is a "something" which remains unchanged and unaffected by the transformations that "it" undergoes. The identification of that which remains untouched by change while undergoing change has traditionally been part of the philosopher's task. If one believes that any correct philosophical analysis of the world must ultimately do justice to our common-sense view of it, the problem becomes singularly acute, for the philosopher is often driven to a picture of the world which is incompatible with this common-sense view. On the one hand, he seems impelled (as Heraclitus presumably was) to maintain that the world is nothing but process and flux and that nothing remains untouched by or immune to change. On the other hand, he is often driven to the position that there must be something which remains exempt from change (Zeno and Parmenides). In the history of this problem the common-sense view stands as a watershed dividing thinkers into two great streams, particularly over the question of whether the world is "really" changing or not. Most of the great theories of antiquity—such as those of Heraclitus, Parmenides,

Zeno, and Plato—fall on one side or the other of this watershed: they affirm either that nothing in reality remains constant or that whatever is real cannot change, and hence that whatever appears to be changing is unreal and illusory. Many other great classical theories (those of Democritus, Aristotle, and Epicurus) may be viewed as compromises attempting to reconcile these conflicting claims, and thus as attempting to justify the common-sense outlook.

Classical views. Difficulties about identity lie at the heart of a vast corpus of seemingly unrelated problems dealt with by writers in the classical and medieval periods. Two broad issues to which they addressed themselves will be discussed here. These issues stem from two differing conceptions of identity—identity interpreted as meaning permanence (amid change) or as unity (amid diversity). These differing conceptions of identity were not always distinguished by early writers, although the two great classical problems to which they gave rise are clearly different from one another. The problem of identity as permanence gave rise to the problem of change, whereas the problem of identity as unity gave rise to the problem of universals. The former problem involves determining what, if anything, remains constant when we say of a certain thing that it changes, but the latter problem may arise independently of any observation of change. We may ask, for example, whether two red spots seen simultaneously in a visual field exhibit the same color when the colors of the spots are indistinguishable from one another. In such a case we are asking whether what appears to be diverse (different things) is really not diverse (is the same thing), whereas in the problem of change we are asking of a certain something whether, after a lapse of time or a transformation in the thing, it is the same thing it was before the lapse of time or the transformation occurred. Each of these problems, in subsequent generations, splintered into a host of related issues, some of them persisting to our own time. The problem of change, for example, gave rise to the problem of substance, problems about the relation between what seems to be so and what is so (appearance and reality), and the problem of personal identity; and the problem of universals gave rise to the problem of individuation and the problem of abstract ideas.

Early modern views. Writers in the seventeenth and eighteenth centuries concerned themselves with five questions about identity: (*a*) how the notion of identity originates; (*b*) what the term "identity" (or "sameness") means; (*c*) whether it is possible for two objects to be identical in all respects and yet differ numerically (the identity of indiscernibles); (*d*) what constitutes personal identity; and (*e*) what is meant by "identical proposition." Personal identity and identical propositions will not be discussed here because these matters are treated at length elsewhere (see ANALYTIC AND SYNTHETIC STATEMENTS; PERSONAL IDENTITY), and the first three topics will be commented upon only briefly, citing the views of representative writers on these topics.

Locke and Hume. Both Locke and Hume treated the problem of the origin of the notion of identity at length and were in considerable agreement in their diagnosis of the origin of the notion of identity. In Book II of *An Essay concerning Human Understanding* (Ch. 27) Locke suggested that the idea of identity originates through a comparison of the "very being" of a thing, observed existing at a determinate time and place, with the same thing existing at another time and place. In *A Treatise of Human Nature* (Book I, Part IV, Sec. 2, "Of Scepticism with regard to the Senses"), Hume proposed a similar but somewhat more subtle analysis that had much the same conclusion. Hume argued that the perception of a single object gives rise to the idea of unity, not of identity, while the perception of a number of objects conveys the idea of multiplicity. Since there can be "no medium betwixt unity and number," the idea of identity can arise neither from the perception of a single object nor from a multiplicity of objects seen simultaneously or in a single moment of time. The solution to the dilemma is to be found in the notion of time, or duration. The notion of identity arises from a propensity of the mind to attribute invariableness or uninterruptedness to an object while tracing it, without a break in the span of attention, through a variation in time. Hume termed such a propensity "a fiction."

Almost all the writers of the period under discussion, from Descartes to Kant, took the term "identity" to mean that an object "is the same with itself" (Hume). These formulations were expressed by the logical principle, regarded as one of the basic laws of reasoning, $[(x)\ x=x]$. In this period queries arose as to the ontological status of this principle—whether it refers to a relation or to a property which all objects possess—a query that was taken up in the writings of Hegel and post-Hegelians (F. H. Bradley, J. M. E. McTaggart) and that became the subject of speculation in the works of Gottlob Frege and Bertrand Russell at the beginning of the twentieth century.

Identity of indiscernibles. The question whether it is possible for two objects to be identical in all respects and yet to differ numerically received elaborate attention in the writings of G. W. F. Leibniz (1646–1716). It is not wholly clear what the common-sense answer to this question would be. If the common-sense view is identified with those distinctions sanctioned by our everyday speech, then the answer would appear to be yes. In ordinary speech we distinguish between "*the* identical automobile" (which may have been taken away for repairs and been returned) and "*an* identical automobile" (an acceptable replacement for one damaged beyond repair). Everyday discourse thus allows for two items to be identical and yet numerically distinct. Still, the ordinary man, if pressed, may be inclined to agree that "an identical automobile" may not be exactly the same as the one it replaces. The Leibnizian response to the query, which emerges from and is demanded by his general metaphysical system, maintains even more strongly that it is impossible for two things to differ only numerically. This response receives expression in his writings in a formal maxim now generally referred to as the principle of the identity of indiscernibles. Leibniz formulated this principle in a number of different ways. In the *Discourse on Metaphysics* (IX) he stated it as follows: "It is not true that two substances may be exactly alike and differ only numerically, *solo numero,*" while in the *Monadology* (9) he wrote, "It is necessary, indeed, that each monad be different from every other. For there are never in nature two beings which are exactly alike and in which it is not possible to find an internal difference, or one

founded upon an intrinsic quality (*dénomination*)." And in his *Fourth Paper to Clarke* (Sec. 4) he wrote, "There are no two individuals indiscernible from one another."

The intuitive idea which these various formulations attempt to articulate is that where two (or more) objects are not identical, it will always be possible to discern a feature, or a set of features, in one of them which the other does not possess. Leibniz' language suggests that he considered this principle to be an empirical law; that if we were to find two items (say two drops of water) apparently possessing exactly the same set of internal features, further investigation (by means of a microscope, for instance) would show that they differed from one another (*ibid.*). According to this interpretation of the principle, "discernibility" is always to be read as "discernibility in principle." But reflection upon his use of the expressions "intrinsic quality" and "internal difference" suggests that he covertly employed the principle as if it were a logical truth, to which no empirical finding would be a counterinstance. This suggestion is reinforced by Leibniz' rejection of the reality of external space. He held that spatial relations are internal properties of substances, and accordingly held that if two items are numerically distinct (are separated in space), they therefore have different internal qualities. It is thus clear that it would be impossible in principle to find two items possessing exactly the same logical properties and yet differing numerically.

It should also be noted that Leibniz invariably formulated the principle of the identity of indiscernibles in a negative way. When so formulated, the principle does not lay down the conditions which any two things, A and B, must satisfy in order to be identical but describes the conditions which must be satisfied when any two things are not identical. Nevertheless, such formulations suggest a corresponding principle of identity; and many commentators regard such a corresponding principle as being merely the converse, or an affirmative formulation, of the principle of the identity of indiscernibles (see Donald Kalish and Roger Montague, *Logic*, New York, 1964, p. 223). Whether such commentators are correct depends on how the positive principle of identity is formulated. If formulated broadly enough, the principle of identity will indeed be the converse of the principle of the identity of indiscernibles (but it should be noted that this positive formulation is not to be found in Leibniz). Benson Mates, in his *Elementary Logic* (New York, 1965, p. 145), gave such a formulation, describing the Leibnizian principle of identity in these words: "If two things are identical, then whatever is true of the one is true of the other." From this principle it does follow that if one thing possesses a feature not possessed by another, the two objects will not be identical. But when the principle of identity is interpreted more narrowly, as involving the coincidence of properties (such as "A and B are identical if and only if all the properties of A are possessed by B and conversely"), then it may be the case that A and B will have all properties in common and yet not be identical. The case where A and B have all internal properties in common, but differ numerically, would be a counterinstance to this formulation of the law of identity, unless spatial relations are also regarded as being internal properties of the objects.

Finally, it should be mentioned that Leibniz used the

term "identical" in at least two other ways. What is sometimes called Leibniz' law (see Mates, *op. cit.*, p. 215) is the principle that "things are identical if they can be substituted for one another everywhere without change of truth-value," a principle which applies to identity of meaning. Second, Leibniz distinguished between "identical propositions" and "contingent propositions" (see *Monadology* 31–35), maintaining that the former are propositions whose "opposite involves an express contradiction," while the latter are propositions whose negation does not involve a contradiction.

Modern views. The work of Gottlob Frege, especially his celebrated paper "Über Sinn and Bedeutung" (translated as "On Sense and Reference"), set the stage for modern researches into the subject of identity. Characteristic of modern approaches to the topic is their connection and involvement with the theory of meaning. From Frege's time to the present, questions about identity or sameness have been interpreted and investigated as questions about the identity of meaning. These questions stem to a great extent from Frege's way of formulating the problem of identity. Frege asked (at the beginning of "On Sense and Reference"), "Is sameness a relation?" and if so, "a relation between objects or between the names or signs of objects?" Frege maintained that identity is to be interpreted as a relation holding between the names or signs of objects. When we utter an identity sentence such as "Venus is the morning star," what we wish to express by this utterance is that the terms "Venus" and "the morning star" both name the same thing, a certain celestial object. If the relation of identity is interpreted as holding between every object and itself, rather than as holding between names referring to a given object, one is faced with the following paradox. It is obvious that the sentences "$a = a$" and "$a = b$" generally have different cognitive significance. For instance, the sentence "The morning star is identical with the morning star" (which is an instance of "$a = a$") is analytic and a truism, while the sentence "The morning star is identical with the evening star" (which is an instance of "$a = b$") is synthetic and represents a "valuable extension of our knowledge." But if a and b are the same object, and identity is taken as a relation holding between this object and itself, then it is impossible to explain how the two sentences can differ in cognitive content, which they obviously do.

Granted that identity is a relation that obtains between the names of an object, how, then, are we to explain how such identity sentences can differ in their cognitive significance? Frege's solution to this difficulty takes us directly into the heart of the theory of meaning. He contended that one must make a distinction between the meaning (*Sinn*) of a term and its referent (*Bedeutung*). His view is that the signs "the morning star" and "the evening star" both denote the same referent, the planet Venus, but the two expressions differ in sense (have a different meaning or connotation). Because they differ in meaning, it is possible for "The evening star is identical with the morning star" to convey information, even though both "the evening star" and "the morning star" have the same referent. The reason why "The morning star is identical with the morning star" is analytic, and uninformative, is that both of the denoting expressions in this sentence not only refer to the same object (Venus) but also have the same sense, or meaning.

The line of research initiated by Frege's seminal paper led, in the early part of the twentieth century, to a widespread agreement among philosophical logicians that the notion of meaning is ambiguous and that a distinction must be made between the meaning of an expression in the connotative or intensional sense and in its referential or extensional sense. Reflection upon Frege's paradox and similar difficulties also led to problems about synonymity (under what circumstances, or in what contexts, expressions have the same meaning). One important consequence of such inquiries was the widespread rejection of the principle that two expressions are synonymous if and only if they denote the same object. A second important result was that Leibniz' law that synonymous expressions may be interchanged in any context without change of truth-value does not generally hold and is true only of extensional contexts. These issues were discussed by Russell in his *Introduction to Mathematical Philosophy* (Ch. 16), where they led to the development of the theory of descriptions; by Rudolf Carnap in *Meaning and Necessity* (esp. pp. 1–68); by W. V. O. Quine in "Notes on Existence and Necessity"; by Nelson Goodman in "On Likeness of Meaning"; by Benson Mates in "Synonymity"; and by others. (The last three papers are reprinted in Leonard Linsky, ed., *Semantics and the Philosophy of Language*, Urbana, Ill., 1952, pp. 77–94, 67–76, 111–138).

An interesting solution to a difficulty analogous to Frege's paradox was proposed by P. F. Strawson in "On Referring" (*Mind*, Vol. 59, 1950, 320–344). Strawson contended that the problem is to explain the difference in the ordinary use of what he calls identification statements. He distinguished between (*a*) That is the man who swam the channel twice in one day and (*b*) That man swam the channel twice in one day. Strawson dismissed the "bogey of triviality," that is, one's apparently referring to the same individual twice over and hence either saying nothing about him or identifying him with himself and thus producing a trivial identity statement. Strawson's view was that the difference between the two statements can best be explained by considering the difference between the circumstances in which one would say (*a*) and one would say (*b*). One would say (*a*) instead of (*b*) if one knew that his hearer knew or believed that someone had swum the channel twice in one day and wondered who did it, whereas one would say (*b*) to someone who did not know that anyone had swum the channel twice in one day. According to Strawson, the solution to the paradox is to be found in the fact that one would say (*a*) to a man "whom you take to know certain things that you take to be unknown to the man to whom you say (*b*)."

Another form of Frege's paradox is called the paradox of analysis, which maintains that all analysis is either false or trivial. The paradox states that if the expression to be analyzed (the analysandum) and the analyzing expression (the analysans) are synonymous, then no information is conveyed by the analysis and it is trivial. If the analysandum and the analysans are not synonymous, then the analysis is false. But since the analysandum and analysans must be either synonymous or not, all analysis is either false or trivial. This difficulty, originally suggested by

C. H. Langford (see "Moore's Notion of Analysis," in P. A. Schilpp, ed., *Philosophy of G. E. Moore*, Evanston, Ill., 1942, pp. 319–342), is dealt with by various writers (Moore, Carnap, Max Black, Morton White, Leonard Linsky); characteristic solutions follow the lines suggested by Frege in distinguishing between the sense and referent of the terms involved.

Under the influence of ordinary language philosophers, the use (uses) of such terms as "identity," "same," and "like" have been intensively studied. Discussions of these notions are found in Ludwig Wittgenstein's *Philosophical Investigations* (Oxford, 1953), John Wisdom's *Other Minds* (Oxford, 1952), J. N. Findlay's *Language, Mind and Value* (New York, 1963, Ch. 1), and J. L. Austin's "The Meaning of a Word" (*Philosophical Papers*, Oxford, 1961, pp. 23–43) and "Truth" (*ibid.*, pp. 85–101). Austin suggested that "same" is one of a group of words ("real," "exists") in which the "negative use wears the trousers." It has no positive meaning but takes its meaning from what it excludes, being a typical device "for establishing and distinguishing the meanings of ordinary words. Like 'real,' it is part of our verbal apparatus . . . for fixing and adjusting the semantics of words" (*Philosophical Papers*, p. 88).

Bibliography

PRIMARY SOURCES, ANCIENT AND EARLY MODERN

Descartes, René, *Philosophical Writings*, translated by Norman Kemp Smith. New York, 1958. Especially *Meditation* III and *Discourse on Method*.

Heraclitus, fragments in G. S. Kirk and J. E. Raven, *The Presocratic Philosophers*. Cambridge, 1957.

Hume, David, *A Treatise of Human Nature*, L. A. Selby-Bigge, ed. Oxford, 1946. Book I, Part I, Sec. 5; Book I, Part IV, Sec. 1.

Kant, Immanuel, *The Critique of Pure Reason*, translated by Norman Kemp Smith. London, 1929.

Leibniz, G. W. von, *Monadology*. 9, 10, 14, 22, 47, 62, 71.

Leibniz, G. W. von, *Discourse on Metaphysics*. 8, 9, 13, 33, 34.

Locke, John, *Essay concerning Human Understanding*. Ch. 27, esp. Secs. 9 and 10.

Parmenides, fragments in G. S. Kirk and J. E. Raven, *The Presocratic Philosophers*. Cambridge, 1957.

Plato, *Parmenides*.

Spinoza, Benedict, *Ethics*. Book I, Secs. 3, 5, 6, 8, 13.

PRIMARY SOURCES, LATE MODERN

Ayer, A. J., *Language, Truth and Logic*. London, 1936. Ch. 7.

Ayer, A. J., *Philosophical Essays*. London, 1954. Pp. 26–35.

Bosanquet, Bernard, "The Philosophical Importance of a True Theory of Identity," in his *Essays and Addresses*. London, 1891.

Bradley, F. H., *The Principles of Logic*, 2d ed., Vol. I. Oxford, 1922. V, VI, Cap. Secs. 4 and 5.

Bradley, F. H., *Appearance and Reality*. Oxford, 1930. VIII, IX, X, XXII, XXIII, XXIV, Appendix C.

Carnap, Rudolf, *Meaning and Necessity*. Chicago, 1947.

Frege, Gottlob, "Über Sinn und Bedeutung." *Zeitschrift für Philosophie und philosophische Kritik* (1892). Translated by Max Black as "On Sense and Reference," in Max Black and P. T. Geach, eds., *Translations From the Philosophical Writings of Gottlob Frege*. Oxford, 1952.

Hegel, G. W. F., *Encyclopedia of Philosophy*, translated by G. E. Mueller. New York, 1959. Secs. 53–75.

McTaggart, J. M. E., *The Nature of Existence*. Cambridge, 1921. Ch. 10, p. 99.

Mill, John Stuart, *A System of Logic*. London, 1843. Ch. 1, p. 201.

Russell, Bertrand, *The Philosophy of Leibniz*, 2d ed. London, 1937.

Russell, Bertrand, *The Principles of Mathematics*, 2d ed. London, 1956. Secs. 24, 64–65, 95, 209, 428.

Russell, Bertrand, and Whitehead, A. N., *Principia Mathematica*, 2d ed. Cambridge, 1962. 13.01, 13.101, 13.12, 13.15, 13.16, 13.17, 13.191, 13.192, 13.193, 13.195.

Wittgenstein, Ludwig, *Tractatus Logico-philosophicus*, translated by D. F. Pears and B. F. McGuinness. London, 1963. Especially 4.241, 4.242, 4.243, 5.53, 5.5301, 5.5302, 5.5303.

ARTICLES

Black, Max, "Identity of Indiscernibles." *Mind*, Vol. 61 (1952), 153.

Bosanquet, Bernard, "The Philosophical Importance of a True Theory of Identity." *Mind*, Vol. 1 (1888), 356.

Bradley, F. H., "On Professor James' Doctrine of Simple Resemblance." *Mind*, N. S. Vol. 2 (1893), 83–88, 366–369.

Chappell, V. C., "Sameness and Change." *Philosophical Review*, Vol. 69 (1960), 351–362.

Church, R. W., "Identity and Implications." *Philosophical Review*, Vol. 43 (1934), 229–249.

Church, R. W., "Bradley's Theory of Relations, etc." *Philosophical Review*, Vol. 51 (1942), 26–46. Reply to Will's article.

Hicks, L. E., "Identity as a Principle of Stable Values." *Philosophical Review*, Vol. 22 (1913), 375–394.

Jones, E. E. C., "Precise and Numerical Identity." *Mind*, Vol. 17 (1908), 384–393.

Lewy, C., "Equivalence and Identity." *Mind*, Vol. 55 (1946), 223–233.

Linsky, Leonard, "Hesperus and Phosphorus." *Philosophical Review*, Vol. 68 (1959), 515–518.

Parker, DeWitt H., "Reflexive Relations." *Philosophical Review*, Vol. 42 (1933), 303–311, and Vol. 43 (1934), 295–300.

Quine, W. V., "Notes on Existence and Necessity." *Journal of Philosophy*, Vol. 40 (1943), 113–127.

Quine, W. V., "Identity, Ostension and Hypostasis." *Journal of Philosophy*, Vol. 47 (1950), 621–633.

Rescher, Nicholas, "Identity, Substitution and Modality." *Review of Metaphysics*, Vol. 14 (1961).

Savery, B., "Identity and Difference." *Philosophical Review*, Vol. 51 (1942), 205–212.

Smith, Norman Kemp, "The Nature of Universals." *Mind*, Vol. 36 (1927), 137–157, 265–280, 393–422.

Taylor, Richard, "Disputes About Synonymity." *Philosophical Review*, Vol. 63 (1954), 517.

Webb, C. W., "Antinomy of Individuals." *Journal of Philosophy*, Vol. 55 (1958), 735–739.

Wiggins, David, "Identity-Statements," in R. J. Butler, ed., *Analytical Philosophy*, 2d series. Oxford, 1965. Pp. 40–71.

Will, F. L., "Internal Relations and the Principle of Identity." *Philosophical Review*, Vol. 49 (1940), 497.

Wilson, N. L., "Space, Time and Individuals." *Journal of Philosophy*, Vol. 52 (1955), 589–598.

Wilson, N. L., "Identity, Substitution and Modality." *Review of Metaphysics*, Vol. 14 (1961), 714.

Woods, M. J., "Identity and Individuation," in R. J. Butler, ed., *Analytical Philosophy*, 2d series. Oxford, 1965. Pp. 120–130.

AVRUM STROLL
Bibliography by D. *Gardiner*

IDENTITY OF INDISCERNIBLES. See IDENTITY.

IDENTITY OF MENTAL AND BODILY STATES. See MIND–BODY PROBLEM.

IDEOLOGY.

"Ideology" did not begin as a term of abuse, and in current usage it often so far escapes any implications of exposé or denunciation that it embraces any subjectively coherent set of political beliefs. In mid-career, however, in the use that Karl Marx gave it, "ideology" signified a false consciousness of social and economic realities, a collective illusion shared by the members of a given social class and in history distinctively associated with that class. It was not only a term of abuse but a term whose abusiveness was amplified by a dramatic and disturbing theory which has not yet been laid to philosophical rest.

The original "idéologistes." At the moment that the word *idéologie* was coined, by Destutt de Tracy in 1796, he and his friends had reason to hope that their "science of ideas"—a program (inherited from Locke) of reductive semantic analysis—would lead to institutional reforms, beginning with a sweeping reform of the schools of France. Like their contemporary Bentham, as much practical reformers in outlook as devotees of theoretical clarification, the *idéologistes* for a time enjoyed a key policy-making position in the Deuxième Classe (moral and political sciences) of the Institut National. It was their fate, unfortunately, to clash with the purposes and the mystique of Napoleon Bonaparte. As a center for sober thinking, the Deuxième Classe could not be tolerated; Napoleon therefore proceeded to abolish it in the course of reorganizing the Institut (1802–1803). He dismissed its members as impractical visionaries and persecuted them with ridicule, allegedly under the name of *idéologues*.

Notoriously, Marx adopted the Napoleonic fashion of using "ideology" with suggestions of contempt, though Marx did not think ideologies were impractical. However, like the *idéologistes* and unlike Napoleon, Marx was a sincere enemy of mystification, and he revived, at the heart of his theory of ideology, a theme congenial to the *idéologistes*. Condorcet, one of the *idéologistes'* friends and chief heroes, had taught that mystification about nature and society originates with specialized intellectuals—priests playing a leading part among them—and that it is foisted on other men in the interest of an oppressive social class. Marx's theory of ideology elaborates this theme with the distinctive addition, to a degree incompatible with the *idéologistes'* expectations but wholly in accordance with their fate, that as mystification is a social phenomenon with institutional causes, it requires an institutional remedy as much beyond the powers of its critics as of its dupes to bring about by argument alone. Only time and economic development can furnish the cure.

Marx's conception. The existence of an ideology—for Marx the mystification to be exposed rather than the method of exposing it—expresses a condition of alienation affecting society as a whole. As Hegel taught, men in such a society mistake their own creations—objectified Mind—for independent external realities, and the intellectual reorientation needed to correct the mistake waits on large-scale historical processes. Society will recover its health and sense of integrity only when the events of economic life visibly embody the rationally coordinated purposes of society and its members. For Marx, though not for Hegel, this happy condition comes about when even the modern state has been superseded by a radical classless democracy preoccupied with industrial administration rather than police work and characterized by thorough-going participant social planning.

The differentiation and alienation of brain-workers from hand-workers is a necessary condition for the existence of an ideology, and hence no ideology would ever have originated if the division of labor—the alienation of man from man—had not taken this direction, which Marx supposed it did very early. But the differentiation of brain-workers from hand-workers is also a sufficient condition for the emergence and continuance in some form or other of the false consciousness of reality embodied in an ideology (and hence both in social institutions and in the ways men think about social institutions). Deprived of physical objects to work upon, the brain-worker's sense of reality is undermined, but *homo faber* still, with his thinking shaped to suit his means and activity of gaining a livelihood, he invents fictitious supersensible objects to work on and discourse about and attaches to them distorted conceptions of the state, of law and morals, of man's relation to nature, of human history and human prospects. These conceptions reflect current economic arrangements—the arrangements for preserving man in society and preparing improvements in his condition—but reflect them so misleadingly as to forestall, for the time being, their conscious and effective social control.

The delusions of theism concerning supersensible reality, together with associated extravagances in idealistic metaphysics, illustrate the lengths to which ideological falsification may be carried. These delusions, in conflicting versions, have been the paramount feature of past ideologies—elaborated in philosophical disputes by brain-workers belonging to multiple social classes; seized upon as rallying points for self-interpretation, self-vindication, and propaganda by multiple social classes differentiating themselves from the submerged hand-workers and from each other. For the emergent bourgeoisie the Calvinist doctrine of predestination was, in Engels' words, "the religious expression of the fact that in the commercial world of competition success or failure does not depend upon a man's activity or cleverness, but upon circumstances uncontrollable by him."

But Marx believed that advanced bourgeois thinkers—the classical British economists, for example—have left most of these delusions behind. Religion no longer counts for much in their ideology. Compared with past ideologies, theirs is a highly simplified one in which what is fundamentally at stake—how current economic relationships are to be conceived—is acknowledged on every hand. The processes of history have made bourgeois ideology ripe for exposure and have eventuated in an especially transparent illustration of ideological distortion. Generalizing from this illustration, it is possible, Marx thought, to look back on history and arrive at a doctrine of the succession of ideologies.

The succession of ideologies. Every ideology embraces, according to Marx, beliefs that motivate the behavior of its adherents, and every social class adhering to an ideology does so because it suits a specific, though transitory, set of economic arrangements. False though it may be in its general appreciation of social realities, it assists the class adhering to it to a period of success; it becomes a blinding handicap only after changing economic conditions have undermined the class's power to maintain itself.

Let F equal the productive forces in characteristic use in a given society—the resources, capital equipment, technology. Let R equal the relations of production—chiefly, the legal relations between members of the society, which define control over the productive forces and determine how the output of given enterprises (and hence of society as a whole) is to be disposed of. Let I equal the ideology prevalent in the society—the beliefs (embodied, generally speaking, in social institutions, in some cases in institutions other than those included in F and R) that motivate members of the society to heed the essential requirements of R in the course of putting F into operation.

According to Marx, (1) given F, certain R's are suitable, and others are not; given a combination of F and R (the basis), certain I's (superstructures) are suitable, and others are not. (2) If F changes, then R changes; if the basis (F and R) changes, then the superstructure (I) changes. (3) A given I attains maximum suitability for a given F and R only at the very time that changes in the F and R are beginning to make this I obsolete. (4) Borne upward by a change in F and R, a new social class rises to dominance, motivated by a new ideology, which it imposes on the whole of society that it (for a time) dominates.

In its own time an ideology serves the interests of the then ruling class by rationalizing the arrangements (R) from which it derives its privileges. Yet in its own time an ideology is more than a rationalization. At its zenith in history the ideology of the dominant class harmonizes actions with opportunities. Accepted wholeheartedly by the dominant class, elaborated by time-serving intellectuals, and at least respected, for want of relevant elaborated alternatives, by the dominated classes, the ideology provides the confidence in incentives that is necessary to make the economic system work.

Thus, the ideology of the bourgeoisie corresponds in an appropriate way to the capitalist system at high noon. This ideology conceives of the laws of the competitive market as natural and impersonal; it accepts the institution of private property in the means of production as natural and permanent; it professes that workers are paid all that in the market they can be paid; and it sanctions without question the expropriation of surplus value by claims founded on private property.

Marx judged this set of ideas false because, like all ideologies, it mistakes contingent historical facts for permanent and immutable ones. But Marx does not deny that if the ideology were repudiated, the incentives of capitalism would disappear. Would the bourgeoisie accumulate capital if they did not consider their savings as permanent acquisitions for themselves and their families? But if they did not save and accumulate capital, the capitalist system would not perform its historic task of accumulating the means of future abundance for society as a whole. Marx believed, just as strongly as any laissez-faire liberal, that economic planning and the incentives offered and required by capitalism are incompatible.

Ideologies distort as much by omitting to ask questions as by affirming false answers. Natural rights advocates issue proclamations that leave their own slaves out of account; bourgeois economists recognize that labor determines exchange value but fail to inquire into the contingency of the institutions that permit capitalists to appropriate what labor has created. These were not glaring omissions for the people who made them. Indeed, how could they have detected them? Once the possibility of mistakes by omission has been suggested, are not the difficulties of detecting ideological errors redoubled?

But it is other people who will do the detecting. Marx believed, optimistically, that current omissions—at least, when they are of social importance—will be identified, just as current mistakes will be corrected, in due time. Optimistically again, he believed that with the identification of the omissions and mistakes characteristic of advanced bourgeois thinkers, the historical process of exposure was nearing its end. Refusing to be diverted from their historical mission by the trivial gains in comfort that trade unions might win for them, the proletariat would complete the work, which the bourgeoisie had carried very far forward, of rationally reconstituting every aspect of life and thought. The class outlook proper to the proletariat could not be dismissed as just another ideology, for the proletariat, unlike previous rising classes, would undertake to reorganize economic relationships so as to dispense with the system of confining men to specific occupations, mental or manual, and of assigning them on this basis to social classes with distinct economic roles. With the abolition (in this sense) of the division of labor and the concomitant disappearance of social classes, alienation would give way to social planning and the occasion for ideological fictions would vanish for good.

The above account is no doubt too flexible to support a rigidly deterministic interpretation of Marx's theory of ideology and too loose to indicate exactly what detailed hypotheses are to be drawn from it. But so is Marx's language. Engels, late in life, indicated that what he and Marx mainly wished to do was simply to insist that intellectual history is not, as ideological versions would have it, independent of the history of economics and technology. Early and late, both of them granted the possibility of interaction—mutual influence—between basis and superstructure, and Engels acknowledged that factors peculiar to different realms of ideology share in determining their development—for example, the notions of consistency and universal application that figure in the development of law.

Ideology today. As a description—a very sweeping description—of social phenomena, Marx's theory of ideology looks less plausible today than it did in his time. It involves discredited prophecies about the imminence of the proletarian revolution. It envisages a prerevolutionary development—bipolarization of the class struggle—that has not taken place. Its picture of latter-day social classes, polarized or not, is obsolete. Nothing easily recognizable as the bourgeoisie and proletariat of Marx's day survive as important social classes; certainly, the division between classes has not been so simplified that only these two remain.

These defects are probably not incurable. The prophecies could be dropped; the conception of social classes could be revised to take into account new complications of class division and new ideological alignments. If individual capitalistic entrepreneurs no longer form anything like a dominant social class, the various groups that have fallen heir to their economic power exhibit many symptoms of ideological conviction. Rallying to cries of "freedom," "peace," and "justice," they rationalize the arrangements associated with their own positions, interests, and incentives as essential to the good of their country or of mankind.

The problem for descriptive theory is to show how such symptoms reflect the economic roles assigned different classes of men by current technology and, more broadly, how the present pattern of beliefs and roles emerged out of past patterns. Sociologists—Marxist or non-Marxist—have done less to refine thinking about this problem and less to prosecute relevant investigations than one might have expected. The problem is still alive, however, and so is the peculiar challenge that the concept of ideology presents to epistemology.

The problem of collective illusion. Where does ideology stop? What standards of truth can be preserved from ideological error and called on to detect it? Some writers—most notoriously Karl Mannheim, discoursing on the sociology of knowledge—have tended to inflate the theory of ideology into an all-embracing doctrine of historical and cultural relativism. Now, such relativism cannot be treated simply as manifesting a hyperbolic doubt of the familiar personal—Cartesian—sort. It may be hyperbolic, but it is not personal; it is a doubt that raises the possibility of collective illusion. Nor can it be refuted—as Karl Popper, understandably impatient with Mannheim, suggested— merely by citing the techniques, leading to collective agreement, that scientists use to correct for personal bias. It is not simply personal bias that is at issue, but a bias that a whole community of scientists may share.

It helps, adopting the treatment of hyperbolic personal doubt in part, to point out that doubts which assume away every means of clearing them up are as perfectly gratuitous as they are perfectly insoluble. This move leads back to Marx. Marx's theory is a theory of limited doubt. He not only allowed for means of resolution but also indicated where the means are to be found. The locus of ideology lies in beliefs of political import about social institutions. To find the distortion and expose its economic connections, Marx would have called in the methods and results of the natural sciences. But even given, under the auspices of some broadly positivistic (or pragmaticist) doctrine, the epistemological primacy of natural-scientific methods, the difficulty remains of distinguishing between well-conceived applications of those methods in the social sciences and ill-conceived ones—possibly ideologically ill-conceived. How, for example, can there be so much disagreement, East and West, and even within the West, about the viability of the market system among economists, all of whom have subjectively coherent and socially shared impressions that their ideas and methods are scientific? While such disagreements continue, with important political issues affecting the livelihood of great numbers of people hanging upon them, one may suspect that the phenomenon of ideology has not disappeared on every side and that neither the sociological nor the philosophical aspects of collective illusion have been fully illuminated.

When they have been, the uses of Marxism will be clearer and so, of course, will the abuses.

Bibliography

Hans Barth, *Wahrheit und Ideologie* (Zurich, 1945), offers a comprehensive scholarly history of the concept of ideology, including an adequate chapter on Destutt de Tracy. F. J. Picavet's *Les Idéologues* (Paris, 1891) remains the fullest treatment of the original *idéologistes*. The main points of Marx's theory of ideology can be gathered from Marx and Engels, *The German Ideology* (written 1845–1846; first published, Berlin, 1932); Marx's preface to *A Contribution to the Critique of Political Economy* (1859); and Engels, *Ludwig Feuerbach and the End of Classical German Philosophy* (1888), especially Chs. 3 and 4.

Secondary works in English on Marxism rarely focus even as much attention on the concept of ideology as the present brief article; for a fuller treatment one does best to resort again to Barth's *Wahrheit und Ideologie*. Georg Lukács's essay of 1920 on class consciousness is an outstanding and exceptional effort on the part of a Marxist writer to develop refinements in Marx's theory; at present, the essay seems to be most easily available in French translation in *Histoire et conscience de classe* (Paris, 1960). In *Sciences humaines et philosophie* (Paris, 1952), Lucien Goldmann supplies an interesting Marxist critique of leading ideological tendencies in Western social science. Karl Mannheim's *Ideology and Utopia* was published in 1936 (London); Karl Popper attacks it in Ch. 23 of *The Open Society and Its Enemies*, 2 vols. (London, 1945; 3d ed., 1957). Inadequate though the chapter may be in some respects, it calls at the end, very much in the spirit of Marx, for social science to rectify its theories by closer association with questions of practical policy.

For discussions of the concept of ideology as an instrument of contemporary non-Marxist social science, see Talcott Parsons, *The Social System* (Glencoe, Ill., 1951), and material contributed by the same author to *Theories of Society*, Vol. II (New York, 1961); see also an essay by Arne Naess in Hadley Cantril, ed., *Tensions That Cause Wars* (Urbana and Champaign, Ill., 1950). The concept is put to use in a major investigation, with instructive and amusing results, in Francis X. Sutton et al., *The American Business Creed* (Cambridge, Mass., 1956).

DAVID BRAYBROOKE

IF. As J. L. Austin, relying on the *Oxford English Dictionary*, has pointed out, the words from which our "if" is descended expressed and sometimes even meant "doubt," "hesitation," "condition," or "stipulation." Because our present uses of "if" are extremely varied and carry, in their manifold contexts, obvious echoes of these origins, it is instructive to attend to these echoes in elucidating the word's various senses.

"Ifs" of doubt, hesitation, surprise, uncertainty. "If" may mean "whether," as in "See if she's here." It may mean "although perhaps," as in "It was an amusing if amateurish cast." It may mean "perhaps even" or "possibly even": "When I was there last, things had, if anything, improved." "If" is often used in solitary conditional clauses to express surprise ("If it isn't Mary!"), indignation ("If that wasn't a stupid thing to do!"), hope ("If the war will only end!"), and so on. It is also used in hypothetical sentences to express skepticism ("If he was embarrassed, he showed no signs of it!") or utter disbelief ("If he succeeds, I'm the king of Siam!"). Finally, it is used in a conditional clause to express doubt or hesitation about some matter relevant to the content, or even the stating, of the main clause. The doubt might concern the hearer's attitude toward what is categorically stated in the main clause

("There's some sherry, if you'd like some") or toward hearing the main clause addressed to him ("I paid you back last week, if you remember"). Although "if" appears in hypothetical sentences in these last uses, it is clear that it does not function as an "if" of conditionality.

"Ifs" of stipulation. "Ifs" of stipulation, which may often be replaced by such expressions as "in the event that" or "in case that," are used in hypothetical sentences to stipulate the conditions under which a thing is to be or will be done (as promised, intended, contracted, commanded, requested, and the like). Examples of this use are "I was to stay home if it rained," "I shall go if the rain stops," "I agree to go if the rain stops." These locutions differ from such related ones as "If it rains, I shall probably stay home" or "I might agree to go if the rain stops" in that the former represent conditional orders, intentions, and agreements instead of hypothetical ones, the latter being orders, intentions, and so on which are not actually given, formed, or made but which will or might be given, formed, or made *if* this or that. Conditional orders, intentions, and the like are, in other words, actual orders, intentions, and so on, but their content is qualified by certain stipulations. That is, they are to be carried out only under the conditions mentioned in the if-clause of the order, statement of intention, and so forth.

"Ifs" of conditionality. "Ifs" of conditionality, which occur in what are called the protases of hypothetical sentences, are often replaceable by such expressions as "on the condition that," "given (or granted) that," "in case that," and "on the supposition that." The main clause, or apodosis, which typically follows the if-clause in these sentences, is often introduced by "then" or "it follows that," these connectives serving to signal the link between the two clauses. The most general remark one can make about this link is that what is stated (granted, supposed, alluded to) in the if-clause purports to provide a condition of what follows in the sense that if the hypothetical is true, sound, or tenable, the apodosis would constitute a reasonable inference from the protasis. Thus, if one knew or had good reason to think that the hypothetical is sound or true, one could justifiably argue, given the premise p, "p, so q," and supposing it to be a known fact that q, one could account for q by affirming "q, because p."

Since reasonable inferences may be of radically different types, hypothetical statements may be of different types as well. Thus, some hypothetical statements purport to state entailments, so that the inference in point is purely deductive; others state definitions (for instance, of such dispositional properties as solubility), lawful relationships ("Whatever has a lower specific gravity than water will float"), causal connections ("If you scratch one of these matches, it will light"), and so on. What is common to these different types of hypothetical is just that if they are true (or sound or acceptable), the corresponding inferences ("p, so q") and explanations ("q, because p") are justifiable.

Although true hypotheticals warrant corresponding inferences, the latter are not always explicitly formulated in those hypotheticals. There are at least two reasons for this. First, the subjunctive form is very commonly used in hypotheticals (for instance, "If it should rain, the crops will be saved"; "If that were put into water, it would dis-

solve"); yet, the terms of the corresponding inference are in the indicative mood (for instance, "It is raining"; "The sugar is put into water"). Second, hypotheticals often have a modal force and may be written with modal terms: "If the premises of a valid argument are true, the conclusion must be true." (Here the warranted inference is from "The premises are true" to "The conclusion is true"; the word "must" simply indicates that the inference is a necessary one.) In general, however, it is possible to rewrite such hypotheticals in a way that makes the terms of the inference explicit. Thus, "If it were to rain, the streets would be wet" may be rewritten as "If it were the case that *it is raining*, it would be the case that *the streets are wet*" (where the italicized expressions constitute the terms of the inference); "If the premises of a valid argument are true, the conclusion must be true" may be rewritten as "It must be the case (or it is necessary) that if *the premises of a valid argument are true, the conclusion is true* as well."

Typically, one who advances or affirms a hypothetical statement does not in any way commit himself to the truth or falsity of the statements related, in the way just indicated, to the protasis and apodosis of the hypothetical, for the truth of the hypothetical is virtually independent of the actual truth-values of these statements, except, of course, in the special case in which the protasis is true and the apodosis is false. Thus, if it is true that Johnny is spanked and false that he cries when spanked, then it is false that if he were spanked, he would cry; otherwise, however, the hypothetical might be true or false, whatever actually happens to be the case with Johnny—that is, whether he happens to be spanked, whether he happens to cry, and so on. For the truth of the hypothetical is determined by the reasonableness of the corresponding inference, by the success of the move from "Johnny is (being) spanked" to "Johnny is crying." (Traditionally, it was insisted that the truth-value of the hypothetical is determined by the "real connection" between the two related propositions or between two possible facts or universals. A reason for putting the point as above will emerge shortly.)

Having related hypotheticals to corresponding inferences and explanations, we can now make an important point about the "ifs" of stipulation and their role in hypotheticals that lack truth-values. Consider the hypotheticals "I order you to take the trip if the weather is suitable"; "I shall go, if the weather is suitable" (where this is an expression of intention); and "Please take the trip if the weather is suitable." Although the "ifs" in these sentences are not "ifs" of conditionality and although the hypotheticals as wholes lack truth-values (as is generally the case with orders, expressions of intention, and requests), there are nevertheless corresponding inferences and explanations of the "p, so q" and "q, because p" patterns. These forms are used chiefly by the agent (the one asked, ordered, or who has the intention) in his practical reasoning about what to do at a given time and in his efforts to explain or justify why he performs a certain action. Thus, corresponding to the three hypotheticals just mentioned, there are three patterns of practical inference: "The weather is suitable, so I must take the trip"; "The weather is suitable, so I will (now) take the trip"; and "The weather is suitable, so I should (out of kindness, decency, or the like) take the trip." Similarly, a corresponding "because" locution is in point as well: "I did take (am taking) the trip because the weather is suitable (and I was ordered, asked, or had formed the intention to take the trip if the weather is suitable)." In other words, just as the moves "*p*, so *q*" and "*q*, because *p*" involve putting a corresponding hypothetical statement to use, so the moves listed above involve putting a corresponding conditional order, intention, or request to work as well.

"Ifs" of truth-functional assertion. Many contemporary philosophers, impressed by the clarity of modern logic, use the locutions "if *p*, then *q*" and "*p* only if *q*" in the sense of "*p* ⊃ *q*" and have therefore established a new use for them. Although there is nothing objectionable in this usage (indeed, it has certain advantages), it is important to see that when "if *p*, then *q*" is used in this way, it does not strictly express a conditional at all—or if it does express a conditional, it is a conditional at the vanishing point. The reason for this is that "*p* ⊃ *q*" means approximately "not-*p* or *q*" or "not both *p* and not-*q*," and there is nothing very conditional about these statements. Besides, if "*p*" is true, then "*r* ⊃ *p*" is true for any "*r*" whatsoever. And to argue "*r*, so *p*" amounts to committing a fallacy of relevance. Thus, the arguments "The moon is made of green cheese, so Socrates was a philosopher" and "Socrates was a philosopher because the moon is made of green cheese" are both jokes, even though "Socrates was a philosopher" is true. Of course, the truth-functional "if" has one property that is essential to conditionality, namely, "if *p*, then *q*" (in this sense) will guarantee the truth of "*q*" if "*p*" is true. But then any equivalence relation on propositions has this property, too: it is possessed, for instance, by "*p* ≡ *q*." The fact is there are 4 relations having this property in a two-valued system and 2,916 relations that have it in a three-valued system.

In spite of all this the practice of using "if" in this "material" or truth-functional sense has some real advantages. For one thing, the detailed logic of the ordinary "ifs" is still somewhat problematic, being a field of controversy for contemporary philosophers of language. Since the logic of the truth-functional "if" is entirely clear and in no way open to dispute, there is an obvious advantage in using this "if" whenever possible. For another thing, if we are asked what must obtain in the natural order (or in the real world) if certain subjunctive or modal hypotheticals are true, we can perhaps give a metaphysically illuminating answer by using a statement involving a truth-functional "if"—one which, like "(*x*)(*fx* ⊃ *gx*)," can be interpreted as merely affirming or denying certain constant conjunctions in nature (for example, that *f*'s are constantly conjoined with *g*'s, and non-*g*'s with non-*f*'s). We may say, in fact, that what justifies a subjunctive or modal "if–then" statement concerning empirical matters is that a certain truth-functional conditional is true and backed by inductive considerations. In other words, the mere fact that, properly understood, "*p* ⊃ *q*" asserts no "real connection" between *p* and *q* may be ontologically illuminating, casting important light on the old battle between empiricist and rationalist interpretations of scientific laws. Of course, because we want to reason about possibilities and eventualities as well as actualities, we will continue to find it extremely useful to employ subjunctive and modal hypotheticals. It may be argued, however, that these statements do not commit us to "real connections" between universals or possible facts. They have the status, roughly, of "inference-tickets," as Ryle has put it, and their factual import can be adequately captured by certain truth-functional conditionals, whose truth is warranted by inductive considerations. (See CONTRARY-TO-FACT CONDITIONAL and LAWS OF SCIENCE AND LAWLIKE STATEMENTS.)

Bibliography

Anderson, A. R., and Belnap, N., "The Formal Theory of Entailment." *Journal of Symbolic Logic*, Vol. 27 (1962), 19–52. This article contains a discussion of the "fallacy of relevance" mentioned in the text.

Austin, J. L., "Ifs and Cans," in J. O. Urmson and G. J. Warnock, eds., *Philosophical Papers*. Oxford, 1961.

Ayer, A. J., "What Is a Law of Nature?" in his *Concept of a Person*. London, 1963.

Burks, A. W., "The Logic of Causal Propositions." *Mind*, Vol. 60 (1951), 363–382.

Kneale, William, *Probability and Induction*. Oxford, 1949.

Kneale, William, and Kneale, Martha, *The Development of Logic*. Oxford, 1962.

Lewis, C. I., and Langford, C. H., *Symbolic Logic*. New York and London, 1932. See p. 228 of this book for a discussion of implication-like relations in three-valued systems of logic.

Mackie, J. L., "Counterfactuals and Causal Laws," in R. J. Butler, ed., *Analytical Philosophy*. Oxford, 1962.

Pap, Arthur, "Disposition Concepts and Extensional Logic," in Herbert Feigl et al., eds., *Minnesota Studies in the Philosophy of Science*, Vol. II. Minneapolis, 1958.

Ryle, Gilbert, "'If,' 'So' and 'Because,'" in Max Black, ed., *Philosophical Analysis*. Ithaca, N.Y., 1950.

Sellars, Wilfrid, "Counterfactuals, Dispositions, and the Causal Modalities," in Feigl, *op. cit.*

Strawson, P. F., *Introduction to Logical Theory*. London, 1952.

BRUCE AUNE

IKHWAN AL-SAFA. See ISLAMIC PHILOSOPHY.

ILLUMINATION. The idea of a divine illumination in the mind occurs in both philosophical and religious contexts. Often it forms one of the links between the two types of thought, and sometimes it bears distinctly religious overtones even in its more philosophical applications. This is one of the characteristic features of the theory of illumination in the thought of Plato, where it played, for the first time in its long history, a major part. Plato, like many other thinkers, creative artists, prophets, and mystics, spoke readily of the sudden flash of understanding or insight in the mind as a flood of light (see, for example, his *Seventh Letter*, 341C, 344B). The image is, indeed, one that occurs naturally in many languages and is especially apt for the description of insight thought to have been achieved as a result of external aid of some kind, of an "inspiration." The language of inspiration is based on the entry of breath, and that of illumination on the entry of light into the mind. The Stoic tradition can be said to have developed the former analogy in its metaphysics; Plato was undoubtedly the father of the philosophical tradition to which the analogy of light is fundamental.

In his *Republic*, Plato employed the analogy of light and vision to describe the process of understanding or of knowledge in general (Books V–VIII). The mind's knowledge of the world of intelligible reality, of the forms or ideas, was held to be analogous to the awareness of material objects accessible to the eye's vision when illuminated by the light of the sun. Plato developed a detailed correspondence between physical and intellectual sight (*Republic* 507 f.), according to which the mind corresponds to the eye and the form to the physical object seen; an "intellectual light" emanating from the supreme form, the Good, and pervasive of the whole intelligible world as well as the mind, corresponds to the sun. Understanding, in terms of this analogy, depends on the intellectual illumination of the mind and its objects, just as vision depends on a physical illumination of the eye and its objects.

A theory of this type, in one or another of many variant forms, became an essential part of a vast body of thought cast in Platonic molds. During the Hellenistic and Roman periods it was widely diffused and incorporated into Jewish and Christian thought. In the Hellenized Judaic milieu of Alexandria the divine wisdom was sometimes spoken of in terms of light, for instance, by the author of the book of Wisdom, who referred to it as "an effulgence of eternal light," which he interpreted as an image of God's goodness (7, 26). Thoughts of this kind found a place in the work of Philo and in the prologue to the Fourth Gospel. Middle-Platonist thinkers, such as Albinus, took the step—perhaps already hinted at by Plato in some passages—of placing the forms within a divine mind and, in effect, identifying the "intelligible world" with the mind of God. In this way a long and rich future was prepared for the theory of illumination within the body of Christian thought.

In Christian thought it is in the work of St. Augustine of Hippo that the theory of illumination is found in its most highly developed form. Like Plato, Augustine thought of understanding as analogous to seeing. Understanding, or intellectual sight, was therefore, he held, conditional on illumination, just as physical sight was; only here the light was the intelligible light that emanated from the divine mind and in illuminating the human mind endowed it with understanding. Understanding, in the last resort, was an inward participation of the human mind in the divine. The scope of illumination was further extended, at the cost of precision, in the work of the pseudo-Dionysius. His favorite designation for God, the absolutely transcendent One, was in terms of light. God is the intelligible light beyond all light and the inexhaustibly rich source of brightness that extends to all intelligence. His illuminating activity gathers and reunites all that it touches; it perfects creatures endowed with reason and understanding by uniting them with the one all-pervading light (*De Divinus Nominibus*, IV, 6). In true Neoplatonic fashion, the pseudo-Dionysius conceived of the cosmos as a hierarchically ordered system, descending in order of reality and value from its source, the One. Illumination, in general terms, is the means by which intellectual creatures ascend and return to unity, and the "hierarchy" (understood as extending through both the cosmos and the church) is defined as the divine arrangement whereby all things, participating in their measure in the divine light, are brought back to as close a union with the source of this light as is possible for them (*De Coelestia Hierarchia*, III, 1). In a more special sense, illumination is the second of three phases—namely purification, illumination, and perfection—of man's return to the One. In this more specialized sense the church's sacramental system and the grades in the ecclesiastical hierarchy concerned with its administration are agencies of divine illumination. Illumination is the intermediate stage of approach to God, between initial purification and final perfection (*De Ecclesiastica Hierarchia*, V, 1, 3). In the most restricted sacramental contexts "illumination" thus becomes synonymous, in accordance with an old Christian usage, with "baptism." In the work of the pseudo-Dionysius the theory of illumination was merged with an inclusive conception of the spiritual life formulated in the language of light and illumination.

The reputation enjoyed by Augustine and by the writings of the pseudo-Dionysius in the Middle Ages assured their views a long future. In the thirteenth century the rise of Christian Aristotelianism provided the first serious alternative theory of knowledge. In this there was no place for the intervention of a divine illumination as an essential constituent of knowledge. Knowledge was accounted for entirely in terms of mental activity and its objects, and no reference to God was necessary to explain it. Nevertheless, the *lumen intellectuale* of the mind was held to be a participation in the *lumen divinum* of the divine mind, since God was present everywhere, in the mind no less than in other things. In this way Christian Aristotelians, such as St. Thomas Aquinas, were able to endorse some characteristically Augustinian statements in spite of the fact that their theories of knowledge were built on a radically different structure. The Augustinian version of the theory of illumination continued to have a vogue among some thinkers of the thirteenth century, such as St. Bonaventura, and even later. It found echoes in the thought of some modern philosophers, such as Malebranche. Increasingly, however, in the later Middle Ages and after, the language of illumination, especially as elaborated by the pseudo-Dionysius, became the special property of mystical writers and writers on the spiritual life.

Bibliography

Allers, R., "St. Augustine's Doctrine on Illumination." *Franciscan Studies*, Vol. 12 (1952), 27–46.

Geach, P., *Mental Acts*. London, 1957. Section 11 and the Appendix include corrections of the standard account of Aquinas' theory of concept formation.

Jolivet, R., *Dieu soleil des esprits*. Paris, 1934. A study of the theory of illumination.

Markus, R. A., "St. Augustine on Signs." *Phronesis*, Vol. 2 (1957), 60–83. Includes a discussion of illumination in Augustine's theory of knowledge.

R. A. MARKUS

ILLUSIONS. Most of the major philosophical problems of perception derive from the fact of illusions. These problems center on the question whether perception can give us true and direct knowledge of the world, and thus they are basic to epistemology. This article will describe illusions and set forth and examine the argument from illusion that perception cannot be trusted as a source of knowledge of the external world but affords direct awareness only of appearances or sensa.

Three kinds of illusory experience. The term "illusion" is used by philosophers to cover a range of phenomena approximately classifiable as follows.

Illusions proper. Illusions proper occur when the percipient is deceived or is liable to be deceived in identifying the object perceived or its properties. Psychologists have produced a number of optical illusions, such as equal lines that appear to be of unequal length; a stationary balloon that when inflated and then deflated seems to advance and then recede; and a specially constructed Distorted Room, in which a man looks smaller than a boy. Diseases or drugs, including alcohol, may produce other illusions, such as double images or the unearthly colors and multiple shapes an object may assume for one who has taken mescaline. Other examples are mirages, mirror effects, and conjurers' tricks. The perception of motion introduces many more: at the cinema a rapid succession of slightly different stills on a flat screen makes us see a scene with a three-dimensional perspective in which people move about; the wheels of a coach may seem to be going backward when really they are moving rapidly forward (stroboscopic effect).

Relativity of perceptions. A round plate that looks elliptical when seen from an angle and a square table that looks diamond shaped illustrate the relativity of perception. The same water may feel cool to one person and warm to another; the same wine may taste sweet or dry, depending on what one has just been eating; green hills may look blue in the distance; and as a train rushes past, the pitch of its whistle may seem to vary. Further examples are color blindness, shortsightedness, and other physical defects that alter the appearance of things. In all these cases the apparent properties of an object vary relative to the position of the percipient, the distance and media between him and the object, the lighting, the state of his health, body, or sense organs, etc. These are not strictly illusions (they usually do not deceive), and they vary around a norm in which the objects are perceived accurately.

Hallucinations. In pure hallucinations—for example, the pink elephant a drunkard sees, the apparitions of delirium, Macbeth's dagger—some physical object is "perceived" when neither it nor anything at all like it is present. In contrast are illusions where the mistake is about the properties, position, or identity of some object actually in view.

Some, perhaps even most, hallucinations are triggered by some perceived feature of a very different character; for instance, a beam of light may be taken to be a person. Many hallucinations are integrated; they fit well with the real background, cast shadows, and vary in size and perspective as they move. One may also class phantom limbs as hallucinations. Pain or other sensations are felt "in the toes," for example, of a leg that has been amputated—the victim still feels he possesses the missing limb.

Argument from illusion. The main aim of the argument from illusion is to show by means of illusions that the senses are not to be trusted and that perception is not direct and certain awareness of the real properties of material objects but awareness of appearances only. In fact, this argument involves three subarguments.

(a) A skeptical claim. However sure we are about our perceiving, it is always possible that we are being deceived by one of the many kinds of illusion or hallucination, since it is characteristic of such states that we cannot tell that we are suffering from them. This may in practice be a negligible possibility, but philosophy is concerned with the highest standard of exactitude, and from this strict position perceiving is not absolutely certain because there is always some theoretical possibility of error. Various conclusions can then be drawn. One is that for certain knowledge we must rely not on the senses but on some other faculty, such as intellectual intuition (as in Descartes); another is that we must abandon common-sense realism (discussed in REALISM and SENSA).

(b) Nature of appearances. In all these illusions there is some thing or quality that does not coincide with the object or object-properties that are in fact present—for example, the apparitions of hallucinations, the elliptical appearance we see when we look at a round plate, the black shape the color-blind man sees when looking at a red box, the oasis of a mirage, and the second bottle in double vision. All these are merely appearances and cannot be identified with real objects or properties. What then are these appearances? In some cases, and probably in all, they must be *sensa*, private, probably mental, objects of awareness quite distinct from external material objects, although no doubt they are caused by or resemble material objects.

(c) Significance of continuity. If one were to change from seeing an appearance, a private and transitory sensum, to seeing a public, enduring physical object ("public" meaning observable by several persons at one time), one would expect a sudden change in the character of one's sensory experience. But no such jump occurs: there is normally an unbroken continuity between situations where we cannot actually be seeing the material object but are aware only of appearances and situations where we think we see the material object. As we move from where the plate looks elliptical to where it looks round, or as the drunkard looks first at the pink rat and then at the real bed on which it sits, there is a smooth transition. Consequently, even in these seemingly genuine or veridical perceptions we must also be aware of appearances or sensa and not directly of the object itself.

We may note three things concerning our subarguments: (1) argument (*b*), unlike (*a*), does not depend on there being error; even if one is not deceived by perspectival distortion, double vision, and so on, the argument that what is really perceived must be sensa is unaffected. (2) The claim in (*b*), that the appearances are private and mental existents, depends to some extent on considerations of continuity. Almost all hallucinations, the dark shapes a color-blind man sees or the results of diseases and drugs, are plausibly private to the percipient. But simple perspectival distortions will be private only to the viewpoint. For instance, the elliptical appearance of the plate is as public as the round one in that many may see it at once; this holds similarly for mirages and reflections. Unless causal considerations are introduced, the supposition that each person is then seeing a numerically different but qualitatively similar elliptical appearance or sensum must rely partly on similarity with cases where the content of illusion is undeniably private and partly on the assumption that if the plate is round, then the elliptical appearance must be something other than the plate; but these are hardly compelling grounds. (3) The charge may be made, How do we know that the plate is round or what its real color is? These points would normally be settled by measurement or by reference to standard lighting conditions, but the argument does not rely on this. To take the plate example, it may be put thus: the plate looks elliptical to *A* and round to *B*; it cannot be both round and elliptical, for that would be a self-contradiction; therefore, one of these appearances at least must be quite distinct from the plate—and perhaps (by continuity) both are.

Criticism of the argument from illusion. The argument from illusion can be countered in various ways.

Certainty. The skeptical claim is often met by stressing the comparative rarity of illusion and the efficacy of the various tests that can be made to remove doubt. We can use one sense to help another. For example, wax fruit may look like real fruit, but touch and taste reveal it; sight, memory, and testimony can show that a phantom limb does not exist; measurement can settle the real shape of an object; confirmation from others can show up many hallucinations, though there are some group hallucinations; we soon learn to discount alcohol and drugs and may generally argue from known causal factors present. But although these tests reduce the possibility of error in a tested perception to extremely slight and in practice negligible proportions, the critic will still say that it is not *absolutely* certain and that only absolute certainty will satisfy the philosopher. To this there are two replies. (1) It is logically impossible that we suffer from hallucinations all the time; if no perception were ever certain, then there would be no way of distinguishing hallucinations and illusions from normal perception. (2) The skeptic is misusing the word "certain"; well-tested perceptions are just the things we refer to as certain. If we say they are only probable we destroy the normal useful distinction between "certain" and "probable." If nothing is certain, the word has no meaning, and we shall just have to invent a new term for that ordinary distinction.

We may comment on these replies. Reply (1) is of no help in deciding whether any particular perception is certain or not—which is one of the main points—and anyhow, a merely approximate certainty would serve to distinguish perceptions from hallucinations. Reply (2) seems to depend on confusing meaning and reference. It is true that perceptions are things we refer to as certain, but that may only be due to our ignorance of the possibility of illusions. The normal meaning of "certain"—without any possibility of doubt—is correctly adopted by the skeptic; he merely argues that it may only be used of the results of intuition or of mathematical demonstration, not of perception; that is he differs only as to the referents of the word. Also, he can still distinguish between "probable" and "practically certain" in perceptual statements. However, a modified reply to the skeptic may be made (3) that he is in fact limiting the word "certain" to cases of logical necessity, to those which it is self-contradictory to deny. This limitation not only has the practical disadvantage of destroying the ordinary certainty–probability distinction but also rules out a priori the possibility of any perceptual statement's being certain; thus the lack of certainty in perception is due not to any defect in perceiving but simply to its not being something quite different from what it is, namely intuition or entailment. It would therefore be much more appropriate to use a relaxed standard in dealing with perception and to allow a perceptual statement to be regarded as certain if it has passed all conceivable or all recognized tests. At any rate, there is no reason to suppose that ordinary perceptions are uncertain in the way that the result of a horse race or the nature of next year's weather is uncertain.

Hallucinations. The argument from the significance of continuity claims (1) that hallucinations are private sensa, not public material objects, and (2) that since they are indistinguishable from the objects of perceptual consciousness, especially when integrated with them, the latter must also be groups of sensa—representations, perhaps of external objects.

(*a*) One answer, based on the usual psychological account of hallucinations, would be that they are not sensa but mental images of an unusually vivid type that are confused with normal perception. To meet point (2), the unusual vividness and the lack of normal discrimination may be stressed and explained by the special circumstances in which almost all hallucinations occur, as when the victim is suffering from fever, drunkenness, drugs, starvation, religious ecstasy, or madness or is influenced by lesser factors, such as fear, acute anxiety, or drowsiness. (In the hallucinations of mescaline the person's mental powers are unimpaired, but he usually recognizes the hallucinations as such and is not deceived into thinking they are real.) It is questionable whether these factors, especially the lesser ones, can account for the integration and triggering of hallucinations—cases in which the continuity argument is strong and imagery would seem to merge with genuine perceptions. Also, to be complete this answer would need to offer an explanation of the nature of mental imagery and of why it resembles perceiving. Probably imagery depends on reactivation of the kinds of brain and nervous activity that occur in perception (or in action, if it is motor imagery), and the occurrence of such activity can be detected during the imagery. However, this involves the causal processes, study of which leads by a different route to the abandonment of common-sense theories.

(*b*) It has been pointed out, by J. L. Austin, for example, that the argument from illusion as applied to hallucinations relies on certain dubious assumptions, namely, that if two things (i.e., an object of genuine perception and an object of hallucination) are not generically the same they cannot look alike, and that they cannot be distinguishable if we in fact fail to distinguish them. The special circumstances cited in point (*a*) may come in here as providing reasons for the victim's failing to distinguish what are in fact distinguishable and quite different experiences. This criticism certainly undermines the argument from illusion as a demonstration; for it to be that, these assumptions would have to be accepted as universally true. But it can be replied that an explanation is still required for the general similarity between the two things (sufficiently close a similarity for people suffering only from anxiety to confuse them); also, we need some general theory of the nature of hallucinations and of their integration and triggering.

Phantom limbs are not covered by these points: one can

hardly say that the pains and sensations involved are images of genuine ones—they are genuine enough—nor are the victims suffering from drugs or delirium. The usual physiological explanation is that the nerves from the toes, for example, remain in the untouched part of the limb and, being irritated at the stump, send impulses to the brain similar to those they would send if the toes were being crushed or the pain and other receptors in the toes were being otherwise stimulated. This seems to confirm that pain and somatic sensations are private sensa and accords with the general causal theory of representative realism. But it is still arguable that such sensations are very different from sight and hearing, so that nothing follows about the nature of the latter.

Illusions and relativity. The argument from the nature of appearances relies on the odd assumption that things cannot look other than they are, that when one apparently sees as elliptical a plate that is actually round, then one cannot really be seeing the plate; one is seeing something, an appearance or sensum, which, being elliptical, cannot be the round plate. But one can simply deny the assumption and say that one is in fact seeing a round plate from such a position that it looks elliptical; its elliptical appearance is not some entity different from it. To treat appearances as entities, as though they were things, is a quite unjustified reification; when we speak of the appearance of something we speak of how it, the original object, appears, not of some other object distinct from it. One may confirm this point by noting that the elliptical shape will appear on a photograph too, so that it cannot be subjective or mental. The same answer may be applied to the various examples of relativity and illusion. The distant green mountains are actually seen but look blue and may be so photographed; in the Doppler effect we still hear the whistle (a "public" noise), and its apparent variation in pitch may be recorded on tape. In the optical illusions we are still seeing lines on paper, balloons, or a man and a boy, and cameras will photograph them with their deceptive appearances. Again, as J. L. Austin has shown in detail, in refraction and reflection we still see the object—the face in the mirror or the stick in the water; even in a mirage we see a real oasis, though it appears many miles nearer than it actually is. It may also be claimed that the color-blind man sees the red box, even if it looks black to him, and that the man with double vision sees the one bottle, but it looks double to him. (This last point is more dubious: it may be said that looking double is not like looking blue for it involves an extra apparent object and not a differing quality of the one object. On the other hand, the percipient is not seeing two bottles in the same way normal people see one: the bottle and the background have a doubled, slightly defocused appearance that perhaps makes it reasonable to say they look double.)

For some people this general answer is immediately convincing, and it seems incredible that the argument from illusion was ever taken seriously. But others protest that it is inadequate and neglects the immediacy of perception; in the various situations mentioned they seem clearly and directly to be aware of an elliptical shape or a blue expanse of mountain, an advancing balloon, two bottles, or, if color-blind, a black box-shaped expanse. Thus to be told that they are aware only of a round plate, green mountain,

stationary balloon, one bottle, etc., is to them unconvincing and fails to do justice to the facts of experience. This feeling for the immediacy of sensory awareness, and the belief that confrontation is so direct that its apparent object must exist as perceived, is at the bottom of the sense-datum theory (see SENSA). The alternative is to dismiss as illusory this apparent direct and mistakeproof confrontation in perception; perceiving is variable in quality, is affected in its accuracy by position, distance, and many other factors, and may thus be inefficient. It is more plausible to suppose that position, distance, and media distort perception of a round or green object or that color blindness and short-sightedness prevent one from seeing it properly than to suppose that these factors give one excellent and perfect awareness of some elliptical or blue sensum different from the object. But this is not a final answer, for if one then seeks to discover how these factors affect the quality of perception, one has to go into scientific details. Angle of sight varies the pattern of light striking the eye, refraction or reflection bends the light rays, dust scatters the light or absorbs some frequencies rather than others, drugs affect the activity of the nervous system, lack of certain retinal pigments alters the eye's response to light, the Distorted Room and other optical illusions rely in their effects on misleading cues. In short, the effects of illusion point beyond themselves to the causal and psychological processes that underlie perception and constitute its most serious theoretical problem (see PERCEPTION).

Bibliography

The argument from illusion is a stock feature of introductions to philosophy and is dealt with in most of the books in the bibliographies for SENSA, REALISM, and PERCEPTION. The books listed below give a fuller treatment of the subject.

Henry Habberley Price's *Perception* (London, 1932) and Charlie Dunbar Broad's *Scientific Thought* (London, 1923) and *The Mind and Its Place in Nature* (London, 1925) develop the argument to support sense data. Alfred Jules Ayer's *Foundations of Empirical Knowledge* (London, 1940) develops it to support the introduction of a "sense-datum language." Price has some second thoughts on perspectival distortion in his article "Illusions," in Volume III of *Contemporary British Philosophy*, edited by Hywel David Lewis (London, 1956), and Ayer's latest views are presented in his clear introductory work *The Problem of Knowledge* (London, 1956).

John Langshaw Austin, *Sense and Sensibilia* (Oxford, 1962), D. M. Armstrong, *Perception and the Physical World* (London, 1961), and Rodney Julian Hirst, *The Problems of Perception* (London, 1959), are critical of the argument from illusion. See also George McCreath Wyburn, Ralph William Pickford, and R. J. Hirst, *Human Senses and Perception* (Edinburgh and Toronto, 1964), which, besides criticism, gives some physiological and psychological details. For other attempts to meet the facts of illusion without postulating sensa, see the works listed under "Perspective realism and the like" in the bibliography for REALISM and under "Sense data" in the bibliography for SENSA.

The neurologists John Raymond Smythies, in *Analysis of Perception* (London, 1956), and Russell Brain, in *The Nature of Experience* (London, 1959), give some useful references and nontechnical information on hallucinations. The psychological details of illusion in general can be found in any good introductory textbook on psychology, such as David Krech and Richard S. Crutchfield, *Elements of Psychology* (New York, 1958).

R. J. HIRST

IMAGES. Aristotle's claim that "it is impossible even to think without a mental picture" (*On Memory and Recollection* 450a) has frequently been echoed by subsequent philosophers. Hume equated thinking with having mental images, since he appears to have considered ideas and images to be the same; for of any sense impression "there is a copy taken by the mind, which remains after the impression ceases; and this we call an idea" (*Treatise of Human Nature*, Book I, Part I, Sec. ii). The sole contents of the human mind are original impressions and these copies of them. Hobbes was stating much the same view when he said, "Imagination therefore is nothing but *decaying sense*" (*Leviathan*, Ch. 2).

Many other philosophers have also accepted the existence of such mental contents without examining their nature; they had assumed that images are things whose nature or existence is obvious to all human beings and that can most simply be described as "copies" or "pictures" of the external world. Views denying the existence of such objects have been rare; the chapter in Gilbert Ryle's *Concept of Mind* that seems to attack the commonly held view of the imagination as the power of producing mental images is felt by many to be contrary to normal experience. The images that Hobbes and Hume were talking of, and that Ryle attacks, are mental existents, depending on our prior experience of the physical world, though they may have objective counterparts in the brain. In this they differ from the Epicurean *eidola* or *simulacra,* which Lucretius defined as "images of things, a sort of outer skin perpetually peeled off the surfaces of objects and flying about this way and that through the air" (*De Rerum Natura*, Book IV, ll. 29 ff.). These images Lucretius thought of as physical objects, albeit rather ethereal ones, whose function is to explain perception as well as images and dreams. When actual existence is attributed to them they are made to resemble the physicists' "real images," which are the representations of objects formed on screens or in space by lenses, or on the retina of the eye by the same mechanism. Physicists also talk of a "virtual image," a visual appearance that cannot be detected by physical means in the place in which it seems to be (for example, the appearance of objects behind the mirror's surface). This usage, which implies that there is something unreal about the image, is nearer to the normal philosophical or psychological use than is that of the term "real image." The connection between "image" and "imaginary" is preserved in ordinary usage.

Images as the meanings of words. Undoubtedly the strongest desire to maintain the existence of mental images has come from the need to provide something to serve as the bearer of meaning for words of our language. Berkeley's attack on Locke in the Introduction to *The Principles of Human Knowledge* is mainly concerned with this question. Against what he took to be Locke's view of the existence of "abstract general ideas," or the meanings of general terms, Berkeley argued that images must be particular. It is, he claimed, impossible for anyone to form a general idea (by which he clearly meant "image") of a triangle, for it would have to be "neither oblique nor rectangle, neither equilateral, equicrural, nor scalenon, but all and none of these at once." Whether Locke had meant this by his argument for abstract general ideas will not be discussed here; the important point is that Berkeley may be said to have shown that in some cases thought may proceed without

images, because there could be no image or "mental picture" to correspond with some terms of our vocabulary.

Nevertheless, it may still be claimed that imagery is an important part of our mental life; this is argued by H. H. Price in his *Thinking and Experience* and elsewhere. Empirical evidence would appear to show that there is considerable divergence in the amount of mental imagery experienced by different individuals; Sir Francis Galton (in *Inquiries Into Human Faculty and Its Development*) stated that imagery tended to be lacking in "scientific" minds and to be common in those of artistic bent. The Würzburg school of psychologists in the early twentieth century maintained that their experiments proved the existence of "imageless" thought. The difficulty here lies at least partially in determining what is to be called a "mental image." Although most people, as has been said, understand the instruction "Picture to yourself a familiar building" and claim to be able to do so, it is obvious that what they do in such a case is not the same thing as looking at a picture or photograph of the object, and it is not clear what connection this ability has with that of using the words of a language.

Wittgenstein's criticism. Wittgenstein argued that if some form of mental picture is needed to "give meaning" to a word, then an actual picture can be used instead; for example, asked to get a red apple, a man could use a color chart that gave a specimen of red opposite the word "red." He could then compare apples with this sample until he found one that matched. Those who think of images as being essential to the use of language are talking as if each person carried such charts "in his head" and proceeded in the same way in the absence of an actual sample. The difficulty with this view, in Wittgenstein's opinion, is that the command "Imagine a red patch" can be given and obeyed; here it is obvious that the "mental sample" will be of no use or will lead to an infinite regress. The image can itself be recognized as red without the use of any intermediary, so there is no reason why a specimen of red should not also be recognized. Most people do, in fact, immediately recognize specimens of the common colors, though they may need a chart for the rarer ones. Wittgenstein summarized his attack on the false picture of recognition as follows:

> It is as if I carried a picture of an object with me and used it to perform an identification of an object as the one represented by the picture. Our memory seems to us to be the agent of such a comparison, by preserving a picture of what has been seen before, or by allowing us to look into the past (as if down a spy-glass). (*Philosophical Investigations*, Sec. 604)

There are two further difficulties about this view of the image as the bearer of meaning. First, it is not clear how an actual picture functions, and second, the comparison of the image with a picture itself gives rise to difficulties.

Functioning of actual pictures. Price has stated that "both words and images are used as symbols. They symbolise in quite different ways, and neither sort of symbolisation is reducible to or dependent on the other. Images symbolise by resemblance" (*Thinking and Experience,*

p. 299). Price's arguments for his weakened version of the imagist theory rest, as the quotation shows, on the assumption that images, like other pictures, are related to their objects by resemblance. Such a view assumes that there is no problem in recognizing a picture of, say, a man as a man. Just as anyone who could pick out a real man could identify a mirror image of a man, so, it is thought, could he pick out a pictorial representation of a man.

But what is to count as a picture of a man here? A child's matchstick man consisting of five lines and a circle? A rough sketch? A "lifelike" portrait by a Royal Academician? A life-size photograph? As the art historian E. H. Gombrich has shown in his *Art and Illusion,* the representation and the recognition of three-dimensional objects on a two-dimensional surface is a sophisticated activity. Our children are taught something of the appropriate techniques at about the same time as they learn their native language. There is no basis for feeling that the procedure of representing objects in these ways is more "natural" than describing them by means of words. It has been said that some primitive peoples find it impossible to recognize a photograph of one of their number because they have not learned to interpret the pattern of black and white in the appropriate way. Yet it would seem that a photograph is the most "natural" representation because it is the product of a purely objective projection of the object; drawings and paintings depend on a variety of learned techniques of representation.

It is necessary to distinguish between the way in which a picture is produced and the use that is made of it. There may be a method of projection, but it is not because of that method that we accept the picture as a likeness. Furthermore, it is not clear from the picture itself, though it may be from the title, what it is meant to be the likeness of. A picture of an oak may be that of a particular historic tree (King Charles' Oak, for example), an example of an oak tree for purposes of identifying the species, an illustration for a general article on trees, a sign for a forest, or a composition to hang on the wall for its "artistic" quality. Without some rule it is impossible to tell what the picture is for and hence what its subject is; its meaning, what it symbolizes, lies in the use we make of it. In the context of a botany class it may be quite clear that the picture of an oak is being shown to enable students to identify specimens of that tree; here the rule is given by the situation in which the picture is used. Similarly, it is clear that the man who carries a photograph of his sweetheart does it to remind himself of her, uses it as a kind of substitute for her presence. Real pictures have a variety of uses.

Images as pictures: objections. A picture may be used to give information; from a picture of the Pantheon it is possible to discover the number of columns in the façade. But as Sartre points out in *L'Imaginaire* (p. 117), an image of the Pantheon may not be sufficiently detailed to enable this, even though before the question was asked the agent thought his image was perfectly clear. If he does not already know the number, then he cannot count the columns in his image. In this the image differs radically from the picture. Furthermore, it is usually known what the image is an image of without the need to inspect it for clues. Even when an image arises in the mind and cannot be

recognized, no closer examination will provide clues to its identity; we have to wait until the name comes to us. In the extreme case of dreaming, we may "recognize" a person even though his characteristics are entirely different from those possessed in real life. A picture, on the other hand, may be identified gradually by the collection of clues. Thus, "having an image" of an object differs from contemplating either the object or a picture of it. The image is not a picture in a special private gallery (cf. Ryle, *op. cit.,* p. 247).

Part of the difficulty, as Ryle stresses, is due to an excessive concentration on the sense of sight; we naturally talk of "picturing" or of "visualizing," but there are also aural, tactual, and olfactory imagery. (A blind man's imagery, presumably, would be entirely of these kinds.) But in these cases there is no recognized means of representing the sound, touch, or smell—what would such a process be like?—and hence no temptation to talk of such images in terms that are drawn from the inspection of physical representations.

We do find it very natural to talk of mental images, and because external objects are normally described in visual terms, these terms are also applied to images.

Images are not always under our control; a person may find he is "haunted" by the image of a street accident or by the cries of the victim. Images do occur and must be accounted for. But to say this need not lead us to think of them as "decaying sense." Such a description would apply to afterimages, caused by staring at a bright light and then looking away. But these are actually perceived and can be physically located, on or just in front of whatever is looked at. Mental images have no location and are not related to public visual space; it is useless to ask a subject, as some psychologists have done, to project his mental image onto a screen, for it is impossible to look at the physical world and contemplate an image at the same time. But the "seeing" of a visual image or the "hearing" of an auditory one is only, in Sartre's terminology, a "quasi observation"; as Ryle puts it, "an imagined shriek is neither louder nor fainter than a heard murmur. It neither drowns it nor is drowned by it" (*op. cit.,* p. 250; despite differences in terminology, there is a measure of agreement between Ryle and Sartre on this topic). The "quasi-observational" nature of our apprehension of images is marked by the device, naturally adopted, of putting quotation marks around "see" and "hear" in this context.

Nevertheless, the question "What is a mental image?" is wrongly posed, for it implies that there is some definite mental content to which the words can be applied. As has been shown above, the similar question "What is a picture?" equally has no definite answer. A picture may be regarded as a pattern of pigment on a piece of canvas, and much can be said about it in this respect. But such a description leaves out of account its function *as a picture,* which may be to recall the face of an absent friend. When it is being used for this purpose its characteristics as a physical object are ignored; the person is seen "through" the painted representation. It is he in whom we are interested. Similarly, when a mental image is being used it is the object that is of interest to us, not the image itself. "When we are thinking, although we must know what our images are of, it is not necessary for us to know what our images are like—even whether they are clear and distinct, or fuzzy and shifting" (D. W. Hamlyn, "The Stream of Thought," 71). Indeed, it is hard to see how it is possible to know "what they are like," for they are described only in terms of their objects. In the case of the portrait there is a public object that can be described in physical terms and serves as the "analogue" of the absent friend.

It has been suggested that there are similar analogues in the case of mental imagery—for example, movements of the eyeballs. These may well occur, but their occurrence is not part of what is meant by having an image. In the case both of the picture and of such movements it is the way in which an existing but absent object is indicated or referred to that constitutes the essence of the representation. Sartre has suggested that we can set up a series of representations, starting with a photograph, continuing with a full portrait, a drawing, a caricature (which may be a few lines on paper or a piece of behavior on the part of an actor). All these are ways of indicating a particular person. The series can be continued with a mental image, and finally with the person's name. These different ways of thinking of him depend on a relation of meaning. "For the contents (images for instance) which accompany or illustrate them are not the meaning or intending. . . . If God had looked into our minds He would not have been able to see there whom we were speaking of" (Wittgenstein, *op. cit.*, p. 217). Or whom we were thinking of. So far from being the vehicles of meaning, images are dependent on a prior ability to mean or intend particular objects for their very existence. In this they are like pictures, but this fact must not lead us into talking of our apprehension of images as if it were the inspection of private pictures.

Bibliography

CLASSIC WORKS

Aristotle, *On Memory and Recollection.*
Aristotle, *On the Soul.*
Lucretius, *De Rerum Natura (On the Nature of Things).*
Hobbes, Thomas, *Leviathan.*
Locke, John, *Essay Concerning Human Understanding.*
Berkeley, George, *The Principles of Human Knowledge.*
Hume, David, *Treatise of Human Nature,* Bk. I.

MODERN WORKS

Flew, Annis, "Images, Supposing and Imagining." *Philosophy,* Vol. 28, No. 106 (July 1953), 246–254.
Furlong, E. J.; Mace, C. A.; and O'Connor, D. J., "Abstract Ideas and Images." *PAS,* Supp. Vol. 27 (1953), 121–158. A symposium.
Furlong, E. J., *Imagination.* London and New York, 1961.
Galton, Francis, *Inquiries Into Human Faculty and Its Development.* London, 1883.
Gombrich, E. H., *Art and Illusion.* London, 1960.
Hamlyn, D. W., "The Stream of Thought." *PAS,* N.S. Vol. 56 (1955–1956), 63–82.
Harrison, Bernard, "Meaning and Mental Images." *PAS,* N.S. Vol. 63 (1962–1963), 237–250.
Humphrey, George, *Thinking.* London and New York, 1951.
Price, H. H., "Image Thinking." *PAS,* N.S. Vol. 52 (1951–1952), 135–166.
Price, H. H., *Thinking and Experience.* London, 1953.
Ryle, Gilbert, *The Concept of Mind.* London, 1949.
Sartre, Jean-Paul, *L'Imaginaire.* Paris, 1940. Translated by Bernard Frechtman as *The Psychology of the Imagination.* London and New York, 1949.
Shorter, J. M., "Imagination." *Mind,* Vol. 61, No. 244 (October 1952), 528–542.
Wittgenstein, Ludwig, *Philosophical Investigations,* translated by G. E. M. Anscombe. Oxford, 1953.

A. R. MANSER

IMAGINATION is generally held to be the power of forming mental images or other concepts not directly derived from sensation. In spite of the popular usage of the term, the majority of philosophers from Aristotle to Kant considered it in relation to knowledge or opinion. They conceived it either as an element in knowledge or as an obstacle to it—as in Plato's attack on art—or as both an obstacle and an element. Hume is a representative of the last view: "Nothing is more dangerous to reason than flights of the imagination, and nothing has been the occasion of more mistakes among philosophers." Yet in the same place he wrote of the understanding as "the general and more established properties of the imagination" (*Treatise of Human Nature,* Book I, Part IV, Sec. vii). The fancy, the power of the imagination to combine ideas in fantastical ways, is to be avoided, but nevertheless imagination is vital to knowledge.

This latter element in Hume's view had its greatest development in Kant's *Critique of Pure Reason,* where the imagination is described as a "blind but indispensable function of the soul, without which we should have no knowledge whatsoever, but of which we are scarcely ever conscious." Kant thought that the imagination has two tasks to perform in giving rise to knowledge, though it is not always easy to separate them. First, it completes the necessarily fragmentary data of the senses: it is impossible to perceive the *whole* of an object at once, yet we are seldom aware of the partial nature of our perception. For example, we cannot see more than three sides of a cube at one time, but we think of it as having all six sides. This completion of perception is the work of the "reproductive" imagination (called reproductive because it depends on prior experience for its operation). Kant contrasted this with the "productive" imagination, which has an even more important role to play.

The two names mark different functions of the imagination, rather than imply that it is twofold. The productive imagination gives rise to the transcendental synthesis of imagination, which combines our experience into a single connected whole. Kant called this operation "transcendental" because it is prior to experience, not subsequent to it; without such a synthesis no coherent experience of a world would be possible. So central is the work of the imagination to the first *Critique* that it is sometimes hard to separate from the understanding; Kant even said in one passage: "*The unity of apperception in relation to the synthesis of the imagination* is the *understanding;* and this same unity, with reference to the *transcendental synthesis* of the imagination, the *pure understanding*" (A 119).

Artistic imagination. In spite of Kant's emphasis on the productive nature of the imagination and the importance he gave to it, his view of it in the first *Critique* is still as a faculty for forming images, images that are at the service of the cognitive powers of the mind. It is our normal apprehension of the world that is mainly at issue in that work. Consequently, it is hard to see how this use of the term is related to that by which we talk of writers and artists as "imaginative." Many critics and philosophers have written as if the artist or writer were a person especially good at imagining, in the sense of visualizing, scenes or events that had not occurred, which he then transmitted to the public by means of his art. The mental operations were of the "fancy" in Hume's sense of the term, the imagination recombining materials it had previously received from the senses into new forms that were not reproductions of previous experiences. The degree to which an artist could do this was the measure of his imaginative powers, while the reader or viewer reproduced in his own mind what the artist had had in his. Two contemporary literary critics have attacked this view:

> But much great literature does not evoke sensuous images, or, if it does, it does so only incidentally, occasionally and intermittently. In the depiction even of a fictional character the writer may not suggest visual images at all. . . . If we had to visualise every metaphor in poetry we would become completely bewildered and confused. (Wellek and Warren, *Theory of Literature*, pp. 26–27)

It has even been suggested that the term "imaginative" has now come to fill the place in the critical vocabulary left by the general abandonment of the term "beautiful" in aesthetics; a "work of imaginative power" would previously have been called "beautiful." Clearly it is inadequate to equate "imagination" with the power of the mind to produce images. Interestingly enough, the germ of a better theory of the imagination might be seen in Kant's discussion of teleological judgment in his *Critique of Judgment:* to think of nature *as if* it had a purpose is an imaginative activity, though there do not seem to be any actual images involved in the process.

Coleridge. One of the most important contributions to the theory of the imagination in the nineteenth century was that of Coleridge, put forward in *Biographia Literaria* and elsewhere. He strongly contrasted the Fancy and the Imagination; the former he defined as "no other than a mode of Memory emancipated from the order of time and place." It operates almost mechanically and is responsible for the production of verse, whereas the Imagination is the source of true poetry. This he divided into two: the Primary Imagination, which is the equivalent of Kant's productive imagination and is responsible for all human perception, and the Secondary Imagination, which is the source of art. Coleridge described the operation of the Secondary Imagination as follows: "It dissolves, diffuses, dissipates, in order to re-create . . . it struggles to idealise and to unify. It is essentially *vital,* even as all objects (*as* objects) are essentially fixed and dead." This vital nature of the imagination meant for Coleridge that it is a way of discovering a deeper truth about the world; he would have agreed with Keats's "What the imagination seizes as beauty

must be Truth," and thus he went beyond the Kantian original of this theory. In this he sided with the romantics, for whom art and science were alternative ways of reaching the real world; previous writers had tended to think of science and philosophy as superior to art in this respect.

Ryle on imagination. Coleridge and those who followed him, including both Croce and Collingwood, still thought of the Imagination as a single faculty or power of the mind. Gilbert Ryle, in his chapter on imagination in *The Concept of Mind,* stresses that there is no one thing that can be called "imagination" but rather a variety of activities that are imaginative, among which are pretending, acting, impersonating, fancying, and so-called imaging. His arguments clearly establish his central thesis, though his subsidiary denial of mental images, which is not essential to the main point, is open to doubt. A child shows his imaginative ability, Ryle maintains, not by what goes on in his head but rather by the way in which he plays—for instance, the manner in which he pretends to be a bear. An actor, again, demonstrates his ability by the way he performs on the stage, his public appearance, to which mental accompaniments are largely, if not entirely, irrelevant.

Many of the activities called "imaginative," Ryle says, are "mock-performances"; he talks of boxers sparring as "making these movements in a hypothetical and not a categorical manner" (p. 261). This is closely connected with supposal, the running over in the mind of a future possibility. Indeed, in ordinary speech the word "imagine" is often synonymous with "suppose" or "think"; the instruction "imagine what it would be like if" is equivalent to "think what it would be like if." In both cases the evidence that the instruction had been carried out would be a report in words; even the operation itself might have been purely verbal, without any "images" passing through the mind. Hence, Ryle can argue that there is no need for an artist or writer—or, indeed, for anybody at all—to have "mental imagery."

Imagination and truth. Because there is such a close connection between "imagining" and "supposing" or "fancying," it is easy to see why what is imagined is often thought to be unreal or false. In fact, "I must have imagined it" is a common form for the admission of a mistake of some kind. Hence, it is natural for epistemologically minded philosophers to assume that all imaginative activity is false or unreal. Ryle, in spite of the over-all excellence of his account, may be criticized on this score: such forms of expression as "mock-performance" and the use of quotation marks stress this element. However, the falsity of the imagination may, by philosophers of other persuasions and interests, be welcomed as a sign of the mind's freedom. Sartre would appear to be of this number. E. J. Furlong, in his book *Imagination,* agrees with Sartre on this point: ". . . to act 'with imagination' is to act with freedom, with spontaneity; it is to break with the trammels of the orthodox, of the accepted; it is to be original, constructive" (p. 25). But, as has already been mentioned, artists and writers about art often want to go further than this, to stress the "truth" of imaginative works. Collingwood, for example, in a section of *The Principles of Art* entitled "Imagination and Truth," has said, "Art is not indifferent to truth; it is essentially the pursuit of truth" (p. 288). It is clear that the truth in question is one somehow connected with the imagination rather than with the ordinary cognitive powers of the mind.

The difficulty of assessing this claim is increased by the fact that the idealist theory of art, of which Collingwood and Croce are the chief representatives, places the locus of the work of art not in its physical manifestation, the painting or poem, but in the imagination of the artist and spectator. The real work of art is an experience in the mind of the artist, and the spectator is moved to re-create the experience of the artist in his own imagination when he contemplates the picture. The picture is thus connected with the work of art but is not the work itself. The main difficulty here lies in the fact that it is an imaginative experience, not a statement, which is said to be true. A subsidiary problem is that such a view leads to the undervaluing of the actual product of the artist, the picture, novel, or poem. But the stress on the part played by the imagination in appreciating art is shared by some writers not normally thought of as idealists. For instance, Sartre says, "In a word, reading is directed creation" (*Situations II*, p. 96). The writer, he argues, has only provided a series of clues that the reader has to "solve" and complete by his own activity. Sartre even goes so far as to talk of reading as a "dream under our own control" (*ibid.*, p. 100), which assimilates the appreciation of art even more closely with activities normally thought of as imaginative—for example, daydreaming.

One aspect of the idealist account of art clearly fits in with our normal thinking on the subject, for a person said to be "imaginative" is frequently one who is capable of appreciating works of art or of fiction. A man who could not read novels because "they are not factual" would be unimaginative. But the antithesis imaginative–factual that is here employed would seem to contradict the idealist claim that art is connected with truth. In ordinary conversation a novel may be described as "true to life" or "realistic." A child pretending to be a bear may also be praised for the realism of his performance, as may a young actor playing the part of an old man. In these and similar instances no one need be deceived by the novel or the performance; the readers or spectators can be fully aware that they are not reading a factual account or seeing a genuinely old man. Indeed, if they were not so aware their reactions would be different. The spectator who responds to the stage performance as to an actual event has made a serious mistake; many events on the stage would be too painful to contemplate if they took place in real life. This kind of awareness has sometimes been described as "aesthetic distance," but it is the same feature that was above described as the "unreality" of the imagination. Sartre expresses this fact by saying that the image "contains a certain nothingness." He continues: "However lively, however affecting or strong an image may be, it is clear that its object is non-existent" (*L'Imaginaire*, p. 26). For Sartre, when someone imagines the face of an absent friend he is supposing that the friend is present to him, which *ex hypothesi* he is not. A person who forgets that he is imagining, that his thought is supposal, not fact, has made the same mistake as the spectator who thinks a real murder has been committed on the stage. The sense in which imagination may provide, in works of fiction, for example, a "truth" that is not conformity to actual fact can thus only be that the world which is supposed is a possible one, in the sense that it is self-consistent. Those who claim that the imagination gives another "truth" must be extending the meaning of the word in a way that requires justification, or at least explanation.

What has just been said also serves to point to a solution of the difficulty of the idealist account, that of the actual mode of existence of the work of art, whether it is in the mind or is the physical object it is ordinarily taken to be. Against the idealist view it is normally asserted that what is criticized in a work of art is the work itself, not its effects on the imagination, which would be private to each person; the critic thinks he is talking about a public object. The solution lies in the ambiguous nature of the work of art, as Sartre stresses, in that a picture, for example, can be viewed either as paint on canvas or as a picture of an absent friend. The picture does not produce an image of the absent person, but, as Sartre says, we respond to the picture in some of the ways in which we would respond to the friend himself, albeit we are aware that he is not present. The ability to respond in this way is the imagination, but the response does not require a flow of imagery in the mind. To have established this is one of the merits of Ryle's account.

Mimesis. It is now possible to see the connection between many of the various, apparently disparate uses of "imagination." The man who is thoroughly immersed in reading a story, who is almost dreaming it, is very like the child who is fully occupied with pretending to be a bear. These are in a position similar to that of the man who is taking the behavior of a young actor on the stage for that of an old man. There is a common element in the behavior of all three, which is shared by the man who is supposing that something is the case, though his activity is less full. This man, again, is not dissimilar to the person having a mental image, who is fancying or supposing that he is seeing or hearing something he is not seeing or hearing, although aware that he is not.

All of these notions are related to an earlier account of art, the Greek *mimesis*, or imitation, although it has often been thought that there was a radical difference between them. Aristotle's idea of an "instinct of imitation" in the *Poetics* (IV, 1) is not entirely unlike Ryle's account of the imagination. In both cases there is something unreal about the activity, as Sartre has tried to indicate by his talk of "nothingness" as a feature of imagination; in these areas the implications of normal life do not hold. Thus, in spite of the apparent diversity of usage, there is a "family likeness," in Wittgenstein's phrase, between the various terms, which makes talk of "the Imagination" legitimate.

Bibliography

CLASSIC WORKS

Aristotle, *On the Soul.*
Aristotle, *Poetics.*
Coleridge, Samuel Taylor, *Biographia Literaria*, J. Shawcross, ed. Oxford, 1907.
Hume, David, *Treatise of Human Nature*, Bk. I.

Kant, Immanuel, *Critique of Pure Reason,* translated by N. Kemp Smith. London, 1929.

Kant, Immanuel, *Critique of Judgment,* translated by J. H. Bernard. New York, 1951.

MODERN WORKS

Cameron, J. M., "Poetic Imagination." *PAS,* N.S. Vol. 62 (1961–1962), 219–240.

Carritt, E. F., *The Theory of Beauty.* London, 1914.

Collingwood, R. G., *The Principles of Art.* Oxford, 1938.

Croce, Benedetto, *Estetica come scienze dell'espressione e linguistica generale.* Bari, Italy, 1902. Translated by D. Ainslie as *Aesthetic.* London, 1922.

Furlong, E. J., *Imagination.* London and New York, 1961.

Gombrich, E. H., "Meditations on a Hobby Horse," in L. L. Whyte, ed., *Aspects of Form.* London, 1951.

James, D. G., *Scepticism and Poetry.* London, 1937.

Koestler, Arthur, *Act of Creation.* London and New York, 1964.

Langer, S. K., *Feeling and Form.* New York, 1953.

Levi, A. W., *Literature, Philosophy and the Imagination.* Bloomington, Ind., 1962.

MacDonald, M., "Art and Imagination." *PAS,* N.S. Vol. 53 (1952–1953), 205–226.

Mischel, T., "Collingwood on Art as 'Imaginative Expression.'" *Australasian Journal of Philosophy,* Vol. 39 (1961), 241–250.

Price, H. H., *Thinking and Experience.* London, 1953.

Ryle, Gilbert, *The Concept of Mind.* London, 1949.

Sartre, Jean-Paul, *L'Imaginaire.* Paris, 1940. Translated by Bernard Frechtman as *The Psychology of the Imagination.* London and New York, 1949.

Sartre, Jean-Paul, "Qu'est-ce que la littérature," in *Situations II.* Paris, 1948. Translated by Bernard Frechtman as *What Is Literature?* New York, 1949; London, 1951.

Shorter, J. M., "Imagination." *Mind,* N.S. Vol. 61, No. 244 (October 1952), 528–542.

Wellek, R., and Warren, A., *Theory of Literature.* London and New York, 1949.

Wittgenstein, Ludwig, *Philosophical Investigations,* translated by G. E. M. Anscombe. Oxford, 1953.

Ziff, P., "Art and the 'Object of Art.'" *Mind,* N.S. Vol. 60 (1951), 466–480.

A. R. MANSER

IMMORTALITY. The literature on the philosophical problems involved in the question of a future life begins with Plato. We cannot therefore do better than start with a quotation from *Phaedo,* the dialogue in which Plato deployed what is put forward as a demonstration of the immortality of the soul. Having heard and apparently accepted the supposed proof put into the mouth of Socrates, Crito asks:

"But how shall we bury you?" "However you please," Socrates replied, "if you can catch me and I do not get away from you." And he laughed gently, and looking towards us, said: "I cannot persuade Crito, my friends, that the Socrates who is now conversing and arranging the details of his argument is really I: he thinks I am the one whom he will presently see as a corpse, and he asks how to bury me. And though I have been saying at great length that after I drink the poison I shall no longer be with you, but shall go away to the joys of the blessed, he seems to think that was idle talk uttered to encourage you and myself." (115C, D)

This passage can be employed to fix two fundamental points by reference to which the main problems can be mapped.

The first point is that the essence of doctrines of personal survival (or immortality)—and precisely this and this only is what gives them their great human interest—is that they should assert that after our deaths we shall continue to exist (forever). Only in this way can they provide the basis for what John Wisdom has called "these logically unique expectations"—that we shall, to put it as noncommittally as possible, have "experiences" after death, that death will be not our terminus but the beginning of a new journey. This has to be underlined both because there have been some famous philosophical doctrines of immortality which have not been of this sort and because there have been other doctrines which either were from the beginning substitutes for, or have been so hedged and interpreted that they have now ceased to be, the genuine article, personal immortality. Thus, whatever one makes of Aristotle on the immortality of the intellect (*De Anima* 429a–431a) or of Spinoza on the eternal element in the mind (*Ethics,* V, xxiii ff.), it is certain that these views do not, nor were they intended to, provide any ground for such "logically unique expectations." Again, the man who urges that we all of us live forever because the ill (and sometimes even the good) men do lives after them indicates by the very irrelevance of his supporting reason that this sort of immortality is not the authentic personal brand.

The second basic reference point is that any doctrine of survival or immortality has one enormous and immediate obstacle to surmount before it can begin to qualify for any further consideration. This obstacle consists simply in our manifest universal human mortality. It is due to this ineluctably familiar fact that "All men are mortal" has become a trite truistic example in logic and that we so use the word "survive" that it is logically impossible for one and the same passenger to be both dead and a survivor after a crash. One can recognize and respect the longing that may lie behind the epitaph "Not dead, but sleeping," yet no one can deny that, literally interpreted, it is false. Indeed, even to consider the contrary possibility would be to enter the ghoulish world of Edgar Allan Poe. This second reference point is, of course, as obvious as the first though the inducement to disregard it is perhaps greater. And both points have to be kept constantly in view.

THREE DOCTRINES OF IMMORTALITY

There seem to be three ways of trying to circumvent the massive initial difficulty confronting any doctrine of personal immortality. If once the initial obstacle could be overcome, the remaining problems would turn out to be not philosophical but factual and practical.

Immortal-soul doctrine. The first of the three doctrines is the Platonic attempt to demonstrate two points. One point is that we are essentially composite beings. Besides the more familiar corporeal element, the body, there is also something else, different in kind—the incorporeal soul. For the duration of a life the soul is somehow attached to—incorporated into or imprisoned in—its body. Although the soul is incorporeal, it is nevertheless a substance, something that could significantly be said to exist independently of anything else. This is precisely the point of Plato's arguments to the conclusion that the soul is not a harmony, for it would not even make sense to suggest that a harmony might survive or, for that matter, precede the elements of which it is a harmony. This is no more possible than that there could be a grin without a face to grin it (*Phaedo* 85E–86D and 91C–95A).

The other point is that the soul must be the person or, at any rate, the real, true, or essential person. This, though it is sometimes neglected, is crucial. Unless it is established that I am my soul, the demonstration of the survival of my soul will not demonstrate my survival, and the news that my soul will last forever could provide me with no more justification for harboring "these logically unique expectations" than the rather less elevated assurance that my appendix is to be preserved eternally in a bottle.

Reconstitution doctrine. The second doctrine is, in its purest form, extremely simple and direct. It consists in urging the resurrection of the body or, more accurately, the reconstitution of the person. Whereas the first doctrine insists that I am the sort of thing that could perfectly well escape unharmed and unnoticed at death ("if you can catch me and I do not get away"); the second recognizes that to be truly a human person, I have to have the corporeal human form. It then relies on an act of sheer omnipotence to produce the immortal me.

Shadow-man doctrine. Considering that the reconstitution doctrine or something approaching it has been part of traditional Christianity, it is surprising to find that Aquinas seems to be the only philosopher of the first rank to have discussed a version of it at any length. (See especially "Treatise of the Resurrection" in the supplement to Part III of the *Summa Theologica*.) But the shadow-man doctrine seems to have received even less attention. It can perhaps best be regarded as an attempt to combine the strong points of the other two doctrines. It is the claim that a person is a kind of shadow man, sufficiently human and corporeal to overcome the problem of identification with the familiar flesh and blood person and at the same time sufficiently ethereal and elusive to have no difficulty in escaping unnoticed from the ordinary earthy body which is destined to be burned or buried. This view is found in some of the Christian Fathers (for instance, Tertullian in *De Anima*). A similar view is also held by some modern spiritualists—"the astral body" detaches itself at death to proceed on its "journey to the summerland." Perhaps the best way of conveying the idea to the modern reader unfamiliar with either patristic or spiritualist literature is to refer to the many films in which a "spirit" is shown as a tenuous shadowy replica of a man that detaches itself from him at death and is thereafter visible to the entire audience but only to favored characters in the film.

Difficulties in these doctrines. At first sight the third doctrine might appear to be the most promising way to avoid the initial difficulty. However, the doctrine is bold precisely where the other two are discreet. By insisting upon the essential incorporeality of the soul, the first neutralizes all the ordinary weapons of empirical inquiry; the second, by deferring the corporeal resurrection to an unspecified time and place, indefinitely postpones any occasion for their deployment. But astral bodies, detaching themselves at death from the other sort, should be empirically detectable here and now. The crucial and probably insoluble dilemma for the shadow-man doctrine is to provide a specification of the nature of an astral body in which an astral body remains sufficiently like an ordinary flesh and blood person to avoid difficulties of identification and at the same time to ensure that the claim that there are such things would be verified or, at least, not immediately falsified by the appropriate factual investigation.

In the time of Tertullian and even in the early days of modern psychical research there may have been some slight basis for believing that this might possibly be done. Tertullian himself appealed not only to purely theological considerations but also to such cases as that of the woman who claimed to have seen "a transparent and lucid figure in the perfect form of a man." The systematic investigation of such phantasms has shown, however, that though they do undoubtedly occur, they belong to the category of purely subjective and hallucinatory experience. (See, for instance, G. N. M. Tyrrell, *Apparitions,* London, 1953.) The third way must therefore be dismissed as a blind alley.

Any reconstitution doctrine confronted with the question "How is the reconstituted person on the last day to be identified as the original me, as opposed to a mere replica, an appropriately brilliant forgery?" There seems to be no satisfactory answer to this question, at least for a pure reconstitution theory. This question is, however, logically prior to all questions about the reasons, if any, that might be brought forward in support of such a doctrine.

This decisive objection seems rarely to have been raised, and when it has been, its force has not usually been felt. No doubt, the explanation lies largely in the fact that the doctrine is scarcely ever found in the pure form, unalloyed with any Platonic elements. There are two defenses that might be offered. It could be urged that God will infallibly ensure that the unending torments and the eternal ecstasies are allocated to the right people—that is, in the one case to the very same people who had incurred his disapproval and in the other case to precisely those who had won his favor. It might also be suggested that though there might indeed be cases in which all other merely human observers must be entirely at a loss, the person himself could not fail to know whether he was the original person rather than a changeling or a replica. These are, in substance, the arguments presented by Locke in developing and defending his own analysis of personal identity; however, that analysis itself was intended to meet difficulties about the identification of the future victims of divine judgment with people now living on earth.

Both these arguments, though they possess a strong appeal, seem to miss the point. Notwithstanding the form of the original question, the difficulty is not one of "How do you know?" but of "What do you know?" The objection is that the reconstituted people could only be mere replicas of and surrogates for their earthly predecessors. Neither the appeal to the cognitive and executive resources of Omnipotence nor the appeal to the supposed special status of the person in question does anything at all to meet this contention.

The point can be brought out better in the case of the argument that the person cannot fail to know who he is. This argument depends on the premises that if I remember doing something, I must have done it and that normal people in normal situations are usually able to remember the most important features of their lives. Both premises are true, but it does not follow from them that if someone on the last day or any other day claims in all honesty to remember doing something, he must in fact have done it. From "He remembers doing that" it follows necessarily that "He did that," just as from "He knows that that is true" it follows necessarily that "That is true." But from "He claims to remember doing that, and he is not lying" it does not follow that "He did that," any more than from "He claims to know that that is true, and he is not lying" it follows that "That is true."

The crux in both cases is the possibility of honest error. However honest and however convinced, claims that you did something do not guarantee that you actually did it. In normal circumstances most such claims are no doubt entirely reliable, and the memories involved can properly be said to constitute knowledge. But the circumstances envisaged by the reconstitutionists are conspicuously not normal. In these circumstances the question of whether any of the ostensible memories enjoyed by the reconstituted people can properly be counted as memories at all must wait on the resolution of the logically prior issue of whether they have any past to remember, of whether, in particular, they are indeed the people they apparently think they are.

Aquinas seems to have appreciated that the immediate objection to any pure reconstitutionist view is decisive. This insight is no doubt one of the reasons that his own view incorporated important Platonic elements. In answer to the objection "that it will not be identically the same man that shall rise again. . . . After the change wrought by death the selfsame man cannot be repeated," Aquinas replied:

The form of other things subject to generation and corruption is not subsistent of itself, so as to be able to remain after the corruption of the composite, as it is with the rational soul. For the soul, even after separation from the body, retains the being which accrues to it when in the body. . . . Consequently there has been no interruption in the substantial being of a man, as would make it impossible for the selfsame man to return on account of an interruption in his being. (*Op. cit.*, IIIa, Supp. 79, 2, *ad* 1)

IMMORTAL-SOUL DOCTRINE

It thus seems that if any headway is to be made toward overcoming the first gigantic obstacle in the way of doctrines of survival or immortality, it will have to be, at least in its first stages, Platonic in an extremely broad sense. In this sense Descartes's views on the nature of the soul and its relations to the bodily machine can be characterized as Platonic (see, for instance, *The Passions of the Soul* I, xxx ff.), and even Aquinas must count as at least Platonizing. For everyone who maintains that the mind or the soul is a substance, in the sense that it could significantly be said to exist alone and disembodied, is thereby Platonizing, and everyone who identifies this putative substantial mind or soul as the real or true person is adopting a fully Platonic position.

Platonizing concerning the nature of the soul seems to be the essential condition of the possibility of any defensible doctrine of personal immortality or even survival. Philosophy that is Platonizing or Platonic in this sense constitutes an enormous field, so this article will concentrate on the views of Plato, Aristotle, and Descartes, making their positions serve as focuses. All three are well suited to serve in this way both because their work has been and is enormously influential and because they can each be seen as representative of a different approach to the problem. Since all three believed in some sort of immortality and since it is scarcely possible to treat their arguments about the nature of the soul without touching on their ideas of immortality, it will be convenient to consider the two together.

Difficulties in the notion of the soul. One great and rather peculiar difficulty of our present subject is that it is very hard and, hence, very uncommon for anyone really to begin from the beginning. The key terms like "body," "mind," and "soul" and their equivalents or near equivalents in other languages are all in a way familiar to all those acquainted with the languages concerned. Though there may be much unclarity about their meanings and perhaps even a certain indeterminacy in their usage, they are not the recognizably fresh coinages that both demand definitions and enable meanings to be prescribed with some confidence that the appropriate usage can be followed consistently by the prescriber and by others. (The point here is simply that speech habits, like other habits, can be very hard to break.)

Again, in the air there always are and always have been vulgar or not so vulgar theories about bodies, minds, and souls and their several natures, destinies, and relations, with no guarantee that these theories can be harmonized with the meanings of such terms as "mind" or "soul" as actually determined by whatever is the accepted correct usage of the culture concerned. For instance, correct usage—and this surely is and must be the only possible standard of meaning—may very well determine that the soul, in the relevant sense of "soul," is not a substance, even though the people concerned entertain fantasies which presuppose that it is. This thesis has been fully developed in this connection by Gilbert Ryle, chiefly in *The Concept of Mind.* The consequence of this is that the issues tend to be presented not as a matter of first giving some suitable sense to the word "soul" or "mind" and then asking whether in that sense the term would in fact have any application but, rather, as an inquiry which presupposing that we have or are souls or minds, asks what is the nature of the soul or the mind. Such a presentation is bound to constitute a temptation to prejudge the question whether, in the sense eventually chosen, we have or are such things. By itself this might give rise to no more and no less trouble than the insistence of the modern analytic philosopher that he is not concerned with the reality of matter, time, or whatever but is merely searching for an adequate analysis of the notions of matter, time, and so on. In the present case, however, there are also the various theories in the background, and these theories happen to be of very different sorts and suited to answering very different questions.

The fundamental distinction needed is that between theories that might serve as answers to philosophical questions about the meanings of the terms "mind," "soul," and the like and theories that offer some sort of explanation of why the creatures that are said to have minds, souls, and the like behave and suffer as they do. Thus, for instance, in reading Aristotle's criticisms of his predecessors (*De Anima* I), we must distinguish—even if they, or he, did not—between those thinkers who said that the soul was a vapor, blood, or something of that order and must to that extent be interpreted as embryonic scientists and those thinkers who urged that the essence of the soul is motion, sensation, or some combination of the two and are therefore to be counted as philosophers.

Another crucial distinction must be made between explanatory and descriptive concepts. Suppose that for some person the meaning of the words "mind" and "soul" is to be given entirely in terms of certain capacities or incapacities and that in his use having a first-class mind is just being able to compass certain sorts of achievement. In his sense of "mind," then, it can be no explanation to say that someone can do these things because he is endowed with a first-class mind, for to say this is, for him, only to redescribe the phenomenon. If his concept of mind is to be explanatory, he must give the word "mind" a meaning such that minds would be, in the terminology already explained, substances.

Plato. There seems to be only one, very brief passage in Plato (*Alcibiades* I 129B–130C) where the argument is explicitly directed toward the justification of the Platonic presupposition that the soul is the person. Even in this passage the first presupposition, that we are composite beings, is very much taken for granted.

Soul as the person. Socrates is talking with Alcibiades, and the question is raised, "What are we, and what is talking with what?" The conclusion is that we are our souls. The argument runs in this way. In speaking, we use words. The user and the thing used are always different. We use our hands, our eyes, our whole bodies. Thus, I cannot be my body. Yet it is agreed that I must be my soul, my body, or a combination of both. However, because the user and the thing used are always different and because I use my body, I cannot be either my body or my body and soul combined. Thus, I must be my soul.

Considering how vital the conclusion is, Plato's argument may seem inadequate. But if, sympathetically, we call in the rest of Plato's writings to provide supplementary evidence, it becomes clear that it has to be taken as the epitome of many arguments. For Plato constantly talked of the phenomenon of self-control and the lack of it and of all those times when we are inclined to speak of being let down or dragged down by the weaknesses or by the excessive strength of the body or some part of it. Few concepts are, in the ordinary narrow sense, more typically Platonic.

In all the innumerable cases of bodily control or lack of it, it is possible to produce arguments of basically the same form, and it is not at all necessary to appeal to the assumption, which may not seem as obvious to everyone today as it did to Plato's Alcibiades, that I must be my soul, my body, or both. Thus, starting from the known fact that our eyes sometimes play tricks on us, we may go on to argue that this shows that we see not with, but through, them, that they are, as it were, built-in optical instruments (com-pare *Theaetetus* 184C ff.). Or, again, noting how natural and entirely proper it is to describe someone on some desperate occasion as "flogging on his protesting body," we may infer that we drive our bodies as we drive our cars. In every case the Platonic conclusion, expressed in a more modern idiom, would be that the personal pronouns, personal names, and all other person words, words which clearly must refer to something and which, it seems, equally clearly cannot refer to bodies, the only available corporeal objects, must therefore refer to some incorporeal objects, the conclusion is that these are the objects to which we apply the term "souls."

This conclusion is wrong, however, and all arguments of this kind are misguided. It is not true that person words are words for any sort of incorporeal objects. People are what you meet. We do not meet only the sinewy containers in which other people are kept, and they do not encounter only the fleshy houses that we ourselves inhabit. It is therefore wrong to suggest that the word "person" is equivalent to the word "soul" in this sense of "soul" and, hence, to imply that it is contradictory to deny that people are incorporeal objects and that it is absurd to say that you can see a person. This basic fact about the meanings of person words is central and fundamental to the entire problem.

To deal in detail here with all the variations on the present argument would be impossible. The mistake involved in all such arguments seems to be that of insisting that because expressions like "that person" are, for one reason or another, not synonymous with "that human body" and because we use all sorts of idioms in which I and my body are spoken of as if they were two substances, there must therefore be a special class of incorporeal objects for person words to refer to. This false conclusion seems to be one more product of the perennially disastrous *unum nomen, unum nominatum* theory of meaning—the misconception that every different class of word must refer to a different class of object. The truth seems to be that in this area we have a vastly rich and idiomatic vocabulary that provides us with all manner of subtle linguistic instruments, all of which we employ to say things about one sort of inordinately complicated but essentially corporeal creature, ourselves.

Argument from reminiscence. Plato's second argument to the conclusion that we are incorporeal souls was his doctrine of reminiscence. This has two forms, each proceeding to the same conclusion from rather different premises. In one form the premise is that we can all be shown to possess some knowledge, which we have not acquired in this life, of a priori truths (*Meno* 81B–86B). In the other it is that we all have certain ideal concepts, such as the ideal of perfect equality, which we cannot have acquired in our lives because they are never fully instantiated in this world (*Phaedo* 73A–77A). In both forms the conclusion is that these facts can be accounted for only in terms of memory. We, or "our souls," must have acquired our knowledge of the conclusion of the theorem of Pythagoras or have been acquainted with the Platonic Idea of equality before this life began.

This argument has never been very popular, partly because of a well-grounded mistrust of both premises and partly because of the fact that the notion of pre-existence involved in the conclusion does not square with the demands of Western orthodoxy. For its force the argument depends on the existence of an important logical link between (true) memory and personal identity. If I really do remember certain truths or being acquainted with certain objects, then it follows that at some time in the past I must have learned them or made that acquaintance. Plato's argument is sound, but he draws the wrong conclusion. The correct conclusion is not that we must be remembering from a former existence but that memory cannot be involved. It cannot be memory for the simple and basic reason that we were not available to acquire knowledge or anything else before we existed, because we are not, what this argument in fact assumes that we are, the sort of incorporeal things which could pre-exist our conception and growth.

It is worth remarking that although to products of Western cultural conditioning pre-existence appears much less credible than immortality, Plato, in insisting on both, was adopting a much less arbitrary position than that of those who assert immortality alone. It was not without reason that in the ancient world Lucretius and other spokesmen for human mortality made much of the comparison between our nothingness before birth and our annihilation in death (see, for instance, Lucretius, *De Rerum Natura* III. 11. 830–842 and 973–977). As Santayana once remarked, "The fact of being born is a poor augury of immortality."

Argument from rationality. Another argument was developed from distinctions embedded in Plato's account of Socrates' intellectual history (*Phaedo* 96A ff.). The Platonic Socrates here tells of his dissatisfaction with Anaxagoras, who apparently wanted to explain how the universe works rather than justify why everything is for the best. Socrates then goes on to contrast the physiological conditions of human behavior with the reasons the agent has for acting as he does. These categorial distinctions could serve as the foundations of an argument to the conclusion that since there are no necessary connections between the concepts of physiology, on the one hand, and the concepts that are peculiar to the distinctively human business of giving reasons for actions, on the other, it must therefore follow that rational agents are of their very nature incorporeal.

It would probably be going too far to attribute the argument in this form to Plato, although the conclusion and all the ideas involved are thoroughly Platonic. It is nevertheless one that needs to be noted here. C. S. Lewis and other contemporary apologists have tried to use these ideas to show that rationality is somehow essentially supernatural and that the bodily occurrences involved in rational behavior cannot be completely compassed in any scientific explanation.

There are two crucial points to be made in reply to this argument. The first is that precisely because the justification and appraisal of actions is so totally different from the causal explanation of physiological events, questions and answers belonging to the one universe of discourse cannot rival those belonging to the other. It is thus entirely possible to be confronted by a series of corporeal events—those, for instance, involved in what would normally be described as the oral development of an argu-

ment—and to ask and to answer both logical questions about the rationality of the whole performance considered as an argument and physiological questions about the causes of all the various glottal, oral, and nervous happenings considered as subject matter for the physiologist.

The second point is that to show that the concepts involved in the rational assessment of conduct are not logically reducible to purely physiological terms is not the same as to establish that agents must be essentially incorporeal. It would be equally impossible by purely logical analysis to translate the statement "Italy declared war" into a series of assertions about individual Italians, but this is no reason for thinking that "Italy" is the word for some incorporeal substance. Nor is the impossibility of a logical reduction any reason for thinking that it could even make sense to talk of incorporeal rational agents' or of Italy's taking part in international affairs if there were no individual Italians.

Life as a substantial soul. The Platonic approaches thus far considered have all involved thinking of the soul as the person; at the same time the person was wrongly thought of as an incorporeal substance. Another approach starts from the notion of a soul as a principle of life. It helps to note some peculiarities of the Greek language. The word ψυχή, translated "soul," is etymologically related to such words as ἔμψυχος, meaning "alive" (literally, "ensouled"), and λιποψυχία, meaning "swooning" or "death" (literally, "abandonment" by the soul). A popular idea to which Plato makes gently contemptuous reference was that death was a matter of the soul's permanently leaving its body; the soul was thought of as a puff of air, an invisible vapor, that would be dispersed in the breeze (see *Phaedo* 77D; compare, for instance, Euripides, *Supplices* 553–554). In this connection we might therefore distinguish two senses of "soul." In the first "to have a soul" means merely "to be alive"; in the second "soul" is the word for a class of supposititious entities, corporeal but elusive.

In the first sense one might speak, rather pretentiously, of the soul as the principle of life. In this sense we do have souls, for to say that a creature possesses a soul in this sense is just a misleadingly substantival way of describing it as alive. At this point Plato took another step, apparently without recognizing that any step was involved and, therefore, without providing the slightest warrant for taking it. He simply assumed what is manifestly false—that the word "soul" in this sense is equivalent to the term "soul" construed as a synonym for "person" (albeit for persons recognized to be incorporeal objects). He unjustifiably equated this "soul as the principle of life" with what the older commentators call "the soul as the bearer of moral values" (see, for instance, *Republic* 353D, a passage that is no less revealing for being found in an argument a little removed from our present concern).

Incompatibility of life and death. The false equation of two senses of "soul" is crucial in the most considerable of Plato's arguments for immortality (*Phaedo* 100B–107A). Of his other arguments the only one that retains more than antiquarian interest is the contention that the soul is something that moves itself and that whatever moves itself must be ingenerable and incorruptible (*Phaedrus* 245C–246A). And the interest of this argument lies mainly in its later theological development. It was the germ of some of the theology of Plato's *Laws*. This theology led to Aristotle's notions of God as the Unmoved Mover. And Aquinas later quarried Aristotelian materials for the first of his five ways—the argument to the First Mover.

This most interesting of the Platonic arguments presupposes Plato's general theory of Ideas, or Forms, especially as expounded in *Phaedo*, in the *Republic*, and elsewhere; in fact, Plato's other arguments derive what plausibility they may have from the theory of Ideas as a background assumption. Plato believed that for every significant word, such as "justice" or "equality," there is a corresponding abstract Idea, or Form. These Ideas are eternal and incorporeal substances, intelligible to the intellect as material things are sensible to the senses. All the many particular instances of some general class of things "participate" in the appropriate unique Idea, and this Idea serves as an ideal standard, itself apparently pre-eminently possessing the characteristic concerned. These Ideas are thought of as providing answers both to questions about criteria—What makes an *X* count as an *X*?—and to questions of a more causal character—What is ultimately responsible for the existence of *X*'s?

The argument to show that life is incompatible with death starts from the notion of the soul as the principle of life, and this is equated, in terms of the theory of Ideas, with the Form of Life. Now, life in the abstract is as incompatible with death as equality is with inequality. Life can never be overcome by Death. Thus, the conclusion is that the soul as the very Idea of Life is essentially deathless and eternal and, hence, "the immortal part" of us is not destroyed by death, for "our souls will exist somewhere in another world" (*Phaedo* 106E and 107A).

The answer to this argument is that since Life and Soul are convertible terms in this context, there is as much or as little reason for saying that the Idea of Soul is eternal as there is for maintaining the eternal reality of any other Form. But, as Plato himself always insisted, the abstract Form is entirely different from the particular individual, whereas the nerve of the entire argument lies precisely in the equation of the Form of Soul with the particular soul. This identification is impossible not merely because, as we have seen, there is no reason to equate souls in the present sense with the souls that are people but, more fundamentally, because in the present sense no meaning has been given to the expression "an individual soul." This vital fact is one of the many that are obscured by the confusion of explanatory and descriptive concepts and by the failure to separate philosophical questions about criteria from factual questions about causes. Once these distinctions are made, it becomes clear that to say that someone has a soul (is alive) is not to say that he is alive only thanks to the presence of some mysterious extra substance, whether corporeal or incorporeal.

Aristotle. Aristotle's *De Anima* is perhaps best approached as a philosophical treatise on life. *Anima* is Latin for "soul" and is the word from which our "animate" and "inanimate" are ultimately derived; the declared aim of *De Anima* is "to ascertain the nature and essence of soul" as "the principle of life" (402a–403b). The fundamental thesis is that life or the soul is "the form of the particular living body." The Aristotelian notion of form is complex and is to be distinguished from the Platonic. R. D. Hicks, the editor of the classic English language edition, stated that by the thesis that the soul is the form of the body Aristotle "so far from favouring materialism, secures once and for all the soul's absolute immateriality" (R. D. Hicks, ed., *Aristotle: De Anima*, Cambridge, 1907, p. xliii). Aristotle does dispose of all ideas that the soul is a lump of stuff. However, Aristotle's basic thesis is quite un-Platonic and leaves no room at all for any doctrine of immortality. An Aristotelian form is no more a corporeal thing than a Platonic Form would be, but it is not an incorporeal one either. In our sense it is not a substance at all. The soul as the form stands to the stuff of the particular body—and the examples are all Aristotle's—as the configuration of the statue to the materials of which it is made, as vision to the eye capable of seeing, as cutting power to the serviceable ax. Whatever else may be obscure, here it is obvious, as Aristotle himself said, that in this view the soul is not separable from the body (413a) and, furthermore, that this inseparability is a matter not of physical but of logical impossibility.

Had this been all that Aristotle said, Aristotle's views could not have been used in support of immortality. He also maintained, however, certain Platonic views which have given rise to much discussion and development, particularly among the Scholastics and others committed to a belief in personal immortality. These views concern the intellectual aspects of man and the corresponding intellectual (functions of the) soul. Despite the enormous labors of the commentators, precisely what Aristotle thought on these points is far from clear, possibly because Aristotle was not very clear in his own mind. There are nevertheless some relevant points that may usefully be made.

Immortal Abstract Intellect. The tradition descending from Alexander of Aphrodisias through Averroës attributes to Aristotle a belief in some sort of Eternal Intellect. This is, however, a doctrine of personal immortality offering "prospect of rewards and punishments," a point emphasized by St. Thomas (*De Unitate Intellectus Contra Averroistes*). Furthermore, since the Abstract Intellect as opposed to the intellects of particular men is necessarily unique, it is not at all the right material to serve Aquinas' own vital theoretical need for bridges between us and our successors in the next life.

Two senses of "eternal." The one kind of reason that might be proffered for saying that the Abstract Intellect (or any other putative Abstract Reality) is essentially eternal is really no reason for saying that anything at all actually goes on forever. In a way it is correct to say that such things as necessary truths and the logical relations between abstract mathematical concepts are somehow timeless and eternal. Yet this is not a matter of the existence of anything imperishable but, rather, of its not making sense to ask temporal questions about the periods during which any of these truths and these relations obtain. From eternity in this sense we can have nothing either to hope or to fear.

This distinction between two senses of "eternity" is fundamental in discussing personal immortality. We are concerned only with a life that would live on forever; the eternity of mere abstractions is not to the point. In the light of this distinction we can better appreciate the significance and the error of Plato's contention that the soul belongs to the same category as the abstract Ideas and, hence, that it is the sort of thing that may be presumed immortal (*Phaedo* 78B–80B).

The presumption that an incorporeal substance would be naturally incorruptible has always been the philosophers' favorite argument for the immortality of the soul. Aquinas appealed to it, for instance, although he, of course, would not have included Platonic abstract Ideas in this category and although he was also careful to insist that souls, like everything else, are sustained by God and would be at once annihilated if he chose to withdraw his support (*Summa Theologica* Ia, 75, 6; *ad* 2). It was perhaps with the same idea in mind that in the *Republic* Plato offered, as if it were a proof, the following unconvincing argument: Because every sort of thing has its one congenital evil, because nothing can be destroyed by anything but its own congenital evil, because the congenital evil of the soul is wickedness, and because wickedness as such is never directly lethal to the wicked man, our souls must be immortal (*Republic* 608E–611A).

Reason not localized. Assuming that Aristotle had really wanted to suggest that it could make sense to talk of an individual intellect's existing separately, then, presumably, a large part of his reason would have lain in his belief that ratiocination, unlike sight or hearing, is not localized in any organ (*De Anima* 402a, 408a, 429a). This belief has, of course, turned out to be erroneous. But even if it had not, the absence of any special corporeal organ provides no justification for assuming that our intellectual attributes must, or even might, be those of special incorporeal substances. The lack of special organs of melancholy or of volition is surely not to be construed as grounds for seeking invisible subjects to which to attribute Eric's feeling glum or Katrina's wanting to go to sleep. These are simply and obviously attributes of the people concerned.

Aristotle himself never employed any argument of this sort. On the contrary, he urged that the intellect, "since it thinks all things must needs, in the words of Anaxagoras, be unmixed with any, if it is to rule, that is, to know" (429a). This dark saying has been construed as an expression of a belief that our intellects are both incorporeal and substances, a belief that might seem to mesh well with the conviction, which Aristotle undoubtedly did have, that pure intellectual activity, abstract cognition, is something rather grand, almost divine, an occupation only for the highest sort of person (see, for instance, *Nicomachean Ethics* 1177a–1179b). Aristotle immediately went on to insist, however, that this pure intellect "has no other nature than this, that it is a capacity," and a capacity is not at all the sort of thing that can significantly be said to exist separately. Again, he seems elsewhere to have dismissed the idea of individual immortality with contempt (*ibid.,* 1111b). And in the whole range of his works there is neither a positive treatment of the subject of a future life nor any promise of such treatment. The most plausible interpretation of Aristotle's view is surely that defended by Pietro Pomponazzi in Chapter 9 of his great polemic *De Immortalite Animae.* He concluded that the soul, including the intellect, "is in no way truly itself an individual. And so it is truly a form beginning with, and ceasing to be with, the body; nor can it in any way operate or exist without the body."

Aquinas. Aquinas, as was mentioned, had urgent theoretical reasons for wanting to show that the soul is a substance, that it is, as he put it, "something subsistent." He was therefore inclined as far as possible to read Aristotle as holding the same view. In his *Commentary on Aristotle's De Anima* he explained the passage considered above (429a) in this way:

> But our intellect . . . must itself lack all those things which of its nature it understands. Since then it naturally understands all sensible and bodily things, it must be lacking in every bodily nature; just as the sense of sight, being able to know colour, lacks all colour. If sight itself had any particular colour, this colour would prevent it from seeing other colours, just as the tongue of a feverish man, being coated with a bitter moisture, cannot taste anything sweet.

If this were indeed what Aristotle meant, he really was confused. For if intellect is, reasonably enough, to be compared with the sense of sight, it is because they are both (cognitive) capacities. But we need no particular argument to show why a capacity, as opposed to the subject that may possess that capacity, cannot itself have any material characteristics. The reason that the sense of sight is not yellow is not that being yellow must render it or its possessor incapable of seeing yellow things but that, generally, it is nonsense to attribute sensible characteristics to a capacity. (It is hard not to regard all this as the product, at least in part, of the bad habit of making nouns out of verbs and then succumbing to the temptation to presume that a substantive must be a word for a substance.)

It might seem that it is upon precisely this argument that Aquinas himself relied in the *Summa Theologica* to establish "that the principle of intellectual operation which we call the soul is . . . both incorporeal and subsistent." He even employed the same example of "a sick man's tongue being vitiated by a feverish and bitter humour," but here he was comparing the soul as "the principle of intellectual operation" with the organ, not the sense, of sight. Having thus supposedly established that "it is impossible for the intellectual principle to be a body," he proceeded:

> It is likewise impossible for it to understand by means of a bodily organ; since the particular nature of the organ would prevent its knowing all bodies; compare the way in which liquid put into a glass vase seems to be of the same colour, not only when some particular colour is in the pupil of the eye but even when it is in the vase. (Ia, 75, 2)

In this version the argument escapes the previous criticism. But it escapes only at the price of removing what was in the commentary on *De Anima* offered as the proof of its major premise, here formulated as the proposition that "whatever knows certain things cannot have any of them in its own nature; because that which is in it naturally would impede the knowledge of anything else." The question arises, "How is this premise known?" The answer seems to be that it is not known, perhaps even that it is known to be false. Take Aquinas' own example of the eye as the organ of sight. The eyes are admittedly material, yet that does not prevent us from using them for seeing material things, including other people's eyes and even—in mirrors—our own. Furthermore, even if the Thomist proposition did fit all the facts about our present sense organs, this would at most suggest that it was a contingent truth about them. But to serve Aquinas' purpose, it must be known to be, if not actually necessary, at least sufficiently universal to apply not only to sense organs but also to "that principle of intellectual operation which we call the soul"—something which he himself is here trying to show to be radically different from anything corporeal.

Descartes. Plato and Aristotle can be regarded as the archetypical protagonists of two opposing views of man. Plato is the original spokesman for a dualistic view, and it seems that it is upon dualism that a doctrine of personal immortality must be grounded if it is to possess any initial plausibility. As a defender of a monistic view, Aristotle was neither so consistent nor so wholehearted. Yet it is still fair to see him at his most characteristic as the philosophical founding father of the view that the person is the living human organism, a view that apparently leaves no room whatsoever for belief in personal immortality. Aquinas, who generally followed Aristotle on this point, characteristically attempted a synthesis that would have opened, had it been successful, the doors to heaven and to hell. In the present perspective Descartes must be placed squarely in the Platonic tradition. Thus, in the final paragraph of Part V of the *Discourse on Method*, after remarking that "next to the error of those who deny God . . . there is none which is more effectual in leading feeble spirits from the straight path of virtue, than to imagine that . . . after this life we have nothing to fear or to hope for, any more than the flies or the ants," Descartes concluded that "our soul is in its nature entirely independent of the body, and in consequence that it is not liable to die with it. And then, inasmuch as we observe no other causes capable of destroying it, we are naturally inclined to judge that it is immortal."

Soul as a thinking substance. Although his conclusions were thoroughly traditional, Descartes was nevertheless a revolutionary thinker. Unlike Plato, his chief intellectual interests were science, in particular physiology. Like Hobbes, the other great metaphysician of his period, Descartes quickly grasped the wider significance of the work of Harvey and Galileo. Harvey's discovery of the circulation of the blood suggested to Descartes that both animals and human bodies might be regarded as machines. Descartes then asked himself how the creatures that we know might be distinguished from living machines. His answer was that with respect to animals there simply was no distinction in principle but that an automaton in human shape, however brilliantly constructed, could always be distinguished from a true human being in two ways. There were two sorts of test which were bound to reveal the absence of the vital rational soul: without a rational soul such an automaton would not be able "to reply appropriately to everything . . . said in its presence, as even the lowest type of man can do," and their lack of versatility would always reveal that the automata "did not act from

knowledge, but only from the disposition of their organs" (*Discourse on Method*, Part V).

One fundamental distinction, often overlooked in discussing these questions, is that between logical and technical impossibility. In Part V of the *Discourse*, his first published treatment, Descartes seems to have been making a purely factual claim "that it is morally impossible that there should be sufficient diversity in any machine to allow it to act in all the events of life in the same way as our reason causes us to act." To make any such would-be factual claim must be both rashly premature and scientifically defeatist. Elsewhere and later, it becomes clear that what Descartes, like so many successors, really wanted to say is that it is inconceivable that any material mechanism could be responsible for certain sorts of things. Thus, in the *Passions of the Soul* he laid down the principle "that all that which is in us and which we cannot in any way conceive as possibly pertaining to a body, must be attributed to our soul" (I, iv). And in his view what has to be thus attributed is thought, in his own rather broad sense of "thought," which seems to include all actions and passions considered to involve consciousness (*ibid.*, I, xvii ff.). "By the word thought I understand all that of which we are conscious as operating in us. And that is why not only understanding, willing, imaging, but feeling also here count as thought" (*Principles of Philosophy*, I, ix).

Descartes was thus insisting that it is inconceivable that matter, however disposed, could in this sense think. This is a notion of the same sort as the idea that purposive and rational beings could not, without benefit of control by some Higher Purpose, have evolved first from creatures of a lower order and, ultimately, from inanimate matter, an idea found in both some objections to evolutionary theory and some versions of the Argument to Design. Presumably, Descartes would have accepted both contentions and many others like them because they fall under the generic principle, which he formulated as the fourth of his "axioms or common notions"; "All the reality of perfection which is in a thing is found formally or eminently in its first and total cause" (Addendum to the Replies to the Second Set of Objections to the *Meditations*).

It has since Kant become the custom to dignify such principles with the title "synthetic a priori propositions." But the one with which we are here concerned, though certainly synthetic, can be described as a priori only in the quite artificial sense that it is wholly arbitrary and unwarranted. Descartes's more specific idea had been forcibly challenged long before by the Epicureans (see, for instance, Lucretius, *De Rerum Natura* II. 865–870 and 875–882). The challenge was later repeated by both Spinoza and Locke even before Hume launched his decisive onslaught on the generic notion that it is possible to know a priori that some thing or sort of thing must be or cannot be the cause of some other thing or sort of thing. The points made, in their different ways, by both Spinoza and Locke were that there is no contradiction in the idea of something material being endowed with thought and that we are in no position to deny dogmatically that there are material creatures so endowed.

Subjectivism. Thus far, Descartes's originality, as against the Platonic tradition, has chiefly been in his positive scientific interests and in his mechanistic ideas about the body. His achievement was to form a new framework of discussion and to provide a metaphysical foundation for the further development of physiology. He was also revolutionary on a second count, for it was he who developed with compelling dramatic power a new approach to questions of mind and matter. For three full centuries this remained part of the accepted philosophical orthodoxy, an orthodoxy which even Hume seems never to have thought to question. This approach can be characterized, though with no intended moral overtones, as self-centered.

Whereas Plato generally—and Descartes, too, when he suggested tests of humanity—approached people from our common public world, Descartes at his most characteristic tried to approach the world from inside the closed circle of his logically private consciousness. Thus, in Part IV of the *Discourse,* having reached his rock bottom certainty in the proposition *cogito ergo sum,* he asked what he was. "I saw that I could conceive that I had no body, and that there was no world nor place where I might be; but yet that I could not for all that conceive that I was not." He concluded that he "was a substance the whole essence or nature of which is to think, and that for its existence there is no need of any place, nor does it depend on any material thing; so that this "me," that is to say, the soul by which I am what I am, is entirely distinct from body, . . . and even if the body were not, the soul would not cease to be what it is" (compare, especially, *Meditations,* II).

Much of the power of the Cartesian argument lies in the use of the first-person personal pronoun and in the idiosyncratic choice of tenses and moods. For there is surely no difficulty at all, even for Descartes, in supposing that Descartes may one day be annihilated or that Descartes might never have been born. The most fundamental objections are founded upon a rejection of his unstated general assumption that (his) words obtain their meaning by reference to (his) logically private experiences. In particular, Descartes mistakenly assumed that all the words for all the things that he comprehended under the term "thinking" are words for such private experiences. Only on this assumption is it possible to assert that there could be—much less that we are—essentially incorporeal beings and, as such, fully capable of every sort of thinking. To insist that this assumption is wrong is not necessarily to adopt either a complete logical behaviorism—saying that all terms of this type refer only to public performances—or Wittgenstein's extreme later position—apparently denying the very possibility of a language's containing words defined in terms of one man's logically private experience. It is sufficient to commit oneself only to the more modest claim that most thinking words refer wholly or partly to various actual or possible proceedings that are necessarily corporeal. To recognize that this is true and could scarcely be otherwise, it is sufficient to reflect for a moment upon the whole context in which we learn to use these terms; consider how we should teach the meaning of "He argued with her" or "She drew her own conclusions." In this perspective it becomes no wonder that, as Wittgenstein said, "The human face is the best picture of the human soul."

Personal identity and parapsychology. The appeal of the Cartesian approach and its influence can be appreciated by considering two examples, both relevant to the question of immortality—first, the discussion of personal identity initiated by Locke and continued by Butler, Hume, and Reid and, second, the investigation of the question of human survival by modern parapsychologists through the study of the possible relevance of the evidence furnished by all types of mediumistic performances.

Both investigations have started from the self-centered Cartesian standpoint and have taken for granted that, essentially, people are bodiless. Thus, the problem of personal identity was generally taken to be one of the identity of an incorporeal thinking thing. Locke tried to provide an analysis of personal identity, so construed, in terms of consciousness (memory). The decisive objection to any such analysis was sharply put by Butler: "And one should really think it self-evident that consciousness of personal identity presupposes, and therefore cannot constitute, personal identity" (Dissertation I, "Personal Identity," appended to the *Analogy of Religion*).

But most of Locke's critics, Butler included, seem to have failed to appreciate just how difficult—even, perhaps, impossible—the problems of the nature of the identity and of the principle of the individuation of such putative incorporeal beings must be. If people are thought of as incorporeal substances having sorts of thinking, in the wide Cartesian sense, as their qualities (the substance, or "pure ego," theory of the self), then the question is how such substances are to be identified, what sense can be given to the expression "pure ego." If, with Hume, one is unable to provide any satisfactory answer to this question, the only alternative seems to be thinking of people as collections of experiences (the serial, or "bundle," theory of the self). Theories of this sort face two difficulties. First, it does not seem to make sense to speak of thoughts or experiences as "loose and separate" without anyone's having them, and, second, there seems to be no string capable of tying the bundles of experiences together while keeping one bundle distinct from another. The first difficulty may or may not be merely grammatical. The second, once the impossibility of using memory as the string is fully realized, appears very formidable. It was the second difficulty in a slightly different form that Hume had to confess to be "too hard for my understanding" (Appendix to *Treatise of Human Nature*).

In parapsychology it seems to have been almost universally assumed that mediumistic material, insofar as it cannot be either satisfactorily explained away in terms of fraud and delusion or conveniently redescribed in terms of telepathic and clairvoyant transactions among the living, can and must be interpreted as evidence for human survival. Yet to interpret such material in this way is not to provide support for, but rather to presuppose, a Platonic–Cartesian view of man. For it is only insofar as a person is essentially incorporeal that it can even make sense to suggest that someone years ago dead, buried, and dissolved is even now communicating with us through a medium.

OTHER ARGUMENTS CONCERNING IMMORTALITY

This article has thus far concentrated on philosophers who have adopted, more or less consciously, a Platonic or Platonizing view of man and who, if they have argued philosophically for any sort of immortality, have urged that the nature of the soul is such that it must be or must be presumed to be imperishable. None of these arguments requires any reference to a deity, and none appeals to any moral premises. This may perhaps be surprising, for most people—at least those in the European cultural tradition—are likely to think that beliefs in God and in immortality must go together. They are inclined to take it for granted that the main if not the only point of immortality—and sometimes perhaps of God, too—is to provide inordinate rewards and punishments. Yet there is no obvious inconsistency in believing in a Creator while denying that he has established a new world in a future life to redress the moral unbalances of the old. Nor does it appear that to assert our immortality is logically either to presuppose or to imply the existence of any sort of god. It may seem odd, but it is not manifestly inconsistent, for such avowedly atheist philosophers as J. M. E. McTaggart and C. J. Ducasse to affirm immortality, McTaggart offering exclusively metaphysical reasons and Ducasse appealing mainly to the evidence of parapsychology.

Moral arguments. The most considerable philosopher to rest his case for immortality on morality was Kant. Unfortunately, this is one of the many cases in which it is difficult to give an account of Kant's position and reasons which is clear, consistent, persuasive, precise, and acceptable to Kant scholars. Kant himself may be at fault here not merely, as usual, because he obscured his thought with cumbrous and idiosyncratic expression but also because he presented imprecise and uncompelling arguments.

But with these warnings it can be said that in the *Critique of Practical Reason* and in the *Critique of Judgment* Kant offered freedom, immortality, and God as the three postulates of practical reason. Practical reason is for Kant the source of the universal imperatives of morality. A "postulate of pure practical reason" is defined in the *Critique of Practical Reason* as "a theoretical proposition which is not as such demonstrable, but which is an inseparable corollary of an a priori unconditionally valid moral law" (translated by L. W. Beck, Chicago, 1949, pp. 225–228). The form of the argument, in the cases of immortality and God, appears to be that something is said to be commanded by the moral law but could be obeyed only on a certain condition; therefore, the conclusion is drawn not that that condition must obtain but that it must be a postulate of practical reason. The first difficulty is to see how Kant, who in and after the *Critique of Pure Reason* regularly denied the possibility of proofs of immortality or of the existence of God, proposed to reconcile this denial with insistence on the validity of the present deductions. The most promising response to this is to suggest that they cannot be rated as proofs of the doctrines that Kant maintained to be unprovable because it has not been and cannot be shown that the moral ideas are indeed soundly based but that they do prove that to act in accordance with moral ideas is to act as if, or to act on the assumption that, these doctrines are true.

The second difficulty lies in the supposed derivations themselves. In the case of the postulate of immortality the conclusion is to be drawn from the premise that the moral law commands us to achieve a perfect correspondence between our will and that law. This is taken to be out of

the question in this life. Thus, what the law really requires is an endless progress toward the ideal, which is possible "only under the presupposition of an infinitely enduring existence and personality of the same rational being." If this is what Kant meant—as it certainly is what he said—then the moral law includes one very strange command. For to reach the proposed conclusion, we have to construe that law not as stating that we should approach as near to perfection as is humanly possible, or, as Kant seemed at first inclined to say, that we must actually achieve perfection, but, rather, that we must forever approach asymptotically this eternally unattainable ideal.

In the case of the third postulate of God the moral premise is that the law requires us to promote the highest good, which involves a perfect correspondence between the morality and the happiness of every individual. But the only guarantee of the possibility of this correspondence would be the existence of God, presumably because God alone would possess the power necessary to achieve it. Consequently, practical reason demands this postulate.

There seems to be a crucial disharmony between the premises of the second and the third arguments. Only at first in the second but throughout the third, Kant apparently wanted to insist that the ideals prescribed by practical reason must be practically and not just theoretically possible. Surely, it is merely the contingent weakness of the flesh that makes holiness something "of which no rational being in the world of sense is at any time capable," whereas if the theoretical possibility of achieving the necessary correspondence was all that was at stake, there would be no call "to assume the actual existence of God." Yet Kant had urged in the second argument that the true imperative is to press ever closer to an ideal which is, it seems, not even theoretically attainable. This is fatal. If it is once allowed that an imperative can be to get as near as is humanly possible to an ideal that may be practically—even theoretically—unattainable, then the whole foundation of both arguments collapses. For such more modest demands could be satisfied in an earthly lifetime and without benefit of God.

Three general points about the Kantian arguments should be particularly noted. First, that the cases for the second and for the third postulate are separate. Second, Kant scrupulously avoided any suggestion that the authority of the moral law is at all dependent on the availability, here or hereafter, of rewards and punishments. Third, Kant was careful not to make the mistake of trying to deduce what is the case from premises affirming only what ought to be. It is not often that any of these things can be said for some more popular arguments for immortality.

For instance, it is often urged—most commonly, perhaps, in Roman Catholic textbook apologetic but elsewhere, too—that the lack of appropriate rewards and punishments would make nonsense of the claims of morality. Thus, the Jesuit M. Maher wrote:

But in the judgement that conduct entailing a sacrifice *ought* to be pursued, there is implied a further judgement that it cannot be ultimately *worse for the agent himself* to do that which is right. . . . The supposition that virtue can finally result in . . . misery for the agent; or that wickedness may effect an increase in the total quantity of his personal happiness is seen to be in conflict with reason, and to be destructive of all morality. (*Rational Psychology*, London, 1940, p. 530)

Maher proceeded to argue that God could not permit this and, therefore, that there must be immortality, with penalties and compensations. He himself believed that the existence of God is independently established by natural theology (p. 533), but "some of the proofs of Immortality are amongst the most forcible arguments for the existence of a Deity" (*ibid.*, pp. 525–526). It is interesting to compare the distress of Henry Sidgwick, who saw the moral situation similarly but was unable to share the supposedly saving religious convictions (*Methods of Ethics*, London, 1874, especially Part IV, Ch. 7).

Even if it were to be allowed that some such view is correct, it certainly does not warrant the suggested conclusions. Suppose we allow that rewards and penalties are indeed morally necessary; at most, this could support a demand not for immortality but for a temporary survival. Nothing has been said in the premises to explain why these necessary rewards and penalties have to be eternal. Indeed, to the secular moralist, to whom no revelation has been vouchsafed, it might seem that to provide eternal penalties for temporal offenses would be to make the universe infinitely worse. More generally, it is essential to insist that no argument from purely gerundive premises—stating only what ought to be or what is in some other way desirable—can by itself either establish or make probable any conclusion about what is actually the case. (Compare J. S. Mill, *Three Essays on Religion*, London, 1874, especially the essay "Theism.")

In any case it is certainly no part of the meaning of moral obligation that the obligation must always accord with the eventual self-interest or the person obliged. The sense in which categorical imperatives can be characterized as essentially rational refers to their universality and impartiality rather than to any implication that obedience must always be ultimately the best-paying policy. If anything, surely, it is part of the very idea of morality that sacrifices are sometimes required.

Argument from desire. Many other arguments have been and are put forward. It is urged, for instance, that the allegedly almost universal belief in survival is somehow evidence of its own truth, a contention rejected by J. S. Mill for the decisive reason that to urge this is not to offer a good ground but, rather, if anything, to concede tacitly that there is none. Again, attempts have been made (by Dugald Stewart, for instance) to make something of the allegedly almost universal desire for immortality or of the existence of human potentialities that cannot be realized in a mere three score years and ten. If the existence of a desire really were a reason for affirming not merely, as perhaps it is, that this desire has some describable object but also, as it manifestly is not, that this object must actually be realized, then the argument could still be refuted by the consideration—pressed by Hume in his essay "Immortality"—that the certainly no less nearly universal fear of annihilation equally demands its real object. Of course, the existence of a desire for immortality, where it is found, does call for—

and can easily be given—a naturalistic explanation. Such a desire, however, begins to be useful to the advocate of immortality only insofar as it can be used in conjunction with some idea of a God who may be relied on to arrange for the ultimate fulfillment of (some of?) the desires and (some more of?) the potentialities that he has arranged for us to have. (The qualification "some of" has, presumably, to be put in to allow for the existence of ambivalent and evil desires; the "some more of" is needed if we are to have an argument that even appears to hold.)

To consider the possibility of establishing the existence of such a God is beyond the scope of this article. Yet it is perhaps worth suggesting that the existence of these ostensibly frustrated wholesome desires and these apparently unfulfilled splendid potentialities must, by itself, count as evidence against, rather than for, the existence of this kind of God. It is, as Hume insisted both in his *Dialogues* and in the first *Enquiry*, very odd—notwithstanding that it is very common—to argue from what in themselves would have to be rated as defects of the familiar world to the conclusion that this world is the work of a being without defect, who will in the future make good all present deficiencies.

ARGUMENTS AGAINST IMMORTALITY

Philosophers opposed to the belief in immortality have generally confined their case to attacking weaknesses in the arguments thought up by immortalists. But some have also advanced arguments intended to show that human beings do not survive the death of their bodies. Thus, in the essay mentioned above Hume was not satisfied with pointing out the flaws in the metaphysical and the moral arguments for immortality but urged a number of considerations "from the analogy of nature" in favor of "the mortality of the soul." Similarly, many other writers who are not materialists and who are not committed to the view about the meaning of person words presented in this article maintain that there are powerful empirical grounds supporting a negative position on immortality. The most popular and impressive of these is what may be called the "body–mind dependence argument," an argument that, according to its more recent exponents, has received powerful confirmation from modern brain research. Bertrand Russell wrote,

> We know that the brain is not immortal, and that the organized energy of a living body becomes, as it were, demobilized at death and therefore not available for collective action. All the evidence goes to show that what we regard as our mental life is bound up with brain structure and organized bodily energy. Therefore it is rational to suppose that mental life ceases when bodily life ceases. The argument is only one of probability, but it is as strong as those upon which most scientific conclusions are based. (*Why I Am Not a Christian*, New York, 1957, p. 51)

Philosophers in the Hume–Russell tradition have also generally insisted that in the case of immortality the onus of proof must lie entirely with the believers. In their view it is quite wrong that we start with an open question. As this article urged at the beginning, the familiar facts of life and death establish an overwhelming presumption of mortality. Given these facts and the fact that person words mean what they do mean, there are massive philosophical obstacles to be overcome before the question of a future life can be shown to be sufficiently open to leave any room at all for appeals to evidence or even to faith.

Of course, there is nothing to stop anyone from giving what sense he likes to the expression "disembodied person." The difficulty is to attach enough sense to the expression so that some discovery about disembodied people could provide us with grounds for believing that we survive death. In their present senses person words have logical liaisons of the very greatest human importance. Personal identity in the present sense is the necessary condition of both accountability and expectation. This is only to say that it is unjust to reward or punish someone for something unless, as a minimum condition, he is the same person who did the deed and that it is absurd to expect things to happen to me in 1984 unless, as a minimum condition, there is going to be a person in existence in 1984 who will be the same person as I. The difficulty is to change the use of person words so radically that it becomes significant to talk of people's surviving dissolution without changing it in such a way that these crucial logical liaisons must be broken.

If this difficulty cannot be overcome—and there seems little reason to think that it can—then the apocalyptic words of the early Wittgenstein are to the point: "Our life is endless as the visual field is without limit. Death is not an event in life. Death is not lived through" (*Tractatus Logico-philosophicus*, London and New York, 1922, Secs. 6.431 and 6.1411).

Bibliography

For a massive survey of the history of the doctrine of immortality, see W. R. Alger, *A Critical History of the Doctrine of the Future Life* (New York, 1871). For surveys of particular aspects of the doctrine, consult the bibliography of Antony Flew, ed., *Body, Mind, and Death* (New York, 1964), an anthology which includes a number of important pieces on immortality. The sources for the views given in the text are cited there.

St. Augustine's *De Immortalite Animae* has been translated by George G. Leckie in St. Aurelius Augustine, *Concerning the Teacher and On the Immortality of the Soul* (New York and London, 1938). Pietro Pomponazzi's *De Immortalite Animae* is available in an English translation by W. H. Hay II, revised by John H. Randall, Jr., in Ernst Cassirer, Paul Oskar Kristeller, and John H. Randall, Jr., eds., *The Renaissance Philosophy of Man* (Chicago, 1948).

Moses Mendelssohn's *Phaedon* (Berlin, 1767) is a famous dialogue on immortality that consciously imitates Plato's *Phaedo*. Hume's "Of the Immortality of the Soul" first appeared in *Two Essays* (London, 1777); it is reprinted in Paul Edwards and Arthur Pap, eds., *A Modern Introduction to Philosophy*, 2d ed. (New York, 1965). The translation of Immanuel Kant's *Critique of Practical Reason* quoted in the text is that of L. W. Beck (Chicago, 1949). Dugald Stewart's *Philosophy of the Active and Moral Powers of Man* is contained in *The Works of Dugald Stewart*, Vol. V (Cambridge, 1829), pp. 366–423. J. M. E. McTaggart's views can be found in *Some Dogmas of Religion* (London, 1906). For C. J. Ducasse's views see *Nature, Mind, and Death* (La Salle, Ill., 1951) and *The Belief in a Life After Death* (Springfield, Ill., 1960). Joseph Butler, *The Analogy of Religion* (London, 1736), Part I, Ch. 1, is a detailed argument for immortality with replies to objections. John Fiske, *The Destiny of Man* (Boston and New York, 1884) and *Life Everlasting* (Boston, 1901); William James, *Human Immortality* (Boston and New York, 1898; 2d ed., with reply to critics, 1917); Harry Emerson Fosdick, *The Assurance of Immortality* (New York, 1926); John Baillie, *And the Life Everlasting* (London, 1934); A. E. Taylor, *The Christian Hope of Immortality* (London, 1938); and Jacques Maritain, *The Range of Reason* (New York, 1952) all present arguments for immortality, as does "Ten Reasons for Believing in Immortality," a sermon by John Haynes Holmes, published in *The Community Pulpit* (1929–1930) and reprinted in Edwards and Pap, *op. cit.* G. T. Fechner, *Büchlein vom Leben nach dem Tode*, translated by John Erskine as *Life After Death* (Chicago, 1906), is a panpsychist defense of immortality. A. S. Pringle-Pattison, *The Idea of Immortality* (Oxford, 1922), holds that if there is personal immortality, it is not the inherent possession of every human soul but must be won by continual effort. E. S. P. Haynes, *The Belief in Personal Immortality* (London, 1913); Chapman Cohen, *The Other Side of Death* (London, 1922); Clarence Darrow, *The Story of My Life* (New York, 1932); and Corliss Lamont, *The Illusion of Immortality* (London and New York, 1932) argue against immortality. Bertrand Russell, *Why I Am Not a Christian and Other Essays* (London and New York, 1957), should be consulted for a representative sample of Russell's arguments against immortality. A negative position similar to that presented in this article is found in C. B. Martin, *Religious Belief* (Ithaca, N.Y., 1959).

C. D. Broad's *The Mind and Its Place in Nature* (London, 1925), though somewhat dated, is perhaps the most valuable work on the problem of mind and body so crucial to the question of immortality. In Section D, Broad argues against the moral argument for immortality.

The source of the discussion of personal identity is Locke's *Essay Concerning Human Understanding*, A. C. Frazer, ed., 2 vols. (Oxford, 1894), Vol. II, Ch. 27. For the contributions of Butler, Hume, and Reid and for later works on this topic, see the Bibliography of PERSONAL IDENTITY.

The classic parapsychological study of immortality is F. W. H. Myers, *Human Personality and Its Survival of Bodily Death* (London and New York, 1903). See also Ducasse, *op. cit.*; C. D. Broad, *op. cit.*, *Religion, Philosophy, and Psychical Research* (London, 1953), and *Lectures on Psychical Research* (London and New York, 1962); Antony Flew, *A New Approach to Psychical Research* (London, 1953); and the Bibliography of ESP PHENOMENA, PHILOSOPHICAL IMPLICATIONS OF. For the investigations of psychical researchers into the nature of the experiences of spirits, see, for instance, G. N. M. Tyrrell, *Apparitions* (London, 1953). J. R. Hick, "Theology and Verification IV," in *Theology Today*, Vol. 17 (April 1960), reprinted in J. R. Hick, ed., *The Existence of God* (New York, 1964), presents a view opposite to the thesis of this article on the difficulty of identifying the reconstituted person with the original person.

F. C. Copleston, *Aquinas* (London and Baltimore, 1955), gives a sympathetic and illuminating account of Aquinas' views on immortality.

For the most important recent criticism of the Cartesian doctrine of the soul, see Gilbert Ryle, *The Concept of Mind* (London and New York, 1949). For a Wittgensteinian criticism see P. T. Geach, *Mental Acts* (London and New York, 1957).

For the view that the bodily occurrences involved in rational behavior can be completely explained only supernaturally, see, for example, C. S. Lewis, *Miracles* (London and New York, 1957), especially Ch. 2. For a fuller development of the view that such occurrences can be the subject matter of the physiologist while logical questions as to the rationality of the performance considered as an argument can be raised and answered, see Antony Flew, *Hume's Philosophy of Belief* (London and New York, 1961), Ch. 5.

ANTONY FLEW

IMPERATIVES. See LOGIC, DEONTIC; MUST.

IMPLICATION. See LOGIC, HISTORY OF; LOGIC, MODERN; LOGIC, TRADITIONAL.

INDETERMINISM. See CHANCE; DETERMINISM.

INDEXICAL SIGNS, EGOCENTRIC PARTICULARS, AND TOKEN-REFLEXIVE WORDS.

Demonstratives, pronouns, and tenses have often been grouped together under a single label, such as "indexical signs," "egocentric particulars," or "token-reflexive words." This article will consider what is involved in these classifications and then go on to show what philosophical importance they have.

Indexical signs. What is there about demonstratives, pronouns, and tenses that warrant their being subsumed under a common label? It is because what they denote is relative to the speaker; to know the referent of "I," "now," "here," and "you," we must know who utters the word and when, where, and to whom he utters it. Thus, knowledge of the speaker and his context is essential in determining the referent of such words. C. S. Peirce called them indexical signs because their referent is determined by its existential relation to the sign, a sign, for Peirce, being anything which represents or signifies an object to an interpretant (a mind which understands the sign). An act of pointing is an indexical sign because its object, or referent, is determined by the spatiotemporal relation between the index finger used in the act of pointing and its object. The symbol "this" is a surrogate for an index finger in an act of pointing; its referent is determined by the existential relation between some object and the sign which is uttered or written by the speaker.

Rather than an indexical sign being used in place of a noun, as is often stated in grammar books, Peirce claimed that it was the other way around, for an indexical sign indicates its object in the most direct way possible and does not rely on any descriptive element, as does a noun. Peirce overlooked the fact that an indexical sign does not always indicate its object directly—for instance, when the indexical sign refers to an object which has been previously named or described in discourse: "Napoleon was a great general. *He* shaped history." Also, it would be an oversimplification to say that the pure index "this" can indicate its object directly without the need of any descriptive symbols; the naked use of "this" is extremely ambiguous, and to cut down this ambiguity, "this" must be accompanied by some descriptive symbol—"this tree," "this color."

There are other difficulties in Peirce's analysis. First, he confused the concept of index with that of grammatical subject when he asserted that all subject terms are indexes. Proper names and descriptions are used as subjects, but it is not thereby shown that they are indexical signs. Second, he claimed that such symbols as "red" and "blue" are indexical signs because indexical signs are used in the ostensive teaching of them, but this confuses the way in which a symbol refers to its object with the way in which it is learned. To teach someone the meaning of "blue," we might point to a blue patch and say, "This is blue," but it does not follow that "blue" is an indexical sign just because the indexical sign "this" was used in teaching its meaning.

Peirce also claimed that a name for a date or place involves indexical signs, and about this there has been considerable controversy, Arthur W. Burks and Arthur Pap defending him and Yehoshua Bar-Hillel attacking his view. But Peirce's point here seems to be not merely that we must use indexical signs in teaching someone how to set up and use a spatiotemporal coordinate system but that every time we specify the coordinate(s) of a position in time or space, it essentially involves an indexical element. If I specify a temporal or spatial coordinate, I must be able to indicate whether the event serving as the origin on my calendar is earlier or later than now and whether the object serving as the origin in my system of spatial coordinates is to the left or right of here. If a definite description is given of this event or object, it does not ensure uniqueness of reference, since it is possible, contrary to Leibniz' principle of the identity of indiscernibles, that more than one event or object could have all of the properties described and since this holds regardless of how detailed and elaborate the description is. Uniqueness of reference can be ensured only through the use of indexical signs, for although it is possible for there to be two or more events that have all of their properties in common, there could be only one of these events that stands in a determinate temporal relation to now and a determinate spatial relation to here.

In his *Brown Book* Ludwig Wittgenstein brought out some interesting differences in the "logical grammar" (rules of use) of indexical signs and names. In the sentence frame "_____is here" or "It is now_____," we can put into the blank a name for a place or time—"The equator is here" or "It is now Valentine's Day"—but it would be nonsense to put "here" or "now" into the blank, since that would result in our saying, "Here is here" or "It is now now." Similarly, in the sentence frame "This is called_____," we can insert into the blank space a name but not the index "this." Therefore, although it is correct to say that "now," "here," or "this" indicates a time, place or object, it would be incorrect to say that they name a time, place, or object.

Use and denotation of indexes. One of the curious features of indexes is that in regard to any index, such as "here" or "this," the referent often changes from one occasion of their utterance to another; in spite of this changing reference, however, each utterance of "here" or "this" means the same thing. This strange fact can be accounted for if we distinguish between (1) the rules or conventions controlling the use of an indexical sign and (2) what is denoted by a particular utterance or inscription of this sign. The rules for using indexes are as follows: "now" is used to refer to a moment of time virtually simultaneous with the utterance of the word "now"; "I" is used by the speaker to refer to himself; "here" is used by the speaker to refer to the place where he is standing; and so on. Every time "now," "I," or "here" is uttered, it has the same meaning, even though the referent may change, in the sense that it is controlled by the same rules of use. If we should find a slip of paper in the street on which was written "I am now tired," we would not know the referent of "I" or the time indicated by "now" and therefore would not know what facts would be relevant to the truth or falsity of this statement. However, since we understand the meaning (the rules of use) of the indexical signs "I" and "now," we at least know that whoever wrote this was asserting that he was tired at the time he wrote it. Therefore, we know what facts would be relevant to determining the referent of these indexes—namely, facts concerning who wrote the sentence and at what time. Because of the changing reference of different utterances of the same indexical sign, the inclusion of an indexical sign in a sentence renders this sentence context-dependent in that it is not freely repeatable—that is, its utterance by different persons at different times, places, and so on will result in statements whose truth-values may not all be the same.

Egocentric particulars. Bertrand Russell called pronouns, tenses, and demonstratives egocentric particulars because what they denote is relative to the speaker. He attempted to reduce all such expressions to the egocentric particular "this," in which "this" is a "logically proper name" for a sense datum experienced by the speaker at the time he makes his utterance. For example, "I" means "the biography to which *this* belongs"; "now" means "what is compresent with *this*." "This" is a strange sort of a proper name because it applies to something different—a different sense datum—every time it is uttered. And yet on each occasion of its use, it is unambiguous, applying to one and only one particular, though, of course, only the speaker can know its referent since it is a sense datum private to him.

As was the case with indexical signs, the inclusion of the egocentric particular "this" in a sentence renders the sentence nonfreely repeatable. For instance, if we translate "It was raining" into "An occurrence of rain is (tenselessly) earlier than *this*," in which "this" is a logically proper name for a sense datum experienced by the speaker at the time he makes his utterance, the second sentence is as context-bound as the first in that both sentences are subject to the same temporal restrictions in their use—that is, they can be used to make true statements only if uttered later than the occurrence of rain. Also, in the second statement "this" functions as a temporal, rather than a spatial, indicator, since it makes sense and is natural to say, "the time at which *this* occurs" but not "the place at which *this* occurs." Herein "this" has the same logic as "now." However, in the statement "The monument is to the west of *this*," "this" has the same role as the spatial index "here."

A fundamental objection to Russell's analysis is that it renders communication impossible not only between different persons but even in respect to a single person at different moments in his history. For example, when I say, "An occurrence of rain is (tenselessly) earlier than *this*," only I can know what event an occurrence of rain is earlier than, for it is a sense datum private to myself. Any analysis of language which entails that communication is impossible is reduced to absurdity (see PRIVATE LANGUAGE PROBLEM).

This objection can be easily met by making a slight alteration in Russell's analysis; instead of having "this" denote a private sense datum, let it have as its referent a publicly observable event that the speaker experiences at the time he makes his utterance. Russell's claim that "this" must denote a sense datum is a result of his epistemological quest for certainty, and by making this alteration, we are separating the analysis of egocentric particulars from this dubious piece of epistemology.

Token-reflexive words. An independent, though in some ways similar, analysis of egocentric words was given

by Hans Reichenbach, who called them token-reflexive words. A word is defined as a class of similar tokens, a token being an individual sign—that is, a set of noises made on some occasion or ink marks on a piece of paper. By similar tokens Reichenbach means tokens that are equisignificant rather than tokens that physically resemble one another. A token-reflexive word is one that refers to the corresponding token used in an individual act of speech or writing. Every token of a given token-reflexive word will refer to a different physical token—namely, itself. All such words can be defined in terms of "this token." For example, "I" means "the person who utters *this token*"; "now" means "the time at which *this token* is uttered." Every token of the phrase "this token" refers to a different token—a different set of noises or ink marks. A sentence containing a token-reflexive word is called a token-reflexive sentence; every token of a given token-reflexive sentence will refer to a different sentence-token.

According to Reichenbach's analysis, we could translate "It was raining" into "An occurrence of rain is (tenselessly) earlier than *this token*," in which "this token" refers to the entire sentence token within which the token of the phrase "this token" occurs. Both sentences are subject to the same temporal restrictions in their use. Also, in the second sentence "this token" is short for "the time at which *this token* occurs" and thus functions as a temporal indicator.

Although the token-reflexive analysis generally agrees with the egocentric particular analysis, it differs from it in making the referent of "this" the physical token occurring in the speech act rather than some other event simultaneous with the occurrence of this token. By doing this, the token-reflexive analysis makes explicit the implicit reference made to the sentence token in the egocentric particular analysis in that the logically proper name "this" denotes an event experienced by the speaker at the time he makes his utterance. Since "this" is a logically proper name for an event occurring simultaneously with the occurrence of the token of "this," we must first be able to locate the token of "this" before we can know what its referent is. By making do only with the token of "this" occurring in a speech act, the token-reflexive analysis as well as the indexical analysis eliminates the need to bring in some event in addition to the occurrence of the token. Therefore, the token-reflexive and indexical accounts are more economical than the egocentric particular one because the egocentric particular analysis must make reference to two events—the occurrence of the token and some event other than the token that is simultaneous with it.

Several attempts have been made to construct ideal languages in which all token-reflexive words would be eliminated, so that all sentences in such a language would be freely repeatable. But such efforts are in vain, for in a language without token-reflexive words we could not say, for example, that some event is now happening, is simultaneous with this token. Reichenbach attempted to eliminate token-reflexive words, such as tenses, by translating "It was (is, will be) raining" into "An occurrence of rain is (tenselessly) earlier than (simultaneous with, later than) theta," in which "theta" is a metalinguistic proper name for the tensed sentence token that precedes it in this sentence. This analysis fails because the statement in the analysans does not convey the same information as does the one in the analysandum, in that the second tells us that the occurrence of rain is now past (present, future) whereas the first merely describes a tenseless relation of precedence (simultaneity, subsequence) between an occurrence of rain and the occurrence of the tensed sentence token named by "theta" without asserting that either event is now past, present, or future. Because of this asymmetry in information between the analysandum and the analysans, it would not be redundant for us to ask someone who utters the sentence in the analysans whether it was (is, will be) raining, whereas this question has already been answered by the statement in the analysandum.

In opposition to Reichenbach's token-reflexive theory, one might question whether language can be token-reflexive or, at any rate, point out that the sense in which a token-reflexive phrase or sentence refers to itself is very different from the sense in which it refers to something other than itself. In ordinary language isolated words and phrases are not self-referring, and if it is legitimate to speak of a sentence as a whole as being token-reflexive, it does not refer to itself in the manner of selecting itself. One could make "this" or any other word or expression token-reflexive merely by stipulating that it shall be. For example, we could stipulate, as Reichenbach does, that any symbol is token-reflexive when written within what he calls token quotes (˃this˂). By writing "this" within token quotes, we make it token-reflexive, but such a move is unilluminating and does nothing to show that the ordinary use of "this" or any other symbol placed within token quotes is token-reflexive.

So-called token-reflexive words are used to refer not to themselves but to something other than themselves, though they do so by the spatiotemporal connection between the token occurring in a speech act and its referent. When I say "you," I am referring to a person in my vicinity, not to the token of "you" that I utter, though in order to know the referent of this token one would have to know the spatiotemporal relation it has to the person in question. When I point and say "this tree," I no doubt attract attention to myself and my utterance token; otherwise, I could not successfully refer to the tree. It would be wrong, however, to say that I refer to myself or the token I utter.

The demonstrative "this," when used alone, is a surrogate for an act of pointing, but for this very reason it can never point to itself any more than a hammer, which is an instrument involved in hammering something, can hammer itself. If I want to refer, for instance, to my index finger's act of pointing, I must point to it with another finger, or I might just hold up the index finger and say "this index finger," but the "this" is a surrogate for my pointing to this finger with another finger. Since the demonstrative "this" is a surrogate for an act of pointing, it follows that a token of "this" is never self-referring any more than an act of pointing is. Therefore, a token of "this token" cannot refer to the entire token (both words). If a perverse radio announcer should say, "The time will be five o'clock when you hear the next token of the words 'this token.' This token," it would not be correct to say that the token of "this token" occurring at the end of his sen-

tence is self-referring, for he denotes or refers to this particular token by the definite description "the next token of the words 'this token'" that immediately precedes it. Another possible counterexample would be to say "this room and everything in it," but here "this" refers not to itself but to a room, for it is not essential that the token of "this" occur in the room referred to. It would not if the speaker were standing outside the room when he made his utterance. But a token-reflexive word, according to Reichenbach's definition, cannot fail in its reference to the token used in an individual speech act. Therefore, this use of "this" is not token-reflexive. Similar considerations can be brought to bear against the counterexample "this token phrase and every token in it." It might be used to refer to a token-phrase immediately preceding or following it.

Thus far, we have shown only that the ordinary use of "this" and "this token" is not token-reflexive in the sense of being self-referring. However, the token-reflexive theory claims not merely that these words, when used alone, are self-referring but also that their inclusion in a sentence renders that sentence as a whole token-reflexive. In this connection consider the following sentences: "This sentence contains five words"; "This sentence is in English"; "This· sentence token is short"; "This sentence token is written in ink." What is wrong with saying that these sentences as a whole are token-reflexive? First, these sentences are not token-reflexive because not every token of them is token-reflexive. In fact, most tokens of these sentences are not token-reflexive because they are used to refer to a sentence token that immediately precedes or follows them—for example, "This sentence contains five words: 'The boy hit the ball.'" Tokens of these sentences are token-reflexive only because there are no other sentence tokens in their immediate vicinity for them to refer to. Second, in cases where a sentence token is token-reflexive, it always refers to some physical properties of the token (the fact that it is loud, written in ink, or the like) and never to the meaning of the token (what it signifies or denotes). It is nonsense to say, "This sentence means what this sentence means."

Philosophical importance. Egocentric particulars and token-reflexive words have played a prominent role in the attempts that have been made by various philosophers to create an ideal language by means of which we could view the universe *sub specie aeternitatis*. In such a language we could describe every fact about the world through the use of sentences that are not in any way context-bound; it would not matter who uttered them or where, when, or to whom he uttered them. To accomplish this, the language must be purged of all token-reflexive words, which render a sentence context-bound. Now, it has already been argued that the statements of such an ideal language could not be adequate translations of token-reflexive statements in ordinary language. A proponent of the timeless way of seeing and talking about the world might grant this but go on to argue that the tensed temporal perspectives of past, present, and future are subjective in the sense of being language-dependent or "linguocentric"; this might be supposed to follow from the fact that tenses are egocentric particulars or token-reflexive words. There is no more a unique now in nature than there is a unique here but, rather, a democratic equality of times and places. Russell used his egocentric particular analysis to justify this when he wrote:

> I think it is extremely difficult, if you get rid of consciousness altogether, to explain what you mean by such a word as "this," what it is that makes the absence of impartiality. You would say that in a purely physical world there would be a complete impartiality. All parts of time and all regions of space would seem equally emphatic. But what really happens is that we *pick out* certain facts, past and future and all that sort of thing; they all *radiate out from* "this". . . . ("The Philosophy of Logical Atomism," Lecture IV, pp. 55–56; italics added)

What is revealing in this quotation is Russell's use of the phrase "pick out." He suggests that the speaker "picks out" some event or moment of time from other moments of time by pointing to it and uttering the word "this." If Russell's way of picturing the selectivity of "this" is correct, it would follow that there is something subjective, in the sense of being language-dependent, about temporal perspectives. But this way of picturing the use or function of the demonstrative "this" is incorrect and rests on a false analogy between a series of temporal events and an order of spatial objects. The crucial point is that the demonstrative "this" is spatially selective, picking out one object in the speaker's visual field from other objects coexistent with it which could have been chosen or selected in its place; however, it is never temporally selective, picking out one event or moment of time from other earlier or later events which could have been chosen in its place. There is no temporal field of vision corresponding to a spatial field of vision, since events which are earlier and later than one another by definition do not coexist. Although it is correct to say that "now" and "this" in the analysans of the egocentric particular and token-reflexive analyses function as temporal indicators or demonstratives, it would be wrong to say that they pick out, select, or choose a moment of time. The basic common-sense belief that man is not temporally free to choose his "now," that he is finite and time-bound, is reflected in the fact that "this" and "now" are never temporally selective.

A parallel argument to Russell's for the subjectivity of temporal perspectives is based on the token-reflexive analysis rather than the egocentric particular analysis. Since, as shown by the token-reflexive analysis, events are past, present, and future only in the elliptical sense of being respectively earlier than, simultaneous with, or later than a given tensed sentence token and since the speaker can choose which sentence token that shall be by his use of the token-reflexive phrase "this token," it follows that temporal perspectives are subjective in the sense of being dependent upon the speaker.

This argument suffers from the same defective premise as Russell's argument—namely, that the speaker picks out the event, in this case the occurrence of a sentence token, which will serve as the point of orientation for the temporal schema of past, present, and future. When a person utters a word which by stipulation is token-reflexive, such as "you" or "this" in Reichenbach's analysis, he in no

sense picks out which particular token of "you" or "this" will be referred to. He has some choice, however, as to which person or object shall be denoted by his token of "you" or "this," assuming that there is more than one person or object in his immediate vicinity. "This," when interpreted in accordance with the token-reflexive analysis, is a very queer sort of demonstrative, for it involves no element of selectivity. In the ordinary use of the demonstrative "this," there is an element of spatial, but not of temporal, selectivity. But if "this" is token-reflexive, even the element of spatial selectivity drops out, for an utterance of "this token," when interpreted in accord with the token-reflexive analysis, does not pick out one token from among other tokens simultaneous with it that could have been chosen in its place. What would it be like for a person to utter a token of the token-reflexive phrase "this token" and not refer to the token he utters? It is impossible for a token of "this token" to refer unsuccessfully—that is, not refer to some physical token. But a person who utters a token-reflexive sentence does not pick out a sentence token. Since the speaker does not choose the sentence token which serves as the origin of his tensed temporal schema when he says "this token," the argument is destroyed for the subjectivity of temporal perspectives based on the token-reflexive analysis, which made it appear that there was something speaker-dependent about past, present, and future.

Bibliography

INDEXICAL SIGNS

C. S. Peirce's treatment of indexes is contained in Charles Hartshorne, Paul Weiss, and Arthur W. Burks, eds., *Collected Papers of Charles Sanders Peirce*, 8 vols. (Cambridge, Mass., 1931–1958). Excellent discussions of indexical signs are found in Arthur W. Burks, "Icon, Index, and Symbol," in *Philosophy and Phenomenological Research*, Vol. 9 (1948–1949), and "A Theory of Proper Names," in *Philosophical Studies*, Vol. 2 (1951); Arthur Pap, "Are Individual Concepts Necessary?," in *Philosophical Studies*, Vol. 1 (1950); Yehoshua Bar-Hillel, "Indexical Expressions," in *Mind*, Vol. 63 (1954). An interesting discussion of indexes is in Ludwig Wittgenstein's *Brown Book* (Oxford, 1958), which is developed in Richard M. Gale's "Is It Now Now?," in *Mind*, Vol. 73 (1964).

EGOCENTRIC PARTICULARS

Bertrand Russell's initial discussion of egocentric particulars, which he then called emphatic particulars, is in "The Philosophy of Logical Atomism," *Monist*, Vol. 28 (1918) and Vol. 29 (1919), Lecture IV, reprinted in R. C. Marsh, ed., *Logic and Knowledge* (London, 1956); his most complete analysis is in Ch. 7 of *An Inquiry Into Meaning and Truth* (New York, 1940). A critical analysis of his theory is in C. D. Broad's *Examination of McTaggart's Philosophy*, Vol. II (Cambridge, 1938), Part I, Section 2.24.

TOKEN-REFLEXIVE WORDS

The classic analysis of token-reflexive words is in Hans Reichenbach, *Elements of Symbolic Logic*, (New York, 1947), pp. 284–287. Other discussions are in F. B. Ebersole, "Verb Tenses as Expressors and Indicators," in *Analysis*, Vol. 12 (1952); Richard M. Gale, "Tensed Statements," in *Philosophical Quarterly*, Vol. 12 (1962), which has been criticized by J. J. C. Smart, " 'Tensed Statements': A Comment," in *Philosophical Quarterly*, Vol. 12 (1962), and by B. Mayo, "Infinitive Verbs and Tensed Statements," and I. Thalberg, "Tenses and 'Now,' " which both appear, along with Gale's reply, "A Reply to Smart, Mayo and Thalberg," in *Philosophical Quarterly*, Vol. 13 (1963). The following philosophers have doubted the possibility of language's being token-reflexive: J. Jørgensen, "Some Reflections on Reflexivity," in *Mind*, Vol. 42 (1953); J. N. Findlay, "An Examination of Tenses," in H. Lewis, ed., *Contemporary British Philosophy*, Third Series, (London, 1956); Richard M. Gale, "The Egocentric Particular and Token-Reflexive Analyses of Tense," in *Philosophical Review*, Vol. 43 (1964); and K. W. Rankin, "Referential Identifiers," in *American Philosophical Quarterly*, Vol. 1 (1964).

RICHARD M. GALE

INDIAN PHILOSOPHY.

There is no single term in Sanskrit corresponding to "philosophy" in the modern Western sense. However, the use of the word *darśana* (literally, "seeing") for a metaphysical system brings out two general characteristics of Indian philosophy. First, it has, from quite an early time, crystallized into a number of traditional systems; and second, these systems tend to have a soteriological or theological focus and are supposed to lead to a vision of the world involving religious or mystical experience. This dominance of religion over philosophy throughout most of Indian classical and medieval thought is formally recognized in the orthodox theory that the ultimate aim of philosophy is *mokṣa*, or release. It also means that it is desirable to understand the reasons, to be found in varying types of religious experience and theological interests, for the structure of the different *darśanas*, or viewpoints.

Nevertheless, there have been, and are, naturalistic and materialistic tendencies in Indian thought; and although religious factors may often explain the central features of the *darśanas*, there are other—such as protoscientific and epistemological—determinants of their structures. Moreover, in the course of the interplay among the viewpoints, there has been a considerable elaboration of philosophical argumentation and some development of logic. It is convenient, therefore, to describe first the origins and structures of the principal metaphysical systems, then to describe the arguments and theories advanced about certain key philosophical topics, and finally to describe developments in modern Indian philosophy (which, unlike traditional work, is written mainly in English).

EARLY HISTORY AND CRYSTALLIZATION OF THE VIEWPOINTS

Because of the religious orientation of most Indian philosophy, the viewpoints are generally classified as orthodox and unorthodox, according to whether they recognize the validity of the Veda. Of these Hindu, or orthodox, scriptural texts, the *Upaniṣads* are the most metaphysical and systematic in style; but there are different, often seemingly conflicting, strands of thought expressed in them. This variety of thought has allowed considerable latitude in their interpretation, so that scriptural orthodoxy has not led to a single viewpoint. Thus, Hindu metaphysicians range in their adherence from religious absolutism and theism to atheism. The chief unorthodox schools are Buddhism and Jainism, which look to their respective scriptures—some of which are notably philosophical and argumentative in style—and also to materialism (*Cārvāka*). Materialism flourished in early times, but for various reasons it failed to survive as a traditional viewpoint and is therefore scarcely represented by any systematic texts.

The Veda originated in north India among the Aryans (the descendants of the Indo-European invaders of India) about 1500 B.C. The scriptural traditions were formed mainly from the eighth century B.C. to the early fifth century B.C. The principal *Upaniṣads* were in process of composition from about 800 B.C.; and the teachings of the Buddha and of Vārdhamāna, later recorded in the unorthodox canons, were formulated in the late sixth century and early fifth century B.C. In the period from 400 B.C. to about A.D. 600, there evolved the basic Hindu texts known as *sūtras* (literally, "threads"). These aphoristic manuals were systematic attempts to order such various branches of knowledge as ritual, grammar, law, and metaphysics. Since they were allusive and mnemonic in character, serving to remind the pupil of the complex arguments lying behind each thesis, they consequently required commentaries. Each viewpoint had its own manual, and later commentators elaborated detailed systems on each manual. Various schools also emerged within Buddhism, ranging from the agnostic pluralism of the Theravāda to idealistic monism in the Mahāyāna. Jainism, which is more conservative and rigid, developed no great metaphysical divisions.

From the eighth to the sixteenth centuries there was a great proliferation of philosophical writings, and the first half of this period was the golden age of Indian metaphysics. The seventeenth and eighteenth centuries were rather sterile; but in the latter part of the nineteenth century, Indian philosophy came into contact with European metaphysics, especially the post-Hegelian forms of British philosophy. The analogy between these and some classical Hindu doctrines has been a factor in the revival of Hinduism during the last one hundred years. Thus, Indian philosophical history may be divided roughly into the following main periods: (1) 800 B.C.–400 B.C., the formation of the main scriptural traditions; (2) 400 B.C.–A.D. 600, the period of the *sūtras*; (3) 600–1600, the period of detailed systematization; (4) 1850 onward, the modern period. Naturally, these dates are intended only as a schema for ordering overlapping material and tendencies. For convenience, the four periods can be labeled the early, classical, medieval, and modern periods.

Traditionally, orthodox *darśanas* are classified into six systems, linked in three pairs: Yoga and Sāmkhya, Mīmāmsā and Vedānta, Nyāya and Vaiśeṣika. Theoretically, the first of each pair is essentially practical, and the second of each pair is the metaphysical basis of the practice. Thus, Yoga is supposed to deal with the techniques of self-control; Sāmkhya, to delineate the structure of the world presupposed by the aims of Yoga. Mīmāmsā is supposed to systematize the exegesis of Vedic ritual texts; Vedānta, to explore the theological ideas lying behind the ritual. But this neat classification does not work out for a number of reasons. First, Yoga, although owing its main structure to Sāmkhya, departs from it in some particulars and thus constitutes a separate metaphysical viewpoint. Second, Mīmāmsā has its own metaphysical assumptions which contradict those of Vedānta. Third, Vedānta itself contains some importantly different subschools which are in some ways more divergent from one another than are, say, Mīmāmsā and Sāṃkhya. The most important of these schools of Vedānta are Nondualism (Advaita, whose main exponent was Śankara); Qualified Nondualism (Viśiṣṭādvaita, developed especially by Rāmānuja); and Dualism (Dvaita, developed especially by Madhva). These titles signify respectively the relationships asserted to hold between the self, soul, and Divine Being. Fourth, there are other Hindu schools lying outside the orthodox classification in terms of the "six viewpoints," notably Śaiva Siddhānta, which expounds a metaphysical theology in the context of Śaivism (the cult of Śiva as Supreme Being).

The literal meanings of the titles traditionally given to the above viewpoints are as follows: Yoga, "harnessing" (of one's faculties, in order to control them); Sāṃkhya, "enumeration" (of the categories used by the system to delineate the structure of the world—though it is not quite certain that this interpretation of the original meaning of the name is correct); Mīmāṃsā, "investigation" (of the meaning of the ritualistic texts); Vedānta, "end of the Veda" (an account of the real import of scriptural teaching); Nyāya, "logical method" (logic and a syllogistic ordering of philosophical inquiry); Vaiśeṣika, "concerned with particular differences" (of individual atomic substances; the school propounds, among other things, a protoscientific atomism).

It is convenient to use "dualism" to mean the doctrine that the self or soul is distinct from, and not identical with, or a mode of, the Divine Being. It is also convenient to use "monadism" to mean the doctrine of a plurality of eternal selves and "pluralism" to mean the doctrine of a plurality of distinct substances or events in nature. Briefly, then, the above systems can be characterized as follows: Sāṃkhya is atheistic, nonpluralistic, and monadistic; later Yoga is virtually theistic but otherwise like Sāṃkhya; Mīmāṃsā, surprisingly, in view of its exegetic and ritualistic preoccupations, is atheistic and monadistic; Vedānta, as noted above varies from nondualism to dualism, and from monism to pluralism and monadism; Nyāya and Vaiśeṣika are both theistic, pluralistic, and monadistic.

In terms of philosophical importance, the chief systems and schools have been the various subschools of Vedānta, the Buddhist schools, Nyāya–Vaiśeṣika (which coalesced virtually into a single system), materialism, and Sāṃkhya. During the classical period, but more particularly during the medieval period, the interplay among these schools generated important arguments on key topics. These will be described after a more detailed examination of the structures of the systems.

SĀMKHYA AND YOGA

The origins of the various viewpoints are hard to trace with certainty. Elements of Sāṃkhya thought are found in two *Upaniṣads* which have a theistic tendency, and prominently in the *Bhagavad Gītā* (c. 200 B.C.). Medieval Vaiṣṇavism (the cult of Viṣṇu as Supreme Being) made use of cosmological ideas derived from Sāṃkhya. For these reasons the thesis has been put forward that originally Sāṃkhya was theistic, and only later acquired its atheistic character. On the other hand, H. Zimmer has powerfully argued (*Philosophies of India, passim*) that Sāṃkhya had

its origins outside the Brahmanical tradition, in close association with such unorthodox movements as Buddhism and Jainism, which themselves did not recognize the existence of a Creator God. The use made of Sāṃkhya and Yoga ideas in the *Upaniṣads* represents, on this view, a synthesis between Aryan and indigenous forms of religion. The first extant work of Sāṃkhya is Īśvarakṛṣṇa's *Sāmkhya-kārikā* ("Concise Verses on Sāṃkhya"), perhaps of the third century. Other important works are the *Tattva-kaumudī* ("Elucidation of Categories") of the ninth century and the commentary of Vijñāna Bhikṣu (sixteenth century). Yoga made use of Sāṃkhya from an early period; for example, in the *Yogasūtras* ("Yoga Aphorisms") of Patañjali (c. second century).

As it emerged in its classical and medieval form, Sāṃkhya held that reality consisted in a unitary material substance (*prakṛti*, or nature) which evolves, on the one hand, into the world as perceived by our senses and, on the other hand, into an infinite number of distinct souls (*puruṣa*). The soul as such is inactive, and only through its association with various mental elements (included here, as generally elsewhere in Indian metaphysics, under the head of matter) does it acquire the attributes normally ascribed to consciousness. The active character of nature suggests that it has an inherent teleology, whereby it subserves, in the long run, the best interests of the souls in their passage toward *mokṣa*, or release from entanglement in the round of rebirth and in the material world.

As in all other schools (apart from Mīmāṃsā), the cosmos is conceived as pulsating—a period of cosmic dissolution is followed by a period in which the cosmos is organized and differentiated; this in turn is followed by a period of dissolution, and so on indefinitely. According to Sāṃkhya, during dissolution certain internal forces of nature (known as *guṇas*—literally, "strands") are in a state of equilibrium. The *guṇas* are characterized respectively as the brightness strand (*tejas*), the force strand (*rajas*), and the mass strand (*tamas*). The first is lucid and adaptable and forms the basis of, among other things, the higher mental functions. The second is volatile and charged with energy. The third is sluggish and is the basis of heavy and dense material objects. The evolution of the cosmos occurs through the disequilibrium of these forces, with the brightness strand initially predominant. Nature thereby precipitates out the substances known as *buddhi*, the intellects associated with souls in the prior cosmic period. The precipitation of the brightness strand releases the energy of the force strand, thus boosting the tendency of the other strands to differentiate themselves. Nature thereby continues evolving on two parallel lines, corresponding roughly to the mental and the physical. On the one hand, a *sensus communis*, the five senses, and five active faculties (including speech, handling, and locomotion) are differentiated in innumerable complexes which become associated with the souls; on the other hand, a preponderance of mass substance gives rise to a material substratum, which then is distilled into infra-atoms that combine and form atoms capable of giving rise to sense impressions.

This complex cosmology exhibits a number of motifs. First, it is a protoscientific attempt to explain the phenomena of the perceptible world in terms of a single unitary substance, nature, evolving according to a rudimentary dynamics. Second, it attempts to show how we have knowledge of the external world, since mental and physical entities evolve on parallel and mutually adapted lines; thus, it opens the way to a correspondence theory of perception. According to this theory, external happenings imprint themselves via the senses and the *sensus communis*, or mind organ (*manas*), on the intellect (*buddhi*). These images are then illuminated by the soul. The mind is, so to say, a screen containing pictures of the outer world, and the soul lights these up. But the soul itself cannot be illuminated and thus perceived introspectively; therefore, its existence is known only by inference (or, in Yoga, by a special state of consciousness). Third, Sāṃkhya cosmology provides a way of accounting for phenomena without appeal to an external Creator. Nevertheless, an inherent teleology in nature is implied by the system; and later theists who made use of Sāṃkhya's cosmological ideas considered it more reasonable to externalize this teleology, in terms of the will of God, than to postulate a mysterious inner drive in nature to adapt itself to the long-term needs of the souls.

Since Sāṃkhya sharply differentiates souls from nature, including psychophysical organisms, there remains the problem of how the latter become associated with the former. The intellect here serves as a bridge. Because of the refinement of the matter composing it, the intellect is well adapted as a medium of consciousness—it is like a translucent substance through which the soul can shine. But it is only in conjunction with a soul that the intellect and the whole psychophysical organism can have experiences. The soul can gain release through discriminatory knowledge (*viveka*), that is, by realizing the essential distinction between itself and nature. In Yoga, contemplative techniques induce a stilling and purification of the mind in which the essential nature of the soul is reflected clearly. Thereby the soul becomes forever detached from any psychophysical organism.

The Sāṃkhya aim of tracing the multiple entities in the world (except souls) back to a single source was reinforced by its doctrine of causation, the *satkāryavāda*, or identity theory, which states that the effect is identical with the cause and is the realization of what was potential in the cause through a process of evolution or transformation (*pariṇāma*). A great deal of discussion about causation in the Indian tradition centered on whether this theory (*asatkāryavāda*), espoused by both the Buddhists and the Nyāya–Vaiśeṣika school, was to be preferred. The Sāṃkhya doctrine implied that the continuous changes in the cosmos (continuous, that is, save in the periods of dissolution) are changes in a single, dynamic (but permanent) substance, while the cosmologies of the atomists and of the Buddhists were pluralistic.

NYĀYA–VAIŚEṢIKA ATOMISM

Although Vaiśeṣika has roots as early as the sixth century B.C. or before, it took shape as a system about A.D. 100 in the *Vaiśeṣikasūtras* ("Aphorisms on Vaiśeṣika") of Kaṇāda. Between the fifth and the tenth centuries, the school coalesced with Nyāya and acquired a theistic (or, perhaps

more properly, a deistic) character. Traditional commentators, however, attempt to project this later theism into the *sūtras*.

Nyāya probably had its origin in the attempt to formulate rules of argument for use in disputations, a feature of Indian philosophical and theological life over a very long period. The *Nyāyasūtras* ("Logic Aphorisms") probably date from the second century and already include atomist elements. This marks the start of the syncretism of the two viewpoints. However, around 1200 the New Logic school (Navyanyāya) was formed, mainly through the influential work of the logician Gaṅgeśa.

The coalescence of Nyāya and Vaiśeṣika is somewhat puzzling. The former is essentially a methodology of argument, while the latter is a fairly elaborate systematization of metaphysical and protoscientific ideas. It happened, however, that certain features of Logic, especially its theory of inductive inference, fitted in with the protoscientific concerns of atomism. The imposition of theism upon atomism probably results from the fact that originally the Logic school's classification of arguments was partly a tool for apologetic and exegetical purposes. The more strictly logical doctrines of the combined viewpoint, together with the developments in the New Logic school, are dealt with in LOGIC, HISTORY OF, section on Indian logic.

The principal feature of atomism is the theory of everlasting atoms which constitute the fundamental structure of the cosmos (but nonatomic selves are also held to exist; these are distinct from one another but all-pervading). In a period of cosmic dissolution the atoms are uncombined; macroscopic objects are formed only during periods of creation or organization. Since atoms were considered to be of infinitesimal magnitude, a problem was posed as to how they could form macroscopic entities. It was argued that two atoms combine in a dyad and that the combination involves a quantum jump; the dyad has a noninfinitesimal magnitude, a "minute" magnitude, regarded as *sui generis*. Dyads then combine in molecules which, through another quantum jump, possess "gross" magnitude. The association of molecules accounts for all macroscopic objects. The reason for postulating a double quantum jump was chiefly the argument that the multiplication of minute quanta ought to produce even *more* minute quanta (the minute being represented by a fraction less than a whole number). The difficulties occasioned by this solution provided the basis for God's existence in later theistic atomism. Although the solution is untidy because it introduces unexplained jumps, there was no theoretical objection from the standpoint of Logic–atomist doctrine of causation, namely the nonidentity theory. Causation occurs when a combination of conditions is followed, according to a law of invariable concomitance, by a determinate effect. Thus, in principle, a set of causes could be followed by any effect whatsoever; and there is no bar to the occurrence of a genuine novelty not pre-existent in the causes.

The Logic–atomist viewpoint, however, was disinclined to account for the idiosyncrasies of macroscopic entities simply in terms of the number, arrangement, and type of the atoms (such as earth atoms and air atoms). For this reason, the school introduced a category of particularity to explain the idiosyncratic: atoms themselves, besides having such universal characteristics as fieriness, have indescribable particularities (the name of the Vaiśeṣika school is derived from the term used here, *viśeṣa*). This is one illustration of a more general feature of atomism, its attempt to synthesize atomic theory with a doctrine of categories (substance, property, particularity, for example) which were presupposed in ordinary knowledge and language. The two theories did not always fit together very neatly.

The atomists listed the following categories: substance (that in which the properties and other categories inhere), property (including what would more naturally be called relations), motion (divided into types according to direction), universality (whereby we can say that two substances have, for example, the *same* color), particularity, and inherence (although inherence could not properly be said to inhere in substances because its existence presupposes the existence of substances). Concerning inherence, it was felt necessary to make the relation between the atoms constituting a substance and the substance itself as close as that between a substance and its properties, since a property inhering in a macroscopic substance also in some sense inheres in the constituent atoms. Thus, the notion of inherence was extended to cover the cause–effect relation. (The effect inheres in the cause; thus, the table inheres in the combination of atoms causing it.)

The fact that cause and effect thus are inseparable does not affect the nonidentity doctrine. In principle, any effect can arise from a given cause, and it is a matter of experience to discover the actual laws of nature. Hence, Logic–atomism elaborated techniques of induction; the main aim was to find the invariable antecedents of particular class effects. By a criterion adopted by the school, these antecedents are required to be immediate. This obviates difficulties about tomorrow's sunrise being caused by today's, and other similar problems. It also saves Logic–atomism's radical pluralism, for otherwise everything might turn out to inhere in everything else, and it expresses the principle that there is no causal action-at-a-distance. However, certain entities, such as space, time, and, in theistic atomism, God, are regarded as nonspecific underlying conditions of causality.

In the physical speculations of the atomists, heat atoms or fire atoms, which move rectilinearly at the highest possible speed, play a key part in explaining changes. No doubt this was suggested partly by the way in which light emanates from a source, and partly by the way in which, in cooking and other uses, heat is seen to transform substances. Consequently, the sun was held to be ultimately or mediately responsible for all terrestrial changes.

In common with most other Indian systems, Logic–atomism held that there is a plurality of eternal selves. Although a self is essentially without attributes, knowledge and various kinds of activity and consciousness can inhere in it when the right combination of conditions is present. Thus, release (*mokṣa*) consists in a qualityless condition, which only metaphorically can be considered blissful (there is an absence of pain); this has led some critics to consider release in Logic–atomism's doctrines as equivalent to annihilation. The all-pervasive character of the self involved some modification of the principle of no causal action-at-a-distance (a modification as regards space, not time; at rebirth the self is conjoined to a new series of properties manifested in a different part of space from those manifested in the previous life).

Logic–atomism is thus a syncretistic system which not only combines logical inquiry with a protoscientific metaphysics but also attempts to synthesize atomism with a common-sense doctrine of categories and a traditional concept of the self and of release. It also incorporates theism; the main exposition in Indian literature of the arguments for the existence of God, the *Kusumāñjali* ("A Bouquet of Flowers") of Udayana (tenth century), is a Nyāya–Vaiśeṣika document.

MATERIALISM

Materialistic doctrines flourished in India from the sixth century onward; and there are numerous references, in the Buddhist scriptures and elsewhere, to the circulation of such ideas in the early period. There are references to naturalism (*svabhāvavada*), to Cārvāka (a school named after its legendary founder), to the unorthodox (*nāstika*), and to antisupranaturalism (*lokāyata*). Unfortunately, scarcely any materialist texts have survived, and knowledge of their doctrines is drawn mainly from the accounts of their opponents. In a period of speculative ferment a number of tendencies seem to have combined in a school that came to be called the Cārvāka. First, because of skepticism and (perhaps) social discontent, many people were seeking to undermine the current religious beliefs with counterarguments. Even within the *Upaniṣads* there is evidence of antireligious feeling. Some arguments were directed against certain rites as unethical; others, against the value of testimony, and therefore of revelation, regarded as "what is heard" (*śruti*). Thus, it was argued that ordinary testimony depends upon perception and therefore is otiose; revelation testifies to what is imperceptible and thus to what is unverifiable. Others argued against the belief in a future life with such questions as "Why do people never return to their dear ones?" Second, protoscientific speculation attempted to explain all phenomena naturalistically in terms of the four elements. This presented a problem about consciousness. The materialists argued by analogy with liquor, which, although the combination of certain nonintoxicating substances, is nevertheless intoxicating; likewise, consciousness supervenes when the material elements are combined in a certain way. Third, philosophical skepticism, although liable to inhibit all forms of speculation, was used as a blanket support for antireligious arguments. Not only did some materialists reject testimony as a source of knowledge, but they rejected inference as well (some of their arguments against induction were ingenious). This was doubtless because of the use which the orthodox made of inferences to establish the soul, the transcendent realm, and God. However, such skepticism was two-edged, because the doctrine that everything is composed of material elements cannot be derived from perception. Some materialists (such as Purandara in the eighth century) allowed inference, but only from what is perceptible to what is also in principle perceptible. Atomism, since it involved the thesis that there are unobservable entities (the atoms), was rejected, as was supernaturalism.

The influence of materialism was at one time considerable, and both orthodox and unorthodox metaphysicians, such as the Buddhists, took great pains to refute Cārvāka arguments. But by the latter part of the medieval period, materialism virtually disappeared; and all the surviving Indian schools claimed to have a religious goal of some kind.

MĪMĀṂSĀ

Mīmāṃsā originated from attempts to provide a consistent exegesis of the Vedic scriptures, with the emphasis upon ritual. The earliest exposition is found in the *Mīmāṃsāsūtras* ("Aphorisms of Exegetic Investigation") ascribed to Jaimini, which took their present form between 200 B.C. and A.D. 200. A number of early commentaries have been lost; that of Śabara (c. fifth century) was further commented on by Kumārila Bhaṭṭa (seventh century) and by Prabhākara, a younger contemporary who differed from Kumārila on a number of points. This divergence gave rise to two subschools of Mīmāṃsā that followed these two teachers. Mīmāṃsā was later much influenced by the Navyanyāya (New Logic) school, a logical phase summed up in the work of Nārāyaṇa (sixteenth century); however, Nārāyaṇa's work remains largely unexplored.

The viewpoint is of interest chiefly because its attempt to interpret Vedic texts as a system of ritual and other injunctions led to certain developments in logic. This interpretation of revelation (*śruti*) involved the concept of ritual as potent in itself, the gods becoming otiose. The autonomy of sacrifice and of revelation itself led Mīmāṃsā to deny what all other orthodox systems, as well as Jainism and Buddhism, held—the doctrine of a "pulsating" cosmos: the Veda, being eternal, cannot be destroyed, as the idea of a period of cosmic dissolution would appear to imply.

The extreme fundamentalism of the school led to arguments between it and other schools about the nature of language. For Mīmāṃsā, the meaning of a word is an intrinsic power it possesses, and the sacred Sanskrit tongue is eternally existent and independent of linguistic conventions. Here there is a direct conflict with Buddhism, which insists on the conventional, and often misleading, character of ordinary language. Admittedly, this eternal sacred language becomes apparent to us only because of its manifestation in human use of language; but it nevertheless continues to exist imperceptibly when not in use.

The conservative character of Mīmāṃsā is shown by its rejection, until a relatively late date, of the ideal of *mokṣa*, or release from rebirth. In line with the early Aryan tradition, which did not incorporate belief in reincarnation, the Mīmāṃsā regarded heaven as the goal—it is the reward for the correct observance of religious duties (as elsewhere, heaven is regarded as, so to say, a compartment of the cosmos: *nirvāṇa* and *mokṣa*, on the other hand, are conceived as involving a state which transcends even heavenly life).

Mīmāṃsā thus represents a curious phenomenon in religious thinking. Although it centers on numinous and sacramental religion and has no interest in contemplation and mysticism (it is in this respect the antithesis of Yoga and Theravāda Buddhism), it loses, by a paradox, all genuine interest in the objects of worship and sacrifice. The divine has become superfluous.

THE VEDĀNTA AND OTHER SCHOOLS

Although Vedānta is traditionally classified as a single *darśana*, or viewpoint, it is divided into a number of radically different schools. The principal ones, Advaita, Viśiṣṭādvaita, and Dvaita, have established the main directions for subsequent developments. Also of some importance is the position known as Bhedābheda (Identity-in-Difference, the doctrine that Brahman is both identical with the world and different from it), whose chief exponent was Bhāskara (c. tenth century).

The Vedānta tradition received formal expression in the *Brahmasūtras* ("Holy Power Aphorisms") of Bādārāyaṇa (sometimes known as Vyāsa, the "Arranger"). The chief medieval Vedāntins wrote commentaries on these *sūtras*. Their main point of departure was a consideration of the relation between *Brahman*, the Holy Power spoken of in the *Upaniṣads* and elsewhere as sustaining and/or informing the cosmos, and the self, or *ātman*. Some Upaniṣadic texts, ones that came to be regarded as central to the thinking of the period, asserted that in some sense *Brahman* and *ātman* are one.

Śaṅkara (788 – c. 820) took this to mean numerical identity. It followed, since they are equivalent, that if there is only one Absolute, likewise there is only one Self, not to be identified with the empirical egos which undergo reincarnation. Further, given that *Brahman* alone is real (*sat*), the world (together with empirical egos), considered as distinct from *Brahman*, is an illusion (*māyā*). Śaṅkara's monism not only claimed to give a correct interpretation of central scriptural texts: its impact at the time, and since, is also to be explained by its simultaneous preservation of what he took to be the chief insight of the Veda and the common-sense attitudes appearing to be in conflict with his illusionist doctrine. This was achieved by his concept of two levels of truth, the "higher" truth expressing the mystical experience of release and identification with *Brahman*, and the "ordinary" level used in both popular religion and common-sense descriptions of the world. From the point of view of the ordinary man who has not attained the higher insight, it is correct to say that tables and trees exist (they can be distinguished from hallucinatory objects). It is also appropriate at this level to look upon *Brahman* as the *Īśvara* (Lord), or Creator of the cosmos. Moreover, the two-level doctrine enabled Śaṅkara to give a plausible exegesis of those Vedic passages which appear to refer to a personal God distinct from the world and the self.

Śaṅkara's work was carried on by Maṇḍana Miśra, Sureśvara, Vācaspati Miśra (ninth century), and others. In the twelfth century, Śrīharṣa used dialectical methods to defend Advaita, in the style of the Buddhist Mādhyamika school. In a sense, this was a return to origins, since Mādhyamika ideas, including the two-level doctrine of truth, had influenced Śaṅkara (a reason for his being styled a crypto-Buddhist by his opponents). Another trend among Nondualists was the subjectivist interpretation of the concept of *māyā*. This so-called *dṛṣṭisṛṣṭivāda* ("Subjective Creationism") was expounded by Prakāśānanda (sixteenth century), among others, and involved the thesis that the empirical world consists of perceptions—it is a coincidence that the perceptions of different individuals tend to agree. Although Śankara himself was not strictly a subjective idealist of this kind, there were already elements of such a view in the works of Maṇḍana Miśra.

Rāmānuja (twelfth century) reacted against both Śankara's monism and his two-level doctrine of truth. His reasons for doing so were primarily religious: as an exponent of the supreme importance of *bhakti,* the loving adoration of a personal God, Rāmānuja was highly disinclined to make nonsense of this relationship by agreeing that the soul, or self, and God are identical. He owed something to Bhedābheda (Identity-in-Difference school) but was able to give a more coherent account of how *Brahman* and the cosmos (and selves) are intimately related and yet distinct by using the analogy of the self–body relationship. The chief later Qualified Nondualist was Veṅkatanātha (fourteenth century). Although there were divisions among the followers of Rāmānuja, these were mainly of a strictly theological character: the Vaḍagalai school held that *mokṣa* is achieved by grace alone; the Tengalai, that the individual's active cooperation with grace is a necessary condition (not just a sign) of salvation.

Madhva (thirteenth century) brought about a break with the earlier Vedāntins' attempt to endorse or qualify the identity between *Brahman* and the world and selves. Madhva argued for a strict distinction between them and against the whole concept that perception, for instance, could be a valid source of knowledge at one level of truth and not at another. Madhva's chief successor was Jayatīrtha (thirteenth century), among whose writings those on logic were notable.

Although not Vedāntin, certain Śaivite schools, notably the *Śaivasiddhānta* ("Śaivite Doctrine"), which had its origins in south India, held a general position close to that of Dualism and reflected a similar desire to hold a metaphysics which expressed the presuppositions of devotional religion. The chief writer in this school was Meykaṇḍa (thirteenth century).

Modern developments in Vedānta are described at the end of the article.

JAINISM

For the principal religious doctrines of the school, see JAINISM. Grafted onto them are the philosophical theories of relative pluralism (*anekāntavāda*) and modified skepticism (*syādvāda*). According to *anekāntavāda*, an object can be viewed from a number of perspectives (*naya*); this is in line with the Jain doctrine that perception gives only a partial view of what is perceived. Seven perspectives are categorized. First, we can see an object without distinguishing its specific and generic properties. Second, we can look at it simply as exhibiting its generic properties (we see the flower as an instance of being a flower or of being colored, for example). Third, we can note its individual properties (such as the particular shape of a petal). Fourth, we can advert to its contemporary character, without reference to its future or past history. Fifth, we can contemplate the object in relation to the word or words describing it; thus, one sees how the word or words correctly refer to the object. Sixth, one may note the nuances of the different words. Finally, one considers the correspondence between the meanings and the aspects of the object they describe. This formal list of perspectives indicates that Jainism holds a correspondence theory of truth; hence the preoccupation with the relation between language and objects.

Another sevenfold list is found in the *syādvāda*. About a given object, we may assert (1) "Maybe it is"; (2) "Maybe it is not"; (3) "Maybe it both is and is not"; (4) "Maybe it is inexpressible"; (5) "Maybe it both is and is inexpressible"; (6) "Maybe it is not and is inexpressible"; and (7) "Maybe it both is and is not, and is inexpressible." The *maybe's* here are intended to show that dogmatic assertions are out of place, since a statement is true only of an aspect of what is described and true only in a certain context. The verb "to be" can be used, it should be noted, in both a copulative and an existential sense. The scheme thus can be exemplified as follows. Statement (1) "Maybe this orchid is (exists)" applies; but the object is here treated as an *instance* of an orchid and thereby implicitly as a noninstance of something else. Thus, it implies (2)—"In respect of being a dandelion, it is not." Third, we can combine (1) and (2). The fourth statement is more obscure, but it rests chiefly on the following consideration. On the Jain theory of language, there is a one–one relation between a word and the sort of entity it describes (if a word has more than one meaning, it is counted as more than one word). Thus, there can be no single expression which will cover the respect in which a thing is both an orchid and not a dandelion. Finally, statements (5), (6), and (7) come from combinations of previous judgments.

There are connections between the Jain scheme and the fourfold negation used by the Buddha, as well as between the Jain scheme and early Indian skepticism, which also used multiple negation. However, although it is interesting to see how contextualism and the recognition of the inexpressible were incorporated into Jain doctrine, the metaphysical formulations of Jainism were not directly affected. However, the *syādvāda* was one reason for the considerable interest taken in logic by Jain writers from the ninth century to the twelfth century.

BUDDHISM

The line between religious and philosophical doctrines is even harder to draw in Buddhism than elsewhere in the Indian tradition. This is true partly because the Buddha himself seems to have showed great philosophical acumen in his teachings. For instance, certain questions were ruled by him to be "undetermined." Thus, the question of whether one who has attained *nirvana* in this life (and hence will not be reborn again) persists after death could not be answered by saying "He does," "He does not," "He both does and does not," or "He neither does nor does not." This fourfold negation was used by the Buddha to indicate that the question is wrongly put: he compared it to the question "Where does a flame go (north, or some other direction?) when it goes out?"—which is likewise meaningless or unanswerable. Similar undetermined questions were whether the self is or is not identical with the body, and whether the cosmos is or is not infinite as to space and time.

Fundamental to Buddhist teaching were the nonself doctrine (*anattā*) and that of impermanence (*anicca*). According to *anattā*, the individual is constituted of a complex series of states, both physical and conscious; given this analysis, one can give up the concept of a permanent underlying self, or *ātman*. The Buddhist belief in rebirth requires the series of states to stretch over a virtually infinite time, to be terminated only by the attainment of *nirvana*. According to the doctrine of impermanence, things or substances are likewise analyzed into series of impermanent states. The notions of a permanent self and of permanent substances are illusions fostered by language (Buddhism has always strongly insisted on the conventionality and artificiality of language).

Anattā and *anicca* generated interesting philosophical difficulties which account for some of the developments of Buddhist metaphysics. Thus, the nonself doctrine raised questions about personal identity and about agenthood (to whom should good and evil acts be ascribed if the individual is a congeries of impersonal states?). The personalists (Pudgalavādins), who may have arisen before the second century B.C. as an offshoot of the Theravāda school, postulated a *pudgala*, or person, lying behind the various groups of states that make up the empirical individual. The concept was strongly resisted by other schools as marking a virtual return to the theory of the self which the Buddha had denied. Eventually, after a period of great influence up to the seventh century, the personalists disappeared from the Buddhist scene. Only a handful of texts survive, and for the most part the personalists' position has to be gleaned from the recorded criticisms of their rivals.

The doctrine of impermanence generated problems about causation and related issues. If a substance is a series of short-lived states, it is not unnatural for the conclusion to be drawn that each state is strictly momentary. It was then asked: How, if this is true, could event E_1 bring about E_2, since by the time E_2 is coming into existence, E_1 has already disappeared? Such problems suggested to Nagarjuna, the founder of the Mādhyamika school (second century), that all theories of causation could be shown to be contradictory. More generally, he argued that by applying dialectical methods to all doctrines, in the style of the Buddha's own fourfold negation, all judgments about reality are proved contradictory. The only proper thing to say is that everything is "empty" or "void" (*śūnya*). But the *śūnya* itself was spoken of, in the Mādhyamika school, as though it were a kind of shadowy substance: as it were, the inner nature of everything is The Void, which thus functions as a kind of Absolute, which mysteriously phenomenalizes itself as the Buddha and which is identified with *nirvana*. Thus, Nāgārjuna's dialectic turned out to be other than a form of nihilism.

Parallel to the development of the Mādhyamika school was that of the Vijñānavādin (Idealist), or Yogācāra (Yoga

Practitioner), school, whose first great systematizers were Maitreyanātha (270–c. 350), Asanga, and Vasubandhu (fourth century). An earlier school, the Sautrāntika, had argued that perceptions are reflections or copies of external objects, which can only be known to exist by inference. The idealists argued that since there could thus be no experiential evidence for external objects, they could be dispensed with. This phenomenalistic interpretation of external objects was further developed into the theory of a "store consciousness" (*ālayavijñāna*) which gives rise to perceptual and other experiences in individuals. Mādhyamika and Vijñānavādin absolutism tended to coalesce during the medieval period.

While the metaphysics of the Mahāyāna school developed in the direction of belief in an Absolute (a doctrine coordinated to the religious doctrine of the "Three Bodies" of the Buddha—see BUDDHISM, section on evolution of the Mahāyāna), the conservative Theravāda remained pluralistic and *nirvana* was not identified with any kind of transcendent quasi substance. The most outstanding systematizer of Theravādin teachings was Buddhaghosa (fifth century), an Indian Brahmin converted to Buddhism, whose monastic life was spent in Ceylon. His commentaries, and above all his *Visuddhimagga* ("The Path of Purity"), remain classical expositions of the Theravāda and of the Pāli tradition.

ANALYSIS OF THE MAIN VIEWPOINTS

Although the arguments used by the various schools are of independent interest and often of great subtlety, the main form of the different systems reflect (with one or two exceptions) religious concerns. One can see this in relation to the main polarity in religious life and sentiment during the classical and medieval periods (a polarity which, however, had roots going back to a much earlier time): that between *bhakti*, or devotionalism, and *yoga*, or contemplative mysticism. In the medieval period, this polarity needs qualification, in that yogic techniques were sometimes used to gain an inner illumination which was itself interpreted in devotional terms as gaining knowledge of a personal Lord (*Īśvara*). It is thus useful to introduce a third category, that of devotional meditation. The relative emphasis on the three forms of religious life in the various systems, in relation to certain key concepts in them, can be shown (admittedly crudely) in the following observations.

(1) An element of pure devotionalism (neglecting for the moment devotional meditation) implies some doctrine of a personal Lord, although not necessarily of a Creator. This observation is true of Dvaita, Śaiva Siddhānta, Viśiṣṭādvaita, Buddhist Mahāyāna absolutism (the Buddha, who was given the title Tathāgata, or "Thus-gone," as an object of devotion), and of Advaita (devotionalism being legitimate at the lower level of truth).

(2) Where devotionalism is given some significance but is outweighed in importance by meditative techniques (yoga in the wide sense), there is a doctrine of the Absolute (*Brahman, tathatā*, and so on). This is true of Advaita and of Buddhist absolutism.

(3) Exclusive concentration on meditative and related methods of release is correlated with nontheistic monad-

ism or (in Theravāda Buddhism) with doctrines which emerge from, but transcend, an archaic background of monadism, as in Sāṃkhya, early Yoga, and Jainism.

(4) Where devotionalism outweighs meditation, or is coordinated to devotional meditation, there is the doctrine of a personal Lord as Supreme Being (not as a "lower" manifestation of *Brahman* or as a phenomenalization of the Absolute, as with the Tathāgata) and as Creator, as in Visiṣṭādvaita, Dvaita, and Śaiva Siddhānta.

(5) The doctrine of a personal Lord and Creator is coordinated to that of a plurality of selves in Visiṣṭādvaita, Dvaita, and Śaiva Siddhānta.

Certain comments on these observations are important. Regarding (3), the typical form of Indian mysticism is not—as is often held—monistic (involving the mystic's identification with the one Reality) but monadistic. Monism, whether in the *Upaniṣads*, Buddhist absolutism, or Advaita, is the consequence of the synthesis of yogic religion with that of worship and the numinous. However, it is a synthesis in which the supreme object of worship takes second place and is ultimately transcended. This secondary place is brought about doctrinally by an illusionistic or idealistic theory of the empirical world and of God as related to it in his creative and other activity. Regarding (4), it may be noted that both the *Gītā* and Rāmānuja indicate that the impersonal *Brahman*, that with which the monistic contemplative aims at identification, is an aspect of the supreme personal Lord; this is the reverse of Śankara's absolutism and reflects a difference in priority between *bhakti* and contemplative experience. As to (5), the reason for the coordination of the personal Lord and a plurality of selves is that the religion of worship implies that the worshiper is distinct from the object of worship (hence theistic objections to monistic descriptions of mystical experience) and likewise from the rest of the world; this goes naturally with a realist metaphysics. Realism and soul–God dualism together imply the doctrine of a plurality of selves. This is brought out clearly in the doctrines of Madhva and Rāmānuja and in Śaiva Siddhānta.

This schematic account does not work too well for Nyāya–Vaiśeṣika, later Yoga, and Mīmāṃsā. The former two tacked theistic belief in a Lord onto originally atheistic systems. This was due partly, in the one case, to the coalescence of Nyāya and Vaiśeṣika. In Yoga, under the influence of medieval theism, the practice of devotional meditation upon the Lord was adopted by practitioners as a useful means toward attaining release. But the two cases contrast in spirit: Vaiśeṣika was essentially protoscientific speculation which developed a formal doctrine of God; Yoga was essentially mystical in character. Mīmāṃsā represents a ritualism which became detached from the proper objects of worship and sacrifice (the gods or God).

These considerations help to indicate briefly the determinants of the main doctrinal schemes in the classical and medieval periods.

ARGUMENTS ABOUT THE EXISTENCE OF GOD

Since different schools disagreed about whether a Creator or Lord (*Īśvara*) exists, there was considerable debate on this topic. Some arguments concern the validity of revelation, but others are more analogous to the Western discussions centering on the possibility of a natural theology. Some of the "proofs" of God's existence are dependent on doctrines peculiar to individual schools, some on concepts peculiar to the Indian tradition, and some are more general. The principal arguments and counterarguments in these three categories follow.

Doctrines peculiar to individual schools. It has been noted that the Nyāya–Vaiśeṣika explained macroscopic objects as being combinations of infinitesimally small atoms and had to introduce the concept of quantum jumps to explain how the infinitesimal atoms combine into objects of gross magnitude. What, however, causes the changes from the infinitesimal to the minute and from the minute to the gross? The only factor present, apart from the atoms themselves, is their number. But number, apart from unity, was held to be due to the activity of the mind in holding a plurality of objects together. It is thus mind-dependent. But finite minds could not exist at the earliest point in the re-creation of the cosmos after a period of dissolution (chaos), because they presuppose psychophysical organisms which themselves involve the combination of atoms. It follows, therefore, that at that point an extra-cosmic, bodiless Mind is required—and this is God. It was counterargued that the introduction of number as the cause of the quantum jump is a sign of the theoretical inadequacy of the explanation; and general arguments adduced against Nyāya–Vaiśeṣika atomism made the deduction doubtful in any case.

Concepts peculiar to Indian tradition. The characteristic Indian notion of *karma*, the notion that an individual's status is determined by his deeds in previous lives, was used as the basis for theistic arguments. The Śaiva Siddhānta advanced two connected considerations. First, the doctrine implies an apportionment of good and evil in accordance with a person's deeds. But this presupposes a perfect knowledge of the moral law, and thus only the Lord can justly distribute karma. Second, karma is nonintelligent and cannot operate on its own. Nor can selves which are disembodied appropriate karma to themselves; for activity depends upon the psychophysical organism, which would not exist during the period of chaos. Thus, the Lord is required as a regulator of karma. A similar argument is used in theistic Yoga, in rejecting the adequacy of the teleology supposedly implicit in nature according to the Sāṃkhya school. But the concept of a self-regulative karma was too deeply entrenched in the Indian tradition for such arguments to prove persuasive; and attempts to make karma depend on God were criticized as morally unsatisfactory, especially by the Jains and Buddhists, in accordance with their belief that liberation depends upon one's own efforts (although this belief was modified in some Mahāyāna schools).

Arguments based on more general principles. The chief argument of a general nature is analogous to the (Western) Teleological Argument. It is stated in the Nyāya author Udayana's *Kusumāñjali* ("Handful of Flowers," tenth century) and elsewhere and was given a comprehensive critique by Rāmānuja, who held that knowledge about God comes solely through revelation (this was in line with his powerful emphasis on the grace of God). The argument is this: the cosmos has the nature of an artifact because it is made up of parts, as are artifacts, and thus requires an intelligent author. Secondarily, it was argued that the cosmos is similar to a complex organic body whose functioning depends upon an intelligent principle.

Rāmānuja had eight chief objections to this argument. First, experience shows that pots and other vessels, for instance, are made by intelligent beings. But since the material causes of the earth are unknown, and since we have not observed the production of the earth, we cannot legitimately infer to an intelligent agent. Second, even if the inference were legitimate, there is no reason to believe that the cosmos has been produced by a *single* agent. It might have been brought into being by a number of finite selves working together. If it is objected that finite selves would be ignorant of the material causes needed for the production of the cosmos, it can be replied that craftsmen do quite well without full insight into the nature of the materials they use. Third, it is unwarranted to infer that the cosmos came into being all at once, for we have no evidence for this. But if we assume that it came into being in successive stages, we arrive at the wrong conclusion; experience shows that effects produced at different times are caused by different agents. Thus, we ought to infer creation by many finite selves rather than by a single Lord. Fourth, we have no experience upon which to base an inference to an omnipotent, omniscient Being; we have experience only of inferring a finite agent from certain kinds of things—artifacts. We could therefore infer only a finite self, which conflicts with the definition of God. Fifth, agents operate through bodies; but if we ascribe a body to the Lord, we are conceding that something made of parts can be eternal. In that case, why should not the cosmos be so regarded? If, however, we say that God is bodiless, we destroy the basis of the inference, since we have experience only of embodied agents. Sixth, the stronger the proof, the greater the supposed similarity between finite selves and the Lord. But the latter has all excellences, and it is repugnant to religious sentiment to think that the Lord can be closely compared to imperfect beings within the cosmos. Seventh, the existence and functioning of an organic body requires only a specially intimate relation between its parts; it does not require an intelligent principle to keep it in being. Eighth, there is no strong analogy between the cosmos and organisms; for example, mountains do not breathe.

On the other hand, in contrast with the fifth objection of Rāmānuja, a general argument from movement was used; namely, that the paradigm of movement is volitional, as, for instance, when I move my foot. Thus, atoms, being material entities, are in themselves inert; and their combination must be explained by reference to an intelligent being or beings. But since finite beings need bodies, which are themselves combinations of atoms, a Lord must be postulated whose volitions are realized bodilessly (save insofar as the cosmos can be regarded as his body). Nevertheless, atomism of the classical period seems not to have had difficulty in using such concepts as heaviness to explain the falling of bodies. Thus, there was no difficulty in ascribing movement to inanimate entities.

A passage in the *Yogabhāṣya* ("Yoga Commentary," i. 24)

is sometimes seen as an anticipation of the Ontological Argument. It is this: The Lord's pre-eminence is altogether without anything equal to it or excelling it, since whatever might seem to excel it would itself turn out to be that very pre-eminence—and thus that is the Lord wherein we meet the uttermost limit of pre-eminence; further, two equals are impossible, for if they simultaneously need the same thing, one will necessarily be frustrated and thus will not be equal. However, all this differs from the Ontological Argument in a number of ways, chiefly because it is an argument to show that the most perfect being is God and is unique, and because existence as such is not treated as a perfection.

Another Yoga argument is more ambitious. It was argued that there are grades of knowledge and that these grades presuppose an upper limit, omniscience. This must belong to a self, namely to the most perfect being (shown by the former argument to be God). Some objectors (for instance, Mīmāṃsists) found difficulty in the concept. Ordinary perception could not give the Lord knowledge of all events past, present, and future. Hence, some supernatural means of knowledge must be used. But if a self can in principle dispense with the senses, how is it that they appear necessary to finite selves? Again, it was objected that the inference "Omniscience is absent from beings whom we perceive, so it must belong to an unperceived entity, namely God" is no more rational than the inference that the horn of a hare is absent from what we observe, so it must belong to an unobserved entity. This way, all the properties ascribed to chimeras, and peculiar to them, would be realized somewhere.

A few other counterarguments to theistic belief were important in the Indian tradition. Thus, the appeal to contemplative experience or intuition was countered (by the Jains) with the argument that the intuition may arise from the belief in God rather than conversely. The problem of evil weighed heavily on the Buddha and others. Also, it was difficult to understand why an all-perfect Being should have any motive for creating. However, theologians did not necessarily regard the objections as fatal to theism. Rāmānuja appealed to revelation alone, while others considered the proofs unpersuasive by themselves but cogent when taken in conjunction with revelation.

ARGUMENTS ABOUT THE SELF AND CONSCIOUSNESS

The materialists argued that consciousness is an emergent characteristic arising from a certain sort of combination of material elements. (Discussions concerning the truth of the doctrine of rebirth, which stimulated discussions of the self and consciousness, are noted in REINCARNATION.) The materialist thesis was countered with the challenge to show that conscious states do not exist independently of the body with which they are for a time associated. Certainly, some mental states can be described without referring to bodies or to bodily states, and it must therefore remain an open question as to whether such mental states can actually exist independently of a given body. However, this generates inductive difficulties.

Thus, an ingenious Vijñānavādin (Buddhist idealist)

argument ran as follows. The concomitance of mental and physical states can be perceived only by oneself. However, the causal dependence of consciousness on physical states in the early stages of an individual's life cannot be perceived, for the physical states which give rise to consciousness cannot be observed before that consciousness has emerged. Nor can one observe such a dependence in regard to other people, for one cannot observe another person's experiences. Nor can one now, on the basis of observation, tell whether mental states in oneself cease; and a negative observation is impossible on the death of other people. Thus, there can be no normal inductive grounds either for believing or disbelieving in survival and pre-existence.

The Buddhists, of course, although eager to show that not all mental states are totally caused by physical ones (a premise in one of their arguments for rebirth), were strongly critical of the doctrine of an eternal self underlying mental states. Some, such as the Nyāya–Vaiśeṣika school, held that the self could be known to exist by inference. However, as the Advaitins objected, if the inference is supposed to take the form "Here are some experiences; they must belong to some self," one runs into a severe difficulty. I have no assurance that the experiences are *mine,* rather than someone else's. In order to distinguish my experiences from someone else's, I must already recognize them as *mine.* Consequently, Śankara and his followers claimed that the Self is known by an immediate intuition or is "self-luminous." Śankara also argued that doubt certifies a self, for there must be a self in order to doubt. The Qualified Nondualists had further arguments: first, that such locutions as "I know" presuppose a self; second, that in rapt concentration there is no association of experience with the body; and third, that "This is my body" implies that there is something distinct from the body. Unfortunately for the argument, the phrase "my self" also occurs in Sanskrit; but it was countered that it is a conventional and pleonastic phrase, while "my body" introduces two concepts—that of the self and that of the body—and thus cannot be explained away as pleonastic.

The Viśiṣṭadvaitins had not merely to establish that the self exists but also, in opposition to Advaita, that there are *many* eternal selves. They attacked the doctrine of the self-luminous character of the Self as incoherent. If an entity is called self-revealing when it is identified with its mode of manifestation, pains and pleasures should be counted as self-revealing; yet Advaita holds that they have a subject. But then a similar consideration ought to apply to the self-revelation of the Self, namely that we distinguish the subject from the introspective knowledge he experiences; thus the self-revealing self must reveal itself *to* someone. Therefore, if we recognize the existence of even a single Self, we can also recognize a plurality of selves having experience of it.

The principal arguments upon which the Buddhists rested their rejection both of a unitary Self and of monadistic doctrines were as follows. First, introspection reveals nothing other than various mental states. Second, an eternal self could have no causal work to do: it would be without explanatory value. They argued that an impermanent or momentary event could have only an impermanent or momentary effect; and conversely, an eternal cause could have only an eternal effect. Suppose that an eternal cause has an impermanent effect; then there must be conditions for the coming-into-being and going-out-of-existence of the effect. But *ex hypothesi* the cause has not changed, so some extra factor or factors must occur. In this case, however, the extra condition suffices to explain the effect; and the notion of an eternal cause is otiose. Hence, an eternal self could have causal efficacy only if we suppose that its effect is eternal. But mental states and human acts are observably noneternal. Thus, the concept of the self is useless. A like consideration was used against classical Indian atomism, since it involved the doctrine that the atoms are everlasting.

Notions of the self varied somewhat between the different schools. Thus, for Śankara it is essentially pure consciousness; while for the atomists it acquires consciousness only when in conjunction with a psychophysical organism. Again, three views on its extension were held. Jainism, archaically, holds that the life monad expands and contracts according to the size of body it occupies. Rāmānuja considered that it is atomic, while the more common view was that it is all-pervasive. These last two doctrines flow from the presupposition that finite (but not infinitesimally small) entities are liable to change and destruction. The all-pervasive view, moreover, accounted both for the naive grounds for the Jain body-filling view and for the fact that introspection reveals nonlocalized mental events. In addition, it seemed to be implied by the action-at-a-distance presupposed by the doctrine of karma.

It may finally be noted that the soul was normally distinguished from the psychophysical organism, including the *sensus communis* (*manas*), the intellect (*buddhi*), and the sense faculties. Normally, these were regarded as subtle forms of matter which become, as it were, illuminated when conjoined to the self.

EPISTEMOLOGICAL QUESTIONS

Two main areas of discussion about epistemology existed in the classical and medieval periods. First, the schools differed over the number of *pramānas,* sources or bases of knowledge. Perception and inference, for instance, were generally accepted as necessary; and testimony (*śabda*) was accepted by the orthodox (Hindu) schools, mainly because it centrally included the testimony of revelation. Memory was not normally accounted a source of knowledge because "knowledge" was interpreted to mean new knowledge, that is, new to an individual observer. This also accounts for the importance of testimony (in the nonrevelational sense) in Indian discussions. Second, discussions of perception and illusion were highly relevant to certain metaphysical issues, such as the Buddhist idealist denial of an external world.

Inference usually, but not exclusively, meant inductive inference; and there was considerable discussion of its nature and validity. The materialists used various arguments against its validity. First, induction aims at establishing an invariable concomitance between two types of events. However, these events can be known only by perception; and we cannot perceive all past, present, and future members of a given class. Thus, induction is always open to falsification. Second, it is not enough to establish that *A*'s are always followed by *B*'s. One must also show that non-*B*'s are concomitant with non-*A*'s. But the job of examining all things in the universe other than *A*'s is even more formidable than that of examining the positive instances.

Such problems were tackled in a number of ways. The Nyāya–Vaiśeṣika made use of their category of universals. Given a sufficient sampling by the method of agreement and difference, one could validly establish the concomitance of a pair of universals. The Advaitins argued that nonfalsification is the criterion of validity, and thus the concomitance of two classes of events could be affirmed on the basis of a single instance. This doctrine allowed the Advaitins to give a neat account of the two levels of truth, the common-sense and the higher. Within the common-sense world there can be falsification through the negative instance or through discovery that a perception is illusory. On the other hand, the *whole* world picture formed by common sense could be seen to be falsified (that is, to be a grand illusion) in the higher nondual experience of release.

The notion of levels of truth was repugnant to realist metaphysicians, including Madhva and the Qualified Nondualists. Madhva employed two main arguments against it. First, a *pramāṇa* means something which gives us knowledge of things as they are. This being so, it is absurd to speak of a source of knowledge which is ultimately falsified—yet this is how Advaitins treated perception. Second, although doubt can be thrown on individual perceptions, some are certainly veridical. However, the method of agreement and difference and the criterion of nonfalsification both leave room for skeptical doubt; and Madhva held that there must be a final arbiter, namely the "inner witness" (*sākṣi*), which passes conclusive judgment on what is presented by perception. That such a witness exists is borne out by the following considerations. First, the self is aware of pains and pleasures, and there is no room for doubt about such experiences. Second, the apperception of space presupposes some intuitive faculty. Third, methods of induction generate an infinite regress unless a final arbiter is postulated, since the results of experiment and observation require testing by the same methods, and so on. Another solution to the skepticism concerning perception was to employ a behavioristic criterion of doubt: those who doubt on philosophical grounds whether water extinguishes fire nevertheless extinguish fire with water. Again, the Nyāya–Vaiśeṣika school considered that although in theory smoke might always be caused by an invisible demon rather than by fire, there comes a point in inductive testing when doubt becomes merely frivolous.

The Buddhist idealists (Vijñānavādins) used various arguments to show that perception does not yield knowledge of external objects distinct from the percipient. First, the experience of a datum and the datum itself occur simultaneously, but two supposedly different events occurring simultaneously cannot be distinguished and should be treated as identical. Second, the external world supposedly consists of a number of different objects, but they can be known as different only because there are different sorts of experiences "of" them. Yet if the experiences are thus distinguishable, there is no need to hold the superfluous hypothesis of external objects. Third, sense organs are supposedly intermediaries between external objects and consciousness. However, we have sensory experience during dreams, when the sense organs are not functioning; thus, it is feasible to explain the existence of sensations as due to the inner workings of consciousness. The Absolute evolves itself in a way which makes individuals *think* that there is an external world. The saint in the mystical nondual state realizes pure consciousness and sees the misleading character of ordinary experience.

Arguments about testimony as a source of knowledge turned partly on the question of the validity of sacred testimony, or revelation (*śruti*). Śankara considered that in essence revelation is the experience of nonduality, although he also classified this experience as a kind of perception. However, he wished to show that the identity texts in the *Upaniṣads*, such as *tat tvam asi* (That thou art), conveying the essential import of the scriptures, could arouse knowledge without observation. Thus, it was useful to cite cases where ordinary testimony can bring such knowledge—for example, where a number of people are sitting in a group and one is told by an outsider, "You are the tenth person" (a complicated example since, among other things, it involves a person's self-awareness). At all events, the recognition of testimony helped to give a communal character to the concept of knowledge, which was otherwise treated in an individualistic manner.

Related to testimony was the *pramāṇa* of analogy (*upamāna*), accepted by the Mīmāmsa, Advaita, and Nyāya. The stock example is of a person who is going into the forest and is told that a wild ox is rather like a cow. On seeing a wild ox, he correctly identifies it—but not just on the basis of testimony, for he has to perceive the analogy.

Certain other *pramāṇas* were recognized by some schools and subschools. Thus Mīmāmsā held that *arthāpatti* ought to be included. This is "implication," a special type of inference. The stock example was "Devadatta is living, but he is perceived not to be in the house; therefore he exists somewhere outside the house." The reason for differentiating this from inference proper is that to cast it into a normal inferential form would involve the noninductive and tautologous premise "All existent entities which are not in a given place are in some other place." However, Madhva and others subsumed *arthāpatti* under inference proper.

The perception of the absence of something proved to be a problem for the Indian schools. Thus Advaita counted *anupalabdhi* (negative perception) as a basis of knowledge. It was argued that the method of agreement and difference presupposed the capacity to know when one is *not* perceiving *A*, but the absence thereof. On the other hand, the Nyāya–Vaiśeṣika school argued that the absence or nonexistence was of the objectively perceivable and could not be accounted a *pramāṇa*, which is a source of knowledge *about* the objective world. Therefore, they introduced nonbeing (*abhāva*) as an extra category in their list (discussed above), which later was responsible for a number of logical problems. The Buddhist schools, on the other hand, with their emphasis on the conventionality of language, considered that the perception of absence could be analyzed as a situation involving the perception of a state of affairs which is described negatively.

The basic sources of knowledge, then, were perception and inference, plus testimony (although this was rejected by the unorthodox when testimony meant revelation). The other *pramāṇas* were introduced to deal with special difficulties in the main classification.

CAUSATION

While Sāṃkhya affirmed the identity theory of causation (*satkāryavāda*)—that the effect pre-exists in the cause—both the Buddhists and the Nyāya–Vaiśeṣika held the nonidentity theory (*asatkāryavāda*). The reasons for the former view were not merely that nature (*prakṛti*) was conceived as a unitary principle underlying observable phenomena, which are transformations of this substance, but also that the notion of the emergence of something out of nothing was regarded as unacceptable. The converse "Nothing out of something" was likewise, to Sāṃkhya, unacceptable; and thus effects must pre-exist in causes and causes post-exist in effects. The Nyāya–Vaiśeṣika criticized this view as abolishing the distinction between material, efficient, and other causes; but the problem about causation centers on the establishment of immediate concomitances between properties, substances, and so on. The Buddhists took this last principle to its strict conclusion. Although both the atomist and Buddhist doctrines are classified under the head of the nonidentity theory, considerable differences existed between them. To the atomists, cause is a conjunction of properties inhering in persistent substances. To the Buddhists, it is a conjunction of short-lived or momentary events. (In any event, Buddhism rejected the concept of substance, in line with the doctrine of impermanence.) Certain problems occasioned by this analysis opened the way for the Mādhyamika critique of the concept of causation (see NĀGĀRJUNA). Since Buddhism in any case rejected the identity theory, Nāgārjuna was able to argue that both theories, plus intermediate or mixed positions, are incoherent and that thus the concept of causation itself is contradictory.

The principal Buddhist objection to the atomist account was that the underlying substances (atoms) could, like the eternal Self, play no causal role because an eternal entity could have only an eternal effect. Atoms, as conceived by the Vaiśeṣika, are therefore superfluous. This line of argumentation was one support for the doctrine of momentary atomic events. The condition of a simple entity's going out of existence cannot be the occurrence of some other entity because then a simple entity could, in principle, be everlasting. Thus, the condition of its destruction must be its coming-into-existence; and therefore simple entities disappear immediately after their arising.

The difficulties of the Vaiśeṣika atomism were resolved in an interesting way in the Sautrāntika school of Buddhism, by holding that atoms are short-lived, the defect in classical atomism being not the notion of atomicity but the doctrine of the permanence of the atoms. At the same time, the Buddhist realists. (*Sārvāstivādins*) attempted to avoid

difficulties about how momentary causes could have effects (for the causes *ex hypothesi* would have disappeared before the effects came into existence) by holding that in some sense past, present, and future states exist simultaneously, although cause and effect are momentarily manifested at different times. The notion of a moment was also stretched to cover a number of instants, during which an entity manifests different phases.

The atomists and others criticized the identity theory on the ground that it implied an imperceptible power or energy relating cause and effect, which is undiscoverable in experience. Thus, Madhva argued that the concept of nature (*prakṛti*) as an underlying something which is transformed into the observable states of the world has no warrant in experience, and that a license to introduce unobservable entities would equally warrant the affirmation of such entities as the hare's horn (a stock example of the absolutely nonexistent, that is, of something which does not merely happen not to exist). Moreover, if the effect pre-exists in the cause, it must be produced earlier; and production means coming-into-existence. If the effect already exists at t_1 (before t_2, the time when it is supposedly produced), then it must already have been produced at t_1. The Sāṃkhya reply, that the effect is *manifested* at t_2 rather than produced then, is countered by Madhva with the answer that the concepts of manifestation and production are quite different. The former means "being presented to perception," while the concept of production does not imply this. One may therefore ask: If the effect exists before its time of manifestation, why was it not perceptible before that time? And if the manifestation of the effect is a change, then the manifestation ought to pre-exist itself, However, it is absurd to speak of an unmanifest manifestation.

The dualists attempted a synthesis between the two main theories by using the concept of energy (*śakti*). The coming-into-existence of an effect is in part the result of the operation of the energy of one substance upon a second, and thus is the actualization of this implicit energy. The effect is also the evolution or transformation of the second substance brought about by the energy of the first, and as such the effect belongs to the entity (the second substance) that is a partial cause of it. Thus, the effect, it was argued, is both identical with the cause (the transformed substance) and nonidentical with it (the transforming energy). On the other hand, selves and the Lord are essentially changeless and thus capable only of *manifesting* themselves. In this connection, a law of causal inertia was enunciated: Something comes into existence when there are sufficient conditions for it to do so, and likewise goes out of existence when there are sufficient conditions for its destruction. Thus, a thing remains in its *status quo* until something of sufficient energy comes along to disturb it. The selves are such that sufficient conditions for their destruction never arise; thus, they are everlasting. This contrasts with the Buddhist argument for momentariness.

Śankara and his followers espoused a theory often classified as causal, although its main point was theological—namely, the appearance theory (*vivarttavāda*). Śankara, however, referred to his own position as being a form of the *satkāryavāda*. The effect is considered as merely an *apparent* effect. This is a way of describing the relation between *Brahman* and the world appearance. Using the Buddhist principle that an eternal cause must have an eternal effect, the Advaitins argued that there is indeed an eternal Being, but that since perceptible phenomena are manifestly noneternal, they cannot be the genuine effects of *Brahman* but only illusory or apparent effects. Yet insofar as *Brahman* underlies appearances, it can be regarded as the material cause of the world. This is in line with Śankara's doctrine that in perception there is an intuition of being, even though the rest is illusion.

The Rāmānujists objected to this use of the concept of pure being. It is as useful to say that being is the material cause of existent objects as it is to say that nonbeing is the material cause of chimeras. *Being* is merely the most general property ascribable to substances, but it presupposes substances in which to inhere. It is therefore nonsense to speak of pure being as a self-existent entity or substance. Further, the description of *Brahman* as pure being and as featureless was criticized on a number of grounds. For instance, the language of revelation consists in determinate words, which implies that different words stand for different aspects of reality. It therefore follows that scripture could not refer to a totally featureless or indescribable entity. That is, *Brahman* must have some distinct characteristic that differentiates it from other aspects of the universe.

These, then, were some of the issues related to causation debated in the medieval schools. Although, naturally, there was a good deal of discussion on topics other than those of God's existence, the self, epistemology, induction, and causation (the mechanism of perception, the status of language, the nature of illusion, for example), the above areas represent the chief aspects of Indian metaphysical debate.

THE PHILOSOPHY OF VALUE

Traditional Indian discussions in the areas of ethics, politics, and aesthetics at the philosophical level have not been as extensive as might be expected. This is partly because philosophy came formally to be seen as ultimately concerned with the problem of release (*mokṣa*). Traditionally values were categorized as falling under four heads—*dharma* (law or virtue), *artha* (wealth), *kāma* (pleasure), and *mokṣa*. Practical inquiries, except the spiritual quest, thus were generally bypassed in most metaphysical systems. The first three of the four ends, known as the *trivarga* (group of three) tended to be treated separately from the aim of release. Hence, there are treatises separately devoted to expositions of *dharma* (religious and ethical laws), of *artha* (especially considered as political, not just economic, power), and *kāma*. The most famous political tract is the *Arthaśāstra*, legendarily ascribed to Kauṭilya (fourth century B.C.), minister of the Emperor Candragupta. Kauṭilya argues for the advantages of a monarchy over other forms of government and identifies the welfare of the people with that of the monarch. He gives a detailed account of methods of effective government and of political defense and aggrandizement. Such writings were, however, more in the nature of hand-

books of traditional and advantageous practices than metaphysical, critical, or analytic works. But there was some discussion of the relation of the parts of the triad of ends to each other, and between them and *mokṣa*. While power and pleasure are pursued by both animals and men, the pursuit of *dharma* (virtue) is confined to men. The question was raised as to whether *dharma* is merely instrumental to well-being or is an end-in-itself. Some of the Mīmāṃsā school held the latter view for two reasons. First, the view that virtue subserves pleasure implies that man is not distinctive in having the capacity to pursue or reject what he recognizes as his duty but is determined by inclination. Second, it makes virtue inferior (because it is instrumental to) pleasure; and this is contrary to the consensus of wise opinion.

On the other hand, Śankara pointed out that this makes psychological nonsense, for then free virtuous choice has no end in view. Moreover, duty becomes quite irksome—performance of it means toil; nonperformance, future suffering. Although materialists regarded duty simply as subserving worldly interests, other schools, apart from the Mīmāṃsā subschool mentioned above, became generally agreed that the performance of duty is, among other things, a mode of self-purification, which is a necessary preliminary to the higher spiritual life leading to release. Likewise, in Buddhism and Jainism morality is integrated into the path leading to release. However, there appeared in Buddhism some tension between compassion as the key disposition informing good works and the pursuit of virtue as a means toward *nirvana*—hence the Mahāyāna concept of the Bodhisattva's (Buddha-to-be) self-sacrifice in postponing his attainment of *nirvana* to serve the welfare of living beings. (For certain discussions relevant to free will, see KARMA.)

Aesthetic theory became quite highly developed in the medieval period. Earlier, the *Nāṭyaśāstra* of Bharata (c. fifth century), a manual of dance and dramatic art, had introduced the concept of *rasa* (savor), which played a large part in medieval aesthetic analysis. It stands for the feeling or sentiment that pervades a work of art or is aroused in the contemplator. The number of *rasas* varies between eight and ten, according to different writers (the last two of the following list are those in dispute): romantic love, heroism, abhorrence, anger, merriment, terror, compassion, wonder, holy peace, and fatherly affection. Their nature was disputed. Some (such as Bhaṭṭa Lollita, ninth century) held that they reside in the persons represented in drama, for example, or in the objects of the works of art, and secondarily in the performers or artists; but for Sankuka (ninth century) the *rasa* is the intensified emotion experienced by the viewer. According to Bhaṭṭa Nāyaka (tenth century), these views were still, in a sense, too realistic. He held that the *rasa* is a unique form of delight unconnected with a particular ego, whether real or imitated. Aesthetic enjoyment is not related to the aims and concerns of one's daily life and is evoked by art objects which express universal moods in an ideal way. This theory was further developed by Abhinavagupta (c. eleventh century). In accordance with these notions, a distinction was made between the "body" and "soul" of aesthetic works. Thus, a work of art could present information, imaginative thoughts, and savor. The first is unimportant, for art is concerned with what is neither true nor false. The imaginative presentation is a means of evoking the *rasa* in the contemplator; and thus "savor" stands out as the "soul" of art. Although all these views suggested that aesthetic works should not be didactic, nevertheless they have a general spiritual significance. Thus, from the point of view of Advaita, to those who are unable to attain the higher insight and detachment, aesthetic contemplation gives a foretaste of release. Through it, people are taken out of their daily concerns; they see the aesthetic object as hovering between existence and nonexistence (like the illusory world of Advaitin metaphysics, which is seen existentially once a person attains release); and they partake of the delight or bliss which characterizes ultimate reality (the Self or *Brahman*). It may be noted that these developments in aesthetics involved a drift toward a subjectivist account of the essence of art, and thus it was held both that the poet has to use indirect means in evoking the *rasa* (this could not, like imaginative thoughts, be directly communicated) and that appreciation by the viewer is itself a form of creativity.

THE MODERN PERIOD

During the modern period, as previously in the Indian tradition, religious concerns have been prominent, although philosophical speculation has been altered somewhat by the impact of Western culture and philosophy. The establishment of British-style universities in the latter part of the nineteenth century resulted in the teaching of Western philosophy at a time when absolute idealism was the dominant trend in British metaphysics. Its obvious affinities with Vedānta—and especially with Advaita—were one factor in the renaissance of Hindu theology and were reinforced by reform movements sparked in part by the impact of Christian missions and propaganda. The earliest such movement was the Brahmo Samāj, founded by Raja Ram Mohan Roy in 1828; but the one with the most influence has been the Ramakrishna Mission, founded by Swami Vivekananda to continue the work and teaching of the Bengali saint Ramakrishna (1834–1886). Preaching a form of Advaita, the mission stresses the unity of religions and the need for practical social work. It manifests a tendency in modern Hinduism to look to Advaita as an ideology, and the chief exponent of a reconstructed Advaita is Sir Sarvepalli Radhakrishnan. Among Muslims, the most powerful restatement of religious ideas was that of Sir Muhammad Iqbal (1873–1938).

While these movements have been obviously religious in their aim, other, more directly philosophical, work has gone on in the context of the English-speaking culture which has come to pervade Indian intellectual life. The most notable Advaitin metaphysician in recent times was K. C. Bhattacharya (1875–1949), a Bengali. Although orthodox, he held that metaphysics should not turn back to the methods of the medieval period, which tended to involve appeal to scriptures and the criticism of rival systems which are not necessarily of great interest today. Rather, metaphysics should start with a phenomenological critique of ordinary experience. He held that this would bring about a realization of the self as pure freedom.

A radical reshaping of Vedantin ideas has been attempted by Aurobindo Ghose (known as Aurobindo); and among philosophers working in relative independence from the Advaitin tradition is N. V. Banerjee (b. 1909), whose new-style metaphysics is partly Neo-Kantian. The radical changes in English-speaking philosophy have not had a great impact in India, but the new *Indian Journal of Philosophy* (founded in 1958) is a sign of growing interest in analytic investigations and in philosophy as an international pursuit.

In the twentieth century, some distinguished work has been done in the history of Indian philosophy. The outstanding figure has been Surendranath Dasgupta (1885–1952), whose remarkable and monumental *A History of Indian Philosophy* in five volumes has laid a solid foundation in the subject. Among a mass of recent historical works and expositions, the most outstanding are T. R. V. Murti, *The Central Philosophy of Buddhism* (1955) and K. N. Jayatilleke, *Early Buddhist Theory of Knowledge* (1963). Throughout the modern period, moreover, there has been a steady flow of texts and books from Western Indologists.

(See also the following articles on religious movements and theories that have influenced Indian thought: BUDDHISM; HINDUISM; JAINISM; KARMA; NIRVANA; REINCARNATION; YOGA; and ZOROASTRIANISM. Indian mysticism is also treated in the article MYSTICISM, HISTORY OF. See Indian Philosophy in Index for articles on Indian thinkers.)

Bibliography

GENERAL WORKS

Surendranath Dasgupta, *A History of Indian Philosophy,* 5 vols. (Cambridge, 1922–1955), is the most distinguished survey and covers nearly all schools (although Vol. V is incomplete because of the author's death). His aim is clear exposition, rather than comparative philosophy or criticism. Sarvepalli Radhakrishnan, *Indian Philosophy,* 2 vols. (London, 1923–1927), is moderately helpful. Mysore Hiriyanna, *Outlines of Indian Philosophy* (4th impression, London, 1958), is an excellent account of orthodox schools; his *Essentials of Indian Philosophy* (2d impression, London, 1951), a simpler version of *Outlines,* makes an excellent introduction. Giuseppe Tucci, *Storia della filosofia indiana* (Bari, 1957), is devoted mainly to describing discussions of various topics covered by traditional metaphysics. H. Zimmer's posthumously published *Philosophies of India,* Joseph Campbell, ed. (New York, 1957), is important and fascinating, although the author is more interested in psychological aspects of Indian religion than in metaphysical and analytic questions. Karl H. Potter, *Presuppositions of India's Philosophies* (New York, 1963), is excellent and original. Ninian Smart, *Doctrine and Argument in Indian Philosophy* (London, 1964), is an attempt at a descriptive and analytic account of the main schools and issues. Quite a useful selection of texts in English that contains a good bibliography of primary sources is Sarvepalli Radhakrishnan and C. A. Moore, eds., *A Source Book in Indian Philosophy* (Princeton, N.J., 1957). E. Frauwallner, *Geschichte der indischen Philosophie,* 2 vols. (Salzburg, Austria, 1953–1956), is a distinguished work.

SĀMKHYA AND YOGA

Primary sources for Sāmkhya and Yoga are *The Sāmkhyakārikā of Īśvarakṛṣṇa, With the Commentary of Gandapādācārya,* edited and translated by H. D. Sharma (Poona, India, 1933), and the bibliography to YOGA. Secondary sources include A. B. Keith, *The Sāmkhya System,* 2d ed. (London, 1924); S. N. Dasgupta, *Yoga Philosophy in Relation to Other Systems of Indian Thought* (Calcutta, 1930); and Mircea Eliade, *Yoga: Immortality and Freedom* (London, 1958).

NYĀYA–VAIŚEṢIKA

A primary source for Nyāya–Vaiśeṣika is Gaṇganātha Jha and D. S. Nyayapadhyaya, eds., *Nyāyadarśana: The Sūtras of Gautama and Bhāṣya of Vātsyāyana With Two Commentaries* (Banaras, India, 1925), translated by Gaṇganātha Jha (Poona, India, 1939). A. B. Keith, *Indian Logic and Atomism* (Oxford, 1921); S. C. Vidyabhusana, *A History of Indian Logic* (Calcutta, 1921); and B. Faddegon, *The Vaiçeṣika System* (Amsterdam, 1918), are secondary sources.

MATERIALISM (CĀRVĀKA)

For further information on materialism, see Dale Riepe, *The Naturalistic Tradition in Indian Thought* (Seattle, Wash., 1961); Giuseppe Tucci, *Linee di una storia del materialismo indiano* (Rome 1924); and Dakshinaranjan Shastri, *A Short History of Indian Materialism, Sensationalism and Hedonism* (Calcutta, 1930).

MĪMĀṂSĀ

Gaṇganātha Jha, *The Pūrva Mīmāṃsā Sūtras of Jaimini* (Allahabad, India, 1916), and *Pūrva Mīmāṃsā in Its Sources* (Banaras, India, 1942), are primary sources. Secondary sources are A. B. Keith, *The Karma Mīmāṃsā* (London, 1921); and N. V. Thadani, *The Mīmāṃsā* (New Delhi, 1952).

VEDĀNTA AND OTHER HINDU SCHOOLS

For discussions of Vedānta and other Hindu schools, see W. S. Urquhart, *The Vedānta and Modern Thought* (Oxford, 1928); Mukhopadhyaya Govindagopal, *Studies in the Upaniṣads* (Calcutta, 1960); J. Estlin Carpenter, *Theism in Medieval India* (London, 1921); Sarvepalli Radhakrishnan, *The Brahma Sūtra* (London, 1960); S. M. Srinivasa Chari, *Advaita and Viśiṣṭadvaita* (London, 1961); P. M. Srinivasachari, *The Philosophy of Bhedābheda*, 2d ed. (Adyar, India, 1950); B. N. K. Sharma, *A History of the Dvaita School of Vedānta and Its Literature*, 2 vols. (Bombay, 1960–1962); V. Paranjoti, *Śaiva Siddhānta* (London, 1954); and Sarvepalli Radhakrishnan and others, *History of Philosophy Eastern and Western* (London, 1952), Vol. I, Ch. 15. For published scriptures, see the bibliography to HINDUISM. For primary philosophical sources, see bibliographies to ŚANKARA, RĀMĀNUJA, and MADHVA.

BUDDHISM AND JAINISM

See bibliographies to BUDDHISM and JAINISM for primary sources. Secondary sources are K. N. Jayatilleke, *Early Buddhist Theory of Knowledge* (London, 1963); Edward Conze, *Buddhist Thought in India* (London, 1961); T. R. V. Murti, *The Central Philosophy of Buddhism* (London, 1958); Bhikshu Sangharakshita, *A Survey of Buddhism*, 2d ed. (Bangalore, India, 1959); Theodor Stcherbatsky, *Buddhist Logic*, 2 vols. (Leningrad, 1932); H. von Glasenapp, *Der Jainismus* (Berlin, 1925); G. Della Casa, *Il giainismo* (Turin, 1962); and Y. J. Padmarajiah, *A Comparative Study of Jaina Theories of Reality and Knowledge* (Bombay, 1956).

MODERN DEVELOPMENTS

J. N. Farquhar, *Modern Religious Movements in India* (New York, 1919); D. S. Sarma, *Studies in the Renaissance of Hinduism in the Nineteenth and Twentieth Centuries* (Banaras, India, 1944); and Sarvepalli Radhakrishnan and J. H. Muirhead, *Contemporary Indian Philosophy*, 2d ed. (London, 1952), are secondary sources. Other works include Beni Prasad, *The Theory of Government in Ancient India* (Allahabad, India, 1927); W. E. Hopkins, *Ethics of India* (New Haven, Conn., 1924); and Mysore Hiriyanna, *Art Experience* (Mysore, India, 1954). See bibliographies to RADHAKRISHNAN, SARVEPALLI and AUROBINDO GHOSE for primary sources.

NINIAN SMART

INDIRECT REALISM. See REALISM.

INDISCERNIBLES, IDENTITY OF. See IDENTITY.

INDIVIDUALISM. See HOLISM AND INDIVIDUALISM IN HISTORY AND SOCIAL SCIENCE.

INDUCTION. The name "induction," derived from the Latin translation of Aristotle's *epagoge*, will be used here to cover all cases of nondemonstrative argument, in which the truth of the premises, while not entailing the truth of the conclusion, purports to be a good reason for belief in it. Such arguments may also be called "ampliative," as C. S. Peirce called them, because the conclusion may presuppose the existence of individuals whose existence is not presupposed by the premises.

Thus, the conclusion "All *A* are *B*" of an induction by simple enumeration may apply to *A*'s not already mentioned in the finite number of premises having the form "A_i is *B*." Similarly, in eduction (or arguments from particulars to particulars) the conclusion "Any *A* is *B*" is intended to apply to any *A* not yet observed as being a *B*.

It would be convenient to have some such term as "adduction" to refer to the sense of induction here adopted, which is broader than the classical conception of induction as generalization from particular instances. Most philosophical issues concerning induction in the classical sense arise in connection with the more general case of nondemonstrative argument.

In what follows it will be convenient to use Jean Nicod's expression "primary inductions" to refer to those nondemonstrative arguments "whose premises do not derive their certainty or probability from any induction." Problems of philosophical justification are most acute in connection with such primary inductions.

It may be added that "mathematical induction" is a misnomer because the useful types of reasoning so labeled are rigorously demonstrative. Given that the first integer has a certain property and also that if any integer *n* has that property then so does $n + 1$, the next, it follows demonstratively that *all* the integers have the property in question. Inductive arguments, as here conceived, do not constitute mathematical or logical proofs; by definition induction is not a species of deduction.

Types of inductive arguments. In addition to the types of arguments already mentioned, the following are most frequently discussed:

(1) Elaborated induction (as it might be called) consists of more or less sophisticated variations of induction by simple enumeration, typically including supplementary information concerning the mode of selection of the individuals named in the premises and perhaps including reference to negative instances.

(2) Proportional induction is inference from the frequency of occurrence of some character in a sample to the frequency of occurrence of the same character in the parent population—that is, from "m_1/n_1 *A*'s selected by a stated procedure *P* are *B*" to "m_2/n_2 *A*'s are *B*." Here the ratio stated in the conclusion may be other than the one stated in the premise; it is often advantageous to locate the final ratio within a certain designated interval.

(3) Proportional eduction is argument from sample to sample. From the same premises as in proportional induction a conclusion is drawn concerning approximate frequency of occurrence in a further sample obtained by the same procedure or by another one.

(4) Proportional deduction (commonly called "statistical syllogism") is inference from "m/n C's are B" (where m/n is greater than 1/2) and "A is a C" to "A is a B."

In all the above cases modern writers usually insist upon inserting some more or less precise indication of probability or likelihood, either within the conclusion itself or as an index of reliability attached to the mark of inference ("therefore," "hence," or the like). Careful attention to the probability or likelihood attributed to a given inductive conclusion is a distinct merit of modern treatments of the subject.

The foregoing list cannot claim to be exhaustive, nor are its items to be regarded as mutually irreducible. There is no general agreement concerning the basic forms of inductive argument, although many writers regard simple enumeration as in some sense the most fundamental.

History of inductive methods. Interest in the philosophy and methodology of induction was excited by the extraordinary successes of natural science, which tended to discredit the rationalistic conception of knowledge about matters of fact. The classical writers on the subject, from Francis Bacon on, have lamented the powerlessness of deduction to do more than render explicit the logical consequences of generalizations derived from some external source. If recourse to intellectual intuition or to self-evidence is repudiated as a source of factual knowledge, nothing better seems to remain than reliance upon the empiricist principle that all knowledge concerning matters of fact ultimately derives from experience. However, experience, whether conceived as sporadic and undirected observation or as the systematic search for specific answers extorted by planned experiment, seems to supply knowledge only of particular truths. Empiricists are therefore faced with the problem of accounting for the crucial step from knowledge of experiential particulars to reasoned acceptance of empirical generalizations sufficiently powerful to serve as the major premises of subsequent logical and mathematical deduction.

The aspiration of early writers was, characteristically, to demonstrate the conclusions of acceptable inductive arguments as true; not until the end of the nineteenth century did a more modest conception of inductive argument and scientific method, directed toward acquiring probability rather than certainty, begin to prevail.

PROBLEM OF INDUCTION

The celebrated problem of induction, which still lacks any generally accepted solution, includes under a single heading a variety of distinct, if related, problems. It is useful to distinguish the following:

(1) The general problem of justification: Why, if at all, is it reasonable to accept the conclusions of certain inductive arguments as true—or at least probably true? Why, if at all, is it reasonable to employ certain rules of inductive inference?

(2) The comparative problem: Why is one inductive conclusion preferable to another as better supported? Why is one rule of inductive inference preferable to another as more reliable or more deserving of rational trust?

(3) The analytical problem: What is it that renders some inductive arguments rationally acceptable? What are the criteria for deciding that one rule of inductive inference is superior to another?

These problems may be briefly labeled "justification," "differential appraisal," and "analysis." Many writers on induction have also occupied themselves with the task of codification, the formulation of a coherent, consistent, and comprehensive set of canons for the proper conduct of inductive inference. Important as it is, this task is not distinctively philosophical, except insofar as it requires in advance answers to the questions listed above.

In practice the three problems here distinguished cannot be pursued separately; a comprehensive general defense of inductive procedures involves specification, *inter alia*, of legitimate forms of inductive argument, and selection between alternative inductive rules or methods must rely, explicitly or not, upon determination of what, if anything, makes an inductive argument "sound." The *why* of inductive argument cannot profitably be isolated from the *how*.

It is characteristic of much recent investigation of the subject to concentrate on the last two of the problems listed, often in the hope of formulating precise canons of inductive inference (an inductive logic). These comparative and analytical versions of the problem of induction are thought worth pursuing even by writers who reject the general problem of justification as insoluble.

Hume's view of causation. For better or worse, all modern discussion of the philosophy of induction takes off from Hume's celebrated analysis of causation, whose connection with the philosophical problems of induction (a word that Hume never used) arises from his view that all reasoning concerning matters of fact is founded on the relation between cause and effect. Although Hume may be held to have given undue prominence to causation (his skeptical conclusions do, in fact, challenge every kind of nondemonstrative argument, whether or not grounded in causal imputation), it is easy to overlook and to be misled by the special form in which he conceived the problem of justification.

Hume, unlike such later writers as J. S. Mill, was not satisfied to analyze the notion of cause and effect into the notions of spatial contiguity, temporal succession, and joint occurrence; he fatefully added to these the criterion of "necessary connexion." That objects of certain kinds have been conjoined or associated in past experience might be no more than an extended coincidence. Something more is needed before one event can properly be recognized as the cause of the other; we must be able to pass from *post hoc* to *propter hoc*. In predicting a putative effect of a given event we can ensure contiguity and succession by choosing to look only for a spatiotemporally proximate event, and memory (if that can be relied on) will furnish knowledge of constant conjunction in the past. Whether we are truly justified in predicting the occurrence of the putative effect will therefore turn entirely upon whether there is good reason to assert that it is necessarily connected with its neighbor. Hume, in effect, challenged his reader to find anything in the observation of a single case of supposed causal action (for instance, in the favorite example of a collision between two billiard balls) that answers to the required "necessary connexion" between two events. No observation, however attentive, will discover more than contiguity and an internal habit of expecting association. Nor will examination of a series of cases, all exactly alike, help at all: a sum of zeroes is still zero.

But what did Hume mean by "necessary connexion"? Although he did not tell us in so many words, his main proof that we can "never demonstrate the necessity of a cause" rests simply upon the conceivability, and hence the logical possibility, of an event's being bereft of its putative cause. He seems, therefore, to have implied that our notion of a cause and its effect requires the existence of the one to be entailed by the existence of the other. If so, it does not need much argument to show that we can have no impression (direct sensory experience) of such entailment. Hume concluded that necessity cannot reside in the external world but must arise, as an idea, from an internal impression of the mind, a "determination to carry our thoughts from one object to another."

Repeated observation of the association of events leads us to the *habit* of expecting the association to continue "by means of an operation of the soul . . . as unavoidable as to feel the passion of love, when we receive the benefits" (*Enquiry Concerning the Human Understanding*, Sec. 5, Part 1). Our idea of necessary connection is nothing more than an internal response to the habit of expecting effects: "Upon the whole, necessity is something in the mind, not in objects." At this point skepticism is just around the corner; we are on the verge of such famous conclusions as that "all probable reasoning is nothing but a species of sensation" (*Treatise*, Book I, Part 3, Sec. 8).

The reference to habit or custom explains nothing, of course, and is at best only a concise reference to the truism, which according to Hume's view simply has to be accepted, that men do in fact expect events to be accompanied by effects. Without such habits of causal expectation men could hardly have survived—but this reflection, itself based on induction, cannot be a reason for belief in causation. For a philosopher so critical of such allegedly occult entities as power and energy, Hume was strangely carefree in his reliance upon habit or custom as a *vera causa*. In keeping with his own principles he ought to have turned as skeptical an eye on habit as on cause and ought to have concluded that our idea of habit is derived from nothing more than a habit of expecting that a man who acts in a certain way will continue to do so. But now the account looks circular. Have we any better reason to believe in the existence of habits—even if construed, in as reductionist a fashion as possible, as mere constant conjunctions—than we have to believe in causes? And would not everything that tended to show we have no sufficient basis in external experience for belief in the objective reality of causal connection also tend to show, by parity of reasoning, that we have no basis for believing in the existence of those habits that are invoked at least to explain, if not to justify, our ordinary causal beliefs?

It has seemed to nearly all of Hume's readers that his method must lead to a skepticism more sweeping than he himself was perhaps willing to recognize or to accept. If Hume had been correct about the origin of the idea of necessity, he would have been committed to a totally skeptical answer to the general problem of justification. Whether or not we can escape from the bondage of causal expectation, we are at any rate free to see that such a habit can provide no reason, in Hume's sense, for the belief in causal connection. And once we see this, wholesale skepticism concerning inductive inference seems inescapable.

Hume's skeptical conclusions cannot be dismissed on the ground that they originated in an oversimplified psychology of ideas and impressions, for his argument can, with little difficulty, be made independent of any psychological assumptions. Cause and effect are logically independent, not because repeated search fails to find any logical connection, as Hume's own account misleadingly suggests, but because it is a part of what we mean by cause and effect that the two shall be logically separable. It is tempting to say, then, that there is no reason why the separable consequent should follow its antecedent in any particular instance. We can very well imagine or conceive the cause's occurring without its usual consequent, and, in Hume's words, "nothing of which we can form a clear and distinct idea is absurd or impossible" (*A Treatise of Human Nature*, Book I, Part 1, Sec. 7).

Neo-Humean arguments. Even if Hume was wrong in including logical necessity in the idea of causal connection, a Neo-Humean can correct his argument without weakening its skeptical force. It is reasonable to say that what distinguishes a causal connection from a merely accidental association is that empirical rather than logical necessity obtains between the two events. This, in turn, may be rephrased by saying that the observed conjunction is a case of lawful and not merely accidental association. But then Hume's challenge to discover such lawfulness in experience remains as formidable as ever; no matter how many instances of joint occurrence we encounter, we will never observe more than the *de facto* association and will never have ultimate, noninductive grounds for believing in a *de jure* connection.

Thus, Hume's problem can be put into modern dress, without restriction to causal inference, as follows: An inductive inference from an observed association of attributes (A_n-B_n) can justify inference to another case $(A_{n+1}-B_{n+1})$ or inference to the corresponding generalization ("All A are B") only if the association is somehow known to be lawlike, not merely accidental. Yet how can this be known in primary inductions that do not themselves rest upon the assumed truth of other laws? Certainly not by immediate experience, nor a priori, nor, without begging the question, by appeal to induction.

The sharpest form of this version of the problem (called by its author the "new riddle of induction") is that of Nelson Goodman. Suppose all emeralds examined before a certain time t have been green; use the label "grue" for the property of being green up to the time t and being blue thereafter. Then all the evidence supports equally well the competing laws "All emeralds are green" and "All emeralds are grue." Here an instance of the comparative problem is raised in a particularly pointed and instructive way.

Goodman's challenge awaits an answer. Some writers have hoped to defend the received or standard modes of inductive argument by invoking criteria of relative simplicity. But apart from the yet unsolved problem of clarifying what simplicity is to mean in this connection, there seems no good reason why nature should obligingly make correct inference simple; often enough the best-confirmed law is less simple than others that would accord with the given evidence. Goodman's own suggestion to restrict defensible inductions to "entrenched" predicates (roughly speaking, those that have been frequently employed in previous inductive judgments) seems less than satisfying.

From the standpoint of the philosophy of induction the chief significance of Hume's memorable discussion (apart from its tonic effect in disturbing "dogmatic slumber") is that it brought into full daylight the problem of distinguishing between a merely accidental series of associations and the genuine laws that we seek by means of inductions.

Deductive standard of justification. A demand that induction be justified arises, of course, from some supposed deficiency or imperfection. If all were obviously well with inductive argument, there would be no point in asking for any defense or justification. It is therefore of the first importance to be clear about the alleged weakness or precariousness of induction and the corresponding standard of justification to which appeal is covertly made. We need to know what is supposed to be the trouble with induction, for only when the disease is understood will the search for a remedy have much prospect of success.

The root of the trouble is plain enough in the writings of a hundred writers who have trodden in Hume's footsteps. All have been haunted by the supposedly superior certainty of demonstrative reasoning. If valid deduction from premises known to be true transmits certainty to the conclusion, even the best induction will seem inferior by comparison. (Locke said that induction from experience "may provide us convenience, not science"—*Essay Concerning Human Understanding*, Book IV, Ch. 12, Sec. 10.) The nagging conviction that induction somehow falls short of the ideals of rationality perfectly exemplified in valid deductive argument has made the problem of induction needlessly intractable.

If Hume, for instance, did not require that induction be shown as somehow satisfying the criteria of valid deduction, an answer to his question about how "children and peasants" learn from experience would be easy. The method employed, as he himself stated, is that of arguing from similarity of causes to similarity of effects. However, such an answer would obviously not have satisfied him, because this method will not guarantee the truth of the conclusion drawn; that is, it is not the kind of method that would be acceptable as justifying a valid deduction. Hume would have liked an inductive conclusion to follow from (be entailed by) premises known to be true, for anything less would not have seemed genuinely reasonable. Having shown, in effect, that no reason of this kind can be produced for primary inductions, he was forced to regard the question of justification as demonstrably insoluble. This conclusion has the notable inconvenience of leaving the comparative problem also insoluble (while the analytical task vanishes for lack of an object).

Hume's conclusion must be granted if his is the only sense of "reason" in point. If we never have a reason for an inductive conclusion unless we know the conclusion to follow strictly from premises known to be true, then we can have no reason for believing in primary inductive conclusions; it is as reasonable to expect that thistles will bear figs, or something equally absurd, as it is to expect anything else extending beyond past experience. (Whether we can in fact bring ourselves to believe anything so absurd is beside the point.) Only in recent times have serious efforts been made to escape from the spell of the deductive model, used by Hume and his innumerable followers, by inquiring whether there may not be other proper and relevant senses of "reasonable." It will be argued later that belief in induction is reasonable in principle and that belief in one kind of inductive conclusion is more reasonable than belief in another.

The lasting attraction of the deductive model is not hard to understand. The *raison d'être* of deductive argument seems enticingly plain: valid deductions are truth-transmitting and truth-preserving—which, given an interest in obtaining novel truth, seems enough to show the point of deductive reasoning. (That this cannot be the whole story is obvious from the uses of deductive reasoning in exhibiting the consequences of propositions hypothetically entertained—not to mention *reductio* arguments and other uses.) By contrast the *raison d'être* of induction seems unclear and mysterious. It would be easy, although unsatisfying to the genuinely perplexed, to say that sound inductive arguments are "likelihood-transmitting," for likelihood is as unclear a concept as inductive correctness. Thus, it is natural to ask for and to expect a detailed answer to the question "Why should a reasonable man rely upon likelihood in default of truth?" Even if the power of sound induction to confer likelihood upon conclusions is regarded as sufficient to make inductive argument reasonable beyond further cavil, the question how such likelihood is conferred will remain. Attention thus shifts to the analytical task.

It may be added that an enduring source of disquiet concerning inductive argument is its disorderliness and formlessness by contrast with deductive argument. In deductive argument we flatter ourselves upon readily perceiving the underlying principles and their necessary connection with logical form. By contrast with such classic simplicity and order the realm of inductive argument seems disconcertingly complex, confused, and debatable: an inductive argument accepted by one judge may be rejected, on good grounds, by another, equally competent judge; supposedly sound arguments from different sets of true premises may yield opposed conclusions; the very soundness of induction seems not to be clear-cut but to admit of gradations of relative strength and reliability. Given all this, it is not surprising that although many students have labored to introduce order into the field, others, abandoning any hope of so doing, have turned away from induction as a tissue of confusions.

TYPES OF SOLUTION

The answers given in the literature to Hume's problem can be briefly summarized as follows:

(1) Hume's challenge cannot be met; consequently,

induction is indefensible and ought to be expunged from any reasoning purporting to be rational.

(2) In the light of Hume's criticisms, inductive arguments as normally presented need improvement, either (a) by adding further premises or (b) by changing the conclusions into statements of probability. In either case a conclusion's validity is expected to follow demonstratively from the premises, and inductive logic will be reconstructed as a branch of applied deductive logic.

(3) Although inductive argument cannot be justified as satisfying deductive standards of correctness, it may be proved that inductive policies (rather than rules or principles) are, in a novel sense to be explained later, reasonable. Induction can be vindicated if not validated.

(4) Hume's problem is generated by conceptual and linguistic confusions; it must therefore be dissolved, rather than solved, by exposing these confusions and their roots.

These approaches are not all mutually exclusive. Thus (3), the pragmatic approach, is usually combined with (1), repudiation of induction as an acceptable mode of *reasoning*. Apart from (4) all the approaches accept or make substantial concessions to Hume's major assumption—namely, that the only wholly acceptable mode of reasoning is deductive. This is true even of those who hold (3), the "practicalists," who might be supposed, at first glance, to be relaxing the criteria of rationality.

Rejection of induction. The rejection of induction as a proper mode of scientific reasoning is sometimes found in the guise of advocacy of the so-called hypothetico-deductive method. According to such a view, the essence of genuinely scientific reasoning about matters of fact is the framing of hypotheses not established by given empirical data but merely suggested by them. Inference enters only in the control of hypotheses by the verification of their observable consequences: negative instances strictly falsify a hypothesis, whereas positive instances permit its use, pending further experimental tests, as a plausible, if unproved, conjecture. Science, as well as all reasoning about matters of fact aspiring to the reliability of scientific method, needs only the kind of reasoning to be found in deductive logic and in mathematics. Some such position was already adumbrated in the writings of William Whewell. It has at least the merit of drawing attention to the role of hypotheses in scientific method, a welcome corrective to the excessive claims of early partisans of inductive logic.

The most influential, and possibly the most extreme, of contemporary writers following this line is Karl Popper, who has often maintained that what is called induction is a myth, inasmuch as what passes under that title "is always invalid and therefore clearly not justifiable." In his own conception of scientific method such repudiation of induction is linked with the thesis that the purpose of scientific theorizing is falsification (demonstration of error) rather than verification or confirmation (provisional support of an approximation to the truth). Those who agree would rewrite putatively inductive inferences to make them appear explicitly as hypothetical explanations of given facts. (Thus, instead of inferring "All A are B" from premises of the form "A_n is B," the first statement is offered as a more or less plausible explanation of why all the A_n should have been found to be B.)

In spite of its enthusiastic advocacy, it is hard to see where this proposal accomplishes more than a superficial change in the form in which inductive arguments are written and a corresponding alteration in the metalanguage in which they are appraised. Any hypothetical explanation of given empirical data is intended to reach beyond them by having empirical consequences amenable to subsequent tests. If all explanations consonant with the known facts (always an infinite set) were treated as equally unjustified by the evidence, Hume's problem would certainly be set aside, but only at the cost of ignoring what provoked it—namely, the apparent existence of rationally acceptable nondemonstrative arguments. It can hardly be denied that there are nondemonstrative arguments lending reasonable support to their conclusions; otherwise it would be as reasonable to expect manna from heaven as rain from a cloud. Anti-inductivists have seldom been hardy enough to brand all inductive arguments as equally invalid, but as soon as they discriminate between alternative hypotheses as more or less corroborated, more or less in accord with available facts, they are faced, in a new terminology, with substantially the original problems of justification and differential appraisal.

Inductive support for induction. To the layman the most natural way of defending belief in induction is that it has worked in the past. Concealed in this reply, of course, is the assumption that what has already worked will continue to do so, an assumption that has seemed objectionably circular to nearly all philosophers of induction. A stubborn minority (including R. B. Braithwaite and Max Black), however, insists that the appearance of circularity arises only from overhasty application of criteria applicable to deduction. Even in the limiting case, where the rule governing the supporting argument from previous efficacy is the very rule that is to be defended, it can be plausibly argued that no formal circularity is present. Nor is there the more subtle circularity that would obtain if knowledge of the conclusion's truth were needed to justify use of the self-supporting argument. In spite of spirited objections, this line of reasoning has not yet, in the writer's opinion, been shown to be mistaken.

The point that inductive support of induction is not necessarily circular has some importance as illustrating the interesting self-applying and self-correcting features of inductive rules; in virtue of these features, scrutiny of the consequences of the adoption of such rules can, in favorable cases, be used to refine the proper scope of inductive rules and the appropriate judgments of their strength.

A more serious weakness of this kind of defense, if it deserves to be called that, is lack of clarity about what counts as success in using the rule, which is connected in turn with the insufficiently discussed question of the *raison d'être* of induction considered as an autonomous mode of reasoning.

But even if this controversial type of inductive support of inductive rules ultimately survives criticism, it will not dispose of the metaphysical problems of induction. Those satisfied with Hume's conception of the problem are at bottom objecting to any use of inductive concepts and of the language in which they are expressed unless there is deductive justification for such use. They will therefore reject any reliance upon induction by way of defense, however free from formal defect, as essentially irrelevant to the primary task of philosophical justification. It must be admitted that inductive support of induction, however congenial to the layman, does not go to the roots of the philosophical perplexity.

A priori defenses. A few modern writers (notably D. C. Williams and R. F. Harrod) have maintained that certain inductive arguments, unimproved by the addition of supplementary premises or by modification of the form of the conclusion, can be *proved* to be valid. Williams has argued, with surprising plausibility, that the probable truth of the conclusion of a statistical syllogism can be shown to be necessitated by the truth of the premises, solely by reference to accredited principles of the mathematical theory of chances. While admiring the ingenuity displayed in this approach, critics have generally agreed in finding it fallacious. That some modes of inductive argument are certified as sound or acceptable on broadly a priori (perhaps ultimately linguistic) grounds is, however, a contention of some versions of the linguistic approach.

Deductive reconstruction. The effort to provide justification for induction through a reconstruction of inductive arguments so as to make them deductively valid has chiefly taken two forms.

Search for supreme inductive principles. If a given nondemonstrative argument, say from the amalgamated premise P to a conclusion K (where K, for the present, is regarded as a categorical statement of fact containing no reference to probability), is looked at through deductive spectacles, it is bound to seem invalid and so to be regarded as at best an enthymeme, needing extra premises to become respectable. It is easy, of course, to render the original argument deductively valid by supplying the additional premise "If P then K" (this premise will be called Q). In order for induction to be defended in the classical way, however, the premises have to be true and known to be true. Since P was supposed not to entail K, the new premise, Q, will be a contingent statement of fact, knowledge of whose truth is presumably to be derived either by deduction from more general principles or by induction from empirical data. In either case, if the deductive standard of justification is to be respected, the process must continue until we obtain general factual principles, neither capable of further empirical support nor needing such support.

The line of thought is the following: Since K does not follow strictly from P, the fact that the truth of propositions resembling P in assignable ways is regularly associated with the truth of propositions resembling K is a contingent fact about the actual universe. Looked at in another way, if events occurred purely at random, it would be impossible to make successful inductions; conversely, if inductions of a certain sort do systematically produce true conclusions, there must be a contingent regularity in the universe that should be capable of expression in the form of supreme principles or postulates of induction. Only if such postulates are true can inductions be sound; they must therefore be the assumed but unexpressed premises of all sound inductive arguments.

Favored candidates for the role of such enabling postulates have been the principle that the future resembles the past (Hume), a general principle of causation to the effect that every event has a sufficient cause (Mill), a principle of spatiotemporal homogeneity, which makes locations and dates causally irrelevant (Mill again), and a principle of limited independent variety ensuring that the attributes of individuals cluster together in a finite number of groups (J. M. Keynes, C. D. Broad; Keynes's principle, however, was intended to ensure only the probability of inductive conclusions). Any of these, if true, records the presence in the universe of a certain global regularity or order which permits inductive procedures to produce the desired true conclusions. For example, if we somehow knew in advance that a given attribute C of an observed event must have some other attribute invariably associated with it, and if we further knew that the associated attribute must be included in a finite list of known attributes, say E_1, E_2, $\cdots$, E_n, then there would be a good prospect that repeated observations of similar events would eliminate all but one of the possible associations, $E_1 - E_i$. Refinements aside, this is how Mill, for instance, conceived of inductive method; his celebrated "methods" (which have received attention out of all proportion to their merits) reduce, in the end, to deductive procedures for eliminating unfit candidates for the title of necessary or sufficient conditions. (Later attempts to develop eliminative induction follow substantially the same path.)

It is clear that the whole interest of this program rests upon the considerations that can be advanced in favor of the supreme premises. If the supreme premises can be known to be true, the remaining processes of inference become trivial (so that there is no need for an autonomous logic of induction); if not, the entire project floats in the void.

The task of formulating plausible principles of the sort envisaged by this program has proved harder than Mill supposed. However, it may be argued that the search for them is pointless and misguided. For one thing, they would accomplish too much: if known to be true, they would allow the conclusions of selected primary inductions to be demonstrated as true, which is too much to expect. It is generally agreed (and rightly so) that the conclusion of even the best inductive argument may without contradiction turn out to be false—if only through bad luck.

Still more serious is the problem of how, from the standpoint of this program, the desired supreme premises could ever be known to be true. Since appeal to induction is excluded at this point on the score of circularity, and since the principles themselves cannot be analytic if they are to serve their desired purpose, there seems no recourse at all. At this point those who search for supreme inductive principles find themselves with empty hands. Mill, for instance, was compelled to let his whole program rest upon the supposed reliability of simple enumeration (the method he regarded as the weakest), in whose defense he had nothing better to say than that it is "universally applicable" (which, on his principles, delightfully begs the question); Keynes, forsaking his empiricist principles for a half-hearted flirtation with Kant, could do no better than to suggest that the ultimate principles rest upon "some direct synthetic knowledge" of the general regularity of the universe. Induction may indeed beg to be spared such defenders as these; better the robust skepticism of Hume or Popper than the lame evasions of Mill or Keynes.

The conclusion seems inescapable that any attempt to show (as Bacon and many others have hoped) that there are general ontological guarantees for induction is doomed to failure from the outset.

Recourse to probability. A more promising way, at least at first sight, of hewing to the deductive line is to modify the conclusion of an inductive argument by including some explicit reference to probability. This approach, influential since Keynes's spirited exposition of it, still has many adherents. If there is no prospect of plugging the deductive gap between P and K by adding further premises known to be true, then perhaps the same end can be achieved by weakening the conclusion. If K does not follow from P, why not be satisfied with a more modest conclusion of the form "Probably, K" or perhaps "K has such and such a probability relative to P"?

The most impressive projects of this sort so far available have encountered severe technical difficulties. It is essential to Keynes's program, for instance, that the probability of a generalization relative to an unbroken series of confirmatory instances steadily approach unity. The conditions necessary for this to be possible in his program are at least that the generalization have an initial nonzero probability and that infinitely many of the confirmatory instances be independent, in the sense of having less than maximal probability of occurrence given the already accumulated evidence. The supreme ontological principles to which Keynes was ultimately driven to appeal (see the preceding section) hardly suffice to satisfy these conditions; subsequent criticism—for example, by Nicod and G. H. von Wright—has shown that even more rigorous conditions are needed. (Von Wright has argued that the desired asymptotic convergence will result only if in the long run every instance of the generalization is scrutinized—which would certainly render the theory somewhat less than useful in practical applications.) For all his importance as a founder of confirmation theory, the theory advocated by Keynes must be judged a failure.

Carnap's construction. The merits of Carnap's impressively sustained construction of inductive logic, following in the tradition of Laplace and Keynes but surpassing the work of both in elaboration and sophistication, are still in dispute. Taking probability to express a logical relation between propositions, Carnap has shown how, in certain simplified languages, it is possible to define the breadth or logical width of a given proposition. (Roughly speaking, the degree of confirmation given by a proposition x to a proposition y is the ratio of the width of $x \cdot y$ to the width of x.) The definition of logical width depends on the class of possible universes expressible in the language in question. In order to assign a definite measure of logical width it is necessary to adopt some method of weighting the various possible universes ("state descriptions," in Carnap's terminology) compatible with a given proposition. One of the merits of Carnap's analysis is to have shown that there is an entire continuum of alternative weighting procedures and associated inductive methods, each of which is inter-

nally coherent. The arbitrariness thereby recognized in inductive procedure has worried even the most sympathetic of Carnap's readers; still more disturbing is the emergence of what might be called the paradox of the unconfirmable generalization—the impossibility of ensuring, by Carnap's principles, that an unbroken series of positive instances will raise the probability of a generalization above zero. (Carnap retorts that an instance confirmation—that is, the conclusion of an eduction—does acquire progressively increasing probability, but this is insufficient to satisfy those critics who still hope to find a place for authentic generalization within inductive method.) It is too soon to decide whether such problems as these are more than the teething pains of a new subject. The ingenious modifications of Carnap's program suggested by, among others, J. G. Kemeny and Jaakko Hintikka offer some hope for their elimination.

More serious is the fundamental difficulty that flows from Carnap's conception of confirmation statements as analytic. If it is a truth of logic (broadly speaking) that given the selected definition of confirmation, presented evidence confirms a given hypothesis to such-and-such a degree, then how could such an a priori truth justify any rational belief in the hypothesis? Or, again, if someone were to adopt a different definition of confirmation and thereby be led to a contrary belief, then how could he be shown to be in error? Carnap's answer is based on the notion that the bridge between confirmation, as defined by him, and rational belief is to be found in some principle for the maximization of expected utility (due allowance being made, however—in his sophisticated rendering of that principle—for subjective estimates of probabilities and utilities). Yet it seems that because considerations of probability also enter into the calculation of probabilities and expected utilities, a logical circle is involved here. Since Carnap's discussions of this fundamental point are still comparatively rough and provisional, it would be premature to reach any final judgment on the success that he and those who agree with him are likely to achieve in coping with this basic difficulty. (It might be said that difficulty with the connection between probability judgments and practice is not peculiar to Carnap's work, since it arises in one form or another for all theorists of induction who take the trouble to work out in detail the consequences of their principles and assumptions.) It may be held, however, that Carnap's relatively cursory judgments about the justification of induction belong to the least satisfactory parts of his work on inductive logic.

How much the recourse to probability will accomplish depends, of course, upon how the reference to probability is construed. With empirical interpretations of probability, such as those favored by "frequentists" (see PROBABILITY), the probability conclusion still extends beyond the premises by covert reference to finite or infinite sets of events not covered by the given premises. The inductive leap remaining in the reconstructed argument will thus still leave the problem of induction unsolved. If, however, probability is construed in some logical way (as by Keynes or Carnap), the amended conclusion will say less than the premises and will therefore be untouched by subsequent empirical test; the deductive validity of the reconstructed argument will be saved only at the cost of rendering problematic its relevance to prediction and empirical control. In converting a purportedly inductive argument into a valid deductive one, the very point of the original argument—that is, to risk a prediction concerning the yet unknown—seems to be destroyed.

Pragmatic defenses. Answers of the pragmatic type, originally offered by Peirce but independently elaborated with great resourcefulness by Hans Reichenbach, are among the most original modern contributions to the subject. To many they still offer the best hope of avoiding what seems to be the inevitable failure of the attempts so far discussed. The germ of the pragmatic strategy is the reflection that in ordinary life, situations sometimes arise where, in default of reliable knowledge of consequences, problematic choices can still be justified by a "nothing to lose" argument. Faced with a choice between an operation for cancer and a sure death, a patient may choose surgery, not because of any assurance of cure but on the rational ground that nothing is lost by taking the chance.

Reichenbach's "vindication." According to Reichenbach, the case is similar in what he takes to be the paradigmatic inductive situation. Given an antecedent interest in determining the probability of occurrence of a designated character (construed, by him, as the limit, in an infinitely long run of events, of the relative frequency of occurrence of that character), Reichenbach argues that the only rationally defensible policy is to use the already ascertained relative frequency of occurrence as a provisional estimate of the ultimate limiting value. A man who proceeds in this way can have no guarantee or assurance that his estimates, constantly revised as information about the series gradually accumulates, will bring him into the neighborhood of a limiting value of the frequency, for the provisional values of the relative frequencies may, in fact, diverge. In that case no predictive policy at all will work, and successful induction is impossible. However, if this should not be the case and the series really does have a limiting value for the relative frequency in question, we can know in advance, and with certainty, that the policy is bound eventually to lead the reasoner to estimates that will remain as close to the limit as desired. There is therefore nothing to lose by adopting the inductive policy: if the series of events under scrutiny is sufficiently regular to make induction possible, the recommended policy is bound to yield the desired result ultimately (and we know before we start that it will do so), whereas if the series is irregular enough to defeat the standard inductive policy, nothing will avail, and we are no worse off than if a contrary decision had been made.

This type of justification is often called "vindication," as Herbert Feigl termed it. It is claimed that in a sense the type of vindication sketched above resolves Hume's problem by bypassing it. We know for certain that what Hume desired—namely, certification of the soundness of inductive argument by the standard of demonstrative reasoning—cannot be supplied. But it would be fainthearted to leave the matter there. By conceiving the practice of induction as the adoption of certain policies, applied in stoic acceptance of the impossibility of assured success in obtaining reliable knowledge concerning matters of fact, we are able to see that such policies are, in a clear sense,

preferable to any of their competitors. Standard induction is preferable to soothsaying because we know that it will work (will approach limiting values in the long run) if *anything* will.

To these plausible claims it has been objected that the analogy with genuinely practical decisions to act upon insufficient evidence is misconceived, for in the state of perfect ignorance postulated by defenders of the pragmatic approach no method at all can be regarded as superior to any other. Vindicationists have been relatively undisturbed by such general criticism; they have, however, felt obliged to seek remedies for a grave technical flaw that threatens to wreck their entire program. Given the assumption that the best to be achieved by an inductive policy is asymptotic convergence to a limiting relative frequency, it is obvious that no policy for inductive estimation in the short run is excluded as unreasonable. Thus, from the standpoint of pragmatic vindication an unbroken run of *A*'s found to be *B* would not make it unreasonable to predict the subsequent occurrence *in the short run* of *A*'s that are not *B*, provided only that the adopted estimates are chosen so as to converge eventually to the limit (if it exists). But since the long run is in fact never attained, even by immortal beings, it follows that the pragmatic defense yields no criteria for inductive decisions in short-run cases, to which inductive prediction is confined, and offers no differential reasons for preferring one inductive policy to another.

In spite of strenuous attempts (notably by Wesley Salmon) to improve Reichenbach's original conception by providing supplementary reasons for rejecting unwanted nonstandard policies, the prospects for vindicationism remain dubious. Even if some plausible way could be found of assigning, on vindicationist principles, a special status to the standard policy of induction, the approach would be vulnerable to the objection that it conceives inductive method in an eccentrically restricted fashion. The determination of limiting values of relative frequencies is at best a special problem of inductive method and by no means the most fundamental.

Peirce's views. Peirce, whose views on induction have exerted a lasting influence on the subject since the posthumous appearance of his *Collected Papers,* had a more complex conception of scientific method than latter-day vindicationists.

Induction, conceived by him as a process of testing statistical hypotheses by examining random samples, has to be understood in its relations to two other procedures, statistical deduction and abduction.

Statistical deduction consists of inference from the frequency of occurrence of an attribute in a population to the probable and approximate occurrence of that attribute in a sample randomly drawn from it. Given Peirce's definition of probability as limiting frequency and his conception of randomness, it follows demonstratively that most of the samples drawn will have nearly the same composition as the parent population; statistical deduction is thus "valid" in the sense that it generates conclusions that are true most of the time.

Abduction, the creative formulation of statistical hypotheses and the only mode of scientific inference introducing new ideas, is a kind of inversion of statistical deduction. It has almost no probative force, its value being rather that it provides new generalizations needing independent verification and having "some chance of being true."

When the three procedures are used in combination, induction is seen to be a self-correcting method that if indefinitely followed must in the long run lead the scientific community, although not the individual reasoner, indefinitely close to the truth. In such asymptotic convergence to the truth lies the peculiar validity of induction.

Peirce cannot be held to have succeeded in his effort to defend the rationality of inductive policies in terms of long-range efficacy in generating conclusions approximately and for the most part true. Since the intended justification of induction depends essentially upon the randomness of the samples used, it must be objected that there is normally no way of guaranteeing in advance the presence of such randomness. (To this objection Peirce had only the lame and unsupported rejoinder that inductive inference retains some probative force even in the absence of the desired randomness.) The following are among the most obvious weaknesses of Peirce's views about induction.

The self-corrective tendency of induction, which Peirce, in his last writings on the subject, came to view as the heart and essence of inductive method, remains obscure, in spite of his eulogies. That inductive estimates will need, on Peirce's principles, repeated adjustments as further evidence accumulates is clear enough, but that this process will show any convergence toward a limiting value cannot be guaranteed a priori. If the samples to be examined were random in Peirce's severe sense of that term, we could at least count upon an over-all predominance of approximately correct estimates, but even then we should have no reason, in the absence of additional guarantees, to expect the better estimates to come near the end of the testing process. In any case, supposing realistic conditions for the testing of hypotheses (such as our necessary reliance on cases that we are in a position to examine), it seems clear that the conditions for the kind of sampling demanded by Peirce cannot be fulfilled.

Peirce's references to the long run seem on the whole incoherent. Much of the time he seems to have been thinking of what would prove to be the case in an actual but infinitely extended series of trials. Toward the end of his life, however, he appears to have recognized that his definitions of probability and of the validity of induction needed to be construed more broadly, by reference to the "would be" of events, conceived as real general characters or habits. How such general features of events can in fact be disclosed, even by very lengthy series of trials, Peirce never made plain. Yet the need for clarification is great for anybody attracted by his approach. The infinitely long run is a chimera, and to be told that a certain method, if consistently pursued, would in such a long run eventually lead as close as we pleased to the truth is to be told nothing that can be useful for the actual process of verification. All verification is necessarily performed in the finite run, however extended in length, and what would happen if *per impossibile* the "run" were infinite is not relevant to the relative appraisal of given hypotheses. We need a method for adjudicating between rival hypotheses, if not now then in the foreseeable future, and this Peirce's conception cannot provide. Because of his reliance upon the infinitely long run Peirce's pragmaticism, which initially seems so hardheaded in its emphasis upon success and practical consequences, ends by being as utopian as any of the metaphysical conceptions that he derided.

Justification as a pseudo problem. In view of the quandaries which beset all known attempts to answer Hume's challenge, it is reasonable to consider whether the problem itself may not have been misconceived. Indeed, it appears upon examination that the task of logical justification of induction, as classically conceived, is framed so as to be a priori impossible of solution. If induction is by definition nondeductive and if the demand for justification is, at bottom, that induction be shown to satisfy conditions of correctness appropriate only to deduction, then the task is certainly hopeless. But to conclude, for this reason, that induction is basically invalid or that a belief based upon inductive grounds can never be reasonable is to transfer, in a manner all too enticing, criteria of evaluation from one domain to another domain, in which they are inappropriate. Sound inductive conclusions do not follow (in the deductive sense of "follow") from even the best and strongest set of premises (in the inductive sense of "strongest"); there is no good reason why they should. Those who still seek a classical defense of induction may be challenged to show why deductive standards of justification should be appropriate.

Perhaps the retort will be that there is no clear sense in which assertion of a conclusion is justified except the sense in which it is known to follow strictly from premises known to be true, so the burden of argument rests upon anybody who claims the existence of some other sense.

Linguistic approach to the problem. The challenge to the claim that inductive arguments cannot be said to be justified might be met in the following way: Suppose a man has learned, partly from his own experience and partly from the testimony of others, that in a vast variety of circumstances, when stones are released they fall toward the ground. Let him consider the proposition *K*, that any stone chosen at random and released will do likewise. This is, in the writer's opinion, a paradigm case for saying that the man in question (any of us) has a good reason for asserting *K* and is therefore justified in asserting *K* rather than not-*K*. Similarly, this is a paradigm case for saying that the man in question is reasonable in asserting *K* and would be unreasonable in asserting not-*K*, on the evidence at hand. Anybody who claimed otherwise would not be extraordinarily and admirably scrupulous but would be abusing language by violating some of the implicit criteria for the uses of "good reason," "justified," and "reasonable," to which he, like the interlocutor with whom he succeeds in communicating, is in fact committed.

Any man—say, one from Mars—who used these words according to criteria that would really make it improper for him to apply them in the kind of situation envisaged would not, in the end, be *understood* by us. Worse still, he would be trying, if he were consistent, to change our actual concepts of reason and reasonableness so that it would be logically impossible to have reasons for assertions concerning the unknown or to be reasonable in expecting one matter of fact rather than another on the basis of empirical evidence. (He would be behaving like a man who insisted that only stallions deserved to be called horses.) Nor would such distortion achieve anything significant, for the man who proposed to make "empirical reason" as impossible of application as "being in two places at once" would find himself forced to reintroduce essentially the same concept under some such label as "generally accepted as a reason" or "what commonly passes for a reason." The distinction between what ordinary men and what scientists call "good reasons" and "bad reasons" is made for a good purpose, has practical consequences, and is indispensable in practice. Thus, the dispute between the advocate of the linguistic approach and his opponent seems to reduce to a verbal one, ripe for oblivion.

Given the intertwined complexity of the concepts entering into alternative formulations of the problem of induction and the seductive plausibility of the distortions to which such concepts are subject, no brief reply such as the above can be expected to clarify and to expose the conceptual confusions upon which traditional formulations of the problem rest. A full discussion would at least also have to consider the relevant senses of "knowledge" and "possibility" and related epistemological notions. The outline of the strategy is perhaps sufficiently plain; the line to be taken is that close and detailed examination of how the key words in the statement of the problem occur will show that criteria for the correct uses of such terms are violated in subtle and plausible ways. If this can be established, the celebrated problem of justifying induction will dissolve, and the confused supposition that induction needs philosophical justification or remains precarious in its absence will disappear.

The comparative problem and the analytical problem do not dissolve under this attack. Advocates of the linguistic approach can be fairly reproached for having been too often content to show to their own satisfaction that the general problem of justification is rooted in confusion, while neglecting the constructive tasks of rendering clearer the criteria for preferential appraisal of inductive arguments.

To those unsympathetic with the linguistic approach such an attack upon the traditional problem has sometimes seemed to be operating with dubious and insufficiently elaborated theories of meaning or use and to be altogether too glib in its attribution of semantical confusions. Moreover, a number of critics have thought that an appeal to ordinary language cannot be ultimately decisive from a philosophical standpoint. Even if it were established that it is a violation of ordinary language to describe the conclusion of some inductive arguments as supported by less than good reasons, the critics ask, what is there in the nature of things that requires us to continue talking in the ordinary way or to be bound by the encapsulated metaphysical prejudices of those originally responsible for establishing the rules of use to which appeal is now made? The linguistic philosopher necessarily uses such key words as "reasonable" in his polemic against the traditional approaches to the problem. But to use the crucial terms in a discussion of the nature of the inductive problem, it might be urged, is to beg the very question at issue. A lunatic or an eccentric philosopher might well use the expression "good reason" in a way that would be blatantly improper, yet he might be able to prove, by appeal to his own criteria, that he had "good reasons" to use the phrase in the way he did. But are we ourselves in any better position? Are we not obligated to break through the linguistic barrier and at least to show why the alleged criteria for good reasons to which appeal is made should continue to receive our allegiance?

There is no short way of dealing with this type of objection. It may be helpful, however, to sketch the general view upon which the present writer, as a defender of the linguistic approach, would rely.

Defense of the linguistic approach. All normal adult human beings follow the same broad and systematic patterns for drawing inferences concerning the unobserved and apply the same general principles for appraising such nondemonstrative inferences. For instance, all normal persons expect observed cases of association of attributes to be confirmed in further experience unless there are countervailing factors (the principle of simple enumeration), all count increase in the number of independent confirmatory instances of a law as strengthening (or at least not weakening) the probability of the law's truth, and all alike share the inductive beliefs that underpin causal notions. It is, therefore, not fanciful to conceive of all sane adult human beings as participating in a complex system of ways of learning from experience that might be called the inductive institution. Like other institutions (warfare, the law, and so on), it has a relatively fixed, though not immutable, structure, transmitted from one generation to the next and crystallized in the form of prohibitions and licenses, maxims of conduct, and informal precepts of performance. Like other institutions, the inductive institution requires that its participants have mastered a system of distinctive concepts (among them the concepts of good reason, sound argument, and relative likelihood) having both descriptive and normative aspects. Such mastery is shown in capacity to use the corresponding language correctly—which, in turn, implies recognition of, though not invariable obedience to, associated rules for assertion, for evaluation, and for the appraisal of actions. Understanding what people mean by reasons for empirical conclusions requires acceptance of certain types of situations as paradigmatic of empirical evidence; to call given facts sound reasons for some conclusion is to imply the acceptability of certain criteria for judging one reason to be better than another; asserting that some belief about the hitherto unobserved is reasonable commits the speaker to holding that other things being equal, action based on such belief should be approved.

The philosophical problem of justifying induction can arise only for somebody who is a member of the inductive institution and is therefore already bound by its constitutive rules. A man can understand bridge without being a player, but all of us are necessarily players of the "inductive game" before we achieve the reflective self-consciousness characteristic of philosophical criticism.

The constitutive rules of the inductive institution (whose precise delineation remains a still unfinished task for philosophers of induction) are highly abstract, schematic, and limited in their practical usefulness. Indeed, the general principles of inductive inference are about as relevant to practice as the abstract principles of justice are to decisions on concrete legal issues. In particular situations concerning the soundness of empirical hypotheses the reasoner is compelled to fall back upon his specific knowledge of relevant facts and theories. In this way the conduct of concrete inductive inference resembles the exercise of a craft or skill more than it does the automatic application of a decision procedure. Yet the constitutive rules provide important general constraints that cannot be violated without generating nonsense.

To be in command of inductive language, whether as a master of advanced techniques of statistical inference or as a layman constantly and more or less skillfully anticipating future experience, is necessarily to be subject to the implicit norms of belief and conduct imposed by the institution.

The inductive concepts that we acquire by example and formal education and modify through our own experiences are not exempt even from drastic revision. The norms may be usefully thought of as formal crystallizations into linguistic rules of general modes of response to the universe that our ancestors have, on the whole, found advantageous to survival, but the earlier experience of the race never has absolute authority. Piecemeal reform of the inductive institution can be observed in the history of modern science. What is clearly impossible, however, is the sort of wholesale revolution that would be involved in wiping the inductive slate clean and trying to revert to the condition of some hypothetical Adam setting out to learn from experience without previous indoctrination in relevant rules of inductive procedure. This would be tantamount to attempting to destroy the language we now use to talk about the world and about ourselves and thereby to destroy the concepts embodied in that language. The idea of ceasing to be an inductive reasoner is a monstrosity. The task is not impossibly difficult; rather, its very formulation fails to make sense. Yet it remains important to insist that the inductive institution, precisely because its *raison d'être* is learning from experience, is intrinsically self-critical. Induction, like the Sabbath, was made for man, not vice versa. Thus, constantly renewed experience of the successes and failures of the specific inductive procedures permitted within the general framework of the inductive institution provides a sound basis for gradual reform of the institution itself, without objectionable circularity.

Yet even if no feature of the institution is exempt, in principle, from criticism and reconstruction, the entire institution cannot be called into question all at once without destroying the very meaning of the words in which the philosophical problems of induction are stated. Wholesale philosophical skepticism about matters of fact is senseless and must be shown to be so. If this is the "linguocentric predicament," we must make the best of it.

The view here outlined must be carefully distinguished from what is commonly called conventionalism. The argument is not that the constitutive inductive rules hold by convention but rather that the sweeping question "Why should we accept *any* inductive rules?" can be shown to make no sense.

Our sketch may be usefully compared with Hume's view of induction as a habit or custom. Both views agree in regarding inductive practices as being, on the whole, so-cial and contingent facts obtaining at given periods in human history. It is, after all, a contingent fact that there have existed animals sufficiently rational to be able to speak and hence to have inductive concepts. The present conception differs significantly from Hume's, however, in regarding the inductive institution as partly constituted by normative inductive rules to which the philosopher, like every reasoning man, finds himself already committed. Thus, the encompassing social fact of the existence of the inductive institution includes within itself the means for appraisal and criticism of inductive procedures; we cannot regard inductive inference as something merely "given," as a natural fact, like the Milky Way, that it would be absurd to criticize. To understand induction is necessarily to accept its authority. However (to repeat), questions about the general or ultimate justification of induction *as such*, questions of the form "Why should any induction be trusted?" must be recognized as senseless. If we persist in trying to raise them, we come, as Wittgenstein expressed it, to the "limits of language," and we can see that we have done so by perceiving that what we had hoped were important and fundamental questions are no better than nonsense masquerading as sense.

The foregoing will undoubtedly strike critics of the linguistic approach as too facile, for the tangle of philosophical problems that have been dubbed "the problem of induction" constitute, in their depth, their importance, their elusiveness, and their capacity to bewilder and confuse, a very paradigm of philosophical perplexity.

The foregoing survey indicates that no wholly satisfactory philosophy of induction is yet available. The work still to be done may be summarized as follows: for those who recognize the crucial role of probability in inductive inference, to develop a consistent, systematic, and relevant reconstruction of the concept of probability; for those who reject induction as an outmoded myth, to elaborate a detailed and comprehensive account of scientific practice that will be reasonably close to the best actual procedures used in reasoning about matters of fact; for those who pin their hopes on the construction of an inductive logic, to remove the constraints imposed by the study of artificially simplified languages and to show in detail how analytical statements of probability can be relevant to the practice of inductive prediction; for vindicationists, to solve the comparative problem of selecting competing hypotheses and to show how eventual convergence in the long run can bear upon short-run judgment; for those who regard induction as a pseudo problem, to articulate the theory of language presupposed and to demonstrate in convincing detail the origins and the character of the stubborn confusions that have infested the subject.

Bibliography

COMPREHENSIVE STUDIES

The best introduction to the whole subject of induction is still William Kneale, *Probability and Induction* (Oxford, 1949). See especially Part II, "The Traditional Problem of Induction." A shorter and more up-to-date discussion is Stephen F. Barker, *Induction and Hypothesis* (Ithaca, N.Y., 1957), which is especially good on the role of simplicity in inductive inference. Georg Henrik von Wright, *The Logical Problem of Induction* (Oxford, 1941;

2d, rev. ed., 1957), is invaluable for its ample discussion of the history of the subject and also contains penetrating criticism. John Patrick Day, *Inductive Probability* (London, 1961), uses somewhat opaque symbolism but is very comprehensive. *Induction: Some Current Issues*, edited by Henry E. Kyburg, Jr., and Ernest Nagel (Middletown, Conn., 1963), is a conference report containing edited versions of discussions by Black, Braithwaite, Nagel, Salmon, and others.

TERMINOLOGY

For a good brief treatment of terminology, see Kneale, *op. cit.*, pp. 24–48, which includes discussion of Aristotle's uses of *epagoge*. Kneale is good also in his treatment of intuitive induction and mathematical induction.

S. F. Barker, "Must Every Inference Be Either Deductive or Inductive?," in Max Black, ed., *Philosophy in America* (Ithaca, N.Y., 1965), pp. 58–73, answers in the negative; it is an illuminating effort to distinguish criteria for nondemonstrative inference.

HISTORY OF INDUCTIVE METHODS

André Lalande, *Les Théories de l'induction et de l'expérimentation* (Paris, 1929), contains brief discussions of Newton, Herschel, Claude Bernard, and other scientists, as well as of Bacon and Mill. There is no satisfactory general history of inductive methods.

Most students of Bacon confine themselves to Book I of the *Novum Organum* (available in many editions). The best philosophical commentary on Bacon remains R. L. Ellis' General Preface to James Spedding, R. L. Ellis, and D. D. Heath, eds., *The Works of Francis Bacon* (London, 1857). For a lucid and sympathetic appreciation of Bacon's general program—but with comparatively little discussion of Bacon's views on induction—see the commemorative address by C. D. Broad, *The Philosophy of Francis Bacon* (Cambridge, 1926).

For Mill, see *A System of Logic*, 8th ed. (London, 1872), especially Book III, Ch. 3, "On the Ground of Induction," and Ch. 21, "Of the Evidence of the Law of Universal Causation." Ernest Nagel, ed., *John Stuart Mill's Philosophy of Scientific Method* (New York, 1950), is a useful selection from the *Logic*, including part of Mill's *Examination of Sir William Hamilton's Philosophy.* The editor's introduction is helpful.

A serious student of Mill will wish to consult his unjustly neglected critic, William Whewell, whose *The Philosophy of the Inductive Sciences* (London, 1847)—especially Part II, entitled "Novum Organum Renovatum"—is still instructive. A useful summary of Whewell's views is C. J. Ducasse's "William Whewell's Philosophy of Scientific Discovery," pp. 183–217 in Edward H. Madden, ed., *Theories of Scientific Method: The Renaissance Through the Nineteenth Century* (Seattle, Wash., 1960).

For Peirce's views, see the *Collected Papers of Charles Sanders Peirce*, Charles Hartshorne, Paul Weiss, and Arthur Burks, eds. (8 vols., Cambridge, Mass., 1931–1958), especially "Ampliative Reasoning," Vol. II, pp. 272–607. Unfortunately, Peirce's writings on induction are scattered throughout the volumes, out of chronological order. A concise critical examination is Thomas A. Goudge, "Peirce's Treatment of Induction," in *Philosophy of Science*, Vol. 7 (1940), 56–68. Part VI of the same author's *The Thought of C. S. Peirce* (Toronto, 1950) has a fuller treatment, for which the rest of the book provides good background.

For Keynes, see *A Treatise on Probability* (London, 1921). Chs. 18–22 are the most relevant; they include, *inter alia*, Keynes's original ideas concerning analogy. Jean Nicod, "The Logical Problem of Induction," Part II of *Foundations of Geometry and Induction* (London, 1930), contains lucid and trenchant criticisms of Keynes's position. For more recent appraisal, see von Wright, *op. cit.*, pp. 127–132.

Rudolf Carnap, *Logical Foundations of Probability* (Chicago, 1950), is an elaborate treatise which, although still unfinished and in part superseded by Carnap's later studies, remains the most important original source for his views.

The Philosophy of Rudolf Carnap, P. A. Schilpp, ed. (La Salle, Ill., 1963), is now indispensable to the serious student because of its important essays by Carnap's defenders and critics and the detailed comments and replies by Carnap. John G. Kemeny,

"Carnap's Theory of Probability and Induction," pp. 711–738, is an outstandingly successful effort to convey the gist of Carnap's position sympathetically; Ernest Nagel, "Carnap's Theory of Induction," pp. 785–825 (vigorously attacked in Carnap's rejoinder, pp. 989–995), expresses at length the misgivings of those who see in Carnap's view a retreat from empiricism; Hilary Putnam, "'Degree of Confirmation' and Inductive Logic," pp. 761–783, is a highly ingenious attempt to demonstrate that a logic based on confirmation must violate accepted canons of scientific method.

Carnap's "The Aim of Inductive Logic," pp. 303–318 in Ernest Nagel, Patrick Suppes, and Alfred Tarski, eds., *Logic, Methodology, and Philosophy of Science* (Stanford, Calif., 1962), is an important pioneering discussion of the application of inductive logic. Carnap concludes, "Induction, if properly reformulated, can be shown to be valid by rational criteria."

PROBLEM OF JUSTIFICATION

There is no substitute for reading Hume. His own summary, *An Abstract of a Treatise of Human Nature* (London, 1740; reprinted, with Introduction by J. M. Keynes and Piero Sraffa, Cambridge, 1938), should not be overlooked. Pp. 11–20 express the essence of Hume's position. The serious student must, of course, read *A Treatise of Human Nature*, L. A. Selby-Bigge, ed. (Oxford, 1896). See especially Book I, Part 3. Sec. 6 contains the famous skeptical attack on the objectivity of causal connection.

See also Hume's *Enquiry Concerning the Human Understanding*, L. A. Selby-Bigge, ed., 2d ed. (Oxford, 1902), especially Sec. 4, "Sceptical Doubts Concerning the Operations of the Understanding."

Bertrand Russell, "On Induction," Ch. 6 of *The Problems of Philosophy* (London, 1912), is a lucid and concise version of what is basically Hume's skeptical position.

The best statement of the "new riddle of induction" is in Nelson Goodman, *Fact, Fiction and Forecast* (Cambridge, Mass., 1955), Chs. 3 and 4. Goodman's position, with some unpublished improvements, is sympathetically discussed in Israel Scheffler, *The Anatomy of Inquiry* (New York, 1963), pp. 291–326. The same book is valuable for its lucid appraisal of various theories of inductive confirmation.

REJECTION OF INDUCTION

See Karl Popper, *The Logic of Scientific Discovery* (London, 1959), especially Ch. 1. John Oulton Wisdom, *Foundations of Inference in Natural Science* (London, 1952), is written from a Popperian standpoint; Parts II–IV, pp. 85–232, deal with induction. For criticism of Popper's general position, see John Arthur Passmore, "Popper's Account of Scientific Method," in *Philosophy*, Vol. 35 (1960), 326–331.

A PRIORI DEFENSES

Donald C. Williams, *The Ground of Induction* (Cambridge, Mass., 1947), claims to have answered Hume on a priori grounds. For a dissenting verdict, see the extended review by Max Black in *The Journal of Symbolic Logic*, Vol. 12 (1947), 141–144.

Roy F. Harrod, *Foundations of Inductive Logic* (London, 1956), is still another ingenious attempt to show that induction must be successful. For criticism, see Popper's review in *British Journal for the Philosophy of Science*, Vol. 9 (1958–1959), 221–224; Harrod's reply appears in Vol. 10 (1959–1960), 309–312.

INDUCTIVE SUPPORT FOR INDUCTION

Consult Richard B. Braithwaite, *Scientific Explanation* (Cambridge, 1953), Ch. 8, "The Justification of Induction," pp. 255–292.

Abner Shimony's severely critical "Braithwaite on Scientific Method," in *Review of Metaphysics*, Vol. 7 (1953–1954), 644–660, has not been rebutted. On this topic see also H. E. Kyburg, Jr., "R. B. Braithwaite on Probability and Induction," in *British Journal for the Philosophy of Science*, Vol. 9 (1958–1959), 203–220.

A defense of the soundness of self-supporting inductions can be found in Max Black, "Inductive Support of Inductive Rules."

pp. 191–208 in *Problems of Analysis* (Ithaca, N.Y., 1954), and "Self-supporting Inductive Arguments," pp. 209–218 in *Models and Metaphors* (Ithaca, N.Y., 1962). For criticism of Black's views, see Peter Achinstein, "The Circularity of a Self-supporting Argument," in *Analysis,* Vol. 22 (1961–1962), 138–141. See also Black's reply in the same journal, Vol. 23 (1962–1963), 43–44, and Achinstein's rejoinder, *ibid.,* 123–127.

DEDUCTIVE RECONSTRUCTION

See Bertrand Russell, *Human Knowledge: Its Scope and Limits* (New York, 1948). Russell states and defends postulates of scientific inference in the concluding part, pp. 421–507. Arthur W. Burks, "On the Presuppositions of Induction," in *Review of Metaphysics,* Vol. 8 (1955), 574–611, is a persuasive exposition by the ablest contemporary defender of deductive reconstruction. See also Burks's article in Schilpp, ed., *The Philosophy of Rudolf Carnap,* above, and his forthcoming book *Cause, Chance and Reason.* Deductive reconstruction is criticized in most of the articles listed below in the section on induction as pseudo problem.

C. D. Broad, "On the Relation Between Induction and Probability," in *Mind,* Vol. 27 (1918), 389–404, and Vol. 29 (1920), 11–45, is an early and unjustly neglected discussion whose second part is a suggestive development of Keynes's ideas.

PRAGMATIC DEFENSES

Herbert Feigl's views are contained in two of his articles, "De Principiis Non Est Disputandum . . . ?," in Max Black, ed., *Philosophical Analysis* (Ithaca, N.Y., 1950), and "Validation and Vindication," in *Readings in Ethical Theory,* Wilfrid Sellars and John Hospers, eds. (New York, 1952), pp. 667–680. The first paper argues the case for vindication as a special mode of justification, and the second enlarges upon the idea.

Hans Reichenbach, *The Theory of Probability* (Berkeley, 1949), is the *locus classicus* of recent pragmatic defenses; see especially "The Justification of Induction," pp. 469–482. The same author's *Experience and Prediction* (Chicago, 1938) contains a more popular presentation.

Isabel P. Creed, "The Justification of the Habit of Induction," in *Journal of Philosophy,* Vol. 37 (1940), 85–97, and Everett J. Nelson, "Professor Reichenbach on Induction," in *Journal of Philosophy,* Vol. 33 (1936), 577–580, are two thorough appraisals and criticisms of Reichenbach's position.

Max Black, "'Pragmatic' Justifications of Induction," in his *Problems of Analysis* (Ithaca, N.Y., 1954), pp. 157–190, is a full-scale attack upon "pragmatic vindication."

Wesley C. Salmon, "The Short Run," in *Philosophy of Science,* Vol. 22 (1955), 214–221, is an admirable, if ultimately unsuccessful, attempt to avoid reliance upon the infinitely long run. In "Should We Attempt to Justify Induction?," *Philosophical Studies,* Vol. 8 (1957), 33–48, Salmon elaborately defends the pragmatic approach; Black's "Can Induction Be Vindicated?," in his *Models and Metaphors* (Ithaca, N.Y., 1962), pp. 194–208, is a detailed reply to Salmon.

Salmon's "Vindication of Induction," in H. Feigl and G. E. Maxwell, eds., *Current Issues in the Philosophy of Science* (New York, 1961), pp. 245–256, is the latest version of Reichenbach's approach by its ablest contemporary advocate. See also Salmon's contributions to Nagel and Kyburg, eds., *Induction,* above.

INDUCTION AS A PSEUDO PROBLEM

For an introduction to the growing number of studies written from this standpoint, see Alice Ambrose, "The Problem of Justifying Inductive Inference," in *Journal of Philosophy,* Vol. 44 (1947), 253–272; Max Black, "The Justification of Induction," in his *Language and Philosophy* (Ithaca, N.Y., 1949), pp. 59–88; Frederick L. Will, "Will the Future Be Like the Past?," in *Mind,* Vol. 56 (1947), 332–347; and Paul Edwards, "Russell's Doubts About Induction," in *Mind,* Vol. 58 (1949), 141–163. Perhaps the most accessible brief account is Peter F. Strawson, "The 'Justification' of Induction," in *Introduction to Logical Theory* (London, 1952), pp. 248–263. Brief criticism of the "linguistic approach" is to be found in many of the recent works listed above. No satisfactorily broad statement of the position of the "linguists" or their critics is yet available.

BIBLIOGRAPHIES AND SURVEYS

Lengthy bibliographies are supplied in the above-mentioned books by Keynes (to 1921), Carnap (to 1951), and von Wright (to 1955).

Black's "Induction and Probability," in Raymond Klibansky, ed., *Philosophy in the Mid-century* (Florence, 1958), pp. 154–163, is a critical survey of the previous decade's work.

H. E. Kyburg, Jr., "Recent Work in Inductive Logic," in *American Philosophical Quarterly,* Vol. 1 (1964), 249–287, is a highly useful analysis of the main trends, with criticism and an extensive bibliography.

MAX BLACK

INDUCTION, CANONS OF. See MILL'S METHODS OF INDUCTION.

INEFFABLE, THE. It has been held by some philosophers that some things are ineffable (unsayable, inexpressible, incommunicable). By this it has usually been meant either that there are facts or states of affairs, actual or possible, which cannot be linguistically expressed or put into words or that there are things (beings, entities), actual or possible, about the nature of which nothing literal can be said. For example, the fact that Scott was the author of *Waverley* can be put into words (namely, the words "Scott was the author of *Waverley*"), but, some would claim, the fact that we try to express by the words "God is good" cannot be expressed by those or any other words.

The ineffable must not be confused with the unknowable. One may assert, as Kant did about things-in-themselves, that some things are both ineffable and unknowable; nevertheless, the concept of the ineffable is usually so construed that it makes sense to say, "I know something somehow, but I cannot put it into words; I cannot say what I know."

The ineffable in practice must be distinguished from the ineffable in principle. That is ineffable in practice which a certain person cannot put into words. A person may, for example, complain on a certain occasion that he cannot describe how he feels, perhaps because he has forgotten or cannot at the moment think of the words appropriate to describe how he feels; still, how he feels can in principle be described. That is ineffable in principle which no one can put into words, that for which there are and can be no suitable words, that for the expression of which all possible words are unsuitable. Only the ineffable in principle is of philosophical interest.

The thesis that there are things that are ineffable has played a significant part in three areas of philosophy—philosophy of religion, aesthetics, and philosophy of language.

Philosophy of religion. In the philosophy of religion the ineffability thesis is chiefly associated with mysticism and with what is called negative theology. Here the thesis takes something like the following form. Although there is, or may be, something appropriately called God, the one, or the divine, nothing, at least nothing affirmative, can literally be said about its nature; *that* it is can perhaps be said (although some mystical theologians would deny even this), but how it is or what it is like cannot literally be said.

According to one interpretation, this claim—and this

holds for the ineffability thesis generally—is logically unproblematical; according to another, it appears to be paradoxical. Let "*f*" represent some fact, "*x*" some thing. As long as we do not try literally to say what fact "*f*" represents, the statement "There is some *f* that cannot be put into words" is logically unproblematic, for to make the statement is not to put *f* into words. But the statement "There is some *x* about which nothing can literally be said" appears to be paradoxical, for it appears literally to say something about *x*—namely, that nothing can be said about it. But this is merely an apparent paradox. For it seems plain that the ineffability thesis, according to either interpretation, is fundamentally metalinguistic: It holds that a certain class of sentences—namely, all sentences about *x* or that contain (use) the name "*x*"—literally say nothing or literally express no fact (*f*), actual or possible. This is not paradoxical.

The thesis is subject, however, to another difficulty. Consider the sentence "God is good." According to the mystical theologian, this sentence cannot literally be about God, cannot literally express a fact. He would hold, however, that it is not without sense, for metaphorically or symbolically it is about God and does express a fact. Unfortunately, however, "literal" and "metaphorical" are used in such a way that when S stands for some sentence, the statement "S is metaphorical" entails the statement "It is possible that S is literal." Yet, according to the theologian's ineffability principle, it is impossible that the statement "God is good" is literal; hence, it should follow that it is not metaphorical. If this consequence does not follow and if "literal sentence" is in principle inapplicable to "God is good," then the statement " 'God is good' is a metaphorical sentence" can mean no more than " 'God is good' is a sentence."

Aesthetics. Many aestheticians have held that art's sole, or chief, reason for being is that it does something that (ordinary, prose, literal, descriptive, discursive) language cannot do; it accurately expresses feelings and emotions. Every nonartistic linguistic expression of an emotion or feeling fails to express it precisely, whereas every (good, successful) work of art succeeds in doing this. Language generalizes; art particularizes.

We possess at least two contrasting sets of terms applicable to such acts of speech as describing one's emotions and saying how one feels. In one set belong such terms as "general," "abstract," "inaccurate," "imprecise," "inept"; in the other, such terms as "particular," "concrete," "accurate," "precise," "apt." As a metalinguistic claim, the aesthetic version of the ineffability thesis holds that no term belonging to the second set is in principle applicable to anything that would ordinarily count as a description of one's feelings or emotions; the only terms so applicable must come from the second set.

Read as an empirical claim about the way certain expressions are used in known natural languages, this is clearly false. Even though all descriptions of emotions may in fact be inaccurate, an accurate description of an emotion is not a logical impossibility. The phrase "accurate description of an emotion" is not obviously contradictory in the same way that "colorless red object" is.

Read as an a priori claim, reflecting, perhaps, a recommended linguistic innovation, the aesthetic thesis suffers from the same difficulty as its religious counterpart—it is uninformative. For if "precise expression of an emotion" is in principle inapplicable to any member of a certain class of expressions of emotion—for example, to ordinary verbal descriptions of them—and if it is solely applicable, in principle, only to members of another class of expressions of emotion—namely, works of art—then, assuming that works of art are expressions of emotions, the statement "Works of art, at least good or successful ones, express emotions precisely" can mean no more than the statement "Works of art, at least good or successful ones, express emotions." And if the expression theory of art is itself a priori, this statement, in turn, can mean no more than "(Good or successful) works of art are (good or successful) works of art."

Philosophy of language. One of the chief consequences of the theory of language worked out by Ludwig Wittgenstein in his *Tractatus Logico-philosophicus* is that all intelligible discourse is restricted to sentences that express (1) tautologies, (2) contradictions, and (3) descriptive propositions, propositions that assert that certain states of affairs do or do not exist. But tautologies and contradictions "say nothing" (*Tractatus*, 4.461–4.462); hence, sentences that express descriptive propositions—"pictures" of states of affairs—alone have sense or say all that can be said, and these constitute "natural science" (*ibid.*, 4.11, 6.53). This means that many sentences, especially those of the philosopher and even those of the *Tractatus* itself, are without sense (*unsinnig*). What the philosopher means (*meinen*) may be quite correct, only it cannot be said. What cannot be said, however, can (at least in some cases) show or manifest itself or be shown (*ibid.*, 4.1212). For example, "what the solipsist *means* is quite correct; only it cannot be *said* but makes itself manifest" (*ibid.*, 5.62).

Some philosophers (for example, Rudolf Carnap) have found this view inconsistent or inherently untenable on the ground that Wittgenstein himself has said certain things that he holds are unsayable. To be sure, the statement "One cannot say (for example) 'The limits of my language mean the limits of my world'" (*ibid.*) does sound paradoxical; it looks like the utterance of one who says "I do not speak a word of English." But in a statement of the form "One who says S says what cannot be said," there is no paradox if the verb "to say" in its first occurrence means something different from what it means in its second occurrence. In Wittgenstein's view, clearly one can say (that is, utter) the words "The limits of my language mean the limits of my world," but in doing so he is not saying anything—that is, he is not conveying any information about the world or depicting any existent or nonexistent state of affairs. Hence, Wittgenstein's view is not paradoxical. "Philosophical sentences say nothing" is, in the context of the *Tractatus*, truistic. It says no more than that philosophical sentences are philosophical sentences or that what says nothing says nothing. Proponents of the ineffable try to say what the limits of language are, but—and this is a logically necessary truth—such limits cannot be drawn (*ibid.*, 5.61).

Theory of incommunicable content. Some philosophers have held that only the form, or structure, not the content, or material, of a (possible) fact can be expressed or communicated. The argument for this view goes as follows. To express a fact, a sentence must have something in common with what it expresses—namely, the same logical structure or form. "Form" and "content," however, are polar concepts; wherever there is form, there must be content. Nevertheless, only the form of a fact can be communicated; the content or material must be "furnished by the individual himself, derived from his own experience" (Moritz Schlick, *Gesammelte Aufsätze*, p. 164). Why? Because it is possible for there to be "complete understanding between individuals even if there is no similarity between the contents of their minds"; for example, the content which you furnish for the sentence "Her hat is green" may be very different from that which I furnish, and yet we may completely understand one another. Therefore, "understanding and meaning are quite independent of content and have nothing whatever to do with it" (*ibid.*, p. 167).

At least two difficulties confront this view. First, although it is not clear just what Schlick means by the form and content of a fact and of a sentence, it seems plain that the content of our minds is not the polar opposite of the form of a fact or the form of a sentence and, hence, that Schlick's conclusion does not follow. But even if it does follow, since the argument is a priori, the conclusion, as Schlick realized, is "a mere truism," "a tautology" (*ibid.*, p. 169), and is thus uninformative. It does not tell us what is expressible as opposed to what is not expressible. "Form alone is expressible" or "Content is inexpressible" comes to no more than "What is expressible is expressible" or "What is inexpressible is inexpressible." Schlick supposed that in saying that form alone is expressible, he was telling us "what we mean when we use the term 'expression.'" That this is not so is shown by the fact that the following is quite coherent: "That some dogs drink milk and that some cats eat meat are facts that have the same form; but the sentences 'Some dogs drink milk' and 'Some cats eat meat,' although they have the same logical or grammatical form and express facts having the same form, express or communicate different contents."

Bibliography

For a discussion of ineffability in theology, see the writings of the pseudo-Dionysius, particularly *On the Divine Names* and *The Mystical Theology*, in, for instance, *The Works of Dionysius the Areopagite*, translated by John Parker (London, 1897), Vol. I. Also see William P. Alston, "Ineffability," in *Philosophical Review*, Vol. 65 (1956), 506–522.

The aesthetic thesis of the ineffable is discussed in R. G. Collingwood, *The Principles of Art* (Oxford, 1938); John Dewey, *Art as Experience* (New York, 1934); D. W. Prall, *Aesthetic Analysis* (New York, 1936); and Susanne K. Langer, *Philosophy in a New Key* (Cambridge, Mass., 1942), and *Problems of Art* (New York, 1957). For a critique of the thesis, see W. E. Kennick, "Art and the Ineffable," in *Journal of Philosophy*, Vol. 58 (1961), 309–320.

Wittgenstein's views may be found in his *Tractatus Logico-philosophicus* (London and New York, 1961), German text with English translation by D. F. Pears and B. F. McGuinness. For criticism, see Rudolf Carnap, *Philosophy and Logical Syntax* (London, 1935), pp. 37 ff., and George Pitcher, *The Philosophy of Wittgenstein* (Englewood Cliffs, N.J., 1964), pp. 155 ff. Moritz Schlick's views are presented in "Form and Content, an Introduction to Philosophical Thinking," in his *Gesammelte Aufsätze 1926–1936* (Vienna, 1938), p. 151 ff.

For a penetrating study of further philosophical complaints against linguistic adequacy, see Alice Ambrose, "The Problem of Linguistic Adequacy," in Max Black, ed., *Philosophical Analysis* (Ithaca, N.Y., 1950), pp. 15–37.

W. E. KENNICK

INERTIA. See MASS.

INFINITY, AXIOM OF. See RUSSELL, BERTRAND ARTHUR WILLIAM, section on logic and mathematics.

INFINITY IN MATHEMATICS AND LOGIC.

Questions involving the notion of infinity arose very early in the history of Western philosophy and science. It was asked, for example, whether the world was infinite, whether time was infinite, and, more generally, whether anything was or could be infinite in extent. It was also asked whether time or space or matter was infinite in the sense of being infinitely divisible. These difficult questions gave rise to others. Thus, it has been asked whether the idea of something being infinite is internally coherent and consistent. It has been asked, too, whether we really understand the suggestion that such and such a thing is infinite or whether what we call our conception of infinity is not merely that of something that increases indefinitely in some respect while remaining finite.

Some of these questions are discussed by Aristotle in the *Physics*, and one or another of them is adverted to by almost every major philosopher—Aquinas, Descartes, Spinoza, Leibniz, Hobbes, Locke, Hume, Kant, and Hegel. But no attempt will be made in this article to provide a historical account. Instead, we shall proceed in a quite ahistorical way. We shall first explain the revolution of ideas that took place in the nineteenth century as a result of the work of Bernard Bolzano, Richard Dedekind, and Georg Cantor. It will then be seen that clear and apparently satisfactory answers are possible for some of the main questions that have been asked (and, it may be thought, to those that are of most philosophical importance). In addition, we shall discuss some of the objections that have been made to Cantor's ideas and also the distinction (or alleged distinction) between the idea of "the actual infinite" and that of the "potential infinite." We shall also mention briefly some unanswered difficulties about Cantor's theories. In the next section we suggest that some questions about the idea of infinity are best seen as questions about the conditions of applicability of that idea, and we shall try to make this suggestion plausible by means of an extended discussion of some of Zeno's paradoxes of motion.

Some false notions of infinity. An obvious start on the questions first mentioned is to ask what it is supposed to mean to say that something is infinite—that is, what it means to those who claim to understand something by it—and what sort of thing it is of which we may sensibly ask whether it is infinite or not.

It is a striking fact that until the work of Bolzano and Cantor a clear and satisfactory answer had not been provided for these questions. The kind of explanation offered before them can be seen in the *Oxford English Dictionary*, which tells us that something is infinite if it has no limit or end, either real or assignable, or is boundless or unlimited or endless, or is immeasurably great in extent or duration or in another respect. The term is used chiefly, it says, of God and his attributes, but also of space and time; here the use passes into the mathematical. Of this, the dictionary says that a quantity is infinite if it has no limit or is greater than any assignable quantity and that a series is infinite if it can be indefinitely continued without ever coming to an end. Little of this is clear, and what is clear is from a modern point of view wrong. There are many things which are called finite or infinite which do not in any ordinary sense have or lack a limit or a bound or an end. And these phrases are themselves in need of explanation. (Even at the level of common sense, it is not quite clear what is promised as "unlimited hot water" or "unlimited credit.") Nor again are limits and bounds and ends the same thing. What has a limit in the mathematical sense is a sequence, but an infinite sequence may not have a limit. If a sequence has no end (no last term), it is infinite, but the converse is false. It was at one time held that space must be infinite, for if finite it has boundaries (these would be spatial boundaries), but then there would be space on both sides of them. But according to modern physics, space is finite but unbounded.

What according to the *Oxford English Dictionary* is primarily infinite is a quantity. The words "quantity" and "amount" have a double use, like "length." A piece of cloth has a length but is itself sometimes called a length. In the same way, a quantity may be that which we assign, in answering a question of the form "How much . . . ?," but it may be that to which we assign it. Now it is a quite intelligible suggestion that there are things which exist in infinite quantity, for example, that there is infinitely much gold in the universe. But the account suggested of what this means is absurd; a quantity cannot be greater than it is, and surely in saying that there was infinitely much gold we would be assigning a quantity to the gold.

Explanations such as these were criticized by Bolzano in *The Paradoxes of the Infinite* (1851). He also pointed out that the idea of a number is logically prior to that of a quantity. There is infinitely much gold if and only if there are infinitely many ounces of gold (or whatever unit we choose). And one would now say that it is in connection with numbers and classes that the notion of infinity has its primary application. This conception we must now explain.

NUMBERS, CLASSES, AND INFINITE CLASSES

Two classes are said to be equivalent when the members of the one can be paired off with those of the other in such a way that each member of either is paired with just one of the other (formally, when there is a one-to-one mapping from one class to the other). Intuitively, then, two equivalent classes "have the same number of members"; although in explaining what equivalence means we need not appeal to the idea of number at all. Cardinal numbers (those which occur as answers to questions of the form "How many . . . ?") are determined by families of classes with the property that any two classes in the family are equivalent. A "How many?" question is one that asks for the cardinality of some class, its cardinality being that property which it shares with all classes equivalent to it. (Some writers say that a cardinal number *is* a family of classes all

of which are equivalent, but we do not *have* to say that; what is important is the logical connection of the idea of number with that of equivalence of classes.)

One merit of this account of cardinal numbers is that it leaves entirely open the question whether a number can be infinite. The answer will be affirmative if there are classes with infinitely many members. But what does it mean to say that a class has infinitely many members? There are two approaches to this question, one Bolzano's and one Dedekind's. Let us take Bolzano's first.

Bolzano and Dedekind. Let A be some nonempty class, and let $A_1, A_2, \cdots$ be a sequence of classes determined as follows: A_1 contains some arbitrarily selected member of A, and each later class contains everything in its predecessor together with some new thing chosen from A. Now this sequence may terminate because some class A_k contains all the members of A so that a successor for it cannot be constructed. Then A is called finite. In the other case, that in which every class in the sequence has a successor, A is called infinite. The intuitive idea is that a class is infinite when it is not exhausted by any of its finite subclasses. In an alternative formulation (following Bertrand Russell), we can explain the idea of an inductive class by specifying that a class with no members is inductive; then, if B is an inductive class and if there is a class C and a thing x such that everything in C either is in B or is identical with x, then C is also an inductive class. Then we can say that a number is inductive if it is the number of some inductive class and that a number is infinite if and only if it is not inductive.

To the question whether there are classes that are infinite in this sense, Bolzano replied yes: the class of all propositions. In a similar vein, Dedekind said that the class of all possible objects of thought is infinite (if x is a possible object of thought, then the thought of x is so, too, and is distinct from x). Such constructions have an air of artificiality, but we need not stop to consider them, for an obvious example of infinite class is that of the inductive numbers. If we agree to start counting at 0, then each number is the number of those less than itself, and if every number has a successor, no number in the class can be the number of the class. If we wish to say that every class has a number (a cardinality), we must say that there is at least one infinite number, the number of the class of inductive numbers and of any class equivalent to it.

Cantor, who did wish to say that every class has a cardinality, gave the name $\aleph_0$ to this number (Hebrew aleph; the subscript means that $\aleph_0$ is the smallest "transfinite number," as Cantor called them).

The reason why this step was not taken earlier lies in the so-called paradox of Galileo. (It is not now thought a paradox, and it was known to the scholastic philosophers.) Galileo noticed that each number has a double and that each even number is the double of just one number:

$$1, \quad 2, \quad 3, \quad \cdots, \quad n, \quad \cdots$$
$$2, \quad 4, \quad 6, \quad \cdots, \quad 2n, \quad \cdots$$

so that by the criterion of equivalence mentioned before, there are just as many numbers as there are even numbers. But, one is inclined to say, there are "more" numbers than even numbers (indeed, "twice as many"). Galileo (and Leibniz after him) concluded that there could not be infinite numbers. The difficulty is real enough. If we (1) adhere to the equivalence criterion for having the same number, and also (2) allow that if A and B are classes, and B contains everything in A and some things not in A, then the number of B is greater than that of A, we cannot assign a number uniquely to the class of inductive numbers. (If we reiterate Galileo's construction, mapping the even numbers onto those divisible by 4, and then these onto those divisible by 8, and so on, we get an infinite sequence of classes, each of which after the first is a proper subclass of its predecessor, but any two of which are equivalent.)

The solution of the difficulty lies in giving up the general assumption that if A is a proper subclass of B, the number of things in B is greater than the number of things in A. This assumption together with the mapping $n \rightarrow 2n$, the equivalence criterion for sameness of number, and the assumption that every class has just one number, form an inconsistent quadruple. Something had to go, and it was the first assumption that went. We are consoled at its loss by the reflection that it really does hold for finite classes. A class which is equivalent with one of its own proper subclasses is called *reflexive*. Dedekind suggested that "infinite class" be defined to mean reflexive class; this is the second approach of those mentioned before. It is easily seen that an inductive class cannot be reflexive, so that all reflexive classes are infinite in the Bolzano–Cantor sense. (To prove the converse—in effect, that every class is either inductive or reflexive—we have to make certain assumptions about what classes there are.) Returning to the infinite amount of gold, we now see that if there are infinitely many ounces of it, there are also infinitely many tons and infinitely many thousands of tons. This may (conceivably) be a reason for doubting that there is infinitely much gold, but it does not seem to be one for doubting the correctness of the analysis of the proposition that there is.

It was, we may suppose, always obvious enough that if one were asked "How many numbers are there?" and were unwilling to reject the question as improper, one would have to answer "Infinitely many; there is an infinite number of them." But the importance of Cantor's work lies not at all in the fact that he gave a name to that number. Indeed, there would be no point in giving it a name unless there were propositions about it to to be asserted. What Cantor did was to lay the foundations for the arithmetic of transfinite cardinals.

Cantor's theory of transfinite numbers. Cantor showed that it is possible to extend the arithmetical operations of addition, multiplication, and exponentiation and the relation *greater than* to infinite numbers, and indeed in a very satisfactory and natural way. We then have such results as that $\aleph_0 + k = \aleph_0$ (for any finite number k), that $\aleph_0 \cdot k = \aleph_0 k$, and even that $\aleph_0^k = \aleph_0$. However, Cantor was able to show that $2^{\aleph_0}$ is *greater* than $\aleph_0$. The former of these numbers is the number of all functions whose domain is a class having $\aleph_0$ members and whose range is a class having just two members. It is thus readily seen also to be the number of all subclasses of the class of all finite numbers. Suppose, Cantor said, that there are only as many such classes as there are finite numbers. Then there would be a one-to-one

mapping from the classes onto the numbers. Thus, there would be a class x of all numbers which did not belong to their associated class, and, under the hypothesis, that class x would be associated with a unique number. But the class x contains that associated number if and only if it does not, which is a contradiction. We conclude that that number $2^{\aleph_0}$ is not the same as $\aleph_0$ and, since it plainly cannot be smaller, that it is greater. The same argument will show that $2^{2^{\aleph_0}}$ is greater than $2^{\aleph_0}$ and hence that there are infinite numbers greater than $\aleph_0$ and indeed infinitely many such.

Actually, Cantor had another proof that there are infinite numbers greater than $\aleph_0$. To understand it we must turn to Cantor's introduction of transfinite ordinal numbers.

A class is said to be simply (or totally) ordered by a relation if that relation—for example, *precedes*—is transitive, irreflexive, and antisymmetric. It is well ordered by a relation if that relation simply orders it and if, further, for every nonempty subclass there is a member which "precedes" all the other members of the subclass. A class that is well ordered by some relation we shall call a sequence. The inductive numbers in their usual order are a sequence. So are the expressions $a, ab, abb, \cdots$. Two sequences are called *similar* if there is a one-to-one mapping that preserves order. This means that if a goes into a' and b into b', then a precedes b in the one sequence when and only when a' precedes b' in the other. Now, ordinal numbers arise by abstraction from families of similar sequences (ordinals are to sequences and to similarity as cardinals are to classes and to equivalence). Roughly, an ordinal is the measure of the length of a sequence. Finite ordinals turn out to have just the same properties as do finite cardinals, but transfinite ordinals are more interesting. The simplest kind of infinite sequence is that exemplified above; there is a first term, each term has a successor, and every term has finitely many terms before it. The ordinal of this sequence is the smallest transfinite ordinal, and Cantor called it ω (Greek letter omega). Suppose we now reorder the finite ordinals so that 1 comes last: $2, 3, 4, \cdots, 1$. The part of the sequence that comes before 1 is similar to an ω-sequence, because of the mapping $n \rightarrow n + 1$, so that the result is an ω-sequence and a unit sequence end to end. This sequence determines the ordinal $\omega + 1$. The sequence $1, 3, 5, \cdots, 2, 4, 6, \cdots$ has ordinal 2ω, and higher ordinals can be constructed. We may notice that the sequence of all ordinals less than a given ordinal α is itself a sequence having α as its ordinal; thus, the last-mentioned sequence is similar to $1, 2, 3, \cdots, \omega, \omega + 1, \omega + 2, \cdots$.

The ordinal numbers determined by well orderings of the finite numbers Cantor called the second number class (the finite numbers make up the first), and he was able to show that the number of this class is greater than $\aleph_0$. He therefore called it $\aleph_1$. The number $\aleph_1$ determines the third number class of ordinals, and the cardinal of that class is $\aleph_2$. Cantor claimed that there is a least cardinal greater than all of $\aleph_0, \aleph_1, \cdots$, which he called $\aleph_\omega$, and thus a new sequence is generated. In the full theory every ordinal appears as a subscript to some cardinal. There is no greatest cardinal and no greatest ordinal; given Cantor's assumptions, the supposition of either leads at once to a contradiction.

Much of Cantor's theory is now almost universally accepted. There are philosophers who still ask whether there really are infinite numbers, or (a very slight improvement) whether what are called infinite numbers deserve to be called numbers, are numbers in the full, complete, and proper sense of that word. Such questions do not seem very profitable or interesting. As a mere fact of anthropology (but nonetheless interesting for that), one may mention that it is now virtually impossible to instill a general skepticism about infinite numbers among freshmen in philosophy or mathematics who have had a good high-school education. To be struck by the fact that infinite numbers have a different arithmetic from finite numbers is entirely natural, but, as Cantor remarked, this is something one might have expected in the first place.

Actual and potential infinity. Cantor's theory has been called a theory of the actual infinite. He is said (by some philosophers, that is) to have thought of infinite classes as actual, spread out, completed. This reproach, if it is one, seems to cover a number of different things. The notion of an actual infinity is sometimes contrasted with that of a potential infinity, and some philosophers, notably Aristotle and Kant, seem to have allowed the latter idea but not the former. But is is not clear what this contrast, as it occurs in philosophy, comes to.

Aristotle wished to allow that space and time were infinite in extent and also infinitely divisible, but he denied that there could be infinite numbers or a body of infinite dimension. He said, therefore, that the infinite did exist, but in a certain sense potentially. A boy is potentially a man, in the sense that he will or may become a man, but nothing is potentially infinite in that way. But if there is something which comes round again in cycles, like winter or the Olympic games, then we have something potentially infinite. "The infinite exists when one thing can be taken after another endlessly, each thing taken being finite" (*Physics*, Bk. III, Ch. 6, 206a25–30). In the same vein Aristotle says that although mathematicians talk about infinite magnitudes they do not really need such things, but only finite ones, and that geometers do not really need infinite lines; a line never needs to be produced infinitely, but just as much as is required for a construction (*ibid.*, Ch. 7).

It is natural to try to elucidate this in terms of modalities. Let us think of dividing something into parts; we will think of it as homogeneous and forget about its finer physical structure. We bisect it, bisect one of the parts, and continue this indefinitely. The piece of stuff is potentially infinite "by way of division." It is clear that we must distinguish between saying (1) whatever finite number n you take, it is possible for the thing to have been divided into more than n parts, and (2) it is possible that the thing could have been divided into more than any finite number of parts. The second envisages the result of infinitely many acts of cutting; the first says only that however many acts of cutting have been done, we can do more. Clearly, this distinction must be made. But if this is the sort of distinction that stands behind the conception of the infinite as actual and the infinite as potential, it must also be said that it does not justify the rejection of actual infinities in the sense in which Cantor wanted them. This may be seen as follows: Suppose that in dividing our object we agree always to bisect a part

of minimal size. Consider the infinite sequence of rationals 1/2, 1/4, · · · (this sequence will occur again when we discuss Zeno's paradoxes). The infinite sequence is a mathematical representation of the continued (potentially infinite) operations of cutting, the rationals being the points at which in the idealized case the cuts are made. A workman might write down terms of this sequence from time to time to remind himself where his next cut was to be made. But the sequence is also a mathematical representation of what would result if all the infinitely many cuts were made or had been made, and indeed it could not be a representation of the one thing without being a representation of the other. Similarly, to say, as Aristotle did, that winter will *always* return is to say that infinitely many winters lie in the future. There will not, indeed, ever be a time at which it is true to say that infinitely many winters have elapsed between that time and now. But the sequence of winters to come is nonetheless infinite, and in just Cantor's sense.

It does not then seem correct to say that there are *here* two conceptions of infinity, one of it as actual and one of it as potential; nor, then, will it seem correct to say that Aristotle is rejecting the idea of the infinite-as-actual, if this idea is to have any relevance to Cantor's work and to the current mathematical conception. Rather, what Aristotle is rejecting (at least part of the time) is that there could be any physical exemplifications of a certain kind of the denumerably infinite. For example, there could not be any kind of physical thing of which there are now infinitely many, nor could there be any physical body that was infinite in size.

Previous to Cantor's work (and indeed even after it) mathematicians sometimes said that their work involved only the potentially infinite. But they were thinking of infinity only in connection with what they called (in the calculus) variables or "variable quantities," and the word "infinite" was said by them to stand for "the result of increasing a variable without limit." (Similarly, an infinitesimal was said to be "the result of diminishing a variable without limit" without allowing it to become zero.) What these writers called a variable was for the most part what we call a function, but they did not distinguish between the function and its values. The term "variable" is now reserved for letters—"x," "n," "α"—used in a certain way. There are variables in the sense of things that vary, for example, a man's weight. But this conception of a variable is in effect that of a function. The man weighs different amounts at different times, and, for each time while he has a body, his weight is uniquely determined at that time. If we suppose it possible that from some day onward the man weighs twice as much on each day as on the previous day, we have the case described as "increasing a variable without limit," but nothing is infinite except the class of values of the function, whereas the striking fact is that the function diverges. When satisfactory accounts are given of the notions of function, value, and so on, it becomes clear that the calculus did not need the notion of infinity at all.

Difficulties in Cantor's theory. We see, from the account given above, that there do not seem to be any philosophical objections to Cantor's theory. But there are two sets of problematic features about it that must be mentioned briefly here, although each requires a much more extended treatment.

The first set of problems are those of set theory in general. Earlier, we noted Cantor's proof that $2^{\aleph_0} > \aleph_0$ and that his method of proof is here quite general—every class has more subclasses than members. There cannot then be a class of greatest cardinality, or, therefore, a greatest cardinal. It may seem that the class of all classes, which contains as members all of its own subclasses, should have the greatest cardinal. If, however, we try to apply Cantor's method of proof to that class, we come upon Russell's contradiction about the class of all classes that are not members of themselves, and this is indeed how Russell came to discover it. A similar contradiction attends the notion of the class of all cardinal numbers.

Because of this it is sometimes said that Cantor's whole theory in infected with contradictions. This is quite extravagant. If we suppose that there is a class of all classes (or of all cardinal numbers), we find a contradiction. Cantor did not suppose that, nor is there any reason why one should suppose it. (If one asks why, if there is a class of all finite cardinals, there should not be a class of infinite cardinals, one forgets the obvious fact that the former class is bounded above and the latter would not be.) The relevance of the paradoxes is rather this: We cannot suppose in the face of them that to any statable condition on classes there corresponds a class, and we are thus forced to raise the question what classes there are or can consistently be said to be. But Cantor's whole construction depends on the assumption of class existence. Of the proofs that there is a transfinite cardinal greater than the smallest, one of them requires that there *be* a class containing all and only the classes of finite numbers, the other that there be a class of well orderings of the finite numbers. To make assumptions of this kind precise and to trace out their consequences is the task of axiomatic set theory (that is, class theory). Each of the systems of set theory currently known and studied guarantees the existence of very large classes of cardinals and ordinals but is capable of being strengthened so as to give more.

Another question concerns the axiom of choice, which allows us to suppose that any class can be well ordered (that is, that there is at least one well-ordered sequence having just the members of the class). This axiom (itself an assumption of class existence) is necessary for a rigorous proof that of any two cardinals one is greater than the other. But the axiom has for some mathematicians a certain lack of evidence. There is also a question whether $2^{\aleph_0}$ and $\aleph_1$ are the same number. The conjecture that they are was Cantor's continuum hypothesis. One would expect to be able to put $2^{\aleph_0}$ in its right place in the sequence of cardinals or at least to be able to think that it has a right place (that for some unique ordinal α, $2^{\aleph_0} = \aleph_\alpha$). However, in 1940 Kurt Gödel showed that the axiom of choice and the continuum hypothesis could not be disproved on the basis of "standard set theory" (the assumptions of class existence that are most readily acceptable) unless "standard set theory" is itself inconsistent. Quite recently Paul Cohen has shown that if "standard set theory" is consistent, then the continuum hypothesis cannot be proved on that basis either. Thus, it seems possible that there are genuinely alternative theories about what classes there are and hence genuinely alternative answers to some questions about infinite cardinals. (For a discussion of the continuum hypothesis, see CONTINUUM PROBLEM).

It should be mentioned, finally, that there are some problematic features of quantification (in the sense of predicate logic) over infinite classes. If X is a finite class and the question arises whether or not some object in X has some property P (the property being one of which we can decide whether a given object has it), then one would expect the question to be in principle answerable. If X is infinite, however, this may not be the case. (For further details, see the discussion of intuitionism in MATHEMATICS, FOUNDATIONS OF.)

ZENO'S PARADOXES

We have already suggested that at least some of the philosophical problems that have been raised about infinite classes and numbers are properly seen as questions about the applicability of the notion of infinity or about the conditions for applicability. This certainly seems to be true of the earliest philosophical discussions arising out of the so-called paradoxes of Zeno of Elea.

The Achilles and the Race Course. The best known of the paradoxes is the Achilles. Achilles and a tortoise are to race, and the tortoise is allowed a start. Zeno says that before overtaking the tortoise Achilles must get to the place where the tortoise started from—call it T_0. By the time he has gotten there the tortoise will have advanced to another point, T_1, and Achilles must now get to that point, and so on. The suggestion is that Achilles cannot overtake the tortoise, or, less dramatically, that there should be a difficulty about understanding how he does.

According to another paradox, the Dichotomy or Race Course, a man who is to go from A to B must first get to the midpoint of A and B, then to the midpoint of that point and B, and so on ad infinitum. If we think of him as moving along a line of unit length from 0 to 1, he must get to each of the points 1/2, 3/4, $\cdots$. Again, the suggestion is that this should seem impossible. It may be seen that this paradox and that of the Achilles are very much the same. By making suitable assumptions about the tortoise's start and about her speed and Achilles', we can make the points $T_0, T_1, \cdots$ coincide with 1/2, 3/4, $\cdots$, respectively, and the suggestion that Achilles cannot overtake the tortoise becomes the suggestion that he cannot get to 1.

But what is the difficulty in either case? Aristotle said, in effect, that if it is permissible to represent a distance to be traveled as the sum of an infinite number of distances, it should be permissible to represent the time allowed in the same way. (If an hour is allowed, there is half an hour to get to 1/2, three-quarters of an hour to get to 3/4, and so on.) There is then no question of having to run "an infinite distance" in a finite time. But this does not really seem to be the difficulty, nor, apparently, did Aristotle think it was. The difficulty is rather one that arises from the thought that to get from 0 to 1, to perform one task, the runner must perform all of an infinite sequence of tasks. In a way the suggestion that he must perform an infinite number of tasks seems hard to disallow, since he must occupy all the points $1/2, 3/4, \cdots$ (let us call them Z-points) before arriving at 1. But if we do allow it, there is an inclination to say that he is required to do the impossible—at least, some people feel such an inclination: "However many terms of an infinite sequence are taken, others remain, so that to speak of an infinite sequence being completed is a contradiction in terms." We are thus faced with a dilemma.

Infinite sequence of tasks. Let us consider the first horn of the dilemma, that the runner must do infinitely many things. It is plain that to get from 0 to 1 he must pass over every point between 0 and 1 and so must pass over all the points in Z. (One could here raise the question in what sense these points really exist, but let us for the moment leave it.) For just the same reason, he must pass over all the points $1/4, 5/8, 13/16, \cdots$ and all the points $9/10, 99/100, \cdots$. Indeed, we can specify an infinite class of points over which he must pass in infinitely many distinct ways, and among these the class Z is not specially distinguished. However, we are now conceding that the runner must pass over all the Z-points, and the question is why there should be a difficulty in the thought that he can. Let us say that a class of points is "suitable" if it can stand in for Z in a statement of the paradox with the result that the paradox continues to present the same difficulty. It seems that not every infinite class of points between 0 and 1 is "suitable" in that sense. For example, it will not be thought puzzling in the same way if we remark that the runner must pass over all the points between 0 and 1, nor if we say that he must pass over all the points $n/2^m$ ($1/2, 1/4, 3/4, 1/8, \cdots$). Let us take it, then, that a suitable class is one that is *discrete*, in the sense that every point is next to some other point, with none intervening. But this is not enough for a class to be suitable. Consider the discrete class $\cdots, 1/8, 1/4, 1/2, 1$; this class would raise a puzzle about how the runner gets started, so let us say that it is not suitable and draw the conclusion that in a suitable class each point has on its left only finitely many other points in the class (taking the line to have 0 on the left and 1 on the right). Finally, the class $1/4, 5/8, 7/16, \cdots$ is not suitable. For it would raise the difficulty that the runner cannot even get to the half-way point. Of course that difficulty should arise, too, but it is not the same difficulty, and Zeno allows, if only for the sake of argument, that he can get to the half-way mark. A suitable class must then have points arbitrarily close to 1.

If, then, there is a difficulty here, it does not arise simply because the runner must pass over all of an infinite number of points but rather has something to do with the ordinal structure of that class of points. This is obviously true, for it must be possible for someone who proposes the paradox to say that the runner must first do this, then do that, then do the other thing, and so on. But now it is not suggested that there is any of these things that he cannot do. For each finite number n, it is allowed that he can get to the nth point. Each of the Z-points is, we may put it, *unproblematic*, and then each of the points on the line that is to the left of a Z-point is unproblematic, too. What is not allowed to be unproblematic is the point 1. It must be, then, that the difficulty lies in thinking that the runner is somehow confined to the unproblematic points. But if this is the difficulty,

it can be dispelled. The paradox says that to get to 1 the man must pass over all the Z-points. This is indeed necessary, but it is also sufficient. There is no question of his having to pass over all the Z-points and then do something else. It is not even true that he must pass over all the Z-points and then finish. For it is plainly impossible for him to have passed over all the Z-points without having passed over 1. To pass over all the Z-points and to get to 1 are the same thing.

This is, then, the solution of the problem, and it depends only on following out the consequences of those facts that seem to create the problem. Essentially, we have points on a line with the properties that (a) there are infinitely many of them, (b) they are all contained in some finite interval, and (c) each point has only finitely many points on its left. Something has to cross all these points. If the points were not bounded by a finite interval, it really would be impossible to have passed over all of them. But since they are so bounded, there must be a limit point of the class, and, because of (c), this cannot be in the class; and it has the property that to have occupied it and to have occupied all the original points are identical. And in this way the suggestion that to do one thing you must do infinitely many is seen after all to be innocuous.

Completing an infinite sequence. If we turn now to the other horn of the dilemma, the claim that an infinite sequence cannot be completed, we see that it begs the question. It is simply not true that however many of an infinite sequence we take, others remain, but only that whatever finite numbers be taken, others remain. What causes trouble is doubtless that (in the kind of sequence we are talking of) there is no last term, so that one does not see what finishing consists in in such a case. But, in the context of the Race Course anyway, this trouble is illusory; finishing consists in occupying the limit point of the class, and we may suppose that *this is* the last point occupied. (The sequence of points occupied has length $\omega + 1$.)

It is natural at this point to ask whether it is possible to complete an infinite sequence of tasks of some more strenuous kind. Thus, Russell has suggested that it is only "medically impossible" for a man to (for example) call out all the finite numbers, provided that he takes only half the time for each as for its predecessor. There does not seem to be any clear answer to this type of problem. To clarify, suppose we have a physical system S which at each moment is in one of two states, say A and B. We will adopt the convention that when S changes state there is a first moment of the later state. Is it conceivable—apart from the physics of the thing—that S should have changed state indefinitely often in some finite time interval? The difficulty, if there is one, arises about the earliest moment after all the infinitely many changes have been completed. For we naturally think that if S is in one of its states at some time t, either it went into that state at some earlier time t' and remained in it through t or there was an interval bounded by t later in which it was in the other state. This will be false for the time mentioned, and we shall have to suppose that S can at some moment be beginning a period of a state without going into that state from the other state. The suggestion of an infinity of changes of state can then be ruled out if we adopt as an axiom that a period of one state is always preceded by a period of the other. But if someone says that it is a mere prejudice that this must be so, it is not clear what we can say in reply.

Infinite divisibility. Another curious reflection is the following. We have already adverted to the question of infinite divisibility. If we allow it possible that a man should perform all of an infinite sequence of tasks in a finite time, then we allow that something could have been divided into infinitely many distinct parts; there will be, say, a half-sized piece, a quarter-sized piece, ad infinitum. Let us call that a simple division and define a multiple division as follows: In stage 0 we divide something into two parts. At the beginning of stage $n + 1$ we have 2^n parts, and we divide each of them into two parts. After we have completed all the possible stages, what do we have? If we require a "part" to have some size, we do not have any parts. Yet each of these stages requires only finitely many cuts, and to have completed all the stages requires no more cuts than a simple division; if then we think it conceivable that a simple division have been completed, why is it not equally conceivable that a multiple division have been completed?

Kant's difficulty about completing an infinite sequence, as it occurs in his "Antinomies," is, of course, of a different character. If the world did not have a beginning in time (he said), then an infinite number of days would have had to elapse before now, which seems impossible. The difficulty here is not about cardinality but about ordinality. To say that the world did not begin is to say that for each finite n the world was already in existence n days ago. We should then be thinking of a sequence like an ω-sequence but with earlier and later reversed, one similar to $\cdots$, 4, 3, 2, 1. If the world did not begin, then today is, and every past day was, the last day of such a sequence, but none of these sequences had a first day. Any past day can be seen as the first day of a well-ordered sequence, but then this day will be represented in that sequence by a finite ordinal. It is almost as if Kant illicitly replaced the proposition that the world did not have a beginning with the proposition that it did have a beginning which is infinitely remote in time.

The Arrow. Zeno's paradox of the arrow is less interesting than the Achilles or the Race Course. He seems to have said that at any moment in its flight the arrow occupies a space equal to itself and to have concluded from this that at each moment it is motionless. We may take "occupies a space equal to itself" to mean "is just where it is." The argument, then, is that if at some moment a thing is where it is, it is not moving at that moment.

There is, of course, an ambiguity in the idea of "a moment." A moment may be a moment *in* time, something that could be mentioned in reply to the question "When?," and it may be a brief period of time, something whose duration could be mentioned in reply to the question "How long?" It is true that if a thing occupies the same position throughout some moment (period), then it does not move throughout that moment. Let us then take Zeno to have said that if *at* some moment a thing is where it is, it is motionless at that moment.

But why should one want to say that? It is true that from a photograph of a car together with the knowledge of when the photograph was taken one can sometimes tell where the car was at the time, but one cannot generally tell whether it was moving or stationary at that time. In the same way, if we try to imagine the arrow as it is at some moment, we may find ourselves imagining that it is stationary. It is true that motion is something that *takes* time. If a thing is to move from one place to another, some period of time must elapse while it does so. Therefore, it is only of some period of time that it makes sense to ask how much motion went on in that period, how far the thing moved. Yet it makes sense to ask, with respect to some moment in time, whether a given thing was in motion at that time.

Russell, who has discussed Zeno's puzzle on several occasions, has suggested that Zeno's argument refutes the idea of a *state* of motion. The argument shows that if there is such a state, then it is impossible for anything to be in it. If one supposes that for a thing to move it is necessary for it to be in a state of motion, then one will have to say that the argument does refute the possibility of motion. But this supposition (Russell suggests) is itself mistaken. Motion consists merely in the occupation of different places at different times. A thing is at rest throughout some period if it occupies the same place at all times within that period. It is at rest at a time if there is a period throughout which it is at rest and which contains that time not as an end point. And it is in motion at a time if it is not at rest at that time (we may ignore here a complication about times of "momentary rest"). The claim to distinguish between the idea of a thing's moving and its being in a state of motion may well seem wrong. But Russell's account of motion has the merit of making clear that the question whether something was in motion at some time cannot be answered by reference to that time alone but will have to depend for its answer on which places were occupied at other times.

The idea of motion as consisting merely in the occupation of different places at different times seems at first to leave something out. But this may be simply because we are liable to have a wrong notion about the ordinal structure of the places that are occupied when something moves. We must not, for example, think of them as successive or as occupied successively. If the thing occupies such and such a place at such and such a time, there is not a next place that it occupies at a next time. It seems very probable that historically this was the root of the difficulty. The question whether time and space were infinitely divisible was connected with the question whether a line should be thought of as composed of, made up of, points. According to modern conceptions, a line *is* a collection of points—although not every collection of points is a line. We must here refer again to Cantor. Cantor gave necessary and sufficient conditions for a collection of points to constitute a continuum. It turns out that what is important is not so much the number of points in the collection (their cardinality) as the ordering relation in which they stand to each other. One necessary condition is that they be densely ordered, in the sense that between any two there is another and hence between any two an infinity of others. When this is realized, an account of motion like Russell's is less repugnant to our intuitions about the continuity of motion.

We have not attempted here to do more than mention some of the questions about infinity that have been raised by philosophers. But the main conclusion seems to be that some of these questions can now be regarded as definitively settled. Thus, there is no longer any reason to deny that, or even to ask whether, there are infinite numbers and classes. There remain questions and problems about infinite numbers and classes, and some of these may well have important implications for philosophical discussion about mathematical truth and existence. There are also questions about quantification over infinite classes. For the rest, questions that are raised about the concept of infinity seem to be best regarded as questions about its application. Philosophers who maintain that philosophical questions are never settled should perhaps consider the history of this concept.

Bibliography

GENERAL DISCUSSIONS

Aquinas, Thomas, *Summa Theologica.* I, ii, 3; I, vii, 4; I, xlvi, 2 and 7.
Aristotle, *Physics.* Bks. III and VI.
Descartes, René, *Meditations on First Philosophy.* Meditation III.
Descartes, René, *Principles of Philosophy.* Principles XXVI and XXVII.
Hume, David, *Treatise of Human Nature.* Pt. II.
Leibniz, G. W. von, *New Essays Concerning Human Understanding.* II, 27.
Locke, John, *Essay Concerning Human Understanding.* Bk. II, Ch. 17.
Spinoza, Benedict, *Ethics.* Def. 6, Props. 8, 11, 13, 21–23.

NUMBERS, CLASSES, AND INFINITE CLASSES

Bolzano, Bernard, *Paradoxien des Unendlichen,* F. Prihonsky, ed. Leipzig, 1851. Translated by D. A. Steele as *The Paradoxes of the Infinite.* London, 1951.
Cantor, Georg, "Beiträge zur Begründung der transfiniten Mengenlehre." *Mathematische Annalen,* Vol. 46 (1895), 481–512, Vol. 49 (1897), 207–248. Translated with an introduction by P. E. B. Jourdain as *Contributions to the Founding of the Theory of Transfinite Numbers.* Chicago, 1915.
Cohen, Paul, "The Independence of the Continuum Hypothesis," Pts. I and II. *Proceedings of the National Academy of Sciences,* Vol. 50 (1963), 1143–1148, Vol. 51 (1964), 105–110.
Dedekind, Richard, *Stetigkeit und irrationale Zahlen.* Braunschweig, 1872.
Dedekind, Richard, *Was sind und was sollen die Zahlen?* Braunschweig, 1888. Both Dedekind works translated by W. W. Beman in *Essays on the Theory of Numbers.* Chicago, 1901; New York, 1963.
Gödel, Kurt, *The Consistency of the Axiom of Choice and the Generalized Continuum-hypothesis With the Axioms of Set Theory.* Princeton, N.J., 1940.

ON ZENO'S PARADOXES

Black, Max, *Problems of Analysis.* Ithaca, N.Y., 1954.
Grünbaum, Adolf, *Philosophical Problems of Space and Time.* New York, 1963.
Owen, G. E. L., "Zeno and the Mathematicians." *PAS,* Vol. 58 (1957–1958), 199–222.
Russell, Bertrand, *Principles of Mathematics.* London, 1903.
Russell, Bertrand, *Our Knowledge of the External World.* London, 1914.
Russell, Bertrand, *A History of Western Philosophy.* New York, 1945. Pp. 804–806.
Russell, Bertrand, "Mathematics and the Metaphysicians," in James R. Newman, ed., *The World of Mathematics,* 4 vols. New York, 1956. Vol. III, pp. 1574–1596.
Ryle, Gilbert, *Dilemmas.* Cambridge, 1954.
(For additional literature on Zeno's paradoxes, see the bibliography to ZENO OF ELEA.)

JAMES THOMSON

INFINITY IN THEOLOGY AND METAPHYSICS. It would be profitless (even if it were possible) to catalogue every nuance that the word "infinity" possesses in minor, as well as major, thinkers. Fortunately, the dominant strands are clear. Among these the theistic one is the most important both historically and in terms of contemporary debate.

GREEK PHILOSOPHY

Anaximander. The first Western philosopher to speculate on infinity was the pre-Socratic Anaximander. By the infinite (*to apeiron*) he meant a limitless substance from which the limited things that constitute the world have come. This substance is limitless in three respects: it is eternal, not having a beginning or an end; it is inexhaustible; and it lacks internal boundaries and distinctions. But it is not spatially unlimited, for Anaximander (almost certainly) conceived it as a sphere. Also, it is not qualitatively indeterminate, like Aristotle's unformed matter, for it contains nature's basic elements in a fused, nonseparated state.

Pythagoras. The Pythagoreans adopted Anaximander's concept. Some of them identified it with air (which Anaximenes considered to be the basic constituent of the universe). But their main contribution was to posit a limit (*peras*) as a principle that gives structure to the limitless or infinite. This limit was mathematical; the limitless once limited gives the point, twice limited the line, thrice limited the plane, and four times limited the solid. Later writers interpreted Pythagoras theologically. Thus in the *Placita* we are told that he believed in two principles—the monad (God, the Good, the essential nature of the One, *Nous* alone and by itself) and the indefinite dyad (or evil, which is bound up with materiality and multitude).

Plato. Plato's speculations on infinity are contained in his *Philebus.* He gives a fourfold classification of "all that now exists in the universe." The whole world can be viewed in terms of the unlimited, limit, mixture, and the cause of the mixture. This theory is an application of the axiom that the nature (and therefore the good) of anything consists in an intelligible order or proportion. The cosmic cause mixes limit with the unlimited and so imposes structure on the world. In 15D–17A Plato interprets the *peras–apeiron* contrast logically. The unlimited stands for particulars, and the limited for the species into which they can be put. But in 23C–26D the contrast has an ontological significance of a Pythagorean kind. The limitless consists in a collection of opposites (for example, hot and cold, dry and moist). Limit consists in "all that puts an end to the conflict of opposites with one another, making them well proportioned and harmonious by the introduction of number" (25E). This principle of limitation is essential also in the moral realm. Plato affirms that human pleasures (which, in themselves, tend to unlimited excess) ought to be rationally controlled by a law and order that are marked by limit.

Thus, in classical Greek philosophy infinity represents a substratum which is formless, characterless, indeterminate. It is a pejorative word. An entity is good to the extent that it is limited by form. The Pythagoreans indentified this form with numerical ratios. But, as the *Philebus* shows, it can be nonnumerical (such as a universal essence or the personal activity of reason).

An important fact emerges from this survey. Plato could not envisage God (or the divine) as infinite. If God is perfect, he must represent the principle of limit. The cause of cosmic mixture in the *Philebus* is equivalent to the Demiurge in the *Timaeus*. The latter's task is to impose intelligible form on pre-existent matter and thereby make an ordered whole. Otherwise the world would be a vast *apeiron*—a formless, unintelligible chaos. Hence, to say that he is *apeiros*, or that the Forms which he copies are *apeira*, would have seemed self-contradictory.

Plotinus. Plotinus occupies a place between Plato and Christian theologians who, if they are orthodox, regard infinity as the first among God's attributes. Plotinus applied the concept of the infinite, or unbounded (*apeiron* or *aoriston*), to two categories of being. First, he applied it to matter, which is evil because it tends intrinsically to formlessness. In this he developed philosophical tradition. But second, he applied it to the divine hypostaseis. Thus, he called Mind infinite because of its endless power, its complete unity, and its self-sufficiency. Yet while he says that the One is formless, he does not say that it is infinite. The history of *apeiron* prevented him from predicating it of the Absolute. He expressed the infinite nature of the One by denying that any positive idea abstracted from finite experience is applicable to it.

MEDIEVAL AND MODERN PHILOSOPHY AND THEOLOGY

Throughout the postclassical period of Western thought it has been widely assumed that God, or the Absolute, is infinite, or limitless. The division lies between those philosophers (such as Bruno, Spinoza, and Hegel) who interpret God pantheistically and those (especially Christian theists) who hold that he wholly transcends the world. According to the first group of thinkers, the world, being divine, is also infinite (even if particular things and persons reflect its infinity in limited degrees). According to the second group, the whole world is finite (as created), and only God (as the Creator) is infinite.

Pantheism. The clearest example of the pantheistic group is Spinoza. Having posited one substance (God or nature), he affirmed that it must be infinite both in its essence and in the number of its attributes. God must be infinite in his essence because if he were finite, we could suppose the existence of something else by which he is limited, so that he would not be the sole reality. His attributes must be infinite because if his essence is infinite, there must be an infinite number of ways in which it can be conceived.

Hegel's theory is more dynamic and complex. It was based on the conviction that finite and infinite are correlative terms within a single system of thought and reality. The Absolute Spirit (God) is infinite. But it does not exist outside the finite spirits through whom it manifests itself. Since the world is the manifestation of the Absolute, and since the Absolute requires the world for its development, we can predicate infinity either of the Absolute (considered as an identity-in-differences) or of the world (considered as a rational totality). Hegel considered Christianity to be the highest form of religion because it represents a perfect reconciliation between man and God, the finite and the infinite.

Any theory which views the finite as, in some sense, the self-expression of the infinite is exposed to two basic objections.

(1) The world (so the theist claims) is not limitless. It is limited in two main ways. First, it is morally imperfect. The premise of Kant's moral argument for immortality is irrefutable. We cannot in this life bring our wills into complete accordance with the moral law, and even if we could do so, the spatiotemporal order could not fulfill our deepest longings (as A. E. Taylor argued in his Gifford lectures). Second (and this is the core of theism), the world in all its aspects bears the marks of radical contingency, so that its existence cannot be explained unless we suppose it to be derived from a transcendent being who is infinite or absolute.

(2) In any case, the world is full of differences and discordances. How can these be reconciled within a unitary Absolute? How can a set of finite (that is, limited and mutually exclusive) entities constitute a nonlimited and all-inclusive whole? In particular, how can this whole, if it is complete and perfect (as it must be if it is infinite), contain within itself both good and evil? There is no satisfactory answer to these questions. Nicholas of Cusa, in his pantheistic moments, affirmed that in God there is a "synthesis of opposites" (*coincidentia oppositorum*). Similarly, Schelling affirmed that the Absolute is a self-identity in which all differences vanish. But these affirmations are metaphysically vacuous, as Nicholas admitted when, using mystical terminology to conceal a contradiction, he called our knowledge of the all-inclusive Maximum a *docta ignorantia*.

Theism. Theists do not have to face the above problems. Certainly they hold that all perfections pre-exist in God eminently. But they also hold that the mode of this existence is determined by the infinity which God does not share with any creature. God's infinity means that he is "not-finite." He is free from the limitations which affect every other being. There are two fundamental limitations.

First, every other being is a mode of existence (or existing). A man exists in one way, a dog in another. But God is existence *simpliciter*. He does not suffer from the determinations which are reflected in genera and species. We can express this (with deliberate paradox) by saying that he is his own genus.

Second, if God is existence "in itself," he must be self-existent in the sense that he does not derive his being from any other source. Every other being is dependent or derived. It does not contain within itself the cause of its existence. It depends continuously on the creative act of God who alone exists *a se* (that is, by his own intrinsic power).

Both these aspects of God's infinity are affirmed by the scholastic dictum that in him essence and existence are identical. The finitude of any being consists in the lack of this identity at both the points mentioned above. Its essence limits its existential act (or pattern of activity), and this limitation follows from its dependent character. It exists as "this" or "that" by its derivation from a being who is existence in a necessary and perfect form.

This view of God's infinity must be safeguarded by the following assertions.

(1) God's infinity is not to be interpreted as formlessness (as if it were equivalent to Plato's *apeiron*). It is the nature of finite being (at any rate in the subangelic realm) to be a *compositum* of form and matter. The form limits matter. Without some degree of limitation there would be no difference (either generically or individually) between one finite being and another. But since God's essence and existence are identical, his form cannot be a principle of limitation. "Matter," Aquinas wrote, "is perfected and made definite by form. Infiniteness attributable to matter is imperfect and amorphous. On the other hand, form as such is not perfected by matter, but contracted rather; hence infiniteness attributable to form is perfection" (*Summa Theologica* I, 7, 1).

(2) God's infinity is incomprehensible. We cannot imagine or conceive it. We can know *that* God is self-existent. But *how* he is self-existent is utterly unknowable by us in our present state. As soon as we try to represent his infinity through a univocal use of concepts, we commit three errors. We fall into anthropomorphism; we confuse infinity with formlessness; and, finally, we reach a self-contradiction, for the essence of a finite entity (however high it may be on the scale of being) is to possess a form which acts as a limit that excludes other forms.

However, the various attributes that constitute God's character are all deducible from his self-existence. He must be absolutely simple, for if in him essence and existence are identical, his qualities must be coinherent through the whole range of his activity. He must be spiritual and nontemporal, for corporeality entails spatial limitation and temporal successiveness implies divisibility. He must be omniscient and omnipotent, for there cannot be any externally imposed limit to his knowledge or his power. Finally, he must be absolutely good.

Two of these characteristics, spirituality and eternity, call for comment. Since God is nonspatial and nontemporal, the concept of his infinity is unaffected by the views we hold concerning space and time. Whether space and time are limited or unlimited makes no difference to the claims of the theist concerning God's infinity and his relation to the world. Thus, even if the world has existed for an endless length of time, it would still (according to the Cosmological Argument) be endlessly incomplete, so that we should still have grounds for positing a nontemporal act of divine creativity.

Yet the theistic view of God's infinity raises problems of its own. Four are especially urgent. First, if God is infinite and we are finite, how can we speak of him positively (as the Biblical writers and doctrinal theologians do)? Second, Christians affirm that God is personal. But does not the idea of personality conflict with the idea of infinity? (This objection was first urged by Carneades and later elaborated by Hume.) Third, is it not contradictory to say that all God's attributes (for example, justice and mercy) can coexist in a limitless degree? Are not even theists forced to

posit a *coincidentia oppositorum* in the Godhead? Fourth, if God is infinite both in goodness and in power, how can we explain the presence of evil in the world?

The answers which theists normally give to these objections are as follows.

(1) While we cannot speak of God univocally, we can do so analogically. But in applying any analogue to God, we must distinguish between the manner of predication and the object signified. The only positive meaning which we can attach to a term we predicate of God is the one which it has when predicated of finite beings. Yet since God and the creature are ontologically related by an analogy of attribution, we can *affirm that* (although we cannot *know how*) the divine analogate possesses the analogue, according to the analogy of proportionality, in a manner appropriate to his infinite existence (see ANALOGY IN THEOLOGY).

(2) The basic answer to the second question is that we need not equate the essence, or norm, of personality with its human mode. On the contrary, the latter (according to the Bible) is a created image of an infinite archetype. The theist would claim that while we cannot *see how* God can be both infinite and personal, we can *understand that* an infinite existence, so far from being incompatible with personality, would represent it in its most perfect form. At any rate (so the theist would maintain), it is not contradictory to assert that individuality can exist without individuation and that God therefore can have a positive character without possessing characteristics of the kind which differentiate a member of one created genus from a member of another.

(3) If God's attributes were essentially incompatible, they could not be predicated of him infinitely and simultaneously without a logical contradiction which could be solved (as Nicholas and Schelling found) only by an *asylum ignorantiae*. But theists claim that any contradiction is only apparent. Everything depends on how we define our terms. Thus, if we take justice to mean retribution, it is bound to be incompatible with mercy, if both are infinitely conceived. But if we take it to mean the vindication of the moral order, mercy becomes (as St. Paul saw) the primary form of its expression.

(4) Most Christian theists would admit that the fact of evil seems to be incompatible with belief in a God who is infinite both in goodness and in power. But they would also claim that the apparent incompatibility disappears once we recognize first, that since God's power and goodness are inconceivable, his purposes are bound to be largely inscrutable and second, that in Christ he has shown that he not only can but also does bring the greatest good out of the greatest evil.

Bibliography

For literature on Anaximander, see F. M. Cornford, "Anaximander's System," in *Principium Sapientiae* (Cambridge, 1952), pp. 159–186. Plato's views in the *Philebus* are discussed by R. Hackforth in his commentary in *Plato's Examination of Pleasure* (Cambridge, 1945). A. H. Armstrong surveys Plotinus thoroughly in "Plotinus' Doctrine of the Infinite and Christian Thought," in *The Downside Review* (Winter 1954/1955), 47–58. The teaching of Aquinas on God's infinity (together with associated attributes) is collected by Thomas Gilby in his anthology *Philosophical Texts* (Oxford, 1956). Nicholas of Cusa, *De Docta Ignorantia*, is translated by G. Heron, with an introduction by D. J. B. Hawkins (London, 1954). Bruno's theory of infinity can be found in *On the Infinite Universe and Worlds*, which has been translated by D. W. Singer in *Giordano Bruno: His Life and Thought* (New York, 1950). A lucid summary of Hegel and Schelling (with ample references) is given by Frederick Copleston in *A History of Philosophy*, Vol. VII (London, 1963). For a discussion of infinity in traditional Christian theism (and the problems that it raises), see A. M. Farrer, *Finite and Infinite* (London, 1943), and E. L. Mascall, *Existence* and Analogy (London, 1949).

H. P. OWEN

INGARDEN, ROMAN, Polish phenomenologist, was born at Cracow in 1893. He studied philosophy under Kazimierz Twardowski at Lvov and under Edmund Husserl at Göttingen. At Göttingen he also studied mathematics under David Hilbert and psychology under G. E. Müller. Ingarden followed Husserl to Freiburg, where he received his Ph.D. in 1918 with the dissertation "Intuition und Intellekt bei Henri Bergson." The same year Ingarden returned to Poland, where he taught mathematics in high schools. After his habilitation in 1921 he was named *Privatdozent* in philosophy at the University of Lvov. During the German occupation Ingarden was basically preoccupied with writing "Controversy Over the Existence of the World"; universities in Poland were closed at that time. In 1945 he accepted the chair of philosophy at the Jagellonian University at Cracow. During the early 1950s the Polish government barred him from teaching philosophy because of his adherence to "idealism"; and during this period he translated Kant's *Critique of Pure Reason* into Polish. Ingarden regained his chair in 1956 and retired in 1963, but he continues to be philosophically active.

Ingarden was one of the ablest pupils of Husserl. He accepted Husserl's main analytical results and the phenomenological method, but he rejected Husserl's transcendental idealism, showing instead how phenomenology could lead to realism. Max Scheler, Jean Hering, and, in her earlier works, Hedwig Conrad Martius, also exerted some influence on Ingarden. Traces of Ingarden's ideas can be found in the work of Nicolai Hartmann, Herbert Spiegelberg, and Michel Dufrennes, as well as in that of such American aestheticians as René Wellek.

Ingarden's philosophy is a fusion of two traditions: the variety of German speculative metaphysics as represented by Franz Brentano and the restrained and painstaking Polish analytical philosophy. Ingarden has woven grand philosophical designs, but he has woven them with great care and clarity. He has opposed what he regards as the narrowness and one-sidedness of the analytical trend, and he was probably the first to argue (in 1934) that the logical positivist verification principle of meaning, since it is a metalanguage statement, is itself unverifiable; and since it is not analytic, it is therefore meaningless. Ingarden followed this criticism with many others, but he nevertheless acquired and used the skills and techniques of the analytical philosophers. His phenomenology is therefore marked by an intelligibility and clarity rare among metaphysicians and ontologists.

Aesthetics. Ingarden's earliest work was in epistemology, which he conceived of as an independent discipline able to show the certainty of its own conclusions. The center of his investigations later shifted to ontology, which he regarded as a science of pure possibilities. Ontology determines and describes these possibilities in order to provide us with conceptual apparatuses by which we can express various existential situations.

Ingarden has also done significant work in aesthetics. His fully elaborated and original theory of art is perhaps the best-known part of his philosophy. He arrived at this theory through the ontological investigations that were central to his thought, and the theory itself was a preparation for his realistic ontology. One of the possible ways of settling the controversy between idealism and realism is through examining the nature of objects that exist. There seems to be a necessary connection between a mode of being and its formal structure. Ingarden first attempted to investigate this problem through examining works of art, which, in contrast with spatiotemporal objects, are dependent for their existence on the conscious act of the creator but which nevertheless transcend this act and continue to exist in their material shape afterward. What makes them works of art is the intention of the creator to endow them with significance, and it requires another intentional act on the part of the receiver to decipher this significance expressed by physically perceptible signs. Thus, the work of art possesses many strata. In a literary work of art, for example, the following can be distinguished: (1) the visual or phonic stratum; (2) the stratum of the meanings of words and sentences; (3) the stratum of objects described; (4) the stratum of the appearances of these objects. All these strata are polyphonically orchestrated to compose one work of art. In a poem it is not the printed marks in the shape of letters, nor even the actual meanings of particular words, that matter; rather, it is the "poetic significance" achieved through these printed marks and through the meanings of particular words. The intentional act of the creator and another intentional act of the receiver are indispensable for the existence of the work of art. And because of this, works of art are called purely intentional objects.

Ontology. It is customary to link phenomenology with existentialism, as if Husserl, Heidegger, and Sartre were three links in the development of one trend and as if existentialism were an inevitable development of phenomenology. But the linking of phenomenology and existentialism in this manner blurs the fact that for Husserl phenomenology was primarily a cognitive philosophy, seeking to acquire knowledge, whereas for Sartre the main function of philosophy is consolatory, to explain the mystery of man and justify his tragic existence. Ingarden's philosophy is a continuation, development, and restatement of the cognitive core of Husserl's philosophy, and perhaps is closer to its cognitive spirit than any other development of Husserl's doctrine by his numerous pupils. Ingarden perhaps succeeded better than Husserl himself in making his phenomenological inquiries consistent and coherent. Husserl, as Ingarden observed, was entangled in a vicious circle of phenomenology: in order to conduct the phenomenological reductions which are to yield self-evident knowledge, Husserl had to assume that our consciousness is transcendental, whereas it is precisely through application of the phenomenological reductions that consciousness is revealed to be transcendental.

Ingarden attempted to break away from this circle by what he called eidetic analyses, the penetration of the nature of essences in an "objective" way, as opposed to the transcendental approach Husserl used in his later work. Ingarden's objective approach was to clear the ground for philosophy as an independent and self-sufficient discipline. He contended that any reconstruction of our knowledge must start from thorough analyses of the nature of the objects of our knowledge, both existing and possible. Ontology is basic to other philosophical endeavors because the manner of our cognizing is determined by the objects of cognition. It follows that there are as many types of immediate experience as there are types of objects and types of relationships occurring among objects.

Ingarden devoted his principal work, *Spór o Istnienie Świata* ("The Controversy Over the Existence of the World"), to the analysis of these various objects and rela-tionships. According to Ingarden, existence is not that which exists but that by means of which something exists. Not everything that can be distinguished in an object belongs to its attributes: existence is not an attribute of an object. Ingarden attempted to account for the specific role of existence in whatever is, by distinguishing between modes of being (*modus existentiae*) and existential moments (*momentum existentiale*). The real existence (reality) of something, the possibility of something, and the ideal existence of something are examples of modes of being (modes of existence). Nonexistence, however, is not a mode but the absence of any being. An existing object can never be experienced by us without its mode of being. In every mode of being we can distinguish existential moments. The existential moments are the elemental units of the modes and thus are the key to understanding them. Many different existential moments can be distinguished intuitively in each mode of being of something. What we grasp in the object is not existence as such, which is a certain universal idea, but particular existential moments.

Ingarden divided moments of being into mutually exclusive pairs. There are four basic pairs. The first pair comprises existential autonomy and existential heteronomy. "Something is self-existent (is existentially autonomous) if it has its existential foundation *in itself*. It has such a foundation if it is *immanently determined* in itself" (*Time and Modes of Being*, p. 43). Otherwise it is existentially heteronomous. "An object is *existentially original* if, in its essence, it cannot be produced by any other object" (*ibid.*, p. 52). If it can be so produced, it is existentially derivative. "An object is existentially separate if, *for its existence, it does not in its essence require the existence of any other object with which it would have to coexist, because of its essence, within the compass of one and the same whole*" (*ibid.*, p. 82). If it does require such another object, it is "inseparate." The fourth pair of existential moments are existential self-dependence and existential contingency. Existential contingency involves separate objects which, in spite of being separate, require for their existence some other existentially separate object. An existentially self-dependent object, which is also an existentially separate object, does not require such another object.

Ingarden discussed at length both time and causality. In the analysis of time he distinguished further pairs of existential moments, including actuality and nonactuality, persistence and fragility, fissuration and nonfissuration. His original interpretation of the causal relation arose out of his analysis of the moments of existential originality and existential derivation. For Ingarden a causal relation occurs between C and E if: (1) C and E are diverse; (2) C actually conditions E but E does not condition C in the same way; (3) both C and E are events or processes (as far as their form is concerned); (4) the occurrence of E is simultaneous with that of C; (5) both C and E are real (actual).

Modes of being consist of noncontradictory combinations of existential moments. Ingarden distinguished four basic modes, or regions, of being: absolute being, temporal (or real) being, ideal (or extratemporal) being, and purely intentional being. Absolute being is characterized by the existential moments of autonomy, originality, separateness, and self-dependence. The other modes have many subtypes, each of which is characterized by a number of existential moments.

Each of Ingarden's analyses of pairs of existential moments is a small monograph on traditional ontological problems usually rooted in Aristotle and scholastic philosophy. On one level they may appear to be analyses of language, as one linguistic philosopher has pointed out, but they are of a scope not generally undertaken by linguistic philosophers, and Ingarden regarded linguistic analysis as an inadequate tool for the systematic analysis of philosophical problems. The analyses contained in this work were to pave the way for the eventual solution of the controversy between idealism and realism over the nature of the world and our relation to it. They follow in many instances the spirit of Aristotle's analysis of categories, but to be fully comprehended they presuppose familiarity with medieval discussion of pure possibilities.

Works by Ingarden

EPISTEMOLOGY

"Über die Gefahr einer Petitio Principii in der Erkenntnistheorie." *Jahrbuch für Philosophie und phänomenologische Forschung*, Vol. 4 (1921), 545–568.

"Intuition und Intellect bei Henri Bergson." *Jahrbuch für Philosophie und phänomenologische Forschung*, Vol. 5 (1922), 286–461.

"Essentiale Fragen. Ein Beitrag zum Problem des Wesens." *Jahrbuch für Philosophie und phänomenologische Forschung*, Vol. 7 (1925), 125–304.

ONTOLOGY

Spór o Istnienie Świata ("The Controversy Over the Existence of the World"), 2 vols. Cracow, 1947–1948. Vol. I partially translated by Helen R. Michejda as *Time and Modes of Being*. Springfield, Ill., 1964. A German version appeared as *Der Streit um der Existenz der Welt*, 3 vols. Tübingen, 1964–1966. The third volume is not published in Polish.

AESTHETICS

Das literarische Kunstwerk. Eine Untersuchung aus dem Granzgebiet der Ontologie, Logik und Literaturwissenschaft. Halle, 1931.

O Poznawaniu Dzieła Literackiego ("On Comprehending the Work of Literature"). Lvov, 1937.

Studia z Estetyki ("Studies in Aesthetics"), 2 vols. Warsaw, 1957–1958.

"Prace Filozoficzne Romana Ingardena," in *Szkice Filozoficzne Romanowi Ingardenowi w Darze.* Warsaw, 1964. Lists 150 works by Ingarden written between 1915 and 1963.

Works on Ingarden

Gierulanka, D., and Polatowski, A., "Kirunki Badań Filozoficznych Romana Ingardena," in *Szkice Filozoficzne Romanowi Ingardenowi w Darze.* Warsaw, 1964.

Stepien, A., "O Filozofii Romana Ingardena." *Ruch Filozoficzny,* Vol. 22 (1963–1964), 153–159.

Tymieniecka, A. T., "Le Dessin de la philosophie de Roman Ingarden." *Revue de métaphysique et de morale,* Vol. 60 (1955), 32–57.

Tymieniecka, A. T., *Essence et existence: Étude à propos de la philosophie de Roman Ingarden et Nicolai Hartmann.* Paris, 1957.

Tymieniecka, A. T., and others, *For Roman Ingarden. Nine Essays in Phenomenology.* The Hague, 1959.

HENRYK SKOLIMOWSKI

INGE, WILLIAM RALPH (1860–1954), English ecclesiastic and religious thinker, was born at Crayke, Yorkshire. Educated at Eton and Cambridge, he was fellow of Hertford College, Oxford, from 1889 to 1905, vicar of All Saints Church, Knightsbridge, from 1905 to 1907, and professor at Cambridge from 1907 to 1911, when he was appointed dean of St. Paul's Cathedral, London. During his long tenure of this high office, he became one of the best-known Englishmen of his generation. He continued his lifelong studies in philosophy and mysticism, and his penetrating comments on the events of his time, especially on the foibles of contemporary civilization, earned him the sobriquet of "the gloomy dean." He retired in 1934 to Brightwell Manor, Berkshire, where he spent twenty years more of thought and activity before his death.

What provoked Inge's criticism of contemporary culture was its preoccupation with material progress; against this, he pleaded for an end to the separation of fact and value. He maintained that Plato taught an abiding truth when he instructed us to seek reality beyond what is present to the senses, and only a culture that is based on the invisible but eternal values of truth, beauty, and goodness is securely founded. These values are in turn grounded in God, the ultimate spiritual reality, so that Inge's plea was for a religious attitude toward life. The model for such an attitude is provided by the mystic, who penetrates the phenomena of the sensible world to the realm of values and whose soul ascends toward union with God. However, this advocacy of mysticism is not to be understood as escapism or as a denial of the reality of the world of the senses. Inge considered himself in some ways more of a realist than an idealist, and he insisted that any adequate philosophy must take account of the findings of the natural sciences. Mysticism, as he understood it, does not imply emotionalism or irrationalism. Mysticism is itself a kind of spiritual philosophy, a quest for knowledge of the real. If today there is a conflict between the rational and the religious approaches to reality, this is because modern rationalism has become too narrow in its understanding of reason. A genuine rationalism takes account of values as well as of facts; this is the kind of rationalism that flourished in the earlier tradition of Western philosophy, and such a broadly based rational philosophy conduces to the same results as the mystical insights of religion. Both lead, Inge claimed, to "perfect knowledge of the Perfect."

Inge steeped himself in the history of mystical and religious thought, but there was one particular school that seemed to him to approach his ideal of combining genuine rationalism with mystical insight and that therefore strongly attracted him: the Neoplatonism of Plotinus. Inge spoke of Plotinus in terms of almost exaggerated respect as not merely an intellectual teacher but also as a spiritual director, and he studied his philosophy not just as a historical phenomenon but also as the classic statement of the insights that have guided Western culture—and thus as a message for our time. Platonism, Christianity, and Western civilization, Inge believed, are inseparable and interdependent; and a restatement of the philosophy of Plotinus can provide an intellectual basis that, when combined with the spirit of Christianity, can lead to the rejuvenation of the West.

Works by Inge

Christian Mysticism. London, 1899. Given as the Bampton Lectures.

Faith and Its Psychology. London, 1909.

The Philosophy of Plotinus, 2 vols. London, 1918. Given as the Gifford Lectures.

Outspoken Essays, 2 series. London, 1919–1922.

Lay Thoughts of a Dean. London, 1926.

The Platonic Tradition in English Religious Thought. London, 1926.

Christian Ethics and Modern Problems. London, 1930.

God and the Astronomers. London, 1933.

Diary of a Dean. London, 1934.

Mysticism in Religion. London, 1947.

Works on Inge

Fox, Adam, *Dean Inge.* London, 1960.

Helm, Robert M., *The Gloomy Dean.* Winston-Salem, N.C., 1962.

JOHN MACQUARRIE

INGENIEROS, JOSÉ (1877–1925), Argentine positivist metaphysician and ethical philosopher. Ingenieros was born in Buenos Aires. He studied, successively, medicine, psychiatry, axiology, and metaphysics and held appointments on the faculties of medicine and of philosophy and letters in Buenos Aires; he also founded the *Revista de Filosofía.* Ingenieros lived for some years in Germany and Switzerland. He had great influence in Latin America, and some of his works were translated into several European languages.

In *Proposiciones relativas al porvenir de la filosofía* (Buenos Aires, 1918), Ingenieros set forth a prospectus for a metaphysics of the "inexperiential." By the "inexperiential" he did not mean a transcendent object but those parts of the natural world that the limitations of the senses and instruments exclude from present experience. He rejected the "classical" problems of the existence and nature of God, immortality, and freedom, finding them to be not so much meaningless as falsely stated under the influence of theological and ethical orthodoxy. The legitimate problems of metaphysics are those of metacosmology, metabiology, and metapsychology; in metabiology, for example, some legitimate problems are the origin of life, the possibility of life beyond this planet, and the final purpose of life. Because its objects lie beyond experience, metaphysics cannot achieve certainty. Its statements are hypotheses, which must be logically consistent and compatible with experience. Like the sciences, the metaphysics of the future will be antidogmatic, tentative and indefinitely perfectible, and impersonal in the sense that it will be the work of many collaborators.

The ethics of Ingenieros, discussed with visionary enthusiasm in *El hombre mediocre* (Madrid, 1913), is naturalistic, evolutionary, and deterministic. Values or ideals are hypotheses for the perfecting of human life. They arise out of experience, are formulated by the imagination, are tested in the evolutionary process, and are at once relative and a challenge to strenuous philosophy. They are created by exceptional men, or idealists, and are often thwarted, at best conserved, by the mass of mediocre men. For these reasons *El hombre mediocre* is critical of democracy, although it calls for equality under law while asserting an aristocracy of merit.

Works by Ingenieros

Obras completas, 24 vols. Buenos Aires, 1930–1940.
Psicología genética. Buenos Aires, 1911.
Hacia una moral sin dogmas. Buenos Aires, 1917.
La evolución de las ideas argentinas, 2 vols. Buenos Aires, 1918–1920.

Works on Ingenieros

Estrada, Juan Carlos Torchia, *La filosofía en la Argentina*. Washington, 1961. Ch. 9.

ARTHUR BERNDTSON

INNATE IDEAS. The theory of innate ideas, in any of its philosophically significant forms, claims that all morally right judgment or all science, or both, rest upon or consist in a knowledge a priori either of (*a*) universal principles governing reality or (*b*) objects transcending sensory experience. Representative of such universal principles are "From nothing, nothing comes" (*Ex nihilo, nihil fit*); "Equals added to equals give equals"; "It is wrong to murder." Illustrations of transcendent objects are Platonic Forms and God. Concomitantly, the theory attempts to explain the genesis and epistemological status of the conception of such principles and objects. For this purpose it introduces the notion of innate ideas.

Proponents of the theory of innate ideas (henceforth "innatists") would typically agree with empiricists that sensory experience consists of particulars. They would claim, however, that scientific knowledge is knowledge that holds good everywhere and at every time, that such knowledge in fact exists, and that the abstracting and compounding of sensory particulars in empiricist inductions cannot

possibly provide us with such knowledge, but at most only with opinion. Innatists would also maintain, in agreement with some empiricists, that the abstractions and compoundings of sensory particulars described by empiricism as the basis of conception cannot possibly provide us with the conception of such universal principles or transcendent objects as are referred to above. At the same time, innatists would typically disagree with those realists who claim that such conceptions and knowledge are attained through direct perceptions or intuitions of nonsensory reality, or if they did join the theory of innate ideas with a theory of such intuitions, as Plato seems to have done, they would hold that scientific knowledge, though it may conclude in such intuitions, does not commence with them. (To maintain that scientific knowledge commences with such intuitions would be to make the notion of innate ideas methodologically and epistemologically superfluous.) The notion of innate ideas rests, for its philosophical significance, on the assumption that knowledge of reality is not given directly—at least, not in its chronologically first premises—but through representations. Where reality is viewed as something distinct from sensory particulars, innatists are thus representative realists.

Since proponents of the theory of innate ideas deny that such conceptions of universal principles or of transcendent objects as are described above are derived either from sensory experience or from intuitions of nonsensory reality, they are left with the problem of explaining their genesis. This they solve by holding these conceptions to be innate or inborn—to be, in short, innate ideas. But in speaking of innate ideas, proponents of the theory seem to mean two things. By "idea" they sometimes mean an object of awareness, like a mental image. When speaking in this way, innatists must maintain that conceptions of universal principles or of transcendent objects are present in the mind from birth or even prior to it. Innatists then typically explain why children and savages do not seem to be cognizant of the principles or objects in question by holding that these conceptions or representations, though present in the mind, are obscured by the presence of other conceptions or ideas—in particular, sensory ideas or percepts—much as the sound of a flute might be present in the air but be inaudible because of other sounds or noises. Again, innatists sometimes mean by "idea" not an object of awareness but, rather, a disposition of the mind or reason to form a determinate conception under certain conditions or stimuli. In Descartes, for instance, whenever consciousness occurs, there also occurs the conception that something is conscious—namely, oneself—and this is innate in the dispositional sense.

An equally crucial problem for proponents of the theory of innate ideas is to explain the epistemological status of innate conceptions. Since these conceptions are held to constitute the foundation for all science and since science is conceived of as depicting reality, the question arises: How can we know that these conceptions apply to reality?

Again, two answers are traditionally given to this question. One answer, originating in Plato, holds that innate ideas are actually memories. These memories are the representations of direct intuitions of reality experienced before birth. Innate ideas express knowledge, then, in the way that memories do. A second answer, exemplified in Descartes, holds that the truth of innate ideas can be internally validated. Thus, in Descartes we find upon reflection that two innate ideas, the idea that I am and the idea that from nothing nothing comes, possess a special property—they not only involve the immediate assent of reason (their denial being a contradiction of sorts) but they cannot be subjected to doubt, since any possible argument of doubt, as, for instance, appeal to an evil demon as the source of these ideas, must implicitly affirm the ideas in question. Thus, in arguing that an evil demon might be deceiving me, I at the same time affirm that I am and employ the principle that from nothing nothing comes. Taking a stand on these two innate ideas, Descartes then purports to prove the existence of God and God's goodness; by so doing, he thinks to establish clarity and distinctness as both the necessary and the sufficient condition of an idea's being true and thus validate all other innate ideas.

In summary, then, the theory of innate ideas states that certain conceptions of universal principles and nonsensory objects are innate, in the sense of being either images present in the mind at or before birth or inborn dispositions of the mind to form conceptions under certain circumstances. Since these conceptions, taken as either images or dispositions, exist chronologically before sensory experience, they are a priori in the literal, temporal sense of the term. Since they are not composed from or testable in sensory experience but since they provide the basis for all scientific knowledge, they are also a priori in the logical and epistemological senses.

History of the theory. The notion of innate ideas patently lends itself to theological speculation and to systems of metaphysics which locate reality in realms transcending sensory experience. Plato employed the notion as the bridge to the realm of Forms, and similar metaphysical and theological uses of the doctrine occur in the works of the Neoplatonists (Plotinus, for example), as well as in the works of later philosophers and theologians belonging to the Platonic and the Neoplatonic tradition, including St. Augustine in the early period of Christianity, and Ficino in the Italian Renaissance. Outside the strictly Platonic and Neoplatonic line, Descartes, as already noted, employed the doctrine in his proof of God's existence, and it was used in a similar fashion by the ancient Stoics, Herbert of Cherbury, and many other philosophers.

The doctrine of innate ideas also has an intimate relationship with the philosophy of science. Historically, this relationship has minifested itself in the fact that philosophical controversy over the doctrine has been greatest just when philosophers have been most concerned to establish foundations and methods for science. Thus, the existence of innate ideas was especially debated in the fourth century B.C. by the philosophers of the Academy and the Lyceum and in the seventeenth century by the Continental rationalists and the British empiricists.

The question of whether innate ideas exist is not without consequences in the establishment of science. The doctrine of innate ideas favors certain scientific procedures and discourages others. In particular, it favors meditation as opposed to laboratory experimentation and mathematical methods as opposed to inductive methods. It might

seem, however, that philosophical theories concerning the origins and foundations of scientific knowledge could have had, and therefore have had, no actual influence on the establishment of science, just as it has seemed to many philosophers that philosophical theories concerning ethics could have had and have had no actual influence on men's moral behavior. But this view overlooks the failures of would-be science in the seventeenth and eighteenth centuries: on the one hand, the imposing but vacuous systems spun out of the doctrine of innate ideas, and, on the other, the aimless experimentation and observation which Swift, for example, caricatures in parts of *Gulliver's Travels*. The truth would appear to be, not that the doctrine of innate ideas could have had no real influence upon the development of science, but that if it had been strictly and universally adhered to in the seventeenth century and afterward, science would not have been established; but, then, universal adherence to the stricter forms of empiricism would also have been a sterile cause, and so, too, it would seem, would have been an intellectual climate in which neither philosophical empiricism or philosophical rationalism played any part in men's thinking.

Evaluation. The classic attack upon the doctrine of innate ideas is made by Locke in the first book of *An Essay Concerning Human Understanding*. Locke argues that if the doctrine of innate ideas were true, one would expect to find certain ideas, such as the idea of God or the idea that whatever is, is, possessed by everyone and consciously employed in all their reasonings. This is not the case, however. Small children and savages do not possess these ideas, nor do persons consciously employ them in all their reasonings.

Commentators on the theory of innate ideas have sometimes complained that Locke's criticism of the theory sets up a straw man that no responsible innatist has ever cared to defend. In particular it has been claimed that responsible innatists have not held, and have not pretended to hold, that universal recognition and acceptance are corollaries to the existence of innate ideas. But this complaint is beside Locke's point. It is clear, for instance, that if small children everywhere, at the commencement of their discourse with others, appealed explicitly to the idea that whatever is, is, or to the idea of God, there would be good empirical grounds for supposing that innate ideas existed. For these would be at least some of the crucial empirical consequences one would want to deduce from the theory. Since these crucial consequences are not observed but might theoretically be observed, the theory is an empirical theory and, as such, it stands refuted by experience.

It has been argued against the theory of innate ideas that whatever transcendent principles or conceptions the theory pretends to account for can be accounted for more plausibly by supposing them to be constructed from givens of experience or acquired through transcendent intuitions. This argument, however, is not very convincing. It is, for example, impossible to conceive how the concept of infinity could be constructed from givens of experience or acquired through the contemplation of some transcendent realm of entities. But it is not clear, either, how possession of the concept can be accounted for through the theory of innate ideas.

Bibliography

PRIMARY SOURCES

Plato connects the theory of innate ideas with the doctrines of reminiscence and metempsychosis in *Meno* and *Phaedo*. (See *Dialogues*, B. Jowett, ed., 2 vols., 4th rev. ed., Oxford, 1953). He supports this by the case of the slave boy who carries out geometrical demonstrations in a manner suggesting recollection.

Herbert of Cherbury bases his doctrine of natural religion upon a theory of innate ideas. In his *De Veritate*, translated as *On Truth* by M. H. Carré (Bristol, 1937), universal recognition and acceptance are treated as criteria distinguishing innate ideas from other ideas. Pragmatic overtones are introduced: Our common or innate notions are also those that conduce to our preservation, and conversely.

Descartes lays the foundation for most subsequent discussion, pro and con, of the theory of innate ideas in his account of the wax tablet and our judgments of other minds in the "Second Meditation" and in his threefold division of ideas in the "Third Meditation." See *Meditations*, in *The Philosophical Works of Descartes*, translated by E. S. Haldane and G. T. Ross, 2 vols. (Cambridge, 1911, 1931; New York, 1955).

Locke's classic attack upon the theory of innate ideas is given in Book I of the *Essay Concerning Human Understanding* (J. W. Yolton, ed., 2 vols., London, 1961). Locke argues that the theory that all knowledge is acquired from experience can be substantiated in experience; the doctrine of innate ideas is disconfirmed by experience.

Leibniz' *New Essays Concerning Human Understanding* contains an exhaustive examination and critique of Locke's attack upon the theory of innate ideas. See "Specimens of Thoughts Upon the First Book of the Essay on Human Understanding, 1698," "Preface," and "Book I" in the *New Essays* as translated by A. G. Langley, 3d ed. (La Salle, Ill., 1949). In opposition to Locke, Leibniz argues that insensible perceptions exist and that thus Locke's arguments concerning children and savages being unaware of the concept of God or such principles as whatever is, is, do not refute the theory of innate ideas. Contains Leibniz' own version of the theory of innate ideas.

Hume in his *Enquiry Concerning Human Understanding* offers a very brief but penetrating and informative discussion of the theory of innate ideas and its relation to his principle that every simple idea is the copy of a precedent simple impression. See Sec. 2, footnote 1, in the *Enquiry* edited by C. W. Hendel (New York, 1955).

N. O. Lossky connects the historical appearance of the doctrine of innate ideas in the seventeenth century with the failure of empiricists of that era to account for transcendent knowledge, necessary truths, and knowledge of an external world. See Ch. 2 of his *The Intuitive Basis of Knowledge*, translated by N. A. Duddington (London, 1919), where he argues that although the pre-Kantian rationalists seemed able to resolve the difficulties in question by the doctrine of innate ideas, the cost of this resolution was prohibitive. They "had to assume that *the whole of knowledge is innate.*"

R. I. Aaron in *The Nature of Knowing* (London, 1930) discusses innate ideas in connection with his intuitionist theory of knowledge. Although he maintains that all discursive knowledge rests upon a priori knowledge of indubitable or self-evident principles, he denies that the latter are innate ideas.

H. H. Price maintains in *Perception* (London, 1932) that there are a priori innate ideas, but that "we only come to clear consciousness of such concepts . . . when we have already applied them many times."

Lewis E. Hahn's *A Contextualistic Theory of Perception* (Berkeley and Los Angeles, 1942) contains a detailed discussion of the interrelationship of strict sense-data theories of perception, pragmatic theories of perception, and the doctrine of innate ideas. Hahn argues that a strict sense-data theory of perception forces one to accept the doctrine of innate ideas in order to account for one's knowledge and conception of material things, whereas a pragmatic theory of perception does not. He takes this consequence to count in favor of pragmatic theories of perception and against sense-data theories.

John Wild maintains in his *Introduction to Realistic Philosophy* (New York, 1948) that what evidence we possess strongly indicates that rational knowledge does not rest upon innate ideas, but is acquired. This evidence consists in the fact that "first we do not know. Then we know."

SECONDARY SOURCES

Rose, F. O., *Die Lehre von den angeborenen Ideen bei Descartes und Locke*. Berne, 1901.

Sigall, E., *Platon und Leibniz über die angeborenen Ideen*, 2 vols. Chernovtsy, Russia, 1897–1898.

JOHN O. NELSON

INSTRUMENTALISM. See DEWEY, JOHN; LAWS AND THEORIES; PRAGMATISM.

INTENTION. The concept of intention relevant to modern philosophy (in contrast to the medieval notion of the first and second intention of a term) is usually discussed under four chief headings: (1) expressions of intention—"I shall (am going to) do A in circumstances C"; (2) ascriptions of intention—"Jones has the intention of doing A in C"; (3) descriptions of the intention with which some action is done—"His intention in saying that was to embarrass her"; and (4) classifications of actions as intentional or as done with intention—"She shot him intentionally." That these headings are logically related may be seen in the schema "In saying 'I shall do A in C,' Jones expresses the intention that is ascribed to him by 'Jones intends to do A in C'; if having honestly expressed his intention, Jones then does A in C (without changing his mind), he does it intentionally, and the intention with which he does it is that of doing A in C." This schema also makes it clear that the word "intention" is ambiguous in the way, for example, that the word "belief" is ambiguous, for like "belief" the word may refer either to a state or episode (in this case, intending) or to the intentional object of such a state or episode—that is, to that which is intended.

Disposition to action. The basic philosophical problem about intention concerns the sort of state or episode that an intention is and also the manner in which such episodes are related to intentional actions. A fair diversity of opinion has been generated by this problem, but there is marked agreement on one point—namely, that at least one of the things "expressed" by remarks of the sort "I shall (am going to) do A in C" is, other things being equal, a readiness to do, or try to do, things that (one believes) will realize the object or state of affairs intended. This agreement springs from the familiar fact that people, being considerably less noble and well meaning than they like to admit, very commonly profess to have intentions that they really do not have and the fact that there is a standard strategy for refuting such claims. The strategy is arguing that the claimant showed no inclination to do what he allegedly intended to do even though he was fully aware of the circumstances in which he was placed. Thus, if a man who said he intended to do A in C made no move toward doing A when in C, the presumption is that he changed his mind, did not realize that he was in C, or something similar; he could not really have the intention of doing A in C without being actively disposed to do it.

Before considering what else may be involved in an

intention besides the disposition just mentioned, it is essential to appreciate more fully the exact character and complexity of this disposition. To begin with, one cannot have a mere intention to perform an action; one can intend to perform one only at some time, in some place, or under certain conditions. Now, whether the conditions C obtain is always, generally speaking, a matter of judgment, about which one can be mistaken. Hence, the intention to do A in C—even when the action A is a "minimal" one, an action under one's immediate voluntary control, such as a bodily movement—can only entail the disposition to do A when one believes one is in C. If, moreover, the intended action is nonminimal, the knowledge that someone has this intention does not by itself imply any knowledge of the specific actions he is disposed to perform when he believes he is in C. The reason for this is that these specific actions can be determined only by a reference to his beliefs about the preferred means by which his (nonminimal) intention can be realized. Thus, if a man's intention is to murder his employer on a certain date, one cannot reasonably predict the steps he will actually take without further information about his beliefs, preferences, and the like. For although many people might attempt to realize such an intention by firing a gun at the man or by sprinkling poison in his coffee, some might proceed by jabbing pins into a little clay doll or by scratching exotic diagrams in sandy soil. The general point here is that the class of specific actions a man having the intention to do A in C will be disposed to perform can be identified only by reference to his preferences ("Only a savage would use a knife!") and his beliefs concerning (1) what constitutes the obtaining of C and whether it does, in fact, obtain at a certain time and (2) what actions will, when performed in C, constitute the doing of A or will bring it about that A is done. If we define "attempts" to realize A in C as actions in performing which (under certain circumstances) an agent believes he is realizing his complex intention, we can then say that intending to do A in C involves, at least among other things, the disposition (1) to do A when one believes one is in C, if A is minimal, and (2) to attempt to do A in what one believes is C, if A is nonminimal.

Intentionality. Since the disposition characteristic of a minimal intention involves the agent's beliefs concerning the conditions appropriate for its realization and since the dispositions characteristic of more complex intentions involve beliefs concerning the preferred means of realizing them, it is clear that in addition to any purely behavioral disposition an intention will necessarily involve some idea or conception of what is intended. Just how this idea or conception is involved in a state of intending has been a basic problem in recent discussions of the subject. A useful approach to this problem can be made by noting that the locutions used in expressing, ascribing, and describing intentions are nonextensional, possessing the peculiar formal properties that have been called "marks of intentionality." (These marks are purely formal, and far from being peculiar to statements about, or expressions of, intentions, they belong to all statements concerned with distinctively mental phenomena.)

As far as the concept of intention is concerned, there are two marks that are most revealing. First, a statement about a man's intentions, or even his verbal expressions of intention, may use a name or descriptive phrase in such a way that neither the statement nor its negation implies either that there is or is not something to which the name or description applies. Thus, neither "Jones intends to destroy a werewolf" nor its negation implies either that there is or is not a werewolf—which means, less formally put, that a man can intend to destroy a werewolf even if, contrary to his belief, no such things actually exist. Second, a statement of intention may contain a name or descriptive phrase in such a way that one cannot validly make inferences from it in accordance with the logical principle of substitution known as Leibniz' law. Thus, from "Jones intended to assassinate the king" and "The king is the wisest man in Europe," one cannot validly infer "Jones intended to assassinate the wisest man in Europe."

The significance of these purely formal features of statements about intentions is easy to see. The first feature shows not only that intentions are by their very nature the sort of thing that may or may not be realized but also that a man's intentions cannot always be determined by the way he behaves toward the object of his intentions (since the object might not even exist). The second formal property illustrates the familiar fact that an action, such as shooting a man, may be intentional under one description but not under another: "I didn't intend to shoot the wisest man in Europe; I intended to shoot the king, whom I believed to be the dullest man in Europe!" In illustrating this fact, the second feature also reinforces another implication of the first one—namely, that the best way of arriving at certainty about a man's exact intention is to ask him what he intends to do. Considering the earlier remarks about the dispositional aspect of an intention, these last points bring the concept of intention into much clearer focus. For if intentions are essentially the sort of thing that may or may not be realized and if the identity of a man's intention is fundamentally determined by the way in which he conceives and will describe it, having an intention is then largely a matter of envisaging—of conceiving in a particular way—an action or state of affairs while in a state of readiness to do things that will, one believes, directly or indirectly bring about its realization.

Explanation of behavior. Further light can be cast on the concept of intention by relating such cases as Jones's intention to destroy a werewolf to the general fact that the concept of thinking is in part an explanatory concept, used in explaining the peculiarities of intelligent human behavior. Although the best way of determining a man's intention is to ask him what he intends, there is no doubt that when we know his intentions, we can generally understand and explain why he does certain things. In speculating about a man's intentions, moreover, we are typically looking for something that will help to explain his behavior. Thus, the fact that a man dangles a packet of wolfbane on his person and carries a revolver loaded with silver bullets (or, better, nickel bullets which he believes are silver) is the sort of thing that cries out for special explanation, and this explanation is best given by reference to his intention—in this case to destroy a werewolf without being killed in the attempt—and his beliefs about the manner in which his intention can best be realized. That we need to consider his particular beliefs has already been stressed, for they might be highly anomalous and lead him to do things that would not be done by other persons having the same intention. (Supernaturalists might, for instance, regard Jones's efforts as futile on the ground that a silver bullet can destroy a werewolf only when fired by someone who loves him.)

Practical reasoning. Reflection on how explanations of actions by reference to intentions actually work throws still more light on the concept of intention, for what these explanations do is outline, or at least allude to, the steps of practical reasoning that the agent presumably took in deciding what to do in order to realize his intention. In a simple, idealized case a line of such reasoning might begin with an expression of intention, "I shall destroy that werewolf one of these nights," bring in some relevant facts (beliefs), "There will be a full moon tonight, werewolves are vulnerable to silver bullets, and so on," and lead to the decision prompting the concrete steps the agent takes—prowling the garden on a moonlit night, bedecked with wolfbane and armed with a revolver charged with silver bullets. Since the identity of a man's intention is determined in part by the specific terms in which he conceives it and since expressions of intention not only contain these terms but also serve as starting points in the (reconstructed) lines of practical reasoning that account for the actions one takes toward realizing one's intentions, the ideas or thoughts relevant to a certain specific intention may be conceived as having the logical form of an expression of intention. (On the notion of the logical form of a thought see THINKING.) In addition to having the behavioral dispositions already mentioned, therefore, a man who has a certain specific intention is also prone to think thoughts of the form "I shall do *A* in *C*." This does not mean, of course, that a man who has the intention of doing *A* in *C* must constantly be thinking, "I shall do *A* in *C*; I shall do *A* in *C*." On the contrary, he need only have the disposition to think such thoughts, to think them, for instance, when he is deliberating about what to do at a certain time or under certain conditions. In at least one sense, then, having an intention is largely a dispositional matter, a matter of being disposed (1) to make, when deliberating, certain conceptual moves corresponding to the verbal forms used in expressing that intention and (2) to perform various actions which, one believes, will directly or indirectly realize the state of affairs intended.

At the beginning of this article it was said that if a man performs an action with some intention or other, he performs that action intentionally. In view of subsequent discussion it is clear that the reverse is true as well: if a man performs an action intentionally, he necessarily performs it with some intention or other. Thus, if Jones shoots Smith intentionally, he shoots him because he intends to shoot him, because shooting Smith has, as H. L. A. Hart has put it, a place in the "plan of action" under which Jones was operating when he pulled the trigger. Conversely, if Jones shoots Harris, taking him to be Smith, there is a sense in which he shoots him unintentionally—the reason being that shooting Harris has no place in the plan of action he was trying to carry out. Needless to say, Jones shot a man intentionally, for he intended to shoot a man and did so. But the man he shot was not the man he intended to shoot, so, as in the assassination of the wisest man in Europe, we have another case of an action, a shooting, that is intentional under one description but not under another.

Apart from having an intention in the dispositional sense discussed thus far, it is also possible to intend in an occurrent, nondispositional sense—that is, to engage in "acts" of intending. This is possible because resolving is an "act" that counts as a special case of intending—namely, intending as an immediate consequence of deliberation or choice. As dispositions of the sort considered earlier, intentions may form themselves as effortlessly and as unconsciously as beliefs, which they resemble; but sometimes, as in deliberation or choice, one forms an intention explicitly, consciously, and occurrently—in which case one's intending may have the character of a resolve ("So I shall do *A* in *C*"). Here one's intending, as act, is a "practical" thought, serving as the conclusion of a line of practical reasoning. (Resolving is not, of course, the only species of occurrent intending; willing is another, but it is too controversial a case to be mentioned without extensive discussion.) As states or episodes, intentions are, then, both occurrent and dispositional; when they are, for instance, resolves, they are occurrent, and when they are had in the sense in which a belief is "had," they are dispositional.

Contemporary problems. Contemporary philosophers have frequently expressed strong misgivings over the existence of private acts of intending, and it may be helpful to round off this discussion by commenting on the most important of them. There are, first, the misgivings that arise from a general distrust of all private or introspective "mental" phenomena, including even bodily sensations. These misgivings are erroneous because they are based on an overly narrow conception of the limits of empirical discourse. Second, there are the misgivings based on the Humean idea that what is distinguishable is logically distinct and that if intentions, as private or introspective "acts," were distinguishable from the behavioral dispositions mentioned earlier, there would be no logical connection between having an occurrent intention and being disposed to take steps to realize it, a point stressed by A. I. Melden. There are many things, however, such as bugbites, itches, or even knockouts, which, though distinguishable as things or occurrences from preceding or accompanying phenomena, fall under a certain description only insofar as they are preceded or accompanied by these phenomena. Thus, certain abrasions or bites are bugbites only when brought about by a bug, certain feelings are itches only when they make one want to scratch, and certain episodes of falling unconscious are knockouts only when brought about in the familiar way. Similarly, then, the silent thought of doing *A* in *C* is an active or occurrent intention only when it is accompanied by the disposition to do, or to try to do, *A* when one believes one is in *C*. Without this disposition the thought in point is at best the mere thought of a future action on one's part, and it is thus incorrectly described as an active intention.

Bibliography

Anscombe, G. E. M., "Intention." *PAS*, Vol. 57 (1956–1957).
Anscombe, G. E. M., *Intention*. Oxford, 1957.
Aristotle, *Nicomachean Ethics*. Book III.

Chisholm, Roderick, "Statements About Believing." *PAS*, Vol. 56 (1955–1956), 125–148. Reprinted with revisions in Herbert Feigl et al., eds., *Minnesota Studies in the Philosophy of Science*, Vol. II. Minneapolis, 1958.

Davidson, Donald, "Actions, Reasons, and Causes." *Journal of Philosophy*, Vol. 40 (1963), 685–699.

Fleming, Noel, "On Intention." *Philosophical Review*, Vol. 73 (1964), 301–320.

Hampshire, Stuart, *Thought and Action*. London, 1959.

Hart, H. L. A., "Acts of Will and Legal Responsibility," in D. F. Pears, ed., *Freedom and the Will*. London, 1963.

Heath, P. L., "Intentions." *PAS*, Supp. Vol. 29 (1955), 147–164.

Kenny, Anthony, *Action, Emotion, and Will*. London, 1963.

Melden, A. I., *Free Action*. London, 1961.

Passmore, J. A., "Intentions." *PAS*, Supp. Vol. 29 (1955), 131–146.

Ryle, Gilbert, *The Concept of Mind*. London, 1949.

Sellars, Wilfrid, "Imperatives, Intentions, and the Logic of 'Ought,'" in Hector-Neri Castañeda and George Nakhnikian, eds., *Morality and the Language of Conduct*. Detroit, Mich., 1963.

Wittgenstein, Ludwig, *Philosophical Investigations*, translated by G. E. M. Anscombe. Oxford, 1953. *Passim*.

BRUCE AUNE

INTENTIONALITY. The term "intentionality" was used by Jeremy Bentham to distinguish between actions that are intentional and those that are not. It was reintroduced by Edmund Husserl in connection with certain doctrines set forth in Franz Brentano's *Psychologie vom empirischen Standpunkt* (1874). The word is now used primarily in this second sense.

Brentano wrote:

> Every mental phenomenon is characterized by what the scholastics of the Middle Ages called the intentional (and also mental) inexistence of an object, and what we would call, although not in entirely unambiguous terms, the reference to a content, a direction upon an object (by which we are not to understand a reality . . .), or an immanent objectivity. Each one includes something as an object within itself, although not always in the same way. In presentation something is presented, in judgment something is affirmed or denied, in love [something is] loved, in hate [something] is hated, in desire something is desired, etc.
>
> This intentional inexistence is exclusively characteristic of mental phenomena. No physical phenomenon manifests anything similar. Consequently, we can define mental phenomena by saying that they are such phenomena as include an object intentionally within themselves. (*Op. cit.*, Vol. I, Book II, Ch. 1)

This passage contains two different theses: one, an ontological thesis about the nature of certain objects of thought and of other psychological attitudes; the other, a psychological thesis, implying that reference to an object is what distinguishes the mental or psychological from the physical. These two theses are the subject matter of the present article. It should be noted, however, that "intentionality" is also used in connection with certain other related theses of phenomenology and existentialism.

INTENTIONAL INEXISTENCE

The problem that gave rise to the ontological thesis of intentional inexistence may be suggested by asking what is involved in having thoughts, beliefs, desires, purposes, or other intentional attitudes, which are directed upon objects that do not exist. There is a distinction between a man who is thinking about a unicorn and a man who is thinking about nothing; in the former case, the man is intentionally related to an object, but in the latter case he is not. What, then, is the status of this object? It cannot be an actual unicorn, since there are no unicorns. According to the doctrine of intentional inexistence, the object of the thought about a unicorn *is* a unicorn, but a unicorn with a mode of being (intentional inexistence, immanent objectivity, or existence in the understanding) that is short of actuality but more than nothingness and that, according to most versions of the doctrine, lasts for just the length of time that the unicorn is thought about.

Early theories. St. Anselm's ontological argument was thus based upon the assumption that, if God is thought about, he thereby "exists in the understanding." Anselm then proceeded to contrast the perfections of that which "exists in the understanding alone" with that which "exists in reality." Peter Aureol and William of Ockam contrasted the intentional existence of the objects of thought with the subjective existence of the thoughts themselves. The term "objective existence," referring to the existence of something *as* an object of thought, was used by medieval philosophers and by Descartes as a synonym for "intentional existence"; Descartes thus contrasted the formal, or subjective, existence of actual objects with the objective existence in the mind of objects that are merely thought about. The terms "objective" and "subjective," in these uses, had connotations quite different from those that they have now; that which was said to have objective existence (for instance, a unicorn as an object of thought), unlike that which had subjective existence (the idea of a unicorn, for instance), need not exist in fact.

Advantage of the doctrine. The doctrine of intentional existence, or, as Brentano called it, intentional inexistence, had at least the advantage of providing a literal interpretation for the dictum that truth consists in a kind of correspondence between mind and thing: an affirmative judgment is true if the properties of the intentional object are the same as those of the actual object. The very statement of this advantage, however, betrays the fact that the judgment is directed, not upon the intentional object, but upon the actual object, in which case, as Gassendi pointed out, the intentional object would seem to be superfluous.

Intentional reference. The difficulty of the apparent superfluity of the intentional object may be traced, in part, to the fact that the phenomenon of intentionality has two sides. Our intentional attitudes may be directed upon objects that do not exist (Diogenes looked for an honest man), but they may also be directed upon objects that do exist (there is a certain dishonest man whom the police happen to be looking for). The object of the latter quest, obviously, is not a thing having only immanent or intentional existence. But this is also true, as Brentano was later to point out, of the object of the former quest: Diogenes was not looking for an immanent object (for, if the doctrine of intentional inexistence were true, he already had one in his mind); he was looking for an actual, existing honest man, despite the fact that, as we may suppose, no such man exists. Thus, Brentano said, "If we think about a horse, the object of our contemplation is a horse and not a contemplated horse."

In the expression of the ontological thesis of intentionality, "intentional" may be said to refer to a mode of being *within* the mind; but in the expression of the psychological thesis of intentionality, "intentional" is used to describe the direction upon objects that may exist *outside* the mind. It is not inaccurate to say that intentional entities were posited in the attempt to account for intentional reference, but precisely because they were intentional, the attempt did not succeed. Husserl said, in the fifth of his *Logische Untersuchungen*, that the objects of our intentional experiences are never immanent—never intentional objects—but are always transcendent.

Brentano's later views. Thus, for various reasons Brentano abandoned the ontological part of his doctrine of intentionality. In his later writings, he said that "unicorn" in the sentence "John is thinking about a unicorn" has no referential function; a contemplated unicorn is not a type of unicorn. "Unicorn," in such sentences, is used syncategorematically to contribute to the description of the person who is said to have a unicorn as the object of his thought. But this conclusion seems to leave us with our problem. The statement "John is thinking about a unicorn" does not describe *John* as a unicorn; how, then, does "unicorn" serve to contribute to his description?

The ontological problem, therefore, may be said to survive in the question, "How are we using 'unicorn' in 'John believes that there are unicorns'?" There is a temptation to say that the use of "unicorn" in such sentences has no connection at all with the use it would have in "There are unicorns." That this would be false, however, may be seen by noting that "John believes that there are unicorns" and "All of John's beliefs are true" together imply "There are unicorns." Thus, Wittgenstein remarked:

One may have the feeling that in the sentence 'I expect he is coming' one is using the words 'he is coming' in a different sense from the one they have in the assertion 'He is coming'. But if it were so, how could I say that my expectation had been fulfilled? If I wanted to explain the words 'he' and 'is coming', say by means of ostensive definitions, the same definitions of these words would go for both sentences. (*Philosophical Investigations*, p. 130e)

Carnap's theory. In the *Logical Syntax of Language* (London, 1937), Rudolf Carnap suggested that linguistic entities are the objects of our intentional attitudes. "Charles thinks (asserts, believes, wonders about) *A*," he said, might be translated as "Charles thinks '*A*.'" Taken literally, this suggestion would imply, falsely, that a man who wonders whether there are unicorns is a man who wonders whether there is the word "unicorns."

Inscriptional theory. A closely related view has been developed by W. V. Quine and Israel Scheffler. However, these authors, instead of saying that our intentional attitudes have linguistic entities as their objects, suggest instead that certain sentences, which relate people to words or to other linguistic entities, might be used to perform all of the functions of intentional sentences; if this view were adequate, the problem of the status of the intentional object might be avoided. Thus, "John believes-true a Socrates-is-mortal inscription" may be interpreted as a sentence affirming a certain relation to hold between John and a linguistic entity or "inscription," but a relation that is true only under the conditions under which "John believes that Socrates is mortal" is true; hence, if we use the former sentence instead of the latter, we relate John only to inscriptions.

However, it may be held (1) that the plausibility of this approach depends upon the assumption that there are certain semantic sentences (for instance, "The German sentence '*Sokrates ist sterblich*' means that Socrates is mortal") that are true of certain inscriptions and (2) that these semantic sentences are abbreviations for intentional sentences that leave us with our original problem (for instance, "German-speaking people use '*Sokrates ist sterblich*' to express and convey the belief that Socrates is mortal").

This inscriptional approach, moreover, fails to distinguish between such sentences as "Someone is looking for a horse" and "There is a horse that someone is looking for"; these two types of sentence, as noted above, reflect the two different sides of the phenomenon of intentionality. It has been suggested that sentences of the latter sort may be illegitimate, on the ground that they quantify, in effect, into contexts that are referentially opaque, in a sense explained below. To say that such intentional sentences are illegitimate is to imply that the mind is incapable of referring to objects that exist and, hence, that we cannot "get outside the circle of our own ideas."

Response theory. There have been still other approaches to the problem of the intentional object. Some of the American New Realists proposed, behavioristically, that to think about a unicorn might merely be to "put one's unicorn responses in readiness." The thinker, instead of relating himself to unicorns, disposes himself to behave in just those ways in which he would behave if there *were* unicorns. Other psychological attitudes were treated analogously. It would seem, however, that "unicorn responses" cannot be adequately specified except by reference to beliefs and desires that are directed upon unicorns, since the ways in which a man would respond to a unicorn would be, in part, a function of what he otherwise perceives, desires, and believes. More recent revivals of the specific-response theory seem to be subject to similar difficulties.

Church's view. Alonzo Church, in his *Introduction to Mathematical Logic* (Princeton, 1956), proposed that the sentence "Schliemann sought the site of Troy" asserts that a certain relation holds between Schliemann and the *concept* of the site of Troy; Church said, negatively, that the relation is "not quite like that of having sought," but he did not say more positively what it is. This view suggests a return to the medieval doctrine, at least to the extent of viewing the objects of our intentional attitudes as beings of reason.

Analogical theory. Thomas Aquinas seems to have held that "unicorn," in such sentences as "John is thinking about a unicorn," is used *analogically* (*De Potentia* 7c; *Summa Theologica* I, 13, 10). There is ground for questioning whether the doctrine of analogical predication is itself sufficiently illuminating to throw light upon the problem of intentionality, but the fact that we can understand the use of "unicorn" and cannot say just what function the word there performs may, on the other hand, throw some light upon the doctrine.

The most plausible defense of the doctrine of intentional inexistence, therefore, would seem to be that this doctrine, unlike most of its alternatives, *does* provide us with a straightforward account of the use of "unicorn" in "John is thinking about a unicorn": the word is being used simply to designate a unicorn.

PSYCHOLOGICAL THESIS OF INTENTIONALITY

According to Brentano's second thesis, intentionality is peculiar to psychological phenomena and thus provides a criterion by means of which the mental may be distinguished from the nonmental. The problem for the proponent of this second thesis is not so much that of showing that mental phenomena *are* intentional as it is that of showing that physical phenomena are *not* intentional. Some now believe that the thesis can be defended by reference to the language we use in describing psychological phenomena—that the sentences we must use in describing psychological phenomena have certain logical properties that are not shared by any of the sentences we must use in describing nonpsychological phenomena, and that these properties are correctly called intentional. If this view is true, then the basic thesis of physicalism and the unity of science is false. Can we find, then, a logical criterion of the intentional, one that we may then use to distinguish the mental from the physical?

Unsatisfactory criteria of intentionality. It has been suggested that failure of existential generalization yields a logical criterion of the intentional. The intentional "John is thinking about a horse," unlike the nonintentional "John is riding on a horse," does not imply that there are horses. However, existential generalization also fails in application to some of the terms in the following statements that describe physical phenomena: "New Zealand is devoid of unicorns," "That lady resembles a mermaid," and "The dam is high enough to prevent any future floods."

Nonextensional occurrence has also been proposed as a possible criterion of the intentional. A phrase, *p*, may be said to occur nonextensionally in a sentence, *s*, provided that the result of replacing *p* in *s* by any phrase having the same truth value as *p* will be a sentence having the same truth value as *s*. Thus, "Johnson is Kennedy's successor" may replace "Socrates was a philosopher" in "Either Socrates was a god or Socrates was a philosopher," without altering the truth value of the whole, whereas similar replacement is not possible in "Plato believed that Socrates was a philosopher." Nonextensional occurrence, however, is not peculiar to sentences that are intentional; compare "It is necessarily true that if Socrates was a member of the class of philosophers, then Socrates was a philosopher."

Referential opacity has also been proposed as a criterion of the intentional. The occurrence of a substantival expression in a sentence, *s* (for instance, "Truman's successor" in "Joe Martin believed that Dewey would be Truman's successor"), is referentially opaque if its replacement in *s* by another substantival expression (such as "Eisenhower") designating the same individual may result in a sentence having a truth value different from that of *s*. However, referential opacity is not peculiar to the intentional; we may assert "It is necessarily true that if Dewey was Truman's successor, then Dewey was Truman's successor," but not "It is necessarily true that if Dewey was Truman's successor, then Dewey was Eisenhower."

Satisfactory criteria. The failure of nonextensional occurrence and referential opacity has led some to believe that there are no logical characteristics peculiar to intentional statements. However, there are other criteria that do seem to be satisfied only by intentional statements. We may mention two.

Let us refine upon ordinary English in the following way: instead of writing propositional clauses as "that" clauses, we will eliminate the "that" and put the remainder of the clause in parentheses; for example, instead of writing "John believes that there are men," we will write "John believes (there are men)." A simple sentence prefix may be said to be an expression that contains no proper part that is logically equivalent to a sentence or to a sentence function and that is such that the result of prefixing it to a sentence in parentheses is another sentence. We may say that a simple sentence prefix, *M*, is *intentional* if, for every sentence *p*, *M(p)* is logically contingent. Thus, "it is impossible" is not intentional, since when prefixed to "(some squares are circles)," it yields a sentence that is necessary and therefore not contingent; "it is right" is not intentional since, when prefixed to "(there is not anything of which it can be truly said that it is right)," it yields a sentence that is contradictory and therefore not logically contingent.

However, *every* sentence, whether it is itself contingent or not, is such that the result of thus prefixing it by "John believes" is contingent. Similar observations apply to "John questions," "John desires," and to other prefixes referring to intentional attitudes. Thus, we might say that the psychological differs from the nonpsychological in this respect: an adequate description of the psychological requires the use of intentional prefixes.

It may also be argued that some intentional prefixes (for instance, "John believes") are such that the possible ways of inserting them into a universally quantified sentence (for instance, into "For every *x*, *x* is material") and into the corresponding existentially quantified sentence ("There exists an *x* such that *x* is material") yield four statements ("John believes that, for every *x*, *x* is material"; "For every *x*, John believes that *x* is material"; "John believes that there exists an *x* such that *x* is material"; and "There exists an *x* such that John believes that *x* is material") that are logically related in ways in which no corresponding sentences with nonintentional prefixes are related. Thus, it may be said of the four sentences just cited: neither the first nor the third implies any of the others; the second implies all but the first; the fourth implies the third but does not imply either the first or the second; and there is no nonintentional prefix that will yield four sentences that are similarly related. This contention, to the extent that it applies to "John believes," is based upon the assumptions that in believing a thing to have certain properties, one thereby believes that the thing exists; that one may believe falsely, of some nonuniversal set of things (some set comprising less than everything there is), that it comprises everything there is; and that one may believe falsely, of a universal set of things, that it does not comprise everything there is.

There are other psychological sentences—for instance, "He is in pain" and "He is thinking about Jupiter"—that may not satisfy the above criteria of intentionality. The first of these sentences, however, might be said to be intentional if, as some believe, one cannot be in pain if one is not *aware* that one is in pain; or if one does not *believe* that one is in pain; or if, at any one instant, one does not *remember* the pain of previous instants; and analogously for the second quoted sentence. Another possible view, however, is to say that intentionality is at least a sufficient if not a necessary condition of the psychological.

Bibliography

Brentano, Franz, *Psychologie vom empirischen Standpunkt.* Vienna, 1874; 3d ed., Leipzig, 1925.

Brentano, Franz, *Kategorienlehre.* Leipzig, 1933.

Brentano, Franz, "The Distinction Between Mental and Physical Phenomena," translated by D. B. Terrell, in R. M. Chisholm, ed., *Realism and the Background of Phenomenology.* Glencoe, Ill., 1960. Pp. 39–61. Translation of part of Vol. I, Book II, Ch. 1 of Brentano's *Psychologie.*

Chisholm, R. M., *Perceiving: A Philosophical Study.* Ithaca, N.Y., 1957.

Chisholm, R. M., "Notes on the Logic of Believing." *Philosophy and Phenomenological Research,* Vol. 24 (1963), 195–201.

Hayen, André, *L'Intentionnel selon saint Thomas,* 2d ed. Paris, 1954.

Husserl, Edmund, *Ideen zu einer reinen Phänomenologie und phänomenologischen Philosophie.* Halle, 1913. Translated by W. R. Boyce Gibson as *Ideas: General Introduction to Pure Phenomenology.* New York, 1931.

Husserl, Edmund, *Logische Untersuchungen,* 4th ed. Halle, 1928.

Quine, W. V., "Quantifiers and Propositional Attitudes." *Journal of Philosophy,* Vol. 53 (1956), 177–187.

Quine, W. V., *Word and Object.* New York, 1960.

Scheffler, Israel, *The Anatomy of Inquiry.* New York, 1963.

Sellars, Wilfrid, and Chisholm, R. M., "Intentionality and the Mental," in H. Feigl, M. Scriven, and G. Maxwell, eds., *Concepts, Theories, and the Mind–Body Problem.* Minnesota Studies in the Philosophy of Science. Minneapolis, 1958, pp. 507–539.

Spiegelberg, Herbert, "Der Begriff der Intentionalität in der Scholastik, bei Brentano, und bei Husserl." *Philosophische Hefte,* Vol. 5 (1936), 75–91.

RODERICK M. CHISHOLM

INTERNAL RELATIONS. See RELATIONS, INTERNAL AND EXTERNAL.

INTROSPECTION. See MIND–BODY PROBLEM.

INTUITION. The broadest definition of the term "intuition" is "immediate apprehension." "Apprehension" is used to cover such disparate states as sensation, knowledge, and mystical rapport. "Immediate" has as many senses as there are kinds of mediation: It may be used to signify the absence of inference, the absence of causes, the absence of the ability to define a term, the absence of justification, the absence of symbols, or the absence of

thought. Given this range of uses, nothing can be said about intuition in general. Instead, it is necessary to pick out those principal meanings of the term which have played the most important roles in philosophical controversy and to discuss each of these individually.

Four principal meanings of "intuition" may be distinguished: (1) Intuition as unjustified true belief not preceded by inference; in this (the commonest) sense "an intuition" means "a hunch." The existence of hunches is uncontroversial and not of philosophical interest. (2) Intuition as immediate knowledge of the truth of a proposition, where "immediate" means "not preceded by inference." This is a philosophically important sense, since philosophers have found it puzzling that one can have knowledge, and thus justified belief, without having made oneself aware through the process of inference of any justification for this belief. (3) Intuition as immediate knowledge of a concept. "Immediate knowledge" here means, roughly, "knowledge which does not entail ability to define the concept." (4) Intuition as nonpropositional knowledge of an entity—knowledge that may be a necessary condition for, but is not identical with, intuitive knowledge of the truth of propositions about the entity. This sense of "intuition" is exemplified by (a) sense perceptions, considered as products of a cognitive faculty distinct from the faculty of forming judgments concerning the entity sensed; (b) intuitions of universals, or (as in Kant) of such insensible particulars as time and space—intuitions that are necessary conditions of our intuitive knowledge of a priori truths; (c) mystical or inexpressible intuitions that, unlike sense perceptions and intuitions of universals, do not make possible knowledge of the truth of propositions about the entities intuited—such intuitions as Bergson's inexpressible intuition of duration, Fichte's intuition of the Transcendental Ego, and the mystic's intuition of God.

FACULTY AND LINGUISTIC EXPLANATIONS OF INTUITIVE KNOWLEDGE

Intuitive and noninferential knowledge. There is both a strong and a weak sense of "intuitive knowledge that *p*." In the weak sense of this term, *S* knows that *p* intuitively if (a) *p* is true, (b) he is justified in believing that *p*, and (c) his knowledge that *p* is not based upon his inferring *p* from other propositions. The criterion for its not being so based is simply that *S* would deny, for any set of propositions *p** from which *p* follows, that he believes that *p because* he believes that *p** (although he might in fact believe *p** and be willing to adduce *p** to satisfy someone else's doubts about *p*). In this sense of "intuitive," we may know intuitively that we have two legs or two children, but we cannot know intuitively that the Civil War was caused by slavery, or that nothing can move faster than the speed of light. In this sense, the existence of intuitive knowledge is unquestionable; and "intuitive" in this sense is synonymous with "noninferential."

In the stronger sense of "intuition," however, only a certain species of noninferential knowledge is intuitive: *S* knows that *p* intuitively only if (a) *p* is true, (b) he is justified in believing that *p*, and (c) there are no accepted procedures for resolving doubts about the truth of *p*, given *S*'s belief that *p*. Thus we may be justified in believing without inference that we have two legs, but if we have doubts we can undertake such tests as looking and seeing, asking others, and checking the possibility of collective hallucination. Given these tests, so much evidence may appear to show that one leg is missing that it would be irrational to maintain our previous belief. But in certain cases—for example, our belief that we are in pain, or that every event has a cause—there are (at present) no procedures available for resolving doubt. It is never irrational to continue to believe that *S* has a pain once one knows that he believes he does, despite, for instance, the failure of physiologists to find a concomitant neural process. Again, if someone thinks that some events are uncaused, we have no way of testing his hypothesis. Yet we are not willing to give up our claim to know that he is wrong. In both sets of cases—so-called rock-bottom data of perception and introspection, and so-called unquestionable first principles— justified belief is accompanied by the lack of procedures to settle doubt. These are the two paradigm cases of "intuitive knowledge," in the strong sense of the term— first-person statements about those psychological states to which one has "privileged access" and underived a priori truths.

In this stronger sense, too, the existence of intuitive knowledge is unquestionable. Two points should, however, be noted. First, if in formulating the conditions for the application of this sense of intuitive knowledge we had simply said "*p* is indubitable" rather than "there are no accepted procedures for resolving doubts about *p*," then it would have been questionable whether any such knowledge existed. It can plausibly be argued that, under sufficiently peculiar circumstances, it may be rational to doubt one's belief that one is in pain, or that every event has a cause. In general, it can plausibly be argued that there are no intrinsically indubitable propositions, for rational doubt may outstrip the possibility of rationally settling doubt. Second, it is possible for procedures to come into existence for settling doubt in areas where none existed before. Thus we now take *S*'s belief that he was in pain as the best possible evidence for his having been in pain, but advances in physiology may bring about a practice of withdrawing claims to have been in pain when the relevant neural processes have failed to occur. Under these conditions, *S*'s belief that he was in pain would be intuitive in the weak sense, but no longer in the strong sense. Again, some philosophers would argue that, with the rise of quantum theory, we are now in a position to treat "every event has a cause" as an empirical hypothesis, even though it was once the paradigm of an unquestionable first principle. In general, whether a proposition can count as the object of intuitive knowledge (in the strong sense) is a function of the availability of accepted procedures for settling doubt, and it is doubtful that we can know a priori in what areas such procedures will and will not be developed.

"Noninferential" will here be used in place of the weak sense of intuitive, and "intuitive" in place of the strong sense. Both noninferential and intuitive knowledge seemed to philosophers to require explanation because the paradigm of knowledge has, since Aristotle, frequently been taken to be inferential knowledge—the case in which one knows not only that *p* is true but also why *p* is true, and believes that *p* is true because one believes certain other propositions from which *p* may validly be inferred (see Aristotle's *Posterior Analytics* I, 2). Noninferential knowledge has often been explained by being assimilated to this paradigm through the use of the notion of implicit or unconscious inference. Cases of nonintuitive knowledge have been treated as cases in which an inference from intuitively known premises was performed, and cases of nonintuitive, noninferential knowledge as cases in which the knower is not aware of having performed the appropriate inference.

Faculty theory. Various explanations have been given of the existence of intuitive knowledge. As was noted, the objects of intuitive knowledge seem to fall into two quite different groups—such very particular facts as "This looks white" or "This hurts," and such very general facts as "Every event has a cause" or "If *p* implies *q*, and *p*, then *q*." Our knowledge of the particular has often been referred to as sensory intuition, and of the very general as nonsensory intuition. The simplest, most familiar, and least helpful explanation of our possession of these two sorts of intuition is that we possess faculties which produce such knowledge. Accepting this explanation amounts to granting that the presence in our mind of the original starting points of knowledge is inexplicable and must be accepted as a brute fact. Aristotle was content with this solution, and so was Descartes. In Cartesianism this inexplicability was woven into the fabric of a metaphysical dualism, according to which no mental event (such as a coming-to-know) could be caused by any sequence of physical events, and in which the only mental relation that could bring about a coming-to-know was the relation of being inferred from. This picture of the mind required that comings-to-know which were not preceded by inference be treated as uncaused causes, incapable of explanation.

Descartes's extreme rationalism led him to insist that sensory intuitions are not really cases of knowledge at all, and this in turn led him to hold that they are not really mental events but merely physical ones. Thus he did not recognize two intuitive faculties (one sensory and one nonsensory) but only one, the nonsensory. In his view, sense perception is in principle nonessential to attaining complete knowledge, although it is mysteriously necessary in practice. This paradoxical position was criticized by Locke and others. Under the impact of such criticisms, a more moderate rationalistic position was developed, according to which both sense perception and the intellect are sources of genuine knowledge and enjoy equal status as intuitive faculties.

Linguistic theory. The new moderate rationalism was attacked by the immoderate empiricism of Hume, according to which our only intuitive faculty is that of sensory intuition. Hume, however, and such later empiricists as Russell, continued to accept the Cartesian metaphysical framework, thus admitting that no explanation can be given of the fact that a physical event *p* (the modification of one of *S*'s sense organs) is frequently followed by the mental event *M* (*S*'s coming-to-know that *p*). They insisted, however, that an explanation can be given of the acquisition of our nonsensory intuitive knowledge and that consequently it is not necessary to postulate a special faculty that provides us with knowledge of first principles. The alternative explanation (in the form it was given by the logical positivists) was that all such knowledge is knowledge of analytic truths and that the process of acquiring such knowledge is identical with the process of learning the conventions of one's language. This view—sometimes called the linguistic theory of a priori knowledge—held that to know, for example, that all events are caused is simply to know something about the meanings of the words "event" and "cause," and that this knowledge is acquired by easily understandable processes of psychological conditioning. To this suggestion, rationalists objected, first, that the process of learning the meaning of "cause" cannot be accounted for except by invoking a special faculty of intuitive acquaintance with universals; and, second, that the linguistic theory represents a confusion of acquiring knowledge with acquiring the ability to express this knowledge.

Prelinguistic knowledge. The rationalists held, concerning the linguistic theory, that even granted that it would be a violation of linguistic conventions to speak of "uncaused events," the real question is: How do we know that this is the right convention to adopt? Is not this latter piece of knowledge, knowledge of nonlinguistic fact? Are not linguistic conventions adopted on the basis of such prelinguistic knowledge? Such questions, many philosophers thought, show that the linguistic theory does not enable us to dispense with a faculty of nonsensory intuition. As long as the central presupposition of these questions—that S can properly be said to know that p prior to his ability to express p in language—was granted, this rationalist rebuttal created a new deadlock. The influence of Cartesianism, and particularly of the Cartesian notion of sense perception as a special, unanalyzable mental act correlated with certain modifications of sense organs, made it difficult to question this presupposition. Sense perception was, it seemed to most philosophers, a clear example of our ability to know facts without having the ability to express them. If a child, by virtue of his faculty of sensory intuition, can see that a physical object O has the sensory quality Q by a simple, uncaused act, prior to acquiring the ability to express this fact in language, then why cannot the same child see with his mind's eye that every event has a cause and, on the basis of this prelinguistic intuitive knowledge, check the correctness of conventions concerning the words "cause" and "event"?

Behaviorist analysis. The notion of prelinguistic knowledge, and with it the whole Cartesian conception of comings-to-know as mental occurrences, was questioned by Gilbert Ryle, Ludwig Wittgenstein, and their followers. Under the influence of these writers, many philosophers have come to treat "S knows that p" not as a statement about S's mind but as a statement that, besides presupposing the truth of p, asserts that S is disposed to assert p on appropriate occasions, and also either that S is prepared to give good reasons for believing that p or that S is justified in believing p even though he is unable to give reasons for believing that p. The last case covers all noninferential knowledge, both intuitive and nonintuitive. In the case of

S's nonintuitive, noninferential knowledge—that, for example, he has two children, or that there is a house in front of him—the criteria that establish that S is entitled to assert these propositions are of two sorts: those that determine whether he knows the meanings of the terms he uses and those that determine whether his situation and abilities are normal (where "normal" means, roughly, that the sincere reports of persons with these abilities in these situations are usually confirmed when checked by independent means). For example, S would be justified in believing that there is a house in front of him if he knew what a house is (that is, knew what "house" means), had his eyes open, and had normal vision. He would be justified in believing this even if, when asked, "How do you know that that's a house?" he was too unsophisticated to make any reply except "I just know." Whether S satisfies these criteria can be determined by public procedures—testing his grasp of the language, his vision, and his position vis-à-vis the house in straightforward and unmysterious ways.

According to the Cartesian view, what justifies S in believing p in the absence of an ability to produce good reasons for believing p is a special, private, introspectable mental state. S introspects to see whether or not he knows that p, and thus he knows intuitively that he knows that p and has better ground for the belief that he knows that p than anyone else can have. The behaviorist alternative asserts, on the contrary, that the fulfillment of public criteria is not just an external symptom of the presence of an occult mental state called knowledge, but that the statement of such criteria gives a full account of the meaning of "to know." This treatment of such cases of nonintuitive, noninferential knowledge as "I see that O is Q" is designed to replace the Cartesian notion of sense perception as a simple, unanalyzable act with the view that to see that O is Q cannot happen prior to the ability to use correctly the terms "O" and "Q" (or some equivalent expressions). Infants and animals, confronted by O, have sensations but do not have perceptions. They begin to perceive that O is Q when these sensations, and only these sensations, are accompanied by a disposition to assert or assent to "O is Q." Thus, they begin to perceive that O is Q only when their belief that O is Q becomes a reliable indicator of the truth of "O is Q."

This behaviorist analysis of nonintuitive, noninferential knowledge can be used to explain the difference between this case and the case of intuitive knowledge. The difference is that in the case of intuitive knowledge the *only* criterion which S must satisfy in order to be entitled to believe p without being able to offer good reasons for p is that he knows his language. The paradigms of intuitive knowledge—knowledge of "private" psychological states and knowledge of underived a priori truths—are such that if a person claims knowledge of this sort, the only way in which his claim can be refuted is to show that he does not know his language. For example, if someone sincerely believes that he is in pain, we cannot show that his belief is mistaken unless (as in the case of a young child) we can show that his use of "pain" is idiosyncratic. Again, if someone claims to know that every event has (or does not have) a cause, we cannot show that his belief is unjustified unless we discover that he doesn't understand what he is saying (and we discover this by discovering that his use of "event" or of "cause" is idiosyncratic). To know what one is saying is, in certain cases, to know that what one says is true.

Behaviorist analysis also permits an explanation of our possession of intuitive knowledge that dispenses with the notion of intuitive faculties. In the case of sensory intuition, the process of acquiring intuitive knowledge is simply the occurrence of certain sensations in a person who knows a language that contains ways of describing these sensations (that is, contains expressions whose utterance speakers of the language are conditioned to correlate with occurrences of these sensations). In the case of nonsensory intuition, we acquire intuitive knowledge simply by reflecting upon our own linguistic behavior (where "reflecting" means, roughly, "asking ourselves questions about what we would say if . . . "). In both cases, the crucial precondition is knowledge of a language, and the process of acquiring this knowledge is taken to be a matter of psychological conditioning—conditioning whose operations are explicable entirely in terms of a stimulus–response model. Whereas according to the traditional Cartesian faculty view the difference between men and animals is a matter of man's possession of a special *sui generis* power (variously called awareness, consciousness, spirit, reason, and the like), this difference is regarded by many contemporary philosophers as a matter of the ability (due, presumably, to a more complex central nervous system) to respond in more diverse ways to a wider variety of stimuli—as a matter of degree rather than of kind.

Cartesian and Wittgensteinian attitudes. The difference between Cartesian and Wittgensteinian attitudes toward the fact that intuitive knowledge that *p*, such that belief in *p* is justified yet there is no way to settle doubt about *p*, exists may be summed up by saying that for a Cartesian the claim that belief in *p* is justified must reflect a natural fact—for example, some intrinsic feature of that belief (considered as a mental state), such as self-evidence. For the Wittgensteinian, on the other hand, this claim need reflect only a social convention. On the Cartesian view, it is only contingently true that we possess intuitive knowledge, a fact that is to be explained (if at all) by reference to the make-up of our minds. On the Wittgensteinian view, our possession of intuitive knowledge is a necessary truth, built into the use of the word "know." The Cartesian reasons that since there cannot be an infinite regress—and thus justification of beliefs must stop somewhere—there must be certain kinds of belief that are intrinsically of a special sort, such that to have them is to know that they do not require justification. Followers of Wittgenstein reason that since there can be no infinite regress—and thus justification of belief must stop somewhere—one would expect, given our use of the word "know" to mean "justified belief," that there would be certain conventions dictating that certain beliefs are justified even in the absence of good reasons. For the Cartesian, these conventions reflect introspectable facts about the mind or about entities (such as universals) visible to the eye of the mind; for the Wittgensteinian, they do not reflect anything. To ask why we have procedures for settling doubt about *S*'s claim that he sees a house, although we do not have procedures for settling doubt about

his claim that he has a pain, is, according to Wittgensteinians, to ask why we use the words "pain," "house," and "see" as we do. To such questions there is no answer. Nor is there any answer to the question why we use "event" or "cause" in such a way that it does not make sense to ask whether or not a given event was uncaused. We just do. That in certain cases it does not make sense to ask certain questions—for example, the question "How do you know?"—is, on this view, as much a matter of convention as the fact that one normally says "I am in pain" when being tortured but not when being caressed.

Objections to the linguistic explanation. Much contemporary epistemological controversy consists of arguments for and against the behaviorist analysis of knowledge and the linguistic explanation of intuitive knowledge. The principal objections to the linguistic explanation are three: (1) It has been claimed that no behavioristic analysis of "believes" (and thus a fortiori of "knows") can be achieved without recourse to terms that, like "believes" itself, exhibit intentionality (see INTENTIONALITY). (2) It has been argued that the view that there is no awareness, perception, consciousness, or knowledge prior to the acquisition of linguistic ability makes it impossible to understand how we can learn language in the first place. (In rebuttal, it has been argued that to suppose that we learn how words are used by associating certain awarenesses with certain utterances is a misleading backward projection of the way in which an adult learns new words into the original learning of language by the child.) (3) It has been argued that the stimulus–response model is inadequate for explaining the learning of languages, on the ground that one who knows a language is able to produce grammatical sentences he has never heard. This fact has suggested to some theorists that we must postulate innate knowledge in order to explain language-learning.

This article will not attempt to resolve these issues, but will only describe how the linguistic explanation has been brought to bear upon (*a*) the notion of unconscious inference, (*b*) the notion of intuitive awareness of universals, and (*c*) the notion of nonpropositional knowledge.

NONINFERENTIAL KNOWLEDGE AND UNCONSCIOUS INFERENCE

It has traditionally been held that all knowledge which is not intuitive is inferential, and thus that the cases of nonintuitive, noninferential knowledge should properly be regarded as the products of unconscious inference. This view is most familiar in the form of the phenomenalist claim that *S*'s knowledge that, for instance, there is a white house before him is always the result of an inference from propositions concerning the sense data that *S* is currently having or concerning the appearances that the house is presenting to him. Proponents of this view regard *S*'s denial that he made such an inference or believed such propositions simply as evidence of a lack of philosophical sophistication. Such a view results from the assumption that only certain special propositions are suited, by virtue of their intrinsic properties, to be objects of noninferential knowledge. Thus, phenomenalists hold that "That is a white house" is inherently unsuited to be noninferentially known, whereas "I am now having a white sense datum" or "There now seems to me to be something white in my visual field" is inherently suited to be so known. The occurrence of an unconscious inference in *S*, they hold, is guaranteed by the fact that his belief is unsuited to be an expression of direct sensory awareness. No empirical evidence is allowed to disconfirm that such an unconscious inference was performed.

The criterion for being an expression of direct sensory awareness used by sense-datum theorists usually takes one or the other of the following forms:

(1) *p* expresses *S*'s direct sensory awareness if and only if *S* has intuitive knowledge that *p* (if, in other words, there are no procedures available that would provide better evidence against *p* than the fact of *S*'s belief that *p* provides for *p*), and if *S*'s coming to know that *p* is correlated with *S*'s having a certain sensation.

(2) *p* expresses *S*'s direct sensory awareness if and only if a sufficient condition of the acquisition of knowledge that *p* by *S* is that *S* has a certain sensation (so that none of *S*'s antecedent knowledge interferes to provide an interpretation of what his senses give).

These two criteria are often taken as interchangeable by philosophers who have gone in quest of the "given" elements in experience—for, at first blush, such intuitively knowable propositions as "I am in pain" or "I seem to be seeing something white" seem the most promising candidates for satisfying the second form.

The linguistic explanation of sensory intuition attempts to dispense with both the given and unconscious inference. According to the linguistic theory nothing could possibly satisfy the second form, since a sensation is never a sufficient condition for the acquisition of a bit of knowledge. Also, there is nothing paradoxical in saying that a man may simultaneously come to know, without performing any inferences, that this is an airplane, a Boeing airplane, and a B-29 as a result of a single modification of the eyes—the same modification that, in a child, would produce only the knowledge that this is something silver. According to this theory, the man's belief in all these propositions is justified because, roughly speaking, he has been conditioned to utter statements expressing each of them when certain sensory stimuli are received. Some men, as we say, just know a B-29 when they see one, and others do not. An aircraft spotter trained to respond to the appearance of a B-29 by saying "There is a B-29" would have a justified belief in this proposition even if he were unable to list any criteria for B-29-hood (and thus were unable to provide any reasons for his believing the plane to be a B-29).

For those who accept a linguistic explanation of intuitive knowledge, the traditional attempt to identify noninferential and intuitive knowledge by means of the notion of unconscious inference results from a confusion of the context of *S*'s acquisition of the knowledge that *p* with the context of his justifying his belief that *p* to one who doubts *p*. If an argument between *S* and a doubter of an empirical proposition *p* were carried to its ideal limit, *S* might eventually have to retreat to such intuitively known statements as "It seems to me that I remember that *q*" and the like. The ideal empiricist would be the man who never be-

lieves an empirical proposition *p* unless he has previously performed an inference embodying the argument that he would give in defense of *p* when challenged by a die-hard doubter. (The ideal empiricist, in other words, is the ideal Cartesian doubter; he always doubts every proposition he knows how to doubt.) The notion that we are all unconsciously ideal empiricists is a confusion of "*S* would not be able to justify his belief that *p* to a die-hard doubter without appealing to certain propositions that he knows intuitively to be true" with "*S* is not justified in believing *p* if he has not previously justified his belief to himself."

Once we adopt the linguistic explanation of intuitive knowledge, its defenders argue, we see that whereas noninferential knowledge is a matter of one's disposition to make certain statements being a sufficient ground for one's belief that they are true, intuitive knowledge is a matter of that disposition serving as the best possible evidence for their truth. The propositions that can be noninferentially known by *S*, like those that can be intuitively known by him, are determined by *S*'s training, circumstances, and abilities, together with the conventions in force within his linguistic community. The fact that certain propositions are usually known noninferentially, and others usually known intuitively, by normal adults has misled philosophers into thinking that certain special intrinsic properties belong to all those propositions, and only to those propositions, properties detectable by our mental eye. The linguistic theory, freeing us from the "mental eye" model, directs our attention to the factual criteria that we use in deciding whether a certain belief, held by a certain person, is justified.

INTUITIVE ACQUAINTANCE WITH CONCEPTS

A person is said to have intuitive acquaintance with a concept if he is able to understand a large range of propositions that employ a term signifying this concept and is unable to explain the significance of this term. Thus (confining ourselves, for the sake of simplicity, to descriptive concepts) we may say that *S* grasps F-ness intuitively if and only if he can use the expression "F" correctly, and he does not know any noncircular definition of "F," where a "definition of 'F'" is any true statement of the form "*X* is called 'F' (or 'an F') if and only if it is _____," and "noncircular" means that the blank is filled by some expression that neither contains "F" nor contains any word whose definition itself contains "F," nor any word whose definition contains words whose definition contains "F," and so on.

Act of abstraction theories. As in the case of intuitive knowledge that *p*, there is no dispute among philosophers about the existence of intuitive acquaintance with concepts. Rather, as in the former case, controversy arises concerning the explanation of this fact. In this case also, philosophers working within a Cartesian tradition accept a "simple act" theory. On this traditional view, we possess a faculty called abstraction that, for example, peels the whiteness of white objects from these objects and holds the whiteness up before our mental eye; once we have whiteness clearly in focus, we can label it with the term "white" and thus can acquire a knowledge of how to use this term. This act of abstraction, like the act of intuiting that *p*, is specifically mental, simple, and unanalyzable. Within this Cartesian framework, the principal issue is that between rationalists and empiricists: whether such a simple act of abstraction must be postulated to explain only our knowledge of apparently indefinable sensory concepts (like "white"), or whether it is also needed to explain our knowledge of apparently indefinable nonsensory concepts, such as "being," "cause," "necessity," or "good." (See ETHICAL OBJECTIVISM in relation to "good.") Empiricists have traditionally held that these latter concepts are not grasped intuitively. They have claimed either that our knowledge of how to use terms signifying them is a result of our implicitly or unconsciously possessing noncircular definitions of them, or that these terms do not refer to concepts at all but are without meaning. Consequently, they have devoted themselves to proposing such definitions, or to developing theories of meaningfulness that would permit the conclusion that these terms have no meaning. Rationalists, on the other hand, have insisted that certain terms signify a priori concepts, and that none of the definitions of these terms proposed by empiricists (such as Hume's definition of "causation" as "constant conjunction") are adequate.

Linguistic theory of conceptual intuition. The traditional account of our intuitive grasp of concepts contains many of the same elements as the traditional view of intuitive knowledge that *p*. It is again assumed that we need to account for a difference between men and animals (the fact that we can use concepts, whereas animals can merely respond to stimuli) by postulating a simple *sui generis* mental act and that this simple act does not occur in all the cases that, prima facie, are cases of immediate knowledge, but that some such cases are cases of unconscious mediation. Just as recent philosophical thought has turned away from the notion that intuitive knowledge that *p* is to be regarded as such a simple act, and has offered an account of the acquisition of such knowledge in terms of a theory according to which the use of language is a necessary condition of the possession of any piece of knowledge, recent thought has likewise asserted that the ability to use "F" correctly is all that is signified by the phrase "acquaintance with F-ness," and thus that the notion of a prelinguistic grasp of F-ness is incoherent. According to this newer view, no object of acquaintance (such as a concept, conceived of as a sort of mental particular) need be postulated as that with which language learners correlate utterances of general terms. We learn such terms as "white" not by correlating utterances of them with anything but by being subjected to a conditioning process that leads us, after some trial and error, to utter these words in appropriate contexts in appropriate situations. This process need not, at any stage, involve our knowing the truth of any proposition of the form "X is called 'F' only when it is an instance of F-ness."

The older view, in insisting on the necessity of such knowledge, assumes that the process of learning the use of an indefinable word like "white" must parallel the process of learning the use of a word by learning its definition. Just as we might correlate utterances of "bachelor" with situations in which we would be inclined to say "unmarried male," and thus learn the meaning of "bachelor," so (the

older theory holds) we correlate utterances of "white" with situations in which we are aware of whiteness. But, proponents of the newer view object, the only test we have for knowing whether we are aware of whiteness is whether or not we are inclined to utter "white." Nothing is added to an explanation of learning words ostensively by a reference to acquaintance with concepts, save the unverifiable claim to possess a piece of prelinguistic knowledge. If this newer view (largely due to Wittgenstein and his followers) is accepted, then what distinguishes us from the animals is not that they cannot perform the mysterious operation of intuiting concepts but simply that we can respond in much more various ways to a much greater variety of stimuli than they can (and, specifically, we can develop patterns of linguistic behavior). Once again, the difference between men and animals reduces to the possession of language.

One advantage claimed by defenders of this newer view is that, if it is accepted, the old controversy about the existence of a priori concepts that divided rationalists from empiricists is rendered moot. The question of whether we must postulate a sort of nonsensory ostention of such concepts as causality, or an innate grasp of them, no longer arises if the same sort of process that enables us to learn the use of "white" enables us to learn the use of "cause." To acquire the concept of causality is, on this view, to learn the use of the word "cause"; this can be done without correlating utterances of "cause" with anything, but simply by trial and error: Sometimes when we say "This caused that," we are rebuked, and sometimes praised, until gradually we get it right. (Before we got it right, we were said not to know the meaning of "cause," just as we were said not to know the meaning of "white" as long as we called "white" what our parents called "gray.") The question of whether "cause" (and other terms that have been held to signify a priori concepts) is definable without circularity now loses its philosophical interest.

INTUITION AS NONPROPOSITIONAL KNOWLEDGE

The final sense of intuition comes primarily from Kant, who defined "intuition" as "knowledge that is in immediate relation to objects" (see *Critique of Pure Reason*, A19–B34, A320–B377). By "immediate" he here meant "without the mediation of concepts," and he took sense perception as the paradigm of intuition (although he also argued for the existence of pure intuitions of space and time). Kant sharply distinguished immediate knowledge from knowledge of the truth of judgments concerning the objects sensed, since he held that the formation of judgments requires the addition of concepts to intuitions. The former sort of knowledge is a necessary condition of the latter. The knowledge gained in sense perception is expressed by judgments concerning the objects sensed but exists prior to the formation of these judgments. Perceptual knowledge of *O* is, on this view, not reducible to knowledge that *O* has certain properties.

This distinction between immediate knowledge of objects and mediate knowledge of facts about these objects was formulated by Russell, in *The Problems of Philosophy*, as the distinction between "knowledge by acquaintance" and "knowledge by description." He proceeded to explain a priori knowledge by postulating a faculty, analogous to sensation, that acquaints us with universals and with the relations between universals. The assertion of the existence of universals has, traditionally, gone hand in hand with the faculty explanation of our intuitive knowledge of a priori truths and of our grasp of nonsensory concepts. It is still current among contemporary philosophers who resist the linguistic explanation of this knowledge. These philosophers include both such traditional rationalists as Brand Blanshard and phenomenologists who adopt Edmund Husserl's notion of intuition of essences.

The Kantian notion of sense perception as a kind of nonjudgmental knowledge has had the effect of opening the door to the suggestion that we possess a certain sort of knowledge that is like sense perception, or Russellian acquaintance with universals, in being immediate but unlike either in being inexpressible. In other words, it is suggested that we have an intuition of a certain object O even though we do not know the truth of *any* proposition of the form "O is Q." The reason usually given for our failure to have the latter sort of knowledge is that conceptual thought (or language) is inadequate to capture the essence of X. For example, Bergson argued that duration cannot be captured by concepts (nor, a fortiori, expressed in language) because concepts (and thus language) are designed precisely to freeze and stabilize (and thus to distort) the flux of experience, whose essence is duration. Again, God's perfect simplicity—his identity with his own attributes—is held to make it impossible truly to apply any predicate to him, and thus to know any true propositions about him.

Philosophers who adopt the view that there is no knowledge prior to the possession of language, and who construe knowledge in the behavioristic manner, naturally object to the notion of nonpropositional knowledge. On their view, the original Kantian notion of sense perception as a kind of knowledge is based upon a confusion. Once this confusion is dissipated, the analogy to sense perception that is the basis of Russellian accounts of a priori knowledge and of theories of inexpressible intuition will no longer be available, and the notion of knowledge of O that is irreducible to the knowledge that O has certain features will appear as paradoxical as it really is. The original confusion, these philosophers argue, is that of the cause of the belief that some sensed object O has the feature Q with the justification of this belief. Specifically, the fact that knowledge that O is Q is caused by a sensation of O is combined with the assumption that nothing can serve to justify S's claim to know about O except another piece of knowledge about O by S. This produces the conclusion that the mere sensing of O is itself a case of knowing—distinct from, because giving a ground for, the knowledge that O is Q. Since sensing O is construed as a direct relation between the knower and O, whereas knowing that O is Q is construed as a relation between the knower and something distinct from O (a fact or a proposition), it is inferred that there are two sorts of knowing, one of which is primitive and direct and the other derivative and indirect. A causal condition for knowledge is thus confused with a special type of knowledge—knowledge by acquaintance.

Philosophers who deny the existence of such nonpropo-

sitional knowledge by acquaintance argue that the notion of knowledge of O that is not knowledge that O has some feature is neither present in ordinary usage nor part of a useful explanatory theory. On their view, all knowledge of objects is knowledge of the truth of propositions about these objects. This anti-Kantian position is supported by, and supports, the anti-Cartesian behaviorist position, according to which knowledge cannot occur prior to the ability to learn language. Although it is logically possible to hold both that there can be prelinguistic knowledge of facts and that there is no such thing as knowledge of particulars as distinct from knowledge of facts, this position is not popular. Contemporary epistemological thought is, by and large, split between those who adopt both a Cartesian "simple act" explanation of the intuitive knowledge that p and a Kantian notion of nonpropositional knowledge as a necessary condition for intuitive propositional knowledge, and those who reject both of these views in favor of a radically behavioristic approach.

INTUITION OF THE INEXPRESSIBLE

Even philosophers who have remained faithful to the traditional Cartesian and Kantian positions tend to criticize the use of the notion of intuition as nonpropositional awareness made by such philosophers as Fichte, Bergson, and contemporary Thomists. Their criticism is based on the view that the only criterion for knowing whether S has nonpropositional knowledge of O is his knowledge of the truth of propositions about O. Thus both groups reject claims to have knowledge that one is unable to express (except, perhaps, in analogies and metaphors). Anti-Cartesian philosophers, however, argue that it is precisely the Kantian view that sensing is a kind of knowing which opens the gates to claims to intuit the inexpressible (see INEFFABLE, THE). This view leads naturally to the conclusion that even the objects of ordinary sensory acquaintance are incommunicable and inexpressible. No amount of talk by Jones (who has seen O) will suffice to reproduce in Smith (who has not) the sensation Jones had when he was in the presence of O. This failure to reproduce an experience is, given the view that sensing is a kind of knowing, taken as a failure to convey knowledge of O, even though Smith may learn, from Jones's reports, every fact about O that Jones knows. We thus find ourselves adopting a novel, and peculiarly philosophical, sense of "express"—a sense in which an experience would be expressed only if it were reproduced. Whereas in the normal sense of the term, my seeing a white house is completely and adequately expressed by some finite set of such propositions as "That's a white house," in this new sense such propositions are inherently unsatisfactory surrogates. This line of thought, opponents of nonpropositional knowledge argue, plays into the hands of those who, like Bergson, hold that language is inadequate to reality.

The claim that language is inadequate to express one's intuitive knowledge of reality would, in itself, be harmless. However, the danger of adopting this new meaning of "inexpressible" is that we may find ourselves claiming private justification for our moral, philosophical, religious, aesthetic, or other beliefs by saying, "Although I cannot, of course, express (or communicate or put into words) the experience that I had, and hence cannot supply you with reasons for believing that *p*, I am nevertheless entitled to believe that *p* solely on the strength of that experience." The plausibility of this sort of reasoning stems from the fact that, in the case of noninferential belief about physical objects, we sometimes say things like "Since you haven't seen a flying saucer, you have no reason to believe that there are flying saucers; but I have seen one, and so I do believe in them." Here we seem to be justifying a belief solely on the basis of private experience. The difference is that "I saw a flying saucer" is a complete and adequate expression of this experience, in the ordinary sense of "express." The justification is sufficient because the statement that an experience *E* was had analytically implies *p*. (If *S* saw a flying saucer, then there are flying saucers to be seen.) In the former case, however, the statement that an experience *E* was had cannot entail any statement about the object of the experience because the nature of the experience is, *ex hypothesi*, inexpressible. This obvious disanalogy is veiled by the fact that in the second, philosophical sense of "inexpressible," our experiences of seeing houses or flying saucers are just as inexpressible as the Thomists' intuition of Being, or Bergson's intuition of duration. In other words, a tacit shift to a new sense of "express" creates the sophistical argument "Since your sensory experiences are inexpressible, and yet sufficient to justify your beliefs, it is unfair of you not to let my inexpressible nonsensory experiences justify my beliefs." Of course, in the ordinary sense of "express," sensory experiences are as expressible as experiences can be.

In addition to this criticism of the ambiguity contained in the philosophers' use of "inexpressible," a further criticism of such claims to private justification is available if the behaviorist view of the nature of justification of claims to noninferential knowledge is adopted. If this justification is viewed not as a matter of an intrinsic, introspectable property (self-evidence) of certain beliefs but rather as a matter of social convention, then one will hold that we know which of our noninferential beliefs are justified only by knowing which ones our peers would agree are justified. In the flying saucer example, we rightly think that our belief in flying saucers is justified if we think we have seen flying saucers, because we are confident that anyone who had had the sensations we have had would have been disposed to utter "I see a flying saucer." We know that our belief is justified because our peers admit that if they should ever have an experience of the sort we claim to have had, they would share our belief. The only element of privacy lies in the fact that they can have doubts about, for example, whether we are being truthful in claiming that we had this experience, or whether we were sober, or attentive, whereas we cannot. In the "inexpressible intuition" case, however, we cannot tell whether our peers would share our belief if they shared our experience, for we do not know what our experience was. Here we could speak of a private justification only if we had a private language in which we could express to ourselves, although to no one else, what we experienced, and private criteria of justification formulated (in part, at least) in this private language. But, aside from the general difficulties in

the notion of a private language pointed out by Wittgenstein, "private criteria of justification" is an intrinsically paradoxical notion. One can no more have private rules for justifying beliefs than one can have private rules for justifying actions. A criminal has no greater claim on our sympathy if he proclaims that his private ethical code differs from ours, and a believer in untestable beliefs has no greater claim on our attention when he says that his epistemological code is not ours.

Bibliography

The medievals used "intuitive cognition" as we would use "sensory intuition" to refer to knowledge about objects present to the senses. The term was opposed to "abstractive cognition," which included memory and imagination. They also, however, used "intuition" to refer to a vision of God. This use of "intuition" for any sort of knowledge that has the same noninferential character as knowledge of the apparent features of an object present to the senses was continued by Descartes (*Regulae* XII), Spinoza (*Ethics* II, Prop. 40, Note 2), and Locke (*Essay Concerning Human Understanding*, Book II, Ch. 2, Sec. 1). These philosophers used the term as we would use "nonsensory intuition"—to refer to our noninferential knowledge of, for instance, mathematical axioms and analytic truths, and of the validity of valid inferences. Between Descartes and Kant, "intuition" was rarely used in reference to perceptual knowledge, nor was a clear distinction made between propositional and nonpropositional knowledge. Since Kant, however, it has been usual to speak of both nonpropositional perceptual knowledge of a particular, and of the propositional knowledge derived from this nonpropositional knowledge, as cases of intuition.

Whereas Kant had denied the existence of intellectual intuition (nonpropositional knowledge of insensible objects), Fichte asserted it in his *Werke*, edited by I. H. Fichte (Berlin, 1845), Vol. I, pp. 463 ff. However, Fichte argued that he did not really disagree with Kant because the object of this intuition, the Transcendental Ego, was an act rather than a thing. The same strategy is adopted by contemporary Neo-Thomists, who speak of an intuition of Being; what is intuited, they say, is an act rather than a thing or an essence. See Jacques Maritain, *Existence and the Existent* (New York, 1948), Ch. 1, and Étienne Gilson, *Being and Some Philosophers* (Toronto, 1949), Ch. 6. The most influential recent proponent of a faculty of nonpropositional knowledge other than sense perception is Henri Bergson; see his *Introduction to Metaphysics* (New York, 1913). For a criticism of Bergson's notion of intuition, consult G. Watts Cunningham, *A Study in the Philosophy of Bergson* (New York, 1916), Ch. 3. For a discussion of the philosophical importance of the ineffable intuitions claimed by mystics, see W. T. Stace, *Mysticism and Philosophy* (New York, 1960), Chs. 1 and 3.

W. H. Walsh, *Reason and Experience* (Oxford, 1947), contains an account of traditional controversies between rationalists and empiricists concerning intuitive knowledge. For the traditional view that intuitive knowledge of facts about objects sensed is based on a nonpropositional acquaintance with these objects, see Bertrand Russell, *The Problems of Philosophy* (Oxford, 1912), Ch. 5. Criticism of the notion of knowledge by acquaintance, which Russell develops in *The Problems of Philosophy*, is found in H. L. A. Hart, "Is There Knowledge by Acquaintance?" in *PAS*, Supp. Vol. 23 (1949), 69–90; also see the essays by G. E. Hughes and J. N. Findlay on the same topic in the same volume, 91–128, and Wilfrid Sellars, *Science, Perception, and Reality* (London, 1963), pp. 127–196. Additional criticisms of the view that sensing is a form of knowing occur in H. A. Prichard, "The Sense-datum Fallacy," in *PAS*, Supp. Vol. 17 (1938), 1–18; Wilfrid Sellars, "Physical Realism," in *Philosophy and Phenomenological Research*, Vol. 15 (1954–1955), 13–32; and Gilbert Ryle, *The Concept of Mind* (London, 1949), Ch. 7.

The notion of unconscious inference is presented in Bertrand Russell, *The Problems of Philosophy*, Ch. 13, and a defense of this notion in Gilbert Harman, "How Belief Is Based on Inference," in *Journal of Philosophy*, Vol. 61 (1964), 353–359. For the criteria of direct sensory awareness, see Bertrand Russell, "On Verification," in *PAS*, Vol. 38 (1937–1938), 1–20. Russell's *Analysis of Mind* (London, 1921), Ch. 12, states the view that beliefs are introspectable mental occurrences. For criticism of this view, see Gilbert Ryle, *The Concept of Mind*, Chs. 2 and 5. The view that we can introspectively differentiate knowledge from mere belief is found in H. A. Prichard, *Knowledge and Perception* (Oxford, 1950), p. 88. Prichard is criticized on this point by Norman Malcolm in his *Knowledge and Certainty* (New York, 1963), p. 58.

For the contemporary reaction to Cartesianism, see Gilbert Ryle, *The Concept of Mind*, and Ludwig Wittgenstein, *Philosophical Investigations* (Oxford, 1953). An earlier reaction against the Cartesian account of intuitive knowledge is C. S. Peirce's *Collected Papers* (Cambridge, Mass., 1933–1958), Vol. V, pp. 135–189. For the linguistic account of intuitive knowledge of the truth of propositions, see Wilfrid Sellars, *Science, Perception, and Reality*, pp. 164–170. The view that intuitive knowledge of a priori truths is founded upon a nonpropositional knowledge of universals or essences is found in Bertrand Russell, *Problems of Philosophy*, Ch. 10; Brand Blanshard, *Reason and Analysis* (La Salle, Ill., 1962), Chs. 6, 9, 10; and Edmund Husserl, *Ideas* (London, 1931). For critical discussion of this view and of the linguistic account of a priori knowledge, see Arthur Pap, *Semantics and Necessary Truth* (New Haven, 1958).

RICHARD RORTY

INTUITIONISM. See ETHICAL OBJECTIVISM; MATHEMATICS, FOUNDATIONS OF.

IONESCU, NAE (1890–1940), Rumanian logician, metaphysician, and religious philosopher. Ionescu studied at the University of Bucharest and received his doctorate from the University of Munich in 1919 with the thesis *Die Logistik als Versuch einer neuen Begründung der Mathematik*. From 1920 on he was professor of logic, history of logic, and metaphysics at the University of Bucharest. He was also the editor in chief (1924–1928) and director (1928–1934) of the newspaper *Cuvântul*, in which he published more than one thousand articles on religious, political, and economic problems.

Ionescu's scholarly publications were few—some articles on logic, a few prefaces, and a series of articles in the theological journal *Predania* (1937–1938). Nevertheless, his influence from 1922 to 1940 was enormous. His teachings and writings inspired a new interest in metaphysics and religious philosophy in Rumania. Although he was primarily a logician, he strove to understand all forms of human activity. According to Ionescu, the philosopher must take into consideration not only the theoretical expression of historical life—from religion to logic and science—but also its meaningful creations: crafts, arts, biographies, political events, and all others. He approached the history of logic, as well as the history of metaphysics and of religion, as a typology of the human spirit. Such a typology he regarded as always a creation of history and ultimately of life. This seems to imply a radical historicization of the mind's activities, but God, for Nae Ionescu, is present in history through the Incarnation. On the other hand, man's mode of being is completely fulfilled only through death, and death is above all transcendent.

Bibliography

A complete posthumous edition of Ionescu's philosophical works in twelve volumes was announced during World War II, but only three volumes were published: *Istoria Logicei* (Bucharest, 1941) and *Metafizica*, 2 vols. (Bucharest, 1942–1943). See also Vasile Băncilă, "Nae Ionescu," in the Preface to *Istoria Logicei*.

MIRCEA ELIADE

IONIAN SCHOOL. See PRE-SOCRATIC PHILOSOPHY.

IQBAL, MUHAMMAD (1877–1938), Islamic poet and metaphysician, was born in Sialkot, Pakistan. He studied philosophy at Cambridge for three years under J. M. E. McTaggart and James Ward. He received his Ph.D. from Munich University in 1908 for his thesis *The Development of Metaphysics in Persia*.

Inheriting the classical tradition of Muslim mystic poets, both Persian and Urdu, Iqbal was for a long time an admirer of the Spanish Sufi philosopher ibn-'Arabī (1165–1240), the most consistent advocate of pantheism among Muslim thinkers. Very soon, however, he realized that this philosophy was foreign to the simple and invigorating message of Islam as embodied in the Qur'ān and as represented in the dynamic life of Muhammad and his early followers. Under the influence of Jalāl al-Din Rūmī (1207–1273), the great mystic poet, whose philosophical outlook was allied in several important respects with post-Kantian voluntaristic thought in the West, as represented by Nietzsche and Bergson, he evolved a new system of thought that was meant to revitalize the faith of the Muslims of the Indo-Pakistan subcontinent. At first his message, written in verse in the *Secret of the Self* (1915), raised a storm of opposition, but very soon this opposition died its natural death, and the whole subcontinent reverberated with his inspiring melodies. He exerted great influence in molding the pattern of political, social, and intellectual life of the Muslims in the early decades of the twentieth century, an influence which is visible everywhere even now. In 1930, as president of the Muslim League, he proposed the creation of a "Muslim India within India." Pakistan, Iqbal's dream, came into being in 1947, nine years after his death. As a tribute to his memory, the government of Pakistan established in 1951 a statutory body known as Iqbal Academy, in order "to promote the study and understanding of the works of Iqbal."

The system of thought that he evolved may be called theistic pluralism in contradistinction to ibn-'Arabī's pantheistic doctrine of the unity of being, which denied not only the unique personality of the Divine Being and his existence as distinct from the universe but also the existence of human individuals and their partnership with God in constituting the commonwealth of ends.

Kant's negative answer to the possibility of metaphysics provided Iqbal with a basis on which to construct his thought. Human thought, Kant asserted, is circumscribed by the categories of space and time; therefore, the Ultimate Reality, which, by definition, is beyond these categories, cannot be comprehended by pure thought, which is intimately related to and based on the normal level of experience. According to Iqbal, however, time and space are not fixed and unvarying modes, as Kant had thought; their significance may vary with the beings of higher or lower grade, the degree of being determined by greater or lesser psychic powers. Moreover, this normal level is not the only level of knowledge-yielding experience. The level above spatiotemporal experience is revealed by intuition, a form of perception which is allied to ordinary experience in giving objective knowledge but which is quite distinct from it in not being solely dependent upon sense perception; intuitive experience is individual and incommunicable. It is not simple Bergsonian "intellectual sympathy," which implies negation of the perceiver; intuition, according to Iqbal, by bringing the perceiver into contact with the Most Real, has the power to vitally transform his character and to endow him with a new personality, which reveals to him the higher consciousness of his manifold relations with God and the universe. Through his contact with Reality, the individual discovers his uniqueness, his metaphysical status, and the possibility of improvement in that status. The experience of intuition not only serves to confirm his reality and deepen his whole being but also sharpens his will with the creative assurance that the universe is not something to be really seen and known through concepts but rather something to be made and remade by continuous action, by interpreting the intuition of reality as a stimulus to ideal ends and purposes. Conceptual knowledge gives us knowledge of relations, not of reality; it is only through intuition that we can grasp the Real and give a fresh direction to the course of human history.

To Iqbal, ego is the basic reality revealed by intuition as the center of all efforts—a revelation that is vouchsafed not in the barren contemplation of the recluse but in moments of great decision and action, which are expressive of a firm faith in the ultimate purposiveness of the universe. The life of the ego consists in meeting obstruction in its contact with matter and overcoming it. This gives the ego the power to act freely. It is partly determined and partly free, and it reaches fuller freedom by approaching the individual who is most free—God. In other words, the ego is continually moving from a state of lesser freedom to that of greater freedom.

The ego is also immortal. According to Averroës immortality means transindividual eternity of intellect; according to Nietzsche immortality is synonymous with what he calls eternal recurrence, a most "intolerable" conception, as Iqbal put it. Immortality, according to Iqbal, must be individual and personal. He repudiated the pantheistic belief that the self, as a differentiation of the Absolute, will in the end be submerged and lose its identity in the Whole. It was to save man from this fate that Iqbal advocated that immortality is not a gift that every ego will enjoy; rather, it is a hope, an aspiration, depending, of course, upon a particular philosophy of life and a particular ethic that tends to maintain the state of tension in the ego and develop self-reliance, self-respect, self-confidence, self-preservation—even self-assertion, when such a thing is necessary in the interest of life—and the power to stick to the cause of truth, justice, and duty, even in the face of death. Such behavior helps in the integration of the forces of ego, thus hardening it against the forces of disintegration and dissolution. Because the ego, which exists only in the state of tension, is the most valuable achievement of man, he should exert all efforts not to revert to a state of relaxation. We are mortal insofar as we keep ourselves fettered to spatialized

time; as soon as we rise above it and immerse ourselves in what Bergson called duration, we become timeless. It is possible, Iqbal held, to realize this timelessness even in this life, although it be but for a moment. It is the moral duty of man to keep the state of tension intact by repudiating life-negating philosophies and to attain immortality by his ego-sustaining behavior. It is in this sense that attaining immortality, according to Iqbal, becomes a moral duty.

How is the ego related to the world of matter? Iqbal viewed matter, as did Einstein, as "a system of interrelated events" and the universe as an "organism," as did Whitehead. Every atom, however low in the scale of being, is an ego. Mind, with its capacity for self-consciousness, is a higher ego, and body is a combination of subegos. Thus, on this principle the universe is of the nature of life—free, creative, and original. The universe is constantly growing and progressing toward an end—a rationally directed creative life.

How is the Ultimate Ego (God) related to the universe and to the human ego? To the Absolute Self the universe is not a reality confronting him as an "other"; it is only a passing phase of his consciousness, a fleeting moment of its infinite life. Iqbal began with Einstein's view that the universe is finite but boundless and added that it is finite because it is a passing phase of God's extensively infinite consciousness and boundless because the creative power of God is intensively infinite. But the human self is the exception; it is not a mere passing phase in God's consciousness, for it is self-centered and exclusive. It is distinct but not isolated from God. The Ultimate Ego is characterized by the most beautiful names and attributes; he is transcendent and yet immanent, and above all he is a Person who responds to man's inner yearning in "the awful silence of the universe."

Bibliography

Most of Iqbal's works are in verse, Persian and Urdu. Only books available in English are mentioned here. *The Secrets of the Self,* translated by R. E. Nicholson (Lahore, 1950); *The Mysteries of Selflessness,* translated by A. J. Arberry (Lahore, 1953); *Tulips of Sinai,* translated by A. J. Arberry (London, 1947); *The Persian Psalms,* translated by A. J. Arberry (Lahore, 1948); *New Garden of Mystery,* translated by B. A. Dar (Lahore, 1963); *Pilgrimage of Eternity,* translated into English verse by S. M. Ahmed (Lahore, 1961); *Development of Metaphysics in Persia* (London, 1908); *Reconstruction of Religious Thought in Islam* (London, 1951); and *Poems From Iqbal,* translated by V. G. Kiernam (London, 1955).

For literature on Iqbal, see B. A. Dar, *A Study of Iqbal's Philosophy* (Lahore, 1944) and *Iqbal and Post-Kantian Voluntarism* (Lahore, 1956); I. H. Enver, *Metaphysics of Iqbal* (Lahore, 1944); K. G. Saiyadain, *Iqbal's Educational Philosophy* (Lahore, 1938); and S. A. Vahid, *Iqbal, His Art and Thought* (Lahore, 1944).

B. A. DAR

IRRATIONALISM. Like other words in current philosophical use, such as "historicism" and "subjectivism," "irrationalism" is an exceedingly imprecise term that is employed with a wide variety of meanings and implications. Consequently, any attempt to elucidate its sense within the confines of a clear-cut and tidy formula quickly runs into difficulties. It might be said, for instance, that to describe a writer as an irrationalist is to speak of him as denying the authority of reason. But how is the notion of "reason" itself to be understood, and in what respects is its authority supposed to be flouted? It would scarcely be sufficient to reply that denial of reason consists in illogicality or confusion of thought, or that it manifests itself in a tendency to arrive at unacceptable conclusions; for this would apply to the work of many thinkers to whom the label "irrationalist" is clearly inapplicable. In addition, the suggestion fails to identify the primary point of calling a writer an irrationalist. A man may be accused of irrationality if he is prone to make mistakes of a particular kind or to indulge in invalid reasoning; but it is only insofar as he maintains some specific doctrine concerning such things as the status and role of reason or the relevance of rational standards within various domains of experience or inquiry that he can be called an irrationalist. In other words, attention is focused not on an unwitting failure to conform to norms of generally recognized validity, but on the explicit repudiation, or putting into question, of such norms in the light of certain considerations or in relation to certain contexts.

Enlightenment rationalism. A more promising approach to the understanding of irrationalism is the historical. One might try to understand irrationalism by contrasting it with that "belief in reason," that faith in the application of mathematical and scientific procedures, which was so prominent in the thought and speculation of seventeenth-century and eighteenth-century Europe and which provided the inspiration for the Enlightenment. Such a proposal, however, runs the risk of invoking generalities as vague as they are misleading. Seventeenth-century and eighteenth-century theorists interpreted the ideal of rationality in widely differing ways, and they assumed it or sought to realize it at various levels of inquiry—metaphysical, epistemological, ethical, and political. Descartes, Locke, Hobbes, Leibniz, Spinoza, and Hume shared the conviction that in their speculations concerning the nature of the world and our knowledge of it they were conforming to a course acceptable to reason and were applying methods that reason prescribed. But they differed fundamentally concerning both what constituted rational procedure and what types of discovery such procedure was capable of achieving. Similar disagreements may also be discerned at the other levels of investigation mentioned.

Nineteenth-century irrationalism. The diversity of opinion attributable to thinkers who all held a general belief in rationality puts in doubt the notion that irrationalism can be neatly and unambiguously identified by reference to its rejection of a single set of assumptions allegedly shared by philosophers associated with the Enlightenment. Nevertheless, the ideas of those thinkers most typically classified as irrationalists did develop to a large extent in reaction to the ambitious claims made on behalf of reason by Enlightenment theorists and their nineteenth-century successors, however widely such claims may have varied in actual content and formulation. That the world is in some sense a rational or harmonious whole, that the human mind is capable of comprehending it, and that there exist certain communicable and teachable methods by means of which its inner workings can be revealed; that this knowledge can be systematically uti-lized in a manner that will insure the continuous improvement of human society in the foreseeable future; that man is by nature a reasonable and progressive being whose potentialities can be realized through the removal of ignorance and the creation of institutions based upon principles of justice—it has been against views like these that irrationalist philosophies have, in different ways, characteristically protested. Vociferous insistence upon the limitations and weaknesses of reason followed an equally vociferous insistence upon its possibilities and powers.

ONTOLOGICAL IRRATIONALISM

The belief that reality, at least in its innermost nature, represents an intelligible, ordered system whose fundamental character is accessible to the human intellect, is an ancient one; in philosophy, it dates at least from Plato. During its long history it has admittedly been subjected to a number of widely differing interpretations, ranging from the animistic or religious to the mathematical or scientific. Yet the notion of some kind of comprehensible pattern or rational structure to which all that exists or happens can finally be shown to conform retained its hold. From this point of view the world we belong to is not an alien world; on the contrary, it is one in which, by virtue of our own rationality, we can feel at home.

Pascal's skepticism. There have, however, been thinkers to whom the consoling idea of an intelligible world has seemed less acceptable. Thus even in the seventeenth century, the heyday of Cartesian rationalism, Pascal was questioning the conception of reality as a logically coherent whole, transparent to human reason and in which everything, including man himself, can be seen to have its necessary place: "Too much clarity darkens," he wrote with reference to Descartes's famous "clear and distinct ideas." Forcibly impressed both by the contingent character of human existence in an unfathomable universe and by the inadequacies of human reason, Pascal had little use for rational theology with its pretended proofs of God; he eschewed all such forms of ratiocination in favor of an inward religious faith that transcended ordinary methods of argument and justification and that was beyond demonstration.

The world as will. The intense dissatisfaction and disquiet Pascal experienced when he contemplated the world and our situation within it has been echoed in the works of many subsequent writers, although they have not always shared the religious convictions that ultimately sustained him. For some it has appeared necessary simply to acquiesce in the realization that reality, far from representing an intellectually satisfying or morally acceptable system, is in truth devoid of all rational meaning or purpose and that salvation can only be reached through a complete liberation from its trammels. Such an attitude found perhaps its most eloquent and forceful exponent in Schopenhauer. In Schopenhauer's conception of existence there was an explicit and uncompromising reversal of the traditional approach. He made it his object to show, not that the world is governed according to some beneficent teleological principle or that it is the embodiment of certain fundamental rational categories, but that, on the contrary, what lies at its center is something antithetical to all reason and value, namely, a blind unconscious force or striving he termed "will." It is this that constitutes the metaphysical essence of the world, and not (as Hegel and his followers had taught) Absolute Spirit or Mind manifesting itself according to the inner laws of its own rational development. For Schopenhauer, in fact, all forms of rationalism—metaphysical and scientific alike—involve an illicit projection into the ultimate nature of reality of principles whose actual source and spring is the human intellect alone.

The doctrine of absurdity. Schopenhauer's theory rested, in the last analysis, upon a professed knowledge of what "really" lies beneath the phenomenal (and finally illusory) surface of things. Yet there have also been thinkers whose skepticism, although quite as profound as Schopenhauer's, did not derive from claims of this kind but instead took as its point of departure the concrete facts of ordinary experience. Such is the doctrine of *absurdité* in the work of contemporary French existentialists like Sartre and Camus. In some respects Sartre remains firmly within the Cartesian tradition, founding his epistemology upon the conception of man as a thinking consciousness confronted by an external world of unthinking substance. But the world that we are aware of is not, for Sartre, an intrinsically intelligible world whose nature conforms to a determinate logical order and whose existence is guaranteed by a benevolent deity. Sartre's view of material existence is perhaps most succinctly expressed in his first novel, *La Nausée*, a book that contains in embryo many of the cardinal themes that later figure in his impressive philosophical treatise *L'Être et le néant*. The hero of *La Nausée*, Roquentin, is described as experiencing in a peculiarly vivid and horrifying way the brute "contingency" of things, their palpable failure to measure up to the standards of logical rigor and necessity, of clarity and distinctness, that reason of its nature seeks to impose upon or find realized within the world. Roquentin is impressed by the loose and arbitrary character of our modes of classifying objects and by the manner in which existence, in all its rich and pointless superfluity, seems inevitably to elude the network of interpretative concepts and schemes that we try to throw over it. When so perceived, the world can strike us as divested of all significance or value. "The world of explanations and reasons," Roquentin remarks, "is not the world of existence."

The impossibility of trying to reduce experienced reality to a system, whether Cartesian, Hegelian, or some other, had already been accepted by Kierkegaard, who is often regarded as the originator of modern existentialism. But in Sartre's work one is conscious of a more positive and explicit insistence upon the opacity and ultimate unintelligibility of the world and its resistance to the abstract categories of thought. For Kierkegaard there was something eccentric, some element of radical misunderstanding, in the entire project of attempting to explain or justify existence as a whole in rational terms. By contrast, both Sartre in his philosophical works and Camus in *Le Mythe de Sisyphe* are plainly sympathetic to those who demand intellectually or morally satisfying systematic accounts of existence; it is felt to be in some sense an imperfection of

our condition as human beings in the world that such demands are necessarily incapable of being satisfied. The essence of what they call *absurdité* lies precisely in the contrast between the contingent amorphous character of reality, on the one hand, and the understandable requirements of reason that reality so patently fails to meet, on the other.

EPISTEMOLOGICAL IRRATIONALISM

Irrationalism sometimes finds expression, not in the claim that reality itself is devoid of ultimate senses or purpose, but in the distinguishable idea that the customary or scientific methods by means of which we are accustomed to explore its nature and to which we accord the honorific title of "rational," are inherently defective or suspect. There are clearly close connections between this view and the conceptions of ontological irrationalism. For if the world really is irrational in the ways it is sometimes declared to be, this presumably implies that, at some level at least, it is not amenable to those modes of investigation typically regarded as rational. But some philosophers, while agreeing that such methods are incapable of leading us to any finally acceptable and satisfying explanation of the nature of things, have not supposed themselves to be thereby committed to holding that all comprehension of the desired kind is in principle impossible. They have suggested, in other words, that alternative modes of apprehending and understanding the world, free from the limitations that beset standard procedures, remain open. The object of their strictures has been the distortions inherent in these procedures, rather than the world itself.

The limits of rational inquiry. The belief that there exist determinate limits to what we can discover by the resources of ordinary sense and understanding received precise and systematic exposition in the works of Immanuel Kant. To prescribe limits to what rational inquiry can accomplish is not, as such, to impugn such inquiry, and much of the argument in the *Critique of Pure Reason* is, in fact, expressly concerned with establishing and explaining the validity of mathematical and scientific forms of reasoning within the empirical realm. But there were, nevertheless, two strands in Kant's philosophy that led to doctrines far removed in spirit from those Kant himself propounded. One of these was the claim that the fundamental principles in terms of which phenomenal reality is intelligible derive from the human mind and understanding; the other was the claim that there is a "noumenal" realm of things-in-themselves that is necessarily inaccessible to rational investigation.

Subjectivity of criteria of rational inquiry. Kant's description of the means by which phenomenal reality is intelligible gave rise to the suggestion that the criteria of rational judgment and inference we normally accept are not the stable, objectively grounded things we take them to be but are, on the contrary, essentially subjective and even susceptible to change and variation. Thus Fichte, at any rate in his earlier writings, often gave the impression of having thought that the basic principles in terms of which men interpret their experience ultimately fall within the sphere of individual choice or commitment; as prerational posits they cannot be themselves subject to rational assessment and must, instead, be evaluated by reference to the needs and demands of human beings conceived as volitional agents in the world. Fichte ended by taking refuge in the notion of an Absolute Spirit or rational ego that transcended all particular human selves.

Other nineteenth-century thinkers, however, reinterpreted Fichte's initial postulates in a fashion that implied a definite skepticism regarding the claims of rationality. This was true above all of Nietzsche, who—at least in certain aspects of his complex and not always consistent thinking—exhibited a profound suspicion of accredited concepts and procedures. Possibly more sensitive than any previous philosopher to the emotional drives and attitudes that operate beneath the surface of human life and unconsciously influence thought and behavior, he was at times prepared to speak as if the entire manner in which we approach the world were founded upon pervasive myths and fictions. The "lies and frauds" that permeate our cherished forms of scientific investigation and description are not devoid of all value; on the contrary, from a "life-furthering, life-preserving, species-preserving" point of view they are actually indispensable. But insofar as we take them to embody or reveal the truth, we are the victims of deception.

Nonrational cognition. Although his own confident affirmations concerning the limitations of common sense and science might seem to have required it, Nietzsche did not, in fact, postulate a superior form of cognition capable of circumventing the delusive schemes of ordinary thought and experience and of arriving at some clear, unsullied understanding of the world as it is in itself: in the last analysis there could be no escape from particular interpretations and perspectives. But to other thinkers this has not seemed so evident. Schelling, the contemporary of Fichte and Hegel, evolved an elaborate system in which intuition of a mystical or quasi-religious character was accorded a central place and was held to provide access to the ultimate nature of reality. "The nature of the Absolute *itself*," Schelling wrote, "which as ideal is also immediately real, cannot be known through explanations, but only through intuition" (*Philosophie und Religion*, p. 15). Later Bergson also drew a sharp distinction between the intellect, regarded as having a basically practical function and as rationalizing experience through the construction of mechanistic models and hypotheses, and intuition, whereby an inner sympathetic consciousness of the creative flow that underlies and pervades the universe was attainable.

The division between rational and nonrational or suprarational modes of apprehending the world, which these and other writers have stressed, often merges into further, related contrasts; for example, between conventional perception and artistic perception, between scientific and historical understanding, or between technical know-how, which is communicable in words, and a sense of, or feel for, the inward direction and meaning of things, which is not. Rationalists have tended to point out in return that such contentions are open to serious objections. Emphasis is laid upon the "privacy" of the alleged "insight" or "intuition"; but how can such insight aspire to the status of knowledge if no public criteria are available whereby its findings may be tested or confirmed? Again, in what sense can one speak of knowledge or understanding if—as often

seems to be assumed—the intuition is of a kind that precludes conceptualization? Nevertheless, whatever difficulties irrationalist epistemology may present, these have not prevented its adherents from claiming that there are modes of awareness of the deepest significance to which rationalistic theorists have remained perennially blind.

ETHICAL IRRATIONALISM

Questions have also been raised with regard to our claims to moral knowledge and certainty. Quite recently, for instance, a number of writers of an empiricist persuasion (including Rudolf Carnap, A. J. Ayer, and C. L. Stevenson) have adopted views concerning the meaning and function of moral judgments that would seem to deny, or at least put in doubt, the possibility of treating these as the proper subjects of rational argument. Yet such writers would certainly reject the suggestion that they are irrationalists in any of the senses so far distinguished. If they owe a historical debt, it is to David Hume (himself a skeptic concerning the rationality of morals) rather than to Continental sources, and they would in any case claim that their theories are grounded upon purely logical considerations related to the analysis of moral concepts and terms rather than upon alleged discoveries about the nature of the world or the status of human beings within it. Nor would they be likely to admit that what they say entails any dramatic consequences so far as the realm of practical choice and action is concerned; on the contrary, they have tended to contend that their theories, being of a wholly conceptual character, are neutral between particular moral standpoints and outlooks.

Absence of a moral order in the world. Not every challenge to the rationality of morals has, however, been characterized by a comparable detachment. One of the strongest motives in recent times for belief that moral convictions are without basis or justification has been precisely the decay of all-encompassing theological and philosophical interpretations of reality; for these were thought of as providing the moral consciousness with the kind of backing it logically required. Along with the religious beliefs to which it was sometimes allied, the conception of a moral order at the heart of existence, either revealing itself directly to the eye of reason or manifesting itself empirically in the course of human life and history, was already in decline during the nineteenth century. Schopenhauer's theory of all-pervasive metaphysical will was directly expressive of this development, but it was Nietzsche, not Schopenhauer, who drew the radical consequences. According to Nietzsche, it was necessary to recognize, once and for all, that there is no moral order, no system of ready-made values, objectively subsisting "out there" in the world—"there are no moral phenomena, only moralistic interpretations of phenomena," he wrote in *Beyond Good and Evil*. The notion of moral facts is a philosopher's delusion. With such ideas in mind Nietzsche, in effect, did two things. First, he embarked upon a devastating analysis intended to show how traditional moral codes, far from resulting from the operations of contemplative reason, derive instead from deep-lying nonrational forces in the human psyche, from motives like resentment and sadism and fear. Second, he urged that it is now possible for us—since, in his famous phrase, "God is dead"—to create new values, more fitted to preserving the dignity of man and to realizing those human energies and capacities that still await their true fulfillment.

Alternative theories. The claim that it is now possible to determine new values along these lines drew attention to a difficulty that has beset theorists who have denied the possibility of appealing to rational canons within the moral sphere. Nietzsche was a moralist who wished to insist that certain forms of character and behavior were evidently superior to others; at the same time, he was committed to the opinion that, objectively considered, there was nothing to justify preference for one way of life, one system of values, rather than another—*nichts ist wahr, alles ist erlaubt* ("nothing is true, everything is permitted"). If traditional Christian morality is without foundation in fact or reason, then so, likewise, is any alternative ethics with which we may seek to replace it.

Similar tensions and ambiguities underlie other varieties of individualist or existentialist teaching, from Max Stirner and Kierkegaard on. Sometimes it seems to be maintained that sheer intensity and sincerity of commitment is all that ultimately counts from a moral point of view. What is chosen is not a matter for argument, since in the last resort there is no yardstick, no privileged set of criteria, against which rival possibilities may be assessed and evaluated. The vital thing is for a man to assert his essential freedom by refusing to conform his will to forces and agencies external to himself, including the falsely substantialized standards of conventional religion and ethics.

Sometimes, on the other hand, an attempt is made to give the notion of an acceptable mode of living more positive content, the implication being that certain forms of behavior are more appropriate to our situation in the world than others. For beings who find themselves in an alien and meaningless world, which is bereft of purpose or value, there may be virtue, or at any rate fittingness, in conduct that reflects the inescapable absurdity of their condition. Suggestions as to how conduct might be said to do so have for the most part been as vague as they have been various. Living in the present or for the moment, giving spontaneous vent to instincts or passions (as opposed to trying to heed the reasonable dictates of conscience or prudence), indulging in anarchical or incongruous behavior for its own sake, undertaking certain types of useless artistic activity—these are among the proposals that may be extracted from works purporting to show what is meant. Such works often seem to be inspired by a curious form of inverted rationalism; the rational response to an irrational world is to act irrationally. Yet it would be incorrect to imply that this is the only consideration that has been used to justify such behavior. Instead, the recommendation appears to be held by some proponents to follow from a realization of what constitutes our true innermost nature as human beings; and this claim introduces a further dimension of irrationalist thought.

PSYCHOLOGICAL AND SOCIAL IRRATIONALISM

The claim that it is not the human situation which is intrinsically absurd, but that human nature itself is in some fundamental sense irrational, is not confined to philosophers of a metaphysical or speculative persuasion; its adherents also include psychologists, political scientists, social theorists, historians, literary artists, and even statesmen. In this area, above all others, a pervasive departure from certain dominant Enlightenment conceptions may be discerned, involving a shift of outlook that has led to drastic changes in the approach adopted by many writers to problems concerning man and society.

It is difficult neatly to summarize the complex and sometimes conflicting ideas involved here. One underlying theme, however, has been that the *idéologues* of the eighteenth century, together with the utilitarians and progressive radicals who followed them in the nineteenth century, grossly exaggerated the extent to which human behavior is motivated, or is capable of being modified, by rational consideration. It has further been suggested that such overvaluation of reason or intellect caused liberal and democratic thinkers to adopt absurdly optimistic, unrealistic, and naive views concerning the capacity of men to improve themselves and the conditions under which they live.

Individual psychology. At the level of individual psychology it is held to be false that people usually or consistently are activated by calculations regarding their best interests or that they can confidently be expected to respond to considerations of abstract moral principle or general advantage once these are clearly apprehended and understood. Such doctrines are the fictions of philosophical theory and ignore three essential points. First, vast areas of human behavior are, in fact, governed by overriding antisocial passions like pride and cruelty. The indulgence of these is in general detrimental to the agent's long-term advantage, frequently causing as much harm to him as to those against whom his actions may be directed. Second, it is a mistake to write off as mere eradicable superstition the various myths, religious and otherwise, in terms of which men are prone to conduct their lives. These are often attuned to powerful nonrational forces in the psyche that demand expression and that, if frustrated, are likely to seek outlet in other, possibly more dangerous forms. Third, it is important to appreciate how often men are totally unaware of the true motives and drives that determine their actions; human beings are adept at rationalization and self-deception, and their conduct may appear to be guided by reason when, in reality, it is directed by quite different factors. Intimations of these notions occurred in the writings of the Marquis de Sade and Joseph de Maistre at the close of the eighteenth century; and they were subsequently given forceful expression in the works of romantic and postromantic thinkers like Schopenhauer and Nietzsche. More recently, they have been regarded as receiving impressive and detailed corroboration from the advances in psychoanalysis initiated by Freud and Jung.

Political and social thought. In the sphere of political and social theory, insistence upon the irrationality of human nature has tended to be combined with traditionalist, authoritarian, or reactionary conceptions of government. To some, it has seemed obvious that the only enduring way of preserving the integrity of society against the disruptive forces of violence and passion lurking beneath the thin surface of civilized life consists in the use of coercion and suppression. De Maistre, for instance, considered the executioner to be the most significant figure in the state. Stress is laid on the importance of instilling habits of obedience to authority by appeals to supernatural or providential powers and by safeguarding the atmosphere of reverence and awe that surrounds the person of the ruler in established societies—a principal objection to proposals for the reorganization of social life according to egalitarian or consciously utilitarian general principles has been the belief that they can only lead to a loosening of the mysterious ties that hold a political community together. Likewise, attempts to displace unreasoned acceptance of the existing order of things by the propagation of scientifically inspired ideas and policies strike at the root of all that makes for social cohesion.

Edmund Burke was, for these reasons, deeply distrustful of revolutionary theories and plans. He thought that the true sources of political harmony lay below the level of rational reflection and showed considerable prescience concerning the consequences likely to ensue if the checks upon men's passions provided by traditional arrangements were challenged or removed. He did not, however, share the curiously ambivalent attitude toward violent or sadistic human propensities discernible in certain later social thinkers, who saw these as something to be systematically exploited rather than inhibited and for whom the ideas of force and brutality seem to have possessed a powerful emotional appeal. In the case of Vilfredo Pareto, for instance, the approach adopted toward the role of the irrational in human life was not as detached or objective as he tried to present it. Such writers did not merely dismiss humanitarian schemes for social amelioration and improvement as ultimately unrealistic, impracticable, or utopian; it was also strongly suggested in their works that if these schemes were to be realized, this would constitute an intrinsically undesirable state of affairs. It is for pressing the second claim, as well as the first, that fascism is often described as an irrationalist ideology.

Major currents of thought do not originate in a vacuum, and the various components of modern irrationalism have many diverse sources. Among them are the void left by the decay of institutionalized religion, the recurrent failure of large-scale reformist movements (like the French and Russian revolutions) to fulfill the hopes that originally inspired them, and the inability of contemporary industrial society to provide scope for individual self-expression. But it would be a mistake to regard irrationalist trends as purely pathological symptoms or to suppose that they have contributed nothing of value to the development of thought. It is common for Anglo-Saxon critics to denounce some irrationalist claims as having played a pernicious role in the formation of extremist political ideologies and to dismiss others as representing no more than inflated or misleading formulations of familiar logical doctrines—for instance, it has been suggested that the existentialist conception of the world as irrational is (partly at least) a bombastic restatement of the Humean insight that there exist no necessary connections between matters of fact. Up to a point such objections may be justified. On the other hand, it is worth remembering that there are important areas of human consciousness and behavior that theorists of a rationalistic temper have been characteristically prone to

overlook and that it has been largely left to men of a different outlook to explore and define these areas. To say that the task has sometimes been perversely performed is not to say that it should not have been undertaken at all.

Bibliography

MAJOR IRRATIONALIST WORKS

Bergson, Henri, *Time and Free Will*, translated by P. L. Pogson. London, 1910.

Bergson, Henri, *Introduction to Metaphysics*, translated by T. E. Hulme, New York, 1913 and 1949.

Bergson, Henri, *The Two Sources of Morality and Religion*, translated by R. A. Audra and Cloudesley Brereton. New York, 1954.

Camus, Albert, *Le Mythe de Sisyphe*. Paris, 1942.

Dostoyevsky, Fyodor, *Notes From Underground*, translated by Constance Garnett, in his *Works*, 12 vols. New York, 1912–1920.

Heidegger, Martin, *Being and Time*, translated by John Macquarrie and Edward Robinson. New York, 1962.

Kierkegaard, Søren, *Concluding Unscientific Postscript*, translated by D. F. Swenson and Walter Lowrie. Princeton, N.J., 1941.

Kierkegaard, Søren, *Philosophical Fragments*, translated by D. F. Swenson, with introduction and commentary by Niels Tholstrup. Princeton, N.J., 1962.

Maistre, Joseph de, *Les Soirées de Saint-Pétersbourg*, 6th ed. Paris, 1850.

Müller-Freienfels, Richard, *Irrationalismus*. Berlin, 1923.

Müller-Freienfels, Richard, *Metaphysik des Irrationalen*. Leipzig, 1927.

Nietzsche, Friedrich, *The Portable Nietzsche*, edited and translated by Walter Kaufmann. New York, 1954.

Nietzsche, Friedrich, *Beyond Good and Evil*, translated by Helen Zimmern. New York, 1924.

Nietzsche, Friedrich, *The Genealogy of Morals*, translated by H. B. Samuel. New York, 1924.

Nietzsche, Friedrich, *The Will to Power*, translated by A. M. Ludovice. New York, 1924.

Pareto, Vilfredo, *Mind and Society*, translated by Arthur Livingstone. London, 1935.

Pascal, Blaise, *Pensées*, translated by W. F. Trotter. New York, 1954.

Sade, Marquis de, *Selected Writings*, translated by Paul Dinnage. London, 1962. Introductory essay by Simone de Beauvoir.

Sartre, Jean-Paul, *La Nausée*. Paris, 1938.

Sartre, Jean-Paul, *L'Être et le néant*, translated by Hazel Barnes as *Being and Nothingness*. New York, 1956.

Schelling, F. W. J. von. *Philosophie und Religion*, in his *Werke*, M. Schröter, ed. Munich, 1927–1928. Vol. IV.

Schopenhauer, Arthur, *Die Welt als Wille und Vorstellung*, translated by E. F. J. Payne as *The World as Will and Representation*, 2 vols. Indian Hills, Colo., 1958.

Sorel, Georges, *Reflections on Violence*, translated by T. E. Hulme. New York, 1914.

Spengler, Oswald, *The Decline of the West*, translated by C. F. Atkinson. New York, 1947.

Tolstoy, Leo, *Death of Ivan Ilyitch* and *A Confession*, in his *Works*, translated by Louise Maude and Aylmer Maude, 21 vols. Oxford, 1928–1937.

GENERAL COMMENTARIES AND SURVEYS

Aiken, H. D., *The Age of Ideology*. New York, 1956. Selections from nineteenth-century philosophers, with introduction and interpretive commentary.

Ayer, A. J., "Some Aspects of Existentialism." *Rationalist Annual* (1948).

Barrett, William, *Irrational Man*. New York, 1958.

Berlin, Isaiah, *The Hedgehog and the Fox*. London, 1953. This study of Tolstoy's view of history includes a discussion of the antirationalist strains in Tolstoy's thought, and explores some of the parallels between his ideas and those of Joseph de Maistre.

Blackham, H. J., *Six Existentialist Thinkers*. New York, 1952.

Copleston, Frederick, *History of Philosophy*, Vol. VII, *Fichte to Nietzsche*. London, 1963.

Russell, Bertrand, *Power, a New Social Analysis*. New York, 1938. Ch. 16.

Russell, Bertrand, "The Ancestry of Fascism," in *In Praise of Idleness*. London, 1960.

Wolf, L. H. de, *The Religious Revolt Against Reason*. New York, 1949.

Wollheim, Richard, "The Political Philosophy of Existentialism." *Cambridge Journal*, Vol. 7 (1953), 3–19.

PATRICK GARDINER

ISAAC OF STELLA, one of the great monastic thinkers of the Middle Ages, was born in England about 1100. He apparently studied in both England and France before entering the monastery of Cîteaux. After several years at Stella (L'Étoile) in Poitou, where he became abbot, Isaac attempted to found a monastery on the lonely island of Ré, near La Rochelle, but soon returned to Stella, where he died about 1169. His writings include a treatise on human nature (*De Anima*), an exposition of the liturgy (*De Officio Missae*), and 54 sermons, preached either at Ré or at Stella. Through the *De Spiritu et Anima* of Alcher of Clairvaux his psychological theories became widely influential, notably in the Franciscan school of the thirteenth century.

Isaac's mind, schooled in the Biblical spirituality of the Cistercians, was steeped in Scripture, and his writings are full of Biblical allusions. In contrast to many of his contemporaries, however, he was careful and systematic in his use of Scripture. Moreover, although most monastic interpreters were content with the moral lessons derivable from the Biblical text, Isaac was deeply interested in its doctrinal content. Thus, his Biblical exegesis reflects his metaphysical concerns.

As a philosophical theologian, Isaac stood in the tradition of Christian Neoplatonism at the point where it first felt the impact of the Aristotelian renaissance. Both the Greek Fathers and Augustine were extensively studied by the Cistercians, but Isaac's grasp of their teaching was exceptional. Indeed, apart from Erigena no earlier medieval thinker could equal his knowledge of Eastern and Western Neoplatonism. On the one hand, as both his doctrinal tendencies and his extensive use of a Dionysian vocabulary, including at least a dozen Greek terms, indicate, he was well acquainted with the works of the pseudo-Dionysius. On the other hand, he was thoroughly familiar with the philosophical, theological, and mystical thought of Augustine.

Isaac's ambition to reconcile Neoplatonism and Aristotelianism is apparent in his account of human knowledge, which combines the Augustinian doctrine of illumination with the theory of abstraction. In his synthesis reason forms universal concepts by abstraction from sense experience of corporeal objects. Intelligence, however, must be aided by divine illumination in its effort to apprehend incorporeal beings.

The influence of the pseudo-Dionysius can be seen in Isaac's insistence on the negative approach (*via negativa*) to the knowledge of God. It appears also in his emphasis on the hierarchical structure of reality, in his exemplarist doctrine of creaturely participation in the divine perfections, and in his strong interest in liturgical symbolism.

The influence of Augustine's theology is most conspicuous in Isaac's discussion of predestination. With frequent echoes of Augustine's own style, he fully develops the theme of God's initiative in the process of man's salvation. Augustinian influences are obvious also in Isaac's teaching on many points, including the Trinity, the virtue of charity, and the church as Christ's mystical body.

Bibliography

See Louis Bouyer, *The Cistercian Heritage* (London, 1958); G. B. Burch, *Early Mediaeval Philosophy* (New York, 1951); and W. Meuser, *Die Erkenntnislehre des Isaak von Stella* (Bottrop, Germany, 1934).

EUGENE R. FAIRWEATHER

ISLAMIC PHILOSOPHY. In Islam the development of philosophical thought, properly speaking, succeeded earlier schools of dialectical theology (*Kalām*) that began to arise in the eighth century (second century A.H. in the Islamic calendar) through the action of foreign ideas—particularly Greco-Christian—on certain fundamental moral issues raised within the Islamic community. These moral issues clustered particularly around the problems of the freedom of the human will, God's omnipotence and justice, and God's relationship to the world. Although these early schools do not properly belong within the scope of this article, since they are theological rather than philosophical, a very brief characterization of the main groups and their tenets will serve to elucidate the content of the philosophical movement itself. Broadly speaking, there were two theological schools. The so-called rationalist, or Mu'tazila, school maintained the freedom of the will; insisted that right and wrong are knowable through reason independently of, but confirmed by, revelation; and claimed that God's attributes are identical with his essence and that God cannot do what is unreasonable or unjust. However, the Mu'tazilites posed and solved all these problems theologically, not philosophically; their entire thought was theocentric. For example, they did not pose the problem of the will absolutely but discussed it mainly insofar as it is relevant to the concept of a just God. However, their opponents (the Ahl al-Sunnah wa'l-Jamā'ah), who came to constitute the orthodoxy, accused them of stark humanism and opposed them on all these major questions. The orthodoxy, after a long, hard struggle, completely routed the Mu'tazilites as a theological school, but the spark of the Mu'tazilites kindled the purely rationalist movement in philosophic thought.

The work of the original philosophers in Islam was preceded by feverish translation that began around 800 and lasted for about two hundred years; its climax was reached in the time of Caliph al-Ma'mūn al-Rashīd (reigned 813–833). Al-Ma'mūn set up the first official seat of liberal learning in Islam, called the House of Wisdom, whose main function was to translate the works of the Greek masters of science and philosophy. The translations, however, were mostly from Syriac versions and not directly from the Greek. These translations, which were made almost invariably by Arab Christians, covered the entire range of Greek civilization—that is, its thought content—but excluded such specifically cultural aspects as mythology, drama, and literature, which were foreign to the Arabs and to Islam. The Arabs were able to develop a highly technical philosophical diction with astonishing rapidity and to integrate it into the Arabic language so successfully that a philosopher like al-Fārābī (d. 950), who was a Turk and not an Arab, was able to express himself philosophically in Arabic with remarkable facility. All this happened within a span of about 150 years in a language that had previously known no technical philosophical literature whatsoever.

The main character of Islamic philosophy was set by the combination of Aristotle and Neoplatonism that had constituted an important tradition in the late stages of Hellenistic philosophy and that was represented particularly by the Neoplatonic commentators on Aristotle in Athens and Alexandria, such as Simplicius and John Philoponus (sixth century). The Muslim philosophers introduced into this tradition other fundamental concepts in order to adapt it to an Islamic milieu; the most important were the ideas of contingent and necessary being and of prophethood. Despite these fundamental changes, the Muslim philosophers accepted the general cosmological scheme they had inherited from the Greek traditions. Thus, an important place in their cosmology and metaphysics is occupied by the role of the stars and the heavenly bodies, a role that has no place in the scheme of reality of the Qur'ān. This must be attributed to the Greek beliefs about the status of stars and the heavenly bodies and their creative influence on the sublunary sphere, although such a picture of the universe was also quite in harmony with other traditions existing in the Middle East, for instance, Sabaeans and Babylonians.

Al-Kindī. The first important Muslim philosopher was the Arab prince Yaʻqūb ibn-Ishāq al-Kindī (d. after 870). Al-Kindī's philosophic thought is directly connected with, on the one hand, Greek philosophical doctrines transmitted to him through translations and, on the other, with the rationalist theological movement of the Muʻtazilites. He seems to have espoused the Muʻtazilite doctrines *in toto* and to have sought to create a philosophical substructure for them. Thus, the Muʻtazilite dogma of the attributeless transcendence of God must have led him to the somewhat parallel idea of God as absolute and transcendent being, a combination of the Aristotelian concept of God and the Neoplatonic concept of the One. It is this affinity that must have led him further to formulate the doctrine, common to all the great Muslim philosophers, that philosophy and religion, or the rational truth and the revealed truth, not only do not conflict with each other but, in fact, lend support to each other and are basically identical. This recalls the Muʻtazilite doctrine that the source of our knowledge of values is reason confirmed by revelation.

In his philosophy, al-Kindī was more of a Neoplatonist than an Aristotelian. (The Arabs attributed certain Neoplatonic works, such as *De Causis* and *Theologia Aristotelis,* to Aristotle.) He adopted the Neoplatonic doctrine of emanation in his metaphysics and cosmology. Also, in his theory of intellectual knowledge he adopted the doctrine of the active intellect and the passive intellect, originally formulated by Aristotle, later elaborated by the commentator Alexander of Aphrodisias, and subsequently reworked and essentially modified by Neoplatonists. Al-Kindī introduced into the Greek framework of ideas some fundamen-

tal doctrines of Islam. Thus, although he accepted the theory of emanation, he asserted that the first being was created by the sheer act of God's will and out of nothing, an antithesis to the general Greek doctrine that nothing comes out of nothing. Aristotle had postulated two ultimates—one was God, the form of forms; the other, the prime matter—each of which had "existed" independently of the other. Similarly, although the Neoplatonic doctrine of emanation differs vitally from Aristotle's theory of the cosmic movement, it still seeks to avoid having to accept creation *ex nihilo* by postulating the emanatory process. However, it is difficult to see how, in the last analysis, the emanation theory can overcome the difficulties of creation *ex nihilo*. Al-Kindī, however, simply asserted emanationism and creationism side by side without reconciling the contradiction between the two. It was Avicenna (ibn-Sīnā) who later attempted the reconciliation, but it was important to the development of Islamic philosophy that al-Kindī, far from giving up the Islamic requirements of the relationship of God and the world, juxtaposed both the Islamic and the Greek doctrines. In his theory of intellection, al-Kindī was attracted by the ideal of a form of knowledge that would do justice to the demands of reason and revelation, although in his extant works we do not find an elaborated theory of prophethood. This, again, was taken up later by al-Fārābī and Avicenna, but it was al-Kindī who initiated development of the theory of intellection in Islamic philosophy.

Al-Fārābī. With al-Fārābī (875–950) philosophy reached maturity in Islam. Not many of his works have come down to us, but his writings that we do possess reveal an unusually incisive and clear mind. In his cosmology, as well as in his psychology, al-Fārābī was almost entirely Aristotelian, except for the doctrine of emanation. In political theory, which seems to have preoccupied him considerably more than it did other Muslim philosophers, he based himself on Plato's *Republic* and *Laws,* but he adapted the Platonic system to his contemporary political situation with a remarkable ingenuity. He developed the doctrine of the intellect from the point at which al-Kindī had left off, and he constructed a theory of divine inspiration that was to serve as a model for Avicenna. But apart from his original theories, the importance of al-Fārābī lies in his attempt to elevate philosophy to the place of highest value and to subordinate the revelation and the *sharīʻa*, or religious law, to it. In this also he served as a model for both Avicenna and Averroës (ibn-Rushd), but it was precisely this doctrine, in which the *sharīʻa* took an inferior place as a symbolic expression of a higher intellectual truth, that was also ultimately responsible for the fatal attacks on the philosophical movement by representatives of the orthodoxy.

In his religious attitudes, al-Fārābī was a genuinely universalistic spirit who believed that the entire world should have one religion, of which all particular religions would be considered symbolic expressions. However, it would be a mistake to regard al-Fārābī as a relativist. He tells us in no uncertain terms that not all religions are equal either as adequate symbols of truth or as the effective harnessing of men's minds and hearts. Indeed, he believed that there are religious symbolisms that are positively harmful and must be discarded. He did affirm, however, that there are religions which are equivalent in their religious value; and any one of these symbolic systems may be applied in a given milieu, depending upon circumstances. Although al-Fārābī gave no concrete examples of religions or names of prophets, there is little doubt that the prophet Muhammad was fixed in his mind as a paradigm par excellence of a prophet and a lawgiver. This becomes clear in his insistence that the teachings of a prophet should not only be universal but should also be successful in history.

Al-Fārābī's writings give us a full-scale picture of the basic world view of Muslim philosophy. At the apex of his scheme of reality stands God, who is both the One of Plotinus and the First Cause of Aristotle. From him proceeds the first intelligence, which is also the archangel. The first intelligence has a dual nature and gives rise to two further beings: the highest sphere on the physical side and the second intelligence on the spiritual side. This process of emanation continues until we reach the tenth sphere and the last intelligence, identified as the angel of revelation, Gabriel, on the one hand, and as the sphere of the moon on the other. The entire process of the world below the moon is an interaction between the materials emanating from the sphere of the moon and the spiritual influence generated by the tenth intelligence, called the Active Intellect. This interaction generates the world process, and its culminating product is man, with his fully organized body and rational soul.

The goal of man, wherein lies his ultimate bliss, is to develop his rational faculty by his will. The rational faculty is developed by the action of the active intelligence upon it, through which actual thought arises. The end of man, therefore, is to reach philosophic contemplation, and al-Fārābī categorically states that men whose rational faculty remains undeveloped cannot attain immortality but perish with their physical death. The actual activation of man's rational power, however, demands certain practical virtues as well, and this makes it necessary for man to live in organized societies rather than in isolation. People who are ultimately responsible for organizing and directing human societies are those possessed of philosophical wisdom, for it is not possible to enunciate practical laws for mankind without having theoretical wisdom. Therefore, for al-Fārābī the philosopher and the prophet are identical. It is the philosopher-prophet who can formulate the practical principles and laws that will lead men to their final goal of philosophic bliss. Societies governed by such laws are "good societies"; others are "ignorant societies," "misguided societies," or "retarded societies."

At the final stage of the intellective development, the philosophical mind becomes like matter to the Active Intellect, which becomes its form. This is the absolute apogee of human bliss. The prophet is a person who, having attained this philosophical illumination, transforms the philosophic truth into an imaginative myth that moves people to action and can influence societies toward greater morality. It is because of his imaginative power, the power to represent the intellectual truth in the form of a figure or a symbol, that the prophet is able to make laws and to bring revelation. Revelation, therefore, is not philosophic truth but imaginative truth. Only a few gifted philosophi-

cal spirits can pierce the imaginative shell and reach the philosophic truth. In al-Fārābī's theory of prophethood, there seems to be no place for miracles; the accommodation of miracles on a philosophical basis was the work of Avicenna.

Al-Fārābī likened the ruler to the head in the human organism and, like Plato, developed the idea of a hierarchy in which each stratum receives orders from above and issues commands to those below. Just as at the top there is a ruler who is not ruled, so at the bottom there are those who are ruled but do not rule. It is a fully authoritarian view of government, and some scholars have suggested that al-Fārābī was influenced by Shī'ite doctrine. The fact that al-Fārābī was at the court of the Shī'ite ruler is supposed to lend some support to this view. We do not have sufficient historical evidence for such a judgment, but it should be noted that the ultimate ruler of the Farabian state does resemble the Shī'ite Imam, the repository of divine wisdom.

Brethren of Purity. During the tenth century, a secret coterie of popular philosophers known as the Brethren of Purity (*Ikhwan al-Safa*) was formed, and they wrote a series of "epistles," or treatises, entitled Rasā'il Ikhwān as Safā', to propagate their views. The epistles exhibit a thoroughly Neoplatonic character. They seek to formulate a world view culminating in a universalistic religion transcending all organized religions, which, at best, serve as so many different ladders to the ultimate truth. The philosophy preached by the Brethren of Purity is also esoteric, and there are strong reasons to believe that this group was either formed by members of or was connected with the Ismā'īli movement, a religious sect; it is very likely that it was through such channels that Ismā'īlism absorbed those Greek philosophic elements which were rejected by the Muslim orthodoxy but were akin to certain patent Oriental theories and to attitudes about religion and the nature of the ultimate truth. The view of the Brethren of Purity does not constitute philosophy in the strict sense but is a kind of vague and romantic idealism; nevertheless, it is important to note it because its ideas have also influenced the development of another powerful spiritual movement in Islam, Sufism.

Avicenna. The most important and original of Muslim philosophers was Abū 'Alī ibn-Sīnā, known to the West as Avicenna (980–1037). The philosophic movement in eastern Islam comes to its fullest fruition in the thought of Avicenna, who elaborated one of the most cohesive, subtle, and all-embracing systems of medieval history. In the West his ideas had a profound influence on medieval scholastic philosophy, and in the Muslim world his system is still taught in the traditional centers of Islamic learning. The central thesis of Avicenna's metaphysics is the division of reality into contingent being and Necessary Being. In order to formulate this doctrine, whose influence has been so palpable and enduring in both Eastern and Western thought, Avicenna devised his theory of the distinction between essence and existence. In this theory, he refined the implications of the Islamic doctrine of creation, which al-Kindī had crudely asserted, into an integrated philosophic system.

The bases of this theory of essence and existence are set

in Aristotle's doctrine of movement and in the Neoplatonic doctrine of emanation, but in order to achieve the desired results, Avicenna had to effect basic changes both in the doctrine of emanation and in the Aristotelian doctrine of matter and form. Briefly, Aristotle had taught that matter is the principle of potentiality and form the principle of actuality, and that through the interaction of the two the actual movement of the universe takes place, in which potentialities are progressively actualized. Thus, the analysis of any given thing—with the exception of God and prime matter—falls into matter and form. There are, however, grave objections to this view. How can an actual thing come into existence through the interaction of a matter that, according to Aristotle, does not exist and a form that also does not exist? Why should things not remain unactualized in their potentialities, and where is the necessity of movement? Emanation seems to simplify this problem by asserting a single, universal process of outward movement, but it gives no rationale of this movement. Closer examination led Avicenna to posit three factors— matter, form, and existence—and to postulate a Necessary Being as the basis for the world process. There is little doubt, however, that it was not merely these philosophic reasons that led him to formulate this doctrine but also the fact that Islam demanded a fundamental distinction between God and the world. Since Avicenna could not accept the creationism of the Muslim theologians because it implied temporal priority of God over the world, he affirmed that God is distinguished from the world by the fact that his being is necessary and simple; God cannot be composed of matter and form but must be pure existence. From God emanate the intelligences, which, although they have no matter, are nevertheless composites of essence and existence; the material beings are composed of matter and form, which constitute their essence, and the fact of their existence—all existence flowing from God.

Avicenna was thus able to solve, to his own satisfaction, the contradiction that seemed to exist between the Greek philosophic world view and the Islamic doctrine of creationism: in accord with the philosophers he affirmed the eternity of the world and rejected temporal creation, but with the Islamists he made the world entirely and eternally dependent upon God. This solution led him to establish the relationship between religion and philosophy. Since the findings of religion and of philosophy do not contradict one another on this crucial point but are not identical either, they run parallel to one another. From this, Avicenna expounded his further view that religion is a kind of philosophy for the masses: it does not tell the naked philosophical truth but is an endeavor to make the masses come as near to the philosophical truth as possible. The prophets are, then, mass psychologists who launch religious movements as pragmatic endeavors to make people virtuous. Thus, Avicenna reaffirms al-Fārābī's position that revelation is not philosophic truth but symbolic truth.

The possibility of prophethood in Avicenna's system is intimately connected with his theory of knowledge, particularly with his theory of the creative knowledge and of the "internal sense," which appears to be his own contribution to the history of thought. According to Avicenna, all genuine intellectual discovery implies an intuitive act of knowledge, and our ratiocination merely prepares for us this intuitive act. However, there can be—and there are— people who possess a tremendous native intuitive power even without any ratiocination and process of learning. The ultimate limit of such a gifted mind is the prophetic mind, which does not receive knowledge through learning but creates knowledge. This constitutes the prophetic revelation at the intellectual level. But this intellectual power, in a genuine prophet, flows into the imagination or the "internal sense" as well, thus enabling the imaginative faculty to transform the intellectual truth into images and symbols capable of moving people's minds and bodies. It was on the basis of this power of imagination and suggestion that Avicenna explained the possibility of miracles attributed to prophets. He was thus able to accept even the miracle doctrine of the orthodoxy, although he rejected certain miracles as being "impossible."

Al-Ghazālī. Avicenna's system went furthest in integrating the traditional demands of the orthodox religion with the purely Greek rationalism, which explains why his works continue to be studied in the traditional Islamic schools even today. However, his system was made the object of denunciatory criticism by the orthodoxy on certain points: the eternity of the world, the inferior status of the *sharī'a* (religious law) as a mere symbol of the higher truth, and the rejection of the resurrection of the body. The classical criticism was carried out by al-Ghazālī (1058–1111) in his famous work *Tahāfut al-Falāsifa* (*Incoherence of the Philosophers*), which was also rendered into Latin in the thirteenth century under the title *Destructio Philosophorum*.

Averroës. The unrelenting criticism of philosophy as it appeared in Avicenna's system by al-Ghazālī and others led ibn-Rushd, known in the West as Averroës (1126–1198), to defend the claims of philosophy. In the process of doing this, Averroës sought to resurrect the original Aristotelian doctrines from the later Neoplatonic and Muslim accretion as much as possible. He wrote many commentaries on the works of Aristotle, whom he believed to be the philosopher par excellence. He accused both Avicenna and al-Ghazālī of having mutilated philosophical theses and of having confused them with religious doctrines. Averroës, however, did not advocate a theory of two truths, although this may be a logical conclusion of what he said in his work entitled *Faṣl al-Maqāl* ("The Decisive Statement") on the relationship between philosophy and religion.

Averroës rejected Avicenna's distinction between essence and existence. He insisted that existence is, in a way, part of the essence of a thing. The one conspicuous doctrine on which Averroës does not appear to be a faithful follower of Aristotle is that concerning intellect. He declared the passive human intellect also to be eternal and incorruptible and, indeed, to be universal to all mankind, like the Active Intellect. This doctrine of the unity of intellect, besides being apparently unfaithful to Aristotle, was also unacceptable to the followers of the revealed religions. He was thus attacked both by Muslims and, in the West, by Thomas Aquinas, who wrote a special treatise, entitled *De Unitate Intellectus*, against the Averroistic doctrine. It must, however, be pointed out that the common objection raised against Averroes' doctrine of the universality of the intellect ever since Thomas Aquinas' classic formulation of it as *ego intellego* is very superficial. Averroes not only never held that the act of cognition is universal but was, in fact, at pains to prove its individual character. What he seems to be concerned to show is that all thinking, although it occurs individually, becomes in a real sense universal, and that this universal aspect is more intrinsic to human cognition than is the fact that it is the product of such-and-such an individual or individuals. In any case, it is certain that Averroes never denied the individuality of the act of cognition.

Although Averroes believed that religion and philosophy are in two different orbits, he nevertheless felt the necessity of reconciling the two and of so stating the philosophic doctrines as not to offend religion and of so conceiving the religious dogmas that they would not conflict with philosophy. We are, therefore, back at the position of Avicenna. On the question of the eternity of the world, Averroes taught the doctrine of eternal creation. Although he did not reject the religious dogmas of the resurrection of the body, as Avicenna had done, he taught that the numerically same body cannot be resurrected. There was, however, bitter opposition to the doctrines of Averroes, who was also the *qadī* (judge) of Seville, and today very few of his works survive in the original Arabic; they are to be found mostly in Hebrew and Latin translations.

Abu'l-Barakāt ibn-Malkā. In the East we find another important attempt at the *rapprochement* of the content of religion and philosophy in the works of Abu'l-Barakāt ibn-Malkā (also known as Abu'l-Barakāt al-Baghdādī, died c. 1174/1175). A Jew converted to Islam, Abu'l-Barakāt's doctrines show a decisive trend toward Islamic orthodox beliefs. Thus, on the question of the attributes of God, he affirmed all the attributes of the Deity in the positive ense and not as pure negations, as his predecessors had done. His doctrine that the eternal essence of God can be the subject of changing accidents is palpable proof of his conscious orthodoxy. The doctrine is so obviously removed from the teaching of the early great Muslim philosophers and of Aristotle himself that, while it did not seem to have much appeal for the philosophic tradition in Islam, it evoked enthusiastic approval from such orthodox 'Ulamā' (the "learned") as ibn-Taymiya (thirteenth and fourteenth centuries). Similarly, Abu'l-Barakāt taught that the intellectual and the perceptual faculties are not different but are one and the same. He rejected the teachings of the Aristotelians that God does not know the particulars but only the universals, and he obviously did not accept Avicenna's formulation of the doctrine that God knows every particular but "in a universal way" rather than through perception. According to Abu'l-Barakāt, both sense perception and intellective perception belong to the soul and do not intrinsically involve the body. Then he concludes that God knows the particulars just as he knows the universals.

Although further progress of philosophy was cut off by the blows of the orthodoxy, philosophical developments, especially the system of Avicenna, had exerted a rejuvenating influence on orthodox theology (*Kalām*). After al-Ghazālī's refutation of philosophy, the scope of theology was expanded to include all the epistemological and metaphysical questions the philosophers had dealt with but to which theological answers were now provided. The first person to attempt this and who is, in fact, the forerunner of all Islamic theologians is Fakhr ad-Dīn ar-Rāzī (1149–1209). Logic was simply taken over by *Kalām* as a necessary instrumental science. Thus, the official theology set itself up as "the crown of the religious sciences" and began to function as a sufficient substitute for philosophic thought. Rational thought was thus banished from the schools as being redundant; only Avicenna's works (and commentaries and compendia based upon them) were taught, but more in order to be refuted than to instigate independent thought.

Under the attacks of orthodoxy, philosophy went underground, as it were, and lived on in the form of now one theosophy, now another. Instead of continuing as a purely rational expression of the human mind, it emptied its contents into intellectual Sufism. Henceforth, we do not get pure philosophy in Islam but a mystical philosophy. After the activity of the pantheist Sufi theosoph ibn-al-'Arabī (1165–1240), the new philosophic mysticism developed into a closely argued and elaborate system in the works of Ṣadr al-Dīn al Shīrazī, commonly known as Mullā Ṣadrā (1571/1572–1640). Mullā Ṣadrā represents a conjunction of the Shī'ite doctrine, the philosophic tradition of Avicenna, the mystical intellectualism of Suhrawardī (executed at Aleppo in 1192), and of ibn-al-'Arabī. He is a typical representative of the intellectual–spiritual tradition of late medieval Islam. A monist, Mullā Ṣadrā believed in a doctrine of mystic "return" to the First Principle of being. The reality as given is constituted by three levels of "worlds"— the spiritual, the imaginative, and the physical. The "imaginative" world ('*ālam al-mithāl*) is the world of symbols or images that relates the spiritual and the physical realms to one another, and it is the realm essentially relevant to the genesis and interpretation of symbols given in religious experience. This doctrine exercised a very considerable influence on subsequent developments in Islamic thought until the dawn of modern times. The centrality of "the world of symbols," with its religious implications and with its escapism from the external world, is symptomatic of the refined spiritual and intellectual culture of Islam in the later Middle Ages until the impact of Western influence upon it.

The story of philosophic thought in Islam after Averroes still remains to be written. Modern Western students of Islamic philosophy generally stop short at Averroes because the Muslim philosophic movement exerted an influence on medieval Western philosophy until his time. It is a pity that Muslim philosophy has been studied not as an internal whole but essentially from the point of view of its impact upon and relationship to Western philosophy. However, even a thorough account of the influence of Islamic ideas on Western thought is still lacking.

(See also MYSTICISM, HISTORY OF and SUFI PHILOSOPHY for a treatment of Muslim mysticism. See Islamic Philosophy in Index for articles on Islamic philosophers.)

Bibliography

GENERAL WORKS

Boer, T. J. de, *The History of Philosophy in Islam*. London, 1903.
Corbin, Henry, *Histoire de la philosophie islamique*, Vol. I.
Paris, 1964. Paperback.
Menasce, P. J. de, *Arabisches Philosophie*. No. 6 in Bibliographische Einführungen in das Studium der Philosophie. Bern, 1948.
Munk, Salomon, *Mélanges de philosophie juive et arabe*. Paris, 1857; 2d ed., 1927.
Walzer, Richard, "Islamic Philosophy," in Sarvepalli Radhakrishnan and others, eds., *History of Philosophy, Eastern and Western*, Vol. II. New York and London, 1952–1953. Contains a selected bibliography on individual Muslim philosophers.
Watt, W. Montgomery, *Islamic Surveys*, Vol. I, *Islamic Philosophy and Theology*. Edinburgh, 1962.

SUPPLEMENTARY WORKS

In addition to the works listed in the bibliography of the Walzer work, above, the following should be consulted:
"Al-Kindi's Treatise on Intellect," edited and translated by R. J. McCarthy. *Islamic Studies*, Vol. 3, No. 4 (1964).
Averroes' Tahafut al-Tahafut (The ʾIncoherence of the Incoherence), translated with an introduction and notes by Simon van den Bergh, 2 vols. London, 1954.
Corbin, Henry, *Oeuvres philosophiques et mystiques de Sohrawardī*. Paris and Teheran, 1952. Especially *Prolégomènes*.
Masumi, M. S. H., *Ibn Bajjah's ʾIlm al-Nafs*. Karachi, 1961.
Nasr, Seyyed Hossein, *Three Muslim Sages*. Cambridge, Mass., 1963. Discusses Avicenna, Suhrawardī, and ibn-al-ʿArabī.
Nasr, Seyyed Hossein, *An Introduction to Islamic Cosmological Doctrines: Conceptions of Nature and Methods Used for Its Study by Ikhwān al Safā, al-Bīrūnī, and Ibn Sīnā*. Cambridge, Mass., 1964.
Rahman, Fazlur, *Prophecy in Islam*. London, 1958.
Rahman, Fazlur, "Dream, Imagination and ʿĀlam al-Mithāl." *Islamic Studies*, Vol. 3, No 2 (1964).
Sharif, M. M., ed., *A History of Islamic Philosophy*, Vol. I. Wiesbaden, 1963. Published by the Pakistan Philosophical Congress. Essays on all aspects of the history of Islamic thought. Contains much useful information but has scholarship of uneven quality.
Walzer, Richard, *Greek Into Arabic: Essays on Islamic Philosophy*. Cambridge, Mass., 1962. Reprints selected essays of the author, including "Islamic Philosophy."

FAZLUR RAHMAN

ISRAELI, ISAAC BEN SOLOMON (c. 855–955), the first Jewish Neoplatonist, was one of the most distinguished Jewish physicians of the Middle Ages. He was so renowned for his medical competence, both in theory and in practice, that his works were widely circulated in manuscript, translated into Latin, and printed in the early years of the sixteenth century, as *Omnia Opera Ysaac* (Lyons, 1515). This printed edition and the manuscripts on which it was based contained some of Israeli's philosophic writings as well as his scientific treatises. As a result, his name became well-known, beyond his philosophic deserts; indeed, his fame among Christian scholars was second only to that of Moses Maimonides. Yet Maimonides held Israeli's philosophy in no great esteem, referring to him as "merely a physician."

Isaac Israeli was a native of Egypt. He left his native land to study medicine in the intellectual center of Kairouan, in north Africa, under the tutelage of Ishaq ibn-Imram, a Muslim. Later Israeli served as court physician to Ubaydullah al-Mahdi, founder of the Fatimid dynasty in north Africa.

In addition to the philosophic materials in his "Book of Elements" (a medical work), Israeli has long been known as the writer of a "Book of Definitions." Recent studies have added also a "Book of Substances," a "Book on Spirit and Soul," and, probably, a short "Chapter on the Elements," found in a unique manuscript in the Bibliotheca Communale of Mantua and ascribed to Isaac Israeli by A. Altmann. On the basis of these works, Israeli can be confidently classified as a Neoplatonist whose work is akin to that of other Neoplatonists among the Muslim philosophers of his age.

His surviving works do not include any significant discussion of the existence and nature of God but they do describe God as a perpetually active Creator. God's original creative act is a creation out of nothing; later acts of creativity in nature are not of the same order but are "the passing of corporeal substances from privation to existence" in accordance with God's will. Along with this account, however, Israeli also maintained a doctrine of emanation. Thus, on the one hand God creates because of his goodness, while on the other his creativity is a perpetual overflowing. These two accounts of creation are never reconciled in Israeli's thought.

The process of emanation terminates with the emergence of the visible sphere. From this point, Israeli's explanation of the universe is physical and more closely akin to the views of Aristotle. Retaining the classical Greek theory of the four elements, he accounted for everything in the world of our experience by the combination of the elements earth, air, fire, and water. Once again, however, we are confronted with an uncertainty. In the "Book of Definitions," Israeli asserted that the four elements came into being through the movement of the sphere of heaven, but in the "Book of Elements" they are attributed to the power of God. Except by straining the language, these two views cannot be reconciled.

A similar double view emerges in Israeli's doctrine of the soul. Here he spoke of a cosmic soul, which exists independently of body, appearing in three successive stages of emanation—rational, animal, and vegetable—and also of a divine spark within the individual, striving ever upward toward the cosmic soul. Perhaps in this double account of soul we have a reflection of the Neoplatonic doctrine of man as the microcosm. If so, we can understand the emphasis Israeli put on self-knowledge, the road to the knowledge of the universe. Self-knowledge is knowledge of both body and soul; one who knows himself in both soul and body knows everything, and he alone is worthy of the name of philosopher.

Bibliography

English translations of selections from Israeli's philosophic works appear in *Isaac Israeli: A Neoplatonic Philosopher of the Early Tenth Century*, by A. Altmann and S. M. Stern, Vol. I in the series Scripta Judaica (London, 1958), which also contains discussions of his work. For further discussion, see Isaac Husik, *History of Medieval Jewish Philosophy* (New York, 1916); Georges Vajda, *Introduction à la pensée juive du moyen âge* (Paris, 1947); and Joseph L. Blau, *The Story of Jewish Philosophy* (New York, 1962).

I. L. BLAU

ITALIAN PHILOSOPHY. Distinctively national traditions in philosophy—insofar as they exist at all—are not consciously established or accepted. We call problems "philosophical" at least partly because they seem to us to have some kind of eternal significance and universal relevance that transcends historical and geographical boundaries. But the general circumstances of life in any community that manages to maintain itself at the conscious level over a considerable period of time will cause some particular problem or set of problems to occur in the minds of its members with an accent or emphasis which they do not have elsewhere. Thus when Dante Alighieri (1265–1321) set himself, in the *Convivio*, to provide a vernacular manual of Christian moral philosophy, it was exactly because the theories of the Schools seemed to him to have vital relevance for all men. He was dominated by the same fundamental conception of philosophy—as the guide of life and an essential part of the way of salvation—that later caused him to put forward his most original philosophical thesis, the need for a universal empire, in his Latin treatise *De Monarchia*. The philosophical content and argument of his works was to a large extent directly borrowed from the scholastic tradition, especially from Thomas Aquinas. But Dante became the first distinctively Italian philosopher because the subsequent course of Italian history obliged later thinkers, even sometimes rather against their will, to regard the moral and political problems with which he was concerned as the central issues of philosophy.

In the *Divine Comedy*, even more clearly than in Dante's philosophical treatises, the principal source of conflict in Italian philosophy is apparent. It is based on the tension between the two Romes, between the pope and the emperor, between the active life of man in society and the contemplative life of the solitary individual. In the poem Dante appears as a solitary individual, and the superiority of the contemplative life is quite explicitly affirmed. But it is notable that the range of natural reason (symbolized by Vergil as Dante's guide) does not extend beyond purgatory, which seeks to show us how our active lives should be organized and directed. The choice between a social concern with human salvation (with the earthly paradise as its ideal) and a solitary contemplative pursuit of blessedness in a heaven of the intellect was the heritage Dante bequeathed to Italian philosophy, and it has remained the central issue of the Italian tradition ever since.

HUMANISM AND THE RENAISSANCE

For most Italian thinkers the choice between social concern and solitary contemplation was naturally a matter of ultimate emphasis, not a sharply defined or exclusive option.

Platonists: Ficino and Pico. The work of Marsilio Ficino (1433–1499) stands fairly close to the contemplative extreme. He provided one wing of the humanistic movement with a philosophy or theology derived from Plato and from Neoplatonic sources that was mainly conceived as a rational defense for the Christian doctrine of the immortality of the soul, but differed from the older traditions of Augustinian Platonism in its emphasis upon human freedom, human dignity, and even human power. Unlike his medieval predecessors, Ficino knew the whole corpus of Plato and of the Neoplatonists, and he built up his *Theologia Platonica* by fitting Christian doctrines into the framework of his Neoplatonic system (rather than fitting Neoplatonism into Christian doctrine).

An even more ambitious attempt at the reconciliation of all known philosophical and theological traditions in one single system of contemplative wisdom was made by Count Giovanni Pico della Mirandola (1463–1494). The 900 theses he offered to defend against all the scholars of the world shortly before his 24th birthday were drawn from a bewildering variety of sources and authorities, but his central conception of the human soul as an immortal microcosm or image of the universe is essentially Neoplatonic. Pico laid even more emphasis than Ficino on the freedom of man as the true index of his dignity; and this led him to an outright rejection of the general belief in astrology. In his work the purely speculative theology of Ficino gains a practical accent. Philosophy possessed for him a practical mission reminiscent of Dante's program for the establishment of a universal empire of reason. Although his plans for a universal congress of scholars were frustrated by church intervention and, eventually, by excommunication, he never lost his reforming zeal. He died an enthusiastic supporter of Savonarola.

Humanism and science. The Platonizing humanists were in general opposed to the Aristotelian philosophy that flourished at Padua. But it is a mistake to think of this conflict as being simply a matter of Platonists versus Aristotelians, for the "reconciliation" of Plato with Aristotle was a concern of the humanists from Francesco Filelfo (1398–1481) and Pico to Agostino Steuco (1497–1548). Steuco's *On the Perennial Philosophy* (1540) deserves to be remembered not only because the title has passed into common parlance, but also because of its curious doctrine of Adam's perfect knowledge. This doctrine was later used by Malebranche on the one hand to justify the Cartesian contempt for historical knowledge, while Vico on the other hand derived support from it for a "metaphysics of the mind" based on the comparative history of human cultures.

For that matter one did not have to be a Platonist at all to agree with Petrarch's remark about the scientific concerns of the Aristotelians: "Even if all these things were true they are of no value for the happy life" (*On His Own Ignorance*). The essential opposition was between philosophy conceived as the handmaid of theology and the humanities, and philosophy conceived as the handmaid of medicine and the sciences; and the main focus of conflict concerned the status of the human soul. The Paduans saw man as a biological organism, part of the order of living (and dying) nature. But they recognized that man was more than simply a part of that order if he was capable of achieving a true (that is, eternal) knowledge or understanding of it.

Pomponazzi. Pietro Pomponazzi (1462–1525) argued that the human soul was indeed, as Ficino and the Platonists held, a mean between the eternal and the temporal; but it was properly mortal, and only relatively speaking immortal—not essentially so. For "the mean, which is the human intellect, is in none of its operations either totally freed from the body or totally immersed in it; hence it does not need the body as subject, but does as object" (*On the Immortality of the Soul* IX). Pomponazzi, like Ficino and Pico, thought of the world order as a great chain of being—a hierarchy in which every level is occupied. But in Pomponazzi's chain the human link was just one crucial degree lower. Pomponazzi, like Pico and almost all the humanists, taught an ethics of intellectual self-realization. But since man is only a mortal being he will not, if he is truly wise, be essentially preoccupied about his own destiny. The eternal order of physical nature is the proper object of an intelligence dependent on a physical body. Hence the concern of the Padua school with problems which were alien to the heritage of Dante—those of logic and scientific method.

Machiavelli. It is perfectly possible, of course, to adopt the standpoint of a strictly scientific naturalism and yet continue to hold that "the proper study of mankind is man." We can see this clearly in the example of Niccolò Machiavelli (1469–1527), who rejected the Greco-Christian ideal of contemplative knowledge altogether, in favor of the pursuit of mastery over our own fate. Scornful of all the philosophical traditions, he thought of human nature as a sort of mechanism of passions which could be brought under control if it were first dispassionately studied and understood. Like Bernardino Telesio, Machiavelli believed that the immediate rational interpretation of directly observed facts was the only true method, and that by careful attention to the "effective realities" a universal science of human nature could be established. This universal science would be the key to political power and the means of insuring social stability and general prosperity. Because many readers miss this essentially moral purpose of Machiavelli's social science, they are unable to reconcile the apparent moral cynicism of his advice to princes with his admiration for the civic virtues of the Roman republic and his fervent patriotic attachment to the idea of a free and united Italy (which later endeared him to the philosophers of the *risorgimento*). Like the Florentine historian Francesco Guicciardini, Machiavelli remained too much a man of affairs to do more than adumbrate his science, but what he did leave is a completely secular vision of human life as a ceaseless struggle for power, in stark contrast with the religious ideals of universal reconciliation produced by his more pious fellow citizens.

Zabarella. The concern of the Padua school with problems of scientific method culminated in the work of Giacomo Zabarella (1532–1589), the greatest of the Padua Aristotelians. Zabarella developed the terminology of "composition" and "resolution" which Galileo later adopted. We discover the cause of an observed phenomenon by the method of "resolution," an analysis which enables us to identify the essential elements in the process we have observed, so that we can then proceed by the "compositive" method to "demonstrate" the effect from the cause. This may sound trivially circular—as indeed it always did to unfriendly critics—but what we call "prediction" is in fact part of Zabarella's concept of "demonstration"; he was making an important distinction between what is properly termed scientific investigation and the mere accumulation of observations.

THE SCIENTIFIC REVOLUTION

What the Aristotelians totally lacked was an appreciation of the significance of mathematical form and of measurement in scientific investigation. This insight came rather from the Ockhamite logicians of Oxford and Paris, who had some followers at Padua but whose main champion in Italy was that gifted amateur of scientific discovery, Leonardo da Vinci (1452–1519).

Among the academic thinkers influenced by the Ockhamite logic the most important was probably Girolamo Fracastoro (1483–1553), who produced the first "corpuscular" theory of natural processes and moved a long way toward the mechanistic naturalism for which Bacon honored Telesio as "the first of the moderns." ("Corpuscular" theories differed from "atomic" theories in that the corpuscles were not held to be indivisible and no vacuum was admitted.)

Telesio. Bernardino Telesio (1509–1588) rebelled against his Padua teachers for being too interested in their books and theories and not concerned enough with the direct observation of natural processes. He helped to found the first of the scientific academies, the Accademia Cosentina (or Telesiana), at Naples in 1560. In his zeal to be rigorously empirical and to build as far as possible upon direct observation, Telesio produced a philosophy of nature that is reminiscent of the pre-Socratics both in its crudity and in its suggestive power. Everything in nature was ultimately to be explained in terms of three principles: the active forces of heat and cold and the neutral mass of matter. Telesio rejected the Aristotelian conceptions of natural place and of time as the measure of motion, in favor of the absolute space and time with which we are familiar in the work of Newton; and he replaced the Aristotelian "powers" and "forms" with the modern scientific conception of efficient forces.

Man himself was regarded by Telesio as a physical balance of forces, and he explained all human knowledge and experience in terms of sensation (which he regarded as a primitive capacity of all bodies). Man's actions, like those of all living things, are naturally directed toward self-preservation; and the human capacity for self-sacrifice was a proof in Telesio's eyes that God has endowed man with a superadded immortal soul. But he did not concern himself with the possible consequences of this supernatural endowment.

Cardano and Patrizzi. Telesio may have been influenced by his near contemporary Girolamo Cardano (1501–1576), whose conception of the world system as a living whole, in which man is once again the "mean" or microcosm, was inspired by the mathematical mysticism of Cusanus rather than by the Florentine tradition. For Cardano the mathematical understanding of nature was an actual experience of union with God—a view closely akin to that later put forward by Galileo. Thus the new science was reconciled with the older theology and became in Cardano a form of the contemplative journey of the mind to God.

That is what it was also for the Platonist Francesco Patrizzi (1529–1597), He was influenced by Telesio's physics—it was from Patrizzi's work that the doctrine of space as the divine sensorium passed to the Cambridge Platonists and so to Newton. But he rejected the "sensation" theory of knowledge in favor of the Platonic theory of recollection and a Neoplatonic metaphysics of light.

Bruno. In Giordano Bruno (1548–1600) the same tendency was carried to an extreme. Although Bruno lacked firsthand knowledge of the new science, he managed to make it the basis of a sort of personal religious mission. In his long wanderings across Europe he seems to have conformed cheerfully to the religious habits and observances of his audiences, and he showed a similar willingness to conform up to a certain point during his long incarceration by the Inquisition, before he was finally burned at the stake in 1600. But this indifferent tolerance sprang from a burning conviction of the truth of his own vision.

For Bruno, the Copernican theory acted as a sort of catalyst by enabling him to identify his infinity of "living" worlds in endless space with the infinity of God. Bruno drew his ideas from many sources, but his central conception of God as infinite life derives from Cusanus. His theory of knowledge was Platonic, although there is often more of enthusiasm than of logic in his rationalism. In this respect he differs from Spinoza, but like Spinoza he was venerated by the German romantic thinkers for his insistence that reality must be grasped as a whole and for believing that the life of the whole is somehow present in every part. Knowledge therefore must begin not with sense experience but with a rational search for the minima, the monads or units of the divine life. The monad had for Bruno three aspects: in physical reality it appears as the atom, in geometry as the point, and in arithmetic as the unit—for, like Vico and some other rationalists who were not good mathematicians, Bruno found infinite divisibility and incommensurables too paradoxical and scandalous to be admitted. The atoms of the physical world are carried in the ether, which is the universal medium of the divine life and power.

In this rational pantheism the fact of human freedom poses a serious problem. Other living things express the divine nature directly by following the necessary impulses of their own nature, but man can realize his true nature only by moral effort. As a result Bruno's ethics falls into two parts or levels. First there is conquest of self, in which the intellect achieves mastery over the passions and man "drives out the beast." Here all the traditional virtues of moderation and self-control have place, and at this level we appear to have the choice between good and evil. But when we use this freedom as reason dictates, we become aware that we are simply following the urge of our nature toward union with the divine; and the rational man burns with the "heroic fury" of an intellectual love of God that is as different from Spinoza's as the climate of Naples is from that of Amsterdam.

Campanella. In the work of Tommaso Campanella (1568–1639) the new science was seen as the basis for a reformed society. Campanella accepted Telesio's physics and his mechanistic account of sense experience. But although Campanella held that "reason is a kind of imperfect sense" (*De Sensu Rerum* II, 30), he sometimes wavered toward a Platonic theory of knowledge and was, in any case, prepared to place immense trust in the analogical power of reason as a means of empathy with the universal life of things. The universality of sensation that was a necessary postulate of Telesio's mechanism thus became for Campanella the bridge to a Neoplatonic metaphysics in which the mind "senses" the presence of God in the whole of his creation.

In Campanella's *City of the Sun* the scientific ideal of Bacon's *New Atlantis* is combined with the political ideal of More's *Utopia*—except that Campanella is so much more a Platonist than More, or even Plato himself, that he abolishes the institution of the family and of private property not merely for the ruling class, but altogether. His City is governed by a priest called Metaphysics, assisted by three princes: Power, the minister for war and foreign affairs; Intelligence, the minister for science and industry; and Love, the minister for population planning. Campanella saw this conception not as a mere vision but as the goal of a definite program of political action. He was the prophet of a "solar revolution" which would precede the already impending end of the world. The *City of the Sun* was written while he was in prison for conspiracy against the Spanish government of Naples. But unlike Dante, Campanella did not greatly care whether his universal monarchy was established by pope and emperor together or by either one singly; he adapted his program readily to changing conditions in the *Monarchy of Spain* and the *Monarchy of the Messiah*. He wrote ecstatically of the impending conversion of the whole world to "Christianity," but his audience seems always to have realized that for him Christianity was simply the most appropriate set of metaphors for his own natural religion; and it is scarcely surprising that he was under continual suspicion of heresy and did much of his writing in the prisons of the Inquisition.

Galileo. The third great martyr of the new scientific world view, Galileo Galilei (1564–1642), was not primarily a philosopher at all; he was a dedicated scientific investigator. His work has sometimes been presented as the result of a Platonic reaction against medieval Aristotelian science. More recently, and somewhat more plausibly, it has been declared to be the culmination of the scientific tradition of the Padua Aristotelians. But all such generalizations about him seem to be more misleading than enlightening. He was a practical mathematician who was also a sincere Catholic; the Greek thinker who influenced him first and above all was Archimedes.

Galileo's reputation was largely based on his work with the telescope, and it was the fact that men otherwise renowned for their learning failed to see its significance that first drove him into philosophical controversy. He praised Plato for recognizing that philosophy must begin with mathematics, and Aristotle for his concern with the observed facts; but he had a very low opinion of the avowed followers of both philosophers, and it is hard to believe that he owed anything vital to the academics. His world was the world of the engineer, and his main philosophical achievement was to provide a theoretical account of and a justification for the procedure of engineers.

Methodology. Mathematics was for Galileo the science of all that can be; and the proper procedure for a human scientist is to begin with a mathematical hypothesis as a working model that is to be adjusted in the light of observations. If there are no perfect circles or triangles in the world, that is unfortunate, not for the world but for us. It is quite certain even so that everything in the world does have some definite geometrical form, and we can discover it by continually revising our mathematical hypotheses until our calculations correspond always and exactly with our observations. The formulation of the mathematical hypothesis from elementary notions and principles, and the calculation of its consequences, was what Galileo called "composition" or the "compositive method." The terms "resolution" and "resolutive method" he applied indifferently both to the first analysis of observations, which discovers what elements must be included in the composition, and to the subsequent analysis and measurement of observations, which reveals whether they correspond with our calculations.

Mathematics and experience. As a result of his own study of astronomical theories Galileo was keenly aware that rational composition must proceed quite independently of the sensible realm in which resolution takes place. In *The Two World Systems,* "Third Day," for instance, he wrote: "I cannot find any bounds for my admiration, how that reason was able in Aristarchus and Copernicus to commit such a rape on their senses, as in despite thereof to make herself mistress of their credulity." His extremely influential distinction between the primary qualities (figure, magnitude, position, motion, number), which reason requires that bodies *must* have, and the secondary qualities (color, taste, odor, etc.), which depend on our sensory apparatus and must disappear with it, is a philosophical account of what is involved in this "rape of the senses." It is reasonable to suppose, therefore, that Galileo would not have been perturbed by Berkeley's objection that we cannot "conceive" (that is, imagine) an uncolored extension; Galileo held that reasoning should not be concerned with that sort of conception at all but only with mathematical relations. His "geometrical" positivism even caused Galileo to reject the gravitational theory of the tides in favor of a hypothesis of his own, based on the motions of the earth alone and so avoiding the admission of action at a distance.

Faith and reason. In mathematical reasoning, according to Galileo, we possess the standard for God's own knowledge, and whatever we can prove mathematically we know as surely and as perfectly as God does. Thus in the genuinely scientific investigation of nature we possess a revelation equal in authority, though not in importance, to the revelation concerning man's moral duties and destiny that is contained in Holy Scripture. In taking this position, Galileo was only restating in terms of his own mathematical empiricism the essential relation between natural reason and revelation as defined by Augustine and Thomas Aquinas. His more intelligent opponents realized this, but could not understand how, in the name of reason, he could discard with such absolute confidence so much of other men's reasoning.

The church. In 1616 the new science embodied in Copernicus' heliocentric theory, and then in 1633 Galileo himself, were condemned for being mathematical in spirit rather than dialectical; demonstrative, rather than reconciliatory. The church authorities, true to their own conception of reason, stopped short of declaring the Copernican theory to be an outright heresy.

The primacy that Italy enjoyed in European culture until about 1600 could not have been maintained even if the church had not intervened. But the disastrous collision between church authority and the spirit of free thought and free inquiry spelled the end of creative speculation in Italy for two generations and condemned the country to a minor, dependent role in the intellectual exchanges of the new Europe for more than two centuries. Robert Bellarmine (1542–1621), junior member of the commission that condemned Bruno and principal authority in the condemnation of the theory of Copernicus, might well boast that the defenders of the true faith were like "different pens of the same Author" wielded against the many discordant voices of heresy. But his One Author no longer wrote philosophically, as Bellarmine's *Controversiae* rapidly reveals. Only in Pietro Sforza Pallavicino (1607–1667), cardinal and historian of the Council of Trent, did the ranks of orthodoxy produce a philosopher worthy of memory. His treatise *On the Good* contains a theory of artistic imagination that looks forward to Croce's and an interesting analysis of causality as a synthetic a priori relationship on which all empirical knowledge depends.

THE ENLIGHTENMENT

The followers of Galileo and Telesio kept the flame of scientific studies alive at Naples; it is not surprising therefore that Naples became the main center from which the ideas first of Gassendi and then of Descartes gradually spread over the Italian peninsula. In 1663, a group that included Francesco d'Andrea (1625–1698), Tommaso Cornelio (1614–1684), and Leonardo da Capua (1617–1695) as leading spirits founded the Accademia degli Investiganti on the model of the Medici foundation, the Accademia del Cimento, set up in Florence six years before. It was Cornelio who, in 1649, first introduced the works of Descartes into Italy.

Descartes's earliest friends and foes thought of him, as they did of Gassendi, primarily as an ally for the mechanist tradition of Telesio. Thus, Giovanni A. Borelli (1608–1679), the supposed illegitimate son of Campanella and an early member of the Cimento, devoted great efforts to proving Descartes's contention that the animals are machines.

Vico. It was in the intellectual climate of Naples that Giambattista Vico (1668–1744) grew up. Vico is the one great original thinker Italy produced in the long period of isolation. Indeed he is the greatest philosopher Italy has ever produced. For in this awkward, self-taught scholar, all the trends of prior speculation in Italy come together; and it is to him that every later movement in Italian philosophy has appealed. (Vico lived in poverty and obscurity, he was so little recognized that he never obtained a philosophical chair and was obliged to print his life's work at his own expense, in editions that were as difficult to read as they were to understand.) Vico's *Scienza nuova* fulfills Pico's dream of the unity of all traditions in one universal wisdom and confirms the belief of the Platonists from Ficino to Steuco that the history of human thought reveals the existence of a "perennial philosophy." At the same time, it carries through Machiavelli's proposal for a mundane science of human nature and political affairs as dispassionately as Machiavelli would have wished. The abiding preoccupation of the Renaissance humanists with rhetoric and the law receives full justice; and although Galileo's "two new sciences" (mechanics and local motion) and his mathematical method have to yield pride of place to another science and another method, mathematics retains a place of honor. The new scientific naturalism (including even some of its quirks, such as Bruno's belief in metaphysical points) has an important part to play in Vico's own metaphysics and theory of knowledge. The medical tradition alone would appear to have been slighted in his synthesis.

Vico's "new science." Vico's development as an original thinker began after several years of solitary study of classical authors and the Renaissance Platonists. Returning from Vatolla to his native Naples, he came into contact with the Cartesian philosophy; he recognized the Platonic–Augustinian origins of Descartes's theory of knowledge and thus was able to accommodate this new influence. About 1707 he discovered Bacon, and some five years later he read Grotius and Hobbes. These were the main direct influences upon him. But his "new science" was essentially the science of history. The revival of historical scholarship was the one aspect of Renaissance activity that was promoted rather than hindered by the Counter Reformation, with its emphasis on tradition. Thus, for example, Leibniz' achievements on behalf of the house of Brunswick inspired the duke of Modena to appoint Lodovico A. Muratori (1672–1750) archivist and historian of the house of Este, and enabled Muratori to spend half a century in building great monuments of erudition of which the most remarkable was the great collection of *Rerum Italicarum Scriptores* (1723–1751). Vico was from the beginning a devoted student of Roman history, and Tacitus was for him as for many contemporaries the master of political wisdom.

As a philosopher Vico at first took up the Cartesian posture of contempt for historical learning, but with the proclamation of his fundamental principle that "truth coincides with fact," that is, with what is made or done (*On the Most Ancient Wisdom of the Italians,* 1710), his attitude changed dramatically. This principle enabled him to maintain his rationalist faith in mathematical knowledge (as a creative activity of the human mind) and to justify the experimental method in natural science (as the imitation of God's creative activity), while at the same time it showed that the proper concern of the philosopher must be the explanation not of nature but of human affairs. The "certainty" of established historical facts must be replaced by the "truth" of rational understanding.

Historical cycles. Thus Vico was led to his *Scienza nuova* (1725, enlarged ed. 1744) and his theory of an "ideal eternal history," a cycle of development which all human societies must go through because the evolution of human nature itself requires it. First comes the "age of the Gods," typified by the primitive social institutions of religion, the family, and burial; then the "age of the heroes," in which a patriarchal-feudal organization of larger groups is accompanied by peculiarly "mythical" or "poetic" modes of consciousness in language, law, and culture; and finally the "age of men," marked by political democracy, a legal system based on the principles of equity, and a language and culture dominated by the ideal of perfect rationality. The urge toward democratic equality produces political anarchy, and the urge toward rationality destroys religious faith and undermines the primitive social institutions based on it, thus leading to a new barbarism from which the fear of God rouses men to begin the cycle once more.

Recognizing that Vico's doctrine is not one of mechanical recurrence, critics often speak of it as a "spiral" theory, but Vico does not seem to share the Enlightenment faith in progress that this model suggests either. His theory simply shows us how we can and should make progress by self-consciously appropriating the lessons and achievements of the past.

Grace and Providence. What Vico called "Divine Providence" has been presented here simply as the law of human evolution. This is quite in accord with his own views, for he made no distinction between his "proof of Divine Providence" and his "metaphysics of the human mind." But he was also a sincere Catholic, and he distinguished the work of Providence (in the salvation of the Gentile nations) from the work of grace (in the salvation of the Jews and Christians). The distinction caused him little difficulty and even produced advantages, since the only important difference was that the work of grace was more perfect, so that he was entitled to place special reliance on the Biblical record of historical facts. Making a separation between reason and faith as absolute as that of the Padua Aristotelians, he calmly ignored all the mysteries of the faith that were not reconcilable with his historical rationalism; and one cannot help suspecting at times that for him, almost as much as for Bruno and Campanella, Christianity was simply a "mythical" expression of his own "rational" doctrine. This is not to say that there was anything hypocritical about his personal piety, since the first postulate of all his reasoning was that the most primitive and basic of all human experience is religious awe. The essential ambiguity of his religious attitude is thus perfectly explicable within the terms of his theory itself. If, as he himself believed, Dante was the new Homer, then the *Scienza nuova,* the work of the new Plato, deserves the title of "The *Human* Comedy."

French and English influences. Vico's achievement went largely unnoticed, and philosophy in Italy declined more and more into a pale reflection of English and French influences, combined with, or opposed by, a dull repetition of traditional ideas.

The influence of Descartes was succeeded by that of Locke, against whom Vico's friend Paolo Mattia Doria (1666–1742) wrote a book in 1732. Doria had passed from an early interest in Cartesian mechanism to a more Platonic interpretation of Descartes, and from that to a complete rejection of the moderns in favor of Renaissance Platonism. Muratori also studied Locke but remained hostile. The most important critic of Locke (in *Contre l'Examen de Mr. Locke,* 1748), however, and later of Rousseau (in *Anti-Émile,* 1763) was Giacinto Sigismondo Gerdil (1718–1802), who proclaimed himself a disciple of Malebranche and of Padre Giovenale (G. B. Ruffini, 1635–1713, later lauded by Antonio Rosmini as a greater philosopher than Malebranche). These early critics saw in Locke the threatening shadow of materialism. But even Locke's more pious enemies gave him a hearing and gradually he made converts too, though in the end his direct influence can scarcely be distinguished from that of the French *philosophes* and *idéologues.*

Neapolitan school. The first important Italian thinker to be influenced by Locke was a Neapolitan, Antonio Genovesi (1712–1769), who combined the "new way of ideas" with a Leibnizian theory of spiritual monads having innate intellectual powers. There is little of interest in this eclectic theory, but, like Locke, Genovesi was concerned with practical problems. He held the first European chair of political economy, at the University of Naples, and it was in economics and social studies that he and his followers made their most significant contributions. Fernando Galiani (1728–1787) wrote an important treatise, *On Money;* Gaetano Filangieri (1752–1788), a treatise on the *Science of Legislation* in which the name and work of Machiavelli returns at last to honor. Filangieri claimed to have found the right path in Montesquieu, but he also complained that Montesquieu was too interested in tracing the actual development of constitutions and not concerned enough about discovering the ideal principles of morality which should determine all legal systems. Like Melchiorre Delfico (1744–1835), Filangieri was dominated by the Encyclopedists' faith in the perfectibility of man.

As one might expect, the Neapolitan school often sang Vico's praises—especially Mario Pagano (1748–1799), who attempted to harmonize Vico with Rousseau—but they were too preoccupied with their liberal battle against the *ancien régime* to understand Vico properly. Filangieri, however, has the distinction of having brought the *Scienza nuova* to the notice of Goethe in 1787.

Milanese social theory. In the north at Milan another group of social thinkers inspired by the *philosophes* flourished slightly later. They centered round the periodical *Caffè* published by the brothers Alessandro and Pietro Verri. The most important member of this group was Cesare Bonesano, Marchese di Beccaria (1738–1794), whose little book *On Crimes and Punishments* (1764) became deservedly famous. Locke, Helvétius, and Montesquieu provided the inspiration for this work. The central thesis is that punishment should be conceived of as a measure of social defense, not of vengeance; it was deduced from the theory of the social contract, and it proved immensely influential in subsequent movements for penal reform.

Condillac lived in Parma from 1758 to 1767; and in the next generation Milan came under his influence and that of the *idéologues.* Francesco Soave (1743–1806) was the most influential theoretical spokesman of the time; he publicized the new ideas, though he still preferred Locke and brought out a translation of Wynne's abridgment of the *Essay Concerning Human Understanding* in 1775. But the work of Melchiorre Gioja (1767–1829) and Gian Domenico Romagnosi (1761–1835) in social philosophy and economic theory was much more important than Soave's theorizing. These two were philosophers in the style of Bentham, attracted to a simple hedonistic sensationalism because of its utility in the statistical study of social problems and the planning of reforms.

Cuoco. Like the Neapolitan Pagano, Romagnosi had a genuine reverence for Vico. But the truest line of Vico's heritage runs from his son Gennaro to Vincenzo Cuoco (1770–1823). Cuoco scorned the fashionable "ideology" and emphasized the Platonism in Vico's *Scienza nuova,* making the "eternal history" almost a deterministic pattern in which men are merely the puppets of providence. In his *Essay on the Neapolitan Revolution of 1799* he pleaded for a return to the native tradition of speculation. His work thus fittingly marks the end of the Enlightenment in Italy and the dawning of the *risorgimento.*

THE "RISORGIMENTO"

For Italian thinkers of the period from 1740 to 1820, philosophy began with Locke and ended with Destutt de Tracy. In the next fifty years German influences predominated, though both the Scottish school and Victor Cousin had a following. But the attitude of the Italians was more critical and far more independent.

Galluppi. The earliest Italian book on Kant was written by Francesco Soave in 1803; Gioja and Romagnosi also examined the critical philosophy, but could find nothing useful in it. The first really intelligent Italian study was made by Pasquale Borrelli (1782–1849) at Naples; and in the work of Pasquale Galluppi (1770–1846) Kant's influence was seriously felt, if not perfectly assimilated.

Like Kant, Galluppi began with a training in the metaphysics of Wolff; and he passed from that to the study of Locke and Condillac before he came to the *Critique of Pure Reason.* He seems always to have remained attached to Locke's "Plain historical method," and he objected violently to the skeptical tendencies which he detected in Kant and still more clearly in Fichte. The synthetic activity of the understanding was, for Galluppi, a putting together of real elements that are really united in nature; and the subjective categories of substance and cause have objective force because they somehow correspond to reality. In order to maintain this view, Galluppi had to regard sensation itself as an a priori synthesis of subject and object rather than as simply subjective. In much the same spirit of common-sense realism he corrected what he regarded as the excessive rigorism of Kant's ethics, insisting that there was no necessary conflict between duty and pleasure, and laying great stress on the principle "virtue deserves happiness." As against Galluppi's tendency to compromise, Ottavio Colecchi (1773–1847) stood for the most rigid Kantian orthodoxy both in epistemology and in ethics.

Rosmini. A new edition of the *Scienza nuova* was published at Milan in 1801; in 1818 the marquis of Villa Rosa began to issue an edition of Vico's complete works. By this time Antonio Rosmini-Serbati (1797–1855) and Vincenzo Gioberti (1801–1852) were taking their first steps in philosophic studies. Rosmini reacted violently against the "mundane philosophy" of Gioja and Romagnosi, and regarded even the critical empiricism of Galluppi with distrust. He was perhaps influenced more than he realized by the Kantians, but like Gioberti he drew the primary inspiration of his philosophy from the tradition of Italian Platonism.

Subjectivism in all its forms, whether empiricist or transcendental, was to him anathema. In order to escape it he took up again the conception of "the natural light of Reason." The light of reason is our way of participating in Being; thus everything that Kant ascribed to the categorial activity of the understanding became for Rosmini the result of our intuition of Being. Conscious awareness is a primitive synthesis of feeling in which physical sensation is united with this intellectual intuition. Every moment of experience is thus necessarily a fusion of clear knowledge, valid for all eternity, and inexhaustible mystery; this conception of the "fundamental feeling" from which all cognitive experience arises was later one of the most important sources of Gentile's theory of the "pure act." Contemporary critics saw in it, perhaps rightly, the influence of Maine de Biran. But for Rosmini himself the most important consequences were theological rather than psychological, since, when it is pushed to the limit, it yields Patrizzi's doctrine of infinite space as the divine sensorium. Thus, by reflecting upon the foundation of our own experience, we can intuitively perceive how the creation of the infinite world of finite things is an act of the divine love.

The existence of death and evil can similarly be seen to be the necessary price of our existence as beings capable of the free activity of self-perfection. Feeling and life are essentially matters of degree. The practical aspect of sense awareness is the urge toward sensible comfort or pleasure, and similarly the practical aspect of intellectual awareness is the sense of moral duty. To "follow the light of reason" or "to incline the will toward Being" is the basic imperative of human nature.

From this general principle Rosmini managed to derive a whole system of social regulation; and upon it he based the organization of the Catholic Order of the Fathers of Charity, which he founded in 1828. He was an active leader of the more liberal Catholics in the revolutions of 1848, and despite the official condemnation of 40 propositions from his works he has always remained influential in Catholic philosophical circles. He also influenced leaders of thought who were not professional philosophers, notably the novelists Alessandro Manzoni (a grandson of Beccaria) and Antonio Fogazzaro.

Gioberti. Gioberti could not understand how, in Rosmini's system, the sense of actual existence could arise from an idea of pure Being that was explicitly claimed to be the ground of all possibility. This difficulty reflects the fundamental contrast between the two thinkers. Gioberti attached much more importance to actual existence than did Rosmini. He may seem to be close to Rosmini when he sums up his philosophy in the aphorism that recalls Erigena, "Being creates existence, and existence returns to

Being"; but he is actually nearer to the pantheism of Bruno (whom he much admired). Like Rosmini, he began by studying Kant and the Scottish school of common sense; but the whole native Platonic tradition from Bonaventure to Vico, Gerdil, and Rosmini influenced him, and he came at last to see Italy as the providentially appointed guardian of the "perennial philosophy" from the time of Pythagoras onward.

Gioberti was keenly aware of the danger of falling into pantheism, and he believed that Hegel had fallen into it where Vico had not. "Being" in Gioberti is the source not only of light but of life and activity; and the task of philosophy in history is to bring the whole world of existence to a clear awareness of itself as expressing the activity of Being. But, inasmuch as that activity is inexhaustible and the creation of novelty is continual, Being can never coincide with existence.

Mazzini. A similar sense of God as a power at work in history and of the national community as the essential instrument of his activity permeates the writings of Giuseppe Mazzini (1805–1872). Mazzini more or less explicitly (if not quite consistently) identified humanity with God, though he had no clearly worked out ontology or epistemology. But he was, surprisingly, much less chauvinistic about the "primacy" of the Italian nation than Gioberti. He looked forward rather to a consort of nations organized as democratic republics. In this respect his debt to the French Enlightenment is plainly visible. He was much influenced by the radical currents of French religious thought, notably by Félicité de Lammenais; a mystical romantic tendency is evident in his belief—later invoked by Fascist apologists—that individual leaders may be specially inspired and thus possess what he called "the privilege of genius." Slight as Mazzini's philosophical achievement was, he is more worthy of record alongside Rosmini and Gioberti than such academic contemporaries as Terenzio Mamiani della Rovere (1799–1885), who began as an empiricist critic of Rosmini and ended as a Platonist admirer without contributing anything valuable in either role.

Ferrari. The influence of Rosmini and Gioberti on the practical tradition of Romagnosi can be seen in the work of Giuseppe Ferrari (1812–1876), who was forced into skepticism by his inability to reconcile the requirements of reason with the facts of actual experience. The function of thought, he concluded, was properly revolutionary—and he praised Hegel for recognizing this. For a guide to truth he turned to natural instinct; this provided him with a solid foundation for the social ideals of the French Revolution that were his central concern (*Filosofia della rivoluzione*, 1851).

POSITIVISM AND IDEALISM

After Rosmini's death the mundane tradition reasserted itself in the north. In Carlo Cattaneo (1801–1869) the tradition of Romagnosi had a defender more worthy than Mamiani, and more faithful than Ferrari. Like Romagnosi and Ferrari, Cattaneo revered Vico as the thinker who had recognized that the proper concern of the philosopher is with the process whereby men become civilized. The great mistake of previous philosophers, he thought, lay in their concentration upon the individual mind rather than upon social psychology and social interaction. But he held that in seeking to understand man in society, philosophy must accept both method and data from the empirical sciences. From the facts of history and cultural anthropology we must discover by induction the forces that have made us what we are. Inasmuch as he shared the sociological concerns of Comte, Cattaneo should probably be counted as the first of the Italian positivists; and we can plausibly regard the great *Treatise on General Sociology* of Vilfredo Pareto (1848–1923) as a fulfillment of Cattaneo's program, though Cattaneo would scarcely have shared Pareto's fascist sympathies.

The positivism of Comte enjoyed a wide following in Italy. But none of its declared adherents produced anything of note except Roberto Ardigò (1828–1920), a priest who lost his faith without ever losing his vocation, so that he became—like Comte himself—the apostle of a mundane religion. Ardigò criticized Spencer for retaining a shadow of the old God in the shape of the "unknowable," maintaining that nothing was really unknowable, that the answer to any question must in the end be discovered. He was a professor at Padua, and thus it was natural that he should hark back to the naturalism of his fellow Paduan Pomponazzi, which provided him with a ready answer to all spirtualist theories of mental activity. But he liked also to play on Vico's dictum that "truth coincides with fact," which he misinterpreted as a justification for Lockian empiricism. In his ontology he held to a sort of neutral monism in which the concept of "force" served to account equally for all physical and psychical phenomena.

Hegelianism. While the positivists were gathering strength in the north, the circles influenced by Rosmini and Gioberti, along with the Kantians at Naples, were beginning to study Hegel seriously. Augusto Vera (1813–1885) already enjoyed a European reputation as an interpreter of Hegel when he became a professor at Naples in 1861. His training and early career had been in France, and his *Introduction à la philosophie de Hegel* (1855) served its purpose for many readers outside Italy (among them C. S. Peirce). Vera was a zealot for the perfect integrity of Hegel's system, and his very zeal led him to a sort of Platonic dualism in which the completeness and perfection of idea stands opposed to the always imperfect realizations of spirit in history.

The gulf between essence and existence that Vera accentuated appeared to Bertrando Spaventa (1817–1882) to be the great unresolved problem remaining in Hegel's work; and, though his reverence for Hegel was as great as Vera's, he labored long and critically at a "reform of the dialectic" that would resolve the problem. Spaventa found no very clear solution, although Gentile later used his ideas to develop a solution that was more radical than anything Spaventa dreamed of.

Spaventa did apply Hegel's method and general conception of the history of philosophy to the Italian tradition, with results that were both strikingly original and enormously influential. In his conception of "the circulation of Italian philosophy," the native tradition was presented both as the primary source and as the proper culmination of modern philosophy. Thus Bruno prepared the way for Spinoza, but also looked beyond him to the romantics; Campanella anticipated the great struggle between rationalism and empiricism and its resolution by Kant; and Vico foreshadowed the Hegelian synthesis. Rosmini—for all his aversion to foreign influences—was really summing up the achievement of European philosophy from Descartes to Kant, and Gioberti was similarly repeating the development of thought from Kant to Hegel in Italian terms.

Spaventa's view was intended as a correction of the more chauvinist claims of Rosmini and Gioberti. Gioberti, for example, regarded Hegel's philosophy as a degenerate form of Vico's and offered something very like Spaventa's interpretation of Rosmini as a destructive criticism, whereas Spaventa held that Italian thinkers were most fortunately placed to reap the fruits of European speculation and should begin to do so more consciously. Spaventa's approach has produced a great many forced interpretations of Italian thinkers, usually in the interest of inflated claims, but there can be no question of its enormous fruitfulness.

The great *History of Italian Literature* by Spaventa's exact contemporary Francesco de Sanctis provides a perfect example of the sort of marriage between the native tradition and the mainstream of European philosophy that Spaventa hoped for. De Sanctis' work was guided by a general conception of art and culture in which it would be difficult, if not impossible, to distinguish the influence of Vico from that of Hegel. The work of De Sanctis influenced Croce in the construction of a philosophical system that owes more to a re-examination of Vico in the spirit of Spaventa than to any other single source; and Gentile's actual idealism owes as much to Rosmini and Gioberti seen through Hegelian spectacles as it does to Hegel himself.

Marxism. Among Spaventa's disciples, Donato Jaja (1839–1914) is important as Gentile's teacher, and Sebastiano Maturi (1843–1917) as the teacher of Augusto Guzzo. Neither of these men produced any noteworthy work of his own. The one important development for the Hegelian school in the generation that preceded World War I was Marxism, which was perhaps more critically studied and developed as a philosophical system in Italy than anywhere else, probably because in the circumstances of the new nation the parent Hegelian tradition took on a more progressive character than it generally exhibited. First Antonio Labriola (1843–1904) convinced Croce and Gentile that the historical materialism he derived from Marx was a philosophy that deserved serious study; and then in the next generation Antonio Gramsci (1891–1937), founder of the Italian Communist party, repaid the compliment by spending many long hours meditating upon Croce's work in a Fascist jail.

THE TWENTIETH CENTURY

At the beginning of the twentieth century Francesco De Sarlo (1864–1937) was carrying on the best traditions of Italian positivism at Florence. Bernardino Varisco (1850–1933) was moving away from his positivist beginnings toward a monadic spiritualism rooted in the tradition of Rosmini. Filippo Masci (1844–1922) and Piero Martinetti (1871–1943) were carrying on the Kantian tradition, which had outlasted the Hegelian school at Naples. The great flowering of mathematical logic under Giuseppe Peano (1858–1932) produced in Giovanni Vailati (1863–1909) a philosopher of science whose breadth of sympathy and keen historical sense made him well able to integrate the various currents of pragmatism and scientific empiricism in England, Germany, and the United States in a way that would have deserved Spaventa's approval.

But none of these thinkers was destined to have much immediate influence. Varisco's work had one rather independent heir in Pantaleo Carabellese (1877–1948); and Antonio Aliotta has similarly carried on the experimental tradition of De Sarlo in very much his own way. Vailati and his one ally, Mario Calderoni (1879–1914), were both cut off by early death and have only recently become influential, some fifty years later.

Historical idealism. The great upsurge of historical idealism that began with Croce's founding of the journal *La critica* in 1903 overwhelmed all other philosophical movements for forty years.

Benedetto Croce (1866–1952) was the nephew of the philosopher Bertrando Spaventa but never came under his direct influence. Croce possessed independent means and a quite astounding capacity to absorb and marshal concrete historical detail, and he always retained a strong distaste for the disputes of academic philosophers. Although he influenced all of them, he has found few disciples among them. The thinkers who primarily influenced him were men like De Sanctis, Vico, and Labriola, who had applied philosophical principles to the problems of history, economics, and literature. Gentile led him to study the actual works of Hegel carefully; but his idealism was always more a methodology than a metaphysics.

One might fairly say that the fundamental distinction in Croce's philosophy is between a level or range of human activity that is historical and one that is prehistorical or subhistorical. Thus, on the theoretical side Croce distinguished between "intuition," the uniquely individual mode of cognition present in artistic creation and appreciation, and historical understanding, which enables us to comprehend the universal significance of our intuitive experience. On the practical side the basic needs of the living organism make certain institutions and activities (notably natural science and a legal system) into a sort of permanent substructure of all human social life; and on this permanent communal base men are able to realize their peculiar capacities and achieve their moral ideals as free individuals.

Croce found it rather difficult to maintain the distinction on the practical side as he at first envisaged it, because so much of moral action is directed toward political and economic ends. For that matter it was not easy to hold strictly to the view that art has no history, and he found himself obliged eventually to distinguish the literary and technical aspects of art, which were subject to historical analysis, from the pure intuition, which was not. But one can see the value of his conceptual scheme to a working historian, even if the application of it must in practice vary with every particular historical problem to which it is applied.

The "actual idealism" of Giovanni Gentile (1875–1944)

forms a perfect complement to Croce's historicism. Gentile was a pure philosopher, a man for whom a higher destiny than that of a professor of philosophy was scarcely conceivable. Where Croce insisted on distinctions, Gentile's abiding concern was with the essential unity of experience, which is revealed when every activity is seen under its philosophical aspect. If Croce's theory is essentially a methodology, Gentile's is properly a theory of value, though it is also easily transformed into an ontology, which is a fate that can hardly befall Croce's system. For Gentile solved Spaventa's problem of the gulf between the essence and the existence of Hegel's Absolute Idea by identifying human self-consciousness with the Absolute and viewing all of human experience as the dialectical development of the primitive self-feeling. In the dialectic of consciousness two poles are always distinguishable: the subjective, the moment of creative spontaneity that is the source of artistic activity, and the objective, the moment of contemplative passivity that is the basis both of religion and of pure science. These two opposites are synthesized in philosophy, and hence all experience considered integrally or in its concreteness is properly philosophical.

The Hegelian character of this theory is obvious; what is more interesting to note in the present context is that Gentile accepted Vico's view that human consciousness is essentially religious (whereas Croce did not, or at least never did so in his theory). Again, Gentile regarded traditional formal logic as the logic of the objective moment taken in abstraction. Hence scientific research is for him a mode of cognition just as much as of action; and where Croce emphasized its manipulative, pragmatic character, Gentile, like Vico and Galileo, emphasized its mathematical form. In philosophical experience even the distinction between thought and action is overcome, for the most theoretical kind of reflection is, at least, an activity of self-education, and hence part of our progressive creation of our world. All activity is ultimately political because self-consciousness has essentially the form of a dialogue between persons.

Followers of Gentile. Mussolini gave Gentile his long-sought opportunity to reform the Italian school system in 1923; and when the dictatorship began in 1925, Gentile became the chief intellectual voice of the regime while Croce went into opposition. As a result Gentile was perhaps even more influential than he would have been otherwise. Gradually his disciples split into two wings: the "right," led by Armando Carlini (1878–1959), which emphasized the religious and metaphysical side of actual idealism; and the "left," led by Ugo Spirito and Guido Calogero, which emphasized its social and scientific aspects. After the fall of Fascism the two groups moved further apart and began to merge with other traditions.

The right wing became the nucleus of a group of Catholic philosophers, the "Christian Spiritualists," for whom the inspiration of Augustine provided a common ground. This group can fairly be regarded as the direct heirs of Ficino's *Theologia Platonica* and of Rosmini. Currently, the most important of them is probably Augusto Guzzo, whose link with the Hegelian tradition runs through Maturi rather than Gentile.

The left wing has become part of the philosophical

tradition of socialism. This tradition provided the inspiration for Franco Lombardi's critical revision of historicism (*Il mondo degli uomini*, 1935).

Existentialism and analysis. For a few years around 1950 existentialism of various sorts was the dominant fashion on all sides, but it has now declined into a subsidiary influence in most quarters. Lombardi introduced Kierkegaard's work into Italy in 1936, and the remarkable essay of Carlo Michaelstaedter (1887–1910), *Rhetoric and Persuasion*, has received some attention as a sort of protoexistentialist reaction in the era of historicism. The most important declared existentialist in Italy at present is Nicola Abbagnano, but his work is typical of the muted and moderated form that existentialism has assumed in Italy. He has, for instance, been sympathetically associated with the group of younger philosophers, centered round Lodovico Geymonat, who have recently revived the tradition of social scientific philosophy at Milan. They have taken up again the work of Vailati, enriching it with insights from logical positivism and linguistic analysis.

(See also GALLARATE MOVEMENT; HEGELIANISM; HUMANISM; and RENAISSANCE. See Italian Philosophy in Index for articles on Italian philosophers.)

Bibliography

The best general account in English of Italian philosophy down to the time of Galileo is contained in J. H. Randall, *The Career of Philosophy* (New York, 1962); but there are also other histories that treat the Renaissance period fairly adequately, for example, George Boas, *Dominant Themes of Modern Philosophy* (New York, 1957) and A. Robert Caponigri, *History of Western Philosophy* (Chicago, 1903), Vol. III. A fairly complete but extremely biased account of the period from Rosmini to Gentile is provided in Guido de Ruggiero, *Filosofia contemporanea* (Bari, Italy, 1912), translated by A. Hannay and R. Collingwood as *Modern Philosophy* (London, 1921). Angelo Crespi, *Contemporary Thought of Italy* (London, 1926) provides an account of the twentieth century with an opposite bias. The shorter notices in George Boas, *The Major Traditions of European Philosophy* (New York, 1929), are a bit more balanced. No satisfactory account of the period between 1630 and 1830 exists in English. Even Vico has not yet received adequate notice in general histories of philosophy, although he is no longer simply ignored.

Of the works in Italian, Eugenio Garin, *La filosofia*, 2 vols. (Milan, 1947) is well balanced, reliable, and exhaustive. Volumes XI to XXXV of the *Opere complete* of Gentile (Florence) will provide a remarkably unified and continuous account of Italian philosophy in the form of separate monographs.

H. S. HARRIS

ITŌ JINSAI (1627–1705), Japanese Confucianist of the *kogakuha* ("school of ancient learning"). Itō was born in Kyoto, the son of a poor merchant, and spent his life there as an educator. After studying the official Chu Hsi Confucianist doctrine, he rediscovered ancient Confucianism and became its systematizer and, through the Kogidō, a school he founded in 1680, its propagator. The novelty of his teaching aroused the suspicion of the central government in Edo (Tokyo). However, it was not suppressed al-

though his *kogigaku*, or "learning-of-the-ancient-meaning," was gaining a large following. Through the able guidance of his scholarly son, Tōgai, and of his grandson the school was operated until 1871, when all Confucianist schools were abolished in favor of the new Western system.

Itō's philosophy, stemming from a great admiration for Confucius and Mencius, is quite contrary to the Neo-Confucianism of Chu Hsi. Itō is clearly a monist in the sense that he does not admit any priority of *ri*, the principle (reason), over *ki*, the material force, which for him is material energy. A primordial material energy (*ichi genki*), having neither beginning nor end, is the root of everything. *Ri* is but a pattern of *ki*; *ki*, through the motion of the yin–yang, or passive–active, elements, forms the great living organism (*dai-katsubutsu*), the universe itself.

Itō holds with Mencius that man's nature is originally good, and he does not make the usual Chu Hsi distinction between physical and original nature, which he treats as a spurious Taoist influence. Evil in physical nature need not be explained as if it arose from lack of cultivation of the potentialities of human nature. The four sources of virtue (in Chinese, *ssu tuan;* in Japanese, *shitan*) according to Itō are righteousness, humaneness, ritual or propriety, and wisdom. Righteousness is the pivotal virtue of Itō's ethics. Humaneness is benevolent love, or condescension from the superior to the inferior, for in Confucianism universal equalitarian love is practically nonexistent. Morality, the natural Way of things, has a cosmological meaning in addition to the ethical one. The material energy of the universe is manifested in man through humaneness or love. Itō's principles of education centered on forming moral character rather than on imparting knowledge; will is above the intellect.

Itō did not make much of astronomy and mathematics, but he was very fond of history. However, unlike most other Confucianists of the "ancient learning" school, he did not become a nationalist through the study of history. For him China remained the fountainhead of culture. Itō's outstanding merits as a Sinologist were the result of painstaking research in ancient texts, yet he patiently bore the faultfinding of his gifted son and the criticisms of his best pupil, Namikawa Temmin (1679–1718).

Bibliography

Itō's chief works can be found in collections in Japanese, including Inoue Tetsujirō, ed., *Nihon rinri ihen* ("Library on Japanese Ethics"; Tokyo, 1901), Vol. V, pp. 11–181, and *Dai Nihon shisō zenshū* ("Collected Works on the Thought of Great Japan"; Tokyo, 1934), Vol. XLI, pp. 7–249. See also Ishida Ichirō, *Itō Jinsai* (Tokyo, 1964), which is in Japanese.

For works in English see J. J. Spae, *Itō Jinsai, A Philosopher, Educator* and *Sinologist of the Tokugawa Period* (Peiping, 1948), and W. T. de Bary, Ryusaku Tsunoda, and Donald Keene, eds., *Sources of Japanese Tradition* (New York, 1958), pp. 410–422. The second work contains selections in translation with introductions.

GINO K. PIOVESANA, S.J.

J

JACOBI, FRIEDRICH HEINRICH (1743–1819), was a leading representative, with Hamann, of the philosophy of feeling and a major critic of Kant. He was born in Düsseldorf on the Rhine. Jacobi received an education preparing him for a business career, but an inner urge drove him to the pursuit of philosophical studies. He studied the works of Helvétius, Rousseau, Ferguson, and Spinoza, the last of which had a negative influence on him, provoking opposition and criticism; he was also influenced by the English philosophers of feeling—Shaftesbury and others. His friend Hamann, a kindred spirit, lived in his home for a long period, and his influence on Jacobi cannot be overestimated. In 1804, Jacobi was appointed president of the Academy of Sciences in Munich. He was in literary contact with the prominent thinkers of his time—Mendelssohn, Reinhold, Fries, and Goethe. His discussions with his contemporaries are as important for the understanding of his philosophy as are his original works.

Jacobi developed a philosophy of feeling and faith. He was critical of speculations leading to the concept of the prevalence of necessary laws above freedom, hence Jacobi's rejection of Spinoza's pantheism and of the philosophy of Fichte, Schelling, and Hegel in which there are manifest pantheistic tendencies. Because of Jacobi's concept of the primacy of freedom, he found that the actions of man are not to be deduced from his thinking, for thinking is not the primary force in man. The history of man is not the result of his mode of thought; rather, the former determines the latter. Herein is anticipated the method of the historical school of law as it was later developed by Savigny. For Jacobi the immediately given is the determining factor in our cognition of cultural phenomena. Objects have to be given to us through immediate feeling or faith before thought comes into play. The task of discursive thinking is to observe, analyze, compare, and order perceptions by reducing them to their fundamental principles. But unless something real is previously given through feeling, discursive thinking cannot take place.

Jacobi was a master of criticism. His strength lay in grasping a system of thought as a whole and detecting those elements in it which are incompatible. This capacity of critical analysis is manifest in his appraisal of dogmatic rationalism and the critical philosophy. Jacobi subjected both Spinoza and Kant to severe criticism. He pointed to hidden contradictions and inconsistencies in both their systems. The dogmatic rationalism of Spinoza employs the mathematical method in the realm of metaphysics; it accepts as real only what can be proven and deduced mathematically. By this method, however, neither God nor freedom can be maintained. These ideas cannot be deduced by an absolute system of causality, which is the essence of Spinozism. Absolute necessity leads to atheism, and the denial of freedom leads to fatalism. To Jacobi, Spinozism and pantheism were synonymous terms, and pantheism was identical with dogmatic rational atheism. (He ignored the possibility of interpreting Spinoza's system as acosmism instead of as atheism—an interpretation which was first suggested by Maimon and then by Hegel.)

Jacobi's ethicoreligious world view is the background of this criticism of Spinoza. While recognizing the dangers implied in Spinozism, Jacobi and Lessing were the first to acknowledge the philosophical genius of Spinoza. Through Jacobi's discussions with Mendelssohn about Spinozism and Lessing's relation to it, in the course of which the arguments for and against Spinoza were brought forth, Spinoza's philosophy became a force in the intellectual life of the time; it acquired a universal significance (see PANTHEISMUSSTREIT). Spinoza and Kant were two opposing poles of thought for Jacobi. For the former all being, including man, is determined by necessary laws; for the latter freedom and creativity are the essence of man. The whole period of the development of post-Kantian speculative idealism was determined by the two intellectual forces: the dogmatic rationalism of Spinoza and the critical philosophy of Kant. Jacobi was critical of the philosophy of speculative idealism (Fichte, Schelling, and Hegel) for its manifestation of Spinozistic tendencies.

Jacobi on Kant. Jacobi's enthusiasm for Kant's precritical essay *Der einzig möglicher Beweisgrund zu einer Demonstration des Daseins Gottes* ("The Only Possible Ground for a Demonstration of God's Existence") is indicative of his conception of the method by which we can attain knowledge of reality. Kant had shown in this work that the absolute and unconditioned being must be grasped as existing in and through itself, not as a predicate or as a consequence of something else. The attainment of some reality which is simple, insoluble, and immediately given is the ultimate aim in our striving for certainty. Cognition by way of discursive thought cannot attain certainty. A method of deduction of consequences from premises is an endless process which can never attain the original unconditional and primary being. Certainty is acquired only in an immediate perception of a reality not requiring any deduction.

Jacobi admired Spinoza because he had reversed the whole process of philosophizing as it was known since Aristotle. Instead of proceeding from the phenomena of experience, leading gradually to being as such, Spinoza started with a definition of substance as something which is conceived in itself and through itself—that is, a simple and immediately given reality. This simple and indissoluble datum is, however, according to Jacobi, not free from contradiction. Spinoza's substance is not a free, independent, self-sufficient being, but a necessary and causally bound being. The God of Spinoza is nothing else but a manifestation of the logical–mathematical determination of being.

The critical philosophy can be maintained only if it consistently removes all traces of a dogmatic, realistic nature. The concept of a thing-in-itself has to be completely eliminated because it is incompatible with the system as a whole. The Kantian position is, according to Jacobi, pure idealism. As such it cannot retain the concept of things in themselves. The *Critique of Pure Reason* deduces the objects from the constitution of our cognitive capacity. It has therefore to deny objective reality existing independently of and beyond the conditions of cognition. The object has to be completely resolved in subjective presentations of our mind. Kantian philosophy is thus interpreted by Jacobi as pure subjective idealism. Since we perceive the objects through forms of sensibility (space and time) and concepts of understanding, constituting the human capacity of cognition, the "external" objects cannot be beyond us. According to Jacobi, Descartes intended by the principle *cogito ergo sum* to deduce the totality of the inner subjective world from the consciousness of the self as a thinking subject. Self-consciousness of oneself as a thinking being is the primary condition of man's knowledge of the inner world. In a similar manner Kant tried to prove that external objects are likewise conditioned by and dependent on the subject with its forms of sensibility and understanding. Hence, the subjective idealism of Descartes was extended by Kant to encompass the world of objects, too. The Kantian position is thus, according to Jacobi, universal idealism, but since he took Kant to mean that the cognition of things is determined by the individual ego and not by the objective mind as it is presented in scientific thought, universal idealism, according to Jacobi, is a system of absolute subjectivity, which implies a "nihilism" with reference to the objects. This system recognizes only the ego as real; it is thus speculative egoism. Jacobi found this position self-contradictory. Sensibility is a receptive function, according to Kant. But a consistent idealism excludes a receptive capacity in the process of cognition. It is incongruous with idealism to assume the reality of things-in-themselves existing independently of our mind, yet these things are supposed by Kant to supply the material of experience which affects our senses. The first part of the Kantian *Critique* deals with the forms of sensibility as a receptive capacity. Thus, things-in-themselves are assumed, by which our sensibility is affected. "Hence we cannot enter into the *Critique* without assuming things-in-themselves, but we cannot retain this assumption upon leaving the *Critique*."

Since Jacobi understood the Kantian position as subjective idealism, he did not consider the second edition of the *Critique of Pure Reason* an improvement on the first. The Kantian philosophy which Jacobi took to be a form of pure subjective idealism is presented in the first edition of the *Critique,* and this he took to be its genuine and adequate presentation. To Jacobi belongs the priority of recognizing the difference between the two editions, but he was wrong in its evaluation. He failed to grasp the essential characteristic of critical idealism, which is grounded in analysis of objective scientific cognition and not in analysis of the process of cognition of the individual subject. The problem posed by Kant was How are synthetic propositions a priori in mathematics and natural science possible?, not How is cognition of the individual subject as a psychological phenomenon possible? Whereas the Kantian inquiry constitutes the essence of the transcendental method, leading to objective idealism, the investigation of the individual process of cognition appertains to the psychological method, resulting in subjective idealism. The second edition of the *Critique,* which tries to eliminate the psychological sections of the first edition, is the pre-eminent presentation of the transcendental method.

Faith—the sense of reality. In opposition to the critical philosophy, which is, according to Jacobi, absolute subjectivity, he proposed a thesis of absolute objectivity. The objective reality of things-in-themselves existing beyond man and independently of the human cognition is based for Jacobi on an original, immediate certainty which does not require any proof or demonstration. The certainty of the existence of things in themselves is based on faith.

Our consciousness presupposes the reality of things as a necessary correlate of cognition. The idealistic position contradicts an assumption which is inherent in every act of cognition of an object of experience. To be sure, the reality of the things cognized cannot be conclusively derived from the process of cognition as such, which is a subjective phenomenon, but only from the immediate sense of reality accompanying every act of cognition of an object. This sense of reality, which cannot be accounted for logically but is nonetheless present in our mind, is designated by Jacobi by such terms as faith, feeling, and, later, revelation.

With Kant Jacobi recognized that analysis of cognition cannot lead to things-in-themselves, since the validity of the categories is confined to the realm of experience and does not extend beyond it. But the Kantian *Critique* had also shown that reason leads to a realm of faith in addition to mere cognition. Hence, an object which cannot be proven as real on the basis of cognition may still be real on the basis of faith. Kant employed the concept of faith only with reference to the moral and religious realm, but Jacobi extended the scope of faith to include the knowledge of things-in-themselves. In recognizing the validity of faith for the theoretical realm, Jacobi followed Hume, who designated the feeling of reality of the natural human consciousness as faith. The skepticism of Hume showed that the reality of things cannot be derived from sense perception. Analysis of perception cannot lead to cognition of substance and causality; only through faith can we know the reality of things. Hume thus ascribed to faith a positive theoretical function inasmuch as it is a source of knowledge of the reality of the things of experience. The belief in the reality of things, which accompanies our sensuous experience throughout our lives, is incomprehensible, but, according to Jacobi, it commands certainty just as if it were an act of revelation. He understood by revelation a certainty which we are aware of but which we cannot explain rationally. This conception of the belief in the reality of things is radically different from naive realism and common-sense philosophy. The latter does not realize the extraordinary nature and the problematic character of the concept of reality, of things-in-themselves. Naive realism takes for granted that we perceive things as they are. Jacobi, however, realized the miraculous nature of such a belief. The possibility of transition from consciousness to things, from the subject to objects, cannot be comprehended by our understanding. Jacobi was right to affirm the position of critical idealism that we can know of things only what we ourselves put into them. While we cannot cognize things-in-themselves, our belief in their reality can be accounted for as something irrational that is an indispensable ingredient of human consciousness. Our rational thinking cannot lead us to cognition of reality of things-in-themselves. However, the necessary condition of the existence of man as a conscious being is grounded in an incomprehensible and irrational act of faith commanding certainty which is not subject to any doubt. In face of this belief as a necessary condition of human consciousness, the arguments of rationalism, of critical philosophy, and of skepticism are powerless.

Religion. Jacobi's philosophy of religion is grounded in the same principle on which his theory of cognition of reality is founded. The concept of faith as having a theoretical function is the ground of the certainty of real objects beyond us and of a supersensuous reality. This immediate certainty of reality is present in our consciousness of God as it is present in our perception of objects. Through belief man has the capacity of intuiting God. Dogmatic religionists maintain that through an act of faith God reveals himself to man by grace. For Jacobi faith is a mode of cognition or a form of intellectual intuition. And this is not an exclusively religious phenomenon, for through belief man likewise perceives the reality of things of experience. The distinction between the reality of the things and the transcendent, supersensuous reality is that the former reveals itself through an external perception, whereas the latter is intuited through an internal revelation. Both forms of revelation constitute the very essence of human existence as a conscious being.

For Kant, it is impossible through faith to transcend the sphere of the subject, but for Jacobi we are aware through faith of a reality which is not subjective, since in the act of faith the nature of the real thing reveals itself to us. Faith thus commands not only ethical certainty, as Kant held, but also theoretical certainty. To be sure, the transcendent reality cannot be known by the forms of understanding which are confined to the realm of experience. But faith as a function of reason (*Vernunft*) is capable of transcending experience and thus can perceive the supersensuous by an act of intellectual intuition.

Intellectual intuition, which is attained through faith, overcomes the Kantian dualism of sensibility and understanding, which is a necessary condition of cognition of objects of experience. Kant considered intellectual intuition an idea of knowledge of the infinite mind (*intellectus archetypus*), which is not attainable by the finite, human mind. But for Jacobi intellectual intuition is attained through faith, or immediate feeling. Jacobi thus prepared the way for the post-Kantian speculative metaphysicians to consider intellectual intuition a capacity of human reason.

Criticism. By ascribing to belief the function of knowledge of things-in-themselves and of the existence of God and of freedom, Jacobi disregarded the essential difference between the theoretical and the ethical realms. Kant's concept of faith is a new principle of validity but not a mode of knowledge. In the *Critique of Practical Reason* Kant discovered an "unconditioned" in opposition to the conditioned reality of experience. God and freedom as ideas of practical reason are not metaphysical things but principles of ethical conduct. It is the unconditioned of freedom and the "ought to be," not the existence of transcendent reality, which is discovered through faith.

Jacobi is rightly critical of the dogmatic rationalism of the Enlightenment; he realized the limitations of rational thought in face of the endlessness of that which is problematic. But he was wrong in subordinating the realm of science, which is grounded in discursive thinking, to that of feeling and faith. He did not realize the problem involved in his concept of belief and immediate feeling as the highest means of attaining knowledge of reality. The appeal to feeling, belief, and immediate evidence opens up possibilities for abuse and willful arbitrariness. Feeling and immediate sense of reality are subjective, and whenever a capacity of the subject is elevated to a principle of knowledge, objective truth is in jeopardy. The rightful place of faith is therefore the ethical and the religious realm, which is concerned with the "ought," not with being as it is. Theoretical knowledge of reality can be attained only by discursive thinking, which is the scientific method.

Jacobi said of himself that he was a pagan in his mind but a Christian in his heart. He thus recognized the conflict between reason and faith that he caused by the extended role he ascribed to faith. His belief in the reality of things-in-themselves, of a supersensuous being, and of freedom claims not only ethical and religious validity but also pretends to possess the rank of theoretical knowledge; it is therefore in conscious disagreement with reason. The price we pay for extending the scope of faith is its clash with reason.

Works by Jacobi

Jacobi's Werke, F. Roth, ed., 6 vols. Leipzig, 1812–1825.
Über die Lehre des Spinozas, in Briefen an Herrn Moses Mendelssohn. Breslau, 1785.
David Hume über den Glauben, oder Idealismus und Realismus. Breslau, 1787.
Sendschreiben an Fichte. Hamburg, 1799.
Über das Unternehmen des Kritizismus, die Vernunft zu Ver-

stande zu bringen und der Philosophie überhaupt eine neue Absicht zu geben. Hamburg, 1802.

Von den göttlichen Dingen und ihrer Offenbarung. Leipzig, Germany, 1811.

Hauptschriften zum Pantheismusstreit zwischen Mendelssohn und Jacobi, M. Scholz, ed. Berlin, 1916.

Works on Jacobi

Lévy-Bruhl, L., *La Philosophie de F. H. Jacobi.* Paris, 1894.
Schmidt, F. U., *F. H. Jacobi.* Heidelberg, 1908.
Zirngiebl, E., *F. H. Jacobi.* Vienna, 1867.

SAMUEL ATLAS

JAINISM, an Indian religion whose adherents follow the "Victorious One" (*Jina*). This was the title of Vardhamāna, who lived about 500 B.C. and claimed to be the successor of the 23 previous *Tīrthaṃkaras* (literally, "fordmakers," because their teachings enable the faithful to cross the stream of existence and so obtain release). These teachers were supposed to have lived in the immensely distant past. Vardhamāna is also commonly referred to as *Mahāvīra,* or "Great Hero." Although the claim that the religion has been in existence an immense amount of time is clothed in mythology, the archaic elements in Jainism show that it is a tradition older than Vardhamāna, and it is possible that the twenty-third teacher in the sequence, Pārśva, is historical and in fact lived in the eighth century B.C.

The religion, which has affinities with Buddhism and with Sāṃkhya philosophy, had 2,027,000 adherents in 1961, mainly in western India. However, the influence of Jainism on Indian religious and social life has been out of proportion to its present number of followers, partly because of the prosperity of the lay Jains and partly because they were more numerous in medieval times. Like Buddhism, Jainism does not recognize the validity of the Vedic (Hindu) scriptures and thus is considered heterodox in the Indian tradition. It seems likely that its origins are in the pre-Aryan culture of India (see HINDUISM). The main teachings are that there is a sharp distinction between souls and matter, that normally souls are implicated through *karma* in the painful round of Reincarnation, and that through the practice of virtue, meditation, and great austerity the ultimate release of the soul is possible. Jainism is atheistic but does not deny the existence of gods as beings *inside* the cosmos. H. Zimmer therefore has called it "transtheistic," for it regards the worship of the gods as spiritually unimportant.

History. Jain tradition places Vardhamāna's birth in 599 B.C., but more probably it was in 549 or 540 B.C. He came from Vaiśālī near Patna, in Bihar. Like the Buddha, he belonged to the warrior or noble (*kṣatriya*) caste, and at thirty left his wife and child in order to become a wandering recluse. After 12 years of meditation and austerity, he attained omniscience and the assurance of release. His last thirty years were spent in preaching and in reorganizing the order of monks and nuns which, as in Buddhism, constitutes the nucleus of the religion. He died, in what was to become the ideal saintly manner, by self-starvation.

Vardhamāna's followers at an early stage split into two sects, the Svetāmbaras (literally, "white-clad") and the Digambaras ("sky-clad"). The difference lies not in doctrine, but in ceremonial practice and in the fact that the Digambara monks believe in nudism (rarely now practiced in public) as a sign of their independence from worldly customs and attachments. This ideal is represented in the huge standing figures at Sravana Belgola in Mysore, and elsewhere, where the impassive nude saints are represented with creepers climbing up their legs—so long have they stood and so indifferent are they to their environment. The Jain canon, which is quite extensive, is supposed to be based on the teachings of Vardhamāna, but the Digambaras hold that the present corpus is hopelessly corrupt. Nevertheless, the remarkable agreement between the two sects on doctrine indicates the antiquity of the essential teachings.

Cosmology. The universe, according to the Jains, is eternal and uncreated, and contains two types of entities—souls, or life monads (*jīva*), and nonliving matter (*ajīva*). The life monads are infinite in number and are essentially omniscient and blissful; however, these properties are obscured through the association of the life monads with matter, and in particular through the operation of *karma,* which is conceived as a subtle material force. But despite the sharp distinction between life monads and matter, the former are described in a quasi-materialistic way: they expand or contract to fit the bodies they successively animate and are weighed down by *karma,* like invisible bags filled with heavy matter. The aim of the Jain is eventually to annihilate this karmic matter. This annihilation will mean that the life monad, which in a free state has upward gravity, will ascend to the summit of the cosmos, where it will exist motionless, enjoying omniscience and bliss. The transmigrating life monads are classified in accordance with the number of sense organs of the bodies they animate. The elementary atoms (of fire, earth, air, and water) and plants have primitive souls, with only the sense of touch; worms, for example, have touch and taste, and so on. Men, gods, and the inhabitants of the various purgatories have five senses, plus *manas,* the faculty of understanding the data supplied by the other senses (*manas,* too, is conceived as a material entity). Not only do Jains hold that the elements are animated by life monads, but also that even lower in the scale there are clusters of infinitesimally small life monads sharing nutrition and respiration in common. The cosmos is packed with these, and they supply an inexhaustible source of transmigrating souls to make up for those which have attained release.

The inanimate aspect of the cosmos is basically made up of atomic matter; but the Jains also list four other substances—space, time (divisible into atomic instants), the medium of motion (*dharma*), and the medium of rest (*adharma*). Space is not sufficient as a medium of motion, partly because liberated life monads, although they exist in space, are incapable of motion, and partly also because an explanation is needed as to why empty space outside the cosmos cannot be penetrated. Hence, the Jains postulated a kind of ether as the medium in which motion takes place, with a corresponding substance to account for rest.

In accordance with certain primitive elements in the Indian tradition, Jainism pictures the cosmos as being roughly in the shape of a gigantic man or woman. The world inhabited by men is like a huge disc, with the continents arranged concentrically and separated by circular oceans: this corresponds to the waist of the cosmic man. Below there are seven levels, each containing over a million purgatories. Above there is a similar series of heavens, with the gods arranged hierarchically within them. Above these realms is the summit of the universe, corresponding to the top of the cosmic man's head, where the liberated life monads go. In this region there is no *dharma* and therefore no motion. Surrounding the whole are three layers of air, and then infinite empty space. The dimensions of this cosmos are immense. Its height is 14 *rajju*, a unit of length computed as the distance covered in six months by a being traveling at two million miles per smallest unit of time. (Their smallest unit of time is comparable to a microsecond.)

The history of the world consists of an infinite sequence of similar and immensely long aeons, in each of which there is a phase of improvement and a phase of decline. The optimum period in each is a golden age when men are huge and extremely long-lived and when all their needs are supplied miraculously, so that government and property are unnecessary. But at the present time the world is running downhill fast: Vardhamāna is the last "fordmaker" of this era, and gradually the religion will die out, until it is restored in the next aeon.

Philosophy. Jainism has grafted on to the above doctrines the philosophical theories of *anekāntavāda*, or "relative pluralism," and *syādvada*, or "qualified skepticism," for which see INDIAN PHILOSOPHY.

Ethics and religious duties. The attainment of release is immensely difficult, and the monastic life is essential to it. The path prescribed by Vardhamāna has analogies to the techniques of Buddhism and of Yoga, and belongs to the same strand of early Indian religion. But Jainism stresses much more strongly the power of austerity, which can annihilate karmic matter (although the more exhibitionist forms of austerity are discouraged). Severe asceticism is indeed the only effective way of refraining from evil conduct, since the harming, even unintentionally, of living beings and attachment to anything in the world are regarded as intrinsically bad. Thus, monks are expected to walk gently, so as not to crush the living atoms, to filter their water, to wear masks over their mouths so as not to breathe in insects, and so forth. The ideal of death by fasting, following the example of Vardhamāna, is held up to monks who have reached the right degree of self-control. In so doing, they fulfill the central duty of *ahiṃsā*, or noninjury. These austere rules are relaxed for laymen, who are expected to refrain from the generally recognized transgressions, such as dishonesty and promiscuity, and who also on no account must engage in occupations which involve the wholesale destruction of life. This is the chief reason that many Jain laymen are merchants. Alcohol and public entertainments are forbidden, and laymen are encouraged to support the monasteries and temples, as well as to go into retreat for short periods and lead the monastic life.

In addition to austerities, a monk must practice various meditations to purify the understanding. On the one hand, he must make the doctrines alive to himself by thinking of the transitoriness of all beings, including the gods, of the operation of *karma*, of the structure of the cosmos, etc. On the other hand, he should practice going into *dhyāna*, or deep contemplation, in which the mind is rid of images and discursive thoughts.

Like the Buddhas of the Theravādin tradition, the *Tīrthaṃkaras* are incapable of any intervention in the world, but a cult of images of them developed (although not without opposition in medieval times) in iconoclastic movements within the religion. Thus, Jain temples are not essentially different from Hindu ones. Also, the Hindu gods are not repudiated and can be implored for minor boons. Some social ceremonies, such as marriage, are performed by Brahmins. Hence the Jains, although heterodox, have acquired a place within the fabric of Hindu life.

Bibliography

The best recent survey is G. Della Casa, *Il Giainismo* (Turin, 1962). H. von Glasenapp, *Der Jainismus* (Berlin, 1926) and A. Guérinot, *La Religion djaina* (Paris, 1926) are reliable.

In English, there is a dearth of good work, but M. Stevenson, *The Heart of Jainism* (Oxford, 1915) and J. Jaini, *Outlines of Jainism* (Cambridge, 1940) can be consulted.

The best brief introductions are the relevant section (Ch. 7, Sec. 3) of A. L. Basham, *The Wonder That Was India* (London, 1954) and H. Jacobi, "Jainism," in the *Encyclopedia of Religion and Ethics*, James Hastings, ed. (New York, 1959).

H. Zimmer, *Philosophies of India* (New York, 1951; paperback, New York, 1956) has a perceptive account of Jain mythology.

Accounts of the philosophical aspects of Jainism are listed in the bibliography to INDIAN PHILOSOPHY.

Sacred writings are translated by H. Jacobi in Sacred Books of the East, Max Müller, ed., Vols. XXII (Oxford, 1884) and XLV (Oxford, 1893).

NINIAN SMART

JAMES, HENRY (1811–1882), an American philosophical theologian in the Swedenborgian tradition, is perhaps best known as the father of the novelist Henry James and the philosopher-psychologist William James. Although the elder James was physically handicapped from his early teens, an inheritance from his father, a dominant figure in upper New York State real estate provided him with a lifelong income. Henry James was graduated from Union College in 1830 and studied for the Presbyterian ministry at Princeton Theological Seminary from 1835 to 1837. Dissatisfied with the ritual formality and absence of spirituality in what he called "professional religion," he left the seminary and traveled to England, where he came under the influence of the idiosyncratic theology of Robert Sandeman, author of *Letters on Theron and Aspasio*, which James edited for American publication in 1838. Soon afterward, through J. J. Garth Wilkinson, James discovered Swedenborg. During the remainder of his life, he developed his own insights in the language of, and within the broad framework of, Swedenborgian ideas.

Central to James's view was the belief that selfhood (Swedenborg's *proprium*) is the sin of sins. Since the movement of creation is a move away from God, it is during this phase that selfhood flourishes. Religion and morality form, as it were, a reflecting surface from which the individual is "bounced back" toward God, thus initiating the movement of redemption, in which selfhood is replaced by "sociality" as a dominant motivation. Thus, as one of James's titles indicates, society is the redeemed form of man. Selfhood is destructive of the Divine intention with regard to created nature, whereas sociality is reconstructive. The ideal of redemptive society that James envisioned was largely derived from the social theories of Charles Fourier and emphasized social solidarity and democracy.

Because of this double allegiance to Swedenborg and Fourier (an allegiance James shared with many of his contemporaries, including Parke Godwin, Horace Greeley, and Albert Brisbane), James was able to assert that the highest points of European life were reached in Protestantism and constitutional liberty, and that both of these had been raised to still higher levels in America. Beneath the sometimes crude externals of American democracy, he saw "the soul of fellowship that animates and redeems it." Thus, he conceived of democracy as the herald of moral perfection and the means of "preparing the way for the reign of infinite Love." In this way James linked his theology of redemptive society to American democratic practice and to its ideal theory.

Works by James

Moralism and Christianity. New York, 1850.
Lectures and Miscellanies. New York, 1852.
The Nature of Evil. New York, 1855.
Christianity and the Logic of Creation. London and New York, 1857.
Substance and Shadow. Boston, 1863.
The Secret of Swedenborg. Boston, 1869.
Society the Redeemed Form of Man. Boston, 1879.
The Literary Remains of Henry James, William James, ed. Boston, 1885. Contains a lengthy introductory essay.

Works on James

Perry, Ralph Barton, *The Thought and Character of William James.* Boston, 1935. Contains discussions of the elder James.
Warren, Austin, *The Elder Henry James.* New York, 1934. Includes much biographical information.
Young, Frederic H., *The Philosophy of Henry James, Sr.* New York, 1951.

J. L. BLAU

JAMES, WILLIAM (1842–1910), American philosopher and psychologist, was born in New York City to Mary Robertson Walsh James and Henry James, Sr., the eccentric Swedenborgian theologian. James's paternal grandfather and namesake was an Irishman of Calvinist persuasion who immigrated to the United States in 1798 and became very rich through felicitous investment in the Erie Canal. James had three brothers and a sister; one of them, the novelist Henry James, achieved equal fame.

James's early environment was propitious; his father's enthusiastic and unconventional scholarship, his personal and unorthodox religion, his literary association with men like Oliver Wendell Holmes, Sr., and Ralph Waldo Emerson all stimulated free intellectual growth. Even more important was the rather extraordinary respect that the elder James lavished upon the youthful spontaneities of his children; each, he thought, must go his own way and become that most valuable of creatures, himself. There was no strait-laced dogmatism in the James household, and William James was free to accept or reject the ideas of his

father and his father's friends. The thought and sympathies of these transcendentalists and romantic humanitarians of the New England tradition never seemed to James the ultimate answers to his own philosophical and personal problems, but they dealt with genuine issues which he did not evade in his later work.

James's primary education took place at his father's table; its main constituents were the spirited discourse that the family held on every topic and the example of the parents, loving and unworldly. Formal education took place irregularly in various private establishments. From 1855 to 1860 James (often in the company of his younger brother Henry) attended schools in England, France, Switzerland, and Germany. There, as his father said, he and his brother were able "to absorb French and German and get a better sensuous education than they are likely to get here" (Ralph Barton Perry, *The Thought and Character of William James,* p. 59). During this European sojourn James's interest was divided between natural science and art, especially painting.

In spite of his continuing enthusiasm and talent for scientific inquiry, James's interest in painting became so strong by 1860 that he resolved to spend a trial period learning to paint. The elder James was not anxious for his son to become a painter, thereby prematurely cutting himself off from the rest of life's possibilities; any definite vocation, according to the father, was sadly "narrowing" (*ibid.,* p. 171). It was nevertheless arranged that James should begin study with William M. Hunt in Newport. This experiment convinced James that he lacked the ability to be anything more than a mediocre artist, than which there was, he thought, nothing worse. The lesson at Newport permanently discouraged James's pursuit of an artistic vocation, but throughout his scientific and philosophical career he retained the artist's eye, his predilection for concrete sensuous detail, and his concern for style.

In 1861, James entered the Lawrence Scientific School, Harvard, studying first in the chemistry department under Charles W. Eliot, later in the department of comparative anatomy and physiology under Jeffries Wyman and Louis Agassiz. From Wyman he learned the importance of evolution; from Agassiz, an appreciation of "the world's concrete fulness" (William James, *Memories and Studies,* p. 14) and of acquaintance with empirical facts as against abstraction. In 1864, James transferred to the medical school, though without the intention of ever practicing medicine. His medical studies, although fruitful, were attenuated and sporadic.

While at medical school James joined Agassiz as an assistant on the Thayer expedition to Brazil during 1865/1866. In Brazil he contracted smallpox and suffered from sensitivity of the eyes. This was the first serious manifestation of that constitutional failure which was to recur throughout James's life, imposing upon it a pattern of interrupted work and of periodic flights to Europe which were always, at least in part, searches for health.

In 1867 ill health and the desire to study experimental physiology led James to Europe, to Germany in particular. While little formal study of physiology proved to be possible, James read widely and thoughtfully. His first professional literary effort, a revision of Herman Grimm's

Unüberwindliche Mächte, published in the *Nation* (Vol. 5, 1867), dates from this period.

James returned to Cambridge in November 1868 and received his medical degree in June 1869. After a period of illness and retirement, he began teaching anatomy and physiology at Harvard in 1873, psychology in 1875, and philosophy in 1879. This order is very nearly accidental and gives no adequate indication of James's development. Philosophy was an early interest which grew with his scientific studies; for James the more narrowly scientific questions could never be separated, even theoretically, from the more general questions which philosophy considers.

It was indeed a specifically philosophical concern which precipitated James's profound emotional crisis of 1870. He had been suffering from a sense of moral impotence which only a philosophical justification of the belief in the freedom of the will could cure. In the *Essais de critique générale* of Charles Renouvier, James found the basis of the justification he sought. And throughout his life the problem of maintaining free will and the moral attitude in the face of either religious monism or scientific determinism, as well as the problem of legitimating belief despite various intellectual skepticisms, continued to engage James's attention and to influence his mature philosophy. That philosophy, growing out of personal need and agitation, has a strong eschatological flavor. It cannot, however, be reduced either to a scheme of personal salvation or to an apology for some special way of life. James offered a philosophical, not an emotional, defense of free will, moralism, and belief. These topics became important test cases for a general metaphysics which James sought to elaborate not for its own sake but to satisfy interests which were distinctly rational and theoretical.

Having settled into the career of philosopher and teacher, if one may speak of James's settling into anything, he maintained close but not constant association with Harvard until his final resignation in 1907. He married Alice Howe Gibbens in 1878; the marriage seems to have increased his sense of purpose and coincided with a noticeable improvement in James's health. Thenceforth, he led an intensely active life, teaching at Harvard, lecturing widely, and publishing a series of books which became undeniable classics of American philosophy. Three series of James's lectures deserve special mention. He gave the Gifford lectures at Edinburgh in 1901/1902, published as *The Varieties of Religious Experience* (1902); lectures on pragmatism at the Lowell Institute and Columbia in 1906 and 1907, published as *Pragmatism* (1907); and the Hibbert lectures at Oxford in 1908/1909, published as *A Pluralistic Universe* (1909).

Character of James's philosophy. This brief biography gives no indication of that range and richness of James's experience which so struck those who knew him and which entered into everything he wrote. James was a highly social man whose friends formed an intellectual community of great distinction. Chauncey Wright, C. S. Peirce, Shadworth Hodgson, Charles Renouvier, Josiah Royce, George Santayana, John Dewey, Henri Bergson, and F. H. Bradley were a few of those whom James knew as friends and fellow laborers.

From all of these men and others James drew philosoph-ical nourishment, and the very number of sources and influences renders the search for antecedents otiose. James was essentially an original thinker, and he borrowed only what fitted his own design. This must be maintained in spite of James's habitual humility and his characteristic generosity of acknowledgment.

James impressed his friends with his vitality and strength of character, with his open-mindedness and sympathy. His spirit and attitude were admired even by those whose philosophical conclusions differed radically from his own. Santayana, for example, in his witty and condescending memoir *Character and Opinion in the United States* is forced to praise James, at least as an enthusiastic and explosive force. Because James wrote as he talked, much of his vividness and personal style is retained in his works. The majority of James's books are simply transcriptions of lectures; they have all the virtues and vices of spoken discourse, and the circumstances of their presentation must help to determine the kind of analysis to which they can be fruitfully subjected.

James addressed himself to the people, not especially to other philosophers, and he listened to the people to find out what life meant to them. He respected not so much their common sense as their common feelings and hopes and would not allow his philosophy to dismiss cavalierly that which figured largely in the experiences of men. The people listened to James, and his books sold well. By the end of his life he was nearly a legendary figure, and he was generally regarded as the chief representative of American philosophy. Nevertheless, professional philosophers, when they have discussed James at all, have tended to concentrate on those of his ideas which, separated from the body of his work and often distorted, have achieved currency. To this general picture there are important exceptions, such as Ralph Barton Perry, who has done more for James scholarship than anyone else.

To provide a proper perspective for the study of James, three corrective measures must be taken. First, attention must be diverted from his life, however interesting, to his published philosophy. For all its validity the biographical motive can be, and has been, pressed to the point where it precludes philosophical clarity. Second, James must be seen within the general philosophical tradition, in relation to the fundamental philosophical problems that he attempted to solve and not in relation to his position as a distinctly American thinker. To attempt to evaluate James's philosophy in terms of his American background is neither more nor less rewarding than to attempt to evaluate Kant, say, in terms of his German background. Third, the objective aspect of James's philosophy must be stressed. James himself thought that philosophy involved the subjective factors of temperament and personal vision. In the first chapter of *Pragmatism,* he drew a very plausible correlation between tough-minded and tender-minded temperaments and empirical and rationalist philosophical positions. Again, in the essay "The Sentiment of Rationality" James argued that there can be no adequate definition of reason which ignores the feeling of rationality, the ultimate sense of logical fit. James believed that the subjective (or what might better be called the aesthetic) dimension was a feature of philosophy as such. James's philosophy is subjective, therefore, because it is philosophy, not because it is James's philosophy. Objectivity, like truth and reality, was redefined, not abandoned, by James.

The remainder of this article is divided into sections on James's psychology, philosophy of religion, pragmatism, and metaphysics. This arrangement is simply an expository device. If pragmatism is a theory of all belief, then religious philosophy is a subdivision of pragmatism. If pragmatism is a description of what actually happens when men seek truth, then it is part of psychology. If the dualism between human and natural processes is finally inadmissible, then psychology is a chapter of general metaphysics. The interdependence of the various parts of James's philosophy, suggested here, will be exhibited below.

PSYCHOLOGY

The *Principles of Psychology* (1890) is, according to James himself, "mainly a mass of descriptive details"; certainly, this work more than any other justifies Whitehead's remark that James's primary task was philosophical assemblage. The *Principles* "assembles" in two senses. First, there is a brilliant gathering, through extensive quotation and reference as well as careful documentation, of relevant material from the Scottish, English, French, and German schools. Second, there is the exhibition of facts which may never have appeared prominently in any system, either of psychology or of philosophy.

It has become customary, and it is certainly legitimate, to praise the *Principles* for its sensitive evocation of the evanescent inner life. It is indeed a kind of generalized psychic autobiography by a master of introspection, but it is much more than a document of literary psychology. The concrete rendering of experience is an essential element in the development of James's mature philosophy, for when he spoke of the world as "a world of pure experience," he referred to experience as it is described in the *Principles*. If experience had not the ramifications and possibilities so lovingly and exuberantly detailed by James in his "psychological" writings, it could never have become, as it did for James, the central image of complete reality. Moreover, James was not in his early days merely "collecting" facts whose subsequent careers happened to include the incident of being generalized into a total world view. James, as he said himself, "hated collecting" (Perry, *op. cit.*, p. 225). The material of the *Principles* is already thrown into philosophical form, is already illuminated or stained (however one decides the matter) by the foundational metaphysical categories which recur, with greater generality, in the later works.

Description. If the *Principles* is to be regarded as primarily a descriptive work, one must be clear about what is involved in description as James understood it. He was convinced that pure description in the manner of phenomenology is impossible. Description cannot be other than conceptual; concepts, in turn, are tools of classification that have inexpugnable conventional and theoretical elements. Concepts do not passively mirror; they select according to human interests and purposes. Assumptions, James maintained, have a way of establishing themselves "in our very descriptions of the phenomenal facts" (*Principles*, Vol. I, p. 145). Naive phenomenology attempts to eliminate assumptions from descriptive statements. This is an impossible task if for no other reason than that every allegedly assumption-free phenomenology must itself make doubtful assumptions, including the assumption that there can be description without classification. James's own approach was to examine the assumptions involved in all descriptions, making those assumptions "give an articulate account of themselves before letting them pass" (*loc. cit.*). Pragmatism as it appears in the *Principles* consists simply in spelling out what claims our theories and assumptions make for us and in eliminating elements which are superfluous, elements, that is, which can be eliminated without changing the tenor of what we really want to say. Pragmatism here can be fruitfully regarded as a general theory of theory criticism, as an attempt to make clear what we are actually committed to by the theories we entertain. The chapters which criticize the conscious automaton theory (Vol. I, Ch. 5) and the mind-stuff theory (*ibid.*, Ch. 6), respectively, are indeed the first extended exercises in pragmatic criticism.

Science and metaphysics. Purely phenomenological description being considered impossible by James, the question arises as to what is scientific about the *Principles*. The standard interpretation—the interpretation upon which the judgment of its great historical importance is based—finds the work very nearly the first attempt to treat psychology from the standpoint of a natural science—that is, descriptively and apart from metaphysical theories. The sharp distinction which we are likely to draw between scientific theories and metaphysical theories is difficult to sustain from James's own point of view and therefore cannot be used to differentiate the *Principles* from metaphysical treatments of the same subject matter.

A much more pregnant distinction is that between a priori and a posteriori metaphysics. A priori metaphysics was, for James, a totally illegitimate enterprise consisting of vacuous abstractions excogitated apart from any experience of the world. Throughout his work James often referred to a priori metaphysics simply as "metaphysics," and his frequent criticisms of metaphysics must therefore be carefully interpreted in their contexts. The *Principles* is antimetaphysical where metaphysics means "scholastic rational psychology" or "philosophical pyschology."

The more interesting problem is defining the relation between the *Principles* and the kind of metaphysics of which James did approve, a posteriori metaphysics, which is continuous with science and, like science, is both descriptive and theoretical. Here the differentiation must be emphatic rather than absolute. The *Principles* may be regarded as a deliberate (and artificial) restriction of general metaphysical scope. Science, as James saw it, must grow into metaphysics. Explanation must become more complete and more comprehensive even if, as James certainly believed, it cannot become total and absolute. But science must *be* science before it can become metaphysics. In the *Principles* metaphysics is, necessarily, postponed; its positivism is provisional rather than dogmatic and final.

The relative autonomy which science is given in the *Principles* is "for the sake of practical effectiveness exclusively," as James said in his essay "A Plea for Psychology as a 'Natural Science'" (*Collected Essays and Reviews,* p. 317). Science left to itself, with its "convenient assumptions" unquestioned, is best able to accumulate a mass of factual details which lead to the subsequent enrichment and "thickening" of the content of metaphysics. The danger of premature metaphysical reconstruction is thinness, impoverishment of content, and abstraction.

Mental states. The basic assumption of the *Principles* and its "convenient" point of departure is the existence of mental states. The first task of psychology is to describe the conditions of these mental states with as much detail and completeness as possible. Chapter 2 of the *Principles* is an extended examination of the ways in which various brain states condition various mental states. The search for conditions among bodily experiences generally and brain experiences particularly is the only alternative to treating mental states as frankly miraculous. James, the evolutionary naturalist, had to maintain that mental states grow out of physical states, in spite of whatever difficulties this view entails. Since mental states, in addition to arising from physical antecedents, themselves give rise in all cases to changes in the physical world, it seems utterly impossible to create any kind of dualistic ontological chasm between the two types of process, mental and physical. There is indeed a discriminable subject matter of psychology, which James referred to both as "mental states" and as "mental life." This subject matter must be treated autonomously, which means, in practice, guarding against the reduction of mental phenomena to nothing but physical phenomena in the interest of some schematic monism. In this context James at times spoke of "irreducible dualisms," but what he meant to emphasize might perhaps better be called "irreducible dualities," discriminations which remain what they are no matter what supervenient integrations may also be pointed out.

The whole question of the dualism between the physical and the mental is complicated by the fact that James was, even in the *Principles,* developing a view of physical nature at large which departed radically from the familiar deterministic, mechanical model. It is often maintained, for example, that James's treatment of the will as irreducible to antecedent mechanical factors creates a dualistic chasm between natural processes and characteristically human processes. This would be true only if James had retained the customary deterministic model of nature. However, James did not retain this model; he would sooner have conceived of all nature as willful than of man's will as an exception to nature.

James believed that the border line of the mental is vague. Mentality, as James defined it, exists wherever we find the choice of means for the attainment of future ends. Mental life is purposive in a way which involves the overcoming, through suitable invention and appropriation, of any obstacles lying in the way of its purpose. The mind is a tactical power which reveals itself in the struggle with its environment. The only kind of world in which minds can conceivably develop and be found is one in which success is neither automatic nor impossible. An interesting consequence of James's view is that an omnipotent God could not have a mind; neither could a purely contemplative deity. The notion of mind as an instrument within the general economy of purpose and resistance to purpose, a notion which has justly been called "biological" and "Darwinian," is simply an ungeneralized expression of pragmatism.

Although it is necessary to consider mental states as "temporal events arising in the ordinary course of nature" (*ibid.,* p. 319), with emphasis on their natural antecedents and results, it is also necessary to consider mental states in themselves as realities to be described as they are found with their generic particularity and variety intact. Here again, it must be emphasized that James was not attempting a phenomenology of mental life or consciousness. What he was attempting was the provision of adequate description that would not be guilty of gross oversimplification or distortion.

Introspection. Adequate description must, of course, be based somehow upon observation, and, James maintained, the principal method of psychology is introspective observation. Introspection, as an observational process, is similar to other kinds of observation. James could find in introspection no peculiar epistemological characteristic; it is neither more nor less fallible than other kinds of observation. Its frequently alleged infallibility, based on some notion of the immediate relation obtaining between a mind and its contents, is simply contradicted by experience. Even if feeling is unmistakably what it is, our "naming, classing, and knowing" (*Principles,* pp. 189–190) of every feeling share in the notorious general human fallibility. The truth of any observation, introspective or otherwise, is not to be found in the character of the source of observation but in the consequent service, especially theoretical service, which the observation and its correlative preservation in description can be made to render. There is therefore no simple and immediate verification of observations, no once and for all validation of descriptions. For James "the only safeguard [of truth] is the final *consensus* of our farther knowledge about the thing in question, later views correcting earlier ones until at last the harmony of a consistent system is reached" (*ibid.,* p. 192). James's own descriptions in the *Principles* must lend themselves to this kind of pragmatic corroboration.

Thought. The famous "descriptive" chapter, "The Stream of Thought" (perhaps the heart of the *Principles*), cannot be evaluated from a simply empirical point of view. What is described and how it is described are determined by markedly theoretical affinities and avoidances. James singled out five traits of thought in that chapter: (1) Thought tends to be part of personal consciousness—that is, thought is not experienced as simply *a* thought but as *my* thought; (2) thought is always changing; (3) within each personal consciousness thought is sensibly continuous; (4) thought deals with objects independent of itself; and (5) thought is selective and has interests. The metaphysical model which James had in mind here is of a process that is partially determined and partially self-determining—that is, centered or focused and essentially temporal. Although the analysis in the *Principles* is limited to one kind of process, consciousness, the structure of the analysis is similar to that Whitehead offers of all actual occasions. James himself came to believe that all of reality must be describable in terms like those used for human experience. This belief is elaborated in *Essays in Radical Empiricism* as the notion of a world of "pure experience."

Each of the five traits of thought which James distinguishes repudiates some important philosophical position. One dimension of James's work clearly apparent in the *Principles* is a sustained criticism of the "classic-academic" version of mind. No easy summary of what this meant to James is available, but its main features would seem to be the marshaling of instances of mental phenomena according to a priori canons of clarity and rationality, the overwhelming influence of the assertive paradigm (as opposed to the judgments implicit in making and doing) in construing the problems of belief and judgment, and allegiance to the spectator theory of knowledge with whatever passivity is therein involved. These attitudes James attacked in the name of a richer experience, encompassing all the concrete information we possess about the functions of mind. This is the information, so carefully assembled and considered in the *Principles*, which James urged the epistemologist to work into his official model and the philosopher generally to consider in making his pronouncements.

Experience. The appeal to experience is not new in philosophy; James was solidly in the venerable tradition of empiricism. But empiricism in its classic British form is essentially an epistemological position which regards experience as an exclusive witness before a cognitive tribunal in which other sources of evidence are ruled out of court as uncertain or unreliable. The genius of James's empiricism lies precisely in ruling nothing out of court. His theory of experience, the object of so much of James's later labor, is perhaps the first such theory which is cosmological, rather than strictly epistemological, in intention and logical form. This shift of the total frame of reference within which experience is considered has, for better or worse, influenced a subsequent movement in philosophy typified by Whitehead and his disciples. It is this influence which points to the main philosophical significance of the *Principles*.

PHILOSOPHY OF RELIGION

Even in the Introduction to *The Literary Remains of the Late Henry James* (1885), a relatively early work which might be thought no more than an act of filial devotion, James's own ideas about religion were quite clear. There is, of course, a sympathetic exposition of his father's superpersonal theological monism, for William James could honestly admire his father's "instinct and attitude" even if he could not condone the "cold accounts" and abstract formulations of the elder James's system. It is religious experience, rather than religious doctrine, that matters. Unless it is a part of vital experience, religion becomes "fossil conventionalism." Here James shared his father's attitude; his father wrote so much, according to James, because he was dissatisfied with every verbal encapsulation. Writing was a necessary evil and, like the labor of Sisyphus, self-stultifying.

That James could not accept in any unqualified way the religious vision of his father is evident. The difficulty is simply this: "Any absolute moralism is a pluralism; any absolute religion is a monism" (*The Literary Remains*, p. 118). The recognition of the essential opposition of morality and religion was clearly made by the elder James. The logic of his system required him to reject the finite moral agent with his frantic moral efforts. It is certain that James benefited from his father's insight even though he aligned himself with morality and pluralism. The working attitude of the healthy mind must always be, for James, a moral one which takes seriously the difference between good and evil and which commits itself to struggle for the first and against the second. To adopt the religious attitude is to step out of life's fight and to justify that withdrawal by some belief about the character of the world and either the ineffectiveness or superfluity of action within it. For James the character of the world, the nature of reality, does not justify, as a general attitude, the quietism that religion counsels. On the contrary, the world is the kind of place in which moral endeavor is, as a rule, supremely worthy. James neither denied the satisfaction that religion gives to many nor declared that satisfaction illusory. The very fact of pluralism allowed him to suppose at least some aspect, however fragmentary, of reality which justifies the religious option. Religious belief gives us, in James's famous phrase, a "moral holiday." Like any holiday it may be enjoyed for its own sake; more important to James, however, holidays indirectly affect the work week.

Evolutionary theory. James was strongly influenced by the Darwinian theory of evolution and was therefore predisposed to find in all feelings, including religious feelings, clues about what the world is like. Feelings that evolved in the world must somehow reflect the world. The most eccentric fancy, for example, tells us that we have the kind of world in which such a fancy is possible.

Evolutionary theory, as James saw it, begins with the presupposition that each part of reality has a function, that each part is in some way or other good for something or other. The strictly useless, according to such a theory, cannot endure, and all flourishing realities command a certain minimal respect. Religious experience is not especially justified by evolution because nothing is *especially* justified. Religion and irreligion, insofar as they both exist, are exactly equal before the evolutionary tribunal. Belief in evolution, at least as James interpreted that belief, makes simple dismissal impossible; even that which is evil cannot be negligible. The questions must be asked of religion as it must be asked of everything. How is it that it came to be what it is? What is it for?

Antecedents and value of religion. In his major work on religion, *The Varieties of Religious Experience*, James attempted to account for the antecedents and value of religion. The question of how it came to be what it is, is a matter of classifying religious feelings and religious propensities with other kinds of human experience which are found to be similar to them. The initial task, therefore, of *The Varieties* is the provision of a "descriptive survey" beginning with as many and as varied examples of typically religious experience as possible. The emphasis, here as elsewhere, is on spontaneous religious emotions rather than theological interpretations or institutional prolongation and regularization.

James was scrupulously careful to explain religious phenomena by ordinary scientific laws and principles, if at all possible. Accordingly, religious visitations of all kinds are classed as sudden influxions from the subject's own subconsciousness. Conversion is seen as the radical rearrangement of psychic energy around some new center of interest. Examples of this kind of felicitous theorizing could be multiplied.

James, however, was equally concerned with promoting the thesis that nothing said about the history or genesis of religious phenomena can shed the slightest light on the spiritual worth and significance of those phenomena. The older dogmatists attempted to justify religion once and for all by pointing to its privileged origin in some kind of revelation; newer dogmatists—the "medical materialists"—attempted to discredit religion once and for all by pointing to its disreputable origin in some curious bodily state. Neither approach is acceptable. Religion must be judged in the same way that everything else is judged, by proving itself useful (in specifiable ways) in some possible future. Religion must "run the gauntlet of confrontation with the total context of experience" (*The Varieties*, p. 426). This context includes the collection of all our established truths as well as all the exigencies of our affective and intellectual natures. Therefore, the defense of religion that can be found in James is not based on appeals to either mere social utility or subjective feeling. The question of the truth of religion arises only when religion makes some concrete, specific prediction about the world's future. Religion having framed its hypotheses, these hypotheses are supported or refuted in terms set out by James's general theory of belief, known as pragmatism.

Belief. James's notorious defense of the right to believe in the widely read essay "The Will to Believe" and elsewhere, though generally given a limited religious interpretation, is, in fact, not primarily a defense of religious belief but of moral belief, belief in the efficacy of action, including, as an important instance, the active experimentalism of modern science. The point of James's doctrine is its repudiation of the methodological caution epitomized by the Baconian injunction not to "suffer the understanding to jump and fly from particulars to remote and most general axioms" or by the Cartesian rule "that the understanding should always know before the will makes a decision.' James was making a general statement in support of the method of empirical science, with special emphasis upon the initially unwarranted character of every scientific hypothesis. We must at least believe our hypotheses sufficiently to bestir ourselves to test them; without our active interest in and partisanship of belief the enterprise of science would come to a silent, ghostly end. It is the theoretical daring of science which inspired James. His doctrine on the will to believe is no fuzzy *ad hoc* concession to self-indulgent piety but an integral part of his general theory of belief.

The doctrine of the will to believe, with all its genial encouragement of risking belief, is balanced, in James, by an unremitting fallibilism. Belief, however justified originally, is always conditional. Belief must continue to justify itself; there is no possibility of a definitive, once and for all certification. Both the options of practical life and the tenets of religion may be justified as peculiar kinds of scientific hypotheses, the first sort peculiar because of

their limitation to some particular matter or situation, the second because of their elusive generality. There seems to be no difficulty in interpreting the practical decisions of life, with their inherent predictions about relevant future events, as closely analogous to the predictive, if not to the explanatory, activity of science. Religious belief, on the contrary, may seem intrinsically isolated from the arena of confirmation and disconfirmation and, therefore, alien to the scientific pattern. For James all genuine belief, including religious belief, must address itself to the tribunal of experiment. If all possible procedures of verification are irrelevant to some religious doctrine, then that doctrine cannot rightly be the object of any belief; such a doctrine, having no positive content, would be meaningless.

James did, in fact, think that at least a few religious hypotheses were truly empirical, that they made a difference which somewhere could be noticed. James was careful not to prejudice the case against religion by adopting some single restrictive paradigm of verification. If religious belief makes a difference, it is not altogether surprising that we should have to look for that difference with greater sympathy, imagination, and patience than we are used to exercising in more straightforward cases.

James's religious belief. James's own religious belief, expressed without dogmatism in the last chapter and the Postscript of *The Varieties* and again in the last chapter of *Pragmatism*, consists essentially in the affirmation that the world is richer in realities than conventional science is willing to recognize. Religious experience at least suggests that there is what James called a "higher part of the universe" (*ibid.*, p. 516) which, though beyond the immediate deliverance of the senses, is nevertheless effective in the world in a way that makes a noticeable difference. This assertion that the higher part makes concrete and local differences constitutes James's famous "piecemeal supernaturalism" (*ibid.*, p. 520), really only a name for an enlarged and tolerant naturalism. The higher part is perhaps impossible to define given the present state of our knowledge. Certainly, for James it cannot be the infinite and omnipotent God of traditional theism who guarantees the successful outcome of the universe. The higher part is better conceived as a finite power (or perhaps even a polytheistic medley of powers) which, like men, works toward the good and helps achieve it. This is a theological notion compatible with the significance of moral choice in a way that the conventional notion is not.

The vagueness of much of James's treatment, a vagueness he frequently admitted to, has been amply noted by his critics. What must also be noted, however, is the forceful way in which a fundamental idea of our tradition, the idea of God, has been radically reconstructed by James in a manner that makes the idea more consonant with religious experience and that frees it from the congeries of paradoxes associated with the problems, among others, of free will and of evil.

PRAGMATISM

The chief locus for James's pragmatism is, of course, his immensely popular and influential work *Pragmatism: A New Name for Some Old Ways of Thinking*. The origin of pragmatism, however, as James always acknowledged, is found in C. S. Peirce's essay "How To Make Our Ideas Clear," published in 1878. This essay remained generally unnoticed until James's 1898 lecture on pragmatism, "Philosophical Conceptions and Practical Results," at the University of California (in *Collected Essays and Reviews*). This lecture may be taken as the beginning of pragmatism as an explicit, although never a unified, movement, but the essentials of the doctrine as developed by James are found earlier in the *Principles of Psychology* and even in the Introduction to *The Literary Remains of the Late Henry James*. Indeed, James rarely wrote anything, early or late, which did not at least imply pragmatism.

Pragmatism may be approached as a mere method, an eristic device which vouchsafes hints as to either the meaning or truth of propositions or to both together; it may be taken as a theory of meaning or a theory of truth or, once again, as a theory of both meaning and truth. A. O. Lovejoy in "The Thirteen Pragmatisms" insisted upon distinctions such as these and chided James for neglecting them. In fact, though James erred in emphasizing the autonomy of the various aspects of pragmatism, he wished to persuade his readers of the truth of whichever part he was recommending at the moment, and he therefore tended to stress the self-contained plausibility of elements which, if plausible at all, are so only when taken together in the total view.

It is the contention of James's sympathetic commentators that his pragmatism is plausible as nothing less than a theory of reality. It is the descriptive naturalism central to James which saves pragmatism from being merely a convenient device for settling philosophical disputes. The fundamental assumption which generates pragmatism is the assumption that "knowledge," "truth," and "meaning," as well as any other possible object of discourse or any other possible subject matter for philosophical discussion, must be explicable as a natural process or as a functional medley or competition of natural processes. The world, for James, is a plurality of temporal processes related in so many specifiable and concrete ways that it cannot be accounted for by abstract speculation alone.

James believed that a man's personal, peculiar vision counts most in philosophy; not surprisingly, it is vision, not method, which is primary in James. Reality dictates the method by which it may be known. The gross encounter with the world is primary in the determination of what character the world will have for us. Theories of knowledge and of method, existing at a high level of abstraction, are second to the ineluctable fact of experience breaking in upon us.

Truth and meaning. James's pragmatism is an attempt to formulate a metaphysics of truth and of meaning. Logically, such an attempt is exactly on a par with the metaphysical treatment of any discriminable subject matter. By metaphysics James meant the quest for adequate general descriptions either of reality as a whole or of some distinguishable part of it. The descriptions offered by metaphysics are, in principle, continuous with those offered by science, although their range and focus may differ. The distinction between science and metaphysics was not crucial for James; he saw the possibility of unrestricted

intercourse and cooperation exactly where later thinkers are likely to see division and competition for cognitive respectability. It is therefore helpful from James's own point of view to regard pragmatism's description of truth in the same light, say, as geology's description of continental drift. Both are characterizations of natural processes, and both attempt to portray what actually happens.

The metaphysical perspective of *Pragmatism* itself (even apart from the context of James's total work) is so unmistakable that the prevailing interpretation of pragmatism as a set of newly devised rules that serve a certain practical purpose seems totally unjustified. If James was right, men have always unwittingly followed the "pragmatic method." A purely theoretical illumination like pragmatism will indeed clarify practice and improve it; for James no process—least of all, a process where human influence intervenes—is so canalized that modifications are utterly beyond hope. Metaphysics must recognize the plasticity of its subject matter as well as the limits of plasticity.

Pragmatism discusses truth without falling into the epistemological frame of mind habitually assumed by professional philosophers. James's description of actual processes rejects the usual question of what we ought to believe. If there is something we "ought" to believe, the authority of the "ought" itself must be explained concretely. There is no authority which is merely formal. Pragmatism therefore becomes the justification of truth's prestige in terms of the world's exigencies.

One factor discernible in the complex process called "believing truly" is the compulsion of fact or the unavoidability of a residual nonplastic pole in determination of what is true. It is here that we find truth's authority and importance.

Truth, for James, is what we must somehow take account of if we are not to perish. Men cannot in the long run believe what is false not because truth extracts from them a categorical imperative in its own behalf but because reality compels men in spite of themselves, and it is from this that the authority of truth is derived. "Agreement with reality" as a criterion of truth cannot be taken to indicate any fixed structural relation (such as the "copying" relation). The truth relation is characterized not by stasis but by the fluid resourcefulness of functional harmony. The character of the harmony itself may be anything that is compatible with survival. Even in the Darwinian world that James pictured, there is more than one way to survive as truth.

Raw compulsion may account for the authority of truth, but truth is hardly a mute registry of bruises received from the world. Indeed, men create truth, and truth is so exclusively the result of human activity that James's own view has been called "humanism." Central to this humanism is the distinction (so often insisted on by James, so often neglected by his critics) between ideas and objects, between what takes account and what is taken account of. The objects constitute what James referred to as the "unhumanized fringe," the yet to be conceptualized. What must be taken account of is presumably just what it is. Truth and falsity, however, apply not to objects but only to our ideas of objects. Our ideas of objects are mutable in the sense that we can modify ideas or replace one idea by another. In such a situation ideas are to be judged better or worse; such judgments fall between the ideal limits of complete good and complete bad. These are the same limits usually called "truth" and "falsity." Truth is viewed by James as one species of the good. The good is itself interpreted as a plurality of "good fors." In this view ideas are instruments for taking account theoretically, practically, aesthetically, and so on, of reality.

The point of James's view of truth, as Bergson suggests in *The Creative Mind* (p. 256), is that truth is to be described as an invention rather than a discovery. Truth, or propositions which are true, might be compared to cleverly made maps or apt predictions. If they serve us as we expect them to serve us, we have no legitimate complaint. There are, of course, ontological relations between inventions like maps, predictions, and propositions (as well as inventions like light bulbs and cotton gins) and what, in summary fashion, is referred to as reality. Inventions are conventional but not arbitrary. They are not arbitrary because they must somehow take account of reality; they are conventional because they embody one way (among alternatives) for that taking account.

The relationship between two processes within experience constitutes truth—(1) the inventive process or activity of proposing, of framing propositions, and (2) the particular chain of natural processes with which the proposition in question is concerned. The emphasis on the truth relation as a relation within experience and totally construable in terms of "positive experienceable operation" (*Meaning of Truth*, p. x) is one instance of James's general metaphysical position that all relations are within experience. Experience, as it were, forms a cohesive, self-explanatory whole; it hangs together, as James liked to say, and needs no transcendental connectives or supports.

Since the truth relation was taken by James's contemporaries as transcending experience, the strategic function of pragmatism is apparent. It is an extension of radical empiricism, an attempt to place the particularly troublesome truth relation within the total perspective of metaphysical naturalism.

James spoke of true ideas as those which "work," which "lead" propitiously, which give various kinds of satisfaction, and which bring about various kinds of success. He also spoke approvingly of the "cash value" of ideas and thought that meaningful ideas are those which make "practical differences." These highly (and obviously) metaphorical expressions have confused many commentators.

There are those who have found James vague. He intended, however, that all these metaphors should be functionally specific and indeterminate only in respect to instances. "Working," "leading," "satisfying," and "succeeding" are generic terms as respectable and as precise as terms like "copying" and "agreeing." They are, however, functional rather than static. For those who see functions as inherently insubstantial, shadowy, and vague, any functional definition of truth will be unacceptable, but this hardly seems to be an insurmountable objection.

Other commentators have seized upon the prominence of the "practical" in James's account of meaning and truth. Surely, this is a difficult term in James, if for no other reason than that he used it as it is used in ordinary language—that is, variously. His prevailing usage, however,

cannot be equated with some narrow notion of commercial efficiency. Pragmatism is not a philosophical vindication of the businessman's common sense or acumen. It was James, after all, who saw the tendency to worship "the bitch goddess, success," as the principal weakness in the American character. It is especially in our theoretical and moral practice that meaningful ideas, according to James, are to make a difference. Belief divorced from action may well be morally effete, and James set forth this point, though not in its crudely athletic form; his main thesis, however, was that belief divorced from action is *theoretically* inexplicable. James's quest was not for a formula which would rouse his fellows to civic virtue or efficiency of some peculiarly American sort but for criteria which would be descriptively adequate to belief. His philosophical purpose was to find out what it means to believe, what it means to entertain ideas which may be meaningful and true. (For a further discussion of the ideas of James and other pragmatists on the concept of truth see PRAGMATIC THEORY OF TRUTH.)

METAPHYSICS

Although frequently attempted, it is not possible to isolate a final "metaphysical" period in James. The theory of the various kinds of belief, which formed his philosophy of religion and of pragmatism, has as a conspicuous feature the assumption that anything which can be meaningfully said about belief must take into account the grounding of belief in natural processes, particularly human processes. It is possible to formulate a theory of belief apart from a general metaphysics only by adopting an assumption which James explicitly rejected. This is the epistemological assumption that an existentially neutral *logic* of belief can be constructed. In fact, on this assumption existential reference is regarded as the indication of a certain categorial confusion frequently labeled "psychologism." James insisted, even in his least metaphysical passages, that "knowledge," "belief," "truth," and "meaning" indicate discriminable natural existences in the same way that all terms do, or at least all terms that figure as possible subjects of philosophical discussion. This is simply the corrective application of the basic postulate of metaphysical naturalism to the recalcitrant subject matter of epistemology. James regarded the prominence accorded this subject matter since the time of Kant as a distortion of perspective which his own philosophy was intended to correct.

But for the development of James's metaphysics, the psychology—or the treatment of characteristically human processes—was even more important than the theory of belief. His metaphysics was simply the attempt to apply to all reality categories originally framed for human experience. The radical generalization of the concept of experience, so central in James, is necessitated by two ideas. First, James believed that metaphysical dualism is always unacceptable. Whatever dualities or pluralities are distinguished for certain purposes, ultimately the philosopher cannot operate with irreducible categories. Second, if one categorial set or one metaphysical model must be adopted, James believed that this categorial set or metaphysical model must arise from the consideration of our own experience. It is only of human experience that we have anything like "complete concrete data." Anthropocentrism is therefore thought to be a consequence of any genuine empiricism. For James even panpsychism is at least a possible and interesting empirical hypothesis.

In the seminal essay "Does Consciousness Exist?" (1904), James asks us to assume that there is just one "primal stuff" of which everything in the world is made. This stuff, called "pure experience," is not a single entity, like Thales' water; "pure experience" is a collective name for all sensible natures, for all the "that's" which anywhere appear. The monism implied in this concept of the *one* primal stuff is therefore merely formal. Explanatory monism must be accepted before specific metaphysical descriptions may be attempted. In the same essay James provided a sample of metaphysical description. Consciousness is there described as a certain relation of parts of experience to one another. Consciousness is not an unanalyzable substance but simply the name which is given to a certain discriminable function within experience, the knowing function. All other functions are to be explained in the same way as consciousness. Functional explanations in terms of related strands of experience allow the abrogation of traditional dualisms because the same isolable part of experience may enter into many and various relations. What is subject may also be object; what is object may be subject. The knower may also be the known and vice versa, depending on the "context of associates" within which the part of experience so labeled is considered.

James's frequent use of the expression "part of experience" was not meant to suggest that experience has an atomistic constitution. Indeed, James constantly argued against the "pulverization" of experience in British empiricism. We experience not isolated parts but continuities of indeterminate extension. Parts and the relations between parts, both directly experienced, form new functional wholes. The use of the word "part" indicates nothing more than the theoretical and practical need for emphatic focus.

James regarded the "concrete" data appealed to by British empiricism as abstract, intellectual products; he accused that empiricism of committing what Whitehead later called "the fallacy of misplaced concreteness." If James's philosophy is to be classified historically as a criticism of British empiricism, it must also be emphasized that it is self-consciously offered as an alternative to the criticism of empiricism by idealists from Kant to Royce.

If the facts pointed to by the usual empiricism are abstract in the sense of being incomplete, inadequate, or partial, it still cannot be said, as it is said by absolute idealism, that there are no facts at all or that there is just one fact, the immovable "block-universe," as James referred to this notion that he always found slightly ridiculous. There are no general grounds, according to James, for the rejection of the obvious particularity and individuality which characterize the plural parts of experience. James certainly held that any allegedly self-sufficient fact may turn out from some point of view or for some purpose, intellectual or practical, to be partial or abstract. But there are many points of view and many purposes with equal titles to rationality. There are therefore many levels of fact, and words like "part," "whole," "unity," "concrete," "ab-

stract," "particular," and "individual" do not qualify any reality simply or always. These words are definable only within purposive contexts. Absolute idealism, in contrast, sets up a single standard of rationality and develops a characteristic vocabulary which it applies *simpliciter*. This procedure yields a certain clarity and neatness but suffers from "vicious intellectualism" or *"the treating of a name as excluding from the fact named what the name's definition fails positively to include"* (*A Pluralistic Universe*, p. 60).

The notion of self-sufficient centers within experience emphasized by James as particulars or individuals is a generalization of that first trait of the stream of thought referred to in *Principles of Psychology*. Although made familiar by Whitehead, it was James who first used the concept of personal order to replace the traditional concept of some fundamental and thinglike substance.

Other traits of existence which impressed themselves on James are first annunciated in the *Principles* as traits of the stream of thought or of the central human process. So, for example, the doctrine that thought is always changing becomes the doctrine that reality is always changing. Again, human freedom is eventually interpreted as a special case of universal indeterminism. My future, though continuous with my past, is not determined by it. Just so the future of the world; although it grows out of the total past, it is not a mere result of that past. If I am creative—that is, if human freedom is effectual—then the world is creative, if for no other reason than that I am part of the world. What is constant in my behavior is the result of habits which never entirely lose their flexibility. In the same way the constancies charted by the laws of science are only more inveterate habits.

Objections can be raised against all these contentions, especially in the enthusiastic, unguarded form in which James made them. They do, however, add up to a serious philosophical position which has, in fact, borne fruit in the subsequent history of philosophy and is worthy of continuing serious study. (For a general discussion of the development of pragmatism see PRAGMATISM.)

Works by James

Only James's chief works are listed here. For a complete list see Perry's bibliography, below. Secondary literature is copious, and only the most important works are listed here. Those who wish to sample the periodical literature are advised to consult the fifty-year (1904–1953) index of the *Journal of Philosophy* (New York, 1962), under the heading "James."

The Literary Remains of the Late Henry James, with an introduction by William James, ed. Boston, 1885.

Principles of Psychology, 2 vols. New York, 1890. Regarded by many as James's major work, it is a prime source not only for his psychology but also for his metaphysics.

The Will To Believe and Other Essays in Popular Philosophy. New York, 1897. In addition to the title essay, the essay "The Sentiment of Rationality" is, if interpreted in the context of James's total thought, an important source of his basic convictions. The book also contains the famous essay "The Dilemma of Determinism," James's fullest statement of his views on free will.

The Varieties of Religious Experience: A Study in Human Nature. New York, 1902.

Pragmatism: A New Name for Some Old Ways of Thinking. New York, 1907.

The Meaning of Truth: A Sequel to "Pragmatism." New York,

1909. A collection of polemical essays; the Preface is especially important, for it answers certain criticisms of pragmatism and states James's conception of the relation between pragmatism and radical empiricism.

A Pluralistic Universe. New York, 1909. A sustained criticism of absolute idealism and intellectualism; contains chapters on Hegel, Fechner, and Bergson.

Some Problems of Philosophy: A Beginning of an Introduction to Philosophy. New York, 1911. James's last project; it is incomplete. Valuable for its many very clear formulations; three chapters outline his theory of perception.

Essays in Radical Empiricism. New York, 1912. A related series of essays expounding James's mature philosophy; the essays "Does Consciousness Exist?" and "A World of Pure Experience" are especially important.

Memories and Studies. New York, 1912. Fifteen popular essays and addresses selected by James's son Henry James; includes commemorative addresses on Agassiz and Emerson, an essay on Spencer, and several essays on psychical research and academic life.

Collected Essays and Reviews. New York, 1920. Thirty-nine articles, selected by Ralph Barton Perry, extending from 1869 to 1910; many historically important works, including the California lecture "Philosophical Conceptions and Practical Results."

Letters, Henry James, ed., Boston, 1920. Charming letters, primarily of biographical and historical significance, edited by James's son.

Works on James

Aiken, H. D., "American Pragmatism Reconsidered: William James." *Commentary,* September 1962, pp. 238–266.

Bergson, Henri, "On the Pragmatism of William James: Truth and Reality," in his *The Creative Mind,* translated by Mabelle L. Andison. New York, 1946. Brief but provocative development of the thesis that to understand James's pragmatism, we must modify our general conception of reality.

Dewey, John, *Characters and Events,* Vol. I. New York, 1929. Book I, Ch. 12. "William James" consists of three occasional pieces which together provide an informal but penetrating analysis of James's contribution to and place in American philosophy.

Lovejoy, Arthur O., *The Thirteen Pragmatisms and Other Essays.* Baltimore, Md., 1963. In addition to the very influential title essay, there are eight other essays on James or pragmatism.

Moore, G. E., *Philosophical Studies.* London, 1922. "William James' 'Pragmatism'" attempts to refute James from the common-sense point of view.

Perry, Ralph Barton, *Annotated Bibliography of the Writings of William James.* New York, 1920. A listing of 312 items from 1867 to 1920, with helpful indications of each item's content and value.

Perry, Ralph Barton, *The Thought and Character of William James,* 2 vols. Boston, 1935. A massive, richly documented study; the single most important work on James.

Perry, Ralph Barton, *In the Spirit of William James.* New Haven, 1938. A solid and sympathetic philosophical interpretation of James. The chapters "An Empirical Theory of Knowledge" (Ch. 2) and "The Metaphysics of Experience" (Ch. 3) are especially noteworthy.

Royce, Josiah, *William James and Other Essays on the Philosophy of Life.* New York, 1911. An attempt to show James's place in American social history.

Russell, Bertrand, *Philosophical Essays.* London and New York, 1910. See "William James' Conception of Truth" and "Pragmatism."

Santayana, George, *Character and Opinion in the United States, With Reminiscences of William James and Josiah Royce and Academic Life in America.* New York, 1920. Unsympathetic but extremely interesting in its own right.

WILLIAM JAMES EARLE

JANKÉLÉVITCH, VLADIMIR,

French moral philosopher, was born in 1903 at Bourges. He was educated at the Lycée Louis-le-Grand and the École Normale Supérieure.

Having become an agrégé in philosophy in 1926, he took his doctorate in 1933. After teaching at the French Institute in Prague and at various *lycées,* he served as lecturer at Toulouse from 1936 to 1937 and at Lille from 1938 to 1939. He was dismissed by the Vichy government in 1940 but returned to academic life in 1945 as professor at Lille, going from there to the University of Paris as professor of morals and moral philosophy.

Jankélévitch's philosophy is highly individual, though it displays a sympathetic understanding of widely divergent philosophical traditions. In content it has affinities with Christian morality and with the philosophy of Kierkegaard. In expression it is idiosyncratic and always lively.

Jankélévitch's first notable work was *Henri Bergson.* On its first appearance, in 1931, it bore a prefatory note by Bergson himself, praising its "intellectual sympathy." Jankélévitch's own philosophy made its first appearance in his main doctoral thesis, on Schelling's later philosophy, and even more clearly in his secondary thesis, on bad conscience (*La Mauvaise Conscience*). Bad conscience is consciousness directed not unreflectingly forward but regretfully backward toward its own past, which is irremediable because time is irreversible. The problem posed is how to restore the flow of living that tends to be halted by retrospective brooding. How is consciousness freed and time unfrozen? Jankélévitch did not favor the detachment from one's predicament effected by irony, precisely because it intellectualizes and detemporalizes that predicament. Time alone, in its flow, frees us.

In two of his postwar works, *Philosophie première* and *Traité des vertus,* Jankélévitch was perhaps at his best. Just as he rejected intellectual recourse to irony or conceptualization as consolations for the discontent attendant upon self-consciousness, so he showed, in *Philosophie première,* that the concern of metaphysics is not with the world of ideas, eternal truths, or transcendent models, which are ultimately as contingent as the reality that they rationalize, but with the "entirely other Order" of radical contingency. Here, in effect, Jankélévitch suggested that "sufficient reason" is never really sufficient. The instant always brings novelty over and above the schemata that demonstrate its "necessity."

The real importance of this fact is moral and leads to the treatise on the virtues. In this work virtues are classified according to either their intellectual quality of equity or their "non-natural" quality of goodness, to use the language of G. E. Moore. For Jankélévitch the virtues of consistent conduct—the "virtues of the interval," fidelity and justice—are inferior to the creative "virtues of the instant," courage and charity.

Works by Jankélévitch

Henri Bergson. Paris, 1931; rev. ed., Paris, 1959.

La Mauvaise Conscience. Paris, 1933.

L'Odyssée de la conscience dans la dernière philosophie de Schelling. Paris, 1933.

L'Ironie ou la bonne conscience. Paris, 1936; 2d rev. ed., Paris, 1950.

L'Alternative. Paris, 1938.

Du Mensonge. Paris, 1943.

Le Mal. Paris, 1947.

Traité des vertus. Paris, 1949.

Philosophie première. Paris, 1954.
L'Austérité et la vie morale. Paris, 1956.
Le Je-ne-sais-quoi et le presque-rien. Paris, 1957.

Works on Jankélévitch

Barthélemy-Madaule, Madeleine, "Autour du *Bergson* de M. V. Jankélévitch." *Revue de Métaphysique et de Morale,* Vol. 65 (1960), 510–524.
Smith, Colin, *Contemporary French Philosophy.* London, 1964. See pp. 181–201.
Vax, L., "Du Bergsonisme à la philosophie première." *Critique,* Vol. 11 (1955), 36–52.

COLIN SMITH

JAPANESE PHILOSOPHY. After the Meiji restoration in 1868 Japan was reopened to the West, and in 1874 Nishi Amane coined a new term, *tetsugaku,* "science of questing wisdom," to introduce Western philosophy. *Tetsugaku* is now understood as Western philosophy since 1877, the year in which Western professors were called to teach in Japan. The Japanese scholars who took their place kept the tradition and then as now all philosophy, properly so called, has been patterned after Western thought. However, Confucianism as a philosophy of social ethics flourished in Japan from the fifth to the nineteenth century, and it will be treated first. Buddhism, since it is most correctly understood as a religion, will not be discussed in this article (see BUDDHISM and ZEN).

EARLY AND MEDIEVAL CONFUCIANISM

Confucianism entered Japan with the introduction of Chinese script in A.D. 404. Han dynasty Confucianism is evident in almost all the precepts contained in Prince Shōtoku's constitution of 604. With the Taika reform in 646 and other reforms which soon followed it, the influence of T'ang Confucianism was felt. In a college (*daigaku*) of Chinese learning, reorganized in 701, Confucianist philosophy was the most important subject. Mandatory books were the Confucian classics *Filial Piety* and the *Analects;* Taoist books were excluded because they did not foster loyalty to the lord and piety toward parents. Confucianist ideas against the bad ruler were never allowed in Japan. Moreover, education was limited to the aristocracy and the courtiers. The teachers (*hakase*) were a special class of court officials. Nobility and rank took precedence over talent in Japan, although in China the system of examinations for public office was open, in theory at least, to all aspirants. The yin–yang (passive–active) theory, a doctrine of cosmic harmony, spread throughout Japan as it had in China, and it is reflected in the early chronicles of Japan. Famous scholars of that era who expounded Confucian ideas were Kibi no Mabiki (693–755), Fujiwara no Arihira (891–970), and Sugawara no Michizane (845–903), who was also a prominent political figure.

A decline in the study of Chinese culture and of Confucianism as well began in the tenth century after Japan had developed its own syllabary (attributed to the Buddhist monk Kukai, 774–835). Beautiful poetry and prose appeared for the first time in Japanese during those centuries when many bloody feuds were being pursued by the warlike clans. Learning took shelter in the monasteries. Buddhist monks supplanted the lay *hakase.*

Medieval Confucianism in Japan, which dates from the thirteenth to the sixteenth century, is characterized by the introduction of the Chinese Sung dynasty Neo-Confucianism, that is, the doctrines of Chu Hsi (1130–1200). Chu Hsi's great synthesis did not become, at this stage, the *Weltanschauung* of Japanese thinkers because of the strong Zen Buddhist background of the purveyors of Neo-Confucianism. Only in Tokugawa Japan did Chu Hsi become the great master. The Zen monks of Kamakura and Kyoto were more intent on reconciling Buddhism, Confucianism, and Taoism than in extolling Chu Hsi's philosophy; "the unity of the three doctrines" (*sankyō itchi*) is typical of this period. Moreover, during these turbulent years the samurai students were more interested in self-discipline and Zen intuitiveness than in the abstruse aspects of Chu Hsi's thought. His metaphysical doctrine of cosmic harmony was of little help to warriors.

However, Neo-Confucianism became stronger as the Tokugawa era approached. During the period of the Kamakura shogunate (1192–1333), the two scholars Shunjō and Enni, the two Chinese scholars who came to Japan, I'shan and Lan-ch'i, and the great traveler Eisai played important roles in introducing Sung Confucianism. Gen-e explained it at court (1319).

The fourteenth century saw the rise of the Ashikaga shogunate. The school Ashikaga established became a center of Chu Hsi's Confucianism, sending out disciples to all parts of Japan. Buddhist books were not allowed in the school, a sign of the renaissance of Chinese learning and the secularization of Japanese culture. Mentors to the Ashikaga were Gidō (1324–1388) and Hōshū (1363–1424); Hōshū, with Keian (1427–1508), introduced the Japanese diacritical signs for reading Chinese texts, an important element in the diffusion of Sung Confucianism. Keian was a Zen monk who had adopted most Confucian ideas in search of a concept of life that could bring order and peace to Japan.

TOKUGAWA CONFUCIANISM

After the years of unrest of the sixteenth century, the country was finally unified (although it remained a feudal society) under one family: the Tokugawa, who ruled from 1603 to 1867. Ieyasu, the first Tokugawa shogun, was content to leave the profundities of life to the Buddhists, but he believed that the government of the realm must have a more practical basis. He found in Confucianism a suitable means for stabilizing the country.

During the Tokugawa period the Neo-Confucianist Chu Hsi school, known in Japan as *Shushi-gakuha,* became official doctrine, and Japanese Confucianism blossomed. At the same time the Confucian *kogakuha,* or "school of ancient learning," and the Neo-Confucian Wang Yangming school (in Japanese, *Ōyōmei-gakuha*) were also competing for prominence. The intermingling of those schools as Confucianism spread and the rise of a certain rationalism in the eighteenth century made for a complex culture in Tokugawa Japan. Yet some common characteristics of these schools ought to be pointed out. All Tokugawa Confucianists were scholars in the ancient sense in which "scholar" was a name for virtue. The quantity of Confucian literary production is amazing, but originality was considered akin to heresy. Open hostility toward Buddhism is another characteristic of Tokugawa Confucianism. The secularization of Tokugawa culture is a well-known fact, for although the populace clung to the many Buddhist sects, the intellectual strength of Buddhism was on the decline. The medieval temple schools (*terakoya*) lost ground to the private schools (*juku*) set up by the Confucianist teachers (*jusha*), who became the schoolmasters of the nation. The fief schools, too, which spread after 1750, were directed by Confucian scholars.

The peace and order brought to Japanese society by the Tokugawa affected Confucianism in many ways. The samuri became administrators, landowners dealing with a merchant class on the rise, and as a result the practical aspects of Confucianism had to be emphasized at the expense of the metaphysical. Thus the "investigation of things" taught by Chu Hsi became more and more a practical science (*jitsugaku*), which was a blend of administrative and economic philosophy. The lines of class distinction between samurai, rich farmers, and merchants became thinner and thinner. The Confucianist teachers themselves began to come from the lower classes. Ability more than rank tended to prevail. Other reasons for the growth of Confucianism are to be found in the cultural and administrative development of different clans that allowed a variety of trends to arise. However, the general atmosphere of thought in the Tokugawa era became stifling in its uniformity, particularly under Tokugawa Tsunayoshi (1680–1709), who was responsible for enforcing Chu Hsi's orthodoxy.

Chu Hsi Neo-Confucianist school. The *Shushi-gakuha*, or Chu Hsi school, had two early promoters, Fujiwara Seika (1561–1619) and Hayashi Razan (1583–1657). Fujiwara started out as a Zen monk, but contact with Chu Hsi's thought transformed him into a tolerant, if not eclectic, Confucianist. Although concerned about secular affairs, he did not become a bureaucrat in the government of Tokugawa Ieyasu. Fujiwara was an open-minded scholar and a typical representative of the cultural renaissance which was in the offing before the policy of seclusion (1639) cut Japan off from the rest of the world. Hayashi Razan and his son and a grandson were instrumental in making the *Shushi-gakuha* the official social creed of the Tokugawa era. For this purpose a school was set up in Edo (Tokyo) in 1630. In 1691 it became a college under the presidency of Hayashi's grandson, Hayashi Hōkō, with rights of family succession.

However political the reasons may have been for sponsoring Chu Hsi's system in the later Tokugawa regime, Fujiwara, Hayashi Razan, and others were sincerely awed by the intrinsic coherence of that great rational synthesis. Chu Hsi is, after all, a great Confucianist philosopher, if not the greatest. Even recent Japanese scholars, so keen in detecting opportunism, admit that the early Neo-Confucianists were sincerely impressed by Chu Hsi's thought, especially in regard to its theoretical structure. The "great ultimate," rationalized into *ri* (Chinese, *li*), the all-pervading principle (or reason), intrinsically united in the phenomenal world with *ki* (Chinese, *ch'i*), the material force of everything, through the motion of yin and yang, or the passive and active elements, and their five agents— water, fire, wood, metal, earth—forms the order of nature. This order has its counterpart in society in the five human relationships—lord–subject; father–son; husband–wife; older brother–younger brother; friend–friend. Without a doubt the Tokugawa rulers were more interested in the social aspects of Chu Hsi's philosophy, but it is an exaggeration to say that this was the case with the *Shushi* scholars. Ideas have an erratic course; although in Edo Muro Kyūsō (1658–1734) and the Hayashi family were the defenders of strict orthodoxy, the Kyoto circle of the *Shushi* school was more liberal. The most famous of the Kyoto group was Kinoshita Junan (1621–1698), a disciple of Fujiwara and the teacher of the Confucianist statesman Arai Hakuseki (1657–1725). Other notables were Andō Seian (1622–1701), Amenomori Hōshū (1668–1755), and Kaibara Ekken (1630–1714). Kaibara gave voice to his doubts of Chu Hsi doctrine in his book *Taigiroku* ("The Great Doubt"). Another branch of the *Shushi* school developed in the Tosa clan in Shikoku, in the south. Minamimura Baiken (c. 1540) and Tani Jichū (1598–1649) founded this branch; Yamazaki Ansai (1618–1682) was its most famous representative. Yamazaki's pupils Asami Keisai (1652–1711) and Satō Naokata (1650–1719) spread their master's doctrine of "devotion within, righteousness without," although they did not embrace his later turn to Shintoism.

Wang Yang-ming school. The *Ōyōmei-gakuha* (or *Yōmei-gakuha*) has been highly praised by scholars of the past and the present for three reasons: It produced men of strong character; it had an intuitive bent, always esteemed in Japan; it has historical importance as the doctrine held by those who were most active in the Meiji restoration in 1868. Nakae Tōju (1608–1648), the most respected Confucianist of Tokugawa Japan, found in Wang Yang-ming's *liang-chih* (in Japanese, *ryōchi*) the "innate knowledge," a kind of primeval conscience, which guides man in evading the "snares" of Chu Hsi's rationalism. Nake taught the following antipodes as unities: will and intellect, deeds and knowledge, self-cultivation and external behavior. He also taught a kind of theism which instills deep filial piety.

The *Yōmei* school was more monistic than the Chu Hsi school. It virtually identified *ri*, the principle, with *ki*, the material force; and it held mind to be one with external nature. The cultivation of mind is the key to the "investigation of things," the stress being laid upon self-mastery: self-examination in doing things rather than in knowing them. *Yōmei* teaching was addressed equally to all (women not excluded); this universality accounts for its popularity.

Kumazawa Banzan (1619–1691), the most famous pupil of Nakae, was a talented administrator and a fearless advocate of reforms—an exemplification of the *Yōmei* "unity of knowledge and action." Among *Yōmei* followers, Ōshio Heihachirō (1794–1837) is remembered especially because of his part in the Osaka starvation riot of 1837, an uprising against the city magistrates; it cost him his life. Patriots and loyalists to the imperial line like Yoshida Shōin (1830–1859) and Saigō Takamori (1827–1877) were influenced by this school, which fostered nonconformist ideas and thus paved the way for the restoration.

School of "ancient learning." The *kogakuha* ("school of ancient learning") discarded Neo-Confucianism as spurious and tried to go back to Confucius for its inspiration. In spite of this return to antiquity, the old sage's sayings were adapted to the existing society. Yamaga Sokō

(1622–1685) codified *Bushido,* the "way of the warrior," for the samurai of Tokugawa Japan. His strictures on Chu Hsi caused him to be exiled from Edo, and his extolling of the emperor and the imperial line did not ingratiate him with the Tokugawa. Itō Jinsai (1627–1705), a philosopher and a great educator, emphasized the importance of humaneness and righteousness (*jingi*). His son Itō Tōgai (1670–1736) systematized and spread Jinsai's thought. Ogyū Sorai (1666–1728), an accomplished Sinologist, was openly a utilitarian in that he emphasized positive edicts and institutions rather than metaphysical speculation on Heaven's law. Ogyū stressed the social aspect of ethics, thus upholding the importance of rites and ceremonies; his pupil Dazai Shundai (1680–1747) went even further in this direction.

New trends and late Tokugawa Confucianism. After the Kyōho era (1716–1736) the followers of the three main schools of Tokugawa Confucianism scattered to all parts of Japan, intermingling and thus engendering new schools: the *kōshō-gakuha* ("philologico-historical school"), the *setchū-gakuha* ("eclectic school"), and others. Unlike the Confucianists of prior times, however, eighteenth-century Confucianists were not absorbed into any ism. Their open approach, their lack of fanaticism, their individualism, and their positive approach, combined with the spread of education among the merchant class, favored different trends. In 1720 Tokugawa Yoshimune took a more liberal view of Western thought, particularly of Dutch books on medicine and astronomy, than his predecessors, and the impact of Western science was felt. This fomented something which, for lack of a better term, may be called rationalism.

One of the prominent rationalists of the era was Tominaga Nakamoto (1715–1746), who applied historical criticism to Buddhism, Confucianism, and Shintoism to produce "the religion of true fact," a kind of rational ethics. Another was Miura Baien (1723–1789); he came the closest in that age to philosophy in the Western sense. He also developed a kind of dialectic, or "logic of things." Miura, with Kaiho Seiryō (1755–1817), initiated economic thought, and in fact Kaiho equated *ri,* the principle, with the law of buying and selling. Andō Shōeki is another nonconformist thinker of the eighteenth century who harshly criticized the religious and social ideology of his time and who tended toward materialism. Minagawa Kien (1734–1807) showed his positive critical bent in a philological study of the "categories of things." Kamada Ryūō (1754–1817?) approached a realist and materialist epistemology in his thinking; nevertheless, he was also influenced by the *shingaku* ("learning of the mind") school, a very eclectic system of popular ethics founded by Ishida Baigan (1685–1744) that flourished among the merchant class.

The disintegration of Confucianism was also furthered by the *kokugakusha* ("national learning scholars"), guided by Motoori Norinaga (1730–1801) and by Kamo Mabuchi (1697–1769), who extolled the ancient Japanese chronicles containing Shinto mythology at the expense of everything Chinese. The Mito school of Confucianist historians of Japan contributed both to shifting the people's sense of loyalty from the Tokugawa shogunate to the emperor and to making Confucianism subserve Shintoist ideology. No wonder that in 1790 an edict prohibiting "heterodox doctrines" was promulgated in order to uphold *Shushi*

thought, which even at the Hayashi school in Edo was losing prestige. This prohibition had only a temporary effect; in 1841 Satō Issai (1772–1859) became the official Confucianist scholar at Edo. Satō, while teaching Chu Hsi doctrine at the Hayashi school, was propounding his own *Yōmei* thought privately. He also esteemed Western learning highly. At about the same time Takano Chōei (1804–1850) was writing a kind of summary of Western philosophy and, together with many others, was advocating the opening of Japan to the West.

Although Confucianism as philosophy lost much after the Meiji restoration, its impact on the Japanese ethos has been and still is very great. In spite of the mounting nationalism of the years after 1887, it did become the backbone of all Meiji educational reforms. However, it is true that the nationalistic ethic (*shūshin*) enforced by the reforms was more than anything else a political Shintoist ideology. Confucian tenets were incorporated into the Shintoist cult for the emperor in order to foster nationalist expansion.

The Shibun Gakkai (Sinological Society), founded in 1880, and revived in 1918 as Shibunkai, was the center for many scholarly historical studies of Japanese Confucianism. The political activities of the society were one reason for its dying after World War II. Since the war scholarly works have appeared about Confucianism, but there is no sign of its revival as a school of thought.

WESTERN PHILOSOPHY IN JAPAN

Shortly after the Meiji restoration of 1868 and the reopening of Japan to the West that accompanied it, Nishi Amane (1829–1897) introduced Western philosophy into Japan. In 1874 he coined a new term to stand for Western philosophy: *kitetsugaku,* "the science of questing wisdom," which he later shortened to *tetsugaku.* The shorter term is the one that became current; it is understood as meaning Western philosophy since 1877, the year when foreign professors began teaching in Japan. Among these professors were Ernest F. Fenollosa, an American; C. Cooper, an Englishman; and Ludwig Busse, a German. In 1886 the Imperial University of Tokyo was reorganized and in 1893 regular chairs, filled by Japanese professors, were established. In 1887 the first philosophical journal, *Tetsugaku-kai zasshi* ("The Journal of the Philosophical Society") appeared.

Anglo-German idealism. Initially, Western philosophy in Japan passed through stages of positivism, utilitarianism, and materialist evolutionism. Then Anglo-German idealism came to the fore, partly through the influence of the foreign teachers and partly because of the indoctrination with nationalist ethical ideals carried out in Japanese schools. To this task Inoue Tetsujirō (1855–1944), the first Japanese to hold a chair of philosophy at Tokyo University, devoted his long career. Inoue became nationally known for a group of essays published as *Shūkyō to kyōiku no shototsu* ("The Conflict Between Religion and Education"; Tokyo, 1891), in which he attacks Christianity as a religion that places Christ above the emperor. His philosophical contribution was his special brand of German *Identitätsrealismus,* the theory of the identity of the phenomenal world with reality. With this he tried to overcome the realism and materialism of Ernst Haeckel and Katō Hiroyuki (1836–1916), Japan's most famous exponent of materialist evolutionism. Inoue formulated original Japanese terminology second in importance only to Nishi's pioneering work and compiled the first Japanese philosophical dictionary (published 1881). He gained wide recognition for his scholarly works on Japanese Confucianism; he was an ardent advocate of nationalist causes, and national morality became his main interest.

Quite different from Inoue was the stimulating Russian Raphael von Koeber (1848–1923), whose service to Japan in educating several generations of Japanese philosophers at Tokyo University is still honored. Koeber, a Russian of German extraction who had studied under Eduard von Hartmann, came to Japan in 1893; he taught the history of philosophy, stressing the importance of Greek and medieval philosophy. Inoue's successor in the Tokyo chair of philosophy was Kuwaki Gen'yoku (1874–1946), the most thoroughgoing Kantian in Japan. Neo-Kantianism became the general trend during the Taishō regime (1912–1926), although Husserl's phenomenology was introduced in 1921.

Development of the history of philosophy. During the Taishō era Japanese philosophy passed from a stage still smacking of dilettantism to the plane of genuine scholarship. The history of philosophy especially began to be presented in a more scientific form, notably by two men, Ōnishi Hajime (1864–1900) and Hatano Seiichi (1877–1950). Ōnishi, a moral philosopher, was called the Kant of Japan for his critical and independent spirit; nevertheless his ethics is inspired by the Neo-Hegelianism of T. H. Green, an author widely read toward the end of the last century. Hatano began as a historian of Western philosophy and later developed into a somewhat original philosopher of religion. The scientific history of philosophy was also aided by the publication, from about 1910 on, of dictionaries and translations of original source books. The result was strict Neo-Kantianism in the two leading universities, at Tokyo and Kyoto, because Windelband and Heinrich Rickert were the two philosophers read most. Other trends popular during the Taishō era, like the pragmatism of James and the instrumentalism of Dewey, were spread mostly from Waseda University and by such non-academic philosophers as Tanaka Ōdō (1867–1932). Tanaka, who graduated from Chicago University, wrote many books and as philosopher expounded a naturalistic conception of life based on social ideas.

Development of Nishida's school. During the Taishō period Kyoto University's Nishida Kitarō (1870–1945), the greatest contemporary philosopher of Japan, was developing what his pupils were to call "Nishida's philosophy." It was not so well systematized as they thought. Nishida began with *Zen no kenkyū* (1911; translated as *A Study of Good*, 1960); in this and in many other studies, he strove for *basho no ronri*, a "logic of field," or "logic of place." He intended to create an Oriental logic, although the Orient is usually considered bereft of logic. Nishida's logic shows traces of Emil Lask's *Feldtheorie* and is redolent of Mahāyāna Buddhism's nothingness, too; but ultimately it was his own creation.

Another notable philosopher at Kyoto University was Tanabe Hajime (1885–1962), who with other students of Nishida formed the most important philosophic group in prewar Japan, the "Kyoto school." Tanabe distinguished himself with a philosophy of mathematics and general science. He was famous for his *shu no ronri*, "logic of the species" ("species" referring to nation), that mediates between the individual and mankind. After World War II Tanabe was the leader of the intellectuals who urged a thorough housecleaning of theories about nationalism.

Other outstanding students of Nishida were Kōyama Iwao, Kōsaka Masaaki, Nishitani Keiji, and Tomonaga Sanjūrō. Kōyama, Kōsaka, and Nishitani continued to be leading philosophers after the war; Tomonaga (1871–1951) stands out as a Neo-Kantian who described the evolution of recent Japanese philosophic awareness in *Kinsei ni okeru ga no jinakushi* ("A History of Self-Consciousness in Modern Times"; Tokyo, 1916). Takahashi Satomi (1886–1964), an independent thinker, developed a "pan-dialectic" in opposition to Nishida; he never compromised his academic freedom under the pressures of nationalism.

Mutai Risaku and Yamauchi Tokuryū were early spokesmen for Husserl's phenomenology; after 1951 Mutai developed a "third humanism" which shows pacifist tendencies and strives to go beyond Nishida's logic of field and Tanabe's logic of the species. Both Nishida and Tanabe lacked historical perspective, the one being too mystical and the other too abstract. Yamauchi became Japan's best historian of Greek philosophy.

Ethics. Watsuji Tetsurō (1889–1960) wrote *Ethics as Anthropology*, based on the communitarian concept of man. He is also gifted in the field of cultural history; of several works, his *History of Japanese Ethical Thought* is especially good. Among the younger generation of students of ethics are Kaneko Takezō (b. 1905), Furukawa Tetsushi (b. 1912), and Ōshima Yasumasa (b. 1917). The philosophy of Kaneko, who succeeded Watsuji at Tokyo University, is based on Hegel's dialectic of the spirit. Furukawa has cultivated historical studies in Japanese ethics, and Ōshima has studied existential ethics.

Marxist philosophy. Marxism as philosophy entered Japan in 1926; Miki Kiyoshi (1897–1945) was an early explicator, although his post-1930 works manifest no Marxist tendencies. A thoroughgoing communist philosopher was Tosaka Jun (1900–1945). Like Miki, he died in prison.

Marxist thinkers, together with a few Christian liberals, were the only persons opposing the tide of prewar nationalism. The Hegelian philosophers Kihira Masami (1874–1949) and Kanokogi Kazunobu (1884–1949) were the most fanatic nationalists.

For about ten years after 1945 the power of Marxist philosophers burgeoned in academic publications and philosophical congresses. After the war Tokyo University's Aristotelian specialist Ide Takashi created a sensation when he joined the Communist party. Yanagida Kenjūrō, a former pupil of Nishida, is another well-known philosopher who joined the Communist party (in 1960). Though not communists, the historians of Japanese thought Funayama Shinichi and Saigusa Hiroto are materialists.

Other contemporary trends. The second important postwar trend is existentialism in all its forms, from Heidegger and Jaspers to Sartre and Gabriel Marcel. Miyake Gōichi is known for his study of Heidegger's thought, but in the philosophy of mathematics he was influenced by Bertrand Russell. Another trend is a revival of pragmatism through the Association for the Study of American Philosophy guided by Ueda Seiji, a scholar of long-standing authority on Anglo-American thought, who with others had founded the association in the early 1950s. The association includes many specialists on logical positivism, the philosophy of language, analytical philosophy, and the philosophy of science. Shimomura Toratarō (b. 1902) is a well-known philosopher of the history of science. Ikegami Kenzō (1900–1956) is noted for his research in the philosophy of language and his epistemology of culture. His brilliant career at Tokyo University was cut short by cancer.

There are many other strands in contemporary Japanese philosophic studies, ranging from ancient Greek thought and medieval philosophy through the most recent philosophers of all countries. Societies and specialized journals arise in amazing quantity and quality. Then, too, there is comparative philosophy, promoted by Kawada Kumatarō and Nakamura Hajime. Their intent is to find a common ground (still undiscovered) for a dialogue between Eastern and Western philosophy.

An over-all evaluation of Japanese philosophy must take into account the partial lack of academic freedom that was a constant obstacle up to 1945. Negative aspects of Japanese thought are the penchant for dialectic, the relativism, and the noncommitment that foster a special form of eclecticism. However, together with erudite philosophical scholarship, some creative thought has emerged in Japan since 1868 in the work of Nishida, Tanabe, Takahashi, Watsuji, and Hatano. Its specific characteristics include a quest for a special logic, for an ethic of relationship, and for *shutaisei* ("selfhood"). Moreover, a philosophy of culture is arising to place Japan in the main stream of world culture.

(See also BUDDHISM and ZEN for the development of Buddhism in Japan. See Japanese Philosophy in Index for articles on Japanese philosophers.)

Bibliography

BIBLIOGRAPHICAL WORKS

A bibliography of Japanese works on Confucianism and on recent Western philosophy is given in D. Holzman and others, *Japanese Religion and Philosophy: A Guide to Japanese Reference and Research Materials* (Ann Arbor, Mich., 1959), entries 1–119, 545–695, 826–914, and in Kokusai Bunka Shinkokai, ed., *Bibliography of Standard Reference Books for Japanese Studies with Descriptive Notes*, Vol. V-A, Parts I–II, *History of Thought* (Tokyo, 1964–1965).

A bibliography of Western works on Confucianism is given in H. Borton and others, eds., *A Selected List of Books and Articles on Japan in English, French, and German*, rev. ed. (Cambridge, Mass., 1954), entries 1132–1151, and in Bernard S. Silberman, *Japan and Korea, A Critical Bibliography* (Tucson, Ariz., 1962), pp. 36–39.

CONFUCIANISM

On early and medieval Confucianism, see Wajima Yoshio, *Chūsei no jugaku* ("Medieval Confucianism"; Tokyo, 1965).

Tokugawa Confucian texts are available in the collections Inoue Tetsujirō and Kanie Yoshimaru, eds., *Nihon rinri ihen* ("Collected Works on Japanese Ethics"), 10 vols. (Tokyo, 1901–1903). See also

Seki Giichirō, ed., *Nihon jurin sōsho* ("Library of Japanese Confucian Writings"), 6 vols. (Osaka, 1927–1929; 2d series, 4 vols., 1930–1933; 3d series, 3 vols., 1935–1937).

Among the studies of Tokugawa Confucianism are three works by Inoue Tetsujirō: *Nihon Yōmeigakuha no tetsugaku* ("The Philosophy of the Japanese Wang Yang-ming School"; Tokyo, 1900), *Nihon kogakuha no tetsugaku* ("The Philosophy of the Japanese School of Ancient Learning"; Tokyo, 1902), and *Nihon Shushi-gakuha no tetsugaku* ("The Philosophy of the Japanese Chu Hsi School"; Tokyo, 1905). Inoue's trilogy has been summarized in English by Robert C. Armstrong, *Light from the East, Studies in Japanese Confucianism* (Toronto, 1914), and by Walter Dening, "Confucian Philosophy in Japan," *Transactions of the Asiatic Society of Japan*, Vol. 36, No. 2 (1908), 101–152. See also Arthur Lloyd, "Historical Development of the Shushi Philosophy in Japan," *Transactions of the Asiatic Society of Japan*, Vol. 34, No. 4 (1906), 5–80; Ōe Fumiki, *Hompō jugakushi ronkō* ("On the History of Japanese Confucianism"; Osaka, 1944); Bitō Masahide, *Hōken shisōshi kenkyū* ("Studies on the History of Feudal Thought in Japan"; Tokyo, 1961); Sagara Tōru, *Kinsei Nihon jukyō undo no keifu* ("The Pedigree of the Confucian Movement in Early Modern Japan"; Tokyo, 1955, 1964); Ryusaku Tsunoda, William T. de Bary, and Donald Keene, eds., *Sources of Japanese Tradition* (New York, 1958); David M. Earl, *Emperor and Nation in Japan, Political Thinkers of the Tokugawa Period* (Seattle, 1964); John W. Hall, "The Confucian Teacher in Tokugawa Japan," in D. S. Nivison and A. F. Wright, eds., *Confucianism in Action* (Stanford, Calif., 1959), pp. 268–301; William T. de Bary, "Common Tendencies in Neo-Confucianism," *ibid.*, pp. 25–49.

For Confucianism as a political ideology after 1868 see Warren W. Smith, Jr., *Confucianism in Modern Japan* (Tokyo, 1959).

WESTERN PHILOSOPHY

On Western philosophy see Kyoson Tsuchida, *Contemporary Thought of Japan and China* (London, 1927); Masaaki Kōsaka, ed., *Japanese Thought in Meiji Era*, translated by D. Abosch (Tokyo, 1958); Gino K. Piovesana, S.J., *Recent Japanese Philosophical Thought, 1862–1962: A Survey* (Tokyo, 1963). The only yearly journal in English is *Philosophical Studies of Japan*, published in Tokyo; Vol. 1 appeared in 1959.

GINO K. PIOVESANA, S.J.

JASPERS, KARL, one of the architects of contemporary existentialism and one of the first philosophers to use the term "existentialist." He is a prolific writer with a prolix style that is often inelegant, superficial, sentimental, and unclear and that over the years has shown itself to be repetitious. Yet careful and extensive reading of his works shows him to be a rigorous and responsible thinker. Appearances notwithstanding, he is perhaps the most systematic of all existentialist philosophers. His philosophy is neither linguistic analysis nor metaphysics. It can be best characterized as a disciplined and organized description of the critical fringes of human existence, such as impenetrable limits, unmitigated freedom, and the experienced indefinite expanse of space, time, and consciousness. Jaspers fulfills the common-sense image of the philosopher through his vital concern with the contemporary political situation and his trenchant reflections on the threats to man's integrity and fulfillment posed by twentieth-century social, economic, and political institutions. He has spoken with authority to the nonphilosophic mind because of his deep and successful roots in medicine and psychology. He is suspicious of contemporary overconfidence in science and, as an antidote, stresses the irrational in man. As Jaspers sees it, philosophy begins where reason has suffered shipwreck. Philosophy is an activity, a becoming, not a state of being or a body of facts. Philosophy is philosophizing. To appreciate philosophic insights we must—as Socrates and Freud saw—arrive at them ourselves. We must live philosophy, since we cannot meaningfully paraphrase its conclusions. Genuine philosophy arises directly out of the problems confronting the individual philosopher in his existential, or historical, situation. General problems are mere derivatives. Philosophy need not be metaphysics; it can only illuminate some of the potentialities of an individual existence, an existence that is ineffable, unique, and free.

Jaspers was influenced especially by Kant, but also by Kierkegaard and Nietzsche, whom he admired because they were prophets who articulated the structure of their existence, because they were not academic philosophers, because their thinking welled up directly from their personal existence, and because they illustrated the axiom that philosophic thinking begins in the attempt to communicate to another the nature of one's *Existenz*. The influence of Husserl is also apparent, although it is perhaps unconscious, since it is mostly unacknowledged. Jaspers uses Husserl's method of descriptive phenomenology and adopts Husserl's concept of intentionality as a central function of the self. Further nore, Husserl's ideas of the transcendental ego and transcendental consciousness conform to Jaspers' descriptions of the inner self (*Existenz*) and the outermost boundaries of the world (*das Umgreifende*). Jaspers' religious thought, although it ignores Aristotelianism and Scholasticism, is deeply influenced by Plotinus, Bruno, Spinoza, and Schelling and gives a modern phenomenological restatement of many of the classical religious intuitions of mankind.

Life and works. Jaspers was born in 1883 in the East Frisian city of Oldenburg. His father was a banker, constable, and jurist. Jaspers studied law at the universities of Heidelberg and Munich, and medicine at Berlin, Göttingen, and Heidelberg. He received his M.D. from Heidelberg in 1909, upon completion of his dissertation on *Heimweh und Verbrechen* ("Nostalgia and Crime"). Immediately upon graduation he became a volunteer assistant in psychiatry at Heidelberg. His first major work, *Allgemeine Psychopathologie* (*General Psychopathology*, 1913), is a book on methodology showing the merits and limits of various psychological procedures and descriptions. In 1916 he became professor of psychology at Heidelberg. Shortly after World War I he published his *Psychologie der Weltanschauungen* ("Psychology of World Views," 1919), which consists of descriptions of many different attitudes toward life. It is based on Dilthey's *Typologie der Weltanschauungen* and marks Jaspers' transition from psychology to philosophy. He later called it the first genuinely existentialist work. Both of these early works were based on his medical experience.

He received a professorship in philosophy at Heidelberg in 1921, after declining similar offers from the universities of Kiel and Greifswald. In 1932 he published his magnum opus, the three-volume *Philosophie*, which is a detailed development of the notions of transcendence and *Existenz*. In 1937 he was relieved of his duties by the National Socialist regime but was reinstated in 1945. In 1946 he was named honorary senator of Heidelberg University, and

since 1948 he has been teaching at the University of Basel in Switzerland. In 1958 he was awarded the German Peace Prize at the Frankfurt Book Fair. Recently he has been working on his *Philosophische Logik,* the first volume of which appeared in 1947, as well as on a monumental universal history of philosophy. Throughout his life, Jaspers has been greatly concerned with communication. Personal relationships have had great philosophic significance to him. In addition to his parents, particularly significant persons in his life were his teacher Max Weber, his friend Ernst Meyer, and Meyer's sister Gertrud, who became Jaspers' wife. Since she was Jewish, Jaspers lived, through her, the agony of the Jewish people during World War II, and this led him to publish in 1946 his reflections on the question of German guilt, *Die Schuldfrage, ein Beitrag zur deutschen Frage.*

Any classification of Jaspers' views into traditional philosophic disciplines is artificial. For purposes of exposition, however, such an expedient is necessary.

Epistemology. Jasper's method is generally skeptical. It consists of the exploration, description, and analysis of first-person experiences. These form the basic data for philosophical generalizations and are for any person the sole source of his information about reality. Jaspers goes far beyond Descartes in emphasizing the epistemological primacy of subjectivity: my thinking begins and ends with subjectivity, since awareness, as Kant saw, always consists partially of interpretations. Although the results of these descriptions do not form a universal ontology—they apply, strictly speaking, to my own self exclusively—they are nonetheless verifiable inasmuch as egos may compare experiences. Jaspers follows Kierkegaard in describing immediate experiences (which consist not only of sense data but also of love and anxiety, hope and despair) and examining their ontological import. Since he describes fringe states of consciousness, areas of experience that are difficult, perhaps even impossible, to focus sharply, his language necessarily becomes ambiguous.

There is no certainty either in philosophy or in science. I am forced to depend ultimately on the intuitions and decisions of my own ego. Science is not an ultimate form of knowledge because it excludes the observer, because it is replete with unexamined and often erroneous assumptions, and because one method of inquiry is insufficient for a complete world picture. Although the spirit of scientific inquiry is an antidote to dogma in religion, politics, and philosophy, it gives us only surface knowledge, which is, at best, a workable mythology.

Psychology. The nature of the self is discovered through illumination of existence (*Existenzerhellung*), which discloses the possibilities of man, that is, the possibilities of an entity seeking understanding of self and of being. *Existenzerhellung* yields access to the questioner himself. Ordinary modes of perception and cognition, which imply a subject apprehending an object, always bypass the real self (the *Ursprung*). The real and valuable, that is, the authentic, in man is called *Existenz*. *Existenz*, the genuine self, is nonobjective and unique. It is infinitely open to new possibilities and inaccessible to traditional philosophical investigations. Although *Existenz* is that crucial aspect of human existence that cannot be conceptually delimited, it is nonetheless clearly experienced: It can be lived; it is illuminated through philosophical reflection; it can be communicated. *Existenz* is the experience of the total freedom that defines man; it is the experience of the infinity of possibilities for styles of life; it is, finally, the experience of loneliness that cries in the wilderness. *Existenz* is the eternal in man, while *Dasein* (not to be confused with that which Heidegger designates by the same word) is his temporal dimension. *Dasein* is that aspect of man which has describable characteristics and is accessible to theoretical reflection. To confuse mere *Dasein* with the authentic ground of my being, *Existenz*, is crass materialism and leads to shipwreck, while to ignore *Dasein* altogether leads to nihilism. A tension (*Spannung*) between the two is the golden mean.

Man is alienated from his world. He comes from a dim past and goes into an indefinite future. Life is a flux in which he seeks anchor. Existence is rich in mysterious paradoxes and antinomies, such as those of freedom coexisting with dependence, communication with solitude, good with evil, truth with falsehood, happiness with grief, life with death, and progress with destruction. Authentic *Existenz* is disclosed through reason (*Vernunft*), while intellect (*Verstand*) concerns itself with the pragmatic management of existence. *Verstand* is satisfied with practical results, while *Vernunft* engages in endless searching. Man is both *Vernunft* and *Existenz*.

Existenz is limited by impenetrable boundaries (*Grenzsituationen*). To experience these and to exist are one and the same, since despair can be, in the last analysis, a cognitive and elevating emotion. A defining characteristic of man is his finitude, which he experiences as the limits to his existence. Jaspers' analysis of these boundary situations is the existential formulation of the problem of evil and has been most influential. Authentic existence will push back these limits as far as possible and then accept and bear them. Death is one of the most dramatic of these barriers. It is the source of anxiety, but it also elevates the spirit because it emphasizes the urgency of living authentically without postponement. Consciousness of the inevitable presence of death gives man courage and integrity: it gives him an authentic perspective on the things that matter most. Guilt is another important boundary situation. Man not only *feels* guilty but, because of his total freedom, *is* guilty. He always could have chosen otherwise. Ultimate guilt cannot be removed: it must be accepted and can thereby become constructive. Our guilt demonstrates the power that our freedom has over our destiny. The boundary of "situationality" is the fact that we are partially thrust and partially choose ourselves into a particular human condition. We can be inauthentic and inevitably fall into these situations or be authentic and make them happen. Other important boundaries are chance, suffering, and conflict.

Freedom is central to man; it leads to the overriding importance of choice, which becomes the problem of moral responsibility.

Ethics. For Jaspers, ethics is the exploration of the experience and the potential of free will. Freedom is identified with choice, awareness, and selfhood. To choose

means to be free, and man's freedom is his being. I am only to the extent that I choose freely. To be is to be conscious that one is free. I do not choose life's meanings, I do not "define" man, as Sartre contends, since I am limited by my historicity—my past choices bind me. But within these confines my freedom is total. Freedom is experienced as both spontaneity and action; it is thus more important to act and be an *homme engagé* than to observe and be a theoretician. To know and use my freedom is the *raison d'être* of *Existenzerhellung*. Whenever I choose, I act, I am conscious of my action, I am aware of the values involved, I take chances (since the consequences of my choice are often uncertain), and I realize that commitment to some values is unavoidable.

The presence of anguish adumbrates the sacred nature of my freedom. Since each choice carries with it the accumulated weight of previous decisions, the first choice overshadows all others. Consequently, guilt is the inevitable concomitant of my freedom. My original choice (*Urentschluss*) bears down on my subsequent existence and assumes the role of original sin. I am accountable for that first choice, so that to be responsible means to have accepted that guilt. In addition, I am ceaselessly confronted with the choice between sacrificing my integrity for the sake of a longer life or surrendering myself to my authentic existential possibilities. The inherent difficulty of these choices leads to further guilt, which I may alleviate by imagining absolute standards and then approximating them. But in my heart I know there are no fixed standards and that absolutism is therefore a rationalization: the boundary of guilt is indeed impenetrable.

Anguish also appears when I realize I may lose the promise of my possibilities. But that same anguish gives me the urgency and courage to choose with my full being to implement the authentic potential of my *Existenz*. I reach this pedagogically expedient brink caused by anguish when I recognize the limits of scientific thought or when I am faced with critical decisions. Confronted with the abyss, I may accept a philosophic or religious orientation, I may act as if I did not recognize the existence of the abyss before which I stand, or I may adopt the nihilistic position that judges these problems to be meaningless.

Subjectivity is essentially intersubjective. I am only to the extent that another *Existenz* reflects me. Jaspers describes true communication as the feeling that men have known each other since eternity. My own freedom is in essence the search for the "loving strife" of communication with another *Existenz*. In fact, the search for *Existenz* cannot be accomplished in the abyss of absolute estrangement. Existential philosophy is self-disclosure through communication, even being itself, although it can be represented only in ciphers as symbols, is made transparent solely through authentic communication (*Existenzursprung*). Existential communication is neither friendship nor psychotherapy; it is not fusion, esteem, or unanimity; it is, strictly speaking, as with *Existenz* itself, ineffable.

But in the end, human existence is a failure. There is no escape from man's limits (the limit of death in particular), yet man is condemned to endless striving. In this dreadful paradox between finite existence and striving for infinity, man finds the ultimate symbol of his salvation, which is transcendence.

Metaphysics and theology. Jaspers maintains that just as ethical considerations grow out of philosophical psychology, so religious answers emerge from metaphysical descriptions of being.

He follows Kant in criticizing the usual arguments for the existence of God. He rejects theism, pantheism, revealed religion, and atheism alike. All these are but symbols (ciphers), and we are in danger of taking them literally. Phenomenological descriptions of the fringes of inward and outer experiences give us the only accurate understanding of the intuitions that metaphysics and theology have traditionally attempted to articulate.

When man reflects on his freedom, he experiences it as a gift; he dimly knows that he does not stand alone. That gift, in turn, points vaguely to an ultimate horizon as its source and foundation. Awareness of transcendence also originates in the consciousness of our finitude: through our boundaries we recognize the infinite possibilities within us. In general, the world itself points to a region beyond. Transcendence is thus experienced as the intimation of a power by virtue of which man himself exists. Confronted with these clues, man is free to pursue or to ignore them.

Jaspers uses the term "encompassing" (*das Umgreifende*) to designate the ultimate and indefinite limits of being as we experience it in all its fullness and richness, limits which surround, envelop, and suffuse all there is. It is the ultimate experienceable horizon. He uses the expression "being-as-such" to mean the encompassing or the totality of being as it is thought, conceived, or conceptualized, while he reserves the term "transcendence" to mean man's personal, devoted, and committed effort to reach the encompassing. In other words, the encompassing manifests itself in at least three modes: the total encompassing of the world, the encompassing that is the empirical world of ordinary and scientific experience, and the encompassing that is one's own self. Although we are at a loss to describe its essence, we can say of the encompassing that it is. In a sense, I and the world are identical with the encompassing. In it, the severance between subject and object disappears, since both are manifestations of the same encompassing. On similar grounds, the encompassing (and this then applies to Jasper's reinterpretation of God) can never be viewed as one object among many. It is all of being as well as all the differentiations within being. It is likewise beyond idealism, materialism, positivism, and naturalism, since all metaphysical positions are events within the encompassing but do not in any way delimit it. Therefore, in Jaspers' view, God, the unthinkable (*das Undenkbare*), becomes Rudolf Otto's "wholly other." I cannot grasp conceptually the encompassing that I am; similarly, the world is not exactly an illusion, since it is the only language through which the encompassing can reach me. The ultimate encompassing envelops both the I-pole and the object-pole of experience.

Man can search for transcendence by various means. He can explore the world, as science does. In that way he achieves a world view. Or he can search for it by examining the relation between himself and the world, as we find it in epistemology, ethics, and psychology. He thereby achieves illumination of *Existenz*. Finally, he can search for God, in which case he deals directly with the problem of penetrating being itself. But he must never succumb to the error of identifying the encompassing with a particular substance or substratum of the world.

The encompassing manifests itself through the "footsteps of God," through analogical predication, through symbols, or, in Jaspers' own words, through ciphers (*Chiffren*), a notion borrowed from Pascal. The encompassing is like the horizon that is the perennial goal of the sailor: it always shows itself and yet is forever inaccessible. The major purpose of metaphysics is the disclosure of the ciphers that manifest encompassing, but in the end, metaphysical elucidation of the ciphers is a highly personal undertaking. Ciphers may appear suddenly and spontaneously in the presence of empirical facts, for example, an overwhelming mountain. They may appear in art forms, in religious myths and dogma, and in theological disputations; they may become manifest in the symbolism of the history of philosophy and its metaphysical systems; and finally, they may appear through reflection on the mystery of being as well as on the death that awaits every man.

Jaspers' religious prescription is called philosophic faith (*philosophische Glaube*). It consists of the convictions that man is open to transcendence and consequently wills infinity; that there is in fact a transcendence to the ordinary world; that personal freedom is to be maintained and respected; that man, as he finds himself, is inadequate; that man can rely on help from transcendence; and that the world is grounded and supported. To reject faith means to hold that the immediate world is all there is, that man's destiny is fully determined, that man is perfectible and alone, and that the world is self-supporting. Although there are significant similarities between Jaspers' philosophical faith and that of traditional Christianity, he rigidly opposes the absolutism of the latter to the openness and toleration of his philosophic faith. The Bible, for example, is a highly suggestive instrument for his philosophic faith, especially through its ciphers of one God and its emphasis on love, on choosing between good and evil, on the eternal in man, on the ordered and yet contingent universe, and on the image of God as the refuge. Nevertheless, transcendence is discovered through doubt, not reassurance: there can be no rational justification for the final leap of faith, even for a philosopher.

Works by Jaspers

Allgemeine Psychopathologie. Berlin, 1913. Translated from the 7th German ed. by J. Hoenig and Marian W. Hamilton as *General Psychopathology*. Chicago, 1963.

Psychologie der Weltanschauungen. Berlin, 1919.

Die geistige Situation der Zeit. Berlin, 1932. Translated by Eden Paul and Cedar Paul as *Man in the Modern Age*. London, 1933.

Max Weber. Oldenburg, 1932.

Philosophie, 3 vols. Berlin, 1932.

Vernunft und Existenz. Groningen, 1935. Translated by William Earle as *Reason and Existenz*. New York, 1955.

Nietzsche. Berlin and Leipzig, 1936. Translated by C. F. Wallraff and F. J. Schmitz. Tucson, Ariz., 1965.

Descartes und die Philosophie. Berlin, 1937.

Existenzphilosophie. Berlin, 1938.

Die Idee der Universität. Berlin, 1946. Translated by H. A. T. Reiche as *The Idea of the University.* Boston, 1959.

Nietzsche und das Christentum. Hameln, 1946. Translated by E. B. Ashton as *Nietzsche and Christianity.* Chicago, 1961.

Die Schuldfrage, ein Beitrag zur deutschen Frage. Zurich, 1946. Translated by E. B. Ashton as *The Question of German Guilt.* New York, 1947.

Philosophische Logik, Vol. I, *Von der Wahrheit.* Munich, 1947. Partially translated by Jean T. Wilde, William Kluback, and William Kimmel as *Truth and Symbol.* New York, 1959.

Der philosophische Glaube. Zurich, 1948. Translated by Ralph Manheim as *The Perennial Scope of Philosophy.* New York, 1949.

Vom Ursprung und Ziel der Geschichte. Zurich, 1949. Translated by Michael Bullock as *The Origin and Goal of History.* New Haven, 1953.

Vernunft und Widervernunft in unserer Zeit. Munich, 1950. Translated by Stanley Fine-Godman as *Reason and Anti-reason in Our Time,* New Haven, 1952.

Einführung in die Philosophie. Zurich, 1950. Translated by Ralph Manheim as *The Way to Wisdom.* New Haven, 1951.

Rechenschaft und Ausblick. Munich, 1951.

Über das Tragische. Munich, 1952. Translated by H. A. T. Reiche and others as *Tragedy Is Not Enough.* Boston, 1952.

Die Frage der Entmythologisierung, written with Rudolf Bultmann. Munich, 1954. Translated as *Myth and Christianity.* New York, 1958.

Wesen und Kritik der Psychotherapie. Munich, 1955.

Über Bedingungen und Moglichkeiten eines neuen Humanismus. Munich, 1956.

Die Atombombe und die Zukunft des Menschen. Munich, 1957. Translated by E. B. Ashton as *The Future of Mankind.* Chicago, 1961.

Die grossen Philosophen. Munich, 1957. Translated by Ralph Manheim as *The Great Philosophers.* New York, 1962.

Plato, Augustin, Kant. Munich, 1957.

Philosophie und Welt. Munich, 1958.

Freiheit und Wiedervereinigung. Munich, 1960.

Wahrheit und Wissenschaft. Munich, 1960.

For essays on various aspects of Jaspers' thought by various philosophers, see P. A. Schilpp, ed., *The Philosophy of Karl Jaspers* (New York, 1957).

Peter Koestenbaum

JEANS, JAMES HOPWOOD (1877–1946), English physicist and astronomer was educated at Merchant Taylor's School and Trinity College, Cambridge, where he received high honors in mathematics in 1898. He taught mathematics at Cambridge as university lecturer from 1904 to 1905, at Princeton as professor of applied mathematics from 1905 to 1909, and again at Cambridge as Stokes lecturer from 1909 to 1912. In 1912 he resigned all regular offices to live on a private income and later also on the sale of several popular books. He was honorary secretary of the Royal Society, president of the British Association for the Advancement of Science, and professor of astronomy at the Royal Institution.

Jeans was a man of undoubted ability and originality and early won a deservedly high reputation, being elected a fellow of the Royal Society at the age of 28. His main contributions to science were in two fields: the kinetic theory of gases, in particular the equipartition of energy and radiation; and cosmogony, in particular the forms of equilibrium of rotating gravitational masses and the kinetic theories of aggregates of stars. The last constitute perhaps his best and most enduring work.

During the early 1930s Jeans wrote a number of highly successful books popularizing science, and these, together with *Physics and Philosophy* (1942), contain his philosophical writings. His popular expositions of scientific theories are marked by their simplicity of expression and by the striking and illuminating examples and analogies they contain.

Although Jeans contributed nothing substantial to philosophy, his views gained attention because of his eminence in the scientific field and because of their being presented together with expositions of abstruse scientific theories widely agreed to be of philosophical interest. Jeans's writings on philosophy were slight in quantity as well as in quality; even *Physics and Philosophy* contained only about 50 pages of his own views.

His position was never consistently developed and is therefore unclear. Indeed, he seems almost to have felt that it would be against the spirit of philosophy to argue with rigor, clarity, and decent caution. His work is certainly characterized by loose reasoning, and not infrequently by plainly false or confused premises. Broadly, however, his views were that science must connect observables with observables by means of chains of mathematical equations. He held that mathematical formalization is the prime part of physical knowledge and that interpretative models of this formalism are outdated and confusing crutches in coming to know about the world. This was not because Jeans believed that only propositions about observables have a meaning. He was no positivist, despite his claim to be one. On the ground that physical measurement reveals only relations between instruments (including one's eyes and ears) and reality, he believed in a Lockean substratum that is forever hidden from us. He also held that modern science suggests that there is some room for the operation of free will, but it is unclear why he adopted this opinion. His attitude to the common fallacy that the uncertainty relations of quantum physics establish the possibility of free will is quite ambiguous.

The most striking and most widely discussed of Jeans's conclusions is that reality, the Lockean substratum, is mental, not material. This conclusion reaches its most startling form in the final chapter of *The Mysterious Universe*, where Jeans argued that the universe consists of the thoughts of a Pure Mathematician, God.

Jeans asserted—it is hardly an argument—that the universe is shown to be rational by the very fact that a mathematical description of it is possible. He argued that as physics has progressed it has discarded models as an aid to explanation and discovery. Post-Galilean physics discarded the biological model of Aristotle, and modern physics has now discarded mechanical theories and models, being content to present its theories as pieces of mathematical formalism. Jeans put the matter this way: We cannot interpret the multidimensional configuration spaces of quantum physics as material space because material space has but three dimensions. Nor can we interpret the axioms of non-Euclidean geometry, especially the geometry of finite spaces, in terms of the congruences of material rods in material space. (This last claim is simply unwarranted.) Consequently, argued Jeans, the formalism of modern physical theory must be given a pure mathematical interpretation. (However, there is no sense in which we can speak of a pure mathematical *interpretation,* since "pure" here means "*un*interpreted.") Since the subject of pure mathematics is just thoughts, we may conclude, according to Jeans, that the stuff of the universe is mental. It is thought in the mind of God, the Pure Mathematician.

Works by Jeans

Eos; or Wider Aspects of Cosmogony. London, 1928.
The Universe Around Us. London, 1929.
The Mysterious Universe. London, 1930.
The Stars in Their Courses. London, 1931.
New Background of Science. London, 1933.
Through Space and Time. London, 1934.
Introduction to the Kinetic Theory of Gases. London, 1940.
Physics and Philosophy. London, 1942.

Works on Jeans

Milne, E. A., *Sir James Jeans: A Biography.* London, 1952.
Stebbing, Susan, *Philosophy and the Physicists.* London, 1937. Ably criticizes Jeans's views.

G. C. NERLICH

JEFFERSON, THOMAS (1743–1826), third president of the United States, political theorist, and representative of Enlightenment thought. Jefferson was born in Albemarle County, Virginia. He graduated from the college of William and Mary in 1762, studied law under George Wythe, and was admitted to the Virginia bar in 1767. After he entered the House of Burgesses in 1769, public affairs increasingly occupied his time, and he soon became a leading opponent of British oppression of the colonies. *A Summary View of the Rights of British America* (1774), *Declaration of the Causes and Necessity for Taking up Arms* (1775), and the Declaration of Independence (1776), all drafted by Jefferson, made him the major penman of the American Revolution. In 1776 he left the Continental Congress to lead in reforming the laws of Virginia, drafting, among other measures, the famous bill establishing religious freedom. He served as governor of Virginia from 1779 to 1781, retired for two years during his wife's fatal illness, returned to Congress, helped draft the Northwest Ordinance, and went to France, where, in 1785, he succeeded Benjamin Franklin as American minister. He delighted in French culture and conversed with Lafayette and other enlightened Frenchmen about limiting the despotism of the *ancien régime.* He returned to America a warm advocate of Franco-American friendship and in 1790 became secretary of state in Washington's first cabinet. With James Madison, he soon led the opposition against the party and plans of Alexander Hamilton and the spread of British influence in American councils. He resigned in 1793, but during three years of "retirement," he remained politically active—especially in denouncing Jay's treaty. Elected vice-president in 1797, he bitterly opposed the quasi war with France and the alien and sedition laws and wrote the Kentucky Resolutions affirming the right of states to declare void federal laws they deemed unconstitutional. His election as president in 1801 ended Federalist domination of the government. The restriction of the scope of the federal government, the purchase of Louisiana (1803), the failure of reconciliation efforts with Eng-

land (1807), and the Embargo (1808) marked his administrations. He retired to Monticello in 1809, devoting his remaining years to study, farming, a wide correspondence, and the founding of the University of Virginia.

Philosophical views. Jefferson stands with Franklin as the supreme embodiment of the Enlightenment in the United States. His "immortals" were Bacon, Newton, and Locke, each representing a major aspect of his philosophy. He accepted Bacon's empiricism and emphasis on the role of reason in improving society. From Newton he acquired his view that the universe was harmonious, governed by law, and amenable to human investigation. Locke enunciated the political implications of these viewpoints and was, for Jefferson, the pre-eminent philosophical guide. The empirical epistemology of *An Essay Concerning Human Understanding* and the insistence on government by consent in the second *Treatise on Civil Government* undergirded all his thought. Although he read and admired other philosophers of the Age of Reason, especially the French physiocrats, he remained firmly within the English tradition.

True to the Enlightenment, Jefferson was in many respects a universal man. Although not deeply interested in religion and frequently attacked as a freethinker and atheist (especially during the campaign of 1800), he accepted the conventional deism of his day. He admired Christian ethical doctrines enough to arrange them, taken from the Bible, in the volume he titled "Life and Morals of Jesus of Nazareth." Jefferson sought to apply reason and scientific insight to agriculture and plantation life in general; he invented an improved plow, a clock showing days of the week, and the numerous other useful gadgets which add to the fascination of his home, Monticello. He was an outstanding architect and an enthusiastic natural scientist, making especially important contributions to paleontology. In addition, he was a learned philologist, a distinguished bibliophile, a brilliant correspondent, a skilled violinist, and a connoisseur of the visual arts. He showed in his own life what man could do with the birthright of freedom proclaimed by Locke.

Social and political theory. Jefferson's most enduring fame is as the social philosopher of American democracy. If the people were to govern, he held, they had somehow to be rendered "good," lest self-rule prove a curse. Hence, Jefferson favored agriculture because its pursuit fostered self-reliance, diligence, common sense, and other necessary qualities of "governors"; he sought to abolish feudal laws and to promote the right of every man to acquire property and hence independence and responsibility. He made education a key part of his every proposal for government. The statement "that government is best which governs least" became his guide only after he thought existing social and political arrangements would assure an "aristocracy of virtue and talents" and after he came to fear the plutocratic use of power by Hamilton and others. He welcomed authority in governments, especially state and local ones; he accepted checks and balances, believed in the utility of bills of rights, and favored the power of legislatures more than did many of his colleagues. He saw freedom of press and religion as essential to democracy, and he believed it the national interest of the United States to encourage the spead of freedom around the world. Thus he resisted British hegemony in the Western world, encouraged the French Revolution, and supported the Monroe Doctrine. He was, in short, eager to find every device and policy that would prove mankind capable of governing itself in freedom and virtue.

Bibliography

For Jefferson's writings, see Julian P. Boyd, ed., *The Papers of Thomas Jefferson*, 16 vols. (Princeton, N.J., 1950——), and Paul L. Ford, ed., *The Writings of Thomas Jefferson*, 10 vols. (New York, 1892–1899). There are numerous good selected editions of his writings, including Adrienne Koch and William Peden, eds., *The Life and Selected Writings of Thomas Jefferson* (New York, 1944), and Albert Fried, ed., *The Essential Jefferson* (New York, 1963). The standard biography of Jefferson is Dumas Malone, *Jefferson and His Time*, 3 vols. (Boston, 1948–1962), covering thus far his career through 1801. Henry S. Randall, Marie Kimball, Gilbert Chinard, and Claude Bowers have also written useful biographies.

The best studies of Jefferson's thought are Adrienne Koch, *The Philosophy of Thomas Jefferson* (New York, 1943); Daniel J. Boorstin, *The Lost World of Thomas Jefferson* (New York, 1948); Merrill D. Peterson, *The Jefferson Image in the American Mind* (New York, 1960); and Stuart G. Brown, *Thomas Jefferson* (New York, 1963).

RALPH KETCHAM

JEVONS, WILLIAM STANLEY (1835–1882), British economist and logician, was the son of Thomas Jevons, a Liverpool iron merchant, and Mary Anne Roscoe, a lady of some literary note. After early schooling at Liverpool, he attended University College School and University College, London, where he sat under Augustus De Morgan. In 1854 he left London to take up the post of assayer at the mint in Sydney, Australia, but returned five years later to complete his studies. Soon after, in 1863, he secured a junior teaching position at Owens College, Manchester. By this time he had already published various minor papers on meteorology and economics, a statistical study of commercial fluctuations, and a small work, entitled *Pure Logic* (London, 1864, reprinted 1890), reflecting the influence of Boole. His book on *The Coal Question* (London, 1865) attracted the attention of Gladstone and was the first to make him known as an economist. In 1866 he was appointed professor of logic and political economy at Manchester, and in the following year married Harriet Taylor, daughter of the proprietor of the *Manchester Guardian*.

Jevons was a conscientious lecturer, but he neither enjoyed nor excelled at the work; and his laborious habits of study led to recurrent breakdowns of health, which had to be repaired by Continental travel, generally to Norway. In spite of this, he wrote prolifically, publishing *The Substitution of Similars* (London, 1869, reprinted 1890); *Elementary Lessons in Logic* (London, 1870), a widely used textbook introductory to Mill; and *The Principles of Science* (London, 1874; 2d ed., 1877), his most important contribution to scientific methodology, containing, among much else, an account of his celebrated logical machine. *The Theory of Political Economy* (London, 1871; 2d ed., 1879) was an equally important landmark in the development of mathematical economics and the theory of utility, followed soon after by a no less influential work of applied analysis and description, *Money and the Mechanism of*

Exchange (London, 1875). The once-famous speculations on the relation of sunspot cycles to financial crises, posthumously published in *Investigations in Currency and Finance* (London, 1884), exhibit, more curiously, the range of his interests and the originality of his mind.

Wearying of his duties, Jevons resigned his chair at Manchester in 1876 to take up a similar but more congenial post as professor of political economy at University College, London. This he also resigned, however, in 1880. The main works of this later period were *Studies and Exercises in Deductive Logic* (London, 1880) and *The State in Relation to Labour* (London, 1882). In 1882 he accidentally drowned, probably as the result of a heart attack, while bathing off the coast of Kent. His *Letters and Journal*, edited by his wife (London, 1886), gives an interesting portrait of him. His last work, *The Principles of Economics*, appeared, unfinished, in 1905.

Logic. Although marked by no special distinction of style, the writings of Jevons are still worth reading, both for their logical penetration and for their wealth of factual information drawn from many sources of knowledge. His logic (see LOGIC, HISTORY OF, section on Jevons) owes something to De Morgan and a good deal more to George Boole. It represents in the main an attempt to simplify Boole's system by eliminating the more complex and uninterpretable of its mathematical operations and by reducing its procedures of calculation to a mechanical routine. Jevons' own claim to independence in developing his logic as a calculus of qualities, rather than of classes or propositions, is of no great significance; and his method of treating propositions as identities and inferring from them by substitution, though simple enough in its way, is too lacking in subtlety to have become the "logic of the future" that he once hoped it would be. The most successful of his reforms of the Boolean algebra have been the removal of its inverse operations of subtraction and division and the proposal to read the disjunctive symbol ("either . . . or") as including the possibility "both"—a practice now universal and resisted at the time only by the conservative John Venn.

Jevons' most interesting adaptation of Boole is to be seen in his method of indirect inference—the principle underlying his "logical piano" and other mechanical aids to calculation—whereby premises are used to eliminate inconsistent combinations of terms from a matrix listing all the possibilities under which a given set of terms and their negatives can be associated. The machine itself, exhibited at the Royal Society in 1870 and described in the *Philosophical Transactions* for the same year, anticipates in its design a number of the features of modern logical computers, while its mode of operation has some fairly obvious affinities with the use of a truth table, though it can hardly be said that Jevons had much grasp of its applications in that respect.

Induction. The logical machine gave its answers only by displaying the combinations compatible with the information fed to it, leaving to the operator the task of finding a compendious formula to express them. The difficulties of this "inverse process" resist mechanical solution and are comparable, in Jevons' view, to those of induction, which he represents accordingly as the inverse operation of deduction—the problem, that is, of deciphering from a given set of phenomena the hidden laws they obey. The treatment of this problem in *The Principles of Science* is in line with the work of William Whewell and De Morgan and in somewhat embittered opposition to the views of Bacon and Mill. Jevons, in short, is an apostle of the hypothetico-deductive method in science, although, unlike Whewell at least, he does not believe it to be a demonstrative procedure or capable of extending knowledge beyond the range of present or past observation. We are necessarily ignorant of the long-term behavior of the universe at large, and when to this ignorance are added the inevitable deficiencies of observation and measurement, it is evident that inductive conclusions can never be more than probable.

Probability. Jevons was led by the above considerations to give detailed attention to the theories of measurement, approximation, and error and also to bring the whole conception of inductive inference into closer association with the theory of probabilities than was usual with the writers who preceded him. Probability he holds, with De Morgan, to be essentially subjective, though it is a measure of appropriate, rather than of mere actual, belief. It determines "rational expectation, by measuring the comparative amounts of knowledge and ignorance," as represented by the evidence available. That evidence, as nature presents it in the inductive situation, consists of sets of phenomena in combination. Having previously ascertained them (and presumably selected them, somehow, for relevance), we proceed, by more or less intuitive methods (of which Jevons gives no satisfactory account), to erect a hypothesis to explain them. From this in turn we deduce the direct probability of various sets of possible consequences. We then compare these supposed consequences with the known facts in order to determine the probability of their having occurred under the hypothesis in question. This process being repeated for every conceivable hypothesis, we are thereby in a position to assign a probability to each of them by use of the inversion theorem derived, via De Morgan, from Laplace. There is no guarantee that by this method the right answers will be forthcoming; but it justifies the adoption of the most probable hypothesis as a matter of practical policy, and that is the best we can expect.

The mathematical theory of inverse probability is, unfortunately, not equal to the weight that Jevons here put upon it, and his conclusions are accordingly unsound. There is no means of knowing that the a priori probabilities of the rival hypotheses are equal, as the theory requires; and there is still less warrant for its extension, by the "rule of succession," to the prediction of new instances or for the employment, where ignorance is total, of the "principle of indifference" to confer a probability of 1/2 on a proposition merely because knowledge of its truth or falsity is the same (namely, nil) in either case. The fallacies that Jevons committed under this head have since become notorious; the measurement of ignorance is less simple—and nature less like a ballot box—than he was apt to suppose. Errors of conception apart, however, his general view of scientific method has in recent years met with increasing support and is probably his most enduring legacy to the history of thought.

Bibliography

Jevons had no commentators. For a discussion of his logic, see references in bibliography to LOGIC, HISTORY OF. There is an early criticism of his theory of induction in Thomas Fowler, *Elements of Inductive Logic*, 3d ed. (London, 1876), and scattered remarks of value occur in such general treatises as J. M. Keynes, *A Treatise of Probability* (London, 1921); William Kneale, *Probability and Induction* (Oxford, 1949); and G. H. von Wright, *The Logical Problem of Induction*, 2d ed. (Oxford, 1949), and *A Treatise on Induction and Probability* (London, 1951). See also the brief sketch in J. A. Passmore, *A Hundred Years of Philosophy* (London, 1957), pp. 132–136.

P. L. HEATH

JEWISH PHILOSOPHY. The works constituting the Old Testament touch upon various problems that are discussed in philosophical texts, and the literary forms of some of these works, for instance that of the dialogue in the book of Job and that of Ecclesiastes, bear some similarity to those found in certain philosophical writings. However, a conception of philosophy that included Biblical wisdom would lose in clarity and definiteness of outline what it would gain in comprehensiveness. Accordingly, there seems to be a certain amount of justification for considering, as is often done, that the history of Jewish philosophy commences in Alexandria around the beginning of the Christian Era, when the first noteworthy attempt was made to use Greek philosophical concepts and methods to come to terms with facts that in the philosophical view are most peculiar, namely, Jewish history as interpreted in religious tradition and Biblical revelation.

HELLENISTIC PERIOD

Philo. The attempt to apply Greek philosophical concepts to Jewish doctrines was made by Philo Judaeus (fl. 20 B.C.–40 C.E.), a prominent member of the Jewish community of Alexandria—he was part of a delegation sent by this community in the year 39/40, when he was in his own view an old man, to the Roman Emperor Caligula to complain of persecution. Philo, a scholar who combined Greek and Jewish learning, was a most elusive thinker. The immense difficulties that beset any inquiry into Philo's basic conception of the world spring from a variety of sources. Some of the difficulties result from our ignorance of the Greek philosophical authors belonging to Philo's time, for we have only secondhand knowledge of them. Also insufficient is our information about post-Biblical Jewish beliefs and speculations, which may be supposed to have shaped Philo's outlook—at least in part and perhaps decisively. However, Philo seems to have had some acquaintance with the oral law, which was being evolved in his time, mainly by the Pharisees in Palestine, and which much later was set down in writing in the Mishnah and in other works belonging to the Talmudic literature. He also knew of the Essenes, whom he praised highly. Some of the sect's theological doctrines, its ethical lore, and its pseudepigraphic literature may have been adapted by Philo to his own purposes.

In a sense Philo's main life's work was hermeneutic. On the one hand, he provided Jewish conceptions with the hallmark of intellectual (or cultural) respectability by stating them in Greek philosophical terms; on the other, he showed that from the point of view of Judaism many Greek notions were unexceptionable—they could be regarded as consonant with Philo's own Jewish doctrine and with the allegorical sense of Biblical texts. The homiletic character of most of his writings gave him full scope for his labor of interpretation. He had two schemes of reference—Jewish religious tradition and Greek philosophy—and the fact that he took care to stress the primacy of the former may have been more than mere lip service. In many of Philo's religious speculations the Jewish tradition in the particular form he adopted was not interpreted and explained away—as it was by most of the medieval Aristotelians—as being a mere rehash of philosophical doctrines in a language suited to the limited intellectual capacity of most people. It may be argued with a certain amount of plausibility that in central points of his thought, such as his conception of the Logos, Philo used philosophical notions as trappings for an originally nonphilosophical belief.

A main function of the Logos as conceived by Philo is to serve as an intermediary between the transcendent, unknowable God and the world, a view that probably has a close connection with the view of his Jewish contemporaries concerning the Word (Logos) of God, by means of which he accomplishes his designs. It is significant that the Logos of God is said by Philo to be the place occupied by the world of Ideas: this world is also called by Philo the intelligible world (*kosmos noetos*). The conception of Idea intended here is clearly the Platonic one, conceived of as having been "thought out" by God. The expression used by Philo may indicate that in his time Platonistic philosophers already tended, as the Middle Platonists and the Neoplatonists later did—to place Ideas in the mind of God.

Above philosophical and theological speculations Philo placed mystic ecstasy, of which he may have had a personal experience, "when, . . . as at noon-tide God shines around the soul, and the light of the mind fills it through and through and the shadows are driven from it by the rays which pour all around it" ("On Abraham," in *Philo*, 10 vols., translated by F. H. Colson and G. H. Whitaker, Cambridge, Mass., and London, 1929–1937; Vol. VI, p. 63).

Philo's approach, his method of interpretation, and his way of thinking, as well as some of his conceptions, primarily that of the *Logos*, exerted a considerable influence on early Christian thought, but not to any comparable extent upon Jewish thought. Later, in the Middle Ages, knowledge of Philo among Jews was either very slight or, in the majority of cases, nonexistent.

Talmudic literature. Most Hellenized Jews were no doubt absorbed into the Christian communities. On the other hand, such historical catastrophes as the destruction of the Temple and the crushing of the various Jewish insurrections by the Romans may have brought about a spiritual withdrawal of the Jews from the circumambient Greco-Roman civilization, a stressing of their separateness. Moreover, as a result of these disasters the spiritual center of Jewry shifted to Iraq, a country that was part of the Persian Empire and less permeated by Greek culture than the regions belonging to the Imperium Romanum.

Some traces of a knowledge of popular, mainly Stoic, philosophy may be found in the Mishnah, a codification of the oral law composed in Palestine in the second century of the Christian Era, and in the subsequent Talmudic literature set down in writing in Palestine and Iraq. On the whole, these traces are rather slight. Nevertheless, some scholars believe that the influence of Greek philosophy on Palestinian Jewry was far-reaching, but the case, to say the least, is not proven.

Jewish theological and cosmological speculations occur in the Midrashim, which, under the guise of interpreting Biblical verses, propound allegorical interpretations, legends, and myths, and in the *Book of Creation* (*Sefer ha-Yeṣīra*), a work attributed to Abraham, which is a combination of a cosmogony and a grammar. There is no clear evidence of the period in which it was written; both the third century and the sixth or seventh century have been suggested.

MIDDLE AGES

Medieval literature. Hayuye (usually called Hivi) al-Balkhī, who appears to have lived in the ninth century in Muslim central Asia, seems to have been a Jewish representative of a brand of free thought also known in Islam, one that under dualistic influence criticized the God of the Bible, who, in view of the prevalence of evil and the fact of his omnipotence, cannot be just. Al-Balkhī seems to have favored Manichaeism—which at that time had a number of adepts—or at least to have been suspected of this heresy; this inference can be made from a preserved fragment of a polemical work directed against him by Saadia in the tenth century. According to Saadia, "the Lord" of al-Balkhī is being eaten, drunk, burnt, and commingled (v. 54 of *Sa'adia Refutatum*), a description that fits the primeval man of Manichaean mythology and the elements belonging to him.

In the ninth and tenth centuries, after a very long hiatus, systematic philosophy and ideology reappeared among Jews, a phenomenon indicative of their accession to Islamic civilization. There is undoubtedly a correlation between this rebirth of philosophy and theology and the social trends of that period, which produced Jewish financiers—some of whom were patrons of learning and who in fact, although perhaps not in theory, were members of the ruling class of the Islamic state—and Jewish physicians who associated on equal terms with Muslim and Christian intellectuals. The evolution of Islam in the ninth and tenth centuries showed that Greek scientific and philosophic lore could be separated at least to some extent from its pagan associations, could be transposed into another language and another culture; it also tended to show—and many Jewish thinkers learned the lesson—that a culture of which the sciences and philosophy and/or theology were an indispensable part could be based upon a monotheistic, prophetic religion that in all relevant essentials was closely akin to Judaism. The question whether philosophy is compatible with religious law (the answer being sometimes negative) constituted the main theme of the foremost medieval Jewish thinkers.

Approximately from the ninth to the thirteenth centuries, Jewish philosophical and theological thought participated in the evolution of Islamic philosophy and theology and manifested only in a limited sense a continuity of its own. Jewish philosophers showed no particular preference for philosophic texts written by Jewish authors over those composed by Muslims, and in many cases the significant works of Jewish thinkers constitute a reply or a reaction to the ideas of non-Jewish predecessors. Arabic was the main language of Jewish philosophic and scientific writings.

There was little regular teaching of philosophy in the religious universities of Islam (though some taught a brand of Kalām approved by the government) and none in the Jewish schools. Many Jewish philosophers seem to have earned their living or a part of it by practicing medicine, a fact which sometimes influenced their thought. A certain number (among them some physicians) were teachers of and authorities in religious law and active in community matters.

Iraq, a very important center of Jewish thought in the ninth and tenth centuries, counted several Jews among its intellectuals steeped in Greek philosophy. However, by far the most productive and influential Jewish thinkers of this period represented a very different tendency, that of the Mu'tazilite Kalām. Kalām (literally, "speech") is an Arabic term used both in Islamic and in Jewish vocabulary to designate several theological schools that were ostensibly opposed to Greek, particularly to Aristotelian, philosophy; the Aristotelians, both Islamic and Jewish, regarded Kalām theologians (called the Mutukallimūn) with a certain contempt, holding them to be mere apologists, watchdogs of religion, and indifferent to truth. Herein they did not do justice to their adversaries.

Saadia. The Mu'tazilite school formed in the eighth century appears to have had, at certain periods, representatives actuated by a genuine theoretical impulse. Its theology, forged in disputes with the Zoroastrians, the Manichaeans, and the Christians, claimed to be based on reason. This belief in reason, as well as most of the tenets of Mu'tazilite theology, were taken over by Saadia ben Joseph (882–942). He prepared an Arabic translation of the books of the Bible provided with commentaries and composed a number of legal and polemical treatises.

Saadia's main theological work, whose Arabic title, *Kitāb al-Amānāt wa'l'i tiqādāt,* may be translated "The Book of Beliefs and Creeds," is modeled to a considerable extent on similar Mu'tazilite treatises and on a Mu'tazilite classification of theological subject matter known as the "Five Principles." Like many Mu'tazilite authors, Saadia starts out by setting forth in his introduction a list and theory of the various sources of knowledge. It may be noted that in beginning systematic theological treatises in this way the Jewish and Islamic adherents of Kalām approximated not Greek philosophical practice but the custom of Indian philosophical writings, which also normally begin by propounding a doctrine of the sources of knowledge (*pramānāh*). The Organon and the expositions of logical disciplines stemming from it that in the Corpus Aristotelicum and in the treatises of the medieval Aristotelians precede the disquisitions on the natural sciences and metaphysics are very different from these analyses of the sources of knowledge.

Knowledge. Saadia distinguished four sources of knowledge: (1) The five senses, (2) the intellect, or reason, (3) necessary inferences, and (4) reliable information given by trustworthy persons. Concerning the first source, he was aware of the doubts expressed by skeptics about the truth of the sense data but rejected these doubts. He held that as a rule a healthy man, one without disabilities, may trust his senses. Exceptional cases do not carry the weight attributed to them by the Skeptics. In Saadia's sense of the word, intellect or reason (*al-'aql*) means first and foremost an immediate a priori cognition. In "The Book of Beliefs and Creeds" the intellect is characterized as having immediate ethical cognitions, that is, as discerning what is good and what is evil. However, in his commentary on the book of Proverbs, Saadia also attributes to it the cognition of simple mathematical truths. The third source of knowledge concerns inferences that, if we may judge by the examples given by Saadia, are of the type "if there is smoke, there is fire." These inferences are based on data furnished by the first two sources of knowledge. The fourth source of knowledge is meant to validate the teachings of Scripture and of the religious tradition. Teachings of Scripture must be held to be true because of the trustworthiness of the men who propounded them. One of the main purposes of the work is to show that the knowledge deriving from the fourth source concords with that discovered by means of the other three, or, in other words, that religion and human reason agree.

Saadia's "intellect," postulated as the second source of knowledge, has a function quite different from that of the intellect of the medieval Aristotelians, who did not regard even the most general ethical rules as being a priori cognitions. According to them these rules are accepted as true in virtue of a universal consensus; because of this, validity, unlike that of a priori intellectual truths, can be questioned.

In discussing the third source of knowledge, Saadia does not refer to the Aristotelian theory of the syllogism, but this may be because of ignorance; such knowledge of Greek thought as he possessed was derived mainly from compendiums of doxographers translated into Arabic or adapted by Arabic authors. However, unlike the Mu'tazilites and the Karaites, who were atomists, Saadia adopted a number of doctrines resembling Aristotle's physical views. Nevertheless, he had no use for the conception of an eternal order of nature. This position does not necessarily deny all validity to the theory of genera and species, which is a main concern of the Aristotelian syllogistic, but it certainly tends to limit, or in some cases to negate, the relevance of this theory to the actually existing world.

Theology. Saadia did not merely deny the eternity of the world but held, in common with other, less eclectic partisans of the Mu'tazilite Kalām that the demonstration of the temporal creation of the world must precede and pave the way for the proof of the existence of God the Creator. Of the four arguments which he brought forward in favor of temporal creation, the last is the most noteworthy: Creation in time is an inference from the impossibility of supposing that the past (the whole of time which has elapsed up to the present moment) is of infinite duration— for its infinitude would preclude its coming to an end; the present would never arrive.

Given the demonstrated truth that the world has a beginning in time, it can be proved that it could have been produced only through the action of a Creator. It can further be proved that there can have been only one Creator. God's unity means that he is not a body. It also means, according to a conception taken over from the Mu'tazilites, that he has no attributes superadded to his essence. This applies also to the three attributes that Saadia singled out, perhaps rather inconsistently, as belonging to the Creator: he must be held to be living, possessed of power, and possessed of knowledge.

Justice and free will. The theology of Saadia, like that of the Mu'tazilites, hinges on two principles, of which the unity of God is one; the other is the principle of justice, whose formulation in Islam may have been influenced by attacks of dualists similar to those of Hayuye al-Balkhī (see above), who contended that in view of the existence of evil, an omnipotent God cannot be regarded as just.

This principle takes issue with the view (widespread in Islam and present also in Judaism) that the definition of what is just and what is good depends solely on God's will, to which none of the moral criteria found among men is applicable; according to this view a revelation from God can convert an action now generally recognized as evil into a good action. Against this way of thinking, Saadia and the Mu'tazilites believed that being good and just or evil and unjust are intrinsic characteristics of human actions and cannot be changed by divine decree. The notions of justice and of the good as conceived by man are binding on God himself. In the words of a later thinker, Leibniz, he can act only *sub specie boni*. Since, according to Saadia, man has a priori knowledge of good and evil, just and unjust, the fact that human ethical judgments are valid for God means that man's ethical cognitions are also those of the Deity.

This point of view cannot be accorded with strict determinism if one believes, as Saadia professed to do, that men are rewarded for good and punished for evil deeds. It would be contrary to divine justice to condemn or to recompense them for something they cannot help doing; hence, man must be a free agent. For sharing this doctrine with Saadia, the Mu'tazilites were accused of being the dualists of Islam; because of it, they could not regard God as the sole Doer. In Judaism the doctrine of man's free will and free action had very respectable antecedents, and Saadia's position on this point does not seem to have aroused antagonism.

Saadia's simple solution to the problem of reconciling free will with divine prescience seems to be in accord with traditional religious formulas. God has foreknowledge of all the actions that men will perform in the future, but this knowledge does not interfere with human freedom, which enables men to do whatever they wish, both good and evil.

Religious law. The function of religious law is to impose on man the accomplishment of good actions and to prohibit bad ones. Because Saadia believed that man has a priori knowledge of good and evil and that this knowledge coincides with the principles underlying the most important portions of the revealed law, he was forced to ask the question whether this law is not supererogatory. He could, however, point out that whereas the human intellect recognizes that certain actions—for instance, murder or theft—are evil, it cannot by itself discover the best possible definition of what constitutes a particular transgression; nor can it, if it has no other guidance than its own reflections, determine the punishment appropriate for a transgression. On both points the commandments of religious law give the best possible answers.

The commandments of religious law that accord with the behests of the human intellect were designated by Saadia as the "intellectual," or "rational," commandments, According to him they include the duty of manifesting gratitude to the Creator for the benefits he has bestowed upon man. Saadia recognized that a considerable number of commandments, for instance those dealing with the prohibition of work on the Sabbath, do not belong to this category. He held, however, that the obligation to obey them may be derived from the "rational" commandment that makes it incumbent upon man to be grateful to God, for such gratitude entails obedience to his orders.

The Karaites. Saadia's adoption of the "rational" Mu'tazilite theology was a part of his over-all activity, directed toward the consolidation of rabbinical Judaism, which was being attacked by the Karaites. This Jewish sect, which was founded by Anan ben David in the eighth century and which seems to have had some connection or some affinity with earlier Jewish sects of the period of the Second Temple, rejected the authority of the oral Law, that is, of the Mishnah and the Talmud. In the tenth century and after, the Karaites accepted as their guides the Bible and human reason in the Mu'tazilite sense of the word. Their professed freedom from any involvement with post-Biblical Jewish religious tradition obviously facilitated a "rational" approach to theological doctrine. This approach led the Karaite authors to criticize their opponents, the rabbinical Jews, for holding anthropomorphic beliefs based, in part at least, on texts of the Talmudic period. In formulating his theology Saadia had in mind the need to disprove this enlightened criticism.

The Karaites themselves adopted wholesale Mu'tazilite Kalām, including its atomism. The atomism of the Karaite theologians has only a very slight similarity to what is known of the theories of Democritus and Epicurus, although Epicurus' hypothesis concerning *minima*, about which we are ill informed, does bear some resemblance to an important point in Islamic and Jewish doctrines. These doctrines appear to have a certain similarity to a Greek mathematical atomism, about which we possess very scanty information. It may derive from the theories of the Pythagoreans and of Xenocrates. Furthermore—and it is a significant point—Mu'tazilite and Karaite atomism in important points are reminiscent of Indian atomistic theories, those of Buddhism and that of the Nyāya–Vaiśeṣika; a historical connection is not wholly impossible.

The Mu'tazilite atomists, followed by the Karaites, held that everything that exists consists of discrete parts. This applies not only to bodies but also to space, to time, to motion, and to the "accidents"—that is, qualities—which the Islamic and Jewish atomists regarded as being joined to the corporeal atoms (but not determined by them, as had been believed by the Greek atomists). An instant of time or a unit of motion does not continue the preceding instant or unit. All apparent processes are discontinuous, and there is no causal connection between their successive units of change. The fact that cotton put into fire generally burns does not mean that fire is a cause of burning; rather, it may be explained as a "habit," signifying that this sequence of what is often wrongly held to be cause and effect has no character of necessity. God's free will, which is not bound by the nonexistent laws of nature, is the only agent of everything that occurs, with the exception of one category. Man's actions are causes that produce effects—for instance, a man who throws a stone at another man, who is then killed, directly brings about the latter's death. This inconsistency on the part of the theologians was necessitated by the principle of justice, for it would be unjust to punish a man for a murder that was a result not of his action but of God's. This grudging admission that causality exists in certain strictly defined and circumscribed cases was occasioned by moral, not physical, considerations. It may be added that because of the opposition it aroused, the Kalām's denial of the existence of a necessary succession of events seems to have strengthened the conviction of the Muslim and Jewish Aristotelians that such order exists and that it is immutable.

Israeli. Outside Iraq, philosophical studies were pursued by Jews in the ninth and tenth centuries in Egypt and in the Maghreb. Here the outstanding figure is Isaac ben Solomon Israeli, who died in the beginning of the second half of the tenth century—when he was over a hundred years old, if we are to believe his biographers.

Israeli, a famed physician, was the propagator of a type of philosophy that did not satisfy the exigencies of the strict Aristotelians of a later period; Maimonides denied his being a philosopher, saying that "he was only a physician."

In his philosophical works, such as the "Book of Elements" and the "Book of Five Substances," he drew largely upon the Muslim popularizer of Greek philosophy Abū Yūsuf Yaʿqūb al-Kindī and also in all probability upon a lost pseudo-Aristotelian text. The peculiar form of Neoplatonic doctrine that seems to have been set forth in this text had, directly and indirectly, a considerable influence on medieval Jewish philosophy.

According to Israeli, God creates through his will and power. This reference to two aspects of the Deity has been compared to certain passages in Plotinus and in Arabic texts that in a considerable measure derive from Plotinus. It may be noted in addition that power and will are singled out for mention as attributes of God in some Christian texts (see, for instance, Ignatius' *Epistle to the Smyrnaeans*, in Kirsopp Lake, ed., *The Apostolic Fathers*, Vol. I, London, 1959, p. 253, and "Isaac ex Judaeo, *Liber Fidei*, in J. P. Migne, ed., *Patrologia Graeca*, Paris, 1857–1866, Vol. XXXIII, Col. 1543). The two things that were created first are form, identified with wisdom, and matter, which is designated as the genus of genera and which is the substratum of everything, not only of bodies, as was the opinion of the Aristotelians, but also of incorporeal substances. This conception of matter seems to derive from the Greek Neoplatonists Plotinus and Proclus, particularly from the latter. In Proclus' opinion, generality was one of the main criteria for determining the ontological priority of an entity. Matter, because of its indeterminacy, obviously has a

high degree of generality; consequently, it figures among the entities having ontological priority. According to the Neoplatonic view, which Israeli seems to have adopted, the conjunction of matter and form gives rise to the intellect. A light sent forth from the intellect produces the rational soul. The animal soul is an emanation of the rational soul, and in its turn it gives rise to the vegetative soul.

As far as Jewish philosophy is concerned, Israeli's doctrine of prophecy seems to be the earliest theory attributing prophecy to the influence of the intellect on the imaginative faculty. According to Israeli this faculty receives from the intellect spiritual forms that are intermediate between corporeality and spirituality. This explanation implies that these forms "with which the prophets armed themselves" are inferior to purely intellectual cognitions.

Ibn-Gabirol. In essentials the schema of creation and emanation propounded by Isaac Israeli and his Neoplatonic source or sources was taken over by Solomon ibn-Gabirol, a celebrated Hebrew poet of the eleventh century, who seems to have been the earliest Jewish philosopher of Spain.

Ibn-Gabirol's chief philosophical work, "The Source of Life" (or *The Fountain of Life*), written in Arabic, has been preserved in full only in a twelfth-century Latin translation entitled *Fons Vitae*.

Fons Vitae makes no reference to Judaism or to specifically Jewish doctrines; it is a nonironical dialogue between a disciple and the master who teaches him true philosophical knowledge. In the Middle Ages it was criticized with some reason for its prolixity; it is also full of contradictions. Nevertheless, it is a strangely impressive work. Few medieval texts so effectively communicate the Neoplatonic conception of the existence of a number of planes of being that differ according to their ontological priority, the derivative and inferior ones constituting a reflection in a grosser mode of existence of those which are prior and superior.

A central conception in ibn-Gabirol's philosophy is concerned with the divine will, which appears to be both part of and separate from the divine essence. Infinite according to its essence, the will is finite in its action. It is described as pervading everything that exists and as being the intermediary between the divine essence and matter and form. Will was one of a number of traditional appellations applied in various, mainly negative, theologies to the entity intermediate between the transcendent Deity and the world or, according to another, not necessarily incompatible interpretation, to the aspect of the Deity involved in creation. According to a statement in *Fons Vitae*, matter derives from the divine essence, whereas form derives from the divine will. This suggests that the difference between matter and form has some counterpart in the godhead and also that universal matter is superior to universal form. Some of ibn-Gabirol's statements seem to bear out the latter impression; other passages, however, appear to imply a superiority of universal form. The apparent contradiction seems to result from two conflicting approaches: the Aristotelian, which assumes that form (which is held to be *in actu*) is superior to matter (which per se exists only potentially), and the Neoplatonic, which in at least one of its manifestations consistently professed the superiority of matter, which, being indeterminate, could be held to be of a more universal, all-encompassing nature than form.

Form and matter, whether they be universal or particular, exist only in conjunction. All things, with the sole exception of God, are constituted through the union of the two; the intellect no less than the corporeal substance. In fact, the intellect is the first being in which universal matter and form are conjoined. In other words, ibn-Gabirol considered—in accord with Israeli—that the intellect is not one simple substance, as was thought by the faithful disciples of Aristotle; in his view its unity proceeds from a duality. The intellect contains and encompasses all things. It is through the grasp of the various planes of being, through ascending in knowledge to the world of the intellect and cognizing what is above it—the divine will and the world of the Deity—that man may "escape death" and reach "the source of life."

In the twelfth century ibn-Gabirol's system seems to have enjoyed a certain vogue among Jewish intellectuals living in Spain. Thus, Joseph ibn-Zaddik (d. 1149) and Moses ibn-Ezra (c. 1092–1167) were at least to some extent disciples of his. Ibn-Zaddik was the author of the *Microcosm,* a work written in Arabic but extant only in a Hebrew translation, which draws a parallel between man and the microcosm (see IBN-ZADDIK, JOSEPH). However, Abraham ibn-Da'ud (see below) criticized ibn-Gabirol at length, denouncing the feebleness of his argumentation and the incorrect (that is, non-Aristotelian) conception of matter.

Halevi. Judah Halevi (c. 1075–1141), also of Spain, who, like ibn-Gabirol, was a Hebrew poet, has the distinction of being the earliest and the most outstanding medieval Jewish thinker whose theology or philosophy (he would have repudiated the latter term) does not merely take Judaism in its stride, as was largely true of Saadia and the Karaites, to mention only two, but is consciously and consistently based upon arguments drawn from Jewish history.

His views are set forth in an Arabic dialogue whose full title is translated as "The Book of Proof and Demonstration in Aid of the Despised Religion." According to a custom which finds some justification in one of Halevi's letters, this work is usually referred to as the "Kuzari," the Hebrew name of the king of the Khazars who is one of the two protagonists of the dialogue.

Basing his narrative on the historical fact that the Khazars were converted to Judaism, Halevi relates that their king, a pious man who did not belong to any of the great monotheistic religions, dreamed of an angel who said to him, "Your intentions are pleasing to the Creator, but your works are not." To find the correct way of pleasing God, the king seeks the guidance of a philosopher, of a Christian, of a Muslim, and, finally, after hesitating to have recourse to a representative of a people degraded by its historical misfortune, of a Jewish scholar, who converts him to Judaism.

The words of the angel heard in a dream may, in accordance with both religious and philosophical doctrine, be regarded as an (inferior) species of revelation. The use of this element of the story enabled Halevi to suggest that it is not the spontaneous activity of human reason that impels man to undertake the quest for the true religion; for this one needs the gift of prophecy, or at least a touch of the prophetic faculty (or a knowledge of the revelations of the past).

The argument of the philosopher whose advice is sought by the king brings this point home. This disquisition is a brilliant piece of writing, for it lays bare the essential differences—which the medieval philosophers often endeavored to dissimulate by means of circumlocution and double talk—between the Aristotelian God, who is totally ignorant of and consequently wholly indifferent to human individuals, and the God of religion.

Within the framework of philosophical doctrine, the angel's words are quite meaningless. Not only is the God of the philosophers, who is a pure intellect, not concerned with man's works, but the (cultural) activities, involving both mind and body, to which the angel clearly referred, cannot from the philosophical point of view either help or hinder man in the pursuance of the philosophers' supreme goal, the attainment of union with the Active Intellect. This union was supposed to confer knowledge of all the intelligibles. Thus, man's supreme goal was supposed to be of a purely intellectual nature.

In opposition to the philosopher's faith, the religion of Halevi's Jewish scholar is based upon the fact that God may have a close, direct relationship with man, who is not conceived primarily as a being endowed with intellect. The postulate that God can have intercourse with a creature made of the disgusting materials that go into the composition of the human body is scandalous to the king and prevents his acceptance of the doctrine concerning prophecy expounded by the Muslim sage (just as the extraordinary nature of the Christological dogmas deters him from adopting Christianity). It may be noted that the opposition on this point between the king and the philosopher on the one hand and the Jew and the Muslim on the other reflects one of the main points of controversy between pagan authors and the Church Fathers (and some Gnostics in the first centuries of the Christian Era). The moot point is whether a superior kind of man or, as many pagans believed, the souls or spirits ruling the heavenly bodies are the proper intermediaries between God, mankind, and the teachers of the arts and sciences. An echo of this controversy is found in Arabic literature, and Halevi, in developing his point of view, had probably adapted to some extent an older, non-Jewish source, at the same time making extensive use of Jewish religious tradition.

His position is that it is contemplation not of the cosmos but of Jewish history that procures knowledge of God. Halevi was aware of the odium attaching to the doctrine of the superiority of one particular nation; he held, however, that only this doctrine explains God's dealing with mankind, which like many other things, reason is unable to grasp. The controversies of the philosophers serve as proof of the failure of human intelligence to find valid solutions to the most important problems. Halevi's description of the specific Jewish position has also exercised a certain fascination upon several modern Jewish philosophers, such as Franz Rosenzweig.

Halevi's contemporaries. As a speculative author Halevi was by no means an isolated phenomenon. During the period comprising the second half of the eleventh century and the first half of the twelfth century a number of Jewish thinkers appeared in Spain.

Bahya. In this period Bahya ibn-Paquda (second half of the eleventh century) wrote one of the most popular books of Jewish "spiritual" literature, the "Commandments of the Heart," which combines a theology influenced by although not identical with that of Saadia with a moderate mysticism inspired by the teachings of the Muslim Sufis. The commandments of the heart—that is, those relating to men's thoughts and sentiments—are contrasted with the commandments of the limbs—that is, the Mosaic commandments enjoining or prohibiting certain actions. Bahya maintained that both sets of commandments should be observed, thus rejecting the antinomistic position. However, he made clear that first and foremost he was interested in the commandments of the heart.

Bar Hiyya. Abraham bar Hiyya (first half of the twelfth century), an outstanding mathematician, an astrologer, and a philosopher, outlined in *Megillat ha-Megalleh* a view of Jewish history which in some particulars is rather reminiscent of that of Judah Halevi but which does not emphasize to the same degree the uniqueness of that history and is set forth in much less impressive fashion. Living in Barcelona under Christian rule, bar Hiyya wrote his scientific and philosophical treatises not in Arabic but in Hebrew.

Ibn-Ezra. Hebrew was also used by Abraham ibn-Ezra (died c. 1167), a native of Spain, who traveled extensively in Christian Europe. His commentaries on the Bible contributed to the diffusion among the Jews of Greek philosophical thought, to which ibn-Ezra made many, although as a rule disjointed, references.

Abu'l-Barakāt al-Baghdādī. The last outstanding Jewish philosopher of the Islamic East, Abu'l-Barakāt al-Baghdādī (died as a very old man after 1164), sometimes called Abu'l-Barakāt ibn-Malkā, also belongs to this period. Being a borderline case he illustrates a certain indeterminacy in the definition of a Jewish thinker.

Abu'l-Barakāt al-Baghdādī, an inhabitant of Iraq, was converted to Islam in his old age (for reasons of expediency, according to his biographers). His philosophy appears to have had a very strong impact on Islamic thought, whereas its influence upon Jewish philosophy and theology is very hard to pin down and may be practically nonexistent. His chief philosophical work, *Kitāb al-Muʿtabar*, a title that according to Abu'l-Barakāt's own interpretation means "The Book of That Which Has Been Established by Personal Reflection," has very few references to Jewish texts or topics. His theory appears mainly to represent a kind of dialectic development of Avicenna's doctrine concerning the existence of the soul; it is a radicalization that plays havoc with the greater part of Avicenna's psychology and theology. On the other hand, another important work of his, a philosophical commentary on Ecclesiastes, attests his knowledge of and interest in Jewish tradition.

Ibn-Kammūna. Ibn-Kammūna, who lived in the second half of the thirteenth century, may be regarded as the last Jewish philosopher of the Islamic East. There is a possibility that he too was converted to Islam. He wrote a curious treatise, *Tanqīh al-abhāth biʾl-mabhath ʿan al-milal al-thalāth,* dealing, ostensibly impartially, with the three monotheistic religions—Judaism, Islam, and Christianity. His philosophical doctrine seems to derive from Avicenna and his thirteenth-century disciple Naṣīr al-Dīn al-Ṭūsī.

Ibn-Da'ud. With regard to the adoption of Aristotelianism (including such systems as that of Avicenna, which in many essentials stems from, but profoundly modifies, the pure Peripatetic doctrine) there is a considerable time lag between the Islamic East in the one hand and Muslim Spain and the Maghreb on the other.

Abraham ibn-Da'ud (died in the second half of the twelfth century), who is regarded as the first Jewish Aristotelian of Spain, was primarily a disciple of Avicenna. According to a not unlikely hypothesis, he may have translated or helped to translate some of Avicenna's works into Latin, for ibn-Da'ud lived under Christian rule in Toledo, a town that in the twelfth century was a center for translators. His historical treatises, written in Hebrew, manifest his desire to familiarize his coreligionists with the historical tradition of the Latin world, which at that time was alien to most of them. But his philosophical work, *Sefer ha-Emunah ha-Ramah* ("The Book of Sublime Religion"), written in 1161 in Arabic, shows few, if any, signs of Christian influence.

The doctrine of emanation set forth in "The Book of Sublime Religion" describes in the manner of Avicenna the procession of the ten incorporeal intellects, the first of which derives from God. This intellect produces the second intellect, and so on. Ibn-Da'ud questioned in a fairly explicit manner Avicenna's views on the way the second intellect is produced; his discipleship did not by any means spell total adherence.

Ibn-Da'ud's psychology was also, and more distinctively, derived from Avicenna. The argumentation leading to a proof that the rational faculty is not corporeal attempts to derive the nature of the soul from the fact of immediate self-awareness. Like Avicenna, ibn-Da'ud tended to found psychology on a theory of consciousness.

Concerning "practical" philosophy, that is, ethics and political theory, ibn-Da'ud was of the opinion that all that Aristotle discovered in this field of inquiry can be found in the Torah in a more perfect manner.

"The Book of Sublime Religion" was said by its author to have been written in response to a question concerning free will and determinism. Obviously, this problem is closely bound up with the problem of God's knowledge. According to ibn-Da'ud events in this world are in part predetermined by necessity and in part contingent. Insofar as they are contingent, their occurrence or failure to occur may depend on man's actions. The necessary events are known by God as necessary, and the contingent as contingent. With regard to contingent events, he has no certain knowledge of whether they will come about in the future.

Ibn-Da'ud often referred to the accord that, in his view, existed between philosophy and religious tradition. As he remarked, "The Book of Sublime Religion" was not meant to be read either by readers who, in their simplicity, are satisfied with what they know of religious tradition or by those who have a thorough knowledge of philosophy. It was intended for readers of one type only, those who, being on the one hand acquainted with the religious tradition and having on the other some rudiments of philosophy, are "perplexed." It was for the same kind of people that Maimonides wrote his *Guide of the Perplexed*.

Maimonides. Maimonides (Moses ben Maimon, 1135–1204), a native of Spain, is incontestably the greatest name in Jewish medieval philosophy, but it is not because of outstanding originality in philosophical thought, in the proper sense of the term, that his reputation is deserved. Rather, the distinction of Maimonides, who is also the most eminent codifier of Jewish religious law, is to be found in the vast scope of his attempt in the *Guide of the Perplexed* to safeguard both the religious law and philosophy (whose divulgation is, as he was aware, destructive of the law), without suppressing the issues and without trying to impose, on the theoretical plane, a final, universally binding solution of the conflict.

As Maimonides made clear in his introduction to the *Guide*, he regarded his self-imposed task as perilous, and he therefore had recourse to a whole system of precautions destined to conceal his true meaning from the people who, lacking the necessary qualifications, were liable to misread the book and abandon observance of the law. According to Maimonides' explicit statement, these precautions include deliberately contradictory statements meant to mislead the undiscerning reader. It clearly follows that there is no possibility of propounding an interpretation of Maimonides' doctrine which would not be disproved or seem to be disproved by some passage or other of the *Guide*. Nevertheless, a consideration of the system as a coherent whole and of certain indications found in this work appears to suggest that Maimonides' true opinions on certain capital points are not beyond conjecture.

Conception of God. The apparent or real contradictions that may be encountered in the *Guide* are perhaps most flagrant in Maimonides' doctrine concerning God. There seems to be no plausible hypothesis capable of explaining away the differences between the following three views:

(1) God has an eternal will that is not bound by natural laws. Through an act of his will he created the world in time and imposed on it the order of nature. This creation is the greatest of miracles; if and only if it is admitted can other miracles, such as God's interventions, which interfere with the causally determined concatenation of events, be regarded as possible. The philosophers' God who is not free to cut the wings of a fly is to be rejected. This conception is in keeping with the traditional religious view of God and is adopted by Maimonides, if a statement of his is to be taken at its face value, because failure to do so would undermine religion.

(2) Man is incapable of having any positive knowledge concerning God. The ascription to God of the so-called divine attributes—wisdom or life, for instance—should not be regarded as an assertion that God is endowed with a positive quality designated as wisdom or life because it is similar to the corresponding quality found in created beings, for the fact is that their being homonyms is the only resemblance between human and divine wisdom or, for that matter, between man's and God's existence. Contrary to the attributes predicated of created beings, the

divine attributes are strictly negative; they state what God is *not*; for instance, he is not *not-wise*, which, as Maimonides believed, is not a positive assertion.

Negative theology of a similar kind may be found in the writings of Islamic philosophers, such as Avicenna, who are known to have had some influence on Maimonides, but they put much less emphasis on this aspect of their doctrine concerning God. Maimonides used it, *inter alia*, to justify the statement that the only positive knowledge of God possible is that which is known through his acts, identified in the *Guide* as the sometimes beneficent and sometimes destructive operations of the natural order. In other words, human knowledge of God is assimilated into the knowledge of the two sciences that treat of this order, physics and metaphysics.

(3) In accordance with the doctrine of Aristotle, God is an intellect. The formula current among medieval philosophers which maintains that in him the cognizing subject, the cognized object, and the act of intellectual cognition are identical derives from Aristotle's thesis that God cognizes only himself. Maimonides, however, in adopting the formula interpreted it in the light of human psychology and epistemology, pointing out that according to a theory of Aristotle the act of human (not only of divine) cognition brings about an identity of the cognizing subject and cognized object. The parallel drawn by Maimonides between the human and the divine intellect quite evidently implies a certain similarity between the two; in other words, it is incompatible with the negative theology of other passages of the *Guide*. Maimonides' interpretation also implies that God knows not only himself (if the reflexive pronoun is taken to refer to his transcendent essence only) but also objects of cognition, that is, intelligibles held to be outside himself; however, in virtue of the eternal act of cognition, the objects of cognition—which should perhaps be assimilated into the intelligible structure of the world—are identical with God himself.

In view of the relation that it implies between God and the world, the conception of God as an intellect can scarcely be reconciled with Maimonides' negative theology; nor can it be reconciled with his theological doctrine, which is centered on God's will and which asserts that the structure of the world (created in time) came into being through the action of his will.

Prophecy. The enigma of the *Guide* would be nonexistent if Maimonides could be held to have believed that truth can be discovered in a suprarational way, through revelations vouchsafed to the prophets. This, however, is not the case. Maimonides held that the prophets (with the exception of Moses) combine great intellectual abilities, which qualify them to be philosophers, with a powerful imagination. As he put it, the intellectual faculty of the philosophers and the prophets receives an "overflow" from the Active Intellect. In the case of the prophets this "overflow" not only brings about intellectual activity but also passes over into the imaginative faculty, giving rise to visions and dreams. The fact that prophets have a strong imagination gives them no superiority in knowledge over philosophers, who do not have it. Moses, who belonged to a higher category than the other prophets, did not have recourse to imagination. According to another text of

Maimonides, his commentary on the Mishnah, the prophets achieve union with the Active Intellect; hence, they are the supreme philosophers. (For a fuller discussion of Maimonides' doctrine of prophecy and his conception of the role of prophets in political life, see MAIMONIDES.)

The laws and religion as instituted by Moses are intended not only to ensure the bodily welfare and safety of the members of the community but also to facilitate the attainment of intellectual truths by individuals gifted enough to uncover the various hints embodied in religious laws and practices. This does not mean that all the beliefs inculcated by Judaism are true. Some indeed express philosophical truths, although in an inaccurate way, in a language suited to the intellectual capacity of the common people, who in general cannot grasp the import of the dogmas they are required to profess. Other beliefs, however, are false, but "necessary" for the preservation of a public order upholding justice. Such is the belief that God is angry with wrongdoers.

Religious law. As far as the law—that is, the religious commandments—is concerned, two aspects of Maimonides' position may be distinguished. On the one hand, he had to maintain that it is unique in its excellence; there is no basis of comparison between Moses, who promulgated this law, and any other prophet (or any other man) who existed in the past or who may appear in the future and, consequently, the law is valid for all time. This profession of faith, at least with regard to its assumptions about the future, lacked philosophical justification; however, in view of the Muslim polemics and perhaps also in view of incipient tendencies among the "perplexed" to neglect the observance of the commandments, it could be regarded as necessary for the survival of Judaism.

In its second aspect Maimonides' position is characterized by his awareness of the role of historical contingencies in the institution of the commandments. He insisted time and again that Moses had to fulfill two requirements: his law had to be different, but it could not be too different from the customs and ordinances of the pagans among whom the children of Israel lived. The people could not have borne too sharp a break with the way of life to which they were accustomed. For instance, the commandments concerning sacrifice arise from this awareness of the necessities of a specific historic situation. Like nature, which uses many complicated devices in forming a viable organism, the political leader, who must fashion his community, is sometimes compelled to have recourse to a "ruse" or a roundabout method.

Like Aristotle, Maimonides held that the "theoretical life" constitutes the highest perfection possible to man. But he believed (partly under the influence of the Platonic political doctrine adopted by al-Fārābī and others) that certain individuals, for example, the Patriarchs and Moses, are capable of combining contemplation with a life of action. In its supreme manifestation the activity of the prophet-lawgiver imitates that of God or nature.

The thirteenth century. For four or five centuries (and in certain regions for an even longer time), the *Guide of the Perplexed* exercised a very strong influence in the European centers of Jewish thought; in the thirteenth century, when the *Guide* was twice translated into He-

brew, these centers were Spain, the south of France, and Italy. Rather paradoxically, in view of the unsystematic character of Maimonides' exposition, it was used as a standard textbook of philosophy—and condemned as such when the teaching of philosophy came under attack. The performance of this function by the *Guide* was rendered possible or at least facilitated by the fact that from the thirteenth century onward the history of Jewish philosophy in European countries acquired a continuity it had never had before. First and foremost, this development seems to have resulted from a linguistic factor: In Spain, where the Christian reconquest was destroying piecemeal the power of Islam, Jewish philosophers abandoned the use of Arabic as the language of philosophical exposition. The Jews did not, however, switch to Latin, the language of Christian philosophy. They and their coreligionists in other European countries wrote in Hebrew, and they read original and translated texts extant in Hebrew, which were much less numerous and less diverse than those found in Arabic philosophical literature. Owing to the existence of a common and relatively homogeneous philosophical background and to the fact that Jewish philosophers reading and writing in Hebrew naturally read the works of their contemporaries and immediate predecessors, something like a dialogue can be discerned. In striking contrast to the immediately preceding period, European Jewish philosophers in the thirteenth century and after frequently devoted a very considerable part of their treatises to discussions of the opinions of other Jewish philosophers. That many of the Jewish philosophers in question wrote commentaries on the *Guide* undoubtedly furthered this tendency.

The influence of Maimonides' contemporary Averroës, many of whose commentaries and treatises were translated into Hebrew, was second only to that of Maimonides. Indeed, it may be argued that for philosophers, as distinct from the general reading public, it often came first. In certain cases, commentators on the *Guide* tend, in spite of the frequent divergences between the two philosophers, to quote Averroës' opinions in order to clarify those of Maimonides.

The influence of Christian scholastic thought on Jewish philosophy was in very many cases not openly acknowledged in the period beginning with the thirteenth century, but it seems to have been of great significance. Samuel ibn-Tibbon, one of the translators of the *Guide* into Hebrew and a philosopher in his own right, remarked on the fact that the philosophical sciences were more widely known among Christians than among Muslims. Somewhat later, at the end of the thirteenth century and after, Jewish scholars in Italy (Hillel of Verona and others) translated into Hebrew texts of Thomas Aquinas and other Scholastics; not infrequently, although by no means always, some of them acknowledged the debt they owed their Christian masters.

In Spain and in the south of France a different convention seems to have prevailed up to the second half of the fifteenth century. Whereas Jewish philosophers of these countries felt no reluctance about referring by name to Greek, Arabic, and of course other Jewish philosophers, as a rule they refrained from citing Christian thinkers whose views had, in all probability, influenced them. In the case of certain Jewish thinkers this absence of reference to the Christian Scholastics served to disguise the fact that in many essentials they were representative of the philosophical trends, such as Latin Averroism, that were current among the Christian Scholastics of their time.

Albalag. Quite evident is the resemblance between certain views professed by the Latin Averroists and the parallel opinions of Isaac Albalag, a Jewish philosopher who lived in the second half of the thirteenth century, probably in Catalonia, Spain, and who wrote a commentary in Hebrew on the "Intentions of the Philosophers," an exposition of Avicenna's doctrine written by the Muslim philosopher al-Ghazālī. No serious attempt at interpreting Albalag's assertion that both the teachings of the Bible and the truths demonstrated by reason must be believed even if they are contradictory can fail to pose the question whether some historical connections exists between this view and the Latin Averroist doctrine that there are two sets of truths, the religious and the philosophical, and that these are not necessarily in accord.

In most other points Albalag was a consistent follower of the system of Averroës himself (although a few of Albalag's doctrines appear to be in closer accord with ibn-Sīnā). This philosophical position may be exemplified by his rejection of the view that the world was created in time. He professed, it is true, to believe in what he called "absolute creation in time." However, this expression merely signifies that at any given moment the continued existence of the world depends on God's existence, an opinion which is essentially in harmony with Averroës.

Bedersi. Yeda'ya Hapnini Bedersi, of Béziers in the south of France, who lived from the end of the thirteenth century to the beginning of the fourteenth century, appears to have been influenced by the teaching of Duns Scotus, for he believed in the existence of what he called individual forms, which seem by and large to correspond to the *haecceitas* of the Scotists.

Kaspi. One of Bedersi's contemporaries, Joseph Kaspi, a prolific philosopher and exegetical commentator, maintained a somewhat unsystematic philosophical position that seems to have been influenced by Averroës. He expressed the opinion that knowledge of the future, with that of God himself, is like that possessed by experienced people concerning the way in which business transactions or marriages may be expected to turn out—that is, such knowledge is of a probabilistic nature. The prescience of the prophets is of the same nature. It is more than likely that Kaspi's interest in this problem had some connection with the debate about future contingents in which Christian Scholastics were engaged at that time.

Kaspi also held that in view of the vicissitudes of history the return of the Jews to Palestine may on probabilistic grounds be considered likely. As a result he rejected the distinction—which for Judah Halevi, for instance, had been a basic one—between sacred and profane history, the first being the history of the people of Israel and the second that of other nations.

LATE MEDIEVAL PERIOD

Cabala. One of the most urgent problems with which Jewish philosophers were faced in the fourteenth and fifteenth centuries was that of the attitude to be adopted toward the Cabala (literally, "tradition"), a body of mystic and gnostic doctrines, part of which was being elaborated in that period in the countries in which the philosophers lived.

Many of the Cabalists incorporated philosophical doctrines in their writings and claimed Maimonides as a Cabalist but at the same time regarded philosophy as such as an inferior kind of science. This disdainful attitude was reciprocated by some philosophers. Nonetheless, attempts were made to effect a reconciliation between philosophy and Cabala. Such an attempt was made by Joseph ibn-Waqar, a fourteenth-century philosopher of Toledo, who wrote "The Treatise Which Reconciles Philosophy and Religious Law" in Arabic (which in that period and country was atypical for a Jewish philosopher). According to ibn-Wāqar, the opinions of the philosophers are founded on reason, whereas those of the Cabalists owe their validity solely to their having been transmitted by a tradition whose authority guarantees their truth. Although recognizing in theory the superiority of the Cabalistic doctrine to the teachings of philosophy, ibn-Wāqar endeavored to show the basic similarity, masked by a difference of terminology, of the two systems of thought. He also affirmed that knowledge of philosophy increases the aptitude to apprehend the mystic doctrine of the Cabala.

Narboni. Moses of Narbonne, or Moses Narboni, who lived in the south of France in the fourteenth century, was, like many other Jewish writers of this period, mainly a writer of commentaries. He wrote commentaries on Biblical books, on treatises of Averroës, apocryphal treatises, and on Maimonides' *Guide*. In his commentary on the *Guide*, Narboni often interprets the earlier Jewish philosopher's opinions by recourse to Averroës' views. Narboni also expounded and gave radical interpretations to certain conceptions that he understood as implied in the *Guide*.

According to Narboni, God participates in all things because he is the measure of all substances. From another point of view all things exist in God, "the Agent being the essence of the patient." God is the form of the world. In Narboni's interpretation (which, not quite correctly, he opposed to that of Maimonides) this formula means that God is a form which, although it is not in a body, is "with a body": God's existence appears to be bound up with that of the world, to which he has a relation analogous to that existing between a soul and its body (a comparison already made in the *Guide*). As the form of the world, God also determines the fact that the extension of the world is limited. It may be added that, according to a conception of Narboni which runs counter to the views of many Aristotelian philosophers, prime matter has its place in the thought of God. Narboni seems to have been a consistent (and on the whole unusually outspoken) adherent of the Aristotelian tradition that crystallized in the Arabic period of Jewish philosophy.

Gersonides. Gersonides (Levi ben Gerson, 1288–1344), another fourteenth-century Jewish philosopher born in the south of France, wrote the systematic philosophical work *Milḥamot Adonai* ("The Wars of the Lord") as well as many philosophical commentaries. As an astronomer he enjoyed a certain fame among Christian scholars. Gersonides apparently never explicitly mentioned Christian scholastic philosophers; he cited Greek, Arabic, and Jewish thinkers only, and in many ways his system appears to have stemmed from the doctrines of Maimonides or Averroës, regardless of whether he agreed with them. For example, he explicitly rejected Maimonides' doctrine of negative theology (see GERSONIDES). However, a comparison of his opinions and of the particular problems that engaged his attention with the views and debates found in scholastic writings of his period suggest that he was also influenced by the Latins on certain points.

Creation. Gersonides disagreed both with the Aristotelian philosophers who maintained the eternity of the world and with the partisans of the religious who believed in the creation of the world in time out of nothing. He maintained that God created the world in time out of a pre-existent body lacking all form. As conceived by Gersonides this body seems to be similar to primal matter. According to the Aristotelian conception, the "now" separates the past from the future; because of this function its existence at any moment of time entails the existence of a past. Hence, an absolute beginning is impossible, which means that the world is eternal. Gersonides rejected this argument because he believed that it is possible for a "now" to be restricted to the function of beginning or terminating an interval of time. Hence, there is no difficulty in supposing that the existence of a "now" at the instant of the creation of the world in time did not entail the existence of a past. This argument was discussed prior to Gersonides in a Latin Averroistic treatise whose author is unknown, and Gersonides may have been influenced by Latin Scholasticism on this point.

Free will and divine omniscience. The problem of human freedom of action and a particular version of the problem of God's knowledge of future contingents form an important part of Gersonides' doctrine. Gersonides—who, unlike the great Jewish and Muslim Aristotelians, believed in astrology—held that all happenings in the world except human actions are governed by a strict determinism. God's knowledge does not, however, extend to the individual human acts that actually occur. It embraces the general order of things that exist; it grasps the laws of the universal determinism but is incapable of apprehending events resulting from man's freedom. Thus, the object of God's knowledge is an ideal world order, which differs from the "real" world insofar as the latter is in some measure formed according to man's free will.

Political philosophy. In political and social doctrine there is a fundamental difference between Maimonides and Gersonides. Gersonides does not appear to have assigned to the prophets any political function; according to him their role consists in the prediction of future events. The providence exercised by the heavenly bodies ensures the existence in a given political society of men having an aptitude for and exercising the handicrafts and professions necessary for the survival of the community. He remarked that in this way the various human activities are distributed in a manner superior to that outlined in Plato's *Republic.* Thus, he rejected explicitly Plato's political philosophy, which, having been adapted to a society ruled through the laws promulgated by a prophet, had been an important element of Jewish philosophy in the Arabic period.

Gersonides' deviations from this philosophical tradition may have involved various factors, such as the influence of Thomas Aquinas (whose conception of human freedom, to mention but this example, resembles that of Gersonides) or Gersonides' belief in astrology or his pronounced predilection for personal speculation. These deviations did not, however, affect his fundamental allegiance to medieval Aristotelianism.

Crescas. Both Hasdai Crescas (1340–1410), a Spanish Jewish thinker, and Gersonides had thorough knowledge of Jewish philosophy and partial knowledge of Islamic philosophy, and both seem to have been influenced by scholastic thought; moreover, in certain important respects Crescas was influenced by Gersonides himself. However, in Crescas' main work, *Or Adonai* ("The Light of the Lord"), one of his objectives, quite contrary to Gersonides, was to expose the weakness and insufficiency of Aristotelian philosophy. This attitude may be placed in the wider context of the return to religion itself as opposed to the Aristotelian rationalization of religion and the vogue of Cabala, characteristic features of Spanish Jewry in Crescas' time. This change in attitude has been regarded as a reaction to the increasing precariousness of the position of the Jewish community in Spain.

The low estimation of the certainties and the rationalistic arrogance of the medieval Aristotelians coincided chronologically with a certain disintegration of and disaffection toward what may be called the classical Aristotelian Scholasticism. Relevant to this decline were the so-called voluntarism of Duns Scotus, the nominalism of William of Ockham and other Scholastics, and the development, in the fourteenth century and after, of the anti-Aristotelian terminist physics at the University of Paris and elsewhere. It is significant that there is a pronounced resemblance between Crescas' views and two of these trends, Scotism and the "new" physics.

Divine attributes. Crescas accepted Gersonides' view that divine attributes cannot be negative, but unlike his predecessor he centered his explanation of the difference between the attributes of God and those of created existents on the antithesis between an infinite being and finite beings. It is through infinitude that God's essential attributes—wisdom, for instance—differ from the corresponding and otherwise similar attributes found in created beings. In Crescas' as in Spinoza's doctrine, God's attributes are also infinite in number. The central place assigned to the thesis of God's infinity in Crescas' system suggests the influence of Duns Scotus' theology, which is similarly founded upon the concept of divine infinity.

Physics. The problem of the infinite approached from an altogether different angle was one of the main themes of Crescas' critique of Maimonides' 25 propositions; these propositions, concerned mainly with Aristotelian physical doctrines, had been set forth in the *Guide* as the basis of Maimonides' proofs for the existence of God. Crescas' declared purpose in criticizing and rejecting several of these propositions was to show that the traditional Aristotelian proofs (founded in the first place on physical doctrines) were not valid.

In the course of his critique Crescas attempted to disprove the Aristotelian thesis that the existence of an actual infinite is impossible. He held that space is not a limit but a tridimensional extension, that it is infinite, and that, contrary to Aristotle, the existence of a vacuum and of more worlds than one is possible. He also criticized as being impossible the thesis of the Aristotelian philosophers that there exists an infinite number of causes and effects, which have order and gradation. This thesis refers not to a temporal succession of causes and effects which have a similar ontological status but to a vertical series, descending from God to the lowest rung in creation. His attacks were likewise directed against the Aristotelians' conception of time and of matter.

The physical doctrines that emerged in Crescas' critique resemble the "new," mainly "terminist" physics, which was being worked out in the fourteenth century at the University of Paris and other Christian seats of learning and which had a considerable influence on the classical physical theories of Galileo and others. There is no difficulty in supposing that Crescas was acquainted with some of the terminist theses. Crescas may on the whole be regarded as an outstanding representative of the medieval "new physics."

Ascendancy of soul over intellect. Crescas' fundamental opposition to Aristotelianism is perhaps most evident in his rejection of the conception of intellectual activity as the supreme state of being for man and for God. Crescas' God is not first and foremost an intellect, and the supreme goal to which man can aspire is to love God with a love corresponding as far as possible to the infinite greatness of its object and to rejoice in the observance of his commandments. God too loves man, and his love, in spite of the lowliness of its object, is proportionate to his infinity.

Crescas attacked the separation of the intellect from the soul as conceived by the Aristotelians and attempted, perhaps under the influence of Judah Halevi, to refute the Peripatetic doctrine that the actualized intellect, in contradistinction to the soul, survives the death of the body. According to Crescas the soul is a substance in its own right and can be separated from the body; it continues to subsist after the body's death.

Crescas' depreciation of the intellect did not lead to an emphasis on man's freedom of action. Crescas' view concords with that of Avicenna: there is no such freedom; everything in the world is subject to a strict determinism. Man's actions are as predetermined as all other happenings; they depend on his make-up and conditioning and on his reactions to stimuli from the external world. Crescas did not deny man's freedom only with regard to the domain of external action, for he pointed out that a man's beliefs and knowledge are not within his power.

Albo. Whereas Crescas unmistakably regarded the Aristotelian philosophers as adversaries to be criticized or combatted, the attitude of Joseph Albo (c. 1380–1444), who regarded Crescas as his teacher, is much less clearly defined. Albo did not eschew self-contradiction, apparently considering it a legitimate precaution on the part of a philosophical or theological author; indeed, he indulged in it in a much more obvious way than did Maimonides. But whereas the latter's fundamental philosophical position is fairly clear, the problem being how far he was prepared to deviate from Aristotelian doctrine in the interests of religion, there may be valid doubt whether Crescas and the

Jewish religious tradition or Maimonides and Averroës were Albo's true masters. Mainly because of this perhaps deliberate failure to explain to the reader where he really stood, Albo has often been dismissed as an eclectic. He was strongly influenced not only by the authors just mentioned but also by Saadia. He seems to have had a considerable knowledge of Christian theology, even adopting for his own purposes certain scholastic doctrines. He differs from Crescas and to some extent resembles Maimonides in having had a marked interest in political theory.

The proclaimed theme of Albo's magnum opus, *Sefer ha-Ikkarim* (*The Book of Principles*), is the investigation of the theory of Jewish religious dogmas, whose number Maimonides, in a nonphilosophical work, had set at 13, whereas Albo, following a doctrine that in the last analysis seems to go back to Averroës, would limit them to 3: existence of God, providence in reward and punishment, and the Torah as a divine revelation. One section, usually including the philosophical and the traditional religious interpretations side by side, is devoted to each of these dogmas. However, as far as Jewish philosophy is concerned, Albo's principal relatively novel (although in view of the likelihood of a Christian influence, probably not original) contribution to doctrinal evolution is the classification, in his introduction, of natural, conventional, and divine law. Natural law is necessary because man, being political by nature, must belong to a community, which may be restricted in size to one town or may extend over the whole earth. Natural law preserves society by promoting right and repressing injustice; thus, it restrains men from stealing, robbing, and murdering. The concept of "natural law" may have been taken over by Albo from the Christian Scholastics; the term is rarely used in philosophical works written in Arabic, and when it occurs it has an altogether different meaning. Albo did not mention whether natural law accords with human nature; he accounted for the need for and acceptance of natural law on purely utilitarian grounds. He did, however, believe that natural law is the same among all people, at all times, and in all places.

The positive laws instituted by wise men take into account the particular nature of the people for whose benefit they are instituted, as well as other circumstances. This means that they differ from the natural law in not being universally applicable. However, neither natural law nor the more elaborate conventional laws lead men toward true spiritual happiness; this is the function of divine laws instituted by a prophet, which teach men true theoretical opinions.

Contrary to Maimonides, but in agreement with the Scholastics and to some extent with Saadia, Albo believed that men are capable of establishing an orderly society by their own efforts, without the help of prophets.

Whereas Maimonides maintained that Judaism was the only divine law promulgated by a true prophet, Albo considered that the commandments given to Noah also constitute divine law, which ensures, although to a lesser degree than does Judaism, the happiness of its adherents. This position justifies a certain universalism; in accordance with a Talmudic saying, Albo believed that the pious among the non-Jews—that is, those who observe Noah's laws—have a share in the world to come. But he rejected the pretensions of Christianity and Islam to be divine laws.

Renaissance. In the last few decades before their expulsion (1492), the Spanish Jews seem to have freely acknowledged the influence of the Christian Scholastics. A tribute to Christian thought was made not only by Habilla, a translator of several scholastic texts into Hebrew, but also by Isaac Arama and Isaac Abravanel, both of whom immigrated to Italy after the expulsion. Both are critical in various degrees of Aristotelians. Some of the views of Arama (who seems to have influenced Abravanel) mark a return to Judah Halevi. Abravanel's political doctrine is of some interest because it refers to and bestows praise on the regimes of the Italian republics of the period.

The son of Isaac Abravanel, Judah Abravanel, better known as Leone Ebreo (1460–c. 1521), was the author of *Dialoghi d'amore* and as such is one of the outstanding representatives of Platonism in Italy. He is perhaps the first example in postmedieval times of an important Jewish thinker who does not belong primarily to the history of Jewish philosophy (for the conception of Jewish philosophy presupposed in this assertion, see below).

Elijah del Medigo (c. 1460–1493), who was born in Crete, was a Jewish Averroist and a companion of Pico della Mirandola. In his Hebrew treatise *Behinat Hadat* ("The Testing of Religion") he opposed the trend among Jewish philosophers to read philosophical meanings into Biblical texts by means of allegorical interpretations. Del Medigo, like Averroës, did not countenance any attempt to amalgamate religious law and philosophy. The Jewish philosophers who had such an amalgam in mind—it is pretty clear that Maimonides is the foremost object of these strictures—are neither (true) philosophers nor (true) professors of religious law.

MODERN AND CONTEMPORARY PERIODS

The expulsion of the Jews from Spain and Portugal produced a new center of Jewish thought, Holland, where many of the exiled Jews found a new and safer domicile; the tolerance of the regime seemed to provide guarantees against external persecution. This did not prevent, and indeed may have furthered, the establishment of an oppressive orthodoxy that was prepared to chastise rebellious members of its community.

Da Costa. Both Uriel da Costa, or Acosta (1585–1640), and Spinoza (1632–1677) rebelled against Jewish orthodoxy. Uriel da Costa came to Amsterdam from Portugal, where, belonging to a family of Marranos (Jews who had converted to escape the Spanish Inquisition), he had been brought up in the Catholic faith; his philosophical position was to a great extent determined by his antagonism to the orthodox Judaism (the Judaism of "the Pharisees," to use his term) that he encountered in Amsterdam. He was struck by the fact that the commandments as interpreted by his contemporaries did not conform to the text of the Torah, and he formulated a number of theses to prove his point. His growing estrangement from generally accepted Jewish doctrine is attested by his Portuguese treatise *Sobre a Mortalidade da Alma* ("On the Mortality of the Soul"). Apparently under the influence of Michael Serve-

tus, he came to the conclusion that the soul is the vital spirit located in the blood and that it dies with the death of the body, there being no difference in this respect between the human and the animal soul. He considered that the belief in the immortality of the soul has had many evil effects, for it impels men to choose an ascetic way of life and even to seek death. According to him nothing has tormented men more than the belief in an eternal good and evil. God tolerates this opinion merely to torture the conscience of those who have abandoned his truth. At this stage da Costa affirmed the authority of the Bible from which, according to him, the mortality of the soul can be proved.

In his autobiography, written in Latin and entitled *Exemplar Humanae Vitae* ("An Example of Human Life"), he takes a more radical position. He proclaims the supreme excellency of the natural moral law (which, when arguing before the Jews, he seems to identify with the divine commandments to Noah—a comparison may be made with the view of Albo). Accordingly, he denies the validity of the argument that natural law is inferior to Judaism and Christianity, because he believes that both these religions teach the love of one's enemies, a precept which is not a part of natural law. According to da Costa, no good can come of demanding a manifest impossibility.

Spinoza. Although medieval philosophers of Jewish origin for whom Judaism does not constitute a primary philosophical theme are thought of as belonging to the history of Jewish philosophy, a classification of this kind applied to such modern philosophers of Jewish origin as Salomon Maimon, Henri Bergson, Edmund Husserl, and L. I. Shestov might lead to some significant conclusions but would nevertheless seem inappropriate. It would certainly not be in keeping with the intentions of the philosophers themselves, and their views would be taken out of their natural contexts.

These considerations, however, may not, for the following reasons, be quite so valid with respect to Spinoza: (1) It was through the study of Jewish philosophical texts that Spinoza was first initiated into philosophy. (2) It may be argued with some reason that at least in part (if one abstracts the influence of Descartes and of seventeenth-century physics and certain other constitutive elements), Spinoza's system is a radicalization or perhaps a logical corollary to medieval doctrines; although its importance may be contested, the impact of Maimonides and of Crescas is evident. (3) A considerable portion of Spinoza's *Tractatus Theologico-politicus* deals with problems related to Judaism. Reference to some of the views set forth in the *Tractatus* and to their connection with medieval Jewish doctrines may not be out of place here.

Prophecy. As the first chapters of the *Tractatus* show, the doctrine of prophecy is of central importance to Spinoza's explanation of Judaism. These chapters can also provide proof that, as far as this subject is concerned, Spinoza to a large extent used Maimonides' categories, although he applied them to different people or groups of people. In fact, the relationship of Spinoza to Maimonides—although antagonistic—is much closer than that of most of the fifteenth-century Jewish philosophers who did not break with Judaism.

Maimonides held that the prophets combined intellectual perfection, which made them philosophers, with perfection of the imaginative faculty. He also referred to a category of people endowed with a strong imagination but possessing no extraordinary intellectual gifts; this category includes, for example, lawgivers and statesmen. Spinoza took over this last category but applied it to the prophets, whom he described as possessing vivid imaginations but as not necessarily having outstanding intellectual capacities. He denied that the Biblical prophets were philosophers and used a philosophical and historical approach to the Scriptures to show that the contrary assertion is not borne out by the texts.

Spinoza also denied Maimonides' assertion that the prophecy of Moses was essentially different from that of the other prophets and that this was largely because Moses, in prophesying, had no recourse to the imaginative faculty. According to Spinoza the distinctive fact about Moses' prophecy was that he heard the voice of God in a prophetic vision—that is, in a state in which his imagination was active. In this assertion Spinoza employed one of Maimonides' categories of prophecy, differentiated in the *Guide* according to certain characteristics of prophetic dreams and visions. However, Maimonides thought it improbable that the voice of God was ever heard in prophetic vision; he held that this category is purely hypothetical. It seems evident that in his classification of Moses, Spinoza was concerned not with what really happened in history but with pigeonholing the evidence culled from the Bible into Maimonides' theoretical framework in such a way that it fit in with his theologicopolitical purpose.

This purpose made it imperative to propound in the *Tractatus* a theory concerning Jesus, whom Spinoza designates as *Christus*. The category and the status assigned to Jesus are by and large similar to those that Maimonides attributed to Moses. Thus, Jesus is referred to in the *Tractatus* as a religious teacher who makes recourse not to the imaginative faculty but solely to the intellect. However, in following up this hypothesis Spinoza was guilty of an inconsistency. Whereas in the case of the Old Testament prophets he rejected allegorical interpretations predicated on the supposition that the prophets adapted their discourses to the understanding of the general public, in the case of Jesus he adopted this interpretation because he wished to explain away those of Jesus' sayings that he regarded as incompatible with true philosophical doctrine. Both Maimonides' Moses and Spinoza's Jesus are absolutely unique personalities; there is, however, an important difference between them. In the opinion both of Maimonides and of Spinoza, Moses' legislation created the Jewish community and state, whereas Jesus as conceived by Spinoza was not a lawgiver and, as far as his direct activity was concerned, not a statesman, though within Spinoza's blueprint for an ideal State, he is assigned a political function: his authority may be used to institute and strengthen the religion Spinoza called *religio catholica*, which has little or nothing in common with any of the major manifestations of historic Christianity.

Critique of Judaism. The difference between Judaism and Spinoza's *religio catholica* corresponds to the difference between Moses and Jesus. After leaving Egypt the Jews found themselves, in Spinoza's view, in the position of people who had no allegiance to any positive law; they had, as it were, reverted to a state of nature and were faced with the need to enter into a social pact. They were also an ignorant people and very prone to superstition. Moses, a man of outstanding ability, made use of the situation and characteristics of the people in order to make them accept a social pact and a state founded upon it, which, contrary to Spinoza's schema for his ideal communities, were not based first and foremost upon utilitarian—that is, reasonable—consideration of the advantages of life in society over the state of nature.

The social pact concluded by the children of Israel in the desert was based upon a superstitious view of God as "King" and "Judge," to whom the children of Israel owed whatever political and military successes they obtained. It was to God rather than to the representatives of the popular will that the children of Israel transferred political sovereignty. In due course political sovereignty was vested in Moses, God's representative, and in his successors. It should be added that in spite of Spinoza's insistence on the superstitious foundations of the state of the children of Israel in ancient times, his account of its regime was not wholly unsympathetic. He did, however, believe that it contained the seeds of its own destruction and that with the extinction of this state the social pact devised by Moses had lapsed and all the political and religious obligations incumbent upon the Jews become null and void.

"Religio catholica." It could be argued that because the state conceived by Spinoza is based not on superstitious faith but on a social contract originating in rational, utilitarian considerations it does not necessarily need to have its authority safeguarded and stabilized by means of religion. However, Spinoza appears to have held the view—perhaps derived from a purely empirical knowledge of the behavior of the common run of men—that there is a need for religion. In order to fulfill the need for some religion and to obviate the danger of harmful religions, he devised his *religio catholica*, the universal religion, which has the following distinctive traits: (1) Its main purpose, a practical one (which is furthered by recourse to the authority of Jesus), is to impel men to act in accordance with justice and charity. Such conduct is tantamount to obedience to the laws of the state and to the orders of the magistrates, in whom sovereignty is vested. For disobedience—even if it springs from compassionate motives—weakens the social pact, which safeguards the welfare of all the members of the community; in consequence, its evil effects outweigh whatever good it may produce. (2) Although religion, according to Spinoza, is not concerned with theoretical truth, in order to be effective the *religio catholica* requires dogmas, which he set forth in the *Tractatus*. These dogmas are formulated there in terms that can be interpreted in accordance both with the philosophical conception of God that Spinoza regarded as true and with the superstitious ideas of ordinary people. It follows that if they are accepted as constituting by themselves the only creed that everybody is obliged to profess, people cannot be persecuted on account of their beliefs; Spinoza held that such a persecution is liable to lead to civil war and may thus destroy the state. Philosophers are free to engage in the pursuit of truth and to attain, if they can, the supreme goal of man, freedom grounded in knowledge. There can be little doubt that the furtherance of the cause of tolerance for philosophical opinions was one of Spinoza's main objects in writing the *Tractatus.*

Mendelssohn. Moses Mendelssohn (1729–1786) opens what may be called the German period of Jewish philosophy. This period, in which a considerable number of works on Jewish philosophy were written in German and often under the influence of German philosophy, is also marked by the emancipation of the Jews (that is, by the abrogation of discriminatory laws directed against them) and by their partial or complete assimilation. In this period in particular, it appears indicated to apply the term "Jewish philosophy" first and foremost to works whose main purpose or one of whose main purposes consists in proposing a definition of Judaism and a justification of its existence. The second task is often conceived as necessitating a confrontation of Judaism with Christianity rather than with philosophy, which served as a point of comparison for many medieval philosophers. This change seems to have been a result of the demarcation of the sphere of religion in such a way that, at least in the opinion of the philosophers, possible points of collision no longer existed between it and philosophy. This demarcation was largely furthered by the doctrine of Spinoza—from whom Mendelssohn and others took over and adopted for their own purposes certain fundamental ideas concerning Judaism. Like Spinoza, Mendelssohn held (according to his treatise *Jerusalem* and other writings) that it is not the task of Judaism to teach rational truths, although they may be referred to in the Bible. Contrary to what he called Athanasian Christianity (that is, the doctrine set forth in the Athanasian creed), Judaism has no binding dogmas; it is centered on inculcating belief in certain historical events and on action—that is, observance of religious law (including the ceremonial commandments). Such observance is supposed to lead to happiness in this world and in the afterlife. Mendelssohn did not reject this view offhand, as Spinoza would have done; indeed, he seems to have been prepared to accept it—God's mysteries being inscrutable, and the radicalism and what may be called the consistency of Spinoza being the complete antithesis of Mendelssohn's apologetics. Non-Jews were supposed by Mendelssohn to owe allegiance to the law of nature. He did not affirm the superiority of Judaism over this law and was prepared to regard Jesus as a great prophet. He declared his belief that the differences between the various religions are not eternal and that when the whole earth is united in the knowledge of God, the Jews will be permitted to abandon their peculiar rites and ceremonies. But that time has not yet arrived.

Mendelssohn was well grounded in medieval Jewish philosophy and referred quite frequently to the writings of Maimonides and of other Jewish thinkers of the Middle Ages. The three principles on which he held Judaism to be based call to mind those propounded by Albo. They are God, providence, and the divine law.

Formstecher. Whereas Mendelssohn continued the medieval tradition, at least to some extent, or adopted Spinoza's doctrine for his purposes, the Jewish philosophers of the first half of the nineteenth century (except, at least in a certain measure, Solomon Steinheim) may be regarded as disciples of the philosophers of their own time. In *Die Religion des Geistes* ("The Religion of the Spirit,") Solomon Formstecher (1808–1889) was greatly influenced by Schelling in his conception of nature and spirit as manifestations of the divine. There are types of religions that correspond to these manifestations: (1) the religion of nature in which God is conceived as the principle of nature or as the world soul, and (2) the religion of the Spirit which conceives of God as an ethical being. According to the religion of the Spirit, God has produced the world as his manifestation in full freedom and not, as the religion of nature tends to profess, because the world was necessary for his own existence.

The religion of the Spirit, which corresponds to absolute religious truth, was first manifested in the Jewish people. The religious history of the world may be understood as a process of universalization of the Jewish religion. Thus, Christianity propagated Jewish conceptions among the nations; however, it combined them with pagan ideas. The pagan element is gradually being eliminated—Protestantism, for instance, in this respect marks considerable progress. When at long last the Jewish element in Christianity is victorious, the Jews will be right to give up their isolation. The process that will bring about this final religious union is already under way.

Hirsch. The main philosophical work of Samuel Hirsch (1815–1889), entitled *Die Religionsphilosophie der Juden* ("The Philosophy of Religion of the Jews") was decisively influenced by Hegel. This influence is most evident in Hirsch's method and in the task that he assigned to the philosophy of religion—the transformation of religious consciousness into conceptual truth. However, contrary to Hegel, he did not consider religious truth to be inadequate as compared to philosophical truth.

Hirsch believed that man's awareness of himself as an ego is identical with his awareness of his freedom. This freedom is, however, abstract; it became concrete in the various historical religions. Man may renounce this freedom and believe that he is dominated by his senses. This means recognizing the absolute sovereignty of nature regarded as a divine principle, which is the point of departure of the pagan passive religions. If, however, he subordinates his nature to his freedom, his freedom becomes concrete. God is conceived not only as the giver of abstract freedom but as willing man's concrete freedom. This is the principle of Judaism. Christianity was conceived by Hirsch as it was by Formstecher, as being intermediate between Judaism and paganism.

God revealed himself in the first stages of Jewish history by means of miracles and of prophecy. At present he manifests himself in the miracle that is constituted by the existence of the Jewish people. At its beginning in the time of Jesus, Christianity was identical with Judaism. The decisive break between the two religions was caused by Paul. According to Hirsch, when the Pauline elements are eliminated from Christianity, it will be in all essentials in agreement with Judaism, which, however, will preserve its separate existence.

Krochmal. Nachman Krochmal (1785–1840), a native of Galicia (at that time part of Austria), was the author of *Moreh Nebukhei ha-Zman* ("Guide of the Perplexed for Our Time"), a treatise in Hebrew on philosophy of history and on Jewish history, which had a considerable influence.

Krochmal, like Hirsch, was influenced by Hegel and perhaps also by other German philosophers approximately of Hegel's period, such as Fichte. Krochmal's philosophical thought was centered on the notion of "spirit," Krochmal being mainly concerned with the "national spirit," the particular "spirit" that is proper to each people and that accounts for the peculiar characteristics differentiating one people from another in every domain of human activity.

The national "spirits" of all peoples except the Jewish are, according to Krochmal, essentially particular. Hence, the national spirit either becomes extinct with the extinction of the nation or, if it is a powerful spirit, is assimilated by some other nation. The Jewish people has a special relation to the Universal Spirit, who is the God of Israel. This relation accounts for the perpetuity of the Jewish people.

Steinheim. Solomon Ludwig Steinheim (1789–1866), the author of *Die Offenbarung nach dem Lehrbegriff der Synagoge*, ("Revelation According to the Doctrine of the Synagogue"), was apparently influenced by the anti-rationalism of Friedrich Jacobi.

His criticism of science is based on Jacobi's criticism, but he did not agree with Jacobi in opposing discursive reason to our intuitive knowledge of God—Steinheim contrasted human reason to divine revelation. The main point on which the revelation vouchsafed to the prophets of Israel is opposed to reason is to be found in the fact that the God posited by reason is subject to necessity, that he can act only in accordance with laws. Moreover, reason affirms that nothing can come from nothing. Accordingly, God is free to create not a good world but only the best possible world. Revealed religion, on the other hand, affirms the freedom of God and the creation of the world out of nothing.

Cohen. There seems to be little connection between the Jewish philosophers of the first half or two-thirds of the nineteenth century and Hermann Cohen (1842–1918), the head of the Marburg Neo-Kantian school. In a certain sense Cohen may be regarded as a rather unusual case among the philosophers of Judaism of his and the preceding generations, because of the two aspects of his philosophical thought—the general and the Jewish—and the uneasy equilibrium between them. Judaism was by no means the only important theme of his philosophical system; it was one of several and not even his point of departure. There is no doubt that for most of his life Cohen was wholly committed to his brand of Kantianism, in the elaboration of which he displayed considerable originality—it has been maintained with some justification that his doctrine manifests a certain (unintentional) kinship with Hegel's. However, Cohen's idea of God derives from an analysis and a development of certain conceptions of Kant. In Cohen's

view, reason requires that nature be conceived of as conforming to *one* rational plan and that harmony exist between the domains of natural and of moral teleology. These two requirements in turn necessitate the adoption of the idea of God—the word "idea" being used in the Kantian sense, which means that no assertion is made about the metaphysical reality of God. Cohen's theory of ethics stemmed to a considerable extent from Kant's, but he held that the most important ethical principles were discovered by the prophets of Israel, who freed religion from its entanglement with mythology. A harmony also exists between the Messianic notion of the Jewish prophets and the exigency of ethics that the task of coming ever closer to moral perfection be pursued unceasingly. This goal will never be wholly attained. Messianism, too, is an idea in the Kantian sense of the word.

Cohen seems to have changed his attitude in the last years of his life; at least, although he did not explicitly renounce his previous positions, a considerable shift of emphasis can be discerned in his doctrines. The notion of the human individual—an individual who is weak and full of sin—comes to the fore, as well as the conception of a *correlation,* a relationship between God and the individual. This relationship is one of love, the love of God for man and the love of man for God. It is difficult to reconcile the conception of God expounded in Cohen's works of his last period with his Kantian or Neo-Kantian attitude toward metaphysics.

The conceptions of God and the individual and cognate conceptions are set forth in Cohen's posthumously published book *Die Religion der Vernunft aus den Quellen des Judentums* ("Religion of Reason From the Sources of Judaism") and in a series of articles reprinted in his *Jüdische Schriften.*

Rosenzweig. Franz Rosenzweig (1886–1929) published his main philosophical work, *Der Stern der Erlösung* ("The Star of Redemption"), in 1921. This work begins with a rejection of the traditional philosophical attitude that denies the fear of death, maintaining, instead, that this fear is the beginning of the cognition of the All. Man should continue to fear death, despite the indifference of philosophy and its predilection for accepting death. Traditional philosophy is interested exclusively in the universal, and it is monistic—its aim is to discover one principle from which everything can be derived. However, this tendency of philosophy denatures human experience, which knows not one but three separate domains (which Kant had referred to in a different context), namely, God, the world, and man.

According to Rosenzweig, God (like the world and like man) is known through experience (the experience of revelation). In Greek paganism, the most perfect manifestation of paganism in general, every one of these domains subsists by itself: the gods, the cosmos, and man as the tragic, solitary, silent hero. The Biblical religion is concerned with the relation between the three: the relation between God and the world, which is creation; the relation between God and man, which is revelation; and the relation between man and the world, which leads to salvation. The philosophy which renounces the ambition to find one principle for everything that exists and which follows

Biblical religion in centering on the connections between the three domains and between the words and acts that bring about and develop these connections Rosenzweig termed the "narrative" philosophy; the term and the concept were taken over from Schelling, whose influence Rosenzweig repeatedly emphasized.

The Biblical faith brought forth two valid religions, Christianity and Judaism. The first is described by Rosenzweig as the eternal way: the Christian peoples seek in the vicissitudes of time and history the way to salvation. In contradistinction to them the existence of the stateless Jewish people is not concerned with time and history; it is—notwithstanding the hope for final salvation—*already* an eternal life, renewed again and again according to the rhythm of the liturgical Jewish year. Thus, Rosenzweig did not, like Judah Halevi (many of whose poems he had translated and who was very much in his thoughts) oppose the sacred history of the Jewish people to the profane history of the rest of the world but rather to what he considered as the historical existence of the Jews, their involvement in the history of the other nations.

Buber. Since the early years of the twentieth century, Martin Buber (1878–1965) has exercised a powerful influence on both Jews and non-Jews. His theology, centered on the I and Thou relationship, on the conception of a dialogical life, and on the primal importance of the category of "encounter" are discussed in the article BUBER, MARTIN.

In recent years new works dealing with the history of Jewish thought in one of its aspects or in one of its periods appear on the whole to have been more significant than purely philosophical or purely theological Jewish works; in certain cases scholarly works give expression to a personal attitude toward Judaism or toward religion in general. These remarks apply to the two main centers of Jewish philosophical, theological, and scholarly activities, the United States and Israel, as well as to such other countries as France and England. However, it may be too early to attempt to give a definitive summing-up of the tendencies and achievements of a period which verges upon the present.

(See also CABALA and MYSTICISM, HISTORY OF for discussion of Jewish mysticism. See Jewish Philosophy in Index for articles on philosophers in the Jewish tradition.)

Bibliography

GENERAL WORKS

Guttman, Julius, *Philosophies of Judaism.* New York, 1964. Contains extensive bibliography.

Husik, Isaac, *A History of Medieval Jewish Philosophy.* Philadelphia, 1916.

Munk, Salomon, *Mélanges de philosophie juive et arabe.* Paris, 1859.

Strauss, Leo, *Philosophie und Gesetz.* Berlin, 1935.

Strauss, Leo, *Persecution and the Art of Writing.* Glencoe, Ill., 1952.

Vajda, G., *Jüdische Philosophie.* Bern, 1950.

TEXTS

For the works of individual philosophers other than those listed here, see the bibliographies to the articles devoted to them.

Abravanel, Isaac, *Perush l'Moreh Nebukhim.* Vilna, Poland, 1904.

Bar Ḥiyya, Abraham, *Hegyon ha-Nefesh o Sefer ha-Musar,* Y. I. Freiman, ed. Leipzig, 1860.

Bar Ḥiyya, Abraham, *Megillath ha-Megalleh,* A. S. Poznanski, ed. Berlin, 1924.

Cohen, Hermann, *Die Religion der Vernunft aus den Quellen des Judentums.* Leipzig, 1919; 2d ed., Frankfurt, 1929.

Cohen, Hermann, *Jüdische Schriften,* B. Strauss, ed., 3 vols. Berlin, 1924. Introduction by Franz Rosenzweig.

Del Medigo, Elijah, *Sefer Behinat ha-Dat.* Vienna, 1833. Contains commentary and notes by I. S. Reggio.

Ebreo, Leone, *Dialoghi d'amore,* Carl Gebhardt, ed. Heidelberg, 1929.

Formstecher, Solomon, *Die Religion des Geistes.* Frankfurt, 1841.

Heller-Vilensky, S., *Yitzhaq 'Arama ve-Mishnato.* Jerusalem and Tel Aviv, 1956.

Hirsch, Samuel, *Das System der religiösen Anschauung der Juden und sein Verhältnis zum Heidentum, Christentum und zur absoluten Philosophie.* Vol. I, *Die Religionsphilosophie der Juden.* Leipzig, 1842.

Ibn-Da'ud, Abraham, *Sefer ha-Emunah ha-Ramah,* edited with a German translation by Samson Weill. Frankfurt, 1852.

Ibn-Ezra, Abraham, *Yesod Morah v'Sod Torah,* Samuel Waxman, ed. Jerusalem, 1931.

Kaspi, Joseph, *Amuday Kesef u-Maskiyot Kesef,* S. Werbluner, ed. Frankfurt, 1848. Contains two commentaries on Maimonides' *Guide.*

Krochmal, Nachman, *Writings,* S. Rawidowicz, ed. Waltham, Mass., 1961.

Narboni, Moses, *Commentary to the Guide of the Perplexed,* Goldenthal, ed. Vienna, 1852.

Pines, Shlomo, *Nouvelles Études sur Abu'l Barakāt al-Baghdādī.* Paris, 1955.

Saadia ben Joseph, *Polemic Against Hiwi al-Balkhi,* Israel Davidson, ed. New York, 1915.

Steinheim, Solomon, *Die Offenbarung nach dem Lehrbegriff der Synagoge,* 4 vols. Frankfurt, 1835–1865.

Strauss, Leo, *Die Religionskritik Spinozas als Grundlage seiner Bibelwissenschaft.* Berlin, 1930.

Vajda, G., *Isaac Albalag, averroïste juif.* Paris, 1960.

SHLOMO PINES

JOACHIM OF FIORE (c. 1135–1202), Christian mystical philosopher of history, lived in Calabria, Italy, a region characterized by the remote hermit life, yet close to Sicily, the hub of the Mediterranean. This combination of withdrawal from and encounter with the world also characterized Joachim's life. Becoming a Cistercian, by 1177 he was abbot of Curazzo, but he obtained papal permission to retire from monastic administration to a more remote mountainous region, where he founded the order of San Giovanni in Fiore about 1192. Yet he descended to dramatic encounters—in which he prophesied on contemporary events and the advent of Antichrist—with Pope Lucius III (1184), King Richard I of England (1190–1191), and the Holy Roman Emperor Henry VI (1191), and he meditated deeply on contemporary history, especially the two great menaces to Christianity: the infidel and the heretic.

Joachim recorded two mystical experiences: one at Easter, when he was given understanding of the inner concords between the two testaments, and one at Whitsuntide, when he received illumination on the doctrine of the Trinity. Disclaiming the title of prophet, he believed that through the gift of spiritual intelligence he understood the inner spiritual meaning of history.

With papal encouragement, Joachim set out to expound

this belief in his three main works, the *Liber Concordiae,* the *Expositio in Apocalypsim,* and the *Psalterium Decem Chordarum.* His exposition turns chiefly on an interwoven double pattern of twos and threes. The two testaments represent history in two eras, culminating, respectively, in the First and Second Advents and marked continually by concords—for example, twelve Tribes and twelve Churches, seven Seals and seven Openings. History is also trinitarian, growing treelike from the Age (*status*) of the Father (Law) to that of the Son (Grace) to that of the Spirit (Spiritual Understanding), yet in a double "procession" of the third *status* from both the first and the second. This third *status* represents an apotheosis of history, which Joachim equated with the Seventh, Sabbath Age of the traditional Seven Ages, placing it between the worst Antichrist and the end of history. He saw himself on the threshold of the last two generations of the Sixth Age, into which will be crowded the greatest tribulations before the church "crosses Jordan" into the Sabbath of the third *status.*

His strong visual imagination led him to embody this philosophy of history in the remarkable *Liber Figurarum,* through which it was widely disseminated. This doctrine contained revolutionary seeds. Joachim avoided dangerous implications by using his pattern of twos to proclaim that the authority of the Scriptures and church would endure until history ended. His pattern of threes culminated in a spiritual state rather than a historic era. Nonetheless, he almost gave it a starting date—1260—and expected its *Ecclesia Spiritualis,* symbolized in John, to "outlast" the church designated in Peter. This inspired fanatical groups to proclaim the Third Age, the overthrow of existing ecclesiastical institutions, and the transfer of authority to the Eternal Evangel. Joachim's prophecies of two new spiritual orders to lead the church into the Third Age were claimed first by Franciscans and then by Dominicans, Augustinian friars, and even Jesuits.

Condemned as a heretic, revered as a saint, Joachim seldom met with indifference to his views. From the thirteenth to the sixteenth century, when an optimistic expectation of history was proclaimed, it usually drew inspiration from Joachimism.

Works by Joachim

Liber Concordiae Novi ac Veteris Testamenti. Venice, 1519.
Expositio in Apocalypsim. Venice, 1527.
Psalterium Decem Chordarum. Venice, 1527.
Tractatus Super Quatuor Evangelia, E. Buonaiuti, ed. Rome, 1930.
Il libro delle figure, 2d ed., Vol. I, L. Tondelli, ed.; Vol. II, L. Tondelli, M. Reeves, and B. Hirsch-Reich, eds. Turin, 1953.

Works on Joachim

Bloomfield, M., "Joachim of Flora. A Critical Survey of His Canon, Sources, Biography and Influence." *Traditio,* Vol. 13 (1957), 249–311.
Grundmann, H., *Studien über Joachim von Floris.* Leipzig and Berlin, 1927.
Grundmann, H., *Neue Forschungen über Joachim von Fiore.* Marburg, 1950.
La Piana, G., "Joachim of Flora. A Critical Survey." *Speculum,* Vol. 7 (1932), 257–282.
Reeves, M., "The *Liber Figurarum* of Joachim of Fiore." *Mediaeval and Renaissance Studies,* Vol. 2 (1950), 57–81.
Reeves, M., and Hirsch-Reich, B., "The Seven Seals in the Writings of Joachim of Fiore." *Recherches de théologie ancienne et médiévale,* Vol. 21 (1954), 211–247.

MARJORIE E. REEVES

JODL, FRIEDRICH (1849–1914), ranks as one of the most significant representatives of German positivism, although this designation by no means adequately characterizes the full scope of his ideas. Jodl was born in Munich, where in 1880 he qualified as a *Privatdozent* in philosophy. Five years later he was named professor of philosophy at the German University in Prague. In 1896 he accepted a call to the University of Vienna. His many publications ranged over the fields of philosophy and the history of philosophy and ethics, as well as psychology and aesthetics.

Jodl categorically rejected metaphysical speculation. For him, the boundaries of experience were at the same time the boundaries of knowledge; hence, there could be no a priori knowledge, nor any metaphysical cognition of the transcendental. The task of philosophy, he maintained, is to order scientific knowledge systematically and to comprehend it in a unified view of the world. The basis of philosophy, like that of science, can only be experience.

As a consistent empiricist, Jodl criticized phenomenalism, preferring critical realism. The factual existence of a transsubjective reality is guaranteed by the thou-experience, by the existence of one's fellow men. Moreover, without the assumption of an objective external world and without the assurance that we know it as such, natural science would be impossible. Hence, the forms of our intuition and of our thought are not subjective in the sense meant by extreme epistemological idealism; rather, they are also conditioned by the relationships of things. Our knowledge of the world is not subject to a theoretical limit beyond which our consciousness is unable to grasp reality; there is only a frontier that can always be pushed farther back, with the result that the world in its totality constitutes an endless problem, a task for knowledge that can never be definitively solved.

Jodl sought a naturalistic conception of the world, free of religion and metaphysics, such as that of the monistic movement, which he energetically promoted. "We need no other mediator between us and nature except our understanding and a courageous will, nor any mystery behind nature to console us for her; we are alone with nature, and we feel secure because we possess intellect and she behaves according to laws" (*Vom wahren und vom falschen Idealismus,* p. 40).

Jodl treated the problem of God on the basis of this naturalistic monism. Somewhat like John Dewey after him, Jodl, while denying the existence of God in any traditional sense, retained the term "God" as a designation for the highest ideals to which human beings aspire.

In his psychology too Jodl confined himself to the clearest possible presentation of the empirically given facts of mental life, renouncing all metaphysical assumptions. His psychological investigations are unusually rich in acute analyses and genetic explanations. Consciousness is not a substance but an act; it is the inwardness of a living creature. The bearer of consciousness is not an immaterial soul but the living organism; the soul is nothing other than the unified coherence of experience. "Mental" and "physical" are simply two expressions in different languages for one and the same occurrence. Body and consciousness are one; the psychical is the internal, subjective experiencing of neurological processes. An individual experiences as subject the whole complex of his brain processes in internal perception.

In ethics, Jodl was a convinced evolutionist. Ethical values have been subject to continuous transformation; morality is an evolutionary product of the interaction between the individual and society. Jodl made a sharp distinction between the subjective, psychological basis of morality and the objective, axiological criterion for it, although the two, in his view, were most intimately connected. The basis of morality is the will, which rests on social instincts, is influenced by reason, and is aimed at the welfare of the whole. A different question is the establishment of moral norms by which to measure the worth of human attributes and deeds. This requires that one take into account both the motivation and the utilitarian value of an action. In his penetrating studies in the history of ethics, Jodl showed that this discipline has, in the course of its development, increasingly freed itself from metaphysics and has replaced the theocentric foundation with an anthropocentric one.

Jodl, characteristically, was not content with theoretical (historical and systematic) studies in ethics, but sought beyond that to carry out in life a practical, ethical idealism. Imbued with a faith in the value of life and a vigorous optimism in regard to culture and progress, he was an "enlightener" advocating the humanization of culture; an ethically based social life in the spirit of a purely secular, humane morality and freedom of thought. He strongly supported and promoted the system of free popular education and the Ethical Culture movement.

Works by Jodl

Leben und Philosophie David Humes. Halle, 1872.
Die Kulturgeschichtsschreibung. Halle, 1878.
Geschichte der Ethik als philosophischer Wissenschaft, 2 vols. Stuttgart, 1882–1889.
Lehrbuch der Psychologie, 2 vols. Stuttgart and Berlin, 1897.
Ludwig Feuerbach. Stuttgart, 1904.
Der Monismus und die Kulturprobleme der Gegenwart. Leipzig, 1911.
Vom wahren und vom falschen Idealismus. Leipzig, 1914.
Vom Lebenswege, Wilhelm Börner, ed., 2 vols. Stuttgart and Berlin, 1916–1917. Collected essays and lectures.
Aesthetik der bildenden Künste, Wilhelm Börner, ed. Stuttgart and Berlin, 1917; 2d ed., 1922.
Allgemeine Ethik, Wilhelm Börner, ed. Stuttgart and Berlin, 1918.
Kritik des Idealismus, Carl Siegel and Walther Schmied-Kowarzik, eds. Leipzig, 1920.
Geschichte der neueren Philosophie, Karl Roretz, ed. Vienna, Leipzig, and Munich, 1924.

Works on Jodl

Börner, Wilhelm, *Friedrich Jodl.* Stuttgart and Berlin, 1911.
Jodl, Margarete, *Friedrich Jodl, sein Leben und Wirken, dargestellt nach Tagebüchern und Briefen.* Stuttgart and Berlin, 1920.

FRANZ AUSTEDA
Translated by *Albert E. Blumberg*

JOHN DUNS SCOTUS. See DUNS SCOTUS, JOHN.

JOHN OF DAMASCUS or, more commonly, John Damascene (probably c. 674–c. 749) was the last Greek Father of the Church and an important channel of Greek patristic thought to the West. He was one of the few Greek authors known directly to twelfth-century and thirteenth-century European writers (in the Latin translation of Burgundio of Pisa, made around 1150, as well as in that of Robert Grosseteste a century later). Damascene entered the Monastery of St. Sabbas near Jerusalem and eventually was ordained priest. At St. Sabbas he became a prolific writer and gained a reputation for holiness. Both the Eastern and Western churches honor him as a saint, and he was named a Doctor of the Church by Pope Leo XIII in 1890.

His writings include polemics against contemporary heresies, exegesis of Scripture, Greek liturgical poetry, sermons, and dogmatic tracts in theology and philosophy, of which the most important and best known is his "Fount of Knowledge," written after 743. It consists of three parts, entitled in their Latin translations *Dialectica* ("Philosophical Chapters"), *De Haeresibus* ("Concerning Heresies: How They Began and Whence They Drew Their Origin"), and *De Fide Orthodoxa* ("Exact Exposition of Orthodox Faith"). This last tract is the first example of the *summa theologiae,* a genre popular later in the Middle Ages.

As in his other writings, Damascene borrowed heavily from previous Greek writers in "Fount of Knowledge." In the "Philosophical Chapters" his sources include Aristotle's *Categories,* Porphyry, and Ammonius Hermeae, as well as the Greek Fathers from Athanasius the Great to Anastasius the Sinaite, who are not, however, cited by name. In "Heresies," the first eighty accounts are taken verbatim from the "Panarion" of St. Epiphanius. The direct sources of the "Exact Exposition of Orthodox Faith" are an anonymous *De Sacrosancta Trinitate,* Nemesius' *De Natura Hominis,* and Maximus the Confessor's *Epistula ad Marinum* and *Disputatio cum Pyrrho.* Besides these authors, Damascene also called upon Gregory of Nazianzus and Pseudo-Dionysius (who, together with Maximus, were his favorite authors), as well as upon Basil the Great, Gregory of Nyssa, John Chrysostom, Leontius of Byzance, and Anastasius the Sinaite. Nowhere, however, does he show any knowledge of Augustine or other Latin writers except Pope Leo the Great. Nonetheless, he was not a mere compiler; his own outline of doctrine controlled the selection and integration of borrowed texts. Most likely, he merely expressed his own doctrinal positions through the words of his predecessors.

In matters of sacred theology he manifests an accurate and generally clear understanding of most of the dogmas of the Catholic faith. In areas that today are classified as philosophy he perhaps can best be characterized as a "Christian Neoplatonist." He was Christian in his insistence that the universe began in time and through free creation: "Creation . . . was not of the substance of God, but was brought from nothing into being by His will and power and does not involve any change in the nature of God. . . . [Earth] was brought from nothing into being by God on the first day . . . " ("Orthodox Faith," Chase translation, Book I, Ch. 8, p. 178). His view that matter is good and not evil is also Christian. Again, Christianity also led him to affirm that the name best suited for God is "Being," or "He Who Is" (Exodus 3.14).

Nevertheless, he was a Neoplatonist in areas that are not directly treated by divine revelation but that were cultivated by his Greek predecessors (although he does not seem to have been directly acquainted with Plotinus, Proclus, and other pagan Neoplatonists). For example, God's creative (and conservative) operation is likened to "the rays of the sun which warm all things and exercise their force in each in accordance with the natural capacity of each" ("Orthodox Faith," Book I, Ch. 10, p. 191)—a frequent Neoplatonic simile. Moreover, the basic relationship between one creature and another and between all creatures and the Creator is described in Neoplatonic terms of the lower to the higher, with God frequently transcending the order in question. Damascene maintained that an angel is uncircumscribed and undeterminate when compared to corporeal things but circumscribed and determinate in relationship to God, who alone is completely without any circumscription or determination. Or an angel, because relatively immutable, is immaterial in relationship to sensible things but material with respect to God, who alone is totally immutable and, thus, supremely immaterial. Matter has, therefore, become synonymous with mere mutability (*ibid.*, Book II, Ch. 3, p. 205). Again, "to be real" is equivalent to "to be one" (*ibid.*, Book I, Ch. 5), since being real is equivalent to being perfect and valuable and unity is that which contributes perfection and value; the exclusion from God of any essential attributes seems to rest upon this equivalence. If he is supremely real, then he must be absolutely simple—"True reason teaches us that the Divinity is simple and has one simple operation which is good and which effects all things" (*ibid.*, Ch. 10, p. 191)—and, thus, without any attribute that might threaten that stark simplicity. Upon this equivalence, too, rests our inability to predicate any such property of him. We can know that God exists for two reasons: (1) all things are subject to change of some sort, but that which changes must be created; hence there is a creator; (2) "the very harmony of creation, its preservation and governing teach us that there is a God who put all this together and keeps it together" (*ibid.*, Ch. 3, p. 169).

Nevertheless, we cannot know what he is but only what he is not. We can speak figuratively and symbolically of him; we can describe his relations to creatures with such terms as "master," "king," "creator," and "judge"; we can point to his operations or what follows from his divine nature through such adjectives as "good," "wise," "just," and "holy." Such terms, however, do not reveal the divine substance itself but merely what is peripheral to and consequent upon it. At best we have such negative expressions as "incorruptible," "incorporeal," "incomprehensible," "invisible," "ineffable," "eternal," "infinite," and the like.

Bibliography

The works of John of Damascus, edited by M. Lequien, were published as *Opera Omnia* in J. P. Migne, ed., *Patrologia Graeca* (Paris, 1857–1866), Vols. 94–96. A modern edition of the medieval Latin translation, *Saint John Damascene—De Fide Orthodoxa: Versions of Burgundio and Cerbanus*, edited by E. Buytaert, appeared as Vol. 8 of *Franciscan Institute Publications* (New York, 1955). *Saint John of Damascus: Writings*, an English translation by F. Chase, includes a bibliography and was published as Vol. 37 of *Fathers of the Church* (New York, 1958).

For works on John of Damascus, see J. M. Hoeck, "Stand und Aufgaben der Damaskenos-Forschung," in *Orientalia Christiana Periodica*, Vol. 17 (1951), 5–60; M. Jugie, "Jean Damascène," in *Dictionnaire de théologie catholique* (Paris, 1903–1950), Vol. 8; Basilius Studer, *Die theologische Arbeitsweise des Johannes von Damaskus* (Ettal, 1956); Leo Sweeney, S.J., "John Damascene and Divine Infinity," in *New Scholasticism*, Vol. 35 (January 1961), 85–86; Leo Sweeney, S.J., "John Damascene's 'Infinite Sea of Essence,'" in *Studia Patristica*, Vol. 6 (Berlin, 1962), 248–263.

LEO SWEENEY, S.J.

JOHN OF JANDUN (c. 1286–c. 1328), also known as Jean de Jandun and Johannes de Janduno, foremost among the Averroists at Paris in the fourteenth century. He was born in the village of Jandun in the French province of Champagne. The estimate of his date of birth is based on the year 1310, the earliest date found on any writing definitely attributable to him; at the time of this first or very early publication, John would have been a recent master of arts, and reckoning by the age and curricular requirements in effect at the University of Paris in the early fourteenth century, he could not have been much more than 24 years of age. John was active throughout the next decade and a half as master of arts at the Collège de Navarre, in Paris, although he was nominally canon at Senlis—the kind of preferment awarded a practicing teacher and scholar during the Middle Ages. At Paris he lectured on the standard curriculum of the Faculty of Arts: Aristotle's *Physics*, *De Coelo et Mundo*, *De Anima*, *Metaphysics*, *Parva Naturalia*, and *Rhetoric* and Averroës' *De Substantia Orbis*. John's commentaries on these works date from 1310 to 1323. Additional writings from this period attest to his interest in particular problems arising in his lectures and commentaries; there still survive many independent *quaestiones* and *disputationes*, which, in the medieval tradition, supplemented the normal course of studies with special studies and advanced seminars.

By 1324 he was closely associated with Marsilius of Padua, also a master of arts at Paris, in connection with Marsilius' famous and controversial *Defensor Pacis*, published that year. Although John does not seem to have shared in the actual composition of the work, he was apparently an intellectual intimate of Marsilius. The *Defensor Pacis*, a powerful affirmation of the temporal and civil authority over the spiritual and papal, occasioned enough ecclesiastical outrage for John and Marsilius to deem it prudent to leave Paris and seek the protection of Louis IV of Bavaria. Louis was himself embroiled with Pope John XXII on matters of political and spiritual authority and was soon to harbor another intellectual fugitive from Paris, William of Ockham. In 1326 and 1327 a series of papal bulls appeared specifically attacking John and Marsilius, and the final one, dated October 23, 1327, excommunicated them as "heretics and heresiarchs."

The remainder of John's life was brief. He followed Louis in the invasion of Italy and was rewarded with the episcopate of Ferrara. Probably en route to assume his new duties, he died at Todi, not later than August 31, 1328.

Thought. To treat John of Jandun's philosophy, as many historians have done, as a blind recapitulation of the Commentator (the title by which Averroës was referred to throughout the Middle Ages and the Renaissance) and his special views on Aristotle would be an oversimplification. It is true that John did, at one point in his commentaries, call himself the "ape of Averroës," but this was in the context of a particular passage of Aristotle's *Metaphysics*, where John considered Averroës' remarks perfectly adequate. It is also true that John preferred, generally, Averroës' rendering of Aristotle, but it is not illuminating to call him "Averroist" without severe qualifications. Other medieval philosophers (for example, Siger of Brabant) can be termed Averroist, but their speculative positions were sometimes methodologically quite distinct from those of John. It is probably most accurate to place him in the philosophical tradition and method sometimes exemplified in Christian Augustinianism, always recognizing, however, that he was oriented intellectually within the traditions of the Faculty of Arts rather than those of the Faculty of Theology. John's espousal of a *sensus agens* (active principle in the process of sensation), of a plurality of substantial forms in the individual (one for each of the three functions of living: vegetating, sensing, and thinking), of the soul's ability to grasp separate substances (that is, forms) directly, of form as the immanent and essential cause of natural activity, and of other kindred doctrines can be found in the thinking of many Augustinian theologians close to his time, such as Bonaventure, Peter John Olivi, Roger Marston, Duns Scotus, and Peter Aureol. John's own advocacy of these views arose, however, out of the use of Averroës in the analysis of Aristotle for the Faculty of Arts curriculum. Although John's version of Averroism and the tradition called Christian Augustinianism had much in common methodologically, they sprang from different institutional contexts.

John's interpretations of Averroës' commentaries on Aristotle were both acute and influential (as late as the seventeenth century his writings were still used alongside those of Averroës by the Paduan pedagogue Cesare Cremonini), but his place in intellectual history is due less to the conspicuous originality of his thought than to his unusually explicit delineation of the respective domains of faith and reason. Whenever confronted, in his analysis of Aristotle, with a conclusion severely at variance with some doctrine of Christian faith, John appended an apologia of the following kind: "It must be noted that, although the *dicta* are . . . according to the principles of Aristotle and the Commentator, it must be replied firmly according to faith and truth that the world is not eternal." Similar passages abound in John's commentaries; whenever conclusions of reason arrived at in the logic of Aristotle and Averroës differed from the dictates of Christian dogma, John introduced statements proclaiming the consistency of the reasoning but immediately ceding truth itself to the preeminent demands of faith.

Such remarks have had two interpretations. First, John has been indicted, with other so-called Averroists; as holding a theory of "double truth"—that is, that statements of faith, on the one hand, and conclusions of reason, on the other, can be simultaneously true, yet contradictory. This charge has been discounted effectively by Étienne Gilson; no medieval writings maintaining such a self-inconsistent view have yet been found. Medieval thinkers never stated more than the position that although reason can systematically reach certain conclusions, Christian faith is nevertheless the final arbiter of truth when such conclusions conflict with matters of doctrine.

Second, certain of John's disclamatory passages have been interpreted as actually revealing a fundamental religious insincerity. For example, he said:

> This is not known *per se*, nor is it demonstrable by any human proof, but we believe this to be so solely by divine authority and by the Sacred Scriptures. And to the credulity toward things of this kind and similar things, the habit of listening to this sort of thing from childhood adds a good deal.

Or again:

> If anyone knows how to prove this and to make it accord with the principles of philosophy, let him rejoice in this possession, and I will not grudge him, but declare that he surpasses my ability.

And finally:

> although every form inherent in matter is corruptible I say, however, that God can perpetuate it and preserve it eternally from corruption. I do not know the manner of this; God knows it.

Such statements have been interpreted as indicating a radical insincerity in John's thinking, a covert mocking of Christian faith. Thus, some historians have suggested that John was not merely maintaining a "double truth" but actually affirming the superior reliability of the conclusions of unaided reasoning in the mode of Aristotle and could therefore stand as an early precursor of seventeenth-century rationalism and libertarianism.

On close examination, however, John's position on the relation between the claims of faith and claims of reason does not seem to have been distinctively more radical than the thinking of many other medievals. (Similar disclaimers of reason in favor of faith can be found in many commentaries on Aristotle, including those of Thomas Aquinas.) Such discrepancies and apparent conflicts reflect, in small part, a strong institutional rivalry between the faculties of arts and theology and, in large part, a fundamental intellectual crisis occasioned by the confrontation between Greek rationalism and Christian dogma.

Works by John of Jandun

Quaestiones de Anima. Fourteen printings in Venice between 1473 and 1587.

Quaestiones Super Libros Physicorum. Twelve printings in Venice, Paris, and Lyons between 1488 and 1598.

Quaestiones in Duodecim Libros Metaphysicae. Four printings in Venice between 1525 and 1586.

John's most influential writings, the commentaries on Aristotle—including those listed above—can be found only in Renaissance editions. Some lesser writings exist in printed editions published in the fifteenth and sixteenth centuries. All of John's works can be found in manuscript form in various European libraries.

Works on John of Jandun

Gilson, Étienne, "La Doctrine de la double vérité," in *Études de philosophie médiévale*. Strasbourg, 1921. Pp. 51–75.

Gilson, Étienne, *History of Christian Philosophy in the Middle Ages*. New York, 1955.

MacClintock, Stuart, *Perversity and Error*. Bloomington, Ind., 1956.

Valois, N., "Jean de Jandun et Marsile de Padoue, auteurs du *Defensor Pacis*," in *Histoire littéraire de la France*, Vol. XXXIII. Paris, 1903. Pp. 528–623.

STUART MacCLINTOCK

JOHN OF LA ROCHELLE (c. 1190–1245), or de Rupella, was a Franciscan philosopher, theologian, and preacher at the University of Paris. The first clear reference to him (in Thomas of Cantimpré) indicates that in 1238 he was already a friar and a master in theology. From John's own writings, as well as from his knowledge of and interest in philosophy, we may deduce that he had studied and perhaps taught in the faculty of arts before becoming a theologian. His *Summa de Vitiis* ("Summa on Vices and Sins"), which manifests his penchant for ethical questions, is directly dependent on William of Auxerre, Prevostinus, and Stephen Langton, who apparently were John's teachers in the faculty of theology. It seems that only after Alexander of Hales entered the order, in 1236, did John become acquainted with that famous theologian; thereafter John was Alexander's faithful companion and collaborator. Both seem to have taught at Paris until their deaths in 1245.

Though a famous preacher and Biblical commentator, John is known primarily as a "summist" interested in questions of psychology and morals. Both topics are combined in his early *Tractatus de Anima et de Virtutibus* ("Tract on the Soul and the Virtues"), a kind of rambling compilation of definitions of the soul, the divisions of the soul's powers according to the philosophers, and the division of the virtues according to Plotinus, Cicero, Aristotle, and Augustine. Ethical questions predominate in John's proposed *Summa Theologicae Disciplinae* ("Summa of Theological Learning"). As set forth in the prologue to the *Summa De Articulis Fidei* ("Summa on the Articles of Faith"), the larger summa of theology was to include both doctrines and morals. "Morals is divided into two parts: on sins and the remedies of sins. These remedies are four in number: commandments, virtues, the gifts of the Holy Spirit, and the sacraments" (ms. Milan, *Brera A.D. IX. 7*, fol. 75a). Only parts of such a summa seem to have been completed: the "Summa on Vices and Sins," *De Praeceptis et Consiliis* (a tract "On Precepts and Counsels"), *De Virtutibus* ("On Virtues"), and the *Summa de Donis* ("On the Gifts of the Holy Spirit"). The same interest is reflected in the lengthy and influential tract *De Legibus et Praeceptis* ("On Laws and Precepts"), which is probably John's work, and in such Disputed Questions as "The Fall of Human Nature," "On Negligence, Hypocrisy, the Seven Capital Sins," "On Usury," and "On the Just War," all as yet unpublished.

His early "Tract on the Soul" was developed into the more mature *Summa de Anima* ("Summa on the Soul"), which is rightly regarded as the first scholastic textbook of psychology. Beginning with proofs (from Avicenna and Augustine) for the existence of the soul, the first part examines the essence, causes, and properties of the soul and its union with the body (giving a none too clear, yet basically Aristotelian, solution of this latter problem), with a final section on immortality and the status of the soul after death. In the second half John considered at length the problem of the powers of the soul: their relation to the essence and their division according to Pseudo-Augustine (*De Spiritu et Anima*), John of Damascus, and Avicenna. The classification of the external and internal senses, the cognitive and motive powers, follows closely the *De Anima* of Avicenna, with some slight additional material. A comparison with the earlier "Tract" leads us to conclude that the *Summa de Anima* is incomplete. It ends abruptly in the midst of a discussion on the will. The large number of extant manuscripts attests to its popularity in the Middle Ages. If not strikingly original, the summa is of interest also for its use of the philosophers at a time when theologians were inclined to reject their help. John pointedly rejected such an attitude in a university sermon:

> If philosophy is neglected, one may fear lest "there be found no smiths in Israel" (I Samuel 13.19), that is, philosophers who will sharpen our wits like "swords" and with shining "lances" attack the enemy at a distance. The devil himself seeks to stamp out the study of philosophy because he does not want Christians to have sharp minds. (*Collectanea Franciscana*, Vol. 28 [1958], 50)

Last, John is to be considered the primary author or compiler of the first and third books of the so-called "Summa of Alexander of Hales." (See also ALEXANDER OF HALES.)

Works by John of La Rochelle

Tractatus de Anima et Virtutibus, P. Michaud-Quantin, ed. Paris, 1964.

Summa de Anima, T. Domenichelli, ed. Prato, 1882; new ed. in preparation.

Eleven Marian Sermons, K. Lynch, ed. New York, 1961.

Works on John of La Rochelle

Brady, I., "Law in the Summa Fratris Alexandri." *Proceedings of the American Catholic Philosophical Association*, Vol. 24 (1950), 133–147.

Doucet, V., *Prolegomena in Librum III Necnon in Libros I et II "Summa Fratris Alexandri,"* pp. 211–227 and *passim*. Quaracchi, Italy, 1948.

Lottin, O., *Psychologie et morale aux XIIᵉ et XIIIᵉ siècles*, 6 vols. Gembloux, Belgium, 1942–1960.

Michaud-Quantin, P., "Les Puissances de l'âme chez Jean de la Rochelle." *Antonianum*, Vol. 24 (1949), 489–505.

IGNATIUS BRADY, O.F.M.

JOHN OF MIRECOURT (fl. c. 1345) was a Cistercian known as the "white monk" (*monachus albus*). He is notable mainly for the condemnation in 1347 by the chancellor of the University of Paris of fifty articles taken from his commentary on Peter Lombard's *Sentences*. This commentary, which seems to have been his main work, remains unpublished. John's views gave rise to widespread controversy, coming at a time of renewed intellectual ferment at the University of Paris and within a year of similar official action against the writings of Nicholas of Autrecourt. For this reason the two thinkers are often bracketed together. Within certain limits this is justifiable, for they both expressed a like insistence upon the limitations of natural certainty, confining it to the principle of contradiction. But John also stressed the uncertainty which derived from God's absolute freedom to do as he willed, and from this many of his most radical conclusions flowed.

John distinguished between certain knowledge and experience (external and internal). The first, which allowed of no denial, is expressed in the principle of contradiction. Certainty applied to the inner knowledge which each person has of his own existence and thus of the general concept of existence. John followed St. Augustine in concluding that even to doubt one's existence was to affirm it, since to doubt something means that one must be. Experience of the existence of individual things in the outside world, on the other hand, did not provide the same infallibility. While it was also reached directly, by intuition as opposed to mental representations or species, it could nevertheless be illusory, for if God so willed he could create the appearance of something which did not really exist. It was this inherent uncertainty in all contingent being which was at the root of John of Mirecourt's skepticism. It led him, on the one hand, to deny the principle of causality and the validity of inferring the existence of one thing from another (as did Nicholas of Autrecourt), including God's existence. On the other hand, it removed God's actions from human inference in attributing any possibility to God's absolute power (*potentia absoluta*). Thus, John, together with such Ockhamists as Robert Holkot, Adam Woodham, and the earlier Thomas Buckingham, concedes that God could act in such a way that he violated the accepted tenets of moral theology. The conclusions which he drew constituted the main body of the propositions condemned by the chancellor of Paris in 1347. These included the assertion that God could mislead Christ and cause Christ to mislead his disciples and hate God (1–6); that God could cause a man to hate him (31–32); that God was the cause of all human actions and so of a sinner's sin (10–14, 16–18, 33–34); that God predestines men to glory or damnation because he foresees that the good will perform good works and make proper use of their free will and that the evil will not (47–50); and that a being higher than God could be envisaged (46). John was an eclectic, taking different elements from seemingly contradictory sources, as in his views on sin and future contingents. He also upheld the cognitive function of the will. A full assessment still awaits a proper study of his commentary on the *Sentences*.

Bibliography

Chatelain, E., and Denifle, H., *Chartularium Universitatis Parisiensis*. Paris, 1889–1897. Vol. II, 1147, pp. 610–613.

Stegmüller, Francis, "Die zwei Apologien des Jean de Mirecourt." *Recherches de théologie ancienne et médiévale*, Vol. 5 (1933), 40–78, 192–204.

Werner, Karl, *Der Augustinismus in der Scholastik des späteren Mittelalters*. Vienna, 1883.

GORDON LEFF

JOHN OF PARIS (c. 1255–1306), or John Quidort, also known as Surdus or Monoculus, was a Dominican scholastic philosopher and theologian, priest, and author. A native of Paris, John studied and taught philosophy at the University of Paris before entering the Dominican order at St. Jacques prior to 1279. As bachelor in theology he lectured on the *Sentences* of Peter Lombard (1284–1286) and energetically defended the then suspect doctrines of Thomas Aquinas in a famous refutation, *Correctorium "Circa,"* of the *Correctorium* of William de la Mare, which had been officially adopted by the Franciscans. Certain unknown adversaries managed to twist or misinterpret 16 statements delivered in class, and in 1286 they had John denounced to the authorities. Although he ably explained the true meaning of his innocent statements, his academic career was temporarily suspended. In his defense of Thomas, John showed a clear understanding of the Thomistic distinction between essence and existence in creatures, the unicity of substantial form in material substance, the individuation of material substances by matter alone, and the pure potentiality of first matter.

From 1300 on John was again active in Paris, teaching, preaching, and writing. His sermons and treatises testify to the political and social unrest of the times. During the struggle between Pope Boniface VIII and Philip the Fair, John wrote the important treatise *De Potestate Regia et Papali* ("On Royal and Papal Power," 1302), in which, following Aquinas, he defended a middle position between the papalist and imperialist extremes. He clearly distinguished between two autonomous societies in Christendom—church and state—each of which has its independent, legitimate source of authority and its rightful area of concern. For him the source of royal power was not delegation from the pope but the nature of mankind acting reasonably and freely for the common good of society.

In 1304, John was given license to incept in theology, succeeding Raymond Romani as master. In 1305, John presided over a solemn disputation before the bishop of Paris and the faculty of theology, in which he maintained that since the church had not yet defined the doctrine of transsubstantiation, one could hold as equally probable the doctrine that later became known as "impanation"—that is, the continued existence of bread after consecration, now assumed in Christ. This novel view was examined by a number of bishops and theologians, who considered it heretical. John was suspended from all teaching and preaching, perpetual silence being imposed upon him under pain of excommunication. John appealed his case to the papal *curia* at Bordeaux, where he died on September 22, 1306, while awaiting a decision. At the very beginning of the Eucharistic controversy he had publicly expressed his willingness to retract his view should it prove contrary to the teaching of the church.

John was a gifted speculative thinker who, while accepting the basic principles of Aquinas, was anxious to deal with new problems in philosophy and theology.

Bibliography

Glorieux, Palémon. *Répertoire des maîtres en théologie*, Vol. 1, No. 60 (1933), 189–193.

Grabmann, Martin, "Studien zu Johannes Quidort von Paris,

O.P.," in *Sitzungsberichte der Bayerischen Akademie der Wissenschaften zu München*. Munich, 1922.

Käppeli, Thomas, "Praedicator Monoculus." *Archivum Fratrum Praedicatorum*, Vol. 27 (1957), 120–167.

Leclercq, Jean, *Jean de Paris et l'ecclésiologie du XIIIᵉ siècle*. Paris, 1942.

Müller, Jean P., "Les Reportations des deux premiers livres du Commentaire sur les Sentences de Jean Quidort de Paris, O.P." *Angelicum*, Vol. 33 (1956), 361–414.

Müller, Jean P., "La Date de la lecture sur les Sentences de Jean Quidort." *Angelicum*, Vol. 36 (1959), 129–162.

Quétif, Jacques, and Échard, Jacques, *Scriptores Ordinis Praedicatorum*, Vol. I. Paris, 1719. Pp. 500–502.

Roensch, Frederick J., *Early Thomistic School*. Dubuque, Iowa, 1964.

JAMES A. WEISHEIPL, O.P.

JOHN OF ST. THOMAS (1589–1644), Spanish theologian and philosopher, was born John Poinsot, the son of an Austrian, at Lisbon, Portugal, and died at Fraga, Spain. When he entered the Dominican order he took his name from St. Thomas Aquinas. John studied philosophy at Coimbra, Portugal, and theology at Louvain, taught philosophy and theology in Dominican houses of study, at Alcalá de Henares (1613–1630), and from 1630 to 1643 was a professor at the University of Alcalá. Apart from certain Latin and vernacular works of devotion, his writings consist of two series of textbooks, one in philosophy, the *Cursus Philosophicus* (which comprises "Ars Logica," covering logic, and "Philosophia Naturalis," on natural philosophy), the other in theology, the *Cursus Theologicus* (a systematic commentary on Aquinas' *Summa of Theology*).

The "Ars Logica" is fundamentally Aristotelian logic, but John developed the content of the course in two directions: toward a formal theory of correct reasoning and toward a material logic that attends to the meaning of the actual terms of a proposition and thus anticipates some of the problems of epistemology and semantics. John's terminology differs from that of modern logic (*propositio copulativa* is the modern conjunctive proposition; *propositio disiunctiva* the alternative proposition; *bona consequentia* means *implication*). However, it has been claimed, by J. J. Doyle, that the "Ars Logica" and Whitehead and Russell's *Principia Mathematica* are fundamentally similar as formal systems. Concerning material implication, John taught that one may infer from the particular proposition ("Some man is rational") to the universal proposition ("Every man is rational") in cases where the matter is necessary. To some extent he anticipated problems in the philosophy of science and the metasciences and also the theory of induction.

His philosophy of nature is a systematic exposition of a type of Thomism much influenced by the commentaries of Cajetan. Nature is the world of bodies, of being that is subject to change (*ens mobile*), explained in terms of the four Aristotelian causes, substance and accidents, act and potency, matter and form.

John treated certain questions in a novel way—for example, immanent action, the sort of activity that begins and ends within one agent and is typical of psychic functions (see *Cursus Philosophicus*, "Philosophia Naturalis," I, q. 14, a. 3). John had no separate treatise on metaphysics,

but his views on the ultimate character of reality were frequently presented in his explanation of parallel problems (substance, causality, potency) in the "Philosophia Naturalis." The "Theological Course" also contains explanations of problems in speculative philosophy. Cognition, on the sensory and intellectual levels, is explained in terms of a metaphysics of causality (I, q. 1, disp. II, a. 12, n. 4). John was one source of the theory of the distinction between three degrees of knowledge—physical, mathematical, and metaphysical—popularized in the twentieth century by Jacques Maritain.

In his discussion of the gifts of the Holy Ghost (*Cursus Theologicus*, IV, disp. XVII), John had much to say on the relation of knowledge to wisdom. He viewed ethics and political philosophy as speculative sciences and did not write much on practical philosophy. On moral questions he adopted the position called "probabilism"; that is, in moral situations where a person is really in doubt about what he should do, he may solve his doubt by adopting any judgment that has been made by a prudent moralist concerning the proposed action (*Cursus Theologicus*, IV, disp. XII, a. 3, n. 4).

John's writings are useful for their historical information on later scholasticism. He influenced many recent Thomists, notably Maritain, J. M. Ramírez, Joseph Gredt, and Yves Simon.

Works by John of St. Thomas

Cursus Philosophicus, Beatus Reiser, ed., 3 vols. Turin, 1930–1937; 2d ed., 1948.

Cursus Theologicus. Opere et studio Monachorum Solesmensium. Paris, Rome, and Tournai, Belgium, 1933——.

The Material Logic of John of St. Thomas: Basic Treatises, translated by Yves Simon, J. J. Glanville, and G. D. Hollenhorst. Chicago, 1955.

Outlines of Formal Logic, translated by F. C. Wade. Milwaukee, Wis., 1962.

Works on John of St. Thomas

Doyle, J. J., "John of St. Thomas and Mathematical Logic." *New Scholasticism*, Vol. 17, No. 1 (1953), 3–38.

Maritain, Jacques, *Philosophy of Nature*. New York, 1951. See for a reworking of details of John's theory.

VERNON J. BOURKE

JOHN OF SALISBURY (c. 1115–1180), scholar, humanist, and bishop, was born at Old Sarum (Wiltshire), England. After primary instruction from a rural priest he went to France to study in 1136. He read dialectic first under Abelard, during the latter's last period at Paris, then under Alberic and Robert of Melun. In 1138 he began the study of grammar under Richard of Arranches, probably at Chartres, where he also studied under William of Conches; at Chartres too he studied rhetoric and part of the quadrivium. In 1141 he took up theology at Paris under Gilbert of Poitiers and Robert Pullen and made the acquaintance of other masters. He was then probably secretary for a short time to Abbot Peter of Celle (1147–1148). He was a member of the Roman Curia, and in 1148 attended the Council of Rheims, where he knew well both Bernard of Clairvaux and Gilbert of Poitiers. That year he was introduced by St. Bernard to Theobald, archbishop of

Canterbury, with whom he spent a short time. Between 1149 and 1153 John was a member of the Roman Curia in Apulia and elsewhere and was on terms of intimacy with Pope Adrian IV (Nicholas Breakspear). From 1153/1154 to 1161 he was the trusted secretary of Archbishop Theobald and was one of a distinguished household that included Thomas Becket, Roger of Pont l'Évêque, later archbishop of York, and the Italian lawyer Vacarius. He advised and represented the archbishop and wrote his letters, many of which dealt with business of the Curia. After Theobald's death, John entered the service of Thomas Becket, to whom he remained a loyal, although not blind, supporter during Thomas' later controversy with King Henry. Accused by King Henry II of encouraging appeals to Rome, John preceded his patron into exile in 1163 and spent some years in Rheims living with Peter of Celle, then abbot of St. Rémy, and working in Thomas' interest with King Louis VII of France. He rejoined Thomas shortly before the latter's return to England in December 1170 and preceded him to Canterbury. John was at dinner with the archbishop when the knights arrived and was present, although perhaps in concealment, at Thomas' murder in the cathedral. He subsequently worked for Thomas' canonization and, in return, was invited by King Louis in July 1176 to become bishop of Chartres. He attended the third Lateran Council in 1179 and died the following year at Chartres, where he was buried.

John was author of a multitude of letters as well as short lives of Anselm and Thomas Becket, the latter a jejune work that is doubly disappointing in view of the writer's literary skill and intimate knowledge of his subject. His *Historia Pontificalis* is a continuation of the *Chronicle* of Sigebert of Gembloux and covers the years 1148–1152. As a scholar he composed the versified *Entheticus de Dogmate Philosophorum* (1155), a rehearsal of his knowledge of ancient philosophy, as well as the two works on which his medieval reputation rested: the *Policraticus* ("The Statesman") and *Metalogicon*.

The *Policraticus*, subtitled *De Nugis Curialium et Vestigiis Philosophorum* ("Concerning the Vain Purposes of Courtiers and the Traditions of Philosophers"), is a disorderly, rambling work without detailed plan. Dealing in part with such faults and follies of the great as hunting, gaming, dreams, and astrology and with witchcraft, it contains a variety of anecdotes and personal experiences. Books 6–10 deal with the character and duties of a prince, and the work has consequently been called—somewhat misleadingly—the first medieval treatise on political thought. It is, in fact, a sociological study, but it contains a well-known passage on the ministerial function of the prince, who holds the sword in order to perform duties beneath the dignity of the priesthood, which John always considers the superior power, even when emphasizing the virtue of patriotism. The passage shows no clear indication of acquaintance with the almost contemporary teaching of St. Bernard on the possession of two swords by the papacy. In the last book John proclaims the right and duty of citizens to kill a tyrant. The passage has often been quoted in later centuries as authoritative, but it is probably merely an echo of Roman republican rhetoric without any practical application to the world of the twelfth century.

The *Metalogicon* (1159–1160) was written at almost the same time as the *Policraticus*. It is an apologia for true logic, or rather for philosophical training as an introduction to a civilized way of life, contrasted with the technical logic of the schools, which was fit only for sciolists or such careerists as Cornificius, whose name recurs as an unidentified opponent of humane learning. John recounts his own educational experiences (*Metalogicon* II, 10), with a tribute to Bernard of Chartres and a sketch of his methods, and sets out several current opinions on the nature of universals (*ibid.*, II, 17–20). There are the pure nominalists, such as Roscelin, who held universals to be mere words (*voces*), and Abelard (as John understood—or misunderstood—him), who substituted the term *sermones*. There are those who, like Bernard of Chartres, regarded universals as the Ideas of Plato, and with these may be reckoned Gilbert of Poitiers with his "original forms" (*nativae formae*), while others regarded them merely as a group (*collectio*). John himself adopts an Aristotelian position: universals are not independent realities, but mental images (*figmenta rationis*) of real kinds (*genera, species*) into which things can be grouped and from which the intellect can abstract those qualities that resemble those of other members of the group. John wrote no systematic philosophical work and declared himself a tolerant skeptic of the Academy, or of what is now known as Late Platonism. Nevertheless, he had great admiration for Aristotle, whom he called "the Philosopher" par excellence; without his New Logic, John maintained, and especially without the *Topics*, dialectic is doomed to be a hit-or-miss affair (*sine eo non disputatur arte sed casu*). Both these considerable works, the *Policraticus* and the *Metalogicon*, and probably also the *Entheticus*, were dedicated to Thomas Becket.

The *Historia Pontificalis*, written over a period of years and finally revised in 1164, is not professedly concerned with thought, although the controversy between St. Bernard and Gilbert of Poitiers is the most important episode contained in it. John gives the theological position of the bishop of Poitiers at considerable length, although he does not clarify the real point at issue.

John was neither a theologian nor an original thinker. He was rather, in the words of Bishop William Stubbs, "the central figure of English learning," or, perhaps more accurately, the writer of the twelfth century who came nearest to the modern critical attitude toward men and their ideas. His celebrated comparison of St. Bernard and Gilbert is the keenest analysis of character and style to appear between the days of Augustine and those of Petrarch, and this is not the only section of his writing that attains such a high level. Moreover, he is the only writer of the twelfth century to pass in review the schools of the day. He read widely, and his style was perhaps the most classical and idiomatic of all medieval attempts to write in imitation of classical models. He lacks the virtuosity and the emotional appeal of Bernard, and his vocabulary and constructions are at times difficult. He is unable to plan or to discard. But his cool judgment and unemphatic language always satisfy the reader. Similarly, his letters, especially those written during the denouement of the Becket affair, display a caustic wit that does not appear in his longer works. He knew on terms of equality almost all the distinguished men of his day. This width of acquaintance he shared with St. Bernard, but whereas the abbot of Clairvaux saw them as figures in black and white, the objects of his emotion and rhetoric, John saw them with a detached, slightly cynical eye that could observe their foibles as well as their gifts. He has won his reward: we speak of his age and society as the age of John of Salisbury.

Bibliography

The collected works of John of Salisbury were published in Latin as *Joannis Saresberiensis Opera Omnia*, 5 vols., J. A. Giles, ed. (Oxford, 1848). A reprint, edited by J. P. Migne, appears in *Patrologia Latina*, Vol. CXCIX. Individual works include the *Entheticus de Dogmate Philosophorum*, C. Petersen, ed. (Hamburg, 1843); *Policraticus sive de Nugis Curialium*, 2 vols., C. C. J. Webb, ed. (Oxford, 1909); *Metalogicon*, C. C. J. Webb, ed. (Oxford, 1929); and *Historia Pontificalis*, R. L. Poole, ed. (Oxford, 1927).

An English translation of Books 1–4 and parts of Books 7 and 8 of the *Policraticus* may be found in J. B. Pike, *Frivolities of Courtiers and Footprints of Philosophers* (Minneapolis, 1938); a translation of Books 4–6 and parts of Books 7 and 8 appears in J. Dickinson, *The Statesman's Book* (New York, 1927). Other translations are the *Metalogicon*, translated by D. D. McGarry (Berkeley, 1955); and the *Historia Pontificalis*, excellently translated and annotated by M. Chibnall from the Poole edition (Edinburgh and London, 1956).

For works on John of Salisbury, see C. S. Schaarschmidt, *Johannes Saresberiensis* (Leipzig, 1862); and R. W. Carlyle and A. J. Carlyle, *A History of Medieval Humanism in the Life and Writings of John of Salisbury* (London, 1950). A valuable introduction appears in W. J. Miller, H. E. Butler, and C. N. L. Brooke, *The Letters of John of Salisbury*, Vol. I (1153–1161) (Edinburgh and London, 1955).

DAVID KNOWLES

JOHN OF THE CROSS, ST. (1542–1591), or Juan de la Cruz, Spanish mystic and poet, was born at Fontiveros, near Ávila. His family was poor, and as a child he worked in a hospital at Medina del Campo in return for training at the Jesuit school. In 1563 he entered the Carmelite order in Medina, and in the following years he studied at the University of Salamanca. In 1567, the year he was ordained priest, he met St. Teresa of Ávila and planned to start a monastic community in line with the kind of reform she had effected among nuns. Such a community was started in 1568, under the original Carmelite rule and in conditions of great poverty and austerity. This was a prelude to energetic reforming work by St. John and growing opposition on the part of his superiors. In 1577 he was imprisoned at Toledo for eight months and was maltreated. In 1591 he was banished to a lonely monastic house at Úbeda, where he died near the end of that year. His chief prose writings were *The Ascent of Mount Carmel*, *The Dark Night of the Soul*, *The Spiritual Canticle*, and *The Living Flame of Love*. His poems have given him a secure place in the history of Spanish literature.

The best-known feature of St. John's mystical writings is his description of the dark night of the soul (or spirit—*noche oscura del espíritu*). The imagery of night is indeed very prominent in his works and was used by him in a variety of senses. By "the dark night" he principally meant the extreme sense of desolation and despair that overcomes the soul after its first illumination by God. This illumination is not the highest state, for eventually the soul

will achieve a perfect, lasting union with God—the Spiritual Marriage. The earlier illumination, which St. John called the Spiritual Betrothal, is a "high state of union and love." It thus appears that the dark night is brought on by the deprivation felt when the mystical state of illumination ceases.

St. John saw this dark night in relation to what he called the dark night of sense. This is the purgation of the body and of sense experience, in which the contemplative turns inward from the world. This self-discipline, which involves great asceticism and which constitutes the preliminary training needed for contemplation, culminates in the emptying of the mind of discursive thought and mental images. It is in this state that the Spiritual Betrothal can take place. The dark night of the soul which follows this was explained by St. John as follows.

The soul, despite the Betrothal, still has to endure further purgation, which is psychologically rather than physically painful. This is not due to a change of attitude on the part of God but results from the continued impurity of the soul, which is not able to withstand the glory of the divine illumination. In this situation the theological virtues of faith, hope, and love are essential. Faith enables the contemplative to continue undismayed through the "night"; hope turns the soul toward the future rather than to the memory of deprivation; love turns the soul toward God and men. Ultimately, then, the soul will gain the full union of the Spiritual Marriage. This is described as a complete transformation of the soul in God; and St. John tended to use language identifying the soul with God at this stage, which is contrary to theistic orthodoxy. It is interesting that in his commentary on the poem *The Living Flame of Love* he expressed great unwillingness to write about this, the loftiest state which he had experienced. He also said, like other mystics, that the communication of God to the soul is ineffable. However, his use of the imagery of marriage and love indicated that he affirmed the essential distinction between the soul and its Lover.

The attainment of the highest state, according to St. John, is limited to very few persons. Such mystics long for death, after which they may enjoy the Beatific Vision in perpetuity in the next life.

St. John of the Cross and St. Teresa influenced each other, and they are the two most important figures in the history of Christian mysticism in Spain.

Bibliography

St. John's works may be found in *Obras de San Juan de la Cruz*, edited with notes by Padre Silverio de Santa Teresa (Burgos, 1929). The works are translated from the above edition by E. Allison Peers as *The Complete Works of St. John of the Cross*, 3 vols. (London, 1934–1935; reprinted 1953).

Also see E. Allison Peers, *Studies of the Spanish Mystics* (London, 1927), Vol. I.

NINIAN SMART

JOHN SCOTUS ERIGENA. See ERIGENA, JOHN SCOTUS.

JOHNSON, ALEXANDER BRYAN (1786–1867), American philosopher and semanticist. Johnson was born in Gosport, England, of Dutch–Jewish ancestry. He immigrated to the United States in 1801 and settled in Utica, New York, where he achieved wealth and prominence as a banker. His main interests were intellectual, primarily in theory of knowledge and the problem of linguistic meaning. He published works on the politics of his day, on economics and banking, and moralistic tales for the young, as well as a series of philosophical works.

Language and nature. Johnson's preoccupation with language derived from his view that "our misapprehension of the nature of language has occasioned a greater waste of time, effort, and genius than all the other mistakes and delusions with which humanity has been afflicted" (*A Treatise on Language*, p. 300; except where otherwise noted, page references are to the 1959 edition of this work). He found its source in our tendency to interpret nature by language. "My lectures," he wrote, "will endeavor to subordinate language to nature—to make nature the expositor of words, instead of making words the expositor of nature. If I succeed, the success will ultimately accomplish a great revolution in every branch of learning" (*ibid.*, p. 40). A rich harvest of philosophically important insights arose from the detailed application of this principle to a wide variety of topics.

Nature, or reality as it appears to us in objects apprehended, is divisible, according to Johnson, into three irreducible classes—the physical (that is, the sensible), the emotional, and the intellectual (thoughts and concepts, which Johnson called "intellections"). Each class includes several subclasses. Sights, sounds, tastes, (tactile) feels, and smells constitute the physical class; the emotions of joy, pain, fear, awe fall into the second class; and concepts (intellections) such as cause, identity, and infinity fall into the third. Words occurring in discourse constitute a subclass of the physical; insofar as they occur in thinking, they are intellectual in nature. The inevitable discrepancy between the practical infinity of natural existences and the necessarily limited number of words of a language results in a one–many relation between words and things (objects of reference). This ambiguity, along with carelessness and ignorance, accounts for the intellectual confusions whose elimination, or at least marking, was the aim of Johnson's lessons on the nature of language.

The terms "physical," "emotional," and "intellectual" throw no light on the nature of the realities they name, but simply refer to them. Only sensing, feeling, and conceiving can inform us what is so referred to. And as the objects, even within each category, are themselves different, acquaintance with some objects of a given kind will not give knowledge of others not confronted. This is not to deny that distinct elements within a given domain resemble one another sufficiently to justify referring to them by a common term. But we err if we suppose that the word "resembles" refers unambiguously to a unique relation. To know that *A* resembles *B* is not to know how it resembles *B*; this can be learned only by specific experience. The elements—the sights, emotions, intellections—that constitute the ultimate referents of significant words are not thought of as mental in the sense of, say, Descartes or Berkeley. They are precisely what we find when we confront them, and no words or theories can enlighten us as to their natures. Ultimate meanings can only be *shown* or *had*, never

said. To understand language we must pass beyond it to the world. Language does not explain the world; the world explains language.

Words and the multiplicity of nature. Johnson used his theory to throw light on practically the whole body of traditional philosophical puzzles, most of which are the result of projecting upon nature our misunderstandings of our language about it. For example, we impute to nature a oneness corresponding to the unitary words used to refer to it. Finding nature not always in agreement with our verbal predications or imputations, we deem this to be ground for impugning our knowledge of its character. The term "gravity" is a verbal unit, but its referents constitute a multiplicity of diverse phenomena. The discrepancy between verbal unity and phenomenal multiplicity leads us to distinguish between gravity and its appearances or manifestations and finally to the view that what gravity is in itself is a mystery, or unknowable. Similar considerations apply to truth, magnetism, cholera, death, the self, and other concepts. "The word gravity names many interesting and important phenomena; but if, in addition to these, we look for gravity itself, we act as ignorantly as the child at the opera, who, after listening with impatience to the musick, singing, and dancing, said, 'I am tired of these; I want the opera'" (*ibid.*, p. 77).

In the same vein Johnson criticized Berkeley's view that distance is invisible, by pointing out the obvious fact that "distance" names feels as well as sights. The theory that we cannot see distance derives from our often unconscious restriction of the term to the feel.

Similarly, the question "whether seeing can or not inform us of an external universe, depends on the meaning which we attach to the word external. The question relates to language, not to nature" (*ibid.*, p. 63). If "external" is used to refer to what can be tactually felt only, then seeing cannot inform us of an external universe. A sight is not a feel. If we use "external" as referring to a sight, as we frequently and properly do, then seeing can inform us of such a universe.

The origin of theories, according to Johnson, is frequently simply our desire to reconcile these incongruities between what we suppose our language implies and what in fact nature discloses. We invent theories to reconcile the multiplicity of nature to the oneness of language, to supply the unit we suppose must exist but which we fail to find in nature.

Kinds of meaning. In his early writings Johnson assumed that if a word had no sensible meaning (referent) it must refer to some inner feeling, or to some other word; otherwise it would be void of meaning, "an empty salvo." Such words as "love" and "hope," insofar as they do not refer to anything accessible to our senses, would mean other words, their synonyms or definitions, except insofar as they referred to inner feelings. For a person lacking these feelings the word "love" would have only verbal meaning. However, such a person could engage in meaningful discourse involving the word "love" by virtue of being able to explain it by means of other words. He could even have verbal knowledge about love, in the sense that he could make correct verbal deductions from statements containing the term to others entailed by them. In this sense a blind man might have much knowledge of optics, making correct deductions from given premises, even though the sensible meanings, if any, would be beyond his comprehension.

Sensible and verbal space. The distinction between sensible and verbal meaning led Johnson to the difference between physical (sensible) and mathematical (verbal) space, and to the distinction between pure and applied mathematics. The infinite divisibility of space (or matter), not being ascertainable by any of our senses that are cognizant of sensible space, must therefore, he argued, be verbal in nature, since the theory obviously does not refer to any of our inner feelings. Verbal or mathematical space *is* infinitely divisible, our common notion of space entailing such divisibility. The paradox of Achilles and the tortoise is to be explained in terms of this distinction between sensible and mathematical space. In the visual space in which the race is run, Achilles overtakes the tortoise at precisely the moment no light is visible between the two by an observer standing on a line at right angles to the just-touching racers. In mathematical space the process of increasing the denominator of the fraction expressing the "distance" separating them can go on forever. The puzzle is due to our failure to understand that the one-to-one correspondence between the sensible distance and the mathematical distance separating Achilles and the tortoise during the early moments of the race no longer exists at the later stages. When calculation shows that Achilles is one yard behind the tortoise there exists a sensible gap separating them, but when calculation tells us that Achilles is behind the tortoise a distance of one-billionth of an inch nothing in visible space corresponds to this quantity. Hence while still separated in mathematical space they are no longer so in sensible space. The calculations are not faulty. We err in supposing that there must always be a correspondence between the calculated and the observed distance separating them simply because there once was. What is true of mathematical space need not be true of sensible space.

Sensible spaces. Johnson was aware that there are many different sensible spaces having different properties. Visual space is not identical with tactile space. This fact is important in dealing with certain epistemological puzzles, such as the discrepancy between seen distance and felt distance, seen and felt size or shape, seen location and felt location. The well-known skeptical conclusions derive largely if not entirely from a failure to realize or draw the correct conclusions from the fact that what kind of correlations are found to hold between the diverse referents of such ambiguous terms as "size," "shape," "location" is a matter purely of experiences—experiences a sensible man will adjust his theories to, but which do not require that he invoke the two-world theory of appearance and reality.

Qualities. The question whether secondary qualities are located in things in the external, or physical, world or are subjective representations of objective primary qualities is, according to Johnson, the unhappy result of our failure to realize the ambiguity of spatial prepositions. When we ask for the location of something—whether, for example, the green we see is in the leaf, in our minds, or in the brain—we fail to appreciate that there are several different sensible spaces and that visual, tactile, and olfactory space have each their peculiar properties. In the sense appropriate to visual space the term "in" is correctly used when we say that the (seen) color is in the visual leaf. If we speak of the tangible leaf, the color is neither in the leaf nor not in it. All that can sensibly be said to be in it or not in it is a feel. Colors not being feels, there is no sense to the question if it is based on the presupposition that a sight is a feel or can be felt.

Meaning. Johnson thus understood that in some cases it makes no sense either to assert or deny that a certain object has a certain property, and hence that the law of excluded middle breaks down in certain ways. He made this insight the key to his treatment of many philosophical puzzles.

Since our questions and answers involve sentences, not isolated words or phrases, the meaning of such expressions is of fundamental importance. Declarative sentences, possibly expressing theories, such as "Air has weight," invoked to explain the phenomenon of water rising in a vacuum, gain their referential meaning from the facts, if any, to which they refer. To determine which facts these are, we must ascertain to what phenomena the sentences are attached by a given speaker.

> Pressure, like every other word, possesses no invariable signification, nor any inherent signification. Its signification is governed by the existence to which we attach it. When it refers to the effort of my hand against this table, it names a feel; and when applied to the ascent of water in a vacuum, it names the ascent. If we suppose it names also some insensible operation of the air on the water, this is merely our theory, which signifies nothing; or rather it signifies all to which we refer in proof of the pressure. (*Ibid.,* p. 227)

The last clause expresses Johnson's view of statement or propositional meaning. A statement means, for a speaker, whatever evidence he adduces or can adduce in support of it. Speaking of the earth's sphericity, Johnson advises us to pay attention to the evidence given in support of it by an astronomer, such as the earth's shadow in an eclipse of the moon or various calculations, and concludes: "After hearing all that he can adduce in proof of the earth's sphericity, consider the proposition significant of these proofs. If you deem it significant beyond them, you are deceived by the forms of language" (*ibid.,* p. 129).

This principle of the meaning of propositions is of the type now called the "operational" theory of meaning. Johnson's version, by virtue of his concentration on the referential function of language, implies that propositions change their meaning with every accretion of evidence in support of them. Propositions purportedly about the future must in fact refer to what has already occurred, since one cannot refer to what is not, nor can a speaker refer to what he has not experienced. False propositions must be devoid of (sensible) meaning, since they are false precisely because what they purport to refer to does not exist. Since, however, one is rarely—if ever—unable to adduce some kind of evidence in support of one's assertions, genuinely meaningless or false propositions are extremely rare. In fact, Johnson held that "nearly every proposition is true when interpreted as the speaker interprets it" (*ibid.*, p. 133).

Despite the obvious difficulties of this conception of propositional meaning, which needs emendation to allow for what is called "sense" as well as "reference," Johnson was able to suggest some very interesting interpretations of statements that anticipate views now in the center of philosophical controversy.

He held that a theory is a tool whose value is determined by its utility in correlating phenomena already known and enabling us to make true predictions.

He claimed that psychological statements, especially those about other minds, feelings, and thoughts, exhibit duality of meaning. They refer in one interpretation to expressive, that is, external, manifestations; in another to what is supposedly expressed or manifested. This, he held, explains the dispute concerning the possibility of knowing other minds.

He said that true unrestricted universal propositions are such not because they hold in an infinite number of cases, but because the evidence offered in their support is our failure to find an exception. The statement asserting an exception refers to nothing and lacks sensible meaning—hence the unrestricted scope of the universal.

Typical religious or theological propositions have meaning by virtue of their reference to sacred texts or to inner feelings.

It is sensibly, but not verbally, meaningless to assert that the universe either had or did not have a creator.

In his later writings Johnson allowed conceptual as well as verbal meaning to propositions. He came to believe that there are certain "predestinate ideas," concepts or intellections, that express man's intellectual nature. For example, in certain senses of the term, causal connections cannot be sensed, but all men nevertheless think causally. Men likewise impute personal identity to themselves and others, although what is sensibly or emotionally given does not exhibit the implied unity or connection. The verbal meaning that remains when sensible and emotional meanings are eliminated seemed no longer adequate in such cases, and he invoked intellectual meanings, which however are not objective or external; the intellectual words standing in relation to their referents, according to Johnson, as imprecations do to the feelings that give rise to them: "as therefore, the internal organic feeling which prompts an imprecation is the unverbal meaning of the imprecation; so the organism of the intellect that conceives any given words is the unverbal meaning of the verbal conception" (*The Meaning of Words*, p. 202). He thus treated them as expressing certain tendencies of our intellectual nature, though using the language of referential meaning.

The meaning of questions. Johnson's anticipation of a form of the operational theory of propositional meaning was accompanied by a detailed discussion of the topic of the meaning of questions. Like Wittgenstein he arrived at the view that "the riddle does not exist," that there are no unanswerable questions. Corresponding to the verbal meanings of statements are the verbal questions to which the statements are answers. In every interrogation we must make clear the nature of the answer desired, whether verbal, emotional, sensible, or intellectual. For example, the question, "What is life?" may be answered by a definition or a theory, by an inner experience, or by indicating certain forms of overt observable behavior.

Necessary truths. Concerning necessary, analytical, logical truths, Johnson held to a twofold doctrine. These truths express verbal necessities based on meanings assigned to their constituent words, but these definitions or verbal necessities are themselves based on physical, nonverbal necessities.

> Why cannot the same spot be, at the same time, both white and black? Because the word white implies that the spot is not black. But how came white by this implication? Was it arbitrarily imposed by the framers of language? No. The incompatibility of the two colours is a result of experience. If I assert that the same spot cannot be both white and hard, the proposition will be untrue. Why? Because my senses can discover such a coincidence. No other reason exists. (*A Treatise on Language*, p. 195)

The same reasoning applies to the axioms of geometry. For instance, the transitivity of the relations of equality is ultimately based not on verbal but on physical facts. Nothing will explain why two sticks equal in length to a third are necessarily equal in length to each other except what one finds when one tries to construct two sticks equal in length to a third but not to each other.

Aphorisms. Johnson's works are studded with striking and revealing aphorisms:

> The heathen make graven images—we make verbal ones; and the heathen worship not more ardently the work of their hands, than we the work of our pens. (*Ibid.*, p. 205)

> Though we deem any mental phenomenon inexplicable unless we can show it to be analogous to physical operations, we deem the operations of Deity well explained when we can show them to be analogous to mental operations. (*Ibid.*, p. 263)

> We employ words as though they possess, like specie, an intrinsick and natural value; rather than as though they possess, like banknotes, a merely conventional, artificial, and representative value; . . . We must convert our words into the natural realities which the words represent, if we would understand accurately their value. (*Ibid.*, p. 174)

> We can no more exemplify with words that there is a limit to their applicability, than a painter can demonstrate with colours, that there are phenomena that colours cannot delineate. (*Ibid.*, p. 246)

Works by Johnson

The Philosophy of Human Knowledge, or a Treatise on Language. New York, 1828.

A Treatise on Language: or the Relation Which Words Bear to Things. New York, 1836; edited, with introduction and critical essay, by D. Rynin, Berkeley, Calif., 1947; 1947 edition, reprinted 1959.

Religion in Its Relation to the Present Life. New York, 1841; 2d ed., retitled *Morality and Manners*, 1862.

The Meaning of Words: Analyzed Into Words and Unverbal Things, and Unverbal Things Classified Into Intellections, Sensations, and Emotions. New York, 1854; 2d ed., 1862.

The Physiology of the Senses: or How and What We See, Hear, Taste, Feel and Smell. New York and Cincinnati, 1856.

Deep Sea Soundings and Explorations of the Bottom; or the Ultimate Analysis of Human Knowledge. Boston, 1861, privately printed.

Works on Johnson

Johnson's views were ignored in his lifetime and were lost sight of for nearly a century. Despite the recent publication of some of his writings, he remains almost completely neglected. For biographical and bibliographical information and evaluations see the Introduction and the critical essay in D. Rynin's 1947 edition of *A Treatise on Language* and M. M. Bagg's *The Pioneers of Utica* (Utica, N.Y., 1877). The *Dictionary of American Biography* contains a brief entry on Johnson. For an account of Johnson as an economist see Joseph Dorfman's *The Economic Mind in American Civilization* (New York, 1946).

DAVID RYNIN

JOHNSON, SAMUEL (1696–1772), American philosopher, was born in Guilford, Connecticut. He studied and taught at the college at New Haven, later called Yale. One of the first colonials to read Bacon, Locke, and Newton, he introduced their thought into the college program. In 1722, having abandoned the Calvinism in which he had been raised, he went to England to receive orders in the Anglican church. On George Berkeley's arrival in Rhode Island in 1729, Johnson paid him several visits, corresponded with him, and became one of his disciples. At the invitation of Benjamin Franklin, Johnson collaborated in the founding of the University of Pennsylvania. In 1754 he helped found King's College, later called Columbia University; he was its first president (until 1763).

Johnson wrote an autobiography and numerous letters, including correspondence with Cadwallader Colden as well as with Berkeley. His philosophical works include *Synopsis Philosophiae Naturalis*, written about 1714; *Logic*, written in 1714; *Encyclopedia of Philosophy*, written in 1714 and revised in 1716; and *Elementa Philosophica*, published by Benjamin Franklin. The *Elementa* was the first textbook in philosophy published in America. It has two parts, "Noetica" and "Ethica"; the "Ethica" had been published alone under the title *A New System of Morality* (Philadelphia, 1746).

Johnson's early works reflect the scholastic Platonism and Calvinistic theology in vogue in the New England colonies during the seventeenth century. The *Encyclopedia*, also called *Technologia sive Technometria*, was a product of his school days and shows the influence of the method and ideas of Peter Ramus. While using Aristotle's physics, it criticizes his metaphysics and ethics as secular and irreligious. Johnson held that there should be no secular science but that all learning should enter into religion and foster it.

Johnson's reading of Bacon, Locke, and Newton broadened and liberalized his thinking. He became an enthusiastic follower of Berkeley's immaterialism, blending with it elements of Puritan Platonism. The English divines, especially Clarke, influenced him to give up Calvinism and to join the Church of England.

His mature philosophy is contained in his *Elementa Philosophica*. The first part, "Noetica," contains his views on reality and mind; the second, "Ethica," concerns moral behavior. Mind or spirit is defined as intelligent, active being. The objects of mind are ideas or notions. There are no material substances corresponding to our ideas; sensible reality is a system of ideas communicated to us by God as copies of the archetypal ideas in the divine mind.

Arguing against Cadwallader Colden, Johnson maintained that minds are the only agents or active causes; matter is purely passive. Bodies, which are a set of ideas impressed on our minds by God, are entirely inactive and powerless. In Johnson's view, the *vis inertiae*, which Newton attributed to matter, is not a power at all; it is simply resistance, and resistance is the direct action of God on the human mind.

The existence of God is proved by the presence of eternal truths in our minds. Since these truths do not depend on our minds or on the actual existence of things, they must be communications of an eternally existing and necessary mind or God. We know these truths when our minds are illuminated by the divine mind. God is the fullness of being, and consequently he has the positive perfection of infinity.

Johnson defended the freedom of the will on moral grounds. If human actions are not free, then moral laws, rewards, and punishments are meaningless. God is not the only active cause; human minds are also genuine agents, endowed with freedom to choose or to reject, to act or not to act. Johnson accepted Newton's laws as regulating the movement of inanimate nature, but he insisted that the human spirit is not bound by necessary laws. In opposition to his former pupil Jonathan Edwards, he upheld the freedom of the human will and rejected the Calvinist doctrine of predestination as incompatible with genuine human freedom and as destructive of morality.

Johnson's writings are an important source for the condition of philosophy in pre-Revolution America and for the changes it underwent owing to the impact of eighteenth-century English thought.

Works by Johnson

Encyclopedia of Philosophy. London, 1731.
Elementa Philosophica. Philadelphia, 1752.
Synopsis Philosophiae Naturalis. New York, 1929.
Logic. New York, 1929.

Works on Johnson

Beardsley, E. E., *Life and Correspondence of Samuel Johnson.* New York, 1873.

Blau, J. L., *Men and Movements in American Philosophy.* New York, 1952. Pp. 15–17, 39–40.

Schneider, H., *A History of American Philosophy.* New York, 1946. Pp. 7–11, 21–26.

Schneider, H., and Schneider, C., eds., *Samuel Johnson, His Career and Writings,* 4 vols. New York, 1929. Vol. I contains Johnson's autobiography; see Vol. II for his philosophical writings and "The Mind of Samuel Johnson" by H. Schneider.

ARMAND A. MAURER

JOHNSON, SAMUEL (1709–1784), English man of letters, poet, lexicographer, moralist, and humanist, was born in Lichfield, the son of an indigent bookseller. After his early education at Lichfield Grammar School, he tried schoolmastering for a brief period. In 1728 he entered Pembroke College, Oxford, but was compelled to leave the following year because of lack of funds. As a child he had suffered from scrofula and later from melancholia, a mental illness that plagued him throughout life, at times pushing him to the brink of insanity. In 1735 he married Mrs. Henry Porter, a widow who was twenty years his senior. After more futile attempts at schoolmastering, Johnson set out for London on horseback in 1737, taking with him one of his pupils, David Garrick. A journalist and hack writer par excellence, Johnson wrote for the *Gentleman's Magazine* and in addition produced poetry, essays, biographies, translations, a play, a proposal for a new edition of Shakespeare, and a proposal for a new dictionary. As a "harmless drudge" he labored from 1746 to 1755 on the *Dictionary of the English Language*, a work which established the practice of elucidating definition of words by quotations from leading authors. Its appearance brought him fame and belated honorary doctorates from Dublin (1765) and Oxford (1775), but little money. Johnson's famous letter of 1755 to Lord Chesterfield repudiated the system of personal patronage. In 1762, however, despite the fact that he had defined "pension" as "pay given to a state hireling for treason to his country," he set aside his scruples to accept a pension from George III.

The Rambler (1750–1752) and *The Idler* (1758–1760) essays, although acclaimed as literature and as statements on morality, were hardly successful financially. The novel *Rasselas* (1759) was well received, as were the edition of Shakespeare (1765), *A Journey to the Western Islands of Scotland* (1775), and finally, *The Lives of the English Poets* (1779–1781). Johnson's political publications, *The False Alarm* (1770), *Thoughts on The Late Transactions Respecting The Falkland Islands* (1771), and *Taxation No Tyranny* (1775), were, on the contrary, mere diatribes and did him no credit. Yet the charge that they were written as repayment for his pension has no foundation in fact. His general theory of politics was close to that of Burke: conservative, traditional, and distrustful of all popular upheavals.

With a royal pension of £300 a year, poverty and Grub-streeting were over, and Johnson was able to indulge more freely his social proclivities and his desire to travel. The meetings with James Boswell in 1763, and with the wealthy Mr. and Mrs. Henry Thrale in 1764, and the founding of "The Club" in the same year, were happy omens of the new life. Charter members of "The Club" included Joshua Reynolds (who originated the idea), Edmund Burke, and Oliver Goldsmith. Later members of note included Boswell, Garrick, Thomas Warton, Bishop Percy, Sheridan, Fox, Gibbon, and Adam Smith.

Johnson has been immortalized by his great biographer Boswell in *The Journal of a Tour to the Hebrides with Samuel Johnson* (1791), *The Life of Samuel Johnson* (1785), and in present times in the ever increasing number of volumes based upon Boswell's private journals and papers now in the archives of Yale University. Boswell's ability to draw Johnson out in conversation has presented posterity with a wide panorama of the latter's opinions and beliefs. Indeed, it is no exaggeration to say that more intimate details are known about both Johnson and Boswell

than about any other persons of that or any previous age. As he grew older Johnson mellowed considerably; he was no longer the irascible, bitter, and not infrequently rude man of earlier years. Although he loved life, he feared death—despite (or perhaps because of) a deep religious faith. As he once put it, life is everywhere "supported with impatience and quitted with reluctance." He died in 1784 after a prolonged and painful siege of the dropsy. His last words are said to have been, *Iam moriturus,* "I who am about to die." He was buried in Westminster Abbey.

Religion and morality. Johnson acknowledged an early predilection for becoming a metaphysician, but instead he became a philosopher, in the wider sense of a thinking man struggling with the problems of life, death, and immortality. A notable excursion into the realm of metaphysics, however, is his 10,000-word critical review of Soame Jenyns' *Free Enquiry into the Nature and Origin of Evil* (1757). The rationalistic optimism inherent in the Great Chain of Being—an optimism wherein whatever is conceivable must exist (a concept justifying the necessity of evil)—was to Johnson morally monstrous as well as metaphysically illogical. It is illogical because however many links there may be in the Chain, from the Godhead at the one extreme to the lowliest atom at the other, it is always possible to conceive of gaps between the links ad infinitum. The morality of justifying poverty and pain as cosmologically necessary was monstrous to a humanist who had personally suffered both poverty and pain. Although God may move in a mysterious way his wonders to perform, it is idle to be told by a metaphysician that in some mysterious way evil in reality is good. It is small comfort to be complacently informed that poverty is merely the want of riches, and that, just as man has animals for food and diversion, so beings superior to man may be privileged to deceive, torment, or destroy man simply for the sake of utility or pleasure. In short, it was Johnson's belief that "life must be seen, before it can be known." His philosophical novel *Rasselas*, a fictional assault on metaphysical optimism, again exemplifies Johnson's favorite admonition, "Clear your mind of cant."

Johnson never systematized his thinking on morality and religion and consequently exhibits many inconsistencies. An ardent Christian and Anglican high-churchman, although not a regular churchgoer, he was forever seeking further evidence and reasons that would bolster his will to believe. He held that every man is entitled to liberty of conscience, but not necessarily the liberty of talking, preaching, or publishing. It is the prerogative of the magistrate to prohibit what he deems politically injurious to the society over which he presides. If the magistrate is morally or theologically wrong in his prohibitions, then truth may suffer. Consequently, the only way in which religious truth can be established is by martyrdom. In the persecution of a martyr, the magistrate is right politically and the martyr is right morally and religiously.

Johnson was afraid of death not only because he was fond of life (even though he held a tragic sense of life), but also because he was acutely aware of the wages of sin. The occasional sermons that Johnson composed for clerical friends and acquaintances (frequently for a fee) are revealing as expressions of his views on specific theological issues. On a deeply intimate level, the "Prayers and Meditations" (begun in 1729 while he was still at Oxford and continued until a few days before his death) provide poignant evidence of repeated resolutions to reform his mode of living (that is, his habitual indolence), to steel himself against religious doubts, scruples, and fear of damnation, and to purge his mind of morbidity and the dread of recurring insanity.

Johnson claimed that we know the distinction between right and wrong by reason; from experience he also knew the difficulties that man encounters in trying to live the life of virtue. Accordingly, he felt the necessity of a mandate from Christian revelation—but never, to be sure, in the sense of the personal "enthusiasm" of seventeenth-century Puritans or eighteenth-century evangelists. He was thus both a rationalist and fideist, but the former tempered by a healthy empiricism and the latter by the requirement of "works." On the one hand, he had unbounded admiration for the Anglican rationalist theologian, Samuel Clarke (1675–1729), and on the other, for the nonjuring pietist and mystic, William Law (1686–1761), neither of whom qualify as orthodox. The sermons of Clarke provided Johnson with rational treatment of thorny theological problems; for example, Law's *Serious Call to a Devout and Holy Life* (1728) augmented faith through a reason that provides spiritual light. Johnson was sufficiently the ethical rationalist (with the qualifications mentioned above) to oppose the nonrational moralists of sentiment or moral sense, such as Shaftesbury, Francis Hutcheson, Joseph Butler, Hume, and Adam Smith. Johnson, like Hobbes, did not consider benevolence or the will to do good to others a natural instinct. Charity, however, as a requisite Christian virtue, Johnson practiced religiously throughout his life. The desire for fame, he maintained in a *Rambler* essay, is basically the desire of "filling" the minds of others. Johnson achieved fame as a didactic writer and moralist who regarded the end and the rites of religion as divinely instituted for "the perpetual renovation of the motives to virtue." This concept of religious need and Christian stoicism received its most memorable poetical statement in one of Johnson's earliest works, *The Vanity of Human Wishes* (1749); it was a statement that was to be reaffirmed countless times throughout his life.

Bibliography

WORKS BY JOHNSON

The Letters of Samuel Johnson, R. W. Chapman, ed., 3 vols. Oxford, 1952.
The Poems of Samuel Johnson, D. N. Smith and E. L. McAdam, eds. Oxford, 1941.
The Works of Samuel Johnson, 9 vols. Oxford, 1825.
Yale Edition of the Works of Samuel Johnson, Allan T. Hazen, ed., 2 vols. to date. New Haven, 1958—.

WORKS BY BOSWELL

Boswell's Journal of a Tour to the Hebrides with Samuel Johnson, F. A. Pottle and C. H. Bennet, eds. New York, 1936.
Boswell's Life of Johnson, G. B Hill, ed., 6 vols.; revised by L. F. Powell. Oxford, 1934–1950.

MODERN STUDIES

Bate, Walter J., *The Achievement of Samuel Johnson.* New York, 1955.

Cairns, W. T., *The Religion of Dr. Johnson and Other Essays.* Oxford, 1946.
Clifford, James L., *Young Sam Johnson.* New York, 1955.
Hodgart, M. J. C., *Samuel Johnson and His Times.* London, 1962.
Krutch, Joseph W., *Samuel Johnson.* New York, 1944.
Quinlan, Maurice J., *Samuel Johnson: A Layman's Religion.* Madison, Wis., 1964.
Voitle, Robert, *Samuel Johnson the Moralist.* Cambridge, Mass., 1961.
Wahba, Magdi, ed., *Johnsonian Studies.* Cairo, 1962. Pp. 37–113. Six essays treat Johnson's religion and morality.

ERNEST CAMPBELL MOSSNER

JOHNSON, WILLIAM ERNEST (1858–1931), English logician, was born in Cambridge, the son of a schoolmaster. After attending his father's school and then the Liverpool Royal Institute School, he entered Kings College, Cambridge, as a mathematics wrangler. He was eleventh wrangler in the mathematics tripos in 1882 and took first-class honors in the moral sciences tripos in 1883. For many years he was a mathematics coach until he secured a position as lecturer on psychology at the Cambridge Woman's Training College. Johnson held no permanent position until 1902, when he was appointed to a fellowship at Kings College and as Sidgwick lecturer in moral sciences at Cambridge.

Johnson was interested not only in logic but also in economics and indeed published a paper on utility curves in an economic journal. He was a very shy and reserved man, and this and his bronchial troubles handicapped his work. Nevertheless, he had great influence on a whole school of Cambridge logicians, including C. D. Broad and J. M. Keynes. Keynes acknowledged his indebtedness to Johnson in his great work, *A Treatise on Probability*. It was only late in life, at the urging of a woman student, that Johnson published his three-volume work on logic. A fourth volume on probability never appeared, but three articles on the subject were published posthumously in *Mind*.

Johnson's main interest was in what may be called philosophical rather than formal logic. That is, he was interested not in the formal construction of logistic systems but rather in the exploration of what the underlying assumptions of the science or art of logic were. The tendency of British logicians—John Stuart Mill, for example—had been to psychologize logic, treating it as the science and art of reasoning. Johnson was somewhat critical of this tradition, although there was a psychologistic flavor to his own thinking. He defined logic as the "analysis and criticism of thought," where thought is taken to include all judgments, ranging from bare perceptual ones to the most abstract judgments of mathematics. The logician studies the forms of thought that ought to be followed, and in this sense, logic is a normative science. It includes both inductive and deductive inference.

In connection with his investigations of the nature of logic, Johnson made a number of important and interesting points:

(1) In common with most modern logicians, he considered the basic unit of logical analysis to be the proposition, which he took to be the object of a mental attitude such as asserting, denying, or questioning. Propositions were

shown to be all of the same kind, whether primitive (that is, perceptual) or nonprimitive. They all involve an element of abstraction.

(2) Johnson discussed at some length and with great acuity the distinction between an implication and an inference. Formal implication involves a logical relation between two propositions p and q, such that p would imply q. But for this formal implication to be transformed into the valid inference "p, therefore q," there is required not only the hypothetical statement of a logical relation but also the assertion that p is the case. Therefore, although an implication is hypothetical, an inference is categorical.

(3) Johnson showed how logical theory involves conditions which he called epistemic as well as those he called constitutive. Constitutive conditions are, roughly speaking, formal (syntactic or semantic) conditions which must be present if an inference is to be valid. Thus, certain propositions must be true if an inference is to be valid. Epistemic conditions are closer to what we would call pragmatic conditions. Thus, in order for the inference $p \supset q$ to be valid, not only must the proposition p and the proposition "p would imply q" be true (these are constitutive conditions) but epistemic conditions must be fulfilled as well. Thus, both the proposition p and the proposition "p would imply q" must be assertable without reference to the assertion of q. This is clearly a nonformal condition.

(4) Johnson attempted to show that all of deductive logic could be based upon two principles, which he called the implicative and applicative principles. He recognized quite clearly that the difference between logical premises and logical principles (which are not reducible to premises) permitted the making of an implication or, if epistemic conditions were satisfied, of an inference. Although Johnson's main formal concern still remained the syllogism, he recognized the application of these principles to the sentential calculus and to deductions which he called functional and which involved the use of variables.

(5) Johnson believed that inductive inference always rested upon the existence of a causal relation, and therefore he devoted an extensive analysis to the notion of cause and of substance, space, and time, since he believed that all these concepts enter into a proper analysis of cause. Cause, in other words, involves a mode of inference. Inductive inferences are distinguished from deductive inferences in that the conclusion in the first case always follows with a probability less than certainty, while in the second case it follows with certainty. Johnson was committed to an analysis of probability as a logical relation between propositions which is not in all cases numerically determinable or even quantitatively comparable. This analysis was, in fact, very close to the one that Keynes provided. Johnson conceived of causal relations not in the Humean tradition as a succession of events but as a certain kind of connection. He presented an extremely rich discussion of the causal relation, distinguishing very clearly several types of causal connection.

Johnson also made a number of original distinctions and contributed a set of ideas which are of interest even today to philosophers of science and logic:

(1) He distinguished between determinants and determinables. This distinction was in part designed to recast the traditional distinction between universal and particular

and to shed new light on it. Johnson pointed out that adjectival terms can be ordered in relation to each other in regard to the relation of "being more determinate than." This relation bears some analogy to the relation "is a member of" but is not completely similar. A set of determinants falls under a determinable in the way that the determinants "red," "green," etc., fall under the determinable "color." Questions about the nature of intensions, of logical subjects, etc., were dealt with by Johnson with the help of this distinction.

(2) He elaborated a theory of ostensive definition which is of great interest. Meaning, he held, refers to both the connotation and the denotation of a term. Proper names, however, have only denotation. Indeed, they are defined as names which mean the same as what they factually indicate. How, then, do we define them? By an ostensive definition. A proper name applies to an object with a specified spatiotemporal region. The appearance of such an object is a necessary condition for the application of its name. The proper name thus means "the object to which I am pointing." An ostensive definition, then, cannot be given independently of the presence of the object name.

Works by Johnson

Logic, 3 vols. Cambridge, 1921–1924.
"On Probability." *Mind,* N.S. Vol. 42 (1932).

Works on Johnson

A. D., "W. E. Johnson (1858–1931); An Impression." *Mind,* N.S. Vol. 41 (1931), 136–138.
Braithwaite, R. B., "Johnson, William Ernest," in L. G. Wickham Legg, ed., *Dictionary of National Biography 1931–1940.* London, 1949. Pp. 489–490.
Broad, C. D., "William Ernest Johnson 1858–1931." *Proceedings of the British Academy,* Vol. 17 (1931).
Passmore, J. A., *A Hundred Years of British Philosophy.* London, 1957. Pp. 137–138, 345–348.

HOWARD E. SMOKLER

JOUFFROY, THÉODORE SIMON (1796–1842), French common-sense and spiritualist philosopher. He was born at Pontets, near Pontarlier, in the department of Doubs. After his preliminary schooling he entered the École Normale in Paris in 1814 and began teaching there three years later. He was attracted to the study of philosophy by Pierre Paul Royer-Collard and Victor Cousin, who were lecturing on the Scottish school. In 1826, Jouffroy published a translation of Dugald Stewart's *Outlines of Moral Philosophy,* and in 1828 he prepared a six-volume translation of the works of Thomas Reid. Jouffroy's rise in the academic hierarchy was rapid; by 1828 he was lecturing at both the École Normale and the Collège de France, where he was appointed professor of Greek and Roman philosophy in 1833. In the same year he was made a member of the Academy of Science.

Jouffroy's interests were varied, covering psychology, aesthetics, legal philosophy, and epistemology, yet he published very little. He is best known for two volumes of miscellaneous essays, *Mélanges philosophiques,* published in 1833, and *Nouveaux Mélanges philosophiques,* which appeared the year of his death.

Jouffroy's ambition was to found a science of psychology based on Scottish philosophy. A survey of the soul's activity revealed to him six different faculties; basic to each of these is a fusion of love of power, curiosity, and sympathy. Upon this foundation rest sensitivity to pleasure and pain, intelligence, "expression," movement, and volition. The soul is thus a community of faculties, all of which must cooperate if the truth is ever to be discovered. It reproduces in the individual that fusion of human souls which is known in the Scottish philosophy as common sense.

It is common sense that alone possesses absolute truth, access to which is denied individuals. Each of us, Jouffroy believed, should attempt to reach the truth by the use of reasoning, but we must accept its conclusions by "a blind act of faith." For none of our faculties is capable of acting in the name of the collective wisdom of the race. Jouffroy held so strongly to this idea that he regarded individual philosophers as mere mouthpieces for the societies and cultures in which they live. As early as 1827 he showed an interest in society as a being having its peculiar influence on the individuals who compose it, but he was never clear about the nature of this being. Jouffroy maintained that if men understood their dependence on the totality of individuals, they would cease to fight with one another and would form a unified fraternal community. This community would be the explicit embodiment of common sense, which already exists implicitly in all human beings.

Common sense expresses itself in self-evident principles that appear in logic and in the dictates of the moral conscience. They are the source of an all-inclusive philosophy illustrated in natural law, which is that system of moral and political principles that underlies the statutes of all nations. Since this system is always consistent, it can act as a test for all truths. What William James, in his *Varieties of Religious Experience*, called Jouffroy's conversion to skepticism stemmed from this idea. For what man other than a mystic could transcend the limits of his individuality to grasp ideas that were overindividual?

In spite of this, Jouffroy maintained that intelligence can apprehend these self-evident principles, just as conscience can apprehend the difference between right and wrong. Here he departed from his theory that men express the ideas of periods and societies and insisted instead that each man's conscience is his sole guide to the good. For the good turns out to be the accomplishment of a man's destiny and evil the failure to accomplish it. A man's destiny is incorporated in his individuality, no two men having precisely the same goals. In general, however, pleasure and pain indicate to a man whether he is fulfilling his destiny, which is apparently the reason men are pleased by different experiences. Unfortunately, Jouffroy's conclusions on this point are lost. And, indeed, he may not have drawn any conclusions, for he was more given to preparatory analyses than to inferences.

Aesthetics, according to Jouffroy, deals exclusively with the nature of beauty. Just as truth is not the possession of any individual, neither is beauty. Beauty does not reflect the character of our life; it is the sublime that takes beauty's place in experience. "The ideas of our present life," Jouffroy said in his *Cours d'esthétique*, "are more familiar to us than the ideas of a more perfect life, and we are consequently less sensitive to beauty than to the sublime." Though the *Cours d'esthétique* consists of notes

taken by his pupils and hence cannot be regarded as wholly his, it is clear that the metaphor of the whole of which we know but limited parts dominated Jouffroy's thought. Whether the problem was that of truth, goodness, or beauty, he believed it is the nature of the whole that contains the answer and men are condemned never to possess the answer.

Works by Jouffroy

Mélanges philosophiques. Paris, 1833.
Cours de droit naturel, 1st ed., 2 vols. Paris, 1834–1842. 2d ed., with additional notes by Philibert Damiron, ed., 3 vols. Paris, 1843.
Nouveaux Mélanges philosophiques. Paris, 1842.
Cours d'esthétique. Paris, 1843.

Works on Jouffroy

Boas, George, *French Philosophies of the Romantic Period*, pp. 239–250. Baltimore, 1925.
Mignet, F. A., "Notes sur Jouffroy." *Memoires de l'Académie des Sciences Morales et Politiques*, Vol. 25 (1853), 197.
Ollé-Laprune, Léon, *Théodore Jouffroy.* Paris, 1899.
Taine, Hippolyte, *Les Philosophes classiques du XIXᵉ siècle en France.* Paris, 1868.

GEORGE BOAS

JOURNALS, PHILOSOPHICAL. See PHILOSOPHICAL JOURNALS.

JUDGMENTS. See PROPOSITIONS, JUDGMENTS, SENTENCES, AND STATEMENTS.

JUNG, CARL GUSTAV (1875–1961), originator of analytical psychology, was born in Kesswil, Switzerland, studied medicine in Basel, and then became an assistant in psychiatry at Zurich, interrupting his stay there to visit and study under Pierre Janet in Paris. He was a pupil of Eugen Bleuler, and he became Freud's friend and collaborator for a few years, after having been influenced by his writings. He became the first president of the International Psychoanalytic Society in 1911. In 1914 he broke with Freud, founding his own school of analytical psychology. His earlier studies of association tests and of dementia praecox were followed by an attempt to classify types of personality and by the gradual development not only of a theory of the collective unconscious but also of the implications of that theory for the study of culture and especially for the study of mythology and religion.

Jung traveled widely in Africa, America, and India and collaborated with Richard Wilhelm in Chinese studies and with Carl Kerényi in the study of mythology. In June 1933 the German Society for Psychotherapy came under Nazi control. Ernst Kretschmer at once resigned from the office of president, and it is regrettable and noteworthy that Jung took his place. Among many other distinctions, he received honorary degrees from Harvard (1936), Oxford (1938), and Geneva (1945).

Theory of psychological types. Jung, like Kretschmer, distinguished initially between the extraverted type of personality—sociable, outgoing, and optimistic—and the introverted type—more apt to withdraw from external reality, less sociable, more absorbed in his own inner life. This initial distinction was accompanied by a distinction between four functions of personality—sensation, thinking, feeling, and intuition. By "sensation" Jung meant all that we acquire through sense perception. "Thinking" was used in its familiar meanings. "Feeling" was the capacity for making evaluations of oneself and of others. "Intuition" was the perception of realities which are not consciously perceived; it worked spontaneously for the solution of problems which cannot be grasped rationally.

Types of personality were discriminated in terms of which function is dominant and whether the person is extraverted or introverted. For example, the extravert in whom thinking is dominant will be fascinated by facts and concerned to order them rationally, will tend to underrate the emotions and thus be subject from time to time to uncontrolled and perhaps unrecognized bursts of emotion. The introverted thinking type is one in which facts are never of value for their own sake but only in relation to the creative inner theorizing of the thinker. Both types of thinking are accompanied by an undeveloped feeling function, for thinking and feeling are essentially opposite and even inimical. Sensation and intuition are paired in the same way.

On Jung's view one very rarely finds a person who is a pure example of one of these categories. Most often one function is dominant, although modified by the presence of one of the others. In more complex personalities two functions may coexist in dominance, and very occasionally three, but there will always be at least one function neglected and unacknowledged. Jung's classification into types is, of course, a classification in terms of types of conscious response to the world; however, the notion of parts of the self that are unacknowledged requires some reference to the unconscious.

Personal and collective unconscious. The personal unconscious consists of those associated webs of ideas and emotions that Jung named complexes, which have been repressed from consciousness because it found them too painful to acknowledge, and also of those perceptions of reality which have never forced their way into consciousness. Each individual's personal unconscious is thus to some extent explicable in terms of his own life history. Even the personal unconscious, however, has features which are common to every individual and do not derive from his personal history.

Consider the contrast between what Jung termed the "persona" and the "shadow." The persona is the socially accepted and socially imposed mask behind which dwells the true ego. The existence of such a mask is an unavoidable necessity, but the ego can fail to achieve self-realization either by identifying itself too strongly with its persona or by not developing an adequate persona at all. The counterpoint to this accepted and exposed part of the personality is the shadow, the rejected and usually imprisoned set of desires, emotions, and attitudes that we personify in dreams as an unpleasant or hostile figure. The shadow is essentially infantile, for it is untouched by the process of maturation or education. The inability to acknowledge one's shadow is always a potential danger to the personality, for the shadow unacknowledged and unrecognized is stronger and more wayward than the shadow recognized and accepted.

Although every individual has a shadow, since the shadow is the product of what his particular consciousness has repressed, it belongs to the personal unconscious. However, beside it in the personal unconscious is found another major force, the image, the image which constitutes the feminine in a man or the masculine in a woman, termed by Jung "anima" and "animus," respectively. The character of the anima is not determined by a man's private history in the way the character of the shadow is; rather, the anima determines how the opposite sex is perceived or misperceived. The anima is an inherited collective image of woman as such. Thus, what matters to the child is not merely how his mother treats him; his experience of the mother is produced both by the mother's actual behavior and by the way his anima determines his view of and feelings about her. Jung connected the anima especially with the function of feeling, the animus with that of thinking, supposing that thinking is more likely to be dominant in the man, feeling in the woman.

The animus and anima belong to the collective unconscious of mankind, along with persona and shadow. They are among the "archetypes," inherited tendencies of psychic functioning contained in the collective unconscious. Other key archetypes are those of the old wise man, the earth mother, and the self. An archetype plays a variety of roles: not only does it condition the ways in which our conscious experience is formed but also it can appear directly in a number of guises in dreams and phantasies, and the individual may even unconsciously come to be so dominated by one of these images that he might be said to be possessed by it or to identify himself with it. When this happens the personality is itself in danger; it has been taken over and magnified into something that expresses not the individual person but the collective image. This Jung called inflation.

Jung contrasted the self with the ego. The ego is the actual center of consciousness; the self is spoken of by Jung as the center of the unconscious, but clearly it is potentially rather than actually so. Religious visions, dreams, and the magic diagram that Buddhists call the mandala are all images of a possible unity in which the self is at the center. The achievement of this unity by any given individual is a task which belongs especially to the second half of life. In the first half of life the individual is necessarily largely preoccupied with work, marriage, and the bringing up of children; it is when these tasks are mostly accomplished that the individual has to come to terms with himself. Hence the psychological crisis period that occurs in the late forties. At this point the nature of Jungian psychotherapy becomes important.

Psychotherapy. According to Jung a neurotic symptom is never to be explained solely in terms of the patient's past. It always represents something positive in the present, an attempt to solve the problems which confront the patient. Jung was prepared to accept that Freud was correct in ascribing many neuroses to the problems arising out of repressed sexuality and that Adler was correct in ascribing many others to an unrecognized will to power. However, he felt that behind sexuality and the will to power lie other more fundamental causes. Sexuality, for example, is important because it represents the chthonic element in man, an element represented in pre-Olympian Greek religion and in other mythologies. Moreover, the type of neurosis which can be understood correctly, within limits, in Freudian or Adlerian terms belongs characteristically to the earlier part of life. It arises from the inability to carry through the practical tasks of life.

In psychotherapy the patient comes to acknowledge hitherto unrecognized parts of his personality. Jung believed that free association, as practiced by Freudian analysts, leads not toward but away from the complexes of which we need to become aware. However, more is involved in the therapeutic process that ridding oneself of symptoms, as the patient discovers when he brings what was repressed into view, for example through a new awareness of the significance of his dreams, which function, according to Jung, as compensations for deficiencies in the dreamer's waking life. To rid oneself of symptoms, one has to become aware of the process of individuation, of the need for the creation of a harmonious synthesis of the functions in which the nature of the shadow and the power of the archetypes of the collective unconscious have been reconciled with the demands of the conscious personality.

Mythology and religion. Jung used his central theoretical concept, that of the collective unconscious, to explain not only the occurrence in dreams and the awareness in analysis of contents of the unconscious which could not have been repressed into it by the individual psyche but also the widespread recurrence of the same symbols and themes in widely different times and places in mythologies and religions. Thus, Jung found in the dreams and paintings of patients material which closely resembles that in Eastern religious writings, and in literature and art the archetypal images continually recur. Modern man stands, however, in a peculiar relationship to the contents of the collective unconscious.

Jung held that the increase in scientific understanding has led to a dehumanization of the natural and social worlds. A former unconscious acceptance of natural phenomena, which involved endowing them with symbolic power, has disappeared. To treat thunder, for example, not as the voice of a god but as an explicable phenomenon is to have become alienated from external nature. A loss of belief in gods and demons has produced a lack of awareness of the powers within human nature. Modern man is thus specially a prey to psychological disorders.

It follows that men have a strong need for religious beliefs and experiences, since in religious form they are able to encounter and accept the contents of the collective unconscious. Religious beliefs, Jung conceded, cannot be shown to be true; but he held that they cannot be shown to be false, either. Whether to believe or not is thus a matter of choice, on purely pragmatic grounds. Jung regarded with deep suspicion, as essentially one-sided and distorting, the rationalist traditions of scientific thought. Indeed, he dated the disorientation of modern man partly from the original Christian break with paganism, but more importantly from the Enlightenment.

Criticism. Of all Jung's work his classification of types of personality as extravert or introvert has won the widest acceptance. Eysenck has developed this distinction for use in experimental psychology, and it may well be that other

Jungian concepts and theories can also be tested experimentally. However, the linchpin of Jung's theorizing, the concept of the collective unconscious, is so formed that it appears that whereas the existence of the collective unconscious was advanced as an explanatory hypothesis, the question of whether the collective unconscious exists cannot be answered by any possible observation or experiment. That the existence of the collective unconscious is intended as a hypothesis seems clear from the fact that it is avowedly introduced to explain why the same symbols keep recurring in dreams, mythologies, and works of art. However, there are no predictions that we can deduce from this hypothesis other than the vague generalization that such symbols do and will recur—and this, after all, is what the hypothesis was orginally intended to explain. Moreover, Jung is open to criticism for treating the collective unconscious not as a theoretical entity to which reference is made in an as yet untested hypothesis but as something whose existence is an established fact. Jung actually asserted that although the facts about personality and the unconscious are undeniable, they cannot, by their very nature, be formulated in such a way as to satisfy the demands of either science or logic.

At the root of the problem lies an ambiguous set of ontological claims. Jung insisted that the contents of the psyche are as real as what exists in the external world. He clearly meant by this more than the obvious, which nobody would be disposed to deny, for example, that there *are* recurrent patterns of symbolism. But what he meant beyond this remains unclear. Sometimes he seems to have treated the archetypal images as autonomous agents and the collective unconscious as a realm where they dwell. However, his insistence on the inapplicability of the ordinary canons of logic in these matters makes it difficult to press the questions which this seems to raise.

Finally, it is worth noting that we possess no statistical evidence of a worthwhile kind about the efficacy of Jungian psychotherapy. Lacking this evidence, we are forced to conclude that although Jung established a psychological system of some complexity, there are as yet no grounds for believing any of its propositions which go beyond recording empirical data, either as to the nature of personality or as to the process of cure.

Bibliography

Jung's collected works are being published in an English edition. Of 17 planned volumes of the *Collected Works*, 13 have appeared (London and New York, 1953——). See also *Psychological Types,* translated by H. G. Baynes (London, 1923); *Psychological Reflections,* selected and edited by Jolande Jacobi (London and New York, 1953); *Psyche and Symbol: A Selection From the Writings of C. G. Jung,* Violet S. de Laszlo, ed. (New York, 1958); and *The Basic Writings of C. G. Jung,* Violet S. de Laszlo, ed. (New York, 1959).

For literature on Jung, see Frieda Fordham, *An Introduction to Jung's Psychology* (London, 1953); E. Glover, *Freud or Jung* (London, 1950); and Jolande Jacobi, *The Psychology of C. G. Jung* (London, 1942; revised 6th ed., New Haven, 1962), and *Complex/Archetype/Symbol in the Psychology of C. G. Jung* (New York, 1959).

On Jung's concept of extraversion–introversion, see H. J. Eysenck, *Dimensions of Personality* (New York, 1947).

ALASDAIR MacINTYRE

JÜNGER, ERNST, German novelist and cultural critic who, by embracing total war as an exemplary pattern of life, helped to prepare the ideology of the National Socialist revolution of 1933. He was born in Heidelberg in 1895 and educated in Hanover. In 1913 he joined the French Foreign Legion in north Africa in search of "the extraordinary beyond the social and moral sphere . . . a zone in which the war of the forces of nature found its pure and aimless expression." This quest for an exotic life in artificially heightened experience revealed Jünger's metaphysical attitudes and anticipated his later pattern of life. Jünger joined the German army at the outbreak of World War I. He fought on the western front and was commissioned, repeatedly wounded, and highly decorated. To him the war appeared "a means for self-realization, a wild upsurge of life . . . a splendid bloody play which makes the gods rejoice" that offered the key to all essential experience: "ecstasy, sleep and death." After the war Jünger developed his views in a series of brilliant war descriptions: *In Stahlgewittern* (1920); *Der Kampf als inneres Erlebnis* (1922); *Das Wäldchen 125* (1925); *Feuer und Blut* (1925; Hitler annotated his gift copy); culminating in *Totale Mobilmachung* (1930) and *Der Arbeiter* (1932).

Jünger was also fascinated by modern technology, which had transformed the character of warfare and was creating a new form of industrial society. He envisioned the emergence of a new type of technical elite: the worker-soldier in the nationalized, socialist, militarist–imperialist, and dictatorial state of the future. He also discerned a "new consciousness of reality," nihilist in its relations to traditional values. But although he welcomed the rise of technology as a triumph of man, Jünger deplored its mechanization and dehumanization of life. In the Marxian solution of this problem, the common existential experience of the proletariat leads to class solidarity; its mastery of the tools of production leads to the liberation and human autonomy of the proletariat, which represents mankind. Similarly, Jünger's worker-soldier, simultaneously savior and saved, was to achieve the collective salvation of the rotting democratic–humanist society.

However, technology was inseparably bound up with war, "a fiery marriage between the spirit of chivalry and the severe coldness of our forms of work." The world of factories and calculated organization, of production, and of transport finds its true measure in battle. "The battle is a tremendous touchstone of industry, and victory marks the success of a competitive effort which knows how to work more quickly and ruthlessly." The individual worker-soldier finds his liberty in accepting the necessity to be part of "the greater force. Here one can only drift and be formed under the grip of the *Weltgeist*." The worker-soldier type thus replaced the individualist personality of the nineteenth century. Technology became both the means and the end of human endeavor—the means because it procured mastery over others, the end because the old values were dead, and collective power, the product of technology, was equated with value: "Technology and ethos have become synonymous . . . ."

Jünger's "national-Bolshevist" conception of technology provided a scintillating and heady approach to totalitarianism, an approach based also on his belief in inexorable historical trends and his romantic conviction that the individual finds fulfillment only by sacrificial immersion of himself in the whole. Jünger promised redemption for the sacrifice of the obedient soldier but showed scant sympathy for that of the Socratic nonconformist. His *Der Arbeiter* is thus less a sociological interpretation of his times than the revelation of a political myth, a clarion call that exerted a wide influence in Germany among the bewildered generation of the 1920s.

Jünger's misinterpretation and rejection of liberalism prevented his playing a constructive part as a citizen and caused him to be a destructive intellectual force. An anarchic pride in his own independence, however, saved him from effective collaboration with National Socialism. Jünger first parted ways with the Nazi party in 1929, when he backed a terrorist peasant movement opposed by Hitler. Between the lines of his novel *Auf den Marmorklippen* (1939) he criticized the prevailing tyranny, but he took no part in active resistance to the regime. He again fought in the German army in 1940, although he suffered misgivings as a member of the army of occupation in France and Russia. These feelings found expression in *Strahlungen* (1949), Jünger's journals from 1939 to 1949, in which he corrected certain of his former tenets and, in a fashion, held out a hand to Western values and to the Christian religion. In his novel *Heliopolis* (1949) he took up once more the problems raised in *Auf den Marmorklippen*. *Heliopolis* contained an indictment of a closely knit totalitarian order but, at the same time, preserved Jünger's distance from Western rationalism and liberalism. The same theme recurred in *Der Waldgang* (1951); *Gläserne Bienen* (1957), which again expressed Jünger's fascination with technology; and *Der Weltstaat* (1960), which called for international political unity as a historically determined necessity.

Jünger conceived of the writer as a seer and pathfinder. His diagnosis of his times was, however, based on an untrained and intuitive sociological and economic knowledge, poetical and pretentious rather than scholarly. His widely acclaimed concept of the Gestalt, or Typus, of the worker offered no methodological advance and in substance was merely ideological. Jünger's significance was as a spokesman of the powerful romantic strand in the German intellectual tradition that unites elements of *Naturphilosophie,* Neoplatonic mysticism, and a Protagorean theory of knowledge with the negative aspects of Rousseau's and Burke's critiques of society and the Enlightenment. In its modern representatives, such as Jünger and Spengler, such thinking leads to a rejection of the rational, abstract, and mechanical achievements of civilization, the "high-treason of the intellect against life," and to the extolling of the instinctive, oceanic "night side" of life. Although not original, Jünger's philosophy is presented in a highly personal manner and in an evocative style, drawn from military language and a minute observation of nature. As a novelist, however, he did not succeed in creating concrete character.

Bibliography

The collected works of Ernst Jünger were published in a definitive and partly revised edition as *Sämtliche Schriften,* 10 vols. (Stuttgart, 1960–1964).

English translations of Jünger's writings include *The Storm of Steel,* translated by Basil Creighton (London and New York, 1929); *Copse 125,* translated by Basil Creighton (London, 1930); *On the Marble Cliffs,* translated by Stuart Hood (London, 1947; New York, 1948); *Peace,* translated by Stuart Hood (Chicago, 1948); and *African Diversions,* translated by Stuart Hood (London, 1954).

For writings on Jünger, see G. Loose, *Ernst Jünger, Gestalt und Werk* (Frankfurt, 1957), pp. 371–380; Karl O. Paetel, *Ernst Jünger in Selbstzeugnissen,* Vol. 72 in Rowohlt's Monographien (Hamburg, 1962), pp. 168–175; Hans Peter Schwarz, *Der konservative Anarchist: Politik und Zeitkritik Ernst Jüngers* (Freiburg, 1962), pp. 309–315; and J. P. Stern, *Ernst Jünger* (Cambridge, 1953).

H. O. Pappé

JUNGIUS, JOACHIM (1587–1656), of Lübeck, represents the German counterpart to Galileo in Italy, Descartes in France, and Bacon in England as an innovator in science and philosophy. Unlike these men, Jungius did not achieve an international reputation; even among scholars, interest in him has been largely confined to Germans, whose curiosity has been whetted by Leibniz' enthusiastic praise of his merits as a philosopher. But Jungius exercised a wide personal influence in Germany as an active teacher. Furthermore, like Bacon, he envisaged a scientific society that would promote the welfare of mankind: Jungius actually organized a group called the Societas Ereunetica, whose stated objective was to promote sound science and combat false opinions. This group, with its stress on mathematics and logic as an antidote to metaphysical and mystical speculation, invites comparison with the Vienna circle of the twentieth century as well as with the Royal Society. Although Jungius has been linked by legend with the Rosicrucians, there is no evidence whatsoever to support this conjecture, according to Guhrauer.

Jungius studied at Rostock and Giessen before traveling to Italy to take a medical degree from Padua in 1618. During the early seventeenth century, philosophy in the German schools relied to a large extent on Aristotelian compendia drawn up by Melanchthon or by Ramus, supplemented by metaphysics of the Suarezian type. Both traditions were diligently studied by Jungius before he rejected them. Jungius had taught mathematics at Rostock; hence, he must have found the atmosphere of Padua congenial, because of the school's emphasis on a research-oriented natural philosophy, medical training, and mathematics.

On his return to Germany, Jungius resumed his teaching duties, presiding over disputations in which Aristotelian views in physics were mercilessly criticized. He was dissatisfied with the doctrine of the four elements and wished to substitute for it an atomism which, he believed, would be confirmed by future research but which, in any event, offered a more promising hypothesis. Jungius considered atomism more sound from the methodological point of view since it did not require the postulating of entities ("forms") to explain the rise of all sorts of new qualities in things. "Democritus was an Ockhamist," he remarked.

In 1625 Jungius began teaching medicine at Helmstedt, stressing the value of Galen, whose logical empiricism he found congenial. In 1628 Jungius took an unusual step— he left university teaching to assume charge of a secondary school in Hamburg. Jungius rescued the school from the decline into which it had fallen, sending out from it students trained to a high level of critical analysis. For them Jungius composed the famous "Hamburg Logic" (1638), called by Heinrich Scholz "the most significant logic of the seventeenth century," eclipsing the better-known Port-Royal logic. Jungius' critical presentation of traditional logic shows what the more sophisticated Neo-Aristotelian contemporaries of Descartes were thinking about causation, induction, and the nature of scientific demonstration. Jungius was also interested in natural history; he and his students collected plants, minerals, and fossils. His botanical views attracted the attention of Goethe, who planned a monograph about him.

Most of Jungius' writings in manuscript were destroyed by fire in 1691. The works posthumously published under his name, such as the *Doxoscopiae Physicae Minores* (Hamburg, 1662), were compilations made by students. Such writings as we do have bear the stamp of an active and critical mind, free from any mystical leanings and directed toward a scientific reconstruction of philosophy.

Works by Jungius

Logica Hamburgensis, edited by R. W. Meyer. Hamburg, 1957.

Works on Jungius

Guhrauer, G. C., *Joachim Jungius und sein Zeitalter.* Stuttgart and Tübingen, 1850. The definitive biography.

Wohlwill, E., "Joachim Jungius und die Erneurung atomistischer Lehren im 17. Jahrhundert." *Abhandlungen aus dem Gebiete der Naturwissenschaften.* Hamburg, 1887. Vol. X, pp. 3–66.

Neal W. Gilbert

JURISPRUDENCE. See Analytic jurisprudence; Historical school of jurisprudence; Legal positivism; Philosophy of law, history of; Philosophy of law, problems of.

JUSTICE. Although "justice" is sometimes used as a synonym for "law" or "lawfulness," it has a broader sense, closer to "fairness." Questions of justice, according to Hume, Mill, and others, presuppose conflicts of interest; there would be no point in talking about justice, according to Hume, but for the limitations of human benevolence and the competition for scarce goods. Justice presupposes people pressing claims and justifying them by rules or standards. This distinguishes it from charity, benevolence, or generosity. No one can claim alms or gifts as a right. However, although this account is appropriate to questions of distributive justice, where the problem is to allocate benefits, it is not so obviously true of corrective (or retributive) justice. It is farfetched to describe a criminal trial as a conflict between an accused man's interest in being let alone and the community's interest (if it has one) in punishing him. Nevertheless, sentencing criminals and giving judgment in favor of one party to a dispute rather than another have this in common with distribution—that they all may involve overriding a claim and treating one person more harshly than another. All presuppose general principles by which such distinctions are regulated and justified.

Just actions and decisions. Aristotle's analysis of justice is the key to its meaning at the level of the particular act or decision. Justice, he said, consists in treating equals equally and unequals unequally but in proportion to their relevant differences. This involves, first, the idea of impartiality; the honest judge considers only the features of the case that are relevant in law. Justice is no respecter of persons; wealth or status will influence judgment only if it makes a difference in law (for example, in taxation cases or the privilege of a member of Parliament in libel actions). Impartiality implies a kind of equality—not that all cases should be treated alike but that the onus rests on whoever would treat them differently to distinguish them in relevant ways. It is not for a judge to decide the respects in which men are equal but to decide whether the respects in which they are unequal are relevant to the issues in the case. That is what is really meant by the right to equal consideration—to be treated alike unless relevant differences have been proved.

These principles are not limited, of course, to the law. Many philosophers would regard it as characteristic of all moral judgments that the agent places his own interest on the same footing as the interests of others affected by his action, and this distinguishes moral judgments from prudential judgments, in which the agent assumes a position of privilege. The principle of impartiality is closely related, in this regard, to Kant's categorical imperative.

Is there a general duty to act justly? For a judge this is necessarily entailed by his function. Deciding issues according to law means taking account only of those features of a case to which the law attaches significance. But considering the question more generally, the very idea of moral justification implies impartiality and reference to rules. To ask a man why he allots more to A than to B is usually to ask for precisely the kind of justification implied in Aristotle's definition. One might explain a decision by reference to personal preferences; one could not justify it in this way. John Rawls has argued that we are rationally committed to acting justly by our very position as persons engaged with others in joint practices designed to promote common or complementary interests. We cannot reasonably expect other people to respect our interests unless we are prepared to respect theirs, and, as Leibniz put it, a man has grounds for complaint if, should you refuse to do something he asks you to do, he can judge that you would have made the same request in his place. The duty of justice, or fair dealing, according to Rawls, would emerge from the reciprocal recognition by a community of rational egoists that they had similar (and competing) interests and that no one could count on getting his way against all the rest. (Would it follow, however, that a state powerful enough to get its way against all other states would have no obligation to deal justly with them?)

A somewhat similar argument, but couched in a transcendental form, is offered by del Vecchio. Consciousness of oneself as a subject of experience implies, according to del Vecchio, the awareness (and therefore the existence) of objects of experience ("not-self"), but it implies, too, the possibility that one is oneself the object of experience of other experiencing subjects. The very fact of consciousness implies at least the possibility of someone besides oneself who could be a subject of claims. To recognize the existence of another person would therefore be to acknowledge the initial equality or parity of two subjects standing toward each other in this reciprocal experience relationship. It is doubtful, however, whether del Vecchio is entitled to infer from consciousness of another person's existence a duty to respect his interests.

Moral reciprocity—doing to others as one would have them do to oneself and giving an equal return for benefits received—is closely linked to impartiality, for to be impartial between oneself and someone else would mean doing nothing to profit at his expense. From this follow ideas such as a fair wage, a just price, and a fair exchange (what Aristotle called "commutative justice"), as opposed to exploitation and profiteering. It may be difficult, of course, to evaluate benefits exchanged, and the only measure available may be a market price or some conventional standard. For instance, how can one evaluate domestic service without taking for granted a wage structure in which types of work are roughly graded according to accepted standards like skill and responsibility? And for any individual worker the just wage is necessarily related to the idea of "the wage for the job."

Justice considered as reciprocity is often held to require returning evil for evil as much as good for good (*lex talionis*). In this case punishment would be paying back what is due. Mill sought to reconcile retaliative justice with utilitarianism, arguing that the natural impulse to retaliate is moralized as a sentiment of justice by confining it to those cases where the injury is to society at large and where retaliative justice has a useful deterrent function. However, although the duty of reciprocity may spring from our recognition of other men, just as much as ourselves, as persons with interests and claims deserving of respect, we cannot infer from that a duty to *attack* their interests whenever they attack either our own or even those of society at large. (See PUNISHMENT for a full discussion.)

Criteria of a just rule or practice. Although Aristotle respected the law-bound decision as the work of "passionless reason," he held, nevertheless, that because legislators could never foresee all the cases that would fall under a rule, it must be too rigid to do justice on every occasion. The equity jurisdiction of the English Court of Chancery grew up as a way of providing discretionary remedies where none was to be had in law. Again, in some branches of law judges rely on standards rather than strict rules and precedents, enjoying, in effect, wide discretion, or the law authorizes administrators to decide cases on their merits in the light of very general canons of policy, subject only to procedural safeguards of impartiality.

But if the law can be too rigid to do justice, does this not imply some extralegal canons of justice, by which perhaps the rules of law themselves might be assessed? Or again, what help is it to say, as we did earlier, that doing justice consists in making only *relevant* distinctions if the criteria of relevance are themselves in dispute? A judge may enforce a racial segregation law with strict impartiality and yet commit injustice if the distinctions embodied in the law are not themselves relevant.

Legal positivists are skeptical of nonlegal criteria of justice. Alf Ross, for instance, has declared that to use the word "just" as a description of a rule or general order, rather than of a particular decision in accordance with the rule, is merely to express emotion, like "banging on the table." Thrasymachus, caricatured in Book I of Plato's *Republic*, held that justice is simply what is advantageous to the stronger. The modern Marxist is more sophisticated; what is considered just, he holds, depends on the conflicting economic interests in a society, and law reflects those of the dominant class. Hobbes is often said to have been a positivist because he maintained that "just" and "unjust" presuppose a coercive power capable of enforcing obligations and that no complaint of injustice could be made against the sovereign legislator. But since he admitted that the sovereign may act inequitably, that is, contrary to natural law, canons of legal criticism beyond positive law do exist; it is only that the subject is not entitled to use them.

The idea of a law behind the law, the standard of justice to which positive law must conform, is exemplified in the "immutable and unwritten laws of Heaven" to which Sophocles' Antigone appeals against the decrees of Creon. In Stoic philosophy and in Roman jurisprudence this becomes a universal law of nature, equally accessible to all men through reason. Aquinas Christianized this theory by treating human law as the local application of natural law, which was itself an expression of God's rational will guiding the universe. By the early seventeenth century Grotius could argue that even if one could suppose that God did not exist, one would still be bound by the law of nature, since it derived from the two human qualities of sociability and rationality. Our need of society dictates the minimum conditions for social harmony. Natural law thus came to be regarded (for example, by Locke) as a universal test of the justice of positive law.

Classical natural law theory took too little account, no doubt, of the variety of legal institutions and moral standards and of their dependence on social and economic conditions. Modern natural-law theorists admit this. What are constant, they would say, are the formal criteria of justice rather than the substantive rules. They insist, however, that a just law formalizes a pre-existing, objective, juridical relationship, that it does not create justice but recognizes and attaches sanctions to what already exists, and that it can be rationally established independently of positive law. A highly abstract generalized theory of this kind was put forward, in Kantian terms, by Stammler. It is based on the principle that a person subjected to legal norms "must be respected as an end in himself, and treated as a participant in the community." But this is really to abandon the notion of a law behind the law and to offer, instead, formal or procedural criteria for rational criticism of positive law. Justice, in this sense, would be objective in that it would not be a matter of fiat but would be the subject of reasoned argument and justification. But it is doubtful whether there would now be any point in talking about justice as if it were something pre-existent—there to be discovered, like a new galaxy.

Almost as ancient as this kind of theory is the argument of Glaucon in the *Republic* (358–359) and Callicles in the *Gorgias* (483) that justice is conventional. Epicurus, denying that there ever was an absolute justice, declared: "Justice and injustice do not exist in relation to beings who have not been able to make a compact with the object of avoiding mutual harm" (*Doctrines and Maxims*). A compact, however, seems to imply that the duty to act justly stems from the duty to keep a promise, and that, as Hume pointed out, is no easier to establish. The strength of the conventionalist position is illustrated by Rawls's view of a just order as that body of principles that *anyone* might recognize as in his interest to maintain, given that others, on whose acquiescence he depends, have interests that conflict with his own. Although the rules might appear to discriminate against him on some given occasion, he would be able to see the point, nevertheless, of having those rules. This was, broadly, Hume's opinion. Justice, he held, was conventional in the sense of being necessary to society. Though there were discrepancies in detail, men's ideas on justice corresponded in essentials because they arose from needs common to all social situations. These rules were binding by custom and convention but were justified by their public utility.

Hume's view is close, therefore, to that of the utilitarians, which Samuel Butler attacked on the grounds that many acts promoting public utility might yet be acts of evident injustice. To rob Peter to pay Paul would be unjust in Butler's view, even though Paul gained more in happiness than Peter lost. Hume's position, however, is that the rules of justice serve the public interest only if decisions are regularly made in accordance with them, even though in some particular cases the public interest might be better served by departing from them. For the rules give security of expectation, which is their virtue, only if they are practices. Moreover, although one might have one's own views of what the rules ought to be, the just man would not act on them since the public interest is best served by supporting the social order, whatever its faults. Like Bentham, Hume stressed that "public utility requires that property should be regulated by general inflexible rules." This is the approach that Sidgwick called "conservative justice." He said that one could always argue against a change in the rules that people would be treated differently from the way others similarly placed had been treated theretofore. (Perelman has suggested this as a reason why all juridical systems are traditionalist, as in their attachment to precedent.) However, Sidgwick argued that conservative justice cannot be absolute. If the rule is contrary to the public interest, it is not, from a utilitarian standpoint, in accordance with "ideal justice." Nevertheless, it is commonly allowed that if normal expectations *are* disappointed, there ought to be compensation.

Rawls has challenged the view that a practice is just if it answers most fully to wants and interests. Justice is not the outcome but is presupposed by such a calculation. Any interest not compatible with justice ought not to be counted. Classical utilitarianism is at fault, according to Rawls, because it permits one to give as a reason why slavery is unjust that the advantages to the slaveholder do not outweigh the disadvantages to the slave and to society at large. Justice, understood as fairness, would not admit to the calculation the advantages of the slaveholder as such because his role could not be mutually acknowledged as part of an acceptable practice by all parties involved. It would not be thought relevant for one person, engaged with another in a common practice and accused by him of injustice, to answer that nevertheless it allowed of the greatest satisfaction of desire.

Classical utilitarianism is least satisfactory in its treatment of justice. The argument that adhering to rules gives greater general satisfaction than deciding every case on its happiness-producing merits does not meet the objection that a rule would still be unjust which deprived a tiny minority of the basic conditions for a decent life, even though it gave great satisfaction to everyone else. The Benthamite saving clause—"each to count for one and for no more than one"—attempts to write the principle of impartiality into the foundations of the system but does not meet the objection. One has to make the further assumptions that the more desires one has satisfied, the less one values the satisfaction and that there is an interpersonal equivalence of satisfactions all the way up the scale. One might then argue that the cost in satisfaction to a sacrificed minority would be so great that whatever the additional satisfaction to the majority, it must be less. But this is a quite arbitrary postulate, to avoid the conflict between the theory and our moral sentiments.

Criteria of distributive justice. It would be generally agreed that doing justice means treating equals equally and unequals according to their relevant inequalities. Disagreements arise over the criteria of relevance—that is, over the rule to be applied. Distribution (for example, of income, taxation, social service benefits, rations) may be organized on any of at least three principles of justice: arithmetical equality, merit (or desert), or need. Where no good ground can be shown for treating people differently, they clearly ought to be treated alike. This is the procedural presupposition of justice. The principle "one man, one vote" asserts that there are no differences between persons that would justify a differential franchise. This is not the case with progressive taxation, where capacity to pay is taken as a ground for discrimination.

Rewards or earnings are regulated by criteria of merit or desert, varying with the kind of treatment. Athletic prowess, said Aristotle, is rightly rewarded by prizes, nobility of birth and character by political honors and office. Wages are regulated according to skill, responsibility, industriousness, and similar factors. The only kind of reasons one could give for using such criteria, however, would be in the utilitarian terms of public interest, such as stimulating production.

Some social reformers have believed that distribution according to works should be replaced entirely by distribution according to need. Need criteria presuppose some standard condition that a person would fall short of were the need not satisfied and that falling short of it would be a bad thing—a hardship. Special disabilities involve special needs, calling for special treatment if the standard is to be reached. Needs are therefore claims, grounded on a standard to which a person is entitled simply as a person, irrespective of merit or desert. (There are also functional needs, like the plumber's need for tools, which would have to be justified in utilitarian terms.) The working of need criteria in general bears out the criticisms made earlier of utilitarian theories based on the satisfaction of desires. If it is prima facie unjust to give well-fed men television sets while others starve, it is not because

that is not the way to maximize satisfaction. It is, rather, that the degree of urgency of a need depends on how far leaving it unsatisfied deprives an individual of the normal standard to which he is entitled as a person.

Justice and integrity. Justice has been treated here as a particular virtue. Some philosophers, however, have meant by it an all-embracing virtue, closer to righteousness than to fairness. Contact with the narrower sense is to some extent preserved, however, in that justice is thought of as apportioning to each particular virtue or excellence its proper sphere. Plato's just state is that in which every man does the job to which he is best fitted, under the direction of the wisest; the just man is the one in whom the parts of the soul are harmoniously governed by reason. This conception may not be so far from our notion of a just man as one who possesses integrity, who lives according to consistent principles and is not to be diverted from them by consideration of gain, desire, or passion. However, justice in this sense has been the preoccupation of moralists rather than moral philosophers.

Bibliography

RATIONALIST AND NATURAL-LAW THEORIES

Plato's discussion of justice appears in the *Republic;* Aristotle's, in *Nicomachean Ethics;* and Thomas Aquinas' in *Summa Theologica*, Part I. There are selected passages in parallel Latin and English in A. P. d'Entrèves, *Aquinas: Selected Political Writings* (Oxford, 1948). For a Thomist account of justice, see also J. Pieper, *Über die Gerechtigkeit* (Munich, 1953), translated by L. E. Lynch as *Justice* (London, 1957). See also Rudolf Stammler, *Die Lehre von dem richtigen Rechte* (Berlin, 1902–1907), translated by Isaac Husik as *The Theory of Justice* (New York, 1925); Giorgio Del Vecchio, *La giustizia* (Rome, 1946), translated by Lady Guthrie as *Justice*, A. H. Campbell, ed. (Edinburgh, 1952). Both Stammler's and Del Vecchio's analyses are Neo-Kantian.

ANALYTICAL AND POSITIVIST THEORIES

For works concerned mainly with analysis of formal criteria, see Thomas Hobbes, *Leviathan* (1651), paperback edition Michael Oakeshott, ed., with introduction by Richard Peters (New York, 1962), which deals with justice as positive law; and Chaim Perelman, *De la Justice* (Brussels, 1945), translated by John Petrie as *The Idea of Justice and the Problem of Argument* (New York and London, 1963), which distinguishes formal and substantive criteria of justice and investigates the method of reasoning from each. Alf Ross, *On Law and Justice* (London, 1958) presents a positivist, emotivist theory; a relativist approach can be found in Hans Kelsen, *What Is Justice?* (Berkeley and Los Angeles, 1957), which also includes essays on Plato, Aristotle, and Biblical theories of justice. H. L. A. Hart, in *Concept of Law* (Oxford, 1961), explores relations between concepts of law, justice, and morality.

UTILITARIAN AND OTHER THEORIES

For literature on various kinds of utilitarianism, see Jeremy Bentham, *An Introduction to the Principles of Morals and Legislation* and *Principles of the Civil Code*, in *The Works of Jeremy Bentham*, John Bowring, ed. (Edinburgh, 1843), Vol. I, pp. 1–154, 297–364; Bishop Joseph Butler, *The Analogy of Religion . . . to Which Are Added Two Brief Dissertations: On Personal Identity and on the Nature of Virtue* (1736), especially *Dissertation on the Nature of Virtue*, which is in *Butler's Fifteen Sermons and a Dissertation Upon the Nature of Virtue*, W. R. Matthews, ed. (London, 1950); David Hume, *Treatise of Human Nature* (1739 and 1740), especially Book III, and *Enquiry Concerning the Principles of Morals* (1751); J. S. Mill, *Utilitarianism* (1863); Henry Sidgwick, *Methods of Ethics* (7th ed., rev., Chicago, 1962); Hastings Rashdall, *Theory of Good and Evil*, 2 vols. (2d. ed., Oxford, 1924). See also Jonathan Harrison, "Utilitarianism, Universalization, and Our Duty to Be Just," in *PAS*, Vol. 53 (1952–1953), 105–134, also in Frederick A. Olafson, ed., *Justice and Social Policy* (Englewood Cliffs, N.J., 1961), pp. 55–79; John Rawls, "Justice as Fairness," in Peter Laslett and W. G. Runciman, eds., *Philosophy, Politics and Society, Second Series* (Oxford, 1962), pp. 132–157, also in Olafson, *op. cit.*, pp. 80–107; Stanley I. Benn and R. S. Peters, *Social Principles and the Democratic State* (London, 1959), reissued as *The Principles of Political Thought* (New York, 1964), especially Chs. 5–6; and L. T. Hobhouse, *Elements of Social Justice* (London, 1922). Roscoe Pound, *Introduction to the Philosophy of Law* (New Haven, 1922; rev. ed., 1954), includes a useful bibliography.

STANLEY I. BENN

JUSTIFICATION OF MORAL PRINCIPLES. See ULTIMATE MORAL PRINCIPLES: THEIR JUSTIFICATION.

K

KABBALAH. See CABALA.

KAFKA, FRANZ (1883–1924), German author, was the son of a Jewish businessman who had been a peddler in southern Bohemia. The family was German-speaking. Kafka studied law at the German University of Prague and at Munich and became an official of a workers' accident insurance company. He began writing in 1907 but by his own choice published little. About that time he contracted tuberculosis and for some years lived in various sanatoriums. His two engagements ended unhappily. In 1923 he moved to Berlin, where, living with a girl who was in charge of a Jewish orphanage, he achieved what happiness he was to know. He died of a tubercular infection of the larynx in a nursing home at Kierling, near Vienna.

The central experience of Kafka's life, it seems, was a manifold alienation—as a speaker of German in a Czech city, as a Jew among German and Czech Gentiles in a period of ardent nationalism, as a man full of doubts and an unquenched thirst for faith among conventional "liberal" Jews, as a born writer among people with business interests, as a sick man among the healthy, and as a timid and neurasthenic lover in exacting erotic relationships.

Kafka's narrative art is at once immensely original, prophetic, and fragmentary—hence the large number of mutually exclusive interpretations it has received. Several elements of his prose were the stock in trade of the minor literature of his day. His language is unemphatic and prosy and occasionally contains Prague-German provincialisms; some of the subjects of his stories belong to the horror literature of the turn of the century; he shared the modern interest in psychological motivation; and he often used the smaller prose genres cultivated by his contemporaries in Prague and Vienna. But the use Kafka made of these elements is startlingly original, and the compelling gnostic vision of the world which is fashioned from them has become one of the major literary and intellectual influences of our age. In Kafka's work the existentialists' conceptions of absurdity and dread are fully explored. Unlike the later existentialists, he did not derive a positive value from these modes of experience; the value of his writings lies in the intense lucidity of the exploration.

It is obvious from the very titles of many of Kafka's stories—*The Trial*, "The Judgment," "Before the Law," "The Penal Settlement"—that his work is informed by a strong legalistic strain, possibly derived from his Jewish heritage but then secularized. In the famous "Letter to His Father" (1919) he recounted a certain childhood episode which violated his sense of justice. Characteristically, its terror for him lay in his inability to connect the trivial "crime" with the monstrous punishment he received.

The novel *The Trial*, begun in 1914 and published by Kafka's friend Max Brod in 1925, at once challenges and refines our conventional ways of connecting causes and effects through the story of a young man, Josef K, who one day wakes up in his lodgings to find himself arrested without knowing what wrong he has done. He makes various attempts to justify himself against the enigmatic accusation and to influence a number of people who he believes may effect his acquittal. Although offered a chance of repudiating the jurisdiction of the court that is concerned with his case, he ends up by being marched off to his execution, to die "like a dog." The question What has Josef K done? receives a number of detailed answers, the total effect of which is to undermine the reader's notion of guilt. Josef K has lived the unremarkable life of an average young man, a bank clerk. Since in his "ordinary" life he always based his relations with other people on asserting what he believed were his "rights" in this or that situation, it is consistent with his character that he should seek to justify himself before the Law. The only thing he knows about that Law (and the all but unattainable authority behind it) is that it is powerful, whereas he is weak. According to the "inescapable logic" of the world, he must therefore be outside the Law and thus, in some sense, guilty. With his every move the not wholly irrational sense of guilt drags more violently at his soul. At first, this sense is no more than an uneasy "They are sure to have something on me," but gradually it is magnified by all the actions, in themselves trivial, which consitute "normal" behavior in our world, coupled with Josef K's inability to live "outside the Law," which for Kafka amounted to consciousness itself. Simplifying the subtly involuted and complex texture of the novel, we may conclude that "minor guilt + situation of weakness + self-justification = major sense of guilt," which is tantamount to saying that Kafka's dialectical ingenuity is expended on making convincing the equation "[subjective] sense of guilt = [objective] guilt."

Similar dialectical devices are used in the second major work, the unfinished novel *The Castle* (1921–1922, published 1926). K, a land surveyor, has been called to a village that is governed by an authority which resides in a nearby castle. The village and its inhabitants are described only as they are related to K and to his attempts to justify his presence there. His commission, the authority on whose behalf he is to perform it, its relation to himself and to the villagers, the extent of its power, and the morality of its commands—all these are not so much vague as complexly contradictory. (Kafka was prophetically describing the anonymous, muffled workings of a totalitarian ministry as they affect the helpless victim, but since his style is that of an "objective" report, he allowed himself no expressions of pity.) Every assurance that K receives is thrown into doubt either by an oblique contradiction or by K's own unnerved (and, to the reader, unnerving) insistence on exploring its possible ambiguities. Again, the novel elaborates a vicious circle. K uses the people he meets in order to wrest from them hints or indications about his task and status but because he lacks the assurance of a clearly defined status and task, he is an outsider and thus in a position of weakness. He is therefore bound to construe all these hints as hostile and thus distrust them. K does not have enough strength to break the spell that the Castle (like the court in *The Trial*) seems to be casting over him, for he looks to it as the place which, in justifying him, will give him strength. And, to keep alive K's torments of uncertainty, the Castle need do little more than send an occasional hint of a possible way of deliverance.

Leaving aside the various Freudian, Marxist, and Christian interpretations that Kafka's work has received, its fragmentary nature points to a fundamental hiatus. His heroes' desolate quests for justice, recognition, and acceptance by the world are meaningful to us because they invoke our sense of pity and justice, whereas the matter-of-fact ways in which these quests are presented invite us to accept cruelty and injustice as though they were necessary and self-evident modes of life. Thus, the meaningfulness of the quests is impaired. Kafka's writings are indeed prophetic intimations of the logic of the concentration camps; the monstrous insinuation inherent in his prophecies is that the exterminator is not wholly in the wrong, that his hold over his victim is something more than a matter of superior might, for the victim cooperates in his own destruction.

Works by Kafka

Most of Kafka's writings were published posthumously and against his express wishes by his friend Max Brod. The complete edition is *Werke* (Frankfurt, 1952—). The "definitive" English edition, published in London, includes *The Trial,* translated by Willa Muir and Edwin Muir (1945); *Kafka's Diaries,* 2 vols., translated by J. Kresh, M. Greenberg, and H. Arendt (1948–1949); *America,* translated by Willa Muir and Edwin Muir (1949); *In the Penal Settlement: Tales and Short Prose Works,* translated by Willa Muir and Edwin Muir (1949); *The Castle,* translated by Willa Muir and Edwin Muir (1953); *Wedding Preparations in the Country and Other Posthumous Prose Writings,* translated by Ernst Kaiser and Eithne Wilkins (1954); and *Description of a Struggle and The Great Wall of China,* translated by Willa Muir and Edwin Muir and Tania Stern and James Stern (1960). See also Kafka's *Letters to Milena* (Jesenská), translated by Tania Stern and

James Stern (London, 1953), and G. Janouch's *Conversations With Kafka* (New York, 1953).

Works on Kafka

Three biographical studies are available: Max Brod, *Franz Kafka: Eine Biographie* (Frankfurt, 1937), translated as *The Biography of Franz Kafka* (London, 1947); K. Wagenbach, *Franz Kafka: Eine Biographie seiner Jugend, 1883–1912* (Bern, 1958); and P. Eisner, *Franz Kafka and Prague* (New York, 1950).

For critical works on Kafka see G. Anders, *Franz Kafka* (London, 1960); Ronald D. Gray, ed., *Franz Kafka: A Collection of Critical Essays* (Englewood Cliffs, N. J., 1963), which has important contributions by Albert Camus and E. Heller; and Heinz Politzer, *Franz Kafka: Parable and Paradox* (Ithaca, N. Y., 1962), the most recent major addition to the critical literature.

J. P. STERN

KAIBARA EKKEN (1630–1714), or Ekiken, Japanese Confucianist influential in popularizing Confucian ethics among ordinary people. Kaibara was born in Fukuoka. The son of a physician, he became a doctor himself, then left medicine to become a Chu Hsi Neo-Confucianist. His teachers in Kyoto were Kinoshita Junan (1621–1698) and Yamazaki Ansai. At 39 Kaibara returned to Fukuoka, where he spent the rest of his life in the service of the Kuroda fief. Blessed with an extraordinary capacity for work but little originality, he wrote on many subjects. He became an important botanist with the issuing of separate books on the vegetables, the flora, and the medicinal herbs of Japan. His books on education were pioneering works in pedagogy; *Onna daigaku* ("The Great Learning for Women"), the standard book on women's ethics in the Tokugawa era, is attributed variously to him and to his well-educated wife. His books were a great success. Unlike most Confucianists, who wrote in Chinese, he wrote in Japanese; furthermore, his teaching was highly practical, applying Confucian morality to everyday life. His pedagogical ideas were not equalitarian (he assigned to women the role of mere submissiveness and obedience to their husbands), and his botanical studies were not at all scientific in the modern sense, but he played an important role in spreading education.

Kaibara's philosophical importance today rests on his *Taigiroku* ("The Great Doubt"), in which he aired his dissent with the official doctrine of the Chu Hsi school. Kaibara was also critical of the "ancient learning" school of Confucianism and its scholars Itō Jinsai and Ogyū Sorai, and of the Wang Yang-ming school, the rival of Chu Hsi. Kaibara disagreed with Chu Hsi Confucianism in his elevation of *ki,* the material force, over *ri,* the principle immanent in all things. For him *ki* is the "great limit" or the "ultimate" and is an all-pervading life-force. Kaibara does not distinguish the original form of human nature from its acquired form; contrary to Chu Hsi, he is an optimist in his view of man and of the natural world. His cosmology is characterized by cosmic love that embraces all men, born as they are of heaven and earth. Man's indebtedness to nature is limitless, and for him the Confucian virtue of *jen,* "humaneness," comes close to being a religious benevolence, first toward nature and then toward men. His practical bent, however, makes it difficult to clarify his position, which seems to be one of eclectic doubt rather than critical inquiry. In administrative matters Kaibara opposed imitating Chinese ways; rather he was an ardent patriot, loyal in support of the emperor.

Bibliography

Kaibara's works are available in Japanese in *Ekken zenshū* ("Complete Works of Kaibara Ekken"), Ekkenkai, ed., 8 vols. (Tokyo, 1911). A secondary source in Japanese is Inoue Tadashi, *Kaibara Ekken* (Tokyo, 1963).

See also O. Graf, *Kaibara Ekiken* (Leiden, 1942); S. Atsuharu, "Kaibara E. and *Onna daigaku,*" in *Cultural Nippon,* Vol. 7, No. 4 (1939), 43–56; and W. T. de Bary, Ryusaku Tsunoda, and Donald Keene, eds., *Sources of Japanese Tradition* (New York, 1958), pp. 374–377.

GINO K. PIOVESANA, S.J.

KAMES, LORD. See HOME, HENRY.

KANT, IMMANUEL (1724–1804), propounder of the critical philosophy. Kant was born at Königsberg in East Prussia; he was the son of a saddler and, according to his own account, the grandson of an emigrant from Scotland. He was educated at the local high school, the Collegium Fridericianum, and then at the University of Königsberg, where he had the good fortune to encounter a first-class teacher in the philosopher Martin Knutzen. After leaving the university, about 1746, Kant was employed for a few years as a tutor in a number of families in different parts of East Prussia. He kept up his studies during this period and in 1755 was able to take his master's degree at Königsberg and to begin teaching in the university as a *Privatdozent*. He taught a wide variety of subjects, including physics, mathematics, and physical geography as well as philosophy, but nevertheless remained poor for many years. It was not until 1770, when he was appointed to the chair of logic and metaphysics at Königsberg, that his financial stringencies were eased.

Kant's first book, *Gedanken von der wahren Schätzung der lebendigen Kräfte* ("Thoughts on the True Estimation of Living Forces"), was published as early as 1747 (Königsberg), and between 1754 and 1770 he produced an impressive stream of essays and treatises. His earlier works are primarily contributions to natural science or natural philosophy, the most notable being his *General History of Nature and Theory of the Heavens* of 1755; it was not until after 1760 that philosophical interests in the modern sense became dominant in his mind. Kant's publications had already won him a considerable reputation in German learned circles by the time he obtained his professorship. The ten years following his appointment form a period of literary silence during which Kant was engaged in preparing his magnum opus, the *Critique of Pure Reason*. The appearance of the *Critique* was eagerly awaited by Kant's friends and philosophical colleagues, but when it at last came out in 1781 the general reaction was more bewilderment than admiration. Kant tried to remove misunderstandings by restating the main argument in the *Prolegomena to Every Future Metaphysics* of 1783 and by rewriting some of the central sections of the *Critique* for a second edition in 1787. At the same time he continued,

with most remarkable energy for a man of his years, the elaboration of the rest of his system. By 1790 the *Critique of Practical Reason* and the *Critique of Judgment* were in print, and of the major treatises only *Religion Within the Bounds of Mere Reason* (1793) and *Metaphysic of Morals* (1797) had still to appear. Kant then enjoyed a tremendous reputation throughout Germany and was beginning to be known, though scarcely to be understood, in other European countries. In his declining years, however, he suffered the mortification of seeing some of the ablest young philosophers in his own country, among them Fichte, Schelling, and J. S. Beck, proclaim that he had not really understood his own philosophy and propose to remedy the deficiency by producing "transcendental" systems of their own. There is reason to believe that the work on which Kant was engaged in the last years of his life was intended as a counterblast to such critics. But Kant was not able to complete it before his death, and all that remains of it are the fragments gathered together under the title *Opus Postumum*.

Kant's outer life was almost entirely uneventful. He never married. The one occasion on which he might have become politically prominent was in 1794 when, after the appearance of his book on religion, the Prussian king asked him not to publish further on a topic on which his views were causing alarm to the orthodox. But Kant duly promised, and no scandal ensued. For the rest, he fulfilled the duties of his professorship and took his turn as rector of the university; dined regularly with his friends; admired Rousseau and the French Revolution from afar; conversed eagerly with travelers who brought him news of a wider world he never saw himself. Never very robust in body, he carefully conserved his physical resources and was in good health until a relatively short time before his death. He was nearly eighty when he died.

CHARACTER OF KANT'S PHILOSOPHICAL WORK

Kant was the first of the major philosophers of modern times to spend his life as a professional teacher of the subject. He was required by university regulation to base his philosophy lectures on particular texts, and he used for this purpose not the works of major thinkers like Descartes and Locke, but the handbooks of his professorial predecessors, notably Christian von Wolff, Alexander Baumgarten, and G. F. Meier. Wolff and Baumgarten had dressed out the philosophy of Leibniz in what they took to be decent academic garb, presenting Leibniz' thoughts in the form of a system and with an air of finality foreign to the original; Meier did the same for the doctrines of formal logic. Their example had a near-fatal effect on Kant, for he too thought that philosophy must be thorough if it is to be academically respectable—meaning, among other things, technical and schematic. In the *Critique of Pure Reason* he set out his theories in what he later called progressive order, starting from what was logically first and working forward to familiar facts; in that work he also employed an elaborate terminology of his own and an apparatus of "parts," "divisions," and "books" whose titles are alarming and whose appropriateness to the subject matter is not immediately obvious. It is not surprising that his first readers were unable to discover what the work as a whole was about. The *Critique of Practical Reason* and the *Critique of Judgment* were still more pedantic in form, since in them Kant persisted with much of the formal framework already used in the *Critique of Pure Reason*, in each case proceeding from a part labeled "Analytic" to another labeled "Dialectic," uncovering one or more "antinomies" in dealing with the dialectic, and ending with an untidy appendix irrelevantly entitled "Doctrine of Method." The fact that Kant was already an old man when he composed these works doubtless explains his attachment to what some commentators have called his architectonic; it is a major obstacle to the proper grasp and unprejudiced evaluation of his ideas. Yet, as passages in his ethical writings in particular show, Kant was capable of expounding his thoughts with clarity, even with eloquence. He was not by nature a bad writer, but he accepted uncritically the scholastic manner cultivated by his fellow professors.

The first task in reading Kant is thus to cut through the formal academic dress in which he clothes his opinions. When this is done, what emerges is not a provincial pedant like Wolff or Baumgarten, but a person of remarkable intellectual and moral stature. Kant's knowledge of the major European philosophers was often no more than superficial, and his estimate of the work of some of his own contemporaries was certainly overgenerous. But he had, for all that, a sure sense of what was intellectually important at the time; he alone among the eighteenth-century philosophers at once appreciated the greatness of Newton and was fully aware of the challenge for ethics Newton's work presented once its seemingly deterministic implications were understood. To sum up Kant's mature philosophy in a single formula: He wished to insist on the authority of science and yet preserve the autonomy of morals. To achieve this result was a gigantic task, involving consideration of the whole question of the possibility of metaphysics as well as the construction of a theory of scientific knowledge and the elaboration of an ethical system. Nor was Kant one to be content with mere generalities; he sought to work out his position in detail, with many specific arguments, as well as to state a general case. But the obscurities of his language combine with the extent of his intellectual ambitions to prevent the average reader from grasping precisely what Kant was after; individual points are picked up, but the shape of the whole is not discerned. Yet to be fair to Kant the reader must see the individual views in the wide setting in which Kant saw them himself. To estimate their philosophical value without taking account of their position in the Kantian system, as many critics have tried to do, is quite indefensible.

PRECRITICAL WRITINGS

Kant's philosophical career is commonly divided into two periods, that before 1770, usually referred to as "precritical," and that after 1770, usually referred to as "critical." The word "critical" comes from Kant's own description of his mature philosophy as a form of "critical idealism," an idealism, that is to say, built on the basis of a critique of the powers of reason. The precritical period of Kant's thought is interesting primarily, though not exclusively, for its anticipations of his later ideas. Kant was educated by Knutzen in the Wolff–Baumgarten version of Leibniz, and he was, like his master, an independent Leibnizian from the first, although it was many years before he made a decisive break with the Leibnizian way of thinking. The main influence operating against Leibniz in Kant's early thought was Newton, to whose work he had also been introduced by Knutzen. In the more narrowly philosophical field another independent Leibnizian, Christian August Crusius, proved an important subsidiary influence. Just when Hume awakened Kant from his "dogmatic slumber" is uncertain, but it seems likely that Kant had moved some way in the direction of empiricism before that event took place.

Causation. How little the early Kant had learned from Hume can be seen from some of his first metaphysical essays. In the *Principium Primorum Cognitionis Metaphysicae Nova Dilucidatio* (Königsberg, 1755) he discoursed in effect on the subject of causality, discussing at length the relationship of the Leibnizian principle of sufficient reason to the logical principles of identity and contradiction. Kant knew at this stage, as Crusius did, that Wolff's attempt to subordinate the real to the logical was a mistake, but he had only a hazy idea of what he was later to call the synthetic nature of propositions asserting real connections. He moved a step nearer his mature view in the 1763 essay on negative quantities (*Versuch, den Begriff der negativen Grössen in die Weltweisheit einzuführen,* Königsberg) when he pointed out that opposition in nature is quite different from opposition in logic: Two forces acting against one another are quite unlike a proposition in which the same predicate is simultaneously affirmed and denied. But in none of his writings of the time did Kant explicitly raise the question of the sphere of application of the causal principle, as Hume did.

Existence. Kant's failure to press home his questions on causation is paralleled in his otherwise striking treatment of existence in another work published in 1763, "The Only Possible Ground of Proof of God's Existence." He began this work by declaring that even if the proposition that existence is no predicate or determination of anything seems "strange and contradictory," it is nevertheless indubitable and certain. "It is not a fully correct expression to say: 'A sea unicorn is an existent animal'; we should put it the other way round and say: 'To a certain existing sea animal there belong the predicates that I think of as collectively constituting a sea unicorn.'" On these grounds Kant rejected the Cartesian version of the Ontological Argument. But he held, even so, that an alternative conceptual proof of God's existence could be found: Nothing could be conceived as possible unless (as the point had already been put in the *Nova Dilucidatio*) "whatever of reality there is in every possible notion do exist, and indeed, absolutely necessarily. . . . Further, this complete reality must be united in a single being." There must, in other words, be a perfect being if there are to be any possibilities. Kant was to recall this proof in his derivation of the idea of the *ens realissimum* in the *Critique of Pure*

Reason, but he then no longer believed that it had constitutive force. His treatment of attempts to produce causal proofs of God's existence in the *Critique* was also altogether more trenchant than in the precritical works, for though he saw there that the ordinary First Cause Argument was unsatisfactory, he regarded the Argument from Design as generally acceptable, even if not logically compulsive.

Metaphysical propositions. Kant was more successful in another treatise written at the same period, "Untersuchungen über die Deutlichkeit der Grundsätze der natürlichen Theologie und der Moral" ("On the Distinctness of the Principles of Natural Theology and Morals," 1764). The Berlin Academy had proposed the question, Are metaphysical truths generally, and the fundamental principles of natural theology and morals in particular, capable of proofs as distinct as those of geometry? if not, what is the true nature of their certainty? Kant answered by drawing a series of radical distinctions between argument in philosophy and argument in mathematics. The mathematician starts from definitions that are in effect arbitrary combinations of concepts; the philosopher must work toward definitions, not argue from them, since his business is to "analyze concepts which are given as confused." Mathematics contains few unanalyzable concepts and indemonstrable propositions; philosophy is full of them. Then too, the relationship between mathematical ideas can always be observed *in concreto,* whereas the philosopher, having nothing to correspond to mathematical diagrams or symbolism, necessarily works on a more abstract level. The lesson of all this might seem to be that philosophical truths are incapable of strict demonstration, but Kant did not draw this conclusion in the case of natural theology, where he held to his attempted conceptual proof, though he inclined toward it in respect to "the primary grounds of morals." In general, Kant's tendency was to say that metaphysics must be an analytic activity that should follow a method that is fundamentally Newtonian: "It is far from the time for proceeding synthetically in metaphysics; only when analysis will have helped us to distinct concepts understood in their details will synthesis be able to subsume compounded cognitions under the simplest cognitions, as in mathematics" (*Critique of Practical Reason and Other Writings,* Beck translation, 1949, p. 275).

Kant viewed the prospects of attaining genuine metaphysical knowledge with increasing skepticism as the 1760s went on. In the enigmatic *Dreams of a Spirit-Seer* of 1766 he compared the thought constructions of metaphysics to the fantasies of Swedenborg, in a manner that is scarcely flattering to either. Metaphysical contentions are groundless, since metaphysical concepts such as spirit cannot be characterized in positive terms. To survive, metaphysics must change its nature and become a science of the limits of human knowledge. Kant's skepticism about metaphysics was increased by his discovery of the antinomies, which is often dated 1769 although something like the third antinomy is to be found in the *Nova Dilucidatio.* Astonishingly, however, in his inaugural dissertation in 1770 he reverted in some degree to the old dogmatic conception of the subject and argued for the possibility of genuine knowledge of an intelligible world. But the main interest of the dissertation lies in its account of sensory knowledge, which prepared the way for the fundamental criticisms of metaphysical pretensions in the *Critique of Pure Reason.*

THE INAUGURAL DISSERTATION

Kant's Latin dissertation, "On the Form and Principles of the Sensible and Intelligible Worlds," publicly defended on August 21, 1770, was his inaugural lecture as professor of logic and metaphysics at Königsberg. At least one of the themes of the dissertation, the status of the concept of space, represented a long-standing interest. As early as 1747 Kant had argued that the proposition that space has three dimensions is contingent; given a different law of the effects of different substances on one another, "an extension with other properties and dimensions would have arisen. A science of all these possible kinds of space would undoubtedly be the highest enterprise which a finite understanding could undertake in the field of geometry" ("Living Forces," Handyside translation, in *Kant's Inaugural Dissertation and Early Writings on Space,* p. 12). Later, however, he regarded three-dimensionality as a necessary property of space, and used its necessity as a ground for rejecting Leibniz' account of the concept. In a short essay on space published in 1768 Kant had seemed to suggest that Newton's view of space as an absolute reality was the only alternative to Leibniz, but in the dissertation he rejected both theories and widened his treatment of the question so that it covered time as well as space. Despite this extension the dissertation is best viewed as directed mainly against Leibniz.

Space and time. In general, Leibniz had followed the other great rationalists in interpreting perception as a confused form of thinking. Like Descartes, he had treated the deliverances of the senses as sometimes clear but never distinct. In the dissertation Kant developed two main arguments against this position. He maintained in the first place that it could not do justice to the special character of space and time, which are not, as Leibniz supposed, systems of relations abstracted from particular situations and confusedly apprehended, but rather unique individuals of which clear knowledge is presupposed in all perceptual description. The ideas of space and time are intuitive rather than conceptual in character; moreover, they are "pure" intuitions insofar as the essential nature of their referents is known in advance of experience and not as a result of it.

Space and geometry. To reinforce this point Kant brought forward his second argument, that Leibniz' theory could not account for the apodictic character of geometry. There was, Kant supposed, an essential relation between geometry and space, for geometry "contemplates the relations of space" and "does not demonstrate its universal propositions by apprehending the object through a universal concept, as is done in matters of reason, but by submitting it to the eyes as a singular intuition, as is done in matters of sense" ("Dissertation," *ibid.,* Sec. 15 C). But if space is what Leibniz said it was and if, as Kant added, "all properties of space are borrowed only from external relations through experience," then:

> geometrical axioms do not possess universality, but only that comparative universality which is acquired through induction and holds only so widely as it is observed; nor do they possess necessity, except such as depends on fixed laws of nature; nor have they any precision save such as is matter of arbitrary convention; and we might hope, as in empirical matters, some day to discover a space endowed with other primary affections, and perhaps even a rectilinear figure enclosed by two straight lines.   (*Ibid.*, Sec. 15 D)

Kant's own account of space at this stage was that it "*is not something objective and real,* neither substance, nor accident, nor relation, but [something] *subjective and ideal;* it is, as it were, a schema, issuing by a constant law from the nature of the mind, for the co-ordinating of all outer sensa whatever" (*ibid.*). One major advantage of this subjectivist view, in Kant's eyes, was that it explains the possibility of applying geometry to the physical world. Space being a universal form of sensibility, "nothing whatsoever . . . can be given to the senses save in conformity with the primary axioms of space and the other consequences of its nature, as expounded by geometry" (*ibid.*, Sec. 15 E).

Appearance and reality. Kant's view had another, more startling implication, namely that we cannot know things as they really are through sense perception. If space and time are contributed by the knowing mind, spatial and temporal objects will be altered in the very act of being apprehended. It follows that the world known through the senses—the world investigated by the physical sciences and familiar in everyday experience—can be no more than a phenomenal world. Kant was prepared to accept this conclusion in the dissertation, but he balanced it by saying that over and above this phenomenal world is another world of real objects, knowable not by the senses but by reason. Reason lacks intuitive powers—we cannot be acquainted with things as they are. But (and in this the contrast with the *Dreams* is at its strongest) reason possesses certain concepts of its own, among them "possibility, existence, necessity, substance, cause," by means of which it can arrive at a "symbolic cognition" of such things; that is, know some true propositions about them. The intellect, in its real as opposed to its logical use, can form the concept of a perfect being and use this both to measure the reality of other things and for moral purposes.

Achievements. The doctrine of pure intellectual concepts in the dissertation is at best impressionistic and had to be completely rethought in the ten years that followed. But against this may be set Kant's positive achievements in the dissertation, seen from the point of view of his future work. First, Kant had convinced himself that there is an absolute difference between sensing and thinking, and that sense experience need not be in any way confused. Second, he had worked out the main lines, though by no means all the details, of what was to be his mature theory of space and time. Third, he had revived the old antithesis of things real and things apparent, objects of the intellect and objects of the senses, to cope with the consequences of

his views about space and time; in this way he was able to show (or so he thought) that physics gives us genuine knowledge, though only of appearances, and that the task of telling us about things as they really are is reserved for metaphysics. Fourth and last, he had recognized the existence of a special class of concepts, "given through the very nature of the intellect," and had seen that these have an important bearing on the question of the possibility of metaphysics.

What Kant had not done was to pose the problem of metaphysics with all its wider implications. As in the *Dreams,* he treated the question whether we have any knowledge of a world of pure spirit as one that is asked primarily for its theoretical interest. It was intellectual curiosity, that is to say, which at this stage prompted Kant to inquire whether physics and metaphysics could coexist, and, if they could, what should be said of their respective objects. He retained this curiosity when he wrote the *Critique of Pure Reason,* but it was not by then his only motive. For he had seen by 1781 that the question of the possibility of metaphysics was important not only to the academic philosopher, but because of its bearing on the universally interesting topics of God, freedom, and immortality, to the plain man as well; that it was a matter not just of intellectual, but also of moral, concern.

"CRITIQUE OF PURE REASON": THEME AND PRELIMINARIES

Kant's principal task in the *Critique of Pure Reason* was to determine the cognitive powers of reason, to find out what it could and could not achieve in the way of knowledge. The term "reason" in the title was intended in its generic sense, to cover the intellect as a whole; Kant was not exclusively interested in the reason that he himself distinguished from and opposed to understanding. He was, however, particularly concerned with the capacities of "pure" reason, that is, with what reason could know when operating by itself and not in association with another faculty. Kant believed it important to answer this question for two reasons. He saw that there are spheres (mathematics, for instance) in which it is plausible to claim that pure reason is a source of important truths. He also saw that in another field, that of metaphysics, remarkable claims were advanced on reason's behalf: It was alleged that, by simply thinking, we could arrive at ultimate truth about the world, establishing thus a series of propositions whose certainty was unassailable and whose subject matter was of supreme importance. Kant, who had himself made this sort of claim in the dissertation, never doubted that what the metaphysician wants to say matters, but he did question his competence to say it. The fact that reason "precipitates itself into darkness and contradictions" once it enters this field struck him as deeply significant; the "intestine wars," the interminable disputes, of metaphysicians could only mean that their claims were pitched too high. Nor was the scandal of metaphysics—the fact that nothing in metaphysics could be regarded as settled—of concern only to metaphysicians. By failing to make good his proofs, the metaphysician brought doubt on the acceptability of his conclusions, including such fundamental articles of belief as that God exists and that the will is free. In proposing a radical re-examination of the capacities of pure reason, Kant's ultimate motive was to safeguard such convictions by making clear that although they cannot be matters of knowledge, they can all the same be held to as matters of what he called pure rational faith.

Types of judgment. In the preface to the *Critique*, Kant formulates his main question as "how much can understanding and reason know apart from all experience?" (A xvii). (The first edition is customarily referred to as A, the second edition as B.) In the introduction, he takes his first step toward an answer by substituting the formula "How are synthetic *a priori* judgments possible?" Two closely connected sets of distinctions lie behind these celebrated words. First, Kant distinguishes propositions that are a priori from all others; an a priori judgment "in being thought is thought as *necessary*" and is also thought "with strict universality, that is, in such a manner that no exception is allowed as possible" (B 3–4). A priori judgments have the twin characteristics of necessity and universality, neither of which can be found in conclusions from experience.

In holding that experience can present us with no more than contingent truths Kant echoes the views of many of his predecessors. But in his other distinction, between synthetic and analytic judgments, he shows greater originality. A judgment is analytic, he explains, if what is thought in the predicate-concept has already been thought in the subject-concept; a judgment is synthetic if this condition does not obtain. Thus, "All bodies are extended" is analytic because our idea of a body is of something that is extended or occupies space; "All bodies have weight" is synthetic because the notion of weight is not comprised in the notion of body (we learn by experience that bodies have weight). In analytic judgments, again, the connection of subject and predicate is "thought through identity"; or, as Kant puts it elsewhere in the *Critique*, the highest principle of all analytic judgments is the principle of contradiction. It follows from this that every analytic judgment is a priori in that it is true or false without regard to experience; every analytic judgment is either necessarily true or necessarily false, and we establish its truth or falsity by reference only to definitions of the terms it contains and to the principle of contradiction. Synthetic judgments, by contrast, require for their authentication a different sort of reference, since in their case the connection of subject and predicate terms is "thought without identity." In the case of everyday judgments of fact, for example, we need to consult experience to see whether the connection asserted actually holds.

So far Kant's distinction is simply a more elaborate version of Hume's division of propositions into those that assert relations of ideas and those that express matters of fact and existence, a version inferior to Hume's in that it is formally tied to statements of the subject–predicate form. But at this point Kant gives the distinction a fresh twist by asserting that there are judgments that are both synthetic and a priori, thus cutting across the usual classifications. Nearly all the propositions of mathematics answer this description, according to Kant; he also thinks it obvious that *"natural science (physics) contains* a priori *synthetic*

judgments as principles." He gives two examples: "in all changes of the material world the quantity of matter remains unchanged; and . . . in all communication of motion action and reaction must always be equal" (B 17). The very existence of these judgments shows that reason has special cognitive powers of its own, and so lends plausibility to the claims of metaphysicians. But before accepting the claims of metaphysicians, Kant suggests, we need to ask ourselves how (under what conditions) it is possible to assert judgments of this type in the two fields concerned. Only when this question is answered can we decide whether metaphysicians can draw support from the example of mathematics and "pure" physics. This inquiry is what Kant is concerned with in the first half of the *Critique*.

Analytic and synthetic. The terms in which Kant states his problem seem at first sight clear, but the clarity diminishes on closer inspection. There is the criticism that he offers a dual account of the analytic–synthetic distinction, once in psychological and once in logical terms, and the criticism that reference to the principle of contradiction alone is inadequate for the logical formulation of the distinction (he should have referred to logical laws generally). Apart from these two matters, Kant's treatment is marred by a failure to offer any discussion of his key idea, "what is thought in a concept." This omission is the more remarkable because Kant in fact had views on the subject of definition, views that are hard to reconcile with his apparent assumption that every judgment is unequivocally analytic or synthetic. Elsewhere in the *Critique* he states that, according to the real meaning of "definition," an empirical concept "cannot be defined at all, but only made explicit" (B 755). He means that we cannot give the "real essence" (in Locke's terminology) of such a concept, but only its "nominal essence," or conventional signification, which is liable to change as knowledge increases or interests shift. If this is correct, it seems to be only by convention, or provisionally, that the judgment "All bodies are extended" is analytic and the judgment "All bodies have weight" synthetic.

Nor is Kant's other distinction, between a priori and a posteriori, as simple as he pretends. He tries to clarify it by explaining that the first class of judgments have the characteristics of necessity and universality, which serve as criteria that are "inseparable from one another." He fails to notice, however, that the necessity that belongs to synthetic a priori judgments must on his own account differ from that which characterizes analytic judgments. Analytic judgments are, or rather claim to be, logically necessary—to deny a true analytic judgment would be, if Kant is correct, to dispute the validity of the law of contradiction. But though no synthetic judgment can contravene the laws of logic, none can be true in virtue of these laws and of meanings alone. Accordingly, if any synthetic judgment is to be described as necessary, it must be necessary in some further sense.

Kant recognizes in practice that the synthetic a priori judgments he takes to be valid have their own special kind of necessity. In his own terminology, they are "transcendentally" necessary; necessary, that is to say, if we are to have the knowledge and experience we actually have. But he would have done better to acknowledge the ambiguity in his term "a priori" from the outset. It would also have been helpful had he given some elucidation of his statement that, when a judgment is thought with strict universality, "no exception is allowed as possible." He cannot mean that no exception is logically possible, or every a priori judgment would be analytic. But he does not, at least at this early stage, make clear what other sort of possibility he has in mind.

TRANSCENDENTAL AESTHETIC

Kant's next step in the solution of the problem of how synthetic a priori judgments are possible is to examine the two types of case in which, in his view, we undoubtedly can make synthetic a priori judgments, and then to exhibit the bearing of his results on the possibility of metaphysical knowledge. In his short but important *Prolegomena to Every Future Metaphysics* he approaches these tasks directly. In the *Critique* itself his method is more roundabout, since he proposes there to delineate the entire cognitive powers of the mind and so to clarify the background against which synthetic a priori judgments are made. This leads him to undertake an inquiry first into the a priori elements involved in sensory knowledge (the "Transcendental Aesthetic") and then into the corresponding elements involved in thought (the "Transcendental Logic"). The sharp distinction between the senses and the intellect argued for in the dissertation is the obvious basis of this division.

A priori intuitions. It seems at first sight contradictory to say that there might be a priori elements involved in sensory knowledge. According to an old philosophical and psychological tradition, sensation is an essentially passive affair; the senses present us with data and we have no choice but to accept. Kant was quite ready to agree to this as a general account of sensation. But he was persuaded that there are some features of sensory experience that cannot be accepted as empirically given.

Kant identifies these features by a process similar to that in the dissertation: an examination of our ideas of space and time. These ideas, he argues, represent the form of experience rather than its matter; through them we structure the sensory given in the very act of sensing it. To establish this position Kant appeals to a variety of considerations.

First, he insists on the fundamental and ubiquitous character of space and time, as opposed to features like color and sound. Spatial predicates apply to whatever we know through the five senses, temporal predicates both to these and to the immediately experienced flow of our inner lives. Second, he argues that we cannot acquire the ideas of space and time by reflecting on what is empirically given. Some philosophers had said that we come by the idea of space by noticing such things as that one object is adjacent to another, and that we come by the idea of time by observing the way in which events succeed, are simultaneous with, or precede one another. Kant points out that the very description of such situations presupposes familiarity with space and time as such. For to know what is meant by saying that one thing is "next to" or "on top of" another we need to appreciate how the things in question

are situated in a wider spatial framework, which in turn falls within a yet wider spatial system, until we come to the thought of space as a whole. Particular spaces are not instances of space, but limitations of it, and space is accordingly a special sort of particular. The same argument applies to time. Adding to these two points the fact that we know certain things to be necessarily true of space and time (space has only three dimensions, different times are not simultaneous but successive), Kant infers that the ideas of space and time are not only "intuitions," but *a priori intuitions.*

Mathematics. Kant finds confirmation for his view of space and time exactly as he had in the dissertation: in the thought that this view alone can explain the possibility of pure and applied mathematics. Pure geometry is possible because we are able to "construct," or show the real possibility of, its concepts in pure intuition. An experiment conducted in imagination shows at once that a triangle is a real spatial possibility, whereas a figure bounded by two straight lines is not. Applied geometry is possible because whatever is apprehended by the senses must necessarily accord with the forms of sensibility. Kant attempts at various points in his writings to extend his doctrine of the importance of pure intuition for mathematical thinking from geometry to the other parts of mathematics, but it cannot be said that he is ever convincing on this point. His reasons for saying that "seven and five are twelve" is a synthetic proposition were sharply and properly criticized by Gottlob Frege. His account of algebra (B 745, 762) is so sketchy as to be virtually unintelligible. Kant tries to say that in algebra there is a "symbolic construction" corresponding to the "ostensive construction" of the concepts of geometry, but it is not in the least clear what this has to do with the pure intuition of either space or time.

Some critics speak as if Kant's failure to produce a satisfactory philosophy of mathematics invalidated the whole "Aesthetic," and it is true that the central point of this part of his work is destroyed if his main contentions about mathematics are rejected. Kant's explanations fall to the ground if it turns out that there is no intrinsic connection between mathematics and space and time, or if it is held that mathematical propositions are analytic, not synthetic a priori. But it does not immediately follow that the whole Kantian doctrine of space and time must be rejected, for many of his arguments on this matter are independent of his philosophy of mathematics. Nor is it decisive against him that the treatment of space and time in modern physics is very different from his; he claims to be dealing with the space and time of immediate perception.

Significance. Apart from the questions about truth, however, it is vital to appreciate the importance of the conclusions of the "Aesthetic" in the economy of the *Critique of Pure Reason* as a whole. The "transcendental ideality" of space and time carries with it, for Kant, the proposition that whatever we know through the senses (including "inner sense") is phenomenal; Kant's celebrated distinction between appearances and things-in-themselves has its origin, if not its justification, at this point. And the view that space and time are a priori forms of intuition is not only the model on which Kant constructed his theory of categories as concepts embodying the pure thought of an object in general; the view is carried over intact into the "Transcendental Analytic," and plays a crucial part there. To treat the theories of the "Aesthetic" as if they merely embodied a series of views that Kant had outgrown by the time he completed the *Critique,* as some commentators have proposed to do, is not in accord with Kant's own intentions. It is also to ignore a series of arguments that are of independent philosophical interest, and that demand careful notice from anyone writing on the philosophy of perception.

PURE CONCEPTS OF THE UNDERSTANDING

The main contentions of the aesthetic are to be found in the dissertation. Of the doctrine of pure intellectual concepts put forward in that inaugural lecture, on the other hand, almost nothing survives in the *Critique of Pure Reason.*

Objective reference. In the dissertation Kant argues along two lines: First, that pure intellectual concepts are not derived from sense experience (they could not be described as "pure" if they were); and second, that they serve to give us information about things as they really are. Soon after writing this work, however, Kant realized that there was a fundamental difficulty in this position, a difficulty he stated at length in a letter to his friend Marcus Herz dated February 21, 1772. It was that of knowing how "pure" concepts could be said to determine an object of any kind. To elucidate the difficulty, Kant isolated two contrasting types of intelligence, *intellectus ectypus,* "which derives the data of its logical procedure from the sensuous intuition of things," and *intellectus archetypus,* "on whose intuition the things themselves are grounded." The concepts of the first type of intelligence, deriving as they do from objects, have a guaranteed relationship to objects. The concepts of the second type determine objects, because, in this sort of case, thinking itself brings objects into existence in the same way in which "the ideas in the Divine Mind are the archetypes of things." But the human intelligence, as described in the dissertation, answers to neither description, for some of its concepts are not empirically derived and yet none of its thinking is creative in the sense specified. The problem then arises, How can these concepts be said to have objective reference; how can we know that in using them we are thinking about anything actual? It is this problem that Kant professes to have solved in the *Critique of Pure Reason.* Roughly speaking, his solution is that pure concepts can be shown to determine an object if the object is phenomenal. By contrast, when an attempt is made to use them to specify characteristics of "things in general," there is no guarantee that anything significant is being said.

Analytic and dialectic. The details of Kant's explanation of how pure concepts can be said to have objective reference is to be found in the lengthy section of the *Critique* labeled "Transcendental Logic" and divided into two main parts, "Transcendental Analytic" and "Transcendental Dialectic."

The first part contains an inventory of what at this point Kant calls pure concepts of the understanding, or categories, with an account of the function they perform in hu-

man knowledge and a series of arguments purporting to show that, in the absence of such pure concepts, objective knowledge would be impossible for human beings. In addition, the "Analytic" lists the principles that rest on these pure concepts and offers independent proofs of these principles. Transcendental analytic is said by Kant to be a "logic of truth," insofar as "no knowledge can contradict it without at once losing all content, that is, all relation to an object, and therefore all truth" (B 87). It deals, in short, with the proper use of a priori concepts, which is the use they have when they provide a framework for empirical inquiries.

Transcendental dialectic is introduced as if it were merely the negative counterpart of analytic—as if its sole purpose were to expose the illusions generated when dogmatic philosophers, unaware of the sensuous conditions under which alone we can make successful use of a priori concepts, attempt to apply them outside the sphere of possible experience. In fact a large part of the section entitled "Dialectic" is devoted to the exposure of metaphysical sophistries. But insofar as Kant recognizes in this part of his work the existence of a further set of intellectual operations involved in scientific inquiry, he seeks to show that the faculty of theoretical reason as well as that of the understanding has its appropriate pure employment.

Judgment or belief. A good way to approach the central doctrines of the analytic is to see them as an intended answer to Hume. Kant's knowledge of Hume was limited —he had no firsthand acquaintance with the *Treatise of Human Nature*—but he grasped the importance of many of Hume's most challenging points. For instance, Hume had argued that *"belief is more properly an act of the sensitive, than of the cogitative part of our natures"* (*Treatise,* L. A. Selby-Bigge, ed., 1888, Book I, Part IV, Sec. 1, p. 183); in the last resort it is a matter of subjective conviction. It is one of Kant's main objects in the analytic to demonstrate that such a view cannot do justice to an all-important feature of what Hume calls belief and he calls judgment, namely, its claim to be true. When I judge that something is the case I do not merely commit myself to a certain assertion; there is a sense in which I commit all rational persons too, for I purport to state what holds objectively, that is to say for everyone. To make judgment primarily a matter of feeling, something private to an individual person, is to leave out what is most characteristic of it. Similarly, to explain thinking about matters of fact and existence in terms of the association of ideas, as Hume did, is to confuse the objective with the subjective, to put science on the level of idle reverie. Empirical thinking, to deserve its name, must proceed according to rules, and there is all the difference in the world between a rule, which cannot of its nature be private, and association, which is the connecting of ideas on a purely personal plane.

The unity of experience. There are many philosophers who would accept this criticism of Hume but would deny that empirical thinking involves not only rules, but rules that are a priori or necessary rules. To understand why Kant asserts that thinking must proceed according to necessary rules, we must explain his attitude to another of Hume's doctrines, the famous contention that "all our experimental conclusions proceed upon the supposition that the future will be conformable to the past" (*Enquiry Concerning Human Understanding*, Sec. IV, Part II). Kant agrees with Hume that empirical knowledge involves connecting one part or element of experience with another; he agrees too that connection of this sort ("synthesis") proceeds on a principle that is neither analytically true nor empirically probable. But he refuses to follow Hume in deriving the principle from "Custom or Habit," for he sees more clearly than Hume the consequences of adopting this "sceptical solution." If it were really the case that events were as "loose and separate" as Hume supposed, not only should we be deprived of any insight into the connections of things, but we should have no unitary consciousness of any sort. For it is a necessary condition of having a unitary consciousness that we be able to relate what is happening here and now to things and events that lie outside our immediate purview; if the ability to relate is not a real possibility, then neither is unitary consciousness. What Kant calls in one place (A 113) "the thoroughgoing affinity of appearances" (the fact that appearances are capable of being connected in a single experience) thus relates closely to the ability of the observer to recognize himself as a single person with diverse experiences. In fact the relation is one of mutual implication.

It may be useful to cite Kant's explanation as he gave it in the first edition of the *Critique*, in a passage in which all the most characteristic ideas of the "Analytic" appear and which also illustrates Kant's persistent but nonetheless questionable tendency to move from saying that unity of consciousness means that appearances must be capable of connection to the conclusion that they must be capable of connection according to universal and necessary laws.

> There can be in us no items of knowledge, no connection or unity of one item of knowledge with another, without that unity of consciousness which precedes all data of intuitions, and by relation to which representation of objects is alone possible. This pure original unchangeable consciousness I shall name *transcendental apperception*. . . . This transcendental unity of apperception forms out of all possible appearances, which can stand alongside one another in one experience, a connection of all these representations according to laws. For this unity of consciousness would be impossible if the mind in knowledge of the manifold could not become conscious of the identity of function whereby it synthetically combines it in one knowledge. The original and necessary consciousness of the identity of the self is thus at the same time a consciousness of an equally necessary unity of the synthesis of all appearances according to concepts, that is, according to rules, which not only make them necessarily reproducible but also in so doing determine an object for their intuition, that is, the concept of something wherein they are necessarily interconnected. (A 107–108)

Role of categories. If the synthesis of appearances is to proceed in accordance with necessary laws, we must clearly operate not just with empirical but also with a priori concepts. But this must not be taken to mean that some items or features of fact can be known apart from all experience. For the role of an a priori concept is fundamentally different from that of its empirical counterpart.

Categories are concepts of a higher order than empirical concepts; like the ideas of space and time, they have to do with the form of experience rather than its matter. Our possession of categories accordingly supplies no knowledge of particular things; categories are fertile only when brought to bear on empirical data. Thus, because we hold to the a priori concept of cause, we interrogate nature in a certain way; thanks to it, we refuse to believe that there could be an uncaused event. But the answers we get to our interrogation depend primarily not on the form of our questions, but on what turns up in experience. Those who accuse Kant of having believed in the material a priori have failed to understand his theory.

To summarize this part of Kant's argument: If we are to have knowledge (and it is Kant's assumption that we do), various conditions must be fulfilled. The different items that fall within our experience must be capable of being connected in a single consciousness; there can be no happenings that are genuinely loose and separate. But the connections thus demanded must be objective connections—they must hold not just for my consciousness, but for "consciousness in general," for everyone's. An objective connection for Kant is a connection determined by a rule, and a rule is of its nature something that claims intersubjective validity. Finally, if we are to establish the operation of empirical rules we must proceed in accordance with nonempirical rules of a higher order, rules that insure that our different experiences are capable of connection within a single experience.

Judgments. In view of the close relation Kant sees between the making of judgments and the use of a priori concepts, it is perhaps not surprising that he tries to arrive at a full list of such concepts by scrutinizing the formal properties of judgments. In this connection he invokes the doctrines of general or formal logic, a science he believed had been brought to completion at a single stroke by Aristotle. Few scholars have been convinced by this section of his argument, for it seems clear that Kant adapted the list of judgment forms to suit his list of categories, rather than deriving the categories from the judgment forms. In any case, it is not obvious how formal logic, which is a logic of consistency, can supply a clue to the content of what professes to be a logic of truth.

Imagination and understanding. In the first part of the "Analytic" Kant has much to say not only about concepts, judgments, and the understanding but also about the imagination. For example, he remarks in a cryptic passage:

> Synthesis in general is the mere result of the power of imagination, a blind but indispensable function in the soul, without which we should have no knowledge whatsoever, but of which we are scarcely ever conscious. To bring this synthesis to concepts is a function which belongs to understanding, and it is through this function of the understanding that we first obtain knowledge properly so called. (B 103)

The contrasting and, in places, overlapping roles of understanding and imagination are among the most puzzling features of Kant's exposition. The reason why they are both introduced is related to the fact that, in the second edition of the *Critique of Pure Reason* in particular, Kant was concerned with two quite distinct questions. He first asked himself what conditions have to be fulfilled if any sort of discursive consciousness is to have objective knowledge; he then went on to put the question as it relates to the human discursive consciousness, which not only intuits data passively, but does so under the particular forms of space and time. When the first question is uppermost Kant tends to speak of the understanding; when the second is to the fore, he brings in the imagination as well. The passage quoted above, typical of many, suggests that it is the business of the imagination to connect, whereas that of the understanding is to make explicit the principles on which the connecting proceeds. But in one chapter, "Schematism of the Pure Concepts of Understanding," a more satisfying account of the relationship is offered.

Schemata. The problem of the chapter on what Kant called "schematism" is the central problem of the analytic: How can concepts that do not originate in experience find application in experience? At first Kant speaks as if there were no comparable difficulty in the case of concepts originating in experience, although he later makes clear that there are schemata corresponding both to empirical and to mathematical concepts. To possess the concept triangle is to know its formal definition, to be able to frame intelligible sentences containing the word "triangle," and so on; to possess the schema corresponding to the concept triangle is to be able to envisage the variety of things to which the word "triangle" applies. Thus for Kant a schema is not an image, but a capacity to form images or (perhaps) to construct models. Pure concepts of the understanding are such that they "can never be brought into any image whatsoever" (B 181); the thought they embody, springing from the pure intellect, cannot be pictured or imagined. Yet there must be some connection between the abstract idea and the experienced world to which that idea is expected to apply; it must be possible to specify the empirical circumstances in which pure concepts of the understanding can find application. Kant thinks that for the categories this requirement is met by the fact that we can find for each of them a "transcendental schema," which is, he explains, a "transcendental determination of time." Without such a schema the categories would be devoid of "sense and significance," except in a logical (verbal) way. With it, use of the categories is clearly restricted to the range of things that fall within time—meaning, for Kant, restricted to phenomena.

The meaning of this baffling doctrine can perhaps best be grasped through Kant's examples of schemata:

> The schema of substance is permanence of the real in time, that is, the representation of the real as a substrate of empirical determination of time in general. . . . The schema of cause. . . is the real upon which, whenever posited, something else always follows. It consists, therefore, in the succession of the manifold, in so far as that succession is subject to a rule. . . . The schema of necessity is existence of an object at all times. (B 183–184)

It emerges from these cryptic sentences that the transcendental schema is something like an empirical counterpart of the pure category. It is what the latter means when

translated into phenomenal terms. In Kant's own words, the schema is "properly, only the phenomenon, or sensible concept, of an object in agreement with the category" (B 186). A category without its corresponding "sensible concept" would be a bare abstraction, virtually without significance. Insofar as he argues that schematization is the work of the imagination, Kant has found a genuine function for the imagination to perform.

Analytic of principles: pure physics. In the first half of the "Analytic" Kant undertook to produce a "transcendental deduction," that is, a general proof of validity, of the categories. In the second half of the "Analytic" he gives a series of demonstrations of the synthetic a priori principles that rest on individual categories.

The categories are divided, for this and other purposes, into four groups: quantity, quality, relation, and modality. The four sets of corresponding principles are labeled axioms of intuition, anticipations of perception, analogies of experience, and postulates of empirical thought in general. Only one principle falls under each of the first two classes; the third contains a general principle and three more specific principles; the fourth contains three separate though closely connected principles. The first two classes are grouped together as "mathematical" principles; the third and fourth are described as "dynamical." Mathematical principles are said to be "immediately evident" and again to be "constitutive of their objects"; they apply directly to appearances. Dynamical principles are concerned with "the existence of such appearances and their relation to one another in respect of their existence." They are no less necessary than mathematical principles, but must be distinguished from them "in the nature of their evidence" and in that they are not "constitutive" but "regulative."

Behind this formidable façade some interesting ideas are hidden. In the first place, Kant makes stimulating though not altogether convincing remarks on the subject of proving principles of the understanding. The statement that every event has a cause carries strict necessity with it and therefore cannot be grounded on an inductive survey of empirical evidence. But equally it is not analytic, and so not open to straightforward conceptual proof. To be assured of its authenticity we consequently require a different type of argument altogether, which Kant calls a "transcendental" argument "from the possibility of experience." His idea is that only if the principles of the understanding are taken to be operative and in order can we have the type of experience we in fact have. Kant perhaps supposes that this type of proof is logically compulsive, but if so he overlooks the difficulty of setting up the original premise, of being sure that only if such-and-such were true should we have the experiences we have. But even with this defect his procedure has an immediate appeal, and is not without modern imitators.

Axioms of intuition. The details of the particular arguments for the principles corresponding to the categories also deserve careful attention. The principle of axioms of intuition, that "all intuitions are extended magnitudes," is perhaps the most difficult to take seriously, since what it purports to prove has apparently already been dealt with in the "Aesthetic." Kant is once more asking questions about the application of mathematics to the world; in this section of the *Critique* the problem that apparently troubles him is how we know that inquiries about sizes or areas are always appropriate when we are dealing with things that occupy space. His solution is that they must be appropriate, since every such thing can be regarded as an aggregate of parts produced by the observer as he synthesizes his experiences. "I cannot represent to myself a line, however short, without drawing it in thought, that is, generating from a point all its parts one after another" (B 203).

Anticipations of perception. Under the term "anticipations of perception" Kant is concerned with the question of the applicability of mathematics to sensations. What guarantee have we, he asks, that every sensation will turn out to have a determinate degree, in principle quantifiable? Might we not find, for instance, that an object is colored but with no precise depth of saturation, or a smell present in a room but with no specific magnitude? Kant attempts to rule out such possibilities by attention to the formal properties of sensations. We cannot anticipate the matter of sensation, but we can say in advance of experience that every sensation will have intensive magnitude, that is, a determinate degree, because it is possible to think of any given sensation as fading away until it is imperceptible, and conversely as being built up by continuous transitions on a scale from zero to the magnitude it has. Whatever may be the merits of this solution, there can be no doubt of the importance, and for that matter the novelty, of the question Kant asks here.

Analogies of experience. The section on the analogies of experience contains ideas as significant as any in Kant's writings.

The permanence of substance. The principle of the first analogy is that of the permanence of substance: "in all change of appearances substance is permanent; its quantum in nature is neither increased nor diminished." To believe in the permanence of substance is to believe that, whatever happens, nothing goes completely out of existence and nothing totally new is created: all change is transformation. Kant justifies the acceptance of this presupposition (which in his view, it should be remembered, applies only to things phenomenal) by arguing that without it we could not have a unitary temporal system. Coexistence and succession make sense only against a background that abides, and since time itself cannot be perceived, that background has got to be one of permanent things. This does not mean that we can determine a priori what form the permanent will take; empirical scientists are to pronounce on that question, and their answers may obviously change from time to time. All that Kant seeks to rule out is the possibility that there might be no permanent at all. His argument is defective at a vital point here, but presumably he is saying that if things could go completely out of existence, so that it would make no sense to ask what became of them, the establishment of connections between one part of experience and another would be impossible. Experience would be (or at least might be) full of unbridgeable gaps, with the result that no one set of happenings could be integrated with another, and the unity of time would be totally destroyed.

Causation. Kant carries his argument further in his discussion of the second and third analogies, in which he

argues for the necessary operation of the concepts of cause and reciprocity (causal interaction). But just as the notion of substance he justifies is very different from that held by metaphysicians, so is the Kantian concept of cause different from that of, say, Leibniz; it seems at first sight much closer to Hume's idea of a cause as an invariable antecedent. Causality for Kant as for Hume is a relation between successive events; a cause is an event that regularly precedes its effect. But whereas Hume is content to treat the occurrence of regular sequences as an ultimate and entirely contingent fact, Kant believes that without the presumption of sequences that are regular (determined by a rule) there could be no knowledge of objective succession. His reason is that we have to distinguish successions that happen only in ourselves, successions merely in our apprehension, from those that occur in the objective world and are independent of us. We can do this only if an objective sequence is defined as a sequence happening according to a rule. The objective world is a world of events the occurrence of each of which determines the precise place in time of some other event. But though events are necessarily connected in this way, we must not conclude that causal connections can be established a priori; for Kant as for Hume causal propositions are one and all synthetic and empirical. All we can know a priori is that there are such connections to be found, provided we have the skill or good fortune to discover them.

Postulates of empirical thought. One way of expressing Kant's attitude to substance and causality is to say that he thinks the principle of substance licenses us to ask the question, What became of that? whenever something happens, and that the principle of causality licenses the parallel question, What brought that about? If someone tried to say that things might go out of existence altogether, or happen for no reason at all, Kant would say that these were logical but not real possibilities. The contrast between real and logical possibility is explored by Kant in the section "The Postulates of Empirical Thought." This section contains an explanation of the notions of possibility, actuality, and necessity from the critical point of view. By "really possible" Kant means "that which agrees with the formal conditions of experience, that is, with the conditions of intuition and of concepts" (B 265). A two-sided figure enclosing a space is not really possible, though its concept is not self-contradictory, because such a figure does not accord with the formal conditions of intuition. Telepathy and precognition are not real possibilities; they "cannot be based on experience and its known laws" (B 270), presumably because their actuality would violate some principle of the understanding, although Kant fails to make the point clear. The notion of real possibility is for Kant intermediate between logical and empirical possibility. We need it and can use it only because the world we have to deal with is a world that is not independently existent, but has its being in essential relation to consciousness.

Phenomena and things-in-themselves. The distinction between phenomena and things-in-themselves, insisted on in the "Aesthetic" to explain our having a priori knowledge of the properties of space and time, is invoked again in the "Analytic" to account for "pure physics." If the world we confronted were one of things-in-themselves, a priori knowledge of it, even of the very restricted sort for which Kant argues, would be quite impossible. The fact that we have such knowledge—that we possess the principles discussed above—is taken by Kant as proof that the objects of our knowledge are phenomena or appearances. He does not mean by this, however, that they are private objects, at least insofar as they are spatial. The world we know in everyday and scientific experience is common to many observers; if not independent of consciousness as such, it is independent of particular consciousnesses. Parts of it are known only to particular experiencers—my inner life, for example, is accessible only to me—but that does not affect the general point.

Kant's acceptance of the distinction between phenomena and things-in-themselves has met with much criticism. Without the idea of the thing-in-itself, said his contemporary F. H. Jacobi, we cannot enter the world of the *Critique of Pure Reason;* with it we cannot remain inside. At the end of the "Analytic" Kant tries to defend himself against criticism of this sort by arguing that though he says that the objects of experience are phenomena and is prepared to admit that the obverse of a phenomenon is a noumenon or intelligible object, he is committed to noumena only in a negative sense. Having said that the categories, one of which is existence, apply only to phenomena, he cannot with consistency hold any other view. Nor is his position at this stage as devoid of logic as some have tried to make out. After all, to describe things as phenomena he does not need to assert that there actually are things of a different kind; he needs only the idea of such things. To talk about things as they might be in themselves is no more objectionable than to speak of an *intellectus archetypus,* as Kant did in the letter to Herz, or of an intuitive understanding, as he constantly does in both the *Critique of Pure Reason* and the *Critique of Judgment.*

THE ELIMINATION OF DOGMATIC METAPHYSICS

At the end of the section of the *Critique of Pure Reason* devoted to the transcendental analytic, there is a passage that can be taken as summarizing the second stage in Kant's emancipation from Leibnizian rationalism:

> The Transcendental Analytic leads to this important conclusion, that the most the understanding can achieve *a priori* is to anticipate the form of a possible experience in general. And since that which is not appearance cannot be an object of experience, the understanding can never transcend those limits of sensibility within which alone objects can be given to us. Its principles are merely rules for the exposition of appearances; and the proud name of an Ontology that presumptuously claims to supply, in systematic doctrinal form, synthetic *a priori* knowledge of things in general . . . must, therefore, give place to the modest title of a mere Analytic of pure understanding. (B 303)

Kant thus repudiates the possibility of knowledge through pure concepts of things as they really are; in 1770 he had still clung to it. Having disposed of ontology, Kant needed to consider, to complete the negative side of his work, the tenability of the remaining parts of metaphysics (rational psychology, rational cosmology, and natural theology in

Baumgarten's classification), and this he did in the section entitled "Transcendental Dialectic." To complete his own alternative to rationalism he needed to clarify the status of the propositions involved in "pure practical faith." His attempt to meet this requirement is made at the very end of the *Critique,* especially in the chapter "The Canon of Pure Reason" (B 823 ff.).

Reason. Most of the conclusions of the "Dialectic" follow directly from those of the "Analytic," though there are new points of interest. As in the "Analytic," Kant's views are expressed inside a framework that is heavily scholastic. Kant claimed that human beings have an intellectual faculty in addition to the understanding. This additional faculty is reason, and it is equipped with a set of a priori concepts of its own, technically known as ideas of reason. An idea of reason can have no object corresponding to it in sense experience, for the ambition of reason is to arrive at absolute totality in the series of conditions for the empirically given, and in this way to grasp the unconditioned that falls outside experience altogether. However, this ambition can never be realized, and the only proper function for reason in its theoretical capacity is to regulate the operations of the understanding by encouraging it to pursue the search for conditions to the maximum extent that is empirically possible.

The knowing subject. Kant's handling of the "psychological idea" at the beginning of the main part of the "Dialectic" is exceptionally brilliant. He maintains in the "Analytic" that what he there calls the "I think," or the unity of apperception, is the ultimate condition of experience, in the sense of being the logical subject of experience or the point to which all experience relates. All experience is experience for a subject; whatever thoughts or feelings I have I must be capable of recognizing as *my* thoughts or feelings. But the subject here referred to is not something substantial; it is merely a logical requirement, in that nothing follows about the nature of my soul or self from the fact that I say "I think." So far from being "an abiding and continuing intuition" (the sort of thing Hume vainly sought in the flow of his inner consciousness), for Kant the "representation 'I' . . . [is] simple, and in itself completely empty . . . we cannot even say that this is a concept, but only that it is a bare consciousness which accompanies all concepts. Through this I or he or it (the thing) which thinks, nothing further is represented than a transcendental subject of thoughts = *X*" (B 404). The same view is expressed in an earlier passage in the *Critique,* where Kant says that "in the synthetic original unity of apperception, I am conscious of myself, not as I appear to myself, nor as I am in myself, but [I am conscious] only that I am. This *representation* is a *thought,* not an *intuition*" (B 157).

Refutation of rational psychology. These subtleties are unknown to the exponents of rational psychology, who develop the whole of their teaching around a "single text," which is "I think." From the fact that I am the subject of all my thoughts they infer that I am a thinking substance; from the fact that the "I" of apperception is logically simple they conclude that I am, in substance, simple and not composite. The proposition that "in all the manifold of which I am conscious I am identical with myself" is taken by them as implying that I am possessed of continuing personal identity. Finally, my distinguishing my own existence as a thinking being from that of other things, including my own body, is put forward as proof that I am really distinct from such things and so could in principle exist in complete independence of them. None of these inferences is justified, for in each case a move is attempted from an analytically true premise to a synthetic conclusion. As Kant remarks, "it would, indeed, be surprising if what in other cases requires so much labour to determine— namely, what, of all that is presented in intuition, is substance, and further, whether this substance can be simple . . . —should be thus given me directly, as if by revelation, in the poorest of all representations" (B 408).

Mind and body. Kant presents the doctrines of rational psychology in his own idiosyncratic way, but anyone who reflects on the theories of Descartes will see that Kant was by no means attacking men of straw. Kant's treatment of the fourth paralogism, "of Ideality," is of special interest in this connection. Descartes inferred from his *cogito* argument that mind and body were separate in substance, which meant that the first could exist apart from the second. Bound up with this was the view that I am immediately aware of myself as a mind, but need to infer the existence of material things, which is in principle open to doubt. A great many philosophers have subscribed to this opinion, but Kant thought he could show it to be definitively false. In order to say that my inner experiences come one before another I need to observe them against a permanent background, and this can only be a background of external objects, for there is nothing permanent in the flow of inner experience. As Kant put it in the second edition, in which he transposed the argument to the discussion of existence in connection with the postulates of empirical thought), *"The mere, but empirically determined, consciousness of my own existence proves the existence of objects in space outside me"* (B 275). Kant is in no sense a behaviorist; he thinks that empirical self-knowledge is to be achieved through inner sense and declares in one passage that, for empirical purposes, dualism of soul and body must be taken as correct. Yet his commitment to "empirical realism" is quite unambiguous.

The antinomies. Of the remaining parts of the "Dialectic," only the sections on the antinomies and on the existence of God can be discussed here. In the "Antinomy of Pure Reason," Kant first sets out a series of pairs of metaphysical doctrines (which he says have to do with cosmology but which are in fact of wider interest). The two doctrines in each pair seem to contradict one another directly. He then produces for each pair what he regards as watertight proofs of both sides of the case, maintaining that if we adopt the dogmatic standpoint assumed without question by the parties to the dispute, we can prove, for example, both that the world has a beginning in time and that it has no beginning in time, both that "causality in accordance with laws of nature is not the only causality" and that "everything in the world takes place solely in accordance with laws of nature." Thus Kant exhibits in systematic form the famous contradictions into which, as he notes, reason precipitates itself when it asks metaphysical questions. Kant is enormously impressed by the discovery of these contradictions, and it is regrettable only

that he does not sufficiently discuss their formal character or illustrate them with genuine examples.

The only way to avoid these antinomies, in Kant's opinion, is to adopt his own (critical) point of view and recognize that the world that is the object of our knowledge is a world of appearances, existing only insofar as it is constructed; this solution enables us to dismiss both parties to the dispute in the case of the first two antinomies, and to accept the contentions of both parties in the case of the other two. If the world exists only insofar as it is constructed, it is neither finite nor infinite but indefinitely extensible and so neither has nor lacks a limit in space and time. Equally, if the world is phenomenal we have at least the idea of a world that is not phenomenal; and natural causality can apply without restriction to the first without precluding the application of a different type of causality to the second. This is admittedly only an empty hypothesis so far as theoretical reason is concerned, but Kant argues that it can be converted into something more satisfactory if we take account of the activities of practical (moral) reason.

The existence of God. The fourth antinomy is concerned with God's existence. Kant's full treatment of the subject is not in the section on the antinomies but in that headed "The Ideal of Pure Reason," the *locus classicus* for Kant's criticisms of speculative theology. These criticisms have proved as devastating as those he brought against rational psychology.

Speculative proofs. There are, Kant argues, only three ways of proving God's existence on the speculative plane. First, we can proceed entirely a priori and maintain that the very idea of God is such that God could not *not* exist; this is the method of the Ontological Argument. Second, we can move from the bare fact that the world exists to the position that God is its ultimate cause, as in the First Cause, or Cosmological, Argument. Finally, we can base our contention on the particular constitution of the world, as in the "physicotheological proof" (the Argument from Design).

Kant argues that all three types of proof are fallacious. The Ontological Argument fails because it treats existence as if it were a "real predicate," whereas "it is not a concept of something which could be added to the concept of a thing. It is merely the positing of a thing, or of certain determinations, as existing in themselves" (B 626). The First Cause Argument fails on several counts: because it uses the category of cause without realizing that only in the schematized form is the category significant; because it assumes that the only way to avoid an actually infinite causal series in the world is to posit a first cause; finally and most important, because it presupposes the validity of the Ontological Proof, in the step which identifies the "necessary being" or First Cause with God. The Argument from Design makes all these mistakes and some of its own, for even on its own terms it proves only the existence of an architect of the universe, not of a creator, and such an architect would possess remarkable but not infinite powers.

The moral proof. In spite of Kant's criticisms of the classical arguments for God's existence, he is neither an atheist nor even a believer in the principle of *credo quia impossibile.* He both believes in God and holds that the belief can be rationally justified. For although speculative theology is, broadly, a tissue of errors, moral theology is perfectly possible. But the moral proof of God's existence differs from the attempted speculative proofs in at least two significant respects. First, it begins neither from a concept nor from a fact about the world, but from an immediately experienced moral situation. The moral agent feels called upon to achieve certain results, in particular to bring about a state of affairs in which happiness is proportioned to virtue, and knows that he cannot do it by his own unaided efforts; insofar as he commits himself to action he shows his belief in a moral author of the universe. Affirmation of God's existence is intimately linked with practice; it is most definitely not the result of mere speculation. Again, a proof like the First Cause Argument claims universal validity; standing as it does on purely intellectual grounds it ought, if cogent, to persuade saint and sinner alike. But the moral proof as Kant states it would not even have meaning to a man who is unconscious of moral obligations; the very word "God," removed from the moral context that gives it life, is almost or quite without significance. Accordingly Kant states that the result of this proof is not objective knowledge but a species of personal conviction, embodying not logical but moral certainty. He adds that "I must not even say '*It is* morally certain that there is a God . . . ,' but '*I am* morally certain'" (B 857). In other words, the belief or faith Kant proposes as a replacement for discredited metaphysical knowledge can be neither strictly communicated nor learned from another. It is something that has to be achieved by every man for himself.

ETHICS

Kant perhaps intended originally to make the *Critique of Pure Reason* the vehicle of his entire philosophy, but it was clear before he completed it that some of his views, especially those on ethics, could be only touched on there. In the years immediately following its publication he displayed exceptional energy in defending and restating the theories he had already put forth and in extending his philosophy to cover topics he had hitherto not treated, or not treated in detail. By 1788 he had not only published the second, substantially revised edition of the *Critique of Pure Reason*, but had laid the foundations for his ethics in his short but influential *Groundwork of the Metaphysic of Morals* (1785) and had undertaken a more elaborate survey of moral concepts and assumptions in the *Critique of Practical Reason* (1788). He had also, in passing, written his essay *Metaphysical Foundations of Natural Science* (1786), intended as a first step toward a projected but never completed metaphysics of nature. Two years after the *Critique of Practical Reason* he produced yet another substantial work, the *Critique of Judgment,* in which he expressed his views on, among other topics, aesthetics and teleology.

Moral actions. If he had published nothing else but the *Groundwork of the Metaphysic of Morals* Kant would be assured a place in the history of philosophy. Difficult as it is to interpret in some of its details, this work is written with an eloquence, depth of insight, and strength of feeling that make an immediate impact on the reader and put it among the classics of the subject. Kant says that his "sole aim" in the book is "to seek out and establish *the supreme*

principle of morality." He wishes to delineate the basic features of the situation in which moral decisions are made, and so to clarify the special character of such decisions.

The situation as he sees it is roughly as follows. Man is a creature who is half sensual, half rational. Sensuous impulses are the determining factor in many of his actions, and the role of reason in these cases is that assigned to it by Hume; it is the slave or servant of the passions. But there is an identifiable class of actions in which reason plays a different part, leading rather than following. This is the class of moral actions. Such actions have the distinguishing feature that they are undertaken not for some ulterior end, but simply because of the principle they embody.

Intentions and moral judgments. The moral worth of an action, as Kant puts it (*Grundlegung*, 2d ed., p. 13), lies "not in the purpose to be attained by it, but in the maxim in accordance with which it is decided upon." Whether or not I attain my ends does not depend on me alone, and my actions cannot be pronounced good or bad according to the effects they actually bring about. But I can be praised or blamed for my intentions, and I can, if I choose, make sure that the maxim or subjective principle of my action accords with the requirements of morality. To do this I have only to ask myself the simple question whether I could will that the maxim should become a universal law, governing not merely this particular action of mine, but the actions of all agents similarly circumstanced. For it is a formal property of moral as of scientific judgments, recognized in practice even by the unsophisticated, that they hold without distinction of persons; the result is that an action can be permissible for me only if it is permissible for anyone in my situation.

Practical reason. There are difficulties in this position of which Kant seems to have been unaware. In particular, he never asks how I am to decide what is the correct description, and hence the maxim, of my act or proposed act. Nor is it obvious how the theory shows the falsity of Hume's view that "reason alone can never be a motive to any action of the will"—how it can be shown, in Kant's language, that pure reason really is practical. The practical effectiveness of reason is manifested not in the capacity to reflect, which both Kant and Hume allow, but in the power to originate or inhibit action. Kant obviously thinks that the facts of temptation and resistance to temptation, which he sees as ubiquitous in the moral life, have a clear bearing on the question whether reason really has such a power. Recognition that I ought to follow a certain course of action, whether I want to or not, and that anything that is morally obligatory must also be practically possible, is enough in his view to show that I am not necessarily at the mercy of my desires. In favorable cases, at any rate (Kant pays too little attention to the factors that diminish and sometimes demolish responsibility), I am free to resist my sensuous impulses and to determine my actions by rational considerations alone.

Consequences of the moral law. Some commentators have seen Kant as an ethical intuitionist, but this view is clearly mistaken. His "practical reason" is not the faculty of insight into the content of the moral law; it is rather the capacity to act. In determining what the moral law commands, I have initially no other resources at my disposal than the reflection that it must be applied impartially. But in practice this criterion carries others with it. If the moral law applies without distinction of persons, Kant believes it follows that I must treat all human beings as equally entitled to rights under it, and that therefore I must regard them as ends in themselves and never as merely means to my own ends. Further, once I recognize that other people are morally in the same position as I am myself, and that we belong to the same moral community, I recognize both that I can legitimately pursue those of my purposes that do not conflict with the moral law and that I also have a duty to facilitate the like pursuit on the part of my fellows. So though Kant is a formalist in his view of moral reason (as in his view of the theoretical intellect), he sees his ethics as having practical consequences of the first importance. He sets these consequences out in his lectures on ethics and develops them in detail later in his 1797 *Metaphysic of Morals*. To judge him by the *Groundwork* alone, or even by the *Groundwork* and the *Critique of Practical Reason* taken together, is to do less than justice to the scope of his ethical reflection.

Moral imperatives. Previous moral philosophies, Kant writes, whether they put their stress on moral sense or on moral reason, have all been vitiated by a failure to recognize the principle of the autonomy of the will. Utilitarianism, for instance, is a heteronomous ethical theory because, according to its supporters, the point of a moral action is to promote an end or purpose beyond the action, the greatest happiness of the greatest number. Kant is not unaware of the importance of ends and purposes in actions: in the *Critique of Practical Reason* he corrects the one-sidedness of the *Groundwork* by discoursing at length on the concept of "good" as well as on that of "duty." But he holds, even so, that consideration of ends cannot be of primary importance for the moral agent, since a moral action is one that is commanded for its own sake, not with a view to some purpose it is expected to bring about. The imperatives of morality command categorically, unlike those of skill or prudence, which have only hypothetical force (*ibid.*, pp. 39–44). A rule of skill or a counsel of prudence bids us take certain steps *if* we wish to attain a certain end—good health or over-all happiness, for example. There is no "if" about a command of morality; it bids me act in a certain way whether I want to or not, and without regard to any result the action may bring about. It represents a course of conduct as unconditionally necessary, not just necessary because it conduces to a certain end.

Freedom and necessity. The concepts of duty, the categorical imperative, the moral law, and the realm of ends (in which we are all at once subjects and lawgivers) are intended by Kant to illuminate the moral situation. But even when we know what that situation is, there are many features of it that remain mysterious. Morality as Kant expounds it involves autonomy of the will, and such autonomy clearly makes no sense except on the supposition of freedom. But how we can think of the will as free and at the same time regard ourselves as subject to the moral law, that is, as under obligation, has still to be explained. To throw light on this question, Kant invokes the concept of the two worlds, the sensible and the intelligible, to which

he made appeal in the *Critique of Pure Reason*. Insofar as I exercise the faculty of reason I have to regard myself as belonging to the intelligible world; insofar as I exercise my "lower" faculties I am part of the world of nature, which is known through the senses. Were I a purely rational being, possessed of what Kant sometimes calls a "holy will," all my actions would be in perfect conformity with the principle of autonomy, and the notions of obligation and the moral law would have no meaning for me. They would similarly have no meaning if I were a purely sensuous being, for then everything I did would occur according to natural necessity, and there would be no sense in thinking that things ought to be otherwise. The peculiarities of the human moral situation arise from the fact that men are, or rather must think of themselves as being, at once intelligible and sensible. Because I regard myself as belonging to the intelligible order, I see myself as "under laws which, being independent of nature, are not empirical but have their ground in reason alone" (*ibid.*, p. 109). But I am also a natural being, and those laws therefore present themselves to me in the form of commands that I acknowledge as absolute because I recognize that the intelligible world is the ground of the sensible. We can thus see "how a categorical imperative is possible."

What we cannot see, if Kant is to be believed, is how freedom is possible. "All men think of themselves as having a free will. . . . Moreover, for *purposes of action* the footpath of freedom is the only one on which we can make use of reason in our conduct. Hence to argue freedom away is as impossible for the most abstruse philosophy as it is for the most ordinary human reason" (*ibid.*, p. 113–115). Yet freedom remains what it is in the *Critique of Pure Reason*, "only an idea whose objective reality is in itself questionable," and there is a prima facie clash between the claim to freedom and the knowledge that everything in nature is determined by natural necessity. Kant seeks to dissolve the antinomy of freedom and necessity by means of two expedients. First, he insists that the idea of freedom required for morals is not a theoretical but a practical idea. Freedom does not need to be established as a metaphysical fact; it is enough that we find it necessary to act on the assumption that freedom is real, since "every being who cannot act except under the idea of freedom is by this alone—from the practical point of view—really free" (*ibid.*, p. 100). The status of the proposition that the will is free is identical with that of the proposition that there is a God. Both are postulates of practical reason—beliefs that we "inevitably" accept; but they are emphatically not items of knowledge in the strict sense of that term. Second, Kant sees no difficulty in our accepting the postulate of freedom, because there is no contradiction in thinking of the will as free. As an object of theoretical scrutiny I must regard myself as a phenomenon; as a moral agent possessed of a will I transfer myself to the intelligible world of noumena. I can be at once under necessity qua phenomenon and free qua noumenon. But the question of how I can be free leads to the extreme limits of practical philosophy. Freedom cannot be explained, for we lack all insight into the intelligible world; the most we can do is make clear why it cannot be explained. The critical philosophy purports to have performed this task.

Epistemology and ethics. Kant advocates a form of nonnaturalist theory in ethics. But neither his ethics nor his theory of knowledge can be fully understood in isolation one from the other. The two together constitute an over-all theory that is not so much a metaphysics as a substitute for a metaphysics: a theory that argues that human insight is strictly limited, but urges that, so far from being regrettable, this testifies to "the wise adaptation of man's cognitive faculties to his practical vocation" (*Critique of Practical Reason and Other Writings*, Beck translation, 1949, p. 247). If we knew more, we might indeed do as we ought, for "God and eternity in their awful majesty would stand unceasingly before our eyes," but we should not then do things as a matter of duty, but rather out of fear or hope. And thus the world would be poorer, for we should lose the opportunity to manifest "good will," the only thing in the world, "or even out of it, which can be taken as good without qualification."

THE CRITIQUE OF JUDGMENT

None of Kant's other writings is as forceful or original as the first two *Critiques* and the *Groundwork*. The *Critique of Judgment* contains some fresh ideas of remarkable power, but it constitutes a series of appendixes or addenda to Kant's earlier work rather than something wholly new. It should really be seen as three or four separate essays whose connecting link is the concept of purpose.

System of science. The first essay, the introduction, begins with a pedantic discussion of the status of the power of judgment. It then takes up a problem aired in the appendix to the "Dialectic" in the *Critique of Pure Reason*—the problem of the special assumptions involved in the belief that we can construct a system of scientific laws. If we are to have such a system, Kant argues, we must proceed on the principle that nature is "formally purposive" in respect of empirical laws; that nature is such that we can make sense of it not merely in general, but also in detail. Kant's object is to show that this principle is not a constitutive principle of things, but simply a subjective maxim of judgment.

In the *Critique of Pure Reason* (B 670 ff.) Kant argues for what he calls the regulative employment of the ideas of reason: the use of ideas to order empirical inquiries in such a way that we try at once to find greater and greater diversity of form in the material before us and to group different species and subspecies together under ever higher genera. In actual practice we assume that nature will display the unity-in-diversity required for this program to be carried out, but we cannot prove that it will do so as we can prove that whatever falls within experience will conform to the categories. Hence we are concerned not with objective rules, but only with maxims, defined in this connection as "subjective principles which are derived, not from the constitution of an object but from the interest of reason in respect of a certain possible perfection of the knowledge of the object" (B 694).

In the *Critique of Pure Reason* Kant ascribes these maxims to reason. In the *Critique of Judgment,* he assigns them to judgment, in effect the identical doctrine. The difference is accounted for by two facts. First, by the time

Kant wrote the *Critique of Judgment*, the term "reason" suggested to him nothing but practical reason. Second, he had come to think that if the power of judgment is genuinely separate from understanding on the one hand and reason on the other it must have a priori principles of its own. A division within the power of judgment itself, into determinant and reflective activities, had helped to make this last point plausible, at least in the eyes of its author.

Aesthetics. The "Critique of Aesthetic Judgment," the first major division of the *Critique of Judgment*, uses the term "aesthetic" in what has become its modern sense. The discussion is Kant's contribution to the controversies initiated by Lord Shaftesbury and Francis Hutcheson when they made both moral and aesthetic judgments matters of feeling; Kant rejects this view and also explains why he yet cannot approve of Alexander Gottlieb Baumgarten's attempt to "bring the critical treatment of the beautiful under rational principles, and so to raise its rules to the rank of a science" (B 35, note *a*). Kant needs to show, for the purposes of his general philosophy, that aesthetic judgments are essentially different from moral judgments on the one hand and scientific judgments on the other. This need apart, he had a long-standing independent interest in the subject; in 1764, thirty years before the *Critique of Judgment*, he published an essay on the beautiful and the sublime (*Beobachtung über das Gefühl des Schönen und Erhabenen*, Königsberg). Such an interest may seem surprising in view of the obvious limitations of Kant's own aesthetic experience; he had some feeling for literature, especially for satire, but little or no real knowledge of either painting or music. But what he has in mind in discussing the beautiful is the beauty of nature as much as anything, and his main interest is not in making aesthetic judgments, but in deciding on their logical status.

Judgments of taste, as Kant calls them, are peculiar in that they not only rest on feeling but also claim universal validity. That they rest on feeling seems to him obvious: when I ascribe beauty to an object or scene I do so not because I have observed some special character in it, but because contemplation of its form gives me immediate delight. But it is an entirely disinterested form of delight, quite different from that we feel concerning things that are agreeable, or even things that are good. When we take pleasure in something beautiful we are not desiring to possess it, or indeed taking up any attitude toward its existence. The fact that aesthetic delight is disinterested allows us to think of it as universally shared:

> Since the delight is not based on any inclination of the subject (or any other deliberate interest), but the Subject feels himself completely *free* in respect to the liking which he accords to the object, he can find as reason for his delight no personal conditions to which his own subjective self might alone be party. Hence he must regard it as resting on what he may also presuppose in every other person; and therefore he must believe that he has reason for demanding a similar delight from every one. (*Critique of Judgment*, Meredith translation, Sec. 6)

Because they claim universal validity, judgments of taste appear to rest on concepts, but to think that they do is a mistake. The universality attaching to judgments of taste is not objective but subjective; to explain it we must refer to "nothing else than the mental state present in the free play of imagination and understanding (so far as these are in mutual accord, as is requisite for *cognition in general*)" (*ibid.*, Sec. 9). As in the *Critique of Pure Reason*, Kant argues that both imagination and understanding are involved in the apprehension of any spatiotemporal object but that when we simply contemplate any such object aesthetically, no definite concept is adduced; and so the two faculties are in free play. It is the harmony between the faculties in any act of aesthetic contemplation that Kant takes to be universally communicable, and believes to be the basis for the pleasure we feel.

In addition to analyzing judgments about the beautiful, Kant devoted considerable attention in the *Critique of Judgment* to another concept which figured prominently in the aesthetics of his day, that of the sublime. Burke and others had given what was in effect a psychological description of the conditions in which we judge, say, the sight of a mountain range or a storm at sea to be sublime. Kant was all the more anxious to specify more exactly the meaning of such judgments and to establish their transcendental conditions because he was convinced that we here also have to do with a feeling that is held to be universally communicable. The feeling for the sublime, as he explained it, is connected not with the understanding, as is that for the beautiful, but with reason. To put his view somewhat crudely, we are at first abashed by the formlessness of some parts of nature, only to be elevated when we reflect on the utter inadequacy of these objects to measure up to our own ideas, and in particular to our moral ideas. Thus the sublime is not, as might at first sight be supposed, a quality which inheres in natural objects, but a feeling which the contemplation of natural objects provokes in us. It could have no existence for a being totally lacking in culture (a savage might feel fear on observing "thunderclouds piled up the vault of heaven," to use one of Kant's own examples, but could not recognize their sublimity), yet it is not a mere product of culture or social convention. "Rather is it in human nature that its foundations are laid, and, in fact, in that which, at once with common understanding, we may expect everyone to possess and may require of him, namely, a native capacity for the feeling for (practical) ideas, that is, for moral feeling" (*ibid.*, Sec. 29).

Teleology. One of Kant's motives for wanting to avoid making beauty an objective characteristic was that he thought such a view would lend force to the Argument from Design, and so encourage the revival of speculative theology. If things could be said to possess beauty in the same sort of way in which they possess weight, it would be a short step to talking about the Great Artificer who made them to delight us. Arguments of the same general kind were still more vividly present to his mind when he came to write the second main section of the *Critique of Judgment*, the "Critique of Teleological Judgment." Indeed, he ended the book with a lengthy section that underlines yet again the shortcomings of "physicotheology" and points up the merits of "ethicotheology."

Before confronting theology directly, Kant embarked on a detailed and penetrating discussion of the nature and use of teleological concepts. The existence of organic bodies, he argues, is something for which we cannot account satisfactorily by the mechanical principles sanctioned by the physical sciences; to deal with organic bodies we must employ a distinct principle, the principle of teleology, which can do justice to the fact that "*an organized natural product is one in which every part is reciprocally both means and end*" (*ibid.*, Sec. 66). Such a principle cannot be used for cognitive purposes in the strict sense; it can be employed only by reflective judgment to guide "our investigation of . . . [organic bodies] by a remote analogy with our own causality according to ends generally, and as a basis for reflection upon their supreme source" (*ibid.*, Sec. 65). Teleology is a concept that occupies an uneasy intermediate position between natural science and theology. We cannot help using it to describe the world about us, yet we cannot assign to it full scientific status. Kant mitigates the austerities of this position by suggesting in his section "The Antinomy of Judgment" that in the end the mechanical and teleological principles stand on the same level, both belonging to reflective judgment. But it is hard to see how this can be made consistent with the doctrines of the *Critique of Pure Reason*, which ascribes constitutive force to the concepts of "pure physics," or even with the distinction in the *Critique of Judgment* itself between explaining something and merely "making an estimate" of it. We use the categories to explain, but can employ teleological concepts only for the purpose of making an estimate. Kant's underlying attitude to the whole question is revealed most clearly in the passage at the end of Sec. 68 of the *Critique of Judgment,* where he asks why teleology "does not . . . form a special part of theoretical natural science, but is relegated to theology by way of a propaedeutic or transition." He answers:

This is done in order to keep the study of the mechanical aspect of nature in close adherence to what we are able so to subject to our observation or experiment that we could ourselves produce it like nature, or at least produce it according to similar laws. For we have complete insight only into what we can make and accomplish according to our conceptions. But to effect by means of art a presentation similar to organization, as an intrinsic end of nature, infinitely surpasses all our powers. (Meredith translation)

It would be interesting to know if Kant would say the same were he alive today.

OTHER PHILOSOPHICAL WRITINGS

After publishing the three *Critiques*—Kant was 66 when the *Critique of Judgment* appeared—he continued to publish essays and treatises on a wide variety of philosophical subjects. Most of these are in fact contributions to applied philosophy, for he took the view that scientific inquiries and practical activities alike stand in need of philosophical foundations. In many cases he attempts to supply these foundations by means of the principles established in his main works—hence the general shape of his philosophies of science and religion, and of his political philosophy. It would, however, be wrong to see these as no more than mechanical applications of general Kantian conclusions.

For although Kant was deeply and indeed unduly devoted to system, he also had a wide and in some cases penetrating knowledge of many different branches of learning and human activity, and there are few philosophical topics that he touchs without illuminating; in fact, Kant gave the names still in use to most of the branches of applied philosophy he took up.

Philosophy of nature. In the preface to his *Metaphysical Foundations of Natural Science*, Kant argues that the very concept of scientific knowledge is such that we can use the term properly only when dealing with truths that are both apodictically certain and systematically connected. A discipline that is thoroughly and entirely empirical cannot comply with these requirements; hence Kant pronounces chemistry to be no better than "systematic art or experimental doctrine." But the situation is different in physics. Although Kant was as firmly persuaded as any empiricist that detailed knowledge of the physical world could be arrived at only by observation and experiment, he was also sure that physics has an unshakable a priori basis that makes it worthy of the name of science. It owes this, in Kant's judgment, to the fact that its fundamental concepts are capable of mathematical expression, as those of chemistry are not, and to the close connection of these concepts with the categories, the basic concepts of rational thought. The main object of the *Metaphysical Foundations* is to demonstrate the second of these points by means of an examination of the idea of matter. Starting from what professes to be an empirically derived definition of matter, "that which is capable of movement in space," Kant proceeds to a deduction of its main properties in the light of the table of categories. The result is, in effect, a rereading or reinterpretation of then-current physical theory in which all the main doctrines of Newton find their place, but which is distinctive in that the atomism professed by many physicists of the day is rejected in favor of a dynamical theory of matter resembling that of Leibniz. Kant argues in the *Critique of Pure Reason* that only mistaken metaphysics leads scientists to think they must accept the notions of absolutely homogeneous matter and absolutely empty space. In the *Metaphysical Foundations* he works out an alternative conception of matter in terms of moving forces, omnipresent but varying in degree, and puts it forward as both theoretically satisfactory and consistent with the empirical findings.

It is difficult not to see in these views the beginnings of *Naturphilosophie* as it was to be practiced by Schelling and Hegel, the more so if we read the *Metaphysical Foundations* in the light of Kant's further treatment of the subject in the notes published as *Opus Postumum*. But in 1786 at any rate Kant was still far from committing the extravagances of the speculative philosophers of nature. For one thing, he was both more knowledgeable about and more respectful of the actual achievements of physical scientists than were his romantic successors, doubtless because, unlike them, he was something of a physical scientist himself. For another, the lesson he drew from his 1786 inquiries was not how much physical knowledge we can arrive at by the use of pure reason, but how little. To establish the metaphysical foundations of natural science was a useful task, but it was in no sense a substitute for empirical investigation. Despite these differences from *Naturphilosophie*, it must be allowed that *Metaphysical Foundations* testifies, in name as well as in content, to the extent of Kant's commitment to rationalism (his theory of science could scarcely be further from Hume's) and to the way in which he was at least tempted by the constructivism favored by some of his younger contemporaries.

Philosophy of history. Although Kant was quite unaware of the problems about historical knowledge and explanation with which philosophers since Wilhelm Dilthey have dealt, he made an important and characteristic contribution to speculative philosophy of history in his essay "Idee zu einer allgemeinen Geschichte in Weltbürgerlicher Absicht" ("Idea of a Universal History from a Cosmopolitan Point of View," *Berliner Monatsschrift*, November 1784, 386–410). Observing that the actions of men, when looked at individually, add up to nothing significant, he suggests that nature or providence may be pursuing through these actions a long-term plan of which the agents are unaware. To see what the plan may be we have to reflect on two points: first, that nature would scarcely have implanted capacities in human beings if she had not meant them to be developed, and second, that many human intellectual capacities (for example, the talent for invention) are such that they cannot be satisfactorily developed in the lifetime of a single individual. The development of such capacities belongs to the history of the species as a whole. Kant suggests that the hidden plan of nature in history may well be to provide conditions in which such capacities are more and more developed, so that men move from barbarism to culture and thus convert "a social union originating in pathological needs into a moral whole." The mechanism of the process lies in what Kant calls the "unsocial sociability" of human beings—the fact that they need each other's society and help and are nevertheless by nature individualists and egotists—which insures that men develop their talents to the maximum extent, if only to get the better of their fellows, and at the same time necessitates man's eventually arriving at a form of civil society that allows for peaceful rivalry under a strict rule of law. But such a "republican" constitution would be of no value unless it had its counterpart in the international sphere, for the struggles of individuals against one another are paralleled by the struggles of states. We must accordingly conclude that the final purpose of nature in history is to produce an international society consisting of a league of nations, in which war is outlawed and the way is finally clear for peaceful competition between individuals and nations.

The difficulty with this as with other lines of Kant's thought is to understand its relation to empirical inquiries. From what Kant says it seems clear that he intended "philosophical" history to be an alternative to history of the everyday kind, not a substitute for it. Nor did he pretend to be writing philosophical history himself; his essay merely puts forward the idea of or offers a "clue" to, such a history, leaving it to nature to produce someone really capable of making sense of the historical facts as Kepler and Newton made sense of physical facts. It is difficult to see, even so, how Kant could have possessed the idea of history as meaningful without knowing the facts, or alternatively how he could know that the idea throws light on the facts when it was discovered without any reference to them.

Philosophy of law and politics. Kant's views about law and politics, like his philosophy of history, are obviously tied up with his ethics. Kant holds that legal obligations are a subspecies of moral obligation; thus the rational will, and neither force nor the commands of God, is the basis of the law. His standpoint in philosophy of law is thus broadly liberal, though his attitude on many particular legal issues is far from liberal as the term is now understood. He holds, for instance, that if one of the partners to a marriage runs away or takes another partner, "the other is entitled, at any time, and incontestably, to bring such a one back to the former relation, as if that person were a thing" (*Metaphysic of Morals*, Sec. 25). He is notorious as a strong supporter of the retributive theory of punishment and an uncompromising advocate of the death penalty for murder. The explanation of his harshness in these matters is to be found in his legalistic approach to ethics, which leaves little room for sympathy or forgiveness.

In politics also Kant combines a fundamentally liberal attitude with specific views that are conservative, if not reactionary. Following Rousseau, he attempts to explain political authority partly in terms of the general will and partly in terms of the original contract. Insofar as he insists on the contract, which he interprets not as a historical fact but as a regulative idea, he is advocating a version of political liberalism which lays particular emphasis on the rule of law; insofar as he grounds supreme political authority in the will of the people as a whole, he is obviously flirting with more radical doctrines—from whose consequences he is quick to draw back. An admirer of the French Revolution, he nevertheless denies that the subjects of the most ill-governed states have any right of rebellion against their rulers. And though the mixed constitution he favors is one in which citizens can make their voices heard through their representatives, he is for confining the franchise to persons who possess "independence or self-sufficiency," thus excluding from "active" citizenship (according to Sec. 46 of the *Metaphysic of Morals*) apprentices, servants, woodcutters, plowmen, and, surprisingly, resident tutors, as well as "all women." The truth is, however, that Kant's political theorizing was done in a vacuum; in his day there was no real chance for a Prussian professor of philosophy to influence political events.

Philosophy of religion. In the sphere of religion the views of a professor of philosophy could be influential, and Kant's views on this subject were certainly provocative. He treats religion as essentially, if not quite exclusively, a matter of purity of heart—thus dispensing with speculative theology altogether and assigning a meager importance to the institutional side of religion. To adopt the religious attitude, as Kant sees it, is to look on duties as if they were divine commands. But this, he explains, is only to insist on the unconditioned character, the ineluctability, of moral obligation; it is a way of representing morality, not a way of going beyond it. Knowledge of the supersensible, as Kant thought he had shown in the *Critique of Pure Reason*, is impossible; and although moral practice carries with it

belief in God and a future life, the whole meaning and force of that belief is to be found in a persistence in moral endeavor and a determination to repair moral shortcomings. The pure religion of morality needs no dogma apart from these two fundamental articles of belief, which are accessible immediately to the simplest intelligence. Still less has it any need of the external trappings of religion—priests, ceremonies, and the like—although the body of believers must think of themselves as belonging to a church, universal but invisible, and the practices of visible churches sometimes serve to stimulate or strengthen moral effort, in a way which is useful but not indispensable.

The religion of morality is on this account a religion of all good men. Despite this, Kant took a particular interest in Christianity, which he saw as at least approximating true religion though corrupted by the presence of extraneous elements derived from Judaism. His book *Religion Within the Bounds of Mere Reason* (1793) is in effect a commentary on and a reinterpretation of Christian doctrine and practice, written with the object of making this conclusion clear. In this reinterpretation the doctrine of original sin is transformed into a doctrine of the radical evil in human nature, which is the positive source of moral failing; and that of the Incarnation is replaced by an account of the triumph of the good principle over the bad, the part of the historical Jesus being taken by an idea of reason, that of man in his moral perfection. Kant sets aside the historical elements in Christianity as having no importance in themselves: Whatever is true in the religion must be derivable from moral reason. To think of the uttering of religious formulas or the performance of formal services to God as having a value of their own is to fall into the grossest superstition. It is perhaps scarcely surprising that these sentiments, whose attraction for youth can be seen in Hegel's *Jugendschriften*, should have struck the Prussian authorities as subversive and led the orthodox King Frederick William II to demand that Kant refrain from further pronouncements on religion. Though Kant, in his letter acceding to this demand, protested that he had no thought of criticizing Christianity in writing his book, it is hard to take his protest quite seriously, for he had certainly meant to suggest that many of the beliefs and actions of practicing Christians were without value, if not positively immoral. Indeed, the originality and continuing interest of his work on religion connect directly with that fact.

The "Opus Postumum." In the last years of his life—from about 1795 on—Kant was engaged in the composition of what would have been a substantial philosophical work; the preparatory notes for it have been published as *Opus Postumum*. Its original title was "Transition from Metaphysical Foundations of Natural Science to Physics," and in its original form its object was to carry further the process, begun in 1786 in the *Metaphysical Foundations of Natural Science,* of finding an a priori basis for physics. No longer content with the formal structure for which he had argued earlier, Kant thought he had to show that some of the particular laws of nature could be known in advance of experience. The broadest types of physical possibility were determined by the constitution of the human mind; it was this, for example, which explained the presence in nature of just so many fundamental forces, and even of an omnipresent ether. These speculations about the foundations of physics led Kant to epistemological considerations of a wider kind. The whole subject of the relation of the form of experience to its matter, with the question how far the form shapes the matter, arose in his mind anew, doubtless because of the criticisms directed against the formalist position of the *Critique of Pure Reason* by self-professed disciples like Fichte. In 1799 Kant dissociated himself publicly from the views expressed in Fichte's *Wissenschaftslehre*, according to which the subject of knowledge "posits" the objective world and so, in a way, creates nature. Yet the evidence of the *Opus Postumum* is that at this time, or shortly thereafter, Kant was toying with similar ideas and was even using some of the same vocabulary. It is perhaps fortunate for Kant's reputation that he was not able to get his final philosophical thoughts into publishable form.

Works by Kant

COLLECTED WORKS

Gesammelte Schriften, 23 vols., edited under the supervision of the Berlin Academy of Sciences. Berlin, 1902–1955. The standard collected edition of Kant's writings; contains his correspondence and hitherto unpublished notes (including those for the *Opus Postumum*) as well as everything he published. Further volumes covering Kant's lectures are in preparation.

Kants Werke, 10 vols., Ernst Cassirer, ed. Berlin, 1912–1922. Contains the published works, with full indications of the contents of the original editions.

Philosophische Bibliothek series. Leipzig and Hamburg, 1904——. Separately bound editions of all the treatises listed below under the head "Main Treatises," with useful introductions; also includes *Kleinere Schriften zur Geschichtsphilosophie, Ethik, und Politik*.

MAIN TREATISES

Allgemeine Naturgeschichte und Theorie des Himmels. Königsberg and Leipzig, 1755. English translation by W. Hastie in *Kant's Cosmogony* (Glasgow, 1900).

Der einzig mögliche Beweisgrund zu einer Demonstration des Daseins Gottes. Königsberg, 1763. No serviceable translation.

Träume eines Geistersehers, erläutert durch Träume der Metaphysik. Königsberg, 1766. Translated into English as *Dreams of Spirit-Seer* by E. F. Goerwitz (New York, 1900).

De Mundi Sensibilis atque Intelligibilis Forma et Principiis Dissertatio. Königsberg, 1770. Translated into English in Handyside's *Kant's Inaugural Dissertation and Early Writings on Space* (Chicago, 1929).

Kritik der reinen Vernunft. Riga, 1781; 2d ed., Riga, 1787. The first edition is customarily referred to as A, the second edition as B. The most useful modern edition is by Raymond Schmidt (Leipzig, 1926). There are English translations by Francis Heywood (London, 1838); J. M. D. Meiklejohn (London, 1854), F. Max Müller (2 vols., London, 1881), and N. Kemp Smith (London, 1929). Kemp Smith's version is the fullest and most reliable.

Prolegomena zu einer jeden künftigen Metaphysik die als Wissenschaft auftreten können. Riga, 1783. English translations are available by John Richardson (*Prolegomena to Future Metaphysics*, in *Metaphysical Works of the Celebrated Immanual Kant*, London, 1836), J. P. Mahaffy and J. H. Bernard (*The Prolegomena*, London, 1872), E. B. Bax (*Kant's Prolegomena and Metaphysical Foundations of Natural Science*, London, 1883), Paul Carus (*Prolegomena to Any Future Metaphysics*, Chicago, 1902), L. W. Beck (same title as Carus', New York, 1951), and P. G. Lucas (same title as Carus', Manchester, 1953). The Beck and Lucas translations are much the best.

Grundlegung zur Metaphysik der Sitten. Riga, 1785; 2d ed., Riga, 1786. Translated into English by T. K. Abbott as *Fundamen-*

tal Principles of the Metaphysic of Morals (in *Kant's Critique of Practical Reason and Other Works on the Theory of Ethics*, London, 1873), by L. W. Beck as *Foundations of the Metaphysics of Morals* (in *Critique of Practical Reason and Other Writings in Moral Philosophy*, Chicago, 1949), by H. J. Paton (from the 2d edition) as *The Moral Law, or Kant's Groundwork of the Metaphysic of Morals* (London, 1948). All three versions are good; Paton's is the most elegant. Quotations in the text of this article are from Paton's translation; the citations to page numbers in the 2d edition are taken from Paton's marginal notation.

Metaphysische Anfangsgründe der Naturwissenschaft. Riga, 1786. Translated into English by E. B. Bax (in *Kant's Prolegomena and Metaphysical Foundations of Natural Science*, London, 1883).

Kritik der praktischen Vernunft. Riga, 1788. Translated into English by T. K. Abbott, and also by L. W. Beck, as *Critique of Practical Reason* in the books cited for the *Grundlegung zur Metaphysik der Sitten*. The Beck translation is accurate but somewhat clumsy; it has been published separately (New York, 1956).

Kritik der Urteilskraft. Berlin and Liebau, 1790. Translated into English by J. H. Bernard as *Kritik of Judgement* (London, 1892; later reprinted as *Critique of Judgement*). Also translated by J. C. Meredith in two parts, *Critique of Aesthetic Judgement* (Oxford, 1911) and *Critique of Teleological Judgement* (Oxford, 1928), which were reissued together as *The Critique of Judgement* (Oxford, 1952). Both the Bernard and the Meredith versions are of poor quality; Meredith's is slightly the better. Kant wrote an introduction to the *Kritik* which he discarded; it is available as *Erste Einleitung in die Kritik der Urteilskraft*, Vol. V, *Kants Werke* (Berlin, 1922), and in English translation by H. Kabir as *Immanuel Kant on Philosophy in General* (Calcutta, 1935).

Die Religion innerhalb der Grenzen der blossen Vernunft. First part published separately, Berlin, 1792; published complete at Königsberg, 1793. Translated into English by John Richardson as *Religion Within the Sphere of Naked Reason* (in *Essays and Treatises*, London, 1798), by J. W. Semple as *Religion Within the Boundary of Pure Reason* (Edinburgh, 1838), T. M. Greene and H. H. Hudson as *Religion Within the Limits of Reason Alone* (Chicago, 1934; 2d ed., with new matter by J. R. Silber, New York, 1960). The 1960 edition (Greene–Hudson–Silber) is the best.

Zum ewigen Frieden: ein philosophischer Entwurf. Königsberg, 1795. The two best English translations are L. W. Beck's *Perpetual Peace* (in *Critique of Practical Reason and Other Writings in Moral Philosophy*, Chicago, 1949; separately bound, New York, 1957) and C. J. Friedrich's *Inevitable Peace* (New Haven, 1948).

Metaphysik der Sitten, Part I, *Metaphysische Anfangsgründe der Rechtslehre*; Part II, *Metaphysische Anfangsgründe der Tugendlehre*. Separately bound, Königsberg, 1797. Part I translated into English by W. Hastie as *Kant's Philosophy of Law* (Edinburgh, 1887). Part II translated into English by James Ellington as *Metaphysical Principles of Virtue* (Indianapolis, 1964) and by Mary Gregor as *The Doctrine of Virtue* (New York, 1964).

Anthropologie in pragmatischer Hinsicht. Königsberg, 1798. No English translation.

Kant on History. Indianapolis, 1963. Translations by L. W. Beck, R. E. Anchor, and E. L. Fackenheim; contains Kant's minor essays on philosophy of history.

Eine Vorlesung über Ethik, edited from student's notes by P. Menzer. Berlin, 1924. Translated into English by Louis Infield as *Lectures on Ethics* (London, 1930).

Works on Kant

LIFE

The main sources for Kant's life, apart from his letters, are three memoirs published in Königsberg in 1804: L. E. Borowski's *Darstellung des Lebens und Characters Immanuel Kants*; R. B. Jachmann's *Immanuel Kant, geschildert in Briefen an einen Freund*; and E. A. C. Wasianski's *Immanuel Kant in seinen letzten Lebensjahren*. Wasianski's memoir is extensively used in Thomas De Quincey's "The Last Days of Kant" (*Works*, Vol. XII). See also Ernst Cassirer's *Kants Leben und Lehre* (Berlin, 1921), and for a useful short life Karl Vorländer's *Immanuel Kants Leben* (Leipzig, 1911).

COMMENTARIES

Rudolf Eisler's *Kantlexicon* (Berlin, 1930) and Heinrich Ratke's *Systematisches Handlexicon zu Kants Kritik der reinen Vernunft* (Leipzig, 1929) are valuable aids to the Kantian student. The periodical *Kantstudien* has published many important contributions to Kantian scholarship and discussion.

For commentaries on the *Critique of Pure Reason*, see Hans Vaihinger, *Kommentar zur Kritik der reinen Vernunft*, 2 vols. (Stuttgart, 1881–1892), which covers the opening sections only; N. Kemp Smith, *A Commentary to Kant's Critique of Pure Reason* (London, 1918; rev. ed., 1923), which is strongly influenced by Vaihinger's "patchwork" theory; H. J. Paton, *Kant's Metaphysic of Experience*, 2 vols. (London, 1936), which covers the first half only and is sharply critical of Kemp Smith; A. C. Ewing, *A Short Commentary on Kant's Critique of Pure Reason* (London, 1938); T. D. Weldon, *Kant's Critique of Pure Reason* (Oxford, 1945; 2d ed., 1958).

On the theory of knowledge see also H. A. Prichard, *Kant's Theory of Knowledge* (Oxford, 1909); A. C. Ewing, *Kant's Treatment of Causality* (London, 1924); W. H. Walsh, *Reason and Experience* (Oxford, 1947); Graham Bird, *Kant's Theory of Knowledge* (London, 1962); R. P. Wolff, *Kant's Theory of Mental Activity* (Cambridge, 1963).

For commentaries on the *Critique of Practical Reason* and other works on ethics, see L. W. Beck, *A Commentary on Kant's Critique of Practical Reason* (Chicago, 1960), a good source; H. J. Paton, *The Categorical Imperative* (London, 1947), a detailed commentary on the *Grundlegung*; W. D. Ross, *Kant's Ethical Theory* (Oxford, 1954); A. R. C. Duncan, *Practical Reason and Morality* (Edinburgh, 1957); M. J. Gregor, *Laws of Freedom* (Oxford, 1963), which expounds the *Metaphysic of Morals*; P. A. Schilpp, *Kant's Pre-Critical Ethics* (Evanston, Ill., 1938); A. E. Teale, *Kantian Ethics* (London, 1951).

For commentaries on the *Critique of Judgment*, see Konrad Marc-Wogau, *Vier Studien zu Kants Kritik der Urteilskraft* (Uppsala, Sweden, 1938); H. W. Cassirer, *A Commentary on Kant's Critique of Judgment* (London, 1938).

Commentaries on other aspects of Kant's thought are also available. On the precritical writings, see Giorgio Tonelli, *Elementi metafisici e metodologici in Kant precritico* (Turin, 1959). On Kant's philosophy of religion, see C. C. J. Webb, *Kant's Philosophy of Religion* (Oxford, 1926) and F. E. England, *Kant's Conception of God* (London, 1929). On Kant's philosophy of history, see Klaus Weyand, *Kants Geschichtsphilosophie* (Cologne, 1964). On Kant as a scientist, see Erich Adickes, *Kant als Naturforscher*, 2 vols. (Berlin, 1924–1925). On the *Opus Postumum*, see Erich Adickes, *Kants Opus Postumum dargestellt und beurteilt* (Berlin, 1920).

GENERAL STUDIES

S. Körner, *Kant* (Harmondsworth, 1955) is the best general introduction; see also G. J. Warnock's chapter in D. J. O'Connor, ed., *A Critical History of Western Philosophy* (New York, 1964). Edward Caird, *The Critical Philosophy of Kant*, 2 vols. (Glasgow, 1889), criticizes Kant from the Hegelian position. Martin Heidegger, *Kant und das Problem der Metaphysik* (Bonn, 1929) examines Kant as an "ontologist." H. J. de Vleeschauwer, *La Déduction transcendentale dans l'oeuvre de Kant*, 3 vols. (Antwerp, 1934–1937), presents an exhaustive survey of Kant's writings on the problem, and de Vleeschauwer offers a one-volume summary in *L'Évolution de la pensée kantienne* (Paris, 1939), which has been translated into English by A. R. C. Duncan as *The Development of Kantian Thought* (London, 1962). Gottfried Martin, *Immanuel Kant, Ontologie und Wissenschaftstheorie* (Cologne, 1951), translated into English by P. G. Lucas as *Kant's Metaphysics and Theory of Science* (Manchester, 1955), is influenced but not dominated by Heidegger. Richard Kroner, *Kants Weltanschauung* (Tübingen, 1914), translated into English by J. E. Smith as *Kant's Weltanschauung* (Chicago, 1956), stresses Kant's emphasis on the practical. R. Daval, *La Métaphysique de Kant* (Paris, 1951), presents "schematism" as the key idea in Kant's thought.

W. H. WALSH

KANTIANISM. See GERMAN PHILOSOPHY; NEO-KANTIANISM.

KAPLAN, MORDECAI MENAHEM, founder of reconstructionism in Judaism, was born in 1881 in a small town in Lithuania. At the age of nine, he immigrated with his family to the United States, where he received most of his education, both Jewish and secular. At 22, a year after graduation from the Jewish Theological Seminary, Kaplan entered the Orthodox Jewish rabbinate. His intellectual alienation from traditional views of the supernatural had already begun, however, and he was moving toward a new orientation in which conformity to Jewish ritual practice is maintained as far as possible but is combined with novel and modernized intellectual formulations of the meanings attached to these practices. Kaplan called this new orientation reconstructionism; it has been the basis of his writing and teaching and of his work in the rabbinate and in the Jewish community for more than half a century. It is distinctive in that reinterpretation of religion in response to changing circumstances, which has always been an unconscious process, is here transformed into a conscious and deliberate use of all the modern tools of historical, sociological, and psychological research to achieve adaptation without disruption.

Kaplan was deeply influenced by Matthew Arnold's conception of a "God of experience," a Power in the universe that makes for the realization of human ideals. Adopting this naturalistic view, he was also led to reconsider the two other central themes of Jewish thought: the nature of the Torah, including rabbinical teaching, law, and religious tradition, and the character of the people of Israel. He reached the conclusion that the people of Israel are the central reality of the universe of Judaic discourse and that both the idea of God and the conception of Torah must be understood in relation to that central reality. God and Torah are functional concepts within Judaism, which, in turn, is defined as "the folk religion of the Jewish people." Revivifying Jewish religion, then, necessarily requires attention to the secular concerns and interests of the Jewish people.

Kaplan's conception of religion is derived, in large measure, from Émile Durkheim's theory of totemic solidarity. It is an affair of the group, not, as Whitehead claimed, of the individual. Religion is "the sum of those habits and values which give a people the will to live in common, to perpetuate itself and to make the best use of its collective life." In the light of this definition, Jewish religion requires a Jewish people with the will to self-perpetuation. To strengthen Jewish religion, it is necessary to stress the concept of the Jewish people as an organic entity. For this reason Kaplan came to use the term "Judaism" to mean the entire civilization of the Jewish people—everything that unites the Jews to one another and establishes a common identification. In accordance with this definition, he proposed the restoration of Jewish community life on a broad basis that would include those who identified themselves only with the secular life of the Jews as well as those who identified themselves with the religious life. He inaugurated a movement that would make synagogues centers for developing the social solidarity of the Jewish people instead of mere places of worship. The "Jewish center" movement has come about as a consequence of Kaplan's suggestion.

As a teacher of both Jewish teachers and rabbis at the Jewish Theological Seminary of America, Kaplan has had a great deal of influence in the Conservative movement, the original home of reconstructionism, and also in the Reform movement. Even among the many who could not accept his position in every detail, he has been an important stimulus to the rethinking of the meaning of traditional Judaism. However, when Kaplan and his associates published a revised prayer book to express these new conceptions of Judaism, he was excommunicated by the Union of Orthodox Rabbis. As a philosopher of religion, Kaplan has contributed significantly to the working out of the implications of a pragmatic and naturalistic approach to religious phenomena. As a practicing religious leader, he has been most important in such fields as Jewish education, Jewish social work, and the forwarding of cultural and spiritual Zionism.

Works by Kaplan

Judaism in Transition. Toronto, 1936.
The Meaning of God in Modern Jewish Religion. New York, 1937.
The Future of the American Jew. New York, 1948.
Judaism as a Civilization. New York, 1957.
The Greater Judaism in the Making. New York, 1960.
The Purpose and Meaning of Jewish Existence. Philadelphia, 1964.

Works on Kaplan

Agus, Jacob B., *Modern Philosophies of Judaism.* New York, 1941.
Blau, Joseph L., *The Story of Jewish Philosophy.* New York, 1962.
Eisenstein, Ira, and Kohn, Eugene, eds., *Mordecai M. Kaplan: An Evaluation.* New York, 1952.

J. L. BLAU

KAREYEV, NICHOLAS IVANOVICH (1850–1931), Russian historian and philosopher, was educated at Moscow University, where he took his doctorate in history (1884). During the late 1870s and early 1880s he spent several years studying abroad. Kareyev taught modern European history, first at Warsaw University and then at St. Petersburg University. He became a corresponding member of the St. Petersburg Academy of Sciences in 1910 and an honorary member of the Soviet Academy of Sciences in 1929. His main historical studies were devoted to eighteenth-century France, especially the Revolution of 1789.

Although a moderate in politics, Kareyev was deeply influenced by such radical Russian thinkers as Alexander Herzen, Dimitri Pisarev, Peter Lavrov, and N. K. Mikhailovski. Like Lavrov and Mikhailovski, Kareyev was a "semipositivist," but he was less influenced by either Hegel or Marx than Lavrov had been. His views of history echo Herzen's "philosophy of chance." "History," Kareyev declared, "is not a straight line, not a regular design traced out on a mathematical plane, but a living fabric of irregular and sinuous lines, which are intertwined in the most var-

ied and unexpected ways" (*Osnovnyie Voprosy*, Part I, p. 153).

Kareyev's position in ethics, which he called ethical individualism, was even more Kantian than that of Lavrov's early works. He defended individual autonomy against three dominant anti-individualist tendencies: that which breaks down the self into a series of psychic events (Hume); that which turns the individual into an expression of the *Zeitgeist* or *Volksgeist* (Hegel); and that which reduces the individual to a product of socioeconomic relations (Marx). From the point of view of the "human dignity and worth of the individual person," Kareyev insisted, "external [sociopolitical] freedom is a necessary condition for the spiritual growth and happiness of all the members of society" (*Mysli*, 2d ed., 1896, p. 135).

Kareyev rejected the "utilitarian attitude toward the person, which treats him as an object," adding that the "principle of individuality" guarantees the individual's right "not to be an instrument or means for another" or reduced to the status of an organ of a "social organism" (*ibid.*, p. 138). In attributing absolute value to individuals as such, Kareyev said, we take account of both their natural rights and—as Lavrov had stressed—their present potentiality for future moral and intellectual growth. In the name of this absolute value, Kareyev condemned not only political assassination and capital punishment but also euthanasia. On this point he came close not only to Kant but also to Tolstoy, whose philosophy of history, like those of Hegel and Marx, he had criticized perceptively and in detail.

Bibliography

Osnovnyie Voprosy Filosofii Istorii ("Fundamental Problems in the Philosophy of History") was published in Moscow in 1883 (2d ed., in three vols., St. Petersburg, 1887–1890; 3d ed., abridged, St. Petersburg, 1897). "K Voprosu o Svobode Voli s Tochki Zreniya Teorii Istoricheskovo Protsessa" ("On the Question of Freedom of the Will From the Standpoint of the Theory of the Historical Process") appeared in *Voprosy Filosofii i Psikhologii*, Vol. I, No. 4 (1889–1890), 113–142. It was reprinted in *Istoriko-filosofskiye i Sotsiologicheskiye Etyudy* ("Studies in Sociology and the Philosophy of History," St. Petersburg, 1895; 2d ed., St. Petersburg, 1899), pp. 279–304. *Mysli ob Osnovakh Nravstvennosti* ("Thoughts on the Foundations of Morality") was published in St. Petersburg in 1895; 2d ed., St. Petersburg, 1896.

For discussion of Kareyev, see V. V. Zenkovsky, *Istoriya Russkoi Filosofii*, 2 vols. (Paris, 1948 and 1950), translated by G. L. Kline as *A History of Russian Philosophy*, 2 vols. (London and New York, 1953), pp. 374–375.

GEORGE L. KLINE

KARMA (Sanskrit, *karman*; literally, "deed," "action") is an adjunct in Indian religious thought to the doctrine of Reincarnation. In one form or another, it is part of the beliefs of Buddhism, Jainism, and Hinduism. The actions of a living being are regarded as having a special class of causal effects which determine his future spiritual condition, both in this life and in succeeding ones. These effects are known as the "fruits" of the action. Good deeds lead to progress toward liberation (*mokṣa*, nirvana); bad ones, to regress from this goal. Usually caste status, disease, prosperity, and so forth are thought to be the consequences of actions in previous lives. Thus, *karma* is an ethically oriented causal law; and although some Hindus regard *karma* as the work of God, the concept does not necessitate this interpretation, and the award of deserts is as often regarded as an automatic process in nature.

The archaic notion of *karma* seems to have been that action as such binds men to the world (and thereby to suffering and ignorance); hence, liberation must involve suspension of all activity. Thus, in Jainism, which represents a very ancient strand in Indian religion, even a good action, although inducing an influx of meritorious *karma*, ties the person to matter. Indeed, *karma*, as the force determining rebirth, is itself regarded as a subtle form of matter. Also—and hence the emphasis on "noninjury" (*ahiṃsā*)—especially evil effects follow from a person's destroying life, even microorganisms. Such ideas lay behind the heroically quietistic Jain ideal of suicide by self-starvation. Moreover, the concept of *karma* in Vedic literature had the meaning of ritual act, so that combined with the need to refrain from activity there runs through much Indian ascetic thought the notion that even religious acts, although they may bring heavenly rewards, bind men to the cosmos and to rebirth: heaven is part of the cosmos and itself must be transcended.

These ideas presented a number of problems to speculative and religious thinkers: (1) How can liberation ever be achieved if even the effort to be inactive, and inactivity itself, may be forms of binding action? (2) How can the ordinary man, involved in his worldly duties and concerns, have any hope of escaping rebirth? (3) By what mechanism does *karma* operate on future births? (4) Why, if *karma* is what keeps empirical life going, does the saint (*jīvan-mukta*), who has attained serenity and release in this life, keep on living? (5) How can there be any human initiative or free will if our present state is inexorably determined by past *karma*?

Various answers to these questions were given, among them the following: (1) The Jains hold that karmic matter can be annihilated by austerities, so that gradually it can be totally removed from an individual. On the other hand, Buddhism transformed the notion of *karma* by holding that motives, rather than the acts themselves, are what count and that *karma* needs craving (*taṇhā*) as a necessary condition of its effectiveness. Hence, by removing craving through the purification of one's motives, one can find release from rebirth. For the Hindu theologian Śankara, the power of *karma* depends on ignorance, so that the contemplative knowledge that the Self is the sole reality brings liberation from the continuing effects of *karma*.

(2) On the one hand, the ordinary man can hope to become a recluse, monk, or holy man in a future life. On the other hand, theistic ideas introduced grace as a countervailing means of liberation. Thus, in the *Bhagavad Gītā* it is stressed that a man, in performing his duties without regard to their fruits and in sole reliance upon the Lord, can escape the bonds of *karma*. Likewise, in Mahāyāna Buddhism the theory of the transfer of merit involves the belief that the otherwise unworthy individual can be given merit by a *Bodhisattva* (Buddha-to-be) out of the latter's infinite store, acquired through many lives of heroic self-sacrifice on behalf of living beings; thereby the individual qualifies for rebirth in paradise (where the conditions for

attaining nirvana are peculiarly favorable). Thus the operation of *karma* is short-circuited by grace and faith.

(3) It is commonly held that *karma* is *adṛṣṭa*, an invisible force, so that the need to postulate an observable mechanism is evaded. However, among some schools the doctrine that the soul is all-pervasive (and not localized) helps to explain the concept of karmic action-at-a-distance. Traditional medical writings (first or second century) affirm that a person's characteristics are not derived solely from his parents (in this, there is an incipient conflict between modern genetics and the theory of *karma*).

(4) It is generally held that there is a limited continuance of karmic effects, like the running on of a potter's wheel after the potter has stopped turning it—but when the saint's death occurs, there will be no further rebirth for him.

(5) Various positions are adopted concerning the question of free will. The Buddha, for instance, was clearly impressed by the principle that knowledge of causes gives one the opportunity to determine the future, so that a proper understanding of *karma* and its causality should in no way involve fatalistic conclusions. He attacked Makkhali Gosāla, a contemporary teacher, for holding a fatalistic predestinationism, allied to extreme asceticism (which was in no sense a cause of final release, but merely symptomatic of one's progress). The Jains held that theoretically, in its pure state, the life monad or soul is capable of any kind of effort: because of this "omnipotence" it never needs to be subservient to *karma*.

Although some schools argued that, since the effects of *karma* are morally regulated, one must presuppose a conscious regulator, namely God, atheistic and agnostic proponents of *karma* theory held that the difficulties of belief in God are as great as, or greater than, those inherent in assuming the automatic operation of *karma*. Moreover, belief in God generally involves the notion that unworthy people can short-circuit *karma* through calling on God in faith, and this cuts against the concepts of moral responsibility and self-help.

Bibliography

Dasgupta, S. N., *A History of Indian Philosophy.* Cambridge, 1922. Vol. I, Ch. 4.

Paranjoti, V., *Saiva Siddhānta*, 2d ed. London, 1954. Pp. 38 ff.

Parrinder, Geoffrey, *Upanishads, Gītā and Bible.* London, 1962. Ch. 9.

Tucci, Giuseppe, *Storia della filosofia indiana.* Bari, 1957. Part II, Ch. 10.

Zimmer, H., *Philosophies of India.* New York, 1957. Ch. 4, Sec. 7.

NINIAN SMART

KATHARSIS. The most common meaning of the Greek word *katharsis* is purification, especially cleansing from guilt or ritual defilement. Virtually absent from the Homeric poems, such cleansings became important in the following archaic period. They were, above all, a feature of the mystery religions, including Orphism, through which they eventually influenced Christian doctrine and practice. Empedocles wrote a poem, *Katharmoi* ("Purifications"), which must have treated of religious purification, and Plato in the *Phaedo* introduced the idea to philosophy by supposing that the soul must be purified by philosophy from contamination by things of this world in order to prepare itself for a better life. In the Hippocratic corpus we find the term used in the special sense of clearing off of morbid humors by evacuation, whether natural or induced by medicines.

Aristotle in his famous definition of tragedy (*Poetics* 1449b28) used the phrase "accomplishing through pity and fear the katharsis of feelings (*pathemata*) of that kind," and a vast controversy has continued ever since about its meaning. One interpretation maintains that pity and fear remain but are somehow purified; another holds that they are purged and thus removed. In either case there is a psychological experience of value to the spectator. A third interpretation holds that the reference is to something within the action of the tragedy produced upon the plot or the characters. Aristotle does not explain what he has in mind, and in default of further evidence a definite solution is perhaps not very likely to be achieved.

Bibliography

Else, G. F., *Aristotle's Poetics: The Argument.* Cambridge, Mass., 1957.

Moulinier, Louis, *Le Pur et l'impur dans la pensée des grecs.* Paris, 1952.

Pfister, Friedrich, "Katharsis," in *Real-encyclopädie,* A. Pauly and G. Wissowa, eds. Supp. Vol. VI (1935), pp. 146–162.

G. B. KERFERD

KAUTSKY, KARL (1854–1939), was, with the exception of Marx and Engels, the leading theorist of orthodox Marxism before World War I. Born in Prague of Czech and German parentage, Kautsky studied at Vienna and showed much interest in social Darwinism and socialism. As an evolutionist and materialist, he found Marx's combination of dialectical materialism and economic determinism irresistible, and he worked with Engels himself during the 1880s. From 1883 to 1917 Kautsky was the editor of *Die neue Zeit,* the official organ of the German Social Democratic party and the most influential socialist journal of the day. He edited and published the literary remains of Marx after Engels' death. In 1891 Kautsky wrote the famous first, or theoretical, part of the *Erfurter Programm,* the official policy statement of the German party. This document established that the greatest socialist party in history should be orthodox Marxist.

Kautsky, more than any other theorist of repute, accepted Marx's method and conclusions as he found them. The natural laws of economic development resulted in certain inevitable contradictions in capitalism that must necessarily lead to its destruction and replacement by socialism. This would occur, Marx and Kautsky held, because competition and technical improvements, together with the availability of surplus labor, would lead to the concentration of capital and the progressive immiserization of the proletariat, as well as the polarization of society into a few monopolists opposed by vast masses of starving workers. Recurrent depressions and economic catastrophes would finally destroy capitalism. Such crises would be caused mainly by the inability of the workers to purchase the products of their labor. The united proletariat, trained by

its socialist leaders, would see that only social ownership of the means of production could end the contradiction between capitalism's ability to produce wealth but its inability to distribute that wealth through private ownership. Like Marx and Engels, Kautsky held that religion, philosophy, and ethics are reflections of the substructure of class interest and position and that the state is the puppet of the dominant social class.

Kautsky, the "defender of the faith," fought attempts of fellow socialists to make basic alterations in their Marxian heritage. He led the German Social Democratic party in its struggle against Eduard Bernstein and the revisionists, who believed that the facts of European capitalism no longer supported his orthodox views and that parliamentary action and pragmatic flexibility could bring extensive and permanent reform. Kautsky was able to maintain the preeminence of orthodox Marxism in party theory, although the revisionists increasingly dominated party tactics and action. In the early years of the twentieth century, Kautsky and the orthodox centrists had increasingly to contend with the radical left wing of the party under Rosa Luxemburg and Karl Liebknecht. This group held strictly to Marx's economic teachings but rejected orthodox political tactics in favor of more immediately revolutionary doctrines. They hoped for more radical positions on questions before parliament and for greater encouragement of spontaneous revolutionary and general strike activity. Kautsky did not believe that the contradictions of capitalism or the class consciousness of the workers were advanced enough for such tactics. He did join the left in parliament on various crucial questions, notably in its refusal to sanction the continuance of World War I as a war of conquest.

During the Weimar Republic, Kautsky lost his preeminent position as the reformists dominated the party and Leninism captured the left. He was attacked by Lenin and Trotsky for his castigation of their dictatorial and terroristic methods and their conquest of Georgia, then an independent socialist-controlled state. Forced into exile by the Nazis, Kautsky died in Amsterdam.

Works by Kautsky

Das Erfurter Programm. Stuttgart, 1899.

The Social Revolution. London, 1909.

Bernstein und das sozialdemokratische Programm. Stuttgart, 1919.

Ethik und materialistische Geschichtsauffassung. Berlin, 1922.

Die Materialistische Geschichtsauffassung. Berlin, 1927.

Die Geschichte des Sozialismus. Berlin, 1947.

Works on Kautsky

Lenin, Nikolai, *The Proletarian Revolution and Kautsky the Renegade.* London, 1920.

Renner, Karl, *Karl Kautsky.* Berlin, 1925.

Trotsky, Leon, *The Defense of Terrorism: A Reply to Kautsky.* New York, 1921.

JOHN WEISS

KAVELIN, KONSTANTIN DMITRIEVICH (1818–1885), Russian historian and philosopher, was educated at Moscow University, where he was later professor of history. Kavelin also taught at St. Petersburg University and was for a time tutor to the royal family. In addition to nu-

numerous historical works, he wrote essays in psychology, sociology, and ethics. During the 1870s he carried on an active polemic with Vladimir Solovyov, defending a positivist (or "semipositivist") position against Solovyov's criticisms. In politics Kavelin was a moderate liberal; in religion he remained devoutly Russian Orthodox.

Kavelin's main work in ethical theory, *Zadachi Etiki* ("Tasks [or Problems] of Ethics"), appeared in 1844. In it he criticized the then fashionable one-sided "objectivism," which, he charged, blurred the distinction between inner intention and outward behavior, leading to the conclusion that intentions may be "unlawful" or volitions "criminal." From the neo-Kantian viewpoint which Kavelin adopted in this book, such a conclusion is absurd. Intentions and volitions, he insisted, are to be judged only "by their relationship to consciousness, to the understanding and inner conviction of the person in whom they occur" (*Sobraniye Sochinenii*, Vol. III, Col. 907).

When utilitarians equate virtue with utility and vice with social harm they are taking an "outsider's" view of moral experience, the view of a spectator rather than that of a moral agent. In fact, moral virtue may or may not be useful; this depends on the particular social system involved, and the latter is a nonmoral factor. Hence, social utility cannot provide a sound criterion of morality.

It is human individuality as a unique locus of value, Kavelin asserted, which provides such a criterion. However, this assertion raised serious problems for Kavelin's "scientific ethics," since, as he admitted, concrete individuality systematically eludes the abstract generalities of science.

In the end, the "scientific ethics" which Kavelin had been laboring to construct coincided with Christian ethics—the "last word in ethical wisdom" and "an incontrovertible truth of individual spiritual life" (*ibid.*, Cols. 940–941).

Kavelin's attempt to provide a scientific foundation for ethics, like the attempts of other nineteenth-century thinkers, must be judged a failure. However, Kavelin eloquently restated ideas derived from Vissarion Belinski, Alexander Herzen, and the Russian Populists concerning the individual person and his sense of freedom and the role of convictions in morality. His was a genuine, if modest, philosophical contribution.

Bibliography

Vol. III of Kavelin's four-volume *Sobraniye Sochinenii* ("Collected Works; St. Petersburg, 1898–1900) contains Kavelin's philosophical works, including *Zadachi Etiki*, Cols. 897–1018.

For literature on Kavelin, see V. V. Zenkovsky, *Istoriya Russkoi Filosofii*, 2 vols. (Paris, 1948–1950), translated by G. L. Kline as *A History of Russian Philosophy* (London and New York, 1953), pp. 345–348.

GEORGE L. KLINE

KELSEN, HANS, German-American legal philosopher, was born in Prague in 1881. After teaching law and legal philosophy at Vienna, Cologne, and Geneva, he moved in 1940 to the United States, where he lectured at various universities. Kelsen became professor of political science at the University of California (Berkeley) in 1945 and is now retired.

A leading exponent of legal positivism, Kelsen expounds a "pure theory of law" that disregards the specific rules and doctrines surrounding the typical elements of a given legal system, choosing instead to investigate such elements as the concepts of law, legal subject, legal organ, legal person, and legal responsibility—as well as the typical structure of legal systems, the relationship between norms of a system, and the creation of law. The theory is "pure" in two senses. First, it is divorced from any ideological considerations, no value judgments are made concerning any legal system, and the analysis of "legal norm" is unaffected by a conception of just law. Second, the sociological study of law observance and the study of political, economic, or historical influences on the development of law are beyond the purview of the pure theory. Such studies presuppose a prior investigation of the nature of law, in the manner of the pure theory.

The pure theory of law provides the conceptual tools and framework for the rational representation of any given system of positive law. Legal science is one variety of the scientific study of a normative system. In contrast to the causal sciences, which describe their objects of study in "is" terminology, legal science is normative, but it employs normative language ("ought" terminology) in a special way because the jurist is not empowered to issue norms. In order to interpret some act or event as having a legal character (*Rechtsakt*), to explain legal or illegal behavior, or to understand what is meant by saying that the pronouncement of an individual is the issuing of a law, we need the concept of a norm.

A norm is the meaning of an act of will that something "ought to be." However, the "subjective" and "objective" meanings of the act must be distinguished, in the way that we understand the act of the executioner who, with the same blow of his ax, scornfully kills his enemy and executes the sentence of the court. An act of will has objective meaning insofar as its content conforms to the content of some other norm. Norms thus provide a way of interpreting certain acts of will as the issuing of norms and a way of explaining what it means to say that a norm exists, is valid, or ought to be obeyed. The validity of a norm is not to be identified with such empirical facts as its effectiveness or with any kind of social behavior. The concept of "ought" is a simple and unanalyzable notion that in Kelsen's later writings is broadly understood to include not only prescription, but also permission and authorization.

Legal systems, as distinguished from other forms of social ordering, are coercive orders. Legal norms, as represented by the legal scientist, are hypothetical statements stipulating that a given sanction ought to be executed under certain conditions. The connection between antecedent and consequent is one of imputation (*Zurechnung*).

Legal systems are hierarchical in structure (*Stufenbau*). Kelsen treats in detail the relationships of norms within a system, the possibility of conflicts or contradictions between norms, and the nature of interpretation and legislation. He utilizes the notion of a basic norm (*Grundnorm*) to explain the coherence of a plurality of norms as constituting a single system. A basic norm is required for interpreting acts of will as norm-creating acts of a system, but it is not itself a positive legal norm; rather, it is hypothesis or presupposition of the legal scientist. When jurists speak of a legal norm as a valid norm of a system, they intend thereby that the norm is created ultimately in conformity with the basic norm of the system and that the system is effective, which means that behavior, by and large, conforms to the norms. But effectiveness is merely a necessary condition of validity of norms; the ground of validity is the basic norm.

In the pure theory the dualism between law and the state disappears; the doctrine of separation of powers and the traditional distinctions between public and private law and between civil and criminal law all receive fresh interpretations. The concept of sovereignty is analyzed in detail, and the legal character of international law is maintained. Kelsen has defended a monistic view of the relationship between international law and the various national legal orders; but he argues that since legal phenomena may be organized coherently on more than one monistic hypothesis, the choice of a hypothesis can be dictated only by political or moral preferences.

A severe critic of natural law doctrines, Kelsen maintains the logical impossibility of the coexistence of positive and natural law. Natural law doctrines, together with notions of justice, are held to rest upon unscientific, metaphysical bases. Following the broad tradition of positivism and logical empiricism, Kelsen assigns them an emotive origin.

Bibliography

A complete bibliography of Kelsen's writings up to 1960 is contained in *Reine Rechtslehre*, 2d ed. (Vienna, 1960); for works on Kelsen, see the bibliographies in *Reine Rechtslehre*, 1st ed. (Vienna, 1934), and *General Theory of Law and the State*, translated by Anders Wedberg (Cambridge, Mass., 1943).

Other principal works by Kelsen are *Hauptprobleme der Staatsrechtslehre* (Tübingen, 1910); *Das Problem der Souveränität und die Theorie des Völkerrechts* (Tübingen, 1920); *Die philosophischen Grundlagen der Naturrechtslehre und des Rechtspositivismus* (Charlottenburg, 1928), translated by W. H. Krauss and printed as appendix to *General Theory of Law and the State*; *Society and Nature* (Chicago, 1943); *The Political Theory of Bolshevism* (Berkeley, 1948); *The Communist Theory of Law* (New York, 1955); and *What Is Justice?* (Berkeley, 1957), a volume of collected essays.

For studies of the Neo-Kantian background of Kelsen's thought, see R. Treves, *Il fondamento filosofico della dottrina pura del diritto di Hans Kelsen* (Turin, 1934); W. Ebenstein, *The Pure Theory of Law* (Madison, Wis., 1945). See also Harald Ofstad, "The Descriptive Definition of the Concept of 'Legal Norm' Proposed by Hans Kelsen," in *Theoria*, Vol. 16 (1950), 118–151, 211–246; M. P. Golding, "Kelsen and the Concept of 'Legal System,'" in *Archiv für Rechts- und Sozialphilosophie*, Vol. 57 (1961), 355–386; and H. L. A. Hart, "Kelsen Visited," in *U.C.L.A. Law Review*, Vol. 10 (1963), 709–728.

M. P. GOLDING

KEPLER, JOHANNES (1571–1630), the founder of modern astronomy, was born in Weil der Stadt, near Stuttgart. During his life he was a student of theology, teacher of mathematics and astronomy, assistant to Tycho Brahe, imperial mathematicus to the emperors Rudolph II and Matthias, and astrologer to the duke of Wallenstein. His principal scientific discoveries were the three planetary laws named after him, the principle of continuity in geometry, and the Keplerian telescope. He was also responsible for decisive advances in the theory of optics and in work

that led to the development of the infinitesimal calculus, and incidentally he coined a number of terms whose paternity has been forgotten, including "satellite" (for the moons of Jupiter), "dioptrics," "focus" (of a conic section), and "camera obscura."

Significance of Kepler's laws. Kepler's three laws of planetary motion postulate that the planets travel in elliptical orbits, one focus of each ellipse being occupied by the sun; that the radius vector connecting sun and planet sweeps over equal areas in equal times; and that the squares of the periods of revolution of any two planets are in the same ratio as the cubes of their mean distances from the sun.

The promulgation of the three laws was in several respects a turning point in the history of thought. They were the first "laws of nature" in the modern sense: precise, verifiable statements, expressed in mathematical terms, about universal relations governing particular phenomena. They put an end to the Aristotelian dogma of uniform motion in perfect circles, which had bedeviled cosmology for two millennia, and substituted for the Ptolemaic universe—a fictitious clockwork of wheels turning on wheels—a vision of material bodies not unlike the earth freely floating in space, moved by physical forces acting on them. Kepler's laws severed the ties between astronomy and theology and replaced the moving spirits of medieval cosmology by physical causation.

What has come to be called the Copernican revolution was in fact mainly the work of Kepler and Galileo. Kepler's laws and Galileo's studies on the motion of projectiles were the basic ingredients of the Newtonian synthesis. Copernicus' *De Revolutionibus* was published in 1543, nearly thirty years before Kepler was born. Its first edition of a thousand copies never sold out, and it had altogether 4 reprintings in four hundred years. By way of comparison, Christopher Clavius' textbook *The Treatise on the Sphere* had 19 reprintings within fifty years; Copernicus' book had one. This curiosity is mentioned because it illustrates the fact that the Copernican theory attracted very little attention on the continent of Europe for more than fifty years— that is, for the next two generations. *De Revolutionibus* was an unreadable book describing an unworkable system. It revived the Pythagorean idea of a heliocentric universe, first proposed by Aristarchus of Samos in the third century B.C., but it adhered to the dogma of circular motion. As a result, Copernicus was forced to let the planets run on no less than 48 epicycles and eccentrics. He was in fact, as Kepler remarked, "interpreting Ptolemy rather than nature."

Kepler was the first astronomer to raise his voice in public in favor of the Copernican system. His *Mysterium Cosmographicum*, published in 1597, 54 years after Copernicus' death, initiated the controversy; Galileo only entered the scene 15 years later. At that time Kepler—aged 26—knew little of astronomy. He had started as a theologian, but a chance opportunity made him accept the post of teacher of mathematics and astronomy at the provincial school of Gratz in Styria. Three years later, however, he became assistant to Tycho Brahe, whose observational data, of a hitherto unparalleled richness and precision, provided the empirical foundation for Kepler's efforts to determine the orbit of Mars. It took Kepler eight years of nerve-racking labor to succeed. The result was his *magnum opus*, published in 1609, which contains the first and second laws (the third came nine years later). It bears a provocative title:

A New Astronomy *Based on Causation*
or A Physics of the Sky
derived from Investigations of the
Motions of the Star Mars
Founded on Observations of The Noble Tycho
Brahe.

The title is indeed symbolic of the work's revolutionary intent and achievement. Astronomy before Kepler had been a purely descriptive geometry of the skies, divorced from physical reality. Since the observed motions of the planets did not conform to the demands of circularity and uniformity, an increasing number of auxiliary wheels had to be added to the fictitious clockwork to save the phenomena. These wheels were thought to be somehow connected with the eight crystal spheres of medieval cosmology, which were kept in motion by a hierarchy of angels, but any pretense to regard them as a physically workable model had to be abandoned. The situation was summed up in a famous remark by Alfonso X of Castile, called the Wise, when he was initiated into the Ptolemaic system: "If the Lord Almighty had consulted me before embarking on the Creation, I should have recommended something simpler."

Copernicus upset the cosmic hierarchy by placing the sun in its center, but his universe was still cluttered (in Milton's words) "with centric and eccentric scribbled o'er, Cycle and epicycle, orb in orb." It was Kepler who, by banishing epicycles and eccentrics "to the lumber-room" (as he wrote), finally demolished the very scaffolding, as it were, on which the medieval universe rested and replaced its hierarchy of spirit forces with the interplay of physical forces. The tortuous way in which he achieved this may serve as a cautionary tale to scientists and philosophers and represents a significant episode in the history of thought.

Mysticism and empiricism. In Kepler all the contradictions of his age seem to have become incarnate—the age of transition from the medieval to the "new philosophy," as the scientific revolution was called by its founders. One half of his divided personality belonged to the past; he was a mystic, given to theological speculation, astrology, and number lore. However, he was also an empiricist with a scrupulous respect for observational data, who unhesitatingly threw out his earlier theory of planetary motions, the product of five years of dogged labor, because certain observed positions of Mars deviated from those that the theory demanded by a paltry eight-minute arc. He later wrote that Ptolemy and Copernicus had been able to shrug away such minor blemishes in their theories because their observations were accurate only within a margin of ten minutes, anyway, but those who, "by divine kindness," were in possession of the accurate observations of Tycho could no longer do so. "If I had believed that we could

ignore those eight minutes," he wrote in the *Astronomia Nova* (II, Ch. 19), "I would have patched up my hypothesis accordingly. But since it was not permissible to ignore them, those eight minutes point the road to a complete reformation of astronomy."

This newfound respect for hard, obstinate facts was to transform what used to be called "natural philosophy" into the "exact" (or "experimental") sciences and to determine, to a large extent, the climate of European thought during the next three centuries. It provided Kepler with the necessary discipline and put a restraint on his exuberant fantasy, but the primary motivation of his researches was mysticism of a Pythagorean brand. Throughout his life he was obsessed by certain mystic convictions, each of which had the power of an *idée fixe*. The first was the belief that the solar system was patterned on the perfect, or "Pythagorean," solids (Saturn's orbit circumscribed a cube into which was inscribed the orbit of Jupiter; into this was inscribed the tetrahedron that circumscribed the orbit of Mars; and so on down to the octahedron inscribed into the orbit of Mercury). The second was the equally Pythagorean belief that the planetary motions were governed by musical harmonies (the book containing the third law is called *Harmonice Mundi*). Fortunately, both lent themselves to mathematical juggling almost ad lib, until they fitted the data. Far from interfering with his reasoning powers, these irrational obsessions were harnessed to his rational pursuits and provided the drive for his tireless labors. From a subjective point of view, Kepler's fundamental discoveries were in fact merely by-products of his chimerical quest. Toward the end of his life he proudly mentioned in retrospect some of his minor achievements, but there is no mention whatsoever of his epoch-making first and second laws.

Emergence of the concept of force. The apparent paradox of a mystically inspired prejudice acting as a spur to scientific achievement is most clearly exemplified in the circumstances that led Kepler to introduce into astronomy the concept of physical forces. As has already been stated, he started his career as a student of theology (at the Lutheran University of Tübingen). The reason the concept of a heliocentric universe attracted the young theologian was later stated by him repeatedly. Thus, in the "Preface to the Reader" of his *Mysterium Cosmographicum* he explained that he had often defended the opinions of Copernicus in the discussions of the candidates at the seminary and had also written "a careful disputation on the first motion which consists in the rotation of the earth around the sun *for physical, or if you prefer, metaphysical reasons*." (The last phrase is emphasized because it is repeated verbatim in various passages in Kepler's works.)

He then proceeded to explain the nature of these "metaphysical reasons." They were originally based on a supposed analogy between the stationary sun, the stars, and interstellar space, on the one hand, and God the Father, the Son, and the Holy Ghost, on the other. In his first book the young Kepler promised the reader to pursue this analogy in his future cosmographical work; 25 years later, when he was over 50, he reaffirmed his belief in it. "It is by no means permissible to treat this analogy as an empty comparison; it must be considered by its Platonic form and archetypal quality as one of the primary causes" (*Mysterium Cosmographicum*, note to 2d ed.).

He stuck to this belief to the end of his life, as he stuck to the Pythagorean solids and the harmony of the spheres. But gradually his cherished analogy underwent a significant change. The fixed stars were replaced by the moving stars—the planets. The sun in the center of the planets, "himself at rest and yet the source of motion," continued to represent God the Father, and "even as the Father creates through the Holy Ghost" so the sun "distributes his motive force through a medium which contains the moving bodies" (letter to Maestlin, March 10, 1595).

Thus, the Holy Ghost no longer merely fills the space between the motionless sun and the fixed stars. It has become an active agent, a *vis motrix* that drives the planets. Nobody before had suspected the existence of such a force emanating from the sun. Astronomy had been concerned not with the causes of the heavenly motions but with their description. The passages just quoted are the first intimation of the forthcoming synthesis of cosmology and physics. Once he conceived the idea, derived from his analogy, that the sun was the source of the power that makes the planets go round, Kepler hit upon a question no one else had asked before him: why do the planets closer to the sun go round faster than those farther away? His first answer to it, in the *Mysterium Cosmographicum*, was that there exists only one "moving soul" in the center of all the orbits—i.e., the sun—which drives the planets "the more vigorously" the closer they are, but by the time it reaches the outer planets the force is quasi exhausted "because of the long distance and the weakening of the force which it entails."

Twenty-five years later, in the notes to the second edition, he commented that if we substitute for the word "soul" the word "force," "then we get just the principle which underlies my physics of the skies." He continued to explain that he had once firmly believed the motive force was a soul; yet as he reflected that the force diminishes in proportion to distance, just as light diminishes in proportion to distance, he came to the conclusion "that this force must be something substantial—'substantial' not in the literal sense but . . . in the same manner as we say that light is something substantial, meaning by this an unsubstantial entity emanating from a substantial body."

The 25 years that separate these two quotations mark the transition from *anima motrix* to *vis motrix*, from a universe animated by purposeful intelligences to one moved by inanimate, "blind" forces devoid of purpose. For the rest of his life Kepler struggled with this new concept emerging from the womb of animism (its very name, *virtus*, or *vis*, betrays its origin) without ever coming to terms with it. At first he was not aware of the difficulties inherent in it. In a letter to a friend, which he wrote when the *Astronomia Nova* was nearing completion, he outlined his program:

My aim is to show that the heavenly machine is not a kind of divine, live being, but a kind of clockwork (and he who believes that a clock has a soul, attributes the maker's glory to the work), insofar as nearly all the manifold motions are caused by a most simple, magnetic, and material force, just as all motions of the clock are caused by a simple weight. And I also show how these physical causes are to be given numerical and geometrical expression. (Letter to Herwart, February 10, 1605)

Kepler had defined the essence of the scientific revolution. But it turned out to be easier to talk about a "most simple, magnetic, material force" than to form a concrete idea of its working. Kepler's efforts to visualize the nature of the "moving force" emanating from the sun are not only of exceptional interest from the historian's point of view; they also illuminate the philosophical difficulties that were inherent in the concept of "force" from its very beginning. Since no English translation of the *Astronomia Nova* was published by the time this article was written, a few quotations may be found in order. First, Kepler compared the "moving force" of the sun with the light emitted by it:

Though the light of the sun cannot itself be the moving force . . . it may perhaps represent a kind of vehicle, or tool, that the moving force uses. But the following considerations seem to contradict this. First, the light is arrested in regions that lie in shade. If, then, the moving force were to use light as a vehicle, darkness would bring the planets to a standstill. . . .

This kind of force, just like the kind of force that is light, . . . can be regarded not as something that expands into the space between its source and the movable body but as something that the movable body receives out of the space it occupies. . . . It is propagated through the universe . . . but it is nowhere received except where there is a movable body, such as a planet. The answer to this is: although the moving force has no substance, it is aimed at substance, i.e., at the planet-body to be moved. . . .

Who, I ask, will pretend that light has substance? Yet nevertheless it acts and is acted upon in space, it is refracted and reflected, and it has quality, so that it may be dense or sparse and can be regarded as a plane where it is received by something capable of being lit up. For, as I said in my *Optics*, the same thing applies to light as to our moving force: it has no present existence in the space between the source and the object it lights up, although it has passed through that space in the past; it "is" not, it "was," so to speak. (*Astronomia Nova*, III, Ch. 33)

Thus, Kepler's gropings brought him closer to the modern concept of the field than to the Newtonian concept of force, and the modern scientist grappling with the paradoxes of quantum theory will find here an echo of his own perplexities. This may be the reason Kepler, having hit on the concept of universal gravity, subsequently discarded it—as Galileo and Descartes were to discard it.

Gravity and animism. The most precise pre-Newtonian formulations of gravity are to be found in the Preface to the *Astronomia Nova*. Kepler started by refuting the Aristotelian doctrine according to which all "earthy" matter is heavy because it is its nature to strive toward the center of the world—that is, the earth. But all "fiery" matter strives by its nature toward the periphery of the universe and is therefore light. Kepler explained that there is no such thing as lightness, but, rather, the

> matter that is less dense, either by nature or through heat, is relatively lighter . . . and therefore less attracted [to the earth] than heavier matter. . . . Supposing the earth *were* in the center of the world, heavy bodies would be attracted to it, not because it is in the center, but because it is a material body. It follows that regardless of where we place the earth, heavenly bodies will always seek it. . . .

> Gravity is the mutual bodily tendency between cognate [i.e., material] bodies toward unity or contact (of which kind the magnetic force also is), so that the earth draws a stone much more than the stone draws the earth. . . .

> If the earth and the moon were not kept in their respective orbits by a spiritual or some equivalent force, the earth would ascend toward the moon 1/54 of the distance, and the moon would descend the remaining 53 parts of the interval, and thus they would unite. But this calculation presupposes that both bodies are of the same density.

> If the earth ceased to attract the waters of the sea, the seas would rise and flow into the moon. . . .

> If the attractive force of the moon reaches down to the earth, it follows that the attractive force of the earth, all the more, extends to the moon and even farther. . . .

> If two stones were placed anywhere in space near to each other, and outside the reach of force of a third cognate body, then they would come together, after the manner of magnetic bodies, at an intermediate point, each approaching the other in proportion to the other's mass.

In the same passage is to be found the first approximation to a correct theory of the tides, which Kepler explained as "a motion of the waters toward the regions where the moon stands in the zenith." In a work written at the same time — "Somnium—A Dream of the Moon" (an early exercise in science fiction)—he furthermore postulated that the sun's attraction, too, influences the tides—that is, that the gravitational force of the sun reaches as far as the earth.

But here we are faced with another paradox. In the Preface to the *Astronomia Nova*, Kepler, as we have seen, had grasped the essence of gravity and even the idea that its force is proportionate to its mass; yet in the text of *Somnium*, and all subsequent works, he seems to have completely forgotten it. The force that emanates from the sun in the Keplerian universe is *not* a force of attraction but a tangential force, a kind of vortex or "raging current which tears all the planets, and perhaps all the celestial ether, from West to East."

To the question of what made Kepler drop gravity no answer is found anywhere in his profuse writings. Everything points to some unconscious psychological blockage, and we may gather hints about its nature in the writings of the other pioneers of the scientific revolution. Kepler's suggestion that the tides were caused by the moon's attraction Galileo indignantly rejected as an "occult fancy" (*Dialogue Concerning the Two Chief World Systems*). Descartes was equally repelled by the idea of a nonmechanical force acting at a distance and, like Kepler, substituted for it vortices in the ether. As for Newton, his attitude is summed up in his famous third letter to Bentley, in which he said it is inconceivable that "inanimate brute matter" should, without some mediating material substance, act upon other bodies.

> That gravity should be innate, inherent, and essential to matter, so that one body may act upon another, at a distance through a vacuum, without the mediation of anything else, by and through which their action and force may be conveyed from one to another, is to me so great an absurdity, that I believe no man who has in philosophical matters a competent faculty of thinking, can ever fall into it.

Kepler, Galileo, and Descartes did not fall into the philosophical abyss; their thinking was much too "modern"—that is, mechanistic—for that. The notion of a "force" that acts without an intermediary agent and pulls at immense stellar objects with ubiquitous ghost fingers appeared to them mystical and unscientific, a lapse into that Aristotelian animism from which they had just broken loose. Universal gravity, *gravitatio mundi*, smacked of the *anima mundi* of the ancients. Newton overcame the obstacle and made the concept of gravity respectable by invoking a ubiquitous ether, whose attributes were equally paradoxical, and by refusing to speculate on the manner in which gravity worked (his *hypothesis non fingo* refers to this problem, and to this problem only, though it is often quoted out of context). But above all, he provided a precise mathematical formula for the mysterious agency to which gravity referred. That formula Newton deduced from the laws of Kepler, who had intuitively glimpsed universal gravity and shied away from it. In such crooked ways does the tree of science grow.

Synthesis of astronomy and physics. In the Aristotelian cosmos, physical forces operated only among the four elements in the sublunary sphere; the motions of the celestial bodies, made of a fifth element, were due to spiritual agencies and governed by the demands of geometrical perfection. Kepler and Galileo broke down this dualism by postulating that physical causality permeates the entire universe. Kepler's "physics of the sky" we know to have been all wrong. He had no notion of inertial momentum, and he had dropped gravity. In Kepler's universe the sun exerted a tangential force (diminishing in direct ratio with increasing distance), which the "lazy" planets resisted, and the eccentricity of the orbits was accounted for by magnetic forces. (Since the planets' magnetic poles always pointed in the same direction, they would be drawn closer to the sun in the aphelion and repelled in the perihelion).

But though the model was wrong in every detail, his basic assumption, that there were several antagonistic forces acting on the planets, guided him in the right direction. A single force, as previously assumed—the Prime Mover and the allied hierarchy of angels—would never produce elliptical orbits and periodic changes of velocity. These could only be the result of some tug of war going on in the sky, and this dynamic concept, supported by a series of wild *ad hoc* hypotheses, led him in the end, after countless detours, to his three laws.

Kepler's determination of the orbit of Mars became the unifying link between two hitherto separate universes of discourse, celestial geometry and earthly physics. His was the first serious attempt to explain the mechanism of the solar system in terms of physical forces. Once the example was set, astronomy and physics could never again be divorced.

Works by Kepler

Joannis Kepleri Astronomi Opera Omnia, C. Frisch, ed., 8 vols. Frankfurt and Erlangen, 1858–1871.
Johannes Kepler, Gesammelte Werke, W. van Dyck, Max Caspar, and Franz Hammer, eds. Munich, 1938——.
"Somnium, Sive Astronomia Lunaris"—("Somnium—A Dream of the Moon"), translated by Patricia Frueh Kirkwood, in John Lear, *Kepler's Dream*. Berkeley, 1965.

Works on Kepler

Caspar, Max, *Johannes Kepler*. Stuttgart, 1948. Translated by C. D. Hellman. New York, 1962 (paperbound).
Koestler, A., *The Sleepwalkers*. New York and London, 1959.
Koestler, A., "Kepler and the Psychology of Discovery," in Marjorie Grene, ed., *The Logic of Personal Knowledge, Essays Presented to Michael Polanyi*. London, 1961.

A. KOESTLER

KEYNES, JOHN MAYNARD (1883–1946), English economist, the son of a distinguished Cambridge logician and economist, was one of the most brilliant and influential men of the twentieth century. His role as the architect and chief negotiator of Britain's external economic policies in two world wars was only one side of his public life. During his own lifetime, his economic views, contained primarily in two great works, *A Treatise on Money* (London, 1930) and *The General Theory of Employment, Interest and Money* (London, 1936), revolutionized the economic practice, and to a lesser extent, the economic theory, of Western governments.

Keynes wrote only one philosophical work, *A Treatise on Probability* (London, 1921), but it is a philosophical classic. The following account of the book's leading ideas adheres to its own main divisions.

Philosophy of probability. Keynes's philosophy of probability is contained chiefly in Parts I and II. For Keynes, only a proposition can be probable or improbable. A proposition has probability only in relation to some other proposition(s) taken as premise(s). Hence a proposition may have different probabilities on different premises. Nevertheless, the probability that p does have, given q (which Keynes writes as p/q, is perfectly objective. Some probabilities are known to us indirectly—for example, as a result of applying the theorems of the probability calculus; but first, of course, *some* probabilities must be known directly. Where a probability is known to us directly, it is known to us in the way that the validity of a syllogistic argument is

known, whatever that way is. The probability relation is not an empirical one. If it is true that $p/q > r/s$, or that $p/q > 1/3$, or that $r/s = 1/2$, then it is true a priori, and not in virtue of any matter of fact. In particular, the truth of such statements is independent of the factual truth of p, q, r, and s. Finally, $p/q = 0$ if p is inconsistent with q, and $p/q = 1$ if q entails p.

Keynes's fundamental thesis, of which the above statements are developments, is that there are inferences in which the premises do not entail the conclusion but are nevertheless, just by themselves, *objectively* more or less good reason for believing it. This thesis seems to require the existence of different *degrees* of implication. Such degrees are Keynes's probabilities. Thus, for Keynes the study of probability coincides exactly with the study of inference, demonstrative and nondemonstrative. He developed, though somewhat obscurely, a general theory of inference in Chapter X. However, from the axioms and definitions from which he derived the accepted theorems of the probability calculus, he also derived many theorems of demonstrative inference, for example, "if $a/h = 0$ then $ab/h = 0$."

It would be hard to exaggerate the importance of Keynes's fundamental thesis. Classical probability theory of the eighteenth and nineteenth centuries must have presupposed some such thesis. Recent theory on degrees of confirmation presupposes it. To Keynes, as to Laplace and Carnap, this thesis appeared to be necessary as a means of avoiding skepticism about induction. But Hume would presumably have rejected it outright, and it is by no means free from difficulty.

There are two negative theses which distinguish Keynes's philosophy of probability from most earlier or later formulations. One is that probabilities simply do not have a numerical value, except in certain exceptional circumstances, and never in normal inductive contexts. The other is that there are noncomparable probabilities, that is, probabilities that are neither equal to nor greater nor less than one another. For obvious reasons, these theses have contributed to the neglect of Keynes by statistical writers.

Induction. In Part III, Keynes discussed induction. The most important arguments of those which are rational but not conclusive belong to the class of inductions whose conclusions are universal generalizations and whose premises are about instances of the generalization.

Keynes, like Mill, regarded all scientific induction as essentially eliminative induction. His account of the circumstances in which we regard an inductive argument as strong is, in essentials (although not otherwise), a development in detail of Mill's Method of Agreement.

The mere number of confirmations of a hypothesis in itself is of no evidential weight. The important thing is the variety of the instances, in respects other than those which constitute the instances' confirming ones. We regard inductions as being of greatest weight when the evidence approaches the ideal case in which the confirming instances are known to be not all alike in every respect. Various ways in which our evidence can fall short of this ideal are discussed in Chapter XIX. Keynes thought that the extent to which the evidence, by its variety, eliminates alternative hypotheses is the only important factor—not only when our hypothesis is empirical, but when it is, for instance, mathematical or metaphysical.

Keynes very clearly distinguished between the task of analyzing those inductive arguments which we regard as strong and the task of justifying the fact that we regard them as strong.

The latter task, he appears to have assumed, requires a proof of the proposition that relative to instantial evidence, the probability of a universal hypothesis can approach certainty as a limit. It will do so, he purported to prove, if (and one must assume only if) the probability of the instantial evidence supposing the hypothesis to be false can be made small in comparison with the probability of the hypothesis prior to the instantial evidence (its "a priori" probability). To reduce the former probability is the object of "varying the circumstances." The required disparity between the two probabilities will exist, Keynes argued, if (and one must assume only if), *inter alia*, the hypothesis has finite a priori probability. This requires that it be a member of a finite disjunction of exhaustive alternatives.

When the universal hypothesis is an empirical one, this amounts to the assumption that there exists in nature the materials for only a finite number of generalizations linking empirical properties. In other words, the number of the logically independent properties of empirical objects, which a priori might have been constantly conjoined, is finite. This is the famous Principle of Limited Independent Variety (Chapter XX). Hence, the fact that the probability of any empirical universal generalization should approach certainty as a limit requires the assumption of this principle. Or rather, Keynes thought, all that is required for this principle is finite a priori probability, since experience can and does noncircularly support the principle, provided it does have this initial probability.

It does so, Keynes appears to have argued, because we have a *direct* apprehension of the truth of the principle, just as, he thought, we have an apprehension (not independent of experience, yet not inductively inferred) of the truth of the statement, "Color cannot exist without extension."

Statistical inference. The main subject of Part V is those inductive inferences whose premises include a statement of the frequency of a property B in an observed series of A's, and whose conclusions concern B's frequency in the population of A's as a whole, or in a further series of A's, or the probability of the next A being a B.

The theory of statistical inference had been dominated by two methods of making such inferences, both due to Laplace. One is the "rule of succession," according to which the probability of the next A being B is

$$\frac{m+1}{m+n+2}$$

if m out of $m+n$ observed A's have been B. The other is the "inversion" of the great-numbers theorem of Bernoulli. This theorem permits us—under an important restriction—to infer what frequency of B is most probable among observed A's, given its frequency among A's as a whole. Laplace purported to supply a theorem which would guide our inferences in the reverse, inductive direction, i.e., from observed A's to A's as a whole.

Keynes regarded both methods as "mathematical charlatanry." His many criticisms of them cannot be weighed here. Apart from these criticisms, however, he considered it absurd to imagine that we could have exact measures of the probability of statistical conclusions. Statistical induction is subject to all the difficulties that beset inductions with universal conclusions, and to others beside. Moreover, the only evidence taken into account by all methods like Laplace's is numerical. The vital requirement of variety in the instances is neglected. In statistical contexts, the variety of the positive "instances" takes the form of the stability of the observed frequency when the observed series is considered as divided into subseries according to many different principles of division.

Keynes did think that, under a number of extremely stringent conditions, an inversion of Bernoulli's theorem is legitimate. But even to license these inductive inferences, as Keynes interpreted them, the Principle of Limited Independent Variety is required.

Bibliography

Keynes's only philosophical work is *A Treatise on Probability* (London, 1921). On Keynes's life, see R. F. Harrod, *The Life of John Maynard Keynes* (London, 1951).

Valuable critical material on Keynes's theories of probability and induction may be found in the following: Jean Nicod, *Foundations of Geometry and Induction* (London, 1930); F. P. Ramsey, *Foundations of Mathematics* (London, 1931); G. H. von Wright, *The Logical Problem of Induction* (Helsingfors, 1941); G. H. von Wright, *A Treatise on Induction and Probability* (London, 1951); Bertrand Russell, *Human Knowledge, Its Scope and Limits* (London, 1948); and Arthur Pap, *An Introduction to the Philosophy of Science* (New York, 1962). Joan Robinson, *Economic Philosophy* (London, 1962), Ch. 4, is a highly readable brief account of Keynes's place in economic theory.

For another facet of Keynes's many-sided career, see *Essays and Sketches in Biography* (New York, 1956), a varied collection of Keynes's writings on economists, politicians, acquaintances, and himself.

D. STOVE

KEYSERLING, HERMANN ALEXANDER, GRAF VON (1880–1946), German philosopher of life and man, was born in Könno, Estonia. He studied geology and other natural sciences at the universities of Dorpat, Geneva, Heidelberg, and Vienna. In 1902 Keyserling received his doctorate at Vienna where, under the influence of Houston Stewart Chamberlain, he turned to philosophy. He spent the next few years in Paris, interrupting his stay, however, by several trips to England. In 1908, after two years in Berlin, Keyserling returned to Estonia to take over his ancestral estate at Rayküll. He traveled frequently and in 1911 and 1912 took a trip around the world. The loss of his property after the Russian Revolution led to Keyserling's immigration to Germany. In 1920 he founded the School of Wisdom in Darmstadt. Further journeys to North and South America followed. The last years of his life were spent in the Austrian Tyrol.

Keyserling was not a systematic philosopher; instead, he presented brilliant observations, suggestive generalizations, and in vague outline, an image of man. To measure his work by traditional philosophy is to reject his view of the philosophic enterprise. Keyserling wanted to replace the traditional philosopher with the sage, to replace critical examination with immediate appreciation, and to replace the university with his School of Wisdom. He held that, instead of criticizing another position, one should try to empathize with it. His own *Travel Diary* furnishes an example of this approach. Keyserling reduced philosophy to an exercise with the thoughts of other ages and cultures in the hope that such play would lead the reader to an awareness of the spirit that underlies these thoughts. Truth, in the sense of adequacy to fact, was of little concern to Keyserling; intuitive appreciation alone counted. Keyserling used the word "polyphonic" to distinguish his thinking from "homophonic," traditional philosophy. Polyphonic thinking has no definite point of view and presents no definite theses. It is essentially rootless, an exercise with possibilities, designed to reveal a meaning that escapes all philosophic systems.

Keyserling's approach to philosophy bears witness to his understanding of man. Following Schopenhauer, Nietzsche, Dilthey, Bergson, and Eastern thought, he asserted the rights of life in the face of the modern overemphasis on the intellect. His insistence on the protean nature of man anticipated the existentialists' claim that existence precedes essence. Keyserling asked us to intuit, amid cultural and natural diversity, the spirit that finds only inadequate expression in each definite form. Those matters that are truly important cannot be thought clearly but can only be intuited. Critical philosophy was renounced; the philosopher had become an artist. The success of Keyserling's works, particularly of the *Travel Diary*, was symptomatic of the spiritual situation following World War I. Keyserling lent expression to the feeling that many of the traditional answers had become meaningless. But instead of deploring this spiritual homelessness, Keyserling made it a necessary condition of the full life: ideally, man is a traveler.

Works by Keyserling

Die Gesammelten Werke. Darmstadt, 1956——.
Unsterblichkeit. Munich, 1907. Translated as *Immortality.* London, 1938.
Das Reisetagebuch eines Philosophen, 2 vols. Darmstadt, 1919. Translated as *The Travel Diary of a Philosopher,* 2 vols. New York, 1925.
Schöpferische Erkenntnis. Darmstadt, 1922. Translated as *Creative Understanding.* New York, 1929.
Wiedergeburt. Darmstadt, 1927. Translated as *The Recovery of Truth.* New York, 1929.
Das Buch vom Ursprung. Baden-Baden, 1947.
Reise durch die Zeit. Vaduz, Liechtenstein, 1948.
Kritik des Denkens. Innsbruck, 1948.

Works on Keyserling

Feldkeller, Paul, *Graf Keyserlings Erkenntnisweg zum Übersinnlichen.* Darmstadt, 1922.
Noack, Hermann, "Sinn und Geist." *Zeitschrift für philosophische Forschung* (1953), 592–597.
Parks, Mercedes G., *Introduction to Keyserling.* London, 1934.
Röhr, Rudolf, *Graf Keyserlings magische Geschichtsphilosophie.* Leipzig, 1939.

KARSTEN HARRIES

KHOMYAKOV, ALEKSEI STEPANOVICH (1804–1860),

the most versatile of the early Moscow Slavophiles, was born in Moscow of well-to-do Russian gentry and died on the family estate, Ivanovskoe, in the guberniya of Riazan. He early acquired a command of German, French, and English, and also read Latin, Greek, and Sanskrit. During the 1820s he traveled abroad, studied mathematics, and met Ivan Kireevsky, later his collaborator in establishing the Slavophile circle. In this informal group, which included Yuri Samarin, Konstantin Aksakov, and several others, Khomyakov discoursed on religion, theology, and, to a lesser extent, philosophy. Of his philosophical writings two late, unfinished letters to Samarin are especially valuable.

A polemicist, Khomyakov frequently formulated his thoughts as responses to challenges, expressing opposition to Western thought rather than positive Slavophile tenets. The heart of his theology is the doctrine of *sobornost'* (from *sobirat'*, "to come together"), which he considered embodied in the church as a divinely inspired fellowship. Samarin defined *sobornost'* as freedom, mutual love, and organic unity, and stated that for Khomyakov the church was not an institution but a living organism of truth and love. The contrasting individualism, legalism, formalism, and rationalism of Western thought were attributed to Roman paganism, which Khomyakov held had vitiated first Catholicism, then Protestantism and Western philosophy.

Kohmyakov acquired his philosophical training through reading and discussions. Like many of his generation, he experienced the extreme interest in Hegel that has left an enduring impression upon Russian intellectual life. In the Moscow salons he clashed with Alexander Herzen over Hegel and German philosophy. Although he never accepted any Western system, Khomyakov nevertheless esteemed Kant, Schelling, and Hegel, and expressed gratitude for the training and discipline he received from them. He praised "immortal Kant" as the founder of the German school, and Hegel, whom he considered the greatest rationalist, as its consummator. However, Kant's system was intolerable to him, and Hegel had the crucial fault of accepting "the laws of understanding instead of the law of the all-embracing spirit." The defect of the whole German school was its one-sided rationalism, which, in Khomyakov's view, was rooted in German culture and had, in the Reformation, "destroyed the inner calmness of the human spirit" by gradually transferring to philosophy the satisfying of requirements to which faith had responded earlier. Kant was, therefore, the "direct and necessary continuator of Luther." Beyond German idealism and rationalism lay the "infirm hybrid" of materialism.

Schelling, considered more sympathetically by Khomyakov, was the "re-creator of the integrity of the spirit," but in his later thought reason as "elucidated self-consciousness" had usurped the place of reason in its totality, relegating all other principles of cognition to the realm of abstractedness. Khomyakov thus was not a Schellingian, despite his preference for certain aspects of Schelling's thought. Without denying reason, which he and Kireevsky believed had become one-sided and all-important in the West, he professed faith in the integrity of the spirit (*tsel'nost' dukha*). Partly inspired by romanticism but chiefly derived from the Orthodox Church Fathers, this doctrine, never fully elaborated, was Kireevsky's contribution to Slavophilism. It was a concept of harmonious faith and reason. Khomyakov concurred in Kireevsky's belief that the inspiration for a philosophy more nearly complete and more profound than any Western system could be found in the Orthodox faith.

In Khomyakov's thought, faith was accorded primacy over reason, and reason was seen as striving to reach the level of sympathetic agreement with faith. The implications of these concepts were particularly important for Khomyakov's epistemology. Truth was not accessible to any one of man's faculties of cognition (reason, sentiment, aesthetic sense) alone, but to all of them together, illuminated in "the depths of man's soul" by faith.

Zenkovsky has seen transcendentalism in Khomyakov's thought and has suggested that he defended ontologism by the "anti-ontological proposition of transcendentalism." Florovsky has found elements of naturalism; Masaryk has found pantheism; and Chizhevsky, an appreciation for "feeling and will." These diverse interpretations testify to the complex cross currents in which Khomyakov lived, but do not invalidate the importance of the doctrine that he advanced as an integral part of his Slavophile ideology.

Works by Khomyakov

Polnoe Sobranie Sochinenii ("Complete Works"), 8 vols., 4th ed. Moscow, 1911.

Works on Khomyakov

Chizhevsky, D. I., *Gegel v Rossi*. Paris, 1939. Pp. 164–189.

Christoff, P. K., *An Introduction to Nineteenth-Century Russian Slavophilism. A Study in Ideas.* The Hague, 1961. Vol. I, *A. S. Xomjakov.*

Florovsky, G. V., *Puti Russkago Bogosloviia.* Paris, 1937. Pp. 270–281.

Gratieux, A., *A. S. Khomiakov et le mouvement slavophile*, 2 vols. Paris, 1939.

Lossky, N. O., *History of Russian Philosophy.* New York, 1951. Pp. 29–41.

Masaryk, T. G., *Russland und Europa*, 2 vols. Jena, 1913. Translated by Eden and Cedar Paul as *The Spirit of Russia*, 2 vols. London, 1919. Vol. I, pp. 254–266.

Riasanovsky, N. V., *Russia and the West in the Teaching of the Slavophiles.* Cambridge, Mass., 1952.

Zavitnevich, V. Z., *Aleksei Stepanovich Khomiakov*, 2 vols. Kiev, 1902–1913.

Zenkovsky, V. V., *Istoriia Russkoi Filosofii*, 2 vols. Paris, 1948–1950. Translated by G. L. Kline as *A History of Russian Philosophy.* London and New York, 1953. Pp. 180–205.

PETER K. CHRISTOFF

KIERKEGAARD, SØREN AABYE (1813–1855), Danish philosopher and religious thinker, frequently considered the first important existentialist, was the youngest son of Mikaël Pederson Kierkegaard and Anne Sørensdatter Lund, born when his father was 56 years old and his mother was 44. His early childhood was spent in the close company of his father, who insisted on high standards of performance in Latin and Greek, inculcated an anxiety-ridden pietist devotion of a deeply emotional kind, and awakened his son's imagination by continually acting out stories and scenes. Kierkegaard thus felt early the demand that life should be at once intellectually satisfying, dramatic, and an arena for devotion. Confronted with the Hegelian system at the University of Copenhagen, he reacted strongly against it. It could not supply what he needed—"a truth which is true *for me*, to find *the idea for*

which I can live and die" (*Journal*, Aug. 1, 1835). Nor could contemporary Danish Lutheranism provide this. He ceased to practice his religion and embarked on a life of pleasure, spending heavily on food, drink, and clothes. The melancholy which originated in his childhood continued to haunt him, however, and was increased by his father's confiding in him his own sense of guilt for having somehow sinned deeply against God. For Kierkegaard, the question of how a man can be rescued from despair was consequently intensified. He resolved to return to his studies and become a pastor. He finished his thesis *On the Concept of Irony* (1841) and preached his first sermon. He became engaged to the 17-year-old Regine Olsen. But as he became aware of the uniqueness of the vocation which he felt within himself, he found himself unable either to share his life with anyone else or to live out the conventional role of a Lutheran pastor. For him, breaking off his engagement was a decisive step in implementing his vocation. (This cosmic view of the breach does not appear to have been shared by his young fiancée, whose natural hurt pride and rejected affection led to her marriage to Fritz Schlegel, afterwards governor of the Danish West Indies.) From then on Kierkegaard lived a withdrawn life as an author, although he did involve himself in two major public controversies. The first followed his denunciation of the low standards of the popular Copenhagen satirical paper *The Corsair. The Corsair* in turn caricatured Kierkegaard unmercifully. The second sprang from his contempt for the established Danish Lutheran church, and especially for its primate, Bishop Mynster, who died in early 1854. When Mynster's about-to-be-appointed successor, Professor Hans Martensen, declared that Mynster had been "a witness to the truth," Kierkegaard delivered a series of bitter attacks on the church in the name of the incompatibility he saw between established ecclesiastical conformism and the inward and personal character of Christian faith. He died shortly after refusing to receive the sacrament from a pastor. "Pastors are royal officials; royal officials have nothing to do with Christianity."

Kierkegaard's biography is necessarily more relevant to his thought than is the case with most philosophers, for he himself saw philosophical enquiry neither as the construction of systems nor as the analysis of concepts, but as the expression of an individual existence. The epitaph which he composed for himself was simply, "That individual." From his own point of view, any verdict on his thought can only be the expression of the critic's own existence, not a critical assessment which could stand or fall according to some objective, impersonal standard. Hence all attempts at an objective evaluation of his thought were condemned by him in advance. He predicted and feared that he would fall into the hands of the professors. Moreover, the initial difficulty created by Kierkegaard's subjectivism is compounded by his style and manner of composition. Although he attacked Hegel, he inherited a large part of Hegel's vocabulary. Passages of great and glittering brilliance tend to alternate with paragraphs of turgid jargon. Both types of writing often prove inimical to clarity of expression. A great many of his books were written for highly specific purposes, and there is no clear thread of development in them. One device of Kierkegaard's must be given special mention: he issued several of his books under pseudonyms and used different pseudonyms so that he could, under one name, ostensibly attack his own work already published under some other name. His reason for doing this was precisely to avoid giving the appearance of attempting to construct a single, consistent, systematic edifice of thought. Systematic thought, especially the Hegelian system, was one of his principal targets.

The system, the individual, and choice. In Hegel's philosophical system, or rather in his successive construction of systems, the linked development of freedom and of reason is a logical one. Out of the most basic and abstract of concepts, Being and Nothing, there is developed first the concept of Becoming and the various phases of Becoming in which the Absolute Idea realizes itself during the course of human history. Each phase of history is the expression of a conceptual scheme, in which the gradual articulation of the concepts leads to a realization of their inadequacies and contradictions, so that the scheme is replaced by another higher and more adequate one, until finally Absolute Knowledge emerges and the whole historical process is comprehended as a single logical unfolding. It is this comprehension itself that is the culmination of the process, and this point was effectively reached for Hegel in his own philosophy. Thus, in *The Science of Logic* he was able to write that he was setting out not merely his own thoughts, but the thoughts of God—the idea of God being simply an anticipation of the Hegelian conception of the Absolute.

In the Hegelian view, both moral and religious development are simply phases in this total process. In *The Phenomenology of Mind,* Hegel described the moral individualism of the eighteenth century, for example, in terms of a logical progress from the hedonistic project of a universal pursuit of private pleasure, through the romantic idealization of "the noble soul," to the Kantian scheme of duty and the categorical imperative, trying to show how each was brought into being by the contradiction developed by its predecessor. In terms of the Hegelian view, an individual is essentially a representative of his age. His personal and religious views must give expression to his role in the total moral and religious development of mankind—a role which is imposed upon him by his place in the historical scheme. He can at best express, but not transcend, his age.

For Kierkegaard, Hegel dissolved the concreteness of individual existence into abstractions characteristic of the realm of concepts. Any particular conceptual scheme represents not an actuality but a possibility. Whether a given individual realizes this possibility, and so endows it with existence, depends upon the individual and not upon the concepts. What the individual does depends not upon what he understands, but upon what he wills. Kierkegaard invokes both Aristotle and Kant in support of his contention that Hegel illegitimately assimilated concepts to individual existence; he praises in particular the manner of Kant's refutation of the Ontological Argument. But Kierkegaard, in his doctrine of the primacy of the will is, in fact, more reminiscent of Tertullian or Pascal.

Kierkegaard buttressed his doctrine of the will with his view of the ultimacy of undetermined choice. He maintained that the individual constitutes himself as the individual he is through his choice of one mode of existence rather than another. Christianity is not a phase in the total development of man's religious and moral ideas; it is a matter of choosing to accept or to reject God's Word. But choice is not restricted to this supreme decision; it is the core of all human existence. The Hegelian view that human existence develops logically within and through conceptual schemes is not merely an intellectual error. It is an attempt to disguise the true facts, to cast off the responsibility for choice, and to find an alibi for one's choices. Moreover, speculative system building falsifies human existence in another way, for it suggests that although those who lived prior to the construction of the system may have had to make do with a partial and inadequate view of reality, the arrival of the final system provides an absolute viewpoint. But according to Kierkegaard, such a viewpoint must be an illusion. Human existence is irremediably finite; its standpoint is incorrigibly partial and limited. To suppose otherwise is to yield to a temptation to pride; it is to attempt to put oneself in the place of God.

This conclusion is only a special case of Kierkegaard's general doctrine that his intellectual opponents are guilty fundamentally not of fallacies and mistakes, but of moral inadequacy. That Kierkegaard should have thought this not only reflects his unfortunate personality; it was a necessary consequence of his doctrine of choice. Another necessary consequence was his mode of authorship. On his own grounds, he cannot hope to produce pure intellectual conviction in his readers; all that he can do is to confront them with choices. Hence he should not try to present a single position. This explains Kierkegaard's method of expounding incompatible points of view in different books and using different pseudonyms for works with different standpoints. The author must conceal himself; his approach must be indirect. As an individual, he must testify to his chosen truth. Yet, as an author he cannot conceal the act of choice. From these views, it is apparent that Kierkegaard utilized a special concept of choice.

The essence of the Kierkegaardian concept of choice is that it is criterionless. On Kierkegaard's view, if criteria determine what I choose, it is not I who make the choice; hence the choice must be undetermined. Suppose, however, that I do invoke criteria in order to make my choice. Then all that has happened is that I have chosen the criteria. And if in turn I try to justify my selection of criteria by an appeal to logically cogent considerations, then I have in turn chosen the criteria in the light of which these considerations appear logically cogent. First principles at least must be chosen without the aid of criteria, simply in virtue of the fact that they are first. Thus, logical principles, or relationships between concepts, can in no sense determine a person's intellectual positions; for it is his choices that determine the authority such principles have for him. Is man then not even limited by such principles as those which enjoin consistency and prohibit contradiction? Apparently not. For even paradox challenges the intellect in such a way as to be a possible object of choice. The paradoxes which Kierkegaard has in mind at this point in his argument are those posed by the demands of ethics and religion. He is prepared to concede that in fields such as mathematics the ordinary procedures of reason are legitimate. But there are no objective standards where human existence is involved.

The aesthetic and the ethical. In *Either/Or: A Fragment of Life* (1843), the doctrine of choice is put to work in relation to a distinction between two ways of life, the ethical and the aesthetic. The aesthetic point of view is that of a sophisticated and romantic hedonism. The enemies of the aesthetic standpoint are not only pain but also, and above all, boredom. As Kierkegaard wrote of the protagonist of aestheticism in *Purify Your Hearts!*, "See him in his season of pleasure: did he not crave for one pleasure after another, variety his watchword?" The protagonist tried to realize every possibility, and no possibility furnishes him with more than a momentary actuality. "Every mood, every thought, good or bad, cheerful or sad, you pursue to its utmost limit, yet in such a way that this comes to pass *in abstracto* rather than *in concreto;* in such a way that the pursuit itself is little more than a mood. . . ." But just because boredom is always to be guarded against, so its threat is perpetual. In the end, the search for novelty leads to the threshold of despair.

By contrast, the ethical constitutes the sphere of duty, of universal rules, of unconditional demands and tasks. For the man in the ethical stage "the chief thing is, not whether one can count on one's fingers how many duties one has, but that a man has once felt the intensity of duty in such a way that the consciousness of it is for him the assurance of the eternal validity of his being" (*Either/Or*, II, p. 223). It is important to note how intensity of feeling enters into Kierkegaard's definition of the ethical stage. He thought that what his own age most notably lacked was passion; hence one must not be deceived by the Kantian overtones of his discussions of duty. Kierkegaard's categorical imperative is felt rather than reasoned. He is an heir of such romantics as the Schlegel brothers in his attitude toward feeling, just as he is the heir of Hegel in his mode of argument. Kierkegaard is a constant reminder of the fact that those who most loudly proclaim their own uniqueness are most likely to have derived their ideas from authors whom they consciously reject.

In *Either/Or* the argument between the ethical and the aesthetic is presented by two rival characters: an older man puts the case for the ethical, a younger for the aesthetic. The reader, as we should expect, is allegedly left to make his own choice. But is he? The description of the two alternatives seems heavily weighted in favor of the ethical. The difficulty is that Kierkegaard wished *both* to maintain that there could be no objective criterion for the decision between the two alternatives, *and* to show that the ethical was superior to the aesthetic. Indeed, one difference between the ethical and the aesthetic is that in the ethical stage the role of choice is acknowledged. Kierkegaard frames this criticism of the man who adheres to the aesthetic: "He has not chosen himself; like Narcissus he has fallen in love with himself. Such a situation has certainly ended not infrequently in suicide." Remarks like this suggest that in fact Kierkegaard thinks that the aesthetic fails on its own terms; but if he were to admit this, his concept of interested choice would no longer apply at this critical point. In one passage Kierkegaard asserts that if one chooses with sufficient passion, the passion will cor-

rect whatever was wrong with the choice. Here his inconsistency is explicit. According to his doctrine of choice, there can be no criterion of "correct" or "incorrect," but according to the values of his submerged romanticism, the criterion of both choice and truth is intensity of feeling.

This inconsistency is not resolved; rather it is canonized in the thesis that truth is subjectivity. On the one hand Kierkegaard wants to define truth in terms of the way in which it is apprehended; on the other he wants to define it in terms of what it is that is apprehended. When inconsistency results, he is all too apt to christen this inconsistency "paradox" and treat its appearance as the crowning glory of his argument.

Kierkegaard is not consistent, however, even in his treatment of inconsistency. For he sometimes seems to imply that if the ethical is forced to its limits, contradiction results, and one is therefore forced to pass from the ethical to the religious. "As soon as sin enters the discussion, ethics fails . . . for repentance is the supreme expression of ethics, but as such contains the most profound ethical contradiction" (*Fear and Trembling*, p. 147, footnote). What is this but Hegelianism of the purest kind?

Kierkegaard describes the transition from the ethical to the religious differently at different periods. In *Either/Or* the ethical sometimes seems to include the religious. By the time the *Concluding Unscientific Postscript* (1846) was written, the religious seems to have absorbed the ethical. In *Fear and Trembling* (1843), the passage from the ethical to the religious is even more striking than that from the aesthetic to the ethical. One of the heroes of this transition is Abraham. In demanding from Abraham the sacrifice of Isaac, God demands something that, from the standpoint of the ethical, is absolutely forbidden, a transgression of duty. Abraham must make the leap to faith, accept the absurd. He must concur in a "suspension of the ethical." At such a point the individual has to make a criterionless choice. General and universal rules cannot aid him here; it is as an individual that he has to choose. However, according to Kierkegaard, there are certain key experiences on the margins of the ethical and the religious through which one may come to censure oneself as an individual. One such experience is the despair that Kierkegaard describes in *The Sickness Unto Death*; another is the generalized fear and anxiety that is characterized in *The Concept of Dread* (1844). Despair and dread point in the same direction. The experience of each forces the individual to realize that he confronts a void and that he is, in fact, responsible for his own sick and sinful condition. In the state of despair he is brought to recognize that what he despairs of are not the contingent facts (such as the loss of a loved one) that he claims to be the objects of his despair; the individual despairs of himself, and to despair of oneself is to see oneself confronting an emptiness that cannot be filled by aesthetic pleasure or ethical rule-following. Moreover, it is in order to become conscious that one has brought oneself to this point. In analyzing despair, we recognize guilt; so too with dread. Kierkegaard contrasts the fear that has a specific and identifiable object with the dread that is objectless; or rather he identifies the fear which is a fear of nothing in particular as a fear of Nothing. (The reification of negatives into noun phrases is typically Hegelian.) In the experience of dread I become conscious of my bad will as something for which I am responsible, and yet which I did not originate. Original sin is seen as a doctrine deduced from the analysis of experience.

In these works of Kierkegaard it is plain that the existentialist philosophy of choice is in some danger of being submerged in the romantic philosophy of feeling. But the testimony of feeling serves as a propaedeutic to the encounter with Christianity.

Christianity. Kierkegaard regarded his own central task as the explanation of what is involved in being a Christian. Apart from Christianity, the only religions he discusses are those of the Greeks and the Jews, and those only as a foil to Christianity. At first sight, Kierkegaard's doctrines of choice and of truth stand in an uneasy relationship to his allegiance to Christianity. For surely Christianity has always claimed to be objectively true, independently of anyone's subjective commitment, and Kierkegaard recognized this. "Not only does it [Christian revelation] express something which man has not given to himself, but something which would never have entered any man's mind even as a wisp or an idea, or under any other name one likes to give to it" (*Journal*, 1839).

If what we believe depends on the believer's own ultimate choice of rational criteria, then surely all beliefs have an equal moment, or rather equal lack of moment, for claiming objective truth. Kierkegaard, however, tried to evade this conclusion and continued to argue both that ultimate choice is criterionless and that one choice can be more correct than another.

Unfortunately, Kierkegaard never considered the issues raised by religions other than Christianity; for it would clarify our view of his position considerably if we could know what he would have said about an account of Islam or Buddhism that was logically parallel to his account of Christianity, in that it made their claims rest on a doctrine of ultimate choice. But the choices that Kierkegaard discusses are always those that might arise for an educated Dane of the nineteenth century. The foil to Christianity is not another religion, but secular philosophy.

This particular contrast is most fully elucidated in the *Philosophical Fragments* (1844), in which Kierkegaard begins from the paradox posed by Socrates in Plato's *Meno*. How can one come to know anything? For either one already knows what one is to come to know, or one does not. But in the former case, since one already knows, one cannot come to know; and in the latter case, how can one possibly recognize what one discovers as being the object of one's quest for knowledge? Plato's answer to this paradox is that in coming to know, we do not discover truths of which we had hitherto been totally ignorant, but truths of which we were once aware (when the soul pre-existed the body), but which we had forgotten. These truths lie dormant within us, and to teach is to elicit such truths. So Socrates makes the slave boy in the *Meno* aware that he knows geometrical truths which he did not know that he knew.

Suppose, however, Kierkegaard asks, that the truth is not within us already. It will then be the case that we are strangers to the truth, to whom the truth must be brought from outside. It will follow that the moment at which we learn the truth and the teacher from whom we learn the truth will not stand in a merely accidental relationship to us. On the Socratic view, one may learn geometry from this teacher or that, but the question of the truth of a geometric theorem is independent of the question from whom we learned it. Not so, on Kierkegaard's view. There are two possible conceptions of the truth that we must choose between, and the Socratic view represents only one alternative. It is important to note that in the *Philosophical Fragments* (1844) Kierkegaard does not say, as he says elsewhere, that one view of the truth is appropriate in matters of geometrical truth, but another is appropriate in matters concerning moral and religious truth. He speaks of two alternative views of the truth, which apparently cover every kind of subject matter, although for the rest of the book he discusses only religion.

Following Kierkegaard's preferred view of the truth, if the truth is not within us, it must be brought to us by a teacher. The teacher must transform us from beings who do not know the truth to beings who are acquainted with it. It is impossible to conceive any greater transformation, and only God could bring it about. But how could God become the teacher of man? If He appeared as He is, the effect on man would be to overawe him so that he could not possibly learn what God has to teach. (Kierkegaard cites the story of the prince in the fairy tale who could not appear to the swine girl as a prince because she would not have come to love him for himself.) Thus, Kierkegaard argues that if God is to be the teacher of man, He must appear in the form of a man, and more specifically, in the form of a servant. From the standpoint of human reason, the idea that God should come as a teacher in human form is an impossible paradox which reason cannot hope to comprehend within its own categories. But according to Kierkegaard, it is in encountering this paradox that reason becomes aware of the objective character of what it encounters.

To be a Christian is thus to subordinate one's reason to the authority of a revelation that is given in paradoxical form. The Christian lives before God by faith alone. His awareness of God is always an awareness of his own infinite distance from God. Christianity initially manifests itself in outward forms, and Kierkegaard reproaches Luther for having tried to reduce Christianity to a pure inwardness—a project that has ended in its opposite, the replacement of inwardness by an ecclesiastical worldliness. Nonetheless, an inward suffering before God is the heart of Christianity.

As previously mentioned, Kierkegaard saw his own age as lacking in passion. The Greeks and the medieval monastics had true passion. The modern age lacks it, and because of this, it lacks a capacity for paradox, which is the passion of thought.

Criticisms of Kierkegaard. Kierkegaard used Friedrich Trendelenburg's exposition of Aristotle's logic to criticize Hegel. But he never took the question of the nature of contradiction seriously, and hence he never explained the difference, if any, between paradox (in his sense of the word) and mere inconsistency. But without such a clarification, the notion is fatally unclear. The lack of clarity is increased by Kierkegaard's failure at times to distinguish between philosophy, as such, and Hegelianism. Kierkegaard sometimes seems to have thought that any philosophy that claims objectivity must consist solely of tautologies (*Papirer* III, B, 177).

His doctrine of choice raises at least two fundamental questions: Are there criterionless choices? And is it by such choices that we either can or do arrive at our criteria of true belief? Actual cases of criterionless choice usually seem in some way to be special cases. Either they are trivial, random selections (as of a ticket in a lottery) or they arise from conflicts of duties in which each alternative seems equally weighted. But none of these are choices of criteria. Such choices arise precisely at the point at which we are not presented with objective criteria. How do we arrive at such criteria? They appear to be internally connected with the subject matter of the relevant beliefs and judgment. Therefore we cannot choose our ultimate criteria in mathematics or physics. But what about morals and religion? Can one choose to consider the gratuitous infliction of pain a morally neutral activity? We are strongly inclined to say that an affirmative answer would indicate that the word "morally" had not been understood. But what is certain is that Kierkegaard's fundamental positions must remain doubtful until some series of questions such as this has been systematically considered. Kierkegaard himself never tried to ask them.

Works by Kierkegaard

TEXTS

Samlede Vaerker, 2d ed., A. B. Drachmann, J. L. Heiberg, and H. O. Lange, eds., 14 vols. Copenhagen, 1920–1931.
Papirer, P. A. Heiberg, V. Kuhr, and E. Torsting, eds., 20 vols. Copenhagen, 1909–1948.

TEXTS IN ENGLISH TRANSLATION

The following listing is in order of original date of publication.
Either/Or, 2 vols. Vol. I, translated by D. F. Swenson and L. M. Swenson. Princeton, 1941. Vol. II, translated by W. Lowrie. Princeton, 1944.
Fear and Trembling, translated by R. Payne. London, 1939. Also translated by W. Lowrie. Princeton, 1941.
Repetition: An Essay in Experimental Psychology, translated by W. Lowrie. Princeton, 1941.
Philosophical Fragments: Or, A Fragment of Philosophy, translated by D. F. Swenson. Princeton, 1936.
The Concept of Dread, translated by W. Lowrie. London, 1944.
Stages on Life's Way, translated by W. Lowrie. Princeton, 1940.
Concluding Unscientific Postscript, translated by D. F. Swenson and W. Lowrie. Princeton, 1941.
The Sickness Unto Death, translated by W. Lowrie. Princeton, 1941.
The Point of View, translated by W. Lowrie. Princeton, 1941.
Training in Christianity, translated by W. Lowrie. Princeton, 1944.
Purify Your Hearts!, translated by A. S. Aldworth and W. S. Fine. London, 1937.
For Self-examination, translated by W. Lowrie. Princeton, 1941.
The Present Age, translated by A. Dru and W. Lowrie. London, 1940.
Christian Discourses, translated by W. Lowrie. London, 1939.
Works of Love, translated by D. F. Swenson. Princeton, 1946.
The Attack Upon "Christendom," translated by W. Lowrie. Princeton, 1944.
The Journals of Søren Kierkegaard: A Selection, edited and translated by A. Dru. Oxford, 1938.

Works on Kierkegaard

ANTHOLOGIES, BIOGRAPHY, AND CRITICAL STUDIES

Bretall, R., *A Kierkegaard Anthology.* Princeton, 1946.
Geismar, E. O., *Lectures on the Religious Thought of S. Kierkegaard.* Minneapolis, 1937.
Hohlenberg, J. E., *Søren Kierkegaard.* London, 1954.
Jolivet, R., *Introduction to Kierkegaard.* London, 1950.
Lowrie, W., *Kierkegaard.* New York, 1938.
Lowrie, W., *A Short Life of Kierkegaard.* Princeton, 1942.
Swenson, D. F., *Something About Kierkegaard.* Minneapolis, 1941.
Wahl, J. *Études Kierkegaardiennes.* Paris, 1938.

ADDITIONAL BACKGROUND

Barrett, W., *Irrational Man.* New York, 1958.
Blackham, H. J., *Six Existentialist Thinkers.* New York, 1952.
Collins, J., *The Existentialists: A Critical Study.* Chicago, 1952.
Grene, M., *Introduction to Existentialism.* Chicago, 1959.
Shestov, L., *Athènes et Jérusalem.* Paris, 1938.

ALASDAIR MacINTYRE

KINDĪ, ABŪ-YŪSUF YAʿQŪB IBN ISḤĀQ AL- (ninth century), was the first outstanding Arabic-writing philosopher. He was born in the Mesopotamian city of Basra and later held a distinguished position at the caliph's court in Baghdad, where he died shortly after 870. For about a century he enjoyed a reputation as a great philosopher in the Aristotelian–Neoplatonic tradition. He appears to have been the first to introduce the late Greek syllabus of philosophical learning into the Muslim world. It was mainly, though not exclusively, based on the *Corpus Aristotelicum* and its Peripatetic and Neoplatonic commentators. Numerous competent Arabic versions of Greek philosophical texts were available then, and al-Kindī himself commissioned translations of Aristotle's *Metaphysics* and of the so-called *Theology of Aristotle* (in fact a paraphrase of Plotinus) which are extant and available in print.

Al-Kindī's fame, however, was eclipsed by such later philosophers as al-Fārābī and Ibn-Sīnā (Avicenna). Only a few of his numerous treatises reached the Latin Schoolmen, but one recently discovered Arabic manuscript contains 24 of his otherwise unknown philosophical writings.

Two basic tenets of al-Kindī's, concerning prophecy and the creation of the world, were not accepted by his more famous Muslim successors. First, knowledge acquired through revelation in the Scriptures and from divinely inspired prophets is unambiguously superior to any knowledge acquired through philosophical training. In many cases, religious tradition and speculative, dialectical theology (repudiated emphatically by al-Fārābī) lead one to the same conclusions as philosophy and natural theology, which al-Kindī very consciously and proudly introduced for the first time into the Muslim discussion. He maintained, however, that there are certain fundamental tenets of faith that are guaranteed by revelation alone and cannot be demonstrated by human reason.

Second, unlike the later Muslim philosophers, al-Kindī did not proclaim the eternity of the world and an eternal, emanating creation. Rather, he attempted to prove in philosophical terms that the world had been created from nothing, in time, through a divine creator, and that at some future date, according to divine dispensation, it would dissolve again into nothing. In doing this, he appears to use essentially the same arguments that were developed with more sophistication and subtlety by John Philoponus, the Christian Neoplatonic–Aristotelian philosopher, in sixth-century Alexandria. Al-Kindī also disagreed with the leading later thinkers by considering astrology to be a genuine branch of rational and methodical knowledge.

Works by al-Kindī

An Arabic text is *Rasā'il al-Kindī al-falasafiyyah*, edited with an introduction by 'Abd al-Hādī Abū Rīdah, 2 vols. (Cairo, 1950–1953), in which 24 scientific and philosophical texts are printed for the first time. An Arabic text with Italian translation is *Studi su Al-Kindī:* Vol. I was translated by M. Guidi and R. Walzer (Rome, 1940), and Vol. II was translated by H. Ritter and R. Walzer (Rome, 1938). An Arabic text with German translation is "Al-Kindi als Astrolog," translated by O. Loth, in *Morgenländische Forschungen fuer H. L. Fleischer* (Leipzig, 1875), pp. 261 ff. A Latin text with French translation is *Antécédents gréco-arabes de la psychologie*, a translation of *De Rerum Gradibus* by L. Gauthier (Beirut, 1939). A Latin text is found in *Die philosophischen Abhandlungen des Ja'qūb ben Ishāg Al-Kindī*, A. Nagy, ed., which is Vol. II of C. Baeumker, ed., *Beiträge zur Geschichte der Philosophie des Mittelalters* (Münster, 1897).

Works on al-Kindī

Works on al-Kindī are A. Altmann and S. M. Stern, *Ishāq Israeli* (Oxford, 1958), *passim;* F. Rosenthal, "Al-Kindī and Ptolemy," in *Studi orientalistici in onore di G. Levi della vida,* Vol. II (Rome, 1956), pp. 436 ff.; and R. Walzer, *Greek Into Arabic* (Oxford, 1962), *passim.*

RICHARD WALZER

KIRCHHOFF, GUSTAV ROBERT (1824–1887), German physicist, was born in Königsberg and studied at the Kneiphof Hochschule there. His paper on the flow of electricity in a circular plate (1845) 'ed to his being granted a scholarship to Paris, but the revolution of 1848 prevented him from going beyond Berlin. Although he was appointed *Privatdozent* in mathematical physics there, he did not lecture, and in 1850 he became extraordinary professor at Breslau. In 1854 he became professor at Heidelberg, and from 1875 to 1884 he taught at the University of Berlin. Kirchhoff's *Gesammelte Abhandlungen* contains 38 papers, chiefly on electricity and magnetism but also on elastic solids, optics, fluids, heat, and spectroscopy. He made many important discoveries in electricity, and two of his laws concerning the flow of current in an electrical network, which still bear his name, are fundamental to electrical network theory. His work on the chemical analysis of the spectra of incandescent gases (partially carried out in collaboration with Robert Wilhelm Bunsen), although in part anticipated by others, constitutes the true beginning of spectroscopy. His enunciation of the law concerning the emission and absorption of radiation, his linking of the solar spectrum with the spectra of sodium and other gases and the explanation of these spectra by means of this law, and his careful analysis of the solar spectrum together constitute his greatest achievement. Kirchhoff was the author of the four-volume *Vorlesungen über mathema-*

tische Physik. The first volume of this work, *Mechanik* (1876), contains the most important of Kirchhoff's remarks on the philosophy of science.

The nature of mechanics. The first sentence of Kirchhoff's *Mechanik* made an immediate and lasting impact. "Mechanics is the science of motion; we designate as its task to describe in the most complete and simplest manner the motions that take place in nature." This statement must be understood in its context. Eleven years before, in a lecture as rector at Heidelberg, Kirchhoff expressed himself differently and was led to a far more sweeping and Laplacean conception of mechanics. The object of mechanics, he held at that time, is to determine the motions of bodies when the causes of the motions are known. The propositions of mechanics, like the propositions of geometry, are absolutely certain. If we knew the state of matter at a certain time, and all the forces of nature, we could deduce by means of mechanics all the subsequent states of the universe. The highest goal of the natural sciences is the reduction of all natural phenomena to mechanics.

Discussing this conception in the preface to his *Mechanik*, Kirchhoff wrote, "People like to define mechanics as the science of forces, and forces as the causes that tend to produce and sustain motion." But this definition, he commented, suffers from a lack of clarity in the concepts of cause and of tendency, a lack of clarity manifested, among other ways, in differences of opinion over the question whether the laws of inertia and of the parallelogram of forces are derived from experience, are axioms, or are laws that must be derived by the rules of logic. Kirchhoff set as his goal the elimination of such lack of clarity, even if it meant limiting the scope of mechanics. Mechanics could not be the basic science to which all other ought to be reduced, for Kirchhoff now held that mechanics could not explain motions in the sense of pointing out the causes of the motions. By "causes" Kirchhoff had meant "forces." It was because the meaning of force was unclear and engendered controversy that Kirchhoff proposed to give up explanation by means of forces.

Basic notions. Explanation of motions was to be replaced by description of them. The equations of mechanics are expressions of the way motions take place. Kirchhoff seems to have deliberately avoided the epistemological question of what it is that moves. Lenin, in *Materialism and Empirio-criticism,* contrasted the phenomenalism of Ernst Mach with the alleged materialism (which in this context means "realism") of Kirchhoff. Kirchhoff did claim that that which moves is matter. But this is a definition of the role that matter plays in his system rather than an assertion of materialism; he gave no further characterization of what he meant by "matter." In the preface he described mechanics as the science of the appearances by which motion is comprehended, and he stated that it is an assumption in mechanics that matter fills space as it appears to do. It would seem that Kirchhoff did not commit himself to either a realistic or a phenomenalistic conception of the subject matter of mechanics.

Matter, like space and time, was for Kirchhoff simply one of the postulated entities of mechanics. All three notions are necessary if a description of motion is to be given, and these three notions are sufficient for that task. Kirchhoff held that from mathematical axioms concerning these notions, all the universal equations of mechanics can be derived. It is simply a matter of fact that these equations happen to describe what actually takes place in nature. The other concepts used in mechanics, such as force, are auxiliary concepts, used to verbalize concisely mathematical equations that would otherwise be difficult to express in words. "Force" and other such terms should be used only in such a way that any expression in which they appear can be translated into an equivalent expression using only the basic concepts. Thus, Kirchhoff introduced force as the product of mass (matter) and acceleration (motion). It is merely a verbal equivalent of the second derivative of the coordinates of a mass-point with respect to time.

Completeness and simplicity. The task of mechanics, according to Kirchhoff, is not only to describe motions but also to describe them fully and in the simplest manner. Completeness and simplicity are notions whose functions in scientific explanation (to use "explanation" in a more general and more common sense than did Kirchhoff) have generated controversy. The criterion of completeness was only vaguely adumbrated by Kirchhoff: A motion is completely described when all questions that can be asked concerning it have been answered. But he recognized that the notion of simplicity presented difficulties. However, he claimed, we are never in doubt as to which of two descriptions of a phenomenon is the simpler. The utility of the notion of force is that it puts into one word the notion also expressed by the second derivative of the coordinates with respect to time of a mass-point, which experience shows to be the simplest description of the way bodies move. Furthermore, Kirchhoff held, what at one period appears to be the simplest description of a phenomenon may at a later time be replaced by an even simpler one. Thus, Kepler's three laws of planetary motion were brought together by Newton into one equivalent law of greater simplicity. The law that the sun attracts all planets by forces that are inversely proportional to the square of their distance from the sun is, in Kirchhoff's view, obviously simpler, easier to grasp, than the three laws of Kepler. But Newton's one law and Kepler's three laws are only different expressions, different descriptions, of the same motions.

Kirchhoff, Mach, and Hertz. Kirchhoff's program for mechanics has often been compared to Mach's principle of the economy of science. Both attempted to reduce the number of the basic notions of mechanics. However, Mach attempted to define mass, as well as force, in terms of space and time, and his conception of economy is a far more complex and embracing notion than Kirchhoff's claim. It involves considerations concerning the roles of language and mathematics, the relation of thought and reality, an analysis of the role that cause plays in scientific explanation rather than its outright elimination, notions concerning the aesthetic and economical function of simplicity, and a far more thorough analysis of the role of description in science.

Another contemporary of Kirchhoff, Heinrich Hertz, is also noted for his attempt to construct mechanics on the basis of the smallest number of concepts. Like Kirchhoff, he chose space, time, and mass, but he surpassed Kirchhoff in the depth of his analysis of the nature of mechanical explanation. Whereas Kirchhoff stressed the need for completeness and simplicity and neglected to describe either criterion in detail, Hertz presented a description of the relation between concepts and reality and introduced a more complex set of criteria of a good explanation—permissibility, correctness, and appropriateness, with appropriateness expressed in terms of a more precise notion of simplicity. And Hertz described in greater detail than Kirchhoff the nature of these criteria. On the other hand, to compensate for the elimination of the notion of force, Hertz introduced the notion of hypothetical unobservable masses in addition to the observed masses. Because of Kirchhoff's attachment to purely empirical conceptions, he would undoubtedly have balked at this.

Kirchhoff, Mach, and Hertz represent a general trend toward a simplification and clarification of the role and structure of mechanics. Kirchhoff's attempt was neither the earliest—Mach's principle of the economy of science was in great part adumbrated in his brief article "Ueber die Definition der Masse," published in 1868, eight years before Kirchhoff's text—nor the most thoroughgoing. Nevertheless, it was Kirchhoff's tremendous prestige as a physicist that attracted attention to the new views and led to the acceptance of the more elaborate versions of Mach and Hertz.

Works by Kirchhoff

Gesammelte Abhandlungen. Leipzig, 1882.
"Untersuchungen über das Sonnenspektrum und die spektren chemische Elemente." *Berlin Abhandlungen* (1861), 63 ff., and (1862), 227 ff. Translated by H. E. Roscoe as *Researches on the Solar Spectrum,* 2 vols. Cambridge and London, 1862–1863.
Vorlesungen über mathematische Physik, 4 vols. Vol. I, *Mechanik,* Leipzig, 1876; Vol. II, *Mathematische Optik,* Kurt Hensel, ed., Leipzig, 1891; Vol. III, *Electricität und Magnetismus,* Max Planck, ed., Leipzig, 1891; Vol. IV, *Theorie der Wärme,* Max Planck, ed., Leipzig, 1894.

Works on Kirchhoff

Dugas, René, *Histoire de la mécanique.* Neuchâtel, Switzerland, 1950. Pp. 426–428.
Hamel, Georg, *Theoretische Mechanik.* Berlin, Göttingen, and Heidelberg, 1949. Pp. 7 and 411. Discussion of Kirchhoff's view of force.
Helmholtz, Robert von, "Kirchhoff, Gustav Robert." *Deutsche Rundschau,* Vol. 14 (1888), 232–245. Translated by Joseph de Perott in *Smithsonian Institute Annual Report for 1889.* Washington, 1890. Pp. 527–540.
Jammer, Max, *Concepts of Force,* 2d ed. New York, 1962. Pp. 222–223.
Pokkels, F., *Gustav Robert Kirchhoff.* Heidelberg, 1903.
Whittaker, Sir Edmund, *A History of the Theories of Aether and Electricity.* London, 1951. Vol. I, *passim.* Discussions of Kirchhoff's work in electricity and spectroscopy.

PHILIP W. CUMMINGS

KIREEVSKY, IVAN VASILIEVICH (1806–1856), Russian Slavophile, was born in Moscow, where his mother, Elagina, was the center of a literary and intellectual circle. Kireevsky early developed literary tastes. He and his equally young intellectual friends deplored Russia's lag in philosophical studies, and hoped that study of German philosophy would inspire creation of a genuinely

Russian system. In 1830 Kireevsky went to Germany, where he attended the lectures of Hegel, Schleiermacher, and Schelling. After a social evening in Hegel's home he wrote, "I am surrounded by the first-class minds of Europe," but even among these intellectual giants he preserved the critical judgment he had acquired in Moscow. Upon his return home, he faced the complex problems of Russia's "marvelous decade" of the 1830s, when the French rationalism of the Decembrists was giving way to romanticism, utopian socialism, and, particularly, German idealism. At the end of the decade, Kireevsky emerged from this turmoil a confirmed Slavophile. Embracing Orthodoxy as his guide, he chose the elaboration of a Russian philosophy as his lifework. He died in St. Petersburg some 25 years later.

Kireevsky's total output consists of two volumes, and, although he wrote only three philosophical essays, he was nevertheless recognized as the outstanding philosopher of the Slavophiles. He contributed to Slavophilism the doctrine of the "wholeness of the spirit," inspired primarily, if not exclusively, by the Eastern Church Fathers.

Rejecting Western—specifically, the "one-sided" Hegelian—rationalism, Kireevsky stressed the affinity between Aristotle and Western thought. Aristotle had elevated "abstract consciousness of deliberative reason" to a commanding position. Out of the kinship between Aristotle and the West grew Scholasticism within faith, then the reformation of faith, and finally philosophy outside faith. The Scholastics were the first Western rationalists; the Hegelians, their progeny. Kireevsky gave special consideration to German thought, characterizing Schelling, the teacher of Hegel, as such a genius as appears only once in a millennium, but a genius who had doomed his own final system by combining antithetical doctrines. Hegel was a modern Aristotle in his dialectic and in his final, erroneous relating of mind to truth. Thus had Western philosophy, rooted in pagan Greek thought, run its course.

Yet Kireevsky held Greek philosophy to have been invaluable for having educated the mind of pre-Christian man to that neutral position in which it could receive higher truth and for having thereby "prepared the soil for the Christian seed." Where the Byzantine–Greek tradition prevailed, Christian truth remained supreme; consequently, in an Orthodox–Slavophile orientation one could find the basis for a new philosophy, defined as neither science nor faith, but the sum and common basis of all sciences and the "conductor of thought between them and faith." In place of the "self-propelled knife of reason" of the West, Kireevsky proposed "believing thinking" (*veruiushchee myshlenie*), man's infallible guide to wholeness of the spirit. Characteristic of believing thinking was its striving to integrate all of man's spiritual forces into "that inner concentration of existence where reason, will, feeling, conscience; the esthetic, true . . . desirable, just, and merciful; and the manifold manifestations of the mind converge into a living whole . . ." (*Polnoe Sobranie Sochinenii*, Vol. I, p. 275).

Kireevsky's doctrine provided not only the epistemological focus of Slavophilism but also a philosophical–religious concept that has strong psychological and sociopolitical implications. It impressed a number of Russian philosophers and theologians and foreshadowed some later aspects of Western thought, such as Gestalt theory.

Works by Kireevsky

Polnoe Sobranie Sochinenii ("Complete Works"), Mikhail Gershenzon, ed., 2 vols. Moscow, 1911.

Works on Kireevsky

Chizhevsky, D. I., *Hegel in Russland*. Reichenberg, Czechoslovakia, 1934, pp. 151–160.

Lanz, Henry, "The Philosophy of Ivan Kireevsky." *The Slavonic Review*, Vol. 5 (March 1926), 594–604.

Liaskovsky, Valerii, *Brat'ia Kireevskie, Zhizn i Trudy Ikh*. St. Petersburg, 1899.

Lossky, N. O., *History of Russian Philosophy*. New York, 1951, pp. 15–29.

Masaryk, T. G., *Russland und Europa*, 2 vols. Jena, 1913. Translated by Eden and Cedar Paul as *The Spirit of Russia*, 2 vols. London, 1919. Material on Kireevsky in Vol. I, Ch. 10.

Müller, Eberhard, "Ivan Vasil'evič Kireevskij: Reč' Šellinga. 1845 . . ." *Jahrbücher für Geschichte Osteuropas*, N. S. Vol 11 (1963), 482–520.

Setschkareff, Wsewolod, *Schellings Einfluss in der russischen Literatur der 20er und 30er Jahre des XIX. Jahrhunderts*. Berlin, 1939. Pp. 57–66.

Walicki, Andrzej, "Rosyjskie Słowianofilstwo a Filozofia Heglowska." *Archiwum Historii Filozofii i Myśli Społecznej*, Vol. 8 (1962), 53–97.

Zenkovsky, V. V., *Istoriia Russkoi Filosofii*, 2 vols. Paris, 1948–1950. Translated by G. L. Kline as *A History of Russian Philosophy*. London and New York, 1953. Pp. 207–227.

PETER K. CHRISTOFF

KLAGES, LUDWIG (1872–1956), German psychologist and philosopher, was the leading figure in the field of characterology. Born in Hanover, Klages studied chemistry, physics, and philosophy at Munich, receiving his doctorate in chemistry in 1900. As a member of the Stefan George circle, he collaborated with George in the editing of the *Blättern für die Kunst*. In 1905 Klages founded at the University of Munich a *Seminar für Ausdruckskunde*, which soon became Germany's main center of characterological psychology. In 1919 the seminar was moved to Kilchberg, near Zurich, where Klages remained until his death.

Klages was the principal representative in psychology of the vitalist movement that swept Germany from 1895 to 1915. His most important work was directed toward the formulation of a science of character that would reestablish the undifferentiated union of the life forms that had been ruptured by the emergence of ego in the human species. To this end he explored some of the more bizarre pseudo sciences, such as graphology, and attempted to use their insights as the bases for auxiliary disciplines in his study of character types.

In addition to the literary influences of the romantic poets, of Goethe, and of Stefan George, Klages was also influenced by the physiologist E. G. Carus and the psychologist Theodore Lipps and, most important, by the philosopher Friedrich Nietzsche. All of these strands of thought converged in Klages to make of him a major spokesman of a generation of intellectuals consciously dedicated to the repudiation of reason in the name of instinct, and of civilization in the name of life. In short, his work was similar in content and general effect to that of Ernst Jünger, Oswald Spengler, and Martin Heidegger in providing—however unintentionally—an intellectual basis for Nazism.

According to Klages, Nietzsche had perceived correctly that man was distinguished from the rest of animal nature only by his ability to clothe in images the reality given by the senses. But Nietzsche had been wrong, Klages maintained, to regard this image-making ability as necessarily acting in the service of vital forces. In fact, he argued, man's ability to conceive a world in the imagination and to present this imagined world as a project or possible attainment against lived experience was unnatural and, in the end, profoundly hostile to life itself. Human life, for Klages, differed from animal life in general by virtue of the emergence in man of spirit (*Geist*); man's capacity to think and to will provided the source of his estrangement from the world and the cause of his peculiar psychic illnesses.

Animal life is possessed of both body (*Leib*) and soul (*Seele*), whose functions constitute "genuine processes." "The Body finds expression in the process of sensation and in the impulse towards movement, the Soul in the process of contemplation and in the impulse to formation (that is, to the magical *or* mechanical realization of images). . . . " The processes of body and soul express the "eternal" life force, which is characterized by spontaneous creativity and flows beneath individual duration. In man, however, spirit appears, characterized by the "act of apprehension and the act of willing," which are in turn the origin of ego, utterly lacking in animals and impelling man to the "unnatural" desire for immortality "or, more briefly, the urge to self-preservation."

This unnatural urge to self-preservation in man creates the tensions of human life. Man is a field whereon animal consciousness and human consciousness vie for supremacy. The former promotes the impulse to return to nature, expressed in the quest for "eternal life," while the latter promotes the life-destructive impulse to transcend the animal condition, reflected in science, religion, philosophy, and even art. The different quanta of soul and spirit present within an individual account for differences in character. Characterology, which is the study of these differences, constructs a typology of attitudes and structural forms as manifested in different egos. Most men live in the middle range of a spectrum of characterological types that runs from an almost total repression of spirit, as in primitive peoples, to an almost total repression of bodily forces, as in the asceticism of the redemptive religions. But in the science of character, Klages hoped, the true nature of the struggle between life and spirit raging in the individual would be clarified, the disastrous consequences of the triumph of spirit over life would be revealed, and science, art, and religion would be turned upon the spirit, destroy it, and lead to the dissolution of the individual ego in the undifferentiated nature out of which it had unnaturally emerged.

Bibliography

Works by Klages include *Prinzipien der Charakterologie* (Leipzig, 1910), of which the 4th and subsequent editions are entitled *Grundlagen der Charakterkunde* (11th ed., Bonn, 1951). *The Science of Character*, a translation of the 5th and 6th editions of this work, was prepared by W. H. Johnson (London, 1929). Other writings are *Handschrift und Charakter* (Leipzig, 1917); *Die psychologischen Errungenschaften Nietzsches* (Leipzig, 1926); *Der Geist als Widersacher der Seele*, 3 vols. (Leipzig, 1929–1932); *Graphologie* (Heidelberg, 1931); *Geist und Leben* (Berlin, 1935); *Ursprünge der Seelenforschung* (Leipzig, 1942) and *Die Sprache als Quelle der Seelen-Kunde* (Zurich, 1948).

For works on Klages see Max Bense, *Anti-Klages* (Berlin, 1937); K. Haeberlein, *Einführung in die Forschungsergebnisse von Klages* (Kampen, 1934); Herbert Hönel, ed., *Ludwig Klages: Erforscher und Künder. Festschrift zum 75. Geburtstage* (Linz, 1947); Hans Kasdorff, *Um Seele und Geist: Ein Wegweiser zum Hauptwerk von Ludwig Klages* (Munich, 1954); Hans Prinzhorn, ed., *Die Wissenschaft am Scheidewege von Leben und Geist: Ludwig Klages zum 60. Geburtstag* (Leipzig, 1932); Ernest Sellière, *De la Déesse nature à la déesse vie* (Paris, 1931); and Jean Toulemonde, *La Caractérologie* (Paris, 1951).

HAYDEN V. WHITE

KLEIST, HEINRICH VON (1777–1811), German dramatist, poet, and novelist, was born in Frankfurt on the Oder. Following a family tradition, Kleist entered the Prussian military service at 14, but he left, dissatisfied, in 1799. Uncertain what profession to adopt, Kleist prepared himself for the university by studying privately philosophy, mathematics, and classical languages. An intensive study of Kant, or perhaps of Fichte, led to a spiritual crisis in March 1801. The relativity of all knowledge seemed to Kleist to render life, especially a life dedicated to the pursuit of knowledge, pointless. In disgust he discontinued his studies and journeyed to Paris and Switzerland. His decision to pursue a literary career led to a second crisis: afraid that he had no talent, he burned his tragedy *Robert Guiskard* in 1803. A period of restless activity followed. In 1805 he obtained a minor civil service position in Königsberg, which relieved him of his immediate worries. His two comedies, *Amphitryon* and *Der zerbrochene Krug*, were written at this time. Eager to aid the anti-Napoleonic cause he left Königsberg for Berlin, where in 1807 he was seized as a spy and sent to prison in France. After his sister had obtained his release, Kleist made an attempt to establish himself in Dresden from 1807 to 1809. With Adam Müller he founded the literary magazine *Phöbus*, which, however, soon failed. Attempts to help the patriotic cause with his literary efforts (*Hermannsschlacht*, 1808) met with little response. He returned to Berlin, where for a time he published the *Abendblätter*. When this project also failed, partly because of political pressure, Kleist was left without means. On November 21, 1811, Kleist committed suicide with Henriette Vogel near Berlin.

Kleist's reading of Kant taught him that all attempts to penetrate the veil of phenomena were futile, that the world possesses no higher meaning. In his first play, *Die Familie Schroffenstein* (1803), love, the only value, is destroyed by the force of illusion and circumstance—a theme that was to recur in such stories as *Die Verlobung in St. Domingo* and *Das Erdbeben in Chile*. Like Hegel, Kleist saw life as essentially tragic, but unlike Hegel, he saw tragedy in absurdity, in the indifference of the world to man's demands for love and meaning. Kleist's heroes confront this absurdity with demonic defiance. Thus Michael Kohlhaas, in the *novella* of the same name (1810), becomes inhuman in his pursuit of justice; and the heroines of Kleist's plays *Penthesilea* (1808) and *Das Käthchen von Heilbronn* (1810) become inhuman in their pursuit of love—one by being totally aggressive, the other by being totally submissive. In his last play, *Der Prinz von Homburg* (1810), Kleist attempted to oppose the order provided by the state to the uncertainties of the human situation. The prince disobeys orders, wins a battle, and is yet condemned to death. At first incapable of understanding this judgment and driven only by his fear of death, he regains control of himself when made judge of his own actions and freely accepts the verdict.

Bibliography

WORKS BY KLEIST

Werke, 5 vols., E. Schmidt, ed. Leipzig, 1905; 2d ed., 7 vols., G. Minde-Pouet, ed., 1936——.
Werke, 2 vols., H. Sembdner, ed. Munich, 1961.
The Marquise of O, and Other Stories, translated by Martin Greenberg. New York, 1960.

TRANSLATIONS OF PLAYS

"The Feud of the Schröffensteins." *Poet Lore*, Vol. 27, No. 5 (Boston, 1916), 457–576. Translated by M. J. and L. M. Price.
The Prince of Homburg. New York, 1956. Translated by C. E. Passage.
Katie of Heilbronn. Hartford, 1960. Translated by A. H. Hughes.
The Broken Pitcher. Chapel Hill, North Carolina, 1961. Translated by B. Q. Morgan.

WORKS ON KLEIST

Blankenagel, J. C., *The Dramas of Heinrich von Kleist.* Chapel Hill, North Carolina, 1931.
Blöcker, Günter, *Heinrich von Kleist oder Das absolute Ich.* Berlin, 1960.
Cassirer, Ernst, *Idee und Gestalt.* Berlin, 1921.
Fricke, Gerhard, *Gefühl und Schicksal bei Heinrich von Kleist.* Berlin, 1929.
March, Richard, *Heinrich von Kleist.* Cambridge, 1954.
Muth, Ludwig, *Kleist und Kant.* Cologne, 1954.
Silz, W., *Heinrich von Kleist.* Philadelphia, 1962.
Stahl, E. L., *Heinrich von Kleist's Dramas.* Oxford, 1948.
Witkop, Philipp, *Heinrich von Kleist.* Leipzig, 1922.

KARSTEN HARRIES

KNOWLEDGE, SOCIOLOGY OF. See SOCIOLOGY OF KNOWLEDGE.

KNOWLEDGE, THEORY OF. See EPISTEMOLOGY, HISTORY OF.

KNOWLEDGE AND BELIEF. The nature of knowledge has been a central problem in philosophy from the earliest times. One of Plato's most brilliant dialogues, the *Theaetetus*, is an attempt to arrive at a satisfactory definition of the concept, and Plato's dualistic ontology—a real world of eternal Forms contrasted with a less real world of changing sensible particulars—rests on epistemological foundations.

The problem of knowledge occupies an important place in most major philosophical systems. If philosophy is conceived as an ontological undertaking, as an endeavor to describe the ultimate nature of reality or to say what there

really is, it requires a preliminary investigation of the scope and validity of knowledge. Only that can reasonably be said to exist which can be known to exist. If, on the other hand, philosophy is conceived as a critical inquiry, as a second-order discipline concerned with the claims of various concrete forms of intellectual activity, it must consider the extent to which these activities issue in knowledge.

In modern philosophy in the widest sense of the phrase—i.e., philosophy since the Renaissance—theory of knowledge has usually been the primary field of philosophical investigation. Descartes and Locke, Hume and Kant, were all, in the first instance, epistemologists. Epistemological considerations played an important part in the work of Schopenhauer, but they were less central in Hegel and Nietzsche, who were more occupied with the nature of the human mind in general and with the institutions within which it is exercised than with its more narrowly cognitive aspects. With Kierkegaard and his existentialist descendants the focus of interest was man's will rather than his intellect. Anglo-Saxon philosophy, however, has remained epistemological. Mill, Russell, and the analytic philosophers of the present century have continued to work in the area marked out by Locke and Hume. Even the British Hegelians of the late nineteenth century, the school of Green and Bradley, were led into far-reaching epistemological studies by the character of the native tradition they were seeking to overthrow.

Belief has had less attention from philosophers. It has generally been taken to be a more or less unproblematic inner state, accessible to introspection. But there has been disagreement about whether it is active or passive, Descartes having contended that assent is a matter of will, Hume that it is an emotional condition in which one finds oneself. Bain urged that belief should be interpreted in terms of the tendencies to action with which it is associated, and Peirce took the view that it is an unobstructed habit of action which, like health, comes to our notice only when we have lost it. Faith, especially religious faith, and probability, the logic of rational belief, have been thoroughly examined, but belief itself has received surprisingly cursory treatment.

THE DEFINITION OF KNOWLEDGE

According to the most widely accepted definition, knowledge is justified true belief. That it is a kind of belief is supported by the fact that both knowledge and belief can have the same objects (thus, half an hour ago I believed I had left my raincoat in the garage; now I know that I have) and that what is true of someone who believes something to be the case is also true, among other things, of one who knows it. One who comes to know what he formerly believed does not lose the conviction he formerly had.

It is obvious and generally admitted that we can have knowledge only of what is true. If I admit that *p* is false, I must admit that I did not know it and that no one else did, although I may have thought and said so. It is urged, on the ground that beliefs that merely happen to be true cannot be regarded as knowledge, that knowledge must be justified. I may draw a true conclusion by invalid means from false premises or believe a truth on the strength of a dream or the misremembered testimony of a notorious liar. In such cases as these I do not really know the things I believe, although what I believe is true. There are, however, objections to all three parts of the definition of knowledge as justified true belief.

Truth. It has been suggested that the requirement that what is known be true is excessively stringent. Complete certainty of a statement's truth is not to be had; the best we can achieve is very strong grounds for thinking it true. Thus, if knowledge entails truth, we can never attain knowledge or, at any rate, never know that we have done so. This objection is misconceived. If I firmly believe that something is true on what I take to be sufficient grounds, I am right to say that I know it. It may be that the grounds are, in fact, insufficient and that what I claim to know is false. In that case my claim is mistaken, but it does not follow that I was wrong to make it in the sense that I had no justification for doing so.

It has also been argued, with a view to showing that knowledge and belief are quite distinct and unrelated, that whereas beliefs can be true or false, knowledge is neither. This argument exploits the fact that we speak of a belief but not of a knowledge, only of a piece or item of knowledge. Furthermore, since all items or pieces of knowledge are by definition true, we never need to speak of them as true items or pieces in order to distinguish them from false ones.

Belief. It is often objected that knowledge cannot be a kind of belief, even though they can have the same objects, because they exclude each other. If I know that *p*, it would be wrong for me to say that I believe it, since this would suggest that I do *not* know it. If, knowing *p*, I am asked "Do you believe that *p*?," I should reply "No, I know it." This is hardly a serious argument. I should mislead people if I described my wife as the woman I live with, and I might say, "No, she's my wife," if I were asked whether she is the woman I live with. Nevertheless, my wife is the woman I live with. What is true is that I do not *merely* live with her. Likewise, if I know that *p*, I do not merely believe it, but I do believe it all the same. It is often wrong or misleading in certain circumstances to say something that is unquestionably true. The boy who, having taken two jam tarts, answers the question "How many have you had?" by saying "One" has told the truth but not the whole truth.

A more powerful argument against the definition of knowledge in terms of belief is that people can, it seems, know something to be the case and yet refuse, or be unable to bring themselves, to believe it. A woman told by wholly reliable witnesses with a wealth of circumstantial detail that her husband has been killed in an accident might be in this position. One way of getting around this objection is to say that she believes both that her husband is dead and that he is not. It is possible and not uncommon to believe something and its contradictory. It is not possible both to believe something and to not believe it at the same time, and what she will say is, "I don't believe it," although what she means is that she believes it is false.

Another possibility is to say that although she has conclusive grounds for believing that her husband is dead, she does not, in fact, believe it and does not know it either. To have conclusive grounds is one thing; to recognize that they are conclusive is another.

It should be noted that where knowledge and belief overlap, the kind of knowledge involved is propositional knowledge, or what Ryle has called "knowing that." There is also "knowing how" (to skate, tie a reef knot, do long division), where there are no propositions to be true or false and where knowledge can vary in degree. The two kinds of knowledge are connected in that both are the outcome of learning. Belief is always propositional or believing that; there is no believing how that serves as a defective version of knowing how to do something.

Justification. We often express unreasonable hunches or intuitions by saying, "I know," and if they turn out, to our gratified amazement, to be correct, we rejoice by saying, "I knew it." Does this show that true belief can be knowledge even without justification? The emphasis we put on the verb when we use it in such a case suggests that it is an abnormal or marginal use. It is generally accepted that lucky guesses should not count as knowledge.

An important difficulty arises from the requirement that true belief must be justified if it is to be knowledge. What is it for a belief to be justified? One obvious answer is that my belief in *q* is justified if there is some other belief *p* which entails or supports it. It is clearly not enough that this further belief *p* should merely exist. It must also be a belief of mine; I must know it to be true, and I must know that it justifies *q*. But if this is a definition of justification, the original definition of knowledge is rendered circular and generates a regress. It has the consequence that before any belief can be justified, an infinite series of justifications must already have taken place.

How can such a regress be halted? A natural step is to ask whether all justification has to be of this propositional or inferential kind. As Russell has observed, we can define derivative knowledge in this way but must add an account of intuitive or uninferred knowledge. Philosophers have fastened on two forms of intuitive knowledge which, by standing as the uninferred first premises of all inference, can terminate the regress of justification. First, there are self-evident necessary truths, and, second, there are basic contingent statements, immediately justified by the experiences they report and not dependent on the support of any further statable items of knowledge.

In the first group are the axioms of logic and mathematics, such as the law of excluded middle and the principle of the commutativity of addition ($a + b = b + a$), and statements that correspond to familiar verbal definitions, such as that kittens are young cats. Some philosophers hold that such intuitive, necessary truths record the results of intellectual intuition, the direct inspection of the relations of timeless universals; others, that their truth is essentially verbal in character, that a man must accept them if he is to be regarded as understanding the ordinary meaning of the words they contain. To accept an intuitive, necessary truth is to be ready to draw inferences in accordance with it. If I understand and accept the truth of "If (if *p*, then *q*), then (if not-*q*, then not-*p*)," I must regard the deduction of "If he's not over 21, he's not eligible" from "If he's eligible, he's over 21" as valid. By applying such rules of inference to intuitive necessary premises, further demonstrative necessary truths are arrived at.

Intuitive contingent truths have been held to be those that describe the immediate objects of perceptual or introspective experience—for example, "There is a green patch in the middle of my visual field" or "There appears to me to be a green flag here" and "I am in pain" or "I want to go to sleep." Basic statements like these are said to be incorrigible in the sense that they are wholly certified by the experiences they report and are logically immune from falsification by the results of any further experience. There may be no green flag here, but whatever may happen, there does now appear to be one. I may find it impossible to go to sleep once I get into bed, but I still want to go to sleep now. A statement is incorrigible if its truth follows from the fact that it is believed by the person to whom it refers. Thus, although I can make such a statement falsely, I must know that the statement is false when I do so. I cannot be honestly mistaken about my pains or the contents of my visual field.

It has sometimes been denied that there are any contingent, empirical statements that are basic and incorrigible in this sense. Coherence theories of knowledge have been propounded by the absolute idealists of the late nineteenth century and by C. S. Peirce, Karl R. Popper, and W. V. Quine in more empiricist forms in which beliefs are seen as justifying one another but none as in any sense self-justifying. To overcome the apparent circularity of the doctrine, it has been argued that some beliefs are relatively basic in that they can be accepted as true by some kind of convention or posited for the time being but that the element of dogmatism involved is only provisional and is open to revision.

Plato's "Theaetetus." Several of the points raised concerning truth, belief, and justification were first made in the *Theaetetus*, that most modern in spirit of Plato's dialogues. In it three definitions of knowledge are examined, and in the end all are rejected. The three are that knowledge is (1) perception or sensation, (2) true belief, and (3) true belief *meta logou*, translated by Burnet as "accompanied by a rational account of itself or ground." Against the view that knowledge is true belief Plato made the point that lawyers can persuade juries to accept beliefs that are, in fact, true by using rhetorical devices but cannot be said to provide them with knowledge by doing so. Against the third definition, which, in effect, takes knowledge to be justified true belief, he pointed out that it is circular and regressive.

There is an obvious objection to the definition of knowledge as perception. Perception itself must be defined in terms of knowledge—namely, as the acquisition of knowledge about the external world by means of the senses. Plato's meaning here is perhaps better rendered by understanding his first definition to equate knowledge and sensation. Certainly this makes more plausible Plato's identification of this definition with Protagoras' thesis that man is the measure of all things (or that the truth for each man is simply what appears to him to be the case). In fact, Protagoras' thesis would be more accurately interpreted as the view that knowledge and belief are one and the same. This contention has obviously contradictory implications, as Plato pointed out. We all believe some beliefs of others to be truer than our own, and most people believe that Protagoras' theory is false. Something like that theory persists, however, in the view, to which we shall later return, that the foundations of empirical knowledge consist of incorrigible statements about immediate experience. According to this view, what we believe about our current sensations or experiences, whatever we may choose to *say* about them, is true. If it is also correct that such sensations are self-intimating, in the sense that they cannot occur without our knowing them to occur, it follows that every sensation is an item of knowledge though not that every item of knowledge is a sensation.

In his discussion of knowledge as true belief Plato raised the problem of false belief. How can we believe falsely that *X* is *Y* since if the belief is false, there is no *X* that is *Y* to form a belief, true or false, about? A false belief, it seems, is no belief at all. A perhaps oversimple solution to the problem is that we can know a thing *X* well enough to be able to identify it as a subject of discourse without knowing everything about it (whether, for instance, it is *Y* or not-*Y*). This draws attention to the point that the objects of knowledge are not always propositional, that not all knowledge is knowledge that. In addition to the knowledge how emphasized by Ryle, there is knowledge with a direct object, or knowledge of, claimed in such remarks as "I know Jones" or "I know Paris."

A claim to know a person can be intended and understood in two main ways. In saying that I know Jones, I may mean that I have met him and that I could not recognize him (and, usually, that we have had enough to do with one another for him to remember me). On the other hand, I may mean that I know what his character is like, what sort of things he is likely to do. According to the first interpretation, very little knowing that is involved, although I should be expected to be capable of giving some description of Jones's appearance; according to the second, some knowledge that relating to his character is implied, but none about his past history, health, occupation, and so on is. A claim to know a place is ordinarily a claim to knowledge how, to an ability to find one's way about in it. It is not enough simply to have been there. Among other individual objects of knowledge are games, languages, and works of art. The last of these kinds of knowledge can be treated in much the same way as knowledge of persons; the others, as cases of knowing how, as claims to the possession of a skill. In general, knowledge of can be reduced to varying mixtures of knowing how and knowing that, though by no single recipe. It never involves a claim to knowledge that of all the facts involving the individual in question. A further point against Plato is that I can know enough about an individual or a thing to be able to refer significantly and successfully to him or it without being in a position to say that I know him or it *simpliciter*. I know enough about Samarkand to refer to it as a city in the Soviet Union and to ascribe to it a degree of beauty, historical interest, and size, but I do not know Samarkand at all, for I have never been there and could not find my way about in it.

Is knowledge definable? The English philosopher John Cook Wilson (1849–1915), closely followed in this by his disciple H. A. Prichard (1871–1947), strenuously maintained that the concept of knowledge is primitive and indefinable. Against such idealist logicians as F. H. Bradley and Bernard Bosanquet, they argued that judgment is not a genus of which knowledge, belief, and opinion are species. A judgment, said Cook Wilson, is the conclusion of an inference, but some knowledge must be uninferred. Nor is knowledge a kind or species of thinking or a species of belief, for belief rests on knowledge in that it requires that there should be both some known evidence for it and the knowledge that this evidence is insufficient. No doubt, belief usually does rest on evidence or what is taken to be evidence, but it is not, as Cook Wilson supposed, necessary that it should do so. I may believe a woman to be married because I take her to be wearing a wedding ring. The fact that it is not a wedding ring that she is wearing does not in the least imply that I do not really believe what I infer from my mistake.

According to Prichard, knowledge is completely *sui generis* and cannot, as he put it, "be explained." We cannot, he said, derive knowledge from what is not knowledge. This observation, if it is relevant at all, is simply a dogmatic assertion of the indefinability of knowledge. We can certainly define some things in terms of what they are not; for instance, not all cats are kittens, and not all young things are kittens, but a kitten is by definition a young cat. Knowledge and belief, Prichard held, are utterly distinct and cannot be mistaken for each other. We know directly and infallibly whether our state of mind is one of knowledge or belief. If so, knowledge and belief could not be related as genus and species, although they could still be different species of the same genus, another possibility that Prichard ruled out. His view that the two cannot be mistaken for each other seems clearly mistaken. We often claim with complete sincerity to know things which turn out to be false in the end. In so doing, we have taken a belief, mistakenly, to be knowledge.

Is the opposite possibility ever realized? Do we ever take to be mere belief something that, in fact, we really know? Is there a difference between knowing something and knowing that we know it? Spinoza held that there is not. "He who has a true idea, knows at that same time that he has a true idea, nor can he doubt concerning the truth of the thing" (*Ethics*, Part 2, Proposition 43). As Spinoza expressed it, the doctrine is plainly false. I can perfectly well have very little confidence in a belief that is really true if, for example, it has been communicated to me by a notoriously unreliable informant. In other words, I can have a belief that is really true without knowing that it is true. But can I know that something is the case without knowing that I know it? I can certainly have a justified true belief without knowing that that is what it is, for I may not realize that the grounds I have for believing it really do justify it. The question deserves a more thorough investigation than it can be given here.

Rationalist theory of knowledge. Plato's distinction between knowledge and belief has had a greater influence on the subsequent course of philosophy than his penetrating but unsuccessful attempts to find a definition of the concept. His essential point was that knowledge and belief are not only distinct attitudes but that they also have distinct and proprietary objects. Knowledge can be only of what is eternal and unchanging, of Forms, Ideas or universals; belief has for its objects the changing sensible particulars that make up the temporal world. Plato's reflections on mathematics seem to have led him to this conclusion. The propositions of geometry are preeminently objects of knowledge in that they can be established as conclusively true, once and for all, by demonstrative reasoning. Our beliefs about matters of temporal fact, on the other hand, are much more liable to illusion and error. The sensible objects of perceptual belief are infected with contradiction; they undergo change and have contrary properties at different times. But the objects of mathematical knowledge are wholly different. The circles and triangles studied by geometers are exact and perfect; they are ideals which the circular and triangular things we perceive with the senses approximate but always fall short of.

There are three ways in which a circular concrete thing may not be really circular. It may be circular at one time and elliptical at another; it may be other things (for example, green, cold, and sweet) as well as circular; and as concrete and sensible, it may not be strictly or perfectly circular. From these facts Plato concluded that such a thing is not wholly real in the way that the ideal circle of the geometer is. The ideal circle is a genuine object of knowledge, and only such wholly knowable things can be wholly real. From the distinction between knowledge and belief, then, Plato derived a distinction between two sorts of object, each sort constituting a separate world of its own—the abstract world of eternal Forms, which is the knowable reality, and the concrete world of changing particulars, which is only appearance, not nonexistent but not wholly real either, and of which one can have not knowledge but only belief.

Plato's arguments for the unknowability and unreality of concrete, sensible things are not very persuasive. If this once circular mat is now elliptical, it does not follow that it was not really circular before. If this circular object is also green and cold, that does not in any way detract from its circularity. Finally, even if it is not perfectly circular, it may be quite definitely green. In general, there would seem to be many propositions that are known by some people but only believed by others; a mathematician will know the truth of a proposition he has proved, whereas another person will simply believe it on his authority. Some things I now know I used only to believe—for instance, that I should be writing this here today; some things I now only believe I once used to know—for instance, where I bought my raincoat. These considerations show that the objects of knowledge and belief are not wholly mutually exclusive. But it may still be true that there are some things that can be only believed, whereas others can be both believed and known.

At the center of Plato's thinking about this subject is a principle that defines one important sense of the word "rationalism"—the principle that only necessary truths, established by a priori reasoning, can really be known. Something like this principle was accepted by Aristotle, although he rejected Plato's doctrine that Forms or universals occupied a separate abstract world of their own beyond time and space. Aristotle agreed that only the form of things could be known and that the matter that individuated or particularized them was beyond the reach of knowledge. For him true knowledge was to be attained by a process of intuitive induction which discerned the necessary connections between the forms present in concrete things. A science or ordered body of knowledge must consist of propositions deduced from self-evident first principles of this kind.

Descartes's rationalism was inspired by the reflection that ordinary claims to knowledge often prove mistaken. True knowledge, he insisted, must be objectively certain and impossible to doubt. His methodical endeavors to doubt everything were brought up short by the celebrated "I think, therefore I exist." I cannot doubt that I doubt, for in the act of doubting it I prove it to be true; if I doubt, I think; and if I think, I exist. What, he then inquired, is so special about *cogito* and *sum*? What makes them so indubitably certain? His unhelpful conclusion is that they are clearly and distinctly perceived to be true. What he meant by this weakly formulated criterion of certainty can best be discovered by seeing what, in practice, he took it to certify. It appears that two sorts of proposition are clearly and distinctly perceived to be true: (1) necessary truths whose denial is self-evidently contradictory and (2) the immediate deliverances of sensation and introspection about one's own current mental state. Premises of both kinds figure in his first proof of God's existence:

Every event must have an adequate cause.
I have a clear and distinct idea of God.
God alone is an adequate cause for my idea of him.
Therefore, God exists.

In fact, *cogito*, I think, is not a clear instance of either, let alone both, of these two kinds of knowable, and even if it were, it would not follow from its being, on one hand, necessary and immediate and, on the other, certain that anything else that was necessary and immediate was also certain. Descartes's primary certainty was perhaps first thought of on a Thursday, but it does not follow that anything first thought of on a Thursday either by him or by anyone else is certain, too. It is not a necessary truth that I think or exist, for I might not be awake and might never have existed. If this is the case, the facts in question could not, of course, have been expressed in the first person singular.

Locke, despite his justly recognized position as a founding father of empiricism, reached much the same rationalist conclusion as Descartes, although by a very different route. He defined knowledge as "the perception of the agreement or disagreement of two ideas" (*Essay Concerning Human Understanding*, Book 4, Ch. 1, Sec. 2). He went on to distinguish three kinds of knowledge: (1) intuitive knowledge of such things as the fact that red is not green

and the fact of one's own existence; (2) demonstrative knowledge, which includes mathematics, morality, and the existence of God; and (3) sensitive knowledge, which is concerned with "the particular existence of finite beings without us." The third type of knowledge does not conform to his general definition, as he admitted. To become aware of a finite being outside us, we have to infer the existence of something that is not an idea from the ideas of sensation we take it to cause, and in part, to resemble. Locke's definition, as he understood it, restricts knowledge to the domain of a priori necessary truths. In intuition and demonstration there is a direct or indirect awareness of the connection between ideas present to the mind. But in the third case a connection is asserted between an idea of sensation and a physical thing which is not and cannot be directly present to the mind.

Locke did not introduce a special category to accommodate our knowledge of the ideas we passively experience but remitted them in passing to the category of intuitive knowledge. This sort of knowledge is quite unlike his exemplary cases of intuition, being contingent and empirical where the exemplary cases are necessary and a priori, and he might well have introduced a special category of reflective knowledge to accommodate it. It would comprise assertions of the connection of particular ideas, whereas intuition and demonstration would cover the connections of abstract, general ideas. Thus, although Locke's official definition of knowledge confines its application to necessary truths, it could, with a little modification, have been extended to cover a person's awareness of the present contents of his mind. But it could not, by any contortions, have been made to cover sensitive knowledge of real existence, that empirical knowledge par excellence which it was Locke's avowed purpose to justify and explain.

Certainty. The indestructible vitality of the rationalist theory that necessary truths alone or necessary truths and reports of immediate experience are really knowledge is proved by its wide acceptance among empirically minded philosophers of the twentieth century—for example, Bertrand Russell, C. I. Lewis, and A. J. Ayer. In support of it a powerful battery of arguments has been produced, designed to show that despite the subjective certainty we feel in many kinds of belief, they cannot count as knowledge because they are not objectively certain.

Russell has contended that all the sources of what we ordinarily regard as common knowledge of fact are in some degree untrustworthy. Perception is tainted by illusions, hallucinations, and dreams. Memory is notoriously fallible. Testimony, which plays such a large part in building up the social fabric of belief, presupposes an inference to other minds that is inevitably shaky and conjectural. Induction never certifies its conclusions, imparting at best only a measure of probability to them. Even introspection, if it is held to convey information about the self as a continuing personality, goes beyond what is directly present to the mind. Only what is directly present to it—currently occurring thoughts and feelings—is the object of certain, infallible, and indubitable belief.

Lewis generalized Russell's position by distinguishing

expressive judgments that report current states of mind from all other empirical propositions on the ground that they alone are wholly nonpredictive and have no implications about future observable happenings by whose failure to occur they might be refuted. Ayer, at one time, went even further. He held that all contingent, empirical propositions whatsoever, including reports of immediate experience, are uncertain on the ground that every such proposition involves the application of a general predicative term to its subject and thus makes a comparison with previous and perhaps faultily remembered instances of the term's application.

This kind of fallibilism about empirical belief was doggedly resisted by G. E. Moore and, after him, by Wittgenstein, J. L. Austin, and Norman Malcolm. Moore's main point was that the word "certain" is learned and thus acquires its meaning from such situations as that in which a man holds up his hand and makes the perceptual judgment "I know for certain that this is a hand." Some rather subtler arguments are sketched in his book *Philosophical Papers*. Their general upshot is that the rationalists and fallibilists have been working with an unconsidered and excessively stringent concept of certainty. They have simply taken it for granted that for a belief to be certain, it must be impossible to doubt it. Russell, for example, began his search for certain knowledge with the question "Is there any knowledge in the world which is so certain that no reasonable man could doubt it?"

There are at least four senses in which it may be held that a belief cannot be doubted. The first is psychological; a man cannot doubt a belief if he cannot, in fact, bring himself to suspend judgment about it. This kind of certainty will vary from person to person and is of no direct philosophical interest. The second sense is logical. Here "doubt" is taken to mean "suppose false" and "can" to mean "can without logical inconsistency." This yields the strict rationalist view, since only necessary truths cannot be supposed false without inconsistency. A third sense identifies certainty with incorrigibility. According to it, a belief cannot be doubted if its truth follows from the fact that it is believed. Anyone who doubts an incorrigible belief shows that he does not understand the words that express it. The favorite examples of incorrigible beliefs are reports of immediate experience, such as "I am in pain" or "It seems to me now that there is a table here." But the notion would also apply to the more elementary and intuitive kind of necessary truth, such as the law of contradiction. Finally, there is the concept of certainty which, say Moore and his adherents, we actually employ in common speech where it means what cannot *reasonably* be doubted or supposed false. That people make all sorts of mistakes is not, according to this view, a reason for doubting the truth of a particular proposition. What is required to justify doubt is that propositions just like this, made in circumstances just like these and resting on just this kind of evidence, have in the past turned out to be mistaken. In this sense of certainty many beliefs based on perception, memory, testimony, and induction are objectively certain and thus properly regarded as items of knowledge. This view has the merit of allowing that many propositions that are,

in fact, necessary truths are or once were less than certain, and it does not require the theory that there are any incorrigible propositions to be accepted. A further point in its favor is that such surprising theses as the one that no factual belief is certain can surprise us and escape triviality only if they are taken in this sense.

Some modern views. Recent philosophical discussions of knowledge have been much concerned with three distinctions drawn by Russell, Ryle, and Austin which must be briefly mentioned.

Acquaintance and description. In Russell's early writings he drew a distinction between knowledge of things and knowledge of truths, between knowledge of and knowledge that, a distinction marked in French by the verbs *connaître* and *savoir*. Within each kind he also discerned a distinction between an immediate and a derived form. Immediate knowledge of truths is conveyed in intuitive statements—for example, basic judgments of perception and the axioms of logic and mathematics; derivative knowledge of truths, in demonstrable necessary propositions and inferred empirical statements. Parallel to this on the side of knowledge of things is the distinction between knowledge by acquaintance and knowledge by description.

Acquaintance, as Russell defined it, is the converse of presentation; it is the direct and infallible apprehension of some sort of object. But objects of description, unlike those of acquaintance, can fail to exist. Russell held that we are acquainted with present and past particulars and also with universals. This doctrine has led to a good deal of confusion. Certainly we do know things, persons, and places by acquaintance, but to do so is generally to know that something is true of them and is at least to know how to recognize them. The words with which we refer to things we are not acquainted with can be defined or explained in terms of those connected with objects of acquaintance. But this produces understanding rather than knowledge, understanding of singular terms (whether what they purport to refer to exists or not) and of general terms (whether or not there is anything they apply to). Russell's principle of acquaintance ("Every proposition which we can understand must be composed wholly of constituents with which we are acquainted") is really a version of the empiricist theory of meaning. Asserted without qualification, it is highly unplausible. We are not acquainted with anything corresponding to the "if" that occurs in the verbal expression of a hypothetical proposition although we understand the word. In general, to become acquainted with things is to acquire some intuitive knowledge of truths in which they figure, particular objects of acquaintance being the subjects of such truths and universal objects of acquaintance their predicates. In other words, knowledge of things cannot be separated from and regarded as prior to knowledge of truths in the way Russell supposed.

Knowing how and knowing that. Ryle's distinction between knowing how and knowing that has already been mentioned. There is a parallel distinction between remembering how and remembering that (there is also memory *of* past events). Ryle is anxious to correct the intellectualist bias of theorists of knowledge and to draw attention to the dispositional nature of all kinds of knowledge and belief; we speak, after all, of the knowledge and beliefs of those who are fast asleep. He tends to suggest that knowing that is a special, verbal form of knowing how, that it consists in having learned how to answer certain questions and now being ready to answer them.

Performative and descriptive verbs. John Austin's work on performative utterances has interested many philosophers in that class of verbs which are used in the first person present to do things rather than to describe what is being done. Examples of such performative verbs are "promise," "swear," "take thee, *X*, to be my wedded wife," and "name this ship *Y*." A verb ϕ is performative if it follows that I ϕ from the fact that I say, "I ϕ." Austin appears to have thought, wrongly, that "know" is a verb of this kind and that its function is to guarantee or authorize the acceptance of the piece of information that followed it. It is true that to prefix "I know" to a statement of fact does not add much to its content. But *p* and "I know that *p*" are not equivalent, since the former may be true when the latter is false. Austin was right in denying that knowledge is a state of assurance stronger than the most assured belief, though it is not clear that anyone ever supposed that it was. But the correctness of this denial, although it entails that it is not some describable psychological feature of the knower's state of mind that differentiates knowledge from belief, does not entail that the difference is not at all describable and lies, rather, in some nondescriptive function that the word performs.

THE NATURE OF BELIEF

Most philosophers who have in any way adverted to the nature of belief have assumed that belief is an inner state of mind, directly accessible to introspection and distinct from, though causally related to, the believer's behavior. In *The Emotions and the Will* (1859) the Scottish philosopher Alexander Bain proposed that belief should be defined in terms of behavior: "Belief has no meaning except in reference to our actions . . . no mere conception that does not directly or indirectly implicate our voluntary exertions can ever amount to the state in question." In support of Bain's theory is the fact that not only can others check our claims to believe by considering whether we behave appropriately but we ourselves may also take the results of such a test to overrule claims to believe that we have sincerely made. Careful statements of the opposing doctrines have been given by H. H. Price and R. B. Braithwaite. Price's mentalist definition of belief equates it with entertainment of a proposition together with assent. To entertain a proposition is to understand and attend to its meaning; when it occurs by itself, it is neutral and uncommitted as regards the proposition's truth or falsehood. Price breaks assent down into a volitional and an emotional part. He describes the volitional element as a mental act of preferring a proposition to any incompatible alternatives that have occurred to one; the emotional element is a feeling of conviction or assurance and may vary in degree. Braithwaite identifies belief in a proposition with its entertainment together with a dispositional readiness to act

as if it were true. "Being ready to act as if *p* were true" has at first sight a suggestion of circularity, for it seems to mean being ready to act as if one believed *p*. But this can be avoided. I act as if *p* were true if I act in a way which would satisfy my desires if *p* were in fact true.

Against both theories it should be said that "entertainment" is dispensable if the normal sense of "believe" is in question, for we attend consciously to the propositions we believe only at rare intervals. As regards Price, what is to be understood by an act of preferring as opposed to an emotion of preference? It looks very like the silent assertion of the proposition itself, an inner rehearsal of a piece of outward verbal behavior. Second, feelings of conviction do not always attend even the beliefs we consciously entertain. Unless our confident beliefs are actually challenged, our state would seem to be one of easy and unemotional taking for granted.

Against the view of Bain and Braithwaite it has been urged by Mill, Brentano, and Russell that if a belief has behavioral effects different from mere entertainment, it must differ in its intrinsic mental character. This is a misunderstanding. For a behaviorist there is a difference in the dispositions of one who believes and of one who merely entertains a proposition. A more serious difficulty is presented by beliefs that have negligible practical consequences, such as those about remote historical or astronomical events. But even here there is a disposition to verbal behavior, and, again, a disposition can exist without being actualized. There is also the difficulty that my claims about what I believe become, according to this theory, inductive conjectures about what I should do if certain circumstances arose. One reply is that not all inductive conjectures are conjectural to that degree. I need not, for example, feel very hesitant about what would happen if this iron table were dropped on that china teapot. Braithwaite adds that his theory has the merit of making possible rather precise measurements of subjective probability or degree of belief. The numerical probability I attach to a belief can be regarded as the least favorable odds I should accept on its turning out to be correct. Thus, unless I accept an odds-on bet, I do not believe something more than I believe its denial.

There is an interesting and extreme opposition in the history of philosophy between Descartes, who held that assent is a matter of will that can be freely given or withheld, and Hume, who represented us as largely passive in belief, which he conceived as a feeling that we find ourselves with and must put up with whether we like it or not, much as we find ourselves equipped with desires and aversions. Descartes's activism is shown first in his proposal that the philosopher should undertake a course of methodical doubt, suspending judgment about all the beliefs he has hitherto taken for granted. It reaches its fullest development in his attempt to solve the theological problem of error or intellectual evil, to reconcile the fact, on which his whole philosophy depends, that many of our beliefs are false with the goodness of God. The solution he offered is that God has fitted us out with limited intellects, appropriate to our earthly needs, but in his own image, with unrestricted freedom of will. When we make mistakes it is because we have culpably given free assent to propositions beyond the effective reach of our limited intellects.

In Descartes's favor is the fact that we do assess beliefs as more or less reasonable, a practice whose theory is logic and methodology. And the ethics of belief has not always been confined to distinguishing logically reasonable beliefs from others. It has often been held that some beliefs— in the existence of God, for example—are morally obligatory, and some beliefs are often recommended as prudent or useful. Hume himself propounded rules for judging causes and effects whose acceptance, he maintained, will enable us to advance science and avoid superstition. On Hume's side is the fact that it seems no more possible to resolve to believe something one actually does not believe than it is to increase one's height or eradicate one's distaste for endives by a simple effort of will. What one can do is to fortify or undermine one's belief in a proposition indirectly by voluntarily concentrating one's attention on the evidence for or against it.

It is quite commonly said that belief must rest on evidence and sometimes, especially by those who hold knowledge to be indefinable, that it must rest on knowledge. It is certainly usual for belief to rest on something the believer regards as evidence, whether or not it is true and whether or not it lends any support to the belief in question. But a wildly dogmatic or superstitious belief, maintained in the teeth of all the evidence, is still a belief, however unreasonable it may be.

Faith. There is some point to the malicious definition of faith as firm belief in something for which there is no evidence, for faith does involve a measure of risk, a voluntary decision to repose more confidence in a proposition, person, or institution than the statable grounds for doing so would, if neutrally considered, justify. Locke defined faith as resting on authoritative testimony, "the assent to any proposition, not thus made out by the deductions of reason, but upon the credit of the proposer." This applies well enough to the religious faith of traditional Christianity, but it is too narrow to cover the general use of the concept. It is often said that science rests on faith in the uniformity and intelligibility of nature as much as religion does on an undemonstrable conviction that the world is under the direction of a wise and benevolent intelligence. Certainly, science would be wholly sterilized if men were not prepared to consider adventurous and unjustified hypotheses. But it is not obvious that these adventurous conjectures have to be believed by their propounders. The austere maxim of W. K. Clifford—"It is wrong, everywhere and for anyone, to believe anything upon insufficient evidence"—is not strictly incompatible with intellectual enterprise. Yet even Popper, who of all theorists of knowledge is most insistent on the conjectural and fallible nature of science, admits that "our guesses are guided by the unscientific, the metaphysical (though biologically explicable) faith in laws, in regularities which we can uncover."

Bibliography

CLASSIC DISCUSSIONS

Bain, Alexander, *The Emotions and the Will*. London, 1859.
Descartes, René, *Meditations*.

Locke, John, *Essay Concerning Human Understanding*. Book 4.
Plato, *Republic*. Books 5–7.
Plato, *Theaetetus*.

MODERN ACCOUNTS

Austin, John, "Other Minds," in his *Philosophical Papers*. Oxford, 1961.
Ayer, A. J., *The Problem of Knowledge*. London, 1956. Chs. 1–2.
Chisholm, Roderick M., *Perceiving: A Philosophical Study*. Ithaca, N.Y., 1957. Part I.
Hintikka, Jaakko, *Knowledge and Belief*. Ithaca, N.Y., 1962.
Lewis, C. I., *Mind and the World-Order*. New York, 1929. Ch. 9.
Malcolm, Norman, *Knowledge and Certainty*. Englewood Cliffs, N.J., 1963.
Moore, G. E., *Philosophical Papers*. London, 1959.
Popper, Karl R., *Conjectures and Refutations*. London, 1963. See the Introduction.
Prichard, H. A., *Knowledge and Perception*. Oxford, 1950.
Russell, Bertrand, *Problems of Philosophy*. London, 1912. Chs. 5, 13.
Ryle, Gilbert, *The Concept of Mind*. London, 1949. Ch. 2.
Wilson, John Cook, *Statement and Inference*. Oxford, 1926. Part I, Chs. 2, 4; Part II, Chs. 1–3.
Woozley, A. D., *Theory of Knowledge: An Introduction*. London, 1949. Ch. 8.

ANTHONY QUINTON

KNUTZEN, MARTIN (1713–1751), German Wolffian philosopher, studied at the University of Königsberg and became an extraordinary professor there in 1734. Because he was a Wolffian, even though an unorthodox one, he never attained a full professorship in that Pietist-dominated school. However, because he was also a Pietist, Knutzen could never attain such a position in other German universities where Wolffians held the power of appointment.

Knutzen disagreed with Wolff on several significant points. His *Commentatio Philosophica de commercio Mentis et Corporis* ("Philosophical Commentary on the Relation Between Mind and Body," Königsberg, 1735) was an attempt to reconcile Wolff's theory of pre-established harmony with the Pietist doctrine of physical influence. He extended the problem beyond Wolff, from the relation of soul and body to the interrelations of simple substances in general. In this and in a panpsychistic metaphysics, he was closer to Leibniz than to Wolff. Knutzen, in his cosmological work *Vernünftige Gedanken von den Cometen* ("Rational Thought Concerning Comets," Königsberg, 1744), was one of the first philosophers in Germany to accept, at least partially, the Newtonian theory of gravitational attraction. His theological work was derivative and of little significance.

Knutzen's reputation is due more to his having been the teacher of Immanuel Kant than to his own significance. His influence on Kant has been much overrated. Recent research has shown that his influence was confined to the solution given by Kant in his first essay, *Gedanken von den wahren Schätzung der lebendigen Kräfte* ("Thoughts on the True Estimation of Living Forces," Königsberg, 1747), to the problem of the interrelation of substances, and to Kant's acceptance of Newtonian attraction. On the second point, Kant was also strongly influenced by the Berlin circle around Maupertuis, even though Maupertuis himself was reluctant to accept attraction; and in accepting attraction as a real force and in trying to give a metaphysical explanation for it, Kant went beyond the Berlin circle, Knutzen, and Newton himself in his published statements.

Both Kant's "Wolffianism" and his "Pietism" have been attributed by some historians to Knutzen's influence; but although Kant received a Pietist education, he was never either a Pietist or a Wolffian. Kant always opposed Wolff's doctrines, and any Pietist influence came through the general philosophical influence of C. A. Crusius. Even an alleged influence of Knutzen's theology on Kant's religious philosophy has been disproven.

Additional Works by Knutzen

Dissertatio metaphysica de Aeternitate Mundi Impossibili. Königsberg, 1733.
Commentatio Philosophica de Humanae Mentis Individua Natura sive Immortalitate. Königsberg, 1741.
Philosophischer Beweis von der Wahrheit der christlichen Religion. Königsberg, 1740.

Works on Knutzen

Biéma, M. van, *Martin Knutzen, La critique de l'harmonie préétablie.* Paris, 1908.
Bohatec, J., *Die Religionsphilosophie Kants.* Hamburg, 1938.
Erdmann, Benno, *Martin Knutzen und seine Zeit.* Leipzig, 1876.
Tonelli, Giorgio, *Elementi metodologici e metafisici in Kant dal 1745 al 1768,* Vol. 1. Turin, 1959. Chs. 1 and 2.

GIORGIO TONELLI

KOFFKA, KURT (1886–1941), one of the three founders of the Gestalt movement in psychology, was born in Berlin. In 1903 he went to the university there to study philosophy, and he is said to have had a special interest in Kant and Nietzsche at that time. In 1904 he moved to Edinburgh, and in the next few years his interest in psychology became increasingly strong. Soon after receiving his doctorate at Berlin in 1908, he moved to Würzburg, where he served as an assistant to Oswald Külpe and Karl Marbe. In 1910/1911 he taught at the Academy at Frankfurt am Main, and it was during this period, as a result of the joint deliberations of Max Wertheimer, Wolfgang Köhler, and himself, that the central notions of Gestalt theory began to emerge. In 1911 Koffka became a lecturer at the University of Giessen, and from 1919 to about 1927 he was assistant professor.

The early 1920s saw the founding of *Psychologische Forschung,* a periodical in which several of the original articles on Gestalt theory were originally published, and of which Koffka was for many years the editor. During this decade he traveled extensively: a visit to Oxford for the International Congress of Psychology in 1923 resulted in much wider recognition of Gestalt theory than had hitherto been possible, and in succeeding years he was visiting professor at Cornell, Chicago, and Wisconsin. In 1927 he took up permanent residence in the United States, having accepted a professorship at Smith College, Northampton, Massachusetts. In 1932, at the invitation of the USSR State Institute, he joined an expedition to Uzbekistan to carry out ethno-psychological research, but at an early stage he was forced to return because of illness. He remained intellectually active until his death. He is said to

have been a person of considerable kindness and charm, with wide interests which included music, art, and travel. His friendship with Wertheimer and Köhler was lifelong.

To separate Koffka's distinctive contributions from those of Wertheimer and Köhler is not easy, since each was influenced considerably by the other two. Koffka's *The Growth of the Mind* was an attempt to apply Gestalt principles to child psychology, while *Principles of Gestalt Psychology* was a comprehensive account of a wide range of psychological work up to 1935, with detailed theoretical discussion. One of his central claims was that it is possible to take seriously the advances of science while still finding a place for the concepts of meaning and value; indeed, scientific inquiries themselves suffer if one does not do so. An aggressive materialism or behaviorism was quite foreign to him, but the alternative to this for Koffka was a new approach, using the concept of Gestalt, rather than a return to vitalism or Cartesian dualism. In an interesting passage in *Principles of Gestalt Psychology* he called attention to the difference in intellectual climate between Germany and America. The more abstract and speculative ideas, in which many German scholars were interested, had to be kept in the background when Gestalt theory was presented to the Americans, whose "high regard for science, accurate and earthbound" was accompanied by "an aversion, sometimes bordering on contempt, for metaphysics that tries to escape from the welter of mere facts into a loftier realm of ideas and ideals" (p. 18).

Philosophically interesting contributions found in *Principles of Gestalt Psychology* include the distinction between the geographical and behavioral environments, a discussion of the criteria by means of which "things" in the behavioral environment are distinguished from "not-things," and an attempt to reinstate the concept of ego. The behavioral environment is, in effect, the perceived world, the world of common-sense experience, whereas the geographical environment is the world as studied by the physical scientist. There are features in the geographical environment (such as infrared rays) which in ordinary circumstances are not present in the behavioral environment, whereas there are features in the behavioral environment (for example, the fact that two lines are grouped together when someone looks at them) which have no direct counterpart in the geographical environment. Examples of "things" are sticks, stones, clouds, and some types of fog; marginal cases are waves, words, and noises, while "a fog which makes our ocean liner reduce speed and sound its piercing horn is not thing-like at all, as little as the mist from which we emerge when we climb a mountain" (*ibid.,* p. 70). The three characteristics of things are "shaped boundedness, dynamic properties, and constancy." As for the ego, "it has a very definite place in that [the behavioral] world, and well-defined, if variable boundaries. . . . 'In front,' 'to the left and right,' 'behind,' and 'above and below' are characteristics of space which it possesses with regard to an object which serves as the origin of the system of spatial co-ordinates" (*ibid.,* p. 322). In this case science itself is seriously impoverished if the concept of the ego is simply ignored. The study (sometimes called phenomenology) of how the world appears at the common-sense level is logically independent, according to Koffka's view, of any new discovery in physics about what is "really" happening.

Many of the problems that Koffka raised are of current philosophical interest, and as a psychologist he ranks among the greatest of his generation. (For further discussion of his work, see GESTALT THEORY.)

Bibliography

Besides numerous articles published in journals, Koffka's works include *Principles of Gestalt Psychology* (New York and London, 1935); *The Growth of the Mind,* translated by R. M. Ogden (London, 1924); "Mental Development," in Carl Murchison, ed., *Psychologies of 1925* (Worcester, Mass., 1928), pp. 129–143; and "Some Problems of Space Perception," in Carl Murchison, ed., *Psychologies of 1930* (Worcester, Mass., 1930), pp. 161–187.

For discussions of Koffka's work, see G. W. Hartmann, *Gestalt Psychology; A Survey of Facts and Principles* (New York, 1935). See bibliography to GESTALT THEORY for works discussing Gestalt psychology as a whole.

T. R. MILES

KÖHLER, WOLFGANG, German Gestalt psychologist, was born in 1887 in Tallinn, Estonia. He studied first at the University of Tübingen and then at Bonn. He next studied physics under Max Planck and psychology under Carl Stumpf at the University of Berlin, and received his Ph.D. from that school in 1909 for investigations on hearing. In 1911 he became *Privatdozent* at Frankfurt. Max Wertheimer came to Frankfurt in 1912, and in the same year Köhler and Kurt Koffka served as the subjects for Wertheimer's famous experiments on stroboscopic motion that are widely regarded as the beginning of Gestalt psychology.

In 1913 Köhler became director of the anthropoid experiment station operated by the Prussian Academy of Sciences at Tenerife in the Canary Islands, and he remained there, throughout World War I, until 1920. The pioneering studies in the psychology of chimpanzees which he carried out there were published in several papers and in the monograph *Intelligenzprüfungen an Anthropoiden* (*The Mentality of Apes*, 1917).

Köhler's next major work, *Die physischen Gestalten in Ruhe und im stationären Zustand* ("Physical Gestalten in Rest and in the Stationary State"), was published at Brunswick in 1920. It is primarily a work in physics and reveals Köhler's indebtedness to Planck, but its major themes played important roles in his more strictly psychological writings.

In 1921, with Wertheimer, Koffka, Kurt Goldstein, and Hans Gruhle, Köhler founded the journal *Psychologische Forschung,* which served as the leading organ of the Gestalt psychologists until Köhler was forced to suspend publication because of the difficulties of editing it from the United States. In 1922 Köhler succeeded Stumpf as director of the Psychological Institute and professor of philosophy at the University of Berlin. He held a visiting professorship at Clark University in the academic year 1925/1926 and returned to America for another visit in 1929. In the same year his *Gestalt Psychology* was published in English.

Köhler was the only leading member of the Gestalt school who was not Jewish, but he was strongly opposed to the Nazis. He published a letter against them in a Berlin newspaper after they took power and a bit later left Germany. Köhler gave the William James lectures at Harvard in 1934 and published them as *The Place of Value in a World of Fact* in 1938. In 1935 he was appointed professor of psychology at Swarthmore College. His Page–Barbour lectures given at the University of Virginia in 1938 were published in an expanded version in 1940 as *Dynamics in Psychology.* Köhler became professor emeritus at Swarthmore in 1957. In 1959 the school awarded him an honorary doctorate and he became visiting research professor at Dartmouth.

Köhler is correctly thought of primarily as a psychologist. Nevertheless, throughout his career he never hesitated to interpret the results and methodology of the physical sciences and to apply his interpretations to the delineation of the proper task of psychology and to the elucidation of its problems. He admitted a debt to the phenomenology of Edmund Husserl, and his own work was broadly in the phenomenological stream. Both phenomenology and physics influenced his vocabulary, his methods of research, and his theoretical conclusions. Köhler was an ardent controversialist, and he engaged in a continuing polemical defense of the Gestalt theory. He believed that the theory offered a new resolution of the controversy between those who believe in innate ideas or tendencies and those who stress the importance of ideas acquired by learning. He thought that his Gestalt physics could resolve the biological controversy between mechanism and vitalism. He claimed to have dissolved the philosophical controversies between idealism and realism and between monism and dualism, and he advocated a form of epiphenomenalism or even an identity theory of mind and body. Köhler believed that by phenomenological analysis he could demonstrate both the existence and something of the nature of value, and that value, or "requiredness," was more general than moral philosophers and aestheticians believed; thus, he held, the psychologist's investigation of value was of prime importance to the philosopher.

Köhler, then, not only advanced psychological theories and views about the proper subject matter of this science but also presented well-reasoned opinions on speculative problems in biology, physiology, physics, and chemistry, and suggested possibly fruitful lines of research for these sciences to undertake. He also presented theories belonging to such central philosophical disciplines as epistemology, metaphysics, and value theory. This article will discuss some of the philosophically interesting issues raised by Köhler in the physical sciences and psychology, as well as some of his general philosophical positions. It will not attempt to discuss his contributions to Gestalt psychology proper, except for his discussion of isomorphism. (For a connected treatment of Gestalt psychology, see GESTALT THEORY.)

PHYSICS AND PHYSIOLOGY

Köhler has discussed physical concepts and discoveries for at least three main purposes: to demonstrate the existence of physical structures analogous to perceptual Gestalten; to provide a physicochemical theory of perception and other mental functions; and to delineate the proper task of psychology by comparing its present status with the status of physics at various times in its history.

Physical Gestalten. Köhler, like the other Gestalt psychologists, has claimed that a central subject of psychology is the investigation of certain kinds of structures in which "the whole is more than the sum of its parts." An analysis of these Gestalten would explain many puzzling facts of vision, touch, hearing, memory, and understanding. The existence of such structures was denied on the ground that the whole can never be more than the sum of its parts. Köhler sought to show that there are a variety of recognized physical systems in which the whole is more than the sum of its parts. Machines are structures whose movements are strictly determined. From a knowledge of the parts of a machine and their interrelationships, we can know the motions of the whole. Thus a machine, according to Köhler, is no more than the sum of its parts. But in many physical systems it is the state of the whole which determines the state of the parts. Examples of such systems are the distribution of an electrical charge over the surface of a conductor, which varies with the shape of the conductor; the distribution of a current of electricity or fluid in a network of wires or pipes; the distribution of particles of a fluid body whose only constraint is the walls of the container; and a planetary system. The common characteristic of these systems is that the parts interact dynamically rather than mechanically. And in these systems, he claimed, the whole is greater than the parts.

These physical systems all exhibit another characteristic, which Köhler thinks is strikingly analogous to a characteristic of phenomenal Gestalten. When the physical systems are disturbed, the interaction of their parts tends more or less rapidly to restore the systems to a state of equilibrium. They are thus dynamically self-regulating systems. Phenomenal Gestalten are also dynamically self-regulating. The parts of the Gestalten interact with one another to produce, or reproduce, systematic wholes within the perceptual field. Köhler recognizes, following Wertheimer, a set of five factors involved in the recognition of Gestalten. If any of these factors are present, then we tend to perceive a Gestalt, unless inhibiting factors are also present or the factors are so present as to cancel out one another. The five factors are (1) *proximity*: objects which appear close together are more likely to be classed as part of the same Gestalt than those which are far apart; (2) *similarity*: objects which resemble each other tend to be classed as belonging together; (3) "*common destiny*": if objects move or change together, they tend to be perceived as part of the same thing or as belonging together; (4) "*good Gestalt*": forms that are not quite regular tend to be perceived as more regular than they are; (5) *closure*: forms which are in some way incomplete tend to be perceived as complete—for example, a circle with a small arc missing will be perceived as a full circle.

The resemblance between dynamically self-regulating physical systems and phenomenal Gestalten suggested to Köhler that it might be more fruitful to attempt to understand mental phenomena by means of a dynamic rather than a mechanical model, and in fact this model has continued to serve Köhler throughout his career as a fruitful

explanatory hypothesis in psychology. He has been particularly successful in applying it to problems of perception, of memory, and of intelligence or insight—of coming to understand a situation or a problem.

Despite Köhler's apparent success in applying the two notions that in certain physical and phenomenal structures the whole is greater than the sum of its parts and that psychological phenomena should be interpreted dynamically rather than mechanically, they have been widely criticized. Both notions, it is said, are enormously vague. It is not surprising that they seem to "work," for by their very vagueness they can be made to fit almost any body of facts. Surely in some generally accepted sense of "whole" and "part" almost any whole can be shown to be greater than the sum of its parts. But it is not clear that Köhler was applying the two terms univocally in the phenomenal cases he adduced as examples, and it is even less clear that he was using them in the same sense when speaking of the parts of phenomenal Gestalten and of the parts of physical systems. Similarly, although the dynamic model may have aided Köhler in the design of new experiments and the interpretation of many phenomenal facts, it has been claimed that, outside of a certain limited range of cases, the apparent use of a dynamic model can mean no more than a recognition that phenomena change. The substance of the theory is probably Wertheimer's set of dynamic factors, which had in large part been anticipated by earlier psychologists, and there seems no reason to connect them with any specific physical theory.

Isomorphism. Probably the most central concept in all of Köhler's thought is the concept of isomorphism, or similarity of form. He has used this notion for two major and several minor purposes. The two major functions combine into a theory of knowledge which is partly conceptual and partly physicochemical and physiological. Köhler has distinguished between (1) phenomena, or percepts; (2) their cortical correlates, or brain-states; and (3) nature, or the physical world. He has been perfectly willing to believe that percepts and brain-states may eventually be shown to be identical and in this sense does not exclude the possibility of a metaphysical monism. He holds, in opposition to both phenomenalists and new realists, that the phenomenal world and the physical world are not identical, and thus is an epistemological dualist. (These points are discussed below.) It is the theory of isomorphism that serves as the connecting link among these three elements. Percepts, it is claimed, are related to one another within the phenomenal field as their cortical correlates are related to one another in the cortex and as the corresponding physical objects are related to one another in physical space. The structural relations within any of the three realms are reproduced in the others. If a man-percept appears in phenomenal space atop a horse-percept, then in physical space there is a man atop a horse, and in the brain there are two brain processes dynamically related to each other in the cortical correlative of the relation "on top of."

What concerns us here is the isomorphy between the phenomenal world and brain-states. In this connection Köhler formulated the principle of isomorphism for spatial relations (it can be formulated for any type of phenomenal ordering) as: *"Experienced order in space is always structurally identical with a functional order in the distribution of underlying brain processes"* (*Gestalt Psychology*, Mentor edition, New York, 1959, p. 39). The parts of the visual field are not independent of one another; they exhibit structural relationships. If, for example, there is in my visual field a white square on a black ground, then in my brain there are processes corresponding to the white square, the black ground, and the boundary between the two. The topological relations between the brain processes are functionally identical with the corresponding visual relations. Metrical relationships are not preserved, but such relationships as betweenness are. In memory, these relationships are preserved in memory-traces. Thus it is form or structure rather than exact pictorial images that are preserved.

Köhler holds that the physiological processes in the brain which are involved in perception and memory are very probably electrochemical in nature. In the case of the white square, the brain process corresponding to the square-percept contains a higher concentration of ions than the brain process corresponding to the black ground. The two processes are functionally connected at a boundary corresponding to the edge of the square. There is a potential difference across this boundary; an electric flow of ions therefore takes place, and the square is perceived. Changes in the solution leave memory traces, which are subject to alteration in the course of time. These traces are superimposed on one another and thus functionally mirror the order of time of the percepts themselves.

The theory of isomorphism, both in its conceptual outline and in its physiological accompaniment, has been only inadequately outlined here. The physiological element, despite the important role it plays in Köhler's claim that functionally an identity theory of mind and body is at least feasible, is a matter for empirical investigation. Much of what Köhler says sounds rather plausible, but there are difficulties in stating the theory with the proper degree of precision. Although he speaks of a cortical retina, Köhler does not mean that perception involves the reproduction of a (two-dimensional or three-dimensional) image of the object within the cortex. This would be complete isomorphism. On the other hand, almost any set of relationships can represent any other by *some* form of correspondence, and the correspondences, if any, actually involved in perception might be very complex or in some other way not what we would intuitively grasp as a correspondence.

There are other issues involved which can only be raised and not explored here. Suppose it were established that when a certain macroscopic brain-state is observed in people, they generally claim to perceive a certain object. For instance, take any of the reversible figures which appear to an observer now in one way and now in another, such as a Maltese cross, composed of alternating black and white rays, which can be seen in two different ways. In one way of looking at it certain parts appear as the figure and the others as ground, while in the other way what was ground appears as figure and what was figure appears as ground. According to Köhler, each way of seeing the figure corresponds to a different electrochemical state in the brain. Now suppose that one person's descriptions of the

cross fail to correspond, in either a regular or irregular manner, to the descriptions that we have generally found associated with his brain-states. We may wish to claim that he is misdescribing what he is seeing. But how we choose to regard the situation is not merely a matter of fact; it involves at least one conceptual matter, a choice between conflicting criteria of what the person is seeing—the person's description (which is, of course, the only criterion we now have) and our knowledge of his brain-states. And empirical investigation alone cannot settle this conflict.

The same point applies to another example, in which a further factor becomes apparent. There is experimental evidence that when people see two parallel lines close to each other, one of which extends beyond the other at each end, they claim to see shadowy lines connecting the ends of the two lines to complete a trapezoid. Köhler suggests that the shadowy lines are caused by potential barriers in the cortex created by the cortical correlates of the lines actually drawn. Again, if it could be shown that such potential barriers are present in a person's brain although he claims not to see such lines, we might put it down to misdescription. But surely here we are inclined to take him at his word. In the first case we can describe what it means to see the cross in one way rather than another. But in this case we can only point out where the shadowy lines ought to be seen. The achieving aspect of perception is perhaps more obvious here. It is not simply a matter of what is seen but also of how we learn to describe what we see. In most descriptions it is clear what the standards of an accurate description are, and we can understand a proposal for a change in standards. In the present case it is not even clear what the standards are, if there are any. It is this element of conventional standards, which Köhler has omitted from his discussion, that makes his problems of the relationship among percepts, objects, and brain-states not merely a matter of physiological and psychological experimentation but of conceptual analysis.

Isomorphism and language. Köhler has developed an interesting linguistic theory as a corollary of his theory of isomorphism. This corollary, except for Köhler's added complexity, resembles the picture theory of meaning advanced by Ludwig Wittgenstein in his *Tractatus Logico-philosophicus* and seems to have been developed out of similar considerations. If the only way one thing can represent another is by having the same form, then the only way language can represent a situation is through a common form. Since, according to the theory of isomorphism, a phenomenal event has a physiological correlate possessing a similar form, then language represents both the event and the physiological correlate indifferently. A statement ostensibly about an observed phenomenon can be interpreted as a statement about brain-states and vice versa. ". . . language . . . is the peripheral outcome of antecedent physiological processes, among others of those upon which my experience depends. According to our general hypothesis, the concrete order of this experience pictures the dynamic order of such processes. Thus, if to me my words represent a description of my experiences, they are at the same time objective representations of the processes which underlie these experiences. Consequently, it does not matter very much whether my words are taken as messages about experience or about these physiological facts. For, so far as the order of events is concerned, the message is the same in both cases" (*Gestalt Psychology*, p. 40).

Physics and psychology. The third way in which Köhler has used physics is to elucidate what he regards as the proper program for psychology. Physics, in his view, is an old, established discipline whose techniques have been developed and refined over a long period of time. Quantitative methods and pointer readings are appropriate in physics because there are thoroughgoing and widely accepted theories that give meaning to the numbers arrived at. Even in the early days of physics, in the time of Galileo, many of the problems could be investigated quantitatively, because the phenomena investigated had long been known from everyday life and this knowledge provided the necessary qualitative meaning. Where everyday life did not supply the necessary qualitative background, as in the study of electricity, physics had to proceed by qualitative investigations before quantitative ones could be undertaken profitably. The problems of psychology, Köhler claims, are more often like those of electricity than those of Galilean mechanics. In general, in psychology the necessary meaning-giving theory is absent. Intelligence quotients are notoriously hard to interpret. The difficulty in assessing their significance arises out of a lack of any clear notion of what intelligence consists in. Psychology should first try to develop a theory of intelligence before it tries to measure intelligence. Until a satisfactory theory is arrived at, it can hardly be determined whether or not intelligence quotients do measure intelligence and how well they do it.

GESTALT PSYCHOLOGY

Critique of behaviorism. Köhler's attempt to show that qualitative methods are the most appropriate in the present state of psychology arose in the context of his repudiation of behaviorism. His phenomenological view of the nature of the subject matter of psychology was radically different from the notion that psychology is the study of behavior, with its related stimulus–response physiological theory. The behaviorists, according to Köhler, have taken too much to heart one epistemological teaching but ignored its wider context. They seek to limit psychology to the observation of the response of human beings in scientifically controlled situations because they have become aware of the truth that one person cannot directly observe another person's experience. However, the behaviorist cannot avoid the study of direct experience by limiting himself to the observation of human reactions in controlled situations, for the only evidence he has of such reactions is *his own* experience. The behaviorist seeks to be objective, but he confuses two pairs of meanings of the terms "subjective" and "objective." In one sense, observations of another person's reactions are no less subjective than my hearing his statements about what he is experiencing: both are part of my experience. But in the primary sense "subjective" and "objective" refer to differently characterized phenomena within my experience. In this sense there is no reason why I cannot examine both subjective and objective experience; in the first sense I cannot help but investigate subjective phenomena.

Critique of introspectionism. Whereas Köhler has criticized behaviorism for misunderstanding the nature of direct experience, he criticizes introspectionism for distorting the facts of experience to fit a preconceived theory. By "introspectionism" Köhler does not mean the gathering of information from an inspection of one's own experience in general; he has criticized the behaviorists for their refusal to accept information so gathered as unscientific. When he attacks introspectionism, Köhler has in mind certain characteristic theories and procedures of the psychologists of his own and the previous generation who relied on introspection. Philosophers and psychologists long believed, under the influence of geometrical optics, that, for example, a round penny must appear elliptical in most positions or that a white surface under a very low degree of illumination must appear gray, and a darker gray than a black surface under a very high degree of illumination. Experimentation has shown, however, that a "naive" observer tends to describe the penny as round no matter what shape strikes the retina and the white surface as white in almost any circumstances. The naive observer, it was held, could not be seeing what he claimed to be seeing. Introspectionists devised elaborate techniques by which a "trained" observer could be made to claim to see what by the laws of optics he should be seeing. In essence, these techniques consisted in excluding from the visual field of the observer all of the surroundings of the object to be observed. In this way, the introspectionists claimed, all the factors of learning are excluded and the object is seen as it "really" appears, before the process of education has distorted our pristine perceptions.

Köhler rightly points out that by employing this technique of exclusion in the interests of a theory, all other factors that might explain why the round penny looks round have been barred. The Gestalt theory offers an alternative explanation of this fact which does not involve the notion of an elaborate hoax played upon the naive observer, an explanation which cannot even be tested by the exclusionary techniques of introspectionism. The defects of introspectionism were further evidenced, Köhler claims, by the fact that introspective psychology had degenerated into an investigation of minute and trivial facts of interest only to specialists.

Associationism and atomism. Köhler has criticized both the introspectionists and the behaviorists for their psychological atomism or, as he also calls it, their mosaic theory. Closely related to psychological atomism is the theory of associationism, which Köhler likewise regards as inadequate. Psychological atomism is the view that what we perceive is a mosaic of bits and pieces, each independent and essentially unconnected with any other. The parts of the visual and other sensory fields thus lack any sort of relatedness. Yet we do recognize this brown patch and that white patch as belonging together and both as being parts of a dog, rather than one belonging with the ground underneath the dog and the other to the wall behind the dog.

Psychological atomism, according to Köhler, is a theory about the nature of the objects of perception. The theory of association is a theory as to how the experience of order arises out of the unordered psychological atoms postulated by psychological atomism. I have seen white patches associated with dogs in the past, and thus I come to expect that when I see a white patch of a particular kind in the future, it will belong to a dog.

Köhler's answer to psychological atomism is that we do not experience the parts of the visual field, for example, as separate from and unrelated to one another, but that we experience relationships among its parts. Certain wholes separate themselves from other parts of the field, and these wholes are composed of parts related to each other by means of the Wertheimer factors mentioned earlier. If we are in fact led to see things as belonging together by the very structure of experience, then the theory of association is unnecessary. Köhler has gone on to show that it is also inadequate, in that it cannot fully explain all that it was intended to explain.

Many of Köhler's criticisms of atomism and associationism as psychological theories are justified. But he apparently has thought that in arguing against psychological atomism he is also arguing against any epistemological atomism as well. Part of his theory of isomorphism is the claim that the world as experienced contains experienced relationships among its constituents and that the observer does not add this structure to the world. But here, as earlier, conceptual matters are involved: it is not only a matter of experienced relationships but also of learning what it is to experience a relationship. We must learn the established criteria of what is to count as a relationship before we can know that what we are experiencing is a relationship.

Köhler has also believed that the theory of associationism led to a hidden limitation in methods of investigation. According to the associationist, he holds, organization arises out of previous association, whereas, in his view, association depends on previous organization. Sensory Gestalten, melodies, and meaningful sentences are organized wholes, and their parts are readily associated. Totally unrelated visual or auditory objects or nonsense syllables, on the other hand, have first to be organized into some kind of order before they can be recognized or be later remembered as having been associated. Köhler does not deny the facts of association but, rather, that association is a fundamental explanatory category. If it were recognized that order is more easily found than made, then it would be seen that organization should play a role in the design of experiments. As it is, far too many experiments fail. For instance, in experiments designed to test an animal's intelligence the apparatus may be too complex for the animal to grasp the relations of the parts and thus be beyond his capacity, whereas by a slight revision the apparatus could serve adequately in carrying out the experiments.

PHILOSOPHICAL PROBLEMS

Epistemology. Köhler's epistemological views are difficult to organize and apparently are not altogether consistent. Probably the most careful and accurate presentation of his views is found in *The Place of Value in a World of Fact.* His theory is, as he claims, a form of epistemological dualism, here couched in the form of a refutation of both phenomenalism and the new realism and aimed at showing that the body–mind problem is a pseudo prob-

lem. Köhler's theory, both in content and in terminology, is strikingly similar to that developed by Bertrand Russell in *The Analysis of Matter* and *The Outline of Philosophy.*

The body–mind problem, Köhler claims, concerns the location of percepts. Physiology tells us that they are in our interior, in our brains, yet they appear to be outside ourselves. The resolution is that percepts are inside our bodies in one sense and outside our bodies in quite a different sense. We should distinguish between the body as a physical organism and the body as a percept. Percepts depend on processes within the physical organism; without such processes they would not take place. They appear as located outside the body, which is itself a percept. This perceptual body has a definite place in perceptual space, and other percepts have a definite relation to it within perceptual space. There is no more need to wonder why a perceptual dog appears outside of my perceptual body than to wonder why it appears outside of a perceptual house. Relationships in perceptual space say nothing about the location of percepts in physical space.

In some way what Köhler was saying has been recognized at least since Kant's distinction between phenomena and noumena, and Köhler's position seems open to much the same objections as Kant's. What is needed is an account of the relationships between physical space and perceptual space, or between physical object and percept, and this is not what Köhler has given. In physical space percepts are inside the observer's body; in perceptual space they are outside. Here is a radical disparity between spatial relations in the phenomenal and the transphenomenal realms. But Köhler wants to hold that relationships in the phenomenal and the physical worlds are isomorphic. The phenomenal house is between two phenomenal trees; the physical house is likewise between two physical trees. Phenomenal relationships are thus supposed to give us knowledge of physical relationships. And our knowledge of phenomenal relations is the only basis for any knowledge we may have of physical relations. But how do we get from percepts in the physical world to physical objects? And how can we avoid solipsism? Köhler claims that two scientists do not observe the same galvanometer. It is self-evident for him that neither can observe the other's phenomenal world. But physically the percept of each is different, for each is in his own brain. Köhler has not shown how we get from the two percepts to a common physical object.

That Kant spoke of things-in-themselves and Köhler of a physical world, or of nature, should not mask the fundamental similarities of their views. Despite Köhler's belief that the phenomenal world itself gives evidence of a nonphenomenal world, his physical world stands in exactly the same position as Kant's things-in-themselves. They are both unknowable.

Causation. With his emphasis on experienced relationships between the parts of perceived entities, it is not surprising that Köhler denies Hume's claim that we do not experience causal relations. Causation is only a special case of a general characteristic of experienced phenomena which Köhler terms "requiredness," other cases of which are discussed in the section on value. In any of various ways one experience "demands" another for its completion. What Köhler calls insight is the coming to see what is demanded, what is needed to complete a set of factors. Men, and animals to a more limited degree, can have insight into, among other things, what caused a particular event or what will be the probable outcome of a particular line of action. The insight is the experiencing of a causal relation between cause and effect. Köhler concedes that the Humean theory of regular sequence accounts for our practice in various situations of subjecting causal theories to experimental testing after they have occurred to us, but it cannot by itself account for our first recognition of a cause.

Köhler has been criticized by defenders of the regularity theory for confusing psychological issues with logical ones. It may well be the case that in human (as well as in purely physical) situations we frequently arrive at the true answer to a causal problem without any elaborate examination of classes of sequences. From this, however, it does not follow that causation is a "simple" relation like, for example, coexistence which can be given in a single experience. Granting that I may truly judge that A_1 is the cause of B_1 without having performed elaborate controlled experiments, Hume's regularity theory has nevertheless been vindicated as an analysis of the concept of causation if I am prepared to admit that A_1 was not really the cause of B_1 were I to discover that other instances of A are or were not followed by instances of B.

Value. Köhler's epistemological views are developed most fully in *The Place of Value in a World of Fact*. This volume is a contribution to the discussion of axiology which played such a prominent role in American philosophy during the 1920s and 1930s. The argument of the work is long, digressive, and difficult to summarize. The views on isomorphism and on epistemology mentioned above form an integral part of the argument. At the cost of oversimplifying Köhler's views to the point of distortion, it can be said that he holds that we can have direct perceptual knowledge of value. Value is an objective fact of the phenomenal, and hence also of the physical, world. Both phenomenal Gestalten and physical Gestalten spontaneously change in a certain direction. Melodies and visual shapes require completion in certain ways. Very often when we are attempting to remember something, the context in our mind shows us not only the sort of thing we seek to remember but also whether we are getting close to remembering it. Whatever the proper interpretation of these phenomena may be, Köhler believes that they all demonstrate the factor which he terms "requiredness" and that in the case of memory, the requiredness is a characteristic of something outside the present phenomenal situation. Valuation, an assessment of what ought to be, is not a unique phenomenon but another special case of the recognition of requiredness. Köhler does not directly undertake an analysis of valuation but only of requiredness in general. He hoped that his analysis would be of use to philosophers in their own analyses of ethical and aesthetic requiredness.

Mechanism and vitalism. Toward the end of *The Place of Value in a World of Fact*, Köhler returns to two topics which had engaged him earlier, the dispute between mechanism and vitalism and the question of the precise metaphysical classification of his own theory. In the first case, as in many other situations, Köhler argues that the apparent alternatives are not exhaustive. Mechanists, in their treatment of living processes, take the same shortsighted view that they take of the nature of physical processes mentioned earlier. Mechanical systems are not the only kind of physical systems; there are also the dynamically self-regulating systems. The premise that man must be a machine because physics finds only mechanical systems in the world is thus undermined. On the other hand, one does not have to hold to vitalism just because men are obviously different from machines. Living organisms, including man, can quite easily be physical systems without being machines. And in fact, Köhler held, living organisms can be explained quite satisfactorily as dynamically self-regulating systems without postulating some mysterious nonphysical vital force.

Body–mind problem. Köhler seems to advocate an epistemological dualism. He is not, however, a dualist in the sense in which the term is used in connection with the body–mind problem. Other psychologists have labeled him a physicalist, and he does not totally reject the terms "materialist" and "monist" as used to describe his metaphysical views. He finds the label "materialist" misleading because he accepts the modern physicists' account of the world, and this account is very different from any traditional account of matter as composed of solid impenetrable particles. He believes that eventually it may be shown that phenomenal colors are identical with chemical states in the brain and that in this way the physicists' account of reality would be complete. In this sense he does not reject the possibility that monism is true, but in the meantime phenomenal qualities appear so different from any physical correlates that the possibility of the falsehood of monism likewise cannot be ruled out. There is some similarity between Köhler's views on this subject and the recent theory of J. J. C. Smart and U. T. Place that sensations and brain processes are identical. Like Smart and Place, Köhler argues that the undeniable phenomenological differences between colors and chemical states of the brain do not rule out the possibility that, in an important sense, they may nevertheless be identical. However, unlike Smart and Place, Köhler does not claim that such an identity has in fact been established.

Works by Köhler

"Über unbemerkte Empfindungen und Urteilstäuschungen." *Zeitschrift für Psychologie,* Vol. 63 (1913), 51–80.

Intelligenzprüfungen an Anthropoiden. Berlin, 1917. 2d ed. revised as *Intelligenzprüfungen an Menschenaffen.* Berlin, 1921. Translated from the 2d ed. by Ella Winter as *The Mentality of Apes.* London, 1925.

Die physischen Gestalten in Ruhe und im stationären Zustand. Brunswick, 1920; 2d ed., Erlangen, 1924.

"An Aspect of Gestalt Psychology," in Carl Murchison, ed., *Psychologies of 1925.* Worcester, Mass., 1925. Ch. 8.

"Gestaltprobleme und Anfänge einer Gestalttheorie." *Jahresbericht über das gesamte Physiologie und experimental Pharmakologie,* Vol. 3 (1925), 512–539.

"Komplextheorie und Gestalttheorie." *Psychologische Forschung,* Vol. 6 (1925), 358–416.

Gestalt Psychology. New York and London, 1929.

"Some Tasks of Gestalt Psychology," in Carl Murchison, ed., *Psychologies of 1930.* Worcester, Mass., 1930. Ch. 8.

Psychologische Probleme. Berlin, 1933. German edition of *Gestalt Psychology.*

"Zur Psychophysik des Vergleichs und des Raumes." *Psychologische Forschung,* Vol. 18 (1933), 343–360.

The Place of Value in a World of Fact. New York, 1938.

Dynamics in Psychology. New York, 1940.

"On the Nature of Associations." *Proceedings of the American Philosophical Society,* Vol. 84 (1941), 489–502.

"Figural After-effects: An Investigation of Visual Processes." *Proceedings of the American Philosophical Society,* Vol. 88 (1944), 269–357.

IN ANTHOLOGIES

Ellis, W. D., *A Source Book of Gestalt Psychology.* New York, 1938. Contains translation of portions of *Die physikalischen Gestalten in Ruhe und im stationären Zustand.*

Henle, Mary, *Documents of Gestalt Psychology.* Berkeley and Los Angeles, 1961. Contains Köhler's presidential address to the American Psychological Association (1959) and other later papers.

Works on Köhler

Ayer, A. J., *Language, Truth and Logic,* 2d ed. New York, 1946. Pp. 56–59.

Ayer, A. J., *The Foundations of Empirical Knowledge.* London, 1947. Pp. 113–135.

Boring, E. G., "The Gestalt Psychology and the Gestalt Movement." *American Journal of Psychology,* Vol. 42 (1930), 308–315.

Driesch, Hans, "Physische Gestalten und Organismen." *Annalen der Philosophie,* Vol. 5 (1925).

Grelling, Kurt, and Oppenheim, Paul, "Der Gestaltbegriff in Lichte der neuen Logik." *Erkenntnis,* Vol. 7 (1938), 211–225.

Hamlyn, D. W., "Psychological Explanation and the Gestalt Hypothesis." *Mind,* Vol. 60 (1951).

Hamlyn, D. W., *The Psychology of Perception.* New York and London, 1957.

Hartmann, George W., *Gestalt Psychology: A Survey of Facts and Principles.* New York, 1935.

Hobart, R. E., "Hume Without Scepticism." *Mind,* Vol. 39 (1930).

Katz, David, *Gestalt Psychology: Its Nature and Significance,* translated by Robert Tyson. New York, 1950.

Müller, G. E., *Komplextheorie und Gestalttheorie.* Göttingen, 1923.

Nagel, Ernest, *The Structure of Science.* New York, 1961. Pp. 380–397.

Petermann, Bruno, *Die Wertheimer-Koffka-Köhlersche Gestalttheorie.* Leipzig, 1929. Translated by Meyer Fortes as *The Gestalt Theory and the Problem of Configuration.* New York and London, 1932.

Reiser, O. L., "The Logic of Gestalt Psychology." *Psychological Review,* Vol. 38 (1931), 359–368.

Rignano, Eugenio, "The Psychological Theory of Form." *Psychological Review,* Vol. 35 (1928), 118–135.

PHILIP W. CUMMINGS

KORN, ALEJANDRO (1860–1936), Argentine metaphysician and ethical philosopher, was born in San Vicente. He took his doctorate in medicine and directed a hospital for the mentally ill. In 1906 he joined the faculty of philosophy and letters at Buenos Aires. Although he wrote little, he had immense personal influence on Argentine philosophy. His philosophical writing came late in his life: *La libertad creadora* (La Plata, 1930), his major work, is a compilation of five essays dating from 1918 to 1930.

Korn is sometimes called a positivist, a label suggested by his scientific training, his empiricism, the skeptical note in his metaphysics, and his ethical relativism. However, his "Incipit Vita Nova" (1918) set the stage for his own criticism of positivism. In this essay, he maintained that despite the scientific and technological progress of preceding decades, contemporary man is dissatisfied and disillusioned. The cause is the impairment of ethics by the spread of the positivistic doctrine that man is a machine without liberty; the remedy is a libertarian philosophy that subordinates science to ethics. Korn's sources were not Comte or Spencer, but Bergson, Schopenhauer, and Kant.

Korn's methodology rests on an experiential intuition whose objects are concrete particulars of ordinary experience. This common intuition is not passive and its content is not simple. Reason supplies concepts that are merely formal and symbolic but that penetrate intuition; the latter always has discursive elements. There is also a more intimate intuition or vision, which has intellectual, mystical, and aesthetic forms corresponding to metaphysics, religion, and art. Intuition as vision suggests profound convictions and has an important place in the spiritual life of man, but it carries no assurance of truth. For comparative certainty we must turn to the two disciplines of ordinary intuition: science, which has a measurable object in the external world of fact, and axiology, which has an unmeasurable object in the internal world of evaluation. The third great intellectual enterprise, metaphysics, attempts to describe reality through concepts that transcend all possible experience. Metaphysical systems are dialectical poems. We cannot live without metaphysics, but we cannot convert it into a science; it should contain sincere convictions, free from dogmatism.

The external world of science, of the not-self, known through sensations, is spatial, measurable, and governed by strict causal law. The internal world of axiology, of the self, constituted of emotions, volitions, and judgments, is nonspatial, immeasurable, purposive, and free. These are the two halves of one encompassing domain of consciousness, which comprises all that we know and, it seems, all that is real. Common to both halves of consciousness are three further characters: activity or perpetual becoming, which shows that stable things and rigid names are false; relativity, which expresses the fact that every particular act has its reason in another; and time. Most significant in distinguishing the subjective from the objective order is freedom: economic freedom, or mastery of the external world, and ethical freedom, or mastery of self.

The search for an ultimate reality beyond consciousness led Korn to deny monistic realism, dualistic realism, and solipsism, and to affirm a type of absolute idealism. Experienced things, space, and time depend on consciousness, evidently because they involve organizing concepts or forms. A thing lying beyond consciousness and implied as cause of the experienced thing is denied: causality is a creature of our thought. The known object thus depends on consciousness and has its being there. But that does not entail the dependence of objects on my self. The self, or subjective order, is only a part of consciousness; it is not the source of the known world. The further definition of this idealism is through the theory of the *acción consciente:* consciousness as an everlasting, dynamic, and creative process, unknown in itself but manifested as aspiration toward absolute liberty.

This ontological goal is the key to Korn's theory of values. A value is the created object of an affirmative valuation, and valuation is the reaction of the human will to an event. Values therefore are subjective. There are instinctive, erotic, vital, economic, social, religious, ethical, logical, and aesthetic values, none of which can be reduced to any other. Values achieve unity through their common source in human personality and through their common goal in the liberty of man. Creative liberty is the recurring motif of Korn's philosophy.

Bibliography

Obras, 3 vols. La Plata, 1938–1940.
"Influencias filosóficas en la evolución nacional." *Revista de la universidad de Buenos Aires* (1912). Reprinted in *Obras*, Vol. III.
Apuntes filosóficos. Buenos Aires, 1935.

ARTHUR BERNDTSON

KOTARBIŃSKI, TADEUSZ, Polish philosopher and logician, was born in Warsaw in 1886. He studied philosophy and the classics at the University of Lvov, where he obtained his doctorate in 1912. He began teaching at the University of Warsaw in 1918 and soon became perhaps the most influential philosophy teacher in Poland. His enlightened views, integrity, public spirit, and social zeal frequently brought him into conflict with established opinions and with the government, both before and after World War II. Admired by many and respected by all, Kotarbiński commands a unique position of moral and intellectual prestige in his country. He is a member of the Polish Academy of Science and of the International Institute of Philosophy, and he has long been chairman of both bodies. He holds an honorary doctorate from the Université Libre in Brussels and is a corresponding fellow of the British Academy and an honorary member of the Academy of Sciences of the U.S.S.R. and of other foreign scientific organizations.

Concretism. Kotarbiński began his philosophical career as a minimalist. He advocated the abandonment of such terms as "philosophy" and "philosopher" because of their ambiguity and vagueness. The miscellaneous collection of subjects traditionally known as philosophy lacks any factual or logical coherence. These various subjects should be reconstructed as specialized fields of study and thus acquire some recognized criteria of professional competence. "The philosopher" should mean "the teacher of philosophy," and "philosophy" should be used restrictively to denote moral philosophy and logic in the broad sense, which comprises formal logic, the philosophy of language, the methodology of science, and the theory of knowledge. Kotarbiński himself chose logic in this broad sense as the chief subject of his own concern. He wished to transform logic into a science as exact as mathematical logic and he applied himself to the construction of the conceptual apparatus necessary for this task. However, the results of this analytical work, accomplished between 1920 and 1935, exceeded the original design and produced a system known as reism or concretism. Kotarbiński regards it as a program rather than a set doctrine and for linguistic reasons prefers "concretism" to "reism."

Concretism arose from the puzzle about how qualities can belong to or inhere in the things of which they are characteristics. Kotarbiński believes that the puzzle can be resolved if we recognize that whereas things may be hard or soft, black or white, and so forth, nothing is hardness or softness, blackness or whiteness. Thus, the insight underlying concretism can be expressed in the proposition "only concrete individual objects exist." The expression "*a* exists" has the same meaning as "something is an *a*" (ex $a =_{Df} (\exists x)$ x is a) and the meaning of "is" can be explicated as follows:

$$(a,b) :: a \in b. \equiv \therefore (\exists x). x \in a \therefore (x) : x \in a. \supset . x \in b \therefore (x,y) : x \in a . y \in a . \supset . x \in y.$$

This theorem is an early formulation of the single axiom of Leśniewski's ontology and should be read as an implicit definition of the functor "is" in expressions of the type "*a* is *b*," in which "is" has its main existential meaning.

Semantic reism. Concretism is both a metaphysical and a semantic doctrine; as metaphysics its basic characteristic is materialism and as semantics it is nominalism. Nominalism is an essential part of concretism, but materialism is not. For instance, Franz Brentano, although a concretist, was a Cartesian dualist.

If the dyadic functor "is" in expressions of the type "*a* is *b*" has the meaning defined above, then only genuine, empty or nonempty, shared or unshared names are admissible values for *a*. This should be clear in view of the fact that if *a* is *b*, then for some *x*, *x* is *a*, that is, *a* exists (therefore, if an empty name is substituted for *a*, "*a* is *b*" always becomes a false sentence). Semantic reism is a set of linguistic and logical rules that allow us to test the meaningfulness and truth of the expressions of language *L* as determined by their syntactic structure and semantic function.

According to semantic reism, names of concrete objects only, either corporeal or sentient, are genuine names. The names of properties, relations, events, facts, propositions, or classes are objectless and apparent names. Literally understood, sentences involving such fictitious names and implying the existence of properties, relations, events, facts, propositions, or classes are grammatically meaningful expressions, but reistically they are nonsense in disguise or falsehood. Only if, by a suitable transformation, such sentences can be reduced to equivalent expressions involving no apparent names can they become reistically meaningful and either true or false. For instance, in its literal meaning the sentence "the relation *being part of* is transitive" is either false or nonsensical. But if it is regarded as a shorthand statement of the fact that for all *x*, *y*, and *z*, if *x* is part of *y* and *y* is part of *z*, then *x* is part of *z*, the expanded version of this abbreviated sentence expresses a genuine and true proposition.

Ontological reism. Nominalism is the view that the only admissible values for bound variables are entities of the lowest type as understood in the simplified theory of types. To apply this assumption outside logic and mathematics we need operational rules specifying the entities of the lowest type, that is, the referents of genuine names. For this purpose semantic reism must be supplemented by ontological reism; in other words, one's metaphysical commitments must be explicitly stated.

The basic proposition of ontological reism states that

every object is a thing. "Object" is the most general ontological term, synonymous with "something," the name of an arbitrarily chosen thing and thus extensionally equivalent to "thing." "Thing" is a defined term and means a physical or a sentient body, in the nonexclusive meaning of "or." "Physical" means spatial, temporal, and resistant, and "sentient" is defined by the Socratic definition as a term appropriately qualifying such bodies as animals or human beings (and probably also plants). Kotarbiński described ontological reism as somatism rather than as materialism, because for a reist "matter" is an apparent, quasi name, unless it is defined as a metatheoretical concept, in terms of which we speak about material or physical objects identified by the attributes of spatiality, temporality, and resistance and not by material substance. But somatism entails pansomatism, the proposition that every soul or mind (sentient entity) is a body. Therefore, a concretist who accepts pansomatism and asserts that there are only bodies in the universe is a materialist in the sense that he subscribes, speaking loosely, to the identity theory of mind and body. He leaves it to science to discover how it came about that there are sentient as well as physical bodies in the world.

In the theory of knowledge concretism implies the abandonment of the epistemological dualism of the theory of representative perception and the adherence to some form of sensational realism. Since there are no mental images or elements or sense data distinct from the object perceived, a concretist believes that all that is known is apprehended directly and that the so-called perceptual content is part of the physical object.

Imitationism. If reality consists exclusively of bodies, and if the soul or mind is identical with part or the entire organism of a human individual, assertions about mental states and processes are not semantically well-formed sentences; they are objectionable on ontological grounds and consequently false. To be reistically acceptable they must be regarded as assertions of special sorts about persons, reducible, when fully stated, to descriptions of human individuals acting upon their environment and being affected by the external world. This view of the nature of psychological statements, together with the procedure by means of which they can be reduced to statements about persons doing and undergoing things, Kotarbiński called "imitationism." This name is intended to indicate that we come to understand the experiences of other people by imitating their behavior and, in general, that psychological knowledge is acquired not from introspection but by imitation or self-imitation.

Imitationism assumes that every singluar psychological statement is a substitution of the schema "A experiences this: P," where A is a proper-name variable and P is a variable admitting all kinds of enunciations referring to the physical environment of the person whose name is substituted for A. The first part of the schema is the announcement by the experiencing person, EP, or the observer, O, of what its second part expresses by describing the environment in the same way that EP describes or would describe it. If EP and O are two different persons, the announcement refers to the imitation of EP by O and mentions the respect in which EP will be imitated. If EP and O are the same person, imitation becomes self-imitation

and the description of the environment, including EP's own body, is self-description.

Practical philosophy. Kotarbiński has had a lasting interest in practical philosophy. He sees its main task as the formulation of precepts and recommendations concerning the three questions of how to achieve happiness, how to live a good life, and how to act effectively. It is the second and third set of questions to which he has devoted most attention. He is a stanch defender of the autonomy of ethics and approaches its problems deontologically. Inspired both by a theoretical interest and by the desire to help his fellow men, he has produced a general theory of efficient action known as praxeology. Although he had some predecessors, in particular A. A. Bogdanov (1873–1928) and Georges Hostelet (1875–1960), he has accomplished pioneer work and opened a new field of study.

Works by Kotarbiński

Wybór Pism ("Selected Works"), 2 vols. Warsaw, 1957–1958. Includes all important essays and articles published between 1913 and 1954.

Elementy Teorii Poznania, Logiki Formalnej i Metodologii Nauk ("Elements of the Theory of Knowledge, Formal Logic and Methodology of Science"). Lvov, 1929; 2d ed., Wrocław, Warsaw, and Cracow, 1961.

Kurs Logiki dla Prawników ("A Course of Logic for Lawyers"). Warsaw, 1951; 6th ed., 1963.

Traktat o Dobrej Robocie ("Treatise on Good Work"). Lodz, 1955; 2d ed., Wrocław and Warsaw, 1958. Translated as *Praxiology: An Introduction to the Sciences of Efficient Action*. Oxford and Warsaw, 1965.

"The Fundamental Ideas of Pansomatism." *Mind*, Vol. 64 (1955), 488–500.

Wykłady z Dziejów Logiki ("Lectures on the History of Logic"). Lodz, 1957. Translated as *Leçons sur l'histoire de la logique*. Paris, 1964.

"Filozof" ("The Philosopher"). *Studia Filozoficzne* (1957), No. 1, 4–16.

"Essai de réduire la connaissance psychologique à l'extraspection," in *Atti del XII Congresso Internazionale di Filosofia (Venezia, 12–18 Settembre 1958)—Proceedings of the XIIth International Congress of Philosophy*, 12 vols. Florence, 1958–1961. Vol. V (Florence, 1960), pp. 295–299.

"Zasady Etyki Niezależnej" ("Principles of Autonomous Ethics"). *Studia Filozoficzne* (1958), No. 1/4, 3–13.

"Fazy Rozwojowe Konkretyzmu" ("The Stages of the Development of Concretism"). *Studia Filozoficzne* (1958), No. 4/7, 3–13.

"La Philosophie dans la Pologne contemporaine," in Raymond Klibansky, ed., *Philosophy in the Mid-century: A Survey*, 4 vols. Florence, 1958–1959. Vol. I, *Logic and the Philosophy of Science* (Florence, 1958), pp. 224–235.

"Psychological Propositions," in Benjamin B. Wolman and Ernest Nagel, eds., *Scientific Psychology: Principles and Approaches*. New York, 1965. Pp. 44–49.

Works on Kotarbiński

Ajdukiewicz, Kazimierz, review of Kotarbiński's *Elementy Teorii Poznania, Logiki Formalnej i Metodologii Nauk*. *Przegląd Filozoficzny*, Vol. 33 (1930), 140–160. Reprinted in *Język i Poznanie*, 2 vols. Warsaw, 1960, 1965, Vol. I, pp. 79–101. Available in Polish only.

Ajdukiewicz, Kazimierz, "Der logistische Antiirrationalismus in Polen." *Erkenntnis*, Vol. 5 (1935), 151–161.

Grzegorczyk, Andrzej, "O Pewnych Formalnych Konsekwencjach Reizmu" ("On Certain Formal Implications of Reism"), in *Fragmenty Filozoficzne, Seria Druga*. Warsaw, 1959. Pp. 7–14. Available in Polish only.

Jordan Z. A., "Próba Analizy Teorii Zdań Psychologicznych Prof. T. Kotarbińskiego" ("An Analysis of Professor Kotarbiński's

Theory of Psychological Statements"). *Psychometria*, Vol. 2 (1935), 347–375. Available in Polish only.

Jordan, Z. A., *The Development of Mathematical Logic and Logical Positivism in Poland Between the Two Wars*. London, 1945.

Jordan, Z. A., *Philosophy and Ideology: The Development of Philosophy and Marxism–Leninism in Poland Since the Second World War*. Dordrecht, Netherlands, 1963. Pp. 34–38, 195–197.

Lejewski, Czesław, "On Leśniewski's Ontology." *Ratio*, Vol. I (1958), 150–176.

Rand, R., "Kotarbińskis Philosophie auf Grund seines Hauptwerkes: 'Elemente der Erkenntnistheorie, der Logik und der Methodologie der Wissenschaften.'" *Erkenntnis*, Vol. 7 (1937–1938). 92–120.

Z. A. JORDAN

KOZLOV, ALEXEY ALEXANDROVICH (1831–1901), Russian personalist philosopher, was the first major Russian exponent of a pluralistic idealism derived from Leibniz. In his youth Kozlov studied the social sciences and was attracted to the ideas of Feuerbach and Fourier. His socialist views led to a short prison term in 1866 and the loss of his teaching position in a Moscow secondary school. He began to study philosophy seriously only in the 1870s, when, after an initial interest in materialism, he came successively under the influence of Schopenhauer, Eduard von Hartmann, and Kant. In 1876 he became professor of philosophy at Kiev University, where he published the first Russian philosophical journal, *Filosofsky Tryokhmesyachnik*, and began to formulate his own mature position under the influence of Leibniz and his followers—notably Gustav Teichmüller. When illness forced Kozlov to retire in 1887, he moved to St. Petersburg and expounded his views systematically in a private journal, *Svoyo Slovo* ("A Personal Word"), published occasionally from 1888 to 1898.

In Kozlov's metaphysics, which he called panpsychism, there is a plurality of conscious spiritual substances, or monads. Each is an agent whose being consists not only in its substantiality, but also in its (psychic) activities and the contents of these activities. (Thus, Parmenides erred by considering substance alone, Fichte by considering activity alone, and other philosophers erred similarly.) Together, these spiritual substances form a closed totality which is grounded in a Supreme Substance, God, and within which these substances (unlike Leibniz's monads) interact. The human body is a collection of less conscious spiritual substances with which our ego interacts until death. Kozlov suggested that after death the ego is reincarnated by interacting with other spiritual substances to form a new body.

The "material" aspect of the body, as of all supposed "material" entities, is produced by thought in our interaction with other spiritual substances, and is symbolic of these substances. Space and time (to which Kozlov devoted much attention) are likewise products of the thinking subject. Neither is objectively real, but each is symbolic of reality: space is symbolic of the fact that real substances exist in connection, and time of the fact that within this connection there is variety and activity. Thus sense perception, which purports to show us objects in space and time, does not penetrate to the essentially timeless and spiritual reality. Kozlov developed an intuitionistic epistemology, in which knowledge is based upon "primitive consciousness"—primarily consciousness of one's own

ego. Primitive consciousness, however, being simple and immediate, is nonconceptual and ineffable. Knowledge, on the other hand, is complex and mediated; the mind constructs it by relating the elements of primitive consciousness. Thus we are directly conscious of God. Acquiring conceptual knowledge of God, however, is a difficult intellectual enterprise.

Kozlov did not develop his views fully in other areas, but his metaphysics and epistemology influenced many Russian philosophers, including his son, Serge A. Askoldov, and Nicholas Lossky.

Additional Works by Kozlov

Filosofskiye Etyudy ("Philosophical Studies"), 2 vols. St. Petersburg, 1876–1880.

Filosofiya, kak Nauka ("Philosophy as a Science"). Kiev, 1877.

Works on Kozlov

Askoldov, S. A., *A. A. Kozlov*. Moscow, 1912.

Lossky, N. O., "Kozlov: Yevo Panpsikhizm" ("Kozlov: His Panpsychism"). *Voprosy filosofii i psikhologii*, No. 58 (1901), 198–202.

Zenkovsky, V. V., *Istoriya Russkoy Filosofii*, 2 vols. Paris, 1948–1950. Translated by George L. Kline as *A History of Russian Philosophy*, 2 vols. New York and London, 1953.

JAMES P. SCANLAN

KRAUSE, KARL CHRISTIAN FRIEDRICH (1781–1832), German pantheistic philosopher, was born at Eisenberg in Thuringia. He studied at Jena, where he came under the influence of Fichte and Schelling. In 1812 he became *Privatdozent*, but his many efforts to secure a professorship were all unsuccessful. For a time he taught music in Dresden. In 1805 he joined the Freemasons, to further his ideal of a world society. His internationalist leanings were responsible for his failure to be appointed professor in Göttingen, and in Munich his chances were spoiled by the opposition of Schelling. Just as he finally obtained a position, Krause died of a heart attack.

Like several of his contemporaries, Krause claimed to be developing the true Kantian position. His orientation, however, was mystical and spiritualistic. The obscurity of his style is awesome; he expressed himself in an artificial and often unfathomable vocabulary which included such monstrous neologisms as *Or-om-wesenlebverhaltheit* and *Vereinselbganzweseninnesein*—words which are untranslatable into German, let alone into English. He called his system the theory of essence (*Wesenlehre*) and presented an elaborate set of categories, including Unity, Selfhood, Propositionality (*Satzheit*), "Graspness" (*Fassheit*), Unification-in-propositionality (*Satzheitvereinheit*), and so forth. The system was intended to mediate between pantheism and theism; hence Krause called his position "Panentheism," to suggest the idea that God or Absolute Being is one with the world, though not exhausted by it. From this central doctrine Krause derived a theory of man and of history. He regarded all men as part of a spiritual whole, an ideal League of Humanity (*Menschheitsbund*), the actualization of which is the goal of history.

Like Fichte, Krause took self-consciousness as his starting point in the belief that it provides a key to the essence of all things. The ego discovers itself to be both mind and body, enduring and changing; it is an organic, self-sustaining whole. According to Krause, this is the clue to the nature of other beings and of God. Considering its own finitude and that of other beings which it encounters, the ego is led to the idea of an absolute, unconditioned principle upon which it and all other creatures and organizations are dependent. This principle is God, or Essence, whose nature is grasped in a spiritual intuition (*geistigen Schauen*), an immediately certain vision which is the foundation for all subsequent knowledge. God is primordial being (*Orwesen*), the being without contrareity; he is the unity of all that exists. Though he contains the world, he is nevertheless other than and superior to it. The distinction between God and the world is that of whole and part. Krause expressed this by speaking of God as *in himself* Contrabeing (*Gegenwesen*) and Unified Being (*Vereinwesen*), while *as himself,* or qua Primordial Being, he is absolute identity.

The existence of the world follows from an inner opposition in God's actuality (*Wesenheit*). Reason and Nature are two subordinate beings distinguished from, and yet lying within, God. Humanity is a synthesis of these. Humanity and the world, along with numerous basic human institutions, are organisms through which the divine life expresses itself. Thus, every being or group of beings is godlike in essence. Mind and body are integrated in the particular unified being which is man, reflecting the compresence of Reason and Nature in all things. Nature composes all individuals into a single whole. It is a mistake to view nature as a blind, mechanical system without consciousness; for its infinite perpetual activity, which is a pure self-determination, is free. Nature is a divine work of art; at the same time it is itself the artist, fashioning itself. The recognition of this divine character gives meaning and value to life.

Individual human minds together constitute the realm of Reason throughout which mind is organically distributed. But mind does not exist only in man and his institutions. Nature and Reason interpenetrate so fully that even animals are a unification of the two. Among animals, however, the career of each is fixed inexorably, according to the hierarchy of living forms. Man is the supreme unification of Reason and Nature, for he possesses the highest sort of mind joined to the highest sort of body. The individual souls that make up humanity are eternal, uncreated, immortal. Their number can neither be increased nor diminished. Humanity is thus complete at every moment.

What men should strive for is the imitation of the divine life in their own inner lives and in their social organizations. God is good, and men should participate in this goodness. The inner union with God (*Gottesinnigkeit*), or fervor for the divine, is the foundation of ethics, and ethics is the heart of religion. But individuals cannot achieve the moral life alone, since they are what they are only as parts of the whole. The community and its various institutions are thus indispensable.

Ideally, the community is governed by Right, which Krause defined as the organic whole of all of the internal and external conditions necessary for the completion of life that are dependent on freedom. This supernational law is grounded in the nature of the divine; it expresses the right of Humanity, not simply the right of individual human beings. The rights of individuals, groups, and nations can be recognized, but only as subordinate to the right of Humanity as a whole. Humanity is divided into a series of social organisms. There are, Krause speculated, human inhabitants in many cosmic systems. These human beings are subdivided into nations, races, communities, families, and so forth. There is an aesthetic community, a scientific community, a religious community, and a moral community. Each community has rights, although the right of Humanity takes precedence.

Men are all citizens of the universe, which is an infinite divine government. Because he revered the individual as a partial embodiment of the divine, Krause argued against the death penalty and maintained that punishment can be justified only as educative and reformatory. Only a republican form of government, he believed, is entirely compatible with the ideal of justice.

According to Krause's philosophy of history, the development of humanity is the temporal unfolding of a moral ideal. History follows a three-stage pattern, which is mirrored in every individual life as well. The development is not, however, purely progressive. There are two orders, one "ascending" and one "descending," so that the divine life may be presented again and again in the infinitely repeated epochs of history. The three steps in the ascending order are Wholeness, Selfhood, and Whollyunified-selfhood. In the stage of Wholeness, each individual or higher organism exists germinally in the larger whole to which it belongs. In Selfhood, it enters into a free opposition to that whole and strives to develop its unique character. Evil appears as the individual organism tears itself loose from the harmony of the whole. Finally, the organism achieves a loving reunion with other beings (man, for example, becomes reunited with Nature, Reason, Humanity, and God), and with this rediscovery of harmony, all evil is negated. Afterward, however, the historical path leads downward, to a final involution which is both the ending of a career and the birth of a new life. Since the transition is gradual, an older age may survive for a time in a newer age. Each development, nevertheless, exhibits genuine, unforeseeable novelty.

Following this order, the individual man enters the world, proceeds through the stages of embryonic life, boyhood, and youth, and becomes increasingly independent, until he finally achieves the maturity of manhood, from which point he descends in a reverse series. Every human institution and organization pursues the same course of evolution, reflecting the basic laws of the divine organic life. In history, the first stage is marked by polytheism, slavery, caste systems, despotic governments, and a state of war between peoples. In the second period, the age of growth, men recognize the divine as an infinite being standing above all that is finite. This is monotheism, which Krause accuses of fostering theocracy, religious censorship of science and art, and contempt for the world. Finally, in the third stage (to which Krause's own philosophy is supposed to inspire men), humanity comes of age, the finite is reunited with the infinite, and world citizenship, philanthropy, and tolerance become the rule. According to Krause, the transition to this stage began with

Spinoza's discovery of the nature of being, and his own system was to be the development of that theory. He envisaged humanity as arriving at an organic completeness that represents the maturity of the race, and with visionary eloquence he depicted the unification of all mankind, as all men and all associations of men enter into a common life.

Krause's philosophy, while not very influential in Germany, found considerable support in Spain, where, for a time, "Krausism" flourished. This was largely due to the efforts of Julian Sanz del Rio, the minister of culture, who visited Germany and Belgium in 1844 and came into contact with a number of Krause's disciples, notably Heinrich Ahrens in Brussels and Hermann von Leonhardi in Heidelberg.

Bibliography

Krause's most important work is *Das Urbild der Menschheit* (Dresden, 1812), translated into Spanish by Sanz del Rio as *El ideal de la Humanidad* (Madrid, 1860). Included among his other works are *System der Sittenlehre* (Leipzig, 1810); *Vorlesungen über das System der Philosophie* (Göttingen, 1828); and the short *Abriss des Systems der Rechtsphilosophie* (Göttingen, 1828). For Krause's influence in Spain, see Sanz del Rio, *K. C. F. Krause: lecciones sobre el sistema de la filosofía analítica* (Madrid, 1850) and Juan Lopez Morillas, *El Krausismo español* (Mexico City, 1956). See also Hans Flasche, "Studie zu K. C. F. Krauses Philosophie in Spanien," in *Deutsche Vierteljarsschrift für Literaturwissenschaft und Geistesgeschichte*, Vol. 14 (1936), 382–397. Flasche mentions the "left" and "right" wing of Krausism in Spain and, to account for Krause's success in Spain, tries to show (with a tenuous argument) the compatibility of Krause's views with Catholicism. Sharply critical of Krause is Eduard von Hartmann, "Krause's Aesthetik," in *Zeitschrift für Philosophie und Philosophische Kritik*, Vol. 86, No. 1 (1885), 112–130. Sympathetic accounts of Krause are to be found in Paul Hohfeld, *Die Krause'sche Philosophie* (Jena, 1879) and Rudolf Eucken, *Zur Erinnerung an K. Ch. Krause* (Leipzig, 1881). (Hohfeld edited a number of Krause's works, and Eucken studied with a student of Krause.) Clay Macauley, *K. C. F. Krause, Heroic Pioneer for Thought and Life* (Berkeley, 1925) is a eulogistic pamphlet.

ARNULF ZWEIG

KROPOTKIN, PETER (1842–1921), geographer and libertarian philosopher, was the principal exponent of the theories of anarchist-communism. He was born of a line of Russian princes who claimed descent from Rurik, the reputed founder of the Russian empire. His father was a general, and he himself seemed destined for a military career. He was educated in the Corps of Pages and served as personal attendant to Tsar Alexander II. When the time came for him to choose a career, Kropotkin applied for a commission in the Mounted Cossacks of the Amur and went to Siberia because he felt his chance of serving humanity was greater there than in Russia. He had already come under the influence of liberal ideas through reading the clandestinely distributed writings of Alexander Herzen.

In Siberia Kropotkin carried out an investigation of the Russian penal system, which aroused in him a revulsion against the effects of autocratic government. During the early 1860s he led a series of expeditions into the untraveled regions of Siberia and, on the basis of his observations, developed an original and influential theory concerning the structure of the mountains of Asia. He also made important discoveries regarding the glacial ages and the great desiccation of east Asia, which resulted in the onset of barbarian wanderings.

In the solitude of the Siberian wastes, Kropotkin's thoughts turned more and more toward social protest. In 1865 the exiled poet M. L. Mikhailov introduced him to the writings of the French anarchist Pierre-Joseph Proudhon, and in 1866 Kropotkin resigned his commission in protest against the execution of a group of Polish prisoners who had tried to escape.

For some years he devoted himself to science, and in 1871 he was exploring the eskers of Finland when he was offered the secretaryship of the Russian Geographical Society. It was the moment of decision. Kropotkin was already feeling the urge to "go to the people" that affected many of the conscience-stricken Russian noblemen of the 1870s, and he decided to abandon science. In 1872 he visited Switzerland to make contact with exiled Russian liberals and revolutionaries. After listening to many radical views, he went to the Jura, where the watchmakers were fervent disciples of Michael Bakunin. "When I came away from the mountains, after a week's stay with the watchmakers, my views upon socialism were settled; I was an anarchist" (*Memoirs of a Revolutionist*).

In Russia Kropotkin joined the underground circle led by Nicholas Chaikovski. In 1874 he was arrested and imprisoned in the Peter and Paul Fortress. Two years later he made a sensational escape and returned to western Europe, where he became an active worker in the rising anarchist movement. In 1879 he founded *Le Révolté*, the most important anarchist paper to appear since the end of Proudhon's journalistic career in 1850, and in 1881 he took part in the London International Anarchist Congress, which founded the celebrated but short-lived "Black International." In 1882 he was arrested by the French authorities and was tried at Lyons along with a number of French anarchists. He was sentenced to five years imprisonment for alleged membership in the International Workingmen's Association. The sentence aroused wide international protest, and Kropotkin was released early in 1886. He went to England, where he lived until he returned to Russia after the 1917 revolution.

Kropotkin's career in western Europe was sharply altered by his arrival in England. On the Continent, from 1876 to 1886, he had been a revolutionary agitator, conspiring, lecturing, pamphleteering, and taking part in radical demonstrations. His writings were mainly periodical pieces for *Le Révolté*. At first they were topical, but by 1880 Kropotkin was already developing the theory of anarchist-communism in a series of articles later incorporated in two books—*Paroles d'un révolté* (Paris, 1885) and *La Conquête du pain* (Paris, 1892).

Anarchist-communism. The doctrine of anarchist-communism differed from the collectivism preached by Bakunin and his followers in the 1860s in that it considered the need of the consumer rather than the achievement of the producer as the measure for distribution. In the vision of the anarchist-communist, the free-distribution warehouse would replace the earlier systems evolved by Proudhon and retained by the collectivists, which determined the worker's due either by hours of labor or quantity of production. Also, the anarchist-communists laid particular stress on the commune (in the sense of locality), rather than the industrial association, as the unit of social organization. In other respects—their rejection of the state, their stress on federalism, their emphasis on direct rather than parliamentary action, their denunciation of political forms—they did not differ profoundly from other schools of anarchism.

Sources. Although he became its leading exponent, Kropotkin did not originate anarchist-communism. The form of distribution embodied in the theory dates back at least as early as Thomas More's *Utopia* (1515–1516), and it appeared in a modified form in Charles Fourier's Phalansterian communities. The geographer Élisée Reclus, a former Phalansterian, appears to have brought the idea with him when he came to anarchism; it was first developed in writing by François Dumartheray, a Geneva artisan who helped Kropotkin in the founding of *Le Revolté*. But Kropotkin developed the theory and, in *La Conquête du pain,* he tried to show how it would work. This benign vision of an anarchist future reflects not only the optimism of Kropotkin's views, but also the benevolence of his character. For, although he always paid homage to the ideas of violent revolution, he did so against his nature; as Tolstoi shrewdly remarked, "His arguments in favour of violence do not seem to me the expression of his opinions, but only of his faith to the banner under which he has served all his life."

Anarchism and science. When he reached England, Kropotkin moved into a world where he was respected by people in all walks of life. His achievements as a geographer were remembered; he was honored by learned societies; his articles were published in scientific journals; and his books were welcomed by respectable publishers. He did not abandon his ideals, but his role changed from that of agitator to that of writer and libertarian philosopher.

The most important books Kropotkin wrote during this period were his autobiography, *Memoirs of a Revolutionist* (New York, 1899), and *Mutual Aid: A Factor of Evolution* (London, 1902). *Mutual Aid,* together with *Modern Science and Anarchism* (London, 1912), shows Kropotkin attempting to base anarchist theory on a scientific foundation. These books reveal him as a devoted evolutionist, to the extent that he explains revolutions as part of the natural process by which man, as a social animal, evolves. He sees revolutions arising obscurely in the consciousness of the people and punctuating the slow tenor of progress by sudden mutations in social organization, while he views anarchism as a backward trend toward a natural order that has been perverted by the emergence of authoritarian institutions. Man is naturally social, he suggests; therefore he does not need government, which itself perpetuates the unequal conditions that breed crime and violence. In their sociality, human beings resemble the more successful species of animals which depend for their survival on cooperation among their members. This idea is the core of *Mutual Aid,* which is an attempt, based largely on the arguments of K. F. Kessler, to reform evolutionary theory by demonstrating that the Neo-Darwinians wrongly stressed competition as a factor in evolution, to the exclusion of cooperation. In biological terms, his point was well

taken; the appearance of *Mutual Aid* led to modifications in evolutionary theory. But Kropotkin never convincingly welded his ideal of mutual aid to his anarchistic love of freedom, since he ignored the extent to which customs restrict liberty in most societies in which nongovernmental cooperation dominates the pattern of life.

Kropotkin's departure to Russia in 1917 led to tragic disappointment. He found himself out of touch with Russian realities and isolated during the events that led to the October Revolution. He retired to the village of Dmitrov outside Moscow, where he spent his last years writing. He denounced the Bolshevik dictatorship and the terror it imposed. When he died in 1921, his funeral was the last great demonstration against communist rule.

Ethics. Kropotkin's last years were spent on the uncompleted *Etika* (*Ethics*), which was published posthumously in Moscow in 1922. In part a history of ethical theories, this book seeks to present ethics as a science. In developing his naturalistic viewpoint, Kropotkin shows the emergence of morality among animals as an outgrowth of mutual aid and demonstrates its extension into human society, where it acquires a disinterestedness that goes beyond mere equality. He sees morality as the extension of human good will beyond equity and justice. The historical parts of *Ethics* are admirable, but the work is incomplete; Kropotkin's own ethical system is barely worked out.

Bibliography

Other important works by Kropotkin include *The State, Its Part in History* (London, 1898); *Fields, Factories and Workshops* (London, 1898); *La Grande Révolution 1789–1793* (Paris, 1909), translated by N. F. Dryhurst as *The Great Revolution* (London, 1909). *La Conquête du pain* was translated as *The Conquest of Bread* (London, 1906), and *Etika* was translated by Louis S. Friedland and Joseph Piroshnikoff as *Ethics* (London, 1925). See also *Kropotkin's Revolutionary Pamphlets,* edited by R. N. Baldwin, with a brief biography and partial bibliography.

Secondary sources include M. Nettlau, *Der Anarchismus von Proudhon zu Kropotkin* (Berlin, 1927); G. Woodcock and I. Avakumovič, *The Anarchist Prince* (London, 1950); and G. Woodcock, *Anarchism* (Cleveland, 1962).

GEORGE WOODCOCK

KRUEGER, FELIX (1874–1948), German philosopher and psychologist, was born in Posen and received his doctorate in 1897 from the University of Munich, where he studied under Hans Cornelius and Theodor Lipps. After working as an assistant at the Physiological Institute in Kiel he became a *Privatdozent* at Leipzig under Wilhelm Wundt. From 1906 to 1908 Krueger held a professorship at Buenos Aires, where he organized the development of scientific psychology in Argentina and left lasting traces of his views and activities. After returning to Leipzig he was called to Halle to succeed Hermann Ebbinghaus. In 1912/1913 Krueger was an exchange professor at Columbia University. In 1917, after three years of military service, he returned to Leipzig as Wundt's successor. At Leipzig Krueger founded the second Leipzig school of psychology, whose basic principles were designated as a genetic psychology of wholeness and structure (*genetische Ganzheits- und Strukturpsychologie*). In 1928 he received an honorary doctorate from Wittenberg College, Springfield, Ohio. In 1935 Krueger was appointed rector of Leipzig

University. He immediately became involved in political conflicts and was removed from the rectorship and for some time forbidden to lecture; in 1935 he retired prematurely from academic life. Krueger edited two series of psychological works, "Neue psychologische Studien" and "Arbeiten zur Entwicklungspsychologie," from 1914 and 1926, respectively. Early in 1945 he moved to Switzerland.

Krueger's first work, a philosophical one, was *Der Begriff des absolut Wertvollen als Grundbegriff der Moralphilosophie* ("The Concept of the Absolutely Valuable as the Basic Concept of Moral Philosophy"; Leipzig, 1898). In this work he presented a critique of Kant running counter to that of Neo-Kantianism. He tried to show that there was a material vein in the formal ethics of Kant himself, and he stressed that ethical responsibility is moored in the person, in his "energy of evaluation" (*Energie des Wertens*) and in his attitude toward values (*Werthaltung*), which Krueger understood as the "core structure" of personality or character.

After this work Krueger turned to empirical and experimental psychology, in which he became known particularly for his new theory of consonance and dissonance based on the influence of the different tones and for experiments in phonetics and the psychology of speech. In connection with this work he began to develop, as early as 1900, a theory of psychological wholeness, arising from the exhibition of emotional and physiognomic experiencing, which he characterized as a quality of complexes (*Komplexqualität*) parallel to Christian von Ehrenfels' Gestalt qualities (*Gestaltqualität*). Together with his English friend and student (who was, nevertheless, older than he), Charles Spearman, Krueger introduced into psychology the calculus of correlation including the first reflections on factor analysis.

In 1915, in *Über Entwicklungspsychologie, ihre historische und sachliche Notwendigkeit* ("On Developmental Psychology, Its Historical and Factual Necessity") Krueger developed a theory of cultural origins departing from Wundt's psychology of peoples and carried it further in *Zur Entwicklungspsychologie des Rechts* ("The Developmental Psychology of Law"; "Arbeiten zur Entwicklungspsychologie," No. 7, Munich, 1926). In 1918 and (in English) in 1927, Krueger presented sketches for a theory of the emotions, which he defined as the *Komplexqualitäten* of one's total experience, that is, as supersummative qualities not to be confused or identified with Gestalt.

These various strands, including his old moral philosophy, were united by Krueger in 1923 in a theory of structure, which was both critically related to and opposed to the thought of Wilhelm Dilthey. Krueger defined structure as the new scientific conception of the mind, as "the organismic construct of psychophysical wholeness," that is, as the basis of events in experience in the form of disposition, attitude and readiness, inclination, habit, and capability. The existence and individuality of personal structure can be demonstrated particularly in experiences of personal significance and "depth," but also in the subjective predispositions or preconstellations of perception, thought, memory, etc. Structure is the bearer of development and of personal identity. Besides personal structure there are social and "objective" intellectual structures. Formally, the structure of the experienced Gestalt, which exists in

becoming, can be compared to the "actual genesis" (or microgenesis) of the Gestalt. The development of man, like that of animals, arises from qualitatively complex, pre-Gestalt experience and is only gradually differentiated into an articulated Gestalt and into rational clarification. Krueger's last work, *Die Lehre von dem Ganzen* ("The Doctrine of the Whole"; Bern, 1948), began with psychology but culminated in cosmology.

There are four main points in Krueger's philosophical psychology: holism (opposition to associationism, emotionism (or emphasis on feeling and emotion), social evolutionism, and antiphenomenalism (structural personalism). Krueger's genetic *Ganzheitspsychologie* was carried on by many of his outstanding students. Shortly after his death it was characterized as a "re-establishment of the science of the mind" in the full sense of the word, as opposing both mere introspectionism and mere behaviorism. It is the radical rejection of atomism, mechanism, sensationalism, and phenomenalism (psychologism) of traditional psychology, whose loss of credit among academic psychologists is largely due to Krueger. The slogans and basic ideas of *Ganzheitspsychologie* have also stimulated and fertilized related fields, particularly aesthethics and education.

Works by Krueger

IN ENGLISH

"Consonance and Dissonance." *Journal of Philosophy, Psychology and Scientific Method,* Vol. 10 (1913).

"Magical Factors in the First Development of Human Labor." *American Journal of Psychology,* Vol. 24 (1913).

"The Essence of Feeling," in *Feelings and Emotions.* Worcester, Mass., 1927.

IN GERMAN

Zur Philosophie und Psychologie der Ganzheit, E. Heuss, ed. Berlin and Heidelberg, 1953. Writings by Krueger dating from 1918 to 1940, with a complete bibliography.

Works on Krueger

Buss, Onko, *Die Ganzheitspsychologie Felix Kruegers.* Munich, 1934.

Odebrecht, Rudolf, *Gefühl und Gestalt: Die Ideengehalt der Psychologie Felix Kruegers.* Berlin, 1929.

Wellek, Albert, *Das Problem des seelischen Seins: Die Strukturtheorie Felix Kruegers,* 2d ed. Meisenheim and Vienna, 1953.

Wellek, Albert, *Die Widerherstellung der Seelwissenschaft im Lebenswerk Felix Kruegers.* Hamburg, 1950.

ALBERT WELLEK
Translated by *Tessa Byck*

KÜLPE, OSWALD (1862–1915), German psychologist, philosopher, and historian of philosophy. He was born in Kandava, Latvia. After teaching history, Külpe entered the University of Leipzig in 1881, intending to continue in history. However, the lectures of Wilhelm Wundt stimulated his interest in philosophy and psychology, and after further studies in Berlin, Göttingen, and Dorpat (Russia), he returned to Wundt's seminar in 1886, receiving his doctorate the following year. In 1894 he was appointed extraordinary professor at Leipzig but left to accept a full professorship at Würzburg, where he founded a psychological laboratory. Külpe returned to Leipzig in 1896, and he subsequently held academic positions at Bonn and Munich. Primarily because of his work in organizing experimental laboratories, Külpe is regarded as a pioneer of experimental psychology in Germany. He died in Munich during World War I of influenza contracted while visiting wounded German soldiers.

Psychology and epistemology. Külpe's philosophical position, a form of critical realism, was closely related to his work in psychology. He came to regard the positivistic attempts of Ernst Mach and Richard Avenarius to reduce mental processes to sensations as incapable of accounting for the findings of introspective experiments. In one series of experiments, Külpe presented cards with nonsense syllables of varying colors and arrangements to subjects who were asked to report either the color, pattern, or number of items seen. Each person abstracted the features he had been instructed to report, remaining unconscious of the other features of the cards. Külpe concluded that the process of abstraction depends not only on the material presented to sensation but also on the subject's apprehension. This was taken to prove that sensations—as well as physical phenomena—must be distinguished from their apprehension. Thus he questioned the equation of "being" with "being perceived," even at the level of sensation.

Külpe abandoned the sensationalist psychology of contents in favor of a psychology recognizing both contents and acts of mind. Abstraction, he maintained, is a mental act or function that cannot be directly observed, but its occurrence is undeniable, even though it is discoverable only retrospectively. There exist both thought contents (*Gedanken*) and thought processes (*Denken*). The latter include the impalpable acts of thinking, meaning, and judging, which are not merely relations among contents but activities of the ego that transform the actualities (*Wirklichkeiten*) of consciousness into realities (*Realitäten*).

Külpe's position was thus hostile to both naive realism and idealism. Against the former, he argued that thought, although it does not produce the object of knowledge, is nevertheless genuinely spontaneous and creative in contributing to the realization of the object. His argument against idealism held that the facts of conscious experience require the existence of independent objects. When a scientist studies the maturation of an egg, for example, he assumes that this process takes place while no consciousness is directed upon it. Such continuity of development implies the object's independence of its being thought, a presupposition of every science.

Külpe used the word "awareness" (*Bewusstheit*) to indicate that the meanings of abstract words can be discovered in consciousness even when only the words themselves are perceivable entities. This thesis is an application of the theory that there exist impalpable (*unanschaulich*) or imageless contents of consciousness, a theory for which Külpe's "Würzburg school" of psychology was noted. Meanings can be experienced and objectified even without words or other signs. Although we cannot analyze precisely how these contents are given, retrospective acts make the world of meanings accessible to us. Külpe's indebtedness to Edmund Husserl and Franz Brentano is evident. Mental acts provide knowledge of meanings, and the act of meaning (*das Meinen*) may be directed even to such objects as God, the soul, electrons, or atoms, which could not possibly be actualized in consciousness. The capacity for imageless thought is essential if thought is to relate itself to something independent of it. When one wants to imagine a certain structure, the particular image one has in mind is only representative of the structure; the image points beyond itself or is the occasion for such an intentional act.

Aesthetics. In aesthetics, Külpe attempted to support Gustav Fechner's results concerning the golden section. Like Wilhelm Wundt, he maintained that the aesthetic pleasure produced by ideally proportioned objects results from mental economy. When the ratio of a whole to its larger part is the same as that of the larger to the smaller part, the perception involves the least effort combined with the greatest possible diversity.

Külpe attempted to further the development of experimental aesthetics by such methods as asking people to record their reactions to glimpses of slides showing works of art. His findings indicated no sympathetic empathy on the part of his subjects, thus opposing the contention of Theodor Lipps that such empathy (*Einfühlung*) is the basic condition of all aesthetic enjoyment. In the reports of his subjects Külpe found that form, orderliness, symmetry, and harmony were related to attractiveness. However, he recognized the limited validity of his findings, admitting that aesthetically inexperienced people might respond differently than his subjects. This reluctance to claim more for a theory than was warranted by experimental findings was characteristic of Külpe's work in psychology.

Works by Külpe

Grundriss der Psychologie auf experimenteller Grundlage dargestellt. Leipzig, 1893. Translated by E. B. Titchener as *Outlines of Psychology, based upon the Results of Experimental Investigation.* London, 1895.

Einleitung in die Philosophie. Leipzig, 1895. Translated by W. B. Pillsbury and E. B. Titchener as *Introduction to Philosophy.* London, 1910.

Die Philosophie der Gegenwart in Deutschland. Leipzig, 1902. Translated by M. L. Patrick and G. T. W. Patrick as *The Philosophy of the Present in Germany.* London, 1913.

Immanuel Kant. Leipzig, 1907.

Die Realisierung. Vol. I, Leipzig, 1912; Vols. II and III, August Messer, ed., Leipzig, 1920 and 1923.

Ethik und der Krieg. Leipzig, 1915. Külpe's defense of Germany's position in World War I.

Grundlagen der Aesthetik, S. Behn, ed. Leipzig, 1921.

Works on Külpe

Messer, August, *Der Kritische Realismus.* Karlsruhe, 1923.

Ogden, R. M., "Oswald Külpe and the Würzburg School." *American Journal of Psychology*, Vol. 61 (1951), 4–19.

ARNULF ZWEIG

KUMAZAWA BANZAN (1619–1691), Japanese Confucianist of the Wang Yang-ming school. Kumazawa was born in Kyoto and died at Koga, Shimoda Prefecture. Both he and his father were masterless samurai. Deciding to become a scholar, Kumazawa went to Nakae Tōju (1608–1648); in 1642 Nakae taught him the doctrine of Wang Yang-ming (in Japanese, Ōyōmei)—"innate knowledge" and cultivation of the mind. Kumazawa entered the service of Lord Ikeda Mitsumasa of Okayama, but his ideas, contrasting with the officially established doctrine, Chu Hsi Neo-Confucianism, aroused suspicion. However, his character and practical ability were recognized, and Ikeda put him in charge of the fief. For seven years (1649–1656) he successfully brought forth administrative reforms that transformed Okayama into a model fief. Paramount among his accomplishments was his role in organizing the Okayama college. Yet the extreme nature of these reforms, even in monasteries, angered many. Moreover, there were rebellious samurai among his pupils. He decided to retire to the studious life of a teacher in Kyoto, but slander of his teaching forced him to move in 1667; he did pass eight quiet years (1679–1687) at Yadasan near Kōriyama. On the official request of the Tokugawa government, he presented a plan of reform (possibly in his *Daigaku wakumon*). Thereupon his enemies, especially Hayashi, the defender of Chu Hsi Confucianism, succeeded in having him confined at Koga.

Kumazawa is typical of the early Tokugawa nonconformists, who were beset by adversities that multiplied with success. His politico-economic ideas, which were indeed very bold for his times, were the real reason for his difficulties. They are expressed in *Daigaku wakumon* ("Some Questions Concerning the Great Learning"), which is not a commentary on the Confucian classic "The Great Learning" but rather a tract on many subjects concerning how to rule the realm according to the Confucian precept of *jinsei*, or "benevolent rule." Both his unconventional proposals and his pragmatic attitude toward doctrine are striking.

Bibliography

For a guide to primary sources, see bibliography to JAPANESE PHILOSOPHY. See also M. Fisher, "Kumazawa B., His Life and Ideas, *Transactions of the Asiatic Society of Japan*, 2d series, Vol. 16 (1938), 221–259; 259–356. W. T. de Bary, ed., *Sources of Japanese Tradition* (New York, 1958), pp. 384–392.

GINO K. PIOVESANA, S.J.

KUNG-SUN LUNG (b. 380 B.C.?), a dialectician in ancient China, was a native of the state of Chao. His work *Kung-sun Lung Tzu*, in six chapters, has come down to us. His interest in "rectification of names" is largely logical. The central problem discussed is that of universals. In what follows, some of his statements relevant to this central theme will be discussed briefly.

In his "Discourse on the White Horse" Kung-sun Lung makes the statement that "A white horse is not a horse." Owing to the special nature of the Chinese language, this statement may be variously stated as follows:

A white horse is not horse.
White-horse is not a horse.
White-horse is not horse.

The copulative verb "is not" should be understood to mean "not equivalent to." Thus stated, it is obvious that a particular white horse is not equivalent to horse as such, which is a universal; neither is there any difficulty in understanding white-horse as such (a universal) not being equivalent to a particular horse or white-horse as such not being equivalent to horse as such. In other words, a universal given in a particular is not what it is as such. And in the course of discussion Kung-sun Lung also brings out the nonreversibility of an affirmative particular proposition. In excluding a yellow and black horse as an adequate answer to a search for a white horse, he is in essence saying that "A white horse is a horse" cannot be reversed to "A horse is a white horse."

The problem of the universal is further explored in another discourse, "On Universals and Particulars," where he seems to make the following points: A universal does not exist in time and space, but particulars do. The universal is the *raison d'être* of a particular thing, and without the universal the particular thing cannot be. A universal is not a particular, but it is revealed in the particular by means of a name. Although universals do not exist, they must *be* in some sense, since without them there would be no things, and one knows that there are things. Finally, a universal given in a particular is not what it is in itself; it has a being of its own.

The manner in which it has its own being is shown in the discourse "Hardness and Whiteness." Given a white hard stone, one sees the stone to be white and feels it to be hard. The feeling and seeing are two separate functions of two distinct senses. Hence, the qualities of whiteness and hardness must also be separate. If separate and not permeating each other in adhering to the stone, they must have a being of their own. This being-in-themselves Kung-sun Lung calls "concealment" (subsistence?).

In the course of discussion Kung-sun Lung also brings out an interesting observation. Senses by themselves do not function; they are conditioned first by physical elements, such as light for seeing, and then by the mind, without which neither the senses nor the physical elements are adequate to bring about sensory experience. What is most interesting is his insistence that the mind alone is not enough to account for concrete experience. However, he subordinates this epistemological analysis to his main concern of the separateness and self-subsistence of all universals.

Bibliography

Kung-sun Lung's work was translated by Y. P. Mei as "Kung-sun Lung Tzu" in the *Harvard Journal of Asiatic Studies*, Vol. 16 (1953), 404–437. Wing-tsit Chan, *A Source Book in Chinese Philosophy* (Princeton, N.J., 1963), Ch. 10, contains a translation of part of the *Kung-sun Lung Tzu* and an introduction.

For literature on Kung-sun Lung, see Vol. I, pp. 203–215, of Fung Yu-lan, *History of Chinese Philosophy*, translated by Derk Bodde, 2 vols. (Princeton, N.J., 1952–1953).

VINCENT Y. C. SHIH

L

LAAS, ERNST (1837–1885), German philosopher, was born in Fürstenwalde. From 1872 on, he was professor in Strasbourg. His first important book, *Kants Analogien der Erfahrung* (Berlin, 1876), was a critical study both of Kant and of "the foundations of theoretical philosophy"; but in his main work, *Idealismus und Positivismus* (3 vols., Berlin, 1879–1884), he launched a general attack on idealism, including Aristotle, Descartes, Leibniz, and especially Plato as its founder, as well as Kant. His purpose was to provide a remedy for the "discontinuity of philosophy"; that is, its failure to make progress over the centuries and its want of any clear standards. The remedy lay first of all in a new critical approach to the history of philosophy, which in the past had usually been at best merely scholarly and accurate. This new analysis revealed a basic dualism throughout the history of philosophy between the outlooks of Plato and Protagoras; and this revelation, in turn, permitted a revision of the judgment rendered in favor of Plato that had ever since benefited his followers at the expense of their opponents, such as the British empiricists. Laas referred specifically to J. S. Mill and cited approvingly a review of his own book on Kant that had compared it to Mill's *Examination of Sir William Hamilton's Philosophy*.

By "positivism" Laas meant, as was usual in Germany at the time, the tradition of Protagoras and the British empiricists, not the doctrine of Auguste Comte, whom Laas mentioned rarely and with little sympathy. Laas's position might more accurately, especially in English usage, be called neo-empiricism. It proposed to limit knowledge to the data of sense experience, thereby denying both a consciousness independent of the content of perception (insisting on the correlation of subject and object) and objects independent of the process of perception (asserting the instant changeability of objects of perception). At the same time Laas avoided the conclusions drawn by some empiricists, such as Berkeley, by rejecting any version of subjective idealism (which would assert the superiority or exclusive reality of the perceiver *vis-à-vis* the objects of perception or sensation) even more vehemently than he rejected the objective idealism originated by Plato. He identified this idealistic tradition in logic with conceptual realism, in epistemology with a priori deductive rationalism, and in metaphysics with both spontaneous human creativity and superhuman teleology. He associated idealism with a mathematically inspired desire to attain to the knowledge of absolutes and with the doctrines of innate ideas and final causes.

However, in his anxiety to escape from the "monstrous" notions of subjective idealism, as well as from "skepticism," "frivolity," and the "banal philosophy of common sense," Laas came close to a Neo-Kantian position in postulating an ideal or total consciousness. Recognizing, with Mill, that the sum total of *actual* objects of sensation is insufficient to construct an intelligible world, he asserted that the world consists of the sum total of *possible* contents of perception, which would be vouchsafed to an ideal consciousness and which it is the task of philosophy to construct. Since facts (objects) exist independently of consciousness (although not of perception), including this ideal consciousness, Laas claimed in this way to have saved the possibility of scientific investigation of the physical world from "skepticism," even though that world is relative and variable.

Just as he quite openly sided even with idealism (particularly with Kant, whom he often cited sympathetically) rather than with epistemological skepticism, Laas also seeks to defend his ethical doctrine (mainly in Vol. II of *Idealismus und Positivismus*) against any imputation of relying on egoism. Here again, however, his main concern was to overcome what he saw as the Platonic tradition of asceticism founded on a set of absolute and transcendental ideals. For this he proposed to substitute a "positive" ethics for this world, based on its values as revealed by "enlightened self-interest." Laas acknowledged the founders of this ethical doctrine to be Epicurus, Helvétius, and Bentham, but he diverged from them on the crucial point of egoism. He denied the identification of self-interest with egoism and held, rather, that self-interest dictates the performance of duties and the fulfillment of demands and expectations imposed on the individual by his environment. In this way, ethical values are the consequences of a particular social order. They acquire validity when they are judged, in the long run and by a considerable number of people, to be worthwhile. Laas characteristically listed as ethically desirable values security of employment, social harmony, the laws and institutions of the state, and cultural progress. These ethical teachings were the most influential part of his philosophy, affecting, in particular, the ideas of Theobald Ziegler and Friedrich Jodl.

Bibliography

In addition to the works cited in text, see Laas's *Literarischer Nachlass*, B. Kerry, ed. (Vienna, 1887).

For material on Laas, see Nikolaus Koch, *Das Verhältniss der Erkenntnistheorie von Ernst Laas zu Kant* (Würzburg, 1940) and Ludwig Salamonowicz, *Die Ethik des Positivismus nach Ernst Laas* (Berlin, 1935).

W. M. SIMON

LABERTHONNIÈRE, LUCIEN (1860–1932), French philosopher of religion and a leading figure in the modernist movement in the Roman Catholic church, was born at Chazelet (Indre). He studied for the priesthood and was ordained as an Oratorian in 1886. He then taught in various institutions, mainly in the college at Juilly, where he became rector in 1900. Laberthonnière was influenced by philosophies of life and action; he mentions Maine de Biran and Étienne Boutroux as the two philosophers who had most impressed him. Maurice Blondel's philosophy of action was another important formative factor, although Laberthonnière later found it moving too far toward intellectualism. He himself not only advocated a pragmatic point of view but also had an intense distaste for intellectualism and speculative philosophy. In particular, he had no sympathy for the attempted Thomist synthesis of faith and reason, believing that the task is not to conciliate these two but to choose between them. His teachings brought him into conflict with ecclesiastical authorities, and his principal writings were put on the Index in 1906. In 1913 he was prohibited from further publication.

Laberthonnière was not concerned with merely speculative philosophy that is constructed apart from life. He believed that the purpose of all philosophy is to give sense to life, and this motivation underlies even metaphysics, whether or not the metaphysician is aware of it. In the long run, the test of a philosophy must be its viability or its aptness for life, and the criterion of philosophical truth is a pragmatic one. We mistake the character of philosophy if we think of it as a theoretical enterprise resulting in a system of propositions linked together by abstract logical principles. A philosophical doctrine has a moral as well as an intellectual character, so that a worthwhile philosophy has to be worked out by living. The test of its truth is whether it can be illuminating when brought to bear on the problems of life.

Although Laberthonnière apparently held that all philosophy has a pragmatic or existential motivation, even if this remains unconscious, he also believed that some philosophies have been much more successful than others in relating to life. The theme of one of his principal writings, *Le Réalisme chrétien et l'idéalisme grec* (Paris, 1904), is the contrast between two supposedly extreme cases, Greek philosophy and Christian thought. Greek philosophy was concerned with abstract essences, conceived God as static and immutable, and proposed the life of pure contemplation as its ideal for man. In contrast to such idealism or intellectualism, Christianity is presented as a realism. Its concern is with the concrete life of action, and God himself

is conceived as active, the living God of the Bible. Hence, the truth of Christianity cannot be reached by intellectual contemplation, as if it were something external to us. Such truth as Christianity teaches is concrete and intrinsic to life, so that we grasp it only in living and in re-creating this truth in ourselves. These ideas about religious truth had already found expression in Laberthonnière's *Essais de philosophie religieuse* (Paris, 1903), where it is maintained that the doctrines of religion are to be understood not as general truths of the same kind as scientific truths but as concrete truths that must be brought into experience and realized if we are to understand them and know their value.

Although these views lean strongly toward pragmatism, Laberthonnière did not think that religion could be reduced to a purely practical affair or that it could be adequately explicated in naturalistic terms. It is significant that in spite of the harsh treatment that he received from the Roman Catholic church, he remained devoted to it and believed his philosophical views to be compatible with its teaching. If he went far toward abolishing the traditional distinction between the natural and the supernatural, this is not to be understood as the reduction of the latter to the former. Rather, it was Laberthonnière's conviction that the natural is itself already permeated by divine grace. Thus, we should look for God not in some upper or outer realm but in the immediate world, where he is active, and especially in the depth of human life itself.

Bibliography

In addition to the writings mentioned above, Laberthonnière published *Positivisme et catholicisme* (Paris, 1911). His other work, including an important study of Descartes, appeared posthumously in *Oeuvres*, 2 vols. (Paris, 1948–1955).

See also M.-M. d'Hendecourt, "Laberthonnière," in *Revue de métaphysique et de morale*, Vol. 63 (1961).

JOHN MACQUARRIE

LABRIOLA, ANTONIO (1843–1904), professor of philosophy in Rome from 1874 to 1904, was the first Italian Marxist philosopher. He wrote little, but that little was widely publicized by two disciples, Georges Sorel and Benedetto Croce; he exercised his extensive influence through lectures and discussions. Trained as a Hegelian in Naples, he became a Herbartian, more interested in Herbart's ethics and pedagogy than in his metaphysics. He discovered Marxism around 1890 and began a correspondence with Engels that lasted until the latter's death and was published in *Lettere a Engels* (Rome, 1949). This discovery of Marxism was a decisive event in Italian intellectual life, for from it dates the introduction of Marxist theory into Italy's academic culture, where it still occupies a prominent place.

Labriola's articles on Marxism, published in Italy by Croce and in France by Sorel, were first collected in French, as *Essais sur la conception matérialiste de l'histoire* (Paris, 1897). Their publication established Labriola's international reputation as an expositor of Marxism. He wrote Sorel ten letters on the subject, published as *Discorrendo di socialismo e di filosofia* (Rome, 1897). These books were the first exposition of Marxism as an independent philosophy to be made by an academic philosopher. They have been widely used in later efforts to combat all varieties of philosophical revisionism, whether from Neo-Kantian or positivist sources. The "return to Labriola," as recommended by Gramsci and as undertaken in Italy since 1950, has meant going back to the original innocence of a supposedly pure and independent Marxist philosophy, for Labriola claimed not to be an original thinker, and even less to be interested in developing or criticizing Marxism. He wanted to be simply an expositor and systematizer of a philosophy implicit in Marx's work.

The philosophy he found in Marx's work closely resembled the Hegelian views that Labriola had defended in controversies with Neo-Kantians before he had heard of Marx. For example, he held that scientific socialism is not subjective criticism applied to things, but the statement of the self-criticism that is in things themselves. The only criticism of society is society itself, for there is an objective dialectic immanent in history, which progresses by contradictions. Socialism was no longer an aspiration or project (a view soon to be revived by Neo-Kantian revisionists); it was the inevitable result of current contradictions in capitalist society. Labriola stressed the "scientific, objective" status of these assertions, in contrast to mere philosophies of history, which he dismissed as ideology. Historical materialism was no philosophy, but simply a method of research, a guiding thread like the Darwinian hypothesis.

Labriola, Croce, and Sorel were nicknamed the Holy Trinity of Latin Marxism, but the Roman professor came to feel that his spiritual sons were "going too far" in their development and criticism of the doctrine. They lacked that inflexible orthodoxy of which Labriola is the first eminent example in the Marxist tradition, and they touched off the revisionist controversy. That dispute broke out simultaneously in several countries, although Croce gave priority to his own and Sorel's writings. At all events, Eduard Bernstein in Germany, Sorel in France, Croce and Saverio Merlino in Italy, T. G. Masaryk in Prague, and the Fabians in England drew freely on each other's work, and Labriola found himself being quoted by and confounded with the "heretics." In a celebrated dispute, he broke publicly with Croce and Sorel, saying that revisionism was an international conspiracy organized by "scientific police-spies"—perhaps the first appearance of a philosophical terminology that was to become familiar later. Labriola never wrote on Marxism again. His earlier minor works, which include a *Socrate*, have been published by Croce (Bari, 1909) but are of small importance.

Works by Labriola

Opere. Milan, 1959—.
Essays on the Materialistic Conception of History, translated by C. H. Kerr, Chicago, 1904.
Socialism and Philosophy, translated by E. Untermann. Chicago, 1907.

Works on Labriola

Bruzzo, S., *Il pensiero di Antonio Labriola.* Bari, 1942.
Dal Pane, L., *Antonio Labriola: la vita e il pensiero.* Rome, 1935.
Diambrini Palazzi, S., *Il pensiero filosofico di Antonio Labriola.* Bologna, 1923.
Plekhanov, G., "The Materialist Conception of History." *Novoye Slovo* (September 1897). Also published separately. New York, 1940. Originally written as a review of Labriola's *Essays.*

NEIL MCINNES

LA BRUYÈRE, JEAN DE (1645–1696), French author and moralist, was born in Paris, the son of a city official. After some legal training he apparently fell on hard times, but through the influence of Jacques-Bénigne Bossuet he was appointed tutor to the grandson of the great Condé in 1684. After his tutorial functions were ended, he stayed on as librarian. The family seems to have been unpleasant; his colleagues, uncongenial; and the humiliations inflicted on him in this aristocratic society left a lasting mark. Elected to the Academy in 1693 after several unsuccessful attempts, he led a lonely and somewhat frustrated life, never marrying, making few friends, but showing passionate loyalty to those who, like Bossuet, won his respect.

La Bruyère's one famous work, the *Caractères*, reflects his personal experiences. Ostensibly modeled on the Greek *Characters* of Theophrastus, which La Bruyère translated and published in the same volume, the *Caractères* owes more to the quite different genre of La Rochefoucauld's *Maximes* and to the work of such contemporary moralists as Pascal and the Chevalier Antoine Gombault de Méré. Fifteen chapters somewhat arbitrarily group together epigrams (although La Bruyère explicitly disclaimed any intention of producing anything so authoritative as maxims), extended pen portraits (readily, and often wrongly, identified with living people) and brief moral essays, all arranged to cover, with considerable overlapping, the main characteristics and activities of contemporary society, from literary criticism to moneylending, from sex to sermons. The last chapter, which La Bruyère implausibly claimed, constituted the purpose and culmination of the previous 15, is devoted to a defense of religion against the freethinkers. It combines in an agreeable rather than a compelling manner the stock arguments for God's existence from his visible effects in nature with others reminiscent of Pascal and drawn from human psychology. The length of the book more than doubled in the course of nine editions from 1688 to 1696, and it came to include more and more of the concrete and detailed description, based on acute observation and couched in brilliant style, which makes La Bruyère at once a distinctive and a distinguished author.

In La Bruyère's time the splendors of Louis XIV's reign had come to demand too high a price, both economically and morally, of those obliged to maintain it. La Bruyère, a bourgeois himself, soured by personal experience of aristocratic arrogance and temperamentally allergic to worldly frivolity, was unsparing in his criticism of the court, where methodical hypocrisy marked the lives of those enslaved by self-interest and the desire for royal favor.

Like Bossuet, his hero and patron, La Bruyère felt able to combine vehement attacks on social abuses, due certainly in fact (if not in theory) to royal absolutism as currently practiced, with fulsome eulogy of Louis himself, going so far as to assimilate respect for the prince to fear of God. A convinced Christian, he had a genuine social conscience, as is illustrated by his famous remarks about the pitiful condition of the peasants. He contrasted the elegant heartlessness of the nobles with the rough kindliness of the people, with whom, in the last analysis, he would wish to be classed. He was, however, neither egalitarian nor republican, but believed that inequality founded on order is divinely instituted; and it was on moral and religious grounds, not in the name of equality, that he dissociated himself from a society he regarded as irremediably corrupt.

In common with other moralists of the age, La Bruyère was fascinated by the discrepancy between appearance and reality in human behavior. He recorded how skill in playing the social game usurps the name and place of virtue, how fashion makes mock of convictions (a happily married couple finds it socially expedient to simulate infidelity), and how self-interest is the one constant motive of those who disguise it so ingeniously. He was, however, gloomy rather than hopeless about human nature, and did not despair of the potential goodness of men as yet uncontaminated by society. He also believed in the possibility of satisfactory human relationships, speaking with attractive warmth of love and friendship.

Moderate as well as modest, La Bruyère was saved by common sense from the clever cynicism that is purely destructive, and his work is characterized by a positive and humane quality underlying the bitterest criticism. Although the *Caractères* falls short of absolute greatness, it reflects with exceptional accuracy the wane of the *grand siècle*.

Bibliography

La Bruyère's *Les Caractères*, edited by G. Servois, appeared in 3 vols. (Paris, 1865–1882) and was also issued by Bibliothèque de la Pléiade (Paris, 1934). It was translated by H. van Laun as *The Characters* (Oxford, 1963).

Works on La Bruyère are A. Adam, *Histoire de la littérature française au XVIIe siècle* (Paris, 1956), Vol. V, Ch. 6; M. Lange, *La Bruyère critique des conditions et des institutions sociales* (Paris, 1909); P. Richard, *La Bruyère et ses Caractères* (Amiens, 1946); F. Tavera, *L'Idéal moral et l'idée religieuse dans les Caractères* (Paris, 1940).

A. J. KRAILSHEIMER

LACHELIER, JULES (1832–1918), French idealist, was born at Fontainebleau and studied at the École Normale Supérieure in Paris. He received his *docteur ès lettres* in 1871 and held various professorial and administrative positions in the French educational system until his retirement from the post of *inspecteur général* in 1900. Lachelier joined with his teacher Ravaisson-Mollien in founding the neospiritualist movement in French philosophy, a movement opposed to what seemed to be the naive acceptance of science and the scientific attitude in all phases of life. Among those who have acknowledged Lachelier's influence are Émile Boutroux, Victor Brochard, Jules Lagneau, and Henri Bergson.

Lachelier advanced a number of skeptical arguments that tend to reduce objects to phenomena, phenomena to sensations, and, more generally, to resolve the external world into thought. Nevertheless, he retained the conviction that we live in a common, objective world. Accordingly, his philosophy is directed toward the conclusion that the objectivity of our knowledge and experience is derived from mind. He summarized his idealistic philosophy as the discovery of "a thought which does not think, suspended from a thought which thinks itself."

To avoid the pitfalls of both the empiricism and the spiritualism of his day, Lachelier attempted to provide a basis for induction in a philosophy of nature. His procedure consisted of a Kantian reflection upon the necessary conditions for the existence of the world as we know it. He began by observing that, if knowledge is to be possible, sensations must exhibit the same unities that are found in phenomena. By eliminating competing hypotheses, he found that the unifying element within any phenomenon, as well as the unifying element among phenomena, is established by the necessary relations operative in them and is expressed by the law of efficient causes. The necessity of this law cannot be discovered in sensations alone, in phenomena as such, or in their mere juxtaposition; nor can it be isolated in any locus from which mind is separated. It must be regarded, rather, as a kind of unconscious but logical thought diffused throughout nature. The mechanical linkages among events in nature reflect the logical relations in thought. Lachelier concluded that the unity of thought and the formal unity of nature are inverses of each other.

Given a series of phenomena, the law of efficient cause is sufficient to account for their organization in a mechanically interrelated series. But the questions remain: Why do whole phenomena occur? How are several series of mechanically ordered individual phenomenal objects coordinated into groups in order to form complex and recurrent phenomena? The question of recurrence involves the problem of induction and indicates that some principle—in addition to the law of efficient causes—must be found to explain the recurrence of phenomena. If we are neither to stretch the principle of efficient causes beyond reasonable bounds nor to supplement it with some occult principle *ex machina*, then we must suppose that the whole phenomenon—complex yet persistent—contains the reasons for its unity and recurrence. Lachelier, like Kant, recognized a whole to be an end when the whole contained the reason for the organization of its parts. (A whole of this kind is illustrated in a stable chemical compound or in a living organism.)

Thus, in view of the fact that we indisputably are aware of phenomena which are harmonious and recurring complexes or wholes of this sort, Lachelier arrived at a second principle: the law of final causes. By its operation, sensa are grouped into perceptions of which we are actually aware, and thus they provide content and reality for the necessary but empty form of the universal mechanism. This law is to the matter of phenomena what the law of efficient causes is to their form. In these terms the distinction is drawn between the abstract existence of mechanical nature and the concrete existence of teleologically unified but contingent individuals. Since all actual objects are complex, they all presuppose the operation of the law of final causes. This law is, then, prior to the law of efficient causes in respect to actual existence.

These two laws are not on the same logical footing. Lachelier regards the law of efficient causes as proved. The proof is of the Kantian type. Given coherent experiences, this law, which is logic projected into phenomena, expresses the condition under which they cohere and are intelligible. The law of final causes, however, is not reached in the same way. Presumably, simple phenomena might remain logically ordered while being grouped in different ways. Their actual grouping into the harmonious and persistent unities that we experience is the consequence of a law which operates more like an act of will than like a formal or logical requirement. Thus, the law of final causes is said to be regulative only.

The twin laws of efficient and final causes provide the foundation for induction. Induction is thereby "founded" in the sense that it is partly proved or derived from the conditions for experience and partly justified as expressing a teleology of nature. The practice of induction, therefore, may be expected to be partly the logical deduction of events from previous events, and partly a "divining" that natural phenomenona will cooperate with each other in a given way under given circumstances.

This foundation, however, is not ultimate. It does not explain why these two laws alone are the ordering principles of our existent world. Lachelier, in considering this point, observed that some organisms realize to a higher degree than others that harmony toward which nature moves. In fact, the law of final causes entails a whole hierarchy of beings that increase in order and harmony. The more complexly unified organisms in nature are not the chance products of accidentally unified simpler organisms. Rather, the simpler organisms, implicit in the more complex ones, are separated from them by a kind of "division and refraction."

The human being can free himself in thought from the particular mechanical conditions of phenomena. He has the capacity to separate some perceptions from others and, using them as symbols, to represent general properties of things. In his ability to abstract and generalize, the human being, although distinguished from all other things by this capacity, can be said to be in contact with the whole universe. The universe can be discovered again in thought but under a new condition, freedom. In addition, man is free because he can select the means and ends of his activity by reference to ideas. Hence, through man, the realm of final causes and the freedom which is its condition penetrate the organic and mechanical realms. Furthermore, without freedom it would be impossible to conceive of either mechanism or finality. Thus, the laws of efficient and final causality, upon which induction is founded, are themselves founded upon freedom—and freedom is the essential property of thought.

The process of founding induction within a philosophy of nature, therefore, consists partly in a demonstration and partly in a discovery of regulative rules. Finally, the process terminates in a metaphysics that affirms the basic reality of thought. This metaphysics is intended to found the philosophy of nature in the sense of providing a reason for belief in the unity of its laws and in its idealistic source. Lachelier's metaphysics of freedom is further developed in his article "Psychologie et métaphysique" (1885) and is given a religious dimension in "Le Pari de Pascal" (1901).

Works by Lachelier

Oeuvres de Jules Lachelier, 2 vols. Paris, 1933.
Lachelier, la nature, l'esprit, Dieu, Louis Millet, ed. Paris, 1955.
The Philosophy of Jules Lachelier, Edward G. Ballard, ed. The Hague, 1960. Contains an introduction and translations by Ballard of "Du Fondement de l'induction," "Psychologie et métaphysique," "Le Pari de Pascal," and several short writings.

Works on Lachelier

Devivaise, C., "La Philosophie religieuse de Jules Lachelier." *Revue des sciences philosophiques et théologiques* (1939), 435–464.
Mauchaussat, Gaston, *L'Idéalisme de Lachelier.* Paris, 1961.
Millet, Louis, *Le Symbolisme dans la philosophie de Jules Lachelier.* Paris, 1959. Contains a comprehensive bibliography of Lachelier's writings and of the commentaries.
Noël, Georges, "La Philosophie de M. Lachelier." *Revue de métaphysique et de morale* (1898), 230–259.
Séailles, Gabriel, *La Philosophie de Jules Lachelier.* Paris, 1921.

EDWARD G. BALLARD

LALANDE, ANDRÉ (1867–1964), French philosopher, was born in Dijon and entered the École Normale Supérieure in 1885. He took his doctorate in 1899 and taught in *lycées* until he was appointed first to a lectureship and then, in 1904, to a chair of philosophy at the University of Paris.

Lalande was a rationalist whose whole life was devoted to the cause of international communication and the dissemination of knowledge. His constant preoccupation after 1902 was the launching, and subsequent re-editing, of the *Vocabulaire technique et critique de la philosophie*, which aimed at the concise definition and standardization of philosophical terminology. His own philosophical work corresponds to this recognition and promotion of an interdependent humanity.

In his thesis of 1899, *L'Idée directrice de la dissolution opposée à celle de l'évolution,* Lalande challenged Herbert Spencer's thesis that progress is evolutionary and differentiating, and held that, on the contrary, dissolution—or, as he later called it, involution—is more widespread and significant. Involution, or movement from the heterogeneous to the homogeneous, is observable in nature as entropy, or increase of randomness. In human life, however, this movement toward uniformity is fruitful and is served by reason, which, in scientific investigation, leads to the progressive subsumption of more and more classes of phenomena under fewer general laws.

Lalande disapproved of an imposed uniformity, which represents merely the transference from the individual to the group of evolutionary, divisive drives. True reason insures that although people feel differently, they shall think in the same way and thus understand each other even when they do not resemble each other. Lalande's concern was for the individual, whose uniqueness is sacrificed to function in a rigidly specialized and differentiated society. The application of reason to life in the technological field liberates the individual from his functional role, and the application of reason in the cultural field enables men to afford, and to benefit from, the diversity which is their birthright.

In *La Raison et les normes* Lalande restated his involutionist case in the light of recent philosophies of "being-in-the-world." He took cognizance, for example, of the argument that geometrical, objective space is derived from the neuromotor "spaces" of man facing his tasks, but for Lalande the superiority of a common space amenable to conceptualization remained unimpaired. Similarly, he preferred chronological time to the "real" time of naive emotional experience. Lalande reaffirmed his universalist conception of rationality against more recent phenomenological thinking.

Works by Lalande

L'Idée directrice de la dissolution opposée à celle de l'évolution. Paris, 1899; revised and reissued as *Les Illusions évolutionnistes.* Paris, 1930.
Quid de Mathematica vel Rationali vel Naturali Senserit Baconus Verulamius. Paris, 1899. Latin thesis.
Lectures sur la philosophie des sciences. Paris, 1893 and 1907.
Précis raisonné de morale pratique. Paris, 1907.
Les Théories de l'induction et de l'expérimentation. Paris, 1929.
La Raison et les normes. Paris, 1948.
Vocabulaire technique et critique de la philosophie, 8th ed. Paris, 1962.

Works on Lalande

Lavelle, L., *La Philosophie française entre les deux guerres.* Paris, 1942.
Smith, Colin, *Contemporary French Philosophy.* London, 1964.

COLIN SMITH

LAMARCK, CHEVALIER DE (1744–1829), French biologist and formulator of the first comprehensive theory of evolution. Jean Baptiste Pierre Antoine de Monet, Chevalier de Lamarck, was born at Bazentin-le-Petit, a village in northeastern France. As a youth he studied briefly for the priesthood, but later withdrew to follow the family tradition of army service. While in Paris recovering from an injury and intermittently studying medicine, he met Rousseau, through whom he became interested in botany. This interest led to investigations that culminated in the publication of a large work on the flora of France, which brought Lamarck immediate fame and election to the Academy of Sciences. From 1783 to 1793 he held a small post at the Jardin du Roi, which was reorganized and expanded along lines proposed by Lamarck to include a museum of natural history and twelve professorial chairs. The last of these, for the study of invertebrates, went almost by default to Lamarck himself. Hence, at the age of fifty he began his indefatigable labors as a zoologist. These labors led to his conclusion, at some time between 1794 and 1802, that a transmutation of animal species had taken place. He expounded his views in a succession of important works: *Système des animaux sans vertèbres* (Paris, 1801), *Recherches sur l'organisation des corps vivans* (Paris, 1802), *Philosophie zoologique* (2 vols., Paris, 1809–1830, translated by H. Elliot as *Zoological Philosophy*, London, 1914), and *Histoire naturelle des animaux sans vertèbres*, (7 vols., Paris, 1815–1822). The significance of Lamarck's contribution was scarcely appreciated by his contemporaries. When he died at the age of 85,

blind and poor, he had become a forgotten man. His body was buried in a pauper's grave whose exact location is unknown.

System of nature. Lamarck aspired to produce a large-scale "system of nature" set in a deistic framework. He held that nature, "the immense totality of different beings," is neither eternal nor self-explanatory. It is the creation of a "Supreme Author" who brought matter into being and instituted the world order by means of laws that govern whatever happens. Within nature, change is universal. But nature *in toto* is unchangeable and "should be regarded as a whole constituted by its parts, for a purpose which its Author alone knows." This whole, however, is as distinct from the Creator as a watch is from the watchmaker. Hence, nature has productive powers of its own that the sciences can properly interpret in mechanical and materialistic terms. The system that Lamarck originally planned was to have included sections on physics, chemistry, meteorology, geology, and biology. Some of his writings did, in fact, discuss all these topics, but what appeared can hardly be said to form a unified scheme. His attention was increasingly occupied by his reflections on living things, the science of which he named biology in 1802.

Evolution. Lamarck effected a breakthrough to an evolutionary conception of nature by bringing together several lines of thought. His geological studies convinced him that the earth had endured for an immense span of time, during which it had undergone many changes of a gradual sort, especially in its surface features. His observation of fossils supported the conclusion that animal life had existed for a large part of geological time and had also undergone gradual changes. Hence, species must be mutable, and their apparent stability is due to man's limited time perspective. Furthermore, organisms are simply physical bodies whose parts are highly organized. Thus, Lamarck was opposed to vitalism. "Every fact or phenomenon observed in a living body," he held, "is . . . a physical fact or phenomenon, and a product of organization" (*Histoire naturelle des animaux sans vertèbres*, Vol I, p. 53). Accordingly, he accepted the conclusion that a "spontaneous generation" of organisms had occurred. Animals and plants represent two independent lines stemming from two distinct types of spontaneous generation that utilized chemical materials differently. These materials are wholly inanimate and display none of the characteristic properties observed in the organisms they constitute.

Perfecting power in nature. The history of living things on the earth reveals a steady increase in the complexity of their organization, a process by which they have also been perfected. "Nature has produced all the species of animals in succession, beginning with the most imperfect or simplest, and ending her work with the most perfect." Man is the being who exemplifies the highest excellence of bodily organization, and he thereby provides "the standard for judging the perfection or degradation of other animal organizations." Lamarck's thought at this point was influenced by the idea of the "great chain of being," the infinitely graded series of forms from highest to lowest, which was a doctrine congenial to eighteenth-century deism. Since, in his evolutionary approach, the series came into existence from the bottom, Lamarck attributed it to a perfecting power inherent in nature. The postulating of this perfecting power is the feature of Lamarck's evolutionism that separates it most sharply from that of Darwin.

Causes of the power of evolution. If the environment were unchanging, the perfecting power of nature would produce a simple, linear sequence of organisms. But the environment is ceaselessly changing, and, as a result, evolution is "deflected" from a linear path into the "branching" pattern actually found among plants and animals. The mechanism by which the branching pattern is formed consists of a group of causal factors often mistakenly supposed to be the whole of Lamarck's theory, instead of just a part of it.

The causal factors are specified in several "laws"—two in *Philosophie zoologique* and four in *Histoire naturelle des animaux*—whose purport can be summarized as follows. The organs and habits by which animals maintain their adaptation to the environment are controlled by bodily fluids that are constantly in motion. Animals whose structure is so elementary that they have no faculty of feeling are acted on mechanically by environmental changes. New motions of the internal fluids are set up, and these give rise to adaptive alterations in the organs and habits. The case is different with animals whose structure is complicated enough to enable them to feel wants or needs (*besoins*). When the environment of these animals changes, new needs are felt, and each need, "exciting their inner feeling (*sentiment intérieur*), forthwith sets the fluids in motion and forces them toward the point of the body where an action may satisfy the want experienced" (*ibid.*, p. 185). If a suitable organ already exists at that point, it is immediately incited to action. If not, the felt need gradually causes the organ to be generated, "provided the need be pressing and continuous." Everything thus acquired by an individual animal during its lifetime is preserved by heredity (*génération*) and transmitted to that individual's progeny. The operation of these causal factors, superimposed on the general perfecting tendency of nature, accounts for all that has happened in evolution.

Man. Man's place in this theory was a topic that Lamarck understandably treated with caution. He stressed man's "extreme superiority" over other living things because of his possession of reason, although anatomically he differs only in degree from monkeys and apes. Is it not plausible to suppose that the differences have been "gradually acquired" over a long period of time? "What a subject for reflection," Lamarck commented, "for those who have the courage to enter into it!" He himself dared in a short section of *Philosophie zoologique* to outline a hypothetical explanation of how apelike beings might "at length be transformed" into manlike beings, able to walk upright, to use tools, and to develop "the marvelous faculty of speaking." Throughout the process, changed habits would produce new wants and new capacities, until true human beings appeared. "Such are the reflections which might be aroused, if man were distinguished from animals only by his organization, and if his origin were not different from theirs." At this point Lamarck's courage apparently gave out.

Assessment. Despite the comprehensiveness of his outlook, Lamarck failed to formulate a unified theory of evolution. Therefore, he had to conclude that the diversification of plants and simple animals was due to mechanical factors alone, whereas in the case of complex animals an important psychological and teleological factor was operative. He held that no species had ever been totally extinguished, in spite of what the fossil evidence indicated, because he believed that the plan of the Supreme Author of the universe would not allow such wastage. His acceptance of the perfecting tendency obliged him to affirm that there are really two animal series: the grand one from simple to complex, and the particular, branching series that have deviated from it. Above all, his theory demanded not only that modifications acquired by parents during their lifetime should affect their offspring, but also that they should affect the same parts in the offspring as in the parents and should become a permanent hereditary feature in that line of descent, regardless of later modifying factors. Modern genetic research has shown strong, although perhaps not conclusive, reasons for believing that such an "inheritance of acquired characteristics" cannot occur. None of these difficulties, however, can detract from the greatness of Lamarck's contribution. "He first did the eminent service," Charles Darwin remarked, "of arousing attention to the probability of all change in the organic world being the result of law, and not of miraculous interposition."

Bibliography

Cannon, H. G., *Lamarck and Modern Genetics.* New York, 1960.
Gillispie, C. C., "The Formation of Lamarck's Evolutionary Theory." *Archives internationale d'histoire des sciences,* Vol. 35 (1956), 323–338.
Gillispie, C. C., "Lamarck and Darwin in the History of Science." *American Scientist,* Vol. 46 (1958), 388–409.
Landrieu, Marcel, *Lamarck.* Paris, 1909.
Packard, A. S., *Lamarck, The Founder of Evolution.* New York, 1901.
Russell, E. S., *Form and Function.* Cambridge, 1916. Ch. 13.
Wilkie, J. S., "Buffon, Lamarck and Darwin," in P. R. Bell, ed., *Darwin's Biological Work.* Cambridge, 1959. Pp. 262–307.

T. A. GOUDGE

LAMBERT, JOHANN HEINRICH (1728–1777), German mathematician, physicist, astronomer, and philosopher, was born in Mulhouse, Alsace. He taught himself mathematics, philosophy, and Oriental languages; after 1748 he served as tutor in a Swiss family, traveling about Europe with his pupils for several years. He became a member of the Munich Academy in 1759 and of the Berlin Academy in 1764. In 1765 he was appointed by Frederick II as Prussian surveyor of public works. He did research in heat, light, and color and was the founder of the science of photometry. In mathematics Lambert demonstrated that π is an irrational number, and he introduced the conception of hyperbolic functions into trigonometry. In his *Kosmologische Briefe über die Einrichtung des Weltbaues* ("Cosmological Letters on the Structure of the Universe," Augsburg, 1761), Lambert proposed a cosmogonic hypothesis based on Newton's theory of gravitation; it was similar to the nebular hypothesis proposed earlier by Kant in his *Allgemeine Naturgeschichte und Theorie des Himmels* (Königsberg and Leipzig, 1755) but unknown to Lambert.

Lambert's *Neues Organon, oder Gedanken über die Erforschung und Bezeichnung des Wahren und dessen Unterscheidung von Irrtum und Schein* ("New Organon, or Thoughts on the Investigation and Indication of Truth and of the Distinction between Error and Appearance," 2 vols., Leipzig, 1764) was an attempt to reform Wolffian logic. It was strongly influenced by the logical treatises of the Pietist philosophers A. F. Hoffmann and C. F. Crusius, and like their work it widened the field of logic to cover psychological and methodological questions. Although Lambert believed that metaphysics should follow a mathematical method, he assumed, like the Pietists and John Locke, a multiplicity of elementary notions. The a priori sciences (pure theoretical and practical philosophy) should be constructed by combining these elementary notions mathematically. The final section of the *Neues Organon* discusses appearance and gives a theory of experimental and probable knowledge. It contains rules for distinguishing false (or subjective) appearance from true (or objective) appearance, the latter arising from true perception of the phenomenal world. As a blend of Leibnizian, Wolffian, Lockian, and Pietist elements the *Neues Organon* was neither more original nor more influential in its time than several Pietist treatises on logic or J. B. Basedow's *Philalethie*.

The lesser-known *Anlage zur Architektonik, oder Theorie des Einfachen und Ersten in der philosophischen und mathematischen Erkentniss* ("Foundation of Architectonic, or Theory of the Simple and Primary Elements in Philosophical and Mathematical Knowledge," 2 vols., Riga, 1771) was a much more important work. In this work Lambert, dissatisfied with classical German and particularly Wolffian metaphysics, proposed a far-reaching reform through an analysis of the sources, genesis, and development of the basic concepts and axioms of metaphysics and their interrelations. Reacting also against sensationalism, skepticism, and the new schools of common-sense and popular philosophy, Lambert wished to save metaphysics by presenting it in a phenomenalistic manner (as J. N. Tetens and Kant were to do later).

Following Locke, Lambert assumed a certain set of concepts as given and then examined them. Once the analysis was completed, Lambert held, it would be possible to change from an empirical to a rationalistic procedure—the a priori deductive construction, modeled on the procedures of mathematics, of a body of general sciences that are true both logically and metaphysically. The deduced propositions of these sciences would then be applied to experience in the manner of applied mathematics. The joining of such propositions with rules abstracted from observation and experiments would give a foundation for truth in each of the particular sciences.

There were thus two main aspects to Lambert's philosophy, the analytic and the constructive. The former was the predominating interest in the *Anlage zur Architektonik*. This work consists largely of detailed discussions of, and subtle distinctions between, many of the most common simple notions and axioms and elementary interrelations

discussed in traditional metaphysics. This refined analysis, too detailed even to be sampled here, exerted a great influence on Teten's mature work and on the making of Kant's *Kritik der reinen Vernunft*. Kant had earlier been much impressed by the *Neues Organon*, and acknowledged to Lambert in correspondence his interest in Lambert's analyses.

The second, constructive, aspect of Lambert's philosophy was an attempt to develop a mathematical logic (or "intensional calculus") for deducing propositions by an easy and exact method from the simple notions and axioms, once they have been established analytically (see LOGIC, HISTORY OF).

Additional Works by Lambert

Deutscher gelehrter Briefwechsel, 5 vols., Johann Bernouilli, ed. Berlin, 1781–1787. Correspondence.
Logische und philosophische Abhandlungen, 2 vols., Johann Bernouilli, ed. Berlin and Dessau, 1782.
Abhandlungen vom Criterium Veritatis, K. Bopp, ed. Berlin, 1915.
Über die Methode, die Metaphysik, Theologie und Moral richtiger zu beweisen, K. Bopp, ed. Berlin, 1918.

Works on Lambert

Arndt, H. W., *Der Moglichkeitsbegriff bei Chr. Wolff und J. H. Lambert*. Göttingen, 1959. A mimeographed thesis.
Baentsch, O., *J. H. Lambert und seine Stellung zu Kant*. Tübingen, 1902.
Eisenring, M. E., *Johann Heinrich Lambert und die wissenschaftliche Philosophie der Gegenwart*. Zurich, 1942.
Huber, D., *J. H. Lambert nach seinem Leben und Wirken*. Basel, 1829.
Krienelke, K., *J. H. Lamberts Philosophie der Mathematik*. Berlin, 1909.
Lepsius, Johann, *J. H. Lambert*. Munich, 1881.
Zimmermann, R., *Lambert der Vorgänger Kants*. Vienna, 1879.

GIORGIO TONELLI

LAMENNAIS, HUGUES FÉLICITÉ ROBERT DE

(1782–1854), French ecclesiastic and philosopher. He was born in Saint-Malo, Brittany, and died in Paris. Lamennais received the tonsure in 1809 but was not ordained a priest until 1816. His early works in defense of ultramontanism won him the approval of Rome, but it was not long before his inability to compromise in the interest of expediency led to his condemnation. Although never excommunicated, he voluntarily relinquished all sacerdotal functions and died after refusing the last rites.

Ultramontanism. Lamennais's first influential work, *De la Tradition de l'église sur l'institution des évêques* (Paris, 1814), written in collaboration with his brother Jean, was an attack on Gallicanism. Directly inspired by Bonald, it propounded three theses—the supremacy of the Church of Rome, papal infallibility in matters of doctrine, and the basic authority of tradition. It did not, however, grant the pope any sovereign rights in temporal matters. Lamennais's second work, the *Essai sur l'indifférence en matière de religion* (1817–1823) was welcomed enthusiastically in Catholic circles and received the approval of Leo XII. It took as its premises that no beliefs are without influence on the welfare of society and that religious beliefs are of primary importance in this respect. Hence, no man has the right to be neutral in religious disputes. Neutrality may arise from false notions of religion's place in life, from a failure to distinguish between orthodoxy and heresy, or from ignorance, lack of serious purpose, or simple sloth. Since no one can rightly maintain two antithetical ideas, there can be only one religious truth, one mouthpiece for it, and one tradition.

Traditionalism. The traditionalism involved in this led to Lamennais's denial of the individual's rational powers, a denial that he clung to consistently. Our senses, feelings, and reason may lead to the truth, but only accidentally. Certitude can be acquired only by the common reason, that of the human race. One must therefore fuse his opinions with those of his fellow men and find the solution to his problems in faith, authority, and common sense. Trust in one's own insight is madness, as is eccentricity of behavior. But if one asks whence comes the authority of the general reason, the answer is, from God. God has entrusted it to the church, which speaks through the pope. No individual philosopher, even though he be a Descartes, can substitute his method for that based on revelation.

The condemnation. So extreme a form of ultramontanism may have been logical, granted its premises, but it was politically inexpedient. Its anti-Gallicanism alone would have aroused resentment, but it was coupled with violent attacks on the French university system, the Charter, and certain personalities, such as Comte Denis de Frayssinous. Lamennais paid little attention to his critics, turned from them to the Vatican, and was shocked to receive in 1832 the encyclical *Mirari Vos*, which, without mentioning him by name, nevertheless condemned his ultramontanism on the ground that it disrupted the existing harmony between church and state. At the same time, it condemned freedom of conscience and opinion, which could lead only to freedom to err. Lamennais submitted but restricted his submission to questions of religion. During this period he also published his *Paroles d'un croyant* (1834), a series of prose poems that preached fraternity, freedom of association, and confidence in God and in prayer. This work was condemned outright in the encyclical *Singulari Nos* (1834).

Philosophy. In substituting "the Christianity of the human race" for that of the Vatican, Lamennais retained his traditionalism but abandoned his ultramontanism. His point of view was expressed in a three-volume work, the *Esquisse d'une philosophie* (1840), of which he published a fourth volume in 1846. It began with a theology, continued through a philosophical anthropology, aesthetics, and philosophy of science, and was to have been completed with a social philosophy. Lamennais's theology was Trinitarian and made the three persons of the Deity power, intelligence, and love, all interfused. Each realm of being reflected this triune nature, which was undemonstrable but demanded by the very nature of human thought. The work as a whole developed this thesis.

Lamennais's philosophy was Christian traditionalism minus ecclesiasticism, but with a philosophy of nature added. No man, he held, can assent to his own deductions if they are not in harmony with those of the whole human race, and the opinions of the human race will be found in tradition. The inconsistencies of tradition were never dwelt upon. His *Esquisse*, because of its Christian overtones, had no popularity in republican circles and, as for his Catholic associates, they felt little if any need for it.

Works by Lamennais

De la Tradition de l'église sur l'institution des évéques, 3 vols. Liège and Paris, 1814.
Essai sur l'indifférence en matière de religion, 4 vols. Paris, 1817–1823.
Défense de l'Essai sur l'indifférence. Paris, 1821.
Paroles d'un croyant. Paris, 1834.
Oeuvres complètes, 12 vols. Paris, 1836–1837. Not complete.
Oeuvres choisies et philosophiques, 10 vols. Paris, 1837–1841.
Esquisse d'une philosophie, 4 vols. Paris, 1840–1846.
Amschaspands et Darvands. Paris, 1843.

Works on Lamennais

Duine, F., *La Mennais.* Évreux, 1922. The most authoritative work, based in part on previously unpublished material.
Gibson, W., *The Abbé de Lamennais and the Liberal Catholic Movement in France.* London and New York, 1896.
Janet, Paul, *La Philosophie de Lamennais.* Paris, 1890.
Mourre, M., *Lamennais, ou l'hérésie des temps modernes.* Paris, 1955.
Spuller, Eugène, *Lamennais: étude d'histoire politique et religieuse.* Paris, 1892.

GEORGE BOAS

LA METTRIE, JULIEN OFFRAY DE (1709–1751), French physician and philosopher, was born in Saint-Malo, Brittany. After attending the Collège d'Harcourt, he studied medicine at the University of Paris, finally obtaining his doctor's degree from the Faculty of Rheims in 1733. He next went to Leiden to complete his training under the celebrated Dr. Hermann Boerhaave, whose iatromechanist doctrines were to have a decisive influence on his orientation in the philosophical, no less than in the medical, domain. Back in Saint-Malo as a practicing physician, La Mettrie undertook to popularize Boerhaave's teachings by translating into French a number of the latter's principal works. His marriage in 1739 to Marie-Louise Droneau proved unhappy and led before long to a separation. From 1743 to 1745 La Mettrie, as surgeon to the *Gardes Françaises* regiment, participated in several campaigns of the War of the Austrian Succession. The publication in 1745 of his first philosophical work, the *Histoire naturelle de l'âme*, brought him under severe official censure for his materialist views. This circumstance, along with an imprudent satire he wrote on the foibles of his medical colleagues, caused La Mettrie to exile himself to Holland. It was there that he published in 1747 *L'Homme machine*, his best known and most influential book, whose atheistic and materialistic contents aroused even the liberal-minded Dutch to angry protest.

La Mettrie was fortunate enough, at this crucial moment, to find a protector in Frederick the Great, who invited him to Berlin. In Prussia he was appointed a member of the Royal Academy of Sciences, as well as "physician ordinary" and "reader" to the king. Profiting from the security of his position, he brought out, among other writings, *L'Homme plante* (1748), *Le Système d'Epicure* (1750), and *Discours sur le bonheur* (1750), each of which attested, in its own way, to the sort of scandalizing unorthodoxy of thought for which their author had already acquired a unique reputation. His numerous enemies, powerless to suppress either him or his ideas, contented themselves with a plethora of refutations that were too often irrelevant in substance or abusive in tone; in particular, they drew a portrait of La Mettrie himself as a monster of depravity. But apart from his theoretical advocacy and personal pursuit of a frankly hedonistic ideal and his delight in provoking or shocking those of a stiffly bourgeois or pious outlook, La Mettrie's character was actually far from deserving the ignominy heaped upon it. He died in 1751 of what was regarded by his contemporaries, somewhat unkindly, as the effects of overeating—a diagnosis exploited by his foes to prove both the practical dangers of materialism and the providential punishment reserved for atheists. Frederick II composed the eulogy that was read before the Berlin Academy. Besides his philosophical works, La Mettrie wrote several medical treatises of only minor value, a series of polemical and ironical pamphlets aimed at his critics, and three mordant, informative satires on what he considered to be the incompetence and "malpractice" of the doctors of the period, the best being his *Machiavel en médecine* (1748–1750).

"The History of the Soul." In the *Histoire naturelle de l'âme*, directed against the metaphysical dualism of Descartes, Malebranche, Leibniz, and their followers, La Mettrie contended that the soul owes its being to those specific organic forms, produced by a *force motrice* inhering in matter, on which the mental faculties and operations remain dependent. The "history of the soul" thus becomes an aspect of the body's history and falls under the authority, not of the metaphysician or theologian, but of the natural scientist. In this claim we have the fundamental attitude of La Mettrie, from which his originality as a philosopher would spring. His method of inquiry consisted in moving regularly from the empirical sphere of scientific facts and theories to that of philosophy proper—the latter being regarded, at least with respect to epistemological and psychological problems, as the logical extension of such branches of knowledge as anatomy, physiology, chemistry, medicine, and the like. La Mettrie was perhaps the first "medical" philosopher in the complete and true sense—a designation suggesting at once the strengths and weaknesses peculiar to his thought.

In the *Histoire de l'âme*, La Mettrie sought to substantiate his naturalistic conception of the soul by means of two types of evidence, profusely cited, which tend to complement each other. Drawing, on the one hand, from the common fund of Lockean sensationalism (to which he gave, incidentally, a materialist meaning), La Mettrie argued that the contents of the mind—hence the mind itself—have no reality independently of the natural world in which sense impressions originate or of the sense organs by which these are transmitted. Utilizing, on the other hand, the technical data offered by the medical sciences of his time, he affirmed that the sensitive and intellectual activities of what is conventionally called the soul depend essentially on the structure and functions of the central nervous system, in general, and of the brain, in particular. Establishing a natural continuity from the external world through the sensory apparatus to the brain

itself, La Mettrie identified the soul with a physically conditioned process in a way that allowed him to explain the various faculties of the soul, such as memory, reflection, imagination, the emotions, judgment, volition, solely in terms of their related organic causes. However, a special feature of the *Histoire de l'âme* was its exposition of materialism within the conceptual framework of Aristotelian metaphysics. La Mettrie speculated that it is by virtue of the appropriate "material forms" and "substantial forms" that matter, actively organized by an intrinsic *force motrice*, realizes its potential attributes of a "vegetative soul" and a "sensitive soul"; each of these, in turn, he makes the "directing principle" of the biological or psychological functions coming under its sway. In presenting his empirico-physiological theory of mind under Scholastic auspices, La Mettrie intended, no doubt, to lend it some measure of metaphysical support, but probably more important was his wish to disarm the censorship by insisting—as he did throughout—on his theory's conformity with the prevailing orthodox tradition in Western philosophy. His strategy did not succeed very well, however, for the Aristotelianism on which he grafted his opinions served only to render them obscure and confused, yet apparently not quite obscure enough to prevent the authorities from recognizing and suppressing his "heretical" defense of materialism.

"Man a Machine." The thesis of *L'Homme machine*, in asserting and illustrating the material dependence of the states of the soul uniformly on the corresponding states of the body, remains similar to that of the *Histoire de l'âme*, but its mode of expression and exact meaning are appreciably different. Composed in a lively, unmethodical, popular fashion, its exposition of materialism is effected not only without any metaphysical substructure but in a definitely antimetaphysical spirit. Its naturalistic view of man, consequently, is offered mainly as a general heuristic hypothesis necessary in the positive study of behavior, without the need being felt, beyond such a standpoint, to make mental processes reductively identical with their physiological causes. Concurrently La Mettrie proposed an experimental–inductive method, as opposed to the then prevalent apriorist ones, in the search for the principles of psychology. Discussing the organic basis of both vital and psychic events, he insisted on the mechanistic character of the causation involved. This important point was not brought out clearly in *Histoire de l'âme* because of the attempted materialization of the pseudo-Scholastic "souls" and "faculties."

In *L'Homme machine* no essential distinction remained between the conscious and voluntary, as against the merely vital, involuntary, or instinctual activities of the "human machine"; the two types of activity are presumed explainable by the relative complexity of the mechanical structures responsible for their production. Thus La Mettrie could claim that his man–machine theory was the extension to its logical and empirical limits of the Cartesian animal–automaton doctrine. However, he must be credited with conceiving of the "living machine" in a manner that goes beyond the inadequacies of Descartes's passive and inert notion of mechanism. The organic machine that sustains the sensitive and mental life of the individual is defined by La Mettrie as a purposively self-moving and self-sufficient system, consisting of dynamically interrelated parts. It was typical of his empirical procedure that he found proof of the autonomous energy and internal finality of the organism in the physiological data of irritability. Following the pioneering researches of Albrecht von Haller, La Mettrie was among the first to understand the radical value of the capacity for irritability, and he succeeded in interpreting it with particular relevance for his thesis of psychophysical automatism.

Among the subsidiary themes of *L'Homme machine*, the declaration of atheism was a new and significant development. On the one hand, it served a polemical and propagandist aim against the religious enemies of La Mettrie's philosophical position. On the other hand, it was a logical outcome of the universal naturalism in which the man–machine theory was appropriately framed; the traditional belief in an Intelligent Creator was replaced by the concept of an active, self-creating nature.

In epistemology, La Mettrie's characteristic approach was to offer picturable analogies between mind and brain, suggesting (however crudely) the model of a "thinking machine" into which sense perceptions feed ideas in the form of coded symbols that are, in turn, stored, classed, compared, and combined by the cerebral apparatus in order to engender all the known varieties of thought. This mechanical ordering and manipulation by the brain of its symbolically represented contents prompted La Mettrie to consider that the fundamental faculty of the mind is "imagination."

Another feature of *L'Homme machine* is its persistent tendency to assimilate human to animal nature with the aid of evidence drawn from the spheres of comparative anatomy and experimental psychology. The doctrine of free will, of course, becomes meaningless in the light of physiological necessity. The moral aspect of behavior is regarded as no less determined than its other aspects, although it should be noted that the man–machine theory, despite its context of universal determinism, leads to the affirmation of a hierarchy of individual values and capabilities, inasmuch as no two "machines" could ever be identical or equal. The problem of the moral or intellectual perfectibility of man, within the compass of La Mettrie's materialism, becomes primarily a medical problem, for its solution depends on the possibility of perfecting the state of the organism.

"Discourse on Happiness." In the *Discours sur le bonheur*, intended as a refutation of Senecan Stoicism, La Mettrie viewed the *summum bonum* of happiness in a manner no less individualistic than hedonistic. In consistence with his materialist premises, he described happiness as the optimum state of pleasurable well-being of the "man–machine." Underlying his entire treatment of the subject is the assumption that happiness was destined by nature as a benefit to be enjoyed by each and every person, regardless of moral, intellectual, or social preconditions of any sort; that is, the goal of happiness is divorced basically from such traditional considerations as vice and virtue, ignorance and knowledge, social status and responsibility. La Mettrie obviously conceived of the problem of happiness, seen from the perspective of medical ethics, as similar to—indeed, as a special instance of—the more comprehensive problem of health. Accordingly, he diagnosed the greatest threat to felicity to be "remorse," a morbid and "unnatural" symptom, which he proposed, ever faithful to the Hippocratic oath, to alleviate in all and sundry, including even conscience-ridden criminals; he remarked that the practical control of social behavior was a political matter and no business of his.

The *Discours sur le bonheur* was misinterpreted as a cynical inducement to vice and crime and, more than any of his works, gave to the author an enduring reputation for immoralism among philosophes and antiphilosophes alike.

Minor works. Among La Mettrie's minor works, perhaps the most curious is the *Système d'Epicure*. Its concern with ontogenesis and the origin of species represented a broadening of La Mettrie's materialism into an area of biological speculation which, at the time, was just beginning to excite interest. But his description of the "evolutionary" process, in which monstrous and unviable productions are supposed to have been eliminated in favor of the well-constituted types now extant, did little more than revive Lucretian memories.

In *L'Homme plante*, La Mettrie's purpose was to stress the various parallelisms of structure and function between two such seemingly disparate things as the human organism and vegetable life. Reflecting his strong taste for analogical reasoning, it is an extreme confirmation of the "chain-of-being" idea, which it interprets in the sense of a uniform destiny for man and for all other living forms, excluding the possibility of a spiritual transcendence of nature.

Les animaux plus que machines is mainly a polemical piece directed against the school of animistic biology. By elaborating a mock defense of the opinion that a "soul" governs the animal economy, La Mettrie managed to expose, with the support of much physiological evidence, the absurdity and uselessness of such a hypothesis. The inference is that it would be equally ridiculous to claim that the operations of the human machine presuppose the agency of a "soul."

La Mettrie's philosophy, and in particular the man–machine doctrine central to it, has, owing to its very character, grown somewhat obsolete, together with the scientific documentation to which it was so intimately linked. The specific features of his mechanistic theory of mind might, in relation to what is now known or still unknown about neural processes, seem naive, crude, superficial, and pretentious. Nevertheless, his was the first naturalistic rationale for, and technical application of, a consistently physiological method in psychology. And while his philosophic contribution remains circumscribed by the biomedical standpoint that shaped his thinking, the man–machine hypothesis may be said, within its proper limits, to have retained a basic validity and vitality. Despite La Mettrie's bad name in his own age, and the many attempts to suppress, disfigure, or discredit his ideas, he exerted (surreptitiously, on the whole) a considerable influence in the eighteenth-century milieu. Among those indebted to the man–machine conception and to the naturalistic overtones and consequences that accompanied its formulation, the most important were Diderot, Holbach, and Cabanis. Long neglected after his death, La Mettrie has been recognized since the latter part of the nineteenth century as one of the major forerunners of modern materialism. His nonreductive form of materialism may be re garded as an early version of a theory that is widely advocated at the present time by, among others, Ernest Nagel and various American naturalists; and his view that human beings can be fruitfully considered as a certain type of machine has obvious similarities to the principles underlying the science of cybernetics.

Works by La Mettrie

Oeuvres philosophiques, 3 vols. Berlin and Paris, 1796.

L'Homme machine. Translated as *Man a Machine*. London, 1749. A later translation is *Man a Machine; including Frederick the Great's "Eulogy" . . . and extracts from "The Natural History of the Soul."* Translated with philosophical and historical notes by Gertrude C. Bussey. Chicago, 1912.

Works on La Mettrie

Bergmann, Ernst, *Die Satiren des Herrn Maschine*. Leipzig, 1913. On La Mettrie's activities as a satirist.

Boissier, Raymond, *La Mettrie, médecin, pamphlétaire, et philosophe*. Paris, 1931. Mainly on the medical background of La Mettrie's thought.

Lemée, Pierre, *Julien Offray de La Mettrie, médecin, philosophe, polémiste: sa vie, son oeuvre*. Mortain, France, 1954. Best biographical account.

Perkins, Jean, "Diderot and La Mettrie." *Studies on Voltaire and the 18th Century*, Vol. 10 (1959), 49–100.

Pflug, Günther, "Lamettrie und die biologische Theorien des 18. Jahrhunderts." *Deutsche Vierteljahrsschrift für Literaturwissenschaft und Geistesgeschichte*, Vol. 27 (1953), 509–527.

Lange, F. A., *History of Materialism*. London, 1925. Bk. I, Sec. IV, Ch. 2 has a good discussion of La Mettrie.

Poritzky, J. E., *Julien Offray de La Mettrie, sein Leben und seine Werke*. Berlin, 1900. Best general treatment of La Mettrie's philosophy.

Vartanian, Aram, "Trembley's Polyp, La Mettrie, and Eighteenth-Century French Materialism." *Journal of the History of Ideas*, Vol. 11 (1950), 259–286.

Vartanian, Aram, *La Mettrie's L'Homme Machine: A Study in the Origins of an Idea*. Princeton, N.J., 1960. Critical edition with introductory monograph and notes.

ARAM VARTANIAN

LA MOTHE LE VAYER, FRANÇOIS DE (1588–1672), French skeptical philosopher, was born in Paris, the son of a government official. He acquired his father's post when the latter died in 1625. His wife was the daughter of a Scottish intellectual, Adam Blackwood. During his early years, La Mothe Le Vayer traveled widely in Europe. In 1639 he was elected to the Académie Française and in 1647 was appointed preceptor to the duke of Orléans. He was a prominent figure in avant-garde circles in Paris—in the group around Montaigne's adopted daughter, Mlle. de Gournay; in the group of *libertins érudits* with Naudé, Guy Patin, and Gassendi; in the scientific group around Mersenne; and in the literary world of Molière (who jested at La Mothe Le Vayer in *Le Mariage forcé* and other plays) and Cyrano de Bergerac. His numerous writings on skepticism began with *Dialogues d'Oratius Tubero* (1630), followed by the *Discours chrétien de l'immortalité de l'âme* (1637, the year of Descartes's *Discours de la*

méthode), *La Vertu des payens* (1642, published with Richelieu as the sponsor), and a long series of skeptical essays on history and culture throughout the rest of his life.

Although his views were based primarily on those of Sextus Empiricus (whom he called "le divin Sexte" and the author of "notre décalogue") and Montaigne, La Mothe Le Vayer's skepticism represents perhaps the most extreme type of antirationalism in the seventeenth century. He continually offered a wealth of evidence to show the variations in human moral behavior, the diversity of man's religious beliefs and practices, the vanity of scientific study, and the virtues of skepticism. He rarely developed his case theoretically by means of systematic arguments. Instead he usually offered only illustrative materials, followed by a fideistic message that man can find truth only through faith, not through the use of his reason and senses.

In the *Petit Traité sceptique sur cette façon de parler, n'avoir pas le sens commun* (1647), La Mothe Le Vayer contended that man does not understand the nature of even the most obvious things. All of our information is relative to our faculties. Even if there are any instruments for finding the truth about things, we, unfortunately, are unable to discover them. Our senses are unreliable, and we lack any guaranteed criterion for distinguishing veridical experiences from others. Indubitable truths can be known only in heaven, not here and not through any human science.

These views are further developed in his *Discours pour montres que les doutes de la philosophie sceptique sont de grande usage dans les sciences* (1669), where it is claimed, as the title shows, that the great service of pyrrhonian skepticism for the sciences is that it can eliminate any serious concern with scientific research, and that such research is a form of blasphemy. He asserted, without offering any real arguments, that logic is unreliable and physics only a problematical subject about which there are conflicting opinions. Nature is the free manifestation of God's will. Therefore any attempt to restrict God's achievement to what man can measure and understand is an attempt to limit God's freedom, and is, hence, blasphemous. When the scientists realize how uncertain their disciplines are, they should give them up and adopt skepticism, "the inestimable antidote against the presumptuous knowledge of the learned ones."

This complete skepticism should undermine the dogmatist's confidence and pride and lead him to the true faith, Christianity. In his *Prose chagrine* (1661), La Mothe Le Vayer proclaimed that of all the ancient philosophies, "there is no other that agrees so easily with Christianity as skepticism, respectful towards Heaven and submissive to the Faith." Had not St. Paul preached that skepticism was the way to salvation? The true Christian skeptic leaves his doubts at the foot of the altar and lives by faith.

La Mothe Le Vayer's anti-intellectual and destructive attack on human rational knowledge (presented almost obliviously to the scientific revolution going on around him, and especially to the achievements of René Descartes) and his appeal to faith, although not introducing much that was new to skeptical argumentation, carried the Montaignian position to an absurd extreme. He denied any and all value to intellectual activities and left only blind faith. As a result, many commentators from Arnauld on have assumed that he was a pure libertine, undermining all bases for religion, and have classified him, partly on the basis of his risqué work, *Hexaméron rustique* (1670), as an "incrédule volupteux." His views, however, are compatible with his having been either a sincere Christian skeptic or a secret atheist undermining confidence in all views and beliefs—a genuine fideist or an irreligious doubter. His philosophical influence seems to have been more through personal contact than through any serious presentation of philosophical skepticism. As a representative of the skeptical view, he was still important in Bayle's time, but was forgotten for the most part thereafter.

Works by La Mothe Le Vayer

Oeuvres, 15 vols. Paris, 1669.

Works on La Mothe Le Vayer

Bayle, Pierre, "Vayer," in *Dictionnaire historique et critique*. Rotterdam, 1695–1697.
Pintard, René, *Le Libertinage érudit*. Paris, 1943.
Popkin, Richard H., *The History of Scepticism from Erasmus to Descartes*. Assen and New York, 1960; 2d ed. Assen and New York, 1964.
Wickelgren, Florence, *La Mothe Le Vayer, sa vie et son oeuvre*. Paris, 1934.

RICHARD H. POPKIN

LANGE, FRIEDRICH ALBERT (1828–1875), German philosopher, historian, and sociologist, ·was born at Wald near Solingen. Lange studied at Duisberg, in Zurich, where he attended the lectures of a disciple of Herbart, and at Bonn. After receiving a degree at Bonn, he taught high school in Cologne, and in 1851 he became a university instructor at Bonn. His dissertation concerned the relation between theories of education and various world views. From 1858 to 1861 he taught school in Duisberg but resigned because of a government order forbidding teachers to participate in political agitation. Lange remained in Duisberg as a newspaper editor and secretary of the chamber of commerce. His socialist sympathies were not incompatible with a genius for finance. In 1866 he returned to Switzerland and in 1870 became professor of inductive logic at Zurich. He was appointed to a professorship at Marburg in 1873 and remained there until his death. The philosophical poems of Schiller, on which he sometimes lectured, were said to be his final comfort.

Lange's importance in philosophy rests mainly on his brilliantly written *History of Materialism and Critique of Its Present Significance* (1866). This work gave support to the opponents of materialism and helped to stimulate the revival of interest in Kant which led to the Neo-Kantian schools of the last decades of the century. Less important philosophically, but a prominent part of Lange's versatile career, was his concern with social questions, as in *Die Arbeiterfrage* (1865), and his work for constitutional reform in the direction of democratic socialism.

Lange argued that materialistic theories of reality are just as guilty of transcending the proper limits of human knowledge as are the speculative systems of idealism. He appealed to Kant's arguments, rejecting the possibility of any metaphysical knowledge which pretends to take us beyond the sphere of experience. In his view, the attempt to comprehend the world as a whole is doomed to failure. But this criticism applied as much to the materialistic rejection of unobservable spiritual or mental agencies as to their defense. According to Lange, metaphysical theories belong to the realm of art and religion, a field governed by poetizing (*dichten*). This activity is not an illegitimate one, however. It is an essential human need, expressive of men's yearnings for an ideal realm. But religion and the speculative systems of metaphysics do not yield scientific knowledge or any substitute for it.

Lange saw materialism both as a demand for mechanistic explanations of natural phenomena and as a naive realism and dogmatic metaphysics. The first demand he considered valid, but the second, he held, had been refuted by Kant and by the development of physiological psychology. The demand that natural occurrences be explained in terms of material causes is a useful, even indispensable, postulate of scientific method. In attempting to explain human behavior, for instance, it is unreasonable to think of consciousness as intervening somewhere in the series of physical events from stimulus to brain, nerve, and muscular response. Mental processes are not members of this series.

While the only valid categories for science are those which, like space, time, and causality, render nature mechanistically intelligible, these categories have no proper role beyond that of organizing our sense experience. Along with the basic concepts of physics—matter, atom, force, physical object—they are the products of human invention. The Kantian theory of the a priori had shown this, while discoveries in the physiology of sensation proved that our knowledge is sifted through human sense organs. The scientist is not a passive recipient of data; the laws which he discovers are constructions whose objectivity is only an objectivity *for us*. Though the world which science presents is the cognitive realm valid for all men, there is also the individual's world of ideals. To confuse the two worlds is wrong, because each has its significance.

Lange's physiological interpretation of the categories was rejected by his Neo-Kantian successors at Marburg, Hermann Cohen and Paul Natorp. His influence was very strong, however, on Hans Vaihinger, whose pragmatism owes much to Lange's concept of categories as no more than maxims of scientific method. Lange's rejection of all metaphysics placed him also in the positivistic tradition, and it is no surprise that he referred to Comte as "the noble Comte." Though Lange was critical of Feuerbach, whom he regarded as only half emancipated from Hegel, his own sympathetic but noncognitivist view of religion and ideals is akin to the humanism of Feuerbach.

Works by Lange

Die Arbeiterfrage. Winterthur, 1865.
Geschichte des Materialismus und Kritik seiner Bedeutung in der Gegenwart, 2 vols. Iserlohn and Leipzig, 1866. The edition published at Leipzig in 1902 has an introduction and critical appendix by Hermann Cohen. English translation by E. C. Thomas, 3 vols. London, 1877–1879, reprinted with an important introduction by Bertrand Russell, 1 vol. Edinburgh, 1925.

J. S. Mill's Ansichten über die Social Frage. Duisburg, 1866.
Logische Studien, H. Cohen, ed. Iserlohn and Leipzig, 1877.

Works on Lange

Ellissen, O. A., *F. A. Lange.* Leipzig, 1891. Contains letters of interest.
Vaihinger, H., *Hartmann, Dühring, und Lange.* Iserlohn, 1876.
Vaihinger, H., *Die Philosophie des Als-Ob.* Berlin, 1911. Translated by C. K. Ogden as *The Philosophy of "As if."* New York and London, 1924.

ARNULF ZWEIG

LANGUAGE. At many points in his discipline the philosopher becomes involved with problems concerning language. Whenever philosophers turn their attention to any subject matter—science, religion, art, etc.—one thing they try to do is to clarify the concept of that subject matter. Thus, the philosophy of language tries to deal with the question "What is language?"

In attempting to answer this question we can start with relatively obvious features of language. (1) A language is made up of units interrelated in some sort of systematic way. On a common-sense analysis the units are such things as words and syllables; on the more sophisticated analysis of contemporary structural linguistics, they are such things as morphemes and phonemes. For present purposes the common-sense units will do. (2) Units at the word level have meaning by "convention." (3) This system (language) is used for communication. The job of getting clear about the nature of language is largely the job of getting clear as to the nature of the units, the respects in which they form a system, the nature of communication, and what is involved in the system being used for communication.

Language as made up of symbols. Language is sometimes characterized as a system of "symbols," where a "symbol" is something which has meaning by "convention." There are symbols which do not fit into any language, for example, fire sirens, such gestures as a shrug of the shoulders, a red light as a traffic signal, and a deliberately produced cough which means "It's time to go." Where symbols are organized into a system of considerable extent, we have a language. There is a certain amount of truth in this point of view, but it is misleading in two respects.

First, we naturally think of words as the sorts of symbols that are organized into a system when we have a language. But the linguistic analogues of symbols which exist outside language are sentences, not words. This is because an isolated symbol has to be serviceable for performing a complete act of communication all by itself, and within language it is the sentence which has this role. (There are, of course, some one-word sentences, like "Yes," "Now!" and "Fire!") Thus, when the baseball umpire gives the gesture appropriate for calling the base runner safe, he is doing something which, if done linguistically, would have to be done by the sentence "You're safe" or the still shorter sentence "Safe!" rather than by a single word, such as "in," "baseball," or even the *word* "safe," which lacks the intonation contour of the one-word sentence "Safe!" But the basic units of language are words and phonemes, rather than sentences. (This is shown by the fact that there is an indefinite number of sentences in a language,

whereas there is a finite number of words and a much smaller number of phonemes.) A sentence is something which can be constructed for the given purpose at hand out of the elements which make up the linguistic system. Thus, a language is not a system of items which are symbols in the way that nonlinguistic symbols are symbols. It would be better to say that a language is a system which provides the opportunity for constructing an indefinite number of "symbols."

Second, it would be a mistake to suppose that the elements of language, such as words, exist as such apart from the language and that it is just a contingent fact that these "symbols" happen to have been organized into the kind of system which constitutes a language, while other "symbols" have not. To see this, let us consider what a word is. It is clear initially that a word is a relatively abstract entity. The word "in," for example, cannot be identified with any particular sound or visible mark produced at a certain time, for this (same) word can be uttered and written on many different occasions; it must be construed as something repeatable or exemplifiable. We might try to conceive of it as a certain pattern of sounds or visible marks to which particular sounds and marks approximate, more or less. But having selected a paradigm, how do we tell which deviations from the paradigm count as instances of the word and which do not? Consider the word "house." In different dialects this may come out "haus," "hoose," or "hoss." Now why should we count "haus" and "hoose" as variants of the same word but "haus" and "laus" as not, even though "laus" sounds at least as much like "haus" as does "hoose"? This question can be answered only by taking into account the distribution of these forms in the language as a whole. We proceed as we do because the Virginian's "hoose" is distributed in his utterances pretty much in the way the midwesterner's "haus" is in his, whereas the Californian's "laus" does not have the same distribution as the midwesterner's "haus." This shows that we cannot give an adequate account of what makes up a particular word without bringing in the way that word figures in the language. Hence, it is a superficial view to suppose that the word "house" could have still existed as *that word* if the English language had never existed.

Language as a system. Let us try to get some idea of how the elements of a language constitute a system. The preceding discussion should have made it explicit that the kind of system involved is something much more complicated than what we would have if we simply took a number of already functioning, isolated signals and interrelated them by, for example, specifying rules according to which the significance of a given signal depended on what other signals preceded or succeeded it. To get anything like a language we would have to analyze the signals into more elementary constituents which did not themselves have the status of signals. Still following a common-sense analysis of language, we can briefly set out the major respects in which language is systematic. (If we used the more sophisticated kind of analysis which is typical of contemporary linguistics, a much richer system would be revealed.) Words can be grouped into wider and narrower "form classes." The most general form classes are the familiar "parts of speech"—noun, verb, adjective, etc. Each of these can be further subdivided, for example, noun into mass noun ("sugar") and count noun ("table"). It is then possible to discover various restrictions on the number of possible combinations. For example, it is possible to have a sentence constituted as follows: Article + Noun + Copula + Adjective ("The box is heavy"); but we cannot have a sentence constituted as follows: Verb + Article + Preposition ("Lift the in"). Moreover, each word has one or more meanings, and quite often the surrounding linguistic context will make clear which of these is being employed. Thus, in "Did you hear that sound?" the context "Did you hear that _____?" "selects" one item from the range of meanings of the word "sound"; the context "That is a _____ investment" selects another. Furthermore, there are rules according to which the meaning of a whole sentence can be "computed" from the meanings of the constituent words and the order in which they are combined into the sentence. It is important to realize that the meaning of the sentence is not simply a function of the meanings of the constituent words taken as an unordered aggregate; the mode of composition is also important. "The boy hit the girl" has a different meaning from "The girl hit the boy," even though the two sentences are made up of the same semantic constituents. On a more subtle level we may consider the difference in the way the meanings of "copper" and "mine" combine to form the meaning of "copper mine" and the way in which the meanings of "copper" and "kettle" combine to form the meaning of "copper kettle."

Language and communication. So far we have said nothing about the third feature of language, that the system involved in a language is usable in communication. If we look deeply into the matter, we shall see that this feature is not independent of the aspects of the system we have been considering. For to say that a sentence, for example, "Did you hear that sound?," has a certain meaning is to say that it is usable, in accordance with the rules of the language, in a certain act of communication, asking a certain question. In general, for a sentence to have a certain meaning is for it to be usable in expressing a certain attitude, making a certain request, promise, or suggestion, giving a certain piece of advice, blaming someone for something, etc. And digging more deeply, to say that a word has a certain meaning is, in the last analysis, to say that when it is put into a certain slot in a sentence it will partly determine the kind of act of communication for which that sentence is fitted. Thus, depending on whether we insert "song" or "scream" into "Did you hear that _____?," the resulting sentence will be suited to the asking of one or another question. (For a development of this approach to linguistic meaning, see MEANING.)

To be sure, we must remember that language is also used outside the context of *interpersonal* communication, in thought, in soliloquy, and in the spontaneous expression of feelings without regard to the audience, if any. Thus, we must either regard these activities as limiting cases of communication (with oneself), or we must make it explicit that what is essential for language is that it *can* be used for communication, not that it only be actually so used. Even if we adopt the latter, weaker formulation, it would seem to follow that abstract systems created by logicians and mathematicians, for example, the "language" of Russell

and Whitehead's *Principia Mathematica,* are not languages in a strict or primary sense, for it is doubtful that they can be used at all for communication. Perhaps it is best to say that for central or "paradigmatic" cases of languages, interpersonal communication is the central use and that other uses are derivative from this. If one had not first learned to communicate with others verbally, he would not be able to talk to himself. (It is controversial whether this is a logical necessity or a psychological necessity.) Then, abstract systems of logic are best viewed not as languages in any full-blooded sense but rather as logical skeletons of actual or envisaged languages. In any event, there is no suggestion in any of this that language is the only basis of communication. Communication can also be carried on by "isolated" symbols of the sort mentioned earlier, as well as by pictorial representations and in other ways.

Language and speech. It follows from the preceding discussion that a language is an entity of a more abstract order than would appear from many accounts. Language is not a kind of activity, process, or social interaction; still less is it an aggregate of actions, sounds, or other concrete phenomena. It is, rather, a system of abstract elements. It is of the first importance to distinguish between *speech,* the totality of verbal activity in a community, and *language,* the abstract system of sound types and the rules of their combination, which is exemplified in verbal activity and which is discoverable through an analysis of this activity. Every time I speak I add to the sum total of verbal behavior which has gone on in English-speaking communities, but I do not thereby add to or change the English language. The language would change through a general change in some of the linguistic habits of speakers of English. A language is an abstraction from particular activities in something like the way in which a game is. If no one ever hit balls back and forth across a net with rackets in accordance with certain rules, there would be no such thing as the game of tennis. Nevertheless, we cannot identify the game of tennis with such activities, either individually or in the aggregate. Each instance of playing tennis is datable in a way that the game of tennis is not; and the sum total of such activities is constantly increasing, whereas the game of tennis is not. Many philosophers think that if they can get away from talking about propositions, thoughts, and concepts, and talk instead about words and sentences, they will have substituted the concrete and observable for mysterious and dubious abstract entities. Such philosophers do not fully appreciate the extent to which a language and its constituents are themselves abstract.

Primacy of oral language. Linguists customarily restrict the term "language," in its primary employment, to systems of orally produced sounds, and they consider it to apply only derivatively to systems of devices for representing such sound systems, like the system of writing for English or Arabic, and only derivatively again to systems which are introduced via speech or via a derivative of the first sort, such as the notations of various branches of mathematics, the elements and rules of which are initially explained in a natural language. Philosophers find it difficult to understand this restriction. Why could there not be a system of written marks, gestures, or smoke signals, which developed autonomously rather than as a representation of or substitute for oral language? The differing perspectives of linguists and philosophers on this point seem to stem from their respective concentration on the actual and on the logically possible. It is noteworthy that every clear case of an actually existing language is either a system of speech sounds or a derivative of such a system. But this seems to be a result of the contingent fact that as human beings, human society, and human technology have been constituted, vocally produced sounds have been the most readily available, the most efficient, and the most flexible means of communication. The logical possibility remains that there should be a system of elements which have some different sort of physical embodiment, which should not be a derivative of a system of vocal sounds and yet should perform all the functions and have all the distinctive features of what we now recognize as natural languages.

Bibliography

Different philosophies yield different perspectives on language. For a Neo-Kantian point of view, see Volume I of Ernst Cassirer, *The Philosophy of Symbolic Forms*, translated by Ralph Manheim (New Haven, Conn., 1953); W. M. Urban, *Language and Reality* (London, 1939); and Susanne K. Langer, *Philosophy in a New Key* (Cambridge, Mass., 1942).

For the standpoint of logical positivism, see Rudolf Carnap, *The Logical Syntax of Language* (New York, 1937); and N. L. Wilson, *The Concept of Language* (Toronto, 1959).

Ways of viewing language characteristic of contemporary structural linguistics can be gleaned from Leonard Bloomfield, *Language* (New York, 1933); Edward Sapir, *Language* (New York, 1921); A. A. Hill, *Introduction to Linguistic Structures* (New York, 1958); J. B. Carroll, *The Study of Language* (Cambridge, Mass., 1955); H. A. Gleason, *An Introduction to Descriptive Linguistics* (New York, 1961); Noam Chomsky, *Syntactic Structures* (The Hague, 1957) and *Aspects of the Theory of Syntax* (Cambridge, Mass., 1965); and J. A. Fodor and J. J. Katz, eds., *The Structure of Language* (Englewood Cliffs, N.J., 1964).

WILLIAM P. ALSTON

LANGUAGE, ARTIFICIAL AND NATURAL. See ARTIFICIAL AND NATURAL LANGUAGES.

LANGUAGE, PHILOSOPHY OF. What is now called the philosophy of language is a loosely related group of investigations that have little in common beyond their concern with language and their relevance to other philosophical inquiries. Their scope can best be indicated by a review of the main points at which philosophy, as historically carried on, has found itself involved in questions about language.

SURVEY OF LINGUISTIC QUESTIONS

Metaphysics. Metaphysics may be briefly characterized as an attempt to discover the most general and pervasive facts about the world. Many philosophers have supposed that one could discover such facts through a consideration of fundamental features of the language we use to talk about the world.

Plato. In Book X of Plato's *Republic* we find the following: "Whenever a number of individuals have a common

name, we assume them to have also a corresponding idea or form" (596). Here Plato was calling attention to a pervasive feature of language, that a word such as "dog" or "heavy" can be truly asserted of a number of different individual things. Plato assigned a metaphysical significance to such a fact because he thought that this would be possible only if there were some entity *named* by the general term in question—dogness, heaviness—an entity of which each of the individual dogs or heavy things "partakes."

Aristotle. Aristotle argued in his *Metaphysics* as follows:

> And so one might even raise the question whether the words "to walk," "to be healthy," "to sit," imply that each of these things is existent, and similarly in other cases of this sort; for none of them is either self-subsistent or capable of being separated from substance, but rather, if anything, it is that which walks or sits or is healthy that is an existent thing. Now these are seen to be more real because there is something definite which underlies them (i.e., the substance or individual) which is implied in such a predicate; for we never use the word "good" or "sitting" without implying this. (Book Z, Ch. 1)

Here Aristotle began with the linguistic fact that we do not use verbs except in conjunction with nominative subjects, that we do not go around saying "Sits" or "Walks," but rather "He is sitting" or "She is walking." From this he reached the metaphysical conclusion that substances have an independent existence in a way in which actions do not, that substances are more fundamental ontologically than actions.

Logical atomism. Metaphysical argumentation of the sort that Aristotle engaged in was explicitly proclaimed as a program by the twentieth-century movement known as "logical atomism," the chief exponents of which were Bertrand Russell and Ludwig Wittgenstein. The fundamental principle was spelled out by Russell in "The Philosophy of Logical Atomism" (in *Logic and Knowledge*):

> . . . in a logically correct symbolism there will always be a certain fundamental identity of structure between a fact and the symbol for it; and . . . the complexity of the symbol corresponds very closely with the complexity of the facts symbolized by it.

Thus, the program is as follows: First we are to devise a "logically perfect language," or at least to find out what such a language would be like. Then we will be in a position to say what different types of fact-stating sentences there are in that language (for example, simple subject–predicate sentences like "This shirt is striped" or existential sentences like "There is a telephone in that room"), how each sentence is composed of certain types of constituents related in certain ways, and what the logical relations are between sentences of different types. This will enable us to find out what sort of facts reality consists of, how these facts are constituted, and how they are interrelated.

Logic. Concern with language assumes even greater prominence in logic than in metaphysics. Logic is the study of inference or reasoning. Since reasoning is carried on in language, in order to analyze various kinds of inference it is necessary to analyze the statements which figure in it. Moreover, it soon becomes clear that the validity or invalidity of an argument largely depends on the *forms* of the statements in which the argument is formulated. This appears most dramatically in pairs of arguments, one of which is valid, the other invalid, although superficially they look very much alike. Consider the following pair:

(1) The president of the United States is the commander-in-chief of the armed forces. Mr. *Y* is the president of the United States. Therefore, Mr. *Y* is the commander-in-chief of the armed forces.

(2) The president of the United States is elected every four years. Mr. *Y* is president of the United States. Therefore, Mr. *Y* is elected every four years.

The fact that (1) is clearly a valid argument and (2) is clearly an invalid argument shows that there must, despite appearances, be some crucial difference in logical form between the first premises of the two arguments. If one aims to construct a complete (or even very extensive) list of forms of valid inference, he will have to explore fully the conditions under which two statements are or are not of the same logical form. This will entail considerable attention to the varieties of constituents of sentences and the varieties of their interrelation. (In the above example one needs to distinguish different kinds of force which a phrase of the form "the x of y" has.)

Theory of knowledge. The branch of philosophy known as epistemology or theory of knowledge becomes concerned with language at a number of points, the most prominent of which is the problem of a priori knowledge. We have "a priori" knowledge when we know something to be the case on some basis other than our experience. It seems that we have knowledge of this sort in mathematics, and perhaps in other areas as well. The existence of such knowledge has always been a problem for empiricists. It seems that our knowledge that $8+7=15$ is quite independent of sense experience. The statement is not proved by appeal to observation or experiment. It is true that we teach numbers to children by putting objects in piles and counting them, and we might get the idea of addition across to a child by physically adding one pile to another. But our confidence in the arithmetical proposition cited does not depend on the observed result of such manipulations, as is shown by the fact that it is impossible to specify a set of observations which would constitute empirical disconfirmation of the proposition. It seems that whenever the observed result of combining a pile of eight objects with a pile of seven objects was a pile of fourteen objects, we would explain the result in some other way—for instance, in terms of a process by which two of the original items combined to form one—rather than take it as disproving the proposition that 8 plus 7 always equals 15. But then that leaves us with the question of what the basis of our assurance is. A popular answer to this question is that in such cases what we are asserting is true by definition, or true by virtue of the meanings of the terms involved (the linguistic theory of the a priori). According to this view, it is part of what we mean by "8," "7," "15," "+," and "=" (plus the syntactical form in which they are combined) that

$8+7=15$, and to deny this seriously would involve changing the meaning of one or more of these terms. If we take this answer seriously we are led into questions concerning what it is for a term to have a certain meaning.

Reform of language. Language is the chief tool of the philosopher. Philosophy is a much more purely verbal activity than any of the sciences: verbal discussion is the laboratory in which the philosopher puts his ideas to the test. Hence it is not surprising that the philosopher should be particularly sensitive to defects of language and particularly prone to proposing schemes for its improvement. Philosophical complaints about language have taken many forms. Advocates of mystical intuition, notably Plotinus and Bergson, have considered language as such to be unsuited to the formulation of truth. According to these thinkers, the only way to get at real truth is to enjoy a felt immediate union with reality; linguistic formulation can at best give us only more or less distorted perspectives. But most philosophers have been unwilling to abjure discourse, even in theory. Complaints have more often been leveled against some current condition of language, the implications being that steps could be taken to remedy this.

Ordinary language. Philosophers who deal with the reform of language can be divided into two groups. First, there are those who hold that the language of everyday discourse is perfectly suitable for philosophical purposes and that the mischief lies in deviating from ordinary language without providing any way to make sense of the deviation. We find scattered examples of this position prior to this century—for example, in Locke's complaints about scholastic jargon—but it is in our time that it has become the basis of a philosophical movement, "ordinary language philosophy." We find it in its strongest form in the later works of Wittgenstein. Wittgenstein seems to have held that all or most of the problems of philosophy arise from the fact that philosophers have misused certain key terms such as "know," "see," "free," and "reason." It is because philosophers have departed from the ordinary uses of these terms without putting anything intelligible in their place that they have become entangled in insoluble puzzles over whether we can know what other people are thinking and feeling, whether we ever really see physical objects, whether anyone ever does anything freely, and whether we ever have any reason for supposing that one thing rather than another will happen in the future. The proper role of the philosopher is that of a therapist. He must help us, the perplexed, to see the steps by which we have unwittingly slipped from sense into nonsense; he must lead us back to the ordinary use of these words, on which their intelligibility depends, thus relieving the conceptual cramps into which we have fallen.

Philosophical reconstruction of language. In contrast to the ordinary language philosophers are those who hold that the difficulty lies in the fact that ordinary language is inadequate for philosophical purposes, by reason of its vagueness, ambiguity, context dependence, and inexplicitness. This group numbers among its members Leibniz, Russell, and Carnap. Such philosophers see as their task the construction, or at least the adumbration, of a language in which these defects do not appear. Sometimes, as with

Russell, this is combined with the conviction that the chief metaphysical features of reality can be read off from such a language.

Conceptual analysis. We must consider the view of many contemporary philosophers that the primary, if not the whole, job of the philosopher is conceptual analysis. This has always been a prominent part of philosophical activity. Socrates is represented as having devoted a great deal of time to asking questions like "What is justice?" A large part of Aristotle's works is taken up with attempts to arrive at adequate definitions of terms like "cause," "good," "motion," and "know." Usually it has been felt that however important this activity is, it is still only a preliminary to the ultimate task of philosophy—arriving at an adequate conception of the nature of the world and an adequate set of standards for human society and conduct. But recently there has been a growing conviction that although armchair reflection does not provide a sufficient basis for substantive conclusions about what is or ought to be, it *is* fitted to bring about greater clarity and explicitness concerning the basic concepts we employ in thinking about the world and human life.

This shift in the center of gravity of philosophy is particularly relevant to the philosophy of language because of an accompanying shift in the conception of conceptual analysis itself. When an analytical philosopher investigates a topic—knowledge, causality, moral obligation, or whatever—there are three ways in which he may formulate his problem. He may say, taking causality as our example, (1) that he is investigating the nature of causality, (2) that he is analyzing the concept of causality, or (3) that he is trying to make explicit what it is one is saying when he says that one thing causes another (or, alternatively, that he is trying to get at the meaning of "cause"). Increasingly it has come to be felt that (3) gives the most accurate way of specifying what the philosopher is really doing and that (1) and (2) are acceptable only if taken as alternative formulations of (3). If we do not so construe them, (1) is likely to suggest that the task is one of locating and inspecting some entity called "causality," an entity which exists and has a certain nature independent of our discourse. But no one actually has any procedures for investigating such entities. And if we try to take (2) as independent of (3) it would imply that the task is one of introspectively scrutinizing something called a concept and discovering what its parts are and how they are put together (as the word "analysis" suggests). Again it does not seem possible to develop objective techniques for doing such a thing, nor does it seem that this is what philosophers really do under the heading of "conceptual analysis."

If we take (3) as the canonical statement, it follows that insofar as philosophy consists of conceptual analysis it always deals with language in one way or another. This might be taken to imply that philosophy of language is simply the whole of philosophy, and one might choose to use the term "philosophy of language" in such a way that this would follow. But it is more useful, as well as more in accordance with prevailing usage, to restrict the term so that it is applied only when problems concerning language are in the forefront of attention. Thus, when one is trying to decide what he is saying when he utters a sentence of the form "A knows that p," he will be said to be engaged not in the philosophy of language but in the theory of knowledge, since the aim of his inquiry is to resolve not problems about language (the nature of meaning, the relations of various forms of sentences, etc.) but problems about the conditions of knowledge. An analytical philosopher would be said to be working on the philosophy of language only if the expressions he was attempting to elucidate were themselves concerned with language (what is it to say what the meaning of a word is?).

But even if we do not go so far as to place all philosophical analysis within the philosophy of language, it remains true that insofar as conceptual analysis takes the center of the stage the pursuit of the philosophy of language receives a powerful impetus. If conceptual analysis is thought of in the third of our three ways, the analytical philosopher will spend a great deal of his time in trying to decide what a given expression means, whether two expressions mean the same thing, how a given expression is used, and so on. And at many points it is by no means obvious how such questions are to be answered. There are persistent disagreements over such questions as whether "I know that p" means the same as "I believe that p; I have adequate grounds for this belief; it is the case that p," whether "feels sad" means the same in "I feel sad" and "He feels sad," and whether sentences following the form "that A is good" are always used to influence the attitudes of a hearer. Where one's intuitive knowledge of one's language does not provide a clear answer to such questions, the need arises to develop an explicit theory about what it is for a linguistic expression to have a certain meaning, what it is for two expressions to have the same meaning, and what it is for a sentence to be used in order to do so-and-so. Thus, the need for a workable methodology for semantic investigations makes it inevitable that analytical philosophers turn their attention to problems in the philosophy of language.

PROBLEMS IN THE PHILOSOPHY OF LANGUAGE

Semantic questions. On the basis of the foregoing survey we can say something about the content of the philosophy of language. Among the questions into which philosophers are led for the reasons given earlier, those dealing with linguistic meaning are especially prominent. They include:

(1) What is it for a linguistic expression to have a certain meaning?

(2) Under what conditions do two linguistic expressions have the same meaning?

(3) Under what conditions are we justified in saying that a word has two different senses in two different given contexts?

(4) What are the ways in which the meaning of an expression may be more or less vague?

(5) What is the difference between a literal and a figurative use of a term?

(6) What kinds of meaning are there? For example, is there any distinction between cognitive and emotive meaning?

It is easy to see how one can get involved in all these

questions from an attempt to lay down conditions for the adequacy of an analysis of some term. In order to *show* that the two sentence forms in the sample analysis of "I know that *p*" (presented above) have the same meaning one must appeal to an account of what it is for two sentences to have the same meaning; for example, two sentences have the same meaning when they have the same truth conditions. Challenging this involves asking what it is for a sentence to mean what it does. (Indeed, there are philosophers, such as Gilbert Ryle, who deny that it makes sense to talk about a sentence's having a meaning, which then makes it necessary to ask what range of expressions meaning attributions are appropriate for.) If someone objects that the sentence "I know that my redeemer liveth" cannot be analyzed in this way, it may be replied that "know" is being used there in a sense different from the one we are seeking to analyze; if this answer is challenged, we must consider the justification for our having made the distinction. The result may be that there are cases of knowledge claims that cannot be evaluated by general standards for sufficiency of evidence. This may well lead us into asking whether and in what ways the meaning of "know" falls short of perfect preciseness. Someone like John Austin may suggest that knowledge claims have a kind of force which is not captured by the usual kind of analysis, for in saying "I know that *p*," I am *vouching* for the truth of *p*, authorizing people to repeat it on my say-so. If this is admitted, should we call it part of the meaning of "know"? Is it something that we want to capture in an analysis? This leads to questions about different kinds of meaning. And so on.

Other problems in philosophy of language. Although semantic questions are at the heart of the philosophy of language, as practiced today, they do not constitute the whole of it. They do not even exhaust the problems emerging from the concerns surveyed earlier. Thinking back on the attempts to use linguistic facts as a basis for metaphysical argumentation, it is clear that semantic problems are involved. If the Platonist is challenged in his assumption that a common noun can have meaning only if there is a single entity of which it is the name, he will have to rely on an analysis of meaning, presumably one that identifies meaning and naming. But other problems are lurking in this underbrush. Logical atomism is based on the assumption that there is a fundamental similarity between the grammatical structure of an ideal language and the metaphysical structure of the world. Thus, we can add:

(7) What is the relation between the structure of language and the structure of whatever it is used to talk about?

Again, as we have seen, the logician needs an analysis of language into types of statements and types of terms in order to distinguish forms of inference. This leads him into tasks which are much more particularized than the "What is the nature of . . . ?" sort of problem on which we have been concentrating until now, although the logician may avoid coming into direct competition with the empirical linguist by restricting his classifications to a "formal" language, specially constructed for his purposes.

The impossibility of placing any definite limit on the range of topics in the philosophy of language results from the unpredictable variety of questions that may arise in the investigation of the problems already mentioned. For example, if one takes a Wittgensteinian approach to meaning and relates the meaning of an expression to its function, another kind of inquiry becomes necessary:

(8) What are the varieties and interrelations of linguistic acts and uses of language?

Other topics which would normally be thought of as belonging to the philosophy of language are:

(9) What are the special features of the language of religion, poetry, moral discourse, etc.?

(10) What are the special features of kinds of linguistic expressions which are of special interest to philosophers for some reason—for example, proper names and definite descriptions.

PHILOSOPHY OF LANGUAGE AND OTHER DISCIPLINES

Some of the topics lie between philosophy and more special disciplines. The job of distinguishing between different sorts of linguistic behavior might be assigned to psychology. One of the functions of descriptive linguistics is to classify types of linguistic expressions and note the distinguishing features of each. Even if these problems belong in principle to the more special disciplines, they belong to their conceptual foundations, and philosophy has always been concerned with such matters, expecially when the special disciplines are in early stages of development. Some people think of philosophy as the spawning ground of conceptual frameworks which then become the bases for new sciences, and whether or not this is what philosophy *is*, it has been one of philosophy's main functions. It is significant that there are linguistic topics which were treated in the past by men usually regarded as philosophers but which would not now be considered fit occupation for a philosopher. Nineteenth-century discussions of the origin and historical development of language, by such men as Herder and Humboldt, are an example. In contemporary philosophy there are indications that the burgeoning disciplines of linguistics and the psychology of language are on the verge of taking over problems of the sorts just mentioned from the less-specialized philosophers. Whatever the ultimate disposition of these matters, it seems clear that for the foreseeable future philosophers will be concerned with a complex of problems focusing on the basic concepts one uses in thinking about language.

(See also the survey articles LANGUAGE and SEMANTICS, HISTORY OF, as well as the following articles in this area: ANALYTIC AND SYNTHETIC STATEMENTS; ARTIFICIAL AND NATURAL LANGUAGES; CRITERION; DEFINITION; EMOTIVE MEANING; INDEXICAL SIGNS, EGOCENTRIC PARTICULARS, AND TOKEN-REFLEXIVE WORDS; INEFFABLE, THE; LINGUISTIC THEORY OF THE A PRIORI; MEANING; METAPHOR; NONSENSE; PERFORMATIVE UTTERANCES; PRESUPPOSING; PRIVATE LANGUAGE PROBLEM; PROPER NAMES AND DESCRIPTIONS; PROPOSITIONS, JUDGMENTS, SENTENCES, AND STATEMENTS; QUESTIONS; REFERRING; RELIGIOUS LANGUAGE; RULES; SEMANTICS; SIGN AND SYMBOL; SUBJECT AND PREDICATE; SYNONYMITY; SYNTACTICAL AND SEMANTICAL CATEGORIES; VAGUENESS; VERIFIABILITY PRINCIPLE.)

Bibliography

From time to time in the history of philosophy, language has been the center of attention. This can be seen in Plato's *Cratylus*, Aristotle's *Categories*, Book III of John Locke's *Essay Concerning Human Understanding*, and Book VII of George Berkeley's *Alciphron*.

In eighteenth-century and nineteenth-century Germany the philosophy of language became a self-consciously distinct branch of philosophy. The chief names in this movement are J. G. Hamann, J. G. Herder, and Wilhelm von Humboldt. None of the central works of these men have been translated into English. Volume I of Ernst Cassirer, *The Philosophy of Symbolic Forms* (New Haven, 1953), an important twentieth-century work on language in the Neo-Kantian tradition, contains a discussion of their ideas. Other derivatives of the Neo-Kantian tradition include W. M. Urban, *Language and Reality* (London, 1939), and S. K. Langer, *Philosophy in a New Key* (Cambridge, Mass., 1942).

The work of C. S. Peirce in developing a general theory of signs and elaborating a pragmatic theory of meaning has been in good part responsible for the recent interest in the subject in English-speaking countries. Peirce's contributions are to be found in Volumes II and V of his *Collected Papers* (Cambridge, Mass., 1931–1935). Charles Morris, *Signs, Language, and Behavior* represents a development of Peirce's ideas, with heavy influence from the behaviorist movement in psychology.

C. K. Ogden and I. A. Richards, *The Meaning of Meaning* (London, 1923), is historically important, especially for its distinction between referential and emotive meaning.

The logical positivist's interest in language is well represented by Rudolf Carnap's works *Philosophy and Logical Syntax* (London, 1935), *The Logical Syntax of Language* (New York, 1937), and *Introduction to Semantics* (Cambridge, Mass., 1942). Logical positivism, with a variety of eclectic borrowings, is carried on in W. V. Quine, *Word and Object* (New York, 1960).

The approach of logical atomism found its classic formulation in Ludwig Wittgenstein's *Tractatus Logico-philosophicus* (New York, 1922), a work that played a formative influence on the development of logical positivism. Logical atomism is also advocated by Bertrand Russell in *Logic and Knowledge*, R. C. Marsh, ed., London, 1956.

Wittgenstein's later works, *The Blue and Brown Books* (Oxford, 1958) and *Philosophical Investigations* (Oxford, 1953), sparked the development of "ordinary language philosophy." For good selections from discussions of language in this tradition, see V. C. Chappell, ed., *Ordinary Language* (Englewood Cliffs, N.J., 1964). The most important work on language to emerge from this milieu is J. L. Austin, *How to Do Things With Words* (London, 1962).

In recent years an increasing number of philosophers have been using techniques and concepts of structural linguistics in working on problems in the philosophy of language. Some of their essays are collected in J. A. Fodor and J. J. Katz, eds., *The Structure of Language* (Englewood Cliffs, N.J., 1964). Paul Ziff's *Semantic Analysis* (Ithaca, N.Y., 1960) bears clear traces of the influence of structural linguistics. A number of important essays on the subject are collected in Leonard Linsky, ed., *Semantics and the Philosophy of Language* (Urbana, Ill., 1952). For a recent attempt to provide a brief presentation of the field, see William P. Alston, *Philosophy of Language* (Englewood Cliffs, N.J., 1964).

WILLIAM P. ALSTON

LANGUAGE, PRIVATE. See PRIVATE LANGUAGE PROBLEM.

LANGUAGE, RELIGIOUS. See RELIGIOUS LANGUAGE.

LAO TZU (sixth century B.C.?) was the founder of Taoism. The first and standard biography of Lao Tzu (*Shih-chi*, "Records of the Historian"), written about 91 B.C. by Ssu-ma Ch'ien, says that he was Li Erh and post-humously honored as Tan, that he was a curator in the archive in the capital of Chou, that Confucius visited him to ask about ceremonies, and that upon retirement he wrote a book of 5,000 words. There has been considerable controversy about whether Li was indeed his surname, whether Erh, probably meaning "ear," was his private name, and whether Lao was his surname or simply an adjective describing him as an elderly (*lao*) philosopher (*tzu*). A majority of scholars believe that he was the curator whom Confucius visited.

The biography also mentions a Lao Lai Tzu, suggesting that he and Lao Tzu might be the same person, but few have accepted this identification. The biography also gives an account of Grand Historian Tan of the fourth century B.C. and expresses uncertainty whether he was Lao Tzu. Some scholars believe that he was.

The belief has rested not only on the fact that the two *tans* have the same pronunciation and meaning, although written differently, but also on the theory that the so-called 5,000-word classic, the *Lao Tzu*, also called the *Tao-te ching* ("Classic of the Way and Its Virtue"), could have been written only in the fourth century. Scholars of this opinion maintain that Lao Tzu was not mentioned in earlier works, that its style of prose poems instead of dialogues does not belong to the sixth century B.C., that certain terminologies in the book were not known before, that its strong attack on social and political institutions reflects the turbulent fourth century, and that certain ideas, for example, that of the nameless, could have been developed only after the School of Names flourished about 350 B.C.

None of these arguments is well founded because Lao Tzu was in fact mentioned and the terminologies in question existed before the fourth century, and neither a literary style nor specific ideas can be confined to a particular period.

One difficulty in dating the book is that there is not a single date, proper name, or historical event to provide a clue. The book has from 5,227 to 5,722 words, depending on the edition, and is divided into 81 chapters in two parts. The sentences are mostly rhymed, some short and easy and others long and difficult, and are in many places repetitious. Most scholars think that it is a product of many hands over a long period of time, perhaps not assuming the present form until the fourth century but containing the basic doctrines taught by Lao Tzu two centuries earlier.

The chief doctrines of the book are of course those of Tao and *te* (virtue). Of the many characteristics of Tao or the Way, the most important and the unique is that of nothingness. Tao is nonbeing, which is the mother of being, which in turn produces all things. It is nameless, for it is greater than anything that can be named. It takes no action, that is, it leaves things alone. It supports all things but does not take possession of them. It lets things transform themselves. It does nothing and yet all things are thereby done. In short, Tao is Nature transforming itself spontaneously; it is Natural Order.

The word *te* is identical with another *te* which means "to obtain." It is what a thing has obtained from Tao—virtue or power. But in opposition to the concept of virtue of other schools which emphasize elaborate social organization and regulated behavior and aim at power and strength, the *te* of the *Lao Tzu* is characterized by simplicity and weakness. Morality and knowledge are to be understood in their essentials, and life should be so natural as to resemble an uncarved block.

Among the highest virtues is weakness, symbolized by the infant, the female, and water. Water dwells in lowly places but it benefits all things. Although soft, it overcomes the strongest things in time. One should return evil with goodness, just as an army commander often yields in order to advance. Thus, weakness is really strength; it is so because it follows Tao, the Natural Way.

Bibliography

See Wing-tsit Chan, *The Way of Lao Tzu* (New York, 1963), and Arthur Waley, *The Way and Its Power* (London, 1935), both of which are complete translations of the *Tao-te ching* and which contain long discussions and many notes.

WING-TSIT CHAN

LA PEYRÈRE, ISAAC (1594–1676), or Pereira, was born in Bordeaux, France, a Calvinist, of Portuguese New Christian, or converted Jewish, background. He became the prince of Condé's librarian. Apparently he was friendly with leading Parisian avant-garde intellectuals like Gassendi, La Mothe Le Vayer, Grotius, Guy Patin, and Ménage. His first book *Du Rappel des juifs* (1643) deals with the conversion of the Jews, their potential return to Palestine, and the beginning of the Messianic age. In 1644 he went to Denmark and gathered there the material for his *Relation de l'islande* (1663) and *Relation du Groenland* (1647), both written as letters to La Mothe Le Vayer. His most famous works, the *Prae-Adamitae* and the *Systema Theologicum ex Prae-Adamitarum Hypothesi*, apparently written by 1643, were published in Amsterdam in 1655 while he was in the Netherlands with the prince of Condé. Several editions and translations of these works were published almost immediately. La Peyrère argued that the only consistent interpretation of certain Biblical passages, and of the anthropological and historical evidence about the Chinese, Mexicans, Eskimos, and other peoples, is that there were men before Adam and that the Bible deals only with Jewish history, and not world history. The effect of this work was like that of a bombshell to the seventeenth-century intellectual world. (It appeared at almost the same time as Archbishop Ussher's proof, on the basis of Biblical data, that the world was created in 4004 B.C.) La Peyrère was immediately attacked and refuted on all sides. His book was burned in Paris, and he himself was arrested and kept in prison in Belgium for six months until he retracted his views and became a Catholic. He then went to Rome and begged the pope's forgiveness, publishing a formal retraction of his views. In 1659 he entered a religious order near Paris, where he remained until his death. Despite his official retractions, it is believed that he continued to hold to his pre-Adamite views. For example, Pierre Bayle cites a letter in which La Peyrère's religious superior is supposed to have said that "he was always writing books that . . . would be burned as soon as the good man died. La Peyrère was the best man in the world, the sweetest, who tranquilly believed very little."

La Peyrère's revolutionary work on the pre-Adamite theory had tremendous influence on seventeenth- and eighteenth-century thought. In raising the possibility that Biblical data might only apply to Jewish history, he introduced a radical new conception of human development and led people to speculate on the relative merits of various cultures and religions. Further anthropological and geological studies, as well as investigations into comparative religion, soon led to the abandonment of Biblical chronology and history as the framework for understanding all human history and led also to the beginning of higher criticism of the Bible by writers like Spinoza and Richard Simon and to the Enlightenment critiques of traditional religion. Most writers for at least a century after him seem to have been directly or indirectly aware of his pre-Adamite hypothesis and its extraordinary implications.

Bibliography

La Peyrère's *Prae-Adamitae* (Amsterdam, 1655) has been translated as *Men before Adam* (London, 1956).

For works on La Peyrère, see D. C. Allen, *The Legend of Noah* (Urbana, Ill., 1963); Pierre Bayle, "Peyrère, Isaac La," in *Dictionnaire historique et critique* (Rotterdam, 1695–1697); and David R. McKee, "Isaac de La Peyrère, a Precursor of Eighteenth-Century Critical Deists," *PMLA*, Vol. 59 (1944), 456–485.

RICHARD H. POPKIN

LAPLACE, PIERRE SIMON DE (1749–1827), French astronomer and mathematician, famous for his celestial mechanics and theory of probability. Laplace was born in Normandy. Upon coming to Paris, he attracted the attention of d'Alembert, who found him employment in the École Militaire. Here he taught mathematics to trainee artillery officers, among whom was Napoleon. When the revolutionary government established the École Polytechnique, Laplace was one of its founding professors. He served with distinction on many of the great committees of the French Academy of Sciences and of the government. He helped devise the meter, standardized weights and measures, and worked out an ingenious system of sampling to provide an economical and efficient census. The elegance of his mathematical work has yet to be rivaled, and his power of analysis is matched only by that of Newton and Lagrange. His philosophical opinions, especially those in his *Exposition du système du monde* (*The System of the World*) and *Essai philosophique sur les probabilités* (*A Philosophical Essay on Probabilities*), have a bluntness and clarity of expression that ensured their popularity.

Laplace's adult life was passed in conditions of civil strife and sometimes of chaos, but despite his revolutionary affiliations, the restoration of the Bourbons brought him neither poverty nor disgrace; he died honored by all, a newly created marquis. Against this background of political confusion, he came to believe that the theory of probability, properly and widely applied, would reduce most of the problems of society (like the attainment of justice) to something manageable; with the help of probability theory, he believed, a man of delicate intuition and wide experience could find practical solutions to most social difficulties.

Laplace's scientific work had a strong element of tidiness about it. It consisted largely of the final polishing of the Newtonian enterprise, knitting up its loose ends. Using the improved calculus devised by his colleagues, particularly Lagrange, he removed all known errors from, and explained all known anomalies in, the Newtonian cosmology and physics. It seemed to Laplace that there was no phenomenon that the improved and polished Newtonian physics was incapable of handling. He came to regard the enormous explanatory power of the system as practically a demonstration of its truth. New observations would only confirm it further, he thought, and their consequences were as certain as if they had already been observed.

What had produced this remarkable confidence was a series of complete successes. Newton had never been convinced of the stability of the solar system, which he suggested might need divine correction from time to time. Laplace showed, in effect, that every known secular variation, such as the changing speeds of Saturn and Jupiter, was cyclic and that the system was indeed entirely stable and required no divine maintenance. (It was this triumph that occasioned his celebrated reply to Napoleon's query about the absence of God from the theory; Laplace said that he had no need of that hypothesis.) He also completed the theory of the tides and solved another of Newton's famous problems, the deduction from first principles of the velocity of sound in air. Laplace added a very accurately estimated correction for the heating effect produced by rapidity of the oscillation, which was too short to allow the heat of compression to be dissipated

Determinism and probability. Not only was Laplace confident of the Newtonian theory, but he was also greatly struck by its determinist nature. Where one could gather accurate information about initial conditions, later states of a mechanical system could be deduced with both precision and certainty. The only obstacle to complete knowledge of the world was ignorance of initial conditions. Laplace's confidence in Newtonian theory is exemplified in the introduction to his *Philosophical Essay on Probabilities,* in which he envisaged a superhuman intelligence capable of grasping both the position at any time of every particle in the universe and all the forces acting upon it. For such an intelligence "nothing would be uncertain and the future, as the past, would be present to its eyes. The human mind offers, in the perfection which it has been able to give to astronomy, a feeble idea of this intelligence" (*Philosophical Essay*, p. 4).

But this ideal is difficult to attain, since we are frequently ignorant of initial conditions. The way to cope with the actual world, Laplace thought, is to use the theory of probability. The superhuman intelligence would have no need of a theory of probability. Laplace would have regarded as ridiculous the idea that there could be systems that would react to stimuli in only more or less probable ways. He said, "The curve described by a simple molecule of air or vapor is regulated in a manner just as certain as the planetary orbits; the only difference between them is that which comes from our ignorance" (*ibid.*, p. 6). He then defined a measure of probability as follows:

The theory of chance consists in reducing all the events of the same kind to a certain number of cases equally possible . . . and in determining the number of cases favorable to the event whose probability is sought. The ratio of this number to that of all the cases possible is the measure of this probability, which is thus simply a fraction whose numerator is the number of favorable cases and whose denominator is the number of all the cases possible. (*Ibid.*, p. 6.)

This is the definition of probability known today as the proportion of alternatives. Then as now, it involves the very tricky notion of equipossible cases. Laplace deals with this notion by glossing equipossible cases as those that "we may be equally undecided about in regard to their existence" (*ibid.*, p. 6).

This account does have its difficulties. Equal indecision is not at all easy to determine and may, in the end, hinge upon states of mind quite irrelevant to a sound estimate of probabilities. Throughout his study of probability Laplace refers to such subjective factors as honesty, good judgment, and absence of prejudice, which are required in using probability theory. However, he does give a much sounder criterion for its practice; it encourages one to reckon as equally possible those kinds of events instances of which we have no special reason to believe will occur. Equality of ignorance then becomes his criterion for equality of possibility. Laplace is quite happy about this, since he believed—perhaps rightly—that the proper occasion for the recourse to probability is ignorance of the initial conditions, the relevant theory, or both. Actual estimates of probability are made statistically. In his practical examples he appears to depend on a further distinction, which also seems correct. It is the distinction between the meaning of the statement of probability for a certain kind of event (that is, ratio of number of favorable to equipossible kinds of events) and the usual estimate of this probability, which is the relative frequency of actual events of the kind under consideration among all appropriate cases.

Applications of probability. Laplace made several practical applications of probability theory. In science he applied it to the problem of sampling for the census and to the theory of errors; to both of these studies he made valuable contributions. He also believed that probability theory would have great utility in the moral sciences. He studied the optimum size for a jury to give the least doubtful verdict and the voting procedures of assemblies both on candidates for office and on propositions. He discussed the advantages and disadvantages of voting by ranking in order of merit and of voting by the knockout majority system. In this study and in his reflections on what it is reasonable to risk and in what kind of game, one gets the occasional glimpse of Laplace's basic moral principle, "Only bet on a reasonably sure thing."

Philosophy of science. In his philosophy of science and in his views on the nature of scientific method, Laplace expressed himself somewhat along the same lines as Newton, but more liberally. He saw quite clearly that science is not the accumulation of isolated and particular items of information. "It is by comparing phenomena together, and by endeavouring to trace their connection with each other, that he [man] has succeeded in discovering these laws, the existence of which may be perceived even in the most complicated of their effects" (*System*, Vol. I, p. 205). In searching for connections we do not need to shun hypotheses. Laplace said of hypotheses what Newton should have said, considering the use he made of them: that if we refuse to attribute them to reality and regard them merely as the means of connecting phenomena in order to discover the laws (which we correct according to further observations), they can lead us to the real causes or at least enable us to infer from observed phenomena those which given conditions ought to produce.

In fact, it is by excluding on the basis of decisive experiments all those hypotheses that are false that "we should arrive . . . at the true one." Ideally, Laplace sees scientific method as the formulation of generalizations of connection between phenomena, proceeding inductively from phenomena to laws (which are the ratios connecting particular phenomena), and from these to forces. When these forces reveal some general principle, that principle is verified by direct experience, if possible, or by examination of its agreement or disagreement with known phenomena.

Testing consists both of trying to formulate a deductive system based upon the highest hypotheses and designed to explain the phenomena, "even in their smallest details," and of seeing whether the theory agrees with as varied and as numerous phenomena as are relevant to it. If a theory passes these tests, it "acquires the highest degree of certainty and of perfection that it is able to obtain."

Laplace saw that our confidence in predictions had to be based upon confidence in some principle of the uniformity of nature. The sources of his confidence in some principle of uniformity were twofold. First, there is the condition of the absence of interference. If there is no reason why a change should occur, a change will not occur—a principle deeply embedded in Newtonian science. As Laplace put it, "Being assured that nothing will interfere between these causes and their effects, we venture to extend our views into futurity, and contemplate the series of events which time alone can develop" (*ibid.*, Vol. I, p. 206). Second, simplicity was to be regarded as a mark of future reliability. The principle of induction, said Laplace, is that "the simplest ratios are the most common." He said, too, "We judge by induction that if various events, movements for example, appear constantly and have been long connected by a simple ratio, they will continue to be subjected to it" (*Philosophical Essay*, p. 178). The theory of probability supplies a connection between the two sources of confidence, for, said Laplace, we conclude from the fact that a simple ratio is found among quantities in nature "that the ratio is due, not to hazard, but to a regular cause." Thus, if no other causes intervene, we may expect a likeness of effects, in fact, a uniformity of nature.

Summing up scientific method, Laplace said, "Induction, analogy, hypotheses founded upon facts and rectified continually by new observations, a happy tact given by nature and strengthened by numerous comparisons of its indications with experience, such are the principal means for arriving at truth" (*ibid.*, p. 176).

Works by Laplace

Oeuvres complètes, 14 vols. Paris, 1878–1914.
Exposition du système du monde. Paris, 1798. Translated by J. Pond as *The System of the World.* London, 1809. Contains two important conjectures: that the planets might have been formed by

the condensation of a large, diffuse solar atmosphere as it contracted, and the hypothesis, since confirmed, that the nebulae are clouds of stars and that the Milky Way is our view of that nebula of which our sun is a star.

Traité de la mécanique céleste, 5 vols. Paris, 1799–1825. Translated by N. Bowditch as *Mécanique Céleste*, 4 vols. Boston, 1829–1839.
Théorie analytique des probabilités. Paris, 1812.
Essai philosophique sur les probabilités. Paris, 1814. Translated by F. W. Truscott and F. L. Emory as *A Philosophical Essay on Probabilities.* London and New York, 1902; New York, 1951. A semipopular introduction to the *Théorie analytique.*

Works on Laplace

Andoyer, H., *L'Oeuvre scientifique de Laplace.* Paris, 1922.
Whittaker, Sir E., "Laplace." *Mathematical Gazette*, Vol. 33, No. 303 (1949), 1–12.

R. HARRÉ

LAPSHIN, IVAN IVANOVICH (1870–1952), Russian Neo-Kantian philosopher. He was born in Moscow and studied at the University of St. Petersburg under the leading Russian Neo-Kantian, Alexander Vvedensky. Lapshin pursued his studies abroad for some years after 1893, concentrating particularly on Kantianism in English philosophy. With the publication in 1906 of his dissertation and chief philosophical work, *Zakony Myshleniya i Formy Poznaniya* ("The Laws of Thought and the Forms of Cognition"), he received his doctorate from the University of St. Petersburg and in 1913 was made professor of philosophy at that institution. Along with many other noted Russian scholars Lapshin was exiled from the Soviet Union in 1922; he settled in Prague, where he lived until his death. His many writings cover a broad range of topics in philosophy, psychology, literature, music, and art, and include Russian translations of works by William James.

In his chief work Lapshin developed an antimetaphysical position on Kantian grounds, arguing specifically that the "laws of thought" derive their necessity solely from their connection with the forms through which sensory objects are cognized and that, therefore, it cannot be known whether these laws apply beyond the bounds of possible experience. According to Lapshin the law of contradiction, for example, can be understood only in reference to space and time (which, contrary to Kant, he held to be categories of the understanding rather than forms of sensibility); and since the categories of space and time do not necessarily apply to transempirical objects, neither does the law of contradiction. Consequently nothing can legitimately be affirmed of "things in themselves," not even their existence.

Lapshin devoted little attention to problems of ethics and did not accept Kant's transition to a noumenal realm and to religious faith via the dictates of moral consciousness. In general he regarded metaphysics and religion as entirely without epistemological foundation and as obstacles to the progress and vitality of human thought.

Much of Lapshin's later philosophical work was concerned with questions of the psychology of creativity and with the epistemological basis of our knowledge of other minds. His two-volume study of creativity in philosophy (1922) was complemented by a number of other writings on creativity in literature and the arts.

As early as 1910 Lapshin had published a historical account of the problem of other selves, and in 1923 he presented his resolution of the problem in the article "Oproverzheniye Solipsizma" ("A Refutation of Solipsism"). He argued that our sense of the immediate giveness of other selves is an illusion based on the projection of subjective impressions; other selves are hypothetical constructs, which can be called "immanently real" but cannot be shown to have transcendent reality.

Works by Lapshin

Zakony Myshleniya i Formy Poznaniya. St. Petersburg, 1906.
Problema Chuzhovo "Ya" v Noveyshey Filosofii ("The Problem of Other Selves in Modern Philosophy"). St. Petersburg, 1910.
Filosofiya Izobreteniya i Izobreteniye v Filosofii ("Philosophy of Creativity and Creativity in Philosophy"), 2 vols. Petrograd, 1922; 2d ed., Prague, 1924.
"Oproverzheniye Solipsizma" ("A Refutation of Solipsism"), in *Trudy Russkikh Uchonykh za Granitsey,* No. 1. Prague, 1923.

Works on Lapshin

Lossky, N. O., *History of Russian Philosophy.* New York, 1951.
Zenkovsky, V. V., *Istoriya Russkoy Filosofii,* 2 vols. Paris, 1948–1950. Translated by George L. Kline as *A History of Russian Philosophy,* 2 vols. New York and London, 1953.

JAMES P. SCANLAN

LA ROCHEFOUCAULD, DUC FRANÇOIS DE

(1613–1680), French epigrammatist and moral critic, was born in Paris; he was known as the prince de Marcillac until he succeeded his father in 1650. An incurable love of adventure and imprudent women brought him into early conflict with Cardinal Richelieu, who imprisoned him briefly in the Bastille in 1637. Contempt for Mazarin, whose treatment he bitterly resented, led La Rochefoucauld to join the faction of the Cardinal de Retz when the Fronde broke out in 1648, but before the end of hostilities he had gone over to Condé's side and was seriously wounded in 1652. In 1656 he was permitted to return from exile to Paris, where he lived until his death, which occurred after many crippling years of gout. During this period, he became a leading figure in salon society, where his closest friends were Mme. de Lafayette and Mme. de Sévigné, as well as in the Port Royal circle, which included Antoine Arnauld and Mme. de Sablé. Shortly after his return to Paris he began his *Mémoires,* first Books III–VI (covering the Fronde), then Book II (on the years from 1642 to 1649), and finally Book I (on the years from 1624 to 1642). A grossly inaccurate pirated Dutch edition, which appeared in 1662, caused a great scandal, but the authentic text was not published until the nineteenth century. These *Mémoires,* although less ample and distinguished than those by Retz on the same events, are indispensable to an understanding of the *Maximes,* since they show the inconsistency, dishonesty, and superficiality characteristic of the aristocratic *Frondeurs.*

The *Maximes* were begun as a joint enterprise with Mme. de Sablé and Jacques Esprit (of the Port Royal Circle) and reflect a popular salon pastime, but after the appearance of a pirated Dutch edition in 1664, successive authorized editions followed from 1665 to 1678, considerably altering the scope and nature of the work. The contributions of La Rochefoucauld's friends, as well as maxims too closely resembling such models as Seneca and Montaigne, were deleted, and the original brief moral reflections that occupied a page or so were cut up into the present highly condensed epigrammatic form of a few lines.

The *Maximes* deal with human nature from a strictly human standpoint, all references to God and religion having been systematically removed. They give a lucid and penetrating analysis of the manifold forms taken by self-interest, which, according to La Rochefoucauld, is the fundamental motive behind human behavior. He also claims that "reason is most often the dupe of the heart," so that human nature is a mass of capricious and unpredictable passions of physiological origin, and what commonly passes for virtue, when it is not pure accident, is really disguised, or unrecognized, vice. He shows little confidence in the Cartesian program of passions controlled by reason and will, and no confidence whatsoever in any concept of natural virtue such as that held by admirers of the virtuous pagans of antiquity. The *Maximes* stress the importance of self-analysis and being honest with oneself; without these qualities love and friendship are a hollow sham, and even with them they may be no more than exercises in egoism. The predominantly pessimistic outlook reflected in the *Maximes* is partly relieved by the brilliance of the style and the subtlety of the analysis, and also partly by various qualified admissions that true friendship and genuine integrity (*honnêteté*), although rare, may occasionally be encountered. The growing pressure of conformism in a highly artificial society, the author's own experience of pointless heroism and shabby motives in the *Fronde,* and above all his proud and melancholy temperament serve to explain the harsh verdict of the *Maximes.* For all their abiding interest these epigrams remain the direct product and reflection of the age in which they were written.

Some brief essays, portraits, and numerous letters constitute the rest of La Rochefoucauld's work.

Bibliography

La Rochefoucauld's writings may be found in his *Oeuvres complètes,* Bibliothèque de la Pléiade (Paris, 1957). Recent editions of the *Maximes* include an edition edited by J. Vallier (Lausanne, 1962) and the English translations of C. Fitzgibbon (London, 1957) and L. W. Tancock (London, 1959).
For literature on La Rochefoucauld, see E. Magne, *Le Vrai Visage de La Rochefoucauld* (Paris, 1923). There is also an excellent chapter on him in A. Adam, *Histoire de la littérature française au XVIIe siècle,* Vol. 4, Ch. 2 (Paris, 1954).

A. J. KRAILSHEIMER

LAROMIGUIÈRE, PIERRE

(1756–1837), French professor of philosophy, was born at Livignac in the district of Rouergue. As a young man, he was ordained a priest and exercised his ecclesiastical duties for a short period before becoming professor of philosophy successively at Carcassonne, Tarbes, Toulouse, and the Sorbonne. He was a close student of Condillac and an associate of the Idéologues but departed from the teachings of both in certain particulars. Excessively shy, he refused to propose his candidacy to the French Academy, though twice urged to do so, and confined his public appearances to the classroom. He died in Paris, one of the most esteemed and beloved of teachers. Among his more famous pupils were Victor Cousin and Théodore Jouffroy.

Laromiguière's disagreement with the school of Condillac arose over the question of the mind's passivity. He argued that if all our ideas were modifications of sensory material impressed upon us by external causes, it would be impossible to account for attention, comparison, and reason. These, he held, were essentially active. There is a fundamental distinction to be made, he said, between seeing and looking, listening and hearing, and the difference cannot be explained if the soul is a passive recipient of sensory stimuli. Activity was indefinable for Laromiguière, since it had no anterior ideas from which it could be derived. He seemed to believe that anyone hearing the term would grasp its meaning.

The three activities of the understanding were attention, comparison, and reasoning; and the three activities of the will corresponding to them were desire, preference, and freedom—the latter being the power to act or not to act. Laromiguière's insistence on the soul's activity was most welcome to his contemporaries, for it restored to men the autonomy which, they felt, Condillac had destroyed. While disagreeing with Condillac on this point, Laromiguière agreed with his predecessor that the primary business of philosophy was the analysis of ideas. In his best known and extremely popular work, *Leçons de philosophie*, which ran through six editions between 1815 and 1844, he assigned to metaphysics the single task of discovering the origin of all our ideas.

Laromiguière was particularly admired for the perfection of his literary style, the fame of which was acknowledged even by Hippolyte Taine.

Works by Laromiguière

Projet d'éléments de métaphysique. Toulouse, 1793.
Sur les paradoxes de Condillac. Paris, 1805.
Leçons de philosophie sur les principes de l'intelligence. Paris, 1815–1818.

Works on Laromiguière

Boas, George, *French Philosophies of the Romantic Period.* Baltimore, 1925. Pp. 33–42.
Janet, Paul, "Laromiguière, la liberté de penser." *Revue philosophique et littéraire,* Vol. 1 (1848), 253–263, 358–368
Picavet, François, *Les Idéologues.* Paris, 1891. Pp. 520–548, 552–567. Second section referred to deals with Laromiguière's influence.
Taine, Hippolyte, *Les Philosophes classiques du XIXe siècle en France.* Paris, 1868. Ch. 1.

GEORGE BOAS

LASSALLE, FERDINAND (1825–1864), German socialist, was born Ferdinand Lasal in Breslau, Silesia, of a middle-class Jewish family. The young Lassalle—he gallicized his name—was a poor and rebellious student. Quite early he indicated his persistent, but never conflicting, longings both to relieve the oppressed and to achieve aristocratic status. These two desires illuminate the paradoxical nature of a man who championed the causes of oppressed workers and oppressed noblewomen with equal vigor. He corresponded regularly with Karl Marx, defended

the honor of the Countess von Hatzfeldt in a lengthy and celebrated lawsuit, sought the acclaim of Berlin society, founded the Allgemeiner Deutscher Arbeiterverein (the first political party for German workers), dressed fastidiously, and died at the age of 39, from wounds suffered in a duel with Count von Racowitza.

Lassalle attended the universities of Berlin and Breslau, falling under the influence of Hegelian philosophy at the latter. But, although he had philosophic pretensions and sought the acclaim of philosophers, he preferred a life of action to one of theory; and his fame rests chiefly on his founding the Allgemeiner Deutscher Arbeiterverein in 1863, to which German Social Democrats still trace their origin.

Lassalle referred to his exposure to Hegel as his "second birth." He avidly consumed Hegel's works, as well as those of young Hegelians like Strauss and Feuerbach. Hegel's reference to the ancient Ionian philosopher Heraclitus of Ephesus as his forerunner led Lassalle to study Heraclitus; and he sought to demonstrate that Heraclitus had forecast Hegelian ideas. Lassalle also aspired unashamedly to the fame that a major philological and philosophical work would provide for him in German society. He began his research while not yet 20, but did not complete it until 15 years later. Berlin academicians hailed the publication in 1858 of *Die Philosophie Herakleitos des Dunkeln von Ephesos;* but later critics have found grave defects in the work, most notably Lassalle's preoccupation with Hegel rather than Heraclitus.

Hegelian ideas dominated Lassalle's historical and economic thought as well. His historical and economic theories, although not carefully formulated, emerge most clearly from the works of his last years, when he was organizing the Arbeiterverein, especially *Das System der erworbenen Rechte* (Leipzig, 1861); *Arbeiter–Programm* (Berlin, 1862); *Über Verfassungswesen; Die indirekte Steuer und die Lage der arbeitende Klassen* (1863; reprinted Berlin, 1874); and *Herr Bastiat-Schulze von Delitzsch, der ökonomische Julian, oder Kapital und Arbeit* (Berlin, 1864). He shared with Marx the belief that revolutions are not "created" by revolutionaries, but occur as the result of a historical process. Men called revolutionaries are in fact merely the midwives to a new age produced in the womb of time. Lassalle described this process in Hegelian terms. A new social order, when it appeared, would rise on the wings of Hegelian ideas. The bourgeois idea of freedom had destroyed feudal solidarity in 1789. The bourgeoisie had liberated itself by reducing the state to the role of "nightwatchman." The proletariat would in turn liberate itself through association, at first within a political party that would demand and obtain universal suffrage from the state. Having achieved universal suffrage, the proletariat would use the power of the state to form great workers' associations or cooperatives. These would in turn liberate the worker from the cruel "iron law of wages" and achieve freedom for him.

Lassalle worked arduously at organizing the workers into a national political party. He did not intend to overthrow the state, but to use it. The idea of freedom would find eventual embodiment through the state. All previous conflicts would be synthesized in this final stage of history.

Thus Lassalle accepted the Prussian state and perhaps even the Prussian monarchy. His position on the latter, as well as on private property, is ambiguous. Lassalle wrote and agitated under Prussian censorship and was constantly being tried for treasonable activity. His published works and public statements are therefore not always consistent with his private correspondence and conversations.

Lassalle's relationship with Marx waxed warm and cool. Lassalle undoubtedly admired Marx and sought the latter's approval, whereas Marx disapproved of much that Lassalle wrote and did. Marx regarded Lassalle as a friend, an informant, a creditor, a publishing agent, and an immature, pompous plagiarist. They broke off their correspondence before Lassalle's death.

Collected Works of Lassalle

Gesammelten Reden und Schriften, Eduard Bernstein, ed., 12 vols. Berlin, 1919–1920.
Nachgelassene Briefe und Schriften, Gustav Mayer, ed., 6 vols. Stuttgart, 1921–1925.

Works on Lassalle

Baron, S., *Die politische Theorie Ferdinand Lassalles*. Leipzig, 1923.
Bernstein, Eduard, "Ferdinand Lassalle und seine Bedeutung in der Geschichte der Sozialdemokratie," in Ferdinand Lassalle, *Reden und Schriften*, Vol. I. Berlin, 1892.
Brandes, Georg, *Ferdinand Lassalle*. Berlin, 1877. Translated by Eden and Cedar Paul. London, 1911.
Footman, David, *The Primrose Path, a Life of Ferdinand Lassalle*. London, 1946. A good biography.
Oncken, Hermann, *Lassalle*. Stuttgart, 1904. An excellent biography.
Schirokauer, Arno, *Lassalle, die Macht der Illusion, die Illusion der Macht*. Leipzig, 1928. Translated as *Lassalle, the Power of Illusion and the Illusion of Power*. London, 1931. A good biography.
Thier, Erich, *Rodbertus, Lassalle, Adolph Wagner*. Jena, 1930.

STERLING FISHMAN

LATIN AMERICAN PHILOSOPHY. Despite their geographical spread from Mexico and Cuba to Argentina and Chile, and barriers to communication posed by mountains and other natural obstacles, the nations of Latin America have a considerable unity of history and culture, which is reflected in pervasive resemblances in their philosophies.

Almost all these nations use the Spanish language, which they inherited from the Spanish conquerors of the first half of the sixteenth century. Until the nineteenth century they were colonies of Spain, with a history mainly of rigid political control by one of the most conservative countries of Europe. In the second and third decades of that century they struggled for and achieved independence, which was followed by periods of anarchy, tyranny, and civil war that have continued to the present. Catholicism has been virtually the only religion, with political results that have ranged from theocratic authority during the colonial period to anticlerical measures after independence had been consolidated. The original Indians for the most part have survived conspicuously: in some instances with relative purity of race, in many others with general intermarriage. Social and economic problems have been rampant, because of underdeveloped economies, concentration of wealth, and inadequate education. The intellectual classes have turned successively for guidance to Spain, France, and Germany; they have largely ignored or rejected the United States. The principal exception to some of these statements is Brazil, which uses the language of its Portuguese founders and which achieved independence without external or internal struggle.

In intimate relation with these social conditions has been the development of philosophy in the Hispanic nations and, to a lesser extent, in Brazil, where philosophy has not had as vigorous a development. The history of Latin American philosophy may be divided into three main parts. First was the colonial phase of scholastic philosophy, which was promptly introduced from the mother country, soon had university centers in Spanish America, was widely conducted by Jesuits (with influence of Francisco Suárez on the traditional corpus of Aquinas and Aristotle), and was for the most part carefully orthodox. Second was an intermediate phase, which began before independence and expired in the early part of the twentieth century and was influenced by successive currents of French philosophy, including the Enlightenment, ideology and eclecticism, and positivism. And third is the recent phase, which extends from about 1910 to the present. This phase, influenced first by German voluntarism and Henri Bergson and later by José Ortega y Gasset and German phenomenology, has seen the rise of the eminent Latin American philosophers. It is in this phase that Latin American philosophy has come of age, producing original thinkers of scope and system who command the attention of the philosopher as well as of the student of Latin American history and culture.

The several phases of Latin American philosophy may be studied to advantage through the examples of Mexico and Argentina, the main centers of this philosophy.

MEXICO

Scholastic phase. The long history of scholasticism in Mexico may be said to have begun officially with the founding in 1553 of the Royal and Pontifical University. The first professor of philosophy there was Alonso de la Vera Cruz, who had an early exposure to Renaissance humanism, saw some need for reform in scholasticism, introduced the works of Aristotle to Mexico, and wrote books on logic, dialectic, and physics. Shortly before the founding of the university, Erasmus was represented in the *Doctrina Breve* of Juan de Zumárraga, first bishop in the New World; in this form, ideas of that humanist circulated unacknowledged after they had been condemned in overt publication. Scholasticism declined in the seventeenth century, owing to tighter restrictions. In 1681, however, Carlos de Sigüenza y Góngora, a mathematician who had studied Descartes under Jesuit auspices, criticized astrology and defended the doctrine of uniform law in nature. In the latter part of the eighteenth century, a measure of freedom appeared in scholasticism. Benito Díaz de Gamarra was influenced considerably by Descartes. While holding to Catholic dogma, he asserted the autonomy of reason against scholastic authority and emphasized an empirical and objective spirit in natural science. According to Samuel Ramos, the rationalism of Díaz de Gamarra helped to prepare Mexicans for the liberal political ideas which soon became dominant.

Intermediate phase. The intermediate phase of Mexican thought began with the liberal political ideas, which became effective in the revolt against Spain of 1810. Their direct source was the French Enlightenment, with its confidence in individual liberty and social progress under the guidance of a universal natural reason. To this influence was presently added that of the French ideology and sensationalism of Destutt de Tracy and Cabanis, which became the leading philosophy of Mexican schools in the first third of the century. From England came the contribution of Jeremy Bentham's utilitarian ethics and politics. The particularism of sensationalism and utilitarianism, the strife and anarchy that followed independence, and the demand for a complete break with the institutions of the colonial past fostered a strain of romanticism in the middle decades of the nineteenth century, accompanied by a version of liberalism which was less abstract and more local than the theory offered by the Enlightenment. A representative of some of these tendencies was José María Luis Mora, a historian who had considerable influence on Mexican reform and was intimately associated with the ideas of Bentham and Destutt de Tracy. According to Leopoldo Zea, his advocacy of a liberal philosophy suited for the emerging bourgeoisie anticipated positivist ideas.

The initial and leading figure of positivism in Mexico was Gabino Barreda, a physician who in 1867 was selected by President Juárez to reorganize Mexican education. Barreda was a follower of Auguste Comte, whose lectures he had attended in Paris. Positivism for Barreda had two important advantages. In the realm of knowledge, it replaced theology and metaphysics with modern science and the positive philosophy based on it, thus yielding a growing body of certain truths. In the sphere of action, positivism could be used, through universal education, to promote community of thought in Mexico and thereby encourage order and progress instead of anarchy. These considerations led Barreda to make positivism the basis of his educational reforms. Although he had been identified with the liberals of the reform movement, he developed a concept of liberty based not on individual initiative but on behavior according to nature, in which principles of law were conspicuous. The conservative element of positivism became more pronounced in the three decades ending in 1910, during which it was identified with the oppressive regime of Porfirio Díaz. Positivist inspiration shifted from Comte to Herbert Spencer and Charles Darwin. However, the agnostic element in Spencer presently came to the fore in the prominent Spencerian Justo Sierra, whose criticism of the dogmatism of Barreda's scientism was a factor in the transition to the following era.

Recent phase. The recent phase of Mexican philosophy began approximately in 1910, when a group of intellectuals called the Athenaeum of Youth, who were critical of the reigning positivistic temper, sponsored a series of lectures designed to introduce new ideas. Members of the group included José Vasconcelos and Antonio Caso, who subsequently became the principal figures of Mexican philoso-

phy. In his contribution to the series, Vasconcelos criticized Barreda for neglecting poetic intuition and dogmatically overlooking the tentative character of scientific hypotheses. In a series of significant books which began soon afterward and spanned three decades, Vasconcelos developed a philosophy that stresses intuition as well as scientific fact and hypothesis; the primacy of spirit, from intimations of it in recent physics to God, whom he conceived first in pantheistic and later in theistic terms; an ethics which is broadly revelatory; and an aesthetics which has applications both to metaphysics and to ethics. The main source of Vasconcelos' thought was Henri Bergson. The same was true of Caso, also an intuitionist, whose extensive writings occupied the same interval as those of Vasconcelos. Caso's metaphysics emphasizes change, which has a factor of spontaneity in its uniformities; life, which has a unique nature in relation to matter; and spirit, which organizes the data of raw experience in Kantian fashion. His ethics stresses love as the highest value of spirit; his aesthetics identifies art with disinterest and emotional expression; and his social philosophy criticizes totalitarian politics. To these two speculative philosophers may be added the less important Ezequiel Chávez, who began under the influence of Spencer, moved into a theory of intuition and spirit without entirely abandoning positivism, and ended, as did Vasconcelos, with Catholicism.

By 1930 the recent phase of Mexican philosophy began to shift from speculative metaphysics influenced by Bergson to a cultural humanism inspired by Ortega, whose work as editor and publisher introduced contemporary German philosophy to Latin America and whose own writings had great influence in Mexico. According to Samuel Ramos, Ortega's doctrine of vital reason provided a middle ground for younger philosophers who desired neither the intuitionism of Vasconcelos and Caso nor earlier rationalism, and his perspectivism and historicism encouraged these philosophers to direct their serious inquiry to the formation of a philosophy for and about Mexico. To the influence of these strains in Ortega may be added that of the existentialist aspects of his thought, which anticipated the subsequent and greater influence of Heidegger and others. The second half of the recent period has also seen work in ethics and allied fields influenced by Max Scheler and Nicolai Hartmann.

Under the influence of Ortega, Samuel Ramos, historian of Mexican philosophy, has written books directed toward a characterology of the Mexican people and, as a prescription for their ills, toward a humanism that would explore the nature of man, assert objective values, and simultaneously avoid the errors of machine civilization and of the philosophical romantics, Caso and Vasconcelos, whose anti-intellectual looseness contributed to the confusion in Mexico. The historian of positivism in Mexico, Leopoldo Zea, has written discerningly of the influence of Ortega, "despite himself," in Latin America. Following that lead, Zea has asserted the historical and changing nature of man, the circumstantial truth and cultural relativity of philosophy, and the need for Mexico and America to develop a philosophy appropriate to their circumstances. Edmundo O'Gorman has written in the philosophy of history under the influence of Ortega and Heidegger. Other writers who have taken an interest in existentialist ideas are Adolfo Menéndez Samará, a follower of Gabriel Marcel; Agustín Basave Fernández del Valle; and José Romano Muñoz. In his earlier work Romano Muñoz was an initial disseminator of Ortega's works in Mexico; he has also written on ethics and theory of values, with considerable debt to Hartmann. The influence of Hartmann appears likewise in the extensive writing in philosophy of law of Eduardo García Máynez, who has applied to the theory of law a belief in the objectivity of values. Francisco Larroyo is a Neo-Kantian; Oswaldo Robles is a Neo-Thomist who has adopted certain existentialist concepts; and Vicente Lombardo Toledano is a Marxist.

ARGENTINA

The development of philosophy in Argentina resembles that in Mexico, except that the scholastic phase was shorter and less vigorous, the intermediate phase was more clearly defined and its protagonists more conspicuous, and the recent phase has been less speculative and more analytical.

Scholastic phase. Scholasticism had centers in Córdoba, where the university was founded in 1613 and chartered in 1622, and in Bue:ios Aires, where the *Reales Estudios* was founded in 1773. In the latter part of the eighteenth century, some elements of modern science were added to Aristotelian physics, but philosophy generally remained unchanged. Perhaps the most significant figure in the scholastic period was José Elías del Carmen Pereira, a Franciscan active in the final decades of the century, who accepted Cartesian skepticism and ideas of Copernicus and Newton. His contemporary in Buenos Aires, Luis José Chorroarín, was opposed to Descartes and regarded scholastic method as appropriate for the sciences.

Intermediate phase. As in Mexico, the intermediate phase in Argentina began with liberal ideas, imported from Europe, which were the intellectual background of the revolution of May 1810 and of the ensuing efforts of Bernardino Rivadavia and his associates to form a stable and unified government in the independent nation. The first academic school of philosophy after scholasticism was that of ideology, which flourished in the third and fourth decades of the nineteenth century and reflected the liberal philosophy of newly won independence. Juan Crisóstomo Lafinur, a professor of philosophy who died in his twenties, borrowed extensively in his logic from Destutt de Tracy but pursued a more conservative course in metaphysics, in which he accepted the existence of God and the immortality of the soul, with some assistance from revelation. Juan Manuel Fernández de Agüero, first professor of philosophy at the University of Buenos Aires, was influenced by Destutt de Tracy and Cabanis. He felt some sympathy for materialism, thought physiology was important for an understanding of ethics, and admired Bentham's work in philosophy of law. Diego Alcorta, regarded by Torchia Estrada as the ablest of the ideologists in Argentina, was influenced especially by Condillac, from whom he adopted a sensationalist analysis of ideas.

After ideology there came a contrasting school of thought: romanticism. The new movement stemmed from a later generation of French thinkers, including the eclectics Victor Cousin and Théodore Jouffroy and the school of Saint-Simon. The romantic movement in Argentina favored spirit, ethical absolutism, democratic idealism, and philosophy of culture. Most significant in this movement was Juan Bautista Alberdi, whose *Fragmento preliminar al estudio del derecho* (1837) exhibited influences of Jouffroy and other French writers. Alberdi asserted an absolute good, cosmological and religious in scope but independent of religion for its obligatory nature. Morality is conformity with this good; pleasure is not the good but the sensuous reflection of it; law derives from the absolute good. Lesser philosophical contributions were made by Vicente Fidel López, a historian who formulated a philosophy of history which emphasized the ideas of liberty and progress, and by Adolfo Alsina, an admirer of eclecticism, which he found to be the alternative to the absurdity of exclusive systems. On the fringe of philosophy were writings of a kindred romantic spirit, which had great influence on social thought and action in Argentina: the *Bases* of Alberdi, the *Dogma socialista* of Esteban Echeverría, and the *Facundo* of Domingo Faustino Sarmiento.

Positivism came to Argentina in the last two decades of the nineteenth century and survived for at least two decades of the twentieth century. It was influenced by Comte and Spencer but was not confined to these sources. Torchia Estrada believes that the term "naturalism" is more appropriate, although he continues to use the common designation. Comte was most influential among professional educators. Prominent in this group was Alfredo Ferreira, who accepted an evolutionary optimism as the basis for ethics, denied the freedom of the will, and praised Comte's religion of humanity. A variety of influences, including that of Spencer, appeared in the work of Carlos Octavio Bunge. Bunge asserted a positive metaphysics confined to the boundary between the knowable and unknowable; based ethics on biology; and characterized law as the systematization of force. By far the most important of the positivists was José Ingenieros, whose writing indicates the flexibility of this term in the period at hand. His philosophy was naturalistic, deterministic, and evolutionary. He had an extensive background in medicine and psychiatry, and he regarded the sciences as the sole repositories of certain knowledge. However, he conceded to metaphysics a function in the domain of the "inexperiential," by which he meant whatever parts of nature might lie beyond experience at a given time. He also formulated an ethics which was strenuous in its ideal of perfection, which he opposed to the mediocrity of the ordinary man.

Recent phase. The recent phase of Argentine philosophy began in the early years of the twentieth century, when a shift away from positivism began to appear. The principal influence was that of Bergson and the leading figure was Alejandro Korn, whose terse but weighty contributions appeared mainly between 1918 and 1930, when he was elderly. Korn criticized positivism for its deterministic view of man, a view which he regarded as destructive of ethics. He based certain knowledge on an ordinary, or empirical, kind of intuition; regarded reason as formal and constructional; and referred an intellectual intuition to metaphysics, which he regarded as important in the life of man but incapable of certainty. His own metaphysics asserts a universal conscious activity, everlasting and creative. In ethics Korn was a relativist and a pluralist. Accompanying Korn in his development of a new trend in philosophy were Coriolano Alberini and Alberto Rougès. Alberini identified life with the psychical and the psychical with evaluation and purpose; he therefore believed that mechanism, although partly true of living processes, must be supplemented with finalism. Rougès, whose principal work appeared quite late in his life, gave a metaphysical account of time that borrowed elements from Bergson and Plotinus. He ascribed an instantaneous present to matter and a durational present to spirit, which in varying degrees preserves the past and anticipates the future. Eternity is a present that encompasses all past and future time. It is the condition of God, but men move toward it insofar as their lives meaningfully transcend the present.

After 1930 the recent phase of Argentine philosophy moved into a second period, which experienced the pronounced influence of recent German philosophers, including Edmund Husserl, Scheler, Hartmann, and Heidegger. The leading figure of this period is Francisco Romero, who continued in the tradition of Bergson and Korn in philosophy of nature and borrowed from Scheler and Hartmann in philosophy of values and man. The pervasive concept in his thought is transcendence. Because reason is immanent Romero restricts it in favor of an amplified conception of experience, which extends to essences and values. Transcendence develops through four levels of phenomena: the physical, the vital, the psychical, and the spiritual. The theory of man emphasizes the last two levels, including the intentionality of the psychical and the disinterest and the love of the spiritual.

Of kindred interests with Romero in the tradition of Korn are Aníbal Sánchez Reulet and Risieri Frondizi. Sánchez Reulet has written on transcendence and liberty in relation to being and value. Frondizi has formulated a theory of the factors in consciousness, in which, in addition to particular activities, the self is asserted as something relatively permanent but organically related to changing states, and objects are asserted because of the intentionality of activities. Existentialists and Catholic philosophers have also contributed to the most recent period. Carlos Astrada has been influenced by Heidegger, with a recent debt to Marxism. Vicente Fatone has written on Sartre and other existentialists. Miguel Ángel Virasoro has attempted to develop a position at once existential and dialectical. Among Catholic philosophers the leading writer is Octavio Nicolás Derisi, a Thomist.

OTHER COUNTRIES

The philosophy of the twentieth century may be studied further in a number of nations besides Mexico and Argentina. One of the most active nations is Uruguay. Arturo Ardao divides twentieth-century Uruguayan philosophy into five schools. The most prominent is a broadly empirical movement headed by the leading philosopher of Uruguay and a major figure in Latin American thought, Carlos Vaz Ferreira. Vaz Ferreira advocated a plastic reason close to the fluent course of experience and reality. Although this reason contains a factor of skepticism, it sanctions a cautious metaphysics, which in turn understands the strength and limits of science. The same skepticism, accompanied by compassion and insight, marks the ethics of Vaz Ferreira, in which there is an awareness of the clash of ideals and the inevitable exposure of morally alert persons to doubt and crisis. An empiricist of less detached temper is the eminent literary figure José Enrique Rodó, who has developed an evolutionary pantheism and an empirical and naturalistic theory of ethical ideals. Materialism is represented by Pedro Figari, who emphasizes notions of energy and life rather than of mechanistically determined particles, and by the Marxists Emilio Frugoni and Pedro Ceruti Crosa. Idealism—ontological, epistemological, and rationalistic—appears in the works of Emilio Oribe and Fernando Beltramo. Roman Catholic philosophy is advocated by Antonio Castro. A philosopher of culture is Juan Llambías de Azevedo, a follower of Hartmann and Scheler. To the history of Uruguayan philosophy Arturo Ardao contributes lucidity, scholarly precision, and philosophic understanding.

Recent philosophy in Peru is distinguished by the work of Alejandro Deustua, who led the departure from positivism in his country. Under the influence initially of K. C. F. Krause and then more especially of Bergson, Deustua took an interest in liberty, which he identified with spirit and particularly with imagination. The opposite of liberty is nature, but the two are reconciled in beauty, which involves an ideal order created by the imagination out of elements drawn from nature. Liberty is manifest only in order, and it is fully realized only in an order of its own creation. Therefore, liberty is more complete in the aesthetic domain than in any other. A similar emphasis on spirit and its categories appears in the philosophy of Enrique Molina of Chile, who also was influenced by Bergson.

In Cuba the major philosopher is Enrique José Varona. Unlike the other eminent thinkers of Latin America, he was a positivist, although his positivism contained unusual elements. His work appeared mainly between 1880 and 1910. He was impressed with the dependence of the individual on the group and formulated a theory of morality as conformity with social solidarity; he rejected both Kantian and utilitarian ethics.

In Brazil the chief philosopher is Raimundo de Farias Brito, an admirer of Schopenhauer and Bergson. Although his idealistic philosophy contributed heavily to antipositivism in the recent period in Brazil, he did not initiate that tendency; his predecessor, Tobías Barreto, had stood apart from the Comtean philosophy after it became dominant in Brazil in the last three decades of the nineteenth century. Farias Brito asserted the phenomenality of matter, and of force qua physical, since we know matter only from the outside and force only through the motion of material units. Believing that we have direct knowledge in ourselves of an intellectual or psychical force, and that the method of analogy is dependable, he concluded that all force in essence is spiritual. He took pains to make will an attribute and not the substance of spirit, in order that the privation, effort, and suffering of will should not be fundamental in things.

COMMON CONCERNS

The foregoing summary of places, times, and persons has implicit evidence for a high degree of unity in Latin American philosophy. The evidence may be made explicit by considering briefly four themes of the recent phase, as found in the six leading philosophers of Latin America: the ideas of change and power, ideal value, freedom, and intuition, which may be taken as variations on the basic theme of mind.

Change and power. In the field of common experience, the mobile and plastic nature of reality was emphasized by Caso, Vasconcelos, Vaz Ferreira, and Korn. In the area of scientific experience and hypothesis, Vasconcelos pointed to science's replacement of the concept of a rigid elementary body by an "individualized dynamic frequency," and Romero to the same replacement by a *foco activísimo:* the intent of both men was to substantiate the thesis of change with the authority of science. In phenomenal metaphysics, Romero's ideas of transcendence in the four levels of phenomena is a thesis of change, which is fortified by the assertion of the irreducibility of the levels. In ontology, change appears in the notion of the universal *acción consciente* in Korn and in the more modest hypothesis of a universal impetus underlying phenomenal transcendence in Romero. In several of these areas the notion of power accompanies that of change; it is especially conspicuous in the scientific and ontological expositions of change. Although the nature of power has not been analyzed by the Latins, power on the whole is treated as immanent in change, so that the notion of detached substances is rejected.

Value. The centrality of questions of value in Latin American philosophy is generally acknowledged. Theory often is subordinated to practice, individual or social; but practice is approached in terms so wide and basic as to encourage theory of a subtle and speculative kind. In addition to this general emphasis on value, there is a specific affinity for values in an ideal and even a heroic mode. Caso placed the biological values of individuals well below the spiritual values of persons, who are capable of disinterest in art and of love in society. A similar distinction and evaluation was made by Romero in regard to the psychical and spiritual levels of man. A more transcendental approach to ideal values was made by Vasconcelos. In his ethics he stated the high claims of the ethics of Christianity and of Buddhism, with their support of a general and infinite love. In his aesthetics he expounded the value of mystical art, with its sublimation of human passion in the direction of an eternal love. Vaz Ferreira discerningly sketched the condition of the ethically sensitive individual, who pursues perfection amid the doubt and remorse occasioned by the clash of ideals and by the frequent inevitability of evil.

Liberty. The ideas of power and ideal value converge upon the third theme, liberty. In view of the long history of despotism in Latin America, the striking emphasis on freedom indicates that for the Latin American thinkers philosophy is a guide as well as a mirror of society. In the recent period, freedom usually is identified with spirit, and simpler forms of it are ascribed to subhuman nature. Caso and Vasconcelos pointed to evidences of novelty and spontaneity in recent physics. Caso ascribed the highest degree of freedom to persons and criticized totalitarian society as destructive of persons. Vasconcelos believed that the sublimation of passion in mystical art is the key to freedom, which the Dionysian stage of art could not attain because it understood only natural passion and its inevitable disaster. Transcendence in Romero appears to be an impetus toward increasing freedom in the successive stages from the physical to the spiritual. The philosophy of Deustua is based on the concept of freedom, which culminates in art. The idea of freedom also occurs in the several parts of Korn's philosophy: the self is most significantly distinguished from the not-self by its freedom; ethics requires freedom, and the several and unique types of value have a common goal in liberty; and the universal conscious action, in itself unknown, is manifest to us as aspiration toward absolute liberty.

Intuition. The intuitionism of the recent period is intimately related to the preceding themes, for intuition has a plastic nature appropriate to changing objects, an affective potential suited to values, a spontaneity akin to liberty in objects, and a synoptic tendency in which change, value, and liberty can be grasped in organic unity. The intuition of Latin American thought is largely empirical in a broad sense of the word, being an emphasis on activity and maximum individuality in external sensation, and an extension of experience from sensation to introspection and to the immediate grasp of values. Intuition is sometimes metempirical in various degrees, from immediate awareness of life and consciousness in other finite entities, with an emphasis on other persons, to mystical awareness of deity in the world at large or beyond it. It is always opposed to orthodox reason and what it conceives to be reason's apparatus of fixed concepts, static and usually external relations, and discursive analysis. Caso and Vaz Ferreira contrasted the rigidity of concepts with the flow of experience. Romero ascribed to reason factors of homogeneity and transparency, which he assigned to immanence at the expense of transcendence and reality in reason. And Vasconcelos called for an organic logic, which should not analytically reduce particulars to universals but should relate them organically to other particulars. These writers agree with ordinary empiricists that reason of itself yields no knowledge of reality, and with pragmatists that reason has an instrumental value.

(See Latin American Philosophy in Index for articles on Latin American philosophers.)

Bibliography

Ardao, Arturo, *La filosofía en el Uruguay en el siglo XX*. Mexico City, 1956.

Francovich, Guillermo, *Filósofos brasileños*. Buenos Aires, 1943.

Ramos, Samuel, *Historia de la filosofía en México*. Mexico City, 1943.

Romanell, Patrick, *Making of the Mexican Mind*. Lincoln, Neb., 1952.

Salazar Bondy, Augusto, *La filosofía en el Perú/Philosophy in Peru*. Washington, D.C., n.d.

Sánchez Reulet, Aníbal, *Contemporary Latin American Philosophy*. Albuquerque, N.M., 1954. Anthology.

Torchia Estrada, Juan Carlos, *La filosofía en la Argentina*. Washington, D.C., 1961.

Zea, Leopoldo, *El positivismo en México*. Mexico City, 1943; 2d ed., Mexico City, 1953.

ARTHUR BERNDTSON

LAVATER, JOHANN KASPAR (1741–1801), German-Swiss poet, physiognomist, and theologian. Born in Zurich, he studied at the gymnasium there under the literary critics Johann Jakob Bodmer and Johann Jakob Breitinger. Later, in northern Germany, he attended the lectures of the Protestant pastor Johann Jakob Spalding, who, influenced by Shaftesbury and the English moralists, sought to reconcile reason and sentiment and stressed the moral and religious conscience. While in northern Germany Lavater also met Johann Georg Sulzer, Moses Mendelssohn (whom he later tried to convert to Christianity), the dramatist Klopstock, and other persons of note. Returning to Zurich in 1764, he held various posts in churches there from 1769 on. He traveled widely in Germany, was acquainted with many culturally important people, and was one of the most sought-after and famous persons of that time. As a poet, he published a volume of religious verse, *Christlicher Lieder* (1771), and two epic poems in the manner of Klopstock, *Jesus Messias* (1780) and *Joseph von Arimathia* (1794). Because of his opposition to the Zurich government, Lavater was forced to move to Basel in 1796. He returned, only to be wounded during the French capture of Zurich in 1799. He died of this wound in 1801.

Lavater is chiefly known as a physiognomist. His theories were expounded in two main works, *Von der Physiognomik* (Leipzig, 1772) and *Physiognomische Fragmente zur Beförderung der Menschenkenntnis und Menschenliebe* ("Physiognomic Fragments for Furthering the Knowledge and Love of Man," 4 vols., Winterthur, 1775–1778). Herder and Lavater's close and longtime friend Goethe both collaborated on the latter work. Lavater claimed independence from traditional physiognomy dating from the time of Aristotle, but his independence was chiefly a matter of superficial knowledge of the tradition. He supported the classical view that the human body is influenced in shape by the character of the person, and vice versa; but his criteria were inconsistent and confused. There were two main reasons for his unprecedented success: first, his lively and simple manner of exposition that followed the pattern of the "popular philosopher"; and second, the psychology of character at the base of his theory.

Lavater stressed "feeling" and such spiritual qualities as inspiration and creative genius, which were being widely discussed in the eighteenth century. The native language of genius, and of virtue and wisdom, could become known only by studying the human form. Man is the measure of truth. That which harmonizes in form with a man, and is a part of him, is what exists for him. There is no absolute truth, but only a subjective experiencing. Therefore feeling should be cultivated, as it is in the genius. Lavater's psychology of genius, which gave emotions a place beside reason, was an important link between Pietism and sentimentalism on the one hand, and *Sturm und Drang* on the other. Lavater was severely criticized—notably by Georg Christoff Lichtenberg—but his handsomely printed volumes, with their illustrations, and his complimentary analyses of various influential contemporary figures were widely read.

As a writer of religious and devotional literature, Lavater was equally influential. His religious views were based on a belief in inner light, making his subjectivism a mystical and sentimental anthropomorphic theology. God is what satisfies the needs of man. The Bible is historically true but it is to be interpreted subjectively. Lavater was strongly convinced of the magical force of grace and prayer, and was strongly interested in miracles and prophecies. He was therefore drawn to spiritualism and mesmerism.

Additional Works by Lavater

Aussichten in die Ewigkeit in Briefen an Zimmermann, 2 parts. Zurich, 1768–1769; 2d ed. and 3d part, 1773; 4th part, 1778.
Geheimes Tagebuch von einem Beobachter seiner selbst, 2 vols. Leipzig, 1771–1773.
Pontius Pilatus oder die Menschen in allen Gestalten, oder die Bibel im Kleinen und der Mensch im Grossen, 4 parts. Zurich, 1782–1785.
Nathanael, oder die Göttlichkeit des Christenthums. Winterthur, 1786.
Ausgewählte Werke, E. Stähelin, ed., 4 vols. Zurich, 1943.

Works on Lavater

Bracken, Ernst von, *Die Selbstbeobachtung bei Lavater, Beitrag zur Geschichte der Idee der Subjektivität im 18. Jahrhunderts*. Münster, 1932. Dissertation.
Forssmann, J., *Lavater und die religiösen Strömungen des 18. Jahrhunderts*. Riga, 1935.
Janentzky, Christian, *J. K. Lavater*. Frauenfeld, 1928.
Maier, Heinrich, *An der Grenze der Philosophie Melanchton, Lavater, D. F. Strauss*. Tübingen, 1909.
Muncker, Franz, *J. F. Lavater, Eine Skizze seines Lebens und Wirkens*. Stuttgart, 1883.
Vömel, Alexander, *J. K. Lavater 1741–1801. Ein Lebensbild*. Elberfeld, 1923.

GIORGIO TONELLI

LAVELLE, LOUIS (1883–1951), French philosopher, was born in Saint-Martin-de-Villéréal, in southwestern France. He was professor of philosophy at the Sorbonne from 1932 to 1934 and at the Collège de France from 1941 until his death. In a time of reaction against speculative system-building, Lavelle boldly elaborated an extensive system combining elements of the French *philosophie de l'esprit* and existentialism. Convinced that the modern world needs basic security, Lavelle, like other existentialist thinkers, sought philosophical and moral certitude in the experience of the self, "pure inwardness," and "absolute existence." Unlike such philosophers as Sartre, who "disintegrated" the human universe inherited from tradition, Lavelle, like Jaspers and Barth, attempted to "reintegrate" the basic experiences of humanity in a novel form. In his spiritualistic interpretation of the self Lavelle continued the French tradition of Malebranche, Maine de Biran, Octave Hamelin, Henri Bergson, and Maurice Blondel.

Metaphysics of participation. Metaphysics was for Lavelle "the science of spiritual inwardness." According to him, Kant had shown that we cannot find true reality on the side of the object, or thing, because objects and the world they compose cannot have independent existence. The essence of things resides in their relation to a being for whom they are "objects." Consequently, in the search for true or absolute reality we must turn toward the act of consciousness, the "inwardness" of the human being. Thus Lavelle's central preoccupation was to discover and describe the fundamental relation between our innermost being and the Absolute.

Lavelle pointed out that there is a "primitive act" upon which our very being depends, as well as the being of the entire world. It is our primordial experience of being part of the world, in which act we find ourselves also "participating" in something which infinitely transcends us—the Act (Absolute Being, God). From a subtle dialectic description of this spiritual act of "participation" flow the broad lines of Lavelle's doctrine.

Ontology of spiritualistic existentialism. The originality of Lavelle's conception of the nature of beings in their relation to Being consists in his introducing a dynamic and "actualistic" content into the traditional themes of Aristotelian ontology. His approach yields a finalistic and optimistic view of the universe and human destiny.

All experiences of man emerge against the background of the limited individual being, participating in the Absolute Being. By their relation to participation, which is constant and eternal, individual beings establish their relation to the world, and through the notions of essence and existence they establish their spiritual identity. The Absolute Being is pure actuality, the infinite source of existential dynamism, and an endless reservoir of all possible forms or essences, from which individual beings receive their own limited existence. In spite of this direct and continuous dependence of the individual on his source, actualism is reconciled in Lavelle's thought with temporal progression, dynamism with formal immobility, and human freedom is safeguarded by the self-creativity of the individual. Indeed, from the human point of view, participation is a pursuit of an ideal which constantly moves ahead of our efforts. In this pursuit we create our spiritual self, and our experiences, moving onward, progressively acquire a unique form. Our effort in life is meant to discover this form, which has its prototype in the reservoir of Being and is our spiritual essence. The accomplishment of our essence at our death means the radical passage from limited existence into transfinite Being. Thus participation appears as the means of man's ultimate redemption, toward which everything occurring in the universe converges.

The world is the interval which separates pure Act (Being) from the limited act of participation (human existence). Matter, in limiting the spirit, offers the resistance necessary for the self to transcend itself. The world comprises three modes of reality: the world of things, that of ideas, and that of individual beings (consciousnesses). The material world plays the necessary role of separating beings; ideas give spiritual meaning to things. The world of individual consciousnesses is necessarily conscious because the essence of the Absolute Being from which they proceed is itself perfect inwardness; as such it is eternally fecund and intended to communicate the creative act to beings which, in turn, propagate it in self-creation.

Ethics of consent. In Lavelle's moral philosophy an unusual meaning is given to existential themes, such as freedom, human destiny, and solitude. Lavelle had a constructive conception of man's vocation and of the ideal of life.

Freedom is the essence of man. But whereas the Absolute Act is synonymous with absolute freedom, man, the participating act, is limited by the "natural spontaneity" of the instinct. Consequently, the life of the spirit, which he proposed as the ideal of human life, is a fighting toward gradual liberation from the passivity peculiar to instinct. We become fully men by subordinating natural spontaneity to reflection and rational discipline. Human freedom originates in this process; and this conversion of spontaneity into freedom is the real vehicle of participation. The spiritual being, like the Leibnizian monad, is endowed with potentialities for the accomplishment of its pre-established essence. Our vocation is to seek to make our actual selves coincide with the "better part of ourselves," which represents these potentialities. This self-searching and self-controlling effort presupposes an "act of consent" to our vocation of the spirit. In opposition to other existentialist thinkers who glorify the "exceptional instant," Lavelle rehabilitated everyday existence, seeing even in the least significant instant an opportunity for consent to the self-creative effort and, thereby, an opportunity for participation in the Absolute.

Finally, the theme of solitude was reconciled with that of human communion insofar as the ideal of wisdom was seen to lie in the union between a certain asceticism and everyday life and love.

Works by Lavelle

La Dialectique du monde sensible. Strasbourg, 1921.
La Perception de la profondeur. Strasbourg, 1921.
La Dialectique de l'éternel présent, 3 vols. Vol. 1: *De l'Être.* Paris, 1928; Vol. 2: *De l'Acte.* Paris, 1937; Vol. 3: *Du Temps et de l'éternité.* Paris, 1945.
La Conscience de soi. Paris, 1933.
La Présence totale. Paris, 1934.
Les Puissances du moi. Paris, 1939.
L'Erreur de Narcisse. Paris, 1939.
Le Mal et la souffrance. Paris, 1940.
Du Temps et de l'éternité. Paris, 1945.
Introduction à l'ontologie. Paris, 1947.

Works on Lavelle

Delfgaauw, B. M. I., *Het Spiritualistiche Existentialisme van Louis Lavelle.* Amsterdam, 1947.
Foulquié, P., *L'Existentialisme.* Paris, 1946. Pp. 109–122.
Grasso, Pier G., *L. Lavelle.* Brescia, 1948.
Nobile, O. M., *La filosofia di Louis Lavelle.* Florence, 1943.
Truc, G., *De Jean-Paul Sartre à Louis Lavelle, ou désagrégation et réintegration.* Paris, 1946.

ANNA-TERESA TYMIENIECKA

LAVROV, PETER LAVROVICH (1823–1900), Russian philosopher and social thinker, a major theoretician of Russian Populism and the leading exponent of a distinctive form of positivism in nineteenth-century Russian philosophy (also elaborated by Nicholas Mikhailovski). Lavrov was born in Melekhov, the son of a landed gentleman and retired artillery officer. He was sent to the Artillery School in St. Petersburg in 1837 and received his commission upon graduating in 1842. In 1844 he joined the faculty of the Artillery School, and for over 20 years (during which he rose to the rank of colonel), he taught mathematics and the history of science at military institutions in St. Petersburg. At the same time Lavrov read widely in philosophy and gained a reputation as a writer—first for his poetry and after 1858 for his scholarly essays in philosophy. In the 1860s, the increasing liberalism of his social views aroused the suspicion of the tsarist authorities. Arrested in 1866, he was exiled to the provinces in the following year. In 1870 he fled to Paris, where he played an active role in the Commune of 1871. After sojourns in London and Zurich, he settled in Paris in 1877. A friend of Marx and Engels, Lavrov became the voice of Russian socialism abroad and a revered figure in the international socialist movement. He died in Paris.

Lavrov developed an early interest in socialism through reading Fourier and other leading socialists; he was particularly attracted to the ideas of Proudhon and Alexander Herzen. Philosophically, Lavrov's initial scientific orientation evolved in the direction of positivism rather than in the direction of the "materialism" that was prevalent in Russian radical circles of the day, among such thinkers as Nicholas Chernyshevski and Dmitri Pisarev. However, his positivistic philosophy was based more on German models than on Comte. Lavrov did not become acquainted with Comte's writings until the middle of the 1860s; by then his thinking had been given strong direction by a close study of Kant, Hegel, the Neo-Kantian Albert Lange, and "young Hegelians" such as Ludwig Feuerbach and Arnold Ruge.

In his first important philosophical writings, which consisted of several long essays written between the years 1858 and 1861, Lavrov criticized materialism as a metaphysical system that unnecessarily restricts science to matter in motion. Distinguishing between material phenomena, conscious phenomena, and historical phenomena, he maintained that phenomena of the last two classes cannot be dealt with by the methods of the natural sciences. The phenomena of consciousness, in particular, require a "subjective," introspective method, and furthermore, these phenomena must be regarded as scientifically primary, since every investigator must begin from the facts of his own consciousness. Calling this approach "anthropologism," Lavrov developed it into a Neo-Kantian positivism which, while it rejected supernaturalistic metaphysics and religion, did not reject moral imperatives. It stressed the thought and action of the free individual who finds in his own consciousness an absolute sanction to strive toward the realization of moral ideals such as individual dignity and social justice. While material phenomena are governed by universal natural laws, man's conscious conviction that he is free is inescapable and thus may be taken as a foundation for practical philosophy. Moral ideals are ultimately grounded in man's striving for pleasure, but in the consciousness of the cultivated individual they present themselves as nonegoistic, universal imperatives.

In his best-known philosophical work, *Istoricheskiye Pis'ma* ("Historical Letters"), first published serially in the magazine *Nedelya* ("Week") in 1868 and 1869, Lavrov continued his attack upon materialistic reductionism by applying "anthropologism" to history. Arguing that man

can view history only "subjectively" and teleologically, he defined the goal of history as the physical, moral, and intellectual development of the individual. On this basis he maintained that the "critically thinking individuals" who have already achieved such development have a moral obligation to extend the opportunity for development to the masses, whose toil has given the privileged few the leisure and the resources needed for self-cultivation. Lavrov asserted that in coming to understand the defects of existing social institutions and in actively striving to reform them, the "critically thinking individuals" both discharge their "debt to the people" and serve as the moving forces of history. He envisaged a future in which all social institutions will conform to man's natural needs and the coercive institutions of the state will be all but eliminated. The *Historical Letters* had a great impact on the Russian revolutionary youth of the 1870s.

Lavrov was able to develop his socialist program more explicitly abroad, where he was free from tsarist censorship. From 1873 to 1876 he edited the journal *Vperyod!* ("Forward!"), the chief organ of Russian Populist socialism—a form of agrarian socialism, inspired by Herzen and Chernyshevski, which stressed the Russian village commune and the possibility it afforded Russia of moving directly to a socialist order, thus bypassing the evils of capitalism. Lavrov's political theory was further elaborated in *Gosudarstvenny Element v Budushchem Obshchestve* ("The State Element in Future Society"), published in London in 1876. Acknowledging the need for revolution, Lavrov at first stressed the value of preparatory education and propaganda. Later he came to condone revolutionary terrorism and was associated with the Russian extremist party, *Narodnaya Volya* ("The People's Will").

In his later socialist views, which were closer to those of Marx, Lavrov gave more attention to class conflict and to the process of production, but he never adopted a fully Marxist view of history or social dynamics. His emphasis remained moralistic and individualistic, with its focus on the development and activity of the "critically thinking individual." The philosophical outlook reflected in Lavrov's *Historical Letters* remained fundamentally unchanged in his last major work, which consisted of two lengthy introductory volumes of an unfinished intellectual history entitled *Opyt Istorii Mysli Novovo Vremeni* ("Essay in the History of Modern Thought," Geneva, 1894).

Works by Lavrov

Sobraniye Sochineni, 11 numbers. Petrograd, 1917–1920.
Izbrannyye Sochineniya, 4 vols. Moscow, 1934–1935.
Filosofiya i Sotsiologiya, 2 vols. Moscow, 1965.
Historical Letters (selections), translated by James P. Scanlan, in James M. Edie, James P. Scanlan, and Mary-Barbara Zeldin, eds., *Russian Philosophy*. Chicago, 1965.

Works on Lavrov

Knizhnik-Vetrov, I., *P. L. Lavrov*. Leningrad, 1925; 2d ed., Moscow, 1930.
Venturi, Franco, *Il populismo russo*. Rome, 1952. Translated into English by Frances Haskell as *Roots of Revolution*. New York, 1960.
Zenkovsky, V. V., *Istoriya Russkoy Filosofii*, 2 vols. Paris, 1948–1950. Translated into English by George L. Kline as *A*

History of Russian Philosophy, 2 vols. New York and London, 1953.

JAMES P. SCANLAN

LAW, PHILOSOPHY OF. In addition to the detailed survey articles PHILOSOPHY OF LAW, HISTORY OF and PHILOSOPHY OF LAW, PROBLEMS OF, the Encyclopedia includes the following articles in which legal theories and concepts are discussed: ANALYTIC JURISPRUDENCE; HISTORICAL SCHOOL OF JURISPRUDENCE; JUSTICE; LEGAL POSITIVISM; LEGAL REALISM; NATURAL LAW; PROPERTY; PUNISHMENT; RESPONSIBILITY, MORAL AND LEGAL; RIGHTS; SOCIOLOGY OF LAW; and SOVEREIGNTY. See Philosophy of Law, History of, and Philosophy of Law, Problems of in Index for articles on philosophers and legal theorists who have concerned themselves especially with questions in the philosophy of law.

LAW, WILLIAM (1686–1761), English devotional writer, controversialist, theologian, and mystic. He was a fellow of Emmanuel College, Cambridge; as a nonjuro., he refused to take the oath to King George I and thus terminated his career at the university and in the church. For a time he was a tutor in the household of Edward Gibbon, grandfather of the historian. His later life was virtually without incident, and after years of retirement, he died in his native village of King's Cliffe, Northamptonshire.

Law is best known as a devotional writer and especially for his *A Serious Call to a Devout and Holy Life* (1728); but his importance in the history of thought lies elsewhere, in his resistance to latitudinarianism, his defense of morality, his attack on deism, and his mystical writings.

Law was a formidable controversialist, and in his *Three Letters to the Bishop of Bangor* (1717) he brought remorseless logic to bear on Benjamin Hoadly's lax view of the nature of the church. Bernard de Mandeville had contended in the *Fable of the Bees* that private vices are actually public benefits; Law subjected the work to rigorous examination and showed that the canons of morality cannot be understood in terms of such specious sophistries. His most serious and celebrated work was his attack on deism. In *Christianity as old as the Creation*, Matthew Tindal argued that reason is the only test of truth; insofar as Christianity is valid, it rests on rationalist principles that owe nothing to revelation. Law's *Case of Reason* was a closely argued refutation of the prevailing rationalism of the period. Human reason is not able, by itself, to encompass all knowledge, nor is it sufficient to test all truth. Those who exalt natural religion are exposed to the same criticism as those who accept revelation without question. The universe is less simple and the ways of God are more mysterious than the arrogance of rationalism admits. Law shared with George Berkeley and Joseph Butler the credit for terminating the active phase of the deistic controversy.

Law's later writings reflect the profound influence that mysticism (especially as expounded by Jakob Boehme) came to exercise over his thought. He reached the conclusion that real knowledge is "the communion of the knowing and the known." To convey his new insights, Law organized his teaching in the form of "myth." He believed that mysticism gives birth to symbols within which its truth can live. Law felt that he had penetrated to a deeper understanding of human nature and that it could best be interpreted through a grasp of the meaning of the myth of the Fall on the one hand and through an understanding of divine self-communication in love on the other ("Love is the first *Fiat* of God"). Law's mystical teaching about life was related to a restatement of orthodox Christianity. He expounded the atonement with great beauty and insight and believed that the Trinity was the most illuminating way to describe the self-unfolding of the Eternal.

Law's mystical writings were perplexing to thinkers of the eighteenth century (see John Wesley's letter to Law about mysticism), but his *Serious Call* exercised a profound influence at the time (especially on Samuel Johnson and John Wesley) and is still considered a classic work on the Christian life.

Works by Law

The Works of William Law, G. Moreton, ed., 9 vols. London, 1892.

Selected Mystical Writings of William Law, S. Hobhouse, ed. London, 1938.

Works on Law

Cragg, G. R., *Reason and Authority in the Eighteenth Century*. Cambridge, 1964.

Overton, J. H., *The Life and Opinions of the Rev. William Law*. London, 1881.

Talon, H., *William Law*. London, 1948.

GERALD R. CRAGG

LAWS AND THEORIES. It is generally assumed in the literature on the structure of scientific theories that there is an important logical distinction between experimental laws (for example Galileo's law of falling bodies, Boyle's law, the chemical law of constant proportions, and Mendel's laws of heredity) on the one hand, and theories (such as the theory of relativity, the atomic theory, and the theory of evolution) on the other. Familiar terminology is not always a reliable guide to this distinction, for although we may speak of the "law" of conservation of energy, this so-called law has many of the chief characteristics of theories, and on the other hand Newton's "theory" of gravitation may be held to be in all important respects an experimental law. We shall therefore begin by attempting to make the distinctions between laws and theories explicit and examining their importance for the logic of theories.

Observables versus theoretical terms. Apparently the most fundamental distinction between laws and theories is that experimental laws contain only terms that refer to observables or are operationally definable (such terms as "pressure," "velocity of fall," "sulfuric acid," or "proportion of tall sweet pea plants in the sample"), whereas the statements of theories contain at least some terms that do not refer to observables and are not operationally definable. In other words, it is held that experimental laws are immediately intelligible, independent of theories, in terms of the generally understood experimental procedures of science, and that their truth or falsity is epistemologically prior to that of theories since they can be confirmed or falsified directly by carrying out the experimental operations implicitly or explicitly specified in the meanings of their component terms. In the case of theoretical terms, on the other hand, it seems that there are no overt procedures for identifying their referents; "electron," "space curvature," "electromagnetic wave" cannot be pointed to, and hence it is suggested that theoretical statements cannot be directly tested by observation and experiment.

What is generally admitted, even by those who regard this distinction as a real and important one, is that it nevertheless has vague boundaries, and that it may be relative to the current development of science and to the sophistication of the observers. For example, sulfuric acid is not an "observable" to those ignorant of chemistry; "air" might now be said to refer to an observable for most laymen, but for the pre-Socratics it was a debatable theoretical term; and a physicist might say he observed in a cloud chamber the creation of a particle-pair when a layman would see only two white streaks. Furthermore, some terms which must surely be said to be theoretical if any are, such as "the mass of the electron," are also in a sense operationally definable, since one can specify experimental situations in which electrons are present and one can measure their mass. However, the admission that the boundary between laws and theories is vague or shifting does not imply that it is nonexistent. What remains to be considered is whether it signifies a radical difference between laws and theories, and in particular whether the notion of "observable" can be made precise and distinguished from its contrary, or whether the distinction is merely pragmatic and therefore relative to the observer's knowledge, experience, and language. That the distinction is not fundamental has been argued by Paul Feyerabend and Hilary Putnam, in opposition to the more traditional account of Ernest Nagel.

Laws as invariant in truth-value and meaning. The "observable" character of experimental laws may be taken to imply a further characteristic, namely that their truth-value and their meaning are wholly independent of the changing theories that may be used to explain them. Once the statement "The pressure times the volume of a gas at constant temperature is constant" is understood in terms of experimental operations, and once it is tested and found to be confirmed, it becomes and remains an experimental law, whether gases are understood in theoretical terms as continuous fluids or randomly moving particles or in any other way. Experimental laws in this view have a rock-bottom, incorrigible status that is denied to theories. Any theory is subject to revision or replacement, but any subsequent theory, if it is to be acceptable, must be consistent with the experimental laws previously known to be true. Moreover, it is often held that experimental laws derive their support wholly from their observable instances and not at all from theoretical considerations, whereas theories are judged on the basis of experimental laws and sometimes also in terms of such other considerations as internal coherence, plausibility, and simplicity, which have no place in the acceptability of laws.

These apparently sharp distinctions may be challenged, however, for it is not clear that support for experimental laws comes solely from their observable instances. There are cases where a law deduced from a theory may be preferred to one generalized from observable instances, either because the deduction is more accurate than any direct experimental evidence would justify or because it actually corrects a law generalized from data subsequently found to be inaccurate. This occurred, for example, in the case of Kepler's third law, which related the periodic times of the planets with the size of their orbits. The comparatively simple law, which was consistent with the observed data, was found to be inconsistent with Newton's theory and had therefore to be corrected, although the effect of the correction was still within the range of experimental error then involved. Thus it seems that laws as well as theories are subject to revision in the light of theoretical considerations.

Even the alleged invariance of meaning of experimental terms with respect to changes of theories has been challenged (for example, by Feyerabend). Operational definition cannot exhaust the meaning of even an observable term, for if it did we would never find it possible to identify the same observable by means of different operational procedures. Some component of meaning must come from a theory, as when, for example, we identify as a mechanical "velocity" a quantity measured by the red shift of stellar spectra, although this was not one of the methods that originally gave operational meaning to the observable term "velocity." Again, it may sometimes be the case that theoretical considerations make changing the operational definition of an observable appropriate, as when, for example, Descartes's definition of "motion" as "quantity of matter times speed" was transformed by Newton into "quantity of matter times velocity in a given direction" because Newton's quantity, not Descartes's, was found to be conserved.

The deductive hierarchy. Finally there is a group of distinctions between laws and theories which are less controversial but also perhaps less important. Laws are usually expressible as single statements, theories are systems of statements that entail laws. Theories are higher and laws lower in the deductive hierarchy constituted by a systematic science. Theories are therefore more general than laws, covering many qualitatively different phenomena; laws are more restricted in their range of application.

Theories are also sometimes said to be more abstract than laws and to refer to ideal systems, whereas laws refer to concrete entities. Insofar as theories, in virtue of their generality, encompass possible physical systems which are in practice never realized ("ideal gases," "frictionless machines," "the economic man"), they may correctly be said to be more abstract than experimental laws, but if "abstract" is taken in the sense "more formal" or "mathematical," the characterization begs questions about the cognitive status of theories that are discussed below.

THE STRUCTURE OF THEORIES

The structure of explanation in science is discussed in the article EXPLANATION IN SCIENCE in terms of the deductive, or covering law schema, familiarized by the classic article of Carl G. Hempel and Paul Oppenheim on the logic of explanation. Theoretical explanation can be fitted into this schema by regarding the explanation of laws by theories as analogous to the explanation of particular facts by laws. That is to say, just as laws, together with initial or boundary conditions, entail their instances, so do theories, together with boundary conditions, entail the laws they explain. This schema can be maintained in a modified form even if the deducibility relation is questioned in the way discussed above in the example of Kepler's law. For a law *L* that requires theoretical explanation may be replaced by another law *L'* that is deducible from a theory that is in all ways acceptable (except that it is not consistent with *L*), if *L'* is subsequently found to be at least as good an account of the evidence as was *L*. This possibility does not remove the relation of entailment between the theory and the new law *L'*; it shows rather that no law such as *L* can be regarded as incorrigible by a theory.

Correspondence rules. The deductive schema by itself, however, does not take account of the difference of language in a theory and the experimental laws which it explains. Whatever may ultimately be thought about the distinctions between theoretical and experimental languages there is no doubt that theories which purport to refer to unobservables (and henceforth the term "theory" will be used only with this meaning) do employ a terminology which does not appear in experimental laws, and therefore an analysis of theories requires an account of the connection between the theoretical and the experimental language. This connection is usually described in terms of correspondence rules, which link theoretical terms with observables and thus enable directly testable statements to be deduced from theories. Examples of correspondence rules are "The mean kinetic energy of the molecules is the absolute temperature of the gas"; "Electromagnetic radiation of wave length 5900 Å is sodium light"; "Common salt is a cubical crystal lattice of sodium and chlorine atoms." The logical status of these rules has often been debated, for instance by Nagel and by Wilfrid Sellars (in "The Logic of Theories"). Are the rules analytic definition? This, in the light of the examples, seems an implausible suggestion. Are they extra premises of the theory, having the same empirical status as its other premises? Or are they perhaps dependent on a model for the theory which provides an interpretation of both the theoretical and observable terms? In an instrumentalist view of theories the second suggestion is likely to be adopted; in a realist view, something like the third. In general the status given to the correspondence rules will depend on which view is taken of the cognitive status of theories.

Calculus and interpretation. The first extension to the Hempel–Oppenheim deductive schema required to accommodate theoretical explanation is the inclusion of correspondence rules as some kind of bridge between theories and experimental laws. The second extension (suggested by many writers, including Norman Campbell, Richard Braithwaite, and Ernest Nagel), is the distinction between the formal calculus of the theory, and various interpretations or models of the calculus. We can in fact find in the literature specifications for five different ingredients of a fully articulated scientific deductive system:

(1) The formal calculus, or deductive machinery, with no interpretation; for example, a wave equation and its consequences.

(2) The intended interpretation of this calculus (normally called the "theory"), which refers to unobservables,

at least prima facie; for example, a theory of light waves as an interpretation of the formal wave equation.

(3) The correspondence rules, which link some but not necessarily all terms of either the formal calculus or the intended interpretation with terms referring to observables.

(4) The experimental laws, which are deductive consequences of the formal calculus and the correspondence rules taken together, or perhaps of the intended interpretation and the correspondence rules taken together, and which are confirmed by observable instances.

(5) Further interpretation of the formal calculus in a model or models, which may (some writers say *must*) be different from the intended interpretation; for example, waves conceived as oscillations of the particles of a material ether.

Opinions differ about the status of all these ingredients and the relations between them; In the article MODELS AND ANALOGY IN SCIENCE the relations between (1), (2), and (5) are particularly discussed, and it is shown how various views have been held about the meaning of theoretical concepts. Here we shall investigate other, interrelated problems arising from this fivefold account of the structure of theories: the cognitive status of theories, the criteria for the "reality" of theoretical entities, and the validity of the theory–observation distinction itself.

THE COGNITIVE STATUS OF THEORIES

We shall consider three main views of the status of theories: reductionism, instrumentalism, and realism.

Reductionism. Since theories do not refer directly to observables, at least prima facie, and do not make directly testable statements, the first attempt to clarify their status was the suggestion that they make a disguised reference to observables; that is, that they provide some kind of short-hand for observation statements, or that their content can be exhaustively translated into or reduced to observation statements. Writers taking this view have sometimes claimed that the observation statements to which theories are reducible are sense-data statements; however, in later formulations of this view, it was usually claimed that the observation statements are physical-object statements in "ordinary language," such as appeared in P. W. Bridgman's "operational definitions" of scientific concepts. Early examples of the view are Russell's assertion that "physics cannot be regarded as validly based upon empirical data until the [light] waves have been expressed as functions of the colours and other sense-data" (*Mysticism and Logic*, London, 1918, p. 140); and Arthur Eddington's "a physical quantity is defined by the series of operations and calculations of which it is the result" (*The Mathematical Theory of Relativity*, Cambridge, 1923, p. 3).

The view that there could be a definition of every theoretical term in terms of observables was subjected to damaging criticism and has been universally abandoned. It broke down for two main reasons. First, it can be shown that in many existing theories such translations cannot in fact be carried out, and yet no reputable theorist wishes to abandon otherwise satisfactory theories on this ground alone. Second, and more fundamental, it has been demonstrated in detailed artificial examples by Frank Ramsey and Braithwaite and argued in general terms by many other writers that if explicit definitions of all theoretical terms by means of observables could be carried out, theories would be incapable of growth and therefore useless. Theories are required to be general and predictive and therefore capable of assimilating an indefinite number of new observations without themselves radically changing in meaning. Explicit definitions could not leave room for this and could not exhaust the potentially infinite and largely unknown range of observables to which the theory might be relevant.

A weaker form of reductionism is the suggestion that although every theoretical term and statement may not be translatable into observation terms or statements, nevertheless it may be possible to give reduction definitions of all theoretical terms and some theoretical statements in conditional form. The proposal can best be explained by means of an example. Consider the theoretical statement *T*: "Space is curved in the neighborhood of the sun." Understood in terms of a conditional reduction definition of "space curvature," the statement would become: "*T* if and only if light passing in the neighborhood of the sun from a distant star suffers a deflection from its straight path as observed from the earth." But this definition suffers from several shortcomings. First, it says nothing about the meaning of *T* when no light is passing the sun, yet in relativity theory *T* cannot be taken to have meaning only when the sun is accompanied by other luminous bodies. Second, it presupposes a particular theory about the bending of light in a gravitational field, but *T* is not necessarily dependent on the truth of this theory; we might wish to retain *T* for other theoretical reasons even if the correlation with light deflection were refuted. Third, it is by no means clear that *every* theoretical term can be defined even in this conditional form.

For these and other reasons it must be concluded that the attempt to exhaust the meaning of theoretical terms and statements by means of either explicit definitions or reduction definitions, or by the closely similar operational definitions of Bridgman, has failed.

Craig's theorem. A somewhat different approach to the problem of showing that theories are essentially redundant because they are equivalent to sets of observation statements has been made by William Craig. (See CRAIG'S THEOREM.) He proposes not the translation of theories into observation statements but the replacement of the formal theoretical system with another system containing no theoretical terms and having the same empirical content as the theory. He has given a general proof that this replacement is possible if the theory is formalized, but that in general it will require an infinite number of axioms, and that these axioms turn out to be mere reformulations of all the true observation statements entailed by the theory. These two features of the method show that it can only be regarded as a reduction of the theory in a trivial and useless sense.

It must be concluded from all these attempts at reduction that if indeed there is a distinction between theories and observation statements, then it is not possible to show that theories are wholly redundant by showing that they are equivalent in all essential respects to sets of observation statements.

Instrumentalism. Instrumentalists assume that theories have the status of instruments, tools, or calculating devices in relation to observation statements. In this view it is assumed that theories can be used to relate and systematize observation statements and to derive some sets of observation statements (predictions) from other sets (data); but no question of the truth or reference of the theories themselves arises. The suggestion derives some force from the representation of theories in terms of the formal-calculus-plus-correspondence-rules with no interpretation of the calculus as such, for then the sentences of the calculus are neither true nor false. Instrumentalism is also supported by the extreme difficulty in modern physics of finding self-consistent interpretations of the formal calculi of quantum theories and by the fact that different and conflicting interpretations may be used for different parts of a theory, or for one theory under different circumstances (as with the quantum particle and wave models).

There are several reasons, however, why such an instrumentalist view does not seem adequate as it stands. In the first place, we do not use theories in the same way that we use a convenient tool; we are inclined to demand a specific, well-adapted tool for each different purpose—there is no virtue in seeking to fit all purposes to one universal tool. But we do look for universal theories and are not content with convenient but mutually conflicting theories in different domains of phenomena. Furthermore, we do hold theories to be vulnerable to falsification, and theories which are falsified are discarded as serious competitors in scientific explanation even if they continue to be useful as approximations in some contexts. It may also be argued that an extreme instrumentalist view of theories, according to which they consist only of the formal calculus regarded as a "black box" into which data are fed and out of which predictions emerge, is inadequate to account for the explanatory and predictive functions of models of the formal calculus. However, it is sometimes held (for example by Nagel) that all such refinements can be built into the instrumental view without essentially changing it, and that indeed the dispute between this view and the realist view is a merely verbal dispute. We shall return to this point.

Realism and the criteria for reality. Realism is a generic term for a number of views, all holding that theories consist of true or false statements referring to "real" or "existing" entities. Let us consider the various criteria proposed for answering such a question as "Do electrons exist?" Each such criterion generates a different form of realism.

Quine's criterion. W. V. O. Quine's statement that "To be is to be the value of a variable" is based on his proposal that those entities may be said to "exist" which are "among the entities over which our variables range in order to render one of our affirmations true" ("On What There Is," *Review of Metaphysics*, Vol. 2, p. 32). That is to say, if a theory contains a quantified statement $(x)(P(x) \supset Q(x))$, or $(\exists x)(P(x) \supset Q(x))$, where, say, *P* is the property "is an electron" and *Q* is "is charged," then those entities ("electrons") exist which make either of these statements true. This sense of "existence" is expressed in somewhat weaker form by Braithwaite when he says that electrons "exist" if "electron" is a term in true theory having deductive relations with true observation statements (*Scientific Explanation*, p. 79).

Such a criterion for "existence" does not, however, seem strong enough to deal with all the questions that might be asked about theoretical entities, since it embraces all the substitution instances that make theoretical statements true. It is not, therefore, capable of distinguishing between different interpretations of the same formal calculus (and yet two otherwise distinct interpretations, for instance light waves and light corpuscles, cannot both refer to "existing" entities); neither can it distinguish between an interpretation intended as a useful "fiction" (for instance, "heat fluid" as a pictorial representation of certain heat phenomena) and a theory intended to refer to real entities (for example, a dynamic theory of heat as the motions of molecules). The same difficulties are entailed in Braithwaite's reference to "true" theories, for it may be that among alternative interpretations of a calculus just those theories are accepted as true that are already believed to refer to real entities.

Before we can say that a putative theoretical entity "exists," it is certainly necessary that the Quine condition be satisfied. It is of course also necessary that the theory in question should not have been falsified (for example, phlogiston is "nonexistent" not because it is the referent of a theoretical term but because the theory in which it appears is false). But the considerations of the last paragraph suggest that further conditions also need to be satisfied before we have sufficient reason to speak of existence. These further criteria are concerned not with the formal aspects of the theory but with its content, or intended interpretation. The formal criteria alone might be reconciled with some form of instrumentalism, as Nagel suggests; but it is difficult to see how the nonformal criteria can be so reconciled, since instrumentalism is bound to be indifferent as to the various possible interpretations of a theory's calculus. It is Nagel's omission of the intended interpretation from his account of the structure of theories that seems to lead him to hold that the issue between instrumentalism and realism is merely verbal. Three kinds of nonformal criteria for "existence" can be recognized and will now be discussed.

Fulfillment of expectations. An important distinction is made in ordinary language between the "real" and the "fictional" or "illusory" in terms of the further fulfillment of expectations for things of a given kind. Mirages are distinguished from real oases by their subsequent non-fulfillment of expectations for oases; real from fictional characters by their possession of actual birth certificates, addresses, and the like. Similarly, if a theory, such as the dynamical theory of heat, yields expectations and predictions in new experimental situations, this is an indication that, unlike the heat fluid model, it is being taken realistically, and if the expectations are fulfilled, this may be regarded as confirmation of the real existence of the entities to which it refers. Thus to take seriously the model of a theory and to rely upon predictions made from the model

is at least an indication that the model is believed to be the "real" reference of the theory.

Observability and causal efficacy. It may seem a little odd to suggest observability as a criterion of existence for theoretical entities, since it is this characteristic that first led to the distinction between "observable" and "theoretical" terms. But it may be possible so to extend the naive conception of "direct observability" that at least some so-called theoretical entities can be said to exist in the comparatively nonproblematic sense in which observable entities exist. This suggestion arises naturally in contexts such as the magnification of objects by telescopes or microscopes, which sometimes bring "unobservables" into view; and once this possibility is admitted in the case of such instrumental aids, it is difficult to stop short of admitting as observable any entity detected in ways which are in principle similar, however indirect they may appear to be. Thus, for example, radio stars and large molecules may be said to be brought into the domain of observables.

A further step may now be taken. Some experiments which "detect" unobservable entities are more naturally described as rendering observable the effects of these entities rather than the entities themselves. For example, subatomic particles are sometimes detected by the visible tracks in cloud chambers. But if the deductive relation between theory and observation in these cases can be correctly described as a causal as well as a merely logical relation, then surely the causes as well as the effects must be said to exist, and the notion of existence appropriate to observables must be extended again to include entities which may not be observable even in principle (for example, photons), but which have observable effects. This last proposal in fact widens the criteria of existence to the point where any theoretical entity to which we are prepared to ascribe causal efficacy should in principle be included, for if such an entity were to have *no* observable effects, it is not easy to see that it would add anything to the empirical content of the theory, and if it adds nothing it ought not to be included in an acceptable scientific theory at all. However, such a criterion would exclude from the domain of existing entities any models which are deliberately introduced as fictions or instruments, since these would not be said to cause observable effects. On behalf of instrumentalism it may of course be replied that it is never necessary to ascribe causal efficacy to theoretical entities in the sense required in this argument, but a full discussion would require analysis of the notion of causality in science (see CAUSATION).

These considerations tend, of course, to cast doubt on the radical distinction which has been made between the theoretical and the observable, and thus to reinforce the other attacks upon this distinction which were referred to at the beginning of this article.

Substance versus property. Some disputes about "existence" are concerned not with the various senses of "observability" but rather with the logical distinction between substantives and predicates. It is sometimes said (echoing the nominalism of some recent logic) that whereas fundamental particles can be said to "exist" as substances or individuals, the referents of such terms as "energy," "valency," or "species" do not exist because they are properties, relations, or classes. The main interest of this question does not reside in the dispute between nominalism and Platonism, but rather in two questions: how to distinguish between the individuals and the predicates in a theory, and how to distinguish the predicates that are fundamental or primary from those that are derivative or secondary.

The distinction between individuals and predicates cannot in general be decided by looking at the logical formalization of the theory. In the first place, few theories are formalized. More fundamentally, formalization itself cannot give the decision, because formalization presupposes that such a distinction has been made and different preformal interpretations in respect to the individuals and the predicates will yield different formalizations. For example, electrostatics may be interpreted in such a way that mass-charges are the substances, and then space–time positions and force–energy relations are the predicates. But alternatively electrostatics may be given a "real field" interpretation in which either "energy-in-the-field" or space–time points themselves are substantive, and mass and charge are then predicated of certain points of space–time. In deciding which of such interpretations to adopt, there is a tendency to take whatever is "conserved" as substantial; thus, in the history of physics, mass, motion, charge, heat, energy, and mass–energy have been successively taken to be substances. On the other hand, criteria such as P. F. Strawson's for "individuals" (identifiability, reidentifiability, and distinguishability from their like) tend to cast doubt on the substantive status of the fundamental particles of modern physics, which are neither reidentifiable nor distinguishable from their like.

The question "What is real?" may, however, be a request not so much for a list of substances but for "what is really there" as opposed to "what is mere appearance," and thus may be a request for a list of the primary qualities. Seventeenth-century mechanists would have replied in terms of the primary mechanical qualities, in comparison with which secondary qualities have, if not an illusory status, at least a derived one. Thus, this question may involve the issue of which science is the fundamental one to which all others ought ideally to be reducible; should biology be reduced to physics, psychology to neurophysiology, and so on?

A further question is implied in a realist view of theories which cannot be pursued here, namely, how seriously are we to take the proposed realistic use of theoretical language as compared with observation language? Even if these two languages are not essentially different, there still remain questions like the one posed by Eddington: Which is the real table—the hard, solid, brown object of ordinary experience, or the physicist's force-field consisting mostly of empty space? Most instrumentalists will reply that the table of ordinary language is alone real; the other is a fiction. A realist in any of the senses we have discussed will reply either that only the physicist's table is real, or that both tables are real because both languages describe the same table and in spite of appearances the two languages are mutually consistent and interdependent. For exploration of the realist's reply along these lines and its consequent effects upon the traditional distinctions between observables and theories and upon the fivefold structure of theories outlined above, the reader is referred to Feyerabend's article "Explanation, Reduction, and Empiricism" and to the works by Sellars and J. J. C. Smart—all listed in the bibliography.

Bibliography

COLLECTIONS

The following collections are referred to below by the abbreviations indicated.

Colodny, R. G., ed., *Frontiers of Science and Philosophy*. Pittsburgh, 1962. (*Frontiers*)

Danto, Arthur, and Morgenbesser, Sidney, eds., *Philosophy of Science, Readings*. New York, 1960.

Feigl, Herbert, and Brodbeck, May, eds., *Readings in the Philosophy of Science*. New York, 1953. (*Readings*)

Feigl, Herbert, and Maxwell, Grover, eds., *Current Issues in the Philosophy of Science*. New York, 1961. (*Issues*)

Feigl, Herbert, and Scriven, Michael, eds., *Minnesota Studies in the Philosophy of Science*. Vol. I, Minneapolis, 1956. (*Minnesota* I)

Feigl, Herbert; Maxwell, Grover; and Scriven, Michael, eds., *ibid.* Vol. II, Minneapolis, 1958. (*Minnesota* II)

Feigl, Herbert, and Maxwell, Grover, eds., *ibid.* Vol. III, Minneapolis, 1962. (*Minnesota* III)

Linsky, Leonard, ed., *Semantics and the Philosophy of Language*. Urbana, Ill., 1951. (*Semantics*)

Nagel, Ernest; Suppes, Patrick; and Tarski, Alfred, eds., *Logic, Methodology and Philosophy of Science*. Stanford, Calif., 1962. (*Logic*)

Reese, W. L., ed., *Philosophy of Science: The Delaware Seminar*. New York, 1963. Vol. II. (*Delaware* II)

DISTINCTION BETWEEN LAWS AND THEORIES

Alexander, P., "Theory-construction and Theory-testing." *British Journal for the Philosophy of Science*, Vol. 9 (1958), 29–38. Reply to Hesse article "Theories, Dictionaries and Observation."

Alexander, P., *Sensationalism and Scientific Explanation*. London, 1963. Upholds the distinction between observation statements as descriptive and theories as explanatory.

Bridgman, P. W., *The Logic of Modern Physics*. New York, 1927. The classic source of the theory of operational definition of physical terms.

Feyerabend, Paul K., "An Attempt at a Realistic Interpretation of Experience." *PAS*, Vol. 58 (1957–1958), 143–170.

Feyerabend, Paul K., "Explanation, Reduction, and Empiricism," in *Minnesota* III. Pp. 28–97. Attack on Nagel.

Hanson, Norwood R., *Patterns of Discovery*. Cambridge, 1958. Chs. 1–2. A view of observation as "theory-laden."

Hesse, Mary, "Theories, Dictionaries and Observation." *British Journal for the Philosophy of Science*, Vol. 9 (1958), 12–28, 128–129.

Nagel, Ernest, *The Structure of Science*. New York, 1961. See Chs. 5 and 6 especially. The standard presentation of the view that theories and experimental laws are radically distinct.

Popper, Karl R., "The Aim of Science." *Ratio*, Vol. 1 (1957), 24–35. Theories cannot be inductively derived from laws, since they may correct laws.

Putnam, Hilary, "The Analytic and the Synthetic," in *Minnesota* III. Pp. 358–397.

Putnam, Hilary, "What Theories Are Not," in *Logic*. Pp. 240–251.

STRUCTURE OF THEORIES

Beckner, Morton, *The Biological Way of Thought*. New York, 1959. The structure of theories in biology.

Braithwaite, Richard B., *Scientific Explanation*. Cambridge, 1953. See especially Chs. 1–4.

Campbell, Norman R., *Physics. The Elements*. Cambridge, 1920; reprinted as *Foundations of Science*, New York, 1957. The pioneer discussion of theory structure in terms of deductive calculus and interpretation; see especially Ch. 6.

Carnap, Rudolf, *Foundations of Logic and Mathematics*. Chicago, 1939. This is Vol. I, No. 3, of *International Encyclopedia of Unified Science*. Partially reprinted in *Readings*, pp. 309–318.

Duhem, Pierre, *La Théorie physique, son objet, sa structure*, Part II. Paris, 1906; 2d ed., 1914. Second edition translated by P. P. Wiener as *The Aim and Structure of Physical Theory*. New York, 1954.

Hempel, Carl G., and Oppenheim, Paul, "Studies in the Logic of Explanation." *Philosophy of Science*, Vol. 15 (1948), 135–175. Parts I–III reprinted in *Readings*, pp. 319–352. The classic account of the deductive schema for explanation.

Kuhn, T. S., *The Structure of Scientific Revolutions*. Chicago, 1962. Attack on the view of theories typified by Braithwaite's *Scientific Explanation*.

Maxwell, Grover, "Meaning Postulates in Scientific Theories," in *Issues*. Pp. 169–195. With a reply by Wilfrid Sellars.

Nagel, Ernest, *The Structure of Science*. New York, 1961. Pp. 106–117, 336–380.

Sellars, Wilfrid, "The Language of Theories," in *Issues*. Pp. 57–77.

COGNITIVE STATUS OF THEORIES

Nagel, Ernest, *The Structure of Science*. New York, 1961. Pp. 117–152.

Pap, Arthur, *An Introduction to the Philosophy of Science*. New York, 1962. Chs. 2, 3, 18. An introductory account.

Popper, Karl R., "Three Views Concerning Human Knowledge," in *Conjectures and Refutations, The Growth of Scientific Knowledge*. London, 1963, Pp. 97–119.

REDUCTIONISM AND INSTRUMENTALISM

Achinstein, P., "Theoretical Terms and Partial Interpretation." *British Journal for the Philosophy of Science*, Vol. 14 (1963), 89–105.

Barker, S. F., *Induction and Hypothesis*. Ithaca, N.Y., 1957. Chs. 1, 5, 6, 7. Introductory account of the reductionist and formalist view of theories.

Braithwaite, Richard B., "Axiomatizing a Scientific System by Axioms in the Form of Identifications," in L. Henkin, Patrick Suppes, and Alfred Tarski, eds., *The Axiomatic Method*. Proceedings of an international symposium, Berkeley, Calif., 1957. Amsterdam, 1959. Pp. 429–442.

Carnap, Rudolf, "Testability and Meaning." *Philosophy of Science*, Vol. 3 (1936), 420–471; Vol. 4 (1937), 1–40. Partially reprinted in *Readings*, pp. 47–92. Holds that the confirmability of theories requires reduction definitions.

Carnap, Rudolf, "The Methodological Character of Theoretical Concepts," in *Minnesota* I. Pp. 38–76. Abandons requirement of reduction definitions in favor of theoretical and observation languages linked by correspondence rules.

Craig, William, "Replacement of Auxiliary Expressions." *Philosophical Review*, Vol. 65 (1956), 38–55.

Hempel, Carl G., "Problems and Changes in the Empiricist Criterion of Meaning." *Revue internationale de philosophie*, Vol. 11 (1950), 41–65. Also in *Semantics*, pp. 163–185.

Hempel, Carl G., "The Theoretician's Dilemma," in *Minnesota* II. Pp. 37–98. Account and evaluation of Craig's theorem.

Hertz, Heinrich, *Die Prinzipien der Mechanik*. Leipzig, 1894. Translated into English by D. E. Jones and T. E. Walley as *The Principles of Mechanics*. London, 1899; New York, 1956. Hertz's Introduction to this work is an early account of theories and interpretations.

Quine, W. V. O., "Two Dogmas of Empiricism." *Philosophical Review*, Vol. 60 (1951), 20–43. Also in Quine's *From a Logical Point of View*. Cambridge, Mass., 1953. The second dogma includes the alleged reducibility of theories to immediate experience.

Ramsey, Frank P., "Theories," in *The Foundations of Mathematics*. London, 1931. Pp. 212–236.

Rozeboom, W. W., "The Factual Content of Theoretical Concepts," in *Minnesota* III. Pp. 273–357. Claims that the factual content of theories is exhausted by observables.

Scheffler, I., "Prospects of a Modest Empiricism." *Review of Metaphysics*, Vol. 10 (1957), 1–42.

Toulmin, Stephen, *The Philosophy of Science*. London, 1953. Introductory; an instrumentalist view of theories as "inference rules."

REALISM

Carnap, Rudolf, "Empiricism, Semantics, and Ontology," *Revue internationale de philosophie*, Vol. 11 (1950), 20–40. Also in *Semantics*, pp. 208–228.

Harré, R., *Theories and Things*. London, 1961. Introductory; holds that "models" may be shown experimentally to be "real mechanisms."

Harré, R., "On the Structure of Existential Judgments." *Philosophical Quarterly*, Vol. 15 (1965), 43–52.

Hesse, Mary, "On What There Is in Physics." *British Journal for the Philosophy of Science*, Vol. 13 (1962), 234–244. Review of Harré's *Theories and Things*.

Maxwell, Grover, "The Ontological Status of Theoretical Entities," in *Minnesota* III. Pp. 3–27.

Quine, W. V. O., "On What There Is." *Review of Metaphysics*, Vol. 2 (1948), 21–38. Also in Quine's *From a Logical Point of View* and in *Semantics*, pp. 189–206.

Sellars, Wilfrid, "Philosophy and the Scientific Image of Man," in *Frontiers*. Pp. 35–78. Discusses the "manifest" image of common sense and the scientific image, and their relationship.

Sellars, Wilfrid, "Theoretical Explanation," in *Delaware* II. Pp. 61–78.

Smart, J. J. C., *Philosophy and Scientific Realism*. London, 1963.

Strawson, P. F., *Individuals. An Essay in Descriptive Metaphysics*. London, 1959.

MARY HESSE

LAWS OF SCIENCE AND LAWLIKE STATEMENTS. In the sciences a large number of statements of greater or less complexity and of apparently diverse kinds are recognized as laws. Many other statements are recognized as not being lawlike; others, again, are matters of dispute. A dispute about whether a statement is lawlike may deal with either of two questions: first, whether it has strong enough scientific support to justify its being accepted as a law; or second, whether it is of a lawlike kind. The first question is directly for scientists to settle. Although the answer that is given is to some extent related to the answer to the second question, which is the one that philosophers have been primarily interested in, the term "law" is used by scientists with no consistent meaning. It is not one of the technical terms defined by any science, and the scope of its application has varied. Once a statement is accepted in a science, it has not much mattered whether it is called a law, or principle, or theory, or anything else. What has mattered is its function within the body of statements that make up the science. Furthermore, during the period of its use, the term has undergone changes of meaning, especially since it has been associated with the terms "nature" and "natural," which are notoriously vague and ambiguous. There is now, however, agreement that a minimum necessary condition of any scientific statement proposed as lawlike is that it be a universal generalization. It is assumed in the following discussion, and in the controversy to be referred to, that this is a necessary condition of any scientific law.

It is further assumed that what are proposed as laws are either true or false and are confirmable or disprovable by statements of observation. On this assumption the interpretations of laws will differ from the interpretation offered by instrumentalism, for example, according to which laws are neither true nor false but rather devices or instruments useful for a time in explaining, predicting, and enabling men to cope practically with particular matters of fact.

Given these assumptions, the questions to be answered are: (1) What is the complete logical form of laws of science or lawlike statements? (2) What are the differences between them and other kinds of statements?

Many kinds of statements are recognized as not lawlike—for example, mathematical statements, explicit definitions, tautologies, and singular or numerical statements restricted to either individual objects or times. The main characteristics of laws that are lacking in singular and numerical statements are the universal quantifier and the timeless present tense. The other kinds of statements fail to be lawlike because they are analytic. Any claim that a statement *p* is a law entails the claim, at least, that *p* is a true, nonanalytic, universal generalization.

TWO VIEWS ABOUT THE NATURE OF LAWS

The main topic of philosophical discussion has been whether all true, nonanalytic universals are properly called laws, or whether a distinction should be made between some that are lawlike (or "nomic" or "nomological") and some that are not but are merely accidental or *de facto* universals. There are two main views; the first is here called "the necessity view," the second "the regularity view."

According to the necessity view, there is a logical distinction between lawlike and accidental universals, laws being logically stronger than accidental universals, which are coextensive with universals of fact. Laws are appropriately expressed in a modal or apodictic language, whereas accidental universals are appropriately expressed as categorical statements.

By the regularity view it is argued that there are two different distinctions covered by the terms "lawlike" and "accidental," neither of which corresponds to those claimed by the necessity view. The first distinction is between laws as unrestricted universals and accidental universals as restricted ones. The second is made within the class of unrestricted universals, so that laws are distinguished from accidental universals by the kinds of logical relation accepted universal statements have to other statements accepted within a science; in particular, this refers to the kinds of logical support universals have and consequently to the kinds of roles they play in thinking.

The point at issue may be put another way. One of the functions of a lawlike statement is to enable explanations, particularly causal explanations, to be made of specific matters of fact. Consequently, such statements are used for predictions or serve as bases for inference from observed to unobserved matters of fact. It is widely held that not only actual instances but also unrealized possibilities should come within the scope of such explanation and inference. These possibilities are instances that might occur or might have occurred in certain circumstances, although they do not or did not actually occur. According to the necessity view, such explanation is possible only if laws assert something stronger than that certain events or properties regularly occur together or succeed one another just as a matter of fact. Thus, a lawlike statement is characterized by its being necessary, which is interpreted as logical necessity by some writers and in a somewhat weaker sense by others, and its necessity is thought to lie in some connection between its terms. It is this that makes lawlike statements distinct in kind from accidental or factual universals, which, it is claimed, cannot include unrealized possibilities within their scope of application. The regularity view, however, holds that the rational consideration of unrealized instances can be accounted for in a theory asserting that nothing stronger than factual concomitance is conveyed by any universal.

Supporters of the two views. The stronger version of the necessity view can be found in the writings of philosophers who hold idealist positions, such as F. H. Bradley, B. Blanshard, A. C. Ewing, and G. F. Stout. According to this version, laws are ultimately logically necessary. E. Meyerson also supports this view, but from a different standpoint, arguing that the ultimate form of a law is an identity.

According to the weaker, or nonrationalist, version, the necessity of laws is less than logical but cannot be explained by appeal to merely contingent statements. W. E. Johnson, W. C. Kneale, and G. H. von Wright, who take it to be characteristic of laws that they apply to possible instances, explicitly hold this view. C. J. Ducasse also upholds a nonrationalist necessity in causal relations. He rejects the rationalist account of necessary connection but argues that necessary connection is an observable feature of causal situations, emphasizing change rather than constant conjunction. For Johnson and Kneale laws and universals of fact are experientially certified statements, but laws convey a necessity that sets limits to what is possible as actual fact. This is what Kneale means when he speaks of laws as principles of modality. The law "All *X* are *Y*" in principle rules out the possibility of an *X* that is not *Y* or entails that the class of *X*'s that are not *Y*'s is necessarily empty (von Wright), whereas a true universal of fact does not so restrict the possibilities. A similar view of laws is that of K. R. Popper, who speaks of them, for example, as prohibiting certain logically possible matters of fact. Popper has proposed a justification of this from the standpoint of the regularity view, although he attacks the supporters of that view who hold that laws can be established by induction.

The predominantly empiricist temper of twentieth-century philosophy has diminished support for the stronger version of the necessity view, and the dispute is now generally between the nonrationalist versions of the two views. The dispute, for example, between Kneale, on one side, and Popper, R. B. Braithwaite, and A. J. Ayer, on the other, is not about the propriety of using such terms as "nomic necessity"; rather, it is about the interpretation of these terms or the justification of their use. Briefly, the nonrationalist supporter of the necessity view takes necessity to be an intrinsic characteristic of laws, and in some way recognizable as such; in other words, in this context he takes the modal term "necessary" (or "possible" or "impossible," since these terms are interdependent or interdefinable) to be irreducible. For the supporter of the regularity view necessity is not an intrinsic characteristic of laws, nor is it irreducible.

In addition to Popper, Braithwaite, and Ayer, supporters of the regularity view include Rudolf Carnap, R. M. Chisholm, C. G. Hempel, J. L. Mackie, Ernest Nagel, Arthur Pap, Hans Reichenbach, and Bertrand Russell.

Example. A simple example illustrates the difference between the two views. Suppose it is a law, s, that sodium burns when exposed to air. This law, according to either view, can explain why a given piece of sodium burns when exposed to air and can be used to predict that a given piece of sodium will burn when exposed to air. However, it is said, further, that this law should justify both the claim that an actual piece of sodium never exposed to air would have burned had it been exposed and the claim that other substances exposed to air would be burning, or would have burned, had they been sodium. According to the necessity view, s cannot explain these unrealized instances unless it asserts more than that sodium, as a matter of fact, regularly burns when exposed to air. According to the regularity view, s can explain such instances without having to be taken to assert anything more than a factual regularity.

LAWS AS UNIVERSAL GENERALIZATION

A universal generalization may be expressed as "All A's are B's" or "For any x, if x is A then x is B." Here A and B are variables for descriptive terms, such as "pieces of sodium" and "substances that burn when exposed to air," and x is an individual variable. "All A's are B's," then, symbolizes a statement like s above, and the other statement form symbolizes a statement like "If anything is sodium then it is a substance that burns when exposed to air." As interpreted by modern logic, a statement of the first kind does not have existential import. It is equivalent to "There are no A's that are not B's" and is true if, in fact, there are no A's. (Consider "All unicorns are mammals.") A statement of the second kind, as a material implication, is also true if, in fact, nothing is A. This vacuous truth of universals, however, is never allowed as a ground for calling such statements laws, since it would entail that both "All A's are B's" and "No A's are B's" are accounted laws when there are no A's; no two statements of such forms would ever be regarded as both true in the sense in which a law is said to be true.

Some hold that only universals in which the subject term is not empty can be laws, so traditional logicians, believing all categorical statements to have existential import, can agree with modern logicians in supporting the regularity view. There are, however, in developed sciences laws with terms denoting ideal entities, such as "bodies not acted on by external forces." Supporters of the necessity view argue that the regularity view, whether based on the assumptions of traditional or of modern logic about existential import, cannot account for these entities.

By the regularity view the answer is that such laws cannot be understood apart from the body of theory of which they form part. Properly interpreted in context, these laws can be seen either to have instances, though not in the obvious way of terms in empirical generalizations, or to be logically related to statements that do; in either case their character as laws is elucidated by a consideration of their role in a theory and not by the search for some intrinsic necessity. The regularity view admits difficulties in this, but from an empiricist view these do not seem greater than trying to account for a special necessity or trying to reconcile the necessity view with the empirical procedures of science—the testing of laws by observation of matters of fact. The necessity view can be stated most strongly as a criticism of the regularity view, and for that reason the further details of the regularity view will be brought out first.

Restricted and unrestricted universals. The forerunner of the regularity view is Hume's analysis of the causal relation and his denial of cause as necessary connection. Just as Hume emphasized the fact of constant conjunction of cause and effect, so regularity theorists emphasize that the constant conjunction of events or characteristics is all that is asserted by lawlike statements.

They do, however, draw a distinction between kinds of universal statements, namely those that are restricted and those that are unrestricted. It has normally been said that only universal statements which are unrestricted can be lawlike. Those which are restricted are sometimes referred to as accidental universal statements. Arthur Pap, however, drew attention to some apparently restricted statements that are lawlike. He took unrestricted universals to be statements which do not essentially refer to or contain individual constants and restricted ones to be statements which do essentially refer to or contain individual constants. In his account a universal statement such as "All the planets continually revolve around the sun in elliptical orbits" is restricted. But it is also lawlike. The question turns upon the meaning of "restricted" and "unrestricted." Those philosophers who have argued that laws or lawlike statements are unrestricted have normally taken an unrestricted statement to be one in which the subject term does not necessarily denote a finite number of instances and have taken a restricted statement to be one in which the subject term does necessarily denote a finite number of instances. If these meanings are adopted, then Pap's objection to the regularity view may be met.

In any restricted universal statement the restriction is not a function of the universal quantifier, which is always strictly number-neutral. In other words, the quantifier "all" or "for any x" does not entail that there is any particular number of things denoted by the quantified terms. The statement "All A's are B's" is such that there might be a finite or an infinite number of A's, unless A itself entails some limit or restriction on the number denoted.

A universal statement is restricted when it is logically entailed that the term quantified denotes a closed or finite class. There are, for example, certain terms, such as "even prime" or "tallest man," whose sense entails that there can be only one entity denoted (although, as in the second case, there may in fact be no entity satisfying the description). The normal kind of restriction in universal statements is restriction to a specified finite space-time region; with certain other assumptions it is sufficient to say that the class denoted is closed, although it may not entail any particular number. This is normally an implicit kind of restriction that would have to be made explicit in any particular case. Thus, "persons now in this room" is such a restricted term, given that this room is of specifiable maximum dimensions, that persons are of specifiable minimum dimensions, and that "now" refers to a definite time. Universal statements containing these terms, such as "All persons now in this room speak French," are normally the result of summative inductions and are shorthand devices for referring to a finite conjunction of singular statements. In another way, the finite conjunction of singular statements constitutes the ground for asserting the restricted universal.

Someone who is told that A is such a restricted term and that x is an A would be able to conclude that x is a B, given that all A's are B's. If asked to suppose that x is an A when in fact it is not, he could not draw any conclusion about whether it would have been a B, since the restricted statement provides no ground for statements concerning any term not a member of the restricted class. In other words, a restricted statement provides no ground for contrary-to-fact conditional judgments such as "If x had been an A it would have been a B." It is often thought, however, by both necessity and regularity theorists, that such a contrary-to-fact conditional judgment could have been made if A had been unrestricted and if "All A's are B's" had been a lawlike statement.

LAWLIKE AND ACCIDENTAL STATEMENTS

According to the regularity view, all true unrestricted universals, if considered simply in themselves and provided they are not vacuously satisfied, are lawlike. Against this, necessity theorists have objected that there are true statements of unrestricted generality that would be called accidental, not lawlike. For example, "All ravens are black," assuming it to be true, is such an accidental statement. One way of showing its accidental character is by considering well-selected instances that are in fact unrealized; for example, the supposition that ravens have survived in snowy regions, although none in fact have, would show that the statement is accidental, since the contrary-to-fact conditional "If ravens had survived in snowy regions, they would have been black" can be shown to be false. On the other hand, the statement "All species surviving in snowy regions are white" can be shown to be lawlike since it sustains the true contrary-to-fact conditional "If ravens had survived in snowy regions, they would have been white."

More radically, however, it is objected that any statement said to be lawlike, such as the one just given, cannot at once be lawlike and assert merely a factual concomitance. The objection is that the question whether universal statements are lawlike is quite independent of the question whether they assert facts, even of unrestricted generality. Given "All A's are B's" as an unrestricted universal statement of fact, then whether the class A happens to be of finite or of infinite membership, the statement is equivalent to a conjunction of the three statements "All past A's were B's," "All present A's are B's," and "All future A's will be B's." This covers all that the necessity theorist means by universal of fact or accidental universal and is of no use in determining whether, if an A were to occur or to have occurred, it would be or would have been a B.

There are two objections here for the regularity theorist to meet. He meets the first by agreeing that there is an established sense of "law" or "lawlike" in which it seems to mean more than "unrestricted universal," since in this sense a distinction between lawlike and accidental statements is drawn within the class of true statements of unrestricted universality. Scientists do with justification distinguish between laws, on the one hand, and empirical generalizations, on the other, and regard the first as more strongly grounded than the second. The regularity theorist asserts that this is not a distinction between necessary universals and universal statements of fact but is rather a distinction between the kinds of support unrestricted universals have within a theory or a body of theory, between the kinds of evidence there are for accepting a universal as true. In this sense a statement is accidental for which the only or the main support is number of observed instances, especially when these are all very similar. In cases where a statement has the support of direct confirming evidence or observed instances and is, as well, deducible from laws of wider scope, it is regarded as lawlike. Thus, "All ravens are black," having only the support of confirming instances and not following from any statement of wider scope, can be called accidental, whereas "All species surviving in snowy regions are white," having the support of instances as well as following from the principle of natural selection, could be said to be lawlike. It is, however, the logical relations holding among the statements of a science, not the logical features of statements themselves, that determine lawlikeness in this sense. This sense amounts to the view that the characterization of universal statements as laws or lawlike depends on their functions within scientific theory.

There are two subsidiary points to note: first, statements called lawlike in this sense are normally confirmable by a greater variety of instances than those called accidental; and second, laws regarded at any time as ultimate must be recognized as lawlike, not because there are other laws from which they are deducible, since by definition there are none, but rather by the number and variety of the laws deducible from them.

The second objection to the regularity theory is that it cannot account for possible instances. If this charge were indeed well founded, it would be difficult to see how one could avoid the view that natural laws assert some kind of necessity such that they apply in all possible worlds. However, it is not established that a defender of the regularity view cannot give a plausible account of the application of laws to possible instances. He would argue that statements about possible instances stand in the same kind of logical relation to a law as do statements about actual unobserved instances. To the extent that a law enables prediction about unobserved instances, it enables justifiable claims about unrealized possibilities. There is, however, this difference between the two instances: the actual unobserved instance might in fact falsify the supposed law or suggest that it is false, whereas no such possibility of falsification is open with the unrealized instance. Apart from this, the serious consideration of an unrealized instance amounts to a serious consideration of the grounds on which the universal statement, thought to apply to the instance, is held to be true.

Bibliography

Ayer, A. J., "What Is a Law of Nature?" *Revue internationale de philosophie*, Vol. 36 (1956), Fasc. 2. Reprinted in *The Concept of a Person*. London, 1963.

Blanshard, B., *The Nature of Thought*. London, 1939. Book 4.

Blanshard, B., *Reason and Analysis*. London, 1962. Chs. 11 and 12.

Cohen, L. J., *The Diversity of Meaning*. London, 1962. Ch. 10.

Ducasse, C. J., *Causation and Types of Necessity*. University of Washington Publications in the Social Sciences, Vol. 1, No. 2 (1924).

Ewing, A. C., *Idealism, a Critical Survey*. London, 1934. Ch. 4.

Johnson, W. E., *Logic*. Cambridge, 1924. Part III, Ch.1.

Kneale, W. C., *Probability and Induction*. Oxford, 1949. Part II.

Kneale, W. C., "Universality and Necessity." *The British Journal for the Philosophy of Science*, Vol. 12 (1961), 89–102.

Meyerson, E., *Identity and Reality*, translated by K. Loewenberg. London and New York, 1930. Ch. 1.

Popper, K. R., *The Logic of Scientific Discovery*. London, 1959. Ch. 3 and New Appendix 10.

Russell, B. A. W., *Human Knowledge, Its Scope and Limits*. London, 1948. Part IV, Ch. 9.

Stout, G. F., *Mind and Matter*. Cambridge, 1931. See especially Book 4, Ch. 6.

Stout, G. F., et al., "Mechanical and Teleological Causation." Symposium, *Proceedings of the Aristotelian Society*, Suppl. Vol. 14 (1935).

Wright, G. H. von, *Logical Studies*. London, 1957. Pp. 144–162.

See also bibliography for CONTRARY-TO-FACT CONDITIONAL.

R. S. WALTERS

LAWS OF THOUGHT. The term "laws of thought" traditionally covered the principles of identity, of contradiction, of excluded middle, and occasionally the principle of sufficient reason. Whereas these principles were frequently discussed from the time of the Greeks until the beginning of the twentieth century, the term has become obsolete, for at least two good reasons. One is the great and confusing variety of meanings with which it has been used, the other is the now generally acknowledged fact that no viable system of logic can be constructed in which the principles of identity, contradiction, and excluded middle would be the only axioms. Typical discussions of these principles are to be found, for example, in Friedrich Ueberweg's *System der Logik* and in H. W. B. Joseph's *Introduction to Logic*. In the following discussion the principle of sufficient reason, which, unlike the others, cannot be interpreted as a principle of formal logic, will not be dealt with.

The three laws of thought have in the main been conceived of as descriptive, prescriptive, or formal. As *descriptive* laws, they have been regarded as descriptive (a) of the nature of "being as such," (b) of the subject matter common to all sciences, or (c) of the activity of thinking or reasoning. As *prescriptive* laws, they have been conceived of as expressing absolute or conventional standards of correct thinking or reasoning. As *formal* laws, they have been held to be propositions which are true in virtue of their form and independently of their content, true *in* all possible worlds, or true *of* any objects whatsoever, whether these objects exist or not. Distinctions between these conceptions are often blurred, since they depend on implicit and often unclear assumptions about the relations between factual, normative, and metaphysical propositions: It is, for example, rarely investigated either to what extent various kinds of rules depend for their satisfiability on what is the case or to what extent logic is or can be free from metaphysical presuppositions or implications.

All these very different conceptions of the laws of thought are compatible with their traditional formulations, which lack the precision now achievable by means of the axiomatization and formalization of theories. Examples of typical, traditional formulations are: For the law of identity, A is A; everything is what it is; every subject is its own predicate. For the law of contradiction, A is not not-A; judgments contradictorily opposed to each other cannot both be true. For the law of excluded middle, everything is either A or not-A; judgments opposed as contradictories cannot both be false, nor can they admit the truth of a third or middle judgment, but one or the other must be true, and the truth of the one follows from the falsehood of the other. An obvious ambiguity concerning the law of identity is connected with the question whether "is" is to be taken as expressing equality or as the copula between subject and predicate, and, in the latter case, whether or not it implies the existence of the subject. Again, the term "not" admits of different interpretations according to different metaphysical and logical assumptions about negation.

DESCRIPTIVE INTERPRETATIONS

Metaphysical interpretation. For Aristotle, who discussed the laws of thought in his logical and metaphysical works, they are primarily descriptive of being as such and only secondarily standards of correct thinking. It is thus a metaphysical or ontological impossibility that "the same can and cannot belong to the same in the same reference" (*Metaphysics* III, 2, 2), from which it follows as a rule of correct thought and speech that it is incorrect to assert that "the same is and is not" (*Metaphysics* IV, 6, 12). Aristotle produced seven "proofs" to demonstrate the indispensability of the law of contradiction. With a similar intention, formal logicians are nowadays wont to show that its negation implies any proposition whatever (and thus also the law of contradiction itself) by some such reasoning as the following: (1) To assume that the law of contradiction is false is to assume for some proposition p that p and not-p are both true. (2) From the truth of p it follows that "p or x" is also true, where x is an arbitrary proposition and "or" is used in the nonexclusive sense of "and/or." (3) From the truth of "p or x" and the truth of not-p the truth of x follows. But x is an arbitrary proposition for which, for example, the law of contradiction may be chosen.

Aristotle's defense of the law of contradiction as descriptive of "being as such" includes implicitly a defense of the metaphysical principle of identity against Heraclitus, who held it possible for the same thing to be and not to be and who explained the concept of becoming as implying the falsehood of the principle that everything is what it is. Before Aristotle this metaphysical principle had been defended by Parmenides.

Aristotle's arguments for the truth of the principle of excluded middle are again metaphysical. They are connected with his rejection of the Platonic doctrine that attempts to mediate between Heraclitus and Parmenides. The changing sensible and material objects, which in Plato's phrase "tumble about between being and nonbeing," are placed by Plato between the eternal Forms, which fully and truly exist, and that which does not exist at all, that is, they are "a third" between being and nonbeing. The metaphysical principle of excluded middle, as understood by Aristotle, excludes any such third. This principle has sometimes been taken to imply fatalism: since of any two contradictory statements one must be true, of any two contradictory statements about the future one must be true, so that, it is argued, the future is wholly determined. In a famous passage about "the sea fight tomorrow" Aristotle refutes this argument: It is, he points out, necessary that the sea fight will or will not take place tomorrow. But it is not true that it will *necessarily* take place tomorrow or *necessarily* not take place tomorrow. Indeed the logical necessity of a disjunction "*p* or not-*p*" does not imply that either *p* or not-*p* is a necessary proposition (see DETERMINISM).

Metaphysical refutation. Heraclitus, Parmenides, Plato, and Aristotle conceived of the laws of thought as controversial metaphysical principles, and just as Aristotle attempted their justification on metaphysical grounds, so did Hegel, Marx, and Engels attempt their refutation on metaphysical grounds. Hegel's attack was based on his distinction between abstract understanding, which petrifies and thus misdescribes the ever-changing "dialectical" process that is reality, and reason, which apprehends its true nature. Hegel objected to the principle that *A* is *A* or, what for him amounts to the same thing, that *A* cannot at the same time be *A* and not-*A* because "no mind thinks or forms conceptions or speaks in accordance with this law, and . . . no existence of any kind whatever conforms to it" (*Die Encyclopädie der philosophischen Wissenschaften*). For Hegel contradiction is not a relation which holds merely between propositions but one that is also exemplified in the real world, for example, in such phenomena as the polarity of magnetism, the antithesis between organic and inorganic matter, and even the complementarity of complementary colors. With such an interpretation it becomes possible for him to assert that "contradiction is the very moving principle of the world" and that "it is ridiculous to say that contradiction is unthinkable." Aristotle's metaphysics corresponds to a logic in which the metaphysical principles of identity, contradiction, and excluded middle have their logical counterpart in corresponding laws of reasoning. The counterpart of Hegel's rejection of these metaphysical principles is not any traditional logical theory but a "dialectical" logic, or dialectics.

The Hegelian point of view was adopted by Marx and Engels with the difference that they conceived reality not as ideal but as material. Engels, unlike Hegel, did not even acknowledge the law of identity as valid for the ab-

stractions of mathematics. His arguments, based on the alleged structure of the differential and integral calculus, seem—at least today—confused. He held, for example, that under certain circumstances straight lines and curves are literally identical.

Empirical interpretation. From the conception of the laws of thought as descriptive of "being as such," whatever this may mean precisely, we must distinguish the conception of them as empirical generalizations of very high order. This view was most clearly expressed by John Stuart Mill in his *System of Logic* (London, 1843). Thus, he regarded the principle of contradiction as one "of our first empirical generalizations from experience" and as "originally founded on our distinction between belief and disbelief as two different mutually exclusive states" (*System of Logic*, Book II, Ch. 7). He similarly argued that the empirical character of the law of excluded middle follows from, among other things, the fact that it requires for its truth a large qualification, namely "that the predicate in any affirmative categorical proposition must be capable of being meaningfully attributed to the subject, since between the true and the false there is the third possibility of the meaningless" (*ibid.*). Mill's view must not be taken to imply that the laws of thought are psychological laws, describing the processes of thought—a view which rests on a confusion between thinking and correct thinking.

PRESCRIPTIVE INTERPRETATIONS

Regulative interpretation. Another interpretation of the laws of thought regards them as in some sense prescriptive—based on some absolute authority, by analogy with moral laws, or based on conventions admitting of possible alternatives, by analogy with municipal laws. Traces of the former view are, for example, still found in J. N. Keynes' *Formal Logic*, one of the last valuable treatises on traditional formal logic. According to the preface of this work, logic deals with the laws regulating the processes of formal reasoning purely as "regulative and authoritative" and as affording criteria for the discrimination between valid and invalid reasoning.

Conventionalist interpretation. Versions of the conception that all logical principles are based on conventions have rarely been worked out with sufficient care. According to A. J. Ayer's *Language, Truth and Logic* (1936; 2d ed., 1946) every logical principle is based on conventions. Thus "not (*p* and not-*p*)" is logically necessary because the use of "and" and "not" is governed by certain linguistic conventions, which are neither true nor false. Yet given these conventions the proposition "not (*p* and not-*p*)," that is, the law of contradiction, is necessarily true. Ayer and those who have held similar views never consider the question whether, and to what extent, linguistic conventions depend on some nonconventional framework which restricts one's freedom to formulate, accept, or reject them. Can one, for example, by adopting suitable conventions for the use of "or" and "not" really think or speak in contravention of the principle which under the usual conventions is expressed by "not (*p* and not-*p*)"?

Conventionalism is most plausible when it explains the necessity of alternative systems of definitions and of alternative systems of logic as being based on conventions, in the sense of rules whose acceptance is not obligatory. In the case of the law of contradiction no alternative is conceivable, so that the "convention" on which it is based would have to be obligatory in a sense in which the other conventions are not. However, an admission of "conventions obligatory for all thinkers" would bring conventionalism much nearer to views of logic which, at least prima facie, it seems to reject.

FORMAL INTERPRETATIONS

Leibniz and Kant. According to Leibniz there are two kinds of truths, truths of fact and truths of reason, truths of reason being true in all possible worlds and therefore descriptive of facts in such a way that not even God can change them. Leibniz regarded as a necessary and sufficient condition for a truth's being a truth of reason, and thus logically necessary, that its analysis should reveal it to depend wholly on propositions whose negation involves a contradiction, that is, on identical propositions (see, for example, *Monadology*, Secs. 31–35). He even held, in the second letter to Samuel Clarke, that the law of contradiction is "by itself sufficient" for the demonstration of "the whole of arithmetic and geometry." Although the thesis that all logical, as well as all mathematical, truths are demonstrable by means of the law of contradiction alone is, from the point of view of contemporary knowledge, mistaken or at least obscurely expressed, the characterization of logical truths as true in all possible worlds is still the root of the Bolzano–Tarski definition of logical validity (see BOLZANO, BERNARD; and SEMANTICS).

Although Kant opposed the Leibnizian doctrine that the truths of mathematics are logical truths, he adhered to the principle of contradiction as the supreme principle of all logical truths or, more precisely, as the "general and wholly sufficient principle of all analytical knowledge." Since the truth of such knowledge in no way depends on whether or not the objects which are referred to exist, the principle of contradiction is a necessary but not a sufficient condition of factual knowledge. What is true of possible objects must be true of all actual ones—what is true in all possible worlds must be true of the actual one. But since the converse statement is false, the principles of formal logic cannot be an "organon" of any particular science, that is, a means for attaining knowledge of its subject matter. (See *Kritik der reinen Vernunft*, 2d ed., introduction to Part II of "Transcendentale Elementarlehre.")

Contemporary logic. In contemporary logical theory the conception of "true in every possible world" or "true of any objects whatever" has been sharpened into the conception of valid statement forms and valid statements which are well formed in accordance with the precisely formulated syntactical rules of elementary logic—propositional calculus, quantification theory, and theory of identity. A distinction is made between the logical particles, or constants, on the one hand and nonlogical constants and variables on the other. The logical constants are (1) "¬," "∨," "∧," and other connectives, whose intended interpretations are, respectively, "not," "or," "and," etc., conceived as connecting true or false propositions so as to form other true or false propositions in such a way that the truth or falsehood of any compound statement depends only on the truth or falsehood of the component statements; (2) the quantifiers "∀" and "∃," the intended interpretation of which is such that "∀x Px" and "∃x Px" mean, respectively, that for a well-demarcated domain of individuals, which may be finite or infinite, every element x has the predicate P, and that there exists an individual x which possesses P (in addition to such monadic predicates as Px, such dyadic predicates as Pxy and polyadic predicates are also admitted, so that, for example, ∀x ∃y Pxy, ∀x ∀y Pxy, etc., are also admitted); and (3) the sign "=" with the intended interpretation as identity of individuals. The nonlogical constants are (a) names of specific individuals, such as "Socrates" or, indeterminately, "x_0," (b) names of specific predicates, such as "green" or, indeterminately, "P_0," where two predicate names which are truly asserted of the same individuals of the given domain are regarded as naming the same predicate, (c) names of specific statements, such as "Socrates is mortal" or, indeterminately, "p_0." The variables are individual variables such as "x," predicate variables such as "P," and statement variables such as "p." Variables are either free (or, more precisely, free for substitution by names of corresponding constants) or bound by a quantifier so that, for example, "Px" contains a free individual variable and a free predicate variables, whereas ∀x Px contains only a free predicate variable. (For a more precise description of the syntactical structure of elementary logic and its interpretation, see LOGIC, MODERN.)

A well-formed formula of elementary logic which contains free variables is a statement form. A statement form is valid if—with the intended interpretation of the logical constants—every substitution instance of it is valid in every nonempty domain, provided that every individual, predicate, and statement variable is replaced by the same individual, predicate, and statement constant wherever it occurs in the statement form. Clearly the laws of thought are valid statement forms in, for example, the following formulations: Principle of identity: $x = x$. Principle of contradiction: ¬$(p ∧ ¬p)$, ∀x ¬$(Px ∧ ¬Px)$. Principle of excluded middle: $p ∨ ¬p$, $(∀x Px) ∨ (∃x ¬Px)$. It is equally clear that many other well-formed formulas such as ¬¬p ∨ ¬p are valid. Valid statement forms which contain only statement variables have been called tautologies by Wittgenstein.

The great precision and clarity given to the conception of the laws of thought as principles of formal logic has, however, not lifted them out of the range of philosophical controversy. Thus, intuitionist philosophers of mathematics argue that the principle of excluded middle is valid only for finite domains and that the extension of its validity to the nonfinite domain of arithmetic is based on the mistaken notion of an actually infinite domain of natural numbers, a notion which unjustifiably assimilates the number sequence to a finite class of objects. Similarly, they deny the validity of other classically valid statement forms, such as ¬¬p → ¬p. (See MATHEMATICS, FOUNDATIONS OF.)

The results of modern mathematical logic have deprived the laws of thought of their privileged status as the supreme principles of all logical truths. But since these results do not imply that there is only one true logic, the choice between classical elementary logic, intuitionist logic, and perhaps some other logical theories still depends, at least at the present time, on extralogical, philosophical arguments.

Bibliography

Aristotle, *Metaphysics*.

Ayer, A. J., *Language, Truth and Logic*. London, 1936; 2d ed., 1946.

Engels, Friedrich, *Herrn Eugen Dührings Umwälzung der Wissenschaft*. Leipzig, 1878. Translated by E. Burns as *Herr Eugen Dühring's Revolution in Science*. London, 1934.

Hahn, Hans, *Logik, Mathematik und Naturerkennen*. Vienna, 1933. Partially translated by Arthur Pap as "Logic, Mathematics and Knowledge of Nature" in A. J. Ayer, ed., *Logical Positivism*. Glencoe, Ill., 1959. Pp. 147–161.

Hegel, G. W. F., *Die Encyclopädie der philosophischen Wissenschaften*. Heidelberg, 1817. Partially translated by W. Wallace as *The Logic of Hegel*, Oxford, 1873, and *Hegel's Philosophy of Mind*, Oxford, 1892.

Husserl, Edmund, *Logische Untersuchungen*, 2 vols. Halle, 1900–1901. Chs. 4 and 5.

Joseph, H. W. B., *Introduction to Logic*. Oxford, 1906; 2d ed., 1925.

Kant, Immanuel, *Kritik der reinen Vernunft*, 2d ed. Riga, 1787.

Keynes, J. N., *Studies and Exercises in Formal Logic*. London and New York, 1884.

Leibniz, G. W., *Monadology*, in *The Monadology and Other Writings*. Translated by Robert Latta. Oxford, 1898.

Nagel, Ernest, "Logic Without Ontology." in Y. H. Krikorian, ed., *Naturalism and the Human Spirit*. New York, 1944. Reprinted in Nagel's *Logic Without Metaphysics*. Glencoe, Ill., 1956.

Russell, Bertrand, *The Problems of Philosophy*. London, 1912.

Ueberweg, Friedrich, *System der Logik*. Bonn, 1857. Translated by T. M. Lindsay as *System of Logic*. London, 1871.

Wittgenstein, Ludwig, *Tractatus Logico-philosophicus*. London, 1922.

S. KÖRNER

LEBENSPHILOSOPHIE. See PHILOSOPHICAL ANTHROPOLOGY.

LE CLERC, JEAN

(1657–1736), philosopher and Arminian theologian. Although Le Clerc was not a major figure, he had a considerable influence on eighteenth-century French philosophy. He championed rational religion, which was later widely accepted, and was also the first disciple of John Locke, whose work he introduced to Continental audiences. Through his learned reviews, the *Bibliothèque universelle et historique* (1686–1693), the *Bibliothèque choisie* (1703–1713), and the *Bibliothèque ancienne et moderne* (1714–1727), he stated and defended Locke's views.

Raised in Geneva during a period of strife over the Calvinist dogma of predestination, Le Clerc was a confirmed rationalist when he left the Geneva Academy. He believed that the fundamentals of Christianity (God's existence and the divinity of Scripture) are capable of demonstration. Scripture must be rationally interpreted; one cannot believe what conflicts with rational truths, and doctrines over which rational men disagree are not essentials of faith. For this doctrine, Le Clerc was expelled from Geneva in 1683.

He went first to England and then settled permanently in Holland, a haven for political and religious exiles. He found a spiritual home in the rationalistic Remonstrant church and soon became professor of Hebrew, philosophy, and belles-lettres at the Remonstrant College at Amsterdam. At this time Le Clerc met Locke, then in exile, and acquired a systematic philosophy. In 1688, two years before the English publication of the *Essay Concerning Human Understanding*, he printed a long French summary in his *Bibliothèque universelle*. He also helped popularize many other English writers and published a long review of Berkeley's *New Theory of Vision* in the *Bibliothèque choisie* (1711).

Le Clerc's philosophy was purely Lockian. He rejected innate ideas, used the notion of abstract ideas, and continued the critique of the idea of substance. He opposed Descartes, Malebranche, Spinoza, and Leibniz because their theories claim knowledge beyond human ideas. However, whereas Locke was indifferent to the rise of radical skepticism, Le Clerc was quite critical of it. He vigorously asserted the reality of human knowledge, although restricting its scope, and tried to refute each of the leading skeptics (Sextus Empiricus, Montaigne, Pierre Daniel Huet, and Pierre Bayle). He became involved in an acrimonious dispute with Bayle, who argued that the conflict between fundamental Christian doctrines and the principles of reason must be considered as a basis for skepticism regarding reason. To Le Clerc, Bayle's view led to irreligion or fanaticism. He insisted that reason is the criterion of truth and that faith and reason are compatible.

Works by Le Clerc

Vita et Opera ad Annum 1711. Amsterdam, 1711. This work includes the philosophical texts listed separately below.

Logica, sive Ars Ratiocinandi. Amsterdam, 1694.

Ontologia, sive de Ente in Genere & Pneumatologia. Amsterdam, 1694.

Physica, sive de Rebus Corporeus libri quinque. Amsterdam, 1696.

Works on Le Clerc

Barnes, Annie, *Jean Le Clerc et la république des lettres*. Paris, 1938. Contains details on Le Clerc's often stormy career.

Colie, Rosalie, *Light and Enlightenment, a Study of the Cambridge Platonists and Dutch Arminians*. Cambridge, 1957. Contains a discussion of Le Clerc's thought.

Haag, Eugene, and Haag, Émile, *La France protestante*. Paris, 1846. This work and the Barnes mentioned above contain bibliographies of Le Clerc's diverse works on philosophy, theology, history, philology, and Biblical criticism.

PHILLIP D. CUMMINS

LECOMTE DU NOÜY, PIERRE ANDRÉ

(1883–1947), French biophysicist and writer on the philosophy of science. Born in Paris, he studied law at the Sorbonne and had a brief career as a playwright and actor; he then returned to the Sorbonne in 1913 to study physics and chemistry. His friendship with Sir William Ramsay led him to the application of the methods of physics to biological problems. While working with Dr. Alexis Carrel at a front-line hospital during World War I, he discovered a mathematical law that applied to the rate of healing of wounds, and he presented this discovery in a thesis for the doctorate of science at the University of Paris in 1917. From 1920 to 1927 he was a member of the Rockefeller Institute for Medical Research in New York, and from 1927 to 1936 he directed a biophysical laboratory at the Institut Pasteur in Paris. After the German occupation of France, he returned to the United States.

In his earlier years Lecomte du Noüy was an agnostic, influenced by Renan and Taine, but toward the close of his life he became deeply committed to theism. This led him to stress the limitations of science and to deny knowledge in order to leave room for faith.

His most substantial treatment of a philosophical topic occurs in *Biological Time*. Using experimental data and mathematical calculations based on his study of cicatrization, he argued that the standard division into objective (physical or sidereal) time and subjective (psychological) time is not exhaustive. There is a third kind of time, physiological or biochemical, capable of being measured quantitatively by the rate of tissue repair in living organisms. This rate, however, is variable, being—in most human beings—four times slower at age fifty than at age ten. It is as if each person had an internal chemical clock that runs more rapidly as he grows older. "Everything, therefore, occurs as if sidereal time flowed four times faster for a man of fifty than for a child of ten. A year is physiologically and psychologically much longer for a child than for its parents." Lecomte du Noüy then contended, as had Bergson, that objective time is an intellectual construction, not something that exists or flows apart from man. Real time is individual, physiological time, which is variable and granular rather than uniform and continuous. Universal time is "a mere conceptual envelope" for this reality.

In *Human Destiny*, his popular work on evolution, Lecomte du Noüy aimed to refute atheistic materialism by showing that a proper understanding of evolution "leads inevitably to the idea of God." Materialism, on his view, affirms that life evolved by chance alone. But this, he asserted, was demonstrably impossible. Using figures derived from the Swiss scientist C. E. Guye, who had calculated the probability of the formation of a protein molecule by the random coming together of the right atoms as of the order of 1:100[160], he argued that the earth has not existed nearly long enough for such a fantastically improbable event to have occurred. The origin of life must therefore have been due to "anti-chance." Furthermore, the evolution of living beings is in "absolute contradiction" to the second law of thermodynamics, "the keystone of our science." No scientific law can explain the antientropic sweep of evolution toward the production of the human brain and spirit. We are driven to espouse "a teleological hypothesis, that is, a finalism with a very ultimate goal, a *telefinalism*." But telefinalism implies that a supreme, transcendent intelligence, or God, underlies the whole evolutionary process. This concept is needed to fill in the vast blanks contained in the scientific world picture. Science has taught us how little we really know about anything and how much place there is for a religious faith that will help man fulfill his destiny.

Lecomte du Noüy's books cannot be said to have great philosophical value. Even his grasp of scientific doctrines has been questioned. Although *Human Destiny* was a favorite with the general reading public and with apologists for religious orthodoxy, critics have pointed out its gross misinterpretations of probability, thermodynamics, and evolutionary theory.

Works by Lecomte du Noüy

Le Temps et la vie. Paris, 1936. Translated as *Biological Time*. London, 1936.

L'Homme devant la science. Paris, 1939. Translated by Mary Lecomte du Noüy as *The Road to Reason*. London, 1948.

Human Destiny. New York, 1948.

Works on Lecomte du Noüy

Lecomte du Noüy, Mary, *Lecomte du Noüy: de l'agnosticisme à la foi*. Paris, 1955. Translated as *Road to Human Destiny: A Life of Pierre Lecomte du Noüy*. New York, 1955.

Nagel, Ernest, "Pseudo-Science as a Guide to Human Destiny," in *Logic Without Metaphysics*. Glencoe, Ill., 1956. Pp. 419–422.

T. A. GOUDGE

LEGAL POSITIVISM. In many discussions of the nature of law the terms "legal positivism" and "natural law" are assumed to be the names of rival theories. In fact, each of these designations stands for a number of different and logically distinct doctrines, with the unfortunate result that in many disputes between "positivism" and "natural law" the precise point of conflict is unclear and the classification of a legal theorist as a "positivist" may afford very little indication of the nature of his theory. Thus, what is called the imperative theory of law, that is, the view that laws are commands, is usually treated as a central tenet of legal positivism; but although Jeremy Bentham and John Austin held this view, Hans Kelsen (usually regarded as the most uncompromising of modern legal positivists) held neither this view nor its corollary, that international law is not really law but a mere species of morality. Similarly, "legal positivism" is sometimes used as a designation for a thesis concerning the nature of moral judgments, including those made about the justice or injustice or the goodness or badness of human laws. This is the thesis (sometimes termed "noncognitivism") that such judgments cannot be established by reasoning but are merely expressions of human feelings or choices or "prescriptions." Kelsen held this view of moral judgments but Bentham and Austin did not. Bentham and Austin were both utilitarians who considered that moral judgments could be rationally established by the application of the test of utility, which according to Austin was also an "index" of God's commands.

A variety of other doctrines about law, besides those mentioned above, have been described as "positivist." These include the doctrine that although law and morals may often overlap or be causally related, there is no necessary or conceptual connection between them; the doctrine that judicial decisions are or should be deducible by logical means from legal rules and involve no choice or creative activity on the part of the judge; and the doctrine that there is an absolute moral obligation to obey the law, however morally iniquitous it may be.

The etymology of the word "positivism" and cognate expressions offers little guidance to its use in the philosophy of law. Since at least the fourteenth century, the expression "positive law" has been used to refer to laws laid down or made by human beings in contrast to natural or divine law, which is regarded as something discovered and not made by man. But the expression "positive law" has also long been used to refer to any law brought into being by a command or act of will and so includes the law of God as well as human legislation. More recently, the use of the expression "legal positivism" has been colored by the philosophical sense of "positivism" introduced by Auguste Comte. In this sense a "positivist" doctrine is one according to which nothing can be truthfully (or in later versions, meaningfully) said to exist unless it is in principle observable by human beings.

More important for legal theory than the etymology of the word is the identification and classification of the principal issues in relation to which philosophers of law or legal theorists have advanced views commonly styled positivist. Five such issues may be distinguished, and the discussion of these constitutes the remainder of this article.

Positivism as a theory of a form of legal study. Bentham, Austin, and Kelsen, while differing as noted above on certain points, agreed that there is an important branch of legal study distinguished by two features: that it is not concerned with any ideal law or legal system but only with actual or existent law and legal systems; and that its concern with law is morally, politically, and evaluatively neutral. The object of this form of legal study is the clarification of the meaning of law, the identification of the characteristic structure of a legal system, and the analysis of pervasive and fundamental legal notions, such as right, duty, ownership, or legal personality. Bentham, Austin, and Kelsen were all concerned to distinguish such an "analytical" jurisprudence, as this form of legal study is now called, from critical or evaluative studies of the law, and they have stressed the importance of this distinction. However, none of these theorists—though the contrary is sometimes suggested—considered that analytical jurisprudence excluded critical or evaluative studies of the law or rendered them unimportant.

It should be observed that belief in the importance of analytical studies of the law does not strictly entail belief in other forms of legal positivism, though in fact it has usually been associated with one or more of these other forms. It is also true that not all morally or evaluatively neutral studies of the law need take an analytical form. Many sociological descriptions of the operation of law and society, and many sociological theories of the causal connection between law and other social phenomena are also evaluatively neutral, at least in intention. Hence, some of these, too, have at times been regarded as forms of positivism.

Positivism in the definition of law. The definition of law as the command of the "sovereign" is no doubt the most prominent example of a form of positivism. But the expression "positivist" is also used in a wider sense to include any doctrine according to which law is defined as the expression of human will or as man-made, even if it does not take the form of a command. Thus, both the doctrines known in American jurisprudence by the loose title of "legal realism," according to which only decisions of courts and the predictions of such decisions are law, and those theories of international law which insist that it is composed exclusively of rules originating in custom or in agreements between states are usually described as positivist. It is to be noted, however, that both Bentham and Austin, who defined law as the command of a sovereign,

extended the notion of a command to include both customary law and judge-made law. For this purpose they invoked the idea of a "tacit," or "indirect," command resting on the principle that whatever the sovereign permits he commands.

Positivism as a theory of the judicial process. Sometimes the term "legal positivism" is used to refer to the view that correct legal decisions are uniquely determined by pre-existing legal rules and that the courts either do or should reach their decisions solely by logical deduction from a conjunction of a statement of the relevant legal rules and a statement of the facts of the case. This is sometimes referred to as the "automatic" or "slot-machine" conception of the judicial process; but it is doubtful whether any Anglo-American writer who is usually classified as a positivist would subscribe to any such view. It is true, however, that Bentham and Austin thought that the area of choice allowed to judges by a system of case law was excessive and led to great uncertainty, and they claimed that this could and should be drastically reduced by classification and codification of the law in clear and detailed terms. But they were both well aware of the fact of judicial legislation and creative activity, and as noted above, they sought to reconcile this fact with their definition of law as the command of the sovereign by using the idea of a tacit command. The doctrine that a judge should not exercise choice in his decision of cases but should merely be the mouthpiece of previously existing law is to be found in the works of eighteenth-century writers not usually classed as positivists, such as Montesquieu's *L'Esprit des lois*. They looked upon this doctrine as a corollary of the doctrine of the separation of powers and as a protection of the individual against arbitrary decisions, uncertainty, and privilege.

Positivism as a theory of law and morals. It seems that all writers classed as positivists have subscribed to the view that unless the law itself provides to the contrary, the fact that a legal rule is morally iniquitous or unjust does not entail that it is invalid or not law. This view may also be expressed as the claim that no reference to justice or other moral values enters into the definition of law. "The existence of law is one thing: its merit or demerit another" (Austin). "Legal norms may have any kind of content" (Kelsen). Such a denial of a necessary or definitional connection between law or legal validity and morality is perhaps the principal point of conflict between legal positivism and theories of natural law. For nearly all variants of the latter refuse to recognize as law or legally valid rules that violate certain fundamental moral principles. It is, however, important to remember that this denial of a necessary connection between law and morals is compatible with the recognition of many other important connections between them. Thus few, if any, positivists have denied that the development of the law has in fact been influenced by morality or that moral considerations should be taken into account by legislators and also by judges in choosing between competing interpretations or conflicting claims as to what the law is.

Positivism and the obligation to obey law. If positivism has become a pejorative term, it is very largely because it has been identified by some critics with the claim that where a legal system is in operation, there is an unconditional moral obligation to obey the law, however unjust or iniquitous it may be. This claim may be based either on the view that there is a moral obligation to obey law as such or on the belief that the actual existence of a legal system, however oppressive or unjust, provides large numbers of human beings with a minimum of peace, order, and security and that these are values which no individual is morally justified in jeopardizing by resistance to the law. The German legal theorist K. M. Bergbohm, perhaps the best-known legal positivist in continental Europe in the nineteenth century, held this view; but though he in fact also subscribed to other forms of legal positivism described above, this view is logically quite independent of them. Utilitarian positivists, such as Bentham and Austin, held that resistance to law might be justified in extreme cases, but before this step was taken, careful calculations in terms of utility were necessary to ascertain that a balance of good over evil was likely to result. They criticized the doctrine of natural law and natural rights not because they believed that there was an unconditional obligation to obey the law, but because in their view these doctrines presented standing temptations for men to revolt without making such calculations of the consequences.

Works by Legal Positivists

Austin, John, *The Province of Jurisprudence Defined*. London, 1832.

Austin, John, *Lectures on Jurisprudence, or the Philosophy of Positive Law*. London, 1863.

Austin, John, *Essay on the Uses of the Study of Jurisprudence*. London, 1863.

Bentham, Jeremy, *A Fragment on Government*. London, 1776.

Bentham, Jeremy, *The Limits of Jurisprudence Defined*. New York, 1945.

Bentham, Jeremy, *Introduction to the Principles of Morals and Legislation*. London, 1789.

Bentham, Jeremy, *The Theory of Legislation*, 2 vols. London, 1931.

Bergbohm, K. M., *Jurisprudenz und Rechtsphilosophie*. Berlin, 1892.

Kelsen, Hans, *The General Theory of Law and State*. Cambridge, Mass., 1945.

Works on Legal Positivism

Fuller, Lon, "Positivism and Fidelity to Law." *Harvard Law Review*, Vol. 71 (1958), 630–672.

Gray, J. C., *The Nature and Sources of Law*. New York, 1909.

Hart, H. L. A., *The Concept of Law*. Oxford, 1961.

Holmes, O. W., "The Path of the Law," in his *Collected Legal Papers*. Boston, 1920.

Morison, W. L., "Some Myths about Positivism." *Yale Law Journal*, Vol. 68 (1958), 217–222.

Pound, Roscoe, "Mechanical Jurisprudence." *Columbia Law Review*, Vol. 8 (1908), 605 ff.

Roguin, E., *La Science juridique pure*. Paris, 1923.

Ross, Alf, *On Law and Justice*. London, 1958.

Stone, J., *The Province and Function of Law*. London, 1950.

Numerous articles critical of various forms of legal positivism may be found in the *Natural Law Forum*, published since 1955 by the Notre Dame Law School.

H. L. A. HART

LEGAL REALISM. Beginning about 1920, an iconoclastic group of American legal writers, led by K. N. Llewellyn, Walter Wheeler Cook, Jerome Frank, Herman Oliphant, and Underhill Moore, denounced the established legal tradition as formalistic and conservative. That tradition, they charged, wrongly saw the law as a complete and autonomous system of logically consistent principles, concepts, and rules. To apply the law was to unfold the ineluctable implications of those rules. The judge's techniques were socially neutral, his private views irrelevant; judging was more like finding than making, a matter of necessity rather than choice. The realists, by contrast, saw legal certainty as rarely attainable and perhaps even undesirable in a changing society. In their view the paramount concern of the law was not logical consistency but socially desirable consequences. Law was an instrument of government, and jurisprudence should focus less on legal concepts than on social facts.

Basis of legal realism. According to the realists, legal decisions were not compelled; choice was necessary at every step. Just as lawmakers built their ideological preferences into a statute, judges built theirs into their formulation of "the facts" of a case. Legal concepts represented nothing more than tentative decisions to consider diverse cases identical with respect to a given concern. Unless readjusted continually, such concepts could then be rendered irrelevant by changing circumstances and purposes.

Realism meant opposition to illusion or pretense, sometimes to abstractions or appearances. Judges had always made law, but now, the realists insisted, they must know and say that they did. They must acknowledge their responsibility instead of attributing their choices, through tortured technicalities, to the compulsions of legal doctrine. (Oliver Wendell Holmes, the favorite judge of the realists, had said that law becomes more civilized as it becomes more self-conscious.) If the judges' latent motives and official reasons were reconciled, their judgments would be not only more honest but more informed. Moreover, assumptions about the nature of law could then be considered in the light of scientific knowledge of the actual workings of legal institutions, and assumptions about social policy could be seen in the light of scientific knowledge about society. The realists took the possibility of such scientific knowledge for granted. They further assumed that society had its own mechanisms for effecting changes and that, in general, the law should reflect social change, not shape it. Yet the realists avoided the conservative conclusions that usually accompany this view, for being, above all, reformers, they believed that the constant flux of modern society required a legal system flexible enough to match its pace.

Like other iconoclasts, the realists saw rationalization and self-deception beneath traditional claims to objectivity. They "saw through" appearances, theories, and justifications to underlying motivations or functions. They sought complete candor. The natural sciences provided their model; John Dewey, their philosophical vocabulary. They also drew on the tradition of sociological jurisprudence, which in both Europe and America had already prescribed the study of society as the proper way to discover social preferences beneath the neutral forms of the law.

These ideas were more influential in America because of the unique power of American judges to declare statutes unconstitutional. Moreover, the differences among the states in their approach to identical legal problems frustrated belief in inexorable solutions. Thus, Holmes had asserted since the 1870s that "the true grounds of decision are considerations of policy and of social advantage." John Chipman Gray saw the sources of law brought to life only in the crucial act of judicial interpretation; he believed that since courts have the last word, "all law is judge-made law." At the turn of the century Roscoe Pound attacked "mechanical jurisprudence," distinguished "law in action" from "law in books," and conceived of a sociological jurisprudence that would increase legal sensitivity to social needs and to the social effects of legal rules.

The realists were distinctive, however, in their preoccupation with the processes of judicial decision, with how law is made. They put forward a theory of precedent starting from Llewellyn's assertion that "a case stands not for one thing, but for a wide variety of things." Following Dewey, for whom a judgment was always somebody judging something, they stressed the crucial position of the judge who decided whether a case was "the same" as a previous case—that is, which similarities between them should be considered important. Skeptical of principles abstracted from a particular factual context, the realists found support in the common-law tradition that principles should evolve from rather than precede the disposition of particular cases. They trusted the judge's trained reaction to the entire set of facts before him—his "intuition of experience" (Oliphant), which depended on "knowing how" rather than "knowing that"—much more than they trusted the justification he supplied in his opinion. They therefore wanted precedents to be based on what a court actually did in response to a particular set of facts, not on its language. But emphasizing particularity means getting less direction from previous cases, for facts vary enormously. The more that precedent presupposes factual similarity between cases, the fewer its applications; future judges are freer. No two cases are identical, and if any distinction distinguishes, no precedents are possible. Logically, it is always open to a judge to decide either way, to see a previous case as a precedent or not. Some realists therefore concluded that every decision was a "free" moral decision. This conclusion, shorn of the analysis of the logic of precedent behind it and interpreted simply as giving judges greater discretionary power than the traditional view allowed them, was seen by most of the legal community as the essential message of legal realism.

Rise of legal realism. Grant Gilmore has related the realist's view of precedent to the remarkable increase, starting around 1890, in the amount of litigation and in the proportion of cases reported, an increase that threatened to inundate a system depending on "a comfortable number of precedents, but not too many." According to Gilmore, the realists responded to this crisis by allowing fewer cases to count as precedents. In this way, Gilmore has noted, legal realism was part of the major social developments of 1880–1930, notably the rise of urbanism and modern industrialism and technology; during this period realism was not confined to the law. The search for fact, for concreteness, for the truth behind appearances, can be found everywhere—in literature, in painting, in social criticism. Consider, for example, the salient characteristics of a movement quite unrelated to legal theory—progressive education. For both progressive education and legal realism, pursuing "reality" meant going from theoretical formulas to what worked in practice, from books to life, from text to context, from passively and mechanically transmitting a received tradition to actively and flexibly responding to each pupil or case. Both progressive education and legal realism flourished in the 1930s during the New Deal. Both can be seen as to some extent a response to sheer numbers, to universal education and the increase in litigation, respectively.

Influence of legal realism. Throughout the law the realists contributed to greater candor about the social bases of decision. They also suggested specific improvements in practical areas of the law—for example, Charles E. Clark on covenants' running with the land, Walter Wheeler Cook on conflict of laws, Arthur Corbin on contracts, Leon Green on torts, and K. N. Llewellyn on sales. On the other hand, they underestimated the role of generalization and of justification in the law. Dewey had distinguished clearly between the "logic of inquiry" and the "logic of exposition," between an argument's source and its persuasiveness. Yet the realists often pointed to a judge's psychological processes or social background as if they were demonstrating the irrelevance of his justifications or the speciousness of his claim to be applying rules.

Realism is especially inadequate if taken to be the comprehensive explanation or theory of the nature of law suggested by the definitional form of certain central realist slogans. Thus, realists constantly endorsed Holmes's statement that "the prophecies of what the courts will do in fact . . . are what I mean by the law." This remark can be accepted as a paradoxical emphasis on the individual discretion inherent in applying "open-textured" concepts to particular circumstances; accordingly, the exercise of individual discretion becomes part of any adequate concept of law. But Holmes's remark cannot be accepted if it is read as an assertion that the best understanding of legal reality derives from equating law with prediction. A predictive viewpoint obscures the role of legal rules as guides to conduct. As H. L. A. Hart said, " . . . legal rules function as such in social life: they are *used* as rules not as descriptions of habits or predictions" (*The Concept of Law*, Oxford, 1961, pp. 134–135). If the normative character of legal rules were not generally accepted, our concept of law would be entirely different.

However, it may be that attempts, like that of the realists, to jolt accepted habits of thought must rely on paradox and exaggeration. Proudhon said, "Property is theft," knowing full well the immediate sense in which "property" is not "theft" at all. In jurisprudence the very distortion frequently produces the insight; we often learn more from a caricature than from a photograph.

Bibliography

Frank, Jerome, *Law and the Modern Mind,* 2d ed. New York, 1948.

Fuller, Lon, "American Legal Realism." *University of Pennsylvania Law Review,* Vol. 82 (1934), 429–462.

Gilmore, Grant, "Legal Realism: Its Cause and Cure." *Yale Law Journal,* Vol. 70 (1961), 1037–1048.

Llewellyn, K. N., *Jurisprudence.* Chicago, 1962.

YOSAL ROGAT

LEGAL RESPONSIBILITY. See PUNISHMENT; RE
SPONSIBILITY, MORAL AND LEGAL.

LEIBNIZ, GOTTFRIED WILHELM (1646–1716),
German philosopher, scientist, mathematician, historian,
and diplomat. Leibniz was born in Leipzig; his father was
a professor, and his mother was the daughter of a professor
at the University of Leipzig. A precocious child, he read
widely in the library of his father, who died when Leibniz
was six. Although Leibniz studied philosophy and law at
the university, he was not permitted to present himself for
the doctorate of laws in 1666, on the ground that he was too
young. Thereupon he left Leipzig and graduated at Altdorf,
where he was offered a professorship. He declined this, and
went to Nuremberg, where he became secretary of the
Rosicrucian Society. In Nuremberg he met Johann Christian von Boyneburg, a statesman and diplomat who had
formerly been first minister at the court of Mainz but was
now in retirement although still active. Through Boyneburg, Leibniz was introduced to Johann Philipp von Schönborn, elector of Mainz, who took him into his service.
During this period Leibniz wrote a number of papers furthering Boyneburg's schemes and cooperated with Dr.
Lasser, one of Schönborn's lawyers, in revising Roman law.
However, his position as a Protestant in a Catholic court
was never very secure, and in 1672 he went to Paris, partly
on Boyneburg's private affairs and partly for personal reasons. After four years in Paris he went to Hanover (October
1676) in the service of Johann Friedrich, the reigning duke.
He remained in Hanover until his death, serving under
Ernst August after the death of Johann Friedrich in 1679,
and then under Georg Ludwig, who in 1714 became king
of Great Britain. In 1685 Ernst August set Leibniz the task
of writing the history of the house of Brunswick, and to
gather material for this history in 1687 he began a journey
that lasted nearly three years, going through Munich and
Vienna to Italy and returning to Hanover in June 1690. He
succeeded in showing the connection between the houses
of Brunswick and Este.

Sophie, the wife of Ernst August, and her daughter
Sophie Charlotte, who became queen of Prussia, were very
close to Leibniz, and much of his writing, including the
Théodicée, was occasioned by his discussions with them.
While Sophie Charlotte was alive, he frequently visited
Berlin, where in 1700 the Berlin Society of Sciences (later
the Prussian Royal Academy) was founded, with Leibniz
as president for life. However, after Sophie Charlotte's
death in 1705, Leibniz' presence in Berlin was more and
more unwelcome, and by 1711 he had altogether ceased to
go there.

Throughout his life Leibniz sought to promote cooperative activity in scientific and medical research and in the
systematic collection and arrangement of facts already
known, whether about things or about technical processes.
He also sought to bring together Christians of all sects
by presenting a body of doctrine containing everything
essential for Christian faith, on which all could agree. He
wrote innumerable letters to advance these projects and
drafted innumerable prefaces. His later years were marred,
however, by the controversy with the Newtonians over priority in the discovery of the calculus, a strong blow to his
own ideal of scientific cooperation. And, although during a
stay in Vienna from 1712 to 1714 Leibniz was made an imperial privy councilor and given the title of Freiherr, he was
generally neglected. His death passed almost unnoticed by
both his royal patrons and the intellectual world.

EARLY VIEWS

A few general points may be noted in regard to Leibniz'
views before he went to Paris.

He knew of Descartes's work mainly through the writings of some of Descartes's followers; but he was more
familiar with Bacon, Gassendi, and Hobbes. He read very
widely and rapidly, generally assimilating what stimulated
his own thinking; and, although his university studies had
made him thoroughly familiar with the Aristotelian tradition and his own early reading had given him a wide range
of ideas from the Scholastics, he decided strongly in favor
of the modern outlook, with its stress on explanation
through efficient causes, its atomism, and its experimental
approach to the study of nature.

Final causes. Leibniz did not completely abandon
the traditional views, but he thought it possible to harmonize them with the new. In particular, he thought that for ultimate explanations of the nature of things, God's existence
and the consideration of final causes could not be neglected. The world was a harmonious whole produced by
God to serve the divine ends, and although the fundamental workings of things in the world were in accordance
with laws of efficient causes, these laws brought about the
divine ends. Efficient causes did not rule out final causes.

Mind, body, and free will. During this early period
Leibniz did not think of mind and body as being sharply
separated, any more than the Scholastics or atomists, such
as Gassendi and Bacon, did, or than Hobbes did. His inclination to consider body in terms of mind rather than to
read mind in terms of body is epitomized in his statement,
"A body is a momentary mind, but without memory." In
various letters to Johann Friedrich and others, he outlined
the view that the human mind is implanted in an imperishable bodily kernel that remains as the seat of the mind
even when the rest of the body is dissipated. Later, in
some of his Parisian writings, he linked minds with vortices, suggesting that the unity of body comes from minds.
All these speculations were crude, but they formed a natural basis for his more mature views.

Leibniz was greatly interested in what he called the two
most important labyrinths that perplex and imprison the
human mind—that of fate and free will and that of the
continuum.

Logic and the universal language. Leibniz' earliest
philosophical interest, almost before he was in his teens,
was in logic. Here his main emphasis (as was Bacon's) was
on classification; deduction was a natural consequence of
combining classified items into new classes. In an early
academic exercise on the principle of individuation ("De
Principio Individui," 1663) he listed as one of the corollaries on which he was ready to dispute, the principle
"Things are like numbers." By this Leibniz meant that
statements about complex things can be derived from
statements about their simpler constituents by a process of

combination analogous to multiplication of numbers. This was a kind of conceptual atomism that resulted in a fundamental schema for an alphabet of human thought, haunting him throughout his whole life and becoming more and more unrealizable the more he worked on it. Leibniz thought that if man could discover the fundamental concepts involved in all possible existence, the derivation of all possible truths would be within his reach. On the lowest level there would be combinations of fundamental concepts; on the next level (as Leibniz put it) "contenations" or "con3nations"—that is, combinations of concepts taken three at a time, with corresponding combinations at higher levels. It can be seen that the classification is the basis for deduction within this schema.

Universal encyclopedia. Related to Leibniz' notion of a conceptual alphabet was his conception of an encyclopedia of human knowledge. Leibniz held that there already exist vast stores of experience held by groups of skilled workers, or by individuals, that are not fully utilized. These must be collected and systematically arranged, if their full fruits are to be obtained for understanding and practical application. Leibniz thought that the fuller knowledge of the world made available by such an encyclopedia would be conducive to piety by bringing out the richness and variety in the world, and thus testifying to God's wisdom and power. Leibniz desired a fuller knowledge of the nature of things because he believed it would increase piety and devotion to God.

Jurisprudence. During his university years one of Leibniz' fundamental interests was to see how philosophical disciplines could help in the clarification of other studies, especially legal studies, and his academic theses in his legal course were devoted to this. His *Nova Methodus Docendae Discendaeque Jurisprudentiae* ("New Method of Teaching and Learning Jurisprudence," 1667), dedicated and presented to von Schönborn, led to his appointment to assist Dr. Lasser in the work of reforming the corpus juris.

NEW PHYSICAL HYPOTHESIS

Most important to the next step in Leibniz' career was his 1671 work, *Hypothesis Physica Nova* ("New Physical Hypothesis," Gerhardt 1875–1890, Vol. IV, pp. 177 f.), which was divided into two parts: a theory of concrete motion, dedicated to the Royal Society in London, and a theory of abstract motion, presented to the Academy of Sciences in Paris.

Concrete theory. The concrete theory, a hypothesis designed to explain the most important complex phenomena in terms of simpler phenomena, was based on the relative circulation of the ether through and around the materials that made up the earth in its earliest state. In his abstract theory Leibniz showed how all cohesion of bodies depends on the motion of their constituent particles. This motion is due to the impact of the ether upon the particles and is the ultimate explanatory cause of all the physical characteristics of bodies.

Abstract theory. The abstract theory turns on two main lines of thought: Leibniz' study of the labyrinth of the continuum and his reaction to the laws of motion given by Wren and by Huygens in the *Proceedings of the Royal Society*, laws that Leibniz thought could not be fundamental. He also based his idea of continuity in space and time on Hobbes's concept of "endeavor" (conatus), defined by Hobbes as movement over a space less than any given space in a time less than any given time. Leibniz conceived the conatus as unextended but insisted that both points and instants, although unextended, have parts. His account of the laws of motion depended on the view that particles of matter completely at rest offer no resistance to a moving body; it is only because of the inner movements of their parts that bodies have either resistance or cohesion. A moving body, however small, will sweep along with it those parts of a body completely at rest, however large, that stand in its way.

The "New Physical Hypothesis" must be looked upon as a stage, soon to be superseded, in Leibniz' thought about the problems of motion. It was during his stay in Paris that Leibniz first learned to handle competently the problems of the continuum and of motion. He was indebted for his new skill to the encouragement of Christian Huygens, whom he met there and who showed him what he must study in mathematics. Huygens' methods of handling problems of motion gave Leibniz his fundamental principle that in all physical transactions (which he regarded as resulting from impacts) the total effect is equal to the entire cause.

PARIS YEARS

Leibniz' sojourn in Paris (1672–1676) was one of the most profitable periods of his life. He made many important contacts with mathematicians, physicists, philosophers, and men of affairs. The most important of these contacts, after Huygens, were the philosophers Antoine Arnauld, Nicolas Malebranche, and Simon Foucher, canon of Dijon; the physicist Edmond Mariotte; and Walther von Tschirnhaus, who came to Leibniz with an introduction from Henry Oldenburg, secretary of the Royal Society. During these same years Leibniz studied the works of Pascal, Descartes, and Huygens; made discoveries in the calculus that brought him into contact with Sir Isaac Newton and other British mathematicians; and constructed a calculating machine capable of multiplying large numbers.

Philosophical notes. In Paris, Leibniz composed a series of philosophical notes, dating from the end of 1675 to April 1676 (edited by Iwan Jagodinski and published in 1913 as *Leibnitiana Elementa Philosophiae Arcanae de Summa Rerum*). Of the wide range of topics covered, only a few that throw light on his later development can be mentioned here. Leibniz took for granted the notions of the harmony of all things and the perfection of the world as created by God, and utilized them in the discussion of other topics. The greatest possible amount of essence exists and, since thought and perception mirror things, this mirroring increases the variety of the world—and hence increases its perfection. That is why particular minds exist.

Sensation. The harmony of all things is also increased by there being an infinite number of creatures in the smallest particle, and they also have their own perceptions that mirror their world (Jagodinski 1913, pp. 28–40). This later led Leibniz, in the course of a discussion of Descartes, to raise the question as to what our perception assures us of.

He concluded, as Descartes had, that all we can be certain of is that we sense and that we sense things congruous to each other. The difference between dreams and waking life lies in the regularities that are observed in our sensings in ordinary life, so that reasons can be given for them and predictions about further sensings can be made. There is no need to suppose that what different people sense is the same, so long as (as is the case) what each person senses is congruent to himself. Each person's sensings have the same cause and therefore are in conformity. There is no need to posit interaction.

The external world. Leibniz went on to suggest that there is likewise no need to ask whether space and body exist outside our minds. Space, as he put it, is what makes many perceptions cohere among themselves—the perception of space relations among one's perceptions enables one to make predictions about the space relations of new perceptions to the old ones. However, he seemed to imply that there is such a thing as "our" world—that "we" all perceive the same space; and he went on to conclude that other creatures can have other spaces (that is, they can have perceptions that are linked among themselves by spatial laws other than ours), in which case there would be no conformity between them and us. Indeed, to ask whether there can be another world and other spaces is only to ask whether there are other minds that have no communication with ours. It will be seen that Leibniz was assuming that, although two persons need not have qualitatively the same sense experiences, they can and do communicate, and that this communication somehow depends on the nature of the space relations underlying the congruity of each person's perceptions.

Causation. The philosophical notes contain another point very significant in relation to Leibniz' later doctrine. In a paper dated April 1, 1676, and headed "Meditatio de Principio Individui" (Jagodinski 1913, p. 44), Leibniz started from the common notion that an effect involves its cause, so that anyone who understands some effect perfectly would also be able to come to a perfect understanding of the cause. This involves the idea that it is impossible for a particular effect to be produced in two alternative ways by two different causes (as, for instance, a square might be produced either by joining two rectangles or by joining two right-angled isosceles triangles). Leibniz decided that no two things can be alike, but in a material thing there is always something that bears the traces of its earlier state, so that its cause can be discovered in it. This element, he said, is mind, since matter itself is incapable of containing such traces.

Leibniz uses an interesting argument (*ibid.*, p. 46) to show that effect involves cause: "It is true of the effect that it was produced by such a cause. Therefore there is at present in it a quality of such a kind as carries this fact, which even though relative, has something objective"; that is, in the effect itself. The implication of this—that whatever is true of anything is expressed in some way in the thing—is also found in another passage: "When another thing becomes greater than me by increasing, there also occurs some change in me, since a denomination of me is changed . . . and in this way all things are contained in all things" (*ibid.*, p. 122).

These two passages are consistent with the more general view, which Leibniz enunciated later, that if man had a perfect knowledge of the present state of an individual thing, he should be able to deduce its whole past and future states, and even the past and future states of the whole universe. The notion of the individual mirroring the universe was thus given enormous significance. The principle (discussed below) enunciated in the *Discourse on Metaphysics* of 1686—that in the complete notion of an individual is to be found whatever can be said about the individual, past, present, and future—gave a rather special twist to the general thesis, based on the further proposition that all true statements consist in attributing diverse predicates to a complex subject that "in some way" contains them all.

Identity of indiscernibles. The argument showing that effect involves cause also contains one of the main reasons for Leibniz' later principle of the identity of indiscernibles, the principle that there cannot be two things in the universe that are exactly alike. A characteristic expression of this principle is to be found in a paper printed by Couturat (*Opuscules et fragments*, p. 9). The point is that a thing A cannot have a spatiotemporal position different from another thing B without this difference being intimately linked with differences within the natures of the things themselves. The identity of indiscernibles is significantly connected with the principle that in every true proposition the predicate is contained in the subject. Elsewhere (*ibid.*, p. 519) the principle is found connected with the principle of sufficient reason; if there are two different things, some reason for this difference must be present in the natures of the things themselves. The whole complex of ideas is very close to the argumentation in the papers of 1676.

Simple and complex ideas. There are also in the philosophical notes many discussions of simple ideas and of their combination to form complex ideas. Leibniz noted (Jagodinski 1913, p. 124) that there are some complex ideas that represent things that are impossible, such as the swiftest motion or the greatest number. He therefore sought examples of maxima and minima that are possible, and also noted that the ontological proof of God's existence from the concept of the greatest possible being or the most perfect being is incomplete until it is shown that such a being is possible (*ibid.*, p. 112; cf. letter to Oldenburg of December 28, 1675, in Gerhardt 1849–1863, p. 85).

One would expect Leibniz to argue that since (1) all complex concepts are derived from simple concepts, (2) all simple concepts are both purely positive and completely independent of one another, and (3) God is the being to whom all positive attributes belong (if this is possible), it therefore follows that the concept of God is possible and hence that God exists (cf. Jagodinski 1913, p. 122).

Origin of created beings and the creation. However, if Leibniz' account of simple and complex concepts is correct, it is not easy to see how any complex concept could represent an impossible being, or how any negation or incompatibility could arise at all. Yet if some particular things are to exist rather than others, there must be negation and incompatibility. Leibniz never satisfactorily solved this problem. In the Parisian notes he took refuge in the thought that particular things result from forms (simple concepts) combined with a subject. This, he said, involved some kind of modification of the forms, although in what manner this occurred was not made clear. "How things result from forms I cannot explain otherwise than by analogy with numbers arising from unities, with this distinction that all unities are homogeneous whereas forms are different" (*ibid.*). This explanation did not help in the least.

At a later period he referred the distinction between God and created beings to the concept of difference, or negation, which must be a constituent of every thing created; and his analogy then was not with numbers arising from unities but with the fact that in the dyadic notation all numbers are expressible in terms of the two characters 1 and 0. Thus, Pure Being (God) and nonbeing are the two ultimate constituents of all created things, and nonbeing brings about profound modifications in the constituent concepts of things. Leibniz associated nonbeing with imperfection and evil; nonbeing makes it impossible for God to create a completely perfect world, and allows him to create only the best of all possible worlds. It is not clear that Leibniz ever asked himself how nearly the best possible world approaches the perfection of God himself; he would probably have regarded the question as unanswerable by finite beings. In one passage (Bodemann 1895, p. 120) he suggested that the world improves with the passage of time, although it never arrives at fullest maturity. He never even seems to have raised the question of whether the concept of a best possible world is possible, although presumably he would have said that it must be, since that is what God creates. However this may be, it seems clear that there must be an infinite difference between the Creator and any created world.

"PACIDIUS PHILALETHI"

The notes published by Jagodinski are our main evidence for Leibniz' philosophical explorations in Paris. In the early part of 1676 he made an abbreviated translation of Plato's *Theaetetus* and *Phaedo*, and he had a discussion with Malebranche on the question of whether matter is to be equated with extension.

In that October Leibniz left Paris to take up his new position at Hanover, traveling by way of London and Holland, where he visited Spinoza, among others. While delayed on board his boat in the Thames, Leibniz composed a long dialogue, *Pacidius Philalethi* (Couturat, pp. 594 ff.), in the form of a letter from Pacidius to Philalethes, in which Pacidius relates a conversation between himself and some friends. (The title may be translated "Godfrey [or Gottfried], to the lover of truth.") The dialogue shows familiarity with the stock arguments associated with the labyrinth of the continuum.

The fundamental problem of the continuum arises through regarding any motion as analyzable into successive states, in each of which a body occupies a position different from that in the next state. In this analysis there is no way of avoiding the problem of how the body gets from one position to the other, or of avoiding the problem of how the two positions are spatially related. The solution adopted by Leibniz used a form of the principle that the continued existence of material things is their continual re-creation by God. Leibniz used the word *transcreation* in the early part of the dialogue to express the idea that when a body moves, it goes out of existence in the earlier position and is re-created in the later position, there being a gap between the two positions. Motion was thus resolved into a series of rests, without any leaps by any actually existing thing. Leibniz showed that this notion was open to a variety of objections, and he finally arrived at a different conception of transcreation, in which the successive positions are contiguous, without any gaps. However, he still resolved motion into a series of rests, God letting the body go out of existence at one point and re-creating it at the next.

This solution did not satisfy Leibniz, but he could see no way out so long as space and motion were regarded as objectively real (substantial), and he was forced to the conclusion that there is something phenomenal in both. The difficulties of the continuum were thus instrumental in leading Leibniz to the view that motion itself cannot be a real entity, because it never exists; only what can exist in a moment of time can be real. This view was important for his dynamical conception of substance.

NEW FORMULATION OF LAWS OF MOTION

Leibniz appears to have gradually come to accept Huygens' view of the fundamental principles governing the laws of the impact of bodies, and soon after his arrival in Hanover he began to enunciate these principles, although the evidence (as so far published) is scanty and gives only the barest facts. Thus, in December 1676 Leibniz wrote that any effect taken in its totality is equal (quantitatively) to its entire cause (Grua 1948, p. 263). In March 1677 he enunciated two rules of impact: that the motive power of two impinging bodies (taken together) is the same before and after impact, and that the center of gravity of the two bodies proceeds with equal velocity before and after their impact, so that the direction of the aggregate of bodies is the same before and after the impact. "From these we derive the rest" (Bodemann, *op. cit.*, p. 328, Bl. 144). These are Huygens' rules. In January 1678 a paper headed "De Concursu Corporum" began: "Force is the quantity of effect. Hence the force of a body in motion should be measured by the height to which it can ascend" (*ibid.*, p. 328, Bl. 86–91). This rule, which was inspired by Huygens (although not used by him in precisely this form), is based on Galileo's discussion of falling bodies. Huygens, and Leibniz after him, assumed that however a body was moving, it could always—in theory—be supposed to have all its force directed upward, so that the height to which it could ascend against gravity could be measured. Thus, a body moving with velocity v could rise against gravity to a height proportional to v^2 before its active force was used up. Hence, Leibniz took this height as the measure of the force of the moving body in terms of the square of its velocity.

There were two further points for which Leibniz was indebted to Huygens. One was that the center of gravity of a set of mutually interacting bodies cannot be raised through their interactions. If it could, there would be a system making perpetual mechanical motion possible. Leibniz used this principle (for instance, in the *Discourse on Metaphysics*) in his criticism of Descartes's measure of force in terms of mass multiplied by velocity, which he claimed would make perpetual motion possible.

The second point was the use Huygens made of relative motion in what he called his "method of a boat." Leibniz generalized this method, arguing that there was no way of determining, by a mere consideration of the motions of a set of bodies moving relative to one another, which of the motions were the real ones. This point was an additional reason for concluding that there is something not completely real—something phenomemal—in motion, and for deciding that the nature of substance must be found in something other than body (since body gets all its positive attributes through motion).

New conception of substance. Stress has been laid on Huygens' work because it was Leibniz' studies of motion and of the laws of motion that were responsible for what can only be described as a complete about-face on the question of fundamentals of dynamics.

Leibniz had essentially agreed with the outlook of the most modern of his contemporaries, for whom extension, figure, and motion were the outstanding examples of what is clear and distinct, not only making rational investigation possible in science but also justifying the claim that what science was investigating was the nature of reality itself. He had held to this outlook even though in his view the world of nature interpreted in this way was not metaphysically self-sufficient but needed God as creator and sustainer, and even though he sometimes treated bodies in terms of minds, through his notion of the conatus.

Dynamical laws not basic. Toward the end of the 1670s Leibniz began to think of extension, figure, and motion as containing something imaginary, and held that the basic laws of motion cannot be derived from a study of their nature. Nevertheless, he continued to hold that, given basic laws derived from other sources, extension, figure, and motion could provide a means for explaining and predicting the course of phenomena. This is a noteworthy point. For Descartes and for Malebranche extension was real only because one can reason on it. Leibniz was now insisting that one can reason on it even though, like sound or color, there is something imaginary about it.

Activity essential to matter. Metaphysical considerations were now necessary for the basic laws. The question arises, however, of what Leibniz meant by this. In two letters, one to Johann Friedrich, probably written in the autumn of 1679 (Preussische Akademie, Series II, Vol. I, p. 490), and one to the Jesuit Father de La Chaise, Louis XIV's confessor, probably from May 1680 (*ibid.*, p. 512), he spoke of re-establishing substantial forms, and stated that the nature of body does not consist in extension, but in "an action which relates itself to extension" (a remarkable anticipation of the view he expressed in the 1690s). The then current view of matter treated it as inert substance; Leibniz insisted that activity (effort) is essential to substance.

However, there was still much that was obscure in this work, and not until the dynamical discussions after 1690 was there any major clarification.

DOCTRINE OF PROPOSITIONS

A further development of Leibniz' views must be referred to at this point—his generalization in the *Discourse on Metaphysics* that in every true affirmative proposition, whether necessary or contingent, the predicate is contained in the notion of the subject. All the other basic ideas contained in the *Discourse* can be found in Leibniz' writings up to and including 1680, but this doctrine concerning true propositions, and the ideas immediately dependent on it, appear to have been formulated just prior to the writing of the *Discourse*. It emerged from a long series of investigations into logic (Couturat, *op. cit.*). Perhaps it is a natural outcome of Leibniz' early view of knowledge as resulting from combinations of simple concepts, taken with his speculations—already alluded to—about modifications of pure concepts arising through their application to subjects. If *a, b, c,* and *d* are completely simple concepts having no common content (although Leibniz found some difficulty in this), then the proposition *abc is a* is true and the proposition *abc is d* is false. The first is an identical (necessary) proposition, and the second is self-contradictory (impossible).

Contingent propositions. However, there are many propositions that are not of either type—for instance, "Caesar crossed the Rubicon." All such propositions, concerning existing individuals, are contingent. Leibniz constantly asserted that they are ultimately reducible to identities, but he had to admit that such truths of fact are not capable of being reduced to identities by human beings or even, in a straightforward sense, by God. He was also compelled to distinguish these truths from necessary propositions of the type *abc is a*, because he was unwilling to admit that everything that happens, happens necessarily. His studies of the endless discussions of free will had left him insistent on the contingency of what actually exists, and this was combined with stress on the freedom of God as creator of the best possible world and on the freedom of human beings in that world. However, Leibniz was unable to find any ultimate principle of demonstration other than that of the ultimate reducibility of true propositions to identities. He therefore tried to give this principle a form that would not jeopardize contingency.

It is clear that this attempt is not consistent with any account of the ultimate concepts as positive, separate, and containing nothing in common. The formula *abc is a* obviously will not apply to contingent propositions. On the basis of this formula, the predicate must be in the subject literally. In the *Generales Inquisitiones* of 1686 (Couturat, Secs. 132–136, p. 388), he said that contingent propositions are proved by "continued resolution" that is never completed, and in a paper on liberty (Foucher de Careil 1857, p. 182), he stated that this resolution is never completed, even by God, since it has no end. This means that more and more reasons can be given that make it likely that the predicate does belong to the subject. Thus, for God, who sees the infinite, the result is certain, although not necessary. Leibniz compared this continual progress toward identities with the continued approach of a curve to its asymptote. Elsewhere he compared contingent propositions with incommensurable numbers. While all this shows how much he stressed the views that contingent propositions are not necessary, it is incompatible with any formal account that could be given of basic concepts and of complex concepts as simply results of combinations of basic ones.

Possibility. As has been shown, Leibniz had long held the view that every individual, whether person or thing, in some way reflects everything that is happening in the universe. He also asserted that there is an infinity of possible individuals that has never existed and never will, each possible individual being part of a possible universe and mirroring that universe. The Adam in our world was tempted and sinned; there are other possible worlds containing Adams who were tempted and did not sin. From this point of view, one can say that it would not be self-contradictory for the Adam in our world not to sin, although, given all his characteristics up to the time of his temptation, it was certain that he would sin. This makes Adam's sin contingent and not necessary; he could, Leibniz insisted, have refrained.

On the other hand, if the Adam in our world had refrained, our world—and, consequently, all the substances other than Adam in it—would have been different. An Adam without sin would have been possible, but would not have been compossible with the rest of the things in our world. From this point of view, God must be conceived as surveying all the different compossible worlds and decreeing the existence of the one containing the greatest perfection.

Perhaps a remote parallel is to be found in the activity of a dramatist working out alternative developments of his plot, always endeavoring to make characters act freely in accordance with their own natures but not admitting them into his drama if their behavior does not suit his purposes.

The point to be stressed is that the concept of a possible individual is always relative to the concept of a possible world, and cannot be considered independently. The notion of a possible individual in a possible world is a summary of God's complete knowledge of this and all the other individuals in that world, showing the individual's complete behavior but in no way constraining his action.

DENIAL OF INTERACTION

The most important immediate consequence Leibniz derived from his conception of individual substance was the denial of any interaction between substances. In this he was doing no more than the occasionalists had already done, the difference between his view and theirs being that they made God the only immediate agent in the world, while Leibniz made every individual substance evolve in accordance with its own determinate nature, which was admitted into existence by God when he created the world. (For a more detailed discussion of occasionalism, see CARTESIANISM; GEULINCX, ARNOLD; MALEBRANCHE, NICOLAS.)

Attack on occasionalism. In contrast to Malebranche, whose *Méditations chrétiennes* he had studied in 1679 with great interest, Leibniz emphasized the view that individual substances are responsible for their own activity. He told de L'Hôpital in a letter of September 30, 1695 (Gerhardt 1849–1863, Vol. II, p. 299), that his view was a development from Malebranche's doctrine of occasional causes "and it is to him that I owe my foundations on this subject." He also wrote to Wolf on December 8, 1705 (Gerhardt 1860, p. 51), that he would not have discovered his harmonic system if he had not found laws of motion that overturn occasional causes. Thus, it seems that for Leibniz both logic and laws of motion lead to metaphysics.

Appearance of interaction explained. The denial of interaction led Leibniz to an account of the appearance of interaction in terms of the correspondence between all creatures established by God. He held that one could still speak of action and passion; changes in a substance as it evolves are changes in the degree of perfection with which it expresses the universe. A substance can be said to act when it passes to a lower degree of expression. In addition, one substance can be said to act on another when (*a*) it contains a clearer expression than any other substance of the changes that are about to occur in the substance that is said to be acted upon, and (*b*) the latter substance passes to a less perfect expression.

Each soul expresses the universe. The relation between the human mind and the body is explained in terms of the view that the soul, evolving spontaneously, always expresses the entire state of the universe. It does this "according to the relation of other bodies to its own." This expression is contained in its "perception"—Leibniz' word for the most rudimentary awareness, sensuous in nature, of an object. It follows that the perceptions of the soul must correspond most directly to what is happening in its body, and this is what makes it appropriate to call one's body one's own. Monads, as Leibniz said later, have no windows (*Monadology*, Sec. 7) and need none. They know what is going on outside through the effect of the outside world on their own bodies; and, as we have seen, such effects mirror their causes.

Other points. It also follows that our sense perceptions must contain much that is confused, which we are not able to perceive clearly. Leibniz had already noted this in 1676 (Jagodinski 1913, p. 96), and it is the basis of his later doctrine of *petites perceptions*.

There are many points in the *Discourse* that have not been explicitly referred to. Mention must be made of two: the account of the rules governing God's action in the world, which are regular—aside from occasional suspensions for miracles—but are such as to produce the maximum richness of effects; and the discussion of the sense in which man can be said to have ideas of all things. The first point was touched upon very early, but was reinforced and given definition by Leibniz' study of Malebranche's writings in 1679, and the second can be compared with the study "Ideas" ("Quid Sit Idea," Gerhardt 1875–1890, Vol. VII, p. 263).

There is a strong note of piety struck in the *Discourse* in the account of the City of God, of which all rational creatures are members. As has been shown, Leibniz held that the accumulation of knowledge of the universe naturally increases the devotion of men to its creator.

SUBSTANTIAL UNITY OF THE HUMAN BODY

Leibniz sent a paragraph-by-paragraph summary of the *Discourse* to Count Ernst von Hessen-Rheinfels for transmission to Antoine Arnauld. This led to a long correspondence (first published with the *Discourse*, 1846) in which the main points raised by Arnauld arose from Leibniz' account of the concept of an individual substance and of the individual's complete lack of interaction with other substances. Five specific issues may be noted: (1) Arnauld's fear that the derivation of whatever will happen to an individual from his complete notion renders all events necessary and deprives not only the individual but also God of all freedom; (2) the difficulty of understanding how the events in the body can fit in completely with the events in the mind, if both interaction and occasionalism are denied; (3) in what way the human body, which is extended and divisible, can be a substance, which is, on Leibniz' view, unextended and indivisible; (4) the manner in which mind can express what is in the body; (5) of what things there are substantial forms.

Substantial forms. Here only the third issue, that of the substantial unity of the human body, will be treated. Leibniz had no really satisfactory answer to this question. He made it clear that he did regard the human body as forming a true unity with the mind, which is the substantial form of the body; but he was unable to say how mind unifies body. The body is, of course, an organism, but it is body; and everything happens in it according to the laws of motion. In this correspondence Leibniz did not, as he later did, stress the notion of an organism as fundamental to a substance. Assuming that the human being, consisting of mind and body, is a true unity, he extended the notion of organism to cover all beings endowed with substantial forms. A substantial form, for Leibniz, was something analogous to a mind and capable of "perception" (the lowest degree of mental activity, not involving either self-consciousness or thought). It is through its perceptions that any individual "expresses" what goes on in the universe.

Bodies as bodies are mere phenomena. Leibniz insisted that unless bodies are made up of constituents that have substantial forms, they have no reality but are mere phenomena. If there are such substantial forms, then bodies have such reality as belongs to their constituents; but even so, when they are considered only as bodies (the substantial forms not taken into account), they are mere aggregates, phenomenal and not real. This is important because it indicates one of the things Leibniz often had in view when he spoke of something as phenomenal. Take something real, consider some aspect of it that does not directly involve the substantial forms that make it real, and that aspect is phenomenal. Or take a number of real things, aggregate them, and consider the aggregate as a single thing; as a single thing it is phenomenal and not real. The phrase "well founded phenomena" (*phenomena bene fundata*) was used by Leibniz of things that, although phenomenal in the above sense, are based on something real; an example is the rainbow, which is based on light refracted from water drops, which in turn are based on monads.

Substances have organic bodies. The letter to Arnauld dated October 6, 1687, was the last in the series, for Leibniz went traveling. On March 23, 1690, he wrote to Arnauld once more, this time from Venice, sending a résumé of his metaphysics (much shorter than his previous résumé

and, apart from one point, of interest chiefly for its omissions). Bodies are not substances but aggregations of substances—these substances are indivisible, incorruptible, and not capable of being generated, and possess something analogous to souls. This view stresses that these substances have been and will always be united to *organic* bodies capable of diverse transformations. The view that substances are united to bodies was not new to Leibniz, but his stress on the organic nature of these bodies seems to be new.

Nothing was said about substantial forms, about the notion of individual substance, or about bodies apart from forms being phenomena. Substances were still spontaneously active and self-contained, but the new formula was less provocative. "Each substance contains in its nature the law of continuation of the series of its own operations and all that has happened to it and all that will happen to it." The notions of expression of the union of soul and body and of action of one thing on another are explained as in the *Discourse*. The remainder of the final letter corresponds briefly to the sections in the *Discourse* dealing with God as the head of the republic of spirits, with a brief note about physics.

In Leibniz' later writings the stress on every substance's having an organic body, and on the substance's having in it the law of continuation of the series of its operations, predominated. The *notion* of an individual substance was rarely mentioned.

PRE-ESTABLISHED HARMONY

While in Italy, Leibniz saw a review of Newton's *Principia* in the *Acta Eruditorum* of June 1688, and was stimulated by it to develop his own views in a manuscript on dynamics (Gerhardt 1849–1863, Vol. VI, pp. 281–514). He left the manuscript in Florence, to be criticized by friends before publication, but it was not published in his lifetime.

From the time Leibniz returned home, he published aspects of his new views in the various journals. In March 1694 his "First Philosophy and the Notion of Substance: An Emendation" (Gerhardt 1875–1890, Vol. IV, p. 468) appeared in the *Acta Eruditorum*. In this article Leibniz stressed the concept of force as essential to substance, contrasted it with the scholastic notion of power, and called substance by the Aristotelian word *entelechy*. In April 1695 he published his "Specimen Dynamicum" in the same journal (Gerhardt 1849–1863, Vol. VI, pp. 234 f.), giving a more technical and systematic account of his conception of force; and on June 27, 1695, he published his "Système nouveau de la nature et de la communication des substances" (*ibid.*, Vol. IV, pp. 477 f.), containing a discussion of the problem of the relation between mind and body, in the *Journal des sçavans*. In this latter paper, Leibniz expounded his view that every substance is completely self-contained, but did so in consequence of his inability to see how one could solve the problem otherwise, rather than in relation to the doctrine of propositions. Interaction is inconceivable because of the disparity between matter and mind; occasional causes show the power of God but not his wisdom; therefore, Leibniz said, he was led gradually to a view that surprised him: that God created each substance in such a way that everything that happens to it arises from its own nature, in complete spontaneity and without any influence from anything outside, apart from God, and yet in complete harmony with what happens to every other substance. In January 1696 (Gerhardt 1875–1890, Vol. IV, p. 499), he publicly described his hypothesis as "the way of pre-established harmony," a phrase that has provided the most popular description of Leibniz' system (first used in a 1695 paper; see Gerhardt 1849–1863, Vol. II, p. 298).

MONADS

The common term "monad" was first used by Leibniz in 1695 (not in 1696, as popularly held) in a letter (*ibid.*, p. 295) to de L'Hôpital (who in 1696 wrote the first treatise on the integral calculus, using Leibniz' symbols and methods). There were so many examples of the use of the word *monas* in the seventeenth century to signify the unit that it is impossible to say which of them stimulated Leibniz to use it. However, Euclid's word for the unit (*Elements*, Bk. VIII, Def. I) is *monas* and, since Leibniz had recently, in the *Acta Eruditorum*, quoted the *Elements* (Bk. V, Def. V) in his reply to Nieuwentijt's criticisms of the calculus, this may have been an important influence on Leibniz' choice of the term in a letter to a mathematician and thereafter.

Monads and the physical world. Leibniz' fundamental stress was on the unity and spontaneous activity of monads, but he insisted that monads are in the real world and mirror the world only because of their association with their organic body. A monad without a body would be "a deserter from the general order" ("On Principles of Life," written 1705; Gerhardt 1875–1890, Vol. VI, p. 546). Since everything that happens anywhere in the physical world has some effect everywhere else, the body belonging to a monad is receiving such effects at every moment and is in correspondence with these effects—although not as a causal consequence of them—in such a way that the monad is able to mirror what is happening everywhere.

As has been shown, the fundamental physical process is impact, and in order to preserve the law of continuity—which Leibniz claimed to have introduced—all bodies must have some degree of elasticity and some degree of hardness. When two bodies impinge, each gradually changes shape through its elasticity and then rebounds; thus, speeds change gradually. Each body derives the whole of its force of rebound from its own inner structure; it depends on the force of the other body only for the amount of force it itself displays (thus echoing the independence of the monads). Elasticity is possible only because an elastic fluid circulates between the parts of the body, but this fluid in turn can be elastic only by means of an elastic fluid circulating between its parts, and so on ad infinitum, so that we must admit bodies within bodies without end. (Leibniz welcomed such infinite regresses.)

All bodies are moving diversely, and all have effects on the organism of any monad and are thus mirrored by the monad. Although monads are not extended, they nevertheless have a certain kind of situation in extension: ". . . a certain ordered relation of coexistence with all others, through the machine over which they are, though this

situation cannot be designated by precise points" (letter to de Volder, March–June 1703, *ibid.*, Vol. II, p. 253). There is no particle of matter, however small, that is not composed of organisms, each with its dominant monad. When Leibniz was asked the use of this elaboration of organisms—why God could not have been satisfied with monads and their perceptions—he replied that a part of the function of the monad is to express its body, and that without bodies nature would lack the "bond of order" between all things (letters to Foucher, September 1695, *ibid.*, Vol. IV, pp. 492–493; to Jaquelot after September 1704, *ibid.*, Vol. VI, p. 570).

Objectivity of the physical world. Leibniz' view of monads and the physical world is quite in accordance with his account of phenomena, by which matter is phenomenal because the monads that give it reality are omitted from consideration, but it is difficult to reconcile this with any account that makes phenomena entirely subjective. Leibniz quite often spoke as if all that is necessary in the universe is God and individual monads with their inner states, so that the whole appearance of spatiotemporal material objects is entirely within each monad (letters to de Volder, June 30, 1704, *ibid.*, Vol. II, p. 270, and after November 14, 1704, *ibid.*, p. 275).

But what then becomes of Leibniz' stress on organisms as essential to the "bond of order"? The wisdom of God in harmonizing efficient and final causes requires that there should really be efficient causes, and efficient causes require that extended bodies in time have at least some degree of reality. Although space and time considered in themselves are abstractions, extended and enduring things are concrete. Even if they are "phenomenal" (in some sense) when reference to their underlying monads is left out of account, they nevertheless make up the real world, taken along with their monads. In abstracts the wholes are prior to the parts, so that parts are mere limitations of the wholes; but abstracts are derived from concretes, and in concretes the parts are prior to the wholes. Space and time, being abstract, are derived from enduring things; and enduring things, being concrete, are dependent on the monads composing them. Therefore, unless there are unitary monads that themselves have no parts, there are no concretes from which space and time can be abstracted.

This was one of Leibniz' main arguments, many times repeated, in favor of monads other than rational spirits. However, this whole elaborate structure vanishes if material things are merely contents of the perceptions of monads in a modern subjective sense. The student of Leibniz' conflicting writings must make what he can of this topic.

Space and time *considered by themselves* are not real; that is, they are not substances: they are ideal and abstract. Leibniz certainly regarded ideal space as having the structure given to it by Euclidean geometry, and he thought of this structure as being imposed on whatever is spatially extended. Space in this sense is also the form of possible coexistences, as time is the form of possible successive existents.

Organisms and "vis viva." At this point one of the most obscure parts of Leibniz' doctrine is involved. To get organisms into his world even as aggregates, Leibniz somehow had to derive them from his monads. To do this, he stated that (1) every monad is an entelechy (primitive active force) combined indissolubly with primary matter (primitive passive force); (2) derived forces, both active and passive, are modifications of primitive forces; (3) impenetrability of extended bodies is derived from the prime matter (*materia prima*) of monads, as is their inertia, although this in some way involves active force as well; (4) extension presupposes something diffused or spread out—something capable of resistance and which Leibniz further seems to have identified with the prime matters in a multitude of monads, although every such monad is involved as a whole; (5) in this way secondary matter (*materia secunda*) results; this is not just an extended mass of matter, but an aggregate of monads spatially related through their matters.

Derived active force, *vis viva*, belongs to *materia secunda*. Since primary active forces in the monads display themselves as derived active forces to the degree made possible by the interlinking of matter in space, a body can get the amount and kind of movement allowed it only through the moving bodies that environ it (May 1702, *ibid.*, Vol. IV, pp. 393 f., printed also in Gerhardt 1849–1863, Vol. VI, pp. 98 f.; *ibid.*, pp. 235, 247; Gerhardt 1875–1890, Vol. IV, pp. 364, 467; *ibid.*, pp. 510–511; and many other places).

It does not seem that there is any way of making out Leibniz' views in detail. An infinity of monads would have to contribute primary active force toward the *vis viva* of the smallest particle of *materia secunda*. Again, Leibniz always rejected the idea that there is any active power inside a monad that can actually produce a movement, so the link between primary active force and the force said to be derived from it is difficult to understand. Even if the derivation were successful, it would do nothing to justify the existence of organisms (as distinct from mere unorganized bodies); and Leibniz stated that while organisms are not essential to matter, they are essential to matter organized by a supreme wisdom (letter to Lady Masham, June 30, 1704, *ibid.*, Vol. III, pp. 356–357).

There is also the general difficulty of reconciling the dynamical account of monads as active centers of force impeded by primary matter with the psychological account of them as active–passive producers of confused and clear perceptions through appetition; it is hard to see how the monad could be both things, although Leibniz thought that it could (letter to des Bosses, March 11, 1706, *ibid.*, Vol. II, p. 307). Certainly overstress on the psychological account was liable to endanger the entire development based on the dynamical account.

GENERAL PRINCIPLES

Leibniz claimed that his philosophy was based on certain general principles concerning necessary truths and concerning truths of fact, which are contingent.

Principle of identity. The fundamental principle of necessary truths is the principle of identity, which Leibniz always associated with noncontradiction: *A* is *A* and cannot be non-*A*. The opposites of necessary truths are self-contradictory.

Principle of the best. A contingent truth is one whose opposite is not self-contradictory. The fundamental principle of contingent truths is the principle of the best, which arises from the free choice of God in creating the world. God, being perfectly wise, powerful, and good, is obliged to choose the best among possibles if he decides to admit any possibles to existence. However, this is a moral, not a metaphysical, necessity; he could refrain from creating any world, and it would not be self-contradictory (since he chose freely) if he chose to create a world less good than the best, although it is certain he would not do so.

The main difficulty here is that if God's wisdom, power, and goodness are necessary characteristics (and they seem to be if the standard proof of his existence from his essence, as amended by Leibniz, is sound), it is hard to see how there could be even the possibility of his doing something not in accordance with these characteristics.

Principle of sufficient reason. The principle of sufficient reason holds for all truths, but its main application was to contingent truths, since identity is the sufficient reason for necessary truths. It was used by Leibniz to show the impossibility of identical atoms: there would be no possible reason why any one such atom should be where it is rather than elsewhere. He similarly rejected the idea of the world's being created at a particular moment of time, on the ground that there could be no reason why it should not have been created earlier or later than that particular moment. Sometimes he used sufficient reason as the basis of the principle of the identity of indiscernibles. It is not impossible, he told Clarke, that there should be two things exactly alike, but God would not admit two such things into existence because he would have no reason for treating them differently (Alexander 1956, 5th letter, Sec. 25).

Metaphysically necessary principles. There are a number of principles that Leibniz considered metaphysically necessary, although he did not actually reduce them to identities; for instance, that everything possible demands (*exigit*) to exist, and will exist unless hindered. Here it must be remembered that what exists depends on God's will, and that unless possibles demanded existence, God would have no reason for admitting any of them into existence. However, once this reason is given God, he can and does impose conditions of perfection.

Other examples are the principle that activity is essential to substance, which Leibniz thought would hold in any world (Gerhardt 1875–1890, Vol. II, p. 169), and the axiom that a thing remains in its own state unless there is reason for change (*ibid.*, p. 170).

Principles of order. Very important for the understanding of Leibniz' philosophy of science are the laws that he called systematic, or laws of order ("Specimen Dynamicum," Gerhardt 1849–1863, Vol. VI, p. 241). These are the principle of continuity, the principle that every action involves a reaction, and the principle of the equality of cause and effect.

The principle of continuity has a wide range of application, since it covers changes in perception and all changes in degrees of perfection in monads. It also requires that there be no sudden qualitative alterations as an observer goes from one point of space to another. This principle, however, must be linked with an equally general one, that of maximum variety. There are no two locations, however close together, where there is not some divergence in every aspect of every feature. Leibniz also stressed two principles together: *tout comme ici*, and *che per variar la natura e bella*: nature is everywhere the same, everywhere varied (letter to Queen Sophie Charlotte, May 8, 1704, Gerhardt 1875–1890, Vol. III, pp. 343–348). To all these must be added the principle of maximum determination. Nature does not always seek the shortest paths, but always acts in the most determinate way.

Correspondence of efficient and final causes. One other important general point is the correspondence between efficient and final causes. The higher monads act in accordance with what appears their greatest good; final causes apply to them. In matter everything occurs through efficient causation, including the increase and diminution of organisms, although neither the origination nor the destruction of an organism is possible through mechanical means. The two realms of efficient and final causation correspond perfectly and in complete independence, the lower realm being so contrived as to "serve" the higher. The laws of efficient causation cannot be derived from matter, although they are "natural" to it.

Concept of the "natural." The conception of what is "natural" to a thing plays a significant part in Leibniz' system. The natural is intermediate between the essential and the accidental. It is, he held, capable of being derived from the nature of the thing as an explicable modification (Preface to *New Essays, ibid.*, Vol. V, p. 59). What God allows to exist, what he chooses as best, is chosen from natural characteristics, since to give things what is not natural to them would involve a constant miracle. Leibniz came to believe that the natural tendency of a body moving in a curved path is to move along the tangent to the curve; that bodies cannot naturally attract one another; that matter is not naturally capable of thinking; that there is a natural and not a merely arbitrary connection between our perceptions of secondary qualities and the bodily movements giving rise to these perceptions (for instance, *New Essays*, Book IV, Ch. 6, Sec. 7).

There is no clear justification for these views, but they show how anxious Leibniz was to avoid anything purely arbitrary in the construction of the universe. He was sure that God would not do anything merely because he willed it: if there were no objective reason to determine God's will, he would not act at all.

DISCUSSIONS OF CONTEMPORARY PHILOSOPHY

Leibniz was moved by the publication in 1704 of Coste's French translation of Locke's *Essay on Human Understanding* to lay his thoughts in detail alongside those of Locke. Leibniz' *New Essays (Nouveaux Essais sur l'entendement humain)* was not a systematic criticism of Locke's philosophy. It contains occasional discussions of Locke's views, but in general Leibniz expounded his own views, without giving reasons, on the points raised by Locke. The book is thus more valuable as a collection of passages relating to aspects of Leibniz' system than as a

thoroughgoing criticism of Locke. Leibniz had intended to publish the *New Essays* and get Locke's views on them, but Locke died in 1704, the year in which Leibniz wrote them, and he gave up the idea. They were first published at Amsterdam and Leipzig in 1765.

Criticisms of Descartes. Leibniz had also thought of publishing his papers on Descartes, but never succeeded in getting them ready. By comparison with his criticisms of Locke, Leibniz' criticisms of Descartes were much more searching. This was natural, in view of the strength of Cartesianism in France.

Leibniz and Spinoza. Leibniz was never a Spinozist. He thought highly of Spinoza, but held that his view that only what is actual is possible involved a denial of God's providence and of all freedom. His statement to Bourguet (Gerhardt 1875–1890, Vol. III, p. 576)—"Spinoza would be right if there were no monads"—emphasized a further point, the need for a "substantial foundation in things" other than God.

The "Theodicy." Leibniz' only large book on philosophy that was published during his lifetime, *Essais de Théodicée sur la bonté de Dieu, la liberté de l'homme et l'origine du mal* (the *Theodicy*), was the outcome of discussions with Sophie Charlotte on matters concerning free will, evil, and the justification of God's creation, many of which had been raised by Bayle. The *Theodicy*, written in French, was published at Amsterdam in 1710; a Latin translation by des Bosses, at Frankfurt in 1719. In this work Leibniz was at his ease, pouring out his vast learning with an avoidance of technicality and finding no difficulty in replying to objections in such a way as to appeal to Sophie Charlotte, who, while interested and intelligent, was not a professional philosopher. One of the interesting things about the *Theodicy* is the way in which Leibniz' memory unearthed ideas and views from his early years; a lifetime's ideas are in it. It is not to be put aside as mere recreation for a queen; unsystematic though it is, it contains many passages that give clear and explicit expression to many of Leibniz' views.

LATER CORRESPONDENCE

Of Leibniz' philosophic correspondence in his later years three sets may be singled out: that with Simon de Volder, a physicist and philosopher of Leiden and the literary executor of Huygens (*ibid.*, Vol. II, pp. 148 ff.); that with des Bosses, a Jesuit priest of Hildesheim (*ibid.*, pp. 291 ff.); and that with Samuel Clarke. In this correspondence Leibniz showed his mettle, not merely expressing his views but also defending them. De Volder, who forced Leibniz to discuss the notion of substance when Leibniz wanted to discuss the measurement of forces, remained unconvinced by Leibniz' accounts, although he compelled Leibniz to bring out explicitly many points in his view of substance.

The letters between Leibniz and Clarke, which concern Newton's views on space, time, and matter and Leibniz' views on these topics and the principle of sufficient reason, grew in length, and Leibniz died before he could receive Clarke's reply to his fifth letter. These letters went via the princess of Wales, whom Leibniz had known in Hanover, and national pride was at stake on both sides. The situation for Leibniz was embittered by the attack on his integrity that had been begun 15 years earlier by Fatio de Duillier, who charged that Leibniz had used—without acknowledgment—Newton's discoveries on the calculus, an attack that had been fully endorsed by the large-scale inquiry made by the Royal Society. The whole dispute was caused by misconceptions on both sides, and would have been unnecessary had Newton been less secretive and more ready to publish his work.

Des Bosses, in his correspondence with Leibniz, began by expounding certain difficulties he felt with regard to Leibniz' system, but gradually the discussion began to turn on the doctrine of transubstantiation. To explain how the blood and body of Christ could be literally present in the sacramental bread and wine, Leibniz suggested the notion of a substantial bond (*vinculum substantiale*) conferring substantiality on material bodies (such as bread and wine) so as to make them more than mere entities by aggregation (mere phenomena), as they were in Leibniz' system. What Leibniz himself wanted was not to confer substantiality on ordinary material bodies as such, but to show how an organism has unity through the presence in it of its dominant monad. While he never succeeded in showing this, he constantly asserted it (although sometimes he did deny it). However, a substantial bond of the sort discussed in these letters would be somewhat of an excrescence, since it would be affected by the monads but they would not be affected by it. The supplementary note at the end of the letter to des Bosses of August 19, 1715 (*ibid.*, p. 506), containing Leibniz' classification of entities, shows no trace of a need for any such bond.

THE PAPERS OF 1714

Mention must be made of two important papers of 1714, "Principes de la nature et de la grâce, fondés en raison" ("The Principles of Nature and of Grace," first published in *L'Europe savant*, 1718), written for Prince Eugene of Savoy, and the "Monadologie" ("Monadology," which first appeared in Erdmann, *Opera Philosophica*), begun for Remond. These two papers have much in common, although the "Monadology" is more complete and gives references throughout to the relevant sections of the *Theodicy*. Together they give a synoptic view of Leibniz' philosophy. It must be remembered, however, that for the working out of his views in detail, one must go to Leibniz' letters and papers; the synoptic views are insufficient.

Leibniz' general philosophical views could be made out pretty well from the papers published in his lifetime, along with the *Theodicy* and the correspondence with Samuel Clarke, published by Clarke in 1717. These do not, however, enable one to understand the grounds for his views, and without this, misunderstanding is only too easy. Publication of his writings came only slowly. Among the important works are the *New Essays*, published by R. E. Raspe in 1765, the *Discourse on Metaphysics* and correspondence with Arnauld, published by C. L. Grotefend in 1846, and the logical essays, published by Louis Couturat in 1903.

One personal characteristic of Leibniz helps to explain much in his work. He said he had a weak memory but strong gifts of invention and judgment (Guhrauer, *Life*, Vol. II, Appendix, p. 60). Much of his original work was done over and over: "When I have done something, I forget it almost completely in a few months, and rather than hunt for it among a chaos of sheets that I never had time to sort out and index, I have to do the work all over again" (Gerhardt 1849–1863, Vol. II, p. 228). His papers show how true this is. They were never reduced to order in the past, and it is only during the twentieth century, under the auspices of the Berlin and Paris academies, that a systematic attempt has been made to classify and catalogue them.

Bibliography

BIBLIOGRAPHICAL SOURCES

Bodemann, Eduard, *Der Briefwechsel des G. W. Leibniz in der Königlichen Öffentlichen Bibliothek zu Hannover.* Hanover, 1889; reprinted Hildesheim, after September 1965.

Bodemann, Eduard, *Die Leibniz-Handschriften zu Hannover.* Hanover, 1895; reprinted Hildesheim, after September 1965.

Ravier, Émile, *Bibliographie des oeuvres de Leibniz.* Paris, 1937. Corrections and additions by Paul Schrecker in *Revue philosophique de la France et de l'étranger*, Vol. 126 (1938), 324 ff.

WORKS

Opera Omnia, Louis Dutens, ed., 6 vols. Geneva, 1768. Still the most complete collection.

Leibniz's deutsche Schriften, G. E. Guhrauer, ed., 2 vols. Berlin, 1838–1840; reprinted Hildesheim, after September 1965.

Opera Philosophica, J. E. Erdmann, ed., 2 vols. Berlin, 1840; reprinted Aalen, 1958. Still the most useful compact edition.

Oeuvres, Amédée Jacques, ed., 2 vols. Vol. I, Paris, 1845; Vol. II, Paris, 1842.

Briefwechsel zwischen Leibniz, Arnauld und dem Grafen Ernst von Hessen-Rheinfels, C. L. Grotefend, ed. Hanover, 1846. First publication of the *Discourse on Metaphysics* (1685–1686).

Mathematische Schriften, C. I. Gerhardt, ed., 7 vols. Berlin and Halle, 1849–1863; reprinted Hildesheim, 1962. Much valuable philosophical matter.

Nouvelles Lettres et opuscules inédits, L. A. Foucher de Careil, ed. Paris, 1857. Still very useful.

Oeuvres, L. A. Foucher de Careil, ed., 7 vols. Paris, 1859–1875.

Briefwechsel zwischen Leibniz und Wolf, C. I. Gerhardt, ed. Halle, 1860; reprinted Hildesheim, 1963.

Philosophische Schriften, C. I. Gerhardt, ed., 7 vols. Berlin, 1875–1890; facsimile reprint Hildesheim, 1960–1961. Indispensable.

Mittheilungen aus Leibnizens ungedruckten Schriften, G. Mollat, ed. Leipzig, 1893.

Briefwechsel von G. W. Leibniz mit Mathematikern, C. I. Gerhardt, ed. Berlin, 1899; reprinted Hildesheim, 1962.

Opuscules et fragments inédits de Leibniz, Louis Couturat, ed. Paris, 1903; reprinted Hildesheim, 1961. A model of what such an edition should be. Exceedingly valuable for logic and theory of knowledge.

Nachgelassene Schriften physikalischen, mechanischen, und technischen Inhalts, Ernst Gerland, ed. Leipzig, 1906.

Leibniz. Avec de nombreux textes inédits, Jean Baruzi, ed. Paris, 1909.

Leibnitiana Elementa Philosophiae Arcanae de Summa Rerum, Iwan Jagodinski, ed. Kazan, Russia, 1913. Text with Russian translation. In spite of errors, this is a precious record. Review with many corrections by A. Rivaud, in *Revue de métaphysique et de morale*, Vol. 22 (1914), 94–120.

Leibnitiana Inedita. Confessio Philosophi, Iwan Jagodinski, ed. Kazan, Russia, 1915. Text with Russian translation. *Confessio* edited and translated into French by Yvon Belaval. Paris, 1961.

Ausgewählte philosophische Schriften im Originaltext, Herman Schmalenbach, ed., 2 vols. Leipzig, 1915.

Sämtliche Schriften und Briefe, edited under the supervision of the Preussische Akademie der Wissenschaft. Darmstadt and Leipzig, 1923——. Only one volume of the philosophical letters and two of the philosophical writings have appeared so far. The remaining volumes are historical and political.

Lettres et fragments inédits, Paul Schrecker, ed. Paris, 1934.

Textes inédits, Gaston Grua, ed., 2 vols. Paris, 1948. A most useful addition to the published material.

REVISIONS OF TEXTS

Discours de métaphysique, Henri Lestienne, ed. Paris, 1907; 2d ed., 1929; reprinted 1952. This diplomatic edition contains all the variants of Leibniz' drafts.

Lettres de Leibniz à Arnauld, Geneviève Lewis, ed. Paris, 1952. Gives text as received by Arnauld, but Arnauld's replies are not given.

Malebranche et Leibniz, André Robinet, ed. Paris, 1953. Large collection of texts from original sources.

Principes de la nature et de la grâce fondés en raison; Principes de la philosophie ou monadologie, André Robinet, ed. Paris, 1954. Gives all variants.

Correspondance Leibniz–Clarke, André Robinet, ed. Paris, 1957.

COMMENTARIES

Boutroux, Émile, *La Monadologie*. Paris, 1881; reprinted Paris, 1956.

Burgelin, Pierre, *Commentaire du Discours de métaphysique*. Paris, 1959.

Costabelle, Pierre, *Leibniz et le dynamique. Les textes de 1692*. Paris, 1960.

Le Roy, Georges, *Discours de métaphysique et Correspondance avec Arnauld*. Paris, 1957.

ENGLISH TRANSLATIONS

Philosophical Works, translated by G. M. Duncan. New Haven, 1890.

The Monadology and Other Philosophical Writings, translated by Robert Latta. Oxford, 1898.

Discourse on Metaphysics, Correspondence With Arnauld, Monadology, translated by G. R. Montgomery. Chicago, 1902. Contains many mistranslations. Edited with corrections by A. R. Chandler. Chicago, 1924.

New Essays Concerning Human Understanding, translated by A. G. Langley. Chicago, 1916; reprinted 1949. Many errors in translation.

Monadology, translated by H. W. Carr. London and Los Angeles, 1930.

Philosophical Writings, translated by Mary Morris. London, 1934.

Theodicy, translated by E. M. Huggard, Austin Farrer, ed. London, 1951.

Selections, translated by Philip Wiener. New York, 1951. A wide and very representative collection.

Monadology, translated by P. G. Lucas and Leslie Grint. Manchester, 1953; reprinted with minor corrections, 1961. Based on Lestienne's edition.

Leibniz–Clarke Correspondence, H. G. Alexander, ed. Manchester, 1956. Gives Clarke's translation of Leibniz' letters.

Philosophical Papers and Letters, translated by L. E. Loemker, 2 vols. Chicago, 1956. The widest and most useful collection in English, with an admirable selected, annotated bibliography.

GERMAN TRANSLATIONS

Hauptschriften, translated by Ernst Cassirer and Artur Buchenau, 5 vols. Leipzig, 1904–1906; 2d ed., 2 vols., Leipzig, 1924.

Schöpferische Vernunft, translated by Wolf von Engelhardt. Marburg, 1952. A very useful collection, containing much not translated elsewhere; for instance, *Pacidius Philalethi*.

Fragmente zur Logik, translated by Franz Schmidt. Berlin, 1960.

A microfilm negative of unpublished manuscripts in Hanover, selected by Paul Schrecker, is deposited in the University of Pennsylvania Library. Permission for a positive copy to be made must be obtained from the Niedersachsische Landesbibliothek in Hanover.

BIOGRAPHIES

Fischer, Kuno, *Gottfried Wilhelm Leibniz. Leben, Werke und Lehre*, 5th ed., Willy Kabitz, ed. Heidelberg, 1920. Of great value, with appendix containing many new details and corrections.

Guhrauer, G. E., *Gottfried Wilhelm, Freiherr von Leibniz*, 2 vols. Breslau, 1842; 2d ed., 1846; reprinted Hildesheim, after September 1965. The only full-scale life.

Huber, Kurt, *Leibniz*. Munich, 1951.

Merz, J. T., *Leibniz*. Edinburgh and London, 1884; reprinted New York, 1948. Still useful.

Wiedeburg, Paul, *Der junge Leibniz, das Reich und Europa*, Part I, *Mainz*, 2 vols. Wiesbaden, 1962.

INTERPRETATIONS

Belaval, Yvon, *Leibniz, critique de Descartes*. Paris, 1960.

Belaval, Yvon, *Leibniz. Initiation à sa philosophie*. Paris, 1962. Replaces *La Pensée de Leibniz* (1952).

Blondel, Maurice, *Une Énigme historique: Le Vinculum substantiale d'après Leibniz*. Paris, 1930.

Boehm, A., *Le "Vinculum substantiale" chez Leibniz*. Paris, 1934.

Brunner, Fernand, *Études sur la signification historique de la philosophie de Leibniz*. Paris, 1950.

Cassirer, Ernst, *Leibniz' System in seinen wissenschaftlichen Grundlagen*. Marburg, 1902; reprinted 1962. Classical study.

Couturat, Louis, *La Logique de Leibniz*. Paris, 1901; reprinted Hildesheim, 1961. Classical study.

Friedmann, Georges, *Leibniz et Spinoza*. 2d ed., Paris, 1946; 3d ed., 1963. Useful correction of wrong ideas.

Galli, Gallo, *Studi sulla filosofia de Leibniz*. Padua, 1948.

Grua, Gaston, *Jurisprudence universelle et théodicée selon Leibniz*. Paris, 1953.

Grua, Gaston, *La Justice humaine selon Leibniz*. Paris, 1956.

Gueroult, M., *Dynamique et métaphysique leibniziennes*. Paris, 1934. An admirable full-scale study of Leibniz' dynamics.

Hildebrandt, Kurt, *Leibniz und das Reich der Gnade*. The Hague, 1953.

Iwanicki, Joseph, *Leibniz et les démonstrations mathématiques de l'existence de Dieu*. Strasbourg, 1933.

Jalabert, Jacques, *La Théorie leibnizienne de la substance*. Paris, 1947.

Jalabert, Jacques, *Le Dieu de Leibniz*. Paris, 1960.

Joseph, H. W. B., *Lectures on the Philosophy of Leibniz*. Oxford, 1949.

Kabitz, Willy, *Die Philosophie des jungen Leibniz*. Heidelberg, 1909. A very good account.

Le Chevalier, L., *La Morale de Leibniz*. Paris, 1933.

Mahnke, Dietrich, *Leibnizens Synthese von Universalmathematik und Individualmetaphysik*. Halle, 1925. Still one of the best discussions of Leibniz; contains full-scale criticisms of Cassirer, Couturat, and Russell works.

Martin, Gottfried, *Leibniz: Logik und Metaphysik*. Cologne, 1960. Translated by P. G. Lucas as *Leibniz: Logic and Metaphysics*. Manchester, 1963.

Moreau, Joseph, *L'Universe leibnizien*. Paris, 1956.

Naert, Émilienne, *Leibniz et la querelle du pur amour*. Paris, 1959.

Naert, Émilienne, *Mémoire et conscience de soi selon Leibniz*. Paris, 1961.

Piat, Clodius, *Leibniz*. Paris, 1915.

Pichler, Hans, *Leibniz*. Graz, 1919.

Russell, Bertrand, *A Critical Exposition of the Philosophy of Leibniz*. Cambridge, 1900; 2d ed., 1937.

Schmalenbach, Herman, *Leibniz*. Munich, 1921.

Stieler, Georg, *Leibniz und Malebranche und das Theodicee Problem*. Darmstadt, 1930.

Wundt, Wilhelm, *Leibniz*. Leipzig, 1917.

CHRISTIAN UNIFICATION

Baruzi, Jean, *Leibniz et l'organisation religieuse de la terre.* Paris, 1907. The best book on the subject.

LEIBNIZ AS HISTORIAN

Davillé, L., *Leibniz historien.* Paris, 1909.
Schischkoff, Goerge, ed., *Beiträge zur Leibniz-Forschung.* Reutlingen, 1946.

L. J. RUSSELL

LENIN, V. I. (1870–1924), born Vladimir Ilyich Ulyanov, Russian political leader, Marxist theoretician, and, after Karl Marx and Friedrich Engels, the chief architect of the philosophy of dialectical materialism. Lenin was born in Simbirsk (now Ulyanovsk), Russia. He enrolled in the University of Kazan in 1887 but was soon expelled for participating in student disturbances; in 1891 he received a degree in law from the University of St. Petersburg as a correspondence student. He was imprisoned in 1895 for revolutionary activity, was exiled to Siberia in 1897, and from 1900 to 1917 lived abroad, except for the years 1905 to 1907, when he returned to Russia and took an active part in the revolutionary movement. Lenin was the acknowledged leader of the Bolsheviks from the time of their break with the Mensheviks in 1903, and after the Bolshevik revolution of 1917 he headed the government of the Soviet Union until his death.

Lenin's philosophical activity extended from his student days to the revolution, and throughout this period, its character was determined by his devotion to the principles and tactics of Marxist social reconstruction. His writings are strongly polemical, exemplifying the Leninist concept of *partiinost* ("partisanship" or "party spirit") in philosophy. Lenin first studied the writings of Marx and Engels systematically in 1888 and 1889. One of his earliest works, *Chto Takoye "Druz'ya Naroda" i Kak Oni Voyuyut Protiv Sotsial-Demokratov* (*What the "Friends of the People" Are and How They Fight the Social-Democrats*, 1894, distributed in hectographed copies)—directed against the Russian Populists, such as N. K. Mikhailovsky—shows Lenin's general acceptance of dialectical materialism, the materialist conception of history, and the characteristic concepts of Marxist socialism. The distinctively Leninist element already evident is the strong emphasis on action, on the need to combine theory with revolutionary practice. Lenin asserted that the objective, necessary character of the laws of history in no way destroys the role of active individuals in history. Thus, unlike the more "fatalistic" or evolutionary Marxists, Lenin stressed the need for deliberately organizing the revolution and for focusing attention on the proletariat as the leading revolutionary force and viewing the peasantry as an ally of the proletariat. This activist approach was carried further in subsequent works, chiefly *Chto Delat'?* (*What Is to Be Done?*, Stuttgart, 1902) and *Shag Vperyod, Dva Shaga Nazad* (*One Step Forward, Two Steps Back*, Geneva, 1904), in which Lenin elaborated the need for a militant, centralized, and highly disciplined party to unify and direct the proletariat.

Lenin's chief philosophical work, *Materializm i Empirio-Krititsizm* (*Materialism and Empirio-Criticism*, Moscow, 1909), is directed against a group of Russian writers, including Bazarov, Bogdanov, and Lunacharsky, who attempted to supplement Marxism with the phenomenalistic positivism of Avenarius and Mach. Characterizing their position as a form of subjective idealism (and thus as inimical to Marxism), Lenin defended dialectical materialism on the chief points at issue, particularly the status and character of matter and the nature of knowledge. Opposing the view that matter is a construct of sensations, Lenin argued that matter is ontologically primary, existing independently of consciousness. Likewise, space and time are not subjective modes of ordering experience but objective forms of the existence of matter. Opposing the view that discoveries of modern science cast doubt on the "materiality" of matter, Lenin distinguished between scientific conceptions of the composition of matter, which are provisional and "relative" because no components can be regarded as irreducible ("The electron is as inexhaustible as the atom"), and the philosophical conception, according to which matter is simply "the objective reality given to us in sensation." The only property of matter to which philosophical materialism is committed, according to Lenin, is "the property of being an objective reality." In epistemology, Lenin opposed the "hieroglyph" theory of Plekhanov, according to which sensations are noniconic signs of an external reality, and developed a strictly realist position, the "copy theory," according to which sensations depict or mirror the real world. On this basis Lenin defended the possibility of objective truth, emphasizing practice as its criterion.

Dialectics, which Lenin had long considered the heart of Marxism, is treated most fully in the *Filosofskiye Tetradi* (*Philosophical Notebooks*), a collection of notebooks and fragments, published posthumously, dating chiefly from 1914 to 1916 and including Lenin's extracts from, and comments on, a number of philosophical works, above all Hegel's *Science of Logic*. Lenin showed a high regard for the Hegelian dialectic, which he found thoroughly compatible with materialism, and asserted that dialectics, logic, and the theory of knowledge are identical. In his conception of dialectics Lenin departed from Engels in laying greatest stress not on the transition from quantity to quality but on the struggle of opposing ("contradictory") forces or tendencies within every natural object and process; Lenin saw this struggle as the basis of all change ("the self-movement of matter"), and thus as the core of dialectics. Dialectics, Lenin stated, is "the study of contradiction in the very essence of objects."

Lenin's last major works are concerned with questions of historical materialism, in particular with economic and political aspects of the revolutionary transition from capitalism to communism. In *Imperializm, Kak Vysshaya Stadiya Kapitalizma* (*Imperialism, the Highest Stage of Capitalism*, Petrograd, 1916) Lenin argued that capitalism had reached its final, monopolistic phase and was ripe for overthrow, but that, because of the "uneven" development of capitalism in different countries, socialism would not triumph in all or most countries simultaneously, as Marx had expected. In *Gosudarstvo i Revolutsiya* (*State and Revolution*, Petrograd, 1918), directed against the "opportunism" of such Marxists as Plekhanov and Kautsky, Lenin developed the Marxist theory of the state as an instrument of class domination. He laid special stress on a number of points not fully elaborated by Marx or Engels—the need for shattering the bourgeois state machinery, the establishment of the proletarian state or "dictatorship of the proletariat," and the distinction between a lower phase of communism, in which reward is proportional to work and the state is still needed, and a higher phase, in which reward is proportional to need and the state will "wither away" completely.

Contemporary Soviet philosophers consider Lenin a philosophical luminary of the first magnitude and commonly call their over-all intellectual outlook "Marxism–Leninism."

Works by Lenin

The most recent Russian editions of Lenin's writings include *Sochineniya*, 4th ed., 40 vols. (Moscow, 1941–1962); there is a two-volume index to this edition. See also *Polynoye Sobraniye Sochineni*, 5th ed., 49 vols. to date (Moscow, 1958——). Among the most recent English editions are *Collected Works*, a translation of the fourth Russian edition, 20 vols. to date (Moscow, 1960——) and *Selected Works*, 3 vols. (Moscow, 1963–1964).

Works on Lenin

For literature on Lenin, see A. M. Deborin, *Lenin Kak Myslitel'* ("Lenin as a Thinker," 3d ed., Moscow and Leningrad, 1929); M. A. Dynnik et al., eds., *Istoriya Filosofii*, Vol. 5 (Moscow, 1961); Gustav A. Wetter, *Il materialismo dialettico sovietico* (Turin, 1948), translated into English by Peter Heath as *Dialectical Materialism* (London, 1958); Leon Trotsky, *Lenin* (New York, 1925); N. K. Krupskaya, *Vospominaniya o Lenine*, 2 vols. (Moscow and Leningrad, 1930–1931), translated into English by Bernard Isaacs as *Reminiscences of Lenin* (Moscow, 1959); Bertram Wolfe, *Three Who Made a Revolution*, rev. ed. (Boston, 1955); Louis Fischer, *Life of Lenin* (New York, 1964).

JAMES P. SCANLAN

LEONARDO DA VINCI (1452–1519), Florentine artist, scientist, and inventor, was born at Vinci in Tuscany, the natural son of a notary, and died near Amboise, France. At his death he left a sizable collection of notebooks which were subsequently scattered in the various libraries of Europe. From 1881 on, many of these notebooks have been published. They consist of notes and jottings on various topics: mechanics, physics, anatomy, physiology, literature, and philosophy. They contain, moreover, plans and designs for machines that frequently have suggested Leonardo's "precursive genius." There are machines of war and of peace, flying machines based on the flight of birds, a parachute, a helicopter, tools and gadgets of all kinds. Leonardo's notebooks are also full of methodological notations on the procedures of scientific inquiry and philosophical considerations about the processes of nature. Undoubtedly many of the arguments which he discussed were taken from the philosophical literature of the time, especially from the writings of the Ockhamists; however, a coherent and complete philosophical scheme cannot be found in the notes, whose chronological order is extremely uncertain. Duhem held that Leonardo was mainly inspired by the doctrines of Nicholas of Cusa, but recent studies tend to emphasize his dependence on Marsilio Ficino. Leonardo lived in Florence for the first thirty years of his life and subsequently returned there many times.

Leonardo's *Treatise on Painting* (published 1651) reveals the artist and the scientist united in one personality. Painting, which he placed above all other arts, aims at representing the work of nature to the senses. Thus it extends to the surfaces, the colors, and the forms of natural objects, which science studies in their intrinsic forms. The beauty that painting seeks in things is the proportion of the things themselves, and proportion is also the object of the scientific consideration of nature. According to Leonardo, understanding nature means understanding the proportion that is found not only in numbers but also in sounds, weights, times, spaces, and any natural power whatever. Both art and science have the same object, the harmonious order of nature, which art represents to the senses and science expresses in its laws.

Leonardo held that the two pillars on which science stands are experience and mathematical calculation. As an "unlettered man" (as he called himself) he had contempt for those who, instead of learning from experience, claimed to learn from books (the commentators and followers of Aristotle). He contrasted his work as an inventor with their work of "trumpeting and reciting the work of others." "Wisdom is the daughter of experience," he said. Experience never deceives, and those who lament its deceitfulness should lament their own ignorance because they demand from experience what is beyond its limits. The judgment of experience can be mistaken; and the only way to avoid error is to subject every judgment to mathematical calculation and to utilize mathematics unrestrictedly to understand and demonstrate the reasons for the things that experience manifests. Mathematics is therefore, according to Leonardo, the basis of all certitude, since without recourse to mathematics it is impossible to put an end to the verbal disagreements of what he called the sophistic sciences—that is, the philosophical disputes about nature.

The privilege accorded to mathematics was most certainly a legacy from Platonism. Leonardo took from Plato's *Timaeus* and Ficino's commentary on it the doctrine that the elements of natural bodies are geometric forms; thus the efficacy of mathematics as an instrument of investigation was justified for him by the fact that nature itself is written in mathematical characters and that only those who know the language of mathematics can decipher it. This is the major contribution that ancient Platonism made to the formation of modern science. Copernicus and Galileo shared this obviously metaphysical doctrine which, however, strongly contributed to launching science from its origins to its mathematical organization. It helped bring scientific consideration from the domain of quality (of natures or essences) to that of quantity by permitting consideration of the natural object as measurable; that is, in the extremes, by reducing the objectivity of nature to its measurability.

However, if the order of nature is a mathematical order, then it is a necessary order; and this necessity is, according to Leonardo, the only true "miracle" of nature: "O wondrous and awesome necessity! With your law you constrain all effects to result from their causes by the shortest path, and according to the highest and irrevocable law every natural action obeys you with the briefest operation." The phrases "by the shortest path" and "with the briefest operation" refer to another feature of the necessary order of nature: its simplicity. Nature follows the shortest or simplest path in its operations. It does not like useless loitering, and this also reveals the mathematical character of its structures. Necessity and simplicity of nature exclude the presence of arbitrary or miraculous forces, as well as the efficacy of magic and of those forces to which it appeals.

Guided by these criteria, Leonardo could arrive at and formulate important theorems and principles of statics and dynamics. The theorem of the composition of forces, the principle of inertia, and the principle of action and reaction are the most notable of these formulations, which, of course, he did not state in the precise form that they received later from Descartes and Newton. Nevertheless, they demonstrate his genius for moving from the limited work of the inventor to the generalizations of the scientist.

Bibliography

Leonardo's manuscripts have been published with photographic reproductions by Charles Ravaisson-Mollien, 6 vols. (Paris, 1881–1891). They have also been published in G. Piumati, ed., *Codex Atlanticus* (Milan, 1894–1904) and *I manoscritti e i disegni di Leonardo da Vinci*, published by the Reale Commissione Vinciana (Rome, 1923–1930). The best collection of selections is J. P. Richter, *The Literary Work of Leonardo da Vinci*, 2 vols. (London, 1883; 2d ed., 1939). *Leonardo da Vinci On Painting: A Lost Book*, edited and translated from the *Codex Vaticanus Urbinas*, No. 1270, and from the *Codex Leicester* by Carlo Pedretti (Berkeley, 1964), includes a preface by Kenneth Clark and some material never published before.

Works on Leonardo include the following: Pierre Duhem, *Études sur Leonardo da Vinci*, 3 vols. (Paris, 1906–1913); E. Solmi, *Leonardo* (Florence, 1900); C. Luporini, *La mente di Leonardo* (Florence, 1953); Eugenio Garin, *Medioevo e Rinascimento* (Bari, 1954), pp. 311 ff., and *Cultura filosofica del Rinascimento italiano* (Florence, 1961), pp. 388 ff.; and I. B. Hart, *The World of Leonardo da Vinci* (London, 1961).

NICOLA ABBAGNANO
Translated by *Nino Langiulli*

LEONTYEV, KONSTANTIN NIKOLAYEVICH

(1831–1891), Russian writer, religious thinker, and philosopher, was trained in medicine at Moscow University and served as an army doctor in the Crimean War. He gave up medical practice in the early 1860s and entered the Russian diplomatic service, serving in Turkey for eight years. Following a religious crisis, he spent a year (1870/1871) in a Greek Orthodox monastery on Mount Athos. Later Leontyev worked as a journalist in Warsaw and as a government censor in Moscow. He retired to the Optina cloister, in the province of Tula, in 1887 and took monastic vows shortly before his death in 1891.

Leontyev has been called a Russian Nietzsche, but some of his most Nietzschean views were developed independently, and others were suggested by Alexander Herzen, who may himself have influenced Nietzsche.

For Leontyev, aesthetic values were decisively superior to moral, social, or economic values. An early statement (1864) by a character in one of his novels dramatizes the point: "A single century-old, magnificent tree is worth more than twenty faceless men" (*Sobraniye Sochinenii*, Vol. I, p. 306). Much later, in criticizing European tech-

nology, Leontyev added, "Intensification of movement does not in itself indicate intensification of life. The machine runs, but the living tree stands firm" (Letter to V. V. Rozanov, July 30, 1891, *Russki Vestnik*, Vol. 285, 1903, p. 414).

Leontyev, like Herzen, saw a retrogression, a gradual grinding down of the brilliance and intensity of earlier times under the massive pressure of modern mediocrity, reinforced by the egalitarian drift of advanced technology. He was appalled at the thought that

> Moses went up to Sinai, the Greeks built their splendid Acropolises, the Romans waged their Punic wars, the handsome genius Alexander, in a feathered helmet, crossed the Granicus and fought at Arbela, the apostles preached, martyrs suffered, poets sang, painters painted, and knights shone in tourneys—only in order that the French, German, or Russian bourgeois, in his ugly and comical clothing, should sit complacently . . . on the ruins of all this past greatness. (*Sobraniye Sochinenii*, Vol. V, p. 426)

Leontyev sketched the outlines of a philosophy of history, inspired by N. Y. Danilevski, to account for the decay of European civilization: Historical cultures, like biological organisms, proceed from a stage of initial simplicity to a culminating stage of "flourishing complexity" and then sink, through "secondary simplification" and "leveling interfusion," to organic death (*ibid.*, pp. 195 and 197). European culture was far along in this process, having reached its "flourishing complexity" during the Middle Ages. Russian culture, since the time of Peter the Great, had been sinking toward "leveling interfusion"; the task of the nineteenth century was to reverse this process. Leontyev attempted to do just this by sharply attacking European secular humanism, "anthropolatry," and the utilitarian–egalitarian *mania democratica progressiva* as being destructive of hierarchy, unity in diversity, the "despotism of form" (both aesthetic and political), and the free creativity of strong individuals. He defended "the pressure of classes, despotism, danger, strong passions, prejudices, superstitions, fanaticism . . . , in a word everything to which the nineteenth century is opposed" (*ibid.*, Vol. VIII, p. 98). He even posed the rhetorical question: "Which is better—the bloody but spiritually luxuriant period of the Renaissance, or the tame, prosperous, moderate existence of contemporary Denmark, Holland, and Switzerland?" (*ibid.*, Vol. I, p. 414).

The individualism which Leontyev attacked was bourgeois, security-minded, self-enclosed, and egalitarian; that which he defended was aristocratic, risk-seeking, "open," and hierarchical. Nietzsche had made a distinction between Christian *Nächstenliebe* (love of one's neighbor) and anti-Christian *Fernstenliebe* (love of the far-off, that is, of future generations). To love and to help one's neighbor, according to Nietzsche, is to preserve the weak and uncreative, thus undermining the living culture of the future. Leontyev drew a similar distinction, but reversed Nietzsche's evaluations, rejecting love of a "collective and abstract mankind" (*ibid.*, Vol. VIII, p. 207) and "the feverish preoccupation with the earthly well-being of future generations" (*ibid.*, p. 189) in the name of an inclusive compassion which, though evincing a Christian concern for presently encountered, existing human beings, embraces the strong and creative as well as the weak and suffering.

Bibliography

Sobraniye Sochinenii ("Collected Works") was published in 9 volumes in Moscow (1912–1914). "Sredny Yevropeyets kak Ideal i Orudiye Vsemirnovo Razrusheniya" ("The Average European as an Ideal and Instrument of Universal Destruction"), Vol. VI, pp. 1–79 of *Sobraniye Sochinenii*, was translated and abridged by W. Shafer and G. L. Kline and was published in James M. Edie, James P. Scanlan, Mary-Barbara Zeldin, and George L. Kline, eds., *Russian Philosophy* (Chicago, 1965), Vol. II, pp. 271–280.

For literature on Leontyev, see Nikolai Berdyaev, *Konstantin Leontyev: Ocherk iz Istorii Russkoi Religioznoi Mysli* ("Konstantin Leontyev: An Essay in the History of Russian Religious Thought," Paris, 1926), translated by George Reavey as *K. N. Leontiev* (London, 1940); Thomas G. Masaryk, *Die geistigen Strömungen in Russland* (Jena, 1913), translated by Eden Paul and Cedar Paul as *The Spirit of Russia: Studies in History, Literature, and Philosophy* (London and New York, 1955), Vol. II, pp. 207–220: V. V. Zenkovsky, *Istoriya Russkoi Filosofii*, 2 vols. (Paris, 1948 and 1950), translated by G. L. Kline as *A History of Russian Philosophy*, 2 vols. (London and New York, 1953), pp. 434–453.

Georce L. Kline

LEOPARDI, COUNT GIACOMO (1798–1837), Italian poet and prose writer, was one of five children born to Count Monaldo Leopardi and Marquise Adelaide Antici, in Recanati, near Ancona. His brief and anguished existence was plagued both by continuous illnesses (among them rachitis, which made him a hunchback) and the bigotry of his parents, who refused him financial support. A liberal and an agnostic, he yearned to leave the "bodiless, soulless, lifeless" ancestral abode where he had spent all his time devouring books; learning Latin, Greek, Hebrew, and a number of modern languages; and translating and writing critical essays on the classics, history, and astronomy. A fellow philologist, Pietro Giordani, opened to him the world beyond his "savage native town." Afterward, he traveled to Rome, Milan, Bologna, Pisa, Florence, and Naples, never venturing beyond the Alps because of his frail constitution, and even refusing the Dante chair offered to him by the University of Bonn. Often he returned to Recanati, only to leave after a short stay. Nature and beauty offered him moments of precious calm, but these few instants could not dispel the physical and metaphysical oppression which, for Leopardi, seemed to weigh upon the world. Everywhere reality proved a bitter disillusionment. Several devoted publishers and friends offered him various jobs and forms of subsistence, but generally to little avail. The poet both expected and invoked death, which came to him in Naples in 1837, shortly after he had dictated his last poem.

The "Canti." As Elme Marie Caro said, Leopardi wanted to be, deserved to be, and was a philosopher. He did not come to philosophy through poetry, or to poetry through philosophy; his poetry is his philosophy. While Leopardi's prose works (the magnificently cogent *Operette morali*, 1827; the diary called the *Zibaldone*, 1898–1900; and the copious correspondence, or *Epistolario*, published posthumously) reflect the melancholy meditations of a thinker concerned with universal sorrow, the most fulfilling expression of his thoughts is to be found in his poetry, the *Canti* (1831, 1835, 1845). The *Canti* complement and complete the *Operette*, because in expression and content they constitute an organic outgrowth of the nature and orientation of Leopardi's philosophy.

Pessimism. Leopardi's philosophy, which should not be viewed as a methodically pondered and presented system, has been labeled skeptical and pessimistic, a philosophy of despair. Indeed, it dwells upon the triumph of evil over good and of nature over man, the mystery and insignificance of our mortal existence, the anguish of our miseries, the extinction of youth, and the lure of death. As Schopenhauer recognized, "No one has treated these subjects more fundamentally and exhaustively in our day than Leopardi." Given the limited dissemination of Schopenhauer's *Die Welt als Wille und Vorstellung* (1819) at that time, it is unlikely that Leopardi read the work or that he met the author. It is certain, however, that Schopenhauer read Leopardi's poems; yet while he mentions them, he in no way indicates whether they influenced the development of his own thought.

Yet the similarities run deep. Leopardi characterized life—this life we love, not for itself but, erroneously, for its promise of happiness — under the rubrics of sorrow (*dolore*), or unhappiness (*infelicità*), and tedium (*noia*). By means of this perspective, he was able to discard many cherished notions. Assuming the hapless state of humanity, the notions of patriotism and heroism vanish as follies, as does the glory of genius, which the poet had once assiduously pursued and which later, like Eduard von Hartmann, he relegated to the category of illusions. As for love and beauty, they entice soul and senses cruelly, since their ephemerality brands them as colossal deceptions. Nature, which according to Leopardi is the mysterious principle of being, closely related to Hartmann's concept of the Unconscious as a neutral absolute, answers none of man's queries about the secret of things; it is undecipherable, mechanical, unreasoning and unreasonable, and at times brutally hostile toward men. Man, then, is nothing; if he is something, he is so by virtue of being his own greatest enemy. In the *Operette morali*, Schopenhauer's gloomy picture of life as a gory chase in which men scramble for spoils differs only moderately from Leopardi's description of Prometheus' and Momus' journey.

Death as nonbeing is therefore, like love during its moment of existence, a thing of beauty. Death as suicide, however, solves nothing because it constitutes not a negation of existence but rather, as Schopenhauer asserted, an act directed against the accidental portion of unhappiness which creeps into human existence. Moreover, the future holds no promise, and "progress" and "perfectibility" are empty words.

Evil. Leopardian pessimism differs from Schopenhauer's on two questions: the principle of evil and the remedy of evil. Leopardi refused to consider the problem of the necessity of evil and, in any case, would not have ascribed evil to a principle, such as Will or the Unconscious, simply because he believed that evil is an empirical datum and does not require metaphysical or transcendental explanation. He felt the existence of evil and saw only gross arbitrariness in those who attempt to show why it must exist, or who make a transcendent dialectics of the universal law of suffering. Historical pessimism, which stems from the "restless creative mind" of men who boldly oppose unconquerable nature, and cosmic pessimism, through which evil, inherent in nature, subjugates man, are fundamentally interrelated in Leopardi's philosophy and preclude all thought of remedy. The individual's only recourse is stoic dignity—resignation, silence, and scorn. "Of what value is our life, except to despise it?" In this respect, Leopardi was a precursor of German pessimism.

Schopenhauer also upheld Stoic dignity, but for Leopardi dignity was less a remedy for suffering than an instinctive and protective reaction that neither alters suffering nor consoles the sufferer. Schopenhauer even found some consolation in the Buddhist ideal of nirvana, which Leopardi could not. And while Schopenhauer could derive a sense of pride from his belief that the more developed the organism, the greater its misery, Leopardi, even when speaking of man's nobility, could not find in it any basic gratification. The degree to which both men felt a sense of compassion differed: Leopardi's pity, although less central to his ethics than *Mitleid* was to Schopenhauer's, was still less condescending and more sympathetic than Schopenhauer's.

Leopardi held to the inexorability of destiny and nature's blind subservience to it—subservience which fails to take into account man's struggle and misery. Everything, therefore, is deceit; the only truth lies in nothingness. For Leopardi, what counts is the philosophical negation of life, both in its effective pains and in its false felicities. Only in this way can one claim to demonstrate moral consistency—through the affirmation of a negative totality.

Illusions and reality. Reason, then, in Leopardi is tantamount to negation. Illusions are merely dreams, substances insofar as they may be considered "essential ingredients" of living, "half-real things." Since all that is real comes to nothing, Leopardi inverted the concept of reality and asserted that only the illusory is real. In claiming this, he did not suggest that reality is a mere phenomenon concealing a noumenon. On the contrary: the reality of the world in which man lives and which has meaning for him is neither rational nor spiritual, but natural and imaginary; it is a reality that is necessarily maintained by what we call illusions. Beyond it lies complete negation. Hence Leopardi professed the opposite of the instinctive noumenalism of man's mind. The world is real in relation to the absence of those other substances which we seek under the heading of truth. Just as the world is arbitrary, so men's beliefs, desires, hopes, and "certainties" (justice, science, virtue, freedom, idealism) are merely groundless illusions. Leopardi despised theological, dogmatic, spiritualistic philosophies, along with any form of presumptuous optimism.

Religion. The philosophy outlined above precluded religious faith. Leopardi might assent to the Scriptures' theory of man's decadence, but he could not admit Christian Providence or the Resurrection. Yet although he is unhappy (*infelice*), the poet is not irreligious. His "atheism" bespeaks the combined awareness of the necessity and of the absence of God—in short, of the impossibility of hope. Escape into pleasure is self-deceiving

("pleasure is a subjective speculation and is unreal"), for we seek the idea of pleasure more than we seek pleasure itself; indeed, the latter does not exist. The resulting tedium closely approaches Heidegger's *Angst,* which reflects the experience of nothingness.

Value of life. Because Leopardi is an artist and poet, the immensity of his despair loses its bitterness in a melancholy and fraternal contemplation of existence. Despair allows him to understand the value of human life, although in the long run life is a "useless misery." As a measure of exiguous man's infinite desires against the infinity of being, tedium itself (that is, enthusiasm, heroism, and desperation successively experienced and resulting in a sense of nothingness) seemed to him "the greatest sign of grandeur and nobility in human nature." He recognized illusion as a positive value, offsetting negation and "the infinite vanity of all things." This kind of deception is of value to man, since it constitutes his only justifiable pleasure. Despite it, or actually because of it, Leopardi called for brotherly solidarity and compassion, not out of love of God, but out of a desire to combat the cruelty of destiny and of nature.

What Leopardi finally did was to negate negation, thus creating what he called an ultraphilosophy. He developed a philosophy about philosophy (namely, that we should not philosophize) which rejects reason. For, wrote Leopardi, "As Bayle said, in metaphysics and morals reason cannot edify, only destroy." But by denying itself, reason in a sense vindicates its own power and worth. While exposing the pains and infirmities of existence, Leopardi makes us love the very objects of his despair. By glorifying illusion, art, in the pureness of its beauty (which supersedes the misery of all material things), becomes the most important postulate of ultraphilosophy. Art transfigures sorrow and, by not limiting its own strength and freedom, converts that sorrow into human greatness—a greatness that constitutes the triumph of free creative power and of infinite strength.

Works by Leopardi

The critical edition of Leopardi's collected works is *Tutte le opere,* Francesco Flora, ed., 5 vols. (Milan, 1937–1949). For English translations, see *Essays, Dialogues and Thoughts,* translated by James Thomson (New York, 1905?); *The Poems of Leopardi,* a translation of all the *Canti* by Geoffrey L. Bickersteth (Cambridge, 1923); *Translations from Leopardi* by R. C. Trevelyan (London, 1941); *Giacomo Leopardi: Poems,* translated and with an introduction by Jean-Pierre Barricelli (New York, 1963).

Works on Leopardi

For literature on Leopardi, see Giovanni Amelotti, *Filosofia del Leopardi* (Genoa, 1937); Aristide Baragiola, *Giacomo Leopardi: filosofo, poeta e prosatore* (Strasbourg, 1876); Elme Marie Caro, *Le Pessimisme au XIXe siècle* (Paris, 1880); Karl Vossler, *Leopardi* (Munich, 1923); Giovanni Gentile, *Poesia e filosofia di Giacomo Leopardi* (Florence, 1939); Iris Origo, *Leopardi: A Biography* (London, 1935); J. H. Whitfield, *Giacomo Leopardi* (Oxford, 1954); and G. Singh, *Leopardi and the Theory of Poetry* (Lexington, Ky., 1964).

JEAN-PIERRE BARRICELLI

LEQUIER, (JOSEPH LOUIS) JULES (1814–1862), or Léquyer, French philosopher, was born at Quintin in Brittany. He was educated there and in Paris at the *collège* of St. Stanislas and the École Polytechnique. An intensely religious though extremely heterodox Roman Catholic, Lequier devoured the literatures of philosophy and theology, and although none of his own work was published during his lifetime, he wrote voluminously and also translated Sir Humphrey Davy's autobiography. Jean Wahl has made interesting comparisons between certain aspects of the thought of Lequier and Kierkegaard, although neither could actually have influenced the other. However, Lequier directly influenced Charles Renouvier, who always considered him his "master in philosophy," and through Renouvier he attracted the attention of William James. Renouvier later published Lequier's book, *La Recherche d'une première vérité* (Paris, 1865).

Lequier's philosophy aimed at but never achieved systematic wholeness; its essential theses, however, may be restated in four interrelated doctrines. First, Cartesian methodological doubt must be genuine, not feigned, and unless it is employed in good faith, one is likely to err in doubting real evidence, just as, without methodological doubt one is likely to err in allowing unwarranted belief. Accordingly, doubt has no privileged status over belief. Ability to attain truth as well as falsehood must underlie the quest for truth, and freedom is thus a condition of the possibility of knowing truth as well as of being mistaken.

Second, freedom is a "double dilemma." Either causal necessity or freedom is a fundamental truth, and each doctrine must be asserted either necessarily or freely. If necessity is the true doctrine, my affirmation thereof is *eo ipso* necessary, but since neither doubt nor belief relative to evidence would function in that determination, doubt results. If necessity is true but I affirm freedom, then in addition to my inconsistency (for my affirmation is made necessarily), there is only a subjective foundation for knowledge and morality. Given the truth of determinism, erroneous as well as true judgments are necessary, and any supposed distinction between them is illusory. According to the hypothesis of freedom, if I freely affirm global necessity I am fundamentally inconsistent. Finally, if I affirm freedom under the same hypothesis, not only is my affirmation consistent with the hypothesis but I have a foundation for knowledge and morality. Under the double dilemma, the only satisfactory alternative is freely to affirm freedom —Lequier's "first truth." Freedom is essentially the power to add some novel reality to the existing world. Causality must be explained through freedom and not vice versa.

Third, the data that are present to a given event of consciousness arise out of the past relative to that event; they are past actualities but present potentialities for the internal character of that event of consciousness out of which a determining decision is made. Human consciousness is a succession of self-creative events, each of which is given its ancestor selves as well as other data, and each of which is partially *causa sui*, a "dependent independence." Thus, the totality of causal conditions of any human experience does not make this experience necessary, but only possible, while internal decision makes it contingently actual. All choice-making contains some arbitrary element.

Fourth, in extending these doctrines to theology, and taking as axiomatic the concept that freedom, responsibility, and moral and religious values depend upon choice-decisions, Lequier holds that an omniscient God need not know future contingents, since, in relation to any divine experience, they are not yet existent. To be knowable is to be determinate, and if all were known "from eternity," then all would be eternally determinate, and time and choice-making would be illusions. Also, since contingents are unequivocally in part *causa sui*, they are not wholly dependent on divine power. Far from viewing divine power as absolute total control, Lequier insists that the only power worthy of God is the far greater one of creating self-creators. Real choice in the world is incompatible with all-embracing necessity, and it is neither metaphysically requisite nor religiously desirable that God be wholly immutable and eternal. God must have a temporal aspect in order to come to know contingents as they are realized; thus he remains always omniscient in knowing all there is to know. Lequier's theology is thus that of an eternal-temporal being, his omniscience and omnipotence being relative to the irreducible contingency and self-creativity in the world.

Lequier's philosophy bears various striking resemblances to themes in Samuel Alexander, Henri Bergson, Nikolai Berdyaev, Émile Boutroux, William James, Søren Kierkegaard, C. S. Peirce, and A. N. Whitehead.

Bibliography

For works by Lequier, see *Oeuvres complètes*, Jean Grenier, ed. (Neuchâtel, 1952).

Literature on Lequier includes Émile Callot, *Propos sur Jules Lequier* (Paris, 1962); Jean Grenier, *La Philosophie de Jules Lequier* (Paris, 1936); Charles Hartshorne and William L. Reese, eds. *Philosophers Speak of God* (Chicago, 1953), the only material by Lequier now available in English; Adolphe Lazareff, *Vie et connaissance* (Paris, 1948); Xavier Tilliette, *Jules Lequier ou le tourment de la liberté* (Paris, 1964); and Jean Wahl, *Jules Lequier* (Paris, 1948), which contains an introduction and selections.

HARVEY H. BRIMMER II

LE ROY, ÉDOUARD (1870–1954), French philosopher of science, ethics, and religion, was born in Paris and studied science at the École Normale Supérieure. He passed the *agrégation* examination in mathematics in 1895 and took a doctorate in science in 1898. Le Roy became a *lycée* teacher of mathematics in Paris but was soon drawn to philosophical problems through an interest in the philosophy of Bergson. He succeeded Bergson, to whose thought his own was deeply indebted, as professor of philosophy at the Collège de France in 1921 and was elected to the French Academy in 1945.

In a series of articles entitled "Science et philosophie" (*Revue de métaphysique et de morale*, Vol. 7, 1899, 375–425, 503–562, 706–731, and Vol. 8, 1900, 37–72), Le Roy took a pragmatic view of the nature of scientific truth, a view more or less shared by his contemporaries Bergson, Henri Poincaré, and E. Wilbois. Scientific laws and even scientific "facts," Le Roy maintained, are arbitrary constructs designed to meet our needs and to facilitate effective action in pursuit of those needs. Scientific reason, in other words, distorts reality in the interests of practical action. The scientific facts on which induction is based are artificially extracted from the continuous flow of happenings and experiences and built up into convenient (rather than "true") thought structures, which constitute "the grammar of discourse" and enable us to talk about, and deal with, what would otherwise be "the amorphous material of the given." Thus, in reacting against scientific mechanism, Le Roy presented an extreme view of mind as the creator of its own reality.

Le Roy took the same pragmatic view of discursive religious truth in *Dogme et critique* (Paris, 1906). His views were supported by the Catholic modernists and condemned as dangerous in a papal encyclical. Le Roy held that the validity of dogmas cannot be proved, nor do they profess to be provable; they depend upon a rigid and externally imposed authority; their expression and frame of reference is that of medieval philosophy; and they are alien to, and incompatible with, the body of modern knowledge. For these four reasons they are unacceptable to the modern mind as truths. Nevertheless, they possess a pragmatic value; they fulfill a purpose, in this case a moral one. "Although mysterious for the intelligence in search of explanatory theories," Le Roy held, "these dogmas lend themselves nonetheless to perfectly specific formulation as directives for action." Christianity is thus not a system of speculative philosophy, but a set of stated or implied injunctions, a way of life. For example, the belief in a personal God demands that our relation to him resemble our relation to a human person. The doctrine of the resurrection of Christ teaches that we should behave in relation to him as if he were alive today.

Le Roy's misgivings concerning religious dogmas arose because the dogmas seemed to him irreconcilable with a homogeneous system of rational knowledge. In a pragmatic and relativist conception of truth such incompatibility should not be significant. However, the criterion of truth, for Le Roy, was neither use nor coherence, but "life" itself, dynamic and self-developing. Scientific theory is useful distortion, religious teaching a source of moral action, and both are arbitrary in their choice of concepts and symbols. Genuine knowledge is a kind of self-identification with the object in its primitive reality, uncontaminated by the demands of practical need. Intuition, not discursive thought, is the instrument of such knowledge, and the criterion of truth is that one should have lived it; otherwise, according to Le Roy, *one ought not* to understand it. This, as Susan Stebbing rightly pointed out, altogether removes the criterion from rational criticism, since life is both truth and the criterion of truth.

Le Roy's philosophy culminated in moral and religious concerns, as is seen in Volume 2 of his posthumously published *Essai d'une philosophie première* (2 vols., Paris, 1956–1958). His position is similar to Bergson's in *Les Deux Sources de la morale et de la religion*. The *élan vital* which animates us takes the form of an "open," that is, indeterminate, moral demand. This generalized obligation is the essence of the self as a free and self-creating agent. Le Roy stated that "to believe is to perceive a spiritual exigency and to act under its inspiration." The open nature of the exigency "beyond any ideal capable of being formulated" places Le Roy's view in the same category as much recent morality of authenticity. The agent is constantly transcending the determinate in the direction of some necessarily unspecified self-fulfillment. Because morality

implies precepts and precepts imply universalizability, the notion of a morality that cannot be formulated would seem to be self-defeating. In his conception of a moral quest Le Roy, in fact, seemed to presuppose the Christian values to which he subscribed.

Additional Works by Le Roy

Une Philosophie nouvelle: Henri Bergson. Paris, 1912.
L'Exigence idéaliste et le fait de l'évolution. Paris, 1927.
Les Origines humaines et l'évolution de l'intelligence. Paris, 1928.
Le Problème de Dieu. Paris, 1929.
La Pensée intuitive, 2 vols. Paris, 1929–1930.
Introduction à l'étude du problème religieux. Paris, 1944.
La Pensée mathématique pure. Paris, 1960.

Works on Le Roy

Gagnebin, S., *La Philosophie de l'intuition. Essai sur les idées d'Édouard Le Roy.* Paris, 1912.
Olgiati, F., *Édouard Le Roy e il problema di Dio.* Milan, 1929.
Stebbing, L. Susan, *Pragmatism and French Voluntarism.* Cambridge, 1914.

COLIN SMITH

LE SENNE, RENÉ (1882–1954), French spiritualistic philosopher, was born in Elbeuf in Normandy. From 1903 to 1906 he was a pupil of Rauh and Octave Hamelin at the École Normale Supérieure, where he passed the *agrégation* examination in philosophy in 1906. He obtained his doctorate in 1930 with a thesis entitled *Le Devoir* ("Duty"). After holding provincial teaching posts he was appointed to the Lycée Louis-le-Grand in Paris and, in 1942, to a chair of moral philosophy at the University of Paris. He distinguished himself as joint editor, with Louis Lavelle, of the series of works published in the collection "Philosophie de l'esprit." In 1948 he was elected to the Académie des Sciences Morales et Politiques.

The conception of philosophy underlying the "Philosophie de l'esprit" was traced by Le Senne to the Cartesian tradition, which, he held, identified existence with the act of thought and regarded existence as dependent upon a transcendent and infinite being. This tradition, according to Le Senne, was threatened both by positivism, which discounts the self-creating principle that raises man above causally determined physical nature, and by an excessive modern subjectivism, which makes man the measure of all things. Against these threats to the French "psycho-metaphysical" tradition Le Senne and Lavelle launched their series, in what they conceived as a kind of philosophico-moral mission, a reassertion of metaphysical philosophy against antiphilosophy.

Like much of recent French thought, Le Senne's work evokes not so much Descartes as Maine de Biran. The essence of the self is consciousness of action against the resistance and limitation of reality. This could be rendered: I will, or I strive, therefore I am. Thus, personality for Le Senne was "existence as it is formed by the double cogito: hindered by obstacles, elevating itself by and towards value." Man participates in absolute and transcendent value. Although value outruns him and is not wholly his creation, it is made determinate by him in a given, concrete situation.

Reality, then, is at once the organ of self-creation and an obstacle to it. In a sense it degrades value, yet it actualizes value by making it determinate. We are, moreover, called back to awareness of the value-creating source in which we participate. This is a spiritual flow, or upsurge (*essor*). "Some obstacle has to break the continuity of the upsurge before the self, concentrating upon it the body's energy, begins to will." The willing self owes its being and consciousness to the obstacles it encounters. We participate in a world of absolute value and a world of brute reality and create ourselves unceasingly through them.

Works by Le Senne

Introduction à la philosophie. Paris, 1925.
Le Devoir. Paris, 1930.
Le Mensonge et le caractère. Paris, 1930.
Obstacle et valeur. Paris, 1934.
Traité de morale générale. Paris, 1942.
Traité de caractérologie. Paris, 1949.
La Destinée personnelle. Paris, 1951.
La Découverte de Dieu. Paris, 1955.

Works on Le Senne

Paumen, J., *Le Spiritualisme existentiel de René Le Senne.* Paris, 1949.
Pirlot, J., *Destinée et valeur. La philosophie de René Le Senne.* Namur, 1953.
Vax, L., "Pensée souffrante et pensée triomphante chez René Le Senne." *Critique,* Vol. 12 (1956), 142–152.

COLIN SMITH

LEŚNIEWSKI, STANISŁAW (1886–1939), Polish philosopher and logician, was born in Serpukhov, Russia. He studied philosophy at various German universities but eventually came to Lvov in order to complete his doctoral dissertation under Kazimierz Twardowski, receiving his Ph.D. in philosophy in 1912. From 1919 until his death Leśniewski was professor of the philosophy of mathematics in the University of Warsaw. He was one of the founders of, and a dominant figure in, the Warsaw school of logic, and numerous acknowledgments in the writings of his colleagues and pupils bear witness to the scope of his influence.

As a student Leśniewski was impressed by the logic of John Stuart Mill and the logical investigations of Edmund Husserl. Between 1911 and 1914 he published a number of essays on such topics as existential propositions, the ontological principle of contradiction, the principle of excluded middle, and eternity and sempiternity of truth, but he later renounced these papers in his lectures and in print.

Leśniewski's discovery in 1911 of Jan Łukasiewicz's monograph on the principle of contradiction in Aristotle, *O zasadzie sprzeczności u Arystotelesa* (Cracow, 1910), was a turning point in his philosophical career. From this book Leśniewski first learned of symbolic logic, of Bertrand Russell's work, and of the antinomy of the class of all the classes that are not elements of themselves. The problem of antinomies immediately fascinated him and for many years absorbed a large part of his interest. His persistent efforts to solve this problem eventually resulted in the construction of a system of the foundations of mathematics distinguished by originality, comprehensiveness, and elegance.

Mereology. Analysis of the Russellian antinomy convinced Leśniewski that we should distinguish between the distributive and the collective interpretations of class expressions. The expression "*A* is an element of the class of *b*'s," in which the terms "element of" and "the class of" are used distributively, means simply that *A* is a *b*. If, however, we interpret the terms "element of" and "the class of" collectively, then our original expression means that *A* is a part (proper or improper) of the whole consisting of *b*'s, that is, that *A* is a part of the object that has the following two properties: (1) every *b* is a part of it, and (2) every part of it has a common part with a *b*. According to Leśniewski the presuppositions of the Russellian antinomy appear to be true because we fail to distinguish between the distributive and collective interpretations. Once the distinction is made it is evident that on either interpretation some of the presuppositions on which the antinomy hinges turn out to be false. Leśniewski developed his ideas concerning the collective interpretation of class expressions by constructing a deductive theory, first outlined in Polish in 1916. At that time Leśniewski mistrusted symbolic language and formulated his theorems and gave proofs of them in ordinary language. Thus, his theory, which he subsequently termed "mereology" and whose improved version he included in "O podstawach matematyki," does not resemble a formal calculus but reads rather like Euclid. Among the various systems of mereology the one based on "element of" as the only undefined term, with "the class of" introduced by definition, appears to have been most popular with Leśniewski and his pupils.

Ontology. Leśniewski had always been aware that his mereology presupposed certain logically prior theories—a logic of names or noun expressions and a logic of propositions. In 1920 he decided to lay an axiomatic foundation for the logic of noun expressions that he had been assuming in his deductions, and this was the birth of his "ontology." The only undefined term of this theory is the copula "is" (or "is a"), which with two noun expressions forms a true proposition of the form "*A* is *b*" (or "*A* is a *b*,"), provided the noun expression for which "*A*" stands designates exactly one object, which also happens to be designated by the noun expression represented by "*b*." Thus, ontology embodies the distributive interpretation of class expressions. One of the characteristic features of ontology is that its language, which is also that of mereology, makes no categorial distinction between proper names and definite descriptions on the one hand and the common names of ordinary grammar on the other. As a rule Leśniewski used capital letters of the Latin alphabet as nominal variables in propositional functions that would become true propositions only if the variables in question were replaced by proper names or by nonempty definite descriptions. Otherwise he used small letters of the Latin alphabet as nominal variables. This differentiation, however, is not enjoined by the syntax of the language and can be regarded as stylistic license.

In regard to its subject matter, ontology can be described as a general theory of what there is. It comprises the traditional logic in its modernized form and has counterparts to the calculus of predicates, the calculus of classes, and the calculus of relations, including the theory of identity. It has no axiom of choice, and the theorems that in other systems of logic are proved with the aid of such an axiom appear in ontology as consequents of implications in whose antecedents conditions corresponding to the axiom of choice have been embedded. Leśniewski decided against the axiom of choice because its acceptance was inferentially equivalent to postulating that every set, finite or infinite, can be well ordered. Moreover, because ontology admits an unlimited variety of semantical categories (logical types), a single axiom of choice would not suffice as it could not be "transmitted" from a lower semantical category to a higher one. Thus, one would have to provide ontology with a rule of choice in accordance with which one could add to the system a thesis of choice for each of the semantical categories introduced into the system. This, however, turns out to be too strong a measure since the thesis of choice for a higher semantical category can be transmitted to an appropriate lower category. In view of these difficulties Leśniewski preferred to let his ontology be uncommitted to an axiom or a rule of choice.

Protothetic. In the early 1920s. when the axiomatic foundations of ontology had been established, Leśniewski turned to the problem of the logic of propositions, which was presupposed by both ontology and mereology. He desired a highly comprehensive system which would yield at least all the theses derivable within the classical calculus of propositions and also the law of extensionality for propositions. With this aim in view he constructed his "protothetic," or theory of first principles. By means of important discoveries by Alfred Tarski, at that time Leśniewski's pupil, it was possible to base a system of protothetic on the functor of equivalence as the only undefined term. This was a welcome development for Leśniewski because equivalence constituted for him the most intuitive form for definitions.

In many respects protothetic goes far beyond the classical calculus of propositions. It allows for functorial variables, which, like propositional variables, can be bound by an appropriate quantifier. It contains a rule of definition which enables us to extend at will the variety of semantical categories within the theory. The law of extensionality for propositions is embedded in the axiom system, but analogous laws for higher semantical categories are available by virtue of the rule of extensionality. The rule for distributing the universal quantifier binding variables of any semantical category makes it possible to derive, within the framework of protothetic or any other theory which presupposes protothetic, theses which render redundant the usual rules for operating with the universal quantifier. In view of these characteristics protothetic emerges as the most comprehensive logic of propositions ever constructed.

Formalization. By 1923 Leśniewski had become familiar with the results obtained within the province of logic and the foundations of mathematics by Gottlob Frege, Ernst Zermelo, Whitehead and Russell, and others. He regarded Frege's *Grundgesetze der Arithmetik* as the greatest achievement in the long history of inquiry into the foundations of mathematics, notwithstanding the fact that Frege's system had been shown to be inconsistent. He found the system of *Principia Mathematica* deficient largely because of the absence of explicitly stated conditions which, in the opinion of Whitehead and Russell, would have to be satisfied by an expression if it were to be regarded as a definition or added to the system as a new thesis. Zermelo's set theory appeared to Leśniewski to resist any attempts at a coherent interpretation.

Leśniewski was naturally anxious that his system of the foundations of mathematics should be free from such deficiencies. In order to state with sufficient precision the conditions that would have to be satisfied by an expression if it were to be added to the system as a new thesis, he first worked out a general theory of semantical categories, which formally resembles the simplified theory of types but which, in its intuitive credentials, has more in common with the traditional "parts of speech" or with Husserlian *Bedeutungskategorien*. Leśniewski then devised an appropriate symbolism for his theories. After these preliminaries he proceeded to the formulation of "directives," that is, rules of definition, inference, and extensionality. On his own admission this was the most difficult project he had ever undertaken in logic. Beginning with a straightforward vocabulary adapted from ordinary usage he introduced a long series of terminological explanations of ever increasing complexity. He needed 53 such explanations to state the directives of protothetic. These comprise (1) the rule of protothetical definition, (2) the rule of protothetical extensionality, and three rules of inference: (3) distribution of the universal quantifier, (4) detachment, and (5) substitution. Further terminological explanations are required to state the directives of ontology. For we obtain ontology by subjoining to protothetic an ontological axiom system, adapting the directives of protothetic to it, and adding the rule of ontological definition and the rule of ontological extensionality. Mereology is arrived at by subjoining to ontology a mereological axiom system and adapting the ontological directives to it. No additional directives are involved. Mereology is, of course, open to further extensions, but this line of inquiry was not pursued by Leśniewski. Both ontology and mereology have an interpretation in protothetic, which means that the whole system is consistent if protothetic is consistent.

The original axiomatic foundations of Leśniewski's three theories have undergone a series of successive simplifications resulting from Leśniewski's own researches and from the researches of Tarski, Mordchaj Wajsberg, Bolesław Sobociński, and others. As a result of these efforts we now know that the following three propositions constitute sufficient axiomatic foundations of protothetic, ontology, and mereology, respectively:

I. $[pq] :: p \equiv q . \equiv \therefore [f] \therefore f(pf(p[u].u)). \equiv : [r] : f(qr). \equiv . q \equiv p;$

II. $[Aa] : A\epsilon a. \equiv .[\exists B].A\epsilon B.B\epsilon a;$

III. $[AB] ::: A\epsilon \mathrm{el}(B). \equiv :.: B\epsilon B ::. [Ca] :: [D] :: D\epsilon C. \equiv \therefore [E] : E\epsilon a. \supset . E\epsilon \mathrm{el}(D) \therefore [E] : E\epsilon \mathrm{el}(D). \supset . [\exists FG].F\epsilon a.G\epsilon \mathrm{el}(E).G\epsilon \mathrm{el}(F) ::. B\epsilon \mathrm{el}(B).B\epsilon a :. \supset . A\epsilon \mathrm{el}(C),$

with "ϵ" standing for "is" or "is a" and "el" for "element of."

Each of these propositions satisfies Leśniewski's requirements for well-constructed axiom systems, and, with the possible exception of III, offers little hope for further simplifications on the basis of the original directives.

Interpretation. Like Frege, and like Russell in the days when he wrote of "a robust sense of reality" and compared logic to zoology, Leśniewski was an uncompromising critic of formalism for its own sake. Contrary to the fashion prevailing among mathematicians, he intended his deductive theories to be interpreted theories. Moreover, he wanted them to be interpreted in one particular way and be judged in the light of this and no other interpretation. Thus, for instance, the interpretation he had in mind for his ontology was "ontological" through and through, in a truly classical sense. In this theory we have, among others, the concept of object and the various concepts of existence and identity, which are meant to serve the same purpose as their less precise counterparts familiar to philosophers since Parmenides, Plato, and Aristotle. Mereology carries the examination of objects a step further by describing them in terms of such concepts as that of part and whole. In Leśniewski's view mereology provided basic presuppositions for any inquiry into the foundations of geometry in the traditional sense of the term. In other words, the conceptual apparatus of Leśniewski's theories was intended by its originator to be used in philosophical or scientific practice at any level of lower generality. Leśniewski developed his theories because for him they consisted of interesting though extremely general propositions true of reality as we know it from experience. He axiomatized his theories because by axiomatization the theories that interested him could be derived from relatively simple axioms, definitions, or laws of extensionality by a series of irresistibly cogent inferences. He formalized his theories because he knew of no better method of conveying his thoughts on the subject of his investigations. But he insisted most emphatically that his theories did not lose their meaning by being subjected to the process of formalization. Thus, in his inquiries into the foundations of logic and mathematics Leśniewski never ceased to be a philosopher.

Works by Leśniewski

"Podstawy ogólnej teoryi mnogości. I" ("The Foundations of a General Theory of Manifolds"). *Prace Polskiego Koła Naukowego w Moskwie*, Sekcya matematyczno-przyrodnicza, No. 2. Moscow, 1916. A presentation of mereology.

"O podstawach matematyki" ("On the Foundation of Mathematics"). *Przegląd Filozoficzny*, Vol. 30 (1027), 164 206; Vol. 31 (1928), 261–291; Vol. 32 (1929), 60–101; Vol. 33 (1930), 77–105 and 142–170. Contains an improved version of mereology and discussions of the Russell paradox, classes and sets, the interpretation of the *Principia* symbolism, and the meaning of the copula "is."

"Über Funktionen deren Felder Gruppen mit Rücksicht auf diese Funktionen sind." *Fundamenta Mathematicae*, Vol. 13 (1929), 319–332.

"Grundzüge eines neuen Systems der Grundlagen der Mathematik." *Fundamenta Mathematicae*, Vol. 14 (1929), 1–81. Primarily on protothetic.

"Über Funktionen deren Felder Abelsche Gruppen in Bezug auf diese Funktionen sind." *Fundamenta Mathematicae*, Vol. 14 (1929), 242–251.

"Über die Grundlagen der Ontologie." *Comptes rendus des séances de la Société des Sciences et des Lettres de Varsovie*, Classe III, Vol. 23 (1930), 111–132. Contains a statement of the single axiom of ontology and a formulation of the directives of the system.

"Über Definitionen in der sogenannten Theorie der Theorie der Deduktion," *Comptes rendus des séances de la Société des Sciences et des Lettres de Varsovie*, Classe III, Vol. 24 (1931), 289–309.

Einleitende Bermerkungen zur Fortsetzung meiner Mitteilung u. d. T. "Grundzüge eines neuen Systems der Grundlagen der Mathematik." Warsaw, 1938. Primarily on protothetic.

Grundzüge eines neuen Systems der Grundlagen der Mathematik Sec. 12. Warsaw, 1938. Primarily on protothetic. This work and the one above were to have been included in Vol. 1 of *Collectanea Logica*, pp. 1–60 and 61–143, respectively.

Works on Leśniewski

Ajdukiewicz, Kazimierz, "Die syntaktische Konnexität." *Studia Philosophica*, Vol. 1 (1935), 1–27. An informal presentation of Leśniewski's theory of semantical categories.

Gromska, Daniela, "Philosophes polonais morts entre 1938–1945." *Studia Philosophica*, Vol. 3 (1948), 31–97.

Grzegorczyk, Andrzej, "The Systems of Leśniewski in Relation to Contemporary Logical Research." *Studia Logica*, Vol. 3 (1953), 77–95. Contains some adverse criticism.

Jordan, Z. A., *The Development of Mathematical Logic and of Logical Positivism in Poland Between the Two Wars*. Oxford, 1945. Pp. 23–26 and *passim*.

Kotarbiński, Tadeusz, *La Logique en Pologne*. Rome, 1959. Pp. 19–22.

Lejewski, Czesław, "A Contribution to Leśniewski's Mereology." *V Rocznik Polskiego Towarzystwa Naukowego na Obczyźnie* (1955), 43–50.

Lejewski, Czesław, "A New Axiom of Mereology." *VI Rocznik Polskiego Towarzystwa Naukowego na Obczyźnie* (1956), 65–70.

Lejewski, Czesław, "On Leśniewski's Ontology." *Ratio*, Vol. 1 (1958), 150–176.

Luschei, E. C., *The Logical Systems of Leśniewski*. Amsterdam, 1962. A comprehensive survey.

Słupecki, Jerzy, "St. Leśniewski's Prototetics." *Studia Logica*, Vol. 1 (1953), 44–112.

Słupecki, Jerzy, "S. Leśniewski's Calculus of Names." *Studia Logica*, Vol. 3 (1955), 7–76. Discusses ontology.

Słupecki, Jerzy, "Towards a Generalised Mereology of Leśniewski." *Studia Logica*, Vol. 8 (1958), 131–163.

Sobociński, Bolesław, "O kolejnych uproszczeniach aksjomatyki 'ontologji' Prof. St. Leśniewskiego" ("On Successive Simplifications of the Axiom System of Prof. S. Leśniewski's Ontology"), in *Fragmenty Filozoficzne*. Warsaw, 1934. Pp. 144–160.

Sobociński, Bolesław, "L'Analyse de l'antinomie Russellienne par Leśniewski." *Methodos*, Vol. 1 (1949), 94–107, 220–228, 308–316; Vol. 2 (1950), 237–257.

Sobociński, Bolesław, "Studies in Leśniewski's Mereology." *V Rocznik Polskiego Towarzystwa Naukowego na Obczyźnie* (1955), 34–43.

Sobociński, Bolesław, "On Well Constructed Systems." *VI Rocznik Polskiego Towarzystwa Naukowego na Obczyźnie* (1956), 54–65.

Sobociński, Bolesław, "In Memoriam Jan Łukasiewicz." *Philosophical Studies* (Ireland), Vol. 6 (1956), 3–49.

Sobociński, Bolesław, "La génesis de la Escuela Polaca de Lógica." *Oriente Europeo*, Vol. 7 (1957), 83–95.

Sobociński, Bolesław, "On the Single Axioms of Protothetic." *Notre Dame Journal of Formal Logic*, Vol. 1 (1960), 52–73; Vol. 2 (1961), 11–16, 129–148. In progress.

Tarski, Alfred, "O wyrazie pierwotnym logistyki." *Przegląd Filozoficzny*, Vol. 26 (1923), 68–89. Translated by J. H. Woodger as "On the Primitive Term of Logistic," in Alfred Tarski, *Logic, Semantics, Metamathematics*. Oxford, 1956. A contribution to protothetic.

CZESLAW LEJEWSKI

LESSING, GOTTHOLD EPHRAIM (1729–1781), German dramatist and critic, was born at Kamenz in Saxony. The son of a scholarly Lutheran pastor, he was sent to study theology at Leipzig University. There, however, he absorbed the popular rationalism of the Enlightenment, whose leading contemporary exponent was the Leibnizian Christian Wolff, of Halle. Lessing was influenced in the same direction by his friends from Berlin, Friedrich Nicolai and Moses Mendelssohn, and by the writings of the English deists, many of which had been translated into German. Although literature, and especially the drama, became Lessing's supreme interest, he was to return to theology in the last decade of his life. He has no special claim to being ranked as a philosopher of originality and distinction, but with regard to the diffusion of certain ideas and attitudes among educated minds, his historical influence is pre-eminent. He was above all a critic, and his attitude may be described as one of "passionate detachment." His nonconformity made him appear to be perennially restless; he was never permanently satisfied to adopt the conventional opinions of society, always preferring to be in a "minority of one." The movement of his mind carried him beyond his parents' theological beliefs and the commonplace deism of his twenties until, through his invocation of Spinoza, he eventually prepared the way for the romantic reaction against the Enlightenment.

Literature and art. Lessing's approach to the drama was based on his conviction that it was urgently necessary to break the tyrannical dominance over German literature exerted by the established French classicism—a trend that was encouraged by Frederick II of Prussia. In Lessing's eyes, the effect of this French influence was the suppression of the native German genius. In a series of "Literary Letters" (*Briefe, die neueste Literatur betreffend*, Leipzig, 1759–1765), written in cooperation with Christoph Nicolai and Moses Mendelssohn, Lessing exhorted German writers to turn their backs on the artificial perfections of Corneille and Racine; he claimed that they should take as their stylistic model the bold naturalism of Shakespeare, whom Voltaire had characteristically dismissed as a "drunken savage."

Lessing's best-known work of criticism is his *Laokoon, oder, über die Grenzen der Malerei und Poesie* (*Laocoön, or the Bounds of Painting and Poesie*, Berlin, 1766). Judged as constructive thinking about the nature of art, it is a disappointing work, although it is noteworthy in that it contains the first explicit statement of the concept of "art for art's sake." Moreover, its overt thesis—that painting works by forms and colors in space, while poetry belongs to a quite different category in that it sets out to describe successive moments in time—is not only inadequate, since it fails to take account of lyric poetry and indeed of all poetry that describes states of mind, but also much less original than Lessing implied. But it is significant that the *Laokoon* takes the form of a critique of Lessing's German, English, and French predecessors; he could not write well without a target to attack. In the *Laokoon*, Lessing's main critique was directed against Winckelmann and the latter's idealization of "noble simplicity and quiet grandeur." Lessing was prepared to acknowledge that this ideal may hold good for painting, which, he claimed, is exclusively concerned with the beauty of physical form. But he wholly denied its validity or relevance for judging poetry, which is concerned with action and passion. *Laokoon*, like much

that Lessing wrote, has a subtle undercurrent of irony and polemic, the thrust of which, on the surface, is not apparent to the rapid reader. Although Lessing took as his text a famous piece of ancient sculpture, his essay is more an oblique sermon about literature than an aesthetic analysis of the visual arts by a critic with a real understanding of, or even sympathy for, his subject. Its essential thesis is a warning that Winckelmann's neoclassical ideals must not constrict the freedom of the poet, who, unlike the painter, is primarily concerned with passionate action.

Lessing's writings on art and literature do not constitute a serious analysis and critique of aesthetic experience. But his work was directed toward liberating the artist from all the limiting rules and conventions of artificial formality. Lessing was not in any sense a romantic writer, but because of his demand for the free expression of natural feelings and his retrospective interest in antiquity, he occupies an important place among the forces which made German romanticism possible. The significance of Lessing's role as a precursor of the romantic movement emerges even more prominently in his treatment of religious problems. He initiated the endeavor to discover within the immanent order of the world those values that had been derived by traditional Christianity from a transcendental view of the universe.

History and theology. Lessing inherited from his father strong scholarly and historical interests. By temperament antipathetic to all partisan historiography, he published a series of *Rettungen* ("Vindications") in 1754, in which he defended historical figures to whom ecclesiastical historians, for dogmatic reasons, had not been quite fair. These essays are quite characteristic of Lessing's nature and cast of mind. Written with suppressed passion and permeated with a profound sense of engagement, they nevertheless remain uncommitted to any personal judgment either for or against the doctrinal beliefs of those whom he was vindicating. His neutrality toward Christianity never took the form of quasi-Gibbonian irony. He always wrote as one wholly sympathetic to Christian ethical ideals, but coolly reserved toward dogmatic formulas that breed unreasoning prejudice and the negation of humane values.

The turning point of Lessing's life occurred in 1769, when he became librarian for the duke of Brunswick at Wolfenbüttel. In 1773 he began to publish essays on historical theology based on the Wolfenbüttel manuscripts. Earlier, during a three-year residence in Hamburg from 1766 to 1769 as a theater critic, Lessing had met the deist Hermann Samuel Reimarus (1694–1768), whose daughter had lent him the manuscript of an unpublished book by her father entitled *Apologie oder Schutzschrift für die vernünftigen Verehrer Gottes* ("Apology for Rational Worshippers of God"). In 1774, and from 1777 to 1778, Lessing printed extracts from this work as fragments from the writings of an anonymous and unidentifiable deist whose manuscripts had presumably been found in the Wolfenbüttel library ("Wolfenbüttler Fragmente eines Ungenannten," in *Beiträge zur Geschichte und Literatur*). The last and most important fragment precipitated a violent controversy with a Hamburg pastor, Johann Melchior Goeze, and effectively initiated the long nineteenth-century quest for the Jesus of history behind the Christ of faith. Reimarus was a believer in natural religion, but he was skeptical about revelation. His objections to traditional Christianity presuppose that Biblical inerrancy is essential to faith. Lessing sometimes wrote as if he shared this assumption and sometimes as if he did not, so that it is not possible to arrive at a strictly coherent view on this point. In his more cynical moments, Lessing treated liberal theology, such as that represented by J. S. Semler of Halle, with hostile contempt, on the ground that it was deceptively credible; he preferred to "defend" orthodoxy as being so patently absurd that by defense it would be sooner ended. Strictly as a scholar, Lessing was Semler's inferior; nevertheless, Lessing's genuinely scholarly instinct, combined with his inner detachment from the entrenched positions of the contemporary theological schools, as well as from those of the Enlightenment, enabled him to begin the critical study of the sources of the Synoptic Gospels (a fundamental question on which Reimarus had naively said nothing) with his pioneer essay, "New Hypothesis Concerning the Evangelists Regarded as Merely Human Historians" (*Neue Hypothese über die Evangelisten als bloss menschliche Geschichtsschreiber betrachtet*). This was written from 1777 to 1778 and first printed in 1784 in Lessing's *Theologische Nachlass*. Prevented by the duke of Brunswick from indulging in theological controversies, Lessing put his theology into a play, *Nathan der Weise* (*Nathan the Wise*, 1779) which was a plea for religious indifferentism on the ground that what is required of man is not an assent to the propositions of a creed, but sincerity, brotherly love, and tolerance. It is not easy to discover precisely what Lessing's positive beliefs were, so little did he commit himself, either in published writings or even in private correspondence, to any positive avowal of convictions. But he certainly accepted the commonplace thesis of the Enlightenment that the quintessence of Christianity, hidden beneath the accretions of theology, consists in universal brotherhood and a basic moral code. Like many rationalists of his age, he passed for a time into Freemasonry, though he emerged disillusioned with what was for him evidently a pale substitute for Christianity. In one sense, it could be said that Lessing spent his life hoping that Christianity was true and arguing that it was not. But his basic attitude toward religious belief was neither one of affirmation nor of denial; it took the form of an impassioned question.

Lessing was the first modern writer explicitly to emphasize that even if conclusions about historical events were more certain than they are, any religious affirmation based upon them involves a transition to another plane of discourse, that of faith. He was torn between the idea of revelation as the communication of timeless propositional truths, and the untidiness and irrationality of history. "Accidental truths of history can never become the proof of necessary truths of reason" (*Über den Beweis des Geistes und der Kraft*, 1777). Events and truths belong to altogether different categories, and there is no logical connection between one and another. Lessing's statement of this antithesis presupposes on the one hand the epistemology of Leibniz, with its sharp distinction between necessary truths of reason (mathematically certain and known a pri-

ori) and contingent truths (known by sense perception), and on the other hand the thesis of Spinoza's *Tractatus Theologico-politicus*, that the truth of a historical narrative, however certain, cannot give us the knowledge of God, which should be derived from general ideas that are in themselves certain and known. Lessing's own way out of the dilemma was to conceive the role of religious belief in the historical process as a relative state in the advance of humanity toward maturity, a thesis which he argued at length in the tract *Die Erziehung des Menschengeschlechts* ("The Education of the Human Race," Berlin, 1780). Lessing thus became the father both of the "post-Christian" consciousness expressed in nineteenth-century positivism, and of the liberal religion of thinkers such as Coleridge and Frederick Denison Maurice.

There is more relativism than skepticism in Lessing's view. He did not think that absolute truth is revealed; but even if it were, and even if he were capable of apprehending it, he would not have wished to apprehend it. Adapting an aphorism of Clement of Alexandria, Lessing declared:

The worth of a man does not consist in the truth he possesses, or thinks he possesses, but in the pains he has taken to attain that truth. For his powers are extended not through possession but through the search for truth. In this alone his ever-growing perfection consists. Possession makes him lazy, indolent, and proud. If God held all truth in his right hand and in his left the everlasting striving after truth, so that I should always and everlastingly be mistaken and said to me, Choose, with humility I would pick on the left hand and say, Father grant me that; absolute truth is for thee alone. (*Eine Duplik*, Lachmann and Muncker, eds., Vol. XIII, p. 23)

The move to immanentism. Several fragmentary notes found among Lessing's papers, and published in 1784 by his brother Karl in *Theologischen Nachlass*, disclose the extent of Leibniz' influence. Lessing's interest was always most deeply aroused by Leibniz' references to theology and ethics. One of these pieces, written by Lessing about 1753, "Das Christentum der Vernunft" ("The Christianity of Reason"), foreshadowed a section of *Die Erziehung* in its attempt at making a speculative restatement of the doctrine of the Trinity, with the help of Leibnizian ideas on the hierarchy of being and the harmony of the monads. But there is a strong admixture of Spinoza in Lessing's conception of this harmony; he did not think of it as something pre-established by a Creator who is a superobject behind and beyond phenomena, but rather as being itself God, so that the perfect continuum of existents, in which there can be no gap, is indistinguishable from the perfection of the divine being. Similarly, in the brief notes entitled "Ueber die Wirklichkeit der Dinge ausser Gott" ("On the Reality of Things Outside God," written in 1763, published in 1795 in Karl Lessing's *Lessings Leben*) Lessing denied the thesis of traditional theism that the created world exists independently of its Creator, in the sense of being distinct from him. Lessing urged that nothing can be outside the divine mind, and that there need be no hesitation before the conclusion that, since ideas of contingent things are themselves contingent, there is contingency even in God. These aphoristic fragments hardly amount to a coherent system. They show Lessing looking toward Spinoza, whom he had studied in his years at Breslau from 1760 to 1765, for a solution to some of the problems left unanswered by Leibniz.

Leibniz had formally asserted the freedom of the will, though it was doubted by Pierre Bayle and others whether Leibniz's libertarian assertions were in fact fully compatible with his philosophical principles. Lessing agreed with Spinoza that free will is a superfluity and an illusion. In 1776 Lessing published the "Philosophical Papers" (*Philosophische Aufsätze*) of Karl Wilhelm Jerusalem, with the intention of making a protest against Goethe's *Werther*, with its description of Jerusalem's suicide. In a note to Jerusalem's third essay Lessing commented on his wisdom in recognizing that freedom is nothing but a cause of anxiety and fear, and that the recognition of necessity and destiny as beneficent is the only way to true happiness. "I thank my God," Lessing added, "that I am under necessity, that the best must be." The notion that the moralist has anything to fear from deterministic philosophies is just a mistake.

In 1785 at Breslau, Friedrich Heinrich Jacobi published his *Ueber die Lehre des Spinoza in Briefen an der Herrn Moses Mendelssohn* ("Letters to Moses Mendelssohn on Spinoza's Doctrine"), in which he disclosed that at Wolfenbüttel in July 1780, he had been told by Lessing, seven months before Lessing's death, that he could not believe the old transcendental metaphysic, and that he unreservedly accepted the pantheism of Spinoza—"There is no other philosophy." Jacobi was astonished to hear Lessing add that the determinism of Spinoza was no obstacle to him, and indeed that he had no desire for free will. Jacobi's revelations precipitated a furious controversy known as the *Pantheismusstreit* (see PANTHEISMUSSTREIT). The Enlightenment had derived from Bayle's *Dictionnaire historique et critique* such an unflattering picture of Spinoza that Jacobi's attribution of Spinozistic views to Lessing seemed like a shocking libel of a dead man. Moses Mendelssohn was moved to write an irate reply, in which he denied that Lessing was a pantheist and a determinist. Although not all of Jacobi's deductions were correct, the substantial accuracy of his account of what Lessing said is sufficiently vindicated by the fragments found among Lessing's papers. Lessing's final creed was a belief in an immanent destiny, with no room either for the concept of transcendence or for special revelation in any form; he believed in a determined pattern of cause and effect extending not only throughout the physical order of nature, but also to morality and "the realm of ends."

Lessing's legacy to posterity was therefore to give an impetus to the notion of historical inevitability, especially in "The Education of the Human Race," at the end of which he even toyed with speculations about the transmigration of souls—obviously because this concept seemed to him more compatible with his historical determinism than the traditional eschatology connected with the Christian ideas of freedom and of personality.

The strong influence of Lessing is manifested in the history of religious thought in the nineteenth century. It can be traced particularly in the work of Kierkegaard, whose *Concluding Unscientific Postscript* took its starting point from Lessing's statement about the intellectually impossible leap from the contingent truths of history to the necessary truths of divine revelation. The other, more liberal, side of Lessing was reflected in Coleridge, whose work was even suspected of being a plagiarism of Lessing's. In the field of literature and art, Lessing's attack on French classicism opened the way for the romantic ideal of free self-expression and naturalism, while his final theological position of Spinozistic immanentism clearly foreshadowed Schleiermacher's *Speeches on Religion (Reden über die Religion,* 1799). His consciousness of living in an age of humanist maturity anticipated the Hegelian and Comtean estimates of religion as a useful, though now surpassed, stage in the education of humanity toward something higher and truer. Probably Lessing did as much as anyone to encourage among the educated European minds of his time an attitude of critical doubt that would lead to passionate engagement, rather than impersonal remoteness.

Works by Lessing

Werke, Julius Petersen and W. von Olshausen, eds. Berlin, 1925–1935.
Gesammelte Werke, Lachmann and Muncker, eds., 23 vols. 1886–1924.
Lessings Gesammelte Werke, Paul Rilla, ed., 10 vols. Berlin, 1954–1958.
Selected Prose Works, translated by E. C. Beasley and Helen Zimmern. London, 1879.
Hamburgischen Dramaturgie, G. Waterhouse, ed. Cambridge, 1926.
Laocoön, translated by E. A. McCormick. New York, 1962.

Works on Lessing

Aner, K., *Die Theologie der Lessingzeit.* Halle, 1929.
Cassirer, Ernst, *Die Philosophie der Aufklärung.* Tübingen, 1932. Translated by F. C. A. Koelln and J. P. Pettegrove as *The Philosophy of the Enlightenment.* Princeton, 1951.
Chadwick, Henry, *Lessing's Theological Writings.* Palo Alto, Calif., 1956.
Gombrich, E. H., "Lessing." *Proceedings of the British Academy,* Vol. 43 (1957), 133–156.
Hazard, Paul, *La Pensée européenne au 18ème siècle. De Montesquieu à Lessing.* Paris, 1946. Translated by J. Lewis May as *European Thought in the 18th Century.* London, 1954.

HENRY CHADWICK

LEUCIPPUS AND DEMOCRITUS were the earliest Greek atomists. The originator of the atomic theory, Leucippus (fifth century B.C.), must be considered a speculative thinker of the first order, but to Democritus (c. 460–c. 370 B.C.) must go the credit for working out the detailed application of the theory and supporting it with a subtle epistemology. Moreover, the range of Democritus' researches surpassed that of any earlier philosopher, and he appears to have been an original and, for his day, advanced ethical thinker.

We have very little biographical data for Leucippus. Epicurus is even reported to have said that there was no philosopher Leucippus, but the evidence of Aristotle decisively refutes this opinion (if, indeed, Epicurus did not merely intend to deny Leucippus' philosophical importance). Leucippus was probably born at Miletus; reports associating him with Elea or Abdera should be taken as reflecting views concerning his philosophical affiliations rather than as reliable evidence for his birthplace. He was presumably older than Democritus. His book *On Mind* may have been directed partly against Anaxagoras, and according to Theophrastus, Diogenes of Apollonia derived some of his theories from Leucippus. All this suggests that Leucippus was a slightly younger contemporary of Anaxagoras and that his main philosophical activity fell some time within the broad limits of 450–420 B.C.

Democritus was born at Abdera. He described himself in the *Little World-system* as a young man in the old age of Anaxagoras; Diogenes Laërtius says that he was forty years younger than Anaxagoras. On this evidence the date given for his birth by Apollodorus (in the 80th Olympiad, 460–456 B.C.) is generally preferred to that suggested by Thrasylus (the third year of the 77th Olympiad, 470–469 B.C.). He is variously reported to have lived between 90 and 109 years. To judge from the number of his writings, his literary activity extended over a considerable period, but we have no means of assigning different works to different times in his life. His statement that he wrote the *Little World-system* 730 years after the fall of Troy (Diogenes Laërtius, *Lives* IX, 41) is of little value since we cannot tell which of several possible chronologies for the Trojan War Democritus accepted.

Many stories, most of them apocryphal, relating to Democritus' life and character circulated in antiquity. There are the accounts of his saving the Abderites from a plague, of his dying by voluntarily abstaining from food, and of his reputation as the "Laughing Philosopher." The tradition that he traveled extensively is, however, more plausible and better grounded. The authenticity of the fragment (299) in which he claimed to be the most widely traveled of his contemporaries is disputed, and the genuineness of the five books dealing with foreign travel mentioned by Diogenes Laërtius (for example, *A Voyage Round the Ocean*) has also been doubted. But evidence concerning his travels goes back to Theophrastus (see Aelian, *Varia Historia* IV, 20), and the reports that he visited such places as Egypt, Chaldea, and the Red Sea (see Diogenes Laërtius, *Lives* IX, 35) may well have a sound basis in fact.

All that has been preserved of the original writings of Leucippus and Democritus is a poor selection of isolated quotations, most of which derive from the ethical works of Democritus. For the atomic theory itself we rely on reports in Aristotle, Theophrastus, and later doxographers, who were often unsympathetic to the views of the atomists. In most of the principal texts referring to Leucippus, his doctrines are not clearly distinguished from those of Democritus, and the precise contribution of each philosopher is in question. Aristotle, however, undoubtedly treated Leucippus as the founder of atomism (*De Generatione et Corruptione* 325a23 ff.), and we may reasonably attribute both the principles of the physical theory and a fairly complex cosmogony to him. Democritus evidently elaborated the atomic theory and was responsible for the detailed account of sensible qualities, besides going far beyond Leucippus both in the range of his scientific inquiries and in his interest in moral philosophy.

Writings. Only two works are ascribed to Leucippus, *On Mind*, from which our sole surviving quotation comes, and the *Great World-system*, which may be attributed to Leucippus on the authority of Theophrastus (Diogenes Laërtius, *Lives* IX, 46), although Thrasylus later assigned it to Democritus.

Democritus, on the other hand, wrote some sixty-odd works, the titles of which provide valuable evidence of the scope of his interests. The main works were catalogued by Thrasylus into thirteen tetralogies. Two tetralogies are devoted to ethics and four to physics (including *Little World-system, On the Planets, On Nature, On the Nature of Man, On the Senses,* and *On Colors*). These were followed by nine works not arranged in tetralogies—for example, *Causes of Celestial Phenomena, Causes Concerning Seeds, Plants and Fruits,* and three books of *Causes Concerning Animals.* Three tetralogies are classified as mathematics, two deal with music and literature, and two consist of technical works, including treatises on medicine, agriculture, painting, and warfare. Nine other miscellaneous works, mostly concerning travel, are also mentioned by Diogenes Laërtius but are less certainly authentic as they were not included in Thrasylus' catalogue.

Democritus' style is described by Cicero as elegant (*De Oratore* I, 11, 49) and lucid (*De Divinatione* II, 64, 133), and an anecdote recorded by Diogenes Laërtius (*Lives* IX, 40) implies that his works already had wide circulation by the time of Plato.

THE ATOMIC THEORY

The basic postulate of Greek atomism in its original form was that atoms and the void alone are real. The differences between physical objects, including both qualitative differences and what we think of as differences in substance, were all explained in terms of modifications in the shape, arrangement, and position of the atoms. Aristotle illustrates these three modes of difference with the examples A and N, AN and NA, and ⊏ and H.

This theory was already interpreted by Aristotle as an answer to the Eleatic denial of change and movement. Other post-Parmenidean philosophers had countered this denial in different ways, but both Empedocles and Anaxagoras had assumed a variety of elemental substances, on the one hand, the four "roots," on the other, an original mixture containing every kind of natural substance. In postulating a single elemental substance, Leucippus remained closer to Parmenides' own conception. In common with Parmenides' One Being the individual atoms are ungenerated, indestructible, unalterable, homogeneous, solid, and indivisible. Leucippus may be said to have postulated an infinite plurality of Eleatic ones, and he may even have been directly influenced by Melissus' argument (Fr. 8) that "if there were a plurality, they would have to be as the One is." Leucippus also agreed with the Eleatics that without void movement is impossible. Yet whereas the Eleatics denied the existence of the void, or "what is not," Leucippus maintained that not only "what is" (the atoms), but also "what is not" (the void), must be considered real. Leucippus thereby reinstated both plurality and change; the void is that which separates the atoms and that through which they move.

The atoms are infinite in number, dispersed through an infinite void. Their shapes are infinitely various, there being no reason that any atom should be of one shape rather than another. Democritus, at least, also allowed differences in the sizes of the atoms, but whether he thought any atom large enough to be visible seems doubtful. Late sources which report that atoms are unlimited in size as well as number (Diogenes Laërtius, *Lives* IX, 44) or which suggest the possibility of an atom the size of the world (Aëtius, *Placita* I, 12, 6) are difficult to credit in view of the testimony of Aristotle, who apparently believed that for both Leucippus and Democritus the atoms are all so small that they are invisible.

The atoms are in continuous motion. Aristotle, among others, objected that the atomists did not explain the origin of movement or say what kind of movement is natural to the atoms. However, they evidently assumed that the motion of the atoms is eternal, just as the atoms themselves are, and they perhaps drew no clear distinction between original and derived motion. Although Epicurus was later to suggest that atoms naturally fall vertically, the earlier atomists probably did not consider movement in any particular direction prior to movement in any other. Weight for them, it seems, was not a primary property of the atoms nor a cause of their interactions, although in a developed cosmos the atoms have "weight" corresponding to their size (and the weight of compound bodies varies according to the proportion of atoms and void they contain).

The movements of the atoms give rise to constant collisions whose effects are twofold. Sometimes, the atoms rebound from one another; alternatively, when the colliding atoms are hooked or barbed or their shapes otherwise correspond, they cohere and thus form compound bodies. Change of all sorts is accordingly interpreted in terms of the combining and separating of atoms, which themselves remain unaltered in substance. The compound bodies thus formed possess various sensible qualities—color, taste, temperature, and so on—and Democritus undertook a detailed exposition relating these qualities to specific atomic configurations.

Cosmogony. Evidence concerning Leucippus' cosmogony comes mainly from Diogenes Laërtius (*Lives* IX, 31 ff.). The process begins when a large group of atoms becomes isolated in a great void. There they conglomerate and form a whirl or vortex in which atoms of similar shape and size come together. In this vortex the finer atoms are squeezed out into the outer void, but the remainder tend toward the center, where they form a spherical mass. More atoms are drawn into this mass on contact with the whirl, and some of these are ignited by the speed of the revolution, thus forming the heavenly bodies. The earth is formed by atoms that cohere in the center of the mass. The cosmogonical process is not unique. The atomists argued that since atoms and the void are infinite, there are innumerable worlds. These worlds are not all alike, however; Democritus held that some worlds have no sun or moon and that some lack moisture and all forms of life (Hippolytus, *Refutatio* I, 13, 2 f.).

Several features of this account are obscure, and two apparently conflicting criticisms were leveled against it in antiquity—first, that although the atomists asserted that the cosmogonical process came about by necessity, they did not explain what this necessity was (Diogenes Laërtius, *Lives* IX, 33); second, that they maintained that it occurred spontaneously (Aristotle clearly has the atomists in mind when he considered this view, *Physics* 196a24 ff.).

But Aristotle's judgment should be taken as referring primarily to the atomists' exclusion of final causes; in Aristotelian terms the atomists held that the world arose spontaneously because they denied that it was intelligently planned. Leucippus explicitly stated that "nothing happens at random, but everything for a reason and by necessity" (Fr. 2), and throughout their cosmology the atomists not only excluded purpose or design but also assumed that every event is the product of a definite, theoretically determinable cause. Thus, they doubtless conceived the vortex to arise from certain mechanical interactions between the colliding atoms, although it is unlikely that they attempted to say precisely how this came about. Democritus illustrated his doctrine that like things tend to come together with examples drawn from both the inanimate and the animate sphere (Fr. 164). And like many of the pre-Socratics, the atomists constructed their cosmogony in part on an embryological model. The outer envelope of the world was likened to a membrane, and in both Leucippus' cosmogony and Democritus' embryology the process of differentiation apparently takes place from the outside (see Aristotle, *De Generatione Animalium* 740a13 ff.).

Astronomy and biology. Leucippus' astronomical theories are surprisingly retrograde. He accepted the old Ionian picture of a flat earth, tilted toward the south, and he believed that the sun is the most distant of the heavenly bodies. Democritus' theories were generally less crude, and he attempted rational explanations of a wide variety of obscure phenomena. He accepted Leucippus' account of the earth with only minor modifications (Aëtius, *Placita* III, 10, 5) but corrected his notion of the relative positions of the heavenly bodies, observing, for example, that the planets are not equidistant from the earth and placing Venus between the sun and moon. Among other topics on which some of Democritus' theories are recorded are the behavior of the magnet, the nourishment of the embryo, and the relative longevity of different types of plants. Of his biological doctrines the notion that the seed is drawn from the whole of the body (the pangenesis theory) was particularly influential (Aëtius, *Placita* V, 3, 6).

Soul, knowledge, and sensation. Our evidence concerning the atomists' psychological and epistemological doctrines derives very largely from Democritus, although his theory of the soul was probably developed from ideas outlined by Leucippus. This theory was a materialist one in line with the principles of atomism. Democritus conceived of the soul as consisting of spherical atoms, this being the shape best adapted to penetrate and move things. Fire, too, is composed of spherical atoms, and he evidently subscribed to the common Greek belief in the connection between life and heat, now interpreted in terms of the similarity in the shapes of soul atoms and fire atoms. The soul atoms tend to be extruded from the body by the pressure of the surrounding air, but this process is counteracted by other soul atoms which enter the body with the air we breathe; life depends on this continuous replenishment.

Our main source for Democritus' theory of knowledge is Sextus Empiricus. Several of the fragments which he quotes appear to express an extreme skepticism—for instance, "We know nothing truly about anything" (Fr. 7). However, Fragment 11 shows that Democritus was no outright skeptic. There he distinguished between two modes of cognition; the senses provide what is called a "bastard" knowledge but contrasted with this is a "legitimate" knowledge, which operates on objects too fine for the senses to perceive. Clearly, "legitimate" knowledge relates to atoms and the void, which alone are real; the objects of sensation, on the other hand, exist "by convention" (Fr. 9). The doctrine enunciated in the fragments is that sense perception is not trustworthy, and Aristotle's repeated statement that the atomists found truth in appearance (*De Generatione et Corruptione* 315b9 ff.) should be understood as an interpretative comment based on Aristotle's own conception of the distinction between sensibles and intelligibles. Yet although we must rely on reasoning to attain knowledge, Democritus acknowledged that the mind derives its data from the senses (Fr. 125). Not a pure intellectualist like Parmenides, a crude sensationalist like Protagoras, nor a complete skeptic as Gorgias made himself out to be, Democritus advocated critical reflection on the evidence of the senses as our best means of approaching the truth; yet since thought itself, like sensation, involves physical interactions between atoms, it, too, is subject to distortion, and even "legitimate" knowledge is at best, it seems, only opinion (Fr. 7).

Democritus' detailed accounts of the five senses were reported and criticized at length by Theophrastus (*De Sensibus* 49–82). According to Alexander (*In Librum de Sensu* 24, 14 ff.), Leucippus already held that physical objects constantly emit images which effect vision on entering the eye. Democritus modified and complicated this doctrine by suggesting that images from both the object and the eye itself meet and imprint the air in front of the eye. Each of the other senses, too, is produced by contact between the organ and images deriving from the object, and thought was analogously explained as the contact between soul atoms and images coming from outside the body. But not content merely to assert in general terms that secondary qualities are due to differences in the shapes and sizes of the atoms, Democritus also proposed a detailed account relating specific tastes, colors, smells, and so on to specific shapes. Thus, an acid taste is composed of angular, small, thin atoms and a sweet taste of round, moderate-sized ones. Democritus' primary colors—black, white, red, and greenish yellow—were similarly associated with certain shapes and arrangements of atoms, and other colors were derived from combinations of these four. For all its crudities Democritus' theory may claim to be the first fully elaborated account of the physical basis of sensation.

Mathematics. Democritus' interest in mathematics is apparent from the titles of fives works dealing with mathematical subjects, and we are told, for example, that he discovered the relation between the volumes of a pyramid and a prism with the same base and equal height. We have, however, little evidence on the part of his mathematical work that related directly to the atomic theory. The atoms are definitely conceived of as physically indivisible (on the grounds that they are solid and contain no void), but it is not clear whether they are absolute minima in the sense of being mathematically indivisible. Epicurus later distinguished between atomic bodies (which are physically indivisible but logically divisible) and the "minima in the atom." But Aristotle appears to have assumed that Leucippus and Democritus themselves drew no distinction between the limits of physical and mathematical divisibility (*De Generatione et Corruptione* 315b28 ff.), and he considered that their atomic theory necessarily conflicted with the mathematical sciences (*De Caelo* 303a20 ff.). Unless Aristotle has completely misrepresented the atomists, it would appear that Democritus was unaware of any inconsistency in holding both (1) that the atoms have different shapes and sizes and (2) that they are mathematically as well as physically indivisible. But it must be repeated that the evidence on which to convict or absolve Democritus of this gross confusion is scanty.

Ethics. Although serious doubts have been raised concerning the transmission of the ethical fragments of Democritus, most scholars now consider that the majority of those accepted by Diels and Kranz may be used as a basis from which to reconstruct his ethics. There remain, however, wide disagreements on the nature and value of his moral teaching. Alongside the fragments which convey traditional sentiments (for example, on the dangers of fame and wealth if not accompanied by intelligence) we find others which expound notions far in advance of the popular morality of the day, as, for instance, the doctrine that it is one's own consciousness of right and wrong, not fear of the law or public opinion, that should prevent one from doing anything shameful (Frs. 181, 264). And sayings such as Fragment 45 ("The wrongdoer is more unfortunate than he who is wronged") express views more commonly associated with Socrates than with Democritus.

The ethical ideal is termed "well-being" or "cheerfulness," which is to be gained through uprightness and a harmonious life. Although Democritus clearly implied that life without pleasure is not worth living and even said that pleasure is the mark of what is expedient (Fr. 188), it is the higher pleasures of the soul that we should cultivate, not those of the body. Sensual pleasures are condemned as short-lived. He repeatedly stressed that we should moderate our desires and ambitions, become self-sufficient, and be content, in the main, with simple pleasures. Yet Democritus was no quietist. Rather, he recognized that worthwhile objects are to be achieved only through effort (Frs. 157, 182).

One of the salient features of Democritus' ethics is his rejection of supernatural sanctions of behavior. In part, he seems to have rationalized belief in the gods as a mistaken inference from terrifying natural phenomena (Sextus, *Adversus Mathematicos* IX, 24), and yet he did not dismiss notions of the gods entirely, for he appears to have related certain such ideas to images, some beneficent, some harmful, that visit men (Fr. 166). Religious sanctions are, however, rigorously excluded from his ethics. He refuted those who concocted fictions concerning the afterlife (Fr. 297), and he spoke with apparent irony of those who prayed to Zeus as "king of all" (Fr. 30). Equally, he castigated those who invented chance as an excuse for their own thoughtlessness or who failed to recognize that their misfortunes stemmed from their own incontinence (Frs. 119, 234). Throughout his ethics he may be said to have set high standards of personal integrity and social responsibility.

The question of the relation between Democritus' ethics and his physics has been much debated. In some respects, such as in the idea that excesses "cause great movements in the soul"—that is, presumably, in the soul atoms (Fr. 191) —his ethics reflect a psychology which is based on his physical theories. Whether we should expect other aspects of the atomic doctrine to be in evidence in the ethical fragments seems very doubtful. Democritus clearly did not feel (nor need he have felt) that the notion of necessity in his physics (the belief that every event has a definite cause to be sought in the interactions of the atoms) conflicted with his doctrine of moral responsibility in the sphere of human behavior. His denial of supernatural sanctions in his ethics parallels his rejection of teleology in his cosmology. And his ethics have in common with his epistemological theory that he argued against an unreflecting acceptance of the evidence of the senses concerning what is pleasant just as much as concerning the nature of reality as a whole.

Sociology and politics. The only indication we have of Democritus' political leanings is the idealistic but otherwise rather inconclusive Fragment 251: "Poverty under democracy is as much to be preferred to so-called happiness under tyrants as freedom is to slavery." It has, however, been conjectured that the account of the origin of civilization preserved in Diodorus (*Bibliotheca Historica* I, 8) owes much to Democritus. According to this, primitive men originally gathered in groups for the sake of mutual protection from wild animals, and subsequently language and the arts were also invented under the spur of man's needs. It is very uncertain how far this reproduces Democritus' ideas, but there is some evidence in the fragments that he maintained a naturalistic theory of civilization and progress and excluded teleological explanations here, as he did elsewhere in his philosophy. Fragment 144 may be taken to suggest that he believed that the earliest arts (although not some of the later ones) were products of necessity, and in Fragment 154 he argued that man learned many of his skills by copying the behavior of animals.

The theory founded by Leucippus and developed by Democritus was the most coherent and economical physical system of its day, and the history of its influence can be traced from the fourth century B.C. to modern times. Although Plato mentioned neither Leucippus nor Democritus, the *Timaeus* is markedly indebted to their thought. Even Aristotle, who rejected atomism outright, conceded that of all his predecessors Democritus was the most notable physicist. Later, the Epicureans championed atomism against the continuum theory of the Stoics. Leucippus' theory, in origin primarily an answer to the Eleatic arguments against change, was the first clear formulation of the doctrine that matter exists in the form of discrete particles, and as such it may legitimately be considered the prototype of modern theories of the discontinuous structure of matter, even though the nature of such theories, the problems they are intended to resolve, and the methods used to establish them all differ fundamentally from those of ancient atomism.

Bibliography

The extant fragments of Leucippus and Democritus and the principal reports and commentaries in ancient authors are collected in Hermann Diels's *Die Fragmente der Vorsokratiker*, Vol. II, 6th ed., with additions by Walther Kranz, ed. (Berlin, 1952). There is an English translation of the fragments in Kathleen Freeman, *Ancilla to the Pre-Socratic Philosophers* (Cambridge, Mass., and Oxford, 1948).

The best monograph on Leucippus and Democritus is still Cyril Bailey's *The Greek Atomists and Epicurus* (Oxford, 1928). *The Presocratic Philosophers* by G. S. Kirk and J. E. Raven (Cambridge, 1957) has a lucid, brief exposition of their thought. The second volume of *A History of Greek Philosophy* by W. K. C. Guthrie (Cambridge, 1965) contains a full discussion and extensive up-to-date bibliography. Otherwise, the most important general studies are those of Wilhelm Nestle's revised and enlarged edition of Eduard Zeller's *Die Philosophie der Griechen*, 6th ed. (Leipzig, 1920), Part I, Sec. 2, pp. 1038–1194; Wilhelm Schmid in Wilhelm Schmid and Otto Stählin, eds., *Geschichte der griechischen Literatur* (Munich, 1948), Part I, Sec. 5, pp. 224–349; and V. E. Alfieri, *Gli atomisti* (Bari, 1936) and *Atomos Idea* (Florence, 1953).

PHYSICS AND COSMOLOGY

Bury, R. G., "The Origin of Atomism." *Classical Review*, Vol. 30 (1916), 1–4.

Dyroff, Adolf, *Demokritstudien*. Leipzig, 1899.

Fritz, Kurt von, *Philosophie und sprachlicher Ausdruck bei Demokrit, Plato und Aristoteles*. New York, n.d. [1939].

Hammer-Jensen, Ingeborg, "Demokrit und Platon." *Archiv für Geschichte der Philosophie*, N.S. Vol. 16 (1910), 92–105, 211–229.

Kerschensteiner, Jula, "Zu Leukippos A 1." *Hermes*, Vol. 87 (1959), 441–448.

Löwenheim, Louis, *Die Wissenschaft Demokrits*. Berlin, 1914.

McDiarmid, J. B., "Theophrastus *De Sensibus* 61–62: Democritus' Theory of Weight." *Classical Philology*, Vol. 55 (1960), 28–30.

Mugler, Charles, "Sur Quelques Particularités de l'atomisme ancien." *Revue de philologie*, 3d series, Vol. 27 (1953), 141–174.

Sambursky, Samuel, "Atomism Versus Continuum Theory in Ancient Greece." *Scientia*, Vol. 96 (1961), 376–381.

EPISTEMOLOGY

McDiarmid, J. B., "Theophrastus *De Sensibus* 66: Democritus' Explanation of Salinity." *American Journal of Philology*, Vol. 80 (1959), 56–66.

Weiss, Helene, "Democritus' Theory of Cognition." *Classical Quarterly*, Vol. 32 (1938), 47–56.

MATHEMATICS

Luria, Salomo, "Die Infinitesimaltheorie der antiken Atomisten." *Quellen und Studien zur Geschichte der Mathematik, Astronomie und Physik*, Part 2 (Studies), Vol. 2, Sec. 2 (Berlin, 1932–1933), 106–185.

Mau, Jürgen, *Zum Problem des Infinitesimalen bei den antiken Atomisten*. Berlin, 1954.

Philippson, Robert, "Democritea." *Hermes*, Vol. 64 (1929), 175–183.

Vlastos, Gregory, "Minimal Parts in Epicurean Atomism." *Isis*, Vol. 56 (1965), 121–147.

Zubov, V. P., "K Voprosu o Matematicheskom Atomisme Democrita." *Vestnik Drevnei Istorii*, Vol. 4 (1951), 204–208.

ETHICS

Langerbeck, Hermann, ΔΟΞΙΣ ΕΠΙΡΥΣΜΙΗ, *Neue Philologische Untersuchungen*, Vol. X. Berlin, 1935.

Laue, Heinrich, *De Democriti Fragmentis Ethicis.* Unpublished dissertation, University of Göttingen, 1921.

Laue, Heinrich, "Die Ethik des Demokritos." *Sokrates,* N.S. Vol. 11 (1923–1924), 23–28, 49–62.

Luria, Salomo, *Zur Frage der materialistischen Begründung der Ethik bei Demokrit.* Berlin, 1964.

McGibbon, Donal, "Pleasure as the 'Criterion' in Democritus." *Phronesis,* Vol. 5 (1960), 75–77.

McGibbon, Donal, "The Religious Thought of Democritus." *Hermes,* Vol. 93 (1965), 385–397.

Natorp, Paul, *Die Ethika des Demokritos.* Marburg, 1893.

Philippson, Robert, "Demokrits Sittensprüche." *Hermes,* Vol. 59 (1924), 369–419.

Stewart, Zeph, "Democritus and the Cynics." *Harvard Studies in Classical Philology,* Vol. 63 (1958), 179–191.

Vlastos, Gregory, "Ethics and Physics in Democritus." *Philosophical Review,* Vol. 54 (1945), 578–592; Vol. 55 (1946), 53–64.

SOCIOLOGY AND POLITICS

Aalders, G. J. D., "The Political Faith of Democritus." *Mnemosyne,* 4th series, Vol. 3 (1950), 302–313.

Vlastos, Gregory, "On the Pre-history in Diodorus." *American Journal of Philology,* Vol. 67 (1946), 51–59.

G. E. R. LLOYD

LÉVY-BRUHL, LUCIEN (1857–1939), French philosopher and social anthropologist, was educated at the University of Paris and the École Normale Supérieure. He occupied the chair of philosophy at the Lycée Louis-le-Grand from 1885 to 1895, when he became *maître de conférences* at the Sorbonne; in 1908 he was appointed titular professor. In 1916 he became editor of the *Revue philosophique.*

Lévy-Bruhl's early work was devoted to the history of philosophy, particularly that of Auguste Comte. While still under the influence of Comte and also of Émile Durkheim, he published *La Morale et la science des moeurs* (Paris, 1903; translated by E. Lee as *Ethics and Moral Science,* London, 1905). It stressed the need for detailed empirical studies of the diverse moral attitudes and ideas of different societies as well as the adaptation of these ideas to the social structure of the group. He considered such a description and explanation as a preliminary to a possible applied science of morals, which would give men the same power to modify social life as physical technology gives them over natural phenomena.

Lévy-Bruhl did not develop this idea of a moral technology but devoted most of his life to investigating an extremely wide range of anthropological data derived from the reports of other observers. The interest of his work lies in the theoretical ideas that he applied to this material.

Lévy-Bruhl argued that the behavior of men in primitive societies must be understood in terms of Durkheim's concept of "collective representations," which are emotional and mystical rather than intellectual. The primitive man's world is dominated by occult powers, and his thought is "prelogical," following a law of participation and quite indifferent to what civilized man would regard as self-contradictions. For example, the members of a totemic group may regard themselves as actually identical with their totem, as belonging to a continuum of spiritual powers, rather than as existing as distinct individuals. Prelogical concepts imply no systematic unity but "welter, as it were, in an atmosphere of mystical possibilities" (*How Natives Think,* Ch. 3). Space, for instance, is conceived, not as a homogeneous whole, but in terms of the mystical ties

binding each tribe to a particular region, the structure of the ties being understood in terms of the various occult forces to which the life of the tribe is subject.

Primitive man is similarly indifferent to conceptions of causality as understood in civilized cultures. For him there is no natural order within which perceptible phenomena are causally interconnected, but, equally, nothing happens by chance. Events are brought about directly, not through any mechanism of secondary causes; they are effected by the imperceptible denizens of an occult realm who have no definite spatiotemporal location and who may be felt as present in several places simultaneously.

Durkheim's followers have criticized Lévy-Bruhl for failing to bring out the connections between primitive collective representations and social structure. He has also been accused of overstressing the extent of prelogical elements in primitive thought. In attempting to reconcile the existence of fairly highly developed arts and crafts in primitive tribes with his denial that such tribes thought at all in terms of logical and causal connections, he held that such manual skills are not based on reasoning but "are guided by a kind of special sense or tact," refined by experience without benefit of reflection. Lévy-Bruhl's most serious philosophical shortcoming, perhaps, is his failure to see anything problematic about the nature of logic itself and the role it plays in civilized life. His identification of logical thought with the thought of Western civilization prevented him from perceiving many important continuities and analogies between primitive and civilized attitudes and practices.

Additional Works by Lévy-Bruhl

History of Modern Philosophy in France, translated by G. Coblence. London and Chicago, 1899.

La Philosophie d'Auguste Comte. Paris, 1900. Translated by K. de Braumont-Klein as *The Philosophy of Auguste Comte.* London, 1903.

Les Fonctions mentales dans les sociétés inférieures. Paris, 1910. Translated by L. A. Clare as *How Natives Think.* London, 1926.

La Mentalité primitive. Paris, 1922. Translated by L. A. Clare as *Primitive Mentality.* London and New York, 1923.

L'Ame primitive. Paris, 1927. Translated by L. A. Clare as *The "Soul" of the Primitive.* London, 1928.

Le Surnaturel et la nature dans la mentalité primitive. Paris, 1931. Translated by L. A. Clare as *Primitives and the Supernatural.* London, 1936.

La Mythologie primitive. Le monde mythique des Australiens et des Papous. Paris, 1935.

Les Carnets de Lucien Lévy-Bruhl. Paris, 1949.

Works on Lévy-Bruhl

Cailliet, Émile, *Mysticisme et "mentalité mystique." Étude d'un problème posé par les travaux de M. Lévy-Bruhl sur la mentalité primitive.* Paris, 1938.

Leroy, Olivier, *La Raison primitive. Essai de réfutation de la théorie du prélogisme.* Paris, 1927.

PETER WINCH

LEWES, GEORGE HENRY (1817–1878), English journalist, editor, critic, novelist, dramatist, actor, biographer, scientist, philosopher, and psychologist. Lewes was born in London. A man of remarkable talent and versatility, he compensated for his lack of a university education by his capacity and enthusiasm for intellectual activity. In the early 1840s Lewes corresponded with John Stuart Mill, who introduced him to the positivist doctrines of August Comte. Lewes' first book, *The Biographical History of Philosophy* (4 vols., London, 1845–1846), was written with the aim of ousting metaphysics from philosophical inquiry and replacing it with scientific positivism. In 1850 he became editor of *The Leader,* a liberal weekly, to which he contributed, among many other articles, a series on Comte, published in 1853 as *Comte's Philosophy of the Sciences.*

In 1854, after Lewes had separated from his wife because she had committed adultery, he began a long and happy life with Mary Anne Evans (George Eliot, the novelist). He published his famous *Life of Goethe* in 1855, but after 1856 scientific research absorbed his interest. His first scientific work, *Sea-Side Studies at Ilfracombe, Tenby, the Scilly Isles and Jersey* (Edinburgh, 1858), was followed by a number of papers on motor and sensory nerves read to the British Association for the Advancement of Science in September 1859. His *Physiology of Common Life* (2 vols., London, 1859–1860) was followed by *Studies in Animal Life* (London, 1862). His *Aristotle: A Chapter in the History of Science* (London, 1864) remains one of the few analyses of Aristotle's work in physical science. Lewes also contributed scientific as well as political and literary material to the *Fortnightly Review,* which he edited from 1865 to 1866. He wrote articles for practically every important English journal. His scientific work earned him the respect of such scientists as Charles Darwin and Charles Lyell. The outcome of his years devoted to philosophy and science was his five-volume *Problems of Life and Mind* (London, 1874–1879).

Philosophy of science. Although Lewes helped to popularize the ideas of Comte in England, he was not a disciple, and his criticism of some of Comte's views eventually caused unfriendly relations between the two. However, Lewes was impressed by Comte's early theories because of his own uncompromising naturalism. Rejecting transcendental explanations, he held that the positive method of science was the valid means for studying man as a natural being in a natural world. The nucleus of his exposition of scientific method was correctly described by C. S. Peirce as involving an emphasis on verification (*Collected Papers,* Vol. I, Cambridge, Mass., 1931, p. 14). Recognizing that most schools of thought claim to derive their tenets from some type of verification, Lewes noted, however, that their notions of verification were usually fallacious because they were based upon an erroneous view of the kind of experience to be investigated. In his view the experiential manifold consists of an inextricable combination of sensation and inference. Sensation alone cannot give knowledge. To see an apple does not mean that the apple actually exists unless other sensations normally associated with the presence of an apple are recalled, such as the sensation of taste when the apple is eaten. If we wish to know whether some given sense datum is really what we think it is, we must reinstate the sensations that accompanied the occurrence of the given sense datum in the past. Verification is a process of testing these inferred sensations to determine whether they are reducible to those directly given.

Lewes distinguished between the roles of laws and of hypotheses in scientific inquiry. A hypothesis is the first stage in the process of noting similarities among various phenomena and expressing them in a generalized formula. A real hypothesis explains a phenomenon by an agent or agency known to be present in it. An auxiliary hypothesis is a fictitious theory, used to facilitate research, that surmises the effect of an agent not known to be present in phenomena and is scrupulously accounted for in the final tabulation of the data. An illusory hypothesis, such as the theory of creation, substitutes ambiguous phraseology for explanation and is of no value to research.

The possession of more certain knowledge elevates a hypothesis to the rank of law. A real law—for example, Joule's law—gives a mathematical formulation of the reactions of similar phenomena when the inferences made about them are actualized; an ideal law, such as the law of inertia, is an extrapolation from a real law, expressing what the case would be if the conditions implied in the real law were changed. Since the symbols used in ideal laws have been abstracted from the real laws, ideal laws are valid to the degree in which their symbols are derived from empirical data. Thus, one of the most important functions of science is the study of the actual and possible conditions under which a phenomenon can occur, and there is no limit to the store of conditions to be scientifically investigated.

Lewes was so thoroughgoing an empiricist that he considered even so-called self-evident truths to be experientially derived; he defined axioms as ideas generalized in the mind from uniform experiences. He believed so strongly in the efficacy of scientific method that he foresaw the possibility of its application in all fields, even religion. He unequivocally rejected Christianity with its traditional metaphysics and theology and envisioned a religion founded on science.

But Lewes did believe in the existence of genuine metaphysical problems. Through the elaboration of what he called an empirical metaphysics, he tried to indicate how metaphysical problems could be dealt with scientifically. He equated metaphysical issues with the problems of abstract science, which deals with the sensible and logical facts inherent in such general scientific principles as cause, force, life, and mind. Reaffirming Aristotle's view of metaphysics as the "science of the most general principles," Lewes designated the object of empirical metaphysics to be the determination of these general laws. Its role is to help science integrate the data of the sciences in order to achieve the maximum understanding of man and his universe. To accomplish this goal, the traditional concepts of substance, matter, causation, and the dualistic views of reality must be revised.

Mind and body. Dualisms have enlarged the split among the various sciences and have prevented metaphysics from becoming an integrating science. Lewes maintained that no dichotomy exists between the mental and the physical. Every experience presents a "double aspect": real and ideal, particular and general. Regarded in one way, experience is subjective; regarded in another, it is objective. For different purposes it is viewed differently. Material and mental operations are merely different aspects of the same process. Body is merely the objective aspect of the subjective process known as mind. Therefore, metaphysics does not have to solve the mystery of how a material phenomenon becomes a mental phenomenon, nor must it search for answers in a Platonic Form or a Kantian thing-in-itself.

The qualities of matter are our sensations; the properties of matter are the qualities viewed in reference to their effect on other objects rather than their effect on us as feelings. But these properties do not inhere in some thing-in-itself. Since every phenomenal manifold contains a subjective–objective construction, every context is relational; that is, a thing *is* its relationships. To Lewes substance was no more than a name for some cluster of characteristics normally found together. Similarly, the agent or power that science seeks to understand in causation is not suprasensible; it is the relationship of the elements involved. Lewes was one of the first, if not the first, to distinguish between the *resultant,* the antecedently predictable change, and the *emergent,* the antecedently unpredictable transformation. He believed that someday enough would be known about the unseen process that produces emergents to make possible the expression of its action in a mathematical formula.

He analyzed more fully than Darwin or Spencer the significant implications of biological evolution in the field of psychology. He insisted that man, like the animal, must be studied in relation to the natural world. However, since man is also part of a social organism, he can no more be isolated from society than he can be from nature. All psychical activity is therefore the result of interaction of the organism and a physical and social environment. In Lewes' view, mind and body are interdependent; every mental change has a corresponding physical change, and these changes are isolated only as convenient abstractions. Every mental act is carried on by the entire organism; it is not the brain that thinks but the entire man. Personality is a "total." Sensibility is energy manifested as a function of various conditions existent in a neuromuscular mechanism. The "Triple Process" by means of which sensibility is achieved is actually one process involving three kinds of reactions—stimulation, coordination, and discharge, described further as sensation, thought, and will.

Using the terminology of association psychologists, Lewes referred to the sense datum, or neural tremor, as the basic element of experience. Thus, a sensation is a primary grouping of neural tremors; an image (an intermediary grouping) is formed when a sensation is reproduced; an idea is formed when an image loses its original value and becomes a symbol of a different sensation. Sensations represent the objective side of mental phenomena, since they have their origin in objective stimuli external to the organism; images represent the subjective side, for they arise out of excitations within the organism. Through words ideas that substitute for sensations have the power of recalling an absent object or action without the intervention of any sensible qualities. Feelings are products of groupings of images that have become signs or symbols—that is, of ideas. Since ideas are translatable into language, thoughts are primarily social instruments dependent upon the social environment. Both feeling and thought are products of the same kind of operation, differing in the particular combination of elements involved.

Lewes realized that his explanation could be stigmatized as materialism since it employed a material pattern to account for mental phenomena. To refute this charge, he used the double-aspect theory. If sensation were viewed as a physiological phenomenon and thought were considered a mental condition, it would be absurd to relate them in any way. But feeling and thought are both functions of the sentient organism under different aspects. Viewed objectively, feeling and thought are physical states; viewed subjectively, they are mental states. No sensation can exist without involving the functions of thought, nor can any thought exist without involving the functions of sensation.

Lewes further noted that a human organism is a mechanism of a very special kind. Its behavior differs in important ways from that of a machine. First, the human organism is comparable to an emergent in that the properties characteristic of its later development cannot be reduced to or predicted from the properties characteristic of its early development. Hence, its behavior patterns cannot be predicted on the basis of prior knowledge of physical and physiological conditions. But a machine is not comparable to an emergent, and its behavior patterns are always predictable. Second, the emergent nature of organisms makes it possible for them to react in novel ways to different stimuli. But a machine, lacking this quality, cannot react to unexpected situations by devising new plans to meet new problems.

Therefore, Lewes could not accept the strict materialist position. But neither was he an indeterminist. Even though the organism has the potential for new and unpredictable action, it cannot violate any of the physical laws of nature. Human choice is always conditioned by both internal and external stimuli. Free will must be explained in terms of the functioning of the entire organism and its relationship to the environment. Thus, in reality only choices that are compatible with physical laws and behavioral patterns of the organism are possible. Lewes used the following analogy to clarify his view: "Each sailor knows that he moves with the vessel, but knows also that he is free to move to and fro on deck" (*Problems of Life and Mind: The Study of Psychology,* Boston, 1879, p. 103).

In the nineteenth century the cause of science had no more devoted champion than Lewes, and the main principles of his philosophy are taken for granted by contemporary empiricists. However, much of his speculation is dated. He failed, as did John Stuart Mill, to distinguish between logical and empirical validity. At times his empirical metaphysics seems to do no more than confuse metaphysics with physics. His reasoned realism suffers from the same kind of tautological oversimplification that plagues any monistic system. These failings notwithstanding, Lewes elaborated theories that are still of consequence.

As a relativist, Lewes focused attention on the nature of conditions and the type of certainty that is supposed to occur under particular conditions. He anticipated the modern pragmatic theory of truth in his notion of verification. His belief that the intelligibility of an experiential context rests upon certain implicit inferences of future experience has been reaffirmed by John Dewey and C. I. Lewis. Although Lewes did not analyze fictions in experimentation as thoroughly as did Hans Vaihinger, his concept of auxiliary hypotheses was an interesting contribution to scientific theory. His distinction between resultants and emergents was to influence the ideas of later emergent evolutionists. Variations of his double-aspect theory have reappeared in the work of Paul Natorp, Durant Drake, C. Lloyd Morgan, Hans Driesch, Herbert Feigl, and J. J. C. Smart.

Much of Lewes' psychological terminology is outmoded, but certain emphases of his system contain significant contributions to psychology. Lewes fought constantly against metaphysical views that would isolate mental phenomena as independent entities. Because his work includes the most reliable conclusions of the evolutionary hypothesis, Lewes is of special interest to the genetic psychologist. He recognized the need to study man as a complex being, an approach requiring the integration of psychology, biology, and sociology. Finally, his demand that philosophers become scientists has been met in the work of C. D. Broad, Bertrand Russell, and A. N. Whitehead, just as his urgent insistence on the need for unification of the sciences has been confirmed by the efforts of John Dewey, Rudolf Carnap, Ernest Nagel, Charles W. Morris, and Philipp Frank.

Bibliography

Consult G. Grassi-Bertazzi, *Esame critico della filosofia di George Henry Lewes* (Messina, 1906); Gordon Haight, ed., *The George Eliot Letters*, 7 vols. (New Haven, 1954–1955); Alice R. Kaminsky, ed., *Literary Criticism of George Henry Lewes* (Lincoln, Nebr., 1964); Jack Kaminsky, "The Empirical Metaphysics of George Henry Lewes," in *Journal of the History of Ideas*, Vol. 13 (1952), 314–332; Anna T. Kitchel, *George Lewes and George Eliot: A Review of Records* (New York, 1933); Howard C. Warren, *A History of the Association Psychology* (New York, 1921).

Alice R. Kaminsky

LEWIN, KURT (1890–1947), American psychologist who developed topological psychology and applied field theory to psychology and social psychology. Lewin was born in Posen, Germany (now Poznan, Poland), of Jewish parents. He studied under Karl Stumpf at the University of Berlin, where he later rose to the rank of extraordinary professor. He emigrated from Germany to the United States when Hitler came to power. He taught first at Cornell, then at the University of Iowa, where he was in charge of the Child Welfare Research Station, and finally at the Massachusetts Institute of Technology, where he organized the Research Center for Group Dynamics.

Lewin was perhaps the most philosophically oriented of recent psychologists. He was more indebted to the Neo-Kantian philosophers Ernst Cassirer and Wilhelm Windelband than to any psychologist, and all his work was as much related to problems of scientific methodology as to the psychological research of his contemporaries. Chief among the problems he considered were those of explanation in psychology and of the nature of causation. These two questions together led him to his attempted application of topology to psychology.

Explanation. The problem of explanation arose directly out of Wilhelm Windelband's and Heinrich Rickert's distinction between the natural sciences (*Naturwissenschaften*) and the cultural sciences (*Kulturwissenschaften*), each with its appropriate methods of research. The natural sciences are "nomothetic": they seek general laws and rules governing the universe. The cultural sciences, including psychology, are "idiographic": they are concerned with individual cases only. History is the paradigm of an idiographic science, because what happens in history happens but once. Each historical event is unique and unrepeatable, an idiophenomenon.

Under the influence of this view, Lewin placed the single case at the center of his psychology. At the same time, he held, the single case must be tested by general laws. He explained how this was possible by distinguishing three periods in the history of psychology. In the "Aristotelian" stage psychologists were concerned with the "essence" of an event, with its membership in a given class of events. Thus, only recurrent events were regarded as lawful and capable of explanation. In the second, "descriptive" stage, scientists collected facts and described them in detail. It was time, Lewin held, for a new "Galilean," or constructive, stage, in which the concrete situation in its totality would be described conceptually. On this view, every concrete situation, rather than just recurrent events, is regarded as conforming to psychological laws. Each individual case contains in itself all psychological laws, and a complete representation of it would bring with it the completion of the entire task of psychology. Thus, in the Galilean stage representation itself becomes an explanation.

No less significant for Lewin's theory formation was his belief that "past events cannot influence present events." He sought to substitute for the "historical" notion of causation a "systematic" notion, by means of which one could deduce a particular effect from the totality of present events and relevant laws. Lewin's idea of systematic causation strongly reinforced the desire to examine situations as a whole that arose out of his conception of scientific method.

The life space. To see a situation in its totality, Lewin claimed, one must view it as a field. In physics a field is a totality of interdependent facts. Lewin introduced the notion of a psychological field as a totality of interdependent psychological facts. The psychological field, or life space, of an individual comprises his personality and environment in their interrelationships. The individual's behavior is a function of his personality and his environment and, hence, of his life space, defined as the totality of coexisting facts.

Lewin sought to mathematically describe behavior in a life space, but the mathematics appropriate to the physical sciences was not necessarily appropriate to the idiographic sciences. Lewin thought that geometry, and in particular topology, offered several advantages as a formal tool for psychology, and he applied such topological notions as regions, paths, connectedness, and boundaries to the interpretation of psychological situations. Later he even suggested a new conception of space, which he called "hodological" space and in which "direction toward" is distinguished from "direction from." He left to mathematicians the working out in detail of the geometry of hodological space, but he applied the conception to psychological situations which could not be adequately described in terms of topological space.

Lewin did not carry out mathematical operations using

his mathematical terminology to arrive at new psychological conclusions, nor did he show how such operations could be of use to psychology. His "Galilean" attempt to combine examination of the single case in its totality with the elucidation of general laws, together with his attempt to avoid "Aristotelian" class concepts, is an important effort to reconcile the idiographic and the nomothetic approaches perhaps unique in the history of scientific methodology. According to Lewin, the first step in theory formation involves the logico-mathematical concepts, the second step involves the "conditional-genetic" concepts—dynamic concepts which arise out of empirical data—which he sought to substitute for class concepts.

Works by Lewin

"Gesetz und Experiment in der Psychologie." *Symposium,* Vol. 1 (1927) 375–421.
A Dynamic Theory of Personality, translated by D. K. Adams and K. E. Zener. New York, 1935.
Principles of Topological Psychology. New York, 1936.
"Field Theory of Learning," in *Forty-first Yearbook of the National Society for the Study of Education,* Vol. 41, Part II (1942). Pp. 215–242.
"Cassirer's Philosophy of Science and the Social Sciences," in P. A. Schilpp, ed., *The Philosophy of Ernst Cassirer.* Evanston, Ill., 1949.
Field Theory in Social Science. New York, 1951.

Works on Lewin

Feigl, Herbert, "Principles and Problems of Theory Construction in Psychology," in Wayne Dennis, ed., *Current Trends in Psychological Theory.* Pittsburgh, Pa., 1951.
Leeper, R. W., *Lewin's Topological and Vector Psychology.* Eugene, Ore., 1943.
Wolman, Benjamin B., *Contemporary Theories and Systems in Psychology.* New York, 1960. Pp. 443–490.
Wolman, Benjamin B., ed., *Historical Roots of Contemporary Psychology.* New York, 1966.

BENJAMIN B. WOLMAN

LEWIS, CLARENCE IRVING (1883–1964), American epistemologist, logician, and moral philosopher. Lewis was born in Stoneham, Massachusetts, and educated at Harvard University (A.B., 1906; Ph.D., 1910). He taught at the University of California from 1911 to 1920 and at Harvard from 1920 until his retirement in 1953; after 1930 he was the Edward Pierce professor of philosophy. He delivered the Carus lectures in 1945 and the Woodbridge lectures in 1954.

Lewis was a student and critic of modern extensional systems of logic and developed a modal logic based on the notion of strict implication. (See LOGIC, MODAL.) In epistemology and ethics, he was a pragmatic Kantian.

Lewis internalized within himself the great dialogue on knowledge and reality which began with Descartes and continued with the British empiricists, Kant and the German idealists, and the American pragmatists. It may be said that this tortuous development, both in its long history and in the intellectual life of Lewis, is the attempt of the modern mind to achieve consistency and adequacy in its conceptual foundations.

The basic commitments of any philosopher, whether formulated or not, concern the nature and modes of knowledge; they not only determine what is philosophically problematic for him but also determine how intelligibility can be achieved. Lewis modifies the classical certainty theory of knowledge, which maintains that knowing is an infallible state of mind. He contends that it does not make sense to talk about knowledge where there is no possibility of error. Knowing, according to him, is an assertive state of mind that is subject to appraisal as correct or incorrect by virtue of its relationship to what it is about, and also subject to appraisal as justified or unjustified in terms of its grounds or reasons. Thus the apprehension of a sensory given, or, in other words, the occurrence of an appearance, the classical paradigm of empirical knowledge, is not regarded by Lewis as knowledge, for there is no possibility of error. The apprehension of the appearance and its existence are indistinguishable.

Yet Lewis' departure from the tradition is not great. He, too, insists that at the foundation of our knowledge structure there must be certainty and that this is found in knowledge of sensory appearances. This certainty, however, does not reside in the apprehension of the given. Sensory appearances may be linguistically reported in "expressive" language, which denotes and signifies only appearances. Although there can be no error in the apprehension of a given appearance, it is possible to tell lies about it. Therefore, such reports are statements with truth-values. But still there is no knowledge, for no judgment is made in which the person could be in error. Knowledge is born at the level of what Lewis calls "terminating judgments," which are of the form "'S being given, if A then E,' where [in expressive language] 'A' represents some mode of action taken to be possible, 'E' some expected consequence in experience, and 'S' the sensory cue." For example, there being a red patch in my visual field, if I seem to turn my head to the left, the red patch moves to the right. Such a judgment is not merely the apprehension of a given, or the linguistic expression of such. It embodies a prediction that the red patch will be displaced to the right if the specified condition is fulfilled, which Lewis contends is conclusively verified by the occurrence of the mentioned appearances.

Thus Lewis locates certainty in verified terminating judgments, which are about sensory appearances. Furthermore, he claims that all knowledge about the world is grounded in and derived from such certainties. Although this is more sophisticated than the traditional empiricist's account, it comes to much the same subjectivistic conclusion, namely, that the direct objects of knowledge are subjective and private, and therefore falls heir to all the problems of modern subjectivism. Lewis' major works are devoted to the central and toughest of these problems: how to make intelligible, from within these epistemological commitments, empirical knowledge of the objective world; a priori knowledge, including mathematics, logic, and philosophy itself; and value claims and normative judgments.

Empirical knowledge of the objective world. The paradigm of empirical knowledge for Lewis is the verified terminating judgment. It alone can be conclusively verified. All other empirical judgments are nonterminating. They may be shown to be probable but cannot be established with certainty. The probability value they have is conferred upon them by the verification of terminating judgments which they entail. Therefore, a necessary condition for a nonterminating judgment to be confirmable in any degree, and thus meaningful, is for it to entail terminating judgments.

Any statement which purports to be about objects other than appearances, such as physical objects, is nonterminating, and insofar as it is confirmable and therefore meaningful, it entails terminating judgments, which are about appearances only. It would seem that the full meaning of such a statement would be expressible in the terminating statements entailed by it and that, since these statements are about appearances only, the physical-object statement itself would really refer only to appearances. This would be phenomenalism.

Lewis resists this conclusion. He gives two arguments for realism. The first is that although a physical-object statement is intensionally equivalent to an inexhaustible set of terminating statements and the terms in the latter refer only to appearances, the terms in the physical-object statement genuinely denote physical objects. Thus we have two sets of statements, phenomenalistic and physical-object statements. For each physical-object statement there is a set (although inexhaustible) of phenomenalistic statements intensionally equivalent to it. By confirming the phenomenalistic set we confirm its equivalent physical-object statement with the same degree of probability. Yet the two are about radically different kinds of objects, and from knowledge of appearances we derive knowledge of physical objects.

This argument turns upon his theory of meaning. Lewis distinguishes four modes of the meaning of terms: (1) *denotation,* "the class of all actual things to which the term applies" (for example, the denotation of "man" is the class of all actual men, past, present, and future); (2) *comprehension,* "the classification of all possible or consistently thinkable things to which the term would be correctly applicable" (for example, the comprehension of "man" includes not only actual men but those who might have been but were not, like the present writer's sisters, since he has none); (3) *signification,* "that property in things the presence of which indicates that the term correctly applies, and the absence of which indicates that it does not apply" (for example, the property "rationality" is often regarded as included in the signification of "man"), and (4) *intension,* which consists of (*a*) linguistic intension or connotation, all other terms which must be applicable to anything to which the given term is applicable (for example, "animal" must be applicable to anything to which "man" is applicable); and (*b*) sense meaning, the criterion in mind, an imagined operation "by reference to which one is able to apply or refuse to apply the expression in question in the case of the presented, or imagined, things or situations" (for example, the sense meaning of "kilogon" is the imagined operation of counting the sides of a plane figure and the completion of the operation with the count of 1,000). Since he regards "propositions," statements with the assertive factor extracted (for example, "Mary's baking pies"), as terms, these modes of meaning apply to them as well. He further distin-

guishes between the "holophrastic" meaning of a statement, its meaning as a whole, and its "analytic" meaning, the meaning of its terms.

His argument is that although the holophrastic intensional meaning of a physical-object statement is the same as that of a set of phenomenalistic statements, the physical-object statement and its corresponding set of phenomenalistic statements are different in their analytic denotive meaning, the former denoting physical objects and the latter appearances.

Lewis rightly maintains that any two expressions which have the same intension have the same signification. Yet if a term denotes a physical object, it must signify a physical-object property. Therefore such a term could not have the same signification as a phenomenalistic term. Hence it seems that a physical-object statement could not have the same intension as a set of phenomenalistic statements.

Lewis senses this difficulty and seeks to avoid it by speaking of intension, in the form of sense meaning, as "that in mind which refers to signification." Appearances are said to signalize objective properties or states of affairs. Yet he gives no account of how this is possible for beings who can apprehend only appearances. How can appearances, as simple occurrences, be signs of anything other than other appearances? It would seem that the only way out of this subjectivistic trap is to regard appearances not as simple occurrences or objects of apprehension but as intentional in nature, as experiences of physical objects that embody truth claims about them which can be assessed as true or false on the basis of their consistency or lack of it with the claims of other experiences.

Lewis' second argument for realism turns upon the interpretation of "if . . . then . . ." in terminating judgments. He regards it as a contrary-to-fact conditional, that is, he claims that the truth of the conditional as a whole is independent of the truth-value of the antecedent and therefore may be significantly asserted when the antecedent is known to be false. Therefore, since it does not express a logical relation of entailment or a truth-functional relationship, it must express a real connection, perhaps causality, that holds between the facts or states of affairs located or referred to by the antecedent and the consequent of the conditional sentence. Belief in a real world, he maintains, is belief in such contrary-to-fact conditionals.

It is not clear how this is an argument for realism. Why must independent physical objects be assumed to account for the contrary-to-fact character of terminating judgments? Why couldn't the "real" connection hold between kinds of appearances?

Furthermore, if terminating judgments are to be interpreted in the manner of the contrary-to-fact conditional, does this not compromise their conclusive verifiability? It would seem to introduce an element of generality which would transcend any specific sequence of subjective experiences. In fact, Lewis himself, for other reasons, held that no terminating judgment of the form "S being given, if A then E" is strictly entailed by a physical-object statement. The most we can say, he concluded, is "If P [physical-object statement], then when presentation S is given and act A is performed, it is more or less highly probable that E will be observed to follow." Since the statement is inconclusive, it seems that he has given up the terminating character of "terminating" judgments.

Lewis has not, it seems, made a convincing case for realism from within his phenomenalistic foundations. Some have concluded that it is impossible to do so and that the only way out of phenomenalism is to abandon the subjectivistic starting point itself.

A priori knowledge. The a priori disciplines, namely, mathematics, logic, and philosophy, were the stronghold of classical rationalism. They were regarded as yielding knowledge, grounded in rational intuition, about the essential and necessary structure of the world. Empiricists, for the most part, claim that such knowledge is only intralinguistic, that it consists of analytic truths, which are said to be uninformative about the world.

Lewis subscribes to the view that all "a priori truth is definitive in nature and rises exclusively from the analysis of concepts." Unlike many empiricists, however, he is not content with merely characterizing a priori knowledge as analytic. For him, concepts, their logical relations, and their relation to the data of sense and the structure of the world are highly problematic. He regards concepts, logical relations, and a priori truths arising from them as the peculiar characteristics of mind. He sets them in contrast with the given data of sense experience, which he regards as brute fact, unlimited and unaffected by the conceptual structure. But these givens would be unintelligible without the a priori criteria of classification provided by mind, criteria which are involved not only in talk about things but even in the experience of objects. Thus, the necessary connections of concepts are embedded in perception, and analytic truths, far from being trivial and only intralinguistic, formulate the a priori structure of the world as experienced and known.

Our basic conceptual structure, and thus our a priori truths, are not fixed and eternal. They consist of deepseated attitudes grounded in decisions that are somewhat like fiats in certain respects and like deliberate choice in others. There is nothing in our conceptual structure that is not subject to change in the face of continuing experience. This includes such basic decisions as the decision that whatever is to count as real, in contrast with the hallucinatory, must stand in causal relations with other real things. Even the laws of logic, "the parliamentary rules of intelligent thought and action," are subject to change. The only test applicable is pragmatic, the achievement of intelligible order with simplicity, economy, and comprehensiveness in a way that will be conducive to the long-run satisfaction of human needs. Thus, Lewis holds to a pragmatic theory of a priori truth but not of empirical truth.

Philosophy, according to Lewis, is a reflective, critical study of mind and its a priori principles as found in "the thick experience of everyday life," and thus in "the structure of the real world which we know." Although it studies what is implicit in experience, it is analytic and critical in method rather than descriptive. Its function is not only to formulate the conceptual structure built into experience and thought but to sharpen and to correct it. Thus philosophical claims may be analytic in character, like "There is

an intelligible order in the objective world." Lewis takes this statement to be analytic on the ground that an intelligible order is an essential mark of the objective world. Whatever lacks a certain minimum order is only subjective, private experience, like dreams and hallucinations. Philosophical claims also may be critical and revisionary, recommending some change in our categorial attitudes, such as "Only the physical is real."

Lewis' theory of the a priori places the conceptual framework between two sets of givens, the presentations of sense, to which concepts apply to yield empirical knowledge, and the values in terms of which the a priori structure is pragmatically tested. It seems that both sensory experiences and values would have to be free of a priori assumptions in order to serve the function ascribed to them. This is a difficult doctrine to maintain.

Value claims and normative judgments. The ultimate test of the a priori conceptual framework, according to Lewis, is "the long-run satisfaction of our needs in general." It would seem that value judgments would have to be independent of the conceptual framework that is being pragmatically tested if the test is to be clear-cut and not beg the question. But obviously this would be impossible in the case of basic issues. Although Lewis does not face the problem in these terms, he may be said to blunt the criticism by locating values among sense presentations and by invoking unavoidable imperatives which would be operative in any conceptual framework.

Value, in its most primitive sense, has to do with sense presentations. It is not so much a specific phenomenal quality as a mode or aspect of the given, namely, the given as gratifying or grievous. The only thing that is intrinsically good is liked or wanted subjective experience. In addition to the immediately found intrinsic value of an experience, it may be said to have contributory value by virtue of the contribution it makes to the total value quality of the conscious life of which it is a part. Such a life, he contends, is not simply a sum of its parts. So the contributory value of an experience is quite different from its intrinsic value. Objects of experience are said to be extrinsically good or bad according to their capacity to produce experiences which are satisfying or unpleasant.

Thus, for Lewis, value knowledge is a form of empirical knowledge. There are both terminating and nonterminating value judgments. The former are subjective statements of intrinsic and contributory value; the latter are objective statements about extrinsic values. Judgments of right and wrong, however, are not empirical in character. They are determinable only by reference to rules or principles that refer to values in their prescriptions. He regards the basic rational imperative to be so to think and so to act that later you will not be sorry. The only way this can be achieved is for decisions to be guided by objective knowledge rather than merely by the affective quality of immediate experience. In the area of morals, this requires that we respect others as the realities we know them to be, "as creatures whose gratifications and griefs have the same poignant factuality as our own; and as creatures who, like ourselves, find it imperative to govern themselves in light of the cognitive apprehensions vouchsafed to them by decisions which they themselves reach, and by reference to values discoverable to them."

Any attempt to prove the validity of such principles can only appeal to an antecedent recognition of them. They must be recognized by all who make decisions, all who think and act. Genuine skepticism with regard to judgments of right and wrong, good and bad, would be impossible, for on such a basis even doubt itself would be meaningless.

The question remains: Is the conceptual framework in which normative and value knowledge is formulated pragmatically testable, and, if so, just what could such a pragmatic test amount to? If it is not so testable, then it would seem that in the end Lewis is not a pragmatist after all.

Works by Lewis

A Survey of Symbolic Logic. Berkeley, 1918.
Mind and the World-order. New York, 1929.
Symbolic Logic. New York, 1932. Written with C. H. Langford.
An Analysis of Knowledge and Valuation. La Salle, Ill., 1946.
The Ground and Nature of the Right. New York, 1955.
Our Social Inheritance. Bloomington, Ind., 1957.

Works on Lewis

Baylis, C. A., "C. I. Lewis, *Mind and the World-order.*" *Journal of Philosophy,* Vol. 27 (1930), 320–327.
Boas, George, "Mr. Lewis's Theory of Meaning." *Journal of Philosophy,* Vol. 28 (1931), 314–325.
Chisholm, Roderick M., "The Problem of Empiricism." *Journal of Philosophy,* Vol. 45 (1948), 512–517.
Chisholm, Roderick M., Feigl, Herbert, et al., *Philosophy.* Englewood Cliffs, N.J., 1964.
Ducasse, C. J., "C. I. Lewis' *Analysis of Knowledge and Valuation.*" *Philosophical Review,* Vol. 57 (1948), 260–280.
Firth, R., Brandt, R. B., et al., "Commemorative Symposium on C. I. Lewis." *Journal of Philosophy,* Vol. 61 (1964), 545–570.
Frankena, William, "Lewis's Imperatives of Right." *Philosophical Studies,* Vol. 14 (1963), 25–28.
Frankena, William, "C. I. Lewis on the Ground and Nature of the Right." *Journal of Philosophy,* Vol. 61 (1964), 489–496.
Henle, Paul, "Lewis's *An Analysis of Knowledge and Valuation.*" *Journal of Philosophy,* Vol. 45 (1948), 524–532.
Kusoy, B. K., *Kant and Current Philosophical Issues.* New York, 1961.
Pratt, J. B., "Logical Positivism and Professor Lewis." *Journal of Philosophy,* Vol. 31 (1934), 701–710.
Schilpp, P. A., *The Philosophy of C. I. Lewis.* Vol. XIII, Library of Living Philosophers. La Salle, Ill., 1966.
Stace, W. T., "C. I. Lewis: *An Analysis of Knowledge and Valuation.*" *Mind,* N. S. Vol. 57 (1948), 71–85.
White, M. G., "Value and Obligation in Dewey and Lewis." *Philosophical Review,* Vol. 58 (1949), 321–329.

E. M. ADAMS

LIBERALISM. By definition, a liberal is a man who believes in liberty, but because different men at different times have meant different things by liberty, "liberalism" is correspondingly ambiguous. The word was first heard in a political sense in England in the early nineteenth century, when "liberals" were thus named by their Tory opponents. Indeed, they were first called *liberales,* and the Spanish form was used "with the intention of suggesting that the principles of those politicians were un-English" (see *Shorter Oxford English Dictionary*). This was ironical, since the word "liberal" had been adopted by the Span-

iards for policies they regarded as essentially English—that is, the Lockean principles of constitutional monarchy, parliamentary government, and the rights of man. In any event, the Englishmen who were called liberals (though as late as 1816 Robert Southey was still calling them *liberales*) rejoiced in the name, and what was intended to be a pejorative quickly proved to have a distinctly pleasing flavor, perhaps partly because its other significance, the Shakespearean sense of liberal as "gross" or "licentious," had given way to the modern sense of liberal as "bountiful," "generous," or "open-hearted."

English liberalism. Traditional English liberalism has rested on a fairly simple concept of liberty—namely, that of freedom from the constraints of the state. In Hobbes's memorable phrase, "The liberties of subjects depend on the silence of the law." In general, however, English liberals have always been careful not to press this notion to anarchist extremes. They have regarded the state as a necessary institution, ensuring order and law at home, defense against foreign powers, and security of possessions—the three principles Locke summarized as "life, liberty and property." English liberals have also maintained that the law can be used to extend the liberties of subjects insofar as the law is made to curb and limit the activities of the executive government. Thus, for example, the English laws of habeas corpus, of bail, and of police entry and arrest all constrain or restrain the executive and, in so doing, increase the freedom of the people. Some instruments of constitutional law have a similar effect.

The traditional form of English political liberalism naturally went hand in hand with the classical economic doctrine of laissez-faire. Toward the end of the nineteenth century, however, certain radical movements and certain English liberal theorists, such as Matthew Arnold and T. H. Green, developed, partly under foreign, left-wing influences, a different—as they claimed, a broader—concept of freedom, which was, to a large extent, to prove more popular in the twentieth century than traditional English liberalism with its economic gospel of laissez-faire. The central aim of this new school was utilitarian—namely, freeing men from misery and ignorance. Its exponents believed that the state must be the instrument by which this end was to be achieved. Hence, English liberal opinion entered the twentieth century in a highly paradoxical condition, urging, on the one hand, a freedom which was understood as freedom from the constraints of the state and, on the other, an enlargement of the state's power and control in order to liberate the poor from the oppressive burdens of poverty. In the political sphere this contradiction in the liberal ideology ended in the disintegration of the British Liberal party. With the defeat of Prime Minister Asquith, a disciple of the philosopher T. H. Green and an adept at reconciling contradictions, the British Liberal party broke into two, the right-wing, or laissez-faire, element joining forces with conservatism and the radical, *étatiste* element merging with socialism. Only a "rump" remained.

French liberalism. The ambiguity of the word "liberalism" is more marked in French than in any other European language. Some writers hold that as a result of events in France since the time of Louis XIV, the French people have been divided into two political camps: one which supports the Roman Catholic church, traditional social patterns, and the Syllabus of Pius IX (1864) and one which opposes the church and favors parliament, progress, and the rights of man. Historians who see France in these terms call one side *conservateur*, the other *libéral*. Opposed to this view are those historians who see not two, but at least three, continuing traditions in French political thought: on the right, royalism and conservativism; on the left, socialism, anarchism, syndicalism, and communism; in the center, liberalism. In the first of these two analyses, *libéralisme* is understood to embrace all the creeds of the left; according to the second analysis, *libéralisme* is a political doctrine at variance with the creeds of the left.

Again, one can distinguish two distinct—indeed, opposing—schools among French theorists who claim to be liberal. One is the Lockean liberalism of Voltaire, Montesquieu, and Benjamin Constant (in effect, also that of François Guizot and the July monarchy of Louis Philippe)—the liberalism of the minimal state, individualism, and laissez-faire. But there is a second liberalism, represented by the masters of the French Revolution and by the youthful Napoleon, which is democratic, Rousseauesque, and *étatiste*. Whereas Lockean liberalism understands freedom as being left alone by the state, the other liberalism sees freedom as ruling oneself through the medium of a state which one has made one's own.

Both these schools of *libéralisme* contributed something to the ideology of the French Revolution, and the often unperceived contradiction between them may also be said to have contributed to the intellectual confusion of those times. The fall of Napoleon was the signal for a return to the more purely Lockean style of liberalism. Benjamin Constant not only insisted that Rousseau's concept of liberty was an illusory one but also maintained that "*Du Contrat Social* [1762] so often invoked in favour of liberty, is the most formidable ally of all despotisms." Constant and his friends desired only to reproduce in France the Lockean Glorious Revolution of 1688. In 1830 they believed they had succeeded; Louis Philippe was enthroned on the basis of an understanding very like that on which William and Mary had been crowned in England. Politicans like Guizot, who called themselves Libéraux, were put in charge of the kingdom. The result was not inspiring. A new bourgeoisie basked in the liberty the Lockean state introduced; the great were diminished, but the poor were not elevated. A rebellion came from the left in 1848, and the right replied with Napoleon III. Henceforth, there were few self-styled Libéraux of any importance in French politics and no liberal party. When new parties were formed later in the century, the name chosen by the center was Republicain rather than Libéral. This is not to say that liberalism died in France in 1848; rather, the word *libéralisme* thereafter ceased to call to the minds of French-speaking people any clear or distinct idea.

In 1912 Émile Faguet published a celebrated work, *Le Libéralisme*, in which he took a rigidly Lockean position. "The state," he wrote, "is an evil; a lesser evil than anarchy, but nevertheless to be limited to the tasks of securing public order and safety through the justiciary, police and army." Several critics at the time attacked Faguet's

definition as being outmoded; nevertheless, the definition of *libéralisme* in the 1935 edition of the *Dictionnaire de l'Académie Française* is, like Faguet's, thoroughly Lockean; it defines *libéralisme* in terms of the citizen's right to freedom of thought and to protection from government interference in private and business affairs.

One of several French theorists who attacked Faguet's exposition of liberalism (and, by implication, the academy's definition) was Jean de Grandvilliers. "How the word 'liberalism' is perverted by those who treat it as synonymous with individualism!" he wrote in *Essai sur le libéralisme allemand* (1925). "We can only reply by giving the word its true meaning." According to Grandvilliers, the true meaning of liberalism is to be found in a policy of extending the liberty of the people; he maintained that the intervention of the state is not only a useful, but also a necessary, means to achieve that end. Grandvilliers is thus a champion of the *étatiste* school of liberalism, which derived its concept of liberty from Rousseau and which argued that as long as the state belongs to the people, the enlargement of the power of the state is equally an enlargement of the power, and therefore the freedom, of its citizens.

German liberalism. The word "liberal" was first heard in Germany in 1812, going there, as it went to England, from Spain. But the last years of Napoleon's power marked the decline of one tradition of German liberalism and the beginning of a new one. For in Germany, as elsewhere, we may discern not a single doctrine of liberalism but at least two main, conflicting schools, which again may be classified as the Lockean and the *étatiste*. The older German tradition was not merely derivatively Lockean; it also had contributed much to the formulation of Locke's own thought. In the sixteenth century it was a German philosopher, Johannes Althusius, who proclaimed that sovereignty derived from the people, and it was the German *Naturrechts* school of jurists which provided the bridge between the Stoic concept of *jus naturale* and the Lockean doctrine of the rights of man. But Locke, in turn, influenced the eighteenth-century German liberals, among whom Wilhelm von Humboldt was perhaps the most conspicuous. The very title of his book *Ideen zu einem Versuch, die Grenzen der Wirksamkeit des Staates zu bestimmen* ("Ideas Toward an Investigation to Determine the Proper Limits of the Activity of the State," 1792), reveals his preoccupation with limited sovereignty and the minimal state. In this work Humboldt argued that the function of the state is not to do good but to ward off evil, notably the evil which springs from man's disregard for his neighbors' rights. The state, he said, "must not proceed a step further than is necessary for the mutual security of citizens and protection against foreign enemies; for no other object should it impose restrictions on freedom." Eighteenth-century Germany also had several liberal economists, including Christian Kraus, who considered that Smith's *Wealth of Nations* (1776) was the most important book after the Bible.

In the nineteenth century a new school of liberalism, which was first and foremost nationalistic, arose in Germany. The freedom it stood for was the freedom of Germany, and the condition of the realization of this national freedom was the unification of Germany. Thus, whereas the old Lockean liberals were against the state, the new nationalist liberals wanted to create a greater state. The French declaration of 1789 proclaimed the rights of *man*; the German liberals inspired in 1848 a declaration of the rights of the German people. The new German liberals thought in terms of collective, rather than individual, rights. Thus, the *étatiste* German liberals saw nothing incongruous in sending a mission in 1849 from the Frankfurt parliament to Berlin to offer the crown of all Germany to a Prussian monarch, Friedrich Wilhelm, who detested democracy and who, in any event, grandly announced that he did not take crowns from commoners.

The difficulty of understanding in what sense this new German liberalism rested on a principle of freedom is that of understanding what it was that its votaries were demanding freedom from. Indeed, for many German liberals it was not a question of freedom from anything. German metaphysics of the same period was working out a concept of freedom which had nothing to do with resisting constraint. Guido de Ruggiero, a sympathetic Italian historian of German liberalism wrote:

> The eternal glory of Kant is to have demonstrated that obedience to the moral law is freedom. . . . It was the great merit of Hegel to have extracted from the Kantian identification of freedom with mind, the idea of an organic development of freedom, coinciding with the organisation of society in its progressively higher and more spiritual forms. . . . The State, the organ of coercion *par excellence,* has become the highest expression of liberty.   (*History of European Liberalism*)

The idea that true freedom is to be found in obedience to the morally perfected state gave a theoretical justification (of a highly abstract kind) to the nineteenth-century German liberals' pursuit of liberty in submission to a strong and unified nation-state. But these high-thinking theorists never recovered from Friedrich Wilhelm's snub in 1849. Germany got its unity, but it was the imperialists, not the new liberals, who achieved it, and it was Bismark, rather than Kant, who gave the unified nation its political ethos. After the defeat of the Nazi regime in 1945, however, there was some revival of the Lockean type of liberalism in Germany.

American liberalism. In the United States the word "liberal" has never enjoyed the prestige it has in the United Kingdom, for in America there has never been, as there has in England, a national liberal party. The short-lived Liberal Republican party of the 1870s was without a coherent program. Horace Greeley, its presidential candidate, was at once a socialist, spiritualist, vegetarian, and total abstainer; his personality led many Americans of his time to associate the word "liberal" with a visionary crank, and some still do. F. O. Matthiessen wrote in 1948: "In our nineteenth-century political life we had no such formulated division as that between the Conservatives and Liberals in England. . . . The key word seized upon by our native radical movement of the eighties and nineties, that of the Populists, was not 'liberal' but 'progressive'" (*From the Heart of Europe*, New York, 1948, p. 90). Again, whereas in Parrington's *Main Currents in American Thought* the word

"liberal" occurs on almost every page, Parrington's pupil Henry Steele Commager never once uses the words "liberal" and "liberalism" in his continuation volume, *The American Mind* (New Haven, 1950).

Just as in France the word "liberal" had been used by some writers for almost any kind of left-wing opinion, so in America the word "liberal" was widely adopted after the depression as a soubriquet for "socialist." In *The Liberal Imagination*, Lionel Trilling defined liberalism as meaning, among other things, "a belief in planning and international co-operation, especially where Russia is in question." This definition may not have been wholly authorized by common usage, but there can be no doubt that the word "liberal" has come to be associated in the American public's mind with *étatiste* and left-wing ideologies rather than with the Lockean notions of laissez-faire and mistrust of organized power.

Indeed, it was one of Parrington's arguments in *Main Currents in American Thought* that American liberalism, as he called it, had always been concerned with democracy in a way that Locke and his English followers had not. Yet even before the emergence of twentieth-century left-wing liberalism, two rival creeds, both of which could reasonably be called liberal, contended for political supremacy. The first, as Parrington pointed out, was close to the "English philosophy of *laissez-faire*, based on the assured universality of the acquisitive instinct and postulating a social order answering the needs of the abstract 'economic man' in which the state should function in the interests of trade." The second liberalism was Rousseau-esque rather than Lockean. It was "based on the conception of human perfectibility" and looked toward an egalitarian democracy "in which the political state should function as the servant to the common well-being."

The dominant political sentiment of the American tradition derives something from both these kinds of liberalism, for it has combined a Lockean attachment to liberty from the state with a Rousseauesque belief in democracy and equality. Nevertheless, perhaps it is still not quite respectable to be an avowed liberal in America. This may be partly because there has been no traditional support for a liberal party. It is also partly because not only socialists, but also communists and communist sympathizers, have not ceased to assume the title "liberal" rather than a more explicit expression of their political commitment.

A remarkable variety of political structures has been thought by different philosophers to embody liberty, and a correspondingly mixed company has shared the name "liberal." In singling out certain main streams or schools of liberal thought, one has to be mindful of the divergences that exist even among those which can be usefully grouped together. One might broadly divide philosophers of freedom into those who think that to be free is to be able to do what one wants to do and those who think that to be free is to do what one ought to do. By a similar method, one might divide liberals into those who see freedom as something which belongs to the individual, to be defended against the encroachments of the state, and those who see freedom as something which belongs to society and which the state, as the central instrument of social betterment, can be made to enlarge and improve. It remains to be said that some of the greatest names in the history of liberal thought, including John Stuart Mill himself, are strangely poised between these two positions.

Bibliography

Adler, Mortimer J., *The Idea of Freedom*. New York, 1958.
"Alain," *Le Citoyen contre les pouvoirs*. Paris, 1926.
Berlin, Isaiah, *Two Concepts of Liberty*. Oxford, 1958.
Cranston, Maurice, *Freedom*. London, 1953.
Duclos, Pierre, *L'Évolution des rapports politiques*. Paris, 1950.
Faguet, Émile, *Le Libéralisme*. Paris, 1912.
Grandvilliers, Jean de, *Essai sur le libéralisme allemand*. Paris, 1925.
Halévy, Élie, *La Formation du radicalisme philosophique*. Paris, 1935.
Hallowell, John H., *The Decline of Liberalism*. London, 1946.
Hartz, Louis, *Liberal Tradition in America*. New York, 1955.
Hayek, Friedrich A. von, *The Constitution of Liberty*. Chicago, 1960.
Hobhouse, L. T., *Liberalism*. New York, 1911.
Konvitz, M. R., and Rossiter, C. L., eds., *Aspects of Liberty*. Ithaca, N.Y., 1958.
Laski, Harold J., *The Rise of European Liberalism*. London, 1936.
Martin, B. Kingsley, *French Liberal Thought in the Eighteenth Century*. London, 1929.
Neill, T. P., *Rise and Decline of Liberalism*. Milwaukee, 1953.
Parrington, Vernon Louis, *Main Currents in American Thought*, 3 vols. New York, 1927–1930.
Ponteil, F., *L'Éveil des nationalités*. Paris, 1960.
Popper, Karl R., *The Open Society and Its Enemies*, 2 vols. London, 1945.
Ruggiero, Guido de, *Storia del liberalismo*. Bari, Italy, 1925. Translated by R. G. Collingwood as *History of European Liberalism*. London, 1927.
Sartori, Giovanni, *Democratic Theory*. Detroit, 1962.
Schapiro, J. Salwyn, *Liberalism*. Princeton, N.J., 1953.
Thomas, R. H., *Liberalism, Nationalism and the German Intellectuals*. Chester Springs, Pa., 1953.
Trilling, Lionel, *The Liberal Imagination*. New York, 1951.
Waldeck-Rousseau, P. M. R., *L'État et la liberté*. Paris, 1906.
Watson, G., ed., *The Unservile State*. New York, 1957.

MAURICE CRANSTON

LIBER DE CAUSIS (or *Liber Aristotelis de Expositione Bonitatis Purae*). The *Liber de Causis* ("Book of Causes") is a Latin translation of an Arabic work that is derived from the "Elements of Theology" of Proclus (fifth century, A.D.). The author of the Arabic work is unknown; some scholars consider it the twelfth-century composition of David the Jew (Abraham ibn-Da'ud or Avendeath) at Toledo, while others believe it an eighth- or ninth-century product of a school of Neoplatonism in the Near East, possibly stemming from a still earlier Syriac source.

At least one Latin translation appeared before 1187, probably the product of the Toledan translator, Gerard of Cremona. The work then came to be ascribed variously to David, al-Fārābī, or Aristotle. By 1255 the Parisian Faculty of Arts, considering it a work of Aristotle, included it in the curriculum.

Among the many doctrines contained in the 211 chapters, or Propositions, of Proclus' "Elements of Theology," the following should be noted. Proclus uses the term "theology" to mean Neoplatonic metaphysics. The latter describes the necessary procession of the world, or being, from its ultimate origins. The most important of these originative principles are: first, the gods; second, the pure spirits, or Intelligences; third, souls. The supreme god, or the One, is not describable as "being," yet it is the universal cause of every being. Before producing Intelligences, the One effects a pair of opposite principles, Limit and Infinity, and then a series of subordinate gods, or "henads," which have the causal function of Plato's Forms. The immediate effect of each principle, whether the latter be a god, a spirit, or a soul, is an attribute that is both similar to, and yet more specific than, its source. The particularity of the effect is due to its recipient. Consequently, it is difficult for the reader to see how the One can produce all things without the cooperation of its subordinates.

The 32 Propositions of the *Liber de Causis* summarize this material with the following changes: (1) the multitude of deities (Limit, Infinity, and henads) is eliminated and divinity is reserved to the One alone; (2) the first cause is described as "being" and its causality as "creation." These changes suggest that the Neoplatonic author was either Jewish, Islamic, or Christian. Nevertheless, because the causes of Proclus act solely from the necessity of their natures and are mutually interdependent, it is questionable whether the *Liber de Causis* actually presents a monotheistic theory of free creation.

After reading William of Moerbecke's Latin translation of the "Elements of Theology" (*Elementatio Theologica*, 1268), St. Thomas Aquinas noticed for the first time that the *Liber de Causis* was not a work of Aristotle, but a modification of Proclus. Unfortunately, this discovery had to be made again during the Renaissance.

The doctrines in the *Liber de Causis* influenced many thinkers, among them: William of Auvergne, Roger Bacon, St. Albertus Magnus, John Duns Scotus, and Meister Eckhart.

Bibliography

EDITIONS

Bardenhewer, Otto, *Die pseudo-aristotelische Schrift über das reine Gute, bekannt unter dem Namen Liber de Causis*. Freiburg im Breisgau, 1882.
Steele, Robert, *Opera Hactenus Inedita Rogeri Baconi*, Fasc. 102, "Questiones supra *Librum de Causis*." Oxford and London, 1935.

ON THE "LIBER DE CAUSIS"

Anawati, Georges C., "Prolégomènes à une nouvelle édition du *De Causis* arabe (Kitāb al-hayr al-maḥḍ)." *Mélanges Louis Massignon*, Vol. 1 (1956), 73–110.
Doresse, J., "Les Sources du *Liber de Causis*." *Revue de l'histoire des religions*, Vol. 13 (1946), 234–238.
Gilson, Étienne, *History of Christian Philosophy in the Middle Ages*. New York, 1955. Pp. 236–237.

MICHAEL W. STRASSER

LIBERTY. See FREEDOM.

LICHTENBERG, GEORG CHRISTOPH (1742–1799), German satirist, scientist, and philosopher. He studied mathematics and science at the University of Göttingen and was a professor there from 1767 to the end of his life. On two occasions Lichtenberg visited England. His impressions from these visits are recorded in his diaries and letters.

Lichtenberg's original contributions to mathematics and to pure and experimental science are not of great importance. The Lichtenberg figure in the theory of electricity was named after him. He was very successful as a teacher; among his pupils were Alexander von Humboldt and Christian Gauss. It has been said that his fame as a lecturer and demonstrator surpassed that of any other German scientist of his time.

His literary reputation with his contemporaries rested mainly on his satirical criticism of the writers of the *Sturm und Drang* movement and of the Swiss clergyman Johann Lavater's quasi-scientific psychology of character. Lichtenberg's own favorites and models in art were Englishmen: Shakespeare, David Garrick, the actor, and William Hogarth, the painter. His analyses and descriptions of Garrick on the stage and his detailed "explanations" of Hogarth's etchings have become famous. Most of Lichtenberg's literary output during his lifetime appeared in two periodicals, of which he was the editor, the *Göttinger Taschen-Calender* and the *Göttingisches Magazin der Wissenschaften und Litteratur*.

By far the most valuable part of Lichtenberg's literary work, however, consisted of his "aphorisms," or scattered thoughts on psychological, philosophical, scientific, and many other topics. They were written down in notebooks but were never systematically arranged by the author. Nor were they used as raw material to any great extent for the more systematic work that Lichtenberg was constantly planning but never carried out. *Vermischte Schriften*, a comprehensive selection of his remarks, was published soon after his death.

Philosophically, Lichtenberg was not attached to any school or movement. The thinkers who made the deepest impressions on him were Spinoza and Kant. It is noteworthy that Lichtenberg was an early reviver of the great Jewish philosopher and one of the first to understand and acknowledge the revolutionary significance of Kant's transcendental philosophy. Furthermore, the versatility of his philosophical intellect is shown by his acute understanding of the work of Jakob Boehme.

Lichtenberg has had but a modest influence on the development of thought, but it is evident from the observations of Kant and Alexander von Humboldt, among others, that his contemporaries greatly prized his philosophical intellect. Subsequent generations were first made aware of his status as an independent thinker through the observation of Ernst Mach (in his *The Analysis of Sensations*) that Lichtenberg had anticipated the empiriocritical solution of the ego problem with his critique of the Cartesian *cogito ergo sum*. (In another work, "Die Leitgedanken meiner naturwissenschaftlichen Erkenntnislehre"—"The Primary Ideas of My Scientific Epistemology," 1919, p. 5, Mach even hinted that he had been influenced by Lichtenberg.) Moreover, the affinity of Lichtenberg's ideas with modern linguistic philosophy has been indicated by various writers, for example, Friedrich Waismann in the preface to Moritz Schlick's *Gesammelte Aufsätze* and Richard von Mises in *Positivism*.

Philosophy of mathematics. Lichtenberg, in contradistinction to Kant, distinguished sharply between pure and applied mathematics and separated mathematics as a logicodeductive formalism from mathematics as a theory of reality.

The truths of pure mathematics are not only certain in a strict sense but are derived (in principle) independently of experience and empirical observation. A blind man, for instance, could discover the laws of light by means of the calculus, for as soon as the fundamental facts of refraction and reflection are discovered experimentally, "the whole of dioptrics and catoptrics becomes a purely geometrical problem," which can be treated without further knowledge of natural processes. For this reason the ideal form of a scientific theory is that of a logicodeductive system. Lichtenberg stated: "The aim of the physicists is to prepare the way for mathematics."

In his conception of pure mathematics, Lichtenberg approached the notion of the analytical, or tautological, character of mathematical truths. He did not take a positive stand on Kant's view of the synthetic a priori character of mathematics, but it is evident from his remarks that he viewed it with suspicion.

Mathematics shapes its own world. The business of the physicist is to decide which "of the innumerable suppositions possible" is the single true one. The results of mathematical deduction cannot be asserted in advance to agree with the results of physical inquiry. "Their agreement is a purely *empirical* coincidence, nothing else." (It is apparent from his manuscript that Lichtenberg ascribed great importance to this remark.) Thus Lichtenberg renounced all a priori claims concerning the application of mathematics to reality.

Instead of being astounded at the actual success of mathematics in the exploration of natural phenomena, Lichtenberg emphasized the approximate character of mathematical laws of nature and warned of the temptation to read more mathematics into things than is actually there. "All mathematical laws that we find in nature, despite their beauty, are doubtful to me." The forms in which nature covers herself are too manifold and changeable to be comprehended exhaustively by our own conceptual apparatus. These thoughts, which had come early to Lichtenberg, were closely connected with his highly developed talent for observation and his acute feeling for the concrete.

It is characteristic that the work with which Lichtenberg qualified for his professorship was devoted to the study of an alleged discrepancy between theory and experience. This work, "Considerations About Some Methods for Removing a Certain Difficulty in the Calculation of Probability in Gambling" (not mentioned in Keynes's bibliography in his *Treatise on Probability*), concerned a famous problem of the theory of probability, the so-called Petersburg paradox, which engaged many leading mathematicians of the eighteenth century, among others, d'Alembert and Daniel Bernoulli. It is erroneous, however, to see in this problem, as Lichtenberg and others have done, a contradiction between the mathematical calculus and the actual course of events.

Recognition is due Lichtenberg for his scientific genius in being one of the first to see the possibility of denying, without contradiction, the Euclidean axioms. That between two points only one straight line can be drawn is indeed an accepted axiom, but it is by no means *necessary*. One can also conceive of the possibility that several distinct lines might pass through the same two points. The manner in which Lichtenberg attempted to show this possibility was, indeed, less significant: he imagined one could take arcs with the radii ∞, ∞^2, ∞^3, etc., so that they proceed through two fixed points, describing distinct straight lines.

Interestingly enough, Lichtenberg also expressed some thoughts about the deflection of light through gravitation. As an adherent of Newton's corpuscular theory, he assumed that light has mass, from which it follows that a beam of light must deviate from a straight path because of its weight. "Light alone appears to be an exception (viz., to the curved path of most bodies); however, since it is probably heavy, it will be deflected as a result."

Epistemology of the exact sciences. Lichtenberg realized the great significance of the discovery of structural identities among qualitatively different domains of theoretical research into nature. His idea of *paradigmata* (patterns), according to which processes were to be "declined," seems to have approached James Clerk Maxwell's view of the significance of analogy and to have anticipated the concept of isomorphism. Lichtenberg called discovery through *paradigmata* the most fruitful of all the heuristic devices of science. As an example of an application he suggested that one might use Newton's *Optics* as a model in the theory of the calcination of metals.

Lichtenberg had a clear view of the logic of constructing hypotheses: "If we want to understand nature," he said, "we must begin with sensible appearances." Hypotheses that transcend the evidence of the senses may only be constructed insofar as they can be tested within the domain of appearances. Concepts whose presence or absence in the individual case can never be demonstrated but only assumed are not permissible in science. The concept of ether in physics belongs to this category. The ether, which "no one has seen or felt, . . . condensed, rarefied, etc.," is like the notion of the world soul: since it has no experiential consequences, it must be eliminated once and for all from a rational physics.

In spite of his opposition in principle to hypothesis making in physics, Lichtenberg did not agree with the view that all assumptions should be discarded if, although they have testable consequences, they do not literally correspond to sensible reality. Assumptions of this kind may nonetheless ·be useful as pictures of complicated courses of events, and thus facilitate the application of mathematics to nature. (The notion of "picture," reminiscent of Heinrich Hertz's *Principles of Mechanics,* turns up often in Lichtenberg.) "If someone could make a clock that presented the movements of the heavenly bodies as exactly as actually obtains, would he not deserve much credit, even though the world does not operate by means of cogwheels? Through this machine he could discover many things that he would not have believed to be present in it."

In addition to such mechanical models, the two theories of light and atomic theory also belong to this category.

The truth content of scientific assumptions of the type mentioned above is proportional to their explanatory power and to their relative simplicity. Lichtenberg quite aptly noted that with theories as complex as that of light "it can no longer be merely a question of what is true, but of what manner of explanation is the simplest." And he added, "The door to truth is through simplicity." Moreover, his speculation that one could attempt to combine the corpuscular and wave theories sounds very modern.

The falsification of such hypotheses can not be established beyond question by empirical circumstances. A single negative instance does not in general make it necessary to renounce a comprehensive scientific theory which has otherwise been well confirmed. "One should take special note of contradictory experiences," wrote Lichtenberg, "until there are enough of them to make constructing a new system worthwhile."

Soul and matter, realism and idealism. Early in his career Lichtenberg rejected the idea of the soul as a substance. Before enough was understood to explain the phenomena of the world scientifically, spirits were accepted as explanations of phenomena. As our knowledge of the physical world increased, however, the boundaries of the spiritual realm shrank until finally "that which haunts our body and produces effects in it" was the only thing left that required a ghost for an explanation. The case of the "soul" is like that of phlogiston: in the end both substances dissipate into nothingness. What remains is a "bare word" comparable to the word "state" (*Zustand*), to which, however, one may at least attribute heuristic value as a picture and as a type of idea innate in the human being.

According to Lichtenberg, the thesis of materialism is "the asymptote of psychology." In psychology, he linked himself closely with the materialistic–mechanistic association theories of the Englishmen David Hartley and Joseph Priestley. A one-to-one correspondence obtains between the mental occurrence and the state of the brain, so that the former can, in principle, be inferred from the latter.

Lichtenberg, however, did not accept metaphysical materialism. Parallel with his critique of the concept of the soul went a critique of the concept of matter. Soul and inert matter are mere abstractions, he wrote in a letter in 1786; we know of matter and of soul only on the basis of the *forces* (*Kräfte*) through which they manifest themselves and "with which they are identical." We postulate for these forces in one case "an inert receptacle and call it matter." Through such a hypostatization, which is just a "chimera" of the brain, arises "the infamous dualism in the world": the division of being into body and soul, spirit and matter. But in reality everything is *one*.

This acknowledgment of monism still bore a metaphysical character. It is probable that the influence of Spinoza had its effect on the position taken by Lichtenberg in 1786, since the letter of that year referred directly to Spinoza. But we may observe that, much earlier, Lichtenberg had expressed the same opinion almost word for word. However, it is not impossible that the influence of Spinoza was already at work then. Even in his earliest books of aphorisms there were remarks of a Spinozistic character, although the name of the great thinker was not mentioned.

Later, Lichtenberg's monism took a more epistemological turn in that he clearly indicated how the basis of his monistic system should be interpreted. "We are aware only of the existence of our sensations, ideas, and thought," he said and expressed the same thought with the words, "Everything is feeling (*Gefühle*)." We experience a part of our impressions as dependent upon us, another as independent of the perceiving subject: in this way we arrive at the difference between the inner and outer worlds.

To argue from sensations to an "ego" as their bearer, as Descartes does, is not logically warranted. Lichtenberg remarked very perceptively: "One should say, 'There is thinking,' just as one says, 'There is lightning.'" To say *cogito* is to say too much; for as soon as one translates it as "I think," it seems necessary to postulate an ego. Lichtenberg's earlier critique of the idea of the soul culminates here in a critique of the self, somewhat reminiscent of the position of Hume.

It took considerable effort on Lichtenberg's part to attain clarity on the question of how we proceed from our sensations to things outside us. He perceived the significance of the problem from his study of Kant, and in his treatment of it we can generally discern Kant's influence.

At first it was very difficult for Lichtenberg to rid himself of the idea that something in the actual world might correspond to our representations, although we can have "no conception at all of the true nature of the outside world." But later he recognized that the question "whether things outside ourselves really exist and exist as we see them" is in fact "completely meaningless." It is just as foolish as asking whether the color blue is really blue. We are compelled by our nature—this compulsion he termed, with Kant, *die Form der Sinnlichkeit* ("form of sensibility")—to express ourselves in such way that we speak of certain objects of our perception as being outside ourselves and of others as being within us. "What is outside? What are objects *praeter nos*? What is the force of the preposition *praeter*? It is a purely human invention; a name to indicate a difference from other things which we call 'not-*praeter nos*.'" "There is probably no one in the world who does not perceive this *difference,* and probably no such person will ever exist; and for philosophy that is enough. Philosophy need not go beyond this."

Is not this standpoint "idealism"? Lichtenberg clearly perceived that, just as his critique of the idea of the "soul" did not result in metaphysical materialism, so his attitude toward the question of the reality of the outer world should not be confused with metaphysical idealism. Rather his doctrine stood *beyond* idealism and materialism in their traditional senses. "It is truly of little consequence to me whether one wants to label this idealism. Names have no significance. It is at least an idealism which, through idealism, acknowledges that there are things outside us." What more can one ask? For human beings, "at least for the philosophical ones," there is no other reality than the one so constituted. It is true that one is satisfied in ordinary life with some other, "lower station," but whenever one begins to philosophize, one cannot but accept this enlightened point of view. "There is no other alternative," he concluded.

Lichtenberg's conception of philosophy. "Our entire philosophy," wrote Lichtenberg, "is a correction of linguistic usage." What he meant by that is especially evident in his treatment of the question of realism. As indicated above, Lichtenberg's conception should not be understood as an attempt to deny the existence of things outside ourselves. That would have been a senseless undertaking. His intention was only to discover the meaning of the distinction between outer and inner objects by clearly presenting the facts that underlie this distinction. It turns out that the root of the traditional difficulty about the question of realism is that in ordinary life we attach a *contradictory* meaning to the expression "outside ourselves." When we have become conscious of this contradiction and have undertaken the proper correction of our linguistic usage, the difficulty vanishes of itself.

Philosophy, then, is a critique of language. Its goal, however, is not definitions of concepts. Lichtenberg was not of the opinion that one could, for philosophical use, replace the common language with an ideal language, perhaps in the sense of Leibniz' *characteristica universalis*. Attempts to reform the nomenclature of the sciences did not find much favor with him. "To clarify words does not help," he said. Why? Because the interpretation of the clarified concepts takes place, in the final analysis, in the vernacular. But the vernacular, by its nature, is imbued with our false philosophy. The rectification of colloquial usage, which leads to true philosophy, is thus undertaken in the language of false philosophy: "We are therefore constantly teaching true philosophy with the language of the false one." The common philosophy, then, always maintains a certain superiority over the enlightened one, for the former is in possession of the "declensions and conjugations" of our language, and these are not changed by the clarification of meanings of words. "The invention of language preceded philosophy, and it is just this that makes philosophy difficult, particularly when one wishes to make it understandable to those who do not think much for themselves. Philosophy, whenever it speaks, is forced to speak the language of nonphilosophy. . . . Pure philosophy still imperceptibly enjoys the pleasure of love with the impure (and cannot avoid doing so)."

The philosopher, then, speaks with the words of the common language about things that are beyond it. He is thus compelled to express himself, to a certain degree, in metaphors (*Gleichnissen*). He is supposed to direct our attention with his sentences to the false logic of our language, so that we learn to see the world correctly. He does not teach us a new language but helps us to express ourselves clearly with our own. "The peasant," said Lichtenberg, "uses all the sentences of the most abstract philosophy, only they are entangled, hidden, confined, latent, as the physicist and chemist say; the philosopher gives us the pure sentences."

It should be evident from the above that Lichtenberg anticipated the conception of philosophy that has been represented in our times by Ludwig Wittgenstein. Wittgenstein knew Lichtenberg's work well and esteemed it highly. It is hardly possible, however, to speak of Lichtenberg as an influence on the philosophy of Wittgenstein. Nevertheless, a rare congeniality between the two men can be noted—not only in view of their conceptions of philosophy but also in view of their entire intellectual talents and temperaments.

Bibliography

Lichtenberg's works in German include *Vermischte Schriften,* L. C. Lichtenberg and F. Kries, eds., 5 vols. (Göttingen, 1800– 1803); *Physikalische und mathematische Schriften,* L. C. Lichtenberg and F. Kries, eds., 4 vols. (Göttingen, 1803–1806); *Neue Original-Ausgabe,* 14 vols. (Göttingen, 1844–1853); *Aus Lichtenbergs Nachlass,* Albert Leitzmann, ed. (Weimar, 1899); *Aphorismen, nach den Handschriften,* Albert Leitzmann, ed., 5 vols. (Berlin, 1902–1908); *Lichtenbergs Briefe,* Albert Leitzmann and Carl Schüddelkopf, eds., 3 vols. (Leipzig, 1901–1904).

Lichtenberg's remarks on questions of mathematics and physics have been printed only in part. It is most unfortunate that all of his notes from the years 1779–1788 and the greater part of those from 1793–1796, which existed at the time of the first edition of the *Vermischte Schriften,* had been lost when Albert Leitzmann, in the beginning of this century, edited the *Aphorismen, nach den Handschriften.* This loss greatly complicates the task of reconstructing the course of development of Lichtenberg's thought. The selection of aphorisms in the *Vermischte Schriften* shows that some of his most important philosophical remarks were among those subsequently lost.

For literature on Lichtenberg, see J. Dostal-Winkler, *Lichtenberg und Kant* (Munich, 1924); P. Hahn, *Georg Christoph Lichtenberg und die exakten Wissenschaften* (Göttingen, 1927); F. H. Mautner, "Amintors Morgenandacht," in *Deutsche Vierteljahrschrift für Litteraturwissenschaft und Geistesgeschichte,* Vol. 30 (1956); F. H. Mautner and F. Miller, "Remarks on G. C. Lichtenberg, Humanist–Scientist," in *Isis,* Vol. 43 (1952); A. Neumann, "Lichtenberg als Philosoph und seine Beziehungen zu Kant," in *Kantstudien,* Vol. 4 (1900); A. Schneider, *Georg Christoph Lichtenberg, précurseur du romantisme,* Vol. I, *L'Homme et l'oeuvre,* Vol. II, *Le Penseur* (Nancy, 1954); J. P. Stern, *Lichtenberg: A Doctrine of Scattered Occasions* (Bloomington, Ind., 1959); and G. H. von Wright, "Georg Christoph Lichtenberg als Philosoph," *Theoria,* Vol. 8 (1942), 201–217, of which the present article is an adaptation.

GEORG HENRIK VON WRIGHT
Translated by *David H. DeGrood* and *Barry J. Karp*

LIEBERT, ARTHUR (1878–1946), German Neo-Kantian philosopher, was born Arthur Levi in Berlin. The son of a merchant, he spent six years in business after completing his secondary education in 1895. He then entered the University of Berlin, where he received his doctorate in 1908. After teaching at the Berlin Handelshochschule, Liebert lectured at the University of Berlin, becoming extraordinary professor in 1925. From 1918 to 1933 he was coeditor with Paul Menzer of *Kantstudien,* which became under their guidance an instrument of growing international cooperation in philosophy. Forced to leave Germany in 1933, when the National Socialists came to power, he was appointed professor of philosophy at the University of Belgrade and there founded the journal *Philosophia: Philosophorum Nostri Temporis Vox Universa,* which appeared at irregular intervals from 1936 to 1939. When the German armies invaded the Balkans, he found refuge in England, where he published *Das Wesen der Freiheit* (1944) and, together with other refugees, organized the Freier deutscher Kulturbund in Grossbrittanien. At the end of

World War II he returned to his restored professorship at Berlin, but he died shortly thereafter.

Liebert was influenced by the realistic interpretation given Kant at Berlin by Friedrich Paulsen, Alois Riehl, and especially by Wilhelm Dilthey, who stressed the historical aspects of the *Geisteswissenschaften* (cultural sciences). Within this realistic Neo-Kantian orientation, Liebert turned to the ethical problems of value and freedom and to the search for a dialectic movement of ethical and metaphysical categories in history. Many of his writings, particularly in his later years, were devoted to the promotion of world-wide philosophical cooperation as "the free guardian of freedom" and particularly to the development of a philosophical organization, "an Areopagus of mankind," within which the new humanism was to be promoted. This is the theme of "On the Duty of Philosophy in Our Age" (*Von der Pflicht der Philosophie in unserer Zeit*), published during his exile in 1938.

Liebert's philosophical efforts to work out his critical metaphysics as a dialectic were to have taken the form of a large work entitled *Geist und Welt der Dialektik,* of which only the first volume, *Grundlegung der Dialektik,* appeared (Berlin, 1929). To be distinguished from science, philosophy must accept as its field not simply being (*Sein*) but value (*Geltung*), for being not merely *is,* but *is valid* (*gilt*), or validates, itself. In opposition to the Baden Neo-Kantians, Liebert rejected obligation (*Sollen*) as the ground of value, finding a new basis for metaphysics in the Kantian concern for the validation of judgments. "The right of metaphysics and the right to a metaphysics," he wrote, "flow from the idea and right of philosophy itself." The task of metaphysics thus becomes that of a historical "critical phenomenology" that "tests its own possibility and justification and derives its presuppositions and conclusions through reason."

Such a metaphysics does not merely use dialectic as the basis of metaphysical criticism but is itself dialectic. Its categories must include both philosophical ideas and the social and cultural contexts out of which they arise. "The idea of dialectic is at once the a priori condition and the definitive force (*massgebende Kraft*) for the construction of metaphysics, and also the distinctive instrument for penetrating into the nature of metaphysics, and for studying and understanding it." This dialectic must include within the scope of its critical and dynamic movement four motives: the intellectual, moral, aesthetic, and religious. Metaphysics is no longer "ontological–dogmatic" but "actualistic–critical"; the movement of its categorical structures of value combines temporal and supratemporal viewpoints. Its task is apparently never completed, because historical change outgrows the adequacy of every a priori structure. In particular, the modern world with its conflicts prevents a return to the classical humanizing harmonies of thought; the historical–normative dialectic that modern life calls forth must take the form of tragedy.

Liebert's lectures and seminars were devoted to the development and illustration of this conception of metaphysics. The *Grundlegung der Dialektik* provided only an introduction, in which Liebert traced the beginnings of the metaphysical dialectic in the thought of his contemporaries—practitioners of the *Geisteswissenschaften;* metaphysicians and theologians; and Neo-Kantians and Neo-Hegelians.

The Kantian identification of freedom with reason remained for Liebert the fixed a priori point of view of his "actualistic–critical" metaphysics. He persistently attacked the currently popular forms of *Lebensphilosophie* as relativistic, irrational, and sacrificing philosophical freedom. Philosophers were called upon to fulfill their vocation by turning to metaphysics and ethics as guides for individual and organizational action against the forces of irrationalism and cultural decay.

Liebert's thought has received little attention since his death. His most important writings are those in which he sought to formulate the principles of his own historical metaphysics of value.

Additional Works by Liebert

Das Problem der Geltung. Berlin, 1906.
Der Geltungswert der Metaphysik. Berlin, 1915.
Wie ist kritische Philosophie überhaupt möglich? Leipzig, 1919.
Die geistige Krisis der Gegenwart. Berlin, 1923.
Von der Pflicht der Philosophie in unserer Zeit. Zurich, 1946.

L. E. LOEMKER

LIEBMANN, OTTO (1840–1912), German Neo-Kantian philosopher. Liebmann was born at Löwenberg (Lwowek Slaski), Silesia, and became successively *Privatdozent* at Tübingen (1865), extraordinary professor at Strassburg (1872), and professor at Jena (1882). He served as a volunteer during the siege of Paris in 1870 and 1871 and published a memoir of his experiences.

In a *Festschrift* dedicated to Liebmann on his seventieth birthday, various thinkers discussed the aspects of his work which were of particular interest to them. Each interpreted him differently; for example, Bruno Bauch stressed transcendental-methodological aspects, Erich Adickes empirical openness, Wilhelm Windelband critical-metaphysical insight. Such variegated criticism was not without foundation, for Liebmann's thought had many facets and did not evolve so much as oscillate between impulsive outbursts and great restraint, passing from problem to problem.

In his notable early book, *Kant und die Epigonen* (1865), Liebmann swept aside the academic philosophy of his day and preached a return to Kant. He simplified Kantian thought and streamlined the post-Kantian systems. The essence of the Kantian revolution, he claimed, was the discovery of the transcendental, which, however, must be freed from the *caput mortuum* of the thing-in-itself. The systematic effort of the great successors of Kant failed because Fichte's Ego, Schiller's Absolute, Hegel's Spirit, Herbart's "reals," and Schopenhauer's Will all represent the thing-in-itself, whereas J. F. Fries mistook the transcendental for the psychological. For Liebmann the only reality, immanent in consciousness and sufficient, is experience, which is both empirical reality and transcendental ideality. But could such simplified views be unequivocally developed?

In a subsequent essay, *Über den individuellen Beweis für die Freiheit des Willens* (1866), Liebmann dealt with the freedom of the will, in opposition to Schopenhauer.

Are we, it can be asked, on the level of the transcendental or of the individual ego in dealing with this problem? Re-examining the question in 1901 (*Gedanken und Tatsachen*, Vol. II, p. 88), he referred it to the individual.

In *Über den objektiven Anblick* (1869) Liebmann distinguished three factors in perception: the sensitive, the intellectual, and the transcendent. The transcendent factor in perception "is the relationship between an unknown X and a likewise unknown Y, which appears to us as our body, and from which in turn there spring into our consciousness those sensitive qualities which our intellect transforms, according to a priori laws, into perceptible nature, a phenomenon of the external material world" (p. 153). In this work the thing-in-itself is not eliminated; on the contrary, two things-in-themselves—X and Y—are admitted.

Liebmann's major works, *Analysis der Wirklichkeit* (1876) and *Gedanken und Tatsachen* (2 vols., 1882–1907), are collections of problems, not only in the critique of knowledge but also in *Naturphilosophie*, psychology, aesthetics, and ethics. In all of these, self-consciousness recognizes its limits; but the resulting agnosticism is superseded by a program of "critical metaphysics."

In this connection Liebmann denounced as a *doktrinäre Fiktion* the Neo-Baconian ideal (or idol) of pure experience, itself a notion which Liebmann took from Avenarius and from the evolutionary genetic psychology of Herbert Spencer and others. Every experience and every science, Liebmann claimed, is possible only by means of certain nonempirical premises, such as the principles of real identity, of the continuity of existence, of constant causality or legality, and of the temporal continuity of becoming, or, in general, by means of fundamental a priori forms or principles, which constitute the organization of human cognitive powers but from whose transcendental validity by no means necessarily follows its transcendent reality.

Liebmann distinguished three types of theories, which seek explanatory principles in the immediate empirical data, in hypotheses by which the phenomena are deduced, or in absolute metaphysical realities. He rejected the first and third, and admitted the hypotheses, if and as long as the facts confirm them. This is true not only of scientific but also of philosophical theories, especially of critical metaphysics as a "strict discussion of human views, human hypotheses on the essence of things." Liebmann concentrated on the theories of science and their metaphysical pronouncements or assumptions. He claimed, for example, that the biological point of view is more than a mere postulation of an as-if; it is a positive affirmation of entelechies. Darwinism abounds with metascientific problems and teleological claims; but not even the transcendental philosopher can escape the problems posed by nature, with its own immanent logic (*Weltlogik*), its dynamic causality which achieves an increase in perfection, even though he knows that every hypothesis and system is a product of the specifically human thinking apparatus. A study of space and time which Liebmann undertook to come to grips with non-Euclidean viewpoints led him to problems which appeared to Wilhelm Windelband as idle fancies.

In dealing with the problem of the multiplicity of subjects, Liebmann developed but did not elaborate upon a distinction between three conceptions of the ego: the metaphysical substrate, an objective never attained by dogmatic metaphysics; the individual ego, a tacit assumption of psychology; and the transcendental ego, a "typical" subject of the intelligence of the human species and a fundamental condition of the empirical world. The problem of psychophysical parallelism led him to postulate a coincidence of natural and logical laws on the metaphysical plane of *natura naturans*, but he did not draw the necessary methodological distinctions to adequately treat this problem.

Works by Liebmann

Kant und die Epigonen. Stuttgart, 1865; 2d ed., Berlin, 1912.
Über den individuellen Beweis für die Freiheit des Willens. Stuttgart, 1866.
Über den objektiven Anblick. Stuttgart, 1869.
Zur Analysis der Wirklichkeit. Strassburg, 1876; 4th enlarged ed., 1911.
Über philosophischen Tradition. Strassburg, 1883.
Die Klimax der Theorien. Strassburg, 1884.
Gedanken und Tatsachen, 2 vols. Strassburg, 1882–1901; 2d ed., 1899–1904.
Immanuel Kant. Strassburg, 1904.

Works on Liebmann

Meyer, Adolf, *Über Liebmanns Erkenntnislehre und ihr Verhältniss zu Kant.* Jena, 1916. Dissertation.
Zum 70. Geburtstag Otto Liebmanns. A *Festschrift* in *Kantstudien,* Vol. 15 (1910). Contains works by Adickes, Bauch, Driesch, Windelband, and others.

Mariano Campo
Translated by *Robert M. Connolly*

LIFE, MEANING AND VALUE OF. To the questions "Is human life ever worthwhile?" and "Does (or can) human life have any meaning?" many religious thinkers have offered affirmative answers with the proviso that these answers would not be justified unless two of the basic propositions of most Western religions were true— that human life is part of a divinely ordained cosmic scheme and that after death at least some human beings will be rewarded with eternal bliss. Thus, commenting on Bertrand Russell's statement that not only must each individual human life come to an end but that life in general will eventually die out, C. H. D. Clark contrasts this "doctrine of despair" with the beauty of the Christian scheme. "If we are asked to believe that all our striving is without final consequence," then "life is meaningless and it scarcely matters how we live if all will end in the dust of death." According to Christianity, on the other hand, "each action has vital significance." Clark assures us that "God's grand design is life eternal for those who walk in the steps of Christ. Here is the one grand incentive to good living . . . . As life is seen to have purpose and meaning, men find release from despair and the fear of death" (*Christianity and Bertrand Russell,* p. 30). In a similar vein, the Jewish existentialist Emil Fackenheim claims that "whatever meaning life acquires" is derived from the encounter between God and man. The meaning thus conferred upon human life "cannot be understood in terms of some finite human purpose, supposedly more

ultimate than the meeting itself. For what could be more ultimate than the Presence of God?" It is true that God is not always "near," but "times of Divine farness" are by no means devoid of meaning. "Times of Divine nearness do not light up themselves alone. Their meaning extends over all of life." There is a "dialectic between Divine nearness and Divine farness," and it points to "an eschatological future in which it is overcome" ("Judaism and the Meaning of Life").

Among unbelievers not a few maintain that life can be worthwhile and have meaning in some humanly important sense even if the religious world view is rejected. Others, however, agree with the religious theorists that our two questions must be given negative answers if there is no God and if death means personal annihilation. Having rejected the claims of religion, they therefore conclude that life is not worthwhile and that it is devoid of meaning. These writers, to whom we shall refer here as "pessimists," do not present their judgments as being merely expressions of certain moods or feelings but as conclusions that are in some sense objectively warranted. They offer reasons for their conclusions and imply that anybody reaching a contradictory conclusion is mistaken or irrational. Most pessimists do not make any clear separation between the statements that life is not worthwhile and that life is without meaning. They usually speak of the "futility" or the "vanity" of life, and presumably they mean by this both that life is not worth living and that it has no meaning. For the time being we, too, shall treat these statements as if they were equivalent. However, later we shall see that in certain contexts it becomes important to distinguish between them.

Our main concern in this article will be to appraise pessimism as just defined. We shall not discuss either the question whether life is part of a divinely ordained plan or the question whether we survive our bodily death. Our question will be whether the pessimistic conclusions are justified if belief in God and immortality are rejected.

Schopenhauer's arguments. Let us begin with a study of the arguments offered by the pessimists, remembering that many of these are indirectly endorsed by religious apologists. The most systematic and probably the most influential, though in fact not the gloomiest, of the pessimists was Schopenhauer. The world, he wrote, is something which ought not to exist: the truth is that "we have not to rejoice but rather to mourn at the existence of the world; that its non-existence would be preferable to its existence; that it is something which ought not to be." It is absurd to speak of life as a gift, as so many philosophers and thoughtless people have done. "It is evident that everyone would have declined such a gift if he could have seen it and tested it beforehand." To those who assure us that life is only a lesson, we are entitled to reply: "For this very reason I wish I had been left in the peace of the all-sufficient nothing, where I would have no need of lessons or of anything else" (*The World as Will and Idea,* Vol. III, p. 390).

Schopenhauer offers numerous arguments for his conclusion. Some of these are purely metaphysical and are based on his particular system. Others, however, are of a more empirical character and are logically independent of his brand of metaphysical voluntarism. Happiness, according to Schopenhauer, is unobtainable for the vast majority of mankind. "Everything in life shows that earthly happiness is destined to be frustrated or recognized as illusion." People either fail to achieve the ends they are striving for or else they do achieve them only to find them grossly disappointing. But as soon as a man discovers that a particular goal was not really worth pursuing, his eye is set on a new one and the same illusory quest begins all over again. Happiness, accordingly, always lies in the future or in the past, and "the present may be compared to a small dark cloud which the wind drives over the sunny plain: before and behind it all is bright, only it itself always casts a shadow. The present is therefore always insufficient; but the future is uncertain, and the past is irrevocable" (*ibid.,* p. 383). Men in general, except for those sufficiently rational to become totally resigned, are constantly deluded—"now by hope, now by what was hoped for." They are taken in by "the enchantment of distance," which shows them "paradises." These paradises, however, vanish like "optical illusions when we have allowed ourselves to be mocked by them." The "fearful envy" excited in most men by the thought that somebody else is genuinely happy shows how unhappy they really are, whatever they pretend to others or to themselves. It is only "because they feel themselves unhappy" that "men cannot endure the sight of one whom they imagine happy."

On occasions Schopenhauer is ready to concede that some few human beings really do achieve "comparative" happiness, but this is not of any great consequence. For aside from being "rare exceptions," these happy people are really like "decoy birds"—they represent a possibility which must exist in order to lure the rest of mankind into a false sense of hope. Moreover, happiness, insofar as it exists at all, is a purely "negative" reality. We do not become aware of the greatest blessings of life—health, youth, and freedom—until we have lost them. What is called pleasure or satisfaction is merely the absence of craving or pain. But craving and pain are positive. As for the few happy days of our life—if there are any—we notice them only "after they have given place to unhappy ones."

Schopenhauer not infrequently lapsed from his doctrine of the "negative" nature of happiness and pleasure into the more common view that their status is just as "positive" as that of unhappiness and pain. But he had additional arguments which do not in any way depend on the theory that happiness and pleasure are negative. Perhaps the most important of these is the argument from the "perishableness" of all good things and the ultimate extinction of all our hopes and achievements in death. All our pleasures and joys "disappear in our hands, and we afterwards ask astonished where they have gone." Moreover, a joy which no longer exists does not "count"—it counts as little as if it had never been experienced at all:

That which *has been* exists no more; it exists as little as that which *never* been. But of everything that exists you may say, in the next moment, that it has been. Hence something of great importance in our past is inferior to something of little importance in our present, in that the latter is a *reality*, and related

to the former as something to nothing.   ("The Vanity of Existence," in *The Will to Live,* p. 229)

Some people have inferred from this that the enjoyment of the present should be "the supreme object of life." This is fallacious; for "that which in the next moment exists no more, and vanishes utterly, like a dream, can never be worth a serious effort."

The final "judgment of nature" is destruction by death. This is "the last proof" that life is a "false path," that all man's wishing is "a perversity," and that "nothing at all is worth our striving, our efforts and struggles." The conclusion is inescapable: "All good things are vanity, the world in all its ends bankrupt, and life a business which does not cover its expenses" (*The World as Will and Idea,* Vol. III p. 383).

The pointlessness of it all. Some of Schopenhauer's arguments can probably be dismissed as the fantasies of a lonely and embittered man who was filled with contempt for mankind and who was singularly incapable of either love or friendship. His own misery, it may be plausibly said, made Schopenhauer overestimate the unhappiness of human beings. It is frequently, but not universally, true that what is hoped for is found disappointing when it is attained, and while "fearful envy" of other people's successes is common enough, real sympathy and generosity are not quite so rare as Schopenhauer made them out to be. Furthermore, his doctrine that pleasure is negative while pain is positive, insofar as one can attach any clear meaning to it, seems glaringly false. To this it should be added, however, that some of Schopenhauer's arguments are far from idiosyncratic and that substantially the same conclusions have been endorsed by men who were neither lonely nor embittered and who did not, as far as one can judge, lack the gift of love or friendship.

Darrow. Clarence Darrow, one of the most compassionate men who ever lived, also concluded that life was an "awful joke." Like Schopenhauer, Darrow offered as one of his reasons the apparent aimlessness of all that happens. "This weary old world goes on, begetting, with birth and with living and with death," he remarked in his moving plea for the boy-murderers Loeb and Leopold, "and all of it is blind from the beginning to the end" (*Clarence Darrow—Attorney for the Damned,* A. Weinberg, ed., New York, 1957). Elsewhere he wrote: "Life is like a ship on the sea, tossed by every wave and by every wind; a ship headed for no port and no harbor, with no rudder, no compass, no pilot; simply floating for a time, then lost in the waves" ("Is Life Worth Living?," p. 43). In addition to the aimlessness of life and the universe, there is the fact of death. "I love my friends," wrote Darrow, "but they all must come to a tragic end." Death is more terrible the more one is attached to things in the world. Life, he concludes, is "not worth while," and he adds (somewhat inconsistently, in view of what he had said earlier) that "it is an unpleasant interruption of nothing, and the best thing you can say of it is that it does not last long" ("Is the Human Race Getting Anywhere?," p. 53).

Tolstoy. Tolstoy, unlike Darrow, eventually came to believe in Christianity, or at least in his own idiosyncratic version of Christianity, but for a number of years the only position for which he could see any rational justification was an extreme form of pessimism. During that period (and there is reason to believe that in spite of his later protestations to the contrary, his feelings on this subject never basically changed) Tolstoy was utterly overwhelmed by the thought of his death and the death of those he cared for and, generally, by the transitory nature of all human achievements. "Today or tomorrow," he wrote in "A Confession," "sickness and death will come to those I love or to me; nothing will remain but stench and worms. Sooner or later my affairs, whatever they may be, will be forgotten, and I shall not exist. Then why go on making any effort?" Tolstoy likened the fate of man to that of the traveler in the Eastern tale who, pursued by an enraged beast, seeks refuge in a dry well. At the botton of the well he sees a dragon that has opened its jaws to swallow him. To escape the enraged beast above and the dragon below, he holds onto a twig that is growing in a crack in the well. As he looks around he notices that two mice are gnawing at the stem of the twig. He realizes that very soon the twig will snap and he will fall to his doom, but at the same time he sees some drops of honey on the leaves of the branch and reaches out with his tongue to lick them. "So I too clung to the twig of life, knowing that the dragon of death was inevitably awaiting me, ready to tear me to pieces. . . . I tried to lick the honey which formerly consoled me, but the honey no longer gave me pleasure. . . . I only saw the unescapable dragon and the mice, and I could not tear my gaze from them. And this is not a fable but the real unanswerable truth."

These considerations, according to Tolstoy, inevitably lead to the conclusion that life is a "stupid fraud," that no "reasonable meaning" can be given to a single action or to a whole life. To the questions "What is it for?" "What then?," "Why should I live?" the answer is "Nothing can come of it," "Nothing is worth doing," "Life is not worthwhile."

What ways out are available to a human being who finds himself in this "terrible position"? Judging by the conduct of the people he observed, Tolstoy relates that he could see only four possible "solutions." The first is the way of ignorance. People who adopt this solution (chiefly women and very young and very dull people) have simply not or not yet faced the questions that were tormenting him. Once a person has fully realized what death means, this solution is not available to him. The second way is that of "Epicureanism," which consists in admitting the "hopelessness of life" but seizing as many of life's pleasures as possible while they are within reach. It consists in "disregarding the dragon and the mice and licking the honey in the best way, especially if much of it is around." This, Tolstoy adds, is the solution adopted by the majority of the people belonging to his "circle," by which he presumably means the well-to-do intellectuals of his day. Tolstoy rejects this solution because the vast majority of human beings are not well-to-do and hence have little or no honey at their disposal and also because it is a matter of accident whether one is among those who have honey or those who have not. Moreover, Tolstoy observes, it requires a special "moral dullness," which he himself lacked, to enjoy the honey while knowing the truth about death and the depri-

vations of the great majority of men. The third solution is suicide. Tolstoy calls this the way of "strength and energy." It is chosen by a few "exceptionally strong and consistent people." After they realize that "it is better to be dead than to be alive, and that it is best of all not to exist," they promptly end the whole "stupid joke." The means for ending it are readily at hand for everybody, but most people are too cowardly or too irrational to avail themselves of them. Finally, there is the way of "weakness." This consists in seeing the dreadful truth and clinging to life nevertheless. People of this kind lack the strength to act rationally and Tolstoy adds that he belonged to this last category.

Strengths of the pessimist position. Is it possible for somebody who shares the pessimists' rejection of religion to reach different conclusions without being plainly irrational? Whatever reply may be possible, any intelligent and realistic person would surely have to concede that there is much truth in the pessimists' claims. That few people achieve real and lasting happiness, that the joys of life (where there are any) pass away much too soon, that totally unpredictable events frequently upset the best intentions and wreck the noblest plans—this and much more along the same lines is surely undeniable. Although one should not dogmatize that there will be no significant improvements in the future, the fate of past revolutions, undertaken to rid man of some of his apparently avoidable suffering, does not inspire great hope. The thought of death, too, even in those who are not so overwhelmed by it as Tolstoy, can be quite unendurable. Moreover, to many who have reflected on the implications of physical theory it seems plain that because of the constant increase of entropy in the universe all life anywhere will eventually die out. Forebodings of this kind moved Bertrand Russell to write his famous essay "A Free Man's Worship," in which he concluded that "all the labors of the ages, all the devotion, all the inspiration, all the noonday brightness of human genius, are destined to extinction in the vast death of the solar system, and the whole temple of man's achievement must inevitably be buried beneath the debris of a universe in ruins." Similarly, Wilhelm Ostwald observed that "in the longest run the sum of all human endeavor has no recognizable significance." Although it is disputed whether physical theory really has such gloomy implications, it would perhaps be wisest to assume that the position endorsed by Russell and Ostwald is well-founded.

Comparative value judgments about life and death. Granting the strong points in the pessimists' claims, it is still possible to detect certain confusions and dubious inferences in their arguments. To begin with, there is a very obvious inconsistency in the way writers like Darrow and Tolstoy arrive at the conclusion that death is better than life. They begin by telling us that death is something terrible because it terminates the possibility of any of the experiences we value. From this they infer that nothing is really worth doing and that death is better than life. Ignoring for the moment the claim that in view of our inevitable death nothing is "worth doing," there very plainly seems to be an inconsistency in first judging death to be such a horrible evil and in asserting later on that death is better than life. Why was death originally judged to be an evil?

Surely because it is the termination of life. And if something, *y*, is bad because it is the termination of something, *x*, this can be so only if *x* is good or has positive value. If *x* were not good, the termination of *x* would not be bad. One cannot consistently have it both ways.

To this it may be answered that life did have positive value prior to one's realization of death but that once a person has become aware of the inevitability of his destruction life becomes unbearable and that this is the real issue. This point of view is well expressed in the following exchange between Cassius and Brutus in Shakespeare's *Julius Caesar* (III.i.102–105):

CASSIUS.   Why he that cuts off twenty years of life
    Cuts off so many years of fearing death.
BRUTUS.   Grant that, and then is death a benefit:
    So are we Caesar's friends that have abridged
    His time of fearing death.

There is a very simple reply to this argument. Granting that some people after once realizing their doom cannot banish the thought of it from their minds, so much so that it interferes with all their other activities, this is neither inevitable nor at all common. It is, on the contrary, in the opinion of all except some existentialists, morbid and pathological. The realization that one will die does not in the case of most people prevent them from engaging in activities which they regard as valuable or from enjoying the things they used to enjoy. To be told that one is not living "authentically" if one does not brood about death day and night is simply to be insulted gratuitously. A person who knows that his talents are not as great as he would wish or that he is not as handsome as he would have liked to be is not usually judged to live "inauthentically," but on the contrary to be sensible if he does not constantly brood about his limitations and shortcomings and uses whatever talents he does possess to maximum advantage.

There is another and more basic objection to the claim that death is better than life. This objection applies equally to the claim that while death is better than life it would be better still not to have been born in the first place and to the judgment that life is better than death. It should be remembered that we are here concerned with such pronouncements when they are intended not merely as the expression of certain moods but as statements which are in some sense true or objectively warranted. It may be argued that a value comparison—any judgment to the effect that *A* is better or worse than *B* or as good as *B*—makes sense only if *both A* and *B* are, in the relevant respect, in principle open to inspection. If somebody says, for example, that Elizabeth Taylor is a better actress than Betty Grable, this seems quite intelligible. Or, again, if it is said that life for the Jews is better in the United States than it was in Germany under the Nazis, this also seems readily intelligible. In such cases the terms of the comparison are observable or at any rate describable. These conditions are fulfilled in some cases when value comparisons are made between life and death, but they are not fulfilled in the kind of case with which Tolstoy and the pessimists are concerned. If the conception of an afterlife is intelligible, then it would make sense for a believer or for somebody who has not made up his mind to say such things as "Death cannot be worse than this life" or "I wonder if it will be any better for me after I am dead." Achilles, in the *Iliad*, was not making a senseless comparison when he exclaimed that he would rather act

. . . as a serf of another,
A man of little possessions, with scanty means of
  subsistence,
Than rule as a ghostly monarch the ghosts of all
  the departed.

Again, the survivors can meaningfully say about a deceased individual "It is better (for the world) that he is dead" or the opposite. For the person himself, however, if there is no afterlife, death is not a possible object of observation or experience, and statements by him that his own life is better than, as good as, or worse than his own death, unless they are intended to be no more than expressions of certain wishes or moods, must be dismissed as senseless. At first sight the contention that in the circumstances under discussion value comparisons between life and death are senseless may seem implausible because of the widespread tendency to think of death as a shadowy kind of life—as sleep, rest, or some kind of home-coming. Such "descriptions" may be admirable as poetry or consolation, but taken literally they are simply false.

Irrelevance of the distant future. These considerations do not, however, carry us very far. They do not show either that life is worth living or that it "has meaning." Before tackling these problems directly, something should perhaps be said about the curious and totally arbitrary preference of the future to the present, to which writers like Tolstoy and Darrow are committed without realizing it. Darrow implies that life would not be "futile" if it were not an endless cycle of the same kind of activities and if instead it were like a journey toward a destination. Tolstoy clearly implies that life would be worthwhile, that some of our actions at least would have a "reasonable meaning," if the present life were followed by eternal bliss. Presumably, what would make life no longer futile as far as Darrow is concerned is some feature of the destination, not merely the fact that it is a destination; and what would make life worthwhile in Tolstoy's opinion is not merely the eternity of the next life but the "bliss" which it would confer—eternal misery and torture would hardly do. About the bliss in the next life, if there is such a next life, Tolstoy shows no inclination to ask "What for?" or "So what?" But if bliss in the next life is not in need of any further justification, why should any bliss that there might be in the present life need justification?

The logic of value judgments. Many of the pessimists appear to be confused about the logic of value judgments. It makes sense for a person to ask about something "Is it really worthwhile?" or "Is it really worth the trouble?" if he does not regard it as intrinsically valuable or if he is weighing it against another good with which it may be in conflict. It does not make sense to ask such a question about something he regards as valuable in its own right and where there is no conflict with the attainment of any other good. (This observation, it should be noted, is quite independent of what view one takes of the logical status of intrinsic value judgments.) A person driving to the beach on a crowded Sunday, may, upon finally getting there, reflect on whether the trip was really worthwhile. Or, after undertaking a series of medical treatments, somebody may ask whether it was worth the time and the money involved. Such questions make sense because the discomforts of a car ride and the time and money spent on medical treatments are not usually judged to be valuable for their own sake. Again, a woman who has given up a career as a physician in order to raise a family may ask herself whether it was worthwhile, and in this case the question would make sense not because she regards the raising of a family as no more than a means, but because she is weighing it against another good. However, if somebody is very happy, for any number of reasons—because he is in love, because he won the Nobel prize, because his child recovered from a serious illness—and if this happiness does not prevent him from doing or experiencing anything else he regards as valuable, it would not occur to him to ask "Is it worthwhile?" Indeed, this question would be incomprehensible to him, just as Tolstoy himself would presumably not have known what to make of the question had it been raised about the bliss in the hereafter.

It is worth recalling here that we live not in the distant future but in the present and also, in a sense, in the relatively near future. To bring the subject down to earth, let us consider some everyday occurrences: A man with a toothache goes to a dentist, and the dentist helps him so that the toothache disappears. A man is falsely accused of a crime and is faced with the possibility of a severe sentence as well as with the loss of his reputation; with the help of a devoted attorney his innocence is established, and he is acquitted. It is true that a hundred years later all of the participants in these events will be dead and none of them will *then* be able to enjoy the fruits of any of the efforts involved. But this most emphatically does not imply that the dentist's efforts were not worthwhile or that the attorney's work was not worth doing. To bring in considerations of what will or will not happen in the remote future is, in such and many other though certainly not in all human situations, totally irrelevant. Not only is the finality of death irrelevant here; equally irrelevant are the facts, if they are facts, that life is an endless cycle of the same kind of activities and that the history of the universe is not a drama with a happy ending.

This is, incidentally, also the answer to religious apologists like C. H. D. Clark who maintain that all striving is pointless if it is "without final consequence" and that "it scarcely matters how we live if all will end in the dust of death." Striving is not pointless if it achieves what it is intended to achieve even if it is without *final* consequence, and it matters a great deal how we live if we have certain standards and goals, although we cannot avoid "the dust of death."

The vanished past. In asserting the worthlessness of life Schopenhauer remarked that "what has been exists as little as what has never been" and that "something of great importance now past is inferior to something of little importance now present." Several comments are in order here. To begin with, if Schopenhauer is right, it must work both ways: if only the present counts, then past sorrows no less than past pleasures do not "count." Furthermore, the question whether "something of great importance now past is inferior to something of little importance now present" is not, as Schopenhauer supposed, a straightforward question of fact but rather one of valuation, and different answers, none of which can be said to be mistaken, will be given by different people according to their circumstances and interests. Viktor Frankl, the founder of "logotherapy," has compared the pessimist to a man who observes, with fear and sadness, how his wall calendar grows thinner and thinner as he removes a sheet from it every day. The kind of person whom Frankl admires, on the other hand, "files each successive leaf neatly away with its predecessors" and reflects "with pride and joy" on all the richness represented by the leaves removed from the calendar. Such a person will not in old age envy the young. " 'No, thank you,' he will think. 'Instead of possibilities, I have realities in my past' " (*Man's Search for Meaning*, pp. 192–193). This passage is quoted not because it contains any great wisdom but because it illustrates that we are concerned here not with judgments of fact but with value judgments and that Schopenhauer's is not the only one that is possible. Nevertheless, his remarks are, perhaps, a healthy antidote to the cheap consolation and the attempts to cover up deep and inevitable misery that are the stock in trade of a great deal of popular psychology. Although Schopenhauer's judgments about the inferior value of the past cannot be treated as objectively true propositions, they express only too well what a great many human beings are bound to feel on certain occasions. To a man dying of cancer it is small consolation to reflect that there was a time when he was happy and flourishing; and while there are undoubtedly some old people who do not envy the young, it may be suspected that more often the kind of talk advocated by the prophets of positive thinking is a mask for envy and a defense against exceedingly painful feelings of regret and helplessness in the face of aging and death and the now-unalterable past.

The meanings of the "meaning of life." Let us now turn to the question whether, given the rejection of belief in God and immortality, life can nevertheless have any "meaning" or "significance." Kurt Baier has called attention to two very different senses in which people use these expressions and to the confusions that result when they are not kept apart. Sometimes when a person asks whether life has any meaning, what he wants to know is whether there is a superhuman intelligence that fashioned human beings along with other objects in the world to serve some end— whether their role is perhaps analogous to the part of an instrument (or its player) in a symphony. People who ask whether history has a meaning often use the word in the same sense. When Macbeth exclaimed that life "is a tale/Told by an idiot, full of sound and fury,/Signifying nothing," he was answering this cosmic question in the negative. His point evidently was not that human life is part of a scheme designed by a superhuman idiot but that it is not part of any design. Similarly, when Fred Hoyle, in his book *The Nature of the Universe* (rev. ed., New York, 1960), turns to what he calls "the deeper issues" and remarks that we find ourselves in a "dreadful situation" in which there is "scarcely a clue as to whether our existence has any real significance," he is using the word "significance" in this cosmic sense.

On the other hand, when we ask whether a *particular* person's life has or had any meaning, we are usually concerned not with cosmic issues but with the question whether certain purposes are to be found *in* his life. Thus, most of us would say without hesitation that a person's life had meaning if we knew that he devoted himself to a cause (such as the spread of Christianity or communism or the reform of mental institutions), or we would at least be ready to say that it "acquired meaning" once he became sufficiently attached to his cause. Whether we approve of what they did or not, most of us would be ready to admit—to take some random examples—that Dorothea Dix, Pasteur, Lenin, Margaret Sanger, Anthony Comstock, and Winston Churchill led meaningful lives. We seem to mean two things in characterizing such lives as meaningful: we assert, first, that the life in question had some dominant, over-all goal or goals which gave direction to a great many of the individual's actions and, second, that these actions and possibly others not immediately related to the overriding goal were performed with a special zest that was not present before the person became attached to his goal or that would not have been present if there had been no such goal in his life. It is not necessary, however, that a person should be devoted to a cause, in the sense just indicated, before we call his life meaningful. It is sufficient that he should have some attachments that are not too shallow. This last expression is of course rather vague, but so is the use of the word "meaning" when applied to human lives. Since the depth or shallowness of an attachment is a matter of degree, it makes perfectly good sense to speak of degrees of meaning in this context. Thus, C. G. Jung writes that in the lives of his patients there never was "sufficient meaning" (*Memories, Dreams, Reflections*, New York and Toronto, 1963, p. 140). There is nothing odd in such a locution, and there is equally nothing odd in saying about a man who has made a partial recovery from a deep depression that there is now again "some" meaning in his life.

Although frequently when people say about somebody that his life has or had meaning, they evidently regard this as a good thing, this is not invariably the case. One might express this point in the following way: saying that attachment to a certain goal has made a man's life meaningful is *not* tantamount to saying that the acts to which the goal has given direction are of positive value. A man might himself observe—and there would be nothing logically odd about it—"As long as I was a convinced Nazi (or communist or Christian or whatever) my life had meaning, my acts had a zest with which I have not been able to invest them since, and yet most of my actions were extremely harmful." Even while fully devoted to his cause or goal the person need not, and frequently does not, regard it as *intrinsically* valuable. If challenged he will usually justify the attachment to his goal by reference to more fundamental value judgments. Thus, somebody devoted to communism or to medical research or to the dissemination of birth-control

information will in all likelihood justify his devotion in terms of the production of happiness and the reduction of suffering, and somebody devoted to Christianity will probably justify his devotion by reference to the will of God.

Let us refer to the first of the two senses we have been discussing as the "cosmic" sense and to the second as the "terrestrial" sense. (These are by no means the only senses in which philosophers and others have used the word "meaning" when they have spoken of the meaning or meaninglessness of life, but for our purposes it is sufficient to take account of these two senses.) Now if the theory of cosmic design is rejected it immediately follows that human life has no meaning in the first or cosmic sense. It does not follow in the least, however, that a particular human life is meaningless in the second, or terrestrial, sense. This conclusion has been very clearly summarized by Baier: "Your life or mine may or may not have meaning (in one sense)," he writes, "even if life as such has none (in the other). . . . The Christian view guarantees a meaning (in one sense) to every life, the scientific view [what we have simply been calling the unbeliever's position] does not in any sense" (*The Meaning of Life*, p. 28). In the terrestrial sense it will be an open question whether an individual's life has meaning or not, to be decided by the particular circumstances of his existence. It may indeed be the case that once a person comes to believe that life has no meaning in the cosmic sense his attachment to terrestrial goals will be undermined to such an extent that his life will cease to be meaningful in the other sense as well. However, it seems very plain that this is by no means what invariably happens, and even if it did invariably happen the meaninglessness of a given person's life in the terrestrial sense would not *logically* follow from the fact, if it is a fact, that life is meaningless in the cosmic sense.

This is perhaps the place to add a few words of protest against the rhetorical exaggerations of certain theological writers. Fackenheim's statement, quoted earlier, that "whatever meaning life acquires, it derives from the encounter between God and man" is typical of many theological pronouncements. Statements of this kind are objectionable on several grounds. Let us assume that there is a God and that meetings between God and certain human beings do take place; let us also grant that activities commanded by God in these meetings "acquire meaning" by being or becoming means to the end of pleasing or obeying God. Granting all this, it does not follow that obedience of God is the only possible unifying goal. It would be preposterous to maintain that the lives of *all* unbelievers have been lacking in such goals and almost as preposterous to maintain that the lives of believers never contain unifying goals other than obedience of God. There have been devout men who were also attached to the advance of science, to the practice of medicine, or to social reform and who regarded these ends as worth pursuing independently of any divine commandments. Furthermore, there is really no good reason to grant that the life of a particular person becomes meaningful in the terrestrial sense just because human life in general has meaning in the cosmic sense. If a superhuman being has a plan in which I am included, this fact will make (or help to make) my life meaningful in the terrestrial sense only if I know the plan and approve of it and of my place in it, so that working toward the realization of the plan gives direction to my actions.

Is human life ever worthwhile? Let us now turn to the question of whether life is ever worth living. This also appears to be denied by the pessimists when they speak of the vanity or the futility of human life. We shall see that in a sense it cannot be established that the pessimists are "mistaken," but it is also quite easy to show that in at least two senses which seem to be of importance to many people, human lives frequently are worth living. To this end, let us consider under what circumstances a person is likely to raise the question "Is my life (still) worthwhile?" and what is liable to provoke somebody into making a statement like "My life has ceased to be worth living." We saw in an earlier section that when we say of certain acts, such as the efforts of a dentist or a lawyer, that they were worthwhile we are claiming that they achieved certain goals. Something similar seems to be involved when we say that a person's life is (still) worthwhile or worth living. We seem to be making two assertions: first, that the person has some goals (other than merely to be dead or to have his pains eased) which do not seem to him to be trivial and, second, that there is some genuine possibility that he will attain these goals. These observations are confirmed by various systematic studies of people who contemplated suicide, of others who unsuccessfully attempted suicide, and of situations in which people did commit suicide. When the subjects of these studies declared that their lives were no longer worth living they generally meant either that there was nothing left in their lives about which they seriously cared or that there was no real likelihood of attaining any of the goals that mattered to them. It should be noted that in this sense an individual may well be mistaken in his assertion that his life is or is not worthwhile any longer: he may, for example, mistake a temporary indisposition for a more permanent loss of interest, or, more likely, he may falsely estimate his chances of achieving the ends he wishes to attain.

Different senses of "worthwhile." According to the account given so far, one is saying much the same thing in declaring a life to be worthwhile and in asserting that it has meaning in the "terrestrial" sense of the word. There is, however, an interesting difference. When we say that a person's life has meaning (in the terrestrial sense) we are not committed to the claim that the goal or goals to which he is devoted have any positive value. (This is a slight oversimplification, assuming greater uniformity in the use of "meaning of life" than actually exists, but it will not seriously affect any of the controversial issues discussed here.) The question "As long as his life was dedicated to the spread of communism it had meaning *to him,* but was it really meaningful?" seems to be senseless. We are inclined to say, "If his life had meaning to him, then it had meaning—that's all there is to it." We are not inclined (or we are much less inclined) to say something of this kind when we speak of the worth of a person's life. We might say—for example, of someone like Eichmann—"While he was carrying out the extermination program, his life *seemed* worthwhile to him, but since his goal was so hor-

rible, his life *was not* worthwhile." One might perhaps distinguish between a "subjective" and an "objective" sense of "worthwhile." In the subjective sense, saying that a person's life is worthwhile simply means that he is attached to some goals which he does not consider trivial and that these goals are attainable for him. In declaring that somebody's life is worthwhile in the objective sense, one is saying that he is attached to certain goals which are both attainable and of positive value.

It may be held that unless one accepts some kind of rationalist or intuitionist view of fundamental value judgments one would have to conclude that in the objective sense of "worthwhile" no human life (and indeed no human action) could ever be shown to be worthwhile. There is no need to enter here into a discussion of any controversial questions about the logical status of fundamental value judgments. But it may be pointed out that somebody who favors a subjectivist or emotivist account can quite consistently allow for the distinction between ends that only seem to have positive value and those that really do. To mention just one way in which this could be done: one may distinguish between ends that would be approved by rational and sympathetic human beings and those that do not carry such an endorsement. One may then argue that when we condemn such a life as Eichmann's as not being worthwhile we mean not that the ends to which he devoted himself possess some non-natural characteristic of badness but that no rational or sympathetic person would approve of them.

The pessimists' special standards. The unexciting conclusion of this discussion is that some human lives are at certain times not worthwhile in either of the two senses we have distinguished, that some are worthwhile in the subjective but not in the objective sense, some in the objective but not in the subjective sense, and some are worthwhile in both senses. The unexcitingness of this conclusion is not a reason for rejecting it, but some readers may question whether it meets the challenge of the pessimists. The pessimist, it may be countered, surely does not deny the plain fact that human beings are on occasions attached to goals which do not seem to them trivial, and it is also not essential to his position to deny (and most pessimists do not in fact deny) that these goals are sometimes attainable. The pessimist may even allow that in a superficial ("immediate") sense the goals which people try to achieve are of positive value, but he would add that because our lives are not followed by eternal bliss they are not "really" or "ultimately" worthwhile. If this is so, then the situation may be characterized by saying that the ordinary man and the pessimist do not mean the same by "worthwhile," or that they do mean the same in that both use it as a positive value expression but that their standards are different: the standards of the pessimist are very much more demanding than those of most ordinary people.

Anybody who agrees that death is final will have to concede that the pessimist is not mistaken in his contention that judged by *his* standards, life is never worthwhile. However, the pessimist is mistaken if he concludes, as frequently happens, that life is not worthwhile by ordinary standards because it is not worthwhile by his standards.

Furthermore, setting aside the objection mentioned earlier (that there is something arbitrary about maintaining that eternal bliss makes life worthwhile but not allowing this role to bliss in the present life), one may justifiably ask why one should abandon ordinary standards in favor of those of the pessimist. Ordinarily, when somebody changes standards (for example, when a school raises or lowers its standards of admission) such a change can be supported by reasons. But how can the pessimist justify his special standards? It should be pointed out here that our ordinary standards do something for us which the pessimist's standards do not: they guide our choices, and as long as we live we can hardly help making choices. It is true that in one type of situation the pessimist's standards also afford guidance—namely, in deciding whether to go on living. It is notorious, however, that whether or not they are, by their own standards, rational in this, most pessimists do not commit suicide. They are then faced with much the same choices as other people. In these situations their own demanding standards are of no use, and in fact they avail themselves of the ordinary standards. Schopenhauer, for example, believed that if he had hidden his antireligious views he would have had no difficulty in obtaining an academic appointment and other worldly honors. He may have been mistaken in this belief, but in any event his actions indicate that he regarded intellectual honesty as worthwhile in a sense in which worldly honors were not. Again, when Darrow had the choice between continuing as counsel for the Chicago and North Western Railway and taking on the defense of Eugene V. Debs and his harassed and persecuted American Railway Union, he did not hesitate to choose the latter, apparently regarding it as worthwhile to go to the assistance of the suppressed and not worthwhile to aid the suppressor. In other words, although no human action is worthwhile, some human actions and presumably some human lives are less unworthwhile than others.

Is the universe better with human life than without it? We have not—at least not explicitly—discussed the claims of Schopenhauer, Eduard von Hartmann, and other pessimists that the nonexistence of the world would be better than its existence, by which they mean that a world without human life would be better than one with it.

Arguments of a phenomenologist. Some writers do not think that life can be shown to have meaning in any philosophically significant sense unless an affirmative answer to this question can be justified. Thus, in his booklet *Der Sinn unseres Daseins* the German phenomenologist Hans Reiner distinguishes between the everyday question about what he calls the "need-conditioned" meaning of life, which arises only for a person who is already in existence and has certain needs and desires, and the question about the meaning of human life in general. The latter question arises in concrete form when a responsible person is faced with the *Zeugungsproblem*—the question whether he should bring a child into the world. Reiner allows that a person's life has meaning in the former or "merely subjective" sense as long as his ordinary goals (chiefly his desire for happiness) are attained. This, however, does not mean that his life has an "objective" or "existential" (*seinshaft*) meaning—a significance or meaning which "attaches to life as such" and which, unlike the need-conditioned meaning, cannot be destroyed by any accident of fate. The philosopher, according to Reiner, is primarily concerned with the question of whether life has meaning in this objective or existential sense. "Our search for the meaning of our life," Reiner writes, "is identical with the search for a logically compelling reason (*einen einsichtigen Grund*) why it is better for us to exist than not to exist" (*Der Sinn unseres Daseins*, p. 27). Again, the real question is "whether it is better that mankind should exist than that there should be a world without any human life" (*ibid.*, p. 31). It may be questioned whether this is what anybody normally means when he asks whether life has any meaning, but Reiner certainly addresses himself to one of the questions raised by Schopenhauer and other pessimists that ought to be discussed here.

Reiner believes that he can provide a "logically compelling reason" why a world with human life is better than one without it. He begins by pointing out that men differ from animals by being, among other things, "moral individuals." To be a moral individual is to be part of the human community and to be actively concerned in the life of other human beings. It is indeed undeniable that people frequently fail to bring about the ends of morally inspired acts or wishes, but phenomenological analysis discloses that "the real moral value and meaning" of an act does not depend on the attainment of the "external goal." As Kant correctly pointed out, the decisive factor is "the good will," the moral intent or attitude. It is here that we find the existential meaning of life: "Since that which is morally good contains its meaning and value within itself, it follows that it is intrinsically worth while. The existence of what is morally good is therefore better than its nonexistence." (*ibid.*, pp. 54–55). But the existence of what is morally good is essentially connected with the existence of free moral individuals, and hence it follows that the existence of human beings as moral agents is better than their nonexistence.

Unlike happiness, which constitutes the meaning of life in the everyday or need-conditioned sense, the morally good does not depend on the accidents of life. It is not within a person's power to be happy, but it is "essentially" (*grundsätzlich*) in everybody's power to do what is good. Furthermore, while all happiness is subjective and transitory, leaving behind it no more than a "melancholy echo," the good has eternal value. Nobody would dream of honoring and respecting a person for his happiness or prosperity. On the other hand, we honor every good deed and the expression of every moral attitude, even if it took place in a distant land and among a foreign people. If we discover a good act or a good attitude in an enemy we nevertheless respect it and cannot help deriving a certain satisfaction from its existence. The same is true of good deeds carried out in ages long past. In all this the essentially timeless nature of morality becomes evident. Good deeds cease to exist as historical events only; their value, on the other hand, has eternal reality and is collected as an indestructible "fund." This may be a metaphysical statement, but it is not a piece of "metaphysical speculation." It simply makes explicit what the experience of the morally good discloses to phenomenological analysis (*ibid.,* pp. 55–57).

Replies to Reiner. There is a great deal in this presentation with which one could take issue. If one is not misled by the image of the ever-growing, indestructible "fund," one may wonder, for example, what could be meant by claiming that the value of a good deed is "eternal," other than that most human beings tend to approve of such an action regardless of when or where it took place. However, we are here concerned primarily with the question whether Reiner has met the challenge of the pessimists, and it seems clear that he has not. A pessimist like Schopenhauer or Darrow might provisionally grant the correctness of Reiner's phenomenological analysis of morality but still offer the following rejoinder: The inevitable misery of all or nearly all human beings is so great that even if in the course of their lives they have a chance to preserve their inner moral natures or their good will, the continued torture to which their lives condemn them would not be justified. Given the pessimist's estimate of human life, this is surely not an unreasonable rejoinder. Even without relying on the pessimist's description of human life, somebody while accepting Reiner's phenomenological analysis might reach the opposite conclusion. He might, for example, share the quietist strain of Schopenhauer's teachings and object to the whole hustle and bustle of life, concluding that the "peace of the all-sufficient nothing"—or, more literally, a universe without human life—was better in spite of the fact that moral deeds could not then be performed. Since he admits the "facts" of morality on which Reiner bases his case but considers the peace of the all-sufficient nothing more valuable than morality, it is not easy to see how an appeal to the latter would show him to be mistaken. What phenomenological analysis has not disclosed, to Reiner or, as far as is known, to anybody else, is that doing good is the only or necessarily the greatest value.

Why the pessimist cannot be answered. The conclusion suggests itself that the pessimist cannot here be refuted, not because what he says is true or even because we do not know who is right and who is wrong but because the question whether a universe with human life is better than one without it does not have any clear meaning unless it is interpreted as a request for a statement of personal preference. The situation seems to be somewhat similar to what we found in the case of the question "Is my life better than my death?" when asked in certain circumstances. In some contexts indeed when we talk about human life in general, the word "better" has a reasonably clear meaning. Thus, if it is maintained that life for the human race will be better than it is now after cancer and mental illness have been conquered, or that human life will be better (or worse) after religion has disappeared, we understand fairly well what is meant, what facts would decide the issue either way. However, we do not really know what would count as evidence for or against the statement "The existence of human life as such is better than its nonexistence." Sometimes it is claimed that the question has a fairly clear meaning, namely, whether happiness outweighs unhappi-

ness. Thus, von Hartmann supports his answer that the nonexistence of human life is better than its existence, that in fact an inanimate world would be better than one with life, with the argument that as we descend the scale of civilization and "sensitivity," we reach ever lower levels of misery. "The individuals of the lower and poorer classes and of ruder nations," he writes, "are happier than those of the elevated and wealthier classes and of civilized nations, not indeed because they are poorer and have to endure more want and privations, but because they are coarser and duller" (*Philosophy of the Unconscious,* Vol. III, p. 76). The "brutes," similarly, are "happier (i.e., less miserable)" than man, because "the excess of pain which an animal has to bear is less than that which a man has to bear." The same principle holds within the world of animals and plants:

> How much more painful is the life of the more finely-feeling horse compared with that of the obtuse pig, or with that of the proverbially happy fish in the water, its nervous system being of a grade so far inferior! As the life of a fish is more enviable than that of a horse, so is the life of an oyster than that of a fish, and the life of a plant than that of an oyster. (*Ibid.*)

The conclusion is inevitable: the best or least undesirable form of existence is reached when, finally, we "descend beneath the threshold of consciousness"; for only there do we "see individual pain entirely disappear" (*Philosophy of the Unconscious,* Vol. III, pp. 76–77). Schopenhauer, also, addressing himself directly to the "*Zeugungsproblem,*" reaches a negative answer on the ground that unhappiness usually or necessarily outweighs happiness. "Could the human race continue to exist," he asks (in *Parerga und Paralipomena,* Vol. II, pp. 321–322), if "the generative act were . . . an affair of pure rational reflection? Would not rather everyone have so much compassion for the coming generation as to prefer to spare it the burden of existence, or at least be unwilling to take on himself the responsibility of imposing such a burden in cold blood?" In these passages Schopenhauer and von Hartmann assume that in the question "Is a world with human life better than one without human life?" the word "better" must be construed in a hedonistic or utilitarian sense—and the same is true of several other philosophers who do not adopt their pessimistic answer. However, while one may *stipulate* such a sense for "better" in this context, it is clear that this is *not* what is meant prior to the stipulation. Spinoza, for example, taught that the most miserable form of existence is preferable to nonexistence. Perhaps few who have directly observed the worst agonies and tortures that may be the lot of human beings or of animals would subscribe to this judgment, but Spinoza can hardly be accused of a self-contradictory error. Again, Nietzsche's philosophy is usually and quite accurately described as an affirmation of life, but Nietzsche was very careful not to play down the horrors of much of life. While he did not endorse Schopenhauer's value judgments, he thought that, by and large, Schopenhauer had not been far wrong in his description of the miseries of the human scene. In effect Nietzsche maintained that even though unhappiness is more prevalent than happiness, the existence of life is nevertheless better than its nonexistence, and this surely is not a self-contradiction.

It is important to point out what does not follow from the admission that in a nonarbitrary sense of "better," the existence of the human race cannot be shown to be better than its nonexistence: It does not follow that I or anybody else cannot or should not prefer the continued existence of the human race to its nonexistence or my own life to my death, and it does not follow that I or anybody else cannot or should not enjoy himself or that I or anybody else is "irrational" in any of these preferences. It is also impossible to prove that in some nonarbitrary sense of "better," coffee with cream is better than black coffee, but it does not follow that I cannot or should not prefer or enjoy it or that I am irrational in doing so. There is perhaps something a trifle absurd and obsessive in the need for a "proof" that the existence of life is better than its nonexistence. It resembles the demand to have it "established by argument" that love is better than hate.

Perhaps it would be helpful to summarize the main conclusions reached in this essay:

(1) In certain familiar senses of "meaning," which are not usually regarded as trivial, an action or a human life can have meaning quite independently of whether there is a God or whether we shall live forever.

(2) Writers like Tolstoy, who, because of the horror that death inspires, conclude that death is better than life, are plainly inconsistent. Moreover, the whole question of whether my life is better than my death, unless it is a question about my preference, seems to be devoid of sense.

(3) Those who argue that no human action can be worthwhile because we all must eventually die ignore what may be called the "short-term context" of much of our lives.

(4) Some human lives are worthwhile in one or both of the two senses in which "worthwhile" is commonly used, when people raise the question of whether a given person's life is worthwhile. The pessimists who judge human life by more demanding standards are not mistaken when they deny that by *their* standards no human life is ever worthwhile. However, they are guilty of a fallacious inference if they conclude that for this reason no human life can be worthwhile by the usual standards. Nor is it clear why anybody should embrace their standards in the place of those commonly adopted.

(5) It appears that the pessimists cannot be answered if in order to answer them one has to be able to prove that in some nonarbitrary sense of the word "better," the existence of life is better than its nonexistence. But this admission does not have any of the gloomy consequences which it is sometimes believed to entail.

Bibliography

The position that human life cannot be meaningful without religious belief is defended in James Martineau, *Modern Materialism and Its Relation to Religion and Theology* (New York, 1877), and more recently in C. H. D. Clark, *Christianity and Bertrand Russell* (London, 1958), and in E. L. Fackenheim, "Judaism and the Meaning of Life," in *Commentary,* Vol. 39 (1965), 49–55. Substantially similar views are expounded in Paul Althaus, "The Meaning and Purpose of History in the Christian View," in *Universitas,* Vol. 7 (1965), 197–204, and in various publications by Viktor Frankl. Frankl's *Man's Search for Meaning* (New York, 1963) contains a full list of his own writings as well as those of his followers, most of whom may be described as practicing "pastoral psychology." A proreligious position is also advocated by William James in "Is Life Worth Living?," in *The Will To Believe and Other Essays in Popular Philosophy* (New York, 1897), and *The Varieties of Religious Experience* (New York, 1902), Chs. 6 and 7. A milder version of the same position is presented in Chad Walsh, *Life Is Worth Living* (Cincinnati, no date).

Schopenhauer's views about the "vanity" of life are stated in Vol. I, Bk. IV, of *Die Welt als Wille und Vorstellung* (Leipzig, 1818), translated by R. B. Haldane and J. Kemp as *The World as Will and Idea,* 3 vols. (London, 1883), and in several of his pieces included in *Parerga und Paralipomena,* 6th ed., ed. J. Frauenstädt, 2 vols. (Berlin, 1851). Three of his essays that bear most closely on the subject of the present article—"On the Vanity and Suffering of Life," "On the Sufferings of the World," and "The Vanity of Existence"—are available in an English translation by T. Bailey Saunders in Richard Taylor, ed., *The Will to Live—Selected Writings of Arthur Schopenhauer* (New York, 1962).

Eduard von Hartmann's position is stated in Vol. III of *Die Philosophie des Unbewussten,* 3 vols. (Berlin, 1869), translated by W. C. Coupland as *Philosophy of the Unconscious* (London, 1884), in *Zur Geschichte und Begründung des Pessimismus* (Berlin, 1892), and in *Philosophische Fragen der Gegenwart* (Leipzig and Berlin, 1885), Ch. 5. Clarence Darrow's pessimism is expounded in *The Story of My Life* (New York, 1932) and in two pamphlets, "Is Life Worth Living?" and "Is the Human Race Getting Anywhere?" (Girard, Kansas, no date). Tolstoy's views are stated in "A Confession," in *A Confession, The Gospel in Brief and What I Believe,* translated by Aylmer Maude (London, 1940). Gloomy implications are derived from the second law of thermodynamics by Bertrand Russell in "A Free Man's Worship" (1903), which is available in several books, perhaps most conveniently in Russell's *Mysticism and Logic* (New York and London, 1918), and by Wilhelm Ostwald, *Die Philosophie der Werte* (Leipzig, 1913). F. P. Ramsey, in "How I Feel," in *The Foundations of Mathematics and Other Logical Essays* (London, 1931), agrees with Russell and Ostwald about the physical consequences of the second law but does not share their gloomy response. Stephen Toulmin, "Contemporary Scientific Mythology," in Toulmin et al., *Metaphysical Beliefs* (London, 1957), questions whether the second law has the physical consequences attributed to it by Russell, Ostwald, and many others. L. J. Russell, "The Meaning of Life," *Philosophy,* Vol. 28 (1953), pp. 30–40, contains some interesting criticisms of the view that eternal existence could render any human actions meaningful.

The fullest discussions of the questions of the meaning and value of life by contemporary analytic philosophers are Kurt Baier, *The Meaning of Life* (Canberra, 1957), parts of which are reprinted in Morris Weitz, ed., *Twentieth Century Philosophy—The Analytic Tradition* (New York, 1966); Ronald W. Hepburn, *Christianity and Paradox* (London, 1958), Ch. 8; and Antony Flew, "Tolstoi and the Meaning of Life," in *Ethics,* Vol. 73 (1963), 110–118. Baier, Hepburn, and Flew support the position that life can be meaningful even if there is no God and no afterlife. This position is also defended in Eugen Dühring, *Der Werth des Leben* (Leipzig, 1881), Chs. 6–7, and more recently in Bertrand Russell, *The Conquest of Happiness* (London and New York, 1930), Ch. 2; Ernest Nagel, "The Mission of Philosophy," in Lyman Bryson, ed., *An Outline of Man's Knowledge of the Modern World* (New York, 1960); Sidney Hook, "Pragmatism and the Tragic Sense of Life," in *Proceedings and Addresses of the American Philosophical Association,* Vol. 33 (1960), 5–26; Karl R. Popper, *The Open Society and Its Enemies,* 2 vols. (5th rev. ed., London, 1966), Vol. II, Ch. 25; and Kai Nielsen, "Examination of an Alleged Theological Basis of Morality," in *The Iliff Review,* Vol. 21 (1964), 39–49. Sartre and Camus are frequently (and rather inaccurately) described as "nihilists," but in effect they also take the position that although the universe is "absurd," human life can be meaningful.

Sartre's views are found in *Being and Nothingness,* translated by Hazel E. Barnes (New York, 1956), Pt. 4. Camus's views are stated in *The Myth of Sisyphus and Other Essays,* translated by Justin O'Brien (New York, 1955). Views very similar to those of Sartre and Camus are advocated by Flew and R. W. Hepburn in their BBC discussion "Problems of Perspective," which is printed in *The Plain View,* Vol. 10 (1955), 151–166. C. D. McGee, *The Recovery of Meaning—An Essay on the Good Life* (New York, 1966), Ch. 1, contains a lively and detailed discussion of some of the issues treated in the present article. The author reaches similar conclusions but devotes far more attention to the "malaise" which inspires questions about the meaning of life. In a similar vein, Ilham Dilman, "Life and Meaning," in *Philosophy,* Vol. 40 (1965), 320–333, concentrates on the psychological situations that prompt people to ask whether their own lives or the lives of others have meaning. Moritz Schlick, *Vom Sinn des Lebens* (Berlin, 1927), is concerned primarily with psychological questions, arguing that modern life tends to be spoiled by overemphasis on the achievement of distant goals. Freud in several places alludes to the question of the meaning of life and usually dismisses it as senseless and pathological. "The moment a man questions the meaning and value of life," he wrote in a letter to Marie Bonaparte, "he is sick. . . . By asking this question one is merely admitting to a store of unsatisfied libido to which something else must have happened, a kind of fermentation leading to sadness and depression" (*Letters of Sigmund Freud,* translated by James Stern and Tania Stern, E. L. Freud, ed., New York, 1960, p. 436).

The Polish Marxist Adam Schaff deals with some of the issues discussed in the present article in his *A Philosophy of Man* (London, 1963). Schaff's views are criticized from a Christian point of view in Christopher Hollis, "What Is the Purpose of Life?," in *The Listener,* Vol. 70 (1961), 133–136. There is a discussion of the "meaning of life" from the point of view of fascism in Mario Palmieri, *The Philosophy of Fascism* (Chicago, 1936). The "phenomenological" position of Hans Reiner, which was discussed in the final section of this article, is stated in his *Der Sinn unseres Daseins* (Tübingen, 1960). Other recent German works include Richard Wisser, ed., *Sinn und Sein* (Tübingen, 1960); Reinhart Lauth, *Die Frage nach den Sinn des Daseins* (Munich, 1953); and Johannes Hessen, *Der Sinn des Lebens* (Cologne, 1933).

Psychological studies of people who attempted or who committed suicide are contained in Margarite von Andics, *Suicide and the Meaning of Life* (London, 1947); Louis I. Dublin and Bessie Bunzel, *To Be or Not To Be* (New York, 1933); and E. Stengel, *Suicide and Attempted Suicide* (Harmondsworth, England, 1964).

Will Durant, *On the Meaning of Life* (New York, 1932), consists of answers by various eminent men, including Gandhi, H. L. Mencken, Russell, and George Bernard Shaw, to the question of what they take to be the meaning of life.

PAUL EDWARDS

LIFE, ORIGIN OF. As soon as men grasped the fact that the earth has a history and were able to identify some of the earth's occupants as living things, speculations about the origin of life began. Three different conceptions were first proposed. Ancient religions affirmed that living things had been created by a supernatural power. Early philosophical thought tended to hold that they arose from inanimate matter by spontaneous generation. Occasionally it was suggested that they were derived from special seeds or spores of life which always existed. With the growth of geology, biology, and biochemistry, these conceptions ceased to be mere speculations and were confronted with a body of evidence and scientific theory in the light of which they could be refined and tested. Geology made it plain that the first forms of life were structurally simple. Darwinian evolutionary theory showed how a continuous selective process could give rise to complex organisms by natural means. Biochemistry analyzed the components of

living systems in such a way as to suggest lines of derivation from preliving systems. How scientific findings have affected speculations about the origin of life, and what issues of philosophical interest have resulted, will now be briefly reviewed.

Life as eternal. It is possible to hold that, in the universe at large, life is coeternal with nonliving matter and hence had no origin. This conclusion might be supported by appealing to the steady-state theory advocated by some cosmologists, according to which the universe presents the same aspect to every fundamental observer at all places and times. (Hermann Bondi explains this point of view in *Cosmology.*) Yet it is virtually certain that the earth has been able to support life for not more than the past three billion years. If so, one must suppose that the first "germs of life" came to the earth from outer space. These hypothetical germs ("biospores," "cosmozoa," "astroplankton," "panspermia," etc.) are assumed to have been carried either by meteorites or by bits of cosmic dust propelled by radiation pressure, light quanta, or other media. In the nineteenth century Lord Kelvin and Helmholtz defended the meteorite transmission hypothesis. Later, Arrhenius defended the hypothesis of "radiopanspermia." However, difficulties confront this whole approach to the problem. No uncontroversial evidence of such entities as biospores has been found. It is well-known that the intense cold, ultraviolet radiation, and cosmic rays in outer space constitute a threat to all life. They make it highly improbable that viable germs could ever reach the earth from elsewhere in the universe. These difficulties do not prove that life is not eternal. But they have led investigators to prefer other hypotheses about the beginning of living systems on our planet.

Life from nonliving matter. The old belief that organisms such as flies and worms can be generated spontaneously from inanimate matter was refuted by the work of Pasteur. Some took this to mean that organisms can be generated only by other organisms. New light was thrown on the problem by Oparin in his celebrated book *The Origin of Life* (1938), which argued that a long process of biochemical evolution under terrestrial conditions quite different from those which now prevail could have led to the production of primitive living systems from nonliving ones. This scientifically supported version of "spontaneous generation" has been widely accepted.

The account that Oparin proposed is in broad outline as follows. The earth's early atmosphere contained almost no oxygen, and there was no upper ozone layer to act as a shield against ultraviolet radiation. Hence, intense radiation reached the surface of the earth, on which seas or pools of "probiotic soup," rich in chemical elements, existed. Inorganic photochemical and other reactions were set up, as a result of which organic compounds, including amino acids, were formed. Once they appeared on a sufficient scale, chemical selection would set in, because of differential utilization of available energy. Over a prolonged period, biochemical complexity and efficiency would build up in a small number of surviving systems, the immediate precursors (so-called eobionts) of living things. Living things themselves appeared when there were systems that exhibited metabolism and the capacity for self-reproduction. At this stage morphological evolution began to supersede chemical evolution. The altered physical conditions on the planet, including the presence of an oxygenic atmosphere, no longer allowed organic compounds to be formed by purely inorganic synthesis.

Many details of this account remain controversial. Experts disagree about whether the earliest life consisted of genes, or viruses, or macromolecules. But certain misconceptions have been removed. It is no longer held that life arose from inorganic matter; or that it arose in just one way at just one place; or that it must have been microscopic in size; or that a sharp line of demarcation separates the living from the preliving. The idea that a single blob of living substance popped into existence on an otherwise lifeless planet at a particular moment of time is no longer seriously entertained. What happened is to be conceived in statistical and evolutionary terms. The most reasonable supposition is that innumerable molecular aggregates were produced at random in the probiotic soup and, by prolonged trial and error, evolved to form the basis for life.

Life and supernatural creation. Some scientists have contended that the origin of life can only be explained by postulating the action of a supernatural creator, or God. One form of the argument proceeds in part as follows. "A living thing possesses a series of attributes which sever it from the inorganic by a chasm across which there is no bridge. Hence, to account for life we are compelled to admit that . . . at some definite point in past time it was placed upon the planet by the operation of an extra-mundane cause. . . . That cause must have been living, intelligent, personal. But this can only have been God" (G. H. Joyce, *Principles of Natural Theology*, pp. 145–152). The main objection to this argument is that it embodies three of the misconceptions mentioned above. It assumes that there is a sharp separation between the living and the preliving; it assumes that life appeared at a definite moment of time; and it assumes that a naturalistic explanation of the origin of life must derive it from inorganic matter. These assumptions are all unwarranted.

A more sophisticated argument, directed against the view that eobionts could arise by random or spontaneous activity, makes use of some probability calculations of Guye. He estimated that the probability of the spontaneous production of some proteinlike substance is $1:100^{160}$. For such a colossally improbable event to occur on our small planet, something of the order of 10^{243} years would be required. Hence, Guye concludes, not even the universe has existed long enough to allow one protein molecule to arise spontaneously. Accepting these calculations, scientists such as Lecomte du Noüy and Mottram have concluded that life was created by an intelligent, supernatural God, since it could not have arisen by chance.

This line of argument has been subjected to severe criticism. Thus, Pirie contends that it embodies two basic fallacies: "(1) It assumes that there is only one way in which a certain state of affairs, such as life, can exist; and (2) it assumes that the probability of a process can be calculated although its mechanism is unknown" ("Some Assumptions Underlying Discussions of the Origin of Life," p. 370). Others have pointed out that even if the random origin of life was a very improbable event, this does not prove that it *could not* have happened. Indeed, Haldane urges that we take seriously the hypothesis that life originated as the result of a very improbable event, which was nevertheless almost certain to occur given sufficient time and sufficient matter of suitable composition in a suitable state. However, Oparin in his 1957 work, *The Origin of Life on the Earth,* rejects the idea of "the chance development of living molecules" and espouses the idea that they originated by natural necessity. If so, life may well exist at many stations in the cosmos and not just on earth.

From a methodological point of view it is clear that explanations of the origin of life can hardly hope to conclude with a statement about how life *must* have begun. At best an explanation can claim to depict one of the ways in which life *could* have begun. Numerous assumptions are always needed, and it is difficult to formulate them in a manner which permits them to be tested experimentally. Yet even here progress is possible. Recently, for example, Miller (1953; 1957) produced amino acids by circulating over an electric spark gases believed to have been present in the earth's early atmosphere. The structure of arguments used in scientific discussions of the origin of life has just started to be explored by students of the logic of explanation; see, for example, the article "Origin Explanations and the Origin of Life" by Ebersole and Shrewsbury. These arguments have many features that are philosophically interesting. The whole subject, indeed, will continue to excite philosophical interest as scientists map the routes along which life could have proceeded.

Bibliography

Bernal, J. D., *The Physical Basis of Life.* London, 1951. A concise, stimulating discussion by a distinguished physicist. In spite of the title, its main concern is with the *origin* of life rather than with structure, metabolism, or behavior.

Blum, H. F., *Time's Arrow and Evolution,* 2d ed. Princeton, 1955. An original and controversial work centered on the relation of the second law of thermodynamics to the origin and evolution of life. An important book.

Bondi, Hermann, *Cosmology,* 2d ed. London and New York, 1960.

Ebersole, F. B., and Shrewsbury, M. M., "Origin Explanations and the Origin of Life." *The British Journal for the Philosophy of Science.* Vol. 10 (August 1959), 103–119.

Guye, C. E., *L'Évolution physico-chimique,* 2d ed. Paris, 1942.

Haldane, J. B. S., "The Origins of Life." *New Biology,* No. 16 (April 1954), 12–27.

Joyce, G. H., *Principles of Natural Theology.* London, 1923.

Lecomte du Noüy, P. A., *Human Destiny.* New York, 1947.

Miller, S. L., "A Production of Amino-acids Under Possible Primitive Earth Conditions." *Science,* Vol. 117 (1953), 528–533.

Miller, S. L., "On Formation of Organic Compounds on the Primitive Earth." *Annals of the New York Academy of Sciences,* Vol. 69 (1957), 260–275.

Mottram, V. H., "A Scientific Basis for Belief in God." *The Listener,* Vol. 39 (April 22, 1948), 662–663.

Oparin, A. I., *The Origin of Life.* New York, 1938. English translation by S. Morgulis of *Vozniknovenie Zhizni na Zemle.* Moscow, 1936. This work merits the much-abused title of a "classic." An absolutely fundamental book.

Oparin, A. I., *The Origin of Life on the Earth.* London, 1957. English translation by Ann Synge of the 3d revised and enlarged edition of *Vozniknovenie Zhizni na Zemle.* Moscow, 1956. A valuable, up-dated version of the 1938 work.

Pirie, N. W., "Some Assumptions Underlying Discussions of the Origin of Life." *Annals of the New York Academy of Sciences,* Vol.

69 (August 1957), 369–376. Lucid, authoritative, and penetrating. Of particular interest to students of scientific methodology.

Rutten, M. G., *The Geological Aspects of the Origin of Life on Earth.* Amsterdam and New York, 1962. A short, carefully argued work by a geologist on a somewhat neglected aspect of the origin of life.

T. A. GOUDGE

LIFE, SANCTITY OF. See POPPER-LYNKEUS, JOSEF; SUICIDE.

LINGUISTIC THEORY OF THE A PRIORI. In recent philosophy various attempts have been made to explain the peculiar nature of "a priori propositions" (see A PRIORI AND A POSTERIORI) in terms of features of the language or symbolism in which these propositions are expressed. Examples of propositions which it has been supposed are known a priori are "(If today is Monday, then tomorrow is Tuesday) implies (If tomorrow is not Tuesday, then today is not Monday)," "$(a+b)^2 = a^2 + 2ab + b^2$," "Every cube has twelve edges," "Every substance possesses some attribute," and "An all-perfect being necessarily exists." Logic, mathematics, and traditional metaphysics are said to consist entirely or almost entirely of a priori propositions. But these so-called propositions are puzzling for the following reasons. It is evident that the truth of such a proposition is not and cannot be established by appeal to experience; then the problem immediately arises of how such a proposition can have a nonempirical method of validation and what this method is. It has been supposed that the truth of an a priori proposition is ascertained simply by understanding the proposition, either by examining the proposition alone, or by deducing it from other propositions so understood, or by some kind of argument that makes no reference to empirical matters of fact. But then it may be asked, "What is it to examine a proposition?" or "What is the nonempirical form of argument in question?" Moreover, if the truth of an a priori proposition can be ascertained simply by understanding the proposition, it seems that such a proposition could not be other than true. Consequently, it has been supposed that all a priori propositions are necessarily true (see CONTINGENT AND NECESSARY STATEMENTS). But how any proposition can be not simply true but *necessarily* true has seemed deeply puzzling to many of the ablest philosophers.

The effect, and in many cases the intention, of linguistic theories of the a priori has been to repudiate rationalistic conceptions of a priori knowledge—in particular, the notion that this kind of knowledge is the product of intellectual intuition or insight. For the features of language that have been appealed to are known empirically. Nevertheless, not every type of linguistic theory denies outright the existence of a priori propositions. If a proposition is held to be of such a nature that its truth can be ascertained simply by reference to the use of the words or symbols that occur in its expression, without any further appeal to sense experience, then, in the sense in which such a proposition is usually defined, it is an a priori proposition.

Logical truth and analyticity. Ludwig Wittgenstein's early researches into the nature of the propositions of logic provided a powerful stimulus for linguistic theories of a priori knowledge. Wittgenstein devised the thesis that a proposition of logic is a "truth-functional tautology." Any formula of propositional logic—which has been called "the ground floor of logic"—can be shown by the truth-table method to have the value "true" for every possible combination of the values "true" and "false" for its components. For example, the formula corresponding to "(If today is Monday, then tomorrow is Tuesday) implies (If tomorrow is not Tuesday, then today is not Monday)":

$(p \supset q)$	$\supset$	$(\sim q \supset \sim p)$
T T T	T	F T F
T F F	T	T F F
F T T	T	F T T
F T F	T	T T T

The importance of this is that (1) it shows that any proposition that is an instance of the formula can be known a priori, for it provides a nonempirical procedure for determining the truth-value of any such proposition; (2) it shows why any proposition of the form in question is necessarily true, for it shows that the proposition is true for every possible combination of the truth-values of its components, that is, for every possible combination of the corresponding states of affairs in the world; (3) it shows that any proposition of the form in question says nothing about the world, for since the proposition is true whatever the state of the world it does not assert or deny the existence of any particular state of the world; and (4) it shows that the a priori, necessary, and "tautological" (that is, uninformative) character of any such proposition is a consequence of the truth-table, or "extensional," definitions of the logical signs that occur in its formulation—in other words, of the conventions of the symbolism in which the proposition is expressed. Nevertheless, the truth-table method is restricted by the fact that it can be applied only to propositions that are truth-functional compounds of a finite number of component propositions, and besides these there are many other types of propositions that can be known a priori, (for example, propositions corresponding to the formulas of quantificational logic, such as "If all Europeans are white and some Europeans are Muslims, then some white men are Muslims"). Various suggestions have been made for overcoming this limitation—for example, G. H. von Wright, in his articles "Form and Content in Logic" and "On the Idea of Logical Truth," has attempted to extend the truth-table method to "the quantified logic of properties"—but the effectiveness of these suggestions is still a matter of controversy among logicians.

The logical positivists, much influenced by Wittgenstein, claimed that every proposition that can be known a priori is "analytic," in the sense that its truth follows simply from the definitions of the words or symbols that occur in its expression. They held that this alone could explain the fact that the propositions of logic and mathematics can be validated without appeal to experience. Some of the logical positivists allowed that some a priori propositions, such as "Whatever is red is colored," are true not in virtue of the logical signs that occur in their formulation (and hence are not "logical truths" in the narrow sense) but in virtue of the meanings of certain descriptive words, such as "red" and "colored" (and for this reason they are "analytic" in a wider sense). But in general it was stressed that since an analytic proposition is true—and can be known to be true—independently of any empirical evidence, such a proposition has no empirical content and cannot be used to make any factual assertion. The main difficulty with this doctrine, as we shall see, has been to obtain an adequate characterization of the notion of analyticity.

Carnap. Rudolf Carnap, in his book *Meaning and Necessity,* has given an account of logical truth ("L-truth") which is intended as an explication of the vague notion of "necessary" or "analytic" truth. Carnap considers language systems in which the vocabulary of primitive predicates and individual constants makes it possible to give a specification of the atomic sentences of the system in question. A class of sentences in the system which contains for every atomic sentence either this sentence or its negation but not both, and no other sentences, gives a complete description of a possible state of the universe considered by the language. Carnap therefore calls such a class of sentences a state description in the system. All other sentences in the language are constructed from atomic sentences by means of logical signs. A number of rules are given which determine for any sentence in the language whether it "holds" in a given state description—that is, whether it would be true if that state description were true. Carnap can then say that a sentence is "L-true" in the system if it holds in every state description in the system. This account is a formulation of Leibniz' view that a necessary truth is one that is true for every possible world, relativized to a semantic system. It is also an extension of Wittgenstein's thesis, by applying it to languages more differentiated than the language of propositional logic—for example, to languages in which sentences containing quantifiers and other logical signs occur.

Quine. W. V. Quine, in his article "Two Dogmas of Empiricism," remarks that the relevant feature of the logical truth "No unmarried man is married" is not simply that it is true as it stands but that it remains true under any and all reinterpretations of "man" and "married." He therefore characterizes a logical truth as "a statement which is true and remains true under all reinterpretations of its components other than the logical particles." Elsewhere he says that a logical truth is a true statement "involving only logical expressions essentially." Quine's account of logical truth apparently presupposes that the logical constants can only be enumerated, in which case the notion of logical truth is in effect relativized to a particular language; then it may be objected, as it may against Carnap, that the account is lacking in generality—that is, that it explains "logically true in *L*" but not "logically true." What is required to meet this objection is a general characterization of a logical constant, one, moreover, that does not make use of the notion of logical truth; it is not at all clear, however, that such a characterization can be given.

Quine argues that even assuming a satisfactory account of logical truth, an analytic statement such as "No bachelor is married" cannot be represented as a logical truth. To do that we would have to replace "bachelor" with "unmarried man" and thus analyze the statement as "No unmarried man is married." But that would involve substituting synonym for synonym, and according to Quine the only

available accounts of synonymity already make use of "logically necessary" or "analytic." Thus, the wider class of analytic statements cannot be analyzed as logical truths without presupposing an understanding of the term "analytic" or of some other related term that is equally in need of clarification. Quine also contends that an analytic statement such as "No bachelor is married" cannot be explicated as "L-true" by Carnap's procedure. He argues that in the construction of a semantic system not both, for example, "John is a bachelor" and "John is married" can be allowed to be atomic sentences; for if they were, there would be a state description in which both these sentences were true, and then "All bachelors are unmarried"—that is, "No bachelor is married"—would not be true for every state description and hence would not be L-true. But if in the construction of the language system not both of a pair of related expressions, such as "bachelor" and "married," can be allowed as primitive predicates, then it will not be possible to express the statement "No bachelor is married" in the language in question. Hence, Carnap's procedure cannot provide an explication for analytic statements of this kind.

Carnap has attempted to meet this objection in his article "Meaning Postulates." He proposes that in the construction of a semantic system, meaning postulates or rules (for example, "$(x)(Bx \supset \sim Mx)$," that is, "for every x, if x is a bachelor, then x is not married") should be stipulated in such a way as to determine all the logical relations between the intended meanings of the primitive predicates. This, he says, is not a matter of knowing certain logical relations between properties; it is entirely a matter of decision about how the predicates in question are to be used in the system. Supposing that P is the conjunction of all the meaning postulates of L, Carnap says "a sentence S_i in L is L-true with respect to $P =_{\text{Df}} S_i$ is L-implied by P (in L)." S_i is L-implied by P (in L) $=_{\text{Df}} P \supset S_i$ is L-true in $L =_{\text{Df}} S_i$ holds in every state description in which P holds (in L). It may be objected, however, that if "No bachelor is married" is L-true in virtue of a meaning postulate or rule, then for example, "John is a bachelor and John is married" should be meaningless in the language; whereas Carnap surely wishes to be able to regard this sentence as a significant denial of the first sentence and as L-false. Again, if "$(x)(Bx \supset \sim Mx)$" is introduced as a meaning postulate, then, for example, "Ba" entails "$\sim Ma$"—that is, certain atomic sentences are no longer logically independent; hence, state descriptions in which "Ba" and "Ma" are both true are no longer permissible, and this leaves as permitted state descriptions only those in which "$Ba \supset \sim Ma$" is true. Thus, the introduction of the meaning postulate in effect stipulates that the range of possible state descriptions is restricted to those in which substitution instances of "$(x)(Bx \supset \sim Mx)$" are true, and this is tantamount to simply declaring that "No bachelor is married" is L-true (true in every state description). Carnap allows these difficulties in connection with primitive relational predicates, such as "warmer." A meaning postulate for "W," which would give it the sense of being transitive, irreflexive, and asymmetrical, would have the result, for example, that "Wab" entails "$\sim Wba$." Hence, certain atomic sentences would not now be logically independent, and the range of permissible state descriptions would be restricted to those in which "*Wab* ⊃ ~*Wba*" is true. Thus, the introduction of the meaning postulate would have the effect of simply declaring that certain sentences are L-true. Carnap admits that either primitive relational predicates must be prohibited, which would be an unwelcome restriction, or the logical independence of atomic sentences must be sacrificed by the introduction of meaning postulates, and this, he says, is the same as introducing "directly L-true" as a primitive semantic concept. If the second alternative is adopted, Carnap's procedure reduces "L-true in *L*" to "directly L-true in *L*," but it leaves the latter concept undefined.

A large part of the linguistic thesis concerning a priori knowledge consists in giving a linguistic account of the notion of logical truth and of the wider notion of analyticity. As has appeared in the preceding paragraphs, the present position is that none of the available theories of logical truth is entirely satisfactory (for further criticisms, some of which can be answered, see, for example, Arthur Pap, *Semantics and Necessary Truth,* Ch. 6). Moreover, the attempt to give a linguistic explanation of the wider class of analytic statements by reducing them to logical truths has so far not been successfully carried out, mainly because of the lack of a suitable account of synonymity.

Contingent statements about linguistic usage. The simplest linguistic theory of the a priori asserts that what seem to be necessary propositions known a priori are really contingent statements about linguistic usage that are known empirically. The strength of this view is that if it is held, as most advocates of a linguistic theory hold, that it is by empirical observation of verbal usage that we come to know so-called necessary propositions, then apparently the propositions we come to know in this way must themselves be contingent and empirical. But although this view of "a priori propositions" is sometimes discussed in the literature, it is not clear that it was ever held, except for one class of apparently necessary propositions, by any well-known philosopher.

Carnap, in his early book *The Logical Syntax of Language,* held that to say of something *A* (a proposition, fact, circumstance, etc.) that it is logically necessary is a misleading way of saying that the sentence "*A*," in a particular language, is analytic. According to this view, the modal proposition "*A* is necessary," which traditionally would have been regarded as an a priori proposition, is in fact the (meta)statement "'*A*' is analytic (in *L*)"; where "*A*" is a sentence in a natural language, this metastatement would occur in "descriptive syntax" and would be a contingent statement about a certain linguistic usage. But even if this was Carnap's early view regarding certain modal propositions, it was not in general his view of the formulas of logic. At that time he held that logic consists entirely of syntactical conventions and their consequences. According to A. J. Ayer, in the first edition of *Language, Truth and Logic,* sentences that express a priori propositions "enlighten us by illustrating the way we use certain symbols" and "call attention to linguistic usages." But Ayer's intention, as he makes clear in the introduction to the second edition of his book, was not to *identify* a priori propositions with contingent verbal statements. P. F. Strawson, in

his article "Necessary Propositions and Entailment Statements," held that in such statements as "'If John is a bachelor, then he is not married' is logically necessary" and "'John is a bachelor' entails 'John is not married,'" we mention the sentences that occur in them and use the main intensional expression ("is logically necessary," "entails") to make a contingent statement about the usage of the quoted sentences. But although Strawson held this view about intensional statements, which traditionally were regarded as a priori propositions, it was not his view of "necessary propositions." As we shall see, he held that such "propositions" are in effect rules or rule formulas.

The principal objection to holding that, for example, the sentence "No bachelor is married" expresses a contingent statement about a certain linguistic usage is that this sentence evidently does not mention, and hence is not about, the words "bachelor" and "married," or the corresponding words in any other particular language. Assuming that the sentence does express a statement, it is evident that the statement expressed (that is, "what the sentence *says*") would still be true even if the words "bachelor" and "married" in English, or the corresponding words in any other language, had a different usage—and even if English or any other particular language did not exist.

Linguistic rules. Another type of linguistic theory asserts that the sentences that seem to express a priori propositions really express linguistic rules or rules of inference; that is, their function is to prescribe how certain words or symbols are to be used. Wittgenstein, in the *Tractatus Logico-philosophicus,* said "In real life a mathematical proposition is never what we want. Rather, we make use of mathematical propositions only in inferences from propositions that do not belong to mathematics to others that likewise do not belong to mathematics." And at a later time he said "'The colours green and blue cannot be in the same place simultaneously' expresses a rule of (logical) grammar." Moritz Schlick, Hans Hahn, Gilbert Ryle, Karl Britton, Ayer, and Strawson, among others, have at different times held a similar view. Strawson, for example, in "Necessary Propositions and Entailment Statements," said that the sentences that express "necessary propositions" express rules (or rule formulas, if, as in logic and mathematics, they contain variables) "to be repeated as an aid to working, verbal exercises for getting in practice for inference, or occasionally, moves in a game called constructing a deductive system."

The plausibility of this view rests partly upon the following consideration: We can argue "'All bachelors are unmarried, and John is a bachelor,' therefore 'John is unmarried'"; here "All bachelors are unmarried" is a premise of the argument, and the argument makes use of a certain rule of inference. But instead we can argue more simply "'John is a bachelor,' therefore 'John is unmarried'"; in this case "All bachelors are unmarried" is not a suppressed premise but the rule of inference that is followed in passing from the premise to the conclusion. Since the sentence "All bachelors are unmarried" is factually uninformative (compare "All bachelors are selfish," which also could be used as a rule of inference) it seems that nothing more is involved in accepting the sentence as expressing a "necessary proposition" than a readiness to make certain inferences, and in this case the use of the sentence is simply to express a rule of inference. In a similar way the principle of contradiction, which traditionally was regarded as a necessary proposition known a priori, may be understood as the rule "Do not give both the truth-value 'true' and the truth-value 'false' to the same statement at the same time"; that is, "do not contradict yourself."

It has been objected that if the sentences and formulas in question express only rules of inference then they cannot be either true or false, but it is highly implausible to maintain that every sentence like "All bachelors are unmarried"—and every formula of logic and mathematics—does not express anything that is either true or false. Moreover, if any such sentence or formula were simply a linguistic rule, then apparently anyone who understood the constituent words or symbols would understand what is involved in accepting the sentence or formula. But this is not so. Understanding such a sentence or formula, especially in logic and mathematics, very often involves understanding its deducibility relations with other sentences or formulas—and on one view deducibility relations hold only between propositions or propositional formulas. Furthermore, even if the sentences and formulas in question are rules and deducibility relations hold between them, these deducibility relations will be expressed in entailment statements (of the form "'R_1' entails 'R_2'"), and it is widely held that entailment statements are necessary propositions. Finally, it is sometimes objected that a reason needs to be given for the adoption of some linguistic rules rather than others, and although this justification may first be given in terms of convenience, it will sooner or later involve the admission that certain propositions—or perhaps, even, certain nonlinguistic facts—are necessary. For example, it may be argued that the convenience of the linguistic rule that the relational predicate "later than" is to be used in such a way that it is transitive depends not on transitivity's being a contingent feature of time relations but on its being a necessary feature. In opposition to this it may be said that our concepts of time relations depend on there being such expressions as "later than" and on these expressions having a standard use—and to say that an expression has a standard use is to say that it is used in accordance with a linguistic rule.

Linguistic usage and necessary propositions. Some adherents of the linguistic theory maintain that we find out whether a proposition is necessary by empirical observation of linguistic usage and that we use a necessary proposition in order to justify certain inferences and verbal substitutions, but that necessary propositions are nevertheless not to be identified either with empirical propositions about linguistic usage or with linguistic rules. Necessary propositions, it is held, are necessarily true because of certain contingent facts of verbal usage; but they are not descriptive of such usage, for they are not descriptive propositions at all. Necessary propositions are necessary because certain linguistic rules are presupposed, and the sentences that express them characteristically elucidate or exhibit verbal usage; but they are not in effect simply rules, for they are (necessarily) true and not arbitrary, whereas rules are neither true nor false and are in sense arbitrary. According to this view there is a distinct class of

necessary propositions, known not by intellectual intuition but by empirical observation of linguistic usage. This version of the linguistic theory has been held by, among others, John Wisdom, Norman Malcolm, Morris Lazerowitz, Ayer, and Strawson.

Nevertheless, very considerable difficulties are involved. In the first place, it seems that what we find out empirically must itself be an empirical and contingent proposition that is more or less confirmed by the available evidence. It would make no sense to say, for example, that the necessary proposition expressed by "All bachelors are unmarried" is confirmed by the available evidence. Thus apparently what we come to know empirically is not the proposition "All bachelors are unmarried," but either the modal proposition "'All bachelors are unmarried' is necessary" or the linguistic proposition "The sentence 'All bachelors are unmarried' expresses a necessary proposition." The first possibility seems to be ruled out by the following considerations: (1) There are good reasons for holding that the modal proposition "'All bachelors are unmarried' is necessary" is itself necessary. For if this modal proposition were contingent, then it would be possible for the proposition "All bachelors are unmarried" not to be necessary. But it is doubtful whether it makes sense to say of a necessary proposition that it is possible for it not to be necessary. (2) The modal proposition, whether it is necessary or contingent, entails the proposition "All bachelors are unmarried." Hence, if empirical evidence could be relevant to the modal proposition, it could be relevant to "All bachelors are unmarried." But since empirical evidence cannot be relevant to the latter (necessary) proposition, it cannot be relevant to the former (modal) proposition. Thus we are left with the other possibility—that what we come to know empirically is the linguistic proposition "The sentence 'All bachelors are unmarried' expresses a necessary proposition"—that is, the contingent fact that a particular sentence in English expresses a necessary proposition. But this by itself does nothing to explain our knowledge of necessary propositions.

In reply it may be said that a proposition is simply the meaning of a declarative sentence (and of a class of synonymous sentences) and that the meaning of a sentence is given by its characteristic use. But according to the present view the characteristic use of a sentence expressing a necessary proposition is to justify certain inferences and verbal substitutions and to elucidate or exhibit a certain verbal usage. Unlike sentences expressing contingent propositions (and these sentences also elucidate verbal usage), the sentences in question are said to be entirely nondescriptive. It is difficult, therefore, to see how the sentences that are said to express necessary propositions can express anything other than linguistic rules.

The adherents of the present view maintain that the necessity of necessary propositions "rests upon" or "presupposes" certain contingent facts of linguistic usage. But these expressions are vague and do not make clear exactly what relation is supposed to hold between contingent statements about linguistic usage and necessary propositions.

It is, perhaps, possible to account for this relation in the following way. It may be argued that (1) certain contingent statements about English, notably that "bachelor" can be correctly applied to someone only if "unmarried" can be correctly applied to that person, entail that whatever proposition is expressed by the sentence "All bachelors are unmarried," that proposition is necessary; and (2) certain other contingent statements about English, in particular that "bachelor" is correctly applied to someone if and only if that person is a bachelor and that "unmarried" is correctly applied to someone if and only if that person is unmarried, entail that the sentence "All bachelors are unmarried" expresses the proposition "All bachelors are unmarried." But (1) and (2) together entail that the proposition "All bachelors are unmarried" is necessary. Hence it seems that certain contingent statements about English entail that the proposition in question is a necessary proposition. The most serious objection to this account is that an argument of apparently the same form could be given for the words "raven" and "black" and for the sentence "All ravens are black," and it would then lead to the false conclusion that the proposition "All ravens are black" is necessary. There would, however, be an important difference between the two arguments. The second would employ the contingent statement about English that "raven" can be *truly* applied to something only if "black" can be *truly* applied, and this plainly does not entail that whatever proposition is expressed by the sentence "All ravens are black," that proposition is necessary. The first argument makes use of the idea of the *correct* application of a word. The fact that in English "bachelor" can be correctly applied to someone only if "unmarried" can be correctly applied to that person cannot be regarded as the result of a meaning rule of English, as we have seen in connection with Carnap's view. It may be suggested that the fact in question, although not the result of a meaning rule, is nevertheless one that could not be different unless there were a change in the language—that is, it is a constitutive feature of English. The problem that remains is to distinguish the linguistic changes that are due to a change in the constitution of the language from those that are due only to a change in the extralinguistic entities that the language describes.

Other difficulties. Philosophers who hold a "rationalist" view of a priori knowledge maintain that when we think of a necessary implication we are not thinking in extensional terms. For example, when we think that being red entails being colored we are not, according to these philosophers, thinking simply that every red object, past, present, and future, happens also to be colored. We are thinking—or intellectually "seeing"—that there is a necessary relation between two distinct properties. Consequently, it is held that the extensional (truth-table) logic adopted by Wittgenstein and by many adherents of the linguistic theories we have been considering cannot explain our a priori knowledge of such implications.

Further, it is objected that the Wittgenstein–Carnap account of logical truth is circular. For this account says, in effect, that a statement is logically true if and only if it is true for every possible state of the world, but evidently what is meant here is every "logically possible" state of the world, that is, every state permitted by the truths of logic. Philosophers of a rationalist persuasion conclude

that logic is prior to language or symbolism—that logical possibility, impossibility, and necessity are objective characteristics known by rational intuition. In reply it may be argued that in Wittgenstein's account (in the *Tractatus*) his picture theory of elementary propositions ensures that every proposition is either true or false and not both, and given this he can proceed to his theory of logical truth without circularity. In Carnap's account, "L-truth" is defined relative to a particular language system, and it is the conventions of the system that determine the possible states of the world describable by the language. The philosophers we are now considering would object, however, that unless certain fundamental objective necessities are assumed—in particular those expressed by the principle of identity and the principle of contradiction—neither Wittgenstein's nor Carnap's nor any other theory can be even expressed or understood.

It is also asserted (by Blanshard and Ewing) that any attempt to give a linguistic explanation of a priori knowledge can at best apply only to our knowledge of the truths expressed by analytic statements; it is argued that (1) the view that all entailment statements are analytic cannot account for the fact that deductive inference can give us new knowledge about the world, and (2) some entailments are plainly not analytic but synthetic. Those who adhere to the view that all entailment statements are analytic sometimes say that the conclusion of a deductive inference must be "implicit" or "contained in" the premises, because to assert the premises and to deny the conclusion of such an inference is to be involved in a self-contradiction. For example, it would be self-contradictory to assert "All humans are mortal, and Socrates is human" and to deny "Socrates is mortal." To this it is objected that nothing is explained by the expressions "implicit" and "contained in": "implicit" simply means "implied by," and the usual sense of "contained in" is that in which a part is contained in a whole, and evidently this is not what is meant in the present context. Furthermore, in many deductive inferences—for example, the deduction of Pythagoras' theorem from the axioms and postulates of Euclid—the *meaning* of the conclusion cannot be already contained in the *meaning* of the premises, for if it were, then in understanding the premises we should have already understood the unlimited number of conclusions that can be deduced from these premises. In any ordinary sense of "understand" and "know," it is said, we can understand the premises before we know the conclusion. To meet these objections some adherents of the analytic view of entailment statements have tried to distinguish between a psychological and a logical sense of "understand" and "know." They have argued that we can know the premises of a deductive inference without knowing the conclusion only in the psychological sense that we can think of the premises without consciously thinking of the conclusion. But in a logical sense when we think of the premises we are already thinking of the conclusion, since we cannot assert the former and deny the latter without self-contradiction. Nevertheless, it is still objected that some entailments are not analytic but plainly synthetic; some examples given to support this claim are "Whatever is colored is extended," "Nothing can be colored in different ways at the same time with respect to the same part of itself," "Every cube has twelve edges," "If x is later than y, and y is later than z, then x is later than z." As we have already remarked, it is argued that the truths expressed by such statements are not simply a consequence of certain linguistic conventions that happen to be convenient. On the contrary, the conventions of language are convenient because of the necessary features of the world which these statements express. It is concluded that these necessary synthetic truths are known by direct intellectual intuition. It is sometimes added (for example, by Ewing) that the assertion that there are no synthetic a priori statements, if it is not to be simply a consequence of certain arbitrary linguistic conventions (concerning the use of "synthetic" and "a priori"), must itself be a synthetic a priori statement. And in that case an advocate of the linguistic theory assumes the view he is denying in the course of denying it.

However, without entering into a detailed discussion of these objections, it is to be noted that in recent years linguistic philosophers themselves have come to question the distinction between "analytic" and "synthetic" statements. It may be held, for the kind of reasons advanced by Quine, that there is no satisfactory explanation of the distinction. Nevertheless, these philosophers still hold that when we "know" a statement a priori we do so as a result of certain conventions or rules or facts which are at least partly linguistic in character.

Philosophers who are opposed to the linguistic theory of the a priori also argue that by itself empirical observation of linguistic usage could never yield knowledge of necessary statements. Empirical observation of linguistic usage could establish at best that certain expressions in a language are synonymous or partially synonymous—for example, that in English "bachelor" is synonymous with "unmarried man" and partially synonymous with "unmarried." But, it is said, knowledge of the synonymity of "bachelor" and "unmarried man" is not sufficient to establish that the sentence "All bachelors are unmarried men" expresses a necessary statement. To arrive at that conclusion we have to *assume* that "All bachelors are bachelors" expresses a necessary statement and then, on the basis of the established synonymity, replace the second occurrence of "bachelors" with "unmarried men." Moreover, the additional premise that is required—that the sentence "All bachelors are bachelors" expresses a necessary statement—cannot be explained in terms of linguistic synonymity. For example, the synonymity of the two sentences "If anything is a bachelor, then it is a bachelor" and "Nothing is both a bachelor and not a bachelor" does not by itself establish that either of these sentences expresses a necessary statement. It is concluded that we need to know by rational insight the necessary truth of the principle of identity and its substitution instances. As we have seen in a preceding section of this article, those who support the linguistic theory may argue that the principle of identity is simply a general linguistic rule to the effect "Do not give both the truth-value 'true' and the truth-value 'false' to the same statement at the same time." Alternatively, they may argue that the necessity of the statement expressed by the sentence "All bachelors are unmarried" is a result of the *form* of a constitutive feature of Eng-

lish—namely, that in English "bachelor" can be correctly applied to someone only if "unmarried" can be correctly applied to that person.

Against the linguistic theory it is sometimes objected that linguistic considerations can determine at best that a particular sentence in a particular language expresses a necessary statement but that this by itself does not explain either the necessity of necessary statements or our knowledge of such statements. It has also been argued that we can know in advance that any sentence in an unfamiliar language that expresses the statement that all bachelors are unmarried expresses a necessary statement; therefore, it is said, our knowledge of necessary statements is in some sense independent of our linguistic knowledge. Similarly, in support of the view that necessity is an intrinsic property of extralinguistic propositions, it has been argued (by Pap) that (*a*) from the proposition "'There are nine planets' is a true proposition" it follows that there is something that is a true proposition, and (*b*) it does not follow that any language exists and a fortiori that any sentence expressing this proposition exists. Hence a proposition can exist, and be contingent or necessary, even if there exists no sentence that expresses this proposition. This last argument is, however, clearly fallacious. The first step consists of the inference from "'There are nine planets' is a true proposition" to "There is something that is a true proposition," and this inference would be valid only if the sentence in question designated an extralinguistic proposition—which is to assume the point at issue. The second step is that since the proposition "There are nine planets" is about planets and not about sentences, it does not entail that any sentence exists; but similarly, the proposition "There are nine planets" is not about propositions, and so it does not entail that any proposition exists either.

Bibliography

CLASSIC STATEMENTS

Ayer, A. J., *Language, Truth and Logic.* London, 1936; 2d ed., 1946.

Ayer, A. J., "Truth by Convention." *Analysis* (1936–1937).

Black, Max, "Necessary Statements and Rules." *Philosophical Review,* Vol. 67 (1958).

Britton, Karl, "Are Necessary Truths True by Convention?" *PAS,* Supp. Vol. 21 (1947).

Carnap, Rudolf, *Foundations of Logic and Mathematics.* Chicago, 1939. This is Vol. 1, No. 3, of *International Encyclopedia of Unified Science.*

Carnap, Rudolf, "Die alte und die neue Logik." *Erkenntnis,* Vol. 1 (1930–1931). Translated as "The Old and the New Logic" in A. J. Ayer, ed., *Logical Positivism.* Glencoe, Ill., 1959.

Carnap, Rudolf, *Logische Syntax der Sprache.* Vienna, 1934. Translated by Amethe Smeaton as *The Logical Syntax of Language.* New York, 1937.

Carnap, Rudolf, *Meaning and Necessity.* Chicago, 1947.

Hahn, Hans, "Logik, Mathematik und Naturerkennen," in Einheitswissenschaft series, Vol. 2. Vienna, 1933. Secs. 1–4 translated as "Logic, Mathematics and Knowledge of Nature" in Ayer, ed., *Logical Positivism* (see above).

Hempel, C. G., "Geometry and Empirical Science." *American Mathematical Monthly,* Vol. 52 (1945).

Hempel, C. G., "On the Nature of Mathematical Truth." *American Mathematical Monthly,* Vol. 52 (1945). Both Hempel articles were reprinted in Herbert Feigl and Wilfrid Sellars, eds., *Readings in Philosophical Analysis.* New York, 1949.

Ryle, Gilbert, "Why Are the Calculuses of Logic and Arithmetic Applicable to Reality?" *PAS*, Supp. Vol. 20 (1946).

Schlick, Moritz, "Is There a Factual *A Priori?*" *Wissenschaftlicher Jahresbericht der Philosophischen Gesellschaft an der Universität zu Wien für das Vereinsjahr 1930/31.* Translated by W. S. in Feigl and Sellars, eds., *Readings in Philosophical Analysis* (see above).

Wittgenstein, Ludwig, *Tractatus Logico-philosophicus.* London, 1922.

Wittgenstein, Ludwig, *Remarks on the Foundations of Mathematics.* Oxford, 1956.

CRITICISMS OF THE THEORY

Black, Max, "Conventionalism in Geometry." *Philosophy of Science* (1942).

Black, Max, "Logic and Semantics," in *Philosophical Studies—Essays in Memory of L. Susan Stebbing.* London, 1948. Reprinted under the title "Carnap on Logic and Semantics" in *Problems of Analysis.* London, 1954.

Ewing, A. C., "The Linguistic Theory of A Priori Propositions." *PAS* (1939–1940).

Kneale, W. C., "Truths of Logic." *PAS* (1945–1946).

Kneale, W. C., "Are Necessary Truths True by Convention?" *PAS*, Supp. Vol. 21 (1947).

Langford, C. H., "A Proof That Synthetic A Priori Propositions Exist." *Journal of Philosophy* (1949).

Pap, Arthur, "Necessary Propositions and Linguistic Rules." *Semantica.* Rome. 1955.

Pap, Arthur, *Semantics and Necessary Truth.* New Haven, 1958.

Quine, W. V., "Truth by Convention," in O. H. Lee, ed., *Philosophical Essays for Alfred North Whitehead.* New York, 1936. Reprinted in Feigl and Sellars, *Readings in Philosophical Analysis* (see above).

Quine, W. V., "Two Dogmas of Empiricism." *Philosophical Review* (1951). Reprinted in *From a Logical Point of View.* Cambridge, Mass., 1953. Pp. 20–46.

Whiteley, C. H., "Truth by Convention." *Analysis* (1937–1938).

Williams, D. C., "The Nature and Variety of the A Priori." *Analysis* (1937–1938).

DEFENSES OF THE THEORY

Edwards, Paul, "Do Necessary Propositions Really 'Mean Nothing'?" *The Journal of Philosophy* (1949).

Gasking, D. A. T., "Mathematics and the World." *Australasian Journal of Psychology and Philosophy* (1940). Reprinted in A. G. N. Flew, ed., *Logic and Language,* Second Series. Oxford, 1953.

Grice, H. P., and Strawson, P. F., "In Defence of a Dogma." *The Philosophical Review* (1956).

Lazerowitz, Morris, "Logical Necessity," in *The Structure of Metaphysics.* London, 1955.

Malcolm, Norman, "Are Necessary Propositions Really Verbal?" *Mind* (1940).

Malcolm, Norman, "The Nature of Entailment." *Mind* (1940).

Nagel, Ernest, "Logic Without Ontology," in Y. H. Krikorian, ed., *Naturalism and the Human Spirit.* New York, 1944. Reprinted in Feigl and Sellars, eds., *Readings in Philosophical Analysis* (see above). Also reprinted in Ernest Nagel, *Logic Without Metaphysics.* Glencoe, Ill., 1957.

Popper, Karl, "Why Are the Calculuses of Logic and Arithmetic Applicable to Reality?" *PAS*, Supp. Vol. 20 (1946).

Strawson, P. F., *Introduction to Logical Theory.* London, 1952.

Strawson, P. F., "Necessary Propositions and Entailment Statements." *Mind* (1958).

Von Wright, G. H., "Form and Content in Logic," in *Logical Studies.* London, 1957.

Von Wright, G. H., "On the Idea of Logical Truth," *ibid.*

Wisdom, John, "Metaphysics and Verification." *Mind* (1938). Reprinted in *Philosophy and Psycho-analysis.* Oxford, 1953.

ADDITIONAL REFERENCES

Bennett, Jonathan, "A Myth About Logical Necessity." *Analysis* (1961).

Black, Max, "Truth by Convention." *Analysis* (1936–1937).

Black, Max, "The Analysis of a Simple Necessary Statement." *The Journal of Philosophy* (1943).

Blanshard, Brand, *The Nature of Thought.* London, 1939.

Blanshard, Brand, *Reason and Analysis.* London and La Salle, Illinois, 1962.

Kneale, W. C., and Kneale, M., *The Development of Logic.* Oxford, 1962.

Lewy, C., "Why Are the Calculuses of Logic and Arithmetic Applicable to Reality?" *PAS*, Supp. Vol. 20 (1946).

Quinton, Anthony, "The A Priori and the Analytic." *PAS* (1964).

Urmson, J. O., "Are Necessary Truths True by Convention?" *PAS*, Supp. Vol. 21 (1947).

R. W. ASHBY

LIPPS, THEODOR (1851–1914), German psychologist and aesthetician, was born in Wallhalben in the Rhenish Palatinate. He studied in Erlangen, Tübingen, Utrecht, and Bonn. In the course of his studies his interests turned from theology to mathematics, natural science, and psychology. He held academic positions at Bonn (1877–1890), Breslau (1890–1894), and Munich (1894–1914). Lipps founded the Psychological Institute in Munich. In 1896 he was joint president (with Carl Stumpf, his predecessor as professor of philosophy in Munich) of the International Congress of Psychology. He was also editor of *Beiträge zur Aesthetik.*

Philosophy, according to Lipps, rests on an inner experience which is the basis of all the cultural sciences (*Geisteswissenschaften*). These sciences include logic, which Lipps held to be a special branch of psychology, concerned with the normative laws of thinking. Psychology is philosophy made scientific.

Lipps is of interest in the history of philosophy and psychology mainly as a proponent of the theory of empathy (*Einfühlung*). The theory was first presented in his *Raumästhetik* ("Aesthetics of Space," 1893–1897), though the term *Einfühlung* is found in earlier German philosophers (e.g., Rudolf Lotze). Empathy, according to Lipps, is an act of sympathetic projection into objects or persons distinct from the agent. He defined it as "the objectivated enjoyment of self," and meant by this that the agent discovers and identifies himself with "something psychical" in the actual qualities of an object of aesthetic contemplation or in another human being. The subject experiences his own activity, striving, and power in the object, and this is the key to aesthetic experience and to aesthetic production.

The psychological background of Lipps's theory of *Einfühlung* is somewhat complicated. He regarded psychology as the science of conscious experiences and maintained that it is of the essence of consciousness to "reach out" beyond itself. Lipps is sometimes grouped with the Austrians Franz Brentano, Alexius Meinong, and Ernst Mach, since his psychological theory is in some respects more favorable to an "act" than to a "content" psychology. He characterized experiences (*Erlebnisse*) as acts of thought whose image-contents are adequate to their objects. A sensation is the mere having of a sensory content, the content being given to the "eye of sense." When this content is inspected by the "mind's eye," the experience becomes an activity. Activities are stretches of attention or apprehension that end with a simple act of thought whereby the subject disengages an object over against himself from the original content. The "eye of sense" then gives way to the "eye of intellect" (*das geistige Auge*). Here the simple act of thought becomes extended into an activity of "apperception." There are two sorts of apperception: the activity of classifying and the activity of questioning. The first terminates in a simple act of fixation of the intellectual eye. The second type of apperception is more complex. In this activity, the object that I "question" replies to me and thereby makes demands on me, to which I may just listen or which I may positively acknowledge. If I do the latter, the activity ends in an act of judgment. There is then a parallel between apprehension (which terminates in an act of thought) and apperception (which terminates in an act of acknowledgment). If I have only an experience of the object's demands (a *Forderungserlebnis*), I have a receptive experience analogous to the "having" of a sensory content. It is a feeling of constraint or compulsion.

This theory provides the context for Lipps's use of the notion of *Einfühlung,* for the *Einfühlung* in aesthetic contemplation presupposes apperception. The object contemplated is the resultant of two components, the sensuously given and the subject's activity of apperception. The aesthetic object makes a variety of suggestions to me, suggestions which I may either accept or oppose. When I surrender myself to the suggestion and find it in accord with my natural inclinations and needs, I experience a feeling of freedom. Positive *Einfühlung* is the conscious symptom of this agreement between the stimulus and one's inner activity. It is a species of pleasure. If I cannot accept the suggestion and find it in conflict with my inner self, the experience is one of negative empathy, or pain. Where positive empathy is possible, the object is beautiful. Where I am incapable of encountering myself in the object, the form is experienced as ugly and the contemplation of it involves an inward sense of compulsion or hindrance. The laws that indicate the conditions under which a definite "echo" in the mind of the perceiver will occur are objective. The subject must be aesthetically educated to the necessary "surrender" to aesthetic experience, however.

Lipps distinguished four main types of empathy. General apperceptive empathy is shown when we animate the forms of common objects, for example, when we see a line as a movement. Empirical empathy, or empathy in nature, manifests itself when we humanize natural objects, as when we speak of a howling storm, the groaning of trees, a murmuring brook. Mood empathy (*Stimmungseinfühlung*) projects our feelings into colors and music (yellow is joyful, dark blue is serious, music is full of rejoicing, struggle, tears). Empathy for the sensible appearance of living beings is shown when we take other people's gestures, tones of voice, and other characteristics as symptomatic of their inner lives. All four types of empathy are exploited by the artist and utilized by the spectator of a work of art.

Lipps's theory may be regarded as an attempt to avoid the pure subjectivism of some aesthetic theories while granting an active role to the aesthetic perceiver. Judgments of aesthetic worth are, from one point of view, egocentric, while at the same time they need not be arbitrary. Since the object is a material form that is nevertheless expressive of spiritual content, beauty is a function, according to Lipps, of both the object and the beholder.

Works by Lipps

Lipps's main works are: *Grundtatsachen des Seelenlebens* (Bonn, 1883); *Psychologische Studien* (Heidelberg, 1885; 2d ed., Munich, 1905), translated by Herbert C. Sanborn as *Psychological Studies* (Baltimore, 1926); *Der Streit um die Tragödie* (Hamburg and Leipzig, 1891); *Raumästhetik und geometrisch-optische Täuschungen* (Leipzig, 1893–1897), which contains a discussion of over a hundred optical illusions; *Leitfaden der Psychologie* (Leipzig, 1903); *Vom Fühlen, Wollen und Denken* (Leipzig, 1902); *Aesthetik,* 2 vols. (Hamburg, 1903–1906); and a translation of Hume's *Treatise of Human Nature* as *Traktat über die menschlichen Natur,* 2 vols. (Hamburg and Leipzig, 1895–1906).

Works on Lipps

The fullest account of Lipps's psychology in English is given in E. B. Titchener's *Systematic Psychology* (New York, 1929). Lipps's theory of aesthetics is discussed in most histories of aesthetics. A bibliography of Lipps's writings (53 titles) appears in G. Anschütz, "Theodor Lipps," in *Archiv für die gesamte Psychologie,* Vol. 34 (1915), 1–23. See also J. Pikler, *Über Theodor Lipps Versuch einer Theorie des Willens* (Leipzig, 1908) and Heinrich Gothot, *Die Grundbestimmungen über die Psychologie des Gefühls bei Theodor Lipps* (Bonn, 1921).

ARNULF ZWEIG

LIPSIUS, JUSTUS (1547–1606), Flemish humanist, classical philologist, and literary critic, foremost interpreter of Stoicism in the later Renaissance, and the founder of modern Neo-Stoicism, exercised a strong influence on later moral thought. Born near Louvain, he spent most of his life in exile. At the age of 24, he renounced the Catholicism of his native land, accepting the chair of history and eloquence at the Protestant University of Jena (1572). After two years, ne returned—ostensibly as a repentant Catholic and loyal Brabantian. Again forced to flee—this time to the Calvinist Dutch—and abjuring Catholicism a second time, he accepted the chair of history at Leiden (1579). Harassed constantly by political and religious pressures, he went to the University of Louvain, becoming one of its most prominent scholars.

The vicissitudes of his life began during the time of civil war in the Low Countries. His *Tacitus* appeared at Louvain the year after his return from Jena (1575), as did his *Antiquae Lectiones.* These commentaries on Plautus signaled his adoption of a literary style modeled after Plautus, Tacitus, and Seneca. Lipsius was profoundly influenced by the thought and prose style of Seneca and devoted the remainder of his life to the study of Stoicism. This work of Lipsius, in turn, influenced Montaigne, du Vair, and Charron, and in England, Francis Bacon and Joseph Hall.

The victories of Don John of Austria (Gembloux, 1578) caused Lipsius to flee to the home of his friend Christophe Plantin, and then from Antwerp to Leiden, where he became a Calvinist. Here appeared *De Constantia* (1584), an introduction to Stoicism and his most famous work. Another well-known work, *Politicorum Libri Sex* (1589), led to a bitter dispute over its advocacy of severe methods to curb unrest. His position again became intolerable; finally, he made his peace with the Jesuits (and his old friend Martin Delrio) at Mainz (1591) and returned to Catholic Europe. He accepted the chair of history and Latin literature at Louvain (1592) and was also appointed professor of Latin at the Collegium Trilingue. He published several pieces on miracles as testimonials of faith, which added little to his fame. A projected *Fax Historica,* on Greco-Roman history and the histories of the Jews, Egyptians, and others, was never completed, although several parts were published. His last works were *Manuductio ad Stoicam Philosophiam* (1604), a miscellany of Stoic moral doctrines and survey of the *Paradoxa;* and *Physiologia Stoicorum,* a careful study of the Stoic logic and physics (1604). These make clear that Lipsius was responsible for a restored Stoic philosophy and particularly for the re-emphasis on natural philosophy. Although he counted himself more an eclectic than an orthodox follower of any school, Lipsius attempted to show in these works that there was no real difficulty in reconciling the Stoic *fatum* with the Christian emphasis on free will (whereas in *De Constantia,* this possibility had been rejected).

Works by Lipsius

Opera Omnia, 4 vols. Wesel, 1675.
Tvvo Bookes of Constancie, R. Kirk, ed., translated by Sir John Stradling. New Brunswick, N.J., 1939.

Works on Lipsius

Croll, Morris W., "Juste Lipse et le mouvement anti-cicéronien à la fin du XVIIᵉ siècle." *Revue du seizième siècle,* Vol. 2 (1914), 200–242.
Saunders, J. L., *Justus Lipsius: The Philosophy of Renaissance Stoicism.* New York, 1955.
Zanta, L., *La Renaissance du stoicisme au XVIᵉ siècle.* Paris, 1914.

JASON L. SAUNDERS

LITTRÉ, ÉMILE (1801–1881), French linguist and positivist philosopher, was born in Paris. From an early age Littré was interested in medicine and languages; and he received training in both. He is now best known for his *Dictionnaire de la langue française* (4 vols., Paris, 1863–1872) and his edition (with Charles Robin) of Nysten's *Dictionnaire de médecine, de chirurgie, de pharmacie, de l'art vétérinaire et des sciences qui s'y rapportent* (Paris, 1885). He was also prominent in radical political journalism (in *Le National* of Armand Carrel) and in freethinking circles. He became a member of the Académie des Inscriptions in 1838 and of the Académie Française in 1871, the latter over the violent objections of Bishop Dupanloup of Orléans. Littré was elected a deputy in 1871 and a senator for life in 1875.

These various activities and contacts enabled Littré to be unusually successful in his principal philosophical activity, the propagation of Auguste Comte's Positivism. He began to read Comte's *Cours de philosophie positive* in 1840, wrote a series of articles on it in *Le National* in 1844 and 1845 (published separately under the title *De la Philosophie positive* in 1845 and later reprinted in his *Fragments de philosophie positive et de sociologie contemporaine* in Paris in 1876), and for a time became Comte's "principal disciple" and heir apparent as Director of Positivism and High Priest of the Religion of Humanity. However, Littré broke with Comte in 1852 over a combination of personal and political disagreements. Thereafter he took an increasingly independent line on Comte's doctrine as well, forming a loose group of disciples—distinct from the orthodox Comtean school—that found its principal expression in the journal *La Philosophie positive,* started by Littré (with G. N. Vyrubov, the Russian positivist) in 1867. Littré himself contributed numerous important articles to the journal, but his position is stated most clearly in his *Auguste Comte et la philosophie positive* (Paris, 1863). Littré's fundamental proposition was that during the 1840s, partly for personal reasons, Comte had abandoned the positive method for the sake of a "subjective" method that vitiated all his subsequent work. Littré proposed to cleanse Positivism of the "aberrations" of Comte's "second career" by propagating the doctrine in the pure, scientific form of the *Cours.* He insisted that "there is only one stable point and that is science." Positivism as a scientific philosophy is in one aspect a system, "which comprehends everything that is known about the world, man, and societies," and in another aspect a method, "including within itself all the avenues by which these things have become known." It has, however, a practical purpose as well: to provide a "demonstrable rallying point" and a "definite direction" for mankind. Littré differed from Comte in doubting whether Positivism was yet sufficiently advanced to serve as a basis for social and political action. He also, among other things, denied ethics its place at the apex of the hierarchy of the sciences, which Comte in his later years had given it; for Littré, ethics was not an autonomous science at all. On the other hand, Littré was inclined, against Comte, to admit psychology as an independent discipline. Littré remained committed to the evolution of the positivist Religion of Humanity into a "spiritual power" but rejected Comte's prescriptions for its actual institutionalization.

Littré and his group often found it difficult to elaborate a consistent doctrine, largely because Comte's system had in fact been conceived as a unity very early in his career, and it was therefore wrong and illogical to divide his life and work in half.

Bibliography

Littré's important works also include *Conservation, révolution et positivisme* (Paris, 1852; 2d ed., 1879) and *La Science au point de vue philosophique* (Paris, 1873).
For information on Littré, see É. Caro, *M. Littré et le positivisme* (Paris, 1883), which is hostile.

W. M. SIMON

LOCKE, JOHN (1632–1704), English empiricist and moral and political philosopher. He was born in Wrington, Somerset. Locke's father, an attorney and for a time a clerk to the justices of the peace in Somerset, fought on the parliamentary side in the first rebellion against Charles I. Locke was reared in a liberal Puritan family and early learned the virtues of temperance, simplicity, and aversion to display. Though his father was severe and remote from him in early youth, as Locke matured they became close friends.

In 1646 Locke entered Westminster School, where he studied the classics, Hebrew, and Arabic. Little time was given at Westminster to science and other studies, and its harsh discipline, rote learning, and excessive emphasis on grammar and languages were later condemned by Locke.

In 1652 Locke was elected to a studentship at Christ's Church, Oxford. He received his B.A. in 1656 and remained in residence for the master's degree. He was not happy with the study of Scholastic philosophy and managed to inform himself of many new areas of thought. As a master, Locke lectured in Latin and Greek and in 1664 was appointed censor of moral philosophy.

His father's death in 1661 left Locke with a small inheritance and some independence. During these years he became acquainted with many men who were to have a profound influence upon his life. From Robert Boyle Locke learned about the new sciences and the corpuscular theory, as well as the experimental and empirical methods. Confronted with the choice of taking holy orders, continuing as a don, or entering another faculty, Locke chose medicine. Though well trained, he never practiced medicine, nor was he permitted to take the medical degree, which would have permitted him to teach the profession, until 1674, although in 1667 he began to collaborate with the great physician Thomas Sydenham, who deeply influenced him.

In 1665 Locke was sent on a diplomatic mission accompanying Sir Walter Vane to the elector of Brandenburg at Cleves. He subsequently rejected a secretaryship under the earl of Sandwich, ambassador to Spain, and returned to Oxford. It was at this time that his interests began to turn seriously to philosophy. Descartes was the first philosopher whom Locke enjoyed reading and the first to show him the possibility of viable alternatives to the Schoolmen.

Locke had met Lord Ashley, earl of Shaftesbury, in 1662 at Oxford. They found much pleasure in each other's company, and the astute Shaftesbury quickly recognized Locke's talents. In 1667 he invited Locke to live with him in London as his personal physician. Later Locke served him well in many other capacities. Under Shaftesbury Locke found himself in the center of the political and practical affairs of the day. He assisted Shaftesbury in the framing of a constitution for the colony of Carolina. For a time he was secretary for the presentation of benefices and then secretary to the Council of Trade and Plantations. Locke was always at home in the world of practical affairs, and many of his philosophical attitudes reflect this interest. At the same time he became a fellow in the Royal Society, where he continued to be in touch with learning.

Locke, never robust in health, in 1675 went on a prolonged visit to France, where he made many friends and came into contact with the foremost minds of his day. His studies and criticisms of Descartes were deepened under the influence of various Gassendists.

In 1679 Locke returned to an England torn by intense political conflicts. Shaftesbury, who had become the leader of the parliamentary opposition to the Stuarts, alternated between political power and impotence. The close association with Shaftesbury brought Locke under suspicion; he was kept under surveillance. Shaftesbury was tried for treason in 1681, but acquitted. He subsequently fled England for Holland, where he died in 1683. Locke, at Oxford, uncertain of his position and fearing persecution, also fled England, arriving in Holland in September 1683. The king had demanded that Locke be deprived of his studentship at Oxford, and news of this demand caused Locke to prolong his stay. After the death of Charles II and the ascension of James II to the throne, the duke of Monmouth

attempted a rebellion, which failed. Locke was denounced as a traitor, and the crown demanded of the Dutch that he be returned to England. No great effort was made to comply with the demand, and Locke remained in Holland.

During his stay in Holland, Locke again acquired a wide circle of distinguished friends and wrote extensively. He contributed an article as well as reviews to the *Bibliothèque universelle* of Jean Leclerc; these were his first published works. He wrote in Latin the *Epistola de Tolerantia*, which was published anonymously in 1689 and translated as the *First Letter Concerning Toleration*. He also worked assiduously on the *Essay Concerning Human Understanding*, which he had been writing off and on since 1671. In 1688 the *Bibliothèque universelle* published an abstract of the *Essay*.

These activities did not prevent him from being deeply engaged in politics. The plot to set William of Orange on the throne of England was well advanced in 1687, and Locke was, at the very least, advising William in some capacity. The revolution was accomplished in the fall of 1688, and in February 1689 Locke returned to England, escorting the princess of Orange, who later became Queen Mary.

In 1689 and 1690 Locke's two most important works, the *Essay Concerning Human Understanding* and the *Two Treatises of Government*, were published. From 1689 to 1691 Locke shuttled between London and Oates, the home of Sir Francis and Lady Masham, the daughter of Ralph Cudworth. He had declined an ambassadorial post only to accept a position as commissioner on the Board of Trade and Plantations. Apparently his practical wisdom was invaluable, for when he wished in 1697 to resign because of ill health, he was not permitted to do so. He remained until 1700, serving when he could, although his health was extremely poor.

In 1691 Locke made Oates his permanent residence at the invitation of Lady Masham. It was, for the aging Locke, a place of refuge and joy; there he received visits from Newton, Samuel Clarke, and others. These were productive years for Locke. *Some Thoughts Concerning Education* appeared in 1693. The second edition of the *Essay* was published in 1694. In the following year the *Reasonableness of Christianity* was published anonymously. He answered criticism of it in *A Vindication of the Reasonableness of Christianity* (London, 1695) and in a second *Vindication* in 1697. From 1697 to 1699 Locke engaged in an epistolary controversy with Edward Stillingfleet, bishop of Worcester.

However, Locke's health steadily failed him. After 1700, when the fourth edition of the *Essay* appeared, he remained almost constantly at Oates. He was engaged in editing the *Two Treatises of Government*, for no edition which pleased him had yet appeared. In his last years he wrote extensive commentaries on the epistles of St. Paul, which were published posthumously. On October 28, 1704, while Lady Masham was reading the Psalms to him, Locke died. Lady Masham wrote of him, "His death was like his life, truly pious, yet natural, easy and unaffected."

Character. The Lovelace Collection of Locke's personal papers in the Bodleian Library, Oxford, shows that Locke's character and personality were more complex than had been suspected. The great affection and respect which so many men and women had for him are testimony to his charm and wisdom. That he was modest, prudent, pious, witty, and eminently practical was long known. But he was also extremely secretive and apparently given to excessive suspicion and fears. When his lifelong friend, James Tyrrell, voiced his suspicion that Locke had written the *Two Treatises*, Locke was evasive and would not admit the fact. When he suspected that Tyrrell was spreading the report that Locke was the author, Locke angrily demanded an explanation. At the same time, Locke showed great affection for many friends and a real fondness for children. In maturity he could not abide religious intolerance or suffer tyranny. He was passionately devoted to truth and strove constantly to state the truth as he saw it, but always with a caution that distrusted all dialectic, even his own, when it appeared to go beyond common sense.

Influences on Locke. Locke's philosophy is grounded in medieval thought, though he, like Descartes, turned away from it as far as possible. The Cambridge Platonists, notably Ralph Cudworth and Benjamin Whichcote, influenced him greatly with respect to religious tolerance, empirical inquiry, and the theory of knowledge. Locke was indebted to Richard Hooker in his political thought. Hobbes probably influenced him somewhat, though Locke was concerned not to be classed as a Hobbist. The two most important philosophical influences upon him were Descartes and Pierre Gassendi. From Descartes he learned much that is incorporated in the *Essay*, and in Gassendi and the Gassendists he found support to challenge the doctrine of innate ideas and the radical rationalistic realism of Descartes. Gassendi helped to convince Locke both that knowledge begins in sensation and that intellect, or reason, is essential to the attainment of truth and knowledge.

"ESSAY CONCERNING HUMAN UNDERSTANDING"

Locke's position in the history of Western thought rests upon *The Essay Concerning Human Understanding* and *Two Treatises of Government*. He spent long years working out the thought of each, and he carefully and lovingly revised and corrected them for subsequent editions. Locke wrote two drafts of his *Essay* in 1671, and in 1685 he wrote a third. The first edition, though dated 1690, appeared in late 1689. During the years between 1671 and 1689 Locke revised and reorganized many of his original concepts. In response to criticisms of the first edition of the *Essay*, he introduced a number of changes in subsequent editions. This long period of gestation and Locke's subsequent modifications of his initial public statement disclose primarily the refinement and clarification of his philosophy by way of certain important additions, but never by a radical or fundamental departure from his basic position.

From the first appearance of the *Essay* Locke was criticized for being inconsistent in his theory of knowledge, vague in the presentation and development of many of his ideas, and wanting in thoroughness in developing other ideas. But these criticisms have in no way diminished either the importance or the influence of the *Essay* on subsequent thinkers. By no means the first of the British

empiricists, Locke nonetheless gave empiricism its firmest roots in British soil, where it still proudly flourishes. It must be remembered that Locke was also a rationalist, though one of quite different orientation from such Continental thinkers as Descartes, Spinoza, and Malebranche. In Locke many strands of traditional thought are rewoven into a new fabric. Subsequent thinkers, notably Berkeley, Hume, and Kant, perhaps fashioned more coherent and consistent systems, but it is doubtful whether they were more adequate to what Locke might have called the plain facts. Locke's tendency toward inconsistency can be seen in his definition of knowledge as "the perception of the connection and agreement, or disagreement and repugnancy, of any of our ideas" (*Essay*, IV.i.2). This is plainly incompatible with his later contention that we have intuitive knowledge of our own existence, demonstrative knowledge of God's existence, and sensitive knowledge of the existence of particular things. Nonetheless, Locke would not abandon his position for the sake of consistency alone. He was persuaded that common sense and the facts justified his conviction and that whatever faults there were in his position lay in the difficulty of stating a coherent theory of knowledge, not in the reality of things. If this made him an easy prey to a skillful dialectician, like Berkeley, it also left him closer to the common conviction of most of us when we think about anything other than epistemology. It is this viewpoint, almost unique in philosophy, that accounts for the abiding interest in Locke's thought and the great extent of his influence despite the shortcomings of his work.

Purpose of the "Essay." In the "Epistle to the Reader" Locke related that some friends meeting in his chamber became perplexed about certain difficulties that arose in their discourse about a subject (left unnamed). He proposed that before they could inquire further, "it was necessary to examine our own abilities and see what objects our understandings were, or were not, fitted to deal with." This discussion in 1670 or 1671 first started Locke on the inquiries that were to continue intermittently for twenty years. What Locke first set down for the next meeting is not known, unless it was Draft A (1671) of the *Essay*. That the initial suggestion became the abiding purpose of the *Essay* is clear from Locke's assertion that his purpose was "to inquire into the original, certainty, and extent of human knowledge, together with the grounds and degrees of belief, opinion, and assent" (I.i.2). At the same time he disavowed any intention to examine "the physical consideration of the mind, . . . wherein its essence consists, or by what motions of our spirits or alterations of our bodies we come to have any sensation by our organs or any ideas in our understandings, and whether those ideas do in their formation any or all of them depend on matter or no" (I.i.2).

Locke did not, in fact, offer any detailed or explicit accounts of these matters. He would have considered that a subject for natural philosophy. Nonetheless, he did, as indeed he had to, deal with the physical considerations of the mind, as well as all the other matters mentioned.

From the outset Locke was persuaded that our understanding and knowledge fall far short of all that exists; yet he was equally certain that men have a capacity for knowledge sufficient for their purposes and matters enough to inquire into. These convictions, pragmatic and utilitarian, set Locke apart from most of the other major philosophers of the seventeenth century, who, impressed by the new developments in mathematics and the new physical sciences, boldly plunged ahead with a rationalistic realism in the belief that their new methods would enable them in large measure to grasp reality. Locke saw that the very advances made in the new sciences put reality farther from the reach of the human mind. This did not make Locke a nominalist or an idealist in any modern sense; rather, he persistently affirmed the real objective existence of things or substances. What he denied was that the human understanding could know with certainty the real essences of substances. If "ideas" stand between reality and the understanding, it is to link them, even if only under the form of appearances. It is not to obliterate any connection between them or to justify a negation of substance—God, mind, or matter.

Ideas. The key term in Locke's *Essay* is "idea," which he defined as ". . . whatsoever is the object of the understanding when a man thinks, . . . whatever is meant by phantasm, notion, species, or whatever it is which the mind can be employed about in thinking" (I.i.8). Any object of awareness or of consciousness must be an idea. But then how can we have any knowledge of anything other than ideas and their relationships? It is true that Locke spoke of ideas as the "materials of knowledge." Yet knowledge itself, when possessed and made the object of the mind, must be an idea. For example, to perceive that *A* is equal to *B* is to perceive the agreement between *A* and *B*. This agreement as perceived must be an idea, or it cannot be an object of the mind when it thinks. Despite this difficulty Locke clung tenaciously to his term "idea" in his disputes with Stillingfleet. He actually intended something other than he stated, namely, that knowledge is an operation, an activity of the mind, not initially one of its objects. It would have served his purpose better had he spoken of "knowing" rather than of "knowledge," even though this would not have entirely removed the difficulty, since to set the mind at a distance where we may look at it, in order to know what knowledge is, is still to have an idea.

Locke, however, went beyond ideas to assume the real existence of things, substances, actions, processes, and operations. Ideas, except when they are the free constructs of the mind itself, signify and represent, however imperfectly, real existences and events. So deep was Locke's conviction on this point that no argument could shake him, although he constantly tried to remove the difficulties implicit in his definitions of "ideas" and "knowledge." This conviction is evident in the first two books of the *Essay,* in which Locke inquired into the origin of our ideas.

No innate ideas. It was Locke's central thesis, developed extensively in Book II of the *Essay,* that we get all our ideas from experience. The whole of the first book is given to an overlong criticism, at times not germane to the subject, of the doctrine that we have innate ideas and innate knowledge.

Locke contended that there are no innate principles stamped upon the mind of man and brought into the world by the soul. In the first place, the argument that people have generally agreed that there are innate ideas, even if true, would not demonstrate the innateness of ideas. Moreover, there are no principles to which all give assent, since principles such as "Whatever is, is" and "It is impossible for the same thing to be and not to be" are not known to children, idiots, and a great part of mankind, who never heard or thought of them. Locke here assumed that innateness was equivalent to conscious perceiving and argued that to be in the mind is to be perceived or to be readily recalled to perception. Locke allowed that there is a capacity in us to know several truths but contended that this lent no support to the argument that they are innate.

To argue that all men know and assent to certain truths when they come to the use of reason proves nothing, since they will also come to know many truths that are not innate. It would appear, then, that all truth is either innate or adventitious. Again, why should the use of reason be necessary to discover truths already innately in the mind? Locke allowed that the knowledge of some truths is in the mind very early, but observation shows such truths are about particular ideas furnished by the senses; for example, a child knows the difference between the ideas of sweet and bitter before it can speak and before it knows abstract ideas. Even assent at first hearing is no proof of innateness, for many truths not innate will be assented to as soon as understood.

On the contrary, the senses first furnish us with particular ideas, which the mind by degrees becomes familiar with, remembers, and names. The mind subsequently abstracts from these particular ideas and gives names to general ideas. Thus, general ideas, general words, and the use of reason grow together, and assent to the truth of propositions depends on having clear and distinct ideas of the meaning of terms. Locke held it to be evident that particular propositions are known before the more universal and with as much certainty.

We have natural faculties or capacities to think and to reason. This is not, however, the same thing as having innate ideas, for if anyone means by innate ideas nothing but this natural capacity, he uses terms, according to Locke, in a manner plainly contrary to common usage.

In a similar fashion, Locke argued that we have no innate moral or practical principles, for there is no universal agreement about such principles; great varieties of human vice have been at one time or place considered virtues. We all have a desire for happiness and an aversion to misery, but these inclinations give us no knowledge or truth. Locke was persuaded that there are eternal principles of morality, which men may come to know through the use of reason about experience. This, however, is far from proving them innate.

In the third chapter of Book I Locke argued that no principles can be innate unless the ideas contained in them are innate, that is, unless men can be conscious of them. Impossibility and identity are hardly innate, yet without them we cannot understand the supposedly innate principle of identity, that it is impossible for the same thing both to be and not be. Similarly, the proposition that God is to be worshipped cannot be innate, for the notion of God is so diverse that men have great difficulty agreeing on it, while some men have no conception of God whatsoever.

Locke's target. Who was Locke criticizing in his long and repetitive attack on the doctrine of innate ideas? Was the position he denounced held by anyone in the form in which he presented the theory? Why did he examine the question at such length?

Since the *Essay* was first published tradition has held that Locke's target was Descartes and the Cartesians. Certainly Leibniz thought so, as did others after him. In the late nineteenth century, critics pointed to Locke's own rationalism and noted that his recognition of men's natural faculties and innate powers to think and reason is not far from the position of Descartes, who wrote, "Innate ideas proceed from the capacity of thought itself," and "I never wrote or concluded that the mind required innate ideas which were in some sort different from its faculty of thinking." Various other possible objects of Locke's attacks were suggested, the Cambridge Platonists, certain groups in the universities, and various clergymen. Recently R. I. Aaron has argued persuasively that the older tradition, that Descartes, the Cartesians, and certain English thinkers were the targets of Locke's attack, is the correct one and that Locke was not simply striking at a straw man of his own making.

Reasons for attacking innate ideas. Locke suggested that the doctrine of innate ideas lends itself to a certain authoritarianism and encourages laziness of thought, so that the foundations of knowledge are not likely to be examined. The expression "innate ideas" is an unfortunate one and admittedly extremely vague. It carries with it the suggestion that certain ideas and knowledge are, in Locke's sense, imprinted on the mind and are in no way dependent on experience. Certainly there are passages in Descartes which strongly suggest that certain ideas are innately in the mind, and more than a few thinkers took this to be Descartes's meaning. Furthermore, Locke wished to prepare the ground for his own thesis that all ideas and all knowledge are acquired. If he overemphasized the crude sense of the theory of innate ideas, he also showed that even the refined doctrine is unnecessary in accounting for knowledge.

There is another point that Locke discussed later in the *Essay.* Descartes asserted that the essence of the mind is to think. To Locke this meant that the mind could not both be and not think. He argued that the mind does not think always and that its real essence cannot be thinking. If the mind thinks always, either some ideas must be innate or the mind comes into being only after it has been furnished with ideas by experience. Neither alternative was acceptable to Locke.

Source of ideas. Locke, in his positive thesis in Book II, valiantly and sometimes awkwardly endeavored to show that every idea we have is ultimately derived from experience, either from sensation or reflection. Locke began by asserting that a man is conscious of two things, the fact "that he thinks" and "the ideas" in the mind about which he thinks. Locke's initial concern was with the question of how a man comes by his ideas; and he made an assumption in terms of several similes. "Let us then suppose the mind to be, as we say, white paper, void of all characters,

without any ideas. How comes it to be furnished? . . . Whence has it all the materials of reason and knowledge?" (II.i.2). Locke replied to his own questions that we get all our ideas from experience, the two fountainheads of which are sensation and reflection. Our senses are affected by external objects (bodies) and afford us ideas, such as yellow, white, heat, cold, soft, hard, bitter, and sweet. Perceiving the operations of our own minds when we reflect, we are furnished with ideas of perception, thinking, doubting, believing, reasoning, knowing, and willing.

The ideas that are furnished by experience are the materials of reason and knowledge. These materials are either the immediate objects of sense, such as color, or the unexamined but direct awareness of such acts as doubting or knowing. Locke's meaning becomes explicitly clear in his account of solidity. He held that we get the idea of solidity by touch. "That which . . . hinders the approach of two bodies, when they are moving one towards another, I call solidity" (II.iv.1). He sharply distinguished this sense from the purely mathematical use of the term. Impenetrability is an acceptable alternative name for solidity. It is clearly distinct from space and hardness. After an extensive discussion Locke stated, "If anyone asks me what this solidity is, I send him to his senses to inform him. Let him put a flint or a football between his hands and then endeavour to join them, and he will know" (II.iv.6). All philosophical and scientific discourse about solidity, however complex and sophisticated it may be, must ultimately refer back to that from which it began, namely the experience or sensation we have when we put something such as a flint or a football between our hands. Similarly, we cannot by discourse give a blind man the idea of color or make known what pain is to one who never felt it. All knowledge about the physics of light and color or sound refers back to what we perceive when we see and hear. It is in this sense, then, that we get all our ideas from sensation and reflection. Locke nowhere, however, suggested that we can or should stop there. Once the mind is furnished with ideas, it may perform various operations with them.

Ideas and the real world. Throughout the first book of the *Essay* Locke assumed the real existence of an external physical world and the substantial unity of a man in body and mind. He undoubtedly accepted the thesis that the external physical world is corpuscular and acts by bodies in motion that possess only those qualities which Locke called primary. Locke spoke of secondary qualities as powers in bodies to produce in our minds ideas that are signs of these powers but that in no way resemble the powers which produce them. Often he suggested that if we had the means of observing the minute motions of the particles making up gross bodies, we might have a clearer notion of what we mean when we call secondary qualities powers. Locke's position here is physical realism. It is not simply a manner of speaking. The ideas we have do represent real things outside of us and do constitute the links by which we know something of the external physical world.

Identity. Among the bodies that exist are those of plants, animals, and men. Existence itself constitutes the principle of individuation. Identity is not applied in the same way to a mass of matter and a living body. The identity of an oak lies in the organization of its parts, which partake of one common life. So it is with animals. Again, "the identity of the same man consists: viz. in nothing but a participation of the same continued life, by constantly fleeting particles of matter, in succession vitally united to the same organized body" (II.xxvii.6).

Origin of sensation. With these controlling hypotheses in the *Essay* in view, we may return to Locke's invitation to consider the mind as a blank sheet of paper without any ideas. Is a mind without ideas anything but a bare capacity to receive ideas? If we ask what a man is without ideas, we can say he is an organized body existing in a world of other bodies and interacting with them. Experience is a matter of contact of the organized human body with other bodies before it is a matter of sensation or perception. Not every body impinging on our body gives rise to sensation; if it does not, we take no notice of it. However, if some external bodies strike our senses and produce the appropriate motions therein, then our senses convey into the mind several distinct perceptions. How this takes place Locke avoided considering, but that it takes place he was certain; a man, he asserted, first begins to think "when he first has any sensation" (II.i.23).

Simple and complex ideas. Locke proceeded to distinguish between simple and complex ideas. A simple idea is "nothing but one uniform appearance or conception in the mind, and is not distinguishable into different ideas" (II.ii.1). A color seen, a sound heard, warmth felt, an odor smelled, are all simple ideas of sense. Once it is furnished with a number of simple ideas, the mind has the power to repeat, compare, and unite them into an almost infinite variety of combinations; but it is utterly incapable of inventing or framing a new simple idea. Thus, with respect to simple ideas the mind is mostly passive; they are simply given in experience. The ideas are given not in isolation from each other but in combinations, as when we simultaneously feel the warmth and softness of wax or the coldness and hardness of ice; nevertheless, simple ideas are distinct from each other in that the mind may mark off each from the other, however united the qualities may be in the things that cause the simple ideas in the mind. Moreover, only those qualities in things that produce ideas in us can ever be imagined at all. Thus, our knowledge of existence is limited by the ideas furnished by experience. Had we one sense less or more than we now do, our experience and knowledge would be respectively decreased or increased.

We have certain ideas, such as color or odor, from one sense only; others, like figure and number, from more than one sense. Reflection alone provides us with experience of thinking and willing. Other ideas, such as pleasure, pain, power, existence, and unity, we have from both sensation and reflection.

Primary and secondary qualities. Locke made a second basic distinction—between primary and secondary qualities. In doing so he clearly went beyond ideas. He wrote, "Whatsoever the mind perceives in itself, or is the immediate object of perception, thought, or understanding, that I call idea; and the power to produce any idea in our mind, I call quality of the subject wherein that power is" (II.viii.8). Primary qualities, he argued, are utterly inseparable from

body. They are known to be primary because sense constantly finds them there if body can be perceived at all, and the mind by critical reflection finds them inseparable from every particle of matter. Solidity, extension, figure, and mobility are all primary qualities. Our ideas of these qualities resemble the qualities themselves, and these qualities really exist in body, whether or not they are perceived. Berkeley was to show that to speak of resemblance supposes that a comparison, an observation, can be made. Locke was aware of the difficulty, as is shown in his *Examimination of Malebranche.* Apparently he believed it was the only explanation plausible in spite of its difficulties.

Secondary qualities, in Locke's terms, were nothing but powers to produce various sensations. Bodies do so by the action of their bulk, figure, and texture, and by the motion of their insensible parts on our senses. Somehow they produce in us such ideas as color, odor, sound, warmth, and smell. These ideas in no way resemble the qualities of bodies themselves. They are but signs of events in real bodies. Locke also frequently called these ideas secondary qualities. He would have been clearer had he called them sensory ideas of secondary qualities, preserving the distinction between qualities as attributes of a subject and ideas as objects in the mind. A third class of qualities (sometimes called tertiary) is the power of a body to produce a change in another body, for example, the power of the sun to melt wax.

Nowhere is Locke's physical realism more evident than in his distinction between primary and secondary qualities. Whatever epistemological difficulties the distinction might entail, Locke was persuaded that the new physics required it. Indeed, the distinction was made by Boyle, Descartes, Galileo, and others before him and was thoroughly familiar in his day. Admittedly there is a problem in the assertion that a certain motion in body produces in us the idea of a particular color. Nevertheless, Locke was persuaded that it was so. In such difficult cases Locke fell back upon the omnipotence and wisdom of God and the fact that our knowledge is suited to our purpose.

Ideas of reflection. Locke observed that perception is the first faculty of the mind and without it we know nothing else. Hence, the idea of perception is the first and simplest idea we have from reflection. What perception is, is best discovered by observing what we do when we see, hear, or think. Locke added that judgment may alter the interpretation we make of the ideas we receive from sensation. Thus, if a man born blind gains his sight, he must learn to distinguish between a sphere and a cube visually, though he can do so readily by touch. By habit the ideas of sensation are gradually integrated into the unified experience of complex ideas, and by judgment we come to expect things that look a certain way to also feel or smell a certain way. It is worth noting that Locke was persuaded that animals have perception and are not, as Descartes held, mere automatons.

Memory and contemplation. The second faculty of the mind that Locke held indispensable to knowledge is the retention manifested in both contemplation and memory. Contemplation consists in holding an idea before the mind for some time. Memory, however, gave Locke some difficulties. He asserted that "our ideas being nothing but actual perceptions in the mind—this laying up of our ideas in the repository of the memory signifies no more but this: that the mind has a power in many cases to revive perceptions which it has once had, with this additional perception annexed to them, that it has had them before" (II.x.2). The inadequacy of this statement is at once evident. It proposes no more than a kind of subjective conviction that may often be in error. Locke's analysis of memory was more psychological than philosophical. He passed over the consideration of how memory is possible at all and the criteria by which a true memory may be distinguished from a false memory. He did say, however, that attention, repetition, pleasure, and pain aid memory and are the conditions under which memory is strengthened or weakened. Again he asserted that animals have memory.

Other ideas of reflection. Other faculties of the mind are discerning and distinguishing one idea from another, comparing and compounding, naming, and abstracting. Locke considered each point also in respect to animals, holding, for example, that animals compare and compound ideas only to a slight extent and do not abstract ideas at all. At the conclusion of this chapter (II.xi.15) Locke asserted that he thought he had given a "true history of the first beginnings of human knowledge."

Complex ideas. Locke next considered complex ideas. Just as the mind observes that several combinations of simple ideas are found together, so too, it can by its own action voluntarily join several simple ideas together into one complex idea. There are three categories of complex ideas—modes, substances, and relations. Modes are dependencies or affections of substances. Simple modes are variations or different combinations of one simple idea, whereas in mixed modes several distinct ideas are joined to make a complex idea. Ideas of substances represent distinct particular things subsisting in themselves. Complex ideas of relation consist in comparing one idea with another.

This classification is not entirely satisfactory because ideas of modes invariably entail relations in the broadest sense. Locke seems to have been closer to Aristotle than to modern usage in his employment of the term "relation." Under modes Locke included space, duration and time, number, infinity, motion, sense qualities, thinking, pleasure and pain, power, and certain mixed modes. Under substance he placed the idea of substance in general, the ideas of particular substances, and collective ideas of substances. In the category of relation, he considered a number of ideas, including cause and effect, relations of place and time, identity and diversity, and others that he classified as proportional, natural, instituted, and moral.

The greater number of these concepts have in other philosophies been credited with some a priori and extraempirical character. They are not direct objects of sensory experience; and they appear to have a certainty not found in the mere coexistence of sensory ideas. They are more abstract and universal than the simple ideas of sensation and reflection. Locke's broad use of the term "ideas" tends to confuse and obscure the distinction between sensory percept and concept. Nevertheless, Locke undertook to show how the mind actively constructs these complex ideas, abstract and conceptual though they may

be, out of the materials of knowledge, the simple ideas of sensation and reflection. In this undertaking Locke's rationalism was most evident, for he held that while the mind constructs complex ideas, it cannot do so arbitrarily. In this sense, Locke could claim for them an objective reality.

The mode of space. Examination here will be limited to only those complex ideas that are most important and difficult. Among modes, only space, duration, number, thinking, and power will be considered. Locke contended that the modifications of a simple idea are as much distinct ideas as any two ideas can be. Space in its first manifestation is a simple idea, since in seeing and touching we immediately perceive a distance between bodies and the parts of bodies. Though the idea of space constantly accompanies other sensory ideas, it is distinguishable from them. All our modes of the idea of space derive from the initial sensory experience. Thus space considered as length is called distance, considered three-dimensionally is capacity, considered in any manner is termed extension. Each different distance, especially when measured by stated lengths, is a distinct idea, including the idea of immensity, which consists in adding distance to distance without ever reaching a terminus. So too, figure allows an endless variety of modifications of the simple idea of space. Place is distance considered relative to some particular bodies or frame of reference.

Locke disagreed with Descartes's assertion that extension is the essence of matter, although he agreed that we cannot conceive of a body that is not extended. But a body has solidity, and solidity is distinct from the notion of space; for the parts of space are inseparable in thought and in actuality and are immovable, whereas a solid body may move and its parts are separable. Descartes's argument that the physical universe is a plenum was dismissed by Locke as unsound, for there is no contradiction in the conception of a vacuum. If body is not infinite, we can conceive of reaching out beyond the physical limits of the universe to a place unoccupied by matter. The idea of pure space is necessarily infinite, for we can conceive of no limit or terminus to it. Locke professed not to know whether space was a substance or an accident and offered to answer the question when the ideas of substance and accident were clarified. He was more confident of the idea of pure space than he was of the traditional philosophical categories. Locke placed a great load on the simple idea of space, and by the activity of his reason he went beyond the bounds of possible experience.

Duration and time. The idea of duration is broader than that of time. If we consider the train of ideas that passes through our minds, we observe that one idea constantly succeeds another, and so we come by the idea of succession. By reflection we acquire the idea of duration, which we may then apply to motion and sensory ideas. Where there is no perception of the succession of ideas in our minds, there is no sense of time. Locke insisted that motion does not furnish us with the idea of duration, and he directly opposed Aristotle's definition that "time is the measure of motion with respect to before and after."

Once we have the idea of duration, we need a measure of common duration. Time is the consideration of duration marked by certain measures such as minutes, hours, days. The most convenient measures of time must be capable of division into equal portions of constantly repeated periods. We cannot be certain of the constancy of motions or of the time spans they measure. Locke was concerned with liberating time from motion. Consequently, he argued that we must consider duration itself as "going on in one constant, equal, uniform course; but none of the measures of it which we make use of can be known to do so" (II.xiv.21). Once time is liberated from motion, Locke held, we can conceive of infinite duration even beyond creation. Thus we can expand by endless addition the idea of duration to come to the notion of eternity.

Were it not for the implicit realism of Locke's arguments, it would be possible to agree with those scholars who have seen in his arguments about duration and expansion a vague groping for a position somewhat similar to Kant's a priori aesthetic. For both men, space becomes the framework of body, and duration or time the structure of the mind, or the inner sense.

Number. The idea of unity is everywhere suggested to the mind, and no idea is more simple. By repeating it we come to the complex modes of number. Once we have learned to perform this operation, we cannot stop short of the idea of infinity. Locke regarded both finite and infinite as modes of quantity. Because we are able to apply the idea of number to space and time, we are capable of conceiving of them as infinite. The idea of infinity is essentially negative, since we come to it by enlarging our ideas of number as much as we please and discover that there is no reason ever to stop. We may know that number, space, and duration are infinite, but we cannot positively know infinity itself. Locke insisted that however remote from the simple ideas of sensation and reflection these ideas may be, they have their origin in those simple ideas.

The modes of thinking. Locke gave only casual and formal attention to the modes of thinking, such as sensation, remembrance, recollection, contemplation, attention, dreaming, reasoning, judging, willing, and knowing. Equally superficial was his consideration of modes of pleasure and pain, which consisted of little more than definitions of various emotions.

Power. The chapter on power is the longest in the *Essay*, and Locke felt obliged to rewrite portions of it time and again, for each new edition.

It is evident that power is not perceived as such. Locke observed that the mind, taking note of the changes and sequences of our ideas and "concluding from what it has so constantly observed to have been, that the like changes will for the future be made in the same things, by like agents, and by the like ways . . . comes by that idea which we call power" (II.xxi.1). From this it hardly seems that the idea of power is a simple idea, unless Locke meant no more than that the idea of power is only the observation of the regular order and connection of our ideas. But Locke wrote that "since whatever change is observed, the mind must collect a power somewhere able to make that change, as well as a possibility in the thing itself to receive it" (II.xxi.4). Here the idea of power is a necessary idea of reason, grounded in certain other experiences. Locke never made clear this distinction. He admitted that the idea of power included some kind of relation but insisted that it was a simple idea.

Power is both passive and active. Whether or not matter has any active power, Locke pointed out, we have our idea of active power from the operations of the mind itself. We find by direct observation that we have the power to begin, continue, or stop certain actions of our minds and motions of our bodies. This power we call will, and the actual exercise of this power, volition, or willing. Action is voluntary or involuntary insofar as it is or is not consequent upon the order or command of the mind.

Locke proceeded to explore the ideas of will, desire, and freedom in terms of the idea of power. "The idea of liberty is the idea of a power in any agent to do or forbear any particular action, according to the determination or thought of the mind, whereby either of them is preferred to the other" (II.xxi.8). Where this power is absent, a man is under necessity. Locke consequently dismissed as unintelligible the question of whether or not the will is free. The only intelligible question is whether or not a man is free. Freedom is one power of an agent and will is another; one power cannot be the power of another. "As far as this power reaches, of acting or not acting, by the determination of his own thought preferring either, so far is a man free" (II.xxi.21). Freedom then, for Locke, was the absence of constraint. If we distinguish will from desire, we cannot make the mistake of thinking the will is free.

What then determines the will with respect to action is some uneasiness in a man that may be called the uneasiness of desire. Good and evil work on the mind but do not determine the will to particular actions. The only thing that can overcome the uneasiness of one desire is the greater uneasiness of another. The removal of uneasiness is the first and necessary step to happiness. Since it is present desire that moves the will to action, good and evil contemplated and known in the mind can move us to action only when that knowledge is accompanied by a greater uneasiness than any other. Since we have many desires and can have knowledge of desired good in the future as well as feared evil, we can suspend the pursuit of any desire until we have judged it. Thus, government of our passions is possible whenever there is a greater uneasiness in not doing so. This power is the ground on which we hold men responsible for their actions. Good and bad are nothing but pleasure or pain, present or future. Error in choice is usually due to the greater strength of present pleasure or pain in comparison with future pleasure and pain. A true knowledge of what contributes to our happiness can influence a choice only when to deviate from that choice would give greater uneasiness than would any other action. Thus it is possible to change the pleasantness and unpleasantness of various actions by consideration, practice, application, and custom.

Locke's conception of power, like his ideas of cause and effect, was inadequate and vague. It was both a simple idea and a complex one; it was the notion of regular sequence and that of efficacious cause; and it was at once given and a priori. The rational and empirical elements in Locke were at war here. Locke was at his best in showing how the word "power" is commonly used. His analysis of the will and freedom was likewise involved in difficulties.

The will is not free and thus man's actions are determined; but at the same time we can suspend the execution of any desire by our judgment. Locke was aware of these difficulties, but he saw no satisfactory alternative.

Mixed modes. Mixed modes are made by the mind and are exemplified by drunkenness, a lie, obligation, sacrilege, or murder. To a great degree we get these ideas by the explanation of the words that stand for them.

Substance. Of all the ideas considered by Locke none gave him more difficulty than that of substance, and nowhere was his empiricism more in conflict with his rationalism. The diverse trends of Locke's thought concerning substance and the problems he raised prepared the ground for Berkeley, Hume, Kant, and many others who struggled with the same questions. At every opportunity throughout the *Essay* he returned to consider particular substances and the general idea of substance. Locke held that we are conversant only with particular substances through experience; yet his rationalism and realism would not permit him to abandon the general idea of substance.

The mind is furnished with many simple ideas by the senses, and it observes by reflection that certain of them are constantly together. It then presumes that these belong to one thing and for convenience gives them one name. In this way the mind arrives at the complex idea of particular substances, such as gold, which we observe to be yellow and malleable, to dissolve in aqua regia, to melt, and not to be used up in fire. A substance so defined gives us only a nominal definition.

Locke added that "not imagining how these simple ideas can subsist by themselves, we accustom ourselves to suppose some substratum wherein they do subsist, and from which they do result; which therefore we call substance" (II.xxiii.1). This idea of a substratum is extremely vague, and Locke called it a "something we know not what." Our ideas do not reach, and we cannot have, a knowledge of the real essence of substances. Nonetheless, Locke continued to believe that real essences do exist, although our knowledge comes short of them.

Our knowledge of corporeal substances consists of ideas of the primary and secondary qualities perceived by the senses and of the powers we observe in them to affect or be affected by other things. We have as clear an idea of spirit as of body, but we are not capable of knowing the real essence of either. Locke observed that we know as little of how the parts of a body cohere as of how our spirits perceive ideas or move our bodies, since we know nothing of either except our simple ideas of them. Locke even suggested that God could if he wished, as far as we know, add to matter the power to think, just as easily as he could add to matter a separate substance with the power to think.

Even our idea of God is based on simple ideas that are enlarged with the idea of infinity. God's infinite essence is unknown to us. We can only know that he exists.

Relations. The mind can consider any idea as it stands in relation to any other; and thus we come by ideas of relation, such as father, whiter, older. Frequently, the lack of a correlative term leads us to mistake a relative term for an absolute one. Locke distinguished the relation from the things related and appears to have made all relations external. Indeed, he held that many ideas of relation are clearer than ideas of substances; for example, the idea of brothers is clearer than the perfect idea of man.

Though there are many ideas and words signifying relations, they all terminate in simple ideas. There is a difficulty here. If the idea of relation is not a simple idea or a combination of simple ideas, then it is distinct from them. Like the general idea of substance, it is a concept derived from reason. No doubt the mind is capable of comparing the relation of one idea with another, but our perception of this operation must have for its object either a simple idea or the operation itself. On this point Locke was obscure and evasive and avoided the difficulties by the vague assertion that all relations terminate in simple ideas.

Causation. The relation to which Locke first turned was cause and effect. His discussion was inadequate and marked by the duality found in his consideration of other ideas. We observe the order and connection of our ideas and the coming into existence of things and qualities. In pointing this out Locke was on strictly empirical grounds. When, however, he defined cause as "that which produces any simple or complex idea," and "that which is produced, effect" (II.xxvi.1), he went beyond experience and rested his argument on reason. Locke undoubtedly saw the difficulties of his position. He was concerned, on the one hand, to show how we have the ideas of cause and effect from experience. On the other hand, he was not satisfied with a mere sequence theory. The difficulty arose, as it did with power and substance, because he was persuaded that there is a reality beyond the ideas manifest to us. It is a reality, however, about which he could say little in terms of his representationalism.

Identity and diversity. Under relation Locke also examined identity and diversity, by which he meant the relation of a thing to itself, particularly with respect to different times and places. As was stated above, the identity of a plant, an animal, or a man consists in a participation in the same continued life. To this Locke added an examination of personal identity. He argued that personal identity is consciousness of being the same thinking self at different times and places. (For a detailed discussion, see PERSONAL IDENTITY.)

Locke also discussed other relations, such as proportional, natural, instituted, and moral, which are not essential to the main argument of the *Essay* and which will, therefore, not be discussed here.

The remaining chapters of Book II of the *Essay* are devoted to "Clear and Obscure, Distinct and Confused Ideas," "Real and Fantastical Ideas," "Adequate and Inadequate Ideas," "True and False Ideas," and "The Association of Ideas." All of them have merit in clarifying other parts of the *Essay* but add little that is new and not discussed elsewhere. Consequently, they will be passed over.

Language. At the end of Book II of the *Essay* Locke related that he had originally intended to pass on to a consideration of knowledge. He found, however, such a close connection between words and ideas, particularly between abstract ideas and general words, that he had first to examine the "nature, use, and signification" of language, since all knowledge consists of propositions. Book III, therefore, was incorporated into the *Essay.*

The merits of Book III are the subject of some controversy. Most scholars have dismissed it as unimportant and confused. Some, such as Aaron, see many merits in it despite its manifest inadequacies.

The primary functions of language are to communicate with our fellow men, to make signs for ourselves of internal conceptions, and to stand as marks for ideas. Language is most useful when general names stand for general ideas and operations of the mind. Since all except proper names are general, a consideration of what kinds of things words stand for is in order. "Words, in their primary or immediate signification, stand for nothing but the ideas in the mind of him that uses them" (III.ii.2). We suppose they stand for the same ideas in the minds of others. Words stand for things only indirectly. General words stand for general ideas, which become general by separation from other ideas and from particular circumstances. This process Locke called abstraction.

Definition. Definition by genus and differentia is merely a convenience by which we avoid enumerating various simple ideas for which the genus stands. (In this, Locke prepared the way for descriptive definition, which makes no pretense of defining the real essence of things.) It follows that general or universal ideas are made by the understanding for its own use. Thus the essences of so-called species are nothing but abstract ideas. Locke asserted that every distinct abstract idea is a distinct essence. This must not be taken in a Platonic sense, for it is the mind itself that makes these abstract ideas. If essences are distinguished into nominal and real, then with respect to simple ideas and modes there is no difference between nominal and real essence. In substances, they are decidedly different, in that the real essence of substance is unknowable to us.

Names. Locke asserted that the names of simple ideas are not definable. One wonders, Is blue a general idea? If so, what is this blue as against that blue? What is separated out? What retained? Locke never examined these questions, with the result that his conception of abstraction is vague and vacillating. Locke gave several distinct meanings to such terms as "general ideas" and "universal ideas," shifting from one meaning to another and never clarifying them.

Complex ideas consisting of several simple ideas are definable and intelligible provided one has experience of the simple ideas that compose them. Without experience how can a blind man understand the definition of a rainbow?

Simple ideas are "perfectly taken from the existence of things and are not arbitrary at all" (III.iv.17). Ideas of substances refer to a pattern with some latitude, whereas ideas of mixed modes are absolutely arbitrary and refer to no real existence. They are not, however, made at random or without reason. It is the name that ties these ideas together, and each such idea is its own prototype.

Since names for substances stand for complex ideas perceived regularly to go together and supposed to belong to one thing, we necessarily come short of the real essences, if there are any. One may use the word "gold" to signify the coexistence of several ideas. One man may use the term to signify the complex idea of A and B and C. Another man of more experience may add D, or add D and

leave out A. Thus, these essences are of our own making without being entirely arbitrary. In any case, the boundaries of the species of substances are drawn by men.

Connective words. In a brief chapter, "Of Particles," Locke pointed out that we need words signifying the connections that the mind makes between ideas or propositions. These show what connection, restriction, distinction, opposition, or emphasis is given to the parts of discourse. These words signify, not ideas, but an action of the mind. Again a difficulty arises. If "is" and "is not" stand for the mind's act of affirming or denying, then either the mind directly apprehends its own actions in some way or we do have ideas of affirmation or denial. If we do have ideas of the mind's acts, then these words ought to signify the ideas of these acts; if we do not have ideas which these words signify, then either we do not apprehend them or something besides ideas is the object of the mind when it thinks.

The remainder of Book III concerns Locke's thoughts on the imperfection of words, the abuse of words, and his suggested remedies for these imperfections and abuses.

Knowledge. The first three books of the *Essay* are largely a preparation for the fourth. Many scholars see a fundamental cleavage between Book II and Book IV. Yet Locke saw no conflict between the two books, and whatever split existed in Locke's thought runs throughout the *Essay*, as J. W. Yolton and others have pointed out. An effort can be made to reconcile Locke's empiricism and his rationalism, his grounding of all ideas and knowledge in experience and his going beyond experience to the existence of things.

Many of Locke's difficulties stem from his definition of "idea." It is so broad that anything perceived or known must be an idea. But Locke showed, in Books I and II, that we get all our ideas from experience, not in order to claim that nothing exists except ideas, but to show that there is an alternative to the theory of innate ideas. For Locke, experience is initially a contact of bodies and subsequently a reflection of the mind. He never doubted the existence of an external physical world, the inner workings of which are unknown to us.

Sources of knowledge. There are two sources of knowledge—sensation and reflection. The ideas we have from reflection are in some important ways quite different from those we have from sensation. In Book II Locke asserted that the mind "turns its view inward upon itself and observes its own actions about those ideas it has (and) takes from thence other ideas" (II.vi.1). The important point here is that in reflection the mind observes its own action. It is true that Locke spoke of modes of the simple ideas of reflection, such as remembering, discerning, reasoning, and judging. Nonetheless, if the mind does observe its own action, then something more than ideas are the object of the mind in reflection, or else ideas of reflection are somehow importantly different from the ideas of sensation. This point will show up in a consideration of Locke's theory of knowledge.

Propositions. Locke defined knowledge as "the perception of the connection and agreement, or disagreement and repugnancy, of any of our ideas" (IV.i.2). This agreement or disagreement is in respect to four types: identity and diversity, relation, coexistence or necessary connection, and real existence. Perceiving agreement or disagreement is quite different from just barely perceiving the ideas that are said to agree or disagree. Strictly speaking, this perception must be a distinct idea of either agreement or disagreement. Yet this was not Locke's meaning. Where there is knowledge, there is judgment, since there can be no knowledge without a proposition, mental or verbal. Locke defined truth as "the joining or separating of signs, as the things signified by them do agree or disagree one with another" (IV.v.2). There are two sorts of propositions: mental, "wherein the ideas in our understandings are, without the use of words, put together or separated by the mind perceiving or judging of their agreement or disagreement" (IV.v.5); and verbal, which stand for mental propositions.

Judgments. In this view, ideas are the materials of knowledge, the terms of mental propositions. They are, insofar as they are given in sensation and reflection, the subject matter of reflection. If perception of agreement or disagreement in identity and diversity is the first act of the mind, then that act is a judgment. If we infallibly know, as soon as we have it in our minds, that the idea of white is identical with itself and different from that of red, and that the idea of round is identical with itself and different from that of square, we must distinguish between the bare having of these ideas and the knowledge of their identity and diversity. The knowledge of their identity and diversity is a judgment. It is reflective, and in it the mind perceives its own action or operation. There can be no distinction between the judgment and the idea of it. This is perhaps Locke's meaning, which is unfortunately obscured by his broad use of the term "idea." This perception of its own action is quite distinct from the abstract idea of the power of judgment. We may be uncertain as to how the mind makes judgments, what determines it to judge, or in what kind of a substance this power inheres, but we may be sure that in the actual making of a true judgment the mind perceives its own act. This position may be beset with difficulties, but it makes some sense out of Locke's definition of knowledge.

Degrees of knowledge. Locke recognized two degrees of knowledge, in the strict sense of the term—intuition and demonstration. Of the two, intuition is more fundamental and certain. "The mind perceives the agreement or disagreement of two ideas immediately by themselves, without the intervention of any other" (IV.ii.1). Such knowledge is irresistible and leaves no room for hesitation, doubt, or examination. Upon it depends all the certainty and evidence of all our knowledge. Here, clearly, what the mind perceives is not any third idea, but its own act. In demonstration the mind perceives agreement or disagreement, not immediately, but through other mediating ideas. Each step in demonstration rests upon an intuition. This kind of knowledge is most evident in, but is not limited to, mathematics.

A third degree of knowledge is "employed about the particular existence of finite beings without us, which going beyond bare probability and yet not reaching perfectly to either of the foregoing degrees of certainty, passes under the name of knowledge" (IV.ii.14). Locke called this sensitive knowledge. Fully aware of the dialectical difficulty entailed in this position, he grounded his reply to critics on common sense. The differences between dreaming and waking, imagining and sensing, are strong enough to justify this conviction. Hunger and thirst should bring a skeptic to his senses. For Locke, it was enough that common sense supported him, for he always took sensory ideas to be signs or representations of something beyond themselves.

Limits of knowledge. Locke asserted that knowledge extends no farther than our ideas and, specifically, no further than the perception of the agreement or disagreement of our ideas. We cannot have knowledge of all the relations of our ideas or rational knowledge of the necessary relations between many of our ideas. Sensitive knowledge goes only as far as the existence of things, not to their real essence, or reality. Two examples were given. In the first, Locke argued that though we have the ideas of circle, square, and equality, we may never find a circle equal to a square and know them to be equal. In the second, he observed that we have ideas of matter and thinking but may never know whether mere material being thinks. This has been discussed earlier.

In his controversy with Stillingfleet, Locke never abandoned this latter thesis. And throughout this section (IV.iii) Locke showed that many relations of coexistence give us no certainty that they will or must continue to be so. He seemed persuaded that the continued discovery of new knowledge suggests that there are vast horizons of reality that we may advance upon but can never reach. With respect to the relations between abstract ideas we may hope to advance very far, as in mathematics. To this he added the belief that a demonstrable science of morality is possible. On the other hand, he held that we can have no certain knowledge of bodies or of unembodied spirits.

Knowledge of existents. Locke argued that though our knowledge terminates in our ideas, our knowledge is real. "Simple ideas are not fictions of our fancies, but the natural and regular productions of things without us, really operating upon us; and so carry with them all the conformity which is intended; or which our state requires" (IV.iv.4). On the other hand, he argued: "All our complex ideas, except those of substances, being archetypes of the mind's own making, not intended to be copies of anything, nor referred to the existence of anything, as to their originals, cannot want any conformity necessary to real knowledge" (IV.iv.5).

Universal propositions, the truth of which may be known with certainty, are not concerned directly with existence. Nonetheless, Locke argued that we have intuitive knowledge of our own existence. Here the argument is much the same as Descartes's, and it is valid only if we accept the view that the mind in reflection perceives its own acts. This knowledge of our own existence has the highest degree of certainty, according to Locke.

We have a demonstrable knowledge of God's existence, Locke held. He used a form of the Cosmological Argument: starting with the certainty of his own existence, he argued to the necessary existence of a being adequate to produce all the effects manifest in experience. The argument assumed the reality of cause, the necessity of order, and the intelligibility of existence.

Of the existence of other things, as has been shown, we have sensitive knowledge. Locke felt the inconsistency of his position on this matter, yet accepted what he believed common sense required. We know of the coexistence of certain qualities and powers, and reason and sense require that they proceed from something outside themselves. Throughout these arguments about existence Locke went beyond his own first definition of knowledge.

Probability. The remaining portions of the *Essay* are concerned with probability, degrees of assent, reason and faith, enthusiasm, error, and the division of the sciences. Though Locke's treatment of probability is inadequate, he recognized its importance. The grounds of probability lie in the apparent conformity of propositions with our experience and the testimony of others. Practical experience shows us that our knowledge is slight, and action requires that we proceed in our affairs with something less than certainty.

Faith was, for Locke, the acceptance of revelation. It must be sharply distinguished from reason, which is "the discovery of the certainty or probability of such propositions or truths, which the mind arrives at by deduction made from such ideas which it has got by the use of its natural faculties, viz. by sensation or reflection" (IV.xviii.2). Though reason is not able to discover the truth of revelation, nevertheless, something claimed to be revelation cannot be accepted against the clear evidence of the understanding. Thus, enthusiasm sets reason aside and substitutes for it bare fancies born of conceit and blind impulse.

Error. Error cannot lie in intuition. Locke found four sources of error: the want of proofs, inability to use them, unwillingness to use them, and wrong measures of probability. Locke concluded the *Essay* with a brief division of science, or human knowledge, into three classes—natural philosophy, or φυσικὴ, practical action and ethics, or πρακτικὴ, and σημειωτικὴ, or the doctrine of signs.

Influence of the "Essay." Many minds of the seventeenth century contributed to the overthrow of the School philosophies and the development of the new sciences and philosophies. Descartes and Locke between them, however, set the tone and direction for what was to follow. Certainly Locke was the most prominent figure in the early eighteenth century, the indispensable precursor of Berkeley and Hume as well as a fountainhead for the French Encyclopedists. If it is said that the two strains of Cartesian rationalism and Lockian empiricism met in Kant, it can be added that Hume built on Locke's foundation and Kant formalized much that was first a vague groping in Locke. Though Locke was not a wholly satisfactory thinker, his influence on thought in England and America has never completely abated, and even now there appears to be a revived interest in the *Essay*.

POLITICAL THOUGHT

Locke's earliest known political writings were the *Essays on the Law of Nature*, written in Latin between 1660 and 1664 but not known until the Lovelace Collection was examined in 1946. They were first published in 1954 with a translation by W. von Leyden. Though much in these essays appears in the *Essay Concerning Human Understanding* and the *Two Treatises*, there remain many points at which the early essays are in conflict with parts of both later works. This fact and the bother of translating them may have deterred Locke from publishing them, despite the urging of Tyrrell. Since von Leyden can find no evidence of direct influence of these essays on anyone other than Tyrrell and Gabriel Towerson, the student of Locke is referred to von Leyden's publication for additional information.

The "Two Treatises." The *Two Treatises of Government* appeared anonymously in 1690, written, it is said, to justify the revolution of 1688, or, according to the preface, "to establish the Throne of Our Great Restorer, our present King William; to make good his Title, in the Consent of the People." Locke acknowledged his authorship only in a codicil in his will listing his anonymous works and giving to the Bodleian Library a corrected copy of the *Two Treatises*. He never felt that any of the editions printed during his lifetime had satisfactorily rendered his work. Only in 1960 did Peter Laslett publish a critical edition based on the Coste master copy of the *Two Treatises*.

The first treatise. It has long been suspected that the first treatise was written in 1683 and that the second treatise was written in 1689. Laslett has presented much evidence to show that the second treatise was the earlier work, written between 1679 and 1681. If his thesis is correct, it was a revolutionary document, whose purpose was not primarily to philosophize but to furnish a theoretical foundation for the political aims and maneuvers of Shaftesbury and his followers in their struggle with Charles II. Only further scholarly probing will resolve this question.

In his preface, Locke stated that the greater part of the original work had been lost. He was satisfied that what remained was sufficient, since he had neither the time nor the inclination to rewrite the missing sections. The evidence is clear that it was portions of the first treatise that were lost.

The first treatise is a sarcastic and harsh criticism of Sir Robert Filmer's *Patriarcha*, which argued for the divine right of kings. Locke's treatise is more of historical than philosophical importance. It argued that Adam was not, as Filmer claimed, divinely appointed monarch of the world and all his descendants. Neither was the power of absolute monarchy inherited from Adam. Adam had no absolute rights over Eve or over his children. Parents have authority over children who are dependent upon them and who must learn obedience as well as many other things for life. The function of the parent is to protect the child and to help him mature. When the child comes to maturity, parental authority ends. In any case, the relation of parent and child is not the same as that of sovereign and subject. Were Filmer right, one would have to conclude that every man is born a slave, a notion that was utterly repugnant to Locke. Even if Filmer were correct, it would be impossible to show that existing rulers, especially the English kings, possess legitimate claims to their sovereignty by tracing it back to lawful descent from Adam.

The second treatise. Locke began the second treatise with the proposition that all men are originally in a state of nature, "a state of perfect freedom to order their actions, and dispose of their possessions, and persons as they think fit, within the bounds of the Law of Nature, without asking leave, or depending upon the Will of any other man" (II.ii.4). Although Locke sometimes wrote as if the state of nature were some period in history, it must be taken largely as a philosophical fiction, an assumption made to show the nature and foundation of political power, a fiction at least as old as Plato's treatment of the Prometheus myth in the *Protagoras*. It is a state of equality but not of unbounded license. Being rational and being a creature bound by God, man must be governed by the law of nature.

Natural law. Though the concept of the law of nature is as old as antiquity, it flourished in the seventeenth century in the minds of a considerable number of ethical and political thinkers. In general it supposed that man by the use of reason could know in the main the fundamental principles of morality, which he otherwise knew through Christian revelation. Locke was extremely vague about the law of nature, but in his *Essays on the Law of Nature* he held that that law rests ultimately on God's will. Reason discovers it. It is not innate. When, however, Locke spoke of it as "writ in the hearts of all mankind," he suggested some kind of innateness. There are obvious difficulties here, for sense and reason may fail men, even though the law of nature is binding on all. Moreover, the various exponents of the law of nature differ on what it consists of, except that it presupposes the brotherhood of man and human benevolence.

State of nature. In a state of nature, according to Locke, all men are bound to preserve peace, preserve mankind, and refrain from hurt to one another. The execution of the law of nature is the responsibility of each individual. If any man violates this law, he thereby puts himself in a state of war with the others, who may then punish the offender. The power that one man may hold over another is neither absolute nor arbitrary and must be restrained by proportion. The state of nature was for Locke a society of men, as distinct from a state of government, or a political society.

Social contract. There are certain inconveniences in a state of nature, such as men's partiality and the inclination on the part of some men to violate the rights of others. The remedy for this is civil government, wherein men by common consent form a social contract and create a single body politic. This contract is not between ruler and ruled, but between equally free men. The aim of the contract is to preserve the lives, freedom, and property of all, as they belong to each under natural law. Whoever, therefore, attempts to gain absolute power over another puts himself at war with the other. This holds in the political state as well as the state of nature. When a ruler becomes a tyrant, he puts himself in a state of war with the people, who then, if no redress be found, may make an appeal to heaven, that is, may revolt. This power is but an extension of the right of each to punish an aggressor in the state of nature. Unlike Hobbes, Locke was persuaded that men are capable of judging whether they are cruelly subjected and unjustly treated. Since one reason for men entering into the social contract is to avoid a state of war, the contract is broken when the sovereign puts himself into a state of war with the people by becoming a tyrant.

Slavery. Curiously, Locke justified slavery on the grounds that those who became slaves were originally in a state of wrongful war with those who conquered them and, being captive, forfeited their freedom. Apart from being bad history, this argument ignores the rights of the children of slaves. Locke's inconsistency here may mercifully be passed over.

Property. Property was an idea which Locke used in both a broad and a narrow sense. Men have a right to self-preservation and therefore to such things as they need for their subsistence. Each man possesses himself absolutely, and therefore that with which he mixes his labor becomes his property. "God has given the earth to mankind in common." No man has original, exclusive rights to the fruits and beasts of the earth. Nevertheless, man must have some means with which to appropriate them. This consists of the labor of his body and the work of his hand. By labor, man removes things from a state of nature and makes them his property. Without labor, the earth and things in general have but little value. However, only so much as a man improves and can use belongs to him, nor may a man deprive another of the means of self-preservation by overextending his reach for property.

Though the right to property is grounded in nature, it is not secured therein. It is one of the primary ends of the state to preserve the rights of property, as well as to make laws governing the use, distribution, and transference of property. In communities or countries under government, there are fixed boundaries to the common territory, and there is land and property held in common which no one may appropriate to himself and to which those not members of the community have no right at all. Money, being something which does not spoil, came into use by mutual consent, serving as a useful means of exchange. At the same time it made possible the accumulation of wealth greater than warranted by need or use.

Political society. Having established several rights and duties belonging to men by nature and having shown certain inconveniences and disadvantages of the state of nature, Locke turned to political society. The first society consists of the family, whose aims are not initially or primarily those of political society, but which may be included under political society.

In political society "any number of men are so united into one Society, as to quit everyone his Executive power of the law of nature, and to resign it to the public" (II.vii.89). The legislative and executive powers are "a right of making laws with penalties of Death, and consequently all less Penalties, for the regulating and preserving of property, and of employing the force of the community, in the execution of such laws, and in the defense of the commonwealth from foreign injury, and all this only for the public good" (II.i.3). By the social contract men give up, not all their rights, but only the legislative and executive right they originally had under the law of nature. This transference of power is always subordinate to the proper and true ends of the commonwealth, which are "the mutual preservation of their lives, liberties and estates."

Each man must voluntarily consent to the compact either explicitly or implicitly. An individual who at age of discretion remains a member of the community tacitly consents to the compact.

Since the compact is made between the members of the community, sovereignty ultimately remains with the people. The sovereign, in the form of a legislative body, and executive, or both, is the agent and executor of the sovereignty of the people. The community can act only by the rule of the majority, and everyone is bound by it, because an agreement of unanimity is virtually impossible. It is the people who establish the legislative, executive, and judiciary powers. Thus, an absolute monarch is incompatible with civil society.

Locke's theories so far are compatible with either monarchy, oligarchy, or democracy so long as it is recognized that ultimate sovereignty lies with the people. He believed that a constitutional monarchy with executive power, including the judiciary, in the hands of the monarch, and legislative powers in a parliamentary assembly elected by the people was the most satisfactory form of government. The supreme power he held to be the legislative, for it makes the laws that the executive must carry out and enforce. Whenever the executive violates the trust that he holds, no obligation is owed him and he may be deposed. The legislature may also violate its trust, though Locke believed it less likely to do so. Whenever this occurs, the people have a right to dissolve it and establish a new government. For this reason a regularly elected legislative body is desirable.

Rebellion. Locke explicitly recognized, as the events during his lifetime had shown, that men may become tyrants to those whom they were bound to serve. It may be a king, an assembly, or a usurper that claims absolute power. In such cases the people have a right to rebellion if no other redress is possible. Locke was not unmindful of the fact that the executive needs latitude and prerogative so that he may govern, and that the legislative body must deliberate and make laws which they believe to be in the public good. The right to rebellion is warranted only in the most extreme conditions, where all other means fail. Locke did not believe that men would lightly avail themselves of this power, for men will suffer and endure much before they resort to rebellion.

In transferring to the government the right to make and execute law and make war and peace, men do not give up the natural light of reason, by which they judge good and evil, right and wrong, justice and injustice. In specific laws or executive decisions judgment must be allowed to the legislature and the executive. If, however, a long train of acts shows a tyrannical course, then men, judging that the sovereign has put himself into a state of war with them, may justly dethrone the tyrant. On the other hand, the legislative and executive power can never revert to the people unless there is a breach of trust.

The dissolution of government is not the dissolution of society. The aim of revolution is the establishment of a new government, not a return to a state of nature. The dissolution of a government may occur under many circumstances, but foremost among them are when the arbitrary will of a single person or prince is set in place of the law; when the prince hinders the legislature from due and lawful assembly; when there is arbitrary change in elections; when the people are delivered into subjection by a foreign power; and when the executive neglects and abandons his charge. In all such cases sovereignty reverts to the society, and the people have a right to act as the supreme

power and continue the legislature in themselves, or erect a new form, or under the old form place sovereignty in new hands, whichever they think best. On the other hand, "the power that every individual gave the society, . . . can never revert to the individuals again, as long as the society lasts" (II.xix.243).

As theory, Locke's second treatise is full of inadequacies, but its magnificent sweep of ideas prepared the ground for popular and democratic government.

EDUCATION AND RELIGION

Locke's thought on education and religion was not presented in strictly philosophical terms. It was, however, deeply rooted in the fundamental concepts of the *Essay* and the *Two Treatises*. His works in these areas display clearly the liberal bent of his mind as well as his love of freedom, tolerance, and truth. His attitude was pragmatic and based on considerable psychological insight into the motives, needs, passions, and follies of men. *Some Thoughts Concerning Education*, several letters on toleration, and *The Reasonableness of Christianity* profoundly affected educational and religious thought in the eighteenth century and after. Two of these works, *Some Thoughts Concerning Education* and the first *Letter on Toleration*, continue to be fresh and relevant.

Education. When Locke was in Holland, he wrote a number of letters to Edward Clark advising him on the education of his son, a young man of no particular distinction. Locke had in mind the education of a gentleman who would one day be a squire. In 1693 Locke modified these letters somewhat and published the contents as *Some Thoughts Concerning Education* in response to "so many, who profess themselves at a loss how to breed their children." His thought was marked by a ready understanding of, and warm sympathy with, children. Three main thoughts dominate the work. First, the individual aptitudes, capacities, and idiosyncrasies of the child should govern learning, not arbitrary curricular or rote learning taught by the rod. Second, Locke placed the health of the body and the development of a sound character ahead of intellectual learning. In the third place, he saw that play, high spirits, and the "gamesome humor" natural to children should govern the business of learning wherever possible. Compulsory learning is irksome; where there is play in learning, there will be joy in it. Throughout he placed emphasis on good example, practice, and use rather than on precepts, rules, and punishment. The work was an implicit criticism of his own education at Westminster and Oxford, which he found unpleasant and largely useless.

Writing almost as a physician, Locke advised "plenty of open air, exercise, and sleep; plain diet, no wine or strong drink, and very little or no physic; not too warm and strait clothing; especially the head and feet kept cold, and the feet often used to cold water and exposed to wet." The aim in all was to keep the body in strength and vigor, able to endure hardships.

Locke urged that early training must establish the authority of the parents so that good habits may be established. The prime purpose is the development of virtue, the principle of which is the power of denying ourselves the satisfaction of our desires. The child should be taught to submit to reason when young. Parents teach by their own example. They should avoid severe punishments and beatings as well as artificial rewards. Rules should be few when a child is young, but those few should be obeyed. Mild, firm, and rational approval or disapproval are most effective in curbing bad behavior. Children should be frequently in the company of their parents, who should in turn study the disposition of the child and endeavor to use the child's natural desire for freedom and play to make learning as much like recreation as possible. High spirits should not be curbed, but turned to creative use. Curiosity too should be encouraged, and questions should be heard and fairly answered. Cruelty must always be discouraged and courageousness approved.

As the child grows, familiarity should be increased so that the parent has a friend in the mature child. Virtue, breeding, and a free liberal spirit as well as wisdom and truthfulness were the goals set by Locke in all his advice. Affection and friendship were for him both means and ends of good education.

Learning, though important, Locke put last. First, he would have the child learn to speak and read his own language well by example and practice, not by grammar. In the study of all languages, he would put off the study of grammar until they can be spoken well. He would begin the learning of a second modern language early. Reluctantly he would allow a gentleman's son to learn Latin, but he did not recommend much time on Greek, Hebrew, Arabic, rhetoric, or logic, which constituted the curricula of the universities of his day. Rather, time should be given to the study of geography, arithmetic, astronomy, geometry, history, ethics, and civil law. Dancing he encouraged, and music as well, in moderation. He was less sympathetic to poetry. Remarkably, he urged that everyone learn at least one manual trade and make some study of accounting. Finally, travel was valuable if not done before one could profit by it.

If much of this is familiar and even trite, it must be remembered that Locke was among the first to formulate these ideas. His influence on educational thought and practice was enormous and is still very much with us in its fundamental outlook and method.

Religion. Locke saw some merits in all the competing claims of various religious groups. He also saw the destructive force that was released when these claims sought exclusive public dominion at the expense of individual conscience. He looked in several directions at once. This tendency has earned for him the reputation of being timorous and compromising. Nonetheless, it is on this trait of mind that much of his great influence and reputation rests. For Locke, fidelity to the evidence at hand always outweighed cleverness, consistency, and dialectic. It is the chief testimony to his claim that truth was always his aim, even when he might have won an easy victory by dogmatic consistency.

Locke's writings on religion are voluminous. When he died he was working on extensive commentaries on the *Epistles of St. Paul*, as well as a draft of a fourth *Letter on Toleration*. Earlier he had written and published three letters on toleration, *The Reasonableness of Christianity*

(1695), and two *Vindications* (1695 and 1697) of the latter work. Moreover, Locke's three letters to Stillingfleet, the bishop of Worcester, are concerned with religious questions as well as epistemological ones.

Religious tolerance. Locke's first *Letter Concerning Toleration* stated his position clearly, and he never deviated from it substantially. It was originally written in Latin as a letter to his Dutch friend Philip van Limborch. In 1689 it was published on the Continent in Latin, and in the same year a translation of it by William Popple appeared in English.

Locke was not the first to write in advocacy of religious toleration. His was, however, a powerful, direct, and passionate plea. It was linked with the *Essay* by its recognition of the limits of human knowledge and human fallibility, and with the *Two Treatises* by his deep commitment to individual rights and freedom.

Locke took toleration to be the chief characteristic mark of the true church, for religious belief is primarily a relation between each man and God. True religion regulates men's lives according to virtue and piety, and without charity and love religion is false to itself. Those who persecute others in the name of Christ abjure his teachings, seeking only outward conformity, not peace and holiness. Who can believe that in torture and execution the fanatic truly seeks the salvation of the soul of his victim? Moreover, the mind cannot be forced or belief compelled. All efforts to force or compel belief breed only hypocrisy and contempt of God. Persuasion is the only lever that can truly move the mind.

A church is "a voluntary society of men, joining themselves together of their own accord in order to the public worshipping of God in such manner as they judge acceptable to Him, and effectual to the salvation of their souls." It is sharply distinct from a state, or commonwealth. The state is concerned with the public good, protecting life, liberty, and property. It has no authority in matters of the spirit. "Whatever is lawful in the commonwealth cannot be prohibited by the magistrate in the church."

It is to be doubted that any man or group of men possess the truth about the one true way to salvation. In the Scriptures we have all that may reasonably be claimed by Christians to be the word of God. The rest are the speculations and beliefs of men concerning articles of faith and forms of worship. Sincere and honest men differ in these matters, and only tolerance of these differences can bring about public peace and Christian charity. Jews, pagans, and Muslims are all equally confident in their religious faith. Mutual tolerance is essential where such diversity exists. This is most evident when we observe that it is the most powerful party that persecutes others in the name of religion. Yet in different countries and at different times power has lain in the hands of different religious groups. It is physical power, not true faith, which decides who is persecuted and who persecutes.

Throughout Locke's argument the liberty of person and the liberty of conscience are decisive. He limited this liberty only by denying to religion the right to harm directly another person or group or to practice clearly immoral rites. By a curious and probably prudential exception, he denied tolerance to atheists, because promises, covenants, and oaths would not bind them, and to any church so constituted "that all those who enter into it do thereby *ipso facto* deliver themselves up to the protection and service of another prince."

Despite these limitations, Locke's letter moved subsequent generations to a greater spirit of tolerance in religious matters. It is still part of the liberal democratic ideal and transcends the time of its composition.

Faith and reason. The *Reasonableness of Christianity* and the *Vindications* are works more bound to Locke's own time. Locke was probably neither a Socinian nor a deist, even though certain deists and Unitarians found comfort and inspiration in his work. He was a sincere Christian, who tried to diminish the flourishing schisms and sects by proposing a return to the Scriptures and an abandonment of the interminable theological disputes of his day. He accepted the divine inspiration of the Bible. Nevertheless, he held that even revelation must be tested by reason. In the New Testament, Christianity is rational and simple. The core of Christian faith lies in the belief in the fatherhood of God, the divinity of Christ the Messiah, the morality of charity, love, and divine mercy. Justification by faith means faith in Christ, whose essential revelation is that God is merciful and forgives the sinner who truly repents and strives to live a life of Christian morality. The Mosaic law, God's mercy, and Christian morality are all consonant with human reason. Revelation discloses to man what unaided reason could not discover—the mysteries, the Virgin Birth, the Resurrection, the divinity of Christ. But when disclosed, these do not violate the canons of reason. Here as elsewhere, Locke's emphasis on reason was circumscribed, reason must be followed where possible, but it does not carry us far enough by itself.

Locke's influence was wide and deep. In political, religious, educational, and philosophical thought he inspired the leading minds of England, France, America, and to some extent, Germany. He disposed of the exaggerated rationalism of Descartes and Spinoza; he laid the groundwork for a new empiricism and advanced the claims for experimentalism. Voltaire, Montesquieu, and the French Encyclopedists found in Locke the philosophical, political, educational, and moral basis that enabled them to prepare and advance the ideas which eventuated in the French Revolution. In America, his influence on Jonathan Edwards, Hamilton, and Jefferson was decisive. Locke's zeal for truth as he saw it was stronger than his passion for dialectical and logical niceties, and this may account for the fact that his works prepared the ground for action as well as thought.

Works by Locke

Essays on the Law of Nature. Translated from the Latin and edited by W. von Leyden. Oxford, 1954. Also gives an account of the Lovelace Collection.

An Early Draft of Locke's Essay (Draft A), R. I. Aaron and J. Gibb, eds. Oxford, 1936. Valuable as a study of the development of the *Essay.*

An Essay Concerning the Understanding, Knowledge, Opinion and Assent (Draft B), B. Rand, ed. Cambridge, Mass., 1931. Valuable, but superseded by manuscript in Bodleian Library.

Epistola de Tolerantia. Gouda, 1689. Translated by William Popple as *A Letter Concerning Toleration.* London, 1689. Several defenses appeared in the 1690s and fragments of a fourth in 1706.

An Essay Concerning Human Understanding. London, 1690; 2d ed. with large additions, London, 1694; 3d ed., London, 1695; 4th ed., with large additions, London, 1700; 5th ed., with many large additions, London, 1706. Best modern edition, from which all quotes in this article are taken, is a reprint of the fifth edition, J. W. Yolton, ed., 2 vols. New York and London, 1961.

Two Treatises of Government. London, 1690. The critical and collated edition of Locke's corrected copy by Peter Laslett (Cambridge, 1960) surpasses all previous editions.

Some Considerations of the Consequences of the Lowering of Interest and the Raising of the Value of Money. London, 1692. Two additional papers on money appeared in 1695.

Some Thoughts Concerning Education. London, 1693.

The Reasonableness of Christianity. London, 1695. Defenses of this work were published in 1695 and 1697.

A Letter to the Right Rev. Edward Ld. Bishop of Worcester, concerning Some Passages relating to Mr. Locke's Essay of Humane Understanding. London, 1697. Two further letters appeared, in 1697 and 1699.

A Paraphrase and Notes on the Epistles of St. Paul to the Galatians [etc.]. London, 1705.

Posthumous Works of Mr. John Locke, 6 vols. London, 1706.

The Remains of John Locke, E. Curl, ed. London, 1714.

Works of John Locke, 3 vols. London, 1714; 10th ed., 10 vols., London, 1801.

The Correspondence of John Locke and Edward Clarke, B. Rand, ed. Oxford, 1927.

For the remainder of Locke's published and unpublished papers, consult the works listed below by Aaron, Christopherson, von Leyden, Long, Ollion, and Yolton. See von Leyden and Long particularly for the Lovelace Collection.

Works on Locke

BIOGRAPHIES

Bourne, H. R. Fox, *Life of John Locke,* 2 vols. London, 1876. Excellent, but inadequate since Lovelace Collection became available.

Cranston, Maurice, *John Locke, a Biography.* London, 1957. A thorough study of the life of Locke, using all materials available at present.

King, Lord Peter, *The Life and Letters of John Locke.* London, 1829. Not good, but contains original material.

CRITICAL COMMENTARIES

Aaron, R. I., "Locke's Theory of Universals." *PAS,* Vol. 33 (1932/1933). Useful and enlightening.

Aaron, R. I., *John Locke.* Oxford, 1937; rev. ed., Oxford, 1955. Best general commentary.

Adamson, S. W., *The Educational Writings of John Locke.* Cambridge, 1922.

Bastide, C., *John Locke, ses théories politiques et leur influence en Angleterre.* Paris, 1906. Still valuable work on Locke's political philosophy.

Christopherson, H. O., *A Bibliographical Introduction to the Study of John Locke.* Oslo, 1930. Incomplete.

Clapp, J. G., *Locke's Conception of the Mind.* New York, 1937.

Cranston, Maurice, "Men and Ideas; John Locke." *Encounter,* Vol. 7 (1956), 46–54.

Czajkowski, C. J., *The Theory of Private Property in Locke's Political Philosophy.* Notre Dame, Ind., 1941. Useful on the labor theory of value.

DeMarchi, E., "Locke's Atlantis." *Political Studies,* Vol. 3 (1955), 164–165.

Gibson, James, *Locke's Theory of Knowledge.* Cambridge, 1917. Emphasizes Locke's rationalism.

Gibson, James, *John Locke.* British Academy, Henriette Hertz Lecture, 1933.

Gierke, Otto von, *Naturrecht und deutsches Recht.* Translated and edited by Ernest Barker as *Natural Law and the Theory of Society*, 2 vols. Cambridge, 1934. A major study.

Gough, J. W., *John Locke's Political Philosophy. Eight Studies.* Oxford, 1950. Important.

Jackson, Reginald, "Locke's Distinction Between Primary and Secondary Qualities." *Mind*, Vol. 38 (1929), 56–76.

Jackson, Reginald, "Locke's Version of the Doctrine of Representative Perception." *Mind*, Vol. 39 (1930), 1–25.

James, D. G., *The Life of Reason. Hobbes, Locke, Bolingbroke.* London, 1949.

Krakowski, E., *Les Sources médiévales de la philosophie de Locke.* Paris, 1915. One of the few studies of influences on Locke.

Lamprecht, S. P., *The Moral and Political Philosophy of John Locke.* New York, 1918.

Laslett, Peter, "The English Revolution and Locke's Two Treatises of Government." *Cambridge Historical Journal*, Vol. 12 (1956). Interesting and controversial.

Leibniz, G. W., *Nouveaux Essais sur l'entendement humain.* Leipzig and Amsterdam, 1765. Translated by A. G. Langley as *New Essays concerning Human Understanding.* New York and London, 1896. An important critique of Locke by a contemporary.

Leyden, W. von, "John Locke and Natural Law." *Philosophy*, Vol. 31 (1956). A useful examination.

Long, P., *A Summary Catalogue of the Lovelace Collection of Papers of John Locke in the Bodleian Library.* Oxford, 1959.

O'Connor, D. J., *John Locke.* Harmondsworth, England, 1952.

Ollion, H., *Notes sur la correspondance de John Locke.* Paris, 1908.

Polin, R., *La Politique de John Locke.* Paris, 1960. Interesting contrast to Laslett.

Pollock, Sir Frederick, "Locke's Theory of the State," in his *Essays in the Law.* London, 1922. Ch. 3.

Ryle, Gilbert, *Locke on the Human Understanding.* Oxford, 1933.

Smith, N. K., *John Locke.* Manchester, England, 1933.

Ware, C. S., "The Influence of Descartes on John Locke." *Revue internationale de philosophie* (1950), 210–230.

Webb, T. E., *The Intellectualism of Locke. An Essay.* Dublin, 1857. Presents Locke as a precursor to Kant.

Yolton, J. W., "Locke's Unpublished Marginal Replies to John Sergeant." *Journal of the History of Ideas*, Vol. 12 (1951), 528–559.

Yolton, J. W., "Locke and the Seventeenth-Century Logic of Ideas." *Journal of the History of Ideas*, Vol. 16 (1955), 431–452.

Yolton, J. W., *Locke and the Way of Ideas.* Oxford, 1956. A careful study.

Yolton, J. W., "Locke on the Law of Nature." *Philosophical Review*, Vol. 67 (1958), 477–498.

JAMES GORDON CLAPP

LOEB, JACQUES (1859–1924), was one of the most forthright defenders of biological mechanism in recent thought. Loeb was born at Mayen, Germany, and studied medicine at Munich and Strasbourg. As a result of reading Schopenhauer and von Hartmann, he became interested in philosophical questions concerning the nature of will, and it was partly in the hope of throwing light on these questions that he turned to the study of physiological and comparative psychology. After a brief period as assistant in physiology at Würzburg and Strasbourg (1886–1890), he immigrated to the United States, where he occupied academic posts at Bryn Mawr College (1891), the University of Chicago (1892–1902; here he had considerable influence on Thorstein Veblen, among others), and the University of California (1902–1910). From 1910 until his death he was head of the division of general physiology at the Rockefeller Institute for Medical Research.

Loeb gained an international reputation for his skill and originality as an experimenter. His investigations were dominated by the desire to show that all life phenomena can be explained in physicochemical terms. Two sets of experiments that he designed were taken by him to give overwhelming support to a mechanistic doctrine. In one set he studied the responses of insects and other lower animals to such external influences as light, chemicals, and electrical stimuli. These responses, he contended, were forced or automatic reactions of the organism as a whole. He called them "tropisms," extending a term which had previously been applied to the forced movements of plants. Tropisms are wholly mechanical modes of response and can be interpreted quantitatively so as to make superfluous any teleological or vitalistic notions. The second set of experiments involved pioneer work in inducing artificial parthenogenesis by means of chemical reagents. Here he achieved such startling effects as producing normal, free-swimming larvae from the unfertilized eggs of starfish, sea urchins, and other echinoderms by adding various acids to the water in which the eggs were situated. Even pricking the eggs with a needle or shaking them would cause them to begin developing. All this appeared to prove that the function of the male sex cell was purely physicochemical. The theory of biological mechanism was thus given a powerful new impetus.

The philosophical interests that underlay Loeb's researches led him to generalize in a way scarcely warranted by the evidence. For instance, he held that "a mechanistic conception of life is not complete unless it includes a physico-chemical explanation of psychic phenomena." No such explanation is yet available, but the successes achieved in identifying the chemical basis of animal instincts aroused in Loeb the hope that the ultimate triumph of the mechanistic point of view was only a matter of time. Ultimately, we would come to understand that "our wishes and hopes, disappointments and sufferings, efforts and struggles, are comparable to the light instinct of the heliotropic animals." Conditions compel us to feel or act in these ways, just as they compel other organisms to behave as they do. We like to believe that human beings are unique in possessing free will, but this conception expresses nothing more than our ignorance of the orienting forces at work when we perform a "premeditated" act. Loeb held that it by no means followed that all ethical notions are without foundation. Moral behavior is no less "tropistic" than any other kind.

We seek and enjoy the fellowship of human beings because hereditary conditions compel us to do so. We struggle for justice and truth since we are instinctively compelled to see our fellow beings happy. . . . Not only is the mechanistic conception of life compatible with ethics: it seems the only conception of life which can lead to an understanding of the source of ethics. (*The Mechanistic Conception of Life*, p. 31)

The care with which Loeb conducted his experiments was not found in his theorizing. A critical reader encounters many obscurities in "the mechanistic conception of life." Sometimes it appears to be old-fashioned reductive materialism. Yet Loeb also said that "only certain species of animals possess associative memory and have consciousness." The rest are pure automata and so appear to differ in kind.

Few references to biological evolution occur in Loeb's writings. The life sciences for him were experimental, not historical, investigations. He admired Darwin for having insisted "that accidental and not purposeful variations gave rise to the variety of organisms." But the doctrine of natural selection seemed to Loeb much less important for biology than the work of Mendel and Pavlov.

Works by Loeb

The Dynamics of Living Matter. New York, 1906.
The Mechanistic Conception of Life. Chicago, 1912.
The Organism as a Whole. New York and London, 1916.
Forced Movements, Tropisms and Animal Conduct. Philadelphia and London, 1918.

Works on Loeb

Jennings, H. S., *The Behavior of Lower Organisms.* New York, 1906.
Nordenskiöld, Erik, *The History of Biology.* New York and London, 1928. Ch. 18.

T. A. Goudge

LOGIC, COMBINATORY. Combinatory logic is a branch of mathematical logic that analyzes certain processes, such as substitution, which are associated with variables. These processes are taken for granted in most formulations of logic, but they are complex, and since a fundamental part of the resulting theory is recursively undecidable the analysis is not trivial. Combinatory logic contributes to simplifying the ultimate foundations of mathematical logic and to explaining the paradoxes; it contains an arithmetic in which exactly those numerical functions that are partial recursive are representable; and it has potential applications to the deeper study of such areas as logical calculuses of higher order, computer programming, and linguistics.

Before one can define combinatory logic precisely, it is necessary to explain some notions concerning formal systems. This will be done in the next section. In the following section the definition will be given and a plan presented according to which the later sections of this article will develop the subject. Each technical term is defined by the context in which it appears in italics.

FORMAL SYSTEMS

Consider a formal system of the following type: There is a class of formal objects, or *obs*, constructed from certain primitive obs, or *atoms*, by certain *operations*; each ob has a unique such construction. Among these operations a binary one, called *application*, is singled out. If this is the only operation, the system is called *applicative;* otherwise it is *quasi-applicative.* There is a unique unary predicate, symbolized by the sign "⊢" used as prefix; the *elementary statements* are then of the form

(1) ⊢*X*,

where *X* is an ob. The *elementary theorems* form an inductive subclass of the elementary statements; they are

generated from certain initial ones, the *axioms*, by *deductive rules*. The atoms, obs, elementary statements, and axioms are definite classes—that is, it can be effectively ascertained whether a proposed member of one of them is actually a member—but concerning the elementary theorems it is required only that the correctness of a derivation by the deductive rules can be effectively checked. Combinatory logic takes such a system as basis. Other sorts of system exist, but all those ordinarily used in mathematical logic can be reduced to the above type.

Assuming such a system, we observe the following conventions: The application of *X* to *Y* is symbolized as (*XY*). Parentheses are omitted according to the rule of association to the left and also to the rule that outside parentheses are superfluous, so that $XY_1Y_2Y_3$ is the same ob as $(((XY_1)Y_2)Y_3)$. A *combination* of given obs is an ob formed from some or all of them by application alone. The sign "≡" stands for definitional identity; "→" and "⇄" for metatheoretic implication and equivalence, respectively. Finally, "=" is defined, say, by

(2) $$X = Y \rightleftarrows \vdash \mathbf{Q}XY,$$

where **Q** is a specific ob, the axioms and rules being such that equality has the appropriate properties.

With such a formal system one associates two sorts of ontology. On the one hand, some persons insist on describing more definitely what the obs are; on the other hand, one may give a description of the meaning one intends for the elementary statements. The first description will be called a *representation*; the second description will be called an *interpretation*.

For a representation it is customary to state that the obs are words in an object language. We will not do that here—all symbols belong to the *U-language* (metalanguage)—but it can be done quite easily for any given object language with two or more symbols. This permits a certain freedom in regard to use and mention.

An interpretation for combinatory logic may be described as follows (this is for motivation only and does not imply a commitment to any special type of metaphysics): One associates with certain obs *contensive* (known from prior experience) notions called *interpretants*. The fact that *Y* is the interpretant of *X* will be expressed simply as *X* means *Y*. Then if *X* means a function and *Y* means a possible value for the first assignment of that function, *XY* will mean the result of assigning the interpretant of *Y* as value to the first argument of *X*. Thus, if *X* means the addition function of natural numbers and *Y* means the number 1, then *XY* will mean a form of the successor function, and if *Z* means the number 2, then *XYZ* will mean the number 3. This device reduces many-place functions to unary ones without postulating ordered pairs. An elementary statement (1) will mean that *X* means an asserted statement; the interpretation is a valid one when every asserted statement is true.

DEFINITION AND DIVISIONS
OF COMBINATORY LOGIC

The usual formal systems contain a special class of obs, usually atoms, called (*formal*) *variables*. These are so named in the formalization and play a special role, such that arbitrary obs can be substituted for them (perhaps under restrictions). Variables do not have interpretants; obs containing them mean functions in which they stand for arguments. Thus, the elementary statements of *Principia Mathematica*, Sec. 1A, are not about p, q, r but about negation ($\sim$) and alternation (v); the interpretants of its elementary theorems state rather complex relationships, indicated by the variables, between these functions.

Let $\mathscr{H}$ be a system as defined earlier, and let $\mathscr{H}(x_1, \cdots, x_m)$ be the system formed by adjoining $x_1, \cdots, x_m$ as variables —that is, as new atoms—without further changes. As stated above, the natural interpretant of an ob M of $\mathscr{H}(x_1, \cdots, x_m)$ is that function over $\mathscr{H}$ whose value for arguments $a_1, \cdots, a_m$ is the result of substituting $a_1, \cdots, a_m$ for $x_1, \cdots, x_m$, respectively, in M. Let us say that an ob X of $\mathscr{H}$ designates M when and only when

$$(3) \qquad Xx_1x_2\cdots x_m = M$$

is derivable in $\mathscr{H}(x_1, \cdots, x_m)$. The system $\mathscr{H}$ is called *combinatorially complete* when and only when such an X exists for every M. A *constant* (that is, an ob of an $\mathscr{H}$ containing no variables) X is called a *proper combinator* when and only when it designates a combination of variables alone; a *combinator* is any combination of proper combinators.

Combinatory logic may now be defined as that branch of logic which studies combinators. This is tantamount, at least for applicative systems, to studying combinatorial completeness.

There are two methods of achieving combinatorial completeness. The first is to postulate a designator for every M. This idea leads to the *theory of λ-conversion*, which is discussed in the next section. It is a quasi-applicative system with bound variables. The other method is to exhibit all combinators as combinations of certain atomic ones, after which we can get along with an applicative system. This leads to *synthetic combinatory logic*, to which the rest of the article is devoted. The two approaches have been shown to be equivalent.

The subject of combinatory logic divides itself into two parts in another way. In the first part, called *pure combinatory logic*, one introduces no constant atoms except combinators and those atoms necessary to define equality and pays no attention to whether the obs have interpretants. In the second part, called *illative combinatory logic*, one introduces atoms meaning other logical notions, such as implication, quantification, and semantical categories. The question whether an ob has an interpretant, and if so, what sort of interpretant, belongs to the illative theory.

Theory of λ-conversion. In the theory of λ-conversion we postulate that given M, $x_1, \cdots, x_m$, there is an X in $\mathscr{H}$ such that (3) holds. This X, in Alonzo Church's notation, is $\lambda x_1 \cdots x_m M$. It suffices to postulate this for $m=1$, for we can define

$$\lambda x_1 \cdots x_m x_{m+1} M \equiv \lambda x_1 \cdots x_m (\lambda x_{m+1} M).$$

Thus, we need only a binary operation forming $\lambda x M$ from x and M. This operation is the only primitive operation besides application. Thus, x is a variable and is bound (in a natural extension of the usual sense) in $\lambda x M$. One must distinguish, just as in predicate calculus, free and bound occurrences of variables. One understands "ob of $\mathscr{H}$" to include any ob formed from atoms of $\mathscr{H}$ and variables without free occurrences of variables not in $\mathscr{H}$. Further, given an ob M, a variable x, and an ob N, we define $[N/x]M$ (subject to restrictions to prevent confusion of bound variables) as the ob obtained by the substitution of N for x in M.

In view of the intended interpretation, the following are acceptable (subject to the stated restrictions) as axiom schemes:

$$(\alpha) \qquad \lambda x M = \lambda y [y/x] M,$$
$$(\beta) \qquad (\lambda x M) N = [N/x] M.$$

Along with this one has the rules for equality, which give as a special case

$$(\xi) \qquad M = N \rightarrow \lambda x M = \lambda x N.$$

The equality relation is called *convertibility*, and "cnv" is often used instead of "=." We call (β) (as well as η and δ below) a *replacement scheme*. The definition is equivalent to saying that X cnv Y when and only when X can be converted to Y by zero or more successive applications of replacement schemes in either direction. There is also defined a relation of *reducibility*, indicated by "red," in which the replacement schemes can be used from left to right only. An ob is said to be in *normal form* when and only when no replacement scheme can be so applied to it.

There are various modifications of this system. In λI-*conversion* (the original λ-conversion), $\lambda x M$ is defined only when M contains a free occurrence of x; in λK-*conversion* this restriction is dropped. Again the additional axiom scheme (for x not free in U)

$$(\eta) \qquad \lambda x (Ux) = U$$

is acceptable from interpretations which maintain a strong extensionality principle. If it is adopted, the theory is here called λη-*conversion*, in contrast to the original λβ-*conversion*. Finally one may introduce axiom schemes (δ) which single out special constants $\delta_1, \delta_2, \cdots$ and allow constants of the form $\delta_k U_1 U_2 \cdots U_{n_k}$, where n_k is fixed by δ_k and the U_j are in normal form, to be replaced by other constants determined in some uniform manner. Note that (δ) is, in principle, illative.

The various forms of λ-conversion have differences in interpretation. In λI-reduction no component is dropped; hence, if X has a normal form, so does every part of X. This is not true for λK-reduction, a disadvantage if one identifies possession of an interpretant with having a normal form. Again, if one accepts (η), every ob means a function (in some sense), and sometimes this is unacceptable. However, one may prefer to make such distinctions in the illative theory.

The principal result concerning λ-conversion is the Church–Rosser theorem. This states that if X cnv Y, then one can find effectively a Z such that X red Z and Y red Z. Thus, two different combinations of variables are never interconvertible; this establishes consistency. In 1936,

Alonzo Church and J. B. Rosser ("Some Properties of Conversion," in *Transactions of the American Mathematical Society,* Vol. 39, 472–482) proved the theorem for λIβ-conversion; it has since been extended to all forms of λ-conversion.

The decision problem for all equations $X = Y$ was shown by Church in 1936 ("An Unsolvable Problem of Elementary Number Theory," in *American Journal of Mathematics,* Vol. 58, 345–363) to be recursively unsolvable, as was the problem of determining whether X has a normal form. This result was the basis of Church's later proof of the recursive unsolvability of the decision problem for predicate calculus.

Since every kind of λ-conversion is equivalent to a synthetic theory and vice versa, the results described below for the synthetic theory are also results of λ-conversion and in some cases were first so obtained.

Foundations of pure synthetic theory. The table contains a list of special combinators. The names assigned to the combinators are in the first (X) column and the values of m and M to be used in equation (3) are in the second and third columns. The other columns will be explained later. In the various formulations certain of the combinators will be atomic; the corresponding equations (3) will then be assumed as axiom schemes in which 'x_1', $\cdots$, 'x_m' stand for arbitrary obs.

Basic Combinators

X	m	M	*Definition*	FX
B	3	$x_1(x_2x_3)$	**S(KS)K**	$F(F\beta\gamma)(F(F\alpha\beta)(F\alpha\gamma))$
C	3	$x_1x_3x_2$	**S(BBS)(KK)**	$F(F\beta(F\alpha\gamma))(F\alpha(F\beta\gamma))$
I	1	x_1	——	$F\alpha\alpha$
K	2	x_1	——	$F\alpha(F\beta\alpha)$
S	3	$x_1x_3(x_2x_3)$	——	$F(F\alpha(F\beta\gamma))(F(F\alpha\beta)(F\alpha\gamma))$
W	2	$x_1x_2x_2$	**SS(KI)**	$F(F\alpha(F\alpha\beta))(F\alpha\beta)$
Φ	4	$x_1(x_2x_4)(x_3x_4)$	**B(BS)B**	
Ψ	4	$x_1(x_2x_3)(x_2x_4)$		

We seek to define, for arbitrary $M, x_1, \cdots, x_m$, an X such that (3) holds. The X so defined will be $[x_1, \cdots, x_m]M$; this means the same thing as $\lambda x_1 \cdots x_m M$ but is a defined, not a postulated, concept. One way of defining it is to use an induction on m, as above, and then, for $m = 1$, an induction on the structure of M. The latter can be obtained, for instance, by defining X to be KM when M does not contain x, to be I when M is x, and to be SX_1X_2 when $M \equiv M_1M_2$ and we have already defined $X_1 \equiv [x]M_1, X_2 \equiv [x]M_2$. Such an algorithm defines all combinators in terms of I, K, S as atoms; the definitions are very long, but suitable modifications improve matters. The fourth column of the table gives some definitions obtained by suitably modified algorithms. Other modifications give definitions in terms of I, B, C, S for all cases where M actually contains x; these are suitable for an analogue of λI-conversion.

Thus, we get a definition for $[x]M$ compatible with any of the forms of λ-conversion if we postulate schemes (3) as stated, together with the properties of equality. The analogues (with $[x]M$ in place of $\lambda x M$) of (α) and (β) will then hold. But we do not have the analogue of (ξ), nor do we have an extensionality principle

$$(\zeta) \qquad U_1 x = U_2 x \rightarrow U_1 = U_2$$

even under the restrictions which are appropriate for λβ-conversion. One can obtain these properties by adjoining a finite number of *combinatory axioms*. Examples of these axioms are

$$(4) \qquad \mathbf{SK = KI},$$
$$(5) \qquad \mathbf{\Psi SK = BK}.$$

Given a form of λ-conversion, we can choose these axioms so that there is a many–one mapping of the resulting system into the λ-conversion and another one vice versa, such that an equation in either system is a theorem exactly when its image is in the other. Thus, λ-conversion and the synthetic theory are equivalent. Bruce Lercher, in 1963, extended these considerations to include (δ).

It is possible to define, in several ways, a combinator $\mathbf{Y}$ such that for any X, $\mathbf{Y}X = X(\mathbf{Y}X)$. If Γ means negation, then $\mathbf{Y}\Gamma$ means the same as its own negation. For $\mathbf{Y} = \mathbf{WS(BWB)}$, this is the notion at the root of the Russell paradox. Thus, in a combinatorially complete system one cannot exclude the paradoxes; one must explain them in the illative theory.

In the foregoing, equality can be taken as primitive. Then the axioms consist of the combinatory axioms, all instances of the reflexive law, and (3) (for atomic combinators); the rules are the usual rules for equality. When we press the analysis deeper so as to define equality by (2), the schemes (3) become rules; for example, that for $\mathbf{S}$ gives the pair of rules (one in each sense)

$$(6) \qquad \vdash U(\mathbf{S}XYZ) \rightleftarrows \vdash U(XZ(YZ)),$$

whereas reflexivity can come from an axiom. The result is a system with a finite number of axioms (no axiom schemes) and about a dozen rules, each with one or two premises and otherwise no more complex than (6) and such that the premises uniquely determine the conclusion. There are also only a finite number of atoms—variables are used only in the metatheory—and the single operation of application. The structure is therefore very simple. But all functions of variables can be performed therein, and with suitable illative additions it can form a basis for almost any logical system.

Combinatory arithmetic. From the formal standpoint the natural numbers are constructions from a single atom, 0, by a single unary operation, σ. On this basis one can develop the usual recursive arithmetic, and one can explain how to count. Assume that such a system is given, represented, say, in the words in some alphabet with only one letter. These words we shall call the *natural numbers.* Further, let σ be the successor function, δ the predecessor function, τ the ordered-pair function, and μ the operation such that for any numerical function f, μf is the least n for which $f(n) = 0$ and is undefined if there is no such n.

One can find a representation of the natural numbers as combinators; indeed, there are many choices. For any such choice let angle brackets "⟨ ⟩" symbolize the combinatory analogues of the arithmetic notions indicated within them. Thus, ⟨n⟩ is, for any numeral n, the *combinatory numeral* which represents it, $\langle + \rangle$ the analogue of addition, etc. The analogues are often not uniquely determined.

The first representation, by Church in 1933, chose $\langle n \rangle$ so that $\langle n \rangle f$ is the nth iterate of f (the first iterate being f itself). If one has **K**, then $\langle 0 \rangle$ is **KI** and $\langle \sigma \rangle$ is **SB**. Then $\langle n \rangle$ is the $\mathbf{Z}_n$ of H. B. Curry and Robert Feys (*Combinatory Logic*). Further, $\langle + \rangle$, $\langle \cdot \rangle$, and $\langle e \rangle$, where $e(x,y) = x^y$, have simple definitions (for example, $\Phi\mathbf{B}$, **B**, and **CI**, respectively) from which their arithmetical properties follow. There are other proposals for combinatory numerals; one, made by Dana Scott in 1963, has a simple $\langle \delta \rangle$. For the sake of generality, $\langle n \rangle$ is here unspecified, but a **Z** is postulated such that $\mathbf{Z}\langle n \rangle = \mathbf{Z}_n$. If $\langle n \rangle \equiv \mathbf{Z}_n$, then $\mathbf{Z} \equiv \mathbf{I}$.

Next one can define combinators $\mathbf{D} \ (\equiv \langle \tau \rangle)$, $\mathbf{D}_1$, $\mathbf{D}_2$ such that

$$\mathbf{D}_1(\mathbf{D}xy) = x, \qquad \mathbf{D}_2(\mathbf{D}xy) = y.$$

For instance (as Paul Bernays suggested in 1936),

$$\mathbf{D} = [x,y,z].\mathbf{Z}z(\mathbf{K}y)x.$$

For this

$$(7) \qquad \mathbf{D}xy\langle 0 \rangle = x, \qquad \mathbf{D}xy\langle \sigma n \rangle = y,$$

so that $\mathbf{D}_1$ and $\mathbf{D}_2$ can be $[x]x\langle 0 \rangle$ and $[x]x\langle 1 \rangle$, respectively. One can also define **D** in terms of $\langle \delta \rangle$ rather than **Z**.

Next a combinator **R** can be defined such that

$$(8) \qquad \mathbf{R}xy\langle 0 \rangle = x, \qquad \mathbf{R}xy\langle \sigma n \rangle = y\langle n \rangle(\mathbf{R}xy\langle n \rangle).$$

If $x = \langle g \rangle$ and $y = \langle h \rangle$, where g and h are, respectively, k-place and $(k+2)$-place numerical functions, $\mathbf{R}xy$ can be taken as $\langle f \rangle$, where f is the $(k+1)$-place numerical function defined by the "primitive recursion scheme" from g and h. Since the other processes of forming primitive recursive functions have combinatory analogues, definition of **R** will ensure that $\langle f \rangle$ is defined for any primitive recursive f.

Several definitions of **R** exist. The first (given by Bernays in 1936) depends on the fact that $f(n)$ can be obtained (for $k = 0$, as an example) by iterating n times, starting with $\tau(0, g)$, the function ϕ such that $\phi(\tau(x, y)) = t(\sigma x, h(x, y))$ and taking the second member. This leads to the definition (in two stages)

$$Y = [u]\mathbf{D}(\langle \sigma \rangle(\mathbf{D}_2 u))(y(\mathbf{D}_1 u)(\mathbf{D}_2 u)),$$
$$\mathbf{R} = [x,y,z](\mathbf{D}_2(\mathbf{Z}zY(\mathbf{D}\langle 0 \rangle x))).$$

Another possibility is to define a combinator Ω such that for given obs p, q, r, the ob $t = \Omega pqr$ satisfies the conditions

$$(9) \qquad t\langle n \rangle = \begin{cases} p\langle n \rangle & \text{if } r\langle n \rangle = \langle 0 \rangle, \\ qf\langle n \rangle & \text{if } r\langle n \rangle = \langle 1 \rangle, \end{cases}$$

thus:

$$Y \equiv \mathbf{D}(\mathbf{K}p)([u](q([z](u(rz)uz)))),$$
$$\Omega \equiv [p,q,r,x](Y(rx)Yx).$$

For $p \equiv \mathbf{K}x$, $q \equiv [u,z](y(\langle \delta \rangle z)(u(\langle \delta \rangle z)))$, $r = \mathbf{I}$, the ob $[x,y]\Omega pqr$ is an **R**, different from the foregoing, satisfying (8). There are still other ways of defining **R**. Since $\langle \delta \rangle$ can

be defined as $\mathbf{R}\langle 0 \rangle\mathbf{K}$ and **Z** as $\mathbf{R}(\mathbf{KI})(\mathbf{K}(\mathbf{SB}))$, we have any primitive recursive function as soon as we have either **Z** or $\langle \delta \rangle$ and a discrimination for $\langle 0 \rangle$.

We can go further. If we take $p \equiv \mathbf{I}$, $q \equiv [u,z](u(\langle \sigma \rangle z))$, while r is a given function $\langle g \rangle$, then Ωpqr is an $\langle f \rangle$ such that $f(n) = n$ if $g(n) = 0$ and otherwise $f(n) = f(\sigma n)$. This shows that we can define $\langle \mu \rangle$ in terms of the above q as $[x](\Omega\mathbf{I}qx\langle 0 \rangle)$. Consequently, every partial recursive numerical function is definable by combinators. The converse of this thesis follows by the usual arguments involving Gödel numeration.

These conclusions are not greatly affected if one restricts the system to correspond with restricted forms of λ-conversion. The passage from η-conversion to β-conversion hardly makes any difference. The omission of **K** complicates things somewhat—one needs ordered triples instead of ordered pairs. But the main conclusion, that every partial recursive function is definable by combinators and vice versa, stands.

Some generalizations are known. One can define by combinators certain transformations between obs and their Gödel numbers. An extension to recursive functionals of certain types can be obtained by using an analogue of $\langle \delta \rangle$. There is also an extension to certain transfinite ordinal numbers.

Illative theory. By definition illative combinatory logic includes all considerations where there are atoms which neither are combinators nor are necessary to express equality. We consider here those cases in which the new atoms mean ordinary logical notions—for example, Π (absolute universality), **P** (implication), Ξ (relative universality or formal implication), **F** (functionality—**FXYZ** means that Z is a function from X into Y), Σ (instantiality), Λ (conjunction), Γ (negation), Θ (descriptive quantifier), etc. In addition, we need obs meaning semantical categories, such as **E** (the category of all obs—**E** is definable, for example, as **WQ**), **H** (propositions), **J** (individuals), **M** (sets), **N** (numbers), etc.

The meaning of these obs is expressed more precisely by the rules associated with them. For the first four obs these are

RULE Π:	$\vdash \Pi X \ \& \vdash EU \rightarrow \ \vdash XU.$
RULE P:	$\vdash \mathbf{P}XY \ \& \vdash X \rightarrow \ \vdash Y.$
RULE Ξ:	$\vdash \Xi XY \ \& \vdash XU \rightarrow \ \vdash YU.$
RULE F:	$\vdash \mathbf{F}XYZ \ \& \vdash XU \rightarrow \ \vdash Y(ZU).$

These rules, when relevant, are to be postulated in addition to the combinatory rules given earlier; the latter can be summarized as

RULE Eq:	$\vdash X \ \& \ X = Y \rightarrow \ \vdash Y.$

These notions are, of course, interdefinable; in fact, one can take as atoms either **F**, Ξ, or Π and **P** and define the others as follows (there are two possible definitions for Ξ in terms of **F**):

$$\mathbf{F} \equiv [x,y,z](\Xi x(\mathbf{B}yz)),$$
$$\Xi \equiv [x,y](\Pi([z](\mathbf{P}(xz)(yz)))),$$
$$\Pi \equiv \Xi E,$$
$$\mathbf{P} \equiv \Psi\Xi\mathbf{K} = [x,y](\Xi(\mathbf{K}x)(\mathbf{K}y)),$$
$$\Xi' \equiv [x,y](\mathbf{F}xy\mathbf{I}), \qquad \Xi'' \equiv [x,y](\mathbf{F}x\mathbf{I}y).$$

The system based on **F** as primitive is called $\mathscr{F}_1$, or the theory of *functionality;* that on Ξ as $\mathscr{F}_2$, or the theory of *restricted generality;* and that on Π and $\mathbf{P}$ as $\mathscr{F}_3$. With reasonable axioms, these are listed in order of increasing strength.

Although the Church–Rosser theorem shows that pure combinatory logic is consistent, in the illative theory one easily runs into contradictions. Thus, if one were to assume

$$(10) \qquad \vdash \mathbf{P}(\mathbf{P}\alpha(\mathbf{P}\alpha\beta))(\mathbf{P}\alpha\beta)$$

as an axiom scheme, with the Greek letters standing for arbitrary obs, the theory would be inconsistent in the sense that (1) would hold for any X. But (10) is a thesis of the *absolute* (that is, positive intuitionistic) *propositional algebra.* Thus, it is necessary, if the theory is to contain this algebra, that (10) be a theorem scheme with a restricted range for the Greek letters. In its early stages illative combinatory logic will have axiom schemes with such restrictions. Later, perhaps, these schemes will be reduced to axioms by quantifying over a suitable category.

This requires some sort of machinery of categories or types. Such machinery is taken for granted in the usual systems of mathematical logic. It consists of four items: (*a*) a list of primitive categories (such as those listed above), (*b*) devices for forming derived categories, (*c*) assignments of the primitive notions to categories, (*d*) means for determining the categories of composite notions. Of these items (*a*) and (*c*) are special to the theory considered, but (*b*) and (*d*) are general processes which are appropriate for study in combinatory logic. Since composite obs are formed by application alone, one would expect a means of assigning a category to XY when those for X and Y are known; the general principle is that if X is a function from α to β and Y belongs to α, then XY belongs to β. This principle is expressed by Rule **F**, so the basis for this generalized theory of types is $\mathscr{F}_1$.

From the illative standpoint one would expect that each combinator would be assigned a category depending on parameters expressing that it is a function transforming from certain sorts of categories to categories of certain other sorts. Such *functional characters* for some basic combinators of the table are listed there in the fifth column. Assignments of these characters to the atomic combinators would then be axiom (or at least theorem) schemes of $\mathscr{F}_1$. However, these schemes cannot be accepted with the Greek letters standing for arbitrary obs, for if one so accepts **FW**, the theory is again inconsistent. Even $\mathscr{F}_1$ has to be formulated with restrictions on the Greek letters.

The most radical restriction is the requirement that the Greek letters range over an inductive class of F-obs generated from certain otherwise unspecified atoms $\theta_1, \theta_2, \cdots$ by the operation of forming $\mathbf{F}\alpha\beta$ from α and β. One further restricts Rule Eq thus:

RULE Eq′: $\qquad \vdash \xi X \ \& \ X = Y \rightarrow \vdash \xi Y.$

The resulting theory is called the *basic theory of functionality.* In this theory every elementary statement will be of the form

$$(11) \qquad \vdash \xi X,$$

where ξ is an F-ob and X is a combinator. The theory is demonstrably consistent. If X is a *stratified* combinator— that is, if X satisfies (3) and one can derive $\vdash \eta M$ by Rule **F** alone from the axiom schemes and assignments of categories to the variables—then one can derive a statement of the form (11) stating that X has the appropriate functional character. There is a converse to this which is somewhat difficult to state, but it shows that the X's for which (11) can be derived are greatly restricted; in particular, they have a normal form.

There are several "stronger" theories of functionality with less drastic restrictions. A theory in which one uses only combinators that do not repeat variables can be constructively proved consistent without restrictions on the Greek letters. Constructive consistency proofs have been obtained for some other theories of $\mathscr{F}_1$.

All these systems of $\mathscr{F}_1$ are extremely weak. To obtain stronger and natural theories one proceeds to $\mathscr{F}_2$ (or adds assumptions to $\mathscr{F}_1$ which are equivalent to this). In $\mathscr{F}_2$ reasonable schemes $\Xi\mathbf{I}$, $\Xi\mathbf{K}$, etc., with Greek letters restricted to a class of "canonical obs," can be formulated from which the corresponding **FI**, **FK**, $\cdots$ can be derived. Thus, $\mathscr{F}_2$ has a deduction theorem; it also includes the absolute propositional calculus of pure implication. There is a Gentzen-like theory of "verifiability" from which it follows that certain weak forms of the illative theory are consistent.

The study of illative combinatory logic is still in its preliminary stages. Little is known, for example, about $\mathscr{F}_3$. It is clear that ordinary logical systems can be founded on a combinatory basis, but little has been published along this line. On such a basis E. J. Cogan, in 1955, analyzed the foundations of Gödel's set theory and also the predicate calculus and some other calculuses; owing to an unfortunate oversight in the definition of "class," the system was inconsistent, as Rainer Titgemeyer showed in 1961, but the necessary changes are rather minor. Other investigations of this sort are in the process of development or publication. Some authors, such as F. B. Fitch, go in a somewhat different direction.

In illative combinatory logic we are dealing with concepts of such generality that we have little intuition in regard to them. This explains why proposals by competent logicians beginning with Frege (not all combinatory, but the principle applies) have later proved inconsistent. We must, indeed, proceed by trial and error. No doubt we shall continue to find both inconsistencies in weaker systems and consistency proofs of stronger systems. In due course nonfinitary methods will be used, and much is to be expected of them. But the possibility remains that we may always be interested in systems for which neither consistency nor inconsistency is known.

Combinatory logic was inaugurated by Moses Schönfinkel in 1924. He introduced the notion of application, the combinators **B, C, I, K, S** (his Z, T, I, C, S), and an illative notion U. He showed how statements of logic could be expressed in terms of these notions, but he gave no deductive theory of them. He became ill shortly after writing the paper and was unable to do anything further in the subject. Curry, beginning in 1929, produced the first deductive synthetic theory and introduced the terminology used here. The theory of λ-conversion was developed by Church from 1932. Subsequent improvements were made by these authors and by Rosser, S. C. Kleene, Bernays, Fitch, and Paul Rosenbloom. The present state of the subject is the result of an interaction of the work of these authors and their students.

Bibliography

Items listed here either are of broad scope or treat aspects of the subject not included in the text. For sources, details, etc., see the bibliographies in the works cited.

Church, Alonzo, "The Richard Paradox." *American Mathematical Monthly,* Vol. 41 (1934), 356–361. Expounds a system modeling illative notions on the pure theory.

Church, Alonzo, *The Calculi of Lambda-conversion.* Princeton, N.J., 1941; 2d ed., 1951. The standard work on λ-conversion, with references.

Cogan, E. J., "A Formalization of the Theory of Sets From the Point of View of Combinatory Logic." *Zeitschrift für mathematische Logik und Grundlagen der Mathematik,* Vol. 1 (1955), 198–240. Contains a readable introduction and some information on illative theory going beyond Curry and Feys (below). For an inconsistency, see text, section on illative theory.

Curry, H. B., "The Elimination of Variables by Regular Combinators," in Mario Bunge, ed., *The Critical Approach to Science and Philosophy,* in honor of Karl R. Popper. New York, 1964. Pp. 127–143. Contains, on pp. 128–131, a discussion of the "ontology" of combinatory logic, partly in answer to Quine (below).

Curry, H. B., and Feys, Robert, *Combinatory Logic,* Vol. I. Amsterdam, 1958. A monograph, with full bibliography, historical sketch, etc. A second volume is in progress.

Fitch, F. B., "The System CΔ of Combinatory Logic." *Journal of Symbolic Logic,* Vol. 28 (1963), 87–97. A nonfinitary system with consistency proof. Refers to Fitch's other papers.

Quine, W. V., "Variables Explained Away." *Proceedings of the American Philosophical Society,* Vol. 104 (1960), 343–347. An alternative formulation of combinatory logic, to be used in combination with first-order predicate calculus, which, Quine claims, involves fewer ontological presuppositions.

Rosenbloom, Paul, *The Elements of Mathematical Logic.* New York, 1950. Very compact. Departures from standard notations hinder reading.

Rosser, J. B., *Deux Esquisses de logique.* Paris, 1955. A masterly exposition of certain parts of the pure theory.

Schönfinkel, Moses, "Über die Bausteine der mathematischen Logik." *Mathematische Annalen,* Vol. 92 (1924), 305–316. Still readable and interesting for motivation. The statement in the postscript (by Heinrich Behmann) to the effect that parentheses can be eliminated by **Z** (that is, **B**) alone is erroneous.

HASKELL B. CURRY

LOGIC, DEONTIC.

Deontic logic, or the logic of obligation, is that area of thought in which we formulate and systematize such principles as that nothing can be obligatory and forbidden at once and that whatever we are committed to by doing what is obligatory is itself obligatory. It differs from ethics in that it does not pronounce upon questions concerning what is in fact obligatory (the view that our only obligation is to maximize pleasure and minimize pain would be an ethical position rather than one in deontic logic) and from pure formal logic in that it formulates principles that are specific to the concept of obligation and allied problems (the principle, for example, that

whatever is obligatory is obligatory can be established outside deontic logic, being merely a special case of the ordinary logical principle that everything is what it is).

Principles of deontic logic have in the past tended to be merely stated in passing in the course of works on moral theology or casuistry, but even in the Middle Ages it was realized that the logic of the permissible and the obligatory in some ways paralleled that of the possible and the necessary and could be regarded as falling under modal logic in a broad sense. The systematic treatment of modal logic in modern times led naturally to attempts to handle deontic logic in a similar way, such as those of E. Mally in 1926 and Kurt Grelling and Karel Reach in the late 1930s. More extensive studies were stimulated by the work of G. H. von Wright in 1951.

DEONTIC LOGIC AND MODAL LOGIC

Typical principles of modal logic are that whatever is necessary is possible, that what is impossible is necessarily false and vice versa, and that what is necessitated by something necessary is itself necessary. Analogously, it would seem that whatever is obligatory is permissible, that what is forbidden (not permissible) we are obliged not to do and vice versa, and that what we are committed to by something obligatory is itself obligatory. On the other hand, whereas whatever is necessary is actually the case and whatever is actually the case is possible, it does not seem to be true that whatever is obligatory is actually done and whatever is actually done is permissible. It does seem true, however, that it ought to be the case that whatever is obligatory is done. Thus, although we do not have the deontic analogue of the plain "If necessarily *p* then *p*," we do seem to have the analogue of "Necessarily (if necessarily *p* then *p*)."

The structure of deontic logic thus appears to be like that of a fragment of modal logic, and a simple way of presenting it formally would be to take some system of modal logic, replace "It is necessarily the case that . . ." by "It ought to be the case that . . ." and "It could be the case that . . ." by "It is permissible that . . . ," and omit those laws that fail to remain valid after this transformation.

A deontic system of this sort may be fruitfully enlarged by the introduction of ordinary modal concepts as well as deontic ones. We can then formulate such principles as that for a thing to be obligatory it must be possible ("What I ought I can") and that what cannot be done without something wrong being done would itself be wrong to do. Since the converse of this last principle is obviously also true (that is, what would itself be wrong to do cannot be done without something wrong being done—namely itself), if we introduce a constant proposition *S* to mean "Something wrong is being done," we can equate "It is forbidden that *p*" with "It cannot be the case that *p* without *S* being the case"—that is, with "If *p* then-necessarily *S*." With this equivalence many of the typical laws of deontic logic can easily be derived from those of ordinary modal logic.

These derivations are even easier if we introduce a

constant *E* with the meaning "not-*S*" (i.e., "Nothing wrong is occurring") and equate "It ought to be the case that *p*" with "If *E* then-necessarily *p*" (i.e., "If nothing wrong is to occur then-necessarily *p* will occur"). Consider, as an illustration, the principle that if it ought to be the case that *p*, then if it ought to be the case that if-*p*-then-*q*, it ought to be the case that *q*. If "ought" is defined as suggested, this law amounts simply to a special case of the following law of modal logic:

> If *r* necessarily implies that *p*, then if *r* also necessarily implies that *p* necessarily implies that *q*, then *r* necessarily implies that *q*.

The special case is that in which *r* is the "escape clause" *E*. The only major principle of deontic logic that is not thus reducible to a special case of an ordinary modal principle is the law that whatever is obligatory is permissible, or nothing is both obligatory and forbidden. This reads

> If *E* necessarily implies that *p*, then *E* does not necessarily imply that not-*p*.

If *E* were of the form "*p* and not-*p*," it *would* both necessarily imply *p* and necessarily imply not-*p*, so that in ordinary modal logic this law could have exceptions. Such exceptions will be precluded and the law established if we add to modal logic, with the definition of "ought," an axiom to the effect that *E* is not impossible—that is, that we *can* avoid doing something wrong.

This way of simplifying deontic logic was discovered by A. R. Anderson, who in turn derived it from a suggestion of H. G. Bohnert that imperative sentences of the form "Do *X*" may be regarded as indicative sentences of the form "You will do *X*, or else"—that is, "If you do not do *X*, such and such harm will befall you," or "If you are to escape this harm, you will do *X*." In its original form Anderson's theory simply transferred this suggestion to "ought" and stated that "It is obligatory that *p*" means "If *p* is not done then-necessarily some sanction or penalty will be applied." This is open to the objection that it is possible, however regrettably, to do what is wrong or to omit what is obligatory and yet escape the penalty. The essence of the Andersonian system, however, is simply the definition of the forbidden as what necessarily implies the occurrence of a certain bad thing, and the details are the same whatever this bad thing is supposed to be. Indeed, as T. J. Smiley has pointed out, the purely logical interest of Anderson's system, particularly in the form in which the obligatory is defined as what necessarily implied by the "escape clause," is in its exhibiting the logic of being necessitated by a given condition, as contrasted with being simply necessary. This is an important concept even apart from its possible use in deontic logic.

E. J. Lemmon and P. H. Nowell-Smith have argued that even in its most plausible form Anderson's way of presenting deontic logic is open to the following objection: Take any ordinary statement to the effect that something is obligatory—for example, that it is always obligatory to maximize pleasure and minimize pain or that right now a certain person ought to shut a certain window. In general, statements of this sort belong to ethics and do not belong to logic. In a few special cases they may belong to deontic logic—this may be true of the statement that it is obligatory that whatever is obligatory be done—but they certainly do not belong to ordinary logic. On the other hand, a statement that something necessarily implies something else *would* normally be regarded as belonging to ordinary logic. But the Andersonian procedure identifies every assertion of obligation with an assertion of necessary implication. This procedure seems therefore to blur the boundaries between ethics and logic and thus to commit what is often called, after G. E. Moore, the "naturalistic fallacy." One might express this objection by saying that the performance of something which is in fact wrong does in some sense imply that something wrong is being done, but only in the sense that "*X* is being done, and *X* is wrong" implies that something wrong is being done; the plain "*X* is being done," even if *X* is in fact wrong, does not by itself imply that something wrong is being done, which it would have to do if "*X* is wrong" means "The doing of *X* implies that something wrong is being done."

One answer to this objection is to bring against the objector the countercharge of making assertions of obligation merely empirical or contingent. If the objector does not want to do this—and few philosophers do—he must admit that assertions of obligation and forbiddenness are, when true, necessary truths, and if it is a necessary truth that it is wrong to do *X*, then it is a necessary truth that if *X* is done, something wrong is done. If this is not a logical necessity, then there must be other forms of necessity besides, and the laws of modal logic (such as that what is necessarily implied by a necessary truth is itself necessary) apply to those other sorts of necessity also and thus can be used to derive the logic of obligation as a special case of necessary implication.

GRAMMAR OF OBLIGATION STATEMENTS

In the developments of the subject just sketched it is assumed that "It is obligatory that . . ." or "It ought to be the case that . . ." is an expression that is attached to a sentence, in just the same way as we attach "It is not the case that . . ." or "It is necessary that . . ." or "It is alleged that . . ." to a sentence to form a larger sentence. The attached sentence expresses *what* is being said to be obligatory, while the complete sentence states *that* it is obligatory. To this way of constructing obligation statements some writers have objected that what is obligatory is never a sentence but an action. There is a rather crude misunderstanding here. "It is not the case that grass is green" is not a statement about the sentence "Grass is green" but a negative statement about grass. Similarly, "It ought to be the case that you are shutting that window"—that is, "You ought to be shutting that window"—is not a statement about the sentence "You are shutting that window" but a complex one about you and the window. What is said to be obligatory is not the sentence but what the sentence expresses, and this is an action.

There are, however, more serious reasons for considering modifications of the above procedure. In the first place, the term "action" is ambiguous. It may mean a particular performance on a particular occasion, such as John's shutting the window now, or it may mean a type of performance, such as shutting the window or giving people money, and although actions in the first sense seem to be appropriately described by complete sentences, actions in the second sense are not. Von Wright's first deontic calculus was designed to handle the obligatoriness, permissibility, etc., of actions in the second sense and accordingly symbolized actions by letters—*A*, *B*, *C*, etc.—that were *not* thought of as standing for sentences. Action types as well as action instances may be complex; for example, if *A* is "running" and *B* is "walking," not-*A* will be "not running," and *A*-or-*B* will be "running or walking." But we do not get complete sentences until we attach *O* or *P* ("is obligatory" or "is permissible") to these *A*'s, *B*'s, etc.

One consequence of this procedure is that the form "If *A* is obligatory then *A*" will represent not something like "If it ought to be that Jones is shutting the window, then Jones is shutting the window" but rather something like "If shutting the window is obligatory, then shutting the window," so that the principle is to be condemned not as sometimes false but rather as meaningless. In order to express the false principle in a language of this sort, Robert Nozick and Richard Routley (following G. E. Hughes) introduced a special operator meaning that an action is done, the false principle then being simply "If an act of type *A* is obligatory, then such an act is done." If, however, we proceed as in the last section, this complication is unnecessary, and in any case it seems desirable to have a theory about the obligatoriness, etc., of "actions" in the sense of particular doings.

Even if we agree that deontic operators are appropriately attached to sentences, it is arguable that they are not appropriately attached to all sentences, for although some sentences describe actions, many others (for instance, "2 and 2 is 4") do not. The restriction of deontic operators to action-describing sentences can be built into a deontic calculus in a variety of ways. Some quite elaborate mechanisms to achieve this end are developed in von Wright's recent *Norm and Action*. Von Wright first introduced the form *pTq* to express the transformation of the state of affairs *p* into the state of affairs *q* (including as a special case *pTp*, the persistence of the state of affairs *p*) and the forms *d*(*pTq*) and *f*(*pTq*) for bringing about such transformations and forbearing from bringing them about. It is to such "*df*-sentences" that deontic operators like *O* and *P* are attached.

R. M. Chisholm proceeds more simply. He allows "It ought to be the case that . . ." to be attached to any sentences whatever, but he takes sentences to express actions only if they are formed by putting "*x* brings it about that . . ." to other sentences. Obligations in the strict sense are then expressed by sentences of the form "It ought to be the case that *x* brings it about that *p*."

Yet another way of restricting the application of deontic operators has been suggested by certain writers of the school of R. M. Hare. This suggestion is that deontic operators attach not to indicative but to imperative sentences. It is as if we read the deontic logician's *O* as "It ought to be that you . . ." and treated it as forming the sentence "It ought to be that you do *X*" out of the imperative "Do *X*." H.-N. Castañeda regards the sentence thus formed as being itself indicative; it is in effect an assertion that the command is justified, not in the sense that it would be wrong not to give the command, but in the sense that it

would be wrong not to obey it. (The former would be "It ought to be that you command *X*," formed from the higher-order imperative "Command *X*"). Another way of forming indicatives from imperatives is by prefixing an operator with the force of "It is the case that you . . . ," to form the assertion that the imperative is obeyed. Imperatives may then have a special relation to logic in two ways: it may be a law of the system that they are obeyed, as with the imperative "Either do *X* or don't do it," or it may be a law of the system that they are justified, as with the imperative "If it ought to be that you do *X*, do it." It is an interesting feature of this deontic system that it does contain an analogue of the modal principle "If necessarily-*p* then *p*"—namely, the logically justified imperative just mentioned. The same imperative occurs in a modification of Castañeda's system by Hare and Mark Fisher, in which "You ought to do *X*" is itself not an indicative but an imperative, related to the plain "Do *X*" in the same way as "Necessarily *p*" is to the plain *p*.

Even if we drop these complications and simply attach deontic operators to indicative sentences to form other indicative sentences, there remains the question whether we ought to take as fundamental an operator attaching to one sentence or to two. Søren Halldén, for instance, has developed a system in which the basic type of sentence is "It is better if *p* than if *q*," "It ought to be the case that *p*" being possibly definable as "It is better if *p* than if not-*p*." Von Wright, on the other hand, regards this "logic of preference" as being not deontic logic but rather a kind of formal value theory. But even apart from this, deontic logic has to handle the notion of moral commitment. Attempts to define "Doing *X* commits one to doing *Y*" in terms of simple obligation (for instance, as "It ought to be that if one does *X*, one does *Y*" or as "If one does *X*, it ought to be that one does *Y*") have proved in various ways unsatisfactory. Therefore, von Wright, Nicholas Rescher, and others have looked at the possibility of defining simple obligation in terms of an undefined commitment, conditional obligation, or conditional permission. One might say, for example, that one is simply obliged to do that which one is committed to doing by any action or state of affairs whatever. Chisholm defines obligation in terms of the notion of *p*'s "requiring" that *q*, but Chisholm's system is best discussed after an examination of some of the problems that provoked it.

HINTIKKA'S PARADOX

Deontic logic involves problems that concern not merely its grammar but also its content. For example, although it seems clear that what is obligatory must be possible and what is impossible therefore not obligatory, can we say, further, that what is impossible is not even permissible? Most people's moral intuitions have nothing to say about this, but the following argument, in essence that of Jaakko Hintikka, suggests that what is not possible is positively forbidden: It seems clear that (1) to do something which cannot be done without something wrong being done would itself be wrong. But (2) what cannot be done at all cannot be done either with or without something wrong being done—if *X* is impossible and *Y* is wrong, I can neither do both X and Y nor do X-but-not-Y. But by (1), if Y is wrong and doing X-but-not-Y is impossible, it is wrong to do X. Hence, (3) if it is impossible to do X, it is wrong to do it.

There is a case for simply accepting this as a queer but harmless by-product of sound basic principles—harmless because if the impossible is a sin, it is a sin which no one will commit even in ignorance. What cannot be done will not be done, whether it would be wrong to do it or not. However, from Hintikka's principle, together with the principle that what it is wrong to do it is wrong to attempt, it would follow that it is wrong even to attempt the impossible, which seems a more substantial conclusion and a dubious one. It could be argued that no one would attempt the impossible knowing it to be so (for no one could then envisage anything as a step toward the achievement in question), and sins committed in ignorance are excusable. But Roger White has furnished the following case: Suppose a logician does not know whether a certain formula follows from certain axioms, spends a day trying to deduce it from them, fails, and then spends a day trying to show that it is impossible to deduce it. But either it is impossible to deduce this formula or it is impossible to show that it cannot be deduced, so that by the time the second day comes the logician will know that either he was previously attempting the impossible or he is doing so now. No doubt this is not quite the same as knowingly attempting the impossible, but it is near enough to it to reflect a certain doubtfulness upon Hintikka's law.

If we reject Hintikka's law, we must reject one of the premises from which it is deduced—for example, the principle that what cannot be done without something wrong being done is itself wrong. Perhaps the true principle is not this but that what entails the doing of something wrong is itself wrong, in a sense in which "*p* entails *q*" makes a stronger assertion than "(*p*-and-not-*q*) is impossible" (see LOGIC, MODAL). If *p* is impossible, then certainly (*p*-and-not-*q*) is also impossible, but from *p*'s being impossible it does not follow that *p* entails *q* in this sense of "entails," so that when Hintikka's premise (1) is thus modified the analogous modification of his premise (2) will fail, and with it his conclusion.

However, even the principle that what entails the doing of something wrong is itself wrong is open to an objection. For that I am helping someone who is being attacked entails (though it does not bring about) that the person in question is being attacked and so entails that a wrong is being done and would itself be wrong by this principle (this is known as the "paradox of the Good Samaritan"). Perhaps the true principle is simply that one ought not to bring about what ought not to be the case.

It has also been suggested that we can avoid Hintikka's paradox by saying that deontic statements about what is impossible simply do not make sense, because we form genuine sentences by attaching deontic operators to other sentences only when these latter sentences describe not merely actions but possible actions. This ruling, however, would make it impossible to develop deontic logic in any systematic way at all. Presumably anything which contradicts a logical theorem is impossible, so we cannot know whether we can attach a deontic operator to some complex until we know what all the logical theorems are; however, we can develop theorems only if we can formulate them and can formulate them only if we already know to which complexes we can attach deontic operators.

LOGIC OF REQUIREMENT

A second problem about the content of deontic logic is that which R. M. Chisholm has noticed in connection with what he calls "contrary-to-duty imperatives" (the phrase was coined by analogy with "contrary-to-fact conditionals"), duties, such as apologizing and making amends, which are imposed on us by our having failed to do some other duty. The following, Chisholm points out, seems a reasonable principle:

(1) If we ought to do something, say X, and if it ought to be the case that if we do X we do Y, then we ought to do Y.

But suppose that

(2) We ought to do X—for example, go to a neighbor's assistance—but in fact

(3) We are not doing X.

Suppose further that

(4) It ought to be that if we do X we do Y—if we are going to a neighbor's assistance we tell him we are—but that

(5) If we are not in fact doing X we ought not to do Y—if we are not going to our neighbor's assistance we ought not to tell him we are.

By the principle (1) it clearly follows from (2) and (4) that we ought to do Y—that is, tell our neighbor that we are going to his assistance. However, from (3) and (5) it follows that we ought not to do Y—that is, it would be positively wrong to tell our neighbor that we are going to his assistance. Hence, one and the same thing is both obligatory and forbidden on such an occasion, contrary to one of the most elementary principles of deontic logic.

The conclusion that Chisholm draws is that current systems of deontic logic must be radically reconstructed and built on the notion of what he calls "requirement." In sketching this reconstruction we may note first that even apart from the above argument, the principle that nothing can be obligatory and forbidden at once has often been criticized as being superficially at variance with the existence of "conflicts of duty." The inconsistency is removed if, following W. D. Ross, we distinguish prima-facie duties from actual ones, or, as it is sometimes put, claims from obligations. Various features of our circumstances give rise to various claims, or prima-facie duties, and these may indeed be in conflict, but in any given situation there is, as it were, a resultant of these claims, which is what we actually ought to do in that situation. It is with respect to this resultant obligation that we may say that what we are obliged to do we cannot also be obliged not to do.

The relation between a particular feature of our circumstances and the claim it gives rise to is what Chisholm means by "requirement." If the relevant feature of our circumstances is expressed by the sentence *p* and the prima-facie duty to which it gives rise by *q*, his basic form of deontic sentence is not "It ought to be that *q*" but "*p* requires *q*," or more accurately "*p*, if present, would require *q*." And to say that *q* is required in a given situation is simply to say that for some *p*, *p* would require *q*, and it is the case that *p*. We might be tempted to think that if *p* required *q*, then anything that entailed *p*, such as *p*-and-*r*, would also require *q*, but this is not so, for requirements may be overridden by further features of a situation. It may be that *p* requires *q* but *p*-and-*r* does not require *q*. To say that *q* is absolutely obligatory, that it simply ought to be the case that *q*, is to say that for some *p*, *p* is the case, *p* requires that *q*, and this requirement is not overridden (i.e., there is no *r* such that *r* is the case and *p*-and-*r* does not require *q*). Often a requirement which is overridden by a further feature of a situation will be restored by a still further one. If *p*, *r*, and *s* are all the case, it might be that *p* requires *q*, *p*-and-*r* does not require it, and *p*-and-*r*-and-*s* does require it. Then again, *p*-and-*r*-and-*s*-and-*t* may not require it, but if *q* is absolutely obligatory, we shall sooner or later reach a description of the situation sufficiently comprehensive for the requirement of *q* not to be overridden by anything further. In the limit this will be "everything that is the case," but normally we may expect the moral oscillations to stop far short of that, and it may even be, as some moralists have thought, that there are some quite simple requirements (for example, not to torture) which no piling on of circumstances can override.

Bibliography

Von Wright's main contributions are in *An Essay in Modal Logic* (Amsterdam, 1951), Ch. 5, and *Norm and Action* (London, 1963). For earlier treatments of deontic logic, see Kurt Grelling, "Zur Logik der Sollsätze," in *Unity of Science Forum* (January 1939), 44–47; and Karel Reach, "Some Comments on Grelling's Paper 'Zur Logik der Sollsätze,'" in *Unity of Science Forum* (April 1939), 72.

A. R. Anderson's views are developed in *The Formal Analysis of Normative Systems,* Technical Report No. 2, U.S. Office of Naval Research Contract No. SAR/Nonr-609 (16) (1956), and commented on in A. N. Prior's *Time and Modality* (Oxford, 1957) and "Escapism: The Logical Basis of Ethics," *Essays in Moral Philosophy,* A. I. Melden, ed. (Seattle, 1958), pp. 135–146; in P. H. Nowell-Smith and E. J. Lemmon's "Escapism: The Logical Basis of Ethics," *Mind,* Vol. 69 (1960), 289–300; and in T. J. Smiley's "Relative Necessity," *Journal of Symbolic Logic,* Vol. 28, (1963), 113–134.

On the syntax of deontic logic, see Robert Nozick and Richard Routley, "Escaping the Good Samaritan Paradox," in *Mind,* Vol. 71 (1962), 377–382; A. N. Prior, "The Done Thing," in *Mind,* Vol. 73 (1964), 441–442; H.-N. Castañeda, "Un sistema general de lógica normativa," in *Dianoia,* Vol. 3 (1957), 303–333, and "The Logic of Obligation," in *Philosophical Studies,* Vol. 10, No. 2 (February 1959), 17–23; and Rose Rand, "The Logic of Demand-sentences," in *Synthese,* Vol. 14 (1962).

For systems with "better than" as a primitive, see Søren Halldén, *The Logic of Better* (Copenhagen, 1957), and G. H. von Wright, *The Logic of Preference* (Edinburgh, 1963).

Chisholm's main contributions are in "Contrary-to-duty Imperatives and Deontic Logic," *Analysis,* Vol. 24 (1963), 33–36, and "The Ethics of Requirement," *American Philosophical Quarterly,* Vol. 1, No. 2 (April 1964), 1–7.

Most of the main problems are surveyed in Georges Kalinowski's *Introduction à la logique juridique* (Paris, 1965).

A. N. Prior

LOGIC, HISTORY OF. The mainstream of the history of logic begins in ancient Greece and comes down through the Arabian and European logic of the Middle Ages and through a number of post-Renaissance thinkers to the more or less mathematical developments in logic in the nineteenth and twentieth centuries. In the period after the fall of Rome many of the ancient achievements were forgotten and had to be relearned; the same thing happened at the end of the Middle Ages. Otherwise this Western tradition has been fairly continuous. Indian and Chinese logic developed separately. Today logic, like other sciences, is studied internationally, and the same problems are treated in the Americas, western and eastern Europe, and Asia and Australasia. The story of the development of logic will be told here under the following headings:

Ancient Logic
Indian Logic
Chinese Logic
Arabic Logic
Medieval (European) Logic
The Interregnum (between medieval and modern logic)
Precursors of Modern Logic
Modern Logic: The Boolean Period
The Heritage of Kant and Mill
Modern Logic: Frege to the Present

(A. N. P.)

ANCIENT LOGIC

Precursors of Aristotle. Ancient logic began with Aristotle (384–322 B.C.). However, Aristotle had precursors among the earlier Greek mathematicians, rhetoricians, and philosophers.

Inference and proof. The principal contribution of Aristotle's precursors to the rise of logic in the fourth century B.C. consisted in the development and cultivation of a kind of discourse that involved the use of inference and proof. While mathematicians were preoccupied with proving new and interesting theorems, rhetoricians and philosophers were finding themselves compelled to look for ways of refuting the contentions of other rhetoricians and philosophers. This involved analyzing the validity of arguments, and in due course this analysis suggested such stratagems as tentatively accepting the point of view of the adversary and then rebutting it by showing that it implied absurd consequences. The connection between this procedure and *modus tollens* is obvious at once. Forensic controversies must also have provided clever and experienced rhetoricians with tempting opportunities for employing fallacious and confusing arguments. In the fifth and fourth centuries B.C. interest in fallacious arguments was very great, as can be judged from Plato's *Euthydemus* and Aristotle's *De Sophisticis Elenchis*. Indeed, the part played by the various logical puzzles invented by Greek rhetoricians and philosophers is comparable to that played in modern times by the antinomies discovered in the early systems of the foundations of mathematics.

The demand for proof in philosophy seems to have been first occasioned by doctrines that appeared to challenge common sense directly. One such doctrine was the Parmenidean metaphysics of the first half of the fifth century B.C., which conceived of reality as a plenum—one, eternal, indivisible, continuous, immovable, and unchanging. The opposition and criticism which this doctrine provoked was brilliantly met by Zeno of Elea (born c. 490 B.C.), who tried to show that the opposite hypothesis, that the all is many and in motion, implied consequences more absurd than the Parmenidean hypothesis that the all is one and that motion is impossible. It is not surprising that Aristotle regarded Zeno as the founder of dialectic even though we have no evidence that Zeno discovered any logical principles. He was a practitioner of logic and produced actual arguments without attempting to develop that quite different thing, a logical theory. Another celebrated practitioner of the art of close argumentation, Socrates (470–399 B.C.), whom Aristotle credits with having made use of induction and universal definition, also arrived at no logical theory.

Syntax and semantics. Logic, of course, not only is concerned with inferences and proofs but also involves the study of language, its syntax and semantics. In this field, too, Aristotle had predecessors, notably among the Sophists. Both Protagoras (c. 490–c. 421 B.C.) and Prodicus (c. 460–c. 399 B.C.), his contemporary, were greatly interested in the correct use of words, Prodicus giving special attention to synonyms. What is perhaps more important, Protagoras was the first thinker to distinguish between different types of sentences. He recognized prayer ($\epsilon\dot{v}\chi o\lambda\dot{\eta}$), question ($\dot{\epsilon}\rho\dot{\omega}\tau\eta\sigma\iota\varsigma$), answer ($\dot{\alpha}\pi\dot{o}\kappa\rho\iota\sigma\iota\varsigma$), and injunction ($\dot{\epsilon}\nu\tauo\lambda\dot{\eta}$). Alcidamas (fl. fourth century B.C.), a rhetorician and a pupil of Gorgias (before 480–after 399 B.C.), classified expressions into affirmation ($\phi\dot{\alpha}\sigma\iota\varsigma$), denial ($\dot{\alpha}\pi\dot{o}\phi\alpha\sigma\iota\varsigma$), question ($\dot{\epsilon}\rho\dot{o}\tau\eta\sigma\iota\varsigma$), and appellation ($\pi\rho o\sigma\alpha\gamma\dot{o}\rho\epsilon\nu\sigma\iota\varsigma$), which appears to correspond to what we now call ostensive definition.

Linguistic studies of this type were also cultivated in the Academy. In the *Sophist,* for instance, Plato (428/427–348/347 B.C.) discussed affirmations and denials and carried the analysis a little further by distinguishing nouns from verbs. A verb ($\dot{\rho}\eta\mu\alpha$), he pointed out, indicates action, whereas a noun ($\dot{o}\nu o\mu\alpha$) indicates the agent. Neither a series of nouns alone nor a series of verbs alone adds up to a proposition ($\lambda\dot{o}\gamma o\varsigma$), which in its simplest form requires both a noun and a verb. This remark of Plato's, provided it is generalized in an appropriate way, seems to anticipate one of the fundamental principles of the modern theory of semantical categories or logical types. Understandably enough, the division between true and false propositions was of great concern to Plato. He held that a true proposition states facts as they are ($\lambda\dot{\epsilon}\gamma\epsilon\iota\ \tau\dot{\alpha}\ \dot{o}\nu\tau\alpha\ \dot{\omega}\varsigma\ \dot{\epsilon}\sigma\tau\iota$) and that a false proposition states things other than facts ($\dot{\epsilon}\tau\epsilon\rho\alpha\ \tau\hat{\omega}\nu\ \dot{o}\nu\tau\omega\nu$). In other words, a false proposition states things that are not, as if they were ($\tau\dot{\alpha}\ \mu\dot{\eta}\ \dot{o}\nu\tau\alpha\ \dot{\omega}\varsigma\ \dot{o}\nu\tau\alpha\ \lambda\dot{\epsilon}\gamma\epsilon\iota$). These definitions justify our regarding Plato as the originator of the correspondence theory of truth, a view highly characteristic of Greek thought in general. Finally, the writings of Plato contain passages which seem clearly to indicate that the notion of the axiomatic method was already foreshadowed in the Academy as an ideal means of systematizing knowledge, even though the method remained in Plato's thought little more than a program, to be filled out only later by Aristotle and, more prominently, by Euclid.

Aristotle. Although Aristotle's debt to his predecessors, particularly Plato, is by no means negligible, the credit for creating the first logical system is unquestionably his. Aristotle's system, known as syllogistic from the prominence it gives to the syllogism, constitutes an elementary but important part of the logic of terms or, as it would be called today, the logic of nonempty classes. It need hardly be emphasized that the logic of classes is one of the cornerstones in the foundation of modern logic. That the logic of classes—and hence also syllogistic—presupposes a more fundamental logical theory, namely the logic of propositions, was not known to Aristotle.

Aristotelian canon. The logical treatises of Aristotle make up the collection known as the *Organon*—the "tool." The title was adopted by the commentators, who, in accordance with the well-established peripatetic tradition, regarded logic as a tool or instrument of philosophy. The *Organon* contains the *Categories,* the *De Interpretatione,* the *Prior Analytics* (two books), the *Posterior Analytics* (two books), the *Topics* (eight books), and the *De Sophisticis Elenchis.* The arrangement within the collection is meant to be systematic rather than chronological; it may be Aristotle's own, or we may owe it to Andronicus of Rhodes (first century B.C.), who published a new edition of the Aristotelian writings after they had been brought to Rome by Sulla. Their original chronological order can hardly be determined now with any certainty, since Aristotle apparently used later insertions to supplement his original treatises. However, it is generally believed that if we take the dates of the writings as corresponding roughly to their relative logical excellence, we may conjecture that the *Categories,* the *Topics,* and the *De Sophisticis Elenchis* are earlier than the *De Interpretatione* and that this work, in turn, is earlier than the *Prior Analytics* and the *Posterior Analytics.* The chapters on modal logic in the *Prior Analytics* are probably the last that Aristotle added to the body of the *Organon.* Outside of the *Organon,* the fourth book of the *Metaphysics* could be described as a logical work concerned with the principle of contradiction. By our "logical excellence" criterion it would be placed earlier than the *De Interpretatione.*

In the *Categories,* Aristotle distinguished expressions that exhibit propositional unity ($\tau\dot{\alpha}\ \kappa\alpha\tau\dot{\alpha}\ \sigma\nu\mu\pi\lambda o\kappa\dot{\eta}\nu\ \lambda\epsilon\gamma\dot{o}\mu\epsilon\nu\alpha$) from expressions that do not ($\tau\dot{\alpha}\ \dot{\alpha}\nu\epsilon\nu\ \sigma\nu\mu\pi\lambda o\kappa\hat{\eta}\varsigma\ \lambda\epsilon\gamma\dot{o}\mu\epsilon\nu\alpha$). This notion of propositional unity ($\sigma\nu\mu\pi\lambda o\kappa\dot{\eta}$) can perhaps be traced back to Plato, but the treatment of nonpropositional expressions is new and original. Nonpropositional expressions were defined by Aristotle as neither true nor false and were said to signify ($\sigma\eta\mu\alpha\dot{\iota}\nu\epsilon\iota\nu$) one or another of the following: substance ($o\dot{v}\sigma\dot{\iota}\alpha$), quantity ($\pi o\sigma\dot{o}\nu$), quality ($\pi o\iota\dot{o}\nu$), relation ($\pi\rho\dot{o}\varsigma\tau\iota$), place ($\pi o\hat{v}$), time ($\pi o\tau\dot{\epsilon}$), position ($\kappa\epsilon\hat{\iota}\sigma\theta\alpha\iota$), state ($\dot{\epsilon}\chi\epsilon\iota\nu$), action ($\pi o\iota\epsilon\hat{\iota}\nu$), and affection ($\pi\dot{\alpha}\sigma\chi\epsilon\iota\nu$). It is by no means clear whether this classification is to be regarded as ontological or as purely linguistic—that is, whether it is about extralinguistic entities or about words and expressions—and the same ambiguity has been characteristic of practically every other scheme of categories suggested since.

The *Topics* appears to have been intended as a manual for participants in contests that involved argumentation. For the most part it consists of suggestions about how to look for an argument that will establish or refute a given thesis. Some of the suggestions are so general in their application that they sound almost like logical laws or rules. The *De Sophisticis Elenchis,* which deals with fallacies, reads like a sequel to the *Topics.*

Of all the treatises in the *Organon,* the *De Interpreta-*

tione and the *Prior Analytics* are by far the most important from the point of view of logic. Between them they contain (1) the theory of opposition, which establishes logical relations between a simple affirmation and the corresponding simple denial, (2) the theory of conversion, (3) the theory of the assertoric syllogism, and (4) the theory of the modal syllogism. The *Posterior Analytics* is concerned with scientific method rather than with logic proper. It gives the impression of being largely a collection of notes.

Variables. One of Aristotle's most revolutionary contributions to logic was his introduction of variables into logical discourse. Variables enabled Aristotle to express logical principles directly instead of describing them metalogically or illustrating them by means of standard examples. He used these indirect methods in his earlier treatises (including the *De Interpretatione*), but it is in the *Prior Analytics* that the new method becomes prominent. For instance, one of the laws of conversion is first described metalogically: "It is necessary that the assertoric universal negative proposition should convert in respect of its terms." This law is then illustrated with the aid of a standard example: "If no pleasure is good, then no good will be pleasure"; finally, it is expressed directly: "If *A* belongs to none of the *B*'s, then *B* belongs to none of the *A*'s." On other occasions, Aristotle used concrete inferences or inference schemata as a means of referring to a logical principle. Thus, the law of conversion could have been exemplified by an inference, "No pleasure is good; therefore, no good is pleasure," or represented by an inference schema, "*A* belongs to no *B*; therefore, *B* belongs to no *A*." It is a moot point whether or not Aristotle appreciated the difference between "if–then" propositions, or implications, and inferences or inference schemata. In fact, in his exposition of syllogistic (in the *Prior Analytics*) he did formulate the syllogistic laws directly, in preference to representing them by means of inference schemata. Strangely enough, Aristotle made no attempt to explain his use of variables. This may have been merely because he was accustomed to using them in his lectures in the Lyceum. Possibly they were used at an early stage simply for the purpose of abbreviating concrete terms in the standard examples that he employed to illustrate logical principles.

Affirmation and denial. It has already been mentioned that syllogistic presupposes the logic of propositions. Aristotle's own presentation presupposes, in addition, the theory of opposition and the theory of conversion. Both theories are parts of the logic of terms, and unlike the logic of propositions, they had been worked out by Aristotle himself. He referred to them in his systematic exposition of syllogistic.

By way of introduction to his logical theory Aristotle gave a number of syntactical and semantical explanations. In the *De Interpretatione* he began the discussion of simple affirmation and simple denial where Plato left off. Like Plato in the *Sophist*, Aristotle distinguished nouns from verbs and pointed out that a proposition or declarative sentence (ἀποφαντικὸς λόγος or ἀπόφανσις) must have a verb or an inflection of one, but it is evident that he was interested only in simple propositions which use the copula. As a consequence he had no logic of predicates or relations in the modern sense of these terms. Within the class of nouns he seems to have distinguished between

singular names and common nouns, for he referred to a sort of ontological theory according to which some things (πράγματα), for example, man, are universal and some, for example, Callias, are individual. Moreover, it would appear from certain passages in the *Organon* that Aristotle recognized empty singular names and empty common nouns, but again his interest was eventually limited to nonempty common nouns. In the *Prior Analytics* he classified existing things (τὰ ὄντα) into those which cannot be predicated of anything although other things can be predicated of them, those of which nothing can be genuinely predicated but which can be predicated of other things, and those which can be predicated of others and of which other things can be predicated. As a rule, he remarked, it is with this last kind of object that arguments and inquiries are concerned. Linguistically this amounts to saying that for scientific inquiries nonempty common nouns with limited generality are of greater importance than any other kinds of nouns. This appears to be a tacit assumption of the Aristotelian logic of terms.

The various affirmations and denials we can make by using the copula with singular names and common nouns, which latter include adjectives, fall into four classes or types of propositions:

(1) Singular, e.g., "Socrates is white," "Socrates is not white."

(2) Universal, e.g., "Every man is white," "No man is white."

(3) Particular, e.g., "Some man is white," "Some man is not white."

(4) Indefinite, e.g., "Man is white," "Man is not white."

However, for the purposes of syllogistic only universal and particular propositions are required. These propositions are called categorical, and in Aristotle's logic they exhibit a slightly different form if variables occur in them. If, for instance, we let "*B*" and "*A*" stand for "man" and "white," the four types of categorical propositions read: "*A* belongs to all *B*," "*A* belongs to no *B*," "*A* belongs to some *B*," and "*A* does not belong to some *B*." Variants such as "*A* is predicated of all *B*" and "*A* is predicated of some *B*" are also common in Aristotle. In all these examples *A* is, of course, the predicate (τὸ κατηγορούμενον), and *B* is the subject (τὸ καθ'οὖ κατηγορεῖται).

Opposition and conversion. The theory of opposition (ἀντίθεσις) is stated in the *De Interpretatione* in metalogical idiom supplemented by standard examples. A universal affirmation and the corresponding particular denial are said to be opposed as contradictories (ἀντιφατικῶς), and so are particular affirmation and the corresponding universal denial. Of any two such contradictories one must be true and the other false. A universal affirmation and the corresponding universal denial are said to be opposed as contraries (ἐναντίως); they cannot both be true, but their respective contradictories can. It apparently escaped Aristotle's notice that the contradictories of a pair of correlated contraries—in traditional logic these are called subcontraries—cannot both be false. In connection with the theory of opposition it is customary to talk about the laws of subalternation, which say that a universal proposition implies the corresponding particular one. Aristotle referred to these laws in the *Topics*.

The theory of conversion (ἀντιστροφή) is expounded in

the *Prior Analytics*. It is stated in metalogical idiom and illustrated by standard examples, and its principles are then expressed directly in terms of variables. This is followed by a systematic exposition of the theory of the assertoric syllogism.

Syllogism. Aristotle's definition of a syllogism as a "propositional expression (λόγος) in which, certain things having been laid down, something other than what has been laid down follows of necessity from their being so" fails to distinguish syllogism from other types of logical principles (*Prior Analytics* 24b18). An Aristotelian syllogism is, in fact, (1) an "if–then" proposition—i.e., an implication, of the form "If α and β, then γ," where the Greek letters stand for categorical propositions with variable terms—(2) that is true for all values of the variables involved, (3) with "premises" (represented by α and β) which have at least one term in common, while the remaining two terms are the ones occurring in the "conclusion" (represented by γ). In an implication satisfying these conditions the result of substituting concrete nouns for variables, equiform nouns for equiform variables, is also a syllogism. Thus, the Aristotelian version of what is known in traditional logic as the syllogism in Barbara has the form "If A is predicated of all B and B is predicated of all C, then A is predicated of all C." The syllogism in Darii reads "If A belongs to all B and B belongs to some C, then A belongs to some C."

Outside of his systematic exposition of syllogistic in the *Prior Analytics* (Book I, Chs. 4–7), Aristotle occasionally used inference schemata to give expression to syllogistic principles. But it was only after his time that the practice of expressing syllogisms in the form of inference schemata or indicating them with the aid of standard inferences gained currency, probably owing to the influence of the Stoic logicians. This practice was followed by the Roman authors, who transmitted it to the Scholastics. Moreover, Aristotle's somewhat artificial way of formulating categorical propositions was abandoned in favor of a more natural mode of expression, which involved the use of the copula. Accordingly the two syllogisms Barbara and Darii, mentioned above, would in traditional logic be given the form of the following inference schemata:

(1)
>All B is A;
>All C is B;
>Therefore, all C is A.

(2)
>All B is A;
>Some C is B;
>Therefore, some C is A.

The term which occurs in a syllogism as the subject of the conclusion is called the minor term (τὸ ἐλάττον), the predicate of the conclusion the major term (τὸ μεῖζον), and the term which occurs in both premises the middle term (τὸ μέσον). The definition of the middle term is Aristotle's, but the other two definitions are not. They are to be found in the commentary to the *Prior Analytics* by Philoponus (c. A.D. 500). The position of the middle term in the premises gave Aristotle the clue to dividing syllogisms into figures. In the first figure the major term is predicated of the middle term, which in turn is predicated of the minor term. In the second figure the middle term occurs in the premises as the predicate, and in the third figure it occurs in the premises as the subject. The division of syllogisms into figures has, of course, no logical significance. It only aids the systematic examination of all ordered pairs of categorical propositions with a view to establishing which of them, if used as premises, give rise to syllogisms. Indeed, Aristotle began his systematic survey of the first figure by considering the four different pairs of universal premises. He picked out the two which generate Barbara and Celarent and showed, by means of suitable counterexamples, that no syllogisms can be constructed with the help of the remaining two pairs. Then he examined the eight pairs, each consisting of a universal and a particular proposition, and found that two of these give rise to Darii and Ferio. The remaining six pairs can be disposed of by appropriate counterexamples, for which Aristotle suggested terms. Finally, he gave terms for the counterexamples, proving that no pair of particular premises—there are four such pairs—yields a syllogism. The treatment of the second and third figures proceeded by similar stages. However, the four syllogisms of the second figure (Cesare, Camestres, Festino, and Baroco) and the six syllogisms of the third figure (Darapti, Disamis, Datisi, Felapton, Bocardo, and Ferison) were not simply stated to hold; they were "reduced" to syllogisms of the first figure. This reduction (ἀναγωγή), however, is actually proof (ἀπόδειξις), as Aristotle seems to have known. For the most part he provided direct proofs involving the laws of conversion. In the cases of Baroco and Bocardo he had recourse to indirect proofs that presuppose, among other things, some of the laws of the theory of opposition. Sometimes both kinds of proof were given.

It appears that Aristotle at first overlooked the arrangement of premises in which the minor term is predicated of the middle term and the middle term is predicated of the major. This arrangement gives rise to five more syllogisms (Bramantip, Camenes, Dimaris, Fesapo, and Fresison), which in traditional logic form the fourth figure. There is ample evidence that the syllogisms of this figure were known to Aristotle. Perhaps he discovered them at a later stage but did not take the trouble to fit them into his systematic exposition. This was eventually done by his pupil Theophrastus (c. 321–c. 286 B.C.), who incorporated the five syllogisms into the first figure, having redefined it as consisting of those syllogisms whose middle term was the subject in one premise and the predicate in the other. There is no reference in the *Organon* to the "subaltern" syllogisms (Barbari, Celaront, Cesaro, Camestrop, and Camenop). According to Lucius Apuleius of Madaura (second century A.D.) they were introduced by a Peripatetic, Ariston of Alexandria (first century B.C.).

In his exposition of syllogistic Aristotle was concerned with finding out which of the various ordered pairs of categorical propositions could be used as premises in a syllogism. The early commentators on Aristotle spoke in this context about combinations or conjunctions of premises. Later the notion of mood (τρόπος, *modus*) was introduced by ancient logicians to designate an ordered triple of categorical propositions, and in traditional logic one of the major problems was to determine the necessary and sufficient conditions for a mood to yield a valid syllogistic inference.

From the point of view of modern logic Aristotle's system of syllogistic is a deductive system in miniature. The four syllogisms of the first figure, described by Aristotle as perfect, play the part of axioms from which the remaining syllogisms are deduced. In the deductions use is made of the theories of opposition and conversion, and the logic of propositions is implicitly presupposed. Aristotle subsequently simplified the axiomatic foundations of his syllogistic by showing that the syllogisms Barbara and Celarent implied all the other syllogisms.

Modal logic. Modal syllogistic appears to have been Aristotle's last major contribution to logic. He inserted it in the *Prior Analytics,* where it occupies Chapters 3 and 8–22 of Book I. An earlier discussion of some problems belonging to modal logic can be found in Chapters 12 and 13 of the *De Interpretatione.* In very general terms, Aristotle's modal logic involves the study of such notions as necessity (τὸ ἀναγκαῖον), impossibility (τὸ ἀδύνατον), possibility (τὸ δυνατόν), and contingency (τὸ ἐνδεχόμενον). In modal syllogistic these notions are applied to the categorical propositions in a syllogism. Modern logicians have suggested two rival interpretations of modalities, object-language interpretation and metalinguistic interpretation. It is best, however, to examine the characteristic features of Aristotle's modal logic without taking sides in a controversy which, after all, did not exist in his time.

In the *De Interpretatione,* Aristotle attempted to establish logical relations between modal notions. The view that a proposition is not necessary if it is possible led him into a difficulty, which he eventually avoided by laying down the rule that a proposition is possible if and only if its negation is not necessary. Similarly, a proposition is said to be necessary if and only if its negation is not possible. The notion of contingency is treated in the *De Interpretatione* as synonymous with that of possibility, but in the *Prior Analytics* it is also defined in such a way as to imply that a proposition is contingent if and only if it is neither necessary nor impossible. Contingency in this sense is of special interest for modal syllogistic; Aristotle made little use of the notion of possibility as defined in the *De Interpretatione.* Compared with the theory of the assertoric syllogism, the theory of the modal syllogism is far more intricate and by no means free of controversial issues. For instance, Aristotle accepted the syllogism "If it is necessary that *A* should belong to all *B* and *B* belongs to all *C,* then it is necessary that *A* should belong to all *C,*" but at the same time he rejected the syllogism "If *A* belongs to all *B* and it is necessary that *B* should belong to all *C,* then it is necessary that *A* should belong to all *C.*" His arguments for doing so failed to convince Theophrastus and Eudemus of Rhodes (fourth century B.C.), his pupils, who rejected both syllogisms. The problem of syllogisms involving premises with mixed modalities proved to be particularly perplexing. It is known that Alexander of Aphrodisias (fl. c. A.D. 200), a famous commentator on Aristotle's works, wrote a treatise with the title "On the Disagreement Concerning Mixed Moods Between Aristotle and His Friends," but it is not extant.

Logic of propositions. Aristotle was fully aware that besides the laws of the theories of opposition, conversion, and syllogism, there were other logical principles of valid inference. In the *De Interpretatione* he discussed at some length the laws of obversion, and in the *Topics* he illus-

trated a law of contraposition with concrete examples. The *Topics* contains certain generalizations which correspond to simple laws of the theory of identity and difference. In the *Prior Analytics* mention is made of syllogisms from hypothesis, but apparently Aristotle did not pursue the subject. There are a few passages in the *Organon,* however, where Aristotle appears to have been groping after laws of the logic of propositions, and it would be ungenerous to dismiss his fumblings as irrelevant.

Until the emergence of symbolic logic (that is, for more than two thousand years) Aristotle's authority in matters of logic remained unchallenged, and his logic was regarded as a comprehensive system which admitted of no extension. Only in the light of relatively recent developments did it become possible to work out a more realistic assessment of his contribution. We now know that the logic of propositions is a more fundamental logical theory than syllogistic, which presupposes it. This did not occur to Aristotle, and the logic of propositions was not discovered and developed until a generation or so later by Theophrastus, the Megarians, and the Stoics. Aristotle's deductions within the framework of syllogistic do not refer explicitly to any laws of propositional logic, but neither do they violate any of these laws. This fact bears witness to the great reliability of his logical intuition. Modal logic aside, Aristotle's system of the logic of terms contains no errors. It has been reaxiomatized and shown to be consistent and decidable. By appropriate steps it can be strengthened to compare with modern systems of the logic of terms. It would be more than surprising if all these possibilities were seen by Aristotle's immediate successors.

Theophrastus. The logical studies inaugurated by Aristotle were continued by his pupils Theophrastus, Eudemus, and others. Theophrastus of Eresus, who succeeded Aristotle as head of the Lyceum, was the author of several logical treatises, now lost. Our knowledge of his contributions to logic is derived from a number of quotations and references, to be found, for the most part, in ancient commentaries to Aristotle's logical writings. In many of these references Theophrastus' name is linked with that of Eudemus, but our sources are not explicit enough to justify our discussing Eudemus separately.

Refinements of Aristotle. It appears that Theophrastus is to be credited with having improved and developed certain ideas already present in one form or another in the writings of Aristotle. This, of course, does not imply that the innovations made by Theophrastus are of little significance for logic. To begin with, Theophrastus is reported to have equated the meaning of the indefinite proposition with that of the corresponding particular proposition. He is also said to have accepted a wider definition of the first figure, assigning to it every syllogism whose middle term is the subject in one premise and the predicate in the other. This enabled him to incorporate into the first figure the additional five syllogisms that Aristotle mentioned outside his own system of syllogistic.

Theophrastus' innovations in modal logic appear to be more important. In his system contingency is omitted, and as a consequence the rule of the weaker premise is introduced. If we agree that a true or assertoric premise is stronger than a possible premise and weaker than a necessary one, then Theophrastus' rule provides that in respect of modality the conclusion in a modal syllogism follows the weaker premise. The acceptance of this rule simplifies modal syllogistic, but in the opinion of some logicians it raises difficult problems of its own.

Prosleptic syllogism. Of still greater significance, it seems, was Theophrastus' theory of prosleptic syllogism. This theory involves propositions whose structure can be illustrated with the aid of the following examples:

(1) "Whatever entity *B* is universally predicated of, *A* is universally predicated of" (more clearly, "For all *X*, if *B* is predicated of all *X*, then *A* is predicated of all *X*").

(2) "Whatever entity *B* is in every instance predicated of, *A* is in no instance predicated of" (more clearly, "For all *X*, if *B* is predicated of all *X*, then *A* is predicated of no *X*").

To put it very generally, the propositions involved are all of the form "For all *X*, if $\Phi(X)$, then $\Psi(X)$," where both $\Phi(X)$ and $\Psi(X)$ stand for categorical propositions in which the variable *X* occurs as one of the terms. Propositions of this type Theophrastus called prosleptic ($\kappa\alpha\tau\grave{\alpha}\ \pi\rho\acute{o}\sigma\lambda\eta\psi\iota\nu$). He characterized them as having three terms, two of which, *A* and *B* in our examples, are definite, whereas the third—indicated in our paraphrase by the bound variable *X*—is not definite or explicit in the same sense. The position of this indefinite term, which was also called the middle term, suggested to Theophrastus the division of prosleptic premises into three figures. In combination with an appropriate categorical premise a prosleptic premise gives rise to a valid inference. An example is

> For all *X*, if *B* is predicated of all *X*, then *A* is predicated of all *X*;
> *B* is predicated of all *C*;
> Therefore, *A* is predicated of all *C*.

Inferences of this type were called prosleptic syllogisms. On the assumption that in a prosleptic syllogism the categorical premise and the conclusion are of the same type as, respectively, the antecedent and the consequent in the prosleptic premise, the number of different prosleptic syllogisms will be the same as the number of different prosleptic premises. Since every prosleptic premise involves two categorical propositions, with four types of categorical propositions we have 32 different prosleptic premises in the first figure (provided the first figure is understood in the Theophrastian sense) and 16 different prosleptic premises in each of the remaining two figures, the total being 64.

Some prosleptic premises are equivalent to appropriate categorical premises. This was known to Theophrastus, who regarded premises (1) and (2) above as equivalent to "*A* is predicated of all *B*" and "*A* is predicated of no *B*," respectively. This does not mean that every prosleptic premise can be reduced to a categorical one in such a simple manner; the criticism made by some ancient logicians that prosleptic syllogisms are categorical syllogisms in disguise is therefore not justified.

Hypothetical syllogism. Finally, Theophrastus developed a theory of the totally hypothetical syllogism. In this theory three figures also recur. Alexander of Aphrodisias, who is our earliest source on the subject, illustrated the three figures with examples:

First figure:

> If *A* then *B*;
> If *B* then *C*;
> Therefore, if *A* then *C*.
>   or
> If *A* then *B*;
> If *B* then *C*;
> Therefore, if not *C* then not *A*.

Second figure:

> If *A* then *B*;
> If not *A* then *C*;
> Therefore, if not *B* then *C*.
>   or
> If *A* then *B*;
> If not *A* then *C*;
> Therefore, if not *C* then *B*.

Third figure:

> If *A* then *C*;
> If *B* then not *C*;
> Therefore, if *A* then not *B*.
>   or
> If *A* then *C*;
> If *B* then not *C*;
> Therefore, if *B* then not *A*.

This last contribution of Theophrastus' broke fresh ground, for it is clear that totally hypothetical syllogisms—or, rather, the logical principles which make them valid—belong to the logic of propositions. In this connection Theophrastus appears to have been the first to use propositional variables in a systematic way. It may, however, be doubted whether Theophrastus appreciated the significance of his innovation or whether he in fact made any serious study of compound propositions, such as implications or disjunctions, which are the backbone of the logic of propositions. Alexander also showed how the totally hypothetical syllogisms of the second and third figures can be reduced to those of the first. It is very likely that in doing so he repeated the instructions of Theophrastus.

In spite of these promising beginnings, the logic of propositions made little progress in the Lyceum. However, it became the central topic in the inquiries of the Megarian and Stoic logicians.

Megarians. The Megarian school was founded by Euclides of Megara (c. 430–c. 360 B.C.), who was a pupil of Socrates. The second generation of the Megarians was made famous by Euclides' successor, Eubulides of Miletus (fourth century B.C.), the inventor of the paradox of the Liar and several other paradoxes. Two generations later there followed Diodorus Cronus (fourth century B.C.) and his gifted pupil Philo of Megara. No writings of the Megarian logicians have been preserved. In our efforts to reconstruct their doctrines we have to rely on reports by later authors, particularly Diogenes Laërtius, Sextus Empiricus, and Boethius.

Diodorus. Whereas Eubulides followed with distinction the tradition of Zeno of Elea, Diodorus and Philo turned to the study of modal concepts and, for the first time in the history of logic, inquired into the meaning of "if–then" propositions. Diodorus defined the possible as that which either is true or is going to be true, the impossible as that which is false and is never going to be true, and the necessary as that which is true and is never going to be false. Whatever is false or is going to be false is not necessary. Diodorus tried to prove the correctness of his definition of the possible by arguing that it follows from the assumption that everything that is past and true is necessary and that the impossible does not follow from the possible. It is characteristic of the Diodorean modalities that they involve the notions of past, present, and future. The notion of time also enters into Diodorus' definition of truth as applied to implications. According to him an implication is true if and only if it neither was nor is possible for it to have a true antecedent and a false consequent.

Philo. It appears that Philo, who must have been a very independent pupil, did not approve of Diodorus' doctrines concerning modality and the meaning of implication. He thought that the various modalities should be distinguished by whether or not the "intrinsic nature" of the proposition in question admitted of truth or falsity. The notion of intrinsic nature is far too vague to recommend Philo's suggestions; he was more successful in dealing with the problem of implication. He argued that an implication is true in three ways and false in one way: It is true if its antecedent and consequent are (1) both true or (2) both false; it is also true if (3) its antecedent is false and its consequent is true. It is false if its antecedent is true and its consequent false. This is obviously a truth-functional definition of implication. It is not known whether Philo used the same method for the purpose of defining the truth-values of other types of compound proposition, such as the "and" proposition (conjunction) and the "either–or" proposition (exclusive disjunction). Whatever the case may be, both conjunction and exclusive disjunction, along with Philonian implication, occur as truth-functions in the logic of the Stoics.

Stoics. According to tradition Zeno of Citium (c. 336–c. 265 B.C.), the founder of the Stoic school, learned his dialectic from Diodorus Cronus and from Philo, whom he greatly admired. Zeno, however, was not a creative logician, nor was his successor, Cleanthes of Assos (c. 331–232 B.C.). It fell to Chrysippus of Soli (c. 279–206 B.C.), the "second founder" of the Stoa, to bring the logical ideas of the Megarians to fruition. Chrysippus was a prolific author, but his writings, over seven hundred in number, are all lost. Diogenes Laërtius remarked that in the opinion of most people, if the gods used any logic, it would be the logic of Chrysippus, and the quotations and references by later writers fully support Chrysippus' reputation as one of the greatest Greek logicians.

Logic of propositions. As distinct from the Aristotelian logic of terms, that of Chrysippus, and of the Stoics in general, is a logic of propositions. It is a two-valued logic, since the Stoics regarded as fundamental the principle that every proposition is either true or false. In fact, they defined a proposition (ἀξίωμα) as that which is either true or false. They divided propositions into simple and nonsimple. Nonsimple propositions resulted from the combination of two occurrences of the same proposition or from the combi-

nation of different propositions. The combination was, of course, effected by means of appropriate connectives. Among simple propositions the Stoics distinguished simple affirmations and simple denials. They insisted that a denial should be formed by placing the negative particle in front of a proposition. Denial was conceived as a truth-function, since a denial was said to be true if the denied proposition was false and false if the denied proposition was true. Among the nonsimple propositions the Stoics recognized implication (συνημμένον), conjunction (συμπεπλεγμένον), and exclusive disjunction (διεζευγμένον). All these types of nonsimple proposition were defined as truth-functions. Following Philo of Megara, the Stoics held that an implication was false if its antecedent was true and its consequent false. In the remaining three cases the implication was true. They regarded a conjunction as true if each of its conjuncts was true and otherwise as false. An exclusive disjunction was regarded as true if just one of its disjuncts was true; otherwise it was held to be false. There is evidence that inclusive disjunction was also introduced into Stoic logic in due course. An inclusive disjunction was described as false if all its disjuncts were false and otherwise as true.

Logical principles. The logical connectives which occur in the various types of nonsimple propositions give rise to logical principles. The Stoics represented these by means of paradigm inferences (λόγοι) or of inference schemata (τρόποι). The following five inference schemata were, according to tradition, set out by Chrysippus as being in need of no proof:

(1) If the first then the second; but the first; therefore, the second.

(2) If the first then the second; but not the second; therefore, not the first.

(3) Not both the first and the second; but the first; therefore, not the second.

(4) Either the first or the second; but the first; therefore, not the second.

(5) Either the first or the second; but not the second; therefore, the first.

From these indemonstrables (ἀναπόδεικτοι), as they were called by the Stoics, a great number of other inference schemata could be derived in accordance with certain rules (θέματα), which unfortunately are not known to us in full detail. We have, however, a few examples of the sort of derivation the Stoic logicians practiced. From the point of view of logical rigor these examples are beyond reproach. For instance, they showed the schema "If the first and the second, then the third; now, not the third, but the first; therefore, not the second" to be valid by first deriving "not both the first and the second" from the first two premises in accordance with the second indemonstrable and then using this result and the remaining premise to derive the conclusion "not the second" in accordance with the third indemonstrable. This is clearly a specimen of what is now known as "natural deduction." The ordinals "the first," "the second," "the third," . . . were used by the Stoics to stand for propositions; that is, they are to be interpreted as propositional variables.

It should be noted that the Stoics did not formulate their logical principles directly but chose to present them by means of inference schemata. In this respect the Stoics differed from Aristotle, whose syllogisms were direct principles of the logic of terms. Although it may be doubted whether Aristotle appreciated the difference between a direct logical principle and the corresponding inference schema, the Stoics explicitly related the validity of an inference to the corresponding logical principle when they said that an inference is valid if the implication is true in which the conjunction of the premises is the antecedent and the conclusion is the consequent.

After Chrysippus little creative work seems to have been done by the Stoics in the field of logic. It is known that Antipater of Tarsus, head of the Stoa from about 150 to about 130 B.C., was interested in inferences from one premise. This would have been an important novelty, but the extant fragments merely suggest that Antipater argued the legitimacy of certain enthymemes with a second premise suppressed.

Galen and the commentators. As a result of interschool enmities and jealousies there was at first no cooperation in logical research between the Lyceum and the Stoa. The Peripatetics limited their interest to the study of the categorical syllogism, whereas the Stoics did not look beyond those inference schemata which they could derive from the Chrysippian indemonstrables. Consequently, Theophrastus' theory of totally hypothetical syllogisms attracted little attention from either side. It is significant that in discussing logical problems the schools developed differing terminologies. However, after the establishment of the eclectic trend in philosophy, in the second half of the first century B.C., the controversies on logical subjects gradually lost their heat, and the two logical theories, the Aristotelian syllogistic and the Stoic logic of propositions (often described as the theory of the hypothetical syllogism), became part of the syllabus for general philosophical education. Boethus of Sidon (second half of first century B.C.), a pupil of Andronicus of Rhodes and himself a Peripatetic philosopher of considerable repute, went so far as to argue that the hypothetical syllogism was prior to the categorical. Unfortunately, we are not told what sort of priority Boethus had in mind.

Galen (A.D. 129–c. 199) dismissed this problem of priority as irrelevant and applied himself to the study of logic under teachers from both the Stoa and the Lyceum. Galen, who achieved fame as a physician, was one of the best logicians of the period. He wrote a number of essays and treatises on a variety of logical problems, among them critical commentaries on logical works by Aristotle, Theophrastus, and Chrysippus. Galen's *Introduction to Dialectic* is still extant, and we have some information on the contents of his *On Demonstration*. In this last work he not only criticized Theophrastus' theory of the prosleptic syllogism but also expounded his own theory of the compound categorical syllogism in which two middle terms occur. A careful analysis of such syllogisms has shown that they fall into four figures, and it is apparently this fact that Galen discovered. Thus, the tradition connecting his name with the fourth figure of the simple categorical syllogism turns out to be mistaken.

Ancient logical literature after Galen seems to have consisted of either compendia for beginners or learned and lengthy commentaries on the logical treatises of Aristotle. The writing of commentaries on Aristotle had been made fashionable by Andronicus of Rhodes, whose example was followed by a great number of ancient scholars. Andronicus' own commentaries are not extant, but some of the commentaries on various parts of the *Organon* by such authors as Alexander of Aphrodisias (fl. c. A.D. 200), Porphyry (c. 232–c. 301), Ammonius Hermeiou (fifth century), Simplicius (sixth century), and Philoponus (c. 500) have been preserved.

In this connection mention should be made of the Roman authors Cicero (106–43 B.C.), Aulus Gellius (second century A.D.), Lucius Apuleius of Madaura (second century), Marius Victorinus (fourth century), Martianus Capella (fifth century), Cassiodorus (468–562), and Boethius (c. 480–524). They made no original contributions to logic, but we are indebted to them for three things. First, their works occasionally supply information that supplements the Greek sources. Second, they were very successful in devising Latin terminology for logical inquiry. Third, their compendia, translations, and commentaries transmitted the achievements of the Greek logicians to the Middle Ages. Medieval logic would certainly have developed along more modest lines, if at all, had it not been for the informative and stimulating works of Boethius.

CZESŁAW LEJEWSKI

INDIAN LOGIC

The term "Indian logic" may be used to refer to the system of logic (Nyāya) that forms one of the six principal schools of Hindu philosophy. In a wider sense it denotes Buddhist and Jaina logic as well. In a still wider sense it refers to any logical doctrine propounded by Indian scholars. In this article the term is used in the last sense, although Jaina logic is omitted and only some representative doctrines and techniques from other sources are discussed.

The history of Indian logic covers at least 23 centuries, and the number of works by Indian logicians, published and unpublished, is vast. Those available in Western languages or accessible in good editions constitute only a fraction of this material. Attention here is confined to material from some of the published Sanskrit texts. For the study of Buddhist logic translations into Tibetan or Chinese from Sanskrit originals, many of which are lost, must also be utilized.

This survey falls into five parts: (1) Grammar, which was well developed by the time of the Sanskrit grammar of Pāṇini. Its sophisticated logical rules and techniques influenced almost all later scholarly developments in India. (2) Mīmāṃsā, the most orthodox of the six philosophical schools of Hinduism. It dealt largely with problems of textual interpretation and faced a variety of logical problems in the course of its history. (3) Vaiśeṣika and Old Nyāya. Vaiśeṣika, which also embodied a system of natural philosophy, provided a list of categories that set the framework within which logicians of the Old Nyāya school developed their systematic analyses of perception and inference. (4) Buddhist logic, partly a reaction against the Old Nyāya. Some branches of Buddhist logic laid a foundation for formal logic and began to exclude extraneous considerations of ontology, epistemology, and psychology. (5) New Nyāya, the final phase of Hindu logic, both challenged by

Buddhist logic and substantially enriched by it. The New Nyāya began with the work of Gaṅgeśopādhyāya (thirteenth century A.D.) and continues to the present day.

Lack of space prevents discussion of the role of logic in the sciences and of the philosophical schools of the Vedānta, which dealt with logical topics, especially in the later developments within Advaita and Dvaita.

Since more attention will be paid to doctrines than to individual logicians and their works and dates, a chronological table may be helpful in providing a rough outline of their historical context. (In the table, names of writings are in italic.) The table makes it clear that some of the schools which developed simultaneously were in a position to influence each other.

but it produced various attempts to reduce complicated expressions to simpler forms.

For the sake of brevity grammarians not only introduced numerous technical terms but also adopted particular methods for referring to forms of the object language. The technical language thus constructed within the framework of ordinary Sanskrit developed into a metalanguage, the language of grammatical instruction (*upadeśa*). Special rules were required to delineate the domain of the metalanguage and to prevent its elements' being considered elements of the object language. Such rules are themselves metarules (*paribhāṣā*). For example, if the technical metalinguistic term *vṛddhi* denotes, among other things, the sound *ai*, substitution of *vṛddhi* means substitution of *ai*.

INDIAN LOGICIANS AND LOGICAL WORKS

CENTURY	GRAMMAR	MĪMĀṂSĀ	VAIŚEṢIKA AND OLD NYĀYA	BUDDHIST LOGIC	NEW NYĀYA
	(Vedas)				
	(prātiśākhya)	*(ritual sūtras)*			
Fourth B.C.	Pāṇini				
Second B.C.	Patañjali				
First A.D.			Kaṇāda		
Second				Nāgārjuna (?)	
Third		Jaimini (?)	Gautama		
Fourth			Vātsyāyana		
Fifth		Śabara	Praśastapāda		
Sixth				Dignāga	
Seventh	*Kāśikā*	Prabhākara	Uddyotakara	Dharmakīrti	
	Bhartṛhari				
Eighth		Kumārila		Dharmottara	
Ninth			Vācaspatimiśra		
Tenth			Udayana		
Eleventh	Kaiyaṭa				
Thirteenth					Gaṅgeśopādhyāya
Sixteenth		Nārāyaṇa			Raghunātha
Seventeenth	Bhaṭṭojīdīkṣita	Āpadeva			Mathurānātha
					Jagadīśa
					Gadādhara
					Annambhaṭṭa
					Pañcānana
					Maṇikaṇa
Eighteenth	Nāgojībhaṭṭa				

Grammar. The earliest Indian grammarians were mainly preoccupied with the phonology of the Vedic language, a preoccupation that is reflected in the technical literature of the *prātiśākhyas*. With Pāṇini attention shifted to a synchronistic description of spoken language (*bhāṣā*). This led to the elaboration of various methods and distinctions, of which several are of logical interest.

The first is an economy criterion (the principle of *lāghava*), which requires that the description of language omit superfluous elements. "Grammarians rejoice over the saving of the length of half a short vowel as over the birth of a son" (Nāgojībhaṭṭa, *Paribhāṣenduśekhara*, *paribhāṣā* 122). For this reason abbreviations are used, and repetition is eschewed. Since the amount of repetition varies with the order in which grammatical rules are introduced, the order of exposition becomes a major problem of grammatical description. The grammarians generally preferred the shortest possible expressions, and the later logicians adapted the economy criterion to their specific needs by attempting to manipulate a relatively small number of elementary concepts. This did not result in full-fledged axiomatic theories,

Similarly, an infix -*a*- may be accompanied by particular features, which are symbolized by the metalinguistic indicatory sound *ś*. The infix is therefore denoted by *śa*, and if *śa* has to be substituted, this means that -*a*- is substituted. For instance, substitution of *śa* between *tud*- and -*ti* yields *tudati*, but not **tudśati*. On the other hand, if an element occurring in a rule is not a technical term, it belongs to the object language and denotes "its own form" (Pāṇini, *Aṣṭādhyāyī* 1.1.68). For example, if *agni* ("fire") has the suffix -*eya*, the suffix must be attached to the form *agni*- itself. We clearly cannot add the suffix to the embers, Patañjali wrote.

The distinction made here is that between use and mention, which modern Western logicians express with the help of quotation marks. In Sanskrit, quotation is effectuated by the insertion of *iti* at the end of a citation. This facilitates reference to individual words of the object language, as well as to sentences or larger units of discourse. In later philosophy and logic, examples, conflicting views, and views of opponents are quoted in this way.

The grammarians referred to grammatical rules by means

of the term *lakṣaṇa*. Forms of the object language known from common usage (*loka*) are called *lakṣya*. In order to arrive at a grammatical description a *lakṣaṇa* which is co-extensive with *lakṣya* has to be constructed. This is generalized in the Nyāya theory of definition, which studies the relations between the definiens (*lakṣaṇa*) and the definiendum (*lakṣya*).

Patañjali introduced numerous other grammatical concepts with logical connotations—for example, synonyms and homonyms. He also applied logical principles, such as the laws of contradiction and contraposition. His practice of dealing with a grammatical problem by giving both an example (*udāharaṇa*) and a counterexample (*pratyudāharaṇa*) is a forerunner of the later practice of logicians of discussing both *sapakṣa* and *vipakṣa* cases.

Mīmāṃsā. In continuation of the ritual sūtras, Mīmāṃsā systematized the interpretation of Vedic expressions by means of *paribhāṣā* rules, which are often called *nyāya*. The early use of the term *nyāya* as synonymous with *paribhāṣā* suggests that elements and laws of the Nyāya system can be traced back to the discussions on problems of language and metalanguage.

Whereas the grammarians were interested in problems of description (a feature that remains characteristic of most Indian logic and philosophy), the philosophers of Mīmāṃsā were concerned primarily with prescriptions. They interpreted the majority of Vedic utterances as injunctions (*vidhi*). The logical analysis of prescriptions was further utilized in the legal literature of *dharmaśāstra*. To gain an idea of some of the features of this analysis let $N(F(x))$ denote prescriptions of the form "he shall look," where $F(x)$ denotes the description "he looks." In a formal representation of Mīmāṃsā discussions on possible negations of the expression $N(F(x))$, use will be made of a symbol for negation, $\sim$, which is defined in combination with following prescriptions (such as N), descriptions (such as F), or terms (such as x). Now, what is meant by the negation of an injunction? The general Mīmāṃsā answer is that the negation of "he shall look" is "he shall-not look," where (in Sanskrit) the negation is connected with the verb ending. This case, called prohibition (*niṣedha*), can be expressed by $(\sim N)(F(x))$. Stressing the importance of verb endings is a distinctive feature of Mīmāṃsā, since the prescriptive force of injunctions is said to be expressed by the injunctiveness (*liṅtva*) of the verb ending.

In other contexts the negation of an injunction means that the opposite of the description underlying the injunction is enjoined. This kind of negation of "he shall look" is "he shall not-look." Here an activity opposed to looking (*īkṣaṇa-virodhī*) is positively enjoined. This can be represented formally by $N((\sim F)(x))$. The remaining possibility—that is, the negation of "he shall look" as "not-he shall look"—can be represented by $N(F(\sim x))$. In Mīmāṃsā both $N((\sim F)(x))$ and $N(F(\sim x))$ are classified as cases of *paryudāsa* (sometimes translated as "exclusion"). In later grammatical works an analogous distinction is made.

Mīmāṃsā recognized that the law of contradiction, which holds for *niṣedha* negations, need not hold for *paryudāsa* negations; that is, it is not necessary that

$$\sim(N(F(x)) \wedge N(F(\sim x))).$$

These distinctions may lead to interesting variations on other logical laws. An example is provided by the law of double negation

$$N(F(x)) \leftrightarrow (\sim N)F(\sim x),$$

exemplified by the equivalence between "five 5-toed animals are fit to be eaten" and "animals different from these (five 5-toed animals) are not fit to be eaten."

Vaisesika and Old Nyāya. The *Vaiśeṣika-sūtra* ascribed to Kaṇāda gives an enumeration of categories, which are called *padārtha*—that is, a classification of the meanings (*artha*) of words (*pada*) or the things (*artha*) to which words refer. The ambiguity of the term *artha* (like that of the English term "meaning") explains how this logical classification could have ontological implications as well. The categories are *dravya* ("substance"), *guṇa* ("quale"), *kriyā* ("action"), *jāti* ("generic character," e.g., horseness), *viśeṣa* ("ultimate difference," postulated to explain the difference between atoms), and *samavāya* ("inherence," postulated to explain relations between other categories). Later a seventh category, *abhāva* ("absence"), was added, and this gave rise to a host of logical problems.

The partial similarity between these categories and those of Aristotle is easily explained by the common Indo-European syntactical background. A common grammatical background also explains the controversy over the concepts of *jāti* and class, which led to discussions between realists (notably in Mīmāṃsā) and nominalists (notably the Buddhists). According to Nyāya logicians *jāti* is related to each individual (*vyakti*) through inherence. It may be noted here that suffixes forming abstract terms, such as *-tva* and *-tā* ("-ness"), are more easily used in Sanskrit than in other Indo-European languages. In logical texts a common expression for "the pot is blue" is, in literal translation, "(there is) blueness of the pot." Although "blueness" can inhere in many substances, "blue" inheres in one substance only. For this reason *guṇa*, exemplified by "blue" but not by "blueness," is translated as "quale" (inhering in one substance) rather than as "quality" (inhering in many).

In epistemology Nyāya adopted the view that there are four distinct means of valid knowledge, or *pramāṇa*: *pratyakṣa* ("perception"), *anumāna* ("inference"), *upamāna* ("identification," sometimes translated as "comparison"), and *śabda* ("verbal knowledge"). Other schools added other means of valid knowledge; for example, Mīmāṃsā added *anupalabdhi*, which denotes the faculty that perceives *abhāva* ("absence"). However, according to Vātsyāyana the absence of a thing is established by the same means of knowledge as its presence. Later logicians analyzed the perception of absence of a thing in terms of perception of the locus of the thing's absence. The third *pramāṇa, upamāna,* is invoked when a person who has heard what a rhinoceros is sees a wild animal and recognizes it as a rhinoceros by identifying it with the denotation of the concept he knows. The last *pramāṇa, śabda,* which in other systems was needed to safeguard the authority of revelation, was applied by logicians of the Nyāya system to any statement made by an expert (*āptavacana*). In the course of the development of Nyāya, logical research was increasingly devoted to perception and inference.

In the Old Nyāya the basic form of inference was the so-called syllogism consisting of five members, which can be approximately represented by the following expressions:

(1) $\rightarrow G(a)$,
(2) $F(a) \rightarrow$,
(3) $(x)(F(x) \rightarrow G(x))$,
(4) $F(a)$,
(5) $G(a)$.

The not-well-formed expressions, (1) and (2), are called ascripts; the other expressions are assertions. The stock example is

(1)   The mountain possesses fire
(2)   because of smoke;
(3)   Where there is smoke there is fire, as in a kitchen;
(4)   (This mountain) is similar (that is, possesses fire);
(5)   Therefore, (it) is similar (that is, possesses fire).

It has been argued that this syllogism depends for its validity on an example and is therefore a mere argument by analogy. Actually the kitchen appears to play the same role that the figure customarily drawn in geometrical proofs does; it serves no purpose other than to fix the attention. In the proof no use should be made of any special characteristic of the example not appearing in all other examples.

Buddhist logic. Following Dignāga, Buddhist logicians recognized perception and inference as the only means of valid knowledge. Later the main constituent of an inference was called *vyāpti* (denoted by V), a term referring to the relation that holds between the *hetu* ("reason," h) and the *sādhya* ("thing to be inferred," s). Both h and s occur in a locus through an occurrence relation A. For *vyāpti* we have

(1) $V(h,s) \leftrightarrow (x)(A(h,x) \rightarrow A(s,x))$.

In the formulation of Dharmakīrti quantification is expressed by means of the particle *eva* ("only"). Dharmakīrti defined *sapakṣa* ("similar instance") as any locus x such that $A(s,x)$, and *asapakṣa* (later *vipakṣa*, "dissimilar instance") as any locus x such that $\sim A(s,x)$. Then *vyāpti* holds "if there is occurrence of h in similar instances only":

(2) $(x)(A(h,x) \rightarrow (x = sapakṣa))$.

Vyāpti also holds "if there is nonoccurrence in dissimilar instances of h only"—that is, if

(3) $(x)((x = vipakṣa) \rightarrow \sim A(h,x))$.

According to Dharmottara either (2) or (3) implies (1). The latter implication involves contraposition.

The Buddhist logicians made numerous other contributions to formal logic, particularly in connection with negations. Interesting discussions took place on *reductio ad absurdum* (*prasaṅga*). Other topics have become part of the Indian tradition of logic—e.g., infinite regress (*anavasthā*). The Buddhist distinction between the thing itself (*svalakṣaṇa*) to which a word indirectly refers and the mental image (*vikalpa*) the word connotes is reminiscent of the modern Western distinction between denotation and sense.

New Nyāya. In the final development of Indian formal logic, generally called New Nyāya, or *navya-nyāya*, attention centered on the analysis of inference. Formal rules, whose validity depends only on the structure of the sentence expressions, were established. In such expressions variables occur (represented, for example, by relative pronouns) for which constants may be substituted. The formal apparatus so developed is indispensable to later Indian writing on philosophy, grammar, ritual, or science in general and is therefore equally indispensable to the Western student of any of these later developments.

In the analysis of inference the definitions of *vyāpti* occupy a central place. Many of these definitions are discussed and refuted. In each definition two concepts, occurrence and locus, play an important role. The occurrence of x in y will again be expressed here by $A(x,y)$, and $B(x,y)$ will denote that x is the locus of y. Two well-known definitions of *vyāpti*, which were later rejected, are "nonoccurrence of h in the locus of absence of s" and "nonoccurrence of h in the absence of the locus of s."

The first definition can be applied if and only if (1) there is an x such that $x \neq s$, (2) there is a y such that $B(y,x)$, provided that condition (1) holds for x, (3) $\sim A(h,y)$, provided that condition (2) holds for y. The second definition can be applied if (1) there is an x such that $B(x,s)$, (2) there is a y such that $y \neq x$, provided that condition (1) holds for x, (3) $\sim A(h,y)$, provided that condition (2) holds for y. In order to meet specific objections such definitions underwent numerous modifications, many of which resulted in particular expressions for quantification.

The analysis of the fourth means of valid knowledge, *śabda*, led to the logical study of grammatical categories. One branch is called *śaktivāda* ("semantics"), literally "the doctrine of *śakti*," where *śakti* is defined as the relation between a word (*pada*) and its reference (*padārtha*).

The new school also studied multiple negation. Raghunātha formulated laws of multiple negation that have counterparts in intuitionist logic.

Western study of Indian logic is still in its infancy. At present many Indian logical doctrines can be understood only because similar developments have recently taken place in the West. It seems reasonable to assume that a large body of apparently obscure texts is actually ill understood and needs a new formal apparatus for its adequate expression. Although it remains uninfluenced by Western logic and stems from an entirely different tradition, Indian logic offers striking parallels to Western logic. Its study is interesting not only for its own sake but also for the unexpected light it may throw on the vexed problems of the universality of logical principles and the relation between logical structure and linguistic expression.

J. F. STAAL

CHINESE LOGIC

Systematic argument in Chinese philosophy began with the Moist school, founded in the fifth century B.C. by the first anti-Confucian thinker, Mo Tzu (c. 468 – c. 376 B.C.). He laid down three tests for the validity of a doctrine: ancient authority, common observation, and practical effect. At first the controversies of the various schools over moral and political principles led to increasing rigor in argument; then to an interest in dialectic for its own sake, as evidenced in Hui Shih's paradoxes of infinity and in Kung-sun Lung's sophism "A (white) horse is not a horse"; and still later to the antirationalism of the Taoist Chuang Tzu (born c. 369 B.C.), who rejected all dialectic on the grounds that names have only an arbitrary connection with objects and that any point of view is right for those who accept the choice of names it assumes.

Logic of Moism. In the third century B.C. the Moists responded to Chuang Tzu's skepticism by systematizing dialectic in the "Moist Canons" and the slightly later *Ta-ch'ü* and *Hsiao-ch'ü.*

"Moist Canons." The "Canons" confined dialectic to questions of the form "Is it this or is it not?" or, since they assumed that the proposition is merely a complex name for a complex object, "Is it or is it not the case that . . . ?" (The form is distinguished in Chinese by a verbless sentence with a final particle, not by a verb "to be.") In true dialectic the alternatives are paired ("Is it an ox or not?") so that one and only one fits the object. Dialectic excludes such questions as "Is it an ox or a horse?" (it may be neither) and "Is it a puppy or a dog?" (it may be both). Its solutions are absolutely right or wrong; being or not being "this," unlike being long or short, is not a matter of degree, since nothing is more "this" than this is. The Moists further argued that it is self-contradictory to deny or to affirm all propositions: the statement "All statements are mistaken" implies that it is itself mistaken, and one cannot "reject rejection" without refusing to reject one's own rejection.

Names are of three types, distinguished by their relations to "objects," which are assumed to be particular. "Unrestricted" names (such as "thing") apply to every object. Names "of kinds" (such as "horse") apply to every object resembling the one in question. "Private" names (for example, the proper name "Tsang") apply to one object. Whether a name fits an object is decided by appeal to a "standard." There may be more than one standard for an object; for "circle" the standard may be a circle, one's mental picture of a circle, or a compass. Some standards fit without qualification: a circle has no straight lines. Some fit only partially: in deciding whether someone is a "black man" it is not enough to point out his black eyes and hair. The "Canons" began with 75 definitions, evidently offered as "standards," of moral, psychological, geometrical, and occasionally logical terms. An example of a definition of a logical term is " 'All' is 'none not so' " (supplemented in the *Hsiao-ch'ü* by " 'Some' is 'not all' "). The first of the series is "The 'cause' is what is required for something to happen." ("*Minor cause:* with this it will not necessarily be so; without this it necessarily will not be so. *Major cause:* with this it will necessarily be so.") The "Canons" also distinguish the senses of 12 ambiguous terms. Thus, "same" is (1) identical ("two names for one object"), (2) belonging to one body, (3) together, and (4) of a kind ("the same in some respects").

"Ta-ch'ü" and "Hsiao-ch'ü." The Moist *Ta-ch'ü* further refined the classification of names. Names indicating "number and measure" cease to apply when their objects are reduced in size; when a white stone is broken up it

ceases to be "big," although it is still "white." Names indicating "residence and migration" do not apply when the population moves, as in the case of names of particular states ("Ch'i") or of kinds of administrative divisions ("country"). The claim that one knows *X* only if one knows that an object is *X* applies only to names indicating "shape and appearance" ("mountain," but not "Ch'i" or "county").

The *Ta-ch'ü,* and still more the *Hsiao-ch'ü,* also showed a shift of interest from the name to the sentence and to the deduction of one sentence from another. The Chinese never analyzed deductive forms, but the Moists noticed that the formal parallelism of sentences does not necessarily entitle us to infer from one in the same way as from another, and they developed a procedure for testing parallelism by the addition or substitution of words. For example, "Asking about a man's illness is asking about the man," but "Disliking the man's illness is not disliking the man"; "The ghost of a man is not a man," but "The ghost of my brother is my brother." In order to reconcile the execution of robbers with love for all men some Moists maintained that although a robber is a man, "killing robbers is not killing men." Enemies of Moism rejected this as sophistry, on the assumption that one can argue from "A robber is a man" to "Killing robbers is killing men," just as one can argue from "A white horse is a horse" to "Riding white horses is riding horses." The *Hsiao-ch'ü* replied that there are second and third sentence types of the same form, which do not allow such an inference—for example, "Her brother is a handsome man," but "Loving her brother is not loving a handsome man"; "Cockfights are not cocks," but "Having a taste for cockfights is having a taste for cocks." A four-stage procedure was used to establish that "A robber is a man" belongs to the second type:

(1) Illustrating the topic ("robber") with things ("brother," "boat") of which formally similar statements may be made.

(2) Matching parallel sentences about the illustrations and the topic—for instance, "Her brother is a handsome man, but loving her brother is not loving a handsome man"; "A boat is wood, but entering a boat is not entering [piercing?] wood"; "A robber is a man, but abounding in robbers is not abounding in men, nor is being without robbers being without men."

(3) Adducing supporting arguments for the last and most relevant parallels by expanding them and showing that the parallelism still holds: "Disliking the abundance of robbers is not disliking the abundance of men; wishing to be without robbers is not wishing to be without men."

(4) Inferring, defined as "using its [the topic's] similarity to what he [the person being argued with] accepts in order to propose what he does not accept": "Although a robber is a man, loving robbers is not loving men, not loving robbers is not not loving men, and killing robbers is not killing men."

Hsün Tzu. Outside the Moist school only the Confucian Hsün Tzu (c. 313–c. 238 B.C.) left a consecutive treatise on logical questions. According to his "Correct Use of Names" the purpose of names is to point out objects, thereby distinguishing the noble from the base and the similar from the different. Names are fixed by convention and are mutable, but to use them idiosyncratically when their usage is fixed is a crime akin to falsifying weights and measures. Objects are different if they differ in place although not in form; they remain the same if they change in form without dividing. Objects of the same kind are perceived by the senses as similar and are given the same name. Names may be of any degree of generality; we may assimilate objects under the name "thing" or distinguish them as "bird" and "beast." (Like the Moists, Hsün Tzu took for granted a nominalist position.) The sentence is a series of names conveying one idea, and a name is understood when we grasp both the object to which it points and its interconnections in the sentence.

Hsün Tzu distinguished three sorts of fallacies, which he illustrated with unexplained examples (two are explained by his refutations of them in his "Treatise of Corrections"). Fallacies that abuse names are exposed by an appeal to established usage, and fallacies that abuse objects are exposed by an appeal to the evidence of the senses. The first fallacy, "confusing names by misuse of names," Hsün Tzu illustrated by "To be insulted is not disgraceful." This is a violation of the established use of "disgrace" in two senses, for social and for moral degradation. The second fallacy, "confusing names by misuse of objects," was exemplified by "Our genuine desires are few." Hsün Tzu criticized this as a factual error about mankind. The third fallacy is "confusing objects by misuse of names." Kung-sun Lung (born 380 B.C.) had defended the sophism "A (white) horse is not a horse" on grounds which assume that the question is one of identity, not one of class membership. Hsün Tzu would presumably have replied simply that a white horse is commonly called a "horse."

Later logical thought. The classical period of Chinese philosophy ended about 200 B.C. The next important movement, the Neo-Taoism of the third and fourth centuries A.D., revived the study of the sophists and the Moist "Canons." Indian treatises on logic were available in translation from the seventh century on; Buddhists wrote commentaries on them during the T'ang dynasty (618–907), and in Japan they have continued to do so. But there is little evidence of progress by either Taoists or Buddhists. Neo-Confucianism, the main philosophical movement after the Sung dynasty (960–1279), entirely neglected logical inquiry.

Chinese neglect of logic. It is well known that almost all Chinese philosophical "systems" are practical, moral, or mystical philosophies of life, indifferent to abstract speculation. It is therefore not surprising that Chinese thinkers have cared little for the forms of reasoning, except under the pressure of the acute controversies of the third century B.C. What is surprising is the almost exclusive interest of Chinese philosophers in the problem of names and the fact that even those who advanced from the name to the sentence studied the parallelism of sentences rather than their analysis.

A reason for this interest can be found in the Chinese language, which organizes uninflected words solely according to word order and the placing of particles. Without the inflections that expose the structure of Sanskrit, Greek, or Arabic sentences and encourage the simultaneous growth of grammar and logic the Chinese sentence, until recently, almost defied analysis; the Chinese have been lexicographers but not grammarians. On the other hand, strict parallelism of clauses—in which noun is matched with noun, adjective with adjective, adverb with adverb, verb with verb—is part of the ordinary resources of the Chinese language and easily calls attention to the logical dangers of formal parallelism.

A. C. GRAHAM

ARABIC LOGIC

Arabic logic, like the rest of medieval Arabic science and philosophy, is entirely Western and has nothing to do with Oriental philosophy. It developed wholly in the wake of the classical Greek tradition as preserved in and transmitted through late Greek Aristotelianism. The present account briefly traces the evolution of Arabic logic from its inception in the late eighth century to its stultification in the sixteenth century, mentioning only the most important trends, figures, and achievements. Information on individual writers can be found in Carl Brockelmann's monumental *Geschichte der arabischen Litteratur*, cited hereafter as *GAL* (2 vols.—I, II—Weimar, 1890; Berlin, 1902; 2d ed., Leiden, 1943–1949; 3 supp. vols.—SI, SII, SIII—Leiden, 1937–1942).

Transmission of Greek logic to the Arabs. After their conquest of Syria–Iraq the Arabs came into contact with Greek learning as it continued to be nursed by various Christian sects—primarily the Nestorians and the Monophysites, or Jacobites—that had transplanted there (via such centers as Antioch, Edessa, and Nisibis) the Hellenistic scholarship of Alexandria. Thus, the first writers on logic in Arabic were Syrian Christian scholars, and their tradition of logical studies—closely linked to medicine—was transferred to an Arabic-language setting and laid the foundation for the development of Arabic logic.

The Syriac expositors of Aristotelian logic arrived at the following standard arrangement of logical works: *Isagoge* (by Porphyry), *Categories, De Interpretatione, Prior Analytics, Posterior Analytics, Topics, De Sophisticis Elenchis, Rhetoric,* and *Poetics.* These nine works were thought of as dealing with nine distinct branches of logic, each based on its own canonical text. This construction of Aristotelian logic was taken over by the Arabs, resulting in the following organization of the subject matter of logic:

BRANCH	ARABIC NAME	BASIC TEXT
(1) Introduction	*al-īsāghūjī*	*Isagoge*
(2) Categories	*al-maqūlāt*	*Categories*
(3) Hermeneutics	*al-'ibārah*	*De Interpretatione*
(4) Analytics	*al-qiyās*	*Prior Analytics*
(5) Apodictics	*al-burhān*	*Posterior Analytics*
(6) Topics	*al-jadal*	*Topics*
(7) Sophistics	*al-mughālitah* (or *al-safsatah*)	*De Sophisticis Elenchis*
(8) Rhetoric	*al-khitābah*	*Rhetoric*
(9) Poetics	*al-shi'r*	*Poetics*

The totality of this organon was referred to as the nine books of logic, or as the eight books with the *Poetics* (or sometimes *Isagoge*) excluded. The first four of these logical treatises were apparently the only ones translated into Syriac prior to 800 and into Arabic prior to 850. They were called the four books of logic, and they constituted the object of logical studies in the basic curriculum of the Syrian academies.

Arabic translations of Aristotle's logical treatises and of several Greek studies and commentaries on them prepared the ground for the first indigenous Arabic writer on logic, the philosopher al-Kindī (c. 805–873; *GAL*, I, pp. 209–210). His logical writings, however, probably amounted to little more than summaries of the writings of others about the Aristotelian texts.

School of Baghdad. In the late ninth and the tenth centuries Arabic logic was virtually the monopoly of a single school of logicians centered at Baghdad. The founders of this school belonged to a closely knit group of Syrian Christians, including the teachers of Abū Bishr Mattā ibn Yūnus and the teachers of these teachers. Its principal continuators were the pupils of Abū Bishr's pupil Yaḥyā ibn 'Adī and the pupils of these pupils. Virtually all of these men—with the notable exception of al-Fārābī, a Muslim—were Nestorian Christians.

Abū Bishr Mattā ibn Yūnus (c. 870–c. 940; *GAL*, I, p. 207) was the first specialist in logical studies to write in Arabic. He produced the first Arabic translations of *Posterior Analytics* and *Poetics* and translated several Greek commentaries on Aristotelian works (such as Themistius on *Posterior Analytics*). In addition he wrote logical commentaries and treatises of his own, which unfortunately have not survived.

Abū Naṣr al-Fārābī (c. 870–950; *GAL*, I, pp. 210–213) was perhaps the most important logician of Islam. His commentaries, only a fraction of which survive, covered the entire Aristotelian *Organon* in great detail. All later Arabic logicians—even those who, like Avicenna, have opposed al-Fārābī's influence—have seen Aristotle through his eyes. Among the points of special interest in the commentaries of al-Fārābī are (1) a strong emphasis on *ecthesis* (the setting out of terms) as a principle of syllogistic reduction, (2) an increased resort to noncategorical (for instance, hypothetical and disjunctive) types of syllogism, (3) an elaborate treatment of inductive uses of syllogistic reasoning, especially the application of the categorical syllogism in argument by analogy, and (4) a detailed treatment of the problem of future contingency, providing for a reading of Chapter 9 of *De Interpretatione* that does not deny prior truth status to future contingents (anticipating the position of Peter Abelard).

Yaḥyā ibn 'Adī (893–974; *GAL*, I, p. 207), who studied logic and philosophy with both Abū Bishr and al-Fārābī, not only translated Greek works from Syriac into Arabic but also taught virtually half of the Arabic logicians of the tenth century. He wrote various independent works (including a commentary on *Prior Analytics* that devoted special attention to modal syllogisms), almost none of which have survived.

The three principal achievements of this school of Baghdad are (1) completion of the series of Arabic translations of Greek logical works, (2) the masterly commentaries of al-Fārābī (and possibly others) on the logical treatises of Aristotle, and (3) the elaborate study of certain extra-Aristotelian topics by Abū Bishr Mattā and al-Fārābī (for instance, theory of "conditional," or hypothetical and dis-

junctive, syllogisms along lines already found in Boethius, and the syllogistic reduction of inductive modes of argument).

Avicenna and his influence. Despite the demise of the school of Baghdad around 1050, the ultimate survival of logical studies in Islam was assured by the fact that logic had, through the mediation of medicine, become an integral constituent of the Arabic medicophilosophical tradition as taken over from the Syrian Christians. From a quantitative standpoint the eleventh century was a low ebb in the history of Arabic logic. Yet this period produced perhaps the most creative logician of Islam, the great Persian scholar Abū ibn Sīnā, known as Avicenna (980–1037; *GAL*, I, pp. 452–458).

Avicenna made a daring innovation. Although greatly indebted to the school of Baghdad, he had nothing but contempt for it because it regarded logic as the study of the Aristotelian texts. Avicenna disapproved of this orientation toward the text rather than the subject. For him, and for the tradition he dominated, a logic book was no longer a commentary on Aristotle but an independent, self-sufficient treatise or handbook that covered the ground after its own fashion. Avicenna's masterpiece is a series of treatises in his monumental *Kitāb al-shifā'* dealing with the nine parts of the Arabic logical organon.

An example of Avicenna's originality is the following: In Aristotle and in the Stoics one finds a temporal construction of the modality of necessity that construes "All X's are *necessarily* Y's" as "At any time t all X's-at-t are Y's-at-t." This construction works well for, say, "All men are necessarily animals" but clearly not for "All men necessarily die." Avicenna distinguished between such cases as:

(1) At every time during its existence every X is a Y ("All men are necessarily animals").

(2) At most times during its existence every X is a Y ("All men are necessarily breathing beings").

(3) At some time during its existence every X is a Y ("All men are necessarily dying beings").

He then constructed a detailed theory of syllogistic inference from temporally modalized propositions of this sort.

Avicenna styled his own work in logic (and philosophy) as Eastern, in deliberate contrast with the Western approach of the school of Baghdad. This Eastern logic espoused by Avicenna differs from that of, say, al-Fārābī not so much in matters of substance as in emphasis and in willingness to depart from Aristotelian precedent. Thus, Avicenna imported into his logic a certain amount of material derived probably from Galen (including an at least grudging recognition of the fourth figure of the categorical syllogism) and certainly from the Stoics (for example, quantification of the predicate of categorical propositions, elaboration of quality and quantity for "conditional" propositions, and a treatment of singular propositions in the manner of the Stoics).

Avicenna's call to study logic from independent treatises rather than via the Aristotelian texts met with complete success in Eastern Islam. Only in Muslim Spain did the tradition of Aristotelian studies of the school of Baghdad manage—for a time—to survive.

Logicians of Andalusia. During the late eleventh and

the twelfth centuries Andalusia (Muslim Spain) was the principal center of logical studies in Islam. Muhammad ibn 'Abdūn (c. 930–c. 995; Heinrich Suter, *Die Mathematiker und Astronomen der Araber und ihre Werke,* Leipzig, 1900–1902, No. 161; not in *GAL*), a Spanish Muslim who studied medicine and philosophy in Baghdad, was instrumental in transplanting to Córdoba the teachings of the school of Baghdad in Aristotelian logic. In the medicological tradition of Andalusia these teachings stayed alive for over two and a half centuries, surviving well past their extinction in Eastern Islam.

Abū 'l-Ṣalt (1068–1134; *GAL,* I, pp. 486–487) wrote an influential logic compendium that follows al-Fārābī closely; like most other Spanish Arab logicians, he seems to have had special interest in modal syllogisms. The detailed study of the writings of Aristotle was revitalized by ibn Bājja, or Avempace (c. 1090–1138; *GAL,* I, p. 460), who wrote an important series (extant but unpublished) of discussions of Aristotle's works based on the commentaries of al-Fārābī.

Ibn Rushd, or Averroës (1126–1198; *GAL,* I, pp. 461–462) was unquestionably the most important of the Arabic logicians of Spain. His elaborate commentaries on the treatises of Aristotle's logical *Organon* rival (and conceivably surpass) those of al-Fārābī in their detailed understanding of Aristotle's logic. Averroës stands, as he considered himself to stand, heir to the masters of the school of Baghdad and successor to the heritage of al-Fārābī.

Among the points of special interest in the Aristotelian commentaries of Averroës are (1) certain historical data—for instance, regarding Galen's origination of the fourth syllogistic figure—taken from the last writings of al-Fārābī, (2) anti-Avicennist polemics that afford us a view of the points of dispute between Avicenna and his opponents, (3) the detailed account of the Aristotelian theory of modal syllogisms, and (4) in general, his effort to systematize as unified doctrine the teachings of the Aristotelian *Organon.*

After Averroës the logical tradition of Muslim Spain entered a period of decline. Arabic logic became extinct in Spain because there—in contrast to Eastern Islam, where logic achieved a *modus vivendi* with religious orthodoxy—popular and theological hostility toward logic and philosophy as an integral part of "alien learning" continued unabated.

Quarrel of the Eastern and Western schools. Avicenna's criticisms of the school of Baghdad and his shift away from Aristotelian orthodoxy were not received with universal acceptance. A Western school arose to oppose Avicenna's innovations. Its principal exponents were the prolific Persian scholar Fakhr al-Dīn al-Rāzī (1148–1209; *GAL,* I, pp. 506–508) and his followers al-Khūnajī (1194–1249; *GAL,* I, p. 463) and al-Urmawī (1198–1283; *GAL,* I, p. 467). These logicians not only offered detailed criticisms of Avicenna's departures from Aristotle but also wrote handbooks of logic that became standard textbooks both during the lifetime of their school and later.

Opposed to these Westerners, the school of the Easterners, which supported Avicenna, continued to be active throughout the thirteenth century. Its leading exponent was the eminent and versatile Persian scholar Kamāl al-

Dīn ibn Yūnus (1156–1242; *GAL,* SI, p. 859). His position was supported by his pupils al-Abharī (1200–1264; *GAL,* I, pp. 464–465) and Naṣīr al-Dīn al-Ṭūsī (1201–1274; *GAL,* I, pp. 508–512), as well as by the pupils of the last-named scholar, especially the logician al-Qazwīnī al-Kātibī (c. 1220–c. 1280; *GAL,* I, pp. 466–467). These logicians produced polemical treatises to attack the theses of the Westerners, as well as textbooks and handbooks to facilitate the teaching of logic according to their conceptions.

Amid this disputation and textbook writing the logical treatises of Aristotle were completely lost sight of. In effect, Avicenna carried the field before him; in Eastern Islam, Aristotle's logical writings were utterly abandoned. Ibn Khaldūn (born 1322) could lament, "The books and methods of the ancients are avoided, as if they had never been, although they are full of the results and useful aspects of logic." The handbooks of the two thirteenth-century schools provided a basis for all future study in Islam, completely replacing the works of Aristotle. But very little produced at this stage has any significance for logic as a science rather than as a field of instruction.

Final period. The period 1300–1500 may be characterized as the final period of Arabic logic, when its ossification became complete. It was a time not of creative logicians but of teachers of logic writing expository commentaries and supercommentaries on the thirteenth-century handbooks, now basic to all Arabic instruction in logic.

Underlying this development was the effort of al-Tustarī (c. 1270–c. 1330; *GAL,* SI, p. 816) and his disciple al-Taḥtānī (c. 1290–1365; *GAL,* II, pp. 209–210) to effect an arbitration between the Eastern and Western schools. As a result, later Arabic logicians were free to draw on both sectors of the tradition and to use the handbooks of both schools for the teaching of logic. The flood of glosses and supercommentaries on commentaries on the thirteenth-century logic handbooks marks the final, disintegrative phase of the evolution of logic in Islam.

Contributions of Arabic logic. Some of the original contributions made by the Arabic logicians to logic as a science are (1) al-Fārābī's syllogistic theory of inductive argumentation, (2) al-Fārābī's doctrine of future contingency, (3) Avicenna's theory of "conditional" propositions, (4) Avicenna's temporal construction of modal propositions, and (5) Averroës' careful reconstruction of Aristotle's theory of modal syllogistic. Many of the prominent "innovations" of medieval Latin logic are in effect borrowings or elaborations of borrowings of Arabic ideas (for example, the distinction between the various modes of *suppositio* and the distinction between modality *de dicto* and *de re*).

However, in speaking of the "original contributions" of Arabic logic two qualifications are necessary. In the first place, our knowledge of late Greek logic is so incomplete that any "original" item of Arabic work could turn out to be a mere elaboration of a Greek innovation. Second, an emphasis on originality in discussing Arabic logic is somewhat misplaced in that all the Arabic logicians—even Avicenna, the most original of them all—viewed their logical work as the reconstruction of a Greek teaching rather than as an enterprise of innovation.

NICHOLAS RESCHER

MEDIEVAL LOGIC

Although Arabic and Indian logic flourished in the Middle Ages, the term "medieval logic" is customarily used to designate the body of logical doctrine developed in the schools and universities of western Europe between the eleventh and fifteenth centuries. Study of this logical tradition was first undertaken in recent years and is as yet insufficient to permit more than a partial and provisional account of its historical development and doctrinal content. These studies have, however, revealed that in the later Middle Ages formal logic achieved a rich and original development, on a level comparable to that of the Stoic–Megarian and Aristotelian contributions and not surpassed until the rise of mathematical logic, within the past century. A characteristic of medieval logic was its metalinguistic formulation as a quasi-prescriptive systematization of the syntax and semantics of natural language—specifically, of scholastic Latin. Within this framework medieval logicians developed (1) a general theory of reference (*suppositio terminorum*) that was applied both to the semantical problem of use and mention of expressions and to the formulation of what is now called quantification theory, (2) a general theory of implication (*consequentia*) governing a logic of propositions, (3) a well-articulated logic of modalities, and (4) some sophisticated treatments of problems in the philosophy of logic and language, such as those involved in the Liar paradox. In treating medieval logic we shall first describe the stages of its development and then consider its doctrinal contributions in their mature form.

Development of medieval logic. When the Latin West became isolated from Greek culture, after the barbarian invasions and the Muslim conquests, the only works on logic generally available in the monastic schools were those of Boethius (c. 480–524), along with a few handbooks of negligible value, such as the *De Nuptiis Philologiae et Mercurii* of Martianus Capella. The Boethian writings included translations of Aristotle's *Categoriae* and *De Interpretatione* and of the *Isagoge* ("Introduction to the Categories") by the Neoplatonist philosopher Porphyry. In addition to literal commentaries on these texts, Boethius had written treatises of his own on categorical and hypothetical syllogisms and on dialectical and rhetorical arguments (or "topics"), adding to these a commentary on Cicero's *Topics*. The make-up of this heritage was significant for the later development of medieval logic in two respects: First, it conveyed only those elements of Aristotelian logic which bore on the syntax and semantics of language and on syllogistic and topical inferences, dissociating the theory of inference from Aristotle's doctrine of scientific demonstration. Second, it conveyed fragments of the Stoic–Megarian doctrine of implication and of the Theophrastian theory of hypothetical syllogisms. Of equal significance was the fact that in the educational program of the early medieval schools logic was regarded as an "art of language" closely associated with grammar and rhetoric, useful in construing the texts of the Bible and the Church Fathers and in reconciling apparent contradictions found in these texts. These factors tended to shape the medieval conception of logic as a discipline concerned with the syntax and semantics of natural language and with the validity of inference forms.

Logical writings of the early medieval period by Alcuin of York (730–804), Eric of Auxerre (841–876), Abbo of Fleury (died 1004), Gerbert of Aurillac (Pope Sylvester II, died 1003), and Garland the Computist (fl. c. 1040) show only a meager understanding of the Boethian heritage and scarcely get beyond the doctrines of predicables and categories. In the eleventh century a class of professional logicians (or "dialecticians") emerged, and lively controversies arose over the propriety of applying logical criteria to the interpretation of Scripture or of theological doctrines. Peter Damian (1007–1072) questioned the validity of the principle of contradiction with respect to what falls within the power of God, and Roscelin (c. 1050–c. 1120) was condemned as a heretic for applying the logic of identity to the doctrine of the Trinity. He also gained fame for having said that universals are nothing but vocal utterances (*flatus vocis*), for which he has been regarded as a founder of nominalism. St. Anselm (1033–1109) is best known for his "Ontological Argument," but he also concerned himself, in his *Dialogus de Grammatico*, with the distinction between the meaning (*significatio*) and the reference (*appellatio*) of general terms.

Abelard. The first important medieval logician was Peter Abelard (1079–1142), who taught in the schools of Paris in the first half of the twelfth century. His extant writings include detailed and critical literal commentaries on Porphyry's *Isagoge*, Aristotle's *Categories* and *De Interpretatione*, and the *De Differentiis Topicis* of Boethius. Abelard's major work was a five-book treatise entitled *Dialectica*, of which all but the initial portion of the first book has been preserved. In this work he dealt systematically with the "parts," or constituents, of propositions, with categorical propositions and syllogisms, topical arguments and the notion of logical consequence, hypothetical syllogisms, and definition and division. Working only with the Boethian materials, which he supplemented with bits of Stoic logical syntax gleaned from Priscian's *Institutiones Grammaticae*, Abelard carried out a critical reconstruction of the Boethian legacy in which the formal and linguistic approach characteristic of the Stoic–Megarian extension of Aristotelian logic prevailed over the metaphysical interpretations that stemmed from Porphyry and the Neoplatonic tradition.

In dealing with the dispute over universals Abelard held that universality is a property of words or of "common conceptions of the mind" expressed by them, and he rejected all theories which involved the assumption that general terms signify common natures existing in individual things outside of thought. In dealing with inference he distinguished arguments valid by their logical form alone from those whose cogency depends on factual content or meaning, and he held that only the former constitute "perfect," or logically conclusive, arguments. His detailed discussions of the functions of the copula, of quantifying prefixes, of the negation sign (which he treated as a truth-function), and of the conditional and disjunctive sentential connectives laid the ground for many of the developments that became explicit in thirteenth-century treatises on *Syncategoremata* and on the "properties of terms."

"New logic." During the half century after Abelard's death the remaining books of Aristotle's *Organon* became available in translations from Arabic and Greek, and these were quickly followed by translations of Aristotle's *Metaphysics, Physics*, and *De Anima*, along with works by the Arabic philosophers Avicenna and Averroës. The newly received parts of the *Organon* came to be called the "new logic" (*ars nova*), to distinguish them from the previously known portion, the "old logic" (*ars vetus*). Of the new parts the *De Sophisticis Elenchis* had immediate appeal to the twelfth-century logicians because its content had not been conveyed in the Boethian treatises and because the detection and resolution of fallacious arguments was highly germane to the scholastic method of the "disputed question," then becoming established in the schools.

A favorite form of exercise in dialectical skill, already found in such earlier works as the *Ars Disserendi* of Adam of Balsham (written in 1132), was that of propounding paradoxical theses known as "sophisms" (*sophismata*), from which contradictory conclusions appeared to follow, and then resolving them by exhibiting the hidden logical difficulty. Treatises on the art of disputation, known as *Tractatus de Obligationibus*, began to be written at this time; they established rules governing what kinds of premises introduced by one disputant could be rejected as inadmissible by the other and what kinds the other disputant would be obliged to admit.

Logic in the universities. With the formation of the universities of Paris and Oxford at the beginning of the thirteenth century the teaching of logic fell within the province of the lower faculty of arts, but because the philosophical works of Aristotle and of the Arabic writers were considered dangerous to orthodoxy, study of them was reserved for the higher faculty of theology. As a result the development of logic within the arts faculty continued along the formal and linguistic lines that had been established in the twelfth century, enriched with materials drawn from the new translations of the *Prior Analytics, Topics*, and *De Sophisticis Elenchis;* the teachers of the arts faculty seem to have disregarded the *Posterior Analytics*, as if it was irrelevant to formal logic. But the theologians studied the *Posterior Analytics*, and the *Organon* as a whole, in the context of Aristotle's metaphysics and theory of knowledge, and utilizing the works of Avicenna and Averroes, they wrote literal commentaries on the Aristotelian treatises in an effort to recover the "original Aristotle" in authentic form. Such commentaries were composed by Robert Grosseteste (1175–1253), Thomas Aquinas (1224–1274), Robert Kilwardby (died 1279), and Giles of Rome (c. 1247–1316); Albert the Great (died 1280) wrote paraphrases of each book of the *Organon* as part of his encyclopedic enterprise of writing treatises corresponding to every work of Aristotle. With respect to logic there arose in the thirteenth century an Aristotelian "purism" promoted by the theologians, occurring simultaneously with a development of new methods and problems in the logic of the arts faculty. The Aristotelian purism came to be called the *logica antiqua* and the logic of the arts faculty the *logica moderna*.

Representative of the logic taught in the arts faculty of the University of Paris around the middle of the thirteenth century are treatises and textbooks written by William of Sherwood (1200/1210–1266/1271) and Peter of Spain (died 1277). Of these the earlier and more original are those of Sherwood, although it was the *Summulae Logicales* of Peter of Spain that became a standard textbook in the logic curriculum during the fourteenth and fifteenth centuries.

William of Sherwood. Of Sherwood's writings two have been edited and published. A treatise *De Insolubili*, on the Liar paradox, and a treatise *De Obligationibus* are still unpublished. One published treatise is *Syncategoremata*, in which the functions of what we now call logical constants ("not," "and," "if," "every," "some," and so on) are examined. The other, a logic textbook entitled *Introductiones in Logicam*, consists of six treatises, "On the Proposition," "On the Predicables," "On the Syllogism," "On the Dialectical Topics," "On Fallacies," and "On the Properties of Terms." The first five treat in a terse, formal manner the traditional themes of the old logic, with the addition of the material provided by Aristotle's *De Sophisticis Elenchis*, but the discussion of categories is, significantly, dropped. The sixth treatise introduces the notion of the supposition of terms, an original medieval contribution to logic which will be separately considered. Sherwood's treatise on syllogisms contains the first presentation of the mnemonic verses "Barbara, Celarent, . . ." but takes no account of modal syllogisms. The treatise on propositions not only deals with categorical propositions but also gives truth-functional definitions of the sentential connectives "and," "or," and "if," adopting the inclusive sense of disjunction and defining the conditional in what appears to be the Philonian sense. Perhaps the most interesting part of Sherwood's treatment of the proposition is his consideration of doubly general propositions, where he explicitly introduced the notion of the scope of one quantifier extending to include the other. This notion is applied in his treatment of the supposition of terms in the sixth part of his book; it will be discussed in our examination of that doctrine.

Peter of Spain. The *Summulae Logicales* of Peter of Spain, apparently composed at a later date than Sherwood's textbook, contains six tracts on the traditional themes (including the categories) and six tracts devoted to the new doctrines concerning the "properties of terms." This logical textbook enjoyed enormous popularity throughout the later Middle Ages, and more than 150 printed editions, many with commentaries by later logicians, were published in the fifteenth and sixteenth centuries. For all that, Peter's work displays less logical insight than Sherwood's does and was probably less original.

A treatise *De Syncategorematibus*, ascribed to Peter, is contained in some early printed editions, but its authenticity has been questioned.

Late medieval logic. Toward the end of the thirteenth century, it appears, the cultivation of the *logica moderna* shifted its geographical center from Paris to Oxford, where the cult of Aristotelianism was less pronounced. Robert Kilwardby's commentary on the *Prior Analytics*, written at Oxford in the late thirteenth century, exhibits an acute and critical grasp of formal problems, and the works of Duns Scotus, though mostly on theology, give evidence of his familiarity with the logical doctrines of the arts faculty.

Among the inauthentic writings included in the old edition of Scotus' *Opera Omnia* are some treatises on formal logic in which the ideas of the *logica moderna* are developed with the highest skill; these works, now attributed to an unknown author designated the pseudo-Scotus, were probably written in the fourteenth century and may well have been influenced by the work of William of Ockham (c. 1285–1349), whose *Summa Logicae*, composed around 1326, inaugurated the period of maturity of medieval logic.

In this final stage of its development the *logica moderna* provided a framework within which the Aristotelian heritage was absorbed and reconstructed on new foundations. The Aristotelian logic of terms was reconstituted from the perspective of the theory of supposition of terms, and the laws of inference and of syllogism were grounded on a general theory of implication (*consequentia*), in which the logic of unanalyzed propositions was recognized as more fundamental than the logic of predicates. Modal logic was developed far beyond its Aristotelian origins, and various types of *sophismata* involving syntactical and semantical problems of an advanced sort were formulated and investigated, with the Liar paradox receiving an enormous amount of attention.

Although the general form and much of the content of fourteenth-century logic was established by Ockham, other able logicians made significant contributions which served to complete the evolution of medieval logic. Among these may be mentioned Jean Buridan (c. 1295–after 1358), who wrote a *Summula de Dialectica* and treatises on *Consequentiae* and *Sophismata;* Walter Burley (1275–after 1349), who wrote a treatise entitled *De Puritate Artis Logicae;* Albert of Saxony (c. 1316–c. 1390), whose *Summa Logicae* integrated the contributions of Ockham and Buridan with great clarity and elegance; and William Heytesbury, Ralph Strode, and Richard Ferabrich, all of Oxford, whose writings on logic had great influence in Italy in the fifteenth century. From the late fourteenth to the early sixteenth century the logical tradition of Paris and Oxford flourished in the German and Italian universities, where its doctrines were actively debated, apparently without being essentially altered or significantly advanced. The *Logica Magna* of Paul of Venice (died 1429) represents late medieval logic in its advanced form and constitutes a veritable encyclopedia of the whole tradition.

Standing apart from the main tradition of medieval logic was Ramón Lull (c. 1235–1316), who conceived of a combinatory system of elementary concepts, called the *ars universalis,* which he proposed to use to prove the truth of the Christian faith. Lull's choice of elementary concepts was not such as to make the method fruitful, but the basic idea of such a combinatory method had fascination for later generations and may well have suggested to Leibniz his enterprise of constructing a *characteristica universalis.* Lull even designed machines, formed of superimposed rotating discs, by which his calculus could be worked out mechanically—an enterprise which perhaps earns him the right to be called the father of computer programming.

More fruitful for later scientific developments were the efforts of such fourteenth-century logicians as Heytesbury and, especially, Richard Swineshead (the "Calculator") to resolve logico-mathematical problems involved in the notion of the continuum. These problems, treated as a special type of *sophisma,* generated methods of treatment that yielded some basic concepts of modern kinematics and paved the way for the differential and integral calculus.

The reciprocal influences between mathematics and logic in the late medieval period have not been sufficiently investigated. There was a tendency toward axiomatization of logical theory, probably owing to the influence of the Euclidean tradition, but the degree to which logic may have contributed to the algebraic approach to mathematics is an interesting but almost wholly neglected question for historical research.

Supposition of terms. Medieval logicians normally reserved the word "term" to designate the descriptive (or "categorematic") signs which occupy subject or predicate position in propositions, the other components (copula, quantifiers, and so on) being called syncategorematic signs. The treatises composed by Sherwood and Peter of Spain on the properties of terms use the word "term" in this sense and make an initial distinction between the property of being meaningful (*significatio*), which belongs to vocal sounds in virtue of their institution to serve as language signs, and the property of "supposition" (*suppositio*), which is acquired by an already meaningful term when it functions as subject or predicate of a proposition. Since logic is a science of language (*sermocinalis scientia*), it presupposes the existence of meaningful signs as its subject matter, and hence the question of the meaning of "meaning," or of how vocal sounds acquire significance, pertains not to logic but to psychology or metaphysics.

Supposition was defined by Ockham as the "standing for something else" of a term *in* a proposition, "such that when the term stands in the proposition for something, we are using that term for something of which . . . that term . . . is verified" (*Summa Logicae,* Pars Prima, Cap. 63). What primarily determines the supposition, or referential use, of a subject or predicate term in a proposition is the verb or copula; what the affirmative copula indicates is that subject and predicate "stand for the same" in accordance with such conditions as are determined by quantifying prefixes or other syncategorematic signs in the proposition. As applied to general propositions the doctrine of supposition constitutes an interpretation of the logic of quantifiers in terms of a theory of reference rather than a theory of meaning.

Meaning and reference. The concept of supposition was used in another way in connection with the semantical distinction of language levels. Medieval logicians divided the categorematic, or descriptive, terms of the language into two classes: terms of "first intention," which have been instituted to signify things that are not language signs, and terms of "second intention," which have been instituted to signify kinds of language signs. This distinction corresponds to the modern one between object language and metalanguage, the syncategorematic signs being common to both; the terminology of first and second intentions was taken over from Avicenna.

Now, it may happen, in the ordinary usage of language, that a term of first intention occurs as subject of a sentence whose predicate is a term of second intention—for example, "Man is a general term." Instead of treating such sentences as meaningless violations of type restrictions, medieval logicians said that the reference of the subject term of such a sentence could be interpreted in two ways: If interpreted "significatively" for the things to which it applies in virtue of its meaning, it has "personal supposition" (*suppositio personalis*); so interpreted, the sentence "Man is a general term" is simply false. But the term "man" can also be interpreted "nonsignificatively" as standing for itself as a language expression (in which case it has "material supposition") or as referring to the concept or "sense" it expresses (in which case it has "simple supposition"); if interpreted in either of these ways, the sentence "Man is a general term" is true, at least if we allow the word "term" to designate not only the design of the word but also the concept expressed by it. The distinctions made here, between the use and the mention of a language expression and between the normal referent of a term and its "sense" or meaning, are of fundamental importance. But to make these distinctions by assigning different domains of reference to the same symbol instead of enclosing it in quotation marks or introducing separate symbols to serve as names of words or of their meanings was not only clumsy; it also obscured the meaning of the concept of "supposition" by using it for two very different purposes.

Quantification. It was in application to the analysis of propositions whose terms are used significatively or in *suppositio personalis* that the theory of supposition constituted a theory of quantification. Three modes of personal supposition were distinguished:

(1) Determinate supposition (*suppositio determinata*), given to a term in a proposition by the existential quantifier "some," occurs when the term stands for all its individual referents in such a manner that the general proposition is equivalent to a disjunctive set of singular propositions whose subject terms name all of the individuals for which the general term stands and whose predicate terms are the same as that of the general proposition. Thus, supposing that the only men are Tom, John, and Robert, it will follow that if some man is white, then either Tom is white, John is white, or Robert is white.

(2) Confused and distributive supposition (*confusa et distributiva*), given by the universal quantifier "every" to the term immediately following it in the proposition, occurs when the term stands for all its individual values in such a manner that the descent to singular propositions yields a conjunctive set. For example, if every man is white, then Tom is white, John is white, and Robert is white.

(3) Merely confused supposition (*confusa tantum*) occurs when the predicate term of a universal affirmative proposition stands for all its individual referents in such a manner that the reduction to singulars is effected not by a disjunctive or conjunctive set of sentences with the same subject and singular applications of the predicate but rather by a proposition with a "disjunct predicate." For example, if every man is an animal, then every man is either this animal, that animal, or that other animal, and so on, but it does not follow that every man is this animal, or every man is that animal, and so on.

The interest of this "merely confused" type of supposition lies in the fact that it involves recognition by medieval logicians of the problem of multiple quantification and of the extension of the scope of one quantifier to include another. To show the nonequivalence of merely confused supposition with determinate supposition Sherwood con-

sidered the case in which every existing man is looking at himself but at no other man. Then from the true proposition "Every man looks at a man" we cannot infer the proposition "There is a man that every man looks at," although the converse implication would be valid. This is a recognition of the fact that a doubly general proposition of the form $(x)(\exists y)F(x,y)$ is implied by, but does not imply, a proposition of the form $(\exists y)(x)F(x,y)$. Seeing the necessity of differentiating between these two cases, Sherwood and other medieval logicians introduced the third manner of supposition, *confusa tantum*, to take care of the case in which an existential quantifier falls within the scope of a preceding universal quantifier. A further point to be noticed is that the medieval logicians did not regard the quantifying prefixes as quasi-adjectival determinants of only the term following them but conceived of them as also operating on the supposition of both terms or on the proposition as a whole.

Ampliation. Since medieval logic was a tensed logic, the tense of the verb or copula functioned as a temporal operator, but a temporal operator affecting the supposition of the subject and the application of the predicate in different ways. A verb of past time extends, or "ampliates," the range of supposition of the subject term to include not only presently existing things but past things as well, and although the predicate is indicated to stand for any of the things in this range, it is said to have "appellation" (*appellatio*) for them—or, we might say, application to them—only for the time indicated by the verb. For example, in the sentence "Every adult was a baby" the subject "adult" stands for those who are adults not only in their present existence but also in their past existence, and although the predicate also refers to all these individuals, what it asserts concerning them is applicable to them (or "appellative" of them) only for past time—since no person now an adult is now a baby. Because an omnitemporal assertoric verb form was lacking, ampliation of supposition to both past and future time was effected by use of the potential form "can be," and it could also be effected by use of a dispositional predicate. This device had the defect of blurring the distinction between an omnitemporal assertoric proposition and the corresponding modal proposition of possibility.

Inference. Applied to the relations of opposition and subalternation among general categorical propositions, the doctrine of supposition gave existential import to the universal affirmative but not to the particular negative, for if one of the terms of the universal affirmative does not stand for anything at all, then its terms do not "stand for the same," and hence it is false, in which case its contradictory, the particular negative, is true. By the same token the inferences from universal affirmative to particular affirmative and from universal negative to particular negative were regarded as valid, along with the so-called subaltern moods of the syllogism. On the other hand, the doctrine of ampliation of supposition to "what can be," mentioned above, raises questions about what the requirement of existential import amounts to.

Exposition. In addition to its application to the problem of use and mention of expressions and to quantification theory and tensed logic, the theory of the supposition of terms provided a means of analysis of idiomatic forms of statements logically equivalent to hypothetical (that is, molecular) propositions. Such analysis was called "exposition" of the proposition, and special treatises *De Exponibilibus* gave rules for such "ordinary-language analysis." As an interpretation of the syntactical structure of ordinary language by an extensional semantics of reference, the medieval doctrine of *suppositio terminorum* marked an important stage in the development of logic. Its defects were due more to the intrinsic difficulty of formulating the extraordinarily complex syntax of natural languages without benefit of symbolic techniques than to any lack of ingenuity or logical acumen on the part of the medieval logicians.

Implication ("consequentia"). Propositions composed of two or more categorical propositions joined by a sentential connective were called "hypothetical propositions" by medieval logicians. These were classified, depending on the connective involved, as copulative (that is, conjunctive), disjunctive, conditional, causal, temporal, local, etc. The function of the connective was defined, in each case, by stating truth rules; thus, the conjunctive was said to be true if and only if both component propositions were true, and the disjunctive was said to be true if one of its components was true. A true conditional was called a "consequence" and its components distinguished as "antecedent" and "consequent." But there was considerable discussion over the condition of its truth. Sherwood said that for the conditional to be true "it is not required that its parts be true, but only that when [*cum*] the antecedent is true the consequent is true" (*Die Introductiones in Logicam des Wilhelm von Shyreswood*, p. 37). But Peter of Spain said that it was required that the "antecedent *cannot* be true without the consequent," adding that "every true conditional is necessary and every false conditional impossible" (*Summulae Logicales*, I. M. Bocheński, ed., Rome, 1947, p. 8). The later logicians followed Peter of Spain in defining a consequence, or true conditional, in accordance with the formula $p \prec q := : \sim\Diamond(p . \sim q)$. (See LOGIC, MODAL.)

Consequences were divided into two main classes, "formal" and "material." A consequence was called formal if it was valid by the logical form of the component sentences or under all transformations of the categorematic terms or of the "matter," or content, of the propositions. Such consequences included the valid inference forms belonging to the logic of terms, such as the syllogistic forms and the traditional equipollences, subalternations, conversions, and obversions. But they also included theorems of propositional logic, such as those now represented by the following formulas:

$$p . q : \prec p;$$
$$p \prec (p \lor q);$$
$$p . p \prec q : \prec q;$$
$$\sim q . p \prec q : \prec \sim p;$$
$$p \prec q . q \prec r : \prec : p \prec r;$$
$$p . \sim p : \prec q;$$
$$p \prec : q \lor \sim q;$$
$$p \lor q . \sim p : \prec q.$$

To these we may add what are now called the De Morgan laws, which were well known in the fourteenth century.

Material consequences were described as conditionals that satisfy the general requirement expressed by the formula $\sim\Diamond(p . \sim q)$ but that hold not on formal grounds alone but in virtue of the "matter" or content specified by the descriptive terms of the component propositions. Such consequences included enthymemes, which are reducible to formal consequences by apposition of the suppressed premise required for a valid syllogism, but they also included the "paradoxical theorems" that an impossible proposition implies any proposition and that a necessary proposition is implied by any proposition. Material consequences were separated into two classes, "simple" material consequences (*consequentiae materiales simplices*) and "as of now" material consequences (*consequentiae materiales ut nunc*). "As of now" material consequences are conditionals true for a limited time range, or in virtue of a factual condition prevailing "as of now" (or "as of then," if in past or future tense); "simple" material consequences are those such that at no time can the antecedent be true and the consequent false. This distinction corresponds strikingly to that between the Philonian and the Diodorean definitions of implication, and like those, it involves the notion of contingent propositions' being true at one time and false at another, with necessary propositions being of the kind that are "always true."

Material consequences "as of now" included those enthymematic consequences whose reduction to syllogistic form is accomplished by apposition of a true contingent premise, whereas those whose reduction is accomplished by apposition of a necessary premise belonged to the class of simple (or absolute) material consequences. Most of the later logicians also included among material consequences *ut nunc* the paradoxical theorems of material implication—namely, $\sim p \prec : p \prec q$ and $q \prec : p \prec q$. Yet it is questionable whether this constituted a recognition of material implication in the modern sense, since the consequences *ut nunc* were held to be necessary within their restricted time range and to satisfy "as of now" the formula $\sim\Diamond(p . \sim q)$. The paradoxical theorems, whether simple or "as of now," were considered useless for inference, as indeed they are.

The "rules of consequence" formulated in the medieval treatises entitled *De Consequentiis* were all formal in the sense that they specified logically true relations of implication holding between propositions of various forms. However, since logic was conceived of as a metalinguistic formulation of the logical structure of language, use was not normally made of object-language formulas expressed with propositional variables, and the valid forms of consequence were described through metalogical rules. For example, the valid inference form $p \prec q : \prec : \sim q \prec \sim p$ was described by the medieval rule "In every valid consequence the contradictory of the consequent implies the contradictory of the antecedent."

Ockham and the thirteenth-century logicians treated the *consequentiae* in connection with rules of inference discussed in Aristotle's *Topics* and gave separate sections of their works to the syllogism. But the later logicians, such as Buridan, Albert of Saxony, and Paul of Venice, incorporated the doctrine of syllogism in their treatises on *consequentiae,* and in these treatises they developed rules of propositional logic first and used these in proving certain moods of the syllogism, thereby showing recognition of the priority of propositional logic over the logic of terms. The entire theory of deductive inference, assertoric and modal, finally came to be embraced within the theory of consequence, and some effort was made (by Buridan and Albert of Saxony, for instance) to formulate the theory of deduction along axiomatic lines.

To what extent the medieval propositional logic was historically related to the propositional logic of the Stoics is a moot question. Although Boethius, in his treatises on hypothetical propositions and hypothetical syllogisms, conveyed some fragments of Stoic doctrine on the notion of consequence, the medieval logicians seem to have developed their theory of the *consequentiae* in connection with Aristotle's *Topics* rather than in connection with the doctrine of hypothetical syllogisms. It is possible that some fourteenth-century logicians drew ideas from the works of Sextus Empiricus, translated just at that time, but as medieval writers were prone to mention ancient authors used as sources, the absence of any mention of Sextus Empiricus counts against the assumption that his work was utilized.

Logic of modalities. Aristotle treated modal propositions in the *De Interpretatione* and modal syllogisms in the *Prior Analytics*. The earlier medieval logicians, such as Abelard, Sherwood, and Peter of Spain, discussed the structure of modal sentences and their relations of opposition, equipollence, and consequence but did not treat modal syllogisms. Albert the Great, Thomas Aquinas, and other thirteenth-century theologians took particular interest in modal arguments, partly because such arguments were used extensively by Avicenna and Averroës (and by Aristotle in his philosophical treatises) and partly because certain theological questions, such as that of divine knowledge of future contingent truths, involved problems of modal logic. By the end of the thirteenth century Aristotle's doctrine of modal syllogisms had begun to receive systematic treatment from the logicians of the arts faculty, who also developed their theory of *consequentiae* with reference to modal inferences, and in Ockham's *Summa Logicae* the logic of modal syllogisms was given an extended formal treatment.

The fourteenth-century logicians recognized six standard modes, "possible," "impossible," "contingent," "necessary," "true," and "false"; they also considered propositions containing words like "known," "believed," and "doubted" and the validity of arguments containing such propositions. A modal proposition was described as one containing a modal term, but an important distinction was made between two ways in which any modal sentence could be construed: (1) the "composite sense" (*sensus compositus*), where the modal term is taken as a second-order predicate affirmed of the dictum, which is then taken as naming the corresponding assertoric proposition, and (2) the "divided sense" (*sensus divisus*), where the dictum is taken as a proposition whose copula is adverbially modified by the modal term. This distinction corresponds to that between the metalinguistic and the object-language interpretations of modal statements. Abelard, Sherwood, Albert the Great, and Aquinas regarded the object-language interpretation (*sensus divisus*) as fundamental and the metalinguistic sense as derivative. But Peter of Spain,

Ockham, and the fourteenth-century logicians took the metalinguistic interpretation as fundamental and concerned themselves with the task of formulating, in metalinguistic terms, truth conditions for the quantified propositions in which the modal term occurs adverbially. Thus, Albert of Saxony wrote:

> For the truth of a modal proposition in the divided sense it is required that the modal term be verifiable of a proposition composed of a demonstrative pronoun indicating that for which the subject term of the proposition corresponding to the dictum stands, and of the predicate of that proposition corresponding to the dictum. (*Perutilis Logica,* Venice, 1522)

For example, the truth of the sentence "A bachelor can be married" requires not that the sentence "A bachelor is married" be possibly true but only that the sentence "This is married" be possibly true, where "this" refers to the person denoted in the first sentence by the term "bachelor." Where the divided modal is quantified this reduction to metalinguistic form becomes more complicated. For example, "Every star can be seen by me" does not reduce to "'Every star is seen by me' is possible"; rather, it is required that each of a set of singular propositions of the form "This is seen by me" be possible, where the pronoun "this" refers in each case to a different star.

In their formal development of conversions, equipollences, and syllogisms composed of modal propositions the fourteenth-century logicians formulated two distinct systems, for the "divided" and for the "composite" senses. They also worked out rules for the validity of syllogisms in which one premise was modal and the other assertoric and for the validity of syllogisms in which one premise was taken in the divided sense and the other in the composite sense. All possible combinations were considered in a combinatorial manner and the valid forms distinguished from the invalid forms. Ockham formulated 1,368 such combinations and arrived at nearly 1,000 valid modal syllogisms. Since the metalinguistic interpretation of modal propositions governing this whole analysis involved recognition of the fact that modal logic belongs to the logic of propositions and not to the logic of terms, this immense labor of reducing modal arguments in the divided sense found in ordinary language to metalinguistically formulated truth conditions to which laws of modal consequences could be applied bears witness to the difficulties encountered in the enterprise of formalizing natural language and to the great economy of the modern method of developing logic by constructing formal systems.

Philosophical problems. The treatises entitled *Sophismata* composed by Buridan, William Heytesbury, Albert of Saxony, and many other fourteenth-century logicians are among the most interesting works of the period because they raise philosophical problems bearing on foundations of logic and discuss alternative resolutions. Buridan's *Sophismata,* for example, treats the problem of negative existential statements, such as *Chimaera non est* ("There is no chimera"), as well as the question whether sentences designate any extralinguistic entity other than the things designated by their terms. Of particular interest is Buridan's treatment of the problem of the nonsubstitutivity of extensionally equivalent expressions within the scope of "cognitive" verbs such as "believes," "knows," and "desires." He considered such *sophismata* as the following: Let it be assumed that you have not looked into my purse and that on my asking you if the number of pennies in my purse is odd or even you say you do not know. I ask, "Do you know that the number two is even?" Of course, you admit this. Then I argue, "The number of pennies in my purse is two, and you know that the number two is even; therefore, you know that the number of pennies in my purse is even."

The problem known as the Liar paradox, of great significance for logical theory, as Tarski's work has shown, engaged the minds of medieval logicians for two centuries or more. It was called "the insoluble," not because no resolution was thought possible, but because it was difficult. Paul of Venice, in his *Logica Magna,* listed 14 different solutions offered by medieval logicians, but most of these were minor variants of two or three resolutions. Ockham, treating the problem very briefly, held that the subject term of a proposition cannot stand for the proposition of which it is the subject, since it cannot at the same time be used and mentioned; others thought this inadequate because the paradox can arise if one person is saying that what the other is saying is false when the other is saying that what the first person is saying is true. Buridan developed a solution based on the principle that every proposition implies, by the form that constitutes it as a proposition of the language to which it belongs, a metalinguistic proposition in which "true" is predicated of the name of the first proposition. So if the original proposition asserts its own falsity, it implies by its content that it is false, yet by its formal status as a proposition it implies that it is true. But a proposition which implies contradictory consequents is false. The interest of Buridan's solution lies in its apparent recognition of the fact that the truth condition of a proposition depends on the semantical structure of the language to which it belongs, so that it cannot be used to violate the conditions which give it its status as a linguistic expression.

Also of interest is the fact that the logicians of the fourteenth century, in their treatments of the Liar paradox and other semantical issues, sought to resolve such issues within the framework of a theory of reference by distinguishing discourse about language (formulated in a metalanguage) from discourse within the object language referring to extralinguistic objects. Their approach was extensional in its formulation of the semantical as well as the syntactical dimensions of logical inquiry, and to that extent it was independent of the epistemological and metaphysical issues on which medieval philosophers were in disagreement. And since natural language is, and is likely to remain, at the base of the constructed languages of the sciences, this medieval effort to make natural language as well formed as possible has more than archaeological interest.

ERNEST A. MOODY

INTERREGNUM

The interregnum between medieval scholastic logic and modern mathematical logic may be taken as having begun about the middle of the fifteenth century. There is no clear mark of division; the change was a shift away from the characteristic interests of the twelfth to the fifteenth century, with nothing of comparable importance arising to take their place. At the same time, certain less desirable trends in scholastic logic were perpetuated. The result is that formal logic was reduced almost entirely to a very imperfectly presented syllogistic. Medieval influences continued to operate in the early years of the sixteenth century, and medieval authors were still sometimes read in the seventeenth, but by the time that Ockham's *Summa Logicae* was printed at Oxford in 1675, no one had written creatively in the idiom of scholastic logic for many years.

The interregnum was characteristically sterile, a cause for despondency when one thinks of the large place logic continued to occupy in the educational curriculum and of the innumerable writers who put manuals of logic on the market. The tendency to publish at all costs was encouraged by the post-Reformation and post-Tridentine growth of universities, colleges, and seminaries.

Valla. The first author to consider is the humanist Lorenzo Valla (1407–1457), best remembered for his writing on the forged donation of Constantine. In his *Dialecticarum Libri Tres* (1441), Valla gave no definitions of syllogistic figures and moods, evidently assuming that the reader would know about these. His aim was to confine the syllogistic to the first two figures, without the five moods of Theophrastus and Eudemus. To do this he would have had to reject subalternation, conversion, and *reductio ad absurdum*. About subalternation he was inconsistent; conversion he rejected as lacking brevity, ease, pleasantness, and utility; *reductio ad absurdum* he largely neglected. The five offending moods were called "Agrippine births," and of them all the most monstrous was "Frisemomorum, forsooth!" Here we see the common humanist objection to the barbarity of scholastic terminology, but of course Valla was not objecting merely to comparatively recent Scholastics. His fullest invective was saved for the six moods of the third figure, which he thought insane and never found in use, unlike the first-figure and second-figure moods, which he accepted as dictated by nature to everyone, "even peasants, even women, even children." The standard means of reduction are but "remedies for sick syllogisms." The standing of the third figure would remain a point of dispute for a hundred years, until Ramus undercut Valla's argument by declaring that the figure was in obvious fact very commonly used (*Institutionum Dialecticarum Libri Tres*, Paris, 1554). Thus, Philipp Melanchthon (*Compendiaria Dialectices Ratio*, Basel, 1521) could not make up his mind on the subject.

Melanchthon. In Melanchthon (1497–1560), a most influential writer, the rhetorical approach to logic already appeared at a high state of development, although he retained some Aristotelian doctrine. The rhetorical tradition, derived from Cicero and Quintilian, had a place, albeit a very subordinate one, in scholastic logic. We can see it beginning to predominate in the *Dialectica ad Petrum de Medicis* (D. M. Inguanez and D. G. Muller, eds., Monte Cassino, 1943; composed about 1457), by Joannes Argyropulos, who held that the detail of the theory of *suppositio*, which was the distinctive and most original scholastic contribution to logic, offered almost nothing to oratorical practice. Thus, scholastic logic, which in its origins had borrowed considerably from grammar, began to yield to the third member of the trivium, rhetoric. Accordingly Melanchthon declared the fruit of dialectic to be the ability to speak with propriety and exactness on any theme, and he expounded the Ciceronian syllogism, with its five parts—*propositio, approbatio, assumptio, assumptionis approbatio,* and *complexio*—before the Aristotelian. (A century later a similar five-part syllogism, with proposition, reason, example, application, and conclusion, came into favor in the New Nyāya school of Indian logic.) In general, Melanchthon said, the natural reasoning common to the learned, children, and ordinary people is to be preferred to the "rancid commentaries of dialecticians." From this time on it was often felt desirable to include comparative lists of terminology, ancient and modern, as was done by a commentator on Rodolphus Agricola in 1538, by John Seton in 1572, and by John Sanderson in 1589.

Ramus. The syllogistic as a deductive system underwent considerable attrition in the rhetorical treatment of logic, but this cannot be ascribed exclusively to the new interests. John Dolz's *Sillogismi* (Paris, 1511), a work of purely scholastic inspiration, methodically examines arguments in the different moods and figures as though they had nothing to do with one another. Dolz gave 32 sets of objections to Barbara before going on to Celarent "to avoid prolixity." Although logic applied to itself was by no means unknown in Scholasticism, the idea of a closed logical system was little developed, and hence the piecemeal treatment so characteristic of the scholastic *sophismata* was easily extended to encroach on the systematic character of syllogistic. The fact that Aristotle began by presenting syllogisms in lists probably also contributed to this encroachment.

The process of fragmentation was given new impetus by Pierre de la Ramée (Peter Ramus, 1515–1572). This great master of Latin rhetorical style and innovator of educational theory developed a massive attack on the Aristotelian tradition in logic and an alternative corpus of logical material that quickly gave rise to a widespread Ramist scholasticism.

Attack on Aristotelian tradition. Ramus' *Animadversiones Aristotelicae* (Paris, 1556) tells in 20 books how Ramus turned from the clarity of Plato to the comparative chaos of Aristotle. Pretending to be analytical, Aristotle was almost completely deficient in that (Ramist) analysis which consists in systematic definition and division, and his doctrines are not supported by examples (are not, in fact, established by rhetorical syllogisms!). These are the standards Ramus applied as he worked through the *Prior Analytics* in his Book VII, firing off a broadside at every detail of Aristotelian or scholastic doctrine that occurred to him on the way. The typically rhetorical teaching that experience, observation, and usage are the proper guides in logic is prominent. Variables seldom make their appearance in this milieu, but Ramus' express attack on abecedarian examples—which, being examples of nothing, can be adapted to nothing—is remarkable.

Ramist logic. The *Dialecticae Libri Duo* (Paris, 1556) is divided between invention, or discovery, and judgment, a distinction derived immediately from Agrippa and medi-

ately from Cicero and Boethius. This distinction had been recalled among Scholastics—for example, at the opening of Kilwardby's popular thirteenth-century commentary on the *Prior Analytics,* often printed under the name of Giles of Rome. Like Descartes, whose methodological ideas supplanted his own, Ramus could not escape his antecedents. The first book covers topics, or *loci;* the second expounds the Ramist syllogistic, divided into the contracted syllogism (an enthymematic version of the Aristotelian third figure) and the explicated syllogism (comprising the second and first figures, in that order). There are no signs of quantification, all unquantified propositions which are not singular being deemed universal. A mood is general if it contains no singular term, special if it contains one, and proper if it contains two. Examples are taken from classical rhetoric and poetry; the propriety of such sources was vigorously attacked by a little-known anti-Ramist, Thomas Oliver of Bury, in his *De Sophismatum Praestigiis Cavendis* (Cambridge, 1604), on the ground that logic has very little place in poetry or forensic oratory. This whole early version of an ordinary-language approach to logic was admirably countered by Gisbertus Isendoorn (*Cursus Systematicus,* Oxford, 1658). Writing directly against the famous Cambridge Ramist George Downame, Isendoorn said (p. 613): *Observa . . . orationem et popularem discurrendi usum non esse mensuram et normam Logicae, sed rectam rationem et accuratam artem viamque concludendi* ("Mark that popular speech and usage are not the standard and norm of logic, but right reason and an exact method of reaching conclusions").

Manuals of logic. With all the effort of the mid-sixteenth century to simplify logic, it is not surprising that vernacular manuals began to appear, although sparsely, at that time. In England there were Thomas Wilson's *The Rule of Reason* (London, 1551), Ralphe Lever's *The Arte of Reason rightly termed Witcraft* (London, 1573), Abraham Fraunce's *The Lawiers Logike* (London, 1588), and Thomas Blundevile's *The Arte of Logicke* (London, 1599); in France there was Philippes Canaye's treatise *L'Organe* (Paris, 1589). Little further seems to have been published in English until John Newton's *The English Academy* (London, 1677).

Wilson's pioneer effort is interesting chiefly for its novel terminology; for example, the major, minor, and middle terms are called the "terme at large," the "severall terme," and the "double repeate." Blundevile introduced an arithmetical syllogism and used a catechetical method. This method had been used by Matthias Flacius Illyricus in *Paralipomena Dialectices* (Basel, 1558; composed 1550), which gives a very detailed treatment of the venerable *pons asinorum.* Canaye's book was also devoted largely to the *pons asinorum,* being distinguished by the dissection of the traditional rectangular figure into two circular ones. The same subject had been dealt with in Christopher Corner's *Ratio Inveniendi Medium Terminum* (Basel, 1549), which set a new standard of scholarship by appending a Greek text of relevant chapters of Aristotle. Thus, Aristotelian subjects were being pursued, in somewhat new ways, at the same time that the widespread Ramist innovations were taking hold.

Something of the same development can be seen in commentaries on the *Prior Analytics,* from the sixteenth-century editions of Kilwardby, through the work of Lefèvre d'Étaples (Faber Stapulensis), with his emphasis on tabular presentation; that of Agostino Nifo (Niphus Suessanus), who professed to follow the Greek commentators but wrote a long treatise on conversion in the scholastic manner; Burana's urbane commentary, with lengthy appendixes by his teacher Bagolinus and an interesting prefatory glimpse of the logical curriculum in a north Italian university; Monlorius' commentary, relatively brief but careful; to that of Pacius, with its businesslike presentation, schemes, and figures, a work praised by Sir David Ross in his own commentary. Within this developing tradition of Aristotelian scholarship we may also put the *Apparatus Syllogistici Synopsis* of Joannes Albanus (Bologna, 1620), which elaborately examined the crescent-shaped and triangular diagrams that descended from Greek sources to the Aristotelians of the Renaissance.

In a field in which syllogistic occupied so large a place one must note widespread incompetence in the matter of classification by figure. This is, of course, a point settled by definition, as Lorenzo Maiolo (*Epiphyllides in Dialecticis,* Venice, 1497) and John Wallis (*Institutio Logicae,* Oxford, 1687) saw. These two were exceptional, however. Franciscus Titelmans (*De Consideratione Dialectica Libri Sex,* Paris, 1544) found the distinction between major and minor premises a hard thing for youths; Richard Crakanthorp (*Logicae Libri Quinque,* London, 1622) omitted the fourth figure without rejecting it and found it hard to determine the number of moods. The basic trouble was that the later medievals, following a lead given by Boethius, defined the major premise as the first stated, the major term as the extreme therein, and so on, whereas Philoponus had defined the major term as the predicate of the conclusion, the major premise as the premise containing the major term, and so on. Each of the schemes can be worked out consistently, but they give different classifications and are mutually incompatible. This was seldom understood; it was a common fault to speak of indirect conclusions in connection with Philoponian definitions or to define with Philoponus and then take, for example, Balnama as fourth figure, instead of first figure with transposed premises.

In the Oxford logicians one does not find 24 moods in four figures correctly worked out on a Philoponian basis until Henry Aldrich (*Artis Logicae Compendium,* Oxford, 1691; this first edition was anonymous). The principles of the matter remained so little understood that even Augustus De Morgan (*Formal Logic,* 1847) could say, "Consider the fourth and first figures as coincident and the arbitrary notion of arrangement by major and minor vanishes," and W. S. Jevons (*Elementary Lessons in Formal Logic,* 1876) described fourth-figure syllogisms as ill arranged and imperfect and unnatural in form. "Unnatural" as a description of fourth-figure syllogisms was first used by Averroës, and his opinion was reinforced by Giacomo Zabarella (1533–1589); both meant to make a point of genuine formal logic, but they used some phrases that permitted a psychological interpretation. Sir William Hamilton's treatment of the matter (*Lectures on Logic,* 1860, Vol. IV), with lists of authors for and against the fourth figure and indirect moods of the second and third, is useless without knowledge of these authors' definitions and therefore of what they were favoring or opposing. A writer of a very

different style was John Hospinianus (1515–1575), who proceeded on a combinatory basis and found that by admitting singular and indefinite propositions to the syllogistic and by identifying certain moods, he could obtain 36 valid moods out of a possible 512.

Extremely influential on manuals of the eighteenth and nineteenth centuries was *Logique, ou l'Art de penser* (1662; *The Port-Royal Logic*), by Antoine Arnauld and Pierre Nicole. Even Aldrich, who disliked its novel terminology and Cartesian standpoint, may well have been prompted by it to his strict deductive treatment, for he shows no acquaintance with any other likely influence. The authors' epistemological interests certainly contributed much to the psychologism that was soon to infect logic, but such headings as conception, judgment, and reasoning were not new in promoting this tendency. Canaye had already spoken of syllogism as the third operation of the mind, which *leaves* the premises and *arrives* at the conclusion. Such terminology is symptomatic of a change that occurred in the mid-seventeenth century. The Port-Royal section on method—a most popular subject in this period—more explicitly opened the way to the discursive excesses that would soon masquerade as logic, culminating, perhaps, in Henry Kett's *Logic Made Easy, or A Short View of the Aristotelic System of Reasoning, and Its Application to Literature, Science, and the General Improvement of the Mind* (Oxford, 1809).

A book praised by Leibniz and rather above the average, although not completely out of the common rut, is the *Logica Hamburgensis* (Hamburg, 1638), by Joachim Jung, or Jungius. One notable feature of this book is the marking of the lines of a syllogistic demonstration by letters, which are then used as references for showing by what principles which line follows from which others. Such a rather exact method of proof was very exceptional in logic before modern times, but contemporaneously with Jung, Pierre Hérigone introduced a similar method in mathematics (*Cursus Mathematicus,* Paris, 1634–1637). Jung was thoroughly acquainted with the possible use of contraposition as a means of syllogistic proof but was no more successful in his discussion of the fourth figure than so many others had been. Under the medieval heading of consequences he noted the argument *a recto ad obliquum,* which can be found in Aristotle's *Topics* II, 8, 114a18.

Some considerations, usually brief, of such standard medieval subjects as consequences and supposition theory continued to appear—for instance, those of Chrysostom Javellus (*Compendium Logicae,* Lyons, 1580), Robert Sanderson (*Logicae Artis Compendium,* Oxford, 1618), and Henry Aldrich—but these were exceptions. Arnold Geulincx hoped to repopularize such treatises by his *Logica Fundamentis Suis a Quibus Hactenus Collapsa Fuerat Restituta* (Leiden, 1662). He was able to relate alternation, conjunction, and negation by means of their truth conditions according to the laws that are often called after De Morgan or Ockham but that go back, at least in part, to the *Syncategoremata* of Peter of Spain. These laws were also known to the mathematician Gerolamo Saccheri, whose *Logica Demonstrativa* (Turin, 1697) is outstandingly original in its high degree of organization, its reflections on the assumptions necessary to logic, and its use of indirect proof, in the pattern of the so-called *mirabilis conse-*

quentia, to the effect that what follows from its own negation is true. Unfortunately the few signs of revival and advance discernible at the close of the seventeenth century did not produce any general or permanent result, and even the work of Leibniz met with little response.

Ivo Thomas

PRECURSORS OF MODERN LOGIC

Modern logic, or the logic that is loosely called "mathematical," began in a serious and systematic way with Augustus De Morgan's *Formal Logic* and George Boole's *Mathematical Analysis of Logic,* both published in 1847. But a number of earlier writers were already "modern" in spirit, and of these, four stand out especially sharply—Leibniz, Euler, Lambert, and Bolzano.

(A. N. P.)

Leibniz. Gottfried Wilhelm Leibniz (1646–1716) was distinguished in many fields, but in none more than in logic. There, however, his worth was not fully appreciated until the present century. He early began to investigate Aristotelian syllogistic and never completely escaped from the syllogistic point of view. In 1666 he wrote a *Dissertatio de Arte Combinatoria,* a juvenile work that was not free of mistakes, as he later realized, but that showed a new, high sense of organization and a genuine feeling for formal logic, very rare at the time. In one part of this book Leibniz worked out for himself the calculations of Hospinianus (1560) relative to the possible and the valid moods of syllogism. He differed from Hospinianus in making singular propositions equivalent to universal ones, as did Wallis and Euler. He arrived at 24 strictly Aristotelian syllogisms, 6 in each of 4 figures, which he arranged in a neat tableau suggestive of certain deductive relationships. Leibniz' standard method of proof in this context was *reductio ad absurdum,* as suggested to him by his teacher Jakob Thomasius (1622–1684), author of *Erotemata Logica* (Leipzig, 1670), but he also recognized the need for conversion. He wrongly credited Ramus with a method actually known in the thirteenth century, the device of proving laws of conversion and subalternation by means of syllogism and the laws of identity "All *a* is *a*" and "Some *a* is *a*."

Leibniz often returned to syllogistic and was periodically vexed by semantic considerations, namely whether to think of the matter in extension or in intension—whether in "All *a* is *b*" it is the *a*'s which are said to be contained in the *b*'s or the property *a* which contains the property *b*. Leibniz had something of a fixation on the intensional approach, although he often suspected that extension was more effective and logically satisfactory. One thing that pushed him in the direction of extensionality was a fondness for experimenting with spatial interpretations. Thus, we find several attempts at diagrammatic representation, some using ruled and dotted lines and some using circles. He found it impossible to carry through such interpretations when thinking in intension.

Theory of combinations. The theory of combinations is highly relevant to logic. Chrysippus is reported to have shown some interest in combinations, Kilwardby and others in the thirteenth century repeatedly made combinatory

summaries of assertoric and modal syllogistic, and semantic interpretations of logical formulas in finite domains employ the theory. Besides the syllogistic computations described, Leibniz considered how many predicates can be truly asserted of a given subject or how many subjects set under a given predicate. Such problems need some preliminary arrangements, and Leibniz supposed that a composite concept is analyzable into a number of ultimate simples, just as an integer is uniquely decomposable into its prime factors. Correlating the simple concepts with prime numbers, we can say that a predicate is truly attributable to its subject if the product associated with the predicate divides that associated with the subject. The essentials of this idea have been used in modern times to obtain a decision procedure for syllogistic, and unique decomposition into primes plays an essential part in Gödel numbering.

Universal language. The idea of decomposing concepts into "prime factors" suggested to Leibniz the possibility of following up the initial steps toward a universal language taken by John Wilkins (1668), Jean Joachim Becher (1661), George Dalgarno (1661), Athanasius Kircher (1663), and others. He wanted such a language not merely to be practically or commercially useful, as were many of the pioneer efforts, but to be logically constructed so as to have general scientific import. Leibniz later distinguished a universal language from a logical calculus and desired to base his language on a thorough analysis of the communicative function of the various parts of speech, tenses, suffixes, etc. (an anticipation of modern theories of syntactical categories), and at one point (*Analysis Linguarum,* 1678) he envisaged a basic Latin rather in the style of C. K. Ogden and I. A. Richards' basic English.

In saying that nouns express ideas and verbs express propositions Leibniz radically altered the Aristotelian basis of the distinction and gave, in germ, the concept of a propositional function. Such reflections led him to a reductionist program, with adverbs reduced to (derived from) adjectives and adjectives to nouns, and with the copula taken as the only fundamental verb. He recognized that particles, connectives, and prepositions are of especial importance to linguistic structure. In taking us out of the syllogistic area this theory recalls the medieval doctrine of syncategorematic terms and Aquinas' analysis of many prepositions, while it adumbrates the logic of truth-functional connectives and of relations. Leibniz knew that not all arguments are syllogistic, in this matter acknowledging a debt to Jung, but the dominance of a syllogistic point of view in Leibniz' thought is shown by his curious distinction between syllogistic and "grammatical" consequences.

This part of Leibniz' thought constitutes a distinct chapter in the history of the relations between grammar and logic. Grammar had been influential in the constitution of scholastic logic, but in the interregnum it had yielded to the third member of the medieval trivium, rhetoric, as a dominant power. In the projects for a universal and rational language we see grammar reasserting itself. But Leibniz was not content to confine logic to the "trivial" arts.

Logical calculus. The idea that logic might be quadrivial, and notably mathematical, was not new with Leibniz. Leibniz considered Aristotle to have been, in his logic, the first to write mathematically outside mathematics (letter to Gabriel Wagner, 1596). Roger Bacon (thirteenth century)—who also wished to reduce the trivial art of grammar to the quadrivial one of music—stated in his *Opus Maius* that "all the predicaments depend on the knowledge of quantity, with which mathematics deals, and therefore the whole of logic depends on mathematics." It is in the light of this that one should read the statement in his *Communia Mathematica* that "the mere logician cannot accomplish anything worthwhile in logical matters" (*nihil dignum potest purus logicus in logicalibus pertractare*). Ockham had been of the opposite opinion, and in *De Sacramento Altaris* he described mathematicians as among those less skilled in logic. Ramón Lull had written a combinatorial work, *Ars Magna* (which captured Leibniz' imagination, though he soon came to understand its deficiencies), and Thomas Hobbes had elaborated suggestively, if ineffectively, on the theme "by ratiocination I mean computation" ("Computatio Sive Logica," in *De Corpore*"). There is little doubt, however, that Leibniz' ideas, which far outstripped in detail and understanding any earlier hints, were his own spontaneous creation. "While I was yet a boy with a knowledge only of common logic, and without instruction in mathematics, the thought came to me, I know not by what instinct, that an analysis of ideas could be devised, whence in some combinatory way truths could arise and be estimated as though by numbers" (*Elementa Rationis*). He was thereafter constantly occupied with such notions and attempted to contrive an alphabet of thought, or *characteristica universalis*, which would represent ideas in a logical way, not things in a pictorial way, and would be mechanical in operation, unambiguous, and nonquantitative; this alphabet of thought would be a means of discovery, a support to intuition, and an aid in ending disputes. Leibniz regarded his great invention of the infinitesimal calculus (1675) as emerging from such researches, and the calculus led him to reflect still more intently on the properties desirable in such a characteristic. Exactly what he meant by "mechanical" and "calculation" is still in question, and he no doubt underestimated the task he set himself, but the imaginative fervor with which he always wrote of it reveals, as we can now appreciate, a true prophetic instinct. He often used an image from mythology to summarize his intentions, saying that his method was to be a *filum Ariadnes*, a thread of Ariadne. Many authors had long envisaged logic as a Cretan maze in need of such a clue—and that this should be so in an age when logic was scarcely existent does them little credit—but from the pen of Leibniz the allusion was more than a literary elegance and condensed a program of "palpable demonstrations, like the calculations of arithmeticians or the diagrams of geometers." (For Leibnizian references to the *filum*, see Louis Couturat, *La Logique de Leibniz*, pp. 90–92, 124; for other authors, see Ivo Thomas, "Medieval Aftermath.")

Encyclopedia. One may ask what the theory of combinations was meant to combine, what the logical calculus was meant to calculate with, or where the analyses presupposed by the unified language of science were to be found. Leibniz was not content to leave such analysis in the state of a general project. The enormous range of his knowledge and interests, which included unity in religion, interna-

tional relations, cooperation among scientists and scholars, and jurisprudence, as well as the not unrelated ordering of thought, prompted his lasting interest in the construction of an encyclopedia. T. Zwinger's *Theatrum Vitae Humanae* (1565) and Johann Heinrich Alsted's *Encyclopaedia* (1608) provided Leibniz with a basis for early schematisms, and sketches and fragments from about 1668 to the end of his life show an unceasing interest in the plan, which he believed had failed of completion through his own distractions and the lack of younger assistants. Appeals to monarchs and to learned societies met with little response. The project was, of course, a gigantic one, impossible of immediate fulfillment, but it should not be supposed that Leibniz thought it could be perfected quickly. Rather, its elaboration was to proceed gradually, along with that of the universal language and a calculus of logic. In later drafts this calculus took an ever more prominent place.

Structure of the calculus. The main stages (1679, 1686, 1690) of Leibniz' many experiments in logical algebra have often been expounded and commented on. Here only some laws which were constant features will be mentioned.

(1) *a* is *a*;

(2) If *a* is *b* and *b* is *c*, then *a* is *c*.

Propositions of the form "*a* is *b*" are intended as universal affirmatives, "All *a* is *b*," which Leibniz normally thought of as meaning that the property *a* contains the property *b*. Sometimes he wrote "*a* contains *b*" instead of "*a* is *b*." Accordingly, rule (1) is one of the syllogistic laws of identity which, as was said above, he used from the start in syllogistic demonstrations, and rule (2) is the Barbara syllogism. Today we know that by means of the calculus of quantifiers and some definitions all asserted laws of the syllogistic can be obtained from rules (1) and (2) alone. Leibniz lacked those aids, but he admitted negative terms that obey the laws

(3) *a* is interchangeable with not-not-*a*;

(4) *a* is *b* if and only if not-*b* is not-*a*.

Rule (4) is the law of contraposition familiar to the Scholastics and, for Leibniz, most recently given prominence by Jung. From rules (1) to (4), with some definitions and Leibniz' favorite method of *reductio ad absurdum*, the whole syllogistic can be obtained. Leibniz did not use exactly that method but adopted at one time a rather similar one based on a restatement of rule (1), $a = aa$, and rule (5), below. Identity has the substitutive property described below; "*a* is *b*" is made equivalent to "$a = ab$"; and "Some *a* is *b*" is written "$Sa = b$." Compound terms such as *ab* were thought of as signifying the addition of properties *a* and *b*. They obey the laws

(5) *ab* is *a*;

(6) *ab* is *b*;

(7) If *a* is *b* and *a* is *c*, then *a* is *bc*.

It has been pointed out by Karl Popper that if rules (5) and (6) are made the premises of the mood Darapti, we have the conclusion "Some *a* is *b*." This does not render the system inconsistent, but it does show that the system is already more extensive and more trivial than Leibniz presumably intended. From rules (1), (2), (5), (6), and (7) it is easy to deduce, as Leibniz did,

(8) If *a* is *bc,* then *a* is *b,* and *a* is *c,*

which is the converse of (7), and

(9) If *a* is *b,* then *ac* is *bc* (using rules 2, 5, 6, and 7);

(10) If *a* is *b* and *c* is *d,* then *ac* is *bd* (using rule 9 twice and then rule 2).

Rule (10), which was known to Abelard in the twelfth century, Leibniz called *praeclarum theorema,* a very notable theorem.

Identity of terms was introduced in various ways, but always so that it was equivalent to the conjunction of "*a* is *b*" and "*b* is *a*" and so that identical terms could be substituted for one another in all contexts of the calculus. The first definition in the *Non Inelegans Specimen Demonstrandi in Abstractis,* for instance, posits that $a = b$ holds if and only if *a* and *b* can be substituted for each other without altering the truth of any statement. The "only if" part is commonly called the principle of the identity of indiscernibles; for its converse W. V. Quine has suggested "the indiscernibility of identicals." As a principle of general application it has given rise to much discussion, although it is normally accepted in logic. While it is commonly attributed to Leibniz, Aristotle presented it in essentials in the *Topics* (VII, 1, 152a31ff.) and *De Sophisticis Elenchis* (Ch. 24, 179a37 ff.).

An algebraic calculus requires that substitution for variables be possible, and Leibniz explicitly recognized this, in what was certainly the clearest statement in logic of the principle up to his time. Some medievals—Albert the Great, for instance—had shown their understanding of the generality conferred by variables when they called them "transcendental terms." Three more laws important for the calculus were known to Leibniz, following from rules (1), (5), (6), and (7):

(11) *ab* is *ba* (using 5, 6, and 7);

(12) *a* is *aa* (using 5);

(13) *aa* is *a* (using 1 and 7).

In the course of his experiments Leibniz came to see that particular propositions have existential import, whereas universals may not, and it was a puzzle to him what the existential import might be—factual existence or logical possibility—and whether it was built into his system or had to be further provided for. This problem had been raised by medieval logicians from the time of Abelard. One of Leibniz' solutions—that subalternation is invalid if the universal states a relation of concepts and the particular states a matter of fact but holds if we stay in one of those domains—is essentially that of Paul of Venice, who required the subjects of both propositions to have the same *suppositio.*

At a late stage Leibniz used the addition sign in place of, and with the sense of, multiplication; that is, he used $a + b$ instead of *ab.* But he knew that such expressions could be interpreted as logical disjunctions, and there is also an early hint that the calculus could be interpreted propositionally, the antecedent of a conditional being said to contain the consequent. This hint may serve as a summary indication of Leibniz' position in the history of logic. Aristotle had used "antecedent" and "consequent" for "subject" and "predicate"; among medievals (such as Abelard and Kilwardby) it is often hard to tell whether the words were used of propositions or of terms; Leibniz offered a

glimpse of the two domains as distinct but analogous. If his work had not gone long unpublished (we still have no complete edition), we might not have had to wait so long for the full light of Boolean day.

Euler. The noted mathematician Leonhard Euler (1707–1783) is remembered in logic chiefly for his geometrical illustrations of syllogistic, "Euler's diagrams" or "Euler's circles." Similar devices were used by J. C. Sturm (1661), Leibniz (see Bocheński, *History of Formal Logic,* plate facing p. 260), Joachim Lange (1712), and Gottfried Ploucquet (1759), and in a very general way the idea of spatial illustration goes back at least to Juan Luis Vives, who used triangles to illustrate the Barbara syllogism ("De Censura Veri," in *Opera,* Basel, 1555). But because of Euler's fame as a mathematician and the popularity of his charming *Lettres à une princesse d'Allemagne* (the relevant letters are CII ff., dated 1761) such diagrams are traditionally named for him.

Euler used proper inclusion for the universal affirmative proposition, exclusion for the universal negative, and intersection for both the particulars. If his interpretation is followed systematically, it correctly decides the validity or invalidity of all three-term syllogisms with all terms distinct but fails for the laws of identity and contradiction and for degenerate syllogisms depending on them. Apparently nobody developed full syllogistic along these lines until J. D. Gergonne (1816), whose five relations give a complete system and can indeed be defined by three of them (see Ivo Thomas, "Eulerian Syllogistic," and references supplied there), but not by Euler's three. The extensional approach evidenced by Euler's interpretation of the universal affirmative was a healthy influence.

Euler also lent his authority to the doctrine that singular propositions are equivalent to universal ones (*Lettres,* CVII), a thesis propounded by John Wallis (from 1638; see Appendix to his *Institutio Logica,* Oxford, 1687). Bertrand Russell has severely criticized this doctrine as confusing class membership with inclusion, but of course we can get an inclusive proposition equivalent to a membership proposition by taking the unit class of the singular subject.

Lambert and Ploucquet. Johann Heinrich Lambert (1728–1777), German physicist, mathematician, and astronomer, devoted a number of essays to the enterprise of making a calculus of logic, which he evidently thought of in connection with the tree of Porphyry. His standpoint is, as is usual with the early investigators, intensional. Let *a* and *b* be any concepts, $a + b$ their combination into a compound concept, and *ab* their common part. The letters γ and δ can be multiplied with conceptual variables, so that $a\gamma$ and $a\delta$ are read as "the genus of *a*" and "the difference of *a.*" The intended meaning suggests that γ and δ are descriptive operators; yet Lambert sometimes treated them as though they were placeholders for generic or differential concepts. At any rate Lambert, following an elementary intuition, posited $a = a\gamma + a\delta = a(\gamma + \delta)$. Wanting to descend the tree to subordinate species as well as to ascend to superordinate genera and differences, he used the notation $a\gamma^{-1}$ or a/γ, which should mean "the genus under *a.*" Waiving the fact that a concept containing *a* may be an ultimate species, we reflect that although $a\gamma$ is unique, $a\gamma^{-1}$ may not be so. This accounts for the trouble which Lambert found in applying multiplication and division, for $(a/\gamma)\gamma$, "the genus of a species of a," is identical with a whereas $(a\gamma)/\gamma$, "a species of the genus of a," need not be a itself. Lambert used subtraction to obtain the removal of a concept. He did not account for the appearance of coefficients and, in general, did not question the logical appropriateness of the algebraic operations to which his basic intuitions gave rise. Boole met with similar difficulties but reflected on them.

In syllogistic Lambert started not from the Aristotelian relations but from the five that are now attributed to Gergonne. This is feasible, but Lambert failed to achieve a satisfactory notion for the mutual exclusion of two terms. His most promising innovation lay in his attention to the relative product, but he did not develop this in any practical way.

Lambert, like Leibniz, experimented with sets of ruled and dotted lines to illustrate the relationships of syllogistic terms, in part trying to correct the defect in Euler's circles of not allowing for $a = b$. Some stages of his investigations were criticized by his correspondents G. J. von Holland (whose extensional standpoint was remarkable for the time) and Gottfried Ploucquet, both of whom were making their own efforts to evolve a logical calculus. Ploucquet (1716–1790), who was a teacher of Hegel, claimed independence of Euler in his use of closed figures—he used squares (1759)—and seems to have been the first to base his syllogistic on thoroughgoing quantification of the predicate. One of his notations, "$A > B$" for "No A is B," strangely, enjoyed some popularity.

IVO THOMAS

Bolzano. The most important logician of the first half of the nineteenth century was Bernard Bolzano (1781–1848). His views are closest to those of Leibniz, who preceded him by more than a century (Bolzano was sometimes called the Bohemian Leibniz). Although he quoted often and extensively from philosophers and logicians of his own generation and the preceding one, among them Kant, Salomon Maimon, Hegel, J. F. Fries, J. G. E. Maass, and K. L. Reinhold, he did this almost always in order to criticize them, and rightly so from our modern point of view, because orders of magnitude separate Bolzano as a logician from his contemporaries.

One may doubt whether he deserves to be called a forerunner of mathematical logic and modern semantics. His approach is in many respects rather crude and old-fashioned in comparison with those of George Boole and Gottlob Frege, one and two generations later, respectively. But many points first made by Bolzano look strikingly modern. Unfortunately most of these were either not noticed or not understood during his lifetime or were forgotten by later generations.

For Bolzano logic was mainly the theory of science. To investigate science he used a partly formalized language consisting of ordinary German extended by various types of constants and variables, as well as by certain technical terms which for the most part he was at great pains to define as carefully as possible.

The fundamental entities with which logic has to deal, according to Bolzano, are terms and the propositions they constitute. These abstract entities are carefully distinguished from the corresponding linguistic and mental entities. Because a single proposition can be expressed in an indefinite number of ways, Bolzano's first aim was to normalize such linguistic expressions, to reduce all of them to canonical forms prior to their purely formal treatment.

Bolzano's solution was highly idiosyncratic. Deviating radically from tradition, he claimed that all sentences (complex and compound sentences as well as simple ones) are reducible to the single form "A has b," where "A" is the subject term, "b" the predicate term, and "has" the copula. Although this reduction works reasonably well with such sentences as "John is hungry," which can easily be rendered as "John has hunger," it sounds less convincing in the case of reducing "This is gold" to "This has goldness" (although Bolzano presented reasons why such words as "goldness" had not been created in natural languages) and still less so when "John is not hungry" is reduced to "John has lack-of-hunger." The reduction of the compound sentence "Either P or Q" to "The-term-One-of-P-and-Q-is-true has the-property-of-being-a-singular-term" or "The-term-One-of-P-or-Q-is-true has nonemptiness" (depending on whether the original expression "Either . . . or . . ." is interpreted from its context as denoting exclusive or inclusive disjunction) looks rather strange in its verbal formulation, although it looks much less strange in some appropriate symbolism. And reducing "Some A is B" to "The-term-An-A-which-is-B has nonemptiness" may appear fantastic at first sight, although it looks much more familiar when symbolized as $A \cap B \neq 0$. Nevertheless, Bolzano did not attempt to present a full set of rules for such conversions and relied instead on the reader's willingness to believe in the existence of such reductions after being shown how to perform them on certain representative samples, including some rather recalcitrant cases.

This reduction played a small role in the further development of Bolzano's work in logic. His major innovation was his introduction of the technique of variation into what amounts essentially to the logical semantics of language, even though the semantic approach, in its modern sense, was foreign to him. Starting with a proposition, true or false, he investigated its behavior with regard to truth and falsehood under substitution for any of its terms of all other fitting (that is, propositionhood-preserving) terms. (In modern terminology, he investigated all models of sentential forms.) When the number of such variants was finite he defined the degree of validity of a proposition with respect to one or more of its constituent terms as the ratio of the number of its true variants to the number of all variants. When this ratio is 1, the proposition is universally valid; when 0, universally contravalid; when greater than 0, consistent.

After extending these notions to propositional classes Bolzano was able to define an amazing number of interesting, and sometimes highly original, metalogical notions, including compatibility, dependency, exclusion, contradictoriness, contrariety, exclusiveness, and disjointness. By far the most important notion introduced in this way is that of derivability with respect to a given class of terms, defined as holding between two propositions P and Q if and only if *Q* is consistent and every model of *Q* is a model of *P* with respect to this class of terms; with respect to propositional classes it is defined similarly. This definition differs only in the unfortunate consistency clause from Tarski's definition, given in 1937, of what he called the consequence relation.

Kant had defined an "analytic" affirmative judgment as one in which the predicate concept was already contained in the subject concept. Rejecting this definition as clearly inadequate for explicating logical truth, Bolzano defined a proposition to be analytically true when universally valid with respect to at least one of its constituent terms, analytically false when universally contravalid, etc., and as analytic when either analytically true or analytically false. Bolzano was aware that this definition of analytical truth was too broad as an explication of logical truth, and he therefore went on to define a proposition as being logically analytic when (again in modern terminology) all its descriptive (extralogical) constituent terms occur in it vacuously, an anticipation of a well-known definition by W. V. Quine (1940).

Bolzano's views of probability are also strikingly modern. To define the probability of the proposition *M* on the assumptions *A*, *B*, *C*, *D*, $\cdots$ (with respect to certain terms *i*, *j*, $\cdots$) he used the relative degree of validity of *M* with respect to *A*, *B*, *C*, *D*, $\cdots$, which he defined as the ratio of the number of true variants of the set *M*, *A*, *B*, *C*, *D*, $\cdots$ to the number of true variants of the set *A*, *B*, *C*, *D*, $\cdots$. This conception, tenable, of course, only when the numbers involved are finite, is an important refinement of Laplace's well-known conception of probability, standard in Bolzano's time, in that it elegantly sidesteps the problem of circularity involved in the notion of equipossibility.

Yehoshua Bar-Hillel

MODERN LOGIC: THE BOOLEAN PERIOD

The eighteenth-century and early nineteenth-century logicians considered in the preceding section were all Continental Europeans, and those who were also philosophers, namely Leibniz and Bolzano, were representatives of Continental rationalism. The British empiricism of the same period produced no logicians. On the contrary, it was antilogical. The empiricists attacked formal logic—by which they meant the attenuated syllogistic to which much of the science had shrunk during the interregnum—as trivial and sometimes as circular. This antilogicism largely echoed John Locke, whose scornful treatment of logic in his *Essay Concerning Human Understanding* had provoked one of Leibniz' minor defenses of it, in the *Nouveaux Essais*. In the early nineteenth century the common logic was rescued from oblivion by Richard Whately but was not enlarged by him. Its enlargement, however, came soon after and, despite the British antilogical tradition, was at first largely a British affair, spreading later to the United States (C. S. Peirce) and then to Germany (Ernst Schröder).

(A. N. P.)

Hamilton. The nineteenth-century revival of logic in Britain, inaugurated by Whately and continued, among others, by George Bentham, Chrétien, and Solly, owed much of its later impetus to the cosmopolitan learning and reforming zeal of Sir William Hamilton (1788–1856). A severely critical article by Hamilton on Whately and his followers, in the *Edinburgh Review* (1833; reprinted in his *Discussions*, London and Edinburgh, 1852), established his authority in the field, which was chiefly exercised thereafter in oral teaching from his Edinburgh chair. His scattered and largely polemical writings, including even the posthumous *Lectures on Logic* (Edinburgh and London, 1861), give a very imperfect account of his system, which acquired such order as it possessed from the works of his pupils and disciples: William Thomson and H. L. Mansel at Oxford; T. S. Baynes, John Veitch, and William Spalding in Scotland; and Francis Bowen in America. Hamilton's main service was to insist, following Kant, on the formal nature of logic and to break with the prevailing European tradition by exhibiting its forms primarily as relations of extension between classes. He also attempted to maintain a parallel logic of intension (or comprehension) for concepts, as the inverse of extension, but this approach, like others of its kind, was a predictable, if pardonable, failure.

Hamilton's most celebrated innovation, though it was far from being his invention, was the "thoroughgoing quantification of the predicate." By attaching the quantifiers "all" ("any") and "some" to the predicate, he obtained 8 propositional forms, in place of the AEIO of tradition:

(1) All *A* is all *B*.
(2) All *A* is some *B*.
(3) Some *A* is all *B*.
(4) Some *A* is some *B*.
(5) Any *A* is not any *B*.
(6) Any *A* is not some *B*.
(7) Some *A* is not any *B*.
(8) Some *A* is not some *B*.

If "some" is read as "some only," these are all simply convertible and can thus be represented as the affirmations or denials of equations. The syllogisms made up of such propositions arrange themselves, tidily enough, into 108 valid moods, 12 positive and 24 negative, in each of 3 figures (Hamilton rejected the fourth). With this arrangement, a consolidated rule of inference, and a quasi-geometrical symbolism to depict it all, Hamilton claimed to have effected a major simplification—indeed, completion—of the Aristotelian scheme.

These hopes were not borne out in the sequel. His own vacillations in the use of "some" and neglect of the differences between "all" and "any" threw even professed Hamiltonians into confusion, and the status of his propositional forms (not to mention the validity of some of his syllogisms) was much disputed. The first, for example, has no contradictory in the set and appears (on the ordinary view of "some") to be a compound of (2) and (3). The two particular affirmatives, (3) and (4), found acceptance with some writers, such as Thomson and Spalding; but of the new negatives, (6) made few friends, and (8) none at all; since it is compatible with any of the others, it says so little as to be well-nigh vacuous. A more serious objection is that since forms (1) to (5) represent all the possible ways in which two classes can be related in extension (that is, the

Gergonne relations), the last three must necessarily be ambiguous or redundant.

De Morgan. The above criticisms of Hamilton's system are primarily due to Augustus De Morgan (1806–1871), whom Hamilton, in 1846, had misguidedly accused of plagiarizing his quantification. In the famous and protracted controversy that ensued, De Morgan was led into a thorough dissection of the whole system, and subsequent critics, from Mill, Peirce, and Venn onward, have taken most of their ammunition from him.

Though greatly superior as to insight and technical ability, the logic of De Morgan has affinities with that of his rival in that it, too, lays stress on the autonomy of logic and on the extensional point of view. It equally shares Hamilton's interest in reforming and enlarging the traditional syllogistic, an enterprise now outdated, which has caused it to fall into unmerited neglect. Apart from his early *Formal Logic* (London, 1847; 2d ed., Chicago, 1926), the bulk of De Morgan's logical writings are to be found in five memoirs (plus a sixth, still unpublished) contributed to the *Cambridge Philosophical Transactions* between 1846 and 1862. The *Syllabus of a Proposed System of Logic* (London, 1860) gives a cursory account of his scheme, as does his article "Logic" in the *English Cyclopaedia* (*Arts and Science Division*, V, London, 1860, pp. 340–354).

The basis of common logic, for De Morgan, consists in relations of partial or total inclusion, or exclusion, among classes. Where information about a majority of class members is available or where, as in the "numerically definite" syllogism, precise numbers are given, it is possible, as he shows, to draw valid conclusions of a non-Aristotelian type. But these conditions are seldom realized. A more radical departure is the admission into ordinary propositions of negative terms and class names (symbolized by lower-case letters), such that a term X and its "contrary" x between them exhaust the "universe of discourse" (a useful device that has since been generally adopted). Assuming these classes to have at least notional members, it follows that two classes and their contraries can be related in eight possible ways:

(1) All X's are Y's.
(2) All x's are y's.
(3) All X's are y's.
(4) All x's are Y's.
(5) Some X's are Y's.
(6) Some x's are y's.
(7) Some X's are y's.
(8) Some x's are Y's.

These can be rewritten without negative symbols as:

(1) All X's are Y's.
(2) All Y's are X's.
(3) No X's are Y's.
(4) Everything is either X or Y.
(5) Some X's are Y's.
(6) Some things are neither X's nor Y's.
(7) Some X's are not Y's.
(8) Some Y's are not X's.

Of these the contradictory pairs are (1) and (7), (2) and (8), (3) and (5), and (4) and (6). Since the distribution of terms is given or implied throughout, these forms are simply convertible by reading them in reverse. "Contraversion"

(or obversion) is obtained by altering the distribution of a term, replacing it by its contrary, and denying the result. "All X's are Y's" becomes successively "No X's are y's," "All y's are x's," and "Everything is either x or Y." The procedure is the same for the other seven forms, making 32 possibilities in all.

De Morgan's rule of syllogism is either that both premises should be universal or, when only one is, that the middle term should have different quantities in each. Inference takes place by erasing the middle term and its quantities. Since, including the syllogisms of weakened conclusion, there are four basic patterns, and since three terms and their contraries can be paired off, in premises and conclusion, in eight different ways, there are 32 valid syllogisms, of which half have two universal premises and eight a universal conclusion.

To remedy the "terminal ambiguity" whereby the undistributed term in the universal "All X's are Y's" may refer indifferently to some or all of the Y's, De Morgan investigated the complex propositions produced by combining pairs of elementary forms. It is in this connection that he gives the well-known rules for negation of conjunctions which have since received his name—though he did not, in fact, invent them.

In endeavoring to patch up Hamilton's quantified system De Morgan made further distinctions between "cumular" (collective) and "exemplar" (distributive) forms of predication; struggled, unavailingly, to bring the intensional interpretation of terms (as attributes) into line with the extensional and to subsume both under a pure logic of terms (the "onymatic" system); and explored in passing such nontraditional forms of inference as the syllogisms of "undecided assertion" and "transposed quantity." More important is his recognition that the copula performs its function in inference, not as a sign of identity, but only through its role as a transitive and convertible relation.

De Morgan's generalization of the copula leads on, in his fourth Cambridge memoir, to a pioneer investigation of relations in general, which is the foundation of all subsequent work in the field. He there distinguishes a relation (say, "lover of") from its denial, its contrary, and its converse ("loved by"); proceeds to compound relations, or relative products ("*L* of *M* of"), and to quantified versions of these ("*L* of every *M*," "of none but *M*'s," etc.); and discusses a variety of equivalences that hold between these different sorts of relations and the rules for their discovery and manipulation. The purpose of this, typically enough, was to exhibit the syllogism in its most general form, as a series of combinations of relations. Despite the ingenuity and resource with which he treated it, this devotion to the syllogism was something of a weakness in De Morgan's work. It tethered him too closely to tradition, so that it was not until others exploited them that his own most fruitful discoveries were seen for what they were.

Boole. Few major innovators in any science can have had so little to learn from their predecessors as George Boole (1815–1864). Nevertheless, he did owe something to De Morgan, not only for early encouragement but also for the stimulus of the quarrel with Hamilton, which provoked him to the writing of his epoch-making booklet, *The Mathematical Analysis of Logic* (Cambridge, 1847; reprinted, Oxford, 1951). More important than either, perhaps, was the idea—also due to De Morgan, among others—that the laws of algebra can be formally stated without regard for any particular interpretation, for example, in terms of the real positive number system. This led Boole to conceive of a limited algebra, representing (as he supposed) the necessary operations of thought, though it would be truer to describe it as a calculus of classes in extension. In working out this idea, which he did most fully in *An Investigation of the Laws of Thought* (London, 1854), he became the first to devise a practicable symbolic algebra and is thus reckoned (next to Leibniz) as the father of modern logic.

Boole saw that if x and y are used as "elective symbols" to stand for classes formed by selection from a universe of things, $x=y$ will signify their identity of membership, xy the class of members common to both, and $x+y$ the class formed by aggregating them (though in that case, to avoid duplication, it will have to be assumed that they do *not* have members in common). The common class of x and "everything" being plainly the same as x, the symbol 1 is taken to represent the universe (later modified, following De Morgan, to the universe of discourse); so $1x=x$. The symbol 0 stands for the null class (though Boole did not use the term), and $0x=0$. By the same token, however, the class of members common to both x and x can be none other than x and so yields the peculiar, though characteristic, equation of the system, xx (or x^2) $=x$. It might seem equally to follow that $x+x=x$, but this is disallowed by the restriction that an aggregate of classes shall not have members in common. The expression $1+x$ (where $x \neq 0$) is similarly uninterpretable as it stands, but $1-x$ (everything but x) represents De Morgan's negative or complementary class, and $x(1-x)=0$ (Boole's version of the principle of contradiction). It should be noted in passing that, in contrast to addition, subtraction of y from x can properly occur only where y is already part of x and not an independent class; and that since $x+(1-x)=1$, it can be "multiplied" with any other class, z, to yield $zx+z(1-x)=z$—a principle of importance in the further development of the system. Boole also showed that his symbols are distributive: $x(y+z)=xy+xz$, and commutative: $xy=yx$. In this respect they resemble the symbols of ordinary algebra.

Thinking it necessary, for purposes of inference, to introduce the AEIO-propositions of traditional logic as equations under this scheme, Boole was led to adopt the "indefinite" symbols v (and sometimes w), whose function is merely to indicate that there are members in the class to which they are prefixed or equated. We thus have

A	$x=vy$	E	$x=v(1-y)$
I	$vx=wy$	O	$vx=w(1-y)$.

These may be rewritten in various other forms, such as

A	$x(1-y)=0$	E	$xy=0$
I	$xy=v$	O	$x(1-y)=v$.

The procedure for handling syllogisms is, roughly speaking, to maneuver the premises into one or another of these forms, with the middle term, y, on opposite sides in the two equations, and then, by combining the latter, to elimi-

nate y algebraically and solve for the subject term. Since Boole shares De Morgan's tolerance for negative terms, he likewise admits various syllogisms unknown to the Aristotelian canon. His method of working them is by no means foolproof, however, owing to the precautions necessary in handling the symbol v. The real advantages become apparent only in problems more complicated than the syllogism can provide.

It is a striking fact, as Boole himself recognized, that his system is not confined solely to an interpretation for classes. The expression $x(1-x)=0$, or $x^2=x$, though invalid in ordinary algebra, will hold for a restricted case, where the possible values of x are limited to 0 and 1. So long as these are the only values, the operations of the class algebra can all be carried over to this interpretation, although the converse does not hold, since it is quite possible for the product of two classes to equal 0 even though neither of them is itself an empty or a universal class.

A second interpretation, also suggested by Boole, revealed for the first time the affinity between class logic and the calculus of propositions. If 1 and 0 are taken to stand (again exclusively) for truth and falsity and x and y for propositions, then $xy=1$ will assert the truth of their conjunction, $x+y=1$ that of their (exclusive) alternation, and $x(1-y)=0$ the fact that if x is true, y is true. Boole actually treats x and y as elective and wavers as to whether they indicate cases in which, or times during which, the propositions X and Y are true. But on either view, as he points out, the disjunction $xy+x(1-y)+(1-x)y+(1-x)(1-y)$ exhausts all the possible truth cases for a pair of propositions and therefore equals 1. Since the alternatives are also exclusive, the truth of any one of them sets the remainder equal to 0, and the conjunction of any pair will likewise equal 0. The same treatment can be extended to any number of terms and gives a rough indication of Boole's more general procedure for the development, or expansion, of a function in terms of x and y and the method whereby, given any number of propositions with any number of terms, he is able to extract whatever conclusions may be logically contained in them.

Owing to his free use of algebraic operations such as division and subtraction, the success of Boole's general method is offset by the appearance, in his calculations, of numerical and fractional coefficients and of other expressions whose logical significance is, to say the least, uncertain. It was the task of his successors to get rid of these anomalies and so give the system a greater appearance of being what it claimed, a mathematical logic, and not the mere logical mathematics that its opponents suspected it to be.

Jevons. It was the aim of William Stanley Jevons (1835–1882), himself a pupil of De Morgan, to render Boole's calculus more simple and "logical" by removing those of its features that he found "mysterious" and by reducing its operations to mechanical routine. He also professed, officially, to reject the extensional standpoint in favor of a "pure logic" of terms, or "qualities," though the result in practice was still effectively a class or propositional logic, conceived rather in the manner of De Morgan's "onymatic" system. These views are set forth in two pamphlets, *Pure Logic* (London and New York, 1864) and *The Substitution of Similars* (London, 1869; both reprinted in *Pure Logic and Other Minor Works*, London, 1890), and at greater length in *The Principles of Science* (2d ed., London, 1887) and *Studies and Exercises in Deductive Logic* (London, 1884).

Jevons takes over the Boolean notations for conjunction and identity (AB, $A = B$) and admits negative classes, which he symbolizes, like De Morgan, by a small a, but makes no use of 1, the universal class, and dismisses as uninterpretable both the operations of subtraction and division and the various ill-favored symbols—$(1 - x)$, x/y, 0/0, 1/0, etc.—that result from their use. In the case of disjunction (written $+$ or, more generally, $\cdot|\cdot$) Jevons follows the minority view of De Morgan and a few others in proposing to read it inclusively, so that $A + B$ is permitted to have common members, and $A + A = A$ (law of unity). The importance of this reform, almost universally accepted since, is that it abolishes the need for numerical coefficients, establishes the symmetry between conjunction and disjunction exhibited, for example, in De Morgan's laws, $\overline{AB} = a + b$ and $\overline{A + B} = ab$, and makes possible such other useful rules of simplification as the "law of absorption," $A + AB = A$.

Jevons conceives of classes as groups of individuals, and of propositions about such classes, or about qualities, as equations asserting a complete or partial identity between them. Thus, "All A is B" identifies all A's with those that are B—that is, $A = AB$—and the corresponding E-proposition is $A = Ab$. He symbolizes particular propositions, on occasion, by an arbitrary prefix, but pays little attention to them—or, indeed, to the problems of quantification in general. Inference consists merely of what he calls the "substitution of similars"—that is, the replacement of any term by another, stated in a premise to be identical to it. Thus, $A = AB$ and $B = BC$ yield, by substitution, $A = ABC = AC$, the conclusion.

Of more interest is the Jevonian method of indirect inference, based on what he calls the "logical alphabet." This alphabet, which amounts to no more than a Boolean expansion of 1, is constructed by listing all the possible combinations of the terms A, B, C, etc., together with their negatives, thus:

ABC	aBC
ABc	aBc
AbC	abC
Abc	abc

Any given premise, say $A = BC$, on being combined with each line in turn will be found inconsistent with some—that is, will yield an expression equal to 0. These lines being struck out, the remainder give the conclusion, though it still remains to consider the "inverse problem" (which Jevons saw but did not solve) of expressing the results in a single concise formula. Particular propositions are somewhat troublesome to handle on this scheme, which actually works better for propositions than for classes. But with many terms the process soon becomes tedious in either case, and it was to remedy this that Jevons invented his "logical abacus" and "logical piano," contrivances which operate mechanically on the same principle, namely the employment of the premises to eliminate in-

consistent combinations from a matrix already set up on the machine. The development of the modern computer has revived interest in Jevons' pioneer device and in his very able description of its workings (see LOGIC MACHINES). For the rest, Jevons' "equational logic," though famous in its day, is now remembered chiefly for the technical improvements on Boole's procedure which it helped to bring into use.

Venn. The logic of John Venn (1834–1923), sketched briefly in the *Princeton Review* (1880) and more fully elaborated in his *Symbolic Logic* (London, 1881), shows a greater understanding of Boole's intentions and a better acquaintance with the historical background than had yet been displayed by anyone else. Though he did not suppose the new methods to have any great practical advantage over the old, he saw no reason, either, to suspect them of being anything more than a generalization of traditional practices, couched, for convenience, in a mathematical form. He therefore resisted the Jevonian simplifications and was at pains to bring out the logical significance of such operations as subtraction and divison, though the latter is admitted to merit inclusion more on grounds of consistency than for any use made of it in the reasoning of everyday life.

Venn's own account of the matter proceeds from what he calls the "compartmental," or "existential," view of logic, whose purpose is to set out the possible ways in which the four classes designated by x, y, and their negatives, in combination, may have one or more of their components empty. Omitting the case where all four compartments are unoccupied, this yields 15 forms of proposition, compared with the 4 that arise on the traditional, or predication, view, whereby an attribute is asserted or denied of a class, and the 5 that emerge from diagrammatic consideration of the ways in which two nonempty classes may include, exclude, or overlap one another. Each view has its merits, in Venn's opinion, the choice between them being ultimately a conventional one.

This leads Venn to the discussion of another vexed issue, the "existential import" of propositions. Traditional logic must in consistency assume that its classes have members and nonmembers alike, and its universal propositions are thereby rendered hypothetical. To Venn it was clearer what the universal denies than what it asserts, and he therefore proposed to write A, "All x is y," as $x\bar{y} = 0$ and E, "No x is y," as $xy = 0$. These propositions are definite, yet they do not require members in x or y to make them true, since they deny only the existence of members in the common class. Particular propositions do, however, imply the presence of members in each class, since they contradict the universals; they are therefore to be written I, $xy \neq 0$, and O, $x\bar{y} \neq 0$, respectively. This was an improvement on Boole's use of indefinite symbols and has since been generally adopted, though one consequence of it (also noted by Hugh MacColl) is that subalternation ceases to be valid and that the "syllogisms of weakened conclusion" which depend on it have therefore to be rejected.

Venn was not much enamored of the syllogism, but he deserves the gratitude of all beginners in the subject for what is probably his best-known contribution to logic, the diagrams that bear his name. These are, in effect, graphical representations of the algebraic processes introduced by Boole and mechanically illustrated in Jevons' alphabet: the partitioning of a universe in terms of the possible combinations of x, y, etc. and the elimination of those subdivisions inconsistent with the premises given. For two terms a pair of intersecting circles (x and y) on a ground give the four compartments $xy + x\bar{y} + \bar{x}y + \bar{x}\bar{y} = 1$ (Figure 1). Three interlaced circles (Figure 2) depict the eight combinations of

Figure 1

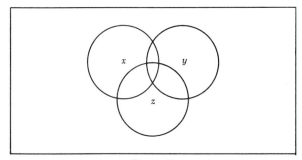

Figure 2

Jevons' table, given earlier. The effect of a universal premise is to declare one or more compartments to be empty, shown by shading the area in question. A particular premise indicates that one or more compartments have occupants, shown by a cross (which may lie ambiguously on the boundary between two areas). The conclusion can then be read off, in various ways, by inspection. By the use of ellipses the same principle can be employed for up to five terms, but it then becomes unwieldy, especially in the "inverse problem" of formulating the outcome, so that one or another of the square diagrams devised by later authors is at that stage generally preferable. With suitable modifications the method can also be extended to the calculus of propositions. Though Venn did not carry this extension far, he was led by it to an early realization of the truth-functional character of the relation of material implication.

The merit of Venn's work lies not in its original departures, which are few, but rather in the light it throws on the obscurities of Boole's procedure and in its very careful and fair discussion of opposing views.

Carroll. The contributions to logic of Lewis Carroll (C. L. Dodgson, 1832–1898) are too slight to deserve much notice; they were not taken very seriously by the author himself. Like Venn, Carroll adopted a "compartmental" view of the subject, and in his books *The Game of Logic* (London, 1887) and *Symbolic Logic*, Part I (London, 1893) he dwelt

chiefly on the merits of this view in the solution of syllogistic problems, using a square diagram and colored counters to mark the presence or absence of members in each class. In addition, Carroll published nine short papers on logic, based on lectures given to women students, and two short pieces in *Mind*. The first of these, "A Logical Paradox" (N.S. Vol. 3, 1894, 436–438), propounds a conundrum about rules governing the exits and entrances of employees in a barber's shop, which has been discussed, *inter alia*, by W. E. Johnson, Bertrand Russell, and most recently A. W. Burks and I. M. Copi ("Lewis Carroll's Barber Shop Paradox," in *Mind*, N.S. Vol. 59, 1950, 219–222; the article gives further references). The second, "What the Tortoise Said to Achilles" (in *Mind*, N.S. Vol. 4, 1895, 278–280), gives amusing and memorable expression to an important point about inference that Dodgson was perhaps the first to recognize, namely that the rule permitting a conclusion to be drawn from premises cannot itself be treated as a further premise without generating an infinite regress. A pro-Achillean rejoinder to this argument has been given by W. J. Rees (in *Mind*, N.S. Vol. 60, 1951, 241–246).

P. L. HEATH

MacColl. Hugh MacColl (1837–1909), a Scotsman who received his B.A. from the University of London, was for most of his life a teacher of mathematics in Boulogne. He became interested in logic while investigating certain problems in probability and the integral calculus. For their solution he invented a logical symbolism which he developed into a full-fledged logical system, expounded in two series of papers and in a book, *Symbolic Logic and Its Applications* (London, 1906).

MacColl's chief contribution, like Frege's, was to base all logic on the logic of propositions, which he called *pure logic*. He employed primitive notation for propositional variables, implication, negation, conjunction, disjunction, and equivalence—without referring, as Boole and Peirce did, to the supposedly analogous relations between classes. In MacColl's symbolism $a:b$ means "a implies b," or "if a is true, b must be true"; a' denotes the denial of a; and ab, $a+b$, and $a=b$ denote, respectively, the conjunction, disjunction, and equivalence of a and b. Little attention is paid to logical economy; in fact, not all of the classical interdefinitions are possible in the system, MacColl being at pains to show that $a:b$ implies but is not equivalent to $a'+b$. His reason was that the implication $a:b$ requires the conjunction of a and b' to be not false but impossible. In fact, he made a fivefold division of propositions into *true, false, certain* (always true), *impossible* (always false), and *variable* (neither certain nor impossible). MacColl's conception of these modalities seems to have been temporal, so that a variable proposition is *sometimes true and sometimes false*. For admitting such propositions into logic he was roundly criticized by Russell, who in his review of MacColl's book in *Mind* (1906) took MacColl's example "Mrs. Brown is not at home" to be not a proposition at all but a propositional function analogous to "x is a barrister." MacColl's premeditated rejoinder was that saying the above proposition "is a *different proposition* when it is *false* from what it is when it is *true*, is like saying that

Mrs. Brown is a *different person* when she is *in* from what she is when she is *out*" (*Symbolic Logic and Its Applications*, p. 19).

MacColl used the symbols a^τ, a^ι, a^ϵ, a^η, and a^θ to denote a's being true, false, certain, impossible, and variable, respectively. Returning to $a : b$, he asserted this implication to be equivalent to $(ab')^\eta$, thus anticipating by some twenty years C. I. Lewis' definition of strict implication (see LOGIC, MODAL). MacColl was aware of the paradoxes of strict implication—that an impossible proposition implies any proposition and that a certain proposition is implied by any proposition—and accepted them. In fact, his system, if presented deductively, would be in many respects identical to Lewis' system S3, but MacColl does not seem to have thought of trying to isolate the axioms from which the true formulas of his system could be deduced. For example, taking "certain" to mean "necessary" and defining a^θ to be $a^{-\epsilon}a^{-\eta}$ (the dash being an alternative symbol for denial), we find that the following laws are all in S3:

(1) $a : b = b' : a'$;

(2) $(a : b)(a : c) = a : bc$;

(3) $(a + a')^\epsilon$;

(4) $a^\epsilon : a^\tau$;

(5) $a^\eta = (a')^\epsilon$;

(6) $(a^\epsilon + a^\eta + a^\theta)^\epsilon$;

(7) $a^\theta = (a')^\theta$;

(8) $(a : b) : (a^\epsilon : b^\epsilon)$;

(9) $\epsilon : a = a^\epsilon$,   where the first "$\epsilon$" denotes an arbitrary certain proposition.

Of these, (6) and (7) represent truths concerning the Aristotelian notion of contingency, which has notoriously resisted treatment in formal terms. The formulas $(a : b) : (a^\theta : b^\theta)$ and $\theta_1 = \theta_2$, the latter asserting the equivalence of any two contingent propositions, were rejected by MacColl and are false in all the Lewis systems.

Perhaps the most interesting parts of MacColl's logic are his definition of class inclusion in terms of implication (Russell in his review corrected his own previous attribution of this innovation to Peano) and his corresponding attempt to base Aristotle's syllogisms upon propositional logic. Take any individual S at random out of the universe of discourse, and let a denote "S belongs to the class A." Then the syllogism Barbara ("If all B is C, and all A is B, then all A is C") will be represented by

$$(b : c)(a : b) : (a : c).$$

Furthermore, since the particular premise "Some A is not B" means "S may belong to A without belonging to B," it will be $(a : b)'$, and the mood Baroco will be

$$(b : c)(a : c)' : (a : b)',$$

easily derived from Barbara by antilogism. These moods are valid in the usual algebra of classes, but certain other Aristotelian moods are not. For instance, Felapton ("If no B is C and all B is A, then some A is not C") is

$$(b : c')(b : a) : (a : c)'$$
namely $$(a : c)(b : a) : (b : c')',$$

which follows from Barbara if $(b : c')'$ ("Some B is C") follows from $b : c$ ("All B is C"). Apparently it was pointed out to MacColl by Venn that the latter implication failed if b was impossible, that is, if B was empty, and this eventually led MacColl to devise a universe of discourse in which no classes were empty—that is, in which every proposition of the form "S belongs to A" was *contingent*. This again got him into trouble with Russell, and led to their celebrated dispute over the null class (see Russell, "The Existential Import of Propositions," in *Mind*, Vol. 41, 1905, 398–401; and MacColl, "The Existential Import of Propositions," in *Mind*, Vol. 41, 1905, 401–402, 578–580), MacColl stoutly defending the presence of nonentities in his universe and denying the truth of "Every round square is a triangle."

The many other idiosyncracies in MacColl's system, such as his calculus of Wa, the weakest premise that implies a, and Sa, the strongest conclusion that a implies (this yields a modal logic like Lewis' S2, but with $SWa = WSa = a$), his notion of causal implication, and his distinction between a and a^τ, still await a competent interpreter.

STORRS MCCALL

Peirce. The logical work of Charles Sanders Peirce (1839–1914) was an unusual blend of the traditional and the modern. His early paper "Memoranda Concerning the Aristotelian Syllogism," read and distributed in 1866, adapted to the second and third syllogistic figures Kant's description of first-figure reasoning as the subsumption of a case under a rule, and in later papers he exhibited analogy and induction as probabilistic weakenings of the second and third figures thus conceived. In 1867, independently of Jevons, Peirce improved Boole's logical algebra by identifying logical addition with the inclusive rather than the exclusive sense of "either–or." In 1870, inspired by De Morgan's pioneer work on the logic of relations, he extended Boole's method of algebraic analogy to this discipline, noticed that there are three-termed as well as two-termed relations, and introduced the sign "$-\!\!\prec$" for class inclusion, considered an analogue of the arithmetical "$\leqslant$."

In 1880, Peirce began to use the symbol "$-\!\!\prec$" indifferently for class inclusion, implication, and the "therefore" of inference. It became one of his persistent themes that the distinction between terms, propositions, and inferences is of little logical importance. For him all propositions are, in the end, implications (this thesis is bound up with his pragmatic theory of meaning) and as such are simply inferences deprived of an element of assertiveness; terms, at least general terms, are propositions deprived of a subject. General terms are "rhemes," or, as we would now say, "open sentences," sentences with gaps where names might go. Such sentences with gaps are in a broad sense relative terms, the number of gaps indicating what Peirce called the "adinity" of the relation. Thus, "— loves —" represents a "dyadic" relation, "— gives — to —" a "triadic" one, and so on. Extending this conception downward, Peirce described an ordinary predicative term, such as "— is a man," as representing a "monadic" relation and a complete sentence, with no gaps at all, as representing a "medadic" one.

As Frege did with his "concepts," Peirce compared his "rhemes" to unsaturated chemical radicals having various valencies. Unlike Frege, however, he did not subsume rhemes under functions, like "The square of —," as the special case in which the value of the function for a given argument is a truth-value. Frege's procedure underlined the resemblance between a completed proposition and a name; for Peirce a completed proposition was rather a special case of a predicate. Nevertheless, Peirce pioneered (in 1885) the use of truth-value calculations in establishing logical laws and also foreshadowed many-valued logic by suggesting that there might be an infinity of degrees of falsehood, with truth as the zero.

A gap in a rheme may be filled, in the simplest case, by what Peirce called an "index." He divided signs into indices, which operate through some physical connection with what they signify; icons, which operate through some resemblance to what they signify; and symbols, which acquire their meaning by convention. An ordinary proper name is an "icon of an index"; it is (when uttered) a noise which resembles the noise that was made when we were introduced to the person named. A simple index would be, for example, a demonstrative pronoun accompanied by a pointing gesture. Peirce regarded the phrase "demonstrative pronouns" as an inaccurate description—it would be more appropriate to call a noun a "pro-demonstrative." A common noun, for Peirce, is only an inseparable element in a rheme (for example, "man" in "is a man").

Instead of directly filling a gap in a rheme with an index, we may say either "I can find you an object such that it —" ("is a man," "loves Susan," etc.) or "Take anything you like and it —" ("is mortal if human," etc.). These are the particular and universal quantifiers, which Peirce introduced into his logic—independently of Frege, but with some debt to his own student O. H. Mitchell—in 1883. He represented them with the mathematical symbols "Σ" and "Π" for continued sums and products. If we write "$a=0$" for "a is false" and "$a>0$" for "a is true," $\Sigma_i a_i$ or "For some individual i, a_i" will have for its value the sum of the values of the possible a_i's and therefore will be >0 (that is, true) if and only if at least one of the a_i's is >0, whereas $\Pi_i a_i$ or "For any individual i, a_i" will have for its value the product of the values of the possible a_i's and therefore will be >0 if and only if all of the a_i's are >0. Peirce was aware of the possibility of putting any quantified expression into what is now called prenex normal form, with all the quantifiers at the beginning. He also, in what he called second-intentional logic, quantified over variables other than those standing for indices.

Every implication, Peirce came to believe, has an implicit or explicit initial quantifier—i.e., is of the form $\Pi_i(a_i \prec b_i)$, "For any i, if a_i then b_i." The i's may be either ordinary individuals *of* which our a and b may be true, or instants *at* which they may be true, or possible states of affairs *in* which they may be true; for example, "If it rains it pours" may mean "For any instant i, if it rains at i, it pours at i" or "For any possible state of affairs i, if it

rains in i, it pours in i." But in the latter case we may consider wider or narrower ranges of possibility, and if we limit ourselves to the actual state of affairs, the quantifier may be dropped.

Peirce made several attempts to define negation in terms of implication, and in 1885 he produced a set of axioms for the propositional calculus with implication accepted as an undefined operator and negation defined as the implication of a proposition from which anything at all would follow. This was the second set of axioms sufficient for the propositional calculus to be produced in the history of the subject (the first being Frege's of 1879) and the first set to use the curious law $((a \prec b) \prec a) \prec a$, now called Peirce's law. But Peirce experimented with other types of systems also, and in 1880 he anticipated H. M. Sheffer in showing that all truth-functions can be defined in terms of "Neither — nor —" and "Not both — and —." The "not" within a proposition (as opposed to "It is not the case that —," governing the whole), which forms the "negative propositions" of traditional logic, he regarded as expressing the relation of otherness, and he worked out what properties of this relation are reflected in traditional logical laws. For example, the law of contraposition, "'Every A is a B' entails that whatever is not a B is not an A," follows from the mere fact that otherness is a relation, for whatever relative term R may be, if every A is a B, then whatever is an R (for instance, an other) of every B is an R of every A.

Peirce thought it desirable that logical formulas should reflect the structure of the facts or thoughts which they express and so be, in his sense, "icons"—that is, signs operating by resemblance to what they signify—and he sought constantly to develop symbolisms that were genuinely "iconic." In his later years he came to regard this as best achieved by a system of diagrams which he called "existential graphs." Typically, he attempted to represent his graph for "If A then B" as basic, but in fact his diagrams are most easily understood as starting from the representation of "and" by juxtaposition and of "not" by enclosure in a bracket or circle or square. $(A(B))$, which is his graph for "If A then B," reads off naturally as "Not both A and not B." Rules of inference are represented as permissions to alter the graphs by insertions and erasures; for example:

(R1) We may insert or remove double enclosures at will, provided that there is no symbol caught between the two enclosures; for instance, we may pass from A to $((A))$, i.e., to "Not not A," and back, but not from $(A(B))$ to AB.

(R2) Any symbol may be removed from an evenly enclosed graph (including a completely unenclosed one) or added to an oddly enclosed one; for instance, we may pass from AB, i.e., "A and B," to A, or from $(A(BC))$ to $(A(B))$, i.e., from "If A then both B and C" to "If A then B," or from (A) to (AB), i.e., from "Not A" to "Not both A and B."

(R3) We may repeat a symbol across an enclosure immediately interior to the symbol's own, and if a symbol is already thus repeated, we may remove it from the inner enclosure; for instance, we may pass from $(A(B))$ to $(A(AB))$, i.e., from "If A then B" to "If A then both A and B," or from $A(AB)$ to $A(B)$, i.e., from "A and not both A and B" to "A and not B."

If a graph is such that these permissions will enable us to transform it into any graph at all, that graph is "absurd" and its negation a logical truth. For example, A(A), "Both A and not A," leads by R2 to A((B)A), where B is any graph you please, and this leads by R3 to A((B)), this by R2 to ((B)), and this by R1 to B. Hence, (A(A)), "If A then A," is a logical truth. For clarity Peirce suggested drawing rectangular enclosures, with evenly enclosed symbols written on the left and oddly enclosed ones on the right. For example, Figure 3 is a representation of (A(B(C)), "If A then (B but not C)." This arrangement makes it clear that Peirce was, in effect, setting up what are nowadays called "semantic tableaux," in the manner of E. W. Beth.

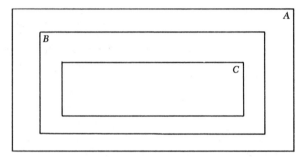

Figure 3

Peirce also thought of logical truth as represented by the blank sheet on which his graphs were drawn and absurdity by an enclosure with nothing but the blank graph sheet inside it. Since by R2 we may inscribe anything whatever in such an otherwise blank enclosure, this enclosure would in fact represent an absurdity in the previous sense of a graph that can be transformed into any graph whatsoever. "If A then absurdity," Peirce's favorite definition of "Not A," would then be strictly "(A(( )))" ("If A then B" is "(A(B))," and here we put "( )" for B), but this assumes that in representing the absurd as "( )" we already understand simple enclosure as negation, and in attempting to modify his symbolism in ways which would avoid this assumption Peirce was led into occasional unnecessary trouble.

Although Peirce was one of the inventors of bound variables, in his graphs for quantified formulas he explicitly dispensed with them in favor of what he called "lines of identity," a device recently put to the same purpose, though informally, by W. V. Quine and Peter Geach. A monadic rheme may be written as "— A" or "A —," the single valency line being close enough to be thought of as part of the symbol and on its own this symbol is read as "Something is A." If "— B" is added to this, the whole, "A —— B," of course, means "Something is A and something is B." But if the valency lines are joined by a "line of identity," to give us "A —— B," this means "Something is A and *that same thing* is B," or "Something is at once A and B." In the common systems this identification of the subjects of which A and B are predicated is effected by attaching these predicates to the same bound variable, thus: "For some x, x is A and x is B." Again, "If anything is A then *that same thing* is B" is distinguished in the common

systems from the more indefinite "If anything is A then something is B" by writing the former with a common bound variable, thus: "For any x, if x is A then x is B." In Peirce's graphs this is done by tightening "(— A (— B))" to "(A(B))" or "(A —+ B))." To give some examples with dyadic rhemes, "Every A is an R of some B" comes out as "(A —+ R — B))"; "Some B is R'd by every A" as "(A —+ R —++B"; and "Every A is an R of itself" as "(A—+⌐R))" or "(A—⌐L+ R))."

This "Beta part" of Peirce's graphs, of course, contains special rules for the transformation of lines of identity. For example, the additions and erasures of terms permitted by R2 may be extended to terms attached to others by lines of identity; thus, we may pass from "A — B," "Something is at once A and B," to the plain "— B," "Something is B." Peirce said that the blank sheet—which is left here when "A —" with its line of identity is removed and which represents accepted truth when considered as a medad—represents an accepted existent when considered as a monad.

Since lines of identity may themselves be treated as dyadic rhemes and subjected to enclosure, the graphs cover identity theory and, therefore, the arithmetic of specific integers, as well as the theory of first-order quantification. For example, "There are at least two A's" will be "A —+⊢ A"—that is, "Something is an A, and something that *is not* that thing is also an A." But the graphs do not readily lend themselves to the representation of higher-order quantifications, such as "Some qualities belong to everything and others to some things only," although Peirce made some rather clumsy efforts in this direction. More successful, but only adumbrated in outline, was his extension of his method to modal logic by using separate sheets for different possible worlds. This procedure is very like that now adopted by S. A. Kripke (see LOGIC, MODAL) and also echoes medieval theories of "ampliation" (see EXISTENCE).

There is probably no logical writer who has been more rich in original suggestions than Peirce, and his papers are a mine that has still to be fully worked. He was, at the same time, more aware than any of his contemporaries of the contributions made by their ancient and medieval predecessors. He held and persuasively supported a theory that Aristotle had anticipated (in a chapter of the *Prior Analytics* (now missing) later derivations of simple conversion from the laws of identity and syllogism, and he saw the significance of the Megarian controversy over the nature of implication and of the distinctions drawn by the Schoolmen in their theory of *consequentiae*.

Peirce's immediate circle in America included two logicians of some distinction: O. H. Mitchell, from whom Peirce derived the germ of his device of quantification, and Christine Ladd Franklin (1847–1930), who used eight "copulae" to construct De Morgan's eight categorical forms and exhibited syllogisms in different figures as derivable from "inconsistent triads," or "antilogisms." An antilogism states that a certain three propositions—for example, "Every Y is a Z," "Every X is a Y," and "Not every X is a Z"—cannot all be true: hence (syllogism 1), the first and second jointly imply the denial of the third; also (syllogism 2), the first and third jointly imply the denial of the second; also (syllogism 3), the third and second jointly imply the denial of the first.

A. N. Prior

THE HERITAGE OF KANT AND MILL

The development of logic, at least of formal logic, in the nineteenth century was largely independent of the general development of philosophy during the same period. Of the logicians considered in the preceding section only Peirce and perhaps Hamilton were of importance in branches of philosophy other than logic, and the persons who were of most importance in other branches of philosophy contributed nothing whatsoever to technical developments of the sort here described. These persons did not ignore logic altogether, however, nor did competent logicians entirely ignore them. It will be helpful, therefore, to break the chronological order at this point and to glance back at these philosophical developments and influences.

In the nineteenth century, as in the eighteenth, there were divergent Continental and British philosophical influences, but the Continental stream, stemming from Immanuel Kant (1724–1804), was now not so much rationalistic as idealistic, and in logic it was increasingly antiformal, antimathematical, and antitechnical. Kant himself could not be described as antiformal; he had a quite exalted view of the place of formal logic in philosophy. Unfortunately, however, he thought of formal logic not as a field for new developments but as the first science to have reached perfection—it had reached perfection, he said, with the work of Aristotle. Even Kant's "Aristotelianism" was of the sadly truncated variety that had been characteristic of the interregnum. Slightly systematizing what he took to be Aristotelian logic, he divided "judgments" according to their "quantity" into universal, particular, and singular; according to their quality into affirmative (X is Y), negative (X is-not Y) and infinite (X is not-Y); according to what he called "relation" into categorical, hypothetical (that is, conditional), and disjunctive; and according to modality into apodictic (asserting necessity or impossibility), assertoric, and problematic (asserting possibility). The division according to quality is particularly absurd; where would one put, for example, the forms "X is-not not-Y" and "Not-X is Y"? More influential was his subdivision of affirmative categoricals into "analytic," in which the predicate concept is implicitly contained in the subject concept, and "synthetic," in which it is not. "Body is extended," for example, is analytic because what is meant by a body is precisely an extended substance.

The empiricism which had characterized British philosophy in the eighteenth century was still in evidence in the nineteenth in the work of John Stuart Mill (1806–1873), but Mill was not, as the eighteenth-century British empiricists had been, antilogical or antimathematical. He did not personally advance the young science of mathematical logic, but he was not hostile to it, and in the later nineteenth century it was possible for J. N. Keynes and W. E. Johnson to develop a logical style that was indebted almost equally to Mill and to the mathematicians.

Mill's own formal logic, like Kant's, was rather thin, and for details he referred his readers to Whately; the greater part of his *System of Logic* (London, 1843) is devoted to what would now be called scientific method. Its first two books, however, contain well-developed theories about the meaning of various types of words and sentences and about the nature of syllogistic reasoning. (Details can be found in LOGIC, TRADITIONAL.) It may be added here that the propositions corresponding to what Kant called analytic judgments were described by Mill as "merely verbal."

In the later nineteenth century there was considerable crossing of geographical and philosophical boundaries. Christoph Sigwart (1830–1904), in Germany, was indebted to Mill as well as to Kant; Franz Brentano (1838–1917), in Austria, owed much to Mill and nothing at all to Kant. The antimathematical logical tradition of Kant and Hegel was carried further in England by Bradley and Bosanquet, just when logic as an exact science was being given in Germany a new impetus by Gottlob Frege.

A. N. Prior

Bradley. Francis Herbert Bradley (1846–1924) contributed to the philosophy of logic, rather than to deductive logic itself, in *The Principles of Logic* (London, 1883; 2d ed., 1922), parts of *Appearance and Reality* (London, 1893; 2d ed., 1897), and *Essays on Truth and Reality* (Oxford, 1914). He sought throughout to show the logical features of such notions as judgment and inference and to distinguish them, for logical purposes, from the feelings and images which accompany some occurrences of judging, inferring, and so on. Inference, he held finally, "is the ideal self-development of a given object taken as real" (*Principles of Logic*, 2d ed., p. 598). This does not merely mean both that we are given a set of premises, regarded as "real" for the purposes of the argument, and that if we are clever we then spot what they logically imply—as if this "unfolding" were the "development," and a self-development, too, because no other premises come in. Bradley meant by the "object" not just the premises but the premises completed by all the conditions needed to guarantee their truth or required to make the conclusion true in virtue of "internal" relations. Internal relations are those without which the thing related could not remain describable in the same terms: if Agatha's husband were unmarried, he logically could not be Agatha's husband (internal relation between "husband" and "married"), but if Giles were unmarried he could still be Giles (external relation between "Giles" and "married"). Bradley held that even if the premises could include all their truth-guaranteeing conditions, these would still be "ideal" or discursive, using terms which falsify reality because they abstract from sensuous detail. We must use logic, but it is metaphysically unsound.

Bradley drew several useful distinctions, although some for doubtful reasons. Discussing validity (*ibid.*, pp. 551 ff.), he distinguished between what is now often called validity (premises entail conclusion, disregarding their truth-values) and soundness (entailment and true premises), but he did so because he had different metaphysical doubts about each. Validity postulates both the completability of truth-guaranteeing conditions, required to complete even the meaning of the premises, and the indifference of the premises to our considering them—an indifference doubted by idealists. Soundness, which Bradley called "validity in the sense of conclusiveness" (*ibid.*, p. 579), postulates some correspondence between the abstractions of even the ideally completed argument and concrete many-faceted reality. Bradley believed various suggested correspondences were incoherent. His doubts may have stemmed partly from misassimilating "the truth" to "the whole truth" and partly from substituting aesthetic for logical criteria (see COHERENCE THEORY OF TRUTH).

Bradley also distinguished between premises and principles of argument (*ibid.*, p. 527) and between logical and psychological novelty in argument—between something new in the conclusion because neither explicitly nor implicitly in the premises and something merely new to us when made explicit (*ibid.*, p. 406). Bradley later withdrew the claim that if there is no psychological novelty, there is no inference (*ibid.*, p. 425). Finally, he denied that the syllogism is the model of all reasoning. He produced valid arguments in which the premises are not of subject–attribute form and cannot be distinguished as major and minor—for example, "*A* is in tune with *B* and *B* with *C*; therefore, *A* is in tune with *C*." Bosanquet's reason for the same claim was the syllogism's disregard for "system." Both writers said there could be no complete list of valid argument forms.

Bosanquet. The logical writings of Bernard Bosanquet (1848–1923) include *Knowledge and Reality* (London, 1885), *Logic* (2 vols., Oxford, 1888; 2d ed., 1911), *The Essentials of Logic* (London and New York, 1895), and *Implication and Linear Inference* (London, 1920). Bosanquet and Bradley acknowledged mutual debts; their logical views are broadly similar. Bosanquet defined inference as "the indirect reference to reality of differences within a universal by means of the exhibition of this universal in differences directly referred to reality" (*Logic*, 2d ed., Vol. II, p. 3). This "universal" is some complex unity remaining constant through the argument, some large region of reality—perhaps the whole, the Absolute—underlying the "system" within which the premises cohere. The premises exhibit or "directly refer to reality" some "differences" or aspects of this whole; in the conclusion we infer ("indirectly refer to reality") other, related aspects of the system.

System was crucial in Bosanquet's thought. The truth of a premise always depends on many conditions, and those conditions depend on further conditions. These conditions form a system from which the premise derives meaning as well as truth (*Implication and Linear Inference*, p. 59; *Logic*, Vol. II, Ch. 6). In workaday logic we treat premises as given and see what follows. For Bosanquet and Bradley this was intellectually unsatisfying: we should ask what supports the premises, what systems contain them. This leads again to idealist metaphysics. Bosanquet's favorite systems were biological organisms, political institutions, and scientific theories; such systems support premises about the liver, or voting, or expanding metals. Bosanquet did not investigate how they differ as systems or how in general the features of system are present in whatever evidence there is for some given proposition.

Bosanquet's notion of "reciprocity," or mutual implication, has been severely criticized. But he did not say we can infer "If *q* then *p*" from "If *p* then *q*." He held only

that the ideally complete hypothetical must be a reciprocal judgment (*Logic*, 2d ed., Vol. I, p. 246). "If *A* is *B*, then it is *C*" implies "If *A* is *C*, then it is *B*" only when taken with other parts of the alleged system or when *A*, *B*, and *C* are so explicable in terms of relations within reality as a whole that we can see the mutual implication. Bosanquet's intellectual ideal was a system in which all relations are mutual implications; he did not show why this should be the ideal for all discursive intellectual enterprises.

Both Bradley and Bosanquet disclaimed expertise in mathematical logic. But their views on the ultimate unintelligibility of abstraction and on the inferential nature of such notions as comparison and recognition challenged logicians to discuss the applicability of interpreted formal systems.

ROGER MONTAGUE

Keynes. John Neville Keynes (1852–1949) was for a large part of his long life registrar of the University of Cambridge. His first contribution to logic was an article in *Mind* in 1879, in which he defended formal logic as a substantial discipline distinguishable alike from the philosophical logic being pursued by the heirs of Kant and Hegel, from the "empirical" (largely inductive) logic developed by the heirs of J. S. Mill, and from the mathematical logic lately started on its career by Boole and De Morgan.

In 1884, Keynes's view of the subject was exhibited in greater detail in the first edition of his *Studies and Exercises in Formal Logic*. This work dealt, in the traditional manner, successively with terms, judgments, and syllogisms, but it had a fourth part in which essentially Boolean material was presented as a logic of categorical propositions with conjunctive, disjunctive, and negative terms and conjunctive and disjunctive compounds of these propositions. Each chapter in the book consisted of a number of well-constructed exercises, sometimes with introductory remarks and often with lengthy comments. Part I, on terms, was much influenced by the treatment of names in Book I of Mill's *System of Logic*. Part II was distinguished by a very judicious discussion, in Chapter 8, of the problems raised by Brentano and Venn about the existential import of categorical propositions (see EXISTENCE).

In successive revisions and enlargements in 1887, 1894, and 1906 the chapters took on the more normal shape of extended discussions with exercises at the end. Part IV (on compound and complex propositions) was transformed into a long appendix, and much new material was incorporated. W. E. Johnson, in the preface to his own logic, was able to refer to the final product as "Dr. Keynes's classical work, in which the last word has been said on most of the fundamental problems of the subject." To this result Johnson himself generously contributed; he and Keynes had frequent and regular discussions of logical problems, and many of the footnotes in Keynes's third and fourth editions express his indebtedness to Johnson. For example, Keynes owed to Johnson the distinction between "conditional" and "true hypothetical" propositions which Russell later dealt with more precisely as one between formal and material implication.

Keynes's literary style was of singular clarity and distinction, and he dealt urbanely but decisively with the many sophistries and confusions which were current, especially among logical writers of a broadly idealist stamp, such as Bosanquet and Bradley. At the same time, he paid attention, particularly in his final edition, to the broadly "intensional" considerations to which these writers were perhaps more sensitive than many whose standards of logical rigor were higher. He handled modal distinctions, for example, with the same neatness and skill which he brought to other topics, and he anticipated C. I. Lewis in drawing attention to what are now called the paradoxes of strict implication (see LOGIC, MODAL).

The development of Keynes's thought from edition to edition, as he brought it to bear on one topic after another, is fascinating to examine. For instance in dealing with what Mill called the connotation and denotation of general names he distinguished even in the first edition between (1) the connotation proper—that is, the set of attributes which we select by convention as those which an object must have if we are to give the name to it—and (2) the totality of attributes possessed in common by all the attributes to which the name applies. In the second edition he suggested that for (2) we might use the Port-Royalists's term "comprehension." Thus, the connotation being selected by convention, objective facts determine the name's denotation, that is, which objects have the attributes entitling them to the name, and further objective facts determine the comprehension, that is, which attributes beyond the connotation these objects have in common. But in the third edition Keynes noted that we might alternatively fix the application of a name by an "exemplification," a selection not of attributes but of objects, with respect to which we decide that we will give a certain name to anything which possesses all the attributes that these objects have in common (making an exception, as Johnson reminded Keynes that we would have to do, of such attributes as that of having been selected for this purpose). When we proceed this way convention fixes the exemplification, and the facts determine the comprehension and then the denotation.

Johnson. Keynes's collaborator William Ernest Johnson (1858–1931) did not publish Part I of his own *Logic* until 1921 (Part II, 1922; Part III, 1924), although he had published a series of three articles titled "The Logical Calculus" in *Mind* in 1892 (Vol. 17, 3–30, 235–250, 340–357) and two titled "The Analysis of Thinking" in *Mind* in 1918 (Vol. 27, 1–21, 133–151). In the first series the variables in Boolean equations were explicitly given the propositional interpretation, the logical product ("x and y") being represented by juxtaposition and negation by a superimposed bar. The logical product and negation being taken as primitive, "If x then y" is defined as "Not (x and not y)"—that is, $\overline{x\overline{y}}$—the logical sum "x or y" as "Not (not x and not y)," and universal and particular quantification as continued logical multiplication and addition. "The Analysis of Thinking" is more philosophical and seems to reflect the influence of G. F. Stout's *Analytic Psychology.*

Johnson's *Logic* exhibits an attractive combination of the formal elegance of his 1892 articles with the philosophical penetration of those of 1918. In some ways—for example, in his extensive discussion of "problematic induction" (that is, scientific generalization)—he played Mill to

Keynes's Whately. His book is now best known for its development of the distinction between "determinables" and "determinates," in Part I, Chapter 11. A "determinable" is one of the broad bases of distinction which may be found in objects, such as color, shape, size. Under each of these fall more or less determinate characteristics, such as red, blue, etc. under color (and scarlet, crimson, etc. as more determinate forms of red). Johnson used this distinction as the basis of many further developments. In Part II, Chapter 10, for example, Johnson discussed what he called "demonstrative induction," in which a universal conclusion is deduced from a singular premise by the help of an "all-or-nothing" proposition. From "Either every S is P or every S is not P" and "This S is P" we can infer "Every S is P." A natural extension is the form of reasoning in which the major premise asserts that every S exhibits the same determinate form of the determinable P (for instance, every specimen of a given element has the same atomic number) and the minor that this S exhibits the determinate form p of this determinable; hence, every S is p. (Cf. Mill on "uniform uniformities" in his *System of Logic,* Book III, Ch. 4, Sec. 2.)

Johnson presented many critical asides concerning Russell's *Principles of Mathematics,* the most valuable being in Part II, Chapter 3, "Symbolism and Functions."

A. N. PRIOR

MODERN LOGIC: FREGE TO THE PRESENT

Twentieth-century logic, and even late nineteenth-century logic, cannot be properly understood without some acquaintance not only with earlier nineteenth-century logic but also with nineteenth-century mathematics. The final section of our survey therefore begins with a sketch of the influence of nineteenth-century mathematics on the major logical developments of both the Boolean and the more recent periods. This will be followed by discussions of particular logicians.

(A. N. P.)

Nineteenth-century mathematics. Mathematics in the nineteenth century was characterized by reorganization in every field, effected both by generalization, which led to the viewing of areas once considered discrete as special instances of the same general case, and by the examination of foundations, either in terms of basic concepts or by an axiomatic approach. Apart, therefore, from any specific contributions that mathematicians made to modern logic, the atmosphere was highly favorable to an explicitly logical investigation both of mathematics in general and of its various branches, including, by the end of the century, mathematical logic itself. At the same time, the growth of abstract algebra encouraged the persistence of Leibniz' ideal of mathematizing deductive logic; his ideas, although most were unpublished, maintained a steady, if at first tenuous, foothold. Thus, the early mathematical logicians, having caught the idea of a new kind of algebra, tended to work on it as a specialized branch of mathematics. By the end of the nineteenth century it had become an instrument sufficiently perfected to be able to discard its traditional algebraic appearance, even to forget momentarily its self-concern, and to apply itself to the articulation of the increasingly well-organized mathematical material. Only in the twentieth century did it catch up to its own axiomatic origins and fruitfully rejoin its algebraic ones.

Peacock. As early as 1821, A. L. Cauchy (1789–1857), in his influential *Cours d'analyse* (Paris, 1821, Introduction, p. ii), attacked the current use of algebraic reasonings in geometry because "they tend to make one attribute an indefinite range to the algebraic formulas, while in reality most of these formulas hold uniquely under certain conditions, and for certain values of the quantities concerned." This thought was adopted, in a more positive version, by George Peacock (1791–1858) in *A Treatise on Algebra* (2 vols., London, 1842–1845), elaborating a work of 1830. Instead of merely rejecting such illegitimate, or at any rate unjustified, extensions of the ranges of algebraic formulas, he distinguished between two kinds of algebra, arithmetical and symbolic.

Arithmetical algebra is the science which results from the use of symbols and signs to denote numbers and the operations to which they may be subjected; those numbers or their representatives, and the operations upon them, being used in the same sense and with the same limitations as in common arithmetic. [In symbolical algebra] the symbols which are used are perfectly general in their representation, and perfectly unlimited in their values; and the operations upon them, in whatever manner they are denoted, or by whatever name they are called, are universal in their application. (Vol. I, Ch. 1)

The relationship of the two is more fully explained in the Introduction:

The generalizations of arithmetical algebra are generalizations of reasoning not of form. . . . Symbolical algebra adopts the rules of arithmetical algebra, but removes altogether their restrictions. . . . It is this adoption of the rules of the operations of arithmetical algebra as the rules for performing the operations which *bear the same names* in symbolical algebra, which secures the absolute identity of the results in the two sciences so far as they exist in common. . . . This principle, in my former Treatise on Algebra, I denominated the "principle of the permanence of equivalent forms."

Peacock expressed his conviction that the convention by which such permanence had been commonly assumed had both delayed the emergence of his symbolical algebra as a science in its own right and resulted in consequent confusion and false reasoning such as Cauchy had complained of. By contrast to arithmetical algebra, "the results of symbolical algebra, which are not common to arithmetical algebra, are generalizations of form, and not necessary consequences of the definitions" which introduce special conditions according as the variables denote lines, forces, periods of time, and so on.

Boole. It is not hard to see the influence of Peacock's thoughts on George Boole. In the Introduction to *The Mathematical Analysis of Logic* (1847), Boole wrote:

Those who are acquainted with the present state of the theory of symbolical algebra, are aware, that the validity of the process of analysis does not depend upon the interpretation of the symbols which are employed, but solely upon the laws of their combination. Every system of interpretation which does not affect the truth of the relation supposed, is equally admissible. . . . That to the existing forms of analysis a quantitative interpretation is assigned, is the result of the circumstances by which those forms were determined, and is not to be construed into a universal condition of analysis. It is upon the foundation of this general principle, that I purpose to establish the calculus of logic, and that I claim for it a place among the acknowledged forms of mathematical analysis, regardless that in its object and in its instruments it must at present stand alone.

In this passage we see mathematical logic struggling to be born, aware of its parentage, but still uncertain, as it continued to be for some time, of its status. Boole himself interpreted his calculus in relation to both classes and propositions. Thus, "The symbol $1-x$ selects those cases in which the proposition X is false" (*ibid.,* "Of Hypotheticals"), and "Let us for simplicity of conception give to the symbol x the particular interpretation of *men,* then $1-x$ will represent the class of 'not-men'" (*An Investigation of the Laws of Thought,* London, 1854, Ch. 3 in Prop. iv).

Peacock's work drew increased attention to the formal properties of operations, and Boole regarded his subject from this point of view.

The laws we have established . . . are sufficient for the base of a calculus. From the first of them it appears that the elective symbols are *distributive,* from the second that they are *commutative;* properties which they possess in common with symbols of *quantity,* and in virtue of which, all the processes of common algebra are applicable to the present system." (*The Mathematical Analysis of Logic,* "First Principles")

These terms actually antedate Peacock; they may have been introduced by F. J. Servois (see *Annales des mathématiques,* Vol. 5, 1814, 93). "Associativity" has been ascribed to Sir William Rowan Hamilton (see Hermann Hankel's *Theorie der complexen Zahlensysteme,* Leipzig, 1867).

Gergonne. The new trend in algebra was already evidenced by the "Essai de dialectique rationelle" (in *Annales des mathématiques,* Vol. 7, 1816–1817, 189–228) of J. D. Gergonne (1771–1859). In this he wrote:

In the same way that an algebraic calculation can be carried out without one having the least idea about the meaning of the symbols on which one is operating, it is possible to follow a course of reasoning without any knowledge of the meaning of the terms in which it is expressed, or without adverting to it if one knows it.

Such a formalistic approach would have been more in order when fields of application were better charted, and Karl Weierstrass was still fighting for this point of view many years later. Gergonne later did important work on duality in geometry, which shows again his ability to distinguish structure from interpretation. He offered a new analysis of the fundamental ideas of syllogistic and used an inverted *C* for inclusion, now standardized as the hook, ⊂.

De Morgan. Augustus De Morgan, a contemporary of Peacock and Boole, took a special interest in the organization of mathematics for didactic purposes. After *Elements of Arithmetic* (1830) he wrote *On the Study and Difficulties of Mathematics* (1831), *First Notions of Logic* (1839), which was designed to help beginning students of geometry, and *Formal Logic* (1847). In *Trigonometry and Double Algebra* he investigated symbolic calculuses. A remarkable text ("On the Syllogism, III") shows De Morgan striking out element after element in the material proposition "Every man is animal" till he is left with *X——Y*, showing the "pure form of the judgment"; thus, he made a start on the extension of the mathematical notion of function, to which Boole, Peirce, and most notably Frege also contributed. De Morgan's right parenthesis, as used in "*X*)" to mean "every *X*", yielding "*X*)*Y*"—that is, every *X* is *Y*—is reminiscent of Gergonne's inverted *C,* although Gergonne's symbol means "is contained in" and operates on two terms rather than one.

Grassmann. One of the creators of a new form of algebra was H. G. Grassmann (1809–1877). Grassmann's *Ausdehnungslehre* (Leipzig, 1844; rev. ed., 1862), fundamental to vector analysis, anticipated W. R. Hamilton's work through its greater generality and influenced Alfred North Whitehead's *A Treatise on Universal Algebra With Applications* (Cambridge, 1898). Giuseppe Peano's *Calcolo geometrico* (Turin, 1888) was written "according to the *Ausdehnungslehre* of H. Grassmann, preceded by the operations of deductive logic."

Non-Euclidean geometry. In geometry the great breakthrough was the effective creation of non-Euclidean systems. The chief figures were János Bolyai (1802–1860), Nikolai Ivanovich Lobachevski (1793–1856), and Bernhard Riemann (1826–1866). Bolyai's work on non-Euclidean geometry was entitled *Appendix Scientiam Spatii Absolute Veram Exhibens; A Veritate aut Falsitate Axiomatis XI Euclidei (A Priori Haud Unquam Decidenda) Independentem.* Written in 1823, it was published in 1833 at Maros-Vásárhely in the second volume of the *Tentamen* of his father, F. Bolyai. Lobachevski wrote *Geometrische Untersuchungen zur Theorie der Parallellinien* (Berlin, 1840), an elaboration of ideas first presented in a lecture delivered at Kazan in 1826. Riemann's inaugural lecture *Ueber die Hypothesen, welche der Geometrie zu Grunde liegen* (1854) was published at Göttingen in 1867. Each seems to have done his work independently of the others, but behind all of them appears the great, although in this matter somewhat enigmatic, figure of Karl Friedrich Gauss (1777–1855), friend of Bolyai's father and of Lobachevski's teacher Bartels and teacher of Riemann. Gauss's correspondence shows him long to have had ideas on the subject, and to him we owe the word "non-Euclidean" (in a letter to Taurinus, 1824).

Bolyai, as the title of his work indicates, simply dropped Euclid's axiom of parallels; Lobachevski adopted its denial. Both required the infinity of the straight line. Rie-

mann, approaching the matter from an analytic point of view, wished to determine the general conditions of spaces in which the measure of distance would remain everywhere constant and figures could move freely without deformation. He was thus led to consider spaces of constant curvature and more than three dimensions, with Euclidean space a special case. Riemann's work was immediately taken up by Hermann von Helmholtz (1821–1894), in *Über die thatsachlichen Grundlagen der Geometrie* (1868–1869) and *Über die Thatsachen, die der Geometrie zu Grunde liegen* (1868), and was further refined by Sophus Lie (1842–1899). Lie was one of the principal developers of the theory of groups, which Felix Klein (1849–1925) applied to geometry in his *Erlanger Programm, Vergleichende Betrachtungen über neuere geometrische Forschungen* (Erlangen, 1872; translated by M. W. Haskell as "A Comparative Review of Recent Researches in Geometry," in *Bulletin of the New York Mathematical Society,* Vol. 2, 1892–1893, 215–249).

Independence. Though Bertrand Russell (in 1897), Alfred North Whitehead (in 1898), and David Hilbert (in 1899) all wrote on geometry, and Hilbert's later foundational work (*Grundlagenforschung*) provided the basis for all subsequent investigations, these pioneers of mature mathematical logic failed to secure independence for their propositional axioms. This is remarkable after all the attention that had been devoted to the independence of Euclid's axiom of parallels. Frege, too, failed in this matter. Alessandro Padoa, in 1901, gave directives for establishing the independence of concepts within an axiom system—an idea that influenced Peano—but no general method for securing the independence of propositional axioms was attained until Jan Łukasiewicz (1925) and Paul Bernays (1926), independently, found the method of interpretation by matrices.

Many-valued logics and proof theory. Non-Euclidean geometries are often mentioned in discussions of the status of many-valued logics, but they appear to have had no direct influence. (Łukasiewicz was brought to the idea by Aristotle's *Peri Hermeneias.*) It is likely that the theory of groups (closed systems of operations)—which was already finding widespread application by the end of the nineteenth century—and the rise of different algebras did much to create the climate of thought in which proof theory, and in general the metalogical investigation of the properties of entire deductive systems, could be developed. Such investigation seems to be one of the most notable characteristics differentiating mathematical logic from the logic of any other period. Proof theory stems mainly from Hilbert.

Schröder. The early, algebraic period of mathematical logic ended with Ernst Schröder (1841–1902). After a paper on algorithms for solving equations (1870) and a textbook on arithmetic and algebra, Schröder devoted himself more and more to the algebra of logic, his two chief works being *Der Operationskreis des Logikkalküls* (Leipzig, 1877) and *Vorlesungen über die Algebra der Logik* (3 vols., Leipzig, 1890–1905). Much of his work was a tidying up of the past. He discarded Boole's subtraction and division, which were subject to too many restrictions to be satisfactory inverse operations; used (as had W. S.

Jevons) the sign of addition in the sense of inclusive rather than exclusive alternation; and introduced at the beginning a sign for inclusion. In this last matter he independently duplicated Frege's abandonment of the algebraic form in *Begriffsschrift* (Halle, 1879), which later became standard with *Principia Mathematica* (3 vols. Cambridge, 1910–1913). But Schröder remained interested in the solution of equations; his results for the Boolean system were taken over by Whitehead in *A Treatise on Universal Algebra*. Like Peirce, Schröder noticed a duality between logical multiplication and addition and similarly between the null and the universal classes. Duality in geometry had been brought to the fore by J. V. Poncelet (1822), enunciated with greater generality by Gergonne (1827), and skillfully exploited by Jakob Steiner (1830).

Schröder explicitly rejected those syllogisms which are invalid when the terms are null, Boole having merely passed them over. Besides using the method of 1–0 evaluation, which goes back to Boole, he developed a process of reduction to normal form. Schröder introduced two novelties. Unlike those of his contemporaries mentioned above, he was interested in independence, wishing particularly to have the distributive law independent of his other axioms, and he was thus brought to perhaps the first idea of a nondistributive lattice. He also had a clear view of the need for a theory of logical types:

> By that process of arbitrary selection of classes of individuals of the manifold originally envisaged, there arises a new, much more extensive manifold, namely that of the domains or classes of the previous one. . . . [It] is necessary from the start that among the elements given as individuals there should be no classes comprising as elements individuals of the same manifold. (*Vorlesungen,* Vol. I, p. 247)

This foreshadows Russell's vicious-circle principle.

Schröder worked on Peirce's algebra of dyadic relatives as an extension of Boole's algebra, but the result was unsatisfactory, and, indeed, by the time Peirce reviewed it Schröder had already abandoned the algebraic form (though not the name) in favor of what is essentially first-order functional calculus. The Schröder–Bernstein theorem, to the effect that if each of two classes is similar to a part of the other, then they are similar to each other, was proved by Schröder in 1896 and independently by Felix Bernstein in 1898.

Peano. Schröder deplored the lack of use for the logical tool he had developed and experimented with the application of his theory of relation to Dedekind's chains. Giuseppe Peano, primarily interested in the rigor of mathematical proof, applied Schröder's instrument to comprehensive mathematical material in successive volumes of his *Formulaire de mathématiques* (5 vols., Turin, 1892–1908). He prefaced the work with a section on mathematical logic (a phrase that he originated), distinguished class membership from inclusion, which Schröder had not done, and expressed all theorems as implications rather than as equations. He still did not isolate propositional logic as a deductive preliminary, but he stated a generalized form of *modus ponens,* to the effect that a true proposition could be suppressed when it occurred as an antecedent or as part of a conjunction of antecedents in a theorem.

Peano had already obtained his five axioms of arithmetic, which contain the principle of mathematical induction, by 1889, when he published *Arithmetices Principia Nova Methodo Exposita.* The year before, J. W. R. Dedekind had reached substantially the same result in *Was sind und was sollen die Zahlen?* (Brunswick, Germany, 1888) with the induction principle provable, however, owing to his having started further back in logic, with sets and projections, rather than with sets, number, and successor. Frege, as Dedekind did not know at that time, had gone still further in the same direction. The fact that Peano, even in 1908, did not refer to either Frege or Dedekind but explicitly left the possibility of defining "number" an open question may indicate that he continued to be interested in logic more as a means of attaining brevity and rigor, and an occasional new insight, than as material from which the basic arithmetical notions might be constructed.

Cantor. Peano did draw on the theory of sets of Georg Cantor (1845–1918), including Cantor's proofs that the algebraic numbers can be put in one-to-one correspondence with the positive integers and that the real numbers cannot be so made to correspond (the "diagonal" proof). Cantor's work had grown out of a reorganization of analysis parallel to that of algebra and geometry. He was influenced, of course, by the work of Cauchy, Riemann, and Hankel on functions of complex variables, but his principal predecessor was Karl Weierstrass (1815–1897), who was greatly interested in foundational matters, especially in regard to irrational numbers and points of condensation of infinite sets. Cantor became convinced that without extending the concept of number to actually infinite sets it would hardly be possible to make the least step forward without constraint. The arithmetic which he thus created was welcomed by Frege; its influence is widely apparent and was acknowledged in Russell's *Principles of Mathematics* (Cambridge, 1903), which plotted the future progress of *Principia Mathematica.*

Ivo Thomas

Frege. Modern logic began with the publication in 1879 of the *Begriffsschrift* of Gottlob Frege (1848–1925). In the *Begriffsschrift* we find for the first time a comprehensive treatment of the ideas of generality and existence, because sentence forms which were hitherto accommodated only by complicated *ad hoc* theories are here provided with an adequate symbolization by the device of quantification, rules for which are adjoined to the first complete formalization of the classical propositional calculus. The result closely approximates a modern formal axiomatic theory. It meets Frege's aim of a codification of the logical principles used in mathematical reasoning, although the rules of inference (substitution and *modus ponens*) and the definition of other logical constants in terms of the primitives (negation, implication, the universal quantifier, and identity) are not explicitly formalized but are mentioned as obviously justified by reference to the intended interpretation. A proof of completeness was not to be had in Frege's day, but he demonstrated the power of his system by deriving a large number of logical principles from his basic postulates and took an important step toward the formulation of arithmetical principles by showing, with the aid of second-order quantification, how the notion of serial order may be formalized.

After the *Begriffsschrift*, Frege's next major work was *Die Grundlagen der Arithmetik* (Breslau, 1884), an analysis of the concept of cardinal number presented largely in nontechnical terms. It opens the way for Frege's theories with a devastating criticism of the views of various writers on the nature of numbers and the laws of arithmetic. Difficulties encountered in the analyses of number find explanation and resolution in the celebrated claim that a statement of number contains an assertion about a concept. To say, for instance, that there are three letters in the word "but" is not, on Frege's view, to attribute a property to the actual letters; it is to assign the number 3 to the concept "letter in the word 'but'". If we now say that two concepts *F* and *G* are numerically equivalent (*gleichzahlig*) if and only if there is a one-to-one correspondence between those things which fall under *F* and those which fall under *G*, we can define the number that belongs to a concept *F* as the extension of the concept "numerically equivalent to the concept *F*." In terms of this definition any two numerically equivalent concepts, such as "letter in the word 'but'" and "letter in the word 'big'", can be seen to determine the same extension, and therefore the same number, and it remains only to specify concepts to which the individual numbers belong. In sketching this and subsequent developments Frege found that the notions used appear to allow of resolution into purely logical terms. He concluded that it is probable that arithmetic has an a priori, analytic status, a view that places him in opposition to Kant, who held that propositions of arithmetic were synthetic a priori, and to Mill, who regarded them as inductive generalizations.

In papers published after the *Grundlagen*, Frege turned his attention to problems of a more general philosophical nature, and the development of his thought in this period led to a revised account of his logic, which is incorporated in his most ambitious work, *Die Grundgesetze der Arithmetik* (2 vols., Jena, 1893–1903), in which he extended and formalized the theory of number adumbrated in the *Grundlagen*. In the *Begriffsschrift* he had rejected the traditional subject–predicate distinction but had retained one predicate, "is a fact" (symbolized "⊢"), which indicated that the judgment which it prefaced was being asserted. In his essay "Über Sinn und Bedeutung" this view was abandoned on the ground that the addition of such a sign, conceived as a predicate, merely results in a reformulation of the same thought, a reformulation which in turn may or may not be asserted. The logic of the *Grundgesetze* is based on Frege's theory of sense and reference, the interpretation of the symbolism of the *Begriffsschrift* being modified accordingly. The formal system of the *Begriffsschrift* is further changed by replacing certain of the axioms with transformation rules, but a more important innovation is the extension of the earlier symbols to cover classes. Corresponding to any well-defined function $\Phi(\xi)$ is the range, or course of values (*Wertverlauf*), of that function, written $\acute{\epsilon}\Phi(\epsilon)$, which Frege introduced via an axiom stipulating that $\acute{\epsilon}\Phi(\epsilon)$ is identical with $\epsilon\Psi(\epsilon)$ if and only if the two associated functions $\Phi(\xi)$ and $\Psi(\xi)$ agree in the values which they take on for all possible arguments ξ. In particular, this axiom licenses the passage from a concept to its extension, the course-of-values notation providing a means of representing classes and foreshadowing Russell's class-abstraction operator, $\hat{z}(\phi z)$. Another device which found a close analogue in Russell's logic is Frege's symbol $\backslash\xi$. If a course of values ξ has a unique member, then $\backslash\xi$ is this member; otherwise $\backslash\xi$ is the course of values ξ itself. In the first case $\backslash\xi$ provides a translation of expressions of the form "the *F*" and so corresponds to Russell's description operator, $(\imath x)(\phi x)$; the second case ensures that when ξ has no unique member, $\backslash\xi$ is nevertheless well defined.

The preliminary development of logic and the theory of classes is followed by the main subject of the *Grundgesetze*, the theory of cardinal number, developed with respect to both finite and infinite cardinals. The theory of real numbers is begun in the second volume but the treatment is incomplete, and Frege was probably loath to advance further in this direction after learning, while the second volume was in the press, that the very beginnings of his theory harbored a contradiction. This contradiction, discovered by Russell, resulted from the axiom allowing the transition from concept to class, an axiom in which Frege had not had the fullest confidence. Russell's communication is discussed in an appendix to the second volume, where an emended version of the axiom is put forward. This emendation was not, in fact, satisfactory, and although Frege apparently did not know that a contradiction could still be derived, he eventually abandoned his belief that the program of the *Grundgesetze* could be carried out successfully and claimed that geometry, not logic, must provide a basis for number theory.

Peano. Giuseppe Peano (1858–1932), professor of infinitesimal analysis at Turin and a prolific writer on a wide range of mathematical topics, contributed to the early development of both logicism and the formalism to which it is partly opposed. His first book, published under the name of a former teacher, Angelo Genocchi, was devoted to the calculus and featured a careful, systematic treatment of the subject which contrasted favorably with customary texts in rejecting loosely phrased definitions and theorems and in substituting rigorous proof for appeals to intuition. Peano was particularly insistent that the acceptability of a mathematical proposition should depend not on its intuitive plausibility but on its derivability from stated premises and definitions, and he devised a remarkable illustration of the way in which what appears evident to intuition may nonetheless be contradicted by formally incontrovertible considerations. This is his well-known space-filling curve, introduced in 1890 in the paper "Sur une Courbe, qui remplit toute une aire plaine" (*Mathematische Annalen*, Vol. 36, 1890, 157–160). About ten years earlier Camille Jordan had defined a curve as a continuous and single-valued image of the unit segment. This definition accords well enough with our intuitive conception of a curve, but Peano showed that a curve in conformity with this definition could in fact pass through every point in a square based on the unit segment and so would appear as a uniformly shaded surface if plotted on a graph.

Convinced that the development of mathematics must proceed independently of intuitive considerations, Peano embarked upon a program of refounding the various branches of mathematics. Not only geometry and analysis, where we are particularly inclined to make an appeal to what can be grasped pictorially, but even elementary number theory was to be purified of common-sense preconceptions. The entities of a mathematical theory (numbers, points, and so forth) would have to enter into the theory not as idealizations of objects given to intuition but as postulated or defined entities, having only those properties which are explicitly listed or which can be grounded on the initial definitions. To ensure the exclusion of misleading intuitive associations, Peano devised a new symbolic language in which to formalize definitions and other postulates. Principles of reasoning employed within mathematics, as well as conceptions forming the substance of mathematical theories, are transcribed into the new notation. It is at this point that mathematical logic enters into Peano's work, and although he did not carry the development of his system very far, the basic ideas and notation were taken over by Whitehead and Russell as a starting point for the system of logic presented in great detail in *Principia Mathematica.*

Also important for subsequent developments was Peano's presentation of arithmetic. It is based on a set of postulates known as the Peano axioms, although, as has been noted, Dedekind had published them earlier. The axioms were intended to free the concept of number from dependence on intuition. The essentials of Peano's treatment are embodied in these five axioms:

(1) 0 is a number.

(2) The successor of any number is a number.

(3) No two numbers have the same successor.

(4) 0 is not the successor of any number.

(5) Any class which contains 0 and which contains the successor of n whenever it contains n includes the class of numbers.

The Peano axioms are commonly taken as a basis for the arithmetic of the natural numbers, supplemented by recursive definitions of such arithmetical operations as addition, multiplication, and exponentiation. Peano himself made considerable use of recursive definition, an analogue, for definitions, of the axiom of mathematical induction given by (5), which allows us to calculate the value of a function $f(n)$ step by step, given an explicit definition of $f(0)$ along with a definition of $f(n')$ in terms of $f(n)$—here "n'" means "the successor of n." Thus, for addition Peano provided the two recursion equations $a+0=a$ and $a+n'=(a+n)'$. Rewriting the second of these as $a+(n+1)=(a+n)+1$, we can see that we have here a particular case of the associative law for addition, $x+(y+z)=(x+y)+z$, which can in fact be derived from the recursion equations by means of axiom (5). Multiplication is defined in similar fashion by means of the equations $a \cdot 0 = 0$ and $a \cdot b' = a \cdot b + a$, and once more familiar arithmetical laws can be extracted by means of induction.

With the assistance of a number of colleagues, including Cesare Burali-Forti, Peano succeeded in reformulating much of existing mathematical theory in accordance with his criteria of rigor and precision, the results of these investigations appearing in the journal *Rivista di Matematica* (later also *Revue de mathématiques* and *Revista de mathematica*) from 1891 to 1906 and in Peano's *Formulaire*

de mathématiques (5 vols., Turin 1892–1908). The detailed coverage of algebra, arithmetic, set theory, geometry, and other branches of mathematics argues convincingly for Peano's approach, but it is questionable whether it vindicates a formalist philosophy of mathematics, since further metamathematical investigation, notably by Thoralf Skolem, has shown that if Peano's axioms are embedded in an axiomatization of set theory, they do not serve to characterize the natural numbers to the exclusion of other progressions. At the same time, it should be noted that Peano was not himself concerned with advancing either a formalist or a logicist philosophy; his approach was determined by a desire for technical improvements in the presentation of mathematics.

Russell and Whitehead. In *The Principles of Mathematics,* published in 1903, Bertrand Russell (born 1872) set out to establish the logicist view that "all pure mathematics deals exclusively with concepts definable in terms of a very small number of fundamental logical concepts, and that all its propositions are deducible from a very small number of logical principles" (2d ed., p. xv) and also to explain "the fundamental concepts which mathematics accepts as indefinable" (*ibid.*). In the *Principles* this program is pursued with minimal recourse to symbolism, the systematic formal presentation being reserved for a proposed second volume. What in fact appeared as the sequel was the classic *Principia Mathematica* (3 vols., Cambridge, 1910–1913), written in collaboration with Alfred North Whitehead. The subject matter of *Principia Mathematica* considerably overlaps that covered by Frege in his *Grundgesetze der Arithmetik,* a work to which the authors acknowledge their chief debt on questions of logical analysis; in some respects, such as the demarcation between logical and metalogical theses, *Principia Mathematica* falls short of the standards of rigor observed in Frege's masterpiece. The symbolism adopted in *Principia Mathematica* derives largely from Peano, and the development of arithmetic and the theory of series is based on the work of Cantor.

We shall concentrate on the most important feature distinguishing *Principia Mathematica* from Frege's work, the attempt to avoid the contradictions which Russell found implicit in the fifth axiom of the *Grundgesetze*. (Details of Russell's logic are given in RUSSELL, BERTRAND, section on logic and mathematics.) This axiom licensed the transition from a concept to its extension and from an extension to the concept, a transition which appears to do no more than give formal expression to a platitude. For instance, the proposition "Stravinsky is a member of the class of composers" appears to be no more than a circumlocution for "Stravinsky is a composer." In general, it would seem reasonable to lay down as a law that x is a member of the class of ϕ's if and only if x is ϕ—in Russellian notation, $x \in \hat{z}(\phi z) . \equiv . \phi x$. But despite its platitudinous appearance, this principle turns out to harbor a contradiction, since corresponding to the concept "is not a member of itself" we have the class of all such things—that is, the class of all classes which are not members of themselves—and if we now ask whether this class is or is not a member of itself, we find that either way a contradiction arises: if it is a member of itself, then it satisfies the defining condition of such members, so it is not a member of itself, and if it is not a member of itself, it belongs to the class of such classes and so is a member of itself.

This contradiction was noted by Russell in 1901, and in subsequent years finding ways to avoid it formed one of his major concerns. His final analysis, incorporated into *Principia Mathematica*, attributed the contradiction, along with a number of analogous paradoxes, to a mode of reasoning involving a vicious circle, a circle which arises when we postulate a collection of objects containing members definable only by means of the collection as a whole. Russell regarded such collections as illegitimate totalities, to be avoided by observing his "vicious-circle" principle, "Whatever involves *all* of a collection must not be one of the collection." Appealing to this principle, Russell claimed that the values of a function cannot contain terms definable only by means of the function, and in place of an indiscriminate application of functions to arbitrary arguments he defined an ascending hierarchy of types, beginning with individuals and progressing through functions of individuals, functions of functions of individuals, and so forth, the only arguments which a function can significantly take being those of the immediately preceding type. In particular, a class cannot significantly be taken as an argument to its defining function, and the derivation of Russell's paradox is accordingly obstructed by ruling out both "$x \epsilon x$" and its negation as ill-formed.

Apart from enabling us to block the derivation of paradoxes, Russell claimed, the theory of types based on the vicious-circle principle has a certain consonance with common sense. However, the principle itself (in the various nonequivalent forms given by Russell) can be challenged on the ground that it rules out circular procedures which are in no way vicious.

If the vicious-circle principle is rejected, it is natural to regard Russell's paradox as no more than a straightforward contradiction, the absurdities resulting from the abstraction schema $(\exists x)(y)(y \epsilon x \equiv \phi(y))$ being no different in kind and requiring no different an explanation from those yielded by $(\exists x)(y)(Fyx \equiv \phi(y))$, where the membership relation is replaced by an arbitrary dyadic predicate. On this view the problem of finding consistent instances of the abstraction schema reduces to the analogous problem for the uninterpreted version, but although such an approach has its merits, it loses sight of an important feature of the system which the vicious-circle principle shapes via the theory of types. That is, the form of theory which the principle determines conforms to a natural conception of classes according to which they are, or at least could be, generated by a step-by-step procedure, the superstructure of classes of classes of classes, etc., resting ultimately on the initial elements of lowest type. On the other hand, although it is natural to conceive of a domain of classes as initially secured by such a procedure, it would seem equally natural to relax this constructivist approach to the extent of allowing the specification of particular classes in the domain to proceed by characterizations in terms of the given totality, provided only that the consequent reflexivity does not embody a contradiction.

Hilbert and formalism. The leading exponent of the formalist philosophy of mathematics was David Hilbert (1862–1943), who pioneered in a development of logic known as proof theory or metamathematics. From the time

of his first papers on the foundations of mathematics, Hilbert stressed the importance of the axiomatic method and its superiority over the genetic approach, by which concepts are extended piecemeal as the need arises. However, once a theory is axiomatized it invites a number of general questions concerning the logical relations holding between its propositions, and Hilbert was soon to consider as central among such questions the problem of establishing consistency, or freedom from contradiction. Hilbert did not himself think that there was any support for the allegations of inconsistency in analysis, as made by Hermann Weyl. Nevertheless, he wished to consolidate once and for all the foundations of mathematics and to give them such clarity that the axiom of choice would be as perspicuous as the simplest arithmetical truth. To this end he needed to devise consistency proofs. He had, in 1899, shown the consistency of Euclidean geometry relative to the theory of real numbers, but proofs of this form do no more than shift the problem of consistency to the system to which the original theory has been reduced. Some new, more direct method seemed to be called for.

Despite his confidence in the consistency of classical mathematics, Hilbert contended that operating in an abstract way with mathematical concepts had proved insecure, and his remedy was to interpret number theory as relating to the observable domain of such signs as 1, 11, 111. Elementary number theory is thereby assured of a concrete interpretation—"$3 > 2$," for example, can be understood as asserting that the concatenation of three strokes extends beyond the concatenation of two strokes. However, the possibility of such an interpretation does not extend to all branches of classical mathematics, for such entities as transfinite cardinals do not allow of representation as sequences of strokes. Hilbert's solution to this difficulty was to treat such numbers as "ideal" elements. Thus, appealing to Kant, he argued that one precondition for the application of logical laws is a domain of extralogical concrete objects, given in actual perception and capable of being exhaustively surveyed. Nowhere in nature is an actual infinity to be found; therefore, whereas for finite numbers a perceptually given basis could be given, transfinite numbers had a place in mathematics only as ideal elements, much like the ideal factors introduced to preserve the simple laws of divisibility for algebraic whole numbers. Such a reduction was, Hilbert claimed, a natural extension of the work of Weierstrass, who had shown that reference to infinity in the context of calculus involved merely a *façon de parler*, replaceable by a theory of limits requiring a potential infinite rather than an actual one. Similarly, the infinities introduced by Cantor, though apparently irreducible, had to be shown to be indispensable, and arguments proceeding via the infinite had to be replaced by finite methods which achieve the same goal. Again, since the transfinite enters with the use of unbounded quantifiers, statements containing these had to be regarded as ideal statements.

With this approach Hilbert hoped to partially vindicate classical mathematics against the attacks of the intuitionists. Complete vindication, however, required a proof of consistency, and the method which Hilbert proposed for obtaining such a proof is closely related to his method for providing elementary number theory with a sound basis.

That is, just as he had considered numbers as sequences of strokes, so he now regarded formulas and proofs as sequences of uninterpreted signs. In this way he provided a concrete subject matter for a proof of consistency, a proof which was to invoke only logical principles whose security and perspicuity are equal to the security and perspicuity of the perceptually given domain on which they are to operate. Thus, the consistency of some given formalization of a branch of mathematics could be unquestionably established if it could be shown by finite combinatorial methods that no manipulation of the symbols which represents a passage from axioms to theorems could result in the derivation of the expression "0 = 1" or of some other concatenation of symbols which, when interpreted, is seen to be an absurdity. The theory itself might contain symbols for transfinite cardinals and other ideal elements, but this would be no obstacle to a consistency proof, since in such a proof we are required only to treat these symbols as perceptually given objects and to show that they will never figure in a formula whose negation is also provable. On the other hand, Hilbert believed that although nonfinitary concepts are allowable within mathematics proper, they are not to be countenanced in the theory of proof which is to ensure consistency.

The formalist school, which included Wilhelm Ackermann, Paul Bernays, and John von Neumann, succeeded in establishing a number of metamathematical results of considerable significance, but without completing Hilbert's original program, for although successively stronger systems of arithmetic were proved consistent, no proof was forthcoming for the full system required by classical number theory. And, indeed, results obtained by Kurt Gödel in 1931 (see GÖDEL'S THEOREM) indicate that no finitary consistency proof is possible, since any proof of consistency must make an appeal to principles which are more general than those provided by the system and accordingly are as much open to question as those principles whose consistency we wish to establish. Attempts were subsequently made to prove consistency by means which were as close to being finitary as possible, notably by Gerhard Gentzen in 1936, but even if "finitary" were thought to apply to the methods used—in this case an application of transfinite induction—it would not follow that classical mathematics had been vindicated against the intuitionists, since to their way of thinking the mere consistency of mathematics would not suffice to confer a clear meaning on the crucial concepts of classical mathematics.

Brouwer and intuitionism. The intuitionist conception of mathematics was developed by the Dutch mathematician Luitzen Egbertus Jan Brouwer (born 1881). According to Brouwer mathematics is not a system of formulas and rules but a fundamental form of human activity, an activity which has its basis in our ability to abstract a conception of "twoness" from successive phases of human experience and to see how this operation may be indefinitely repeated to generate the infinitely proceeding sequence of the natural numbers. In the system of mathematics based on this primordial intuition, language serves merely as an aid to memory and communication and cannot of itself create a new mathematical system; our words and formulas have significance only insofar as they are backed by an essentially languageless activity of the mind. In particular, the wording

of a theorem is meaningful only if it indicates the mental construction of some mathematical entity or shows the impossibility of the entity in question. Brouwer's conception of proof as essentially mental is useful as a corrective to a narrow formalist account which would construe proof as proof in a given formal system, although his psychologism is philosophically questionable—Ludwig Wittgenstein's work has rendered more than doubtful the thesis that language is only an incidental accompaniment to thought, required solely for purposes of memory and communication. What is important in intuitionism is not so much its psychologistic features as its emphasis on constructibility and the form of mathematics which its criterion of meaningfulness determines.

Implicit in classical mathematics is the notion that to know the meaning of a statement it is sufficient to know the conditions under which the statement is true or false, even though these conditions may be such that we could never be in a position to determine whether or not they held. The possibility of a gap between what can be meaningfully stated and what can be recognized either as true or as false is not admitted by the intuitionists. On their theory we can know the meaning of a statement only when we can recognize a proof of it; indeed, to understand a statement simply *is* to know what constitutes a proof or verification of that statement. This emphasis on verification leads to an explanation of the logical constants and of a number of mathematical concepts which results in the rejection or reinterpretation of large parts of classical mathematics. Thus, whereas in classical mathematics the truth-table definition is adequate to giving the meaning of the constant "∨" ("or"), for the intuitionist we can explain the meaning of a statement of the form "$A \lor B$" only by indicating under what conditions we should be warranted in asserting such a statement. These conditions, are that we should be warranted in asserting A or that we should be warranted in asserting B, and it is clear that neither condition may hold, even when A is the negation of B. Assume, for instance, that A is an existentially quantified statement, $\exists x P(x)$, with the quantifier ranging over the natural numbers. To suppose that this holds is to suppose that we can actually construct a number with the required property. On the other hand, what is it to suppose that $\exists x P(x)$ is false? It cannot mean that a case-by-case examination of the numbers will provide a refutation of the statement, since a case-by-case investigation of an infinite totality is not a real possibility—it is a picture to which the classical mathematician is wedded by a mistaken analogy with finite totalities. But if $\sim\exists x P(x)$ is to have a meaning which we can grasp, it can mean only that there is a contradiction in the idea of a number's having the property P. Given this explanation of the sense of the proposition and its negation, we are obliged to abandon Aristotelian logic as no longer trustworthy in this context, for asserting the disjunction $\exists x P(x) \lor \sim\exists x P(x)$ is tantamount to asserting that we either are in a position to construct a suitable number or can show the impossibility of such a construction. We are not entitled to assert a priori that at least one of these possibilities must obtain, but to do so would simply be to commit ourselves to the unfounded belief that all mathematical problems are solvable.

This insistence on the identification of existence with

constructibility can be traced back to Leopold Kronecker (1823–1891), and a precise formulation of principles of intuitionist logic was carried out in 1930 by a pupil of Brouwer's, Arend Heyting (born 1898). Several branches of mathematics have been redeveloped from the intuitionist standpoint, but the reconstructions are often complicated, and in some cases, particularly where set-theoretic notions are involved, there has been a question of outright rejection, rather than reconstruction, of classical mathematics. Thus, impredicative definitions, hierarchies of transfinite numbers, and nonconstructive postulates such as the axiom of choice (and hence the well-ordering theorem), while important classically, are rejected *in toto* by the intuitionists, a rejection which has led many mathematicians to discount the claims of intuitionism without giving sufficient attention to the arguments, admittedly often obscurely expressed, on which they are based.

Post. Besides provoking reactions in the form of rival philosophies of mathematics, the work of Whitehead and Russell stimulated new technical developments. For example, although Whitehead and Russell made free use, in *Principia Mathematica,* of the notions of truth-value and truth-function, they failed to incorporate these notions into a systematic technique for evaluating formulas of the propositional calculus. Such a technique, the method of truth tables, was presented by Emil Post (born 1897) in his dissertation of 1920, published as "Introduction to a General Theory of Elementary Propositions" in *The American Journal of Mathematics* (Vol. 43, 163–185) in 1921, the year in which Wittgenstein independently presented the same method in his *Tractatus Logico-philosophicus.* The method dates back, in fact, to Peirce, but Post considered truth tables in their application not only to classical logic but also to systems in which any number of values are allowed, the primitive connectives of *Principia Mathematica,* "~" and "v", having in these systems the generalized analogues "$\sim_m$" and "v_m", where $\sim_m P$ takes the values $t_2, t_3, \cdots, t_m, t_1$ as P takes the values $t_1, t_2, \cdots, t_m$, and $P v_m Q$ takes that of the two values assigned to P and Q which bears the lesser subscript. Classical two-valued logic is accordingly a particular case of the many-valued logics so constructed. Post provided definitions of consistency and completeness, and for the first time a formulation of the propositional calculus was proved to have these properties, the method of truth tables providing a basis for the proofs.

In his 1920 dissertation Post showed how both truth tables for classical logic and associated postulate sets may be generalized. These postulate sets were treated as uninterpreted formal systems, an approach which Post maintained and extended in the direction of even greater generality in later works, where the derivation of theorems from axioms is represented as the production of strings—that is, finite sequences of symbols—from certain other strings of specified form. Most mathematical theories can be transcribed into the canonical forms admitted by Post, and he was able to show that the rules of any theory so expressed can be reduced to productions of a particularly simple type, a reduction which greatly simplifies investigations into the syntax of formal systems. This approach leads directly to a formulation of recursive enumerability (a set is recursively enumerable if its members can be generated as the values of an effectively calculable function) and thence to one of recursiveness (a set is recursive if both it and its complement are recursively enumerable); Post provided illuminating proofs of results concerning decidability and related topics and introduced and developed a number of important concepts in this field. In 1947 he showed the recursive unsolvability of the word problem for semigroups. That is, he proved that it is impossible to determine whether or not two arbitrarily given strings are equivalent (where A and B are equivalent if B can be obtained from A by starting with A and applying a finite sequence of specified operations prescribing the production of one string from another). This result, published independently and in the same year by A. A. Markov, is an interesting example of the resolution, by techniques of mathematical logic, of an outstanding problem in the field of mathematics proper.

Wittgenstein. The truth-table method for evaluating formulas of the propositional calculus was published independently of Post in the *Tractatus Logico-philosophicus* (reprinted, with translation, London, 1922) of Ludwig Wittgenstein (1889–1951). This Austrian-born philosopher, one of the most original and influential thinkers of the twentieth century, is of importance in the history of logic chiefly for his theories on the nature of logic and mathematics.

The system of logic presented in the *Principia Mathematica* of Whitehead and Russell plays a central role in the *Tractatus.* This system is considered both as a reflection, in symbolic form, of the logical structure of the world and as a system to which all a priori reasoning, including mathematics, can be reduced. Frege and Russell maintained that mathematics was reducible to logic, but Wittgenstein went a step further, reducing predicate logic, and thus also mathematics, to the apparently more restricted system of the propositional calculus. He effected this further reduction by taking a universally quantified formula, "Everything is F," as an abbreviation for an infinite conjunction of atomic formulas, "a_1 is F & a_2 is F & $\cdots$ & $\cdots$"; similarly, "Something is F" represents an infinite disjunction of such propositions. On this view mathematics consists solely of "tautologies"—Wittgenstein's term for formulas which come out true under any assignment of the values *true* and *false* to the component propositions.

With the subsequent development of Wittgenstein's general philosophical position his views on logic and mathematics underwent a corresponding alteration, and in *Remarks on the Foundations of Mathematics* (Oxford, 1956), a posthumously published selection from manuscripts written between 1937 and 1944, the earlier preoccupation with an ideal language gives way to an investigation of logic and mathematics conceived of as belonging to the natural phenomena of language games. A dominant theme of the *Remarks* is the relation between the logical and the empirical—how a proof differs from an experiment, what makes for the unassailability of mathematical propositions—and the position which Wittgenstein adopted is one of extreme conventionalism: the laws of logic and the steps in a proof are not inexorably dictated to us; the necessity to be found in the propositions of logic and mathematics is one we impose on our language, assigning to these propositions a role which conflicts with that of an empirical proposition, which sets them beside the rules of grammar rather than the laws of science. On the other hand, the applicability of mathematical propositions rests on the fulfillment of empirical conditions: propositions expressing the result of numerical computations are usable only to the extent that our actual experience in counting yields consistent results.

The extreme constructivism espoused by Wittgenstein places him closest to intuitionism among philosophies of mathematics. He had no sympathy with attempts to provide a foundation for mathematics and, in fact, was hostile to mathematical logic, describing its invasion of mathematics as a "curse." This hostility is particularly evident in his discussion of certain proofs and concepts, such as Gödel's theorem and Dedekind cuts; indeed, on formal questions Wittgenstein's observations have generally been felt to be less convincing and in some cases simply to embody misunderstandings. His more illuminating remarks bear on topics which relate closely to his general philosophical position.

Ramsey. Frank Plumpton Ramsey (1903–1930), a brilliant Cambridge philosopher and logician, attempted to give a satisfactory account of the foundations of mathematics in accordance with the method of Frege, Russell, and Whitehead, defending their view that mathematics is logic while proposing revisions in the system of *Principia Mathematica* suggested by the work of Wittgenstein.

According to Russell pure mathematics consists of "the class of all propositions of the form '*p* implies *q*' where *p* and *q* are propositions containing one or more variables, the same in the two propositions, and neither *p* nor *q* contains any constants except logical constants" (*The Principles of Mathematics*, p. 3). Ramsey agreed with this definition insofar as it characterizes the generality which is a feature of pure mathematics, but he claimed that it takes no account of an equally important mark of mathematics, its tautological character. The term "tautological" in the relevant sense derives from Wittgenstein, who applied it to formulas of the propositional calculus which come out true no matter what combinations of the values *true* and *false* are assigned to the component propositions. Ramsey extended the term to apply to valid formulas of the predicate calculus. Thus, the formula "$(x) . \phi x : \supset : \phi a$" is tautological, since "ϕa" expresses one of the possibilities which go to make up the possibly infinite conjunction abbreviated by "$(x) . \phi x$". Admittedly we cannot write down the fully expanded versions of quantified formulas, but this inability does not affect the tautological character of truths formulated in the compressed notation. Similarly, Ramsey maintained, the inability of human beings to list the members of an infinite class is no bar to our conceiving of classes whose members could be indicated only in this way and not via the specification of a defining predicate. Indeed, the possibility of such indefinable classes is an essential part of the extensional attitude of modern mathematics, and Ramsey regarded the neglect of this possibility in *Principia Mathematica* as one of the work's three major defects. Thus, as interpreted in the system of *Principia Mathematica* the multiplicative axiom (axiom of choice) is logically doubtful, but on an extensional view of classes it is, according to Ramsey, an evident tautology.

The second major defect which Ramsey found in *Princi-*

pia Mathematica concerns Russell's attempt to overcome the paradoxes, in particular his postulation of the axiom of reducibility. Ramsey accepted the simple theory of types as an unquestionably correct measure for avoiding the logical contradictions, such as Russell's paradox and the Burali-Forti paradox, but he claimed that the contradictions which the hierarchy of orders had been introduced to avoid are of no concern either to logic or to mathematics. These contradictions—for instance, the Richard paradox and Weyl's contradiction concerning the word "heterological"—cannot be stated in logical terms alone but contain some further reference to thought, language, or symbolism. Rejecting Russell's conception of orders, Ramsey put forward a less restrictive theory based on his extensional view of propositional functions. Just as "$(x) . \phi x$" represents an infinite conjunction of atomic propositions "$\phi a . \phi b \cdot \cdot \cdot$" so "$(\phi)\phi a$" expands to "$\phi_1 a . \phi_2 a \cdot \cdot \cdot$" and similarly with disjunctions replacing conjunctions for existential quantifiers. Accordingly, if we start with truth-functions of atomic formulas, then no matter how often or in what respect we generalize upon them, we shall never pass to propositions significantly different from these elementary truth-functions; the only difference will lie in the notation introduced with the quantifiers. There is consequently no need for the axiom of reducibility—which, Ramsey claimed, could anyhow be false—and although the resultant theory countenances definitions of propositions in terms of totalities to which they belong, such definitions are in Ramsey's eyes no more vicious than an identification of a man as the tallest in a group of which he is a member.

The third great defect in *Principia Mathematica* which Ramsey proposed to rectify concerns Russell's definition of identity, according to which it is impossible for two objects to have all their properties in common. Ramsey held that this consequence shows that identity has been wrongly defined, and he advanced a definition of "$x = y$" designed to render the phrase tautological when x and y have the same value and contradictory otherwise.

Carnap. From its beginnings in the works of Frege modern logic was developed primarily as an adjunct to or a basis for mathematics. To Rudolph Carnap (born 1891), a philosopher and logician of the Vienna circle who subsequently immigrated to the United States, we owe the extension of the techniques of modern logic to epistemology, physics, and a variety of other disciplines of importance in the philosophy of science. Carnap's elaborations of formalized languages are pioneering works in constructionalism, and although many philosophers do not sympathize with his approach, or with the logical empiricism of the Vienna circle, interest in his ideas is not confined to adherents of the logical empiricist school. Thus, although Carnap believed that all meaningful sentences belong to the language of science or, if philosophical, are simply part of the syntax of that language, his detailed attempts at formulating philosophically interesting sentences within this framework—for example, sentences in indirect speech, sentences involving modal terms—are of importance to any philosopher concerned with an understanding of the concepts in question. The wide interest of Carnap's investigations is in part due to his adoption of a "principle of tolerance," according to which he was prepared to countenance any forms of expression, despite the philosophical problems surrounding their interpretation, provided only that sufficient logical rules governing their use were given. In his early works of a logical nature, such as *Logische Syntax der Sprache* (Vienna, 1934; translated by Amethe Smeaton as *The Logical Syntax of Language,* London, 1937), Carnap was concerned in the main with syntactical questions—questions concerning derivability and other conceptions involving structural properties of formalized language, as well as the larger problem of expressing the syntax of a language within that language itself. Here his dominant influences were Frege—whose lectures he had attended at Jena—Russell, Hilbert, and Gödel. In later works Carnap, aided by results and ideas developed by Alfred Tarski, has extended his metatheoretic investigations to semantic notions, such as truth and meaning, which previously he did not consider amenable to a formal analysis, and once more his analyses have provided a starting point for much subsequent inquiry.

Gödel. Kurt Gödel (born 1906), a major figure in the history of logic, is best known for his celebrated incompleteness theorem presented in "Über formal unentscheidbare Sätze der Principia Mathematica und verwandter Systeme I" (*Monatshefte für Mathematik und Physik,* Vol. 38, 1931, 173–198) and his associated proof of the impossibility of establishing the consistency of customary formulations of arithmetic by methods formalizable within the systems themselves. In addition to these results (discussed in GÖDEL'S THEOREM), Gödel has made important contributions to several other branches of logic, and prior to his 1931 paper he had already presented the first completeness proof for the first-order functional calculus (in "Die Vollstandigkeit der Axiome des logischen Funktionkalküls," *Monatshefte für Mathematik und Physik,* Vol. 37, 1930, 349–360). Making use of a normal form devised by Thoralf Skolem, Gödel elaborated a proof along lines that were followed by Jacques Herbrand to a similar end in a publication of the same year (*Recherches sur la théorie de la démonstration,* in *Travaux de la Société des Sciences et des Lettres de Varsovie,* Classe III, No. 33, 1930, 33–160), but he went further than Herbrand in his method for showing how any unprovable formula may be falsified.

Intuitionistic as well as classical logic has been one of Gödel's major concerns, and his results in this field are of importance to an understanding of the formalizations of this logic initiated by Arend Heyting in 1930. The intuitionist propositional calculus is naturally thought of as a subsystem of classical logic, obtained by omitting from the latter those theses which are intuitionistically unacceptable. Gödel indicated that this picture could in a sense be reversed, since it is possible to define all two-valued truth-functions by means of the connectives for negation and conjunction, and he was able to show that any formula involving only these connectives is provable within intuitionistic logic if it is provable classically. Gödel showed, further, that even classical number theory, if suitably interpreted, can be thought of as included within intuitionistic number theory. He also proved that the intuitionist propositional calculus has no finite characteristic matrix. That is, although the two-valued truth tables for classical logic serve to verify all and only those theses provable in

this logic, it is impossible, according to Gödel's result, to devise truth tables having any finite number of values which will perform the same service for the intuitionist system.

Two propositions which have been at the center of much investigation and controversy are the axiom of choice and Cantor's generalized continuum hypothesis. It was Gödel who proved that both are consistent with the axioms of set theory provided only that these axioms are themselves consistent. The axiom of choice is a highly nonconstructive axiom licensing the selection of an unspecified element from each of a (possibly infinite) family of sets and the formation of a set comprising just the elements so selected. The generalized continuum hypothesis, which in fact implies the axiom of choice, states that $2^{\aleph_\alpha} = \aleph_{\alpha+1}$; that is, starting with $\aleph_0$, which is the number of the natural numbers, the series of increasingly higher cardinals is successively generated by raising 2 to the power of the preceding aleph. The system Σ of set theory which Gödel used derives from John von Neumann and Paul Bernays. Gödel showed that if it were possible to derive a contradiction from the axiom of choice and the continuum hypothesis in Σ, then the axioms of Σ alone would suffice for the derivation of a contradiction. This result is obtained by constructing a model Δ within Σ itself, where Δ is such that the propositions asserting that the axioms of Σ hold for Δ are demonstrable in Σ and the similar relativizations to Δ of the axiom of choice and the generalized continuum hypothesis are likewise demonstrable in Σ. Paul J. Cohen showed, in 1963, that the negations of these propositions are also consistent with the axioms of set theory. In other words, the axiom of choice and the generalized continuum hypothesis are now known to be independent of the other axioms of set theory.

Löwenheim. A number of significant results concerning the first-order functional or predicate calculus (with identity) date from a paper published in 1915 by Leopold Löwenheim (born 1878), a mathematician of Schröder's school. In this paper, "Über Möglichkeiten im Relativkalkül" (*Mathematische Annalen,* Vol. 76, 1915, 447–470), Löwenheim showed how the problem of deciding the validity of formulas in this calculus reduces to the problem of determining the validity of formulas in which only two-place predicate letters occur. Since (from the point of view of decidability) such formulas are accordingly no less general than arbitrary formulas of the calculus, we know from a later result, by Alonzo Church, that the decision problem for this class is unsolvable. However, Löwenheim was able to provide a decision procedure for a more restricted class of formulas, those in which only one-place predicate letters occur. He also showed that no formula of this restricted class could be valid in every finite domain, yet not be valid in an infinite domain, and his most famous result, known as Löwenheim's theorem, states that any formula of the full calculus which is valid in a denumerable domain is valid in every nonempty domain.

Although it is not difficult to show that if a formula is valid in a given domain, it is valid in any smaller domain, we cannot in general claim that validity in a given domain establishes validity in a larger domain. But as Löwenheim recognized, a formula may be valid in every domain comprising only finitely many of the natural numbers, yet not be valid in the domain of all natural numbers. The significance of Löwenheim's result is thus that validity in a denumerable domain guarantees validity not simply in any smaller domain but in domains which, like that of the real numbers, are of even greater cardinality than the set of natural numbers.

Skolem. The Norwegian mathematician Thoralf Skolem (1887–1963) made extensive contributions to the development of logic, maintaining a steady output of important papers from 1920 until his death. Skolem's first major result was an extension of the above-mentioned theorem of Löwenheim that if a formula of the first-order functional calculus (with identity) is valid in a denumerably infinite domain, it is valid in every nonempty domain and that, equivalently, if such a formula is satisfiable at all, then it is satisfiable in a domain comprising at most a denumerable infinity of elements. In 1920, Skolem generalized this theorem to the case of classes (possibly infinite) of formulas, establishing that if a class of formulas is simultaneously satisfiable, then it is satisfiable in a denumerably infinite domain. Skolem's proof makes use of the axiom of choice and the Skolem normal form of a formula—a type of prenex normal form in which no universal quantifier precedes an existential quantifier—but both these devices were subsequently dropped, and a more constructive version of the proof was given in 1928, a version which led to the developments of Herbrand and to Gödel's completeness proof.

Skolem was led by his work on Löwenheim's theorem to consider set-theoretic concepts as in a certain sense relative. This view derives from the fact that suitable axiomatizations of set theory can be written in the notation of first-order logic, the only symbol foreign to this logic—the epsilon of membership—being replaced by a dyadic predicate letter. The result is a set of formulas which, if consistent, has by Löwenheim's theorem an interpretation within a denumerably infinite domain. On the other hand, within the system of set theory we can establish, by Cantor's theorem, the existence of nondenumerably infinite sets. This apparent conflict between the magnitude of the sets in the axiomatic theory and the more limited domain in which it is modeled is known as the Löwenheim–Skolem paradox. Skolem's way out of this paradox was to suggest that the distinction between denumerable and nondenumerable be taken as relative to an axiom system, a set which is nondenumerable in a given axiomatization perhaps being denumerable in another.

The possibility of an enumeration not available within the original axiom system has led to the description of Löwenheim's theorem as the first of the modern incompleteness theorems, but Skolem's resolution of his paradox does not represent the only possibility. In the first place, it is not clear how the required enumeration could be devised even outside the system in question. To take an analogous case, Cantor's theorem shows that the members of a set containing three elements cannot be paired off with the members of the power set of this set. Since the power set in this case contains eight elements, Cantor's result is in no way surprising, but there is no inclination to say that further mappings might be devised which would yield a one-to-one correspondence between the three-member set and the eight-member set. In the second

place, Löwenheim's theorem does not require us to suppose that the axiomatized theory guarantees an enumeration of the sets, since the reinterpretation of the original symbolism with respect to a denumerable domain results in a revision of the propositions implying or asserting the existence of a nondenumerable infinity of sets. By hypothesis, such propositions go over into propositions which hold in the denumerable model, but although their truth is preserved, their original meaning is altered: they could not without contradiction assert the nondenumerability of the new model.

The set-theoretic relativism which Skolem inferred from the Löwenheim–Skolem theorem led him to doubt whether mathematical concepts could be completely characterized axiomatically, and in 1934 he published a result confirming these doubts by demonstrating that no categorical system of postulates for the natural numbers can be expressed in the notation of quantification theory. Any attempt to give a unique characterization of the natural numbers by means of propositions expressed in this notation is bound to fail, even if a denumerable infinity of such propositions is allowed, since there will always be other systems of entities conforming to the structure so defined. Although this result was uncongenial to those who had hoped to delineate the numbers from a formalist standpoint, the nonstandard models which are yielded by such proofs have become increasingly important, and their application to such topics as independence proofs and mathematical analysis promises to be fruitful.

Skolem also made important contributions to the theory of recursive functions. His work in this field dates from a pioneering paper of 1923, in which he sought to develop arithmetic in a logic-free calculus. Essentially this meant the elimination of quantifiers, an elimination which Skolem proposed to effect by the extensive use of recursive definitions. For instance, instead of defining "$a < b$" as "$(\exists x)(a + x = b)$," we can avoid the use of the existential quantifier by means of the joint stipulation of (i) $-(a < 1)$ and (ii) $a < (b+1) \leftrightarrow (a < b) \vee (a = b)$. In this and subsequent papers Skolem advanced such reductions as part of a finitistic program for securing the basis of arithmetic.

Also important are Skolem's contributions to set theory. The Zermelo–Fraenkel system is commonly presented with his modifications, and in his last years he took up the study of set-theoretic contradictions from the standpoint of systems of many-valued logic.

Herbrand. Despite a tragically short life—he was killed in a mountaineering accident in 1931 at the age of 23—Jacques Herbrand made substantial contributions to the development of mathematical logic, especially to investigations in the metatheory of logic which were the particular concern of Hilbert and his school. The bulk of Herbrand's contributions is to be found in his University of Paris dissertation of 1930, *Recherches sur la théorie de la démonstration* (published in *Travaux de la Société des Sciences et des Lettres de Varsovie*, Classe III, No. 33, 1930, 33–160). This work has much in common with the later "Untersuchungen über das logische Schliessen" of Gerhard Gentzen, but the presentation of proofs and explanations is much less perspicuous than Gentzen's, and even now some aspects of Herbrand's work await further clarification and elaboration. Herbrand's starting point is the system of classical propositional logic presented in Whitehead and Russell's *Principia Mathematica,* but the extension of this to functional calculi of first and higher orders is effected by the addition of further rules in place of axioms. The resultant calculi, in which mathematical theories may be embedded, are investigated from a Hilbertian proof-theoretic viewpoint, with emphasis on such syntactic notions as derivability and to the exclusion of semantic questions which cannot be given a finistic interpretation. New proofs are given of a number of results already known, such as those concerning solvable cases of the decision problem, and for the first time the idea and proof of the deduction theorem is presented for a particular system of logic. That is, Herbrand showed that a necessary and sufficient condition for the derivability of a proposition P in his theory with hypotheses H is that $H \supset P$ should be derivable in the logic without hypotheses.

Herbrand's most powerful result concerns the necessity and sufficiency of certain conditions for the provability of a quantificational schema. He showed, in fact, that such a schema is provable if and only if a quantifier-free tautology of a prescribed form is constructible from it. The proofs of the various theses that go to make up this result are somewhat complicated, but the form of tautology which is associated with a provable formula can be indicated in the following way: First, a given quantificational schema is so transformed that each quantifier has its minimum scope or, alternatively, each has its maximum scope. Taking just the first case, then, all the quantifiers are placed initially and have a scope which extends to the far right of the formula. Suppose we are given a schema in this form—for example, $\exists x \, \exists y \, \forall z \, [Fx \rightarrow (Fy \, \& \, Fz)]$—which we shall call "$A$". The necessary and sufficient condition of A's holding is that it be false that for any x and y there is a value of z for which the matrix of A is false. Accordingly, if x and y both take the value a_1, say, there must be some value a_2 of z which results in the falsity of the matrix if A is to be false; further, if x takes the value a_1 and y takes the value a_2, then for some value a_3 of z the matrix must be false; again, if x takes the value a_2 and y takes the value a_1, the matrix must be false for some value a_4 of z, and so on. But if we find that at least one of the substitution instances of the matrix so generated must be true, we have shown the failure of a necessary condition for the falsity of A. In fact, this is the outcome of the present example, since the disjunction of the cases so far considered, $[Fa_1 \rightarrow (Fa_1 \, \& \, Fa_2)] \vee [Fa_1 \rightarrow (Fa_2 \, \& \, Fa_3)] \vee [Fa_2 \rightarrow (Fa_1 \, \& \, Fa_4)]$, is a tautology—thus, if Fa_2 is true, the first disjunct is true, and if Fa_2 is false, the last disjunct is true.

Herbrand showed how such disjunctions can be constructed from a formula in prenex normal form with the quantifiers occurring in any number and order. He showed, too, that the original formula can be retrieved from such a disjunction by the application of a few simple rules, without use of *modus ponens.* And, indeed, it is clear from the example given that the only rules required for the derivation of the original formula from the tautology are rules allowing for the insertion of quantifiers before the disjuncts and a rule allowing us to erase repetitions of identical disjuncts. The final result allows us to assert that the constructibility of a tautologous disjunction is both a necessary and a sufficient condition for the provability of the associated quantified schema.

In addition to shedding considerable light on the structure of quantification theory, Herbrand's theorem is the source of a number of important metatheoretic results. Löwenheim's theorem is an immediate consequence—accepted by Herbrand only when reinterpreted finitistically—and certain cases of the decision problem allow of simple resolution. Important for Herbrand's aims was the application of his theorem to the question of the consistency of arithmetic, and he was able to show that if we have a model for a set of hypotheses, an interpretation with respect to some domain under which all these hypotheses are true, then no contradiction can arise in the theory deduced from the axioms. Suppose hypotheses H_1, H_2, $\cdots$, H_n give rise to a contradiction while having a true interpretation within the model. Since $H_1 \, \& \, H_2 \, \& \cdots \& \, H_n$ comes out true in the model, the model brings the negation of this conjunction out false, and if a formula is false in some domain, it is not associated with a quantifier-free tautology. If, on the other hand, H_1, H_2, $\cdots$, H_n yield a contradiction, then $\sim(H_1 \, \& \, H_2 \, \& \cdots \& \, H_n)$ is provable and thus is associated with a tautologous disjunction. This form of consistency proof was discussed further by Herbrand in his later article "Sur la Non-contradiction de l'arithmétique" (*Journal für die reine und angewandte Mathematik,* Vol. 166, 1931, 1–8), and the same idea appears in Gentzen's "Untersuchungen über das logische Schliessen."

Church. From the beginning of the twentieth century questions concerning the decidability of logical and mathematical theories have held a special interest for logicians, mathematicians, and philosophers. A number of important concepts and far-reaching results in this field have come from Alonzo Church (born 1903), author of a definitive text on logic and noted writer on the history of logic.

The notion of decidability is not one which a beginner in mathematics could explicitly formulate, but both this and related notions, such as that of effective calculability, have a place in the description of the most elementary mathematical concepts. Often our understanding of a particular numerical predicate is inextricably tied to our ability to determine whether or not an arbitrary number satisfies that predicate, and in many cases terms expressing the result of a calculation or computation can be fully grasped only by one who has the ability to carry out the sorts of computation in question. Thus, with the division of numbers into odd and even there is intimately associated a technique for determining which of these predicates applies to an arbitrary whole number; similarly, a person's grasp of the concepts of sum and product is measured by his ability to calculate sums and products. But although the grasp of concepts and the mastering of techniques may go hand in hand in many cases, the symbolism of arithmetic allows us to formulate propositions whose truth-value may resist determination by any obvious methods of computing or reasoning in general, a situation which frequently arises with the introduction of unrestricted quantification. Consider, for instance, the proposition P, "There is at least one odd perfect number." A perfect number is a number which is equal to the sum of its divisors, itself excluded. Thus, 6 is perfect, being equal to the sum of 1, 2, and 3; so is 28, being equal to the sum of 1, 2, 4, 7, and 14. Like "x is odd," the predicate "x is perfect" is a decidable predicate, in the sense that given any number n, we can, after a finite number of steps, respond with an unambiguous *yes* or *no* to the question "Is n perfect?" But although both of the predicates entering into P are decidable, the infinitude of the positive integers is an obstacle to an immediate determination of the truth-value of P which would make use of the decidability of these predicates together with a case-by-case examination of the integers. Indeed, proposition P, along with Fermat's last theorem, Goldbach's conjecture, and many other propositions of elementary number theory, has as yet been neither proved nor disproved. Accordingly we may well wonder whether it is possible to devise a technique which, when applied to an arbitrary proposition of this class, would enable us to determine the truth or provability of the proposition. Now, for all we know, any one of these outstanding problems may eventually be resolved, but Church showed that no general technique could be devised which would allow us to ascertain in an effective manner the truth or provability of an arbitrary arithmetical proposition. By a direct application of the method of diagonalization (a procedure whereby a hypothesized function is shown to differ from each member of a class of functions of which it must be a member if it is to exist), Church demonstrated not simply that such a technique has proved elusive but that the supposition of its existence involves an absurdity. In this respect arithmetic constrasts with the propositional calculus, but although the propositional calculus does have a decision procedure—the method of truth-tables—Church showed that the first-order functional calculus fares no better than arithmetic, it being impossible to find a method which allows us to recognize as provable or refutable an arbitrary formula of this calculus. It may prove—indeed, in many cases it has already been shown—that fragments of these systems are decidable, but Hilbert's aim of a general technique which would banish ignorance from mathematics appears to be unattainable.

In demonstrating his theorem Church was obliged to provide a formal counterpart of the intuitive notion of effective calculability, and he proposed that this notion be identified with that of recursiveness. The notion of a recursive function (of positive integers) was introduced by Gödel, acting on a suggestion of Herbrand, and was analyzed in detail by S. C. Kleene. A function is said to be (general) recursive (a generalization of the notion of primitive recursive) if, roughly speaking, its value for given arguments can be calculated from a set of equations by means of two rules, one allowing the replacement of variables by numerals, the other allowing the substitution of equals for equals. As Church remarks, the intuitive status of effective calculability rules out any complete justification of his proposal (since known as Church's thesis), but he adduces reasons for regarding the identification as plausible, and the plausibility of his thesis has subsequently been reinforced by the discovery that despite their apparent dissimilarity, various alternative attempts to characterize the intuitive concept have all proved equiva-

lent to that of general recursiveness. Thus, at the time Church put forward his thesis the Church–Kleene notion of λ-definability was already known to provide an equivalent, and Turing's "computability," Post's "1-definability" and "binormality," and Markov's "computability" provide alternatives defined with respect to machines and combinatorial operations. It should be mentioned, however, that Church's thesis has not met with universal support; a summary and criticism of a number of objections can be found in Elliot Mendelson's "On Some Recent Criticism of Church's Thesis" (in *Notre Dame Journal of Formal Logic*, Vol. 4, 1963, 201–205).

Gentzen. The first systematic formulations of the propositional and predicate calculi were presented axiomatically, on the analogy of certain branches of mathematics. In 1934, Gerhard Gentzen (1909–1945), a logician of Hilbert's school, published a formalization of logical principles more in accordance with the way in which these principles are customarily applied. (A similar approach was developed independently by S. Jaśkowski; see below, section on Polish logicians.) In illustrating his technique Gentzen considered how we might establish as valid the schema $(X \vee (Y \& Z)) \supset (X \vee Y) \& (X \vee Z)$. Assuming that the antecedent holds, either X is true, or $Y \& Z$ is true. In the former case we can pass to each of $X \vee Y$ and $X \vee Z$ and hence to their joint assertion. Assuming now $Y \& Z$, we may infer Y, whence $X \vee Y$, and likewise Z, whence $X \vee Z$. In this case the conjunction is once more derivable. Since it is derivable from each disjunct of the original assumption, we may assert the implication unconditionally.

In this simple form of argument the justification of the schema has been broken down into a series of uncomplicated steps, each involving either the introduction or the elimination of a logical connective. Extracting the rules which were applied and supplementing them with similar rules governing the use of the other connectives, we arrive at a system of "natural" deduction—either *NJ* (intuitionist logic) or *NK* (classical logic). Gentzen considered the former more natural than the latter, but whichever we opt for, it appears that the resultant codification of logical principles is more natural, on at least two counts, than a codification presented in axiomatic fashion. In the first place, we avoid the devious moves which may be necessary to establish a logical principle from an axiomatic basis and follow more closely a pattern of reasoning which we should intuitively adopt. In the second place, the conception of logic as a system of axioms and theorems adjoined to some given subject matter appears inappropriate, since, in their application to, say, a branch of mathematics, principles of logic function not as true statements forming part of the theory in question but as rules of inference allowing us to establish relations of consequence between propositions of the theory.

In addition to the systems *NJ* and *NK*, Gentzen devised related formalizations of logic, the *L*-systems, in which derivable formulas are shown to possess a particularly direct form of proof. These systems contain the "cut" rule, a generalized form of *modus ponens* which, like *modus ponens*, has the disadvantage that we cannot work back from a schema to premises from which it could have been derived. However, although the cut rule is crucial in showing the equivalence of the *L*-systems with the earlier *N*-systems, Gentzen showed that the cut rule can be eliminated from any proof in the *L*-systems. This powerful metatheorem simplifies the reconstruction of proofs of valid formulas, yielding a decision procedure for the propositional fragments of *LJ* and *LK* and greatly facilitating the search for proofs in the full calculi. Gentzen further applied his *Hauptsatz* to proofs of consistency; in particular, he showed one formalization of arithmetic to be noncontradictory. The formalization in question does not contain a schema of unrestricted induction, but in later works Gentzen remedied this defect, overcoming the obstacle to such proofs presented by Gödel's results by making use of a principle of transfinite induction which cannot be reduced to ordinary induction within the system. It is a matter of controversy whether such a proof represents the attainment of one of Hilbert's goals, a finitary consistency proof for classical number theory.

Quine. Willard Van Orman Quine (born 1908), author of numerous essays and several books distinguished by their elegance of style and of logical technique, has made important contributions to the development of set theory. According to naive set theory there corresponds to any predicate ϕ a class containing just those objects x for which ϕ holds—in symbols, $(\exists x)(y)(y \epsilon x \equiv \phi)$, with the proviso that x does not occur free in ϕ. This proviso is necessary in order to block the immediate contradiction obtained by taking ϕ as "$y \notin x$", but the schema, known as the axiom schema of abstraction, still allows the derivation of inconsistencies. The most notable consequence is that there is a set x such that $x \epsilon x$ if and only if $x \notin x$, which is Russell's paradox. To avoid this contradiction Russell introduced the simple theory of types, according to which "$x \epsilon y$" is accounted as meaningful only if "y" is of a type one higher than "x". The substitutions yielding "$x \epsilon x \equiv x \notin x$" are accordingly illegitimate, but although contradictions are avoided in this way, the system has a number of disadvantages. For instance, it allows an infinite series of null classes corresponding to the infinitely many distinct types, and this results in an equal duplication of the natural numbers.

In "New Foundations of Mathematical Logic" (*American Mathematical Monthly*, Vol. 44, 1937, 70–80), Quine put forward a system which preserves the spirit but not the complexities of the theory of types. The conception of a hierarchy proceeding through individuals, classes of individuals, and so on is retained but is required only when particular cases of ϕ in the abstraction schema are considered. More precisely, Quine calls a formula stratified if it is possible to substitute numerals for the variables in such a way that "ϵ" occurs only in contexts of the form "$n \epsilon n+1$". Abstraction is accepted with the condition that ϕ be stratified, but unstratified formulas may enter into the system via other routes. The resultant theory, known as *NF*, avoids the reduplications of Russell's system while having considerable power to generate sets—for instance, no additional axiom of infinity is needed. On the other hand, the theory is not without its drawbacks; in particular, mathematical induction of unstratified conditions, often necessary for arithmetic, is not generally provided for.

In a later work, *Mathematical Logic* (New York, 1940;

2d ed., Cambridge, Mass., 1953), Quine presented a system superior in this and other respects. (His original system, in fact, allowed the derivation of the Burali-Forti paradox, as J. B. Rosser showed in 1942. A revised version, offered in 1951, contains a modification suggested by Hao Wang.) In this system, *ML*, the class-existence axiom of *NF* is replaced by the schema $(\exists x)(y) [y \epsilon x \equiv (\exists z)(y \epsilon z . \phi)]$, provided ϕ does not contain x. The condition $(\exists z)(y \epsilon z)$, reminiscent of von Neumann's approach, restricts membership here to elements—that is, entities for which membership in some class is assured. Thus, Quine provides for the existence of the class of all elements that satisfy any condition ϕ, stratified or not. Stratification still enters into *ML*, since there is a rule allowing as elements in *ML* all classes existing for *NF*.

Although *ML* appears to be more liberal in its classes than *NF*, Wang has shown that it is consistent if *NF* is. The relations between these and other systems of set theory are traced in Quine's recent *Set Theory and Its Logic* (Cambridge, Mass., 1963).

Schönfinkel and Curry. In a paper published in 1913, H. M. Sheffer observed that all the connectives of sentential logic could be defined in terms of one primitive, written "$|$", where "$p|q$" is interpreted as the conjunction or, alternatively, the disjunction of $\sim p$ and $\sim q$. This reduction was carried a stage further by Moses Schönfinkel, who in 1924 proposed an extension of this operator to the expression of quantifiers, a step which he achieved by affixing a variable to the stroke function and defining "$Fx|^x Gx$" as "$(x)\sim(Fx . Gx)$". The existential quantifier can now be introduced by further use of this operator, and its application to formulas without free "x" is preserved by allowing vacuous occurrences of the variable in the operator. This reduction is of some interest, but Schönfinkel went on in the same paper to propose a more far-reaching simplification of logical symbolism, a simplification which showed how, at least in the object language, even variables could be dispensed with. This step marks the beginning of a new branch of logical research, combinatory logic (see LOGIC, COMBINATORY), which, by elucidating the processes of substitution and the concept of a function, has proved to be an important instrument in foundational investigations.

Schönfinkel's method of eliminating variables requires an extension of the notion of a function. Ordinarily such operations as multiplication and addition are thought of as two-place functions of the general form $F(x,y)$. Schönfinkel's procedure was to regroup the terms of such a formula so that it comes to be regarded as representing the application of a one-place function Fx to the single argument y. So envisaged, multiplication, for instance, would be expressed as the application of the one-place function "x times . . ." to the argument y, not as the application to x and y of the two-place function ". . . times . . .". Similarly, a function $Gxyz$ is treated as signifying the successive application of one-place functions: Gx to y, and the result of this to z. Schönfinkel then introduced a number of equations defining certain fundamental functions: $Ix = x$, $Cxy = x$, $Tfxy = fyx$, $Zfgx = f(gx)$, $Sfgx = fx(gx)$. Although variables still figure at this stage, the relations between these functions can be arrived at by using as arguments the functions themselves, and in this way the variables are reduced in number and finally disappear. For example, we have $Ix = x = Cxy$, and since y is arbitrary, we can give it the value Cx while preserving the identity. This step yields $Ix = Cx(Cx)$, and by using the definition of S we may derive $Ix = SCCx$, an equation containing only the inessential final variable, which may now be dropped. The resultant equation, $I = SCC$, demonstrates the possibility of defining I in terms of S and C, and Schönfinkel showed how the operators T and Z may also be defined in terms of these two. If we now define $Fx \,|^x Gx$ as Ufg, we can write any logical formula using only C, S, and U.

The further development of combinatory logic is due in large part to Haskell B. Curry (born 1900), who in 1930 systematized the theory sketched by Schönfinkel, though with a slightly different set of primitive operators as the basis. Curry's subsequent writings, complemented by investigations of S. C. Kleene and J. B. Rosser, have furnished a detailed and extended application of combinatory concepts, and Church's calculus of λ-conversion, based on an operation of functional abstraction, provides an independent development of a closely related theory.

BEDE RUNDLE

Polish logicians. One country in which logic particularly flourished between the two world wars was Poland. The study of logic was pursued in a number of centers, led mainly by a group who had been pupils of Kazimierz Twardowski and Jan Łukasiewicz at Lvov. At Warsaw there were Łukasiewicz himself, Stanisław Leśniewski, and Tadeusz Kotarbiński; remaining at Lvov was Kazimierz Ajdukiewicz. A new generation grew up under this group, its most distinguished member being Alfred Tarski. Others were A. Lindenbaum, Mordchaj Wajsberg, S. Jaśkowski, and Bolesław Sobociński. At Cracow, working somewhat independently of the rest, were J. Sleszynski and, later, Leon Chwistek, who simplified Russell's theory of types and was the first to use the device (later modified by Łukasiewicz) of writing logical operators before instead of between their arguments, thereby dispensing with parentheses. Many Polish mathematicians, such as Wacław Sierpiński and Kazimierz Kuratowski, were interested in the logical foundations of their subject; Kuratowski is best known for his definition of relations as classes.

After World War II the Poles' vigorous pursuit of logic continued, both in Poland and elsewhere. Apart from Tarski, who immigrated to America in the 1930s, the major Polish logicians now working outside the country are Sobociński, Czesław Lejewski, I. M. Bocheński, Władysław Bednarowski, and Henry Hiż. Of these the first two are the most notable; former students of Leśniewski, they devote much of their energy to expounding his work and carrying it forward. Lejewski has devised a set of diagrams, analogous to Euler's five for Aristotelian terms, for exhibiting the possible extensional relations between the "names" used in Leśniewski's ontology. He has also produced a new solution to the old problem of defining negation in terms of implication by enlarging the concept of definition to cover a particular type of implicational axiom. Sobociński, in

addition to his Leśniewskian productions, has worked on the foundations of mathematics and on the axiomatics of modal and many-valued systems.

Within Poland the most outstanding contemporary logician is Andrzej Mostowski. Mostowski's interests lie in the philosophy of mathematics, where he has worked on undecidable systems and on the metamathematical properties of many-valued predicate calculi. Younger logicians in Poland include A. Grzegorczyk (recursive function theory), H. Greniewski (the logic behind computer design, for which he introduced functions representing time delay), R. Suszko, J. Łos, H. Rasiowa, and K. Szaniawski. Influential figures from the prewar period who continued to work in Poland include Kotarbiński, Ajdukiewicz, and Jaśkowski. A lively school—including Ludwik Borkowski, Witold Pogorzelski, and Tadeusz Kubiński—has grown up around Jerzy Słupecki and Maria Kokoszyńska at Wrocław, in Silesia.

The range of topics dealt with by these writers and their colleagues is very wide, and details are best gathered from other articles (see CORRESPONDENCE THEORY OF TRUTH; LOGIC, MANY-VALUED; LOGIC, TRADITIONAL; NEGATION), but we may demonstrate here how the thought of such men as Leśniewski and Tarski has been carried further by others, both within Poland and elsewhere.

The boundary between logic and linguistics has been illuminated by studies stimulated by Leśniewski's theory of "semantic categories." Ajdukiewicz, who preferred to call these categories "syntactical" (they are, roughly, parts of speech), devised for them a system of indices which has been used by many writers—Suszko, for example—as the basis of a mathematical treatment of language structures. Taking names, of index n, and sentences, of index s, as basic, we may represent an expression which forms a sentence from a name, that is, an intransitive verb, as s/n; one forming a sentence from two names, that is, a transitive verb, as s/nn; one forming a sentence from two sentences, that is, a conjunction, as s/ss; and so on.

But what, in all this, is to be understood by "name"? Lejewski, in a recent investigation into this question, listed four major possibilities. Leśniewski made no syntactical distinction between common and proper nouns, and "names" in his sense might be applicable to one object, to several, or to none. Aristotelian "terms" are in general common nouns, excluding (at least for syllogistic purposes) those without application. Fregean and Russellian individual names are syntactically distinct from common nouns (which are absorbed into verbs) and have meaning only if they have application (to exactly one object). Lejewski explored a fourth possibility, perhaps the closest of all to common speech, namely the use of singular names which may apply to one object or to none, common nouns being absorbed into verbs as in the case just preceding. One of the main differences between this last alternative and the Russellian is that the law of identity "$x = x$" has exceptions, namely where x has no application. Alternatively we may say that the system requires two relations of identity, the "strong" one just mentioned and a weaker one in which the above law holds but "x is identical with y" is automatically true if both x and y are nonexistent.

A device, rather than a theory, of Leśniewski's that has recently been revived (with a few modifications) by Słupecki and Borkowski is that of "suppositional proof." In effect Leśniewski proved an implication by just laying down all the conjunctive parts of the antecedent and then deducing a long or short conjunction in which the later conjuncts are proved from what was laid down or proved earlier, and the final consequent is the consequent of the implication to be proved. Suppose, for example, that we have a rule (R1) entitling us to pass from "If X then Y" and "If Y then Z" to "If X then Z," and we wish to prove the following theorem:

If (if p then q) and (if q then r) and (if r then s) then (if p then s).

We may set out the proof thus:

> If (1) if p then q and
> (2) if q then r and
> (3) if r then s
> then (4) if p then r (from 1 and 2 by R1)
> and (5) if p then s (from 4 and 3 by R1).

The underlying principle here is that if (5) is deducible from (1), (2), and (3) and so is true given these, then "If (1), (2), and (3), then (5)" is true unconditionally. The same principle is reflected in a different way in the method of suppositional proof devised by Jaśkowski in the late 1920s and published in 1934. In this method of proof we list the suppositions from which we start, and deduce consequences from them by given rules, noting on which suppositions each consequence depends. We then "discharge" these suppositions one by one by a "rule of conditionalization," according to which if a consequence C follows from a supposition S and perhaps some others and so is true given all these, then "If S then C" can be laid down as true given only the others. For example (using *modus ponens* to get 3 from 1 and 2):

> (1) p (supposition).
> (2) If p then q (supposition).
> ∴ (3) q (given 1 and 2).
> ∴ (4) If if-p-then-q then q (given 1; 2 discharged).
> ∴ (5) If p then if if-p-then-q then q (true unconditionally; 1 discharged).

Logical laws are propositions which we may assert without assuming anything at all, like (5) above.

Jaśkowski developed his method of "natural deduction" independently of Gentzen, whose very similar methods are better known in the West. His rule of conditionalization has affinities with the "deduction theorem" that was suggested to Tarski by an early paper of Ajdukiewicz. In the 1920s, Tarski formalized metalogic by producing a calculus in which the objects reasoned about are entire deductive systems, considered as sets of sentences closed under the relation of logical consequence—that is, as infinite sets of sentences such that all the logical consequences of a given set are members of the set. This involved laying out axioms characterizing the relation of logical consequence, such as the axioms stating that any set of sentences X is included in the set of X's consequences (from which it follows that any sentence is a consequence of itself and of any set in which it is itself comprised) and that the consequences of the consequences of a set of sentences X are included in X's consequences. Principles like these are independent of the logical structure of the sentences in X. Other principles may characterize, in terms of logical consequence, particular sentential structures. An example is the axiom that a conditional sentence with y as antecedent and z as consequent is a consequence of a set of sentences X if and only if the plain z is a consequence of the set consisting of X together with the sentence y; roughly, we may conclude to "If y then z" from X if and only if we may conclude to the plain z from X together with y. Given such axioms for the relation of consequence, a logical truth may be defined as a consequence of the empty set of sentences. This, as Tarski showed, is equivalent to defining a logical truth as a sentence which is a logical consequence of any arbitrarily chosen set of sentences whatever. Compare Jaśkowski's definition of a logical truth as a sentence which depends on no underlying suppositions.

In 1928, Tarski produced simple characterizations, in the above sense, of implication and negation, which yielded as logical truths all theses of the classical propositional calculus. In 1960, Słupecki and Pogorzelski produced similar characterizations of implication, conjunction, alternation, and negation which yielded the intuitionist calculus of Heyting and characterizations of strict implication, conjunction, and negation which yielded the Lewis modal calculus S5 (see LOGIC, MODAL). These writers and others have also put Tarski's "calculus of systems" to its original use of proving very general theorems in metalogic.

Another member of the Wrocław school, Borkowski, has followed up a quite different suggestion of Tarski's, namely that numbers are primarily elements in the "numerical quantifiers" which introduce such sentences as "For exactly 53 x's, x is an A" (that is, there are exactly 53 A's). These additions to the ordinary quantifiers "For some . . ." and "For all . . ." may be matched, Borkowski pointed out, by others of a nonnumerical kind, including those which are followed, after their associated variable, not by one but by two or more open sentences. For example, we may regard "For any x, if x is A then x is B" as constructed by the quantifier "For any . . . , if" out of the variable x and the open sentences "x is A" and "x is B." Borkowski constructed many interesting functions which may be satisfied by quantifiers thus generalized. Of Tarski's numerical quantifiers Borkowski observed that we may regard numerals themselves as such quantifiers and can thereby simplify much of Russell's type theory.

Borkowski's work on quantifiers, however, involves radical modifications in the standard Leśniewskian theory of semantic categories, and the consequences of these have yet to be worked out. Leśniewski used only one quantifier, the universal (represented by square brackets around the variables it binds), and placed it outside all semantic categories (like a medieval "transcendental"); he also regarded variables as having the same category as the corresponding constants. But Borkowski categorizes quantifiers as forming sentences from a variable of any category followed by a specified number of sentences, the category of a quantifier varying with the number of sentences that follow but not with the category of the bound variable. This cuts right across Leśniewski's principles of classification; it would be difficult, for example, to give a Borkowskian quantifier an Ajdukiewicz index.

A relative consistency proof of Borkowski's version of arithmetic has been provided by Kubiński, who constructed a model for it in a language for axiomatic set theory that has room for infinitely long sentences. Tarski has recently investigated some of the metalinguistic properties of languages of this sort.

Polish logic has never been tied to a single philosophical school. The majority of its practitioners have been, in a broad sense, positivistic (Kotarbiński, for example, has used Leśniewski's theory of semantic categories to formulate a variety of positivism which he calls "reism"). However, there is also a notable sprinkling of Neo-Thomists, some of whom have attempted to bring up to date the logic used in theology, and both Thomists and others have done valuable work in the history of logic, correcting the oversharp contrast that is often drawn between ancient and medieval logic on the one hand and modern logic on the other. Particularly notable are Łukasiewicz's rehabilitation of the logic of the Stoics and systematization of Aristotle's syllogistic, K. Michalski's work on references to three-valued logic in William of Ockham, Bocheński's work on the logic of Theophrastus, and, more recently, Lejewski's work on propositions κατὰ προσληψιν in Aristotle and other ancient writers.

A. N. Prior

History of Logic

(In general, texts by and studies on individual logicians are listed only if they do not appear in the bibliographies to the separate articles on these people. Most works cited in the body of this article are not repeated below.)

GENERAL WORKS

Bocheński, I. M., *Formale Logik*. Freiburg and Munich, 1956. Translated and edited by Ivo Thomas as *History of Formal Logic*. Notre Dame, Ind., 1961. Contains extensive bibliographies.

Enriques, Federigo, *L'Évolution de la logique*. Paris, 1926.

Kneale, William C., and Kneale, Martha, *The Development of Logic*. Oxford, 1962.

Kotarbiński, Tadeusz, *Wykłady z Dziejów Logiki* ("Lectures on the History of Logic"). Lodz, 1957. Translated into French as *Leçons sur l'histoire de la logique*. Paris, 1964.

Prantl, Carl, *Geschichte der Logik im Abendlande*, 4 vols. Leipzig, 1855–1870; reprinted (3 vols.), Graz, 1955. Covers the history up to 1600, with numerous quotations from the sources.

Scholz, Heinrich, *Abriss der Geschichte der Logik*. Berlin, 1931. Translated by K. F. Leidecker as *Concise History of Logic*. New York, 1961.

WORKS ON POST-MEDIEVAL AND LATER DEVELOPMENTS

Jørgensen, Jørgen, *A Treatise of Formal Logic*, Vol. I, *Historical Development*. Copenhagen and London, 1931.

Jourdain, P. E. B., "The Development of the Theories of Mathematical Logic and the Principles of Mathematics." *Quarterly Journal of Pure and Applied Mathematics*, Vol. 41 (1910), 324–352; Vol. 43 (1912), 219–314; Vol. 44 (1913), 113–128.

Lewis, C. I., *A Survey of Symbolic Logic*. Berkeley, Calif., 1918; reprinted, New York, 1960.

Nidditch, P. H., *The Development of Mathematical Logic*. London, 1962.

Prior, A. N., *Formal Logic*, 2d ed. Oxford, 1962.

Shearman, A. T., *Development of Symbolic Logic*. London, 1906.

Ancient Logic

TEXTS

Philodemus, *On Methods of Inference*, P. De Lacy and E. A. De Lacy, eds. Lancaster, Pa., 1941.

Stoicorum Veterum Fragmenta, H. von Arnim, ed., 4 vols. Leipzig, 1903–1924.

SECONDARY STUDIES

Becker, A., *Die Aristotelische Theorie der Möglichkeitsschlüsse*. Berlin, 1933.

Bocheński, I. M., *La Logique de Théophraste*. Fribourg, Switzerland, 1947.

Bocheński, I. M., *Ancient Formal Logic*. Amsterdam, 1951.

Łukasiewicz, Jan, "Zur Geschichte der Aussagenlogik." *Erkenntnis*, Vol. 5 (1935), 111–131.

Łukasiewicz, Jan, *Aristotle's Syllogistic*, 2d enl. ed. Oxford, 1957.

Mates, Benson, *The Logic of the Stoa*. Berkeley and Los Angeles, 1953; 2d ed. (titled *Stoic Logic*), 1961.

Patzig, Günther, *Die Aristotelische Syllogistik*. Göttingen, 1959; 2d ed., 1963.

Indian Logic

The chief historian of Indian logic is S. C. Vidyābhūṣaṇa, whose main work is *A History of Indian Logic* (Calcutta, 1921). Recent articles can be found in the *Wiener Zeitschrift für die Kunde Sud-und Ostasiens und Archiv für indische Philosophie;* see especially those by Erich Frauwallner and Gerhard Oberhammer. The following are general works and some items not listed in Bocheński, *Formale Logik,* above.

Biardeau, Madeleine, "La Définition dans la pensée indienne." *Journal asiatique*, Vol. 245 (1957), 371–384.

Biardeau, Madeleine, "Le Rôle de l'exemple dans l'inférence indienne." *Journal asiatique*, Vol. 245 (1957), 233–240.

Brough, John, "Theories of General Linguistics in the Sanskrit Grammarians." *Transactions of the Philological Society* (1951), 27–46.

Brough, John, "Some Indian Theories of Meaning." *Transactions of the Philological Society* (1953), 161–176.

Edgerton, Franklin, "Some Linguistic Notes on the Mīmāṃsā System." *Language*, Vol. 4 (1928), 171–177.

Faddegon, Barend, *The Vaiçeṣika System, Described With the Help of the Most Ancient Texts*. Amsterdam, 1918.

Foucher, Alfred, *Le Compendium des topiques*. Paris, 1949.

Ingalls, D. H. H., *Materials for the Study of the Navya-nyāya Logic*. Cambridge, Mass., 1951.

Kunjunni Raja, K., *Indian Theories of Meaning*. Madras, 1963.

Kuppuswami Sastri, S., *A Primer of Indian Logic*, 3d ed. Madras, 1963.

Nakamura, Hajime, "Buddhist Logic Expounded by Means of Symbolic Logic." *Journal of Indian and Buddhist Studies*, Vol. 7 (1958), 375–395.

Potter, K. H., *The Padārthatattvanirūpaṇam of Raghunātha Śiromaṇi*. Cambridge, Mass., 1957. Text and translation.

Robinson, R. H., "Some Logical Aspects of Nāgārjuna's System." *Philosophy East and West*, Vol. 4 (1957), 291–308.

Ruegg, D. S., *Contributions à l'histoire de la philosophie linguistique indienne*. Paris, 1951.

Sen, S., *A Study of Mathurānātha's Tattva-cintāmaṇi-rahasya*. Wageningen, Netherlands, 1924.

Sreekrishna Sarma, E. R., ed. and trans., *Maṇikaṇa: A Navya-nyāya Manual*. Adyar, India, 1960. Reviewed in *Journal of the American Oriental Society*, Vol. 82 (1962), 237–241.

Staal, J. F., "Correlations Between Language and Logic in Indian Thought." *Bulletin of the School of Oriental and African Studies*, Vol. 23 (1960), 109–122.

Staal, J. F., "Formal Structures in Indian Logic," in B. H. Kazemier and D. Vuysje, eds., *The Concept and the Role of the Model in Mathematics and Natural and Social Sciences*. Dordrecht, Netherlands, 1961. Pp. 279–286.

Staal, J. F., "Means of Formalisation in Indian and Western Logic," in *Proceedings of the XIIth International Congress of Philosophy X.* Florence, 1960. Pp. 221–227.

Staal, J. F., "The Theory of Definition in Indian Logic." *Journal of the American Oriental Society,* Vol. 81 (1961), 122–126.

Staal, J. F., "Contraposition in Indian Logic," in Ernest Nagel, Patrick Suppes, and Alfred Tarski, eds., *Logic, Methodology, and Philosophy of Science: Proceedings of the 1960 International Congress.* Palo Alto, Calif., 1962. Pp. 634–649.

Staal, J. F., "Negation and the Law of Contradiction in Indian Thought: A Comparative Study." *Bulletin of the School of Oriental and African Studies,* Vol. 25 (1962), 52–71.

Stcherbatsky, Thomas, *Buddhist Logic,* 2 vols. Leningrad, 1930–1932.

Chinese Logic

For critical commentary, see Vol. I of Fung Yu-lan, *A History of Chinese Philosophy,* translated by Derk Bodde (Princeton, 1952). There has been no complete translation of the Moist documents since a largely obsolete version by Alfred Forke, *Mê Ti des Sozialethikers und seiner Schüler philosophische Werke* (Berlin, 1922), Chs. 40–45. Nearly the complete *Hsiao-ch'ü* is translated in D. C. Lau, "Some Logical Problems in Ancient China," *PAS,* N.S. Vol. 53 (1952–1953), 189–204. A complete translation is in A. C. Graham, "The Logic of the Mohist *Hsiao-ch'ü*," in *T'oung Pao,* Vol. 51 (1964), 1–54. "The Correct Use of Names" is included in *Hsün Tzu, Basic Writings,* translated by Burton Watson (New York, 1963), pp. 139–156.

Arabic Logic

A complete bibliography of Arabic logic can be found in Nicholas Rescher, *The Development of Arabic Logic* (Pittsburgh, 1964). On the transmission of Greek logic to the Arabs, see Max Meyerhof, "Von Alexandrien nach Baghdad," in *Sitzungsberichte der Preussischen Akademie der Wissenschaften,* Philosophisch-historische Klasse, Vol. 23 (1930), 389–429. The conflict between logic and Islamic religion is detailed in Ignaz Goldziher, "Stellung der alten islamischen Orthodoxie zu den antiken Wissenschaften," in *Abhandlungen der Königlichen Preussischen Akademie der Wissenschaften,* Philosophisch-historische Klasse, Jahrgang 1915 (Berlin, 1916). For the Arabs' familiarity with Aristotle's logical works, see R. Walzer, "Arisṭū" ("Aristotle"), in *Encyclopedia of Islam* (London, 1960), Vol. I; and Ibrahim Madkour, *L'Organon d'Aristote dans le monde arabe* (Paris, 1934).

Some representative Arabic logical texts accessible in European languages are D. M. Dunlop, translations of several logical *opuscula* of al-Fārābī in *Islamic Quarterly,* Vol. 2 (1955)–Vol. 5 (1959); Nicholas Rescher, *Al-Fārābī's Short Commentary on Aristotle's "Prior Analytics"* (Pittsburgh, 1963); A. M. Goichon, *Avicenne: Livre de directives et remarques* (Paris, 1951); Mohammad Achena and Henri Massé, *Avicenne: Le Livre de science,* Vol. I (Paris, 1955); *Aristotelis Opera cum Averrois Commentariis* (Venice, 1550 and later; 1562–1574 ed. reprinted photographically, Frankfurt, 1962).

Substantive study of the contributions of Arabic logicians has only begun. In addition to Prantl, *Geschichte der Logik im Abendlande,* Vol. II, above, consult T. J. de Boer, "Mantik," in *Encyclopedia of Islam,* 1st ed.; and Nicholas Rescher, *Studies in the History of Arabic Logic* (Pittsburgh, 1963).

Medieval Logic

TEXTS

Abelard, Peter, *Dialectica,* L. M. de Rijk, ed. Assen, Netherlands, 1956.

Adam of Balsham, *Adam Balsamiensis Parvipontani Ars Disserendi,* L. Minio-Paluello, ed. Rome, 1956.

Burley, Walter, *De Puritate Artis Logicae Tractatus Longior,* Philotheus Boehner, ed. St. Bonaventure, N.Y., 1955. With a rev. ed. of the *Tractatus Brevior.*

Consequentiae Strodi cum Commento Alexandri Sermonetae.

Venice, 1517. Contains the *Consequentiae* and *Obligationes* of Ralph Strode, the *Consequentiae* of Richard Ferabrich, and the *Consequentiae* of William Heytesbury, with later commentaries on these works.

Heytesbury, William, *Tractatus . . . de Sensu Composito et Diviso. Regulae Solvendi Sophismata . . . .* Venice, 1494.

Peter of Spain, *Petri Hispani Summulae Logicales,* I. M. Bocheński, ed. Turin, 1947.

William of Ockham, *Summa Logicae,* Philotheus Boehner, ed. *Pars Prima,* St. Bonaventure, N.Y., 1951; *Pars Secunda et Tertiae Prima,* St. Bonaventure, N.Y., 1954.

William of Sherwood, *Die Introductiones in Logicam des Wilhelm von Shyreswood,* Martin Grabmann, ed. *Sitzungsberichte der Bayerischen Akademie der Wissenschaften, Philosophische Historische Abteilung,* Jahrgang 37, Vol. 10. Munich, 1937.

For a very complete list of editions of medieval works on logic up to 1956, see Bocheński, *Formale Logik,* above.

SECONDARY STUDIES

Boehner, Philotheus, *Medieval Logic.* Manchester and Chicago, 1952.

Matthews, Gareth B., "Ockham's Supposition Theory and Modern Logic." *Philosophical Review,* Vol. 73 (1964), 91–99.

Moody, Ernest A., *The Logic of William of Ockham.* New York and London, 1935.

Moody, Ernest A., *Truth and Consequence in Medieval Logic.* Amsterdam, 1953.

Salamucha, J., "Logika Zdań u Wilhelma Ockhama." *Przegląd Filozoficzny,* Vol. 38 (1935), 208–239. Translated into German by J. Bendiek as "Die Aussagenlogik bei Wilhelm von Ockham." *Franziskanische Studien,* Vol. 32 (1950), 97–134.

Interregnum

Dürr, Karl, "Die Syllogistik des Johannes Hospinianus (1515–1575)." *Synthese,* Vol. 9 (1952), 472–484.

Hamilton, William, "Logic: The Recent English Treatises on That Science" (1833), in *Discussions on Philosophy, Literature, Education and University Reform.* London and Edinburgh, 1852. Pp. 116–174.

Howell, W. S., *Logic and Rhetoric in England, 1500–1700.* Princeton, N.J., 1956.

Ong, W. J., *Ramus, Method, and the Decay of Dialogue.* Cambridge, Mass., 1958.

Risse, Wilhelm, *Die Logik der Neuzeit,* Vol. I (1500–1640). Stuttgart and Bad Cannstatt, 1964.

Thomas, Ivo, "The Setting of Classical Logic." *Notre Dame Scholastic,* Vol. 101 (1960), 16–17.

Thomas, Ivo, "Medieval Aftermath: Oxford Logic and Logicians of the Seventeenth Century," in *Oxford Studies in Honour of Daniel Callus.* Oxford, 1964.

Thomas, Ivo, "The Later History of the Pons Asinorum," in *Contributions to Methodology and Logic in Honor of J. M. Bocheński.* Amsterdam, 1965.

Thomas, Ivo, "The Liar: A New Historical Detail." *Notre Dame Journal of Formal Logic,* Vol. 6 (1965), 201–208.

Precursors of Modern Logic

LEIBNIZ

Baylis, C. A., review of various articles on the identity of indiscernibles. *Journal of Symbolic Logic,* Vol. 21 (1960), 86.

Couturat, Louis, *La Logique de Leibniz d'après des documents inédits.* Paris, 1901; reprinted, Hildesheim, 1961.

Dürr, Karl, *Leibniz' Forschungen im Gebiet der Syllogistik. Leibniz zu seinem 300. Geburtstag.* Berlin, 1949.

Kauppi, Raili, *Über die Leibnizsche Logik mit besonderer Berücksichtigung des Problems der Intension und der Extension.* Helsinki, 1960.

Rescher, Nicholas, "Leibniz's Interpretation of His Logical Calculi." *Journal of Symbolic Logic,* Vol. 19 (1954), 1–13. Reviewed by M. A. E. Dummett in *Journal of Symbolic Logic,* Vol. 21 (1960), 197–199.

EULER

Faris, J. A., "The Gergonne Relations." *Journal of Symbolic Logic,* Vol. 20 (1955), 207–231.

Gardner, Martin, *Logic Machines and Diagrams.* New York, 1958.

Hamilton, William, *Lectures on Logic.* London, 1860.

Hocking, W. E., "Two Extensions of the Use of Graphs in Elementary Logic." *University of California Publications in Philosophy,* Vol. 2, No. 2 (1909), 31–44.

More, Trenchard, "On the Construction of Venn Diagrams." *Journal of Symbolic Logic,* Vol. 24 (1959), 303–304.

Thomas, Ivo, "Eulerian Syllogistic." *Journal of Symbolic Logic,* Vol. 22 (1957), 15–16.

Thomas, Ivo, "Independence of Faris-rejection-axioms." *Notre Dame Journal of Formal Logic,* Vol. 1 (1959), 48–51.

Venn, John, *Symbolic Logic,* 2d ed. London, 1894.

LAMBERT AND PLOUCQUET

Bök, F. A., ed., *Sammlung der Schriften welche den logischen Calcul des Herrn Professor Ploucquet betreffen.* Tübingen, 1773.

Dürr, Karl, "Die Logistik Johann Heinrich Lamberts," in *Festschrift . . . Dr. A. Speiser.* Zurich, 1945.

Venn, John, *Symbolic Logic.*

BOLZANO

Bolzano, Bernard, *Wissenschaftslehre,* 4 vols. Sulzbach, 1837; Leipzig, 1929–1931 (W. Schulz, ed.).

Bolzano, Bernard, *Grundlegung der Logik.* Hamburg, 1964. A useful selection by Friedrich Kambartel from the first two volumes of the *Wissenschaftslehre.*

Bar-Hillel, Yehoshua, "Bolzano's Propositional Logic." *Archiv für mathematische Logik und Grundlagenforschung,* Vol. 1 (1952), 65–98.

Berg, J., *Bolzano's Logic.* Stockholm, 1962.

Scholz, Heinrich, "Die Wissenschaftslehre Bolzanos." *Abhandlungen des Fries'schen Schule,* N.S. Vol. 6 (1937), 399–472.

Modern Logic: The Boolean Period

Appraisals of Hamilton's logic are to be found in John Venn, *Symbolic Logic;* C. I. Lewis, *A Survey of Symbolic Logic;* Jørgen Jørgensen, *A Treatise of Formal Logic,* Vol. I; and A. N. Prior, *Formal Logic.* Hamilton's principles, if not his practice, have found a recent defender in P. T. Geach, *Reference and Generality* (Ithaca, N.Y., 1962); his quantification has been analyzed in some detail by Władysław Bednarowski, "Hamilton's Quantification of the Predicate," in *PAS,* Vol. 56 (1956), 217–240.

Except for *Formal Logic,* all the works by De Morgan cited in the section on him are reprinted in *On the Syllogism, and Other Logical Writings,* Peter Heath, ed. (London, 1965). The best modern accounts of De Morgan are to be found in Lewis, *op. cit.;* Jørgensen, *op. cit.;* and Prior, *op. cit.*

On Boole, see Lewis, *op. cit.;* Jørgensen, *op. cit.;* and William C. Kneale and Martha Kneale, *The Development of Logic.* The best earlier expositions are by P. E. B. Jourdain, in "The Development of the Theories of Mathematical Logic and the Principles of Mathematics"; Venn, *op. cit.;* and Alexander MacFarlane, in *Principles of the Algebra of Logic* (Edinburgh, 1879). A. T. Shearman, *Development of Symbolic Logic,* is also useful.

Jørgensen, Lewis, and Jourdain all give some account of Jevons. For earlier criticism, see Shearman, above, and F. H. Bradley, *Principles of Logic* (London, 1883). On Jevons' machine, see Wolfe Mays and D. P. Henry, "Jevons and Logic," in *Mind,* Vol. 62 (1953), 484–505; and Martin Gardner, *Logic Machines and Diagrams.*

There are appraisals of Venn in the works by Jørgensen, Jourdain, and Shearman. On Venn diagrams, see Lewis, *op. cit.;* Prior, *op. cit.;* Gardner, *op. cit.;* J. N. Keynes, *Studies and Exercises in Formal Logic,* 4th ed. (London, 1906); and almost any elementary logic text.

In addition to his book, MacColl published a series of seven papers, "The Calculus of Equivalent Statements," in *Proceedings of the London Mathematical Society* (1877–1898); a series of eight papers, "Symbolic Reasoning," in *Mind* (1880–1906); and "The Existential Import of Propositions," in *Mind,* Vol. 30 (1905), 401–402, 578–580. On MacColl, see Jourdain, *op. cit.;* Prior, *op. cit.;* and Bertrand Russell's review of MacColl's *Symbolic Logic and Its Applications,* in *Mind,* Vol. 30 (1906), 255–260.

Most of Peirce's logical writings are to be found in Vols. II, III, and IV of his *Collected Papers,* Charles Hartshorne, Paul Weiss, and Arthur W. Burks, eds., 8 vols. (Cambridge, Mass., 1931–1958), but there is a discussion of logical paradoxes in Vol. V, Book 2, Paper 3, and one of the history of logic in Vol. VII, Book 2, Ch. 3, Sec. 10. His most developed and comprehensive logical paper is "On the Algebra of Logic: A Contribution to the Philosophy of Notation," Vol. III, Paper 13. "The Critic of Arguments," Paper 14 in the same volume, is comparatively easy reading and has a purple patch on rhemes and demonstratives. Peirce's existential graphs, which he thought were his most important contribution to logic, are the subject of Vol. IV, Book 2. The *Collected Papers* do not include some of Peirce's contributions to the *Century Dictionary,* such as the very suggestive article "Syllogism."

The Heritage of Kant and Mill

TEXTS

Hegel, G. W. F., *Wissenschaft der Logik:* Vol. I, *Die objektive Logik,* 2 vols. Nuremberg, 1812–1813. Vol. II, *Die subjektive Logik.* Nuremberg, 1816. Translated by W. H. Johnson and L. G. Struthers as *The Science of Logic,* 2 vols. London, 1929.

Kant, Immanuel, *Kritik der reinen Vernunft.* Riga, 1781; 2d ed., 1787. Translated by Norman Kemp Smith as *Critique of Pure Reason.* London, 1929.

Lotze, R. H., *Logik.* Leipzig, 1880. Translated by Helen Dendy as *Logic.* Oxford, 1884.

Mill, J. S., *A System of Logic.* London, 1843; 8th ed., 1872.

Mill, J. S., *An Examination of Sir William Hamilton's Philosophy,* 2d ed. London, 1865.

Sigwart, Christoph, *Logik,* 2 vols. Tübingen, 1873–1878. Translated by Helen Dendy as *Logic,* 2 vols. London, 1890.

WORKS ON JOHNSON

Acute and careful, as well as captious, criticism of Johnson is contained in H. W. B. Joseph's "What Does Mr. W. E. Johnson Mean by a Proposition?," in *Mind,* Vol. 36 (1927), 448–466, and Vol. 37 (1928), 21–39. Johnson's views are also discussed in A. N. Prior's "Determinables, Determinates and Determinants," in *Mind,* Vol. 58 (1949), 1–20, 178–194. There is a fine informative obituary of Johnson by C. D. Broad in *Ethics and the History of Philosophy* (London, 1952).

Nineteenth-century Mathematics

R. C. Archibald, "Outline of the History of Mathematics," in *American Mathematical Monthly,* Vol. 56 (1949), cites standard histories of nineteenth-century mathematics. See also the general histories of logic listed above, as well as Robert Bonola, *Non-Euclidean Geometry* (New York, 1955); Alonzo Church, "Schröder's Anticipation of the Simple Theory of Types," in *Erkenntnis,* Vol. 9 (1939), 149–152; Georg Cantor, *Contributions to the Founding of the Theory of Transfinite Numbers,* translated, with an introduction, by P. E. B. Jourdain (Chicago, 1915); Ettore Carruccio, *Mathematics and Logic in Contemporary Thought,* translated by Isabel Quigly (London, 1964); H. B. Curry, *Foundations of Mathematical Logic* (New York, 1963); and Giuseppe Peano, *Formulario Mathematico* (Turin, 1908; facsimile reprint, Rome, 1960).

Modern Logic: Frege to the Present

(Secondary material on the logicians discussed in the final section of the article is to be found mainly in the first two parts of the bibliography.)

Carnap, Rudolf, *Foundations of Logic and Mathematics.* Chicago, 1939. This is Vol. I, No. 3, of *International Encyclopedia of Unified Science.*

Carnap, Rudolf, *Introduction to Semantics.* Cambridge, Mass., 1942.

Carnap, Rudolf, *Meaning and Necessity,* 2d, enl. ed. Chicago, 1956.

Church, Alonzo, "A Note on the Entscheidungsproblem." *Journal of Symbolic Logic,* Vol. 1 (1936), 40–41. See also the correction, *ibid.,* 101–102.

Church, Alonzo, "An Unsolvable Problem of Elementary Number Theory." *American Journal of Mathematics,* Vol. 58 (1936), 345–363.

Church, Alonzo, *Introduction to Mathematical Logic,* Vol. I. Princeton, N.J., 1956.

Frege, Gottlob, *Translations From the Philosophical Writings of Gottlob Frege,* Peter Geach and Max Black, eds. Oxford, 1952.

Gentzen, Gerhard, "Untersuchungen über das logische Schliessen." *Mathematische Zeitschrift,* Vol. 39 (1934), 176–210, 405–431. Translated into French, with commentary, by R. Feys and J. Ladrière as *Recherches sur la déduction logique.* Paris, 1955.

Gentzen, Gerhard, "Die Widerspruchsfreiheit der reinen Zahlentheorie." *Mathematische Annalen,* Vol. 112 (1936), 493–565.

Gentzen, Gerhard, "Neue Fassung des Widerspruchsfreiheitsbeweises für die reine Zahlentheorie." *Forschungen zur Logik und zur Grundlegung der exakten Wissenschaften,* N.S. Vol. 4 (1938), 19–44.

Gentzen, Gerhard, "Beweisbarkeit und Unbeweisbarkeit von Anfangsfällen der transfiniten Induktion in der reinen Zahlentheorie." *Mathematische Annalen,* Vol. 119 (1943), 140–161.

Gödel, Kurt, articles on intuitionist logic and number theory. *Ergebnisse eines mathematischen Kolloquiums,* Vol. 4 (1933), 34–38, 40.

Gödel, Kurt, *The Consistency of the Axiom of Choice and of the Generalized Continuum-hypothesis With the Axioms of Set Theory.* Princeton, N.J., 1940; rev. ed., 1951.

Gödel, Kurt, "What Is Cantor's Continuum Problem?" *American Mathematical Monthly,* Vol. 54 (1947), 515–525.

Herbrand, Jacques, "Sur le Problème fondamental de la logique mathématique." *Comptes rendus des séances de la Société des Sciences et des Lettres de Varsovie,* Classe III, Vol. 24 (1931), 12–56.

Hilbert, David, *Gesammelte Abhandlungen,* 3 vols. Berlin, 1932–1935.

Hilbert, David, and Bernays, Paul, *Grundlagen der Mathematik,* 2 vols. Berlin, 1934–1939.

Post, Emil, "Formal Reductions of the General Combinatorial Decision Problem." *American Journal of Mathematics,* Vol. 65 (1943), 197–215.

Post, Emil, "Recursively Enumerable Sets of Positive Integers and Their Decision Problems." *Bulletin of the American Mathematical Society,* Vol. 50 (1944), 284–316.

Post, Emil, "Recursive Unsolvability of a Problem of Thue." *Journal of Symbolic Logic,* Vol. 12 (1947), 1–11.

Quine, W. V., *Set Theory and Its Logic.* Cambridge, Mass., 1963.

Ramsey, F. P., *The Foundations of Mathematics and Other Logical Essays,* R. B. Braithwaite, ed. New York and London, 1931.

Skolem, Thoralf, "Logisch-kombinatorische Untersuchungen über die Erfüllbarkeit oder Beweisbarkeit mathematischer Sätze nebst einem Theoreme über dichte Mengen," in *Skrifter Utgit av Videnskapsselskapet i Kristiania, I. Matematisk-naturvidenskapelig Klasse 1919,* No. 4. Oslo, 1920. Pp. 1–36.

Skolem, Thoralf, "Einige Bemerkungen zur axiomatischen Begründung der Mengenlehre," in *Wissenschaftlicher Vorträge, gehalten auf dem Fünften Kongress der Skandinavischen Mathematiker in Helsingfors 1922.* Helsinki, 1923. Pp. 217–232.

Skolem, Thoralf, "Über einige Grundlagenfragen der Mathematik." in *Skrifter Utgit av det Norske Videnskaps-akademi i Oslo, I. Matematisk-naturvidenskapelig Klasse,* No. 4. Oslo, 1929. Pp. 1–49.

Skolem, Thoralf, "Über die Unmöglichkeit einer vollständigen Charakterisierung der Zahlenreihe mittels eines endlichen Axiomsystems." *Norsk Matematisk Forenings Skrifter,* Series 2, No. 10 (1933), 73–82.

Skolem, Thoralf, "Über die Nicht-Charakterisierbarkeit der Zahlenreihe mittels endlich oder abzählbar unendlich vieler Aussagen mit ausschliesslich Zahlenvariablen." *Fundamenta Mathematicae,* Vol. 23 (1934), 150–161.

Wittgenstein, Ludwig, *Philosophische Bemerkungen,* Rush Rhees, ed. Oxford, 1964.

Polish Logicians

Zbiegniew Jordan's *The Development of Mathematical Logic and of Logical Positivism in Poland Between the Two Wars* (Oxford, 1945) is an excellent survey of its field; it finds illustration in Alfred Tarski's *Logic, Semantics, Metamathematics* (Oxford, 1956), a collection of papers translated by J. H. Woodger. Other translated classics of Polish logic are Tarski's *Elementy Logiki Matematycznej* (Warsaw, 1929; 2d ed., 1958), translated by Olgierd Wojtasiewicz as *Introduction to Logic* (Oxford, 1941); and Jan Łukasiewicz's *Elements of Mathematical Logic* (London, 1963) and *Aristotle's Syllogistic* (Oxford, 1951).

Much current work appears in the journal *Studia Logica,* published at Poznan, and, outside Poland, in the *Notre Dame Journal of Formal Logic,* edited by Bolesław Sobociński. *Studia Logica* has printed many papers by members of the Wrocław school, including Jerzy Słupecki, Ludwik Borkowski, Witold Pogorzelski, and Tadeusz Kubiński. See Czesław Lejewski's "On Leśniewski's Ontology" (presenting Lejewski's system of diagrams), in *Ratio,* Vol. 1 (1958), 150–176; "On Implicational Definitions," in *Studia Logica,* Vol. 8 (1958), 189–211; "On Prosleptic Syllogisms," in *Notre Dame Journal of Formal Logic,* Vol. 2 (1961), 158–176; and "A Theory of Non-reflexive Identity and Its Ontological Ramifications," to be published in the proceedings of the Sixth Forschungsgespräch organized by the Institut für Wissenschaftstheorie in Salzburg, September 6–10, 1965.

Among the important postwar publications are Andrzej Grzegorczyk, *Zarys Logiki Matematycznej* (Warsaw, 1961); Tadeusz Czeżowski, *Logika* (Warsaw, 1949); Andrzej Mostowski, *Logika Matematyczna* (Warsaw, 1948); Kazimierz Kuratowski and Andrzej Mostowski, *Teoria Mnogości* (Warsaw, 1952); Jerzy Słupecki and Ludwik Borkowski, *Elementy Logiki Matematycznej i Teorii Mnogości* (Warsaw, 1963); and Tadeusz Kotarbiński, *Kurs Logiki dla Prawników* (Warsaw, 1955).

(This article is the work of several authors. Connecting material was supplied by A. N. Prior.)

Edited by *A. N. Prior*